Unger's Commentary on the Old Testament

Unger's Commentary on the Old Testament

Volume I
Genesis — Song of Solomon

by
Merrill F. Unger

MOODY PRESS
CHICAGO

CONTENTS

Abbreviations

AASOR	*Annual of the American Schools of Oriental Research*
AB	Anchor Bible
AMJV	*Alexander Marx Jubilee Volume*
Amp	Amplified Bible
ANET	*Ancient Near Eastern Texts,* edited by J. B. Pritchard
ARI	*Archaeology and the Religion of Israel,* W. F. Albright
ASV	*American Standard Version*
BA	*Biblical Archaeologist*
BASOR	*Bulletin of the American Schools of Oriental Research*
BBC	*Broadman Bible Commentary*
BDB	Brown, Driver, and Briggs, *Hebrew-English Lexicon of the Old Testament*
BE	*Biblical Expositor*
BETS	*Bulletin of the Evangelical Theological Society*
BrBC	*Broadman Bible Commentary*
BRL	*Biblisches Reallexikon,* K. Galling
BS	*Bibliotheca Sacra*
BV	*Berkeley Version in Modern English*
CBC	*Clarke's Bible Commentary*
CBSC	*Cambridge Bible for Schools and Colleges*
CWCB	*Christian Worker's Commentary on the Whole Bible*
ECB	*Ellicott's Commentary on the Whole Bible,* edited by C. J. Ellicott
GNB	*Good News Bible*
GVI	*Geschichte des Volkes Israel,* Rudolph Kittel
HoSB	*Holman Study Bible*
HSB	*Harper's Study Bible*
IAT	*Les Institutions de l' Ancien Testament,* R. deVaux
IB	*Interpreter's Bible*
ICC	*International Critical Commentary*
IDB	*Interpreter's Dictionary of the Bible*
IEJ	*Israel Exploration Journal*
ISBE	*International Standard Bible Encyclopedia*
JAOS	*Journal of American Oriental Studies*
JBL	*Journal of Biblical Literature*
JFB	Jamieson, Fausset and Brown, *A Commentary, Critical and Exploratory on the Old and New Testaments*
JNES	*Journal of Near Eastern Studies*
JPOS	*Journal of the Palestine Oriental Society*
JPS	*Jewish Publication Society Version of the Old Testament*

JTS	*Journal of Theological Studies*
KBL	Koehler and Baumgartner, *Lexicon in Veteris Testamenti Libros*
KD	Keil and Delitzsch, *Commentaries on the Old Testament*
KJV	King James Version
KS	*Kleine Schriften zur Geschichte des Volkes Israel,* A. Alt
LBC	*Layman's Bible Commentary,* edited by B. H. Kelley
LXX	Septuagint
MLB	*Modern Language Bible*
MT	Masoretic text
NASB	*New American Standard Bible*
NBC	*New Bible Commentary*
NBD	*New Bible Dictionary*
NEB	*New English Bible*
NIV	*New International Version*
OAB	*Oxford Annotated Bible*
OTC	*Old Testament Commentary,* edited by H. C. Alleman and E. E. Flack
PEQ	*Palestine Exploration Quarterly*
RB	*Revue Biblique*
RSB	*Ryrie Study Bible*
RSV	*Revised Standard Version*
UBD	*Unger's Bible Dictionary*
UBH	*Unger's Bible Handbook*
VT	*Vetus Testamentum*
Vulg	Vulgate (Latin)
WBC	*Wycliffe Bible Commentary*
ZA	*Zeitschrifte für Assyiologie*
ZAW	*Zeitschrift für die alttestamentliche Wissenschaft*
ZDPW	*Zeitschrift des deutschen Palästina-Vereins*
ZPEB	*Zondervan Pictorial Encyclopedia of the Bible*
ZPBD	*Zondervan Pictorial Bible Dictionary*

GENESIS

INTRODUCTION

Place in the Canon. Genesis is a book of origins. As such, it is foundational and introductory to the entire *canon* ("the books accepted as Holy Scripture"). Correctly and logically, it stands at the head of the whole body of sacred Scripture. It records the beginning of time ("in the beginning"), the beginning of the heaven and the earth (at least as they are related to time), the beginning of all plant, animal, and human life, as well as all human institutions and social relationships. It is also the doctrinal seed plot from which all subsequent teachings and divine revelations spring and from which they are developed.

Name and Relation to the Pentateuch. The book takes its name from the title it bears in the Septuagint, which is derived from the heading of its ten parts, "these are the generations" (*he biblos geneseōs*, 2:4; 5:1; 6:9; 10:1; 11:10; 11:27; 25:12; 25:19; 36:1; 37:2). Following the custom of designating a book by its opening word or words, the Jews named it *Bere'shith*, "In the beginning."

Genesis not only heads the Hebrew Scriptures; it also forms a unit with the Pentateuch (the first five books of the Bible), making the Pentateuchal books more broadly foundational and introductory to the entire body of revealed truth. Therefore, Genesis may be called "the foundation of the foundation," the bedrock upon which the Pentateuch (and all Scripture) rests. As such, the book is uniquely indispensable. It is conceivable that certain others of the sixty-six canonical books might not have been given by God without His divine revelation suffering too much loss, but it is hard to see how Genesis could have been omitted without a serious gap in the whole.

Scope of the Book. Genesis is an account, we believe, of the re-creation of a chaotic, sin-scarred heaven and earth for the latecomer, man (1:1-2 being apparently circumstantial to 1:3). When God said, "Let there be light" (1:3), the chaotic condition of 1:1-2 was not the background for the creation of light, but for its separation from chaotic darkness.

Man was created and placed upon the re-created earth as the special order of creation through which God would demonstrate to the entire universe how He would deal with sin and rebellion in His creatures. The beginning of time is presented in the opening chapters of Genesis (cf. "in the beginning," "evening and morning," day and night, etc.). The intimation is that sin began *before time* in eternity past, in connection with Satan and the fallen angels. (Cf. 3:1-10, where Satan and sin are presupposed, *not* introduced, with Job 38:4-7; Isa. 14:12-14; Ezek. 28:11-19.)

To facilitate the divine demonstration of how God would deal with sin and rebellion in His creatures, man was created innocent, fell, and called forth the gospel (3:15), setting forth the divine plan of salvation by grace through faith (3:21; 4:4). Cain and his descendants represent the rejection of the true gospel of salvation by faith for the false gospel

1

of salvation by works (4:1-5). This rejection and its consequent lawlessness led to the judgment of the Flood (chaps. 6-9), and afterward to the confusion of tongues at Babel (11:1-9).

The first division of Genesis (chaps. 1-11) concludes with the introduction of Abraham, the great protagonist of salvation by grace through faith (15:6; Rom. 4:1-5, 9-25). The book's second division traces God's redemptive program through Abraham, Isaac, Jacob, and Joseph (chaps. 12-50), under the promises of the Abrahamic Covenant and the coming Redeemer.

Authorship. Both Scripture and tradition attribute the book's authorship to Moses, who was eminently qualified both in the divine and human plan to compile the book (cf. Acts 7:22). Many oral and written records were available to this eminent Hebrew sage and man of God, plus the fact that he had intimate communion with Deity in the desert. What information Moses could not obtain on the natural plane to write Genesis, God gave him by revelation on the supernatural plane.

Critics deny Mosaic authorship of both Genesis and the other books of the Pentateuch. They present a so-called Documentary Theory, making the book a product of composite sources, welded together centuries after Moses' lifetime. The narrative sections (J and E) were supposedly fitted into the skeletal history of the origin of the Jewish nation, called the Priestly Code (P), in the late exilic or postexilic period.

The Documentary Theory, though highly developed and deceptively plausible, is a product of rationalistic skepticism and is at variance with clear lines of historical and scriptural evidence supporting the unity of the Pentateuch.

OUTLINE

COMMENTARY

I. PRIMEVAL HISTORY OF THE RACE. 1:1—11:32.

A. PROLOGUE: REMAKING THE EARTH FOR MAN. 1:1—2:3.

1. REMAKING THE EARTH. 1:1-31.

Point of Beginning – A Chaotic, Judgment-ridden Earth. 1:1-2. **1. In the beginning.** These opening words of divine revelation have been almost universally assumed to describe the original creation of the earth and the universe in eternity past, as in John 1:3 and Colossians 1:16-17. But there are cogent reasons to believe a *relative* rather than an *absolute* beginning is envisioned. This view sets God's creative activity of the earth in a much later geological period in preparation for the latecomer, man. The meaning of "in the beginning" depends on the context. For example, in John 1:1 the phrase predates the time in Genesis 1:1, even if the latter is interpreted as original creation ex nihilo. The Hebrew word *bārā'* ("to create") may mean "ex nihilo," but it may also mean "to fashion or make of existing material." Man, for example, was not created out of nothing, but out of the dust of the earth (1:26; 2:7).

The heaven that God created (remade) was evidently *not* the sphere of the planets and stars, but the immediate atmospheric heaven surrounding the earth, as the re-creative activity of the first four days suggests (1:4-19). Light on the first day was solar. But light from the heavenly bodies, which God *had* made in eternity past (v. 16), could not penetrate the chaotic shroud that enveloped the earth. Verse 2 in the Hebrew is apparently circumstantial to verse 3. It tells the earth's condition *when* God began to re-create it, and specifically to separate light from chaotic darkness. It "was" a chaos of wasteness, emptiness, and darkness. God did not create it in this state (Job 38:4, 7; cf. Isa. 45:18). It was reduced to this condition because it was the theater where sin began in God's originally sinless universe in connection with the revolt of Lucifer (Satan) and his angels (Isa. 14:12-14; Ezek. 28:13, 15-17; Rev. 12:4).

The chaos was the result of God's judgment upon the originally sinless earth. If Genesis 1:1-2 describes original creation, a theological problem arises. Where did Satan and sin originate (cf. 3:1-15)? There is no room in the seven days for the creation of angels, much less the angelic fall producing original sin and the fallen angels or demons. Also, a scientific problem arises. If Genesis 1 describes original creation, how can the account be reconciled with the earth's great antiquity and man's comparative late appearance on earth? Genesis 1, we conclude, describes the beginning of *man's* earth and the *history of man upon it.*

The First Day. 1:3-5. In forming a unit, verses 1 and 2 must not be separated from verse 3, for they constitute an introduction to what transpired during the seven days. The fact that "the Spirit of God was moving" (v. 2, NASB) upon the chaotic mass demonstrates that God

5

had not utterly given up the earth, ruined by the sin of its former angelic inhabitants (Isa. 14:13-14; Ezek. 28:12-15; cf. Gen. 6:1-6). Sin began on the earth. God would deal fully and finally with it upon earth, in and through a new order of created beings to live on the earth. Therefore, He undertook to prepare the earth for man and man for the earth. In making the earth the stage for enacting the drama of redemption, the Creator-Redeemer would demonstrate to all created intelligences how He would deal with sin and rebellion in His creatures. At the same time, His goal of an eventual sinless universe would be realized.

What is meant by the term "day"? The seven days represent either (1) literal twenty-four-hour days of re-creation, or (2) literal twenty-four-hour days of the divine *revelation* of re-creation to man, or (3) extended geologic ages preparatory to man's eventual occupation. If one assumes Genesis 1:1 posits original creation ex nihilo, then the same possibilities of interpretation exist, since the Genesis account itself is indecisive.

E. A. Speiser's perceptive rendering of 1:1-3 not only shows the close connection of 1:1 with 1:2, but 1:1 with 1:3. "When God set about to create heaven and earth—the world being then a formless waste, with darkness over the seas and only an awesome wind sweeping over the water—God said, 'Let there be light'" (*Genesis*, AB, p. 3). If this original creation was made out of nothing, why would God start with chaos rather than with nothing? Chaos represents the result of sin and rebellion (cf. 1 Cor. 14:33). God's creative activity moved to bring cosmos out of chaos.

3. God said. By divine fiat God willed and effected the penetration of the chaotic darkness of the earth's atmosphere by the sun's rays. **Let there be light.** This is not the original creation of light (the sun) in the unfathomable past. Scripture gives no inkling when our solar system or the vast solar systems of the universe were created (John 1:1-3; Col. 1:16). Certainly it is presumed by Genesis to be *before* 1:1. The light of 1:3 is obviously from the sun, which does not become visible and function normally with respect to the renewed earth till the fourth day (vv. 14-18). **4. God divided the light from the darkness.** Light (day) and darkness (night) could now follow in succession as the earth turned daily on its axis, and the sun could pierce the gloom as the chaotic shroud was dissipated.

The Second Day. 1:6-8. **7. God made the firmament,** the vault or arch of the sky (Heb., *rāqîa',* that which is "beaten" or "spread out," as the expanse of heaven was thought of). What took place was the separation of the atmospheric waters that had been chaotically mixed with the terrestrial waters. This suggests that dense fogs had shut out all sunlight, enshrouding the judgment-ridden planet in the darkness described in verse 2, precluding any idea of heaven or sky in the primeval chaos.

The waters which were under the firmament were separated from **the waters which were above the firmament.** The chaotic celestial water mass condensed to unite with the land water chaos. The result was the formation of the atmosphere through which the light of the heavenly bodies could penetrate (vv. 14-19). The condensation was only partial, because the resulting climate evidently prevailed till the Noahic Flood. Then the forty-day diluvial downpour apparently further reduced the vapor content of the firmament (7:11-12; 9:11-15). The sign of the rainbow further suggests this.

The Third Day. 1:9-13. **9.** The terrestrial waters were collected together **into one place** (NASB) or specified area. This produced the ocean, the whole body of salt water that covers nearly three-fourths of the surface of the globe and connects with fresh-water lakes by rivers that flow into it. This of necessity was accomplished by gigantic volcanic upheavals that formed vast hollows into which the waters rushed (Psalm 104:6-9). **10. God called the dry land Earth; and the gathering together of the waters called he Seas.** The formation of continents and islands made possible luxuriant tree and plant life, evidently interrupted by chaos, but now resumed in the new order established.

The Fourth Day. 1:14-19. The work of the first and second days prepared the way for what transpired on the fourth day. The separation of light from a chaotic mixture with darkness and the condensation of the chaotic water blanket that enveloped the earth's atmosphere not only produced "the heaven" of 1:1. It also permitted the luminaries (sun, moon, and stars) to be seen from the earth and illuminate the earth. "Let there be light" (v. 3) means "let light have an objective existence; let it have reality or actuality" in distinction to its previous chaotic admixture with darkness (1:2). **14.** Similarly, **Let there be lights** does not mean "let the sun, moon, and stars be created out of nothing," but "let them have real, discernible existence" by becoming visible on the earth as a result of the newly constituted atmosphere effected on the second day.

16-17. God made . . . God set the sun, moon, and stars in the heavens signifies that He "prepared" these bodies by the work of the first and second days and "appointed" them for their normal function in time in reference to the planet earth. That function is "to distinguish between night and day" and "to mark the fixed times, the days and the years" (Speiser, AB, p. 3), literally, "serve as signs and seasons," a hendiadys ("the expression of an idea by two nouns connected by *and*") for "signs for the fixed time periods," namely, "the days and the years" (Speiser, AB, p. 6). That original creation ex nihilo is *not* in view, as suggested by the previous separation of light from chaotic admixture with darkness and the establishment of day and night already on the first day (vv. 3-5). The terms "Day" and "Night" (v. 5) refer only to time (not eternity) and to the earth alone. They are meaningless apart from the existence of the sun and the rotation of the earth, already assumed in verse 5 on the first *day*.

The Fifth Day. 1:20-23. **20-21.** Sea life and birds were **created**, evidently not out of nothing but out of existing material, as man was. The restoration of the judgment-ridden planet proceeded in an orderly fashion. It was to be readied for God's highest earthly creature and to sustain him when he would come forth from the Creator's hand.

The Sixth Day. 1:24-31. **24-25.** Land life and man were created. Man is revealed to have been *created* by God (not evolved). He appeared as the crown and goal of all the divine activity in re-creating the earth as man's home. **26. God said, Let us make man.** The name *God* (Heb., '*elōhîm*) appears no less than thirty-five times in this opening section (1:1—2:4). This, the first of the primary names of Deity, is a plural noun. Implicit in '*elōhîm* from the first verse of divine revelation is the Trinity.

The expression "let us" intimates the Triune God's counsel and activity in man's creation (cf. John 1:3; Col. 1:16), embracing also the divine foreordained plan of human redemption (Eph. 1:4-6).

The triune nature of God is latent in the Old Testament, patent in the New Testament. It is, therefore, not sufficient to construe this term as a mere plural of majesty or greatness. Nor is it enough to confine the meaning to God calling the angels in court to witness the divine deliberation to a matter fraught with such importance as man's creation.

In our image, after our likeness. Two facts concerning man are declared: (1) He was *created*; he did not evolve (v. 27; cf. Matt. 19:4; Mark 10:6). (2) He was made in God's image and likeness. He, like his Creator, possessed personality and moral holiness. Man could not lose his personality, but he forfeited his moral holiness by the Fall. Although God is infinite and man finite, nevertheless man possesses the elements of personality similar to those of the divine Person—the ability to think (2:19-20; 3:8); feel (3:6); will (3:6-7); and act with moral responsibility (cf. Eph. 4:23-24; Col. 3:10). Since "God is spirit" (John 4:24, NASB), man's resemblance to God is spiritual and is found in the elements of personality.

Let them have dominion. Man (*'ish*) may be singular, "a man," or collective, "men" or "mankind." God's counsel was to make the first *man*. But in him, as federal head of the race, all men (i.e., mankind) were comprehended. Subject to his Creator, man was to have sovereignty over the earth (vv. 28-30; Psalm 8:5-8). **27. God created man in his own image.** This passage stresses the unity of the divine essence (cf. 3:22) in contrast to verse 26, "Let us make man in *our* image . . . *our* likeness," which stresses the plurality of the divine personality. (See note on *'elōhîm*, v. 26, and other divine names, Gen. 2:4; 14:18; 15:2; 17:1; 21:33; Exod. 34:6; 1 Sam. 1:3; Mal. 3:18.)

28. God blessed them. This marks the beginning of God's dealing with man in certain periods of time called "dispensations." God inaugurated each of these periods with a specific revelation of His will, giving man a stewardship to obey the disclosure of the divine will. During each time period or age, the particular revelation (called a covenant) that was made to introduce it became the dominant criterion for testing man's obedience to God.

The first dispensation was Innocence. Man was created sinless, untried and untempted by sin, but with free moral choice to sin. Tempted by Satan, man chose to sin (1 Tim. 2:14). The stewardship of innocence ended with judgment. Man was expelled from Eden and denied access to the tree of life (3:24). (For other dispensations, see Gen. 3:7; 8:15; 12:1; Exod. 19:1; Acts 2:1; Rev. 20:4.) The dispensation of Innocence, based on the Edenic Covenant (vv. 26-28) between the Triune God (first party) and newly created man (the second party), governed man's life in Edenic innocence and stipulated his dominion and subjugation of the earth. It presented a simple test of obedience, with death the penalty of disobedience (2:15-17), and it ended as a specific time period when man fell. (For other covenants, see Gen. 3:14-19; 8:20—9:1; 12:1-3; Exod. 20:1—31:18; Deut. 30:1-10; 2 Sam. 7:4-17; Jer. 31:31-33.)

But man's disobedience and Fall did not nullify the covenant's stipulations. **Be fruitful . . . multiply . . . fill the earth . . . subdue it.** These elements of the covenant remained in force. Man's Fall into sin would alter the divine blessing. Nevertheless, man was to procreate and populate the earth. As a rational personality, he also was to develop his God-given capabilities and "subdue" (*kibᵉśû*, "to tread down, bring under control") the earth. Man was to acquire mastery over his material environment. By use of his mental powers, he was to harness the potential built in the earth by the Creator for his comfort and welfare. This God-ordained basis for all scientific and material progress has been followed by fallen man, with mixed blessing. Sin always introduces the element of the curse.

31. The sixth day. Remarkable similarities and differences exist between the Genesis account of creation and the Babylonian account in *Enuma elish,* which confounds divine spirit and cosmic matter, making them coexistent and coeternal. In Genesis, the divine Spirit preceded and was independent of cosmic matter. In *Enuma elish, Tiamat* ("chaos") was enveloped in darkness; in Genesis, darkness covered the "deep" (*tᵉhôm*, a common noun with no mythological connotation). The order of creative (re-creative) phases is identical in both accounts. *Enuma elish* says light emanated from the gods, while Genesis says light was made to appear. Both say the firmament and dry land were made and man was created. The luminaries were created in *Enuma elish*; they were made to appear in Genesis. In *Enuma elish,* the gods rested and celebrated, but in Genesis, God rested and set apart the seventh day. Evidently the two accounts go back to a common source. *Enuma elish* represents a polytheistic corruption. By divine inspiration, the Genesis account captures the original pure form these creation traditions must have assumed.

2. THE SEVENTH DAY. 2:1-3.

The Seventh Day. 2:1-3. This section is part of the foregoing account of creation (re-creation). The unfortunate chapter division (dating from the sixteenth century) obscures this fact and disturbs the story's inner unity. **1. Thus** (Heb., *waw,* "consecutive") expresses logical result. As a result of the divine activity of the six days, **the heavens and the earth were finished, and all the host of them.** The King James Version and the *New American Standard Bible* reflect the Hebrew word order that violates idiomatic English. **Host** "designates the total made up of the various component parts" (Speiser, AB, p. 7).

2. On the seventh day God ended his work . . . and he rested. Since the creation (re-creation) was finished on the sixth day, the text can scarcely declare that God concluded it on the seventh day. The difficulty may be resolved (1) by translating the pertinent verb as a pluperfect: "On the seventh day God had ended his work . . . and rested"; or (2) by giving the Hebrew preposition *beth* a specialized meaning: "By the seventh day God completed His work" (NASB); or (3) by assuming the verb carries some more particular shade of meaning: "On the seventh day God brought to a (gratifying) close the work that he had been doing" (Speiser, AB, p. 8). A. Heidel (*The Babylonian Genesis*, p. 127) proposes "declared finished." God "rested" (Heb., *shābăt*) means He "stopped" or "desisted" from His work. The language is boldly anthropomorphic "ascribing human form or attributes," since the infinite God never gets weary or faint (Isa. 40:28).

3. God blessed the seventh day, and sanctified it. He instituted the Sabbath (*shăbbāt*, lit., "a resting or ceasing from work") for unfallen man. The Creator could "rest" in His re-creation because it was "very good" (1:31). But when sin entered (chap. 3), it became very bad. God's creation rest was broken by man's Fall. God stopped resting in a "very good" creation and began working in redemption for sinful man's salvation (3:15, 21; cf. John 5:17). Hence, the Sabbath *was not imposed upon fallen man*, except in the case of the nation Israel. This is the reason for the silence concerning it from Adam to Moses. At Sinai it reappears with startling suddenness (Exod. 20:8-11), not only being imposed upon the elect and typically saved nation Israel (Exod. 20:1-2), but also made the unique and dominant feature of the Mosaic Covenant (Exod. 31:12-18).

When God "blessed" the seventh day, He attached special benefit to it and "sanctified" it by setting it apart as especially sacred from all the other days of the week. It was a reminder to fallen man that God had created him free of sin, and though he had fallen into sin, that God would eventually redeem him through the coming seed of the woman (3:15), the virgin-born, Israel-begotten Messiah. God would remind the fallen race that His creation rest would one day be restored through the Israelite nation.

B. THE EARLIEST HISTORY OF HUMANITY. 2:4—4:26.

1. THE ACCOUNT OF EDEN. 2:4-24.

The Title of This Section. 2:4a. **4a. These are the generations of the heavens and of the earth.** H. C. Leupold (*Exposition of Genesis*, 1:109) is correct in maintaining that 4*a* gives the simple and correct heading of the section 2:4*b*—4:26. His translation is also pointed: "This is the story of the heavens and the earth at the time of their creation." The Hebrew word *tôlᵉḏôṯ* means literally "generations" or "begettings" in the sense of a genealogical line. Since it deals with much more than a genealogical succession and includes events that happen to people, animals, and things, it has the common derived meaning of a "story, an account, or history."

This is the significance of the term in the ten headings that constitute the literary framework of Genesis. The "generations" of Adam (5:1—6:8); Noah (6:9—9:29); Noah's sons (10:1—11:9); Shem (11:10-26); Terah (11:27—25:11); Ishmael (25:12-18); Isaac (25:19—35:29); Esau (36:1—37:1); and Jacob (37:2—50:26) constitute in each case the story or history of these people. Moreover, in each instance it gives the title or superscription. Never is it a colophon or finis of the preceding section, 1:1—2:3.

"These are the generations" in the sense of "origins" is misleading. The term *tôlᵉḏôṯ* never tells how persons or things come into existence, but it describes what transpired after they appear on the scene. "The story of the heavens and the earth" denotes "the history of the chaotic earth and the immediate atmospheric heavens that envelope it" after they were remade for man's abode as the result of the divine creative activity recounted in 1:3-31.

Accordingly, 2:4-25 (4:26) is not another creation account from a source (J) diverse from the first account, 1:1—2:3 (P), as higher critics contend. It is simply a continuation of the Mosaic history of the re-created earth. The reason the details of man's creation are given in supplementary form is obvious. Such detail would have marred the symmetry and poetic brevity of the account of the seven days. Moreover, man was the goal of the entire divine program for re-creating the earth. Hence, his creation and testing in a perfect environment were of the utmost importance as an introduction to his Fall and the divine plan of redemption as cataloged in chapter 3. All these elements could not have been compressed into the one creation account without making it heavy and unbalanced.

10

The Earth Awaits Man's Creation. 2:4b-6. **4b-6.** These verses are excitingly anticipative of man's creation and assumption of full possession and care of his domain. Verse 4 is usually translated as a unit, but it is best to take 4*a* as a title and to combine 4*b* with verse 5, as does Leupold (1:111). Translated literally, the Hebrew says, "At the time [*b*e*yôm,* "when"] the LORD God made heaven and earth, then no field shrub was as yet in the earth, and no field shrub was yet sprouting forth." This passage goes back to the work of the third day, when plant life appeared (1:11-12), giving details that could scarcely have been inserted there. It says that the particular plants singled out, which needed man's attentive care, did not sprout and grow on the third day, but awaited man's creation and care on the sixth day. Evidently they were specific shrubs for man's special interest and delight.

5-6. The Lord God had not caused it to rain. . . . But there went up a mist. Most commentators (Lange, Leupold, etc.) assume that the mist was a precursor to rain. But there is the suggestion that the pre-Flood earth was watered not by rain, but by vast subterranean sources of water. The "mist" (Heb., *'ēd,* and Akkadian, *edû*) means "a flow" (E. A. Speiser, BASOR 140 [1950]: 9 ff.) or "subterranean stream of fresh water" (W. F. Albright, JBL 58 [1932]: 102-3).

Verse 6 translated literally reads, "So an underground stream of water kept rising from the earth and kept watering all the surface of the ground." If this is true, why would rain be needed? (For full discussion, see comments on 7:11-12.) LORD God (YHWH *'elōhîm*), a compound name of Deity, indicates that the mighty Creator of Genesis 1 is Jehovah (Yahweh), the One who enters into covenant relation with mankind. YHWH means "He is" ("exists eter-

nally," see Exod. 3:14) or "He causes [all things] to be." It is the personal, ineffably holy name, not pronounced by pious Jews. (For other names of Deity, see Gen. 1:26; 14:18; 15:2; 17:1; 1 Sam. 1:3; Mal. 3:18.)

The Manner of Man's Creation. 2:7. **7. The Lord God formed man.** The power of God (*'elōhîm*) is not only displayed in the creation of man, but in His covenant mercy and love (Yahweh). The Yahweh character of God is emphasized by the verb employed, *formed* (*yāṣar,* "to mold, to fashion," as a potter fashions clay; see Jer. 18:2-6). Jehovah God betokens His tender care and personal attention in His creature, man, by molding him as He does. He not only "created" (1:27) and made man (1:26). In molding him, He displayed His infinite interest in him as His highest and dearest earthly creature.

The dust of the ground does not only refer to dry, pulverized earth (cf. 3:19). Here it indicates "a damp mass of the finest earth" (Leupold), hardly a dry, hard clod, much less mud. Man was simply molded out of soil or dirt (Heb., *'āpār*). The Hebrew words *'ādām,* "man," and *'adāmâ,* "soil or ground" (vv. 5, 7) present an obvious play on words and indicate man's close kinship to the earth. What a combination he is of grandeur and dignity (made in God's image) and lowliness (formed of common dirt). Yet into the divinely fashioned soil God **breathed . . . the breath of life**—not air or human breath, but His own vital life, which caused man to live physically and breathe air, as well as to live spiritually and eternally in fellowship with Jehovah *'elōhîm.*

By breathing into man the breath of life, God bestowed upon him what He had not bestowed on any beast—a rational soul to think and will, and a sentient spirit to know his Creator and communicate in fellowship with Him (cf. 1 Thess. 5:23; Heb. 4:12). Adam's soul and spirit were a direct creation, as was his body. Whether man's nonmaterial nature in the successive generations of Adam has been created by God in each case or humanly propagated is not known; it has been the subject of debate throughout the centuries.

The Home of Unfallen Man. 2:8-9. Again Jehovah God's concern and care for His highest creature are underscored. **8.** For the man whom He had tenderly and skillfully "formed," even as a potter fashions a choice vase, He also thoughtfully **planted a garden** (*gān,* "a protected enclosure"). The term *paradise,* borrowed from the Persian by the Septuagint translators, suggests a "royal park," which in a sense it was. As a place of particular beauty, it reflects, as do so many details of this chapter, God's favor toward His chief creature. **Eastward** (*miqqĕḏĕm*) does not mean "from the east" but "in the east," the Hebrew (*min*) here being locative (Speiser, AB). *Eden* (Heb., *'ēḏĕn*; Akk., *edinu*) comes from the Sumerian *eden* ("plain, steppe"). This Akkadian-Sumerian loan word, together with the word for "flow" ("mist," v. 6), harks back to the oldest cultural strata of lower Mesopotamia and points to the location of Eden somewhere at the head of the Persian Gulf.

Doubtless the early Sumerians got their word *eden* ("a plain") from the fact that the original Eden was a flat, fertile tract. In Hebrew, Eden became associated with the homonymous noun for "enjoyment" or "pleasure" (*'ēḏĕn*). **There he put the man.** That man was created (made, formed) *outside* the garden and then placed *in* the garden shows that God at the outset made a distinction between the garden and all the land outside it. How God accomplished all this is not specified. We may be sure it was done in a manner befitting Him.

9. God made to grow in the garden **every tree that is pleasant to the sight, and good for food.** This verse is undoubtedly an amplification of verse 5. Added are **the tree of life** and **the tree of knowledge of good and evil.** The tree of life would have served its purpose in the event that man had remained sinless. Its position in the center of the garden attests the importance of its provision for man's good. Having never been used, it understandably recedes into the background and is not mentioned again till after the Fall (cf. 3:22). It was intended to confirm unfallen man in physical life and to render physical death an impossibility.

Spiritually, it of necessity had a symbolic or sacramental purpose. It was a sign of eternal life and heavenly fellowship with God, to which man was destined once his period of probation was happily consummated. Man in his unfallen state was to eat freely of its fruit, but it was not the fruit that by some magical means nurtured his spiritual life. It was the divine blessing granted him as he through obedience remained in his pristine state of innocence in covenant relation to his Creator.

"The tree of [the] knowledge of good and evil" also possessed a sacramental or symbolic character. It was a test of obedience by which man was to be tried to see whether he would be good or bad, obey God or defy His command. Whether this tree in itself was harmless is beside the point. As the symbol of the divine will, its fruit was strictly forbidden under severe penalty (cf. v. 17).

The Location of Eden. 2:10-14. Latest archaeological research demonstrates that the name Eden, as a geographical designation (cf. v. 9), as well as the physical background pictured in the account, is authentic (E. A. Speiser, "The Rivers of Paradise," in *Festschrift Johannes Friedrich*, pp. 473-85). All four streams once converged near the head of the Persian Gulf to create a rich garden land, captured here by inspiration and reflected in Mesopotamian religion as the land of the blessed.

10. A river flowed out of Eden (NASB), or better, "rises *in Eden* to water the garden; outside it forms four separate branch streams" (Speiser). Apparently the river of Eden emptied into a confluence of the four rivers named. **11. The name of the first** [stream] **is Pishon,** which winds (*sbb*, "twists and turns") through **the whole land of Havilah,** a region noted for its fine **gold** and **bdellium** (an aromatic gum?) and lapis lazuli (*'ĕbĕn hashshohăm;* see Speiser, *Festschrift...,* pp. 480-81).

13. The second river is [the] **Gihon,** which winds through **the whole land of Cush** (Babylonia). **14. The third river,** the Tigris (Sum., *Idigna*; Akk., *Idiglat;* Heb., *hiddĕqĕl*) flows east of Assyria (its eponymous capital) and is well known. **The fourth river is Euphrates.** With mention of the Euphrates, no doubt is left that the approximate locale of the Garden of Eden was in the cradle of civilization, southern Mesopotamia, the extreme eastern end of "Breasted's Fertile Crescent" (W. F. Albright, *From Stone Age to Christianity,* p. 6). Cush refers to the country of the Kassites (spelled *Kuššû* in the Nuzi documents) in Babylonia. There is no reference here to *Ethiopia,* the homonymous biblical term for Cush. The erroneous identification with African Cush has played havoc with the correct geographical view of this passage.

The Edenic Covenant. 2:15-17. A covenant is a sovereign pronouncement of God by which He establishes a relationship of responsibility between Himself and mankind or part of mankind. The first covenant, the Edenic Covenant, stipulated the following responsibilities for Adam: (1) to propagate the race (1:28); (2) to subdue the earth and the animal creation (1:28); (3) to care for the garden and eat its fruits (2:15-16); and (4) to abstain from eating of the tree of the knowledge of good and evil on penalty of death for disobedience (2:17). (See comments on 1:28 and references to the other covenants.) The penalty of death was certain.

17. Thou shalt surely die. The penalty was threefold: (1) immediate spiritual death or loss of fellowship with God; (2) eventual physical death or separation of the body from the soul and spirit; and (3) inevitable eternal death in separation from God in Gehenna. This threefold death passed upon all Adam's posterity as a result of his Fall.

The Creation of Woman. 2:18-22. **18-20.** God, who had pronounced each part of His re-creative work "good," realized it was **not good that the man should be alone,** literally, "in his separation" (singleness). Man needed a counterpart, someone to complement him physically, intellectually, and spiritually. **I will make him a help fit for him** (Heb., *kᵉnĕgdô,* "as in his presence," meaning "one like himself" in physical makeup and constitution). The LORD God's concern for Adam is further emphasized. The Creator formed the animals to show man that he also needed a helpmeet. Adam's naming them indicates man's superior intelligence as a specially created personality with abilities far superior to the lower creatures.

21-22. The Lord God caused a deep sleep to fall upon Adam. The sleep was a divine anaesthetic for the operation that was to produce woman. **He took one of his ribs** and out of it **made . . . a woman.**

The word for "rib" (*ṣĕlā'*) usually means "side"; so the Septuagint renders the term by *pleura*, denoting a piece of his side. The word "made" literally means "built" or "constructed," suggesting extraordinary skill, care, and taste in the plan and proportions of the structure. Therefore, from a part of the side of man, the LORD God fashioned a woman.

Man was created perfect physically and intellectually. Woman, his counterpart, was created subsequently from man. This fact establishes the divine order of the headship of man over woman and husband over wife (cf. 1 Cor. 11:3), exposing the essential unsoundness of the modern women's liberation movement. What beauty and dignity are accorded woman in this account! No casual or hasty production of nature, she was the finished result of the labor and skill of the divine Artificer.

Finally, she was brought with special honor to the man as the Creator's last and most perfect work. As R. Payne Smith so aptly declares, "Every step and stage in this description is intended for the ennoblement of marriage. Woman is not made from the adamah but from the adam ... and while for Adam there is simply the closing of the cavity caused by her withdrawal, she is moulded ... and built up into man's counterpart. She brings back more than the man parted with, and the Creator Himself leads her by the hand to her husband" ("Genesis," in *Ellicott's Commentary on the Whole Bible*, 1:22).

Institution of Marriage. 2:23-24. Adam had long studied the natural world. Each animal had responded to his call and joined his company, but not one of these creatures had he found answering to his needs and responding to him with articulate speech. At last, however, awakening from his trance, he found someone standing by him, whom he at once recognized as his second self. **23.** Welcoming her joyfully, he cried, **This is now** (*pă'ăm*, "this time" or "at last") **bone of my bones, and flesh of my flesh,** that is, "She is my very own self, my counterpart," not merely in physical feelings (flesh), but in the higher realm of the intellectual and spiritual (bones).

The Hebrew word for "bone" (*'ĕṣĕm*) signifies not only "body" or "frame" but also "essence" or "self." "Your bones shall flourish" (Isa. 66:14) means "you in your whole being shall prosper" (cf. Prov. 3:8; 14:30; and 15:30 with Psalms 6:2-3; 35:10). **She shall be called Woman** (*'ishshâ*), **because she was taken out of Man** (*'ish*). The assonance in the Hebrew reflects the original designation of the woman as derivative from and hence of a kind with the man (cf. 2:18b, 20). (Cf. the Old English *wifman, wif,* "wife," "woman," plus *man,* "human being," from which "woman" developed in Middle English and modern English.

24. Therefore shall a man leave his father and his mother. These are the inspired words of Moses as narrator, hence, the words of God Himself (Matt. 19:5) solemnly sanctioning marriage as a divine ordinance and establishing the home as the basic unit of the social order. He who at the beginning made them male and female (Matt. 19:4) declared that sexual union was God-ordained within the holy bonds of marriage. A man was to be monogamous. He was to **cleave unto** (hold fast to and cling to) **his wife** (*not* wives). Polygamy was never in the divine order for man. Adultery and fornication obviously were ruled out as violations of the Creator's holiness and the creature's dignity.

Sex was not regarded as evil, for sexual union was ordained before man fell

(1:28). Even after the Fall, sex was not regarded as evil, but as a God-given impulse to draw man and woman together in marriage, when by their sexual union they became **one flesh.** Such a union was not only for the purpose of the procreation of the race by establishing the family. It was also for the physical, emotional, and mental exhilaration of husband and wife, constituting one of the many joys of marriage and the godly home.

2. THE TEMPTATION AND FALL OF MAN. 2:25—3:24.

The Original Sinless State of Man. 2:25. **25.** This verse does not conclude the marriage section. Actually, it belongs to chapter 3 and introduces the subject of the temptation and the Fall presented there. **They were both naked ... and were not ashamed.** In their childlike innocence, they as yet knew neither good nor evil. Their guileless simplicity was in contrast to the guileful subtlety of Satan's tool, the tempting serpent. This is emphasized by paronomasia ("a play upon words"). Man was "naked" (*'ārôm*). The serpent was crafty (*'ārûm*).

The Temptation. 3:1-5. **1.** The agent of the temptation was **the serpent,** apparently an upright creature and the most cunning and beautiful of the animal creation, not a writhing reptile, which was the result of the divine curse (3:14). The real tempter, however, behind the serpent was Satan. The serpent was merely his tool. Satan comes into view here; his creation, Fall, and the entrance of sin presumably antedated Genesis 1:1-2 (cf. Ezek. 28:12-19; Isa. 14:12-14; Rev. 12:9), for Satan appears without previous introduction. He is identified, however, by subsequent revelation (Job 2:7; 1 Chron. 21:1; Zech. 3:1; Luke 10:18; 2 Cor. 4:4; 1 John 3:8; Rev. 20:2).

His subtlety is shown by choosing the woman as the object of his attack. She was the weaker vessel, apparently having existed only a short time, and therefore more limited in knowledge and experience than the man.

The tempter also used the art of seduction, cunningly opening his barrage. Gradually, in the most adroit manner, he insinuated doubt that Eve might have gotten a wrong notion of the divine command. William Gesenius's rendering reflects more strictly the original: "Is it even so that God has said, You shall eat of no tree in the garden?" (*Gesenius's Hebrew and Chaldee Lexicon to the Old Testament Scriptures*). In other words, "It is impossible that a Being so good and kind could have so restricted you. You must have misunderstood." To suggest the unreasonableness of the divine command, the tempter perverted it, applying it not to one tree but to all, thus most insidiously sapping the foundation of the woman's faith.

2. And the woman said unto the serpent. Eve's reply was wise and corrected the tempter's distortion. **3.** But she did add to the command, **neither shall ye touch it.** Apparently she was beginning to distrust God's goodness, as the tempter was trying to persuade her to do. Moreover, her closing words, **Lest ye die,** seem to ascribe the prohibition to the dangerous nature of the tree itself rather than to the real peril of disobeying God. The evil one was quick to seize the advantage offered by a weakened faith to interject his outright lie.

4. Ye shall not surely die. This was a deliberate denial of God's word (2:17) and a plea to Eve's pride. Not only did the "liar, and the father of it" (John 8:44) assure his eager listener of complete impunity, but he brazenly held out

15

assurance of invaluable benefits from eating the fruit of the forbidden tree. **5. Your eyes shall be opened, and ye shall be as God** (*kē'lōhîm*, "like God"). What could be wrong in acquiring knowledge? Nothing, if it were acquired in the will of God and according to His word. But the knowledge the tempter offered Eve was contrary to both. Eve was tricked into a false or occult knowledge of the evil world of supernaturalism that would bring with it sorrow and misery (1 Tim. 2:14).

The Fall. 3:6. **6. The woman saw ... took ... and did eat.** These words summarize the history of every temptation and sin. First the outward object of attraction was presented, followed by the inner disturbance of the mind, generating increase and triumph of lust or passion, resulting in degradation and shame. There was appeal to (1) the lust of the flesh (carnal appetites)—**good for food**; (2) the lust of the eyes (indulgence of the tastes and affections of the animal spirit)—**pleasant to the eyes**; and (3) the pride of life (the gratification of the intellect's nobler faculties)—**a tree to be desired to make one wise** (cf. 1 John 2:16).

She ... gave ... unto her husband ... and he did eat. Adam, unlike Eve, was "*not* deceived" (1 Tim. 2:14, italics added). He deliberately sinned in siding with his wife against God and the divine commandment, evidently deciding it was impossible to face life without Eve. In disobeying God, he became the first but not the last man to court disaster by putting his wife before the word and will of God. As a free moral agent, Adam's sin was deliberate and presumptuous; moreover, the temptation was from without. As an innocent creature, there was no sinful tendency within him to dictate his sinful action. Eve listened to the tempter; Adam listened to his wife.

The Era of Moral Responsibility. 3:7. **7. The eyes of them both were opened.** They now knew evil experientially, with all of its attendant guilt, sorrow, shame, and misery. Hence, **they knew that they were naked.** The age of innocence ended (see comments on 1:28), and a new era of conscience and moral responsibility began. Fallen man was to abstain from all known evil and was accountable to do all known good. This meant that he, as God's creature, was obliged to keep the eternal moral law of God. To show man that as a fallen creature he could not keep the moral law to the degree necessary to meet the divine standard, approach to God by animal sacrifice was instituted. This emphasized man's helpless lost estate and pointed to the necessity of the finished work of Christ for man's salvation. These provisions were set forth in the Adamic Covenant (3:14-21; see v. 15). Man failed the specific test given him in this dispensation at the Flood (6:5), but the dispensation continues coterminous with other dispensations till the end of time (see 1:28).

They sewed fig leaves together. They displayed the natural bent of fallen men to cover rather than confess their guilt and to offer some sort of human activity or merit rather than trust in God's grace alone. Contrast their pitiable expedient with God's gracious undertaking anticipating redemption (3:21). The verb rendered "sewed" (Heb., *tāpăr*) means simply "to weave or plait" (Job 16:15). The "aprons" were simple girdles or loincloths (cf. 2 Sam. 18:11). The practice of sewing or pinning leaves together is common in Bible lands even in the present day. Umbrellas, baskets, mats, and other items are made of leaves woven or pinned together. What sort of leaves were used by Adam and Eve is not known for certain. Many conjectures have been made, but the fig leaf, because of its lobed nature, is not ideally adapted for the purpose.

God's Concern for Fallen Man. 3:8-14. **8-9. They heard the voice of the Lord God.** The LORD spoke. His voice was heard as He walked in the garden and made known His presence. **The Lord God called unto Adam.** He spoke and questioned Adam. The LORD discoursed freely with both Adam and his wife. How gracious was the "LORD God" to the first sinners. This was possible because He was beginning to work in redemption, signified by the coupling of His covenant-redemptive name, Jehovah (Yahweh; vv. 8, 13), with His creative name, God (*'Elôhîm*). This contrasts saliently with Satan's and Eve's use of only the name *'Elôhîm* in the temptation scene (3:1-6). The description of **the Lord God walking in the garden** is expressively anthropomorphic, as is the entire representation of Deity in the passage. It is fitting that the infinite God, in revealing Himself redemptively to finite man, should accommodate Himself to frail and faulty creatures. Only in this simple way could they understand Him.

Adam and his wife hid themselves. This was natural, for their fallen sinful nature was now uneasy in God's holy presence; their guilt and shame were laid bare. A room may appear clean under drawn shades, but when curtains are pushed aside and sunlight floods the place, every cobweb and speck of dust becomes glaringly visible. Fallen man from the beginning has been hiding from God's presence. Apart from trust in God's grace in Christ, sinners are uncomfortable when God manifests Himself. This is one reason why Gehenna, the eternal isolation ward for all sin and sinners (Rev. 20:11-15), is a necessary feature of the divine plan and purpose of the ages. Heaven would be hell for Satan, demons, and unregenerate men. In fact, if admitted, they would soon make heaven a hell. Because of this obvious fact, they will not be admitted (Rev. 21:8, 27; 22:11).

Where art thou? The divine interrogation was intended to show man *where* he was as a lost sinner, that he might see his need of the divine Savior. Jehovah-Elohim would impress upon fallen man from the start that the first step toward salvation is to see oneself utterly lost and helplessly undone in sin. Lost men today desperately need to realize *where* they are under divine condemnation, that they may see the need of divine pardon and justification.

10. I was afraid ... I was naked ... I hid myself. Adam confessed the plight of the fallen race. Sinners are fearful because they stand guilty and condemned before an infinitely holy God. They are, at best, uncomfortable and embarrassed in the divine presence; at worst, hostile and hateful. In any case, they are estranged from God and seek to avoid contact with Him. This is the natural result of spiritual death (2:17) into which the race was plunged by Adam's sin (Rom. 5:14-21).

11. Hast thou eaten of the tree ...? The divine questioning was continued further to bring Adam to a full confession of guilt, which he tried to avoid by evading any reference to the *cause* of his guilt by attracting attention to the *effect*. But his innocence could only have been forfeited by himself. The loss of it and his manifest shame proclaimed his transgression, and yet he tried studiously to palliate his own conduct. He had to be forced to make a tardy admission, and then it was only partial. He shoved the blame on the woman, apparently willing to make her the scapegoat to save his own hide.

GENESIS 3:11-15

It was undeniably true, of course, that she had offered him the fruit and urged him to partake of it, but that was no excuse for him to disobey God deliberately. Besides, he was not deceived, as the woman was (1 Tim. 2:14). His reference to his wife's influence to lessen his guilt was unmanly, as it was ungenerous. He sealed the proof that he was indeed a fallen sinful being by adding bold impiety to his already sad testimony.

12. The woman whom thou gavest to be with me. Adam even dared to attempt to throw the blame of his Fall upon God Himself! He subtly insinuated it was God's fault in giving him the helpmeet He did. Had he been permitted to live in his original state of solitude, he would have remained steadfast in his integrity, free from the elements of temptation and moral danger that existed as he was allied to his wife. It is not surprising that the divine Judge did not reply to Adam. His words were too foolish and groundless to merit a reply. Instead, God turned to the woman to hear what she would offer in her own defense.

13. The serpent beguiled me. The Hebrew verb in the causative stem means to "deceive, seduce, to trick into temptation and sin." No attempt was made at denial. Although Eve was not caught in the act of plucking and eating the fruit, the evidence was undeniable. At least she tacitly admitted her guilt. But following the sad example of her husband, to screen herself from the heavy penalties of her transgression, she pushed the blame for the whole tragedy upon the serpent. In doing so, she joined her husband in giving indubitable proof of the depravity into which the race had fallen as a result of succumbing to temptation to disobey God.

This juncture in the divine plan for the ages is of great significance. The sin and rebellion of Lucifer and the angels had left open the question of how God would react toward fallen creatures. He was to demonstrate His reaction in creating a new order called "man." He made man innocent. He would allow him to fall. Through man's Fall, God would provide a Savior. Through saved humanity the divine plan is to eventually establish a *sinless universe,* with all fallen angels and wicked men isolated in one place forever. Never again will sin arise to disturb the bliss of unfallen angels and redeemed and glorified men in happy fellowship with their Creator. A sinless eternity with all sin and sinners confined in Gehenna will be God's demonstration to all created intelligences of how He in infinite love and holiness dealt with the sin problem.

The Adamic Covenant. 3:14-19.
14-19. The Edenic Covenant (see 2:17) having been abrogated by the Fall, God placed fallen humanity under the Adamic Covenant. This covenant regulates the life of fallen man. Its conditions must remain, at least in part, as long as unglorified humanity is upon the earth. The Kingdom age will see a partial lifting of the curse (Rom. 8:21), but the full deliverance will not come until the new heaven and new earth (Rev. 21:1—22:5) of the eternal state.

The elements of the covenant are: (1) Satan's agent of the temptation of man was cursed (v. 14). From what apparently was the most beautiful, upright, highly intelligent creature among the Edenic animals, the serpent was degraded into a loathsome crawling reptile (Rom. 16:20; 2 Cor. 11:3, 14; Rev. 12:9), becoming a graphic warning in nature of the effects of sin. (2) The first enunciation of the gospel of grace was made with the promise of the coming Redeemer (v. 15). The Messianic line was begun in Abel and then in Seth, and then

18

went through Noah (6:8-10), Shem (9:26-27), Abraham (12:1-4), Isaac (17:19-21), Jacob (28:10-14), Judah (49:10), and David (2 Sam. 7:5-17), to Immanuel (Isa. 7:10-14; Matt. 1:20-23).

(3) The state of the woman was changed (v. 16). Her conception of offspring was multiplied (Eve evidently had many sons and daughters not mentioned in the abbreviated Genesis account). Motherhood was to be attended by sorrow and pain. The headship of man, necessitated by sin, was established (cf. 1:26-27; Eph. 5:22-25; 1 Cor. 11:7-9; 1 Tim. 2:11-14). (4) The delightful occupation of unfallen man in Eden was changed to rugged labor (3:18-19) as a result of the curse upon the earth (3:17). (5) Life was to be attended by inescapable sorrows (v. 17). (6) The aging process, eventuating in physical death, began and was passed on to the entire race (v. 19; Rom. 5:12-21). Spiritual death (alienation from God) and eternal death were also implied in the Adamic Covenant (2:17; Rev. 20:11-15), calling forth the promise of the coming Redeemer.

The Protevangelium Illustrated. 3:20-21. In verse 15 the protevangelium was announced, and in verse 21 it was dramatically typified for all posterity. God had rested (2:2-3) in a creation He had pronounced "very good" (1:31), but His creation rest was broken by man's Fall. God stopped resting in a perfect creation and began working to redeem a creation ruined by sin (cf. John 5:17; 9:4; 17:4). His redemptive work was initiated by the first announcement of the gospel (Lat., *protevangelium,* "original evangel"), which envisioned the tremendous opposition of Satan and his agents to the Good News of God's redeeming grace. God declared He would put "enmity" between Satan and the woman and between her descen-

dants and Satan's descendants.

The Hebrew word *'ēbâ* ("hostility") is derived from the verb *'ayab* ("to hate, to treat as an enemy, to be hostile to"). The very first enunciation of the gospel of grace through faith was cradled in a warning of conflict. It foreshadows the incessant activity of satanic powers to oppose the salvation of lost mankind and to resist the Good News by which the fallen race is to be rescued from sin and the power of Satan and demons.

The Savior would come through the woman's progeny (the Messianic line to Christ). "The seed of the woman" comprehends the children of God, and "the seed of the serpent" denotes the wicked unregenerate segment of the race (Matt. 23:33; John 8:44; 1 John 3:8). But since "the seed of the woman" focuses on an individual, whose miraculous birth gave Him a preeminent title to be called "the seed of the woman" (see Gal. 4:4), the designation constitutes the first great prophecy of the coming virgin-born, incarnate Son of God and Savior.

The intense conflict between good and evil and light and darkness centers in Him and Satan. "He" (Heb., *hû'*, "he, himself") is a personal pronoun, masculine gender (not "it") and stands in emphatic contrast to "thou" (*'attâ*), referring to Satan. So verse 15 should read, "He shall bruise thy head." The imagery reflects the snake's insidious habit of biting its victim in the heel or somewhere else behind it, and the victim's retaliation of striking at a serpent's head with a club to crush it. The same verb (*shûp,* "to lie in wait to attack, to strike suddenly," Job 9:17; Psalm 139:12 [NASB, marg.]; cf. Rom. 16:20) is employed to describe the attack upon the head and the heel in order to demonstrate that destruction was aimed at by both parties.

Wounds were to be received on both

sides, but Satan's utter defeat was assured. The bite of a serpent on a man's heel, when the poison infects the blood, is dangerous but not incurable. On the contrary, the crushing of the serpent's head spells destruction. Satan's head was potentially crushed at Calvary (Col. 1:13; 2:15). The believer's position "in Christ" is the basis of triumph over him now. At Christ's coming he will be cast into the abyss with the demons (Zech. 13:2; Rev. 20:1-3). During his last revolt after the Kingdom age, he will be cast into Gehenna (Rev. 20:10).

The effect of the protevangelium upon Adam was to produce faith. **20. And Adam called his wife's name Eve** (Heb., *ḥǎwwâ*, "life"). Actually, his wife must have appeared to be the mother of death, since her deception ended in her husband's disobedience, which introduced threefold death—spiritual, physical, and eternal death—into the human family. But by faith comprehending a better hope to come through her, Adam called her Eve ("life"), because the word signifies **the mother of all living.** The name envisioned especially Christ and all who live by Him (John 1:4). Thus, Eve's name compressed in itself the history of redemption and preserved for early mankind the blessed hope of a Redeemer in fulfillment of "the seed of the woman" assured in the protevangelium.

21. The Lord God (did) **make coats of skins, and clothed them.** Beautifully and dramatically portrayed in this gracious act is the divine undertaking in redemption to remove from man the guilt and shame of sin and clothe him with the divine righteousness (cf. 1 Cor. 1:30). This grand transaction to make man fit for the divine presence would necessitate the shedding of blood, for apart from the shedding of blood there could be no remission of sin (Heb. 9:22). Hence, the Lord God had to slay an

animal and thus shed blood to obtain the "coats [coverings] of skin" necessary to clothe the first sinners.

Here at the dawn of redemptive history God not only announced the one true gospel of salvation by grace through faith apart from human merit (Eph. 2:8-9), but He also illustrated it graphically for all the generations of lost, helpless sinners to follow. This one true and only gospel of salvation would be the target of satanic malignity and attack. God would make it plain for all in simple illustration that men might resist the devil's attempts to deny or pervert it by substituting his false gospel of works. Moreover, this occasion undoubtedly introduced animal sacrifices. Prefiguring the coming Redeemer, the sacrifices impressed upon fallen man the fact that God could only be approached by shed blood. They illustrate the gospel and show the necessity of simple faith in the coming Redeemer and His salvation. The highly perverted blood-sacrifice rituals in both ancient and modern polytheism hark back to the original institution of this approach to deity established by God Himself.

The Expulsion from Eden. 3:22-24. Tenderly and compassionately God lamented the sad condition into which man had lapsed by the Fall. **22. Behold, the man is become as one of us** is better rendered, "Behold the man! He was one of us!" Made originally in Our image and likeness, he was a holy and happy being, but look at him now. Look what sin has done to him. Look how tragic his state is! **To know good and evil.** This knowledge, as absolute, is an attribute of God (3:5), who is omniscient. But man, created with only the knowledge of good, acquired the experiential knowledge of evil through pride and disobedience, and in this manner fell into a state of sin and misery.

And now, lest he . . . take . . . of the tree

of life. By his Fall, man lost all claim to this tree. As a sacramental sign or pledge of that immortal life, which was to be the reward for obedience, fallen man might have deluded himself by thinking that eating the fruit would perpetuate his physical life and arrest bodily deterioration. Or he may have been tempted to continue eating it as an empty ordinance, which would have been a sacrilege, since it could not impart spiritual virtue to sinful man.

Therefore, the LORD God sent fallen man from the garden, for his earthly immortality would have been a curse instead of a blessing. With his corrupted nature and unlawful passions, man's cares and labors, sorrows and miseries, and endless existence in this world would have become intolerable. It was an act of mercy as well as justice on God's part, therefore, to remove man from all access to the tree. The very sight of it would have tended to fill his mind with bitter memories and constant disappointment.

23-24. Therefore the Lord God sent him forth . . . drove out the man. The first Hebrew verb means "to dismiss, expel, or eject." The second verb, which is somewhat more forceful, means "to drive away or expel." The combination of the two emphasizes ejection and dismissal under the influence of moral displeasure. There also is a suggestion that fallen man resisted the divine will and had to be forcefully ejected. **To till the ground.** The verb "till" (*'ābăḏ*) means "to serve, to labor in servile work, to cultivate the soil," which had been cursed, to make it produce (cf. 3:17-19). **From where he was taken** apparently refers to the original composition of man's body, formed from the soil (2:7), which he was now to cultivate to earn his living (3:18-19).

He placed ... cherubim, probably sphinxes or human-head lions, as an-cient Near Eastern iconography suggests (cf. Akk., *keribu,* which designates celestial interceding beings; see S. Langdon, *Epic of Creation,* p. 190, n. 3). The cherubim guard the divine, unapproachable holiness. They vindicate the divine righteousness (Exod. 26:1; 36:8), the divine mercy (Exod. 25:22; 37:9), and the divine government (1 Sam. 4.4; Psalm 80:1; Ezek. 1:22). In the most holy place, the divine glory took up residence between the outspread wings of the cherubim (Exod. 25:10-22).

And a flaming sword (lit., "the flame of a sword," that is, by the figure of *enallage,* "a swordlike, pointed flame"). **Which turned every way** (the Hebrew participle means "constantly turning or revolving in every direction"). It was continuously darting its flashing beams on every side to form an effective barrier to all access to the garden. The purpose was **to guard** (*shāmăr*) **the way** (*dĕrĕk,* "access") to **the tree of life,** protecting it against impious intrusion by sinful man "lest he put forth his hand, and take . . . of the tree of life, and eat, and live forever" (see v. 22). In this way fallen man would have perpetuated his misery endlessly, besides pursuing a course inconsistent with the economy that God was about to establish in the world for His fallen creatures. The curse, which entailed physical death, could only be removed by divine redemptive grace—not by fallen man's ingenuity or presumption.

3. CAIN AND ABEL—FALSE RELIGION VERSUS TRUE. 4:1-16.

The First Family. 4:1-2. **1. And Adam knew Eve . . . and she . . . bore Cain.** The Hebrew word translated "knew" is employed in the common Semitic sense (as in Akkadian) of knowing sexually. "And she . . . bore Cain" (Heb., *qăyĭn,* i.e., "gotten" or "acquired" from the verb *qānâ,* "get or gain"). Some stress the assonance in the original: Eve said, "I have acquired an acquisition." This view would indicate the ardor of Eve's joy in becoming a mother. She uttered the name in pious gratitude, indicating she viewed her child as a "possession" of great value. If this view is correct, then the name was given at birth, which is likely. Children normally retained the name given them, which often memorialized some incident surrounding their birth.

I have gotten a man from the Lord. (The Hebrew *'ēt* is used in the rare sense of meaning "from, by, or with"; see 49:25; Deut. 34:1; cf. Akk., *Itti-Bēl-balatu*, "With Baal is life.") There is good reason to believe, however, that Eve expressed the far deeper hope that her firstborn might be the Redeemer, the seed of the woman (3:15) promised the fallen race. "I have gotten a man . . . the LORD" (Heb., *Yahweh* or *Yahaweh*, "the coming One"; cf. Rev. 1:8). The objections to this interpretation that this name of God would in this case be invented by Eve, since Hebrew was not yet in existence at this primeval period, is pointless. Certainly if our first parents walked and talked with God and could comprehend the protevangelium, they could comprehend the names of God, no matter in what language their Hebrew equivalents were originally given. The use of *'ēt* in this case would be the sign of the definite accusation (before the proper name), a usage very common in contrast to the very rare use proposed by the King James rendering.

2. And she again bore his brother (lit., "she added to bear"), meaning she once more conceived and gave birth to Cain's brother. **Abel** (*hĕḇĕl*) means "a breath" or "breeze," or metaphorically, "vanity" or "transitoriness" (Psalm 39:5; Rom. 8:20). If the name was given at birth, it probably reflects Eve's painful sense of the short-lived existence and misery that sin had brought upon her offspring. Or if the name was bestowed upon Abel after his death, it would refer to his murder by his brother. In that case it would become the only name by which he was thereafter known. What he was called during his lifetime would then be presumed to be unknown.

How old Abel was in relation to Cain, or how many, if any, sons and daughters were born to them during the period of Abel's lifetime is a moot question. But there is every presumption that Adam and Eve had many sons and daughters, doubtless even during the first twenty-five years after the Fall. This would be in accord with 3:16: "I will greatly multiply thy . . . conception; . . . thou shalt bring forth children" (cf. 1:28; 3:20).

The First Occupations. 4:2b. Farming and cattle raising appear as man's earliest occupations. **Abel was a keeper of sheep,** literally, "one tending or feeding a flock" (*ṣō'n*, "a herd," which always included both sheep and goats in Bible lands). **But Cain was a tiller of the ground,** literally, "one serving the soil" (*'ᵃḏāmâ*, "red earth, arable land"). Cain's daily work was particularly reminiscent of the curse of sin (3:18-19). Moreover, he was the first (but not the last) to allow his occupation to turn him away from God and true worship of Him. Rationalistic objections against primitive man's inability to follow pastoral and agricultural pursuits at such an early period lose sight of the fact that God taught man all that was necessary to supply his needs (2:20). Adam certainly brought with him the experience he had acquired in Eden, as well as the implements he had used when he was expelled "to till the ground from whence he was taken" (3:23).

False Worship Versus the True.

4:3-4a. Man's Fall, with his consequent succumbing to sin and the power of Satan and demons (Col. 1:13; 2 Cor. 4:4), soon manifested itself in Cain's rejection of the divinely ordained method of sinful man's approach to God by blood sacrifice (3:21) in prospect of the coming Redeemer (3:15). Cain's apostasy illustrates the primeval working of these evil spiritual powers at the very beginning in turning men away from the *one* true gospel of salvation by grace through faith to Satan's counterfeit gospel of salvation by works (cf. Eph. 2:8-9; 1 Tim. 4:1-6; 1 John 4:1-6). Cain's false worship with a counterfeit gospel demonstrates the early rise of "doctrines of demons" (1 Tim. 4:1, NASB) in the sphere of religion (2 Cor. 11:3-4). This represents an activity demonic powers have carried on unceasingly and with tragic success from the dawn of human history.

3. In process of time (lit., "at the end of days," the original phrase denoting either an indefinite considerable length of time, 1 Kings 17:7, or a definite determinate period, 2 Sam. 14:26; 2 Chron. 21:19; Dan. 12:13). Here the occasion was some sacred anniversary. Doubtlessly by this time Adam's sons had large families of many sons and daughters, as well as grandsons and granddaughters, and appeared as the priestly representatives of their respective clans according to patriarchal custom (cf. 8:20; 12:7-8; 13:18; 26:25; 33:20; 35:6-7). The very fact that ungodly Cain chose to unite with godly Abel in a joint act of worship at the primitive sanctuary suggests that the time was divinely appointed to commemorate a holy season well known to both.

Cain brought of the fruit of the ground. The ground had been cursed because of sin and its produce wrung out of it only by dint of the sweat and toil of fallen humanity. From this that bore the taint of sin and the pollution of human works, Cain presented to the LORD **an offering** (*mĭnḥâ*). This was an unbloody "gift" of vegetables or grain by which he manifested himself at the start as a type of the unregenerate, natural man of the earth, destitute of any adequate sense of sin or need of atonement (2 Pet. 2:1-22).

Cain finds his counterpart in the unsaved religionist who believes in God and religion, but after his own will, and who rejects the gospel of salvation by grace through faith in Christ's blood (Jude 11). At the outset of redemptive history Cain became Satan's dupe to believe and promote the false gospel of salvation by human works. Cain's false worship represents the fountainhead of all spurious religion, the essence of which is man's approach to God in his own way rather than in God's prescribed way.

4. And Abel ... brought of the firstlings of his flock and of the fat thereof. Speiser's rendering captures the Hebrew: "For his part, Abel brought the finest of the firstlings of his flock" (AB, p. 29), literally, "the firstborn, namely, the fattest of them." As Keil and Delitzsch note, "the fattest of the firstlings, and not merely the first good one that came to hand" (KD, 1:109). But Abel's offering was more excellent than Cain's because it was a sacrifice in which atoning blood was shed (Heb. 9:22). It evidenced at once Abel's confession of sin and constituted an expression of his faith in a substitute eventually to be supplied.

That Abel simply brought these choicest lambs as a living present without slaying them is unthinkable in the light of the fact that "he obtained the testimony that he was righteous, God testifying about his gifts, and through faith, though he is dead, he still speaks" (Heb.

11:4, NASB). Abel declared to men everywhere and for all time that salvation is by faith alone in divine grace, totally apart from human works or merit, and is grounded in expiatory sacrifice.

Beginning with the Fall, Jehovah God decreed that sinful man could only approach Him through shed blood. This is clearly intimated in the coverings of skins with which God clothed the first sinners (3:21), which obviously came from slain animals. That Cain shed the blood of the lambs he presented is also indicated by the practice of the godly line through Noah (8:20-21), Abraham (12:7-8), Isaac (26:25), Jacob (31:54), and through the Levitical priesthood of the Mosaic economy. All these sacrifices reminded fallen man that he was a sinner and could draw near to God only on the basis of a substitutionary sacrifice. This was God's way for sinful man after the Fall.

The Divine Evaluation of Worship. *4:4b-5.* **4b. The Lord had respect unto Abel and to his offering.** The Hebrew verb *shā'â* means "to gaze at in scrutiny" and, on the basis of examination, "to show (or not show) regard for." The Akkadian cognate signifies "to look closely into." **5. But unto Cain and to his offering he had not respect.** How the LORD showed His favorable reaction toward Abel's offering and His unfavorable response toward Cain's offering is not revealed. Since the issue involved the true gospel and the right approach to God in contrast to the false gospel and the wrong approach to God, the occasion was momentous and merited a dramatic sign, which would be instructive to all future generations and serve as a warning against deception in the religious realm (cf. 1 Tim. 4:1-2; 1 John 4:1-2; cf. 2 Cor. 4:4; 11:3-4). It would seem a fair inference, therefore,

that the divine approval was displayed by the miraculous descent of fire, kindling the wood on the altar and utterly consuming the sacrifice, as was frequently the case in later times (15:17; Lev. 9:24; Judg. 6:21; 1 Kings 18:38; Psalm 50:3).

Cain was very angry. He keenly resented the divine disapproval of his worship and demonstrated his unregenerate condition in "having a form of godliness, but denying the power thereof" (2 Tim. 3:5). No doubt the incident transpired in the presence of congregated descendants over whom the fathers were priests, and so the rejection of his offering was construed as a public affront and severely wounded Cain's pride. It would be natural to vent his jealous rage against his brother, whose worship God had accepted. **His countenance fell.** His inner resentment was reflected outwardly.

The Basis of the Divine Evaluation of Worship. 4:6-7. **6. Why art thou angry?** The LORD remonstrated kindly but firmly with Cain, pointing out exactly why his offering had been disapproved: he had not brought a sin-atoning offering. Had he done so, he would have been accepted exactly as his brother Abel had been. The LORD was saying to Cain, and to the entire fallen race in Adam, **7. If thou doest well** (i.e., what is right in bringing the sin-atoning offering requisite for all lost sinners of Adam's fallen race as a token of faith in the divine redemptive grace), **shalt thou not be accepted? And if thou doest not well** (i.e., refuse to bring the right offering and thus to signify you do *not* believe the one true gospel of salvation by grace through faith), sin unatoned and unforgiven, like a wild beast, is couching (lurking) at the door of your heart. Or "sin is a *demon* (Akk., *rabiṣum*, "demon") at the door" (Speiser, AB, pp. 32-33). In this case

24

rōbēṣ would be an Akkadian loan word signifying "an evil spirit," not a participle meaning "couching."

And unto thee shall be his desire (sin personified or presented as an uncontrollable, beastlike "demon" of hate and murder). In other words, "He shall overmaster you and shortly cause you to murder your own brother in cold blood. This will be a dramatic reminder that you have rejected the expiatory blood of firstling lambs, and allowed sin to drive you to its inevitable end, that your case might illustrate how 'exceeding sinful' sin can become (cf. Rom. 7:13), and how utterly imperative it is that it be atoned for by the shedding of blood." To ward Cain off the dangerous course he was following, the LORD warned: "Unto thee" (emphatic) is sin's "desire" (*tᵉshûqâ*, from the root, *shûq*, "to run after with desire"). Or, "It will pursue you with intense promptings to do evil."

And thou shalt rule over him (sin personified as a beastlike demon). The Hebrew is stronger, the verb having imperative force, in which the divine warning is crystallized: "*But you* [emphatic] rule over him [i.e., over sin]." Or, "Do not let the demon of sin, with which you are dallying by refusing God's remedy, to get the upper hand in your life." The Hebrew word translated "accepted" means literally "a lifting up" (i.e., of the countenance, an infinitive from *nāśāʾ*, "to raise, lift up"), the index of a good conscience (Job 11:15). This would be the result of approaching God in the divinely prescribed way, as Abel had. Cain's anger at God's rejection was written on his face in his "fallen" countenance (v. 6). His faith, like his brother's, would bring the divine approval, which would be evident in the restoration of a cheerful facial expression.

Passages such as this and 3:15, 21 indicate how Jehovah Elohim from the very beginning revealed the true approach of fallen man to Himself through the medium of an animal's shed blood which, when viewed in faith, became a picture and a promise of a better sacrifice to come. From this primitive revelation the faithful—through Abel, Seth, Noah, Abraham, and others—carried on the great truth of salvation by faith in the coming Redeemer. Cain's posterity, rejecting the true gospel of faith for salvation by human works and merit, prostituted this originally pure system of sacrifice. The result was the perverted sacrificial systems of paganism so amply attested by ancient history and profusely illustrated by the findings of modern archaeology.

The Result of the Rejection of the True Gospel. 4:8-10. The divine rejection of his worship constituted a serious threat to Cain's status as priest as the firstborn of Adam's family, now increased to considerable numbers. Jealousy, rage, and hate rankled in his breast and grew to such proportions that demonic powers took over and drove him to the first murder. **8. And Cain talked with Abel his brother.** The Hebrew reads literally, "And Cain *said* to Abel his brother, 'Let us go in the field.'" The Masoretic text omits what Cain said, but this is recorded in the Samaritan Pentateuch, the Septuagint, the Syriac, and the Latin Vulgate. Apparently the original contained Cain's statement, which was accidentally omitted in the Hebrew, owing, no doubt, to the repeated clause "in the field" (cf. Speiser, AB, pp. 30-31).

Cain rose up against Abel, his brother. He rose up against Abel in the sense of falling violently upon him to kill him. **And slew him.** The frequent repetition of the words "his brother, Abel" (vv. 2; cf. 8, 9, 10, 11) highlights the unnatural atrocity of Cain's crime, the enormity of it increased by its being perpetrated in the name of religion. Abel not only became the first murder victim; he was the first martyr for the cause of the Word of God as revealed truth. By its Fall the human race came under the control of sin, Satan, and demons. Cain exposed himself to the domination of these evil powers by failing to accept God's redemptive grace and get the upper hand over sin (v. 7). Accordingly, sin through the advantage gained by Satan got the upper hand over Cain. He yielded to him who was "a murderer from the beginning" (John 8:44), to the extent of murdering his own brother.

9. Where is Abel, thy brother? Cain naturally would try to conceal all traces of his crime by burying the corpse. It is easy to imagine his pretending ignorance of what had happened to, or the whereabouts of, his brother and even joining a searching party. It is conceivable that he even engaged in religious observances at the established place of worship to allay suspicion. Under these circumstances he was challenged by the Shekinah presence itself. **I know not.** Cain's barefaced lie displayed him as a religious person under the power of him who is a liar and a murderer (John 8:44; 1 John 3:12). Cain is an illustration of the control that demonic forces exert in false religion (1 Tim. 4:1-2; 1 John 4:1-2), not only to turn away men from the truth, but to pervert the truth itself.

Cain was not only the first murderer; he was the first religious persecutor. He is an example of how wickedness and false religion often go hand in hand. The extent of his inward apostasy from God is indicated by his gross spiritual blindness (2 Cor. 4:4), which deluded him into the belief that he could escape the divine Omniscience. **Am I my brother's keeper?** Defiance grows with sin. Adam

and Eve had the fear of God in their hearts and owned their guilt, but Cain boldly denied it and displayed the deepest hatred and rebellion, coupled with a callous selfishness that evidences a sin-seared conscience (cf. 1 Tim. 4:2). At the moment when Cain revealed the depth of his wickedness, God charged him with his crime.

10. What hast thou done? The interrogative form emphasizes the gravity of Cain's crime. **The voice of thy brother's blood crieth unto me from the ground.** Literally, "thy brother's *bloods* crieth out," the plural of intensity implying that each drop of blood, shed so violently, kept screaming out its testimony of Cain's guilt. Every sin, as a violation of the divinely established moral order, cries out to the infinitely holy God for punishment. The violent effusion of human blood, being one of the severest violations of God's ordained economy, especially cries out for divine vindication. Added to this is the fact that the death of one of His saints is "precious in the sight of the LORD" (Psalm 116:15; cf. Heb. 11:4). Although the incriminating cry of sin may not be heard by the hardened transgressor himself, nevertheless it always reaches the ears of the supreme Judge of the universe (18:20-21; 19:13; Exod. 3:7).

The Curse of Redemptionless Religion. 4:11-14. **11. And now art thou cursed.** These words, so signally true of Cain, also apply to every lost member of Adam's race, whether religious or irreligious. In the case of Cain, they show what crimes religious people are capable of when they reject the divinely revealed way of access to God. Cain's curse, because of the severity of his crime, was pointedly specific. He was to be cursed **from the earth** (ᵃdāmâ, "the soil, the ground, humus"), which is personified as opening "her" mouth (since the word *earth* is feminine in Hebrew) to receive Abel's blood. This most naturally means that the soil, which Cain cultivated as a farmer, having imbibed innocent blood, will withhold its productivity in indignation at the frightful crime of fratricide. But since the word *'ᵃḏāmâ* may also mean "land" or "country," the sentence may be rendered, "Cursed art thou from *the land*," that is, "Your native haunts will no longer be safe for you; you will become a roving exile and seek asylum in distant lands." This view is supported by the latter part of verse 11, as the preceding interpretation is supported by the formed part of the verse and the preceding verse. Actually, both ideas form parts of the curse, which is, as it should be, very severe.

12. Cain was to be **a fugitive** (a participle from the verb *nûăʻ*, "to move to and fro, to rove, to wander," denoting one continually on the move) **and a wanderer** (a participle from the verb *nûḏ* "to move to and fro, to wander, to flee, to shake," signifying one constantly wandering about in trepidation and danger). The two participles form a hendiadys meaning "a restless wanderer."

13. No wonder Cain's reply to the LORD was **My punishment is greater than I can bear.** That the King James rendering is correct is suggested by the callously impenitent and hopeless attitude of Cain, generated by his unbelief and rejection of all offers of grace. This is true despite the fact that the primary meaning of the word translated "punishment" (*'āwôn*) is "iniquity, sin." Hence, the King James marginal reading, following the Septuagint and a majority of versions, has "Mine iniquity is greater than that it may be forgiven" (*nāśâ*, "to take away" when applied to God; "to bear" when applied to man). The Hebrew infinitive permits either the rendering "(I) can bear" or "(God) can

forgive," hence, the possibilities of translation and interpretation. Since Cain was not overwhelmed with the sense of the greatness of his guilt, but with the severity of the sentence, apparently the King James reading is to be followed.

Cain, therefore, proceeded to outline the chief elements included in the divine punishment. First, he was driven out (*gārăsh*, "forcibly expelled, ejected") from his native land (*'ᵃḏāmâ*, the same word as in v. 11, *q.v.*). Second, he had forfeited spiritual life as God's free gift on the basis of faith in redemptive grace, and so he was punished with spiritual death. **14. From thy face shall I be hidden.** He was to go on living as a mere natural, unregenerate man, separated from the symbols of the divine presence at the gates of the forfeited paradise. Third, he was penalized to be **a fugitive and a wanderer in the earth** (see comments on v. 12). Expelled from his home, he was to be banished as a solitary wanderer in hostile, uninhabited regions. Fourth, he was to be the object of the same hate and potential fate he had inflicted upon his innocent brother, Abel. **Any one that findeth me shall slay me** (*hārăg*, "kill with purpose and premeditation, murder," the same word as in v. 8).

He hated and murdered his own brother; others would hate him and seek to murder him. This can scarcely be restricted to the nearest kinsmen of Abel, even if the idea of the kinsman-redeemer (*gôʾēl*) is presumed to have existed at this primitive period. It is possible Cain was speaking under a morbid sense of fear and hopelessness generated by his deep apostasy and sin. Or, it is not impossible that the divine Judge, who Himself presided over the trial of the first murderer, in order to set the pace for future cases, would have caused men—who by this time had greatly multiplied on the earth—to have adopted this attitude toward the first murderer as a part of his punishment. In any case, Cain apparently represented this element, whether real or supposed, as an intrinsic part of the divine punishment.

But why was the sentence of death (capital punishment) not imposed upon Cain (cf. 9:5-6)? In this primeval state of society, his preservation as a special monument of the divine displeasure undoubtedly resulted in stamping a deeper brand of horror on the crime of murder than the forfeiting of Cain's life would have done. Then, too, the penalty of a long, lingering life of painful exile would be more severe than an instantaneous death. Sometimes he who dies is happier than he who lives and suffers many deaths.

God's Test Decision Against Murder. 4:15. **15.** The King James Version follows the Masoretic text, **Therefore** (*lākēn*), which links closely with Cain's contention that everyone finding him would kill him (v. 14). However, the Septuagint and most of the other ancient versions understood the Hebrew to be *lō' kēn* ("not so"), which would mean the LORD denied Cain's contention that everyone would kill him. The reason is the stiff penalty God imposed upon murder for all time as a result of the divine decision in the *first* case. "Not so. **Whosoever slayeth** (*hārăg*, the same word as in vv. 8, 14) **Cain, vengeance shall be taken on him sevenfold.** He shall be punished to the absolute limit, to the fullest extent, which can only signify capital punishment.

In this passage "sevenfold" intimates that anyone who would dare avenge Abel's death, or commit any act of murder whatsoever, would in the face of the once-for-all divine decision handed down to the race, be considered guilty of

a far more aggravated crime and be condemned to a far more summary and unrelenting punishment than the first murderer, who had no precedent of the divine decision and sentence.

And the Lord set a mark upon Cain. Various types of protective signs existed in the ancient biblical world (cf. Exod. 13:6-9; Deut. 6:8; 11:18; Ezek. 9:4). This sign *'ôt* ("mark, token, symbol, badge, warning") was some sort of symbolic figure or stamp, like a tattoo or brand, which carried with it the divine warning against murder. It served as a "memorial" of the original test decision rendered in the world's first murder trial. Guesses as to what it was are a dime a dozen. The truth is, we do not know what it was, whether a brand of the cherubim or of the fiery sword at Eden's gate (3:24), or something else. If it were essential to know, God would have revealed it. The sign was not to protect the murderer himself, but the divine warning against the heinousness of the crime of murder that the murderer represented. Hence, the sign was not for Cain's personal protection, because the law of capital punishment of Genesis 9:6-7 had not yet been enacted (see note on 4:15 in *New Scofield Bible*, p. 9).

As the law against murder existed before its inclusion in the Mosaic Decalogue (Exod. 20:13) and reflects the *eternal* moral law of God, as eternal as God is eternal, so the law of capital punishment—in connection with the institution of human government under the Noahic Covenant—represents God's unchangeable character and was in force from the beginning of the human race, as is revealed here. In Genesis 9 it was formally instituted as the basis of human governmental authority so man might curb violence by the God-sanctioned principle that he who willfully takes another's life shall forfeit his own life. This divine principle, widely rejected today, must realistically be faced by governments that would control crime.

Cain's Departure from God's Presence. 4:16. **16. Cain went out from the presence of the Lord.** Literally, "Cain went forth from the face [appearance] of the LORD." Condemned to be a restless wanderer, no longer could or would Cain remain near Eden, where the cherubim and the revolving fiery sword had symbolized the divine presence, and where God, somewhere in the general vicinity, had revealed Himself to his brother Abel and so patiently and condescendingly reasoned with Cain concerning true religion and the right approach to God. Cain's unbelief and rejection of the gospel of faith and salvation by divine grace sealed him in spiritual death, and God's face in His revealed presence was no longer comfortable or desirable.

The curse of sin had its final effect on him. When he had every opportunity to know God, he glorified him not as God, neither was thankful, but became vain in his own imagination and his foolish heart was darkened (see Rom. 1:21). **And dwelt in the land of Nod.** Literally, "the land of wandering" was the symbolic place name for Cain's retreat beyond Eden. The retreat of the Mesopotamian flood hero, Utnapishtim, is similarly located "faraway, at the mouth of the rivers" (*Epic of Gilgamesh*, Tablet II, l. 196), east of the head of the Persian Gulf (see 2:10-14).

4. CAIN'S LINE—THE EARLIEST CIVILIZATION. 4:17-24.

The First City. 4:17. With the progeny of Cain began the satanic world system, which consists of humanity organized under the evil principles of greed, selfishness, ambition, force, and pleasure.

Cain's departure from God's presence, and the godlessness that this move engendered in his descendants, gave Satan the hold upon the human race that made possible the beginnings of this evil system, which the New Testament so solemnly warns against (cf. 1 John 2:15-17).

17. And Cain knew his wife. She, of course, was one of the many daughters of Adam or of Adam's numerous sons. Marriage among relatives was necessary in the infancy of the race, and such unions were not harmful when the race was young and virile. Hence, no laws against incest existed and were not promulgated till much later (Lev. 18:9), when the need arose for them.

And she ... bore Enoch: and he builded a city. Enoch became "the founder of a city," literally, "and he became one building a city" in the sense of establishing or beginning to construct it. The "city" or village (*'îr*, "town, hamlet") was doubtless a settlement of rude huts made of boughs, plastered with clay, and thatched with grass. But this simple hamlet was the precursor of all later towns and the harbinger of all civilized city life. Its settled mode of life initiated a new stage in the development of human society, stimulating the invention of arts and crafts mentioned in connection with Cain's line. Cainite civilization, given here in bird's-eye view, was destroyed by the Flood. Archaeologically, no definite traces of it have been found, but it may have been as splendid as Greece and Rome. But it was godless, and its moral, not its material, state (Rom. 1:18-23) brought it to ruin, for it was the criterion of divine judgment (6:5-7).

Cain's Family to Lamech. 4:18. **18. Enoch ... Irad ... Mehujael ... Methushael ... Lamech.** No details are given of these pre-Flood patriarchs. The bare mention of their names reveals how little estimation God places upon worldly and ungodly greatness and power. Important parallels exist between the lists of antediluvian patriarchs, recorded here and in the following chapter, and Mesopotamian traditions preserved in the Sumerian list (see Thorkild Jacobsen, *The Sumerian King List*, pp. 70 ff.). The very fact of similar compilations and the sharp diluvian division are significant common features. The purpose of such data is quite similar in both instances. Just as the Sumerian list aimed at bridging the gap between creation and the Flood, the Genesis account sought to trace the generations between Adam and Noah. The connecting thread was important to the ancients. Archaeology has shed light on these names. Methushael, for instance, is now known to be Akkadian, reflecting *mutu-să-ili* ("man of God"). Lamech is literally Lemech, the Hebrew pausal form of the name having been adopted by the English translators instead of the actual name.

Lamech's Family, and Cultural Advance. 4:19-22. **19.** The cultural advance is associated with the introduction of polygamy and moral decline. **Lamech took unto him two wives.** This is the first recorded instance of polygamy. He is the only descendant of Cain of whom any memorials have been preserved. Both notations concerning him are very significant. First, his bold innovation on the original monogamous institution of marriage produced a serious demoralizing effect on the pre-Flood world and hastened its ruin. Second, his heading a family that achieved great fame in the arts and sciences demonstrates how scientific progress, as in our day, is often accompanied by spiritual ignorance and moral decline. **Adah** ("beauty") and **Zillah** ("shadow") were Lamech's wives. Their names give an

inkling of the position of a primary and a secondary wife. Mesopotamian king lists, as here in the Cainite line from Adam to the Flood, sometimes interrupt their bare statistics to present similar incidental comment about a specific entry.

20. For example, the Khorsabad List (JNES 13 [1954]: 210 ff.) enumerates the first seventeen rulers as "dwelling in tents," using an analogous participial form (1. 10), as occurs in the notice that **Jabal ... was the father** (ancestor) **of such as dwell in tents ... and ... have cattle.** The stem "dwell in" in Hebrew applies to *keeping* "both tents and cattle" (Speiser, AB, p. 35), so Speiser renders it, "who keep tents and cattle." Lamech's wife Adah also bore **Jubal** (v. 21). He was the ancestor "of all who handle lyre and pipe" (Speiser). The lyre was an ancient stringed instrument, while the pipe was a wind instrument.

22. And Zillah, she also bore Tubalcain, "a forger of all kinds of implements [*hrsh*] of copper (bronze) and iron" (literal trans.). The Hebrew word *lāṭăsh* means "to whet, sharpen, forge." Brass was a late discovery, the Hebrew *neḥōshĕt* originally denoting copper, hardened with alloy to form "bronze." Iron (*bărzĕl*) did not come into general use till after 1200 B.C., so many critics think this is a chronological error. But meteorite iron was known in very early times. Besides, it is not impossible that the Cainite civilization might have discovered the secret of making iron, and that it was lost as a result of the Flood.

The Song of Lamech. 4:23-24. This passage constitutes the most ancient piece of verse in existence, perhaps suggesting that poetry and literature in general had their origin with Lamech as part of the invention of the arts and sciences that came into being in the line of Cain. But the passage has greatly perplexed expositors, for it is commonly construed as neither containing doctrine nor fact worthy of historical preservation. But this assumption is doubtless the reason for its true meaning not being understood. Apparently the poem deals with the subject of murder and its punishment. Lamech, who had committed murder in self-defense, defends his action as perfectly justifiable in contrast to the premeditated, cold-blooded murder Cain committed:

A man I killed because he wounded me.
A young man because he assaulted me.
If Cain be avenged sevenfold,
Then Lamech seventy-sevenfold [author's translation].

If anyone would attempt to murder Lamech because he accidently in self-defense killed a man who attacked him, let him remember the case of Cain (v. 15). If anyone who killed Cain, a murderer guilty of the premeditated act, was to be punished sevenfold, how much more grievous will be the punishment of anyone who would kill Lamech, who was not guilty of premeditated murder. In the case of Cain, God's punishment was more severe than death and Cain's life was to be a perpetual reminder of the seriousness of the crime of murder and the sanctity of human life. In Lamech's case, the distinction is made between accidental, unpremeditated killing in relation to the sanctity of human life.

The sanctity of Lamech's life furnishes the example of the sanctity of anyone else's life. The "seventy-sevenfold" (cf. seventy times seven, Matt. 18:21-22), meaning "to the fullest," can signify nothing less than the death penalty for killing another premeditatively and in cold blood. Anyone who would kill Lamech would be punished in the most absolute sense, that is, he would incur the sentence of capital punishment.

5. SETH'S LINE—THE GODLY SEED. 4:25-26.

The Parentage of the Future Redeemer. 4:25-26a. The son whom Eve bore to replace the promised seed in Abel was named *Seth* (Heb., *shēt*, "appointed," in assonance with *shat*), whom God "set" in the place of Abel. Eve acted in faith, being prompted by some divine intimation that this newborn son was to be the heir of the promise (Gen. 3:15). How tenderly God undertook to dispel the despondency of the parents, doubly bereaved of two of their children—of Cain by banishment and Abel by violent death. Seth's birth apparently took place only a comparatively short time after Abel was murdered and long before the events narrated in connection with the six generations of the Cainites. This was necessary to avoid a break in the account, which would have impaired its symmetry.

26. To Seth . . . there was born a son . . . called . . . Enosh. Seth's son was Enosh (*'enôsh*, meaning "man as a weak, mortal being," from *'ānāsh*, in the passive, "be ill, weak, sick, sorrowful"). The very name that Seth chose for his son denotes his comprehension of man's sinful weakness and his need for divine redemption and the promised Redeemer.

The Godly Seed Manifests Its Faith. 4:26b. **Then** refers to the establishment of the godly line in Seth and Enosh and its manifestation of faith. This stands in contrast to the ungodly line of Cain, who "went out from the presence of the LORD" (v. 16), and evidenced its unbelief in the lost and helpless condition of fallen man and the promise of redemptive grace through the coming Redeemer.

31

Then began men to call upon the name of the Lord. Literally, the sentence is: "Then it was begun to call upon the name of the LORD." The impersonal construction is better translated as a passive: "Then the name of the LORD was begun to be called upon" by the godly Sethites. Appropriately, it is the name of Jehovah (Yahweh) that is invoked, the personal name of Deity as revealing Himself in covenant and redemptive relationship to men. The occurrence of the names God (Elohim) and Jehovah (Yahweh) in verses 25 and 26 shows the groundlessness of the higher critical theory of different authors employing the different names of Deity, J (Jehovah) and E (Elohim). Neither is this usage of Jehovah in this passage at variance with Exodus 3:14 and 6:3.

Critics contend that these latter passages indicate "that the name Yahweh had not come into use until the time of Moses" (Speiser, AB, p. 37). But critics confuse the use of the name Yahweh from the beginning with the redemptive revelation of that name in the deliverance from Egyptian bondage. The fact that with the reestablishment of the godly line (after Abel's murder) in Seth and Enosh, men "*began . . . to call* upon the name of the LORD," must mean that there was a spiritual revival in Enosh's day. Both Adam and Seth had called on the name of Jehovah, that is, they believed in, loved, trusted, and obeyed Him. There was a quickening of faith in Enosh's time among the godly. Some think this signifies that numerous Cainites returned to the worship of Jehovah.

C. DEATH REIGNS FROM ADAM TO NOAH. 5:1-32.

The Record of Adam's Family. 5:1-5.
1. This is the book of the generations of Adam, that is, the record of the line of Adam. For meaning of "generations" (Heb., *tôleḏôt*), see comments on 2:4. The Hebrew word *sēp̄er* ("book") also means a "register or record." A résumé of Adam's creation **in the likeness of God**, a subject already presented in the opening section of Genesis (1:26-27; 2:7), is given here to supply a few more details and to prepare the reader for the tragic story of man's moral collapse and judgment in the Flood. How could he who was made in "the likeness of God" (in the general similitude of Deity) fall to such abysmal depths of sin and godlessness, which would require his being wiped out in catastrophic punishment?

2. Male and female created he them. The Hebrew word *'āḏām* ("Adam"), like the Latin *homo* and the English "person," is generic, including both sexes (1:26; 2:7, 21, 23; 6:7). It was originally an appellative (a descriptive or character name). But by frequent use it came to be applied as the personal name of the first man, being in Hebrew commonly prefixed by the definite article. Even in Genesis 3:17, where the article does not occur, "Adam" clearly designates the progenitor of mankind (5:3). Other parts of Scripture clearly have the same reference (Luke 3:38; Rom. 5:14; 1 Cor. 15:45; 1 Tim. 2:13-14; Jude 14). This revelation refutes false theories that deny that the human race sprang from *one* pair, or that claim it developed or evolved from lower forms of life, working its way out of ignorance and barbarism. Adam, as the natural head of the human race (Luke 3:38), is a contrasting type of Christ, the Head of the new creation (Rom. 5:14; 1 Cor. 15:21-22, 45-47).

3. Adam lived an hundred and thirty years. These were lunar years (7:11; 8:5; cf. comments on 8:14 in *New Scofield Reference Bible*). **And begot a son in his own likeness.** Both physically and mor-

32

ally Seth inherited the corrupt fallen nature of Adam, as all men do (cf. John 3:6). This fact is particularly noted because of its vast theological importance. Even though Seth took the place of righteous Abel and was in the godly Messianic line, he nevertheless was a part of fallen humanity and needed redemption as much as the ungodly Cainites and all men. The genealogy of chapter 5, which is drastically curtailed, gives only the name of that person who formed the connecting link in the chain of direct Messianic descent.

Since Adam and the fathers in this list were all quite advanced in life at the time of the birth of the son who is recorded, the presumption is that they were already heads of a very numerous family when he was born and that he is singled out only because of his lineal connection with the coming Redeemer. Born in his father's 130th year, Seth was certainly among the youngest of Adam's very large family. Other heirs of the promise (3:15), such as Isaac, Jacob, and Judah, were younger sons.

5. Adam lived ... nine hundred and thirty years. The relatively high figures of the biblical genealogy turn out to be exceptionally moderate in comparison to the extrabiblical sources imbedded in Mesopotamian traditions, which are attested as early as the third millennium B. C. (cf. Jacobsen, *The Sumerian King List*) and as late as the third century B. C. by the Babylonian priest Berossus in his Greek work on Babylonian history. In these accounts the number of rulers (including the flood hero) varies between nine and ten (sometimes less). Their respective reigns run from 18,600 to almost 65,000 years. For the same period the Cainite list, which gives no ages, records eight patriarchs. The Sethite genealogy catalogs ten.

The extremely modest numbers of the biblical account, comparatively speaking, not only reflect the actual life-span of pre-Flood men, but capture by inspiration the actual line of the Redeemer to come. Actually there is no connection between the two, either in the names presented or the persons (patriarchs in the biblical account in contrast to kings in the cuneiform accounts), but both accounts illustrate the ancients' persistent interest in genealogies. Unbroken lineage meant a secure link with the remotest past as well as a firm basis from which to face the future.

And he died. With this doleful refrain the notice of each of the pre-Flood patriarchs is concluded. Their long lives might have appeared to exempt them from earthly mortality. Yet the experience of all of them attested the certainty of the divine pronouncement that "In the day that thou eatest" of the tree of the knowledge of good and evil "thou shalt surely die" (2:17). It also proved how base was the serpent's lie, "Ye shall not surely die" (3:4).

Record of Seth's Posterity. 5:6-8. Seth was 105 when he begot Enosh (see comments on 4:25-26). Certainly Seth had many sons (and daughters) before he reached the advanced age recorded for the birth of Enosh. But Enosh alone is reported because he was to be in the line of the promised Redeemer (3:15). In contrast to the Cainite patriarchs, who had no part in redemptive history and whose family was soon to be extinguished, the line of the Sethites is carefully traced in its Messianic aspect to demonstrate God's fidelity to His promise concerning a Savior. Seth died at the age of 912, living 18 years less than Adam, his father.

Record of Enosh's Posterity. 5:9-11. Enosh was 90 when his son Kenan (cf. Luke 3:37), who was to be in the Messianic line, was born. After the birth of

Kenan, Enosh lived 815 years and begot sons and daughters. Enosh lived 905 years, 7 years less than his father and 25 years less than his grandfather, Adam.

Record of Kenan's Posterity. 5:12-14. When Kenan ("acquisition") was 70, he fathered Mahalalel ("praise of God"), who was to be in the promised line. Perhaps his faith glimpsed this in the name he gave the child. After Mahalalel's birth he lived 840 years, and during this long span had additional sons and daughters. He lived 910 years, 20 years less than Adam and 5 more than his father, Enosh.

Record of Mahalalel's Posterity. 5:15-17. Mahalalel was 65 when he begot Jared ("descent"), the son who was to carry on the redemptive line. After the birth of the promised seed, Mahalalel lived 830 years and had more children. His whole life-span was 895 years.

Record of Jared's Posterity. 5:18-20. When he was 162, Jared fathered Enoch, the most celebrated of the pre-Flood patriarchs. Jared lived 962 years, just 7 years less than Methusaleh, the oldest man recorded in the Bible.

The Account of Enoch's Translation. 5:21-24. Enoch's name apparently means "dedicated" and bespeaks his early godly upbringing and devotion to the LORD's service. The inspired record in cataloging this patriarch departs from the set form employed of all the rest in two remarkable features. Instead of noting that he lived so many years after the birth of the son in whom the promised seed was continued, it declares that he "walked with God." Also, in place of the stereotyped ending of each entry that "he died," it is said, "he was not," that is, he *lived*. He "was translated that he should not see death" (Heb. 11:5).

22. Enoch walked with God, literally, "*the* God," that is, the (one true) God, a

Person who deigns to have fellowship with His creatures. The figure of walking, taking one step at a time, admirably describes the process of living a life. Twice repeated (vv. 22, 24), this feature of Enoch's life is emphasized by repetition. His "walking with God" is predicated after the birth of the son in whom the redemptive line was to be realized. It signifies his occupation with God's redemptive grace and the divine purpose for the ages, for his is the earliest recorded revelation of the second advent of Christ (Jude 14-15).

24. He was not; for God took him. The idiom means Enoch disappeared from the earthly scene (cf. 37:30; 42:13; Job 7:8; Jer. 31:15). The reason? God *took* him, the Hebrew word *lāqăḥ* meaning "to seize or take hold of and snatch away." It is the same idea as to be raptured: "be snatched away or suddenly caught up" (Gr., *harpageomai*, 1 Thess. 4:17). Enoch, who was raptured (caught up out of the world) and "translated" (changed in the sense of receiving a glorified body) "that he should not see death" (Heb. 11:5) before the Flood, is a type of church saints who are to be translated before the Tribulation judgments (1 Thess. 4:14-17).

The Record of Methusaleh's Posterity. 5:25-27. Methusaleh's name means "man of sending," evidently referring to water (cf. Siloam, "sent," John 9:7, the name given to a pool at Jerusalem). Apparently his godly father Enoch gave him this name as prophetically anticipative of the Flood as a judgment upon sinful humanity (cf. Jude 14-15). His life-span (969 years) is the longest recorded of any other person in the Bible. His son Lamech, born when he was 187, constituted the Messianic link.

The Record of Lamech. 5:28-31. Lamech begot Noah in the line of the promised Redeemer when he was 182. Noah's name, denoting "rest" (from *nūăḥ*, "to rest"), demonstrates Lamech's faith, suggested by the confident tone with which the father explained the import of his son's name. **29. This same shall comfort us.** We would expect "give us rest" (as the Septuagint renders it), but the Hebrew has "comfort" (*piel nīḥam*, "console") us. Hence, Jewish interpreters, who regard this as explanatory of the name Noah ("rest"), but not as indicative of its etymological significance, are evidently correct.

They also contend that Noah invented instruments of agriculture and in some measure rescued the soil from the barrenness of poor tillage. In this way, they hold, Noah "comforted" men from the work and the toil of their hands **because of the ground which the Lord hath cursed.** In support of this view, it is said this is why Noah, after the Flood, was called "a husbandman" (Heb., "a man of the soil," i.e., "a farmer," 9:20). Noah's father, Lamech, lived 777 years.

Record of Noah. 5:32. Noah was a half century old before his son Shem, who was to be the link in the Messiah's lineage, and his other two children, who were destined to survive the Flood, were born. Certainly Noah had other children before his advanced age of 500 years. Like the other pre-Flood patriarchs, they were passed over in this drastically shortened list, which still runs into a chapter of considerable length.

It is possible in these genealogies in the regularly recurring formula "A lived ___ years and begat B. And A lived after he begat B ___ years and begat sons and daughters." B may not be a literal son of A, but a distant descendant. If so, and this is in perfect accord with Hebrew idiom involved in the usage of such terms as *beget, bear, father,* and *son,* the age of A is his age at the birth of the child from whom B was descended. Many centuries, therefore, may intervene between A and B (see J. Raven, *Old Testament Introduction,* pp. 132-35; and M. F. Unger, *Introductory Guide to the Old Testament,* pp. 193-94). The purpose of the genealogies is *not* chronological, but to trace the thread of the promised Redeemer (3:15).

32. Noah begot Shem, Ham, and Japheth. Although Shem ("name, fame") in this record has precedence over Japheth, Japheth was the oldest and evidently Ham was the youngest of the three (cf. 10:21; 11:10). Shem stands first because he was in the Messianic line. In his posterity the knowledge of the true God was to be preserved, assuring him the "fame" or "renown" his name prophetically anticipated. Japheth is derived either from *yāpâ*, "beauty" or "fairness" of complexion, corresponding to the physical features of the Japhetic or Indo-European races, or *pātâ*, "open," in causative stem "to make wide, spread abroad."

Ham is from the root *ḥāmăm*, "be hot," perhaps containing the idea of being hot blooded sexually (cf. 9:21-25). S. P. Tregelles (*A New Hebrew-English Lexicon,* p. 285), however, construes Ham's name as pointing to the fact that his descendants occupied the southern or hot regions of the earth (10:6-20). Some scholars compare the Hebrew root with the Coptic word denoting "sunburned, swarthy, black," and explain Ham's name as the ancestor of those who should inhabit torrid regions.

D. NOAH AND THE FLOOD. 6:1—8:22.

1. JUDGMENT UPON FALLEN MAN'S SIN. 6:1-22.

The Wickedness of Antediluvian

Mankind. 6:1-4. **2. The sons of God saw the daughters of men ... and they took them wives.** This extremely puzzling and difficult passage has a very pointed connection with the Flood. It gives the basic example of the fearful moral lawlessness that occasioned the catastrophe. This was the comingling of "divine beings" (lit., "sons of God," which inescapably denote "angels," Job 1:6; 2:1) with "daughters of men," a Hebraism meaning simply "human daughters." "Here ... the main stress is on 'immortals' as opposed to 'mortals'" (Speiser, AB, p. 44).

Scholarly efforts to make "sons of God" pious Sethites and "the daughters of men" ungodly Cainites simply do not come to grips with the difficulties of the passage. The sample sin plumbs the depths of pre-Flood wickedness. It was far more serious than mixed marriages between believers and unbelievers. It was a *catastrophic outburst of occultism* such as will precipitate the return of the days of Noah at the end of the present age at the glorious advent of Christ (Matt. 24:24, 37-39). The awful invasion from the realm of evil supernaturalism by the *fallen* angels precipitated *incubi* and *succubae* phenomena of Satanism and extreme spiritistic cults. It is true the elect, unfallen angels are sinless. They neither marry nor are given in marriage (Matt. 22:30; Mark 12:25). But who will assert that the fallen angels cannot cohabit with "human daughters" (females of the human race)?

3. My Spirit shall not always strive with man. This construes the Hebrew form *din* to mean "to judge, render a judicial decision against one," and agrees best with the context. The meaning is to be taken in the sense of the Holy Spirit bringing a judicial charge of guilt against the pre-Flood sinners through the ministry of God's servants warning them of their lawlessness. This ministry of God's Spirit convicting of sin, righteousness, and approaching judgment (cf. John 16:8-11) would soon be terminated by Noah's condemning that wicked world through his faith (Heb. 11:7). By His Spirit, God in Christ had been inspiring Enoch, Noah, and doubtless other contemporary prophets (1 Pet. 3:18-20; 2 Pet. 2:5; Jude 14-15) to proclaim repentance to the antediluvians. But now the Spirit would cease His work. These reprobates would be given up to their sin (Hos. 4:17; Rom. 1:28) to face inevitable doom (Rom. 1:18; 2 Thess. 1:7-9; Rev. 20:11-15).

For that he also is flesh is better translated "since he is but flesh" (AB), or "because they [men] are flesh" (Septuagint, Syriac, Targum Onkelos). Adopting this reading, the meaning would be: "My Spirit will not always strive with man [mankind] since he is but flesh." In belonging to an order created "a little lower than the angels" (Psalm 8:4-6; Heb. 2:7, 16), man's sin of cohabiting with fallen angels constituted such flagrant rebellion against God's ordained order of creation, and produced such confusion, that He had to destroy man from the earth. Unless He had done so, the *entire* race would have become a mongrel breed. Satan would have become triumphant.

Only through a godly remnant and a new start would the human race be preserved so that the Messiah eventually would come to identify Himself with the *human* race to redeem it. The occult invasion of humanity that precipitated the Flood was a satanic attempt to take over the earth and banish the name of God and His Christ from this planet. This is the basic cause of the Flood given succinctly in this passage, which is introductory to the great cataclysm nar-

36

rated in detail from 6:5 to 8:22. **Yet his days shall be an hundred and twenty years.** This statement refers to the limitation God's grace set in deferring judgment to that period (cf. 1 Pet. 3:19-20).

4. There were giants in the earth. Literally, "It was then that the *Nephilim* appeared on earth." The Nephilim (*nepīlīm*, "fallen ones," from *nāpăl*, "to fall") were the spirit-human, angelic-demon offspring of the sons of God (angels) and daughters of men (human females). The King James rendering "giants" of the Hebrew *Nephilim* reflects the Septuagint rendering (*gigantēs*, "earth born"). The thought is of spirit beings (fallen angels, demonic powers) cohabiting with women of the human race producing what later became known in pagan mythologies as demigods, partly human and partly superhuman.

This is *not* mythology but the truth of the intermixture of the human race with the angelic creation from which later mythology developed "the Titans" (giants, partly superhuman). Greek mythology (Hesiod, Pseudo-Apollodorus) recalls such beings. Zeus, one of the great gods, had to battle with a group of giants known as Titans. Phoenician lore (earlier than the Greek) also echoes a similar tradition. Hittite texts containing Hurrian myths have been discovered that carry the idea back even earlier to the source of all of this in the revealed facts given in 6:1-4. Gilgamesh, the hero of the Babylonian flood story, was himself a demigod, partly human, partly divine, or superhuman.

The sons of God came in unto the daughters of men. This means it was when the angelic beings had united with human daughters that the Nephilim appeared on earth. **And also after that.** The Nephilim are mentioned as a giant race later (Num. 13:33). The context seems to imply, however, that the people found by the spies were like the very Nephilim of old. The expression "came in unto" refers to the male who visits a woman's quarters (cf. 30:16; 38:16). Angelic beings are sexless (never spoken of as female). But *fallen angels* can in a manner incomprehensible to man in the natural realm assume maleness and have sexual intercourse with females of the human species.

Occult literature is replete with such suprahuman phenomena illustrating the general lawlessness of occultism, here seen in perversion of God's ordained orders of creation and the laws that govern sex in the human order (cf. 1:27-28; 2:21-24). **Mighty men** were heroes or warriors, superior physically and intellectually as demigods. **Men of renown** or "fame" (Heb., "men with a name"). (Cf. *Gilgamesh Yale Tablet*, col. 5, l. 7.) "A name that endures will I make for myself."

Announcement of Coming Judgment. 6:5-7. **5. And God saw that the wickedness of man was great.** The depth of man's wickedness is revealed by what has already been described—the invasion of the sphere of the natural by the realm of evil supernaturalism, which is occultism. Other features are added. **Every imagination of the thoughts of his heart was only evil continually.** Satan and demonic powers first captured the thinking processes and then dominated the conduct of the antediluvians (cf. vv. 11-12; 2 Cor. 4:4; 2 Tim. 3:8). God is dramatically represented anthropomorphically: "God *saw* ... it repented the LORD [Jehovah] ... it *grieved* him at his heart ... the LORD *said*" (vv. 5-6, italics added). This is a literary device to give vividness to the narrative. God cannot change (Num. 23:19; 1 Sam. 15:29; Mal. 3:6; James 1:17), nor can He, like His human creatures, be affected by sorrow. But the language is an accommodation to finite minds. In terminology suitable to human nature, God announced His divine displeasure at man's colossal sin and His intention to destroy the degenerate race from the earth. Clearly God (Elohim), the Creator of man, is identified here and throughout the entire narrative with Jehovah (Yahweh), the God of covenant and redemption.

7. I will destroy man ... from the face of the earth. The verb *māḥâ*, "to rub over or wipe away," signifies God would wipe man off the face of the earth (cf. 7:4). "I will wipe [destroy] Jerusalem as a man wipeth a dish, wiping it, and turning it upside down" (2 Kings 21:13).

Indication of Divine Grace. 6:8. **8. But Noah found grace in the eyes of the Lord.** He "found" in the sense that he "experienced" God's grace. This was wholly on the basis of faith, and it intimates that he approached God by bloody sacrifice (cf. 8:20-21), envisioning the coming Redeemer (3:15, 21). He found acceptance in God's infinitely holy presence because he confessed his sinfulness and looked forward to God's provided righteousness (cf. Rom. 3:25). His exemplary conduct and holy life (v. 9) were the outward evidence (not the basis) of his acceptance before the Lord (Heb. 11:7).

This is the first mention of "grace" in the Bible, and with it ends "the generations of Adam" (5:1). This section has traced man from the Creator's hands until his wickedness became so terrifying that divine justice demanded its punishment, but it concludes with a gleam of hope. Jehovah's purpose was not extermination but regeneration; a new start would assure the promise of the coming Savior. Hence, with the termination of "the generations of Adam"

a new section is introduced with "the generations of Noah" (6:9). This portion of the interwoven genealogical framework of the book of Genesis extends from 6:9 to 9:22 (see comments on 2:4*a*). In Noah the new beginning would be made. The Messianic line would run through him, and ultimately it would provide the world's Savior from sin.

The Character of Noah. 6:9-10. **9. Noah was a just man.** "Just" (*ṣǎddîq*) means "righteous" in the sense of approaching God by faith and being declared acceptable on the ground of trust in God's grace, which would provide salvation through the Redeemer to come (cf. 15:6; Gal. 3:1-12; cf. Gen. 8:20-21). Noah manifested his justification before God by faith alone (Rom. 3:25-26), and before men by works (James 2:14-26). **Perfect** (*tāmîm*), which signifies "sound, healthy, blameless," does not convey any notion of sinlessness, but of spiritual maturity and integrity (Deut. 18:13; Psalm 18:25). Noah was spiritually robust **in his generations**, that is, "among his contemporaries" (fellowmen). **Noah walked with God** (cf. 5:22). Noah's outward walk was a demonstration of the reality of his inner faith. His faith and integrity of life were manifest in his three sons, Shem, Ham, and Japheth, who shared his faith in God's grace and were preserved from the judgment of the Flood.

The Corruption of the Earth. 6:11-13. The earth's wickedness is contrasted with Noah's godliness. Six times the word "earth" appears in this section, indicating that the Flood was to be worldwide and not local. Three times the verb "to corrupt" occurs, emphasizing the complete degeneracy of mankind. Twice the word "violence" (*ḥāmās*, "lawlessness") is found, showing the result of the universal moral putrefaction. The inevitable fruitage of

38

any society that exposes itself to invasion of the powers of darkness is blatant lawlessness—"murders" (violence); "sorceries" (occultism); "fornication" (sexual immorality); and "thefts" (Rev. 9:20-21). Pre-Flood corruption will be repeated in the Great Tribulation preceding Christ's advent in glory (Matt. 24:37-42).

13. The end of all flesh is come before me. The metaphor is taken from the custom of earthly kings. Before a decree is executed it is presented to the king. After he examines and approves it, he gives a signal with his hand by which token it becomes law and is forthwith executed. The term "all flesh" denotes "humanity," the flesh of men, but it does not exclude the flesh of animals, fish, and fowl (cf. 1 Cor. 15:39). **I will destroy them with the earth**—not the verb "destroy" in the sense of "obliterating or erasing," as in verse 7, but "devastate or bring to ruin," the same root used six times in this context to set forth man's terrible degeneracy. "With" (*'ĕṯ*) is the sign of the definite accusative; it is better translated, "*even* the earth." The meaning is, "I will bring them to ruin, even the entire order of earthly things."

Directions to Construct the Ark. 6:14-16. The command to build the ark came directly from God. In contrast, the Babylonian flood hero received his instructions in a dream. **14. Make thee an ark**, literally, "Make for yourself an ark" (*tēḇâ*, like *ekallu, Gilgamesh Epic*, 11:96), denoting a floating "palace," which indeed the Flood vessel was (cf. 7:18; 9:18), the word occurring in Egyptian hieroglyphics. **Gopher wood** is some resinous, highly rot-resisting timber as yet unidentified. "Gopher" (*gōp̄er*) simply transliterates the Hebrew word. **Rooms shalt thou make** (lit., "nests, cells, or compart-

ments"). **Pitch** (*k^ep̄ār*) **it within and without with pitch** (*kōp̄er*; Akk., *kupru*, "asphalt or bitumen"). The verb means "to cover, smear, or tar" a ship. The play on the words (paronomasia) dramatizes the underlying typology.

The ark is a type of Christ, the Preserver of His people from judgment (Heb. 11:7), specifically of the remnant of Israel who will return to the Lord during the Great Tribulation (Isa. 2:10-11; 26:20-21). "To pitch" is the same word rendered "to make atonement" (a covering for sin, Lev. 17: 11). The atoning work of Christ keeps out the waters of judgment. Bitumen or pitch also appears prominently in the Babylonian flood story unearthed at Kuyunjik (Nineveh) in 1853. This version describes a boat five times larger than Noah's ark. Noah's boat was 300 cubits (450 feet) long, 50 cubits (75 feet) broad, and 30 cubits (45 feet) high, with a displacement of 43,300 tons. The Babylonian account of the Flood is one of the most striking of all extrabiblical parallels that have come down to us from antiquity. It presents a problem to critics who deny the authenticity of the Bible account. If there was no flood of such an extent, how did it and all the other nonbiblical accounts arise?

16. A window (skylight) **shalt thou make to the ark.** This was to be terminated within a cubit of the top. Also a "door" (entrance) was to be made to the ark, with lower, second, and third stories. Sufficient detail is given to present a general idea of the ark. But it is impossible from the sparse data to specify the boat's exact displacement or precise construction and plan for light, ventilation, and cleaning.

Divine Covenant with Noah. 6:17-21. Vividly and dramatically God announced to His servant the precise manner in which His judgment against the pre-Flood sinners was to be executed. It was to be by water. **17. I ... do bring a flood of waters.** The Hebrew word *măbbûl* ("deluge, catastrophic flood") is employed only one other time in the Bible (Psalm 29:10) outside of the actual Flood narrative (cf. 9:15). Apparently the word stems from the root *nēbĕl* ("moisten"), as of the "sweating" of a porous vessel, and refers to "the celestial store of water jars," a figurative designation of "the heavenly ocean" (Albright, JBL 58:98) that condensed to furnish part of the water for the Flood. Luther appropriately calls the Deluge a *Sintflood* ("sin flood"). The Bible gives a definite moral cause for it, in striking contrast to the extrabiblical traditions incorporated in the Gilgamesh Epic, which present no plausible reason except the whim of the gods.

18. With thee will I establish my covenant. God entered into solemn agreement with Noah in the first mention of the word *covenant* in Scripture. He arranged to save Noah and his family through the ark, but the rest of the race was to be wiped out by the Deluge. Also, God arranged that animals would be spared by taking pairs of each species aboard the vessel. Evidently marine life was to be preserved in and through the catastrophe apart from the ark. Food and provisions were to be taken aboard the boat to sustain the life of its occupants amid universal destruction.

The Obedience of Noah. 6:22. The faithful, thoroughgoing nature of Noah's response to God's command is emphasized by repetition and by specific detail: **22. Thus did Noah; according to all that God commanded him, so did he.** This terse summary describes what was really one of the most heroic acts of faith in the history of the race (Heb. 11:7). What he was called to do was a task of herculean magnitude involving immense expenditure of time, skill, and labor. It also demanded resolute fortitude to meet the ridicule that would be heaped upon it for well over a century. But persuaded of the LORD's fidelity to His word and covenant (6:18), Noah not only prosecuted it with unflinching diligence, but also warned of the approaching judgment as a preacher of righteousness (1 Pet. 3:19-20).

2. NOAH SHELTERED IN THE ARK. 7:1-24.

Command to Enter the Ark. 7:1-4. **1.** Seven days before the catastrophe, the LORD directed Noah and his immediate family to enter the ship. The reason they were spared is because Noah was reckoned **righteous** (cf. 6:9) before God by virtue of his faith in divine grace, which was manifested in view of the promised Redeemer (3:15; 15:6). Noah's saving faith was attested by the provision for sacrifice on leaving the ark (8:20-21), and even conceivably aboard ship during the Flood.

2. Of every clean beast ... take ... by sevens. This was the purpose of the clean beasts (animals acceptable for sacrifice), of which seven of each were taken aboard. Ten such animals are listed in the Levitical Law (cf. Lev. 11:1-47). But the distinction between clean and unclean animals, like the Ten Commandments, was not a Mosaic innovation; it existed from the dawn of the race. It is significant that these specific orders typifying God's plan of redemption are given in the divine redemptive and covenant name (Jehovah Yahweh) not Elohim, as in the case of most of the Flood narrative.

4. Forty days and forty nights were to be the duration of the period for the condensation of the watery canopy that apparently covered the pre-Flood globe. Afterward "forty" became the sacred number of trial and patience both in the

40

Old Testament (Num. 14:33-34; Deut. 25:3, etc.) and the New Testament (Matt. 4:2; Acts 1:3, etc.). **Every living thing.** The word "living" should be deleted, not being found in the Hebrew. The word translated "thing" ($y^eq\hat{u}m$, "whatever stands erect") is a rare word occurring only here and in 7:23 and Deuteronomy 11:6. **Will I destroy.** Thus, God "destroys" (Heb., $m\bar{a}h\hat{a}$, "blots out"; see 6:7) not man and beast only, but the entire established order of things **from off the face of the earth**—the $^a\underline{d}\bar{a}m\hat{a}$, "the portion subdued to his use by the *'adam*, man" (R. Payne Smith, in Ellicott's commentary, vol. 1, p. 41).

Noah's Obedience. 7:5-10. **5. Noah did according unto all that the Lord commanded.** Noah's full compliance with the LORD's instructions is stressed (cf. 6:22). His obedience was the outward manifestation of his saving faith (Heb. 11:7; cf. James 2:24-26). **7. And Noah went ... into the ark.** Noah's complete performance of all God's instructions is further amplified. The patriarch obeyed all the divine instructions with regard to clean and unclean beasts. But the animals were taken in by God—by implanted instinct (vv. 9, 15), which was only part of the whole divine undertaking. God, who planned it, took care of the details, which are inexplicable on a purely natural and rationalistic basis. The Flood is a proving ground of faith to all men, as it was to Noah.

The Source of the Flood Waters. 7:11-16. **11. In the second month**, of the civil year which began in September at the autumn equinox, the Flood struck. Accordingly, the cataclysm began on November 7 (the seventeenth day of the second month, Marchesvan) and lasted till spring. The principal sources of the Flood waters were **the fountains of the great deep** ($t^eh\hat{o}m$, "the primeval ocean"; cf. 1:2; 49:25). This refers to the "part of the primitive water driven downward" (1:2, 9), so that it lay beneath the earth and communicated water by secret fountains to the solid land and the sea (A. Dillmann, *Genesis*, 1:278). Violent earthquakes alone could have split open these fountains, releasing their vast supplies of subterranean water upon the land areas. These tremendous upheavals involved the sinking of land areas and the raising of sea bottoms.

And the windows of heaven were opened. Violent forty-day precipitation was only a contributory and secondary source of the vast quantities of water needed, occasioning radical climatic changes. Apparently the pre-Flood earth was watered by the subterranean fountains and ascending mist (2:5-6). Atmospheric conditions evidently did not exist to produce rain or a rainbow (9:13), as in the post-Flood world. Apparently the vast quantities of global water vapor (1:6-7), which in large part condensed to furnish the forty-day downpour, gave the pre-Flood earth a warm climate from pole to pole. This was radically changed into the present order of "cold and heat, and summer and winter" (8:22). The apostle Peter clearly infers that the antediluvian world was radically different climatically and geologically from the "heavens and the earth which are now" (2 Pet. 3:7). Advocates of local flood theories (cf. Robert Jamieson, JFB, 1: 98-99) can scarcely reconcile their views with the scope of the catastrophe in the Bible account.

12. And the rain was upon the earth forty days. This violent downpour is called the *măbbûl* or "flood" (cf. 6:17; 7:17). But it is not said that after this 40-day period the rain ceased *entirely*. Rain likely continued to the 150th day (7:24). During this time the waters

41

kept rising, or at least kept their maximum height. After that the waters began to recede (cf. 8:1-3). **13-16.** When Noah had his immediate family and all the animals aboard **as God had commanded him** (cf. 7:5-10), **the Lord** (Jehovah, the God of covenant and grace) **shut him in**, saving and protecting him—because of his faith manifested by obedience—from the awesome judgment on unbelieving sinners.

The Extent of the Flood. 7:17-24. That the Flood was globe-engirdling is inescapable from the terminology used. **17-19. The water increased ... the waters prevailed, and were increased greatly ... the waters prevailed exceedingly.** Stressed in this graphic repetition is the fact, as Peter declares, "the world that then was, being overflowed with water, perished" (2 Pet. 3:6). The apostle means not only antediluvian civilization, but the antediluvian world climatically and geologically. **And all the high hills ... under the whole heaven** can signify nothing less than a universal deluge. **20. Fifteen cubits** (22½ feet) indicates the least depth of the water at any spot on the globe, meaning evidently above the *highest* **mountains**, since these **were covered**.

3. NOAH'S FAITH AND GOD'S GRACE. 8:1-22.

The Flood Recedes. 8:1-5. **1. God remembered Noah.** (Cf. comments on 6:8-9, 22; 7:5.) **1. The waters subsided** is better translated, "the waters became quiet" (*shākăk*), referring not to the ebbing or decreasing (*hāsēr*, v. 3), of the waters but to their becoming calm after the violent currents precipitated by the bursting forth of the subterranean seas. The primary sense of the verb appears in the causative stem in Numbers 17:5 and denotes the *quieting* of popular commotion. The distinction between this word and *hāsēr* is important in determining the stages of the Flood.

2. The fountains ... of the deep ... were stopped "can mean only one thing; the land level was shifted again, so that the sea went back to its former place, or nearly so" (Harry Rimmer, *The Harmony of Science and Scripture*, p. 240). Then **the windows of heaven were stopped**, which means the vast quantities of water above the firmament remained on the earth with the evaporated water forming the clouds, rain, and rainbow of the new order.

3. And the waters returned from off the earth. This backward motion of the water apparently indicates a vast settling of the earth that lowered seabeds, which previously had been raised by earthquakes. Three stages in the recession of the water occurred: first, the quieting of the waters; second, an almost stationary period with the whole decrease of seventy-three days (vv. 4-5) being only fifteen cubits (cf. the submergence of the hills, 7:20) and their reappearance on the first day of the tenth month; and third, the more perceptible subsiding of the waters expressed in verse 3.

4. The ark rested ... upon the mountains of Ararat, that is, "the Ararat range," the allusion not being to a particular peak (Speiser, AB, p. 53). Mount Ararat rises 16,945 feet above sea level in Armenia, where today the frontiers of Turkey, Iran, and the Soviet Union converge in the general area of the Caspian and the Black seas (cf. 2 Kings 19:37; Jer. 51:27).

Noah Sends out the Birds. 8:6-12. Noah first sent out a raven, and then a dove was released on three occasions. The raven's flying back and forth from the ark and its failure to return inside showed that although the waters had declined to some extent, and the outside world was not too inhospitable for a sturdy carrion-eating bird, yet it was still unfriendly. Sending out three doves at intervals of seven days, the dove being gentle and timid, was ideal for Noah's purpose. The return of the first showed the lowlands were still inundated. The return of the second, with a fresh-plucked olive twig, indicated that the valleys, where the olive grows, were dry, but that the bird still preferred the hospitality the ark afforded. The failure of the third dove to return showed it had found a comfortable night's lodging in the lowlands, and it was soon time for the ark's inhabitants to disembark.

This detail of the Flood story furnishes one of a number of striking similarities to the Babylonian version found in the eleventh book of the *Epic of Gilgamesh*. There Utnapishtim in the seventh day after the landing of the boat on Mount Nisir, east of the Tigris River, sent out a dove, then a swallow, and finally a raven. The sending out of the raven last is pointless, as are many other details of the perverted extrabiblical versions of the Flood.

The Flood Dries Up. 8:13-14. Modern criticism views the biblical account as composite and contradictory, especially in its data of the Flood's duration. However, if the narrative is considered as a unit, the facts can be explained reasonably and harmoniously. The days total one year and eleven days (371 days). Taking into account certain peculiarities of Jewish reckoning of time, a case can be made for the Flood lasting exactly a solar year. Multiply the 12 months of 7:11 and 8:14 by the 29½ days of a lunar month. Adding to this total of 354 days the 11 days (17th to 27th of the second month, 7:11; 8:14) gives a total of 365 days, one solar year. In the Babylonian and Sumerian accounts, the catastrophe lasted only about a week.

A New Beginning. 8:15-19. **15-18. And God spoke unto Noah ... Go forth ... And Noah went forth.** To Noah and his family, going forth from the ark represented an absolutely new beginning. The total destruction of all that had previously existed is emphasized by the repetition of the primeval command (cf. 1:22) to **be fruitful and multiply upon the earth.** In fact, a new economy of God's dealing (a dispensation) was inaugurated. It was to be characterized by the administration of human government, attested by the right to enforce capital punishment in order to maintain law and order under the Noahic Covenant (see 9:1-19). For the other divine economies (dispensations), see: Innocence (Gen. 1:28); Conscience and Moral Responsibility (Gen. 3:7); Promise (Gen. 12:1); Law (Exod. 19:1); Church (Acts 2:1); Kingdom (Rev. 10:4).

Noah's Worship in Faith. 8:20-22. **20. Noah builded an altar,** as did the faithful adherents to the one true and only gospel of salvation by grace through faith, beginning with the Fall of man (cf. Gen. 12:8; 22:9; 35:1; Exod. 17:15; 20:24; 2 Sam. 24:18) until the nation Israel took up the hope of the coming Redeemer in the Levitical sacrificial system. **And offered burnt offerings.** This ritual looked forward to Christ offering Himself without spot to God as a substitute for man's sin (cf. Lev. 1:1-17). These offerings were not invented by Moses, but were instituted from the Fall of man (3:15, 21; 4:4). This is also intimated by the stipulation of clean animals fit for sacrifice (cf. 7:2-3, 8). The Babylonian flood story also describes acts of worship by the hero after his deliverance. Utnapishtim offered sacrifices when he left the boat, and "the gods smelled the goodly savor." (Compare v. 21).

21. And the Lord smelled a sweet savor. The language is boldly an-

43

thropomorphic to dramatically emphasize the infinitely holy God's acceptance of Noah by virtue of his faith in the coming Redeemer. The sacrifice was a confession of Noah's thankfulness for sparing him as a *saved* sinner, but a sinner nevertheless, from the judgment of the Flood. Jehovah (not Elohim) appears in this section as the God of covenant and redemption. His grace now shines through as the dark scene of judgment recedes. **The Lord said in his heart** (Heb., "to his heart," that is, "determined with himself," cf. 17:17). Literally, He "came to the settled purpose" that, despite man's inveterate proneness to sin (cf. 6:5), He would never again strike the whole earth with an utterly decimating judgment, destroying all life, as He had done.

22. While the earth remaineth. This verse almost certainly refers to the new climate and the changes it brought on the antediluvian earth. If the Flood caused new atmospheric conditions that prevail today and was partly the result of the condensation of a great celestial watery canopy, alteration in the earth's climate resulted. Greater extremes of heat and cold, distinct seasons of summer and winter, and more pronounced times of sowing and reaping were the result. It may well be that day and night became more pronounced as the atmosphere cleared and the solar rays were less diffused.

E. NOAH'S LATER LIFE. 9:1-29.

God's Covenant with Noah. 9:1-7. This divine agreement and contract conditioned life in the new antediluvian earth. The arrangement was meant to bless Noah and his posterity. **1. God blessed Noah.** The benefits bestowed upon the second father of mankind (vv. 1-2) were precisely parallel to those

given to our first father, Adam (1:28-29; 2:16-17). However, an important addition was growing out of the history of the race up to that time. It was the provision to guard the sanctity of human life, which had evidently become a cheap thing in the frightful violence that precipitated the Flood (cf. 6:5-6, 13).

This was done in five ways: (1) *By prohibiting the eating of blood*, although allowing the eating of flesh (vv. 3-4). The blood, representing the life (Lev. 17:11-14), was to be held sacred in token of the sacredness of human life (v. 4). (2) *By stipulating the responsibility of both man and beast in destroying human life*—life was required for a life (v. 5). (3) *By instituting the law of capital punishment* (v.6a). **6. Whoever sheddeth man's blood** (commits murder) **by man shall his blood be shed.** His life would be required by the constituted government as a punishment and as a deterrent against the wholesale violence that had necessitated the Flood.

(4) *By pointing out the reason for the sanctity of human life.* God made man in His image (v. 6b; Gen. 1:26) as a personal, rational, and moral being, with not only a body and soul, but with a spirit that may know God and have fellowship with Him. Man's life, therefore, unlike that of an animal, is to be regarded as inviolable. Murder is therefore a shocking affront to God, not only a terrible crime against one's fellowman. (5) *By emphasizing the divine purpose for man to multiply and fill the earth* (v. 7). Violence and murder were diametrically at odds with the divine purpose and calculated to frustrate it. For notes on other major covenants, see Edenic (Gen. 2:16); Adamic (Gen. 3:15); Abrahamic (Gen. 12:2); Mosaic (Exod. 19:5); Palestinian (Deut. 30:3); Davidic (2 Sam. 7:16); and New (Heb. 8:8).

The Covenant Established. 9:8-17. In solemn language God announced *His* covenant with Noah and his posterity. **9. I establish my covenant with you, and with your seed.** This agreement also included the animal world. **10. And with every living creature. 11.** The repetition of the words: **I will establish my covenant with you** (cf. v. 9) is a device of Hebrew grammar to denote emphasis. **12. This is the token of the covenant which I make.** In order that man would not have to live in constant fear of another flood, God gave a reminder that He would never again destroy the earth in this manner. The sign or symbol of His mercy is the rainbow (9:8-17 harks back to 6:18). Although most commentators assume the pre-Flood existence of the rainbow, if the catastrophe involved vast changes in the atmosphere with condensation of the waters above the firmament, there is at least presumptive evidence that the bow was a new natural phenomenon, the result of radical climatic changes effected by the Flood.

13. I do set my bow. The bow thus speaks of covenant mercy set upon the storm clouds of judgment. It illustrates the cross of Christ, where judgment, never to be repeated, was visited upon the believer's sins (Gal. 3:10-14; Heb. 10:14-18). **17. This is the token of the covenant.** The idealization of the rainbow is found in many extrabiblical traditions. In Babylonia it was Marduk's bow with which he killed Tiamat. In India it is the battle bow of Indra. Among the Arabs it is the bow of Kuzah, which he suspended in the sky. In Greece it was the radiant messenger of Olympus. But the covenant significance occurs only in the Bible account.

Noah's Descendants. 9:18-19. **18-19.** The importance of Noah's progeny is emphasized (1) by the frequent repetition of their names throughout the Flood narrative (5:32; 6:10; 7:13; 8:18; 10:1); (2) by the fact that **of them was the whole earth** (the earth's population) **overspread** (from *pûṣ*, "to scatter, disperse," probably, to be more pointed or specific, *nifal*, "was scattered," i.e., "populated"; cf. 11:4); and (3) by the fact that the development of the human race in germinal form is prefigured in the character of these three sons.

Noah's Moral Lapse. 9:20-23. **20. Noah began to be a farmer** is better rendered, "Noah, as husbandman (man of the soil), began to plant a vineyard" (Delitzsch, Keil, Lange). Agriculture interrupted by the Flood, he resumes and makes it more complete by means of the new culture of the vine. Armenia, where the ark landed, has been famous from antiquity for its vineyards (Xenophon. *Anabasis.* 4.4.9).

21. He drank of the wine, and became drunk. None other than the new father of the race became the glaring example of the snare that lies behind the use of all intoxicating beverages (Prov. 20:1). The fact that Noah erred in ignorance did not preserve him from the damage intoxicants can inflict. This is a solemn warning to the race of how even good and righteous men can be ensnared by alcoholic beverages, especially to commit sexual sin. Noah, as he lay unguarded in his tent, exposed himself contrary to the law of modesty and morality (Lev. 18:6-19). The error of the father revealed itself in the character of the sons.

22. Ham ... saw the nakedness of his father. He displayed his lascivious bent by neither looking away nor covering his father's "nakedness" (*'ĕrwâ*, "pudenda"). Instead, he evidently took carnal delight in the episode, or at best treated a very serious matter with levity, and **told his two brethren outside** the tent. In connection with this revealing incident, Ham is described as **the father of Canaan**, "father" being used in the broader Semitic sense of "ancestor" or "progenitor of."

Ham's descendants, the Canaanites, developed into seven nations of people in Canaan (Deut. 7:1). They were idolatrous (Deut. 29:17); occult-ridden (Deut. 18:9-10); and enslaved by gross sexual immorality wedded to their debased religion. Both Scripture (Lev. 18:27) and archaeology (the Ras Shamra Tablets from Ugarit in north Syria discovered from 1929 to 1935) attest to the wickedness of the Canaanites.

23. And Shem and Japheth took a garment ... and covered the nakedness of their father. In contrast to the shameless conduct of Ham, the act of the two other brothers presents a beautifully vivid image of delicacy, being at the same time an act of modesty, piety, and filial reverence. "Out of the virtues and vices of the family come the virtues and vices of nations" (Lange, 1:336).

Noah's Prophecy. 9:24-29. **24. And Noah awoke from his wine**, that is, "from his intoxication from wine" (cf. 1 Sam. 1:14). When he became sober, he realized **24. what his younger son** (lit., "his son, the little or the less") **had done unto him.** This can only mean "his *youngest* son," not "younger," the reference evidently being "not to Noah's youngest son, but Ham's; and on the evidence of 10:6 that individual was Canaan" (Speiser, AB, p. 62). Ham's licentious bent shows up in his son's base deed (the nature of which is not indicated in the brief narrative).

25. Cursed be Canaan. As the youngest son of Ham, he was also Noah's youngest son. In Semitic idiom, grandsons, as well as all the descendants of a man, are called "sons" (cf. "sons of Israel"). Everything points to Canaan as the *youngest* son, at that time, of all

Noah's family. The curse of *abject* subjugation and servitude (**a servant of servants shall he be**) was pronounced upon *him* and not upon Ham. Hamites are connected with the earliest empires both in Asia and Africa, not with servitude (see M. F. Unger, *Archaeology and the Old Testament*, pp. 82-94). Scripture contains no allusion to any such sweeping malediction involving all of Ham's descendants. In striking contrast, the result of the curse upon Canaan is dramatized by the Israelite conquest of the land of Canaan in the days of Joshua, and the reduction of the surviving Canaanites to "hewers of wood and drawers of water" (Josh. 9:21, 23, 27).

26. Blessed be the Lord God of Shem. Or preferably, as the Hebrew may also be read, "Blessed of Jehovah, my God be Shem." The prophecy is that Shem's posterity would know and serve the one true God of creation and redemption and that the Messiah-Savior in His humanity would come through the Semitic line.

27. God shall enlarge (*yăpt*) **Japheth** (*yĕpĕt*), a play on the name. The use of the generic *ʾelōhîm* implies that the proper name Jehovah "was the peculiar property of the Shemites" (John Skinner, *Genesis*, ICC, p. 185). The Japhetic line is predicted to enjoy not only expansion in temporal possessions, but spiritual blessing as well. **And he** (Japheth) **shall dwell in the tents of Shem.** Christianity has had great outreach upon the Japhetic peoples of Europe and America. But the Hebrew may preferably be read, "But He [God] shall dwell in the tents of Shem," that is, by His Shekinah, another reference to the spiritual blessing on the Israelites as a Shemitic (Semitic) people.

F. NOAH'S DESCENDANTS. 10:1-32.

Introduction to the Table of the Nations. 10:1. Actually Noah's prophecy (cf. 9:20-29 with 10:1) forms a preface or introduction to the remarkable geographic-ethnographic survey of the ancient biblical world that figures in redemptive history and has been remarkably illuminated by modern archaeological research. The table is eponymous, with the geographical areas being defined in connection with prominent names of Noah's posterity. Japhetic names roughly designate the north and west, Ham the south, and Shem the east (H. C. Alleman, "The Book of Genesis," OTC, p. 183). Underlying the table, which is unique in ancient records, is a moral and spiritual principle which shows that in divine dealings the moral character of a thing cannot be understood unless its source is known.

In God's mind, Israel was the medium of redemptive blessing to the world. Therefore, it was necessary for the nation to comprehend the source from which the various nations that surrounded her sprang in order that she might have an insight into their character by which to guide her attitude and conduct toward them. Accordingly, the table of the nations furnishes a background of world history for the call of Abraham (chap. 12).

The Sons of Japheth. 10:2-5. **2. Gomer** (Assyrian, *Gimirraya*, the Cimmerians). They are listed by Ezekiel as residing "in the uttermost parts of the north" (Ezek. 38:6, margin). By the seventh century B.C. they had settled in Asia Minor in the general region of Cappadocia and are mentioned in the annals of Esarhaddon and Ashurbanipal. **Magog** is the land of Gog (Ezek. 38:2), who has been compared with Gyges of Lydia, who was contemporary with the Assyrian campaigns against the Cimmerians in the seventh century B.C. **Madai** represents the Medes (2 Kings 17:6; 18:11; Isa. 21:2). They settled in the mountainous region east of Assyria and south of the Caspian Sea. Their history is extrabiblically elucidated by Assyrian inscriptions from the ninth century B.C. till the fall of Assyria in the late seventh century B.C.

Javan represents the Greeks, particularly the Ionians of Homer and more particularly the Asiatic Ionians of the coast of Caria and Lydia, whose cities were important commercial emporiums two centuries before those of the Peloponnesus. Javan is the name by which the Greeks are known in the Old Testament (Ezek. 27:13; Isa. 66:19; Joel 3:6; Zech. 9:13; Dan. 8:21). First mentioned by Assyrian Emperor Sargon II (721-705 B.C.), who encountered them in a naval battle, they were prominent in later centuries of Jewish history. **Tubal, and Meshech** are the Tabali and Mushki of the Assyrian records, whose home in Assyrian times was in eastern Anatolia (cf. Ezek. 27:13; 38:2; Isa. 66:19). **Tiras** perhaps represents the Tursenoi, who in ancient times dwelt on the north shores and islands of the Aegean Sea and were dreaded by the Greeks as pirates.

3. The sons of Gomer: Ashkenaz is equivalent to Assyrian Ashkuz, the Scythians, a barbaric people who periodically overran extensive territories; in Jeremiah's day they dwelt in the vicinity of Ararat and Minni (the "Mannai" of Assyrian inscriptions southeast of Lake Van). **Riphath** is evidently preserved in the Riphaean Mountains, supposed by the ancients to skirt the north shore of the world (John D. Davis, in *Westminster Dictionary of the Bible*, revised and rewritten by H. S. Gehman, 1944, p. 516). **Togarmah** is Tegarama in southwestern Armenia (W. F. Albright, "The Old Testament and Archaeology," OTC, p. 138; cf. Ezek. 27:14; 38:6).

4. The sons of Javan: Elishah is Kittim or Cyprus, the Alashia of the Amarna Letters (Ezek. 27:7). **Tarshish** represents a Phoenician copper-smelting center either in Sardinia or in Tartessus, Spain (cf. Ezek. 27:12). **Kittim** denotes the Kitians, the people of Kit or Kiti of the Phoenician inscriptions, connected with Cyprus through Kition, an ancient city on the southern coast, present-day Larnaka. **Dodanim** may be the Dardana (Dardanians) of Asia Minor, although Rodanim is in the Septuagint and the Samaritan text, as well as in the Masoretic text of 1 Chronicles 1:7. In such a case, Rhodes and the adjacent islands of the Aegean Sea are intended.

The Sons of Ham. 10:6-7. In the Hamitic line is traced the rise of earliest imperial world power, first under Nimrod in Babylonia, and later in such capitals of empire as Asshur and Nineveh on the Tigris River and Egypt on the Nile. **Cush** is presented first, and was originally connected with Babylonia. It is doubtless to be equated with the ancient city-kingdom of Kish in lower Babylonia, where emperors of the third millennium B.C. took their title as "kings of the world" (W. F. Albright, "Recent Discoveries in Bible Lands," in *Young's Analytical Concordance*, p. 32). Only later was Cush connected with Egyptian Kosh or Nubia.

Mizraim is ancient Egypt, Mizri of the Amarna Letters, the Hebrew dual preserving the ancient divisions of the country, Upper Egypt (above Memphis) and Lower Egypt (the Delta). Egypt's brilliant history extended through thirty dynasties (c. 2900 -332 B.C.). **Put** (Phut) is located in Cyrenaica in North Africa, west of Egypt, according to the inscriptions of the Persian monarch Darius I the Great (522-486 B.C.). The posterity of **Canaan** was originally Hamitic (9:22-27), but by racial intermixture it later became predominantly Semitic, as archaeology has shown.

7. The sons of Cush principally

peopled Arabia. **Seba** (Southwest Arabia) is a dialectic variation of Sheba. **Havilah** is in south central Arabia. **Sabtah** is generally identified with Shabwat, the ancient city of Hazarmaveth (10:26) in south Arabia. It is still called Hadramant. **Raamah, Sabteca,** and **Dedan** also represent people of the Arabian Peninsula.

Hamitic Imperial Power. 10:8-10. This section portrays the moral character in which earthly imperial power first appeared in human history. That it was evil is obvious from the following: (1) The earthly kingship first developed among the Hamites, upon one branch of which there was a prophetic curse; in the entire line there was an absence of divine blessing (9:25-27). (2) Nimrod is presented as the founder of the kingdom of Babylon, which is invariably presented in Scripture as an evil system in type and prophecy (Isa. 21:9; Jer. 50:24; Rev. 16:19; 17:5; 18:2).

(3) The name Nimrod "no doubt suggested to the Israelites the idea of 'rebel' ... against God" (A. Dillmann, *Genesis*, 1:350), which is true despite the fact that the name did not have this connotation in Hamitic speech. (4) Nimrod is described as **a mighty hunter before the Lord.** The LORD took note of Nimrod's royal character as a hunter instead of the divine ideal of a shepherd (cf. 2 Sam. 5:2; 7:7; Rev. 7:17). A hunter gratifies himself at the expense of his victim. A shepherd, by contrast, expends himself for the good of the subjects under his care.

10. The beginning of his kingdom was Babel ... Erech ... Accad ... Calneh, in the land of Shinar. Shinar is lower Babylonia, the entire alluvial plain between the Tigris and the Euphrates rivers, in about the last two hundred miles of their ancient course. All of these cities, resurrected by archaeology, are now known. **Babel** (Akk., *bab-ilu*, "gate of God") dates from prehistoric times, but it did not become an imperial capital until the time of Hammurabi (1728-1686 B.C.).

Erech (Akk., Uruk) is modern Warka, located one hundred miles southeast of Babylon, where the first temple tower (ziggurat) and earliest cylinder seals have been recovered (Jack Finegan, *Light from the Ancient Past*, pp. 19-23). **Accad** was the ancient name of northern Babylonia, taken from the name of the city of Agade, which Sargon the Great brought to prominence as the capital of his Semitic empire, which dominated the Mesopotamian world (c. 2360-2180 B.C.). **Calneh** is still obscure and may be a shortened form of Hursagkalama (Kalama), a twin city of Kish.

The Sons of Ham Resumed. 10:11-20.
11. Out of that land (Shinar) **went forth Asshur.** Babylonia was the oldest seat of civilization, and Assyria (Asshur) was colonized from it; this is in accord with archaeological findings. The city of Ashur on the west bank of the Tigris River, about sixty miles south of Nineveh, was the earliest capital and center of Assyrian power. It was named after its chief god, Ashur. Its modern site, Qalat Sharqat, has been excavated (1903-14). Ashur's occupation antedates 3000 B.C.

Builded Nineveh ... Rehoboth ... Calah. Nineveh (modern Kuyunjik) is sixty miles north of Ashur and was the great capital of the late Assyrian Empire. It has been rescued from oblivion by modern archaeology. It consists of a complex of cities, including Rehoboth (Rebit-Ninua west of the capital) and **Calah**, eighteen miles south of Nineveh. **12. Resen** was a part of the Ninevite metropolis, but it remains obscure archaeologically.

13-14. The descendants of **Mizraim** (Egypt) were **Ludim**, a tribe bordering Egypt, which Albright construes as a copyist error for Lubim (Libyans), people west of the Delta. As Hamitic tribes bordering Egypt, the **Anamim, Lehabim, Naphtuhim,** and **Casluhim** remain obscure. The **Pathrusim**, however, were clearly the inhabitants of Pathros, Egyptian Ptores, Upper Egypt. The **Caphtorim** were the inhabitants of Caphtor (Kaptara, Crete). The **Philistines** came from Caphtor (Crete) (Amos 9:7; Jer. 47:4); therefore, **out of whom came the Philistines** apparently was misplaced by a copyist and belongs after Caphtorim. The monuments indicate that the Peleste (Philistines) invaded Palestine in the first half of the twelfth century B.C. and eventually gave their name to the country (Palestine) from Philistia (Joel 3:4).

15-17. The descendants of Canaan. **And Canaan begot Sidon ... Heth ... the Jebusite ... the Amorite ... the Girgashite ... the Hivite ... the Arkite ... the Sinite ... the Arvadite ... Zemarite ... the Hamathite. Sidon**, the oldest Phoenician city, hence called Canaan's **first-born**, was located on the Mediterranean coast twenty-two miles north of Tyre. In the early era Phoenicians were called Sidonians (eleventh-eighth centuries B.C.). **Heth** is the reputed head of the Hittites, whose imperial civilization has been uncovered by archaeology. The Assyrians named Syria-Palestine *mat Ḥatti*, "the land of the Hittites."

The **Jebusite** settled in Jebus, the name of Jerusalem when this Palestinian tribe held it (Josh. 15:63; Judg. 19:10). Not until David's reign were they driven out of the citadel of Jebus (2 Sam. 5:6-7; cf. 1 Kings 9:20). The **Amorite** was a powerful race in Palestine. Under five kings they held the hill country of Judah (Josh. 10:5) and a large district east of the Jordan (Deut. 3:8; Judg. 11:22). The

Girgashite as a tribe of Canaan (15:21; Deut. 7:1) as well as the **Hivite** (Horite?) (Exod. 3:17; Josh. 9:1) remain archaeologically obscure. However, the Horites (Hurrians) have been discovered by archaeology as an important people of western Asia.

The **Arkite** is represented by present-day Tell Arka, eighty miles north of Sidon at the foot of Lebanon. It is called Arkantu (fifteenth century B.C.), Irkata in the Amarna Letters. The **Sinite** connects with Assyrian Siannu, a city on the coast mentioned by Tiglath-pileser III (738 B.C.). The **Arvadite** refers to the residents of Arvad, the most northerly of the coastal Phoenician towns (the Arwada of the Amarna Letters). The **Zemarite** (Semarite) refers to a people of the city-fortress of Simura, a half dozen miles south of Arvad (Sumur of the Amarna Letters).

The **Hamathite** refers to the city-state of Hamath on the Orontes River (present-day Hama) often mentioned in the Old Testament and the Assyrian monuments. Verse 19 delimits the territory of the Canaanites from Zidon on the north coast to Gerar (Tell el Jemmeh) and Gaza in Philistia on the south; Sodom and Gomorrah on the east at the south end of the Dead Sea, and **Lasha** on the northern interior, probably to be identified with Laish-Dan (Judg. 18:29), the most northerly Israelite city.

The Sons of Shem. 10:21-32. **21-22.** Last but not least the descendants of Shem are given. **Unto Shem also . . . even to him were children born.** The Hebrew is emphatic in order to dramatize that from this line would come blessing (9:26), which would culminate in the Messiah-Savior. **Elam** is Susiana, east of Babylonia, with the capital city Susa (Heb., Shushan; Neh. 1:1; Esther 2:8) uncovered by archaeology. **Asshur** is Assyria. Asshur and Nineveh were

founded by Hamites (10:11), but were conquered and overrun by Semites. **Arpachshad** (Arrapachitis ?) of the Greeks was east of the Tigris in the upper Zab River country. **Lud** denotes the Lydians, who later settled in western Asia Minor. **Aram** heads the Aramaeans who figure so prominently in Old Testament history. Aramaean states (Zobah, Maacah, Geshur, and Beth-rehob) gradually emerged and were conquered by David.

23. The children of Aram: Uz is located in the Syrian Desert between Damascus and Edom (Job 1:1). **Hul** and **Gether** are unknown. **Mash** is obscure, but evidently it refers to some part of the great Syro-Arabian Desert. In this sense it occurs in Assyrian records as Mat (country of) Mash (S. R. Driver, *The Book of Genesis*, pp. 129-30).

24-25. The children of Arpachshad. Shelah is listed as the son of Arpachshad who begat **Eber**, the progenitor of the Hebrews through his son Peleg and of thirteen Arabian tribes through **Joktan** (Arabia). Eber's name (*'ēbĕr*) means "one who passes over" and is the same as the Hebrew *Habīru* and as such was employed later to designate wandering Semitic seminomads.

Eber's son **Peleg** (*pĕlĕg*, "division, watercourse") lived when the earth was divided. This enigmatic statement has been subject to numberless interpretations: (1) It refers to a separation be-.ween roving Arabs (a dialectal variant of Eber ?) under Joktan and those who settled down to semisedentary lives on "irrigated land" (Akk., *palgu*) under Peleg. (2) It refers to Noah's formal allocation of the earth to Shem, Ham, and Japheth (Deut. 32:8; Acts 17:24-26) about a century after the Flood at the birth of Peleg, whose name was a memorial to that event. (3) It refers to widespread geological landslips separating

50

continents. (4) It refers to the dispersion of the human race occasioned by the confusion of languages at Babel (11:1-9). Perhaps (2) above is most likely.

26. Joktan, brother of Peleg, is the progenitor of Arabian tribes. Most of his descendants are unknown outside the Bible, but south and southwest Arabia may be postulated. Modern tribes of South Arabia claim that pure Arabs are descendants of Joktan. **Hazarmaveth** occurs in the Sabaean inscriptions and is now Hadramaut in south Arabia east of Aden. The names in verse 27 are obscure. **28. Sheba** with its capital at Mariaba (Saba) is located some one hundred miles north of modern Aden in southwest Arabia. The name is well known in the Old Testament (1 Kings 10:1; Jer. 6:20, etc.). **29. Ophir,** which is of uncertain location, is sometimes placed in southwest or southeast Arabia, or the northeast African coast (Somaliland, Egyptian Punt; see W. F. Albright, *Archaeology and the Religion of Israel,* pp. 133-35, 212), or in India Supara, sixty miles north of Bombay.

G. The Confusion of Languages. 11:1-9.

The Sin of the Babel Builders. 11:1-4. This narrative continues from 9:29 (chap. 10 being a parenthesis). **1.** The writer takes a retrospective glance at the descent of the race from a single family. Having a common origin, it is reasonable to conclude mankind had a common language. The sacred historian undertakes to describe the origin of the various languages of the world as a punishment for man's sin of rebellion against God in failing to obey the divine imperative contained in the Adamic Covenant (1:28) and renewed in the Noahic Covenant (9:1) to "be fruitful . . . multiply, and *fill the earth*" (italics added). In opposition to God's will, man attempted

to settle down and establish a world state to offset the divine rule.

2. As they journeyed from the east (not "eastward," but cf. 13:11). This evidently means that some of Noah's descendants left their primeval residence in the highlands of Ararat and pushed on into the hilly country east of the Tigris (later called Susiana or Elam). There they altered their course, turning westward. Attracted by the great fertility of the alluvial plain between the Tigris and Euphrates rivers in the last two hundred miles of the course (anciently called "Shinar"), they **dwelt there** (*yāshāḇ,* "sit, settle down, remain"). Extremely fertile soil, with plenty of water for irrigation, would require little dependence on God. No more "journeying," literally, "pulling up stakes (tent pins)."

3. Come is used with interjectional force to incite or exhort (2 Kings 5:4-5). **Let us make brick.** The soft alluvial mud of the Tigris-Euphrates Valley, whether baked in the torrid sun or in the kiln, offered a ready and inexpensive source of building material. It was a substitute for stone (either the limestone of Palestine or the marble of other regions which were nonexistent in Shinar) and much more plentiful. **Slime** (bitumen) **had they for mortar.** Apparently the bitumen (pitch) industry originated in Babylonia, where the most important deposits of this substance known in antiquity were found (R. J. Forbes, *Bitumen and Petroleum in Antiquity*). The word for bitumen (*ḥēmār*) used here and in 14:10 singularly is not the word *kōpĕr* (Assyr., *kupru*), used of the pitch with which Noah caulked the ark (6:14), or the word *zĕpĕt,* the insulating material of Moses' ark of bulrushes.

4. Let us build us a city and a tower. The city and especially the tower are more clearly understood in light of Mesopotamian structures, particularly the later temple-towers called "ziggurats." The Assyrian-Babylonian word *ziqquratu* denotes a "pinnacle" or "mountaintop." They were gigantic artificial mountains of sun-dried bricks. The oldest recovered one is that at Uruk (Erech; 10:10), modern Warka (dated c. 3800 B.C.). But the structure is not called a ziggurat but a simple tower (*mīgdāl*). Apparently it was the first such edifice attempted and, despite the divine judgment pronounced upon it, the prototype of all subsequent imitations of it, which seem "to constitute an attempt to deflect any possibility of divine punishment" by their customary consecration "to the guardian divinity of the city" (Leupold, *Exposition of Genesis*, 1: 385).

Whose top may reach unto heaven. It is probably something more than hyperbole when it is said the top of this tower might "reach unto heaven." It was customary in later Babylonian ziggurats to regard the highest stage (usually the seventh) as "the entrance to heaven" (T. K. Cheyne, *Genesis*, ICC, p. 226), the abode of the patron deity. **Let us make us a name**, that is, "acquire lasting renown" (cf. 2 Sam. 7:23; Jer. 32:20). **Lest we be scattered** or "be spread" **abroad** (10:18) if *nifal*, but if *qal*, "lest we disperse," depending on how the Hebrew grammar of the passage is construed. The tower was rebelliously intended to be a center and rallying point. They did not wish to obey God.

The Punishment of the Sin of the Babel Builders. 11:5-8. **5. And the Lord came down** is a vivid way of saying by the use of anthropomorphism, "Jehovah interposed" or "intervened" (cf. Exod. 3:8; Num. 11:17). This was not a descent in visible fashion to deal with men face to face (as in Exod. 19:20; 34:5; Num. 12:5), for these were bold, hardened sinners who had openly repudiated the Noahic Covenant (9:1) and were rebels ripe for judgment (6:3). **To see** (an infinitive of purpose) **the city and** (particularly) **the tower, which the children of men** (*beṇ̂e 'āḍām*, "sons of Adam") **builded** (had made). These mere creatures of dust (2:7; 3:19; 6:2) dared defy their Creator to oppose His arrangement of dividing to the nations their inheritance when He separated the sons of Adam (Deut. 32:8).

6. The people (*'ăm*, "union, common bond," from *'āmăm*, "to bind") **are one, and they have all one language.** Easy communication and boldly wicked plans presaged the most daring God-opposing undertakings. The city and the tower were but the beginning of their daring enterprises. **And now nothing will be withheld from them, which they have imagined** (devised, purposed) **to do** (cf. Psalm 2:1-4).

7. Come is in ironical imitation of impious man's wicked determination (vv. 3-4). **Let us go down.** The triune God is speaking (as in 1:26; 3:22). Divine determination counters human resolve. "We *will* go down" (Delitzsch). God is spoken of as Jehovah (Yahweh) because of the mercy He displays in preventing the race from executing its rebellious purpose. He will actively interfere in what He has thus far tolerated. He will "confuse" or "confound" in the sense of mix or mingle (Heb., *bālăl*, used of mixing cakes or flour with oil; see Exod. 29:40; Lev. 2:5; 14:10). Precisely how Jehovah confused their one language and vocabulary into many different languages and mixed dialects is not revealed.

8. So the Lord scattered them. They themselves refused to scatter (v. 4), so Jehovah in mercy scattered or dispersed them. This was for their own good in the long run, even though the confusion of languages was a punishment. **9. Therefore is the name of it called Babel** is a play on words. It was dubbed *Babel* because there Jehovah made a *babble*. From the verb *bālăl* ("mix, confound") comes the form *balbel*, contracted to Babel ("confusion, mixture"). This represents the actual origin of the name of this famous (biblically infamous) city. The Akkadian derivation of Babel from *bab-ilu* ("gate of God") is a polytheistic perversion of the original name of the city, as the ziggurat was a similar polytheistic misunderstanding of the original "tower" (11:4).

H. THE ANCESTRY OF ABRAHAM. 11:10-32.

The Line of Shem. 11:10-26. This is the redemptively important line (9:26) through which Christ was to come. Hence, it is last but not least in the table of nations (10:21-31). All previous history has been skeletonized in order to focus upon the redemptive promise through Shem. **10. These are the generations** (see 2:4) **of Shem.** A new and pivotal turning point is introduced in the divine dealing. Up to now the history recorded, telescopic as it was, concerned the whole Adamic race, with no distinction between Jew and non-Jew (Gentile nations). Now with the call of Abram and the creation of the nation Israel, the divine redemptive promise (3:15) is to be realized.

Shem ... begot Arpachshad two years after the flood. Although the genealogy spans the period from the Flood to Abraham, it does not give data to date the Flood (see 5:30-32). The Hebrew word translated "begot" does not necessarily mean "became the father of," but in these *drastically abbreviated* lists it means "became the ancestor of." When Shem was one hundred years old, his wife bore a child who was either Arpachshad or an ancestor of Ar-

pachshad. The Flood certainly occurred before 4000 B.C. The long interval between it and Abraham's birth (2161 B.C.), probably at least two thousand years, is evidently covered by this brief genealogy. To have listed all the links would have resulted in an impossibly long and cumbersome text, which would have marred the simplicity and appeal of Genesis 1-11, the introduction to the story of redemption.

18-23. Peleg ... Reu ... Serug ... Nahor. Indications of Hebrew residence in northwestern Mesopotamia (called "Paddan-Aram," Aramaic, *paddana*, "field or plain" or Aram, 25:20) appear archaeologically in Abraham's forebears, whose names survive in towns near Haran: Serug (Assyr., *Sarugi*), Nahor (Nahur in the Mari Tablets of the eighteenth century B.C.; cf. 24:10) and Terah (*Til Turakhi*, "Mound of Terah," in Assyrian times). Peleg recalls *Paliga* on the Euphrates River just above the mouth of the Habur River (W. F. Albright, *The Archaeology of Palestine and the Bible*, p. 210). Reu also corresponds to later names of towns in the middle Euphrates Valley (Albright, JBL 43 [1924]: 385-88). The town of Haran (11:31) is still in existence on the Balikh River. The name appears as Harranu ("road") in cuneiform sources from the nineteenth and eighteenth centuries B.C.

The Line of Terah. 11:27-32. **27. Now these are the generations** (see 2:4) **of Terah: Terah begot Abram.** At last the great representative man of faith (15:6; Rom. 4:11) and the most illustrious ancestor of the promised Redeemer (3:15) is introduced. All that precedes (chaps. 1-11) focuses on him, whose descendants through Isaac and Jacob are destined to become the nation Israel. This tiny nation was to be called to be a witness to the one true God amid universal idolatry (Deut. 6:4). It was to be a testimony to the world of the blessedness of serving Him (Deut. 33:26-29). It was chosen to receive and preserve the revealed Word of God (Deut. 4:5-8) and to be the human channel through which the promised Redeemer would come (21:12; 28:14; 49:10). No wonder Abram is dignified with a name meaning "high [exalted] father."

28. Haran died ... in Ur. Terah emigrated from southern Babylonia with his sons, Abram and Nahor. A third son, Haran, died in Ur, a city resurrected by archaeology since 1854 and now one of the best-known ancient sites of the region. When Abram migrated, the city was idolatrous, given over to the worship of the moon deity Nannar and his consort Nin-Gal; a sacred area and ziggurat were devoted to this idolatry.

Significantly, Nannar, the moon god, was also adored at Haran, to which Terah emigrated (cf. Josh. 24:2). It seems Abram's own father was an idolater. From universal polytheism God called Abram as a purge to be an exponent of the gospel of salvation by grace through faith and the blessing of knowing and serving the one God, the Creator and Redeemer of man.

31. They went forth ... from Ur of the Chaldeans, to go into the land of Canaan. Apparently Terah's idolatry caused him, as family head, to settle down in Haran. Not until his father died, did Abram move on and obey the divine call to go on into Canaan (12:1). Idolatry has a terrible fascination; only faith in God can break its charms and free one from its tentacles. Canaan is the more ancient name of Palestine, apparently derived from Hurrian, meaning, "belonging to the land of red purple," the dye the early Canaanites or Phoenician traders peddled far and wide. It was obtained from the murex shells found on the Mediterranean (Phoenician) coast.

II. PATRIARCHAL HISTORY OF ISRAEL. 12:1—50:26.

The primeval history of man (1:1—11:32) set the stage for the patriarchal history of Israel in the land of Canaan. This small country was situated as a bridge between the great ancient empires of Babylonia and Assyria on the Tigris and Euphrates rivers and the Hittites on the Halys River on one hand, and the great Egyptian power on the Nile on the other. This location of God's people was providential. Their calling was to be a testimony and a witness of the true God, who revealed Himself to Abraham and his descendants, so that they might make Him known to those who crossed the bridge between ancient empires.

1. GOD'S PROMISE TO ABRAHAM. 12:1-20.

A. THE HISTORY OF ABRAHAM. 12:1—25:11.

The Abrahamic Covenant Given. 12:1-3. The covenant was confirmed (13:14-17; 15:1-7; 18-21; 17:1-8). It included three unconditional promises of blessing: (1) *To the nation Israel:* **2. I will make of thee a great nation**—through Isaac and Jacob (Israel) of the Old Testament. But the promise awaits fulfilment in the Kingdom age when Israel will be the *head* nation, not the tail (Deut. 28:13). The nation is to inherit a specific territory forever (15:18-21; 17:7-8).

(2) *To Abraham personally:* **I will bless thee,** fulfilled temporally (13:14-15; 15:18; 24:34-35) and spiritually (15:6; John 8:56); **and make thy name great,** fulfilled in recognition by all who honor God's written Word, the Bible; **and thou shalt be a blessing,** fulfilled in Israel's becoming the channel of divine revelation and the vehicle through whom the

54

Savior was to be born (Gal. 3:16).

(3) *To the nations*: **3. I will bless them that bless thee.** Those who have persecuted the Jew have fared ill. Those who have protected and befriended him have prospered (Deut. 30:7). **In thee shall all families of the earth be blessed**, fulfilled in Christ, "the son of David, the son of Abraham" (Matt. 1:1), and all who are saved by grace through faith in the Redeemer of mankind. On other major covenants, see Edenic (Gen. 2:16); Adamic (Gen. 3:15); Noahic (Gen. 9:16); Mosaic (Exod. 19:5); Palestinian (Deut. 30:3); Davidic (2 Sam. 7:16); and the New (Heb. 8:8).

The Abrahamic Covenant initiated the Administration (dispensation) of Promise. As a specific era of testing, this administration ended with the Israelites' acceptance of the Law and Mosaic Covenant at Sinai (Exod. 19:8). However, the promises of this covenant were never set aside, and they span all succeeding ages until the dawn of eternity, like the previous administrations of Moral Responsibility and Government. For these administrations, see: Innocence (Gen. 1:28); Moral Responsibility (Gen. 3:7); Government (Gen. 8:15); Law (Exod. 19:1); Church (Acts 2:1); Kingdom (Rev. 20:4).

Blessing in the Land. 12:4-9. Blessing was promised in the promised land (12:1-2). **4-5.** It began when **Abram ... departed out of Haran** (see 11:31) **... and ... went forth to go into the land of Canaan.** Therefore, this thought is emphasized in connection with the Abrahamic Covenant—**into the land of Canaan they** (he and his relatives) **came.** (On meaning of "Canaan," see comments on 11:31.) **6. And Abram passed through the land** to survey with the eye of faith the place where God had sent him (12:1) and was about to give him and his descendants *by faith*. **Shechem** (Tell

Balaṭa) was in the center of the land at the east end of the valley running between Mount Ebal on the north and Mount Gerizim on the south.

7. And the Lord appeared unto Abram, initiating the place as a holy rallying point of many later historical associations. There Jehovah manifested Himself to the patriarch and gave him the staggering promise of the land as the possession of his descendants. **There builded he an altar.** Like Abel (4:4) and Noah (8:20), Abram offered sacrifices on the altar, proclaiming his trust in the promise of the coming Redeemer (3:15, 21) and his subscription to the one true gospel of salvation by grace through faith based on the shedding of blood in token of fallen man's need of a divine Redeemer.

8. From Shechem Abram moved to the Bethel-Ai region, still in the central highland ridge about a dozen miles north of Jebus (later Jerusalem). He showed his vibrant faith by again building **an altar unto the Lord** and calling on the **name of the Lord.** The divine appearance in theophanic form at Shechem stirred the patriarch's faith to build another altar and, through blood sacrifice befitting fallen humanity, to enter the sanctum of fellowship in prayer with the Holy One, who later became known as the "Holy One of Israel" (2 Kings 19:22; Psalm 71:22; Isa. 1:4; Jer. 50:29, etc.). **9. And Abram journeyed ... toward the Negev.** His faith spurred him on to see the *whole* land to which Jehovah had called him and promised to give to him (v. 1) and his posterity. But in what sense could the land be said to be actually given to Abram, especially when it is said that **the Canaanite was then in the land** (v. 6)? In approximately 2086 B.C. (biblical chronology) when Abram entered Canaan, archaeology has shown that the hill country was still unoccupied by a sedentary population, so the patriarchs were free to roam the hills of central Palestine and the dry lands of the south (the Negeb), where there was still plenty of room for them (Albright, OTC, p. 140; and *Archaeology of Palestine and the Bible,* pp. 131-33).

Forfeiture of Blessing Outside the Land. 12:10-13. Although the Abrahamic Covenant was gracious and unconditional, immediate blessing for Abram, as for all of God's people, was dependent upon faith proved by obedience. **10. There was a famine in the land.** Abram's faith was seriously tried. He failed to remain in the land, the place of promised blessing. Instead of Canaan, which is a type of separation from the world for the believer who is in communion with God (cf. vv. 7-8), under testing he substituted Egypt, a type of the world, which the believer is to shun (1 John 2:15-17).

And Abram went down into Egypt. Even the greatest men of faith fail through unbelief. True, he intended only to **sojourn there** (*gûr*; cf. Arabic, *jārā*, "turn aside, stay as a temporary resident, stop over"). But good intentions often turn out badly, so the word in the Old Testament often approximates "abide," nearly or quite equivalent to "dwell" (Jer. 43:5; 50:40; Isa. 11:6). This was Abram's peril and the temptation of everyone who "goes down" (*yārăḏ*, "descend, take a downward course") from the mountain heights of Canaan to the lowland of Egypt. Spiritual declension opens the life of the best to the worst of sins.

11. When he was come near to enter into Egypt. His decision, dictated by unbelief, made the fruits of disobedience appear. He contrived a lie or, what is worse, a half-truth. **13. Say ... thou art my sister.** Sarai was indeed his half sister on his father Terah's side (20:12). Get-

ting out of God's will always exposes believers to temptation and sin to which they are immune when in spiritual victory. If Sarai passed for his sister, her honor would be endangered, but his life spared. Disobedience brought a dilemma. The Hebrew women were fairer than all others and were sure to be coveted by foreigners. But so sacred was the marriage bond that even a foreigner, to take the wife, must first kill the husband (T. K. Cheyne, *Genesis*, ICC, pp. 248-49).

The Faithfulness of God. 12:14-20. Although Abram became unfaithful, God remained faithful. "He cannot deny himself" (2 Tim. 2:13). He had made a covenant with His servant, promising him the land of Canaan. But when he was out of the place of blessing, Abram was filled with fear of being killed. God had promised him and his posterity blessing through the coming Redeemer; yet Abram exposed Sarai, through whom the promised seed would come, to dishonor. But God interposed to keep His word, despite His servant's failure. **15-17. The woman was taken into Pharaoh's house .... And the Lord plagued Pharaoh and his house with great plagues,** literally, "punished [struck] him with great punishments," or in English idiom, "punished him severely."

18. Pharaoh ... said, What is this that thou hast done unto me? This is the familiar case of a backslidden believer being rebuked by a worldling. Compare disobedient Jonah rebuked by the pagan shipmaster: "What meanest thou, O sleeper?" (Jonah 1:6). The idolatrous Pharaoh displayed more moral awareness at the moment than the man of God. Had not God interfered, Abram might have been tempted to stay in Egypt and forget God's call and promise (cf. Psalm 105:13, 15). **20. And Pharaoh commanded ... and they sent him away.** The term *pharaoh* is the common title in the Bible for the kings of Egypt. Derived from the Egyptian word meaning "great house," it originally denoted the royal palace and court. Gradually, however, it came to denote "His Majesty," the king, becoming an honorific title. A wayward child of God is a liability to sinners; they are glad to be rid of him.

2. ABRAM AND LOT. 13:1-18.

Abram's Return to the Place of Blessing. 13:1-4. **1. And Abram went up out of Egypt.** Palestine being a highland country, the return from Egypt through its southern boundary is geographically a continual ascent. More significantly, the return to Canaan represents spiritually a far greater ascent. The Negeb (*nĕgĕḇ*, "the dry") embraces the semiarid lands of the south, covering about 4,520 square miles, nearly half the area of the modern Israeli State. **2. Abram was very rich.** This fact is stressed as he returned to fellowship with God and prepared himself for covenant blessings (cf. "I will bless *thee*," 12:2, italics added). **Silver** and **gold** were rare among pastoral peoples and probably the result of the sale of cattle in Egypt. **3-4. And he went . . . to Bethel . . . Unto the place of the altar.** He was completely restored from his lapse in Egypt. Recalling the LORD's appearance to him there (12:8), he once more **called on the name of the Lord** (cf. 12:8; 21:33). Certainly he fully confessed his unworthy conduct in Egypt and found full restoration of fellowship with Jehovah. This spiritual undergirding was a necessary step for the tough decision of faith he was to face shortly.

Abram's Separation from Lot. 13:5-9. **5-6.** Lot (*lôṭ*, perhaps "covering") was Abram's nephew, the son of Haran, Abram's youngest brother. He prospered materially, but not spiritu-

ally. Doubtless his defective spiritual life had appeared before the present episode. **7. There was a strife between the herdsmen of Abram's cattle and the herdsmen of Lot's cattle.** For believers to quarrel was a poor testimony to the native pagan inhabitants of the land; therefore, it is recorded that **the Canaanite and the Perizzite dwelt then in the land** (c. 2050 B.C., biblical chronology). **8. Let there be no strife . . . for we are brethren.** Literally, "We are men, brothers." Or, "We have a common tie in Jehovah, and 'strife' (*mᵉrîḇâ*, "contention," cf. Exod. 17:7; Num. 27:14) is not fitting for brothers, adult men, who ought to realize the incongruity of such conduct as a reproach upon the God we serve."

9. Is not the whole land before thee? Abram's conduct was unselfish and nobly nourished by faith. He had a right to dictate, but he gave the freedom of choice to Lot. **Separate thyself.** All God's servants who would walk by faith and not sight and avoid strife and contention and other temptations to sin must separate themselves not only from sinners (Exod. 6:6; 2 Cor. 6:17) but also from believers who walk disorderly (1 Cor. 5:5-7; 2 John 10-11).

Lot's Steps in Backsliding. 13:10-13. **10. Lot** made the choice of sight rather than faith. He **lifted up his eyes, and beheld** (saw) **all the** *plain of Jordan.* Although geographically Lot actually looked down from the height of the hill east of Bethel, yet curiously the idiom is, "he lifted up his eyes" in selfish anticipation, jumping at the chance to make the best choice, and thus yielding to temptation in the form of "the lust of the eyes" (1 John 2:16; cf. Eve, Gen. 3:6).

The plain (circle, round) **of Jordan** was the Jordan Valley as it existed before the catastrophe that destroyed the

57

cities of Sodom and Gomorrah, now buried under the shallow waters of the southern end of the Dead Sea. The violent earthquake and explosion evidently changed this whole region, which previously was **well watered,** evidently by numerous springs. So fertile and beautiful was it that it is compared to **the garden of the Lord** (Eden) and **the land of Egypt**, where the life-giving waters of the Nile are channeled through the fields to irrigate them.

11. Lot chose him all the plain of Jordan. In so doing, he **separated** himself from God's people and yielded to the temptation to settle down and live with sinners (see 13:10; 19:1, 33). This was Lot's second step in backsliding. Lot's choice of sight rather than faith weakened him for his final step of backsliding. **12. Lot ... pitched his tent toward Sodom.** Although a good man, his wrong choices exposed him to grave temptations and perils. **13. But the men** (people) **of Sodom were wicked and sinners before the Lord exceedingly.** They impudently flouted the eternal moral laws of the Creator, later reflected in the Mosaic Decalogue (Exod. 20:1-10), especially those regulating the distinction between the sexes and the different orders of God's creatures (angels and men; cf. 19:5-11).

Abram's Faith Brings Covenant Promises into Clear Focus. 13:14-17. The gift of Canaan was assured Abram and his natural posterity in perpetuity (12:2; Rom. 11:26). Separation from unbelief and carnality results in God's voice, announcing the fulfillment of His promise (cf. 15:5). The promise of the land is inseparable from the promise of peoples. **16. And I will make thy seed** (posterity) **as the dust of the earth.** This figure symbolizes the earthly natural descendants of Abram (28:14) in contrast to "the stars" of heaven, the spiritual or

heavenly progeny (15:5). Faith initiates God's directive to view the land (v. 14) and to walk through it to appropriate it as God's gift (v. 17).

Abram's Faith Brings Spiritual Prosperity. 13:18. Abram maintained his separated pilgrim character. He **removed his tent** (cf. Heb. 11:9). The Hebrew verb means "to take down or set up a tent." He moved to higher ground. Hebron, nineteen miles southwest of Jerusalem, is 3,040 feet above sea level, dominating a beautiful and fruitful area. Ancient oaks (terebinths) graced the place. Evidently a grove of the stately trees belonged to Mamre, a confederate of Abram at Hebron (14:13). Abram's faith also manifested itself in a fresh tribute of devout gratitude to Jehovah in token of the renewal of the covenant promise (vv. 14-17), for he **built there an altar unto the Lord.**

3. ABRAM AND MELCHIZEDEK. 14:1-24.

Lot's Capture: Another Test of Abram's Faith. 14:1-12. **1-3.** The historical difficulties, with which this chapter bristles, have detracted from its relevance to Abram's faith, which contrasts saliently with his worldly nephew's unbelief. Lot's worldly choice (13:10-13) got him into the predicament described in these verses. Abram's unselfish valor in rescuing Lot shows that a man of faith can be a brave hero and act the part of a warrior if the need arises.

The four invading kings were from Elam (v. 9), east of the Tigris River, and the alluvial plain country of lower Mesopotamia called Shinar (see 11:2). Although these rulers cannot be definitely placed as yet in the frame of contemporary history, the Hebrew Bible chronology places them around 2086 B.C. Chedorlaomer, an Elamite name, headed the invading alliance, which had subdued the five petty city-states of the

Jordan Valley some fourteen years previously.

4. Twelve years they served Chedorlaomer, and in the thirteenth year they rebelled. 5. In the fourteenth year ... the kings launched a punitive expedition, subduing the **Rephaim**, a primitive people of this region in **Ashteroth-karnaim**, cities of Hauran (Bashan), archaeologically attested for this early period. **Ham** is identified with a modern place by the same name in eastern Gilead. Also authenticated is the general line of march down from Hauran through eastern Gilead and Moab to southeast Palestine by a road later called "The King's Highway."

8. The vale of Siddim ("valley of bitumen pits") was the area now comprising the whole southern portion of the Dead Sea, where the cities of the plain lie buried beneath the shallow waters since the destruction of Sodom and Gomorrah. To indicate this is the purpose of the gloss in verse 3, "the valley of Siddim (that is, the Salt Sea)" (NASB).

Abram, the Warrior. 14:13-16. **13-14.** As a descendant of Eber in the chosen Messianic line (10:21), Abram is called a **Hebrew**. As a patronymic this designation has a peculiar propriety to distinguish the man of faith and promise from his allies, who are called Amorites. Although Lot was a backslider, Abram recognized him as a fellow believer, and so a **brother** (cf. 2 Pet. 2:7-8) in a deeper sense than merely a kinsman (nephew). Both by natural and spiritual ties, Abram was bound by ancient Semitic custom to hasten to help Lot, being his nearest kinsman (*gō'ēl*). He was **confederate** with the local Amorite chieftains of Hebron, for they were participants in a compact under solemn oath for mutual help and protection. Accordingly, they joined Abram in the expedition to rescue Lot (v. 24).

Hearing the news that his kinsman Lot had been captured, Abram called up **his trained servants** ("retainers," T.O. Lambin, JAOS 73[1953]:160) **born in his own house**, as opposed to slaves obtained through purchase. Hence, this class ranked close enough to family members to be entrusted with great responsibilities. The number 318 is not too small for a surprise attack and shows Abram as a powerful sheik. **Pursued** (gave chase to) **them** as far as **Dan**, modern Tell el-Qadi, near one of the sources of the Jordan, a modernization of the earlier name, Laish (Judg. 18:29) or Leshem (Josh. 19:47), appearing as Lusi in Egyptian texts (nineteenth century B.C.).

15. Pursued them unto Hobah (site unknown) **on the left hand** (of one facing east, hence to the north) **of Damascus.** This ancient city lay east of the Antilebanon Mountains overshadowed by Mount Hermon. **16.** Abram's faith and courage were rewarded with success. He recovered **all the goods, and ... his brother** (kinsman), **Lot.**

Melchizedek and Abram. 14:17-24. This passage displays Abram's gratitude to God for giving him victory over the invading kings from the east. **17. The king of Sodom** went out to meet the returning hero, for he had much to gain materially from Abram's military success. **18. Melchizedek** ("My king is righteousness"; cf. Heb. 7:2), **king of Salem** (Uru-salem, Uru-salimmu of the cuneiform inscriptions, the ancient site of Jerusalem) also welcomed the victorious warrior of faith. Returning from Damascus to Hebron, it would have been natural for Abram to stop over at Jerusalem.

The king-priest of Salem ("peace, safety") prefigures our Lord in His royal priesthood. The type looks forward to the Kingdom age when Christ, as the result of His death, resurrection, and second advent, will reign as King-Priest (Zech. 6:12-15), bringing in an era of universal peace based upon righteousness (Isa. 9:6-7). Then "righteousness and peace" shall kiss "each other" (Psalm 85:10). **Bread and wine** are memorials of Christ's sacrificial death and look forward to His coming again (1 Cor. 11:26). Jehovah is known to a Gentile king-priest as **the most high God** (*El Elyon,* "God the highest," a title of Deity now well known from the Ugaritic texts, fifteenth century B.C.).

19. The distinctive attribute of Deity under this designation is **possessor of heaven and earth** by virtue of creation and redemption. When Christ returns in glory as King and Lord supreme (Rev. 19:16) to set up His righteous and peaceful Kingdom, this title will be realized in its full prophetic connotation (Josh. 3:11; Zech. 14:9; Rev. 11:4). **22.** Abram had made a solemn oath that if **the Lord, the most high God, the possessor of heaven and earth**, gave him victory over the invading foes, he would not enrich himself. **24.** He did, however, allow **Aner, Eshcol, and Mamre,** who in covenant with him had assisted him in rescuing Lot, their portion of the booty.

4. THE COVENANT CONFIRMED. 15:1-21.

Abram's Shield and Reward. 15:1. **1. After these things** (the defeat of the invading kings and Abram's rejection of the offers of the world) **the word of the Lord came . . . in a vision.** Such a revelation banished all fear that Abram had done a foolish thing in refusing the patronage and "the goods" of Sodom. The LORD Himself gave him assurance He would be his **shield** against both his spiritual and natural foes, as well as his **exceedingly great reward**, both for time and eternity—a vivid contrast to the cheap and tainted emoluments Sodom's

king offered him. Faith manifested in works opens our eyes to envision God as our Protector and our incomparable reward, preparing us to face the greatest barriers that seem to lie in the way of the fulfillment of God's promises.

The Pivotal Issue of Sonship and Salvation. 15:2-6. **2.** Divine encouragement was designed to enable Abram to face this burning question upon which the covenant promise hinged. **Lord God** (*Adonai Jehovah,* my lordship, Jehovah), **what wilt thou give me, seeing I go childless . . .?** Wilt Thou be "my exceeding great reward" and give me a son and an heir? "And the son of possession" (Heb. idiom for "the possessor of my house," i.e., "my heir") "will be this Damascene, Eliezer" (Gesenius). Abram had followed the common Mesopotamian custom, archaeologically well attested, of childless couples adopting an heir (sometimes a former slave). It was stipulated, however, that if a natural son were subsequently born, he would replace the adopted son as heir. God's reassurance was offered in the context of the customary law of the period 2000 to 1500 B.C.

4. And, behold, the word of the Lord came unto him. Even a strong faith like Abram's needed assurance. It was one thing to trust God for a son and an heir when he was young; it was another thing to believe when he and Sarai had grown old. But God declared explicitly that not Eliezer but Abram's very own son would be his heir. **This shall not be thine heir; but he that shall come forth out of .thine own loins.** God showed Abram in a vision the star-studded sky, promising him an innumerable spiritual progeny (Rom. 4:18) as well as a natural progeny (cf. Heb. 11:12).

6. And he believed in the Lord (Rom. 4:3-6, 20-25). **And he counted** (reckoned, imputed) **it to him for righteousness.**

Abram's faith was a saving, justifying faith because its object was the coming Savior-Redeemer, whom he believed God would supply. For the first time he clearly and implicitly received, embraced, and rested in the promise of a seed—a son, an heir, and consequently, a Savior. His faith appropriated not merely the promise of salvation, but the specific offer of a Savior. He espoused the one true gospel of salvation by grace through faith. God is the Justifier of him who believes in Jesus (Rom. 3:26).

The transaction which took place under the starry sky is regarded in the New Testament as the pattern of a sinner's justification (Rom. 4:3-5, 21-25). Possessing no inherent righteousness of his own, Abram had the righteousness of Another (not at that time revealed to him) set to his account. Accordingly, he was declared righteous before the infinitely holy God. The condition was solely on the ground of faith in the divine promise of a son, an heir, and a Savior (Rom. 4:2-5).

Abram's faith rested in the naked word of God. He was "fully persuaded that, what he had promised, he was able also to perform" (Rom. 4:21). God has only one way of salvation—faith in God's grace revealed in Christ. This is the true gospel that is the same for all ages and dispensations. It is directed toward utterly lost and undone sinners, who can only be saved by faith in God's grace revealed in His Word.

The Covenant Guaranteeing the Land. 15:7-21. The gift of the land was modified by predictions of three dispossessions and three restorations: (1) the Egyptian (vv. 13-14, 16); (2) the Babylonian (Jer. 24:5-6); and (3) the worldwide, from A.D. 70 to present times (Deut. 28:61-65; 30:1-3). Israel was then in the third dispersion. From this global dispersion the nation will be restored at the advent of the Messiah-King under the terms of the Davidic Covenant (2 Sam. 7:16; Ezek. 37:21-25; Luke 1:30-33; Acts 15:14-17). The covenant was ratified here by divine oath, and afterward by human oath (Gen. 17). Such procedures are illustrated archaeologically by suzerain-vassal treaties and oaths of the times (NBC, p. 95).

7. I am the Lord who brought thee out of Ur. This divine treaty, opening with God's redemptive initiative, is paralleled by the preamble of contemporary treaties. The royal covenant-Maker proclaimed His title and deeds (cf. Exod. 10:2). **9-10. Take me an heifer ... she-goat ... ram ... pigeon.** The ritual confirming the oath was customary in the world of that era.

12. A deep sleep ... an horror of great darkness presaged the Egyptian bondage lasting four generations (better, "life-spans," calculated to last about one hundred years each). This passage foresaw the Egyptian sojourn in round numbers (400 years, v. 13). The exact period is recorded as 430 years to the day (Exod. 12:40), placing the entrance into Egypt at about 1870 and the Exodus at about 1440 B.C., according to the underlying chronology of the Hebrew Bible (cf. 1 Kings 6:1).

16. But in the fourth generation they shall come here again. This was a remarkable prediction of the entrance into Canaan (c. 1400 B.C.), followed by the conquest of the Canaanites, here categorized under the general term **Amorites** (cf. 48:22; Josh. 24:15). The moral debauchery of the Canaanites at the time of the Israelite conquest is shown by the Ras Shamra tablets from Ugarit (c. 1400-1375 B.C.) which bear out the declaration that the iniquity of the Amorites was **not yet full** (c. 2000 B.C.), but became full (c. 1400 B.C.), forfeiting the right of the inhabitants to the land (Lev. 18:24-30; 20:22-24). The time comes in the degeneration caused by persistent immorality that God's patience ends and His grace gives way to wrath and judgment (2 Pet. 3:9-12).

17. A smoking furnace (firepot) speaks of Egypt and the tribulations through which the sons of Israel were to pass (Deut. 4:20; 1 Kings 8:51). The **burning lamp** signifies God's presence with His people in their distresses. **18.** The boundaries of the land secured to Abram's descendants (through Isaac and Jacob) are given. **The river of Egypt** is not the Nile but a small stream south of Gaza on the Egyptian border known as Wadi el Arish. **19-21.** The ten nations, summarized by one (v. 16), are sometimes summarized by three (Exod. 23:28), or by six (Exod. 3:17), or by seven (Josh. 24:11; Acts 13:19).

5. ABRAM'S FALTERING FAITH. 16:1-16.

Temptation to Unbelief. 16:1-3. Great men of faith are tempted by unbelief, and even the greatest sometimes fail. Abram was no exception, and Scripture is faithful to show the seamy side of even the most outstanding saints. **1. Now Sarai, Abram's wife, bore him no children.** This was the divine side of Abram's testing. In the face of Sarai's barrenness, God's promise was that as Abram's "shield" and "exceedingly great reward" (15:1), *He* would give him the promised seed (3:15) and a spiritual progeny (15:4).

And she had an handmaid, an Egyptian, whose name was Hagar. This was the human side of Abram's testing. Most likely Hagar entered Abram's household as a result of his lapse when he forsook the land of promise and went down into Egypt. Worldly actions and choices tend to haunt us like ghosts and appear to ensnare us in our moments of weakness.

2. And Sarai said.... And Abram hearkened to the voice of Sarai. Unbelief, manifested in impatience with God's delay, appeared first in Sarai. Like a cancer, it spread to Abram. Sarai's suggestion represents a human makeshift to help out God. Sarai, *in faith* trusting God alone for the promised seed, the Savior, is a picture of the covenant of grace procuring salvation by grace through faith, totally apart from the works of the Law (Eph. 2:8-9; Gal. 4:24-25). Hagar is a picture of the covenant of the Law, which offers God some human resource or merit for acceptance with Him in the place of complete reliance upon His power and unmerited favor both to save and to keep through the promised seed.

Results of Unbelief. 16:4-16. **4.** Abram yielded to unbelief. **He went in unto Hagar** (had sexual relations with her). The human expedient apparently worked, for **she conceived.** Family tension and unhappiness followed. **5.** Sarai **was despised** (belittled) by her own maid servant, an Egyptian to boot (cf. 1 Sam. 1:6-7). **5.** Family turmoil was further increased when Sarai realized her husband had wronged her. **The wrong done me** (objective genitive). She blamed him, although it had been her idea. **Be upon thee . . . the Lord judge between me and thee.** She also realized that the LORD (above all) had been dishonored, His holy commandment flouted (Exod. 20:14).

6. The lapse of faith brought out the worst in both Abram and Sarai. He cowardly shirked his husbandly duty and delivered Hagar, an innocent victim, to Sarai. Sarai, in turn, displayed harshness and injustice in dealing with Hagar. Literally, she "oppressed" her (*'innâ*, "to mistreat, deal harshly with"). Even Hagar was forced to do another wrong thing (in addition to shamefully being required to submit sexually to Abram). She **fled** from Sarai's cruelty.

9-11. Little wonder God's grace was so signally vouchsafed to Hagar. The angel of the LORD appeared to her at a fountain of water in the wilderness of Shur, beyond the Wadi el Arish, on the border of Egypt. Probably Hagar had planned to go back to Egypt. Directed to return to her mistress, she was promised a child and a numerous posterity. Ishmael ("God has heard"), the child of Sarai's and Abram's unbelief, became the progenitor of the Arabs, Israel's traditional enemies. Also from this line came Muhammad and Islam, one of the most demonic of religions and a foe of Christianity (cf. v. 12). **13-14. The well ... Beer-la-hai-roi** means "the well of him who lives and sees me" (24:62; 25:11). **16.** Abram's faith in the promised seed was to be tested for fifteen more years (cf. 21:5).

6. THE SIGN OF CIRCUMCISION. 17:1-27.

Revelation of God as El Shaddai. 17:1-3. By the time Abram was ninety-nine years old the thought of an heir by Sarai was humanly so remote as to be a laughing stock (cf. 17:17; 18:12). Abram's sorely tested faith needed bolstering by a theophanic appearance of the LORD, revealing Himself as the *Almighty God* (*El*, the mighty One, *Shaddai*, all-powerful, hence, "all-sufficient") to meet the most humanly hopeless and most desperate needs of His people.

1-2. To a ninety-nine-year-old man, "as good as dead" (Heb. 11:12), He declared, **I am the Almighty God** (*El Shaddai*) **... I will make my covenant ... and will multiply thee exceedingly** (18:18; cf. 28:3-4). The patriarchs were familiar with the name Jehovah; however, their experience of God from Abraham on

was largely that of Him as *El Shaddai*, the mighty Provider for all their needs (see Exod. 6:3-4). Such a wonderful revelation demanded proper human response.

Walk before me (live as in My presence) **and be thou perfect** (i.e., be blameless—genuinely and unreservedly confident in the integrity of My word and promise; cf. 6:9). Contemporary treaties began with the titles of the great king and the duties of vassals (cf. 15:7). **3.** Abram's response to God's voice is proper: man on his face, God on His throne. Only in this posture can God really talk to us.

Abram Becomes Abraham. 17:4-5. As the patriarch's faith was strengthened to grasp God's all-sufficiency to keep His promise by his talk with El Shaddai, his name was changed to signify faith's appropriation of God's word. **5. Neither shall thy name any more be called Abram** ("high father") **but ... Abraham ... father of many nations.** The name results from a sound play, "high father of a multitude" (Heb., *'āb -rām hᵃmôn*, "exalted progenitor of a concourse"). This name is prophetic of the hosts of all nations who would become Abraham's spiritual posterity by sharing his covenant faith through the promised redemptive seed (Gal. 3:29).

The Covenant Reconfirmed. 17:6-8. From this line, as to the flesh, Christ would come, following His Old Testament precursors, the kings of Judah (Meredith G. Kline, "Genesis," NBC, p. 96). Therefore, the promised line would be royal. **6. Kings shall come out of thee. 7-8.** Through Abraham's Messianic seed the covenant would be eternal (cf. Gal. 3:16). Christ's Kingdom would stand forever (Dan. 2:44). The covenant would also guarantee the land of Canaan in perpetuity, as a possession of those who would come into the redemptive blessing the Messiah would bring.

The Covenant Ratified by Circumcision. 17:9-14. As the rainbow was made the sign of the Noahic Covenant (8:20-22; 9:13), circumcision was divinely appointed the sign of the Abrahamic Covenant. As such, it represents that quality of faith in the promised seed, upon which the covenant rested, to justify and separate from the worldliness of sin ("the reproach of Egypt"; cf. Josh. 5:2; Gen. 15:6; Rom. 4:11). Spiritually, it is reckoning dead the deeds of the body through the Spirit (Rom. 8:13; Gal. 5:16-17; Col. 2:11-12) by virtue of union with Christ in death, burial, and resurrection (Rom. 6:11).

10. The practice of circumcision, found earlier among other peoples, was adopted to serve as the sign of incorporation into the covenant. Ancient covenants were ratified by oaths. Oath-curses, pronounced for violation of the covenant's terms, were dramatized in symbolic rites (cf. 15:6-17). A characteristic curse cut off the vassal to destruction and represented cutting off his name and posterity. Accordingly, circumcision was the knife rite by which the Abrahamic Covenant was ratified (lit., "cut").

14. Therefore, **the uncircumcised male** was to **be cut off from his people** for violation of the covenant seal. On the other hand, the person circumcised and bearing in his flesh the token of the covenant was "cut off" from the results of unbelief, which marked those who were not in covenant relation. For him, faith in the coming Redeemer brought him the justifying faith of Abraham (15:6), which cut him off from the unrighteous.

The Covenant Confirmed as Everlasting. 17:15-22. **15-16.** Promise was given concerning Isaac, in whom the Messianic line is to run to confirm the covenant as an everlasting agreement. In token of the divine power to be manifested through Sarai, her name was changed to **Sarah**, a variant of Sarai ("princess"). Curiously, the meaning of the change is not indicated, except that more specifically she is significantly designated as being in the royal Messianic line. The name Isaac ("he laughs") memorializes the humor of the situation. The union of aged Abraham and Sarah would produce what was utterly laughable from the human standpoint.

17. Then Abraham ... laughed. But his laughter was not yet in the free abandon of full faith, as his request of God shows. **18. Oh, that Ishmael might live before thee!** Abraham could laugh at God's joke, but the ridiculousness of the whole promise, humanly speaking, staggered his faith when the humor wore off. Abraham was quite willing to settle for Ishmael as the covenant heir. The terminology used is illustrated in contemporary vassal treaties. The aspirant to a vassal throne was made to "live" if the great king established him on the throne, especially when he had been rejected in his claims by rivals (i.e., killed).

19. I will establish my covenant with him (Isaac, not Ishmael) **for an everlasting covenant** (cf. v. 13). In the Messianic seed through Sarah, the Kingdom would stand forever (Gal. 3:16). **20. As for Ishmael, I have heard thee.** Ishmael as a patriarch would head a dynasty over an amphictyonic league (an association of neighboring tribes united for mutual protection and the worship of a common deity), though not over the Messianic line to be realized in the twelve tribes of Israel. **21.** The promised seed would come through Sarah's son, to be born **at this set time ... next year.** Isaac would be heir. A natural son, even if born after a son of a slave-wife, became chief heir in contemporary law.

The Covenant Sealed by Circumcision. 17:23-27. Abraham's faith was manifested by obedience. The sign of the covenant was now in the flesh of his household as a reminder of the promise of the coming Redeemer and the spiritual blessing through Him.

7. ABRAHAM, GOD'S FRIEND AND INTERCESSOR. 18:1-33.

Abraham, God's Friend. 18:1-8. **1. The Lord appeared unto him** in a theophany (cf. 12:7; 26:2; Dan. 10:5). **2. Three men stood by him.** Apparently these were the preincarnate Word, who was with God and was God (18: 1, 17, 22, 33; cf. John 1:1-3), and two angels (Heb. 13:2). The two angels appear again in 19:1. **3-8.** Abraham showed himself to be God's friend (cf. John 3:29; 15:13-15) by his demonstration of warm, typical Oriental hospitality.

Promise of Isaac's Birth Repeated. 18:9-15. (Cf. 17:15-19.) The promise was based upon God's word and power (v. 14). Both Abraham and Sarah were long past the age of childbearing. Abraham was ninety-nine years old (cf. 21:5), and Sarah was similarly advanced in age (21:7). The promise was so utterly impossible from the human standpoint that Sarah laughed inwardly, as if it were a joke. But her laughter concealed real faith (cf. Heb. 11:11).

Sin of Sodom and Gomorrah. 18:16-22. Abraham as God's friend was apprised of the divine judgment to be poured out upon the wicked "cities of the plain" (13:12-13). God's covenant with him, assuring Messianic blessing to all mankind (v. 18) and Abraham's domestic integrity (v. 19) were the reasons the patriarch was taken into the divine confidence. **20. The cry of Sodom and Gomorrah** was the outrage of their grievous sin registered before the infinite holiness of the Creator, before whom Abraham stood after the two angels departed to Sodom (v. 22).

Abraham, the Intercessor. 18:23-33. The patriarch as the friend of God under the control of the Spirit of God appears nobly as a go-between in between the sinners of Sodom and the outraged holiness of their Creator. The love and grace of God, manifested to him as a justified sinner (15:6) were appealed to in behalf of unjustified sinners endangered by death—physical as well as eternal. Certainly Abraham's intercession also had in mind his nephew Lot, a justified sinner and his kinsman (cf. 2 Pet. 2:6-9).

23. Wilt thou ... destroy the righteous with the wicked? In Hebrew, the interrogative grammatically expresses a strengthened negative: "You will surely *not* destroy the righteous with the wicked!" **25. Shall not the Judge of all the earth do right?** (I.e., "He most assuredly will do right!") Deep in the consciousness of the man of God was the inescapable conviction that the eternal Word, who was with God and was God, was absolutely fair, just, and impartial (cf. Rom. 2:5-11; Rev. 20:12-13). Contrast the divine judgment with the frequent partiality of human judgment (James 2:1-13).

27. Behold now, I have taken upon me to speak unto the Lord (*Adonai*)**, who am but dust and ashes.** The patriarch's deep humility and self-abnegation reveal his oneness with the mind of God in the matter. **28-32.** From **fifty righteous** the intercessor pleaded until the number was reduced to **ten.** God does hear the intercession of His own; He does spare His covenant people. He does punish sinners, but their punishment is in accord with their works, that is, their response to His eternal moral Law, which is as eternal as He is, being a reflection of Himself.

8. THE DESTRUCTION OF SODOM.
19:1-38.

The Moral Degeneracy of the City. 19:1-5. **1.** The **two angels** who came to Sodom in the evening were the celestial visitants of Abraham (18:22), dispatched to rescue the righteous before doom (cf. Matt. 24:31). **Lot sat in the gate of Sodom.** The gate with its open space and built-in wall chambers was the usual meeting place of the elders (Deut. 21:19-20). Lot had become a great man in a city of vile sinners doomed to destruction, the inevitable result of his former steps in backsliding (13:10-13). Lot's reverential reception and offer of customary Oriental hospitality displayed him as a believer at odds with his ungodly surroundings (cf. 2 Pet. 2:7-8). **3. Unleavened bread**, which Lot baked, speaks of the haste with which the righteous were to be delivered from the wicked, even as Israel was from Egypt (Exod. 12:8-12).

4-5. The depth of shameless depravity to which Sodom (and by clear intimation the other cities of the Pentapolis) had sunk is revealed. The moral permissiveness and the so-called new morality of these last days (2 Tim. 3:1-8) have their ancient parallel. Homosexuality and sexual perversion were rampant, shameless, and ripe for judgment (cf. 13:13; 18:20; Rom. 1:27), representing the present-day "new morality" in its same ancient dress.

Apparently the angels had assumed human form and could eat and sleep, functions possible for a glorified human body (cf. Luke 24:28-43). Being unfallen angels, sexual functions with humans was impossible, since they were confirmed in holiness. The sin-blinded Sodomites evidently thought they were merely men, or conceivably fallen angels, who by contrast are capable of unnatural sexual relations with humanity (cf. 6:1-4). The scope of this passage seems to necessitate the conclusion and give support to the same depth of wickedness that precipitated the Noahic Flood. **Know them** is a euphemism for sexual intercourse (cf. 4:1).

Lot's Powerless Testimony. 19:6-14. **7.** His pleas, **do not so wickedly**, fell on hostile ears. He was torn between the sacred duty of hospitality to protect his guests at any cost and the chastity of his daughters. His shocking offer to turn over the girls to the Sodomites betrayed his blurred moral sensibilities. What a price his compromise was extorting!

9. But they said, "Stand aside" (NASB; i.e., "Get out of the way!") **"This one came in as an alien** (a visitor or newcomer, for Lot had only recently settled down in Sodom) **and already he is acting like a judge; now we will treat you worse than them"** (NASB). This was a vivid display of the world's contempt for a world-conforming believer. They did not have the slightest regard for what he said. Instead, they attempted to break down the door and invade the privacy of his home with their wickedness and violence.

10-13. The angels had to forcibly pull Lot back into the house out of danger and then strike the Sodomites with blindness to thwart their plans so that Lot and his family might be delivered from impending judgment. **14. And Lot went out and spoke to his sons-in-law**, who evidently were betrothed (not yet married) to his daughters (cf. v. 8). **Who married** (lit., "were taking to wife") **his daughters.** But the language "also allows that the marriages had already taken place and that Lot, therefore, had daughters living with their husbands in addition to the two daughters with him"

(Kline, NBC, p. 98). Lot's bankrupt testimony is again underscored. **He seemed as one that mocked** (jested, joked) **unto his sons-in-law.**

Lot's Deliverance. 19:15-23. Vacillating, hesitating, world-conforming Lot was delivered only by the grace of God. **16. He lingered** (hesitated). **17.** He was warned to escape for his life, not to look back, but flee out of the plain into the mountain. But so infatuated was he with the world, so blinded to the judgment-ripe nature of Sodom's awful sin, so bereaved of a sense of his own immediate peril, that he refused to face reality. **18. Oh, not so, my Lord!** (lit. Heb., "Let it not be, my lords.") Apparently he was addressing the two angels, unless the angel of the covenant (Deity) had reappeared. **19.** So confused was Lot by compromise with evil that he contradicted himself. He acknowledged the mercy shown him in the sparing of his life; yet, through a strange lack of faith and gratitude, he could not believe that He who interposed for his rescue could protect him in a mountain solitude. Backsliding robs one of reason and common sense. How could He who saved him from so great an impending calamity not deliver him from lesser dangers? **20.** Even while this compromising believer was saved out of the world, the world had entrenched itself in his heart. **Behold now, this city is near to flee unto, and it is a little one.** City life had so bedazzled him that he had lost his pilgrim character. What a contrast his impulse of self-interest was to Abraham's intercession for Sodom, which sprang from unselfish love and sympathy. But Lot had to learn the hard way that it is always better and wiser to follow divine directions implicitly. **22. I cannot do anything till thou be come there.** Justified believers are saved

and safe before God in His eternal reckoning in Christ. They will never partake of God's wrath. So the church of Christ of the New Testament will not go through the Great Tribulation (Rev. 3:10; cf. 1 Thess. 1:10). Not until Lot was safe in Zoar (also called Bela, 14:2) did God destroy the cities of the plain.

Sodom's Destruction. 19:24-29. **24. The Lord rained upon Sodom and upon Gomorrah brimstone and fire.** The "cities of the plain" (v. 29), are now under the shallow waters of the southern part of the Salt (Dead) Sea. About 2065 B.C., this region was fertile and populous. But about 2050 B.C., the salt and abundant free sulphur of the area, which is now a burned-out region of oil and asphalt (14:10), were mingled miraculously, apparently by an earthquake. The violent explosion hurled the red hot salt and sulphur into the air, literally raining fire and brimstone over the whole plain.

26. But his wife looked back (her heart was in Sodom) **and she became a pillar of salt** (Luke 17:32). The great salt mass called Jebel Usdum ("Mountain of Sodom"), a five-mile-long elevation at the southwest end of the Dead Sea, testifies to what took place in that area. **27-29.** Abraham, the friend and intercessor of God, surveyed the destruction, but he saw the answer to his prayers in Lot's deliverance.

Lot's Final Phase of Backsliding. 19:30-36. At the very outset Lot discovered his mistake in fleeing, contrary to the divine direction, to Zoar (cf. vv. 17-23). He thought he would be afraid if he followed God's plan, but he experienced fear in his own way. Even when he switched to God's original plan, it was in self-will and self-interest, resulting in gross sin. **31-33.** His daughters displayed their father's weakness of character and choice of expediency rather than that which was morally right. The cost of Lot's compromise was colossal. He "pitched his tent toward Sodom" (13:12) and became a great man there (19:1), but as a result he lost his family, his daughters accepting the morals of Sodom. **33-36.** The sequel is a shameful episode of the twin sins of drunkenness and incest (the basest form of fornication, cf. 1 Cor. 5:1-5).

Origin of Moab and Ammon. *19:37-38.* Conceived in wickedness, these relatives but inveterate foes of Israel, "have a history of shame" (A. C. Gaebelein, *Annotated Bible*, 1: 53). **Moab** (Heb., *mô'āḇ*) is equated with *mē'āḇ* ("from father"). **Ben-ammi** ("son of my kin or people") is equated with "children of Ammon" (Speiser, AB, p. 144).

9. PROTECTION OF THE PROMISED SEED. 20:1-18.

Abraham's Lie. 20:1-2. Even God's greatest men in their unglorified state are but weak, sin-prone men, capable of serious lapse. The patriarch of faith, repeating the weakness of a former year (12:10-20) lied about his wife, Sarah. What a demonstration of the sinfulness of the fallen race. The near-recipient of the redemptive promise, soon to be fulfilled through Isaac, revealed himself to be a needy subject for God's grace. Negev means "the south country" (see comment on 12:9).

Evidently **Kadesh** is Kadesh-barnea in the northeast part of the Sinai Peninsula, while **Shur** lay on the frontiers of Egypt (cf. 16:7, 14) "between the present line of the Suez Canal on the west and the River of Egypt (Wadi el-'Arish) on its east" (NBD, p. 1183). **Gerar** has been commonly identified with Tell Jemmeh eight miles south of Gaza. More recently Tell Abu Hureira, a mound eleven miles

southeast of Gaza, has been suggested, as evidence shows a prosperous occupation in the patriarchal era. **Abimelech ... sent and took Sarah** into his harem, thus imperiling the promised line through Isaac. "Abimelech" ("father-king") was a title for the Philistine kings (21:22; 26:1; Psalm 34:1), as "Pharaoh" was for the Egyptian (12:15) and "Hamor" for the Shechemite rulers. These early Philistines preceded by many centuries the great wave that came with the invasion of the Sea People in the twelfth century.

Abimelech's Peril. 20:3-8. **3. But God** (*'ᵉlōhîm*) **came to Abimelech in a dream.** This is the usual method employed by Elohim in self-revelation toward pagans (41:16; Dan. 4:5). **Behold, thou art but a dead man** (Heb., "Behold, Thyself dying," i.e., "You're as good as dead!"). By this time the king was suffering from the malady that had fallen on his house (v. 17). **For** (because of) **the woman whom thou hast taken** (into thy harem); **for she is a man's wife** (*bᵉ'ulāṯ*, *bā'āl*, "married to a husband, under lordship to a master"; cf. Deut. 22:22).

4. Abimelech had not come near her. Apparently he was divinely restrained by the disease inflicted upon him. Such an action was necessary in view of the approaching birth of Isaac, who might not have been declared the child of Abraham, but of a Philistine king. **And he said, Lord,** (*Adonai*, 15:2) **wilt thou slay also a righteous nation?** At this early period, these tribes were comparatively virtuous. Anticipating that the stroke of divine judgment was about to fall on his people as well as on himself, Abimelech pleaded their innocence. It is evident that the Philistine king, like the Egyptian pharaoh, shrank from the sin of adultery. **5. In the integrity of my heart and innocency of my hands have I done this**, assuming my royal prerogative to take unmarried women into my harem.

6-7. In the divine communication, the king was told of God's intervention to preserve Sarah's chastity, and he was commanded to **restore the man his wife.** The reason: **For he is a prophet** (*nābî*, probably from Akk., *nābū*, "to announce, appoint"; "one appointed by God to speak for Him"). "As mediator of God's covenant, Abraham ... had peculiar access for intercession" (Kline, NBD, p. 98). **And he shall pray for thee** (cf. v. 17) **and thou shalt live** (an imperative meaning "Live thou!" to express lively certainty). **And if thou restore her not ... thou shalt surely die** (cf. 2:17), **thou, and all that are thine. 8. Therefore Abimelech rose early,** which was evidence of the terror of having incurred God's displeasure and in token of his earnest desire to obey the divine instructions. His household showed the same humility as their God-fearing king.

Abraham's Excuse for His Conduct. 20:9-13. **9.** Abimelech's words to Abraham imply a severe reproach (cf. 12:18-19). How tragic when men of God by sin compromise their testimony and invite rebuke from the world (cf. Jonah 1:6). **10.** Abimelech, identifying himself with his people, demanded an explanation from Abraham for his conduct. **What didst thou have in view ...?** ("Did you see any of my people committing adultery or murder?") The patriarch offered three apologies: (1) He had concluded (wrongly) that the fear of God was not in Gerar, and they would murder him to get Sarah. (2) He uttered a half-truth. Sarah apparently was her husband's half sister (Terah's daughter by another wife than Abraham's mother; cf. 12:11-13). (3) He acted in conformity to an old pact made between himself and Sarah. Wherever they went, she was to call him her brother. But Abraham's conduct was inexcusable.

He displayed himself as accepted by God on the basis of pure grace, as Lot also was, and as *all* justified sinners are.

Abimelech's Generosity. 20:14-16. The Philistine king showed more nobility than Abraham. Besides giving Abraham a munificent gift, he invited the patriarch to settle in his country (vv. 14-15). **16. And unto Sarah he said, Behold, I have given thy brother a thousand pieces of silver: behold, he is to thee a covering of the eyes** to everybody who is with you; you have been publicly vindicated.

Abraham's Prayer. 20:17-18. **17. So Abraham prayed unto God** (better, "interceded with God"). **God healed** "restored full health to Abimelech, namely his wife and maidservants, so that they could bear again" (Speiser, AB, p. 144). The whole incident emphasizes the supreme importance of the promised seed through Sarah to the outworking of the divine redemptive program for the salvation of mankind.

10. ISAAC'S BIRTH AND ISHMAEL'S EXPULSION. 21:1-34.

Birth of Isaac. 21:1-8. The fulfillment of God's word is stressed (vv. 1-2*b*; cf. 3:15; Heb. 11:19). **2.** Miraculously, **Sarah conceived, and bore Abraham a son in his old age. 3.** The name **Isaac** ("he laughs"; cf. 18:10-15) presages the joy the child of promise was to bring not only to his aged parents but to all the redeemed through the greater Isaac, Christ. Sarah, Isaac's mother, typifies grace, "the freewoman," and "Jerusalem which is above" (cf. 17:15-19; Gal. 4:22-31).

On the other hand, Isaac is typical in a fourfold sense: (1) of Christ as the Son "obedient to death" (22:1-10; Phil. 2:5-8); (2) of Christ as the Bridegroom of a called-out Bride (chap. 24; Matt. 16:18); (3) of the believer's new nature as "born after the Spirit" (Gal. 4:29); and (4) of the church as composed of the spiritual posterity of Abraham (Gal. 4:28). **4. Abraham circumcised ... Isaac.** This observance of the sign of the Abrahamic Covenant (17:9-14) was a sure evidence of the patriarch's faith in God's redemptive grace to be manifested through the promised seed.

Expulsion of Ishmael. 21:9-21. Current law provided that Ishmael was entitled to a share of the inheritance, but a son by a slave woman could forego his inheritance claim in exchange for freedom. **10. Cast out this bondwoman and her son.** Sarah, in her determination that Isaac should be sole heir, compelled Hagar and Ishmael to go free (cf. Gal. 3:18; 4:30; 1 Tim. 1:7-10). In contrast to Isaac (a type of the new nature), Ishmael is a type of the old nature. "It was not *Ishmael changed, but it was Isaac born*" (C. H. Mackintosh, *Notes on the Book of Genesis*, p. 218). The birth of Isaac did not improve Ishmael; it merely brought out his real opposition to the child of promise. Similarly, "that which is born of the flesh is flesh; and that which is born of the Spirit is spirit" (John 3:6). Ishmael might dwell in the wilderness, become a mighty archer, and beget twelve princes (25:12-18), but he was the son of the "bondwoman" all the while. Likewise, the old nature must be renounced, while the new nature in Christ must be nurtured by faith in the power of God. No matter how weak or depressed Isaac might have been, he was the son of the "freewoman." His position and character, like the new nature at regeneration, were from the LORD.

Covenant with Abimelech. 21:22-32. This incident attests the power and influence of Abraham under God's blessing. The Philistine king, though politically and militarily superior, was nevertheless impressed by the divine protection that guarded Abraham. The name *Beersheba* reflects three features of their treaty: $b^{e_9}\bar{e}r$, "well"; $sh\bar{e}b\check{a}^\varsigma$, "seven"; and $n\bar{\imath}shb\check{a}^\varsigma$, "swear."

Abraham's Worship. 21:33-34. **33. And Abraham planted a grove** ('ĕshĕl, "tamarisk tree") **in Beersheba,** about forty-eight miles southwest of Jerusalem, present Tel-es-Seba. The tamarisk tree was probably a token of the pact made. **Called there on the name of the Lord, the everlasting God** ('ēl 'ôlām). The Hebrew 'ôlām is employed of an indefinite time or age (Lev. 25:32; Josh. 24:2); hence, the term expresses the eternity of God: "from everlasting to everlasting" (Psalm 90:2). The original form of the name was apparently 'El dhu °Olami, "God of Eternity" (cf. W. F. Albright, *Bibliotheca Orientalis* 17 (1960):742).

11. ABRAHAM'S SUPREME TESTING. 22:1-24.

The Test. 22:1-2. **1. After these things ... God did test Abraham** (i.e., put him under trial to see if he would obey in faith; cf. Heb. 11:17-19). This, the greatest crisis of the patriarch's life, was made possible by three other preparatory crises or tests: (1) his surrender of country and kindred (12:1); (2) his separation from Lot, a fellow believer and potential heir (13:5-18); and (3) his yielding up of his own plans for Ishmael (17:17-18). The Hebrew is inverted for emphasis, and the effect is heightened by the definite article with Elohim. "The idea is thus conveyed that this was no ordinary procedure, but that God had a peculiarly important objective in mind" (Speiser, AB, p. 162). **2. Take now thy son, thine only son** (yāḥîd, "the unique one, the one and only") **Isaac, whom thou lovest.** This is the first use of the word *love* in Scripture (cf. John 5:20).

Abraham's Obedience. 22:3-10. **2-3.** The whole incident is fraught with deep spiritual meaning. Abraham prefigures the Father, who "spared not his own Son, but delivered him up for us all" (Rom. 8:32). Isaac is a picture of Christ being "obedient unto death" (Phil. 2:8). The ram illustrates substitutionary atonement through Christ offered as a burned offering in our place (Heb. 10:5-10). Abraham's faith even contemplated physical resurrection (v. 5), as Hebrews 11:19 confirms. **Moriah** is certainly to be connected with the vicinity of the Temple area at Jerusalem (cf. 2 Chron. 3:1). **6-10. Abraham took the wood . . . the fire . . . a knife . . . . And Abraham . . . took the knife to slay his son.** What a magnificent demonstration of unfaltering faith manifesting itself in works (James 2:21-23).

God's Provision. 22:11-14. As in Genesis 16:7, **the angel of the Lord** is not a celestial being who is subordinate to God, but the LORD Himself, the eternal Word who was with God and was God, the preincarnate Christ. What dignity was accorded Abraham in the moment when his faith met God's test. The preincarnate Christ addressed him: **Lay not thy hand upon the lad . . . for now I know that thou fearest God.** You reverentially and completely trust Him (see Psalm 19:9). What a dramatic scene! He Himself, who would in time become the Lamb of God to take away the sin of the world, provided **a ram caught in a thicket . . . for a burnt offering,** a picture of Himself as the vicarious Atoner for the sin of mankind (cf. vv. 7-8; 4:4; Exod. 12:3-11, 27; Heb. 10:18).

14. And Abraham called the name of that place Jehovah-jireh ("Jehovah sees," or "sees to," i.e., "provides"; cf. v. 8, which is literally, "God will see

to a lamb for himself," i.e., "provide for himself a burnt offering"). **In the mount of the Lord it shall be seen** (*yērā'ĕh*, Masoretic text; or, "it will be provided," NASB). "On Yahweh's mountain there is vision" (Speiser, AB, p. 162).

The Covenant Reconfirmed. 22:15-19. Abraham's passing the severest test of faith with flying colors called forth the most solemn ratification of the covenant, indicated by six points: (1) There were the appearance and voice of the preincarnate Christ (the eternal Word with God, who was God, John 1:1-2; cf. Gen. 22:11). (2) This constituted a second appearance, Deity doubly honoring the occasion. (3) The covenant was sealed with a most solemn declaration—swearing by Himself, there being none greater (Psalm 105:9). (4) It clearly intimated that Abraham *had done* what God asked him, namely, to offer his only son as a burnt offering. **16.** "Isaac was *virtually dead* from the time Abraham commenced his journey to Moriah, hence the apostle speaks of his having been offered (Heb. 11:17 cf. Js. 2:21)" (JFB, p. 177). **18. Because thou hast obeyed my voice.**

(5) It expanded the scope of covenant blessing. In the earliest annunciation of the promises, Abraham was assured that he individually would be a source of world blessing (12:3; 18:18); now it is in "thy seed" (v. 17), repeated to Isaac (26:3) and Jacob (28:14). But even this expanded blessing centered in Christ, the coming seed (see Gal. 3:16; cf. John 8:56), and could only be realized in Him. (6) It promised victory over enemies: "Thy seed shall possess (take over) the gate of his enemies (v. 17; cf. 24:60; Num. 24:17-19), comprehending more deeply spiritual foes (Matt. 16:18; Eph. 6:10-20; Col. 1:13; 2:15). The "gate" meant access to a walled city, and "pos-

sessing" it meant control of the town (cf. 24:60).

Aramaean Kin Through Nahor. 22:20-24. **23. Milcah did bear to Nahor** forms a connecting link with the narrative that follows and the genealogical chain broken at 11:29. It is resumed here to give the background of Isaac's marriage. Nahor remained at Haran (see 11:31-32). Rebekah, Isaac's wife-to-be, was the daughter of Bethuel, the son of Milcah, Nahor's wife (24:15).

12. SARAH'S DEATH AND BURIAL. 23:1-20.

Sarah's Death. 23:1-2. **2. Sarah died in Kiriath-arba,** the older name of Hebron (Josh. 14:15; 15.13; Judg. 1:10). The reference to **Canaan** (see comment on 11:31) is necessary because of Sarah's burial. Abraham was still a mere sojourner in the promised land, not the lord or even a small property owner. He might have followed whatever burial procedure was allowed foreigners, but he displayed his faith in God's promises of ultimate reception of the inheritance beyond death (Heb. 11:13, 19). A family sepulcher would not be a legal claim to the possession of Canaan, but it would constitute a prophetic sign. **Abraham came to mourn . . . and to weep** (bewail), a reference to formal rites. Nuzi adoption documents specify that "when A dies, B shall weep for him and bury him" (*Joint Expedition . . . at Nuzi*, no. 59, ll. 19-23).

Purchase of a Sepulcher. 23:3-18. **4. Give me a possession of a burying place.** ("Allow me to acquire cemetery property in perpetuity.") **5. The children of Heth** (Hittites) at this early date belonged to the pre-Israelite population of the land (v. 7; see comment on 10:15). **6. Thou art a mighty prince,** literally, "a prince of God." The wealthy and sizable Abrahamic household with its godly head was regarded as God's protectorate (cf. 21:22). Yet Abraham was merely "a stranger and a sojourner [settler]" (v. 4), a hendiadys for "a resident alien."

Although a long-term resident, he nevertheless lacked the normal privileges of a citizen (12:10; 19:9), notably the right to own land. For this right he was asking for the cave of Machpelah, a tract (vv. 17, 19) in which the grotto was located. Evidently the patriarch desired only the cave, to avoid responsibility for dues, which according to Hittite law would be attached to the whole parcel if purchased. The cave became the tomb of Sarah (v. 19); Abraham (25:9-10); Isaac (35:29); Rebekah (49:31); Jacob (50:13); and Leah (49:31).

14-16. The sale price was 400 shekels of silver, about $260, a shekel being worth about 65 cents. **18. The gate of his city** (cf. v. 10) was the place where the elders conducted business and the sale contract was made legal.

Sarah's Interment. 23:19-20. In a typical sense Sarah is a picture of the nation Israel. Her death prefigures the death of the nation Israel after the events typified in the preceding chapter (the death and resurrection of the true Isaac, the promised seed, the Lord Jesus Christ). Israel, like Sarah, is buried among the Gentiles, while Isaac takes a bride (chap. 24), typifying the present church period. Afterward, Israel will be restored.

13. A BRIDE SECURED FOR ISAAC. 24:1-67.

Abraham Commissions His Servant. 24:1-9. **1. Abraham was old . . . and the Lord had blessed Abraham.** Sarah's death and Abraham's advancing years suggested the timeliness of securing a wife for Isaac to guarantee to him the covenant blessings of land and descendants. Underlying all these events is the typical mosaic that previews God's program to be realized through the Abrahamic Covenant and the promised seed through Isaac. Abraham (vv. 1-4) prefigures God the Father, who would make a marriage for His Son (cf. Matt. 22:2; John 6:44).

The unnamed servant furnishes a picture of the Holy Spirit, who does not "speak of himself" but takes the treasures of the Bridegroom to win the Bride (John 16:13-14), who enriches the Bride with the Bridegroom's gifts (1 Cor. 12:7-11; Gal. 5:22), and brings the Bride to the Bridegroom (Acts 13:4; 16:6-7; 1 Thess. 4:14-16). Rebekah prefigures the church, the called-out virgin Bride of Christ (24:16; 2 Cor. 11:2; Eph. 5:25-32). Isaac typifies Christ, whom the Bride loves through the testimony of the unnamed servant (1 Pet. 1:8), and who goes out to meet and receive His Bride (24:63; 1 Thess. 4:14-16). **2. Put ... thy** (right) **hand under my thigh,** refers to the reproductive organ to seal the utter solemnity of the oath (cf. 47:29) and probably had some connection with the significance of circumcision as the sign of the covenant (see 17:9-14). The object of the oath was to guarantee that the son would not leave the father's side (repeated twice, vv. 6, 8). The bride was to be gotten and brought to the son, not the son to the bride (cf. John 14:3; Acts 15:14-15; 1 Thess. 4:13-18).

The Servant's Obedience and Success. 24:10-56. The servant's faithfulness and his prayer (vv. 10-14) and its answer (vv. 15-21) beautifully bespeak the Holy Spirit's work in calling out and giving gifts to the church of this age (vv. 22-33). The servant's testimony concerning the father (Abraham) and the son (Isaac, vv. 34-52) dramatically illustrates the Holy Spirit's ministry in calling out the Bride of Christ (cf. John 16:13-14). The second bestowment of gifts (v. 53; cf. v. 22) portrays the Spirit's rich endowment of the church (cf. 1 Cor. 12:1-6).

The Bride Brought to Isaac. 24:57-61. Rebekah offers a rich and full illustration of the church. Her beauty, virginity, kindliness, and energy already have been stressed (vv. 15-19; 2 Cor. 11:2; Eph. 5:25-27). **57-58.** Now her love for her unseen bridegroom is shown in her willingness to go to him. **59-60.** The blessing pronounced upon her was wonderful as she left home and kin (cf. 1 John 4:19).

Isaac Meets and Takes His Bride. 24:62-67. **62-66.** Rebekah was brought to Canaan (type of the heavenlies to which the church will be taken by translation or rapture). Even as the servant presented the bride to Isaac, so the Holy Spirit will present the church to Christ (Eph. 5:25-27). **67. Isaac brought her into his mother Sarah's tent ... she became his wife ... Isaac was comforted.** The church comforts the divine Isaac upon the national death and setting aside of Israel. The union of Christ and the church will take place in heaven (Rev. 19:7-9).

14. ABRAHAM'S DEATH. 25:1-11.

Abraham's Marriage to Keturah. 25:1-4. The typical teaching of chapters 22 through 25 springs out of the fact that the blessings set forth are connected with the Abrahamic Covenant and, accordingly, with the patriarch and his life. His marriage to Keturah, which took place after Isaac's marriage, shows that after the church is completed and the present age ends, all families of the earth will be blessed (12:3). This is prefigured by Abraham's descendants from Keturah. These prefigure millennial nations. The Keturah tribes settled in northwest Arabia (cf. 17:5).

Isaac the Heir. 25:5-6. **5-6. Abraham gave all ... unto Isaac.** He alone was heir. The others received only gifts and were sent away. So the divine Isaac is "heir of all things" (Heb. 1:2).

Abraham's Death and Burial. 25:7-11. Abraham died at the age of 175, living apparently till Jacob and Esau were 15 years old. He was buried beside Sarah in the cave of Machpelah (cf. 23:3-18). He was "gathered to his people." This sequel to death does not refer to burial of the body, but to the abode of the soul and spirit after death. It is employed only of six persons— Abraham (25:8); Ishmael (25:17); Isaac (35:29); Jacob (49:29-33); Aaron (Num. 20:24); and Moses (Deut. 32:50).

B. THE HISTORY OF ISAAC.
25:12—28:9.

1. THE DESCENDANTS OF ISHMAEL.
25:12-18.

Ishmael's Posterity. 25:12-18. **12. Now these are the generations of** means "this is the history of" (see comment on 2:4). Abraham was promised fatherhood of many nations (17:4, 6, 16) besides Israel. As **Abraham's son,** Ishmael was to beget "a great nation" (17:20). Jehovah, Lord of the Abrahamic Covenant, it must be noted, is God of all the earth. He directs *all* history by His sovereign providence.

16. By their towns, and ... encampments, distinguishing the more settled princes from those who were more roving. **18.** The nomadic sphere of the Ishmaelites (Arabs) was far flung across the northwest Arabian wilderness. The great chapter on the millennial Kingdom (Isa. 60) mentions Kedar and Nebaioth (v. 7), showing that when Israel is restored to blessing in the land, Ishmael's

posterity will not be forgotten. Like later Israel, the Ishmaelites were organized into twelve tribes, each with a tribal prince.

2. ISAAC'S TWO SONS. 25:19-34.

Isaac's Family. 25:19-21. **19.** The fact that Isaac was **Abraham's son** was emphasized, as that was the basis of the redemptive line. **20.** His wife, Rebekah, and her Aramaean lineage are stressed. Her barrenness presented another serious test to the realization of the divine promise, as Sarah's similar situation had done. **21.** Isaac showed faith in casting himself upon divine omnipotence in prayer.

Birth of Esau and Jacob. 25:22-26. **22. And the children struggled together within her,** ominously presaging the conflict between them even in the prenatal condition. **If it be so, why am I thus?** ("If this is how it's going to turn out, why did God let me become pregnant?") She demonstrated her faith by seeking God's answer in prayer. The answer she got reveals God's sovereignty, here solemnly made known (cf. Rom. 9:11-13). The·struggle recalls the clash between the two seeds, Ishmael and Isaac, in Abraham's household (21:9-21) and the clash between the spiritually renewed man of faith (Jacob) and the unrenewed natural man of the earth, destitute of faith (Esau).

23. The elder shall serve the younger. God knew the two boys before they were born and chose Jacob according to His sovereign will and purpose. Only after the defiant character of Edom had been fully established did God declare, "I hated Esau" (Mal. 1:3). Then the term *hate* is employed relatively, not absolutely. The good things done for Jacob in comparison with those done for Esau were like loving and hating (cf. Luke 14:26).

74

25. The first came out red (*'aḏmōnî*, a play on the word *Edom*) **all over,** literally, "like a mantle of hair" (*śē^cār*, a play on the word *Seir*, "hair," a synonym of Edom). **And they called his name Esau**, an indirect word play and eponym of *Edom* and popularly construed as meaning "hairy" (27:11). **26. His brother came out, and his hand took hold on Esau's heel.** The word for "heel" (*'āqēḇ*) is employed as a pun for *Jacob* (*yă^caqōḇ*), found also in extrabiblical sources with the meaning, "may he [God] protect" (*ya^{ca}qōḇil*; see Kline, NBC, p. 101).

Esau Sells the Birthright. 25:27-34. The divine oracle, confirmed by the birth omen, began to be fulfilled in the character of the two boys, who were opposites. **27-28.** Tension in the home developed as a result of parental favoritism. Esau's sale of the birthright shows him as a representative of the natural man of the earth (Heb. 12:16-17), destitute of faith and interested only in carnal pleasure and satisfaction. The birthright conveyed a double share in the inheritance, in this family the full "blessing of Abraham" (28:4).

The Nuzu letters record the transfer of a prospective inheritance from one brother to another for a few sheep. It may be only this double share that Jacob could get by barter. But certainly Esau's unbelief and despising of spiritual blessings cost him (1) the honor of being in the direct line of the promised Satan-bruiser (3:15) and the Abrahamic promise of the earth-blesser (12:3); (2) the exercise of the domestic priesthood, for until the Aaronic priesthood was instituted, the family head was the priest; and (3) the dignity of the family headship and the highest paternal blessing. **29.** When Jacob was cooking a stew, Esau came in famished from the field. **30.** Esau said, "Give me a swallow of

that red stuff" (*hā-'āḏōm*), which is why they named him Edom ("red," another play on "Edom"; cf. 25:25). **31-33.** Although Jacob took advantage of Esau's hunger and carnal appetite to gain the birthright, nevertheless his desire for it evidenced faith.

34. Esau, for a momentary fleshly gratification, **despised** (*bāzâ*, "to treat with contempt") this invaluable spiritual benefit. Esau and Jacob illustrate the entirely different ground that faith and unbelief occupy. In spite of Jacob's unworthy behavior, he had faith, which opened up his faulty experience to the electing grace and love of God (Mal. 1:2-3). Unbelief barred Esau from spiritual blessings.

3. EPISODES IN ISAAC'S LIFE. 26:1-35.

The Abrahamic Covenant Confirmed to Isaac. 26:1-5. **1-3.** As Abraham was tested by famine (12:10), so was Isaac. As a pilgrim alien, Isaac went to Abimelech (evidently a Philistine dynastic title) at Gerar (see comments on 20:1-10; cf. 1 Sam. 21:10-11 and the heading of Psalm 34). The LORD's appearance, prohibiting Isaac to trust in the arm of Egypt, compelled him to look to God. As a result the Abrahamic Covenant was confirmed to him (vv. 3-4). Since Isaac is the type of Christ risen from the dead (22:5) and Egypt is a type of the world, this command is very significant. Isaac was separated from Egypt, even as Christ and His people are separated from the world and share a heavenly position in Him (Eph. 1:3). **4.** Noteworthy in this connection is the prophecy that his posterity would be **as the stars of heaven** (the spiritual seed; cf. in Abraham's case "as the dust of the earth," 13:16, with stress on the natural descendants; but cf. 15:5, since the spiritual progeny was also included in Abraham's descendants). **5.** "All be-

75

cause Abraham heeded my call and kept my mandate: my commandments, my laws, and my teachings" (Speiser, AB, p. 198). "Mandate," *mǐshmĕrĕṯ*, "charge" (KJV) is "something to be scrupulously observed" (Speiser, AB, p. 201). The three nouns that follow spell out the contents of the mandate.

Isaac's Lapse in Gerar. 26:6-11. In Gerar, Isaac failed just as his father had (20:1-18). While Sarah had been taken into the royal harem, Rebekah was not touched or separated from Isaac, presaging the glorious fact that Christ and His church are inseparable. In one case God undertook to protect the promised seed. In the other case He demonstrated His care of His own despite their unfaithfulness; "He abideth faithful; he cannot deny himself" (2 Tim. 2:13).

Isaac's Prosperity. 26:12-16. Isaac was shown to be under the LORD's protectorate. **13.** "Isaac grew richer all the time, until he was very wealthy" (lit. Heb. trans.). God blessed him despite the famine and Philistine harassment. **16.** As a pilgrim alien, he eclipsed the native city-state.

Isaac the Well-Digger. 26:17-22. In the laborious work of well-digging, Isaac's patience displayed his character and further revealed him as a type of Christ, "who, when he was reviled, reviled not again" (1 Pet. 2:23). The encampments at *Esek* ("contention") and *Sitnah* ("enmity") resulted in enlargement, peace, and "room" (*Rehoboth*).

God Appears to Isaac at Beersheba. 26:23-25. Sacred because of God's appearance to Abraham there (21:31-32), Beersheba became a holy place to Isaac also as the LORD revealed Himself and renewed the covenant's guarantees. Isaac built an altar and dug a well, receiving divine blessing in both.

Isaac's Treaty with Abimelech.

26:26-33. This covenant renewed the former agreement with Abraham (21:23). God's blessings in grace to Isaac, whose life was opened to the divine favor by faith, were witnessed by the Philistines (v. 3). Again Isaac showed his long-suffering and patience in allowing his visitors to gloss over the Philistine harassment diplomatically. He even consented to a parity treaty, ratified by a covenant meal and mutual oath. **33. Shebah** is a form of the number seven. Isaac thus confirmed the name originally given the place by Abraham.

Esau's Wives. 26:34-35. Taking foreign pagan wives demonstrated Esau's profane and carnal nature. Such a course could only bring domestic tension and grief to Isaac and Rebekah.

4. ISAAC DECEIVED. 27:1-46.

Isaac's Determination to Bless Esau. 27:1-29. The patriarch knew the word of God, "the elder shall serve the younger" (25:23), but he was set on blessing Esau. This constituted failure on his part, perhaps attributable in part at least to the infirmities of old age. **2. Behold now, I am old.** This was legal terminology employed in introducing final testaments. At that time Isaac was 137 years old, and he lived 40 years longer (cf. 35:28). Isaac's self-will invited a whole chain of sins, including Rebekah's wily scheme to divert the blessing to Jacob (vv. 5-17), and Jacob's indefensible deception (vv. 18-25). As James M. Gray aptly notes, "Surely the goodness of God is of grace, and these things show that He has a plan to carry out in which He is simply using men as He finds them and subsequently conforming them to Himself as His sovereign will may determine" (CWCB, p. 42). Yet, despite the deception, Isaac blessed Jacob by faith (Heb. 11:20).

Isaac Discovers the Ruse. 27:30-40.

30. As soon as Isaac had finished blessing Jacob, ... Esau ... came in. The Nuzi letters reveal that oral wills made by a dying father and cited in court were binding. **33. Yes, and he shall be blessed.** Therefore, the blessing given to Jacob, although meant for Esau, was irrevocable, especially since it had the character of an oath "before the LORD" (v. 7; cf. v. 37). **33. Isaac trembled**, justifiably stunned as he realized that, despite his own purpose to the contrary, the prenatal declaration of God's purpose (25:23) had been made effective through the inspired testament he had spoken in irreversible legal form. In this bitter moment, Isaac realized what he should have realized from the start: that God's will for his sons was better than his own will for them.

34. Esau ... cried. Dramatically poignant was Esau's unavailing remorse (cf. Heb. 12:16-17), the fruit of his own unbelief and world conformity (cf. 26:34-35). **36. Is not he rightly named Jacob** (*yă'ªqōḇ*, "supplanter")? **For he hath supplanted** (*yăqªḇēnî*, "take by the heel, cheat, deceive," a pun on "Jacob") **me. He took away my birthright** (*bªḵōrātî*); **and ... my blessing** (*biŕḵātî*), another play on words in the Hebrew. **38. Hast thou but one blessing, my father?** Pathetically tragic was Esau's loss of spiritual blessings and the recognition of the fact when it was too late (Heb. 12:17).

40. Esau's "blessing," correctly translated, was a far cry from Jacob's: "Your home shall be far from the earth's riches, and the dew of heaven above. By your sword you shall live and your brother you shall serve. But as you grow restive, you shall throw off his yoke from your neck" (Speiser, AB, p. 208). The prophecy was historically fulfilled in Edom.

Sequel to Sin. 27:41-46. **41. Esau hated Jacob.** Terrible hatred and vengeance were engendered in Esau toward Jacob. **42-45.** Rebekah, so wily at deception, advised Jacob to flee. Although she commendably wanted to comply with the divine declaration, her unholy measures to aid God cost her the unity of her family. **46.** Rebekah also was reaping misery in Esau's Hittite wives. Family turmoil is the firstfruits of sin.

5. ISAAC SENDS JACOB AWAY. 28:1-9.

Isaac's Charge to Jacob. 28:1-5. **1.** Isaac's solemn injunction was that Jacob was not to take a wife from the Canaanites. Esau's wives were grief enough. Besides, such a procedure would be in direct violation of the covenant blessings so recently conferred upon him. **2. Go to Paddan-aram** (see 25:20), the "field" or "plain" of Aram, the area around Haran in Upper Mesopotamia, identical with "Aramnaharaim, Aram of the two rivers" (24:10, NASB margin). **3-4. God Almighty** (*'El Shaddai*) **bless thee ... and give thee the blessing of Abraham** (26-24). *'El Shaddai* was the name by which God revealed Himself to the patriarchs before the redemption out of Egypt (Exod. 6:3-4; cf. comments on Gen. 17:1). To them He was the all-powerful, all-sufficient One while they wandered as pilgrims and aliens in a land that was not theirs but was promised to be theirs ultimately through their posterity. The blessing of Abraham was the full sweep of the provisions of the Abrahamic Covenant (see 12:1-3).

Esau's Choice of Another Wife. 28:6-9. Esau's choice of an Ishmaelite woman (cf. 26:34-35; 36:3), while showing some regard for his father, Isaac, was still in line with his naturalistic, fleshly character. The experience of being cheated of the blessing had not changed him. Then he claimed a blessing to which he had no right before God and man, and showed that he still had no right.

C. THE HISTORY OF JACOB. 28:10—36:43.

1. JACOB'S VISION AND VOW. 28:10-22.

Jacob's Vision. 28:10-19. At this point Isaac fades out and Jacob takes the stage. **10. And Jacob ... went toward Haran** (see comments on 11:31-32; cf. 27:43; 29:4). Jacob's departure from Canaan prefigures Israel's expulsion from their own land, till they will be brought back again to inherit in the Kingdom age what was promised to them in the Abrahamic (12:1-3); Palestinian (Deut. 30:1-10); and Davidic (2 Sam. 7:4-17) covenants. In Jacob's sufferings in Paddan-aram is reflected the divine governmental dealing with Israel to restore them to blessing.

11. Stones ... for his pillows were a harbinger of God's severe dealings, which were a prelude to the dream that was prophetic of Israel's final regathering for Kingdom blessing. **12. A ladder** (staircase) **set up on the earth, and the top of it reached to heaven and ... the angels of God ascending and descending on it** speak of the comingling of angelic beings and the glorified saints of the Old Testament, church, and Tribulation with the redeemed unglorified men in the millennial reign of Christ. This is why our Lord saw the angels "ascending and descending upon the Son of man" (John 1:51), the Representative of glorified humanity. Then He will be "King of Israel" (John 1:49), but much more than that, "KING OF KINGS, AND LORD OF LORDS" (Rev. 19:16).

13-14. The Lord stood above it (the staircase), declaring Himself to be **the Lord God of Abraham ... and ... Isaac,** solemnly renewing the promise of the gift of the land and assuring blessing to **all the families of the earth.** This envisions the Kingdom age, when the Kingdom will be established over Israel (Acts 1:7; Rev. 20:4). How appropriate the assurance was as Jacob pillowed his head on a stone during his flight in fear from Canaan. Would he ever return again? Would God keep His promises?

15. Behold, I am with thee ... I will not leave thee, until I have done that which I have spoken to thee of. All was of sovereign mercy. Jacob had done nothing to merit this. **16-19.** Jacob recognized God's presence and called the place **Bethel,** meaning "house [abode of] God," the name afterward extended to the nearby town of **Luz** (cf. Josh. 16:2; 18:13), already called Bethel in Abraham's day by anticipation.

God's covenant disclosure at Bethel contained the standard treaty features of the day—a preamble with identifying title, the divine self-identification (God of Abraham, Isaac), and a virtual historical prologue recalling God's mercies. Already conveyed through Isaac's inspired blessing, the full-orbed covenant inheritance was ratified by the LORD in heaven.

Jacob's Vow. 28:20-22. For God's protection and supply, Jacob promised complete devotion to the LORD as his God, and a tithe of his income. **22. Stone ... for a pillar ... God's house.** Extrabiblical evidence also points to stone pillars associated with covenants and called "house of God" (cf. 35:7, 15).

2. JACOB IN HARAN. 29:1-35.

Jacob's Arrival in Padan-aram. 29:1-14. **1. The people of the east,** a general expression (11:2), is specifically applied here to the Aramaeans. Jacob's meeting with Rachel at the well was as dramatic as Abraham's servant finding Rebekah under similar circumstances

(24:10-21). **11.** Jacob's watering the sheep for Rachel, then kissing her in a burst of tears as he introduced himself, was apparently love at first sight. **13.** Laban, Jacob's uncle, received the newcomer cordially, claiming him as his **bone and ... flesh.**

Laban's Deception. 29:15-30. During Jacob's twenty-year exile in Padan-aram, the LORD did not manifest Himself to him, even as Israel dispersed among the nations today has no communication from the LORD. Jacob was severely disciplined, reaping in a sense what he had sowed. He deceived his father, Isaac. Now Laban deceived him in different ways, notably by substituting Leah for his beloved Rachel. A week after he received Leah, Rachel was given to him. But he had to serve seven more years for her (v. 30). His wily uncle conveniently got fourteen years of service from him.

Leah's Sons. 29:31-35. Reuben ("see, a son"), Simeon ("hearing"), Levi ("joined"), and Judah ("praise") were born. The circumstances surrounding the origins of the twelve tribes demonstrate the purely gracious character of Israel's election.

3. GROWTH OF JACOB'S FAMILY. 30:1-43.

Bilhah's Sons. 30:1-8. **1-2. Am I in God's stead** (in the position of God), **who hath withheld from thee the fruit of the womb?** In her barrenness, Rachel became unreasonable. Jacob's exasperated retort reveals a sense of reliance upon the God of the covenant. **3. Upon my knees.** To place a child on one's knees was to acknowledge it as one's own, as in the Hurro-Hittite tale of Appu (ZAW 49[1956]; 220, l. 5). The intent of the reference here is to establish the adoptive mother's legal right to the child, although the act was normally performed by the father.

4. She gave him Bilhah, her handmaid (maid) **as his wife** (i.e., as a concubine, *'ishshâ*, normally "woman, wife"). But the emphasis in this passage is on *connubium* (cf. 16:3), since Jacob was to cohabit with her. **6. God hath judged** (vindicated) **me ... therefore called she his name Dan** ("vindicate"). **7. Bilhah ... conceived again. 8. Rachel said, With great wrestlings have I wrestled with my sister, and I have prevailed: and she called his name Naphtali** (*năptûlê 'elōhîm nĭptăltî*, "wrestlings of God I have wrestled").

Zilpah's Sons. 30:9-13. **9. Leah ... took Zilpah ... and gave her to Jacob as his wife** ("concubine," cf. v. 4). **11. Leah said, Good fortune!** (i.e., "How propitious!" *bāgād*, "luck has come," the MT and the KJV take *gad* to mean "troop," or "a troop comes"). **12. Zilpah ... bore Jacob a second son. 13. Leah said, Happy am I** (*be'ŏshrî*, "with my happiness") **and she called his name Asher** ("happy").

Leah's Other Children. 30:14-21. **14-19. Mandrakes** (an aphrodisiac) were a part of Rachel's strategy to overcome her barrenness. Not only was this plan ineffectual, but it boomeranged to her rival's advantage. She bought Leah's mandrakes at the price of Leah's cohabiting with Jacob, which resulted in the birth of Issachar ("hire, pay") **for surely I have hired thee** (*śākōr śekărtîkā*, lit., "for I've indeed paid for you") **with my son's mandrakes.** (Cf. *śekārî*, "my hire," or "reward," v. 18.) **God hath given me my hire** (reward), **because I have given my maiden to my husband ... she called his name Issachar.**

20. Six sons ... Zebulun (*zebādănî, zēbĕd*, "God has given me a precious gift," from the root *zbd*, in assonance with Zebulun, from the root *zbl*). "This time my husband will bring me presents *yĭzbelēnî*, another pun on Zebulon"

(Speiser, AB, p. 229). The link in this etymology comes from the Akkadian word *zubullû*, "bridegroom gift" (*z^ebŭlûn*), so the name is given a double etiology. The play on the name was an important thing in Hebrew names, etiology rather than strict etymology. **21. She bore a daughter ... Dinah** (cf. 34:1-31; 37:35; 46:7).

Rachel's Joseph. 30:22-24. Another double etiology is found in the naming of Joseph: "God has removed," *'āsāp*, in assonance with *yōsēp* (Joseph). **24. She called his name Joseph**, meaning, "May the LORD add *yōsēp*" (i.e., "another son to me").

Jacob's Outwitting Laban. 30:25-43. **25.** Having first tricked Jacob into a double bride payment, crafty Laban then sought to extend the profitable arrangement. This time his greed was to be repaid in kind. The oppressor was to be despoiled. Meanwhile, with the birth of Joseph, Jacob's thoughts turned toward Canaan, where his inheritance through Isaac and the Abrahamic Covenant awaited him. Continuing on in Laban's employ became less wise. Natural sons born to Laban (cf. 31:1) were replacing Jacob as chief heir (cf. 15:4; 29:14-20). **26. Let me go.** Legally, Laban's permission was necessary for Jacob to leave with the family he had paid for by his services. The situation was not unlike that of a departing slave (Exod. 21:2-6). It is possible Jacob was under the relationship of an adopted son and the service contracts were subordinated to it. In such a case Jacob's independent proprietorship was contingent on Laban's death.

27-31. Laban's greed prompted him to insist on an arrangement for continued service. Jacob's wages would be the dark spotted lambs appearing among the normally white sheep, or any kids with white markings among the normally

dark goats. **34-36.** Since such deviations from the normal were rare, Laban thought he had another sure bargain. But the LORD stepped in on Jacob's side, overruling the dubious biological theory of prenatal conditioning by visual impressions. It was God's grace, not Jacob's scheming, that accomplished the miracle. Laban was being punished for his greed. Jacob was being blessed by divine grace in accordance with the divine promise (31:9-13).

4. JACOB'S RETURN TO CANAAN. 31:1-55.

Pressures upon Jacob to Return. 31:1-16. **1-16.** Four things urged Jacob to leave: (1) complaints and dissatisfaction among Laban's sons, who accused Jacob of taking away their father's wealth and their inheritance (v. 1); (2) Laban's altered attitude toward Jacob (v. 2); (3) the LORD's direct command: **Return unto the land ... and I will be with thee** (v. 3; cf. vv. 10-13; 28:15; 32:9; 46:4); and (4) the willingness of Rachel and Leah to leave their father (vv. 4-16). Laban's greed was so obvious that even his own flesh and blood could not be blinded to it. But Laban's treatment of their husband was not the only thing; his treatment of them was just as bad, if not worse. He showed no intention of bestowing on them any part of the bridal price, the wealth that accrued to them through Jacob's services, as was customary in their area (vv. 14-16). It was only natural for them to conclude that what God was now taking from their father and giving to their husband was no more than what actually belonged to them (v. 16).

Jacob's Flight. 31:17-24. **17-19.** Laban's absence and precautions provided Jacob with the opportunity of escape. Rachel showed her exasperation with her wily father by stealing **the images** that belonged to him. These were household gods (*tĕrāpîm*, statues venerated in the domestic circle). Adoption tablets stipulate that the chief heir should receive the father's gods. Possession of them implied legal advantage in respect to inheritance. Such images, moreover, belonged to actual sons born after adoption. Laban was not only outwitted by Rachel regarding these religious figurines, but the contemptuous treatment she gave them constituted a judgment of Laban's gods along with him (cf. v. 34). **24.** God's admonition to Laban in a dream (cf. vv. 29, 42) warned the wily Aramaean against pressing any legal claims against Jacob in any way (either good or bad). Actually, the LORD was assuming the role of a Kinsman-Protector, securing release for the virtual slave (cf. the six years, 31:41; Deut. 15:12).

Jacob's Confrontation with Laban. 31:25-42. Laban overtook Jacob in Mount Gilead in Transjordan southwest of the Sea of Galilee. His pursuit covered about three hundred miles, and Jacob had a three-day start and some ten days to cover this distance. Laban's upbraiding of Jacob was groundless, for his conduct had forefeited any more consideration than had been accorded him. The stir he created over the teraphim demonstrated their importance legally and, in Laban's eyes, religiously. Laban's frustration in trying to prove his allegations opened up the opportunity for Jacob to "tell him off" and prove the moral case in his favor.

A Mutual Nonaggression Pact. 31:43-55. **43. All ... is mine.** Laban bluntly stated the case. Under Hurrian law, Jacob's status in Laban's household would normally be tantamount to self-enslavement. However, if Jacob was recognized as an adopted son who had married the master's daughter, that position would be altered. Possession of

the household gods very probably made the difference. Afraid of pressing his claim legally (with the teraphim no longer in his possession) and in the face of divine warning, Laban took the next best step—a treaty guaranteeing each of them protection from the other's malice. The covenant Witness was God (vv. 49-53), while the **pillar** (*stele*) and **heap** (*cairn*, "mound of stones," vv. 45-52) were symbolic witnesses, named by each of the bilingual participants in his native language: *Jegar-sahadutha* (Aramaic for "mound of testimony") and *Galeed* ("mound of witness").

49. Mizpah ("watchtower"), for he said literally, "May the LORD keep watch [set a guard] between you and me when we are out of sight of each other." **53.** "May the God of Abraham and the god of Nahor [their respective ancestral deities] maintain order between us" (lit. trans.). **And Jacob swore** (took oath) **by the fear** (*pāḥāḏ*, "the awesome one") **of ... Isaac.** A sacrifice and covenant meal concluded the treaty.

5. JACOB RENAMED ISRAEL. 32:1-32.

Jacob Met by Angels. 32:1-2. **1.** As Jacob proceeded back to Canaan, the land of promised blessing, **the angels of God met** (encountered) **him.** The LORD graciously gave him this sustaining token of His presence and protection. **2. Jacob ... said, This is God's host** (*māhᵃnēh*, "army, camp, encampment, troop"). **And he called the name of that place Mahanaim,** a dual form meaning "two hosts" or "bands." The visible band was Jacob and his servants; the invisible band (momentarily visible to the patriarch) was God's angels (cf. 2 Kings 6:13-17). How welcome was this meeting in the light of the impending encounter with Esau.

Jacob's Quandary. 32:3-12. **4-6.** Jacob did all that he was capable of in his customary craftiness to assuage Esau's possible rage and revenge, including sending messengers to humbly beg Esau's favor. The messengers returned with the most disconcerting news, literally, "We reached your brother Esau; he himself is on his way to meet you, accompanied by four hundred men." **7.** Badly frightened, Jacob divided his retinue into two camps, figuring that if Esau should come upon the one camp and attack it, the other camp might still survive.

9. Jacob also prayed, but there was no holy and elevated trust in God. He had learned too little about God at Bethel and too much about man at Haran. True, God was with him, for nothing can hinder the outshinings of divine grace, but his prayer (vv. 9-12) was uttered only after his own schemes and plans were exhausted. He was still the "supplanter," although his prayer was impelled by faith in God's grace and faithfulness. He appealed to God's promises made to Abraham and Isaac and confirmed to him, confessing his utter unworthiness and God's goodness to him (v. 10). He pleaded for deliverance according to the promise that his seed would be **as the sand of the sea** (v. 12; cf. 22:17), but his cry to God was a plea to bless his plan.

Jacob's Present to Esau. 32:13-21. Not only did Jacob give Esau a munificent gift, but he dexterously planned its presentation to Esau in installments, to assuage Esau's anger (vv. 13-19). **20. For he said, I will appease** (propitiate) **him with the present that goeth before me, and afterward I will see his face; perhaps he will accept of** (forgive) **me. 21.** Jacob was really leaning on his own scheme. If it failed, he wanted to be sure of God's help, but only as a last resort. His eye was filled with his own planning; hence, he was not prepared to see God

acting for him. He was asking God to bless his plans, not submitting to God for His deliverance.

Jacob Becomes Israel. 32:22-32. That night with his immediate family, Jacob crossed **the ford, Jabbok** (Num. 21:24), the stream flowing into the Jordan about twenty-one miles north of the Dead Sea. **24. Jacob was left alone** to face himself before God in his wily self-planning and insubmission to God. He had to be brought to the end of himself as well as the end of his plans. Before entering the land of inheritance, he had to undergo an experience of utter yieldedness to God that would seal him as a man of God and a man of faith—not a wily self-planner and schemer, piously asking God to bless his plans.

There wrestled a man with him. This was the angel of the LORD, the captain of the LORD's host (the preincarnate Christ; Josh. 5:13-14; Hos. 12:2-4). The word "wrestled" ($wayy\bar{e}'\bar{a}\underline{b}\bar{e}q$) is a word play on *Jabbok*. The purpose of the contest was to break Jacob's will into submission to the divine will—to bring him to see what a poor, feeble, worthless creature he was. **25. He touched** ($n\bar{a}\underline{g}\breve{a}'$ b^e, "smote"). God in His omnipotence needs only to touch us. **The hollow of Jacob's thigh was out of joint.** The sentence of death must be written over self and the flesh before we can walk in the full victory that grace longs to give us.

26. Only when the source of his strength was touched did Jacob learn to say, "I will not let *Thee* go." The spiritual crisis enabled him to cling to God *alone*, so that the story of his life might be more characterized by holy elevation above the circumstances through which he might pass. **I will not let thee go except thou bless me** is the secret of all true spiritual strength. Jacob could not say this until his long struggle in the flesh was abandoned and his reliance upon the flesh renounced. He had to become weak before he became strong. Like Job, Jacob could say, "I have heard of thee by the hearing of the ear, but now mine eye seeth thee. Wherefore I abhor myself, and repent in dust and ashes" (Job 42:5-6). **28. Israel**, normally, means "God strives" (cf. RSV margin), but a different sense is assigned here (i.e., "he strives with God"). Actually God strove with Jacob, and he fought back until God broke him. Only then, when fully surrendered *to* God, did he prevail *with* God. **31. Peniel** ("face of God") is the same as the older place name *Penuel*. The vision of God alone can supply a true vision of self (Isa. 6:1-5); the sight is never pleasant.

6. JACOB MEETS ESAU. 33:1-20.

The Groundlessness of Jacob's Fears. 33:1-15. **1-3.** Despite his experience at Peniel (32:25-32), Jacob still appeared fearful and was still planning. The tail end of his carnal precautions after Peniel (vv. 1-3) were just as elaborate as those before his encounter with God. He still anticipated vengeance from Esau and took special pains (so characteristic of him) to expose those about whom he cared least to the first stroke of that vengeance. Had he been leaning upon God, he never could have anticipated destruction for himself and his family. Even though he was now to move mainly in the Israel role, instead of the scheming role of Jacob, he was to learn how difficult it is for the human heart to repose calmly in the presence and the promises of the infinitely gracious God. **4-5. Esau ran to meet him . . . fell on his neck, and kissed him.** All Jacob's carnal anxiety had been useless—the present, the plan, all the precautions. God "ap-

peased" Esau as He had already appeased Laban. Instead of Esau's sword, Jacob received his kiss; instead of conflict, tears. Such are God's wonderful ways to be realized by those who trust Him. It is obvious, however, that "Jacob" did not all at once cease to dominate the walk of "Israel." **14. Until I come unto my lord unto Seir** constitutes a promise that Jacob had no apparent intent to keep. His future did not lie in Seir, and he was not about to sacrifice his best interests when once he had recovered from the fright into which he had been thrown by Esau.

Jacob at Succoth. 33:17. He **built . . . an house, and made booths** ("arbor shelters," Heb., *sŭkkōt*). Despite God's manifested grace, Jacob settled down at Succoth ("booths") as if he were not a pilgrim and as if this were his final destination. How long he stayed at Succoth is not indicated. However long it was, it was too long.

Jacob at Shechem. 33:18-20. Located in the heart of the promised land at the commercial crossroads of Canaan in the pass between Mount Ebal and Mount Gerizim, Shechem figured prominently in the divine promise of the land to the patriarchs (cf. 12:6). To this sacred spot Jacob came "safely" (NASB; i.e., "in peace," Samaritan Pentateuch; RSV). Evidently he regained his pilgrim character. **He . . . pitched his tent** (encamped) **before the city.** His purchase of the land from **the children of Hamor**, the ruling clan of the city (Judg. 9:28), and his erection of an altar (like Abraham, 12:7), intimated that he at least recognized his return from Padan-aram (24:10; 25:20; 28:2; 31:18) as a fulfillment of the covenant promise. Employing his new name (Israel), Jacob confessed that El was distinctively his God (cf. 28:21). Now, at least on occasion, Jacob's "Israel" character could be discerned—but how faintly and inconsistently.

7. JACOB'S FAMILY DISGRACED. 34:1-31.

Jacob's New Sorrows and Disciplines. 34:1-12. Although Jacob's altar at Shechem proclaimed God to be his God, it was obvious he had not received the power of the name. He was still walking in his own ways. His house at Succoth (33:17) and his purchase at Shechem (33:18) attested this fact. As a result, further divine disciplinary dealing was necessary. **1.** This came through **Dinah, the daughter of Leah** (30:21; 46:15). She "represents the young women of today who want to see the world and have their fling" (James M. Gray, CWCB, p. 46). She **went out to see** (visit) **the daughters** (women) **of the land** (i.e., Canaanite women). Her father should not have violated his pilgrim character by settling down in Shechem, thus exposing his daughter to mixing with Canaanites.

2. The rape of Dinah by **Shechem, the son of Hamor** was a peril Jacob could well have anticipated, had he maintained the separation to which all God's people are called to practice (12:1-2; Lev. 26:12; 2 Cor. 6:14-17). **3-12.** There can be only condemnation for the crime of Shechem, but the reparation he and his father offered to make was honorable from the viewpoint of human morality. Yet even this was contrary to the separation demanded of the LORD's people, especially with reference to marriage.

The Grievous Crime of Jacob's Sons. 34:13-29. Again Jacob reaped what he had sown. The duplicity of the father was reflected in the deceit of his sons. Utterly reprehensible was their lying and base demeaning of the covenant sign of circumcision (cf. 17:9-14). The Abrahamic Covenant in their flesh (cf.

17:13) made circumcision binding upon Israel only. What a base ruse to enforce it upon the Shechemites in order to murder them (vv. 25-26). As if that foul crime were not enough, the plundering of the city by Jacob's sons added to the dark outrage (vv. 27-29). Simeon and Levi took the initiative in this horrible atrocity, because they were full brothers of Dinah.

Jacob's Reaction. 34:30-31. Not the insult to his daughter or the blot on his family, but the consequences with reference to himself seemed to have affected Jacob most. **30. Ye have troubled me to make me odious** (stink) **... and I being few in number, they shall gather ... together against me and slay me; and I shall be destroyed, I and my house.** Was this faith or unbelief speaking? God's Spirit or self talking? It was not that Jacob was not in the main a man of faith; he assuredly was (Heb. 11:21). Yet he frequently exhibited sad failure from not walking by faith. Could faith have led him to say, in the light of what God had said to him (28:14-15), "I shall be destroyed, I and my house"? It was not Jacob's faith, but God's grace carrying him on despite his unbelief, that was most remarkable about this man.

8. JACOB RETURNS TO BETHEL. 35:1-29.

The Divine Admonition. 35:1-5. **1.** God's command to **go up to Bethel** was a reproof to Jacob, who had gravitated to low ground spiritually. This is shown by five things: (1) *By the reference to his "fleeing" from the face of Esau*, which was occasioned by his deceptive stealing of the blessing (27:1-33). (2) *By the reference to God's former appearance (manifestation) there*, promising him protection, safe return, and possession of the land of Canaan from which he was fleeing (28:13-15)—all of which Jacob all too often had forgotten in the interim of

84

perhaps more than thirty years.

(3) *By God's reminding the patriarch of the pledge he had failed to redeem in performing his vow* (28:20-22). God had kept His part of the bargain, but had Jacob? He had been in the land for at least seven years, and yet he had *not* gone up to Bethel. (4) *By the immediate effect the reproof had upon Jacob.* **2. Then Jacob said unto his household ... Put away the foreign** (strange) **gods ... be clean.** Had Jacob gone directly to Bethel, the taint of idolatry would have been purged away more promptly and his children would have escaped the de-filement and tragedy of complicity with idolatry and its concomitants: lust and murder. Not only did Jacob and his household put away the idols (certainly the teraphim Rachel had stolen), but also **their earrings** (amulets) connected with idol worship (Exod. 32:2; Hos. 2:13). He buried those idolatrous trappings, separating himself from them completely. (5) *By the manifest power of God upon Jacob and his household.* **5. The terror of God** fell upon the Canaanites, so that they did not pursue after Jacob to take vengeance for the atrocity Simeon and Levi had perpetrated upon them.

Jacob's Obedience. 35:6-8. **6.** He returned to Luz (28:19), the earlier Canaanite name of Bethel. Faith, producing obedience, resulted in the building of an altar and true spiritual worship of El-Bethel ("the God of Bethel"), who had manifested Himself so wonderfully to Jacob when he fled in mortal terror of Esau's vengeance (cf. 28:19). Compare Abraham's similar restoration after spiritual lapse (13:3-4). **8.** The death of Deborah, who was Rebekah's nurse, and Rachel (v. 19) marked the severing of Jacob's connections with Paddan-aram.

Jacob's Restoration to Divine Bless-

ing. 35:9-20. Jacob's restoration is typical of Jacob's descendants, who will receive divine favor after their worldwide wanderings at the end of the age prior to Kingdom blessing. Then eight things will happen: (1) God will appear to Jacob *again* as He did at Bethel when Jacob left the land (28:11-17). (2) Jacob's posterity will realize the power and blessing of the new name *Israel*, when all idolatrous contamination shall be purged out (v. 10; Zech. 13:1-6). (3) Restored Israel will enjoy the sustaining power of God Almighty (El Shaddai, 17:1) with prosperity and Kingdom dignity (v. 11). (4) Israel will realize the full possessing of the *promised* land (v. 12). (5) Israel will realize the joy of the fulfillment of the Abrahamic Covenant. The stone pillar (v. 14), as the customary covenant witness (cf. Josh. 24:26-27), plus the drink offering poured upon it, speak of the blessing Israel will receive in the Kingdom as the result of Christ's life poured out in death (Psalm 22:14; Isa. 53:10) for their salvation and the realization of the covenant promises. (6) Israel will come to Ephrath (Bethlehem, "the house of bread") when they realize that He who was born there is God incarnate, their Redeemer, the true Bread of Life. (7) Israel will recognize their Messiah in His suffering and death (*Benoni*, "the son of my sorrow") and in His Kingdom glory as *Benjamin* ("son of my right hand," vv. 17-18). (8) Then Israel will journey (v. 21). In millennial blessing, they will move in the dignity of their new name.

The Line of Blessing. 35:22-29. The conclusion of the section on "the generations of Isaac" rounds out the record of the twelve tribes. Reuben's crime is mentioned (v. 22) to show why he forfeited the birthright (v. 23; cf. 49:3-4). The twelve sons are listed according to their mothers (vv. 23-26), with reference to legal rather than chronological priorities. Isaac's death (vv. 27-29) marks Jacob's succession as the covenant patriarch. How mistaken Isaac was concerning his death (27:2), living forty-three years longer (twelve more years after the reunion of father and son at Mamre, near Hebron).

9. ESAU'S DESCENDANTS. 36:1-43.

Esau Settles in Edom. 36:1-19. Edom (called Seir, v. 8) is the rugged mountainous country extending from the Dead Sea to the Gulf of Aqabah. Esau had already occupied Edom when Jacob returned from Haran (32:3; 36:6-8). Edom is not fertile but has cultivable areas. Esau not only intermarried with the Canaanites, displaying his profane nature, but also multiplied his wives. He therefore passed off the stage of spiritual blessing and left the land of promise. Yet before the history of the central line of Jacob is related, a survey of Esau's branch is made, carrying out God's revealed purposes concerning him (25:23) and Isaac's inspired blessing on him (27:39-40).

The Horite Line in Seir. 36:20-30. This section traces the Horites, whom the LORD dispossessed before Esau (cf. Deut. 2:12, 22) and with whom Esau's descendants intermarried (v. 2). They are the Hurrians, whose ruins modern archaeology has resurrected. They settled in large numbers in north Mesopotamia and Syria-Palestine before 2000 B.C.

Kings of Edom. 36:31-39. Israel had no kings until the time of Saul (c. 1020 B.C.), but Abraham and Sarah were promised that kings would be among their descendants. Edom's kings were elective, not dynastic.

Tribal Chieftains. 36:40-43. The importance of these chieftains appears in this additional list, arranged with special attention on geographical and administrative divisions.

D. JACOB'S SONS, ESPECIALLY JOSEPH. 37:1—50:26.

1. JOSEPH AND HIS BROTHERS. 37:1-36.

Jacob's History Resumed. 37:1-2a. **2. The generations of Jacob** (37:2—50:26) constitute the last genealogical division of Genesis. It covers the period of Jacob's patriarchal authority, which was begun upon his return to Isaac in Canaan as a coregency with his aging father. Joseph, although elevated to be the preserver of the covenant community, nevertheless remained subordinate to Jacob within the covenant structure. Meanwhile, Jacob, under the blessing of his new name, Israel, became the progenitor of a community of faith, united by the divine promise of a Redeemer, called "the sons of Israel," that is, Israelites.

Jacob's Favorite Son. 37:2b-4. **2b.** Early indications of Joseph's future preeminence made him the object of jealousy and hatred. He was particularly despised by the four sons of the handmaids, who ranked lowest (cf. 30:3-13; 33:2). His bringing an unfavorable report of the conduct of these brothers to their father further fanned the flame of their resentment.

3. Israel's love for Joseph and his obvious unwise show of favoritism further aggravated the family division. He doted on him because he was **the son of his old age**, the youngest, except for Benjamin, and the offspring of his beloved Rachel after her prolonged childlessness. The **coat of many colors** (taken from the Septuagint and Vulgate rendering) was rather an "ornamental tunic," like the *kitû pišannu* of the cuneiform inventories (cf. JNES 8

(1949):177; Speiser, AB, p. 290), which was a robe with gold or other ornamental appliqué. The paternal intent was evidently to honor Joseph with the birthright forfeited by Reuben (cf. 35:22; 1 Chron. 5:1-2). For Joseph as a type of Christ, see comments on 41:46-57.

Joseph's Prophetic Dreams. 37:5-11. Sensing a divine predestinating disclosure, Joseph's brothers were upset and their hatred increased. Dream interpreters are common in ancient Near Eastern literature, including works on dream symbols and their meaning. It was enough that the dream of the sheaves should suggest that Joseph's brothers would bow down to him (cf. 42:6; 44:14); but when it was suggested in the second dream that his father and mother, as well as his brothers, would bow to him, even Jacob took offense. He could not foresee that Joseph's dominion over him would operate within the confines of the enforced stay in Egypt and would not entail usurpation of his patriarchal authority.

The Plot to Kill Joseph. 37:12-22. **12-13.** Continuing divine protection over Jacob's family was evident in the pastoral activity in the Shechem area without harassment from the outraged Canaanites (cf. 34:30). **14.** Little did Jacob surmise that sending his beloved Joseph to visit his brothers would result in the greatest sorrow and testing of his sorely tried career. **17.** Joseph found his brothers at Dothan, modern Tell Dothan, about a day's journey north of Shechem. **18. When they saw him afar off ... they conspired** (lit., "sought or weighed clever schemes") **to slay him** (cf. Matt. 21:38; 26:3-4). **20.** They **cast him into some pit** (water hole or cistern). **22.** Reuben's countersuggestion was accepted only because it still appeared to entail eventual death for Joseph.

Joseph Sold into Egypt. 37:23-36.

25-27. First Joseph was **cast ... into a pit,** then sold to the **Ishmaelites** at Judah's suggestion. At a distance the approaching caravan was identified by the racial term "Ishmaelites," of which "traders" was apparently a secondary meaning. When these traders came closer it was discerned that they were Midianites (Medanites), Midian and Medan being sons of Abraham by Keturah (25:1-2). The return to the term *Ishmaelites* (or "traders," v. 28*b*) underscores the heartless treatment accorded Joseph.

28. And they (Joseph's brothers) **lifted up Joseph out of the pit** (45:4-5), **and sold Joseph ... for twenty pieces of silver,** which was less than the price of a common slave (Exod. 21:32; Lev. 27:3-5; cf. Matt. 26:15). **And they** (the Midianites) **brought Joseph into Egypt.**

31-32. The rankling robe (vv. 3-5) became legal evidence to transfer Joseph's inheritance to his rivals (cf. 31:39; Exod. 22:13). **33.** Jacob, a former cruel deceiver, was himself cruelly deceived. But the God of grace was overruling evil for good. **34-35.** The very son whose death Jacob mourned would one day mourn his death with all Egypt's splendor (50:11-13). **36. Sold him ... unto Potiphar**, an Egyptian personal name meaning, "One whom Re (the sun-god) has given." Potiphar was **an officer** (courtier) **of Pharaoh's** (see comments on 12:15-17) **and captain of the guard**, that is, "chief steward" (lit., "chief or master of the cooks," but the title had become a generalized term).

2. JUDAH'S SIN. 38:1-30.

Judah's Alliance with Idolaters. 38:1-5. **1. Judah went down** (both geographically from the heights of Hebron to the Philistine hill country, and morally from the high covenant standards to low practices of the Canaanites). This meant separation from his brothers (God's covenant people) and joining pagans, creating disunity in his father's house. He settled down with Canaanite **Hirah**. There he met a Canaanite woman **Shua** and had three sons by her—Er, Onan, and Shelah. Such flagrant compromise with sin could only bring tragic sorrow. **Chezib** is apparently Achzib (Josh. 15:44; Mic. 1:14).

Results of the Idolatrous Alliance. 38:6-11. **6.** Judah got a Canaanite wife named **Tamar** for his son **Er.** But Er, guilty of some unspecified sin, suffered premature death at the LORD's hand. **8.** Judah requested his second son, **Onan,** to perform the rite of a husband to his brother's widow, to maintain his brother's line. Such levirate marriages were common, as attested by Hittite and Middle Assyrian law codes and later regulated for Israel in the Mosaic code (Deut. 25:5-10), to perpetuate a brother's posterity.

9. But Onan, knowing that the seed would not count as his, let it go to waste on the ground every time that he cohabited with his brother's widow, so as not to contribute offspring to his brother. This had nothing to do with masturbation ("onanism"). It was selfish greed and counted as a very serious sin (cf. "the sin unto [physical] death (1 John 5:16; cf. 1 Cor. 5:5). Onan coveted the firstborn's portion for his own name, since the firstborn of the new marriage was reckoned as the deceased brother's heir, carrying on his name. The LORD killed him also. **11.** Judah himself also conspired against Tamar's right and Er's name. Although he sought to live up to the practice of levirate marriage, he shrank from risking the life of his last surviving son.

Tamar's Ruse. 38:12-26. Tamar, convinced that her father-in-law, now a widower, was temporizing, tricked him into leaving her with child by waylaying him in the disguise of a harlot (*q^{e}dēshâ*, "votary, cult prostitute," according to the debased Canaanite fertility cults where both males and females were devoted to sexual immorality as a part of religion). **18.** The **pledge** Tamar demanded was literally "a signet and cord" (a cylinder seal worn on a cord about the neck, a uniquely personal item of identification. The **staff,** another distinctive item of identification, was an object resembling a pestle that changed hands to symbolize the conclusion of a transaction (Old Babylonian, *bukānum*).

24. Let her be burned. Judah had tried to get rid of Tamar by sending her to her father's house (v. 11). Now a new opportunity to be free of her presented itself. When she was found to be pregnant by harlotry, Judah jumped at the chance to have her burned (cf. Lev. 20:14; 21:9), although stoning was the penalty for a case like Tamar's as betrothed to Shelah (Deut. 22:20-21).

26. But Judah's guilt, proved by the pledge, forced his confession: **She hath been more righteous than I.** Both had practiced deception: she, to secure her legal rights; he, to circumvent his legal paternal obligations.

Divine Grace Displayed. 38:27-30. Despite the sordid sin of Judah and Tamar, both of their names, as well as those of their two sons, are in the genealogy of Christ (Matt. 1:3). **29. Perez** became an ancestor of the Davidic line (Ruth 4:18-19; 1 Chron. 2:3-15).

3. JOSEPH IN EGYPT. 39:1-23.

Joseph's Promotion in Potiphar's House. 39:1-6. The Joseph narrative, broken by the account of Judah's sin, is resumed from chapter 37. **1. Potiphar**

88

... **bought him** (see 37:36). Archaeology attests the presence of many Asiatics on Egyptian estates, mostly through capture in war, but also through slave sales. The pharaoh was most likely of the Twelfth Dynasty (1991-1786 B.C.). **2.** Divine providence was at work to preserve Joseph, who in turn was to become the preserver of his people, who had rejected him. **4-6.** Joseph's designation as **overseer over his** (Potiphar's) **house** reflects a common Egyptian title. Archaeological evidence shows that Semitic slaves in Egypt sometimes were elevated to positions of great domestic responsibility (cf. 41:39-40).

Joseph Falsely Accused. 39:7-18. **7-8.** Potiphar's wife represents a typical wealthy pagan woman willing to sacrifice another's welfare to gratify her lust. **9. How . . . can I . . . sin against God?** Joseph's moral integrity sprang from his knowledge of God and the operation of divine grace through covenant relationship. Sin might invade the chosen line, as in the case of Judah's lapse (Gen. 38), but God's grace would provide a holy witness to the nations through Jacob's posterity. Joseph realized that breaking the moral law of God was sinning against *God* as well as his own body (cf. Exod. 20:14; 1 Cor. 6:18). This was **great wickedness** (Lev. 20:10). **10. He hearkened not . . . to lie by her, or to be with her.** He realized strict avoidance of sin was the only way to escape its snare.

12. Even when the temptress determined to seduce him by cunning subtlety, he **fled, and got out.** He did what can only be done with fornication—he *fled* from it (1 Cor. 6:18). **He left his garment** (vv. 15, 18) **in her hand.** Once again Joseph's garment was made to lie wickedly about him (37:31-35). **13-18.** Potiphar's wife displayed the venom of a wicked woman, repulsed and outwitted in her lustful self-will. Her use of the term **Hebrew** (cf. 14:13) reflects a derogatory flavor and an Egyptian bias against Asiatics.

Joseph Put in Prison. 39:19-23. **19.** Assuming that his wife had told the truth, Potiphar's rage in casting Joseph in prison was perfectly understandable. Death was the normal penalty, but the same divine grace that had elevated Joseph in Potiphar's house was providentially at work to place him among the crown prisoners and give him favor with the chief jailer. Adversity was God's way to prosperity. His way up is often down, as in the case of our Lord, of whom Joseph is a type (see 41:46).

4. JOSEPH IN PRISON. 40:1-23.

Joseph Interprets the Cupbearer's Dream. 40:1-15. How wonderfully God's providence continued to work to fulfill the divine plan through Joseph— first, through the imprisonment of two high officials of Pharaoh (vv. 1-4); second, through their dreams (vv. 5-19). **2. The chief of the butlers** ("chief butler" or cupbearer) corresponds to the title of an Egyptian officer, who was a royal confidant and adviser. **The chief of the bakers** ("chief baker") was another high courtier, who attended Pharaoh. **4. The captain of the guard** (*săr ṭăbbāḥîm*) head of the royal bodyguard (*KBL,* 346) **charged Joseph with them . . . he served them.** Actually, Joseph, although placed over the prison's administrative affairs, was still Potiphar's duly acquired slave and accustomed to serve people of high rank.

8. Do not interpretations belong to God? (cf. Dan. 2:20-22). He told the Egyptian courtiers not to be upset because they did not have access to their favorite dream interpreters from Pharaoh's court. The young Hebrew

89

slave suggested tacitly that those professionals were mere charlatans in comparison to God, who alone can give the true interpretation of dreams.

13. Lift up thine head, an expression with opposite meanings, was used purposely by Joseph to indicate the cupbearer's pardon and restoration (2 Kings 25:27, KJV; Jer. 52:31) and the beheading of the chief baker (v. 19). The same terminology was employed in a third sense (v. 20) "to give attention to (the pending cases)" (BASOR 149 [1958]:17-18). **14-15.** Joseph pleaded with the cupbearer to remember him to Pharaoh when he was reinstated in favor, defending his innocence in being **stolen** (kidnapped) from **the land of the Hebrews** and landing in jail in Egypt.

Joseph Interprets the Baker's Dream. 40:16-23. **16. I had three white** (wicker) **baskets on my head.** Such baskets permitted birds to pick at the pastries both from the sides and top. **19. Yet within three days shall Pharaoh lift up thy head** (behead) **... thee, and shall hang** (impale) **thee.** Aside from other evidence, a beheaded man is not hanged (cf. v. 22), because he no longer has a head.

Joseph Forgotten. 40:24. The chief butler forgot Joseph, but God did not forget him. He often waits that He may be more gracious to His own.

5. JOSEPH EXALTED. 41:1-57.

Pharaoh's Dreams. 41:1-36. **1-4.** Pharaoh's first dream involved seven handsome and sturdy cows coming up out of the Nile River and grazing in **a meadow** (reed grass), and seven ugly and gaunt cows that came up out of the river and devoured them. **8.** Agitated, Pharaoh **sent ... for all the magicians of Egypt.** These were occult practitioners in contact with the realm of evil supernaturalism with clairvoyant and other demon-energized powers. **9-13.** Their

inability to interpret royal dreams furnished the occasion for the chief cupbearer to recall Joseph's gift, resulting in his being called before Pharaoh.

14-32. Joseph's interpretation of the dreams, indicating seven years of plenty followed by seven years of famine, was of extreme importance for the welfare of the country. **33-36.** Joseph's suggestion was to appoint a man of discernment and wisdom and to "organize" or "regiment" (*ḥmsh*, "to divide into five parts") the whole country to gather and conserve the grain of the seven good years in anticipation of the seven years of famine.

Joseph's Exaltation. 41:37-45. **38-39.** (1) Pharaoh confessed Joseph to be **a man in whom the Spirit of God is** and, despite the idolatrous religion of Egypt, discerned that God had showed him that which the gods of Egypt were powerless to reveal. **40-42.** (2) Pharaoh placed him not only over his palace but over all the land of Egypt, his high position being indicated by his putting the royal signet ring on Joseph's hand, making him his second-in-command (cf. 2 Chron. 28:7), a title referring to the grand vizier, who was also the royal seal-bearer (vv. 42-43). The robes of fine linen and the gold neck chain were official Egyptian dress of the one who was **to ride in the second chariot** of the Pharaoh's second-in-command. **43. Bow the knee** (if *'ăḇrēk* is construed as a Hifil infinitive absolute from *bārāk*, "bend the knee," doubtless adopted from an Egyptian word with a similar meaning).

45. Pharaoh named Joseph **Zaphenath-paneah** (probably "God speaks—He lives") and gave him **Asenath** ("belonging to [the goddess] Neith"), **the daughter of Potiphera** (see 39:1), priest of On (Heliopolis, the cultic centre of Re, the sun-god, seven miles northeast of modern Cairo; cf. v. 50;

90

46:20; Ezek. 30:17, NASB). Although his Egyptianization seemed complete with a change of name and his marriage to a priest's daughter, Joseph's bold faith in God demonstrated that he in no sense was compromising his spiritual position. Critics have frequently doubted the possibility of the elevation of a foreigner to high office in Egypt. Contemporary records, however, show that such an occurrence was rare, but by no means unique.

Joseph as a Type. 41:46. Joseph was plainly a prefigurement of Christ. Like Christ: (1) He was the special object of his father's love (37:3; Matt. 3:17). (2) He was hated by his brothers (37:4; John 15:25). (3) He was rejected by his brothers (37:8; Matt. 21:37-39; John 15:24-25). (4) He was in intent and figure slain by his brothers (37:24, 28; Matt. 27:35-37). (5) He became a blessing among the Gentiles and gained a bride (41:1-45; Acts 15:14; Eph. 5:25-32). (6) He eventually reconciled his brothers to himself and was exalted over them (45:1-15; Deut. 30:1-16; Rom. 11:25-26).

Birth of Manasseh and Ephraim. 41:47-57. **51.** Two sons were born to Joseph and Asenath during the gathering of huge stores of grain preceding the seven years of famine. The firstborn was **Manasseh** ($m^e n\check{a}shsh\check{e}h$ is apparently meant to be a piel participle with the suffix "one" making **me forget** from $n\bar{a}s\hat{a}h\hat{a}$, "forget"). **52. Ephraim** ($\bar{e}pr\bar{a}y\check{i}m$, "double fruitfulness") refers either to the increase in Joseph's family or to the seven years of plenty, from the verb $p\bar{a}r\hat{a}$, "to bear fruit." **For God hath caused me to be fruitful** ($h\check{i}pr\bar{a}n\hat{i}$, causative stem, "made me prosperous").

6. THE BROTHERS MEET JOSEPH. 42:1-38.

Jacob Sends His Sons to Egypt. 42:1-5. God was working mysteriously to perform His wonders. The famine drove the inhabitants of all the neighboring lands to Egypt, the granary of the ancient world. Among the first to be driven to this necessity would be those of south Palestine, "where at best there is but a hand-to-mouth existence, (Alleman, OTC, p. 202). **3. Joseph's ten brethren went down to buy grain in Egypt.** Monuments show Asiatics arriving in Egypt to barter for grain or other commodities (Karl Lepsius, Denkmäler, 2:133). **4.** Jacob would not risk sending his youngest son, Benjamin. He was still haunted by the fear that the fate that overtook Joseph would overtake him also.

Joseph Tests His Brothers. 42:6-35. **8. Joseph knew** (recognized) **his brethren, but they knew** (recognized) **not him.** Undoubtedly Joseph's dress, speech, and clean-shaven body were among the reasons, contrasting silently with the brothers' beards and Hebrew dress. **9. Ye are spies; to see the nakedness of the land.** According to Herodotus, Egyptians showed a disposition to distrust foreigners, because attacks came from the north in the direction of Palestine-Syria. **Nakedness** (Heb., $'\check{e}rw\hat{a}$) is used metaphorically here of things (lack of defense) "that are meant to be hidden" from "potential enemies" (Speiser, AB, p. 321).

15. Hereby ye shall be tested, not as to whether they were spies, of course, but whether they had repented of the dastardly crime of enslaving their brother, whom they described as **is not** (v. 13). **By the life of Pharaoh,** that is, "I swear by Pharaoh." An oath in this august name meant that Pharaoh was thought of as a god, for oaths were usually a solemn appeal to divine authority (R. D. Wilson, JNES 7 [July 1948]:129-56).

17-20. He put them ... into prison, letting them "sweat it out" for **three days.** Meanwhile, he gave testimony to prick their conscience: **I fear God** (cf. 20:11). **21.** Joseph's purpose was accomplished as the brothers confessed their guilt in selling him. **22.** At the same time, Reuben, the oldest, revealed his attempt to save Joseph. All this Joseph heard dramatically with his own ears and wept. **24.** Because Reuben had saved his life, Joseph required Simeon, the next to the oldest, to remain as hostage. Moreover, he ordered the others to bring Benjamin, his full brother and the youngest, to Egypt (v. 20).

25-28. Joseph's strategy in returning the money paid for the grain in each brother's sack was effective in convicting them more thoroughly of their wicked conduct toward him. **What is this that God hath done unto us?** They were beginning to see their sin against God and His just punishment of them. Evidently this was also Joseph's purpose. **29-35.** Apparently, not until they had reported to their father did they discover that each brother's money had been returned to his sack. Then their fear reached its height.

Jacob's Remorse. 42:36. **36. All these things are against me.** This demonstrates how hard it is for even a man of faith to bow unquestioningly under the hand of Providence when the going becomes rough. By an apparent gift of discernment, Jacob acted and spoke as if he somehow sensed that it was by some fault on the part of his sons that Joseph and Simeon were no more and that they likewise would **take Benjamin away** (cf. 43:14).

Reuben's Assurance. 42:37-38. Reuben's suggestion to slay his two sons was extreme and unwarranted. Certainly he never seriously expected his father to accept it. Its purpose was purely to accentuate the extreme care that would be taken of Benjamin. Little did Jacob know that God was testing

him, too (Heb. 12:7-8), and that all those things he thought were against him actually were working together for his good (Rom. 8:28).

7. THE SECOND MEETING WITH JOSEPH. 43:1-34.

Preparations for Another Trip to Egypt. 43:1-15. **1-2.** The severity of the famine soon became a pressure upon Jacob to send his sons to Egypt for new food rations. **3.** Judah reminded Jacob of the necessity of sending along Benjamin. "The man warned us sternly" (MLB), is expressed in Hebrew by the infinitive absolute. The whole experience with Joseph was as much of a testing of Jacob because of his favoritism as it was of his sons for their evil deed. **6-7.** Jacob's turmoil belied the fact that he was not really looking to "God Almighty" (v. 14), but at circumstances and difficulties.

8-9. With deep sincerity Judah pleaded that Benjamin be allowed to go along, promising to accept all responsibility. **I will be surety** (guarantee against loss or damage) **for him.** This is a technical use of the verb *'ārāḇ*, very common in Akkadian legal terminology. **11-12.** Jacob scarcely manifested his **Israel** character of complete reliance upon God. Even the present of **the best fruits in the land** (cf. 37:25), and **the double money**, though manifesting worldly wisdom, scarcely highlighted faith. **14.** Yet deep down under the veneer of carnal worry was his trust in **God Almighty** (*'El Shaddai* 17:1; 35:11; 48:3).

Joseph's Kindness. 43:16-34. **16-17.** When the brothers arrived in Egypt, to their surprise they were kindly received and invited to dinner. **18-22.** Even this positive turn of affairs filled them with apprehension, prompting them to make a complete explanation to **the steward of Joseph's house. 23.** The steward's words again stressed the fundamental motif of the story—the operation of divine Providence. Then he **brought Simeon out unto them** (cf. 42:24), another token of God's working. **26. When Joseph came home, they ... bowed themselves to him to the earth. 28.** A few moments later they again prostrated themselves and **made obeisance.** The hendiadys stresses their doing in the most humbling manner possible that which they had declared they would never do (cf. 37:8-11, 19-20). **29-30.** When Joseph **saw his** (own full, uterine) **brother Benjamin, his mother's son,** Rachel's offspring, as he was, **his heart yearned** (he was overcome with feeling; lit., "his emotions boiled over"). **He sought where to weep ... and wept there** (cf. 42:24; 45:2, 14-15). **31. Set on bread** (food), idiom for "serve the meal." **32.** It was **an abomination unto the Egyptians** to eat with the Hebrews, because the latter ate the cow, which was sacred to Isis. **33-34.** Joseph's high preferment of Benjamin (cf. 35:18) had a larger design than to test the feeling of his brothers, as the sequel shows.

8. JOSEPH'S ULTIMATE TEST OF HIS BROTHERS. 44:1-34.

The Purpose of the Test. 44:1-13. **1-2. Put my cup ... in the sack's mouth of the youngest.** The design was to bring Benjamin into a situation of peril, to see how far his brothers would go in risking their own necks to seek his deliverance. The purpose of the restored money was partly at least to prevent any injurious impressions of Benjamin's character, the sight of the money in **every** man's grain bag pointed to the conclusion that Benjamin was just as innocent as they. And if guiltless of this, he would very likely also be guiltless of the theft of the cup. **5. Is not this it** (the silver cup) **in which my lord drinketh, and whereby ... he**

diveneth? The value of the cup lay principally in its occult use in prognostication. Divination (foretelling the future) by means of liquids is well attested in Mesopotamia (cf. J. Hunger, *Becherwahrsagung bei den Babylonieren*; J. Vergote, *Joseph en Egypte*, pp. 172-73). Oil or water was poured into a receptacle, and then omens were based on the appearance of the liquid inside the container (v. 15; cf. Num. 24:1). **9. With whomsoever of thy servants it** (the cup) **be found, both let him die, and we also will be my lord's slaves. 10-13.** So sure were they of their innocence, that the penalty they suggested was extreme. Yet what agony overwhelmed them as the cup turned up in Benjamin's sack.

The Brothers' Confession of Guilt. 44:14-17. **16. God hath found out the iniquity of thy servants.** Since the brothers acknowledged their collective guilt, Judah's words may not only refer to the theft, but also to their treatment of Joseph in his youth. **17. The man in whose hand the cup is found, he shall be my servant.** Joseph centered his test on Benjamin to see whether, as in his own case, they would let his brother go into slavery and return to their father to justify the loss of another of his sons.

Judah's Magnificent Plea. 44:18-34. **18-27.** Judah's dramatically moving speech summarizes the whole sequence of events with soul-stirring pathos. His portrayal of Jacob's plight is superbly touching. **28-29.** When the plea turned to Joseph's fate in relation to Benjamin's present peril, the tenseness of the scene must have been well-nigh unbearable. **33. Now therefore ... let thy servant abide instead of the lad a slave to my lord; and let the lad go.** At this crescendo point, Joseph's severe testing of his brothers reaped its highest benefit as his brothers proved their moral and spiritual transformation. So will Israel's coming trials in the Great Tribulation result in the conversion of a remnant for Kingdom blessing.

9. JOSEPH REVEALS HIMSELF TO HIS BROTHERS. 45:1-28.

The Disclosure. 45:1-15. **1-2.** The return of all his brothers and the artless expression of Judah's heroic self-sacrifice completely unnerved Joseph. He **could not control himself.** In one dramatic moment he found himself forced to bring his painful trial to a swift close. He had heard enough to convince him that time, grace, and the painful trials that he himself had put his brothers through had had a happy effect on the improvement of their character. **3. I am Joseph.** The self-disclosure typifies that future day when the greater than Joseph in His exaltation at His second advent will make Himself known to the Israelite remnant purged through the Great Tribulation (see Joseph as a type of Christ, 41:46).

4-7. Joseph emphasized divine Providence working through all the dark events. **Be not grieved ... for God did send me before you to preserve life.** He emphasized that five more years of famine remained in which there would **neither be plowing nor harvest. And God sent me before you to preserve you ... and to save your lives.** Joseph displayed his deep faith in the omniscience and omnipotence of God, overruling Satan, demonic powers, and wicked men to work out His sovereign will and unfrustratable plans (cf. Rom. 8:28). **8. It was not you that sent me here, but God.** Faith lifted the whole sordid crime of the brothers out of the pit of misery and self-recrimination and placed it on the mountain peak of divine sovereignty, where God's forgiving grace not only wipes away the past but also heals the wounds inflicted by sin of bygone days.

9-15. Faith also saw God's hand in the present exaltation and prosperity Joseph was enjoying and the future purpose of God to preserve His people a remnant on earth through which to effect not only their salvation, but eventually that of the world. "At once, with the clear purpose that marked all his actions, Joseph sets forth his plans for the rest of the family of Israel" (H. C. Leupold, BE, 1:90). **10. Goshen** (cf. 47:6) is the fertile grazing land in the eastern section of the Nile Delta, where the Israelite flocks could prosper.

Pharaoh's Invitation to Egypt. 45:16-28. Joseph's plan was enthusiastically endorsed by Pharaoh and his court. Wagons were provided for comfort, consonant with the honorable estate of those who were now members of the vizier's household and not common Asiatics, with men riding on asses and the women carrying their burdens and following on foot, as depicted in Egyptian reliefs (Alleman, OTC, p. 204).

10. JACOB MIGRATES TO EGYPT. 46:1-34.

Jacob Leaves Canaan. 46:1-7. **1.** From Hebron (37:14) Jacob went first to Beer-sheba, the shrine associated with Isaac (26:23-25; 28:10) and the spot marking the southernmost place of the promised land (cf. Judg. 20:1). A momentous event, comparable to the migration of the Pilgrim fathers to New England, was taking place. Should the man of faith and promise leave the land of promise? Would Jacob not call to mind the boding prophecy given Abraham (15:13)? It was only natural that he should seek God's guidance at the shrine of his fathers. **2-3.** The divine permission was given. The assurance that his posterity were to grow into nationhood in Egypt heartened Jacob to proceed.

Catalog of Jacob's Descendants.

94

46:8-27. The vast import of the emigration to Egypt for the history of Israel and the working out of the divine plan of redemption called for a formal genealogical listing at this point. The total migrants of Jacob's own issue, not counting the wives of Jacob's sons, numbered sixty-six. **26.** This number did not include Joseph's two sons (v. 27), or Jacob and Joseph apparently. In any case the complete total was seventy, however the calculation was made (Exod. 1:5), a full round number being aimed at in the final reckoning.

The Settlement in Egypt. 46:28-34. Judah was sent ahead because he was the chief spokesman (37:26; 43:3-10; 44:18-34). Goshen was what is now a part of the Wadi Tumilat (cf. 45:10). **29.** What a dramatic scene as Joseph, in regal splendor in his chariot, was reunited with his aged father of great patriarchal dignity. **30-34.** Joseph advised his brothers to testify that they were shepherds. There in Goshen they would be near him and still be more or less isolated from the Egyptians and their idolatry, both geographically and socially, since the shepherd's occupation was an abomination to the Egyptians, who lived in the interior. This arrangement was undoubtedly providential and necessary for the Israelites to be protected from pagan influence and to increase and become a powerful people, distinct from the Egyptians.

11. JACOB SETTLES IN GOSHEN. 47:1-31.

Presentation to Pharaoh. 47:1-6. **2-4.** Five brothers as representatives were introduced to Pharaoh, and Goshen was confirmed as the place of settlement. **6.** Pharaoh also invited able Israelite men to take charge of his cattle. Egyptian sources attest that the pharaohs possessed large herds and bred cattle.

Jacob Blesses Pharaoh. 47:7-12.

Presumably Jacob's blessing of Pharaoh consisted of general welfare and long life. **9.** Jacob told Pharaoh his age was 130 years. He called his days **few and evil,** reflecting the view that there was an increasing shortening and troubling of man's life (see 5:4-5). Ages decreased from 900 to 1000 years (Adam to Noah), to 200 to 600 years (Noah to Abraham), to 100 to 200 years (the patriarchs), to the normal 70 years (Psalm 90:10). **11.** Goshen was further described as **the best of the land . . . the land of Rameses,** either named anticipatively after the later Rameses II or, as some critics surmise, a gloss added by an editor to define precisely where Goshen was located (cf. a similar definition, Ur "of the Chaldeans," 11:31).

Joseph's Land Policies. 47:13-26. The agrarian program, which was initiated as a result of the exigencies of the famine, effected a change in the Egyptian land ownership. **14.** First the Egyptians spent all their money for grain (cf. 41:56). **15-17.** Next, in their desperation, they exchanged their cattle. **18-19.** Finally, they sold themselves and their land to Pharaoh. **20-26.** The result was that the whole population became Pharaoh's tenants, farming the land for him and, as a tax, paying him one-fifth of the produce. Priests and temple property were excluded (v. 22). Such a feudalistic system was later inaugurated between 1700 and 1500 B.C., as Egyptian sources attest, and apparently appeared in this earlier era. Joseph's wisdom was lauded in saving the people. No sanction of absolutism is suggested.

Joseph's Promise to Jacob. 47:27-31. **27-28.** For seventeen years Jacob dwelt in Goshen and saw the remarkable growth and prosperity of his people, dying at the age of 147. **29-30.** He charged Joseph by solemn oath not to bury him in Egypt. **But I will lie with my**

fathers (cf. 50:5-13; Heb. 11:21). Putting the hand **under** (the) **thigh,** an ancient form of oath-taking (cf. 15:2-4; 24:2), sprang from the notion that the seat of reproductivity was sacred to deity. Jacob "died in faith" (Heb. 11:13). His insistence on burial at Machpelah evidenced his attachment by faith to the Abrahamic Covenant and his resting in the divine promises concerning Canaan (cf. 49:28-33). **31.** His worship was an expression of his faith; he **bowed himself upon the bed's head**, that is, "at the head of the bed" (*miṭṭâ*, MT), but the Septuagint has *mǎṭṭěh*, "staff" (cf. 32:10; Heb. 11:21).

12. JACOB'S LAST DAYS. 48:1-22.

Jacob Blesses Joseph's Sons. 48:1-16. Jacob's deathbed scenes are of great significance to the history of Israel. Therefore, they are described in detail, becoming the occasion of the blessing of the twelve tribes. **5-6.** Jacob's benediction upon Joseph's sons explains why Ephraim and Manasseh ranked as two independent tribes. Jacob adopted them by the ceremony of taking them between his knees (v. 12). His blessing them was based upon the divine promises made to him at Luz (Bethel; 28:13-17; 35:10-12). **7.** The allusion to Rachel was prompted by the honoring of her son Joseph. **13.** Joseph expected to have Jacob bless his elder son by positioning him so that Jacob's right hand would rest upon his head. **14.** But Jacob by divine guidance accorded the place of preeminence to Ephraim instead of Manasseh. This blessing of Joseph's sons is the most impressive blessing in the Old Testament. **15-16.** Jacob first referred to God as *Elohim*, before whom his fathers had walked; next, as a *Shepherd*, who had watched over Jacob all his life; and third, as the *divine presence* who was Jacob's *Go'el* (Redeemer), delivering him from all evil (cf. Num. 6:24-26).

Joseph Objects. 48:17-22. But Jacob was guided by the Spirit of prophecy that foresaw the future. Manasseh and Ephraim, situated in the hill country, were powerful tribes in the early history of the nation. However, during the period of the Judges and the early monarchy, Ephraim gained the preeminence over the "first-born" tribe, which once ranked first in power. **20.** So the order became Ephraim and Manasseh, as Jacob foresaw. **22. Moreover, I have given to thee one portion** (*shekěm*, "shoulder," evidently a play on Shechem, the important city that was located in the territory of Joseph, cf. 12:6).

13. JACOB'S PROPHETIC TESTAMENT. 49:1-33.

Prologue. 49:1-2. **1-2.** In this poem Jacob appears not preeminently as a saint or man of faith, but as a prophet. He gathered **his sons** about his deathbed to tell them what was going to happen to them **in the last days** (Deut. 4:30; Num. 24:14; Isa. 2:2; Mic. 4:1). Although the phrase sometimes refers specifically to the time of the second advent and the establishment of the Kingdom over Israel, evidently here it comprehends the indefinite future from Jacob's time to Kingdom blessing.

Reuben. 49:3-4. **3.** The **first-born,** the father's eldest son, normally would have enjoyed **the excellency of dignity, and the excellency of power** by right of primogeniture. But because of his atrocious crime (35:22), he lost the privileges of his birthright (a double portion of the inheritance, the priesthood, and the Kingdom, according to Jewish writers). The first was conferred on Joseph, the second on Levi, and the third on Judah. **4. Unstable as water**

96

(boiling or gushing up with lust and passion, cf. 35:22; 1 Chron. 5:1). **Thou shalt not excel**—he was destined for mediocrity—no judge, prophet, or ruler would arise from the Reubenites.

Simeon and Levi. 49:5-7. **5-6.** These brothers in crime showed their true colors the day they cruelly massacred the Shechemites (34:26). Jacob called them **brothers** (NASB) in the sense of being "a pair or two of a kind." "Their wares" (from the root *mkr*, "to sell, trade") were "the tools of lawlessness" (Speiser, AB, p. 361). "For they killed men in their fury, and maimed oxen at their whim." **7.** "I will disperse them in Jacob, scatter them throughout Israel" (Speiser). Levi, once a full tribe, came to be a priestly class (Exod. 32:26-29; Deut. 10:8-9). Simeon was eventually absorbed into the tribe of Judah.

Judah. 49:8-12. Judah ("praise") received the first unqualified commendation. "He would emerge as the powerful leader of a people who could enthusiastically admire and praise him" (Kyle M. Yates, Sr., "Genesis," WBC, p. 45). "He crouches like a lion recumbent, a lion's breed—who would dare rouse him?" (Speiser). Judah's glories were predicted to be (1) military exploits (v. 8*b*); (2) lionlike courage (v. 9); (3) Messianic realization (v. 10); (4) a flourishing grape industry (vv. 11-12).

10. This verse is patently Messianic and, despite interminable discussion, the general sense is clear—Judah was to retain the scepter (political sovereignty) until the Messiah (Shiloh or Sheloh) appeared. **Shiloh** ("peaceful" or "peacemaker") agrees with the title given the Messiah by Isaiah (9:6) and is the reading of the Hebrew Bible (MT). *Sheloh* literally means, "whose it is" if construed as an Aramaic form. Even if not taken as a proper name (as in the RV, "until he come to whom it be-

longs"), the Messianic import is inescapable.

James M. Gray's observation is to the point: "Both Jews and Christians agree that Shiloh ... applies to Christ, in which regard it is noticeable that the tribe of Judah maintained at least the semblance of government in Israel until after the crucifixion, while since that time she has had no national existence. It is in connection with Judah ... we have the clearest prophecy of the Redeemer since that of Eden (Gen. 3:15)" (CWCB, p. 52). **10b.** This verse should read: "And to Him shall be the obedience of the peoples." All peoples shall obey Him in the coming Kingdom. **12.** The allusion to **eyes ... red with wine ... teeth white with milk** speaks of Judah's fine vineyards and grazing lands. The prophecy concerning Judah prefigures Christ's kingship.

Zebulun. 49:13. Zebulun is not described. His geographical position on the sea (lit., "seas") seems to place his tribe between the Mediterranean (the Great Sea) and the Sea of Chinnereth (the Lake of Galilee). Evidently the tribe of Zebulun was not able to hold its original maritime position (cf. Judg. 5:18).

Issachar. 49:14-15. Issachar is described as a beast of burden. His position in the Valley of Esdraelon (an important crossroad) made him an easy prey of foreigners, and he had a disposition to sacrifice freedom for material profit and ease (cf. Judg. 1:28-32).

Dan. 49:16-18. Dan was to judge the people of his own tribe, that is, maintain his independence by his prowess. The reference to the snake **that biteth the horse heels** is probably a figurative description of guerilla warfare employed by the tribe in its rise to power. **18. I have waited for thy salvation, O Lord.** This sudden outburst was evidently elicited by the reference to the serpent, recalling the first mention of the gospel (3:15). Jacob envisioned the true people of God (particularly the godly remnant of the Tribulation period), awaiting divine deliverance by the seed of the woman (Christ) from the wrath of the seed of the serpent (the Antichrist). If, as some surmise, Antichrist will arise out of Dan, then this prophecy will receive its fulfillment in the time of Jacob's trouble.

Gad. 49:19. Gad would be exposed to attacks by raiding bands, but he would turn upon them and rout them.

Asher. 49:20. Asher's yield would be so rich that he would furnish dainties for kings.

Naphtali. 49:21. Naphtali is compared to a hind let loose, suggesting the freedom, agility, and vitality of this tribe (cf. Deut. 33:23).

Joseph. 49:22-26. Joseph is portrayed as a strong and prosperous tribe, apparently envisioning the period before "the house of Joseph" was divided into the tribes of Manasseh and Ephraim, as in Deuteronomy 33:13-17. Joseph's spiritual blessings are suggested by the numerous appellations of God: (1) **the mighty God** (One) **of Jacob** (cf. Isa. 1:24; 49:26), a title of "the God of the fathers"; (2) **the Shepherd, the stone** (Rock) **of Israel**; (3) **the God of thy father**; (4) **the** (God) **Almighty** (El Shaddai), the name under which God revealed Himself to the patriarchs (see 17:1; 28:3; 35:11; 43:14; 48:3; Exod. 6:3). **25. Blessings of heaven** (rain and sunshine) **... blessings of the deep** (rivers and springs) (*Harper Study Bible*, p. 80). Joseph forecast Christ's millennial reign.

Benjamin. 49:27. Benjamin is compared to a "wolf," envisioning the fiercest and most warlike of the tribes (cf. Judg. 19:16; 2 Sam. 2:15-16; 1 Chron. 8:40; 12:2; 2 Chron. 17:17). Heroes of this tribe were marked by ferocity and wolflike treachery—Ehud (Judg. 3:15-22); and Saul (1 Sam. 22:17-20). Benjamin adumbrates Christ as the terrible Warrior (Isa. 63:1-3; Rev. 19:11-15).

Jacob's Death. 49:28-33. **29-32.** Jacob's charge to Joseph concerning his burial in Canaan (47:29-31) was repeated before all his children. The family sepulcher at Machpelah (23:1-20) was specified. **33. Jacob ... died** ("breathed his last," RV), **and was gathered unto his people** (see comments on 25:8).

14. JACOB'S BURIAL AND JOSEPH'S FINAL YEARS. 50:1-26.

Jacob's Burial. 50:1-14. **2. Joseph commanded his servants, the physicians,** to embalm his father. Embalming was an ancient Egyptian custom for people of prominence and wealth. Moreover, it was necessary in this case if Joseph was to keep his oath and bury Jacob's body in Canaan. Numerous mummies have been found, often in a remarkably preserved condition. **3.** So elaborate was the process that it required forty days. **The Egyptians mourned ... threescore and ten** (seventy) **days,** indicating that they, out of respect for Joseph, gave Jacob a royal funeral, since it was customary to bewail a pharaoh's death seventy-two days. **10-11. The threshing floor of Atad** is not mentioned elsewhere and the site is unknown. It was renamed **Abel-mizraim** ("meadow" or "mourning" of Egypt). Joseph **made a mourning** (lamentation) **for his father seven days,** the normal period for wailing among the Hebrews (cf. 1 Sam. 31:13). There in Transjordan the Egyptian escort evidently returned home. The idea that Jacob was interred in Transjordan has no basis either in the Bible or in tradition (v. 5 refers to Machpelah; cf. v. 13).

Joseph's Kindness to His Brothers.

50:15-21. **15-16.** The brothers had never forgiven themselves for their treatment of Joseph. Consequently, they could not quite believe that Joseph had forgiven them. Their anxiety took the form of a petition. **17-21.** Once more Joseph manifested his noble character. He asserted that only God can forgive and testified once more to God's overruling providence (cf. 45:4-7).

The Death of Joseph. 50:22-26. **22.** Joseph lived to be 110 years old, representing the Egyptian ideal of a complete life. **24-25.** Like Jacob, Joseph never looked on Egypt as his home or final resting place. So he made his family solemnly swear that they would carry his body back to the land promised them. **God will surely visit you.** Joseph eloquently expressed prophetically the same faith that Jacob had in the covenant God and the covenant hope (cf. 47:29-31; Heb. 11:22). **26. So Joseph died ... and they embalmed him, and he was put in a coffin in Egypt.** But faith had assured him that his bones would not remain there, but be buried in Canaan (Exod. 13:19; Josh. 24:32).

EXODUS

INTRODUCTION

Title. Whereas Genesis is the book of beginnings, Exodus is the book of redemption. Rescued out of Egyptian bondage, the newly constituted nation was given the Law, priesthood, and a system of sacrifice as provision for the worship and government of a redeemed people. The name Exodus comes from the Vulgate through the Septuagint. It means literally, "going out" or "departure" (cf. 19:1; Heb. 11:22). The book focuses upon the great experience of redemption from Egypt, setting it forth as a type of all redemption.

As a book of redemption, Exodus is one of the most helpful spiritual books of the Old Testament. The LORD, heretofore connected with the Israelites only through His covenant with Abraham, Isaac, and Jacob, now brings them to Himself nationally through redemption and puts them under the Mosaic Covenant with the tabernacle, priesthood, and the Shekinah glory of His presence. The entire book is highly typical of the person and finished redemptive work of Christ. Especially the tabernacle and the priesthood, as well as the sacrificial ritual, show meticulously the work of our Lord Jesus Christ in salvation.

Called the "second book of Moses," Exodus follows Genesis in the closest possible relation. The book is second to no other in the Old Testament in the history of redemption. Moses is set forth as the great deliverer and lawgiver, a type of Christ.

Higher Critical View. Higher critics make the book along with Genesis a late compilation of popular traditions (Jehovistic, c. 850 B.C.; Elohistic, c. 750 B.C.; and priestly, c. 500 B.C.), these being allegedly combined with the original Mosaic tradition. Under such a rationalistic view, Exodus is adjudged non-Mosaic in authorship, unreliable historically, and traditional rather than factual in the miracles and events it contains.

But the elements of the book are so intimately and closely interwoven in such harmony with the other Pentateuchal books and the Bible as a whole that the higher critical view appears to be at variance with clear lines of historical and scriptural evidence supporting the unity of the entire Pentateuch. Redemptive typology is woven throughout the book like a magnificent mosaic. It portrays God's great redemptive plan running through the entire Scripture from Genesis to Revelation. This internal evidence of inspiration strongly argues against the naturalistic views of the Pentateuchal partitionists.

Historical Background. Although this second book of the Pentateuch covers a long span of years (430 according to Exod. 12:40), the author treats this extended interval with extreme brevity. The entire period, except for the last year, is covered in the first two chapters. That one year, in which occurred the climactic events of Israel's deliverance out of Egypt and the inauguration of a new relationship with God, occupies the remaining thirty-eight chapters of the book.

Following the chronology embedded in the Pentateuchal books, the Egyptian sojourn lasted from about 1871 to 1441 B.C. Evidently the patriarchal period in Palestine was contemporary with a strong Middle Kingdom in Egypt under the Twelfth Dynasty (2000-1780 B.C.). Joseph became the prime minister for, and Jacob stood before, one of the powerful rulers (Amenemes I-IV or Senwosret I-III) of this line of kings. Under this chronology, Israel lived in Egypt during the Hyksos period of foreign domination (1780-1546 B.C.), was oppressed by the great warrior Thutmose III (1482-1450 B.C.) of the Eighteenth Dynasty, and left the country under Amenhotep II (1450-1425 B.C.).

Many scholars, however, place the Exodus and the conquest under the Nineteenth Dynasty under Rameses I (c. 1319), Sethi I (c. 1319-1299), Rameses II (c. 1299-1232), and Merenptah (c. 1232-1222). In the latter's famous stele, Israel is mentioned for the first time in Egyptian records: "The people of Israel is desolate; it has no offspring."

OUTLINE

EXODUS

E. The Golden Calf. 32:1-35.
F. Renewal of the Covenant. 33:1—34:35.
   1. The Lord's Guidance. 33:1-23.
   2. The Second Table of the Law. 34:1-35.
G. Erection of the Tabernacle and Institution of the Priesthood. 35:1—40:38.
   1. Gifts and Workmen. 35:1-35.
   2. The Tabernacle Materials. 36:1-38.
   3. The Tabernacle Furniture. 37:1—38:31.
   4. The Priestly Garments. 39:1-43.
   5. The Assembling and Dedication. 40:1-38.

COMMENTARY

I. ISRAEL IN EGYPT. 1:1—12:51.

A. EGYPTIAN BONDAGE. 1:1-22.

Historical Link with the Past. 1:1-7. The book of Exodus connects immediately with Genesis and actually begins with a parenthesis. Verse 8 is in immediate sequence to Genesis 50:26 and is the natural beginning of the book. Verses 1-5 are a recapitulation as an introduction to a new section of what had been stated before concerning the sons of Jacob. The reference is to Genesis 46:8-26, where the sons are listed according to their mothers. There it is said, "All the souls were threescore and six" (v. 26), and "All the souls ... were threescore and ten" (v. 27). The "souls that came with Jacob" (v. 26) were sixty-six. "All the souls of the house of Jacob" (v. 27), constituting the entire family of Jacob, were seventy. With Joseph and his two sons, already in Egypt, they totaled sixty-nine; and, adding Jacob himself, the total was seventy.

The account of Joseph's death is narrated in Genesis 50:24-26. **7.** The period of the sojourn in Egypt, during which the Israelites were **fruitful, and increased abundantly, and multiplied,** is given as 430 years in Exodus 12:40 (cf. Gal. 3:17). In generalized terms, it is given as 400 years (Gen. 15:13). **The land** was the land of Goshen (cf. Gen. 47:4), called Rameses (Gen. 47:11), and located in the eastern delta of the Nile River.

The New Pharaoh's Policy. 1:8-14. **8.** **A new king ... who knew not Joseph.** The new king, doubtless under the powerful Eighteenth Dynasty, came to power. The phenomenal increase of the Israelites is graphically portrayed in verse 7. This picture of expansion precedes heartless oppression (vv. 8-14). By forced labor Pharaoh built **Pithom** (Tell er-Ratabeh) **and Raamses** (Avaris-Tanis) in the delta. The miraculous increase of the Israelites produced the first outcroppings in history of anti-Semitism. But that increase always has taken place under oppression and persecution. When they were oppressed, God's time for deliverance drew near. The oppression in Egypt was also permitted for their own good, because the idolatry of Egypt was a great snare (cf. Josh. 24:14; Ezek. 23:8). **12. Grieved because of** should be translated "felt a loathing for."

13-14. The pharaoh was an absolute monarch, and the corvée had been in practice since the pharaohs had become builders. The Israelites were taken from their free life as shepherds and subjected to hard service **in mortar, and in brick.** Typically, Pharaoh becomes a picture of Satan, the enslaved Israelites become pictures of sinners, and their hard labor becomes a picture of the wages of sin. From Thutmose III of the Eighteenth Dynasty comes a picture from Thebes, the great capital, showing Asiatic slaves making bricks, and bearing the inscription, "A taskmaster says to his laborers, 'The rod is in my hand, be not idle.' " **Service in the field** was probably irrigation and agricultural work in the delta.

Planned Extinction. 1:15-22. Hebrew midwives were ordered to kill all male Israelite babies, but they disobeyed Pharaoh and were blessed by the LORD. The two midwives were very likely representative names of many midwives, perhaps supervisors. **16.** The birth **stool** is well illustrated in ancient sources. In Mesopotamia and in Egypt and among the Hebrews, women customarily crouched down in childbirth on a pair of bricks or "stones" (*'ŏḇnāyim*, 1:16) or on a birth stool of similar form. The Egyptian word *msi'* ("to give birth") was frequently followed by the hieroglyphic of a crouching woman in the act of giving birth. In one late text the figure is actually shown crouching on two bricks or stones (NBD, p. 821). The word *pharaoh* (lit., "great house") is a title, not a personal name. Failing in this strategy, the king ordered the people to drown every male Hebrew baby in the Nile River. Satan's attempt to destroy the promised seed and the Jewish people can be traced from Cain's murder of Abel to the time of Christ (cf. 2 Chron. 21:4; 22:10-11; Esther 3:13; Matt. 2:16).

B. THE DELIVERER RAISED UP.
2:1—4:31.

1. MOSES THE DELIVERER. 2:1-25.

Birth of the Deliverer. 2:1-10. Moses' parents, Amram and Jochebed (6:20), were of the tribe of Levi, later designated as the priestly line. The ark of Moses was made of papyrus reed, woven together and plastered with bitumen, a well-known product from the Dead Sea. About 2600 B.C., Sargon of Agade was also saved from danger in infancy by being placed in a basket of rushes sealed with pitch and floated on a river. Moses' **sister stood afar off.** Her name was Miriam (Num. 26:59). Was the Pharaoh's daughter Hat-

shepsut or one of the fifty-nine daughters of Raamses II, forty-five of whose names have been preserved? The Hebrew *mōsheh* (Moses) is an active participle meaning "the one drawing out," because Pharaoh's daughter drew the infant out of the water. But this is the interpretation given by the sacred writer. Probably the name was Egyptian *Mase*, pronounced *Mose*, meaning "the child" (cf. Ahmose, "son of Ah, the god of light," and Thutmose, "son of Thot").

Flight to Midian. 2:11-23. **11-14.** At age forty (Acts 7:23), Moses cast his lot with his countrymen (Heb. 11:24-25). He needed divine preparation, as is shown by his killing an Egyptian taskmaster in anger. God was dealing with the future deliverer, and many lessons from the school in the desert were prepared for him. **15. Midian,** to which Moses fled, was the habitat of a northwest Arabian tribe descended from Abraham by Keturah (Gen. 25:1-4; cf. Gen. 37:28; Judg. 6:2-3).

16. The priest of Midian was the head priest of the tribe and the secular head of the clan. He evidently had two names (Jethro, 3:1; 4:18; and Reuel, 2:18; Num. 10:29 margin), as did some Sabaean kings and priests. The scene of Moses watering the flocks of Jethro's daughters is related to show how he won Zipporah ("bird") as his wife. To them was born a son, Gershom ("a sojourner there").

God Remembers the Covenant. 2:24-25. **God heard . . . God remembered . . . God looked upon the children of Israel . . . God knew their plight.** What a picture of the great God of grace demonstrating His interest and His love in His oppressed people, and all the while planning graciously for their deliverance (cf. 6:4-5; 19:5-6; 34:10).

2. MOSES' CALL TO DELIVER ISRAEL. 3:1-22.

The Burning Bush. 3:1-3. God was at work to prepare His servant for a great ministry of deliverance. As Moses looked, a common desert thorn bush was afire; yet it was not consumed. The prickly shrub pictures the sinful enslaved Israelites, since thorns are the result of the curse of sin (Gen. 3:16-18). The fire symbolizes their suffering and tribulation. The unscathed bush shows that all the persecutions visited upon the people could not annihilate them.

The appearance of the angel of the LORD (the preincarnate Christ) out of the flaming bush indicates God's people are preserved by divine power. Moses received this great revelation as a shepherd, a vocation the Egyptians despised, showing that he shared the reproach of Christ (Heb. 11:26). Mount Horeb, or Mount Sinai (the former term usually denotes the mountain range, and the latter term identifies the particular peak), has been identified in ancient tradition with Jebel Musa, located some sixty miles from the tip of the Sinai Peninsula.

The Call. 3:4-12. **4-10.** Moses' vision was followed by his call. The One who called him revealed Himself as the God of Abraham, Isaac, and Jacob. Moses, who had already removed his sandals because the place on which he was standing was holy ground, then hid his face, for he was afraid to look on God's presence. God's message was one of sovereign grace. He saw the helpless condition of the Israelites and was moved to deliver them. The salvation that the LORD was undertaking typified the future incarnation of the Word who was God (John 1:1, 14-15) for the redemption of sinful man.

11. Who am I, that I should go . . . ? In answering God's call, Moses announced distrust in himself. Forty years before, he had undertaken the work of deliverance in complete self-confidence and had revealed his human weakness. Now the vision and voice of God revealed him as he actually was. God's reply was sufficient. **12. I will be with you.** To bolster faith, God gave Moses a sign of His deliverance and power. One day, redeemed out of Egypt, the Israelites would serve God upon this very mountain where He revealed Himself to His servant.

Revelation of the Name Jehovah (Yahweh). 3:13-14. God revealed His name to the inquiring deliverer as I AM THAT I AM. This was a revelation of the eternal Creator and Consummator of redemption. The name is derived from the Hebrew *hāyâ* ("to be"); thus, "He who was, is, and shall be." He is "I *was* who I was," "I *am* who I am," and "I *shall be* who I shall be." All these translations are possible in the original to describe the eternally existing One "who is, and who was, and who is to come, the Almighty" (Rev. 1:8).

Directions for Deliverance. 3:15. The human deliverer was to go in the name of Jehovah (Yahweh), the divine Deliverer. He was to go under the aegis of the eternal One, who had come to fulfill His covenant with and keep His promise to the afflicted descendants of Abraham, Isaac, and Jacob.

Moses to Gather Together the Elders of Israel. 3:16-20. **16-17.** Moses was to lay before them the revelation he had received at the bush and disclose God's purpose to deliver them from Egypt. **18-20.** They were then to ask Pharaoh for permission to make a three days' journey into the wilderness to sacrifice to their God. The wilderness was the broad, dry plateau known as *et-Tih*, a barren terrain extending from the eastern border of Egypt to the south of Palestine. Although the request was not unreasonable, it surely would arouse Pharaoh's suspicions and be refused. This was an initial test of the monarch to see how he would react to God's plan. The request was hardly intended as an excuse to get a good start for subsequent flight. This would be a clear case of deception, although some scholars understand this as a reflection of Oriental psychology, which maintains that the end justifies the means. In any case, the king would refuse and God's hand of deliverance would be revealed in mighty miracles.

Provision of Jewels and Raiment. 3:21-22. **21. When ye go, ye shall not go empty.** A persistent ancient Near East tradition, experienced by those who have servants, is that the servants borrow from their employers in addition to receiving their wages. The coveted articles they get are called a "gift." Neither dishonesty nor unfairness is implied (cf. H. C. Trumbull, *Studies in Oriental Social Life*, pp. 330-31). In this way the Israelites would make their exit recompensed properly for their long and arduous slavery among the Egyptians (cf. 11:2-3; 33:6).

3. MOSES' RETURN TO EGYPT. 4:1-31.

Confirmatory Signs. 4:1-9. Despite the wonderful divine assurances of 3:18-20, Moses continued his objections. He had already pleaded no ability (3:11) and no divine authority (3:13-14). Next he argued that the Israelites would not believe him or listen to his voice. In early Israel a prophet's credentials were his wonderful deeds (Judg. 6:36-40; 1 Sam. 12:17; 1 Kings 17:14). To enable him to be the deliverer he was called to be, Moses was endowed with power to perform three signs, which were to serve as credentials to the people: (1) the

rod, Moses' shepherd's staff, now a symbol of authority, was to be at his command and become a serpent when thrown on the ground; (2) **his hand** was to become as white as snow—leprous (cf. Num. 12:10; 2 Kings 5:27)—when placed in his bosom; and (3) he would be able to change **water** (into) **blood** (cf. 7:19).

Moses and Aaron. 4:10-17. **10-13.** Moses offered a fourth objection: he was not gifted in speech (literal Heb., "a man of words"). The divine reply to this was that the God who made man's mouth would be with him and teach him what to say. **14-17.** God also promised Moses that He would give him his brother, Aaron, who could **speak well** and would be a mouth to Moses, that is, he would speak for him. But Moses would retain the authority of leadership and be as God to Aaron.

Return to Egypt. 4:18-23. Moses went back to Jethro, his father-in-law, and requested permission to return to Egypt. Through his marriage to Zipporah, Moses had become a member of her clan, of which Jethro was head. Tribal law in such a case required permission to leave. After Moses set out with his wife and sons, he received further assurances that it was God's will to deliver His people from Egypt, though there would be a great struggle.

22. Israel is my son, even my firstborn. These words, clearly connected with Moses' sons, reveal that what a son of Moses was to him, so Israel was to Jehovah—*I am that I am*. The concept of sonship was a favorite with the prophets (cf. Isa. 63:16; Jer. 31:9; Hos. 11:1). However, the sonship referred to in this passage is not individual sonship, as in the New Testament, but a relationship of a people, who would shortly become a nation, to the LORD.

Moses' Wife. 4:24-26. Zipporah, apparently objecting to her son's circumcision, had hindered Moses in performing this rite that was so closely connected with the Abrahamic Covenant (Gen. 17:9-14) and the redemption of Israel back to the land of promise. This was a serious matter inasmuch as Moses was returning to Egypt to be God's instrument of deliverance, the human medium through whom the Abrahamic Covenant would be eventually realized. The sin was very grievous (cf. sin unto death in the New Testament, 1 Cor. 5:5; 11:30-32; 1 John 5:16). Accordingly, Zipporah circumcised her son, apparently unwillingly and angrily.

Moses' Meeting with Aaron. 4:27-28. Meeting Aaron must have been very dramatic. The LORD began to work in Aaron's heart, even as He had done in calling and commissioning Moses.

Performance of Signs. 4:29-31. The signs signaled the progress of the redemptive plan. **The people believed.** It was a thrilling realization that **the Lord had visited** His people (cf. 3:16; 13:19) and **looked upon their affliction** (3:7; Deut. 26:7).

C. STRUGGLE WITH PHARAOH.
5:1—11:10.

1. MOSES BEFORE THE KING OF EGYPT.
5:1-23.

First Appearance Before Pharaoh. 5:1-19. In obedience to the LORD, Moses and Aaron presented themselves before Pharaoh and asked permission for the Israelites to keep a three-day feast in the wilderness. The word for feast (*ḥăg*) comes from the verb *ḥāgăg* ("to dance, to move in a procession"; hence, keep a festival). The cognate Arabic word is the same as that still used by the Arabs for their pilgrimage to Mecca. The Semitic concept of worship envisioned a shrine and a pilgrimage.

The three days' journey would take the Israelites completely out of Egypt; therefore, there was no deceit in what Moses said. By starting out with the smallest demand upon Pharaoh, did it not give the ruler the least possible occasion to harden his heart? **2.** The contemptuous Pharaoh, whose absolute power was enforced by his deification in the Egyptian religion, knew many gods, but he was ignorant of this God (the LORD). Therefore, the request made in His name carried no authority with this proud monarch.

3. Lest he fall upon us with pestilence. The idea of Israel's God was still largely that of El Shaddai (cf. 6:3, the Almighty One). They were yet to learn of Him as the covenant God of their redemption. **4. Wherefore do ye, Moses and Aaron, loose the people from their works?** The king, without taking any notice of what they had said, treated them as turbulent demagogues who were appealing to the people's superstitious feelings to stir up rebellion and to light the fuse of a spirit of discontent. Pharaoh cruelly imposed heavy burdens upon the people, requiring the same number of bricks, but compelling the Israelites to gather their own straw. Both straw-made bricks and pure clay bricks have been found at Pithom and Tanis.

This description of brick-making is amply illustrated in Egyptian monuments, such as wall paintings in the tomb of the Grand Vizier of Thutmose III, which portray the building of the temple of Amun by taskwork. Men are depicted drawing water from a tank to moisten the mud and carrying mud in baskets. Others are kneading the mud with their feet or placing it in molds. Some stand under the slave driver. The inscription reads: "The taskmaster says to his laborers, 'The rod is in my hand, be not idle.'" In an Egyptian papyrus, these words occur: "I am not provided with anything. There are no men for making bricks, and there is no straw in the district," illustrating the Egyptian custom of using straw in brick-making.

Israel's Complaint and Moses' Prayer. 5:20-23. The deliverer of Israel soon discovered that his obedience to the word of the LORD apparently only aggravated the evil he wished to remove. Instead of receiving the gratitude of his countrymen, Moses was loaded with reproaches. His faith and obedience were being tested. No great work of God is ever accomplished without severe testing, and Moses' career was no exception. He wisely went to the LORD and poured out his heart before Him. In chapter 5, Moses appeared before Pharaoh; in 6:1-13, the deliverer was before the LORD.

2. MOSES BEFORE THE LORD. 6:1-30.

Revelation of the Divine Deliverer. 6:1-13. The LORD reminded Moses of His covenant with the patriarchs under the name El-Shaddai (God Almighty, Gen. 17:1). **2-3.** Now that He was about to deliver them from Egyptian bondage (sin), Pharaoh (Satan), and Egypt (the world), He was about to reveal the meaning of His personal redemptive name, Jehovah (Yahweh). Contrary to common higher critical theory, the implication is not that the name Yahweh was not previously known in Genesis, for it occurs there many times. What is meant is that its meaning had not yet been revealed. The reason is simple because redemption from Egypt, typical of redemption in Christ, was not wrought in Canaan but was to be wrought in Egypt.

Note that this passage does *not* concern itself at all with the occurrence or nonoccurrence of the divine name Jehovah in the pre-Mosaic era. Rather, it concerns itself solely with the *declaration of the revelation* of that name. To make the revelation of a name identical with its first occurrence is a subtle fallacy obscured by the plausibilities of the partition theory of the Pentateuch. The peculiar biblical idiom "to know a name" means to experience the particular character, grace, and power of God that are implicit in that name.

The people, through the revelation of the name Yahweh, were to see the mighty manifestation of God's *grace* and *power* in redeeming His people from Egypt, the very attributes the name denoted. That God was so known by the patriarchs, therefore, can indicate nothing as to the existence of the name Jehovah in the earlier period. But it simply means that while tokens of God's almighty power under the name El Shaddai had been granted them (Gen. 17:1; 28:3; 35:11; 43:14; 48:3), no such disclosure had been made of the divine redemptive faithfulness indicated by His name Jehovah as was now to be vouchsafed to their posterity (see 3:13-14 for the meaning of the name).

6. I will redeem you. Exodus as a book of redemption presents a type of all redemption, which is (1) wholly from God (Exod. 3:7-8; John 3:16); (2) through a Person (Exod. 2:2; John 3:16-17); (3) by blood (Exod. 12:13, 23, 27; 1 Pet. 1:18-19); and (4) by power (Exod. 6:6, 13; Rom. 8:2). The blood of Christ redeems the believer from the guilt and penalty of sin (1 Pet. 1:18-19), and the power of the Holy Spirit delivers from the dominion of sin on the basis of Calvary (Rom. 8:2; Gal. 5:16).

7. Ye shall know that I am the Lord your God, who bringeth you out from under the burdens of the Egyptians. This is the essence of the revelation of the name Jehovah (Yahweh, cf. vv. 2-3). God, who said, "I will bring you out"

(v. 6), also said "I will bring you in" (v. 8). God's salvation is *out* of Egypt and its bondage in sin, and *into* the land of Canaan, typical of a believer's victorious life. Salvation not only involves deliverance from the penalty of sin, but from its power. It is not only deliverance from the thralldom and burden of sin, but also means entering into rest and joy in the Lord.

8. Salvation and redemption spring out of the promises of the Abrahamic Covenant. **I am the Lord** (Yahweh) is a name that prefigures the Lord Jesus Christ in His saving ministry. In this redemptive work no condition is specified. The salvation of the Israelite slaves, like ours, was "not of works" but solely by grace. It sprang from God's love as its source (Deut. 7:7-8). The LORD was to demonstrate that deliverance was His work, not theirs. At last they were to know the name of the LORD in a vital salvation experience. They were to be taught by God's interposition that there is only one true gospel, only one way of salvation—that of utterly helpless captives being delivered from sin by the grace and power of God in response to faith.

The Genealogy. 6:14-27. The genealogy that follows records **the heads of their fathers' houses.** As a further indication of divine grace, God called His enslaved people by name. He was acquainted with their heavy burdens, and His love did not only extend to them as a whole, but to each one of them. The genealogy, however, is obviously selective and abbreviated.

A Renewed Commission. 6:28-30. The deliverer himself also needed constant encouragement. **30.** He again complained of **uncircumcised lips** (cf. v. 12), which is a vivid way of saying that Moses was a man poor in speech (4:10-16).

3. FIRST OF THE TEN PLAGUES. 7:1-25.

Moses and Aaron Assured. 7:1-7. **1. A god to Pharaoh** means that Moses' words were to be God's words, and Moses' acts were to be supernatural acts of God working through him with regard to his contact with Pharaoh. **Aaron, thy brother, shall be thy prophet.** Aaron was to be Moses' appointed spokesman (cf. 4:16).

3. I will harden Pharaoh's heart. (*Harden* is from the causative of the Hebrew *qāshâ*, "to be hard, heavy, harsh, severe, difficult," and so, in the causative stem, "to harden, to make heavy, difficult, or obstinate.") God's overruling providence is another way of saying that God overruled the natural unbelief and stubbornness of Pharaoh's heart to accomplish His redemptive purposes. **6. Moses and Aaron did as the Lord commanded.**

The Sign of the Rod. 7:8-14. Egyptian religion was full of idolatry, which is connected with demonism (1 Cor. 10:20). The LORD in speaking to Moses anticipated the fact that he would ask for the demonstration of a miracle. "Magic, i.e., demonic miracle" was the only language the Egyptians understood in the realm of religion. The magicians of Egypt were famous throughout the ancient world; hence, when Moses and Aaron approached Pharaoh, they had to communicate with him in a language that he understood. Moses and Aaron were provided with miracle-working power that was their credential to get his attention. The rod first appeared in the hand of Moses (4:4) and was employed by him to convince the elders of the people, who had long been under the spell of Egypt. Now it was in the hands of Aaron, the official head of Israel's religion, to be an expression of the power of the LORD.

The question is, Was the action of the magicians, who duplicated the miracles, real or merely juggling? Snake charming was carried on in ancient Egypt. However, these magicians were obviously the instruments of Satan and exponents of occultism. They performed lying wonders (2 Thess. 2:8-10). Two exponents of demonized religion, Jannes and Jambres, are mentioned in 2 Timothy 3:8. Such manifestations of demon power are prominent today in spiritualism and in other forms of occultism. These forms of demon power will be accentuated at the end of this age (2 Thess. 2:9-12). Pharaoh's heart was hardened, first by his own actions and then judicially by God, because he willfully rejected the signs given.

The First Plague. 7:15-25. In verses 14-19 the plague was announced. In verses 20-25 the judgment was executed. **20. The waters ... were turned to blood.** Egypt was a country two to thirty miles wide, situated along the course of the sacred Nile River. Egypt was the Nile, and the narrow ribbon of fertile alluvial land the river deposited was watered by an annual inundation, making it the breadbasket of the ancient world. Very early the river was deified, first as Hapi, "the giver of life," and then as Osiris, the embodiment of fertility. The Nile, therefore, was vitally essential to Egypt. Pharaoh had gone out to the Nile, doubtless to perform some religious ceremony. There he was met by Moses and Aaron. The Nile waters were smitten by the rod and turned into blood.

21. The fish ... died; and the river stank (became foul), **and the Egyptians could not drink ... water of the river.** The miracle evidently was in the intensification of natural phenomena, a mixture of the natural and the supernatural. "The wonder" consisted in the dreadful severity of the visitation and the opportune time of its occurrence. Often in August the river turns a dull red, and fish die and the water is unpalatable. God used a phenomenon with which the people were familiar to show His mighty power by intensifying it and punishing the people. The plagues were blows from God to strike the prestige of Pharaoh and his gods. The first blow had struck. Although the magicians were able by demonic power to duplicate this miracle to some extent, it was evident that the God of Moses, Aaron, and the Israelites was beginning to work wonderfully.

4. PLAGUES TWO TO FOUR. 8:1-32.

The Second Plague: Frogs. 8:1-15. As in the case of the other plagues, this was a miraculous intensification of a frequent natural phenomenon. With the inundation of the river in July, the recession of the waters leaves numerous pools that become stagnant. These are places where frogs breed in August and September. Ancient classical writers referred to plagues of frogs in Egypt. The frog itself was often worshiped as a symbol of Hekt, a form of the goddess Hathor. The Egyptian magicians were able to produce frogs, but they could not take them away; so Pharaoh called on Moses and Aaron to intreat their God to remove them.

The Third Plague: Gnats. 8:16-19. **17. All the dust of the land became lice.** Lice (Heb., *kinnîm*; "gnats" or "sand flies") means some kind of stinging insect. Stinging insects are notorious in Egypt. **18.** The magicians tried with their secret arts to bring forth gnats, but they were unable; so there were gnats, it is said, on man and beast. **19.** At this point, the magicians had to acknowledge **the finger of God.** Occultism can only go so far. God permits Satan and demonic powers to perform certain supernatural phenomena in occultism, but God is sovereign and His "finger" is stronger, as it were, than the entire body of Satan.

The Plague of Flies. 8:20-32. The fourth plague of flies demonstrated God's purposeful and discriminating activity, which was behind all the plagues. **22-23.** The Hebrews living in Goshen were clearly exempted from this plague. **24-26.** Again Pharaoh made a superficial response, saying he would permit the people to sacrifice **in the land.** This was refused. After complete permission was given, it was withdrawn as soon as the flies were removed by God in answer to Moses' prayer. Pharaoh made his objection, as Satan makes his, to a full and complete deliverance of God's people from Egypt, a type of the world.

28. From permission to sacrifice in the land, he made a compromise that they must **not go very far away.** In 10:9-11 he decided that the men could go, but the rest of the people and their belongings were to stay behind. In the final compromise (10:24) Pharaoh asked that only their flocks and herds remain behind. In these compromises we read Satan's attempt to keep God's people ensnared by the world and thus hold them under his control and power. In this strategy he has succeeded highly in Christendom.

5. PLAGUES FIVE TO SEVEN. 9:1-35.

Fifth and Sixth Plagues: Murrain and Boils. 9:1-12. **3.** The cattle were stricken with **a very grievous plague**, which means destruction, murrain, and pestilence (cf. Lev. 26:25; Deut. 28:21; 2 Sam. 24:13). The disease was possibly anthrax. **6. All the cattle of Egypt died.** Not absolutely every beast was killed, for some were mentioned later (vv. 19-21), but a great many of each herd died. These plagues were directed

against Ptah (Apis), the god of Memphis, represented as a bull, as well as other gods represented by the goat, the ram, the cow, and other animals.

8-12. The next plague came without warning, unannounced. Moses and Aaron sprinkled the **ashes of the furnace,** and it became boils upon man and beast. The magicians apparently attempted to do the same, but the boils broke out on them. **The furnace** speaks of Egypt in its fiery persecution of Israel. The suffering afflicted upon the people of God by the Egyptians was to boomerang upon them. This plague was the first that endangered human life; therefore, it was the forerunner of the death of the firstborn, which would bring Pharaoh to the end of himself.

The Seventh Plague: Hail. 9:13-25. The plague of hail came from the sky. Jehovah is the Lord of heaven as well as of earth, and so the hail would impress the Egyptians, who had a different god for each phenomenon of nature. **14. That thou mayest know that there** is *none like me in all the earth.* These words are a comparison between Jehovah and other gods (cf. 8:10; 12:12). Verse 15 ought to be rendered, "For by now I could have put forth my hand and struck you and your people with pestilence, and you would have been cut off from the earth" (RSV).

15. Cut off from the earth. Never again did Egypt rise to the height of power and glory reached in that Eighteenth Dynasty. **16. For this cause ... made thee to stand** (ASV). God's sovereign moving in world history, as well as in redemptive history, is declared. Hail, rare in Egypt, occurred in January, for the barley was in bloom (vv. 31-32). It appears throughout that each of the plagues was seasonable, but miraculous.

6. PLAGUES EIGHT AND NINE. 10:1-29.

The Eighth Plague: Locusts. 10:1-20.

1-3. The purpose of the locust plague was not to win Pharaoh, whose heart was hardened, but **that ye may know that I am Jehovah** (ASV) Locusts are a common phenomenon in Palestine, but not so common in Egypt. Joel 1 and 2 give a classic description of a locust plague. In February 1915, Palestine was visited by an extraordinary plague of locusts. (For a description, see *National Geographic* magazine, Dec. 1915.) The locusts were brought by an east wind and carried away by the west wind. The fact that the wind blew a day and a night before bringing the locusts demonstrates that they were brought from a great distance. This proved to the Egyptians that the LORD's omnipotence reached far beyond the borders of Egypt and ruled over every land.

Darkness. 10:21-29. Darkness followed the preceding plague with no introduction, request, or warning. Apparently the same wind that carried away the locusts brought a dreaded sandstorm from the desert. This terrible wind, called *Khamsin*, prevails twenty-five days before and the twenty-five days after the vernal equinox. It is a blinding sandstorm and creates a darkness one can feel. At the end of three days Pharaoh sent for Moses and offered another compromise. The women and children might go, but the flocks and the herds were to remain. Moses refused the offer, demanding complete and free departure, which demonstrated redemption—a complete break from Satan, typified by Pharaoh. This alone would satisfy God's demands. There remained only a fearful looking for judgment by the Egyptians.

7. THE TENTH PLAGUE: DEATH OF THE FIRSTBORN. 11:1-10.

Favor with the Egyptians. 11:1-3. **1.** The LORD told Moses that He would bring **one plague** (*nĕgă‛*, lit., a "blow" or "stroke") **more upon Pharaoh, and upon Egypt.** After that Pharaoh would let the people go out; in fact, he would not merely give them leave, without any conditions, but he would push them out. ("Drive you out from here completely," NASB.)

2. Moses also was directed to notify the people publicly that **every man ask** (*šā’ăl*, "request") **of his neighbor, and every woman of her neighbor,** articles of silver and gold. **3.** Moreover, **the Lord gave the people favor** and Moses esteem, both **in the sight of Pharaoh's servants, and in the sight of the people.**

Death of the Firstborn Announced. 11:4-8. Verses 4-8 constitute a parting warning to Pharaoh following 10:29. **4-5.** The LORD through His servant, Moses, announced that about midnight He would go through the midst of Egypt, and **all the first-born in the land of Egypt** would die. This was catastrophic because "the firstborn represented the whole race of which he was the strength and bloom" (KD). **6.** There would be **a great cry** in all the land of Egypt, such as there had never been before nor ever will be again.

7. But against any Israelite **a dog shall not even** *bark* (NASB). (Lit., "a dog shall not sharpen his tongue.") The purpose was that the distinction between Israel and Egypt might be strictly maintained (8:22). **8. All these nobles of yours shall come down to me and bow deeply to me, begging of me, Do go out; you and all your followers! And after that I will go out** (Berkeley).

End of Moses' Negotiations with Pharaoh. 11:9-10. Verse 9 should be translated, "The LORD had said to Moses: Pharaoh will not listen to you, so that My mighty works may multiply in the land of Egypt" (BV). **10. And Moses and Aaron performed all these wonders before Pharaoh; yet the Lord hardened Pharaoh's heart, and he did not let the sons of Israel go out of his land (NASB).** The word "hardened" means, literally, made stiff, strong (cf. 4:21; 10:20, 27). Pharaoh first hardened his own heart; then God judicially hardened it.

D. DELIVERANCE FROM EGYPT. 12:1-51.

A New Beginning. 12:1-2. Redemption and the birth of a nation required a change in the calendar, which was announced. Redemption marked a new life and a new beginning. **2. This month shall be unto you the beginning of months: it shall be the first month of the year to you.** In 13:4 it is given its Canaanite name, Abib ("ripening ears"). Its later Babylonian name was Nisan (Neh. 2:1; Esther 3:7). It came the latter part of March and the first part of April. The middle of this month, corresponding to our Easter, occurred the first Sunday after the first full moon following the vernal equinox.

The Feast of Tabernacles came at the "end of the year." According to 23:16 and 34:22, the beginning of the new year came, therefore, with the month Tishri (Sept.-Oct.). This is the Jewish New Year to this day. The new calendar became identified with the ecclesiastical year, while the old Canaanite calendar is preserved in what is called the "Civil Year." The months were strictly lunar, with the year of 12 months, consisting of 354 days. In order to make up the extra 11 days, an intercalendar month called "Second Adar" was necessary.

The Passover Instituted. 12:3-13. The Feast of Passover commemorates the rescue out of Egypt. When it was instituted, the Israelites were directed to take a one-year-old male lamb without blemish for each family. It was to be killed in the evening on the fourteenth day of the first month. Its blood was to be sprinkled with a bunch of hyssop on two sideposts and lintel of the door of the Hebrew houses. When the LORD passed through Egypt on the fateful night and saw the blood on the doorposts, He would spare the firstborn within. The flesh of the lamb was to be roasted and then eaten with unleavened bread and bitter herbs. None was to be left until the morning. The Israelites were to eat the feast with girded loins, fully shod and staff in hand in complete readiness to leave Egypt. This memorial feast was to be kept perpetually by Israel (v. 14).

The slain lamb is a type of the Lamb of God, whose blood was shed at Calvary. The hyssop, a common plant of the field, typifies faith. Applying the blood to the doorposts of the Israelites' houses in Egypt symbolizes our applying Christ's shed blood to our hearts by faith. As the Israelites were sheltered from the death angel, even so the believer is shielded from God's wrath as a result of salvation (1 Cor. 5:7). The roasted lamb symbolizes the sufferings of Christ under the wrath of God. The unleavened bread demonstrates the essential separation of the Israelites in Egypt and their hurried departure from it. The bitter herbs are reminiscent to the redeemed of their bondage under Pharaoh.

The Feast of Unleavened Bread. 12:14-28. The lamb slain on the fourteenth day at sunset was followed immediately by the putting away of all leaven for seven days. Leaven, in Scripture an illustration of sin, is referred to as "malice and wickedness" (1 Cor. 5:8). The experience of being redeemed (the Passover) is to be followed by separation from sin and the living of a holy life. A holy life and walk should immediately follow the experience of salvation. The seven days symbolize the entire life of a believer after his experience of redemption. The institution of the Passover and the Feast of Unleavened Bread are appended by a command given for its celebration by the people about to be delivered (vv. 21-28).

Execution of the Tenth Plague. 12:29-43. **29-32.** The death of the firstborn, from the firstborn of Pharaoh on the throne to the firstborn of the captive in the dungeon, is recounted. A great cry of distress arose in Egypt. Moses and Aaron were summoned by night and urged to leave the country. Pharaoh even urged them to bless him also. **33-36.** The people departed swiftly, richly laden with Egyptian treasure. Raamses (cf. 1:11) and Succoth (13:20) were the starting places on Israel's journey (Num. 33:5). **37-42.** A great company, approximately 600,000 men, besides women and children, was accompanied by a mixed multitude. Israel left Egypt after a 430-year sojourn there.

Further Instructions Concerning the Passover. 12:43-51. **43-45. No foreigner** shall eat of it. Only the LORD's covenant people or those admitted to covenant relationship by circumcision were to partake of it. **46. In one house shall it be eaten.** It was to be a family observance. **Neither shall ye break a bone of it** was fulfilled in our Savior's death (John 19:36). **48.** Circumcision, as a token of the redemptive covenant, was absolutely necessary for an alien. **51.** The Exodus was the great redemptive feast of Israel, signifying that the LORD brought the children of Israel out of Egypt by their armies.

II. ISRAEL IN THE WILDERNESS. 13:1—18:27.

A. THE EXODUS AND PURSUIT. 13:1—15:21.

1. CONSECRATION OF THE FIRSTBORN. 13:1-22.

Command Concerning the Firstborn. 13:1-2. God's command called for the dedication of that which had been redeemed. While it literally referred to the firstborn of man and beast, it was intended to symbolize and apply to the whole nation, which was God's firstborn son (cf. 4:22-23). Redemption calls for dedication (cf. Rom. 12:1-2). Those whom the Lord redeems, He claims for Himself (1 Cor. 6:19-20).

Connection with the Feast of Unleavened Bread. 13:3-10. Basic to holiness, both positional and experiential, is redemption from bondage (the penalty and power of sin). Salvation is unto a holy life. This is the reason Moses emphasized the importance of the Feast of Unleavened Bread (cf. 12:15-20) as a perpetual ordinance stressing holy separation of the redeemed. The ritual of this feast was to be followed by a perpetual ordinance in connection with the celebration of the Passover. The unleavened bread, as noted in connection with the Passover, typifies holiness and separation of life. The redeemed are to be a holy people.

9. Putting away evil was to be a **sign** on their hand and as a **memorial** between their eyes. God meant that the people were to diligently observe His commandments concerning separation. Jews originated their ordinance of phylacteries based on Exodus 13:9, 16, as well as Deuteronomy 6:4-9 and 11:13-21. The Egyptians had words written on strips of cloth that they wore as amulets. A similar custom was practiced later by Jews when at prayer. Phylacteries were attached to the head and to the left hand. They contained handwritten copies of Exodus 13:1-10, 11-16; and Deuteronomy 6:4, 9; 11:13-21. This became a later custom preceding New Testament times, but here (vv. 9, 16) it appears as pure metaphor evidencing the essential inward reality of true religion in the Old Testament.

Requirements for the Redemption of the Firstborn. 13:11-16. **13.** The ass, taken as a representative of the unclean animal and valuable as a beast of burden, was either to be redeemed or destroyed. The alternatives were plain: either dedication or destruction. **14-16.** Redemption of firstlings was a memorial to Israel of their own redemption.

Redemption by Power. 13:17-22. Redemption by blood is followed by redemption by power. The meaning of the shedding of the blood of the pascal lamb in Egypt was realized in the experience of the people by their being removed from Egypt. This has its parallel in the life of the Christian. Cleansed from sin through faith in the blood of Christ, the believer through the power of the Holy Spirit is delivered from sin manifested in the flesh, through the world and the devil and typified in the Egyptian bondage. **17.** The direct route to Canaan was the way of the land of the Philistines. Apparently a roundabout route was dictated by God's knowledge of the weakness and fickleness of the people. To bring them safely home, He guarded them from trials that would prove too much for their faith (cf. 1 Cor. 10:13).

18. The Red Sea is Hebrew *yăm-sûp*, the "Sea of Reeds"; the "Red Sea" translation comes from the Septuagint. Reference is apparently to the Bitter Lakes region north of the Gulf of Suez. These lakes were filled with sea water when the Suez Canal was built, after having lain dry for centuries, but they were known as bodies of water in ancient Egyptian sources. The Reed or Papyrus Sea, another possibility, is referred to in an Egyptian document of the thirteenth century B.C. It was located near Tanis, which may be the site of Israel's deliverance. The great miracle at the Reed Sea was the most dramatic and far-reaching manifestation of divine power in the Old Testament and the most memorable event in Israel's national history.

19. Joseph died in faith, and the prediction concerning his bones (Gen. 50:25) came true (cf. Heb. 11:22; 12:22). The cloud of glory, which later became known as Shekinah ("abiding" or "dwelling"), was called by various names in the Old Testament: "my glory" (29:43); "the cloud" (34:5); "the pillar of cloud" (33:9-10); "the cloud of the LORD" (Num. 10:34); "my presence" (33:14-15). Shekinah was to guide Israel (13:21; Neh. 9:19) and to defend Israel (14:19; Psalm 105:39). The cloud of glory appeared at other times both in the Old and New Testaments (cf. Matt. 17:5; Acts 1:9). The Shekinah glory will light up the heavens at Christ's second advent (Luke 21:27; cf. Acts 1:11).

2. CROSSING THE RED SEA. 14:1-31.

The Lord's Directions. 14:1-4. **1-2.** The LORD gave specific directions to the Israelites to make camp at a very definite place facing Pihahiroth between Migdol and the sea. From the human standpoint, it seemed God had led the people into a trap. But His sovereign wisdom and grace were working to redeem them by power and to be glorified through His great redemptive act for all subsequent generations.

3. Divine, overruling, sovereign wisdom knew Pharaoh would conclude that the Israelites had lost their way in the desert and that he and his army would pursue them. In this way overruling Providence would be honored. The Egyptians would learn what God meant when He declared, "I am the LORD." They still needed this final and fatal lesson.

Pharaoh's Pursuit. 14:5-9. The Egyptians decided to pursue the Israelites with their chariotry and army. Six hundred choice chariots are mentioned. Sample chariots of Egypt are preserved in the Cairo Museum. They were swift-running, light vehicles made famous in the campaigns of Thutmose III.

Moses' Faith. 14:10-14. **10.** When the Israelites looked up, they saw the Egyptians marching behind them and became frantic. Some evidently cried out to the LORD, while others severely criticized Moses. **11. Because there were no graves in Egypt, hast thou taken us away to die in the wilderness? 13-14.** Moses' faith displayed itself and showed him a worthy leader. **Have no fear; be steadfast and watch how the Lord will be your salvation today. As for the Egyptians whom you see today, you will never, never see them again; the Lord will fight for you while you keep still** (BV).

The Lord's Encouragement. 14:15-18. **15. Wherefore criest thou unto me? Speak unto the children of Israel, that they go forward.** God was encouraging Moses' great faith. Responsible leaders in an emergency need great faith. Moses was directed to lift up his staff and stretch out his hand over the sea, which would be divided, and then they would go over on dry ground. The Egyptians would know that the LORD was God, and they would be overthrown in the sea.

Israel's Deliverance. 14:19-31. **19-20. The angel of God,** previously mentioned

as the LORD Himself, the preincarnate Christ (13:21), moved ahead to deliver His people. How beautiful that the manifestation of God in the preincarnate Christ, who had gone before the camp of Israel, **removed and went behind them,** coming **between the camp of the Egyptians and the camp of Israel,** being **a cloud and darkness** to the Egyptians but giving **light** to the Israelites.

21. A mighty east wind blew the waters back, making a wide path for the Hebrews to go through. This wall of water was not perpendicular; it bulged. All pictures that portray it as a perpendicular wall of water are false to the Bible passage. God miraculously used the wind to make a pathway for Israel through the sea, which was to be a deathtrap to the pursuing Egyptians. The great miracle was not a reversal of natural forces, but a shift of them so that they saved the Hebrews and destroyed the Egyptians. In other words, the LORD did not reverse the law of gravity, but He used the wind to force the water into a certain position. **23.** The Egyptian chariots, attempting to follow, got bogged down in mud and sand. Then the wind dropped, and the waters flowed back and overwhelmed them. There were also torrents of rain, thunder, and lightning (Psalm 77:17-19).

24. The LORD terrified the Egyptians in **the morning watch.** The Hebrews divided the night into three watches. This one was from 2 to 6 A.M. What a demonstration that the God of Israel was mightier than the gods of Egypt and that Moses was a greater leader than Pharaoh. The people accepted the leadership of Moses from that moment forward.

Typology. The Egyptian redemption, the wilderness wandering, and the entrance into the land of Canaan are types or shadows of spiritual truths applicable

118

to New Testament saints (1 Cor. 10:1-15). Moses prefigures Christ (1 Cor. 10:2). Israel passing through the cloud and the sea illustrates the baptism of the Spirit into Christ (Rom. 6:3-4). The redeemed Israelites prefigure New Testament saints (1 Cor. 10:11). Therefore, the deliverance through the Red Sea pictures *our position* in Christ, separated by the waters of the Red Sea from Pharaoh and slavery to sin by being united to Moses (Christ) in deliverance and destiny (1 Cor. 10:2). The wilderness experience pictures the failure of the redeemed to claim their position by faith and enjoy it in their experience. Entrance into the land signifies counting on our position and by faith converting it into our *experience* of salvation (Rom. 6:11).

3. THE SONG OF THE REDEEMED. 15:1-21.

Israel Celebrates Deliverance. 15:1-19. Saved people are filled with praise and gratitude; they sing to the LORD. The great victory wrought was celebrated as the LORD's triumph (vv. 1-10), because "Salvation is of the LORD" (Jonah 2:9). **11-13.** The LORD's power, holiness, and steadfast love were praised, because as a result of these attributes of God, salvation, as a great work of God, is wrought. The people were completely unable to help themselves. Had it not been for the LORD, they would have been decimated by Pharaoh and his army. Their deliverance was by God's power alone.

14-16. The terrifying effect of this great deliverance on Philistia, Edom, Moab, and Canaan is described. **17.** Appended is a sure promise that the Redeemer would also bring them into Canaan: "Thou wilt bring them and plant them in the mountain of Thine inheritance, the place, O LORD, which Thou

hast made for Thy dwelling, the sanctuary, O LORD, which Thy hands have established" (NASB). **18. The Lord shall reign forever and ever** (NASB). The closing verse looks forward to not only the millennial reign of Christ, but to His eternal reign in the eternal state (cf. "the throne . . . of the Lamb," Rev. 22:1, 3).

The Women's Chorus. 15:20-21. A chorus was conducted by Miriam, the prophetess, the sister of Aaron. She played a tamborine, and all the women followed her with tamborines, to which they danced while Miriam taught them to sing God's praises of deliverance.

B. JOURNEY TO SINAI. 15:22—17:16.

1. GOD TESTS ISRAEL. 15:22-27.

Israel Tested. 15:22-27. The redeemed soul faces testing. Scarcely had the joyful singing subsided than the people advanced into the desert of Shur. For three days they traveled in the wilderness without finding water. Arriving at Marah, they could not drink the bitter waters. Israel came to those bitter waters while walking in the very path of the LORD's leading. God has a purpose in educating His people. The tree which healed the waters is an illustration to the Christian that the cross of Christ can take the bitterness out of all such experiences (cf. Rom. 15:3-4; Gal. 3:13). Blessing and growth follow a trial that is accepted as the Father's will (v. 27; cf. Psalms 1:3; 92:12).

26. The LORD made a healing covenant with Israel. He promised that if they would obey Him, first He would keep physical disease away from them; and second, if they got physically ill, He would heal them. **I am the Lord that healeth thee.** The nationally elect people, Israel, were under this healing covenant until they were temporarily set aside nationally when they rejected Christ and turned away from the gospel (cf. Acts 28:23-28). This is one reason for the dramatic healings in the first nine chapters of Acts. The healing of the crippled man (Acts 3:1-10; cf. 4:30; 5:16-22) was evidence that Israel had come into contact with the God of Abraham, Isaac, and Jacob. The covenant promise of physical healing to that people was still operative.

Such a healing covenant has never been made to the Christian church, wherein physical healing is conditioned (1) by chastisement, and (2) by refinement of Christian character. God heals physically today according to His will, but He is under no direct covenant agreement with His people to heal them physically. Not physical healing, but spiritual healing is in the atonement, guaranteeing a glorified body (Isa. 53:5; Matt. 8:16-17; 2 Cor. 12:7-9; Rev. 21:4).

2. MANNA FROM HEAVEN. 16:1-36.

The Redeemed Tested by Hunger. 16:1-13. The most likely route for the Israelites was in a south-southeasterly direction from five to ten miles east of the Gulf of Suez to Marah and then to Elim. The wilderness of Sin lies in the southwestern portion of the Sinai Peninsula, evidently the wide plain of Markha beyond Elim, where the desolation presented a genuine food problem. In fertile Goshen, with two crops a year, there had never been any lack of food. Now bread from heaven and quails were to be providentially supplied. But the people preferred food to liberty, and even to life itself.

The common quail migrated across the Red Sea in large numbers at this time of the year (v. 13). Faint after a long journey, they could be caught with ease. The miraculous element consisted in the time of their arrival. The birds came in fulfillment of God's promise (v. 12) and constituted a luxury, not a staple part of the people's diet. However, they furnished additional evidence that it was the LORD who brought them out of Egypt. Their murmuring was against Him and not His servant (v. 8). What God furnished as a blessing could, however, become a curse if not received in the right spirit (Num. 11:4-7, 31-35).

Manna from Heaven. 16:14-30. The word "manna" (Heb., *man-hu'*) means "What is it?" Moses explained it was bread from heaven. The manna foreshadows Christ, the food of God's people (cf. John 6:33-35). **14.** Each morning after the dew there appeared on the ground a **fine flake-like thing** (NASB) like frost. It had a sweet taste like honey. The Sinai Peninsula furnishes several parallels to this phenomenon. Insects that produce a honeylike dew leave sweet drops on tamarisk twigs. However, the parallel is only partial, and the manna known to the Israelites is wholly in the realm of the supernatural. The fact that the manna bred worms every day except on the seventh day was to prove that trust for each day's need was necessary, and obedience regarding the Sabbath would be rewarded. **18. An omer** is approximately four pints.

Manna Kept for Memorial. 16:31-36. These verses are in anticipation of the erection of the tabernacle. A jar of manna was to be placed with the tables of the Law in the Ark of the Covenant. The Sabbath is a type of salvation rest and of Israel's Kingdom blessing (Heb. 4:8-9). It was enjoined upon Israel in connection with the gathering of the manna. Those who feed upon God's Word will enjoy salvation rest and discern God's plan and purposes for time and eternity, as recorded in His holy revelation.

3. REPHIDIM: WATER FROM THE ROCK. 17:1-16.

The Redeemed Tested by Thirst. 17:1-4. Rephidim is probably the Wadi Feiran on the natural route to Sinai. Probably barred from springs by the Amalekites marching up the valley, the Israelites suffered thirst and rebelled against the LORD and Moses.

Water from the Rock. 17:5-7. The smitten rock beautifully illustrates the death of Christ resulting in the outpoured Spirit because of an accomplished redemption (Acts 2:1-4). Water gushing out of the rock beautifully typifies Christ, the Giver of the Spirit (John 7:37-39). *Horeb* here may stand for the entire Sinaitic Peninsula. More conceivably it denotes the same mountain range in which the Sinai mountain peak is found. *Massah* ("proof") and *Meribah* ("strife") were the names given to the place where the Israelites tempted the LORD and were in conflict with Him.

A Struggle with Amalek. 17:8-16. The Bedouin tribe of Amalek descended from Esau (Gen. 36:12) and was Israel's implacable foe. Wherever the Amalekites might have been when the Hebrews entered the peninsula, they would have been in possession of the Oasis of Feiran, a choice spot in the whole Sinaitic area. It had to be fought for. Joshua is mentioned here for the first time (v. 9). Hur, like Joshua, is introduced without description (v. 10). He was the grandfather of Bezalel (31:2). Amalek ("born after the flesh," cf. Gal. 4:22-29) is a type of the flesh in the believer (Gal. 4:29). But this conflict illustrates the resources of the man under Law rather than the believer under grace.

Man under Law could fight and pray (vv. 9-12). Man under grace has the Holy Spirit, who gains the victory over the flesh in the believer's behalf (Rom. 8:2-4; Gal. 5:16-17). But this victory is realized only as a believer walks in the Spirit by faith. If the Israelites had acted in independence and disobedience, Amalek would have gained an easy victory (Num. 14:42-45).

15. And Moses built an altar, and called the name of it Jehovah-nissi, meaning "Jehovah is my banner," my "ensign of victory" as a believer. He is my victory over Amalek and every fleshly desire. **16. Jehovah hath sworn** (ASV). The Hebrew is literally, "A hand upon the banner of the LORD!" The *Revised Version* margin reads, "A hand is lifted up upon [against] the throne of the LORD!" This was, evidently, Amalek's presumptuous sin, and God, who does not give His glory to another, struck him (NBC, p. 130).

C. VISIT OF JETHRO. 18:1-27.

Jethro's Visit. 18:1-12. Jethro was Moses' father-in-law (3:1). Impressed by what he had heard of the deliverance of the Israelites from Egypt, he visited Moses and brought Zipporah and his sons to him. Having found it unsafe for his family, with Pharaoh so hostile, Moses had sent his wife and children back to Midian from Egypt (18:2). Moses had named his elder son Gershom (2:22) and his second son Eliezer (cf. 18:4). Eliezer means "my God is my help" and is probably the same name as Eleazar, one of Aaron's sons (28:1).

The meeting between Jethro and Moses was very dramatic. It illustrates how the people of God, delivered out of Egypt, were a testimony to the power and the glory of God (vv. 7-9). "They" (v. 11) refers to the gods of Egypt. **11.** Jethro's testimony was, **Now I recognize that Jehovah is greater than all the gods; so much so that their impudence went against them** (BV). Here it is shown that a people and their idols stand or fall together.

12. Jethro, Moses' father-in-law, took a burnt offering and sacrifices for God. A burnt offering was a common Oriental sacrifice of thanksgiving in which the offering was wholly consumed by fire (cf. Lev. 1:3-17). The sacrifice Jethro offered was due to his position as head of a tribe. Sacrifice was known before Sinai; in fact, it was instituted from the very fall of the race (Gen. 4:4).

Government of the Redeemed. 18:13-27. God graciously supplied governmental administration, as He had previously supplied redemption (12:37—13:18); guidance (13:19-22); deliverance (14:1—15:21); temporal provision (15:22—17:7); and victory in war (17:8-16). Jethro not only was moved to praise God for all that He had done, but he also proceeded to counsel Moses on how he could lighten his burden of ruling the people. The greatest and most widely used men of God can learn from other men of God, for none is so wise or useful that he is not able to learn from others (vv. 15-16). Moses' answer was important because it showed that the people wanted a decision from God and that Moses could give it to them in connection with the immediate dispute; it also proved that he could impart moral statutes (vv. 15-22).

Jethro's answer did not do away with Moses' prime office, but it made provision for others to deal with minor cases (vv. 23-24). This arrangement was proposed to Moses and not coerced upon him. The whole was submitted to God for approval. Often men who are greatly used by God get the idea that they are indispensable. This is a trick of Satan. It is always good to share responsibility and service so that others may develop their spiritual gifts and that God's servant may not overdo.

III. ISRAEL AT SINAI. 19:1—40:38.

A. GOD GIVES THE LAW. 19:1—20:26.

1. THE GIVING OF THE LAW. 19:1-25.

The Wilderness of Sinai. 19:1-2. The site of Sinai is evidently Jebel Musa, located toward the center of the southern tip of the Sinaitic Peninsula about sixty miles from the actual tip. It is marked by the monastery of St. Catherine. However, some scholars favor Jebel Serbal near the oasis of Wadi Feiran. **1-2.** The Israelites reached Sinai in the third month after they left Egypt, and they stayed there for nearly a year (Num. 10:11). The **wilderness of Sinai** was the open land before the mountain.

The Lessons to Be Taught. 19:3-4. At Sinai in the giving of the Law, Israel was to be taught these great truths: (1) that God is infinitely holy; (2) that man is utterly lost, abysmally sinful; (3) that sinful, fallen, helpless man can only be saved by the glorious grace of God exemplified in provisions of priesthood and sacrifice; (4) that saved mankind can no more keep itself saved by its works and self-effort than it can be saved initially by works and self-effort; and (5) that both salvation of soul and sanctification of life are by "grace . . . through faith . . . not of yourselves, . . . not of works, lest any man should boast" (Eph. 2:8-9).

Israel was to be taught that salvation is "from faith to faith" (Rom. 1:17), beginning in faith and consummating in faith, totally apart from human works and self-effort. Israel, in entering into the legal arrangement, was herself to be taught these lessons. The Law was to be a hard teacher that was to underscore the great truth that there is only one gospel, the gospel of salvation by God's grace through faith plus nothing. Centuries would be required in teaching, but the nation was not only to learn the lesson herself, but to teach it to all the nations of the world.

3. And Moses went up unto God and the Lord called unto him out of the mountain. 4. Divine redemptive grace is a revelation from God, manifested by the deliverance out of Egypt by blood, by power, and by God's bearing His people **on eagles' wings**, bringing them to Himself in separation from sin and sinners (Gen. 12:1; Exod. 33:16; 2 Cor. 6:14-17).

God uses a beautiful figure of speech that is expressive of His care for His people (cf. v. 4; Deut. 32:11-12; also examine Rev. 12:14, where His care for Israel in their coming Tribulation at the end of this age is spoken of in similar terms). The parent eagle, in teaching its nestlings to fly, sweeps gently past them as they are perched on the ledge of a rock. When one, venturing to follow, begins to sink with dropping wing, the mother eagle glides underneath it and bears it aloft again. This is a picture of the God of grace in educating and disciplining His people under grace. But the people, in total ignorance of the weakness of the flesh and the sinfulness of fallen man, were very willing to give up God's gracious dealing with them by grace through faith alone and instead accept a legal principle that in and of themselves they were not able to follow.

God's Purpose Revealed. 19:5-6. At Sinai the Israelites had shown that they were a people set apart by God as His saved ones to do a peculiar work. Since they were to be the recipients of divine revelation for the benefit of all mankind, the laws and regulations about to be given to them differed from those of all other nations. God has a specific purpose for this people. His plan for Israel is founded upon the idea of a theocracy. The LORD Himself is to rule over them

as a sovereign. **6.** In no other way could they be a **kingdom of priests, and an holy people.** God's glorious dealing with them, by grace (v. 4) is to be appropriated and lived out under the terms of the Theocratic Covenant (v. 5). Israel accepted the terms of the Law, and the theocracy was solemnly established.

The Dispensation of the Law. 19:7-8. This age stretches from Sinai to Calvary—from the Exodus to the cross. **8.** When the people answered, **All that the Lord hath spoken we will do,** they meant well and no doubt spoke sincerely from the heart. But they were ignorant of the weakness of the flesh and of the fact that even redeemed man can only keep the word of God and enjoy the power of God in his life by faith and not by human effort. They were leaving the sure ground of faith alone in God's grace and looking to themselves and what they were in themselves instead of looking entirely to God and what they were in Him.

The history of Israel from that moment on is one long record of violation of the Law. It is a glowing illustration of Romans 7 and of the defeat of the redeemed soul trusting in himself instead of in the Lord. The testing of the nation under Law resulted in failure and in the judgment of the captivities. But the dispensation itself came to an end at the cross. For the other six economies of God's dealing, see: Innocence (Gen. 1:28); Conscience (Gen. 3:23); Human Government (Gen. 8:20); Promise (Gen. 12:1); Grace (John 1:17); Kingdom (Eph. 1:10).

The People Under Law. 19:9-23. **9.** To a people under the Law, God was in a **thick cloud**, and the people were to sanctify themselves in preparation to envision the theophany. **12.** A people under the Law were to keep their distance. Bounds were to be set. They were not to go up into the mountain or touch its border. **Whosoever toucheth the mount shall be surely put to death.** People depending upon themselves and their own efforts find that God is a consuming fire and that their unholiness in His presence can only bring the threat of death. **16.** A people under the Law face the **thunders and lightnings** of Mount Sinai. Under Law, people tremble at God's presence. The appearance of God in theophanic form from Mount Sinai was to give them an audiovisual lesson of His infinite holiness and their abysmal sinfulness. The mountain, aflame and filled with smoke, and the thunder and lightning were evidence that the people needed God's grace and that only through faith in His grace could they live lives to please Him, deriving the strength and power from Him to live as they had agreed as His called people and "peculiar treasure."

The Mosaic Covenant. 19:24-25. Through Moses, God gave the covenant to Israel as a theocratic nation. Note that this covenant was in operation during the legal age; it was given only to Israel. The rest of the human family was under the Age of Conscience (Gen. 3:23), Human Government (Gen. 8:20), and Promise (Gen. 12:1) that the Abrahamic Covenant would bring blessing to the entire human race.

The Mosaic Covenant is in three divisions: (1) the commandments, expressing the righteous will of God (20:1-26); (2) the judgments, governing the social life of Israel (21:1—24:11); and (3) the ordinances, governing the religious life of Israel (24:12—31:18). These three divisions form "the Law" as that phrase is employed in the New Testament (cf. Matt. 5:17-18). The commandments and the ordinances constitute one religious system. The commandments express the eternal moral law of God, which men

were to keep outwardly as a basis of human beings living together; but as far as being able to bring favor with God, they were a "ministration of condemnation" and of "death" (2 Cor. 3:7-9). The ordinances in the person of the high priest provided a representative of the people with the LORD. In the sacrifices they gave a "cover" (cf. atonement, Lev. 16:6) for their sins in anticipation of the cross (Heb. 5:1-3; 9:6-9; Rom. 3:25-26).

The Christian is not under the conditional Mosaic Covenant of works, the Law, but he is under the unconditional new covenant of grace (Rom. 3:21-27; 6:14-15; Gal. 2:16; 3:10-14, 24-26; 4:21-31; Heb. 10:7-17). The other seven covenants are: the Edenic (Gen. 1:28); Adamic (Gen. 3:15); Noahic (Gen. 9:1); Abrahamic (Gen. 15:18); Palestinian (Deut. 30:3); Davidic (2 Sam. 7:16); New (Heb. 8:8).

2. THE DECALOGUE. 20:1-26.

The Nature of the Ten Commandments. 20:1. The Ten Commandments, or Ten Words, as they were known to the Hebrews, constitute the moral law of God. The "first table" (vv. 1-12) outlines duties to God, while the "second table" (vv. 13-17) gives duties to men. The commandments did not originate at Sinai. They existed from the beginning, even before the Fall of man, because they are an expression of the eternal moral nature of God. In a sense, they govern the life of all men as God's creatures, unsaved as well as saved men. As creatures of God, men are required to keep God's laws. The fact that man fell and was unable to keep these moral laws did not excuse him. Although man changed, God remained unchangeable.

Man was required to keep these laws outwardly as a basis of life among men. God's redemptive purpose was to regenerate man so that he might keep the laws by God's power internally and in reality. But as a basis of all relationships between God's creatures, all mankind is held accountable to keep the moral law of God, and each person, saved as well as unsaved, will be judged according to his response to that moral law. These enactments were never intended to serve as a basis for man's self-justification (as the legalists of Christ's day supposed). They were to guide the life even of unsaved people from the very beginning, but they were specifically directed for the saved, who love God and seek to please a divine Redeemer and carry out His will. The Decalogue had its origin and source in God.

1. And God spoke all these words, saying (cf. 31:18; Acts 7:53). God used Moses and angels to mediate the Law (John 1:17; Gal. 3:19; Heb. 2:2; cf. Deut. 32:2; Psalm 68:17). By nature the Law is not grace (Rom. 10:5; Gal. 3:10; Heb. 10:28). It is holy, righteous, good, and spiritual (Rom. 7:12, 14). In its ministry it declares and proves all men guilty (Rom. 3:19). Yet it justifies no one (Rom. 3:20). It cannot impart righteousness or life (Gal. 3:21). It causes offenses to abound (Rom. 5:20; 7:7-13; 1 Cor. 15:56). It served as an instructor until Christ appeared (Gal. 3:24). In relationship to the believer, the Law emphatically does not save anyone (Gal. 2:21). A believer does not live under the Law (Rom. 6:14; 8:4), but he stands and grows in grace (Rom. 5:2; 2 Pet. 3:18). The nation, Israel, alone was a recipient of the Law (Exod. 20:2).

All the laws of the Decalogue, except the fourth commandment concerning the Sabbath, were written in the hearts of men everywhere from the beginning and are found on legal codes of antiquity and are the basis of human government today. The Ten Commandments are

thus an epitome of man's duties toward God and his neighbor. That an unregenerate man could not perform these duties internally really does not excuse him from keeping them outwardly and superficially.

Unsaved man will be judged in eternal hell for his response to the moral law of God, while saved people will be judged in heaven, also for their response to the moral law of God. But the point is, no unregenerate man can keep the Law in order to be saved. He must be saved by grace through faith. The Law was given to emphasize this fact and also to show the regenerate believer that only by virtue of his regeneration and the power of God could he keep these commandments internally and live a life pleasing to God.

The Giver and the Recipients of the Commandments. 20:2. In their Mosaic dress in connection with the Mosaic Covenant the Ten Commandments were given to the theocratic nation of Israel. But as existing from the beginning, they are operative upon all mankind. Only by keeping these commandments could Israel keep the Mosaic Covenant and be the LORD's own possession among all peoples and be "a kingdom of priests, and an holy nation" (19:5-6).

But Israel had to learn that they could not keep the commandments unless they were redeemed, and then only by faith in their Redeemer's gracious interposition. The priesthood and the sacrificial system were part of the Mosaic economy to show them they were saved by grace and were to live sanctified lives by grace through faith. They could no more be saved by self-effort than they could be sanctified in life and experience by self-effort. The Law was a schoolmaster to show them this, and to demonstrate through them, as an example to all nations, that offering salvation by grace through faith is God's only method of dealing with fallen humanity to bring it back to fellowship with Himself.

Most of the commandments are negative: "Thou shalt not." They mainly constitute a prohibition against fallen man's will and natural tendency to sin. Man is a sinner, and the Law was given to fully demonstrate that fact (Rom. 5:12-14; 6:6-13; Gal. 3:19-29). The Law's righteous requirements are fulfilled in those who walk according to the Spirit by faith, as they also were fulfilled by Old Testament saints who walked by the Spirit in faith. The commandments illustrate God's right to command, which is grounded in His self-revelation (v. 1), His character as Creator (v. 2a), and His role as Redeemer (v. 2b), and it centers in His role as Sanctifier (v. 2c).

2. I am the Lord thy God, who have brought thee out of the land of Egypt, out of the house of bondage. Although salvation puts believers in the sphere within which they can keep the Law of God, they cannot keep it by self-effort or human strength. Sinai instructs that observance of the Law can no more give believers victory over sin and self (Rom. 7:7-24) than it can justify sinners before God (Rom. 3:21—5:11).

The Law demonstrates for all time that the believer's salvation, sanctification of life, and victory over sin are the result of faith producing the fruit of the Spirit (Gal. 5:22-23), and not of self-effort producing "the works of the flesh" (Gal. 5:19-21). See Deuteronomy 5 for the relation of the commandments to the covenant treaty.

The First Commandment–Against Idolatry. 20:3. **3. Thou shalt have no other gods before me.** "No other gods before me" means "as antagonists in My eyes, as casting a shadow over My eternal being and incommunicable glory in the eyes of the worshiper." The primary reference is to the idols of the heathen. They did not really worship the idols, but the gods that the idols supposedly represented. These were not real gods, for there is no other God save One; rather, they were demons (Lev. 17:7; Deut. 32:17; Psalm 106:37; 1 Cor. 10:19-20).

How terrible that in occultism and occult-vitiated religionism there are professing Christians (not to mention the pagans) who worship demons through spiritism, clairvoyance, séances, and other forms of evil supernaturalism (Deut. 18:9-22). The emphasis, however, is not on the first commandment of outer conduct, but on inner motives and acts of the spirit (cf. Christ's Sermon on the Mount, Matt. 5:20-48; and Rom. 7:7-11). Hence, there may be idolatry without visible idols, without worshiping demons in any form. Seeking happiness in the creature rather than the Creator is a very subtle form of idolatry. Covetousness, or love of money and material gain, is especially signaled out as idolatry (Col. 3:5). This commandment enjoins love of God, in fact supreme love to God, based on His gracious self-revelation (v. 2a) and His redemption (v. 2b). These sound the death knell to idolatry (v. 3). As Creator-Redeemer, the LORD said to Israel, "I am the LORD, thy God" (v. 2a).

The Second Commandment–Against Representations of God. 20:4-6. The opening injunctions guard the unity and spirituality of God against idolatry. All likenesses or images of God are taboo. God is said to be "jealous," not in the sense of a human passion, but in the sense of the feeling of an infinitely holy Being against evil and any insult to His spirituality (Deut. 32:21). Had not Israel been delivered out of the gross idolatry of the Egyptians? Were the multitudinous images and gods of Egypt not a lesson? Had not their persecution been by idolatry-ridden people? Was not the nation now reaping what had been sown then?

5. Those who **hate me** are idolaters. The iniquity of those who practice idolatry runs down through a family tree. This is especially true of occult religionism, which is honeycombed with idolatry. Spiritism, witchcraft, astrology, and all forms of occult-religionism are filled with demonism, and this demon power and demon domination run through family trees of those who worship demons (1 Cor. 10:20) as God-haters, that is, idolaters. Yet in response to faith in God's grace, mercy is shown "to a thousand generations" (Deut. 7:9).

The Third Commandment—Against Profanity. 20:7. **7. Thou shalt not take the name of the Lord thy God in vain.** Literally, "Lift up the name of the LORD ... in vain," meaning in vanity, falsehood, lying, and particularly wickedness in the sense of connection with idolatry. The Semitic conception gave almost material reality to a name. God's name is a revelation of Himself. Any idle or irreverent use of His name would be lifting it up "in vanity."

All profanity is forbidden. Compare James 5:12: "Above all, my brothers, do not swear, either by heaven or by the earth or any other oath; but let your yes be yes, and your no, no; so you may incur no judgment" (BV). How contrary the blasphemy and profanity of those who interlard their speech with such expressions as "God," "Lord," "Christ," "the Lord knows," "oh, my goodness," "oh, heavens," and the like (cf. Matt. 5:33-37). The third commandment is of the same gravity as the preceding two. It guards the deity of

God as the others guard His unity and spirituality.

The Fourth Commandment—Against Disloyalty and Secularism. 20:8-11. **8. Remember the sabbath day, to keep it holy.** This commandment is unique in the Decalogue. This moral law, like all the moral laws set forth in the Ten Commandments, had been revealed and was operative upon the human race from the beginning. This is the sole commandment that had been enjoined *only upon unfallen man* (Gen. 2:2-3). When man fell into sin, God's creative rest was broken. He immediately began working in redemption (Gen. 3:15, 21; John 5:17). As a result, God could not impose a memorial upon His fallen race *when the very thing commemorated by it had been destroyed by sin*. Although God never enjoined the Sabbath upon fallen mankind (but only upon the race before it fell into sin and broke His Sabbath creation rest), it is apparent that from Adam to Moses, men without divine sanction attempted to observe the seventh day, as archaeology has shown.

Moreover, this commandment of Sabbath-keeping was never imposed upon any nation or people except Israel (v. 9). All the other nine commandments express omnitemporal moral principles binding upon *all* God's creatures from the beginning. They are *never* to be abrogated in any age or dispensation. This is evident in the fact that all the moral principles thundered as stern law from Sinai find expression under grace in the New Testament church epistles, except the commandment to keep the Sabbath.

Nowhere is Sabbath-keeping ever enjoined upon a Christian in this age of grace. Indeed, the very opposite is true (Gal. 4:9-10; Col. 2:16-17; Heb. 4:4). Moreover, the practice of setting apart the seventh day degenerated as a fallen race strayed from God and lapsed into idolatry. In giving Israel the fourth commandment, the LORD accordingly took a well-known day that paganism regarded with ill omen and popular superstition, and then sanctified it by restoring it to its original significance. It commemorated the Creator and His perfect creation, enjoining it upon His people who had just been redeemed out of Egypt (vv. 1-2). It was a unique sign that Israel was the LORD's blood-bought people separated from the pagan nations and unto the LORD, their Redeemer (31:13-17).

What the LORD never commanded fallen man or the nations, He imposed upon this one nation, which He selected to be an example of His redemption to all idolatrous nations. This Sabbath commandment was imposed upon Israel to show the necessity of the complete separation of God's people from idolatry and sin. "But the seventh day is the sabbath of the LORD thy God" (v. 10). As LORD, He was Israel's Redeemer out of Egypt (vv. 1-2). As God, He was Israel's Creator, who in six days had made the heaven and earth (v. 11).

Even as circumcision had been given as a token of the Abrahamic Covenant (Gen. 17:9-13), the keeping of the Sabbath was instituted as a symbol of the Mosaic Covenant to Israel (31:13). It was a distinguishing mark of the LORD's elect nation, chosen to be an example to all the other nations of the earth, showing the blessing of salvation and dedication to the LORD.

Because the Sabbath was a sign between the LORD and His people—that He had established a perpetual covenant with them—profanation of the day was a direct violation of the covenant. Therefore, observance of the Sabbath was rigidly enforced. Breaking it denoted crass disloyalty (31:14-15; Num. 15:32-35). By breaking the sign of the covenant, the offender broke the covenant itself. By doing so, he denied that God's people were different from the unsaved.

This commandment was given Israel as a reminder that God's creation rest would be restored through that nation (v. 11). Israel's Sabbath had a double role. It looked back and memorialized God's creation rest (Gen. 2:2-3); and at the same time, it looked forward to Israel's future as a Messianic nation through which God's creation rest would be restored.

Christ's redemption appropriated by that nation and mediated by her to all the nations of the earth in the future Kingdom age would accomplish its restoration (Isa. 11:10-16; 60:1-22; Acts 1:6; Rom. 11:26-36). The Sabbath "now in abeyance" (cf. Hos. 2:11) will be reestablished upon the completion of God's present purpose in the church. In the Tribulation (Matt. 24:20) and in the Kingdom set up at Christ's return (Rev. 19:11-21), the Sabbath will be reinstated (Deut. 30:8; Isa. 66:23; Ezek. 46:1). As a sign of a perpetual covenant (between the LORD and Israel), it will point to the great consummation of God's purpose for the earth.

This will center in Israel and restore Israel's ministry to the nations of the earth as Christ rules in the millennial Kingdom, and on into eternity when He puts all enemies under His feet and delivers the Kingdom to God the Father, that God may be all in all (1 Cor. 15:24-28). Then God's creation rest will be restored by the redemption brought to mankind through His elect, redeemed nation, which was set apart from all other nations by the mark of the Sabbath observance. Meanwhile, Christians are to celebrate the Lord's Day in honor of Christ's resurrection (John 5:18).

The Fifth Commandment–Against

Dishonoring God by Dishonoring His Vicegerents. 20:12. This commandment asserts that honoring one's parents is more than a social virtue. Parents are God's representatives, God's vicegerents; honoring them is honoring God. This commandment is the basis of the home, the primary unit of society. Paul called it the first commandment with promise (Eph. 6:2-3).

The Sixth Commandment–Against Murder. 20:13. **13. Thou shalt not kill,** literally in the Hebrew, "thou shalt not commit murder." Murder is a crime, for we cannot restore life. Man is created in God's image, and God's creatorship is insulted by deeds of violence (cf. Matt. 5:21-22).

The Seventh Commandment–Against Adultery. 20:14. This commandment, like the commandment to honor parents, guards the sanctity and inviolability of the home. Since it involves extramarital sex between married people, it is a direct peril to the integrity of the family. The penalty, therefore, was very severe: death (Lev. 20:10; Deut. 22:22). This commandment has a deeper inner meaning (cf. Matt. 5:27-28).

The Eighth Commandment–Against Theft. 20:15. This injunction asserts the sanctity of property, of which Genesis 1:26-28 is a title deed. The right of each person to the fruits of his toil and labor are to be guarded. Theft is a threat to society. A society of thieves means moral and social chaos. The home, the state, and every other agency of society are hurt by theft.

The Ninth Commandment–Against Falsehood. 20:16. **20. Thou shalt not bear false witness against thy neighbor** (cf. Lev. 19:18). This is a primary reference to testimony in courts of law (cf. Deut. 19:16-19). It has a broader connotation and prohibits everything in men's dealings with one another that is not according to the truth (cf. Psalm 15:2; Prov. 19:9; Col. 3:9). In its broader meaning the commandment embraces all lying and falsehood, all equivocation of the truth, whether telling a lie or concealing the truth.

The Tenth Commandment–Against Covetousness. 20:17. To covet means to earnestly desire or long after. The feeling may not be sinful in itself, for its sinfulness appears in longing for anything unlawful or longing to an inordinate degree for that which is lawful. This commandment goes from deeds and words to the thoughts and intents of the heart, the fountainhead of sin, the spring of human life (cf. Rom. 7:7-14).

The Laws of the Covenant. 20:18-26. In verses 18-20 the fear of the people is portrayed. In verses 21-26 the first law of the covenant is given—the law of the altar. As an exposition of the moral law of God, the people were prohibited from making any type of material image. This high requirement of monotheism called for repeated expression (v. 23; cf. Lev. 19:4; Deut. 4:15-18). Actually, verses 21-26 begin a discussion of the laws of the covenant in setting forth the law of the altar. The first enunciation from the infinitely holy God was a stern warning against idolatry (vv. 21-23). A simple altar of earth (v. 24) or, at best, unhewn stone furnished a deterrent against idolatrous customs (v. 25) and immoral immodesty (v. 26).

B. SOCIAL AND CEREMONIAL LAWS. 21:1—23:33.

This body of laws (chaps. 21-23) is closely associated with the Ten Commandments (the moral Law). The regulations are called judgments ("ordinances," v. 1). They constitute "the book of the covenant" (24:7), which bears striking resemblance to the Hittite

Code and particularly to the Code of Hammurabi, which reflects legal procedure throughout the whole of western Asia (c. 1700 B.C.). These ordinances constitute an application of the Ten Commandments to Israel at that time and in the early period of their history, when they should have inhabited Canaan. Actually, the laws of the covenant begin at 20:22-26 in the prohibition of images and regulations regarding altars. This is an expansion of the first and second commandments.

Laws Concerning Slaves. *21:1-11.* **1-11.** The Mosaic economy did not outlaw slavery, which was a universal institution at the time. It did, however, regulate and elevate it, imbuing it with kindness and mercy and, like Christianity, announcing principles that would ultimately abolish it (cf. Lev. 25:39-40; Deut. 15:12-18). Such was the law requiring liberation of a Hebrew slave after six years of servitude, as well as the regulations concerning his wife and children. The servant whose ear (the organ of hearing and obedience) was bored (pierced) is a moving type of the Lord Jesus Christ (Psalm 40:6-8). These provisions are a natural expansion of the fifth commandment, the master being substituted for the parent in the same way that the parent substitutes for God.

Laws Concerning Murder. 21:12-17. **12-14.** Careful distinction was made between premeditated and unpremeditated murder. The former was a capital crime, incurring death without mercy. **15.** Striking one's parents was tantamount to striking God (in whose place parents stand to their children) and was punishable by death. **16-17.** The same was true of cursing one's parents. Manstealing (kidnapping) was also a capital crime. These injunctions, as well as the noncapital offenses that follow, are an expansion of the sixth commandment.

Laws Concerning Noncapital Offenses. 21:18-32. **18-19.** Forfeiture of life would result only if the victim of assault died. Otherwise, the guilty person had to pay the damage incurred to his victim. A master who struck his slave so that he died was to be punished (in an unspecified manner). If the slave survived several days, he was to go unpunished, the economic loss to the master evidently considered to be sufficient punishment. The book of the covenant, in its encouragement of humane treatment of slaves, moves on a higher plane than contemporary laws (cf. vv. 26-27).

In the case of the woman who suffered a miscarriage through injury as the result of a brawl between two men, the *lex talionis* ("law of retaliation") furnished the principle of compensation (vv. 22-25; cf. Matt. 5:38). This law of retaliation often has been misunderstood by those who have felt it encouraged revenge. Rather, it envisions the execution of justice through magistrates (v. 22). The law of retaliation was in accord with widespread ancient usages, but the Israelites modified it somewhat (vv. 24-26; cf. Lev. 24:19-20).

In the case of an ox goring a free person to death, the ox was to be stoned to death. Its flesh was not to be eaten, for it was contaminated by the guilt of blood. If the owner of the ox was morally responsible, he had to forfeit his own life. However, he might be able to satisfy the avenger of blood (the deceased's kinsman), by paying a stipulated ransom (v. 30; cf. Psalm 49:7; Isa. 43:3). The owner of an ox who gored a slave to death had to pay the slave's master *thirty shekels of silver*, the average price of a slave (Matt. 26:15).

Laws Concerning Property Rights 21:33–22:15. Compensation was to be paid to anyone who suffered property loss through the fault or negligence of another (cf. the tenth commandment). **2. If a thief be found breaking in** at night, and was killed, no murder charge could be lodged against the one who killed him. But this was not true in daylight, when a thief was more easily and less dangerously caught. Penalties varied— for stealing an ox fivefold, a sheep fourfold (cf. 2 Sam. 12:6), the former being more valuable in farming. **3.** Inability to pay exposed one to be sold into slavery, which is an amplification of the eighth commandment. **4-6.** These verses deal with losses of property suffered through carelessness or neglect; full restitution had to be made.

7-15. These verses concern losses incurred through breach of trust. In a primitive society, before the advent of banks, valuables were deposited with friends or neighbors, or buried in the ground (Matt. 13:44). Theft in such cases was punished by double restitution when the culprit was apprehended. If the thief was not caught, the person entrusted with the valuables had to appear before God (the judges). In the Israelite theocracy, the magistrates represented God and spoke directly for Him (as will be the case in the restored millennial Kingdom). Hence, each was called God (cf. John 10:34-36; Psalm 82:6), and the decision of the judges— regarded as God's decision—was final. Breach of trust is further illustrated by other cases, with penalties stipulated.

Law Shielding a Virgin. 22:16-17. **16-17.** A man who seduced an unbetrothed virgin had to compensate her father for the loss of her virginity as well as marry her. If the girl refused marriage, the seducer still had to pay the marriage price (not the dowry) of fifty shekels (Deut. 22:28-29). Seduction of a betrothed virgin drew the death penalty (Deut. 22:23-25).

Crimes Punishable by Death. 22:18-20. **18.** A sorceress (a woman who practices witchcraft and occultism) was not permitted to live, because in practicing the occult arts she was breaking, in particular, the first two commandments, thus insulting God and His omniscience. At the same time she was in communication with evil spirits or demons (Lev. 19:31; 20:27; Deut. 18:9-11; 1 Sam. 28:9), going to demonic powers instead of to God for knowledge and power from the supernatural realm.

19. Bestiality was a degenerate sin of pagans, utterly out of keeping for a human being, much less for God's redeemed and holy people. One who dared to break the first commandment and insult God by sacrificing to any god except Jehovah (YHWH) was to "be utterly destroyed" (v. 20, i.e., "put under the ban," or "devoted to destruction"; cf. Deut. 2:34; 1 Sam. 15:3).

Various Regulations. 22:21-31. **21.** Injunction was given against wronging or oppressing a stranger (alien). There was reason enough, for Israel had been strangers in Egypt for 430 years! **22-24.** Solemn warning was made against afflicting (causing distress to) **any widow, or fatherless child** (Deut. 24:17-18), the most helpless members of society, especially open to abuse by the unscrupulous. The LORD's dramatic espousal of their cause was warning enough. **25-27.** Lenders of money to the poor of God's people were not to charge interest or act the role of a creditor. If a mantle or outer robe was taken in pawn as a pledge, it was to be returned by evening, since this was the only covering the poor man had against the chill of the night. **28.** Judges and rulers, as God's theocratic representatives, were not to be abused or spoken ill of. **29-30.** God was to receive the first part of their substance. **31. Neither shall ye eat any** flesh ... **torn of beasts.** Such flesh was rendered unclean because not properly drained of its life blood (Lev. 7:24; 17:15). **Dogs** were symbolic of all that is unholy and outside the covenant.

Regulations Administering Common Justice. 23:1-9. These laws of veracity correspond to the ninth commandment. **1. Thou shalt not raise** (*nāśā'*, "lift up, bear, carry") **a false report** (20:16; Deut. 19:16-21). **2.** This should be read: "You shall not follow a multitude in doing evil, nor shall you testify in a dispute so as to turn aside after a multitude in order to pervert justice" (NASB).

3. Nor shall you be partial (*hādǎr*, "honor") **to a poor man in his dispute** (NASB). One would expect *gādôl* ("great man") rather than *dǎl* ("poor man," MT), since favoritism is more likely to be accorded the rich and influential. **4.** Common integrity was inculcated upon them in returning stray property to whom it belonged. **5.** Helping an enemy was taught in order to "overcome evil with good" (cf. Rom. 13:9-10; 12:21). **6.** Justice due to the poor was not to be "wrested," in the sense of being "twisted" or "distorted." Because he was poor and helpless was no reason to take advantage of him legally.

7. Keep far from a false charge, and do not kill the innocent or the righteous, for I will not acquit the guilty (NASB). **8.** "A gift" given to affect justice is **a bribe.** It blinds the eyes of even wise men and distorts the words of the righteous. **9.** Oppressing **a stranger** (*gēr*, "foreigner, sojourner, visitor") was utterly incompatible with an Israelite, who had been a sojourner for so long in Egypt (cf. 22:21).

Regulations for Festal Celebrations. 23:10-19. **10-11.** The Sabbatic year of rest for the land was commanded (Lev. 25:2; cf. the fourth commandment).

Field labor was to cease. The produce of the earth was to be common property, debts were to be remitted, Hebrew servants set free, and the Law was to be read publicly (Lev. 25:4-7; Deut. 15:1-13; Neh. 10:31). Failure in observing the Sabbatic year and Sabbath day eventually led to captivity. Three great feasts were commanded (v. 17): Passover (Unleavened Bread, 12:1-28), Pentecost, and Tabernacles (Lev. 23:4-44).

19. Thou shalt not boil a kid in his mother's milk (34:26; Deut. 14:21) constitutes a protest against a Canaanite fertility cult practice of preparing a sacrifice. Milk so boiled was sprinkled on the earth to insure good crops. The idea was that the new life of a kid added to its mother's milk produced double fertility. God's people were to abhor such rites of occult religion and look to God to bless the soil. This principle comprised all other heathen practices, which were to be outlawed.

Conclusion of the Covenant Code. 23:20-33. **20.** The **angel** is the theophanic appearance of the preincarnate Christ, the eternal Word who was with God and was God (John 1:1; cf. Gen. 16:7; on the name, see Gen. 32:27). The victory will be the LORD's. **28.** The **hornets** were evidently meant to be taken literally (Deut. 7:20; Josh. 24:12).

C. THE RATIFICATION OF THE COVENANT. 24:1-18.

The Ceremony of Ratification. 24:1-8. **1-2.** Moses alone was directed to come near the LORD. Aaron, Nadab, and Abihu, with the seventy elders of Israel, were to worship at a distance. They constituted the people's divinely chosen witnesses and representatives. The people were to remain at the foot of Mount Sinai, while the representatives were to ascend part way up the mount.

Only Moses went to the clouded fiery summit; he was a type of Christ in his exclusive privilege.

3. Moses formally presented the body of laws to the people, who in turn agreed to observe them. Hence, the laws received the designation "the book of the covenant" (v. 7). **4.** In the ratification of the covenant, Moses set up, in accordance with the regulations (chaps. 20-24), **an altar ... and twelve pillars,** representing the twelve tribes. **5.** He then commissioned certain **young men** to offer sacrifices.

6-8. He himself, however, sealed the covenant by sprinkling blood upon the altar, the book, and the people (cf. Mark 14:24; Heb. 9:19-20). The blood, denoting life given, was a solemn warning that the penalty of disobedience would be death. At the same time the offerings and the blood point to Christ, who would come and take the curse of the Law upon Himself.

The blood was first sprinkled upon the altar (representing God, v. 6), for the primary need was propitiation, the quieting of the divine wrath against sin. When the people committed themselves to obedience (vv. 3, 7) the blood was sprinkled upon them, for when God's people attempt to walk in holiness they become aware of the need of the atoning blood (cf. 1 John 1:7; 2:2).

The Revelation of God's Glory. *24:9-11.* The legal covenant placed man at a guilty distance from God (cf. vv. 1-2). Only Christ, prefigured by the sacrifices offered (the sin offering and the peace offering, Lev. 1, 3) and establishing the covenant of grace, brings man near to God. **9-10.** Thus, the elders, typically cleansed and entirely submissive symbolically in confession and consecration, beheld the glory of God in theophanic form. Yet they did not incur death. **11. Yet He did not stretch out His hand against the nobles of the sons of Israel** (NASB).

Moses Called to Receive the Law. *24:12-18.* **12-14.** Apparently Moses and the elders returned to the people before this call summoned him to the summit to receive the Law. His servant, Joshua, accompanied him, but only so far. **14.** Moses delegated his administrative authority to Aaron and Hur while he was absent on the mountain.

D. THE TABERNACLE AND PRIESTHOOD INSTRUCTIONS. 25:1—31:18.

1. THE TABERNACLE: ARK, TABLE, LAMPSTAND. 25:1-40.

The Tabernacle. The importance of the tabernacle in the history of redemption appears (1) in the strict pattern divinely given for its instruction in minute detail; (2) in the large space devoted to its description (thirteen chapters); (3) in the unusual preparation required on man's part for the reception of its specifications (cf. 24:9-18); (4) in its significance as a divine object lesson portraying in vivid fashion the one true gospel of salvation by grace through faith totally apart from human effort, works, or merit; (5) in its portrayal typically of the person and redemptive work of the Savior, Christ Jesus; (6) in its priesthood demonstrating man's access to God and fellowship with God; and (7) in its purpose as God's "dwelling place" (*mīshkān*) and sanctuary (*mīqdāsh*).

The People's Offerings. *25:1-9.* The pattern of the tabernacle was divinely given, but it was to be constructed through the people's free will gifts. **2. Giveth it willingly with his heart,** literally, "whose heart moves him" (*ndḇ,* "to incite, stir up," cf. 35:4-9; 2 Cor. 8:11-12). God's work is to be supported by God's people giving willingly (not by the unsaved). The Israelites came out of

133

Egypt with wealth (12:36) and were further enriched by the conquest of Amalek (17:13).

The Ark. 25:10-16. The first and foremost article, forming the heart of the Tabernacle, was the Ark of the Covenant. This box, 3¾ feet long, 2¼ feet wide, and 2¼ feet high, was made of acacia wood, grown in the desert out of the dry ground (Isa. 53:2), speaking of Christ's humanity. The gold that covered it portrays His deity. It held the Ten Commandments engraved on stone (cf. 31:18). The moral law was to be basic in all God's dealings with His people; hence, it was given the central place in the sanctuary (v. 16; cf. Heb. 9:4).

The Mercy Seat. 25:17-22. The mercy seat was the sacred center from which proceeded a description of the various parts of the Tabernacle. The mercy seat rested upon the ark. The Israelites called it *kapporeth* (kăppōrĕṭ, "covering, propitiatory, place of forgiveness," or "atonement," from the root *kāpăr*, "to cover, pretermit sin"; cf. Rom. 3:25). It was a solid slab of gold, supporting two cherubs of beaten gold, one on each end facing each other with outspread wings. These creatures (evidently winged lions with human heads, according to contemporary iconography) portrayed the guardianship of the holiness of God's throne. Atoning blood (typical of Christ's death for sinners) transformed the throne of judgment into a throne of grace.

Above the cherubim was enthroned the Shekinah glory presence of God (deity denoted by the gold). The mercy seat was the meeting place between God and His people, between the infinite divine holiness and sinful man. Concentrated in the Ark, the mercy seat, and cherubim "are all the connotations of the covenant of law and gospel, judgment and mercy, revelation and re-

demption" (H. C. Alleman and E. E. Flack, OTC, p. 234).

The Table of Showbread. 25:23-30. Made of acacia wood, which was hard and durable, the table of showbread was 3 feet long, 2¼ feet high, and 1½ feet wide, and overlaid with pure gold. Like the ark, it looked forward to the coming of the divine-human Redeemer, the God (gold)-man (acacia wood), who would fulfill all the symbolism of God's object lessons for Israel and humanity. The "face bread," "bread of presence" was made of fine wheat flour baked in twelve loaves, renewed every Sabbath and to be eaten by the priests only. This aspect of the object lesson envisioned Christ, the Bread of Life, Nourisher of the believer as a Priest (1 Pet. 2:9; Rev. 1:6; John 6:33-58).

The Golden Lampstand. 25:31-40. Made of pure gold, the seven-branch lampstand, portraying Christ our light, shone in the fullness of the Spirit, for natural light (cf. 1 Cor. 2:14-15) was excluded from the Tabernacle (John 1:4, 9; 8:12; 9:5). The decorational almond motif pictures Christ in resurrection (Num. 17:8), installed in heaven's glory, giving the Holy Spirit, seen as the sevenfold Spirit in the lampstand (Rev. 1:4, 13, 20; 3:1; 4:5), making us "sons of light" (1 Thess. 5:5). The lampstand was made of a talent of gold, which weighed 98 pounds, 12 ounces.

2. THE TABERNACLE: GENERAL CONSTRUCTION. 26:1-37.

The Typology of the Tabernacle. The general authority for the typical significance of the Tabernacle is found in Hebrews 9:1-24. Having the assurance that the building, its furnishings, and its priesthood are typical, the details of necessity must have typical significance also, or at least be richly illustrative of the person and work of the Savior and the salvation He came to bring. The New Testament explains that the tabernacle is typical (1) of Christ (Heb. 9:4); (2) of the church as the habitation of God through the Spirit (25:8; Eph. 2:19-22); of the believer (2 Cor. 6:16); and (4) as a figure of things in the heavens (Heb. 9:23-24).

The Linen Curtains. 26:1-6. **1.** The **ten** (a perfect number) **curtains of fine-twined linen** speak of the sinless life of Christ, fine linen portraying personal righteousness (Rev. 19:8). **Blue** signifies Christ's heavenly origin. **Purple** suggests His royal lineage as David's Son. **Scarlet** indicates His sacrificial blood shed for fallen mankind. The **cherubim** are symbolic of God's infinitely holy presence and unapproachability apart from Christ's sinless efficacious sacrifice (cf. Gen. 3:24; Exod. 36:8, 35). The perfect joining and hanging of the curtains speak of the heavenly grace and divine energy that enabled Christ to combine and perfectly adjust the claims of God and man as the one Mediator, who never for one moment marred the unity of His character.

The Coverings. 26:7-14. **7.** The **curtains of goats' hair** formed the outer tent that protected the inner tent or dwelling proper from the weather. This outer tent had other coverings of ram skins dyed red and badger skins. **9.** These eleven curtains were to be joined together into two sections of five and six curtains each, the **sixth curtain** forming an overlap in front at the entrance. These coverings hid the outward appearance of Him who had "no form nor comeliness . . . no beauty that we should desire him" (Isa. 53:2).

The Boards. 26:15-30. **15-30.** Made of acacia wood (as the ark and the table), the boards illustrate Christ and His people united through redemption. The boards rested in sockets of silver (the

ransom money, 30:11-13; 38:25-28), the whole framework of the Tabernacle anchored in what speaks of atonement. The believer's standing is in Christ, separated from the world as the boards were separated from the earth by the sockets of silver.

The Veil. 26:31-35. **31-35.** Designed to separate the holy place from the most holy place, the veil typifies the sinless humanity of Christ (Heb. 10:20). Barring entrance into the holiest, it was eloquently expressive of the truth that "by the deeds of the law there shall no flesh be justified" (Rom. 3:20; cf. Heb. 9:8). Torn supernaturally from top to bottom when Christ died (Matt. 27:51), it gave instant access to God to all who come by faith in His Son. The priests must have replaced the divinely split veil, for the Temple ritual continued for almost forty years. The substitute veil illustrates Galatianism—the attempt to make salvation anything other than by grace through faith (Gal. 1:6-9).

The Entrance Veil. 26:36-37. **36-37.** The hanging for the door of the tent also signifies Christ as "the way" to God (John 14:6). **37.** The **five sockets of bronze,** however, show that redemption not only displays divine mercy (silver), but also vindicates the divine righteousness in manifesting mercy (bronze symbolizing divine righteousness in judgment, Num. 21:9). Those who enter by God's way through Christ have all judgment (condemnation) removed (Rom. 8:1).

3. THE TABERNACLE: BRONZE ALTAR, COURT. 27:1-21.

The Bronze Altar. 27:1-8. Located at the threshold was the great altar for the sacrifice of animals, measuring 7½ feet square and 4½ feet high. There sacrificial blood was shed (atonement made), which is the prerequisite to man's approach to God. It is typical of the cross (death) of Christ, our whole burnt offering, who offered Himself without spot to God (Heb. 9:14). The bronze (brass) speaks of manifested divine judgment (Num. 21:9; John 3:14; cf. Exod. 26:36-37). At Calvary, Christ met the burning heat of divine justice against sin. Upon this altar the burnt offering was completely consumed, portraying Him who "knew no sin" yet was "made ... sin" for us, enduring the full wrath of God (2 Cor. 5:21).

The Court. 27:9-19. **9-10.** Surrounding the Tabernacle was a large uncovered **court** (150 feet long and 75 feet wide). It was enclosed with fine **linen** (canvass) **hangings** fastened with silver hooks and held in position by bronze **pillars,** pegs, and sockets. The hangings are symbolic of God's righteousness. The fine linen (cf. 26:1) in the hangings of the court illustrates the measure of righteousness that God demands of those who would approach His presence. This righteousness is found only in Christ; hence, all sinners are barred (Rom. 3:19-20; 10:3-5), the white linen speaking of God's infinite holiness (no colors being inwrought).

16. The only way of approach is the **gate** (cf. John 10:9), that is, Christ. Therefore, the colors reappeared in the veil (26:31) and in the curtains of the dwelling place itself (26:1-6). The fillets and hooks holding up the linen were made of silver, which portrays redemption (cf. 26:15-30; 30:11-13; 38:25-28). It is through His redemptive work that Christ is our way of access, and not by virtue of His righteous life (symbolized by the fine linen). However, the pillars of the court rested upon brass sockets, not silver as in the case of the boards (cf. 26:19), the brass symbolizing God's righteousness in judgment (Num. 21:9). Redemption not only demonstrates

God's mercy; it also vindicates His righteousness in displaying mercy (Rom. 3:21-26).

Oil for the Lampstand. 27:20-21. **20. Bring ... pure olive oil ... for the light ... to burn always.** The Holy Spirit is symbolized (John 3:34; Heb. 1:9). In Christ the oil-fed light burns perpetually, for He is "the light of the world" (John 8:12). However, the light does not refer here to the believer's testimony to the world, but to his communion and worship as a believer-priest in the most holy place of God's presence (Heb. 10:19-20). Our access to God's presence is by blood, but our communion and transformation into Christlikeness are by the Spirit (Eph. 2:18; 1 Cor. 2:14; 2 Cor. 3:18). Only as we are filled with the Spirit (Eph. 5:18) do we truly "walk in the light" (1 John 1:7).

4. THE TABERNACLE: PRIESTHOOD. 28:1-43.

The Priestly Line. 28:1-5. **1.** The priesthood is to be taken from Aaron and his sons. Aaron, the high priest (Heb., "great priest"), typifies Christ, who discharges His office after the Aaronic *pattern* (Heb. 9:1-11), but after the Melchizedek *order*, in that He is an eternal deathless High Priest (Heb. 5:5-10). Aaron's sons portray types of believers. Nadab and Abihu represent false worshipers (Lev. 10:1-2) and Eleazer and Ithamar true worshipers (1 Pet. 2:9; Rev. 1:6).

Ideas of priesthood, ritual, and sacrifice were not confined to Israel, as both history and archaeology attest. But the regulations of Israel were unique in their revelation, institution, redemptive meaning, and God-ordained practice. Founded upon God's redemptive program for a sin-ruined race, they belong intrinsically to Exodus as the book of redemption.

3. The holy **garments** for Aaron, the high priest, stand for the glory and beauty of the antitype, Christ, as our great High Priest. The various colors of gold (deity), blue (heaven), purple (royalty), scarlet (blood), and white (purity) in verses 5, 6, 13, and 33 portray various aspects of our Savior's person and redemptive work (cf. 26:1, 26).

The Ephod. 28:6-14. **6. The ephod** was a short linen garment of the same exquisite material and workmanship as the Tabernacle veil, since it represented our great High Priest. It was apronlike and constituted a vestment worn under the high priest's breastplate. It was worn over a robe (v. 31). **7-8.** The ephod was joined at the shoulder, and the two open sides were bound together by a girdle. Its beauty appears from 39:2-3, portraying Him who is altogether lovely.

9-10. Two onyx stones were encased in gold and engraved with the names of the Israelites, **six . . . on one stone and six . . . on the other stone.** In Aaron's bearing the names of God's people on his shoulders (symbolic of strength), Christ is envisioned in His present high-priestly intercession (cf. Heb. 7:25). **11.** The names engraved on the precious stones set in gold were ineffaceable, speaking of our security in Christ, our divine Lord and Savior.

The Breastplate. 28:15-29. **15-21. The breastplate** was gorgeously embellished with precious stones engraved with the names of Israel's tribes. **28-30.** This demonstrates what great value God sets on His people, whom Christ bears **upon his heart, when he goeth in unto the holy place.** The heart is the place of affection. Twice (for emphasis) the divine love for His redeemed is stressed. In no way does God's love for His own appear finer than in Christ's perpetual intercession for them, assuring their security in

Christ—the engraved gems being set "in gold enclosures" (v. 20, BV). What a blessed truth that Christ carries His people upon His heart of love. The breastplate was securely fastened to the ephod (vv. 26-28), being attached by a **lace of blue** so that it could not possibly shift. Nor is there any possibility that His love for His own can diminish. His love and power are inseparably joined.

The Urim and Thummim. 28:30. **30. The Urim and the Thummim** ("lights and perfections") were placed in the breastplate. They seem to have been two gemstones, used oracularly to ascertain God's will in difficult decisions (cf. Num. 27:21; 1 Sam. 14:37-42). Israel did not need to stumble in darkness. Neither do we who possess the Holy Spirit and God's completed revelation.

The Robe of the Ephod. 28:31-35. **31.** A cassocklike vestment woven entirely of blue, **the robe of the ephod** was seamless and sleeveless, but with armholes. It was to be drawn over the head and worn underneath the ephod. Its color speaks of our heavenly High Priest. **33.** The **bells of gold** on the hem speak of Him who went in to God after His priestly work on earth was completed, and the Holy Spirit came to set the gospel bells of testimony ringing. The **pomegranates** speak of the fruitfulness in the salvation of souls that followed. The bells also rang when Aaron came out from God's presence. Fruitfulness will follow Christ's second advent and the fresh testimony that will then be heard.

The Gold Headplate. 28:36-38. **36. A plate of pure gold** bore the inscription: "HOLINESS TO THE LORD," a Hebraism for "Holy is the LORD," and was fitted to the front of the linen miter or turban. The crown of holiness was meant to symbolize the acceptance of the high priest as the representative of the people before God in bearing their iniquity. **38. So that Aaron may take on him the guilt connected with the sacred gifts which the Israelites dedicate** (Berkeley). This is prophetic of our Lord's taking "on him the iniquity of us all" (Isa. 53:6). "In the Great High Priest God and His people are brought together in perfect reconciliation and communion" (Alleman & Flack, OTC, p. 237). This is true despite the emphatically stressed holiness of deity (the plate of pure gold, v. 36).

Garments of the Regular Priests. 28:39-43. **39-40.** The ordinary vestments of the high priest and the regular priests, over which the special high-priestly regalia was placed in the case of the high priest (vv. 39-43), were also **for glory and for beauty.** This indicates that the glory and beauty that characterized Aaron (Christ) also, in a definite sense, is shared by his sons (believer-priests in the church of this age). **42.** The linen trousers to cover the naked flesh of the priests "set forth the righteousness of Christ imputed to the believer, the *sine qua non* of approach to God in a priestly capacity" (M. F. Unger, BE, 1:113).

5. CONSECRATION OF THE PRIESTS.
29:1-46.

The Washing. 29:1-4. **1-3.** The materials for the sacrifices and offerings that typify the redemptive work of Christ (Lev. 1-7) are enumerated first. **4.** The reason is that the washing of **Aaron and his sons ... with water** symbolizes regeneration (John 3:5; 13:10; Titus 3:5), which is based upon Christ's atoning death and resurrection. Aaron had part in the washing, because he was a sinner and needed it. Our Lord as the spotless Lamb of God (Heb. 7:26-28) did *not* need it. Nevertheless, He submitted to John's baptism at Jordan to identify Himself with sinners and to fulfill the Aaronic pattern (Matt. 3:13-17).

Aaron's Clothing and Anointing. 29:5-7. Clothed with his splendid garments (vv. 5-6) and anointed (v. 7), symbolic of Christ's enduement with the Holy Spirit (Matt. 3:16; Acts 10:38), Aaron alone was anointed *before* the blood was shed (cf. v. 21). This distinguishes him as a striking picture of Christ, who was anointed with the Holy Spirit by virtue of what He was in Himself in His deity and sinless humanity. How different the case of all believers (typified by Aaron's sons) who are anointed by virtue of redemptive grace, symbolized by the elaborate ritual accompanying the priestly ordination.

Aaron's Sons' Clothing. 29:8-9. That Aaron's sons were clothed for priestly service immediately after Aaron and before the blood was shed and before their anointing points to the fact that all true believers are one with Christ, as Aaron's sons were one with Aaron, and were priests of God as he was. The great Reformation truth of the priesthood of *all* believers appears this early in divine revelation.

9. Gird ... with girdles symbolizes service (Luke 12:37; 17:8; John 13:4; Rev. 1:13). **Consecrate** means "fill the hands," placing the sacrifices that follow (vv. 10-46) in the priests' hands, so that by the offering of them they were not only sanctified but also installed into their offices.

The Sin Offering. 29:10-14. The sin offering dealt specifically with the forgiveness of sin and restoration of fellowship with God (Lev. 4:1—5:13). The presentation of this offering was to remove the legal disqualifications from Aaron and his sons on account of sin. The life in the blood of the sacrificial animal made atonement for the Aaronic priests, whose lives, like the lives of all of us, were forfeited through sin (cf. the antitype, 1 John 1:7).

The Burnt Offering. 29:15-18. The burnt offering presents Christ offering Himself spotless to God (Lev. 1:1-17; Heb. 9:11-14; 10:5-7). Identification of the offerer with his offering is seen in placing the hand upon the head of the victim.

The Peace Offering. 29:19-37. The peace offering prefigures Christ's work on the cross in the aspect of procuring peace for the sinner (Lev. 3:1-17). God is propitiated; the sinner is reconciled (Col. 1:20; Eph. 2:14; Rom. 5:1). This offering is inseparable from the burnt offering, since it was offered on the altar of burnt sacrifice. Peace with God springs from the death of Christ and is a prerequisite to dedication and all priestly consecration, service, and communion prefigured in the ordination ritual (vv. 20-37).

Atonement (vv. 33, 36). At the root of the Hebrew term *kāpăr* is the idea of "covering." Mosaic sacrifices "covered" sin from God's sight in view of Christ's future redemptive work. Thus the sinner's forgiveness was secured by God's passing over or pretermitting (Rom. 3:25) sin. Not until Christ died was sin finally "put away" (Heb. 9:15) and actual atonement (at-one-ment) made between God and man (see Lev. 16).

The Daily Sacrifice. 29:38-46. Provision for the sacrifice of a lamb (Christ's death) and the presentation of a meal offering (Christ's sinless humanity) and drink offerings (Christ's life poured out in death, Psalm 72:14; Isa. 53:12) each morning and evening kept alive the ritual that pointed to the coming Redeemer. The LORD consequently promised to sanctify the tent of meeting by His presence (based on atonement, see vv. 33, 36) to commune with His people, to reveal His will to them, to perpetuate a holy priesthood for them

(fulfilled in Christ), and to demonstrate to them that He was *their God*.

6. THE ALTAR OF INCENSE AND WORSHIP. 30:1-38.

The Altar of Incense. 30:1-10. The altar of incense was important in true worship and is described first in this great chapter on worship. **3.** It was constructed of acacia wood (bespeaking Christ's humanity) and **pure gold** (symbolizing His deity). It was 1½ feet square, 3 feet high, and equipped with rings and staves for transporting it. It had horns on its four corners, like the altar of burnt offering.

The horns on the Tabernacle's altars evidently symbolized God's power as the "horn of . . . salvation" (2 Sam. 22:3; Psalm 18:2; Luke 1:69) and therefore were regarded as places of refuge (1 Kings 1:50-51; 2:28-32) (NBD, p. 537). The incense altar was positioned in the holy place before the veil. It portrays Christ our Intercessor in heaven (John 17:1-26; Heb. 7:25), through whom our prayers and praise (incense) ascend to God (Heb. 13:15; Rev. 8:3-4).

7-9. Aaron was to offer incense twice daily, showing how important prayer and praise are. There was to be no "strange incense" that was "unprescribed" or improperly compounded (cf. 30:34-38), speaking of "will-worship" (Col. 2:23), or purely ritual treadmill performance. See "strange fire" (Lev. 10:1-3). For the cleansing of the altar, Aaron was to apply atoning blood to its horns annually (cf. Lev. 16). **10.** On "atonement," see 29:33.

The Ransom Money. 30:11-16. The altar of incense sets forth what true worship is. The rest of the chapter points the question: Who may worship? The answer: (1) the redeemed (vv. 11-16; cf. 15:1-21; Psalm 107:1-2); (2) the cleansed (vv. 17-21); (3) the anointed (vv. 22-33);

139

and (4) those who offer spiritual (not sensuous) service to God (vv. 34-38; cf. John 4:24). The ransom money was not only a means of providing for the tabernacle worship; it also was a somber reminder of the absolute necessity of redemption of a fallen, lost race. "Here is a confession of the fact that all are lost, all are on equal footing, and all need redemption" (A. C. Gaebelein, *The Annotated Bible*, 1:167).

The ransom money amounted to a half shekel of silver (about one-fifth ounce). It was to be levied in connection with the taking of a census (cf. Num. 1). So crucial was this ransom money in demonstrating fallen man's helplessly lost estate apart from divine redemptive grace that ignoring payment of it, when the census was taken, invited severe divine punishment (*plague*). Accordingly, silver became symbolic of redemption (cf. 26:19; 38:27; Num. 3:44-51).

The Laver. 30:17-21. **18.** The laver was a washbasin set between the altar and the door. It was used by the priests to cleanse their hands and feet, being symbolic of the "washing of water by the word" (Eph. 5:25-27; cf. Heb. 10:22; John 13:3-10; 1 John 1:9). True worship demands continual cleansing from daily defilement. The **laver** points to Christ cleansing the believer from the daily defilement of sin. **19.** The priests could not enter the holy place after serving at the bronze altar till their hands and feet were cleansed. **20-21.** To attempt to come into God's presence uncleansed meant courting physical death.

The Anointing Oil. 30:22-33. The anointing oil speaks of the Holy Spirit for worship and service (John 4:23; cf. Acts 1:8; Eph. 2:18; 5:18-19). The various fragrant substances mixed in a hin of olive oil (between one and two gallons) speak of the fragrance and beauty of Christ produced in the believer by the

Holy Spirit. **23. Myrrh** is now identified with the "balm of Mecca." The **sweet cinnamon** is an aromatic plant, but otherwise uncertain (Prov. 7:17; Song of Sol. 4:14).

24. The same is true of **cassia.** The **olive oil** was to consecrate the tabernacle and its furniture and the priests. **32-33.** But the oil was not to be poured on the flesh or be imitated. Since the flesh is utterly corrupt, the Holy Spirit can have nothing to do with it. Counterfeits, so common today, must be avoided.

The incense. 30:34-38. **37.** Carefully compounded, the incense was not to be imitated, but used only in betokening prayer and praise to God. **38.** God's worship is to be spiritual, not sensuously appealing to the natural man. The incense speaks of Christ's wonderful fragrance to God, the focal point of all true worship.

7. THE WORKMEN AND THE SABBATH. 31:1-18.

The Craftsmen. 31:1-11. Not only skilled men, but spiritual men as well, were needed, chosen, and endowed by God to execute the directions given Moses. Bezalel ("in the shadow of God") and Oholiab ("tent father") were selected by God for the task. God's call is His enablement.

The Sabbath. 31:12-31. Because of its extreme importance as a sign between the LORD and Israel, Sabbath-keeping is repeated and emphasized throughout the Pentateuch. It was first mentioned with regard to Israel in connection with the giving of the manna (16:23-29). Shortly afterward it was included in the moral laws of the Decalogue in the fourth commandment (for full exposition of its meaning, see 20:8-11).

The Lord's Day (Sunday) does not represent a mere change from the Sabbath (Saturday). Rather, it is a new day

140

to commemorate a new order. It memorializes a new creation and the resurrected Christ as its Head. The Sabbath by contrast is related to the old creation, recalling God's rest from His creative work of fashioning the earth (Gen. 1:1—2:3). God could "rest" because man and everything else He had created were "very good" (Gen. 1:31). Hence, He "rested on the seventh day" and "blessed" and "sanctified" it for *unfallen* man (Gen. 2:2-3).

However, man's Fall made it impossible for God to impose Sabbath observance upon fallen man. The very thing commemorated, namely, the divine rest in a "very good" creation, had been destroyed by the entrance of sin into the human family. This explains the silence of revelation concerning the Sabbath from Adam to Moses.

17. Then at Sinai, Sabbath observance was not only made a part of the Mosaic code (20:8-11), but also was made its *unique* and dominant feature as a **sign** between the LORD and Israel. The Sabbath, accordingly, is a Jewish institution, the *quintessential badge of the Mosaic Covenant*. Its infraction was, therefore, understandably punishable by death (vv. 14-15; cf. Num. 15:32-36), since it was tantamount to breaking the covenant.

The termination of the Mosaic economy at Christ's death (cf. Matt. 27:51) signified the new purpose of God in the church (Lev. 23:11; Psalm 118:22-24; Matt. 28:1; Acts 4:11-12; Col. 2:16-17; Heb. 4:4; Gal. 4:9-10). Meanwhile, the Sabbath is in abeyance (cf. "for a perpetual covenant," v. 16). It will be reinstated for Israel in the Tribulation (Matt. 24:20) and in the Kingdom (Isa. 66:23; Ezek. 46:1).

Moses Receives the Tables of Stone. 31:18. This is a fitting interlude that connects the importance and sanctity of the Sabbath with the breaking of the covenant that follows (chap. 32). **18. Finger of God** graphically declares the divine origin of the Law, though mediated by angels (Acts 7:53) and men.

E. THE GOLDEN CALF. 32:1-35.

The People's Sin. 32:1-14. What a revelation this scene is of the exceedingly wicked nature of sin and the helplessness of man apart from faith in the grace of God not only to be redeemed, but after being redeemed, to live a holy life consonant with his redeemed status. The people demonstrated their utter inability in their own strength to keep the legal covenant, which they had so glibly accepted. Their rebellious and callous conduct was incredible, especially their shocking return to the bull worship of Egypt.

Deliberately breaking the first two commandments of the Decalogue, they brought the wrath of the broken Law upon themselves (vv. 7-10). Aaron abetted the people's sin by building an altar and prostituting a feast of the LORD, who was thought to be worshiped under the guise of a calf, evidently as invisibly enthroned on the animal, as is seen later in the case of Jeroboam's golden bulls at Dan and Bethel. **6.** The outcome of such perverted worship was not holiness but **play** (orgiastic dance), which fit in with the immorality of pagan religion (cf. 1 Cor. 10:6-7).

The scene between the LORD in His wrath (v. 10) and Moses in his intercession (vv. 11-14) affords a striking contrast between Law and grace. God's infinite holiness, reflected in the Law, could only demand the destruction of the people. Moses' intercession is a reminder of Christ's advocacy (John 17) and the grace that provides "an advocate with the Father," whose propitiatory sacrifice never loses its efficacy (1

John 2:1-2). Where Law condemns, grace justifies and forgives.

The People Are Punished. 32:15-29. Wrath may not be outpoured, but sin is not excused. Grace disciplines. Moses met Joshua (cf. 24:13). Coming down the mount with the Law of God in his hands, Moses shattered the tablets to bring home to the people the depth of their sin. The whole episode shows the inability of the Law, itself good, to make men good. Depraved man is never saved by Law-keeping, but by faith. Faith alone is the way to justification and salvation in every age, as well as the way to sanctification of life.

The Law was a pedagogue to uncover man's sin and guilt so that he might cast himself in faith upon God's grace and power to save and to sanctify. Calling on those who were on the LORD's side, the Levites leaped up and slew three-thousand of the worst offenders. Verse 29 evidently laments a blessing the backsliding people had forfeited.

Confession and Intercession of Moses. 32:30-35. This is a sublime portrayal of Moses' concern for God's people (cf. Rom. 9:1-3). **32. Blot me, I pray thee, out of thy book** (i.e., "take my physical life"). The expression comes from the practice of keeping registers of citizens and removing the names of those who die in a time of judgment (cf. Psalm 69:28; Isa. 4:3). **35.** God's grace is manifested to His people, but He chastens and scourges disobedience and rebellion of His own (Heb. 12:5-11).

F. RENEWAL OF THE COVENANT. 33:1—34:35.

1. THE LORD'S GUIDANCE. 33:1-23.

God's Presence Withheld. 33:1-6. Despite His people's utter unfaithfulness (chap. 32), the LORD remained faithful. He cannot deny Himself (cf. 2

Tim. 2:13). **1-3.** He confirmed His promise of the land of Canaan. Yet He reminded His **stiffnecked** people that He could not accompany them Himself lest His holiness consume them. By sending His angel or alter ego (cf. 32:34), He would not forsake them as they assumed the place of self-judgment and acknowledged broken fellowship with the Holy One. **4-6.** This they did, by stripping off their jewelry.

The Tent of Meeting. 33:7-11. This was a pretabernacle structure, portable like ancient Arabic tent shrines. The Hebrew *'ōhĕl mô'ēḏ* means "tent of assembly or appointment." **7.** Moses was accustomed to pitch this tent **outside . . . afar off from the camp** in contrast to the Levitical tabernacle, which was to stand in the middle of the camp. This tent was a place where those **who sought the Lord** resorted.

9-11. Joshua was the minister, in contrast to the later tent where the Levites officiated. When **Moses entered into the tabernacle,** the **pillar** of cloud **descended and stood at the door,** while the **Lord talked with** him (cf. Psalm 99:7) **face to face** (Num. 12:8; Deut. 34:10), that is, closely and directly rather than at a distance or indistinctly, as through a dream or vision (cf. 1 Cor. 13:12). The tent of meeting was a simple substitute tiding Israel over until the Levitical tabernacle could be erected.

The Promise of God's Presence. 33:12-17. **12-13.** Moses pleaded for a clear apprehension of God's leading and favor. Without this would it not be better to remain at Sinai, where he had repeated assurances, than to venture on without such assurances and with such a rebellious people to deal with? "Truly Sinai at its worst with God was better than Canaan at its best without Him" (Alleman & Flack, OTC, p. 241). **13.** Moses' plea was based on God's electing love of Israel as His nation (cf. Rom. 11:1-12). **14-17.** The LORD's reply assured Moses of His presence and rest (Deut. 12:10). **I will give thee rest** (causative of *nûăḥ*, "settle down, dwell"), hence, "to cause to settle down and dwell quietly" in the land promised them.

New Vision Sought. 33:18-23. **18-19.** Moses had already seen God's glory at Sinai (24:16-17), but he needed a new vision for a new task if he was to launch out in the unknown wilderness beyond Sinai. God's wonderful grace, so sorely needed after the debacle of the golden calf, was revealed. **22.** God allowed Moses to behold His glory as He put His servant **in a cleft of the rock** and covered him **with** His hand as He passed by (Song of Sol. 2:14; Isa. 49:2; John 10:28-29). **23.** But Moses was allowed to see only God's **back** (cf. v. 20; John 1:18; 2 Cor. 4:6).

2. THE SECOND TABLE OF THE LAW. 34:1-35.

The New Tables Prepared. 34:1-5. The promised vision of the covenant God was based upon the renewal of the covenant broken by the lapse into idolatry. The renewal was effected by the repromulgation of the law of the covenant. Moses prepared the tablets, but God wrote the Decalogue upon them, for Moses ascended the mount alone.

The New Vision. 34:6-9. **9.** The purpose of this manifestation of the divine splendor was to answer Moses' request that he and God's people might know they had **found grace** in God's sight (33:12-13, 16; cf. 34:9). To find grace (favor) in the divine presence is not to earn or merit it, but to have it freely bestowed because God "knows" us in His electing call (cf. 3:1-22). **5-7.** What grace and love are revealed here in the name of the LORD (YHWH, the God of

covenant love and redemption)—**the Lord, Lord God, merciful and gracious, long-suffering, and abundant in goodness and truth, keeping mercy for thousands, forgiving iniquity and ... sin.** But let those who presume upon that grace take warning, especially those who reject the gospel of grace and whose sin will be visited upon them in divine wrath (cf. 20:5-6).

The Renewal of the Covenant. 34:10-27. **10.** Evidently this was a renewal of the covenant broken by idolatry (cf. v. 27). God promised to perform unprecedented **marvels** (*nĭplā'ōt̲*, "wondrous deeds, miracles, astonishing acts"), such as sustaining over two million people in the desert with food and water, which modern critics deny. **For it is an awe-inspiring thing** (*nôrā'*, "wonderful, stupendous deed"), "something to view with reverence and fear," which the LORD was going to do with His people to manifest His work among the surrounding nations among whom they were to be a testimony through godly separation from their sins (vv. 11-17).

13. Destroy their altars ... their images ("pillars," upright stones representing the abode of deity). **Cut down their groves** (*'ăshērîm*, "sacred posts, symbolizing Asherah," the mother goddess of Canaanite religion; cf. Judg. 2:13). Canaanite altars were places of abhorrent fertility-cult rites (cf. 2 Kings 17:10; 18:4). **14.** The LORD's **name is Jealous,** that is, His infinitely holy character can tolerate no rivals for His people's devotion (20:5; Deut. 4:24).

18-26. Other regulations fundamental to the renewed covenant relation were: (1) **the feast of unleavened bread** to be observed in the month Abib (March-April), the earing month, Abib (Deut. 16:1) marking the Exodus from Egypt (cf. 12:14-28; 23:15); (2) the offering of the firstborn, providing for redemption of children instead of giving them as human sacrifices; (3) the Sabbath observance (cf. 20:8-11; 23:12; 31:13-16; 35:2-3); (4) **the feast of weeks ... and ... of ingathering** (cf. 23:16); (5) the appearance of all adult males at the three great feasts (cf. 23:17); (6) restrictions on the use of leaven; (7) the offering of the firstfruits to the LORD; and (8) prohibition concerning the boiling of **a kid in his mother's milk** (cf. 23:19).

The Shining of Moses' Face. 34:28-35. Moses' countenance glowed with borrowed splendor because the second giving of the Decalogue was mixed with divine grace and glory (33:5-9). This was in contrast to the receiving of the first tables, when no glow appeared on Moses' face, for that giving was altogether legal. He had to cover his face with a veil, however, as grace and mercy are covered in the Law. This veil is done away in Christ, in whom grace and glory shine forth (2 Cor. 3:18). The same veil remains upon unbelieving Jews in rejecting Christ (2 Cor. 3:14-16). But at Christ's glorious second advent, the veil will be removed when they will turn to Christ (Rom. 11:25-36; cf. Zech. 12:10—13:1).

G. ERECTION OF THE TABERNACLE AND INSTITUTION OF THE PRIESTHOOD. 35:1—40:38.

These chapters narrate the execution of the divine instructions for the setting up of the Tabernacle and its priestly ritual given in chapters 25-31. The purpose of this repetition is to emphasize the importance of the tabernacle and its ritual in the history of redemption as foreshadowing the person and work of the coming Redeemer and pointing to the glorious gospel of salvation by grace

through faith that He would provide for a lost race.

1. GIFTS AND WORKMEN. 35:1-35.

The Sabbath Again Emphasized. 35:1-3. (Cf. 16:23-29; 20:8-11; 23:12; 31:13-16; 34:21.) Before any work was begun, the law of the Sabbath was reemphasized. Rest in the LORD must precede work for Him. Worship of the LORD must spring from obedience to Him. Loyalty to the quintessential requirement of the covenant had to be the basis for enacting other instructions pertaining to the fulfillment of the covenant. Violation of Sabbath rest was so basic that it was punishable by death (Num. 15:32-36).

Importance of Giving to God's Work. 35:4-29. (Cf. 25:1-8.) **29.** The people **brought a willing offering ... whose heart made them willing.** An unwilling offering is an insult to God (vv. 21, 22, 26, 29).

Importance of Workmen. 35:30-35. (Cf. 31:1-11.) The principal craftsmen were signalized again and their divine endowments noted.

2. THE TABERNACLE MATERIALS. 36:1-38.

Restrained from Giving. 36:1-7. So liberally and spontaneously did the people give that they had to be stopped. **7. Sufficient ... too much** is the happy outcome when the true spirit of giving takes over.

Materials Donated. 36:8-38. The materials were now supplied and the things for which directions had been given (cf. chaps. 25-31) were made ready: the linen curtains (vv. 8-13; cf. 26:1-6); curtains of goats' hair (vv. 14-18; cf. 26:7); covering of rams' skins (v. 19; cf. 26:14); boards (vv. 20-23; cf. 26:15); silver sockets (vv. 24-30; cf. 26:19); the bars (vv. 31-33; cf. 26:26);

gold overlay (v. 34; cf. 26:29); the inner and outer veils (vv. 35-38; cf. 26:31, 36).

3. THE TABERNACLE FURNITURE. 37:1—38:31.

The Most Holy Place. 37:1-9. **1-5. The ark** (cf. 25:10). **6-9. The mercy seat** (cf. 25:17).

The Holy Place. 37:10-28. **10-16.** The table of showbread (cf. 25:23). **17-24. The lampstand** (cf. 25:31). **25-28. The incense altar** (cf. 30:1).

The Anointing Oil. 37:29. (Cf. 30:23-38.)

The Altar of Burnt Offering. 38:1-7. (Cf. 27:1-8.)

The Laver. 38:8. (Cf. 30:18-21.)

The Courts. 38:9-31. (Cf. 27:9-19.)

4. THE PRIESTLY GARMENTS. 39:1-43.

Making the Priestly Regalia. 39:1-31. **1.** The materials. **2-6. The ephod** (cf. 28:6-29). **8-21. The breastplate** (cf. 28:15-28). **22-26. The robe of the ephod** (cf. 28:31-34). **27-31.** The rest of the garments (cf. 28:39, 40, 42).

Moses Inspects and Blesses the Completed Work. 39:32-43. Everything was given willingly and executed obediently. Moses, therefore, blessed the completed work and the workers.

5. THE ASSEMBLING AND DEDICATION. 40:1-38.

Command to Erect the Tabernacle. 40:1-33. **1-15.** Meticulously, step by step, God gave the directions for how His worship and service were to be conducted. The whole detailed and seemingly repetitious account of the institution of the Tabernacle and priesthood emphasizes how utterly essential it is in matters of salvation and ministry to follow and obey the Word of God undeviatingly. Failure to do so has resulted in the babel of cults and heresies that plague pure, biblical, historical Christianity today. **16-33.** Hence, Moses' obedience is stressed.

Result of Obedience. 40:34-38. **34-35. The glory of the Lord filled the tabernacle.** Always when God's commands are honored and His Word given priority, His pleasure is shown and His manifest power and blessing are experienced. A motley multitude of slaves in Egypt transformed into an emancipated nation in fellowship with God and Canaan-bound gives the synopsis of Exodus, truly "the book of redemption" (Merrill F. Unger, *Unger's Bible Handbook*, p. 105).

LEVITICUS

Name of the Book. The name Leviticus is derived from the contents of the book, which presents the law of the Levites, the descendants of Levi, the priests. It is adopted from the Septuagint (*Leueitikon*) and the Vulgate (Leviticus) and sets forth this portion of Scripture as a handbook of the worship and ritual of the old covenant, centering in the Levitical priesthood (cf. Heb. 7:11).

Nature of the Book. Leviticus is the book of atonement and holy living. All that precedes in divine revelation is preparatory. Genesis, the book of beginnings, presents man lost and ruined. Exodus, the book of redemption, presents him redeemed and restored. Leviticus, the book of atonement, presents redeemed man in separation from sin and walking in fellowship with God. Such a walk demands holiness. Approximately half of the book of Leviticus emphasizes the holiness of God. The other half stresses the truth that God's holiness demands holiness in us if we are to walk in fellowship with Him.

The minute ritual of the Levitical code has the distinct purpose of effecting a keen consciousness of *sin* as a barrier to approach to God. Every Levitical ceremony is a sermon on sin; every sacrifice is a homily on sin acted out. *Salvation from sin* is the underlying theme. The infinitely holy God offers salvation to fallen, sinful man on the basis of pure grace through faith; thus, Leviticus is an object lesson of the one true gospel of God, theologically expounded in the New Testament in the book of Romans. *Atonement* is the means of salvation and, accordingly, is set forth in Leviticus. Man cannot save himself, for he is fallen and sinful; therefore, he is to gain life by the death of a substitute. As a result, *a Savior-Substitute* becomes an absolute necessity. For this reason, all that is dramatically enacted ceremonially in the book is a typical picture of Christ, in whom alone these requirements could be met. Thus, the book of Hebrews constitutes the best commentary on the book of Leviticus.

Background of Levitical Sacrifices. The religious ceremonies in Leviticus were not pulled out of a vacuum. They represent basic truths regarding the approach to God from the beginning. When man fell, the way of access to God by grace through faith was made known. Fallen man thought to approach God by self-righteous works, portrayed by Adam's and Eve's making garments of fig leaves to cover their nakedness (Gen. 3:7). God corrected them by showing that the guilt of sin only could be covered by shedding the blood of a victim (Gen. 3:21). Accordingly, divinely revealed and divinely ordered sacrifice is recorded in the case of Cain and Abel. Cain, presenting his own works, disregarded God's way of approach in worship and was rejected. Abel was accepted into God's presence on the basis of the gospel of salvation by grace through faith (Gen. 4:1-7; Heb. 11:4).

Likewise, Noah (Gen. 8:20), Abraham (Gen. 12:8), Isaac (26:25), Jacob (31:54), and the rest of God's people down to the eve of the Exodus knew the way of access to God and practiced it (Exod. 10:25). At the Exodus the sacrificial system, which had at least in part existed from the Fall, was broadened, given fresh meaning in the light of redemptive experience, organized, codified, and recorded by inspiration in the ritual codes of Exodus and Leviticus.

The Witness of Archaeology. The original revelation and institution of sacrifice, as the sinner's approach to God, was corrupted and perverted by man's lapse into paganism and was reflected in the religious ritual honeycombing the ancient biblical world. Ancient Sumerian, Babylonian, Hittite, Egyptian, and Amorite records show the prevalence of sacrificial systems similar to the Hebrews in the Old Testament. The Ras Shamra religious texts, found at the site of ancient Ugarit in north Syria (1929-37 and later), have particular value in demonstrating both the likeness and the differences between Israelite and Canaanite sacrifices.

The Witness of Theology. Archaeological findings bear out the intimations of revelation and the reasonings of theology that the sacrifices were ordained by God when man fell into sin. This is true because of the character of God, who is infinitely holy, yet gracious in His redemptive love (Gen. 3:15). It also is a fact because of the nature of man, who is a fallen, helpless sinner, totally unqualified to come near God in his own merits or to devise a means of approach by his own ingenuity.

Authorship. Internal evidence warrants the conclusion that Leviticus, as well as the other Pentateuchal books, was committed to writing by Moses himself, or under his command and supervision. Over and over again these laws are declared as being given through him. The phrase "and the LORD said to Moses" occurs some thirty times. Once Mosaic authorship is abandoned, a fruitless search yields only imaginary authors, who only exist as figments in the imagination of the partitionist scholars.

OUTLINE

I. ACCESS TO GOD. 1:1—16:34.
   A. Access to God: By Sacrifice. 1:1—7:38.
      1. The Burnt Offering. 1:1-17.
      2. The Meal Offering. 2:1-16.
      3. The Peace Offering. 3:1-17.
      4. The Sin Offering. 4:1-35.
      5. The Trespass Offering. 5:1-19.
      6. The Law of the Burnt, Meal, and Sin Offerings. 6:1-30.
      7. The Law of the Trespass and Peace Offerings. 7:1-38.
   B. Access to God: By Priesthood. 8:1—9:24.
      1. Consecration of the Priesthood. 8:1-36.
      2. The Priests' Ministry. 9:1-24.
   C. Access to God: By Priestly Obedience. 10:1-20.
   D. Access to God: By Avoiding Defilement. 11:1—15:33.
      1. A Holy People—Their Good. 11:1-47.
      2. A Holy People—Childbirth. 12:1-8.
      3. A Holy Priesthood—Leprosy. 13:1-59.
      4. A Holy People—Cleansing from Leprosy. 14:1-57.
      5. A Holy People—Personal Defilement. 15:1-33.
   E. Access to God: By Atonement. 16:1-34.
II. FELLOWSHIP WITH GOD. 17:1—27:34.
   A. Fellowship with God: By Separation from Sin. 17:1—22:33.
      1. Warning Against Idolatrous Taint. 17:1-16.
      2. Unholy Practices Forbidden. 18:1-30.
      3. Holiness in Human Relationships. 19:1-37.
      4. Separation from Occultism and Immorality. 20:1-27.
      5. Prescriptions for Priestly Holiness. 21:1-24.
      6. Priestly Separation and Obedience. 22:1-33.
   B. Fellowship with God: By Observing the Festivals. 23:1-44.
   C. Fellowship with God: By Obedience and Reverence. 24:1-23.
   D. Fellowship with God: By Observing the Sabbatic Year and Jubilee. 25:1-55.
   E. Fellowship with God: By Heeding God's Promises and Warnings. 26:1-46.
   F. Fellowship with God: By Keeping Vows and Paying Tithes. 27:1-34.

COMMENTARY

I. ACCESS TO GOD. 1:1—16:34.

A. ACCESS TO GOD: BY SACRIFICE. 1:1—7:38.

1. THE BURNT OFFERING. 1:1-17.

The Bullock. 1:1-9. **1. The Lord called unto Moses.** It is stressed that these sacrifices and the ones that follow were divinely revealed and commanded. The revelation was given **out of the tabernacle of the congregation,** probably "the tent of meeting" (ASV), where God met with Moses (cf. Exod. 33:7-11) before the erection of the tabernacle.

3-5. The burnt sacrifice or offering, 'ōlâ, "that which ascends" (from 'ālâ, "go up, rise"), doubtlessly from the altar in smoke, was called the *whole* burnt offering because *all* the flesh was consumed on the altar. It speaks of Christ offering Himself without spot to God in delight in the Father's will, even in death. **A male without blemish . . . the bullock** speaks of the perfection and sinlessness of Christ (cf. 22:19-25). The placing of the offerer's **hand upon the head** of the victim demonstrated his identification and acceptance with the offering. It illustrated the believer's faith in accepting and identifying himself with Christ (Rom. 4:5; 6:3-11). In this offering, although the offerer offers himself and his life to the LORD, he does so on the basis of shed blood and priestly ministry, as well as identification with the offering.

6-9. The flaying and cutting, as well as the burning of the sacrifice with fire, portray the sufferings and death of Christ effecting antitypically expiation of sin, the Old Testament "covering" or atonement (v. 4). The fire symbolizes God's holiness (cf. Heb. 12:29) in judgment upon that which He utterly condemns (cf. Gen. 19:24; Mark 9:43-48; Rev. 20:15).

The Sheep or Goat. 1:10-13. **10. The sheep** (lamb) portrays Christ in complete obedience to the death of the cross (Isa. 53:7; John 1:29; Phil. 2:6-8). Again **the male without blemish** speaks of the sinless life of Christ. The **sweet savor** (smelling) **offering** prefigures Christ in His perfection devoting Himself to the Father's will, even to death, and thus as the delight of the Father.

The Turtle Dove or Pigeon. 1:14-17. The bird suggests sorrowing innocence (Isa. 38:14; 59:11; Heb. 7:26) and poverty (Lev. 5:7). Portrayed is He who "became poor" that we "through His poverty might become rich" (2 Cor. 8:9, NASB). If the offerer was too poor to bring a sheep or goat, he could bring a fowl. Whether he brought much or little, in God's sight it was acceptable if brought in faith, in dependence upon divine grace (cf. Luke 2:24).

2. THE MEAL OFFERING. 2:1-16.

Significance. 2:1-3. **1-3.** Second only to the burnt offering, which prefigures Christ's atoning death and is inseparable from it, this **meal** (cereal) **offering** speaks of His perfect sinless life. The **fine flour,** evenly milled, signifies the perfection that was blended in every part of Christ's humanity, as the perfect Man. The **oil** poured upon the fine flour suggests Christ's perfect humanity immeasurably anointed by the Holy Spirit (Luke 3:21-22; John 3:34). The offering is a **sweet savor** (smell) offering, because Christ incarnate was the Father's beloved Son, in whom He was "well pleased" (Matt. 3:17; cf. Isa. 42:1; Matt. 17:5; Mark 9:7; Luke 9:35; Eph. 1:3-6). The fragrance speaks of the acceptance before God of Christ's testing by suffering, even under divine wrath, to the point of death, as man's sin-bearer.

Aaron and his sons (prefiguring New Testament saints) shared the offering, suggesting our feeding spiritually upon Christ, the Bread of Life (John 6:51-54). Therefore, this portion of the meal offering was **most holy of the offerings ... made by fire,** for it looked forward to the death of the sinless One made sin for us (2 Cor. 5:21) as a satisfaction of the holy wrath of God against sin. For this reason **the memorial** of this part of the meal offering (cf. 1 Cor. 11:25-26) was burned upon the altar, pointing forward to the expiatory death of Christ.

The Meal Offering Baked. 2:4-11. **4-7.** Whether in the **oven,** in **a pan,** or **frying pan,** this offering suggests Christ's sufferings in His preglorified incarnate state. The oven speaks of His inner unfathomable sufferings in Gethsemane (Matt. 26:47-54), and when the Father turned away from Him as the sinless One upon whom the world's guilt was laid (Psalm 22:1; Matt. 27:46). The pan betokens Christ's outward and more evident sufferings, as His rejection by His own, His hunger, weariness, and so forth.

The **unleavened cakes of fine flour** emphasize that no taint of insincerity or untruth (the symbolic meaning of leaven, 1 Cor. 5:8) tainted our Lord's perfect humanity as "the truth" (John 14:6). As **unleavened wafers anointed with oil** speak of the anointing of Christ's sinless humanity, so the **fine flour unleavened, mixed with oil** suggests Christ as conceived by the Holy Spirit (Matt. 1:18-23; Luke 1:35).

8-10. Again from the meal offering made by fire **a memorial** (cf. v. 2) was to be taken, and the remaining portion was to be eaten by the priests (cf. vv. 2-3). No meal offering, since it illustrates the sinless humanity of Christ, was to be tainted with leaven (a type of evil, Matt. 13:33; 1 Cor. 5:8). **11. Ye shall burn no leaven.** Although Christ was made sin, He Himself was sinless in life as well as in death. No **honey,** symbolic of purely natural sweetness, portrays the perfect divine-human excellencies of Christ's character.

Offering of the Firstfruits. 2:12-16. Although the firstfruits offerings look forward to Christ's person and redemptive work, they were intended to call forth similar devotion to God's will as would characterize Him when He came. The best was not too good for God. **13. Salt,** which stands for permanence and incorruption, was to be used with all the offerings, hence the expression **the salt of the covenant with your God** (cf. Num. 18:19; 2 Chron. 13:5). Salt was the opposite of leaven. The offering of the firstfruits apparently connects Christ's sinless humanity, tested unto death, with bodily resurrection (cf. 23:9-14; 1 Cor. 15:20-23).

3. THE PEACE OFFERING. 3:1-17.

Offering of the Herd. 3:1-5. **1.** The **peace offering,** like the burnt offering and meal (cereal) offering, was a sweet-savor (smelling) offering. These offerings are so named because they envision Christ in His infinite perfections completely devoted to the Father's will. They are in contrast to the nonsweet-savor offerings, which picture Christ bearing the whole demerit of the sinner.

152

The peace offering is really *zĕḇăḥ šᵉlāmîm* (lit., "offering of peace blessings"), denoting "the entire round of blessings and powers, by which the salvation . . . of man in his relation to God is established and secured" (Paul I. Morentz and H. C. Alleman, OTC, p. 249). The German *Heilsopfer* ("salvation offering") comes closer to the idea of the original.

Salvation is understood here as being brought into right relation to God and the realization of that relation in conduct. Hence, the whole work of Christ in relationship to the believer's peace is in view—Christ our peace (Eph. 2:14), making peace (Col. 1:20), and proclaiming peace (Eph. 2:17). The many blessings flowing from this position and experience of peace point to Christ prefigured in the victim **without blemish before the Lord,** with whom the offerer is identified by the imposition of hands.

2-3. Christ's death (**kill it**) and its expiatory value (**sprinkle the blood . . . an offering made by fire**) appear as the means by which God and the sinner meet in peace. God is propitiated; the sinner is reconciled. Both are satisfied in what Christ accomplished redemptively. But the price is **blood** (death) and **fire** (enduring the wrath of God against sin).

5. The peace offering cannot be separated from the burnt offering, for it was offered **on the altar upon the burnt sacrifice.** Salvation and its blessings spring from Christ's complete dedication to God's will, "unto death, even the death of the cross" (Phil. 2:8) in redeeming the fallen race.

Offering of the Flock. 3:6-17. Peace *with* God (justification) is the basis of the peace *of* God, expressed in thanksgiving and fellowship. This constitutes the peace offering in a large sense to be a thank offering (7:11-12) in which the believer shows his gratitude for the "salvation blessings" this offering adumbrates.

4. THE SIN OFFERING. 4:1-35.

The Lord's Second Utterance. 4:1-2. In the LORD's first utterance (1:1-2) out of the glory that filled the completed tabernacle, He gave His directions for the sweet-savor offerings (see their meaning in contrast to the nonsweet-savor offerings, 3:1-2). The last two (nonsweet-savor offerings)—the sin and trespass offerings—are the subject of the second utterance.

The Sin Offering for the Priest. 4:3-12. **3.** The high priest is especially in view, but all the priests were anointed (Exod. 40:15) and evidently were included. The anointed priest, as a representative of the people, occupied a very important position. Hence, his sin brought guilt upon all of them. A young bull **without blemish unto the Lord** was to be brought **for a sin offering.** This offering symbolizes Christ loaded with the believer's sin, absolutely in the sinner's place as a substitute, and not appearing in His own perfection, as in the sweet-savor offerings.

Christ's death is portrayed here symbolically, as in Psalm 22:1-21; Isaiah 53:1-10; Matthew 26:28; and 1 Peter 2:24; 3:18. But though He was "made . . . sin for us" (2 Cor. 5:21), His absolute sinlessness is emphasized (Lev. 6:24-30). The sin offerings for the various classes (priest, congregation, ruler, one of the common people) was in every case expiatory, substitutionary, and completely efficacious (vv. 12, 29, 35). Hence, there was identification of the offerer with his offering (v. 4*a*), death of the victim (v. 4*b*), sprinkling of the blood (vv. 5-7) and its inseparable connection with the burnt offering (vv. 8-10), and the burning of the carcass outside the camp (vv. 11-12).

The latter feature prefigures the cross of Christ pointing to our sin offering. Renouncing anything religious that denies Christ as our sin offering is a going forth to Him "outside the camp" (Judaism then, legalistic Christianity now, Heb. 13:13). The cross of Christ is envisioned symbolically as a new altar in a new place. The redeemed assemble there as believer-priests to offer spiritual sacrifices (Heb. 13:15; 1 Pet. 2:5), utterly rejecting any claim of the least merit in themselves. All merit goes to Him who died for them and bore away all the guilt and penalty of their sin forever.

The Sin-Offering for Others. 4:13-35. Whether for members of the congregation, a ruler, or the common people, the sin offering was efficacious. Sacrifices varied according to the person (*nĕpĕš*, "individual") who sinned. A ruler's sin, involving others more directly, like the priest's sin, was more serious. But irrespective of position, all were sinners and were shut up to the sin offering, as sinners are utterly shut up to the grace of God revealed in Christ.

5. THE TRESPASS OFFERING. 5:1-19.

The Sin Offering for Special Offenses. 5:1-13. Cases that required a sin offering are specified: (1) refusal to testify as a witness (v. 1); (2) contracted ceremonial uncleanness (vv. 2-3; see chaps. 11-15; Num. 19:11-13); and (3) uttering a rash oath (v. 4). Confession of sin was necessary and had to precede the ritual, for the sacrifice looked forward to God's grace and was not a magical means of atonement (vv. 5-6). A supplement (vv. 7-13; cf. 4:27-35) covered the case of the poor who could not afford a costly animal (cf. 1:14-15). See Hebrews 13:10-13.

Trespass Against the Lord. 5:14-19.

This offering looks forward to Christ atoning for the harmful effects of sin, that is, in injury done to God and man. **15.** The offering consisted of an unblemished **ram** (cf. v. 18; 6:6), pointing to the sinless, sin-bearing Savior, who on the cross not only bore the guilt and penalty of man's sin (the sin offering), but also the harmful effects of sin (the trespass offering) both to Himself (**sin ... in the holy things of the Lord**) and to man (6:1-7). Whether the sin is that of omission (v. 15) or commission (v. 17), and done in ignorance, the infinite holiness of God sets the standard; hence, such a trespass cannot be passed over, except as His grace operates to satisfy His infinite holiness.

This occurred at Calvary, where God gained more by redemption than He ever lost by the Fall, for Christ also atoned for the wrong done by sin. He has forgiven us "all trespasses" (Col. 2:13), as well as sin. However, the sin must be confessed, and evidenced by restitution made (one-fifth part, v. 16*a*). Then fellowship with God is restored and shown by forgiveness obtained (v. 16*b*; cf. 1 John 1:5-10). God becomes the gainer by redemption (v. 18), as the fifth part is paid to Him through His representative, the priest, because the trespass was against Him (v. 19).

6. THE LAW OF THE BURNT, MEAL, AND SIN OFFERINGS. 6:1-30.

Trespass Against Man. 6:1-7. These verses actually belong with chapter 5. In this case, restitution plus the addition of a fifth part of the whole were paid to the man defrauded, evidencing confession of sin and forgiveness (restoration to fellowship with God), based on atoning sacrifice (vv. 6-7).

Law of the Burnt Offering. 6:8-13. (See 1:1-17.) Two matters, the disposal of the ashes (v. 11) and the tending of the fire (v. 12*a*), were important, for the animal was totally consumed on the altar. This continual burnt offering, with the divinely kindled fire that burned constantly, pictures Christ presenting Himself before God on our behalf as the One in whom all believers are guaranteed full acceptance. His presence in the heavenly sanctuary is ceaseless and infinitely efficacious. Our answer to the burnt-offering aspect of Christ's redemption work must be full devotion to God's will in imitation of His devotion to death. **12.** The burning of **the fat of the peace offerings** on the altar of burnt offering shows that all the blessings of salvation spring from Christ's death on the cross.

Law of the Meal Offering. 6:14-23. See 2:1-16. **15.** The portion of the meal offering burned upon the altar speaks of the death of Christ and the memorial of that death. This looks forward to the Lord's Supper celebrated by New Testament saints, whom the Old Testament priests typified (1 Cor. 11:25-26). The portion eaten by the priests looks forward to feeding spiritually upon the Christ as the Bread of Life (John 6:53). **16. With unleavened bread shall it be eaten in the holy place.** Only in separation from sin (unleavened) in the *holy* place is the eating of the heavenly bread enjoyed. **19-23.** The priest's offering was to be **wholly burned ... not ... eaten,** prefiguring the truth "that Christ gave Himself, entirely and completely, as the offering. This type refers to the Savior alone, not to His people" (Andrew Bonar, *A Commentary on the Book of Leviticus*, p. 128).

Law of the Sin Offering. 6:24-30. (See 4:1-5, 13.) **25.** The sin offering was to be killed (death of Christ) in the same place the burnt offering was killed, thus emphasizing the supreme importance of the death of Christ and showing that sub-stitutionary atonement cannot be separated from the sinless perfections of the Substitute.

26. The eating of the sin offering by the priest who offered it shows Christ's identification with believing sinners as their sin-bearer. Elaborately set forth and guarded is the supreme holiness of the sin offering. **29.** It was called **most holy.** Although Christ was "made ... sin" (2 Cor. 5:21) as the sin offering, He Himself was absolutely sinless.

7. THE LAW OF THE TRESPASS AND PEACE OFFERINGS. 7:1-38.

The Law of the Trespass Offering. 7:1-10. (See 5:14—6:7.) Since this offering portrays Christ atoning for sin in its harmful effects (i.e., injury done), the animal was always an *unblemished* ram (5:18; 6:6), prefiguring the sinless sin-bearer. **1.** Hence, like the sin offering of which it is a variation, it was also to be regarded **most holy,** again emphasizing the fact that the antitype (Christ) was to be sinless and spotless (Psalm 22:3; Heb. 7:26).

2. Also like the sin offering, it depended upon death (shed blood) as the only means of forgiveness and cleansing. It was inseparable from the burnt offering, prefiguring Christ offering Himself without spot to God in delight to consummate the Father's will, even to death, and so was to be killed **where they kill the burnt offering. 5-9.** The reward for ministering in the priest's office is stressed. Blessings invariably accompany the believer's service for God and spring from Christ's atoning death bringing redemption (the fire offerings).

The Law of the Peace Offering. 7:11-38. See 3:1-17. This offering, which previews all the blessings Christ's salvation brings, is here taken out of its place as the third of the sweet-savor offerings and is placed alone *after* all the nonsweet-smelling offerings. In revealing the offering, the LORD works from Himself out to the sinner (see note in *New Scofield Bible* on Exod. 25:10). First, the whole burnt offering is set forth as what is due the divine requirements. The trespass offering is revealed last as meeting the simplest aspect of sin—its injuriousness.

In contrast, the sinner starts with what lies closest to a newly awakened sense of sin—the realization that he is in a state of enmity against God. He first needs peace with God. It is the order of 2 Corinthians 5:18-21, "the word of reconciliation" (v. 19) first, and then the trespass and sin offerings (v. 21). Experience accordingly reverses the order of revelation.

The peace offering was the only one of the sacrifices of which the offerer was permitted to partake, for it represented all the benefits of his salvation. Consequently, the LORD's portion (the fat, considered the best and burned on the altar) was specified (vv. 22-25); the priest's portion was the **breast** and **thigh** (vv. 30-34, NASB). The rest was the portion of the offerer. However, no *fat* (vv. 23-25) or *blood* (vv. 26-27) was to be eaten, under penalty of excommunication. "The unique excellence which attaches to the Person of Christ is very jealously guarded by God, and also the unique value of His blood as making atonement" (C. A. Coates, *An Outline of the Book of Leviticus*, p. 94).

The note of thanksgiving and joyous fellowship (v. 12) is prominent in this offering and looks forward to the Lord's Supper (1 Cor. 10:16—11:32), recalling the blessings of salvation. The unleavened cakes (v. 12) point to the perfect sinless humanity of Christ and His glorious person as the God-man. The leavened bread (v. 13) points to the fact that, though we are redeemed, we still have an old nature and so cannot say we are sinless (1 John 1:8).

Peace with God for the justified believer, opening up the experience of the peace of God in joyous communion and thanksgiving, is the preeminent emphasis of this offering, all the blessed details of which center in the finished redemptive work of Christ. Significantly, the divine origin of the laws of the offerings is emphasized (vv. 35-38).

B. ACCESS TO GOD: BY PRIESTHOOD. 8:1—9:24.

1. CONSECRATION OF THE PRIESTHOOD. 8:1-36.

The Consecration. 8:1-13. (See Exod. 29:1-46.) Since access to God is the subject of the first half of Leviticus (chaps. 1-16), and that access is based upon the offerings reflecting the person and work of Christ in redemption (chaps. 1-7), resulting in the priesthood of the believer, the latter subject is now introduced in its typical connotations (chaps. 8-9).

Aaron appears throughout as foreshadowing Christ, while his sons speak of individual believers of this age. Their priesthood was dependent upon their relation to Aaron, as ours is based on our relation to Christ. The repetition of this consecration (cf. Exod. 28:1—29:46) emphasizes the importance of the priesthood in all access to God and particularly to the access of the New Testament believer to God, a doctrine resurrected by Luther and the Protestant Reformation.

6-12. Three things were done in consecrating the priests: (1) They were **washed** (v. 6), symbolizing regeneration (John 13:2-11; Titus 3:5; Heb. 10:22; see comments on Exod. 29:1-4). (2) They were **clothed** (vv. 7-9; see Exod. 28:1-43). (3) They were **anointed** (vv.

10-12; see Exod. 29:5-25). The high priest as a prefigurement of Christ is differentiated from the regular priests' prefigurement of believers in two pivotal aspects. The high priest was anointed *before* the consecration sacrifices were killed, in striking contrast to the priests, in whose case the application of the sacrificial blood preceded the anointing.

As the sinless One, Christ of course required no cleansing from sin in preparation for the anointing oil (the Holy Spirit). Moreover, only upon the high priest was the anointing oil **poured** (v. 12), for only upon Christ's spotless humanity could the Holy Spirit have been outpoured in immeasurable fullness (John 3:34; Heb. 1:9).

The Offerings of Consecration. 8:14-30. Featured was the sin offering (vv. 14-17), setting forth Christ symbolically burdened with the believer's sin, standing absolutely in the sinner's place, by His death removing the guilt and penalty of sin forever (see 4:1-35; 6:25-30). Also featured was the burnt offering (vv. 18-21), looking forward to Christ offering Himself spotlessly to God in delight to fulfill the divine will even to death (1:1-17; 6:8-13).

Also offered was a consecration offering, a ram (vv. 22-29), which is the only sacrifice not mentioned previously. It shows that *all* believer-priests are to voluntarily dedicate *their bodies* to God because of His "mercies" in redemption (Rom. 12:1-2). **23-24.** This is beautifully set forth by Moses applying the blood of the ram of consecration to the **ear ... thumb ... and ... great toe** of Aaron and his sons.

Next the priests' hands were filled (vv. 27-29). "To fill the hands" is the technical term for investing with office (lit., *millŭ'îm*, "fillings"; cf. Exod.

29:24). The priestly ministrations were to be performed with the hands; so they were *filled* with the fat, the choice parts of the sacrifice, unleavened bread, and so forth, all of which speak of the person and finished work of Christ. Then that which filled their hands was burned, speaking of Christ's death, the basis of the priestly believers' consecration and ministration. Then Moses anointed the priests and their garments (v. 30).

The Sacrificial Feast. 8:31-36. The eating of the sacrifices and the bread illustrates the necessity of believer-priests feeding upon Christ (John 6:50-55) and remembering the benefits of His death through partaking of the Lord's table (1 Cor. 11:25-27). The seven-day span of the feast may envision this present age, when a heavenly priesthood (the church) is spiritually feasting on Christ.

2. THE PRIESTS' MINISTRY. 9:1-24.

Inaugurating the Priestly Ministry. 9:1-22. **1.** The priests began their ministry **on the eighth day** after the week of priestly ordination (8:1-36). Apparently the priestly position of believers in this age is prophetically portrayed, followed by a series of new offerings of the priests in which the future priesthood of converted Israel, as a high-priestly nation, is prefigured (cf. Zech. 3:1-10).

The eighth day seems to represent the Kingdom age when Christ as King-Priest at His second advent will appear in glory to His people Israel, and they will become what they were destined to be: "a kingdom of priests, and an holy nation" (Exod. 19:6; cf. Zech. 3:1-10; Isa. 61:6). The sin offering, burnt offering, peace offerings, and meal offering demonstrate that this future restoration of the Kingdom to Israel (Acts 1:6) will be on the basis of Christ's sacrificial work on the cross during His first advent

157

(vv. 5-22; cf. Zech. 12:10—13:1; Rom. 11:25-36).

The Divine Glory Manifested. 9:23-24. **22.** After all the sacrifices had been offered, Aaron blessed the people, very probably with the words recorded in Numbers 6:22-27. When all that Christ has wrought for us redemptively is appropriated, nothing but blessing can result. **23.** Then **Aaron and Moses went into the tabernacle.** Afterward they **came out, and blessed the people** the second time, as Christ will do to Israel at His second coming.

Moses as leader (king) and Aaron as priest foreshadow Christ's second advent in the dual role of King-Priest (cf. Zech. 6:9-15). This will mean glory for God, for Israel, and for all the earth in the coming Kingdom age. **24.** The divine glory will be revealed to all peoples, as when falling upon the altar it **consumed ... the burnt offering and the fat** (the LORD's portion). God's plan for Israel and the nations (as well as the church) will be prophetically accomplished on the basis of redemptive sacrifice.

C. ACCESS TO GOD: BY PRIESTLY OBEDIENCE. 10:1-20.

Punishment of Sacrilege. 10:1-11. **1. Nadab and Abihu,** the two older of Aaron's four sons, committed a very serious sin in acting in the things of God without ascertaining the mind of God. The **strange fire** was fire they kindled in self-will on the altar of incense by some means they had devised, instead of by God Himself (cf. 1 Kings 18:38-39) or by His direction.

Apparently it was the LORD's intention to kindle the fire Himself, as He had done on the altar of burnt offering (9:24), the flame of which the priests were to feed perpetually (6:12-13). The elaborate detail regulating every facet of the tabernacle, offerings, and priesthood

(Exod. 20:1—Lev. 9:24) should have been warning enough that in the revelation of God's way of access to and fellowship with Himself there is no room for self-will on the part of lost, defiled humanity.

2. Fire from the Lord (cf. 9:24), which doubtlessly would have ignited the incense at the proper moment, struck the two priests dead for their flagrant "will-worship" (Col. 2:23). Theirs was a presumptuous sin unto physical death (cf. Acts 5:5-6, 10; 1 Cor. 5:1-5; 11:29-30; 1 John 5:16). It was official, hence serious. The incident comprehends any unscriptural means used to kindle religious fervor, a sin so prevalent today.

The seriousness of the sin is indicated (1) by the sudden death of the guilty; (2) by the declaration that in the penalty exacted, God's holiness was guarded against sacrilege and He was glorified before the people (v. 3); (3) by Aaron's holding his peace (v. 3); (4) by the quick removal of their bodies in their priestly dress out of the camp (v. 4); (5) by the strict prohibition not to mourn for them (v. 6); and (6) the command to remain in the tabernacle under pain of death.

7. The anointing oil was upon them, typical of the Holy Spirit empowering and blessing believer-priests in priestly service and worship. His ministry is not to be vitiated by alien spirits that energize the will worship that Nadab and Abihu thought to initiate (cf. 1 Tim. 4:1-2; 1 John 4:1-2). Demonic powers not only operate in false prophets but also in false priests. **8-11.** The appended command against intoxicating liquor may well offer a clue at least to part of the reason for Nadab's and Abihu's failure.

The Priesthood Encouraged. 10:12-15. **12-15.** Moses assured Aaron and the remaining priests in the face of the terrible judgment that had been visited on their house. Man may fail; God never! Believer-priests may be unfaithful; God remains faithful (2 Tim. 2:13). He gives eternal life; He never takes it away. He saves through the merits of Christ, removes all human demerit, and guarantees heaven by grace and grace alone.

Therefore, the priests were to go on with their priestly duties and appropriate their priestly dues and blessings. The person and redemptive work of Christ, pictured in the sacrificial offerings, were to be their encouragement and hope. Believer-priests are to feed on Christ and enjoy the blessings that are theirs in Him, undiscouraged by others' failure and chastening.

Failure Forgiven. 10:16-20. This entire chapter is clearly intended by the Holy Spirit to be a detailed and emphatic warning, not only against will worship (Nadab and Abihu), but also against ignoring or setting aside the Word of God in *any* matter of priestly faith and practice. Moses, "faithful in all his house" (Heb. 3:2), displayed great zeal in this matter for God's honor. **16. He diligently sought the goat of the sin offering.** It should not have been burned, but eaten (6:26-30).

17. Besides, Moses perceived that by this deviation from the prescribed order they had lost a privilege—**seeing it is most holy, and God hath given it you,** and meant to be a token of God's kindness and tenderness at such a time of sorrow and bereavement. As no blood had been taken into the sanctuary, there was no reason why the flesh of the sin offering should not have been eaten (9:15).

Moses construed the laws concerning the sacrifices with characteristic literalness. Aaron knew the laws but approved the delicacy shown by his sons in foregoing their privilege on a day when the

LORD's judgment was so signally visited upon their brothers. **20.** Moses showed his appreciation of Aaron's comprehension of the spirit of the sacrificial laws as well as the letter and **was content.**

D. ACCESS TO GOD: BY AVOIDING DEFILEMENT. 11:1—15:33.

Up to this point the theme of Leviticus has been atonement. But atonement and the salvation prefigured can only be appreciated and appropriated by those who realize man is lost, utterly sinful, and utterly unable to save himself. So this section deals with sin—its existence in the world around us, its transmission (chap. 12), its vileness (chap. 13), its cleansing (chap. 14), and its utter deformity (chap. 15). A sinful world is totally shut up to redemption through Christ.

1. A HOLY PEOPLE—THEIR FOOD. 11:1-47.

Clean and Unclean Food. 11:1-23. In this section (chaps. 11-15) the laws regarding uncleanness are set forth. Redemption through Christ's death (chaps. 1-7), constituting us a holy priesthood (chaps. 8-10), requires a holy walk in separation from that which is "unclean" (defiled). This is the conspicuous word in this group of chapters, occurring more than one hundred times. The detailed emphasis on the ceremonial is meant to stress the necessity of moral separation, not only for Old Testament saints, who were called to be "a kingdom of priests" and a "holy nation" (Exod. 19:6), but also for New Testament saints called to holiness (2 Cor. 7:1).

The Mosaic Law was a schoolmaster to drill unforgettable lessons into the student, often employing symbolisms and visual aids (cf. Gal. 3:24). Such is the case here in the distinction between clean and unclean food. The purpose is to create a loathing of polluting sin so that the sinner may through atonement approach God and the believer through atonement may keep away from sin to maintain fellowship with God.

Four classes of animals are presented: (1) *Quadrupeds* (vv. 2-8). Only those animals that divided the hoof and chewed the cud could be eaten. Animals not meeting the requirements are listed (camel, rock badger, hare, and swine). (2) *Sea food* (vv. 9-12). Only fish with fins and scales could be eaten, ruling out eels, shell fish, crabs, lobsters, oysters, and so forth. (3) *Birds* (vv. 13-19; cf. Deut. 14:11 for "clean" birds). The list is completely negative. (4) *Insects* (vv. 20-23). All winged insects that go on all fours are banned (i.e., those that walk or crawl like a quadruped, for *six* legs are characteristic of insects), except for four classes of the locust family, with large jumping legs.

Though there was nothing morally different between one beast and another or one insect and another, God put a difference between them that the people had to regard. In this way, constantly and in every facet of life, they were to be taught God's discernment of sin, the stigma He set upon it, and the necessity of atonement for it and separation from it.

Defilement by a Dead Body. 11:24-42. Death defiled a person because it was connected with sin, the Fall, divine wrath, and the curse (Gen. 2:17; 3:19). Again the Law, using the effective teaching device of visual aid and vivid symbolic illustration, drives home a very necessary truth: he who approaches, communes with, and serves "the *living* God" must be "cleansed" from "*dead* works" (Heb. 9:14, italics added).

Sin is not only all around us as that which we may commit either consciously or unconsciously, so that we must continually be reminded to differentiate between the clean and unclean (the lesson brought by taboo foods, vv. 1-23), but it lurks all around us in order to defile us by touch and unconscious contact. Death is therefore illustrative of that which is purely in the natural realm and has no place in the experience of one who is redeemed and has access to the *living* God.

The man defiled by the touch of death (vv. 25-27) represents a sinner's state. **28.** His washing symbolizes employing the appointed cleansing, typically in the sacrifices, antitypically in Christ's death. Waiting **until the evening,** before the effects of death and sin are annulled, represents the justified believer, fully aware of his cleansed state, yet also conscious of the old nature and its proneness to sin in a body not yet glorified and made sinless. Verses 29 to 38 enlarge upon verses 20 to 23 and emphasize how subtle sin is and how its defiling nature must be meticulously avoided.

The Necessity of Holiness. 11:43-47. Man's relation to the animal kingdom, over which he was given dominion, is followed by a call to holiness (separation from the unclean and separation to the Holy One of Israel). Why? (1) I am your Creator-Redeemer, your God (Creator), the LORD (Redeemer), who brought you out of the land of Egypt; and (2) I am holy. "Ye shall therefore be holy, for I am holy" (cf. 1 Pet. 1:15-17). This is the reason for the detailed (almost wearisome) distinctions in this chapter, which are summarized in verses 46 and 47.

2. A HOLY PEOPLE—CHILDBIRTH. 12:1-8.

Childbirth and Uncleanness. 12:1-5. **1-3.** The LORD declared through Moses that a woman was made unclean by the birth of a child, because the child was born in sin, transmitted from its forebears in Adam (Psalm 51:5; Rom. 5:19; cf. Isa. 43:27). On **the eighth day** a male child was to be **circumcised.** Iniquity was imputed to the mother for having brought a sinner into the world.

4. After the boy was circumcised (received into the covenant with Abraham's God, Gen. 17:9-14), her imputed sin was reckoned removed in some degree. But although she shared to some extent in the benefits her child received from the covenant of circumcision, she was not to touch anything hallowed or walk on holy ground for thirty-three days. How deeply must the lesson of his depravity been impressed upon the child when in later days his mother told him of her forty-day defilement.

5. Birth of a female child rendered the mother unclean double the time period of the male child. The reason in part was probably because "the woman . . . was in the transgression" (1 Tim. 2:14) and led Adam into it. The regulation kept alive the memory of the Fall and the first sin. Christ's salvation removes such restrictions because it takes away the curse of sin (Gal. 3-13, 28).

Removal of the Uncleanness. 12:6-8. The mother's sin, brought to the altar at the termination of the forty- or eighty-day period, was to be atoned for by a yearling lamb for a burnt offering and a fowl for a sin offering, or two fowls if she was poor and could not afford a lamb, as in the case of Mary, mother of our Lord (Luke 2:23-24). The pigeon or turtle dove was emblematic of the child's tender years and apparent innocence, though guilt lay hidden within. How eloquently was the mother taught that her infant needed cleansing in redeeming blood. Then the mother returned home rejoicing, to train her child in

God's ways for the LORD, who had accepted her, and had taken her pledge that she would rear her offspring for Him.

3. A HOLY PEOPLE—LEPROSY. 13:1-59.

Recognizing Leprosy. 13:1-44. Leprosy, a common and much dreaded disease of the Orient, forms a graphic illustration of indwelling sin working through the old nature (Matt. 15:19). Particularly emphasized is its horrid features as manifested in the believer (Rom. 6:12-14; 1 John 1:8) when he yields to the flesh and fails to confess his sin in self-judgment and claim cleansing (1 John 1:9).

1. The Lord spoke to Moses. Leprosy has been divinely chosen to become a classic symbol of sin because of its loathsome manifestations, its progressive character, the separation of its victims from association with their fellows, and its being incurable by human means. Leprosy represents "the breaking out of the lawlessness of the flesh in acts or words so as to call for priestly discernment and pronounced judgment of the saints. It renders one unfit to occupy one's tent, or to partake in the privileges of the congregation of God" (Coates, *Outline of . . . Leviticus*, p. 140).

The detailed typical instruction with which such a condition is set forth shows how varied and common is the leprosy of sin among God's people. In fact, leprosy in the Bible includes a broader range of skin diseases (see note on Matt. 8:2, NIV). Moreover, the account emphasizes the fact that the LORD wanted His priests to be skilled in the ability to discern and deal with it, as it cropped up, and to be qualified to render all the service needed for cleansing when divine mercy had effected healing.

17-44. From a general diagnosis (vv. 1-17), three specific cases are considered: (1) leprosy arising from a **boil** (vv. 18-23); (2) leprosy from a **burn** (vv. 24-28); and (3) leprosy on the **head** or **beard** (vv. 29-44). The first two categories refer to such manifestations of indwelling sin working through the old nature as bad temper, jealousy, ill-will, malice, and so forth. Such manifestations may be short-lived and not serious, so as not to be classified as leprous. Then again, they may increase, generate hatred, and become an extreme threat to the welfare of God's people, and so they are to be diagnosed as leprosy. In such a case the saint was to be quarantined till healing by God and cleansing by the priest were effected.

It is noteworthy that only in connection with leprosy in **the head** (v. 30) was the man declared **utterly unclean** (v. 44). This graphically demonstrates that the will of the flesh, taking form in thoughts and teaching, constitutes the most serious manifestation of leprosy. Head leprosy is frighteningly common today—wrong thoughts of God, Christ, the Holy Spirit, the gospel of grace, salvation, and so forth. Much of this is the result of human infirmity and ignorance, but a great deal of it is purely demonic!

The Plight of the Leper. 13:45-46. What a picture the leper is of how giving in willfully to the old nature reduces a believer to a pitiable state of defilement, tragedy, and isolation from God's people (cf. 1 Cor. 5:5). But still the leper was to be the subject of priestly solicitude and care. His tent was a perpetual reminder that he was of the LORD's people. The spirit of chapters 13 and 14 is that there would always be the desire that the leper might be healed, cleansed, and restored to his tent and his privileges among the redeemed.

Leprosy in Garments. 13:47-59. **47-50.** The symbolism here represents sin working not exactly in the believer, but as closely identified with his person, such as his possessions, occupation, habits, or associations. In such a case the believer was not leprous, but his **garment** lay under suspicion and had to be **shown unto the priest.** What an illustration of the care that must be taken by a believer to avoid inlets to sin as to where he permits himself to go or what he allows himself to do, or what associations and alliances he permits himself to make.

52. Any garment tainted with leprosy was to be **burned in the fire**, illustrating how rigidly sin is to be put away in a believer's associations. The people of God are to "cleanse" themselves "from all filthiness of the flesh and spirit, perfecting holiness in the fear of God" (2 Cor. 7:1). They are to hate "even the garment spotted by the flesh" (Jude 23), and keep themselves "unspotted from the world" (James 1:27). Any habit or association hindering fellowship with God should be subject to priestly scrutiny and care and put away as leprous and burned in the fire.

4. A HOLY PEOPLE—CLEANSING FROM LEPROSY. 14:1-57.

God's Cleansing. 14:1-8. The cleansing ritual assumed that the leper had been healed by God. The type presents a beautiful illustration of the gospel of grace: (1) The leper does nothing but believe, shown by his submission to the cleansing ritual (Rom. 4:4-5), all of which points to the person and redemptive work of Christ. (2) The priest seeks the leper (vv. 2-4), not the leper the priest (Luke 19:10). (3) The cleansing is based upon the death (the bird killed) and resurrection of Christ (the bird dipped in blood and let loose, vv. 4-7), presenting our Lord in two aspects—"delivered for our offenses, and . . . raised again for our justification"(Rom. 4:25).

It was the blood that purified from the leprosy of sin (1 John 1:7), both in positional purification at regeneration and in experiential purification by confession of sin and holy living. The living bird in its upward flight bore the blood heavenward upon its outstretched wings as the badge of a finished redemptive work (Heb. 9:22).

The blood of the slain bird (typifying the atoning blood of Christ) was sprinkled with hyssop (denoting appropriating faith, Exod. 12:22), evidently bound by a scarlet cord (denoting faith in the blood) with cedar wood (Num. 19:6; Heb. 9:19), perhaps suggesting the preservative qualities and keeping power of God's salvation (vv. 4, 49-52). The earthen vessel in which the one bird was slain suggests Christ's humanity, and the running water typifies the Holy Spirit as "the Spirit of life" (Rom. 8:2; cf. 1 Pet. 3:18; John 7:37-39).

The Believer's Cleansing Himself. 14:9-20. God's cleansing (vv. 1-7) is to be followed by the believer's cleansing himself, which he does by separating himself and keeping separate from sin, thus giving evidence of the reality of his faith in God's cleansing (cf. 2 Cor. 7:1). The second part of the ritual, performed the next day within the camp, required that after seven days of isolation, the recovered leper was to shave off all his hair and wash his clothes and flesh (v. 9).

On the eighth day he was to offer the following sacrifices as evidence that his faith in God's cleansing was not a mere ritual routine, but that *he was cooperating with God in cleansing himself* from the leprosy of sin: (1) a male lamb for a guilt offering, along with meal and oil; (2) a ewe lamb for a sin offering; (3) a male lamb with flour for a burnt and meal offering (see chaps. 1-7). The application of blood (v. 14) to the tip of the right ear, right thumb, and great toe of the right foot typify that the cleansed man, as a believer, must learn anew to listen to God's commandments and walk in His will.

Concession to the Poor. 14:21-32. For the poor, doves were substituted for animals, and less flour was prescribed. God's grace excludes no sinner, however poor. "Whosoever will may come" (Rev. 22:17). "Whosoever believeth in him shall not perish, but have everlasting life" (John 3:16).

Leprosy in Homes. 14:33-53. How practical this section is in a day when the leprosy of sin is attempting to destroy the family and the home on a colossal scale. When a house was suspected of being leprous, it was to be vacated and sealed for a week (vv. 33-38). If, on further inspection, the infection was still there, the mortar was to be scraped off and the stones removed (vv. 39-42). If the leprosy taint reappeared, the house was condemned. The ritual for its cleansing was identical with that for the leper (vv. 4-7, 49-53).

Importance of the Law of Leprosy. 14:54-57. The law of leprosy was designed to emphasize what is clean and unclean in the eyes of the infinitely holiness of God, and to warn *both* sinner and saint concerning the heinousness of sin.

5. A HOLY PEOPLE—PERSONAL DEFILEMENT. 15:1-33.

Man's Uncleanness. 15:1-18. **1-2.** A holy God, demanding a holy people, gave directions for cleansing from bodily secretions. called **a running issue out of . . . his flesh.** Represented symbolically are those defiling things of what we are naturally. This chapter presents the converse of chapter 11. There most meticulous directions are given as to what may be eaten in connection with clean and unclean food, that is, what we receive into our moral being. Here the emphasis is on the defiling things that come out of us (cf. Matt. 15:19-20).

The lesson is that if we would maintain moral purity consonant with God's tabernacle (cf. v. 31), there must be rigid control of manifestations of what we are naturally. We have a new nature, it is true, but we are still possessed of the old Adamic nature. All the bodily secretions mentioned (vv. 3, 16-18), both voluntary and involuntary, normal as well as pathological, evidence the inveterate sin inherent in the flesh in human nature, even in redeemed humanity.

14-15. Revealed is the utter necessity of continual cleansing by water (the Word of God, see vv. 5, 6, 7, 8, 10, 11, 12, 13, etc.) on the basis of the shed blood of Christ (1 John 1:9). Believers must learn, if they are to retain liberty in what is spiritual, that they must maintain restraint in what is natural.

Woman's Uncleanness. 15:19-33. Fallen human nature is hopelessly defiled. God's Word holds up a faithful mirror to proud humanity. Nothing is left for the flesh to boast of before an infinitely holy God. Woman, like man, is defiled, even in the secret involuntary operation of the flesh. A vivid New Testament photograph is the woman with the bloody issue (Matt. 9:20-22).

19-27. The striking feature of human defilement is that not only the person is defiled, but that everything a person touches or contacts is defiled. **28-30.** How *important*, therefore, is cleansing by the Word in appropriation of the finished work of Christ (John 13:10; 1 John 1:9) if we would not be defiled our-selves and constantly defile others.

E. ACCESS TO GOD: BY ATONEMENT. 16:1-34.

Importance. 16:1-2. The Day of Atonement (23:27-32; 25:9) is the most important of all the holy ordinances presented in Leviticus, the climax of access to God under the old covenant. It was on that day that an atonement ("covering") was made for *all* the sins of *all* the congregation of Israel. **1. The Lord spoke unto Moses**, indicating the *divine* institution of this significant ritual. The time of the divine communication through Moses accents the utter need for atonement—**after the death of the two sons of Aaron** (cf. 10:1-2), when serious failure in the priesthood highlighted the sinfulness of man in the flesh.

2a. The unfitness of fallen man to approach God is further demonstrated in the declaration that even Aaron, the high priest himself, was not to enter the holiest place except at the *one* appointed time yearly, **that he die not. 2b.** Another indication of man's desperate need for atonement appears in the LORD's declaration, **I will appear in the cloud upon the mercy seat.** The LORD is there in His holy, unapproachable light, before which polluted sinful man with his unatoned sin cannot stand (1 Tim. 6:16).

The question raised by the ritual concerns the grounds on which a sinful priesthood and congregation can be with God in having His dwelling among them in infinite holiness. The question was typically raised and answered "once a year" for Israel, but the repetition of it year after year showed that the question was not really settled. It could not be settled until the greater Aaron appeared, entering the holiest with His own blood to obtain eternal redemption for us (Heb. 9:9-12, 24-26; 10:3-4).

The Atonement-Portraying Ritual.
16:3-10. **3-4.** Aaron did not enter the sanctuary to make atonement in the "garments ... for glory and beauty" (Exod. 28:2-38), which set forth Christ as the One who, having died and rose again, ever lives in God's presence to make intercession for us (Heb. 7:25), but in the simple white linen **holy garments.** These bespeak the personal holiness of "Jesus Christ the righteous" (1 John 2:1-2), the predicted "Holy One" (Psalm 16:10), whom Peter called "the Holy One of God" (John 6:69, NASB).

Expiation of sin in priestly activity in atoning (covering) sin is in view here. Therefore, Aaron washed himself in water. He was a sinner needing cleansing, in contrast to our sinless High Priest, who did not need it. Nevertheless, Christ submitted to baptism in order to identify Himself with sinners (Matt. 3:13-17) as He entered upon His mediatorial ministry as Priest, prophetically looking forward to His own death and resurrection, which alone could "fulfill all righteousness" (Matt. 3:15).

3-6. Aaron offered a **bullock for a sin offering** that was **for himself, and for his house,** the ground of expiatory blessing for the priestly family (antitypically the church as associated with Christ). By contrast, he took **two kids of the goats for a sin offering** for **the congregation of the children of Israel** (antitypically the nation Israel in the coming Kingdom age, but the value of which is also known by church saints).

7-8. Lots were cast for the goats. **9.** The **Lord's lot** was the goat that was slain, portraying the expiatory aspect of Christ's death that vindicates the holiness and righteousness of God as expressed in the Law (Rom. 3:24-26), realized by church saints first, but particularly applicable to Israel when they will believe on the Messiah at His sec-

ond advent (Isa. 53:1-10).

10. The scapegoat ... presented alive before the Lord ... (and) **let ... go ... into the wilderness** typifies that aspect of Christ's work that puts away our sins from before God, but with special focus upon Israel's sins at the second advent (Heb. 9:26; Rom. 8:33-34; 11:26-36). Verses 6-10 apparently are a general statement, followed by the details.

The offering of the bullock for the priestly family (vv. 11-14) came before the offering of the goats for Israel (vv. 15-19), even as the blessings of Israel will come in *after* the blessing of the church (cf. Heb. 11:10, 40). Whether the heavenly blessing of the church or the earthly blessing of millennial Israel, all is secured by the atoning work of Christ as the High Priest and sacrifice (Heb. 9:1-14).

Atonement for Aaron's House.
16:11-14. **11-12.** After the sin offering was killed (stressing the utter necessity of the death of Christ for the expiation of our sin), Aaron took **a censer full of burning coals of fire** (cf. Isa. 6:6-7) **from off the altar** of incense **before the Lord,** and with **his hands full of sweet incense beaten small** (cf. Exod. 30:34-38) he went **within the veil** (the holiest place).

13. There he put **the incense upon the fire before the Lord.** The resulting **cloud of incense** covering the Mercy Seat represents the sweet aroma of Christ's infinitely fragrant life of obedience to death Godward when tested to the utmost possible degree by the holy fire of suffering, pain, death, and the divine wrath against sin (Psalms 22:1-21; 40:6-12; Isa. 53:1-12; Matt. 26:36—27:53). The incense cloud covering the Mercy Seat betokens God's delight in His beloved Son in manhood satisfying all the claims of the divine glory with regard to sin.

It is understandable how the cloud of incense preserved Aaron from death.

The man after the flesh, even when represented by Israel's high priest, cannot live in God's presence. He is displaced by another, whose merits and perfections are reckoned to him on the basis of atonement. **14.** The blood of the bullock was then sprinkled in front of the Mercy Seat and **before the mercy seat ... seven times** (*full* expiation). Only the blood of the sin offering was brought into the Holy of Holies, to assure us of the removal of all sin and our access into God's very presence.

Atonement for Israel. 16:15-28. **15.** Likewise, **the goat of the sin offering** was killed for the people of Israel (cf. v. 5). The blood was sprinkled **upon the mercy seat, and before the mercy seat.** This is Israel's great Yom Kippur, when the pierced One (Zech. 12:10) is revealed to them and Christ's salvation comes to the nation (Zech. 12:10—13:1). **16.** Then all that the Day of Atonement looks forward to will be realized when Israel enters into the blessings springing from the **atonement for the holy place** wrought by Christ. There **the uncleanness** of Israel and **their transgressions in all their sins** will be washed away and the nation saved (Rom. 11:26-32). **17.** No one except the high priest was to be in the tabernacle when he went into the Holy of Holies to make atonement. It was to be evident that the high priest *alone* made atonement and *none* else, looking to one great High Priest, who alone would accomplish *eternal* redemption (Heb. 9:12). **18.** Aaron's leaving the Holy of Holies to go out **unto the altar** to cleanse it prefigures Christ *in* His second advent when He will come out to Israel and they will be converted and restored. The altar cleansed was most likely the altar of burnt offering, which had so much connection with sin. The cleansed altar advertised that Christ continues sinless.

Now Christ is still in the holiest. Meanwhile, believers of the church age, as a holy priesthood, enter into the Holy of Holies where He is (Heb. 10:19-22; 1 Pet. 2:9).

Having reconciled the holy place, the tabernacle, and the altar, Aaron sent forth the scapegoat into the wilderness, after laying his hands on the goat's head and confessing the sins of Israel upon it. This prefigures Israel's entering into the blessing of Christ's vicarious substitutionary atonement when they will believe in the Savior at His second coming. The *scapegoat* (vv. 8-10, 16-20; cf. Isa. 53:4-6) is best interpreted to stem from the root *'āzăl* ("to remove") and *'ªzāzēl*, signifying "a removal" (of sin).

23-24. Aaron's putting off his white linen garments and donning *his* glorious **garments**, his splendid high-priestly regalia (cf. Exod. 28:3-38), portrays Christ in resurrection and His present priestly intercession in heaven, after having done away with sin in putting it away by the sacrifice of Himself—a type of Jesus laying aside the likeness of sinful flesh and ceasing from all connection with sin. In His redemptive glory He will appear to Israel as their Savior, sin-bearer, and glorious King. **27-28.** Eternal redemption having typically been illustrated and accomplished, all relics of the type were removed.

Israel's Hope in Christ's Redemption. 16:29-34. **29-34.** Yom Kippur, the Day of Atonement, on the tenth day of the seventh month (Sept./Oct.) was to be a most solemn time of self-affliction, mourning, and absolute refraining from all work. It was to be **a statute forever ... an everlasting statute**, a permanent reminder of their sinfulness and lost estate before God and their utter need of divine redemption, which alone could bring them true rest. Thus, the day is referred to as **a sabbath of rest** ("sabbath of sabbaths"), "a sabbath of solemn rest" (NASB), looking forward to Him who alone could say, "Come unto me, all ye that labor and are heavy laden, and I will give you rest" (Matt. 11:28). One day regathered and saved Israel will experience that "sabbath of solemn rest" in the restored Kingdom (Acts 1:6; Rev. 20:4-9).

II. FELLOWSHIP WITH GOD. 17:1—27:34.

Access to God through sacrifice, priesthood, and atonement (chaps. 1-16) opens up the way to fellowship with God. Since the way to fellowship with God is holiness of life, the dominant note of this section is holiness to the LORD. "Ye shall be holy; for I, the LORD your God, am holy" (19:2; cf. 11:44-45; 1 Pet. 1:16).

A. FELLOWSHIP WITH GOD: BY SEPARATION FROM SIN. 17:1—22:33.

Various regulations concerning the place of sacrifice and the sanctity of blood (chap. 17), the personal relationships of the redeemed people (chaps. 18-20), and the priesthood (chaps. 21-22) are set forth.

1. WARNING AGAINST IDOLATROUS TAINT. 17:1-16.

Regulation Concerning Animal Food. 17:1-9. **3-6.** Warning was given against pagan practices concerning eating meat. All animals slaughtered (such as oxen, sheep, or goats) were to be brought to the LORD at the tabernacle and sacrificed as **peace offerings unto the Lord.** This speaks of fellowship with God in the things we enjoy. (After the central altar was established, killing animals at home was permitted, cf. Deut. 12:15.) Idolatry breaks that fellowship and runs the risk of fellowship with demons (cf. 1 Cor. 10:14-22).

For a man to kill an animal without bringing it to the tabernacle meant he was going to have a feast in which God had no part. **He hath shed blood** was reminiscent of redemption (chap. 16), but with no thought of God. Such an act was tantamount to murder and was so serious that it merited being excommunicated from God's people. There was no sacrificial character to an animal slaughtered apart from the altar, for it did not speak of atonement or of Christ at all. Rather, it only represented that which God had given providentially being used for self-gratification.

7-9. It was sacrificing to **demons** (*śe'îrîm*, "goat-gods, satyrs"), evil spirits that empower idolatry (1 Cor. 10:20). So important was this to fellowship with God and His people that it was to be a **statute forever**, both for Israelites and sojourners.

Regulations Guarding the Sanctity of Blood. 17:10-16. The commandment against eating blood was renewed. First given to Noah (Gen. 9:4), it was repeated in Leviticus 3:17 and 7:26. The reason was stated: **11. The life of the flesh is in the blood.** When poured out, it shows atonement, for it expresses the life taken. But why is life taken? Why is death required? Because, in essence, sin is an attack on God's holy throne and His very existence. It is, therefore, repelled by God by crushing the sinner's life. Jesus bore even this for man. "You killed the Prince of Life" (Acts 3:15, BV). However, when our Lord fulfilled the type, He abrogated that law (John 6:53). We *live* by blood now, as we drink the poured-out life of the Son of Man.

13-14. Even the hunter had to reverence the blood that spoke of God's atonement for man, reverently pouring out the blood of an animal before the LORD and covering it from the unholy gaze of men or the voracity of other beasts. If anyone ate of any animal from which the blood was not properly drained, he was unclean. He had to wash his clothes and his person, and remain unclean until evening. If he failed to wash, he incurred guilt (cf. Acts 15:20).

2. UNHOLY PRACTICES FORBIDDEN. 18:1-30.

Holiness of Life Prescribed. 18:1-5. The basis of the holiness required was the LORD's holiness. The words "I am the LORD your God" and "You shall be holy, for I the LORD your God am holy" occur over and over again in chapters 18-22. **3-5.** The practices of Egypt, where Israel had dwelt, and the practices of Canaan, to which God promised to bring them, were honeycombed with idolatry and immorality. Hence, Israel was to be separated from this iniquity and devoted to the LORD their God.

Unnatural Marital Unions. 18:6-18. Impurity of life was clearly specified. **6.** First considered were unnatural unions, introduced with the general injunction: **None of you shall approach to any that is near of kin to him.** The idiom **uncover the nakedness of** means "to have marital relations with." The list begins with the nearest kinships and closes with the most remote. **7-11.** The first five relationships comprise mother, stepmother, sister, granddaughter, and half sister.

12-18. The second five include aunt, daughter-in-law, sister-in-law; a woman and her daughter or granddaughter; and a wife's sister (while the wife is still living). The last instance suggests that "uncover the nakedness of" refers to actual marriage and marital union. Adultery would come under that heading and be condemned as such (Deut. 22:13-30). The use of such an expres-sion, instead of the usual phrase "to take a wife," probably stresses the fact that such unions cannot be true marriage and are the result of passion rather than holy affection.

Avoiding Uncleanness in Sexual Intercourse. 18:19. This law apparently concerns a husband who was prohibited from intercourse with a woman (his wife) during the period of uncleanness, whether the brief period monthly or the longer period following childbirth (cf. 12:4-5). All uncleanness violates holiness and breaks fellowship with God.

Unlawful Lust. 18:20-23. **20.** Adultery was strictly prohibited (Exod. 20:14; Lev. 20:10; cf. Prov. 6:15-33). It defiles a man. **21.** The reference to Molech (cf. Acts 7:43), the Ammonites' debased god to whom human sacrifices were offered (20:2-5; Deut. 12:31; 2 Kings 16:3), implies that the unnatural vices denounced here were associated with idolatrous worship.

22. Homosexuality was flatly prohibited and listed in a context of degrading sins connected with the most depraved idolatry (an abomination). The present-day trend to justify it cannot be squared with God's Word (20:13; Rom. 1:27), despite widespread attempts, even by professing Christians to do so. **23.** Bestiality is also denounced as **confusion,** that is, chaotic setting at nought the different divine orders of creation, constituting insult to God's image in man (Gen. 1:26-27).

Prophetic Warning. 18:24-30. The nations of Canaan, to which God was leading His people, were to be dispossessed because of their defilement with these sins. Their land was to be given to Israel. The LORD's people were to take warning to keep clear of these sins, so that the land would not *vomit* them out. The Ras Shamra religious literature from Ugarit in north Syria (discovered

168

in 1929 and the years following) proves the utter immorality of the Canaanites and their completely debased religion of debauched gods and lewd goddesses abandoned to lust and violence.

3. HOLINESS IN HUMAN RELATIONSHIPS. 19:1-37.

Basis of Fellowship with God and His People. 19:1-18. **1-2.** This chapter is unique in Leviticus in that its precepts were addressed to **all the congregation of the children of Israel.** The people were viewed as forming a moral whole, observing in unity all God's statutes and ordinances. The gist is given of what is to characterize those who revere God and His sanctuary. It is comprehended in the oft-repeated words, **Ye shall be holy; for I, the Lord your God, am holy** (cf. 11:44-45; 1 Pet. 1:16), giving as does Exodus 20:2, the ground on which all the precepts set forth rest.

3. The commandment to honor parents and observe the Sabbath is a repetition of Exodus 20:12 (see Lev. 20:8-11). **4.** The commandment prohibiting idolatry repeats Exodus 20:4-6 (cf. Exod. 34:17). **5-8.** The law of the peace offering, bespeaking the fellowship and praise of those redeemed (cf. 7:15-18) is repeated. It was the one sacrifice that was eaten (in part) by the people. We belong to a holy assembly, for it is God's holy church. Each one is required to maintain that holy character and the resulting fellowship. **9-10.** The law of gleaning (cf. Deut. 24:19-21) inculcates loving concern for the needy.

11-12. The commandments forbidding theft, lying, perjury, and profanity repeat the Decalogue (Exod. 20:7, 15-16). **13-14.** Humanitarian treatment of neighbors, especially if handicapped or inferior, was important in fostering the fellowship of the saints. **15.** The principle of **righteousness** (*ṣĕḏĕq*) was to be

the standard of neighborly conduct, without partiality to social status or wealth.

16. A **talebearer** (gossip or slanderer) was denounced (cf. Prov. 11:13; 18:8; 20:19). **Neither shalt thou stand against the blood of thy neighbor**, that is, "you shall not bear a false charge which would endanger a person's life," an exposition of the ninth commandment (Exod. 20:16). Hatred and vengeance were not to be nursed (1 John 2:9; 3:15). If a brother's conduct deserved reproof, he was to be warned and rebuked in an effort to salvage him (cf. Gal. 6:1). **18.** Summing up all that precedes, the most exalted concept of human relations under the old covenant was stated—that which Jesus quoted as the second great commandment—**Thou shalt love thy neighbor as thyself** (Matt. 19:19).

The Importance of God's Statutes. 19:19-37. **19.** God's statutes are to be obeyed, if for no other reason than God's people are to realize that their lives are to be holy and minutely regulated by God's Word. Therefore, mixing such things as God has separated in nature is forbidden. **20-22.** The principle is applied to slavery, which was then the natural world order.

23-25. Firstfruits were for Jehovah. Probably as a reminder, the fruit of newly planted trees was not to be eaten for four years. The circumcision of a tree was its ceremonial stripping. **26.** Blood was not to be eaten, for the reason outlined in 17:10-16. **26-29.** Occultism was renounced because it insults God's deity and holy name (cf. v. 31; Exod. 20:1-7). It is connected with demon-energized idolatry, as are tattooing of the flesh and prostitution.

30-31. Sabbath observance (see Exod. 20:8-11) and reverence for the LORD's sanctuary were safeguards against idolatry and spiritualism (spiritism). Such occultism defiles because it is energized by demons (familiar spirits, divining demons), who operate through a spiritistic medium or *wizard*, "a knowing one," endowed with the supernatural knowledge of the controlling evil spirit. Nothing is more unholy and destructive of the fellowship of God's people than pollution by occultism. **32.** Age is to be honored in the LORD. **33-34.** Sojourners must not be harassed, but loved as oneself, an expansion of the regulation already given in verses 17 and 18. **35-37.** Dealing fairly with one's neighbor in all business transactions is the only conduct worthy of the LORD's people.

4. SEPARATION FROM OCCULTISM AND IMMORALITY. 20:1-27.

Separation from Occult Religion. 20:1-8. (Cf. v. 27.) **1-2.** The penalty complicity with the worship of Molech, "the abomination of the Ammonites" (1 Kings 11:5) was death by stoning and being cut off by the LORD from His people. **3.** The distinctive feature of this horribly cruel form of demonized religion was offering infants to the polluted deity, a practice so wicked that it defiled God's sanctuary and profaned His holy name. So depraved was the cult that the Israelites who did not kill the Molech worshiper would be cut off with their families by the LORD. Such a demonic religion required a person to destroy those who turned to it or to be destroyed himself.

4-6. The connection of Molech worship with demonism (cf. 1 Cor. 10:20) is also suggested by the stern commandment against spiritism and witchcraft that immediately follows. The persons who turned to **such as have familiar spirits** (lit., "in whom are familiar spirits" ['*ōḇōṯ*, "divining demons"]) **and after wizards** (*yĭdde'ōnîm*, "knowing

ones," because they are energized by demons possessing superhuman knowledge) were to be cut off from God's people. They had flouted their marriage, as it were, to the LORD and played **the harlot** in demonized religion.

The spiritistic medium, "a man or a woman in whom is a divining demon" (v. 27, lit. Heb. trans.) was to be put to death by stoning. Occult traffic is so iniquitous before God because it insults His deity by breaking the first two commandments of the Decalogue (Exod. 20:1-7). These practices grossly violate God's holiness and call for rigid separation. **7-8. Sanctify yourselves . . . I am the LORD who sanctifieth you.** God sanctified them by His call and redemption. They were to sanctify themselves by keeping themselves true to His call and redemptive grace.

Crimes Carrying the Death Penalty. 20:9-21. See chapter 18, where all the crimes except cursing one's parents (v. 9) are mentioned. Here the crime is repeated for emphasis, and the penalty is added to put teeth in the laws.

Concluding Exhortation. 20:22-27. This exhortation is similar to 18:24-30 (*q. v.*). **24.** The basic feature of these exhortations is: **I am the LORD your God, who have separated you from other people.** Holiness demands rigid separation from sin and sinners. Israel's conduct had to correspond to the nation's call (Exod. 19:6). **27.** See comments on verses 4-6 above.

5. PRESCRIPTIONS FOR PRIESTLY HOLINESS. 21:1-24.

Holiness of Ordinary Priests. 21:1-9. **1-5. Speak unto the priests, the sons of Aaron.** The preceding laws (chaps. 17-20) were directed to the *holy* nation. These special laws regulated the holiness of the priests, guaranteeing a ministry beyond reproach (cf. 2 Cor.

6:3-10). Since the sons of Aaron are illustrative of believers of this age in their priestly capacity, the various injunctions demonstrate the importance of separation from sin on the part of the Christian believer-priest (1 Tim. 3:12; Titus 2:7-8; 1 Pet. 5:3). Note these four points:

(1) Priests could not defile themselves by contact with the dead (vv. 1-4; cf. Num. 5:2; 6:6; 19:11-20). Death being the penalty of sin, contact with it was defiling, as was any "dead work" performed without true faith (Heb. 9:14). Failure to include the wife when referring to close relatives meant that her position of being "one flesh" (Gen. 2:24) made a specific mention of her superfluous. (2) Priests had to strictly avoid pagan practices, such as mourning, that were connected with occultism (v. 5; cf. Lev. 19:27-28; Deut. 14:1).

6. (3) They could not profane **the name of their God**, for they offered that which speaks of divine atonement to be made by the Savior who would suffer and die, symbolized by **the offerings . . . made by fire**. Also, they offered **the bread of . . . God** (Lev. 3:11; Num. 28:2). The fat of the peace offering is called "the food [bread] of the offering made by fire unto the LORD" (3:11, 16). Because the priest was one who ministered to the satisfaction of God in bringing Christ before Him, he had to remember that he was required to minister that which God could feed upon. This demanded rigid separation from sin.

7-9. (4) The priest's domestic life had to be above reproach. He could not marry a harlot or a divorcee, but only a virgin or a widow. His household had to be exemplary. A priest's daughter who yielded to lewdness was to be burned (probably after being stoned).

Holiness of the High Priest. 21:10-15. The standard was higher still for the high

priest, for he is a type of Christ, the anointed and consecrated One; the crucified, risen One, ever living and installed in the holiest of the heavenly tabernacle to make intercession for us (Heb. 4:14; 7:25; 9:24). (1) *He was, therefore, to be absolutely undefiled, with no contact whatever with death.* Nor was he to even mourn for the dead (v. 10; cf. 10:6-7), as a type of our great High Priest, who was "holy, harmless, undefiled, separate from sinners" (Heb. 7:26).

(2) *He was not to go out of the sanctuary* while the anointing oil was upon him, even to mourn the death of his closest kin (cf. 10:7). He is a type of Christ, the Anointed, whose presence sanctifies the heavenly tabernacle, where He never leaves God's holy presence in His constant intercession for us. (3) *He was to marry only a chaste virgin,* bespeaking the church, "espoused . . . as a chaste virgin to Christ" (2 Cor. 11:2) in the present age, or a companion of virgin character in the faithful remnant of His people in other ages.

Unholy Defects of Ordinary Priests. 21:16-24. **17-20.** These defects are remarkably definite and stated specifically. They symbolize any imperfection, blemish, or handicap that reduces one's ability to do priestly service for God. The "defect" may not necessarily be a believer's own fault; it might be the result of bad teaching leaving him unconfirmed in grace and in a stage of immaturity. Then, again, it may be the believer's fault, the result of his own lack of yieldedness, prayer, or diligence (cf. 2 Pet. 1:9-10; Heb. 12:13). **21-23.** In any case, a defect does not in itself make one unclean, for the believer with the defect may eat of **the bread of . . . God** (see v. 6). The defect simply disqualifies someone for priestly ministry; this pictures the perfection of the person and finished redemptive work of Christ.

6. PRIESTLY SEPARATION AND OBEDIENCE. 22:1-33.

Priestly Separation. 22:1-8. **1-3.** Priestly separation was not only to be from unholy things but from any violation of **holy things** and the strict rules governing them. These rules state that no priest could approach the holy things (offering sacrifices or eating of them) if he was unclean (ceremonially defiled, vv. 1-7). The priests, typifying believers, were "compassed with infirmity" (Heb. 5:2; cf. 7:28); yet they were to be conscious of the polluting nature, not only of sin committed, but of death as the result of sin contacted. The dead works (activities not produced in faith by the life of the Spirit) are just as defiling to the conscience as sins that are actually committed, and they need continual confession and cleansing to serve the "living God" (Heb. 9:14; cf. 1 John 1:7).

4-7. A priest who may have contracted leprosy or had an issue or touched an unclean animal, was unclean till sundown and could not eat of the holy things **unless he wash his flesh with water** (cf. John 13:2-10). Christ cannot have communion with a defiled saint, but He can and will cleanse him. **8. That which dieth of itself** signifies a source of food that was not sanctified by sacrifice, and what is **torn** suggests food made available through violence. Both were forbidden as food for priests, for there was nothing for God's glory in it and some of it was the fruit of violence being done to that which is due Him.

Holy Things Restricted to the Priestly Household. 22:9-16. The household had its own privileges, for all who were in it could eat the holy thing (the slave, those born in the house, the daughter at home), but no stranger—only those in the household by purchase or birth (picturing the genuinely redeemed and born again) could partake of the priestly food. **13. But there shall no outsider eat thereof** (i.e., a stranger, "not of the seed of Aaron," Num. 16:40, picturing the unregenerate).

Nature of the Sacrifices. 22:17-25. **19.** The sacrifices had to be physically perfect because they point to the moral perfections of Christ. The oxen, sheep, or goats had to be **without blemish. 20-21.** Strict prohibition against any animal with a blemish (cf. Deut. 15:21) is given. **It shall be perfect to be accepted. 22-24.** The imperfect is spelled out—so important was it that Christ's unblemished character be emphasized. Nor could the blemished sacrifices be offered by a foreigner (apparently a proselyte), because corruption and blemishes were in such sacrifices, no matter who offered them.

Supplementary Regulations. 22:26-33. **26-27.** The sacrificial animal had to have lived a definite length of time (**seven days**). Not until the **eighth day** and thereafter was it acceptable for offering. This precept guards Christ as the antitype, who was not to be offered in infancy. Only when He began to be thirty years of age was He to begin His public priestly ministry. This was to culminate in His rejection and death as an **offering made by fire** and of that which the fire speaks (suffering and death under God's wrath). **28.** The regulation that a **cow or ewe** could not be killed the same day (cf. Deut. 22:6-7) no doubt discouraged cruelty, but had a deeper typical lesson that God "spared not his own Son, but delivered him up for us all" (Rom. 8:32). He "so loved the world, that he gave his only begotten Son" (John 3:16). The Father was to give up the Son, but in a sense the Son was to be torn from the

Father's hands by wicked men. **29.** Directions for offering **a sacrifice of thanksgiving** stressed willingness, sincerity, and spontaneity. **30-33.** As the peace offerings represented communion with God experienced by the reconciled sinner, so the sacrifice represented communion enjoyed with pure delight by the reconciled one at his feast. It had to be eaten only on this occasion to celebrate this *specific* blessing. Five motives for close obedience are set forth: (1) *God is* their covenant God, and His authority backs up the regulations: **I am the Lord**; (2) His holiness is to be guarded: **I will be hallowed among the children of Israel**; (3) His appeal is to His people as Israelites: **I am the Lord who halloweth you**; (4) His right is that of Redeemer: **Who brought you out of ... Egypt**; and (5) His prerogative is being His people's God: **Your God.**

B. FELLOWSHIP WITH GOD: BY OBSERVING THE FESTIVALS. 23:1-44.

The Weekly Sabbath. 23:1-3. The Sabbath is basic to the Mosaic Covenant and Israel's religion. Therefore, it introduces the entire festal cycle, although it is not one of the sacred seasons ("set times" for honoring the LORD). (For the full meaning of the Sabbath, see Gen. 2:3; Exod. 20:8-11; 31:13; Matt. 12:1.)

The Passover. 23:4-5. This was the initial feast ("set season") of the Jewish calendar, celebrated on the fourteenth day of the first month Nisan (Abib), that is, March and April. In Hebrew, it is called *pĕsăḥ* ("a passing over"), commemorating redemption from Egypt, the type of all redemption, when the LORD "passed over" the blood-covered dwellings of Israel. As the first feast, the Passover is basic to all spiritual blessing, because it is grounded in sinful man's redemption by Christ (1 Cor. 5:7; 1 Pet. 1:19; see Exod. 12:1-28; Num. 9:1-5;

28:16-25). Dispensationally, the Passover especially describes Israel's age when blood was poured out to atone for (cover) sin.

Unleavened Bread. 23:6-8. Immediately following the Passover, **unleavened bread** (*măṣṣōt*) was to be eaten **seven days,** demonstrating that the entire span of the believer's life on earth is to be lived in fellowship with Christ in separation from sin. The bread speaks of communion. The leaven betokens sin (1 Cor. 5:7-8; 2 Cor. 7:1; Gal. 5:7-9). The festival commenced on the fifteenth day of Nisan (Abib) and continued a week. The order set forth is redemption and then holy living.

Firstfruits. 23:9-14. The sheaf of the firstfruits of the barley harvest first typifies Christ in resurrection, and then those who are His at His coming (1 Cor. 15:23; 1 Thess. 4:13-18). It was celebrated on the sixteenth day of Nisan in the same week as Passover and the Feast of Unleavened Bread, stressing that the foundation of holy living and future glorification lies in redemption. Jesus arose on the third day after Passover, and this has become our rest ever since. The Father was waiting for His presentation (His sheaf "being waved") after His resurrection, and He stood before the empty tomb and then in God's presence, not for Himself personally as much as for us. The **first fruits** were a pledge of the coming harvest. Christ's acceptance is the basis of our acceptance.

Pentecost, Feast of Weeks. 23:15-22. As the Passover symbolizes the Old Testament era, so Pentecost foreshadows the church age that follows. **15.** The **seven sabbaths** represent the period of full development of the Old Testament dispensation. **16.** At the close, fifty days after Firstfruits, the **new meal offering** of the wheat harvest was presented, look-

173

ing forward to the church.

17. The two wave loaves (a loaf, not a sheaf of separate grains) **baked with leaven**, anticipate the Holy Spirit's ministry of baptizing the Jew (Acts 2) and Gentile (Acts 10) into union with one another in the risen, glorified Christ (1 Cor. 12:12-13). This was made possible by the Spirit's advent at Pentecost (Acts 2:1-4; John 14:20; 16:12-13). The loaf was baked with leaven because evil crops out in the church, because it is not yet glorified.

18-20. Many sacrifices attended this celebration of Pentecost, reminding us that *all* our blessings are the fruits of Christ's atonement. Hence, there were: (1) a very complete burnt offering (Lev. 1), (2) with the usual inseparable meal offering (Lev. 2), (3) and the drink offering (Exod. 29:38-42), with the meal (cereal) offering stressed (Num. 6:17; 15:1-12), and (4) the sin offering (Lev. 4), and (5) a special peace offering consisting of two young lambs waved over the two loaves, exhibiting peace between God and His church through Christ's redemption (Rom. 5:1; Isa. 53:5). The various elements of "salvation," denoted by the different offerings, are actually inseparable. Peace and fellowship through blood are the experience of the church.

22. Love to God and man, taught in all these feasts, is to be demonstrated in practice. The poor and the stranger "are always to be thought of when God's people are reaping the rich harvest of their blessings in Christ" (Coates, *Outline of . . . Leviticus*, p. 253).

Trumpets. 23:23-25. **23-24.** The blowing of the trumpets prefigures Israel's age-end regathering from worldwide dispersion at the consummation of the church age (Matt. 24:31; cf. Isa. 18:3, 7; 27:12; Ezek. 37:12-14). **The seventh month** brings spiritual com-

pletion in which the feasts find prophetic consummation at "the end of the year" (Exod. 23:16). The long interval between Pentecost and the Feast of Trumpets answers to the church age. Then the gifts and calling made to the nation Israel will be fulfilled (Rom. 11:29), for God once more will receive His restored people (Acts 1:6). The blowing of trumpets will alert the remnant of Israel to their coming King (Matt. 25:6). This signal (cf. Num. 10:1-10) was **a memorial** (better, "a reminding" of what was about to happen), an awakening of the people to repentance in prospect of the approaching great Day of Atonement (or expiation), confession, and pardon, introducing the most joyful of all the feasts, the Feast of Tabernacles.

The Day of Atonement. 23:26-32. This solemn occasion on the tenth day of the seventh month (Tishri) prefigures the repentant sorrow of Israel at her conversion at the second advent. See chapter 16, where the meaning of the day is expounded. Israel's great coming time of self-humiliation and conversion is described in Zechariah 12:10—13:1. This was the most solemn day of the festal cycle, and it will be the coming highlight of Israel's history. The whole nation will be saved when "there shall come out of Zion the Deliverer ['Redeemer,' Isa. 59:20-21], and shall turn away ungodliness from Jacob" (Rom. 11:26).

Tabernacles. 23:33-44. **34.** This Feast of Tabernacles or Ingathering was the last and most joyous feast of the Jewish year. **36-37.** The **offerings made by fire** look forward (and then, in retrospect, backward) to Christ's sufferings until death as the basis of Israel's future salvation and restoration in millennial blessing. **39.** It was prospective in that it presaged the Kingdom rest of Israel. The solemn eighth day looks forward to a blissful eternity after the millennial reign. **43-44.** It was retrospective in that it commemorated redemption from Egypt as the people built booths of branches and dwelt in them for seven days.

C. FELLOWSHIP WITH GOD: BY OBEDIENCE AND REVERENCE. 24:1-23.

Oil for Tabernacle Light. 24:1-4. **1-4.** The LORD gave directions through Moses concerning the private official duties of the priest withdrawn from men in the holy place (cf. 1 Tim. 3:15). The people were to bring the **pure olive oil** (cf. Exod. 25:6), which was clear, unmixed, **beaten**, and carefully prepared. They were to feel that they, as much as the priests, had an interest in the activities of the holy place. They had to realize that the seven-lamp golden candlestick (speaking of Christ, the shaft, supporting His church, the seven branches, supplied by the light and life of the Spirit, the oil) burned for them also.

Three times (vv. 2, 3, 4) it is emphasized that the priest was to set the lamps **to burn continually.** What a picture of Christ causing His people to receive light and life daily through the Spirit in order to manifest it to a sin-darkened world (Matt. 5:14-16; 1 John 2:27). What a reminder to Israel that they were to manifest the LORD to the darkened pagan nations around them. The constantly shining light illuminated the golden table of showbread (a picture of Christ who died for us) and the golden altar and its incense (portraying Christ exalted in resurrection and His acceptance in God's presence). As the candlestick was the only light in the tabernacle, so was Israel the only light in the Old Testament (and so is the church in the New Testament) to a sin-darkened world.

The Showbread. 24:5-9. **5-6.** The bread of presence (*lĕḥĕm hāppānāyim*, i.e., bread fit to be set in the divine presence) was to be prepared carefully, exhibited, and then eaten by the priests strictly according to divine directions. Each of the twelve loaves (picturing the twelve tribes of Israel) was to consist of two-tenths of an ephah of flour (about six quarts). They were to be placed in **two rows** ("arrangements"; hence, the name "bread of arrangement," 2 Chron. 2:4; Neh. 10:33). These loaves lay on a **pure table** (cf. Exod. 25:24) made of acacia wood (the humanity of Christ) overlaid with pure gold (the deity of Christ), the food of our souls being the Son of Man from heaven.

The bread of presence was set before God in the holy place, just as the incense on the golden altar was offered there to God. Thus it was a type of Christ, on whom the Father's delight was placed, so that Christ might be said to be the food of heaven on whom God figuratively feasted with delight. The **twelve cakes** (loaves) advertised the truth that for each name on his breastplate, the high priest had a full supply (double the need for one individual's need, v. 5; cf. Exod. 16:16) so that the believer has no lack before God in any aspect of salvation.

7. The **frankincense** (cf. 2:15-16) denoted acceptance before God. It was burned at the week's end (instead of the loaves) in order that Aaron's sons might feast on the loaves, as we do memorially of Christ's death and second coming in the Lord's Supper. **8.** The bread of presence was renewed weekly so that it was always fresh. So is the Antitype— always refreshing as the dew and stimulating as we feed upon Him daily (cf. Exod. 16:14, 19-20).

Blasphemy Dealt With. 24:10-16. **11.** This is the case of the blasphemy of **the**

name, the ineffable name Jehovah (Yahweh; cf. v. 16; Exod. 3:14-15; Phil. 2:9) by the son of a Danite woman and an Egyptian husband. The incident served to confirm the authority of the Mosaic laws both to the Israelites and the "mixed multitude" (Exod. 12:38) among them. **12.** The blasphemer was to be placed in ward until the LORD's will was ascertained.

14-16. The severe death penalty served as an example of the culprit's contempt for God's salvation itself. Israel's own national crime in rejecting the LORD when He became incarnate is foreshadowed. Judaism's superstitious reverence in refusing to pronounce the holy name Jehovah (Yahweh) on the strength of this passage, was no substitute for their own blasphemy in rejecting the Lord incarnate when He came.

The Lex Talionis ("the law of retaliation"). 24:17-24. The blasphemer's crime is still in view in this law of retaliation. The first table of God's moral law, requiring reverence for God, has been vindicated. The second table, requiring kindness to one's fellowman, is now commanded. The law of an eye for an eye and a tooth for a tooth is not an expression of man's revenge (Matt. 5:38), but of the righteousness of the Holy One of Israel (cf. Exod. 21:23; Deut. 19:21). But it is also an expression of the LORD's grace to men, for by it He draws a fence around their lives to protect them from violence and death. As He was jealous for His own name, so He is concerned about His people's physical as well as spiritual safety. The connection of all this with the crime of the Danite woman's son is shown in verse 23.

D. FELLOWSHIP WITH GOD: BY
OBSERVING THE SABBATIC YEAR AND
JUBILEE. 25:1-55.

The Sabbatic Year. 25:1-7. The Sabbath of days was extended to a Sabbath of years (Exod. 23:10-11; Deut. 15:11). **2.** The Sabbatic year was primarily a recognition of God's sovereignty over the land, which He was to give them (cf. 26:32-35). **6.** Restoration of the soil and provision for the poor on what grew from the untilled fields were prominent features. It was called *shăbbăṯ shăb-bāṯôn* ("a sabbath of sabbaths," i.e., "a very special sabbath," "a sabbath of solemn rest").

The sixth year, ordered and blessed by God, would be sufficient for the year of rest (vv. 18-22). The year was to be consecrated to God (Deut. 31:10). Failure to keep the Sabbatic year resulted in forfeiture of the land. The institution prefigures the coming Kingdom rest and prosperity (vv. 20-23).

The Year of Jubilee. 25:8-22. **8-9.** Seven Sabbatic years (forty-nine years) were to be followed by the year of jubilee, inaugurated by the blowing of the jubilee trumpet on the Day of Atonement on the tenth day of the seventh month (see chap. 16). Prefigured is Israel's entrance into the blessings of the Kingdom reign of the Messiah, foretold so glowingly by the prophets, but it foreshadows even wider blessing for the entire earth (Rom. 8:19-23). The trumpet that was blown was the "horn" (*qěrěn*) of the "ram" (*yôḇēl*), so the ram's horn was abbreviated *yôḇēl*, from which the name "jubilee" is derived, and became synonymous with the trumpet (cf. Exod. 19:13, 19, where both *shōp̄ār*, "trumpet," and *yôḇēl* are used).

10-13. The year is one of liberty, a return to one's possessions and family. **15-17.** It was a humanitarian institution inculcating love for God and one's neighbor. **18-22.** The LORD promised prosperity and security in the observance of this year. **23-24.** Jubilee was a reminder that the land really belonged to the LORD; therefore, it was not to be held oppressively without due consideration of others.

The Law of Redemption. 25:23-34. **23.** The principle underlying the Sabbatic cycle and jubilee is that the land belongs not to any man but to God. Men are not owners but **strangers and sojourners.** They are no more than tenants by courtesy, tenants at will—the will of God (Exod. 22:21; Deut. 10:19). **25-28.** Redemption of the land could be made by a relative, the man himself, or automatically by divine institution in the jubilee year. **29.** An exception was cited in town property because it had no immediate connection with the land and its tenure. **31.** Village houses came under the provision, probably because farmers and shepherds lived in them. **32-34.** The Levitical order came under a special class.

Treatment of the Poor and Non-Israelites. 25:35-46. The prospect of the jubilee year was never to supersede present duty for the Israelite, nor should it for us in prospect of the Lord's coming and the greater jubilee marking the consummation of our redemption. **35-37.** The poor, even a non-Israelite, are to be helped (cf. Matt. 25:34-45), with no interest or profit demanded on a loan, because of the fear (reverential trust) of the LORD (cf. Psalm 19:9). Redemption must open the heart of God's people to be sensitive to others' needs. **38-41. I am the Lord your God,** who has shown you grace and mercy; therefore, show others the same, including those reduced to slavery because of poverty.

42-43. A fellow Israelite had to be treated as a hired servant, and even as such he was to be held no longer than the jubilee, for the LORD declared, **They are my servants. 44-46.** However, an Israelite could have pagan slaves and retain them permanently. This was not sanction of slavery, but a punishment of the Canaanites and others for their sins. But

the antitype looks forward to Israel's exaltation under the Messiah in His Kingdom reign (Psalm 149:7-9; Isa. 61:5; Rom. 8:21; Rev. 2:26).

Redemption of the Poor Brother. 25:47-55. **47-49.** This passage prefigures Christ as our Kinsman-Redeemer. The word *go'el* is used to indicate the "redeemer," the one who pays, from *ḡā'ăl*, meaning "to release, ransom, deliver" by fulfilling the duties of a relative. Comfort abounded for God's ancient people in the hope of the jubilee. If a wealthy foreigner purchased an Israelite who had fallen into debt, the LORD desired that such bondage should not continue. It was the duty of friends to redeem him. At worst, no foreigner was to hold him beyond the jubilee. Pictured also is the LORD's determination to deliver His own from oppression and sorrow. **54.** In the great jubilee the whole family of God shall be completely released from all sorrow, bondage, and death (cf. Rev. 21:4). Joy, therefore, is the keynote of the jubilee.

E. FELLOWSHIP WITH GOD: BY HEEDING GOD'S PROMISES AND WARNINGS. 26:1-46.

Gist of the Warning. 26:1-2. The features of the warning are solemn injunctions (1) against idolatry, prohibiting making *any* image of the invisible God (cf. Exod. 20:1-7); (2) against Sabbath desecration, thus violating the quintessential stamp of the Mosaic Covenant and the sign between the LORD and His people Israel (Exod. 31:12-17); (3) against irreverence toward the tabernacle with all that it prefigures concerning God's grace and righteousness as operative in the redemption of sinful man.

The Blessings of Obedience. 26:3-13. **3-13.** Four great promises were made to Israel if they would **walk in God's statutes, and keep His commandments:** (1)

bountiful harvests (vv. 4-5); (2) peace and security (vv. 6-8); (3) fruitfulness and increase (vv. 9-10); the harvest would be so great that what was left in storage from the preceding year would have to be disposed of before the new harvest could be hauled in (v. 10); and (4) the LORD's manifested power and presence (vv. 11-13). Through the tabernacle (Exod. 29:45-46), God would be their God and they His people, enjoying freedom and liberty as His redeemed.

The Curses of Disobedience. 26:14-26. **14-15.** Breach of the covenant would be tantamount to open rebellion against God's statutes and commandments. **16-26.** Severe chastisement would be the result: (1) terror, distress, defeat (vv. 16-17); (2) drought, scarcity, **heaven as iron ... earth as bronze** (vv. 18-20); (3) plagues and desolation by wild beasts (vv. 21-22; Deut. 32:24; Ezek. 14:21); (4) war and death, not because of the strength of the enemy but on account of their own weakness (vv. 23-26). **Seven times** was the *full* measure of severity (cf. Amos 4:6-13). Bread would become so scarce that one oven would be sufficient for the baking of ten families, with rationing required.

Persistent Rebellion. 26:27-39. **29-31.** The penalty would be (1) horrible famine (v. 29; cf. 2 Kings 6:28-29); (2) severe desolation (vv. 30-31); and (3) dispersion (v. 33; cf. Psalm 44:11). **34-39.** Violation of the Sabbath, the Sabbatical year, and the jubilee would be repaid by the land resting while its people were in captivity (cf. v. 43). The small remnant that would be left would be pitifully fearful, stricken, and defeated.

Confession and Restoration. 26:40-45. **40-42.** As definite as the threats, so were the promises of blessing, upon confession, and the restoration to fellowship. The Abrahamic Covenant remained with its unconditional promises. **43.** The desolate land would enjoy her Sabbath (see v. 34). **44-45.** God's mercy would follow His people in captivity. **46.** A summary statement was given concerning the laws and statutes God made with Israel. All look forward to His plans for the redemption of mankind.

F. FELLOWSHIP WITH GOD: BY KEEPING VOWS AND PAYING TITHES. 27:1-34.

Special Vows. 27:1-8. These special vows involved persons dedicated to God. Each, according to age and sex, had a different estimation (valuation) as set by the LORD. The rate was the same in the different categories for persons of all ranks. Since those in the prime of life had the greatest potential for service, they were rated highest. Were the shekels of silver paid by the offerer to free him from his vow, or were they an addition to the offering (person) to seal the sincerity of the dedication? Apparently the latter was the case. Hence, Jephthah's daughter could not be redeemed (Judg. 11:30), for she was God's property. The idea is that of buying one's admission into the LORD'S service to demonstrate how valuable *to us* such service is. Although the act is itself entirely voluntary (a vow of dedication), that which we dedicate is ourselves (2 Cor. 5:15), tangibly, our "bodies" (Rom. 12:1).

Vows Involving Animals. 27:9-13. Nothing dedicated to God is to be regretted. **9.** It is **holy** and is to be reckoned such. **10.** It is not to be changed or exchanged for something else, either better or worse, valuable or less valuable. If it is exchanged, both it and **the exchange ... shall be holy.** The lesson taught is that our highest feelings are never wrong in their intensity when God is the object.

11-12. If an unclean beast (such as a camel) was dedicated to God, then its **value** had to be offered, as determined by the priest.

13. But if he (the one who made the vow) would **at all redeem it** (wish to retract and substitute another animal), he could do so. But a fifth part of the value of the original gift had to be added to the animal substituted, because declension is manifested and is treated somewhat like a trespass. As in the trespass offerings, one-fifth was specified as a fine in addition to the restitution made, showing that the LORD abhors retraction in the matter of dedicatory zeal.

Vows Involving Houses. 27:14-15. Sanctifying a house meant setting it apart to the LORD by a vow. The priest's evaluation of it stood. If the person who set it apart wanted to buy it back, he had to add a fifth, as in the case of animals.

Vows Involving Land. 27:16-25. **16-17.** In the case of a parcel of land, the estimate was the amount of seed required to sow it with barley. **18-19.** The time to the jubilee year was also a computing factor. The penalty for buying it back was again one-fifth of the original dedication. **20-21.** Under certain conditions the field became unredeemable and reverted to the LORD at the jubilee, becoming the priests' property. **22-24.** We must give to the LORD what belongs to us, not what is borrowed or rented. Willing self-denial is the object taught. **25.** The law of the sanctuary is to regulate all—a perfect weight and a just balance (cf. 1 Sam. 2:3). The LORD's all-righteous wisdom is that which weighs all thoughts and actions of His people, who dedicate themselves or their property to Him.

Other Regulations. 27:26-27. First-lings of beasts were already the LORD's, so they could not be vowed. Animals outside this category, since they were unclean and could not be sacrificed, were redeemable, but a fifth was added to show there was something in the nature of a trespass in the man who wanted an unclean firstling. A double use of one thing must not color our devotion to God.

The Ban. 27:28-29. **28-29.** The **devoted thing** (*ḥĕrĕm*), doomed or given over to destruction by the LORD (not by men) should be rendered "from among men" (*min hā'āḏām*). "Among people no one who is under human doom can be bought off; he must certainly be executed" (BV). This instance is the LORD's exercising His sovereignty in displaying His wrath against sin (cf. Josh. 6:17; 1 Sam. 15:3; 2 Sam. 1:21).

Concerning the Tithe. 27:30-34. **30-31.** Tithes were holy to the LORD. If redeemed (such as the tithe of seed) a fifth was added to show the LORD is jealous and marks anything that might be a retraction. **32-33. Passeth under the rod** refers to counting cattle (cf. Jer. 33:13). The tenth was tithed and taken inalienably. The LORD seeks only what is His due, *every* tenth animal, good or bad. With this note the "Pictorial Gospel of the Old Testament" (Bonar, *Leviticus*, p. 505) concludes with God's claims upon us and His expectations of our service and willing devotion. He who has done so much for us certainly is justified in expecting nothing short of our best in return.

NUMBERS

Title. The name "Numbers" comes from the Latin *Numeri*, a translation of the Greek Septuagint *Arithmoi*. The book was so titled because of the two numberings of the Israelites in chapters 1 and 26 and the considerable attention devoted to numbers throughout the book. The Hebrew title is "In the Wilderness" (*bᵉmiḏbār*, 1:1), which is much more descriptively appropriate, for the substance of the book is a record of the events *between* the first and second censuses. Indeed, Numbers is a history of the wilderness experiences of Israel.

Purpose. Numbers continues the history of Israel as "a kingdom of priests, and an holy nation" (Exod. 19:6), where Exodus stops. As Genesis is the book of beginnings, Exodus the book of redemption, Leviticus the book of holy worship and fellowship, so Numbers is the book of the service and walk of God's redeemed people. Commencing with the events of the second month of the second year (Num. 10:11) and ending with the eleventh month of the fortieth year (Deut. 1:3), the intervening thirty-eight years concern God's discipline of His people to bring them into closer fellowship with Himself and thus enrich their lives as His own purchased possession. In the light of this, Charles Erdman calls the book "a commentary on the nature and providences of God ... a Drama of Divine Discipline" (*The Book of Numbers*, p. 9).

But the book has a far larger ministry. Its highest service is found by regarding it as a book of symbolic illustrations and object lessons designed for the instruction of believers today. In referring to Israel's experiences in the wilderness, the apostle Paul gives the clue to the most meaningful interpretation of the book. "Now *all* these things happened unto them for examples, and they are written for our admonition, upon whom the ends of the ages [world] are come" (1 Cor. 10:11).

Authorship. As one of the traditional five books of Moses, Numbers, until comparatively modern times, has been attributed to Israel's great lawgiver and leader. Modern theories that deny this position, however, are not satisfactory substitutes for the view that holds to essential authorship by Moses himself of not only Numbers but of the entire Pentateuch. Robert Dick Wilson's summary is still valid, "The Pentateuch as it stands is historical and from the time of Moses ... Moses was its real author, though it may have been revised and edited by later redactors, the additions being just as much inspired as the rest" (*A Scientific Investigation of the Old Testament*, p. 11).

The inescapable impression the book of Numbers gives is that the laws and events cataloged stem from the wilderness wanderings (e.g., 9:1; 15:1-13, 32-41). Moses is the central personality throughout the book. Clearly and repeatedly it is stated that the laws and regulations it sets forth were given through his agency and that of Aaron (1:1; 3:44; 6:1; 8:1, etc.). Numbers and the other Pentateuchal books are best viewed as Mosaic in origin. That the books, however, had a history, in fact, a very long history, and were doubtless edited and even amplified does not detract from their Mosaic origin.

Modern Views of Authorship. Those who deny Mosaic authorship contend that Numbers is composed primarily from the Priestly Source and JE, resembling Exodus in literary structure. The first ten chapters are taken as a long extract from P, as well as various laws scattered throughout the book. JE is supposed to reappear by the side of P, but as a rule is not thought to be so intimately interwoven with it. At best, such a view is highly artificial and is largely based upon plausible but inconclusive assumptions.

OUTLINE

183

COMMENTARY

I. LEAVING SINAI. 1:1—10:10.

A. THE CENSUS OF THE TRIBES. 1:1-54.

The People Ordered to Be Numbered. 1:1-16. **1-3.** By blood redeemed out of Egypt (Exod. 12:12-36) and by divine power given the Law, the tabernacle, and priestly ritual (Exod. 12:37—15:21), all of which speak of the person and redemptive work of Christ, God's people Israel, as believers, were called to prepare for inevitable warfare (cf. Eph. 6:11-20). Hence, the LORD ordered a military census through Moses. This numbering comprised the males by their polls (i.e., "head by head") **from twenty years old and upward**, all who were **able to go forth to war.** Some nine months previously a census had been taken in connection with the atonement money (Exod. 30:11-16). The same total of 603,550 men is given (1:46; cf. Exod. 38:25-26). Necessary to spiritual warfare is ransom (Exod. 30:12), of which the half shekel of silver spoke.

Those numbered for warfare had to declare their lineages (v. 18). They alone had a rightful place among God's people and were fitted to conduct warfare. The new birth (regeneration), which gives us a place among God's people, is our lineage and prerequisite for spiritual warfare. A careful distinction, therefore, had to be made between the LORD's people and "the mixed multitude" (11:4; Exod. 12:38), representing the unsaved who often claim the name of the LORD but have no experience of salvation or qualification for spiritual warfare. To facilitate the census-taking, one chief man of each tribe (except Levi) was appointed to assist Moses and Aaron in the task.

The Census Taken. 1:17-46. **17-18.** On the basis of lineage, showing the care taken about genealogies, the numbering was made. This was not only to differentiate the true people of God from the untrue, but also to keep the Aaronic order intact and, more vitally, to preserve the Messianic line of the Redeemer distinct. **27.** The tribe of Judah was most numerous (cf. Gen. 49:8-10). **32-35.** Jacob's prophecy (Gen. 48:17-20) finds fulfillment in Ephraim's growth and strength over Manasseh.

The Levites' Position. 1:47-54. **47-50.** The Levites were not numbered by their ancestral tribe along with the other tribes since they were not required for military service. Their task was to care for **the tabernacle of testimony,** so designated because it housed the two tables of stone on which the Decalogue was inscribed (cf. Exod. 31:18; 40:20). The term *testimony* (*'ēḏŭṯ*) means literally, "prescription, precept, law" and refers to the "covenant stipulations." **51.** The death penalty was imposed on any non-Levite who dared to assume Levitical functions. **52-53.** Whereas the other tribes pitched their tents around their standards, the Levites encamped around the tabernacle. **54.** God calls to specific service, and His Word must be strictly obeyed in performing that service.

B. THE TRIBES ARRANGED. 2:1-34.

The Divine Direction. 2:1-9. **1-9.** The

LORD gave His people instructions for their encampment and movements while they were still in the wilderness, but the instructions actually were in regard to their tribal positions in relation to the tabernacle. Judah was on the east (vv. 3-4), flanked by Issachar and Zebulun (vv. 5-9) **These shall first set forth** (cf. 10:14).

Symbolized are the saints in their spiritual associations with one another in central relationship to the divine service and testimony. The LORD's directions for our journey through the wilderness of this world are specific. Both *where* we encamp and the *time* and *place* we serve are to be oriented to the central position to be accorded Christ's redemptive work (symbolized by the tabernacle). Every movement, as well as every association with other saints, is to be under divine direction.

In the New Testament, every believer has his appointed place in the Body of Christ (the church), with Christ as the Head (1 Cor. 12). Carefully specified were the leaders of the tribes, for it is God who gives both the gifts and the gifted men to His people (Eph. 4:8-11). It is He who instructs us how we ought to conduct ourselves "in the house of God" (1 Tim. 3:15) and in relation to one another.

The Details of the Divine Order. 2:10-31. The truth is emphasized that nothing is casual or accidental in our movements for God or our relations to His people. **10-16.** Everyone is to encamp by his **standard,** according to his army (the focus is spiritual conflict). The standard, moreover, was connected with a **camp,** of which there were four, rather than with each local tribe. **On the south side** was **Reuben** (vv. 10-11), flanked on the east by **Simeon** (vv. 12-13) and on the west by **Gad** (vv. 14-16), with their marching movements indicated

(cf. 10:11-28). **17.** At the center were the Levites and the tabernacle.

18-24. On the west side was **Ephraim** (vv. 18-19), flanked on the south by **Manasseh** (vv. 20-21) and on the north by **Benjamin** (vv. 22-24). They were to go forward in the **third rank**, that is, "set out third on the march" (RSV). **25-31. On the north side** was **Dan** (vv. 25-26), flanked on the west by **Asher** (vv. 27-28) and on the east by **Naphtali** (vv. 29-31). They brought up the rear (cf. 10:25). God's people are thus shown in their unity (cf. 1 Cor. 12:12-26).

Even while in the most local setting, the tribes encamped as warriors; and they journeyed in oneness with their brothers, demonstrating the utter necessity of unity for victory in warfare and in protection of the tabernacle and all that its testimony stands for in divine redemption. The number twelve, in relation to the total tribes, conveys the idea of completeness of administration with regard to *all* God's people. In New Testament truth it illustrates the fact that whereas each assembly has its local place and responsibility, it must recognize its oneness in Christ with *all* other assemblies universally in its conduct of spiritual warfare. God's people are to fight against the common enemy, not against one another (Eph. 6:12).

The Strength of God's Warriors. 2:32-34. The total of warriors was large—603,550 (cf. 1:46; 601,730 in 26:51, a decrease of 1,820, representing all who perished in the desert, except for two, Joshua and Caleb). Some critics suggest that the Hebrew word translated "thousand" (1:21, 23, etc.) is an old term for a subsection of a tribe (31:14) rather than a later developed meaning of 1,000 men. This would drastically reduce the total to 5,550.

But the testimony of Scripture is that the LORD marvelously increased Abraham's descendants (Exod. 1:7) by at least two million. But how could the Sinai Peninsula support such a multitude? (1) Miraculous supplies of food and water had to be reckoned with, for acts of divine intervention form an integral part of the Pentateuchal narratives. (2) Perhaps the climate of the region has changed in the course of almost three millennia. (3) Possibly the people scattered over the peninsula and occupied fertile oases beside Kadesh-barnea.

C. THE LEVITES' WORK IN GENERAL. 3:1-51.

The Priests. 3:1-4. **1.** The priests and Levites were expressly excluded from the military census (chap. 1) in order to distinguish saints in their capacity as warriors from their ministry as priests and servants in holy ministrations. The priests (Aaron and his sons) were mentioned first because their ministry *was* basic to *all* other ministry and because the other Levites were given to them and had to serve in every detail under their authority. **These ... are the generations** (i.e., "the account"; cf. Gen. 2:4) **of Aaron and Moses,** meaning "not only the families which sprang from Aaron and Moses, but the Levitical families generally, which are named after Aaron and Moses because they were both of them raised into the position of heads or spiritual fathers of the whole tribe ... at the time when God spoke to Moses upon Sinai" (KD, 3:19). **2-3.** Named were Aaron's four sons, **who were anointed, whom he consecrated** ("ordained"; lit., whose hand he filled, i.e., to whose hand he entrusted) **to minister in the priest's office. 4.** The sin and death of Nadab and Abihu (see Lev. 10:1-2) were alluded to in order to show that the exercise of the priesthood continues despite failure. Priesthood repre-

sents access to God and the highest spirituality and was to direct *all* Levitical service.

The Levites as Servants of the Priesthood. 3:5-10. **5-10.** The Levites were divinely given to the priests to be directed by them in every detail of their service, which was meticulously spelled out. Priestly duties were strictly confined to the Aaronic order. No Levite, much less a layman, could approach the priestly office except on pain of death (v. 10; cf. 18:6-7). Emphasized is the great truth that Levitical service (the mechanics or ritual of religion) had to be directed and empowered by priestly ministry (access to God on the basis of the redemptive work of Christ).

The reason is that Levitical ministry as **the service of the tabernacle** dealt with that which was "the example and shadow of heavenly things" (Heb. 8:5), "the pattern of things in the heavens" (Heb. 9:23). Hence, it demanded a priestly basis of contact and empowerment by "the living God" (Heb. 9:14). As Levites, saints are called to serve in relation to a system that is heavenly in character and requires direction by Christ, as the true Aaron, and by His sons, who prefigure that which is genuinely spiritual in God's people.

Significance of the Levites. 3:11-16. As representatives of the hallowed firstborn (Exod. 22:29-30; 34:19-20), the Levites picture the saints composing "the church of the first-born ... written [enregistered] in heaven" (Heb. 12:23), having no earthly inheritance, but a heavenly place and service. **12. The Levites shall be mine** (cf. 8:14; 1 Cor. 6:19-20).

14-16. Moses alone numbered the Levites—**every male from a month old and upward**, prefiguring believers being hallowed to God through the redemptive value of Christ's blood, long before they could account for themselves (cf. Acts 9:15; Gal. 1:15; 1 Tim. 1:18). The Levite was not matured as a servant till he was thirty, but all he would be was in prospect from the beginning (cf. Rom. 8:29; Eph. 1:4). When it was a question of military service, maturity was in view (chap. 1) and the numbering was from "twenty years old and upward" (1:3).

The Families of the Levites. 3:17-39.
17-20. Sons of Levi ... Gershon ... Kohath ... Merari. "Levi" signifies "united," and no family of his sons served independently of the other families. Nor were any of them to serve apart from the priests (4:18-19). They formed a unity, thus prefiguring the oneness of God's people in every age (cf. 1 Cor. 12:12-26). Each had a different gift and function, but ministry was grounded in priestly sacrifice and intercession.

21-26. The Gershonites encamped **behind the tabernacle westward** under the divinely appointed leadership of Eliasaph. They were in charge of all the tabernacle coverings, curtains, and cords (cf. 4:24-28). Their God-ordained work concerned not the making of these things but their continuance in connection with the movement of the testimony. On the march they followed Reuben (cf. 10:17).

27-32. The Kohathites encamped on the south side of the tabernacle under the leadership of Elizaphan. They were charged with the most sacred objects (the ark, the table, the lampstand, the altars, the vessels, and the screen separating the holy place from the most holy). Hence, their service was in "the most holy things" (4:4).

33-37. The Merarites (**Mahlites** and **Mushites**, the families of Merari), under the leadership of Zuriel, camped on the north side of the tabernacle. They had charge of the tabernacle boards, pillars, sockets, pins, and cords. Each Levite had his specific work, divinely given and outlined. Faith alone, producing obedience, was necessary. This is also the situation in the church, the Body of Christ (1 Cor. 12:4-6). Each believer has his gift, each his distinctive place, each his specific calling and work to do. **38.** But *all* service must proceed out of worship and fellowship with God based upon the sacrifice of Christ, illustrated by the priority of the priesthood. Hence, everything Levitical had to be subordinated to that which was priestly.

Redemption of the Firstborn. 3:40-51.
40-43. The census of the firstborn in Israel totaled 22,273. The Levites numbered 22,000, the difference of 273 required some compensation if the LORD claimed the Levites instead of the firstborn of Israel. **44-47.** Compensation was achieved by the payment of redemption money (five shekels of silver for each of the 273 Israelites not matched by a Levite; cf. Lev. 27:6). **48-51.** This **redemption money** was given to Aaron and his sons. By this token the Levites were placed in a position hallowed to the LORD and representative of the whole camp of Israel.

Every saved person must realize he is a **first-born,** set apart for God, and such service is due from him as is illustrated in the tribe of Levi. If any of the firstborn were not personally represented in Levitical service, they had to be ransomed (*pāḏâ*, "to redeem, rescue"), "a term from commercial law referring to money paid to liberate persons or things which have fallen into the possession of another" (NBC, p. 174). The youngest believer must realize his value in the divine estimation in view of the service due from him, even though he may be too young to assume it in any practical way.

D. THE LEVITES' DUTIES IN PARTICULAR. 4:1-49.

Duties of the Kohathites. 4:1-20. **2-3.** This census was for those **from thirty years ... until fifty years old,** contemplating full maturity for service viewed as too holy and important to be entrusted to novices. Contrast chapter 3, which is about equating Levites with the firstborn and the numbering was "from a month old," taking into account those who were potentially available for service. A babe in Christ might be fresh in affection and fervent in spirit, but something more is needed for service of a spiritual high order. Maturity alone will suffice for the latter.

4-15. This particular service involved ministry when the testimony moved **forward** under wilderness conditions (vv. 5, 15). Each believer had his particular work to do and had to avoid trying to do someone else's. The Kohathites were entrusted with the transport of **the most holy things,** including the **veil** separating the holy place from the most holy (Exod. 26:31; Heb. 9:3; 10:20); **the ark of testimony** (v. 5; Exod. 25:10, 16); **the table of showbread** (v. 7; Exod. 25:30); **the lampstand** (v. 9; Exod. 25:31-38); **the golden altar** (v. 11; Exod. 30:1-5); and the **altar** of burnt offering (vv. 13-14).

But *before* any carrying forward of the testimony was attempted by the Levites, the Aaronic priesthood had to perform its functions of taking down the veil and covering the ark and all the holy furniture according to minute directions (vv. 5-15). Only **after that** were the **sons of Kohath** to come and **bear** (carry) it. Indeed, the Levites were not to see or **touch** any **holy thing, lest they die.**

How emphatically is the truth symbolized that all carrying forward of the testimony of God's saving grace in Christ (typified in the holy furniture) in the wilderness of this world *must be preceded by priestly ministry.* Unless one is a partaker himself of saving grace, and himself constituted a priest in fellowship with God, he cannot bear a testimony for God. Only he who is a priest can be a Levite, and the combination also makes a warrior (cf. their numbering for military service, 1:3, 20, 24).

The careful way the holy furniture was wrapped by the priests highlights the fact that in our testimony we must meticulously guard the holy things of our faith as jealously as the priests and Levites guarded the sacred things of the tabernacle. How easy it is to mar our testimony by inconsistent priestly exercise. That is why proper priestly exercise *had to* precede Kohathite service.

The **cloth ... of blue** (vv. 6, 7, 9, 11) speaks of guarding the heavenly nature and origin of Christ, (1) the ark (v. 5) reflecting Him in whom God has made good everything that is now the subject of testimony; (2) the table of showbread (v. 7) presenting Him as the Bread that came down from heaven; (3) the golden lampstand (v. 9) setting Him forth as the heavenly light; and (4) the golden altar of incense (v. 11) portraying Him as our heavenly Intercessor through whom our prayers and praises ascend to God.

The **cloth of scarlet** (v. 8) suggests sacrifice, guarding the complete efficacy of the redemptive work of Christ. The **purple cloth** (v. 13) spread on the altar of burnt offering after **the ashes** were removed bears witness to the royal kingship of Him who was crucified. The **badgers' skins** (*tăḥăsh*) are probably those of the dolphin (Arabic, *tuhasun*; cf. Exod. 25:5; Ezek. 16:10). Dolphin skin, which was precious, guarded the sacred things from the hostile elements of the pilgrim journey.

16. Eleazar, Aaron's son, was to have personal supervision over the sacred supplies of the sanctuary and the sanctuary itself, again stressing that priestly service had to precede Levitical witness (bearing the tabernacle testimony). **18-20.** But the two functions are rigidly separated in type that they might be *inseparably united* in the antitype (cf. 1 Sam. 6:19).

Duties of the Gershonites. 4:21-28. These duties are the same as those outlined in 3:25-26. Their service, like that of the Merarites, had to do with the tabernacle itself rather than what was enshrined in it. Gershonite service means carrying forward in testimony every divine thought illustrated by the curtains, coverings, and hangings of the tabernacle. The Gershonites were under Ithamar, Aaron's son.

Duties of the Merarites. 4:29-33. These duties also were under the direction of Ithamar and are the same as in 3:36. The Merarites carried such things as the boards, bars, pillars, and bases, speaking of that which is necessary to support the witness which the tabernacle as a whole bears. Levitical service was manifold and exceedingly varied, but it always depended upon and was efficaciously operative only as springing from priestly service.

The Results of the Census. 4:34-49. The number of Kohathites subject to active service was 2,750; the Gershonites, 2,630; the Merarites, 3,200, totaling 8,580. *Every* believer is called to Levitical service, based upon priestly service as a prerequisite.

E. SANCTIFICATION OF THE CAMP. 5:1-31.

Separation from the Unclean. 5:1-4. The camp had to be holy because the LORD was in the midst of it. All that defiled belonged outside of it. The ritually unclean included those afflicted with leprosy, a type of indwelling sin

(see Lev. 13-14), and those defiled by physical secretion (Lev. 15), or by contact with physical death (Lev. 11:24-47). These were to be ostracized from the camp (cf. Rom. 12:2; 1 Cor. 5:13; James 4:4; 1 John 2:15-17).

The journey through the wilderness of this world, which lies in the power of the wicked one and is stamped by death, defiles one and incapacitates him to serve the living God (Heb. 9:14). God's people, therefore, must cleanse themselves from "all filthiness of the flesh and spirit, perfecting holiness in the fear of God" (2 Cor. 7:1).

Confession and Restitution. 5:5-10. **6-7.** Sin committed calls for confession (Psalm 32:5; 1 John 1:9). If the sin was against a brother, restitution was required. According to the law of the trespass offering, a fifth part was to be added (cf. Lev. 6:1-7). Unconfessed sin cannot be tolerated among the Lord's people (James 5:16).

The Seriousness of Adultery. 5:11-31. If a man and woman committed adultery, the sin was punishable by the death of both (Lev. 20:10; Deut. 22:22). A sanctified camp placed great importance upon the preservation of the marriage estate. Not only was the Law severe on adultery, but it provided that a husband who suspected his wife of marital infidelity could subject her to an elaborate ritual ceremony in which the LORD would decide the case. However, the elaborate details of the trial by ordeal point to a deeper meaning. Israel was the wife of the LORD in the Old Testament (Hos. 2:2), as the church is betrothed to Him in the New Testament (2 Cor. 11:2). The episode illustrates testing those of God's people who are professedly faithful and against whom there is no contrary evidence.

God would have the unfaithful state, here represented by the defiled woman, become detestable among His own. He would have them inwardly and vitally faithful to Him. The testing typified is not merely a dealing with conscience; rather, it is a process that brings to light whether there are spiritual sensibilities and true appreciation of God's word and the grace of Christ in the very depths of the soul. Here is where the true sanctification of the camp of God's people is ascertained (cf. Heb. 4:12-13).

F. THE NAZIRITE. 6:1-27.

The Person. 6:1-2. **2.** The term **Nazirite** (sometimes spelled *Nazarite*, Heb., *nāzîr* from *nāzăr*, "to separate, abstain, consecrate") denoted an Israelite of either sex who separated himself wholly to the LORD (cf. 16:20-21; 2 Cor. 6:14—7:1). The **vow** taken was of a special nature in that it represented a distinct setting apart of the person to God as the outcome of a definite movement of the heart toward Him (1 Sam. 1:11; Psalm 66:13-14). Appropriately, the law of the Nazirite was added to the preceding enactments (chaps. 1-5), which concern the sanctity of the holy nation, to which status Israel was called (Exod. 19:6). That sanctity found its highest expression in the Nazirite vow.

God knew there would be unfaithfulness in His people (5:1-10), necessitating trial even by ordeal (5:11-31) to bring self-judgment and realization of the value of the person and death of Christ in the depths of the soul. Such a condition is graphically symbolized by the "clean" woman (5:28). Faithfulness in the affections leads to fruitfulness. The Nazirite is the moral offspring of such inner faithfulness of the heart and in the aggregate represents the faithful remnant God has always had, even in days of deepest apostasy (Isa. 1:9; Rom. 11:5).

The Vow. 6:3-8. The vow was threefold: (1) *It included abstention from wine* (vv. 3-4). Since wine was the symbol of mere natural joy (Psalm 104:15), not drinking it expressed a *complete* dedication that found all its joy in the LORD (Psalms 87:7; 97:12; Hab. 3:18; Phil. 3:1, 3; 4:4, 10). **3-4.** To accentuate the thoroughness of his consecration, the Nazirite was not only to abstain **from wine or strong drink** but from **vinegar, whether made from wine or strong drink . . . grape juice . . . [even] fresh or dried grapes . . . anything . . . produced by the grape vine, from the seeds even to the skin** (NASB). (2) *It included long hair* (v. 5; Judg. 16:17-22; 1 Sam. 1:11; Ezek. 44:20). Naturally a reproach to man (1 Cor. 11:14) uncut locks were at once the visible sign of the Nazirite's separation and his willingness to bear worldly rejection and reproach for the LORD's sake.

(3) *It included rigid separation from ceremonial uncleanness* (vv. 6-8; Lev. 21:1-3; Num. 19:11; Heb. 9:14). Death is the result of sin and the curse (Gen. 2:17; 3:19). Contact with it, even accidentally, symbolized contact with the curse of sin and resulted in defilement. Even good deeds, religious acts, and high morality, which are devoid of faith that honors the *living* God, are "dead works" and require cleansing (Heb. 9:14).

Failure in Performing the Vow. 6:9-12. **9.** Unwatchfulness, apparently due to some degree of self-confidence, brought defilement to the **head** (of uncut hair), the visible symbol of the Nazirite's consecration. Therefore, the Nazirite was required to **shave his head** (Lev. 14:8-9) on the seventh day, denoting that his vow had to begin all over again. He underwent seven days of purification, after which his head was shaved again (v. 18).

10-12. On the eighth day the least expensive form of offering, **two turtledoves, or two young pigeons,** were brought for a **burnt offering** and for a **sin offering,** because the sin was unwitting. The fleshly element that marred his initial consecration is now judged as having come under divine purifying of the death of Christ. Hence, something new results. Consecration is renewed on the grounds that what is fleshly has been judged in Christ's death, and a wholly new basis of acceptance results. In beginning again, the Nazirite brought a yearling **lamb** for a **trespass offering,** in type showing that his breakdown has been so serious that nothing but Christ's sacrifice could make amends for it.

Success in Performing the Vow. 6:13-21. **13-17.** The Nazirite typically gives up all reliance on the flesh and begins again as a self-judged believer, relying solely on Christ's death. Christ's sinless birth, life, and death are portrayed beautifully in type (see the typical meaning of the offerings, Lev. 1-6).

18. The Nazirite shaved his consecrated head **at the door of the tabernacle** and then put the hair **in the fire . . . under the sacrifice of the peace offerings,** his separation becoming in a peculiar way a sacrificial offering to God. The Nazirite's identification with the peace offering stresses the separation of the saints in their fellowship. The excellencies of Christ are symbolically offered to God in the holy fire. Here they are seen being reproduced in the Nazirite and therefore completely acceptable (Rom. 12:1-2).

19-20. It was really a priestly act, so the priest put on the Nazirite's hands what spoke only of Christ and then waved it before the LORD for His delight, evidently by placing his hands under those of the Nazirite (cf. Lev. 7:30). **After that the Nazirite may drink**

wine. This looks forward to the joy when Christ will drink the fruit of the vine in the coming Kingdom (Matt. 26:29; Mark 14:25; Luke 22:18). We drink the "new wine" of that Kingdom already realized in the shining upon us of God's love and favor in Christ (Rom. 14:17).

The Blessing of Fulfilled Naziriteship. 6:22-27. Nazirite separation ministers to what is priestly (cf. vv. 18-21), and what is priestly ministers to the blessing of *all* God's people. **23-26.** This beautiful benediction speaks of the blessing that the true Aaron, as well as "His sons," bestows. The priestly and the spiritual of God's people (the Nazirite remnant) are in the light and grace of this gracious pronouncement, ever seeking to bring it in power and enjoyment into the hearts of the Israel of God. Especially do they declare the keeping (preserving) power of Christ's salvation (John 17:12, 15), its unforfeitable quality made possible because God in Christ has caused His face to shine upon us and has been gracious to us in giving us eternal life.

G. THE GIFTS OF THE TRIBAL HEADS. 7:1-89.

Presentation of the Offerings. 7:1-3. **1-3.** When Moses had set up and fully consecrated the tabernacle and all its appurtenances (Lev. 8:10-11), the tribal chiefs brought offerings **before the Lord.** These offerings: (1) were purely voluntary and spontaneous, without any commandment, giving spiritual leadership to God's people, which was both appropriate and pleasing to God (cf. 2 Cor. 9:7; Heb. 13:16); (2) displayed a beautiful spirit of cooperation in the work of the LORD; (3) showed a fine appreciation of the spiritual character of what had been set up in the tabernacle; (4) evidenced care that the holy things of God be guarded and protected (cf. 4:6-28), for they brought **covered wag-**

ons; (5) perceived God's intention that His testimony should always be accompanied by exercise and movement, for they gave **oxen** to draw the **wagons** (or were they covered "litters"? cf. Isa. 66:20).

The Lord's Direction. 7:4-10. **4-5.** Moses was divinely instructed to receive the wagons and oxen for the service of the tent of meeting and to give them to the Levites. **6-9.** They were given to the Gershonites and Merarites but not to the Kohathites, who were entrusted with the most holy things (4:1-20), which they were to honor by transporting them on their shoulders.

Further Gifts of the Tribal Heads. 7:11-88. Although the gifts of each tribal prince (representing the tribe) were identical, each was recorded in detail. How beautifully this dramatizes the truth that the LORD takes note of the gifts of His people, since giving is an individual matter. The order of the princes was that assigned to them in chapter 2.

One day was allotted for the gifts of each tribe through its prince, totaling twelve days in all. This shows how important giving was for **the dedicating of the altar.** Prefiguring, as it does, "the mercies of God" evidenced in the finished redemptive work of Christ (Rom. 1-11), it calls for presenting our redeemed bodies to God (Rom. 12:1-2), that is, giving our redeemed selves to Him who gave Himself in death for us.

13-88. This is a unique offering and of special interest; the first things presented were silver and gold vessels. (1) The **silver** vessels (v. 13, etc.) represented saints redeemed to God (Exod. 30:12-16; 38:25-27; cf. 1 Pet. 1:18-19), and who willingly and spontaneously give themselves to their Redeemer. (2) **Gold** (v. 14, etc.) speaks of deity in manifestation and comprehends those who

are "in Christ" and have the divine righteousness imputed to them, and the divine nature imparted to them (1 Cor. 12:12; 2 Cor. 5:21; 2 Pet. 1:4).

(3) The **fine flour mixed with oil** (v. 13, etc.) symbolizes Christ as conceived by the Holy Spirit in the virgin's womb (Matt. 1:20; Luke 1:31, 35) and sinless in His incomparable life in which every moral perfection was in even balance (see the meal offering, Lev. 2). (4) The **spoon** [cup] **... of gold full of incense** (v. 14, etc.) prefigures what we are *positionally* (as God sees us) in Christ and in the new creation in Him (2 Cor. 5:17-18). The incense symbolizes prayer as it rises to God from those in Christ, viewed as united to Him apart from what we are naturally in the flesh (cf. Paul's great prayers, Eph. 1:15-23; 3:13-21).

(5) The **bullock ... ram** (and) **lamb ... for a burnt offering** (v. 15, etc.) speak of comprehension of Christ in His sacrificial character, so important in the dedication of the altar that features atonement (covering of sin). (6) **One kid** [buck] **of the goats for a sin offering** (v. 16, etc.) speaks of sin dealt with by the forsaken One (Psalm 22: 2 Cor. 5:21) as the basis of all God does for the sinner in sovereign love.

(7) **A sacrifice of peace offerings** (v. 17, etc.) speaks of food and fellowship, with the offerings diversified and extended, showing that communion with the altar has a very special place in God's mind. All the offerings were males (vv. 15-17, etc.), denoting energy of apprehension and excluding feeble thoughts of Christ's redemptive work.

Manifestation of the Lord's Pleasure. 7:89. **89.** The LORD manifested His pleasure when Moses, entering the tabernacle from the dedicated altar to speak to God (12:8; Exod. 33:9, 11), heard **the voice of one speaking unto him from off the mercy seat.** It was more than prayer; it was holy converse, such as Christ has with God, and we, in union with Him, also have with God. **And he spoke unto him.** The conversation did not end with the voice speaking from the mercy seat, for there was a holy two-way conversation. There always is when Christ's person and glorious redemption are apprehended and appropriated by His people.

H. CONSECRATION OF THE LEVITES. 8:1-26.

The Lighting of the Lampstand. 8:1-4. **1-3.** The lighting of the lamps of the lampstand was cited as a feature of the inauguration of the tabernacle service (in addition to the dedication of the altar, chap. 7). The former, as noted, speaks of the movement of the heart Godward, aroused by appreciation of Christ in His personal perfection and atoning sacrifice. The latter presents the provision God has made to keep the glorified One brightly in view of those who love Him during their pilgrimage through the dark world.

The seven lamps (cf. Exod. 25:37; 40:25) **shall give light over against the lampstand,** its gorgeous work of beaten gold representing the glorified Christ in the heavenly sanctuary (Exod. 25:31-40). The true Aaron lighted **the lamps** when He ascended on high into the heavenly tabernacle (Heb. 8:1-2) and sent the Holy Spirit (the oil in the lamps) to bear witness of Himself (John 15:26-27) and to glorify Him (John 16:7, 14, 15).

The Consecration of the Levites. 8:5-22. This ceremony consisted of setting them apart for service in eight ways: (1) *By cleaning them by sprinkling water of purifying upon them* (v. 7a; cf. 19:9, 17; Psalm 51:2; Heb. 9:13-14). The ashes of the red heifer (type of Christ coming under the all-consuming judgment of

sin) were mixed with water (symbol of both the Spirit and the Word, John 7:37-39; Eph. 5:26), to form the water of purification. *Sprinkling* with this cleansing agent portrays the perfect cleansing effected by Christ's death and now applied by the Spirit through the Word to the believer as a Levite or worker for God (19:13, 20-21). Upon the basis of this once-for-all positional cleansing by the death of Christ, the believer confesses any sin that may come in to becloud fellowship, and it is forgiven and cleansed on the basis of Christ's death (1 John 1:9; cf. John 13:3-10).

(2) *By their shaving all their flesh* (skin) (v. 7b; cf. Lev. 14:8-9). This signified a drastic dealing with and disallowance of *all* that is the outcome of the flesh. It is the human response to the divine undertaking symbolized by sprinkling with the water of purifying. (3) *By their washing their garments* (v. 7c). All had to be cleansed (both internally and externally) in view of the new life a Levite worker for God was about to enter (Isa. 1:16).

(4) *By an atonement being made for them* (vv. 8-12). **8-12.** The two young bullocks, one for a **sin offering** and the other for a **burnt offering,** illustrate the fact that those who undertake holy service for God can only do so as they are identified with Christ in His sin-offering and burnt-offering character. (5) *By identifying them with the whole assembly as their representatives* (vv. 9-10). Individual responsibility rightly enters into all service. But every Levite had to serve in unity with *all* his fellow servants in performing a service due from *all* Israelites. So today it is God's will that each serve for the *whole* church's benefit.

(6) *By presenting them to the LORD as an offering from all the Israelites* (vv.

11-13). They were to be separated *from* the Israelites and *unto* the LORD as being uniquely His possession (vv. 11-14; cf. 1 Cor. 6:19-20; 2 Cor. 8:5; Eph. 2:10). (7) *By subordinating the Levites to the preists* (v. 13). They were given to God and, through Him, to Aaron (cf. 4:5-9, 19, etc.), showing that the priestly activity was basic and preliminary to all Levitical service (cf. Col. 1:7; 4:12). (8) *By commemorating the fact that they were wholly given to the LORD instead of the firstborn* (v. 16; cf. 3:5-13).

Period of Levitical Service. 8:23-26. **24.** From twenty-five to fifty years was the age for Levitical service. The five-year period between twenty-five and thirty was evidently an apprentice stage (cf. 4:3; 1 Chron. 23:3). Preparation for Levitical work was necessary, and the necessity of full competency was hinted at. Also suggested was a time limit for active service (cf. John 9:4); and when arduous labor was no longer permitted, the person was to retain an honorable status.

I. GUIDANCE FOR THE REDEEMED. 9:1-23.

Commemoration of Redemption. 9:1-5. With the people numbered for war, the tribes arranged for camping and journeying, and the priesthood, Levitical service, and tabernacle testimony set up, how appropriate for the redeemed to commemorate the basic blessing that made all this possible— redemption out of Egypt. **1-3.** The divine command came through Moses: **Keep the passover at its appointed season** (cf. Exod. 12:3-28; Lev. 23:4-5; Num. 28:16), which they did. The next recorded celebration of the Passover took place in Canaan (Josh. 5:10-11).

Problem of Defilement. 9:6-14. **6-7.** Certain Israelites were rendered cere-monially unclean (19:11-12) and could not keep the Passover at its appointed time (cf. Lev. 7:21). Apparently on the basis that their uncleanness was not their fault, they appealed to Moses and Aaron concerning why they should be shut out from celebrating the feast.

8-14. As was the custom, Moses inquired of the LORD (cf. 15:34; 27:5; Lev. 24:12). The answer came as a token of God's grace and provided for a supplementary Passover in the second month to be kept by those who for any valid reason could not keep it at the regular time. However, this concession was safeguarded from abuse. **Cut off from ... his people** apparently means "the sin unto [physical] death" (1 John 5:16; cf. 1 Cor. 11:30).

Guidance of the Redeemed. 9:15-23. The fiery cloud was both a symbol of the divine presence and a guide to the Israelites as they traveled through the wilderness (cf. Exod. 13:21-22; 40:34-38). As they were about to leave Sinai and face the uncertainties of the journey to Canaan, the divine leadership, so important to every redeemed one, was reemphasized. This manifestation of God's presence was miraculous, as is His leading us by His Spirit through His Word (John 16:13; Acts 13:2-4).

J. THE SILVER TRUMPETS. 10:1-10.

The Silver Trumpets. 10:1-10. **1-2.** The trumpets, like the fiery cloud, were tokens of divine leading. Two in number, they were made by divine command for assembling the people or warning that camp was to be broken. The trumpets were the last things mentioned that had been divinely ordered for the tabernacle, and they formed a very distinctive part of the priestly equipment (31:6).

They were made of silver, which was connected prominently with redemption and atonement (Exod. 30:12-16; 38:25-27; cf. 1 Pet. 1:18-19), suggesting that they were symbols of divine grace and faithfulness. Whether they were used to assemble the congregation or the tribal leaders, or to set the camp in movement in time of war or in peaceful celebration, the **trumpets** ($h^a\bar{s}\bar{o}\bar{s}^e r\hat{a}$) **of silver** sounded in a priestly way the assuring note that the LORD had redeemed His people and would be "for them" and faithful to them (Rom. 8:31). **3.** When one long blast on the two trumpets was blown, **all the assembly** was to gather before Moses **at the door of the tabernacle of the congregation.** This meant the trumpets called *all God's* people to God's Word and authority. **4.** If the long blast was blown only on one trumpet, the leaders assembled before Moses. It is clear how wonderfully these trumpets were meant to call the people and their leaders to God's word mediated through Moses. What a need exists today for such a priestly ministry to call the Lord's people and their leaders back to the Bible out of error, priestism, cultism, and apostasy to apprehend the full free salvation by grace through faith alone in the redemptive work of Christ! **5.** A special kind of blast, an **alarm,** gave warning when the camps were to go forward. The first alarm was for the camps **on the east parts** (lit. Heb., "toward the sun-rising"; cf. 3:38). Evidently the testimony and movement of the LORD's people were oriented in God's mind with reference to the coming Redeemer, "the Sun of righteousness" who would "arise with healing in his wings" (Mal. 4:2). **6-7.** When the alarm was sounded the second time, the camps of Reuben on the south side were to move. They represent believers who occupy a favored position to the testimony, but have not

the sun's rising so distinctly in view. But they enjoy God's present favor and do not desire to lose it by dropping behind. The camps on the west and north are not mentioned in the Hebrew text (although they are in the Greek Septuagint). Dan represents the most tardy in spiritual movement. **9-10.** Another entirely different purpose of the silver trumpets was that the people in conflict with enemies might be **remembered before the Lord ...** [and] **saved,** and in **the day of ... gladness** on festal occasions their burnt offerings and peace offerings might be to them a **memorial before ... God.** Yet how appropriate are these uses of the silver trumpets, symbolic as they are of God's redemptive grace and faithfulness to His redeemed people. The words, **ye shall be remembered ... that they may be ... a memorial** in no sense imply that the LORD had forgotten His people, but rather, that Israel would not presume upon His gracious faithfulness, even though He might declare **I am the Lord your God.**

II. WANDERING IN THE WILDERNESS. 10:11—20:29.

A. THE JOURNEY CONTINUED. 10:11-36.

Departure from Sinai. 10:11-28. **11.** When Israel had been at Sinai just under one year, in the second year after leaving Egypt, the cloud (9:15-23) moved on. **12.** The **cloud rested in the wilderness of Paran,** probably Et-tîh in the north center of the Sinai Peninsula (cf. Gen. 21:21; Num. 12:16). **13-21.** The movement of the camp was **according to the commandment of the Lord by the hand of Moses,** according to chapter 2, except that the tabernacle was **taken down** and borne after Judah in order to be ready to receive **the sanctuary** when it followed

the camp of Reuben. The direct service of God is the important thing. Outward order should be looked at in relation to the holy service and all it stands for in relation to the person and redemptive work of Christ.

Hobab Plans to Return Home. *10:29-32.* **29-32. Hobab** was **the son of Raguel** (Heb., Ruel), the Midianite, Moses' father-in-law (Exod. 2:18). Apparently Hobab was Moses' brother-in-law (cf. Judg. 1:16, 4:11; Heb., *ḥōṯēn,* evidently used here in a broad sense for "in-law"). While Hobab declined Moses' first invitation to go with the Israelites as a guide, nothing is said as to whether he declined the second appeal. It seems somewhat incongruous, however, that Moses should have planned to rely on Hobab's knowledge of the desert when God was so signally guiding by the cloud and by the Ark of the Covenant going before them "to search out a resting place for them" (v. 33).

The Ark Leads On. 10:33-34. **33.** The **three days' journey** is probably a technical expression for such a distance as could not be traversed in a single day, and therefore not without intervals of encampment and due provision (cf. Gen. 30:36; Exod. 3:18; 15:22). The usual place of the ark during the march was in the center of the host (see v. 21; 2:17). Here, when the Israelites were setting out for the land, and in Joshua 3:6, when they were entering it, the ark preceded the people to symbolize divine leading on the journey (cf. Deut. 9:3).

The ark of the covenant of the Lord was given this title for the first time. This most sacred piece of furniture of the tabernacle speaks of Christ as the witness and pledge of divine love and faithfulness, who goes before His flock as Leader and Shepherd, charging Himself with the care of His people so they

will be led aright to a resting place (rest; cf. Matt. 11:28).

Song of the Ark. 10:35-36. The song is based upon the conviction that the ark was the LORD's throne, upon which He was invisibly seated as holy war was waged against His enemies (Josh. 3-4; 1 Sam. 4:3-22; Psalm 24:7-10).

B. THE PEOPLE COMPLAIN. 11:1-35.

Discontent at Taberah. 11:1-3. **1. The people complained.** Israel's murmuring in the wilderness was chronic and continual (Exod. 16:2-3; 17:3; 32:1-4; Num. 12:1-2; 14:2-3; 16:13-14; 20:2-13; 21:4-5). They grumbled about their hardships. In the face of all that the LORD had done for them and promised them (cf. 10:29), their discontent displayed base ingratitude. Divine discipline was necessary.

The fire of the Lord that **burned among them** was not a natural phenomenon, but a revelation of Him who to sinners is "a consuming fire" (Heb. 12:29; cf. Lev. 10:2). Some destruction was done in the outlying parts of the camp! **2.** The people **cried unto Moses,** who interceded with the LORD, and **the fire was quenched. 3.** The place was called Taberah ("burning," from the root *bā'ar,* "to burn, to be consumed by fire").

Complaints About the Manna. *11:4-9.* **4-6.** Complaints about the manna originated with the **mixed multitude** (Exod. 12:38), the rabble or spiritual riffraff who were not of the Israel of God but soon infected true Israelites. They **fell to lusting.** They began to have a strong craving for flesh and recalled their Egyptian diet of fish, cucumbers, leeks, onions, and garlic, which contrasted sharply with the austere desert food with its staple element of manna. The Israelites **wept again** (cf. Exod. 16:2-3), unbelief remanifesting itself as the natural unspiritual cravings of the old nature despised God's food and lusted for the things of the world (Egypt).

7-9. The **manna** is described (see Exod. 16:14-21, 31). Although the manna (Heb., *măn hû'*, "What is it?") was totally miraculous in supply, it may have been a natural substance from the *Tamarix gallica mannifera*, a tree exuding a sweet, sticky substance that falls by night to the ground like **coriander seed**; grayish yellow in color like **bdellium**, it is a resinous gum (see Exod. 16:35 for *manna* as a type of Christ, "the bread of life," John 6:35, 48-51; Josh. 5:11).

Moses' Expostulation and the Lord's Answer. 11:10-25. **11-15.** What a picture this is of an overwrought leader whose faith was severely tested by the unbelief of the LORD's people. (On Moses' impatience, see Exod. 17:2-4.) **The burden is too heavy** (RSV; see Exod. 18:17-18, 24-25). **16-25.** Moses' load was lightened by investing **seventy elders** with authority to assist him (cf. Exod. 18:21-23). The LORD graciously **took of the Spirit** that was upon Moses and endowed the seventy elders with it, so that they prophesied, that is, under the extraordinary impulse of the Holy Spirit they proclaimed God's praises and declared His will, as a sign to the unbelieving, murmuring Israelites that they were divinely selected and empowered to aid Moses. **They prophesied, and did not cease** (lit. Heb., "and added not," i.e., "they prophesied once, but not again," BV). Their gift was only temporary, and its purpose was strictly to mark their entrance into their sacred office.

Eldad's and Medad's Prophesying. 11:26-30. **26. Eldad** and **Medad** were **of them that were written** (or registered, i.e., "enrolled" as representatives of the community with the seventy). However, they had failed to go out to the tabernacle (cf. Exod. 33:7). Yet the Spirit came upon them, too, and **they prophesied in the camp. 28.** When this was reported to Moses, Joshua urged Moses to make them stop, as if they were detracting from Moses' power or glory.

29. Moses' rebuke of Joshua manifests the realization of the truth, so important to all leaders in the LORD's work, that the Spirit enabling him was not his own but God's, and therefore not motivated by any thought of self-sufficiency or self-glory. God's servants must be jealous of God's glory, not their own.

The Judgment of the Quails. 11:31-35. **31-33.** The LORD's punishment of the people's unbelief in complaining about the manna is recounted. "There is nothing at all, besides this manna, before our eyes" (v. 6). The wind from the sea bringing the quails was to relieve their whining, but at what a cost! Like the manna, the quails (Exod. 16:13) are a natural phenomenon of the Sinai Desert. They migrate over the region in enormous numbers and, when exhausted, are easily caught. This visitation, however, was a miracle.

A wind from the Lord . . . brought (the) **quails.** Also, the time, the place, and the abundance of the birds were elements in the miracle. Keil and Delitzsch (3:73) are doubtless correct in concluding that the passage can be understood in no other way than in Psalm 78:27-28, namely, "that the wind threw the quail about over the camp, so that they fell upon the ground a day's journey on either side of it, and that in such numbers that they lay . . . in places . . . as much as two cubits (3 feet) deep."

32. Only in that sense could the people gather them for two days and a night, so that the *least* amount that anyone gathered was ten homers (over one hundred bushels). **And they spread them all abroad,** that is, to preserve them by drying. The verb "spread out" (*shāṭāḥ*) occurs in some verses with the second and third consonants transposed, making the verb *shāḥāṭ* ("slaughter"). If this reading is accepted, it means the freshly killed birds were gluttonously devoured, occasioning the **plague. 35.** Evidently many people died, for the place was commemorated as **Kibroth-hattaavah** ("graves of lust"), possibly Ruweis el-Ebeirig, northeast of traditional Sinai. **Hazeroth** is possibly Ain Khudra, the next logical stopping place.

C. VINDICATION OF MOSES' UNIQUE POSITION. 12:1-16.

Miriam's and Aaron's Attack. 12:1-3.
1-3. Miriam was the instigator of a bold challenge of Moses' unique relation to God, as is indicated by her name preceding Aaron's and the verb being in the feminine gender in the Hebrew. Miriam was a prophetess (Exod. 15:20), and Aaron was high priest. Both were honored by God and held preeminent positions (Mic. 6:4), but within each was an unjudged root of evil that had to be searched out. The occasion was Moses' marriage to a Cushite (probably Ethiopian) woman of Hamitic descent (Gen. 10:6).

It is probable that Zipporah (Exod. 2:21) had died, and Miriam may have expected to have greater influence than ever with her brother. Consequently, her disappointment at this second marriage precipitated her attack on Moses, and Aaron followed her, being no more able to resist his sister's suggestion than he had formerly been able to resist the people's desire for a golden idol (Exod. 32).

Both are examples of how eminent and gifted saints, if not wary, can give

place to the flesh, just as the Israelites had done in complaining of desert hardships and the manna (chap. 11). Both were proud of their own prophetic gifts (cf. Exod. 15:20; 28:30), and in their pride they abused the gifts of God in their brother.

And the Lord heard, for in speaking against Moses they were actually speaking against the LORD Himself, who had given Moses his unique position. To speak against one whom in a distinctive way the LORD has declared "My servant" (vv. 7-8) is a serious sin. It is really in antitype challenging the rights of God and of Christ as Son over God's house (Heb. 3:5).

3. Moses' declaration of meekness is not self-adulation. "It is simply a statement which was indispensable to a full and correct interpretation of all the circumstances and which was made quite objectively with reference to the character which Moses had not given to himself, but had acquired through the grace of God" (KD, 3:77).

The Lord's Interposition. 12:4-10.
4-5. Solemnly God intervened in behalf of Moses, pointing out that His servant was uniquely preeminent. He was supreme in authority and nearness to God. **6-8.** He received *direct* communications from the LORD, as God's special **servant,** faithful to all God's house (Israel). With him God spoke **mouth to mouth ... plainly ... not in dark speeches** (obscurely). Moreover, he saw **the similitude** (the form or likeness) **of the Lord** (cf. Exod. 33:20-23).

Twice the LORD declared him **My servant.** Moses' uniqueness had been demonstrated still further by the transfer of the Spirit that was upon him to the seventy elders (11:25). Was all this not enough to inspire fear in Miriam and Aaron in their attack upon their brother? **9.** Little wonder **the anger of the Lord**

was kindled against them and He abruptly **departed** (cf. Psalm 105:15), leaving the evidence of His wrath.

10. The cloud of His presence **departed from off the tabernacle; and, behold, Miriam became leprous.** Leprosy was nothing short of a living death, a poisoning of the springs of life and a little-by-little dissolution of the whole body, so that one limb after another actually decayed and fell away. This is an apt illustration of indwelling sin and its manifestation in the flesh. Their sin lay fully exposed in the flesh where it was lodged.

Confession and Restoration. 12:11-16. **11.** At that moment Aaron must have greatly appreciated the sin offering (Lev. 4:3). How vividly must the ceremony for the cleansing of the leper have leaped into his mind (Lev. 14:1-57). In pleading to Moses in acknowledgment of his God-ordained position, he was really acknowledging the divine order established in Christ, of whom Moses is a type.

12-13. Convicted of the most awful working of the flesh in themselves, having realized its full condemnation has been borne by Another, and having seen it judged there, the way was then open for healing and restoration. The Spirit of Christ became active in intercession, and God heard. **14.** But discipline was not shelved; otherwise the work of restoration might have been aborted. Time was required, not for God to forgive, but for the moral lesson to be ingrained in the life. If her earthly parent had treated Miriam contumely (cf. Deut. 25:9), she would have felt humiliated for a time. How much more when God had chastised her.

15. Moreover, the whole assembly was detained in order to learn the lesson Miriam had to learn. Seeing the flesh judged in Miriam, the people had an opportunity to judge it in themselves. **16.** When this was done, God's people were ready to move on in the pilgrim march.

D. ISRAEL'S TEST AT KADESH-BARNEA. 13:1-33.

The Scouts Sent Out. 13:1-16. **2-3.** Although sending scouts was by divine direction, it originated in the unbelief of the people (Deut. 1:22-23). The LORD ordered it as a testing, not that He might know the state of their hearts, but that they might know (cf. John 6:5-6). The scouting expedition would have been quite unnecessary for a people who truly believed what God had said.

It is noteworthy that there is no description of the land, simply **the land of Canaan, which I give unto the children of Israel** (contrast Deut. 8:7-10). As the expedition was to be a test, it was left entirely to the people to form their own estimate and to make their own decision. The Israelites were to be represented by the **heads** (princes, chiefs; Heb., *nāśi'*, "one lifted up, exalted") of each tribe (vv. 4-16). **The land** speaks figuratively of what God in His love and grace has in His heart for His people. For this reason it became a greater test than the conditions in the wilderness. Hence, failure in this case was fraught with more serious consequences than any previous probing (cf. 14:32-33).

16. It is of the utmost significance that at this point **Moses called Hoshea** ("salvation, deliverance") **Joshua** (Jehoshua, "the LORD is salvation"). By the Spirit of prophecy, Moses was looking beyond all the dismal unbelief and failure, which were about to be manifested in the people, and envisioned One, the greater than Joshua, in whom the divine plan would be realized and the greatness of God as Savior would be experienced. It was a blessed hint that the land would be pos-

200

sessed in the power of a salvation which is wholly of God.

Joshua first appeared as an army captain (Exod. 17:9-10), then as Moses' servant or minister (Exod. 24:13; 32:17), and finally as Moses' successor (Num. 27:18-23). Typically, he prefigures Christ, by whom a place is secured for us in the land in the greatness of God's salvation (Heb. 3:6).

The Commission of the Scouts. 13:17-24. **17-21.** The scouts were to enter the land from the south (Negev) and proceed up the central highland ridge to the extreme northern limits to **Rehob** (2 Sam. 10:6-8), near the sources of the Jordan River, and continue onward to the vicinity of Hamath on the Orontes River. They were to ascertain the lay of the land, the strength of the people, and the nature of the cities. **The time** was the season **of the first-ripe grapes,** which was the end of July or the first of August.

22-24. Hebron was featured in the reconnaissance in Canaan. The town was founded seven years before **Zoan** (Tanis or Avaris), the capital of the Hyksos rulers in Egypt (c. 1720-1570 B.C.). Descendants of **Anak**, a great warrior, lived there. At the **brook** (valley) **of Eshcol** they cut a branch **with one cluster of grapes,** so big that two men had to carry it on a pole. They also brought **pomegranates, and ... figs** as evidence that God's land was fertile, fruitful, and wonderful.

The Report of the Scouts. 13:25-33. **25-27.** The spies returned to **Kadesh** (evidently 'Ain Qudeirat, some five miles northwest of 'Ain Qudeis), where there is ample water and which is eleven days' travel from Mount Sinai (Deut. 1:2), as confirmed by Yohanan Aharoni (*The Holy Land: Antiquity and Survival,* 2:289-90; cf. also Num. 20:1, 16; 32:8; 33:36; Deut. 1:19; Josh. 14:6). First

they showed the people the evidence of the land's fertility, and then they described it as a land that **floweth with milk and honey,** so richly pastured that it supported an abundance of milk cows, and so fertile with flowers and blooming shrubs that it was filled with honey-producing bees.

28-29. But despite the evidence of the goodness of God and of the land He was giving them, ten of the twelve scouts refused to believe God. The unbelief that took over, producing confusion, fear, and rebellion, saw only the walled cities, the giants, the Amalekites, Hittites, Jebusites, Amorites, and Canaanites.

30. In Caleb, however, faith spoke boldly and confidently. (1) His faith had a quieting and stabilizing effect upon the confusion gendered by unbelief, for **Caleb stilled** (quieted) **the people before Moses.** (2) Faith in Caleb was keen to see and seize the opportunity to obey the LORD and claim His blessing: **Let us go up at once, and possess** the land. His reason? **We are well able to overcome it.** The LORD, who promises it to us, is with us. If He is "for us, who can be against us?" (Rom. 8:31).

31. (1) But unbelief in the leaders, spreading like a cancer to the people, flatly contradicted faith and transformed the people into confused cowards and intolerable insurgents against God. The rebels were right in declaring, **We are not able to go up against the people,** because they left God out of the picture. Unbelief contradicts faith because it operates in a totally different sphere—that of the flesh, with God left out.

(2) Unbelief also blinded the vision to the fertility of the land (our inheritance in Christ), causing them to see only the difficulties in the way of their possessing it (enjoying our inheritance in our ex-

perience). **32-33.** Unbelief not only occupies itself with the difficulties, but magnifies and exaggerates them, so that spiritual defeat (Rom. 7) rules out victory (Rom. 8).

E. ISRAEL'S FAITHLESSNESS AT KADESH-BARNEA. 14:1-45.

The Sad Results of Unbelief. 14:1-4. **1-2.** The camp of the LORD's people was transformed into a place of despair, with murmuring against Moses and Aaron. This illustrates how all that Christ is as Mediator (Moses) and Priest (Aaron) may be nullified by the unbelief of those who belong to the LORD (1 Cor. 10:1-5; Heb. 3:7-19) when they are presented with their inheritance in Christ (Eph. 1:11, even as Israel was shown the land of Canaan), but then refuse to reckon by faith on what they are in Him (Rom. 6:11) and what He has provided for them here and now in His great salvation (Heb. 2:3; Eph. 1:15-23; 3:13-21).

For the believer, the choice is inevitable—either he must go forward in Christ (to possess the land, 13:30), or go back to the world (Egypt), or die in defeat in the wilderness (vv. 2-4). Against this unbelief and its dire results are directed *all* the warnings of the book of Hebrews (2:1-4; 3:7-19; 5:11—6:12; 10:19-39; 12:25-29).

The Assurance of Faith. 14:5-10. **5.** In spite of the tragic state of unbelief in the people, the LORD then brought into evidence the faith that reflects the salvation that is of Himself (Jonah 2:9) and is assured by divine, not human, faithfulness. This appears in the prostration and earnest pleading of Moses and Aaron before the people, prefiguring the mediatorial ministry of Christ and His pleading not only before God on our behalf (Heb. 4:14-16; 7:25), but also through us by the Spirit's ministry (Rom. 8:26).

6-9. So Joshua and Caleb came forth to voice faith in the land, which is typical of our spiritual inheritance, to be entered and enjoyed experientially here and now by those who know that they are "in Christ" (Rom. 6:1-10) and count upon their position by faith (Rom. 6:11).

God, both then and now, in the midst of general unbelief is a Witness to the power and completeness of His salvation. Joshua is a type of that salvation (Heb. 4:8), while Caleb sets forth God's work in a believer, so that there is in him "another spirit," that is, the spirit of faith (v. 24; cf. 2 Cor. 4:13). The two together give a full idea of a divine salvation wrought by Christ and in Christ, totally apart from what man is in the flesh.

As the land tested God's ancient people and brought out their unbelief or their faith, so does our "so great salvation" test God's people today. Unbelief neglects it (Heb. 2:3). Faith appreciates and appropriates it and enters into Canaan rest (Heb. 4:3). **10.** The congregation's declaration that Caleb and Joshua should be stoned was the last provocation to reveal what unbelief really is, and to seal its doom. No wonder that with this terrible challenge **the glory of the Lord appeared.**

Moses' Intercession. 14:11-25. **11-19.** Moses' intercession was based on the LORD's threat to smite the people with instant physical death (cf. 1 Cor. 5:5; 11:30; 1 John 5:16) and to disinherit them by taking away their reward because of their unfaithfulness (1 Cor. 3:9-14; 2 Cor. 5:10), not their salvation, as they were unchangeably redeemed out of Egypt (2 Tim. 2:13). Moses' noble intercession presents the man of God as a striking type of Christ, our Mediator: (1) he was jealous for God's glory alone (vv. 13-16); and (2) he pleaded God's power, long-suffering, mercy, and justice (vv. 17-18) as the basis of His forgiving His people (v. 19).

20-21. The LORD forgave and consequently did not immediately and totally wipe out the people by physical death. But alongside this dominant principle of grace is the principle of divine government. In the case of saints under grace, sin invites divine chastening, scourging, and even physical death in this life and the loss of reward in heaven in the life to come (1 Cor. 11:30; 2 Cor. 5:10). In the case of the unsaved, who are not under grace, the iniquity of the fathers is visited upon their descendants to the third and fourth generation (v. 18; cf. Exod. 20:5) and is fully punished in Gehenna to the degree that the moral law of God has been broken (Rev. 20:12-13).

In the eternal state, when the "government of God" has fully dealt with sin, the divine glory will fill the earth, because all sin and sinners will be relegated to Gehenna (Rev. 20:13-15). **22-25.** The LORD's unbelieving people were punished by being shut out of the land and, by forfeiture of their status as pilgrims, became aimless wanderers until they perished in physical death in the wilderness.

The Lord's Sentence. 14:26-38. **26-34.** What the LORD had said to Moses in his intercession was communicated to the people. The penalty was wandering in the wilderness for forty years, a year for every day that the spies viewed the land of Canaan. **37-38.** The ten tribal leaders, so directly responsible for the people's unbelief, were visited by the ultimate in divine chastening (immediate physical death; cf. 2 Sam. 12:13-23; 1 John 5:16).

The Presumption of Unbelief. 14:39-45. **39-43.** Unbelief had produced confusion, cowardice, and rebellion. Then it gendered pure presumption. The

people were afraid to go up with God, but they were not afraid to go up without Him. **44-45.** But **they presumed** (lit., "were headstrong, reckless"), and were completely defeated, chased as far as **Hormah** (meaning "complete destruction," from the root *hărăm*, "put under the ban of complete destruction").

F. THE LORD'S FAITHFULNESS REFLECTED. 15:1-41.

Offerings in the Land. 15:1-16. The instructions of this chapter speak of the LORD's faithfulness in stark contrast to His people's unfaithfulness (chap. 14). **1-2.** In the foreground of these regulations was eventual settlement in the land. This fact points out the comforting assurance that, despite all the failure of His people, the LORD would not fail them. While the great mass would die in the wilderness, the rest were assured that the LORD would take them into the promised land.

3-11. Then they would present the offerings outlined. These offerings present (as in Lev. 1-4) various aspects of the person and redemptive work of Christ. But here they prefigure the believer's *fuller apprehension* of the aspects as those believers who are settled in rest in the land, who not only have a position before God by being redeemed and saved out of Egypt (Rom. 6:1-10), but who also by faith have laid hold of the meaning of that placement before God and are enjoying it in their experience (Rom. 6:11).

Four things are stressed in this *fuller* apprehension: (1) *The perfections of Christ's sinless humanity* are portrayed by the **meal offering** of between **a tenth part of flour to three tenth parts** (vv. 4, 6, 9), which suggests an increasing measure of the victorious believer's spiritual understanding of Christ, although such knowledge is limited in our unglorified state. (2) *The perfections of Christ's sinless humanity* are also emphasized by the fine **flour mixed with . . . oil** (vv. 4, 6, 9), typifying the fact that as the God-man He was conceived by the Holy Spirit in the virgin's womb (Isa. 7:14; Matt. 1:18-25; Luke 1:35). Whether we consider His redemptive work as the sacrificial lamb, ram, or bullock, His virgin birth is the basis of any knowledge of Christ that is spiritual, as the sinless, spotless sin-bearer.

(3) *The joy of Christ in being poured out in the service of God for our redemption* is portrayed in the **wine** of the **drink offering** (vv. 5, 7, 10). The wine of the drink offering was a pouring out of joy in the sanctuary (see Phil. 2:17-18; cf. Psalm 40:8; John 15:11; 17:13). (4) *The infinite delight and supreme satisfaction of Christ's redemptive work Godward* is set forth in the **sweet savor** offerings (v. 3), which all these offerings (vv. 3-16) are (*not* sin offerings; cf. Lev. 1-3).

Leviticus 1 begins with the largest comprehension and goes down to the smallest, because there God's grace is pictured as descending step by step to make provision for the smallest and feeblest. But here there is an ascending scale, contemplating a spiritual increase on the part of the people, from the lamb to the ram and then to the bullock. It demonstrates the increasing ability of those who have entered into God's rest (Heb. 4:1) to reflect Christ (i.e., in their experience) before God's presence for His delight. **14-16.** These verses comprehend the blessings of God's salvation rest extended to non-Jews (cf. Luke 2:32; Eph. 3:6). God's plan would have all men know how acceptable Christ is to Him. The Gentiles will come in to offer to God (cf. Acts 15:14-15).

Cake for a Heave Offering. 15:17-21. A portion of the first coarse meal was to be taken from the threshing floor and made into a cake. This was to be presented as a **heave offering unto the Lord.** This refers to a "lifting up" or removal of a portion of it for the LORD, an act that betokened the fact that all the grain came from the LORD and was His by right. But it has a deeper Christ-centered meaning, as do all the offerings of the Pentateuch.

The bread of the land speaks of Christ as risen and *spiritually fed upon* by those who experience rest in the land. In proportion as we have entered into what it was to God to give Him up to death (the offerings, vv. 3-16) shall we comprehend the delight of God in receiving Him out of death in resurrection. God is to have His **cake . . . first.** His satisfaction in it is to be paramount in our thoughts. If God gets the first cake, what a wonderful thought it gives of the character and value of "the bread of the land," the food eaten by saints who enjoy salvation rest (cf. Heb. 4:1-9).

Sins of Ignorance. 15:22-29. **22-29.** The sins of ignorance may be committed even by saints viewed in the aggregate (**all the congregation**, v. 26) and in the land, hence, enjoying the rest of faith. But there is a marked difference between the provision for the sin of ignorance in Leviticus 4:13-21 and in this passage. In Leviticus there is no burnt offering, oblation, or drink offering. Here, however, these precious tokens of Christ's atoning work come first.

Customarily when the sin offering and burnt offering occur together, the sin offering precedes. But here the burnt offering comes first. This evidently points to the safety and security of the saint "accepted in the Beloved" (Eph. 1:6). The true way to forgiveness in the church is to stand on the ground of our union with Christ eternally. The **sin offering** follows (v. 24), showing that forgiveness is on the basis of the finished redemptive work of Christ, which is foreseen as being extended to Gentiles.

Presumptuous Sins. 15:30-31. **30-31.** Presumptuous sin refers to persistent, willful sin that prefigures the "sin unto [physical] death" (1 John 5:16; cf. 1 Cor. 5:5; 11:30). **That soul** (person) **shall utterly be cut off,** which seems to embrace more than mere excommunication from the church or from the congregation of Israel, which points to the church.

The Sin of Sabbath Breaking. 15:32-36. This example furnishes an illustration of presumptuous sin (vv. 30-31). It is introduced here to illustrate how the lawlessness of man would set aside the most blessed provisions of divine grace set forth in redemption out of Egypt and placement in the land of Canaan solely on the basis of *faith in God's grace.* This Sabbath rest of salvation (Eph. 2:8-9) means ceasing from our "own works, as God did from his" (Heb. 4:10). What God has provided in the gospel of His Son is beautifully set forth in the Sabbath. He did everything in the six days of creation, and "it was very good" (Gen. 1:31). So He "rested" in the completion and perfection of His own work (Gen. 2:2-3).

But sin came in, God's Sabbath rest was broken, and He began working in redemption. Therefore, we hear no more of a Sabbath until after God had a redeemed people (Exod. 15:2). Man was to rest, not to work, on the Sabbath (Exod. 20:4-7), that through Christ's redemption he might enter the rest of salvation, a perpetual Sabbath-keeping (Heb. 4:9). Indeed, the present period of grace is a prolonged Sabbath in which God will not allow human works to be introduced.

But men break the Sabbath by violating the gospel of grace, as did the Gala-

tians in espousing "another [different] gospel" (Gal. 1:6-9). People would rather work for blessing than *rest in* Christ as God's Sabbath. The man gathering sticks represents figuratively the legal spirit that produced such chaos in the Galatian assemblies (cf. Gal. 4:29; 5:15, 26). **35-36.** The severity of the punishment by stoning **outside the camp** corresponds to "the anathema" of Galatians 1:9, and shows that legalism has no place among the redeemed and is a presumptuous sin against God's grace revealed in Christ.

The Wearing of Tassels. 15:37-41. **38.** The **fringes** ("tassels," NASB) at the corners of the Israelites' garments, with an attached **cord** (lace) **of blue,** illustrate God's mind that His people's conduct and testimony shall ever be characterized by what is heavenly in color and character (cf. Col. 3:1-3). **39-41.** These were to be constant reminders of the divine commands (Exod. 20:1-19) and a warning against spiritual infidelity against Him who emphatically declares: **I am the Lord your God, who brought you out of the land of Egypt.**

G. REBELLION AGAINST DIVINE AUTHORITY. 16:1-50.

Korah's Uprising. 16:1-11. **1-2. Korah,** the leading insurgent, was a Kohathite Levite (Exod. 6:21; Jude 11) and therefore had the most honorable charge of all the Levites in transporting the most holy things of the tabernacle (4:15). Yet he was not satisfied, for he aspired to the priesthood (v. 10). Perhaps, too, he regarded himself as mistreated, since Elizaphan, who belonged to the youngest branch descended from Uzziel (3:27), was made "head ... of the families of the Kohathites" (3:30). Dathan, Abiram, and On joined the rebellion. As descendants of the firstborn, Reuben, they

claimed the right to give orders. Probably On realized his error and withdrew
from the conspiracy, for his name is not
mentioned again. The wicked pride of
these men was a dreadful leaven that
infected 250 princes (cf. 1:16).

3. The revolt was against the divine
authority delegated to Moses; hence, it
was against Christ as Lord, of whom
Moses was a type, and against Aaron
and the priesthood, which was divinely
invested in him. Therefore, it was
against Christ and His gracious service
as priest. This is prophetic of the apostasy of the last days (see Jude 11). These
lawless rebels had to clothe their rebellion with some semblance of piety, for
they were intruding into a sphere where
divine light shines. Yet it was the language of those who were setting themselves up against the divine authority
exercised in grace. They meant to
overturn what the LORD had established
to usurp a place for themselves that He
had not given them (Heb. 5:4).

4-5. Moses prostrated himself in
humility and placed the case wholly in
God's hand (cf. vv. 22, 45; 2 Tim. 2:19).
Ecclesiastical priestism denying or en-
croaching upon the priesthood of all believers (typified by Aaron and his sons)
is the modern analogy (1 Pet. 2:5; Rev.
1:6).

*Dathan's and Abiram's Rebellion.
16:12-15.* **12.** Dathan and Abiram were
rebelling laymen who flouted God's
authority vested in Moses by refusing to
appear when summoned. Just as there
was a grasping at religious power by
Korah, so a rejection of divine authority
appeared in Dathan and Abiram. One is
ritualism exercising usurped authority
under a sacerdotal caste that lays claim
to priesthood. The other is *rationalism*,
which exalts human intellect and will
not submit to the authority of the LORD
or of the Holy Scriptures. Both are

prominent in latter-day apostasy and are
forms of rebellion against Christ. **14.
Wilt thou put out the eyes of these men?**
means "throw dust in the eyes" of these
men? or "blind them to the fact that you
(Moses) keep none of your promises."

*The Judgment of the Rebels.
16:16-35.* **16-19.** The command given to
Korah (vv. 6-7) is repeated. All religious
pretensions face testing by the LORD
Himself, no matter how popular with the
majority. **20-21.** Evil developed to the
full calls forth God's glory in judgment.
Only the priestly grace, as seen in Moses
and Aaron, saved the people from being
consumed. **22.** Their intercession
speaks of Christ's high-priestly work
before God (Heb. 7:25). What the
people had actually rebelled against was
their only hope. The divine proposing to
consume the people in a moment was a
test for Moses and Aaron to see whether
they were imbued with the spirit of
grace, of which the priesthood was a
blessed witness. They passed the test
with flying colors.

23-26. But the LORD quickly commanded Moses to order the congregation to separate themselves from all
contact with the rebels (cf. 1 Cor. 5:1-5;
2 Tim. 2:19-21; Rev. 18:4). The insurgents were ripe for ruin, even as Sodom
was when Lot was ordered to flee from
the doomed city (Gen. 19:15). **30.** In this
solemn scene, where the divine authority and grace were so flagrantly flouted,
the LORD is seen to **make a new thing,**
literally, "create a creation." **31-33.**
Apparently this took the form of a
supernatural earthquake, as the ground
opened and swallowed up the rebel
leaders with their families.

35. Fire from the LORD then **consumed**
the 250 who had **offered incense.** But
even in wrath God remembered mercy,
for the children of Korah were
preserved (26:11). Evidently they had

learned God's holiness by the awful fate of their father and could be trusted to guard God's house from the intrusion of anything out of keeping with its sanctity (cf. 1 Chron. 6:54-67; 9:19-32; 26:1-20; 2 Chron. 23:3-4).

The Efficacy of the Divinely Appointed Priesthood. 16:36-50. **36-38.** Divine judgment upon the humanly concocted priesthood of Korah and his fellow rebels furnished the occasion for the LORD's attestation of the Aaronic order and that which it typifies of Christ and His priestly redemptive work. This is shown by three things: (1) It was attested by the LORD's direction concerning what should be done with the censers desecrated by the insurgents. A duly consecrated Aaronic priest, Eleazar, was to **take up the censers out of the burning** of the fire that had consumed the false priests. Moses, in type vindicating God's Word and the lordship of Christ, was to **scatter . . . the fire,** for it with the censers had entered the sanctuary and so it was hallowed, belonging to the LORD.

(2) It was attested by the fact that the censers were not to be destroyed or put to a profane use, since they had been set apart for the LORD, even though wrongly used. **39-40.** Accordingly, Eleazar was commanded to have the censers beaten into plates for the altar of burnt offering. Thus, they were to serve two purposes: first, to cover the altar (figuratively vindicating and protecting God's Word and its witness concerning Christ's priesthood work in atonement); and second, to serve as a reminder for generations to come of the God-ordained character of the Aaronic priesthood and its adumbration of Christ's gracious service as priest. Korah's rebellion was a blatant attack on God's Word and its testimony concerning this great truth.

46-50. (3) It was attested by Moses commanding Aaron to run to the sanctuary to bring his censer with the legitimate fire and incense to provide an **atonement** (covering) against the judgment (plague) that was justly decimating the people *for their high-handed unbelief.* The plague was halted as Aaron **stood between the dead and the living,** one of the most dramatic portrayals of the glorious priestly ministry of Christ, the greater than Aaron, and His "so great salvation" (Heb. 2:3) that is found anywhere in the Old Testament (cf. 2 Cor. 2:14-17).

H. FINAL VINDICATION OF AARON'S PRIESTHOOD. 17:1-13.

The Direction Concerning the Rods. 17:1-5. **1-2.** The final attestation of the God-ordained position and purpose of the Aaronic priesthood, so wickedly challenged in Korah's rebellion (chap. 16), is now presented. The LORD directed the positive test that would settle for all time the question broached by the insurgents. A rod was to be taken for each tribe with the tribal name inscribed on it. **3.** Aaron's name was inscribed on the rod of Levi. **4.** The rods were then placed in the tabernacle before the ark of the testimony (Exod. 25:16), where the LORD met with His people.

5. The divine word was: **the man's rod, whom I shall choose shall blossom** (cf. 16:5) **and I will make to cease from me the murmurings of the children of Israel.** Murmurings arise from the flesh wanting a place with God and refusing to admit that it is under death and judgment before Him. This was the cause of the rebellion of Korah, Dathan, and Abiram. The gracious testimony God gave of Aaron's priesthood, and through him antitypically to Christ's priestly work, is designed to open the way to end the activities of the flesh.

The Rods Before the Lord. 17:6-7. **6. Every tribal prince gave Moses a rod apiece ... even twelve rods.** In this way all the Israelites were brought representatively before the LORD. And Aaron's name was inscribed on the tribe of Levi to show the distinctive calling of the high priest over the priesthood, and the priesthood over the Levites, and in turn the Levites over the other tribes. **7. And Moses laid up the rods before the Lord** for the confirmation of Aaron's high-priesthood before the testimony (the Ark of the Covenant, v. 4) from which the divine revelation proceeded (Exod. 25:21; 29:42) in the tabernacle of witness.

Aaron's Rod Blossoms. 17:8-9. **8.** Aaron's rod was made alive by a miracle. This foreshadowed the resurrection of the greater than Aaron, by which He became our heavenly High Priest, securing the fruit of life in service Godward. All the rods were absolutely dead, with not a sign of life in any of them. Only Aaron's rod was quickened with superabundant life, attested by **buds ... blossoms, and ... almonds** (cf. Rom. 6:4).

The almond tree is the first of all trees to bud and bloom after the winter season, furnishing even in a natural way an apt illustration of resurrection. Although Christ was a priest in the days of His flesh, He did not become a priest officially until He died, rose again, and ascended to heaven. Numbers 17 portrays Him as our "great high priest" who through resurrection has "passed into the heavens," making intercession for us and bidding us to "come boldly unto the throne of grace" (Heb. 4:14-16). As such, He "hath an unchangeable priesthood. . . [and] is able also to save them to the uttermost that come unto God by him, seeing he ever liveth to make intercession for them"

(Heb. 7:24-25). Korah's rebellion would set aside the divine order that foreshadowed all this in the redemptive priestly work of Christ.

9. Moses brought out all the rods from before the Lord unto all the children of Israel to prove to them that the divinely ordained priesthood ran through the Aaronic line alone.

The Lesson of the Rods. 17:10-13. **10.** The lesson must not be forgotten, and so Moses was instructed to permanently deposit Aaron's rod **before the testimony ... for a sign against the rebels** and to **take away their murmurings from me, that they die not.** Only through the death and resurrection of Christ and a resting in the efficacy of His high-priestly ministry in heaven will the believer be delivered from murmuring. Aaron's staff kept before the testimony was an abiding witness to the power and life of the risen heavenly High Priest. His life is continually active on our behalf so that by His grace and support, as we realize the deadness of our own rods, we appropriate His life and victory as our own. Only then are we delivered from the death that characterizes the flesh and from the murmuring it produces. Only then can we come *near* unto the tabernacle of the LORD in a living way.

12. The lesson of death that characterizes the flesh had been learned by the people, at least in a negative way, when they cried, **Behold, we die, we perish, we all perish. 13.** Without knowledge of our risen heavenly High Priest and faith in the efficacy of His ministry for us, **we** (shall) **be consumed,** as the murmurers in the wilderness were, **with dying.**

I. DUTIES AND DUES OF PRIESTS AND LEVITES. 18:1-32.

Duties of the Priests and Levites. 18:1-7. The Aaronites having been divinely established in their distinctive

208

priestly position and the Levites in their special sphere of service (chap. 17), in logical sequence the duties of each and their dues from each other and the people are set forth. **1.** The Aaronites were to **bear the iniquity of the sanctuary** by being responsible for any neglect or offense relating to approaching God in the priesthood and tabernacle ritual (cf. Exod. 28:38). This was to avoid further calamities of unauthorized persons intruding into the sanctuary and priesthood, as in Korah's rebellion.

2-5. The task of the rest of the tribe of Levi was to minister to Aaron and his sons while they officiated in the sanctuary (see 3:5-10; 4:15-20). Violation of Aaron's special high-priestly status is typified in setting aside Christ's unique high-priestly position and the one way of approach to God by His death and resurrection (John 14:6). Violation of the God-ordained status of Aaron's sons prefigured the rejection of the priesthood of the believer and his access to God through the atonement of Christ. This is why wrath came upon the rebellious Korahites (8:19). In figure, human sin was left unatoned and exposed to the infinite holiness of God and, therefore, to His wrath.

7. I have given your priest's office unto you as a service of gift meant that the office of the priest was a privileged gift granted by God Himself to prefigure His saving grace, which was to be manifested in due time in the person and redemptive work of Christ.

Priests' Dues from the People. 18:8-19. The priesthood was to be maintained by a wide range of offerings from the people. The offerings typify the believer-priest's sacrifice of praise and thanksgiving to God (Heb. 13:15), as well as doing good and sharing material bounty by giving to God and His work (Heb. 13:16). **8.** The offerings lifted up or waved before God—**heave offerings** —included what was to be reserved of the offerings presented to God for the priests by reason of their anointing (Lev. 8:10-12, 30), prefiguring the anointing of every believer-priest (2 Cor. 1:21) by virtue of his identification and union with Christ (1 Cor. 12:12), our great High Priest. It is the anointing that puts us on a priestly footing with God.

9-13. Also included was whatever was not consumed on the altar fire—every cereal offering, every sin offering. These are described as **most holy things** because (1) they were never to leave the sanctuary; (2) they were to be eaten by the priests alone; (3) they speak of the person and redemptive work of Christ; and (4) they show how God's people are to comprehend the importance of the priestly ministry and to cultivate and support it perpetually by giving the best to God both spiritually and materially (Heb. 13:15-16) in the form of a **wave offering**, that is, every portion "lifted away" from an offering.

14-18. Also all **devoted** things, that is, items banned from common use, such as war booty (Josh. 6:17, 19), were to be consecrated to the LORD alone and given to the priests, as well as the firstborn of man and unclean beasts, which had to be redeemed (see Exod. 13:2, 12, 15; 34:20; Luke 2:22-24). The food of the priests as seen in this chapter, coming from the offerings of the people, has in view what goes out from the people to God. It is the expression of their spiritually enriched hearts toward Him or as a result of their moral exercises induced by their presentation of sin and trespass offerings. In view is *not* the downflow of blessing from God, although that is the producing cause, but the upflow of offering Godward, which is the result of His priests being well nourished.

19. All the heave offerings of the holy things were secured for the priests in perpetuity under **a covenant of salt** (Lev. 2:13), sealed with that which preserves, so as never to be broken (2 Chron. 13:5; Ezek. 43:24; Mark 9:49-50; Col. 4:6).

Levites' Dues from the People. 18:20-24. **20.** In return for their service in connection with the tabernacle, the Levites were supported by the tithes of the people, for they had no inheritance among the tribes. It is significant that the staff of Aaron was "for the house of Levi" (17:8). All Levitical service is to take character from Christ as the living Priest, ordained by God, and it is all to be inseparably united to what is priestly and to minister to what is priestly. Its basic object is that God may be served in relation to the tent of meeting and all it stands for in approach and service to God.

Priests' Dues from the Levites. 18:25-32. A tithe of the tithes, which they received from the people, was to be given by the Levites to the priests. **29.** This was to be **the best** (lit., "fatness") of the gifts, **the hallowed part** as a contribution to the priests. This plainly shows that every movement toward God is meant to benefit what is priestly. All service had to yield its tithe to the priest. **32.** Otherwise, if it was not centered in contact with the living God through the divinely ordained priestly approach, it would be merely dead ritualism and fleshly works (the subject of chap. 19), which would **pollute the holy things** and result in physical death.

J. CLEANSING FROM FLESHLY DEFILEMENT. 19:1-22.

Provision for Cleansing. 19:1-10. **1-8.** This cleansing provision was strictly according to the LORD's direction and commandment. The **red heifer** is a type of Christ's sacrifice as the basis of the believer's cleansing from the defilement of sin manifested through the flesh. It emphasizes (1) the color *red*, speaking of sacrificial blood, and (2) the perfections of Christ as the sacrifice, stressed by the particularity of description, **without spot** (blemish) strengthened by the negative **no defect** (NASB; cf. Lev. 22:20-25; 1 Pet. 1:18-20), indicating absolute perfection demanded, and the words, **upon which never came yoke**, illustrating the perfect obedience of Christ and His complete yieldedness to the will of God and His total freeedom from any form of fleshly servitude (Deut. 21:3; 1 Sam. 6:7).

While the **ordinance of the law** of the red heifer was given to Moses and Aaron, Eleazar, not Aaron, had to do with the red heifer becoming **unclean until the evening.** This suggests he is not to be viewed here as a type of Christ, but as a priestly condition in the saints being divinely helped (*Eleazar* means "God's helper"), by which they would understand what was necessary to meet defilement contracted in the wilderness journey. Eleazar would not **slay** or **burn** the heifer, but these actions would take place **before his face ... in his sight.**

It is evident that priestly exercise in the saints produces understanding of the utter necessity for the death and judgment-bearing of Christ, not only for justification but also for purification from uncleanness. Eleazar's sprinkling the blood before **the tent of meeting seven times** (v. 4, NASB) illustrates faith's recognition of the complete value and efficacy of Christ's blood to cleanse from sin manifested in the flesh (1 John 1:7), the life of the flesh being symbolically poured out in the sacrificial ritual (Lev. 17:11; cf. Heb. 10:4).

In our Lord's case, His death was vicarious and signified the fact that the believer's life in the flesh has come to an end in Christ's death. Consequently the flesh can have no place in the believer's approach to God. The burning of the heifer, even to its blood and excrement, eloquently emphasizes the unmitigated judgment under which Christ came when He was "made . . . sin for us" (2 Cor. 5:21). Upon the cross He identified Himself, and was identified by God, with the state of sinful flesh in which the believer is by nature, and He came under its condemnation in the most complete way (Rom. 6:10; 8:3).

As priests we should contemplate divine wrath falling fully upon Him, which should impress upon us the necessity of seeing and acting upon the fact of the complete defilement of the flesh. The moral effect that is to follow immediately is portrayed in the priest's casting **cedar wood . . . hyssop, and scarlet . . . into the midst of the burning of the heifer**, prefiguring things in which a believer might naturally pride himself (cf. Gal. 2:20; Phil. 3:3-11).

The spiritually minded believer, viewing Christ's judgment-bearing, must cast everything of the flesh into the burning. Even though the priest had not actually been defiled, his washing and bathing indicate that God wants to arouse believers to the consciousness of the sinfulness of their flesh, necessitating a self-judging cleansing process. The priest was **unclean** until the **evening.** A certain period of exercise of soul is necessary to realize at least fully the defilement of one's own flesh, not by actual failure, but in view of Christ's suffering in bearing its condemnation.

9-10. The same sort of exercise was performed by the **man who** was **clean,** who gathered up **the ashes of the heifer** so they would be available for the cleansing of others. He had to realize the defilement of the flesh. With the priest, he represents saints who have not allowed

the flesh to act, but who must never forget, through what Christ suffered, the utter defilement of their own flesh. The sacrifice was reduced to ashes, which were preserved as a memorial of the sacrifice. The ashes (a type of Christ's death, as bearing the defilement of sin in the flesh) were mixed in turn with water (type of both the Spirit and the Word; John 7:37-39; Eph. 5:26). The Spirit uses the Word of God in its testimony to Christ's death to convict the believer of sin in the flesh. Instead of despairing, the convicted believer judges and confesses the sin (1 John 1:9) and is forgiven and cleansed (John 13:3-10; 1 John 1:7-10).

General Rules for Cleansing. 19:11-13. **11.** Anyone who touched a **dead body** was unclean for seven days. This illustrates a believer's allowing some working of the flesh. **12-13.** In such a case, purification could be effected by a moral process that took time—**on the seventh day he shall be clean.** The responsibility to use the appointed means (the "water of separation," v. 9; cf. 8:7) rested on the defiled person (cf. 2 Cor. 7:1; 1 John 3:3). When one became conscious of having allowed the flesh to manifest itself, exercise was to begin at once, but during two days nothing could be done in the way of purifying. The type suggests the seriousness of fleshly defilement and its results.

But **on the third day** the defiled person **shall purify himself with it** (i.e., the "water of separation" from sin, called the "water of purifying," 8:7). By neglecting to cleanse himself (lit., "de-sin" or "un-sin" himself), a man defiled the tabernacle, or dwelling of the LORD, and incurred excommunication from God's people (cf. 1 Cor. 5:5; 1 John 5:16-17).

Special Rules for Cleansing. 19:14-22. **14.** Sin in the flesh may extend its defiling effects even to the place one occupies among God's people (cf. 1 Cor. 15:33-34). When the flesh manifests itself, it has no place in "the tents of the righteous" (Psalm 118:15, NASB). Yet it is like "a little leaven" that "leaveneth the whole lump" (1 Cor. 5:6; Gal. 5:9) when it appears. **15.** Open vessels with no cover were unclean.

16. The saint was constantly exposed to sources of uncleanness, and so it was imperative that he should not be open to receive solicitation to fleshly indulgence. **17.** If he was, the water of purification, freshly prepared with **running water** ("living water," speaking of the vitality of the Spirit's ministry through the Word; cf. John 7:37-39) was to be applied as stipulated (vv. 12, 19).

18-22. The services of the brethren had an important place in purifying, for the ministry of a clean man was necessary to sprinkle the water on one who was unclean (cf. Gal. 6:1). The priesthood of the believer does not support any contention that the saint can have private sin, for sin hurts God's people and His service. God's people often neglect their ministry of purifying the assembly, but a believer must not think he can help restore a brother without going through a personal humbling exercise (1 John 1:8).

K. FINAL EVENTS IN THE WILDERNESS. 20:1-29.

Miriam's Death. 20:1. Miriam died at Kadesh in the wilderness of Zin, apparently in the fortieth year after the Exodus (cf. 14:33-35; 33:3, 37-39). It is sad that she died almost within sight of the land, never entering into the rest it prefigured (cf. Mic. 6:4; Heb. 4:1). The incident of her rebellion (12:1-16) reflects a subtle working of the flesh that disbarred her from the life of victory, which the entrance into Canaan prefigures.

Moses' Sin. 20:2-13. **2-5.** Once again the shortage of water presented a test (cf. Exod. 17:1-7; Deut. 32:51). And again the people, longing for the abundance of Egypt, contended with Moses and Aaron (cf. 11:4-6), protested that it would have been better to have died with their brethren (cf. 16:35). But the LORD's purpose in testing His people at this time was not to expose their unbelief (although that was revealed incidentally), but to show them in dramatic fashion the value of the priesthood, which was divinely set up on their behalf, betokening the grace of God that would see them into the land.

7-12. This appears in the divine command, **Take the rod** (Aaron's priestly staff in the ark, which in budding had spoken of Christ in resurrection and heavenly priestly intercession, 17:9-10). **Speak ... unto the rock** (Christ, 1 Cor. 10:4) **before their** (the people's) **eyes; and it shall give forth its water.**

Moses' sin in the light of the typical symbolism was threefold: (1) *Moses sinned in presumptuous disobedience.* He should have merely spoken to the rock as commanded, not struck it once, much less twice (vv. 10-11). The rock (Christ, 1 Cor. 10:4), once smitten in death, does not need to be smitten (put to death) again. Moses' act of disobedience implied typically that one sacrifice was ineffectual, thus setting aside the eternal efficacy of the blood (Heb. 9:25-26; 10:3, 11, 12). The abundant water speaks of divine grace through the Spirit reaching the needs of God's people, despite the error of their leader. Antitypically it points to our great heavenly High Priest responding through "the throne of grace" to the infirmities of His people on earth (Heb. 4:14-16).

The **rod** was the first thing in God's mind, and the very unbelief of the people served to highlight its virtue and value before Him. Their unfaithfulness accented His faithfulness in grace (2 Tim. 2:13). Wonderfully set forth is the fact that God's people *have* a great High Priest in the heavenly tabernacle (Heb. 4:14; 8:1; 10:21).

(2) *Moses sinned in his failure to sense the divine grace.* Although Moses and Aaron went from the complaining people and in a right attitude fell on their faces before the LORD, neither of them was transformed into correspondence with the glory of the LORD that appeared to them (v. 6). Neither comprehended the LORD as the One who was hallowing Himself in all the grace that the priesthood expressed, and which had the fulfillment of His own purpose in view (cf. Rom. 8:33-35). Moses, representing the Law, ready to denounce the people as **rebels** and strike in double condemnation, as it were, in the context of the manifestation of God's grace through the priesthood, was an untrue witness to the divine glory before the congregation. Hence, he was disqualified to bring the people into the land (v. 12).

(3) *Moses sinned in his self-exaltation.* Assuming authority that was not his, Moses should not have said, "Must *we* fetch you water?" and presumptuously put himself and Aaron in God's place (v. 10, italics added; cf. Psalm 106:32-33).

Edom's Hostility. 20:14-21. The descendants of Esau, the brother of Israel (Jacob) showed heartless cruelty in denying passage through their territory (cf. Gen. 25:20-24). But such conduct may often be expected of kindred people, whom it is right that we recognize as brethren, but who are characterized, like Esau, by what is natural and fleshly and who despise the true birthright of the saints. We must not expect them to facilitate our movements toward Canaan rest, but to resist our true spiritual progress on "the king's highway" (v.

17), marked today by ancient sites along the modern road, hoary already when the Roman road was laid in the pre-Christian centuries.

Aaron's Death. 20:22-29. **25-28.** Aaron's death on Mount Hor (Jebel Harun), some fifty miles south of the Dead Sea, offered clear intimation that "the Levitical priesthood" could not bring the people of God into the spiritual rest God had in purpose for His people (Heb. 7:11-28), typified by Canaan. Aaron's death marked the end of the wanderings. From then on Israel marched or encamped, but did not wander. God's grace carried them through to the land, which was typical of the spiritual rest we enter by faith (Heb. 3-4). Mount Hor became the place of special instruction for the whole assembly as Aaron ascended it to die.

29. All the congregation saw that Aaron was dead. But there is another Priest "of whom it is witnessed that he liveth" (Heb. 7:8). He is of that order which alone can bring the people of God into all that His love has purposed for them. The priestly office, represented by the holy garments, has passed from Aaron to Christ. God's ancient people could not possibly have comprehended the spiritual significance of all these prefigured events. But *we* can, and ought to, because "these things happened to them as types, and have been written for our admonition, upon whom the end of the ages have come" (1 Cor. 10:11, literal Gr.)—a sufficient scriptural authority to defend a detailed typology of the Pentateuch.

III. JOURNEYING TOWARD CANAAN. 21:1—36:13.

A. THE BRONZE SERPENT. 21:1-35.

Foretaste of Victory. 21:1-3. **1. King Arad ... in the Negev** (Negeb), the sparsely watered region south of

Beersheba extending south and south-west beyond Kadesh-Barnea, attacked Israel and took some of them prisoners. He was a Canaanite and among Israel's enemies that had to be vanquished in order to reach the land. In an illustrative sense, these foes represent certain fleshly principles that stand in opposition to what is spiritual in God's people. Since Canaanite ($k^e n\check{a}^{ca} n\hat{i}$) denotes "a tradesman" (cf. Isa. 23:8), originally of red purple wool, the foe suggests the peril that material prosperity and desire for worldly gain presents to God's people, some of whom were taken prisoner by this king.

2. Israel's vow marked a vigorous devotion not common in Numbers. Viewed typically, it is the result of drinking water from the rock and the investiture of Eleazar (20:11, 26-28), whose office speaks of divine grace and whose name betokens divine help. The apprehension of God's purpose for His own and of Christ as Priest in relation to that purpose invigorates the soul. It assures us that God is for us, so who can be against us? (Rom. 8:31-32).

3. True to her vow, Israel **utterly destroyed** Arad and its villages south of Hebron, calling the place **Hormah** ("destruction," from the root $h\check{a}r\check{a}m$, "utterly destroy as under a curse"). It was a holy war conducted to illustrate the spiritual principle that everything that opposes the will of God is under the ban of Him who is Lord of history and whose infinite holiness is working out His moral principles.

The Bronze Serpent. 21:4-9. **4-5.** But the victory won apparently threw the people off guard. The hardships of the journey to circumvent Edom gave the flesh an opportunity to manifest itself. The people traveled south by way of the Red (Reed) Sea, here denoting the right arm of the Red Sea, now called the Gulf of Aqaba. The LORD had to teach them the lesson of Romans 7, that the flesh is inveterately sinful and at enmity with God. The believer must learn to judge the flesh, and to understand how God has secured its complete condemnation, if he is to experience the victory of Romans 8.

6. The fiery serpents the LORD sent among His people symbolize the fact that the venom of sin in fallen humanity is satanic in origin (Gen. 3:1, 15; cf. Rev. 12:9), and its manifestation in human nature takes on a burning and destructive character, producing death. The physical death of the Israelites foreshadows spiritual death, as evidenced by broken fellowship with God and His people (1 John 1:3, 7).

7. When provision for cleansing by Christ's propitiatory work on the cross (the bronze serpent lifted up) is not appropriated in confession (1 John 1:9), eventual physical death may result (1 Cor. 11:30; 1 John 5:16).

8-9. The divine command was **Make thee a fiery serpent. . . . And Moses made a serpent of bronze** (brass), prefiguring Christ "made . . . sin for us" (2 Cor. 5:21; cf. Psalm 22:1; Matt. 27:46). The form of bronze was that of the fiery serpent without the poison. So Christ appeared in flesh, yet without sin. The serpent **set . . . upon a pole** (cf. John 3:14; 12:32) portrays how Christ in being lifted up upon the cross came to be identified with what the serpent brought in (Gen. 3:1-15). The bronze symbolizes judgment (in the bronze altar, of divine judgment, in the bronze laver, of self-judgment). It was the divine purpose that the lawless principle of sin, expressing itself so fully in fallen man (cf. Matt. 27:27-31), should be judged and condemned in man, the God-man, Christ Jesus (Rom. 8:3).

In type, the serpent was lifted up in

the fortieth year after the Exodus. But in the antitype, the believer may know and appropriate by faith the blessing of the truth that all that he is morally in the flesh has been judged in Christ as a sacrifice for sin on the cross. Looking at the serpent of bronze for healing of the snake bite emphasizes the truth that faith is always the prerequisite for the manifestation of divine grace in salvation (Isa. 45:22; John 3:16; Eph. 2:8-9).

When anyone bitten by a serpent beheld the serpent of brass, **he lived.** For the Israelites it meant faith resulting in physical life, which would enable them to enter Canaan—a type of enjoying the rest and victory that divine salvation provides for us in this life, in knowing our *position* in Christ and converting it into our experience of Christ (Rom. 6:11). But God's purposes of love to us transcend time and envision eternity. Hence, the life in antitype also comprehends eternal life (John 3:14-18).

Joyful Journey to Transjordan. 21:10-20. After healing at the cross, and in figure the judging of sin in the flesh, victory and joyful singing are the order of God's people, who as the army of the LORD then moved relentlessly on toward Canaan. The spiritual sequence is significant: (1) *victory* over indwelling sin (vv. 8-9; cf. John 3:14-16; Rom. 8:3); (2) *identification of the LORD with them in battle* by reference to the book, "*The wars of the LORD*" (vv. 14-15); (3) *water*, speaking of the Spirit given (v. 15; cf. John 7:37-39) and *a well* (vv. 16-18), suggesting the Spirit surging up within *the believer* (John 4:14); (4) *joy and singing* (vv. 17-18; cf. Rom. 14:17); and (5) *high ground*—Pisgah, one of the elevated peaks of the Moabite plateau, jutting out toward the Dead Sea and presenting a fine view of Canaan on the west (vv. 19-20).

Defeat of the Amorite Kings.

21:21-35. Still greater victories were won, for the LORD was now identified with His people in battle. Sihon, king of the Amorites (vv. 21-31), and Og, the giant who was king of Bashan (vv. 33-35), were completely defeated and their lands possessed. Both represent the principles and powers of darkness in their resistance to God's people. **23.** Sihon was defeated at **Jahaz**, identified with Khirbet Umm el-Idham, five miles north of Dibon. Heshbon (vv. 27-30), originally a Moabite town, had been taken by Sihon and made his royal city. **33.** The defeat of the Amorite kingdom north of the Jabbok took place at **Edrei**, possibly modern Der^{c}a, forty miles east of the Jordan.

B. BALAAM THE PROPHET. 22:1-41.

Balak's Desire to Curse Israel. 22:1-4. **1.** On the threshold of the promised land, God's elect people Israel faced an unseen peril. **2-3.** Balak, king of Moab, terrified at what Israel had done to the Amorites (21:21-35), was utterly dismayed at the number and the strength of the nation. **4. Now shall this company lick up** (shear off) **all that are round about us, as the ox licketh up** (shears off) **the grass of the field.** Balak as king is closely identified with Moab, which represents unregenerate man's pride (Isa. 16:6; Jer. 48:42). In view is not a natural but a spiritual warfare (Eph. 6:10-20). It is the spirit of Satan, the accuser of the brethren, to proudly curse what God has blessed. It is madness to attempt such a thing, but it is the pride of man's heart that opens the door to such folly (cf. Rom. 8:31-35).

Balaam Hired by Balak. 22:5-20. Balak sent for Balaam ("people's devourer") from Pethor, a city of Mesopotamia (Deut. 23:4). Balaam was originally a pagan magician of a common class of religious occultists, who had mediumistic divinatory powers. He evidently had some sort of conversion experience; but, like Simon the sorcerer, he carried over his mediumistic gifts and attempted to use them in the service of the LORD (Acts 8:9-24; cf. Matt. 12:27). As in such cases in modern church history, covetousness was the impelling motive that blinded Balaam to the peril of such a ministry in which the demon spirit dares to intrude into the realm of the Spirit of God.

6. That Balaam had real demonic power is evidenced by Balak's declaration, **for I know that he whom thou blessest is blessed, and he whom thou cursest is cursed** (cf. 23:7; 24:9). As a corrupt, money-loving prophet, Balaam became the prototype of false teachers, especially those of the last days (2 Pet. 2:15-16; Jude 11).

7-14. He was dazzled by **the rewards of divination**, but the LORD pleaded with him and urged him away from the evil course toward which the glitter of gold was impelling him. **15-20.** Yet greater rewards and worldly honor were promised him, but the directive will of God had been made known to him. Balaam should have dropped the matter, but he was lured on by his love of money.

Balaam a Perverse Servant of God. 22:21-35. **21.** Rejecting the directive will of God (v. 12) left the prophet to follow his own selfish inclination, as he preferred the permissive will of God. By the latter, God had in mind the testing of the prophet, so that he might become an example and a warning to future generations. **22-23. The angel of the Lord** (the preincarnate Christ, Judg. 2:1; cf. Gen. 31:11-13) with drawn sword (cf. Josh. 5:13) was seen by the dumb animal, but not by the money-blinded prophet. The case of the ass speaking is an instance of divine omnipotence.

28-31. The Lord opened the mouth of the ass . . . then the Lord opened the eyes of Balaam. 32. The LORD dramatically showed Balaam that his **way** was **perverse** and that fact, along with his spiritual resistance weakening with every step of the way he was going, tragedy was inevitable, unless his spiritual senses were aroused. So Balaam was directed to go, because God had a message to give posterity. **35.** However, the command was stern: **But only the word that I shall speak unto thee, that thou shalt speak** (cf. v. 38).

Balaam Sees Israel. 22:36-41. **41. The utmost part** (extremity) **of the people** comprehends the end of the encampment—those most remote from the sanctuary. Balak's thought was that those in such a position were more likely to come under the curse than *all* the people. How greatly the enemy would take advantage of the sins and failures of the Lord's people to bring them, if possible, under a curse (cf. 11:1). But Balak had to learn, as all must, that not even "the extremity" of God's people can be cursed. As God's elect, they are justified from all things, and no accusation against them will stand.

In all this, Balaam is the type of the mercenary prophet, ambitious to exploit his gift in a monetary way ("the *way* of Balaam," 2 Pet. 2:15, italics added). The "error of Balaam" (Jude 11) is the diviner-prophet's blunder in reasoning that God *of necessity* must curse His people because of their sin. Balaam was ignorant, as are those who are contaminated by occult religionism, of God's electing love of His people and the immutability of His choice (Rom. 11:29). He failed to see how God can be "just, and the justifier" of the believing sinner through the death of Christ (Rom. 3:26), to which *all* Israel's sacrificial and priestly ritual pointed. The "doctrine of Balaam" (Rev. 2:14) was the teaching of the covetous seer to abandon a separated pilgrimage for worldly conformity (31:15-16; cf. James 4:4).

C. BALAAM'S FIRST TWO PROPHETIC PARABLES. 23:1-30.

Parable One. 23:1-12. Presented first is the sacrificial preparation (vv. 1-6). This was certainly suggested by some knowledge that Balaam had acquired of the sacrifices God had prescribed to be offered by His people (v. 4). **3.** However corrupt the motives that moved Balaam and Balak, it was doubtlessly ordered by God that what they offered spoke to Him of Christ—**the burnt offering**, the ground of blessing, *not* cursing. The sacrificial preparation, therefore, furnished the basis for the prophetic parable itself (vv. 7-10).

It was impossible for Balaam to curse or condemn Israel, whom God had blessed (vv. 8-9), for Israel's *standing* (as *God* saw them) as a redeemed people was immutable in the light of the water out of the rock (20:11) and the serpent lifted up (21:5-9). Israel's *state* (as the people actually were) was morally reprehensible. But this called for the LORD's disciplinary action, not His judgment or curse upon them (Rom. 11:29; cf. 1 Cor. 5:1-5; 11:30-32; Heb. 12:3-17).

9-10. From the top of the rocks ... from the hills I behold him. Balaam saw the people of God from God's lofty vantage point of electing grace. **The people shall dwell alone** (cf. Deut. 32:8; 33:28), a chosen nation, different from all other nations, destined for ultimate unforfeitable blessing. Balaam's parables bring out what God is doing in His sovereign grace and power for His people, whom He will have for Himself despite the enemy's accusations and in spite of what the flesh is (cf. Acts 15:14-17; Acts 18:10; Gal. 1:4; Phil. 1:6).

11-12. Balak, the accuser and condemner of God's people, can only be answered by the word of God. That every true believer is eternally saved and safe is the testimony of that word as spoken even by Balaam, who did not want to declare this truth, but had to speak what **the Lord ... put in** [his] ... **mouth.**

Parable Two. 23:13-30. **13-14.** Those who deny the blessed security of true saints doggedly pursue their denials (cf. 1 Tim. 4:1-2). Balak's strategy throughout was not to let Balaam see the whole host of the LORD's people (cf. 22:41). In bringing Balaam **to the top of Pisgah,** Balak tried to correct what he apparently considered a blunder (22:41). But upon getting a superb panoramic view of the whole camp, the hireling had to utter a grander word in the second parable (vv. 18-24) than in the first (vv. 7-10). This he did again against the background (the **seven altars** and the burnt offering of **bullock and ram on every altar**) of that which spoke to God of Christ (see v. 3).

19-24. The second parable stresses: (1) The LORD is absolutely faithful to His Word and His unchangeable purpose of grace toward His elect people (v. 19; cf. Rom. 11:29). (2) His view of His people is in their unforfeitable blessing (v. 20), in which they are justified from all things through His grace, as typified in their sacrificial and priestly ritual (v. 21*a*). (3) His presence is with His people (v. 21*b*; cf. Exod. 29:45-46), and they are promised certain triumph over their foes (v. 21*c*). (4) God is their Redeemer with great power (v. 22), His power being symbolized by the **wild ox,** a buffalo-type animal with a huge horn in which its strength was concentrated. (5) The satanic and demonic malignity that are against them, manifested in the occult religion of Balak and the occult contamination of Balaam, cannot harm them (v. 23*a*). (6) As the recipient of divine salvation by grace, Israel's testimony is: **What hath God wrought!** (v. 23*b*; cf. Psalm 31:19; 44:1; Jonah 2:9, "Salvation is of the LORD," the theme of divine revelation). Eventually, when the Kingdom is restored to Israel and the nation is saved (Rom. 11:26), the *universal* testimony will be, "What has God done!" (7) Because the Messiah-King will one day rule over the restored nation, Balaam declared, **The shout of a king is among them** (v. 21).

D. BALAAM'S LAST TWO PROPHETIC PARABLES. 24:1-25.

Parable Three. 24:1-14. As in the previous parables, and with similar import, the third parable (vv. 5-9), was prefaced by Balak's unrelenting zeal to curse Israel (23:27-28) and a description of the sacrificial ritual (23:29-30), which, as in all four parables, foreshadows Christ and furnishes the basis for the testimony through Balaam of God's grace toward Israel. **1.** Also introductory to this parable is the account of Balaam's abandonment of occult practice, **enchantments** (properly, "omens," *neḥāshîm*, i.e., looking to auguries). He therefore turned his face westward to the steppes of Moab, where Israel was encamped. **2-4.** This time he was placed by the Spirit of God in an ecstatic state so that **he saw** the substance of the third parable "with his inward mental eye, which had been opened by the Spirit of God" (KD, 3:186).

In beautiful figures he foretold three things: (1) He foretold Israel's future Kingdom glory (vv. 5-7). **7.** His king, ultimately realized in the Messiah, **shall be higher than Agag,** the traditional name for the king of Amalek (1 Sam. 15:8), Israel's inveterate enemy, and suggestive of the Antichrist and all anti-Semitic forces. But since the ora-

cles are to be construed as both literal, with regard to Israel, and illustrative, with regard to the church, they also envision the "righteousness, and peace, and joy" of the Kingdom of God (Rom. 14:17), the victory in Christ we now know (Rom. 8:37; 16:20; 1 Cor. 15:57).

(2) He foretold the ultimate triumph of God's people in conquest over their foes as the final outworking of God's redemptive grace toward them (vv. 8-9*a*). (3) He foretold the consummation of the Abrahamic Covenant of blessing to Israel and to all God's people with the defeat of their foes (v. 9; cf. Gen. 12:3; 27:29). Balak's anger at Israel's blessing (vv. 10-11) was met by Balaam's reply, the result of divine overruling that makes the wrath of men to please Him and the perverseness of the covetous prophet to glorify Him (vv. 12-14).

Parable Four. 24:15-25. **15-16.** By special inspiration, as in the case of the third parable, Balaam uttered the last and most remarkable prophecy, which refers to "the latter days" (vv. 14, 17). **17.** (1) This final parable envisions the Messiah as the **Star out of Jacob,** and **Scepter . . . out of Israel.** The thought is conveyed that all He is and will be as the "Star" and the "Scepter" at His coming is already cherished in the hearts of His saints, so that in this twin role He can be regarded as their Savior, Champion, and Deliverer to set aside everything hostile to God and to them. To us, He is the "morning star" (cf. 2 Pet. 1:19; Rev. 2:28; 22:16-17), who is imminently coming to introduce the day of His Kingdom reign.

The "Star" represents the LORD appearing to be the consummation of all that is cherished in the hopes of the saints by virtue of Christ's redemptive work. The "Scepter" envisions the LORD coming to rule the earth as absolute King and Lord (Rev. !9:16). The

"Scepter" is owned first in Zion (Psalm 110:2) and extends to the ends of the earth when Shiloh comes (Gen. 49:10; Psalm 45:6-17; Isa. 11:9-10). Although the royal insignia "star" and "scepter" include David, they only find their fulfillment in the greater David at His second advent and Kingdom.

(2) Balaam's final parable also envisions the judgment of Israel's enemies and all they stand for at the second advent (vv. 17-19). **Moab** and **the children of Sheth** (likely the ancient inhabitants of the country known from early Egyptian records as the "Shutu people"), represent human pride (Isa. 16; Jer. 48). **18. Edom** represents man's wisdom rendering him independent of God (Jer. 49:7; Obad. 8). **20. Amalek** portrays the inveterate opposition of the natural man to what is of God (Exod. 17:16). **21-22. The Kenites** seem to set forth the disposition of the godless to seek security as earth dwellers. **Asshur** (Assyria) speaks of vaunting pride and cruelty (Isa. 10).

23. Balaam's exclamation, **Alas, who shall live when God doeth this!** envisions the terrible Tribulation judgments, which will purge out the wicked preparatory to Kingdom blessing (cf. Rev. 1:7; 6:1—19:16). **24. Kittim** is Cyprus (Gen. 10:4). The descendants of **Eber** (Gen. 10: 21-30) evidently include God's people, the Hebrews (Israelites). This supplementary parable seems appended to show that God not only acts in judgment upon the world, but also disciplines and judges His own people that they may enter into the blessings He plans for them (Matt. 25:1-46).

E. ISRAEL'S SIN WITH BAAL-PEOR. 25:1-18.

The Sin. 25:1-3. **1.** The enemy, having completely failed to bring a curse upon the people of God by working through Balak and Balaam, changed his tactics.

If Balaam could not curse, he would try to *corrupt* (31:16). The latter satanic ruse has frequently been proved to be more successful, as at **Shittim** ("Acacia Trees"), probably Tell Kefrein, the last stopping place before crossing the Jordan (cf. Josh. 2:1; 3:1).

2. There Moabite women **called** (invited) **the people unto the sacrifices of their gods.** The friendliness and invitations of the world are more subtlely deceptive than its curses. Accepting the invitation to share in the religious festivals of the local Baal worshiped on the height of Peor, the last place from which Balaam blessed Israel (23:28), God's people fell into both spiritual and physical harlotry (vv. 1-3). God's blessing is frequently the prelude to satanic temptation. Satan's snare is not only set for the young and immature, but for the seasoned and mature.

Here the typical picture is of God's people at the end of the wilderness sojourn, when they were about to enter Canaan rest and victory (Heb. 3), and had made a great deal of spiritual progress. It is not to "little children" but to strong "young men" that the appeal is made: "Love not the world, neither the things that are in the world" (1 John 2:15). **3. And Israel joined himself unto Baal-peor** and the grossest immoral idolatry, breaking the first commandment of the Decalogue (Exod. 20:1-7; Psalm 106:28-29; Hos. 9:10).

The Punishment. 25:4-5. Sin in believers always calls forth the divine disciplinary healing (vv. 3-4; cf. Heb. 12:3-17). Serious sin is "sin unto [physical] death" (1 John 5:16; cf. 1 Cor. 5:5; 11:30). Hence, the divine chastening was in proportion to the offense. **4-5.** Moses was ordered to hang the ringleaders in the affair **against the sun,** that is, "publicly" in broad daylight (cf. 2 Sam. 21:9). Moses ordered the

judges of Israel to slay every guilty man who had fraternized with Baal-peor (cf. Exod. 32:27). The LORD also sent a plague in the camp (vv. 3, 8) as an expression of His **fierce anger.**

The Zeal of Phinehas. 25:6-9. **6.** One of the princes of Israel, in plain view of Moses and the entire Israelite community while they were penitently weeping at the sin of those who had fallen into idolatry, appeared and introduced a woman of Midian to his relatives. His shameless attitude before the people and his impenitent complicity with idolatry were a brazen affront to God (cf. v. 11).

7-9. Phinehas, the son of Eleazar the priest, stirred up by this impudent impenitence, seized a spear and pursued the prince and the woman **into the tent** (the prince's tent or bed chamber). There he slew both of them, halting the plague, but not until twenty-four thousand had died (Psalm 106:30). In 1 Corinthians 10:8, the number is stated to be twenty-three thousand; this does not include the one thousand who, according to Jewish tradition, perished when the leaders were executed.

The Reward of Phinehas. 25:10-15. **11-12.** (1) Phinehas was given the LORD's **covenant of peace** (Isa. 54:10; Ezek. 34:25; Mal. 2:5). This prefigures not only effecting "peace with God" in a *positional* sense, through atoning priestly sacrifice (Rom. 5:1), but also "the peace of God" (Phil. 4:7) in an *experiential* sense, on the basis of the believer's position through priestly ministry.

13-14. Phinehas's zeal typifies the zeal of Christ as a Priest for God's righteousness (Heb. 10:11-12) in reference to seriously sinning saints, represented by the Simeonite prince, Zimri, who was guilty of presumptuous idolatry and fornication, and yet was an honored member of the LORD's congregation. Christ's priestly intercession for the saints never ceases or diminishes because of their sins (Rom. 8:34; Heb. 7:25), no matter how serious they are, thus guaranteeing *all* believers an eternal, unforfeitable salvation.

Yet the One who is greater than Phinehas is zealous and jealous for the Father's infinite holiness. Accordingly, He cannot allow serious sin to pass without severe chastisement. The ultimate in such chastisement is physical death (1 Cor. 5:5; 11:30-32). This is what was incurred by the "saints turned idolaters" in general, and by the brazen and audacious Simeonite prince, **Zimri, the son of Salu** in particular, who incurred the ultimate in God's punishment in His own (physical) death (1 John 5:16).

(2) Phinehas also was given an **everlasting priesthood** (cf. Exod. 40:15). The promise looked forward to the eternal priesthood of Christ, which would be characterized by the same priestly concern for God's infinite holiness in relation to the experience and conduct of sinning saints, as so saliently marked Phinehas's ministry.

Command to Smite the Midianites. 25:16-18. The Midianites were descendants of Abraham (Gen. 25:2) and represent the influence that those persons who are physically related to us may have to draw us into worldly and idolatrous associations. **17-18.** Separation from such associations called forth the command: **Vex** (*ṣārăr*, "harass, trouble, show hostility toward")...**and smite them** (cf. 2 Cor. 6:14—7:1) **for they vex** you. Idolatry must be fled from (1 Cor. 10:14) or fought against and exterminated. Israel failed to flee and were vexed; thus they had to adopt the second alternative and exterminate the idolaters and their idolatry.

F. THE SECOND CENSUS. 26:1-65.

The Command and Commission. 26:1-4. Eleazar, the priest, assisted Moses in this numbering, for Aaron had died (20:28). This numbering has in view the people's entrance into their inheritance (cf. vv. 53-54). From this point onward this thought is in the mind of God for His people. The inheritance was a very definite thing before Israel, but it is illustrative of a much greater spiritual heritage of the believer today (Acts 26:18; Eph. 1:11). Repeatedly we are spoken of as "heirs of God" and "joint heirs with Christ" (Rom. 8:17). When we experience the rest that the entrance into the land prefigures (Heb. 3:1—4:16), our heritage in Christ now and hereafter becomes a faith-appropriated reality (Heb. 9:15).

The Record of the Census. 26:5-51. This census was similar to the first census (chap. 1), but it differed in being much more a *family* numbering than a *military* numbering. The military aspect is mentioned here only once (v. 2), in contrast to the first numbering, where it is mentioned in connection with each tribe. This suggests that while military service may be required to gain or hold the inheritance, the enjoyment of it is in family relationships. It was to develop this family character in God's people that their divine education in the wilderness was directed. The LORD would have them move together more and get closer to each other in affection (as in 1 John, the family epistle) to develop conditions most favorable to the enjoyment of the inheritance.

Hence, in this numbering, in addition to the name of the tribe, a record was made of the leading family divisions, designated by the names of the leading tribal patriarchs. In the case of the tribes of Reuben (vv. 5-10); Judah (vv. 19-22);

Manasseh (vv. 28-34); Ephraim (vv. 35-37); Benjamin (vv. 38-41); and Asher (vv. 44-47), these family designations were carried to the third generation. In the case of each tribe there follows the number of men above the age of twenty who were fit for military service, for enjoyment of the rest and the inheritance did not exempt them from conflict (Eph. 6:10-20).

In the record, five tribes had decreased in numbers (Reuben by 2,770 men; Simeon by 37,100; Gad by 5,150; Ephraim by 8,000; Naphtali by 8,000). The other tribes increased. The total count was 601,730, or 1,820 less than at Mount Sinai. Simeon's large decrease was evidently due to more culpable complicity with the defection at Baal-Peor and the consequent more severe punishment in the plague (cf. 25:14). Manasseh's increase, which was the largest (from 32,200 to 52,700), tallies with evidences of this tribe's interest in having and holding the inheritance (cf. 27:1-11; 36:1-13).

Instructions for Dividing the Inheritance. 26:52-56. Two regulations were set forth: (1) The size of the allotment was to be determined in proportion to the size of the tribe indicated by the census (vv. 52-54). This emphasized that fairness and impartiality had to mark the distribution of the inheritance. (2) Yet the application of this general rule of equity was to be determined by lot (vv. 55-56). "Notwithstanding it seems thus to be left to the prudence of their princes, yet the matter must be finally reserved to the providence of their God, in which they must all acquiesce" (Matthew Henry).

The method of the lot was adopted not only to preclude jealousies and disputes, but also so that the several tribes might regard the territories as determined for them by God Himself (cf. Prov. 16:33).

The "tribes" represent saints in assembly (church) order, and this is directed by sovereign divine grace and regulation (e.g., the place of women in the church, 1 Cor. 11:1-16; the distribution of spiritual gifts, 1 Cor. 12:6-7; Eph. 4:4-7).

The Census of the Levites. 26:57-62. As God's special tribe supplying the personnel for the atoning sacrificial ritual, priestly access to God, and the care of holy things, Levi was not numbered with the rest, but by itself. **62.** The reason was that **there was no inheritance given them** because the LORD was their inheritance (for explanation, see 3:11-16).

An Observation Concerning the Census. 26:63-65. The fulfillment of the divine judgment pronounced in 14:28-35 was emphasized. Eleazar and Phinehas (Josh. 14:1; 22:13) and perhaps other Levites entered the land. The sentence of exclusion did not apply to that tribe, which, in contrast to the other tribes, did not send a spy into Canaan; nor does it appear that it concurred in the general murmuring, which the report of the spies occasioned.

G. LOOKING TOWARD ENTRANCE INTO THE INHERITANCE. 27:1-23.

A Question of Inheritance. 27:1-5. **1-3.** The five daughters of Zelophehad of the tribe of Manasseh presented a problem of inheritance to the leaders of Israel. Their father had died in the wilderness as a result of the general punishment of that generation of unbelief (14:28-29; 26:64-65). They were now concerned about inheriting familywise, for their father had left no male heir. Hence, there was no male representative of the family who could record his name in the census registry. **4.** This meant there was no prospect of an inheritance allotment of land for the family by which its name could be perpetuated to posterity. **5.** The problem was presented to the LORD.

The Answer. 27:6-11. The daughters of Zelophehad were justified in their claim. Not only were they given an inheritance, but the law was instituted to guarantee that the land inheritance could never pass out of the possession of the family. If a man died without a son, his possession would go to his daughters. If he was childless, it would pass to his brothers; if there were no brothers, it would go to his father's brothers. If, finally, there were none of those, it would go to his nearest relative (v. 11). This law secured an extended territory for Manasseh (cf. Josh. 17:5-6).

But this family inheritance could not conflict with the tribal inheritance, sovereignly imposed by lot (chap. 36). It is important to the LORD how we conduct ourselves in God's family (see 1 John). But this walk must not violate how we walk together in the local church (the tribal character). Illustrating this aspect of the believer's testimony are the Pauline epistles (cf. 1 Cor. 14:37).

Moses' Imminent Death, and Prayer for a New Leader. 27:12-17. Moses, like Aaron, was denied entrance into the promised land because of the sin committed at Meribah (20:12). Nevertheless, as Israel's great leader, he was permitted to have a view of Canaan from the top of Mount Abarim, a mountainous plateau in northwest Moab, called Mount Nebo (Deut. 32:48-52), or Mount Pisgah (the specific peak; Deut. 3:27; 34:1). **13.** After Moses had seen the land, the LORD said: **Thou also shall be gathered unto thy people** (see Gen. 25:8, 17; 35:29; 49:29, 33).

15-17. Moses' beautiful prayer for the new leader addressed the LORD as **the God of the spirits of all flesh** (cf. 16:22), ascribing to Him the origin and source of

all life. If the LORD sustained a relationship to *all flesh* that was beneficial and
providential, could He possibly fail to
provide a true shepherd-leader for His
own people (cf. 1 Kings 22:17; Zech.
10:2; Matt. 9:36; Mark 6:34)? What a
transformation of spirit from Meribah,
when he angrily cried to the people, "Ye
rebels!" He had come over to the side of
God's unfailing faithfulness and was
counting on it to raise up suitable leadership to possess the inheritance.

Joshua's Appointment. 27:18-23. **18.
Take thee Joshua ... a man in whom is
the Spirit, and lay thine hand upon him**
(cf. Deut. 34:9). Moses and Joshua are
both types of Christ. The former represents Christ's authority as LORD, as
known in the wilderness. The latter represents Christ as the Shepherd-Leader
conducting the LORD's people into the
land. Joshua, Spirit-indwelt, indicates
that it is in the power of the Spirit that
Christ leads into that sphere of spiritual
blessing where salvation rest is known
and enjoyed (Heb. 3-4). Caleb's having
"another spirit" in him (14:24) portrays
how God can bring about in His people a
state that appreciates the "exceedingly
good land" (14:7, KJV) and the full enjoyment of salvation rest that it illustrates.

**19-21. And set him before Eleazar, the
priest, and ... he shall stand before
Eleazar, the priest.** Aaron's priesthood,
as seen in Exodus and Leviticus, is a
type of Christ in His sacrificial work on
the cross. Eleazar, Aaron's successor,
prefigures the resurrection-heavenly
priesthood of Christ. Accordingly,
Joshua foreshadows Christ in heaven,
who acts in and through His people on
earth by the Holy Spirit conducting
them into salvation rest. Therefore,
Joshua had to stand before Eleazar, the
priest, depending, as it were, upon him,
as the work of the Holy Spirit in the

believer is dependent on the priesthood
of Christ in glory (cf. Heb. 4:14-16).

But Joshua was not only to be set
forth before Eleazar the priest but also
before all the congregation. The
presentation of Christ as the greater
Joshua, the Leader of salvation, leading
His own into all that He has provided for
them in salvation rest, is for "the whole
congregation" (assembly) today.
Moreover, "the whole assembly" was
to be **with** Joshua, that is, identified *with*
him (cf. Rom. 6:1-11), so that whether
they went out or came in, they were to
move *with* him. To move with him in
whom the Spirit was, they would need to
have the Spirit too (cf. Rom. 8:11), the
Spirit of sonship and heirship (Rom.
8:14-17).

The close association of the leader
with the priest demonstrates how the
two offices of Christ stand in relation to
each other before God. The leader was
to receive light concerning God's mind
from the priest through the Urim in the
priestly breastplate (see comment on
Exod. 28:30). So God has made communication by Jesus Christ, that
through the Spirit He may show what
He has communicated to His servants
(Rev. 1:1).

God's people are to follow their
leader, who goes ahead of every spiritual movement, to bring them into the
full blessings of salvation rest. Spiritual
leaders are to be followed, as they follow Christ. Hence, spiritual leadership
has great significance in God's ways (cf.
1 Cor. 16:15-19; 1 Thess. 5:12-13; Heb.
13:7, 17). Only those who fully follow
the LORD like Caleb and Joshua are capable of leading God's people into the
exceedingly good land of salvation rest.

H. GOD'S DUE FROM THOSE WHO
POSSESS THEIR INHERITANCE. 28:1-31.

Portion from the Daily Offerings.

28:1-8. God's grace in Christ has provided a wonderful inheritance for His people (Deut. 4:20; Eph. 1:11, 14; 5:5; Col. 1:12; Heb. 9:15). Chapters 28 and 29 unfold what is due God from those who enter into and enjoy their inheritance, that is, the salvation rest (Canaan), which the One who is greater than Joshua has provided for us and into which He conducts us by the Spirit (see 27:18-23).

2. The key is the LORD's command: **My offering, and my bread for my sacrifices ... shall ye observe to offer unto me in their due season.** Humanly speaking, God's heart feeds upon Christ. Hence, the sweet-savor (smell) offerings, symbolizing the matchless worth and complete devotion of Christ (Lev. 1-3), are prominent. Those who enter into salvation rest offer to God their full appreciation of the glorious person and completed redemptive work of Christ, which is their due and God's delight.

Possession of the land (enjoyment of salvation rest) results in God's people having increased ability to minister to Him, and they are obligated to do so. There are no voluntary offerings in this chapter and the next. They are to be spontaneous, but nevertheless are definite obligations **in their due season** (at their set time).

3. The daily burnt offering was basic to all the other offerings. Day by day God would have us delight Him with the keen sense that we stand before Him in identification with the sweet aroma of Christ (see Exod. 29:38-42).

The Sabbath Offerings. 28:9-10. **9-10.** These offerings consisted of two additional **lambs ... besides the continual burnt offering.** When God gives rest, it is to have us yield to Him increased perception of the excellencies of Christ and His all-sufficient redemptive work. The Sabbath is a figure of the believer's rest (Heb. 4:3). Although we observe the Lord's Day in honor of the resurrection of Christ, by which our redeemed lives have become a perpetual spiritual Sabbath, surely God is due more on that day than on any other day of the week in terms of worship, praise, prayer, and testimony.

The Monthly Offerings. 28:11-15. God would remind us that we have months as well as days and years in our spiritual history to "offer the sacrifice of praise ... the fruit of our lips giving thanks to his name" (Heb. 13:15). The months point to the year, which represents the whole cycle of God's gracious dealing with us in time (cf. Isa. 62:2; Luke 4:19). He would remind us in a special sense at these appointed times of how important it is to praise and thank Him for His marvelous provision of salvation, as well as its outworking in His plan for time and eternity, to which the set feasts also point. The importance of the monthly commemoration of these great truths is emphasized by the increased offerings. (For the meaning of the offerings, see detailed exposition in Exodus and Leviticus.)

The Passover Offerings. 28:16-25. The spiritual "beginning of months" for Israel was when the people were delivered from Egyptian bondage (see Exod. 12:1-28; Lev. 23:4-8; Num. 9:2-3). It was a wonderful "beginning of months" for us when Christ became our Passover and took the penalty of sin and death for us. The offerings on this occasion were meant in a special sense to point to His death and our appreciation of it in the praise and thanksgiving we present to God.

The Firstfruits Offering. 28:26-31. The offerings for the Feast of Unleavened Bread (v. 17) were the same as for the day of firstfruits (Pentecost). These occasions are typical of the present period. We are called to celebrate the Feast of Unleavened Bread in a spiritual manner (1 Cor. 5:7-8), and we are to celebrate the Feast of Weeks by offering our praises and thanksgiving to God as present vessels of the Holy Spirit, fully envisioning all the excellencies of our Redeemer and the marvelous redemption He has wrought. The details of the offerings speak of this.

I. God's Due from Regathered and Converted Israel. 29:1-40.

The Offerings of the Feast of Trumpets. 29:1-6. Prophetic of the end-time regathering of Israel (Lev. 23:23-25; Isa. 11:10-16), the offerings specified here point to Christ as He will be revealed to and received by the Jewish remnant preceding His second advent (Zech. 12:10—13:1; Rom. 11:25-36; cf. Ezek. 36:25; Joel 2:28-29).

The Offerings of the Day of Atonement. 29:7-11. Prophetic of the nation's conversion when they will see the returning Christ (Zech. 12:10—13:1; Rom. 11:26-36), these offerings speak of the redemptive work of Christ as it will be appropriated by His people Israel (Isa. 61:8-11; Jer. 31:31-34).

The Offerings of the Feast of Tabernacles. 29:12-38. This festival is prophetic of Kingdom blessing. The enlarged account of the offerings (twenty-eight verses in all, contrasting with only twelve verses devoted to the feast in Lev. 23:33-44) looks forward to millennial praise, worship, and joy, commemorating a finished redemption (cf. Num. 14:21; Psalm 72:17-19; Hab. 2:14). The seven days of the feast, with their different sacrifices, are described.

Noteworthy is the decrease from thirteen bullocks on the first day to seven on the seventh day. This suggests that there will be gradual spiritual deterioration in the Kingdom age, a fact

also revealed in Revelation 20:7-9. **35.** The eighth day of solemn rest points to the dawn of the eternal state. The precious work of Christ will never be forgotten throughout the eternal ages to come (cf. Rev. 22:1, 3).

Summary Statement. 29:39-40. The offerings set forth as due to the LORD were to be over and above *all* other sacrifices and vows. The latter are the spontaneous fruit of devotion in the hearts of His people and are the subject of chapter 30.

J. Regulation of Vows. 30:1-16.

Vows of a Man. 30:1-2. A vow is a solemn promise to God by which a believer binds himself to an act, service, or condition (see Lev. 27:2; Deut. 23:21; Judg. 11:30, 35; Eccles. 5:4). The vow was very sacred in Israel. A man who made a vow had to keep it.

Vows of a Woman. 30:3-16. By contrast, a woman might be absolved from a vow (1) in the case of a daughter still living in her father's house, if her father raised objection to it (vv. 3-5); or (2) in the case of a daughter who married while the vow was still unfulfilled, if her husband raised objection to it (vv. 6-8). In the case of the vow of a married woman, the vow was inviolable if she was a widow or divorced (v. 9). But the vow of a married woman living with her husband was subject to his approval (vv. 10-15).

The whole chapter, except one verse that deals with the man, is occupied with the *woman* who vows. The illustrative symbolism points to Christ, the One in whom the spirit of the vow was manifested in absolute perfection. In perfect obedience, He became incarnate, with the wondrous words upon His lips: "Lo, I come; in the volume of the book it is written of me, I delight to do thy will, O my God; yea, thy law is within my heart" (Psalm 40:7-8); and, "Mine ears hast thou opened" (Psalm 40:6). As in the case of the Israelite man, everything stood that went out of His mouth.

From a lad of twelve concerned with His "Father's business" (Luke 2:49; cf. John 9:4), till His obedience to death, even the shameful death on the cross (Phil. 2:8), He was a living embodiment of the sacred vow that bound Him to do only God's will. In Him the sacredness of the vow in Israel found *complete* expression. In ancient Israel the vow in its inviolable character, with reference to the male, pointed ultimately to Him. On the other hand the woman, in the deeper meaning of the passage, represents the nation Israel.

At Sinai, Israel made a vow (Exod. 19:8), which she could never keep. When the offer of redemption was made, she refused to accept it, tenaciously holding to her broken contract. Someday the vow under which Israel has put herself will be disallowed, and the nation will be restored to favor. **12. And the Lord shall forgive her.**

K. WAR AGAINST MIDIAN. 31:1-54.

Command to Avenge the Midianites. 31:1-6. **1-2.** As the last official act of his leadership, Moses was instructed by the LORD to avenge the Israelites of the wrong done them by the Midianites. Anything that causes damage to the people of God in their relations to Him, as did the events at Baal-Peor (25:1-3), is a very serious matter to Him. It is something to be punished (25:16-18) as a wrong done to Him and to them; hence, it has the character of a holy war. It is fitting that Moses, as a type of Christ as LORD, should order the attack. Recognition of Christ as LORD, and true subjection to His authority, will assure execution of divine vengeance on influences that have ensnared His people.

3-5. Every tribe was to participate, so **twelve thousand** were sent. All God's people are to recognize the lordship of Christ and act concertedly in obedience to the divine word of authority (1 Cor. 14:37). **6.** The spiritual character of this holy war is emphasized. **And Moses sent ... Phinehas ... the priest, to the war** with the vessels of the sanctuary, possibly the ark (cf. 10:35-36; 14:44; 1 Sam. 4:4; 2 Chron. 5:5) and the trumpets of alarm (cf. 10:9). The whole matter was to be conducted in a priestly way, with true consideration for what was due to God as a holy exercise in keeping with the LORD's sanctuary. Now all Israel was to be identified with Phinehas (25:7-8) in an act of unsparing vengeance upon that which beguiles and debauches God's people.

Incomplete Obedience to the Command. 31:7-15. **7-9.** Although they slew all the males, including the five kings of Midian and Balaam, they took the Midianite women captive. It can scarcely be imagined that Phinehas was party to this. **14.** It rightly called forth the wrath of Moses as a type of Christ as LORD. All of God's people rarely carry out God's will in every detail, but the overcomers do (Rev. 2:7, 11, 17, 26; 3:5, 12, 21; cf. 2 Cor. 6:11—7:1), separating themselves from every association that hinders enjoyment of fellowship with God in holy service, while they submit uncompromisingly to the lordship of Christ.

Necessity of Cleansing. 31:16-24. **17-18.** When Moses saw that the warriors had spared the women, who in particular had caused the seduction of Israel at Baal-peor, he ordered all of the women, except the virgins, as well as all the male children to be put to death. **19-20.** Then he enforced the law of purification (see 19:14-19) on warriors and captives alike, on anyone who had slain a person or come in contact with a dead body. It is a defiling thing to touch what is evil, even though it is to judge it, and purification is necessary if fellowship with the LORD in a priestly manner is to be restored.

21-24. This truth is further emphasized by amplification of the law of purifying made by Eleazar. Every metal object and everything indestructible by fire was to be cleansed by fire and then purified by water. The final act of purifying ("de-sinning") took place on the seventh day with the washing of all garments (cf. John 13:2-15).

The booty taken from Midian represents that which is really God's but has been appropriated by His enemies and used in a way He never intended. In the hands of God's people, it is restored to its rightful place. But it must first be purified to be employed for His service and glory. It must be taken up in relation to the death of Christ and cleansed "with the washing of water by the word" (Eph. 5:26).

Distribution of the Spoil. 31:25-47.
25-27. Moses ... Eleazar ... and the principal fathers of the congregation were divinely directed to ascertain the spoil and divide it equally between those who went to war and those who remained at home (cf. 1 Sam. 30:24-25). **28-29.** In any spiritual conflict those who bear the brunt of it (in this case the twelve thousand) will be the largest gainers, but the congregation shared proportionately with the fighting force. The LORD's portion was that given to the priests, which was one part out of five hundred (one-fifth of 1 percent) of the warriors' half. Given to Eleazar, it represents that which ministers to the direct priestly service of God, the result of spiritual energy in overcoming corrupting influences. It has top priority with God.

30. The Levites' portion, representing the general service of the tabernacle, was taken from the whole congregation and specified as **one portion of fifty,** or 2 percent (cf. vv. 42-47). Although the priests received only one-tenth as much as the Levites, quality of service, not quantity, is in view. It is possible to do a great deal to expedite the work of God in Levitical service with little concern about priestly access and actual fellowship with God. But the type stresses that which is most vital and occupies first place in the mind of God. The large amount of the booty taken (vv. 32-47) illustrates the truth that when believers judge corrupting Midianite (worldly) associations, large spiritual spoil results (2 Cor. 6:17-18).

The Officers' Oblation. 31:48-53.
48-49. The army officers, upon reviewing their respective divisions, discovered to their joy that not one man had been lost in the war. **50-52.** In gratitude, they brought 16,750 shekels (about 600 pounds) of gold jewelry as an offering to the LORD. They said, **We have ... brought an oblation for the Lord ... to make an atonement** (covering) **for our souls before the Lord.** (Cf. Exod. 30:12-16.) Apparently what they meant was that they wanted to be before God in the sense of being under the protective cover of all that He Himself was and had manifested Himself to be in giving them such a signal victory over the Midianites.

The Memorial of Gold. 31:54. Moses and Eleazar **took the gold ... and brought it into the tabernacle of the congregation, for a memorial.** The tabernacle already had a memorial of silver (Exod. 30:11-16; 38:25-27), which spoke of redemption. Now a memorial of gold **before the Lord** was to be laid up. The *gold* symbolizes what is purely of God, here representing something that has been in the hands of the world to promote human pride and idolatry, but retrieved and purified for the glory of God alone. Things thus recovered through spiritual conflict on the part of the saints become a suitable memorial for them before God.

L. PORTION OF REUBEN, GAD, AND MANASSEH. 32:1-42.

Reuben's and Gad's Request. 32:1-5. **1-5.** Having become cattle raisers, the tribes of Reuben and Gad found the land just conquered very suitable for their needs. So they requested it for their possession and asked that they not be required to cross over Jordan. It is called **the land of Jazer** (cf. 21:32) and **the land of Gilead,** designating the territory between the Arnon and the Yarmuk rivers (Deut. 3:12; Josh. 12:2-5).

How easy it is for God's people to get so near to what is God's purpose for them and yet be diverted from it by what is expedient from a worldly standpoint. "Let us, therefore, fear lest, a promise being left us of entering into his rest, any of you should seem to come short of it" (Heb. 4:1). Redemption out of Egypt and baptism into Moses in the cloud and the sea signify salvation in the aspect of being baptized by the Spirit into our *position* in Christ by identification with Him in death, burial, and resurrection (Rom. 6:1-10; 1 Cor. 10:1-11). Crossing the Jordan symbolizes reckoning on that *position* by faith, thus converting it into an *experience* of victory and rest in the land (Rom. 6:11).

The nearer we come to these great experiential realities of our salvation rest, the more powerful and persuasive will be the influences that tend to hold us back from the actual realization of them. Especially is this true of the good and providentially advantageous things of this life that in themselves are by the mercy of God, but which, if we settle down in them, become the "good" that is the enemy of the "best" that God has for us. This is what happened to Reuben and Gad with regard to their **very great multitude of cattle** and their desire to settle down in the place that was **a place for cattle,** but not the place of full blessing God had promised them. They are illustrations of believers who never realize what they are when identified with Christ; or if they do, they never reckon on this death-to-sin and alive-to-God position, seeing it blossom into Spirit-filled victorious living.

Moses' Rebuke. 32:6-15. Moses rebuked them (1) for shirking war and settling down in worldly advantage (v. 6); (2) for being a poor example of discouragement to their brethren (v. 7); (3) for repeating the sin of unbelief (cf. Heb. 3:7—4:11) of their forefathers at Kadesh-barnea and refusing to *wholly* follow the LORD (vv. 8-13; cf. 14:24; Deut. 1:36; Josh. 14:8-9); and (4) for endangering God's people to follow their example not to cross the Jordan (v. 5) and so expose Israel to God's anger, in which case they would be instruments of destruction of God's people (vv. 14-15).

Reuben's and Gad's Promise. 32:16-19. **16-17.** Reuben and Gad were quite willing to go **armed before the children of Israel** until they had **brought them unto their place** of inheritance. **18-19.** But they themselves had no desire to inherit the land with them (cf. v. 33; Josh. 12:1; 13:8). This is illustrative of the fact that many saints are prepared to contend for the truth of *positional* identification with Christ without having the faith or the desire to claim it as an experiential reality in their lives.

Moses' Conditions. 32:20-38. Moses agreed to the proposal made by Reuben and Gad. If we refuse God's best through unbelief, we should not expect

God to compel us to enter anything out of which we shut ourselves. He allows us to take lower ground if we refuse the higher. He allows much in our lives that comes short of what His love has provided. If we choose Gilead, He will not force us into Canaan; but we are always the losers. But, in His tender love, the spiritual and the eternal can be entered into *now* and enjoyed in a way that they will never be known again. The worldly decision of Reuben and Gad was stressed by the mention of the cities they built (vv. 34-38).

Inclusion of the Half Tribe of Manasseh. 32:39-42. The fact that part of the tribe of Manasseh claimed land outside of Canaan is explained by the conquest of Gilead by three clans from the tribe. Later Manasseh also had a share west of Jordan (Josh. 17:14-18).

M. SUMMARY OF THE JOURNEY FROM EGYPT. 33:1-56.

Introduction to the Itinerary. 33:1-4. **1-2.** By divine command Moses had kept a written log or record of Israel's various journeys (or stages; Heb., *măssăᶜ*, "a plucking up" of tent pins; hence, striking of the camp). Those stages are described according to their starting points or **goings out**. The log represents the people surveyed from God's viewpoint. This condensed history is marked by stress upon energy of movement from place to place, stage to stage. All these "goings out" had in a sense a liberating and instructive character.

3-4. They emancipated and separated the people from Egypt and finally brought them to an inheritance in their own land (typifying the positional and experiential aspects of salvation), all the while instructing them in various aspects of that salvation. They departed from Rameses (Zoan-Tanis, Exod. 1:11) **with an high hand** (triumphantly), while

the dazed Egyptians were recovering from the tragic events of the Passover night.

From Rameses to Sinai. 33:5-15. (See Exod. 12:37—19:2.) **5-6. Succoth** (probably Tell el Maskutah) and **Etham** lay in a southeasterly direction from Rameses, the latter situated in the vicinity of the Bitter Lakes (one of which was doubtless the Red or "Reed Sea" crossed by the Israelites). **7-11.** From this point the journey followed a route from five to seven miles inland along the eastern shore of the Gulf of Suez to **Marah** (ᶜAin Hawara, some twenty-five miles down the gulf to **Elim**, i.e., the oasis of Wadi Gharandel).

12. Dophkah may be Serabit el-Khadim. **13-14. Alush** is southeast of Dophkah, and **Rephidim** is likely Wadi Refayid (Exod. 17:1; 19:2). **15.** Mount Sinai is Jebel Musa, at the foot of which is the Monastery of St. Catherine.

From Sinai to Kadesh-barnea. 33:16-36. (Cf. 10:11—20:1.) How blessedly God's watchful eye follows the journeys of His people. Despite failure, they are His people and His elect whom He leads to a promised goal. Most of the place names are not as yet identifiable. Ezion-geber is modern Tell el-Kheleifeh on the Gulf of Aqaba. From there to Kadesh the distance is about fifty miles.

From Kadesh to the Plains of Moab. 33:37-49. See 20:22—22:1. Many years elapsed before Israel left Kadesh. Aaron's death is noted (vv. 38-39; cf. 20:22-29), and passing allusion is made to the king of Arad (v. 40; cf. 21:1). Then the itinerary is taken up (vv. 41-49). **42-43. Punon** is apparently present-day Feinan. **44. Iye-abarim** along the Wadi Zered is likely modern Maḥay (cf. 21:10-12). **45-46. Dibon-gad** is mentioned in the Moabite stone as Mesha's capital. **49. Beth-jeshimoth** (Tell el ᶜAzimeh) and **Abel-shittim** (Tell Kefrein) are both located opposite Jericho in the Jordan Valley.

Final Instructions Before Entering Canaan. 33:50-56. **52. Drive out** (dispossess) **all the inhabitants ... destroy all their stone idols** ("carved stones," illustrated by the Astarte plaques from the period; cf. W. F. Albright, *The Archaeology of Palestine*, fig. 27; also see comments on Exod. 23:23-33; Lev. 26:1-46). **55-56.** The idolatry of Canaan posed a terrible danger and had to be destroyed or it would eventually destroy God's people. It was a special affront to God, violating the first two commandments of the Decalogue (Exod. 20:1-7), and it was demon-energized (cf. 1 Cor. 10:20). Canaan, accordingly, although prefiguring salvation rest, represents at the same time the sphere of conflict (Eph. 6:10-20). Crossing Jordan and entering the land (reckoning on what we are in Christ) always arouses satanic opposition. Victory can only be realized by a total break with idolatry and everything else that is satanic.

N. The Allotment of the Inheritance. 34:1-29.

The Boundaries of the Inheritance. 34:1-15. The borders of the land of Canaan are divinely specified: the southern border (vv. 1-5); the western border (v. 6); the northern border (vv. 7-9); the eastern border (vv. 10-12). The people had not yet entered the land, but it was the LORD's pleasure to give them an appraisal of the exact extent of the inheritance into which He was about to bring them. This is beautifully illustrative of the fact that "the inheritance of the saints in light" (Col. 1:12), into which He is waiting to bring His sanctified people, is clearly outlined in His Word (cf. Acts 26:18; Eph. 1:11, 14; Col. 3:24; 1 Pet. 1:4).

This is not heaven after we die, but our portion in Christ now (Col. 3:1-4); it has definite borders in the spiritual sphere of light, so it is clearly marked off from everything outside those borders (all darkness, see 1 John 1:5-7; 2:8-11; cf. 1 Pet. 2:9). It can only be enjoyed by those who claim the deliverance "from the power of darkness" (Col. 1:13) and who "keep ... [themselves] from idols" (1 John 5:21; cf. Num. 33:52-56) as they "walk in the light, as he is in the light" (1 John 1:5-7).

Just as Israel never took full possession of the land as here given by God, so many believers never claim their full inheritance as "saints in light." But the nation Israel, through God's faithfulness, shall do so in the coming millennial Kingdom (Acts 1:6; Rom. 11:26-36; Rev. 20:7-9). Also because of God's faithfulness, all church saints will be glorified, but some will forfeit inheritance in the eternal Kingdom (1 Cor. 6:9-10; cf. 3:11-15). Reuben, Gad, and the half tribe of Manasseh illustrate those believers who never claim their full inheritance in Christ (vv. 13-15; see 32:1-42).

Appointees to Allot the Land. 34:16-29. **17-18. Eleazar ... Joshua** and **one prince of every tribe** were divinely appointed to distribute the land. This clearly demonstrates that there was a God-ordained arrangement for the allocation of the inheritance. Eleazar and Joshua are prefigurative of Christ in the exercise of priestly and shepherd activities that have as their goal the enjoyment of the inheritance by the LORD's people. Significantly, Eleazar the priest is mentioned first (cf. Josh. 14:1; 19:51; 21:1), pointing to the fact that what is priestly and pertains to access and fellowship with God must always have top priority (cf. 27:21). When the priestly element has its proper place in service, shepherd ministry and care will be evident.

The tribes, illustrating individual assemblies as well as the spiritual people of God in general, will be found entering into and enjoying their heritage of salvation rest in Christ. Moreover, Eleazar and Joshua represent the distribution from God's side, under the hand of Christ, and ministered giftwise through the Spirit. The tribal heads, on the other hand, portray the man's side, setting forth human leadership in appropriating and administering what is given. Both sides are necessary.

If the inheritance is to be possessed and enjoyed, there must be the setting forth in power giftwise of what God intends to give us, as well as spiritual energy on the part of believers to claim their inheritance allotment. The "prince" of each tribe, moving energetically to claim the inheritance and stimulate others to do so, would correspond to the overcomers in each assembly (cf. Rev. 2-3).

O. The Levitical Cities. 35:1-34.

The Levitical Cities. 35:1-8. **1-5.** The LORD through Moses ordered the Israelites to give the Levites cities and suburbs (pasturelands for their cattle), because they were not entitled to a tribal inheritance (Lev. 25:32-34). Since they could not all be occupied at the central sanctuary at one time, they were allotted forty-eight towns among the tribes. Apparently on each side of every city there was an area of land that extended five hundred yards outward from the wall and one thousand yards in length for pasturage and perhaps gardening. These **environs** or suburbs (v. 3, KJV), attached to each city, intimate that the Levites, who were taken instead of the firstborn (see 3:40-51), thus representing the "church of the first-born" (Heb.

12:23), were to have only as much temporal supply as was needed, since they were especially set apart for the service of God.

Levites are a picture of saints in the capacity of ministering in duties not directly priestly, but as being dependent upon priestly ministry. Actually, believers are in antitype a priest-Levite combination, since both the priests and the Levites were representative of all the congregation of Israel, which prefigures the saints in general.

The thought of "city" or "cities" is very prominent in this chapter, even as it is in God's thought (cf. Heb. 11:10, 16). In the eternal city, the Levitical aspect will continue, for "his servants shall serve him" there (Rev. 22:3). Cities with a Levitical character are meant to typically express an aspect of God's ultimate plan for a city. Wherever His people are together in dedication to His service, this will happen.

The Cities of Refuge. 35:9-34. In ancient times when one man killed another, whether accidentally or deliberately (vv. 16-19), the blood of the victim was avenged by a kinsman (Gen. 9:6). **13-15.** Six cities were set apart where a killer might flee from the avenger (*gō'ēl*, "kinsman" of the slain) and seek asylum until he came before the congregation for judgment.

25. In cases of accidental homicide, the congregation declared the man's innocence and allowed him to live in one of the cities until **the death of the high priest. 26-28.** But if the man ventured beyond the boundaries of the city, he might be slain by the avenger. **29-34.** In any case, justice was to be practiced and murderers were to be put to death, in order that the land might not be defiled (Exod. 29:45-46).

Illustratively, this ordinance has special reference to Israel, who "killed the

Prince of life'' (Acts 3:15). But the nation in God's grace will be treated as a slayer, not as a murderer (cf. Josh. 20:1-6; Luke 23:34; Acts 3:17). For this bloodguiltiness the people of Israel have been deprived of their inheritance. Yet they have had their city of refuge and will be set free on the basis of the death of the High Priest (Christ) when He returns as the King-Priest to establish the Kingdom over Israel (Acts 1:6). The cities of refuge speak in a general sense of Christ sheltering the sinner from judgment (Heb. 6:18-19).

P. THE SECURITY OF THE INHERITANCE. 36:1-13.

Threat to the Security of the Inheritance. 36:1-4. When the question of the inheritance of the daughters of Zelophehad was first broached (27:1-11), it was decided that daughters might inherit their father's estate when there were no sons. Now a further problem arose in the case of such heiresses as subsequently married. The heads of some of the families of Manasseh were concerned about the inheritance being diverted to ''another tribe'' (v. 9) by marriage.

The Security of the Inheritance Established. 36:5-12. Moses, obtaining the will of the LORD, ruled that women should marry only within the tribe of their father, thus precluding the loss of the inheritance of that tribe to another tribe. The daughters of Zelophehad subsequently married within their own tribe (vv. 10-12). They showed faithful adherence to God's original order. Since the tribes in the underlying symbolism represent local assemblies (churches), Zelophehad's daughters prefigure a remnant that is faithful in maintaining the original divine order governing the inheritance of each local assembly. No part of what God gave was to be permitted to pass from any one of the ''tribes.''

By each ''tribe'' holding its full portion (compare each assembly holding its full portion in Christ), the whole inheritance would be held in a divine way, and the universal unity and strength of God's people would be maintained unimpaired. Any action of self-will, or any acquiescence to what God has not prescribed, will result in loss of some of the inheritance that rightly belongs to our local ''tribe.'' Everyone has to learn the lesson of Zelophehad's daughters to be zealous for the tribal inheritance and to be in subjection to divine directions that govern it. Only in this way will our ''tribe'' (local church) not suffer loss.

Closing Subscription. 36:13. This is an epilogue surveying the body of laws covered by the closing chapters of the book (either chaps. 22-36 or chaps. 27-36; cf. Lev. 27:34).

DEUTERONOMY

INTRODUCTION

Name of the Book. The name *Deuteronomy* in our English version stems from the Septuagint through an inexact rendering of Deuteronomy 17:18, which should be translated, "This is the copy (or repetition) of the law." Accordingly, the book does not set forth a "second law," distinct from the Sinaitic legislation, as the name *Deuteronomy* (*deuteros*, "second," and *onomos* "law") implies. It simply consists of a partial restatement of previous laws to a new generation that had grown up in the wilderness. In the Massorah, it is called *Mishneh Torah* ("repetition" or "copy of the law," 17:18).

Nature of the Book. Completing the Pentateuch, the book occupies a logical place. Deuteronomy is the book of obedience. Obedience in the spirit of love, flowing from a blessed and enjoyed relationship with the LORD, is the constant demand made upon God's people. All that precedes in the divine revelation is preparatory. Genesis, the book of beginnings, presents man lost and ruined. Exodus, the book of redemption, presents him redeemed and restored. Leviticus, the book of atonement, presents man cleansed, worshiping, and serving. Numbers presents the redeemed as tested and disciplined. Deuteronomy calls the tested and disciplined to an obedient walk (cf. 4:30; 8:20; 11:27-28; 13:4; 30:2, 8).

Christ's Use of the Book. Our Lord Jesus quoted exclusively from Deuteronomy in repelling Satan's temptations, quoting 6:13, 16; 8:3; and 10:20. This clearly implies that He considered it the Word of God, authentically presented historically. As the book of obedience, it was highly significant that He who had come to be perfectly obedient, even to the death of the cross, resorted to this book, which features obedience, to demonstrate His own submission to the Father's will. Incidentally, in doing so He bore witness to the very character of the book, as being genuine and in no sense a forgery, as modern criticism has tended to make it.

Deuteronomy Reflected in the New Testament. Comparison of the Scriptures in the following table will not only show how the book was employed in the New Testament, but also furnish aid in understanding the book itself.

Deuteronomy	New Testament
1:16-17; 16:19	John 7:24; James 2:1
4:2; 12:32	Matt. 5:18; Rev. 22:18-19
4:7	James 4:8
30:6	Matt. 22:37
5:5	Gal. 3:19
7:8	1 John 4:10
9:7, 24; 10:16	Acts 7:51
9:15, 19	Heb. 12:18
10:17	Acts 10:34; 1 Tim. 6:15
13:14	2 Cor. 6:15
14:2; 26:19; 28:9	1 Pet. 2:9
15:11	Matt. 26:11; John 12:8
16:20	1 Tim. 6:11
17:6; 19:15	Matt. 18:16; 2 Cor. 13:1
18:15	Acts 3:22; 7:37
18:19	Luke 10:16; John 12:48; 17:7-8
19:21	Matt. 5:38
21:6	Matt. 27:24
21:23	Gal. 3:13
22:22	John 8:4
23:25	Matt. 12:1
24:1	Matt. 5:31; 19:3
24:14	James 5:4
25:3	2 Cor. 11:24

Book of Prophecy. Moses was a prophet par excellence (34:10; cf. Exod. 33:11; Num. 12:6, 8). Among his great prophecies in this book are: (1) the prediction of the Messiah the Prophet (18:15-18; cf. Acts 3:22); (2) the past, present, and future of Israel (chaps. 28-29); (3) the dispersion of Israel (30:1); (4) future repentance of Israel (30:2); (5) the second advent of Christ (30:3); (6) the restoration of Palestine (30:5); (7) Israel's future national restoration and conversion (30:5-6); (8) the judgment of Israel's enemies (30:7); and (9) national prosperity (30:9). The song of Moses (chap. 32) is wholly prophetic and spans the plan of God for the ages.

Authorship (Critical Theory). The book holds a strategic place in the Graf-Wellhausen Theory of the origin of the Pentateuch. It is claimed to be the product of an anonymous writer (who imitated Moses) and a product of the seventh century B.C. (time of Josiah or a little earlier). Supposedly, only after this date does history bear incontrovertible evidence of the existence of the book.

Biblically Sound View. The book is authentically Mosaic and dates from the time of Moses. (1) This is supported by the striking parallels that exist between the Sinaitic Covenant (Exod. 20), renewed forty years later for the new generation of Israelites, and the suzerainty treaties of the Mosaic period (see G. E. Mendenhall, "Law and Covenant in Israel and the Ancient Near East," *BA* 17 [1954]:50-76). Meredith Kline finds the five parts of the contemporary suzerainty treaties—preamble, historical prologue, stipulations, treaty ratification, and succession arrangements—in the literary structure of Deuteronomy (*Treaty of the Great King*, 1963; and *The Structure of Biblical Authority*, 1972). Suzerainty treaties of the later period (seventh and sixth centuries) do not parallel the literary structure of Deuteronomy. In the preamble (1:1-5) Moses identifies the parties in the covenant. In the historical prologue (1:6—4:49) he reviews the relation between God and Israel, since the covenant was made at Sinai. Chapters 5-26 contain the covenant stipulations. Chapters 27-30 catalog the covenant ratification by the new generation. Moses then arranges for a successor to insure covenant continuity. (2) There is archaeological attestation that such treaties were carefully committed to writing in the Mosaic period and were not dependent upon oral tradition, as the higher critics of the eighteenth and early nineteenth centuries had supposed (see Kenneth A. Kitchen, *Ancient Orient and Old Testament*, p. 136). In the Mosaic era, archaeology attests at least five scripts that were available—Akkadian cuneiform, Egyptian hieroglyphics, Sinaitic pictographs, Byblian alphabet, and Ugaritic alphabetic cuneiform, a sister script of Hebrew. Such scientific evidence warrants considering Deuteronomy as an authentic document written substantially by Moses, with possibly a few post-Mosaic additions, and constituting not a forgery, but an outstanding religious communication for all times (see Samuel Schultz, "Did Moses Write the Pentateuch?" *Christianity Today* [Sept. 25, 1975], pp. 12-16).

OUTLINE

I. MOSES' FIRST DISCOURSE (HISTORICAL). 1:1—
4:43.
   A. From Sinai to Kadesh-barnea. 1:1-46.
   B. From Wilderness Wandering to Conquest. 2:1-37.
   C. Further Conquest. 3:1-29.
   D. Call to Covenant Obedience. 4:1-43.

II. MOSES' SECOND DISCOURSE (LEGAL). 4:44—
26:19.
   A. Conquests Summarized. 4:44-49.
   B. The Renewal of the Covenant. 5:1-33.
   C. Exposition of the First Table. 6:1-25.
   D. Separation from Sin. 7:1-26.
   E. The Lord's Chastening. 8:1-20.
   F. Divine Grace Versus Self-Righteousness. 9:1-29.
   G. Divine Grace and Covenant Renewal. 10:1-22.
   H. The Necessity of Obedience. 11:1-32.
   I. God-Directed Worship. 12:1-32.
   J. Peril of Occult Contamination. 13:1-18.
   K. Avoiding the Semblance of Idolatry. 14:1-29.
   L. Demonstrating God's Love to Others. 15:1-23.
   M. Commemorating God's Love. 16:1-22.
   N. Honoring God in Government. 17:1-20.
   O. Honoring God Through Vital Service. 18:1-22.
   P. Judicial Asylum—God's Grace in Operation.
      19:1-21.
   Q. The Law of Warfare. 20:1-20.
   R. Expiation for Murder and Other Laws. 21:1-23.
   S. Laws Governing Conduct Toward Others. 22:1-30.
   T. The Sanctity of the Lord's Congregation. 23:1-25.
   U. Divorce and Other Laws. 24:1-22.
   V. Various Other Laws. 25:1-19.
   W. God Confessed as Redeemer-King. 26:1-19.

III. MOSES' THIRD DISCOURSE (PROPHETIC).
27:1—30:20.
   A. Ratification Ceremony in Canaan. 27:1-26.
   B. Proclamation of the Covenant's Sanctions. 28:1-68.
   C. Summons to the Covenant Oath. 29:1-29.
   D. The Terms and Challenge of the Covenant. 30:1-20.

IV. MOSES' FINAL WORDS AND ACTS (COVENANT
    CONTINUITY).
     A. Carrying on the Covenant. 31:1-30.
     B. The Song of Witness. 32:1-52.
     C. The Blessing of the Tribes. 33:1-29.
     D. Moses' Death—Dynastic Succession. 34:1-12.

COMMENTARY

I. MOSES' FIRST DISCOURSE (HISTORICAL). 1:1—4:43.

A. FROM SINAI TO KADESH-BARNEA. 1:1-46.

Introduction. 1:1-5. Moses rehearsed the LORD's dealing with Israel since the departure from Sinai (Horeb). **1.** Apparently some of his **words** were uttered on the route from Horeb to Kadesh-barnea (cf. Num. 33:18-20), south of Edom. **2.** How striking that these preliminary words were interrupted with the declaration that a journey that took **eleven days** was prolonged to forty years because of disobedience and unbelief (cf. Num. 14:23). Horeb was the place where the LORD spoke to His people of what He had in heart to give them. **3-4.** He continued through Moses to speak to them after the long interruption. Now they were ready to hear after **Sihon, the king of the Amorites,** and **Og, the king of Bashan** (who represent the enmity and energy of the flesh in opposition to God) had been conquered. **5. In the land of Moab, began Moses to declare** (*bē'ēr*, "explain, elucidate") **this law** to the new generation, who needed an exposition of it on the threshold of the promised inheritance.

In Deuteronomy, Moses is typical of Christ, not as Lord, but as Teacher and Instructor of His saints (Matt. 23:8, 10; cf. Eph. 4:20-21), tutoring them to prepare them for their inheritance provided for them by His love and faithfulness. This book is a review of the experiences the people of God have passed through

and their behavior in them under the tutelage of Moses (Christ), with the purpose of their being conformed to the features proper to children and heirs (cf. Rom. 8:14-16).

In its spiritual meaning, this great book does not comprehend what will be enjoyed in a heavenly future, but what God's inheritance holds for His people in a heavenly *present* as salvation rest (Heb. 3:1—4:16) is entered into under the figure of entering and possessing the promised land. But while it is our privilege as the LORD's people to enjoy the sovereign grace of God, and thus in our position before God to come in contact in a spiritual sense with things that are outside responsibility, we ourselves, as long as we are in the flesh and insofar as our experience of our position is conceived, are never outside responsibility with all of its sobering obligations. Therefore, the government of God operates in relation to His people. The way in which it acts constitutes a prominent feature of Deuteronomy.

The Command to Possess the Land. 1:6-8. The command to possess the land was connected with Horeb, the sacred mountain, and with the wondrous divine revelations there. It also linked the preceding generation, which failed to obey and consequently fell under grievous chastisement, with the present generation, which was ready to obey. The LORD would have had them depart from Horeb and go straight into the land, possessing it to its fullest limits (cf. Gen. 15:18; 2 Sam. 8:3). Therefore, they had to realize that the delay had been caused entirely by their unbelief and disobedience.

Synopsis of Moses' Mediatorship and Israel's Leaders. 1:9-18. The leaders were held up to the nation to inspire it to loyalty to its new leadership, which would soon replace Moses, whose loving care for Israel shines forth so resplendently (vv. 10-11). Moses' limitation as a burden-bearer (vv. 9, 12; cf. Num. 11:4) contrasts saliently to Christ, the never failing burden-bearer (1 Pet. 5:7), but it is an encouragement to the Lord's people in their role in this area (cf. 1 Cor. 9:9; 12:25; 2 Cor. 11:28; Gal. 6:2).

13-15. In a wonderful sense, even as Moses represented God to the people, so did the **wise men**, whom he appointed to assist him in governing and judging the people. He pointed out that they were wisely welcomed by the people (v. 14) and that their judgment was recognized as being of God Himself (v. 17; cf. Psalm 82:6; John 10:34-35), since such judges and spokesmen for God were styled "gods" (Exod. 21:6, literal Heb. trans.). **18. And I commanded you at that time all the things which ye should do.** Moses illustrates the lordship of Christ over His people in their wilderness experiences (v. 19).

Failure to Possess the Land. 1:19-46. **20-21.** The LORD through Moses as mediator directed the people at Kadesh-barnea to **go up and possess** the land. **22.** The people's request to send out scouts to search out the land (Num. 13:1-3) was actually a step of unbelief; they should have been willing to take God's word for it. **23.** Moses confessed that he went along with the proposal and dispatched the spies (Num. 13:2).

24-46. He summarized the dismal failure at Kadesh-barnea (Num. 14:1-39) and the presumption of the people at Hormah (Num. 14:40-45). This warning

lesson from the LORD's mouthpiece was a necessity for the new generation on the eve of their entry into the land. The punishment for this blatant unbelief was reemphasized.

B. FROM WILDERNESS TO CONQUEST. 2:1-37.

From Kadesh to the Land of the Amorites. 2:1-23. **1.** With solemn brevity the terrible years of wilderness wandering were alluded to. **2-6.** The command to circumvent Edom was rehearsed (Num. 20:14-21). **7.** Yet God's gracious love and care were tenderly pointed out, demonstrating the unfailing faithfulness of God, even to that rebellious generation (cf. 2 Tim. 2:13). **8-13.** The journey past Moab was mentioned. **14-15.** The fulfillment of God's word (Num. 14:23-34) was recounted. How imperative it was for the new generation to be reminded of the finality and sure fulfillment of the Word of God (Isa. 40:8). **16-23.** Now that God's Word was vindicated, the people were free to proceed to the land of the Amorites.

The Command to Possess. 2:24-25. Battle would now ensue, but Israel was promised victory because the LORD would fight for her.

Sihon's Defeat. 2:26-37. (See Num. 21:21-32.) Again the importance of God's word and obedience to it for victory over the flesh was stressed (v. 37). How this lesson needs to be indelibly impressed upon God's people who would claim their inheritance in Christ (Heb. 3:1—4:13, especially 4:11-13; cf. Deut. 3:1-11).

C. FURTHER CONQUEST. 3:1-29.

The Conquest of Og. 3:1-11. (See Num. 21:33-35.) Both Sihon and Og portray aspects of the flesh that must be overcome by obedience to the Word of God before our spiritual inheritance (salvation rest) can be experienced (see Deut. 2:26-37).

Transjordan Possessed. 3:12-20. (See Num. 32:33-42; Josh. 13:8-32.) The failure of Reuben and Gad did not lie in taking possession on the east of Jordan, but in being content to have their inheritance *on that side only*. They failed to value what was God's delight to bestow. They were solicitous of what they wanted to receive, rather than of what God wanted to give (cf. Num. 32:5). What they received was good, but what they refused to receive was better. Many believers appropriate the truth of justification by faith (Rom. 3-4), but they never recognize their position in Christ (Rom. 6:1-10) and claim the power of it (Rom. 6:11).

Joshua to Take Moses' Place. 3:21-29. **21.** The conquest of Sihon and Og was a precursor of the victories that God's people would realize when they entered the land of their possession. **22.** As Joshua was to lead in these victories, he was encouraged in the task. **25-26.** Moses' request to **go over and see the good land** was not only rejected, but he declared to the people, **The Lord was angry with me for your sakes.** Moses did not speak here of suffering the governmental consequences of his own failure, but of suffering on account of the people.

This incident has typical reference to what Christ suffered vicariously when, as the holy sin-bearer, He was not heard (Psalm 22:1-2; Matt. 27:46). Prefiguring our Lord according to the flesh, Moses could not enter the land. He had to come under divine wrath on account of the people and endure, as it were, the suffering of death for their sakes.

But by this means, under the figure of Joshua, Christ came forth as the risen, ever living One to go before His people and conduct them into the promised possession. In this blessed character, Joshua portrays the risen Christ (v. 28). Moses, however, was permitted to see the whole land from the summit of Pisgah (v. 27). This illustrates how the whole range of purposed blessing for man was in Christ's purview before His death (John 14-17). But our Lord's death was a divine prerequisite—the Jordan that lay between Him and the fruition of all the purposes of His love for His own.

D. CALL TO COVENANT OBEDIENCE. 4:1-49.

The Covenant and the Purpose of the Law. 4:1-13. **1. Now therefore hearken, O Israel, unto the statutes and . . . ordinances.** It was imperative that the new generation be taught the importance and the design of the Law, which with the statutes and ordinances was, as it were, the charter of the covenant. Moses as mediator of the old covenant prefigures Christ, the Mediator of the new covenant, the latter resting upon an accomplished redemption (Matt. 26:27-28; 1 Cor. 11:25; cf. Jer. 31:31-40; Heb. 8:7-13).

The old covenant, declared in Horeb, covered all that God proposed to do for Israel and the conditions requisite on their side if they were to enter in and enjoy all that He proposed. The new covenant, sealed by Christ's death on Calvary, graciously assures to all who believe an unchanging position in Christ before God and the experience of that position as the prescriptions of grace for holy living are observed. What was outwardly a dispensation of Law envisioned Christ and the new-covenant conditions as its end (2 Cor. 3:13).

2-3. Those who keep the prescriptions of grace never fall into the snare of idolatry resulting from idolatrous associations, as did Israel at Baal-peor (see Num. 25:4-9). **6-9.** Neither will they endanger their testimony for **wisdom and ... understanding in the sight** of sinners, as Israel was warned against doing in the sight of the nations.

10-13. At Horeb the injunction was: **Hear my words ... fear me,** enforced by the sight of **the mountain** that **burned with fire,** with the LORD speaking out of **the midst of the fire,** declaring **his covenant ... even ten commandments,** reflecting the eternal moral law of God. All of these injunctions, except the fourth commandment of Sabbath observance, are included under the prescriptions of grace in the New Testament and represent principles that guide human conduct in all ages.

The Covenant and the Peril of Idolatry. 4:14-40. The appearance of the LORD without similitude at Horeb (vv. 13-14) was to be an unforgettable warning against making idolatrous images of any kind or in worshiping the creature or the creation rather than the Creator (vv. 15-19). **20.** As the LORD's people, redeemed **out of the iron furnace** of Egypt, they were to recognize the LORD's ownership and, as such, be **a people of inheritance,** completely free of idolatry.

21-22. Moses' death (cf. 1:37; 3:26), typical of Christ's death, was to be a necessary prelude to their entering into their possession, as Christ's was to our entering ours. **23-24.** In both cases idolatry must be sedulously guarded against (1 John 5:21), for God is a consuming fire (9:3; cf. Heb. 12:29), a jealous God (Exod. 34:14), who can brook no rivals.

25-28. Moses solemnly warned against covenant infraction by idolatry and the severe divine chastening that would result. **29-30.** Repentance, however, will bring restoration to divine favor, especially during the Great Tribulation of the end-time, which Moses prophetically envisioned (Jer. 23:20; Hos. 3:5). **31-40.** The love, mercy, holiness, and gracious self-revelation of God are incentives to obedience on the part of His people.

The Cities of Refuge. 4:41-43. This is not a disconnected parenthesis, but a deeply significant typical reference to the solemn fact that, as foreknown by God, Israel would be the slayer of Christ. Yet divine mercy would be extended, accounting it to be done "unawares" (v. 42, KJV; cf. Luke 23:34; Acts 3:17). **42.** It is as true of us, as it will be for Israel in the coming day, that the inheritance can only be possessed on the grounds of pure mercy (Rom. 9:23; Eph. 1:7).

Typically, this chapter glimpses the glory of the coming age of Israel's restoration silhouetted against the backdrop of the Mosaic era, inaugurated by divine speaking and writing. Thus, there follows a warning of departure through man's unfaithfulness, followed by restoration effected by God's faithfulness, so that those who are to **live** do so on the basis of divine mercy and grace alone.

II. MOSES' SECOND DISCOURSE (LEGAL). 4:44—26:19.

A. CONQUESTS SUMMARIZED. 4:44-49.

Introduction to Moses' Second Discourse. 4:44-49. As a transition passage, this section presents a summary of the Trans-Jordanic conquests (vv. 46-49) and serves as a conclusion to Moses' first discourse as well as an introduction to his second discourse. The latter gives the stipulations of covenant life in line with contemporary suzerainty treaties (see Introduction).

Just as treaty stipulations customarily began with the fundamental and general demand for the vassals' absolute allegiance to the suzerain, and then proceeded to various specific requirements, so Moses began by setting before

Israel, the covenant people, the primary requirement for loyalty to the LORD (5:1—11:32), followed by the more detailed stipulations for the covenant people (12:1—26:19).

B. THE RENEWAL OF THE COVENANT. 5:1-33.

The Preface to the Decalogue. 5:1-5.
1. The covenant at Horeb was commemorated so that the new generation might realize its responsibility to **hear ... learn ... keep, and do** the Ten Commandments, which form the essence of the covenant (cf. Exod. 20:1-17), as well as **the statutes and ordinances** (cf. Exod. 20:18—23:33), comprising the social and religious regulations.
3. This responsibility was further emphasized: **The Lord made not this covenant with our fathers.** It was a conditional covenant, and that rebellious generation—representing those who walk after the flesh—by their rebellious unbelief forfeited it altogether, as well as the inheritance it held out through faith and obedience. By contrast, the new generation of those who were there **alive** that day, representing those quickened and who walk after the Spirit, stood ready to enter the land (cf. Heb. 8:9).
4-5. The mediatorial character of the covenant was emphasized (cf. v. 27). The old covenant prefigured the new (Jer. 32:38-41; Luke 22:20; Heb. 8:8-13), with Moses, as mediator of the old, looking forward to Christ, the Mediator of the new.

The Decalogue. 5:6-21. **6-10.** *The first and second commandments* (see Exod. 20:2-6) present the basic issue of faithfulness to the covenant through idolatry-free loyalty to the divine Suzerain—God as Redeemer, Savior, and Deliverer from bondage. Reading the old covenant purely in the letter of it discloses it to be a ministry of death and

condemnation. But seeing Christ as the Spirit of what Moses wrote, removes the veil and gives clear vision that the end it had in view was the new covenant based on the death and resurrection of Christ. **Showing mercy unto thousands** looks forward to Christ's death, from which fountain *all* mercy to lost sinners springs, and from which the love of God for sinners flows, engendering love for God in return. The cross divides mankind into sinners and saints—haters of God and lovers of God—those who keep His commandments and those who do not.
11. *The third commandment* separates the **name of the Lord** from all that is untrue and iniquitous (cf. 2 Tim. 2:19; Exod. 20:7). **12-15.** *The fourth commandment* is keeping the Sabbath. In Deuteronomy this envisions rest brought to God's people in grace through divine deliverance from every kind of bondage, so that it leads to gracious consideration for others. In Exodus, Sabbath-keeping is connected with creation (Exod. 20:10-11; Gen. 2:3) and that which secures what is restful to Himself in the manifestation of salvation rest in His own.
16. *The fifth commandment,* honoring parents, is actually honoring God, in whose place they stand in the life of the child. God intends for the father and mother to be illustrations of His own parental love, as expressed in the "household of God" (Exod. 20:12). **17.** *The sixth commandment* not only forbids murder (cf. Exod. 20:13) but comprehends the hatred and vengeance that lead to the act (Matt. 5:21-31; 1 John 3:15).
18. *The seventh commandment* forbids adultery and extramarital intercourse, protecting the family and home, which constitute the basic unit of society (cf. Exod. 20:14). **19.** *The eighth*

commandment forbids any unlawful appropriation of what belongs to another (Exod. 20:15; cf. Matt. 19:18; Mark 10:19; Rom. 13:9). **20.** *The ninth commandment* rules out all forms of slander, defamation, and misrepresentation (cf. Exod. 20:16; John 18:37; Eph. 4:21). **21.** *The tenth commandment* prohibits coveting anything that belongs to another, preparing believers for the gracious desire to enrich and add to another (Exod. 20:17; cf. 1 Thess. 2:8).

The Necessity of a Covenant Mediator. 5:22-33. **22-24.** The manifestation of God's glory at Horeb caused the people to realize that they were sinners. **25-26.** But they needed a mediator between a holy God and themselves, lest they die. **27-33.** Their request for such a mediator (Moses) pleased the LORD, because it pointed to Christ, the one Mediator between God and man (1 Tim. 2:5; Heb. 8:6).

C. EXPOSITION OF THE FIRST TABLE. 6:1-25.

Preface to the Exposition. 6:1-3. **1-3. The commandments, the statutes, and the ordinances** (the latter two are not actually given until chap. 12) were to be taught and put into practice so that Israel in the land might **fear** the LORD (hold Him in godly reverence).

The First Commandment. 6:4. (Cf. Mark 12:29-30.) This commandment involves duties to God of the first table or tablet of stone. Called *Shema*[c] by orthodox Jews, after the first word, "Hear," this famous passage supports the Trinitarian concept of deity—The LORD [Jehovah] our God [Elohim] is one LORD," the *one 'ĕḥād*, expressing *compound unity*, not *yāḥīd*, meaning a *single* one. He alone to whom the name of Jehovah (Yahweh, "the self-existing One") belongs is absolutely God. It is at

once a testimony against Unitarianism as well as polytheism.

Because He is the one and only God, of one eternal, uncreated essence, yet manifested tripersonally as Scripture shows, He must be loved by the creature with the whole being: heart, soul, and might (v. 5), Jesus adding the "mind" (Mark 12:30). We who believe today know this same Jehovah, Israel's Redeemer, as our Redeemer, who in process of time became incarnate and died in our place. "We love him, because he first loved us" (1 John 4:19). "This is the love of God, that we keep his commandments" (1 John 5:3).

Duties Springing from the First Commandment. 6:5-25. Israel is to love Him, obey Him, and serve Him supremely (vv. 5-25; cf. Matt. 22:37). Love is one of the exalted themes of Deuteronomy, because the book envisions the outpoured, divine, redemptive love. It is appropriate for a people ready to enter their salvation rest, about to realize their redeemed position before God in their experience of that redemption before men, typified by their impending entry into "the good land" (v. 18) to love God and His redeemed.

6-9. What was meant to be carried out spiritually is literally practiced by orthodox Jews. These words are inscribed on parchment and put in little boxes, which are bound to their foreheads and upon their hands. Also, they are placed in metal boxes and nailed to their houses. What a constant reminder! **10-14.** How solemn the divine warning against idolatrous forgetting of the LORD in days of blessing and prosperity! **16.** The warning, **Ye shall not put the Lord your God to the test** (tempt) was quoted by our Lord to rout the devil (Matt. 4:7; Luke 4:12). Tempting God is expecting Him to do something contrary to His Word and will. At **Massah**

("testing" or "proving," Exod. 17:7), Israel tempted God by questioning His presence among them in the face of many tokens of His manifested power and the promises of His Word.

21-23. The basis for Israel's love for the LORD is their redemption **out of** Egypt and **in to** the promised land. God has solemnly sworn to give the land to them (vv. 10, 18, 23). The people were not to doubt His faithfulness to keep His oath, despite the formidable enemies they would face (v. 19; cf. 7:1), which are figurative of the powers of darkness the believer in the land (appropriating salvation rest) faces (2 Cor. 10:4; Eph. 6:12).

D. SEPARATION FROM SIN. 7:1-26.

Separation Commanded. 7:1-5. **1.** Those who enter God's inheritance of salvation rest will face enemies (powers of darkness, Eph. 6:12). But divine grace will cast out these foes and give the redeemed victory over them, despite their great power (cf. Col. 1:12-13). **2-4.** When the LORD delivers these foes into the hand of His people, they are to completely exterminate them, make no affinity with them, nor intermarry among them.

The idolatry and immorality of the Canaanites made them ripe for ruin (cf. Gen. 15:16; 1 Cor. 10:14). It was a question of destroying them or being destroyed, being separate or fatally polluted and ruined. Therefore, both idolaters and their idolatry were to be mercilessly wiped out. The Ugaritic religious literature recovered from Ras Shamra (Ugarit) on the north Syrian coast (1929-37) fully authenticates the moral depravity of the Canaanite civilization around 1400 B.C. and supports the biblical notices and the justness of the divine severity that ordered their extermination.

Separation Necessitated. 7:6-11. **6-10.** Separation was necessary because: (1) the Israelites are **an holy people**, who must not be besmirched by contact with gross unholiness (v. 6a; cf. Exod. 19:6); (2) they are a **chosen** (elect) **people** (v. 6b; cf. 10:15; 1 Pet. 5:13); (3) they are **a special people** unto the LORD **above all people** (lit., "a people for his own possession"; v. 6c; cf. Exod. 19:5; Deut. 14:1-2; Titus 2:14; 1 Pet. 2:9); (4) they are a people upon whom God **set his love** and toward whom His faithfulness is sworn (vv. 7-8a); (5) they are His **redeemed** (v. 8b); (6) they are the ones with whom he **keepeth covenant** and shows mercy as they keep covenant with Him by keeping His commandments (v. 9); and (7) God recompenses to everyone according to his works (v. 10; cf. Prov. 24:12; Rom. 2:6; Rev. 20:12-13). He **repayeth them who hate him to their face.**

Separation Rewarded. 7:12-26. (1) Covenant mercy will be assured (v. 12). (2) God's love will be manifested in prosperity and blessing (vv. 13-14). (3) Physical health will result (v. 15; cf. Exod. 9:14; 15:26; Deut. 28:27, 60). (4) Victory over enemies will be assured (v. 16; figurative of conquest of spiritual foes, Eph. 6:10-20). (5) Faith in God's delivering power will be engendered (vv. 17-19). (6) Divine deliverance will be vouchsafed—"thy God will send the hornet among them" (v. 20). (7) Supernatural courage will be given, "for the LORD thy God is among you, a mighty God and awesome" (v. 21). (8) God will exterminate the idolatrous inhabitants (vv. 22-24). (9) God's people will destroy their idols and their idolatry (vv. 25-26).

E. THE LORD'S CHASTENING. 8:1-20.

The Purpose of Chastening. 8:1-6. **1-6.** The divine disciplinary dealing in the wilderness was intended: (1) to produce obedience to the LORD's commandments (v. 1*a*); (2) to guarantee both physical life (bodily well-being and longevity, 5:16; 6:2; cf. 1 Cor. 10:30-32) as well as spiritual vitality (fellowship with God and experience of covenant love and mercy, v. 1*b*; cf. 4:10; 8:3; Heb. 12:9); (3) to assure both material and spiritual prosperity by bringing God's people *into* the land—**multiply, and go in and possess the land** (v. 1*c*; cf. 6:23), for divine discipline purposes that redemption be followed by experiential sanctification and growth in grace; (4) to vindicate God's promises, **which the Lord swore to give** (v. 1*d*); (5) to **humble . . . test . . . to know** what is in the heart of His people (v. 2; cf. 2:7; 29:5; Exod. 15:25; 20:20); (6) to teach His people that man cannot live by material things alone, but must cultivate the spiritual by feeding upon the Word of God (v. 3; cf. Matt. 4:4; Luke 4:4); (7) to demonstrate His paternal love and care for His children (vv. 4-5; cf. Psalm 89:30-33; Prov. 3:11-12; Heb. 12:5-7; Rev. 3:19); and (8) to produce practical piety and reverential respect toward God (v. 6; cf. 10:12; Psalm 19:9).

The Fruit of Chastening. 8:7-20. **7-9.** (1) Chastening brings God's people to experience their gracious position before God in covenant relationship with Him, illustrated by this lovely description of the **good land.** The **brooks of water, of fountains and depths** (springs) speak of spiritual life and refreshment for those who know their "so great salvation" (Heb. 2:3) and who enter into enjoyment of the inheritance it brings (John 4:14; 7:37-39; Eph. 5:18).

The resources and wealth of the land portray illustratively both the material and spiritual benefits with which God's people are blessed as they enter their inheritance. "Now no chastening for the present seemeth to be joyous, but grievous [the wilderness testing] nevertheless, afterward it yieldeth the peaceable fruit of righteousness unto them who are exercised by it" (Heb. 12:11).

10-18. (2) Chastening also fortifies God's people against the perils of prosperity (vv. 10-18), forgetting the LORD (6:12; 28:47; Prov. 30:9; Hos. 13:6), and high-mindedness and self-sufficiency (vv. 14, 18), sins utterly incompatible with the status of those so graciously redeemed out of sin and bondage and so patiently disciplined and educated in the wilderness (Exod. 17:6; Num. 20:11; 21:6).

19-20. (3) Chastening also holds out warning of the ultimate punishment in divine dealing with disobedient and rebellious believers—the "sin unto [physical] death" (cf. 1 John 5:16 with 1 Cor. 5:5; 11:30-32). **Ye shall surely perish . . . so shall ye perish.**

F. DIVINE GRACE VERSUS
SELF-RIGHTEOUSNESS. 9:1-29.

Warning Against Self-Righteousness. 9:1-6. **1-3.** God's grace and mercy are exalted above any meritorious claim, because both salvation and experiencing salvation rest (entering and possessing the possession) are realized entirely on the basis of "grace through faith . . . not of yourselves . . . not of works, lest any man should boast" (Eph. 2:8-9). Here in question is the enjoyment of salvation rest, involving formidable obstacles and strong foes, which only God can overcome (cf. Eph. 6:10-20). Dependence upon Him in simple faith alone will **bring . . . down** these foes before their face through the LORD as **a consuming fire** (cf. 4:24; Heb. 12:29), so that His people may **drive them out, and destroy them quickly** in obedience to His command.

4-5. The reason the LORD will drive

out these nations is emphatically *not* because there is any self-righteousness or merit in His people (cf. 8:17; Rom. 11:6, 20; 1 Cor. 4:4, 7), but because of the **wickedness of these nations** (cf. Gen. 15:16) and to perform the **word which the Lord swore unto . . . Abraham, Isaac and Jacob** (cf. Gen. 50:24). Salvation with the enjoyment of salvation rest is the gift of God (John 1:12-13; Eph. 2:8). **6.** If this were not so, a **stiff-necked people** (cf. 31:27; Exod. 34:9) like Israel would have had no chance.

Historical Witness Against Any Claim to Self-Righteousness. 9:7-24. Israel's history from their departure out of Egypt till the threshold of their entrance into Canaan is summarized as a continual provocation to God's wrath and an unbroken story of rebelling against the LORD. Specifically cited is the terrible idolatry in Horeb when "they made a calf . . . and worshiped the melted image" (Psalm 106:19; cf. Exod. 32:4), so that the Lord almost destroyed them (vv. 7-14). He would have done so (vv. 15-17) except for Moses' prayer (vv. 18-20), prefiguring Christ's intercession for His own (cf. John 17:1-20). Other citations include Taberah, where "the fire of the LORD burned among them" (Num. 11:3), because of their murmurings "and consumed . . . the farthest parts of the camp" (Num. 11:1) and Massah, where they tempted the LORD by saying, "Is the LORD among us, or not?" (Exod. 17:7).

Also mentioned is Kibroth-hattaavah (Num. 11:34), where the people who lusted were buried in the graves of lust after eating the quail. But the most tragic testimony against any claim to self-righteousness is the woeful tale of unbelief at Kadesh-barnea (Num. 14:23), which precipitated the forty-year wandering and death in the desert. The historical witness closes (v. 24) as it had opened (v. 7) with a general summation of the people's total lack of merit and their being shut up to God's mercy alone to enter, possess, and enjoy the good land.

Moses' Intercession. 9:25-29. Moses' action beautifully sets forth the safety and security of God's people as the subjects of His saving grace (cf. vv. 18-20). **26.** The basis of Moses' plea was the same as the basis of Christ's intercession for His own. They are the LORD's **inheritance . . . redeemed** by His grace and power. He sees them as such and never sees them otherwise, even when they behave badly.

27. They are the elect of God, the called of God, through the ancient promises of God made through covenant with Abraham (Gen. 12:1-3) and his descendants. How touching to see that Moses' intercession (and Christ's) was made on the basis of what is true in the mind of God concerning His people. If we lose cognizance of it, our great Intercessor does not (cf. Rom. 8:27; Heb. 7:15).

G. DIVINE GRACE AND COVENANT RENEWAL. 10:1-22.

Divine Grace Reconfirms the Broken Covenant. 10:1-5. The purpose of this passage is to state in a comprehensive and general way (in line with contemporary international suzerainty treaties) that God had mercifully reconfirmed the covenant with the rebellious vassals (the calf-worshiping Israelites). In accordance with the legal customs of that era, the duplicate covenant texts were to be deposited in the respective sanctuaries of the two covenant parties so as to be under the surveillance of the oath deities. In this case only one sanctuary was involved, since God, the covenant Suzerain, had His sanctuary in Israel (see Meredith Kline, WBC, p. 168).

The two *new* treaty tablets contrast with the two broken old ones. Four times (vv. 1-4) reference is made to the *first* tables and the *first* writing, referring to what Scripture connects with the natural, while "the second" connects with the spiritual (1 Cor. 15:45-49). The golden-calf episode illustrates how everything connected with the natural man breaks down in perversity and rebellion. The first table sets forth Law, apart from grace, broken by the people and condemning them to death.

Only Christ (typified by Moses) could carry the unbroken Law in His two hands. But because there was no answer to God's Law in fallen man, Moses was constrained to cast it out of his hands and break it in the sight of all the people (9:17). This demonstrated to them that they were under the curse of the broken Law (see Exod. 32:1-29; 34:1-35). The new tablets envision the new covenant, with the "law" of God engraved upon human hearts as the result of Christ's redemption and the giving of the Spirit (Jer. 31:33-34; 2 Cor. 3:3-7; Heb. 8:10).

3. The new tablets were to be placed in **an ark of acacia wood,** which suggests preservation of the covenant in the suitable vessel of Christ's humanity (Psalm 40:7-8). But when God's "good pleasure" or "law" is envisioned as in the heart of Christ, we are at once conducted far beyond the letter of the Law, which only gave the knowledge of sin to the spirit of it, which embraces God as Redeemer, Deliverer, known by "thousands" as the object of their love and obedience (5:10; Exod. 20:6; 34:7).

"The ark of the covenant overlaid round about with gold" (Heb. 9:4) symbolizes Christ in His personal unique glory. But the simple "ark of wood" (vv. 1, 3) suggests Christ in that aspect in which what is true in Him can also be true in His own, as those who are in Him

positionally and abide in Him experientially (Rom. 7:22; 1 John 2:7-8). The covenant will be realized in Israel's heart in a future day, as it is made good in this, the Spirit's day. Where are the tablets now? **5. There they are,** in those who know God and abide in Christ.

Divine Grace Provides Suitable Priesthood. 10:6-7. This parenthesis is of the utmost spiritual importance. In it the Spirit of God calls attention to two events that took place long after the episode of the golden calf and the renewal of the covenant. They are inserted here because of their intimate connection with divine grace foreshadowed in the second tablets of the Decalogue. The first event is the death of Aaron, who represents Christ exercising priesthood in relation to wilderness needs and weakness. The second event is the priesthood succession of Eleazar, who prefigures Christ as Priest in relation to the inheritance and, from the Deuteronomic standpoint, represents all that is summarized as "good things to come" (Heb. 9:11).

Joshua was to stand before Eleazar, who would inquire for Joshua before the LORD (Num. 27:21). In the Eleazar aspect of His priesthood, Christ has complete knowledge, according to divine light, of "the divine inheritance" and allots to all His people and to each assembly their appointed place in the inheritance, as Eleazar did for all Israel and for each tribe. **7. A land of rivers of waters,** to which they came after the transfer of the priesthood to Eleazar, speaks of the Spirit as an abundant source of refreshment for God's people, even as viewed before crossing Jordan to experience salvation rest (cf. John 4:14; 7:37-39).

Divine Grace Is Manifested Through Priestly Ministry. 10:8-9. The separation of the tribe of Levi shows divine grace in action producing dedication to the LORD in preserving what is of God and due God (cf. Exod. 32:26). The priests represented in Israel the direct service of God, which is greater than the inheritance, the LORD being their inheritance (v. 9; cf. Num. 18:20, 24).

8. Their duties were distinguished from the inheritance and represented what the inheritance was to support. They were: (1) **To bear the ark of the covenant of the Lord.** They carried in their holy service what symbolized the glory of God shining out in the fullness of the grace of Christ. (2) **To stand before the Lord to minister unto him** in the sanctuary service—caring for the lamp, burning incense, and presenting offerings and sacrifices, all of which speaks of access to God and worship through Christ. What serves God is all-important, and the inheritance is bestowed to sustain that worship and service. (3) To **bless in his name** as a result of having access to Him by priestly privilege and intercession.

Divine Grace Is Revealed Through Priestly Intercession. 10:10-11. **10.** The LORD listened to Moses' intercession and would not destroy the sinning Israelites, even as He heeds Christ's intercession and preserves us (cf. Heb. 7:25). **11.** As a result of divine grace, God's people are conducted onward to inherit the promises and the inheritance.

Divine Grace Admonishes Believers to Godly Conduct and Service. 10:12-22. **12-13.** Grace requires and stimulates our godly fear, love, dedicated service, and obedience (cf. Titus 2:11-13). **14-16.** Grace teaches that God owns us by virtue of creation and redemption and that we are to give ourselves to Him whose we are. **17-19.** His love toward us is to stir up love for others, especially the helpless and destitute. **20-22.** His role as

Redeemer is to stir up our role as His servants.

H. THE NECESSITY OF OBEDIENCE. 11:1-32.

The Reasons for Obedience. 11:1-12. The application was made of the great truths of Israel's election and consequent responsibility (v. 1). God's people were to be obedient because: (1) They had experienced the LORD's chastisement for disobedience, the display of His greatness and power in redemption out of Egypt (vv. 3-4) and His disciplinary dealings in the wilderness (v. 5). (2) They saw the divine punishment meted out against the rebellion of Korah in his setting aside the divine order of the priesthood (v. 6; Num. 16:1-33; 26:9-10; 27:3; Psalm 106:17)—a terrible example that God will not tolerate insubjection to Christ (Jude 11).

(3) They had the positive promises of blessing for obedience—possessing of the inheritance and longevity in the land (vv. 8-9). (4) They had a preview of the very land's dependence upon the LORD for its fertility, and consequently the necessity of their obedience to the LORD to share the blessings of its fertility (vv. 10-12).

The Rewards of Obedience. 11:13-25. **13-15.** God promised: (1) To give **the rain . . . in its due season, the first** (early) **rain** in the autumn at the time of sowing, and **the latter rain** in the spring, helping the crops toward maturity, ready for harvest in May or June (cf. 28:12; Jer. 5:24; Joel 2:23; James 5:7). **16-17.** Idolatry would incur God's wrath and withholding of the rains. **18-21a.** (2) To give them peaceful and prosperous longevity in the land. Even today on the houses of orthodox Jews one can see on the outside doorpost a *mᵉzûzâ* (lit., "doorpost"), a small receptacle containing a copy of Deuteronomy 6:4-9 (*q.v.*).

21b. (3) To grant them **the days of heaven upon the earth** (cf. Psalm 72:1-8; 89:29; Matt. 6:10). Obedience will produce heavenly conditions upon the earth. Entering into salvation rest and victory is like experiencing heaven before we get there. **22-25.** (4) To **drive out** all their enemies and give them peaceful possession of the land (Josh. 1:3; 14:9), figurative of faith-producing obedience, enabling the believer to triumph over all his spiritual foes (Eph. 6:10-20; Col. 1:13).

The Curse of Disobedience. 11:26-32. **26-28.** The blessing of obedience was offset by the curse of disobedience (cf. 28:2-14; 30:1, 15). **29-32.** The warning was to be memorialized in the land, the sight of Mount Ebal and Mount Gerizim ever bringing to mind the importance of doing all that the LORD commands.

I. GOD-DIRECTED WORSHIP. 12:1-32.

The Overthrow of False Worship. 12:1-4. The section 12:1—26:19, giving detailed commandments, has its counterpart in contemporary international treaties consisting of obligations imposed upon the vassal. Here Moses set forth the regulations for the religious and social life in the land (12:1—16:22), governing worship and holy living. **1.** The phrase **in the land** envisions immediate entry into Canaan, honeycombed as it was with gross and degraded idolatry. The first thing required for true worship of the LORD was the complete extermination of pagan cults, cult objects, and cult shrines (vv. 1-4; cf. John 4:24; 1 John 5:21). Possession of our inheritance necessitates the most rigid dealing with idolatry.

The Establishment of True Worship. 12:5-32. True worship involves eight things: *(1) Worship must be in spirit and in truth, free from idolatrous contaminations* (vv. 1-4; cf. John 4:24). (2) *Wor-*

ship must recognize the unity of all the people of God in their approach to God. As all Israel was to worship at a central sanctuary selected by the LORD (vv. 5, 11, 14, 18; cf. Exod. 20:24; 1 Sam. 2:29), so approach to God is universal in character, there being one Body, one church, and one way of approach for all His people, wherever they may be found (1 Cor. 12:13; Eph. 4:4-5).

Of old, God put His name at Shiloh (1 Sam. 2:29), and ultimately at Jerusalem (v. 11; 26:2; Josh. 9:27; 1 Kings 8:29; 2 Chron. 7:12; Psalm 78:68). Today He has put His name in the church, the Body of Christ. The church as the Body of Christ is not to be ignored in its expression and administration in the local church, nor is the individual believer to violate the order and administration divinely committed to the local assembly (vv. 13-14). The principles of the unity and purity of the church are to balance one another.

(3) Worship must minister to the pleasure of God. Believers are to appear before Him at the place where He puts His name, with acceptable gifts and offerings (vv. 6-11). This prefigures such things as spiritual sacrifices of prayer, praise, and the offering of substance in the public assembly (Heb. 13:15-16), as well as partaking of the Lord's table (v. 18; 1 Cor. 11:23-26). *(4) Approach to God must be in the manner He has appointed* (v. 8). Will worship is utterly inconsonant with the enjoyment of the inheritance (vv. 9-14).

(5) Worship with the enjoyment of God's blessings in one's "gates" (home) is to be preparatory to worship and blessing in the place where He sets His name (vv. 15-17). Householdwise, we are to enjoy all we can of spiritual good in our mutual fellowship as saints, but we must not despise or forget the assembly of God.

248

(6) Worship in the place the LORD chooses is to be marked by consideration of what we give to God, and not only by what we get from Him (vv. 7, 12, 18). His blessing upon us in our gates calls forth the presentation of gifts, burnt offerings, peace offerings, and choice vows in grateful worship and dedication. Presenting to Him His portion, we shall not fail to receive our portion. Holding what we receive from Him in a right relation to Him and His assembly brings the fullest enjoyment. When God's people view their blessings being held in common to the glory and praise of God, they enjoy the greatest expression of joy.

Grain, wine, and oil (v. 17), representing things we gather by the work of our hands in the inheritance, are to be tithed, and the tithe carried to the place where God causes His name to dwell. The communion found where God dwells in the midst of His people is always to be sustained by what the saints gain individually or householdwise. The tithes were to be eaten at the central sanctuary. True worship of God results not only in direct ministry to God, but ministering indirectly to the communion of His saints before Him.

(7) Worship of the LORD must ever hold in view the value of shed blood to make expiation for sin (vv. 16, 23-24; see Lev. 7:26; 17:10-16; 1 Pet. 1:18-19). *(8) Worship of the LORD must be rigidly separated from all idolatrous contamination* (vv. 29-32), an emphatic repetition of the warning with which this chapter opened (vv. 1-4).

J. PERIL OF OCCULT CONTAMINATION. 13:1-18.

Peril of False Prophetism. 13:1-5. **1.** False prophets and clairvoyants contaminated by demon-energized occult-ism were warned against. **2.** By communication with the realm of evil supernaturalism (cf. Eph. 6:12; 2 Thess. 2:9-10), these protagonists of occult-ridden idolatry have evil powers of prognostication to lure their victims away from the LORD (cf. 1 Cor. 10:20; 1 Tim. 4:1; Rev. 9:20-21). **3-4.** They are to be tested rigidly by God's Word and rejected. God allows them their restricted sphere of power to test the loyalty of His people (1 John 4:1).

5. Because such traffic in the occult arts is an insult to God and breaks the first two commandments of the Decalogue (Israel's covenant), such false prophets were to be purged out by the death penalty (18:20) to protect the LORD's redeemed from the snare of idolatrous contamination (cf. 17:5; 1 Cor. 5:3).

Necessity of Dealing Mercilessly with Idolatry. 13:6-18. No pity was to be shown toward enticers to idolatry. **6-10.** One's **son,** even **the wife of** one's **bosom** (cf. Luke 14:26) was not to be spared. **But thou shalt surely kill him ... thou shalt stone him ... that he die. 11.** Such was the seriousness of turning the redeemed from their Redeemer that a public example had to be made of it. **12-16.** In the case of a city contaminated with idolatry, the whole town was to be utterly destroyed and made **an heap forever** (cf. Josh. 7:26).

K. AVOIDING THE SEMBLANCE OF IDOLATRY. 14:1-29.

Pagan Mourning Customs Prohibited. 14:1-2. In addition to actual rebellion against God through occult complicity, the very semblance of heathenism also had to be avoided (1 John 5:21). **1.** Mourning customs employed by idolaters who held the dead in reverential awe were therefore forbidden, especially so in self-mutilation in which blood was shed or hair cut off in token of a covenant or as a propitiatory gift for the dead (cf. Jer. 16:6; 41:5). Compare the parallel law (Lev. 19:28; 21:5) concerning the priests.

Diet of Idolaters Prohibited. 14:3-21. The clearest distinctions between the LORD's people and idolatrous pagans had to be maintained, even in what was eaten. God's people had to practice separation from what was idolatrous and defiling (cf. Lev. 11:2-23). Certain animals and specific kinds of sea food and fowl (vv. 7-10, 12-19) were to be carefully identified and avoided, the interdict being principally religious. Either these creatures were totems of surrounding paganistic peoples or they had some association with pagan rites. For a holy people, separation was imperative (cf. 2 Cor. 6:14—7:1; Eph. 5:5; 1 John 5:21).

3. The prohibition of **any abominable thing** as food is well known in the case of Peter, who was at last set free in accordance with the principles of Christian liberty (Acts. 10; cf. Gal. 2:11-19). **21.** The heathen custom of boiling a kid in its mother's milk was a common pagan practice, the milk subsequently being poured out as a charm upon the soil to insure its fertility (cf. Exod. 23:19).

Practice of Pure Religion Inculcated. 14:22-29. These negative requirements were prerequisite to the positive demands of Israelite faith. First among these was the tithe annually due to the LORD at His sanctuary (vv. 22-27). One-tenth of the land's produce was to be required by God to be offered annually at His house. God's people were stewards of the land that belongs to the LORD. Therefore, tithes of produce had to be offered annually at the harvest festival (16:9-12).

A special Deuteronomic provision allowed the tithe to be converted into

specie ("silver" or "gold"). Food was then to be purchased at the shrine, and the feast held there (vv. 24-27). Every three years the householder's tithe went not to the sanctuary and its established priests, but to the Levites (cf. 18:6-8), the poor, the sojourner (foreigners in Israelite employ), and the orphans and widows (vv. 28-29; cf. 26:12-15; James 1:27). Possessing our inheritance means giving God top priority and not forgetting to show charity to those in need.

L. DEMONSTRATING GOD'S LOVE TO OTHERS. 15:1-23.

By Observing the Sabbatic Release from Debt. 15:1-6. **1-3.** In Exodus 23:10-11 the Sabbatic year was for the sake of the poor; in Leviticus 25:1-7 it was a fallow year for the sake of the land. Here it is a charitable regulation for the remission of debts. Possessing our possessions in Christ means sharing our blessings with others and showing mercy and grace to others as God has shown His love to us. **4-6.** This brings spiritual enrichment, as it was promised to bring material prosperity to Israel (cf. Matt. 6:14-15; Luke 11:4; Eph. 4:32; Col. 3:13).

By Cultivating Charitable-Mindedness. 15:7-11. The above-mentioned statute was the springboard from which Moses pleaded for sincerity in benevolent giving. No one who possessed the inheritance was to fail in loving concern for others. **7-9.** God will regard the cry of the poor as a witness against the hardhearted. **10-11.** Practical demonstration of a merciful attitude is necessary, for the **poor shall never cease out of the land** (cf. Matt. 26:11; Mark 14:7; John 12:8).

By Observing the Sabbatic Liberation of Slaves. 15:12-18. **12.** The release enjoined upon creditors (vv. 1-6) was to apply also to owners of Hebrew slaves (see Exod. 21:2-11 for the law on Hebrew servitude). **13-15.** Love was to be exemplified in the requirement that such a manumitted slave was not to go out **empty** (i.e., "empty-handed"). **15.** The nation's gracious deliverance from Egyptian bondage and the spoil of the Egyptians granted the escaping people had to remain a perpetual reminder that God's love was showered upon them and that they were to manifest it to others in bondage (Exod. 6:6). The humanitarianism that has flowed from Christianity has its roots in Deuteronomy, because the possession of the divine inheritance and enjoyment of the salvation rest that Christ came to bring are envisioned.

16-17. In the servant who chooses to remain in servitude appears a beautiful type of Christ (cf. Psalm 40:6-8; also see explanation of Exod. 21:1-11). In this passage, male and female slaves were put on the same level, unlike the older law, showing how the manifestation of God's grace in Christ would liberate womanhood (cf. Gal. 3:27-28). The lesson for us in this passage is that whatever obligation a brother (or sister) may have come under, he is to be treated with brotherly love and with a bounty worthy of God (cf. Gal. 6:1-2; James 5:19-20).

Commemorating God's Love— Presenting Firstlings. 15:19-23. Actually these verses belong to chapter 16 (*q.v.*). The hallowed firstborn (v. 19; cf. Exod. 13:2, 12; Num. 3:13) was a memorial of God's love in securing Israel as His firstborn (Exod. 4:22) for Himself through redemption out of Egypt. In sovereign love He gave His people the position of sonship as their primary distinction—"to whom belongs the adoption [sonship]" (Rom. 9:4, NASB).

The truth that Israel was God's son, His firstborn, underlies the Passover (Hos. 11:1). Sonship properly belongs to

the land. In the wilderness, God acted toward Israel as a father. But they, on their side, were not addressed as sons until Deuteronomy 14:1 (cf. Gal. 3:26). God's purpose is to place His sons as heirs of the inheritance in order to enjoy all the wealth of it in happy realization of the position they have for His delight.

The firstling envisions "him, whom the Father hath sanctified and sent into the world" (John 10:36), the Beloved, Savior, and Redeemer, who was to become "the firstborn among many brethren" (Rom. 8:29), and by His death give birth "to the ... church of the firstborn" (Heb. 12:23). Since it looked forward to the coming One, the firstling was not to be worked or sheared (v. 19) and was to be perfect and unblemished (v. 21), pointing to the spotless Lamb of God.

20. Eating the firstborn **before the Lord** in the central sanctuary speaks of God's delight in His Firstborn and in all those who share the exalted position of sonship in union with Him. Prefigured is the communion of saints in the church (the assembly). Such fellowship cannot be experienced in our gates (v. 22), but only in the place that He chooses. We must bring one firstling to the place where all Israel brought theirs to teach us that what is for God's delight embraces all His sons. Sonship is both individual and collective. The collective aspect is in view here (Rom. 8:29; Gal. 3:26, 28; Eph. 1:5). The pleasure of God is found in His people being together before Him in the communion of sonship.

M. COMMEMORATING GOD'S LOVE.
16:1-22.

By Presenting Firstlings. 15:19-23. See above.

By Observing the Passover. 16:1-8. The clear testimony of Scripture is that

God was acting in love through the Passover for the redemption of His people in manifesting His wondrous purposes of favor toward them (7:8; Isa. 43:1, 4; 63:9; Hos. 11:1). Israel's annual observance of the feast was to commemorate God's redemptive love. The feast was obligatory (like Pentecost and Tabernacles), calling for obedience attesting faith and proper response to that love.

1-2. Two things are peculiar to the account of the Passover in Deuteronomy: (1) *The place* where the feast was to be kept: **in the place which the Lord** thy God **shall choose to place his name there** (vv. 2, 6, 7). Prefigured is the entrance of God's people into the inheritance (salvation rest) and, as in the case of the offering of the firstlings (15:19-23), their communion as saints and sons in the assembly (church), particularly in partaking of the Lord's table and thus remembering His death (see 1 Cor. 11:26). "God would gather His beloved people around Himself, that they might feast together in His presence, that He might rejoice in them and they in Him and in one another" (C. H. Mackintosh, *Deuteronomy* 2:222).

(2) *The mode* of celebration: those redeemed out of Egypt (the world), are mentioned three times (vv. 1, 3, 6), which emphasizes that redemption is more than shelter, for it secures a people delivered out of the world for God's pleasure and saved *to* (not *by*) personal holiness.

3. Featured is **unleavened bread** (vv. 3, 4, 8), typical of holiness of heart and life, which is so indispensable to true communion with God (1 Cor. 5:8; 11:27-32). Called **the bread of affliction,** unleavened bread speaks of meditating on what it cost our Lord to redeem us from sin; and so "if we would judge ourselves" in that light, "we should not

be judged" by being "chastened of the Lord" (1 Cor. 11:31-32).

Leaven permitted deals a deathblow to the fellowship of the saints, destroys true worship, and does despite to the manifestation of God's love in redemption. Absolutely essential was the keeping the Feast of Unleavened Bread, which was inseparable from the Passover. It is one thing to know and believe He died for us, and quite another thing that we died in Him—died to sin, the world, and the flesh (Rom. 6:1-10). Knowing and believing the latter enables us to keep the Feast of Unleavened Bread (Rom. 6:11).

By Observing the Feast of Weeks. 16:9-12. **9.** This feast was called the "Feast of Weeks" because it was celebrated **seven weeks** after Passover and the Feast of Unleavened Bread, marking the beginning of the wheat harvest, even as Passover marked the beginning of the barley harvest (see Exod. 34:22; Lev. 23:15-16; Num. 28:26). Therefore, the Feast of Weeks was related to presenting *firstfruits*—first, of the barley harvest at the beginning of it, as typical of Christ risen and those who arose after Him (cf. Matt. 27:52-53); and second, of the wheat harvest at the end of it, as typical of those at Pentecost who received the gift of the Spirit (Acts 1:8, 13; 2:1-4). Thus pictured is the period that began with the resurrection of Christ and ended with the pouring out of the gift of the Spirit. The seven weeks were to be carefully numbered or counted.

To keep the Feast of Weeks: (1) There must be a reckoning in a definite way from Christ's resurrection. As we "count," God works in us so that we become before Him as "the first fruits of [the] wheat harvest" (Exod. 34:22)—a company of people in this world identified in mind and affection by the power of the Holy Spirit with the risen Christ, like the disciples at Pentecost (Acts 2:1-4).

10. (2) We offer **a tribute of a freewill offering ... according as the Lord** our **God hath blessed** us. Liberality in both spiritual and material sharing with God and with one another will abound. This is graphically illustrated in Acts 2:42-47. **11.** (3) We *rejoice* before the LORD (Acts 2:46-47), which pictures the joy of the Holy Spirit manifested in the church (1 Cor. 12:26). Realized are "tidings of great joy, which shall be to all people" (Luke 2:10)—**son ... daughter ... manservant ... maidservant ... the Levite ... the sojourner ... the fatherless, and the widow ... in the place which the Lord thy God hath chosen to place his name** (the church of Jesus Christ). **12.** (4) We remember, as God's redeemed, the slavery of sin from which we have been rescued.

By Observing the Feast of Tabernacles. 16:13-15. **13.** The third annual pilgrimage was related to a harvest festival, conveying the fullest thought of blessing and joy with which the typical year ends. **14-15. Thou shalt rejoice ... thou shalt surely rejoice** (be wholly joyful). The time for being "wholly joyful" has not yet come publicly, as it will in the Kingdom age. But this joy is anticipated in the church, where it is possible for us to know fullness of joy, even though outward circumstances are not yet changed.

The Deuteronomic aspect of this feast is limited to seven days (no "eighth day" as in Lev. 23:39). Contemplated is the fullness of joy realized in the present time, not in eternity. However, for Israel the seven days would correspond to the Millennium, while the "eighth day" looks on to what is eternal. Pictured here are the completeness of God's blessing and the fullness of joy that it affords saints who are in the land, possessing their inheritance (salvation rest), enjoying its wealth, and keeping this **solemn feast unto the Lord ... in the place which** He **shall choose** (the local church, where assembly communion in joyful worship and praise is realized).

By Responding Fully to the Lord's Blessing. 16:16-17. **16.** The three feasts—Passover, the Feast of Weeks, and Tabernacles—were obligatory upon *all* males, who were representing *all* Israel, and signifying today *all* the people of God (the church, 1 Cor. 12:13). The three obligatory pilgrimage feasts of the Israelites can be compared to the Hittite treaties, where vassals had to appear in the suzerain's capital once a year. **They shall not appear before the Lord empty** ("empty-handed," NASB). To come into the LORD's presence "empty" would deny that we were full of the LORD's blessing. It would constitute the sad evidence of failure to cultivate the inheritance (work out our "so great salvation," Heb. 2:3; cf. Phil. 2:15) in faithful response to His manifested love.

By Just Judgment Among God's People. 16:18-20. **18.** It is God's will that there should be among His people those who **shall judge ... with just judgment** (cf. 1 Cor. 6:1-8). Judgment is not to be distorted; persons are not to be "respected," or bribes taken. Cases are to be decided according to God's Word that everything that would interfere with the true fellowship of saints and their possession and enjoyment of the land might be removed. A mere legal settlement is not to be sufficient for this. Making the heart and motives right is necessary, which is the real issue in practically all cases that call for judicial decision among God's people.

By Extirpating Pagan Customs. 16:21-22. Pagan customs, such as **a grove** (Heb., *'ashērâ*) and the Canaanite goddess, Asherah, were an affront to

253

God's love. In Ugaritic literature, Asherah is called the "Goddess of oracles" (*Keret*, pp. 201-2). The cultic Asherah and pillar apparently were symbols associated with judicial oracles (cf. Prov. 16:10) as well as religion (cf. 2 Cor. 6:14—7:1).

N. HONORING GOD IN GOVERNMENT. 17:1-20.

By Just Judgment Among God's People. 16:18-20 (see above).

By Extirpating Pagan Customs. 16:21-22 (see above).

By Owning God's Absolute Lordship in Judicial Matters. 17:1-7. Since the LORD was both God and King in Israel, all theocratic institutions, including the judicial, were religious. Accordingly, there was an extension of religious practice beyond the sanctuary into the administration of government. Moreover, the priests possessed the dominant judicial voice because the book of the law, containing the covenant stipulations, was committed to them at the central sanctuary in order for them to guard and expound it. The priests also had access to the direct divine oracles through the Urim and Thummim.

1. So the stipulations that only unblemished offerings were to be sacrificed unto the LORD showed that the religious aspect of judicial procedure must be characterized by the same reverence for the LORD's holy name that was required in all Israel's sacrificial ritual (cf. 15:21; Lev. 22:17-24). In judicial matters, as in all others, approach to God must be on the basis of the perfections of Christ, of which the unblemished animal speaks (cf. Lev. 22:17-24).

2-7. The first concern of the judges was to maintain what is due to God by exclusion of everything idolatrous or imperfect in His service and govern-ment. Idolatrous apostasy constituted a capital offense because it violated the first two commandments of the Decalogue and struck at loyalty to the LORD, which was at the very heart of the covenant relationship. Hence, the severe penalty by stoning. But such a judgment was not to be executed without thorough inquiry on the testimony of at least **two witnesses.**

This is an important principle of judgment in the church (2 Cor. 13:1; cf. Mark 14:56-59; John 8:17). Things pertaining to the LORD's people are to be judged in the light of divine revelation and of approach to God on the basis of the perfection of Christ. God through Christ's perfect sacrifice forgives us; therefore, we are to be forgiving (Eph. 4:32; cf. Matt. 6:12, 14, 15).

By Utilizing God's Ultimate Court of Appeal. 17:8-13. **8-10.** Any case that proved to be **too hard** (lit., "too wonderful"; cf. Job 42:3) for the local officials was to be taken to the central sanctuary (cf. 19:16-18). There **the priests . . . and . . . the judge** were to render judgment. In the New Testament our Lord puts the church (the local assembly) in precisely this position (Matt. 18:15-19), corresponding in the Old Testament to **the place which the Lord thy God shall choose** to place His name. But our Lord sets forth the spirit in which believers are to act toward each other in their own gates *before* they bring any case before the assembly (Matt. 18:1-16). Only after the heart-searching procedure is outlined, did our Lord direct: "Tell it to the church; but if he refuses to listen even to the church, let him be to you as a Gentile [heathen man] and a tax-gatherer" (Matt. 18:17, NASB).

As the LORD vested His authority at the central sanctuary, and absolute obedience to the judicial sentences handed down there was necessary for His Old Testament people (vv. 10-13), so He has vested His authority in the church (Matt. 18:18), even in its simplest form (Matt. 18:19-20). In the place that the LORD chooses, everything is judged according to the name that dwells there, the name of ineffable grace. If a believer's conduct is not according to grace, it will assuredly be visited governmentally by God. He who spurns the voice of grace, voiced by the assembly, shows that he is a spiritual outlaw, not to be recognized as one of God's people (Matt. 18:17).

By Heeding God's Ideal of a King. *17:14-20.* **14.** In this section the mind of God concerning a king is revealed. It anticipates the future in the land. **15.** The five requirements were stipulated: (1) He was to be God's choice (cf. 1 Sam. 9:15; 10:24; 16:12; 1 Chron. 22:10). (2) He was to be an Israelite, a covenant person, not a foreigner or a pagan (cf. 2 Cor. 6:14—7:1). "It is noteworthy that in the secular suzerainty treaties, a similar oversight of the vassal's choice of a king is exercised" (Kline, WBC, p. 179). In surrounding nations, the king was often considered a god. In Israel, God was King (cf. 33:5; Exod. 15:18; 19:5-6).

(3) He was to be God's servant and representative. He was never to forget his own and his people's divine election and redemption from Egyptian bondage. **16.** Hence, he had to avoid lust for horses, such as the Pharaoh had (cf. 1 Kings 10:28-29; Isa. 30:2), for that would prove a snare to compromising worldliness, as was the case with Solomon (1 Kings 10:26-29; 11:1-8). **17.** (4) He was not to have numerous wives or amass great worldly wealth (1 Kings 11:1-8; 10:14). **18.** (5) He was to make **a copy of this law** (the enactment relating to the king and his duties) and read and

ponder it all the days of his life. In contemporary suzerain treaties, a duplicate copy was provided for each vassal king. The LORD's copy, the original, was deposited at the central sanctuary (31:9).

O. HONORING GOD THROUGH VITAL SERVICE. 18:1-22.

Nourishing a Priestly Ministry. *18:1-5.* **1-2.** "The priests, the Levites—the whole tribe of Levi" (literal Heb. trans.) represented *all* Israel as the people of God in the capacity of ministering to the LORD in a priestly way (in access to God) or in a Levitical way (in furthering His service among the people). In figure, they speak of New Testament saints possessing their inheritance in enjoyment of salvation rest, God Himself becoming their inheritance.

2. The Lord is their inheritance. Hence, in Deuteronomy the official service of the priest and Levite was not in view, but rather, their personal portion—that which as food gave them strength for their holy service. Their sustenance depended on offerings, tithes, and firstfruits brought by the people, who were to cultivate and gather the produce of the land to contribute to the nourishment of what was priestly. This in figure means ministering to what is priestly in oneself as a saint in order to minister what is priestly in the place (the assembly) where God chooses to place His name.

Inheritance with Israel speaks of what God has given His own in Christ. But this passage stresses the fact that, as a result of enjoying their God-given portion, there is a *portion for God*, which He calls **his inheritance.** What was given to the priests and Levites in tithes was in a distinct sense God's portion. They were to live on that (10:9; 1 Cor. 9:13).

The saints viewed in their priestly capacity are privileged to have what is for God as their portion; as priests they live upon that. They feed upon Christ, whose perfections are prefigured in **the offerings of the Lord made by fire,** which they were to eat.

3-5. The priest's due from the people (cf. Lev. 7:32-34; Num. 18:11-12) further illustrates the nourishing and strengthening of the priestly ministry by feeding upon Christ, whom the sacrificial animals (**ox** and **sheep**) typify as Savior and Redeemer. Feeding on the **shoulder** (strength, cf. Isa. 14:25) speaks of being nourished by contemplation of His firm unfaltering devotion to God's path (Psalm 16:8; John 8:29).

The two cheeks (jaws), where the food was masticated, suggest our LORD delighting and *meditating* (ruminating) in God's Law "day and night" (Psalm 1:2). The **stomach** gives the idea of digestion and assimilation (cf. 8:3; Matt. 4:4; John 6:52-59). Essential for the vigorous discharge of the priestly ministry are the comprehension and appropriation of Christ, symbolized by the shoulder, cheeks, and stomach of the sacrificial animal.

The first fruits (a foretaste of more to come) indicates what is new and fresh in spiritual apprehension. The firstfruits of **grain** (the Word, Matt. 13:22), of **wine** and **oil** (the Holy Spirit in fresh, living operation, Eph. 5:18; Psalm 45:7), and of **fleece** (wool as being warm and comforting the priest) indicate that vigorous priestly service must minister the Word in the power and joy of the Spirit with spiritual warmth and comfort.

Volunteering a Levitical Ministry. 18:6-8. The service of the Levites dealt with the mechanics or ritual of religion. The Levites were strictly under the priests (see Num. 5:5-10), for the latter had access to God on the basis of the redemptive sacrifice, and since all work for God (including the Levitical) demands a priestly basis of contact and empowerment by the *living God* (Heb. 9:14). **8.** Entrance into the inheritance (salvation rest) being envisioned, the Levite here appears as one whose soul senses the holy privilege of ministering at the place where God puts His name (cf. Psalm 84:10), and who gladly and spontaneously offers his services at some personal sacrifice—he sold his patrimony. What a picture of the New Testament believer who willingly devotes himself to the multifarious places of service for God in the local church. This is availing oneself of assembly privilege and reaping great benefits.

Outlawing Occultism. 18:9-14. God is grossly dishonored by all traffic in the occult arts. Hence, all pagan modes of inquiring after supernatural counsel were banned from the LORD's people. "The list given here is well-nigh exhaustive of what either the Scripture or anthropology knows as substitutes for divine revelation" (Charles M. Cooper, "Deuteronomy," OTC, p. 317). Occultism is basically an appeal for knowledge and power from demonic powers, instead of from God. An offshoot of pagan idolatry, it insults God by openly breaking the first two tables of the Decalogue, thus violating the heart of the covenant relationship with the LORD (Exod. 20:5), involving traffic with demons (cf. 1 Cor. 10:20). It is to be absolutely proscribed by God's people. Molech worshipers sacrificed the firstborn by the cruel practice of passing through the fire (12:31; Lev. 18:21; 20:2; Jer. 7:31; 19:5).

10-11. A consultor of mediums (familiar spirits or demons) is a spiritistic medium (see Lev. 19:31; 20:6; 27; 1 Sam. 28:1-25). **A witch** is "one who inquires of a divining demon" (Heb., *'ôḇ*, "a fortune-telling spirit"), and a **wizard** (*yidde'ōnî*, "a knowing one") is one who possesses supernatural knowledge through communication with the evil world of supernaturalism. A **necromancer** (literal Heb., "a seeker among the dead") is a medium who professes to communicate with the dead, but who really has communication with evil spirits that ape the dead. This practice is called "spiritualism" today; actually, it is "spiritism" (traffic in spirits). Occultism was part and parcel of the debauched Canaanite religion, which was honeycombed with demonism, sexual perversion, and violence, as the Ugaritic literature recovered from Ras Shamra (ancient Ugarit) attests.

Esteeming True Prophetism. 18:15-19. This section contains the great Messianic prediction of the Messiah as the Prophet par excellence, as interpreted by Jesus and the apostles (John 1:21, 45; 7:40; Acts 3:22-23; 7:37). Christ was the great Prophet toward whom the Old Testament prophetic institution pointed. But inasmuch as this "Prophet" is introduced as the legitimate counterpart of the occult oracular institutions of Canaan (vv. 9-14), the figure of the prophet has both a corporate and an individual connotation. This fact further appears when the problem of differentiating true and false prophetism is also broached in this context (vv. 20-22). False prophetism is the outcome of contamination by occultism or occult religionism, the snare that beset the people of God in Canaan and made the proscription of *all* such practices absolutely necessary.

18. The Prophet (Messiah) to be raised up was to be, Moses declared, **like ... me**, meaning, "like me at Horeb, mediating a fresh and normative revelation of God" (R. K. Harrison, NBC, p. 221). As a type of Christ as Prophet,

Moses was like our LORD in seven aspects: (1) His life was spared in infancy (Exod. 2:1-10; Matt. 2:1-23). (2) He emptied himself (Phil. 2:5-9), for he renounced a royal court to identify himself with his enslaved brothers, becoming a deliverer and a savior (Exod. 2:1-15; 3:10-12). (3) He was faithful (Heb. 3:2), and full of compassion and love (Num. 27:17; Matt. 9:36). (4) He spoke with God face to face, reflecting the divine glory (Exod. 34:33-34; Num. 12:8; 2 Cor. 3:7). (5) He was a mighty prophet in word and deed (cf. Luke 24:19), a revealer of God's will and purpose (6:1; Rev. 1:1). (6) He was a mediator of the covenant (29:1; Heb. 8:6-7). (7) He was a leader of the people (cf. Isa. 55:4).

Ferreting out False Prophetism. 18:20-22. The false prophet can and must be distinguished from the true prophet. (1) The false prophet leads into some form or variation of idolatry (13:1-5; cf. 1 John 5:21). (2) He speaks his own words instead of God's, and speaks in the name of other gods (v. 20), although he may masquerade under God's name (v. 22). (3) His prophecies are fake or half true, in distinction to God's bona fide prophets, who speak *only* God's word (Isa. 8:20) and whose predictions are completely true (1 Kings 22:28; Jer. 28:9). Compare the New Testament test of a prophet (1 John 4:1-7), which centers in the person (and work) of our Lord.

P. JUDICIAL ASYLUM—GOD'S GRACE IN OPERATION. 19:1-21.

Cities of Refuge in Canaan. 19:1-10. For the general significance of the cities of refuge, see 4:41-43 and Numbers 35:9-34. The stress here is upon God's grace manifested in the provision of asylum for cases when the normal enjoyment of the land is no longer possible. God graciously gives these cities (v.

1) in the land He Himself provides (v. 2), in the place He enables His people to inherit (v. 3). In giving them, the divine goodness is magnified against the dark backdrop of the divine severity (cf. Rom. 11:22)—grace to His own, severity toward unrepentant sinners (the Canaanites).

The unintentioned manslayer (v. 4), illustrated by the woodsman whose ax head accidentally kills his neighbor (v. 5), represents an individual Israelite who is guilty of unpremeditated homicide. As a result, he has lost the right to the normal enjoyment of the inheritance. But in a larger sense, he represents (1) Israel corporately (the nation), who in "ignorance" slew "the Prince of life" (Acts 3:15, 17), thereby forfeiting their right to the earthly inheritance; as well as (2) the Gentiles, who had no earthly inheritance to lose.

In both senses the slaying of Christ was done in ignorance (Luke 23:34; cf. Acts 3:17 with 4:27-28). Both Jew and Gentile became totally shut up to God's grace in Christ and to a *heavenly* inheritance, as those described in Hebrews, "who have *fled for refuge* to lay hold upon the hope set before us ... which entereth into that within the veil, where the forerunner is for us entered, even Jesus" (Heb. 6:18-20, italics added).

The people of God at the present time must not center their hope in any inheritance upon the earth, but they must flee for refuge to those things that lie within the heavenly veil. The highest and richest blessings that God has to give today are available in the cities of refuge, for the cities represent a divine provision not only for sinners, but for the people of God as well.

When conviction comes to God's people that there has been a terrible departure from the normal conditions in which the land was originally held and that they themselves have unwittingly struck blows against God's truth and the brethren, they will find that the city of refuge is always available for them to flee to. Although many may forfeit much blessing, the inheritance can still be enjoyed by those who assume the place of refugees. Moreover, God graciously provides for spiritual enlargement by increased provision for refugees (vv. 8-9).

Penalty for Murder. 19:11-12. A real murderer fleeing to a city of refuge would find no asylum there, for he would be extradited by the city elders to the proper blood avenger. *Blood for blood* is the rigid law. God's severity is just as real as His grace (Rom. 2:4-5).

Removal of Landmarks. 19:14. **14.** One's **neighbor's landmark** (27:17) or boundary was not to be removed, because it was divinely set and appointed. The inheritance is common to all God's people, but each has his assigned portion, his particular gift and calling (1 Cor. 3:5; 12:11; Gal. 2:7-9; Eph. 4:7). If our neighbor has his landmark removed, not only does he suffer, but we suffer too. Landmarks give to each one his true spiritual place in the inheritance for the glory of God and for the benefit of all (cf. 2 Cor. 10:13-16; Phil. 2:4).

Law of Witnesses. 19:15-21. **15. At the mouth of two ... or ... three witnesses** stipulates the general regulation in criminal cases of the same law that had been declared for capital cases (17:6; Num. 35:30). **16-21.** The perjured witness in a court violating the ninth commandment is dealt with (see 5:20; Exod. 20:16; 23:1). The central court determines the **false witness**, and his punishment is severe, demonstrating the utter heinousness of the sin of perjury.

Q. THE LAW OF WARFARE. 20:1-20.

Trust Must Be Placed in the Lord. 20:1-4. **1. When thou goest out to battle**

... be not afraid. The inheritance could not be held apart from conflict (cf. 7:18; Eph. 6:10-20), but faith in the LORD would dispel fear. God's people are not to be occupied with what they see with their physical sight (the **horses, and chariots, and a people more than thou**), but what they can see with the eye of faith (cf. 2 Cor. 5:7). Two reasons will aid them to "fight the good fight of faith" (1 Tim. 6:12): (1) God is with them. (2) He redeemed them and will preserve them.

2-4. Faith in the LORD would also be evidenced by hearkening to the voice of **the priest,** who represented that element of the people that has an approach to God and has clarity of spiritual vision. Any conflict that is not led by priestly access to God will not be "the battles of the LORD," but some fracas of our own.

Certain Exemptions Are to Be Allowed. 20:5-9. Not every one was prepared and ready for conflict. This is true in the natural (a soldier must be trained) as well as in the spiritual (God's soldiers must be prepared). **5.** The man who **built a new home** but had **not dedicated it** was almost ready for military duty, but not quite. He had claimed his inheritance, settled down in it, and even completed his home in it. He was like the Ephesian saints, who knew their position and possessions in their inheritance in Christ (Eph. 1-3); but in not having dedicated his house, he was unlike them. He had not yet reckoned on his exalted position (cf. Rom. 6:11), converting it into experiential reality (Eph. 4:1—6:9), thus making him ready for conflict (Eph. 6:10-20).

6. The man who **planted a vineyard** and who had **not yet eaten of it** had not tasted the joy of the inheritance as a fruit of his own cultivation of it (cf. Eph. 5:18), and so he was not ready for conflict (Eph. 6:10-20). **7.** The man who had

betrothed a wife, and hath not taken her envisions bringing forth a generation to occupy and enjoy the land, resulting in the increase of God's people. Entering into and appropriating all the blessing God has for us should precede going to battle. There are conditions by God's appointment that not only precede conflict but provoke it. Divine order and not mere humanitarian considerations govern our going to battle for the LORD.

8. The **fearful and fainthearted** were instructed to return from conflict, for their example would have a negative effect. They failed to listen to priestly ministry (vv. 2-3). Compare Paul's acting in this capacity to Timothy (2 Tim. 1:6-7). Contrast Paul's acting in the role of an "officer" to John Mark (Acts 15:38).

Rules for Siege and Battle. 20:10-20.
10-11. Peaceful offers were to be made before a city was besieged. If the offer of peace was accepted and the city opened its gates, the inhabitants would become bond servants (cf. 2 Sam. 20:18-22). **12-14.** If resistance was made and the city was besieged, every male was to be slain with the sword, but the women, children, cattle, and spoil were to be spared. Service to God is viewed here as warfare (cf. Num. 4:3; 2 Tim. 4:7), a kind of warfare that has in view the addition of something of value—even extending the message of God to non-Israelites. **15.** These rules applied only to foreign powers outside Canaan.

16-17. By contrast, the nations occupying the inheritance were to be completely exterminated (7:1-5), because they were hopelessly corrupt and insidiously corrupting (cf. 18:9-15). **19-20.** Fruit-bearing trees were not to be cut down, even to meet the exigencies of war, since they furnished food. Conflict must not be undiscerning and indiscriminate. Something that is of God and of abiding value may be found even among adversaries; it must not be destroyed, for it has lasting value.

R. EXPIATION FOR MURDER AND OTHER LAWS. 21:1-23.

Expiation for a Case of Unpunished Murder. 21:1-9. **1-4.** Bloodguiltiness of this sort had to be atoned for by killing a heifer in a deserted valley. **5-6.** Meanwhile, the elders of the nearby city, in the presence of the priests, washed their hands over the slain heifer, confessing their innocence of the crime. This furnishes an illustration of Israel's guilt in putting the Messiah to death at His first advent (Matt. 27:24-25), together with the nation's cleansing on the basis of Christ's death at the second advent, when they will turn to Him (Zech. 12:10—13:1).

Here the heifer (cf. Num. 19) appears as a type of Christ in the character in which He is to be apprehended to make atonement for the guilt of slaying Him: (1) The heifer had not been worked, nor had it drawn the yoke—Christ never came under man's influence in any way, nor did He serve man's purposes at all. He strictly served God's will and was slain "by the determinate counsel and foreknowledge of God" (Acts 2:23).

(2) As to man's responsibility, He was found slain; but on the divine side, He was the heifer brought down into **a rough valley**—"a valley with running water" (NASB) of God's blessed activities in grace, an ever flowing stream, altogether independent of man, and existing in spite of man's wickedness. This appears to be what is suggested by the ever running watercourse in the valley that was neither **plowed** nor **sown**. Only in this region can Christ be apprehended through the Word (Eph. 5:25*b*) as having died to

effect expiation for those under bloodguiltiness.

5-6. Only by washing one's hands **over** the slain heifer (Christ is the One whose death has wrought expiation) can those guilty of innocent blood be cleansed. Contrast Pilate, who washed his hands of the heifer to be slain, but *not* over the slain heifer to expiate his guilt (Matt. 27:24), with those convicted under Peter's preaching who believed and were saved (Acts 2:38-39), and could declare, *"Our hands have not shed this blood* directly, but indirectly. We were therefore under bloodguiltiness. But we have been cleansed and saved." The principle here enunciated of divine grace flowing through the death of Christ has a wider bearing in **every controversy and every stroke** (assault). If something fatal to the enjoyment of the inheritance arises, all the people of God are affected. All have to prove themselves clear of the matter through priestly and judicial trial.

8-9. When that element is operative, things are determined according to the Word of God in light of the death of Christ and the unceasing operation of divine grace and not merely in a legal way. Intercessory prayer is to play a large part in this procedure. In any case, God's people must be relieved of any implication in wrongdoing in order to continue in priestly blessing. Moreover, it is the community's responsibility to seek atonement for the crime (vv. 2-3).

Law Concerning a Captive Woman. 21:10-14. **12-13.** A captive woman could be taken in marriage after being given opportunity for the due performance of mourning. **14.** In the event the marriage proved unsatisfactory to the husband, her freedom to **go wherever she wishes** (NASB) was guaranteed her. The ancient law illustrates the nation Israel, the wife of the LORD (Ezek. 16; Hos. 2:16-23).

The LORD desired Israel and proposed to have her for Himself in covenant relationship, separated from all that marked her natural origin. But the thought is suggested that, after having gotten her, the man might **have no delight in her.** He might have to "let her go wherever she wishes." This in germ gives a synopsis of what actually happened. The LORD did not delight in Israel because of her infidelity. He has let her go "whither she will" (KJV). How tragic her position in being let go! How tragic when any of God's people are similarly let go (cf. John 6:66; 2 Tim. 1:15; 4:10; Rev. 2:4, 14, 20; 3:16).

The Inalienable Rights of the Firstborn. 21:15-17. This law put the right of the firstborn above family rivalry or preference (cf. Gen. 25:29-34). The firstborn represents what is the result of divine working, the fruit of the operation of divine grace and power. The firstborn for earthly blessing will be brought forth from Israel (Rom. 11:25-36), but now God's firstborn for heavenly blessing is being called out from the Gentiles (Acts 15:14-15). When "the times of the Gentiles" have run their course (Rom. 11:25), then Israel—today in the position of the hated wife (Hos. 2:1-13)—will be restored (Hos. 2:14-23), according to divine grace and the unchangeableness of the divine purpose (cf. Exod. 4:22-23).

The Rebellious Son. 21:18-21. **19-20.** Flouting parental authority is tantamount to flouting God's authority and strikes at the heart of the covenant order as a manifestation of God's lordship. **21.** It is punished by the ultimate sanctions of theocratic law (cf. Exod. 21:15, 17; Lev. 20:9; Deut. 27:16). But the intractable son illustrates what turned out to be

Israel's case and is very largely the case in Christendom today. As God's firstborn, Israel would not obey or respond to paternal discipline (v. 18). So he was turned over to the elders of the city (judicial punishment) and condemned to death by stoning, even as rebellious Israel was judicially given over to captivity and death. Divine election, however, assures ultimate blessing (Rom 11:7) as the firstborn, the result of divine grace and calling. But the rest reveals Israel's true character, which is yet to come under full judicial judgment during the Great Tribulation (Jer. 30:5-7).

Disposition of a Criminal's Corpse. 21:22-23. **22-23.** This case takes the judicial process a step beyond the execution to the exposure of the corpse as a public warning that justice has been satisfied. The condemned is revealed to be guilty of offenses declared to be accursed in the covenant sanctions. As one put to death, he would visibly embody the curse of God poured out in an ultimate sense (cf. 2 Sam. 21:10; Rev. 19:17-21). That this law foreshadows the ignominious death on the cross suffered by our Lord in His being accounted the lowest criminal is shown by the quotation of verse 23 in Galatians 3:13 (cf. John 19:31). Joshua observed this law in the burial of the king of Ai (Josh. 8:29).

S. LAWS GOVERNING CONDUCT TOWARD OTHERS. 22:1-30.

Duty of Brotherly Love. 22:1-8. **1-4.** It is important to act from a spirit of love toward one's neighbor. Only in this way can God's requirements be met. Guarding and preserving another's property constitutes a good test of our loving him. **5.** The law forbidding one sex to wear the clothes of the other sex was primarily aimed at preserving God's ordained order. God created them male and female with distinctive natures and functions.

In the divine arrangement, man is head of the woman, as together they reign over the earth. To abrogate the divine order of the sexes, as in present-day sanction and practice of homosexuality and so-called women-liberation movements, is a species of anarchy fraught with confusion and many ill effects. An "abomination" is that which sets aside God's supreme authority, and thus violates all gradated authority, springing from this fundamental concept, God, Christ, husband, wife, children (cf. 1 Cor. 14:34-35; Eph. 6:1-5; 1 Tim. 2:11-12).

6-7. The law concerning the bird's nest shows that in the enjoyment of God's inheritance, even the smallest details are important and teach us lessons. In this case this is especially true, for a significant promise of spiritual prosperity is connected with it: **that it may be well with thee, and that thou mayest prolong thy days.** The dam (a female parent of the bird) represents an element among God's people which is to be **let . . . go** (permitted to remain active, free, and uncurtailed). It is the maternal instinct of tender care for its young that makes a bird an apt illustration of God's concern for His people (cf. Exod. 19:4; Deut. 32:11; Psalms 17:8; 36:7; Matt. 23:37). That same spirit should dominate the concern of saints for those under their spiritual care (cf. Phil. 2:20; 1 Thess. 2:7-8; Heb. 13:23). The "dam" beautifully illustrates our Lord's devotion for others (Matt. 23:37).

8. When we build (cf. 1 Cor. 3:10-15), we must do so for the safety and security of our brothers in the Lord. A **parapet** on the roof must be installed to protect others. Those who do such things as build in a party spirit or fail to proclaim

pure grace endanger the spiritual welfare of others.

Laws Enforcing Separation. 22:9-12. **9.** The need for separation from all evil in uncontaminated devotion to the LORD (cf. 1 Cor. 6:11—7:1) is stressed by the commonest distinctions in everyday life. Four illustrations are used: (1) A vineyard, from which a man derives joy (Judg. 9:13), is not to be sown with two different kinds of seed if an unmixed joy is to be experienced (cf. Lev. 19:19). A great deal of "joy" claimed among people in the inheritance springs out of doctrine that cannot be squared with God's Word, and so is suspect.

10. (2) **Thou shalt not plow with an ox and ass together.** This is an illustration of being "unequally yoked together with unbelievers" (2 Cor. 6:14; cf. 1 Kings 8:53; Ezra 6:21). **11.** (3) A garment of different materials, such as **wool** and **linen**, is not to be worn. Wool causes body sweat and was not to be worn by the priests (Ezek. 44:17-18). The warmth of nature has its proper sphere in natural affections and the like, but it must not be mixed with that which in character should be wholly spiritual.

12. (4) **Fringes** (tassels) were to be made on the four corners of garments. These "tassels" imply something distinctive that should mark God's people in every aspect of their conduct before men. But more than mere outward correctness, which can be imitated, is meant. Spontaneity of divine life from within is basic (1 Pet. 3:3-4). The tassels illustrate those who "have put on Christ" (Gal. 3:27) and, being clothed with Him, as having possessed the inheritance, "adorn the doctrine of God" (Titus 2:10). Mark the contrast (Matt. 23:5).

Law Against False Accusation of Infidelity. 22:13-21. **13-17.** Proof of a bride's virginity is often actually displayed in Oriental lands on a bloodstained sheet or garment used on the wedding night. This evidence is adduced in the case of a libel by an estranged husband. **18-19.** If the charges of the husband proved false, he was punished by a beating and a fine, together with the stipulation that he would maintain this wife the rest of her days (cf. 24:2). This is an illustration of the utmost importance of preserving the virgin character of God's people from reproach. This can only be done by presenting the true tokens of such virginity, namely, "minds" uncorrupted "from the simplicity that is in Christ" (2 Cor. 11:2-3), resulting in the eventual presentation to Himself of "a glorious church . . . holy and without blemish" (Eph. 5:25-28).

Other Laws Governing Sexual Relationships. 22:22-30. **22.** The death penalty was prescribed for adultery in the case of a guilty man or woman (cf. John 8:5-11, where the sex of the offender brought before Jesus is not in point). Cases of seduction were considered (vv. 23-29). **23-24.** A betrothed woman had the same status as a married woman under the law of adultery.

25-27. But if no clear proof of sin could be presented through witnesses, such a woman was considered a victim of rape and not an adulteress. The seducer of an unbetrothed girl was to be fined and the pair married (cf. Exod. 22:16-17). **30.** The law against marriage with a stepmother was given (cf. Lev. 18:8; 20:11). The Hebrew expression **uncover his father's skirt** is an euphemism for sexual union.

T. THE SANCTITY OF THE LORD'S CONGREGATION. 23:1-25.

Constitution of the Congregation of the Lord. 23:1-8. **1-2.** The **congregation** (*qāhāl*, "assembly") **of the Lord** (Yhwh), like the New Testament church (*ecclesia*), consisted of those who were in covenant relationship to the LORD by redemption and hence had a fixed and unalterable position and a changing experience. Therefore, it was to be separated from *everyone* and *everything* that violated its position before the LORD and its witness to and enjoyment of that position before men (2 Cor. 6:11—7:1).

It was thus a prefigurement of the New Testament church, to which only the truly regenerate and hence positionally clean belong (cf. John 13:10 with 13:3-15), and whose fellowship and privileges are enjoyed only by those experientially cleansed by the Word (Eph. 5:26). For this reason the necessity of the new birth (cf. John 3:7-10) is symbolically underscored by the reference to mutilated regenerative organs (v. 1) and the very severe stricture against a person of blemished birth (v. 2).

3-6. Separation of true believers from what is fleshly and opposed to God is stressed by the exclusion of the Ammonites (cf. Neh. 13:1-3) and Moabites (see 2:27-30; Num. 22:5-6), both of whom were also the offspring of incestuous unions (Gen. 19:30-38), as well as implacable foes of God's people. **7-8.** The Edomite represents those to be regarded as brethren, who have an assigned portion from God (Heb. 11:20), but who nevertheless stop short of His full purpose for His people. The Egyptian represents the man of the world who might eventually desire to share in God's inheritance and receive a new status (believe and be saved) and do so (Col. 3:1-4).

Cleanliness of the Camp. 23:9-14. **9-13.** Especially imperative was the strictest separation from the defilement of sin in time of war. Why? **14. For the**

Lord thy God walketh in the midst of thy camp, to deliver thee ... therefore shall thy camp be holy. Enunciated is the truth that spiritual conquest and victory (Eph. 6:10-20) are only possible by separation from complicity with Satan and demonic powers. Only then will the LORD **give up thine enemies** (to defeat) **before thee.**

Runaway Slaves. 23:15-16. God's people are to show evangelical grace to any fugitive from slavery (prefiguring bondage to sin, the world, or Satan). God would have His people known as liberators, for they themselves have been liberated. Onesimus, the runaway slave, partakes of the spirit of this passage. He is sent back to his master "not now as a servant [slave] but above a servant [slave], a brother beloved" (Philem. 16).

Law Against Prostitution. 23:17-18. **17.** Sexual vice under the garb of religion, as was the case in Canaan, is abominable in the extreme. The **harlot** (Heb., *qᵉdēshâ*, "female religious prostitute") and the **sodomite** (*qādēsh*, "male religious prostitute") were "holy," in the sense of "sacred," being dedicated to the polluted fertility goddess Astarte (Ashtoreth) (cf. 22:21; Lev. 19:29). Such immorality, thinking to honor the deity, was abominable in the extreme. **18.** Any money tainted by such depravity, **the price of a dog** (*kĕlĕḇ*), the fee paid to a male cult prostitute or catamite (Lev. 18:22; 20:13) was not to be brought into **the house of the Lord** (cf. Rev. 22:15).

The Law Against Usury. 23:19-20. Taking interest from foreigners was permitted, but not from fellow Israelites. The latter would concern loans made to the needy (cf. Exod. 22:25; Lev. 25:35-37) and presumably had nothing to do with business credit in general commerce.

The Law Concerning Vows. 23:21-23. A vow was a sort of promissory oath made to God to perform some act of dedication in return for the LORD's special help in some venture or deliverance. Discharge of a vow was extremely important (cf. Gen. 28:20; Judg. 11:30; 1 Sam. 1:11; on this subject, see also Lev. 27:1-34; Num. 30:1-16).

Law Concerning Eating Fruit. 23:24-25. This is a generous regulation to govern the LORD's own as a generous people. The practice is illustrated by Jesus' disciples (Mark 2:23-28). **25.** But the boundary between liberty and license is carefully marked.

U. DIVORCE AND OTHER LAWS. 24:1-22.

Mosaic Concession on Divorce. 24:1-4. **1.** The right to divorce was limited in the Old Testament to the husband. This right was not a commandment, but a concession to human frailty (cf. Matt. 19:7-8). Moses allowed divorce because of the hardness of the Israelites' hearts. This contrasts with Jesus' view of marriage and its permanence (cf. Matt. 5:31-32; 19:3-12; Mark 10:4-5; Luke 16:18). Compare Paul's statement (1 Cor. 7:10-15).

Exemption for Newlyweds. 24:5. A further gracious provision was given, emphasizing the sanctity of the family relationship and especially concerned with the welfare of the woman within it. **5.** This law might be called "a honeymoon exemption from war and business," so that the newlywed husband would be **free at home** to **cheer up his wife.** Prefigured is the interval between the union of the bride (the church) and the bridegroom (Christ; John 14:2-3; 1 Thess. 4:13-18) and the second advent of Christ to "make war" (Rev. 19:11; cf. Psalm 110:1).

Millstones Exempt as Security. 24:6. Nothing necessary to a man's very existence was to be taken as security for

264

a debt. Such was a millstone (Exod. 22:26) with which the grain for one's daily bread was ground. This speaks in the higher sense of spiritual bread (8:3; Matt. 4:4) made by grinding the seed of the Word and converting it into an edible form of bread. This is even more essential than daily physical bread. Nothing must deprive a man of this necessity.

Law Against Man-stealing. 24:7. Kidnapping for enslavement was punishable by death (cf. Exod. 21:16). But there are other ways of enslaving a brother. One may employ personal influence over him and mislead him so that he is deprived of spiritual freedom in the inheritance. Compare Absalom's deception (2 Sam. 15:1-6), Jesus' warning (John 10:10-13), and Paul's ominous words, "from among your own selves men will arise, speaking perverse things, to draw away the disciples after them" (Acts 20:30, NASB). Men-stealers had been at work in Galatia and elsewhere; they were legalists who were depriving the saints of their freedom in Christ and reducing them to bondage.

Laws of Leprosy. 24:8-9. As a type of the defilement of sin, meticulous observance of the laws of leprosy was required of people who would enter and enjoy the LORD's inheritance. (See Lev. 13-14, where the various types of the disease are dealt with.) Miriam's case (Num. 12:9-15) was memorable. The directions referred to are alluded to by Jesus (Luke 17:14).

On Taking Pledges. 24:10-13. (See also v. 6.) The LORD's people possessing the inheritance are to display love and unselfish concern for their brothers. Especially is this to be evidenced where they are tested most severely—in the sphere of business. Nothing must be done in selfish disregard of another brother's welfare or comfort or in detriment to one's testimony before him. The

same idea is presented in negative form in Exodus 22:25-27, where God promises to hear the cry of the oppressed. **13.** The **righteousness** mentioned is that which evidences faith and covenant relationship, *not* human works (cf. 6:25).

Treatment of Hired Servants. 24:14-15. Nothing tarnishes a testimony for the LORD so much as niggardliness or unfairness toward servants or employees (cf. 15:7-18; Lev. 25:35-43; 1 Tim. 5:18.).

Law of Personal Responsibility. 24:16. This principle of being responsible for one's sin is a variation of the universal law that every human being, saved as well as unsaved, will be judged for his works, issuing in degrees of punishment in eternal hell (Rev. 20:12-13) and degrees of reward in heaven (1 Cor. 3:9-15; 2 Cor. 5:10; cf. Prov. 24:12; Rom. 2:6, 11; Rev. 2:23; 22:12). This Deuteronomic law was obeyed by Josiah (2 Kings 14:6) and amplified by Jeremiah (31:29-30) and Ezekiel (18:25-32).

Justice and Generosity for the Poor. 24:17-22. Nothing short of being just and generous to the poor is consonant with God's people entering their inheritance. God's redeemed are always to remember God's love and compassion toward them (vv. 18, 22) as an incentive for stirring up their fair dealing, love, and compassion toward others (vv. 17, 19-21; 15:9-10; cf. Lev. 19:9-10).

V. VARIOUS OTHER LAWS. 25:1-19.

Corporal Punishment. 25:1-3. **1-2.** One of the duties of judges was to oversee the infliction of penalties imposed in civil cases (17:8-13; 19:16-18). A merciful provision limiting scourging to forty lashes was given (cf. Luke 12:48). This regulation protected the testimony of God's people from the odium of cruelty that was attached to paganism. Paul was punished five times in this manner (2 Cor. 11:24).

The Ox. 25:4. The ox was not to be muzzled when he treaded out grain at the threshing floor, but he was to be allowed to eat freely while he worked. So the toiling servant of the LORD is worthy of his remuneration (1 Cor. 9:7-9; 1 Tim. 5:18; cf. Luke 10:7).

Levirate Marriage. 25:5-10. Marriage of a sonless widow to her brother-in-law (Latin, *Levir*) had as its purpose supplying an heir to the deceased man's estate. This custom was pre-Mosaic (Gen. 38:8-11). It finds its outworking in the kinsman-redeemer theme of the book of Ruth (*q.v.*). Failure to comply with this custom evidenced a lack of fraternal affection and was publicly stigmatized (vv. 8-10). Taking off the shoe (v. 9; cf. Ruth 4:7) arose from the custom of walking on the soil, declaring one's right to ownership.

The law was not obligatory (vv. 8-9), but its spirit is intended to influence us in our brotherly relations. Our brother's name is to be maintained in the inheritance, even at some personal sacrifice. The unbrotherly spirit manifested in the scribes and Pharisees of Jesus' day had little concern for others in distress. But the genuine brotherly spirit found perfect expression in the true Kinsman-Redeemer, the divine Boaz. Even as Boaz married Ruth "to raise up the name of the dead upon his inheritance" (Ruth 4:10), so Christ came in to perform a true Kinsman's part for those dead in trespasses and sins and utterly resourceless in themselves.

Against Foul Play. 25:11-12. This passage deals with the dignity of God's covenant servant. In his circumcision (see Gen. 17:9-14) he bears in his body the sign of the covenant. It is contempt for the covenant sign, and not just indecency, that accounts for the severity of the punishment. Both involve mutilation. Apart from this instance, only the *lex talionis* (19:21) imposes such penal mutilation.

Against Dishonest Weights. 25:13-16. Actually this law is a phase of "love thy neighbor as thyself" (Lev. 19:18). Practical demonstration of this commandment would rule out two sets of weights to cheat one's neighbor (cf. Lev. 19:35-36; Amos 8:5). **15-16.** Long life and blessing will be the reward of honesty as love is manifested, but cheating is an **abomination**, something heinous in God's sight.

Extinction of Amalek. 25:17-19. How can this follow an injunction that inculcates love? While this law of love summarizes intertheocratic relationships (dealings with the LORD's people) we now deal with the avowed enemies of the LORD's people. Therefore, no repudiation of the mandate of conquest (cf. 7:1-26; 20:16-17) is to be imagined, nor is there any contradiction involved. "For though God requires love of neighbor, those who set themselves to destroy the people of the typical OT theocratic kingdom removed themselves from the neighbor category, just as those doomed with Satan in eternal perdition are not the neighbors of the inhabitants of the heavenly theocracy" (Kline, WBC, p. 189). To love God is to love whom He loves and to hate whom He hates. Amalek represents the flesh, which God hates and we must hate. Conflict against the flesh is a holy war in the spiritual realm and merits no mercy (see comments on Exod. 17:8-16; Num. 24:20).

W. GOD CONFESSED AS REDEEMER-KING. 26:1-19.

Offering of Firstfruits. 26:1-11. The lengthy section giving the stipulations of covenant life (chaps. 5-26) draws to a close with the ritual offering of firstfruits (vv. 1-11), prayer at the offering of the triennial tithe (vv. 12-15), and the declaration of the ratification of the covenant (vv. 16-19). Destruction being pronounced upon man after the flesh as a vessel and tool of Satan's inveterate antagonism to what is of God (25:17-19), those begotten of God enter the divine inheritance.

1-2. As they come into possession and cultivate their lots, the fruits begin to be gathered. The first of these fruits, a token of God's right to all, is to be offered to God at the central place of worship. This prefigures priority to assembly worship, praise, and service (as in chaps. 12, 14, 15, 16). This is to assure spiritual freshness that cannot be set aside by liturgical ritual.

4. The priest serves Godward in presenting the basket of firstfruits **before** the altar. It is not placed on the altar. The service here is not sacrificial, as it so often is in Leviticus, for it is not concerned with sin or acceptance. Rather, it is a witness that the brethren are in grateful and worshipful possession and enjoyment of the inheritance God has given them.

5-10. The prayer offered (vv. 5-10*a*) acknowledged five things: (1) Their lowly ancestry and helplessness (v. 5). A **Syrian** (Aramaean) **ready to perish was my father** (Gen. 25:20; Hos. 12:12). (2) Their bondage in Egypt (v. 6), bespeaking their hopeless enslaved condition. (3) Their wonderful redemption by God's grace (vv. 7-8). (4) Their glorious inheritance, prefiguring their salvation rest (v. 9). (5) Their acknowledgment of God's redemptive grace and blessing by presenting the firstfruits as a token. He is LORD of all and is to be gratefully worshiped. **11.** As a result, they rejoice in all that God's grace has done for them.

Prayer at Offering of Triennial Tithe. 26:12-15. The distribution of the tithe in the third year had been ordered previously (14:28-29). This was the climax of instruction about "the land." Not only was God known and responded to as the Giver (in offering the firstfruits), but His people, enriched by His grace, became givers also (in the triennial tithe). This envisions God's people as being formed in His blessed nature and expressing it in gracious ways, which are a reflex of His own. It is an illustration of God's character being reproduced in His children (cf. Eph. 5:1; 1 John 4:7-8, 11, 12). It is the picture of God's own people walking in love, in deed, and in truth, and being able to say so before God (1 John 3:18-22), and as a result being able to claim His promised blessings (vv. 13-15). So vital is this gracious activity that nothing must be permitted to interfere with it—neither sorrow, defilement, nor sin of any type.

Declaration of the Ratification of the Covenant. 26:16-19. Central in the covenant ratification in contemporary suzerain-vassal treaties was the oath of allegiance the vassal took to his lord in response to the declaration of the covenant stipulations and sanctions. Israel had taken such an oath at Sinai (Exod. 24:7). Now the new generation had to do the same in the plains of Moab (cf. 29:10-15).

Surely if the wilderness sojourn was a time of Israel's "love as a bride" (Jer. 2:2, RSV), this passage would indicate the consummation of the marriage bond between the LORD and Israel, so often referred to by the prophets and so shamefully rejected by the nation. But the divorced nation will be restored at the second advent, and the wonderful words of Isaiah will be fulfilled (Isa. 62:4-5). Israel still awaits the consummation of what God's love has purposed. Meanwhile, saints of the church can take up spiritually what is illustrative for us of New Testament truths. As C. A. Coates says, "Deuteronomy is, for us, a book of heavenly instruction" (*An Outline of the Book of Deuteronomy*, p. 326).

III. MOSES' THIRD DISCOURSE (PROPHETIC). 27:1—30:20

A. RATIFICATION CEREMONY IN CANAAN. 27:1-26.

The Prescribed Ceremony of Covenant Ratification. 27:1-8. This ceremony was to be inaugurated on Mount Ebal and Mount Gerizim, overlooking the city of Shechem in the heart of the land. The historical performance of what is prescribed here is described in Joshua 8:30-35. **1.** Moses on this solemn occasion associated **the elders of Israel** with himself, all of them representing the intelligent responsibility of the people in order to promote respect for what was commanded by God.

2-3. The command was: **set thee up great stones ... and write upon them all the words of this law.** The will of God concerning His people in the land had been presented to the people in the ministry of Moses. Now for their part, *they* were to write it on "great stones," dramatizing their expressing it in a stable and permanent manner. Passing over the Jordan (cf. Josh. 4:1) is the experiential counterpart of the position Israel obtained by passing through the Red Sea. There they were separated from Pharaoh and Egypt and "baptized into Moses" (1 Cor. 10:1-2, NASB; cf. Rom. 6:1-10), figuratively, "into Christ" (1 Cor. 10:4). Passing over Jordan into the inheritance is reckoning on that position and enjoying it in actual experience (Rom. 6:11).

8. The old covenant required God's Law to be written on stone **very plainly.** But concerning the new covenant to which it points, operative now for the church and for Israel in the future day of her conversion, the word is: "I will put my laws into their mind, and write them in their hearts" (Heb. 8:10). The "great stones," upon which the word of God was to be written "very plainly," illustrate what Paul calls "the new man" (Eph. 4:24; Col. 3:10). The "old [unrenewed] man" as controlled by the flesh can never have the Law written on it or be an expression of it. This can be true only of the "new man" controlled by the Spirit.

The stones being plastered (vv. 2, 4) illustrates the truth that the "one new man" views the saints collectively set together to present one great and legible expression of God's will. Only in realization of this truth can we joyfully take up our place of acceptance with God (offer burnt offerings, v. 6) and get along in blessed fellowship with our brethren (offer peace offerings and eat there, v. 7).

5. The **altar of stones**—whole stones uncut by the hand of man (Exod. 20:25)—portrays how God's people are to regard their whole portion of blessing before God, secured without human works or merit, totally on the basis of God's grace foreshadowed in Christ.

The Priests' Call to Attention. 27:9-10. **9.** Moses and the priests next prepared to rehearse the prescribed ritual by calling all Israel to be silent and pay attention, as if listening to the LORD Himself. It was **the priests** (not the elders) who now joined Moses, which indicates that the people, identified with their elders, had intelligently committed themselves to the responsibility of carrying out what was commanded. Now

268

the priests, speaking along with Moses, demonstrated priestly concern that those who had formally taken the place of God's people (cf. 16:18) should obey Him. To assume responsibility for God without priestly prayer and exercise is to court failure (Col. 1:3, 9-11; 2:1; 4:12). *The Rehearsal of the Curses. 27:11-26.* Moses alone spoke in this section concerning the government of God, involving a curse upon what was contrary to the divine will and a blessing upon what was in line with the divine will. **12-13.** Six tribes were to stand upon Mount Gerizim **to bless the people** and six upon Mount Ebal **to curse** the people, showing that God's people are to love righteousness and hate lawlessness. **14-26.** Love for good is to be balanced by hatred for evil. What is abhorrent to God must be abhorrent to His people. He who does not say a hearty *Amen* to the curse is not morally qualified to say a sincere *Amen* to His blessings.

Blessings and curses are *everywhere* in Scripture (cf. Rom. 8:13; 1 Cor. 16:22; Gal. 6:8; Heb. 6:8). God's people who are possessing their spiritual possessions in Christ need to realize that everything that displeases God must be repudiated (vv. 15-26) if communion with God and with one another (vv. 6-7) is to be enjoyed (cf. 1 John 1:1—2:2). But why were the blessings that were to be uttered upon Mount Gerizim not mentioned? The omission points to an important truth. Israel in the flesh and under divine government could never on that ground inherit the spiritual blessings Christ was to bring. But the great stones, the altar, the burnt offerings, and the peace offerings on Mount Ebal pointed to the fact that where disobedience and the curse prevailed, God, by the redemption of Christ and His working in His people, would secure the realization of all that He promised regarding His saving grace.

B. PROCLAMATION OF THE COVENANT'S SANCTIONS. 28:1-68.

The Blessings. 28:1-14. **1-2.** These benefits (in contrast to the curses) were to be the result of obedience to the LORD in the promised land. (Blessings and cursings were also important elements in contemporary Hittite treaties.) Moses announced them in the land of Moab and so continued to present the sharp contrast between the results of obedience and disobedience. Christ, our divine Instructor to whom Moses points, has done the same. The overall blessing is that **God will set thee on high above all the nations of the earth. 2.** The verbs **come on** (upon) and **overtake** ("to catch up with," cf. Zech. 1:6) show that righteousness, as well as iniquity, catches up with us.

3. Blessings **in the city** speaks of the common and mutual interests of God's people, which we enjoy as "fellow citizens with the saints" as members "of the household of God," a "building" growing into "a holy temple in the Lord ... an habitation of God through the Spirit" (Eph. 2:19-22). Blessings **in the field,** involving sowing, planting, watering, reaping, and waiting for the harvest (James 5:7), speak of each receiving his own reward according to his own labor (1 Cor. 3:8). These various blessings are the result of faith and have no affinities with a religion of works for salvation. Obedience will bring Israel on top in every military and commercial encounter with other nations (vv. 7-8); assure her a wonderful testimony for God (vv. 9-10; cf. Num. 6:27); prosperity (vv. 11-12); and headship in position among the nations (vv. 13-14). *The Curses. 28:15-68.* These curses form an amazing prophecy of Israel's tragic career of unbelief and disobedience. Moses was a prophet (18:15), and nowhere does the Spirit of prophecy rest upon him so signally as in his foreseeing the sufferings, tribulation, and worldwide dispersion of God's ancient elect nation. Reflected in the prewritten history are the sieges by the Assyrians, Babylonians, and the Romans (vv. 49-62) and Israel's present worldwide Diaspora (vv. 63-68). The twentieth century has witnessed the initial stages of the predicted restoration. The curses of this chapter also play a prominent role in the prophetic books.

C. SUMMONS TO THE COVENANT OATH. 29:1-29.

Definition of the Covenant. 29:1-15. **1.** This covenant was not the Sinai Covenant of Law, which Israel completely broke and under which they could not enter the inheritance. Neither was it the Abrahamic Covenant of grace, for under it they would not have been turned out of the land. Neither was it the new covenant, because Christ had not yet come to ratify it in His own blood (Jer. 31:31-34; Heb. 8:8-13). It was the Deuteronomic or Palestinian Covenant, governing Israel's tenure of the promised land.

2-6. It was distinct from the Sinai Covenant, but it was based upon it—redemption by divine power and miracle from Egypt and disciplinary education in the wilderness, revealing God's goodness and faithfulness to them. Yet in all this manifestation of divine power and grace, they remained without understanding and faithful appropriation of the wonderful position God had given them in calling them and constituting them as His people and His elect nation.

7-8. But on occasion, where they did so, as in their defeat of **Sihon, the king of Heshbon, and Og, the king of Bashan,** they were gloriously victorious. The Palestinian Covenant was a restatement of the Sinai Covenant, based upon a new perception of Israel's position not only as redeemed *out of Egypt* but *into* the promised land. Now as they were on the eve of actual entrance into the possession, it was eminently essential for them to clearly comprehend their position (Rom. 6:1-10) as they were by faith about to convert it into *experiential* reality (cf. Rom. 6:11).

Therefore, Deuteronomic law is not a mere repetition of the Sinaitic legislation. It is the Law of God adapted to salvation by grace and accommodated to those who have come into the land, that is, those who have entered into the rest of faith (Heb. 4:1-9) and have "ceased" from their "own works" (Heb. 4:10). It is God's commandments worked in the fabric of grace, seen so beautifully in the New Testament epistles.

12-13. The Deuteronomic Covenant, as far as the position and possession of God's people are concerned, has its antitype in Romans 1-12. The dedication it calls for is that so powerfully appealed to in Romans 12:1-2. **14-15.** This dedication exempts *no* child of God.

Reiterated Warning Against Disobedience. 29:16-28. **16-18.** The pull away from loyalty to the LORD was persistent and powerful (Heb. 12:15; cf. Deut. 32:32; Acts 8:23). **19.** But God's people, possessing their possession, must steadfastly resist violation of the covenant stipulations, especially through self-deception. **20-21.** God's sternest chastening will be visited upon His disobedient people (cf. 30:17-20), for God's grace must not be trampled upon. His "gifts and calling" are irrevocable (Rom. 11:29), but His chastisement of sin in His own is certain.

270

22-28. The barren and desolate condition of Palestine from the fall of Jerusalem in A.D. 70 until comparatively recent times furnishes mute fulfillment of these verses (cf. Gen. 19:24-25; Isa. 1:9; Ezek. 19:12-13; Hos. 11:8).

God's Triumphant Grace. 29:29. **29. The secret things** that **belong unto the Lord our God** are what God would do, in spite of Israel's shameful failure—the provisions of His mercy and grace to be displayed, despite their utter dereliction under both the Deuteronomic and the Sinai covenants (30:3-10). **Those things which are revealed** are the things plainly made known to Israel to do (cf. 27:1-8), but the people did not do them. Though the "secret things" were hidden from Israel in the plains of Moab, they have been fully and clearly revealed to us for our profit and edification (1 Cor. 2:9-11; 10:11). The Holy Spirit was given at Pentecost (Acts 2) to lead the disciples into "all truth" (John 16:12-13); and with the completion of the canon of Scripture (cf. 1 Cor. 13:10), *all* the purposes and counsels of God are *fully revealed* (1 John 2:20).

D. THE TERMS AND CHALLENGE OF THE COVENANT. 30:1-20.

Conditions of the Tenure of Palestine. 30:1-10. **1-2.** Moses under the Spirit of prophecy prefixed the terms of the covenant with a panoramic prediction of the curse of the Exile and the ultimate restoration of the nation. The divine redemptive program is not to be frustrated. God's grace will provide a remnant to fulfill the promises of restoration. Israel's disobedience and failure will not avail to overthrow God's purposes of grace.

The Palestinian or Deuteronomic Covenant (see 29:1-15) contains the following promises and warnings: (1) Dispersion of the nation for disobedience (v. 1, described in 28:63-68); (2) Israel's future repentance while in the dispersion (v. 2); (3) the second advent of Christ (v. 3; cf. Amos 9:9-14; Acts 15:14-17); (4) the restoration of the land (v. 5; cf. Isa. 11:11-12; 35:1-10; Jer. 23:3-8; Ezek. 37:21-25); (5) Israel's future national conversion (v. 6; cf. Hos. 2:14-16; Rom. 11:26-27); (6) the judgment of the nations, Israel's foes (v. 7; cf. Isa. 14:1-2; Joel 3:1-8; Matt. 25:31-46); and (7) the national prosperity of the restored nation (v. 9; cf. Amos 9:11-14).

For the relation of the Palestinian Covenant to the other covenants, see 29:1-15. For discussion of other major covenants, see Edenic (Gen. 2:16); Adamic (Gen. 3:15); Noahic (Gen. 9:16); Abrahamic (Gen. 12:2); Mosaic (Exod. 19:5); Davidic (2 Sam. 7:16); and the new covenant (Heb. 8:8).

The Way of Spiritual Recovery. 30:11-14. Recovery was not only indicated actually for the nation Israel in the land or out of it, but also typically for *all* the people of God everywhere (Rom. 10:5-13). Israel's possessing and enjoyment of the land betokened spiritual blessing, even as it illustrates our enjoyment of salvation (Heb. 4:1-10). Forfeiting the enjoyment of salvation (not salvation itself!) as a result of disobedience is tantamount to being exiled from the land and dispersed over the earth.

11-14. Regathering and restoration to the land indicate spiritual recovery. This is possible because **the word** is not far away, but on the contrary is **very near unto thee, in thy mouth, and in thy heart.** "The word" is **this commandment**, meaning the Word of God, which the people were commanded to observe. The apostle Paul, speaking antitypically, defines it as "the word of faith," centering in confessing Christ as Lord

271

and believing in the "heart that God hath raised him from the dead" (Rom. 10:8-10). In these words he presents the way of spiritual recovery for God's people who forfeit the enjoyment of their inheritance in Christ by disobedience. Not until Israel confesses the lordship of Christ in His resurrection from the dead will the restoration and spiritual recovery spoken of in the Palestinian Covenant be realized. Not until a backslidden church does the same, will a restoration to the enjoyment of the inheritance result.

Call for Decision. 30:15-20. The section of the treaty dealing with covenant ratification (chaps. 27-30) concludes with a call for radical decision. **15.** Moses had reminded the people that they could not plead ignorance of God's demands (vv. 11-14), and here he pressed upon them the fact that the alternatives set before them were so momentous as to involve **life** and **death** (vv. 15-20). He was speaking to a people in covenant relationship, typically redeemed, and about to enter the inheritance (salvation rest). The death, therefore, was forfeiture of the enjoyment of the inheritance—loss of fellowship with God, and the curse incurred by being carnally minded and disobedient (Rom. 8:6; Heb. 6:7-8).

19. Moses called **heaven and earth** to witness. This is reminiscent of the secular suzerainty treaties of the Mosaic period. The standard divisions in these treaties contain an invocation of the deities worshiped by the lord and vassal as witnesses of the covenant oath. The parallel is interesting (cf. 4:26; 31:28; 32:1), although the LORD is, of course, the divine Witness as well as the Suzerain of this covenant. From an archaeological viewpoint, this fact helps show that Deuteronomy is a genuine product of the Mosaic era and not a fabrication of the seventh century B.C., as higher critics have contended.

IV. MOSES' FINAL WORDS AND ACTS (COVENANT CONTINUITY). 31:1—34:12.

A. CARRYING ON THE COVENANT. 31:1-30.

Moses' Charge to Israel. 31:1-6. The final section deals with the succession of the covenant relationship. Joshua was Moses' successor in the office of mediatorial representative of the LORD. This corresponds in the extrabiblical suzerainty treaties to the prominence of the royal succession. The reasons Moses gave for his retirement were: (1) his advanced age of 120 years (v. 2*a*; cf. Exod. 7:7; Deut. 29:5); (2) his loss of stamina essential to shepherd the whole flock of Israel, particularly to conduct the campaign of conquest facing the nation (v. 2*b*; cf. Num. 27:16-17; Deut. 34:7). (3) the LORD's refusal to allow him to cross Jordan (v. 2*c*; cf. 3:23-28; 4:21-22; Num. 20:12); and (4) the fact that the LORD, through Joshua, His new mediatorial representative, would complete the conquest in Canaan, already successfully begun by Moses in Transjordan (vv. 3-6).

Moses' Charge to Joshua. 31:7-8. Moses publicly charged Joshua to his task to which the new leader already had been ordained by Moses before Eleazar (see 1:38; Num. 27:18-23). The promise of the LORD's presence was repeated (v. 8; cf. Josh. 5:13-15).

Moses' Charge to the Priests. 31:9-13. In assigning the priests and elders the duty of periodically republishing the Law of the covenant, Moses was wisely associating these leaders with Joshua in regard to the responsibility of shepherding God's people. More important, the entire covenant community

272

of the people and their leaders was placed under the lordship of the Giver of the Law and the Suzerain of the covenant. Also emphasized was the necessity of priestly activity in the ministry of the Word of God.

10. The septennial reading of the Law to Israel at the Feast of Tabernacles (cf. 16:13-17) in the year of release (15:1-11) looks forward to Israel's eventual establishment in Kingdom blessing after her dispersions and regatherings (see Exod. 23:16; Lev. 23:33-34). **11-13.** The last reference to the central sanctuary stresses how vital instruction in the Word of God in ancient Israel was and anticipates the importance of the ministry of teaching and preaching of the Word in the New Testament assembly. The reading of the Law is archaeologically illustrated in the contemporary suzerainty treaties of the nations. Directions were included for reading them to the vassal peoples from one to three times annually.

The Commission to Write and Teach the Song. 31:14-23. **14-15.** God appeared to Moses and Joshua in **the tent of meeting . . . in a pillar of cloud** (NASB), confirming Moses' ominous prophecies of Israel's future disobedience and infraction of the covenant (v. 16), so that the LORD would hide His face from them for their gross infidelity (vv. 17-18). **19-21. Therefore, write this song for you . . . a witness for me against the children of Israel . . . this song shall testify against them as a witness.** The dominant note of the song was divine faithfulness in the face of the people's failure, ending in the triumph of divine grace on the ground of atonement. It corresponds with those parts of the New Testament that foretell the future of the Christian profession (e.g., 2 Timothy; 2 Peter; Jude; Revelation 2-3).

The Storing of the Book in the Ark.

31:24-29. **24.** A complementary covenant witness, along with the song, was the treaty document written by Moses. **26.** It was called **the book of the law** and represented the will of God, the divine Suzerain, in its entirety. With "the song" it formed a twofold witness for Himself against the predicted infidelity of the people. Regarding both the "book" and the "song," Moses wrote and spoke the words "until they were finished" (v. 24) and "until they were ended" (v. 30).

Set forth is the complete manner in which God has disclosed both His plan and purpose for His people, as well as His ultimate end of grace and love for them. He has reached the conclusion of all that He has to say. Paul declared that he was "made a minister, according to the dispensation [stewardship] of God . . . to fulfill [make full] the word of God" (Col. 1:25). It is a wondrous privilege to live in a day when the canon of Scripture is completed (cf. 1 Cor. 13:10), but it involves an awesome responsibility.

Introduction to the Song. 31:30. The song begins with verse 30. The song itself is a poetic resume of the Deuteronomic treaty.

B. THE SONG OF WITNESS. 32:1-52.

The Witnesses Invoked. 32:1-3. **1.** Heaven and earth were solemnly called upon to witness the covenant (cf. 31:28; Isa. 1:2). The intimation is that "the words of this song" (31:30) contain what is beneficial and instructive for both the heavenly and earthly people of God. **2.** Divine communication is like rain upon the earth, manifesting what we really are by the way we receive it in our hearts (cf. Heb. 6:7-8). Moses' reference to **my doctrine . . . my speech** looks forward to the doctrine and word of Christ (of whom Moses was a prefigurement), in whom all God's "wisdom" centers (1 Cor. 1:30).

Covenant Preamble. 32:4-6. This preamble gives the purpose of the song as being a theodicy, that is, a vindication of God's dealings with His people. Celebrated is the greatness of God in stability, perfection of working, righteousness, and faithfulness. **4. The Rock** is an appellative or descriptive name of God, who is steadfast and immovable in all His glorious attributes and a reliable refuge for His people. The term *Rock* occurs six times in the song (vv. 4, 15, 18, 30, 31, 37). God's righteousness is dramatically contrasted with the perversity of the Israelites.

5. They who were presumably called to sonship (14:1; 32:18; Exod. 4:22-23) are here literally and dramatically denominated His **not ... children,** that is, "non-sons" (literal Heb. trans.). Compare His "not ... [non] people" (v. 21). Prefaced to the main burden of the song is the declaration that Israel's sin was the completely adequate explanation of all the calamities that would engulf them. **6. Is not he thy father who hath bought thee ... and established thee?** (i.e., by election and redemptive calling out of Egypt and formation into a theocratic nation).

Historical Prologue. 32:7-14. **7.** This section is introduced by an injunction, **Remember the days of old,** and embraces a panoramic sweep of divine providence that goes back as far as the events of Genesis 10 and 11 (cf. Psalms 44:1; 78:5-8). **8.** This explains the words: **When the Most High divided** (Gen. 11:8; Acts 17:26) **to the nations their inheritance ... he set the bounds of the people according to the number of the children of Israel** (not "sons of God," following the Septuagint, Qumran fragments, RSV).

9-14. The whole point of the passage is that all of God's providential disposition of things in this world is according to His purpose for His elect people. They are His portion, and **Jacob** (Israel) was that people in the Old Testament (cf. 7:6; 10:15; Gen. 10:32). He redeemed Israel, encircled him, cared for him **as the apple of his eye** (Jer. 2:6; Zech. 2:8; Hos. 13:5). He taught and led His people as the eagle teaches her young to fly (vv. 11-12) and lavished every blessing and tender care upon them (vv. 12-14). Let the song of God's goodness be a witness against their perverseness!

Record of Rebellion. 32:15-18. **15. Jeshurun** ("Upright One") is a poetic appellative of "Israel," designating the people under their ideal character, but here, by contrast, it is employed ironically and reproachfully. Fattened in a rich pasture, Israel turned into an unruly beast, abandoning his Creator and despising **the Rock of his salvation** (see v. 4). **16.** God had wonderfully and graciously led him so that there was "no strange god with him" (v. 12), but what a contrast now! The gods to which they sacrificed were not gods, but demons worshiped under the guise of the idol image (Psalm 106:37; 1 Cor. 10:20). **18. Of the Rock who begot** them, they became crassly **unmindful** (cf. v. 6).

Curses on the Rebels. 32:19-25. Stern warning against idol images characterized the Sinaitic Covenant (Exod. 20:1-6). The LORD warned that He was jealous and would brook no rivalry or infidelity (5:9; Exod. 20:5). **21.** His jealous anger parallels that of a husband of a wife who plays the harlot (Rom. 10:19). **22.** It will **burn unto the lowest sheol,** the underworld abode of departed spirits. **23-25.** It will result in the most terrible chastisements.

Mercy Mingled with Judgment. 32:26-43. **26-28.** The LORD would limit the enemy's overrunning Israel so that he would not misinterpret his victory over God's people and fail to accord the honor due to Israel's God (cf. Isa. 10:12-15). **29-31.** Israel's foolish foes should have known that their easy victory over Israel was due to the displeasure of the Suzerain of heaven and earth with His covenant protectorate. How else could **one chase a thousand, and two put ten thousand** (of Israel) **to flight . . .?** The only explanation was that **their Rock had sold them** (cf. Judg. 2:14; Psalm 44:12) **and the Lord had shut them up** ("given them up," NASB). Even the foolish enemies of Israel could discern that "their rock," the puny deities they trusted in, were a far cry from Israel's **Rock**, that is, the Lord, the sovereign Suzerain of heaven and earth (cf. Exod. 14:25; Josh. 2:9-10; 1 Sam. 4:8). Furthermore, if Israel's enemies were wise, **they would consider their latter end** (cf. Matt. 25:31-46; Rev. 19:11-21).

32-33. If the Lord judges His own in fiery wrath, what must the wicked nations and persecutors of Israel expect when God begins to judge them? The greatest wickedness of the enemies would be that they had attacked God's people. **34-36.** Therefore, their guilt was laid up as a treasure in God's storehouse, to be visited upon them in divine **vengeance** and **retribution** (NASB) as a vindication of **his people** and a display of His gracious compassion for His servants (cf. Rom. 12:19; Heb. 10:30). **37-38.** Then He will say, "Where are their gods, the rock in which they sought refuge? . . . Let them rise up and help" (NASB).

39-40. Identifying Himself as the one and only absolutely sovereign God (cf. 4:35, 39; 5:6; Isa. 43:11-13), He declares, **I lift up my hand to heaven.** As in the case of the Abrahamic Covenant, the Lord added oath to promise in the Palestinian Covenant. He swore by Himself, for there is no other (cf. Gen. 22:16-18; Isa. 45:22-23; Heb. 6:13), that His punishment would be fearful against His enemies (Isa. 63:1-5).

43. The song ends with a call to the nations to rejoice because God will **avenge the blood of His servants,** and **render vengeance on His adversaries,** thus expiating all guilt **for His land and His people** (NASB). This represents the establishment of the Kingdom over Israel (Acts 1:6) in fulfillment of this and a vast segment of Old Testament prophecy.

Moses' Last Words. 32:44-47. **44.** Moses and Joshua taught the song to all Israel, as they had been instructed (cf. 31:19). **46-47.** After a final exhortation, much like his first (cf. 4:1), Moses' addresses were concluded.

The Arrangement for Moses' Death. 32:48-52. The manner of Moses' death had already been revealed to him at the outset of his addresses in Moab (cf. 3:27-28). Here an account is given of the actual command to ascend Mount Nebo and meet the death prearranged by God (cf. 34:7). Typically foreshadowed is the death of Christ, foreknown and fore-planned "from the foundation of the world" (Rev. 13:8).

C. The Blessing of the Tribes.
33:1-29.

Moses' Testament. 33:1. As a spiritual and theocratic father of the twelve tribes, Moses, according to ancient Near Eastern customs, pronounced a blessing on them just before his death. Such a final blessing constituted an irrevocable legal testament (cf. Isaac, Gen. 27; and Jacob, Gen. 49). In the case of the biblical patriarchs, the Spirit of prophecy speaking through them added authority and potency to their last utterances. Israelites, as God's adopted sons and heirs, were heirs of the covenant blessings that were dispensed through Moses. Inasmuch as promised redemptive blessings are not inheritable apart from the promisor's death, the covenant includes the testamentary principle.

Introduction. 33:2-5. **2-5.** The glory of the LORD was portrayed as He declared His kingship in making His theocratic covenant with Israel in her ideal character poetically called Jeshurun, "the Upright One" (see 32:15), with Moses called the **king in Jeshurun.** Thus, the whole scene has a historical aspect. The appearing of the LORD as the King of kings in radiant sunrise glory over the eastern mountains of the Sinai Peninsula, together with **ten thousands of saints,** also has a prophetic view. It looks forward to the second advent in glory of the "King of kings" (Rev. 19:11-16) to set up His earthly Kingdom over Israel, then converted and regathered, to fulfill the gracious promises of the covenant and to realize the prophetic scope of the name Jeshurun—Israel cleansed by the blood of Christ and constituted "the upright one" indeed in Kingdom glory (Zech. 12:10—13:1; Rom. 11:25-36; Rev. 20:1-9). That is why this chapter is filled with unmixed blessing. It presents the operations of divine grace and glory, for God will yet be glorified in Israel, and Israel will be fully and forever blessed in God. "The gifts and calling of God are without repentance" (Rom. 11:29).

The Blessings of the Tribes. 33:6-25. The contrast between Jacob's prophetic testament (Gen. 49) and Moses' (chap. 33) is marked. Jacob viewed his sons in their personal history; Moses viewed them in covenant relationship with the LORD. Hence, Jacob presented human failure and sin, while Moses told of divine faithfulness and loving-kindness. Jacob told of human acts and the judgment on them, but Moses gave divine counsels with unmingled blessing flowing from them, issuing in the future restoration, blessing, preeminence, and glory of the twelve tribes of Israel in their own land.

6. *Reuben.* **Let Reuben live,** that is, not suffer tribal extinction: **let not his men be few.** As the firstborn, God's grace would be manifested to him even though he had lost the rights of the firstborn through sin (cf. Gen. 49:3-4). **7.** *Judah.* Moses' prayer for Judah was that the kingly tribe might be enabled to accomplish the royal task of conquering adversaries so that Judah might return to his people to receive their obedience. The prayer will be answered when "the Lion of the tribe of Judah" (Rev. 5:5) returns to the earth to dispossess His enemies and to establish the Kingdom.

8-11. *Levi.* The name of *Simeon* was omitted to make room for the two sons of Joseph. He doubtlessly was considered to be reckoned with Judah, having his portion in the land within the territory of Judah. Levi was presented as tested for the priesthood (Exod. 32:26-29; Num. 20:1-13; Deut. 6:16; 9:22; 32:51) for the privilege of access to God, receiving special divine revelation, teaching the covenant Law (v. 10a), and officiating at the altar (v. 10b). Levi's blessing included a petition that his priestly ministry in behalf of the covenant people would prove efficacious. Prophetically, this will have its ultimate realization in Christ's King-Priest role at His second advent to establish the Kingdom (Zech. 6:12-15), when Israel will become a priestly nation (Zech. 3:1-10).

12. *Benjamin.* The name of Benjamin appears here by the grace of God to be manifested in Israel's future day (Rom. 11:25-37) as **the beloved of the Lord** (Psalm 60:5; Jer. 11:15). Contrast his untransformed character (Gen. 49:27). He is to "dwell in security by Him, who shields him all the day, and he dwells between His shoulders" (NASB; cf. Exod. 28:12). Again the safety and blessing of Israel in the Kingdom age are envisioned as the ultimate fulfillment of this prophecy.

13-17. *Joseph.* Moses confirmed the precedence Jacob gave Ephraim over Manasseh (v. 17), blessing Joseph with military power and temporal gifts (vv. 13-16; cf. Gen. 49:22-26). The source of all this benefit was **the favor of Him who dwelt in the bush** (NASB), the reference being to the God of Abraham, Isaac, and Jacob, who had spoken to Moses out of the burning bush (Exod. 3:2-6). The phrase **separated from his brethren** (KJV), or "distinguished among his brothers" (NASB) is rendered by the Revised Standard Version, "prince among his brothers." In any case, Joseph's preeminence is stressed, as in verse 17. **As the first-born of his ox** (denoting strength), **majesty is his** (NASB). Joseph's strength is emphasized by the figure of the horn of a species of ancient buffalo (*re'ēm*, "wild ox"). Now extinct, this species had a huge frontal horn in which all its brute strength was concentrated. He will **push the people ... to the ends of the earth.** Evidently this prophecy reaches to the Kingdom age both by context and by the scope of the passage itself.

18-19. *Zebulun* and *Issachar* were united in this blessing (cf. Gen. 49:13-15). Zebulun was assured prosperity in his commerce by sea (**going out**) and Issachar would be successful in domestic and agricultural pursuits (**in thy tents**). However, both **shall draw out the abundance of the seas** (NASB). Doubtless in the Kingdom age the resources of the seas will be greatly developed. **20-21.** *Gad* had chosen the **ruler's portion** (NASB) as his inheritance in Transjordan, the firstfruits of the conquest. Then he faithfully joined his brothers to secure them their portion in Canaan.

22. *Dan.* **Dan is a lion's whelp, that leaps forth from Bashan** (NASB; cf. Gen. 49:16; Ezek. 19:2-3) is an apt figure describing the adventurous spirit of the Danites (cf. Judg. 18:27-31). **23.** *Naphtali.* The divine favor upon Naphtali was to be shown in the fertility and beauty of his inheritance, especially the southern part skirting the Sea of Chinnereth (cf. Gen. 49:21). **24-25.** *Asher.* **May he dip his foot in oil** (NASB). Asher's fertile territory was famous for its olives. His mountains yielded **iron** and **bronze** (copper).

The Conclusion of the Blessing. *33:26-29.* **26.** The blessing ended with a panegyric of praise extolling **the God of Jeshurun** (Israel redeemed, regathered from final dispersion, and established as the "Upright One" in Kingdom blessing). Moses extolled God, the true source of the benefits of this covenant. It is He who **rideth upon** the heavens (Psalms 18:10; 68:33-34) to help His people.

27-29. In the Kingdom age **the eternal God** will in a very emphatic sense be **a dwelling place** (NASB) and **underneath** will be the **everlasting arms** (cf. Psalm 90:1-2). **Who is like unto thee ... ?** Realization of Kingdom blessing will bring into full focus the uniqueness of Israel's Savior-Lord-King (v. 29; cf. 26a). **He shall thrust out the enemy from before thee** (Rev. 19:11-16) and say, **Destroy** (Rev. 19:17-21).

Israel then shall dwell in safety alone (Jer. 23:6; 33:16; Num. 23:9). **Grain ... wine ... dew** speak of millennial prosperity (cf. Amos 9:13-15). Then it shall truly be said of Jeshurun, **Happy art thou, O Israel! Who is like unto thee ... ?**

(Cf. 4:32-34.) **So your enemies shall cringe before you** (cf. Psalm 66:3) **and you shall tread upon their high places** (NASB; cf. 32:13; Num. 33:52).

D. MOSES' DEATH—DYNASTIC SUCCESSION. 34:1-12.

Moses' View of the Land. 34:1-4. **1-3.** The great lawgiver, obedient to the command of the LORD (cf. 3:27; 32:49), dramatically ascended Mount Nebo and, from the peak of Pisgah, surveyed the whole extent of the promised land. **4.** The LORD graciously recalled His promise to the patriarchs to give them and their posterity the land, but Moses was reminded that he would **not go over there** (cf. 1:37; 3:26; 4:21-22; 32:52).

Moses' death. 34:5-8. **5. So Moses . . . died there in the land of Moab.** The testator must die before the testament is in force (Heb. 9:16-17). Accordingly, the Deuteronomic Covenant in its testamentary aspect would not become operative until after Moses' decease, as "king in Jeshurun" (cf. 33:5). Only then would Joshua succeed in the dynastic succession in the role of vicegerent of God over Israel. Only then could the tribes, according to God's plan, enter the Canaan inheritance. Moses' death was necessary to notarize the treaty, just as Christ's death was necessary to purchase salvation rest and notarize the new covenant (Jer. 31:31-34; Heb. 8:8-13). In due time the latter was to be introduced to make possible the grace and glory promised in the Deuteronomic Covenant.

6-7. Moses' age is again given (cf. 31:2; Exod. 7:7). He did not expire of old age, but by the command of God, who gives life and takes it away (34:5), for it is said, **His natural force** (*lēăḥ*, "freshness"; physical and mental "vigor") had not **abated** (*kāhᵃṭâ*, "become weak or feeble"). God distinguished the great lawgiver by burying him, and the Israelites honored him by a thirty-day mourning period, the same as for Aaron (Num. 20:29; cf. Gen. 50:3).

Joshua's Succession. 34:9-15. **9-10.** Joshua had been divinely chosen and ordained as the dynastic heir by the laying on of hands, which symbolized commissioning and conferring of spiritual gifts, notably the gift of governmental wisdom (31:7-8; Num. 27:18-23). **The children of Israel hearkened unto him.** In assenting to the accession of Joshua, they were acting in accord with their oath of obedience to the LORD's will, sworn in the Deuteronomic ceremony (cf. 26:17; 29:12). But in accepting Joshua, the people had to realize that he was not Moses' equal. God spoke directly to Moses, **face to face** (Exod. 33:11; Num. 12:8). Joshua, on the other hand, had to discover the will of God through priestly mediation. Joshua proved to be Moses' divinely chosen successor by crossing the Jordan River on dry ground and triumphing over Canaan's armies.

11-12. But Moses had a unique record of delivering Israel from Egypt through **all the signs and the wonders** connected with the Exodus **and . . . the mighty power and . . . all the great terror which Moses performed in the sight of all** Israel (NASB). None was like him as God's instrument to display His redemptive might.

JOSHUA

INTRODUCTION

Title and Place in the Canon. The book takes its name from the great leader whose exploits it recounts. Joshua (*yᵉhôshûă'*, Heb. equivalent of "Jesus") means "Jehovah [YWHH] saves," aptly describing the nature of the great Israelite warrior and soldier of the LORD. The book is distinct from the Pentateuch. There is no ancient Jewish tradition or manuscript evidence that the book ever formed a unit with the five books of the Law to substantiate the critical claim for a so-called Hexateuch (see E. J. Young, *Introduction to the Old Testament*, pp. 157-59). Yet Joshua is linked in the closest possible manner with the Pentateuch in carrying forward the history of Israel as it unfolds the story of divine redemption.

The book opens the second great division of the Hebrew Old Testament called the Prophets, consisting of Joshua, Judges, Samuel, and Kings (four books, the former prophets) and Isaiah, Jeremiah, Ezekiel, and the Twelve (four books, the latter prophets). These books were so called by the ancient Jews because their authors were held to be prophets by office.

Authorship and Date. That the book was composed in substance by Israel's great general, or so soon after his time that the history it contains is authentic, is supported by four points of internal evidence: (1) Parts of the book, at least, were written by Joshua, namely, the covenant made with the people (24:26), embracing his last charge to Israel (24:1-25). (2) Large portions of the book were apparently penned by an eyewitness (cf. 5:2, 6; 15:4) and described with such vividness that participation in the events is suggested. Such is the case with the sending out of the spies (chap. 2), the passage of the Jordan (chap. 3), the siege and capture of Jericho and Ai (chaps. 6-8), the alliance with the Gibeonites and the victory at Gibeon (chaps. 9-10). For that reason the book has traditionally been substantially ascribed to Joshua. (3) Numerous indications in the narrative point to a very early date of composition. Rahab the harlot was still living (6:25). Canaanite cities are mentioned by their archaic names (cf. 15:9; 18:16, 28). The Gibeonites were still employed around the tabernacle (9:27; cf. 2 Sam. 21:1-9). (4) Although early substantial authorship by Joshua is suggested, the account in the form it has come down to us contains minor details that were added, such as the account of Joshua's death (24:29-30) and the transmigration of the Danites to the north (19:47; cf. Judg. 18:27-29).

Purpose in Redemptive History. Joshua continues the account of all those events that happened to God's ancient people as "ensamples" that "are written for our admonition, upon whom the ends of the world are come" (1 Cor. 10:11, KJV). The book continues the detailed redemptive typology of the Pentateuch (q.v.). Deliverance of Israel out of Egypt is expanded to include the consummation of redemption into the promised land, the latter typifying not heaven but the *heavenly position* of the believer as identified in death, burial, and resurrection with the risen Christ (Col. 3:1-4), to whom Joshua points (Heb. 3:7—4:11). In a spiritually illustrative sense, Joshua is to the Old Testament (Josh. 21:43-45) what Ephesians is to the new—a picture of conflict and conquest (Eph. 6:10-20) as the "heavenly places" (1:3) of our placement in Christ are appropriated by faith and translated into our experience of victory in Christ (4:1—6:9).

Authenticity and Credibility. Unbelieving critical scholarship of necessity must explain away the large number of miracles in the book as legends and treat the history as idealized, as they also must do with the Pentateuch. That is why they have lumped Joshua with the Pentateuch in a so-called *Hexateuch* and subjected it to analysis on the basis of the same late literary sources. That is but a rationalistic attempt to explain away the miraculous element. There is no need, however, for the Christian scholar, who experiences God's miraculous power in every phase of his life, to resort to tenuous theories of literary composition to reduce the miracles of the book to legends, or to deny that the narrative rests on solid historical grounds.

Moral Problem in Israel's Warfare. Many people find it difficult to reconcile God's command to utterly destroy the Canaanites with the revelation of the Father given in the Son in the New Testament. That God's holiness in those instances is not at variance with His love is shown by the fact that the destruction of the Canaanites is presented as a religious duty that was essential to carry out God's government of His moral universe and to illustrate symbolically for all believers the utter necessity of total uncompromising warfare with the powers of darkness that the wicked Canaanites portray (cf. Eph. 6:10-20). Moreover, as far as the moral problem is concerned, God waited four hundred years until Canaan's iniquity was full (Gen. 15:16). Jericho, for example, with its inhabitants was "accursed," that is, "devoted" or "put under the ban" (Josh. 6:17, see NASB and RSV; Heb., *hĕrēm*; "devoted to the LORD for destruction," 6:18, RSV; "devoted things," 7:1, RSV). Clearly the ban had a religious significance in that it got rid of everything that might imperil the spiritual life of the community by putting it out of the way and prohibiting it from human use. That dramatically and indelibly taught God's people the necessity of complete separation from evil and, in particular, the abominable idolatries and immoralities of the Canaanites and their religion.

Date of the Conquest. See the date of the Exodus under *Historical Background* in the Introduction to the book of Exodus.

OUTLINE

COMMENTARY

I. THE LAND CONQUERED.
1:1—12:24.

A. PREPARATION TO ENTER THE LAND.
1:1-18.

Joshua Is Commissioned. 1:1-9. **1-2.** In spite of Moses' death the work had to go on. Hence, Joshua was called to the task he was to perform as Moses' successor (cf. Deut. 34:9). Joshua is called Moses' **minister** (*me shārēṯ*, the Hebrew term referring to official rather than menial service, and suggesting special religious ministry; cf. Exod. 33:11, since the term commonly refers to Old Testament Temple ministrations). Moses prefigures Christ in the aspect of His death and burial, delivering His people from bondage and sin, enabling them to realize the promise of inheritance.

3-5. Joshua prefigures Christ in the character of His resurrection and ascension, leading His people into possession of their inheritance. Under Moses the people obtained the position of a redeemed people (Rom. 6:1-10; 1 Cor. 10:1-4). Under Joshua they realized the experience of that position as they entered the land (Rom. 6:11) to enjoy its wealth and its fruits—illustrative of our present enjoyment of our heavenly position of union with our resurrected and exalted Joshua-Jesus (Col. 3:1-4; cf. Rom. 6:11). **6.** Joshua was to **be strong and of good courage** (Eph. 6:10; Phil. 4:13) to apportion **the land** promised to Abraham and his posterity (Gen. 12:6-7; 13:14-15; 15:18-20).

7. The promise was then fulfilled, but strict obedience to do **all the law** commanded them through Moses (cf. Deut. 5:32; 1 Cor. 9:26-27) was enjoined. **8.** Rigid adherence to **this book of the law** (Deut. 31:24, 26) was stressed (Josh. 8:34). They were to **meditate** (*hāgâ*, "muse, ponder") **therein day and night** (cf. Psalm 1:2-3; Deut. 17:18-20), so that their minds would be saturated with God's Word in order to **observe** (*shāmăr*, "keep, pay heed to") it. **9.** That would insure prosperity and good success, boosting their morale in assuring them of God's presence and help, thus preserving them from fear and dismay (cf. 2 Tim. 1:7).

Joshua Assumes Command. 1:10-11. **10-11.** Joshua ordered the mobilization of **the host**, by then a well-disciplined and united army ready to undertake the LORD's battles. **The officers** (*shōṭe rîm*, "writers" or "scribes") who kept records and issued administrative orders (Exod. 5:6-19; Num. 11:16; Deut. 16:18) received Joshua's commands and transmitted them to the people. **Prepare food supplies** (*ṣêḏâ*, "food, provisions"). Other food now being available, they no longer were to depend on manna, which soon was to cease (cf. Josh. 5:12). Manna speaks of Christ in the flesh before His death and burial, since it is connected with the career of Moses, who typifies our Lord's earthly life.

Joshua's assumption of command envisions the resurrected and ascended Christ through the Spirit continuing "to do and teach" what He, prefigured by Moses, merely began in His earthly career (Acts 1:1). Therefore, the words for within three days (the number of resurrection) ye shall pass over this Jordan ... to possess the land (picture of experiencing our heavenly position as identified with the risen Christ, Rom. 6:11; 2 Cor. 5:15; Col. 3:1-4) are significant. As Israel could not possibly go forward to "fight the good fight of faith" (1 Tim. 6:12) and overcome the Canaanites except as identified with Joshua and his command, so we cannot possess our possessions in Christ apart from assurance of our acceptance before God and appropriation by faith of our union with Christ in death and resurrection.

The Faithfulness of the East Jordanic Tribes. 1:12-18. **12-15.** At their own request, the East Jordanic tribes had received their allotment of land east of the Jordan (cf. Num. 32:1-42). In consideration of that concession, those tribes had agreed to assist the other tribes in the conquest of the land west of the Jordan (Deut. 3:12-20). They had been given **rest**, not from warfare, but in possession of the land, so they had to realize that God's people cannot enter their inheritance without conflict (Eph. 6:10-12).

Although already allotted their portion, they not only had to bear their share in the conquest of Canaan, but also had to take the lead in the fighting. **Ye shall pass before your brethren armed** (*ḥᵃmǔšîm*, "in five parts," front, rear, body, and two wings, i.e., in full battle array). **16-18.** Complete faith and obedience marked Reuben, Gad, and the half tribe of Manasseh. Those who would spearhead spiritual conquest must be completely identified with the greater Joshua and strengthen themselves in Him and "the power of his might" (Eph. 6:10).

B. THE SPIES SENT OUT. 2:1-24.

Rahab Hides the Spies. 2:1-7. In sending out the scouts, Joshua was not compromising but, rather, manifesting faith in God by an active, persevering use of means (James 2:22), since he had not yet been informed how the LORD would deliver the fortified city of Jericho. He also had divine precedent for his action (Num. 13:1-2). Jericho was situated some five miles west of the Jordan, and Shittim ("Acacias") was approximately the same distance east of the river.

Accordingly, the spies had to travel about fourteen miles to reach the fortress city, which guarded the pass leading to central Palestine. Therefore, the capture of the fortress was necessary to the invasion of the land from the east. The spies, moreover, were to be God's agents to discover the right path for Israel to take (cf. Deut. 1:22, 32-33). They brought back a report of the state of affairs in Jericho that encouraged the people to go forward.

1. And they went, and came into an harlot's house. How wonderfully such an unlikely character as Rahab illustrates God's sovereign grace. Even in a depraved city, doomed to destruction, a wicked individual could experience grace by turning to God in faith (cf. Rom. 5:20; Heb. 11:31). Such grace magnifies God and renders unnecessary the attempt of many expositors to explain Rahab as a hostess or innkeeper to remove the stigma of that name from an ancestress of the Savior (Matt. 1:5).

But the propriety of the term *harlot* (*zônâ,* f. part. from *zānâ,* "to play the harlot, commit whoredom") is attested (1) by scriptural usage (Lev. 21:7-14; Deut. 23:18; Judg. 11:1; 1 Kings 3:16); (2) by the authority of the Septuagint; (3) by the New Testament (Heb. 11:31; James 2:25); and (4) by Oriental custom, according to which *khans* ("public inns") were never kept by women.

Providence was directing to salvage a sinner from a cesspool of sin and to connect that display of divine mercy with the love and grace of God to be manifested in the coming of Jesus Christ.

2-3. It was told to the king (*mělěk*), a proper designation for the mayor of such a strategic fortress-town as Jericho was. At such a time of threatened invasion, sentinels would be posted everywhere. Their strict duty was to report to headquarters. **4-6. The woman took the two men, and hid them** (lit., "him," i.e., each of them in separate places). The king's sentinels did not barge in to search, but asked the woman to bring out the foreigners. Oriental custom accords an almost superstitious respect to a woman's apartment. She **hid them with the stalks of flax.** The flat roofs of Oriental homes afford an excellent place for drying flax and other vegetable products. Providentially, those luxuriant stalks presented an ideal hiding place.

Rahab's lie, of course, was morally wrong. "She failed to fully trust the LORD, and the fear of man brought a snare. He whose angels had smitten the men of Sodom with blindness (Gen. 19:11) and who had slain the fifty men sent to lay hands on His prophet (2 Kings. 1:9-12), could have prevented those officers finding the spies" (Arthur W. Pink, *Gleanings in Joshua*, p. 59). God overruled Rahab's falsehood; yet that did not exonerate her of her fault. **7. As soon as they who pursued after them were gone out, they shut the gate** to insure the capture of the spies, should they still be hiding in the city.

Rahab's Justifying Faith. 2:8-14. The harlot is an apt illustration of the power of the gospel of grace to save a sinner by faith and faith alone. "*By faith* the harlot, Rahab, perished not with them that believed not" (Heb. 11:31, italics added; cf. John 3:16). She was justified *before God* totally by faith. **9-14.** She attested her saving faith, that is, was justified *before men* by works, (1) "when she had received the spies with peace" (Heb. 11:31), "when she had received the messengers, and had sent them out another way" (James 2:25); (2) when she declared, **I know that the Lord hath given you the land, and that your terror is fallen upon us** (v. 9; cf. Deut. 1:8; 2:25; Josh. 9:9-10); (3) when she rehearsed the divine redemptive power at the Red Sea and the miraculous deliverance from Sihon and Og, the Amorite kings (v. 10); (4) when she witnessed to the sole deity of Israel's God both **in heaven above, and in earth beneath** (v. 11); (5) when she became a soul-winner and showed concern for the salvation of her loved ones (vv. 12-13); (6) when she persevered in faith until full assurance of salvation became her portion (v. 14).

Rahab's Covenant with the Spies. 2:15-21. **15.** Rahab let the spies down **by a cord** (*ḥěḇēl*, "a rope"; 2 Sam. 17:13; Jer. 38:6-13). That was possible since her house was built on the wall. **16. Get you to the mountain.** (Cf. v. 22.) Towering limestone cliffs, fifteen hundred feet high and dotted with numerous caves, skirt the edge of the Jordan Valley and provided an admirable hiding place.

17-20. We will be blameless of this thine oath (i.e., released from it), if the following conditions were violated: (1) **This line of scarlet thread,** furnished by one of the spies, being a sign and pledge of safety to Rahab's house as the bloody mark on the lintels of Israelite houses in Egypt betokened redemption by blood (Exod. 12:12-13) had to be displayed at the window through which the spies escaped (v. 18). By that means the two living witnesses (spies) gave Rahab assurance of salvation, illustrating the glorious truth that our assurance is in

Him "who was delivered for our offenses, and was raised again for our justification" (Rom. 4:25).

(2) All who were to be spared were to be gathered into Rahab's house (vv. 18-19), protected by the line of scarlet, a symbol of divine redemption apart from which there is no salvation (Acts 4:12). (3) Rahab's faith had to be genuine and her word firm (v. 20; cf. v. 14). Saving faith is always attested by works, as hers was.

The Return of the Spies. 2:22-24. After three days of hiding in the hills and caves around Jericho, the spies returned with their faithful report of the utter consternation of the Canaanites and with assurances of their impending overthrow.

C. THE JORDAN CROSSED. 3:1-17.

Arrival at the Jordan. 3:1-6. **1. They ... came to the Jordan,** which like the Red Sea in a similar crisis, at flood stage stood in their way as an insuperable barrier, barring their entrance into the land. It was a moment of immense spiritual import in which only divine omnipotence and faithfulness could carry God's people forward to fulfill the promises made to the patriarchs (e.g., Gen. 12:1-3; 13:14-17; 15:1-7; 28:13-15). God had to perform a miracle and the people had to prepare for conflict.

2-3. Preparations for a holy war of complete extermination of the enemy energized by satanic powers (cf. Eph. 6:10-20) were signaled by **the ark of the covenant** leading the way, and the call for consecration to the LORD for the **wonders** (*niplᵉʾ ôṯ*, "wondrous things, miracles") He was about to perform. The ark (Exod. 25:10-22), one of the most comprehensive object lessons of Christ in the Old Testament, leading on into the swirling waters of the Jordan, beautifully portrays our Lord going through the billows of death to make a way for His people to advance experientially into victorious possession of their salvation rest. He went through death.

Pictured are His people going through death with Him, being buried with Him, and coming out of the waters of death with Him into resurrection life. Passing through the Red Sea, the people secured a *position* of death-burial-resurrection when their redemption from Egypt was accomplished and salvation obtained (1 Cor. 10:1-13; cf. Rom. 6:1-10). Passing through Jordan, their position before God then became an *experience* before men (Heb. 4:1-11; cf. Rom. 6:11).

Although Israel had a position before God, they failed miserably in the wilderness to live up to that position. The Law given at Sinai only brought to light that the people were "carnal, sold under sin" (Rom. 7:14), operating in the flesh and serving "the law of sin" (Rom. 7:25). Their *condition*, as far as their experience of their position was concerned, was just as absolute an obstacle to their entering Canaan as were the waters of Jordan.

But God's gracious power undertook to remove that difficulty and take them through Jordan on dry ground to enter salvation "rest" by ceasing from their own "works" and fleshly strivings (Heb. 4:10) and by relying completely on their position of death to sin and resurrection to righteousness. The spiritual counterpart is "reckon ye ... yourselves to be dead indeed unto sin, but alive unto God through [*ĕn*, "in union with"] Jesus Christ, our Lord" (Rom. 6:11). They possessed the dead-to-sin, alive-to-God position. The crossing of Jordan illustrated its being made real in experience.

4. Strict distance was to be kept between the Ark (as illustrating our Lord going into the waters of death) and the

286

people. (The fact is emphasized that our Lord had to accomplish that work alone, cf. John 13:36.) That was done through priestly ministry, for the priests bore aloft the Ark in the sight of all the people. There was no one with Christ when He opened this "new and living way" of victory over sin in the flesh (Heb. 10:20).

But having opened the way gloriously, He takes *all* His people through death into resurrection life for victory over sin and all enemies in this life and for the realization of glory in the life to come. It is the way **ye must go** to experience salvation rest (Col. 3:1-4). Until the Ark opened up the Jordan and Christ opened up the path to victorious living for His own, it could be said, **Ye have not passed this way heretofore** (cf. John 14:6).

Joshua Begins to Be Magnified. 3:7-8. When the LORD's people cross the Jordan and illustratively enter the *experience* of their position in Christ, they begin to obey and thus exalt the divine Joshua, the Captain of their salvation (4:14).

Joshua Directs the Crossing. 3:9-13. **10.** Joshua assured them **the Living God**, the one true God of miracle and power, would prove His presence among them (cf. Deut. 31:8, 17) by driving out the debauched inhabitants of the land, who illustrate the spiritual foes of the believer (Eph. 6:10-20). **11.** But the prelude to all the conquest was that **the ark of the covenant of the Lord of all the earth passeth over before you into the Jordan.** The secret of spiritual victory is *faith* in what Christ has accomplished for us by His passing through the waters of death for us, and resting in the merits of His death enjoyed by us as we are identified with Him. That opens *the way* (see v. 4) for the experience of resurrection power in our enjoyment of salvation rest in the

land through the conquest of all our enemies.

13. Shall not He who is **the Lord** (*'āḏôn*, "master") **of all the earth** be able to subdue our foes? How appropriate that Zechariah employs that appellative in describing the time when Israel will be established in coming Kingdom blessing (Zech. 4:14) after all her enemies have been judged (6:5) and the Messiah, by right of creation, redemption, and conquest, is absolute King and Lord, not only over Israel but over the nations as well in the millennial earth.

The Crossing Is Made. 3:14-17. The mighty miracle of the parted waters was wrought by "the living God" (cf. v. 10), that is, Deity in manifested omnipotence. That is true whether or not the Creator employed an earthquake at Adam (Adamah), a town eight miles north of Succoth overlooking the Jordan. Specialists have maintained that the dozen miles between Adamah and Zarethan comprise the only stretch in the Jordan Valley where such a damming up and going over on dry ground could have taken place. Parallels to such a temporary blocking of the Jordan have been adduced. In A.D. 1266, near Tell ed-Damiyeh in that vicinity, the bed of the Jordan was left dry for ten hours as the result of a landslide. In 1927 an earthquake near Adam (Adamah) stopped the Jordan's flow for twenty-one hours.

D. THE TWELVE MEMORIAL STONES SET UP. 4:1-24.

The Two Memorials. 4:1-18. Such a momentous event as the crossing of the Jordan, with such far-reaching spiritual repercussions (see chap. 3), had to be commemorated. **2-9.** Accordingly, when the crossing had been completed, Joshua took the twelve men, whom he had already appointed (cf. v. 12), and sent them back to where the priests were standing with the Ark to take out of the river twelve stones to be set up as a memorial at Gilgal. Joshua then set up another twelve stones in the midst of the Jordan where the priests' feet had stood.

The two sets of stones, **unto the number of the tribes of the children of Israel**, emphasized that all twelve tribes had been redeemed out of Egypt, had been in the desert together, and had all entered the land at the same time. The truth of the unity of God's people in every age must not be obscured or violated (cf. 1 Cor. 12:12-26; Eph. 4:4-5). **12-13.** To stress that fact, a note was inserted that the eastern tribes crossed the Jordan with their fellow Israelites.

14. When believers realize their oneness and strive to maintain that unity, Joshua is exalted as well as the greater than Joshua, the Captain of our salvation (cf. 3:7; 1 Chron. 29:25; Eph. 1:20-23). **15-18.** With the completion of the crossing, **the waters of the Jordan returned unto their place** at full spring flood level, occasioned by the melting snows on Mount Hermon.

What Mean These Stones? 4:19-24. **19. The people came up out of the Jordan on the tenth day of the first month** (Abib, i.e., "green ears," later called Nisan) four days before the celebration of the fortieth anniversary of the first Passover, the very day the paschal lamb was set apart (Exod. 12:3). **20. Gilgal** ("circle" or "rolling"), the site of Israel's first encampment in Canaan, and their headquarters for the war of conquest, was two or three miles northeast of Jericho. There the twelve stones taken from the Jordan were set up as a memorial, and the site became a shrine in Israel (cf. 1 Sam. 7:16; 10:8; 15:21; Hos. 4:15; Amos 4:4).

21. When future generations visited the great historical site, an answer was to be given to their question, **What mean these stones? 22-24.** They were to be told how the LORD dried up the waters of the Jordan, as He did the Red Sea. But that climactic event was to be a spiritual lesson of the LORD's redemptive power, not only to the Israelites, but to **all the people of the earth.** By it God would illustrate His great salvation that He would eventually bring to all peoples of the world. Israelite history would thus be uniquely redemptive history, investing it with an inestimable and abiding value for all mankind.

The twelve stones erected at Gilgal (vv. 1-8, 20) speak of that aspect of Christ's death that brings God's people *into* the land of inheritance and into the sphere of *experience* of victory and conquest. The message is: let us reckon on that death and enjoy the life and victory that spring out of it in the sphere of salvation rest (Rom. 6:11).

The stones left in the swirling Jordan to be overwhelmed by its waters (v. 9) are mementoes of Christ's death under judgment in the believer's place (Psalm 22:1-18; 42:7; 88:7; John 12:31-33). The message is: we *died* in Christ (Rom. 6:1-10), and the life of the flesh has been put to death and buried forever in Jordan, that the life of the Spirit might be manifested in conquest from military headquarters at Gilgal (for the spiritual significance, see comments on chap. 5).

E. ISRAEL AT GILGAL. 5:1-15.

A Fear-Stricken Enemy. 5:1. **1.** Doubtlessly relying on the flooded Jordan as a certain though temporary barrier, the morale of the Canaanites completely collapsed when they learned that the river had completely dried up, giving incontestable truth that the LORD of the invading people was indeed the actual powerful "living God." A people who a generation ago had so terrified God's unbelieving people (Num. 13:32-33) now were themselves terrified before them as they advanced in faith in what their God was doing through them. A redeemed people reckoning on their "death to sin and the flesh" position in Christ *always* strike terror to the enemy.

Circumcision Performed. 5:2-9. **2. Make thee sharp knives** (lit., "knives of flint," cf. Exod. 4:25), an evident survival of an ancient custom due to religious conservatism, since bronze had long supplanted stone for use in making cutting instruments. **Circumcise again ... the second time.** That does not mean that they had been circumcised already, but that they were returning to their former condition as a circumcised nation in covenant relation with God.

4-8. During the period of almost forty years of wilderness wandering, the rite of circumcision had not been performed because the disobedient people had been under divine judgment (cf. Num. 14:34). If the people had been circumcised during that period, it would have appeared that all was well and that the covenant blessing had never been suspended. Now, however, having passed through the Jordan, illustrative of death to the flesh experientially, they once more were to bear in their bodies the seal of the Abrahamic Covenant (see Gen. 17:9-14; Exod. 4:24-26), which speaks of the execution of the sentence of death upon the flesh.

Christ's death is set forth as a spiritual circumcision for His people (Col. 2:11). But the fact that believers are dead to sin by the circumcision of Christ, and thus have a death-to-sin *position* in Him (Rom. 6:1-10), furnishes the basis for appropriating faith to translate that position into a death-to-sin experience (Rom. 6:11) by applying the sharp knife

to the flesh and its lusts (v. 2; cf. Gal. 5:16-26).

9. The Lord declared, **This day have I rolled away** (*găllôṯî*) **the reproach of Egypt from off you**. That reproach was the shame and disgrace of uncircumcision (Gen. 34:14). During the latter years of the Egyptian bondage, that separating sign had been neglected (see Exod. 4:24-26), but those who left Egypt had been circumcised (v. 5; cf. Exod. 12:44) as the redeemed and as those prepared to eat the Passover, which spoke of redemption.

Wherefore the name of the place is called Gilgal. The new significance of "rolling" was connected to the old name, which literally meant "circle" (of stones), to serve as a reminder to the Israelites of their deliverance out of Egypt into the promised land. Their circumcision was a token of the Lord's faithfulness to His promise to them. Thus, Gilgal stands for the place of death to the flesh.

The Passover Kept. 5:10. This is the third Passover recorded. The first was held in Egypt (Exod. 12:1-15); the second on the first anniversary of its institution (Num. 9:5). For many years the disobedient people had been out of covenant relationship and uncircumcised, and so they could not keep the Passover.

Canaan's Food. 5:11-12. **11. And they did eat of the old grain of the land**, doubtless barley being harvested in the fields and stored in granaries abandoned by the Canaanites, who had fled into Jericho for safety. In faith the people took the first step of entering into their inheritance, which was theirs by covenant. "The corn of the land that Israel ate, speaks to us of Christ risen from among the dead, and all the harvest of heavenly blessings in Him, which through grace are our portion" (H. Forbes Witherby, *The Book of Joshua*,

p. 104). That is the proper food of those who pass through the waters of Jordan (reckoning on their death-to-sin position), are circumcised (pronouncing death upon the flesh), and keep the Passover (relying wholly on Christ's redeeming blood and entering the experience of salvation rest).

Illustrated is the glorious spiritual truth: "I am crucified with Christ: nevertheless I live; yet not I, but Christ liveth in me; and the life which I now live in the flesh I live by the faith of the Son of God, who loved me and gave himself for me" (Gal. 2:20). God gave His people a food that had been unknown to them in Egypt, the grain of the land of Canaan, the food available in the possession of salvation rest. A heavenly, glorified Christ as the God-man passed through this sin-stained world in spotless humanity (the unleavened bread), and in that same humanity passed through the fire of judgment (like the parched corn); now, having entered the glory through resurrection, He sits as man at the right hand of God.

12. And the manna ceased on the next day (see 1:10-11). Israel ate it no more. It was wilderness food, reflecting Christ in humiliation giving His flesh that the believer might have life (John 6:49-51). To feed on manna is to meditate upon the Lord Jesus as He lived among men, doing only the Father's will (John 6:38-40). "Indispensable and most blessed as it is that the remembrance of it should remain ... still as food it is transitory and suited to the journey which comes to an end" (H. L. Rossier, *Meditations on the Book of Joshua*, pp. 43-44).

The Captain of the Lord's Army. *5:13-15.* **13.** Conflict was about to begin; yet the Captain of the host had not yet appeared. He revealed Himself at the last moment, but precisely at the needed time, **when Joshua was by Jericho**. Faith can count on Him in the time of need. He comes to fight for His people (cf. Eph. 6:10) **with his sword drawn in his hand** (cf. Num. 22:23; 1 Chron. 21:16). He is none other than the Angel of the Lord, the Lord Himself (Exod. 23:20-21), the preincarnate Christ in visible form to undergird Joshua and to show Him that He who marshals the armies of heaven is fighting for His people.

14. The divine character of the Captain was disclosed by His accepting the homage of worship (cf. Acts 10:25-26; Rev. 19:10) and by His command. **15. Loose thy shoe** (sandal) **from off thy foot.** If God is holy in *redemption* (Exod. 3:5), He is not less holy in *combat*. We can successfully engage in combat only after having loosened the shoes off our feet.

F. JERICHO TAKEN. 6:1-27.

The Divine Instructions. 6:1-16. **1-2.** Verse 1 is a parenthesis inserted to introduce the divine plan for the overthrow of Jericho set forth by the Captain of the Lord's army (vv. 2-5). The Lord (under the appearance of the Captain of the Lord's army, 5:15) unequivocally assured Joshua of complete victory (cf. Deut. 2:24; Josh. 8:1). If the Lord promised the divine, supernatural destruction of Jericho as the pledge of the conquest of all the land, there was absolutely no need for Joshua to devise a plan of his own. He believed God and humbly accepted the divine plan, however fantastic, even though it might have seemed ridiculous from a human point of view, particularly from the military angle (cf. 1 Cor. 1:25).

3. The city was to be circled once every day for six days. Faith was to be tested by patience to have its perfect work. **4. Seven priests** were to **bear before the ark seven trumpets of rams'**

horns. God marshaled His people in conflict around the Ark of the Covenant, prefiguring Christ (Exod. 25:10-22). In all spiritual conquests Christ is to be lifted up in priestly service. In exalting Him, the Word of God is at the same time lifted up, for the Ark contained the Law of God, even as Christ, the living Word, embodied in His life the written Word of God.

The armed men that preceded the written Word were its executioners. The priests who blew the "trumpets of jubilee" were its heralds, announcing the arrival of the LORD as King, whether to His people, to consummate His covenant or proclaim release and liberty, or to His enemies, to judge and smite them (cf. Lev. 25:8-54; 27:17-24; Num. 36:4). It was their LORD and His Law that had brought Israel over Jordan. That Law was about to be established in Canaan and take vengeance on its flagrant transgressors. The seven days' march around Jericho plus the seven times on the seventh day were well calculated to impress upon the inhabitants the "forbearance ... of God" (Rom. 2:4) and to fill them with terror and consternation, for divine judgment was about to fall (cf. Gen. 15:16; Lev. 18:1-30).

The Capture of Jericho. 6:17-21. The formidable walled city offered a real obstacle to Israel in the conquest of the land. It is illustrative of the world that the believer must overcome if a life of victory is to be realized (John 16:33; 1 John 5:4-5). Remains of the massive walls and the city that fell to Joshua (c. 1400 B.C.) have largely eroded. Kathleen Kenyon's excavations (1952-58) revealed that most of the extant mound is sixteenth century or earlier. Apparently the Late Bronze Age Canaanites reused the Hyksos rampart, upon which they built their own mud brick wall not long before its overthrow by Joshua.

21. The completeness of the destruction (cf. v. 24) plus the following five centuries of erosion until Hiel rebuilt the town (1 Kings 16:34) no doubt explain the absence of corroborating archaeological remains. The mound itself was evidently not large, comprising about nine acres, which could easily be circumvented in about a quarter of an hour. Rahab's house, set on the wall, furnishes an indication of the crowded condition of the walled city.

17. The city shall be accursed (*ḥĕrĕm*, i.e., "devoted to ... destruction," RSV, put under the ban of extermination as the firstfruits of Canaan's conquest and belonging to the LORD, Lev. 27:28-29). Having belonged to the Baal of the land, it could become the LORD's only by being obliterated. Being utterly reprobate, it had to be totally destroyed to prevent contamination of the LORD's people, to teach them the absolute necessity of separation from idolatry, and to meet the requirements of outraged divine holiness against a people whose sin was full (Gen. 15:16), whose doom was sealed, and who (except Rahab) had no claim to divine redemptive grace. Hence, there is no clash with Christian ethics, as God's wrath in every age is revealed against such sinners (Rom. 1:18-32), and He may use His holy angels (Rev. 16:1-21), or even His own people, as His executioners against them (cf. Rom. 13:1-4).

Rahab Saved. 6:22-25. Here the principle of the ban or curse is seen in reverse in the principle of saving faith effecting identification with the people of God (Gal. 3:16-17). Unbelief results in judgment and death. As Joshua saved Rahab because of her faith (2:12-21), so the greater Joshua saves all who place their trust in Him (John 11:25). **23.** As Gentiles, Rahab and her family were set **outside the camp** because they were ceremonially unclean. When they were cleansed from the defilement of their idolatries and the men were circumcised, they became one with the people of God, Rahab becoming an example of true faith (Heb. 11:31; James 2:25; cf. Eph. 3:6).

Curse upon Jericho. 6:26-27. The placing of Jericho under the ban and the pronouncing of a curse upon anyone who would afterward rebuild it furnish an illustration of the destruction of the satanic world system ripe for judgment at the end of the age when Christ will return. Then trumpets of jubilee will usher in the time of blessing for the earth when Israel returns to the land and her enemies are destroyed. Compare the prominence of the number seven (vv. 2-5) with the context of the doom of the satanic world system under the seven seals, seven trumpets, and seven bowls of the book of Revelation (Rev. 6:1—20:10). Hiel, the Bethelite, disregarded the ban on Jericho at the cost of the lives of his two sons (1 Kings 16:34).

G. ACHAN'S SIN. 7:1-26.

Cause of the Defeat at Ai. 7:1-5. **1.** Despite the brilliant victory so recently enjoyed over Jericho (chap. 6), this chapter opens with the registry of a humiliating defeat. The sin that led to defeat at Ai was due to three things: (1) The sin was due to Achan's deliberate disobedience, for which the LORD held the people corporately responsible (cf. v. 11). The unity and solidarity of God's people are stressed (cf. 1 Cor. 12:12-26). The sin of one involves all. Specifically, Achan's sin was a breach of the covenant in failing to obey the command of separation from the **accursed thing** (*ḥĕrĕm*; see 6:17-19), that is, from Jericho (the world), ripe for destruction under the sentence of divine judgment (cf. James 4:4; 1 John 2:15-17).

(2) The sin was due to a sinful dependence upon human strength rather than upon God, manifested by deciding to send only a few men, because the city was small (v. 3; cf. 8:25). **2.** The trouble began when Joshua sent men **from Jericho**, which was not the true point of departure. He forgot Gilgal, where Israel learned what the flesh was (cf. 5:2-9), and in the victory at Jericho he apparently found an opportunity for trusting in self. In sending **men . . . to Ai**, he repeated what he had done in the case of Jericho (2:1). But now a former act of faith became a fleshly expedient in the light of the report of the spies after their their return from reconnoitering Jericho (2:24).

(3) The sin was due to the absence of any record of consulting God for directions in taking Ai, in contrast to the case of Jericho (6:1-5). **4-5.** The defeat resulted in thirty-six men being slain when they were ignominiously routed before Ai's gate and chased **unto Shebarim**, which means the "broken places," that is, there were defiles, narrow passages or gorges, in the cliffs in the course of the steep descent.

Archaeological problems exist concerning the exact location of Ai, commonly identified with Et-Tell, but this site was unoccupied from about 2400 to 1200 B.C. and does not fit the picture. Et-Tell may actually be Beth-Aven, and the real evidence for Ai ("the ruin") may yet await further research. Wherever Ai is pinpointed, it was situated strategically on the eastern edge of the central ridge, commanding the main route from Gilgal into the heart of Canaan.

Joshua's Prayer and God's Answer. 7:6-15. **6-7.** Joshua, who appears as a type of Christ by His Spirit working in the believer to bring him into possession of his privileges and into conquest over his foes, pleaded for God's people in their moment of defeat (cf. 1 John 2:1). The tone of his pleading was that of bold remonstrance and complaint, and the typical Joshua, as in all typological characters of the Bible, frequently disappears to make room for Joshua, the mere man. Forgetting for an instant his own commission (1:5), he imagined that God had forsaken Israel, and his human infirmity was revealed (cf. Exod. 5:22; 14:11; 16:3; 17:3; Num. 21:5). **8-9.** Yet a high tone of advocacy, reminiscent of that of Moses for Israel (Exod. 32:12; Num. 14:13), shines through, indubitably pointing to the spirit of the greater Joshua.

10-15. The LORD's answer was in the nature of a mild rebuke. Joshua was not to dwell on the defeat, but its moral cause. **Israel hath sinned, and ... also transgressed my covenant.** The offense was serious because it involved outright disobedience of the divine command (cf. 6:17-18), presumptuous participation in the **accursed thing** (open complicity with evil), bold theft, and flagrant hypocrisy (cf. Acts 5:1-2; Heb. 4:13). Achan's sin appears analogous to the "sin unto [physical] death" (1 John 5:16; cf. 1 Cor. 5:5; 11:30-32). Such tolerated sin brings slander upon the LORD and specifically jeopardizes His people (v. 15; cf. vv. 1, 11), exposing them to defeat at the hands of their enemies.

Achan's Sin Judged. 7:16-26. **16-18.** By means of the sacred lot (evidently inscribed objects; cf. 1 Sam. 10:20-24; 14:41-42; Prov. 16:33), which was cast solemnly, Achan of the tribe of Judah was identified as the culprit. **19.** Joshua instructed him to **give glory to the Lord God of Israel** by confessing his sin and confirming the divine accuracy in naming the transgressor. **20-21.** This he did, declaring, **I saw ... I coveted ... [I] took,** indicating the steps in temptation and

fall (cf. Gen. 3:6-7). The **beautiful Babylonish garment** was literally "one fine mantle of Shinar." The **shekels of silver** were lumps or rings of the metal, whose value was computed by weighing. The **wedge** ("tongue" or "ingot") **of gold** has been illustrated by examples recovered from Palestinian sites.

In stealing objects under the ban, Achan placed himself under the "doom" (*ḥĕrĕm*) of destruction. Members of his entire household, living under the same tent, could not help but be accomplices, and therefore were cursed with him (cf. Deut. 13:12-17). He was partaking of that which typified the world ripe for judgment and under the immediate and irrevocable sentence of divine vengeance. "The whole episode, like the deaths of Saul, Ananias and Sapphira, and others, was not an illustration of the loss of salvation, but a warning of the discipline which befalls a sinning saint, even to the point of physical death" (M. F. Unger, *Unger's Bible Handbook*, p. 161).

24-26. Hence, **the valley of Achor** ("trouble") where Achan was put to death through God's redemptive grace, became "a door of hope" (Hos. 2:15). Did Achan's family share in his death? Apparently, but compare Deuteronomy 24:16, which clearly prohibits an innocent person from being put to death for a relative's crime. The plural pronoun **them** (v. 25) may refer grammatically only to Achan's possessions, and Joshua 22:20 may refer to the thirty-six men who perished because of his sin. Korah's relatives were spared (Num. 16).

H. AI TAKEN. 8:1-35.

Renewed Encouragement. 8:1-2. **1.** The revelation of the LORD's fear-dispelling presence and His assurance of victory always follow confession of sin and self-judgment. Divine directions can then be clearly given, understood, and obeyed. **All the people of war** (fighting men) were to be taken in the renewed attack to restore the nation's shattered morale. **2.** Observe that in the case of Ai, all the spoil and cattle were to be given to the Israelites. Achan would have been rewarded instead of liquidated if he had obeyed the LORD and had put his expectation in Him.

Strategy of Attack. 8:3-17. The complexity of the attack at Ai contrasted with the simplicity of the plan at Jericho (cf. 6:1-5); yet the same LORD gave the directions in both cases. The difference was that at Jericho the LORD was acting in response to the faith of His people to teach them His power. At Ai, on the other hand, although they had judged themselves and put away sin, He wanted to teach them their own weakness.

How little the people knew themselves after the Jericho victory. Though the LORD had taken great pains to prove to them that all the victory was of Him, what self-sufficiency they displayed at Ai. The result was that not only did they suffer humiliating defeat, but, even after self-judgment and restoration, the path they had taken made it difficult for them to see their own weakness, already apparent to their enemies.

But the same power that smote Jericho was with Israel at Ai. God had not changed, though the army had to maneuver and separate into two corps, five thousand men lying in ambush, while the rest lured the defenders out of their stronghold. What a contrast! At Jericho it was not a question of human means. But at Ai there were all sorts of contrivances and schemes. How could the same God order two such different battles? In one case, His purpose was to instruct His people in His power; in the

other, to teach them their own weakness.

Realization of Victory. 8:18-29. The fall of the city was by divine power. Israel's activity was blessedly characterized throughout by Joshua's presence (vv. 3, 9, 13, 15, 21, 26), even as spiritual victory in the case of the believer is always characterized by Christ, both positionally (Eph. 6:10) and experientially (Eph. 6:11-20). **18-26.** At the LORD's command Joshua stretched out the spear that he had in his hand toward the city. **For Joshua drew not his hand back ... until he had utterly destroyed all the inhabitants of Ai.** His hand remained stretched out till conflict was turned to triumph.

Dramatically illustrated also are the unity and diversity of God's people. The Israeli ambush captured Ai and set it afire, while the twenty-five thousand fled before their enemies, until signaled by the smoke from the burning city to turn back upon them. Just as they began to fight, those who had come out of the city in the ambush joined the battle (v. 22). Then all Israel returned to Ai to smite it with **the edge of the sword** (v. 24; cf. John 11:52; 1 Cor. 12:4-26).

The Covenant as Law of the Land. 8:30-35. The altar at Ebal in the Shechem area, which was sacred to the patriarchs, commemorated the faithfulness of the LORD both to His promises (Gen. 12:6-8) and to His displayed power in the destruction of Jericho and Ai. It was also an act of obedience to Moses' command (Deut. 27:2-8). The Law copied on stones, whether the Decalogue or the blessings and cursings of Deuteronomy or the summary of the Pentateuch, was to be the law of the land. The custom of inscribing law codes on stone was a very ancient practice, going back to Sumerian and Babylonian times. The Code of Hammurabi (c. 1700 B.C., with its prologue, 282 sections, and epilogue) is one of the better-known examples.

I. THE GIBEONITE RUSE. 9:1-27.

Enemy Resistance. 9:1-2. **1-2.** The kings of the central highland ridge, including Jerusalem and Hebron, of the Shephelah (the low, receding hills falling off to the plain), and of **the borders** (shores) **of the Great Sea** (Mediterranean) or Maritime Plain, formed a confederacy against Israel. Victorious advance of God's people (Eph. 1:1—6:9) always challenges and arouses the powers of darkness (Eph. 6:10-20). The book of Joshua offers a study in "the rules or strategems of the devil," who knows how to wage war, as well as how to feign peace, employing subterfuge and craft to deceive.

But God overrules Satan's victory and turns it into His school for the righteous, who are taught the claims of divine holiness and to seek their safeguard in the Word of God and find their deliverance in the power of God (cf. Eph. 1:19; 3:16, 20; 6:10). In that conflict God uses two classes of vessels to glorify Himself—those so weak that their only resource is to depend on Him (cf. 1 Cor. 1:27-28), or those so strong in themselves and before men that He must completely smash them to use them (cf. Acts 9:15-16). The consciousness of believers' nothingness as instruments in complete dependence on God is the way to power. Satan attempts to turn them from a posture of dependence by turning their attention upon the enemy's confederation to strike fear in them.

Failure to Rely Wholly on the Lord. 9:3-15. **3-4.** Hearing **what Joshua had done unto Jericho and to Ai**, the Gibeonites worked **wilily** (*bᵉ'ŏrmâ*, "with cunning, craftily"). Gibeon (ej-Jib) was located five miles northwest of Jerusalem.

The Gibeonites were Hivites, a little-known ethnic group of Palestine, perhaps a subsection of the Horites (Hurrians), now well-known people of the ancient Middle East. **4-13.** They pretended to be friends. Their clever lie that they had come a long way to make an alliance, witnessed by their old wineskins, moldy bread, and worn sandals, completely deceived the Israelites.

14. God's people were tricked into making a treaty with the enemy. The reason was that the Israelites **partook of their provisions, and did not ask direction from the Lord** (RSV). They abandoned their dependence and acted apart from reliance on the Word of God. The Gibeonites came with all sorts of good intentions and confessions. How little did the Israelites suspect at that moment that the Gibeonites were the very Canaanites they were divinely commanded to drive out. They neglected to inquire of the LORD and, as a sign of fellowship, they accepted **their provisions** of food.

Hence, the treaty was concluded and the world introduced into the congregation of the LORD's people by means of a subtle strategem of Satan, suggesting the introduction of the world into the camp as a means of conquering the enemy. That sad episode in the history of God's ancient people has found all too frequent illustration in the New Testament church and the damage incurred by alliances and compromise with the world in the course of the centuries (cf. Rev. 2:13).

The Sad Mistake Commemorated. 9:16-27. **16-18.** The blunder was discovered too late to rectify it, but God's grace is seen in operation. Though evil was introduced into the congregation, it was not developed. God graciously delivers us from some consequences of our sin, allowing others to remain. God's people had to undergo the mournful experience of keeping the Gibeonites among them as a lasting reminder of their failure. Having begun by complaining against their leaders, the people of God were brought eventually to a truer sense of their duty. They had to bear having the Gibeonites among them, while keeping them in the place that the curse had put them. **23. Now, therefore, ye are cursed,** Joshua said to them. God's people could only view them as enemies and of an accursed race.

24-26. The judgment of Ai and its king was pronounced, not executed, upon them. **27.** They were, however, reduced to a servile status in connection with **the altar of the Lord.** That was meant to be a perpetual reminder to the LORD's people that they had to bear the consequences of their unfaithfulness and to be humbled by the evil that had insinuated itself into God's house. But by being genuinely sensitive to their shame, they would yet, if faithful, be able to differentiate what was of God from that which merely bore His name outwardly. God's Word reveals the mixture; and faith leaves the religious world under the curse, but at the same time it acts with grace toward it, a principle King Saul grossly violated (2 Sam. 21:1-14; cf. Deut. 19:9-12), as have the professing people of God who have slain one another as heretics, real or supposed, falling prey to Satan's deception as "an angel of light" (2 Cor. 11:14).

J. CONQUEST OF SOUTHERN CANAAN. 10:1-43.

Adoni-zedek and His Alliance. 10:1-5. **1-6.** The name of Adoni-zedek, an enemy Jebusite king, means "my lord is righteousness" and occurs in connection with the first mention in the Bible of "Jerusalem," ancient "Salem"

(Gen. 14:18), or "Jebus" (Judg. 19:10). This king headed an evil coalition against Gibeon and Israel. Behind the movements of these enemies of God's people can be seen the subtle and often hidden operations of the powers of darkness of this world system, frequently working so deviously that it is difficult to determine who is right or which is the good cause in the terrific struggle that ensues.

When Israel entered Canaan (c. 1400 B.C.), more than two dozen and a half city-states existed (cf. 12:1-24). But by 1390 B.C., Israel had swallowed up many of them. According to the Amarna Letters, by 1375 B.C. there were only four main independent states in the south—Jerusalem (Urusalim); Shuwardata; Gezer (Tell Jezer), about eighteen miles west of Gibeon; and Lachish (Tell ed-Duweir), twenty-seven miles southeast of Jerusalem. Jarmuth is Khirbet Yarmuk, sixteen miles southwest of Jerusalem. Eglon is perhaps Tell el-Hesi, some seven miles west of Lachish.

The Victory at Gibeon. 10:6-15. The Gibeon battle was a decisive one in the history of the conquest. **6-10.** The Israelites were covenant-bound to assist the Gibeonites in their urgent appeal for help. **8.** But the circumstances were providential (cf. 1:5) and would eventuate in a great victory. **9-10.** Joshua conducted a forced all-night march in the moonlight from Gilgal (about twenty-five miles) in order to surprise the besieging Amorites by daylight, and thus be in a position to rout them from Gibeon and chase them northwestward by the way of **Beth-horon** to the Shephelah. From there the enemy fled southwestward to **Azekah** (Tell ez Zakariyeh), commanding the Valley of Elah, about three miles west of Jarmuth (Khirbet Yarmuk), and went on to **Makkedah** (probably Khirbet el-Heishum, two miles northwest of Jarmuth). The fleeing foe tried in vain to reach Jarmuth, about nineteen miles southwest of Gibeon.

11-13. As the Amorites fled in confusion down the deep descent between Beth-horon the upper, whose altitude is 2,022 feet, to Beth-horon the lower, at an altitude of 1,210 feet, the LORD sent a terrific storm of darkness and hail, the hailstones killing **more ... than they whom the children of Israel slew with the sword.** That great event is supplemented by a quotation from **the book of Jasher,** a collection of poems celebrating Israelite heroes, doubtless similar to "the book of the wars of the LORD" (Num. 21:14-18). The great miracle was not that God prolonged the day, but that by means of a violent thunderstorm He provided shade and refreshment by rain for Joshua's severely overtaxed army, and at the same time He sent darkness and death by hailstones upon their enemies.

Note these four points: (1) For the sun to cease from the grain harvest through the summer months of the long dry season in Palestine was miracle enough (1 Sam. 12:17). E. W. Maunder, "The Battle of Beth-Horon," ISBE, 1:449, places the battle in July. (2) Joshua's troops, exhausted by their all-night march and steep climb to Gibeon, did not need more sunlight but, rather, relief from the sun's merciless rays. (3) If the sunlight had been extended a dozen or more hours, the stupendousness of the miracle would have dwarfed the crossing of the Red Sea or the Jordan. It would have been noted in ancient records, and it certainly would have been referred to explicitly elsewhere in the Bible (cf. Hab. 3:11).

(4) The true explanation of the miracle is found in the correct translation and interpretation of the poetic terminology in which it is couched. The word *dôm*, translated **stand thou still**, means basically, "be dumb, silent, still," and then "rest" or "cease" from usual activity (as in Job 30:27; 31:34; Psalm 35:15; Lam. 2:18). In Babylonian cuneiform astronomical texts, the root means "to be darkened." Thus, when the sun is said to be "dumb" or "silent," it is merely a poetical way of saying it "stops shining," its "words" or "speech" denoting its sending forth rays of light and heat (Psalm 19:2-6). Similarly, the synonym *'āmăḏ*, rendered **stayed** and **stood still**, often has the connotation of "cease" (Gen. 30:9; 2 Kings 4:6; Jonah 1:15).

So the passage simply means the sun was "dumb" (stopped shining) at Gibeon, and the moon likewise ceased to shine in the Valley of Ajalon, their light being blotted out by the thick, black clouds of the miraculous hail and rainstorm that the LORD sent to discomfit Israel's foe. So **the sun stood still** (ceased shining) **... and** (i.e., although it) **hastened not to go down** (set) **about a whole day.** It did *not* set earlier than normal; yet there was darkness during the more than twelve-hour day. Properly translated and interpreted, the passage states categorically that the miracle was not the sun's "standing still" (cessation of the earth's rotation around the sun), but the blotting out of its light by thick, black storm clouds from its normal shining for a whole day.

14. The day was utterly unique because **the Lord hearkened unto the voice of a man,** that is, to Joshua's prayer (v. 12), and answered (v. 13) because he and Israel were in the path of self-judgment and dependence upon the LORD. So we read that the LORD spoke to Joshua (v. 8), and Joshua spoke to the LORD (v. 12), the LORD in turn answering him in the great victory at Gibeon. The LORD could fight for Israel (vv. 11-14) because Israel was in the place of self-judged dependence upon Him and in fellowship with Him.

Execution of the Five Kings. 10:16-27. **16-19.** The five kings fled and hid in a cave at Makkedah, but the pursuers did not halt to deal with them. **21-23.** Afterward they were brought out. **24.** Before executing them and hanging their corpses on a tree in token of shame and reprobation, Joshua's field commanders placed their feet upon their necks. That symbol of complete subjugation is pictured frequently on the monuments of ancient kings, notably of Egypt and Assyria. **25.** Since Joshua himself was encouraged by the word of God (v. 8), he could encourage the people. **27.** The cave where the vanquished kings had fled was employed as their tomb.

Completion of the Southern Campaign. 10:28-43. **28-40.** With Joshua and Israel in right relationship to the LORD, nothing arrested their victorious progress. Makkedah, Libnah, Lachish, Gezer, Eglon, Hebron, and Debir were their victorious stages. Joshua's strategy seems to have been campaigns of destruction and extermination, not of occupation by immediate settlement. **41.** The limits of the conquest (cf. 11:13; 13:2-13; 15:63) are defined **from Kadesh-barnea . . . unto Gaza, and all the country of Goshen, even unto Gibeon. 42.** Those great victories, in which **the Lord God of Israel fought for Israel**, were possible because Joshua and the warriors went forth to those wars "from Gilgal" (v. 9), the place of circumcision (5:2-11), symbolizing the cutting off of the flesh and the renunciation of all self-confidence in favor of complete trust in the LORD. **43.** They also returned to Gilgal, the same place of self-renunciation before the LORD from which they had

gone forth to possess their possessions.

K. CONQUEST OF NORTHERN CANAAN. 11:1-23.

The Northern Coalition Against Israel. 11:1-5. **1-3.** Israel's success in the invasion of southern Canaan led to the formation of a huge confederacy in the north to prevent a takeover of the entire country. It was spearheaded by Jabin, king of Hazor (Tell el Qedah), a 170-acre mound five miles southwest of Huleh, the largest and strongest fortress of the region (c. 1400 B.C.). But the call to muster their military forces was not confined to Jabin's nearest neighbors. It included kings of the northern hill country, the Arabah south of Chinneroth, an area northwest of the lake of Galilee, and the defeated armies of the south.

4. The strength of the coalition was formidable numberwise (cf. Judg. 7:12; 1 Sam. 13:5), and more so since it had **horses and chariots very many. 5.** The huge army encamped **at the waters of Merom**, lying between Lake Huleh and Lake Tiberias, **to fight against Israel.** Thus, the stage was set for the decisive battle by which the whole land was laid open to Israelite occupation.

Possessing the land of Canaan, the main subject of the book of Joshua, prefigurative of the believer's *experiencing* his position and possessions in the risen Christ (Eph. 1:3; Col. 3:1-4), calls forth intense conflict and the enemy's determined and fierce resistance. So the believer who would possess *all* of His inheritance in the risen Christ faces formidable spiritual opposition (Eph. 6:10-12).

The foe seeks to overwhelm God's people by numbers. It is now the open and avowed enmity of the world against the people of God. No longer is it a question of artifices; it is open assault. That is what God's people must face whenever, in a humble spirit of obedient dependence to the Word, they have baffled Satan in his wiles. It is then he stirs up the world to fight against them.

Defeat of the Northern Confederacy. 11:6-15. **6.** Victory was assured because Joshua and his army were in fellowship with God and trusting in Him. Israel was directed to burn the chariots and hamstring the horses so they would continue to trust in the LORD rather than in man (cf. Deut. 20:1; Josh. 10:8; 2 Sam. 8:4; Psalm 20:7). **7-8.** Swift and unquestioned obedience brought a miraculous victory. In a sudden attack the enemy was taken by surprise, routed, and pursued to **great Sidon**, the larger mainland town opposite the islet city of Little Sidon, on the Mediterranean Coast about twenty-two miles north of Tyre. **Miśrephoth-maim** (Khirbet el-Mushrefeh) is located just south of "the ladder of Tyre," a promontory still farther north on the coast from Sidon. The enemy was pursued eastward and northeast to **the valley of Mizpeh** at the western foot of Mount Hermon (cf. vv. 3, 17; Judg. 3:3). Joshua and his forces **smote** the enemy **until they left them none remaining**. Sweeping victory was Joshua's because the Word had taken its rightful place in his heart and the hearts of the people, as in chapter 10.

9-12. Joshua did to the enemy **as the Lord bade him.** He **utterly destroyed them, as Moses … commanded** (cf. v. 15). Notice how the Word of God instructs believers to judge every natural source of strength, a truth that appears in Joshua's obedience in hamstringing the horses, burning the enemy's chariots, and burning Hazor (vv. 11, 13). The enemy's capital could not be turned into a center for Israel. The principles of the world and its governing power must be a judged thing for all God's people, things in which they must have no part.

13. The other towns were not burned **in their strength** (*'ăl tĭllăm*), on their *tells* or mounds. They were allowed to exist, and Israel took spoil from them, affirming their God-given right to take full possession of the land of Canaan. **14. Every man they smote with the edge of the sword.** Looked at in its spiritual application, faithfulness will lead the believer to deal unsparingly with all that is of man. It can have no part in conflict that results in victory in possessing the blessings God has for His own.

Summary of the Conquest. 11:16-20. **16-18.** Joshua **made war a long time** to conquer the land completely. Possessing our spiritual possessions in an experiential sense (Rom. 6:11) is a matter of continuing faith in what we are in Christ and what He has done for us and stirs up enemy opposition (Eph. 6:10-20). But faith is the victory that overcomes the enemy.

Cutting off the Anakim. 11:21-23. **21-22.** After defeating all their enemies, Israel found in their pathway the Anakim, who had struck terror to their hearts and caused them to fall in the wilderness (Num. 13:33). But now with the Word of God ascendant and their trust in the flesh abandoned, what impression could giants make? **Joshua … cut off the Anakim … and … destroyed them utterly with their cities** (cf. Deut. 9:1, 3). How small and petty are former fears when God is relied upon! What are giants before "the most high God, possessor of heaven and earth" (Gen. 14:22), "the Lord of all the earth" (Josh. 3:11, 13; cf. Rom. 16:20)? **23. And the land rested from war.** Peace follows victory. God not only gives His people victory, but He causes them to experience the fruits of it in enjoyment of peace in the inheritance.

L. LIST OF THE CONQUERED KINGS. 12:1-24.

Conquered Kings East of the Jordan. 12:1-6. **1-6.** The territories of Sihon and Og, conquered under Moses, are reviewed (see Num. 21:1-35; Deut. 2:24—3:17). This list of conquered kings summarizes the main truth enunciated in the book, presenting divine grace through Joshua (prefiguring Christ in the power of the Spirit) obtaining possession for God's people of promised blessings in the land.

Conquered Kings West of the Jordan. 12:7-24. With the goal attained, the enumeration of victories is in order. Thirty-one kings are listed. They were autonomous princes of city-states. The Amarna Letters reveal numerous such city-states in Syria-Palestine during the general period (1400-1375 B.C.). **14. Hormah** evidently was originally Zephath (Judg. 1:17) in the territory of Judah (Josh. 15:30; Num. 14:45). **Arad** is located about twenty miles south of Hebron (Num. 21:1). **16. Bethel** is earlier Luz (Gen. 28:19), ten miles north of Jerusalem. **21. Taanach** and **Megiddo** are located in the area of the Plain of Esdraelon. **23. Goiim** in Gilgal is to be read "Goyim of Galil" (Galilee). **24. Tirzah** is most likely Tel el-Farah, a half dozen miles northeast of Shechem.

II. THE LAND DIVIDED. 13:1—22:34.

A. ASSIGNMENT OF THE EASTERN TRIBES. 13:1-33.

The Divine Command to Apportion the Land. 13:1-7. **1.** Joshua's aging constituted a special reason for entering on the immediate discharge of his duty to allocate the inheritance. He was 110 years old the year he died (24:29), so he must have been more than 90 years old at this time. **3.** This verse, from ar-

chaeological and historical evidence, seems to be an editorial note to explain that in Joshua's day the territory that later came under Philistine control belonged to the Canaanites. The **Shihor** is the Wadi el-Arish on the borders of Egypt.

The Portion of the Transjordanic Tribes. 13:8-33. In apportioning the land, the Holy Spirit took minute care to define the place and the limits of each tribe, so that each might see and realize his exact lot in the inheritance. That is illustrative of the place each believer is appointed in the Body of Christ (1 Cor. 12:18-31; Eph. 4:11-16). Reuben, Gad, and the half tribe of Manasseh, having already received their portion in Transjordan, then had their precise boundaries fixed. Reuben was placed in the south, Gad in the center, and Manasseh in the north (cf. Num. 32; Deut. 3:12-17). **14. Only unto the tribe of Levi . . .** Joshua **gave no inheritance** (cf. v. 33; Num. 18:20). Their inheritance on one hand was "the LORD God of Israel," and on the other, "the sacrifices of the LORD God of Israel made by fire."

Similarly, God's people today, seen in union with Christ in death and resurrection, have their portion in Him and all that springs from His glorious divine-human person as He endured God's wrath as our sin-bearer and Substitute on the cross. Moses had left instructions for the allocating of cities to the Levites (cf. Num. 18:20-24; 35:1-8; cf. Heb. 13:14), but they were to have no tribal area. The appointment of their cities is dealt with in chapter 21.

B. CALEB RECEIVES HEBRON. 14:1-15.

Method of Allocating the Land. 14:1-5. **2.** The land was allocated **by lot** (see Num. 26:55; 33:54; 34:13; cf. Psalm 16:5-6). **3.** The account of the

300

separate land given to the tribes of Reuben, Gad, and the half tribe of Manasseh is repeated.

Caleb Claims His Inheritance. 14:6-15. **6.** The claim of Caleb to the highland region of Hebron was founded on a solemn promise of the LORD and Moses forty-five years previously (Num. 14:24; Deut. 1:36). To claim what was rightly his, Caleb took some of his brothers with him as witnesses to the equity and propriety of his conduct. **8.** Caleb is an outstanding man of faith, manifested in the fact that he **wholly followed the Lord.** He illustrates how faith reaps its reward in the area of its severest testing.

12. Now, therefore, give me this mountain. It was faith that had so signally honored God (Num. 13:30), when the spies who had searched out the land so signally dishonored Him (13:31-33), that now became vocal and came forward steadfastly and firmly to claim its inheritance. The great and fortified cities and the giants at Hebron had terrified unbelief but challenged Caleb's faith. Now that same faith perseveringly claimed its object and never forgot the grapes at the Brook Eshcol (Num. 13:22-25).

In conquering Hebron, Caleb rendered God's people a valuable service. His faith continued to manifest its vitality when he yielded his city to the Levites and lived in the suburbs (Josh. 21:12). He is called the son of Jephunneh, the Kenizzite (vv. 6, 15), because his father of Kenizzite extraction had married a daughter of Hur of Judah (1 Chron. 2:9, 18, 19, 50). **13.** Joshua **gave unto Caleb ... Hebron for an inheritance.** That bestowal superseded the lot, for Joshua recognized the justice of Caleb's claim and granted it with his blessing.

Six salient characteristics signalize Caleb as a victorious believer: (1) Caleb's name was connected closely with that of Joshua (Num. 14:30, 38; 26:65; 34:17-19; Deut. 1:36, 38; Josh. 14:13), which illustrates the inseparable union of the victorious believer with the greater Joshua, risen from the dead, manifesting His resurrection power through the outpoured Spirit. (2) A special object (Num. 13:23-25) had so won his affections and possessed his heart that he never forgot it along his desert pathway (cf. Phil. 3:10-14).

(3) His faith enabled him to realize his hope in possessing his inheritance (Josh. 14:13-14). (4) His purpose of heart to wholly follow the LORD (emphasized by repetition, vv. 9, 14) crowned his perseverance with ultimate success and reproduced the same spirit or purpose of heart in his family circle (15:16; Judg. 1:12-13). (6) He realized divine strength and blessing as he mistrusted self and trusted in the LORD (Josh. 14:10).

C. JUDAH'S INHERITANCE. 15:1-63.

The Boundary of Judah. 15:1-12. The southern border began from the shallow bay of the Dead Sea below the el-Lisan Peninsula, along Wadi Fiqreh to the Ascent of Akrabbim (Scorpions) to the wilderness of Zin, south of Kadesh-barnea, there curving northwestward to Wadi el-Arish and the Great Sea (the Mediterranean). Portions of Judah were later designated as the possession of Simeon (19:1). Judah's inheritance was the largest in Canaan, with only the half tribe of Manasseh east of the Jordan being allotted a larger territory.

Caleb's Possession. 15:13-19. **13.** Compare chapter 14. Hebron was earlier named Kiriath-arba ("tetrapolis"; Gen. 23:2), and **the city of Arba** ("city of the four"). **14.** As a victorious believer who "wholly followed the LORD" (14:9, 14; cf. Num. 13:28-33), **Caleb drove out**

301

from Hebron the **three sons of Anak** (Num. 13:22; Judg. 1:10, 20). Saints who are wholly committed to God conquer every obstacle to possession of their inheritance and lay hold of the choicest blessings of their exalted position in Christ. Hebron produced the huge bunch of grapes (Num. 13:22-23) and was the most elevated town of the promised land, located 3,040 feet above sea level. It was a sacred place, sanctified by the faith of Abraham, and it was where he, Sarah, Isaac, Rebekah, Jacob, and Leah were buried (Gen. 49:30-31; 50:13).

16. Caleb, the overcomer, challenged others to overcome and to reap the rewards of overcoming. **He that smiteth Kiriath-sepher** ("book-town," LXX, or "scribe town") **... to him will I give Achsah, my daughter, in marriage**, a common Oriental custom (cf. 1 Sam. 17:25). **17.** Othniel, **the son of ... the brother** (perhaps the nephew) **of Caleb**, answered the challenge and won the reward (cf. Judg. 1:12-13).

18-19. Achsah, Caleb's daughter, exemplified another side of overcoming faith, when Caleb inquired, **What wouldest thou?** Her reply was **Give me a blessing** (*berākâ*, "a benediction, benefit, favor"); **for thou hast given me the Negev** ("south land," i.e., "the dry land," the southern part of Palestine, which is naturally arid). **Give me also springs of water.** Faith asked that which sustains life and received not only **the upper** but also **the lower springs** as well. Overcomers and the offspring of overcomers receive the choicest benefits from God (cf. Rev. 2:7, 11, 17, 26-28; 3:5, 12, 21).

Cities of Judah. 15:20-63. **20-62.** The cities of Judah are listed by twelve districts in four geographical areas: (1) the cities of the Negev (Negeb, vv. 20-32); (2) the cities of the Shephelah (vv.

33-47); (3) the cities of the hill country (vv. 48-60); and (4) the cities of the wilderness (vv. 61-62). The Spirit of God lists these almost 150 names to stress that the Lord distributed the inheritance to His people and placed them in it as it pleased Him (cf. 1 Cor. 12:11-26).

63. Failure of the tribe of Judah to dispossess the Jebusites from Jebus (Jerusalem) is noted (cf. Judg. 1:8; 2 Sam. 5:5-10). The enemies were all conquered, but not all were driven out. God's people allowed to remain among them those who would continually cause them to fail. If the enemy is not destroyed, he will destroy God's people by corrupting them (cf. Josh. 13:13; 16:10; 17:12; Judg. 1:17-36).

D. EPHRAIM'S INHERITANCE. 16:1-10.

The Portion of Ephraim. 16:1-10. **1-10.** The territory of the tribes of Joseph was drawn as one allotment. Afterward it was divided between Ephraim (southern part) and the half tribe of Manasseh (northern part). Ephraim's boundaries are outlined first, although that tribe was smaller (Num. 26:34, 37), because the birthright had been accorded to Ephraim (Gen. 48:9-20).

Ephraim's southern border (vv. 1-4) extended from the Jordan, past Naarah (v. 7) at the springs just north of Jericho ('Ain Duq and 'Ain Nu'eimeh) into the hill country south of Bethel (Luz, v. 2) to Beth-horon the lower (v. 3; cf. 10:10-11) down the Valley of Ajalon past Gezer to the Yarkon River and the Mediterranean south of Jaffa (Joppa). The boundary continued northward to Michmethath (v. 6, probably Tell Arshuf six and a half miles north of the Yarkon). The northern border continued southeastward from Shechem to Taanath-Shiloh (six miles east-southeast of Shechem) to the Jordan Valley.

Failure to drive out the inhabitants of Gezer is noted (cf. notes on 15:63). The method of defining the boundaries of the Israelite tribes in Canaan is paralleled at that same period in history by the treaty between the Hittite king, Suppiluliuma, and the vassal ruler, Niqmadu of Ugarit on the Syrian coast (Claude Schaeffer, *Le Palais Royal d'Ugarit*, 4:10-18).

E. MANASSEH'S INHERITANCE. 17:1-18.

The Portion of Manasseh. 17:1-6. **1-2.** Notice is given of Manasseh's inheritance in Canaan, besides the portion of the tribe in Transjordan (i.e., Gilead and Bashan; cf. Num. 32:33-40; Josh. 13:29-33). The Samaritan ostraca, dated about 770 B.C., containing records of tax payments and discovered in the palace of Jeroboam II, attest the clan divisions of Manasseh's territory. Those records include the names of Abiezer (as a district, cf. Judg. 6:34; 8:2), Helek, Shechem, Shemida, Noah, and Hoglah (see Num. 26:28-34; 27:1-11; 36:1-13). **3-6.** The son of Hepher, Zelophehad, had no sons (Num. 27:1-11). His five daughters are enumerated again. They exemplified the courage of faith and laid claim to the inheritance the LORD had given them.

Manasseh's Borders. 17:7-13. **7-10.** Manasseh's northern border (shared with Asher and Issachar) was defined less precisely because Manasseh, as a stronger tribe, was allotted the resisting Canaanite fortresses, so that the interest of the more powerful tribes would be served by completing the conquest of the territory assigned to the weaker tribes. **11-13.** Stress is laid on certain city-states from which the inhabitants were not driven out. Megiddo, for example, did not fall to Israel until after 1150 B.C., as excavations reveal. In every age the lack of faith and courage has hindered God's people from possessing the inheritance that belongs to them through divine grace.

Manasseh's Complaint. 17:14-18. **14.** Selfishly, people of Manasseh made a demand for more land. **15.** Joshua's reply, demonstrating tact and firmness, challenged their own proud assessment of themselves (cf. 1:3). **16-18.** But Joshua's challenge only served to bring out their unbelief. They saw only the **chariots of iron**, not the lush pasture and farmlands of the Valley of Jezreel, which was theirs by promise and which Joshua urged them to take. What a contrast was their lack of faith to the bold, intrepid spirit of Caleb (Num. 13:30; Josh. 14:6-15).

F. BENJAMIN'S INHERITANCE. 18:1-28.

The Site of the Central Sanctuary Chosen. 18:1-10. **1-7.** The tabernacle was set up at Shiloh (Seilun, ten miles north-northeast of Bethel and eleven miles south of Shechem). The site was an abandoned Middle Bronze Age town, selected for its central location. It was named **Shiloh** ("peace, security"), after the Messianic usage of that title (Gen. 49:10), since the ark symbolizing God's presence was to remain there, and to commemorate the subjugation of the land. **And the land was subdued before them. 8-10.** Shiloh was to become the center of Israel's loose tribal confederation (amphictyony), from which the official operations then proceeded (cf. 19:51; 21:2; 22:9, 12). From that central point Joshua sent out a reconnaissance expedition **to describe the land ... into seven portions** (parts) for the purpose of assigning them to the remaining tribes. The Levites were to have no portion (see Num. 18:20; Deut. 10:8-9; 12:12; 14:27-29; Josh. 13:14; 14:3).

The Territory of Benjamin. 18:11-28. The whole remaining territory was divided into seven parts by the casting of lots at Shiloh. Benjamin's portion was allotted between that of Judah and Ephraim (cf. Deut. 33:12), the latter serving as a link between the two most powerful and naturally rival tribal groups.

G. INHERITANCE OF THE REST OF THE TRIBES. 19:1-51.

Simeon's Territory. 19:1-9. Simeon's allotment was taken out of the possession of Judah, which had proved too large for Judah. The tribe was ultimately absorbed into Judah, in fulfillment of the curse pronounced by Jacob on Simeon and Levi (Gen. 49:7).

Zebulun's Territory. 19:10-16. The territory of Zebulun consisted of a landlocked district in lower Galilee bordered by Asher on the west, Manasseh on the south, Issachar on the southeast, and Naphtali on the north and northeast. Zebulun was traversed by "the way of the sea" (Isa. 9:1), a widely traveled route to the Mediterranean coast.

Issachar's Territory. 19:17-23. The tribal inheritance for Issachar reached from Mount Tabor on the east to the southern tip of the Sea of Galilee and embraced the fertile plain of Jezreel.

Asher's Territory. 19:24-31. From just south of the coastal city of Dor, Asher embraced the Mediterranean seacoast north to Tyre and theoretically to Sidon and extended inland ten to fifteen miles. Asher's location there is corroborated by Egyptian inscriptions from the reigns of Seti I and Ramses II (c. 1310-1250 B.C.).

Naphtali's Territory. 19:32-39. Occupying the hinterland east of the coastal tribe of Asher, Naphtali extended to Dan and the sources of the Jordan River on the north and to the southeastern extremity of the Sea of Galilee to the borders of Issachar and Zebulun on the south.

Dan's Territory. 19:40-48. Dan was originally located on the seacoast at Japho (Joppa) between Judah and Ephraim. That area was too small for them (v. 47), so the majority of the tribe migrated later to the far north and settled in Leshem (Laish), north of the territory of Naphtali, a full account being given in Judges 18.

Joshua's Inheritance. 19:49-51. After all the land had been apportioned, Joshua selected his own inheritance in Timnath-serah (Khirbet Tibneh, eleven miles west-southwest of Shiloh in the mountainous district of his tribe). As Joshua, prefiguring the greater Joshua, received an inheritance from his people, so Christ has received an inheritance in His own (Eph. 1:18). His own also have an inheritance in Him, as Israel had in their great leader in the conquest and apportionment of Canaan (1:11).

H. CITIES OF REFUGE PROVIDED. 20:1-9.

The Ordinance Reviewed. 20:1-6. The main points of the Mosaic regulations are enumerated (see Num. 35:9-14 and Deut. 19:1-10 for the value of the cities of refuge in illustrating redemptive history). Moses had set apart three cities east of the Jordan (Deut. 4:41-43). Later he directed three more to be provided when Israel took possession of the land. He made provision for a third group of three, if they should ever prove necessary, which they never did (Deut. 19:1-10).

The Cities Designated. 20:7-9. The six cities were then set apart and specified, three on each side of the Jordan River, and located strategically in the north, in the center, and in the south. Kedesh was in northern Galilee, Shechem in the heart of the land, and Kiriath-arba (Hebron) in the south of Judah. In Transjordan, Golan was in

Bashan in the north, Ramath in Gilead in the territory of Gad was in the center, and Bezer (unknown) was in the south in the territory of Reuben, probably east or northeast of the Dead Sea.

I. LEVITICAL TOWNS ALLOTTED. 21:1-45.

The Allotment of Levi. 21:1-8. After all the tribes had received their inheritance, the Levites, as representatives of Israel's faith and ministers of its worship, claimed the cities promised them by Moses (see Num. 35:1-8). To fulfill their calling it was essential that they maintain their distinctive position and be scattered throughout the nation. To realize those objectives they were allotted forty-eight cities out of all the tribes, together with pasturelands around each one of them (see Num. 18:23-24; Deut. 12:12; cf. Lev. 25:32-34). Possibly the pastureland, as distinct from farmland, was meant "to be a reminder of the simple life which Israel had lived in the wilderness, and a constant recall to the simple religion [faith] with which that life was linked" (Hugh Blair, "Joshua," NBC, p. 249).

The Cities Assigned. 21:9-42. These cities were assigned in anticipation of complete subjugation of the land (cf. Gezer, v. 21, which did not come under Israelite control till Solomon's reign). For Taanach (v. 25) and Nahalal (v. 35), see Judges 1:27-30. It appears that God's intention was that the conquest be completed rapidly (cf. Josh. 9:24-27). But Israel's terrible apostasy during the long period of the Judges forfeited God's perfect will.

Summary of the Conquest and Apportionment. 21:43-45. **43-44.** God's promise made to the fathers was fulfilled (cf. Gen. 12:7; 26:3-4; 28:4-13; Num. 33:53; Josh. 1:11). **The Lord gave them rest**, for the land as a whole had been subdued. Although the Canaanites had not been exterminated or wholly driven out, nevertheless they were humbled and rendered so powerless that they could not hope to dispossess the tribes of Israel of their inheritance. **45. There failed nothing of any good thing which the Lord had spoken unto the house of Israel** (Num. 23:19; Josh. 23:14; 1 Kings 8:56; cf. 1 Cor. 1:9; 1 Thess. 5:24; Titus 1:2). God never fails His own.

J. THE EASTERN TRIBES SENT HOME AND AN ALTAR ERECTED. 22:1-34.

Return of the Transjordanic Tribes. 22:1-9. **1-3.** Joshua called and commended the Transjordanic tribes for their obedience to God's commands as mediated by Moses and him (cf. Num. 32:20-22; Josh. 1:12-18). **4-5.** He then instructed them to return home, earnestly exhorting them to cleave faithfully to the LORD and His commandments (cf. Deut. 10:12; 11:13, 22). **6-9.** So Joshua blessed them and **sent them away** with much wealth in spoil taken in the battles for Canaan.

The Altar Erected at the Jordan. 22:10-12. **10-11.** Apparently the altar, a large structure (Heb., "an altar great to the sight"), was erected west of the Jordan in the land of Canaan **at the frontier of the land of Canaan, . . . on the side belonging to the children of Israel.** If it was thus erected west of the river, rather than in the territory of the Transjordanic tribes, it was meant to be a *witness* to the western tribes that the two and one-half tribes east of the Jordan regarded themselves as an integral part of the nation, with the right to worship at the central shrine at Shiloh.

12. But the rest of Israel, hearing of the edifice, interpreted it to be a token of a separate if not idolatrous worship by Reuben, Gad, and the half tribe of Manasseh, which would have been in violation of the law of the one central sanctuary (Exod. 20:24; Lev. 17:8-9; Deut. 12:5-14), and they were ready to go to war about it.

A Deputation Sent. 22:13-20. **13-15.** The western tribes exhibited great zeal for the LORD and His Word. But at the same time they displayed wisdom and restraint, sending Phinehas, distinguished for his loyalty to the LORD, and ten princes to investigate the supposed apostasy. **16.** It was made clear that the delegates did not come as separate individuals but in the name of **the whole congregation of the Lord.** Their query was **What trespass is this ... ?** To erect an altar for idolatrous worship would constitute an act of rebellion against the LORD that would be punishable by death (Deut. 13:13-15). To erect an altar as a rival to that at Shiloh would violate the unity of Israel's worship (Lev. 17:7-9).

17-20. Would the sin at Peor and the trespass of Achan at Ai be repeated, incurring divine wrath against the people of the LORD as one body (Num. 25:1-15; Josh. 7)? **If the land of your possession be unclean,** that is, if they regarded it as polluted because it was separated by the Jordan from the other tribes where the tabernacle was located, **then pass ye over,** that is, cross over to Canaan and inherit with us. It was a generous invitation, for it would reduce their own inheritance.

An Explanation Made. 22:21-34. **24-27.** Astonished, the eastern tribes solemnly denied any thought of rebellion or disunity. **28-29.** Rather, their purpose was just the opposite: to cement their unity and their right to worship at the central shrine of Israel. **33.** Pleased, Phinehas and the delegation returned and reported to the congregation of Israel, who **blessed God** and abandoned any thought of going to war.

34. The altar was called **Ed** (*'ēḏ*), "a witness" to the real unity of the LORD's people (cf. 1 Cor. 12:12-26; Eph. 4:1-6). How desperately the LORD's people who are one in their position before God (John 17:20-21) need to exemplify that unity before men in a genuine testimony of its power—not a man-made monument, but the outshining of genuine faith in God's Word exemplifying spiritual vitality from within the heart.

III. JOSHUA'S FAREWELL ADDRESSES. 23:1—24:33.

A. JOSHUA'S FIRST ADDRESS. 23:1-16.

What God Had Done, and What Israel Had to Do. 23:1-16. **1-16.** If Joshua's address was made in the last year of his life, he was 110 years old (24:29) and had been residing in his home at Timnath-serah (19:50). Verse 2 is best translated "Joshua called together all Israel; namely, their elders and heads, their judges and officers." In his address the aged leader outlined (1) what God had done (vv. 3, 4, 9, 14), that is, what they themselves had seen Him do—He fought for them, gave them an inheritance, drove out their foes, enabled them to be victorious against overwhelming odds, and proved Himself utterly faithful to His promises; and (2) what God would do (vv. 5, 12-13, 15-16). His continued help was promised and assured, but it was contingent on Israel's fidelity to the covenant. Breaking the covenant and turning to apostasy would change the good they had received into terrible evil (cf. Lev. 26:14-39; Deut. 4:24-28; 28:15-68). The responsibility of Israel was fourfold: (1) She had to be obedient to God's Word (v. 6). (2) She had to separate herself from the idolatrous Canaanites and not intermarry (vv. 7, 11-12). (3) She had to be loyal to the LORD (v. 8). (4) She had to **love the Lord** (v. 11).

B. Joshua's Last Message and Covenant Renewal. 24:1-33.

Preamble to the Covenant Renewal. 24:1-2a. **Thus saith the Lord God of Israel.** These words identify the Author of the covenant in His relationship to His vassal people, illustrating a standard form of covenant known in contemporary treaties of the Hittite Empire with its vassal states from 1450 to 1200 B.C. (see G. Mendenhall, *Law and Covenant in Israel and the Ancient Near East*, pp. 24-44).

Historical Prologue. 24:2b-13. **2b-13.** In this section it is the LORD speaking, not Joshua, outlining His theocratic dealings with His covenant people from the call of Abraham to the conquest of Canaan. In the Hittite vassal treaties the king carefully described the benevolent deeds the sovereign has performed for the benefit of the vassal. The LORD, in reviewing His past beneficence to His people, proceeded from Abraham's call (vv. 2-4), to the deliverance from Egypt (vv. 5-7), the defeat of the Amorites (v. 8), the frustration of Baalam's wicked purposes (vv. 9-10), the crossing of the Jordan and the destruction of Jericho (v. 11), and the defeat of the Canaanite coalitions (vv. 12-13). Thus, the history of the LORD's interposition on behalf of His people was brought up to date. **12. The hornet** is doubtless a reference to a literal scourge of the insect (cf. Deut. 7:20-23), or conceivably "a figurative expression for the panic-producing power of God" (J. Rea, "Joshua," WBC, p. 230).

Treaty Stipulations. 24:14-24. Israel's prime obligation under the treaty was to renounce all foreign relations with other gods (vv. 14, 15, 23). Likewise, in contemporary Hittite suzerainty treaties the first stipulation was prohibition of foreign alliances outside the Hittite Empire. Since the scene at Shechem was a renewal of the Mosaic Covenant, rather than the execution of a new covenant, a complete text of the formal covenant renewal was omitted for the sake of brevity, and no other stipulations needed to be listed.

Depositing the Covenant. 24:25-28. **25-26.** The covenant renewed by Joshua was recorded by him **in the book of the law of God** (cf. 1 Sam. 10:25), which was deposited "in the side of ['beside,' NASB] the ark of the covenant" (Deut. 31:24-27). Likewise, among the Hittites the treaty was viewed as being under the protection of their deity and was deposited as a sacred thing in the sanctuary of the vassal state. Moreover, Joshua inscribed the stipulations of the covenant renewal on a large stele set up beneath the terebinth tree, a place sacred to the LORD near Shechem (Gen. 12:6; 35:4).

Death of Joshua. 24:29-33. **29-31.** Joshua died at 110 years of age and was buried in his inheritance by the people. Moses died at 120 years of age and was buried by the LORD (Deut. 34:5-7), doubtless a hint that someday the LORD would put away death, the curse of the broken Law (cf. Gal. 3:13). Joshua reached the same age as Joseph some 400 years before. **32.** The burial of Joseph's bones (cf. Gen. 50:25-26; Exod. 13:19; Heb. 11:22) may have taken place long before Joshua's decease. The Holy Spirit records the burial here to accentuate the central theme of the book of Joshua, namely, the faithfulness of God to His promises.

33. The death of **Eleazar**, the son and successor of Aaron, is recorded along with the death of Joshua, to mark the close of an era. The deaths of these two figures, who foretold and manifested the grace of God that eventually would be revealed in the world's Redeemer, were a warning to the people that divine grace was their only resource. But the people would not have it so (vv. 16-26), and a great stone, an image of the Law, was set up in testimony of judgment against them (vv. 26-28). This judgment will remain until the day when they will once more become an object of God's grace and faithfulness, as shown in the book of Joshua, and be restored to the land and restored to fellowship with the LORD in Kingdom blessing.

JUDGES

Title. The book of Judges receives its name from the divinely called and empowered leaders (*shōpᵉṭîm*) who delivered Israel from a series of foreign oppressors during the time between the death of Joshua (c. 1370 B.C.) and the beginnings of the monarchy (c. 1020 B.C.), a period of approximately three and one-half centuries. The term *shōpēṭ* has a wider connotation than the English *judge*, exercising authority under God first in military matters in the conquest of enemies, and afterward, in civil matters rendering legal decision when occasion arose (4:4-5). In Canaanite literature from Ugarit the term *judge* is employed in parallel relation to *king* (Baal 5., 5. 32). However, in the premonarchic period in Israel, when a definite antipathy existed toward the kingship (cf. Judg. 9:8-15), a distinction had to be made. God Himself was regarded as Israel's King (1 Sam. 8:7), and the *šōpēṭ* did not have that connotation, the sin of the people often reducing the ideal of a theocracy with its "judges" to the state of anarchy (21:25). In fact, the God of Israel is called "the Judge" (*hăshshōpēṭ*, 11:27).

Date and Authorship. The book itself is anonymous, like others of the Old Testament historical books. Critics commonly view the bulk of the work as consisting of old hero tales taken from two ancient independent sources (J and E). Those were supposedly combined in the seventh century by a redactor. In the sixth century a Deuteronomist (a zealot of the book of Deuteronomy who allegedly first published them) imposed upon the whole a pragmatic religious interpretation. Other minor redactions, it is claimed, were made until the book reached its present form (c. 200 B.C.). Internal evidence and tradition, however, suggest an origin during the early years of the monarchy in the time of Saul (c. 1020 B.C.) or in the early reign of David, before the conquest of Jebus (Jerusalem, cf. 1:21) in the seventh year of his reign (cf. 2 Sam. 5:6-8). The expression "in those days there was no king in Israel, but every man did that which was right in his own eyes" (17:6; 18:1; 19:1; 21:25) points to the same conclusion. Hebrew tradition makes Samuel the author, and that may well be the case (Baba Bathra 14*b*). The spirit of the book of Deuteronomy does pervade the book, but that is not a late superimposition; rather, it is the result of the existence of the book as a genuine product of the Mosaic age.

Chronology of the Period. The book has chronological problems that are to be solved on the supposition of the synchronous rule of the judges. On that basis their combined rule (if sequential, it totals 410 years) can easily be restricted to 300 to 350 years. According to 1 Kings 6:1, the fourth year of Solomon's reign was 480 years after the Exodus from Egypt. Allowing 40 years in the wilderness, 25 years for Joshua in Palestine, 40 years for Eli, 40 years for both Samuel and Saul, 40 years for David (2 Sam. 5:4), and 4 years for Solomon, a total of 189 years is the result;

subtracting that from the 480 years from the Exodus to Solomon's fourth year, leaves only 291 years for the judges. That this is the result of the simultaneous rule of some of the judges is indicated by 11:26, which places the entrance into Canaan to Jephthah's second year (cf. 10:8; 11:4, 9) as 300 years. Adding approximately 144 years from Jephthah to Solomon's fourth year (5 years for the rest of Jephthah's reign, 40 years for Samson, Samuel 20 years, Saul about 15, David 40, Solomon 4), a total of 482 years is reached, which closely approximates the 480 of 1 Kings 6:1. It is clear that Samson and Jephthah ruled contemporaneously, since one delivered Israel from the Ammonites and the other from the Philistines (cf. Judg. 10:7). This approach to the chronological difficulties of the book is the correct one, and there are not discrepancies due to the welding together of conflicting documents. J. Garstang (*Joshua, Judges*, pp. 51-61) is right in showing that the underlying time scheme of the book tallies with the early date of the Exodus and fits into the frame of contemporary history.

Purpose of the Book. The book continues the history of the LORD's people through the era intervening between Joshua's decease (c. 1370) and the time of Samuel (c. 1070 B.C.), approximately three centuries. Judges demonstrates that although God's people may enter experientially into their promised inheritance (i.e., in the New Testament parallel, by faith to reckon on their position in the risen Christ, Rom. 6:11; Col. 3:1-4), unless they continue to believe in their placement as God's own in separation from sin and sinners, terrible declension and apostasy result, requiring the sternest divine disciplinary dealing. The book is a sober warning of the monotony and misery of sin, as manifested through the believer's old nature. Yet at the same time it is a portrayal of God's grace working in behalf of His erring people to rescue them from their enemies and oppressors and to restore them to fellowship and a place of blessing with Himself.

OUTLINE

COMMENTARY

I. ISRAEL'S SIN AND SERVITUDE. 1:1—2:23.

A. FAILURE TO DRIVE OUT THE CANAANITES. 1:1-36.

Judah's Incomplete Obedience. 1:1-20. **1.** The **death of Joshua** apparently prompted the Canaanites to take advantage of that event to attempt to recover their lost position; so the Israelites were obliged to renew the war. Wisely, they sought God's counsel regarding that important matter. **2-3. The Lord said, Judah shall go up.** The predicted preeminence (Gen. 49:8) is seen conferred upon this tribe by divine direction in being selected for the honor of taking the lead in executing the divine command to possess all the land and utterly drive out the inhabitants.

Judah's victories as a result of faith and obedience were meant to be an example to animate the other tribes to similar action. Yet, despite the LORD's unequivocal promise, **Behold, I have delivered the land** (Judah's portion) **into his hand**, even Judah, after signal victories (vv. 4-20), displayed faulty faith by relying on **Simeon** and failed to drive out "the inhabitants of the valley, because they had chariots of iron" (v. 19; cf. Josh. 17:18). Were the iron chariots too formidable for the LORD?

Judah's victories demonstrate how God's people may prevail to a praiseworthy degree and yet fail to accomplish all of God's purpose by halting short of complete faith and obedience in the face of clear divine direction and promise. But God's grace highlights the victories of faith, at the same time warning of the defeats of unbelief and their eventual dire consequences (the theme of the book of Judges).

Judah's five conquests are recounted: (1) **4-6.** Judah won a victory over Adoni-bezek in Bezek (a Judahite town near Jerusalem, otherwise unidentified). The enemy was **found**, that is, surprised and routed, in a pitched battle. Taken as prisoner, he suffered mutilation in punishment for his cruel mutilation of others. He fully recognized that divine retribution, according to the lex talionis (law of retaliation), "eye for eye . . . hand for hand, foot for foot" (Exod. 21:24; cf. Lev. 24:20; Matt. 5:38-45), had overtaken him.

7. The **three score and ten kings** were petty princelings and political figures who **gathered scraps of food under** [his] **table.** The practice of feeding captives on scraps is paralleled in Ugaritic literature, where the Canaanite god El invites other gods to a banquet. Those who acknowledge him are offered food, but those who do not are regarded as enemies and "gate crashers," who are ordered to be "beaten with a stick [till they sink] under the table" (*Ugaritica*, ser. 5, 1:6-8).

(2) **8.** Judah conquered Jerusalem. Evidently the unfortified southwest hill is meant, rather than the fortified Jebusite stronghold on the southeast hill (see R. Pearce S. Hubbard, *Palestine Exploration Quarterly* 98 [1966]: 136-37). The realm of Jerusalem suffered a breakup in the period after Joshua's death (see Z.

Kallai and H. Tadmor, *Eretz Israel* 9 [1969] : 138-47). "And the city they sent up in flames" presents the picture of holy war, in which the LORD goes before "as a consuming fire" (Deut. 9:3; see P. Miller, *Catholic Biblical Quarterly*, 1964). While Judah was able to sack "Jerusalem," that is, the unfortified southwest hill, the Benjamites, who shared the border with the Jebusite fort on the eastern hill, faced a more formidable opponent. Thus, despite initial successes (1:8), Judah failed to clear out the Jebusites (Josh. 15:63), and Benjamin was no more successful (Judg. 1:21).

(3) Judah conquered Hebron and Debir, the story of which is repeated (see Josh. 15:16-19) to fill out the account of Judah's victories (vv. 10-15). (4) Judah made additional conquests (vv. 16-21). **16. The Kenite** refers to a tribe related to Israel through Moses' marriage to Zipporah (cf. Exod. 2:21; cf. Num. 10:29-32). They came up from **the city of palm trees**, the Jericho oasis (Deut. 34:3; Judg. 3:13), and settled in the region **south of Arad** (Num. 21:1), modern Tell Arad, seventeen miles south of Hebron. **17.** The Kenites' destruction of Zephath, later called Hormah (*hŏrmâ*, "ban-town"), memorializing the ban (*hĕrĕm*) under which the place was put, refers to an earlier event in Mosaic times (cf. Num. 21:1-3).

18. Also Judah took Gaza ... Ashkelon ... and Ekron. Because Judah was unable to hold these towns, they later were occupied by the invading Sea Peoples, the Philistines, early in the twelfth century. **19.** The Canaanites with their **iron chariots** continued to maintain occupation of the lower ground. Israel did not acquire the knowledge of iron smelting, derived from the Hittites and Mitanni, until the time of Saul after 1050 B.C.

Benjamin's Disobedience. 1:21. **21.** The tribe of Benjamin failed to trust the LORD and to obey the clear command to drive out *all* the inhabitants of the land, including the Jebusites, apparently an Amorite group that settled on an earlier Hittite foundation (cf. Josh. 15:63).

Ephraim's Conquest of Bethel. 1:22-26. **22-26. The Lord was with** Ephraim, and their taking of the city by spying and a ruse is reminiscent of the spies at Jericho and Rahab's being spared (cf. Josh. 2:12; 1 Sam. 30:15). Bethel ("house of God") was called Luz in prepatriarchal times (cf. Gen. 28:19).

Manasseh's Disobedience. 1:27-28. **27. Neither did Manasseh drive out the inhabitants of ... Beth-shean ... Taanach ... Dor ... Ibleam ... Megiddo** (cf. Josh. 17:11-12). These were strongly fortified towns guarding access through the Plain of Esdraelon, separating the tribes of Joseph from the northern tribes. Bethshean guarded the approach through Esdraelon from the east and Megiddo from the west and southwest. Dor was on the Mediterranean coast, south of Mount Carmel.

Ephraim's Disobedience. 1:29. **29.** The result of Ephraim's disobedience was that they could not, and did not, drive out the Canaanites from Gezer, guarding the pass from Joppa to Jerusalem, some eighteen miles northwest of Jerusalem. Excavated Gezer reveals stout walls fourteen feet thick. Not until Solomon's reign did it become a part of the Israelite realm (1 Kings 9:16).

Zebulun's Disobedience. 1:30. **30.** Zebulun failed to **drive out the inhabitants of Kitron ... nor ... of Nahalol**, sites not yet positively identified.

Asher's Disobedience. 1:31-32. **31-32.** Asher failed to dispossess the inhabitants of **Acco** (modern Acre, on the Bay of Acre, north of the Carmel Ridge). **Sidon** was the Phoenician city north of

Tyre, famous from Homeric times, and later overshadowed by Tyre. Ahlab is unidentified, but **Achzib** is situated on the coast about ten miles north of Acco. **Helbah**, northeast of Tyre, is Mahalliba of the Assyrian records. Aphik is uncertain. **Rehob** is Tell Berweh, seven miles inland from Acco. Israel never dispossessed the Phoenicians along the northern coast.

Naphtali's Disobedience. 1:33. **33.** Naphtali failed to dispossess **the inhabitants of Beth-shemesh**, "house of the sun," evidently a shrine-center of Canaanite worship of the sun-god and **Beth-anath**, "house of Anath," a center of worship of Anath, Baal's consort and sister to the Canaanite goddess of fertility. The sparing of such centers of polluted religion were to prove a snare to Israel and tell the sad story of the lawlessness of the period of the Judges.

Dan's Disobedience. 1:34-36. **34.** The results of Dan's disobedience appear in the Amorites (i.e., "westerners" from the Akkadian viewpoint, who had invaded parts of Palestine from the east several centuries before Israel's arrival) who **forced the children of Dan into the mountain.** As the territory became too small, the main body of the tribe migrated to Laish, at the headwaters of the Jordan, and renamed that place Dan (Judg. 18). **35-36.** Although the tribe of Joseph did reduce the Amorites to servitude, the presence of these people, with their debauched idolatry, presented a perpetual peril of contamination and spiritual ruin.

B. ISRAEL'S TRAGIC PLIGHT. 2:1-23.

Israel Rebuked for Disobedience. 2:1-10. **1.** The personage who came up **from Gilgal**, the place where the nation was circumcised and dedicated itself to covenant faith and obedience (see Josh. 5:2-12), was not *an* angel of the LORD,

but *măl'ăk yhwh, the* **angel of the Lord**, the preincarnate Word, who was in time to become the incarnate Redeemer and the world's Savior (cf. Gen. 16:7), apparently called "the angel of the covenant" (Mal. 3:1, NASB margin). He is clearly identified with the LORD Himself in His preincarnate self-manifestation to men (cf. Gen. 31:11-13; Exod. 3:2-6). **Bochim** ("weepers") was apparently situated between Bethel and Shiloh. **I made you go up out of Egypt.** The LORD's redemptive mercies should have elicited a grateful response of faith and obedience to the covenant's stipulations.

2. Ye have not obeyed my voice. They failed to keep themselves separate from the idolaters of the land and to destroy their altars (cf. Exod. 23:32; 34:12-13). **3.** As a result of deliberate disobedience, the nation forfeited the divine help that would have enabled them to obey God's command. **4.** The divine rebuke anticipated the sad history of defeat and miserable bondage that characterized the period of the Judges. **The people lifted up their voices and wept**. But their weeping was not true repentance (2 Cor. 7:9-11), for the nation did not really turn away from its disobedient course. **5.** The name of the place **Bochim** ("weepers") became a standing witness against the nation's lack of genuine repentance even in the face of the divine Presence. **6-10.** These verses are inserted here to give the reasons that called forth such a strong rebuke from the angel of the LORD and are a repetition of Joshua 24:29-31.

The Wickedness of the New Generation. 2:11-15. **11-13.** A résumé of the moral and spiritual conditions that prevailed during the period of the judges is given. Failing to obey the prime covenant stipulation of separation from idolaters, the people lapsed into idolatry and served **Baal** (the local varieties of the chief Canaanite fertility deity) **and Ashtaroth** (the local varieties of Ashtoreth, singular form of Ashtoroth or Ashtart, the Greek Astarte, Baal's consort. In peacetime there was a powerful pull toward Baal worship, since it was considered effective in insuring good harvests, Baal personifying the rain and fertility forces of nature. **14.** The LORD had to chasten the people with foreign invasion and war to wean them away from the alluring attractions of Baalism. That cult so weakened and divided the LORD's people that they **could no longer stand before** (withstand) **their enemies**. As a result, they incurred divine displeasure and chastisement (cf. Lev. 26:14-26; Deut. 28:15-68).

The Manifestation of God's Grace. 2:16-19. **16-17. Nevertheless the Lord raised up judges.** In His loving care God never forsook them, although they in their infidelity turned their backs upon Him. **They played the harlot** (in committing spiritual adultery) **with other gods**, breaking their vows of loyalty to the LORD. **18.** The judges were the agents through whom the LORD manifested His unchanging love toward His erring people. **19.** Upon those Israelite tribesmen the LORD laid the burden of Israel's apostate and oppressed condition as He raised them up and manifested His delivering power through them.

The Divine Overruling Wisdom. 2:20-23. **20-21.** Israel greatly provoked the LORD's anger by transgressing His covenant (Josh. 23:16), thereby causing the LORD to resolve not to **drive out any from before them of the nations which Joshua left when he died** (Josh. 23:4, 13). **22-23.** Yet the LORD used the disobedience of the people to **test** (prove) them concerning their fidelity to Him. God knows what is in the heart of man, but He demonstrates that knowledge before

men by testing them in their moral experience (cf. Deut. 8:2).

II. GOD'S GRACE AND DELIVERANCE. 3:1—16:31.

A. DELIVERANCE BY OTHNIEL, EHUD, AND SHAMGAR. 3:1-31.

Deliverance Through Testing. 3:1-7. **1-2.** This general section (2:20—3:7) presents four reasons why the LORD did not drive out the Canaanites completely but allowed them to remain in the land alongside Israel. (1) He was chastening His people for their disloyalty to His covenant (2:3, 20-21). (2) He was testing His people's fidelity to Him (v. 4; cf. 2:22). (3) He was providing His people with experience in warfare (v. 2), illustrating the inescapability and necessity of knowing and successfully waging the spiritual conflict that faces every believer who would possess his possessions in Christ (cf. Eph. 6:10-20; Phil. 1:30; Col. 2:1; 1 Tim. 6:12; 2 Tim. 4:7; Heb. 10:32). (4) He was preventing the land from becoming overrun with wild beasts, a reason presented in Deuteronomy 7:20-24.

3. Of the enemies left were the **five lords of the Philistines**, who about 1190 B.C. invaded Palestine from Caphtor (Crete; cf. Amos 9:7). They appear on the monuments wearing feathercrowned helmets, typically Carian (cf. 2 Sam. 20:23, ASV margin, where they are called "Carites" [$k\bar{a}r\hat{i}m$], inhabitants from Caria in Asia Minor). Their other name, "Cherethites" (1 Sam. 30:14; 2 Sam. 8:18), connects them with Crete in their southward migration to southwestern Palestine.

All the Canaanites are included in the list of enemies in Judges 1:27-33. **The Sidonians** were Phoenicians on the coast, so called because in that early period their chief town was Sidon (cf.

1:31). The **Hivites** were likely a branch of the Horites (Hurrians), now a well-known ethnic group, who established the kingdom of Mitanni in Upper Mesopotamia around 1500 B.C. and in the following several centuries spread into Canaan, which at one time was called Huru-land by the Egyptians. **Mount Baal-hermon** (later Mount Hermon) is the more easterly range parallel to Lebanon. **The entrance of Hamath** ("Labô of Hamath") is identified with present-day Lebweh, fourteen miles northeast of Baalbek (Baal-god, cf. Josh. 13:5).

5-7. Israel soon failed the test. First **they dwelt among the Canaanites**; then they intermixed and intermarried, utterly disregarding the divine command of separation (Exod. 34:15-16; Deut. 7:3-4; Josh. 23:12; cf. 2 Cor. 6:11—7:1); finally, they **served** their gods, the last step in their downward trend, forgetting **the Lord their God** and serving Baalim (Baals) **and the idols** (*'ᵃshērôt*, "Asheroth") the female counterpart to the Baalim. The goddess Asherah was Baal's consort, as in the Ugaritic literature. That debauched religion of male and female deities sank to sordid depths of immorality (see Judg. 2:11, 13).

The First Apostasy–Deliverance by Othniel. 3:8-11. This is the first of a number of episodes illustrating Israel's idolatry, its chastisement, and the manifestation of divine love in deliverance during the period from about 1375 to 1075 B.C. The first oppressor, **Cushan-rishathaim**, meaning "doubly wicked Cushan," likely represents an epithet assigned to this tyrant by those he oppressed, or conceivably it may be a Hebraized place name. This invader is represented by the Masoretic text as coming from Aram-naharaim, "Aram of the Two Rivers," that is, Mesopotamia, between the Euphrates and Tigris rivers

(see Gen. 24:10; Deut. 23:4; Psalm 60:1).

Apparently he was an obscure Hittite prince who had a chance to invade Palestine after the Hittites had overrun Mitanni, the northern Mesopotamian state that acted as a buffer between the Hittite and Assyrian kingdoms. However, many scholars read "Edom" for Aram, viewing Naharaim as a later interpolation. If this reading was the original, it would explain the fact that Othniel, the deliverer, came from Judah, which is contiguous to Edom (cf. 1:13-15). **9.** Othniel is called **a deliverer** (*môshĭă'*, "a savior") because God through His Spirit worked through the human instrument to rescue His people from oppression, illustrative of deliverance from the slavery of sin.

The Second Apostasy-Deliverance by Ehud. 3:12-30. **12-13. Eglon, the king of Moab**, was the chastening rod the LORD used to whip His erring people. Moab lay east of the Dead Sea. Eglon and his allies invaded Canaan by the same route the Israelites had used, crossing the Jordan and occupying **the city of palm trees**, evidently indicating a temporary occupation of the oasis at Ain es-Sultan, no doubt near the ruins of the city that fell to Joshua and which remained a ruin until the ninth century (1 Kings 16:34; cf. Judg. 1:16). Eglon, king of Moab, and Ammon and Amalek represent the temptation of the world, the flesh, and the devil, which enslave God's people when they backslide.

15. Under the pretense of bringing tribute, **Ehud, ... a Benjamite, a man lefthanded** (cf. 20:16), portraying the weak human agent God often uses in His deliverances, laid out a careful plan to assassinate the Moabite king. **16.** He provided himself with a sword, with which he planned to kill the oppressor.

The **dagger** was a cubit (eighteen inches) in length and had **two edges**.

17-20. Allaying suspicion by dismissing the large retinue of men required to bear the tribute (paid in cattle and other bulky items, besides silver and gold), the deliverer (savior) himself turned back at **the quarries** (*pᵉsîlîm*, "stone carvings, graven images") **that were by Gilgal**. A message was dispatched to Eglon requesting a private audience: **I have a secret errand unto thee . . . a message from God unto thee** (emphatic by repetition), meaning "I have a divine oracle for your execution." The king stood up out of respect for the oracle, ordering his courtier attendants to retire. **Keep silence** (*hās*, which seems to require "depart, leave"; cf. Amos 6:10; Hab. 2:20). "He said, Depart! And all those attending him went out" (R. Boling, *Judges*, AB, p. 84).

21-22. As Eglon stood up, Ehud reached with his left hand to draw the dagger from his right thigh, and then he plunged it into the king's belly. Even the hilt went in after the blade, and the fat closed over the blade, as the weapon was not withdrawn. **And the dirt** (excrement) **came out. 23.** Ehud made his escape **through the porch** (*mîsdᵉrôn*, "a platform with pillars," E. G. Kraeling, JBL 54 [1935]: 208). Instead of going out the way he came in, Ehud went over the side of the porch, after using Eglon's own key to bolt the door to the roof garden from the inside.

24. When Eglon's attendants went in, they found the doors locked to the roof garden. They said, **"Surely he covereth his feet"** (a euphemism, i.e., "He's no doubt relieving himself in the palace restroom," Boling, AB, p. 85; cf. 1 Sam. 24:3). **25.** They waited **till they were ashamed** (Heb., *bôsh*, in the sense of being "at their wits' end," C. F. Bur-

ney, *The Book of Judges*, p. 74; cf. 2 Kings 2:17; 8:11).

26. Meanwhile, Ehud had escaped **while they tarried** (the Hebrew word suggests consternation and confusion as well as delay). By the time Eglon's attendants had discovered his corpse, Ehud had passed Seirath (unidentified) and reached safety in the highlands of Ephraim. **27.** There **he blew a trumpet** to muster men to battle (cf. 1 Sam. 13:3-4). **28-30.** Amassing an Israelite force that took **the fords of the Jordan**, they cut off any Moabite retreat, slaughtering the finest of the Moabite warriors, thus breaking the Moabite yoke on Israel.

This gory story dramatically sets forth a pivotal spiritual message. The two-edged dagger represents the Word of God (cf. Heb. 4:12), while the hand that grasps it illustrates how faith is to employ the Word. The sword of the Spirit must be plunged into that which is of the world—the lust of the flesh, the lust of the eyes, and the pride of life. Into Eglon's fat belly—the center of all that is of the world and which the flesh serves—sinks Ehud's sharp sword. The result is that its true nature is fully exposed as "excrement" (cf. Phil. 3:8). Only after the flesh is judged can the trumpet of victorious conquest be blown and deliverance come.

Deliverance by Shamgar. 3:31. **31.** Shamgar is a foreign (Hurrian) name. Like Samson, he delivered Israel from Philistine oppression. He is called **the son of Anath** (the name of the Canaanite goddess of war and sex, a consort of Baal); so the expression may be an appellative, meaning "the warrior." With a simple **oxgoad** he annihilated a Philistine brigade. The oxgoad was a farm tool from six to eight feet in length, with a spike on one end, used to urge on a lethargic dray animal, and on the other end was a chisel-shaped blade to clean a plow. That the LORD might be glorified, He used one man and this simple instrument, emblematic of His Word, to magnify His name (cf. 1 Cor. 1:27). Other illustrations of God's using humble things to glorify Himself are a nail (Judg. 4:21); trumpets, pitchers, lamps (7:20); a millstone (9:53); and the jawbone of an ass (15:15).

B. DELIVERANCE BY DEBORAH AND BARAK. 4:1-24.

Third Apostasy and Servitude. 4:1-3. **1-2.** This lapse into idolatry was followed by oppression under Jabin, king of Hazor. He is to be distinguished, of course, from the Jabin of Hazor, who was defeated in an earlier generation by Joshua (Josh. 11:1-14). He illustrates the fact that old foes can be resurrected in new forms to vex and enslave the LORD's people who lapse into former sinful ways.

Jabin, meaning "he understands," illustrates the corrupted wisdom of the world, which opposes God and His revelation (cf. 1 Cor. 2:4-16; 2 Cor. 10:5) and presents a serious peril to God's people. Hazor (Tell el-Qedah, some five miles southwest of Lake Huleh in Galilee) was reoccupied by the Canaanites. **The Lord sold them into the hand of Jabin**, a figure quite consistent with Israel's freed-slave relationship to the LORD when redeemed out of Egyptian servitude (Judg. 2:14; 3:8; 1 Sam. 12:9).

Jabin's commander in chief was Sisera, whose name (neither Hebrew nor ancestral Canaanite) possibly can be connected with the invasion of Sea Peoples in the thirteenth and twelfth centuries (R. D. Barnett, "The Sea Peoples," *Cambridge Ancient History*, vol. 2, chap. 28; and W. F. Albright, JPOS 2 [1922]: 60-62). Sisera's home, **Harosheth** (lit., Harosheth of the Gentiles), is commonly identified with Tell

'Amar, located near the place where the Kishon River runs through a narrow gorge as it enters the Plain of Acre about ten miles northwest of Megiddo. **3.** Sisera commanded a force of **nine hundred chariots of iron** (cf. 1:19). The arrival of the Philistines inaugurated the iron age in Palestine, and they and other Canaanites held a strict monopoly on the smelting secrets, which were not broken by Israel till after Saul's time. For **twenty years** the Canaanites severely oppressed the Israelites by their domination of the strategic Plain of Esdraelon.

Deborah the Prophetess-Judge. 4:4-9. Deborah ("honeybee" by popular etymology) was a prophetess and judge, a variety of female prophets having political involvements being illustrated in the ancient world by the records from Mari (Huffman, BA 31 [1968]:101-24). **4. She** (KJV, emphatic in the Hebrew) **judged** (functioned in a recognized office) **at that time.**

5. Deborah dwelt (better, "sat" or "presided"; cf. Isa. 28:5-6) **under the palm tree of Deborah** (cf. Gen. 35:8). That she had a tree named for her suggests a setting in which she inquired of the LORD oracularly for the people, who resorted to her **for judgment** (lit., "the judgment," *hămmĭshpāṭ*, meaning her decision in reply to a specific inquiry or as arbitress in a particular dispute). The tree associated with her judgeship was between **Ramah** in Benjamin, about six miles north-northwest of Jerusalem, and Bethel, about four miles northwest of Ramah, the seat of Samuel's later judgeship (1 Sam. 7:16).

6. Deborah, acting in her oracular role and as judge, summoned Barak ("lightning") from Kedesh-naphtali (Khirbet Qedish in southeastern Galilee) to muster Israelite forces at Mount Tabor in the northeastern part of the Plain of Esdraelon. **7-9.** She spoke prophetically as one whom God had assured victory, even informing Barak of the detailed outcome of the battle.

The Victory of Deborah and Barak. 4:10-24. **10-11.** The two northern tribes of Zebulun and Naphtali were mustered by Barak, for they had the direct responsibility of meeting the threat from Sisera on their borders. Ten thousand men were **at his feet** (i.e., "under his command"; cf. 5:27). **Heber, the Kenite** (*qēnî*, "smith" or "metal worker"; cf. 1:16) had separated from his clan and pitched **his tent** under a grove of oaks, or terebinths, in the upland valley of Kedesh. He is introduced because his wife, Jael, figures prominently in the story as the person into whose hands the LORD delivered Sisera (vv. 17-21).

13-16. Sisera's defeat is narrated. A hint of how the **Lord routed** him is given in the poetic version of the battle (5:21-22; cf. Deut. 7:23; Josh. 10:10). God sent heavy cloud bursts, the Wadi Kishon becoming a raging river overflowing the plain, causing Sisera's vaunted chariotry to be mired in the mud. **17-20.** In confusion, the great general fled ignominiously on foot, while his entire army was annihilated. His flight to the vicinity of the Kenites indicates he was headed for the northern Kedesh, perhaps already renowned as a city of refuge (Josh. 20:7).

21-24. His end came at the hands of a loyal worshiper of the LORD and defender of the covenant, who was called, as a result, "Blessed above women" (5:24). From the Israelite point of view, Jael was a heroine, and the nation's peril was viewed as justifying the violation of the immemorial law of hospitality. God, acting through the historical process, employed the good and overruled the evil to accomplish His ultimate purposes (cf. Psalm 76:10; Acts 2:23-24).

C. DELIVERANCE CELEBRATED IN SONG. 5:1-31.

The Character of the Poem. 5:1. **1. Then sang Deborah and Barak.** Chapter 5 gives the poetical version of the events of chapter 4. This famous masterpiece was apparently preserved in some such a collection as "the book of Jasher" (Josh. 10:13) or "the book of the wars of the LORD" (Num. 21:14). It belongs to the genre of the victory hymn now well known in examples from fifteenth- to twelfth-century Egypt and Assyria. Particularly instructive are the following: Hymn of Victory of Thutmose III and that of Merneptah (J. B. Pritchard, *Ancient Near Eastern Texts*, pp. 373-78), that of Ramses III (W. F. Edgerton and J. A. Wilson, *Historical Records of Ramesses III*, pp. 111-12) and that of Tukulti-Ninurta I of Assyria (c. 1234-1197 B.C.; K. Ebeling, *Mitteilungen der Altorientalischen Gesellschaft* 12 [1938]:3, 37-38).

Introduction: Praise to the Lord. 5:2-3. **2-3.** The ode opens with a call to praise the LORD **for the avenging of Israel, when the people willingly offered themselves.** Better, "Bless the LORD" (1) "that the leaders led in Israel" (*pārā'*, "take the lead," and *pᵉrā'ôt*, "leaders"); (2) "that the people volunteered" (NASB). The call to enlist in the spirit of covenant unity went out to the northern and central tribes. It was left to the various communities to decide whether to respond. Due to the LORD's gracious moving, the people responded gladly.

Invocation of the Lord. 5:4-5. **4.** Portrayed is the LORD in the storm, coming as a delivering Warrior from Seir and Edom, the region where He had first revealed Himself to His people (cf. Deut. 33:2; Psalm 68:7-9; Hab. 3:3-6). The awesomeness of the LORD's activity in behalf of His people is set forth with poetic fervor. **The earth trembled (quaked) and the heavens dropped** (rained water, $n\bar{a}\underline{t}\breve{a}\underline{p}$, lit., "dripped, flowed"), **the clouds also** ($g\breve{a}m$) **dropped** water. Interpreting Hebrew $g\breve{a}m$ as "sound, voice, thunder," following M. Dahood's analysis of the Ugaritic cognate, the translation runs, "With thunder the clouds rained water" (*Biblica* 45 [1964]:399; cf. Boling, "Judges," AB, p. 108).

5. The mountains melted (better, "shook," reading $n\bar{a}z\bar{o}ll\hat{u}$, from the root *zll*, *nifal* "to quake") "Before Yahweh, The One of Sinai, Before Yahweh, God of Israel!" (AB, p. 101). **Even that Sinai** (KJV) or "yon Sinai" (RSV) are not wholly satisfactory. "The One of Sinai" is "God of Israel" and assumes that an archaic pronoun ($\underline{d}\hat{u}$) lies behind both the element $z\breve{e}$ in this verse and the '^{a}*shĕr* in the formulaic names of Yahweh in Exodus 3:14 (see F. Cross, *Harvard Theological Review* 55[1962]:239, n. 61, and pp. 255-56). The imagery of this theophany resembles that of the divine appearance in Exodus 20:18-21.

Desolation Under the Oppressors. 5:6-8. **6. In the days of Shamgar, the son of Anath**, that is, the Anathite (conceivably meaning that this deliverer was from the town of Beth-anath in Galilee, but see comment on 3:31) **in the days of Jael** (anticipating her role in 4:17-21; 5:24-27), such was the sad state of Israel because of oppressing foes that **the highways** (main roads) **were unoccupied** by Israelite travelers, who had to resort to **byways** (lit., "crooked paths," circuitous bypaths unfrequented by the enemy) to get to their destination. The Canaanites, who had gotten control of the main roads, banned Israelite travel at will.

7. "Villagers" ($p^e r\bar{a}z\hat{o}n$, "people who lived in settlements outside walled towns") **ceased** (to exist). So uncertain were the times that they had to move into walled cities. **Until I** (or "thou," as the archaic *qamtî* may also be read), **Deborah, arose, a mother in Israel** (cf. 2 Sam. 20:19), a poetical term dramatizing a woman rendering singular service to her nation, as a mother does to her child.

8. They chose (indefinite third person singular), better rendered, "new gods were chosen." **Then** (at that troubled period) **was war in the gates,** enemy raids reaching the very entrance of Israelite cities. Forfeiting divine help by gross lapse into Canaanite idolatry, Israel opened herself wide to enemy harassment and oppression. To make matters worse, Israel did not have adequate weaponry of iron, because the Canaanites, particularly the Philistines, held a monopoly on iron smelting. **Was there a shield or spear seen ... ?** is a use in Hebrew of expressing an emphatic negative by employing the particle '*îm*, meaning "Neither spear nor shield was to be seen among the forty thousand (contingents) in Israel."

Expression of Praise to the Lord. 5:9-11. **9.** This verse commemorates the poet's gratitude for Israel's leaders, who faithfully responded to meet the crisis that arose (cf. v. 2). **10.** The wealthy who **ride on white** (tawny) **asses** (cf. 10:4; 12:14) and **sit in judgment** (as judges), as well as the poor who **walk by the way** on foot—all had cause for thanksgiving. **11.** Boling in the Anchor Bible renders this verse: "Attend to the sound of cymbals, between watering troughs." Keil and Delitzsch render it: "With the voice of the archers among drawers of water, there praise ye the righteous acts of the LORD." Evidently portrayed is a scene of victory in which the warriors, returning from the conflict, mingle among the women at the watering troughs, recounting to them the triumphs of the LORD by which He intervened for His people to give them salvation and victory.

Mustering of the Tribes. 5:12-18. **12. Awake, awake, Deborah . . . arise, Barak** (cf. Psalm 57:8). This stirring call introduced the mobilization of the tribes and the ensuing conflict and victory. **Lead thy captivity captive**, that is, "parade your prisoners in triumphal procession" (JFB, p. 161; cf. Psalm 68:18; Eph. 4:8). **13. Then he made him who remaineth** (the surviving remnant) **have dominion** (better, "Then the survivor went down to the nobles: Yahweh's troops went down against the knights for me," AB). The knights (*gibbôrîm*) were adult males prosperous enough to equip themselves for warfare. There were so few of them that those who failed to respond to the muster were singled out (cf. 5:23; 6:11-12; 11:1; 18:2; 20:46).

14-18. These verses review the performance of various tribal contingents at a later victory celebration. Verse 14 should read, "Those of Ephraim have taken root in Amalek." The Amalekites settled in certain sections of Ephraim, and this people, representing in a spiritual sense the flesh in the believer (see Exod. 17:8-16; Num. 24:20; Deut. 25:17; 1 Sam. 15:2), hindered Ephraim from joining in the victorious conflict.

Machir, a poetic usage singling out western Manasseh (C. F. Burney, *Joshua*, p. 135), took part, but the Transjordanian tribe of **Gilead** was censured for staying home, as well as **Reuben**, who preferred squatting between hearths and listening to pastoral piping in domestic tranquillity to facing dangerous conflict. **Zebulun, Issachar, and Naphtali** were praised, but Dan and Asher were chided for lack of participation. Singularly, Judah was not mentioned.

The Victorious Battle. 5:19-22. **19.** The conflict took place "at Taanach by

Megiddo's stream" (AB). Taanach, located five miles southeast of Megiddo, was an ancient fortress town guarding one of the pivotal passes to Esdraelon. The Wadi Kishon and its tributaries are referred to poetically as **the waters of Megiddo.** Megiddo commanded the pass between Esdraelon and the Plain of Sharon, and the nearby plain was the scene of other great battles (6:33; 1 Sam. 29:1; 31:1; 2 Kings 23:28-30). **They took no gain of money**, that is, they got no plunder.

20. The stars in their courses fought against Sisera. The LORD intervened and employed the forces of nature to overthrow the Canaanites. A fearful tempest with cloud bursts reduced the plain to a sea of mire, in which the Canaanite chariots became a liability instead of an asset, and the small stream became a raging torrent that swept away the defeated foe (cf. Josh. 10:12-14). F. Cross and D. N. Freedman make the obscure *qᵉdûmîm* read *qiddᵉmām*, "overwhelmed them" (*Studies in Ancient Yahwistic Poetry*, pp. 29, 35). So the passage would read: "The Wadi Kishon swept them away; the Wadi overwhelmed them—the Wadi Kishon." The horses, in their desperate attempt to escape, "stamped" (JPS) the earth.

The Curse upon Meroz. 5:23. **23.** The town of **Meroz** was singled out for a curse, as was Jael, Sisera's executioner, for a blessing (v. 24). Meroz, perhaps Khirbet Marus, located between Kadesh and Hazor in Naphtali, did not come to the aid of Israel **against the mighty** (*băggibbôrîm*, better, "with knights"). Meroz was evidently a wealthy town in which a number of citizens were able to equip themselves for war (see v. 13). It represents the utter indifference of some believers, which amounts to high treason against the LORD and His cause. Such conduct not only forfeits spiritual blessing, but invites the curse (cf. Deut. 28:14-48).

The Death of Sisera. 5:24-27. **24-25. He asked water** but in subtlety **she gave him milk** (i.e., "curds"; cf. 4:19), modern "lebben," which had a marked soporific effect to prepare her victim for her bloody act. She brought the curdled milk in a **lordly bowl,** large and fit for a lord, to insure enough of the potion to put Sisera into a sound sleep. **26.** With her left hand Jael grasped a tent peg and with her right hand a workman's mallet. **27.** Accustomed as a woman to drive a tent peg, her first blow was all that was needed.

The Scene with Sisera's Mother. 5:28-30. **28.** From the latticed window Sisera's mother is pictured looking vainly for the sight of her son's chariot returning from battle. **28-30.** Trying to encourage her when he does not return as the hours drag on, the wisest of the ladies that waited on her suggests they are looting and dividing the spoil, **to every man a damsel** (maiden) **or two.** Ironically, however, instead of joyfully dividing the spoils as victor, Sisera lay dead at the foot of the woman who had murdered him.

Epilogue. 5:31. **31. So let all thine enemies perish, O Lord** (cf. Num. 10:35; Psalm 68:1-3), the poet prayed as the graphic account of Sisera's fate was concluded. Benediction was at the same time pronounced upon the LORD's friends. **Let them who love him be as the sun** (Psalms 37:6; 89:36-37) **when he** (it) **goeth forth in his might** (Psalm 19:5). **Rest** for **forty years** resulted as the land enjoyed peace after Sisera's defeat.

D. DELIVERANCE BY GIDEON. 6:1—8:35.

1. MIDIANITE OPPRESSION AND GIDEON'S CALL. 6:1-40.

The Midianite Menace. 6:1-6. **1-3.** God's people repeat the weary cycle of sin and chastisement. They **did** evil

(2:11; 3:12; 4:1). The whip God used to punish them was Midian. The Midianites were nomads from the desert areas east and southeast of Palestine. They were the first people who employed camels on a large scale, making long-distance raids possible. They were able to make waterless journeys of several days, which earlier nomads using asses were unable to do. The Midianites (Gen. 25:1-2; Num. 31:1-39) were descendants of Abraham through Keturah (Gen. 25:2), but the Israelites had been divinely bidden to maintain a deadly hostility against them because of their shameful worship of Baal-peor (see Num. 25:1-18). Midian thus stands as an illustration of the world and its lusts as the avowed enemy of God and His people. The Midianites were also joined by **the Amalekites, and the children of the east** (*bᵉnê qĕdĕm,* "easterners").

Amalek in a spiritual sense represents the flesh in the believer (see Exod. 17:8-16; Num. 24:20; Deut. 25:17-19; 1 Sam. 15:2; cf. Gal. 4:29). The world and the flesh overrun God's people and despoil them and are routed only by the same faith as was manifested by Gideon's three hundred men. So severe were the Midianite raids that Israel had to flee for refuge to mountain caves, if there was no room for them in **strongholds** (fortified walled towns). **4-6.** The plundering Bedouin would wait till harvesttime and then swoop down like an army of locusts and carry away everything, leaving the land and its inhabitants utterly destitute.

Divine Rebuke. 6:7-10. **7-10.** Midianite oppression drove the sinning Israelites to cry to the LORD (see 3:9, 15; 4:3; Psalm 107:13; Hos. 5:15—6:1). This show of repentance (v. 6) brought a gracious answer from the LORD through **a prophet.** He reminded the people of the LORD's delivering them from Egypt and its slave barracks and from all their oppressors to give them the land. The LORD's words in verse 10 may be rendered, "I am the LORD your God. Do not ever be afraid of the gods of the Amorites (westerners) in whose land you are living. But you have *not* obeyed my voice!" Here the term *Amorites* ("westerners") denotes all the Canaanites (cf. Josh. 24:15).

Gideon's Call. 6:11-18. **11.** Deliverance is promised as repentance is begun. The Angel of the LORD (Deity) appeared to Gideon ("hewer") of Manasseh, a member of the small clan of Abiezer (cf. v. 15) as he was beating out the wheat in the narrow confines of the winepress, instead of the usual place on the hilltop, to hide it from the voracious eyes of the marauding invaders. Specification of the **oak** suggests that Gideon's father, Joash, was proprietor of a place of oracular inquiry, which was, however, Baalist not Yahwist (cf. Deut. 18:9-11).

12-13. The Lord is with thee (singular). Gideon missed the point and replied concerning the current plight of **us**. Deity addressed Gideon as a **mighty man of valor**, evidently evaluating the young man not as to what he was in himself, but what he would be and what God would make him as a ready instrument through whom the divine power would work. God's calling is His enabling.

14. Go in this thy might, and thou shalt save Israel. . . . Have not I sent thee? (cf. Josh. 1:9). Gideon was slow to realize that the visitor was God, that the chastisement He had brought upon His people showed His presence with them and His love for them, and that with the divine aid "he would overcome the Midianites as easily as if they were but one man" (JFB, p. 162). **15. Wherewith shall I save Israel?** Gideon's attitude of humility reminds us of Moses, Isaiah, and Jeremiah (Exod. 3:11; Isa. 6:5; Jer.

1:6). **17.** Like Moses, he required a sign (cf. Exod. 4:1-7).

The Sign That God Was Commissioning Gideon. 6:19-24. **19-20.** Gideon's present of a kid, unleavened bread, and broth was brought out to the heavenly visitor under the oak (terebinth) (see v. 11). Gideon was directed to lay the meat and the unleavened cakes upon a nearby rock, which served as an improvised altar (cf. 13:19), and the broth was used as a libation (cf. 1 Kings 8:33-34).

21-23. Gideon was given incontrovertible proof that the angel was God in the form of a theophany when the visitor's staff caused fire to come out of the rock and consume the present (cf. Judg. 13:21). He feared death when he realized he had seen God in angelic form **face to face** (cf. Gen. 32:30; Exod. 33:20; Judg. 13:22), but was assured he would not die. **24.** To memorialize the appearance of God to him in angelic form, Gideon erected **an altar . . . unto the Lord**, calling it Jehovah (Yahweh) Shalom, "the LORD our peace," *shālôm* denoting welfare in its broadest connotation, including peace of mind, health of body, salvation of soul, comfort in distress, and success in life).

Gideon's Repudiation of Baalism. 6:25-32. **25-26.** Face to face contact with the LORD, the one true, living God, was followed by the divine command addressed to Gideon to destroy his father's **altar of Baal** and to **cut down the images** ("grove," wooden representation of the goddess Asherah, the consort of Baal; see Deut. 16:21; Judg. 2:2; 3:7). Here is an example of the prior claim of obedience to God rather than to parents, who stand in the place of God, when obeying parents would be tantamount to disobeying God (cf. Exod. 20:12; Matt. 15:4; 19:19; Mark 7:10; Eph. 6:2-3).

Doubtlessly by using the stones from the altar of Baal that he had demolished, Gideon was ordered to build an altar to the LORD atop the rock where the divine fire had consumed his present. He was to take his father's **second** (better, *shāmēm*, "fat") young bullock, especially kept for sacrifice (cf. Luke 15:23), and offer it as a burnt offering to the LORD, using the wood of the images of Asherah for the fire. **27.** At great personal risk, Gideon complied with the LORD's command.

28-29. Since demonic powers are the dynamic behind idolatry, notably the debauched fertility cults of Canaan (cf. Deut. 18:9-11; 1 Cor. 10:20; 1 John 4:1-2), the fierce rage of the men of the town is understandable. **30-32.** Gideon's father, Joash, although a Baal-worshiper, showed superior common sense in dealing with a very ticklish situation in which the life of his son was at stake (cf. Deut. 13:6-9). **If he be a god, let him plead for himself** (cf. 11:24; 1 Kings 18:27). And **he** (one) **called him,** better, "He was called (styled)" **Jerubbaal,** meaning "Let Baal strive" (*yārēb bā'āl*). Later, when the wickedness of Baal worship was realized in times of spiritual awakening, the custom prevailed of replacing the *bā'āl* element in personal names with *bĕshĕt* or *bôshĕt,* meaning "shame" (2 Sam. 11:21), as in Ishbaal (Ishbosheth, Merribaal, Mephibosheth).

Gideon's Fleece. 6:33-40. **33. Then all the Midianites** and the Amalekites (see note on v. 3) **encamped in the valley of Jezreel** (the Plain of Esdraelon). The southern part of the Jordan Valley (the Ghor) is very deep, and the ascent by the wadis in that area very difficult. That is why the eastern invaders entered by the northern wadis of the Ghor opposite Jezreel. **34. The Spirit of the Lord came upon Gideon** (lit., "clothed himself with Gideon"; cf. 1 Chron. 12:18; 2 Chron. 24:20; or "took complete possession of him"). **He blew** a trumpet to muster an army (Judg. 3:27) and practically all northern Israel responded. **35.** Ephraim, however, the most powerful of the central tribes, is not listed.

36-40. After the first sign (vv. 17-24), it seems strange that Gideon should have asked for another one. But the task was formidable (v. 33) and, since the LORD was patient with Gideon's faltering faith, we should be also (cf. Exod. 4:10-17). Gideon would (1) strengthen his own faith, and (2) have evidence to strengthen the faith of the people that he was really God's instrument.

2. THE VICTORY OF GIDEON'S THREE HUNDRED. 7:1-25.

Gideon's Army Selected. 7:1-8. **1-4.** Gideon ("hewer"), now also called Jerubbaal, with faith strengthened by the sign of the fleece, pitched camp by **the well of Harod,** that is, "the spring of trembling" (Heb., *hārēd,* "fearful"), which connects with the message to the people: **whosoever is fearful and afraid** (*hārēd*), **let him return and depart early from Mount Gilead** (cf. Deut. 20:8). The site is 'Ain Jalud, which springs from the foot of Mount Gilboa (cf. 1 Sam. 29:1).

The hill of Moreh (Jebel Nebel Dahi) was located some four miles away across the valley. There the Midianites were encamping. That God might have the glory and the Israelites might not **vaunt themselves against** the LORD (*yĭtpā'ēr,* "glorify themselves" rather than the LORD), those of the volunteers who were **fearful and afraid** (a hendiadys meaning "really scared") were urged to **return and depart early from Mount Gilead.**

The only Mount Gilead known is in Transjordan. Was there one in Naphtali? C. F. Burney (*The Book of Judges*, pp. 207-8) proposes the modern name of the Spring of Harod (Ain Galud) as preserving the ancient name, clarified from the Akkadian *galadu*, "to be afraid." The passage would then read: "Whosoever is downright afraid, let him turn back. Let him decamp [Arab., *ḍafara*] from Mount Fearful" (cf. Boling, "Joshua," AB, pp. 142, 145). **Twenty and two thousand** departed, leaving only **ten thousand. 7-8.** The divine test at the water further reduced Gideon's force to **three hundred.** Lapping water like a dog, however it was done, separated the vigilant and watchful from the less alert and those who were concerned about natural comforts and less fired by faith to spot the enemy and press on to victory. The LORD selected the three hundred who lapped water. Evidently they bent over, but kept their heads erect to see any possible movement of the enemy.

Meanwhile, bringing their hands in contact with the stream, they threw the water up into their mouths, lapping it in with their tongues. "The wandering people in Asia, when, on a journey or in haste, they come to water, do not stoop down with deliberation on their knees, but only bend forward as much as is necessary to bring their hand in contact with the stream, and throw it [the water] up with rapidity, and at the same time such address, that they do not drop a particle" (JFB, 2:91).

The Encouraging Dream. 7:9-14. **9-12.** How graciously the LORD worked with Gideon to encourage him in the face of the formidable task he was called to perform (cf. 6:25). **13.** In the dream of the Midianite that Gideon overheard, the cake of barley bread represented Israelite farmers and homesteaders, reduced to scanty fare, since this grain was usually the food of the poor. The tent that the barley loaf struck and flattened represented the nomadic invaders. **14.** The interpretation of the dream gave Gideon absolute assurance.

The Victory of Faith. 7:15-25. **15-18.** Gideon worshiped and then proceeded with a strategem to utterly terrify the enemy. The clay pitchers were empty to contain the torches. Easily broken, they allowed the sudden blaze of the held-up lights, together with the blasts of the trumpets and the shout, **The Sword of the Lord, and of Gideon**, to utterly confuse the Midianite hordes and precipitate their indiscriminate slaughter of themselves in their hasty flight.

19. Gideon struck at **the beginning of the middle watch**, at about 10 P.M. **21-25.** The Midianites fled toward the Jordan and crossed it at points where their hasty retreat could be cut off by the Ephraimites. The slaughter of Midian at the rock Oreb is remembered by Isaiah (Isa. 10:26), and "the day of Midian" is commemorated in Isaiah 9:4.

3. GIDEON'S JUDGESHIP. 8:1-35.

The Complaint of the Ephraimites. 8:1-3. **1.** Victory over the world and the flesh (routing Midian and Amalek) soon faces the test of the reality of such conquest. There are always believers who are tempted with jealousy and whose wounded pride introduces dissension. The Ephraimites thought that the failure to enlist their aid at the outset was intended to deprive them of sharing in the glory of victory.

2. Despite their vigorous argument with him, Gideon answered them wisely and courteously. **What have I done in comparison with you? Is not the gleaning of the grapes of Ephraim better than the vintage of Abiezer?** (Is not the mop-up work done by your tribe, 7:24-25, more vital to the total victory than what my small contingent has done?). How beautifully Gideon illustrates Philippians 2:1-5. All strife among believers begins with self-seeking and vain glory. The remedy is "in lowliness of mind let each esteem others better than themselves."

Punishment of Flagrant Compromise. 8:4-17. **4-5.** A greater test and victory challenged Gideon after he overcame internal strife. He and his three hundred warriors, after wearily giving chase on the trail of the fleeing Midianite kings, Zeba and Zalmunna, implored food of the men of Succoth (apparently Tell Deir 'Alla in the Jordan Valley a short distance north of the Jabbok).

6. The princes of Succoth insolently refused with the taunt, "Do you have in your hand [i.e., in your possession] the hand of Zeba and Zalmunna, that we should give your army food?" They derisively scorned Gideon's success with a play upon two Hebrew words for "hand," hinting at the practice of mutilating prisoners (cf. 1:5-7), and demonstrating that they were secret allies of Midian.

7. Gideon promised stern chastisement. "For that," said Gideon, "when the LORD surrenders Zebah and Zalmunna into my hand, I will flail your flesh with the desert thorns and thistles" (lit. Heb. trans.). **8.** The men of Penuel answered Gideon in similar fashion. **9.** He promised to tear down their tower on his victorious return. **10-17.** After he had captured the two kings, Gideon kept his word and did exactly as he threatened to do to the men of Succoth and Penuel. He was carrying out the divine will against weak, vacillating Israelites who were compromising with the Midianites, the oppressors of God's people who illustrate the enslavement that the world and the flesh impose and with which there must be no compromise on the part of a victorious warrior like Gideon.

Complete Victory over Midian. 8:18-21. **18-19.** The Midianite kings, we learn here, had put to death Gideon's brothers at Tabor. By that act the Midianites imposed upon Gideon the duty of blood revenge (Deut. 19:6). Gideon explained that they were his full brothers, with the same father and mother. **20.** Requesting his son to slay the Midianite kings, which would have added to their humiliation, the boy refused. **21.** Haughtily, the Midianites challenged Gideon to kill them himself, which he did without delay. Thus, he accomplished his mission fully in freeing his fellow Israelites from the oppression of Midian and Amalek.

Gideon's Failure. 8:22-35. **22.** Gideon had proved himself a man of God endued with the Spirit of God in bringing victory over the Midianites. **23.** He showed his loyalty to the LORD also by refusing the kingship by adhering to the theocratic ideal stressed throughout the book of Judges. **24-26.** But his failure began by requesting for himself the earrings taken from the conquered Midianites, the weight being seventeen hundred gold shekels, not including the crescents, pendants, and purple garments and ornaments on the camels' necks.

27. That mistake led to a more serious lapse. **And Gideon made an ephod thereof.** This was an important item of the high priest's garments, being a short outer garment (Exod. 28:6-30; 39:1-21; Lev. 8:7-8). It was of gold, blue, purple, scarlet, and fine-twined linen (Exod. 28:6). It consisted of two pieces, front and back, united by two shoulder pieces and by a band at the bottom. Two onyx stones, set in gold and engraved with the names of the twelve tribes of Israel, were on the shoulders (Exod. 28:7-9, 12, 22). On occasion, it was consulted oracularly (1 Sam. 23:9-12; 30:7-8).

It is possible Gideon had an image made to wear the ephod, which became an idolatrous snare to Israel. Its erection marked the tragic end of a truly great man. He refused the kingship but fell prey to the priesthood. He assumed an honor that did not belong to him. Both he and Israel forgot that the glory belonged to God alone. His act illustrates the usurpation by a false priesthood of the place the LORD alone should have, a mistake that has been repeated so often in the name of Christianity. Gideon reaped a sad harvest in his family, most of his sons suffering death because of the desire of one of them to be king (9:5).

30-31. The many wives of Gideon and his concubine at Shechem show how he himself, who had vanquished Midian and Amalek, fell snare to the world and the flesh, which these enemies portray in a spiritual sense (see 6:1-6). **33-35.** No wonder after Gideon's death the fifth apostasy set in, with Israel serving Baal-berith, who had a shrine at Shechem (9:4).

E. DELIVERANCE FROM ABIMELECH'S USURPATION. 9:1-57.

Abimelech Becomes King of Shechem. 9:1-6. **1. Abimelech** ("my father was king") claimed what his father had rejected and **went to Shechem** (modern Balatah) **unto his mother's brethren.** He was considered part of his mother's family since he was the son of a secondary wife. The offspring of such a union belonged to the wife's clan. Moreover, the wife customarily stayed with her own clan and was visited periodically by her husband. **2.** Abimelech sought help for his arrogant and unfounded claim to kingship from his maternal clan. Degraded by foul Baal worship and insensitive to the moral issues involved, the Shechemites fell for Abimelech's wicked and empty claim as he appealed to their local pride.

3-4. Baalism had stripped them of any sense of loyalty to the LORD as king or to His covenant as binding. So they concluded Abimelech was their **brother** and that they should support him, even financing his monstrous pretensions from money taken out of the temple of Baal-berith (cf. 8:33). This designation of the chief Canaanite deity means "lord of the covenant" and refers to the confederacy in which Shechem, the natural capital of Palestine, was associated with her neighbors.

5. With the money he got, Abimelech hired some idle mercenaries. With these scoundrels he went to his father's house at Ophrah, and in a mass public execution **upon one stone** he slew the seventy sons of Gideon. Only Jotham, the youngest, escaped by hiding. **6. All the men** ("lords") **of Shechem** are referred to as **all the house of Millo** (Beth-millo, *bêt-millô*), identifying them by their place of assembly for deliberation, which was evidently erected on a huge earth fill (*millô*; see G. E. Wright, *Shechem*, pp. 80-102; cf. 2 Sam. 5:9; 1 Kings 9:15). These lords (*be'ālim*) **went, and made Abimelech king, by the oak** (terebinth) **of the pillar.** Joshua had set up a monument there as a witness to the covenant between the LORD and His covenant people (Josh. 24:26).

Jotham's Message. 9:7-21. **7.** From a promontory on Mount Gerizim, which forms a natural pulpit with marvelous acoustical qualities that enable a person who is shouting to be heard in the valley below, where Shechem was located, Jotham, the only surviving brother of the usurper, in a clever fable dramatically denounced the perfidy of Abimelech. **8-14. The trees went forth ... to anoint a king. The olive ... the fig tree,** and **the vine** were all too busy with worthwhile occupations to seek to usurp authority over others and become king. **15.** But the useless **bramble** or thorn bush, representing the scoundrel usurper, said absurdly, **Put your trust in my shadow**, as if it could offer anything but pain and misery. With an even more disgusting show of self-importance, this miserable mass of ugly, prickly thorns with inconceivable effrontery basely threatened to **devour the cedars of Lebanon** if the other trees did not accord it deference. All the good the thorn was capable of was to be the start of destructive fires.

16-20. Jotham made a pointed application to his parable. **If ye have done truly and sincerely, ... rejoice ye in Abimelech, ... But if not, let fire come out from Abimelech**—this bramble king of yours! Not only would this bramble king prove destructive to the men of Shechem, but the men of Shechem would devour Abimelech. **21. And Jotham ... went to Beer** ("well"), probably El-Bireh between Shechem and Jerusalem, or possibly to distant Beer-Sheba. But however far he went was scarcely far enough to be from a scoundrel like Abimelech.

Abimelech's Quarrel with the Shechemites. 9:22-25. **22-24.** When Abimelech had reigned three years, **God sent an evil** (demon) **spirit** between him and the men of Shechem. God used demonic powers to punish Abimelech, for his usurpation of kingship against the divine will and his atrocities to Gideon's family, and the men of Shechem, for crowning such a wretch as their king (cf. 1 Sam. 16:14; 1 Kings 22:21). **25.** The ambush the men of Shechem set up in the mountains deprived Abimelech of tribute and tolls from caravans using the important road through the heart of the land.

Gaal's Conspiracy. 9:26-49. **26-29.** The conspiracy of Gaal was an insurrection of the original Canaanites headed by Gaal, who urged the people to serve **the men of Hamor, the father of Shechem** (cf. Gen. 33:19) and thus revive the ancient Shechemite aristocracy. The season of grape gathering, the Shechemite counterpart of the Feast of Ingathering (Tabernacles) with the ensuing season of merrymaking, was chosen as the time for the revolt.

30-33. Abimelech's governor, Zebul, sent warning of the revolt to Abimelech, who resided at Arumah (v. 41). **34-45.** The result was that Abimelech destroyed Shechem and sowed it with salt, rendering the very soil of the city sterile. **46-49.** Then he set fire to the stronghold of the temple of Baal-berith, where about a thousand men and women had fled. They perished in the flames.

Abimelech's Death. 9:50-55. **50-51.** Apparently as a member of the Shechem confederacy, Thebez (probably modern Tubas, thirteen miles north of Shechem) had joined the revolt. Thebez had a strong tower inside the city. **52-53.** It was while Abimelech was attempting to take the inner tower that a woman threw an upper movable millstone from the wall that struck Abimelech. **54.** Since death at the hands of a woman was regarded as a disgrace, Abimelech had his armor-bearer slay him.

The Moral of the Episode. 9:56-57. **56-57.** God requited the Shechemites for their evil. Both the destruction of Shechem and the death of Abimelech were just recompense for the atrocities perpetrated against Gideon's family. The curse of Jotham (v. 20) was realized. Both Shechem and Abimelech were devoured as Jotham had predicted.

F. DELIVERANCE BY TOLA, JAIR, AND JEPHTHAH. 10:1—12:7.

1. TOLA AND JAIR AND THE AMMONITE AND PHILISTINE OPPRESSION. 10:1-18.

Tola and Jair. 10:1-5. **1-2. Tola** was a tribal name. A son of Issachar bears that name (Gen. 46:13; cf. Num. 26:23). Tola dwelt in Shamir, which is unknown, except that it was in Mount Ephraim, probably in the vicinity of Jezreel. W. F. Albright describes the minor judges as "intertribal arbiters." They were perhaps like Samuel, who later journeyed from place to place judging Israel (1 Sam. 7:15-17). 3-5. Jair was from Gilead. He is said to have had thirty sons. That they rode upon ass colts was a mark of wealth and distinction (cf. 5:10; 12:14), as well as the notation that Jair had thirty cities ... called Havoth-jair ("villages of Jair"). Kamon, Jair's burial place, is probably Qamm in Gilead.

The Ammonite Oppression. 10:6-18. 6. The weary cycle of Israel's evildoing and lapse into idolatry is repeated (cf. 6:1; 13:1). They served Baalim and Ashtaroth (see 2:13), as well as the gods of Syria (Aram), including Hadad and Rimmon, and the gods of Sidon (Baal, Anath, Asherah), Moab (Chemosh), Ammon (Molech), and the Philistines (Dagon and Baal-zebub).

7-8. In His anger the Lord ... sold them (see 4:2) into the hands of the Philistines (cf. 13:1) and the Ammonites (cf. 13:12-13). 9. The Ammonites were not only a scourge in Gilead, but invaded Judah, Benjamin, and Ephraim. 10. In their distress the Israelites cried out (cf. 6:6) and confessed their sin (cf. Num. 21:7). 11-14. The LORD's reply reviewed past deliverances and chided the people for their present infidelity, threatening an end to His gracious deliverances (cf. Deut. 31:17; 1 Kings 9:9). 15-18. Genuine repentance moved the LORD to undertake once more for His oppressed people.

2. JEPHTHAH AND HIS VOW. 11:1-40.

Jephthah Chosen as Leader. 11:1-11. 1-2. Jephthah was a Gileadite, a native of Gilead in north Transjordan. His name is abbreviated *yiptāḥ-'ēl,* "God opens (the womb)" (cf. Josh. 19:14, 27). He is called a mighty man of valor (*gibbôr ḥāyil*), a knight, like Gideon (6:11-12) trained in upper-class combat, who furnished his own equipment, as well as that of a unit of soldiers. He was the son of a prostitute. When his father's legitimate sons grew up, they expelled him.

3. He went to Tob, northeast of Gilead (cf. 2 Sam. 10:6-8), a frontier district where worthless ("empty") men, that is, "wild and reckless" men, in contrast to "respectable" members of society, were attracted to him, doubtless as mercenaries. 4-8. War with the Ammonites was the event that led to Jephthah's recall as the official leader of Gilead. 9-10. Jephthah accepted on the terms that his sovereignty be accepted, if the LORD gave victory through him over the Ammonites. 11. The exact location of Mizpeh is uncertain.

Jephthah's Diplomacy. 11:12-28. These verses present the only narrative account of Israelite diplomacy toward a neighbor state in the book of Judges. The bulk of the unit (vv. 15-27) is a sane factual refutation of the Ammonite claim to Israelite territory from the Arnon to the Jabbok and to the Jordan (v. 13). 15-22. Jephthah clearly showed that Israel left Ammon undisturbed when the people came up out of Egypt. 23-24. Jephthah then bade them to be satisfied with what Chemosh, their god, had given them and not to interfere with what the LORD had given His people. 25. Was the present king of Ammon better than Balak, king of Moab, who could not stop the onward march of Israel then? (cf. Num. 22:1—24:25).

26. Why had the Ammonites waited three full centuries before asserting claim to the territory? Heshbon (*ḥešbôn,* "device") was originally a city of Moab, but it was taken by Sihon,

the Ammonite king, and made his royal city (Num. 21:26). After his defeat it was allotted to Reuben (21:21-24; 32:37), and later to Gad (Josh. 21:39). **Aroer**, the southernmost city of Israel east of the Jordan, lay on the north bank of the Arnon River (Wadi Môjib, at modern 'Ara'ir, about fourteen miles east of the Dead Sea; see D. Baly, *The Geography of the Bible*, p. 237, fig. 72; and Nelson Glueck, AASOR 14 [1923]:3, 49-51).

Jephthah's Vow and Victory. 11:29-40. **29.** Jephthah was a Spirit-anointed leader, not an opportunist. He was enabled by God to lead the Gileadites to victory over their oppressors (cf. 6:34; Heb. 11:32). **30-31.** He vowed a vow unto the LORD (cf. Gen. 28:20; Num. 30:2; 1 Sam. 1:11). **32-40.** Did he actually offer his only child, an unmarried daughter, as a human sacrifice? On the eve of battle the warrior vowed that whoever was the first to come forth from his house to meet him on his victorious return would be the LORD's. He would offer him up for a burnt offering.

His vow apparently involved an actual human sacrifice for these seven reasons: (1) It fits in with the lawless spirit rampant in the era of the Judges (cf. 17:6; 21:25). (2) It was in line with the half-pagan background of Jephthah, and he would have been following a pagan custom and would not have known or been deterred by the Mosaic Law, which forbade such a practice (Lev. 18:21; 20:2-5; Deut. 12:31; 18:10). The closest biblical parallel is Mesha's sacrifice of his eldest son (2 Kings 3:27). (3) Jephthah's great grief bears witness that the sacrifice (*'ôlâ*, always "wholly burnt") actually took place. (4) There is no suggestion in the account that Jephthah's conduct was sanctioned by the LORD.

(5) The daughter pleaded for time to **bewail** (lament) her **virginity**, because no greater misfortune could befall a Hebrew woman than to die unwedded and childless. The absence of motherhood cut off from her, as a Hebrew maid, and in this instance, from her house, the hopes of mothering the Messiah. (6) The declaration that her father **did with her according to his vow** constitutes a euphemism with which the narrator drops the veil over the terrible sacrifice offered. (7) It became a *custom* to lament Jephthah's daughter, apparently local, for no other allusion is made to it.

3. JEPHTHAH PUNISHES THE EPHRAIMITES. 12:1-7.

Jephthah Fights with the Quarrelsome Ephraimites. 12:1-7. **1.** The tribe of Ephraim, located west of the Jordan, displayed a similar contentious spirit toward Gideon (cf. 8:1). **2-3.** Unlike Gideon (8:2-3), Jephthah decided to fight fire with fire instead of gentle words. **4.** The Ephraimite taunt suggests that the tribes in Transjordan who traced their ancestry from Joseph were deserters from Ephraim and Manasseh. **5.** The Gileadites defeated the Ephraimites in battle and seized the fords of the Jordan to prevent the latter from slipping back to their own country.

6. The Ephraimites spoke a slightly different dialect of Hebrew and could easily be spotted by their inability to pronounce the "sh" sound in "Shibboleth," meaning "ear" or "head of grain." Forty-two thousand who pronounced the password as "sibboleth" were massacred. Jephthah's spirit was one of proud exaltation, for he employed the pronoun "I" or "me" eleven times in his answer to his brothers (vv. 2-3). How many "shibboleths" have been invented as a result of a sectarian and fleshly spirit to divide and work havoc among the LORD's people! **7.** Jephthah died and was buried **in one of the cities** of Gilead.

G. DELIVERANCE BY IBZAN, ELON, AND ABDON. 12:8-15.

Judgeship of Ibzan. 12:8-10. **8-10.** All that is told about **Ibzan**, a minor judge (see 10:1-5), is the place of his birth and death (not Bethlehem in Judah, but apparently Bethlehem in Zebulun, some seven miles west-northwest of Nazareth (Josh. 19:15), and the size of his family. Ibzan evidently practiced polygamy. He was an influential man who sought additional influence by intermarriages with other clans and families.

Judgeship of Elon. 12:11-12. **11-12.** The name **Elon** means "terebinth" (*'ēlôn*) and constitutes a play on the word *Aijalon* (Ayalon, *'āyālôn,* "gazelle"). The place of his burial was doubtlessly named for him; otherwise it is unknown.

Judgeship of Abdon. 12:13-15. **13. Abdon** was a native of Pirathon in Ephraim (possibly Fer'ata, six miles southwest of Shechem). He was **the son of Hillel** ("praising"), the first occurrence of a later famous name in Jewish theology (cf. Hillel, the rival of Shammai, shortly before the time of our Lord). **14.** His **forty sons** and **thirty grandsons** rode on seventy asses, a mark of high rank (see 10:4). **15.** His burial **in the hill country of the Amalekites** (NASB) suggests the era of Amalekite oppression (cf. 3:13; 5:14).

H. DELIVERANCE BY SAMSON. 13:1—16:31.

1. BIRTH OF SAMSON. 13:1-25.

Philistine Domination. 13:1. **1.** This is the seventh recorded apostasy in the book of Judges (see 3:5-7; 3:12-14; 4:1-3; 6:1-2; 8:33-35; 10:6-9). **Israel did evil again** (cf. 2:11) . . . **and the Lord delivered** (gave) **them into the hand of the Philistines.** The Philistines were a non-Semitic people, often referred to as "the

uncircumcised" (14:3; 1 Sam. 31:4; 2 Sam. 1:20). They migrated from Crete and settled in the southwestern part of Palestine along the coast. Israel's deliverance into their power lasted forty years, during which there was no recorded cry of repentance. This is the last recorded apostasy in the book and presumably the deepest.

The Philistines were intensely religious, celebrating their victories in the house of their deities (1 Sam. 31:9), frequently carrying their idols to battle (2 Sam. 5:21). Their principal deity was Dagon, a grain god (1 Sam. 5:4; see W. F. Albright, ARI, pp. 74, 220, n. 15). They also adored Ashtaroth (1 Sam. 31:10), a fertility goddess analogous to Assyrian Ishtar, and Baal-zebub ("lord of flies"), a mocking distortion of Baalzebul ("lord of the divine abode," see 2 Kings 1:2). Beelzebub in Jewish theology became "the prince of the demons" (Matt. 12:24). Accordingly, Philistinism represents mere empty ritualism without regenerating or sanctifying power, since the Philistines were uncircumcised and therefore had no covenant knowledge of God, atoning sacrifice, forgiveness of sins, or assurance of salvation.

Prophecy of a Nazirite Deliverer. 13:2-14. Philistinism (see notes on 16:3) appears versus Naziritism. Who was to be raised up to deliver Israel from the Philistines? A Nazirite ("separated one"). See the spiritual significance of the Nazirite vow (Num. 6:1-21). Not only was the deliverer to maintain Nazirite separation from Philistinism from birth, but his parents were likewise to be separated; and as a result of the vision of God, they were to place their trust in God.

2-5. The angel of the Lord who appeared to Manoah's wife was the preincarnate Word (Christ), the same who

332

revealed Himself to Moses in the bush (Exod. 3:1-8), to Joshua outside Jericho (Josh. 5:13-15), and to Gideon at Ophrah (Judg. 6:22-24). To the **barren** wife of Manoah (which means "rest," so longed for in those troublesome days) was promised a child, who would **begin to deliver Israel.** Complete deliverance was not promised, for deep repentance is not recorded. The Philistine scourge would crop out periodically until the time of David.

6-7. Manoah's wife told her husband of the angelic visitation and the promise of a Nazirite deliverer. **8.** Manoah prayed the angel might appear to both of them to teach them what they were to do to **the child that shall be born. 9-14.** The prayer was answered, and the regulations concerning the Nazirite stipulations were stressed again (cf. 16:17). The mother was to share for a time in part of the Nazirite vow. Even the eating of grapes was forbidden, since they were the chief symbol of the culture and religion of the Canaanites (Num. 6:3-5), besides being symbolic of mere natural joy (Psalm 104:15). Naziriteship was the expression of devotion that found all its joy in the Lord (cf. Psalms 87:7; 97:12; Hab. 3:18; Phil. 3:1-3; 4:4, 10).

The Angel of the Lord Reveals Himself. 13:15-23. **15-19.** Manoah sought to detain the celestial stranger to show him hospitality, but he was told, **I will not eat of thy food.** The angel (Deity) notified him that if he would offer food, it had to be in the form of a **burnt offering ... unto the Lord,** prefiguring divine grace to be manifested toward sinful man through Christ's death. Gideon prepared food for one whom he later recognized as the angel of the LORD (Deity); the food was then converted into an offering (cf. 6:18-22).

17. What is thy name ... ? Manoah desired to know so that he might do him honor, especially by a gift (Num. 22:17), since he as yet did not perceive that the stranger was divine. **Why askest thou thus after my name, seeing it is wonderful?** (*pěli'y*, "incommunicable," i.e., "ineffable," beyond human capacity to comprehend; an adjective from the root *pālā'*, "to be a singular, extraordinary, wonderful"; cf. Isa. 9:6). The angel **did wondrously** (*măplī'*, a play on the root pālā', "be surpassing," in the causative, "work a wonder," AB).

20. As the fire ascended from the altar, the angel of the LORD ascended in the flame, while Manoah and his wife looked on. The revelation of Deity caused them to automatically fall face downward to the ground (cf. Lev. 9:24; Num. 14:5; Ezek. 1:28). **21-22.** Manoah, realizing he had seen God, was struck with fear of death (cf. Gen. 32:30; Exod. 33:20; Deut. 5:24). Gideon had a similar reaction (Judg. 6:22). **23.** Manoah's wife's argument was both sensible and practical. **If the Lord were pleased to kill us,** she argued, He would not have received our sacrifice or promised us a child, who would deliver Israel.

Birth and First Exploits of Samson. 13:24-25. The child was born and called **Samson** ("sun"). Although not an idolater, Manoah evidently gave his son a name common in the vicinity, for not far away from Manoah's home was Beth-shemesh ("house of the sun") where the sun-god was honored. Was that a harbinger of Samson's later compromise? **The Spirit of the Lord began to move him** (*pā'ăm*, "incite, stir"; lit., "beat" or "strike" him) in **the camp of Dan** (Heb., *Mahaneh-Dan*), between **Zorah** (Sorᶜâ on the north side of the Wadi al-Ṣarar, "the valley of Sorek," Zarkha in the Amarna Letters, cf. Josh. 15:33) and **Eshtaol** (Josh. 19:41, a town on the border of Dan in the lowlands).

2. EARLY EXPLOITS OF SAMSON. 14:1-20.

Samson Kills a Lion. 14:1-9. **1-2. Samson went down to Timnah**, which like Zorah and Eshtaol was located on the boundary between Judah and Dan (cf. Josh. 15:10; 19:43). It is modern Khirbet-Tibneh, three miles southwest of Beth-shemesh. Samson took his first step in compromising his Nazirite vow by going **down** to a Philistine city, where he met temptation (a Philistine woman) and succumbed to it. **Get her for me as my wife. 3.** There is a note of stubborn self-will in Samson's point-blank directive to his parents, emphasized in the repetition of his insistent demand, **Get her for me; for she pleaseth me well** (lit., "she is right in my eyes"). The Nazirite was being ensnared by Philistinism, the lust of the eyes and the flesh.

4. Parental remonstration availed little. Samson's insistence that his parents arrange for his marriage to the Philistine woman (cf. Gen. 21:21) illustrates the truth that God may overrule such mistaken decisions to accomplish His purposes, in this case to deliver Israel from the Philistines. But in no sense did that excuse Samson from his responsibility for his wrong decision.

5-6. On his way back to Timnah with his parents, Samson turned aside and went into the Timnah vineyards, where suddenly a young lion attacked him. **The Spirit of the Lord came mightily upon him** and he tore it open, like tearing a kid, with his bare hands. By virtue of Samson's Nazirite status, the Spirit was enabled to work through a holy vessel set apart for God. But while the Nazirite did exploits and conquered Satan, as it were (cf. 1 Pet. 5:8) on one front, he was falling a victim to the strategems of Satan on another front in becoming infatuated with the Timnite woman.

7. And he went down, and talked with the woman. Apparently his father and mother had preceded him to make the betrothal arrangements, otherwise Eastern custom would not have permitted him to talk to her. **8. After a time** (a betrothal might last a year) Samson returned, apparently to take the woman to his own home after the bridal feast, unless it was merely to visit her as her husband. **He turned aside to see the carcass of the lion** (i.e., "the skeleton," *măppĕlĕt*, "remains," by then thoroughly dried out by the intense heat of the sun. To his surprise, there was a **swarm of bees and honey in the carcass of the lion.**

9. He took thereof in his hands, thus breaking the express conditions of his Nazirite vow in touching a dead body (Num. 6:6). That perhaps explains why he did not tell his parents that he had taken the honey out of the dead lion. It is possible, too, that Samson already had hatched the riddle in his head and was careful to avoid divulging any clue to its solution.

Samson's Riddle at the Wedding Feast. 14:10-14. **10-11. So his father went down unto the woman** formally to claim her as his son's bride. **Samson made there a feast**, as was universally customary in biblical times (Gen. 29:22; Rev. 19:9). In the era of the judges it was the bridegroom's evident responsibility to provide the feast. The **thirty companions** were "the sons of the bridechamber" (Matt. 9:15); however, they were selected by the Philistines and would prove to be his enemies if anything went wrong.

12-14. The **riddle** in Hebrew takes the form of a rhythmical couplet, the two lines having three beats each: "Out of the eater came something to eat. And out of the strong came something sweet" (Boling, AB). The wages Samson offered were "thirty linen garments

and thirty changes of fine clothing"
(AB), a handsome prize, showing he had
some wealth and was a free spender.
The Philistines could not tell what the
riddle was, because it was insoluble
without the key.

Samson's Wife's Treachery.
14:15-20. **15-17.** On the fourth day of
the seven-day feast, after vainly trying
to solve the riddle, the Philistines
threatened to burn Samson's wife and
her father's house if she did not wheedle
the solution to the riddle from her husband. After weeping and nagging constantly, she finally got her husband to
tell her the answer, which she told her
countrymen. **18. What is sweeter than
honey? And what is stronger than a lion?**
Samson said to them, "If you had not
plowed with my heifer, You would not
have solved my riddle" (AB).

**19-20. And the Spirit of the Lord came
upon him** (*tişlāḥ*, "pervaded, passed
through, came over, fell upon in empowerment," same as v. 6). **And he went
down** to Ashkelon (modern Asqaḷon on
the Palestinian coast between Jaffa and
Gaza). There **he ... slew thirty men** and
with their **spoil** (gear) he discharged his
wages. In fierce anger Samson returned
to his father's house, his bride becoming
the wife of his "best man" (lit., "his
friend," the friend of the bridegroom,
John 3:29).

3. LATER EXPLOITS OF SAMSON. 15:1-20.

*The Philistines Slay Samson's Wife
and Father-in-law. 15:1-8.* The marriage
that Samson contracted with the Timnite woman was an ancient type in
which the husband only **visited his wife**
periodically. This visit was **in the time of
wheat harvest** (about May, near the festival of Pentecost). He brought **a kid** to
appease her for leaving so abruptly at
the wedding festivities. It was on this
visit that Samson discovered that his
father-in-law had given his wife in marriage to Samson's "best man."

2. Samson was enraged when he was
offered **her younger sister** instead (cf.
Gen. 29:23-30; 1 Sam. 18:19-27). **3. This
time I shall be blameless in regard to the
Philistines, when I do them mischief**
(RSV). His second act of vengeance
would at least have more excuse than his
assault on the men of Ashkelon (14:19).
He was reaping the bitter fruit of a Nazirite making alliances with the Philistines, which is analogous to the believer
forgetting his call to separation from
Philistinism and worldliness (cf. 2 Cor.
6:17—7:1).

4-5. In retaliation against Philistine
perfidy, Samson **caught three hundred
foxes** (or possibly "jackals," as some
maintain), joined them in pairs by their
tails, and fastened oil-soaked torches to
their tails. Then he lighted the torches
and released the frenzied animals in the
wheat fields of the Philistines (cf. v. 1),
destroying their grain and olive orchards. **6.** Placing the blame for the
calamity upon Samson's wife and
father-in-law, the brutal Philistines
burned her and her father with fire.

7. The extermination of the family of
Samson's wife was not a sufficient recompense for Samson. **Though ye have
done this, yet will I be avenged of you. 8.**
With that **he smote** (struck) **them hip and
thigh with a great slaughter.** The expression (lit., "leg on thigh") apparently was
a wrestling device, illustrated by Gilgamesh on Babylonian cylinder seals,
which means Samson struck the Philistines with decimating ferocity. Then
Samson **went down and dwelt in the top**
(cleft) **of the rock of Etam,** possibly near
the town of Etam in Judah, about two
miles southwest of Bethlehem.

*The Philistines Attempt to Punish
Samson. 15:9-13.* **9-10.** From the Philistine Plain the Philistines went up to the

Judean hill country to find Samson in order to punish him. **11-13. Three thousand men of Judah**, realizing Samson had enraged their Philistine overlords, went down to Samson to the cleft of the rock of Etam, and notified him that they would have to bind him and hand him over to the Philistines, to appease their anger and ward off their certain reprisals. Samson's only plea was **Swear unto me that ye will not fall upon me** (i.e., "kill me") **yourselves.** Having secured the promise, he allowed himself to be bound by his fellow Israelites **with two new cords** (ropes).

Samson Punishes the Philistines. 15:14-17. **14. And when Samson came to Lehi** (*lᵉhî*, "jawbone," vv. 9, 15, 16), **the Philistines shouted against him; and the Spirit of the Lord came mightily upon him** (see 14:6, 19), endowing him with superhuman strength, so that the ropes with which he was bound became **as flax that was burnt with fire, and his bands** (bonds) **loosed** (were melted) **from off his hands.**

15. He found **a new jawbone of an ass** (donkey), literally "a moist jawbone," that is, of an animal recently dead and before the bone had chance to dry out and become brittle. In this instance, Samson doubtless felt himself absolved from the rule of ceremonial uncleanness, which forbade him as a Nazirite to touch a dead body (Num. 6:6).

16. Samson's exultation over his remarkable feat found expression in a punning couplet with four beats to the line:

With the jawbone of a donkey
One heap! Two heaps!
With the jawbone of a donkey
I have laid low a thousand men.
(Lit. Heb. trans.)

Moffatt renders the first two lines: "With the jawbone of an ass I have piled them in a mass," which presents the essential thought and word play.

17. After his feat, Samson **cast away the jawbone ... and called that place Ramath-lehi**, that is, "the lifting up of the jawbone" or "casting away of the jawbone"; in the first instance deriving Ramath from *rûm*, "to be high," and in the second instance from *rāmâ*, "to cast away." Perhaps the simple meaning "the hill (height) of Lehi" is the more natural meaning. Boling renders it: "He threw the jawbone away, naming that place Jawbone's Height" (AB).

In discarding the jawbone, faith is seen in operation. It was a feeble thing he used (cf. 1 Cor. 1:27-29), boasting being excluded. What a snare to exalt the poor, foolish instrument God in His goodness may use. Put the poor jawbone where it belongs, lest it detract from the glory of Him to whom all glory alone is due.

Samson's Prayer and the Answer. 15:18-20. **18.** After Samson's victory, **he was very thirsty**, since he was in the heat of harvest and exhausted from his slaughter of the Philistines. So he cried out to the LORD, "You have granted by your servant's hand this great deliverance. Shall I now die of thirst and fall into the hand of the uncircumcised?" (lit. Heb. trans.). **19.** This verse should read: "And God broke open the Mortar which is at Lehi (jawbone). Water flowed out of it and he drank. His spirit revived and he came alive!" The rest of the verse is a note of explanation: "That is why it is called *En-hakkore* ('spring of the caller'), which is at Lehi ('Jawbone') to this very day." "The Mortar" "hollow place," KJV; Heb., *măktēsh* was a spring in the form of a mortar, so called from its peculiar resemblance to a hollow dish. (Cf. "the mortar," *măktēsh*, Prov. 27:22; Zeph. 1:11.) **20.** This verse forms a conclusion to the account of Samson's victory over the Philistines at

Lehi, as well as the conclusion to the entire story of his exploits (16:31).

4. SAMSON'S WEAKNESS AND FALL. 16:1-31.

Samson's Moral Weakness. 16:1-3. **1.** Samson went to Gaza (Josh. 15:47), evidently the most important city of the Philistine pentapolis, or five-city confederation (cf. Judg. 1:18; 14:19), which also included Ekron, Ashdod, Gath, and Ashkelon. As a Nazirite he had no business going to Philistia, where temptation again overcame him and he grossly violated his separation to God by uniting himself to a harlot (cf. 1 Cor. 6:16). His physical strength was in contrast to his moral weakness.

2. The men of Gaza learned that their enemy was within the city, and they waited in hiding for him all night at the city gate. **3.** Excavation of city gates of early Iron Age sites reveals how Samson could have slipped past the Gazites, because the latter assumed that they could wait "in the city gate," that is, in the guardrooms flanking the tunnellike opening outside the rooms. Samson's physical prowess is featured because he is portrayed taking hold of the doors of the gate and the two gateposts and carrying them eastward **to the top of an hill ... before Hebron**, meaning not the thirty-nine miles to the city itself, but probably (as the local tradition holds) to El Montar (a hill eastward in the direction of Hebron), from which the mountains of Hebron are visible in the distance.

The carrying away of the gate of his enemies in Bible lands would be understood as a very peculiar insult. Pliny (*Natural History* 7.19) adduces instances of colossal strength, but the biblical narrative depicts Samson's physical strength as not only a supernatural gift but as analogous to spiritual strength

arising from Nazirite separation from the world and dedication to God.

Moreover, Samson's exploits are illustrative of spiritual achievement as the result of dedication to God that opposes Philistinism (see 13:2-14), which is characterized by (1) religious ritualism with no knowledge of efficacious sacrifice that takes away sin, leaving uncertainty as to sins forgiven and the reality of salvation; (2) principles that bind the energy of faith in God and His Word, substituting human works and merit; (3) claims to sole authority over God's Word, which is then tightly shut up, as the Philistines treated Abraham's wells; (4) teaching of some other way into the land of blessing except by the Red Sea and the Jordan (the cross of Christ); and (5) the introduction of carnal principles and ideas, which the flesh can approve, into the things of God.

Samson and Delilah's Deception. 16:4-14. **4.** This third involvement with a Philistine woman brought Samson to a tragic end. Like him, believers can commit "a sin unto [physical] death" (1 John 5:16; 1 Cor. 5:5; 11:30). King Saul is another example (1 Sam. 28:19), also falling victim to the Philistines. Samson **loved a woman in the valley of Sorek** ("vineyard valley," "wadi [*năḥăl*] of choice vines"), present-day Wadi-es-Sarar running along the north end of the Philistine plain. **Delilah** is best explained as meaning "flirtatious," related to the Arabic *dallatum*, "flirt." She is an excellent illustration of the world, the fair, alluring, pleasure-loving religious world, which aims, as she did, to rob the true Nazirite of his separation as the real power of the spiritual life.

5. The Philistine **lords** (*sᵉrānîm*, "tyrants," a technical, political term relating the Philistine pentapolis to an Aegean homeland; cf. 3:3), implored Delilah to **entice** (*păttî*, "persuade, seduce, deceive") **him and see** (*băměh*) **wherein** (in what) **his great strength lieth** (is), and how they might tie him up to torture him. As superstitious idolatrous religionists, they likely attributed Samson's great physical prowess to some occult means, such as a hidden amulet worn on his person. Their bribe of fifty-five hundred pieces of silver, eleven hundred from each of the Philistine tyrants, was enormous; it reflects the high price the world of Philistinism (see vv. 1-6) is willing to pay to rid itself of true Spirit-empowered servants of God, who threaten its very existence.

6. Flirting with Delilah ("flirtatious"), Samson was like a moth attracted to the fire, though burning awaits it. From the very start he knew his temptress was bent on his destruction. In fact, she as much as told him so: "Please tell me in what your great strength is and how (lit., "by what") you may be tied up to be tormented" (lit. Heb. trans.). His fatuity was almost incredible. Only in the light of the subtlety and cunning deception of the world and its blinding effect upon its dupes, whom it infatuates, can Samson's folly be understood. The irresistible lure of the world of Philistinism is so dramatically portrayed here in story form to be a vivid warning to all subsequent generations of believers.

7. And Samson said . . . If they bind me with seven green cords . . . then shall I be weak. What is meant is "seven pieces of fresh gut" prepared from animal viscera, behind which there is some obscure reason (magic perhaps) for using the physically inferior unprocessed product. Archaeology suggests the possibility that Samson may have been jestingly demeaning the maledictory elements in his oath of office as a judge of the LORD. The official in the Hittite "Soldier's Oath," in the middle of a maledictory

barrage, throws "sinews and salt . . . on a pan" and declares: "Just as these sinews split into pieces on the hearth—whoever breaks these oaths . . . let the oaths seize him" (ANET 3:353-54). Was Samson's idle jesting an ominous precursor that he was so grossly violating his oath as a warrior of Yahweh that he was about to be dishonorably discharged from military service? (cf. Boling, "Joshua," AB, p. 249).

11-12. Samson continued his teasing and lying to Delilah. This time he jestingly suggested **new ropes.** "If they were to tie me securely with new ropes that have not been used (for work), then I would be weak and be like any other human being (lit. Heb. trans.). But the new ropes had been anticipated by the extradition incident with the men of Judah (15:13), and there, as here, Samson threw them off with ease.

13-14. In the third round, the crafty and relentless Delilah brought Samson closer and closer to the brink of ruin. **And he said to her, "If you weave the seven locks of my hair** (lit., head) **with the web [and fasten it with a pin, then I shall become weak and be like any other man." So while he slept, Delilah took the seven locks of his hair and wove them into the web]. And she fastened it with the pin** (NASB; the bracketed words are found in the Greek, but not in any Hebrew manuscript).

Delilah must have had the sleeping Samson's head in her lap (as in v. 19), while she deftly wove his hair into the warp and then beat it up into the web with a pin (a flat piece of wood); thus, his hair was intertwined with the woven material. As Moore points out, "We are to imagine the simplest kind of an upright loom" (G. Moore, *Judges*, ICC, p. 354). When Samson awoke, he went off, loom and all fixed to his hair, dragging the upright posts out of the ground (F. F. Bruce, NBC, p. 272).

Samson Divulges the Big Secret. 16:15-20. **15-16.** Wheedling, coaxing, pressuring, and nagging, Delilah finally accomplished her goal. He **was vexed** (exasperated) **unto** (to the point of) **death. 17-19.** So **he told her all** (that was in) **his heart.** He explained the Nazirite vow (cf. Num. 6:2-21) and that he had been God's Nazirite from conception (cf. Judg. 13:5, 7). The tragic thing about Samson was that the rule of the Nazirite warrior meant so little to him that he could jest about it and put it in the same category with common superstitions. There was nothing superstitious, however, about his uncut hair, since it symbolized his willingness to be separated to the LORD and to endure reproach by being different from the world. Nor is there anything superstitious about the cutting of his hair, since that represented his discharge from active duty according to the divinely given legislation (Num. 6:13-21). Samson's trouble was not a broken vow, but a vow that had never been taken seriously.

20. The whole sad story crystallizes in his revealing statement after his locks were shorn and his strength gone: **I will go out as at other times before, and shake myself** (i.e., shake myself free). **And he knew not that the Lord was departed from him** (cf. Num. 14:43; 1 Sam. 16:14). His strength was not in his hair, but only in the dedication to God of which it was the symbol.

Samson's Humiliation and Death. 16:21-31. **21-28.** Samson's humiliation by the Philistines and his chastening by the LORD, whom he had so signally dishonored, are succinctly described: (1) The Philistines **took him** captive. (2) They **put out** ("bored" or "gouged" out) **his eyes,** a most effectual degradation (2 Kings 25:7). (3) They **brought him**

down to Gaza, where his relationship with the harlot had previously brought him (v. 1).

(4) They **bound him with fetters of bronze** (lit., "two bronzes," *nᵉḥushtă-yim,* "a pair of bronze fetters"). (5) **He did grind in the prison house.** Grinding meal between millstones was the task of a beast or slaves and women (Exod. 11:5; Isa. 47:2; Matt. 24:41), not the honorable employ of the mighty hero Samson! (6) He became the cause of praise to the Philistine deity Dagon, the fish god, and the cause of insult and blasphemy to the LORD God of Israel. (7) He was reduced to entertaining the Philistines, evidently by strong-man acts.

But amid that scene of divine chastening, the LORD displayed His love for His own. "For whom the LORD loveth he chasteneth, and scourgeth every son whom he receiveth" (Heb. 12:6; cf. Prov. 3:11-12). Samson's hair **began to grow again** after he was shaven (lit., "after it was cut or snipped off"; *gŭllāh,* "sheared, cut"). The symbol of his Nazirite dedication to the LORD and empowerment from Him began to reappear.

Samson's prayer shows his confession of sin and return to his place of trust in and yieldedness to the LORD. His chastening was "grievous" but it was yielding "the peaceable fruit of righteousness" to one who had been trained and corrected by it (Heb. 12:11). Yet even at that point Samson, although once more conscious of his mission, did not move on a high spiritual level, but instead prayed for vengeance on the Philistines because of the loss of his eyes.

They made him (Samson) **stand between the pillars** (NASB). The main hall of a recently excavated Philistine temple at Tell Qasile is "a long room whose roof was originally supported by two wooden pillars set on round well-made stone bases, placed along the center axis" (A. Mazar, BA 36 [1973] : 43). While Samson was forced to **make sport for** (entertain) the Philistines, he asked the boy who led him to conduct him to the central pillars.

29-30. Putting an arm around each pillar, and bending forward to force them out of the perpendicular, he literally "brought the house down," the weight of the crowd on the roof facilitating the climactic feat. His name, despite his failures and sins, is mentioned in Hebrews 11:32 as one who gave his life to vindicate God before the blasphemous pagans. In spite of his carnal life, he had justifying faith, which saved him. **31.** Samson's burial in the family plot was simple, but honorable. His judgeship in a civil capacity, if any, is not treated in the narrative.

III. EXAMPLES OF ISRAEL'S LAWLESSNESS. 17:1—21:25.

A. RELIGIOUS CONFUSION. 17:1—18:31.

1. MICAH'S IDOLATROUS PRIESTHOOD. 17:1-13.

Micah's Image. 17:1-6. **1-4.** Micah ("Who is like Yahweh?") by his very name implies that Yahweh is incomparable. Yet, ironically, he made a molten image. And there **it was in the house of Micah** (NASB margin; in the house of "Yahweh-the-Incomparable")! Micah's name is paraphrased to give full force to the insult his idolatry was to the LORD. What a scene of religious apostasy is introduced—the thieving son, the cursing mother. He, for fear of the curse in a spirit of superstition (not true faith), restored the money. She, in a spirit of religious ignorance, neutralized

the curse by invoking a blessing, presuming to mix light and darkness and identify the temple of God with idols (cf. 2 Cor. 6:14—7:1). In that spirit she declared, **I had wholly dedicated the silver unto the Lord from my hand for my son** ("my son," vocative; see AB).

Yet she nullified such alleged dedication by the grossest lawlessness in her announcement of the purpose of the dedication—**to make a graven image and a molten image** (a hendiadys, $p\bar{e}s\check{e}l$ $\bar{u}$-$m\check{a}ss\bar{e}\underline{k}\hat{a}$, lit., "sculpture and something poured out," meaning "a molten figure," one carved out of wood and overlaid with silver; cf. Exod. 20:4, 23; 34:17). This hendiadys explains the singular form of the verb in verse 4, which should be translated, "He returned the money to his mother, and his mother took two hundred of silver and gave it to the smith, and he made of it a molten figure. There *it was*, in the house of Micah."

5. And the man Micah had an house of gods ($b\hat{e}t$ $^{\prime e}l\bar{o}h\hat{i}m$, "an idolatrous shrine"; cf. 18:24) and added to his syncretistic system—a lawless mixture of Yahwism and paganism—**an ephod**, an elaborate priestly vestment used for divinatory purposes (cf. 8:27), **and teraphim** (images used as household gods; cf. Gen. 31:30; 1 Sam. 19:13; 2 Kings 23:24; Ezek. 21:21; Hos. 3:4-5; Zech. 10:2). He **consecrated** ("installed, filled the hand of") **one of his sons** (Exod. 28:41; 29:9; Lev. 8:31-33), **who became his priest** (cf. Num. 3:10). That was forbidden by the Mosaic Law upon pain of death and represents utter religious anarchy.

6. No wonder the recurring notation is inserted: **In those days there was no king in Israel,** but every man did that **which was right in his own eyes** (cf. 18:1; 19:1; 21:25; Deut. 12:8). It summarizes the spiritual lawlessness of the cultic opportunist (Micah) and introduces an aspiring religious careerist (Micah's Levite). What a pointed illustration this is of ritualistic, humanly concocted worship that ignores the Word of God. A man-made god, a man-made worship, and a man-made priest have often characterized ritualistic Christendom, as well as lawless cults.

Micah's Priest. 17:7-13. **7.** He came from Bethlehem in Judah and was a Levite **and he sojourned there,** that is, was "a resident alien," reflecting the fact that technically the Levites were considered aliens, resident in the various tribes, but with no tribal allotment of their own. **8-9.** This Levite left Bethlehem in Judah **to sojourn where** (wherever) **he could find** (something), that is, discover some new opportunity to further his ecclesiastical career. He journeyed into the hill country of Ephraim and appeared at Micah's house (Beth-micah; cf. 18:14-15, a later place name).

10-11. Micah invited him to stay with him. **Be . . . father and . . . priest.** Apparently the title "father" emphasizes the priest's role as cultic diviner (as in 18:4-6) in the syncretistic cult that Micah set up. That Micah's "house of gods" (shrine) was well known for that reason is suggested by the equipment it contained. Compare Deborah as the "mother in Israel," being renowned for having the right answers to oracular and other questions (5:7). The Levite accepted Micah's invitation for board, room, clothing, and a yearly stipend.

12-13. Micah concluded he would be blessed by the LORD, **seeing I have a Levite as my priest** (cf. Deut. 10:8-9). This is a striking illustration of all apostasy. False priesthood was exalted while Micah completely departed from the revealed will of God concerning worship and priestly access to God (cf. Num.

3:10, 38; 4:15, 19-20). As the people of God, we have one Priest, through whose infinite grace all believers are constituted priests with Him (Heb. 10:4-16; Rev. 1:6). We are a holy and royal priesthood (1 Pet. 2:5; Heb. 10:19-22). Any other priesthood is a wicked assumption that has corrupted Christianity.

The hireling, too, in commercialized religion is represented in this scene. Micah's priest found a home where he should have been a stranger. Support and salary blinded him to the idolatry of the place over which the halo of the LORD's name was thrown. It was a manufactured priesthood for manufactured gods, all covered with the mantle of professing godliness, with men doing with great satisfaction what was right in their own eyes.

2. THE DANITE MIGRATION. 18:1-31.

Summary and Transition. 18:1. **1.** This verse connects the story of Micah's idolatrous priesthood (chap. 17) with its sequel, the Danite migration and the establishment of a heretical sanctuary at Dan as further evidence of the religious lawlessness of the period. **In those days there was no king in Israel.** What is lamented as producing these sad instances of religious apostasy was the failure to acknowledge the LORD's kingship in Israel. At that time the Danites were seeking for themselves a place to live, since **all their inheritance had not fallen to them among the tribes of Israel.** The Philistines and the Amorites (1:34) had been pressing them relentlessly in their narrow tribal strip located west of Jerusalem and south of Joppa.

The Danite Scouts and Micah's Priest. 18:2-6. **2-3.** The Danites dispatched from their clan five **men of valor** (*'ănāshîm benê-ḥăyil*, "prosperous men") able to fit themselves out militarily and trained in upper-class combat, like Gideon (6:12) and Jephthah (11:1), **to spy out** (reconnoiter) **the land, and to search** (explore) **it.** The five scouts came to the Ephraimite hill country to (*'ăd*, "as far as") **the house of Micah** (Beth-micah) and **lodged there** overnight.

There they **recognized the voice** (the accent) **of the young man, the Levite.** His accent was Judahite (southern) like their own, not Israelite (northern). Their triple question betrayed their excitement at running into the priest. **Who brought thee here? And what makest** (doest) **thou in this place? And what hast thou here?** (i.e., "What business do you have here?").

4-5. When he told them that Micah had hired him as his priest, they were eager for him to inquire of God that they might know whether the mission they were on would be **prosperous** (*tăṣlîăḥ*, "completely successful," an elative use of the Hebrew verbal form to give emphasis to the root idea). **6.** The priest's reply was in line with his man-made priesthood and his essential disregard of the Word of God. **Go in peace; before the Lord is your way**, meaning "Go confidently; the mission you are pursuing has Yahweh's approval." Like all hirelings and false priests, he who had made "his own way" (cf. 17:8) glibly made a pronouncement concerning their way; he illustrates the groundless optimism that frequently characterizes protagonists of empty, ritualistic religion that disregards the Word of God.

The Favorable Report Brought Back. 18:7-10. **7.** The five Danite scouts departed from Beth-micah and went to Laish (18:29; also called Leshem, Josh. 19:47), appearing as Lus(i) in Egyptian texts of the nineteenth century B.C., located in the most northerly part of Israel near the sources of the Jordan River.

They observed the people who were there, how they were living securely (*lābĕṭāḥ*, "without anxiety"), meaning perhaps, "without defenses," as has been borne out by excavations at Tell el-Qadi (Arab., *qadî*, "judge"; cf. Heb., *Dan*), which indicate that the city was unwalled in that period (A. Biran, IEJ 19 [1969]:122-23).

The calm and confident inhabitants of Laish were **far from the Sidonians**, the trading Phoenicians in their coastal emporium and **had no business with any man** (*'ādām*, "anyone"), although most critics read it, with certain LXX and Syriac manuscripts, "and they had no treaty [*dābār*] with Aram ['*ªrām*]." **8-10.** Returning to **their brethren to Zorah and Eshtaol** (cf. v. 2; see Josh. 19:41; Judg. 13:2, 25; 16:31), the report of the spies urged immediate migration to their newly found home.

The Plunder of Micah's Shrine. 18:11-26. **11-12.** Six hundred Danites set out, fully armed, pitching camp on the way at Kiriath-jearim, a city of Judah, eight miles west of Jerusalem, the place afterward being called **Mahaneh-dan** ("camp of Dan"; cf. 13:25). **13.** From there they passed through the Ephraimite hill country and **came unto the house of Micah** (Beth-micah). **14.** There the five spies who had gone to reconnoiter the territory (Laish) spoke up and said to their brothers: **Do ye know** (realize) **that there are in these houses** (Micah's shrine complex) **an ephod, and teraphim** as well as **a molten image** (KJV; see 17:3-4). The suggestion was brutal, but it was in line with the moral and spiritual bankruptcy of the era. **Now, therefore, consider** (make up your mind) **what ye have to do** (cf. Deut. 13:6-18).

15-20. Under cover of the six hundred fully armed Danites, who had stationed themselves at the entrance of the gate, the five spies who had gone to reconnoiter the land went in and expropriated the figure, the ephod, and the teraphim (cf. v. 20). When the priest saw what they were doing, he apparently retrieved the cult items from the five with the glad decision to go along, taking up a safe position surrounded by the troops. As a compromising hireling and ecclesiastical career-climber, he had no real convictions or principles to stand or fight for. **Hold thy peace** was an unnecessary injunction. His tongue was silent regarding any opposition, particularly after their offer to make him a more important and wealthier **father** (an ecclesiastical term like "papa, pope"; cf. 2 Kings 2:12; 5:13; 6:21; Isa. 22:21). **21-26.** So the group with their new hireling priest and syncretistic cult moved out, putting the youngsters, the cattle, and the **possessions** (heavy baggage, $k^e \underline{b}\hat{u}dd\hat{a}$, "heavy stuff") in front to keep the warriors between the loot and the victims (Micah and his men), who might (and did) give chase. Their utterly callous treatment of Micah is a detail that emphasizes the complete moral and spiritual insensitivity into which apostates can sink in the prosecution of dead religion.

The Conquest and Settlement of Laish. 18:27-31. **27.** The conduct of the Danites in regard to Micah was dastardly enough, especially in the name of religion. But then, Micah was reaping the harvest of the seeds of lawlessness he himself had sown. But the action of the Danites in massacring the quiet and unsuspecting people of Laish and burning their city was even more reprehensible. **28-29.** Rebuilding the city and settling there, they renamed the town Dan in honor of their tribal head.

30. Micah's stolen image was set up and the heretical sanctuary of Dan was founded, the whole tribe becoming idolatrous and presenting a picture of thoroughgoing apostasy. A line of priests whose genealogy went back to Gershon, the son of Moses, officiated at the Danite sanctuary. The reading of **Gershon, the son of Manasseh**, is based on a scribal notation in which the raised letter *nun* was inserted in *mōshěh* (Moses) to make it read Manasseh in order to remove the name of Moses from this idolatrous association.

Was Jonathan the name of Micah's Levite (17:7)? This alien priesthood, in violation of the Deuteronomic law of the central sanctuary (see Deut. 12) lasted **until ... the captivity of the land** (the deportation of the people when Tiglath-pileser overran northern Israel in 733-732 B.C. (2 Kings 15:29). Some scholars amend the text to read, "the carrying away of the ark" (1 Sam. 4:5) by the Philistines (c. 1050 B.C.). Others view this verse as having been inserted in a later edition. **31.** The Danites ignored Shiloh as the central sanctuary (1 Sam. 1:3) and maintained their own idolatrous shrine. After the secession of the northern tribes, Jeroboam set up golden calves (bulls) at this ancient seat of illegitimate worship (1 Kings 12:29).

B. MORAL DEGRADATION. 19:1—21:25.

1. THE CRIME AT GIBEAH. 19:1-30.

The Levite and His Concubine. 19:1-9. **1-2. In those days ... there was no king in Israel.** This statement is repeated here (cf. 17:6; 18:1; 21:25) because an appalling crime is about to be related that could never have been committed under strong central government headed by a king. In fact, the LORD was King, but the people had departed so far from His kingly rule that the results appeared in the awful corruption and violence so faithfully recorded in this chapter. In those lawless times there was a Levite living as a resident alien in

343

the remote hill country of Ephraim. His concubine from Bethlehem in Judah, whom he had taken, ran back home to her father's house in Bethlehem as the result of a quarrel. She was there four months.

3. Then her husband went to her to effect a kindly reconciliation. **4-9.** The Levite's father-in-law welcomed him and detained him for four days in a most hospitable manner, no doubt to win back the Levite's heart to his erring daughter and to be thoroughly assured that the Levite was not concealing his feelings and did not desire to inflict some sanguinary retribution on his wife, which was permitted a husband in Eastern lands in punishment of conjugal unfaithfulness.

The Journey Home. 19:10-21. **10.** Finally, toward late afternoon on the fifth day, the Levite set out with his concubine, his servant, and a pair of saddled donkeys. **11-13.** Refusing to spend the night at Jebus (Jerusalem), the Levite and his party determined to press on to Gibeah or Ramah. **14-21.** Darkness overtook them at Gibeah, and so they turned in there. They were taken in and entertained by a resident alien of Gibeah, an old man from the Ephraimite hill country. He happened to run into them as they sat in the town plaza when he was returning from his day's work in the field.

The Fate of the Concubine. 19:22-26. **22-23.** Meanwhile, **the men of the city, certain sons of Belial** (i.e., "worthless scoundrels, hell-raisers," "Belial" being one of the most maleficent characters of the mythical underworld; cf. Psalm 18:4-5; Deut. 13:13; 1 Sam. 2:12) **beset** (surrounded) the house and demanded that **the man,** the Levite who was a guest, be brought out that they might **know** (*yāḏaʿ*, euphemism for having sexual relations with) him. It is

evident that the Benjamites of Gibeah had sunk to the same level as the Sodomites (Gen. 19:1-14).

The neglect and gross violation of the very first duty of hospitality of Oriental countries are proof of the base condition into which Gibeah had fallen (cf. Rom. 1:26-32; 2 Tim. 3:1-5). Adopting Canaanite ways, Israel sank into the cesspool of Canaanite violence and immorality, which were wedded to the Canaanite religion with its degraded gods and goddesses. Similar immorality attends the present-day worldwide apostasy of the end time (Luke 17:28-30). **25-26.** The rape and murder of the Levite's concubine show what happens in any society that turns its back upon God and His Word.

The Levite's Action. 19:27-30. **27-29.** The Levite was affected more deeply than it appears from verses 27 and 28. He put the corpse on his donkey and when he arrived home he systematically dismembered it into twelve pieces and sent one piece to each tribe. **30. And it came about that all who saw it said, "Nothing like this has ever happened or been seen from the day when the sons of Israel came up from the land of Egypt to this day. Consider it, take counsel and speak up!"** (NASB). In the absence of a regular constituted government, an extraordinary step like this was warranted. No method could have been imagined to be more certain of arousing public horror than the Levite's terrible summons to decisive action.

2. THE WAR WITH BENJAMIN. 20:1-48.

The Tribes Meet—The Levite Describes the Crime. 20:1-7. **1-2.** The outrage yielded a harvest of war and bloodshed (cf. Gal. 6:7). Israel assembled representatively **as one man,** united because of the immense revulsion the horrible tragedy at Gibeah produced. All

Israel, **from Dan even to Beersheba** (1 Sam. 3:20; 2 Sam. 3:10), except Jabesh Gilead, appeared as delegates. The place of convention was **Mizpah**, situated on the confines of Judah and Benjamin (Josh. 15:38; 18:26). **The assembly of the people of God** gathered **unto the Lord** to consult the divine oracle.

3. The Benjamites heard that **the children of Israel were gone up to Mizpah.** They had doubtlessly been sent the summons betokened by a piece of the murdered victim's body. Since Mizpah was only three miles from Gibeah, they knew what was happening, but chose to defend Gibeah. **4-7.** The Levite told the assembly what had happened. He called the **men** (citizens) **of Gibeah** ($b^e\bar{a}l\hat{\imath}m$, "masters, lords, nobility"), doubtless in sarcasm. "These noble men of Gibeah" committed such a foul crime! (cf. 9:2; 1 Sam. 23:11-12; 2 Sam. 21:12, where the same term is used of prominent citizens, with a sarcastic, ironic tinge). The Levite concluded his testimony with a pointed challenge: "Therefore, all you Israelites, give your word and counsel, right here!" (AB).

The People's Decision to Punish Gibeah. 20:8-48. **8-11. The people arose as one man** (see v. 1; cf. 1 Sam. 11:7) and determined to go up against Gibeah by lot, taking one-tenth of the fighting force to supply provisions for the army. They determined to render exact retribution for the senseless disgrace the Benjamites had committed in Israel. **12-13.** Couriers were sent throughout Benjamin asking for the surrender of the **children of Belial** (KJV; "scoundrels, hellraisers"; see 19:22) that they might be put to death and the evil they had perpetrated put out of Israel.

14-17. The Benjamites, however, mustered for battle, showing their total lack of moral sensibility to the issue in-

volved, evidently self-confidently relying on their prowess in warfare. **18.** In consulting the lots, the Israelites went up **to the house of God**, that is, Bethel ($b\hat{e}\underline{t}'\bar{e}l$), rather than Shiloh. Evidently the high priest was not prevented by any scruples from taking the ephod and the Urim and Thummim to any place they were needed. Judah was directed to go up against Gibeah first. **19-25.** The first and second encounters were disastrous.

26-28. When the Israelites humbled themselves before the Lord and offered sacrifices at Bethel and inquired again of the Lord at the hands of Phinehas of the Aaronic line (Num. 25:7, 13; Josh. 24:33), victory was promised. **29-46.** And victory was won. The battle strategy resembles the battle at Ai (Josh. 8:4) and at Shechem (Judg. 9:43). The army of Benjamin was drawn away from the city to the main roads and Gibeah was ambushed, taken, and burned.

47-48. Some six hundred Benjamites escaped to the Rimmon Rock, where they survived for four months. The men of Israel returned and killed even the beasts, burning the towns that were implicated. Although the story is one of horror, it illustrates the wrath of God against the outrageous sin and moral degradation that precipitated it. God is infinitely holy, and when the iniquity of a people is brim full (cf. Gen. 15:16), divine vengeance must fall, as it did upon Sodom and Gomorrah (Gen. 19:24-26), and as it must fall upon ageend wickedness during the coming time of the Tribulation (Rev. 4:1—19:16). The record tallies well with the character of Phinehas, the priest-warrior who was zealous for the glory of God and the holiness of his people (Num. 25:7-8; 31:6).

3. THE RESTORATION OF BENJAMIN. 21:1-25.

Remorse at the Extirpation of a Tribe.

345

21:1-15. **1.** With quick change of mind, the Israelite tribes realized that Benjamin was on the verge of extinction. Not only had they massacred the entire tribe, except for the six hundred men who had escaped, but they had taken an oath at Mizpah that no man among them would give his daughter in marriage to Benjamin. It is evident from the sequel (v. 18) that it was not only an oath, but also "a vow under a curse," as in Acts 23:14.

2. The people came to the house of God (Bethel, 20:18, 26-27), and **wept bitterly** (with great lamentation). **3. Why is this come to pass . . . ?** The answer, of course, was because of their departure from God and their sins. The question is often broached in our times, as people behold scenes of war and destruction, "Why is this?" Many are even ready to blame God instead of facing sin and its curse.

The threefold wail **Israel . . . Israel . . . Israel** shows that the nation had not yet lost its sense of corporate oneness as the people of God, even though that unity had been torn apart by civil war. **4.** An altar was built at Bethel and the people presented **burnt offerings and peace offerings**, showing that their faith reached out to the grace and mercy of God to meet them in their failures and excesses (cf. 2 Sam. 24:25; 1 Kings 3:4).

5-9. Another item, omitted up to this point, was the **great oath** concerning those who did not respond to the muster against Benjamin at Mizpah. This anticipates verse 8, where it is recorded that none came up from Jabesh-gilead, two miles east of the Jordan, present-day Tell Abu-Kharaz, on the north side of the Wadi Yabis (N. Glueck, BASOR 91 [1943]:8-9). To secure wives for the surviving Benjamites, it was determined to place Jabesh-gilead under the curse (as upon Meroz, 5:23, "because they came not to the help of the LORD").

How awful in these lawless times appears the force derivable from a vow and the wicked folly of fierce vows rashly made in moments of uncontrolled passion. It is apparent that the vow taken concerning the Benjamites had in mind the tribe's annihilation. Then the foolhardiness of that vow dawned upon the people and they were pressed to counteract it with other violent measures to secure wives for the Benjamite survivors.

10-15. Jabesh-gilead was to be placed under the ban. **Ye shall utterly destroy** (tăḥªrîmû, "you shall devote to destruction"), except for the four hundred young virgins who were found there and later brought to the camp at Shiloh. Evidently the camp had been moved there as the normal and central seat of the tabernacle at that period (18:31).

Restoration of Benjamin as a Tribe. 21:16-25. **16.** The question that then confronted **the elders of the congregation** was how to provide **wives** for the Benjamites who had survived — the two hundred men above the four hundred at the Rock Rimmon (20:47; 21:13). **17-18.** Some way had to be found to circumvent the oath that had been taken to not give wives to the Benjamites (cf. v. 1; 1 Sam. 14:24). **19. Then they said** to the two hundred who were still left without wives, **Behold, there is a feast of the Lord in Shiloh yearly.** It was a local variety of the Feast of Tabernacles (Lev. 23:33-44), held specifically to mark the ingathering of the year's vintage (cf. Judg. 9:27).

20. The Benjamites were instructed to **Go and lie in wait in the vineyards** until they spotted the young women dancing (cf. 11:34). **21.** Then each man was to come out of hiding and **catch . . . every man his wife.** It was hardly anything but rape, in a sense a revival of the ancient practice of marriage by capture; but it relieved the Israelites of any charge of violating their oath, for it could not be said that their daughters were "given" to the Benjamites, but rather they were "taken" by them.

22-23. In case opposition would come from the relatives of the girls, the Israelites gave their assurance to the Benjamites that they would support their cause. In this way wives were provided for a tribe that was reduced to the brink of destruction. **24.** After saving the tribe of Benjamin from extinction, the Israelite assembly dispersed. **25.** The book concludes with a notation that is especially appropriate to the account of the horrible crime of Gibeah and its punishment as well as to the period of the judges in general (quoted from 17:6; cf. 18:1; 19:1).

RUTH

Title. The book of Ruth takes its name from its heroine, a woman of Moab, who after she was widowed left her native land with Naomi, her widowed mother-in-law, to cast her fortunes with the people of God at Bethlehem in Judah. There she found marital happiness and, as the wife of Boaz, Naomi's relative, she became the ancestress of King David (Ruth 4:18-22) and of Jesus the Christ (Matt. 1:1, 5).

Place in the Canon. In the Septuagint and the Vulgate, as in our English Bible, the book of Ruth follows Judges. In Hebrew Bibles, however, Ruth appears in the third section called the Writings. There it is the second of the five so-called Scrolls (Megilloth), which were used liturgically in the synagogue services by the sixth century A.D. Ruth was read at Pentecost because of its background of the wheat harvest. Apparently the book was first placed among the Writings and was later placed in its historical setting between Judges and Samuel. It was highly regarded by Jews in antiquity, and its canonicity was never doubted.

Date and Authorship. The real author of Ruth, as of all the canonical books of Scripture, is God the Holy Spirit. But the human author and the precise date when he wrote are unknown. However, some general indications of the time of composition are found in the book, suggesting a probable date sometime in the reign of David. For example, Sol-omon's name would very likely not have been omitted in the genealogy (4:17-22) had the book been written as late as his reign. On the other hand, the book was written late enough so that the author considered it necessary to explain certain customs that by his time had fallen into disuse. Higher critical views on insufficient evidence frequently date the book in later preexilic times, some even in the postexilic era (R. Pfeiffer, *Introduction to the Old Testament*, p. 718). The Talmud (Baba Bathra 14*b*) attributes the book to Samuel, but without any concrete evidence. The book itself gives full evidence of a reliable historical account of events that have peculiar relevance to the divine redemptive ways. It fits into the picture of David's day, when there was a happy relation between Israel and Moab.

Nature of the Book. From a literary standpoint, the book has been called "the most charming short story in the Old Testament" (G. W. Thatcher, *Ruth*, New Century Bible, p. 175). It is indeed a delightful idyll of faithfulness, love, and high devotion. But it is much more than a lovely pastoral tale inculcating virtue and morality. In its rich underlying typology it is an illustration of the divine redemptive plan for the salvation of the fallen race. In a specific sense it presents the Kinsman-Redeemer in that aspect of His glorious character as it will affect *Israel*, His elect nation, in its future salvation and restoration. To this end it presents an important link in the redemptive line through the house of David, from which the Messiah-Savior was to come more than a millennium later. Although the book in its illustrative purpose specifically relates the truth of kinsman redemption to Israel, it embraces the prospect of salvation for all mankind. Ruth the Moabitess, a Gentile, becomes the ancestress of David, in whose veins Gentile blood ran, and the Davidic ancestry ultimately produced the Savior.

OUTLINE

COMMENTARY

I. RUTH'S DECISION OF FAITH. 1:1-22.

Naomi's Misfortunes. 1:1-5. **1.** The story is laid **in the days when the judges ruled**, precisely when is uncertain. However, the events must have transpired in one of the periods when the land enjoyed a protracted period of peace (cf. Judg. 3:11, 30; 5:31). The story that unfolds is a lovely tale teaching moral lessons. But it is much more than that, since it deals with redemption. As the romance of redemption, it prefigures, in an underlying illustrative sense, God's dispensational ways with the nation Israel. The message of the book is expounded from that point of view, treating it as a phase of the divine redemptive love for the world.

2-4. Naomi ("pleasant one") married to **Elimelech** ("my God is king") portrays Israel's prosperity in the land, married to the LORD, faithful to Him, and enjoying His grace and favor. The griefs that came upon Naomi as a result of the famine speak of spiritual failure and chastisement in the land in Bethlehem ("house of food"), the place where He who is the Bread of Life was to be born later. "Judah" is added to distinguish this Bethlehem from the Bethlehem in Zebulun (Josh. 19:15). Ephrath was the older name of Bethlehem (Gen. 35:19).

The migration to Moab, a pagan nation, is illustrative of Israel's worldwide dispersion. The death of Elimelech, Naomi's husband, in a foreign land illustrates Israel's national rejection during the many centuries of her absence from the land, her widowhood and separation from her Husband, the LORD (cf. Isa. 50:1-3). The deaths of **Mahlon** ("sick") and **Chilion** ("pining") in a foreign country speak of the woes and tragedies that have overtaken Israel ("Naomi") among the nations. **5. The woman was bereft.** During the decade of sojourn in Moab, death wiped out all the male members of the family; so that all that was left of the once-happy circle were three women—Naomi and her two daughters-in-law, Ruth and Orpah.

Ruth's Decision of Faith. 1:6-18. **6-7.** Naomi's hearing that **the Lord had visited his people** and her plan to return to the land suggest the time when Israel in her dispersion will set her face homeward. Naomi's afflictions turned her heart back to the LORD, and doubtless her conscience troubled her for distrusting the God of Israel in leaving the promised land in the first place.

8-15. Both of her daughters-in-law clearly intended to accompany Naomi, but only Ruth's faith enabled her to make the final choice. Orpah ("fawn, hind"), who decided to remain in Moab after Naomi's unselfish decision, is a picture of the unbelieving mass of the nation that will choose to stay among the nations in the time of Israel's return to her ancient homeland. Ruth ("friend"), however, holding fast to Naomi, beautifully portrays the believing remnant of the nation, which will espouse the hope of Israel (Ezek. 37:11; Zech. 8:7-8) and ultimately come into saving relationship with the mighty Kinsman-Redeemer, through whom they will inherit the blessings promised to their fathers.

Both Orpah and Ruth signify the nation in unbelief in the same condition as the Gentiles, $l\bar{o}$'-'ǎmmî ("not my people") (Hos. 1:9). Orpah chose to remain in that condition. Ruth, however, took the step of faith that resulted in her being incorporated among the Lord's people ('ǎmmî, "My people"), and in her becoming the ancestress of Christ. **16-18.** Ruth's protestation of loyalty to Naomi and her God constitutes a classic passage in world literature. Ruth's words, **The Lord do so to me, and more also**, imply a solemn vow, meaning, "May the Lord punish me severely if I do not keep my vow."

Arrival in Bethlehem. 1:19-22. **19-21.** Naomi's and Ruth's arrival created quite a stir. **Is this Naomi?** Her appearance as a childless widow bore testimony to the hardships that had befallen her. **Call me not Naomi** ("pleasant one") **call me Mara** ("bitter one"). **The Almighty** (El Shaddai, see Gen. 17:1; 28:3-4; Heb. 12:10) **hath dealt very bitterly with me** (*hēmǎr*, "has caused me to become *Mara*, "the bitter one," a play in Hebrew on the root *mārâ*, "to be bitter"). El Shaddai, the name under which God had revealed Himself to the patriarchs promising blessing in the land, would have Naomi realize she had forfeited blessing by leaving the land. **22.** Naomi and Ruth arrived in Bethlehem **in the beginning of the barley harvest**, ordinarily falling about the end of April, being the earliest ingathering of grain (Exod. 9:31-32). In the underlying symbolism, the harvest signifies the end of the age (Matt. 13:30, 39). When that end comes after the church has been glorified, Israel (like Naomi), with a believing remnant clinging to her (represented by Ruth), will return to the land (cf. Isa. 6:13; 10:21-22; Mic. 4:7; Zeph. 2:7).

II. RUTH'S APPROPRIATION OF GRACE. 2:1-23.

Boaz's Kindness to Ruth. 2:1-17. **1.** Boaz is presented as a relative of Naomi and thus a potential kinsman-redeemer and **a mighty man of wealth.** His name, **Boaz**, means "in him is strength." He is typical of our Lord Jesus Christ, "the wealthy One." As he "in whom there is strength," Boaz aptly portrays the Kinsman-Redeemer.

2. Ruth's character, appearing in her desire to glean in the fields of Boaz, shows the sterling character of she who represents the longing of the Israelite remnant of the end time to seek the Lord, the Kinsman-Redeemer, and to search the Scriptures to find Him in grace. **Let me go now ... and glean ... after him in whose sight I shall find grace.** She did not turn away from hard work, nor was she too proud to condescend to a work that might be accounted servile. Nor did she hanker after her old home in Moab and the plenty there. When the Jewish remnant returns at the end of the age, they will turn their back on the wealth of the nations and choose the land and its stringency to obtain ultimate blessing.

3. She happened to come. A seeming chance occurrence was actually a clear example of her steps being divinely guided by unseen hands, so that God's purposes might be worked out. When the times of the Gentiles have run their course (Rom. 11:25) and the divine purpose to restore Israel has come, God will work to consummate His plans for Israel's restoration through their Kinsman-Redeemer (cf. Rom. 11:26-33).

4-7. Boaz appeared in a spirit of true courtesy and friendliness toward his servants. The steward gave a special account of Ruth. As a Moabite **damsel** (young woman), she was a foreigner and as such had a *special* claim to the gleanings (Lev. 19:9-10). Boaz recognized that there was a newcomer in his field, doubtless by her dress and appearance, which were different from the girls that he normally observed gleaning after the reapers. The overseer over the reapers gave a good report to Boaz concerning Ruth—how she requested to be allowed to glean after the reapers, and how she worked tirelessly all day, except that **she tarried a little in the house** (a rude brush shelter, a protection from the sun). The LXX, however, reads "and she did not rest in the field" (v. 7).

8-10. Boaz's generosity overwhelmed Ruth. He urged her to remain and glean in the fields, promising her special protection. Evidently she could not take for granted that she would be respected, nor did she have any right as a foreigner to the precious water, which had to be brought from the well. As Ruth found grace in Boaz's eyes and prostrated herself before him, the Jewish remnant in the end time will find favor in the sight of the divine Kinsman-Redeemer.

As a Moabitess, a foreigner, representing the *lō'-'ammî* character of Israel ("not my people," Hos. 1:9), set aside in its national election and fallen practically into the same condition as the Gentiles, the remnant will be incorporated into the Lord's people as they come under the grace of the divine Boaz, as He shows His concern for them as they return to the land. Boaz's words of grace to Ruth and provision for her illustrate that future day when Israel will be restored to her national election of grace (cf. Zech. 12:10; 13:1; Rom. 11:25-36).

11-12. Boaz had inquired about Ruth and her faith in leaving her own land and kin. Recognizing that he could not adequately repay her by himself, he prayed that **a full reward** (would) **be given** (her) **by the Lord God of Israel,**

under whose wings she had **come to trust** ("to take refuge"; Psalms 2:12; 91:2; Heb., *hāsâ*, one of the characteristic words in the Old Testament expressing faith or trust). The thought is of a young chicken that finds protection under the wings of the mother hen (cf. Matt. 23:37; Psalms 17:8; 91:4).

13-15. Ruth, deeply affected by Boaz's concern, could understand his kindness to the maidens, but she realized that his kindness to her as a foreigner from a pagan background was pure grace. At mealtime Boaz invited Ruth to partake and gave her abundance of the new grain, roasted on the spot, so that she had some in reserve for her mother-in-law (v. 18).

16-18. He even **let fall ... some of the handfuls on purpose for her.** These extraordinary marks of favor were not only given out of a kind heart, but from regard to Ruth's good character and devoted attachment to her mother-in-law. Ruth **beat out what she had gleaned.** The quantity was **an ephah,** roughly a bushel, so a stick was used to beat out the grain when the amount was small.

Ruth Learns About Boaz. 2:18-23.
18-20. When Ruth returned, Naomi told her all about Boaz. **The man is near of kin unto us, one of our next kinsmen** (Heb., "one of our kinsmen redeemers"), on whom it devolves to protect us and marry you, there being only one other very near relative having the precedence. Ruth thus was informed that Boaz was "one of our kinsmen redeemers," but not that he would be *the* kinsman-redeemer. This latter disclosure Ruth would learn only from Boaz himself. So Israel will not receive the full revelation of the divine Boaz until He makes Himself known in grace and power to the remnant of Israel at His second coming (cf. Zech. 12:10—13:1; Isa. 60:1-22; Hos. 6:1-11; Rom. 11:26-36).

III. RUTH'S FINDING THE REDEEMER. 3:1-18.

Ruth's Obedient Faith. 3:1-6. **1.** Naomi desired rest for Ruth (cf. 1:9), that is, a home and security, beautifully illustrating the rest of faith in a completed redemption, the rest that remains "to the people of God," who know their Redeemer and repose their faith *wholly* in Him and His redemptive work (Heb. 3:9-12).

2. She therefore instructed her daughter-in-law in the custom of kinsman redemption. This was in accordance with the stipulations of Leviticus 25:25-28 and marriage to a brother-in-law (Deut. 25:5-10). Naomi's plan, made known here to Ruth, was calculated to awaken the kinsman-redeemer to action to perform his duty according to the Mosaic Law. She was fulfilling the function of parents, who customarily arrange marriages in Eastern countries.

She seems to have believed that Boaz was the nearest kinsman, apparently yet unaware of a nearer one (v. 12). Consequently, it was the duty of Boaz to marry Ruth and raise up descendants to Elimelech. Boaz would be winnowing barley **in the threshing floor**, which usually took place from about 4 P.M. till after sunset, when a cool breeze from the sea blew strong enough to separate the chaff from the wheat. Boaz, in all probability, remained at the threshing floor over night for the purpose of guarding the grain from theft.

3. Get thee down to the floor . . . make . . . thyself known to the man. Naomi's explicit instructions suggest that behind them lay some accepted custom. The whole incident is described with so pure a heart that no thought of evil can logically obtrude. **4. Uncover his feet** (lit., "lift up the clothes that are on his feet,"

LXX and Vulgate). Owners who slept on their threshing floors lay with their clothes on, but with their feet covered with a mantle.

5-6. Ruth's obedience displayed her faith, already signalized by her leaving her native land to rest under the wings of the God of Israel. She knew the relationship Boaz sustained to her family and the duties attaching to the relationship (2:20; 3:9). Faith acting on God's Word made her fearless. Strong in conscious innocence, she risked the misinterpretation some might put on her loyalty to duty.

Boaz's Acceptance of a Kinsman's Duty. 3:7-14. Naomi's plan, executed by Ruth, ran into no difficulty. **8-9.** When Boaz suddenly awoke to find a woman at his feet, did he surmise that Naomi might try to claim the rights of kinship? When Ruth asked him to spread his **skirt** (cloak) over her, that is, be her redeemer, she was following an ancient Oriental custom according to which a man spread his cloak over a woman as a token of marriage (cf. Ezek. 16:8).

10. Moreover, Boaz commended Ruth for not seeking the companionship of the youthful men, who normally would have been more attractive to her. He apparently was an older man, likely belonging to her father-in-law's generation. Boaz not only put the best possible construction on Ruth's action, but knowing her virtue and unselfish faith, invoked a blessing upon her for all her acts of kindness. Her circumspect behavior toward Naomi and her family and in the harvest field had not escaped him, nor the community as a whole.

11-14. Boaz definitely assured Ruth that he would discharge the responsibility of a redeemer (*gō'ēl,* "one who releases, delivers, marries the childless widow of an older brother"), provided the one who was a nearer kinsman than he (4:4; cf. 4:1) refused to discharge his obligation. **Lie down until the morning. . . . And she lay at his feet.** Boaz's promised redemption resulted in Ruth's resting at his feet, illustrating the truth that rest can be found only at the feet of the Redeemer, both for the individual believer (Luke 10:38-42) and the converted remnant of Israel as that nation experiences the deliverance of their great Kinsman-Redeemer at His second advent and enters into His Kingdom rest (Isa. 59:20; Rom. 11:23-29). Boaz's occupation of winnowing at the threshing floor, when Ruth sought him, foretells the work of the divine Boaz (Matt. 3:12), who at His second advent will separate His people (25:1-13) from among the believing remnant, who, like Ruth, will seek the place of rest at the feet of the Redeemer.

Ruth's Report to Naomi. 3:15-18. **15-17.** Boaz's vow to perform the duty of a kinsman-redeemer was sealed by a gift of **six measures of barley**, placed in Ruth's **cloak**, or "mantle" (Isa. 3:22). It was also intended for Naomi as a token of recognition of her responsibility for Ruth's action. Naomi's question to Ruth when she arrived was, **How hast thou fared?** or, "How did things go with you?" **18. Sit still** (*sheḇî*, "wait quietly") was an admonition to have faith, much as in the sense to calmly "wait on the LORD" and let Him work out the matter. Faith that honors God does all it can and should do on the human plane and then leaves the rest to God. Reporting to Naomi, Ruth quietly looked for the promised redemption.

IV. RUTH'S REST IN REDEMPTION. 4:1-22.

The Nearer Kinsman Renounces His Right. 4:1-8. **1.** Boaz went up **to the gate**, the normal place for transacting busi-ness (Gen. 23:10, 18), and confronted the nearer kinsman with his responsibility of acting as a kinsman-redeemer. **2. He took ten men of the elders of the city** as witnesses, two or three being sufficient to attest an ordinary bargain. But in cases of importance, such as the transfer of property, matrimony, or divorce, ten witnesses were customary (1 Kings 21:8).

For some reason the nearer kinsman was not named, but simply called **such a one** (so-and-so, Heb., *pelōnî 'almōnî*), perhaps suggesting the anonymity, from a spiritual point of view, into which those persons fall who are not in a position to avail themselves of the choice of faith. In this case the offer involved the glory of being the ancestor of David and eventually of Christ, who was to be born in the far-off centuries.

3-5. Boaz informed the kinsman-redeemer (*gō'ēl*) that the **plot of land**, which belonged to Elimelech, Naomi **has sold** (*māḵerâ*, not "selleth"). Naomi had, so far as it was possible for an Israelite to part with a family estate, sold the land to obtain the means of livelihood. Although the property would revert to the family at the year of jubilee, Boaz proposed to the kinsman that he should redeem the property at once.

The *gō'ēl* was willing enough to redeem the land as a good investment, until reminded that it also involved marrying Ruth, which he declined to do. The kinsman said, **I cannot redeem it . . . lest I mar** (*'ăshḥît*, "injure, ruin") **mine own inheritance** by investing in land that would belong not to him but to a son of Ruth, who would still legally be the son of Mahlon, Ruth's deceased husband. It would be tantamount to mortgaging one's own estate for the benefit of another.

The unnamed redeemer, who could redeem the land but could do nothing for the poor foreigner, Ruth, represents the Law of Moses, ten witnesses attesting its inability. For the Law required that "an Ammonite or Moabite shall not enter into the congregation of the LORD; even to their tenth generation ... forever" (Deut. 23:3). The Law could only keep Ruth out, much less bring her in. The symbolic act of taking off one's shoe (sandal) and giving it to another seems to denote transfer of property, symbolizing the right of the owner to set foot upon and take possession of the land (Psalm 60:8; cf. Josh. 1:3; Deut. 25:8-10).

Boaz Exercises His Right. 4:9-12. **9-10.** Boaz made a public announcement that he had purchased the property and acquired Ruth as his wife by a levirate marriage **that the name of the dead** (deceased) **be not cut off,** that is, that Mahlon's name be not obliterated. Being **cut off ... from the gate of his place** means from the city hall, the place of records, which the gate of an Oriental city was.

11. The elders and people in the gate affirmed the transaction and added their blessing. The reference to Rachel and Leah implies a hoped-for fertility of the marriage, for those two wives of Jacob, with their handmaids, bore him twelve sons. **12.** The story of Judah and Tamar, unsavory as it is, is mentioned because it refers to levirate marriage; but, whereas Tamar had been tacitly refused, Boaz had honored the obligation. Then, too, Perez, who was born of Tamar as a result of her strategem, was an ancestor of Boaz (v. 18; cf. Gen. 38:6-29; Matt. 1:3). Ephratah was the older name of the district of Bethlehem.

Birth of Obed. 4:13-17. **13.** The marriage of Boaz and Ruth was blessed by the birth of a child. The marriage was made at the city gate, but it was also a union sealed by divine sanction. It represents the consummation of the redemption of both the land of Israel and the people of Israel, when through the great Kinsman-Redeemer the redeemed remnant will enter the blessings of Kingdom rest (cf. Isa. 4:1-6; 11:1-16; Zech. 8:6-8). **The Lord gave her conception** (cf. Gen. 29:31; 33:5; cf. 30:2).

14. The women's blessing (cf. Luke 1:58; Rom. 12:15) upon Naomi constitutes a beautiful evening song to a sorrowful life, expressing joy in divine mercy and faith in God's promises. The child was to be a restorer of life to Naomi, for, with her sons dead, she had no hope of continuing her family line. Ruth's union with Boaz brought hope to Naomi, picturing a far larger hope in Israel's future restoration, since the child born was in the Messianic line.

15. No wonder it was said, **Thy daughter-in-law ... is better to thee than seven sons** (cf. 1 Sam. 2:5; Job 1:2). Not only would Naomi find consolation for the loss of her own sons in her daughter-in-law's son, but through his line would come the world's great Kinsman-Redeemer. **16-17. Naomi took the child ... and became nurse unto** the child who was born of an unselfish mother and dedicated to bless and serve others. **Obed** means "a servant," that is, of God.

Messianic Genealogy. 4:18-22. The Holy Spirit through the inspired author of this little book had the special object of illustrating divine redemption in general and Israel's specific restoration in particular. For that reason the Messianic line is given in abbreviated form from Perez, the forefather of the royal family of Judah (Gen. 38:29), to David. The latter prefigures the true theocratic King, the Messiah (cf. 1 Chron. 2:5; 9:4; Matt. 1:3-6).

FIRST SAMUEL

INTRODUCTION

The Name. The two books of Samuel really form one book. In the Hebrew manuscript they constitute one individual work called "the book of Samuel." Modern editions of the Hebrew Bible, following the Septuagint and the Vulgate, divide the book into 1 and 2 Samuel, and that arrangement appears in the English Bible. But that division of the book is not older than the sixteenth century. The contents of both books, in a sense, may be referred to Samuel. Even the deeds of Saul and the early life of David may be connected with Samuel, since both men were anointed by him and were, so to speak, his protégés. The name Samuel apparently means "heard of God"—"I have asked him of the LORD" (1 Sam. 1:20), with the resultant meaning, "God has *heard* my request."

The Date and Authorship. As in the case of other Old Testament books, the date and authorship are not certainly known. Samuel may have written parts, but portions of the two books deal with events that occurred after Samuel's death and were written by a later unknown inspired author, who either added to Samuel's work or used it as a source. That author cannot have written before the death of Solomon, since the divided kingdom is referred to in terms that indicate more than one king had succeeded Solomon (1 Sam. 27:6). A date between 910 and 850 B.C. would be likely, the quality of the Hebrew and the absence of Aramaisms pointing to an early date for the sources as well as the completed work.

Character of the Books. The books are more than a mere historical account of Israel's transition from the lawless era of the Judges to the more advanced and stable period of the early monarchy—more than vivid biography of such leaders as Samuel, Eli, David, Saul, and Jonathan. They have a deep religious overtone and purpose. Throughout them, Samuel was the human agent of the divine inworking. Saul was called and anointed as king, and prospered as long as he obediently represented the LORD to the people. But the moment he disobeyed God and went his own way, God's Spirit departed from him; as a result, he, his family, and his realm forfeited peace and prosperity and took a downward course, eventuating in ultimate disaster.

David, Saul's divinely appointed successor, was constantly assisted to higher heights by the Almighty hand in his first and subsequent triumphs until, without plotting or crime, he mounted his fallen predecessor's throne. Moreover, David prospered as he honored God, but he suffered severe chastening for his sins. Prominent, too, in 1 and 2 Samuel is the rise of the order of the prophets, under whose influence and communion with God, the books of Samuel came into existence.

Messianic References. The prophetic song of Hannah gives a clue to the interpretation of the Kingdom predictions contained in the books. "The LORD," she declared, "shall judge the *ends of the earth*," meaning the Messiah's Kingdom shall be established in *all nations*. "He shall give strength unto his king, and exalt the horn of his anointed"—the Messiah (1 Sam. 2:10, italics added; cf. Psalms 2:8-9; 21:1, 7; 89:24; 96:13; Matt. 25:31-32; 28:18). In setting forth the Davidic Covenant (2 Sam. 7:8-17), 2 Samuel is the first book of Scripture to declare that the incarnation of Christ as King would be effected in the particular family of David and that the kingdom founded in him, raised up from his posterity, would be universal and everlasting.

In Samuel the king is a picture of "the Messiah," the LORD's anointed One. Over and over again, as the pregnant germ of a great future for Israel, the thought occurs with marked prominence. David's portrait appears as its center, as of one in whom the Messiah's features were marked in outline— indeed feebly and imperfectly, but with the certainty that a Messiah would come who would fill up with glorious beauty that faint, blurred sketch.

OUTLINE

COMMENTARY

I. SAMUEL'S CAREER. 1:1—7:17.

A. SAMUEL'S BIRTH AND BOYHOOD. 1:1-28.

Elkanah and His Two Wives. 1:1-8. **1.** Attention is focused on Samuel's parents, Elkanah and Hannah, who resided at **Ramathaim-zophim**, a longer form of the usual Ramah (v. 19), identified with Beit Ramah, a dozen miles west of Shiloh. Zuph was an ancestor of Elkanah; and Ramah, Samuel's home, was located in Zuph (9:5).

2. Elkanah **had two wives**, polygamy being tolerated under the Law of Moses (cf. Deut. 21:15-17), although it was not the original divine order (Gen. 2:24; cf. Matt. 19:3-6), and often occasioned much unhappiness. Hannah ("grace") was childless, which was considered a disgrace for a Hebrew woman. But Peninnah ("pearl, coral") had children.

3. Elkanah went up annually to Shiloh, the religious center of Israel until its destruction by the Philistines (c. 1050 B.C.; cf. Jer. 7:12-13), when Nob replaced it. **The Lord of hosts** (armies) is the title of God under which Elkanah worshiped and is the distinctive name of Deity available for Israel's help and comfort in the time of need (cf. 1:8-11; 1 Kings 22:19; Isa. 10:16; Jer. 27:4-8).

4-5. Elkanah ... gave ... portions. The offerer received back the greater part of the peace offerings, which were customarily eaten at a social feast "before the LORD" (cf. Lev. 3:7; Deut. 12:12). Out of those consecrated parts, Elkanah gave portions to all members of his family. The **worthy portion** (*ʾăppā-*

yim, "one portion for two," "double portion") he gave Hannah, showing his special love for her (cf. Gen. 43:34; 1 Sam. 9:23-24).

6-7. Peninnah **her adversary ... provoked** (*kīʿēs*, "irritated" or "angered") **her relentlessly** as she taunted her childlessness. This incident furnishes an example of the bitter fruits of polygamy. **8.** Elkanah tried to assure Hannah by his tokens of love for her. **Am not I better to thee than ten sons?**—that is, "than *many* sons?" The round number expresses this general idea.

Hannah's Interview with Eli. 1:9-18. **9.** After the solemn sacrificial meal, in which the whole family participated, Hannah got up from the table and went to present her case before the LORD in prayer. **Now Eli** ("my God") **the priest, sat upon a seat.** He was a descendant of Ithamar, Aaron's younger son (cf. 1 Chron. 24:3).

The seat upon which Eli sat was evidently the official high-priestly bench where the high priest sat to administer justice and transact business, while his sons took care of ritual tasks (v. 3). The door **post** and the phrase "doors of the house" (3:15) suggest a permanent home had been erected for the sanctuary. **The temple** (palace) **of the Lord** was so called because at times the visible glory (Shekinah) of Israel's King was pleased to manifest itself there.

10-12. Hannah's prayer and vow contained two solemn promises: (1) She pledged the son for whom she prayed to the service of the LORD all the days of his life. (2) She consecrated him to be a

Nazirite all his life (for the spiritual significance, see Num. 6:1-21; cf. Judg. 13:5). **13-14.** Eli's unworthy suspicion that Hannah was intoxicated was in line with the low morality of the time, when such heartfelt prayer as Hannah prayed was so uncommon as to have been mistaken for drunkenness, which was very common (cf. 2:12-17, 22, 25).

15-16. Hannah laid bare her heart to Eli and protested the insinuation of being a **daughter of Belial** (KJV; a surrogate for Satan, 2 Cor. 6:15). The Hebrew *băt beliyă'ăl* ("daughter without profit") denotes a "good-for-nothing female, a base woman," as "sons of Belial," used to describe Hophni and Phinehas (1 Sam. 2:12, KJV), signifies "scoundrels" or "good-for-nothing males."

17. Eli was quick to see he had harshly misjudged a blameless woman. Nobly retracting his accusation, he displayed real generosity and patriotism in his graceful words of farewell and in his fatherly wish that seems to take the form of a prophetic pronouncement from **the God of Israel**, promising the birth of the future prophet-judge. **18.** Eli's words fired the soul of Hannah with faith, so that **her countenance was no more sad.** The incident is also a fine example of the composing power of prayer.

The Birth of Samuel. 1:19-20. Returning to their home in Ramah, the common abbreviated name of the city, Ramathaim-zophim ("the Ramahs of the watchers"; see 1:1), Hannah conceived and in due time gave birth to Samuel (*shemû'ēl*, "heard of God," the result of God's hearing Hannah's prayer).

The Dedication of Samuel. 1:21-28. **21-24.** Elkanah also had vowed a vow to the LORD; so he and Hannah were agreed on the dedication of their offspring. Hannah decided not to go up to Shiloh until the boy was **weaned.**

Weaning among Israelites customarily did not take place until the child was three years old (cf. 2 Macc. 7:27). Hence, Samuel was old enough to be left permanently **before the Lord**, as a gift dedicated to His service, when his mother finally took him **unto the house of the Lord in Shiloh.** After being weaned, Samuel, a Levite, began at once to minister as a lad, assisting the priests as Levites were commissioned to do. As a weaned child, he was fretless and quiet to wait upon God (cf. Psalm 131:2).

Apparently all **three bullocks** (young bulls), which Hannah **took ... up with her** when she dedicated Samuel, were offered—one for the vow of the child (v. 25); one for the yearly burnt offering; and one for the yearly thank offering. However, the Septuagint reads: "And she went up with him ... with a three-year-old calf" (cf. v. 25), understanding the verse to refer to only one offering, the dedicatory sacrificial animal.

The **ephah** (bushel) **of flour** (cf. Lev. 2:1-16; 6:14-23) prophetically symbolizes the sinless humanity of the Redeemer who was to come, and the wine looks forward to His death; so, together with the slain bullocks, they envision divine redemption. Compare Genesis 14:18, where the "bread" and "wine" are presented as memorials of sacrifice by Melchizedek as king-priest, bespeaking Christ's priestly work in resurrection (see 1 Cor. 11:26).

25-28. Hannah beautifully gave back to the LORD what He had so graciously bestowed upon her. **Therefore ... I have lent him** should be rendered, "Therefore I also make him one asked of the LORD; all the days he lives he is asked of the LORD" (lit. Heb. trans.), meaning, "The LORD gave him to me and now I have returned him, whom I obtained by prayer, to the LORD as one asked or demanded." **And he** (the boy Samuel)

worshiped the Lord there, showing that a three-year-old can be taught to worship and seal a parent's dedication of him to God.

B. HANNAH'S ODE AND ELI'S WICKED SONS. 2:1-36.

The Song of Hannah. 2:1-10. **1. And Hannah prayed** (*tĭtpăllēl*, "conversed with [God]"), not in the sense of asking for anything, but praising and giving thanks for all that God had done for her. **My heart rejoiceth** (*'ālăṣ*, "exults") **in the Lord** (cf. Phil. 4:4). Had she not at last received the blessing of motherhood that all women in Israel longed for? (cf. Gen. 3:15; 4:1; 30:1). **Mine horn is exalted.** The figure is that of strength (2 Sam. 22:3; Psalm 92:10). She considered herself strong in the gift of a child from the LORD. Just as an animal's strength is concentrated in its horns, so Hannah's strength lay in the LORD's goodness to her in giving her a son, who was not only an answer to prayer, but as prophet-judge would be a far-reaching blessing in Israel.

2. Neither is there any rock like our God, a favorite simile among Israel's inspired poets, where the rocks of Sinai and Palestine supplied an ever present picture of God's unchangeable majesty and of the eternal safety found in Him. Notably the term *rock*, as applied to God, is first found in the song of Moses (Deut. 32:4, 15, 18, 30, 31, 37), where its connection with salvation (Deut. 32:15) seems to indicate that Hannah was acquainted with this national hymn of Israel's great lawgiver.

3-4. The LORD is described as **a God of knowledge** by whom **actions are weighed.** The figure of the balance as the means of testing human worth (Prov. 16:2; Dan. 5:27) occurs extrabiblically in the Egyptian Book of the Dead, where the heart of the deceased is weighed on a scale

against the symbol of truth and right before the deceased is admitted to the domain of Osiris. God reverses human conditions, bringing low the wicked and exalting the righteous. **The bows of the mighty** heroes (i.e., "the heroes of the bow") the symbol of human power was put first instead of the bearer of the symbol. While the heroes rejoicing in their strength are shattered, the weak are by God made strong for conflict (see Judg. 3:31; 1 Cor. 1:27).

5-9. The LORD's sovereign wisdom and power in dealing with humanity are further illustrated, setting forth the principle that **by** (human) **strength shall no man prevail** (cf. Zech. 4:6; 2 Cor. 12:9). **10.** This verse looks forward to the climactic judgment of the wicked during the Great Tribulation preceding the King-Messiah's second advent and establishment of the Kingdom. This is the first Old Testament reference to "His Anointed" (His Messiah) and has been rightly comprehended by many Jewish and Christian expositors as looking to Christ (see "Messianic References" in Introduction to 1 Samuel).

The Dissolute Life of Eli's Sons. 2:11-17. **11-12.** Samuel's service as a young lad is incipiently introduced to furnish a contrast throughout the narrative to the wicked conduct of Hophni and Phinehas (vv. 12-17). They are called **worthless men** ("sons of Belial," KJV; i.e., "sons of worthlessness, no-good rascals"; see 1:16), the expression being used some nine or ten times in the records of Samuel (1 Sam. 10:27; 25:17, 25; 30:22; 2 Sam. 16:7; 20:1; 23:6). **They knew not the Lord**, being unbelieving religionists, spiritually dead, morally corrupt, and examples of an unregenerate, worldly, rapacious clergy of all ages.

13-17. These verses present an illustration of the summary of Hophni's and

Phinehas's worthless character as summarized in verse 12. The **custom** of these reprobates was plainly a bold one. They extorted from the offerer what rightly belonged to his own sacrificial feast. Not being content with the share of the offerings assigned to them by the Mosaic Law (see Lev. 7:31, 35; Deut. 18:3), they took all the fork would hold (vv. 13-14), and they also greedily demanded the best cuts of the raw meat, ostensibly to cook them fresh for themselves before the fat and the blood were presented in sacrifice (v. 15). This was even more serious, being a grave insult to the LORD. This fat was not to be taken or eaten by anyone, but was God's portion to be burned by the priest on the altar (Lev. 8:16; 7:23-31).

In insisting, even by force (v. 16), that their servant attendants grab the best pieces before the offerings were made, they were doing despite to that which symbolized the holiness of God and His redemptive grace to sinful man. That is why **the sin of the young men was very great** ("exceedingly serious"). In affronting God's love and grace toward sinners, they turned people away from that love until the people **abhorred** (*nī'ₐṣû*, "despised, derided, scorned") **the offering** (*mĭnḥâ*, "sacrificial gift") presented to the LORD, and also what the offering symbolized, namely, gratitude for divine redemption.

The Ministry of the Child Samuel. 2:18-21. **18-19. But** (setting forth the contrast to Eli's wicked sons) **Samuel ministered** (*mᵉshārēṭ*, "did service as a priest, attended or waited on the LORD"), **girded with a linen ephod**, a light, outer, religious garment worn by priests and occasionally by other eminent persons acting in an ecclesiastical capacity (2 Sam. 6:14). The **little coat** (*mᵉ'îl*; cf. Exod. 28:31) was a sort of loose, sleeveless robe worn over the tunic by prophets (1 Sam. 15:27) and kings (1 Chron. 15:27) as well as priestly ministers. That unusual attire was doubtlessly arranged by Eli, Samuel's protector and guardian.

20-21. And Eli blessed Elkanah and his wife (cf. Luke 2:34), a benediction that soon was manifested in Hannah's fruitfulness **for the loan which** (she) **lent to the Lord**, better, "The LORD give you by this woman offspring in the place of the one you have returned to the LORD" (BV; see 1:27-28). The blessing also was evidenced in Samuel's development. He **grew before the Lord** (cf. 3:19-21). He developed physically, mentally, spiritually, and socially in fellowship with God and under the blessing of God in service for God, as Jesus did (Luke 2:52), the thought being repeated (v. 26) for emphatic contrast to Hophni's and Phinehas's progressive degeneration.

Eli Rebukes His Sons. 2:22-26. **22-24.** Weak and indulgent as Eli was as a father, the writer of Samuel seeks to treat him in the kindest light possible, and excuse is made in the statement: **Now Eli was very old.** His remonstrances with his wicked sons fell on deaf ears. Their disgraceful conduct is further amplified (cf. vv. 13-17) in their sexual offenses **with the women who assembled at the door of the tabernacle of the congregation.** These women are mentioned as performing service (Exod. 38:8), and there is no evidence to conclude that Eli's sons had introduced Canaanite cultic prostitution into the Shiloh tabernacle, as some suppose.

But their lawless conduct did lead the LORD's people to transgress. Their sin was **against the Lord**, as was that of Ananias and Sapphira (Acts 5:4; cf. Num. 15:30; Psalm 51:4, 16), and constituted "a sin unto [physical] death" (1 John 5:16; 1 Cor. 5:5; 11:30), for which no prayer or entreaty could avail, because **the Lord would slay them**, that is, deliver them to physical death (cf. 1 Sam. 4:17; Jer. 7:16). Amid this unchecked evil, the boy Samuel "all the while . . . increased in stature and in favor with the LORD and with men" (v. 26, BV).

Divine Prediction of Doom upon Eli's House. 2:27-36. **27-29.** The announcement of doom was made by an unnamed **man of God**, a designation applied to Moses (Deut. 33:1; Josh. 14:6) and to various prophets some forty times in the books of Judges, 1 and 2 Samuel, and 1 and 2 Kings. Besides those whose names we know, many of his kind must have borne witness to God. He appeared suddenly at Shiloh, announced his message of doom to Eli and his house, and disappeared. The questions the man of God asked constitute a rhetorical device aimed at an emphatic appeal to Eli's conscience.

The sin of Eli's house was underscored by four things: (1) It was underscored by the word of God through the man of God: **Thus saith the Lord.** (2) It was underscored by the historical review of the divine revelation to and gracious choice of Levi for the priesthood. **The house of thy father** was the house of Aaron, the first high priest, from whom (through Ithamar, Aaron's fourth son) Eli was descended (1 Chron. 24:3). **Did I [not] choose him . . . to wear an ephod before me,** including, besides all the privileges of priestly sacrifice and praise, the inestimable privilege of the high priest entering the Holy of Holies and also the privilege of finding the will of the invisible King of Israel by means of the Urim and Thummim.

(3) It was underscored by the base ingratitude of Eli's house. **Wherefore trample ye** (*tiḇ‘aṭû*, "be refractory"; "kick back") **upon my sacrifice.** The image is taken from everyday life—the pampered, overfed ox or ass becomes unmanageable and refuses to obey its kind master (cf. Deut. 32:15). (4) It was underscored by the gross insult that the conduct of Eli's sons was to God. **And honorest thy sons above me.** In indulging his wicked sons, Eli affronted God.

30-36. The punishment of Eli's house is outlined. (1) The flagrant sin of his sons had forfeited the gracious promise that envisioned the perpetuity and blessing of Eli's house through Ithamar, Aaron's fourth son (v. 30). (2) The power and strength of that house (denoted by the "arm"; cf. Job 22:9; Psalm 37:17) would be cut off; sickness and sword would consume its members, and none would attain old age (vv. 31, 33-34), which was fulfilled in the massacre at Nob (22:11-19). (3) Eli would live to see something grievous and horrible. **And thou shalt see an enemy** (or "the affliction of the tabernacle"; v. 32), apparently a reference to the capture of the ark and the death of Eli's sons at the hands of the Philistines (cf. 4:12-18).

(4) A worthy, faithful priest would be raised up (v. 35). This prophecy is connected with Samuel and later with Abiathar of the house of Eli, who was deposed from the high priesthood during Solomon's reign to make room for Zadok. However, the prophecy is comprehensive and goes beyond Samuel and Zadok and embraces in the farthest sweep its ultimate fulfillment in Christ, who in Israel's Kingdom blessing will be the King-Priest and at last exemplify in Israel the perfect harmony between the kingship and the priesthood (cf. Zech. 6:9-15). (5) Menial tasks and humiliation would face Eli's posterity (v. 36).

C. SAMUEL'S CALL. 3:1-21.

The Lord Appears to Samuel. 3:1-10. The prophecy of 2:27-36 started to be fulfilled as Eli began to fade into the background and the lad Samuel emerged into prominence. **1. And the word of the Lord was rare** (*yāqār*), that is, the will of the LORD announced by a man of God was extremely infrequent because of the lawlessness of the times. There was *no* **frequent** (*niprāṣ*, "spread abroad, diffused, common") **vision**, such as the revelations and manifestations of Deity vouchsafed to Abraham, Moses, Joshua, Gideon, and Manoah. That significant silence was due to the deep corruption into which the priesthood and, through their example, the nation had fallen.

2-4. Before the lamp of God went out ... the Lord called Samuel. The seven-branched lampstand was filled with just enough oil to burn through one night (Lev. 24:2-3), so the time of Samuel's call was early in the morning. However dark the world may become, God never allows His witness to be extinguished or His remnant to be cut off completely (cf. Rom. 11:4-5). Samuel, sleeping in a cell in the **temple** area, evidently near the Ark, received his call from the LORD. In the Ugaritic Epic, Keret received a revelation in the sacred tent.

5-7. Three times the boy thought his old, half-blind master was summoning him. **8.** Then **Eli perceived that the Lord had called the child** when it was apparent the voice had come from the same direction, only at the extremity of the tabernacle behind the veil where the Ark was. No doubt the glory of the LORD was shining there, and the voice probably proceeded from that sacred golden throne as of old. **9-10. And the Lord came, and stood**, undoubtedly in theophanic manifestation, but here the specific form, whether angelic or human, is not indicated.

The Lord Announces a Message. 3:11-14. **11.** The prophecy received by Eli (2:27-36) was rehearsed, but in dif-

ferent words. The thing the LORD declared He would do in Israel would make **the ears of everyone that heareth it ... tingle** (from the root *ṣālal*, "vibrate, quiver" at calamitous news; cf. 2 Kings 21:12; Jer. 19:3). The reference is to the capture of the Ark by the Philistines. That the sacred symbol of the presence of their invisible King should fall into the hands of the uncircumcised Philistines, the hereditary foes of God's people, would be a calamity of unparalleled proportions.

12-14. Full judgment would be meted out upon Eli's house. **His sons made themselves vile** (*meqălelîm*, "made themselves contemptible and accursed"), and he **restrained them not** (*kihâ*, "did not rebuke, discipline" them). The enormity of the sin was its insult to God in the aspersion it cast upon the priestly sacrifice and offerings, and upon the divine redemptive grace that they foreshadowed (see 2:25). Thus, it constituted a sin "unto [physical] death" (1 John 5:16) and could not be prayed for or atoned for, but it necessitated the death of Hophni and Phinehas and the other judgments announced upon Eli's house.

Samuel Announces the Doom of Eli's House. 3:15-18. This first experience of having unwelcome truth to tell to those he loved was Samuel's initiation into the duty of a prophet and the cross-bearing it required. **15-18.** Out of fear to tell Eli the vision, Samuel kept to his couch till morning. Only after he had **opened the doors of the house of the Lord** (the sanctuary being enclosed in a house or permanent structure), and Eli had interrogated him and urged him to tell all, did he do so. Eli submitted resignedly to the bitter truth, convicted no doubt that he had acted wrongly in failing to deal sternly with his wicked sons.

Samuel Established as a Prophet.

3:19-21. This résumé of Samuel's early life contrasts him with Eli, his predecessor in the judgeship. **19-20. The Lord was with him, and did let none of his words fall to the ground.** Either Samuel let none of God's words fall to the ground (in contrast to Eli), or the LORD did not let any of the words of Samuel fall to the ground, but established him as a bona fide prophet, whom all Israel recognized, from Dan, in the farthest northern extremity, to Beersheba, in the extreme south of Israel. **21.** Moreover, the LORD appeared again in Shiloh and **revealed himself to** Samuel there.

D. THE JUDGMENT OF ELI'S HOUSE. 4:1-22.

The Philistines Defeat Israel. 4:1-2.
1a. And the word of Samuel came to all Israel. This verse apparently belongs to chapter 3 (as printed in the RSV). If it actually belongs in chapter 4, as some scholars contend (e.g., H. Spence, *Ellicott's Commentary on the Whole Bible,* 2:307), the crushing defeat at the hands of the Philistines was the result of the summons of Samuel, at the LORD's direction, to humble the sinning nation. **1b.** The Philistines encamped at Aphek, which was situated due west of Shiloh on the edge of the coastal plain. Having dominated the lowlands, they were making inroads into the hill country. Israel encamped at **Ebenezer** ("rock of help") and endeavored to drive the invader out of the hills, but they were routed, with some four thousand casualties. Later, when the nation had been chastened and restored to fellowship with the LORD, Ebenezer was the scene of victory over the Philistines (7:12).

The Ark Is Taken. 4:3-11. **3.** The elders and the people had enough perception to realize that it was the LORD, not the Philistines, who had really smitten them. But they showed how far they were from understanding why the LORD had forsaken them when they said, **Let us fetch the ark of the covenant ... that ... it may save us.** Like all spiritually dead religionists, who hold to forms when the Spirit has departed, they mistook the symbol of God's presence for the presence of God Himself. Their defeat occasioned no repentance, no self-judgment, no crying out to the LORD.

4. So the people sent to Shiloh, that they might bring from there the ark ... of the Lord of hosts (armies of heaven), **who dwelleth between** (better, "above") **the cherubim.** They imagined that the Ark's visible presence would bring the aid of the LORD and His angelic armies to gain the victory for them. The note that the wicked priests, Hophni and Phinehas, **were there with the ark** as its guardians was sufficient to account for Israel's terrible defeat. **5.** The **great shout** that rang from the Israelites as the Ark arrived was doubtless the war cry of former days—"Rise up, LORD, and let thine enemies be scattered, and let them that hate thee flee before thee" (Num. 10:35).

6-7. When the Philistines heard the shout and understood that the Ark had been brought into **the camp of the Hebrews,** the name used of the Israelites by foreigners, they were terrified. Since they were polytheists, they assumed that the Israelites were also. **8.** At the same time, they had a warped knowledge of Israel's previous history. **9-10.** God used the Ark, wrongly used by His sinning people, to bring about their disastrous defeat and humiliation. **11.** The supreme tragedy was the capture of the Ark. The death of the two wicked priests fulfilled prophecy (2:34; 3:14).

The Glory Departs from Israel. 4:12-22. The account does not dwell on the misery Israel suffered as a consequence of the great defeat, nor does it relate the subsequent destruction of Shiloh by the Philistines. Our knowledge of the latter tragedy comes from Jeremiah (7:12; 26:6), corroborated by archaeological diggings at Seilun (the modern site) by Danish expeditions from 1926 to 1929, and in 1932.

12-20. The real disaster presented is not Eli's death or the death of his two sons, or the death of Phinehas's wife in childbirth, but the capture of the Ark. Even the name of Phinehas's newborn son recalls this tragedy. *I-chabod* (*'ikābōd*), best construed as a simple negative, means "not glory," that is, "there is no glory." However, it may be taken as an interrogative, "Where is the glory?" The answer is "It is nowhere!" or, in an exclamatory sense, "Alas! the glory," expressing bitter grief. **21-22. And she said, The glory is departed** (*gālâ*, "gone into exile"; cf. Psalm 78:60-61).

E. THE ARK AMONG THE PHILISTINES. 5:1-12.

The Ark at Ashdod. 5:1-7. **1-2.** The Philistines took the Ark from its place of capture to **the house** (temple) **of Dagon** in **Ashdod** (cf. Judg. 16:21-23), a city in the coastal plain due west of Jerusalem and some half-dozen miles from the sea (cf. 6:17). Dagon was a fertility deity worshiped widely from southern Palestine to Mesopotamia. A temple was also dedicated to him at Ugarit, where Baal was called "son of Dagon."

The Philistines set the Ark **by** (*'ēṣĕl*, "in proximity to, beside") **Dagon**, whose image was a human head with shoulders, arms, and the whole upper part of a man, but whose lower portion below the hips was in the form of a fish, to represent a merman. Whether Dagon was connected with "fish" (Heb., *dăg*) or with "grain" (*dāgōn*), he was undoubtedly connected with the fertility and productivity of nature.

3-4. In their blindness the Philistines imagined that their god had conquered Israel's God. They concluded that it was an accident when the next morning they found Dagon fallen face downward before the Ark. Pitiably, they had to **set him in his place again**, only to find a worse humiliation the next morning. Dagon again lay prone on the temple floor, with his head and the palms of his hands **cut off.**

5. There the parts of the idol lay severed **on the threshold**, which became taboo because it had come in direct contact with the idol. The curious memory of this disaster to Dagon's image in the Ashdod temple persisted among the god's devotees. Zephaniah (1:9) in the seventh century B.C. refers to this idolatrous custom: "In the same day also will I punish all those who leap on [over] the threshold." Although the God of Israel had demonstrated His power over the Philistine gods, these darkened idolaters continued to venerate the threshold where the fragments of their impotent, man-made deity had lain. (See comments on Judg. 16:1-3 on the spiritual blindness of Philistinism.)

6-7. Severer punishments came upon the Ashdodites. They were afflicted with **tumors** (boils, piles, most likely hemorrhoids), although the plague of field mice that destroyed fields and harvest (6:4, 11, 18, and also included in this verse in the LXX) suggests the possibility of bubonic plague, an epidemic spread by rodents, and of which swollen lymph glands in the groin are characteristic. Yet the Philistines did not repent of their sins, but carried the Ark about as a superstitious relic. Philistinism avidly clings to outward forms and traditions long after apostasy and

370

idolatry have rendered them meaningless.

The Ark at Gath and Ekron. 5:8-12.
8-12. The **lords of the Philistines** were the rulers of the five cities. They were independent but were capable of efficient concerted action. **Gath** (site uncertain) was one of the five cities, as was **Ekron** (modern Khirbet al-Muquana'). Since both cities suffered calamities, the Philistines were glad to get rid of the Ark.

F. THE ARK RETURNED TO ISRAEL. 6:1-21.

The Philistines Take Counsel. 6:1-12.
1. After a period of seven months, the Ark was returned to Israelite soil. **2.** In their consternation, the Philistines called their priests and diviners to find out what to do with the fatal trophy of which they had been so proud. **3.** The advice, **Send it not empty,** was to propitiate the powerful Hebrew Deity, whom they imagined as having been insulted by being placed in an inferior position in the Dagon temple. Since He had shown Himself powerful enough to punish His insulters, the insults had to stop and He had to be appeased with rich offerings.

4-5. Following ancient pagan custom, the heathen priests and diviners directed that the Ark should be sent away with votive offerings of gold representing what had plagued them, namely, **five golden tumors** (hemorrhoids) **and five golden mice,** likenesses of the diseased parts and of the rodents that devoured their harvests. This is the first mention of the mice in the Hebrew text, but the Septuagint mentions them throughout. The plague, which was nationwide, required a single offering from all five cities, one for each town (cf. vv. 17-18).

6. The Philistine priests knew something of God's judgments upon Egypt.

Therefore, they added an admonition: "Why harden your hearts as the Egyptians and Pharaoh hardened their hearts? Did they not let them go when He had made them feel His power, and they went out?" (BV). The plagues of Egypt had occurred four centuries previously, but those divine acts were still remembered among Israel's neighbors.

7-9. The plan suggested was to prove whether or not the Ark, representing Israel's God, had brought the serious catastrophe upon the Philistines or whether "it happened by chance" (BV). **10-12.** The results proved conclusively that it did not happen by chance, but that the LORD, the God of creation, who was supreme and above all natural instincts, had sent the plagues. The milk cows, unaccustomed to a yoke, nevertheless took the new cart (cf. Num. 19:2; 2 Sam. 6:3) with its sacred burden (cf. Mark 11:2; Matt. 27:60) directly away from where their calves were shut up. By God's direction the dumb beasts did what the idol priests and diviners scarcely considered possible.

The Ark at Beth-shemesh. 6:13-19.
13-15. Taking the straight road to Beth-shemesh, a priestly city near the Israelite border (Josh. 21:16), the cows (while the Philistine lords watched in amazement) did not stop till they came into the **field of Joshua,** where there was a **great stone,** in all probability a natural rock protruding out of the soil.

The presence of **Levites,** among whom doubtlessly there were priests, was natural in a Levitical city. The sacrifices offered constituted no transgression of the Law, because the Ark, the throne of God's presence before which the sacrifices were really offered, was present. The burnt offerings speak of divine redemption through the atoning substitutionary death of Christ offering Himself without spot to God in delight to do the Father's will (see Lev. 1:1-17).

16-18. The Philistine lords witnessed this demonstration of the LORD's sovereignty and His redemptive grace in the precise terms that they themselves had chosen. Yet they clung to their idolatry and went back, in spite of everything, to worship the humbled Dagon. Such is the blindness of idolatrous Philistinism.

The Sin of the Beth-shemites. 6:19-21. **19.** The men who were smitten with death were guilty of breaking the law of Numbers 4:20 by looking into the Ark. As a symbol of God's presence, it was to be handled wholly according to divine direction. The Ark was as equally dangerous to Israelite laymen (as opposed to the priesthood) as it was to the Philistines (cf. 2 Sam. 6:1-11). It taught that access of fallen, sinful man to God's infinitely holy presence was through priestly sacrifice alone, specifically through the high priest, looking forward to Christ's priestly sacrifice through which we are constituted individual priests. Apparently seventy died, the additional fifty thousand (cf. RSV, BV) being a copyist error, illustrating the relatively poor condition in which the Hebrew text of 1 Samuel has been transmitted.

G. SAMUEL AS JUDGE. 7:1-17.

The Ark at Kiriath-jearim and Revival in Israel. 7:1-4. **1-2.** These verses actually belong to chapter 6 and conclude the sections on the fortunes of the Ark. The Ark finally came to rest in the house of Abinadab in Kiriath-jearim (Baalah, identified with Tell el-Azhar, about nine miles northeast of Beth-shemesh). Eleazar, Abinadab's son, was consecrated to keep the Ark during its twenty-year stay there.

And all the house of Israel lamented after (*wăyĭnnāhū*, "was seriously

seeking") **the Lord.** This "hungering after the LORD" was the result of severe divine chastening, which they were enduring at the hands of the Philistines, and Samuel's unwearied labors (cf. 3:19—4:1) to call them back to God from their idolatrous contamination. That involved the polluted pantheon of the Canaanites, including the utterly degraded female deity, Ashtoreth (pl. Ashtaroth), denoting various forms of the mother goddess (Assyr. Ishtar; Gr. Astarte) with aspects of fertility, sex, and war. **3. Prepare your hearts unto the Lord, and serve him only** (cf. Deut. 6:4-5); **and he will deliver you out of the hand of the Philistines. 4.** Israel did so (see Judg. 2:11).

Samuel Calls a Solemn Assembly. 7:5-6. **5.** The object of the assembly was to pray for divine help. **I will pray for you**, declared the man of prayer (cf. 8:6; 12:19, 23; Psalm 99:6; Jer. 15:1). The place of the national assembly was Mizpah ("watchtower"; perhaps Nebi Samwil, an eminence about five miles north of Jerusalem; cf. Judg. 20:1; 1 Sam. 10:17), although some scholars identify the site with Mount Scopus ("watchman"), the height northeast of Jerusalem.

6. At Mizpah they **drew water, and poured it out before the Lord.** The nearest parallel is the pouring out of water from the pool of Siloam on the solemn last day of the Feast of Tabernacles as a reminder of the water from the rock in the desert. However, the pouring out of the water here was apparently a symbolic act indicating deep repentance, attesting the helpless and undone condition of Israel (cf. 2 Sam. 14:14; 23:16).

Samuel appeared at Mizpah, beginning his great national ministry. He **judged . . . Israel in** Mizpah, his function being twofold—civil (cf. Exod. 18:16) and military, doing what Othniel, Barak, and Gideon had done in previous times. He mustered and organized the army of Israel and led them to victory against their oppressors.

Deliverance from the Philistines. 7:7-14. **7-8.** The national assembly at Mizpah provoked the Philistines to action and caused Israel, in fear of the enemy, to beseech their great leader to **cease not to cry unto the Lord our God for us**, indicating their genuine repentance and renunciation of the flesh. In the natural there was just cause for fear— Philistine military power with its monopoly of iron-smelting and consequent superior striking power (cf. Judg. 1:19; 1 Sam. 13:19-22).

9. Genuine repentance is followed by faith in the forgiving grace and mercy of God, demonstrated as Samuel offered a whole burnt offering to the Lord, speaking symbolically of approach to God on the merits of shed blood by the lamb, looking forward to the future when the Lamb of God would offer Himself without spot in delight to do the divine will even to death (Lev. 1:1-17).

10. While the smoke of the slain lamb was still ascending, the first detachment of the Philistine army began to appear. With a people prepared by repentance, faith, and prayer, the LORD Himself fought for His people. A terrific thunderstorm, as at Gibeon (Josh. 10:10-14), burst over the Philistine army, with wind, rain, and lightning striking them down and terrifying them. **11.** Israel pursued the disorganized, fleeing Philistines to Beth-car (site unknown, perhaps a Philistine fortress where the wretched remnant was able to rally and defend itself).

12. Samuel set up a victory memorial between Mizpah and Shen (*hăššēn,* "the tooth," probably denoting a prominent peak or crag), calling it

Ebenezer (*'ĕben hā'ēzĕr,* "the stone of help") in memory of the LORD's interposition for His people. It is possible that the earlier Philistine victory (4:1-10) occurred near a different Ebenezer. If so, Samuel would erase the former defeat by connecting it with a glorious victory.

13-14. So the Philistines were subdued; *not* that they did not pose a constant threat, but they were potentially defeated by a new spirit of faith in the LORD that animated Israel during Samuel's lifetime. It made God's people unconquerable and enabled them to regain cities that had been taken by expanding Philistine power in the days of Israel's sin. There was also **peace between Israel and the Amorites** ("westerners"), a composite designation for all the non-Israelite inhabitants of Canaan.

Résumé of Samuel's Judgeship. 7:15-17. **15.** Samuel served as Israel's circuit judge throughout his life. **16-17.** Annually he made the rounds to hold court at Bethel ("house of God"), where judgment must begin; at Gilgal ("rolling"), where Egypt's reproach was rolled away and the flesh judged (Josh. 5:1-12); and at Mizpah ("watchtower"), where vigilance was constantly exercised against foes. Ramah ("heights"), where Samuel had his home, suggests that the great prophet-judge of Israel lived on a high spiritual plane, which is confirmed by his general life and accomplishments.

II. SAUL'S CAREER. 8:1—15:35.

A. ISRAEL'S DEMAND FOR A KING. 8:1-22.

Incentive for the Demand Furnished by Samuel's Sons. 8:1-5. The monarchy was to be established in Israel through the deliberate self-determination of the people. One of the motives for the demand for a king, besides the advancing age of Samuel, was the unfitness of his sons. **1.** The great leader Samuel made the mistake of making his sons judges. Because he was God-called as judge-prophet and had success in his calling did not mean that his sons were called and were to follow him in the same capacity. God does not ordinarily transmit a gift and calling from father to son. Apostolic succession and traditional authority are man-made inventions that produce great corruption in spiritual matters.

2. Joel and Abijah were judges in Beersheba, in the southern extremity of the nation; the city was located on an important road and accessible, although inconvenient. **3.** They turned aside for **money** (*bāṣă'*, "gain" by wrongdoing or violence; "money" selfishly or dishonestly acquired), **took bribes** (Exod. 23:6-8; Deut. 16:19), and hence, **perverted** ("wrested, distorted," lit., "caused to turn aside") **justice.**

Samuel's Direction from the Lord. 8:6-9. **6.** But the request for a king **displeased** (Heb., *yēră'*, "was evil in the eyes of") **Samuel.** The change from the theocracy ruled by the LORD, the invisible King from heaven, had been foreseen by Moses (Deut. 17:14-20). The people had found by sad experience that such an exalted government was unsuited to their unspiritual state, and they eventually descended to the level of ordinary people, represented by the nations surrounding Israel, all of which had kings. Even so, it was a bitter thought for Samuel that God's people, as the subjects of the eternal King of the universe and directly ruled by Him, should depart from the splendid Hebrew ideal of the theocracy. Despite his own disappointment, Samuel as a man of God submitted the matter to the LORD in prayer for the LORD's will.

7-9. Samuel was to do two things. (1) He was to listen to the people, for they had not rejected him, but the LORD. The people should have asked for a new judge, through whom the LORD could work as He had through the great prophet-judge. Instead, as if God were not their King, they asked for a king "like all the nations" (v. 5). That was but another example of their forsaking the LORD and serving other gods as they had done ever since they had been redeemed out of Egypt. (2) He was to solemnly warn them of what would happen to them for exchanging the theocracy for the monarchy.

Samuel's Warning Concerning a King. 8:10-18. **11-17. This will be the manner of the king ... he will take your sons, ... your daughters ... your fields, ... the tenth of your seed, ... your servants ... and ye shall be his servants.** This is a historically accurate portrayal of the despotic governments of the ancient biblical world, as archaeological evidence from such sites as Alalakh and Ugarit shows. In spite of the restrictions prescribed by the Mosaic Law, the Hebrew monarchy gradually slid into the condition predicted by Samuel, especially during Solomon's reign.

19-20. The people, however, declined to heed Samuel's warning and persisted in their plan to be **like all the nations,** "though it was their glory and happiness to be unlike other nations in having the LORD for their King and Lawgiver" (JFB, p. 180). **22.** The demand of the people was divinely conceded, so Samuel dismissed the representative assembly convened to consider the matter of a monarchy.

B. SAUL CHOSEN AS KING. 9:1-27.

Saul and the Lost Donkeys. 9:1-17. **1-2.** Introducing and anticipating Saul's future greatness, his genealogy is given,

374

but in abbreviated form (cf. Gen. 46:21; 1 Sam. 14:51; 1 Chron. 7:6-8). Saul's father, Kish, is called **a Benjamite, a mighty man of power** (*gĭbbôr ḥăyĭl*, "a man of influence") strong by virtue of physical and material resources (cf. Josh. 10:2; Judg. 5:13, 23), valiant and able to equip himself for war (Judg. 6:12; 11:1).

The description of Kish's son, Saul ("asked"), shows that he was exactly what the people were looking for. God gave them what they wanted and had "asked"—**a choice young man** (*bāḥûr*, "choice," in the sense of being in the prime of life and chosen for military service, 2 Chron. 25:5), **handsome** (*ṭôḇ*, "well built"), and none was **more handsome ... than he**, towering head and shoulders above his peers.

3-5. The story of the strayed asses (female donkeys) constitutes an example of providential leading to bring Saul and Samuel together at Ramah. Saul and a servant, a trustworthy dependent of Kish's household, not a slave, went on a fruitless search to recover the lost animals. The route cannot be traced in detail, but they wound up in **the land of Zuph** (cf. 1:1), where Ramah, Samuel's hometown, was located (cf. 7:17). Thus, in the divine leading, Saul found himself in Samuel's hometown at the very moment the great prophet-judge, advised by the LORD, was looking for a king.

6. Yet Saul was virtually ignorant of Samuel and was urged by his servant to seek him out with a trivial request about the lost donkeys. **7-10.** Saul was willing enough to go to the man of God for counsel, but he was troubled about a present for him—an illustration of the tendency of the natural man to give in order to get from God. Saul and his servant were anxious to know the outcome of their quest. Their imagined mission was a couple of stray asses. However, in the dramatic irony of the situation, their real but quite unsuspected goals were a throne and a kingdom. **11-13.** The maidens at the well told Saul and his servant that the seer was in the city to **bless the sacrifice. 14.** They arrived at the very moment Samuel was coming out right in front of them.

15-16. Now the Lord had told Samuel (lit., "had uncovered the ear of Samuel") all about Saul. The figure is taken from the action of pushing aside the headdress to whisper a confidential message into the ear. Saul was to be anointed **captain** (*nāḡîḏ*, "prince, leader") over the LORD'S people to be a deliverer from Philistine oppression. When Samuel saw Saul, the LORD whispered into his ear: **Behold, the man ... the same shall reign over** (shall control, restrain) **my people**, envisioning a stern and severe rule.

Saul as Samuel's Guest. 9:18-27.
18-19. Samuel invited Saul to the sacrificial meal at the **high place** (the public place of sacrifice), together with his servant. That was a signal honor for one of Samuel's rank to accord to an unknown transient like Saul. **20.** Samuel thoughtfully relieved Saul's mind about the lost donkeys, and then he told him the thrilling news that on him and his house was **all the desire of Israel** (i.e., all that Israel possessed of what is precious or worth desiring; "the best in Israel," Luther). **21.** Such words from the revered seer, holding out a prospect of undreamed of glory, naturally amazed Saul as a member of an obscure family of the smallest of the Israelite tribes.

22. Samuel's purpose was to wean Saul's thoughts from the trivial (the lost donkeys) and fasten them on his high destiny. Therefore, he conducted him to **the parlor** (the "chamber" or "room") attached to the edifice on the high place where the sacrificial feast was to be held. All the details of the sacrifice and the feast had been prearranged by Samuel according to the revelation made to him the previous day, that Israel's future king would appear. **23-24.** Following the Syriac and the Hebrew, **the cook** is correctly read as the "speaker" in verse 24, indicating how completely Samuel had foreseen Saul's coming and provided for every detail.

25-26. The prophet-judge also detained Saul as his honored guest overnight in Ramah, sending him away at **about the dawn of the day. 27.** At **the end of the city** ("the town limits"), Samuel instructed Saul to bid his servant to go on ahead. But Saul was to **stand . . . still a while**, that Samuel might acquaint him with God's message.

C. SAUL'S ANOINTING AS KING.
10:1-27.

Saul's Anointing. 10:1. **1. Then Samuel took a vial** (flask) **of oil, and poured it upon** Saul's **head.** Anointing was an ancient custom, practiced in Egypt and elsewhere, including pre-Israelite Palestine, according to the Amarna Letters. In this case it apparently was not common oil but that which was used in the consecration of the priests, the tabernacle, and sacred vessels (Exod. 29:7; 30:23-33), rich in symbolic significance of God's Spirit resting on the person anointed over God's inheritance. God's people have an inheritance in Him, and He has an inheritance in them (cf. Eph. 1:11, 18; Psalms 28:9; 94:14). Samuel kissed Saul, undoubtedly an act of homage to the new king, and a token of congratulations (Psalm 2:12), rather than personal affection, which scarcely would have had time to develop.

Signs to Saul Confirming His Kingship. 10:2-8. Saul was astonished at the anointing and quite incredulous at the honors bestowed upon him. Samuel outlined the three signs that would confront the future king as he departed from Ramah to his father's home in Benjamin, each of which was designed to strengthen his faith in God's call.

(1) **2.** At Rachel's sepulcher, near Ramah north of Jerusalem (cf. Jer. 31:15), he would encounter two men, who would assure him his father's donkeys had been found. Traditionally, Rachel's tomb is located near Bethlehem, south of Jerusalem, but all that Genesis 35:16, 19 indicates is that Rachel died somewhere between Bethel (north of Ramah) and Bethlehem (cf. Matt. 2:16-18). (2) **3-4.** At the **oak of Tabor** (cf. Judg. 4:5) he would encounter three men going up to sacrifice to God at Bethel; they would providentially give him of their sacrificed provisions of food and wine.

(3) **5-7.** After that, when he came to **the hill of God**, where a Philistine garrison was quartered, he would meet **a company of prophets**, who would be singing, playing music, and prophesying (cf. 19:20). There **the Spirit of the Lord** would come upon him, and he would prophesy with them. Then he would be **turned into another man**, divinely endowed with character and courage for kingship, and a true successor of the judges, who were all impelled by God's Spirit. **8.** Samuel directed Saul to go to Gilgal, a place of deep spiritual import (see Josh. 5:2-12). There Saul was to be tested, and there he was to fail initially (cf. 13:7-14).

The Signs Fulfilled. 10:9-16. **9-10.** The story is abbreviated. The fulfilment of the first two signs is taken for granted. The all-important fact is stressed: Samuel's choice of Saul as king was clearly by divine revelation and approval. Only the third sign is mentioned specifically. **God gave Saul another**

heart, transforming him into a great leader and warrior. **The Spirit of God came upon him mightily**, (NASB; *tiṣlāḥ*, "rushed upon him"; cf. Judg. 14:6, 19; 1 Sam. 11:6; 16:13), indicating a sudden and full possession by the Spirit of Elohim.

11. Saul's conduct was so unusual for a worldling that the saying **Is Saul also among the prophets?** was equivalent to a worldling getting religion (cf. 19:24). **12.** Instead of **Who is their father?**, the Septuagint reads, "Who is *his father*?," referring to Saul, the son of Kish. **14-16.** The story of the lost donkeys is not only rounded off, but the passage shows that Saul's kingship was still a secret, even to his own family.

Saul Publicly Installed as King. 10:17-27. **17-18.** Samuel once more summoned a national assembly at Mizpah (cf. 7:5), reminding the people of the LORD's redemption of the nation out of Egypt and His care over them. **19-22.** In insisting on a king, they were warned that they had rejected their God. Therefore, the lot cast was an outward, empty ceremony. When the lot fell on Saul, he could not be found. Why did he hide? Was it humility and modesty? Scarcely. Rather, it was a lack of faith, as the harbinger of his future failure, despite the tokens of divine power already vouchsafed him.

23-24. A wave of fleshly enthusiasm swept over the people when Saul was presented. They looked on the outward form and figure, towering head and shoulders above the other people (cf. 16:7), and shouted, **God save the king** (lit., "Let the king live [long]"). **25-26.** Samuel rehearsed **the manner of the kingdom** (taken from Deut. 17:14-20), wrote it in a roll, and solemnly laid it up in the nation's archives. He dismissed the representative assembly, and Saul went home to Gibeah with a **band of**

men, whose hearts God had touched. **27.** But certain **worthless fellows** ("children of Belial, good-for-nothing people") despised him. Saul, as a wary man of the flesh, kept quiet about their insult.

D. SAUL'S CONFIRMATION AS KING. 11:1-15.

The Ammonite Insult. 11:1-3. The unstated purpose of this chapter is to show how the incipient opposition to Saul was overcome and how the king proved himself kingly, at least initially. **1. Nahash** ("serpent") **the Ammonite** came up and **encamped against** (besieged) **Jabesh-gilead**, no doubt to avenge the long-standing shame they had suffered at the hands of Jephthah (cf. Judg. 11:1-40). **2-3.** Feeling their isolation from the rest of the Israelite tribes, the citizens of Jabesh in Gilead were willing for expediency's sake to make a treaty and to pay tribute.

But the price of bodily mutilation, making the people unfit for warfare, was too great and the ignominy too deep. Affinity with Ammon, illustrative of compromise with the world and the flesh, always exacts a high toll spiritually and incapacitates the LORD's people for effective warfare and service. The appeal for a seven-day respite shows that although ancient warfare was cruel and relentless, it was conducted according to certain rules of etiquette and honor.

The Appeal of Distress and Saul's Response. 11:4-8. **4.** Although the beleaguered city sent messengers to all the tribes, the reaction of the Benjamites of Gibeah and the action taken by Saul are alone recorded. The assumption is that this was the first city contacted, not only because of their ancient friendship with Benjamin (cf. Judg. 21:1-25), but because Gibeah was the home of Saul, the newly elected king. The weeping of the people of Gibeah attests their longtime friendship with Jabesh-gilead.

5-6. Saul's appearance on the scene was providential, and his reaction was the result of the fact that the Spirit of God **came upon** (*tiṣlăḥ*, "rushed upon") him (see 10:6). **7.** He cut up a yoke of oxen (cf. Judg. 19:29) and sent the pieces throughout the tribes, with a threat that whoever would not come forth after him and **Samuel, so shall it be done unto his oxen.** Under divine anointing, Saul showed himself capable of great leadership and deliverance like that effected by Gideon, Barak, Jephthah, and Samson. The people likewise responded under the same divine inworking (cf. Judg. 20:1). **8.** They assembled at Bezek, southwest of Bethshan west of the Jordan, opposite Jabesh east of the river. The numbers appear huge (cf. Judg. 20:15-17; 2 Sam. 24:9), but if they were corrupted, it took place very early, for the LXX's figures are even larger.

Saul's Victory and Jabesh's Deliverance. 11:9-11. Saul employed Gideon's strategem (Judg. 7:16). He conducted a nocturnal forced march, fell upon the Ammonites while they were sleeping, and slew them in consternation and disarray.

Saul's Confirmation as King. 11:12-15. **12-13.** Saul showed constraint in opposing the people's rash wish to kill his opponents (cf. 10:27; Luke 19:27; 2 Sam. 19:22), and he gave God the glory for the victory. **14-15.** But it is ironic that he who should so soon signally fail to exemplify what Gilgal stood for spiritually should be confirmed in the kingdom there, the place in Israel's history connected with death to the old nature and the putting off the sins of the flesh (see Josh. 5:2, 12; 1 Sam. 13:7-14; Col. 2:8-10).

E. SAMUEL'S FAREWELL ADDRESS. 12:1-25.

Samuel Attests His Integrity. 12:1-5. **1-3.** This public address of Samuel's was made at Gilgal after the solemn confirmation of the kingdom to Saul and before the representative assembly dispersed. He protested his integrity as prophet-judge. **4-5.** His claim was sustained by the people, by the LORD's anointed (Saul), and by the LORD Himself, that they had **not found anything in his hand** (cf. Exod. 22:4), that is, anything acquired by bribery or dishonesty.

Samuel Reproves the People for Ingratitude. 12:6-15. **6-11.** Samuel reviewed the LORD's past deliverances of Israel, from the Exodus through the period of the judges ("Bedan," v. 11, should be read "Barak," in accordance with the Greek and Syriac, and "Samuel" here probably should be "Samson"; cf. Heb. 11:32). **12-15.** The people's reasons for choosing a king were sinful. Their unbelief made them distrust their heavenly King for an earthly one (1 Sam. 8:5, 19-20; Judg. 8:23; Psalm 59:13). But if they and their king would obey the LORD, then all would be well; however, disobedience would result in the LORD's hand being against them, **as it was against** their fathers.

The Lord Demonstrates Israel's Sin in Asking for a King. 12:16-19. **16-18. Thunder and rain** during the wheat harvest (last of June and early July) were so rare as to be miraculous, especially without any prior indications and when wholly foretold by the Word of God as announced through the prophet (cf. 7:10; Ezra 10:9). The **great thing** that the LORD did before their eyes incontrovertibly proved their sin to the people. **19.** They cried out to Samuel, **Pray ... that we die not.** Reference is evidently to the "sin unto [physical] death" (1 John 5:16; cf. 1 Cor. 5:5; 11:30-32).

Samuel's Final Plea. 12:20-25. **20-21.** Although the people had **done all this wickedness**, they were not to fear, but diligently follow the LORD in order to keep free of apostasy and idolatry. **22.** Moreover, the LORD **will not forsake his people** (cf. Deut. 7:6-11; 31:6; Isa. 43:21). **23.** Meanwhile, Samuel promised to pray unceasingly for them (cf. Rom. 1:9). To fail to do so would be to **sin against the Lord**, for they were the LORD's people, His elect, and to fail to intercede for them would be an affront to Him who chose them by His grace. **24. Only fear** (reverence) **the Lord ... serve him.** The motive? **For consider how great things he hath done for you**, "the LORD of all the righteous acts ... which he did to you and to your fathers" (v. 7). **25.** Persistence in wickedness, however, would bring ruin.

F. SAUL'S FIRST GREAT FAILURE. 13:1-23.

The Israelites Muster for Battle. 13:1-7. **1-3. Saul was ... years old**, the numeral for his age having been lost in the Hebrew text very early, so that conjectures of between thirty to forty years have been made for Saul's age when he began to reign. The events of this chapter evidently occurred in the second year of his rule. By then Saul had an adult son, whereas he himself was called a "young man" (9:2) when he became king. Evidently Saul, according to common custom, had married early and could have been in his thirties and still have had a son able to bear arms.

In this second year of his reign, Saul was tested severely regarding his fitness to be king by a formidable invasion of the Philistines. Would he trust the LORD and obey His word through Samuel? Jonathan ("the LORD has given"),

Saul's noble son and a striking contrast to his father, did so. But Saul revealed his real character by his flagrant unbelief and disobedience in intruding into the priest's office at Gilgal (of all places! see notes on Josh. 5:2-12).

Jonathan, with **a thousand** men who were with him, attacked and routed the **garrison of the Philistines ... in Geba**, a village in Benjamin nine miles north of Jerusalem. The Hebrew word $n^e \bar{s} \hat{i} \underline{b}$ may also denote "a prefect" or "official," and the passage would then denote the assassination of this representative of the Philistines and signal general revolt. **Saul blew the trumpet throughout all the land**, the usual Hebrew war summons.

4. Jonathan's action showed the Philistines that Israel was going to attempt to throw off their yoke. A general muster in Israel was ordered at the old camping ground at Gilgal near the Jordan and hence more removed from Philistine attack. **5.** The seriousness of the Philistine peril is indicated in the description of their army, the thirty thousand Philistine chariots evidently meaning the men fighting in them (cf. 2 Sam. 10:18; 1 Kings 20:21; 1 Chron. 19:18), or else the number has suffered corruption in transmission. **6-7.** The trial was to test all Israel, especially their leader.

Saul's Self-Will. 13:8-10. **8-9.** In disobeying the Word of God spoken by Samuel (10:8), Saul's excuse was that sacrifice had to be offered to guarantee success in battle. Meanwhile, as Samuel delayed his appearance, Saul's army was deserting him. Not to offer sacrifice before battle would have shattered the army's morale. Saul was in a quandary. He waited until the seventh day, but could not bring himself to wait till it was over.

And he offered the burnt offering. He, a Benjamite, offered that which only a

Levite and a priest might offer (cf. Num. 16:1-40). The act was a direct violation of God's Law, an act of rebellion against God by God's representative, which was proof of the unbelief of his heart and his essential unfitness to be king over the LORD's people. **10.** No sooner had Saul committed this sin than Samuel appeared and **Saul went out to meet him** so that Samuel **might bless him** (cf. 15:13).

Saul's Rejection Announced. 13:11-14. **11-12.** Saul's excuse to Samuel only set his unbelief and disobedience in bolder relief. **13.** Samuel's rebuke was stern. **Thou hast done foolishly** (*nĭskăltā*, "thou hast shown thyself a fool"; cf. 26:21; 2 Chron. 16:9). **14.** The penalty was the eventual loss of the kingdom to another, **a man after** God's **own heart** (cf. 16:1; Psalm 89:20; Acts 13:22). Saul's subsequent career demonstrates the futility of attempting to do God's work without obedience in gratitude for divine electing grace and blessing.

Israel Helpless Before the Philistine Foe. 13:15-23. When the leaders of God's people fail, God's people suffer. **15.** Saul's forces had dwindled away to a fraction (cf. v. 2), and Samuel's displeasure may well have occasioned further desertions. **17-18. And the spoilers** (raiding bands) came **out of the camp of the Philistines in three companies. 19-22.** Serious depletion of Israel's armies and their inadequate arms encouraged the invaders to plunder the countryside. The Philistines had the secret of iron smelting and had a virtual monopoly on iron weapons, a circumstance that enabled a comparatively small nation to rule over most of Palestine for a time.

Verse 21, as is now known from archaeology, should be read, "And the price of the filing was a pim for the mattocks." A *pim* was a weight about one-quarter of an ounce, approximately two-thirds of a shekel. Hebrew weights discovered at Lachish and elsewhere are marked with the word *pim*. It was a natural thing for the Philistines to charge an exorbitant fee for sharpening weapons that might be used in warfare against them. **23.** The entrenchment of the Philistine garrison in the pass of Michmash was proof enough of their threat to Israel.

G. JONATHAN'S HEROISM. 14:1-52.

Jonathan's Victory of Faith. 14:1-15. **1. Jonathan, the son of Saul**, is one of the most beautiful characters of the Bible. With a spirit kindred to that of his armor-bearer, he bravely attacked the outposts of the Philistines. **But he told not his father. 2-3.** The king was surrounded by a small company, together with the descendants of Eli, the priest. Neither Saul nor the priests nor the people were aware that Jonathan had left the camp. **4-5.** Sharp crags were on both sides of the pass through which Jonathan tried to cross to reach the Philistine post. One was called **Bozez** ("heighten") and the other **Seneh** ("pointed rock").

6-7. Jonathan, his armor-bearer, and their conversation are simple and blessed illustrations of true faith. Jonathan knew the LORD and recognized that He loves His people and therefore would overthrow their enemies. His words to his armor-bearer show his faith: **It may be that the Lord will work for us; for there is no restraint to the Lord to save by many or by few** (cf. Deut. 32:36; Judg. 7:4, 7; 2 Chron. 14:11; Rom. 8:31).

8-10. Jonathan's plan reveals that he cast himself wholly upon the LORD for His help. **11.** When he and his armor-bearer showed themselves to the Philistine garrison, the Philistines mockingly taunted them, "Look, the Hebrews have come out of the holes in which they have been hiding" (BV; cf. 13:6). Just as the term "these uncircumcised" (v. 6) was an uncomplimentary term to describe the Philistines, so the "Hebrews" was an uncomplimentary designation of the Israelites.

12. When **the men of the garrison** answered Jonathan and his armor-bearer, **Come up to us, and we will show you something**, Jonathan knew the Lord had answered. Faith became vocal in the young son of Saul: **Come up after me; for the Lord hath delivered them into the hand of Israel. 13.** Jonathan's strategy lay in making the Philistines believe that the Israelites, who had hidden in the caves, had come out to fight. With this ruse established, Jonathan and his armor-bearer started the battle.

The Philistines began to fight back, and every Israelite in sight, including those who for one reason or another had joined the Philistine army (perhaps by force, or some may have been traitors), was suspected as being one of those who had come out from hiding. Actually, Jonathan and his helper were the only enemies there. The fight, therefore, was actually within the Philistine army itself.

The Philistines thought they were fighting Israel, but actually they were fighting the Lord God of Israel. God used this to punish an apostate element in Israel (Israelites in the Philistine ranks) while Saul's army was suffering no harm. The Philistines were felled by Jonathan and then killed by his armor-bearer, who was fighting behind him. In this battle all Hebrew fighters, beginning with Jonathan's armor-bearer, had to arm themselves with the weapons of fallen Philistine fighters.

14. The first slaughter by Jonathan and his armor-bearer numbered about twenty Philistines **within . . . an half acre of land, which a yoke of oxen might plow** (i.e., the area a yoke of oxen could plow

in one day). **15.** Then terrible panic struck the army garrison, and there also was an earthquake; so the whole proceeding became a terror sent by God.

Subsequent Victory of Israel. 14:16-23. **16-17.** Meanwhile, in Saul's camp at Gibeah it was discovered that Jonathan and his armor-bearer were missing. **18.** Saul told Ahijah, one of the priests, to bring the ark of God, because the king was particularly anxious for divine counsel, which might be furnished with the aid of the priest's ephod. **19.** However, while Saul was talking to the priest, the commotion in the Philistine camp grew worse and worse, and Saul said to the priest, **Withdraw thine hand.** In that remark Saul again showed the weakness of his character. His desire for divine guidance was really hypocritical.

20-23. When he saw the Philistines in disarray and confusion, Saul was quite ready to break off praying and take advantage of the situation. These verses show how the Lord undertook because of Jonathan's faith and gave great victory to Israel that day. The battle even **passed over** (spread out) beyond Bethaven (*bêt āwĕn*, "house of iniquity," i.e., "place of idolatry"), a town located near Ai (Josh. 7:2) and east of Beth-el. The site served as a boundary mark for Benjamin's allotment (Josh. 18:12).

Saul's Rash Command. 14:24-35. **24-26.** In the crisis of Israel's troops that day, Saul had put the people on oath, saying, **Cursed be the man who eateth any food until evening, that I may be avenged on mine enemies.** Saul's action was completely unnecessary and made in self-will. The oath by which he bound the people was simply the manifestation of the natural man. In his blindness, he thought he could help along and complete the defeat of the enemy by his legal injunction and fleshly expedient. But, on account of his foolish oath, the people were in great distress. Legalism and man-made injunctions always put a burden and distress upon God's people.

27-31. Saul's own son, Jonathan, ignorant of his father's command, took a bit of honey on the end of his staff and received physical refreshment from it. Honey illustrates natural things and their sweetness. Their use in strict moderation and in the right way is not forbidden by God. Like Jonathan, the man of faith, we must partake of them only in strict moderation. Had Jonathan filled himself with all the honey he could have eaten, it would not have refreshed him, but instead incapacitated him for the conflict. Jonathan was strengthened physically by the honey he took, while the people fainted in physical weakness.

32-35. But a worse result of Saul's legal enactment occurred. The famished people ate voraciously of meat, together with the blood. God's original command to Noah, with His reason for it (Gen. 9:4-6), applied to the Hebrews and was reiterated by the church (Acts 15:20, 29; see Lev. 17:10-14; 19:26). Saul's restriction of a lawful thing led to the breaking of a divine command.

Jonathan's Guilt Discovered. 14:36-46. **36-42.** Following the victory, Jonathan was naturally the idol, doubtlessly even of his father. But Saul gave one demonstration after another that he had more zeal than sense in declaring a fast (v. 24), which acted as a boomerang. The fighting army needed strength that could not be gotten by fasting, and then Saul had foolishly overlooked the fact that Jonathan was away and did not have any knowledge of the order. While Jonathan's absence was against orders, it turned out to be a case in which disobedience was better than obedience. Then, too, the penalty of death imposed for breaking the fast had been too severe.

45. A near tragedy was averted when the people interceded to prevent Jonathan's execution. It was obvious that the successes wrought through Jonathan that day were proof that the LORD had favored him above Saul's arbitrary plan. Although Saul had the outward pretentions of an ardent worshiper of the LORD, a builder of altars (v. 35), and even a man of prayer, all that was superficial. Saul's disobedience and innate self-will got him in trouble almost every time he undertook religious activity. His decision showed the king's impetuous and stubborn heart. Self-righteous and self-willed, he was ready to slay his own son, even in the moment of his son's great feat in delivering the LORD's people. The people showed more wisdom than the king in rescuing Jonathan from his hands. What humiliation for him who was supposed to be the leader of the LORD's people!

Saul's Wars. 14:47-48. **47-48.** Despite this display of Saul's essential unfitness to be king and the LORD's representative to his people, nevertheless the deliverances wrought through him are mentioned. God often uses unlikely vessels to work deliverances for His people. Saul is no exception, but he who could have been a very great blessing proved to be a great disappointment to the LORD.

Saul's Family and Army. 14:49-52. **49-52.** After listing the important members of Saul's family, it is indicated that throughout Saul's life there was heavy fighting against the Philistines. The fact is featured that whenever Saul noticed any brave and athletic man, he personally drafted him for his army.

H. SAUL'S SECOND GREAT FAILURE. 15:1-35.

Saul's Commission to Exterminate the Amalekites. 15:1-5. **1-2.** Samuel presented Saul with the LORD's clear command. In communicating the plan, Samuel used the title **the Lord of hosts.** He who marshals the angelic armies of heaven and who fights for His people on earth issued the clear command to one who supposedly represented Him on earth and was to be strictly obedient to the heavenly orders. Dramatically, the LORD announced, **I remember that which Amalek did to Israel, how he laid wait for him in the way, when he came up from Egypt** (cf. Exod. 17:16).

3. The command was to **utterly destroy** (*ḥērēm*, lit., "devote" to Jehovah) Amalek. The primal meaning of *ḥērēm* is that the object is dedicated to the LORD, and so it is proscribed from common use. Amalek, the great foe of the LORD's people, in a spiritual sense denotes the flesh and its lusts (see Exod. 17). Israel was to have war with Amalek from generation to generation, and the remembrance of Amalek was to be completely blotted out. Likewise, the flesh is always the enemy of the people of God; it is enmity against God. Saul was to war against and utterly destroy such an enemy. **4-5.** Saul gathered the people together in **Telaim** (probably Telem, Josh. 15:24, located a few miles south of Beersheba).

Saul's Disobedience and Rejection. 15:6-11. **6.** Saul warned the Kenites of the attack and instructed them to separate themselves from among the Amalekites lest they be destroyed with them (cf. Num. 24:21; Judg. 1:16; 4:11-22; 1 Chron. 2:55). The Kenites were also nomads and had always been well disposed toward Israel. These people had accompanied Israel to Jericho and then had gone to dwell with the Amalekites in the desert south of Judah. Famous among the Kenites was Jael, whose husband, Heber, had migrated to north Palestine (Judg. 4:11; 5:24).

7. Saul struck down the Amalekites from Havilah (Gen. 25:17-18) to Shur, east of Egypt. *Shur* means "wall." The name seems to be derived from "the wall," a line of fortifications that in ancient times defended the northeast frontier of Egypt (Exod. 15:22; 1 Sam. 27:8). **8.** Saul captured Agag alive but doomed all the people to complete destruction with the sword.

9. With Agag, Saul also spared the choicest sheep and cattle and the fattest lambs, everything of high value. They utterly destroyed only the lesser-quality cattle and the worthless. Is it not easy in dealing with the flesh and its lusts to judge a multitude of things and spare the worst of all, Agag? How easy it is to spare things that minister to the lusts of the flesh if only they are not what would usually be considered vile.

10-11. In the face of this open disobedience to the Word of God, the LORD spoke through Samuel, **It repenteth me that I have set up Saul to be king.** God is said to "repent" when a change in the character and conduct of those with whom He is dealing leads to a corresponding change in His purposes and plans toward them. Samuel was so deeply upset that he cried to the LORD all night. It is painful to see a life once headed in the right direction finally choose the wrong way (cf. Exod. 32:11-13; 1 Kings 11:1-8).

Samuel's Rebuke of Saul. 15:12-23. **12.** In the morning it was told Samuel that Saul had come to **Carmel** (25:2; Josh. 15:55), where he erected for himself a "monument." The monument was an indication of his egotism and fleshly vanity. Undeniable evidence of his leniency with Amalek on the pretense of piety (vv. 13-15) proved his guilt and called for divine rejection despite his self-defense (vv. 16-23). Saul went down **to Gilgal** (cf. 13:13-14). In the very same place where Saul's kingdom had been confirmed upon him (11:14-15), it was to be taken from him. **13-15.** Saul blamed the people for his disobedience. Like Aaron at Sinai (Exod. 32:22) and Adam and Eve in Eden (Gen. 3:12-13), he tried to shift the personal responsibility to others. Clear evidence was accumulating that Saul was an unfit king. Rather than ruling as a vicegerent of the LORD, he was displaying himself as a weak tool of the people.

17. Samuel reminded the rejected king that when he was little in his own sight he had become a prince of Israel's tribes, and that he had forgotten that the LORD had anointed him king over Israel. **19.** "Why then, did you not listen to the LORD's voice, but flung yourself on the loot and did evil in the LORD's sight?" (BV). **22. Behold, to obey is better than sacrifice** (cf. Eccles. 5:1; Hos. 6:6; Matt. 9:13; 12:7). Faith in God's Word that produces obedience to God's will delights the LORD. **Burnt offerings and sacrifices** may indicate mere external religionism or even hypocrisy, but obedience to God springs out of the heart. **23. For rebellion is as the sin of witchcraft** (divination, which is connected with paganistic idolatry). The sin of divination (see Deut. 18:9-14) consists in sin against the Word of God by consulting some other being in opposition to God, or by neglecting God's Word.

Saul's Confession. 15:24-31. **24.** Although Saul confessed, **I have sinned** (cf. 26:21; Josh. 7:20), even his confession reveals his true character. His basic weakness was that he **feared the people, and obeyed their voice** more than God's. His confession was merely superficial. It did not reach his heart. **27.** As Samuel turned around to leave, Saul seized the border of his robe, which tore off. **28.**

That act turned out to be a representation of the fact that the LORD had torn the kingship of Israel away from him and given it to a neighbor, David, who was better than he. **30.** Saul's main concern was his fear that the breach between himself and Samuel might become a public scandal and weaken his kingly authority.

Agag Exterminated. 15:32-33. **32.** Samuel **said** (demanded) that Agag, the Amalakite king, be brought to him. **And Agag came unto him cheerfully** ("delicately," KJV), since he concluded that the bitterness of death had passed. **33.** Yet Samuel, the man of God, **hewed Agag in pieces** before the LORD in Gilgal. Death alone must be pronounced upon the flesh and all that pertains to it if the Word of God is to be obeyed (Rom. 8:13; Col. 3:5). Only such a course brings spiritual victory and joy. At Gilgal, Israel was circumcised and the token of death to the flesh administered—a proper place for Agag to be executed (see Josh. 5:2-9).

Samuel's Break with Saul. 15:34-35. **34.** Samuel returned to his home in Ramah (cf. 7:17). And Saul returned to his rustic palace at Gibeah (cf. 11:4), excavated by W. F. Albright and dating about 1015 B.C.

III. DAVID'S EARLY CAREER. 16:1—31:13.

A. DAVID ANOINTED AS KING. 16:1-23.

Samuel Instructed to Anoint Another King. 16:1-5. **1.** And the LORD said unto Samuel, **How long wilt thou mourn for Saul ... ?** Even the godly Samuel was inclined to grieve for Saul, despite the fact that the LORD had renounced him as king over Israel. Saul was indeed the king after the people's heart and attracted love and admiration despite his failures and weaknesses. His rejection was followed by the choice of the king after God's own heart, whose exile and sufferings are told in chapters 16 through 31.

Like Jonathan, David was a man of faith, every inch a king and in complete subjection to the LORD. He was to be the type of the true King who would come from Bethlehem of Judea ("praise"), the royal tribe (Gen. 49:10). Like his great antitype, his sufferings were to precede future glory. So the new king was to suffer greatly before ascending to the throne. The narrative of David's anointing is not unlike that of Saul's (cf. 9:1 — 10:1), involving the private anointing of an unsuspecting young man to the royal office.

2-3. Offering sacrifice at Bethlehem may well have been routine for Samuel, the town being a major city of Judah situated five miles south of Jerusalem. Here for the first time appears a hint of the suspicious and vindictive nature of Saul's character. Samuel expressed fear that if Saul heard of his going to Bethlehem, he would kill him. That is understandable since the route from Ramah to Bethlehem passed through Saul's capital, Gibeah.

4. The elders ... trembled. Perhaps they feared that Samuel had come to their town in his capacity as a judge to hold court and to punish their offenses (cf. 7:16). Perhaps they suspected bad news from Saul. **5.** Samuel told them to consecrate themselves and share the sacrifice with him, for which purpose he had come. As directed by the LORD, he also consecrated Jesse and his sons and invited them to the sacrifice.

The Anointing of David. 16:6-13. **6.** As Jesse's sons came in, Samuel scrutinized each one. Eliab, like Saul, was of splendid height. Samuel thought surely the LORD's anointed was before him. **7.** But Saul was proof enough that

one should not look on a person's countenance, or on the height of one's stature. **For the Lord seeth not as man seeth; for man looketh on the outward appearance, but the Lord looketh on the heart** (1 Kings 8:39; 2 Cor. 10:7; John 2:24-25). **8-9.** Neither Abinadab nor Shammah was the LORD's chosen one. **10.** Jesse made seven of his sons pass before Samuel, but Samuel said to him, **The Lord hath not chosen these.**

11. In masterful story-telling fashion, holding the reader in suspense, the historian keeps secret the name of David, the youngest. Jesse described him as keeping **the sheep** (cf. 2 Sam. 7:8; Psalm 78:70-72). David was sent for and appeared before Samuel, who had declared that they would not sit down to the official feast until the youngest son of Jesse had arrived. **12.** And the LORD said (that is, to Samuel), **Arise, anoint him; for this is he** (cf. 9:17).

David Called to Saul's Court. 16:14-23. **14-15.** As the Spirit of God came upon David, the Spirit departed from Saul, and **an evil spirit**, that is, a demon, began to torment the rejected king by the LORD's permission. Divine sovereignty controls evil forces for God's purposes. Believers who stubbornly reject God's Word and go on in self-will and rebellion expose themselves to demon control to a greater or lesser degree (cf. Matt. 12:43-45; 1 Tim. 4:1; 1 John 4:1-4). Saul is patently a case of demonization (commonly called demon possession).

16-23. David's skill in performing on the harp, that is, the lyre, was called upon to refresh the harassed king. Demonic powers notoriously hate spiritual music. David's sweet psalms of trust in God soothed the troubled monarch. When he was no longer needed, David returned to his father's sheep (cf. 17:15, 55-58). Evidently the preoccupied Saul did not bother to ascertain the lineage of this young musician until David was about to become his son-in-law.

B. DAVID SLAYS GOLIATH. 17:1-58.

Goliath Defies Israel. 17:1-11. **1-3. Now the Philistines gathered together their armies to battle.** The invading Philistine army moved into the hills of west Judah, and Saul sent his own army to meet them. **Socoh** (modern Shuweikeh) is located some fourteen miles west of Bethlehem. The name has been found on jar handles in the vicinity. The Israelite army encamped **by the valley of Elah.**

4-11. The enemy decided on a fight between champions. In ancient battle tactics, many conflicts were decided by a contest between two warriors; for example, Achilles and Hector agreed to a duel to decide the outcome of the Trojan War. Goliath of Gath, the Philistine champion, proposed that the differences between Israel and the Philistines be settled by himself and an Israelite warrior. Goliath was over nine feet tall, wore a bronze helmet, and was armed with a bronze coat of mail that weighed two hundred pounds. His legs were protected with bronze leggings, and he carried a bronze javelin on his shoulder. His spear shaft was the size of a weaver's beam. The head of his iron spear weighed twenty-five pounds. His armor-bearer went ahead of him. This proud, taunting pagan struck fear and alarm into Saul and the Israelites in his impious defiance of the LORD's people and the LORD Himself.

Goliath furnishes an apt illustration of Satan, as the giant who defied and terrified God's people through Philistine doctrines and practices. Note the prominence of the number six, the number of man under satanic sway and opposition to God. Compare another giant (2 Sam.

21:20); Nebuchadnezzar's image (Dan. 3:1); and the number of the Antichrist, a triple six (Rev. 13:18), representing the acme of satanic opposition to God.

David Challenges Goliath. 17:12-30. In the deeper spiritual sense, David reminds us of the Lord Jesus. His being sent by his father, Jesse (vv. 12-19); his obedience (vv. 20-27); and his being misunderstood and unfairly accused by his own brothers (vv. 28-30) are details reminiscent of Him whom the Father sent into the world and of His treatment by His own. **12.** Jesse is called an Ephrathite, that is, from Ephratah, evidently a district adjoining Bethlehem (cf. Mic. 5:2). **13.** Only the three oldest sons of Jesse are named, as in 16:6-9.

15. David's arrival on the battle scene was due to divine intervention, for at that time he was not acting as Saul's musician and armor-bearer. **17-18.** Jesse sent his son David to his brothers in the army to take them a bushel of roasted grain, ten loaves of bread, and also ten cheeses for their colonel. The object was to see how the brothers were faring, and David was to bring back some reminder from them to show that he had actually visited them.

20-22. David went enthusiastically to fulfill his father's commission. Arriving at the camp, he left his pack of food in care of the commissary and hurried toward the ranks. **23-24.** While he was asking his brothers about their welfare, Goliath, the Philistine champion, came out from the Philistine army across the valley and repeated the insolent daily challenge, which David heard. He saw the terror of the men of Israel as they faced the giant. **25.** David was told that the king would richly reward the one who slew the giant and would give him his daughter in marriage and exempt his father's family in Israel from such burdens as taxes and involuntary services, which the common man had to meet. It amounted to almost being raised to nobility.

26-30. In a jealous rage, David's oldest brother sternly reproved David for conversing with the men in the army. Young David, fresh from the field, from the pasture, and from conversing with God, was astonished at the fear and trembling among the troops, occasioned by Goliath's appearance. His faith and intrepidity, expressed in his words, were noted and repeated to Saul.

David's Great Victory. 17:31-54. **31-33.** Having heard of what David said, King Saul sent for him. David urged Saul to let no one lose courage on account of this giant and volunteered to fight with the Philistine. Saul warned the lad of the danger and the impossibility of his fighting and conquering the champion. **34-37.** David, however, in utter naiveté and with a vision of God's help uncontaminated by unbelief, recounted his experiences tending his father's sheep. When a lion or a bear came and seized his sheep, David related, he went after him, struck him, and rescued the sheep from his jaws. When the animal turned on him, he caught him by his chin whiskers, wounded, and killed him. David professed his utter faith in God. The same God who rescued him from the paws of the lion and bear, he said, would rescue him from the hand of the Philistine. Dramatically, Saul told David to go and the LORD be with him.

38-39. Typical of his trust in himself and in human means, Saul dressed David in his own suit of armor. But David, a man of faith who trusted and obeyed God, realized he could not move freely in it, having never tried it. He got rid of it. **40.** David put his faith in God. With his staff in his hand, he selected five smooth stones from the brook, and put them in his bag that he had with him

(the shepherd's food bag). Holding the sling in his hand, he went out to meet the Philistine, girded with the power of God because of his faith in Him, and completely unafraid of the Philistine giant.

41-47. Conversation between David and his giant adversary was part of the etiquette of ancient warfare. Again David stressed the fact that he was acting as champion, not so much for Israel but for God Himself (cf. vv. 26, 36). What aroused David was that the Philistines were ultimately scorning the LORD, the God of Israel, not just the Israelite army. David's words to the Philistine show how kingly the young lad was and how firmly he trusted in the LORD. **I come to thee in the name of the Lord of hosts, the God of the armies of Israel, whom thou hast defied** (cf. v. 10). David spoke with a certainty of faith in God, assured of the utter defeat of the Philistine **that all the earth may know that there is a God in Israel** (cf. Josh. 4:24; 1 Kings 8:43; 18:36; 2 Kings 19:19; Psalm 46:10; Isa. 52:10). **The Lord saveth** is the keynote not only of this story, but of the entire revelation of God. *Salvation history* is the term rightly used by modern biblical scholars (cf. Psalm 44:6-7; Hos. 1:7; Zech. 4:6).

48-50. The manner in which David prevailed over the Philistine **with the sling and with a stone** was calculated to bring all the glory to God. **51.** When David ran and beheaded the stunned Philistine, the Philistines fled (cf. Heb. 11:34). **52-54.** In pursuing the routed foe, the Israelites won a great victory, and **David took the head of the Philistine, and brought it to Jerusalem.** Jerusalem was still a non-Hebrew city (2 Sam. 5:4-6). Somewhat later we learn that the sword of Goliath was at Nob (1 Sam. 21:9). Some scholars think that Nob is intended here. However, it was only the citadel on Mount Zion that was in the control of the Jebusites, and during this period Hebrews did 'live in Jerusalem (cf. Josh. 15:63; Judg. 1:8).

Saul's Question. 17:55-58. **55-58.** This section contains a notable difficulty. Various ingenious explanations have been suggested to solve it. Actually, the purpose of Saul's inquiry was *not* to find out who David was—he knew that already—but to ascertain the position and general circumstances of the young hero's father. Saul had not been previously concerned about becoming intimately acquainted with the origin and family connections of the lad, who merely served as his musician and bore his arms. But when David was on the point of becoming his son-in-law, he naturally wanted to acquire a more accurate knowledge of David's personal history.

Some persons attempt to solve the difficulty by noting that an indefinite length of time had elapsed since David's last visit to the court, and as he was then in very early manhood, he had, so to speak, grown in a comparatively short space of time out of Saul's memory. Some even suggest the mental state of Saul, when David played before him, was so disturbed that the king failed to recognize him on the present occasion, and that Abner had not seen him before.

C. DAVID'S FRIENDSHIP WITH JONATHAN. 18:1-30.

The Friendship of David and Jonathan. 18:1-4. **1-3.** By the time David had finished speaking with Saul after the great victory over Goliath, Jonathan's soul was knit with that of David. **And Jonathan loved him as his own soul**, that is, "as himself" (cf. Gen. 44:30; Deut. 13:6). The noble friendship begun here is beautifully silhouetted against the dark background of Saul's

demonic jealousy. The young prince had taken little note of David as a minstrel, but his heroism and modesty, his piety and high endowments, his valorous bearing and conduct had kindled the flame, not only of admiration, but of deep affection in the congenial mind of Jonathan. On that day Saul retained David and did not let him return to his father's home. **3.** A covenant of friendship such as that which Jonathan and David made between themselves is frequent in the Orient. Such covenants, ratified by specific ceremonies in the presence of witnesses, state that the persons covenanting will be sworn brothers for life.

4. Jonathan gave evidence of his great devotion and, as an outward token of the covenant, **stripped himself of the robe that was upon him, and gave it to David.** Clothing possessed something of the wearer's personality; so, each man gave himself symbolically to the other. To receive any part of the dress that had been worn by a sovereign or his oldest son and heir was deemed the highest honor that could be conferred on a subject (cf. Esther 6:8-9). Jonathan, the king's son, gave all the material gifts. David, the poor man's son, gave only his love and respect.

Saul's Jealousy of David. 18:5-16. David's troubles then began to tread on the heels of his triumphs. Sometime after the victory over Goliath, Saul went on a triumphant procession through the cities of Israel that were near his home in order to receive the congratulations of the country. **6-7.** When he made his public entry to any of the places, the women were most anxious to show him respect, which was normal in public triumphs. Singing and dancing to tambourines and making joyful music with cymbals, the women sang responsively,

Saul hath slain his thousands, and David his tens of thousands. 8. That, of course, made Saul very angry. Jealousy, like a wild beast, sprang up in his heart. **9.** From that day on, Saul kept an envious eye on David.

10-11. The next day **the evil spirit from God** came upon Saul (lit., "rushed" upon him), that is, he fell into the demonized state, the demon in him taking over and manifesting itself. He **prophesied** (*yiṭnăbbē'*, "raved") under the control of the indwelling demon, while David, as usual, was playing the harp (lyre). Saul threw the spear he held in his hand, intending to pin David to the wall. As God's anointed king, David was a likely target for the demon. Twice David escaped out of Saul's presence.

12-13. Saul could plainly see that the LORD was with David and that He had departed from himself. Therefore, he removed David from his presence and made him colonel of a regiment. **14-16.** In that public capacity David behaved himself wisely in all his undertakings, and it was evident to everyone that the LORD was with him. Under demonic power, and noticing David's efficiency and how he was highly thought of as a leader by Israel and Judah, Saul's attitude turned to dread.

David Loses Merab but Marries Michal. 18:17-30. **17.** The story proceeds to illustrate Saul's demonic jealousy and his base treachery toward David in regard to his daughter Merab. Saul had promised her to Goliath's slayer, whoever he might be. But in promising her to David, Saul's ulterior motive was to get rid of David by having him fall in the battles with the Philistines, making a condition, **Be thou valiant for me and fight the Lord's battles** (cf. 25:28). But Saul was using the term "the LORD's battles" hypocritically.

18. David's magnanimity appeared in his humility. **Who am I . . . that I should be son-in-law to the king? 19.** When the time came for Merab to be given to David, she was given to Adriel, the Meholathite, in marriage (2 Sam. 21:8). **20-21.** Saul proved as utterly unscrupulous in the case of his younger daughter, Michal, who loved David. Saul was pleased to give her to David for his wife, with the ulterior motive again, that he might fall at the hand of the Philistines.

Saul then said to David, **Thou shalt this day be my son-in-law in one of the two** (i.e., "with the second one"). Saul continued his dark plot to get rid of David. Could he not endanger the hated life, while seeming to wish to keep the old promise that he made when Goliath was slain? David considered himself too poor and insignificant to be the king's son-in-law. The king was quick to let David know that he wanted no dowry (cf. Exod. 22:17), except the one hundred foreskins of the Philistines to take vengeance on his enemies. Saul was under demon power (cf. 16:14, 23) as is suggested by this trick, through which he intended to have David fall by the hand of the Philistines.

David's bravery came to the fore. Before the fixed time, he got up and went out with his men and slew two hundred Philistines and presented their foreskins to Saul. The savage, half-barbarous state of the age, however, comes prominently into view when we reflect upon the ferocious cruelty of such an offer being made and accepted and carried out with more than the required number of victims. Saul fully realized that the LORD was with David, and he feared him more than ever. His jealousy became an uncontrolled demonic passion. David achieved more success than all Saul's captains in encounters with the Philistines when they went to war.

D. SAUL'S RENEWED ATTEMPT TO KILL DAVID. 19:1-24.

Jonathan Placates Saul. 19:1-7. **1.** Saul's demonized state became worse and worse as he yielded to jealousy and hatred toward David. So unprincipled had the monarch become that he even attempted to get Jonathan to kill David in the face of the tender love that existed between the two (cf. 18:1). That desire to bring about David's death became an overpoweringly evil obsession.

2. But prizing David highly, Jonathan warned him that his father was intending to kill him. He urged him to be on guard until the morning and go in hiding to some secret spot. **3.** Meanwhile, Jonathan would engage his father in conversation in the nearby field so that David might hear firsthand and know how the matter stood.

4-5. Jonathan then pleaded with his father on behalf of David. Not only had David not wronged the king, but on the contrary he had conducted himself admirably toward him. Jonathan pointed out how he had slain the Philistine and the LORD had wrought a great deliverance for Israel, which his father was glad to see. Why then was Saul determined to be guilty of innocent blood by killing David without due cause?

6. Under Jonathan's eloquent appeal, dictated by love, Saul was touched. He had a better self when he was not in the demonized state. He made an oath: **As the Lord lives, he shall not be put to death** (BV). **7.** Then Jonathan told David of Saul's change of behavior. Saul took David back in his service.

Saul's Renewed Attempt on David's Life. 19:8-10. **8-10.** David's fresh successes with the Philistines, defeating them with such heavy losses that they fled before him, stirred up Saul's jealousy and hatred more than ever before. Then, after he had lapsed into the demonized state, he tried to kill David by pinning him to the wall with his javelin while David was playing the lyre before him. David dodged away from Saul and **slipped away** in escape. Saul is an illustration of a backslidden believer in rebellion against God, allowing sins of the flesh or spirit (here notably the spirit, jealousy and hatred) to go unconfessed. Demon power took such a hold on him, until he was goaded by an insatiable desire to express his hatred in murder.

Michal Helps David Escape. 19:11-17. **11.** Saul dispatched agents to David's house to guard him, with the intent of killing David in the morning. But David's wife, Michal, told her husband that unless he saved himself that night, he would be killed the next day. **12.** Michal then lowered David from the window, and he escaped. Apparently Michal's house was situated on the city wall (cf. the escape of the spies from Jericho, Josh. 2:15; and of Saul from Damascus, Acts 9:25).

13. Then Michal took an **image** (i.e., "teraphim," KJV margin) and laid it in David's bed as a ruse to deceive the agents sent by Saul to take David. Michal took a goat's hair pillow at the head and covered it with a garment to simulate David. **14.** When Saul's agents arrived, Michal lied and said David was sick. **15.** Saul sent the messengers back to David ordering them to bring him on his bed so he could kill him. **16.** But when the agents went in, there was only the image in the bed with the goat's hair pillow at the head.

17. Saul asked his daughter why she had deceived him and let his enemy go. Michal again lied, saying he had threatened her and said, "Let me go;

why should I kill you?'' Michal realized she had to defend herself; otherwise, Saul's rage might have been vented upon her, and in his demonized condition he could have easily killed her.

Saul Goes to Naioth and Prophesies. 19:18-24. **18.** David fled to Ramoth, Samuel's home. He settled at a suburb of Ramoth named Naioth. **19-21.** Upon hearing that, Saul sent his secret agents to arrest David. But when they saw a group of the prophets, they were moved by the Spirit of God and, led by Samuel, the Spirit of God came upon Saul's officers until they prophesied. This was under God's Spirit, not the demon spirit; so it was not raving, which Saul did when he was in the demonized state, but a genuine manifestation of the Holy Spirit.

22-24. Even Saul himself went to Ramoth. The Spirit of God also took hold of him. Saul, being under the Spirit of God, also prophesied as he neared Naioth. Stripping off his outer garments, he too kept prophesying in Samuel's presence like the rest. Here in the abode of the prophets, where the prophetic school was flourishing under Samuel, Saul prophesied despite himself.

This incidence shows that the Spirit of God can work in a seriously backslidden servant of the LORD even though at times that servant may be dominated by an evil spirit. Thus God, in His sovereignty and making the wrath of man to praise Him, preserved the lives of all the prophets, frustrated all the evil purposes of Saul, and preserved the life of His anointed, David.

E. DAVID PROTECTED BY JONATHAN. 20:1-42.

David Consults with Jonathan for His Safety. 20:1-10. **1.** While Saul was being supernaturally detained at Naioth under the Spirit of prophecy, David hurried away and came to Jonathan to discuss what should be done. Evidently David was prompted to go to Gibeah by a most generous desire to inform his friend of what had recently taken place.

2. Jonathan could not be persuaded that there was any real danger after the oath his father had taken. Perhaps his father's experience at Naioth had really changed his feelings toward David. In any event, he felt assured his father would do nothing without telling him. Filial affection naturally blinded Jonathan to the defects of his father and made him reluctant to believe he was capable of such an atrocity as to break his oath.

3. David, who was more realistic, repeated his unshakened convictions of Saul's murderous purpose, but in delicately chosen terms. He knew there was but one step between him and death as far as Saul was concerned. **4.** Jonathan inquired of David what he wanted him to do. **5-10.** Evidently David's plan was a made-up story to test Saul. He asked to be excused from the king's table at the celebration of the new moon the next day. David was to hide in the field till the evening after that. If Saul asked about him, he was to be told that David had been given permission to go to his Bethlehem home to observe an annual sacrifice with his family.

If Saul grew angry, they would know he had definitely decided upon evil. Thus, they created an opportunity to ascertain Saul's reaction to David's nonappearance. The time and place were set for Jonathan to report to David. But since the circumstances might make another interview perilous, they decided to communicate by a specific signal.

Renewal of the Covenant Between David and Jonathan. 20:11-23. **11.**

Jonathan said to David, **Come, and let us go out into the field.** The private conversation, given here in full, presents a beautiful exhibition of the two noble friends. **12-15.** Jonathan was led by the circumstances to be the chief speaker. His pure unselfishness, his warm piety, his prayer to God, and his solemn oath all show the nobility of this prince. What a story of selfless love. The heir to the throne, far from being jealous or envious of David, who in a sense was a rival to the throne, loved him as himself (cf. 18:1).

Jonathan himself was a hero, as his brave triumph over the Philistines proved (chap. 14). He also possessed a sterling character worthy of being a king. He grasped the wonderful truth that God's will is best and that God had ordained David to be king, to which he bowed with admirable self-effacement. Jonathan's devotion to his rival is a superbly noble story, one of the finest in history. With calm and full expression, Jonathan set forth his conviction that his own family was, by God's will, to be disinherited and that David would be elevated to the throne. **16.** The covenant entered into with David on behalf of his descendants and its implication denounced the one who would violate his part of the stipulated conditions.

17. The repetition of the covenant on both sides was to make it indissoluble. Such magnetic attractiveness in David's character and noble feeling in Jonathan's heart make this interview unrivaled in the records of human friendship in terms of dramatic interest and moral beauty. **When thou hast stayed three days** (either with your family at Bethlehem or wherever you find it convenient), **come to the place where thou didst hide thyself when the business was in hand.** That is, when the same matter was under investigation before

(19:2). **19-23. Remain by the stone Ezel** ("the stone of the way"), a milestone that directed travelers. He was to hide near that spot.

Jonathan Placates Saul Concerning David's Absence. 20:24-29. **24-26.** At the new moon, David's place was vacant at the table, but Saul never said a word. He supposed something had happened to David so that he was not purified, was **not clean**, that is, he was virtually impure due to something unforeseen, and therefore ineligible to take part in the sacrificial meal (cf. Lev. 15:16; Deut. 23:10). **27-29.** But since such impurity lasted only until nightfall, on the following day it became clear to Saul that David's absence was not explainable. When David's place was still vacant on the day after the new moon, Saul inquired of Jonathan why David, whom he demeaningly called **the son of Jesse**, had not come to dinner either that day or the day before. Then Jonathan gave the made-up story to placate his father.

Saul's Quarrel with Jonathan. 20:30-34. **30-32.** Then Saul's anger burst out violently against Jonathan. He denounced him as **the son of a perverse, rebellious woman**, almost equivalent to "a son of Belial," meaning a good-for-nothing wretch. The term at best is one of extreme disapproval. Maybe Saul's wife, Ahinoam, sided with Jonathan and tried to persuade Saul to be fair toward him. Saul was hitting a low blow when he stooped to depreciate Jonathan's mother, that being more of an insult to his son than any personal reproach. **33-34.** Undoubtedly that insult was the main cause of **the fierce anger** the noble prince displayed as he left the table without tasting a morsel. Saul's casting a javelin at his son is sad proof of the demonic frenzy into which the unhappy monarch was transported. It was also proof to Jonathan that it was a hopeless task to try to placate his father concerning David.

Jonathan Warns David. 20:35-42. **35-38.** The reason for the ploy with the arrows becomes evident with Jonathan's being accused of disloyalty to the crown. He might easily be spied on. No suspicion would be aroused by Jonathan's going out with his bow since he was a warrior and presumably often practiced archery. Jonathan yelled after the lad, **Make speed, haste, stay not**, speaking words that were really intended for David's ears. **39-40.** The boy picked up the arrows and came to his master without sensing what it was all about. Jonathan handed him his archery equipment and told him to take them to town.

41-42. Utterly grateful for Jonathan's loyalty, displayed at great risk, David threw himself prone on the ground before him, bowing down three times. This most dramatic and sad parting of these two staunch friends constitutes a classic in the annals of human friendship. **They kissed one another, and wept one with another, until David controlled himself** ("but David more," NASB; i.e., David exceeded Jonathan in the expression of his deep grief). The two men parted from one another, consoled only by the thought of their sworn oath in the name of the LORD. The LORD would be Mediator between them and their posterity forever.

F. DAVID FLEES SAUL'S WRATH. 21:1-15.

David at Nob. 21:1-9. **1.** At that time the tabernacle and legal worship were at Nob, a priest's city (cf. 22:19) located a short distance northeast of Jerusalem, between Anathoth and Jerusalem (Isa. 10:30, 32). David's purpose in going there was partly to supply his physical

necessities, and partly for spiritual comfort and counsel after fleeing Saul's realm. Ahimelech was called Ahijah (1 Sam. 14:3), and also Abiathar (Mark 2:26). **Ahimelech was afraid at the meeting of David.** He evidently suspected something unusual by David's sudden appearance and in the fact that David's attendants had been left behind.

2. David's story—that the king had commissioned him on a strictly confidential task and therefore his attendants were not with him—was a pure fabrication David invented out of fear. Hungry, weak in body, and undefended by weapons, David was naturally severely tried. In his rejection and fugitive condition, hunted like a wild animal, he almost seemed to be another person, no longer the man of joyous faith. His conduct must be viewed with those facts in mind.

3. Hungry and completely exhausted, David asked for five loaves of bread, or as much as could be spared. **4.** The priest explained that he had no ordinary bread on hand, but he did have consecrated bread. It was old showbread, or bread of the presence, which had been removed the previous day and was reserved for the priests (Lev. 24:9). Before giving the bread lawfully to David and his men, the high priest seems to have consulted the oracle (22:10). If that was the course followed in this emergency, a dispensation to use the consecrated bread was specially granted by God Himself. Then David and the men who were with him ate of the showbread, the bread of presence (cf. Matt. 12:1-8; Mark 2:23-28; Luke 6:1-5).

Employing this incident in David's life, our Lord justified the conduct of His disciples in plucking and eating grain on the Sabbath, for it also was the Sabbath when David arrived at Nob. Our Lord was willing to set aside Jewish legal ordinances to give His own the true Bread of Life, of which the bread of the presence speaks (see Psalm 52). The account of David's lapse in faith and deception shows the Scripture's fidelity in presenting the seamy side of human character. What a contrast he was to the greater David (1 Pet. 2:1, 22).

5-6. The priest had reminded David that the bread was consecrated (cf. Exod. 25:30; Lev. 24:5-9; Matt. 12:4), and that the young men themselves had to be consecrated to eat it (cf. Exod. 19:14-15). David replied that they had been consecrated **about these three days**, no doubt hiding in the adjoining caves and consequently reduced to great extremities of hunger during that time. Therefore, they had kept themselves sexually abstinent and were ceremonially clean to partake of the consecrated bread. So the priest gave David hallowed bread.

Removal of the old and the substitution of the new bread was done on the Sabbath (Lev. 24:8), the loaves being kept warm in an oven heated the previous day. When David said, **The bread is in a manner common, yea, though it were sanctified this day in the vessel**, apparently he meant, "Though it is an unholy [ceremonially illegal] procedure [to take the showbread], it is sanctified [today] through the instrument [David or Ahimelech]." Either Ahimelech, a sacred person because he was the high priest, or David, the appointed messenger of the LORD's anointed, was the instrument here that sanctified.

7. The presence of Doeg the Edomite at the tabernacle brought ominous results. Doeg may have entered the service of Saul after the Israelite campaign against Edom (14:47). He was **detained before the Lord**, which means he was kept at the sanctuary in some way, perhaps by a vow or suspicion of leprosy or some other impurity.

8. David not only needed food in his utterly famished condition, but in his unarmed state he needed a weapon. **9.** (On the sword of Goliath, see 17:51-54.) **Behind the ephod** signifies a place where the sacred vestments were kept. The giant sword had been placed in safe custody as a memorial of the divine goodness in delivering Israel. David said, **There is none like that,** not only in its size and superior workmanship, but in its being a pledge of divine favor to him. Here it would act perhaps as a stimulus to his faith. David's lapse and lack of faith produced certain absurdities in his conduct. It seems almost ridiculously humorous that David should enter Philistine territory wearing Goliath's sword and resort to the home city of the conquered giant.

David at Gath. 21:10-15. **10.** David fled for refuge to Achish, king of Gath, one of the five cities of the Philistine Pentapolis. But the extreme peril of David's condition warns us against judging him too harshly in his present conduct. **11.** The servants of Achish said to him, **Is not this David the king of the land?** Their feeling was one of pitiful admiration mingled with amazement at seeing the doer of such splendid achievements in poverty and in exile.

They used the term "the king" in a vague sense, since they knew nothing of the sacred anointing of Samuel at Bethlehem. They simply meant, "Is not this the renowned warrior, the greatest man in Israel of whom the people sang?" They remembered the popular ditty that the women had chanted, "Saul hath slain his thousands," but they judged this one greater still who had slain his "ten thousands" (18:6-8).

12-15. Their words struck fear in David's heart (cf. Psalms 34:4; 56:3). His faith sank to a low ebb, and he **feigned himself mad in their hands** and scribbled, or **made marks on the doors of**

the gate, and let his spittle fall down upon his beard. It is little wonder that Achish thought David was insane. Such an indignity, whether done by another or by oneself, to the beard is considered an intolerable insult in Bible lands.

The ruse succeeded as David hoped it would, and he hurried out of Philistine country. In antiquity the insane were looked upon as persons in some peculiar way possessed by, and therefore under the more immediate protection of, deity. Therefore, the life of the hunted fugitive was perfectly safe from the moment the Philistines considered him mad.

G. DAVID AT ADULLAM. 22:1-23.

David in the Cave at Adullam. 22:1-2. **1.** David got away as soon as possible from Gath and escaped to **the cave of Adullam.** Adullam was a Canaanite city (Gen. 38:1-2) in the territory of Judah (Josh. 12:15), located in the western Judean hills not far from the Philistine border. It has been identified with Tell-esh-Sheikh Madhkur, located midway between Jerusalem and Lachish. Large and small caves dot the nearby hills (cf. the inscription of Psalms 57; 142).

Of course the whole clan to which David belonged soon felt the weight of Saul's anger against the prominent hero of their country. Dreading the fate that often overwhelms whole families for the faults of one of the more distinguished members, they fled from their homes and joined David and his armed force of outlaws.

2. Those **in distress,** those **in debt,** and those **discontented gathered themselves** unto David. **He became a captain** over them (Judg. 11:11; Heb. 2:10). They numbered about **four hundred men** (1 Sam. 25:13; 23:13). These needy people, doubtless under Saul's suspicion, were attracted to the rejected David. It was a foreshadowing of the greater David, to whom all can gather who are in distress

and who feel their debt, sinfulness, sorrow, and need. These people with their captain, the LORD's anointed, had been "outside the camp" (Heb. 13:13). Those who gathered around David, whose rejection and suffering they shared, were especially remembered later (2 Sam. 23:8-39; cf. 2 Tim. 2:12).

David in Moab, and Gad's Message. 22:3-5. **3-4.** From Adullam, David went to **Mizpeh of Moab,** perhaps a Moabite fortress since *Mizpeh* means "watchtower." In taking his parents there, he saved them from Saul's vindictiveness. David displayed his faith, for he left his parents in the care of the Moabite king **till I know what God will do for me.** Through David's lapses, his faith shone through. He might have failed, but his successes were certain because basically his trust was in the LORD.

5. David was not without prophetic assistance. The prophet Gad advised him not to remain in Mizpeh but to move out to the Judah country. David moved to the Hereth Woods, located a few miles east of Adullam. Ruth the Moabitess had left the land of Moab to dwell in Israel. Her great-grandson David left the land to dwell in Moab. It was good of the LORD to send the prophet to direct the distraught David and to build up his morale and his faith. The LORD does not forsake His own when they flounder and fall. David was in the LORD's hands, not Saul's.

Saul's Murder of the Priests at Nob. 22:6-19. **6-8.** The activities of David and his band having been detected by Saul's spies, Saul conducted a public council under an oak tree, or terebinth, at Gibeah on the high place, no doubt near his rustic palace. He downgraded David by referring to him as the **son of Jesse.** He addressed his council members as **Benjamites,** revealing that he showered most of his favors upon the members of his own tribe.

Saul's party-spoils policy furnishes another index into his character. He insinuated that David would be as narrow in his tribal affiliations, not giving those Benjamites a chance in his court. However, David in his magnanimity went the other way, even risking losing the loyalty of his own tribe, Judah. Saul's demonic suspicions and vengeful binges were no longer directed only at David. Even his own men felt the jealous whiplash of his tongue, and the innocent priests at Nob were to be slaughtered.

9-19. Doeg the Edomite, the chief of Saul's herdsmen (21:7), told Saul of David's visit to Nob. He openly and viciously accused Ahimelech of treason against Saul. When the demonized Saul ordered the terrible slaughter of the priests, even his servants refused to participate in the bloody work. Doeg was so wicked and lawless that he suggests the coming man of sin (2 Thess. 2:3-12). Ahimelech's eloquent self-defense at the same time furnished a noble defense of David (vv. 14-15). While David was not blameless for the tragedy, we see regret in him.

Abiathar, who alone escaped the massacre, knew whom he could trust and support. It may be concluded that Abiathar's escape and support of David were providential, for he carried the ephod with which David could repeatedly inquire of the LORD, which was so important. One such occasion occurred very shortly (cf. 23:2). Zadok and Abiathar later officiated at David's tabernacle in Jerusalem (cf. 2 Sam. 15:24).

Saul's slaughter of the priests at Nob constituted an act of barbarity unparalleled in Jewish history. The evident sequel to that terrible atrocity was Saul's slaughter of the Gibeonites (cf. 2 Sam. 21:1). They were "hewers of wood and drawers of water" for the tabernacle (Josh. 9:21-27). In that wholesale destruction of men, women, children, and cattle, the Gibeonites perished. What an illustration of an anointed servant of the LORD falling into persistent sin and becoming so demonized as to be capable of such foul crimes.

David Receives Abiathar. 22:20-23. **20-23.** Apparently Abiathar had remained behind at Nob to perform the necessary functions in the sanctuary. When he heard of the death of his father and his brother priests, he made his escape and eventually joined David. Exactly when the meeting between David and Abiathar took place is uncertain. Probably it did not occur immediately after the massacre at Gibeah or even directly after the destruction of Nob (cf. 23:6).

Throughout David's reign, Abiathar continued to be his faithful friend and the holder of an important office. But he fell into trouble during Solomon's reign. Evidently the prophecy delivered to Eli (2:31-36), which speaks of the calamity that would befall the priestly family with but one to escape, is connected with the massacre of the priests of Nob.

H. DAVID LIBERATES KEILAH. 23:1-29.

David Frees Keilah. 23:1-6. **1-2.** Keilah (Khirbet Qila) was a walled town southeast of Adullam in the west Judean hills, not far from the Philistine border (Josh. 15:44). The Philistines were robbing the threshing floors, which were commonly situated on the hills and were open to the winds (Judg. 6:11; Ruth 3:2). **David inquired of the Lord**, most probably through Gad (2 Sam. 24:11-14; cf. 1 Sam. 22:5; 1 Chron. 21:9), who was in David's camp. No doubt David wondered how far his duty should extend against a public enemy, without the royal commission. Therefore, he asked and obtained divine permission. **3-4.** A

.

visit to David by his men prompted him to renew the consultation for their satisfaction.

5. After being fully assured of his duty, he encountered the aggressors and by a signal victory delivered the people of Keilah from further attacks. The incident was certainly providential. It shows that David, though legally an outlaw, was not considered so in his own estimation or in the minds of some of the people. He held the public confidence militarily.

Despite Saul's hatred, he had not lost his care for the God-given duty to defend his people. However, the liberating of Keilah only brought David into greater peril from Saul, the LORD's anointed, whom he could not fight in open battle. He himself could not be killed or dare to kill Saul. Hence, when Saul planned to kill him in Keilah, David was forced to leave.

David Escapes from Saul at Keilah. 23:7-15. **7.** Hearing that David had moved inside Keilah, Saul thought God had handed David over to him by causing him to enter a town with gates and bars. **8.** Saul summoned all the people (evidently all those in his own district) for war, to march on Keilah and besiege David and his men.

9-12. When David discovered that Saul was planning evil against him, he ordered Abiathar the priest to bring the ephod to consult the LORD. David himself prayed, and the LORD told him Saul would come down and that the men of Keilah would surrender him to Saul. From a human standpoint, that would be prudent action on the part of the men of Keilah because a siege by the Hebrews, especially under those conditions, would likely be far worse than one by the Philistines, from whom they had been delivered by David. **13.** Consequently, David and his men, now

grown to a company of about six hundred, left Keilah and went wherever they could go. When Saul heard that David had escaped, he abandoned that particular trip.

14-15. David stayed in desert strongholds and remained in the mountainous parts of the Ziph Desert. That desert region is connected with Tell Zif, southeast of Hebron. **The forest,** or Horesh, was a place in the nearby wilderness of Judah.

Jonathan Visits David. 23:16-18. **16-18.** Jonathan paid David a visit in the forest, or Horesh, and **strengthened his hand in God.** This act represents courage, faith, and moral grandeur that are difficult to praise adequately. No one ever cleared himself from complicity with guilt more completely than Jonathan. Never was a friend thrown into greater temptation to betray another friend than he. Never did a faithful son have a more unfaithful father. Yet not one undutiful word escaped the lips of this valiant man. How wonderful were his words when he exhorted David to have no fear. How sublime was his expressed assurance that the hands of Saul, his father, would not reach David. David would indeed be Israel's king, and he, Jonathan, would be next to him.

The two then strengthened the covenant they had already made in the LORD's presence. When we think of what it must have cost Jonathan to speak in this fashion, and again of the sad fate that was so soon to overtake him, there is a deep pathos about this brief interview that is almost unequaled in Holy Scripture. What a contrast Jonathan offers to the ambitious hopes of James and John, the sons of Zebedee (Mark 10:35-40).

The Ziphites Attempt to Betray David. 23:19-29. **19-20.** To curry favor with the king, the Ziphites went to Saul at Gibeah and reported David's hiding place. **21.** Hypocritically, Saul said, "The LORD bless you for having sympathy with me" (BV). **22-25.** The Ziphites were engaged to work with Saul to ferret out David. Meanwhile, David and his men had gone to the **wilderness of Maon** (cf. 25:2).

Khirbet Ma'in, eight and a half miles south of Hebron, marks the ancient site of Maon. Surrounded by pastureland, it is probably the Wilderness of Maon, where David sought refuge from Saul. The Maonites were descendants of the Calebite branch of the tribe of Judah. There David was providentially saved from the Philistine raid. **26-27.** That diverted Saul from encircling David, capturing him, and no doubt killing him. **28.** Saul then gave up pursuing David and marched against the Philistines. Therefore, the place was named **Sela-hammah-lekoth**, meaning "the Rock of Escape" (NASB).

I. DAVID SPARES SAUL'S LIFE. 24:1-22.

David Cuts off Saul's Skirt at Engedi. 24:1-6. **1.** En-gedi, meaning "spring of the goat," is located by a fresh-water spring on the west of the Dead Sea; it bears the same name in modern times. The fertility of the area in the midst of the barren country made it an ideal place for an outlaw to find food (Song of Sol. 1:14) and hiding places, since many caves were available. Nothing but demonic hatred and blindness could have driven the king to pursue his outlawed son-in-law among the craggy, perpendicular precipices and inaccessible hiding places of that region. **2.** The large, select force Saul took with him seemed to promise success in finding David. But the overruling providence of God frustrated Saul's plan. His army went **to seek David and his men in front of the Wildgoats' Rocks** (RSV).

3. Saul, in pursuit of David, went into one of the caves **to cover his feet**, that is, to relieve himself (Judg. 3:24). David and his men were in the same cave. **4.** Then David arose and stealthily cut off the skirt of Saul's robe. **5-6.** Even for that act David's heart smote him (cf. 2 Sam. 24:10). David had several opportunities to slay Saul, but he reverenced God's anointed. He was willing to wait for the fulfillment of God's will and God's way, and he did not practice the kind of morality that argues that "the end justifies the means." God's will performed in God's way leads to God's blessing.

David Protests His Innocence. 24:7-15. **7-8.** When Saul arose and moved out of the cave, David followed and called to him. **9-11.** David pleaded with Saul, asking why he listened to people who told him that David was scheming evil against him. He reminded Saul that it has always been difficult for a king to get the truth because no one is supposed to point out his mistakes, presumably because he makes none. In sparing his father-in-law's life, David protested to Saul that he had done nothing against him, but all the while the king intended to take David's life.

12. David allowed the LORD to judge between him and Saul, and he let the LORD grant justice regarding him. But he declared, "My hand shall not be against you." **13.** The ancient proverb David quoted, **Wickedness proceedeth from the wicked** (cf. Matt. 7:16-20) reminds one of an ancient Greek proverb, "From a bad raven comes a bad egg."

14. David's referring to himself as **a dead dog** and **a flea** shows how he humbled himself in his protestations of loyalty. What a comparison between the king of Israel and his grandeur and power and a poor dead dog, an object held in special loathing by the Hebrews (cf. 2 Sam. 9:8; 16:9), and a single flea, that is, "one flea" not easily caught; and, if caught, it is poor game for a royal hunter (cf. 26:20). **15.** David vowed that he was content to wait God's leisure and remain in the sad condition that he was in till it would please the LORD to bring him out of it. In no case would he lay hands on the LORD's anointed.

Saul's Seeming Repentance. 24:16-22. **16-18.** Saul's weeping and his protestation to David, **Thou art more righteous than I** (cf. 26:21) revealed that he was acting in his better self, the un-demonized state. The wicked spirit that had been impelling him was not over-powering him. **19.** Saul even said, **The Lord reward thee with good for what thou hast done unto me this day. 20.** He even went so far as to protest that he knew perfectly well that David would surely be king and that the kingdom of Israel would be established in his hand. He beseeched David to make an oath that when he became king he would not cut off Saul's posterity after him or destroy his name out of his father's house. **22.** Magnanimously, David swore to Saul, and the two men parted. We are given an insight into David's lofty and noble character. Truthfully, he was a man after God's own heart. Although he fell into certain sins and at times his faith ebbed very low, he had a great soul and was thoroughly on God's side and, therefore, God was wholly for him. What a contrast his character and that of Jonathan were to Saul's.

J. DAVID AND NABAL. 25:1-44.

The Death of Samuel. 25:1. **1. Samuel died.** Since Moses, none so great as Samuel had arisen. He died full of years and honor. Through his life and testimony the Law of Moses, in great measure, had been restored in the affections of the LORD's people. He reinstated the forgotten laws of Moses, by the keeping of which Israel had once become great

and powerful; and by the creation of an earthly monarchy he welded into one the separate interests of the twelve tribes so that from Dan to Beersheba there was but one chief and one standard.

Perhaps Samuel's greatest work was the foundation of the schools of the prophets in which men were trained to be the teachers and guides of the people of God. **All the Israelites,** that is, representatively, **were gathered together, and lamented him.** They **buried him in his house at Ramah,** meaning the court or garden attached to the prophet's home in his native town.

Evidently just after Samuel's death, David moved to the **wilderness of Paran** (cf. Gen. 21:21; Num. 10:12). Paran is the wilderness to the south of the Arabian Peninsula west of Sinai, now comprising the vast pastureland known as Et-Tih. The Greek *Vaticanus* reads "Maon" instead of "Paran." This may possibly be the correct reading since Nabal lived in Maon (v. 2).

Nabal's Rebuff of David. 25:2-13. **2.** Living in Maon (cf. 1 Sam. 23:24) was a man (Nabal) whose possessions were in **Carmel** (cf. Josh. 15:55), identified with present-day Khirbet el-Karmel, about seven and one-half miles southeast of Hebron in a rolling pastural region (cf. Dennis Baly, *Geography of the Bible*, p. 164). It is not to be confused with the famous Mount Carmel in the north. The wealthy rancher, the subject of the story, was a descendant of Caleb. The Calebites at the time of the conquest obtained large possessions in the valley of Hebron and the south of Judah.

The exact number of Nabal's flocks is given, evidently to emphasize the churlishness of his reply when David asked for some return for the protection his armed bands had given him. The occasion of David's mission to Nabal was the annual sheep shearing of the rich sheep master, always an occasion of great festivity.

3. The name **Nabal** means "fool," denoting not merely stupidity but moral perversity, befitting the role in which he appears in this account. His wife's name was Abigail, meaning "whose father is joy," no doubt giving a clue to her sunny, joyous, and gracious personality. Just the opposite of her husband, she was generous, kind, and lovely.

4-9. David had every right to expect the little help he asked. **10.** But Nabal was an unbeliever, displaying the folly of unbelief. He did not believe in David as the LORD's anointed king, and his reply to David's servants revealed that fact. **Who is David? And who is the son of Jesse? There are many servants nowadays who break away, every man from his master. 11.** He asked contemptuously whether he should give his food, wine, and meat to persons whom he considered utter strangers. **12-13.** Insulted, David's men returned and related all that had occurred. Immediately David set out with four hundred of his men to punish Nabal for his insult.

Abigail's Noble Conduct. 25:14-31.
14-17. Being told of her husband's shameful conduct, Abigail at once proceeded to try to undo the insult and damage caused by Nabal's folly. The circumspect behavior of David's men all the more highlighted the outrageous behavior of Nabal, **a worthless fellow** (a true "son of Belial," KJV; see 1:16; 2:12; 10:27). Outlaw bands, such as David headed at this period of his life, lived in caves and had to depend upon plunder if their requests were denied, or their rights to earn what they needed were spurned.
18-20. Abigail wisely realized that fact and hurriedly got together an ample supply of food and proceeded to take it to David as a conciliatory gesture.

21-22. Meanwhile, David, vowing the death of every male, was advancing to punish Nabal for scorning his protection and so rudely rebuffing his overtures of kindness.

23-26. Abigail's humble prostration before David saved the day and won David a wife. Abigail played upon the meaning of Nabal's name to accent his folly. "Let my master pay no attention, I beg of you, to this worthless man Nabal ['foolish, wicked'], for as his name, so is the man. He is named Nabal; he is a fool" (BV).

Abigail also declared that when the Lord had restrained David from bloodshed and from taking the law into his own hands, as he was compelled to do in his present state, "May your enemies and all who plan against my master fare like Nabel" (BV). Coming, as she did, without her husband, and speaking against him ran counter to the accepted customs and morality. But under the circumstances, her uncommon wisdom and sound judgment showed her that this was the only prudent course to take.

27-31. Abigail's speech displayed remarkable insight into God's promises to David (cf. 2 Sam. 7:8-15) and faith in God that He would fulfill them. Note especially her reference to the Lord setting up for David a sure house (i.e., a lasting dynasty) that would reach out and comprehend the kingship of Christ (Psalm 2:1-12; Rev. 19:11-16). Her statement, **but the soul of my lord shall be bound in the bundle of life with the Lord thy God,** is truly remarkable (cf. Psalm 66:9; Mal. 3:17; Col. 3:3). She meant that God would keep David safe. His life, as it were, was bound up with the very life of God in a precious bundle that no one (not even insane Saul) could touch.

David's Reply to Abigail. 25:32-35.

32-34. David congratulated and thanked Abigail for her good judgment in restraining him from the guilt of bloodshed and taking the law into his own hands. **35.** He accepted her gift and assured her of his protection.

Nabal's Death. 25:36-38. **36-37.** After Nabal's drunken spree, Abigail told him what had happened. **His heart died within him. 38.** After ten days the LORD **smote** (struck) **Nabal** (cf. 26:10; 2 Kings 15:5) so that he died.

Abigail Becomes David's Wife. 25:39-44. The whole episode of this chapter may be used to illustrate deeper spiritual truth. Abigail, beautiful and understanding, illustrates the believer. Nabal, to whom she was bound, illustrates the flesh, the old nature. Nabal's death and Abigail's marriage to David may be used to illustrate the believer's death to sin and his union with Christ (Rom. 7:4).

K. DAVID AGAIN SPARES SAUL'S LIFE. 26:1-25.

The Treachery of the Ziphites. 26:1-5. **1-2.** Ziph was a town in the hill country of Judah (Josh. 15:55), identified with Tell Zif, southeast of Hebron. **Jeshimon** (*yeshimōn*, "a waste") was the Wilderness of Judah. This was the second time the Ziphites betrayed David (cf. 23:19), showing their extreme malice toward him and their officiousness to curry favor with Saul. Saul's earlier good intentions (24:17-20) were blown to the wind by the report of the Ziphite traitors. Speedily snatching the information, he resumed his insane search for David with three thousand men.

3-4. David, told of Saul's movements, acted defensively. He **abode in the wilderness**, seeking his own safety, not Saul's ruin. He had spies inform him of Saul's arrival, scarcely believing that Saul could be so base after his recent

protestations of David's innocence (24:17). **5.** With his own eyes he observed Saul and his encamped forces. Saul, who was lodging with his general, Abner, the son of Ner, was lying inside the wagon barricade, with the troops encamped around him. **In the trench**, or "in the midst of his carriages" (KJV margin), means that the king lay down within the barricade or rampart formed by the baggage wagons.

David Spares Saul's Life Once Again. 26:6-12. **6.** Deciding to go down to Saul's camp, David turned and asked who would go with him. Abishai, his nephew, volunteered for the hazardous undertaking. He was the son of Zeruiah, David's sister. Zeruiah was not Jesse's daughter, but she and David had the same mother, who had been the widow of Nahash before marrying Jesse (cf. 2 Sam. 17:25; 1 Chron. 2:16). Zeruiah was also the mother of Joab, another nephew of David.

7. David and Abishai invaded the camp of Saul by night. Inside the barricade Saul lay asleep, his spear stuck in the ground by his head, and Abner and the soldiers lying around him. **8.** In reckless gallantry and intense devotion to David, Abishai offered to kill Saul with one fell stroke of his spear. **9.** But David warned against such action, knowing that no one with impunity could assault the LORD's anointed.

10. David expressed an important fact in Israelite theology: God has reserved some things to do Himself, while He has committed other things to men. David had learned to wait on the LORD and trust in Him. He was a striking contrast to Saul in religious matters. Both in self-will and fleshly activity, Saul committed trespasses and mistakes whenever he intruded into religious things. But David, with a heart of faith, honored God in those things.

11-12. Instead of killing Saul when he was in his power, David took his spear and water jug and got away as soon as possible. Verse 12 literally translated from the Hebrew reads: "And none saw and none knew and none awaked." Apparently the **spear** was Saul's special sign of royalty. Its removal from near Saul's head as he slept was an omen of the transfer of the royalty to David.

The **cruse of water** is also significant. According to a common custom in antiquity, a high official always was in charge of a costly urn for the king's necessary ablutions, and it was his special duty to take it with him and set it before the king during campaigns or on other journeys. Its disappearance would be almost as great a disgrace to the king as the loss of his scepter (cf. H. E. Ewald, "David," *History of Israel*, 2:3). All that happened, of course, was by God's direction, for a **deep sleep from the Lord was fallen upon them** (cf. Gen. 2:21; 15:12).

David's Words to Abner. 26:13-16.
13. After taking the royal spear and cruse of water, David and Abishai crossed the deep ravine and ascended the opposite hill or mountain. Therefore, a deep gorge was between them and Saul's encampment. **14.** From that vantage point, David yelled to the people and Abner. Abner answered, **Who art thou who criest to the king? 15.** David taunted Abner, the great, valiant man, for being so careless about protecting the king's life. **16.** Actually, he rebuked him: **This thing is not good that thou hast done.** He even insinuated that Abner was worthy of death for his unwatchfulness.

David's Words to Saul. 26:17-20.
17-18. In contrast to his stern rebuke of Abner, David's whole address to Saul was intensely reverent and even affectionate. As dawn broke, the conspicuous trophies of his late night raid were in his hand, providing proof upon proof that he was not seeking Saul's life. **19.** David's words are difficult to interpret, but apparently they mean, "If the LORD has stirred you up against me for any fault of mine, let me know my offense and I am ready to make an offering for it to the LORD that I may be forgiven."

But most scholars understand the words in their plain, literal sense, namely, "If the LORD has stirred you up to do this evil thing, let Him accept ['smell'] an offering." The Hebrew word for "offering" is *minḥâ*, referring to the meal offering, which signifies yieldedness and devotion to the LORD's will. In other words, "If you feel that God incites you to take this course against me, the innocent one, pray to God that He may take the temptation—if it be a temptation—from you."

But David went on to say that if the cruel, unjust thoughts were the result of the envy and hatred of the men who were his enemies, might the LORD punish them as they deserved. If the king's accusations were unfounded and merely the calumnies of men whispered in his ears, they had driven David into exile. They had violently bidden him to go and serve strange gods. He meant that far away from the only country where the LORD was loved and honored, he and his followers would be tempted to serve pagan deities and share in the foul heathen worship of the nations surrounding Israel. **20.** Again David esteemed himself as no more than **a flea** (cf. 24:14). A partridge hunted alone in the mountains might be found in coveys in the fields. How foolish for Saul to waste his time on a single partridge (David), combing hill and rocky crag.

Saul's Confession and David's Reply. 26:21-25. **21.** Saul's declaration, **I have sinned** (cf. 15:24; 24:17; 2 Sam.

12:13), **I have played the fool** (cf. 2 Sam. 24:10), on the surface bespeaks real repentance. But such protestations only represented Saul's better self when he was not under strong demonic influence. His persistence in jealousy and hatred had exposed him to extreme demon power. When that subsided, as the result of some extraordinary exhibition of goodness, Saul spoke in his old self. But he was undependable because he had exposed himself to the tyranny of demonic powers that took over and crushed his best wishes and desires (cf. 1 Sam. 16:14, 23). **25.** As a result of this dramatic experience, Saul was speaking from his better self when he declared to David, **Thou shalt both do great things, and also shalt still prevail** (cf. 24:20).

L. David Loses Heart. 27:1-12.

David Joins Achish. 27:1-4. **1. And David said in his heart,** that is, to himself, **I shall now perish one day by the hand of Saul** (cf. 1 Chron. 29:28). The man of faith again lapsed into unbelief and became despondent. His plaint is understandable on the human plane in light of Saul's grueling hounding. The king's demonized state had grown sharper and more terrible. The circle of Benjamites he had gathered around him had good reason to fear that if Saul fell, their future would be bleak. No doubt they goaded the insane king on and incited him more and more against David.

David calculated correctly that he would doubtless be more secure among the warlike Philistines than among his own people. However, in his determination to go to Philistia, nothing is recorded of prayer or of consultation with prophet or priest. No wonder a dull despair engulfed him and deprived him of faith and hope. How quickly the heart forgets the LORD's benefits and deliverances when the believer begins to look on circumstances and on things in the natural.

2-3. Once more David took his case out of the LORD's hands and fled to Achish, king of Gath (cf. 21:10-15). The former visit, when he feigned insanity and the Philistine king had driven him away, also had been in unbelief. Now he was welcomed by Achish, for he brought a small army of six hundred men with him. **4.** When it was reported to Saul that David had fled to Gath, he did not hunt for him anymore. Thus, David's human reasoning brought the results he had anticipated—respite in a foreign land from Saul's relentless rage.

Achish Gives David Ziklag. 27:5-7. **5.** David requested space to reside in one of Achish's small towns. **Why should thy servant dwell in the royal city with thee? 6.** Achish magnanimously gave him Ziklag, a city situated only twelve miles north of Beersheba, to live in. Once a city of Simeon (cf. Josh. 19:5), it had been taken by the Philistines, but afterward it became crown property in Judah. **7.** David resided with the Philistines a full year and four months (cf. 29:3).

David's Raids. 27:8-12. **8-11.** Unbelief produced other evil fruits to discourage the LORD's anointed, who had gone over to the enemies of the LORD's people, lived with them, and settled down in the very city from which Goliath, the giant he had slain by faith, had come. To court Achish's trust, David lied concerning the object of his military raids. Surely he was leaning upon the arm of flesh and was out of fellowship with the LORD.

At the same time, David made raids upon the enemies of God and His people. He fought against the nomadic desert tribes who frequently raided the neighboring settled populations, namely, the Geshurites, Gerzites, and

Amalekites. The Geshurites were probably a colony from Geshur, between the Hermon and Bashan mountains. David was living a lie before Achish by pretending he had attacked Israelites or their friends, such as Judah, the Jerahmeelites, or the Kenites (cf. 30:26-31), who lived in the Negev, a dry portion of southern Palestine.

David's activity was not a real work for God, but the result of a self-centered heart; his aim was selfishness and self-protection, demonstrating that a person whose heart is out of touch with God may outwardly be engaged in fighting evil for selfish reasons. Achish shared in the spoils; yet David deceived the king of the Philistines as a result of the unbelief that dragged him lower and lower. The incident warns that the greatest men of God, unless they have their eyes fixed upon the LORD, may fall into serious unbelief and live a life utterly unworthy of the testimony of a believer.

12. Achish, however, trusted David's reasoning and was deceived. He thought that David had doubtless brought himself into such bad repute with his people that he would remain permanently in his service. Often unsaved people demonstrate better conduct than God's people who are out of fellowship with Him and living a life of hypocrisy and deceit.

M. SAUL AND THE MEDIUM AT ENDOR. 28:1-25.

The Philistines Muster for War Against Israel. 28:1-2. **1-2.** The Philistines planned an all-out attack to overrun Israel. Their power is attested by the invasion of the Plain of Esdraelon. Marching eastward, they took up strong positions on the slopes of one of the groups of mountains that enclose the broad plain of Jezreel toward the east near the town of Shunem. Saul quickly assembled the fighting men of Israel and took up his position opposite the Philistines, with only a few miles separating the two armies, on the slopes of another group of mountains known as Mount Gilboa, lying to the south of the Philistine position.

David's complicity with Philistinism (chap. 27), resulting in his compromise and deception, brought him into a quandary. When it came to warfare against his own people, Israel, he could only comply. There is dramatic irony in Achish of Gath making David and his men his bodyguard. Not many years later, Gittites (men of Gath) were to provide David's bodyguard. Affiliation with Philistinism will eventually maneuver a believer into fighting against the LORD and the LORD's people. What a spectacle! The LORD's anointed was made a **keeper of the head** of a Philistine king, an enemy of the LORD's people.

God Does Not Answer Saul. 28:3-6. **1-3.** Samuel had died (cf. 25:1) so he was not available for consultation by Saul, and Saul himself had put away those who were mediums and wizards out of the land (cf. Exod. 22:18; Lev. 19:31; Deut. 18:10). In outlawing occultism, Saul was simply following the Mosaic injunctions. **4-5.** The mighty hosts of the Philistines mustered in the Plain of Jezreel in Shunem (Josh. 19:18; 2 Kings 4:8), making it imperative that Saul get divine guidance. His fear and trembling aggravated the situation. **6.** Saul inquired of the LORD but received no answer, either by dreams (cf. 1 Sam. 14:37) or by the Urim, the sacred lots, or by the prophets. He had disregarded the LORD, and now the LORD disregarded his cry.

Saul Resorts to the Spiritistic Medium at Endor. 28:7-14. **7.** In resorting to occultism, Saul said in effect, "If God will not answer me, then the devil will." Accordingly, he who himself was demonized consulted demonic powers to ascertain what to do about the battle. That the woman of Endor was identical with the modern medium appears in Saul's command to his servants to seek him out **a woman who is a medium** (KJV, "that hath a familiar spirit," *'ēshĕṯ bă'ălăṯ-'ôḇ*, lit., "a woman controlling, or mistress of, a divining demon"), and also in his initial request of the medium herself.

8. Divine unto me as a medium ("by the familiar spirit, *bā'ôḇ*, by means of the divining demon") **and bring me him up, whom I shall name unto thee. 11.** Saul asked that Samuel be brought up, that is, from the realm of the spirits, because he knew there was none like the venerable prophet and judge who knew God's mind and future events so well. The woman doubtlessly began her customary preparations for her control to take over, entering into a trancelike state to be used by her control or divining demon, who would then proceed to impersonate the individual called for.

12. The startling thing, however, was that the usual occult procedure was abruptly cut short by the sudden and totally unexpected appearance of the spirit of Samuel. Transfixed with terror, the woman screamed out with shock as she perceived that God had stepped in. By God's power and special permission, Samuel's actual spirit was presented to pronounce final doom upon Saul. Ecclesiasticus 46:20 agrees on Samuel's actual appearance: "After death he [Samuel] prophesied and showed the king his latter end."

The medium's terrified conduct at the appearance of a real spirit of a deceased person constitutes a complete scriptural disclosure of the fraudulency of all spiritistic mediumship. The woman, to be sure, had the power to communicate with wicked spirits. Such deceiving demons represent themselves to their mediums, and through them to their clients, as the spirits of the departed dead. But actually their messages do not emanate from the deceased at all, but from themselves as lying spirits who cleverly impersonate the dead.

The woman's divining demon had nothing whatever to do with Samuel's sudden appearance. She and her spirit accomplice were completely sidetracked. God stepped in and brought up Samuel, who pronounced doom upon Saul. When the medium was exposed and her craft was laid bare as a fraud by her unseemly fright at the appearance of Samuel, the whole proceeding quickly passed over to a conversation between Samuel and Saul.

13. At first, apparently, only the woman could see Samuel's spirit, whom she described as **a god** (Elohim) **coming up out of the earth** (ASV). The term *god*, as used here, refers (in accordance with a well-established Hebrew usage) to a "judge" or a "prophet," as those "unto whom the word of God came" (John 10:35; Psalm 82:6). God consequently dignified such men with the authority to bear His own name (Exod. 21:6; 22:8). The designation was preeminently apropos of Samuel, God's representative as judge and prophet. **14.** The woman's further description of Samuel was that of **an old man . . . coming up . . . wrapped with a robe** (NASB; cf. 1 Sam. 15:27). Saul seemed to have glimpsed the spirit of Samuel also, for **he bowed with his face to the ground, and did obeisance** (ASV).

Samuel Pronounces Doom upon Saul. 28:15-19. **15-19.** The conversation then proceeded directly between Saul and Samuel, without any further employment of the woman. Samuel's pointed and stinging rebuke to Saul is added evidence that his spirit had actually appeared and that it was not an impersonating demon. In severest terms Samuel announced that the LORD had wrested the kingdom from Saul and that Saul and his sons would die the next day.

When Samuel said, **Tomorrow shalt thou and thy sons be with me**, it meant that at the time of their death Saul and his sons would go to be where Samuel was, that is, to the paradise section of Hades, where all the spirits of the righteous dead went in Old Testament times (Luke 16:19-31). Saul is a type of the child of God who is disobedient and under divine discipline. Saul's last act of lawlessness—resorting to necromancy—resulted in his untimely end on the battlefield. This is typical of the believer's "sin unto death" (1 John 5:16), and is equivalent to being delivered "unto Satan for the destruction of the flesh, that the spirit may be saved in the day of the Lord Jesus" (1 Cor. 5:5).

The Medium Feeds Saul. 28:20-25. **20.** Saul's terrible fear at the news from Samuel, plus the fact that he had eaten no food all that day and night, made him a sad spectacle. **21-24.** The woman very hospitably had prepared food for the distraught monarch. **25.** Saul and his servants ate before going away that night to face imminent death.

N. DAVID KEPT FROM FIGHTING AGAINST ISRAEL. 29:1-11.

The Philistines Dispute David's Fighting with Them. 29:1-5. **1.** The Philistines amassed all their forces at Aphek, where they had captured the ark in the days of Eli (4:1b). The Israelites encamped by a fountain in Jezreel. That fountain is still active. The Jezreel Valley, which has been a natural battlefield for many nations, was later known as the Plain of Esdraelon by the Greeks. There Gideon had routed the Amale-

kites and the Midianites. Jezreel lay at the foot of the Gilboa range.

2. When the **lords of the Philistines** (a special term for the rulers of the Philistine Pentapolis, of whom Achish was one) were marching to the Battle of Gilboa by companies and regiments, Achish and the Philistine commanders and David and his men formed the rear. **3.** The Philistine commanders were quite upset about **these Hebrews**, the term being used here in contempt by non-Israelites (cf. Gen. 39:14; 43:32; 1 Sam. 4:6). Achish staunchly defended David as his loyal servant (1 Sam. 27:6).

4. The Philistine lords were angry with Achish. They insisted that **this fellow**, a derogatory term, be dismissed and ordered to return to the place Achish had assigned him. They did not want David to be allowed to join in the battle, for fear that in the fighting he would turn against them. They claimed that David could more readily gain favor with his master (King Saul) by presenting to him the heads of Philistine soldiers (1 Chron. 12:19-20). **5.** The Philistine lords still remembered the song of bygone days when David triumphed against them. So they feared treachery (cf. 18:7; 21:11).

Achish Dismisses David. 29:6-11. **6-11.** Achish displayed his admiration for David, showing him respect by swearing by David's God and pronouncing him blameless in his sight **as an angel of God.** Under the circumstances, however, he was almost compelled to yield to the will of his colleagues, the Philistine lords.

David's reply, asserting his willingness to stay with the Philistines and fight against the LORD's people, reveals how deeply unbelief can plunge a believer into inconsistency and spiritual treason. Only God's grace restrained David from plunging deeper into the shame that unbelief always brings. This chapter resumes the sad story of David's lapse of faith, begun in chapter 27.

God's servant not only found himself among the enemies of the LORD's people, but he was nearly put in a deplorable situation of having to fight against them. Unbelief makes a sad spectacle of any believer. So much so in this case that David, as a result, became a persona non grata as far as the Philistine lords were concerned. It is incredible that David should call the Philistine Achish **my lord, the king** when his own people Israel, whose anointed king he was, were **the enemies** to whom he referred.

What perils face a child of God who compromises with Philistinism as David did (see note on Philistinism, Judg. 13:2-14). David not only became a vassal of the Philistines, but he also was willing and loyal to them, even as many believers today, who have lost vital contact with God, diligently serve a religion of Philistinism and are loyal to ecclesiasticism rather than to the Lord Jesus Christ.

O. DAVID'S CHASTENING AND RESTORATION. 30:1-31.

The Amalekite Raid on Ziklag. 30:1-6. **1-3.** Ziklag was about eighty miles south of Aphek, a grueling two-day march through rough terrain. David's arrival proved opportune, but it also was a manifestation of the chastening hand of the LORD upon him for his unbelief and compromise with Philistinism. A sad sight met his eyes. The Amalekites had burned the town with fire and had taken captive the women and all the others who were in it, intending to sell them as slaves. There was one ray of light: the marauding Bedouin had killed no one. **4. Then David and the people who were with him lifted up their voice and wept.** They wept until they could weep no more for the tragedy that had befallen them. **5.** David's two wives were also taken captive.

6. David was **greatly distressed.** The people spoke of **stoning him.** They were persuaded that his behavior had brought upon them the disaster and that he, like Achan of old, deserved severe punishment (cf. Josh. 7). It was in that deep valley of humiliation that David turned to the LORD. Chastening from the LORD is for that purpose (cf. Heb. 12:4-10). The essential difference between David and Saul is found in the fact that David **encouraged himself in the Lord his God** (Psalms 18:6; 25:1-2; 34:1-8; 40:1-2; 42:5-11; 56:1-4; Isa. 25:4), while Saul characteristically looked to himself and trusted in the flesh.

David Pursues the Raiders. 30:7-10. **7-8.** David manifested his restoration to fellowship with the LORD by consulting the LORD through the ephod and Abiathar the priest (cf. 23:6). The LORD answered His erring child graciously, in contrast to His silence toward Saul (cf. 28:6-7). The answer was plain that David was to pursue the marauders, that he would overtake them, and that he would recover everything. **9-10.** At the brook Besor, south of Ziklag, David's troops were so exhausted that they could not go on. Two hundred had to remain behind because they were too weary to cross the brook.

An Egyptian Leads David to the Amalekites. 30:11-15. **11-15.** An Egyptian, the servant of an Amalekite, illustrates the needy sinner. Amalek illustrates the old nature and the flesh in the unsaved (see Exod. 17:8-16), the one not born again who is of the world and the slave of Amalek, serving the flesh under the old nature and Satan's dominion. The physical condition of this young Egyptian also illustrates the spiritual condition of the unsaved.

David, who had returned to fellowship with God, prefigures Christ in showing the Egyptian mercy. The young man's confession and the bread and water given to him bespeak how the greater than David supplies needs for those who come to Him. Accepting David's grace, the slave of the Amalekite became a servant to God's anointed king.

David Smites the Amalekites. 30:16-20. **16-17.** Restored to fellowship and trusting in the LORD, David again truly waged the battles of the LORD. **18-19.** He recovered all that the Amalekites had taken and rescued his two wives. **20.** He also captured all the flocks and herds, which were reserved as **David's spoil** (cf. vv. 26-31).

David Divides the Spoil. 30:21-25. **21-22.** David then appeared as a conqueror by the power of the LORD. He was reinstated in favor with the LORD's people. **23-24.** In distributing the spoil with the exhausted men who were unable to proceed to the battle, David showed how fair-minded he was. Those who stayed with the baggage were to share alike with those who fought in the battle. **25.** From that day forward the king made this equitable distribution of spoils a perpetual statute and an ordinance for Israel. David's action in fairness and the sweetness of grace in distributing the spoil among the different cities of Judah is a reminder of the greater David's victory, in which His people will share with Him through infinite grace. David repaid hospitality and no doubt squelched any potential Nabals (cf. chap. 25), distributing booty among all the places where he and his men had roamed in rejection and exile in order to repay those who had befriended him in his rejection.

P. SAUL'S DEATH. 31:1-13.

Saul and His Sons Fall in Battle. 31:1-7. **1-3.** The events of this chapter follow closely upon the episode of Saul's séance with the medium (28:3-25). The details of the battle are given. The Israelites fortified themselves near the summit of the hill, but the Philistines successfully overran their position and totally defeated them. Three of Saul's sons were killed, and Saul was badly wounded. Worsted in battle, the Israelite troops fled to the safety of the hills. However, many of them, including Saul and Jonathan, were overtaken by the pursuing Philistines. This is the tragic ending of one of the most tragic stories of the Bible. The Philistine archers made Saul their target and badly wounded him.

4-7. Saul commanded his armor-bearer to draw his sword and run it through him so that **these uncircumcised**, a derogatory term, might not run him through and have their sport with him. Repelled by the horror of such a deed, the armor-bearer refused. Saul then took his own sword and threw himself upon it, thus committing suicide. Biblical suicides are rare (cf. 2 Sam. 17:23; 1 Kings 16:18; Matt. 27:5). Immediately Saul's armor-bearer also committed suicide.

Saul Decapitated. 31:8-13. **8-9.** Saul had escaped capture in life, but not in death. The Philistines cut off his head and carried his armor into their temple. They shamefully tied up his body to the walls of Bethshan, the fortress guarding the entrance to the Valley of Jezreel from the east. The LORD's enemy gleefully sent messengers throughout the land of the Philistines to carry the good news to their idols and to the people.

10. They put the armor in the temple of Ashtaroth, apparently located in Bethshan, which the Philistines seem to have occupied. Or was it a temple back in Philistia? **11-13.** The men of Jabesh-gilead then had their opportunity to show their gratitude for what Saul had done for them (chap. 11). The bones of Saul and his sons were buried under the tamarisk tree in Jabesh. Some critics consider the reference to being **burned** (v. 12) as a transcriptional error (cf. 2 Chron. 16:14).

SECOND SAMUEL

INTRODUCTION
See Introduction to First Samuel

OUTLINE

COMMENTARY

I. DAVID'S REIGN OVER JUDAH. 1:1—4:12.

A. DAVID LAMENTS THE DEATH OF SAUL AND JONATHAN. 1:1-27.

The News Brought by an Amalekite. 1:1-10. **1-10.** This account is not contradictory to that recorded in 1 Samuel 31:1-6, as many critics claim, but is merely supplementary. First, Saul was severely wounded by Philistine archers and begged his armor-bearer to kill him. Refused, Saul fell upon his own sword, followed by his armor-bearer, who in turn fell upon his sword and died. Saul's attempt at suicide was not completely successful. He was transfixed in death anguish and held upright by his own sword when in the turmoil of battle an Amalekite came by. Apparently, at Saul's plea, the Amalekite killed him and took his crown and bracelet and hurried from the battle to go to David.

Of course, it is possible that the Amalekite lied to curry favor with David, but that was not a necessity. Saul's great sin was in sparing Amalek (cf. 1 Sam. 15; cf. 28:18). An Amalekite made an end of him. Coddled sin eventually destroys. David's slaying the Amalekite was dictated largely by his view of the inviolability of the person of a God-appointed leader.

David's Reaction to the News. 1:11-16. **11-13.** David and his men **tore** their garments (13:31), and **mourned** (3:31) and **wept** and **fasted** until evening (cf. 1 Sam. 31:13). The Amalekite had described himself as a **son of a sojourner**, (a stranger, a resident alien; that is, a foreigner living in Israel and enjoying protection but not full civil rights). **14.** Even under these extreme conditions David inquired how this Amalekite was not afraid to stretch forth his hand **to destroy the Lord's anointed** (cf. 1 Sam. 26).

David's Elegy for the Slain. 1:17-27. **17. David lamented.** Customarily lamentation for the dead was made by professional mourners (2 Chron. 35:25), usually women (Jer. 9:17). **19.** David, employing his great gifts as a poet, personally lamented the deaths of Saul and Jonathan. Here is presented great lyric poetry from a skilled musician (1 Sam. 16:23) and a talented poet (cf. the many Davidic psalms), who was also a man of God and a steadfast friend, even in the face of such treatment as Saul gave him. The words **Thy glory, O Israel,** and **how are the mighty fallen** refer primarily to Saul and Jonathan.

20. Gath (1 Sam. 27:2; Micah 1:10) and **Ashkelon** (1 Sam. 6:17; Jer. 25:20) were two prominent cities of the Philistine Pentapolis. The rejoicing of **the daughters of the Philistines** is reminiscent of the custom of employing women to celebrate personal victories by singing and dancing (cf. 1 Sam. 18:6). **The daughters of the uncircumcised** is a term of disgrace.

21. No dew or **rain** upon the mountains of Gilboa, which would produce terrible drought, expresses the greatest calamity that the lacerated feelings of the mourning poet could conjure. To cast away the shield was counted a national disgrace; yet on the fatal day of Israel's defeat by the Philistines, many of the Hebrew soldiers who had displayed valor in former battles threw away their shields and fled from the field. Cowardly conduct is alluded to with exquisitely touching pathos.

The **shield of Saul—no longer rubbed with oil** (NIV), poetically described by David, was lying upon the mountains, no longer shining and polished and ready to be worn for action, but cast aside as worthless and neglected. Ancient custom records how shields were kept well oiled to preserve their good condition.

22. The bow of Jonathan evidently gives the name to this poem. Jonathan was famous for his skill in archery, while Saul was celebrated for the use of the sword. Saul's sword **returned not empty.** Behind the expression is the figure of the sword devouring flesh (Deut. 32:42). **23.** David celebrated the wonderful character of Jonathan, who could remain loyal to his father despite his father's weakness and his own love for David, whom Saul had come to hate so violently. Yet in death these men were **not divided** (cf. 1 Sam. 31:2-4). The swiftness of an eagle (Hab. 1:8) and the strength of a lion were prominent characteristics of ancient heroes.

24. This verse indicates how successful Saul had been in his wars against the Philistines. He took great spoil, bringing prosperity to his kingdom. **25-26.** These verses comprise a special tribute to Jonathan. David said his love to him was wonderful, **passing the love of women. 27. The weapons of war** is a metaphorical description of Saul and Jonathan.

B. DAVID'S ANOINTING AND ABNER'S REVOLT. 2:1-32.

David Anointed King over Judah. 2:1-7. **1-3.** After David's lamentation over Saul and Jonathan, the first thing recorded concerning him is that he inquired of the LORD by Urim (1 Sam.

23:6, 9; 30:7-8). He would not take a single step toward claiming the kingly rights, which belonged to him, without waiting upon the LORD. With all his faults and in contrast to Saul, David was in submission to the LORD. He sought His guidance and desired to follow Him. He prefigures our Lord Jesus Christ. The answer came at once that he was to go up to the cities of Judah from Hebron, an ancient town (cf. Gen. 13:18; 23:2; Judg. 1:10). **4.** His being anointed king over Judah was quite unostentatious.

5-7. His first act as king showed his magnanimity as well as his political sagacity. He thanked the men of Jabesh-gilead for their kindness in burying Saul's body. Strategically, it was very important for David to cultivate ties of friendship with these Transjordanic people, among whom Saul had been popular and where he had done so much good for the people (1 Sam. 11). Saul's enmity toward David would normally have made them unfriendly toward the new king.

Abner Makes Ishbosheth King. 2:8-11. **8-10.** Abner, a general of Saul's army, took Ishbosheth, Saul's son, and made him king in Mahanaim. Ishbosheth's original name was Eshbaal (1 Chron. 8:33; 9:39), the heathen *baal* part of the name being supplanted by *bosheth,* the Hebrew word for "shame" because of its connection with idolatry. Mahanaim (cf. Josh. 21:38; 2 Sam. 17:24), located in Transjordan on the border between Gad and Manasseh (Gen. 32:2), was a territory that was friendly to Saul. Ishbosheth was not in the battle in which Saul was killed. The tribes over which he ruled are all well recognized except for Ashur. **Ashurites** is a misspelling for Asherites (Judg. 1:32).

Beginning of War Between David and Ishbosheth. 2:12-17. **12-13.** Abner proceeded from Mahanaim to Gibeon in

Benjamin. This furnishes an inkling of his purpose. Apparently he planned to proceed from there against Judah in order to bring the people of Judah under the rule of Ishbosheth. However, David's general, Joab, evidently anticipated that move, and so the two of them met there with their troops.

14-15. A battle began after it was agreed that it should be fought by twelve picked men from either side. Abner's suggestion anticipated a decision from single combat by champions, thus avoiding much bloodshed (cf. Goliath's offer, 1 Sam. 17:8-9). **16.** Each of the champions caught hold of his opponent's head, stabbing his sword into his side so that all of them fell. The place was called "Field of the Sword Edges" in Gibeon. **17.** A general engagement followed, in which Abner's forces were defeated.

Abner Slays Asahel. 2:18-32. **18-23.** Asahel, one of Joab's brothers, pursued after Abner. Anxious to avoid a blood feud with the powerful Joab, Abner tried to persuade Asahel to stop the chase. Abner slew him when he refused. **24-32.** Joab and his group pursued the remnant of Abner's forces, until Joab finally yielded to Abner's plea to break off hostilities. Exactly why the battle was broken off is not disclosed. Possibly it was David's set policy to have as little conflict with the house of Saul as possible.

The skirmish at the reservoir of Gibeon was the beginning of a long, bitter strife between the forces of Ishbosheth and David. It must have lasted nearly seven years, since David's rule over all Jerusalem began when he moved to Jerusalem, making the whole of his reign in Hebron contemporary with Ishbosheth's reign in Mahanaim.

C. ABNER'S DEFECTION AND DEATH. 3:1-39.

David's Dynasty Described. 3:1-5.

1-4. The list of David's sons is given (1) to show that while David's house increased, Saul's decreased; and (2) because vast divine promises centered in David's house (cf. 8:4-15), and everything that happened to it was important and could not be omitted. This was especially true of notations concerning genealogy, which formed a part of the line of descent of Jesus Christ, the greater David, the King of kings, in whom the divine promises for the dynasty of David were to be established.

Even the bad things David did served in their way to glorify the building of his house by demonstrating the excellence of the divine Builder, who could use even that material (e.g., his polygamy and yielding to the flesh, and self-indulgence in his many marriages, having six sons by six different wives). That sowing to the flesh was to reap a sad harvest of great domestic turmoil and unhappiness.

Many of his sons became a deep sorrow to David—**Amnon** (cf. chap. 13); **Absalom**, a still greater trial (15:7—18:33); and **Adonijah**, who became a rival of Solomon (1 Kings 1:5). **Chileab** was called Daniel (1 Chron. 3:1), the former meaning "like his father," apparently a nickname because of his resemblance to his father. **5. Eglah,** the last wife mentioned, is called **David's wife**, probably referring to Michal, David's first and most rightful wife who had no child after she taunted David, although she may have had one before (cf. 2 Sam. 6:20-23).

Abner's Defection to David. 3:6-16. **6-7.** During the civil war between the houses of David and Saul, Abner, who had been the general of Saul's army, was strengthening his own position to a point where it threatened the dynasty of Saul itself. As a pretender, Abner's act toward Rizpah and the royal harem was evidence of usurpation of royal power, indicated by the possession of court women (cf. David's insistence on the return of Michal, v. 13; Absalom's usurpation of David's concubines, 16:21-22; and Adonijah's desire for Abishag, 1 Kings 2:21-22). **8.** Stung by the accusation of Ishbosheth, Abner wrathly retorted, **Am I a dog's head?**, reading ''Am I a dog's head of Judah?'' To this day in the Orient the dog is viewed as a despised and unclean beast (cf. 1 Sam. 24:14; 2 Sam. 9:8; 16:9; 2 Kings 8:13). **9-10.** Abner apparently saw the futility of trying to establish Ishbosheth on the throne and decided to switch over to David's side. He demonstrated an unprincipled willingness to support whatever party best advanced his own interest (cf. v. 6; 2:8-9). **11.** Ishbosheth showed his utter helplessness by being afraid of Abner.

12. Abner's offer to David, of course, was another factor why Saul's house grew weaker and weaker and David's grew stronger and stronger. **13-14.** David naturally concurred to such a politically expedient move to strengthen his position in the war against the house of Saul. He required one condition—that Michal, Saul's daughter, be restored to him.

15-16. So Ishbosheth sent and had Michal taken from her husband, here called Paltiel (cf. 1 Sam. 25:44, where the name has a shorter form, Palti). Although Michal's husband evidently loved her dearly, she was still David's first and rightful wife, and actually belonged to him. This was another politically expedient move on David's part, contributing to the fact that his house grew stronger while Saul's grew weaker.

Abner Visits David. 3:17-21. **17-18.** Abner consulted with the **elders of Israel**, who evidently were representatives of all the tribes. He realized that he was the one impediment standing between popular acceptance of David. Both on the divine and the human side, David was the choice. **19-21.** Abner himself addressed the people of Benjamin, because that tribe was most naturally attached to the Benjamite house of Saul. Then Abner went to tell David personally at Hebron. No doubt in this very important move of bringing all Israel to David, Abner expected some great reward, such as his being the general of David's forces.

Joab Murders Abner. 3:22-30. **22-24.** Dramatically, at this point David's commander in chief, Joab, came in from a raid, bringing huge amounts of plunder. When Joab, flushed with victory and self-importance, heard that Abner had visited King David and had gone away in peace, he immediately saw the danger in which his position stood. He hated Abner, first, because of the existing blood feud (he had killed his brother Asahel); and second, because David's peace with Abner was a threat to his power as the head of David's army.

25. No doubt Joab was sincere in mistrusting the sincerity of Abner, counting him as a spy. **26-27.** Calling Abner back to Hebron, Joab slew him in the gate where business was transacted, fatally stabbing him in the abdomen. **28-29.** David, of course, was horrified at the deed, but he proclaimed that he and his kingdom were innocent before the LORD forever of the blood of Abner, the son of Ner. He pronounced the act as a boomerang on the head of Joab and all his father's house, invoking a curse upon them.

David Laments Abner's Death. 3:31-39. **31.** David instantly proclaimed a state mourning for Abner, instructing the people to tear their clothes and put on sackcloth and mourn for the slain man. King David himself walked behind the bier. **32-34.** Abner was buried in Hebron, and the king lamented over him. This was not political expediency but sincere evidence of David's heart. He lamented the fact that Abner had to die as a fool dies. He was never bound or fettered, but he fell as one who falls before the wicked. Also, all Israel wept over Abner.

35-37. David gave full proof that he was innocent of the death of Abner, so crucial an event in the continued increase of his house. **38.** He pronounced him **a prince** and **a great man ... in Israel.** He complained that the sons of his sister, Zeruiah, were too harsh (19:22) for him. **39.** David resigned the terrible crime to the LORD for His recompense.

D. ISHBOSHETH'S DEATH. 4:1-12.

The Murder of Ishbosheth. 4:1-8. **1-3.** It is quite understandable that when Ishbosheth heard that Abner had been murdered in Hebron, he lost heart. All Israel fell into confusion. Only the assassination of Ishbosheth himself remained to complete the process of the collapse of Saul's house. The text emphasizes that the murderers of Ishbosheth were from Beeroth, a town that was a part of Benjamin then.

The town of Beeroth is linked with Gibeon (Josh. 9:17). Its inhabitants may well have suffered along with the Gibeonites (cf. 2 Sam. 21:1) at Saul's hands. This may be the explanation of the basic enmity to the house of Saul in citizens of Beeroth like Baanah and Rechab. Beerothites had been expelled by Saul (21:1-2) and had fled to Gittaim. Their town of Beeroth had passed into the possession of Benjamin. The town is identified with el Bireh, a village some nine miles north of Jerusalem.

4. The reference to Mephibosheth is not irrelevant, but rather focuses the picture on the nearest of kin to Saul

apart from Ishbosheth. It lays a foundation for chapter 9. The original form of **Mephibosheth** ("he who spreads shame") was Meribbaal ("he who strives for the LORD"; 1 Chron. 8:34; 9:40). The change in the name is due to the fact that the *Baal* element, being a possible reference to the Canaanite fertility god, Baal, was changed to the Hebrew word *bosheth* ("for shame"; cf. 2:8).

5-8. The murderers slew Ishbosheth as he slept **on a bed at noon** during the normal siesta from twelve till three or four o'clock in the afternoon. It appears that the king's prestige had so deteriorated that he did not even have a sufficient bodyguard. The murderers used the clever ruse of the delivery-man approach. They had entered the house, apparently to take out some wheat, when they mortally stabbed the king. Shamefully, they decapitated the king, took the head, and traveled by way of the Jordan Valley all night and brought the gory evidence of Ishbosheth's death to David at Hebron.

The Punishment of the Murderers. 4:9-12. **9-11.** It was now perfectly evident that David would be the new king. So the sons of Rimmon concluded that the best way to curry favor with him, since Ishbosheth's power was ended, was to slay the archcontender to the throne. They failed to apprehend David's policy, which was to spare life wherever possible. In view of Ishbosheth's utter weakness, it certainly would have been possible to spare him without any danger to the kingdom.

12. David summarily executed the murderers, the evidence being in their own hands. The cutting off the hands and feet of criminals convicted of treason was an ancient Oriental custom. Ignominiously, the murderers were hanged up over the pool in Hebron. Exposure of the mutilated bodies was meant not only to be a punishment for their crime, but also proof of David's abhorrence of the violence. The head of Ishbosheth was buried in Abner's sepulcher in Hebron. In all of these events David acted with great sagacity as well as humanity, proving himself every inch worthy of the kingship.

II. DAVID'S REIGN OVER ALL ISRAEL. 5:1—10:27.

A. DAVID MADE KING OF ALL ISRAEL. 5:1-25.

David Anointed as King. 5:1-5. **1.** At last God's king came into his own. All Israel, representatively, came to Hebron to turn the kingdom of Saul over to David (cf. 1 Chron. 12:23-40). The deep conviction of the people was that David was their **bone and** their **flesh**. David's sojourn among the Philistines during the latter years of his persecution by Saul had cast doubt in some that he was truly an Israelite at heart. But his subsequent acts and policies as king of Judah, his political sagacity, and his deep Yahwistic faith disspelled any uncertainty that he was one of his people, Israel.

2. The second great conviction of the people was that he was really their deliverer and their leader, even under Saul's kingship. Moreover, they were deeply convinced that he was the LORD's choice as king (cf. 1 Sam. 16:11-13, where the divine appointment of David to the throne is recorded). He was to **feed**, that is, "shepherd" God's people and be **a captain** (*nāgîd*, "prince") over them (cf. 1 Sam. 10:1). Here is the first reference to the shepherd role (*rā'â*, "feed a flock, govern") applied to a king in Scripture.

3. The people, therefore, **anointed David king over Israel** (cf. 1 Sam. 10:1).

The **league** or "compact" that David made with the people in the presence of the LORD is not recorded. It was the formal declaration of the constitution as well as a defining of the limitation of the royal power and prerogative. Such agreements were made chiefly at the beginning of a new dynasty or at the restoration of a royal family after usurpation (2 Kings 11:17), though circumstances sometimes led to the compact being renewed on the accession of any new sovereign (1 Kings 12:3-4). David's solemn coronation at Hebron foreshadows that day when Israel's long-rejected King, the Messiah, the Son of David (Matt. 1:1), will return in glory to be the Shepherd King of Israel. The great feast of rejoicing, alluded to in 1 Chronicles 12:39-40, offers a faint foregleam of what Israel's joy will be when her true King is enthroned (cf. Isa. 25:6-9).

Jerusalem Becomes David's Capital. 5:6-10. **6.** Jerusalem, the town of Jebus, called Uru-salim ("city of peace") in the Amarna Letters, was Hittite-Amorite in its background (cf. Ezek. 16:3, 45). The town had been taken in the time of the judges (Judg. 1:8), but not the stronghold of the Jebusites on the southeastern hill. The stronghold was so impregnable that the Jebusites claimed that the blind and the lame could defend Jerusalem.

7-8. David perceived that the water shaft could be climbed and the city taken. The impregnable southeastern hill was located above the Gihon spring. Some scholars still maintain David's men gained access to the water shaft, which was dug by the Jebusites to get water inside the city (cf. 5:8, RSV). Early researches of the Palestine Exploration Fund under the direction of Sir Charles Warren yielded important discoveries concerning this Jebusite water system. However, W. F. Albright maintains the wall was scaled by a grappling hook, which is the meaning of the word, instead of "water shaft," as shown by Aramaic and Arabic.

The capture of the southeastern hill of the Jebusites was politically important, providing the kingdom with a neutral capital, situated between Judah and Israel, but belonging to neither. **9.** David called the occupied new fortress the **city of David.** He also did construction work around the fortress from Millo, an inner rampart-fill that was used as a fortification.

David's Alliance with Tyre. 5:11-12. **11-12.** Hiram I of Tyre (c. 969-936 B.C.) displayed friendship to David. He appears in Phoenician records both as a conqueror and a builder. These ties of amity continued through Solomon's reign (1 Kings 9:10-14). This paved the way for the importation of Phoenician arts, skills, and labor, the beautification of the city of Jerusalem, and especially for the later construction of the Temple.

Sons Born to David in Jerusalem. 5:13-16. **13-16.** David increased his harem, displaying the fleshly indulgent aspect of his nature (cf. 3:2-5; 1 Chron. 3:1-9). The most important name among these sons born in Jerusalem is that of Solomon.

David Wars Against the Philistines. 5:17-25. This passage reports two campaigns against the Philistines, the first in verses 17 to 21, and the second in verses 22 to 25 (cf. 8:1; 21:15-22 for later campaigns). **17.** Whenever these battles occurred, it was evident that the Philistines were hard put to stop David's expanding power, which threatened them. As Israel had at times carried the Ark of the Covenant into battle, so the Philistines carried their gods (cf. v. 21). Thus, the contest became a showdown between the LORD and the Philistine gods.

18-19. David showed his usual faith by inquiring of the LORD, **Shall I go up to** (against) **the Philistines?** The LORD's promise was clear. When God's anointed king reigned according to God's will, the enemies of the LORD were destroyed. **The valley of Rephaim** (cf. v. 22; 23:13; 1 Chron. 11:5; 14:9, 13) marks the southwest entrance to the Jerusalem area. This shows how determined the Philistines were to frustrate David's plan to capture the city and make it his capital and thus unite the twelve tribes.

20. In the first campaign David struck down the Philistines, and the place was called Baal-perazim, meaning "master of the breakthroughs." **21.** The Philistines abandoned their idols, and David and his troops carried them off and burned them (1 Chron. 14:12), as required by the Law (Deut. 7:5, 25).

22-25. In the second repulse of the Philistines, David was instructed not to go up against the enemy but to encircle them from the rear and come upon them opposite the mulberry (balsam) trees. When they heard the sound of marching in the tops of the trees, they were to plunge immediately into the battle, knowing that the LORD had gone out before them to overwhelm the Philistine army. David did as he was ordered, and he struck down the Philistines from Geba (that is, Gibeon; 1 Chron. 14:16; Isa. 28:21) to Gezer, meaning the entire highland region, the Philistines being pushed back to the Shephelah and the Maritime Plain.

B. THE ARK BROUGHT TO ZION. 6:1-23.

The Ark Is Brought by David. 6:1-5. **1-2.** Wisely planning to make Jerusalem not only the political but also the religious capital of his realm, David with a great band of chosen men of Israel and the people with him marched to Baale-Judah, also known as Baalah and Kiriath-jearim (1 Chron. 13:6), to bring up the ark of God from there. The ark had remained there in the house of Abinadab for more than half a century, following its capture by the Philistines at the first battle of Ebenezer and its subsequent return (1 Sam. 7:1; cf. 14:18, which the LXX translates, "the ephod," cf. vv. 3, 41, instead of "the ark of God").

The ark—containing the tables of the Law (1 Kings 8:9), the golden pot containing manna, and Aaron's rod (Heb. 9:4)—was the most expressive symbol of the presence of the infinitely holy God, and it presaged God's eventual revelation of Himself through the divine-human Christ for the redemption of the world. David's determination to fetch the ark witnessed his faith in the Creator-Redeemer. **3-5.** The ark was transported on a new cart, in the Philistine manner, while David and all the house of Israel were dancing before the LORD with all kinds of instruments made of cypress, and with lyres, harps, tambourines, castenets, and cymbals.

The Sin of Uzzah. 6:6-19. **6-7.** Two infractions of the Law of God combined to produce the event recorded here. First, the ark should never have been transported on a cart, but instead, carried by authorized carriers, the priests. The penalty for that infraction was death (Num. 4:15). Second, the ark itself was to be transported on staves and was not to be touched even by the authorized carriers, the priests, on pain of death (Num. 4:15). Uzzah's being struck dead did not involve, of course, his salvation. It was "a sin unto [physical] death" (1 John 5:16; 1 Cor. 5:5). The place of the tragedy is called **Perez-uzzah** and means the "breaking out upon Uzzah."

8-11. David's carelessness in this matter, shown in his failure to follow the prescriptions of the Word of God, filled him with fear. He was unwilling to move the ark into the city of David, but redirected it to the house of Obed-edom, the Gittite (i.e., a former resident of the city of Gath). There it remained for three months, and the LORD prospered Obed-edom, a Levite of the family of Korah of the clan of Kohath (1 Chron. 26:1, 4). So the requirements for a caretaker of the ark were met. **12-19.** After an interval, the ark was brought up to Jerusalem. David pitched a tent for it, and the king offered burnt offerings and peace offerings, all of which looked forward typically to the coming Redeemer and His atoning work for a sinful race.

Michal's Sin. 6:20-23. **20.** David's dancing before the LORD showed his sincere love for the LORD and his humility. But Michal, not called the wife of the king here, but the **daughter of Saul**, despised David. **21-22.** She looked upon his holy joy as indecent humiliation for such a prominent person as he. The contrast between David's humility and the pride of Saul and his house, is signally evident in his daughter. **23.** For her sin Michal was punished with the severest possible punishment for an Oriental woman: she had no child.

C. THE DAVIDIC COVENANT. 7:1-29.

David's Desire to Build the Temple. 7:1-3. **1-2.** David's worthy ambition was to build a house for the LORD. However, God's will was to build a house for David. Man's best and noblest plans for God are often not His will. **3.** The prophet Nathan himself was so taken up with David's suggestion that he expressed his own will rather than the Word of God.

The Davidic Covenant. 7:4-17. **4-10.** The great covenant God made with David (vv. 8-17) was introduced by the word of the LORD through Nathan, reminding David that the LORD had not dwelt in any house since the Egyptian redemption. Neither had He commanded His people to build Him such a house. **11-13.** This great covenant of kingship, centering in Christ, provided (1) a Davidic "house," that is, a family line or posterity through which the Messiah, the Savior of the world, would eventually be born (Matt. 1:1, 16; Luke 3:23); and (2) a perpetual kingdom and throne.

14. This kingly covenant had only one condition: divine chastisement for disobedience in the kingly Davidic line. **15-16.** The covenant itself, however, was not to be abrogated, but was to be **established forever.** It was renewed to Mary by the angel Gabriel (Luke 1:31-33; Acts 2:29-32; 15:14-17). Since the Babylonian Captivity, only one King of the Davidic line has been crowned at Jerusalem and He with thorns. However, He will yet be given the throne of His father, David, and sit on His own throne, even as He now sits with the Father on His Father's throne (Rev. 3:21). That throne will be of the millennial Kingdom and will merge into the everlasting Kingdom of the eternal state (Rev. 21:1-8).

Solomon entered into the immediate covenant. His birth was predicted (v. 12), but he was not promised a perpetual seed; he only was assured that he would build an house for the LORD's name (v. 13). His kingdom would be established (v. 12), and his throne of royal authority would endure forever. If Solomon sinned, he would be chastened, but not deposed. Continuance of Solomon's throne, but not his posterity, shows the accuracy of the prediction. Israel had nine dynasties; Judah had but one. Christ was born of Mary, who was not of the Solomonic line (Jer. 22:28-30); He was the descendant of Nathan, another son of David (cf. Luke 3:23-31).

On the other hand, Joseph, the husband of Mary, was descended from Solomon, and through him the throne legally passed to Christ (cf. Matt. 1:6, 16). Thus, it is evident that the throne, but not the posterity, came through Solomon, which is in precise fulfillment of the LORD's promise to David.

In contrast to the irrevocable promise of perpetual fulfillment made to David, Solomon illustrates the conditional character of the Davidic Covenant as applied to the kings who followed him. Disobedience in this line resulted in chastisement, but not in the annulment of the covenant (2 Sam. 7:14; Psalm 89:20-37; Isa. 54:3, 8, 10). So chastisement fell first in the division of the kingdom under Rehoboam and finally in the captivity (2 Kings 25:1-21).

But the Davidic Covenant is immutable (Psalm 89:20-37), and the LORD will yet give to the thorn-crowned One "the throne of his father, David" (Luke 1:31-33). For other major covenants, see the Edenic (Gen. 2:16); Adamic (Gen. 3:15); Noahic (Gen. 9:16); Abrahamic (Gen. 12:2); Mosaic (Exod. 19:5); Palestinian (Deut. 33), and the New (Heb. 8:8).

David's Prayer. 7:18-29. David's prayer (cf. 1 Chron. 17:16-27) breathes a deep note of worship, gratitude, thanksgiving, praise, and complete submission to the will of God. By faith, God's servant grasped the wonderful scope of this prophecy and bowed before the LORD God in humble submission.

D. THE EXTENSION OF DAVID'S KINGDOM. 8:1-18.

David's Conquests. 8:1-14. The great kingdom promises of the Davidic Covenant and David's prayer were followed by far-reaching conquests and victories. Divine promises appear to have been partially realized immediately, although chronologically many of the campaigns, given here in summary form, took place before Nathan's prophecy (cf. 7:1).

1. First mentioned are the Philistines, whom David humbled. **David took Metheg-ammah** ("the bridle of their mother [city]"), which refers to Gath (1 Chron. 18:1), at that time the chief city among the five main Philistine cities. **2.** David's striking down Moab suggests some hostile action on their part, considering the earlier friendly relations (cf. 1 Sam. 22:3-4). Evidently David made their fighting men lie on the ground and measured them with a line, designating two parts for death and one part to be spared alive, thus reducing the nation to a tributary status.

3-4. Hadadezer's domain of Zobah, an Aramaean principality north of Damascus, was the next to fall under David's power. That trouble started when the army of Hadadezer went to help the Ammonites against David (cf. 10:6). The horses were not to be multiplied in Israel, and all but one hundred of them were hamstrung in order to be useless for military purposes. **5-12.** When the Aramaeans of Damascus came to the aid of Hadadezer, David conquered them and stationed garrisons in the city of Damascus. So Syria, or Aram, became a subject people to David, paying tribute.

Great quantities of gold and bronze, won as booty in these conquests over the Aramaeans, were used later by Solomon in building the Temple (1 Chron. 18:8). David also accumulated other materials for the Temple (1 Chron. 22:2-5, 14-15). He won a great diplomatic victory with Toi, king of Hamath, a city on the Orontes River about one hundred miles north of Damascus. **13-14.** He also won striking victories over Edom in the **valley of salt** south of the Dead Sea. David garrisoned Edom

and extracted tribute from them.

David's Reign. 8:15-18. **15.** In David's reign over all Israel, he executed justice and maintained righteousness for all his people. The king's great victories and his equitable and just reign look forward prophetically to the greater than David, who will conquer and reign as King of kings and LORD of lords over the millennial Kingdom at His glorious second advent (Rev. 19:11—20:4).

16-17. Leading officers of the kingdom are also mentioned. Joab was the general and commander in chief of the army, Jehoshaphat was the recorder, Zadok and Ahimelech were priests, and Seraiah was the scribe. Benaiah was in charge of the Cherethites and the Pelethites, foreign mercenaries who were related to Cretans and Philistines (cf. 1 Sam. 30:14).

18. David's sons were priests (NASB margin). Keil, noting the different wording of 1 Chronicles 18:17 ("chief officials," RSV) renders the Hebrew expression as "confidants." Could David himself, as king in Jerusalem, have been thought of as having inherited some priestly functions from Melchisedek? If so, those functions may well have been delegated in whole or in part to his sons. When the true Kingdom is established, which all of this foretells, there will be those who co-rule with the King and be in charge of five or ten cities (cf. Luke 19:17-18). David's sons, who ruled with him, may be compared to true believers who are the sons of God in Christ and who will be fellow heirs and rule with Him in the coming millennial Kingdom.

E. DAVID'S KINDNESS TO MEPHIBOSHETH. 9:1-13.

Mephibosheth Brought to David. 9:1-4. **1-4.** The account of Mephibosheth is the first thing mentioned after David's royal government had been fully established. The story reveals the gospel of God's grace in a dramatic way, especially the kindness of God, which is manifested to all sinners, particularly in the coming Kingdom. Mephibosheth beautifully illustrates the sinner and his condition. He was helplessly crippled in both feet, having become lame as a result of a fall as a child (4:4). The incident is a reminder of fallen man and the helpless condition of sinful humanity.

David's desire to show kindness for Jonathan's sake (1 Sam. 20:14-16; 2 Sam. 21:7) illustrates the kindness and love of God our Savior (Titus 3:4). Ziba, Saul's servant, introduced Mephibosheth to David (cf. 2 Sam. 16:1-4). Ziba said Mephibosheth, Jonathan's son, resided in Lodebar, apparently Ummed-Debar, ten miles south of Lake Tiberias in Transjordan (F. M. Abel, *Géographie de la Palestine*, 2:304).

David's Mercy to Mephibosheth. 9:5-13. 5-8. When the helpless cripple was carried into the presence of King David (cf. 19:24-30), he illustrated repentance. He fell on his face reverently and professed himself to be a **dead dog**. Real repentance involves (1) seeing God as He is — infinitely holy; (2) seeing ourselves as we are — hopelessly sinful and lost; and (3) seeing sin to be exceedingly sinful. Mephibosheth thus confessed his shame and nothingness, calling himself a dead dog (cf. 1 Sam. 24:14; 2 Sam. 16:9), less even than a live dog, which was little enough esteemed in those days.

9-13. David, for Jonathan's sake (illustrating God's wonderful grace), lifted the poor cripple to a place at the king's table as one of the king's sons, restoring his inheritance to him. Similarly, the gospel of Christ lifts us out of our shame, constituting us sons of the living God and giving us an inheritance in the saints.

F. War with Ammon and Aram. 10:1-19.

Hanun's Affront. 10:1-5. **1-2.** David's foreign policy was, first, to win friends by diplomacy, and, failing that, to wipe out enemies by war. When the Ammonite king died and his son ascended the throne, it was David's opportunity to cultivate diplomacy. Nahash, king of the Ammonites, whom Saul had defeated at Jabesh-gilead, **showed kindness** (unrecorded) to David, whom he must have regarded as Saul's foe. It was quite natural then for David on the accession of the Ammonite king's son to send an embassy of consolation to the Ammonite capital.

3-4. Foolishly, **the princes** persuaded the young king that the embassy was one of espionage and that the ambassadors should be insulted. Mutilation of the beard — a badge of masculine honor — and an enforced shameful exposure were heinous insults. **5.** David told the men to **tarry** (remain) **at Jericho** until their beards had grown, and then to return.

The Ensuing War. 10:6-19. **6-8.** The insult triggered the Ammonite-Aramaean war. **Beth-rehob, Tob** (cf. Judg. 11:3, 5), Zobah and Maacah were all Aramaean principalities located on the northeast border of David's realm. **9-12.** By clever battle tactics, Joab turned possible defeat into a great victory. The general did what he could and left the rest up to God (cf. 1 Sam. 3:18), illustrating supporting faith by works. **13-14.** Joab broke up the coalition. But the Ammonites retired into their capital city, while Joab broke off the war because it was the wrong time of the year to begin a siege of the Ammonite capital (cf. 2 Sam. 11:1).

15-16. Hadadezer and the Aramaeans, feeling the importance of the defeat they had sustained, made an effort to rally all their forces and even called their vassal tribes from across the Euphrates. Their rallying point was **Helam**, which was apparently located in Transjordan despite tenuous evidence from Ezekiel 47:16 (LXX), which places it on the border between Hamath and Damascus. **17.** David, being informed of the great Aramaean rally, then took the field in person. Joab may have been with him, but more likely he was in the south, holding the Ammonites in subjection and preventing them from joining their confederates.

18. In this campaign David delivered a crushing blow to his foes, slaying the riders of a hundred chariots (1 Chron. 19:18 has seven thousand, which is apparently a corruption; it also has forty thousand footmen, while here it is forty thousand horsemen. Numbers in the Old Testament have suffered corruption because of difficulty in transmitting them). **19.** After that, the Aramaeans, including Hadadezer of Zobah, acknowledged the suzerainty of David, and later of Solomon, and became tributary states.

III. DAVID'S SIN AND ITS CHASTISEMENT. 11:1—20:26.

A. DAVID'S TERRIBLE SIN. 11:1-27.

David Commits Adultery with Bathsheba. 11:1-5. **1. After the year was ended** (lit., "at the return of the year"; cf. 10:14), that is, in the spring after the rainy season, war with Ammon was resumed. Rabbah, the capital of Ammon, present-day Amman, the capital of Jordan located twenty-two miles east of the Jordan, was again besieged. **But David tarried** (remained) **still at Jerusalem.** This was a danger signal, a prelude to his

sin. He belonged with his warriors on the battlefield, but he was where he should not have been.

2. From his royal palace David saw a woman bathing. **3.** Upon inquiry, he found out she was Bathsheba, **the daughter of Eliam, the wife of Uriah, the Hittite. 4-5.** David had his messengers fetch her. She came to him; he lay with her. Under the Law, she was unclean until the evening (cf. Lev. 15:19-24). Therefore, she remained in David's palace, concerned about that detail, while certainly not unconscious of committing a capital crime and a high offense against God, because her sin would become known, and by the Law (Lev. 20:10) both adulterers should have been punished with death.

David Sends for Uriah. 11:6-13. **6-8. Send me Uriah.** David tried the expedient of sending for Uriah to cover up his crime. When Uriah appeared before the king, David told him to go down to his house and wash his feet (rest) and spend the night with his wife, to hide David's sin. There **followed him a present** ("mess of meat," KJV) **from the king** (cf. Gen. 43:34), no doubt referring to some choice dish sent by the king to the guest whom he wished to honor.

9-10. But Uriah did not go to his home. Instead, he lay at the door of the king's house, probably in the guard chamber at the palace entrance (cf. 1 Kings 14:27-28). **11.** Uriah protested to the king that he could not go down to his house and enjoy the comforts of civilian life while **the ark, and Israel, and Judah,** remained **in tents.** Apparently the ark, as a symbol of the Creator-Redeemer's presence with His people, was still carried into battle. (Note 15:24-25; 1 Sam. 4:3.) **12-13.** By retaining Uriah and feasting him and making him drunk, David took every conceivable means of covering up his sin, but all failed. Uriah faithfully observed the strict continence required of soldiers consecrated to war by religious sanction (1 Sam. 21:4-5).

David Has Uriah Murdered. 11:14-27. This is an illustration of the terrible fact that one sin leads to another. The way of the transgressor is not only hard but downward. **14-15.** David ordered Uriah to be put in the heat of the battle and to be abandoned so that he might **be smitten, and die. 16-17.** It is clear that Joab joined David in this treacherous crime.

18-25. Joab anticipated David's anger at his apparent rashness and charged the messenger that when David should mention it, to tell him of Uriah's death. This was intended to allay suspicion in the messenger, as it would appear to him rather as an effort on Joab's part to throw the blame from himself upon Uriah as the leader of the assaulting party. Reference to Abimelech (Judg. 9:53) attests to the Israelites' familiarity with their past history. David showed that he not only could commit adultery and murder, but also practice deceit very subtly and apparently very successfully.

26. Bathsheba **mourned for her husband**, probably the usual period of seven days (Gen. 51:10; 1 Sam. 31:13), although in the case of a widow it may have been longer. **27.** Bathsheba **bore** David **a son.** Several months must have passed since the beginning of David's course of sin, but his conscience was utterly dulled to the seriousness of it. Possibly he was left so long without being brought to a conviction of his sin in order that his guilt might be proved openly, beyond all possibility of denial, by the birth of the child—the result of the sinful union. It is scarcely credible that David's conscience was not bothering him in the interim. The whole incident shows how a true believer may

backslide and fall into terrible sin that warrants physical death (1 Cor. 5:5; 1 John 5:16).

B. DAVID'S CONFESSION AND CHASTISEMENT. 12:1-31.

David's Sin Exposed. 12:1-7a. **1-4.** God's grace toward the sinner is wonderful. Here his grace toward his sinning saint was even more wonderful. **The Lord sent Nathan unto David.** The prophet, who was already on intimate terms with David, apparently was the court prophet at that time (cf. 7:1-17). Nathan's parable was planned to awaken the sleeping conscience of the offender. The parable does not make reference to any special sins of David, but to the meanness and selfishness of the act portrayed. Similar use of parables is made in other places (cf. 14:2-11; 1 Kings 20:35-41).

5-7a. David's generous impulses and his warm sense of justice readily cried out against the offender in the famous parable of the ewe lamb. He quickly expressed himself in anger: **The man who hath done this thing shall surely die,** that is, "is worthy to die." **7a.** With incisive boldness and suddenness, Nathan cried out, **Thou art the man!** The shock was so great that it at once aroused David's slumbering conscience. Despite his sin, the king was not a bad man. The driving purpose of his life was to do God's will, but he had yielded to temptation. His efforts to conceal his sin had stupified him to the horror of all that now suddenly flashed upon his mind. (Similar prophetic rebukes of royal offenders occur in 1 Sam. 15:21-23; 1 Kings 21:20-24; Isa. 7:3-25; Matt. 14:3-5.)

The Divine Chastisement Announced. 12:7b-12. **7b-8. The Lord God of Israel** reminded David that He had anointed him king over Israel and delivered him out of the hand of Saul. **I gave**

427

thee thy master's house, and thy master's wives. We are told of only one wife of Saul (1 Sam. 14:50); we read of no other. The prophet is apparently referring to the Oriental custom that the new king had a right to the harem of his predecessor. **9.** David had slain Uriah with the sword (two different words being used, with one indicating "to kill," and the other "to murder"). The crime was murder in the eyes of the LORD, although it was accomplished by the sword of the Ammonites. **10.** Therefore, the sword should now never depart, that is, during David's lifetime, from his house. **11-12.** He had taken Uriah's wife, and now others would take his wives. He had done it secretly, but the LORD said, **I will do this thing** (openly) **before all Israel.**

David's Confession Made. 12:13-19. **13-14.** David made an open and full confession: **I have sinned.** Saul had employed the same words (1 Sam. 15:24, 30), but in a totally different spirit. David's deep repentance and travail of soul are found in Psalm 51. The expression of his penitence after the visit of Nathan is found in Psalm 32, where he sets forth his experience after the assurance of divine forgiveness.

The repentant king gave his testimony for the warning and comfort of others. David was assured that the LORD had put away his sin, that is, had forgiven it. It was not to be a sin unto physical death (1 John 5:16; 1 Cor. 5:5; 11:30-32), although he had committed two crimes for which the Law imposed the penalty of death—adultery (Lev. 20:10) and murder (24:17). And inasmuch as he had given great occasion for people to blaspheme or ridicule, that is, speak evilly of God's people and God's salvation by grace through faith, chastisement had to follow. He was to suffer the natural consequences of his sin, which flowed from it according to the immutable laws of God's moral government.

15-19. God took the life of the child of the illicit union. David pleaded before God for the child. Apparently his great desire was to avert the death stroke, the sign of God's displeasure, in the hope that he might be able to discern in the baby's preservation the proof of divine favor consequent to his restoration to divine fellowship.

The Fruits of Divine Chastisement. 12:20-25. **20.** David's reaction to the death of the child is an illustration of Hebrews 12:11 (BV), "Of course, all discipline seems at the time not enjoyable but painful; later on, however, it affords those schooled in it the peaceful fruitage of an upright life." So David arose from the earth, washed himself, anointed himself, changed his apparel, and went into the house of the LORD and worshiped. Obediently and humbly he yielded to the lash of God's whip.

23. David's words, **I shall go to him**, scarcely can be interpreted any other way than that he was conscious of a life beyond the grave and that he, justified by faith, would go where the innocent child went, who had not yet reached the age of accountability. **24.** David was not only comforted himself, but he was able to comfort his wife. The illustration of divine favor is shown in that God gave him and Bathsheba the child Solomon, meaning "peaceable."

Solomon was actually the fourth child of David and Bathsheba (1 Chron. 3:5); so at least three years must have separated the birth of the child that died from that of Solomon. Peace had come to David's heart. The child born was called Jedediah, meaning "beloved of the LORD." He is a picture of God's own Son, who is our peace, "the Beloved" (Eph. 1:6).

Rabbah Taken. 12:26-31. **26-29.** The fall of Rabbah is another indication of God's gracious forgiveness of David. He was called to participate in its fall. **The city of waters** does not refer to the city itself but to the covered passage linking the city with its water supply. The water supply being cut off, the city was doomed. **30. Their king's** (Heb., *Malkam*) is evidently understood by the Septuagint as the name of the Ammonite deity Milcom (cf. Malcom, Zeph. 1:5) and is so rendered by the *Jerusalem Bible*. However, "their king" (RSV) seems preferable. The great weight of the crown (a talent of gold) is calculated to be as much as ninety-two pounds.

31. Most modern translations and commentaries favor hard labor as the understanding of this verse: "He ... set them to labor with saws ... and made them toil at the brickkilns" (RSV). If the King James Version is correct, it was a cruel fate, to say the least. For a Bedouin to be put to hard labor was extreme cruelty. If the King James' reading is followed, this excessive cruelty, nowhere else recorded to have been practiced by the Hebrews, was an act of special retributive justice for the people who were infamous for their cruelties (1 Sam. 11:2; Amos 1:13).

C. DAVID'S FURTHER CHASTISEMENT. 13:1-39.

Amnon's Passion for Tamar. 13:1-5. Now David began to reap what he had sown by committing evil in Uriah's household. The LORD's sentence against him began to be fulfilled: "Behold, I will raise up evil against thee out of thine own house" (12:11). The evil he had committed in his own heart and the passion that he had allowed to possess him broke out in his own family.

1. Amnon, David's firstborn son (3:2), conceived an illicit passion for his half sister Tamar, who was his brother Absalom's full sister. Absalom and Tamar were children of Maacah, daughter of Talmai, king of Geshur, an Aramaean principality northeast of the Sea of Galilee, south of Maacah, and north of Tob. **2.** Amnon was so frustrated that he fell ill for Tamar. Since she was a virgin and hence protected in the harem, it seemed impossible for Amnon to have any physical contact with her. **3-5.** However, Jonadab, a shrewd person who was the son of David's brother Shimeah, suggested a scheme for Amnon either to seduce or rape Tamar.

Amnon Violates Tamar. 13:6-22. **6-7.** It is ironic that Amnon used his father, King David, as a tool to accomplish his deceitful plan, for it was David who **sent home** (lit., "into the house") to Tamar, that is, to the private apartment of the women, the harem. **11-13.** Finding herself utterly deceived and alone in the power of her half brother, Tamar endeavored to escape by reasoning. She even quoted the nation's history to recall the king's son to a sense of right, quoting the very words of Genesis 34:7, 12.

She then spoke of the shame of the act and that the sin would meet her everywhere. Such an act would also make Amnon **as one of the fools in Israel**, that is, as one who casts off all restraint regarding the fear of God and any sense of decency. In desperation, she urged Amnon to **speak unto the king**. However, the marriage of half brothers and sisters was strictly forbidden in the Law (Lev. 18:9, 11; 20:17). It was unthinkable that she thought the king would violate the provisions of the Law for Amnon. But she used any suggestion and grabbed at a straw to gain time to escape the pressing danger.

14-17. That Amnon's passion for Tamar was animal lust and not love is shown by the fact that after committing his vile deed of incest, he hated Tamar exceedingly. Amnon's base conduct was more reprehensible then than at the first. Now under obligation to protect and comfort Tamar, he treated her scornfully, as if she were to blame. The baseness and brutality of his actions were almost incredible. **18-19. The garment of several colors** was a symbol of a royal virgin. As Tamar departed from Amnon's house, she **went on her way crying.** In doing that, she expressed her real feelings and also adopted the proper posture to advertise the wrong done to her, in order to obtain justice.

20-22. Absalom understood the situation at once and made a solemn decision to wreak revenge on his unprincipled half brother. Throughout all of this David showed his weakness and leniency because of his own failures and his giving in to the lusts of the flesh. **He was very angry**, and the Greek adds, ''But he vexed not the spirit of Amnon, his son, because he loved him, because he was his firstborn.''

Absalom Murders Amnon. 13:23-36. **23-25.** It was at sheep-shearing time, a time of great feasting and merriment (cf. 1 Sam. 25:2), two full years later that Absalom determined to kill Amnon. Absalom invited the king, apparently merely to allay suspicion of his ominous purpose. **26-27.** He then asked that if the king himself would not come, that Amnon, his oldest son and the heir apparent, might represent him at the feast. David could hardly refuse without acknowledging suspicion.

28. Absalom had commanded his servants. It was quite customary for the servants of a prince to obey any orders without question, the entire responsibility resting upon their master. **29.** The blow was too sudden, too unexpected, for the other princes to interfere. After the murder, all the king's sons arose and rode away hurriedly, each upon his mule, an animal still being ridden by persons of distinction (18:9; 1 Kings 1:33, 38). The Law forbade the breeding of mules (Lev. 19:19), but they became common through trade (1 Kings 10:25).

30-31. A report reached the king that Absalom had killed all the king's sons, and **not one of them** (was) **left.** This exaggeration caused the king and his servants to manifest the deepest mourning by tearing their garments and putting dirt on their heads. **32-33.** Meanwhile, the wily, scheming Jonadab consoled the king, realizing that only Amnon was dead and that Absalom had determined to kill him from the day Amnon violated Tamar. **34-36.** Jonadab, who had been used so demonically in the whole situation, appears in a strange role as a comforter to the king, who was relieved to learn his other sons were not killed and were returning.

Absalom Flees to Geshur. 13:37-39. **37.** It was a blow for David to lose his firstborn, and he **mourned for his son every day. 38.** Absalom fled to his grandparents' home where he remained three years. **39.** The meaning of this verse is that ''David desisted from going forth against Absalom'' (ECB) which is further proof of his parental weakness, for he failed to have his son apprehended and punished for murder, which was both fratricide and high treason, since Absalom had murdered the heir apparent. Absalom's flight to Geshur made his capture difficult, and David's own moral weakness let the matter slip. As time went by, the king was comforted concerning his firstborn, Amnon, and gradually gave up the thought of punishing Absalom.

D. DAVID AND ABSALOM. 14:1-33.

Joab's Ruse to Effect Absalom's Re-

call. 14:1-17. **1.** Joab perceived that the king's heart **was toward Absalom.** This statement, like the last verse of the previous chapter, should be understood in either of two opposite senses. Either David's heart was "for, to, unto," or it was "against" Absalom, the Hebrew preposition *'al* having a wide meaning. If the king's heart was actually "against Absalom," that would explain Joab's strategem to obtain his recall, which otherwise would have been quite unnecessary.

2-3. To accomplish his purpose, Joab sent to Tekoah, about five miles south of his native town of Bethlehem, for a wise woman. The parable Joab put in her mouth was purposely contrived to resemble the case of Absalom, but not too closely or it would defeat its purpose. **5-7.** The parable is recounted.

8-11. In the conversation between the king and the woman, the king, as judge, exonerated the woman's son, who had killed his brother in a violent quarrel. Actually, the case presented was that of an unpremeditated crime, which would not have been sufficient to urge the king to forgive Absalom. Therefore, the woman prevailed upon David to grant a pardon for a more serious guilt and to confirm it by an oath to stop any avenger of blood, that is, a relative who might take the punishing into his own hands (Num. 35:16-21) and thus add to the slaughter and destroy her son.

13. Then the woman told the king that in pronouncing the judgment he had just given, he had condemned himself, because he did not bring back his own son whom he had driven away. **14.** She stressed the fact that life is short and all must die, like water spilled on the earth, which cannot be recovered. If the king did not seek to bring Absalom home soon, he might never be able to do so. **17.** In pleading for his decision, the woman said the king was as **an angel of God**, referring not to Deity but to a created being.

The Strategem Discovered. 14:18-20. **18-19.** David perceived **the hand of Joab.** Perhaps it was only the wiley courtier's interest in the heir apparent. Doubtlessly Joab had made the same request before. When the woman perceived that the king had seen through the whole ruse, she freely told all. **20. And my Lord is wise, according to the wisdom of an angel of God.** Again, as in verse 17, referring to a created angel as an order characterized by excellence in wisdom.

Absalom Recalled. 14:21-24. **21.** So David made his decision to bring Absalom back. **22.** Joab prostrated himself before the king and expressed his gratitude. **23.** Joab was dispatched to Gesher and brought Absalom back to Jerusalem. **24.** Still, the king directed that he **turn** (aside) **to his own house**; he was not to see the king's face. Halfway forgiveness is worse than no forgiveness at all (cf. v. 32). David's attitude at this point indicates that it is doubtlessly correct to understand 14:1 as being "the king's heart was against Absalom." David allowed Absalom's return in weakness and forbade him from seeing his face out of a sense of justice.

Absalom's Beauty. 14:25-27. **25.** Absalom's physical beauty is stressed, particularly his magnificent head of hair. **26.** The statement that his hair weighed two hundred shekels (roughly five pounds) represents a scribal error of twenty shekels (one-half pound). Fleshly attraction and appeal made him a good leader for rebellion. The deed he had done in avenging the crime against his sister was most likely interpreted by most of the people as a noble and heroic act.

Absalom Pressures Joab to See King

David. 14:28-32. **28-30.** Behind Absalom's handsome exterior there was a proud, evil, and violent spirit, evidenced in his setting Joab's barley field on fire when his request to see the king was ignored. **32.** Absalom demanded, **Let me see the king's face; and if there be any iniquity in me, let him kill me.** The proud, unrepentant heart of Absalom made no acknowledgment of having done wrong. He simply declared that his state of half reconciliation was intolerable and demanded either to be punished or fully pardoned.

David Forgives Absalom. 14:33. **33.** Absalom's feigned humility in bowing himself to the earth before the king again shows his weak character. David's kiss meant full forgiveness and reconciliation, which proved to be a horrible mistake because justice was violated and no good could come from it.

E. ABSALOM'S REVOLT. 15:1-37.

Absalom's Treachery. 15:1-6. **1.** Absalom **prepared him chariots and horses** (cf. 1 Kings 1:5). To carry out his plans for rebellion, it was necessary to impress the people with his wealth and splendor, which were signs of assuming royal power (1 Sam. 8:11). David again displayed his weakness in failing to handle firmly his domestic problems created by his failure to check his son (cf. 1 Kings 1:5, where Adonijah did the same thing).

For the first time horses and chariots were used as part of the regal pomp. Since Absalom was the natural heir to the throne (cf. 14:7), why would he revolt during David's lifetime? Primogeniture was a normal practice in Israel (1 Sam. 2:8-10; Deut. 21:15-17), but there were exceptions (1 Chron. 5:1-2; 26:10). David's failure also was manifested in failing to lay down a law of

succession (1 Kings 1:17) for establishing a new dynasty.

Absalom's disfavor with his father may have goaded him on to his action out of fear that it would occur again; or perhaps, like Amnon, he simply was too immature to wait for what he wanted so desperately. **2-6.** His lament, **there is no man deputed of the king,** attacked another weakness of the royal administration—the failure to establish a judiciary system to hear cases. Evidently David was more adept as a military leader than as a peacetime administrator.

Absalom's Rebellion. 15:7-12. **7.** After **four years** (the reading found in the Syriac; most manuscripts of the Vulgate are probably correct). During this four-year period the conspiracy was carefully nurtured. Absalom could have worshiped in Jerusalem and paid his vow there, but he probably found disaffection among the people in Hebron over the loss of its status as a capital city. **8.** Absalom's vow is certainly an index to the deep hypocrisy of his soul.

9. David's naiveté concerning his children and his indulgence of them appears again. **10.** The pretender **sent spies,** dispatched to various parts of the land to sound out the people to further the conspiracy. **11.** The two hundred guests whom Absalom had invited to take part with him in his sacrifice at Hebron were doubtless prominent and influential citizens of Jerusalem. They **went in their simplicity,** completely ignorant of Absalom's purposes, showing the extreme secrecy with which the affair was conceived.

12. Absalom **sent for Ahithophel.** Giloh, the hometown of Ahithophel, was one of several towns just south of Hebron (Josh. 15:51). Ahithophel had gone there in readiness to be summoned by Absalom. Why he deserted David is not told. Perhaps he, like many others in the tribe of Judah, was alienated from David because of the rapidly growing empire that had diminished its relative importance. It is significant that the rebellion was cradled in Judah. Psalm 41 seems to have been written on this occasion, and perhaps also Psalm 55, reflecting Ahithophel's treachery. **While he offered sacrifices**, doubtless with pomp and circumstance, and continued there several days, time was made available for the conspiracy to strengthen.

David's Flight. 15:13-23. **13-15.** David fled from Jerusalem, perhaps feeling that he would have an advantage by fighting in the open country. No doubt he also doubted the loyalty of some of those around him. By leaving he would soon discover who would follow him regardless of circumstances. At the same time he could leave behind him his agents to work secretly for him in the city (cf. the superscription of Psalm 3). The sequel abundantly proved the wisdom of David's course, by which much of the horror of civil war was averted.

16. David left ten concubines to keep the palace. Large harems were customary at that time (cf. Judg. 8:30-31) and increased the ruler's prestige. David's was very modest compared to Solomon's (1 Kings 11:1-4). **17.** The king **halted at the last house** (RSV), which was probably a definite place on the outskirts of the city known by that name. There David mustered his forces and made the arrangements for his flight. **18-22.** The Cherethites, the Pelethites, and the six hundred Gittites are mentioned, with the incident of Ittai the Gittite contrasting the wonderful fidelity of the Cretan-Philistine foreign mercenaries and bodyguards with the fickleness of many of David's own people. **23.** The people's weeping indicates that the king must have retained much popular support. The brook Kidron marked the eastern boundary of Jerusalem.

The Ark Returned to Jerusalem. 15:24-31. **24-29.** Throughout this severe ordeal David recognized that he was suffering under the disciplinary hand of the LORD, on whom he cast himself entirely (cf. 24:14). He was therefore loathe to have the ark carried with him, lest he should appear to be compelling the divine presence and blessing. He knew that if God so willed, he would be brought again in peace; but, if not, he still would submit himself completely to God's ordering. Therefore, the king directed Zadok and Ahimaaz, his son, and Jonathan, the son of Abiathar, to return with the ark to Jerusalem. **30.** David and the people went up Mount Olivet and wept as they went with their heads covered. **31.** It was reported to David that Ahithophel was among the conspirators with Absalom. David prayed, **O Lord, ... turn the counsel of Ahithophel into foolishness.**

Hushai Sent Back to Jerusalem. 15:32-37. **32.** When David reached the summit where God was worshiped, Hushai the Archite came to meet him. Hushai's place of residence is referred to in Joshua 16:2. It was on the border between Ephraim and Benjamin. Hushai's arrival marked the beginning of the answer to David's prayer (v. 31).

33-37. In his direction to Hushai, David's counsel involved fraud and treachery, and Hushai willingly accepted the role given to him. The purpose was to frustrate Ahithophel's counsel and destroy Absalom's rebellion. The narrative simply states the facts without justifying the actions.

While the morality must be condemned, it must be remembered that such frauds have always been practiced in times of war. Also, David and Hushai did not have the full revelation of the Word of God, as we have, to condemn us and keep us clear of such practices.

F. DAVID IN FLIGHT AND ABSALOM IN JERUSALEM. 16:1-23.

Ziba Slanders Mephibosheth. 16:1-4. **1-2.** Who should meet the exiled king with provisions and help but Ziba, the steward of Mephibosheth! **3-4.** Ziba grossly slandered his master, undoubtedly for the purpose of gain, as it appears in verse 4. This is evident from the sequel of the story (19:24-30). It seems almost incredible that David should have believed Ziba's lie. Could a poor helpless cripple of the house of Saul benefit by Absalom's rebellion? David's weariness, frustration, and his gratitude for Ziba's large contribution to his necessity blinded him to Ziba's libel.

Shimei Curses David. 16:5-14. **5. When King David came to Bahurim** (modern Ras et-Ṭmim) to the east of Mount Scopus in Jerusalem, he was met by Shimei **of the family of the house of Saul**, that is, "of the family" in the larger sense of the tribe. Since the royal power had passed from their tribe, it was natural that many Benjamites should feel aggrieved. Hence, they were ready to show their opposition to David's regime whenever opportunity afforded.

6-8. Shimei's hatred and his actions were almost childish. He threw stones at the fugitives. He taunted them, calling David a **bloody man**, holding him responsible for **the blood of the house of Saul**, especially in the cases of Ishbosheth and of Abner and the execution of Saul's seven descendants at the demand of the Gibeonites (21:1-9). **9-10.** David's humble submission to

God's chastening was shown throughout this ordeal, especially when he said, **So let him curse.** The king did not mean, of course, to justify Shimei's conduct; but insofar as his sufferings were concerned, the insults were by divine appointment, and so he could not resent them. **11.** David's own son sought his life. How much more did the Benjamite have the right to do so! David accused Absalom of seeking not only his throne, but his very life. **14. The king, and all the people that were with him, became weary, and refreshed themselves** (the Greek adding "at the Jordan").

Absalom Enters Jerusalem. 16:15-19. **15-19.** Absalom and his large following entered Jerusalem with Ahithophel. Hushai, David's friend, greeted Absalom with the salutation, "God save the king," literally, "Let the king live." Absalom was amazed at Hushai's presence and was inclined to distrust him for having deserted his former friend and master, but Hushai artfully explained that his case was based on the principle of loyalty to the government, whatever form it might take. Since Absalom's government had the divine authority, he said, he would transfer his former faithfulness to the present government.

Ahithophel Gives Counsel. 16:20-23. **20-23.** Ahithophel's advice was that Absalom should make a complete breach with his father. Absalom followed his counsel and appropriated his father's harem in front of all Israel, showing the people that he had crossed the Rubicon (the line of no turning back), as it were, and claimed the kingship completely. Thus, Nathan's prophecy was literally fulfilled (12:11-12). The concubines being royal property, Absalom's taking them was a sensational means of showing the people that he had assumed the king's office and prerogatives (3:7; 15:16; 1 Kings 2:17-25).

**G. Hushai Thwarts Ahithophel's
Counsel. 17:1-29.**

Ahithophel's Counsel. 17:1-14. The
first plan of Ahithophel certainly had led
to success for Absalom (cf. 16:23).
However, Hushai's plan gave the advantage to David, enabling him to collect his forces for a form of battle in
which his military skill and experience
would be decisive. Ahithophel's counsel was aimed only at the person of
David, but he had not reckoned with
David's Lord, who loved him. Although He was chastening David, He
was still preserving him. Actually it was
not Hushai who defeated the counsel of
Ahithophel, but the Lord Himself, in
answer to David's prayer (15:31).

The Lord gave His counsel through
Hushai; then He overruled the contrary
advice of Ahithophel so that Absalom
and his men would follow Hushai's advice. Thus, the Lord overrules to confound the wisdom of wicked men. **7.**
When Hushai said to Absalom, **The
counsel that Ahithophel hath given is not
good at this time**, he implied that his
previous advice (16:21) had been wise.
Thus, he disarmed his hearers with the
appearance of candor. **8-13.** Hushai's
advice played dramatically upon the irresistible power of uniting all of Israel
and the certain success of the plan,
which dazzled the imagination of the
vain, self-centered Absalom and
pleased his vanity.

Hushai's Warning Saves David.
17:15-22. **15-16.** Hushai's advice, **Lodge
not this night**, had been followed for the
moment. Absalom might have decided
at any time to swing over to
Ahithophel's advice. In any case, there
was imminent danger. Hushai urged
David to pass over the Jordan without
delay. **17.** Jonathan and Ahimaaz stayed
at En-rogel, a fountain just outside the
city (Josh. 15:7; 18:16) located near the

southeast corner of Jerusalem, now
called Job's well. A maid servant hurried the news to them, and they carried it
to David.

18-19. Seen by a boy who had reported them to Absalom, they quickly
escaped to a man's house in Bahurim
(see 2 Sam. 16:5), where they were hidden in a well. **20.** Thus, Absalom's servants could not find them and returned
to Jerusalem. **21-22.** When they came up
out of the well, they reported to David,
and David and all the people moved out
of danger by crossing the Jordan. By
daybreak not one had failed to get to
safety.

Ahithophel's Suicide. 17:23. **23.**
When Ahithophel saw that his recom-
mendations had not been followed, he
saddled his donkey, went to his own
city, made arrangements for his household, and hanged himself. He recognized that the delay, which enabled
David to consolidate his forces, would
assure the undoing of Absalom's cause.

Absalom Pursues David. 17:24-26.
24-25. David reached **Mahanaim** (cf.
2:8) in Transjordan. The same reasons
that had made it a favorable place for the
capital of Ishbosheth also made it a
place of refuge for David and a rallying
point for his forces. Meanwhile, Absalom had crossed the Jordan, having
appointed Amasa in Joab's place over
the army. Amasa was Joab's cousin;
their mothers were half sisters of David
(cf. 1 Chron. 2:17). **26.** Thus, Israel and
Absalom were camping in the land of
Gilead.

David Succored. 17:27-29. **27-29.**
While David was at Mahanaim and Absalom was gathering his forces, assistance came to David from grateful
sources. Among those who gave
supplies was **Shobi, the son of Nahash of
Rabbah, of the children of Ammon.**
Shobi was doubtless David's deputy in
Ammon. His father, Nahash, had been

its king (cf. 10:1). It is very possible that after the dismantling of the royal city, David had left Shobi as governor over the conquered territory. Now he came forward to express his gratitude.

Machir, the son of Ammiel, was a protector of Mephibosheth (cf. 9:4). David reaped a reward for his kindness to the crippled son of Jonathan. **Barzillai,** apparently a non-Israelite because of his Aramaean name, joined those who brought supplies and relief to David. Psalms 61 and 62 have this period of David's life in Transjordan as their setting.

H. ABSALOM'S DEATH. 18:1-33.

David Prepares the People for Battle. 18:1-5. **1. He numbered the people.** Here "numbered" means "mustered." **2-3.** In arranging the army into three divisions, David was following a common strategy (Judg. 7:16; 1 Sam. 11:11). **Ittai, the Gittite** (i.e., Ittai of Gath), a Philistine, was a foreigner in David's service who had proved his sterling honesty. The king's desire to go out in person to the battle met with opposition from the people: "You are worth ten thousand of us" (BV). They told him it would be better for him to be in a position to send them support from the city of Mahanaim.

4. The king aquiesced and took up his post beside the city gate, where all the troops marched by in hundreds and thousands to battle. Absalom's delay gave opportunity for many of the sturdy frontiersmen of Transjordan to come to his aid. But those rough recruits were no match for David's standing army. **5.** As the troops were leaving, the king strictly ordered Joab, Abishai, and Ittai to **deal gently** with the young man, Absalom, and all the people witnessed his order.

Joab Slays Absalom. 18:6-17. **6.** The battle was joined in the **forest of**

Ephraim, this being the only mention of this forest in Transjordan. The locale certainly must not have been too distant from Mahanaim. **7.** In the bloody battle, Absalom's forces were overthrown, with heavy casualties totaling twenty thousand men. **8.** Rough wooded terrain caused more destruction to the Israelite army that day than the sword did, illustrated by what happened to Absalom.

9. Riding his mule, Absalom was suddenly confronted by David's forces. As he fled, Absalom's hair evidently became entangled in the branches of a large tree, so that he hung suspended between heaven and earth, while his mule ran on. **10.** A certain man saw it and informed Joab. **11.** Joab was horrified that the informer had not struck Absalom dead on the spot; if he had, Joab would have given him ten pieces of silver and a belt. **12-13.** The man, however, insisted that he would not have taken a thousand pieces of silver, because of the king's command to deal gently with Absalom.

14. Joab, once more showing his impetuous and vengeful character, took three **darts** (RSV) and drove them into Absalom's heart while he was still hanging alive in the center of the tree. **15.** The ten young aides who carried Joab's armor gathered around and struck Absalom. His body must have been grossly mutilated. **16. Joab blew the trumpet** (cf. 2:28; 20:22) and the battle was called to a halt. With the death of Absalom, the rebellion was at an end, and Joab stopped further slaughter.

17. They cast Absalom's body into a great pit in the forest, over which they heaped a large pile of stones. Thus came the inglorious end of the man who put his own lust for power ahead of the Law of God (Josh. 7:26). Everyone was ordered **to his tent**, an expression derived from the life in the wilderness and

436

meaning that everyone returned to his home (Deut. 16:7; Josh. 22:4-8; 1 Sam. 13:2; 2 Sam. 19:8; 20:1, 22).

Absalom's Monument. 18:18. **18.** In his lifetime, Absalom had set up a pillar in **the king's dale** (cf. Gen. 14:17). The exact location of the king's dale or valley is not known. The "tomb of Absalom" is still to be seen in the Kedron Valley, but it dates from Hellenistic-Roman times and has no connection with Absalom's original monument.

The News Is Brought to David. 18:19-32. **19-20.** Ahimaaz, the son of Zadok, pleaded with Joab to let him run with the news to the king. **21.** But Joab turned to a man from Cush and let him run. **22-23.** After the Cushite had departed, Joab yielded to Ahimaaz's pleading and allowed him to run also. **24-27.** David was sitting between the inner and outer gates of Mahanaim ("twin camps"), while the sentinel had gone up to the roof of the gateway by the wall. The sentinel discerned the two runners coming and recognized Ahimaaz. **28-30.** Ahimaaz arrived first, proving himself a fleet runner, but he was a slow narrator of the news. **31-32.** While he was trying to tell the news, the Cushite arrived and more quickly blurted out Absalom's fate.

David's Grief. 18:33. **33.** David's grief as a father was not for his firstborn son, but for his son slain in the very act of outrageous sin, a fact of which he doubtlessly was conscious. Actually, his overwhelming sorrow was the result of his own terrible sin (cf. 12:10). His grief was genuine, but David in one sense was abysmally weak in allowing his feelings to completely outweigh his sense of justice and royal duty. In managing and controlling his family, this great man, like many great men, showed great weakness.

I. DAVID'S REESTABLISHMENT AS KING. 19:1-43.

Joab Reproves David. 19:1-7. **1-2.** David's excessive grief turned the day's victory into gloom and sorrow. **3.** Instead of the troops being welcomed with joy and shouting, they slunk furtively back into the town like people who were ashamed of having been routed in battle. **4-7.** Meanwhile, the king's covering his face as a gesture of deep mourning and crying aloud in lamentation for his son, Absalom, so angered Joab that he broke in on David and severely reprimanded him.

The striking essence of Joab's character appears saliently in his conduct on this occasion. In harshest terms, with his hands still red with the blood of David's beloved son, he reproached the bereaved father for giving way to his grief. With great hauteur and with insolent superiority, he counseled the king. Yet he did so for the king's welfare, and for that of the kingdom, as a wise and loyal statesman.

He accused the king of loving his enemies and hating his friends. For **I perceive that, if Absalom had lived and all we had died this day then it had pleased thee well.** Had Absalom succeeded, he would no doubt not only have slain David, but also, following the common Oriental custom, would have done away with all rival claimants to the throne (cf. Judg. 9:5; 1 Kings 15:29; 16:11; 2 Kings 10:6-7; 11:1).

David Restored to the Kingdom. 19:8-14. **8-10.** Joab's advice was timely, if rude. All the people were in strife, blaming each other and the spirit of disunity that was rife among the tribes of Israel. They realized what David had done for them, but he had fled the country on account of Absalom and was still away from the government. They were asking each other about their hesitation in bringing the king back. **11.** Then the king directed Zadok and Abiathar, the priests, to go to the elders of Judah to inquire why they were so slow about restoring him to his palace, when **all Israel** (i.e., all the other tribes) had come to him to ask for his return. **12.** He told them they were his brothers, his very **bones and . . . flesh.** So why was Judah asked to bring back the king? The reason, of course, was that they had taken a leading part in Absalom's rebellion. The revolt had been fomented in one of their principal cities, Hebron.

13. Therefore, David began political maneuvering to appoint Amasa as the army commander to replace Joab. Amasa, like Joab, was David's nephew. It was a bold, unjust policy to appoint a rebel general, for Amasa should have been punished, not rewarded, for his treason. The move was sure to provoke jealousy and hostility in Joab, whose overbearing conduct, climaxing in the murder of Absalom, had made David more determined than ever to be rid of him. David also took advantage of the opportunity to win over to himself what remained of Absalom's military organization. **14.** Judah invited the king back.

David's Mercy to Shimei. 19:15-23.
15. David began his trip homeward and met with the representatives of Judah at Gilgal (cf. Josh. 5:9) in the vicinity of the fords near Jericho. **16-23.** David's forgiveness of **Shimei, the son of Gera** (cf. 16:5), had in view securing the allegiance of the rebel army, as well as Joab's demotion. David thought Shimei's friendship was necessary to his stability on the throne at that time. Here David was certainly compromising, not trusting the LORD, to say nothing of his failure to inquire of the LORD in the matter. **When he was come over**, rather, "as he was coming over," that is, as David was about to cross, Shimei and

Ziba met the king on the east of the Jordan at its crossing, as David's crossing is not spoken of until verses 31 through 40. Shimei was not strictly of the house of Joseph, but of Benjamin, the name "Joseph" standing for all the tribes outside of Judah (cf. 1 Chron. 5:1-2; Amos 5:15). The king's oath assuring immunity to Shimei was a transaction made purely from a political viewpoint. It was a rash act on David's part to confirm a traitor by an oath in such a way that he was unable to punish any of Shimei's subsequent treasonable acts (1 Kings 2:8-9, 44).

Mephibosheth's Joy. 19:24-30.
24-28. Mephibosheth came to the king when David had arrived back in Jerusalem. David had heard and believed the story of Mephibosheth's ingratitude and treachery (16:3-4). Now it dawned upon David that he had misjudged Mephibosheth, for Jonathan's son gave complete proof of his innocence. **29.** David's conduct toward the lame Mephibosheth cannot be justified. He told Mephibosheth that he and Ziba should divide the land, which was an injustice. Ziba's deception had deserved punishment, but not only was he not punished, he was rewarded. **30.** Mephibosheth's answer to the injustice was beautiful, a sweet echo of Jonathan's love for David. It breathes a very high note of love and devotion almost unequaled in Holy Scripture. **Yea, let him take all, forasmuch as my lord, the king, is come again in peace unto his own house.**

It is obvious in all of these actions that David was operating as a natural man and a mere politician, not guided by the spirit of the LORD. His object was to make himself more attractive to his people and conciliate the different factions. Had he acted in faith, honoring the LORD and calling upon Him, and remembering that He who had called him into the kingdom was able to keep him, he would not have compromised in the fashion he did in this chapter.

Barzillai and Chimham. 19:31-40.
31-40. One high note in this section is the action of the aged and unselfish Barzillai. The rank, the great age, and the beautiful devotion of this Gileadite chief win our admiration. His declining to go to court, his recommendation of (his son?) Chimham, his convoy across the Jordan, and his parting scene with the king present a very elevating and uplifting scene. The mark of royal favor was bestowed upon Chimham. It is very probable that David gave a great part of his personal patrimony in Bethlehem to him and his heirs in perpetuity (cf. Jer. 41:17).

Judah and Israel Quarrel. 19:41-43.
41-43. This silly quarrel, an ominous harbinger of the coming rift between Judah and the other tribes, arose because only a part of the northern tribes had decided to renew their support of David. They therefore took offense at Judah welcoming back David without their consent. They show how easily petty jealousies creep in among the LORD's people and destroy their unity.

J. SHEBA'S REVOLT. 20:1-26.

Sheba's Treachery. 20:1-2. **1.** Sheba, a worthless son of the family of Becher, the second son of Benjamin, took advantage of the serious quarrel that ensued between the men of Judah and the other tribes. His cry, **Every man to his tents,** called the people to war and rebellion (cf. 1 Kings 12:16) and signaled revolt from the house of David. **2. The men of Judah remained steadfast toward their king.** Apparently David's negotiations with Judah knitted that tribe to him. The tribe in whom the rebellion originated, and who had been slow in returning to its allegiance, was now staunch in its loyalty.

The Ten Concubines Isolated. 20:3.
3. Widowed queens of Hebrew kings were not allowed to remarry, but were obliged to spend the rest of their lives in strict seclusion. David treated his harem in the same manner after the outrage committed to them by Absalom.

Amasa's Failure and Death. 20:4-10.
4-5. David had promised Amasa the generalship of his army to supplant Joab. Revolt of the ten tribes in all likelihood hastened the public appointment that he hoped would be popular. Amasa was ordered within three days to levy a force from Judah that would be sufficient to put down the insurrection. The appointment was a blunder and the king soon saw his error. For some reason Amasa could not muster the troops in the required three days.

6-7. Therefore, the king gave the commission to Abishai and not to Joab—a new affront that no doubt wounded the pride of the nation's venerable general. Joab, however, went on with his detachment of soldiers as a second to his brother, determined to take the first opportunity of wreaking his vengeance on his successful rival.

8-10. Amasa went before them. At Gibeon, true to his bloody career, Joab violently killed Amasa. As he went forward to greet Amasa, his sword, fastened to his belt, fell to the ground. Stooping to pick it up, Joab took Amasa **by the beard with the right hand to kiss him**, the customary greeting among some Orientals even to this day. Amasa, completely thrown off guard, was immediately stabbed by Joab. Amasa did not see the sword in Joab's left hand, with which Joab smote him under the **fifth rib** and disemboweled him. Then Joab and Abishai joined in the pursuit of Sheba.

Joab's Craftiness and Sheba's Death. 20:11-22. **11.** One of Joab's men, who was stationed over the body of

Amasa, called to the troops brought up by the dead general: "Whoever favors Joab, whoever is for David, follow Joab" (BV). **14.** Meanwhile, Sheba had marched on toward Abel of Beth-maachah, a town also known as Abel-maim ("meadow of waters"; 2 Chron. 16:4), located about twelve miles north of Lake Huleh and four miles west of Tell el Kadi (Dan) at the site of the village of Abil. **15.** Joab **cast up a mound against the city** so his army could reach a high point of the wall in order to break it down and force an entrance. Similar scenes are depicted on the bas-reliefs of the siege of Lachish.

16-21. A wise woman of Abel suggested to Joab that before he began the siege and possible destruction of the town, he should inquire of the inhabitants as to whether they intended to fight for Sheba or deliver him over (cf. Deut. 20:10-15). Cleverly, the woman suggested to Joab that the city could be spared if the head of Sheba were thrown over the city wall. **22.** Sheba was promptly beheaded and his head thrown to Joab. Calling off the siege, Joab returned to Jerusalem.

David's Officials. 20:23-26. **23.** Joab is listed as the commander in chief of the army. Benaiah, the son of Jehoida, is listed as being over the foreign mercenaries called the Cherethites and the Pelethites, equivalent to "Cretans and Philistines" (cf. 15:18; 20:7; 1 Kings 1:38, 44). **24.** Adoram (Adoniram) was over the forced labor gangs. He held the office till the time of Rehoboam (1 Kings 4:6; 12:18).

IV. HISTORICAL APPENDIX TO DAVID'S REIGN. 21:1—24:25.

A. The Famine and the Philistine Wars. 21:1-22.

The Famine and Its Cause. 21:1-14.

Chronologically, this event must have preceded the Mephibosheth incident of chapter 9, when no sons of Saul except a crippled grandson remained. **1.** The occasion was a three-year famine. Palestinian famines, always due to deficient winter rains, were not uncommon. But a three-year famine was alarming enough to awaken attention and to suggest some special cause. Inquiring of the LORD, the answer came that the reason was Saul and his **bloody house**, better rendered, his "blood-guilty house."

According to the universal ideas of the times, Saul's family and descendants were regarded as having shared in his guilt. Saul had killed the Gibeonites, an atrocity that involved the gross breaking of a solemn covenant relationship sworn before the LORD, as narrated in Joshua 9:3-27. The actual event is nowhere recorded in the Bible, but evidently it occurred as a part of Saul's slaying the priests of Nob (1 Sam. 22:6-19). Apparently Saul was highly intolerant of non-Israelite elements in his kingdom, which the Gibeonites were, in contrast to David's inclusive policy (cf. 2 Sam. 15:24-37).

2. David heard the complaint from the Gibeonites, which he took as the voice of God connecting the crime with the famine. Saul, in trying to consolidate his kingdom, had sought to slay them by rooting out Canaanite enclaves among his people. Saul's act was reckoned as unexpiated murder, since it constituted the breaking of a covenant, which according to Deuteronomy 21:7-9 defiled the land.

3. David inquired of the Gibeonites what they would accept in settlement for their injury: **Wherewith shall I make the atonement ... ?** The literal meaning of the Hebrew expression "to make atonement" is "to cover." The covering was viewed as a hiding of the offense from the eyes of the offended party and as a withdrawing of the guilt of the offender from the eyes of God, who avenged the wrong. Sometimes a settlement was made by money, commonly called "blood money" or by application of the law of revenge.

4-7. The Gibeonites' requirement was that seven of the male descendants in Saul's house would be handed over to them to be put to death and that their corpses would be exposed to the LORD in Gibeah of Saul. These male descendants of Saul were executed for their father's sin (cf. Num. 35:33; Deut. 24:16). The king agreed to hand over the required number of men, but he spared Mephibosheth because of the LORD's oath between himself and Jonathan (1 Sam. 20:12-17).

8. The king took the two sons of Rizpah, Saul's concubine, and five sons of Saul's daughter Merab, whom she had born to Adriel, the son of Barzillai the Meholathite. Merab (not Michal) is the reading of the more correct manuscripts (cf. 1 Sam. 18:19). **9.** David delivered them up to the men of Gibeon, who exposed their broken corpses on the hill in the presence of the LORD. They were put to death in the first days of the barley harvest, which was immediately after the Passover (Lev. 23:10-11) and therefore about the middle of April. **10-11.** The rains of autumn began in October, so Rizpah's watch must have been for about six months. She spread a rough shelter of sackcloth during the long watch. Not until the heavy rains began in October were the people assured of divine forgiveness. Hence, the bodies of the executed were left unburied until then. **12-14.** And David **took the bones of Saul and ... of Jonathan ... and they gathered the bones of those who were hanged** and buried them. He showed his essential merciful and gracious nature

and, moved by the dramatic story of Rizpah's tender care and wishing to display that he cherished no enmity against the house of Saul, had the remains of Saul and his descendants buried honorably.

First Samuel 31:10 says they fastened the body of Saul "to the wall of Beth-shan." It is noted here that the men of Jabesh-gilead took it secretly from **the street.** These two statements are not contradictory, for the exact place where the Philistines hung up the bodies of Saul and his sons to public view was a broad place or square just inside the gate, and they were taken from that same place. The Septuagint adds, "And they were taken down and Dan the son of Joa, of the descendants of the giant, took them down."

David gave an honorable burial to the house of Saul **in Zelah,** a town of Benjamin (Josh. 18:28) near Gibeah. This whole horrible scene of the slaughter of Saul's descendants was evidently the result of David erring in inquiring of the Gibeonites instead of the LORD and in acquiescing to their demand, resulting in the breaking of the Law when the children were executed for the sins of their parents (Deut. 24:16).

Exploits of the Philistine Wars. 21:15-22. In these excerpts of the records of the Philistine battles, four giants are mentioned. They represent the powers of darkness that are behind Philistinism, which the people of God must overcome. **15-17.** The first incident tells of Abishai's rescue of David from a Philistine giant who had attacked him and would have killed him.

18. The second incident is of Sibbecai (1 Chron. 20:4; cf. 11:29), who was captain of the eighth division of David's army. **19.** The third incident is that when **Elhanan, the son of Jaare-oregim, ... slew the brother of Goliath.** This passage has been corrupted in transmission. According to 1 Chronicles 20:5 it should be emended to read, "and Elhanan, the son of Jair, slew Lahmi, the brother of Goliath." Therefore, David slew Goliath (1 Sam. 17), and Elhanan slew the brother of Goliath. This is an example of the fact that the text of 1 and 2 Samuel has suffered more than any other part of the Old Testament, except perhaps Ezekiel, in textual transmission (for more discussion see D. F. Payne, NBC, App. 5, pp. 318-19). **20-21.** The six-fingered and six-toed giant, who haunted Israel, was killed by David's nephew Jonathan, the son of his brother Shimei.

B. DAVID'S PROPHETIC PSALM. 22:1-51.

Praise to the Lord. 22:1-4. **1.** The sacred historian places this psalm in the career of David. The LORD had delivered him from the power of all his enemies, including the power of Saul. He connects the psalm with 2 Samuel 7, written after the LORD'S great Messianic promise to David, delivered through Nathan. David later made slight alterations in it so that it would be better adapted to public worship, and it is included as Psalm 18 of the Psalter. It was customary for certain Old Testament authors or editors to insert poems in prose books for an artistic and religious effect (cf. 1 Sam. 2:1-10). This ode is prophetic and looks beyond the sufferings and triumphs of David to David's Son and LORD, our Lord Jesus Christ. **2-3.** Because the LORD had assured his deliverance, David celebrated the fact that the LORD was his **rock ... fortress ... deliverer ... shield ... horn ... high tower ... refuge,** and **savior.**

The Lord's Presence and Intervention. 22:5-20. **5-7.** When he was in peril of being swept away by the breakers of death and the floods of the wicked, he cried to the LORD in anguish. God heard his voice **out of his temple,** meaning out of "heaven," as in Psalm 11:4. **8-17.** These verses form a description of the LORD'S descent from His heavenly temple like a storm, as at Mount Sinai (Exod. 19:16-20). This great scene was taken up in later poetry (cf. Deut. 33:2; Judg. 5:2-5). However, in this context it is symbolical of God's deliverance of David by less spectacular means.

The Lord's Reward and Approval. 22:21-28. **21.** The LORD rewarded him, David said, for his righteousness, according to the cleanness of his hands (cf. 1 Sam. 26:23; Job 17:9). **22.** He had **kept the ways of the Lord** and had not **wickedly departed from** his God. **24. I was also upright before him,** David said. These words, of course, go beyond David himself to the greater than David.

The Lord's Judgment upon David's Enemies. 22:29-43. **29.** David claimed the LORD as his **lamp** (Psalm 132:17) who turned his darkness to light. **30.** By Him, he says, he ran through a troop. **By my God have I leaped over a wall** (2 Sam. 5:6-8). **31-32.** He praised God for His perfection (Matt. 5:48) and the perfection of His Word (Psalm 12:6), His salvation, and deliverance. **34. He maketh my feet like hinds' feet. 38-40.** David praised God for teaching him to fight against and to defeat his enemies, and for being his shield. He gave God the glory for his military exploits. **43.** With God's help he was able to beat his enemies **as small as the dust of the earth** (2 Kings 13:7). He trampled them **as the mire of the street.**

David's Exaltation over His Enemies. 22:44-49. **43-44.** He praised the LORD also for deliverance from domestic and social problems. He had delivered him from **the strivings of** (his) **people** (3:1). **45.** Foreigners submitted themselves to him. **47.** In all this, God was his rock, **the** rock of (his) **salvation. 48-49.** God avenged him and brought down the people under him. He brought him forth from his enemies. He also had lifted him up on high above those who rose up against him. All of this speaks of Him as David's LORD, who will come in His second advent as the King of kings and LORD of lords, King supreme, Lord supreme, conquering His enemies (cf. Rev. 19:11-15; Psalm 2:1-10).

Praise to the Lord. 22:50-51. David sang praise to the LORD among the nations. He praised God for his great success. The psalm is a prophetic paean of praise to God for His faithfulness in fulfilling the grand terms of the Davidic Covenant (7:1-29), eventuating in the coming Kingdom over Israel (Acts 1:6), merging into the glorious Kingdom extending forever to the new heaven and the new earth of Revelation 21 and 22.

C. DAVID'S LAST WORDS AND HIS HEROES. 23:1-39.

David's Last Words. 23:1-7. **1.** These are the **last words of David.** Both the divine and the human elements of inspiration are stressed to show that this is more than just a farewell. The human author is described as **the man who was raised up on high** (7:8-9). He is called the **anointed of the God of Jacob** and the **sweet psalmist of Israel,** literally, "he that is pleasant in Israel's psalms," that is, because of the composition and arrangement of the liturgical music of Israel, he is called "pleasant" (*nāʿim*, "lovely, sweet, agreeable").

2. The divine aspect of David's last words is emphasized by the fact that the Spirit of God spoke through David, and God's Word was **in** (his) **tongue. 3-4. The God of Israel said.** Like the final blessing of Jacob (Gen. 49), this ode is an inspired prophecy of the Messiah to come and of the saving covenant of which He would be the Mediator, foretold in the grand Davidic Covenant given through Nathan in chapter 7. David prefigures a righteous Ruler over men, a Ruler **in the fear of God,** compared to **the light of the morning** when the sun rises. He is compared to a **morning without clouds, as the tender grass springing out of the earth by clear shining after rain.**

5. David's own house was not like that with God; yet, by wonderful divine grace, God made **an everlasting covenant** with him (cf. chap. 7). **6.** The worthless people, that is, the sons of Belial, wicked sinners, will all be as castaway thorn bushes. **7.** The man who touches them must have iron and the shaft of a spear, and they shall be utterly burned with fire in their dwelling. This speaks of the greater David's conquest over His enemies at His glorious second advent (Rev. 19:11-15; 20:3). In form, this ode of David shows similarity to the prophetic parabolic message of Baalim (Num. 24:15-24).

His Mighty Men. 23:8-39. **8-39.** In line with this last great prophetic utterance of King David, quickly glimpsing the greater than David, are recorded the names of the mighty men of David. They were the men who loved the king and stood by him, displaying their valor and loyalty. Others are given of whom we read no definite deeds. The last name is Uriah the Hittite. A spiritual illustration is not hard to find. Before the judgment seat of Christ, when God's own are rewarded, all will be made manifest (2 Cor. 5:10; cf. 1 Cor. 3:11-14; Rev. 22:12). The divine David comes to be the righteous Ruler to bring in the millennial period—the "morning without clouds" (v. 4). The loyal and the devoted will be remembered. Every person will be judged according to his works, the righteous as well as the unrighteous. Then the righteous, those who have been faithful to the greater David, will receive the rewards of their fidelity. This passage is a continuation of 21:15-22. See 1 Chronicles 11:11-47, where it is also preserved, with some variation in the names and details.

D. DAVID'S FAILURE AND ITS PUNISHMENT. 24:1-25.

The Sin of Numbering the People. 24:1-9. **1. And again the anger of the Lord was kindled against Israel.** The word *again* clearly refers to chapter 21, thus placing this event after the three-year famine because of wrong done to the Gibeonites. The LORD's anger was not because of the numbering of the people, since that had been provided in the Law (Exod. 30:12) and had been repeatedly carried out by Moses (Num. 1, 26). Sin must then be sought in David's motive. It was clearly a military census, not made through the priests and Levites, but through Joab and the army captains.

Prosperity and power had generated pride in David's heart. For the time being, his humble dependence upon the LORD was forsaken and he had a desire to organize his kingdom as a worldly power among the nations of the earth. It was a desire to turn Israel aside from being a simple theocracy (cf. Jer. 17:5). It is stated here that the LORD incited David to take the census, whereas in 1 Chronicles 21:1 Satan is said to be the motivating agent. This is an instance of God using Satan to consummate His purposes. The powers of darkness are frequently used in the sovereign purpose of God. In such instances, whatever comes about under God's permission is attributed directly to God. **2. From Dan even to Beersheba** (Judg. 20:1) describes the entire realm from its northern to its southernmost limit. **That I may know the number of the people.**

These words express the worldliness and pride into which David had allowed himself to fall. **3.** Even the unscrupulous Joab could see the wrong of David's action. Joab's strong objection demonstrated that David's course was obviously wrong. **4.** Joab's objections were sustained by his subordinate officers, but David showed his self-will and selfishness by his insistence on the census.

5. The military men began in Transjordan at Aroer, located on the north bank of the Arnon River (Wadi Mojib; Dennis Baly, *The Geography of the Bible*, p. 237). The site is modern Aro'ir, about fourteen miles east of the Jordan. The census began on the east of the Jordan at the extreme south. From there it passed northward through the eastern tribes and, crossing the Jordan, passed southward through the western tribes. Jazer was a boundary city of Gad (Josh. 13:25). **6.** If Kadesh, Zidon, and Tyre were included, the census must have been taken after David's Syrian campaign (8:3-12; 10:15-19). But these cities were not truly Israelite, even when under the control of David. **9.** Numbers of the census were, in part, mere estimates. Joab undertook the work unwillingly and performed it imperfectly (cf. 1 Chron. 21:2-6).

Here Israel is said to have 800,000 fighting men, while in Chronicles the total is 1,100,000. But no doubt the latter figure includes an estimate of the omitted tribes of Benjamin and Levi, and perhaps portions of other tribes. Judah is said to be 500,000, a round number like all the rest, and in Chronicles, 470,000, the difference being due to any number of imaginable factors.

The Sin Acknowledged and Gad's Message. 24:10-14. **10. David's heart smote him**, meaning that his conscience severely troubled him. This occurred without recorded prophetic rebuke, as in the case of Uriah. Still, it took at least ten months (cf. v. 8) before David became conscious of his sin. He confessed freely before the LORD that he had sinned greatly and asked forgiveness for his foolish course of action.

11-13. After his confession, the LORD undertook by sending the prophet Gad to him. All along Gad had probably been one of David's counselors, but the last time he was referred to was in regard to his warning David to return to the land of Moab (1 Sam. 22:5). It is not until after David had confessed his sin and prayed for pardon that the word of God came to him through the prophet.

Three choices were opened to David. The first was **seven years** of famine. Here the Septuagint reading is to be adopted, agreeing with Chronicles ("three years"), which would also be more in accordance with the "three" months and the "three" days. The second choice was three months of flight before his enemies; and the third was three days of pestilence in the land. **14.** David was in a quandary. A spirit of faith and of dependence upon the LORD returned to him. He placed himself in God's hands rather than come under the punishments in which the will of man seemed to have a greater share.

The Punishment. 24:15-17. **15.** Accordingly, the LORD sent pestilence upon Israel from the morning **even to the time appointed.** This is taken in the King James Version to refer to the three-day period of the plague. However, the phrase may be translated "from the morning until assembly time," referring doubtlessly to the evening sacrifice (Exod. 29:39). In that case, the epidemic of sickness would have been confined to a single day. **Seventy thousand men** died throughout Israel.

16. And when the angel stretched out

his hand to destroy Jerusalem, the LORD felt grief regarding the calamity. The LORD gave orders to the angel, who was causing the destruction to the people, to stop. This occurred when the angel was by the threshing floor of Araunah, the Jebusite (called Ornan in Chronicles).

17. When David glimpsed the angel decimating the people, he cried to the LORD, confessing his sin and admitting that he had acted wickedly. **But these sheep, what have they done?** David employed a common figure, comparing a leader and his people to a shepherd and his sheep (cf. 5:2; Psalm 23). David cried out that the hand of the LORD might be against him and his father's house.

The Altar on Araunah's Threshing Floor. 24:18-25. **18-19.** The threshing floor of Araunah was on the lower hill of Mount Moriah, which afterward became the site of the Temple, this event doubtlessly determining the later Temple site. David at once proceeded to obey the command of the LORD through the prophet Gad to build an altar on the threshing floor. **20-23.** Araunah generously offered to give David the threshing floor for the altar, as well as the sacrificial animals.

24. But David would not consent. **Neither will I offer burnt offerings ... unto the Lord my God of that which doth cost me nothing.** For fifty shekels of silver David bought the oxen and the threshing floor. First Chronicles 21:25 specifies "six hundred shekels of gold by weight." Probably this text speaks of fifty shekels, not of silver, but of money, and the chronicler means that these were of gold in value equal to six hundred shekels of silver. But that does not solve the difficulty completely. In one of these texts the price must have been altered in transcription.

25. Upon the altar ascended the scent

of the burnt offerings and the peace offerings as a sweet savor to the LORD. The LORD answered by fire (1 Chron. 21:26). David before the altar, buying and offering sacrifice in this way and thus meeting the claims of God, prefigures our Lord, who bought us with a great price and offered Himself to God.

It is significant that this book closes with the LORD being merciful to His land and His people. So will Israel under the greater David receive and enjoy His mercy at His second advent. It will be the result of the one great sacrifice, which all the Old Testament sacrifices prefigure.

FIRST KINGS

INTRODUCTION

Title. The two books of Kings logically form a unit and really constitute one book, not two. In the division into two books in the Septuagint, where the twofold division first occurs, Kings is entitled "Of the Kingdoms, 3" and "Of the Kingdoms, 4," with the two divisions of Samuel forming the first and second books of the "Kingdoms." These books continue the "holy" or "prophetic" history (history as recorded through the eyes of the prophet) begun in the preceding books of Samuel. They cover the period from Solomon's accession to the Babylonian Captivity.

Authorship and Date. The precise author is unknown. Although it is possible he may have been Jeremiah, as the Mishnah surmises (Baba Bathra 15*a*), the unknown historian was at least a contemporary of Jeremiah and, like him, a prophet, living under the same influences. That Israel's historians were, for the most part, men who occupied the prophetic office is suggested by the position of 1 and 2 Kings in the second part of the Hebrew canon called "The Prophets" (*neḇi'îm*), along with Joshua, Judges, and 1 and 2 Samuel. The most satisfactory conclusion seems to be that the books of Kings were written by an unidentified prophet in Babylon at about 550 B.C., since the conclusion of 2 Kings reveals remarkable familiarity with events that took place there at that time.

The author was also a compiler who employed a number of sources written by other authors, including (1) "the acts of Solomon" (1 Kings 11:41); (2) "chronicles of the kings of Judah" (1 Kings 14:29); (3) "chronicles of the kings of Israel" (1 Kings 14:19). Specific authors of the firsthand sources are named in the parallel passages in 1 and 2 Chronicles. They include Nathan the prophet, Ahijah the Shilonite, and Iddo the seer (2 Chron. 9:29); Shemaiah the prophet (2 Chron. 12:15); Isaiah, the son of Amos (2 Chron. 26:22; 32:32); and Jehu, the son of Hanani (1 Kings 16:1). The fact that the sources are prophetic and not mere annalistic accounts, which did not dare displease the reigning king, assures a forthright and spiritually instructive account of the kings' reigns, which makes it uniquely a history in which the Holy Spirit could superintend the creative mind of the author-compiler.

Purpose and Aim. The author-compiler set out to convey a message, not merely to record history. His goal was to outline the fortunes of the nation under its various kings in the light of their response to the covenants with the LORD, particularly the Deuteronomic Covenant (Deut. 30:1-11) and the Davidic Covenant (2 Sam. 7:8-15). Since the ruler represented the nation, the author-prophet chose to evaluate each king on the basis of his reaction toward his covenantal responsibility to the Law of the LORD. That was the acid test of whether he "did evil" or "that which was right in the eyes of the LORD" (cf. 14:22; 15:11).

Deuteronomy and the Books of

447

Kings. Undeniably, the religious point of view of Kings and Deuteronomy are similar. Therefore, many scholars hold that Deuteronomy was written in this era (the time of Josiah) to establish the primacy of the Jerusalem Temple. The story that the ancient Mosaic book was recovered in that period, having been lost and utterly forgotten in the deep apostasy of the period (especially during the long and wicked reign of Manasseh), was not fabricated, but instead, it is supported by several fundamental considerations: (1) the pious forgery that the above view makes of a book that is a part of God-breathed Scripture (2 Tim. 3:16); (2) the inability of such a view to explain the complete absence from the book of the name of Jerusalem; (3) and the failure of the theory to account satisfactorily for the detailed Mosaic dress and authentic wilderness background of Deuteronomy.

It is our conviction that the only correct and God-honoring view, reflected in the exposition, is that the authentic book of Deuteronomy, as an essential product of Moses, continued its influence at least to the Davidic-Solomonic era and that the Deuteronomic reforms of Josiah (2 Kings 22-23), as well as the work of the so-called "Deuteronomist" in writing and compiling Kings, were the result of finding Deuteronomy in the Temple during Josiah's reign.

Text. The Dead Sea Scrolls from Qumran, although fragmentary on the text of Kings, give evidence that there was a Hebrew prototype (much earlier than the Masoretic text) that was closer to the Greek Septuagint. This is a warning against blind subscription to the present Hebrew (MT) text, but should encourage critical use of all textual evidence to try to get back to the original Hebrew. A comparison of the Masoretic text with the Septuagint and the Vulgate gives evidence of some editorial alteration and displacement of the text of Kings. It has been seen that the Hebrew text of 1 and 2 Samuel has suffered corruption in places in its transmission. Only on the basis of comparison with all available textual evidence can the original Hebrew be reconstructed. This is the important domain of lower (textual) criticism.

Chronology. The chronological difficulties that arise when the total length of the reigns of the kings of Judah are tallied with those of the kings of Israel are due to several factors not indicated in the text. First, there are a number of coregencies (overlappings in time computations when the successor's reign is calculated by including the years he ruled as coregent). Second, in some instances the accession year was not reckoned, the counting beginning with the new year. In other cases the accession year was counted (see Edwin R. Thiele, *The Mysterious Numbers of the Hebrew Kings*; and "Coregencies and Overlapping Reigns," *Journal of Biblical Literature* 93 (1974): 174-200).

CHRONOLOGY OF FIRST AND SECOND KINGS

by Edwin R. Thiele

Jeroboam	931-910	Rehoboam	931-913	Sheshonq I	945-924
		Abijam	913-911	Tabrimmon	915-900
Nadab	910-909	Asa	911-870	Benhadad I	900-860(?)
Baasha	909-886			Ethbaal I	898-866
Elah	886-885				
Zimri	885			Benhadad I (?)	900-843
Tibni	885-880			Benhadad II (?)	860-843
Omri	880-874	Jehoshaphat	873-848*		
Ahab	874-853	Jehoram	853-841*	Shalmaneser III	859-824
Ahaziah	853-852			Battle of Qarqar	853
Jehoram	852-841	Ahaziah	841	Hazael	843-796
Jehoahaz	841-798	Joash	835-796		
Jehoash	798-782	Amaziah	796-767	Benhadad II (III)?	796-770
Jeroboam II	782-753	Azariah			
		(Uzziah)	791-736*		
Zechariah	753-752			Rezin	750-732
Shallum	752			Tiglath-pileser III	747-727
Menahem	752-742				
Pekahiah	742-740				
Pekah	740-732	Jotham	750-736*	Fall of	
				Damascus	732
Hoshea	732-722	Ahaz	736-716	Shalmaneser V	727-722
Fall of					
Samaria	722	Hezekiah	716-687*	Sargon II	722-705
		Manasseh	696-642*	Sennacherib	705-681
		Amon	642-640	Taharqa	690-664
		Josiah	640-608	Ashurbanipal	669-627
		Jehoahaz	608		
		Jehoiakim	608-597	Nabopolassar	626-605
		Jehoiachin	597	Nebuchadnezzar II	605-562
		Zedekiah	597-586		
		Capture of		Psammeticus II	595-589
		Jerusalem	586		
		Destruction		Apries (Hophra)	589-570
		of Jerusalem	586		
		Jehoiachin			
		Released	562	Amel-Marduk	562-560

*Overlapping coregencies

OUTLINE

COMMENTARY

I. THE UNITED KINGDOM UNDER SOLOMON. 1:1—11:43.

A. SOLOMON ANOINTED AS KING. 1:1-53.

David's Declining Years. 1:1-4. **1. King David was old.** Although only in his seventieth year (2 Sam. 5:4-5), he was prematurely aged. His physical condition is introduced here because the succession to the throne is the subject broached. The king's strenuous life, the exposures and hardships of his youth, the cares and anxieties of his reign, the chastenings through which he had passed on account of his great sin, and many other things were responsible for his enfeebled condition. His last years offer an illustration of the rigid law that "what a man sows, that shall he reap." **2.** The expedient, recommended by David's physician, is still practiced in some Oriental countries, not merely to rekindle lost sexual vigor, but to restore physical vitality in general, under the supposition that inhalation of young breath will give new life and vigor to the exhausted frame. **3.** Abishag, a Shunammite (1 Kings 2:17) was found. She was from Shunem in the land of the tribe of Issachar (Josh. 19:18); Shunem, present-day Sulam, was situated on an eminence on the Plain of Esdraelon five miles south of Tabor. Clearly, Abishag was made a concubine or secondary wife of David (cf. 1 Kings 2:22). **4.** Despite that fact, the king knew her not, meaning he did not have sexual relations with her. The passage only states that the king could not get warm physically, but it implies that he was too weakened to be aroused sexually.

Adonijah's Bid for the Kingship. 1:5-9. **5.** Adonijah ("my Lord is Jehovah") was David's fourth son, born in Hebron (2 Sam. 3:4). As the oldest living son, he laid claim to the throne (cf. 1 Kings 2:22). Amnon and Absalom were dead, and very likely Chileab, or Daniel, was also (cf. 2 Sam. 3:3; 1 Chron. 3:1). David had previously proclaimed publicly that Solomon would succeed him (1 Chron. 22:1-19; 28:1-8); so Adonijah plotted to seize the throne by a coup d'etat. Adonijah, reminiscent of Absalom, showed his intention of being king by employing a bodyguard of fifty men and the maintenance of chariots and horsemen, as Absalom had done (2 Sam. 15:1). **7-9.** Pointing to the same thing was the festal sacrifice with the support of two important leaders in peace and war, Joab and Abiathar, who sided with Adonijah. But Zadok the priest, Benaiah (2 Sam. 8:18; 1 Kings 2:25), Nathan the prophet (cf. 2 Sam. 12:1), and others did not support Adonijah. En-rogel is present-day Bir Ayyub, that is, Job's Well, a spring located at the junction of the Kidron and Hinnom valleys, southeast of Jerusalem. It was considered a sacred place, appropriate for affairs of that kind (cf. 2 Sam. 17:17).

Nathan's Intervention in Behalf of Solomon. 1:10-27. **10-11.** Realizing the gravity of the situation, Nathan knew immediate action must be taken. That neither Solomon nor Benaiah nor he had been invited to Adonijah's feast was a plain enough indication that they were marked for death. This prophet, who had appeared earlier to announce to David the great royal covenant, to tell him that he must postpone the construction of the Temple (2 Sam. 7), and to reprove him for his great sin (2 Sam. 12; Psalm 51), now secured the kingdom for David's son Solomon. He did so by exposing Adonijah's plot to the proper authorities, in this case Solomon's mother, Bathsheba.

12-14. Nathan's plan was for Bathsheba to appeal directly to the king to name his successor before his death. While Bathsheba was talking to the king, the strategy was that Nathan would appear to corroborate her fears. **17-21.** Bathsheba pleaded with David to make a forthright and immediate declaration, saying, **The eyes of all Israel are upon thee. 22-27.** At the precise moment, Nathan appeared on the scene to support Bathsheba's account of Adonijah's rebellion, repeating substantially what Bathsheba had just said.

The Intervention Succeeds as Solomon Is Anointed King. 1:28-40. **28-30.** Bathsheba, who had discreetly retired, was called back by the king. In the presence of Bathsheba and Nathan the prophet, David solemnly swore that Solomon, Bathsheba's son, should be king after him and occupy his throne in his place. **31.** Bathsheba fell on her knees with her face to the ground and paid homage to the king.

32-35. Then David gave a command that Zadok the priest, Nathan the prophet, and Benaiah, the son of Jehoida (2 Sam. 8:18), should put Solomon on the king's own mule and take him down to Gihon, now called the Virgin's Fountain or Mary's Spring, just a short distance north of En-rogel (v. 9),

but out of sight of the latter, because of a curve in the Kedron Valley, in which they are situated, but well within earshot (cf. v. 41). Gihon was the principal source of water for Jerusalem (2 Chron. 32:30); therefore, it was a place of special significance.

36-38. The king's orders were immediately carried out. The Cherethites and the Pelethites (the royal bodyguard) accompanied Solomon's group. **39.** Zadok, the priest, took the horn of oil from the tent and anointed Solomon. Then the trumpet was sounded and all the people shouted, "Long live King Solomon!" (BV). **40.** As the people were shouting and playing flutes, **the earth split with the sound of them.**

The Collapse of Adonijah's Plan. 1:41-50. **41.** Outmaneuvered, Adonijah's plot collapsed. Adonijah and his guests heard the shouting just when they had finished eating. **42-48.** Jonathan, the son of Abiathar the priest, brought the news that David had made Solomon king. **49-50.** Adonijah's guests scattered, while the pretender himself was so fearful of Solomon that he, too, arose and fled and laid hold of the horns of the altar, a place of refuge (Deut. 19:1-13) according to the law of asylum (Exod. 21:12-13; Num. 35:6).

Adonijah's Life Spared. 1:51-53. **51-52.** Solomon then received the report that Adonijah was pleading with the king that he would spare his life. Solomon replied that not one of his hairs should fall to the ground, if he proved worthy. But if evil were found in him, he would die.

B. SOLOMON ACCEDES TO POWER. 2:1-46.

David's Last Charge and Death. 2:1-11. David's final charge was twofold. **1-4.** The first part concerned Solomon. He strictly enjoined Solomon to follow the Law of Moses, particularly the injunctions of Deuteronomy (cf. Deut. 4:40; 5:1; 11:1 — 12:32; 17:14-20). Critics, who make Deuteronomy a pious fraud of Josiah's era, view this as an insertion by a later editor. But Deuteronomy was the Law of Moses and most assuredly in existence from the time of Moses. David lived up to his responsibility to know and to transmit the material in Deuteronomy (cf. Josh. 1:1-9; see Introduction).

5-6. The second part of David's charge was concerning his enemies. These were not decisions made by Solomon and ascribed to David, as some critics maintain. Joab had blatantly murdered David's two generals in time of peace. Abner (cf. 2 Sam. 3:27) and Amasa (cf. 2 Sam. 20:8-10) had both fallen under the hand of Joab. Keil is correct in maintaining that David was unable to punish Joab and therefore committed the responsibility to his son Solomon. Doubtlessly David was also looking to Solomon's welfare, it is true. But retribution was in order for those who had done wrong, and a purge was needed for those who had shown disloyalty to Solomon.

7. David's order to **show kindness** to the sons of Barzillai (2 Sam. 19:37-40) stands out in pleasant contrast. It appears that David had given Barzillai's son, Chimham, an inheritance near Bethlehem, David's own birthplace (cf. Jer. 41:17). **8-9.** A virtual withdrawal of the pardon freely granted to Shimei long before (cf. 2 Sam. 19:18-23) shows that an old grudge still rankled in David's heart, perhaps the result of the bitterness of old age (cf. Psalm 49). Perhaps this order was partly dictated by policy, for the notice of Shimei (2 Sam. 16:5-8; 19:17) revealed him to be a powerful, dangerous champion of the fallen house of Saul. David had kept his oath, but Solomon was under no such oath. **10.**

The king was buried **in the city of David**, evidently Mount Zion (cf. Neh. 3:16, which speaks of the "sepulchers of David"; also see Ezek. 43:7, 9).

Solomon Ascends the Throne. 2:12. **12. And Solomon sat on the throne of David his father, and his kingdom was firmly established** (NASB). This is a summary statement of what follows; it is more fully set forth in 1 Chronicles 29:23-25.

Adonijah's Request. 2:13-25. **13-15.** Adonijah had the effrontery to come to Bathsheba and declare, "You know that the kingdom was mine and that all Israel expected me to be king; however, the kingdom has turned about and become my brother's, for it was his from the LORD" (NASB). His declaration, of course, did not agree with the facts. Bathsheba surely knew it, but she never displayed real moral stamina.

17. Adonijah's request to Bathsheba was that she ask Solomon to give him David's nurse, Abishag. **19-22.** Solomon understood the request to be a claim on the throne (cf. 2 Sam. 3:6-11). According to the common custom of the period, the appropriation of a royal harem was the prerogative of the new king (cf. 2 Sam. 16:21-22). Solomon had a throne chair set beside his throne and sat his mother on the right hand, the place of honor and authority. **23-25.** But her request was denied, and Adonijah was put to death, having made himself vulnerable by his request (2 Sam. 3:6-11; 16:21-22).

Abiathar Deposed. 2:26-27. **26-27.** Abiathar was banished to his hometown of Anathoth, close by modern 'Anata, about three miles northeast of Jerusalem (cf. Jer. 1:1), since as a priest he was sacrosanct. It probably was not Abiathar's character that saved him, but the remembrance of his long friendship with David in adversity (cf. 1 Sam.

22:20-23; 23:8-9). Solomon's dismissal of Abiathar was a fulfillment of the word of the LORD uttered concerning the house of Eli in Shiloh (cf. 1 Sam. 2:27-36).

The Death of Joab. 2:28-35. **28.** When the news came to Joab, he fled to the tent of the LORD and took hold of the horns of the altar (cf. 1:50). **31-33.** Solomon refrained from making any reference to Joab's supporting Adonijah. He referred only to the old crimes dwelt upon in David's dying charge, possibly to bring Joab's case within the emphatic declaration of the Law, that no sanctuary should protect the willful murderer and that innocent blood so shed and left unavenged should not pollute the land (Exod. 21:14; Num. 35:33).

Verses 28 through 34 are an eloquent commentary on the power of the monarchy when a distinguished soldier with a career of faithful service only once tarnished by disloyalty, was condemned to death and apparently accepted the fact without a single act of resistance or word of remonstrance, even though it was at the hands of an as yet young and untried king.

The End of Shimei. 2:36-46. **36-38.** The king called Shimei (cf. v. 8) and placed him under house arrest, warning him that if he left Jerusalem, crossing over the brook Kidron, he would surely be put to death and his blood would be upon his own head (cf. 2 Sam. 15:23; cf. 1:16). **39-46.** But when Shimei went to Gath in Philistia, ignoring the royal warning, Solomon used that as an occasion to fulfill David's command (vv. 8-9; cf. 2 Sam. 19:23). The king's statements, **Solomon shall be blessed, and the throne of David ... established forever,** involved the direct action of Solomon to invalidate Shimei's terrible curse of 2 Samuel 16:7-8 (cf. J. Gray, "Blessing

and Curse," in *Hastings' Dictionary of the Bible*, pp. 109-11).

C. SOLOMON'S PRAYER FOR WISDOM. 3:1-28.

Marriage to Pharaoh's Daughter. 3:1-2. **1.** Solomon made **a marriage alliance with Pharaoh,** literally, he "made himself a son-in-law of Pharaoh." This pharaoh was evidently one of the weak rulers of the twenty-first dynasty ruling in lower Egypt. Solomon brought his Egyptian princess into the **city of David,** on the southeast hill (2 Sam. 5:7). He had not yet finished his own house (cf. 1 Kings 7:1) or the Temple (chap. 6) or **the wall of Jerusalem** (9:15). The marriage was obviously a political arrangement. The dowry was the city of Gezer (9:16), which a number of scholars consider a scribal error for Gerar.

2. Solomon's foreign marriage was not openly denounced, but the danger it invited is hinted at, as well as the peril of worship on the high places (Lev. 17:3-5; Deut. 12:13-14; 1 Kings 11:7-8). This practice of using commanding elevations for altars was very ancient (cf. Gen. 12:7-8; 22:2-4; 31:54). Because these natural sanctuaries were similar to those used for sacrifices to false gods, they were forbidden in the Mosaic Law.

First, the prohibition was to guard against all local corruptions of God's service and all idolatry, such as worshiping Him (as at Bethel) under visible form. Second, it was to prevent the breach of national unity by the rallying of separate tribes around local sanctuaries. Third, it furnished spiritual education for the worship of the invisible God without the aid of local and visible emblems of His presence in preparation for the more perfect spirituality that was to come in the future.

Sacrifice and Dream at Gibeon. 3:3-15. **3-5.** Solomon's love for the

LORD is stressed, but the peril of sacrificing at the high places is hinted at (cf. 11:4, 6, 38). Gibeon (el-Jib), some six miles north of Jerusalem (cf. 9:2), was a renowned high place (cf. 1 Chron. 16:39; 21:29). In His appearance to Solomon, the LORD said, **Ask what I shall give thee.**

6-9. Solomon's reply emphasized the "covenant love." Both David and Solomon had kept the covenant (2 Sam. 7:14-15); hence, the LORD manifested His love toward David in giving him a son to sit on his throne. Therefore, Solomon made his request, prefacing it with **I am but a little child**, or, "a mere lad" (BV). This is an Oriental figure expressing humility, not to be pressed into undue literalism (1 Chron. 22:5; Jer. 1:6-7).

Another figure is **I know not how to go out or come in** (Num. 27:17; 2 Sam. 5:2), also expressing inexperience. In view of his responsibility to the great people the LORD had chosen, Solomon requested an **understanding heart** (lit., "a hearing heart"), meaning a discriminating, open mind Godward, the Orientals viewing the heart as the seat of the intellect and understanding.

10-13. Because the request pleased the LORD, He not only gave Solomon a wise and understanding heart (cf. 4:29, 31; 5:12; 10:24; Eccles. 1:16), but He also gave him what he had not asked for: wealth and honor, so he would be unique in those matters as a king (cf. 1 Chron. 29:12; Prov. 3:16; Matt. 6:29). **14.** The LORD also promised that if Solomon would remain true to Him, He would lengthen his days.

15. Returning to Jerusalem, Solomon made a feast for all his servants. Such a feast customarily followed a sacrifice (cf. 2 Sam. 6:17-19). The king stood before the Ark of the Covenant in the Jerusalem tabernacle, which then constituted a second and probably a still more sacred place of worship. This great sacrifice was distinctly a thank offering.

The Divine Gift of Wisdom Illustrated. 3:16-28. **16-28.** A typical case is now adduced to illustrate the wisdom that God had given Solomon. It was wisdom in a practical sense (cf. v. 28). Solomon received intuitive sagacity, the ability to cut the Gordian knot of a hopeless difficulty—which woman was the mother of the dead infant, and which was the mother of the living infant? Each woman who appeared before him claimed the living child as her own. The problem was solved by Solomon's appeal to maternal instinct. He set a trap for the woman who was not really the child's mother, and she fell into it. Wisely, he awarded custody of the child to the real mother.

D. SOLOMON'S ADMINISTRATION. 4:1-34.

Solomon's High Officials. 4:1-6. **1.** The statement that Solomon was **king over all Israel** looks back retrospectively from the time of the divided kingdom, the period after which the writer-compiler wrote. **2-6.** The officials described belong to two classes: those attached to Solomon's court, and those invested with local authority. **The princes** were the chief officers, which is evident from the fact that two of them married Solomon's daughters.

Azariah, the son of Zadok, the priest, was actually the "prince," as the Hebrew word *kōhēn* frequently signifies (cf. Gen. 41:45; Exod. 2:16; 2 Sam. 8:18, ASV margin). The honor due the priest apparently belonged to another Zadok (cf. 2:35), Abiathar (v. 4) having been deposed (2:27). Azariah, from his precedence in this list, seems to have been a prime minister, the highest office next to the king.

The **scribes** were the secretaries of

state. During David's reign there had been only one. Under Solomon, three dignitaries in that department indicate either improved relations by the division of labor or a great increase in business and prosperity with more extensive diplomatic correspondence with other countries. **The recorder** was the court analyst, which was an office of great significance in Oriental courts. His duties were chronicling everyday occurrences.

Benaiah, who was **over the host**, was the commander in chief of the army, having replaced Joab (1 Kings 2:35). He had been renowned among "the thirty" of David's mighty heroes (2 Sam. 23:20-23; 1 Chron. 11:22-25). **Zadok and Abiathar were the priests**, with Zadok alone discharging the sacred functions, for Abiathar had been banished to his hometown of Anathoth and retained the title of high priest only in name.

Azariah, the son of Nathan, was **over the officers**, apparently the provincial governors enumerated in verses 7 through 19. **Zabud . . . was principal officer, and the king's friend**, apparently a member of the privy counsel and Solomon's confidential friend or favorite. Evidently he was the son of Nathan the prophet. **Ahishar** was the palace steward, while **Adoniram** (Adoram, 2 Sam. 20:24; or Hadoram, 2 Chron. 10:18) **was over the forced labor** (cf. 5:13-14).

Solomon's Administrative Districts. 4:7-19. **7-19.** These districts did not conform to the old tribal boundaries. Some scholars think that this was the reason for the revolt at the end of Solomon's reign, especially since Judah (v. 19) seems to have been exempt from the taxation mentioned in verse 7. The royal revenues were raised by produce of the soil rather than in money payments, which would have been a difficult job. So, to facilitate the work, Solomon appointed twelve officers, each of whom had charge of a particular district, from which the supplies for the maintenance of the king's household were drawn in monthly rotation.

The supplies were first deposited in the "store cities," which were built throughout his kingdom (cf. 9:19; 2 Chron. 8:4, 6). Some of these officials are named after their fathers. For example, Ben-hur is the son of Hur, and Ben-deker is the son of Deker. This practice of not designating persons by their own names but rather as the sons of their fathers still persists into modern times in parts of the Near East.

Solomon's Prosperity, Wisdom, and Poetic Gifts. 4:20-34. This passage summarizes Solomon's greatness. **20.** The happiness and prosperity of the kingdom are stressed. **21.** The extent of the kingdom is described as from **the river**, that is, the Euphrates (cf. 8:65), to the land of the Philistines and the borders of Egypt in the extreme southwest of Palestine (cf. Gen. 15:18). **22-23.** Solomon's food supply for one day consisted of 195 bushels of fine flour, 390 bushels of meal, 10 fat cattle, 20 pasture-fed cattle, and 100 sheep, besides deer, gazelles, roebucks, and fattened fowls.

24. His dominion extended from the Euphrates River, from Tiphsah (Thapsacus), an important crossing or ford on the west bank of the Euphrates River, to Philistia, the other extremity of Solomon's realm being Gaza, a Philistine city. **25.** Solomon prefigures the Lord Jesus Christ in millennial glory, indicated by many details of this narrative, especially the universal peace and prosperity, with Judah and Israel dwelling safely, **every man under his vine and under his fig tree** (cf. Mic. 4:4; Zech. 3:10, where the terminology has clear prophetic millennial connotations).

26. Archaeological excavations at Megiddo, Hazor, and Gezer verify the biblical notations of Solomon's building operations there, especially at Megiddo, the great thirteen-acre mound in the Valley of Esdraelon that was the headquarters of Solomon's fifth administrative district. There notable discoveries dating from Solomon's era have been made. A group of stables, capable of housing at least 450 horses and about 150 chariots, has been uncovered.

Similar groups of stables from Solomon's time at Hazor and Tell el-Hesi add other evidence of Solomon's splendor and military power. Biblical evidence, substantiated by archaeology, is that Solomon was the first king of Israel to employ horses and chariots in fighting. The amassing of chariots and horses was a dangerous practice (Deut. 17:16).

29-30. Solomon's wisdom was God-given and excelled the wisdom of **all the children of the east country**, that is, "Easterners," as well as **all the wisdom of Egypt** (cf. Isa. 9:11-12; Acts 7:22). Egypt was also renowned as a seat of learning and science in antiquity, as existing monuments show. **31.** Solomon is said to have been **wiser than all men**, that is, than all his contemporaries, either at home or abroad, including **Ethan**, or Juduthun, of the family of Merari (1 Chron. 6:44); and **Heman**, who is referred to in 1 Chronicles 15:17-19. Ethan composed Psalm 89, and Heman, Psalm 88. They, with **Calcol, Darda,** and **Zimri** are referred to in 1 Chronicles 2:6 as five famous brothers of the tribe of Judah.

32. Solomon's proverbs embody his moral sentiments and sage observations on human life and character, some of them being preserved in the book of Proverbs. His poetic gifts are evidenced by a thousand and five **songs** (or "psalms"; cf. Psalms 72, 127, 132) and the "Song," "Canticles," or the "Song of Songs" (i.e., "*The* Song par excellence"). **33.** Solomon also had a deep knowledge of botany. Few of the fruits of his gigantic mind have come down to us, only the portion that was divinely inspired being preserved.

E. PREPARATIONS TO BUILD THE TEMPLE. 5:1-18.

The Help of Hiram of Tyre Enlisted. 5:1-12. **1.** Hiram I (c. 969-936 B.C.) ruled at Tyre and bore the official title "King of the Sidonians" (cf. the expression "Sidonians" in 11:1, 33). From the twelfth to the seventh centuries B.C., Tyre and Sidon existed as one political entity. Consequently, Hiram was a rich and powerful ruler. In winning and maintaining his friendship, Solomon gave a demonstration of his proverbial wisdom. Hiram must have been a very young ruler (perhaps coregent) in the latter part of David's reign (c. 1011-971 B.C.). Yet David, in line with his general foreign policy, carefully cultivated ties of friendship with him (cf. 2 Sam. 5:11-12).

2-6. Solomon reminded Hiram that his father, David, had purposed to build a temple to the LORD, but that he was unable to do so because of the incessant wars of his reign; now, with peace all about him and his enemies conquered, Solomon expressed his intention to build the house for the name of the LORD his God. He agreed to furnish Hiram agricultural products (v. 9), so needed by the Phoenicians, in exchange for timber and other materials for the Temple.

7-10. Hiram received Solomon's message with delight and commended Solomon's wisdom. He sent back word that he was ready to cooperate and would furnish cedar and cypress lumber from the Lebanon region to be floated to the sea to be received at the port of Joppa (Jaffa). **11.** In exchange, Solomon gave Hiram twenty thousand measures or cors (one cor equals fifty gallons dry measure) of wheat for his household and twenty thousand measures or cors (one cor equals 58 gallons) of pure olive oil annually. **12.** Solomon and Hiram made a treaty.

The Corvée in Israel. 5:13-18. **13.** Solomon raised a battalion from all Israel of conscripted laborers, totaling thirty thousand men. **14.** Each month ten thousand of them went by turn to Lebanon. This harsh measure became workable because one month in Lebanon was alleviated by two months at home. **Adoniram** was in charge of the corvée. He was also called Adoram and Hadoram (2 Sam. 20:24; 2 Chron. 10:18; cf. 1 Kings 4:6; 12:18). One reason for the later breaking up of the kingdom was forced labor (cf. 12:4).

15-16. Solomon also had seventy thousand men who carried burdens and eighty thousand stone cutters in the mountains, where the stone was cut for the Temple. Thirty-three hundred foremen directed the work. **17.** The king ordered that costly stones be quarried to lay the foundation of the Temple with squared (dressed) stone. **18.** From Gebal, present-day Byblos, thirteen miles north of Beirut on the Mediterranean coast, came workers who quarried stone and prepared both timber and stone for the Temple's construction. Thus, in planning the Temple, Solomon drew upon the skill of the Tyrians, that is, the Phoenicians, plus the slave labor of conquered peoples and the enforced labor of Israelites.

F. THE BUILDING OF THE TEMPLE. 6:1-38.

The Date of the Undertaking. 6:1. **1.** The fourth year of Solomon's reign would be in the vicinity of 967 B.C. (following Thiele's chronology). This would place the Exodus at 1447 B.C. Late date theorists, who argue for a date a century and a half later, reject this verse as a gloss, but on insufficient grounds. The early date, substantiated by this passage, is undoubtedly the true one, since it underlies the whole time scheme of the Pentateuch during the early history of Israel until the time of Solomon. The month of Ziv came in the spring (April-May).

The Design of the Temple. 6:2-13. **2-6.** The Temple itself was in all of its proportions an exact copy of the tabernacle, with each dimension being doubled; therefore, the whole structure was a cubicle eight times larger than the tabernacle (cf. Exod. 26:16-23). Calculating eighteen inches for the cubit, the dimensions would be ninety feet long, thirty feet wide, and forty-five feet high. Even if the larger cubit (around twenty-one inches) were employed, the size would still be comparatively small.

The structure had three rooms: the vestibule, or entrance hall, about thirty feet wide and ten feet deep; the nave or main room, about sixty feet long (v. 17); and the inner sanctuary, or Holy of Holies, a perfect cube of about thirty feet (v. 20). The side chamber surrounded the nave and the inner sanctuary, but not the vestibule. **7. Neither hammer nor axe . . .** (was) **heard,** a provision made with due regard for reverence. The project involved much labor and skill.

9. This verse suggests that the house was roofed with cedar. Archaeology has revealed that the Solomónic plan of the edifice was characteristically Phoenician, as would be expected, since it was built by a Tyrian architect (7:13-15). Similar ground plans of sanctuaries of the general period from 1200 to 900 B.C.

have been excavated in northern Syria, for example, at Tell Tainat in 1936, and demonstrate that the findings reveal the Solomonic structure to have been pre-Greek and authentic for the tenth century B.C.

Like Solomon's Temple, the shrine at Tell Tainat was rectangular with three rooms, a portico with two columns in front, a main hall, and a cella or shrine with a raised platform. It was two-thirds as long as Solomon's Temple and was in all likelihood lined with cedar. The New Testament expands the typology of the tabernacle, but not the Temple, in the book of Hebrews.

The Interior of the Edifice. 6:14-22. **15-16.** The interior walls were paneled in cedar from the floor to the rafters. The floor was done in cypress. **18.** The cedar in the interior of the Temple was carved in the form of gourds and open flowers. **20.** The inner sanctuary was overlaid with pure gold. **22.** In fact, he overlaid the entire inside of the house with pure gold, including the altar. (For the typical symbolism, see comments on the tabernacle in Exodus.)

The Cherubim. 6:23-28. **23-28.** The cherubim were characteristically Syro-Phoenician, the latter being a winged lion with human head, that is, a winged sphinx. This hybrid animal, however, was not a Solomonic innovation. It was inherited from the tabernacle and appears hundreds of times in the iconography of western Asia between 1800 and 600 B.C. Many representations are found with a deity or king seated on a throne, supported by two cherubs.

In Israel, the Deity and His throne, both invisible, were similarly supported by symbolic cherubim (W. F. Albright, OTC, p. 148; and *Archaeology and the Religion of Israel*, p. 216, n. 65). Archaeology greatly illuminates the meaning of the cherubim in Solomon's Temple and in the early tabernacle and enables us to translate 1 Samuel 4:4 thus: "the ark of the covenant of the Lord of hosts who is *enthroned above the cherubim.*"

The cherubim were symbolic of God's holy presence and unapproachability. They are celestial beings who guard and vindicate the righteousness of God (see Gen. 3:24; Exod. 26:1, 31; 36:8, 35); the mercy of God (cf. Exod. 25:22; 37:9); and the government of God (cf. 1 Sam. 4:4; Psalms 80:1; 99:1; Ezek. 1:22, 26). In the Holy of Holies God's glory resided between the cherubim (Psalm 80:1; cf. Exod. 25:10-22). The cherubim (cherubs) stood ten feet apart in the sanctuary, with the intermediate space used for the Ark of the Covenant (cf. 1 Kings 8:6-7). The cherubim were made of olive wood overlaid with gold (see tabernacle symbolism in Exodus).

Decorations and Doors. 6:29-36. **29.** All the walls of the house were carved with figures of cherubim, palm trees, and open flowers. **30.** The floor of the house was overlaid with gold in the inner and outer rooms. **31-32.** The doors to the entrance of the inner sanctuary were made of olive wood overlaid with gold. **33-34.** Two folding doors were made of cyprus wood. **35.** The decorations were of cherubim, palm trees, and open flowers overlaid with pure gold, evenly applied upon the carved work. Simple decorations, such as open flowers, palmettes, and also the cherubim were characteristically Syro-Phoenician.

The Date of Completion. 6:37-38. **37-38.** It took seven years to build the Temple, which was finished in the eleventh year in the month of Bul (the month of rain, Oct.-Nov.).

G. THE DETAILS OF THE TEMPLE DESCRIBED. 7:1-51.

The Palace Complex. 7:1-12. **2-8.**

This section describes the building of the royal palace, including the hall of state or **the House of the Forest of Lebanon** with its porches, **the Hall of Pillars, the Hall of the Throne** or **Hall of Judgment** (RSV), the royal residence, and the queen's residence. These buildings evidently constituted the large group of edifices enclosed in a great court situated on the western hill opposite the Temple on Mount Moriah.

Jachin and Boaz. 7:13-22. **13-14.** Solomon sent to King Hiram for a man skilled in working on the various parts and furnishings of the Temple. Hiram was sent (cf. 2 Chron. 2:7, 13-14). Hiram's mixed parentage would enable him to enter into the spirit of the Israelite worship and yet put into it his practical skill as a famed Phoenician craftsman and artist.

15-22. Described here are the two pillars set up at the entrance of the Temple, one called **Jachin** ("He shall establish") and the other **Boaz** ("in Him is strength"). Like the north Syrian shrine discovered at Tell Tainat, Solomon's edifice had two columns that stood within the portico. Such pillars flanking the main entrance of a temple were common in the first millennium B.C. in Syria, Phoenicia, and Cyprus.

In Solomon's Temple, following a common Oriental custom, they bore the distinctive names of Jachin and Boaz. It has been convincingly demonstrated that the names of the two columns represented the first words of dynastic oracles that were ascribed upon them (cf. R. B. Y. Scott, JBL 58 (1939): 143 ff.; and Paul L. Garber, "Reconstructing Solomon's Tabernacle," BA 14 (Feb. 1951): 8-10). The Jachin formula may have been something like "Yahweh will establish [*yākîn*] thy throne forever." The Boaz oracle, on the other hand, may have run, "In Yahweh is the king's strength [*bō'ăz*]," or a similar formula.

The best interpretation of these columns is not that they were obelisks, stylized trees, or cosmic pillars (like the pillars of Hercules), but, rather, gigantic cressets or fire altars. Each of the shafts of the two pillars is said to have been crowned with a *gŭllāh* ("oil basin") of a lampstand (cf. v. 41; Zech. 4:3). Thus, following Phoenician models, these lofty incense stands graced and illuminated the magnificent facade of the Temple on Moriah, reminding worshipers of the pillar of fire and cloud that had led Israel through the wilderness wanderings.

The Molten Sea. 7:23-26. **23-26.** Solomon went far beyond the chaste, divinely ordered simplicity of the tabernacle with its symbolic ritual and furniture. Instances of this are not only Jachin and Boaz, but also the great copper sea set on twelve bulls and oriented toward the four quarters of the compass, a new feature of the sanctuary court. This immense basin took the place of the simple laver of the tabernacle. It was ornately decorated with **knobs** ("gourds") and bunches of **flowers**, with fruits in relief. **38.** The relation of the "sea" to the portable lavers that Solomon made, which correspond to Phoenician portable lavers found on the island of Cyprus, was similar to that between the "sea" (*apsû*) and the portable basins of water (*egubbê*) in Babylonian temples (cf. W. F. Albright, *Archaeology and the Religion of Israel*, p. 149).

Solomon's heavy indebtedness to Syro-Phoenician religious architecture and practices presented the peril of religious syncretism, which manifested itself in intermittent conflict between religious assimilators and separatists in subsequent centuries. Evidently Solomon first succumbed to the dangerous precedent in allowing shrines and altars of foreign deities to be built in the immediate environs of Jerusalem itself (cf. chap. 11).

The Ten Bronze Lavers. 7:27-39. **27-29.** Following his ambitious plans, Solomon made ten bases (stands) of bronze ornamented with lions, oxen, cherubim, and wreaths of beveled work. These ten stands were highly decorated bronze wagons; on each of them was placed one of the ten lavers or washbasins. **30.** Each stand had four wheels and axles of bronze, and at its corners were supports for a laver. **31-37.** The construction of these portable lavers and their decoration are described. **38-39.** The size of the stands and the lavers is specified, as well as their position—five on the south side of the house and five on the north, with the sea (the huge laver) on the southeast.

Other Castings. 7:40-47. **45.** The skilled technician, Hiram, also made pots, shovels, basins, and other articles of burnished bronze for the Temple. **46.** In the plain of the Jordan, the king had them cast in the clay ground between Succoth and Zarethan (cf. Gen. 33:17; Judg. 8:5, 16). Succoth is modern Tell Akhsâs or Tell Deir Allah in the Jordan Valley. Zarethan is identified by Nelson Glueck (*The River Jordan*, pp. 154-55) with Tell al-Sa'idiya.

The Vessels of Gold. 7:48-51. **48-49. The altar of gold** is the altar of incense (see Exod. 30:1-10). The table of showbread (see Exod. 25:23-30; 37:10-15) was also made of gold (for the showbread itself, see Lev. 24:5-9). Whether the ten candlesticks of pure gold were to supersede the one seven-branched lampstand made for the tabernacle (Exod. 25:31-40; 37:17-24) or were to be used in addition to it is not specified. These articles of worship and the furniture of the Tabernacle, which speak so eloquently of the deity of Christ, the coming One, were made of pure gold (symbolic of deity). **51.** The things that David had dedicated (see 1 Chron. 18:7-8, 10-11; 22:3-5, 14-16; 28:14-18; 29:2-5) were stored by Solomon in the Temple's treasuries. That which was dedicated by a father to the LORD ought not to be alienated from the LORD by his children.

H. THE DEDICATION OF THE TEMPLE. 8:1-66.

The Ark Brought into the Temple. 8:1-11. **1-2.** Solomon brought to Jerusalem all the elders of Israel, all the heads of the tribes, and all the princes or leaders of the clans to transfer the Ark of the Covenant of the LORD from the city of David to its new abode in the splendid Temple. **The city of David**, or **Zion**, was south of the Temple area in the city's southeastern quarter. The month of Ethanim, or Tishri, occurred in the autumn (Sept.-Oct.). Therefore, the dedication of the Temple was postponed for eleven months (cf. 6:38) in order to make it part of the great autumnal Feast of Tabernacles.

3-9. The great feast of ingathering (Lev. 23:33-44) was both memorial and prophetic. It was memorial of redemption out of Egypt (Lev. 23:43), and prophetic as to the Kingdom rest of Israel after her regathering and restoration, when the feast will again become memorial, not for Israel alone but for all nations (Ezek. 34; Zech. 14:16-21; cf. Rev. 21:3).

The Ark of the Covenant was then transported out of the tabernacle to the most holy place in the Temple. This symbol of the LORD's presence was carried by the Levites according to the instruction of the Law (cf. 2 Sam. 6:6-11). A great sacrificial ceremony took place. The Ark had at last found its permanent resting place (Psalm 132:8). The staves by which the Ark had been carried were drawn out, but not removed (Exod. 25:15). They remained as a memorial of Israel's journey and the LORD's faithfulness in bringing them into the promised rest.

Especially note that nothing was in the Ark except **the two tables of stone.** This emphasis, repeated in 2 Chronicles 5:10, seems intended to make it evident that "nothing else was ever in the ark" (JFB, 2:315). The various things laid up "before the testimony"—the pot of manna (Exod. 16:33-34), the rod of Aaron (Num. 17:10), the copy of the Law (Deut. 31:24-26), but *not* the Ten Commandments engraved on stone— were not *in* the Ark, according to what is actually stated in each case, but were "at the side of the ark." This clear statement must be determinative in the interpretation of Hebrews 9:4, in which no stress need be laid on the literal accuracy of the word "wherein" (KJV).

The purpose of the passage is simply to present a general description of the Temple, its chief parts, and its most sacred furniture. The fact that the tables of the Law written on stone were placed in the ark (cf. Exod. 25:16; 40:20) points to the moral nature of God, His being very truth and righteousness. His purpose for all His creatures, especially His redeemed creatures, is to write His Law on their hearts and minds (Jer. 31:33). The very name of the coming Messiah, to whom all the religious ritual looked, was *YHWH ṣidqēnû* ("Jehovah, our righteousness," cf. Jer. 23:6). **10-11.** **The cloud** of God's presence was manifested; thus, **the priests could not stand to minister** (cf. Exod. 40:35).

Solomon's Speech. 8:12-21. **12-13.** The thick darkness refers to the fact that the inner sanctuary had no windows, causing total darkness except when the door was open on rare occasions. The

poetic prologue, according to the Greek version, was taken from the book of Jasher (Josh. 10:13). **15-21.** The king's address to the people stressed the fulfillment of God's word to Solomon's father, David, and to himself. The LORD had set him on the throne and enabled him to build the Temple.

Solomon's Prayer. 8:22-66. Throughout all this account, especially in the bringing of the sacrifices, Solomon apparently assumed the full character of a priest. He acted as king-priest, another Melchizedek, king of Salem, in which he foreshadowed our Lord in His Kingdom role of King-Priest, when He shall be the "Priest upon his throne" (Zech. 6:13). Now our Lord is upon the Father's throne, a Priest and an Advocate of His people (Rev. 3:21). When He comes at His second advent in glory, He will have His own throne and occupy it as a priest. Despite Solomon's subsequent failure, his reign of peace and prosperity, and especially his great work of building the Temple foreshadow the coming fulfillment of the Davidic Covenant in the enthroned Christ on the millennial throne of His father David.

43. This verse looks forward to the ingathering of the nations into the Kingdom, when the nations shall be joined to restored Israel (cf. Zech. 2:11; 8:23). **65.** The conjunction of the dedication of the Solomonic Temple with the Feast of Tabernacles is prophetic of that time when the Lord Jesus Christ will occupy the throne and build the temple of glory (Ezek. 40-44). The nations will then seek after Him (Isa. 2:1-4). While the king prayed and blessed the people, the people—full of happiness and joy— blessed the king. Heaven and earth rejoiced, as will be the case during the Kingdom reign. This climax of Israel's history in the land prefigures the future millennial restoration when the Davidic Covenant will be fulfilled, the Kingdom restored over Israel (Acts 1:6), and the millennial Temple built (Ezek. 43:1-5; cf. Num. 14:21).

I. THE LORD APPEARS TO SOLOMON A SECOND TIME. 9:1-28.

The Lord's Appearance and Warning. 9:1-9. This portion constitutes the conclusion of the detailed narrative of the preceding chapter. **1-2.** At the height of Solomon's prosperity and power the LORD appeared to him the second time in promise and solemn warning (cf. 3:5). **3-9.** Solomon was told his prayer was heard and that the LORD had put His name in the Temple **forever**. These words simply marked the Temple as the settled habitation for the divine presence to abide in permanently (cf. 8:13) in contradistinction to its changing abode in the movable tabernacle. However, that the word "forever" had a wider significance is plainly declared to be dependent on Israel's fidelity (cf. vv. 7-8). Nothing is declared in this communication to contradict the original declaration that even in case of sin, the mercy of God would chastise but not forsake the house of David (2 Sam. 7:13-14; Psalm 89:30-37). In case of disobedience, the Temple itself would be destroyed and the dynasty of David interrupted, but the throne actually would be perpetuated forever.

Again and again in prophecy, captivity is announced as the penalty for Israel's sin. But the hope of the restoration of the Israelite nation is always held out (cf. Amos 9:9-11; Acts 15:14-15). It is plain, therefore, that part of the Davidic Covenant is conditional, envisioning the penalty of apostasy—the interruption of a Davidic incumbent on the throne, the destruction of the Temple, and the carrying away of the people into captivity. However, the unconditional elements of the Davidic Covenant will be fulfilled by the greater than Solomon, the Lord Jesus Christ. He will establish a Kingdom forever, a throne forever, and a people forever in the coming millennial age. Then restored Israel will be the nation through which He will reign as King-Priest over all the nations of the earth, His Kingdom finally merging into the eternal state, following the millennial age (Rev. 21-22).

Solomon's Relations with Hiram. 9:10-14. **10-11.** Because Hiram of Tyre had supplied Solomon with cedar and cyprus timber and as much gold as he wanted, enabling him to finish his building operations, Solomon transferred twenty cities in Galilee to Hiram. This transaction of delivering Hebrews to pagans was certainly contrary to God's will. Thus, God's blessing was not upon the move.

12-13. Hiram complained about the cities, calling them **the land of Cabul.** The city of Cabul is mentioned in Joshua 19:27; it was in the territory of Asher, evidently on the Tyrian frontier. Perhaps Hiram took this name and applied it to the whole territory, by a play of words upon it, signifying his discontent with Solomon's gift. Ewald proposes a Hebrew derivation of the word meaning "as nothing, as nought." Hiram's displeasure does not necessarily mean that he did not keep the cities (cf. Prov. 20:14). However, it appears that they were afterward restored to Israel (2 Chron. 8:2), although no reason is given.

14. The **six score** (120) **talents of gold** (more than 5½ tons) is a large amount, though little more than a sixth of Solomon's yearly revenue (cf. 10:14), and apparently it refers back to verse 11 and explains the amount of gold Hiram had sent. The amount was considered a payment in acknowledgment of the gift of the cities. But Hiram evidently reckoned the gold he gave Solomon to be of greater value than the Israelite cities he had been given as compensation for it.

The Corvée and Its Purpose. 9:15-23. **15. This is the reason** ("the account") **of the forced labor** (cf. 5:13-18; 2 Chron. 8:3-10; Josephus *Antiquities* 8. 6. 4). The corvée involved pressing non-Israelites into slave labor. Apparently as Solomon's regime declined, Israelites were also forced into service. The forced labor was used to build the huge construction projects in Jerusalem and elsewhere. The **Millo** was a defense work in Jerusalem built upon a mound or fill. Outside Jerusalem, Solomon used the corvée to build Hazor in northern Galilee and Megiddo, one of the most important fortifications controlling a pass between the Plains of Jezreel (Esdraelon) and Sharon. Archaeology reveals the fortifications at each site.

16. The pharaoh who took Gezer, burned it, and gave it as a present to his daughter, Solomon's wife, is unidentified. Scholars are inclined to emend Gezer to Gerar (see 3:1). **17. Beth-Horon the lower** controls one of the approaches to Jerusalem. **18. Baalath** (cf. Josh. 19:44) is southwest of Beth-Horon (Josh. 15:11) in the original tribe of Dan. **Tamar** is evidently in **the land of Judah** (RSV), not Tadmor or Palmyra in the Syrian Desert, and was located on the southeastern limits of the land (Ezek. 47:19; 48:28).

22. It is specifically said that Solomon did not make slaves of Israelites (cf. 5:13; 11:28). Archaeology has illuminated Solomon's building operations at Gezer, Hazor, and Megiddo, especially the latter, which was the headquarters of Solomon's fifth administrative district. His stables, housing at least 450 horses and about 150 chariots, have been excavated at Megiddo.

Pharaoh's Daughter's House and the Millo. 9:24. **24.** See 2 Chronicles 8:11, which gives the following reason for the removal of the queen from Egypt out of the city of David to the house that Solomon had built for her (cf. 1 Kings 3:1): "My wife shall not dwell in the house of David, king of Israel, because the places are holy, to which the ark of the LORD hath come." In the present passage, the notice of the queen's withdrawal is apparently connected with the building of "the Millo" (cf. v. 15). Perhaps that encroached upon her former quarters in the city of David.

Solomon's Offerings. 9:25. **25.** Whether or not Solomon actually assumed the role of a priest, his role here appears as that of a king-priest, prefiguring the greater Solomon's millennial role as King-Priest during the Kingdom age. No doubt these offerings were made at the three great annual feasts, the Passover, the Feast of Weeks, and the Feast of Tabernacles (cf. 8:63).

Solomon's Red Sea Fleet. 9:26-28. **26.** Ezion-geber is Elath (Eloth), Israeli Eilat, at the northern extremity of the present-day Gulf of Aqaba. This harbor served as a terminal port for Solomon's Red Sea (Tarshish) trading fleet to Ophir and Arabia. Solomon developed copper and iron mining and smelting in the Arabah, north of Ezion-geber at Tell el-Kheleifeh, a few miles west of Aqaba (old Elath). **28.** Ophir is probably located in south Arabia, or in Punt on the east coast of Africa, or in India, as some scholars suggest. Iron and raw copper were used in trading exotic wares from distant lands. This trading venture was immensely profitable. A talent of gold consisted of three thousand shekels (about ninety-two pounds).

J. THE VISIT OF THE QUEEN OF SHEBA. 10:1-29.

The Queen and Her Entourage.

10:1-5. **1. Sheba** is likely Saba in southwest Arabia (modern Yemen), mentioned in cuneiform sources from the eighth and seventh centuries B.C. Though queens played little part in the later history of south Arabia, they ruled large tribal confederacies in north Arabia from the ninth to the seventh centuries B.C. Some scholars identify this queen with the colony of Sheba in north Arabia. Solomon's ships plied the Red Sea, his caravans penetrating far into Arabia. His wide commercial outreach must have offered competition to the famous queen.

2. So the queen's strenuous journey to Jerusalem by camel, perhaps traversing over twelve hundred miles of inhospitable terrain, was certainly dictated by business reasons as well as by the desire to see Solomon's splendor and to test him with perplexing questions.

3. In biblical times it was customary royal sport for rulers with a reputation for some skill to test each other's abilities. The visit must have involved delimitation of spheres of commercial interest and arrangement of trade treaties to regulate the equitable exchange of the products of the Arabah and of Palestine for the gems, spices, and incense of the desert areas.

4-5. When the queen became fully aware of Solomon's wisdom and splendor, **there was no more spirit in her**, meaning she was "breathless" with amazement. It is difficult to define what is meant by Solomon's **ascent by which he went up unto the house of the Lord.** Perhaps this was a viaduct crossing the valley from the palace to Mount Moriah and forming the royal entrance into the Temple (cf. 2 Kings 16:18; 1 Chron. 26:16), apparently a unique and remarkable structure.

However, the Septuagint, the Vulgate, and other versions render it, "the burnt offerings, which he offered in the house of the Lord," and Josephus follows the same interpretation. Certainly the magnificent scale of Solomon's sacrificial offerings was noteworthy (cf. 8:63). It is undeniably natural that this point should not be left unnoticed in the wonders of Solomon's court. This is the literal rendering of the Hebrew: "And his burnt offerings which he offered at the house of the Lord" (RSV), and is very likely correct.

The Queen's Words and Gifts to Solomon. 10:6-10. **6-9.** The queen highly praised Solomon's wisdom and prosperity and congratulated him and his court. Her words in verse 9 are an echo of the Davidic Covenant and are actually Messianic in their content (cf. Psalms 2, 110; Isa. 9:6-7; 11:1-5). **10.** The gift of 120 talents of gold weighed about 5½ tons. South Arabia was famous for spices. The visit was remembered particularly for the abundance of spices that the queen brought.

Solomon's Gifts to the Queen. 10:11-13. **11-12.** The wealth brought to Solomon by his fleet (cf. 2 Chron. 9:10-11; Josephus *Antiquities* 8. 71) is not a break in the story of the queen's visit; the parallel in Chronicles has the same thing. This note is introduced to accentuate Solomon's fabulous wealth and to show that he was able to give the queen whatever she might desire. Almug wood (also spelled "algum"; cf. 2 Chron. 2:8) may possibly have been red sandalwood. It was made into supporting beams and musical instruments. **13.** Solomon's gifts to the queen are hinted at, but not expressly described. Introductory verses suggest that they were very great and costly.

Solomon's Wealth. 10:14-21. **14.** Solomon's annual income of gold was 666 talents, or more than 25 tons. **15.** Besides that he had a large income from the incense and precious-stone trade with the kings of Arabia and the governors of the land. **16.** Solomon also made 200 **bucklers** or large shields of beaten gold, each shield containing 600 shekels, or about 18 pounds, of gold. **17.** His 300 smaller shields of beaten gold contained three minas, or about 3¾ pounds, of gold in each shield. These were placed in the house of the forest of Lebanon.

18-20. The king's great ivory throne, overlaid with the finest gold, had six steps decorated with lions (symbols of kingship), and at the back of the throne was a calf's head, denoting service and indicating that he who was king was also God's servant as well as the people's servant. Also, a motif of lions adorned the side of each armrest. **21.** So wealthy was Solomon that all his drinking vessels were of gold, for silver was not accounted as being of much value in his day.

Solomon's Navy. 10:22-25. **22.** Solomon's **navy** or "Fleet of Tarshish" (*'ŏnî ṭărshîsh*) was a "smeltery" or "refining" fleet that brought smelted metal home from the colonial mines. Phoenician boats used to ply the sea regularly, transporting smelted ore from the mining towns in Sardinia and Spain. One of these descriptions from Nora in Sardinia contains the name Tarshish immediately before the name Sardinia, indicating that the Phoenician name of Nora was "Tarshish," meaning "the refinery."

As a result of Solomon's copper mining in the Araba, refined copper became the king's principal export from his Red Sea port and his merchants' main stock in trade (cf. Nelson Glueck, *The Other Side of Jordan*, p. 98). Coming out from Ezion-geber laden with smelted ore, Solomon's "Tarshish fleet" brought back in exchange other valuable goods obtainable in Arabian ports or from the nearby coast of Africa. The products were gold, silver, ivory, apes, and peacocks and two species of baboons (see BV).

Solomon's Horse and Chariot Trade. 10:26-29. **26.** Solomon amassed fourteen hundred chariots and twelve thousand horses, which were quartered in chariot cities or in Jerusalem with the king. This practice was expressly forbidden by the Law (Deut. 17:16). **28-29.** In the light of archaeological research and following the Septuagint and the Vulgate, these verses ought to be translated thus: "Solomon's horses came from Egypt and Cilicia [*Qwh*]. The royal merchants brought them from Cilicia [*Qwh*] at the prevailing price—an Egyptian chariot for $400 in silver and a horse for $100—and so they delivered them by their hand [that is, by their agency] to all the Hittite and Syrian kings."

This reading interpretation makes Solomon the commercial middleman between Egypt and Asia Minor, with a complete monopoly on the horse and chariot trade (cf. 2 Chron. 9:28). Solomon turned the lucrative Egyptian horse and chariot industry into a profitable source of income for himself, as well as a means of augmenting his military power.

K. SOLOMON'S SIN AND DECLINE. 11:1-43.

His Foreign Wives and Apostasy. 11:1-8. **1-7.** To insure the future peace and security of his kingdom, Solomon succumbed to the common custom of the times and made many domestic alliances with subject races and tribes by marrying foreign women. Instead of securing the kingdom, this evil expedient led to spiritual decline, gross idolatry, and the eventual disruption of the nation.

Of the numerous deities to which the foreign wives turned his heart, perhaps the best known in the ancient world was Ashtoreth, called **the abomination of the Sidonians**, since her cult was established early among the Phoenicians. A fertility goddess, she was known as Astarte among the Greeks, and Ishtar in Babylonia. Her degrading cult encompassed many types of immorality. This goddess of sexual love and of war in Babylonia and Assyria is pictured on seal impressions found at Bethel, and her name is given in hieroglyphic characters.

The fact that the foreign marriages were with *pagan* women, rather than that Solomon had so *many* wives, seems to be the point of criticism. The **seven hundred wives ... and three hundred concubines** (cf. Song of Sol. 6:8) are scarcely hyperbolic, considering Solomon's splendor. There are numerous instances of sultans and kings of antiquity having many more wives and concubines in their harems than Solomon.

Milcom (v. 5) and Chemosh (v. 7) were the national gods of the Ammonites and Moabites, respectively. Solomon even went so far as to build a high place for Chemosh and Molech on **the hill that is before Jerusalem. 8.** He did the same thing for all his foreign wives, who burned incense and sacrificed to their gods. Solomon committed these abominations on the hill east of Jerusalem, the Mount of Olives (in 2 Kings 23:13, it is called "the mount of corruption").

The Divine Warning. 11:9-13. **9-10.** The LORD's anger against Solomon is stressed, particularly in the light that the LORD had appeared unto him twice and had specifically warned him against idolatry. **11-13.** Part of the kingdom would be torn away from Solomon, but not in his lifetime. The Davidic dynasty and the city would both continue. The

one tribe mentioned is Judah, possibly thought of as absorbing Simeon.

Hadad and Divine Chastening. 11:14-22. **14.** The LORD raised up **an adversary** (Heb., *śāṭān*, "an opposer") in the person of Hadad, an Edomite of the ruling family of Edom. **15-18.** He had fled while a young child to Paran when Joab murdered his family after Judah's conquest of Edom. **19-20.** During his refuge in Egypt he married the pharaoh's daughter, and his son, Genubath, was brought up at the Egyptian court. **21-22.** When Hadad heard of the death of David and Joab, he returned to Edom and plotted against Solomon.

Rezon Raised up as a Foe. 11:23-25. **23.** Rezon, a son of Eliada, had fled with a band of followers when David attacked Hadadezer of Zobah (2 Sam. 8:3). **24-25.** He occupied Damascus and became its ruler. He was an adversary of Solomon in alliance with Hadad of Edom. Later he **reigned over Syria** and is thus thought to have outlived the united Hebrew monarchy and to be identified with Hezion, the father of Tab-rimmon and grandfather of Benhadad I. If that is correct, Rezon was the founder of the dynasty of Aram, which ruled at Damascus and opposed Israel so relentlessly.

Jeroboam Opposes the King. 11:26-40. **26-39.** Jeroboam also lifted up his hand against Solomon. He was an Ephraimite, the son of Nebat, and became a persona non grata because he was told that he would be king of Israel. He was an efficient worker whom Solomon, while building the Millo, set in charge of the work force of the northern tribes. Being informed by the prophet Ahijah of the royal destiny, which by divine appointment awaited him, his mind took a new turn.

40. Although the prophet from Shiloh took every precaution to make his announcement to Jeroboam completely secret, nevertheless the story and the prediction connected with it probably reached the king's ears; thus, Jeroboam became a marked man. Doubtlessly his aspiring ambition led him to form plots and conspiracies and compelled him to flee to Egypt. Divinely selected, he would not wait the course of God's providence; therefore, he incurred the death penalty by his criminal rebellion.

Solomon's heavy exactions and forced labor, which he imposed upon his subjects at the end of his reign when his foreign resources began to fail, had prepared the greater part of the kingdom for a revolt, especially under a popular demagogue such as Jeroboam. Shishak, who harbored and encouraged the rebellious refugee, was of a different dynasty from that of the father-in-law of Solomon.

Solomon's Death. 11:41-43. **41. The book of the acts of Solomon** is otherwise unknown. **42.** Solomon reigned from about 970 to 931 B.C.

II. THE DIVIDED KINGDOM UNTIL AHAB'S DEATH. 12:1—22:53.

A. REHOBOAM AND THE REVOLT. 12:1-33.

Rehoboam Seeks Coronation by the Northern Tribes. 12:1-5. **1.** Rehoboam was the oldest, if not the only, son of Solomon. Doubtlessly he had been designated as heir. He went to Shechem, which at that time was a chief town of the northern tribes (Josh. 24:1, 32). There Rehoboam needed to be confirmed as king in order to hold the allegiance of the northern tribes. **All Israel was come to make him king.** It was not to make him king merely by submitting to him and to his authority as the divinely chosen and rightful heir, but rather to renew the conditions and stipulations to

which their constitutional kings were subject (cf. 1 Sam. 10:25). **2.** Meanwhile, Jeroboam, the son of Nebat, was recalled from Egypt (cf. 11:40). **3-5.** Jeroboam and the congregation of Israel pleaded with Rehoboam to lighten Solomon's grievous service, promising him their loyalty if he would do so. The splendor of Solomon's court and the vastness of his commercial undertakings involved him in financial difficulties despite the huge income from his commercial ventures so that he had to resort to heavy taxation and oppressive corvée labor.

Rehoboam's Folly. 12:6-15. **6-10.** The incredibly foolish advice of the young men was followed by Rehoboam. His counselors were the spoiled children of the effete and luxurious regime of Solomon's despotism. Their inane suggestions could only succeed if the popular disaffection was superficial, which it certainly was not at that point. **11-15.** Rehoboam's reply was not only utterly foolish, but offensively insulting. **I will chastise you with scorpions** refers to a whip, each lash of which was loaded with weights and sharp points like the Roman flagellum. Rehoboam's folly is only comprehensible under the explanation given: **the cause was from the Lord** (cf. v. 24; Judg. 14:4; 2 Chron. 10:15; 22:7; 25:20). The LORD was overruling in events to fulfill His word spoken by Ahijah of Shiloh (cf. 11:29).

Revolt of the Northern Tribes. 12:16-20. **16.** At this point one of the greatest tragedies in the life of the twelve tribes was enacted. The cry **to your tents** is an idiom, meaning "Let's go home" (cf. 2 Sam. 20:1). **18.** Continuing his blind folly, Rehoboam sent Adoram, who headed the corvée; he was promptly stoned to death. He was called Adoniram (1 Kings 4:6) or Hadoram (2 Chron. 10:18). **20.** Meanwhile, the northern tribes made Jeroboam their king (cf. 2 Kings 17:21).

Rehoboam Divinely Forbidden to War Against Jeroboam. 12:21-24. **21-24. Shemaiah, the man of God,** brought God's message that no war was to be fought. The whole procedure was the result of God's overruling providence to fulfill the word of God: **This thing is from me.** God's word is inviolable and must be fulfilled (Isa. 55:10-11) and obeyed. Rehoboam had enough reason left to submit to the divine order.

Jeroboam Consolidates the Northern Tribes. 12:25-33. **25. Jeroboam built Shechem.** He enlarged and fortified the town to make it his capital. Shechem (Tell Balata) is located at the east end of the valley running between Mount Ebal on the north and Mount Gerizim on the south, some thirty-one miles north of Jerusalem. **Penuel** is in Transjordan at the fords of the Jabbok. Evidently its fortification was to keep the Transjordan areas from Rehoboam.

26-30. Jeroboam's evil plan encompassed building two shrines to the LORD, one at Bethel in the southern part of the country, a bare dozen miles north of Jerusalem, and the other at Dan, at the headwaters of the Jordan in the north. Both were ancient cultic centers. The two golden bull calves were scarcely intended as representations of the LORD in the form of a bull god. But like Israel's pagan neighbors, the deity was represented as standing (invisibly, in Israel's case) on the back of an animal, a throne borne by animals. Archaeological research suggests that the LORD was to be thought of as invisibly enthroned above the animal (cf. 1 Sam. 4:4; 2 Kings 19:15). However, the bull affiliations of Baal made this purely political plan dangerous and wicked.

31. Jeroboam also was guilty of establishing high places and appointing priests who were not from the Levites. The **lowest of the people** is more accurately translated "the mass" or "the whole range of the people." **32-33.** Jeroboam also changed the date of the Feast of Ingathering from the seventh month to the eighth month. The whole plan was first political, then religious. He was determined to consolidate his realm and turn his people away from the house of David and from Jerusalem as a center of worship.

B. DENUNCIATION OF JEROBOAM'S IDOLATRY. 13:1-34.

Jeroboam Rejected by the Man of God. 13:1-10. This chapter continues the condemnation of Jeroboam begun in chapter 12. **1.** The unknown **man of God** out of Judah was the agent of the condemnation. He appeared at the altar at Bethel while Jeroboam was burning incense. He did not rebuke Jeroboam, but addressed himself to the altar, uttering a remarkable prophecy.

2-5. The amazing thing about this prophecy is that **Josiah** is mentioned by name. Normally, predictive prophecy in the Old Testament is by principle and not by specific details. Isaiah's prophecy concerning Cyrus (Isa. 44:28; 45:1) is a notable exception, as is this prophecy. There is no need, however, to conclude as do many scholars, even some conservatives, that the names are later additions. Biblical prophecy in all of its aspects is marvelous, and the wonder of it is not to be limited by man's unbelief, only by God's power and omniscience.

The unnamed prophet told Jeroboam that the altar he consecrated would be desecrated. Idolatrous worship will not continue, but the Word of God will endure forever. If the offering was an abomination to God, how much more the offerers themselves had to fall under

God's wrath. Jeróboam knew that all this would be accomplished by a branch of the house of David. The family that Jeroboam and his kingdom had despised and treacherously deserted would recover enough power to demolish the altar that he thought to establish.

That Josiah would burn the bones of the priests on Jeroboam's false altar was fulfilled in 621 B.C. (2 Kings 23:15-17). The sign (an attesting miracle), given for the confirmation of the truth of this prediction, was that the altar would be shaken to pieces by an invisible power, and the ashes of the sacrifice scattered, which came to pass immediately. This was proof that the prophet was sent by God. He confirmed the word with this sign following (cf. Mark 16:20). Moreover, Jeroboam's hand withered when he stretched it out to seize or smite the man of God.

6. The sudden healing of Jeroboam's dried-up hand upon his submission was evidence of God's grace toward him. This was proof enough that blessing had not come from the golden bulls he had set up, or his own sacrifice of incense, but from the LORD Himself, whom he was insulting by his idolatrous worship. **7-10.** The prophet's refusal of Jeroboam's invitation of reward was in obedience to the divine command for clear-cut separation from evil and evildoers (cf. 2 Cor. 6:14-18; Eph. 5:11; 2 John 1:9-11).

The Man of God Betrayed into Disobedience. 13:11-19. **11-19.** This incident shows how a true prophet of God (the man from Judah) may be misled by a compromising false prophet of God (the man from Bethel; cf. 1 John 4:1-2). Apparently the old prophet had fallen into compromise under the influence of a lying spirit (cf. 1 Kings 22:22-23). The prophet of Judah also presents a warning. That he was a messenger of God is certain, but his heart was not altogether right with the LORD. When the old prophet announced his coming judgment (v. 21), there is no evidence that he turned to the LORD with confession and prayer.

The Man of God Dies for His Disobedience. 13:20-32. **20-32.** Then the predicted fate overtook the prophet of Judah as a solemn warning, showing how important it is to obey the Word of God. The lion that had killed the disobedient prophet remained for a time with the body without touching it, which was a demonstration of the divine character of the judgment. Some think that a man of God cannot become a false prophet. Believers who compromise, and thus ignore or deny the Word of God, degenerate into false prophets. Satan's strategy is to cause true men of God and preachers of the Word of God to depart from biblical truths. They fall into some cult or error and propagate that error. They do not cease for that reason to be believers, but they become believers who preach and practice wrong doctrine and, hence, become false prophets and cultists.

Jeroboam Continues in His Evil Way. 13:33-34. **33-34.** Jeroboam continued in his obstinate idolatry. Someone was found who dared to repair the altar that had been thrown down, and Jeroboam offered sacrifice on it again. This time he was more bold, because the prophet who had disturbed him earlier was dead (cf. Rev. 11:10), and the prophecy uttered would not be fulfilled for a great while to come.

Various methods used to reclaim Jeroboam—threats, signs, judgments, and even divine mercies—fell on deaf ears. By demonic power he became insulated against truth and wedded to his calves, demonism being the dynamic of the idolatry into which he fell (cf. 1 Cor.

10:20). Jeroboam himself did not reform, nor did his priesthood, but he ordained whoever wanted to be a priest, no matter how illiterate or immoral he was or to which tribe he belonged. He who deceived himself into thinking that his golden calves would secure the crown to his family was to see that God's judgment falls on all who flout His word.

C. THE REIGNS OF JEROBOAM AND REHOBOAM. 14:1-31.

Sickness of Jeroboam's Son. 14:1-5. The prophecy of the destruction of Jeroboam's house is outlined in this chapter from verse 1 through verse 16. **1.** The sickness of Jeroboam's son was the occasion of the prophecy. **2.** Jeroboam instructed his wife to disguise herself so no one would know who she was, and then go to Shiloh to Ahijah, the prophet who had announced that Jeroboam would be king over Israel. Jeroboam did not want his people to know that when he was in trouble he needed God.

3. He was playing the role of a godless hypocrite. He had perfect assurance that the prophet would **tell** (reveal) how the lad would fare. **4.** How absurd Jeroboam's hypocrisy was in the light of the fact that Ahijah could not see, his eyes being dimmed by age. **5.** Graciously the LORD informed Ahijah that Jeroboam's wife was coming and instructed him what to say to her when she arrived pretending to be another woman.

The Prophecy of the Destruction of Jeroboam's House. 14:6-16. **6-11.** Ahijah, who had encouraged Jeroboam to revolt in the first place (11:29-31), by God's direction was turned against the king in bitter disappointment to prophesy his doom and that of his house. The word of God to Ahijah stripped away the hypocrisy and deceit practiced by Jeroboam and opened the way for the message of judgment. Jeroboam's disobedience is contrasted strongly with the obedience of the house of David. The king's terrible idolatry was excoriated. The calamity that was to be brought on the house of Jeroboam was to be visited upon every male descendant. Jeroboam's posterity was to be swept away as refuse.

12. The mother was told that while her feet were approaching her hometown, her child would die. **13.** However, he would be buried honorably and would be lamented, because in him was found **some good thing toward the Lord God of Israel.** This incident ought to comfort those who have mourned the loss of a child, realizing that God may be keeping the loved one away from a trouble-filled life by calling him home early.

14. The prediction that the LORD would raise up a king over Israel who would cut off the house of Jeroboam was fulfilled in Baasha (15:27-29). **15-16.** These verses span the whole history of the Northern Kingdom until it was carried away into captivity in 721 B.C. **beyond the river**, that is, the Euphrates. It is prophecy, *not* history interpreted by a writer in about 600 B.C., who knew how short-lived the house or dynasty of Jeroboam was and how the Northern Kingdom fell in 721 B.C., as many scholars contend.

The **idols** (or "groves"; cf. Deut. 16:21) were wooden poles, symbols of the Canaanite fertility goddess Ashera. However, this first prophecy of Israel's future captivity did not rule out the free moral agency of future generations. Although it may seem impossible for us in our finite human reasoning to comprehend, the fact remains that God's foreknowledge does not preclude man's freedom and responsibility.

The Death of Jeroboam's Son. 14:17-18. **17.** When Jeroboam's wife arrived home in Tirzah, the child died. The city was Jeroboam's place of residence after Shechem (12:25), thus becoming the capital of Israel (15:33) until Samaria was built (16:24). It is probably Tell el-Far'ah, about seven miles northeast of Nablus, excavated by R. de Vaux.

Summary of Jeroboam's Reign. 14:19-20. **19-20.** Scriptural record passes over all else and fully commemorates Jeroboam as the son of Nebat "who made Israel to sin" (v. 16). It is an example of how much evil one man is capable of under the guise of religion that rejects God's Word.

Rehoboam's Reign. 14:21-24. **21-23.** As a foolish son of Solomon, immorality and spiritual decline in Rehoboam's reign were to be expected (cf. 2 Chron. 11:5—12:16). The terrible pollution of Canaanite religion swept in. So we read of **high places ... pillars, and Asherim** (RSV), the latter being wooden poles, symbols of the Canaanite fertility goddess, Asherah. **24.** The **sodomites** were male cult prostitutes (*qᵉdāšîm*, "those set apart for religious cult prostitution"). Just as the word *holy* may mean to be separated unto the LORD and to holy things, so *sodomites* is also used as being set apart to that which is idolatrous and unclean (cf. 1 Kings 15:12; 22:46).

Rehoboam's Defeat by Shishak. 14:25-28. **25-28.** This pharaoh (founder of the twenty-second dynasty) is dated from about 940 to 920 B.C. (Albright). He took advantage of the division of the kingdom and the internal wars of Israel to invade the land. His Karnak inscription lists about 150 places that he "captured." He despoiled the Temple before he agreed not to ravage Jerusalem completely.

Rehoboam's Death. 14:29-31. **29.** **The book of the chronicles of the kings of Judah** is mentioned as a source, as are the chronicles of Shemaiah the prophet and of Iddo the seer in 2 Chronicles 12:15. These are the sources for Rehoboam's reign. **30.** The war alluded to is not hinted at elsewhere, but the meaning may be simply that there was continual hostility between the two kingdoms. **31.** The idiom **slept with his fathers** is a euphemism for death, certainly intimating, although vaguely, a future life (cf. 1 Cor. 11:30; 15:51; 1 Thess. 4:13-15).

D. ABIJAH, ASA, NADAB, AND BAASHA. 15:1-34.

Reign of Abijah. 15:1-8. **1-2.** Abijah (or Abijam, KJV; cf. 2 Chron. 13:1-12) had an unworthy three-year reign (913-911 B.C.). His mother was **Maacah, the daughter of Abishalom.** Abishalom, called Absalom (2 Chron. 11:20), was in all probability the rebel son of David, and his mother (2 Sam. 3:3) was also named Maacah. Of the many wives of Rehoboam (2 Chron. 11:21-22), Maacah seems to have been the favorite; and Abijah was the favorite son. Evidence seems to place her as the granddaughter of Absalom. Her influence was evil because of her propensity to idolatry (cf. v. 13).

3. Despite Abijam's representation of himself as a champion of the Temple and of the priesthood against the rival worship of Jeroboam (cf. 2 Chron. 13:4-12), he followed the sins of his father, Rehoboam. Loyalty to the LORD was only superficial. **4.** For David's sake, however, the LORD gave him **a lamp in Jerusalem,** that is, a testimony for the LORD for David's sake. This was in fulfillment of the promise made to David (2 Sam. 7:12-16). **6-7.** These verses stress the fact that there was war between the Northern and Southern Kingdoms. It was tragedy enough that they had split; the greater tragedy was that God's people fought one another as enemies.

Reign of Asa—His Reforms. 15:9-15. **9-10.** Abijah's son, Asa (911-870 B.C.) had a long and good reign over Judah. His mother's name was Maacah. Actually, she was the grandmother of Asa, apparently having retained the place of "queen mother" to the exclusion of the real mother of the king. **11.** Asa **did that which was right.** He was able to strengthen his kingdom spiritually, as well as economically and militarily (cf. 2 Chron. 14-15), as the result of repelling a formidable invasion from Egypt under "Zerah, the Ethiopian" in his fifteenth year.

13. Asa demonstrated his loyalty to the LORD by removing **his mother** (the queen mother, his grandmother) because she had made **an idol in a grove**, correctly translated, "had an abominable image made for Asherah" (RSV). Asa destroyed her vile image of the Canaanite fertility goddess and burned it at the brook Kidron. **14.** Asa attempted to root out the high places (cf. 2 Chron. 14:5), but the craving for local and visible sanctuaries, which tragically had been degraded by gross idolatry, was too strong for even the most thoroughgoing reformers to cope with. **15.** He replenished the Temple's treasury, which had been plundered in Rehoboam's reign as a result of Shishak's invasion, doubtlessly with spoils from his own victory over the Egyptian army and his father Abijah's victory over Jeroboam.

Asa's Wars with Baasha. 15:16-22. **16-17.** Baasha of Israel built Ramah, properly "the Ramah" ("the elevation," Josh. 18:25), as a city of Benjamin, situated about five miles north of Jerusalem (see Josephus, *Antiquities* 8. 1.12. 3.), probably to be identified with the village known as Er-Ram. **18-19.** The evils of the disrupted kingdom are highlighted. Not only did God's people fight one another, but they also called upon pagans to fight against the other people of the LORD. Such a course of action deserved prophetic rebuke (cf. 2 Chron. 16:7-9).

20. Ben-hadad, king of Syria, was glad enough to accept a treaty involving Israelite arrayed against Israelite. Part of the country attacked was later overrun in the Assyrian invasion (2 Kings 15:29). It is a mountainous region near the sources of the Jordan near Dan, which was the most exposed tribe on the northeastern border. Attacked were **Ijon** (probably modern Tell el-Dibbin), **Abel-beth-maacah** (modern Tell Abil near Lake Huleh), and **Chinneroth** (Tell el-'Ureimeh, Deut. 3:17, which lay on the northeast shore of the lake of Chinnereth (Sea of Galilee).

22. Asa's **proclamation** represented an unusual levy or corvée. The purpose was to destroy the fortifications at Ramah and build others at Geba and Mizpah. **Geba**, meaning "hill," perhaps refers to Gibeah, although the name can be applied to a number of sites. **Mizpah** undoubtedly refers to a city of Benjamin (Josh. 18:26) and includes the broad ridge that forms the continuation of the Mount of Olives to the north and east, from which the traveler gets his first view of Jerusalem.

Summary of Asa's Reign. 15:23-24. **23.** Mention of Asa's **might** (not employed of Rehoboam or Abijah) indicates the prosperity and increased power of Judah under his reign. **The cities which he built** (see 2 Chron. 16:6) were aimed at protecting his realm. Exactly what disease inflicted Asa in his declining years, whether dropsy or something else, is not stated. However, there was a deterioration in his character. Second Chronicles 16:12 says he sought not the LORD, but the physicians. He also defied prophetic authority and imprisoned Hanani, the seer (2 Chron. 16:10).

Reign of Nadab. 15:25-32. **25-26.** Nadab, Jeroboam's son and successor (910-909 B.C.), reigned over Israel only two years. He followed the evil ways of his father. **27-28.** He was assassinated by Baasha during the siege of Gibbethon (Tell el-Melat), a few miles west of Gezer (Josh. 19:44; 21:23). The implication is that Philistine Gibbethon revolted against the enfeebled power of Israel. Occupation of Gibbethon commanded a pass from the Plain of Sharon to the interior.

29. Baasha destroyed the entire house of Jeroboam, thus fulfilling the word of the LORD by His servant Ahijah of Shiloh (cf. 14:10-14). The tragic fact that there was war between Asa and Baasha all their days underscores the terrible harm sin causes in dividing God's people and causing them to fight one another.

The Reign of Baasha. 15:33-34. **33-34.** Baasha (909-886 B.C.) followed the evil tradition of Jeroboam and the idolatrous worship at Dan and Bethel.

E. ISRAEL FROM BAASHA TO AHAB. 16:1-34.

The Prophet Jehu Warns Baasha. 16:1-4. **1-4.** Jehu, the son of Hanani, calmly warned Baasha in scathing terms. He must have been very young at the time for he seems to have been the seer of Judah in the reign of Asa (2 Chron. 16:7) who is recorded as rebuking Jehoshaphat after the death of Ahab, and who also wrote the annals of Jehoshaphat's reign (cf. 2 Chron. 19:2; 20:34). The prophet resumed the theme of condemnation upon the idolatrous followers of Jeroboam, already made

familiar by Ahijah the Shilohite (cf. 14:7-11).

Summary of Baasha's Reign. 16:5-7. **7.** The second reference to Jehu's prophecy seems to be added chiefly for the sake of the last clause, **because he killed him,** that is, killed Nadab, the son of Jeroboam. Baasha's crime, though foretold, was not excusable, even though he was the executor of divine punishment.

Reign of Elah. 16:8-10. **8-10.** Elah (886-885 B.C.) reigned over Israel at Tirzah and was treacherously assassinated by Zimri, **his servant.** Apparently Zimri was a high officer in special charge of the palace and the king's purse. Most of the army was fighting at Gibbethon (see 15:27). As a result of Zimri's base treachery, his name passed to posterity as a byword for unusual treachery (cf. 2 Kings 9:31).

The Reign of Zimri. 16:11-20. **11-12.** Zimri (885 B.C.) immediately destroyed the house of Baasha completely, according to the prophecy of Jehu (Hanani, vv. 1-4). **13.** The sins of Baasha and of Elah were the result of their provoking the LORD God of Israel to anger with their **vanities** (i.e., "their idols"; cf. Deut. 32:21; 1 Sam. 12:21; Isa. 41:29; Jer. 8:19). These were not only the golden bulls (idols) at Dan and Bethel. Grosser abominations crept into Israel's life as a result of Jeroboam's apostasy.

15-16. While the army was besieging Gibbethon (cf. 15:27), news came of the assassination of the king. Thereupon **all Israel** made Omri, the commander in chief of the army, king over Israel that day in the camp. **17.** Then Omri went up from Gibbethon and besieged Tirzah. **18.** This verse should be translated, "And when Zimri saw that the city was taken, he went into the citadel of the king's house, and burned the king's

house over him with fire, and died''
(RSV).

Omri Becomes King. 16:21-28. **21-23.**
Although Omri had been chosen by the
army, the people followed an unknown
upstart named Tibni. So civil war broke
out, lasting at least five years. Finally,
by 880 B.C., Omri's forces had won, and
he was made king. Omri (880-874 B.C.)
became the founder of a new and powerful dynasty in Israel.

24. After reigning six years in Tirzah,
he followed the common custom of establishing a new city for his new
dynasty. Jeroboam had set an example
in building Shechem, and evidently
Baasha had done so too in building Tirzah. The word *Samaria* (Heb., *Shôme-
rôn*) means ''a watchtower,'' apparently
having a double derivation from its
natural position on a high hill as well as
from the owner's name from whom it
was purchased.

25-26. Omri was an able, strong ruler,
but he carried on the evil idolatrous
tradition of his predecessors. Hence, he
is dismissed briefly but under severe
condemnation in the biblical account.
Extrabiblically, he appears as an important name in Assyrian inscriptions.
From the time of Shalmaneser III to the
time of Sargon, Israel was referred to as
''the land of the house of Omri.'' His
name also occurs prominently on the
famous Moabite stone. **27.** The biblical
record does note the might that he
showed, but divine revelation has no
special interest in his merely human
greatness, so tarnished by flagrant idolatry.

Ahab and Jezebel. 16:29-34. **29.**
Omri's son, Ahab (874-853 B.C.) began
his reign in Samaria. **30-31.** Like his
father, Omri, he **did evil in the sight of the
Lord above all who were before him**, his
worst sin being his marrying into the
pagan house of Ethbaal, king of the

Sidonians. This led him into Baal worship. Ahab was perceptive, sagacious,
wicked, and idolatrous, and he out-
stripped all his predecessors in wickedness and shrewdness.

32-33. The erection of an altar to Baal,
the great northwest Semitic fertility god,
and the construction of a temple to Baal
in Samaria, as well as his making an
Asherah, a wooden pole symbolic of the
Canaanite fertility goddess, Asherah,
were but three of the idolatrous outrages
of this monarch who led God's people
far away from the LORD. The only reason Ahab's reign is given in detail from
17:1 to 22:40 is because of the tremendous religious crisis it precipitated in Israel.

34. The rebuilding of Jericho has been
confirmed by archaeological diggings,
as there is no evidence of occupational
levels from Joshua's time to Ahab's era,
when small ruins from that century point
to Hiel's rebuilding the site. Hiel's rebuilding of Jericho furnishes an indication of the prosperity and extent of
Ahab's power and shows the ignorance
in his apostate day of the Word of God
and of the old curse that Joshua had
pronounced upon any would-be builder
of the city (Josh. 6:26).

F. ELIJAH'S PROPHECIES AND MIRACLES. 17:1-24.

*Elijah's Prediction of the Drought.
17:1.* **1.** Elijah is introduced with dramatic suddenness and brevity. He is
presented like a flash of lightning preceding a thunderstorm. The approaching tempest was the struggle between
the LORD and Baal. It is presumed at the
outset that Elijah had a long struggle
with the house of Ahab. Now it was
coming to a climax.

The prophet is presented as **Elijah, the
Tishbite.** The term ''Tishbite'' describes
him as a native of Tishbe in Gilead. The

Hebrew text adds **of the inhabitants of Gilead** to distinguish the place from a Tishbe or Thisbe in Naphtali (Tobit 1:2). The LXX renders it "of Tishbe in Gilead." **Gilead**, properly "the rocky region," was in Transjordan and was comparatively uninhabited and well adapted to the recluse or dweller in the desert.

Baal, the Phoenician god of the storm, was believed by Ahab, Jezebel, and his other devotees to control the rain. Elijah (Heb., *Elijahu*, meaning "my God is the Lord") abruptly announced to Ahab that the Lord would be proved to be the One who does so. In his abrupt address to Ahab, the rugged prophet reminded the monarch that the Lord God of Israel is not a dead god like Baal, but He lives. He is the living God before whom the prophet stood as His servant, to be sent wherever the Lord willed.

With this adjuration (cf. 18:15; 2 Kings 3:14) Elijah boldly announced that there would **not be dew nor rain these years, but according to my word**, which was the Word of God. It was the withholding of rain that again and again was referred to as a penalty for apostasy in Old Testament times (cf. Lev. 26:19; Deut. 11:17; 1 Kings 8:35; James 5:17). That is what is noted as the answer to the prophet's prayer, bringing down judgment upon the land.

Elijah at Cherith. 17:2-7. **2-3.** Divine instruction directed the prophet to go eastward from Samaria, where he had evidently encountered Ahab, in order to go into hiding **by the brook, Cherith.** This is the Wadi Yabis in Transjordan, actually in a northeastern direction from Samaria between the Yarmuk and the river Jabbok.

4-6. Soon the Lord, whom Elijah served, promised to feed him through the instrumentality of **ravens.** Old Testament miracles are neither commonplace nor the product of the imagination. They occur in critical periods when the very power of God is needed in order to maintain His people and their testimony, such as in the Exodus from Egypt, the sojourn in the wilderness, and the entrance into Canaan.

Here was another critical period in Israel's history. The occasion was the great Baal apostasy witnessing the struggle of Elijah and Elisha against it. Even the brook of which Elijah drank dried up. God's word through Elijah that there would be no rain was to be the Lord's answer to the false prophets of Baal, the vaunted rainmaker.

The Widow at Zarephath. 17:8-16. **8-9.** Almost as wonderful as being fed by the ravens, Elijah was directed to go to Zarephath in the pagan land of Phoenicia, from which Jezebel came, to be sustained by a widow there. This city is the Sarepta of the Septuagint and of the New Testament (Luke 4:26). It is present-day Sarafand between Tyre and Sidon on the Phoenician coast. What a striking instance of the providence of God that the prophet would find refuge and a welcome in a pagan country, the native place of his deadliest enemy, when his own homeland was apostate and unsafe.

10-12. Elijah met a widow gathering a few sticks to prepare her last meal. **13-16.** What faith was displayed by the pagan woman as she heeded the advice of the prophet, **Fear not; go and do as thou hast said, But make me of it a little cake first, and bring it unto me . . . afterwards, make for thee and for thy son.** Here, indeed, was found faith such as was not found in Israel.

The woman did as Elijah requested. The promise was **the barrel of meal shall not be used up,** that is, not be exhausted, **neither shall the cruse of oil fail** (become empty), **until the day that the Lord send-**

eth rain upon the earth. And she went and did according to the saying of Elijah. Action proved her faith in the God of Israel, and faith was rewarded.

The Widow's Son Restored to Life. 17:17-24. **17.** The widow's son became seriously ill and apparently stopped breathing. **18.** Facing this emergency, the woman revealed growing recognition of the true God of Elijah and the experience of His wonder-working power, as a result of her contact with the prophet. She also came to a deeper realization of her own sinful condition, but her sorrow, strangely enough, made her unreasonable. She felt that her misfortune was a just punishment. In a confused manner, she cried out against the presence of the prophet, as if he were the actual cause of the judgment on her sin. As a matter of fact, it was simply a means used by God to bring it home to her conscience.

20. Elijah's petition and his prayer to the LORD, **Hast thou also brought evil ... ?** reveals the prophet's half-presumptuous impatience (more fully revealed in chap. 19) that his presence as a hunted fugitive had even brought trouble upon the household that sheltered him. **21.** The act of stretching himself upon the child apparently implied healing virtue imparted in a measure to the person of the prophet. That virtue belongs to the LORD alone (Luke 8:45-46; cf. 2 Kings 4:34; 13:21; Acts 20:10). The power to heal is distinctly the LORD's and is definitely made conditional on prayer (James 5:14-15). **22. The Lord heard the voice of Elijah.**

24. Meanwhile, note the woman's progressive faith and increased apprehension of God. She spoke first as an outsider, "The LORD, thy God" (v. 12). Then she came to see Him as God (v. 18). Finally she not only believed that the prophet was a "man of God," but

she confessed that the **word of the Lord** was in his mouth as the **truth.** Undoubtedly the widow was converted to the LORD. Similar stages of faith can be observed in the nobleman at Capernaum (John 4:47, 50, 53).

G. ELIJAH AND THE CONTEST WITH BAAL. 18:1-46.

The Lord Versus Baal Crisis. 18:1-2. **1-2. In the third year,** that is, evidently from the time of Elijah's first appearance to Ahab when he announced the beginning of the famine (17:1), including the period of the prophet's sojourn with the widow at Zarephath, the LORD directed him to appear a second time unto Ahab. **And I will send rain upon the earth.** The terrible 3½-year drought (cf. Luke 4:25; James 5:17) was about to end. The great question was "Who withheld and who would send the rain—the great Baal, god of the thunder and the rain, or the LORD?"

Obadiah Seeks Water. 18:3-6. **3-4. Obadiah** ("servant of the LORD") was a steward of Ahab's household. He is presented as a God-fearing man who had protected the prophets of the LORD when Jezebel was seeking to kill them. Those **prophets of the Lord** possibly included the "sons of the prophets" or "the school of the prophets" (cf. 1 Sam. 10:5-13; 2 Kings 2:3-5). This is the only reference to this persecution. **5-6.** Ahab had given orders to Obadiah, who was a steward of his house, to find water and grass in order to save the horses and mules. Assyrian sources refer to two thousand horses furnished by Ahab in a Syrian coalition against Shalmaneser III at the Battle of Qarqar in 853 B.C.

Obadiah Encounters Elijah. 18:7-16. **7-8.** In the search for water Obadiah met Elijah, who instructed him to go tell Ahab, his master, **Elijah is here. 9-14.** The relentless search for Elijah mentioned in verse 10 does not square with Ahab's halfhearted enmity. It doubtlessly represents the underlying work of Jezebel in Ahab's name, as in the murder of Naboth.

Obadiah was terror stricken at Elijah's command. He was afraid that if he told the king Elijah had appeared, the Spirit of the LORD would carry Elijah away (cf. 2 Kings 2:16; Acts 8:39). Obadiah concluded that Elijah had been removed from persecution for such a long time only by a miraculous agency, and that after emerging for even a brief period, he would again be swept away to his hidden refuge. **15-16.** Only after Elijah swore before the LORD to show himself that very day to Ahab, did Obadiah muster courage to inform Ahab.

Ahab and Elijah Meet. 18:17-19. **17.** When Ahab caught sight of Elijah, he said to him, "Is it you, O troubler of Israel?" (lit. Heb. trans.; cf. Josh. 6:18; 7:24-26). **18.** Elijah's retort was keen and piercing as his words flew back into Ahab's teeth. Ahab and his house were the real troublers in Israel, because they had abandoned the commandments of the LORD (Exod. 20:1-17) and had followed the Baals, the local versions of the great storm and sky god, Baal.

There was only one Baal, but there were many variations of him. He was the principal god of the Canaanite pantheon, whose worship included ritual prostitution involving a kind of sympathetic magic to achieve fertility of the ground. In Canaanite religion, Baal both owned and fertilized the land.

19. Elijah hurled the challenge before Ahab to assemble all Israel at Mount Carmel, a prominent mountain ridge rising to an elevation of about eighteen hundred feet. Carmel is mentioned (Josh. 19:26). It became one of the high places, and an ideal spot for the show-down between the LORD, the true God, and Baal, the false god of the Canaanites. Elijah called for the 450 prophets of Baal and the 400 prophets of Asherah, the consort of Baal. How ironic that Elijah should give orders to the king; but he was God's messenger, and the king felt he had to obey God.

The Contest on Mount Carmel. 18:20-29. **20-21.** Elijah cried out the challenge to all the assembled people, "How long will ye halt between two opinions?" (Heb., "to waver in opinion" or "to hesitate"). "How long will you go limping (*pāsaḥ*) with two different opinions?" (RSV). Elijah was characterized by a righteous impatience with the "halting" (that is, "limping to and fro between two opinions").

It was a dangerous situation because it was an easier course than open apostasy. It was Ahab's attitude and probably that of the mass of the people (cf. Ezek. 20:31, 39). Elijah realized that such compromise would mean the extermination of Yahwism and the eventual triumph of Baalism. A showdown had to come and a clear-cut decision had to be reached.

22-24. Elijah called for a bold sign from heaven (cf. Lev. 9:24; 1 Chron. 21:26; 2 Chron. 7:1). God, who answered by fire, would be recognized as the true God. **26.** The Baal-worshipers frantically called on the name of Baal from morning even until noon. They tried to coax Baal (lord of the heavens and the rain) to answer by fire. **27.** Elijah mocked them with the deepest irony and sarcasm. He jested, taunting them that Baal might be sleeping or off on a hunt. The loud cries and frenzy of the Baal-worshipers and their self-mutilations are all manifestations of demon-energized religion, as in the case of all idolatry (cf. 1 Cor. 10:20).

God Answers by Fire. 18:30-40.

30-31. Elijah said, **Come near unto me.** Then Elijah **repaired the altar of the Lord** that had been thrown down and desecrated by the fanatical Baal devotees (cf. 19:10, 14), selecting twelve stones, one for each of the tribes of Israel. Though these tribes were politically and socially divided, in the mind of God they were still one people, with one LORD and one Messianic expectation. Explicitly, Elijah's action was a rebuke of the sin of the people and their consequent division. The prophet insisted on making the test as difficult as possible for God to meet so that the divine response might stand out in bolder relief against the utter powerlessness of Baal and his prophets.

36-39. Elijah's prayer was made in the name of "Jehovah, the God of Abraham, of Isaac, and of Israel" (ASV). He called upon the LORD, the only true God, to utterly discredit Baal. When the fire from the LORD came down, it burned up the sacrifice, the wood, the stones, and the dust. It even licked up the water in the trench. When the people saw it, **they fell on their faces**, exactly as others had done in Leviticus 9:24. This demonstration gave indubitable proof that the LORD God was the true God and that Baal was a fraud.

40. Then Elijah ordered the prophets of Baal to be seized and brought down to the brook Kishon, where he slaughtered them. It was the only way a false religion could be dealt with. The whole episode on Mount Carmel was a powerful indictment of religious compromise and syncretism. Yahwism and Baalism could not exist together; they were mutually exclusive. Either one or the other had to be destroyed.

The Drought Broken. 18:41-46.
41-42. The end of the drought could now come because, first, Baal was utterly discredited as the lord of the rain and of the sky, and second, the people would know that the drought was not merely an unfortunate coincidence of nature, but a direct disciplinary dealing from God. It ended as it had begun—at the command of the man of God (James 5:18).

43. So Elijah and his servant went up on Mount Carmel, and Elijah commanded him to look toward the sea (the Mediterranean). Six times the servant was sent to look, and the seventh time he returned with a report: **There ariseth a little cloud out of the sea, like a man's hand. 45-46.** The heavens grew black, and there was a tremendous rain, proving that not Baal, but the LORD, the God of Israel and Creator of the heavens, was the God of the storm and the rain. While Ahab rode in his chariot back to his summer capital at Jezreel northwest of Mount Gilboa, Elijah, in celebration of the triumph of God, **ran before Ahab.** Elijah was not only fearless to fight for God; he was unashamed to be enthusiastic and zealous for Him.

H. ELIJAH'S FLIGHT FROM JEZEBEL. 19:1-21.

Jezebel's Threat. 19:1-3. **2-3.** Elijah had entered Jezreel full of hope, but the threat of the enraged queen struck fear in his heart. She swore by her evil gods that she would kill the prophet, even as he had killed the prophets of Baal. Very likely even she could not have laid violent hands on the LORD's servant because of the mood the people were in at the time. To vent her anger, she purposely threatened him because she could do no more.

However, the threat produced its desired effect. Elijah fled from the kingdom into the southernmost part of the territories of Judah. Although **Beersheba** is on the southern extremities of Judah, the prophet did not think he was safe even there. Dismissing his servant, he resolved to seek refuge among the mountain recesses of Sinai. Since Judah was in a half-dependent alliance with Israel and King Jehoshaphat was a friend of Ahab, Elijah might not be safe there. However, his servant stayed there without danger.

Elijah's Flight. 19:4-8. **4.** Elijah fled a day's journey into the desert. There he **sat down under a juniper tree.** It was actually a broom tree that flourishes in desert wadis, sometimes attaining the height of ten feet. The prophet's conduct was the result of being left to himself, and being exalted above measure (2 Cor. 12:7-9), looking to himself instead of to the LORD, as any great man may be tempted to do. For that reason he failed.

5-7. God did not forsake his fugitive servant. He watched over him, miraculously ministering to his needs. God sent one of His angels to minister to the tired prophet. Elijah rested and awoke again. He was again provided with food and drink. **8.** From the strength of that meal, he traveled forty days and forty nights to Horeb, the mount of God. Forty days was more than ample time to cover the two to three hundred miles from Beersheba to Horeb. Evidently the prophet took the journey in slow stages.

God Meets with Elijah. 19:9-14. **9.** When Elijah arrived at Horeb, he lodged in **a cave.** This may have been the identical "cleft of the rock" where the LORD appeared to Moses (Exod. 33:21-23). Thus, the account is reminiscent of Moses' experience at Sinai. The LORD's question, **What doest thou here, Elijah?** may have been a rebuke, but the LORD may simply have been giving Elijah a chance to express his feeling.

10. Whether Elijah's reply was simply an expression of fleshly despair or even of complaint against the LORD, it furnished an illustration of the candid-camera type of photography the Bible

presents of its characters. It photographs people as they are—their points of strength, as well as their points of weakness. Here the prophet's weakness appeared (cf. Rom. 11:3). What a demonstration of what a man, even a great man of faith and a great man of God, can become when left to himself, apart from the grace of God.

Although Elijah had been very **jealous for the Lord God of hosts,** he boldly hinted that the LORD Himself was not jealous for His own name, allowing Baal worship to sweep Israel and the people to forsake His covenant, throw down His altars, and slay His prophets. What momentary blindness to suppose that he alone remained faithful and that they were seeking to take away his life.

11-13. By means of a terrifying exhibition of divine power, Elijah was made aware of the divine Speaker, who addressed him. The LORD was not in the wind, the earthquake, or the fire, but He was in the voice that came to Elijah, saying, **What doest thou here, Elijah?** — the very same question asked initially in verse 9. The **still, small voice,** "the voice of a light breath" (LXX), brought to the prophet the realization of God's presence, as indicated by the veiled face of reverence. **14.** Despite all of that, Elijah, being singularly true to his fallen nature, mechanically repeated the same old complaint.

God's Vindication of His Jealousy for His Name. 19:15-18. In his complaint the overwrought prophet practically accused the LORD of infidelity. Elijah was saying in essence: "I am very zealous for the LORD God of Israel, for You, O LORD God of Israel, but You have not been very zealous for Your own name."

15-18. God spoke in a "still, small voice," the voice indicating the LORD's holiness and zeal, which were to be manifested in the threefold commission given Elijah: (1) to anoint Hazael king over Syria (cf. 2 Kings 8:7-15); (2) to anoint a new king for Israel, Jehu, son of Nimshi (cf. 2 Kings 9:1-10); (3) to appoint his own successor, Elisha, the son of Shaphat. These three individuals would vindicate the holiness and zeal of the LORD by humbling and punishing the house of Ahab.

Elijah Casts His Mantle on Elisha. 19:19-21. **19.** Elijah's casting his mantle upon Elisha ("my God is salvation") is a symbolic act indicating that Elijah's power and authority were to rest upon the younger prophet. **20.** Elijah's words meant, "Go, and return to me, for I have done something very important to you." Elisha's request to kiss his father and his mother must be evaluated in the light of Oriental farewells, which sometimes occupied days and even weeks; also, it is to be viewed in the light of the rigid requirements of discipleship. Elisha's dedication was so evident that the younger man was permitted a brief farewell to his family, since there was no danger of his putting his hand to the plow and looking back (cf. Luke 9:57-62).

21. The food prepared for the occasion was doubtless to honor the senior prophet, Elijah, as well as being in the nature of a family farewell. Thus, at Sinai, Elijah was to learn the deeper lesson of God's holiness and zeal for His holy name, a lesson the Israelites had learned at the same place when the Decalogue was given there under Moses some six hundred years previously.

I. AHAB'S WARS WITH THE SYRIANS.
20:1-43.

Ben-hadad's Insolent Demands. 20:1-6. **1-2.** The two expeditions of this chapter concern Ben-hadad of Syria (Aram), his name meaning "son of Hadad" (Heb., *hᵃḏāḏ*, and Assyr.,

Ḥaddu, "the thunderer," the Amorite equivalent of Baal, "the god of the storm"). This Ben-hadad is probably Ben-hadad II (c. 860-843 B.C.), the son of Ben-hadad I (c. 900-860 B.C.), although many scholars insist on one Ben-hadad during this period. He, with thirty-two allied kings, invaded and besieged Samaria. They were small independent kings, petty rulers of small independent towns.

Ben-hadad seems to have been the common title of Aramaean kings. He was the "son of Hadad," the name of their national god. An inscription from Zinjirli makes reference to a coalition of thirty kings, and so this passage is not unreasonable. **3-6.** The contemptuous demands of the Aramaean king demonstrate how strong this power centered at Damascus had become. It seems that Ahab was in a sense in a tributary state to the Aramaeans. His vascillating reply seems almost cowardly, and he appears to have accepted the status, at least for the moment.

Ahab's Reply. 20:7-12. The tone of this chapter seems to indicate that a spiritual revival must have taken place in Israel after the manifestation of the LORD on Carmel. **7. The elders of the land** were most likely the older men, the heads of the families of all the various tribal regions. **8.** The advice of the elders to Ahab was **Hearken not ... nor consent**, that is, "Pay no attention to him; do not give in." **9.** Ahab refused to fully give in to the demands of Ben-hadad. **10.** Ben-hadad boasted that there was not enough dust in Samaria to provide each of his warriors with a handful. **11.** Ahab displayed himself as a wise and astute political leader, quoting an apt proverb, **Let not him that girdeth on his armor boast himself as he that putteth it off.** The maxim means, "Let not the one who starts a fight boast prematurely of winning it." **12.** Ben-hadad heard it while he and his kings were drinking in their tents. In a drunken stupor he ordered his troops to take their positions against the city.

Ahab's Victory. 20:13-21. **13-14.** An unnamed prophet appeared to Ahab to encourage him to face the great number of the enemy and be assured of deliverance. This gracious promise of deliverance was not grounded, of course, upon Ahab's fidelity, but simply on God's loving care for His people, who doubtlessly had turned to the LORD since the great victory on Carmel.

15-16. Calling together an army of about seven thousand men and following the LORD's direction, they struck strategically at noon. The Syrians were in their tents eating and drinking. **20-21.** The surprise attack threw the Syrian army into confusion, and they were utterly routed. Ben-hadad barely escaped on his horse, and his army was destroyed.

Second Syrian Invasion Foretold. 20:22. **22.** Graciously, God again sent the unnamed prophet to Ahab to warn him that the Syrians would return the following year.

Ben-hadad Defeated. 20:23-34. **23-25.** Meanwhile, the servants of Ben-hadad advised him to gather an identical army, horse for horse and chariot for chariot, to fight in the plain rather than on the hills. The polytheistic Syrians displayed their utter ignorance regarding the omnipresence of the one true God. The LORD Himself was to correct the strange insinuation that Israel's God was confined to the hills.

26. At the coming of the year, that is, in the spring, Ben-hadad invaded Samaria once more and went up to Aphek (Fiq or Afiq at the head of the Wadi Fiq, east of the Sea of Galilee). **27.** The Syrians filled the country, while the Israelites encamped in front of them **like two little flocks of goats** (RSV).

28. Again the man of God came to the king of Israel and told him that because the Syrians had said that the LORD was a mountain God and not a valley God, He was going to give this vast army into their hand in order that they might know that He was God. **29-33.** On the seventh day the Israelites slew a vast number of the Syrian foot soldiers, the rest fleeing to Aphek where a wall fell on twenty-seven thousand of those who remained. Ben-hadad fled to the city, where he was captured by Ahab, who spared his life.

34. Ben-hadad II (?) said he would return the cities his father, Ben-hadad I, had captured from Ahab's father, and that Ahab might establish **streets** (bazaars) for himself in Damascus, like Ben-hadad I had done in Samaria. Ahab declared that with that agreement he would let him go. So he made a covenant with him and let him go.

God's Judgment for Sparing Ben-hadad. 20:35-43. **35-37.** Then one of the members of the prophetic guild was compelled, doubtlessly by the LORD's Spirit, to deliver a message of rebuke to Ahab in a parable. Therefore, he requested a colleague to strike him. The colleague refused and, as punishment, was slain by a lion. The prophet requested another associate to smite him, which he did, wounding him.

38-40. The wounded prophet then disguised himself with a headband over his eyes and went to await Ahab at the roadside. He called to the king and told him that when he had gone out into the heaviest part of the battle, suddenly a man turned and brought another man to him, ordering him to guard him with his life or he would be fined a talent of silver (about $1,500). The servant said that while he was tending to other things, the prisoner disappeared. Immediately

Ahab answered, "That is your sentence; you have given it yourself" (lit. Heb. trans.). **41.** Then the man quickly removed the bandage from over his eyes. The king of Israel instantly recognized him as one of the prophets.

42. Then the prophet pronounced the LORD's condemnation on Ahab because he had permitted the man whom the LORD had destined for destruction to get away. Ahab's life would be for his life and Ahab's people for his people (22:31-39). **43.** The king of Israel, without genuine repentance and submission to God, went home to Samaria embittered and angry, his weak character running true to form (cf. 21:4).

J. AHAB AND NABOTH'S VINEYARD. 21:1-29.

Ahab Covets the Vineyard. 21:1-4. **1.** Naboth, an inhabitant of the city of Jezreel, owned a vineyard that adjoined Ahab's winter palace northwest of Mount Gilboa on the Plain of Esdraelon. Ahab was king at Samaria, but on occasion he lived in his Jezreel residence. **2.** Coveting the vineyard and vegetable garden, Ahab requested Naboth to sell it to him for cash or to exchange it for another vineyard.

3. The owner refused, not because of disloyalty or disrespect to the king, but because he was solely concerned with God's word out of conscientious regard for the divine Law (Lev. 25:10-34), which for important reasons prohibited the sale of a paternal inheritance. Even if, through extreme poverty or death, the land was assigned to someone else, conveyance was made on the condition that it was redeemable at anytime.

In any event, it had to be returned to the original owner at the year of jubilee; it could not be alienated from the family. On those grounds Naboth refused to comply with the king's demands. **4.** Therefore, Ahab's childish and sulky demeanor (cf. 20:43) was purely the result of a spirit of selfishness that could not tolerate any disappointment in possessing what he coveted. He **turned away his face** and refused to eat.

Jezebel's Twin Crimes of Murder and Theft. 21:5-16. **5-6.** When Ahab explained to his wife, Jezebel, the cause of his bitterness and disappointment, she at once displayed the utter ruthlessness of her wicked character. **7.** Caustically she taunted her weak husband, **Dost thou now govern the kingdom of Israel?** or "What a fine king you are! Do you even use your power to take what your heart desires?"

8-10. With calm viciousness she **wrote letters in Ahab's name, and sealed them with his seal.** The seal ring bore the name of the king and gave validity to the documents to which it was affixed (Esther 8:8; Dan. 6:17). By permitting his unprincipled wife to use the signet ring, Ahab passively consented to Jezebel's proceedings. Sealed in the royal name, the letters possessed the character of a royal edict. From Samaria, Jezebel sent the letters to the elders and nobles who were in Jezreel, Naboth's home city.

11-12. The unprincipled magistrates, wicked tools of Jezebel, followed the orders. They pretended that a heavy guilt lay on somebody in their city who was charged with blaspheming God and the king. Insinuating that Ahab was threatening vengeance on the whole city unless the culprit was discovered and punished, they assembled the people to observe a solemn fast. This action was common on extraordinary occasions, if the public interest demanded it (2 Chron. 20:3; Ezra 8:21; Joel 1:14; 2:15; Jonah 3:5).

Proclaiming a fast, the corrupt rulers

and officials in Jezreel had in mind giving an external appearance of justice for their crooked proceedings. They insinuated that Naboth's crime amounted to treason against the king's life. **They set Naboth on high**, either in exaltation of pretended honor, or in the sense of "lifting up his head" (Gen. 40:20) for accusation.

13. There came in **two men** who were **worthless** (i.e., "sons of Belial," KJV; or scoundrels, cf. Judg. 19:22; 20:13; 1 Sam. 1:16; 2:12; 10:27; 25:17, 25; 30:22; 2 Sam. 16:7). The two rascals were good-for-nothings who had been bribed to swear a falsehood. This procedure required two witnesses in capital offenses (Deut. 17:6; 19:15; Num. 35:30; Matt. 26:60). Cursing God and cursing the king were offenses closely connected in the Law (Exod. 22:28), for the king of Israel was viewed as an earthly representative of God.

They carried Naboth **out of the city, and stoned him.** The Law does not specify the exact mode of the penalty for this offense. Either custom or Jezreel's authorities decided a proper punishment would be stoning, which was always inflicted outside of the city (cf. Acts 7:57-58).

15. Jezebel said to Ahab, **Arise, take possession.** Naboth's property then became forfeited to the crown, not by the Law, but by traditional custom (cf. 2 Sam. 16:4). Naboth's family was involved in the same fatal sentence (2 Kings 9:26). **16.** When Ahab got news that Naboth was dead, he **rose up to go down** from Samaria to Jezreel to claim the vineyard.

Elijah Reproves Ahab. 21:17-29. **17-19.** The LORD directed Elijah the Tishbite (17:1) to go and pronounce doom upon Ahab and his house for so basely expropriating Naboth's vineyard. **20-26.** When Ahab saw Elijah, he said, **Hast thou found me, O mine enemy?** The appearance of the prophet at such a time was fraught with evil for Ahab. Elijah's language was appropriately ominous (cf. Ezek. 45:8; 46:16-18).

Because Ahab had **sold** himself **to work evil**, that is, allowed sin to acquire unchecked and complete mastery over him (cf. Gen. 4:7; 2 Kings 17:7; Rom. 7:11), his house was to be destroyed (cf. 1 Kings 15:29; 16:8-12). Jezebel, though included among the members of Ahab's house, had her own ignominious fate expressly foretold (cf. 2 Kings 9:30-37). This was because of her special wickedness.

27. But Ahab, unlike Jezebel, was not obdurately unrepentant. The terrible judgment pronounced on him and his house made a deep impression on the king. The tearing of his clothes, wearing sackcloth, fasting, walking **softly**, that is, barefoot, with a deeply sorrowful attitude were manifestations of the deepest sorrow. **28-29.** However, God's mercy shines through this dark scene, and the threatened punishment, although assured, was deferred.

K. AHAB'S DEATH. 22:1-53.

Ahab and Jehoshaphat in Alliance. 22:1-4. **1-4.** During the three years of peace between them, Syria and Israel had formed a military alliance and successfully fought, together with other allies, against the invading Assyrians at Qarqar (853 B.C.). Now with the Assyrian menace in abeyance, Ahab formed an alliance with Jehoshaphat of Judah, marrying his daughter, Athaliah, to the son of the king of Judah (2 Kings 8:16-18). Old enmity, temporarily set aside because of the mutual threat of the king of Assyria, was stirred up anew over a quarrel concerning the possession of the town of Ramoth-gilead, east of the Jordan (cf. 1 Kings 4:13; Deut. 4:43). Although the alliance was politically advantageous for Jehoshaphat, spiritually it was a very dangerous expedient. It was to lead to tragic results.

The Lying Prophets Predict Victory. 22:5-16. Although Jehoshaphat was helping the ungodly and loving them that hated the Lord, he would pay dearly for what he was doing (cf. 2 Chron. 19:2). **5.** Essentially a good king who feared the Lord, he therefore required that they first consult the word of the Lord.

6. The king of Israel gathered together the prophets, about four hundred men. All of them were false prophets, that is, they spoke what was expedient to speak or what they were paid to speak, in some cases what they were demonically inspired to speak. They were obviously prophets of the Lord and not of Baal. Yet, they were paid by the king; therefore, they said what he wanted to hear. They told him to go to war because the king wanted to go to war.

7-8. Jehoshaphat, otherwise a godly man, had doubts about their predictions. So Ahab called Micaiah, the son of Imlah. But Ahab protested that he hated him because he never prophesied good concerning him, but only evil. That was inescapable since Ahab's evil ways constantly deserved divine chastisement. **10.** Ahab and Jehoshaphat, officially robed, each sat on his throne at **a threshing floor** by the entrance of the gate of Samaria; and all the prophets prophesied before them. The "threshing floor" had been a name that was a hangover from the time before the city was built, when the place had actually been a threshing floor.

11. A false prophet, Zedekiah, made horns for himself (cf. Deut. 33:17; Zech. 1:18-21) and asserted that with the horns of iron the Syrians would be gored until

they were annihilated. **12.** All the prophets prophesied as men pleasers, declaring exactly the opposite of the Lord's will.

13. The messenger who was sent for Micaiah warned him that all the prophecies were favorable and that he should be careful that his was also. **14.** Micaiah showed his true credentials as a true prophet of the Lord, saying, **As the Lord lives, what the Lord says to me, that I will speak** (NASB). **15-16.** Micaiah aped the "yes men" of the king, but even Ahab suspected that his answer was not from the Lord.

Micaiah's True Prophecy. 22:17-28. **17-18.** Micaiah's vision of all Israel scattered over the mountains, as sheep without a shepherd, was a plain warning to Ahab that disaster awaited him at Ramoth-gilead. Yet he was determined to have his own way; since he was sealed for doom, no warning could affect him.

19-23. The celestial scene depicted by Micaiah is very revealing theologically, disclosing the power of Satan and demons to influence prophets of God, who ought to speak the truth by the Spirit of God, but for one reason or another compromise the Word of God and open themselves to demonic deception, and thus become false prophets.

The spirit that came forth, standing before the Lord, said he would be a spirit of deception (v. 22), speaking to all Ahab's prophets. This is one of the few passages in the Old Testament where the curtain to the supernatural world is lifted and an insight is given of the satanic and demonic powers operating there, affecting the actions of wicked men (cf. New Testament passages, 1 Tim. 4:1-6; 1 John 4:1-7; Rev. 16:13-16). Here is an Old Testament illustration of the truth that behind all false doctrine and all perversions of the truth are demon powers working in those who will not obey and follow the Word of God.

24. The insolent pride and blindness of compromising prophets were displayed in Zedekiah as he struck Micaiah on the cheek, saying, "How did the Spirit of the LORD pass from me to speak with you?" (BV). **27.** Ahab showed the mean spirit of all persecutors and opposers of the Word of God. Micaiah was ordered back to prison, to be fed short prison rations "until," Ahab declared, "I return in peace" (BV). No persecutors are so relentlessly cruel as those who are religious and at the same time reject the Word of God. In them demonic blindness is complemented by demonic hatred of the truth against those who would dare to speak the truth.

Ahab's Defeat and Death. 22:29-40.
29. Despite the solemn warning of the prophet of God, Jehoshaphat, like all compromisers, was blinded to the reality of the truth. Compromise always deludes people to take a tragic course. The king of Israel did so and **went up to Ramoth-gilead. 30.** Apparently, on approaching the scene of action, Ahab's courage failed. Hoping to bypass the thrust of Micaiah's prophecy by a secret strategem, he took on the uniform of a subordinate, while he advised Jehoshaphat to fight in his royal attire. **31.** The Syrian king, with a view either to put the speediest end to the war or perhaps to wipe out the shame of his own humiliation (20:31), had given special instructions to his generals to single out Ahab and to either take or kill him. **32-33.** The officers at first directed their attack on Jehoshaphat. But, becoming conscious of their mistake, they desisted. Jehoshaphat was miraculously saved.

34-36. Ahab, on the other hand, was miraculously killed. A soldier drew a bow at a venture and struck the king of Israel between the scale armor and the breastplate. The arrow was guided by a higher hand and found the disguised king of Israel. God's word is sure; it must come to pass.

37-38. Ahab's body was taken back to Samaria and buried. His chariot was washed by the pool of Samaria, where the prostitutes washed themselves, while the dogs licked his blood, **according unto the word of the Lord which he spoke** (cf. 21:19). The text renders this, **They washed his armor.** However, the consonantal text of the Hebrew can be rendered, "and the harlots washed themselves there." If this reading is correct, the dogs came to lick up Ahab's blood; the harlots came to wash. It was a double curse, showing the extreme divine displeasure against a man who had so despised the Word of God.

39. The **ivory house** refers to Ahab's palace in Samaria, decorated with ivory inlay and containing furniture decorated with ivory. Archaeological excavations at Samaria (cf. 10:22; Amos 3:15) brought to light some of these decorated inlays.

Judah Under Jehoshaphat. 22:41-50.
41-43. Succeeding a godly father, Jehoshaphat himself was a godly man. **44.** His main mistake was that he aligned himself with Ahab of Israel (cf. 2 Chron. 17:1—21:1). Thus, he violated a very important principle of Scripture found in 2 Corinthians 6:14—7:1. **46.** Jehoshaphat's moral reforms included the eradication of male prostitutes remaining from the days of his father.

47-48. Jehoshaphat controlled Edom (2 Chron. 20), wishing to imitate Solomon in maritime operations (cf. 1 Kings 9:26-28; 10:22). He constructed a fleet of **ships of Tarshish** (cf. 10:22), that is, a fleet bearing raw copper or smelted copper from the Arabah as stock in trade in exchange for wares from foreign lands, such as gold from Ophir.

Israel Under Ahaziah. 22:51-53.

51-53. Ahaziah, the son of Ahab, followed in the evil ways of his parents, as a Baal-worshiper. The account of his reign is continued in 2 Kings 1.

SECOND KINGS

INTRODUCTION
See Introduction to 1 Kings

OUTLINE

COMMENTARY

I. THE DIVIDED KINGDOM TILL THE FALL OF SAMARIA. 1:1—17:41.

A. ELIJAH AND AHAZIAH. 1:1-18.

Moab's Rebellion. 1:1. **1.** David had reduced Moab to servitude (2 Sam. 8:2). The famous Moabite stone recounts the war of liberation that Mesha, king of Moab, successfully waged against Ahab's successors. Moab's revolt is mentioned here parenthetically, the subject being resumed in 3:4-27.

Ahaziah's Illness and Sin. 1:2. **2.** Ahaziah sustained serious injury as the result of having fallen through a latticed window to the court below. In seeking an oracle from Baal-zebub, Ahaziah demonstrated that he was following closely in the footsteps of his apostate father, trying to syncretize Baal worship with the worship of the LORD.

His action was an insult to the LORD and constituted a deliberate spurning of the covenant. So it precipitated a contest between the LORD and Baal. **Baal-zebub** ("lord of the flies") was **the god of Ekron,** doubtlessly a deliberate alteration of the Hebrew form of the name, scorning the Canaanite Baal-zebul ("lord of the high place"). Ekron was one of the five chief Philistine cities.

Elijah's Message of Judgment. 1:3-8. **3-4. The angel of the Lord,** evidently the LORD Himself (Gen. 22:15-16; Judg. 2:1), spoke to Elijah the Tishbite (cf. 1 Kings 17:1), directing him to confront the messengers of Ahaziah. God Himself took up the challenge. Ahaziah's open, flagrant apostasy from God incurred the sin of physical death (cf. 1 John 5:16). **Thou ... shalt surely die. 5-6.** The messengers returned to Ahaziah and related the message of doom. **7-8.** The king recognized that Elijah was the one who fitted the description: **a hairy man with a leather girdle bound around his loins** (BV).

The Lord's Contest with Baal. 1:9-15. **9.** Displaying his wicked rebellion against God's covenant, Ahaziah sent a captain with his company of fifty to punish or arrest Elijah. The army of Israel was organized by thousands, hundreds, and fifties, and each unit had its captain (*śar*; cf. Num. 1:16; 10:36; 1 Sam. 8:12). The insolent command of the king's soldiers to Elijah to come **down** from the hill dishonored the LORD's covenant by dishonoring His prophet.

10. The **fire from heaven** that consumed the captain and his fifty men demonstrated the power of the LORD in contrast to the powerlessness of Baal. It is futile to argue over the morality or immorality of this action. Elijah could do nothing but obey. The act was that of a sovereign, infinitely holy, infinitely jealous God, showing His wrath against corrupting idolatry. **11-12.** Repetition of the incident shows the terrible rebellion and demonic blindness that is inflicted upon idolaters. Scripture clearly teaches that demonism is the dynamic of idolatry (1 Cor. 10:20).

13-14. The third captain was sent with his fifty, but he fell on his knees before Elijah and begged for mercy. **15.** The angel of the LORD instructed Elijah to go down with the captain from a hill near

495

Samaria and not to be afraid of the wicked Ahaziah, but to face him boldly in the name of the LORD.

Elijah Before the King. 1:16. **16.** Fearlessly, the man of God stood before the king and pronounced judgment, reading the earlier message given to the messengers (vv. 4, 6).

Ahaziah Dies—Jehoram Becomes King. 1:17-18. **17. So he died.** The Word of God stands sure; it must be fulfilled (cf. Isa. 55: 10-11). Ahaziah died without a male heir. His brother Jehoram, another son of Ahab, succeeded him. The synchronism referring to the **second year of Jehoram** involves a coregency in Judah (see 3:1 and Introduction; also see chronology chart in 1 Kings).

B. ELIJAH TRANSLATED; ELISHA SUCCEEDS HIM. 2:1-25.

Elisha Follows Elijah to the Jordan. 2:1-6. **1.** The time for Elijah's departure had come. His faithful LORD, whom he had served so faithfully, would **take** him **up** (lit., "cause him to go up" or "ascend") **into heaven** (cf. Gen. 5:24) **by a whirlwind**, indicating a tempest of wind. Elijah and Elisha left Gilgal, obviously not the place in the Jordan Valley near Jericho, but the town in Ephraim near Shiloh, modern Jiljulieh. It was a seat of worship contaminated by Baalism (Hos. 4:15; Amos 4:4).

2. Elijah told Elisha to tarry (remain) in Gilgal while he went on to Bethel, because Elijah was not certain whether it was God's will that Elisha should accompany him (cf. v. 10). Elisha's three-time refusal to leave the venerable prophet settled the doubt. Elisha's determination to follow the prophet was expressed by a solemn and emphatic oath, meaning literally, "By the life of the LORD, and by the life of thy soul," that is, "of thyself," **I will not leave thee.**

3-6. Elisha was to visit the three schools of the prophets to fortify them against the inroads of Baalism. These schools of the prophets were Old Testament theological seminaries. The spiritual hope of the people resided in them. **The sons of the prophets** were students and disciples of the prophets. Older men taught the younger men, who in turn exercised a teaching ministry to the people (cf. 1 Sam. 10:10; 19:20; 1 Kings 20:35).

The Spirit of the LORD had revealed to the prophetic college that Elijah was going to depart from this life. **The Lord will take away ... today.** "Today" is emphatic in the Hebrew; so it should read, "Knowest thou that this day the LORD is about to take away thy lord **from thy head**?" (that is, "from his position of superiority over you as your teacher and master"; 1 Kings 19:21; Acts 22:3). "I, too, know," replied Elisha (lit. Heb. trans.), **hold ye your peace** (Heb., *hĕhᵉshû*, simply "hush, be still"). He evidently meant that the subject was too painful, both to him and to his beloved master, and too exalted to discuss freely.

The Miracle of the Parted Waters. 2:7-8. **7.** Fifty men of the prophetic guild came and stood some distance from Elijah and Elisha while both of them stood by the Jordan. They were eager to see how the two would cross the stream at a point where there was no ford. **8.** Then Elijah took **his mantle**, the hairy outer garment, which characterized him as a prophet (cf. Zech. 13:4), and wrapped it together (Heb., "rolled it up") and struck the waters of the Jordan. This symbolic action was like that of Moses' smiting the rock or stretching out his staff over the sea. The waters were divided, and they went over on dry land (cf. Exod. 14:16, 21-22; Josh. 4:22-24).

Elisha's Request. 2:9-10. **9.** Elisha

besought Elijah for a **double portion of his spirit** (the Holy Spirit, vv. 15-16) to **be upon me.** In doing this, Elisha was asking to be treated as a firstborn among the sons of the prophets (cf. Deut. 21:17). Consequently, he received twice as great a share of the prophetic blessing and power of his master as any of the rest. In asking to be the firstborn among the prophet's spiritual sons, Elisha was thinking of the paternal blessing of a departing father (Gen. 27:4, 12); see "my father, my father" (v. 12). **10.** Elijah explained that he had **asked a hard thing** because only God could do what was asked or give what was asked. The prophet attached a condition that would be entirely dependent upon God's will.

Elijah's Translation. 2:11-12. **11.** It happened as they were going on farther and farther, talking as they went. Where they were going, we are not told, probably to some height on the mountains of Gilead, Elijah's native country (cf. Num. 20:28; Deut. 34:1, 5); **Behold, there appeared a chariot of fire** (or, "chariots of fire," the Hebrew word *rĕkĕb* generally meaning collective "chariots" of fire and horses of fire (cf. 6:17). The fiery chariots and horses came between Elijah and Elisha, the flaming war host separating the two (cf. 6:17).

Elijah **went up by a whirlwind into heaven.** "Whirlwind" is properly a "storm blast" (Job. 38:1; Ezek. 1:4; Nah. 1:3). This was not the death of Elijah, but his translation without seeing death. Like Enoch (Gen. 5:24), he appeared with Moses on the mount of transfiguration. The transfiguration scene foreshadows the power and coming of our Lord Jesus Christ, according to Peter's exegesis (2 Pet. 1:16-21). In the transfiguration scene, Elijah represents the saints who will be caught up in the clouds to meet the Lord in the air without dying (1 Cor. 15:51-53; 1 Thess. 4:13-18). Moses is representative of those saints who will die and be raised again.

12. And Elisha ... cried. (Lit., "And Elisha was seeing, and *he* [emphatic] was shouting.") Great joy overwhelmed him because he had seen his master taken away, and he consequently would receive the double portion of the firstborn son. **The chariot of Israel, and its horsemen** describes what Elijah was to the nation. In that era, chariots and horsemen constituted an important part of the military arm, as is known from extrabiblical sources, particularly Assyrian accounts of battle. Horses and chariots were indispensable for the struggle against the Aramaean states (1 Kings 20:1; Psalm 20:7; cf. 2 Kings 7:6; 10:2; 13:14). Elijah's spiritual power and influence were Israel's greatest national defense. As a token of great sorrow, Elisha ripped his own garments in two from top to bottom, realizing the loss the nation had sustained (cf. 1 Kings 11:30).

Elisha's First Miracle–The Waters Parted Again. 2:13-14. **13-14.** Elisha took Elijah's mantle, which had fallen upon him, and struck the waters of the Jordan. The mantle was the symbol of the prophetic office. Standing on Jordan's brink, he cried, **Where is the Lord God of Elijah?** Had He left the earth with His prophet? If not, let Him now display His power and show that He has granted my request (v. 9; cf. Jer. 2:6, 8). Verse 14 does not mean that Elisha struck the waters of the Jordan twice. The *Revised Standard Version* is preferred here: He "struck" the water, saying, "Where is the LORD, the God of Elijah? And when he had struck the water, the water was parted to the one side and to the other."

The Request of the Sons of the Prophets. 2:15-18. **15.** The group of the prophets, who had seen Elisha from the other side of the river, realized **the spirit of Elijah** rested **on Elisha**, that is, it had alighted and settled down to remain on him. The proof was that Elisha had just repeated his master's miracle.

16. After Elisha had recounted the translation of Elijah, they selected fifty strong men, doubtlessly attendants of the teachers and students in the theological seminary. Their being valiant men was important, for they determined to search for Elijah in the mountains of Gilead, which involved great danger.

Although the sons of the prophets acknowledged Elisha's succession and belonged to the faithful remnant in Israel, they were filled with doubt about Elijah's translation. They thought that the Spirit might have transported the prophet to another locality on earth (cf. 1 Kings 18:12; Ezek. 3:14; 8:3; Acts 8:39-40).

17-18. They disobeyed Elisha's command and urged him to such a degree to send out a search party that he became ashamed and yielded. After three days of unsuccessful searching, they returned and confessed their mistake. They were like the disciples of our Lord, slow to believe (cf. Luke 24:25), and like many believers today who do not really believe in the translation of the church.

Elisha's Second Miracle. 2:19-22. **19.** Elisha's second miracle was a miracle of mercy. The citizens of Jericho, not the sons of the prophet, complained about the bad water that made the land sterile. **20-22.** Salt, symbolizing healing, was to be placed in a new cruse, the holy purpose to be accomplished requiring a vessel uncontaminated by use (cf. Num. 19:2; 2 Sam. 6:3).

Today the finest spring in Jericho is commonly called "Elisha's Fountain." Jericho pictures the world under the curse (see Josh. 6). He who is greater than Elisha, and is prefigured by Elisha, will return in glory to heal the earth, now under the curse of sin and death. When that curse is removed, healing will come to the earth as it came to Jericho.

Elisha's Third Miracle. 2:23-25. The third miracle was one of judgment. **23.** Individuals, translated **youths**, were males anywhere between the age of six and twenty. Therefore, those who mocked, that is, derided or jeered (cf. Hab. 1:10), were young men. They were from Bethel and no doubt were associated with the syncretistic worship established there (cf. 1 Kings 12:25-33). They were infidels and scoffers and made fun of Elijah's translation and made a joke of Elisha. In doing so, they were despising the Word of God and casting aspersion upon the covenant of God.

24. Avenging the honor of the LORD was the issue at stake. The curse of the prophet was an inspired prediction of punitive disaster. Their dishonoring the new prophetic leader was an affront directed at the LORD, which called for the judgment predicted in Leviticus 26:21-22. Wild beasts were common in Palestine in those days, and two female bears (cf. Hos. 13:8; Amos 5:19) became the instruments God used to vindicate His prophet. It is idle to criticize the morality of this episode. Mockers and rejecters of the Word of God in every age will receive their punishment in due time (cf. 2 Pet. 3:3-7).

C. ELISHA AND JEHORAM. 3:1-27.

Jehoram's Reign over Israel. 3:1-3. **1-3.** Jehoram attempted a partial reformation. He reigned from 852 to 841 B.C., **and he wrought evil.** Surely he "did evil" **in the eyes of the Lord.** He maintained worship of the bull at Bethel, thus adhering to the sins of Jeroboam (cf. 1

Kings 12:28; 16:2, 26). **He put away the image of Baal that his father had made.** The image was more exactly a "pillar" (cf. 2 Chron. 34:4). The Septuagint, Vulgate, and Arabic read "pillars." They had paganistic fertility-rite connotations.

The Rebellion of Moab. 3:4-20. **4.** The account of the Moabite war, presented from the viewpoint of King Mesha of Moab, is preserved on the famous Moabite stone, discovered in 1868 and housed in the Louvre. Mesha was **a sheep breeder** (Heb., *nōqēd*, Amos 1:1). Annual tribute to Israel was paid in kind and consisted of one hundred thousand fatted lambs and one hundred thousand rams and their fleece. **5.** It was a very heavy burden on such a small country as Moab so the country **rebelled**, that is, refused payment of the annual tribute.

6-7. So Jehoram **numbered all Israel**, that is, mustered an army and enlisted the help of Jehoshaphat of Judah. **8.** Jehoshaphat joined the unholy alliance in spite of the prophetic rebukes of his alliance with Ahab and Ahaziah (cf. 2 Chron. 19:2; 20:37). His reply to Ahab's son was similar to that given in 1 Kings 22:4. Jehoram **said, Which way shall we go up?** Jehoshaphat's reply was **The way through the wilderness of Edom.**

9. Thus, the king chose to march south around the southern end of the Dead Sea through the northern borders of Edom. He chose that way because the northern borders of Moab at the north end of the Dead Sea were well fortified, as is known from the Moabite stone. **They made a circuit of seven days' journey** means they went around the Dead Sea, a journey of seven days. They were joined by **the king of Edom,** a vassal king, appointed by Jehoshaphat (1 Kings 22:47). The coalition soon ran into trouble. There was no water for the army and the cattle that followed them,

that is, the herds and flocks brought along for food.

10-11. Jehoshaphat's conscience was troubled by this ungodly alliance; so he inquired for **a prophet of the Lord**, as he had done in 1 Kings 22:7. But while he turned to the LORD, the godless Jehoram fell into a fit of despair. One of the **king of Israel's servants**, who like Obadiah (1 Kings 18:3) was doubtlessly a friend of the LORD's prophets, reported that Elisha was among the troops, and is described as having poured water on Elijah's hands. This is an allusion to the well-known Oriental custom of a servant pouring water from a vessel on his master's hands to wash them, signifying general personal attendance.

12-14. The two kings consulted Elisha. Valorously and uncompromisingly, Elisha refused to have anything to do with Jehoram, but he honored Jehoshaphat. Jehoshaphat, who knew the LORD but was in evil company, was tacitly rebuked, while Jehoram was openly reprimanded. **15.** The Spirit of God was grieved, and Elisha lacked the power to prophesy. First he needed a minstrel to calm his own agitated spirit and get into the condition of soul to give the needed oracle. Jehoshaphat should have been affected and humbled by the fact that after calling for a prophet of the LORD, the divine mouthpiece was unable to prophesy at once. Unholy alliances and attachments hinder the manifestation of the Spirit of God. How grieved and quenched the Holy Spirit is when God's children fraternize and form alliances with ungodly people.

16-20. Then the ditches or trenches, which had been dug in obedience to the command given to Elisha, were miraculously filled with water. It was a supernatural gift of water that came **when the meal offering was offered** (cf. 1 Kings

18:29, 36). According to the Talmud, the morning sacrifice was offered in the Temple the moment it became light. This recalls a spiritual truth that God has supplied the water of life through our Lord Jesus Christ, who is the true meal offering.

The Defeat of Moab. 3:21-25. **21.** Meanwhile, the Moabites mobilized the entire male population for the defense of their country to stand on their frontier. **22.** And the Moabite camp **rose up early** on the frontier mountains. The rising sun tinged the water to make it look bloodred (*'āḏōm*). No doubt the water was further reddened by the red earth of Edom. **23.** The Moabites concluded that this was the blood of the kings who had fallen upon one another and killed themselves. So the order was given for Moab to rush to the spoil.

24-25. The onrushing Moabites were utterly surprised by the Israelites, and Elisha's prediction was fulfilled in the utter defeat of the Moabites and the devastation of their land. **Only in Kir-hareseth left they its stones.** Work of destruction stopped only before the walls of the principal stronghold of the country. Called Kir of Moab (Isa. 15:1), Kir-heres (Isa. 16:11) is Kerak ("castle"), which stands on a steep cliff of chalk some twenty miles northeast of the southern extremity of the Dead Sea.

The Lesson for Israel. 3:26-27. When the king of Moab saw that he was losing the battle, seven hundred swordsmen tried to break through to the king of Edom, whom he thought would have less zeal for the war since he was a vassal of Judah. But they failed. Mesha took his firstborn son, who would have been king in his place. Following the sheer brutality of paganism, he offered him up as a sacrifice on the wall.

This was a clear-cut, vivid demonstration to God's people of how utterly abominable heathen religion was to

God. A never-to-be-forgotten object lesson was presented to Israel as to why they should abandon idolatry. **There was great indignation against Israel.** The *Revised Standard Version* renders this "great wrath upon Israel." The true translation should be "great indignation in Israel" (the Heb. prep. *'al* here has the sense of "in," not "against" as in the KJV).

This abominably shocking act, performed before the eyes of all the army, aroused such terrible indignation in the people of God (cf. Lev. 18:21; 20:3) that, in utter revulsion the kings broke off the siege and returned to their land. The question may well be asked, though, Why, if Israel was so deeply moved in this case, was she not jolted out of her foolish infatuation with idolatry? Idolatry is backed by demon delusion and demon power and is not easily thrown off (1 Cor. 10:20; Rev. 9:20-21).

D. ELISHA'S MIRACLES. 4:1-44.

The Widow's Oil Multiplied. 4:1-7. The prophetic ministry of Elisha is highlighted from chapters 4 through 8. It is designed to demonstrate that God cares for His people and sovereignly undertakes for them. There is no need, personal or national, that He cannot meet.

1. The widow of one of the members of the prophetic guild (school of the prophets; cf. 1 Kings 20:35) appealed to Elisha. She had been left in an impoverished state at the death of her husband, and **the creditor** had come to claim her two sons in payment for the debt. According to the Law, they would have to continue in servitude until the year of jubilee (Lev. 25:39-40). **2.** In asking what he might do for the woman, Elisha inquired what she had in the house. She replied that she only had a small jar of oil.

3. The prophet directed her to borrow vessels from all her neighbors. They were to be empty vessels and **not a few**; she was not to stint in borrowing. **4.** When she had done so, she was to shut the door upon herself and her sons, that is, shut herself in privately in the presence of God, who was to demonstrate His love and kindness to her and her family (cf. Luke 8:51, 54). The visitation by God was to be a sort of Holy of Holies upon which profane eyes and unbelieving hearts were not to gaze.

5-6. When the vessels were all filled, the woman called for another vessel. Her son replied, **There is not a vessel more.** Gracious is the LORD. He is the Father of the widow and the Friend of the orphan, as is beautifully set forth in this miracle. What a grand lesson of faith! The vessels had to be produced to be filled. The greater their faith, the greater number of vessels they would gather. If there had been more vessels, the oil would have filled them all. The limitation was not in the supply of oil but in the lack of empty vessels to be filled. We can always come in faith to God's abundance of grace with our empty vessels to receive of His fullness of grace. When there were no more vessels, the oil stopped flowing (Heb. "stood," i.e., "halted" or "ceased"; cf. Luke 8:44). **7.** The woman was directed to sell the oil, a common staple of Hebrew life and easily sold, and pay her debt and live on the rest.

A Son Promised the Shunammite Woman. 4:8-17. **8.** One day Elisha crossed over the Plain of Jezreel, which he had to do to pass Shunem, situated on the slope of Little Hermon. The **great woman** was a woman of high rank or wealth (cf. 1 Sam. 25:2; 2 Sam. 19:32). She persuaded Elisha to stay for lunch, and after that he went into her house for refreshment as often as he passed that way.

9-10. The woman recognized him as a holy man of God. She and her husband

decided to make an upstairs guest chamber with a bed, table, chair, and lamp in it for him, that whenever he might visit he could rest there. **11-13.** One day as he came by he stopped to rest in the roof room. He ordered his servant, Gehazi, to communicate with the woman, thinking that she would express herself more freely to his servant than to him.

As a token of his appreciation of her hospitality, Elisha through Gehazi asked the woman what favor might be done for her: **Wouldest thou be spoken for to the king,** or any favor she might desire from the king or from the army's commander in chief, the next most powerful person to the king. The answer of the woman, **I dwell among mine own people,** meant that she did not need any particular favor, since her relatives would take care of her if she had any need.

14-15. After Gehazi had reported that the woman had no children, which to a Hebrew woman was a misfortune and a reproach (cf. Gen. 30:23; 1 Sam. 1:6-7, 27), the Shunammite was summoned into the presence of the prophet himself. She stood reverently at the door. **16.** Elisha announced that the next season, about this time, she would **embrace a son.** The woman was so overcome with emotion that she cried out, **Do not lie,** that is, "Do not delude me" (cf. Sarah's reaction, Gen. 18:12-13).

The Son of the Shunammite Raised from the Dead. 4:18-37. **18-20.** On a day after the child had grown up, he went out to his father and the harvesters. Suddenly he complained of a severe headache. The child was carried home by a servant, evidently the victim of a sunstroke. He died upon his mother's lap at noon.

21-22. She carried him up to the guest chamber (the prophet's room), and laid him on the bed of the man of God and told her husband to call for a servant and donkey to make a quick trip to the man of God. **23.** It seemed strange to her husband that she wanted to visit the prophet when it was neither the new moon nor the Sabbath. It implies that the faithful in Israel were accustomed to resort to the prophets on these holy days for the sake of religious instruction. **24.** The woman's instruction, **Slacken not thy riding for me** means, "Do not stop or slow down."

25. Elisha was at Mount Carmel (cf. v. 9), which apparently served as a fixed center of prophetic teaching for the north, as Gilgal, Bethel, and Jericho did for the south. **27-29.** When the woman arrived, Elisha directed Gehazi to take his staff and hurry to the child and lay it on his face. **30.** The woman knew and Elisha knew that no staff would suffice. She refused to return without the prophet, knowing that the case required the warmth of the personal touch, which life from God always requires.

34. The flesh of the child became warm. The life of the divine Spirit was imparted miraculously by contact with the lifeless body (cf. Gen. 2:7). **35. The child sneezed seven times.** The first signs of restored respiration were seen. They are described in successive steps. Miracles sometimes were performed instantaneously; in some cases they advanced progressively toward completion (cf. 1 Kings 18:44-45; Mark 8:24-25). The comment of the writer to the Hebrews is: "Women received their dead raised to life again" (11:35; cf. 1 Kings 17:22).

The Poisonous Pottage Made Harmless. 4:38-41. **38.** Elisha returned to Gilgal, where there was a school of the prophets. He used the famine (cf. 8:1) to teach the danger of subscribing to false teaching. He ordered a big kettle to be put on the fire and a stew made for the sons of the prophets.

39. The wild gourds that poisoned the stew were mistaken for edible gourds. **40.** The young theological students, warned by the familiar bitter taste, realized there was **death in the pot. 41.** The meal, which Elisha placed in the pot before the sons of the prophets, pictures the true Word of God centering in the God of the Word, the Word incarnate, our Lord Jesus Christ.

It is only by the true Word of God, centering in the Word of God incarnate, that the effect of poisonous doctrine can be nullified. Ministers of the Word must be able to detect true doctrine and distinguish it from the false. The truth of the Word can counteract the error of false teaching. The "three measures of meal" (Matt. 13:33) symbolize the truth of the Word, with the leaven representing false doctrine (Matt. 16:11-12; Mark 8:15; 1 Cor. 5:6; Gal. 5:9).

The Miraculous Feeding of a Hundred Men. 4:42-44. **43-44.** This miracle has a striking parallel in Christ's feeding the multitudes (cf. Matt. 14:13-21; 15:32-38). It is symbolic of the abundant wealth of divine grace. Perhaps Baal-shalishah is a place about fourteen miles north of Lydda in the Plain of Sharon (cf. 1 Sam. 9:4). God's power is operative **according to the word of the Lord.** His Word alone can satisfy the deepest hunger of the soul (Matt. 4:4; Deut. 8:3).

E. ELISHA AND NAAMAN'S HEALING. 5:1-27.

Naaman's Leprosy. 5:1. **1.** Naaman ("pleasant") aptly portrays the natural man who enjoys the highest and best but is still unregenerate. He is described as being **a great man with his master** (cf. Gen. 10:9), that is, a man of influence and prestige in the world. He was also called **honorable** (lit. Heb. trans., "lifted up of face"). It is even said that the

LORD worked with him and had **given deliverance unto Syria.** It is not said that Hadad or Rimmon had given victory; rather, the LORD did. Naaman also was a mighty man in valor (i.e., "a brave warrior"). **But he was a leper.** Leprosy vividly illustrates sin, man's fallen and lost state in Adam.

The Testimony of the Israelite Girl. 5:2-4. **2-3.** In contrast to Naaman was the little captive maid, taken from Israel to live at a far distance from her home and her family. However, in her captivity she was happy because she knew the LORD and knew that the prophet in Samaria represented the LORD, who could heal leprosy. She knew and she believed.

She also had a great desire to see the mighty and important Naaman healed. The same grace of God that gave her concern for others also gave her the strength to bare witness for God. In Israel, lepers were excluded from society. Cleansing from leprosy meant being restored to normal life. Hence, the term **cure** means "receive back." Receiving back the leper came to mean "healing the leper" (cf. Num. 12:14-15).

The Message of the Syrian King to the King of Israel. 5:5-7. **5.** It is not known who the king of Israel was, or the king of Syria. The LORD was pleased to use a simple testimony of a servant. The king of Syria heard it and wrote a letter to the king of Israel, telling him to cure Naaman of his leprosy. Naaman took a handsome reward with him of 10 talents (about 920 pounds) of silver, plus 6,000 shekels (about 184 pounds) of gold. The episode probably took place in the reign of Jehoram.

6-7. When the king of Israel received the letter requesting him to cure Naaman of his leprosy, he tore his clothes as if he had heard blasphemy (cf. Matt. 26:65). Did the king of Syria think

that he was God, **to kill and to make alive** (cf. Deut. 32:39; 1 Sam. 2:6)? Leprosy was a kind of living death (cf. Num. 12:12). All the Israelite monarch could think of was that the king of Syria was seeking a quarrel with him.

Elisha Prescribes Healing for Naaman. 5:8-14. **8.** When Elisha heard of the consternation of the king of Israel, he said, **Let him come now to me, and he shall know that there is a prophet in Israel. 9.** The great man of the world with his horses and with his chariot stood before the door of the man of God. **10.** No doubt Keil is correct in suggesting that Elisha did not come out to Naaman because he wished to humble his pride, to impress upon him that worldly self-importance and pride could keep him from being healed. Though some say there is no trace of such a spirit in Naaman, his later conduct at Jordan proves that his ego surfaced.

11. Naaman thought that the prophet would at least come out, stand, and call upon the name of the LORD, his God, waving his hand over the place of the leprosy and heal him, so that he might forthwith be on his way. **12.** In contempt, Naaman contrasted the muddy Jordan with the Abana (modern Barada, which rises in the Antilebanon mountains eighteen miles northwest of Damascus and flows through the city) and the Pharpar, the present Nahr el-Awaj, which flows down from the Great Hermon and skirts Damascus on the south. Both of these rivers are crystalline-clear mountain streams, a striking contrast with the turbid Jordan. Naaman, like the natural man, wanted to be healed and saved in his own way, not God's way. **So he turned and went away in a rage.**

13-14. The servants, however, showed great wisdom. Naaman was desperate enough to listen to them and, as a result, went down and dipped himself seven times in the Jordan. This act does not represent the means of salvation and cleansing, but constitutes the test of saving faith. Through simple faith in the Word of God, as spoken by the prophet, Naaman's body was miraculously made well, like that of a little child, and **he was clean.** What a beautiful picture of "the washing of water by the word" (Eph. 5:26; cf. John 15:3; 17:17).

Elisha Refuses Any Payment. 5:15-19. **15.** Naaman gave indubitable proof, not only of being cleansed from leprosy, but being regenerated, and being made a child of God. The statement that he now knew **there is no God in all the earth, but in Israel** shows that he was really converted.

16. Elisha would not accept the gift that Naaman sought to press upon him, in order to impress upon the new convert that salvation is by grace through faith (Eph. 2:8-9), a free gift of God, not purchased with money or price (Isa. 55:1; 1 Pet. 1:18). Naaman had to learn that he was nothing but a poor, lost sinner, a helpless leper, and all his silver and gold could not purchase his cleansing.

17. However, the new convert did request **two mules' burden of earth** (lit., "a load of a yoke of mules [in] earth"). He, of course, was not all at once divested of pagan thoughts. He wanted to take soil from the Holy Land back to his home so he could build an altar upon it and worship the LORD. He further showed the genuineness of his experience by swearing off all contact with idolatry.

18. He had only one reservation, however. It would be necessary for him to accompany his king into the house of Rimmon (or Hadad), god of Damascus. Whenever he did so, he wished to be pardoned by the LORD. Hadad was the Syrian equivalent of the god of the

storms, the Canaanite Baal of the Ras Shamra texts. Rimmon, the Syrian *Ramanu* (from *ramamu*, "to thunder"), was another name of Hadad. The service Naaman rendered his sovereign as his attendant is indicated by the idiom **leaneth on my hand. 19.** Elisha made no comment on Naaman's declared course of action, neither approving nor disapproving it; he simply gave the parting benediction. His prophetic commission did not extend to any other country but was confined to the conversion of Israel from idolatry.

Gehazi's Covetousness and Punishment. 5:20-27. **20-25.** Gehazi, in running after Naaman, committed the serious sin of covetousness. Bad conduct had a very serious negative effect on the reputation of the office of the true prophet of the LORD. Gehazi also sinned by deliberately lying to Naaman and Elisha.

26-27. But the severity of the punishment, as a result, had a far more serious effect. The LORD would protect the glorious gospel of salvation by grace through faith alone from any act or word that would becloud this great truth. Accepting anything from Naaman on the part of Elisha or his servant would give the impression that Naaman's healing, symbolic of salvation, was in some measure purchased. Simon of Samaria thought he could obtain the gift of God with money (Acts 8:20; cf. Isa. 55:1). Gehazi's case was accepting money for that which God gave to Naaman freely and graciously—faith attested by obedience.

F. ELISHA AND THE SYRIANS. 6:1-33.

Recovery of the Lost Ax Head. 6:1-7. **1.** The history of Elisha's mighty miracle-working ministry is continued. This particular miracle concerns the prophet's causing an iron ax head to float in the Jordan River. It illustrates how God helps in small, personal troubles as well as in great ones of larger scope. At that time, the sons of the prophets had consulted with Elisha about their living quarters becoming too small for them.

2. The prophet agreed that they should go to the Jordan River and each take from there a log and construct for themselves a place to live. **3-4.** The theological students desired their prophet-professor to go with them, which he did. **5.** One of the young prophets was cutting down a tree when his ax head fell into the water. No doubt this was no small calamity for the young man, who, like most theological students, was doubtlessly low in funds. This was aggravated by the fact that the ax was borrowed and its owner had to be repaid.

6. Elisha inquired where it fell. When the place was pointed out, he cast a twig in the water and caused the ax head to float. The iron ax head did not "swim," but simply rose to the surface. Elisha's throwing in the stick (twig) was aimed at helping those who stood by to realize that the coming up of the iron ax head was not a natural but a supernatural phenomenon brought about by God Himself, simply through the prophet's instrumentality.

As in the case of the salt thrown into the spring at Jericho (2:20-22), and the meal put in the poison pottage (4:41), the stick symbol was appropriate to the occasion. It indicated that iron could be made to float like wood by the sovereign power of the LORD, who made the world and established natural law, and who for special purposes could set it aside.

Elisha Discloses Syrian War Plans. 6:8-10. **8-10.** Syria's war plans, supposedly deep secrets, were revealed to the man of God to inform the king of

Israel. So the king of Israel, aided by the prophet of God, sent to the place of which the man of God had informed him. As a result, Elisha warned the king of Israel to avoid an ambush, and he avoided being waylaid **not once or twice** (i.e., three times or more; cf. 2 Chron. 19:10; Ezek. 3:19). In contrast to the previous miracle of the ax head, which involved an individual of relative unimportance, this miracle concerned a nation and its king. God moves providentially in little things as well as in big things.

Elisha Strikes the Syrians Blind. 6:11-23. **11.** The king of Syria was so upset about his war plans being made known to the enemy that he suspected espionage among his own people. **12.** However, one of his servants told him it was Elisha the prophet who had told the king of Israel what the Syrian king said in the privacy of his bedroom.

13. The Syrian king commanded him to find where Elisha was so he might arrest him. He was told that Elisha was in Dothan, a town situated on a hill about ten miles northeast of Samaria on the caravan route from Gilead to Egypt (cf. Gen. 37:17). **14.** The king sent chariotry and a powerful army to Dothan. They arrived at night and surrounded the city.

15-16. In the morning Elisha's servant saw only the great army of horses and chariots besieging the city, but Elisha glimpsed the invisible angelic armies of heaven surrounding them and knew they had no cause for fear. **17.** Then Elisha prayed for the LORD to open the eyes of his servant. The prophet did not pray for the heavenly hosts to come; they were already there. The servant had not been aware of them. **The Lord opened the eyes of the young man, and he saw.**

Similarly, the LORD had opened

Elisha's own eyes to see a vision of heavenly glory when Elijah had been taken away (2:10, 12; cf. Num. 22:31). The Syrians had horses and chariots. God had horses and chariots of fire, fire being the well-known symbol of the divine presence (Gen. 15:17; Exod. 3:2; 13:21; Isa. 29:6; 30:30). Fiery chariots and horses parted Elijah from Elisha (2 Kings 2:11), and the same heavenly army surrounded and protected Elisha.

The fact that the LORD was present and could maneuver the Syrians so easily was meant to teach these men of God, and through them the nation of Israel, that the LORD could protect them from their enemies, as well as enable them to overcome their sins. **18.** Elisha prayed to the LORD that He would afflict the enemy with blindness, and they suddenly lost their powers of recognition. **19-20.** Elisha told them this was neither the way nor the city, and he led them on to Samaria, where he prayed that their eyes would be opened.

21-23. The king of Israel was ready to cut down the army, but Elisha would not allow it, since they were not prisoners of war. Elisha pleaded for them, and they were feasted and then sent away. Evidently the Syrians were taught that Israel's God fought for them and this humiliating experience of His power over them made them see the futility of attacking Israel. This evidently explains the words, **So the bands of Syria came no more into the land of Israel.**

Elisha and the Siege of Samaria. 6:24-33. **24.** Later, however, Benhadad, king of Syria, mustered all his army and besieged Samaria. This was apparently Ben-hadad I of 1 Kings 20 and 2 Kings 8:7. The inscription on the Melkart Stele has been reliably dated at about 850 B.C. (W. F. Albright, BASOR 87 [Oct. 1942]: 23-25; and G. Levi Della Vida, BASOR 90 [April 1943]: 30-33),

although some scholars make him Benhadad II. The famine (cf. Lev. 26:26-29; Deut. 28:51-53) and the siege were chastisements from the LORD to punish His people for violating the covenant (cf. 1 Kings 11:38 for normal covenant requirements).

25. The siege caused such a scarcity of food that even defiling food, such as an **ass's head** and **dove's leavings,** sold for a huge price. The meaning here is a small grain. The Arabs speak of a small plant (*herba alcoli*) as "sparrow's dung." So scarce was the food that a donkey's head brought fifty dollars in silver and a pint of dove's dung about three dollars in silver.

26-29. As he was passing by on the wall, the king of Israel heard a horrible story of famine, demonstrating the terrible straits to which the people of Samaria were reduced by the siege. **30-31.** Although the king was wearing sackcloth, which the people saw as he rent his clothes, and that was a symbol of repentance, his repentance was not real. He vowed vengeance on Elisha in the same breath as he professed to humble himself before God.

32-33. Meanwhile, Elisha realized the king of Israel was the **son of a murderer** (a base assassin) and was sending a messenger to attempt to kill him. The messenger was not admitted. The king arrived and gave full vent to his wicked unbelief: **This trouble is from the Lord! Why should I wait for the Lord any longer?** (RSV). In other words, "Should I not now surrender to the Syrians and slay the prophet, who has so long deluded me with vain hopes?" Here the infidelity of the Israelite king appears in plain view.

G. ELISHA AND THE SIEGE OF SAMARIA. 7:1-20.

Elisha's Startling Prediction. 7:1-2.

1. When the worst had come—Samaria starving to death, the king utterly despondent and viciously rebellious, and Elisha's life threatened—then the mercy and kindness of God were revealed once more. The prophet announced the good news of salvation and deliverance. **Tomorrow ... shall a measure of fine flour be sold for a shekel.** In contrast to 6:25, where the prices were enormously high, here they were unbelievably low. A measure (*se'â*) was about one-tenth of a bushel; a shekel, about sixty-four cents.

2. Then a lord ("captain"; Heb., "third man"; see 1 Kings 9:22) replied to Elisha's prophecy in a tone of scoffing unbelief. Even granting the very improbable supposition that the LORD would make windows in the heavens (Gen. 7:11), sending down supplies through them, the promised cheapness of the provisions could hardly be realized so soon. Elisha answered the voice of unbelief with a stern prediction that would involve the doubter's violent death (cf. vv. 19-20).

The Four Lepers and Their Discovery. 7:3-8. **3-5.** To fulfill His Word, the LORD used four lepers outside the city gate. They faced a quandary. Death faced them if they looked to the city, and death faced them if they went to the camp of the Syrians. They decided on the latter course. These four tragic figures, facing certain death, were the first to discover God's victory for them and the people.

Great need led them to find the needed salvation. The prophet had announced the good news of salvation and deliverance, which is illustrative of the gospel of grace. The courtier who had rejected the good news and refused to believe it represents those who reject the gospel. Great victories, like our salvation, are accomplished by the Lord alone.

6-7. The unseen celestial chariots had frightened the Syrian camp and put the soldiers to flight (cf. 6:20-21). They supposed the king of Israel had hired the **kings of the Hittites, and the kings of the Egyptians** to attack them. Hittites as mercenary bands were common and available, although their empire had long since fallen. Egyptian mercenaries, however, were neither common nor available, nor were the pharaohs called kings of Egypt.

Hebrew consonants, translated "Egyptians," should almost certainly be rendered "Musrians." Shalmanezer III enumerates Musri among his foes at the famous Battle of Qarqar in 853 B.C., and the Musrians are known to have been in alliance with Damascus in 849 and 846 B.C. (NBC, p. 353). **8.** The spoil of the enemy—the bread, water, silver, gold, and raiment—was God's provision for a starving, dying people (cf. Isa. 55:1).

The Day of Good News. 7:9-15. **9.** The poor lepers, who had their fill first and had tasted of God's great salvation, could not hold their peace. They realized, **This day is a day of good tidings ... come ... tell the king's household.** **10-11.** They first told the gatekeepers, who in turn told the good news to the city. **12.** The unbelieving king, who had threatened Elisha's life and still was afflicted with unbelief, concluded that the Syrians had retired to trick the Israelites into coming outside the walls, that they might kill them. He had heard Elisha's promise, but he did not believe it any more than his courtier did. **13-15.** The suggestion of one of the king's servants, who was wise and discreet from a worldly standpoint, perhaps worthy of a courtier, nevertheless was not born of faith.

507

Elisha's Prediction Fulfilled. 7:16-20.
16-20. So the starving people rushed out of the city to partake of the bounty and the deliverance provided by the LORD. Everybody, including the king, saw how wonderfully the word of God, spoken by Elisha, had been fulfilled. But the unbelieving official, who had scoffed at the Word of God, perished violently, being trodden underfoot to his death by the populace as it rushed out of the gate to get the food. What a warning against the wickedness of unbelief, that he who does not believe must die in his sin. The repetition of the Word of God as well as the words of the unbeliever recorded at the beginning of this story prove the peril of rejecting the Word of God, particularly the gospel of grace.

H. ELISHA AND HAZAEL, JEHORAM AND AHAZIAH. 8:1-29.

Prediction of the Famine. 8:1-6. **1.** Evidently the story of Elisha's further aid to the woman of Shunem was continued from 4:8-37; so apparently the intervening material is in the nature of a parenthesis, since the background probably occurred before Gehazi was smitten with leprosy (cf. 5:20-27). The LORD's call **for a famine** was one of His chastisements upon His sinning people (cf. Ezek. 14:21).

2. The woman received the warning of the prophet and went to sojourn seven years in **the land of the Philistines**, the coastal plain not being as subject to droughts as the limestone highlands of Israel (cf. Gen. 12:10; 26:1). **3.** The woman returned to her home after seven years. **She went forth**, that is, from Shunem to Samaria, **to appeal unto the king**, a legal term for presenting an appeal to a sovereign. She pleaded for her house and for her land, which had been taken in her absence by some private

persons or else confiscated by the crown.

4-6. Providentially, the woman came into the king's presence while he was listening to all the great things Elisha had done and at the precise point when Gehazi was telling the king how Elisha had restored the dead to life. Before them appeared the very woman whose son he had restored to life. The woman confirmed the incident. Then the king provided an official for her, ordering him to return all her property, together with all its produce from the time she had left the land until that moment, showing that the land must have reverted to the crown (cf. Exod. 21:2; 23:10-11).

Elisha Anoints Hazael King of Syria. 8:7-15. **7-8.** Afterward, Elisha went to Damascus. Precisely why is not said. If this king was Ben-hadad I, which archaeological evidence seems to suggest, he was indeed an elderly man. His long and energetic reign came to an end in 842 B.C. When he was informed that **the man of God** had come there, the king instructed his closest and most powerful official, named Hazael, to go to meet the man of God and inquire through him whether he would recover from his illness.

9. Forty camels' burden notes a not unusual gift made by a royal suppliant when an oracle was desired of their gods. Here Ben-hadad was, of course, speaking of the God of Israel. **10-11.** These verses should be translated, "Elisha said to him, 'Go, tell him, "You will surely recover." However, the LORD has shown me that he shall surely die.' And he [Elisha] made his face stand [fixed his gaze], and set [it upon Hazael]." That is, "He looked at him fixedly till he [Hazael] was ashamed [disconcerted]." Hazael, conscious that Elisha had read his thoughts, shrank back from the piercing prophetic gaze (cf. 2:17). Then Elisha wept.

12. When Elisha foresaw the evil that Hazael would do to the people of God, he wept. This was fulfilled in 10:32-33; 13:3-4. **13.** Hazael answered in a tone of pretended amazement and self-depreciation, **What is thy servant, a dog, that he should do this great** (i.e., terrible) **thing? 15.** Hazael smothered the king to death. Shalmaneser III (860-825 B.C.) of Assyria says of him: "Hazael, son of a nobody, seized the throne." This plainly states that Hazael was a usurper, not of the royal line.

The Reign of Jehoram of Judah. 8:16-24. **16-18.** The abbreviated history of Jehoram and his successor, Ahaziah, shows how Baal worship tragically infested Judah. Jehoram's reign began as a coregency with his father. The reign is to be dated between the coregency from 853 to 841 B.C. Jehoram's reign is described as evil, for he had married Athaliah, the daughter of Ahab. Jehoshaphat's ungodly affiliation with the Ahab dynasty brought many evil consequences.

19. The **lamp** (RSV) was symbolic of the permanence and Messianic hope of the Davidic dynasty (cf. 2 Sam. 21:17; 1 Kings 11:36; 15:4). **20-22.** The rebellion of Edom, a vassal of Judah, was one of the divine chastisements upon the sinning king and kingdom. **Libnah**, which was in the proximity of Philisitia, also rebelled (cf. 2 Chron. 21:16). Sin in God's people is always chastised.

The Reign of Ahaziah of Judah. 8:25-29. **25.** In 841 B.C., Ahaziah, Jehoram's son, became king of Judah. **26.** His mother was Athaliah, **daughter** (actually "granddaughter" in our idiom) **of Omri,** king of Israel. **27.** She was contaminated with Baalism, and her husband, Jehoram, was son-in-law to the house of Ahab. **28.** Ahaziah joined Joram, son of Ahab, to war against Hazael, king of Syria, at Ramoth-gilead. That action was the immediate cause leading to Ahaziah's death (cf. 9:16), since he was under judgment pronounced upon the "house of Ahab."

I. JEHU ANOINTED KING OF ISRAEL. 9:1-37.

Jehu's Anointing. 9:1-13. **1-3.** Elisha then proceeded to execute the second and only unfulfilled command of the "still, small voice" at Horeb (cf. 1 Kings 19:12, 15-16; 2 Kings 8:7-15). He dispatched one of the sons of the prophets to Ramoth-gilead to anoint Jehu, whose name means "the LORD is He." He reigned from 841 to 814 B.C. The young prophet was not to **tarry**, so as to avoid all questioning and to give greater force to the act of anointing.

4-5. When Elisha's minister arrived at Ramoth-gilead, he went into Jehu's headquarters, where the military captains were sitting in counsel with Jehu. **6-10.** The act of anointing was accompanied by the command to exterminate the house of Ahab and Baalism. A rough instrument like Jehu was necessary for the bloody task assigned him, for Baalism was so unspeakably and viciously cruel that only a person of his relentless thoroughness could deal with it.

Jehu's commission involved avenging the blood of the LORD's servants, the prophets (cf. 1 Kings 18:4, 13), **at the hand of Jezebel** (cf. 1 Kings 21:15). Ahab's house was to be made like the house of Jeroboam (1 Kings 14:10; 21:22), and the house of Baasha, the son of Ahijah (1 Kings 16:3-4). Verse 10 reads in the Hebrew, "And Jezebel [emphatic by position] the dogs shall eat" (cf. 1 Kings 21:23).

11-13. Jehu's colleagues realized that he had been anointed king over Israel.

509

They hastily took their outer garments and laid them as a carpet for Jehu to walk upon (cf. Luke 19:36), an act that intimated King Joram had been very unpopular with the army. They were glad for a new leader.

Joram's Injury and Death. 9:14-26. **14-16.** Having been wounded at Ramoth-gilead, Joram was recuperating at Jezreel. Jehu was very careful to get assurance that no one would slip away from Ramoth-gilead, held by the Israelites, to take news of his anointing to Jezreel. Jehu planned to take Joram and the house of Ahab by surprise in order to more quickly expedite his commission.

17. When the watchman standing on the tower of Jezreel caught sight of Jehu's company approaching, Joram ordered a horseman to be sent down to meet them with the greeting, **Is it peace?**, meaning "Is all well?" **18-19.** Jehu rebuffed the horseman and made him swing around behind him. He did the same thing with the second horseman that the king sent out. In answer to the question "Is it peace?", Jehu replied, **What hast thou to do with peace?** His commission involved war and not peace.

20. The watchman reported, **The driving** of the charioteer **is like the driving of Jehu, the son of Nimshi; for he drives furiously** (RSV). **21.** Joram's command, **"Make ready"** (lit., "bind"), means "Hitch the horses to the chariot." Both Joram and Ahaziah, the king of Judah who was visiting Joram, went out to meet Jehu in Naboth's vineyard, which had become a part of the pleasure grounds of the palace (cf. 1 Kings 21:16).

22. When Joram said, **Is it peace, Jehu?**, he meant, "Is everything all right at the war?" Jehu's reply left no doubt of his intentions to wipe out the house of Ahab. Literally translated, it is, "What

is peace during the harlotries of thy mother and her many witchcrafts?" **Harlotries** stand for spiritual infidelity, that is, idolatries. **Witchcrafts** means sorceries, the various forms of occultism manifested among Semitic idolaters and plainly prohibited by the Law (cf. Exod. 22:18; Deut. 18:10-11). Occultism abounded in the ancient Semitic world. Innumerable Assyrian tablets contained magical formulas, incantations, and exorcisms.

23. Joram **turned his hands**, that is, turned the horses around (cf. 1 Kings 22:34). Joram, at once realizing that there was treachery, shouted words of warning to Ahaziah, and both attempted to escape. **24.** When Jehu **drew a bow with his full strength** (lit., "And Jehu had filled his hand [with an arrow] on the bow"). To "fill" a bow means to stretch it (Zech. 9:13). Jehu proved himself an excellent marksman. **25-26.** Then Jehu ordered Bidkar, his attendant, to cast Joram's corpse contemptuously in the portion of the field of Naboth, the Jezreelite. Jehu at the same time recalled that when he and Bidkar were riding in the back of the chariot with Ahab, the LORD had uttered this oracle against him.

Ahaziah's Death. 9:27-29. **27.** While Ahaziah, king of Judah, fled in mortal terror **in the direction of Beth-haggan** (RSV), Jehu ordered him to be pursued and slain too, although that was going beyond orders. Ahaziah was shot down near Ibleam (Khirbet Bel'ameh, about ten miles southeast of Megiddo). He died at Megiddo, the fortress city guarding the southeastern approach to the Plain of Esdraelon.

Jezebel's End. 9:30-37. **30.** When Jehu arrived at Jezreel, Jezebel had already heard of the slaughter of the two kings. She **painted her face** (lit., "her eyes"). She painted her eyebrows and eyelashes with a pigment composed of antimony and zinc. She **attired** her head with a tire, or headdress (cf. Isa. 3:18, KJV) and put on her royal robes in order to die like a queen. She looked out of the window opening upon the square below, within the city gate, or perhaps a window looking down in the courtyard of the palace. **31.** Her scornful greeting of Jehu as he entered the gate was **Is it peace, you Zimri, murderer of your master?** (RSV). Her intent was probably to stop Jehu by reminding him of the quick death of the infamous traitor and regicide, Zimri (1 Kings 16:8-18).

32-33. Jehu called on the onlookers to take sides. The palace workers, or eunuchs, quite likely were glad enough to take vengeance on Jezebel. So they threw her down into the courtyard, and the chariot horses trampled her underfoot. **34-37.** Jehu's feasting, during which he forgot that Jezebel had not been buried, was providential to fulfill the Word of God (cf. 1 Kings 21:23; Psalm 83:10; Jer. 8:1-3). **So that they shall not say, This is Jezebel** means that they were no longer able to recognize her mangled remains.

J. JEHU MASSACRES THE HOUSE OF AHAB. 10:1-36.

Ahab's Seventy Sons Beheaded. 10:1-11. Although Jehu was the instrument chosen for judgment, that did not excuse his wickedness and ruthless cruelty. Satan, demons, and wicked men are often employed as the agents of divine retribution and punishment. The hint that Jezebel had given Jehu concerning Zimri, suggesting the possibility of a later rebellion against him (9:31), had been a contributing factor on the human plane that influenced Jehu to completely exterminate the descendants of Ahab.

1-5. Seventy sons, a Semitic idiom, in-cludes grandsons and their offspring. Jehu concocted a clever scheme by which the elders of Samaria and the guardians of the grandsons of Ahab were forced to capitulate to him. He cleverly and ruthlessly tricked them into capitulation. **6-8.** The second part of his scheme involved the atrocity of beheading Ahab's seventy sons (descendants). The heads of the king's sons were laid in **two heaps** at the entrance of the city gate so that all the citizens would see them and know that the house of Ahab had been exterminated.

9-10. Then Jehu hypocritically appeared before the people and attempted to shift the blame of the atrocity to others, including the LORD. Jehu forgot that although the LORD had foretold the destruction of Ahab's house and used him as His agent, that in no wise excused his guilt and ruthless wickedness. **11.** This verse includes other atrocities. In Jezreel, the seat of the court, Jehu wiped out all those who owed their advancement to Ahab.

Forty-two Relatives of Ahaziah Slain. 10:12-14. **12-14.** On his way to Samaria, after all effective opposition had ceased, Jehu met the relatives of Ahaziah of Judah. He commanded that they be taken alive, and he slew every one of the forty-two persons in the company, none of them knowing a thing about the revolution.

Jehonadab Slays the Rest of the House of Ahab. 10:15-17. **15.** Jehonadab was a **son of Rechab**, a leader of the Rechabites, a people who dramatically maintained the old desert way of life, believing that only in that way could they properly worship the LORD (1 Chron. 2:55; Jer. 35). Jehu said to him, **Is your heart true to my heart as mine is to yours?** (RSV). **16.** Jehu gave him his hand and took him up into his chariot, saying, **Come with me, and see my zeal** for the Lord. **17.** When the two of them came to Samaria, they exterminated all who remained to Ahab.

The Worshipers of Baal Destroyed. 10:18-27. **18-21.** After eliminating all sympathizers with the royal family, Jehu proceeded to exterminate the Tyrian Baal worship and its devotees. Posing as a patron of the Baal religion, he proclaimed a great festival to which every Baal worshiper was invited. **22-23.** To make sure that no **servants of the Lord** participated in the festival, special garments were given to the Baal worshipers.

25-27. Even Jehu himself offered sacrifice, thus allaying all possible suspicion. When the festival was at full height, Jehu gave the order for the massacre. Baal worshipers were killed and the temple of Baal was broken down. He burned the pillar that was in the house of Baal (cf. 1 Kings 18:40).

Résumé of Jehu's Reign. 10:28-36. **28-29.** Although Jehu wiped out Baal worship from Israel, he failed to forsake the sins of Jeroboam, the son of Nebat. Like Baasha (1 Kings 15:34) and Omri (16:26), Jehu retained the golden calves. **30-31.** Extirpation of Baal worship and the house of Ahab was divinely commended. That did not mean that the LORD approved of the ways and means Jehu used, nor did He condone Jehu's motives. The LORD overruled the wickedness of Jehu to accomplish His purposes of righteousness and to fulfill His word.

K. ATHALIAH'S REIGN AND JEHOIDA'S REVIVAL. 11:1-21.

Athaliah's Wicked Reign. 11:1-3. **1.** Althaliah was the wicked daughter of Ahab and Jezebel; the widow of Joram, king of Judah; and the mother of Ahaziah, slain by Jehu. She arose and destroyed **all the seed royal** (lit., "the

seed of the kingdom"), meaning all who might set claim to the royal succession. Her vicious cruelty stamped her as a worthy daughter of the wicked Jezebel. Her aim was to seize sole authority.

It was a horrible deed, satanically inspired, and one of the many attempts made by the powers of darkness to exterminate the male offspring of the Messianic line and to nullify the divine promise of the coming One, the promised Savior, the Seed of the woman (Gen. 3:15). Had Athaliah's plan succeeded, the divine redemptive plan would have been thwarted (cf. Rev. 12:1-5).

2. But Jehosheba, King Joram's daughter and Ahaziah's sister (but not the daughter of Athaliah), hid Ahaziah's son Joash (Jehoash) so that he was not killed by Athaliah's agents. Jehosheba hid him in **the bedchamber**, the storeroom in the palace where mattresses and bed clothing were kept. **3.** He was there with Jehosheba, his aunt, and then was taken to the house of the LORD, where he was hid for six years while Athaliah was reigning over the land.

Joash Proclaimed King. 11:4-12. **4-8.** In the **seventh year**, when doubtlessly the discontent with Athaliah's tyranny had reached a peak, Jehoiada, the high priest and the husband of Jehosheba, presented the king's son, the rightful heir to the Davidic throne, and called together the military authorities. He made a covenant with them to protect the king and to have him set upon the throne of Judah. Revolt against Athaliah was thus led by Jehoiada.

9-12. Jehoiada's plan was perfectly executed. The king's son was brought into the Temple in all safety, the crown was placed upon his head, and he was handed **the testimony**, that is, the Law from Mount Sinai, again to be the law of the land. Joash was proclaimed king with clapping of hands and shouting, **God save the king!** (cf. 1 Kings 1:25). This crisis in the succession of the Davidic line foreshadows the coming Messianic Savior, the Lord Jesus Christ. Joash under Athaliah's reign was doomed to death and, in a figurative sense, he died. His subsequent appearance and presentation as king is like the dead coming to life. The true Heir of the throne of David will be so hidden till the present age is completed. And when the seventh year comes, prophetically illustrating the coming Kingdom age, He will be brought forth, as Joash was brought forth from his hiding place, and crowned King of kings.

Athaliah's Death. 11:13-16. **13.** Athaliah, hearing the commotion of the bodyguard and the people, came into the house of the LORD. **14.** She saw the king standing **by a pillar**, that is, "the king was standing on the stand," apparently a dais reserved only for the king that stood before the great altar at the entrance of the inner court (2 Chron. 23:13; cf. 6:13). At once Athaliah realized there had been a conspiracy against her, and she cried, **Treason! Treason!,** the word meaning "conspiracy" and the repetition signifying emphasis, so the sense is "Base treason!"

15. Then Jehoiada the priest ordered the military to bring her outside the Temple between the ranks of guards; so that if anyone came out with her, he was to be killed with the sword. She was not to be slain in the house of the LORD, for that would be a profanation of the holy precincts. **16.** Instead, she was conducted to the royal stables, which adjoined the palace, where she was put to death in a proper place.

Jehoiada's Revival. 11:17-21. **17.** A great revival followed. A covenant was made by Jehoiada between the LORD and the king and the people **that they should be the Lord's people. 18. The people of the land** were the common people, who had remained loyal to the LORD. They broke down the temple of Baal, its altars, and its images, and they killed Mattan, the priest of Baal, before his altars. **19.** Jehoiada also took the captains, the Carites (foreign mercenaries), the guards, and all the people, and together they brought the king down from the house of the LORD. He ascended the throne of the kings. **20.** All the people rejoiced, and there was peace.

Since the whole episode involved the royal line of the Savior-King, the Redeemer of the world, the history presents a faint foreshadowing of what is yet to come when the usurper is cast out and the true King of kings is crowned (cf. Zech. 13:2). Then Israel, restored in Kingdom blessing, will truly be the LORD's people. Idolatry will cease out of the land, and universal peace and prosperity will result (Psalm 2:7-12; Isa. 11:4).

L. JOASH OF JUDAH'S REIGN. 12:1-21.

Résumé of Joash's Reign. 12:1-3. **1-3.** Joash's reign (835-796 B.C.) began well. The young king did that which was right in the sight of the LORD as long as Jehoiada, his uncle, was priest. What happened after the departure of Jehoiada? The answer is hinted at in verse 3 and fully given in 2 Chronicles 24:17-22. After he had received such kindness from Jehoiada, he ordered the stoning of Jehoiada's son (or grandson?) Zechariah, because he had delivered a fateful message to the king against his idolatry. Neither did the king remove the high places (cf. 1 Kings 15:14; 22:43; 2 Kings 14:4).

The Priests Fail in Their Duty. 12:4-8. **4-5.** His uncle being high priest and his instructor, Joash was naturally interested in repairing the Temple. So the king instructed the priests to receive the monetary offerings, both those that were assessed and those that were voluntary, for the purpose of repairing the house of the LORD, wherever any need of repair was discovered. **The money of every one who passeth the account** was the "current money," which was needed to pay the bills incurred by the workmen employed in the repairs. **The money that every man is rated at** (assessed) included every kind of redemption money, paid in the case of the firstborn (Num. 18:16) or for a vow (Lev. 27). Money **that cometh into any man's heart to bring** refers to the freewill offerings of the people. **7. Acquaintances** (cf. v. 5) were probably "assessors," possibly to help the priests fix the cost or value of the sacrificial animals and other offerings. The term is technical and occurs in the Ugaritic texts. The clause **breaches of the house** refers to the damage, delapidation, and despoilment of the Temple, caused, not so much by time, for it had stood only about 130 years, but as a result of the neglect and the attacks of Athaliah and her sons (2 Chron. 24:7), who had also diverted the revenue of the sanctuary to the support of Baal worship.

The Temple Repaired. 12:9-16. **9-15.** The assignment of all the Temple revenues to the priests on the condition that they would keep the Temple in repair had proved a failure. Therefore, the priests were relieved of that obligation and also of the privilege of collecting the money. The king ordered that all collections were to be put in a chest and placed next to the altar. **10-12.** From time to time **the king's scribe** (secretary) and **the high priest** were to count the money and turn it over to those who were in charge of the work of upkeep and repair. The plan was effective.

16. However, two classes of offerings—the guilt offering and the sin offering—were not channeled into that fund, but remained for the priests. This was called **trespass money** and **sin money** (Lev. 5:15-18; 25-29; Num. 5:8). The priests were not deprived of their lawful revenues by the new arrangement. They received their ancient dues from the trespass and sin offerings. The new order provided that from that time forward, gifts intended for the sanctuary itself were to be kept separate from those intended for the priesthood.

Joash Buys off Hazael. 12:17-18. **17-18.** Hazael's invasion and exaction of tribute were judgments from the LORD because of Joash's (Jehoash's) sin (cf. 2 Chron. 24:15-22).

The Death of Joash. 12:19-21. **20.** Joash was assassinated as the result of a conspiracy. He had aroused great hatred among his courtiers because he had put to death Zechariah, probably the grandson rather than the son of Jehoiada (2 Chron. 24:25). **21.** Jehozabad ("Zabad," 2 Chron. 24:26) is written in error for Zacar, contracted from Jehozacar (Jozacar).

M. JEHOAHAZ AND JOASH OF ISRAEL. 13:1-25.

The Reign of Jehoahaz. 13:1-9. **1-2.** Jehu's son, Jehoahaz (c. 814-798 B.C.) reigned over Israel in Samaria. He persisted in the sins of Jeroboam (1 Kings 12:26-32). **3.** As a result, the anger of the LORD was stirred against Israel so that the Israelites were constantly delivered into the hands of Hazael, king of Syria (2 Kings 8:12), and Ben-hadad, son of Hazael (c. 796-770 B.C.). This was Ben-hadad III (or II). An Aramaean king is also mentioned on the contemporary stele of Zakir, king of Hamath, and Lu'ash.

4-5. Jehoahaz besought the LORD's favor, the LORD listened to him (cf.

Psalm 78:34). **The Lord . . . saw the oppression of Israel** (Exod. 3:7; Judg. 2:18) and gave His people **a savior** (i.e., a "deliverer"). Evidently Joash (vv. 19, 25) and later Jeroboam II (v. 13; cf. Neh. 9:27) are meant. However, there are scholars who believe that the unnamed *deliverer* of Israel at this time is a veiled reference to the intervention by the Assyrian emperor, Adad-nirari III, against Aram (cf. W. Hallo, BA 23 [1960] : 42, n. 44.).

6. Despite this deliverance, the LORD's people, Israel, did not depart from the idolatrous calf worship at Dan and Beersheba (cf. v. 2). There **remained the idol also in Samaria.** This was the Ashera, a symbol of the Canaanite goddess of fertility (1 Kings 14:15; 18:7-19). How sad it is to see how often the LORD's people backslid and were reduced by sin and chastening. They failed to really confess their sin and return to the LORD.

7. Mention of so small a number as fifty horsemen and ten chariots shows the pitiable state of weakness to which sin had reduced the LORD's people. The whip the LORD used to chastise His disobedient people was the king of Syria, Hazael (cf. 2 Kings 10:32-33), and his 'son, Ben-hadad. The Aramaean scourge (cf. Jer. 49:27; Amos 1:4) made Israel **like the dust by threshing** (Amos 1:3).

The Reign of Jehoash (Joash) of Israel. 13:10-13. **10-11.** Jehoash (Joash) (c. 798-782 B.C.) succeeded his father, Jehoahaz. He also continued in the sin of the golden bulls at Dan and Beersheba (cf. vv. 2, 6). **12. The rest of the acts of Joash** (14:8-15) are recorded in **the book of the chronicles of the kings of Israel. 13.** Jehoash was succeeded by his son, Jeroboam II (c. 782-753 B.C.).

Elisha and Joash. 13:14-19. **14.** Joash came to see Elisha the prophet in his last sickness. He called him **father**, a title from antiquity for a man of religion (cf.

Judg. 17:10; 2 Kings 2:12). Mentioning **the chariot of Israel, and its horsemen** (see 2:12), Joash's scant faith was at least mouthing what Elisha meant concerning Elijah when he was translated. The meaning is that Elijah was more important and more powerful to Israel's welfare and salvation than chariots and horsemen (cf. 13:14). Even a man of Joash's scant faith could realize that Elisha's death would be a great loss to the nation. He wept, but his words were still the words of unbelief, just as if with Elisha's death the chariots of Israel and the horsemen thereof would signify that the protection and blessing of Israel would come to an end.

15-19. The king entered heartily into that which Elisha instructed him to do. But his lack of faith, indicated by his smiting the ground only three times, made complete victory over the Assyrians impossible. "Three times did Joash beat him," that is, Hazael's son, Ben-hadad, "and recovered the cities of Israel" (v. 25).

Elisha's Death. 13:20-21. **20-21.** Elisha died and was buried. Raiding bands of Moabites used to come into the land every spring. Once when some Israelites were burying a corpse, they saw such a band and hastily cast a man into Elisha's grave. As soon as the man touched the bones of Elisha, he revived and stood on his feet. This final postmortem miracle of the great prophet bears a vital testimony. As Elisha's ministry of grace foreshadowed the greater Elisha to come, the miracle furnishes an illustration of the truth that by the death of the coming One, the sinner is to receive life and be raised from the dead (cf. Job 19:25; 1 Cor. 15:52). To touch Him, who died and rose again, in faith, means to live spiritually as well as eternally. Moreover, the man who was raised by coming in contact with Elisha in death illustrates how Israel is yet to live when she comes in contact with Him who "was dead; and . . . [is] alive for evermore" (Rev. 1:18; cf. Isa. 53:1-12; Ezek. 37:1-28; Zech. 12:10— 13:1; Rom. 11:26-36; Rev. 20:4-9).

Joash's Victories over Syria. 13:22-25. **22-23.** The frightful oppression of Hazael, king of Syria, is referred to. Only the LORD's mercy and His covenant with the patriarchs preserved Israel. **24-25.** But in the days of Benhadad, Hazael's son, Jehoash retook the cities from Ben-hadad that the Syrian king had taken in a war with Jehoahaz, Joash's father. Joash was able to strengthen his kingdom for his son, Jeroboam II (782-753 B.C.), who restored Israel to great power and prestige.

N. AMAZIAH OF JUDAH AND JEROBOAM II. 14:1-29.

Events of Amaziah's Reign. 14:1-7. **1-3.** Amaziah of Judah (c. 796-767 B.C.) did that which was right in the sight of the LORD, **yet not like David**, the ideal king of Israel. **4.** The popular **high places** were not done away with. Did the people sacrifice to God there? Even if they did, it was syncretistic. Moreover, His revealed will prescribed priestly sacrifice at the one ordained sanctuary in Jerusalem (cf. Deut. 12:1-14). **5-6.** As soon as he had established himself securely on the throne, Amaziah brought to justice those who had assassinated his father. He spared the children of the murderers in accordance with Deuteronomy 24:16 and Ezekiel 18:4, 20. **7.** Amaziah subdued Edom in a victorious battle in the **valley of salt.** Probably meant is the depression south of the Dead Sea (Salt Sea) that had to be crossed in invading Edom (cf. 2 Chron. 25:5-16). He captured **Sela** (or Selah, "crag" or "rock"), the capital of Edom,

later called Petra (cf. 2 Kings 8:20-22; Isa. 16:1; 42:11).

Amaziah Wars Against Jehoash of Israel. 14:8-14. **8.** Amaziah's message to Jehoash of Israel, **Come, let us look one another in the face,** was an insolent, ill-advised challenge to war. The incident showed a streak of foolhardiness and immaturity that doubtlessly resulted in Amaziah's later assassination. He had become cocky because of his victory over Edom (cf. v. 10), and he probably was aiming at recovering the ten tribes for the house of David. **9.** Joash's reply in a fable shows how utterly loathsome Amaziah had made himself in the eyes of the people of the Northern Kingdom. The miserable, little thistle (Amaziah) tried to make himself equal to a fine cedar of Lebanon and was badly trampled on as a result. In his hearty rebuff Jehoash was both the cedar and the wild beast that trampled down the thistle. Similar parabolic representations occur (cf. Judg. 9:7-15; 2 Chron. 25:18; Zech. 11:7-14). **11-14.** Amaziah's stubborn folly was manifested. So the two kings clashed in battle at Beth-shemesh (modern Ain Shems), situated in a valley of the hill country facing west, located fifteen miles west of Jerusalem. Judah was defeated, and Jehoash **took** (captured) Amaziah. He came to Jerusalem, breaking down the wall for a space of four hundred cubits, or about two hundred yards. The Ephraim gate was on the north wall. The corner gate was actually the northwest angle of the wall. The Temple treasury was plundered (cf. 12:18; 16:8), and **hostages** ("sons of sureties") were taken to insure Amaziah's future good behavior.

Jehoash's Death. 14:15-16. **15-16.** These verses duplicate 13:12-13.

Amaziah Replaced by Azariah (Uzziah). 14:17-22. **17-19.** Doubtlessly

Amaziah was assassinated by those who resented the punishment he had meted out to his father's assassins (v. 5). His foolhardiness, witnessed by his unprovoked war with Israel, was obviously another cause. **21-22.** Azariah's restoration of Elath on the Gulf of Aqaba, the eastern arm of the Red Sea, was again possible because Edom had again been subdued (cf. 8:20-22; 1 Kings 22:47-50).

Jeroboam II's Reign. 14:23-29. **23-24.** Jeroboam's reign was long and prosperous, as is known from the contemporary prophets, Amos and Hosea. However, the prosperity of the period led to grave moral and social degeneration. **25.** The international scene favored Jeroboam's widespread influence. The inactivity of Assyria and the decline of power at Damascus enabled Israel to expand greatly. Jeroboam ruled from the Dead Sea (Sea of the Arabah) as far as Solomon's northern limits (1 Kings 8:65). **The entering of Hamath** was the opening south of the fortress city of Hamath on the Orontes River into the great Syrian valley between the two Lebanon ranges. Labo of Hamath, modern Lebweh, fourteen miles northeast of Baalbek, is probably meant. In any case, the ideal northern boundary of Israel was intended (Num. 34:8; Josh. 13:5; Amos 6:14).

Jeroboam's contemporary was the prophet Jonah, the son of Amittai, of Gath-hepher (modern el-Meshhed, three miles northeast of Nazareth in Galilee). **26. The Lord saw the affliction of Israel** (cf. Exod. 3:7; 2 Kings 13:4; Psalm 106:44) in their extreme chastisement (cf. Deut. 32:36). **27.** "And the LORD did not say that He would blot out the name of Israel" (NASB; cf. 13:23).

O. AZARIAH AND JOTHAM; ZECHARIAH TO PEKAH. 15:1-38.

Judah Under Azariah. 15:1-7. **1-2.** Azariah's (Uzziah's) long reign (c. 791-736 B.C.) was calculated under the principle of overlapping coregencies. He had a long and prosperous rule, like Jeroboam II of Israel (cf. 2 Chron. 26:6-15). **3. He did . . . right in the sight of the Lord** (cf. 14:3). **4.** But he did not remove the high places (see 14:4).

5. The LORD **smote him** (struck him in chastisement) because he intruded into the priests' office (2 Chron. 26:16-21). As a result of his leprosy, he **dwelt in a separate house** (*bēt ḥŏpsît*, lit., a "house of release" or "freedom"), a royal residence outside Jerusalem (Lev. 13:46; 2 Kings 7:3). The special residence had an apt name because lepers were emancipated from all social relations and duties. Because the king was a leper, his son Jotham acted as regent, **was over the house**, during the later years of the king's reign (c. 750-736 B.C.).

The Assyrian emperor, Tiglath-pileser III, refers in his "Annals" to *Azriyau, of Yaudu*, that is, "Azariah of Judah" in connection with a western coalition of kings. A limestone inscription found in Jerusalem from the first century A.D. reads, "Hither were brought the bones of Uzziah, king of Judah—not to be opened."

Israel Under Zechariah. 15:8-12. **8.9.** Zechariah was a son of Jeroboam II. Like all his predecessors, he persisted in the sin of the golden bulls at Dan and Beersheba. **10.** He had reigned only six months when he was slain by Shallum, son of Jabesh (the father's name is uniformly given in case of usurpers). He was struck down **before the people.** However, the *Revised Standard Version*, following the Septuagint, renders it, "in Ibleam" (present Khirbet Bil'ameh, about ten miles south of Megiddo) on the road to Bethshan (9:27). **12.** Zechariah was the last of the dynasty of Jehu (cf. 10:30). His assassination initiated a period of civil war like that which preceeded the founding of the Omride Dynasty (1 Kings 16:15-22).

Israel Under Shallum. 15:13-16. **13-14.** Shallum came into power in 752 B.C., but was quickly murdered by Menahem, who was Zachariah's general and the **son of Gadi**, or "a Gadite." **16.** Menahem plundered **Tiphsah**, an otherwise unknown city in that area, unless we follow the *Revised Standard Version* reading, "Tappuah." He also plundered **Tirzah** (probably Tell el-Far'a) about seven miles northeast of Nablus. His violent atrocities were perpetrated because those towns did not open their gates to him. He resorted to the common hideous cruelty of disemboweling pregnant women (cf. 8:12; Hos. 13:16; Amos 1:13).

Israel Under Menahem. 15:17-22. **17-18.** Menahem ruled from about 752 to 742 B.C., doing evil and tolerating bull worship, as had his predecessors. **19-20.** **Pul** (another name for Tiglath-pileser III), **king of Assyria** (745-727 B.C.), **came against the land.** To retain his kingship, Menahem was forced to pay a huge sum to the Assyrian overlord. **A thousand talents of silver** (a talent weighing about ninety-two pounds and containing three thousand shekels) would require sixty thousand **men of wealth**, each taxed fifty shekels of silver. Tiglath-pileser refers to this event in his annals, "As for Menahem, terror overwhelmed him. Like a bird alone he fled and submitted to me. To his palace I brought him back and silver ... I received as his tribute." Menahem of Samaria ("Menihimmu of Samerina") is also mentioned in the annals with Raṣunnu (Rezin) of Aram.

Israel Under Pekahiah. 15:23-26. **23-24.** Pekahiah was a son of Menahem and ruled from about 742 to 740 B.C. He did evil, as had his predecessors. **25. Pekah**, the son of Remaliah, an army officer, and fifty Gileadites assassinated Pekahiah in the **palace** (better, "citadel" or "keep") of the king's house (cf. same word in 1 Kings 16:18). **Argob** and **Arieh**, who were slain with him, were probably officers of the royal guard.

Israel Under Pekah. 15:27-31. **27.** Pekah is said to have **reigned twenty years** (but this is far too long, the numbers here having suffered corruption in transmission). His reign was approximately from 740 to 732 B.C. **28.** He **did ... evil**, as had his predecessors. **29.** In his reign, Tiglath-pileser (see v. 19) overran the northern and northeastern part of Israel in his campaigns from 733 to 732 B.C., when the Assyrian emperor took punitive measures against Pekah for plotting against Assyira (v. 37; cf. 16:5, 7-8). He also put an end to the Aramaean kingdom of Damascus (16:9). Tiglath-pileser in his annals claimed to have helped in the overthrow of Pekah by Hoshea, indicating that Hoshea clearly began his reign with a pro-Assyrian policy.

Judah Under Jotham. 15:32-38. **32-35.** Jotham was a son of Uzziah. He did that which was right, except that he did not remove the high places. He built the **higher** (upper) **gate** (see 2 Chron. 27:3; Jer. 20:2; Ezek. 8:3, 5; 9:2; 40:38-43). **37.** In his day, the LORD began to send Rezin of Syria and Pekah of Israel **against Judah**—on the human side, to force Judah into an alliance against Assyria (cf. 16:5-9); and on the divine side, to chasten Judah for her sins.

P. AHAZ OF JUDAH AND THE ASSYRIAN MENACE. 16:1-20.

Ahaz's Idolatry. 16:1-4. **1-2.** Jotham's wicked son, Ahaz, reigned from about 736 to 716 B.C. He not only did evil, but gloried in his lawlessness. **3. He walked in the way of the kings of Is-**

rael. "He even burned his son as an offering" (RSV; cf. 17:17; 2 Chron. 28:3; Psalm 106:37-38), reviving the barbarous custom of human sacrifice (cf. 2 Kings 3:27; 21:6), common in ancient paganism and not unknown in Israel (Exod. 22:29-30; Judg. 11:30-31; 1 Kings 16:34), and condemned by the Word of God. Such **abominations of the nations** ("heathen"; Deut. 12:31) were the result of demonic forces working in occult religion (Gen. 22:12; Exod. 34:20; Deut. 18:10). **4.** Ahaz's religion was a corrupt syncretism, involving worship on the **high places, and on the hills, and under every green tree** (cf. 1 Kings 14:23; Hos. 14:8), because the shadow was good and protected from the hot sun, and the elevated terrain caught the cool breezes.

Ahaz Besieged by Pekah and Rezin. 16:5-6. **5.** See the note on 15:37 and Isaiah's prediction of the coming virgin-born Savior in connection with this event (Isa. 7:1-17; 8:1-8). **6.** Edom seized the opportunity to throw off control of Judah and to gain control of the Red Sea port of Elath (cf. 1 Kings 9:26-28; 22:47-50; 2 Kings 8:20-22; 14:22).

Ahaz's Appeal to Assyria. 16:7-9. **7-8.** Utterly disregarding the advice of Isaiah (Isa. 7:4, 16-17; 8:4-8), Ahaz sought the aid of Tiglath-pileser III (see 15:19, 29), bribing the slaughterer and deporter of the LORD's people with treasures taken from the LORD's house. **9.** Pleased to be so munificently rewarded for what he intended to do anyway, **the king of Assyria** brought to an end the Aramaean power in Damascus by killing Rezin and deporting his people to Kir in Mesopotamia, from which locality the Aramaeans had originally come (Amos 1:5; 9:7). The king of Assyria also devastated northern Israel (see 15:29). These events are mentioned in the annals of Tiglath-pileser III.

Ahaz's Idolatrous Altar and Innovations. 16:10-18. **10-11. Ahaz went** to Damascus to pay homage to his overlord, the **king of Assyria.** There he saw an altar, and his idolatrous folly led him to have this pagan altar, probably of Assyrian style, to be duplicated and placed in the Temple in Jerusalem. Ahaz was following the popular fad to syncretize the worship of the LORD with the contaminated cults of foreign deities.

Urijah, the priest, is probably the same as Uriah (Isa. 8:2); he demonstrated his apostasy by obeying the king in making a new altar and removing the old altar, made according to the LORD's instructions (vv. 12, 16). The old altar was made of bronze (brass), while the new, and much larger, Assyrian type was probably made of stone.

12-16. At the dedication, Ahaz performed further impieties by usurping the function of the priest (cf. the punishment of Uzziah's similar sin, 2 Chron. 26:16-21). Ahaz flagrantly set aside God's word and God's order. This wicked conduct has been duplicated many times in apostasy that has invaded the Christian church through the centuries. **17-18.** Ahaz's apostasy was costly. He had to confiscate some of the valuable bronze of the Temple and other treasures to pay the heavy tribute to Assyria. The **covered place** (covering) **for the sabbath** is not clear, but it probably was a passage providing protection for the Temple worshipers.

Ahaz's Death. 16:19-20. **19-20.** Ahaz was a stubborn, inveterate idolater who sold his country into vassalage. From Ahaz's time on, with the exception of two or three uprisings, Judah was a vassal state of Assyria; and worse still, a slave of false religion.

Q. THE FALL OF THE NORTHERN KINGDOM. 17:1-41.

Hoshea, the Last King of Israel.

17:1-2. **1.** Described as **the son of Elah**, Hoshea was an assassin and a usurper, having slain his predecessor, Pekah, to reign in his place (cf. 15:30). His reign extended from 732 to 722 B.C. and was partly coterminous with the reign of Ahaz of Judah. **2.** He **did . . . evil in the sight of the Lord, but not as the kings . . . before him.** There is no hint that he abandoned the bull worship at Bethel, but he may have opposed Baalism. In any case, though he was the last ruler in a falling monarchy, he was not the worst.

Hoshea's Vassalage to Assyria. *17:3-4.* **3.** Hoshea evidently attained his throne by Assyrian aid. In his annals, Tiglath-pileser boasted that he had appointed Hoshea to the throne. Shalmanezer V (727-722 B.C.) came up against Hoshea, and he became **his servant** (vassal) **and gave him presents** (paid him tribute). **4.** The Assyrian overlord found treachery in Hoshea, which was to be expected in one who had gotten his throne by murder and conspiracy (15:30). Hoshea foolishly and disastrously plotted with Egypt (cf. Hos. 7:11) and discontinued his tribute payment to Assyria. Apparently he left his capital to plead for mercy, and he was imprisoned when his overtures to **So, king of Egypt,** were discovered. So was possibly Osorkon IV, reflecting a popular abbreviation, or else he was a lesser king or army commander under Osorkon IV.

The Siege and Fall of Samaria. *17:5-6.* **5.** In the spring or summer of 725 B.C., Shalmanezer marched against Samaria, besieging the city for three years. **6.** However, its capture, late in 722 or possibly in 721 B.C., was claimed by Sargon II (722-705 B.C.; cf. Isa. 20:1), in whose Khorsabad Inscription it is recorded: "Samaria, I besieged. I captured. 27,290 of her inhabitants I carried away." Some scholars believe it was Shalmanezer V and not Sargon II who took the city, despite the latter's claim (cf. J. P. Free, *Archaeology and Bible History*, pp. 199-200).

The Israelites were carried away **into Assyria** (i.e., the Assyrian Empire), specifically to **Halah** (unlocated), which some identify with Calah (Gen. 10:11); **Habor**, a tributary of the Upper Euphrates (cf. 1 Chron. 5:26); **Gozan** (Assyr., *Guzanu*, present-day Tell Halaf, on the upper Habor River); and **the cities of the Medes**, northeast of Nineveh. Assyrian policy was to deport peoples in order to control subject nations.

Israel's Sins That Brought Judgment. *17:7-22.* These sins of Israel are detailed from the divine viewpoint, because the fate of the Northern Kingdom was to serve as a stern warning to the Davidic dynasty. The disaster that befell Israelites of the Northern Kingdom was due to five facts: (1) **7.** They sinned against **the Lord their God**, their Redeemer, and **feared** (worshiped) **other gods**, their destroyers (cf. Judg. 6:10). (2) **8-12.** They fell into the idolatry of the surrounding nations (cf. Lev. 18:3; Deut. 18:9), building high places (v. 29; cf. Judg. 3:7; 2 Kings 3:2) and setting up idolatrous images (Exod. 34:12-14; Deut. 16:21).

(3) **13-14.** They rejected God's warning through the prophets (cf. Exod. 32:9, 33; Deut. 31:27). (4) **15-17.** They abandoned God's covenant, forsaking His commandments (Exod. 20:1-17; 1 Kings 12:28), and lapsing into all the abominations of Baalism and the allurements of occult religion. (5) **18-23.** Their sin aroused God's anger and chastisement, with Judah failing to take warning.

The So-Called "Ten Lost Tribes." *17:23.* **23.** Removal of the bulk of the people composing the Northern Kingdom did not mean that the ten tribes were lost and that only two tribes continued in the land. In the divine view, all the tribes were represented in the Southern Kingdom of Judah and constituted God's continuing with Israel under the Palestinian and Davidic covenants (Deut. 30:1-10; 2 Sam. 7:8-17). This does not mean, however, that the tribes taken into captivity by Assyria are excluded from any promised future return to the land (Isa. 11:11-13; Ezek. 37:15-28).

Before the Assyrian Captivity, substantial numbers from the twelve tribes during reformation, invasions, and other crises identified themselves with the Southern Kingdom in allegiance to the Davidic house, the true worship of the LORD, and the covenants and promises (cf. 2 Chron. 19:4; 30:1-10, 25-26; 34:5, 7, etc.). The remnant that returned from Babylon was representative of the whole Israelite nation, not merely of the two tribes. Our Lord offered Himself to the entire nation (Matt. 10:5-6).

Other tribes than Judah are mentioned as being represented in the land (Matt. 4:13, 15; Luke 2:36; Acts 4:36; 26:7; Phil. 3:5; James 1:1). Israel, long in worldwide dispersion but preserved distinct from all other peoples, has partially been restored to Palestine as a nation. In their worldwide scattering, they still continue as a people known to God, though not knowing Him. This includes the so-called "Ten Lost Tribes."

The Origin of the Samaritans. *17:24-41.* **24.** The Syrian emperor, Sargon, imported peoples from Babylon, Cuthah (Akk., *kutu*, modern Tell Ibrahim northeast of Babylon), Avva (Tell Kefr 'Aya) and Hamath, both on the Orontes River in Syria, and from Sepharvaim near Hamath. This verse is confirmed by Sargon's own records: "The cities I set up again ... peoples from lands I had taken I settled there."

The name **Samaria** was given to the land of Israel, and its inhabitants were called Samaritans. **25-27.** The **lions,** which had a chance to multiply during the unsettled conditions, formed the basis for the appeal of the inhabitants for a savior-priest, which was granted. **28.** Then **one of the priests** who had been deported was sent back to teach the people how they should fear the LORD. **29-41.** The result was a syncretistic religion, worse than pure paganism, and the intermarriage of different peoples, which produced the mixed-race Samaritans, who were a combination of Gentile, pagan, and Jew. These people were despised by later Jews (Ezra 4:1-3; Luke 10:33; 17:16-18; John 4:9).

II. THE KINGDOM OF JUDAH TILL THE CAPTIVITY. 18:1—25:30.

A. HEZEKIAH AND SENNACHERIB'S INVASIONS. 18:1-37.

Summary of Hezekiah's Reign. *18:1-8.* **1-2.** Hezekiah's reign (c. 716-687 B.C.) involved overlapping coregencies; so previous to 716 B.C. he was reckoned as reigning with his father, Ahaz. He was the godly son of an ungodly father. **3-5.** His rule is given unqualified praise, he was compared very favorably with David, Israel's ideal king, and he was lauded for his trust **in the Lord God of Israel; so that after him was none like him.** This statement does not contradict what is said of Josiah (23:25). Hezekiah was preeminent for his faith in the LORD, and Josiah for his zeal for the Mosaic Law.

He removed, better, *"he* it was who removed" **the high places,** making the Jerusalem Temple the sole place for the public worship of the LORD (cf. v. 22; 2 Chron. 29:3-36). Removing the high places, he did what none of his predecessors had been able or willing to do. Also, he **broke the images** (i.e., "shattered the pillars," *mǎṣṣēḇōt*), which were stones with the idolatrous association of fertility rites forbidden in Israel (Lev. 26:1; Deut. 16:22; cf. 1 Kings 14:23; 2 Chron. 14:3; Hos. 3:4).

He cut down **the idols** (representations in the form of wooden poles, symbolic of the lewd fertility goddess, Asherah; cf. 1 Kings 14:9). He also destroyed **the bronze serpent**, a relic of the Mosaic era (Num. 21:6-9) that had invited idolatrous abuse, since the serpent was one of the symbols of fertility employed in Baal worship.

The words **he called it Nehushtan** may mean Hezekiah called it such to indicate "a mere piece of bronze," or "one called it," that is, "it was called Nehushtan" by the people from ancient times. In any case, it involved a play on similar-sounding words in Hebrew— the name "serpent" (*nāḥāš*) of bronze (*neḥōšet*). **6.** Adherence to the LORD and His commandments resulted in Hezekiah's prosperity. **7-8.** He rebelled against Assyria, refusing to pay the tribute Ahaz had incurred, and reduced the Philistines to **Gaza**, the southernmost part of the Philistine territory.

The Fall of the Northern Kingdom. 18:9-12. **9-12.** Apparently Samaria's fall occurred while Hezekiah was still regent under Ahaz, but it is repeated here (see 17:3-6). A contrast is drawn between the utter overthrow of the stronger kingdom and the deliverance of the smaller and weaker kingdom because of Hezekiah's faith in the LORD (v. 5). The overthrow of Israel was meant to be a stern, unforgettable lesson to the Davidic kingdom of the danger of defection from the LORD, outlined in verse 12 (cf. 17:6-23).

Sennacherib's First Invasion of Judah. 18:13-16. **13.** On this occasion Jerusalem was saved by appeasement. Sennacherib had succeeded his father, Sargon II, in 705 B.C. At that time revolt was common among the tributaries of Assyria. In 701 B.C. a rebellion against Assyria, in which Hezekiah took part, broke out in Palestine. Sennacherib acted quickly at Eltekeh, a village east of Ekron where the Philistines and their ally, Hezekiah, were defeated. Judah was invaded and many of her cities were captured.

14. While Sennacherib was still at Lachish, the most important fortress in the Shephelah, Hezekiah sued for terms of peace. **I have offended. Withdraw from me.** Hezekiah promised to pay whatever tribute was put or placed upon him. Sennacherib set the price as **three hundred talents of silver** and **thirty talents of gold. 15.** To gather that huge sum, Hezekiah stripped the house of the LORD and the treasures of the king's house. **16.** Taking the gold off the doors of the Temple and the pillars to make up this tribute to the king of Assyria marked the third time the Temple had been despoiled (cf. 12:18; 16:17-18).

Sennacherib's Second Invasion. 18:17-25. **17.** This second campaign of the Assyrian emperor took place some thirteen or fourteen years after the events of verses 13 to 16. Sennacherib was at Lachish. But instead of Hezekiah asking for peace, Sennacherib sent a detachment to Jerusalem trying to frighten Hezekiah into submission. The date is determined by the reference to Tirhakah, king of Ethiopia (19:9), who did not become coregent until 689 B.C. In 701 B.C., when the previous invasion took place, Tirhakah was only nine years old, since he was born in 711 or 710 B.C.

The expeditionary force that Sennacherib sent against Jerusalem was headed by Tartan, Rabsaris, and Rabshakeh, which are not names, but official Assyrian titles. Tartan means a commander in chief; Rabsaris, the chief of the eunuchs; and Rabshakeh, a high military official. Apparently from atop the ancient wall of the city, at a now unidentified place, these representatives of the Assyrian emperor conversed with Hezekiah's official representatives.

18. Eliakim, Hezekiah's major domo; Shebna, the secretary of state; and Joah, the recorder and historian, were given a message for their sovereign. **19-22.** The Assyrians argued that Hezekiah should realize his weak position and not count on his army or on Egypt or on his God, the LORD. Hezekiah had destroyed the high places out of the land. From the Assyrian viewpoint, Hezekiah had insulted the LORD by the centralization of worship in Jerusalem (cf. v. 4). **25.** How true was the boast of the arrogant invader that the LORD had told him to go up against this land to destroy it. But it was in a sense that lay far above his pagan apprehension to comprehend (cf. Isa. 10:5-7).

The Assyrian Attempt to Persuade the People to Surrender. 18:26-37. **26.** To prevent a further bad effect upon the people, Hezekiah's officials requested that any further conversation be conducted in the **Aramaic language**, the lingua franca of the ancient world. Already the language of diplomacy and commerce, it had not yet become the common tongue of the people. **27-28.** However, the Assyrian addressed the strongest appeal to the people **in the Jews' language**, Hebrew. **29-30.** They taunted them, saying that neither Hezekiah nor the LORD would deliver them. **Let not Hezekiah deceive you. 31.** The Assyrians called for **an agreement**, that is, for surrender.

33-35. These verses show how absurdly the Assyrians misunderstood their conquests and the hand of the LORD in them. **Hamath** (cf. 17:24) was a city-state on the Orontes River, in north Syria. **Arpad** is present Tell-Erfad, thirteen miles north of Alepo. **Hena** and **Ivvah** were in the same general area of the north Euphrates, east of Hamath. **36. The people held their peace** (cf. Isa. 36:21). The purpose was to let God speak for them and act for them. **37.** Their clothes were rent or torn because of sorrow for the blasphemies uttered by the Assyrians against the LORD.

B. HEZEKIAH AND ISAIAH. 19:1-37.

Hezekiah's Message to Isaiah. 19:1-5. **1.** Hezekiah expressed his grief over the Assyrian insult to the LORD, recounted in chapter 18, by tearing his garments. He expressed his deep repentance by wearing sackcloth, and going in humility to the **house of the Lord. 2-4.** Hezekiah's message to Isaiah was delivered to the prophet through Eliakim, palace manager; Shebna, the secretary of state; and the senior priests, heads of the priestly caste.

Hezekiah called the experience with the haughty, blasphemous Assyrians **a day of trouble** (distress) **and of rebuke** (i.e., chastisement), for the king recognized it as divine punishment for sin (of **blasphemy**, provocation), because God had been dishonored and provoked to anger by the Assyrians' taunts. **Children ... come to the birth ... not strength to bring forth** is a proverbial expression to denote the utter collapse of all human resources (cf. Hos. 13:13).

Hezekiah and the delegation to Isaiah acknowledged the prophet's closeness and access to God in the statement **It may be the Lord, thy God, will hear thee.** The seriousness of the Rabshakeh's sin was that he had reproved the living God, in contrast to the dead deities of the pagans (cf. 1 Sam. 17:36). Isaiah was requested to **lift up . . . prayer for the remnant who** were **left,** since Sennacherib had captured most of the cities of Judah, and Jerusalem was indeed blessed to have been spared.

Isaiah's Comforting Reply. 19:6-7. **6. Be not afraid of the words . . . with which the servants of the king of Assyria have blasphemed me.** The Hebrew word for "blasphemed" here means "to grossly insult deity" (Num. 15:30; Psalm 44:16; Isa. 51:7). **7. I will send a blight,** better, "I am about to put a spirit [impulse or inclination] upon him" (cf. Num. 5:14; Isa. 19:14; 29:10), showing that God was sovereignly overruling the enemy's movements. **He shall hear a rumor** (or report), specified in verse 9, and return to his own land and fall by the sword in his own land.

Sennacherib's Blasphemous Letter to Hezekiah. 19:8-13. **8.** The Rabshakeh left Jerusalem and found Sennacherib warring against **Libnah** (Tell es-Safi) in the Shephelah, ten miles north of Lachish (cf. Josh. 10:29). Evidently Lachish had fallen. An excavated relief from Nineveh portrays Sennacherib seated before Lachish, receiving its tribute. **9.** He heard a report (cf. v. 7) that Tirhakah, king of Ethiopia, was advancing. This occurred after 688 B.C.

10. Sennacherib's attempt to frighten Hezekiah into immediate surrender and gain Jerusalem without a battle is evident. His words in this letter were couched in even more vaunting and blasphemous style than in the speech of the Rabshakeh. He reached the acme of blasphemy in attributing deception to the LORD, and thus sealed his doom (cf. v. 7).

11-13. See 18:34 for the cities that Sennacherib boasted of having destroyed utterly, that is, by putting them under the ban, solemnly devoting all that lived in them to extermination. **Gozan,** Assyrian Guzanu, is modern Tell Halaf on the Habor River. **Haran** is the ancient town on the Balikh River. **Rezeph** is present-day Rusefah, northwest of Tadmor (Palmyra). **Eden** is Bit-Adinni of the inscriptions, located west of the Balikh River. **Telassar** is in the same general region. **The king of the city** (Heb., *lā'îr*) is now known to be the Assyrian town of La'ir, Assyrian Lahiru (see F. W. Albright, BASOR 141 [Feb. 1956]: 25; and D. D. Luckenbill, *Ancient Records of Assyria,* 2: 252).

Hezekiah's Prayer. 19:14-19. **14.** Hezekiah spread out Sennacherib's blasphemous message **before the Lord,** leaving Him whom he trusted so implicitly to punish the blasphemy it contained. **15-18.** Most humbly and earnestly, the king cast himself upon the LORD and sought His mercy and power, although he freely granted the truth of Sennacherib's claims (vv. 12-13) concerning the "dead" gods conquered. What made the difference was that Hezekiah was serving the one true "living" God (v. 4), **who dwellest between** the cherubim, rather "sittest above," invisibly enthroned above the cherubim (cf. Exod. 25:22; 1 Sam. 4:4; Psalm 18:10; Ezek. 1:26).

The Lord's Answer Through Isaiah. 19:20-28. The LORD's answer took the form of a taunt song or ode of derision pronounced against the Assyrian king (see RSV and NASB). It was given to the prophet in answer to Hezekiah's prayer (vv. 14-19). **21. The virgin . . . daughter of Zion** is a poetic personification of Jerusalem as a mother of her inhabitants, the term *virgin* signifying the inviolable security of the fortified city.

22. Sennacherib had reproached and blasphemed **the Holy One of Israel,** the

524

favorite expression of Isaiah, occurring twenty-seven times in his prophecy and only five times elsewhere in the Old Testament. **23-24.** The overweaning boasting is characteristic of Assyrian inscriptions. Sennacherib compared his invincible campaigns to ascending the heights and remotest parts of Lebanon, and his victories as felling the tallest cedars and choicest cypress trees (symbols of kings, princes, and nobles, and all that is highest and most stately).

I have digged and drunk strange waters. The scarcity of water was no barrier to the victorious Assyrian's advance. Where fountains and cisterns had been stopped up or covered (2 Chron. 32:3), he boasted that he had dug new wells, tasting strange (foreign) waters. He even exulted that rivers were no barrier to his progress. **With the sole of my feet I dried up all the rivers of Egypt** (NASB; cf. Isa. 19:5).

25-26. Sennacherib's proud effrontery was squelched by the LORD's humbling reminder that it was He, the omnipotent, omniscient God, who not only planned the Assyrian monarch's disciplinary action against Israel, but executed the plan that the so-called "great king" (18:28) should "turn fortified cities into ruinous heaps" and that "therefore their inhabitants were short of strength . . . dismayed and . . . were as . . . grass on the housetops . . . scorched before it is grown up" (NASB). **27-28.** The omniscient God foreknew every move of the Assyrian, and his raging arrogance against the LORD. So the LORD said, **I will put My hook in your nose, and . . . turn you back by the way which you came** (NASB; cf. Ezek. 38:4).

A Sign Given Hezekiah of the Promised Deliverance. 19:29-31. **29.** In two years the peaceful pursuits of farming would be interrupted by the enemy's presence. The third-year peace would

enable them to till and reap normally. **30.** The surviving **remnant**, those who escaped death in Judah during Sennacherib's invasion, would take root and prosper. **31. The zeal** (jealousy) of **the Lord** for His people **. . . shall do** (perform) **this** (cf. Isa. 9:7).

The Promise and the Deliverance. 19:32-35. **32.** Jerusalem would escape attack or siege. **33.** Sennacherib would return by the way he came. **34.** The LORD promised to defend the city for His own sake and David's sake. **35.** Judgment fell upon the Assyrian army. The angel of the LORD (cf. Exod. 12:12-13, 23; 2 Sam. 24:15-17) struck the army, and wholesale death resulted; perhaps on the human plane the means used was the bubonic plague spread by a scourge of mice.

Herodotus recounts that the Assyrians suffered a defeat on the border of Egypt because their bowstrings were chewed to pieces by a sudden onslaught of field mice (*History* 2. 141; cf. 1 Sam. 6:4-5). Prophetically foreseen is the last great invasion of Israel from the north during the Great Tribulation when Gog, whom the Assyrian prefigures, will be destroyed on the hills of Palestine (see Ezek. 38-39).

Sennacherib's Death. 19:36-37. **36. Sennacherib . . . dwelt at Nineveh,** that is, stayed there, implying he did not again invade the west. **37.** His assassination did not take place till 681 B.C., six or seven years after this campaign. The murderers fled to Armenia or Ararat (Assyr. *Urartu*), the plain of the Araxes River. Esarhaddon, Sennacherib's son and successor, reigned from 681 to 668 B.C.

C. THE LATER YEARS OF HEZEKIAH'S REIGN. 20:1-21.

Hezekiah's Illness and Isaiah's Message. 20:1-7. The expression **in those**

days definitely sets the time of the Assyrian invasion. Hezekiah's illness was terminal. As a result, the prophet Isaiah appeared and told the king to set his house in order. The King James Version's marginal reading is correct: "Give charge concerning thine house" (i.e., "Get your last will and testament in order"; cf. 2 Sam. 17:23).

2. The king **turned his face to the wall** to seek the LORD in prayer and to avoid being disturbed in his communion with the LORD. **3.** The good king lamented his untimely death, normally thought of as the punishment of the wicked (Prov. 10:27). **4-6.** Before Isaiah had gone out into the middle court (i.e., the courtyard) of the palace, he was bidden to return to the ill king and tell him that he would recover.

Hezekiah was addressed very respectfully as **the captain** (*nāgîd*, "leader of the LORD's people"), an honorific designation (cf. 1 Sam. 9:16; 10:1; 1 Kings 1:35). Assurance was given from the LORD that He would heal the king, and on the third day Hezekiah would go up to the house of the LORD. Fifteen years would be added to his life. Deliverance from the king of Assyria also was promised. The LORD promised to defend Jerusalem for His own sake and for His servant David's sake, according to the promise of the Davidic Covenant (2 Sam. 7:8-15), guaranteeing the LORD's grace and mercy to His erring people.

7. The prophet was ordered to take **a lump of figs** (i.e., figs pressed into a cake to make a poultice; 1 Sam. 25:18). The figs were not a remedy, but a sign or symbol of the cure the LORD would effect, like the water of the Jordan in the narrative of Naaman (2 Kings 5:10). The king recovered (Heb., "lived"), the result being mentioned by anticipation.

The Sign of the Shadow. 20:8-11.

8-10. To certify such a great miracle, the king asked for a sign or a visible assurance. Then, in answer to the offer made to him, he asked that the shadow on the sundial should recede ten degrees. **11.** It was a wonder wrought by the power of God, as evidenced by Isaiah's crying out to the LORD and by the fact that the LORD brought the shadow ten degrees backward after it had gone down on the dial of Ahaz.

Keil is correct in assuming "a miraculous refraction of the rays of the sun, effected by God at the prophet's [Isaiah's] prayer" (C. F. Keil, *The Books of the Kings*, KD, pp. 464-65). However, it is not necessary to assume that the refraction was anything but local (cf. 2 Chron. 32:24). It is not said the sun moved backward, but that the shadow of the sun did. Precisely how this stupendous miracle was effected, the narrative does not in any way disclose. The same omnipotence that brought about Hezekiah's cure turned the shadow backward on the sundial for Hezekiah to see from his sickroom.

Hezekiah's Folly Before Merodach-baladan. 20:12-15. **12. Merodach-baladan** (Marduk-Apaliddin or Merodach-baladan) was twice king of Babylon (722-710, 703-702 B.C.). He was dethroned by Sargon about 710 B.C. But after Sargon's death in 705 B.C., he regained power once again. His visit came in Hezekiah's fourteenth year, during the course of Sennarcherib's first invasion. Merodach's purpose was to make an alliance with Hezekiah.

13. Hezekiah hearkened unto them, and showed them all the house of his precious things. In showing off his wealth and might, Hezekiah displayed vanity, which was to cost the kingdom of Judah a great price in later years. **14.** Isaiah dauntlessly encountered the king with the words, **What said these men? 15.**

Hezekiah's reply was undeniably naive: **All the things that are in mine house have they seen; there is nothing . . . that I have not showed them.**

Isaiah's Rebuke and Prophecy. 20:16-19. **16-18.** A true prophet of the LORD, Isaiah predicted what would happen, namely, the Babylonian Captivity (cf. 24:13; 25:13; Jer. 27:19-20). He even foretold that the posterity of Hezekiah (i.e., the house of David) would be taken away and would be eunuchs in the palace of the king of Babylon.

19. Hezekiah received the prophetic rebuke mildly, saying, **Good is the word of the Lord.** The king displayed pious acquiescence to the will of God (cf. 1 Kings 2:38). The severity of the prophetic word, however, was tempered with divine mercy in that Hezekiah himself was to be spared. However, Hezekiah's attitude can hardly be rated higher than a shortsighted expression of a "peace in our time" policy.

Summary of Hezekiah's Reign. 20:20-21. **20.** Hezekiah's **might** or strength is stressed. The conduit and pool brought water into the city (cf. 2 Chron. 32:2-4, 30). The king cut the rock-hewn conduit from the Gihon Spring to the Siloam reservoir, 1,777 feet long, which is one of the most amazing devices for water supply in the biblical period. It is comparable to tunnels at Megiddo and Gezer.

In addition, Hezekiah constructed a new and larger reservoir called the Pool of Siloam (John 9:7-11), identical with the "Pool of Shelah" (Neh. 3:15, RSV). The Siloam Inscription, discovered in 1880, is a six-line piece of writing in classical Hebrew that was cut beautifully on the wall of the conduit, about nineteen feet from the Siloam end of the aqueduct. It describes the completion of the engineering feat, as workmen with wedge, hammer, and pickax, digging from opposite ends, finally met.

D. MANASSEH'S AND AMON'S REIGNS. 21:1-26.

Manasseh's Wicked Reign. 21:1-9. **1-2.** A very good king had a very bad son, Manasseh being among the worst. His reign was as long as it was wicked. He ruled from about 696 to 642 B.C. He followed the **abominations of the nations** (heathen; cf. Deut. 29:17; 1 Kings 11:5), the pagan nations whom the LORD cast out before the children of Israel (cf. Deut. 18:9-13).

3. Hezekiah had torn down the high places; Manasseh rebuilt them. He reestablished Baalism. He made an **idol** ("grove," KJV; that is, an Asherah, an image of the polluted female deity, the Canaanite goddess of fertility). He is to be compared to his wicked Israelite counterpart, Ahab. He also established planetary worship.

4. He constructed idolatrous altars in the house of the LORD, wickedly defiling Jerusalem, where the LORD said He would put His name (cf. 1 Kings 14:21). **5.** He built his idolatrous altars **in the two courts.** He even defiled in this horrible manner the inner or more sacred court, where the sacrificial offerings were presented to the LORD.

6. He made **his son** (the Septuagint, as well as Chronicles, has his "sons") **pass through the fire,** stooping to the most abominable and cruel of all idolatrous practices (Lev. 18:21; Deut. 18:10). He dealt with **mediums** (familiar spirits), that is, he had intercourse with demons through occult religion with its spiritists and necromancers (Lev. 19:31; 20:27), formally appointing a necromancer, or spiritist, as a court official (cf. 1 Kings 12:31; 2 Chron. 33:6).

7. Lawlessness and subscription to occult religionism reached their peak when he made a **carved image of the idol** (cf. v. 3) and placed it in the house of the LORD, the abomination being erected within the Temple itself, probably in the holy place, constituting an act of intolerable and terrible blasphemy (cf. Jer. 7:30-32; Ezek. 43:7). **8.** The LORD had promised, **Neither will I make the feet of Israel move any more out of the land.** But that promise of permanent possession of the land depended upon faithfulness to the covenant of the LORD.

9. Manasseh led the people astray from the Mosaic Law to such an extent that the idolatry of Judah became worse than that of the Canaanites. Pagans worshiped only their national gods. Judah, on the other hand, forsook the one true living God and was ready to adopt any foreign cult that came its way (Jer. 2:11). Those who sin against the greatest light fall into the deepest darkness.

The Divine Denunciation of Manasseh's Wickedness. 21:10-15. **10.** The LORD gave sentence against Manasseh through His prophets, or spokesmen (cf. 17:13). **11.** Manasseh had done **wickedly above all that the Amorites did.** The name Amorites, or "westerners," is a comprehensive term for the native inhabitants of Canaan as a whole. Manasseh's indictment has been sustained by archaeology, which has revealed the utter depths of degradation into which Canaanite paganism had sunk. **12.** The LORD said He was going to bring upon Jerusalem and Judah **such evil** that he who heard it, **both of his ears shall tingle.** The truth would be so terrible that he who heard it would experience a ringing sensation in his ears, as when someone hears a sharp, piercing sound (cf. 1 Sam. 3:11; Jer. 19:3).

13. The figure of the measuring line suggests the destruction that will level the city (cf. Isa. 34:11; Lam. 2:8; Amos 7:7-9). The destruction of the people would be so thorough that it would be like a person who wipes a dish clean. **14.** The LORD said He would forsake the remnant of His inheritance (Jer. 6:9), with special reference to the Northern Kingdom, which had already been destroyed, and they would **become a prey and a spoil** (cf. Isa. 42:22; Jer. 30:16).

Summary of Manasseh's Reign. 21:16-18. **16.** Manasseh had **shed innocent blood very much**, being a murderer of the prophets of the LORD and their followers. It is tragic even to think of the terrible struggle under this wicked king for those who followed in Hezekiah's footsteps. **17.** For the rest of the acts of Manasseh, see 2 Chronicles 33:11-19, for the story of his captivity, repentance, and restoration. **18.** This wicked king was buried in the garden of his own house, apparently not the palace built by Solomon, but another that Manasseh had built for himself.

Amon's Reign. 21:19-26. **19.** Amon, the son of Manasseh, reigned only two years in Jerusalem (642-640 B.C.). **20-21.** He followed in the lawless footsteps of his father. **22. He forsook the Lord**, giving himself over with abandon to foreign superstitions. **23. The servants of Amon**, his courtiers or palace officials, conspired to murder him (2 Chron. 33:24). **24. The people of the land**, through their elders and heads of clans in general assembly, gave orders to put to death all those who had conspired against the king. They made Josiah, his son, king in his stead. Here the scene is reversed, for the wicked king was followed by a very good son, Josiah.

E. JOSIAH'S REIGN AND THE REVIVAL. 22:1-20.

The Faithfulness of Josiah. 22:1-2. **1-2.** Josiah (640-608 B.C.) was a good and faithful king who **walked in all the way of David**, his father. He and his great-grandfather, Hezekiah, are the only kings receiving unqualified praise. They were worthy in every sense to sit upon the Davidic throne, to claim the full blessings of the Davidic Covenant (2 Sam. 7:8-15).

The Repair of the Temple. 22:3-7. **3-4.** In the eighteenth year of his reign (622-621 B.C.), Josiah instructed his main officials to go up to the high priest, Hilkiah, to tell him to **reckon the amount of the silver** in the offering chest. The account of the Temple repair naturally resembles that under Joash (cf. 12:9-16, esp. v. 9). The **keepers of the door** had collected the offerings in the chest or box that Jehoiada the priest had placed there two centuries earlier (12:9). **5-6.** The unminted money was to be weighed out to workmen and masons for any necessary repairs of the Temple. More than two hundred years had elapsed since Joash had repaired the building, and evidently it had undergone many defacements under paganistic kings such as Ahaz, Manasseh, and Amon (cf. 2 Chron. 34:11).

The Recovery of the Book of the Law. 22:8-10. **8-10.** In the course of the extensive repairs, Hilkiah, the high priest, found the **book of the law**, the Law of Moses. Evidently it was the entire five books of Moses, the Pentateuch, and not just Deuteronomy or part of Deuteronomy. It was a Temple copy, which had been laid beside the ark in the most holy place (cf. Deut. 31:25-26). During the long, ungodly reign of Manasseh, and even perhaps under his predecessor, Ahaz, this scroll and also the ark had been removed from their places (cf. 2 Chron. 35:3).

Somehow this precious document had been lost and found again during the repair of the Temple. Hilkiah gave a copy to Shaphan, the scribe, which was subsequently shown and read before the king. Apparently the particular passage that excited the king was a portion of Deuteronomy 28 to 30, in which are recorded the renewal of the national covenant and a list of the terrible threats and curses announced against all who would violate the Law covenant, either the king or the people. Possibly during Manasseh's long, idolatrous orgy, the ancient Scriptures had become rare.

The Effect on Josiah. 22:11-14. **12-13.** **The king commanded** that inquiry be made before the LORD concerning the guilt under which he and the people lay because of the infraction of the Law contained in the newly discovered book. He immediately sent a deputation of his principal officers to one endowed with prophetic gifts. Sent were Ahikam, a friend of Jeremiah (Jer. 26:24); Achbor (or Abdon, 2 Chron. 34:20), a man of influence at the court (Jer. 26:22); Shaphan, the scribe; and Asaiah, an official.

14. It is strange that this delegation was not sent to Zephaniah (Zeph. 1:1), or to Jeremiah, who probably was away at his home in Anathoth, but to Huldah, a woman in Jerusalem known for her prophetic gifts. She probably was a widow at the time. Her husband, Shallum, was or had been **keeper of the wardrobe** (probably a priestly wardrobe), and he probably was a Levite. Huldah resided in Jerusalem **in the second quarter** of the city, a particular suburb of Jerusalem. This woman was held in high veneration, as is shown by her being sought out for such an important mission.

The Message of Huldah the Prophetess. 22:15-20. **15-17.** Huldah delivered an oracular response. In it judgment was blended with mercy. She announced impending chastisements that in the near future would overtake the city and its inhabitants. **18-20.** Good news for the king was that the threatened punishment would not occur during his reign on account of his faith in the LORD and penitential zeal for the divine glory and worship.

F. THE RESULTS OF JOSIAH'S REVIVAL. 23:1-37.

The Law Read. 23:1-3. **1-2.** Josiah called together a great concourse of **all the elders**, that is, the representatives of the nation; **and the prophets**, numerous members of the prophetic order who at that time constituted a distinct class (cf. Jer. 2:8; 5:31; 6:13); as well as the general population. **He read** (doubtlessly the priests did this; cf. Deut. 31:9-13).

3. Josiah stood **by a pillar** (better perhaps, "on the stand" or "dais"; cf. 11:14). He **made** ("cut") **a covenant** before the LORD (11:17) to perform all of His commandments. All the people **joined in** ("stood to," KJV) **the covenant.** "Stood to" (lit. Heb.) probably describes the actual ritual of standing within the covenant's symbols, the people taking the same pledge as the king (cf. 18:28).

A Great Reformation Instituted. 23:4-20. **4.** Josiah initiated a widespread, thorough destruction of pagan cult places and objects (cf. 2 Chron. 34:3-4, 7, 33). Hilkiah, the high priest, and the **priests of the second order** or rank (i.e., the high priest's deputies, 25:18), and the **keepers of the door** (doorkeepers) were charged with cleansing the Temple.

These officials brought out of the Temple all the vessels that were made for Baal and for the idol (i.e., Asherah, the Canaanite fertility goddess) and all the objects used in planetary worship. They burned them **outside of Jerusalem,** as utterly unclean and defiling to the "holy city" (cf. Neh. 11:1, 18; Matt. 4:5; Rev. 21:2). They were burned in the fields of Kidron, east of the city where the Kidron Valley widens (cf. Jer. 31:40).

5. He **put down** (deposed) and did away with the **idolatrous priests** (the $k^e m \bar{a} r \hat{i} m$), whom the kings of Judah had ordained to burn incense in the high places in Judean cities. They also rooted out those who burned incense to Baal, the sun, the moon, and the planets (i.e., the signs of the Zodiac). **6.** They brought out the **idol**, the image of Asherah, from the house of the LORD and burned it at the brook Kidron and ground it to powder (Exod. 32:20). **7.** They destroyed the houses of the **sodomites** (male temple prostitutes dedicated to the foul worship of the Canaanites; cf. 1 Kings 14:24; 15:12; Hos. 4:14). The allusion to the women who **wove hangings** (tents) for the Asherah refers to the pavilions, or screens, where they conducted their foul rites.

8. Josiah brought all the priests from the local sanctuaries of the LORD to Jerusalem. He **defiled** (desecrated) the high places in order to eliminate them from further use. The goal of the reformation was to root out worship contrary to the Law of the LORD once and for all from **Geba,** present-day Jeba, near ancient Ramah (1 Kings 15:22), the northernmost point in Benjamin, to Beersheba, the southernmost point, representing the farthest limits of the king's realm. Beersheba was an especially famous high place (Amos 5:5; 8:14; cf. 2 Chron. 34:6). **The high places of the gates** contained altars erected within the city gates (places of trade) so that people might make an offering to insure financial success. **Joshua, the governor of the city**, is unknown otherwise. **9.** For some reason, Josiah's plan did not work, for the priests of the high places did not come up to the altar of the LORD in Jerusalem (cf. 1 Sam. 2:36;

Ezek. 44:10-14). They did not enter into priestly duties, but enjoyed priestly sustenance.

10. He desecrated Topheth in the Hinnom Valley, infamous for its idolatry (see v. 8), laying it in ruins in order to root out the cruel practice of offering children to Molech, the cruel Ammonite deity. **11.** Josiah destroyed **the horses . . . given** (presented) **to the sun.** The horses, which drew the **chariots of the sun** in solemn procession held in honor of the sun deity (cf. Herodotus 1. 189), also were sacrificed to the sun. In antiquity, the figure of the sun's course as a fiery chariot drawn by steeds, as pictured here, was common. **12.** The king destroyed the idolatrous altars of Ahaz and Manasseh (Jer. 11:13; Zeph. 1:5). **13-14.** He cleansed **the mount of corruption,** a name given to the southern summit of the Mount of Olives because of the gross idolatry practiced there (1 Kings 11:5-7). **15.** Josiah made a clean sweep of the idolatry at Bethel (cf. 1 Kings 12:28-33). **16.** He desecrated the bones of the sepulchers in the vicinity, and burned them upon the altar, utterly destroying the high place and fulfilling God's Word in 1 Kings 13:2. **17-18.** Then he noticed the gravestone or monument of the man of God who had foretold his actions (1 Kings 13:1-32), and he ordered that the man's grave be not disturbed. **So they let his bones alone** (i.e., "rest"), **with the bones of the prophet who came out of Samaria** (cf. 1 Kings 13:31-32). **19.** Chapels or temples, called **houses . . . of the high places,** also were destroyed. Josiah could do those things in Samaria because the Assyrian Empire was about to fall, and perhaps the Assyrian emperor took no notice of the king's proceedings in the west.

The Passover Celebrated. 23:21-23. **21-23.** The Passover was the high point of the reformation and was held according to Deuteronomy 16:1-8 (cf. 2 Chron. 35:1-19).

Josiah Cleans out Occult Religion. 23:24-27. **24.** Josiah put away the mediums, those who trafficked in demons. Demonism is the dynamic of idolatry (cf. 1 Cor. 10:20). **Wizards** were people endowed with fortune-telling abilities, because under demon instruction they were paraded as prognosticators or prophets with supernatural powers. **Images** and **idols** were intimately connected with occultism and demon worship, since behind the idol was the demon or the false god.

25. So thorough was Josiah's compliance with the Law of Moses (cf. Deut. 18:9-12) that no king, even Hezekiah, excelled him. Hezekiah excelled in trust in the LORD, Josiah, in devotion to the Law of Moses. Nevertheless, the doom of Judah was sealed. **26-27.** Even this great revival was not deep enough and far-reaching enough to spare the kingdom.

The Death of Josiah. 23:28-30. **29.** Pharaoh-neco (609-594 B.C.) **went up to** (NASB; not "against," KJV) the king of Assyria. This military operation was to aid the Assyrian monarch against Nabopolassar, king of Babylon (see Edwin R. Thiele, BASOR 143 [Oct. 1956]: 25). Josiah was tragically slain at Megiddo. The Chaldean thrust westward was not stopped, because Josiah's ill-advised campaign weakened Neco and resulted in the fulfillment of 20:17 and the sudden emergence of the Neo-Babylonian Empire.

The Reign of Jehoahaz. 23:31-33. **31-32.** Jehoahaz succeeded his father in 608 B.C. Despite the great purge Josiah had effected, Jehoahaz **did . . . evil,** that is, he broke the covenant. **33.** He was taken captive by Pharaoh-neco to Riblah.

The Reign of Jehoiakim. 23:34-37.

34-37. Jehoiakim, another son of Josiah, reigned from 608 to 597 B.C. The reigns of Jehoahaz and Jehoiakim were the beginning of the end of the kingdom of Judah.

G. JEHOIAKIM, JEHOIACHIN, AND ZEDEKIAH. 24:1-20.

Jehoiakim and the First Capture of Jerusalem. 24:1-7. **1.** The Battle of Carchemish in 605 B.C. (Jer. 46:2) witnessed the defeat of the Assyrians and the Egyptians by the Chaldeans (the Neo-Babylonians). The result was that Egyptian control of Judah collapsed, and Judah came under the dominance of the Chaldeans. Jehoiakim, who had been a vassal of Egypt, then became a paltry puppet of the Chaldean Empire. After three years Jehoiakim revolted against Nebuchadnezzar. **2.** Because of Judah's sin, the Word of the LORD was fulfilled as spoken by God's **servants, the prophets** (cf. 20:17; 21:12-14). There came against Jehoiakim, in addition to the Chaldeans, bands of Syrians, Moabites, and Ammonites.

3-4. The sacred record shows that the LORD could not pardon the bloody orgy of Manasseh, especially the **innocent blood ... shed** under him (the God-fearing people he had butchered). God's holiness had to be vindicated. **6.** Jehoiakim **slept with his fathers** (a euphemism for death), and Jehoiachin, his son, reigned in his stead. Jehoiachin is also called Jeconiah (1 Chron. 3:16) and Coniah (Jer. 22:24). This eighteen-year-old youngster took over the tottering throne in 597 B.C.

Jehoiachin and the Second Capture of Jerusalem. 24:8-17. **8-12.** Almost at once the young King Jehoiachin surrendered to Nebuchadnezzar (the more correct form, frequently used in Jeremiah, is Nebuchadrezzar, Jer. 21:2). This took place in the spring of 597

B.C., Nebuchadnezzar's seventh year (Jer. 52:28), as related in the Babylonian records. Since Jehoiachin's father died before he could be punished, Nebuchadnezzar came and besieged Jerusalem.

13. In surrendering to the king of Babylon, the young king gave up all the treasures of the Temple and the palace. **14-16.** The Babylonians carried away ten thousand captives, including all the princes, all the mighty men of valor, and all the craftsmen. They left only the poorest of the land. Jehoiachin was deported to Babylon. **17.** The king of Babylon made Mattaniah, Jehoiachin's uncle, king in his place, changing his name to Zedekiah.

Zedekiah's Reign. 24:18-20. **18-19.** Zedekiah reigned eleven years and did evil, as Jehoiakim, his brother, had done. **20.** The LORD's anger was raised to such a pitch that He cast His people out from His presence.

H. THE FALL OF JERUSALEM AND THE EXILE. 25:1-30.

The Siege of Jerusalem. 25:1-7. **1-2.** Zedekiah (597-586 B.C.) revolted against the king of Babylon. In spite of his oath of allegiance to Nebuchadnezzar (2 Chron. 36:13; Ezek. 17:13), Zedekiah began to plot with Egypt and other nations against the Chaldeans (Jer. 27:3-7; Ezek. 17:15). His rebellion precipitated the last siege and the fall of Jerusalem.

3-4. As a result of terrible privation (cf. Deut. 28:52-57; Lam. 4:10), the city fell in the eleventh year of king Zedekiah (586 B.C.). Zedekiah and all his men of war fled by night through a breach made in the city wall. **5.** The Chaldeans pursued Zedekiah to the plains of Jericho, where all his army was scattered from him. **6.** The Chaldeans captured the king and took him to the king of Babylon at Riblah, located south of Hamath on the Orontes River. Nebuchadnezzar passed sentence upon him. **7.** They killed Zedekiah's sons before his eyes and then put out the king's eyes. Then they bound him with fetters and took him to Babylon.

The Temple and the City Destroyed. 25:8-17. **8-9.** The Babylonians burned the Temple, the palace, and all the houses of Jerusalem. **10-11.** The walls were broken down, and the second deportation was carried out. **12.** Only the poorest of the people were left to be vinedressers and plowmen (Jer. 39:10; 40:7). **13-17.** All the valuable equipment of the Temple was transported to Babylon (Jer. 52:17-23). The Chaldeans broke up the bronze and took it to Babylon, as well as all the gold and silver (Jer. 27:19-22).

The Leaders of the People Put to Death. 25:18-21. **18-20.** The remaining leaders, all of whom were linked with Zedekiah's rebellion, as well as the chief priest, the second priest, and the keepers of the threshold, plus many other officials, were taken to the king of Babylon at Riblah and sentenced to death. **21.** The doleful dirge rings out: **So Judah was taken into exile out of its land** (RSV).

Gedaliah Made Governor. 25:22-26. **22-24.** Gedaliah swore to the people of the land that remained, saying, "Do not be afraid because of the Chaldean officials; dwell in the land, and serve the king of Babylon, and it shall be well with you" (RSV). **25.** But Ishmael of the royal family came with ten men and killed Gedaliah together with the Jews and the Chaldeans who were with him at Mizpah. Gedaliah was well disposed toward Jeremiah the prophet (Jer.

39:14; 40:6) and enjoyed the confidence of his fellow citizens (Jer. 40:11-12). The dastardly assassination of this good man by a deposed member of the royal family brought about utter chaos and ruin (Jer. 40:13—41:18; cf. 44:1-14). **26.** This tragedy precipitated a general exodus to Egypt out of fear of reprisals from the Chaldeans.

Jehoiachin Set Free in Babylon. 25:27-30. **27-30.** After being a political prisoner thirty-seven years in Babylon, Jehoiachin was released by Nebuchadnezzar II's successor, Evil-merodach (Amel-Marduk, Akk., "man of Marduk," 562-560 B.C.). A vase from Susa attests this king and reads: "Palace of Amel-Marduk, king of Babylon, son of Nebuchadnezzar, king of Babylon."

Babylonian records list "Yaukin, king of the land of Yahud" (i.e., "Jehoiachin, of Judah") as one of the recipients of royal rations. He was still considered the king of Judah, even by the Babylonians themselves. Jar handles from Tell Beit Mirsim and Bethshemesh, found from 1928 to 1936, are stamped "Eliakim, steward of Yaukin" (Jehoiachin), showing that the exiled king was recognized as the rightful sovereign by the people of Judah also.

Thus, the book of 2 Kings ends in a gracious note of kindness toward the house of David. Through the dark tragedy to which sin had brought them, the grace of God shines through to give them hope, even in the darkest hour. "For God's gifts of grace and His calling are irrevocable" (Rom. 11:29, BV) are words that not only mark God's ancient people, Israel, but also *all* of God's people of every age and time.

FIRST CHRONICLES

INTRODUCTION

Title. Chronicles originally existed as a single composition. The Hebrew title is *dibrê hăyyāmîm,* meaning "Events or Annals of the Days" ("times"; cf. 27:24). In the Hebrew, the two books were originally one great historical work. The twofold division made by the Septuagint in the second century B.C. was not introduced into modern Hebrew Bibles until the printed edition of Daniel Bomberg in 1517. The Septuagint inaccurately named the two books *Paralipomena,* "things passed over or omitted" (from the books of Samuel and Kings), as if Chronicles were merely a supplement to those works. The book of Chronicles occurs in the third division of the Hebrew canon. Accordingly, our Lord in Luke 11:51 referred to all the martyrs from Abel in the first book, Genesis (chap. 4) to Zechariah in the last (2 Chron. 24). English Bibles follow the Septuagint and the Vulgate in placing Chronicles immediately after Kings.

Purpose. The books of 1 and 2 Chronicles present a history of priestly worship from the death of Saul to the end of the Babylonian Captivity. They are concerned with the working out of what God has ordained; therefore, they represent the *priestly* standpoint. This is in contrast to Samuel and Kings, where the *prophetic* standpoint is set forth, describing how God dealt with His people and so made Himself known to them in His disciplinary ways. The writer sets in prominence only those aspects of history that illustrate the cultivation of the Mosaic ritual as a medium of spiritual blessing and prosperity in the kingdom. Accordingly, great prominence is given to priestly genealogies, to the tribes faithful to the Davidic throne, and to those kings who were favorable to the true worship of the LORD at Jerusalem. Special emphasis is accorded David and Solomon because of their paramount role in establishing the Temple service. All of this looks forward to the coming of the Messiah and the still-future setting up of the Davidic Kingdom, with David foreshadowing Christ's first advent, and Solomon foreshadowing Christ's second advent. The reasons for the writing of Chronicles are evident. The postexilic community had to be made aware of the pivotal fact that the roots of its existence lay in the past, that it was a true continuation of the preexilic kingdom, and that the restoration Temple and its services had their foundation in the Law of Moses and in the institutions of the Davidic and Solomonic kingdom.

Authorship and Date. Tradition considers Ezra the author of Chronicles. Though this cannot be proved, evidence is not lacking to support the validity of the traditional position. W. F. Albright has espoused the thesis that the chronicler was Ezra and that he wrote between 400 and 350 B.C. (JBL 40 [1921]: 104-24). The more negative critics place the book later, between 350 and 250 B.C. (cf. Robert H. Pfeiffer, *Introduction to the Old Testament,* p. 812). Late-date critics stress the variation of Chronicles from Samuel and Kings, especially in the use of larger numbers. However, archaeology is vindicating the historical value and trustworthiness of these books, which Albright has pointed out (BASOR 100 [1945]:18).

Sources. The chronicler makes use of various writings that supplement the history he recounts. These fall into two categories. The first category displays a similarity in the titles, suggesting that a single set of records is referred to. Mentioned are: "the book of the kings of Judah and Israel" (2 Chron. 16:11; 25:26; 28:26; 32:32); "the book of the kings of Israel and Judah" (27:7; 35:27; 36:8); "the book of the kings of Israel" (20:34); "the acts of the kings of Israel" (33:18, ASV). The second category of sources is connected with certain prophets. For David's reign there is "the words of Samuel ... Nathan ... and ... Gad" (1 Chron. 29:29, KJV margin); for Solomon's reign, "the words of Nathan," "the prophecy of Ahijah," and "the visions of Iddo" (2 Chron. 9:29, ASV margin); for Rehoboam's reign, "the words of Shemaiah ... and of Iddo" (12:15, KJV margin); for Abijah's reign, "the story of ... Iddo" (13:22, KJV); for Jehoshaphat's reign, "the words of Jehu" (20:34, KJV margin); for Manasseh's reign, "the history [words] of Hozai" (33:19, ASV). There are two references to Isaiah (26:22; 32:32).

The Hebrew Text and the Septuagint. The translation of Chronicles in the Septuagint is carefully and skillfully done. It is strictly literal and one of the best works of those translators, far surpassing the books of Samuel and Kings, which were translated by someone else. In many passages the Septuagint preserves an unquestionably better reading than that of the Masoretic recension. The unsatisfactory condition of the Hebrew text, due perhaps to the fact that Chronicles was never so highly valued as other portions of the canon, may in part be remedied by a careful comparison of the data of the Septuagint, as well as other books of the Old Testament.

OUTLINE

COMMENTARY

I. GENEALOGIES FROM ADAM TO DAVID. 1:1—9:44.

A. FROM ADAM TO ISRAEL (JACOB). 1:1-54.

Adam to Noah. 1:1-4. In accordance with his priestly approach, the chronicler begins his work with the most extensive genealogical records in the Bible. His purpose is to connect the divine redemptive plan with the human race and its origin in the fall of Adam. It therefore focuses all lines of redemptive history in David, as foreshadowing the greater David, David's Son and Lord (cf. Psalm 110:1).

The great emphasis on the dedication and services of the Temple and the Levitical ministry, all of which symbolize the person and work of the coming Messiah, also points to the focus of redemptive history in the greater David. These genealogies look forward to those of our Lord recorded in Matthew 1:1-17 and Luke 3:23-38, the latter going back to Adam, and the former to Abraham, with both names also highlighted in these genealogies.

1-4. These verses trace the Messianic line in ten generations from Adam (cf. Gen. 1:27; 2:7; 5:1-2, 5) through Seth (cf. Gen. 4:25-26; 5:3-4, 6-8) to Noah (cf. Gen. 5:28—10:1). The Cainite line is omitted, in full conformity with the chronicler's purpose. Verse 4 gives priority to Shem (cf. Gen. 10:22-31) as being in the Messianic line to Abraham (cf. 1 Chron. 1:24-28), but then reverts in verses 8 to 28 to the order in Genesis 10.

The Sons of Japheth. 1:5-7. The Japhethites were in general the ancestors of the Indo-European races. For the ethnic and geographic identifications in the light of linguistic and archaeological research, see Genesis 10:2-5. This opening chapter of genealogy seeks to define the place of God's chosen people in relation to contiguous nations of antiquity, presenting some background for the broad picture of redemptive history.

The Sons of Ham. 1:8-16. The Hamites were in general the dark-skinned races of Africa. The term *Hamitic* is largely restricted today to the peoples and languages of ancient Egypt. For the ethnic and geographic identifications, see Genesis 10:6-20.

The Sons of Shem. 1:17-23. These are the "Shemites" or Semites (see Gen. 10:21-32), the group to which the Hebrews (**Eber,** vv. 18-19) belonged and through which Abraham, Isaac, and Jacob of the redemptive line ran. **19.** In the days of **Peleg** ("division"), one of Eber's sons, **the earth was divided** (cf. Deut. 32:7-9). Jacob Myers (AB) renders it, "divided into districts" (cf. Akk., *puluggu, pulungu,* meaning "district"; see Gen. 10:25).

Shem to Abraham. 1:24-28. **24-27.** The genealogical register now comes to focus on Abraham, breaking off abruptly from all the families of Noah's descendants except that of Arpachshad (Arphaxad), from whom the Messiah was to descend. This chapter emphasizes the fact that God had "made of one blood all nations of men" (Acts 17:26), stemming from one Adam, one Noah. "Have we not all one father? Has not one

God created us? (Mal. 2:10, RSV).

It also highlights the truth that redemption of a fallen race is to come through one Man, the second Adam, who is to appear through the line of Abraham, the representative man of faith (Gen. 15:6; Rom. 4:1-25) and the recipient of the Abrahamic Covenant, guaranteeing salvation by grace through faith (cf. Gen. 12:1-3). **28.** But the line is to run through Abraham's son, Isaac, the younger son, not Ishmael, the older. Therefore, the younger is mentioned before the older, as God's purposes must take the place of preeminence.

The Sons of Ishmael. 1:29-31. **29-31.** It is noteworthy that the sideline is followed first, as if to get it out of the way, so that the main line may proceed, just as in the case of Japheth and Ham (vv. 5-16), being treated before Shem, although Shem was initially given first place (v. 1). Abraham's posterity through Ishmael closely follows the source (Gen. 25:13-16). The Ishmaelites were north Arabians (see J. A. Montgomery, *Arabia and the Bible,* index, for names and possible identification of the Ishmaelites).

Keturah's Sons. 1:32-33. **32-33.** Genesis refers to Keturah as Abraham's second wife, taken after Sarah's decease. The chronicler views her as a **concubine,** though her children are the same as those in the Genesis list (Gen. 25:2). The descendants of Dedan are passed over (cf. Gen 25:3-4), as are numerous groups in these selected and abbreviated lists. Keturah's sons were south Arabians.

The Sons of Isaac. 1:34. **34. And Abraham begot Isaac** (note that Sarah's name, unlike Keturah's, is omitted), this all-important fact in the redemptive line is emphasized by statements in the briefest possible manner and by repetition (cf. v. 28). **Esau,** as the firstborn, is

named first. But Jacob, to whom the birthright was sold by Esau, is listed as **Israel,** the name of spiritual promise and Messianic blessing.

As the genealogies come to Abraham and his descendants (v. 28), all the other nations and peoples—as those not the LORD's and having no portion with His people—have been taken off. The story narrows to the chosen people, the elect, holy nation, which is to become the subject of the sacred history. Accordingly, all the seed of Abraham except the posterity of Jacob (Israel) is set aside to make room for the redemptive line and nation through whom the Redeemer was to come.

The Sons of Esau. 1:35-54. **35-42.** The Edomites were the inveterate enemies of Israel, God's people. Yet, because they were descended from Isaac's son, Esau, they are mentioned in their genealogies. **43-54.** The list of Edomite kings and chiefs is taken from Genesis 36:31-43 and shows the position of Edom while Israel was struggling to maintain itself in the period of the Judges. Such variations as the spelling are due to changes in pronunciation and other things over many centuries.

B. THE LINE OF JUDAH. 2:1-55.

The Sons of Israel. 2:1-2. Presented is the register of the family of Jacob (Israel) and his twelve sons. The previous genealogies prepared the way for this presentation. These twelve sons and their posterity become prominent in the sacred history as God's elect people and nation, who were to "dwell alone, and . . . not be reckoned among the nations" (Num. 23:9) and from whom, through Judah, the Messiah-Savior was to come (Gen. 49:10).

The Family of Judah and the Ancestors of David. 2:3-17. **3.** Judah ("praise") was the tribe most praised, most increased, and most honored, for it was producing the Davidic-Messianic line. Therefore, its genealogy is given first and is the most detailed of all. Yet, opening the register are the names of several persons of blemished character. Despite that fact, the Abrahamic Covenant, confirmed to Isaac and Jacob, was operative on their descendants because of its being of free grace and not of works (Mal. 1:2-3; Eph. 2:8-9).

Er, Judah's firstborn was "wicked in the sight of the LORD; and the LORD slew him" (Gen. 38:3-7). **Onan** was no better and fared no better (38:8-10). **4. Tamar** appears, with whom Judah, her father-in-law, committed incest (38:12-30; cf. Num. 26:19-22). **6.** Also appearing in the register are those who were very wise and good, such as the descendants of Zerah, and those who were preeminent because of their wisdom, such as **Zimri ... Ethan ... Heman ... Calcol, and Dara** (1 Kings 4:31).

7. Listed also is **Achar** (Achan), **the troubler of Israel,** who partook of the accursed thing (Josh. 7:1-26; 22:20).

10-11. Also appearing are some who were very great, such as **Nahshon, prince of the children of Judah** (Num. 1:7), who led the vanguard in that glorious march in the wilderness, and **Salma** (Salmon; cf. Ruth 4:21; Matt. 1:5), who occupied that post of honor when Canaan was entered.

13-17. Particular account is given of the family of **Jesse** for the sake of **David,** and David's Son and LORD, the "rod out of the stem of Jesse" (Isa. 11:1). It here appears that David was the seventh son and that his three great military leaders, **Joab, Abishai, and Asahel,** were sons of **Zeruiah,** one of his sisters; and that **Amasa** was the son of **Abigail,** another of his sisters (cf. 2 Sam. 17:25).

Hezron's Line to Asshur. 2:18-24.

18-20. The Calebites are listed, probably in connection with Bezalel, who was prominent in the construction of the tabernacle furniture and equipment (Exod. 31:2-11; 35:30-35; 38:22; 2 Chron. 1:5), which was transferred to the Solomonic Temple. This Caleb is not the spy (Num. 13:6). Hur is associated with Judah (Exod. 31:2; 35:30). **21-24.** Hezron's line is named (vv. 5, 9-10; cf. Gen. 46:12; Num. 26:21; Ruth 4:18-19).

Jerahmeel's Line. 2:25-41. **25-41.** Little is known of Jerahmeel's line, except that traditionally Jerahmeel early became associated with Judah, probably in an amphictyony (an association of neighboring states) with the center at Hebron (M. Noth, *Die Israeliten und ihre Nachbarstämme,* p. 340).

Other Descendants of Caleb (2:42-49). **42-49.** The Calebites were a southern group, like the Jerahmeelites (1 Sam. 30:14), and were Kenizzites (Num. 32:12; Josh. 14:6, 13; Judg. 1:13). They early became closely identified with Judah and occupied Hebron (Josh. 14:13; 15:13; Judg. 1:20).

The Line of Caleb Through Hur. 2:50-55. **50-54.** Caleb's line was connected with three localities: Kiriath-jearim, Bethlehem, and Beth-gader. **55. The families of the scribes** *(sopherim)* were possibly scribal guilds. For **Rechab,** see 2 Kings 10:15; Jeremiah 35:2.

C. THE LINE OF DAVID TO THE EXILE. 3:1-24.

David's Sons Born at Hebron and Jerusalem. 3:1-9. When the Jews returned from Babylon under the Persians, they were allowed no king, the prophetic word indicating that no purely human descendant of David would ever again occupy the Davidic throne (Jer. 22:30). But postexilic interest continued in the Davidic line, for through it Scripture predicted a greater Son of David, a man, but more than a man, God's "fellow" (Zech. 13:7), through whose death (12:10) would come redemption (13:1) and the Kingdom of God on earth (14:9), with Israel restored as a high-priestly nation (3:1-10) to be the light of the world under the Messiah-King-Priest (4:1-14). Hence, the chronicler, who wrote in the postexilic era, traced the royal Davidic line to the general period in which he lived. The Davidic line is traced from the sons born in Hebron (vv. 1-4) and in Jerusalem (vv. 5-9).

1. Daniel is also called Chileab (see 2 Sam. 3:3). For the parallel list, see 2 Samuel 3:2-5; 5:14-16; and 1 Chronicles 14:4-7. **5. Bathshua** is Bathsheba (2 Sam. 11:2-7). **9.** The sons of David's **concubines** (cf. 1 Kings 11:3) are not named; nor are the offspring of Tamar, who was raped by Amnon (2 Sam. 13).

David's Line to Zedekiah. 3:10-16. All of these kings are well known from the books of Kings. **11.** From a succession of fifteen monarchs, Athaliah, the usurper, is omitted between Ahaziah and Joash. **15.** With Josiah, the regular succession by primogeniture is interrupted. The firstborn, **Johanan,** never ascended the throne, probably dying early. He cannot be identified with Jehoahaz, who was two years younger than Jehoiakim (2 Kings 23:31, 36), and therefore could not have been the firstborn of Josiah.

For some reason the order of verse 15 does not follow strict seniority or actual order of succession, the latter being (1) Shallum (Jehoahaz, 2 Kings 23:30; Jer. 22:11); (2) Jehoiakim (Eliakim, 2 Kings 23:24; Jer. 22:18); (3) Jeconiah, son of Jehoiakim (Jehoiachin, Jer. 22:24); (4) Zedekiah (Mattaniah 2 Kings. 24:17). Jeconiah (Coniah, an abbreviated form, Jer. 22:24, 28) was taken into captivity by Nebuchadnezzar (see notes on 2 Kings 24:15). Zedekiah, his uncle, be-

came king in his place. Apparently Jeconiah (Jehoiachin) also had a son named Zedekiah, although many scholars construe "son" in the loose Hebrew sense of "royal successor" or "relative," Zedekiah actually being Jeconiah's uncle.

David's Postexilic Line of Descent. 3:17-24. **17-18.** These verses should be read, "The sons of Jeconiah, the captive ['ǎssîr, "prisoner"], were Shealtiel, his son, then Malchiram, Pedaiah, Shenazzar, Jekamiah, Hoshama, and Nedabiah"—a total of seven sons (see Myers, AB, p. 18). This means that all seven were born while Jehoiachin was in exile (see W. F. Albright, BA 5 [1942]:50; cf. 2 Chron. 36:9).

The Weidner texts, recovered from Babylon, speak of five sons of Jehoiachin who received rations from Babylonian authorities. These texts date from 595 to 570 B.C., the crucial one from Nebuchadnezzar's thirteenth year (c. 592); so the oldest son of Jehoiachin was born not later than 597 B.C.

Since Pedaiah falls third in the list of seven, and reckoning twenty-five years for a generation, Albright concludes he was born in about 595 B.C. (JBL 40 [1921]:110-11). On that basis the genealogy (vv. 18-24) runs to about 405 B.C., with the approximate date of the birth of each person that forms a link in the chain of Davidic descent as follows: **18.** Pedaiah (c. 595 B.C.); **19.** Zerubbabel (c. 570 B.C.); **21.** Hananiah (c. 545 B.C.); **22.** Shecaniah (c. 520 B.C.); Shemaiah (c. 495 B.C.); **23.** Neariah (c. 470 B.C.); **24.** Elioenai (c. 445 B.C.); Hodaviah (cf. 420 B.C.); Anani (the last son; c. 405 B.C.).

This construction would date the chronicler at about 400 B.C. Pedaiah is listed as the father of Zerubbabel (instead of Shealtiel, as in Ezra 3:2; Neh. 12:1; Hag. 1:12). This fact is doubtless to be explained on the basis of a levirate marriage in the family. The names occurring are common for the period and are attested by such sources as the Elephantine papyri, Lachish Letters, seals, and stamps.

D. THE FAMILY OF JUDAH AND SIMEON. 4:1-43.

Judah's Descendants. 4:1-10. The chronicler further demonstrates his preeminent interest in the tribe of Judah. With its appendages of Simeon, Benjamin, and Levi, it made up the kingdom of Judah, which not only long survived the other tribes, but, when Chronicles was written, had returned from the Exile and was looking forward dimly but surely (cf. the wonderful Messianic prophecies of Haggai, Malachi, and Zechariah) to the glorious future promised the elect nation.

1-2. These verses present the sons of Judah and Shobal, constituting an expansion of Judah's progeny through Shobal mentioned in 2:50, 52. The purpose of the supplement is to explain the background of the Zorathites. (2:53) because of their importance (cf. 2 Chron. 11:10; Neh. 11:29). **3-9.** To the descendants of Hur (vv. 3-4) and Ashur (vv. 5-8) is attributed Jabez's prayer and its answer (vv. 8-9). His name means "He causes sorrow."

10. He prayed for blessing, increase, fellowship with the LORD, preservation from evil, and **that it may not grieve me** (lit., "that I may have no more sorrow," an allusion to the meaning of his name). Whatever the occasion, God heard his faithful cry and answered his prayer, furnishing the centuries with an example of the faith in God and His redemptive grace that existed in the hearts of many Judahites. "This little pericope is theological in meaning, though it may have been intended as a comment on

2:55, where Jabez is a place name" (Myers, AB, p. 28).

Additional Genealogical Lists of Judah. 4:11-23. Problems exist in the clan relationships of the ten leaders listed in these verses, due perhaps to gaps in the genealogical records, which were available to the chronicler, and also to corruption of the text, attributable to copyists' slips through many centuries of transmission. Further elaboration on the Calebites (vv. 11-15) and the Judahite-Calebite clans (vv. 16-20) is given. **21-23.** A brief note on the descendants of Shelah, Judah's third son, is an afterthought expansion of 2:3 rather than a displacement.

Simeon's Descendants. 4:24-43. **24-33.** The interest in the tribe of Simeon is doubtless due to the chronicler's concept of the ideal Israel, comprising all the tribes (Ezra 6:17; 8:35). The notation that Simeon was not so prosperous as Judah reflects its early absorption by Judah (Josh. 19:1, 9; cf. Gen. 49:5-7), suggested, too, by its absence in the blessing of Moses (Deut. 33) and its exclusion from the list of places to which David sent booty (1 Sam. 30:27-31). The Simeonite family list (vv. 24-27; cf. Num. 26:12-13; Josh. 19:1-8) is followed by Simeonite towns and cities (vv. 28-33; for identifications, see Albright, JPOS 5[1925]:149-61; F. Cross and G. E. Wright, JBL 75[1956]:214-15).

34-43. The concluding section describes the movements of Simeonite leaders and clans, who for natural reasons (need for pasture for flocks) sought sustenance elsewhere. One group went westward toward **Gedor** (Gerar?; cf. Josh. 15:58; LXXB), whose lands were controlled by Egyptian puppet rulers (cf. Albright, JPOS 4[1924]:146-47). The second movement was in the opposite direction and displaced the Amalekites inhabiting the Akaba region among the Edomites, since they were scattered in Saul's reign (1 Sam. 15:7-8) and in the Davidic era (30:18).

E. THE DESCENDANTS OF REUBEN, GAD, AND THE HALF TRIBE OF MANASSEH. 5:1-26.

Descendants of Reuben. 5:1-10. **1.** The chronicler's zeal for the position of Judah, the tribe of David, as the center of national religious institutions and Messianic hope did not cause him to lose sight of the other tribes. This furnishes a sidelight on his concept of Jerusalem as the true center and Judah as the true perpetuator of Israel, being representative of all the tribes.

In setting forth Reuben's descendants, the chronicler recognized Reuben as Jacob's oldest son (Gen. 29:32; 35:23; 49:3; Exod. 6:14), but he noted his sin (Gen. 35:22; 49:4) and presented it as the reason for the priority of Joseph's sons (Ephraim and Manasseh). For that reason Reuben was no longer reckoned according to birthright in the genealogy.

The preferential status of the oldest son meant that he received the first or double share (the birthright plus another share), thus sharing equally with the other brothers in the remainder. With twelve sons, the oldest would get the birthright and then share with the other eleven, thus producing thirteen shares in all (see I. Mendelsohn, BASOR 156 [1959]:38-40). In the allocation of Canaan, however, the number of shares was reduced to twelve, with Levi given no tribal inheritance.

2. The chronicler, though conceding that the birthright was Joseph's, concluded that it had been nullified in favor of Judah by the apostasy and captivity of northern Israel and by the subsequent growing superiority of Judah and the shift to her of blessing and power in God's choice of David as the leader or messiah (cf. 2 Sam. 7:8-15; Psalm 78:67-70). **4.** How **Joel** is related to Judah is not stated. **6.** Evidently the chief interest centers upon the Reubenite prince Beerah, whose clan was carried into captivity by Tiglath-pileser III (745-727 B.C.) or Pul (v. 26; cf. 2 Kings 17:6), furnishing added evidence of a shift of blessing from Joseph to Judah.

9-10. Apparently some of the Reubenite clans remained in Gilead, migrating north in the wake of Moabite and Ammonite pressure until the time of the Assyrian conquest. These Reubenite groups were early absorbed by Gad, since the Mesha Inscription (c. 850 B.C.) mentions the latter but not the former. They remained as seminomadic herdsmen, roaming the entire territory indicated. The Hagrites were Arabs (cf. Psalm 83:6), whom these Reubenite clans conquered in Saul's era.

Descendants of Gad. 5:11-22. **11-16.** Gad's descendants resided in Bashan, the area northeast of the Jabbok to beyond the Yarmuk River, roughly the same as Gilead, which later included more or less all of Transjordan. Sharon and Salecah are unidentified, but are here located in the general area. This list of Gad is doubtless from an unknown source, having no connection with the biblical lists (Gen. 46:16; Num. 26:15-18; 1 Chron. 12:9-13). References to many cattle and broad pasturelands fit the geographical locale. **17.** This list was official in the time of Jotham and Jeroboam II (c. 750-745 B.C.). **18-22.** These verses describe this tribe's Transjordanic wars with Arab peoples. Trust in God brought victory and great spoil.

Descendants of the Half Tribe of Manasseh. 5:23-26. **23.** The region of occupation runs northward from Bashan to Mount Hermon, Senir being the old name of Hermon (cf. Deut. 3:9). **24-26.** The list describes a period of Israelite supremacy and then the loss of the region in the westward advance of Tiglath-pileser (-pilneser) in 734 B.C., whose Babylonian name was Pul, and who carried the people into captivity. The chronicler stresses the divine hand in these historical events (cf. 2 Kings 15:19, 29; 17:6; 18:11).

F. THE DESCENDANTS OF LEVI. 6:1-81.

The High Priests. 6:1-15. **1-15.** This is the preexilic high-priestly line, giving the descendants of Levi (vv. 1-3; cf. Gen. 46:11; Exod. 6:16; Num. 3:17; 26:57) and presenting the descendants of Eleazar, the son of Aaron (vv. 4-15), twenty-two generations. The chronicler's interest is in the Aaronic line, which was to prefigure the priesthood of Christ by contrast (Heb. 7:11—8:13). This list is obviously selective; for example, it omits the Shilonite high priests of the house of Eli, doubtlessly because of Eli's moral weakness, and Urijah (2 Kings 16:11) because of his sacrilegious acquiescence to Ahaz's idolatry. This list begins with Eleazar, who came out of Egyptian bondage, and concludes with Jehozadak, who went into Babylonian bondage.

The Levitical Line. 6:16-30. **16-30.** The priests and Levites were especially concerned to preserve their pedigree and to be able to prove it, because their office depended upon their descent. Hence, the **Gershom** line is followed for seven generations (vv. 17, 20), **Kohath** (vv. 18, 22) for ten generations, and **Merari** for seven (v. 29). Significant is the fact that Samuel was reckoned among the Levites, doubtlessly because of his special divine calling (cf. 1 Sam. 3:15), and service to priestly duties (2:11, 26; 7:9-10; cf. W. F. Albright, *Ar-*

chaeology and the Religion of Israel, pp. 109-10).

The Levitical Singers. 6:31-47. **31.** The chronicler presents David as the organizer of the Levitical musical guilds (cf. 15:16; 25:1-7; 2 Chron. 29:26-30; Neh. 12:46-47). David, as a talented musician, was eminently fitted for this task (1 Sam. 16:14-23; 2 Sam. 6:5), as the Psalter attests. Solomon continued the practice of composing songs (1 Kings 4:32).

Other Levitical and Priestly Officials. 6:48-53. **48-53.** This section was designed to confirm the position and duties of the line of Zadok, connecting it with the Aaronic house. (On this difficult problem, see K. Möhlenbrink, ZAW 52 [1934]:202-3; and H. H. Rowley, JBL 58[1939]:113-41.)

The Levitical Cities. 6:54-81. The list, as in Joshua 21, combines the cities of refuge with the Levitical cities. Because the Aaronite line is represented by Kohath, the allotment follows with that line listed first, followed by Gershom, the oldest, and Merari, the youngest, of Levi's sons. (On the cities of refuge, see Num. 35; Deut. 19:1-10; Josh. 20.)

G. THE DESCENDANTS OF THE NORTHERN TRIBES. 7:1-40.

Genealogy of Issachar. 7:1-5. **1-5.** Jacob compared the tribe of Issachar to a "strong ass crouching down between two burdens" (Gen. 49:14); they were an industrious people who rejoiced in their tents (Deut. 33:18). They are presented as a valiant tribe, **men of might,** that is, "warriors," **chief men.** In the Davidic period they numbered 145,000 men fit for war (cf. 2 Sam. 24; 1 Chron. 27:24). (For the census list, cf. Gen. 46:13; Num. 26:23-25; and for the problem of numbers involved, see G. E. Mendenhall, JBL 77[1958]:52-66.)

Genealogy of Benjamin. 7:6-12. **6-12.**

This is a preliminary account of the tribe of Benjamin, with a much larger report given in chapter 8. The warriors of Benjamin ready for combat numbered about sixty thousand. Benjamin was foreseen by Jacob to "consume as a wolf" (lit., "a wolf that tears"; Gen. 49:27).

Genealogy of Naphtali. 7:13. The list for Naphtali is taken from Genesis 46:24 and Numbers 26:48, but it closely follows the former. The fathers of the tribe are named, reflecting the abbreviated nature of many of these genealogical lists.

Genealogy of Manasseh. 7:14-19. **14-19.** Much of the genealogy of Manasseh concerns the situation in Transjordan (cf. 5:23). Intermarriage with the Aramaeans is noted. For the sources of this genealogy, see Numbers 26:29-33; and Joshua 17:1-13.

Genealogy of Ephraim. 7:20-29. **20-21.** This excerpt tells of a tragedy that struck the tribe of Ephraim when the inhabitants of Gath killed some of them. **22-23.** A descendant was named **Beriah** ("in trouble") evidently to commemorate this misfortune. It is good to reflect on the misery that chastening has brought, that we may be *humbled* (Lam. 3:19-20) and walk circumspectly before God. **24.** In the Ephraimite roster is listed a daughter of Ephraim, **Sheerah** by name, who when Israel settled in the land built some cities, one which bore her name. **27.** Joshua, son of Nun (Exod. 33:11), who was the Israelite leader in the conquest of Canaan, is listed as a famous son of Ephraim.

Genealogy of Asher. 7:30-40. **30-31.** The first part of Asher's genealogy, to Malchiel, follows Genesis 46:17 (not Num. 26:44-46). **32-40.** But the remainder of the list is without parallel, indicating a special source. Their fighting men (warriors) totaled only twenty-six thousand in all, extremely low in com-parison to those in Numbers (1:40-41; 2:27-28; 26:47).

H. THE DESCENDANTS OF BENJAMIN. 8:1-40.

Benjamites in Geba. 8:1-7. **1-7.** A larger catalog of Benjamin (cf. 7:6-12) is presented because it was the tribe of Saul, the first king of Israel, to whose story the chronicler is hastening (chap. 10). **Geba** is present-day Jiba, a half-dozen miles north of Jerusalem.

Many difficulties and perplexities exist in the Benjamite genealogies, as well as many of the other lists. But they preserve the names of God's ancient people ("the Lord knoweth them that are his," 2 Tim. 2:19), while the names of multitudes of illustrious worldlings are buried in oblivion. These lists all center in the unity of God's ancient people, Israel, and in the fulfillment of His redemptive purposes for Israel and the world through David of the tribe of Judah, and the greater David, the Lord Jesus Christ.

The difficulties in the genealogies are due to eight factors: (1) Sources that already had a long history of scribal transmission were used. (2) Scribal errors unavoidably crept in. (3) Changes occurred in spelling and pronunciation over the centuries. (4) Abbreviated and often highly selected lists were used. (5) There was the frequent importation of topographical, historical, geographical, religious, and census data. (6) The genealogies were an evidence of faith in the fulfillment of the LORD's promises to His people, for in Babylon they might have said, "Of what use are these lists now?"

(7) When the people returned from Babylon, the genealogies were suffi-cient to direct the returned captives to settle as nearly as possible within their own families in the places of their former

residence, and at the same time keep in mind the covenants and promises (Rom. 9:3-5) made to their fathers, and *thus to them* as their undisputed descendants.

(8) The imperfections of these genealogies is employed by the Spirit of inspiration to reflect the imperfections of the names recorded (although God's people) that God's grace might be manifested in His plan of salvation for the lost race, as it will be in the Lamb's book of life and those inscribed in it (Rev. 20:15).

Benjamites in Other Localities. 8:8-32. **8-32.** Benjamites in Moab and the west are listed (vv. 8-12), as are those in Gath, Aijalon, and Jerusalem (vv. 13-28); and those residing at Gibeon and Jerusalem (vv. 29-32), showing that Benjamites and Judahites coalesced after the fall of the Northern Kingdom; so Judah's captivity and return represented the other tribes as well, or Israel in totality.

The Family of Saul. 8:33-40. Note that there is no mention in any of the chronicler's genealogies of the kings of Israel after their defection from the Davidic house, for since they were all idolaters they cut themselves off from the line of redemptive promise and blessing. **33.** But a particular account is given of Saul's family, which was the royal family before the elevation of David. Saul's lineage is carried to his grandfather, Ner, who in turn was the son of Abiel (1 Sam. 14:51). Kish, Saul's father, was the son (i.e., grandson) of Abiel (9:1); so the order is Abiel, Ner, Kish, Saul (cf. 14:51).

34-39. Of Saul's sons, only Jonathan's posterity is traced for about ten generations because of his high character and kindness to David (cf. 1 Sam. 20:15, 23, 42). **40.** This genealogy terminates in Ulam, whose offspring were prolific and

became famous in the tribe of Benjamin for their valiant and skillful archers.

I. THE ISRAELITES WHO RETURNED FROM EXILE. 9:1-44.

Summary and Conclusion of the Genealogies. 9:1. **1.** This verse, logically concluding chapter 8, summarizes the purpose of the genealogies of chapters 1 to 8. It is to inform us that "all Israel had been officially registered and recorded in the chronicle of the kings of Israel and Judah [when] they were exiled [to Babylon]" (see Myers, AB, p. 59). The clause, "[when] they were exiled" emphasizes that the LORD knew His people by name as they went into exile, and He knew them by name as they returned to Jerusalem after the Exile.

The book of the kings of Israel and Judah (KJV) was not our canonical books of Kings, but another civil record used as a source by the chronicler. Emphasized also is that the LORD's people were **carried away to Babylon for their transgression** (defection), which is a warning to posterity to take heed of those sins that brought on this calamity.

The First Returnees. 9:2-9. **2-3.** These verses form an introduction to the roster of names of those who returned and took up residence in Jerusalem. Four classes are specified: (1) **Israelites** (laity), (2) **priests,** (3) **Levites,** and (4) **Nethinim** (the Temple slaves, who appear in Ugaritic literature as a class; C. H. Gordon, *Ugaritic Handbook,* 2:169; and E. A. Speiser, IEJ 13 [1963]:70 ff.).

4-9. The returnees from Judah are listed (vv. 4-6), as are those from Benjamin (vv. 7-9). The general name of "Israelites" is used (v. 2) because evidently all the tribes were represented (v. 3). Some had escaped to Judah when the ten tribes were taken captive as a body to Assyria, or they had returned to Judah during the revolutions in Assyria, and so they went into captivity with Judah and also returned with them from Babylon (cf. Ezek. 37:22; Hos. 1:11). On the other hand, many from both Judah and Israel remained in captivity in Babylon, but some from both groups returned. (See 2 Kings 17:23 for note on the so-called ten lost tribes.)

The Priests Who Returned. 9:10-13. **10-13.** The priests came with the first returnees, and it was to the credit of the people that they would not return without them. Who but the priests could conduct the Temple ritual, looking to the divine redemptive plan, and bless the people in the name of the LORD? One priest is called **the ruler** (better, "chief custodian") **of the house of God.** They were **very able men,** "experts in the ministerial service of the house of God" (AB).

The Levites Who Returned. 9:14-16. **14-16.** The **Levites** assisted the priests and were very necessary to the service in the postexilic tabernacle or tent that had to serve until the Temple was rebuilt by Zerubbabel.

The Gatekeepers. 9:17-26a. **17.** Four gatekeepers' names are listed (cf. v. 26), while in Nehemiah 11:19 only two names appear. **18.** Their duties are specified (cf. vv. 23-26). **19-26a.** Shallum, as gatekeeper of the east gate, occupied an especially honored position (cf. Ezek. 46:1-3), since that gate faced the entrance of the sanctuary, and by it the king entered the Temple.

The gatekeepers were Levites, but were distinguished from them (v. 26; cf. 23:3-5). The status and duties of the gatekeepers are outlined. David (and Samuel before him) had appointed them in the tradition of Phinehas, who was a zealous guardian of God's house (Num. 25:6-13; 31:6). The four chief gatekeep-

ers had general supervision of all four gates and resided in Jerusalem; their assistants resided in compounds, serving from time to time for seven days.

Levitical Duties. 9:26b-32. **26b.** The Levites had oversight of the rooms and supplies of the house of God. **27.** They spent the night about the house of God to guard it, and they opened it morning by morning. **28-29.** Others were responsible for the cultic implements and supplies. **30.** But the priests mixed the ointments. **31-32.** Some were in charge of baking, and others of preparing **the showbread** (cf. Exod. 25:30) every Sabbath.

The Musicians and Singers. 9:33-34. **33.** These specially talented Levites lived in the Temple chambers, free from other responsibilities, because they were on duty around the clock.

Ancestors and Descendants of Saul. 9:35-44. **35-44.** These verses closely follow 8:29-38, where the list concludes the genealogy of Benjamin. Here the data introduces the story of Saul. Matthew Henry thinks the repetition was an ancient copyist's blunder, the copyist, having written verse 34 ("These dwelt at Jerusalem"), inadvertently cast his eye on the same words, "These dwelt at Jerusalem," in 8:28, and so proceeded with what followed there, instead of going on with what followed here. And when the copyist perceived his mistake, he was loath to erase; and so he let it stand.

II. THE REIGN OF DAVID.
10:1—29:30.

A. THE DEFEAT AND DEATH OF SAUL. 10:1-14.

Saul's Death. 10:1-7. **1-5.** It is David, not Saul, who occupies the interest of the chronicler. Saul's end in Gilboa is included strictly as background material to prepare the way for the presentation of David's kingship and career, to which the chronicler hastens with the greatest possible speed. But having said this, the question still remains why he began his history with David rather than with Abraham or even Adam.

The answer undoubtedly is that he looked upon the history of his people till the time of David as authentic, fixed, and canonical, as it indeed was. Apparently he intended his treatise to be the official history of Judah and the subsequent commonwealth of Israel. Certainly he did not believe that the history of Israel began with Saul, as his numerous references to "the God of the fathers," that is, the God of the patriarchs and their successors show (cf. 12:17; 29:20; 2 Chron. 11:16; 13:12; 14:4, none of which are from the Samuel-Kings source).

The story of Saul's death is taken almost verbally from 1 Samuel 31:1-13 (*q.v.*). The Philistine advance against Saul was God's doing, but on the human side it was provoked by Saul's cutting off the trade routes. Though the Philistines were victorious at Gilboa, David's forces already were making effective progress against them in the south (IDB, 1:771-82).

6. The chronicler states that not only did Saul and his sons die together, but also **all his house.** The passage in 1 Samuel omits "his house," and instead has "his armor-bearer, and all his men." The chronicler deliberately ignores the survival of Ishbosheth (Ishbaal), who headed the kingdom for a time (cf. 2 Sam. 2-4). No doubt he viewed these details as unnecessary to his purpose.

Philistine Abuse of Saul's Corpse. 10:8-12. **10.** Significantly, the chronicler omits "Ashtaroth" (1 Sam. 31:10), and substitutes **their gods** (or "god") and **fastened his head** (skull) in the temple of

Dagon, an ancient Akkadian vegetation deity. At Ugarit he was viewed as Baal's father and had a temple there. The Samuel passage is silent concerning the exposure of Saul's skull, but it does speak of the impaling of his body to the walls of Bethshan. Evidence from the Dead Sea Scrolls (Qumran) shows that Chronicles was based upon a Hebrew text, which was much closer to the Septuagint than to the Masoretic text.

11-12. The citizens of Jabesh-gilead showed their devotion to Saul by providing decent funeral rites, but the Chronicles passage says nothing about the cremation of the corpses, a practice offensive no doubt to the chronicler, since it was practiced only in the case of certain criminals (Lev. 20:14; 21:9; Josh. 7:25). The great respect the men of Jabesh-gilead had for the fallen king was demonstrated by their seven-day fast (cf. 2 Sam. 1:12).

Reasons for Saul's Downfall. 10:13-14. The chronicler gives his theological interpretation. Three charges, evidently involving the "sin unto [physical] death" (1 John 5:16; cf. 1 Cor. 5:5; 11:30-32) are laid against Saul: (1) Saul was characterized by persistent disobedience and self-will, inexcusable in a theocratic king, who was strictly to represent God and His will to the people. He failed to await Samuel's coming to offer sacrifice, intruded into the priest's office (1 Sam. 13), and flatly refused to carry out divine orders regarding the destruction of the Amalekites (1 Sam. 15).

(2) He resorted to occultism and necromancy (1 Sam. 28), which were sternly forbidden by the Mosaic Law (Lev. 19:31; 20:6, 27; Deut. 18:9-10), and which practices he himself had earlier banned (1 Sam. 28:3). (3) He did not consult the LORD, his chronic self-will having shut him out of any access to the

divine will (cf. 1 Sam. 28:6); his attempt to do so was a mere manifestation of hypocrisy and desperation, and no real inquiry at all. The penalty of Saul's disobedience was physical death and forfeiture of the kingdom to David, furnishing a lesson in God's ultimate measure employed in chastening a seriously sinning saint.

B. DAVID'S RISE TO POWER. 11:1-47.

David's Anointing as King. 11:1-3. See 2 Samuel 5:1-5. **1-3.** Having disposed of purely introductory matters dealing with the end of the kingdom of Saul (cf. chap. 10), the chronicler launches at once into his theological ideal—the establishment of the kingdom of David in which the Messianic hope, not only of Israel but of the world, is to be realized.

Because of the vast importance of his theme, the chronicler resolutely bypasses all events he considers irrelevant to his lofty purpose, for example, the struggle of David with Saul (1 Sam. 16-26) and the vestiges of Saul's moribund kingdom (2 Sam. 2-4). Moreover, he commences his account with the gathering of **all Israel** at Hebron to anoint David as king (cf. 2 Sam. 5:1), stressing the unity of the kingdom, which represented all the tribes.

The period of David's rule over Judah at Hebron is omitted, except that it is assumed in the notice that **all the elders of Israel** came **to the king at Hebron,** hinting that David was already king. The reference to **the word of the Lord by Samuel** assumes the details of David's anointing by the prophet (cf. 1 Sam. 16:1-13). The length of David's reign (2 Sam. 5:4-5) is also passed over until later (cf. 1 Chron. 29:27), and then is mentioned without reference to his reign over Judah alone. But note the reference to the latter in 3:4.

Jerusalem Becomes David's Capital. 11:4-9. See 2 Samuel 5:6-12. **4-5.** Again the chronicler stresses the unity of all the tribes in the capture of Jerusalem, important because the city became the capital of the realm and the location of the Temple, making it the religiopolitical center of the kingdom. He says, **David and all Israel** took **Jerusalem** or **Jebus, the stronghold of Zion,** that is, the fortified and practically impregnable southeast hill (cf. Judg. 1:21; 19:10-11), the abode of the Jebusites. Second Samuel 5:6 merely says "the king and his men" took the fortress.

6-7. The allusion to Joab's feat is not in 2 Samuel; it fits into the chronicler's view of David's commander in chief as his right-hand man, with never a reference to the curse that hung over him (1 Kings 2:5-6). **8.** David built the city around the **Millo,** a fortress that some scholars think connected Zion (David's city) with the mountain of the house of the LORD (the Temple) to the north (cf. K. Galling, BRL, 7:300). Joab is recorded as restoring the remainder of the city. **9.** The reason why David prospered is of special interest to the chronicler, who sees the hope of Israel and the world in what David and his kingdom represent Messianically (cf. 2 Sam. 7:4-17).

David's Heroes. 11:10-47. See 2 Samuel 23:8-39. **10.** In Samuel the list forms a sort of addendum. But here the names are worked into the story of David to give prominence to the king and to emphasize the aid he had from others to execute **the word of the Lord concerning Israel.** When the true King of kings, adumbrated by David, returns to begin His earthly reign, those who have been loyal to Him will be commemorated, as were those who were faithful to David.

These men **strengthened themselves**

with him. In strengthening him, they strengthened themselves and their own interests, as do all those who support the Kingdom of the Son of David. What made these men honorable was the good service they performed for the king and his kingdom. The honors of Christ's Kingdom are prepared for those who "fight the good fight of faith."

11-14. Before listing the thirty, the writer describes the heroic exploits of two of them, **Jashobeam** and **Eleazar,** and perhaps three, Shammah apparently being omitted by a copyist's error (cf. 2 Sam. 23:10-12 with vv. 13-14). These men slew numerous Philistines. **15-19.** The valiant three also displayed the deepest devotion to David. In response to his mere wish (not command), they broke through the Philistine line at Bethlehem to fetch David water. They were so ambitious to please David that they were ready to risk their lives for him (cf. 2 Cor. 5:9). The greater David longs for refreshment from His own who are eager to please Him.

But David's greatness shone forth as he **poured out** the water **to the Lord,** showing his own devotion to the LORD. He considered the water from Bethlehem's well too good and precious to satisfy his own appetite; so he poured it out as a *drink offering,* signifying that God must have the best. This act also displayed David's greatness in refusing to be prodigal of the blood of those in his employ, but to be tender and considerate of them.

20-47. In the wonderful exploits of the thirty (vv. 20-41*a*) and the others (vv. 41*b*-47), the power of God had to be acknowledged. How, except by God's enablement, could one man slay three hundred (v. 11), and another the same number (v. 20); another, two lionlike men (v. 22); and another, an Egyptian giant (v. 23; cf. Josh. 23:10)? One of

these worthies was an **Ammonite** (v. 39); another, a **Moabite** (v. 46); yet, they had so proved themselves that the Law was dispensed with (Deut. 23:3), and they were admitted to "the congregation of the LORD," a foregleam that the Son of David would have heroes among the Gentiles and that the day would come when there would be neither Greek nor Jew (Gal. 3:28-29).

C. THOSE WHO JOINED DAVID. 12:1-40.

Followers from Benjamin. 12:1-7. **1-7.** In all likelihood these twenty-three men are listed first because their defection from Saul, a Benjamite, bestowed a special honor on David. Also, they were extremely skillful warriors and very valuable to David. These defectors to David came from eight localities in Benjamin—Gibeah (tell el Ful), the center of Saul's kingdom; Hizmeh, six miles northeast of Jerusalem; Anathoth (Ras el-Karrubeh), three miles east-northeast of Jerusalem; Gibeon (el-Jib), some eight miles north of Jerusalem; Gederah (apparently Jedireh near Gibeon); and the rest are unknown.

Followers from Gad. 12:8-15. **8-13.** The eleven men from Gad probably defected to David when he hid from Saul in the hills and caves in the Engedi region (1 Sam. 24:1). These Gadites were unusual warriors, skillful in combat, **whose faces were like the faces of lions,** that is, "like lions in appearance and as nimble as gazelles upon the mountains" (AB). **14.** These courageous men were of such superb quality as warriors that they became leaders who could hold at bay a multitude of opponents; each one "could match a hundred lesser ones, the greatest a thousand" (AB). **15.** They manifested their skill and valor in crossing the Jordan at full flood stage in the spring of the year (cf. Josh. 3:15; 4:18-19). These men recognized David as a superb leader and the LORD's chosen instrument. They illustrate overcomers who will reign with Christ in the coming Kingdom (2 Tim. 3:12; Rev. 2:7, 17, 26; 3:5, 12, 21).

Followers from Benjamin and Judah. 12:16-18. **16.** These also joined David at **the stronghold** (fortress). **17.** David warned them against perfidy, his suspicions naturally being aroused because he had previously been betrayed on three occasions—by Doeg the Edomite (1 Sam. 21-22); by the inhabitants of Keilah (1 Sam. 23); and by the Ziphites (1 Sam. 3). **18. Then the Spirit came upon** (*lāḇ^eshâ*, "clothed, wrapped up") **Amasai** to utter a message of dedication to David's cause that must have cheered the king's heart. How much more such words cheer the heart of the greater David, whose we are and whom we serve.

Followers from Manasseh. 12:19-22. **19.** The defection of these seven chiefs from Manasseh occurred just before Saul's disastrous defeat at Gilboa. **But they** (the chiefs of Manasseh) **helped them not** (the LXX reads, "he [David] did not help them"), **for the lords** (tyrants) **of the Philistines upon advisement** (in counsel) sent him away, fearful that he would defect to Saul **to the jeopardy of** their **heads** (see 1 Sam. 29:4-5). **20-21.** David made good use of this opportunity to consolidate his position around Ziklag in the southwest, and the Manassites helped him in those activities (1 Sam. 30:1-20). **22.** David's leadership with the assurance of the LORD's presence was a magnet that attracted **a great host** (camp), **like the host** (camp) **of God** (Josh. 5:13-15).

Israelites Who Made David King at Hebron. 12:23-40. **23-37.** Described here is the wonderful gathering from all the tribes to anoint David king of all Israel, an immense throng totaling 339,600 men and 1,222 chiefs (evidently an expansion of 11:1). Mendenhall, in his research on the large numbers occurring in census lists and for military units, thinks the Hebrew *'ĕlĕp* ("thousand") stands for a tribe, part of a tribe, or a unit, and is based on social structure (JBL 77[1958]:52-66); thus, verse 24, for example, would be rendered, "The sons of Judah who bore shield and spear numbered six units with eight hundred men with military training" (instead of 6,800 men).

38-40. The people who came had one purpose: **to make David king.** There was not a dissenting voice. A great feast was kept, and there was great rejoicing. How much greater will be the joy when the greater David is made King, not alone over Israel, but over all nations as "KING OF KINGS, AND LORD OF LORDS" (Rev. 19:11-16).

D. THE ARK REMOVED FROM KIRJATH-JEARIM. 13:1-14.

The Consultation About the Ark. 13:1-5. **1-3.** David's consultation with the military commanders and **every leader** (chief) to **bring again the ark of our God** to its proper place in Israel attests that he was a man of faith, devoted to God's will and Word. He realized the immense spiritual significance of this central symbol of the LORD's presence among His people and of the revelation of Himself to them in His infinite holiness and grace, pointing, as it did, in the gold (deity) and the acacia wood (humanity) out of which it was made to the divine-human Redeemer who was to come to bring salvation to Israel and the world (see Exod. 25:10-22; and R. de Vaux, *Les Institutions de l' Ancien Testament,* 2:127-33). David reminded the people that they should restore for themselves the Ark of their God, to which they had failed to inquire **in the**

days of Saul. By this reference he tactfully implied that the reason for Saul's unfortunate career was his neglect of the sacred symbol of the LORD's presence.

4-5. Unanimous agreement greeted David's proposal; so the king assembled **all Israel** from the southeastern extremity of the land to the northernmost boundary. **Shihor** is Egyptian Si-hor ("waters of Horus") and here refers to the Wady el Arish, the boundary between Egypt and Canaan (Josh. 13:3), although the Shihor sometimes refers to the Nile (Isa. 23:3; cf. Jer. 2:18). The **entrance of Hamath** on the Orontes was in the extreme north. **Kiriath-jearim** ("city of forests"), present-day Tell el-Azhar, lay about eight miles west of Jerusalem (1 Sam. 6:1—7:2).

The Ark Removed. 13:6-8. **6.** Israel went to fetch **the ark of God, the Lord, who dwelleth between** (better, "above") **the cherubim,** invisibly enthroned there as the Shekinah glory, the cherubic wings guarding the divine holiness (see Exod. 25:22; Psalm 80:1; Isa. 37:16). **Where the Name is called on** is better rendered "upon which [the Ark] the Name [of the LORD] is called," that is, "which is called by the name [of the LORD]", being often called "the ark of the LORD" (15:3). **7.** Transporting the Ark in a **new cart** was a Philistine expedient (see notes on 2 Sam. 6). **8.** Despite all the singing, music, and rejoicing, David did not conform to God's Word, which directed that the Ark was to be carried by staves on the shoulders of the Levites (Num. 4:5, 15), not in a cart.

The Sin and Punishment of Uzza. 13:9-14. **9-10.** At the threshing floor of Chidon (Nacon; 2 Sam. 6:6), Uzza put out his hand to steady the Ark because the oxen almost overturned it. The divine anger flared up against Uzza, for he had violated the strict prohibition that only an authorized person might ap-proach, much less touch, the sacred box (i.e., the high priest, and he only by sprinkling blood on the mercy seat once a year on the great Day of Atonement, Lev. 16:15-16). This shows that a sinner cannot approach the infinite holy God (much less contact Him) apart from atoning blood. To attempt to do so brings physical death (cf. Num. 4:15).

11. David's displeasure because the LORD **had broken forth upon** (against) Uzza was noted by naming the place **Perez-uzza** (i.e., "the breaking forth against Uzza"). **12.** No wonder David **was afraid of God** that day. Attempts of sinful man to touch the infinitely holy God except through Christ's priestly work of sprinkling the Mercy Seat with His own blood can only strike fear to the human heart, even the regenerate heart.

13. David's fear kept him from taking the Ark to Jerusalem; for the time being he deposited it in **the house of Obed-edom, the Gittite,** a Levite apparently of Gath-rimmon, a Levitical town (Josh. 21:24). Obed-edom belonged to the clan of Kohath (cf. 1 Chron. 26:1-4), which was charged with transporting the Ark (Num. 4:15). **14. And the Lord blessed ... Obed-edom** (cf. 2 Sam. 6:12; 1 Chron. 26:4-8; Psalm 127).

E. DAVID'S KINGDOM ESTABLISHED. 14:1-17.

Hiram's Mission. 14:1-2. **1.** Hiram reigned from about 969 to 936 B.C. so that his mission to David with materials and craftsmen was in the latter part of David's reign. It is possible that David had a treaty with Hiram's father, Abi-baal, which was renegotiated with Hiram and continued on into Solomon's reign, but this cannot be proved at present. **2.** But David's success within his kingdom and the support of the Tyrian king were evidence to him **that the Lord had confirmed him king over Israel.**

David's Family Expansion. 14:3-7.
3-7. This passage is inserted here as another evidence of the divine blessing upon the king and his kingdom. The list of thirteen sons closely follows the catalog in chapter 3 and differs somewhat from the recording in 2 Samuel 5:14-16. To the chronicler, family growth was important to attest the blessing of the LORD upon the theocratic king.

The Philistine Wars. 14:8-17. See 2 Samuel 5:17-25. **8.** These victories are recorded as evidence of the solid establishment of David's kingdom. Stress is laid upon the fact that the Philistine advance came after the Philistines had learned that David had been made king of **all Israel. 9. The valley of Rephaim,** the place they attacked, is thought to be southwest of Jerusalem (cf. Josh. 15:8). **11. Baal-perazim** ("master of the breakthroughs") received its name from the battle.

12. The defeat of the enemy caused such pandemonium that the routed foe abandoned **their** gods, which David's men **burned with fire,** as required by the Law (Deut. 7:5, 25). **15. The sound of marching in the tops of the mulberry** (balsam) **trees** was a God-given signal (cf. 2 Kings 7:6) for David to spring his ambush. **16.** These successes broke the Philistine threat as the entire central highland was cleared of the enemy from Gibeon to Gezer on the border. **17.** David's fame spread far and wide as a result of his kingdom's success.

F. THE ARK BROUGHT TO JERUSALEM. 15:1-29.

David's Preparations to Bring up the Ark. 15:1-15. See 2 Samuel 6:12-20. **1.** While the Ark remained in the house of Obed-edom (13:14), David arranged a place **for the ark of God** (for symbolic significance, see 13:1-5) and set up a tent

to receive it. The chronicler, according to his purpose of highlighting the worship in the restored Temple of his day, features the permanent centralization of the religion of Israel in Jerusalem. Therefore, his account in chapters 15 and 16 considerably amplifies the parallel description in 2 Samuel 6:12-20. The king's elaborate preparations to avoid any mishap, such as aborted his previous attempt, are listed (vv. 1-15).

2. David then determined to follow to the letter the divine directions for transporting the ark (see Num. 4:5-15; Deut. 10:8). His reference to the Law was a tacit admission that on the former occasion (13:7-10) it had not been observed. That the ark was properly transported is stated in the older account (2 Sam. 6:13), though the fact that the Levites were Kohathites is not expressly declared. **3.** David's assembling **all Israel,** which signifies a full representation of the people, is used by the chronicler throughout his work to stress that the postexilic community represented the whole nation, not merely part of it (Judah and Benjamin).

4-10. The list of priests and Levites called to help in the ceremony amplifies how David planned to adhere strictly to the Law for transporting the ark, as alluded to in verse 2. The section also specifies the family connections of the Levites mentioned in verse 11. In addition to the three regular Levitical branches—Kohath (Kehath), Merari, and Gershom—three others are added—Elizaphan, Hebron, and Uzziel, the latter three being offshoots of the Kohathite branch (cf. Exod. 6:22; Lev. 10:4; 1 Chron. 6:18). **11-13.** In summoning the religious leaders, David put upon them the full responsibility of properly transporting the ark to Jerusalem, to avoid being thwarted as before (cf. 13:9-14). **14-15.** The full compliance with the Mosaic Law is outlined (cf. Exod. 25:13-15; Num. 7:9; 4:15).

David's Provision for Musicians and Singers. 15:16-24. **16-17.** At David's request, the Levites appointed their brothers as singers and instrumentalists. For a description of "Musical Instruments in Israel," see O. R. Sellers (BA 4 [1941]:33-47). **18-24.** The chronicler emphasizes the fact that David was the originator of the musical guilds and services in the worship at Jerusalem (cf. 16:4-6, where the actual appointments are described). Vocalists and instrumentalists are the two categories named. The latter included those who performed on the cymbals, harp, and zither, the priests being the trumpeters.

The three Levitical families were represented—Heman (the Kohathites), Asaph (the Gershonites), and Ethan (the Merarites). Also listed are thirteen of secondary status, some of whom ministered in the dual capacity of porter and musician. Four are mentioned as **doorkeepers** ("porters," *shō'ărîm,* "warders") **of the ark.** Evidently in the procession two walked in front of the ark and two behind to guard against any unauthorized approach to it.

The Joyful Procession. 15:25-29. **25. David . . . went . . . with joy** (cf. Psalm 24, which he apparently composed for this occasion). **26.** The whole company **offered seven bullocks and seven rams,** prefiguring the coming Redeemer and His glorious redemption, the various facets of which the ark itself prefigured. David's offering alone is recorded in 2 Samuel 6:13. **27.** David (as well as all the Levites who carried the ark, and the singers) was **clothed with a robe of fine linen,** a loose, sleeveless, outer garment ("a mantle of byssus" or flax). David also wore **an ephod,** a surplice or priestly

cape worn in worship (Exod. 28:6; 1 Sam. 2:18). In his joyous praise, David evidently removed his outer garment. **28-29.** The joy of David and the people contrasts sharply with the rigid, contemptuous reaction of Queen Michal, Saul's daughter (cf. 2 Sam. 6:20-23).

G. THE ARK SET IN THE TENT AT JERUSALEM. 16:1-43.

The Ark Placed in the Tent. 16:1-3. See 2 Samuel 6:17-19. These verses belong to chapter 15, logically concluding it. **1-2.** And they offered **burnt sacrifices and peace offerings.** And when **David had finished offering the burnt offerings** (Heb., "the burnt offering," prefiguring the *one* offering of Christ to be effected in time), **he blessed the people** (cf. Num. 6:22-27; 1 Kings 8:14, 55; Deut. 33:1).

Blessing to God's people springs out of Christ's offering Himself spotlessly to God in complete submission to the Father's will in substitutionary death, of which the burnt offering speaks (Lev. 1:1-17). The peace offerings prefigure the whole work of Christ in relation to the believer's peace (Eph. 2:14, 17; Col. 1:20), "peace with God" (Rom. 5:1) and "the peace of God" (Phil. 4:7) being one of the greatest blessings of God.

3. Spiritual blessings are portrayed in the parceling out to all Israelites **a loaf of bread,** symbolizing feeding on Christ (John 6:33-34, 51), and a **portion** (*'ĕshpār*) **of meat** (i.e., of the animal slain for the "peace offerings"), speaking of fellowship with God (see Lev. 7:31-34); and a **cake of raisins** (i.e., a mass of dried grapes," cf. Isa. 17:6; Hos. 3:1; Matt. 26:26-29; 1 Cor. 11:23-28), suggesting the joyous exhilaration of being filled with the Spirit (Eph. 5:18).

The Institution of the Ministry Before the Ark. 16:4-6. The appointment of the priests and Levites for the occasion of moving the ark to Jerusalem in the preceding chapter (15:15-24), evidently a temporary arrangement, seems to have proved so satisfactory that David confirmed it on a permanent basis.

4. So David **appointed certain . . . Levites** to minister before the ark (1) to **invoke** (*hăzkîr,* "to record, remind, bring to remembrance," a technical term for chanting the psalms accompanying the sacrificial burning of the meal offering on the altar, Lev. 2; cf. the titles of Psalms 38 and 70); (2) **to thank,** to perform psalms expressing gratitude for favors received; and (3) **to praise the Lord,** to sing and play hymns of hallelujah such as Psalms 146 to 150. Each verb expresses a specific kind of duty in the sense of music and song. Thus, by divine command (2 Chron. 29:25) David established Levitical singers and musicians, who soon became an important feature of the worship at Jerusalem. The musical service was added to the traditional Mosaic ritual and in no way conflicted with it.

5-6. The names of the persons appointed — ten Levites and two priests — were in the procession that brought the ark to Jerusalem, except for Jahaziel (cf. 15:19-21). David elevated Asaph over Heman. Asaph and his descendants in the course of time composed twelve psalms of the Psalter (Psalms 50; 73-83).

The Dedicatory Psalm of Praise. 16:7-36. **7.** **Then on that day** (after the ark had been placed in its tent and the minstrels were appointed) David for the first time committed to the hands of Asaph and his associates the giving of thanks to the LORD. The verse asserts that this was the occasion when the musical appointees were first charged with the duties outlined in verses 4 to 6.

8-36. The model songs, with which David provided them, consist of several psalms: verses 8 to 22 (Psalm 105:1-15);

verses 23 to 33 (Psalm 96:1*b*-13); and verses 34 to 36 (Psalm 106:1, 47-48). These psalms are anonymous in the Psalter, and it seems that David is meant to be considered their composer. In the light of these facts, the meaning of the title to many of David's psalms, "To the chief musician," can be understood. For exposition of the psalm, see the component psalms in the Psalter.

Ministrations at Jerusalem and at Gibeon. 16:37-42. The narrative suspended at verse 7 is resumed. **37-38.** These verses form a résumé of the institution of the Levitical singers and musicians in the Jerusalem tent. **39-40.** The narrative changes in locale from the tent in Zion to the Mosaic tabernacle at Gibeon (cf. 1 Kings 3:4). The inauguration of a new national sanctuary at Jerusalem did not mean that the old one at Gibeon (el Jib, about six miles north of Jerusalem) was abandoned. On the contrary, David either instituted or formally recognized the priesthood of Zadok there.

Zadok was **the priest** (i.e., the high priest; 1 Sam. 1:9; 2:11; 2 Kings 11:9, 15). Although Gibeon was a **high place,** the worship there was strictly Mosaic, the **burnt offering** being offered morning and evening, with its food offering and drink offering being made strictly according to the Law (Exod. 29:38-44; Num. 28:3-10).

41. This verse returns to the principal subject — the Levitical music. With Zadok and his associates were **Heman** and **Jeduthun,** two masters of song who ministered at Gibeon in the same capacity as Asaph did at Jerusalem, with **the rest . . . chosen . . . mentioned** (expressed, enrolled) **by name** (12:31; cf. 15:19-24). Thus, at Gibeon a similar Levitical musical program was introduced as that inaugurated by David at Jerusalem.

H. THE DAVIDIC COVENANT MADE. 17:1-27.

David's Desire to Build the Lord a House. 17:1-2. **1.** After the Ark had found its resting place in a tent, David became deeply concerned about building a permanent abode for the sacred symbol of the LORD's presence. This concern was made more acute as he contrasted his own fine house of cedar with the humble dwelling of the Ark (cf. 2 Sam. 7:1-3; 1 Chron. 14:1). **2.** Nathan the prophet, in giving advice in matters that pertain to God before consulting God, showed how wrong such a pronouncement may be.

The Lord's Promise to Build David a House. 17:3-15. **3.** That night the LORD had to straighten out Nathan and send him to the king with His message (vv. 4-14) to correct the prophet's erroneous advice. **4. Thou shalt not build me an house** (lit. Heb. trans., "It is not you who shall build me *the* house"), the chronicler referring to the famous Temple of Solomon.

10-14. Rather, the opposite was true: God was going to build David **an house,** that is, a royal line that would not only produce Solomon, but Him to whom Solomon pointed, David's Son and David's Lord as well (Psalm 110:1). In Christ alone, the Son of David, is secured the great covenant promise, "a house" or posterity, a **throne,** that is, royal authority, "a kingdom" or sphere of rule—all in perpetuity—**forever** (see 2 Sam. 7:8-17).

The promises of this great (Davidic) covenant are still to be fulfilled. All is yet future, for the Son of David, rejected by His own, does not yet sit upon the throne of His father, David. He now sits with His Father on His Father's throne (Rev. 3:21; cf. Luke 1:32-33; Matt. 19:28; Acts 2:30, 34; 15:14-16).

When He comes as King of kings, He will sit upon the throne of David, His own throne (Matt. 25:31; Rev. 19:11-16; 20:6), and rule in the earthly kingdom restored over Israel (Acts 1:6; 15:16), which will finally merge into the eternal Kingdom in the new heaven and new earth (Rev. 22:1, 3, 5). The time is coming when, in fulfillment of the Davidic Covenant, "the Lord God shall give unto him [the Lord Christ] the throne of His father, David, and he shall reign over the house of Jacob forever; and of his kingdom there shall be no end" (Luke 1:32-33).

David's Prayer of Praise. 17:16-27. **16-27.** What words of grace David poured out to Him whose glorious grace had made such promises. Humility, faith, and joyful confidence welled up within him in response to the promises of divine grace. See notes on 2 Samuel 7:18-29.

I. THE FULL ESTABLISHMENT OF DAVID'S KINGDOM. 18:1-17.

The Philistines and Moabites Subdued. 18:1-2. The chronicler, close upon Nathan's restraining prophecy (17:4), now gives an account of David's wars (chaps. 18-20), since it was because David was "a man of war," who shed much blood, that he was not permitted by the LORD to build the Temple (22:8; 28:3). Hence, the author groups the whole series of David's wars together; and, because they are extraneous to his purpose, he passes over the chapters in 2 Samuel dealing with David's domestic woes. After the glorious revelation of the Davidic Covenant (chap. 17), it is not surprising that David was fired with zeal as Israel's warrior-king to conquer the enemies of the LORD's people.

1-2. He first **smote** the Philistines (2 Sam. 8:1). Taking the offensive, he captured **Gath and its towns** (evidently the meaning of "Metheg-ammah," 2 Sam. 8:1; see A. Alt, ZAW 54 [1936]: 149-52), since it was the nearest Philistine center to David's base of operation. Moab, too, was subdued, but the details of 2 Samuel 8:2 are omitted.

Hadarezer and the Syrians Subdued. 18:3-8. **3-4.** The Aramaean state of Zobah, situated between Hamath on the north and Damascus on the south (J. Bright, *A History of Israel,* pp. 181-83), under its powerful leader, Hadarezer (Hadadezer, 2 Sam. 8:3), clashed with David's expanding empire. The figures for the captured chariots, horsemen, and footmen have, as is true of many numbers in the Old Testament, suffered through copyists' errors during centuries of transmissions (cf. 2 Sam. 8:4).

5-6. The intervention of Damascus also resulted in further triumphs for David. **7-8.** Large quantities of gold, and also copper, were taken from Hadadezer's cities, Tibhath and Cun (also called Betah and Berothai, 2 Sam. 8:8). The copper was especially employed by Solomon in furnishing the Temple.

Hamath's Friendship. 18:9-10. **9-10.** King Tou of Hamath, on the Orontes River north of Zobah, was delighted with David's subjugation of his enemy, Hadadezer, and sent his son with large presents to congratulate David.

David Dedicates the Spoil to the Lord. 18:11. **11.** Numerous other conquered nations are listed in the description of the solemn dedication to the LORD of the booty taken and gifts presented. In this manner David collected the large amounts of metal— gold, silver, and copper—needed for the construction of the Temple.

Edom Subdued. 18:12-13. **12-13.** Notice is also taken of the victory of Abishai (David's nephew and Joab's

brother) over Edom, and the stationing of garrisons there. David did not incorporate these nations into an empire, but put them in a tributary status (A. Alt, KS, 2:1-75).

David's Officialdom. 18:14-17. **14.** David's kingdom expanded rapidly and called for administrative machinery to continue his policy of honesty and integrity. **15.** Joab, David's nephew and a renowned warrior, was army commander in chief. Jehoshaphat was **recorder** (*măzkîr,* "the spokesman or chief of protocol," deVaux, RB 48 [1939]: 394-405), an office similar to the Egyptian royal herald, whose duties included such things as admitting people to royal audience, regulating palace functions, acting as intermediary between king and people, and serving as personal secretary.

16. Zadok and Abimelech were priests. Shavsha was secretary, in charge of the royal correspondence, an office that also corresponded to an Egyptian office, upon which David's administrative machinery was modeled, as is now known (cf. J. H. Breasted, *Ancient Records of Egypt,* 2:763-71). **17.** Benaiah headed the **Cherethites** and **Pelethites.** (2 Sam. 8:18), who formed the royal bodyguard staffed by foreign mercenaries.

The sons of David are described as **chief about the king** (Heb., "the first at the king's hand," rather than *kōhᵃnîm,* "priests," the common and only word for "priest" having just occurred in v. 16. Written from a later age, the chronicler paraphrased the term "priest" in order to avoid the misunderstanding that high secular offices, rather than sacerdotal status, were meant).

J. THE AMMONITE-SYRIAN CAMPAIGN. 19:1-19.

The Ammonite Affront and Its Result. 19:1-15. See 2 Samuel 10. **1-4.** David's foreign policy was to show kindness and friendliness first, and to use force only as a last resort. However, in dealing with Hanun, the suspicious son of Nahash, his overtures of kindness were rudely repulsed. **5.** Even so, David planned no immediate reprisals. **6-7.** The Ammonites were not so foolish to suppose that David would not act at the opportune moment. Accordingly, they enlisted the aid of their northern neighbors. All the Aramaean states responded, except Israel's ally, Hamath.

Aram Naharaim was the region **beyond the river,** the Euphrates; **Maacah** lay north of Lake Huleh and south of Beth-rehob; Beth-rehob was situated north of Dan in the Antilebanon region; **Zobah** lay north of Damascus and Tob; and Tob lay north of Ammon in Transjordan. Tob and Beth-rehob are not mentioned here, but are named in 2 Samuel 10. The Aramaean contingents encamped **before Medeba,** about sixteen miles east-southeast of the northern end of the Salt Sea. **8-15.** David dispatched Joab and the army; by cunning strategy, Joab routed the Aramaeans, while the forces under Abishai, his brother, defeated the Ammonites.

David Subdues the Aramaeans. 19:16-19. **16.** Their defeat only made the Aramaeans more determined. They sent for reinforcements from beyond the Euphrates River. **17-18.** David crossed the Jordan with a large army and engaged the Aramaeans in a final encounter that completely defeated them for any further resistance. **19.** They **made peace** and became tributary states under David.

K. DAVID'S OTHER WARS. 20:1-8.

Rabbah of Ammon Taken. 20:1-3. See 2 Samuel 11:1; 12:26, 30-31. **1.** Joab was in command, while David remained in Jerusalem. It was at this juncture that David committed his great sin with Bathsheba, which the chronicler passes over, because it was not in line with the scope of his work—the divine redemptive plan and purpose through David and his posterity for Israel and the world. The chronicler also abbreviates the actual story, omitting Joab's call to the king to partake of the actual capture of the city.

2. The placing of the huge crown weighing about a talent of gold (more than ninety-two pounds) must have been symbolic. David received the crown, consummating the account of his victorious wars, even as our Lord will one day appear as King of kings, crowned with many crowns (Rev. 19:12, 16). **The crown of their king from his head** should certainly be rendered, "From the head of Malcom," the national deity of the Ammonites (following the LXX, Vulgate, and Arabic). **3.** And he **cut them with saws** (*wăyyāśăr*) should be corrected to "He put them to work (*wăyyāśĕm*) with saws, and with picks of iron, and with axes." Second Samuel 12:31 adds, "and made them toil at the brickkiln."

Further Conflict with the Philistines. 20:4-8. Three episodes of heroism are recounted of how three Israelite warriors slew three Philistine giants. **4.** The first occurred at **Gezer** (corrupted to Gob, 2 Sam. 21:18) when Sibbecai (see 1 Chron. 11:29; 27:11) slew Sippai (Saph) **of the children** (*yᵉlîdê,* "offspring") **of the giant** (the Rephaites, descendants of Rapha, the tribal designation of the gigantic Rephaim, Gen. 14:5; Num. 13:22; Josh. 15:14).

5. The second episode occurred when **Elhanan, the son of Jair, slew Lahmi, the brother of Goliath, the Gittite,** which text should correct the obviously corrupt text of 2 Samuel 21:19, which states that Elhanan slew Goliath. The obvious original of both passages indicates that Elhanan slew the brother of Goliath, and

David slew Goliath (1 Sam. 17).

6-7. The third episode cited is when David's nephew killed the last of the giants, the six-fingered, six-toed giant at Gath, prefiguring the final culmination of apostate Philistinism realized in the false prophet (Rev. 13:11-18). These giants were the special instruments of the powers of darkness and the foes and taunters of God's people (cf. 1 Sam. 17:8-11, 26). In them we see in bold relief the delusions that are to be found in systems of error such as Philistinism depicts, the ecclesiastical mystery of lawlessness that reaches its height in the end-times (2 Thess. 2:6). For the spiritual meaning of "Philistinism," see notes on Judges 13:2-4; 16:1-3.

L. DAVID'S SIN IN NUMBERING THE PEOPLE. 21:1-30.

David's Sin. 21:1-7. See 2 Samuel 24:1-9. The reason the chronicler, contrary to his usual procedure, includes this incident revealing the uncomplimentary side of David's character, is because it is necessary background material for his main subject of the preparations for the Temple. So the narrative, unlike the episode in 2 Samuel, is not presented as a story in itself, but simply as an account of how the site of the future Temple came to be acquired.

1. Satan stood up against Israel, while in 2 Samuel 24:1 it is said the LORD "incited David against them." There is no contradiction. The Old Testament revelation of Satan is that of a fallen creature, yet an angel of God, and His servant, with only duties and powers such as God entrusts to him (cf. Job 1-2; Zech. 3:1-2). God is the primary mover and cause, who may use a secondary agent, which may be good or evil, to accomplish His sovereign purposes, which, however, are *always* good.

Again, it is said, "the anger of the LORD was kindled against Israel" (2 Sam. 24:1) and "Satan stood up against Israel"; yet in both cases David was moved or provoked to sin in order that the LORD's people, in turn, might be chastized for their sin. What this sin was on Israel's part or on David's part is not specifically defined, but the sin was there because the LORD's anger was provoked against both Israel and David. Apparently the direct cause of the divine displeasure was a proud, satanically induced, self-sufficient spirit that came over David to trust in his own strength and the power and strength of his kingdom instead of wholly relying upon the LORD.

2. Possibly David's pride in numbers was a reflection of a similar attitude on the part of his prosperous nation as a whole. In any case, the king persisted in his determination to take a census of Israel, in disregard of God's will. **3.** Even Joab realized David's course was not of faith and, therefore, of sin and would be **a cause of trespass to Israel,** cognizant that leaders cannot sin without involving a nation in trespass and guilt.

4-7. Joab performed the task unwillingly, accounting David's command **abominable** (*nit'ăḇ,* "abhorrent"). The results of the census were 1,100,000 men fit for military service, of whom 470,000 belonged to Judah. Second Samuel 24:9 lists a total of 1,300,000 or 200,000 more than the chronicler records, because Levi (Num. 1:49) and Benjamin were not included in the latter's reckoning.

Alternatives of Punishment. 21:8-14. **8.** Although David repented, demonstrating he was truly regenerated and, therefore, could not go on practicing sin because of the presence of the new nature (cf. 1 John. 3:9), he nevertheless faced chastisement for his sin. **9-12.** Gad the prophet presented him with three alternatives of punishment—**three years' famine,** three months of defeat before enemies, or three days of pestilence.

13-14. David cast himself upon the LORD directly, trusting in the divine mercy, and chose three days of pestilence, in which seventy thousand died, an appropriate punishment for David's apparent pride in numbers and human strength. This illustrates one of the mysteries of life—to be solved only at the future judgment of men for their works (2 Cor. 5:10; Rev. 20:11-15)—of how frequently many suffer for the sins of a few or even one. This is especially so when that one stands in a representative capacity, as David did to his people as the king of a theocratic kingdom.

The Agent of the Punishment. 21:15-18. **15-18.** God used (1) angelic ministry to effect punishment, as so often occurs in the book of the Revelation (7:1; 8:1—10:1; cf. 2 Kings 19:35); (2) obstruction (cf. Num. 22:22-24), to keep David and his company from going to Gibeon (cf. 1 Chron. 21:28-30), hindering them by the angel of the LORD; and (3) revelation (Num. 22:35) to inform David of the divine will through the prophet Gad (cf. Zech. 1:9; 2:3-4).

The angelic agent of divine punishment **stood by the threshing floor of Ornan** (called Araunah, 2 Sam. 24:16), because the pestilence was to lead to the divine appointment of Jerusalem as the religious center of the kingdom (in the place of Gibeon). Hence, David there glimpsed **the angel of the Lord,** not only standing **between the earth and the heaven** with **drawn sword** (cf. Num. 22:23) poised to strike Jerusalem, but also standing **by the threshing floor,** showing that it was to be the exact spot where sacrifice and confession were to be made to avert the plague upon the capital.

That David and the elders were **clothed in sackcloth** shows that they were in deep penitence and on their way to entreat the LORD's forgiveness at the nearest religious center. As Israel's shepherd (king), David pled for the **sheep,** his subjects (cf. 1 Chron. 11:2; Psalm 23), exhibiting a praiseworthy spirit, although the nation itself was not guiltless (cf. v. 1).

The Purchase of Ornan's Threshing Floor. 21:19-25. **19.** David obeyed the angel of judgment, who had told Gad to instruct him to set up an altar in the threshing floor. **20-23.** Ornan was prepared for David's request by his glimpsing **the angel,** thus being informed that the whole transaction was from the LORD, not only to stop the plague, but as it turned out, to furnish the exact location for the future Temple as the religious mecca of the nation.

Accordingly, Ornan not only gladly received David's request, but munificently offered his threshing floor as a gift, with the oxen for the burnt offerings, the wooden threshing instruments for the fire, and even **the wheat for the meal offering.** This is in accord with the Mosaic stipulation that a meal offering was to be included with every burnt offering (Exod. ·29:38-42; Num. 15:1-4), demonstrating that Christ offering Himself without spot and vicariously in atoning death (the burnt offering) must never be separated from His sinless humanity (the meal offering, see Lev. 1-2).

24. David's refusal to offer burnt offerings **without cost** (illustrative of that which cost God so much in redemption) shows that God finds no delight in the redeemed who offer Him only what involves no sacrifice; He implores us to give Him our very selves (Rom. 12:1; 2 Cor. 8:5). **25.** The **six hundred shekels of gold** David gave Ornan (about fifteen pounds), doubtlessly was for the whole future Temple site, while 2 Samuel 24:24 ("fifty shekels of silver," about twenty ounces) gives the price of the rocky threshing floor. The site for the altar to offer sacrifice to stop the plague had to be paid for at once. Somewhat later, the rest was bought at a much higher price, for then there was no plague to be stopped. Characteristically, the chronicler fuses the two events.

David's Offering and the Staying of the Plague. 21:26-27. **26.** David built an altar there. His offering burnt offerings (and meal offerings, see v. 23) and peace offerings on it, pointing forward to the finished redemption to come and the peace that would ensue, brought the divine acceptance and forgiveness attested by the fire from heaven (cf. Judg. 6:21; 1 Kings 18:38; 2 Chron. 7:1). **27.** The LORD's response indicated that His wrath was appeased and the plague had stopped.

How Jerusalem Became the Nation's Religious Center. 21:28-30. **28-29. At that time** the Mosaic tabernacle and the altar of burnt offering were in Gibeon (cf. 16:39-40). The answer by fire from heaven (v. 26) was an unmistakable sign that Ornan's threshing floor was thenceforth to be the central sanctuary. **30.** Evidently David and his counselors were on their way to Gibeon to consult the LORD when they were intercepted by the angel of destruction. The whole episode—David's numbering of the people, the plague, the buying of the threshing floor, and the offering—are intended to show how Jerusalem was chosen for the Temple.

M. DAVID GATHERS MATERIAL FOR THE TEMPLE. 22:1-19.

Materials Gathered. 22:1-5. **1.** This verse, which logically belongs to chapter 21, expresses David's conclusion that the LORD had interposed and transferred the religious center of Israel and the Mosaic tabernacle service from Gibeon to Jerusalem (see 21:18-28; 2 Sam. 24:18-25; 2 Chron. 3:1; Deut. 12:5-7), where the sacred ark had already been transported.

2. An account is given of David's preparations to gather materials for the future construction of the Temple. He ordered into public service **the sojourners** (*gērîm,* "resident foreigners"; cf. Gen. 15:13), the Canaanite population of the land, who were liable to forced labor for the government, if need arose (cf. 1 Kings 9:20-21; 2 Chron. 8:7-8). These he appointed to **hew ... stones.**

3. He gathered large quantities of **iron,** which was possible because his victories over the Philistines, who held the secret of iron smelting, had resulted in breaking their monopoly on that metal (cf. 1 Sam. 13:19-22). His conquests had yielded a vast quantity of **bronze** (brass or copper) **beyond weight** (cf. 18:8). **4.** The Phoenicians furnished timber (cf. 1 Kings 5:6; 1 Chron. 29:1-2). **5.** David's ambitious plans for the Temple required much preparation because the edifice was to be **exceedingly magnificent** (RSV) and world famous. Moreover, Solomon was **young and tender** (inexperienced) and needed help.

David's Instructions to Solomon. 22:6-16. **6.** David's charge to Solomon, as summarized by the chronicler, features the command to build the Temple. Nothing is recorded here of the counsel concerning Joab, the sons of Barzillai, or Shimei (cf. 1 Kings 2:1-9), nor is there the stress on fidelity to the Mosaic Law, that charge assuming an almost secondary place here (vv. 12-13).

7. David's desire and intent to build the Temple are emphasized. **8.** The reason why he was not permitted to do so was because he **shed blood abundantly ... shed much blood** upon the earth in the LORD's sight (lit., "for torrents of blood [pl.] you have shed earthward before Me" (cf. Gen 9:5-6; Amos 1:3; 2:1). **Thou ... hast made** (waged) **great wars.** It was not that war had not been necessary and right (cf. 14:10; 19:13), but David had gone too far and had been guilty of needless bloodshed (cf. 2 Sam. 8:2).

In David's role as a warrior-king, slaying his foes to establish his kingdom (chaps. 18-20), he foreshadows the greater David, who to establish His Kingdom at His second advent will fearfully slaughter His enemies at Armageddon with the sharp sword that proceeds out of His mouth (Rev. 19:15). As a result, the birds of the heaven will be called to "the great supper of God" to gorge themselves with the flesh of the slain (Rev. 19:17-21, KJV).

9. God promised that David's son Solomon ("peaceable," 2 Sam. 12:24) would be a **man of rest,** that is, a man who would not engage in wars. Solomon foreshadows that aspect of the Messiah's second advent when He will reign in peace over the millennial Kingdom, after all enemies have been put under His feet (cf. Isa. 9:6-7; 11:6-9). **10.** This verse echoes the Davidic Covenant (see 2 Sam. 7:13-17; 1 Chron. 17:12-13), which looks to its ultimate fulfillment in the earthly Davidic kingdom that will finally merge into the everlasting Kingdom in the eternal state.

14. In my trouble—"by my hard labor I have amassed for the LORD's temple," (BV) **an hundred thousand talents of gold, and a million talents of silver** (13,100,000 pounds of gold and 116,400,000 pounds of silver). Some critics brand these numbers as Oriental hyperbole, but it must be remembered that David's victorious wars netted him vast amounts of booty, especially in metals (cf. 18:7-8).

David's Charge to His Officials. 22:17-19. **17-19.** The officials were exhorted to support and help Solomon in building the Temple. They were to set their minds and hearts to seek the LORD, in order to bring the ark of God from its temporary abode on Mount Zion (15:1), together with the **holy vessels of God** (at Gibeon, 21:29), **into the house that is to be built** on the site of Ornan's threshing floor.

N. THE ARRANGEMENT OF THE TEMPLE SERVICE. 23:1-32.

David Makes Solomon King. 23:1-2. **1. When David was old ... he made Solomon ... king.** The chronicler passes over the disputed succession and the details of Solomon's taking power (cf. 1 Kings 1:1—2:46; 1 Chron. 29:22). **2.** The notice of David's summoning all the **princes** *(sārîm,* "nobles, heads") together with the **priests and the Levites** forms an introduction to this chapter as well as to the next four chapters (24-27), which are devoted the the Temple service and its personnel. In characteristic fashion, the chronicler gives preeminence to the religious emphasis. He also follows his regular pattern of citing Temple functionaries in reverse order of their priority—Levites, then priests.

The Numbering of the Levites. 23:3-5. **3-5.** David numbered and appointed the Levites to their respective offices. The census revealed a total of thirty-eight thousand, of which twenty-four thousand were supervisors, six thousand officers and judges, four thousand gatekeepers, and four thousand musicians (cf. Amos 6:5). For the subordination of Levitical service to the priestly ministry and its import, see Numbers 4.

The Organization of the Levites. 23:6-24. The Levites were organized on the basis of the three Levitical families, in the order followed by all the lists (Exod. 6:17-18; Num. 3; 1 Chron. 6). Those who minister in the LORD's house are to be organized, each having his assigned place and function, according to his birth in the family of God. **13.** Noteworthy in this account of the families of the Levites is that Moses' posterity stood upon the same level as the common Levites, while Aaron's descendants were advanced to the priests' office to **sanctify the most holy things.**

The leveling of Moses' family and the elevation of Aaron's demonstrate that the LORD determines our place and honor in His service. He puts down one and exalts another. Sometimes this is the result of reward; but sometimes it is apparently only the exercise of His sovereign will, to which the believer is to submit confidently. **24.** David lowered the age when a Levite might serve from thirty years (cf. Num. 4:3; or twenty-five years? see 8:24) and numbered for service those from twenty years and upward.

Duties of the Levites. 23:25-32. **25-26.** Now that the central sanctuary was to be established at Jerusalem, there would no longer be a need for the Levites to transport the tabernacle and its equipment. Hence, the duties of the Levites were altered, being assigned particularly the furnishing of music for the services (chap. 15). In any case, whatever their Levitical service, it was subordinated to priestly service, since all Levitical ministry must proceed from priestly approach to God through sacrifice. Otherwise it consists of mere dead works, which cannot be performed before the living God (cf. Heb. 9:14). **28.** The Levites were to wait upon the priests and do the menial work (if any work for God can be called menial) of the house of God, such as keeping the courts and chambers clean, guarding the

holy things from defilement, and preparing the showbread and the meal for the offerings, so the priest might have everything at hand. **29.** Those who were judges and officers took care of all weights and measures.

30-31. At the regular morning and evening sacrifices (Exod. 29:38-39) they were to present themselves to give thanks and praise to the LORD "and [to present themselves] at the offering of burnt offerings" (AB). Only the priests could actually officiate at the altar; anyone else would do so at the penalty of death (cf. Num. 4:20).

O. CLASSIFICATION OF THE PRIESTS. 24:1-31.

The Twenty-four Courses of the Priests. 24:1-19. David not only organized the Levites (chap. 23), but the priests as well. Accordingly, to him is attributed the highest ecclesiastical activity. **1-2.** The Mosaic order is recorded in Numbers 3:2-4 and repeated here (cf. Lev. 10:1-6; Num. 26:60-61; 1 Chron. 6:3). **Eleazar, and Ithamar** executed the priest's office because of the death of Aaron's two oldest sons.

3. David, with the help of Zadok, of the descendants of Eleazar, and Ahimelech, of the sons of Ithamar, **distributed** (allocated) the priests to their ministry in accord with their official classification. The allocation was for the purpose of dividing their work among them for its more easy and efficient discharge. God is the God of order, whether in the Old Testament Temple service or the New Testament church (cf. Rom. 12:4-5; 1 Cor. 12:12).

4. Since the sons of Eleazar were found to have more **chief men** (headmen) of their house (sixteen) than the house of Ithamar (with only eight), they **were divided by lot, one sort with another** (lit., "these with those"), that is, the sons of

Eleazar with those of Ithamar, the clans of each standing together and apart from those of the other, and the lots being drawn alike for each alternately. The object was in no sense to change the liturgical functions, which were the same for all, but merely to determine the question of precedence in the order of ministry (cf. Luke 1:5, 8-9).

5. The decision was referred to the **lot** in order that the outcome might be determined by the LORD, obviating any quarrel, and because there were distinguished heads belonging to both priestly houses. They are called **governors** (princes) **of the sanctuary** (equivalent to "princes of the priests," 2 Chron. 36:14; Isa. 43:28) and **governors** (śārê hā'elō-hîm, i.e., "princes") **of the house of God,** probably denoting the high priests. **6.** The public notary who registered the names and drew the lots was **Shemaiah.**

7. The method used for drawing lots was to place in one urn the sixteen chief names of Eleazar, and in another the eight for Ithamar. The lots probably were drawn out alternately as long as those of Ithamar lasted, and then they were taken only from Eleazar's urn. Or perhaps two were drawn for Eleazar for every one for Ithamar throughout the procedure.

10. Note that among the twenty-four courses, the eighth was that of Abijah or Abia, referred to in Luke 1:5 as the course to which Zechariah, the father of John the Baptist, belonged. The twenty-four elders (of Rev. 4:4; 5:8) are apparently an allusion to the Davidic arrangement of the priests for the Temple service under the Solomonic reign, which foreshadows Christ's millennial reign. Hence, the twenty-four elders, clothed in white and crowned and enthroned upon twenty-four thrones, are interpreted to symbolize Old and New Testament saints in glory.

Allocation of Other Levites. 24:20-31. **20-30.** Most of the Levites listed here were mentioned previously in connection with their attendance upon the priests in the service of the house of God (23:7-23). **31.** They are listed again as heads of the twenty-four courses of the priests. They **likewise cast lots even as** ("just like," "in the same way as") **their brethren ... the priests.** The purpose was to determine, in the case of the Levites, the rotation order in which they were to serve. Note that the priests are spoken of as **their** (the Levites') **brethren.** So they were not to lord it over their colleagues (cf. 1 Pet. 5:3).

In order that the whole proceeding might be by God's direction, **the heads of the fathers' houses** (clan leaders) of the Levites and his younger brothers alike also cast lots in the presence of David, Zadok, Ahimelech, and the heads of the priestly and Levitical families, just as the sons of Aaron had done. Thus, the whole procedure was not by seniority, but as God directed through the lot. Before God, age is not the badge of acceptance, but faith and sincerity of heart.

P. ARRANGEMENTS MADE FOR TEMPLE MUSIC. 25:1-31.

The Musicians and Singers. 25:1-7. **1-7.** Having arranged the courses of the Levites, who were to attend the priests in their service, David then proceeded to classify those appointed to be singers and musicians in the Temple. First to be introduced were the musical personnel—Asaph, Heman, and Jeduthun, and their sons and other talented Levites (v. 7), whom David and **the captains of the host** ("the princes" of 24:5-6) of the LORD's army (not the regular military officers) **separated** to the service of music.

Asaph, Heman, and Jeduthun headed

three guilds of sacred musicians, who were famous subsequently as witnessed by the headings of many psalms. Apparently Asaph was related to the tribe of Gershon, Heman to that of Kohath, and Ethan-Jeduthun to that of Merari; thus, the musicians represented all branches of Levi (see 6:33-48).

These musical Levites were **separated** or set apart (Num. 16:9; cf. Acts 13:2) to **prophesy** (to perform musically under a spiritual influence). The instruments they played were **harps** (lyres), **psalteries** (a harplike instrument), and **cymbals.** They were called **workmen** (men of work, the good work of praising God). The fathers, Asaph, Heman, and Jeduthun, presided in the musical services (v.1) , and the children were **under the hands of their father** (cf. vv. 2-3).

The Twenty-four Orders. 25:8-31. **8-31.** Asaph had 4 sons (v. 2); Jeduthun had 6 (v. 3); and Heman had 14 (v. 4), for a total of 24. These musical families were allocated by lot to twenty-four courses of 12 men each, using 288 men in all, with each course serving a week in turn. Yet these men were but a small number in comparison with the 4,000 David appointed to praise the LORD (23:5). Perhaps this larger number ministered throughout the country. The psalms could be sung anywhere, but the Mosaic sacrifices were only to be offered at one place.

Q. ARRANGEMENTS MADE FOR GATEKEEPERS, TREASURERS, AND JUDGES. 26:1-32.

The Courses of the Gatekeepers. 26:1-19. David's revival of religion opened up a place of honor and usefulness to the Levites, which they had not had during the long era of the Judges and during Saul's erratic reign. Recorded here are the Levites set apart to be porters (gatekeepers). Their duties included such things as guarding the Temple and all approaches to it, shutting and opening the outer gates, directing and instructing worshipers, and excluding the ceremonially unclean. Hence, able men for the task are described as **mighty men of valor** (v. 6), strong men (v. 8), and one was called **a wise counselor.**

4-8. Obed-edom's eight sons and his family line, which numbered sixty-two, are listed. He had faithfully kept the ark (2 Sam. 6:10-11; 1 Chron. 13:13-14) and was rewarded for it. He had eight sons, **for God blessed him,** and his sons were placed in positions of trust in the sanctuary.

10. Of one Levite it is said that **though he was not the first-born, yet his father made him the chief,** not meaning in inheriting the estate (that was forbidden by the Law, Deut. 21:16-17), but doubtlessly in service requiring special personal qualifications. **12-19.** The gatekeepers, like the musicians, had their posts assigned by lot. Their names total about twenty-four, and so it is reasonable to assume they were allocated to as many companies.

The Levites Appointed as Treasurers. 26:20-28. **20-25.** The Levites had charge of the **treasuries of the house of God,** monetary gifts as well as provisions of food and supplies to be bought. **26-28.** In addition, there were **the treasuries of the dedicated things,** laid up mostly from the spoils of battle (v. 27), as a grateful acknowledgment of divine protection (cf. Num. 31:50; 1 Chron. 18:8-11; Heb. 7:4). Special mention is made in this connection of Samuel, Saul, Abner, and Joab. Over these treasures were set treasurers, who would faithfully manage them and guard them, keeping accounts of all received and dispensed.

The Levites as Officers and Judges. 26:29-32. **29.** These Levites were officials and judges entrusted with public affairs, and the account opens a new section dealing with David's civil and military arrangements (26:29—27:34), having nothing to do with the Temple and its worship, with which 23:1 to 26:28 are concerned.

The Izharites and the Hebronites were placed in charge of secular activities. The former were entrusted with **outward business over Israel,** that is, duties falling properly under royal jurisdiction. In the time of Jehoshaphat, priests and Levites were appointed as judges (2 Chron. 19:4-11). Josephus (*Antiquities* 4. 8. 14) refers to two Levites being appointed for each judge and refers this practice to Moses, which must have been ancient at his time.

30-32. The Hebronites were assigned administrative duties in connection with the Transjordanic tribes, taking care of the **affairs of the king** (which probably included taxes, though none are explicitly mentioned) as well as the **business of the LORD** (tithes), the civil and the sacred being happily interwoven and advanced. There were twenty-seven hundred Levites employed in Transjordan, with only seventeen hundred on the west side. Probably the Transjordanic tribes lacked judges of their own; or being more distant from Jerusalem and more exposed to the idolatry of surrounding nations, they needed more help from the Levites to prevent corruption. The chronicler places these governmental provisions in David's **fortieth year,** which was the last part of his reign. What good we do we must do now, even though the hour is late.

R. MILITARY AND CIVIL OFFICERS APPOINTED. 27:1-34.

The Twelve Army Corps and Their Commanders. 27:1-15. **1.** This verse constitutes the heading introducing the list that follows in verses 2 to 15. The phrase **after their number** refers to the twelve courses of 24,000 warriors each, totaling 288,000 (12 times 24,000) and is in line with the chronicler's dream of a marvelous future Kingdom toward which *all* Old Testament prophecy directs the eye of faith.

The number *twenty-four* occurs again and again in the chronicler's scheme and has already been applied to the Temple personnel (23:4-5; 24:4; 25:9-31). Now it is extended to the military and other groups. *Twelve* in Scripture numerology has governmental significance; twice twelve, that is, *twenty-four,* would suggest a perfect and complete government, such as will be set up when the future Davidic King of kings and King of glory is enthroned.

The courses (each corps of 24,000 men) **... came in and went out month by month,** indicating that the nation had a reserve army of 288,000, composed of twelve corps, each corps of 24,000 actively serving one month, and rotating each month throughout the year. All were subject to call, but only 24,000 were on duty at one time, unless an emergency developed. Thus, national security was guaranteed with the minimum of time and expense.

2-15. The reference to Asahel (v. 7) shows that this military organization existed early in David's reign, for Asahel was killed when David was king in Hebron (2 Sam. 2:19-23). The list of divisional commanders of each monthly corps corresponds closely to that of David's heroes (11:11-47; cf. 2 Sam. 23:8-39). The mention of **Benaiah, the son of Jehoiada, a chief priest** (v. 5; cf. 12:27; 1 Kings 2:25, 29, 34, 46) has led some scholars to suspect the words "a chief priest" as being a scribal error, based on association of ideas with 2 Samuel 8:18.

The Tribal Chiefs. 27:16-22. **16-22.**

Originally the tribal chief was a leader in war, as well as chief authority in times of peace. Apparently David made the important change of appointing the chief commanders himself, as the list (vv. 1-15) suggests. Levi had two princes (v. 17), one for the tribe and one for the influential Aaronic branch.

The Incomplete Numbering. 27:23-24. **23-24.** The reference here is to the census of chapter 21, one of the main objects for the military and political organization described. Two reasons are given why David restricted the census to those above twenty: (1) the promise of the LORD to Abraham of His increase of Israel (cf. Gen. 15:5; 22:17); and (2) God's wrath, which fell on account of the numbering (1 Chron. 21:7-13). Joab never finished the task, and the part that was completed was not **put in** (*'ālâ,* "entered") in the king's official annals.

The Administrators of Crown Property. 27:25-31. **25-31.** David's expenditures evidently were met by the proceeds from crown property, as there is no specific indication of taxation in his kingdom. As a result of military conquests, royal holdings of land, cattle, and other property increased, and so the management of those extensive holdings employed large numbers of people. Storehouses for spoils of war also were established in Jerusalem and in the provinces. (On the crown property of Israelite kings and its management, see M. Noth, ZDPV 50 [1927]:217, 230-40.)

Personal Counselors. 27:32-34. **32-34.** These counselors were in addition to public counselors and administrative officials (cf. 18:14-17; 2 Sam. 8:15-18; 20:23-26). **Jonathan,** David's uncle and a counselor, is referred to only here. He and **Jehiel,** otherwise unknown, were in charge of the upbringing of the king's sons. **Ahithophel** was the royal counselor (2 Sam. 15:12, 31;

16:23). **Hushai** the Archite was **the king's companion,** a title doubtless borrowed from Egyptian officialdom (see A. Erman, *Life in Ancient Egypt,* p. 72; H. Donner, ZAW 73 [1961]: 269-75; and A. H. Gardiner, *Ancient Egyptian Onomastica,* 1:20, n. 74). Only this passage relates that Ahithophel's successor after his suicide was Jehoiada, the son of Benaiah.

S. DAVID INSTRUCTS SOLOMON.
28:1-21.

David's Address to the Great Assembly. 28:1-8. This chapter resumes the thread of narrative from 23:1, where it was said that David was old and that Solomon was made king. The intervening chapters set forth David's preparations for the building of the Temple and the arrangement of its personnel and service. Now the thread of narrative is resumed.

1. The account of the calling of the representative convocation (already mentioned in 23:2) is now expanded. This great gathering was composed of "all the officials of Israel ... the tribal chiefs, the divisional chiefs in the royal service, the captains of the thousands and the hundreds, and the overseers of all the property and cattle belonging to the king and his sons—including the court officials, the mighty men, and every man of standing" (AB).

2-3. The words David addressed to the assembly were similar to his private address to Solomon (see 22:6-19). He repeated his intention to build the Temple and the reason why he did not. **4-6.** He reviewed the divine choice of himself and his house for the kingship, with Solomon as his successor and Temple builder.

7-8. He stressed the promise of the perpetuity of the kingdom, emphasizing, however, only the conditional aspect of the Davidic Covenant (cf. 2 Sam. 7:8-16) in order to warn the people to **keep and seek for all the commandments of the Lord . . . that ye may possess this good land, and leave it for an inheritance for your children after you forever.**

David's Public Charge to Solomon. 28:9-10. **9.** David solemnly called on his son and successor to **know** (*dāʿ*, "have experiential knowledge of") and **serve** (*ʿābad*, "to work as a humble servant or faithful slave") the LORD, though he would be an exalted king. Such faithful and lowly service for God and His people would be the essence of the greatness of his rule. Such service is most certainly demonstrated externally, but it is primarily a matter of the heart and thoughts, which the LORD alone searches and understands. **If thou seek him, he will be found by thee** (Jer. 29:13); **but if thou forsake him** (*ʿāzab*, "leave, abandon"), **he will cast thee off forever** (Deut. 31:17).

Presentation of the Temple Plan to Solomon. 28:11-21. The transmission of the Temple plan was not simply an oral communication; it was also written (v. 19). David transmitted three things to Solomon: **11-18.** (1) David gave Solomon a model of the building. A pattern of the tabernacle had been divinely revealed to Moses (Heb. 8:5), and David had received that pattern **by the Spirit** (not "spirit," KJV).

Since the Temple, like the tabernacle, was to typify Christ, it could not be left to man's invention, but to God's direction. Hence, particular details are mentioned of the **porch** (portico), the holy place, and the most holy **place of the mercy seat** (propitiatory), the **courts . . . the chambers, the treasuries,** and other places in which the dedicated things were stored, specifications **for the courses of the priests and the Levites,** and for all the service and vessels and the

plan of **the chariot of the cherubim** (see Exod. 25:10-22 for meaning). The cherubs are here called "the chariot" with reference to such passages as "He [God] rode [charioted] upon a cherub" (Psalm 18:10; cf. Psalm 99:1). Comparison is also to be made to Ezekiel's vision (1:4-21), called "The Chariot" by the Jews.

(2) David gave Solomon materials (gold and silver). These were by far the most costly of the Temple vessels and furnishings. They were weighed out so that they might be made no less than the patterns. The tabernacle's one golden lampstand (candlestick) would give way to ten in the Temple (1 Kings 7:49), besides silver ones (perhaps hand lampstands). In the tabernacle there was only one table of the bread of the presence, but in the Temple there were ten others for other uses (2 Chron. 4:8), besides silver tables. The gold for the altar of incense was specially **refined,** for nothing is more pure and perfect than that which prefigures Christ's intercession.

20-21. (3) David gave Solomon directions for help in this great undertaking. Solomon was to be courageous and resolute in the work of building the Temple, for the LORD—from whom his help was to come—was with him. He had everything needful both in Temple personnel and skilled artisans for the completion of the task.

T. GIFTS GIVEN FOR CONSTRUCTING THE TEMPLE. 29:1-30.

David's Example in Liberal Giving. 29:1-5. **1-5.** David pressed the people to contribute to the Temple to their full ability for six reasons: (1) Solomon was still **young and tender** (*rak*, properly, "thin, weak," so "immature, inexperienced") and needed the encouragement of the people's enthusiasm and liberality. (2) **The work** (task) **is great** (colossal), requiring extraordinary giving.

(3) **The palace is not for man, but for the Lord God;** therefore, the people were to be especially liberal, because they were actually giving to God (cf. 2 Cor. 8:5). (4) The king himself was enthused about planning the Temple. He made zealous preparation, laying up gold, silver, bronze, iron, wood, and stones—both precious stones and others—"large quantity of carnelian with fillings, blocks of hard mortar with mosaic pebbles, all kinds of precious stones and alabaster" (v. 2, AB).

(5) The king was deeply interested in the Temple. As a result, he donated his personal possessions of gold and silver, over and above all that he had collected otherwise. That amounted to three thousand talents of fine gold from Ophir (located perhaps in southeast or southwest Arabia or northeast Africa; cf. 1 Kings 10:11; 2 Chron. 8:18; Job 22:24; Psalm 45:9) and seven thousand talents of silver, vast sums with enormous purchasing power in antiquity.

(6) The artificers and craftsmen were ready. **Who, then, is willing to consecrate his service** ("fill his hand"), a technical expression used in inducting a candidate into the priestly office, as in Exodus 28:41, but here employed metaphorically of offering willingly, like one devoting himself to the priesthood (see ICC; cf. 2 Cor. 9:6-9).

The Joyous Response of the People. 29:6-9. **6-7.** The leaders came to the fore in munificent giving, offering **willingly** (2 Cor. 9:7) **of gold five thousand talents** and **ten thousand drams** (Pers., "darics"). So the chronicler used the gold *daric* of his day to describe this offering made in about 970 B.C. The bronze (18,000 talents, or 920,000 pounds troy) and the iron (100,000 talents, or 1,656,000 pounds troy) were both much rarer and

more valuable in antiquity than today.

8. Jehiel the Gershonite was the chief Temple treasurer (26:21-22). **9.** That the people **offered willingly** is repeated for emphasis, for this is the heart of godly giving (cf. v. 6), which is always inseparable from godly joy (cf. Judg. 5:1-31; 2 Cor. 8:5), producing spiritual hilarity (2 Cor. 9:7).

David's Prayer of Thanksgiving. 29:10-20. **10-13.** David **blessed** the LORD. To "bless" the LORD is to ascribe grateful praise to Him. David did so in the name of the **Lord God of Israel** and referred to **Israel** (Jacob) as the **father** of the nation. God's gracious dealing with the patriarch is reflected in His wonderful working with his descendants.

Praise was ascribed to God **forever and ever** (i.e., "from eternity even to eternity," cf. Psalms 41:13; 103:17; 106:48) in one of the greatest outbursts of praiseful worship found in the Old Testament, and it is even reflected in the Lord's Prayer (Matt. 6:13). David ascribed **greatness ... power ... glory ... victory ... majesty,** universal ownership, sovereignty, and exaltation to God. **14-16.** He abased himself and the people, giving all glory to God. **17-18.** David referred to the divine testings and chastenings, of which he himself knew so much, and which are often so necessary to keep the **thoughts of the heart** of His people upon Him.

19. David concluded his great prayer by beseeching the LORD to give Solomon **a perfect heart** (*lēb shālēm,* "a sound, whole, healthy mind or attitude," 1 Kings 8:61; Phil. 3:12) to keep the LORD's commandments and **to build the palace** (for the divine dwelling), for which he had made provision. **20.** Then the whole assembly blessed the LORD, as David had done and bowed down and paid homage to the LORD and to the king, foreshadowing the future fulfillment of Psalm 110:3.

The Accession of Solomon. 29:21-25. Following his normal procedure of cataloging the history of the Davidic kingdom from a religious viewpoint, the chronicler in detailing Solomon's enthronement follows a straight line rather than detours that would detract from his purpose. He took a positive approach and hence omitted events like Adonijah's rebellion (cf. 1 Kings 1:9, 19, 25), which would blur his objective.

21-22. After the great sacrifice and the ensuing sacrificial meal, **they made Solomon . . . king the second time,** the first time being briefly noted in 23:1. **23.** When Solomon was made king the first time he was anointed with oil (1 Kings 1:39) and acclaimed as king, but he did not occupy the kingly throne. But when he was made king the second time, he sat upon the throne **and all Israel obeyed him.**

24. All . . . submitted themselves unto . . . the king. Two similar anointings occurred in the case of David (1 Sam. 16:13; 2 Sam. 5:3). Both David and Solomon are typical of the Lord Jesus Christ, the two anointings pointing to His first and second advents. He was anointed King at His first coming (Matt. 3:16), but He did not receive the throne. When He comes the second time, "the Lord God shall give unto him the throne of his father, David. And he shall reign over the house of Jacob forever" (Luke 1:32-33).

25. Then shall be bestowed upon Him such royal **majesty** so that which was bestowed upon Solomon will be but a dim figure. "Royal majesty" is literally "glory of kingship" (cf. Psalm 72:1-19). Only three kings (counting Ishbosheth) had preceded Solomon (cf. 1 Kings 3:12; 2 Chron. 1:12), but the greater Solomon will have had *all* twenty-two kings of the Davidic dynasty from David to Zedekiah, preceding Him; but the glory of His kingship, as "KING OF KINGS" (Rev. 19:11-16) shall far eclipse their combined splendor. In this scene (v. 22) the kingship and priesthood, of course, are separated, with Solomon anointed as king and Zadok as priest. But in the "glory of kingship" in the Kingdom age, these two offices will be combined in Christ (Zech. 6:9-15).

Résumé of David's Reign. 29:26-30. **26-28.** The chronicler's interest focused on David's reign over **all Israel** and the unity of all the tribes, as he looked forward to the full fruition of the kingdom when the entire nation will be restored and blessed through the Messiah *as a nation,* not part of a nation. His blessings were from the LORD. **29-30.** The historical sources for the events of his reign are listed (see Introduction).

SECOND CHRONICLES

INTRODUCTION
See Introduction to First Chronicles

OUTLINE

I. SOLOMON'S REIGN. 1:1—9:31.
    A. The Beginning of Solomon's Reign. 1:1-17.
    B. Hiram of Tyre and the Temple. 2:1-18.
    C. Construction of the Temple Begun. 3:1-17.
    D. The Temple's Furnishings. 4:1—5:1.
    E. The Placing of the Ark in the Temple. 5:2-14.
    F. Solomon's Dedication of the Temple. 6:1-39.
    G. God's Dedication of the Temple. 7:1-22.
    H. Solomon's Fame and Splendor. 8:1-18.
    I. The Queen of Sheba, Solomon's Revenue and His Death. 9:1-31.

II. THE HISTORY OF JUDAH. 10:1—36:14.
    A. The Division of the Kingdom. 10:1-19.
    B. Rehoboam Fortifies Judah. 11:1-23.
    C. Rehoboam's Apostasy and Shishak's Invasion. 12:1-16.
    D. Abijah's Reign. 13:1-22.
    E. Asa's Early Reign. 14:1-15.
    F. Asa and the Prophet Azariah. 15:1-19.
    G. The Later Years of Asa's Reign. 16:1-14.
    H. Jehoshaphat's Early Reign. 17:1-19.
    I. Jehoshaphat's Alliance with Ahab. 18:1-34.
    J. The Prophetic Rebuke and Jehoshaphat's Reforms. 19:1-11.
    K. The Latter Part of Jehoshaphat's Reign. 20:1-37.
    L. Jehoram's Reign. 21:1-20.
    M. The Reign of Ahaziah and Athaliah's Usurpation. 22:1-12.
    N. The Deposition of Athaliah. 23:1-21.
    O. Joash's Reign. 24:1-27.
    P. Amaziah's Reign. 25:1-28.
    Q. Uzziah's Reign. 26:1-23.
    R. Jotham's Reign. 27:1-9.
    S. Ahaz's Reign. 28:1-27.
    T. Hezekiah's Reign. 29:1-36.
    U. Hezekiah's Passover Celebration. 30:1-27.
    V. Hezekiah's Further Reforms. 31:1-21.
    W. Hezekiah and the Assyrian Invasion. 32:1-33.
    X. The Reigns of Manasseh and Amon. 33:1-25.

COMMENTARY

I. SOLOMON'S REIGN. 1:1—9:31.

A. THE BEGINNING OF SOLOMON'S REIGN. 1:1-17.

The Theme of the Book. 1:1. **1.** This verse resumes the thread of thought (1 Chron. 29:24) and strikes the keynote of 2 Chronicles. **Solomon ... was strengthened in his kingdom, and the Lord ... magnified him exceedingly.** The chronicler's central purpose is to highlight Judah's greatness and the gracious divine dealing with the Davidic dynasty, presaging its far-reaching Messianic realization for Israel and the world as promised through the Davidic Covenant (2 Sam. 7:8-15; 1 Chron. 17:3-15).

The theme of 1 Chronicles (genealogy and history through David) lays the foundation for the great king (Solomon), who in turn foreshadows the greater than Solomon, the Lord Jesus Christ, in His rule of peace and splendor in the millennial Kingdom (cf. Psalms 2:7-12; 72:1-20; Isa. 9:7; 11:1-10; 12:1-6; 35:1-10). The chronicler thus presents religious or ecclesiastical history, or shall we call it "redemptive history," since it is channeled into the line of Messianic descent and Kingdom promise built upon the divine plan of redemption. Therefore, he repeats much of what had been given previously and in line with his purpose, adds to it.

At the same time he omits that which has no direct relevance to his plan, such as the woeful apostasy of the Northern Kingdom, which for his purpose did not constitute the true people of God, or the true kings or earthly kingdom of God. In the present context, Adonijah's rebellion is bypassed as being extraneous to the writer's aim (cf. 1 Kings 1:5-31).

Solomon at Gibeon 1:2-6. **2-3.** The first move of the new king was to call the officialdom and people to a religious service at Gibeon, an important religious center seven miles northwest of Jerusalem (Josh. 10:2). When Saul destroyed Nob, the tabernacle was transferred to Gibeon, where it remained till the Solomonic Temple was built (1 Chron. 16:39; 21:29; cf. 1 Kings 3:4).

4-5. David built a special tabernacle to house the ark at Jerusalem when it was brought from Kirjath-jearim (2 Sam. 6:2-12; 1 Chron. 13:5-14; 15:1-2, 28-29). But the Mosaic tabernacle and the bronze altar (Lev. 17:8-9) remained at Gibeon (cf. Exod. 25:1-27; 35:4—36:38), details of which are presented to remove any thought of the illegitimacy of the national worship ceremony at the celebrated high place. Hence, the notation here is of the altar at Gibeon (cf. 1 Chron. 16:39-40; 21:29) as the one made by Bezalel (Exod. 31:2-11; 38:1-2).

As long as the Temple, as the central place of worship ordained by God (Deut. 12:11), was not yet built, the worship of the LORD at Gibeon was not illegitimate. Only after the Temple had been built would public worship there be unlawful. Other high places were taboo because they had been sullied by association with idolatry.

6. Upon the Mosaic altar at Gibeon, Solomon (through the priests) **offered a thousand burnt offerings** (cf. Num. 7:1-89; Luke 21:1-4) as an expression of godly generosity and thankfulness that looked forward to divine grace to be manifested in the coming Redeemer in perfect devotion in sacrifice unto death, this being that which the burnt offering symbolized (Lev. 1:1-17; cf. 1 Kings 3:4-5).

The Lord's Appearance to Solomon. 1:7-13. **7.** That night God appeared to Solomon (1 Kings 3:5) and gave him the choice to ask what he would like the LORD to give him. **8-10.** Like a true son of David, he chose spiritual blessings rather than temporal benefits. Because of divine mercy to David, his father, and to himself, plus the promise made in the Davidic Covenant (2 Sam. 7:8-15; 1 Chron. 17:3-15), he asked for **wisdom and knowledge,** necessary to accomplish what was promised so that he might **go out and come in before this people** (an expression taken from a military usage, cf. 1 Sam. 18:13; 1 Chron. 11:2), in this context meaning "to govern the people adequately and with dignity befitting a king" (J. Myers, AB, p. 4).

11-12. In answer to his God-glorifying prayer, Solomon received a gracious answer. God gave him the wisdom he asked for, because it glorified God by expressing loving concern for His people. God gave him the wealth and honor he did not ask for, because he sought the Kingdom of God first and so the rest was added (cf. Matt. 6:33). **13.** Solomon was then divinely prepared to assume the duties of kingship.

Solomon's Wealth. 1:14-17. **14.** As a sign of his wealth, Solomon amassed horses and chariots, which were forbidden in the Mosaic Law (Deut. 17:16). His **chariot cities** (9:25) have been attested by archaeology, particularly at Megiddo, where one stone stable capable of accommodating about four hundred horses has been uncovered. **15.** The chronicler's description of the royal

wealth is graphic. He **made silver and gold ... as stones** (Palestine is notoriously stony) **and cedar trees ... as the sycamore trees ... in the Shephelah,** the low, descending hills between the central highland ridge and the maritime plain.

16-17. These verses (cf. 1 Kings 10:28-29) describe one of the most lucrative of Solomon's many commercial ventures—his horse and chariot trade with Egypt and Cilicia, acting as middleman to the kings of the Hittites and Aram. The correct rendering is: "And Solomon's horses were imported from Egypt and from Kue [Cilicia]; the king's traders procured them from Kue for a price. And they imported chariots from Egypt for 600 shekels of silver apiece [about $500], and horses for 150 apiece [about $125], and by the same means they exported them to all the kings of the Hittites and the kings of Aram" (NASB). Kue is Cilicia, as is now known from Assyrian inscriptions, Cilician horses being famous (Herodotus *History* 3. 90).

B. HIRAM OF TYRE AND THE TEMPLE. 2:1-18.

Solomon's Resolve to Build the Temple. 2:1-2. **1.** Solomon **determined** (lit., "said," i.e., "purposed, resolved," as in 1 Kings 5:5) to construct **an house for the name of the Lord** (the Temple) and **an house for his kingdom** (a house for his royalty), meaning, as the Vulgate renders, "a palace for himself" (cf. v. 12; 7:11; 8:1), but the chronicler does not relate the building of it (cf. 1 Kings 7:1-2). **2.** Solomon's levy of Canaanite laborers is described (cf. vv. 17-18; cf. 1 Kings 5:15). He **counted out ... men** (lit., "bearers of burdens ... hewers ... overseers," as in v. 18).

Solomon's Request of Hiram. 2:3-10. **3-5. Huram** (Hiram, originally Ahiram) had first sent an embassy to congratulate Solomon upon his accession (cf. 1 Kings 5:1-11). Through these goodwill ambassadors, Solomon then made his request for men and materials for the construction of the Temple, pleading (1) his father's friendship with Hiram and the kindness he had accorded him (v. 3); (2) his own high purpose of dedicating the building to God's service, mentioning the features of the priestly and sacrificial worship, all of which pointed to the saving grace of God (v. 4); and (3) his own testimony of his exaltation and veneration for the God of Israel **above all gods**—all idols, and above all, rulers (v. 5).

Idols are nonentities, rulers are insignificant at best, and both are under the dominion of Israel's God. Therefore, the house had to be great, at least in feeble measure, to reflect the infinite greatness of Israel's God. **6.** Yet, however great it might be, the Temple could never be a habitation for the omnipresent One who, unlike the deities of the nations, does "not dwell in temples made with hand" (Acts 17:24, NASB). Even **the heaven of the heavens** (Hebraism for "the highest heavens"; cf. 1 Kings 8:27) cannot contain Him.

The Temple was designed merely for the convenience of God's worshipers as a suitable place to approach Him through priestly sacrifice and worship. Though a mighty prince, Solomon suitably accounted himself as unworthy of such an undertaking. **Who am I, then, that I should build him an house . . . ?** His words presented a good witness of the God of Israel before Hiram.

7-8. Solomon requested a skilled artisan in metals and other materials, including cedar, fir, and algum wood. The latter was a precious wood, employed in Solomon's palace and Temple construction and in making fine furniture. It

occurs in an inventory list from Ugarit. **9.** It was Solomon's intent to make the Temple **great and wonderful** ("great and glorious," LXX). **10.** He himself would maintain the workmen with the best of food—wheat, barley, wine, and oil.

Hiram's Reply to Solomon's Request. 2:11-16. **11.** Hiram congratulated Israel on having such a king as Solomon, which he construed as a token of the LORD's love for Israel. **12.** He blessed God for raising up such a successor to David, his action showing what a powerful effect a good testimony has upon the unsaved, even idolaters. It seems that the LORD was known to the polytheistic Phoenician by the title "Maker of heaven and earth" (cf. Gen. 14:19).

13. This verse should be rendered: "I have just now sent a trained man, endowed with good judgment, namely Huramabi" (AB), or "Huram, my master [craftsman]" (Heb., *'āb,* "father," sometimes denoting "adviser, master, preceptor"; cf. Gen. 45:8; Judg. 17:10; 18:19; 2 Chron. 4:16, so LXX and Vulgate).

14. The Tyrian king declared his master (craftsman) to be the son of a Danite woman, whereas in 1 Kings 7:14 Hiram is called "a widow's son . . . of Naphtali." The probable explanation is that his mother was a Danite by birth, married into the tribe of Naphtali, was widowed, and as a Naphtalite widow married a Tyrian, by whom she had a son, Huram. It is possible, however, that the words **daughters of Dan** may reflect a corruption in the Hebrew text, which originally read "Naphtali." **16.** The chronicler is more precise in Hiram's agreement to cut and ship the lumber **in floats** (by rafts) to Joppa (Jaffa), the port nearest Jerusalem (cf. 1 Kings 5:9), mentioned extrabiblically as early as Thutmose III (15th century B.C.).

Solomon's Corvée. 2:17-18. **17-18.** A levy was raised out of **all the sojourners** (resident aliens, indigenous Canaanites; cf. Gen. 23:4; Exod. 22:21; Lev. 17:8) to a total of 153,600. In 1 Kings the levies worked in relays of three months, as did corveés in Egypt where they were based on the duration of the Nile inundation (see H. Kees, *Ancient Egypt,* p. 55).

C. CONSTRUCTION OF THE TEMPLE BEGUN. 3:1-17.

Site and Date. 3:1-2. **1.** Here the exact place of the Temple is specified—**at Jerusalem in Mount Moriah,** which is to be compared to "the land of Moriah," the place where Isaac was to be sacrificed (Gen. 22:2). The verse should be rendered: "Then Solomon began to build the house of the LORD [in Jerusalem in Moriah], who [i.e., the LORD] appeared to David, his father."

Clearly, the chronicler alludes to the etymology of "Moriah" as signifying the "appearance of Jah [Jehovah]" (Gen. 22:14), and so the resultant translation is: "who appeared in the mount of the Appearance of Jah, who appeared unto David his father . . . in the threshing floor of Ornan" (cf. 1 Chron. 21:28; 22:1). **2.** The beginning of the construction of the Temple is dated in **the second month** (April/May) in the **fourth year,** 966 B.C. (Thiele's dates; cf. 1 Kings 6:1).

The Temple Itself. 3:3-17. This chapter, like 1 Kings 6, describes the Temple as a whole. The Temple's main features, like those of the Mosaic tabernacle, which was placed within it (1 Kings 8:4) and upon which it was modeled, supply typical illustrations of the person and redemptive work of Christ. **3-4.** The measurements that Solomon fixed for the construction of **the house of God** were given in cubits **after the first**

measure (i.e., "according to the old standard"). The measure adopted later by Ezekiel and employed in Solomon's time was not the shorter measure of 17.49 inches, but the longer 20.405 inches (Ezek. 40:5; 43:13). So the house would measure approximately 105 by 35 feet. The portico was in the form of a lofty tower (120 cubits high, over 200 feet) if these words do not reflect an ancient scribal error.

5. The **greater house** was the nave or holy place, which Solomon paneled with cypress wood and overlaid with gold and decorated with palm and chain designs. **6.** He garnished ("covered" in the sense of "decorated") the house beautifully with **precious stones** and with **gold of Parvaim,** evidently "el Farwaim" in southeast Arabia (H. E. Medico, VT 13 [1963]:156-86).

7. The entire interior of the house was overlaid with gold, which was engraved on the walls with **cherubim** (cherubs), angelic creatures, symbolic of the divine presence (cf. v. 14; Gen. 3:24; Ezek. 1:5-6), who guarded the divine holiness. **8. The most holy house** ("the Holy of Holies," the special dwelling place of the LORD) was twenty by twenty cubits, or thirty-four by thirty-four feet. He overlaid it with **fine** (genuine) **gold,** weighing 600 talents (over 22½ tons). **9.** Apparently each of the gold **nails** for fastening the sheets of gold to the walls weighed fifty shekels (about 1½ pounds). The **upper chambers** of the oracle are not mentioned elsewhere.

10-13. The two cast cherubs for the Holy of Holies, with a total wingspread of twenty cubits—five cubits for each of their two wings, were set side by side with their wing tips touching the wall and each other as they faced the nave (on the cherubs, see W. F. Albright, BA 1 [1938]:1-3). These cherubs, not to be confused with the cherubim on the ark, were two large, gold-plated figures of olive wood (1 Kings 6:23) and filled the oracle (d^{e}bîr; cf. 2 Chron. 3:8); also, with the cherubim, they overshadowed the ark, symbolically guarding it as the place of the revealed presence of God.

14. The veil (see Exod. 26:31-33), the curtain that sealed off the Holy of Holies from the holy place, is not noticed in 1 Kings, or in Ezekiel's Temple, but probably fell accidently out of 1 Kings 6:21b in the course of transmission of the text. The veil was emblematic of the fact that the way to God was not yet open (Heb. 9:8), and would not be until Christ's body would suffer death and fulfill the anticipatory forms of the old dispensation (Matt. 27:51).

15-17. The two pillars, **Jachin,** "He establishes," and **Boaz** "in Him is strength" (see 1 Kings 7:15-22) are prophetically symbolic of Christ's firm and stable government of the earth in the glorious millennial Kingdom prefigured by Solomon and the splendid house he built.

D. The Temple's Furnishings.
4:1—5:1.

The Bronze Altar. 4:1. **1.** This altar of burnt offering (roughly thirty by thirty by fifteen feet) is not directly mentioned in the parallel material in 1 Kings, but it is, of course, assumed (cf. 1 Kings 8:22, 64; 9:25), and probably was deleted from the original through a copyist's slip. It was the first piece of ritual paraphernalia encountered in the Temple court, and it served as a perpetual reminder that sinful man can only approach God through sacrifice, which looked forward to the vicarious substitutionary death of Christ (Heb. 8:2-3; 9:12). The bronze altar of Bezalel in Gibeon, upon which Solomon had offered sacrifices (2 Chron. 1:5-6), was

certainly the model for this altar (see ANEP, fig. 627, for a good illustration of ancient platform altars of Bible lands).

The Cast-Metal Sea and Basins. 4:2-6. **2-6.** The purpose of the sea was for **priests to wash in,** showing that priestly activity demands continual cleansing (Exod. 30:21), and pointing to the necessity of constant confession and cleansing through the blood of Christ if priestly fellowship and service are to be maintained (1 John 1:3-10; cf. John 13:10; 2 Cor. 7:1; James 4:8).

The circumference of the sea was approximately 30 cubits (over 51 feet) and the diameter 10 cubits (over 17 feet). It was 5 cubits in depth (8½ feet), and could hold three thousand baths (a bath equaled more than six gallons, totaling more than eighteen thousand gallons) when completely filled; but normally two thousand baths, or twelve thousand gallons (1 Kings 7:26), were in it, because it was not usually filled to the brim, if the latter reading is also the original one.

The twelve oxen forming the base of the sea evidently represented the twelve tribes of Israel and their allocation around the tabernacle in the wilderness (see Num. 3). In Ezekiel's vision of God's glory, the four faces of the four living creatures prefigure four aspects of God's self-revelation when He incarnated Himself in the human family as the Messiah—on the right the lion, denoting the King (Matthew); on the left the ox, symbol of the Servant (Mark); the face of a man (Luke); and the eagle symbolizing deity (John). Here the ox may denote Christ's servantship and His obedience unto death to purchase our cleansing from sin (the sea laver).

The sea was **an handbreadth** in thickness (about three inches). This huge laver supplied ten smaller lavers on their wheeled bases (v. 6, cf. v. 14; 1 Kings

7:27-39), showing that through Christ's redemptive work, cleansing from sin is readily available according to the unlimited provision of God's grace in Christ.

The Lampstands, Tables, and Bowls. 4:7-8. **7.** The Temple was equipped with **ten lampstands** in contrast to the one in the tabernacle. The lampstands prefigure the perfection of Christ (sevenfold) as "the light of the world" (John 8:12) and the reflected glow with which His people are to shine for Him (Lev. 24:2-3; Matt 5:14; Phil. 2:15) through the oil of the Holy Spirit (cf. Zech. 4:2-6), as they minister as believer-priests (Lev. 24:4; Eph. 5:8).

8. Ten tables likewise took the place of the one; yet, apparently only one table at a time held the showbread (cf. 13:11; 29:18). The tables symbolize the sustaining communion with God of the believer (Lev. 24:8; cf. Exod. 24:11), especially in the Kingdom age, upon which Solomon's reign and the Temple focus (Luke 14:15). **The basins of gold** were bowls for pouring libations (*mizrāqim,* Amos 6:6; cf. 1 Kings 7:45, 50).

The Courts and Position of the Sea. 4:9-10. **9.** An inner and higher area was constructed as **the court of the priests,** where they could minister more effectively (1 Kings 6:36; Jer. 36:10), and was separated from **the great court,** the outer court. This distinction emphasizes the fact that under the Old Covenant there did not yet exist that universal priesthood of believers to be realized when Christ came and opened up free access to the Father (Jer. 31:34; Heb. 4:14-16).

Huram's Works in Bronze. 4:11-18. **11.** This Huram is the Phoenician master craftsman, not the Phoenician king (1 Kings 7:13; 2 Chron. 2:13-14). He made the **pots** (ash containers) **... the shovels, and the basins** (bowls). **12-13.** He also

executed the detailed adornment of the twin pillars, Jachin and Boaz (see 1 Kings 7:21-22), with their oil **bowls** (*gŭllôt*), and **capitals, which were on the top of the two pillars,** apparently fire cressets to illuminate the facade of the Temple by night. Each of the gratings covering the oil bowls was adorned with two hundred pomegranates.

14-18. Huram also executed the ten portable lavers and their bases, the sea with its base of twelve oxen, as well as all the utensils of polished bronze. **Huram, his father** (i.e., "his [Solomon's] master craftsman") made them for the king, and the casting was done **in the plain of the Jordan ... in the clay ground** ("in the earthen foundaries"; see Nelson Glueck, BASOR 90 [April 1943]:13-14), between **Succoth and Zeredah** (Zarthan, 1 Kings 7:46), identified with Tell es-Sa'idiyeh, east of the Jordan about ten miles north of the point that the Jabbok flows into the Jordan near the town of Adam.

Summary of the Furnishings and Equipment of Gold. 4:19-22. See 1 Kings 7:48-50, which closely parallels this. For **the golden altar** of incense, see Exodus 30:1-10 (cf. R. de Langhe, *Biblica* 40 [1959]:476-94). For the **tables of showbread,** see Exodus 25:23-30; for the **lampstands,** see Exodus 25:31-40. Gold symbolizes deity. The lavish employment of it in Solomon's Temple attests that it was meant to honor the one true and only God.

Moving the Gifts into the Temple. 5:1. **1.** This verse dealing with the moving of the gifts into the Temple really concludes chapter 4 and prepares for the transition to the subject of the dedication of the Temple. David's consecrated gifts (1 Chron. 18:11; 26:26) were transferred into the Temple's treasuries, which probably were connected with the "upper chambers" (2 Chron. 3:9) and the side chambers (1 Kings 6:5-6).

E. The Placing of the Ark in the Temple. 5:2-14.

The Ark Brought into the Temple. 5:2-10. **2.** A great assembly of Israelite elders, tribal heads, and family princes was convened by Solomon to bring up **the ark of the covenant of the Lord** from Zion to its permanent abode in the Temple. The Ark of acacia wood overlaid with gold, with its blood-sprinkled Mercy Seat (see Exod. 25:10-22), was the most sacred of all the Tabernacle-Temple furnishings, because it centered in expiation of sin and approach to God. Therefore, it most wonderfully foreshadowed the person and redemptive work of the coming Messiah. But the prophetic panorama here looks forward to the Kingdom age, when another house will once more stand in Jerusalem and the covenant promise made to David will be realized in the enthronement of the coming King as King-Priest upon the holy hill of Zion (Psalm 2:6-12; Zech. 6:9-15).

3. The dedication of the Temple did not take place until the **seventh month** (Sept.-Oct.) after the work was completed (v. 1) in the eighth month (Oct.-Nov.) of Solomon's eleventh year, 960 B.C. So the Temple was not dedicated till eleven months had elapsed (959 B.C.), at the annual **feast** of Tabernacles (cf. 7:8-10), as this great harvest festival looked forward to the Kingdom age and the fulfillment of the Davidic Covenant (see exposition on the Feast of Tabernacles, Lev. 23:33-44).

4-5. The Levites took up the ark (1 Chron. 15:2, 15) according to the directions of the Law of Moses (Num. 3:31; Deut. 10:8; 31:25). **7.** The Levites bore the ark, but the priests actually placed it in the most holy place under the wings of the cherubim. **9.** The poles by which it was carried were so long that they could be seen in front of the sanctuary, though they could not be seen from the outside.

The chronicler quoted his source when he noted, **There it is unto this day,** for the Ark was destroyed with Solomon's Temple in 586 B.C. **10.** Only the two tables of the Mosaic Decalogue, reflecting the eternal moral law of God, remained, the golden pot of manna (Exod. 16:32-34) and Aaron's rod (Num. 17:10-11; Heb. 9:4) having disappeared.

The Glory of the Lord Appears. 5:11-14. **11-12.** On this grand occasion **all the priests . . . were sanctified, and did not then wait by course,** representatives of all the 24 courses (1 Chron. 24:3-19) assisting 120 of them (i.e., 5 for each of the 24 courses or divisions) officiating. **13-14.** The Levitical singers, garbed in linen, stood on the east side of the altar with cymbals, harps, and zithers. With them stood those priests who were trumpeters (1 Chron. 15:24).

The harmony between the trumpeters and singers was so perfect that one melody was audible as they **praised the** LORD. What a magnificent scene as they sang, Praise the **Lord . . . For he is good; for his mercy** (*hĕsĕd,* "His covenant-keeping gracious faithfulness") **endureth forever** (cf. Psalms 65:1; 147:12). This glorious scene foreshadows the future praise of Israel in the Kingdom that the Messiah will establish when He comes again.

Then **the glory of the Lord** was manifested, representing the preincarnate Christ (Exod. 14:19; 23:20-23). The cloud of His presence had conducted the people out of Egypt (13:21-22), had later filled the Mosaic tabernacle (40:34-35), and now filled the splendid Solomonic Temple. Israel's sin was subsequently to drive this cloud away from the land (Ezek. 10:18-19). It marked Christ's first coming (Matt. 17:5) and will herald His glorious second advent (Rev. 1:7; 14:14; cf. Matt. 24:30).

F. SOLOMON'S DEDICATION OF THE TEMPLE. 6:1-39.

Solomon's Dedicatory Address. 6:1-11. **1-2.** In this speech the king gave God all the glory for the Temple and mentioned three specific things about it. (1) Solomon said the Temple was built for the LORD as a **house of habitation** (*bêt-zᵉḇŭl,* "a house of elevation," an exalted house; see W. F. Albright, JPOS 16 [1936]:17-20). In response to the withdrawal of the priests from the sanctuary because of the LORD's manifested presence, Solomon uttered the words that **the Lord ... would dwell in the thick darkness,** that is, His infinite glory would be veiled from human gaze, as at Sinai (Exod. 19:9; 20:21) and in the veiled holy place of the tabernacle (Lev. 16:2). Solomon referred to the Temple as God's **place for ... dwelling forever** (not mentioning the human condition of Israel's faithfulness, 7:20; Matt. 23:37-38). But Christ will yet reign in the restored Kingdom over Israel (Matt. 23:39; Acts 1:6; Rom. 11:26; cf. Psalm 2:6-12).

3-8. (2) Solomon blessed the LORD for fulfilling His promise to his father, David, in choosing Jerusalem to place His name there, and through him, as David's son, to build the Temple there. **9-11.** (3) Solomon said he built the Temple in performance of the word of God. God had said, **Thy son ... shall build the house for my name.** And now he had done it, placing in it the ark containing **the covenant of the Lord ... made with the children of Israel.**

Solomon's Dedicatory Prayer. 6:12-42. **12-13.** This noble prayer was delivered from a **bronze platform** (*kîyôr,* "pan" or "basin," a platform

shaped like an inverted basin and attested archaeologically both in Egypt and Syria; cf. W. F. Albright, ARI, pp. 152-53). **14-15.** The first part of the prayer (vv. 14-21) consists of praise to the LORD for His faithfulness to His covenant and promises, especially those made to David. **16-17.** This is coupled with a petition that the promises made to David might remain true forever.

18. Then follows an ascription of praise to the LORD, whom **heaven** itself, or the **heaven of heavens** (the highest heaven), cannot contain. How, then, could the infinitesimal Temple contain Him? This suggests why the chronicler refers seven times in this chapter to the LORD's hearing "from heaven" (cf. vv. 21, 23, 25, 30, 33, 35, 39). Although the writer follows his source closely (cf. 1 Kings 8), yet according to his priestly slant (in contrast to the prophetic emphasis of 1 and 2 Kings), he presents Solomon in a mediator-king-priest role, prefiguring the future Kingdom's conditions (cf. Zech. 6:9-15) under the Messiah. **19-21.** It is also noteworthy that he stresses the house of the LORD as the place where prayer is offered and answered, not only for the king, but also for the LORD's people, Israel.

22-40. The seven petitions deal almost entirely with the nation as a whole. The *first* (vv. 22-23), on oath-taking, on the surface appears to be individual, but it actually involves the preservation of community order. The *second* (vv. 24-25) concerns sin and repentance in relationship to defeat at the hands of their enemies, and restoration to their land. The *third* (vv. 26-27) concerns drought; and the *fourth* (vv. 28-31) famine and pestilence, and the relationship of those chastisements to repentance and prayer at the Temple. The fourth (vv. 32-33) also embraces the Gentiles and points to the blessing restored Israel will be to the world in the Kingdom age (cf. Zech. 8:20-23).

The *fifth* (vv. 34-35) deals with God's help in battle against enemies in answer to the prayer of the LORD's people. The *sixth* (vv. 36-39) has to do with sin and consequent bondage and captivity, in relation to repentance and restoration to divine fellowship and the land of blessing. The *seventh* petition (v. 40) is a general plea that God will hear prayer **in this place.**

41-42. The conclusion of the prayer was added by the chronicler from Psalm 132:8-10, emphasizing his priestly interest and looking forward prophetically to the enthronement of the Messiah as the Priest-King and the wonderful *rest* (peace) that shall prevail in that coming era, which will see the fulfillment of these promises made to David and Solomon. Psalm 132 is a royal psalm centering about the enthronement of the king (cf. H. J. Kraus, *Psalmen,* 2:876), which will find its fulfillment in the Messiah's earthly Kingdom.

G. GOD'S DEDICATION OF THE TEMPLE. 7:1-22.

The Manifestation of the Lord's Presence. 7:1-3. **1. The fire came down from heaven ... the glory of the Lord filled the house,** as it had filled the most holy place when the Ark had been placed there (cf. 5:13-14). This is a fuller manifestation of the LORD's acceptance of Solomon's work in connection with the Temple and his prayer, the divine presence dedicating the building as no ritual could.

The same phenomenon had occurred when David offered sacrifices on the same spot (1 Chron. 21:26). Compare God's acceptance of Moses (Lev. 9:24), Gideon (Judg. 6:21), and Elijah (1 Kings 18:38). The fire did not descend as the result of the killing of the sacrifices, but

was due to the praying of the prayer. This fire intimated that God was both glorious and gracious, consuming the sacrifices, not His people, signifying that He accepted their offering and them through their offering, even as He accepts us through Christ's atonement.

2. The priests could not enter, the glory of the LORD pointing to that greater Priest and the priesthood that He would bring to all believers, who one day would become priests. **3.** The people's response was solemn worship; they burst into the strains of the psalm just sung (see 6:41-42). So all Israel will one day see the glory of the LORD at His second advent and Kingdom and will worship Him (Zech. 12:10).

The Sacrifices. 7:4-7. **4-7.** The abundance of the sacrifices attested to the king's piety and the people's appreciation of the LORD's great tokens of favor. This magnificent scene, with white-robed Levitical singers and musicians and priestly trumpeters with praise ascending to God, foreshadows the coming joy of the Kingdom, when the blessings of Christ's redemptive sacrifice will be rejoiced in worldwide.

The Feast of Tabernacles. 7:8-10. **8-10.** The Feast of Tabernacles was celebrated in connection with the consecration of the altar, and *all* Israel was present (i.e., all males, Deut. 16:16) from the extreme north (**entrance of Hamath**) to the extreme south of the realm (the Wadi of Egypt, 1 Kings 8:65). This great festival finds its antitype in the restoration of Israel to Kingdom blessing at the second advent (cf. Lev. 23:33-44; 2 Chron. 5:2-3).

The Lord's Second Appearance to Solomon. 7:11-22. **11-12.** The LORD's first appearance to Solomon was at Gibeon (cf. 1 Kings 3:5; 9:2). This appearance betokened the acceptance of his work, not only the Temple, but the whole complex, including the palace and other structures (cf. 1 Kings 7; A. Alt, KS, 2:100-115). The Temple itself was apparently a royal chapel, as the king occupied a special place in Israel as God's representative to His people and their representative before the LORD. Hence, the house of the LORD being located adjacent to the royal palace was quite fitting.

13-14. The LORD graciously assured the king that if He chastised His people by drought, locusts, or pestilence, and they humbled themselves, sought His face, and turned from their wicked ways, He would **forgive their sin, and . . . heal their land. 19-22.** The warning pronounced has passed into history and found its literal fulfillment.

H. SOLOMON'S FAME AND SPLENDOR. 8:1-18.

The Building and Fortification of Cities. 8:1-6. **2. The cities which Huram . . . restored to Solomon** apparently were those that Solomon had originally given the Phoenician monarch in exchange for gold and lumber (1 Kings 9:10-14), which never pleased Huram (Hiram). Perhaps the cities were used as collateral and when Solomon paid off, he got the cities back and **caused the children of Israel to dwell there,** that is, colonized them with Israelites.

3. The capture of Hamath-zobah is not mentioned in 1 Kings 9. Apparently Solomon had assigned the oversight of Zobah to his friendly ally Hamath, and Zobah revolted against Hamath. At any rate, Solomon seized it. **4.** He incorporated it formally in his empire and at the same time fortified **Tadmor in the wilderness,** the famous trading center northeast of Damascus, as well as **the storage cities** he had built in Hamath. **5.** Solomon also built Upper Beth-horon and Lower Beth-horon (Beit el-

Foqa and Beit 'Ur et-Tahta), located some ten miles west-northwest of Jerusalem (Josh. 18:13). Those sites were enlarged and fortified because they formed a strategic gateway to the hill country. **6. Baalath** was located in Dan (Josh. 19:44). **The chariot cities** are not specified by the chronicler, but Kings mentions Hazor, Megiddo, and Gezer, where Solomon's building activities are attested by archaeology (cf. R. S. Lamon and G. M. Shipton, *Megiddo,* 1:8-16; for Gezer, see G. E. Wright, BA 21[1958]:103-4; for Hazor, see Y. Yadin, BA 21 [1958]:46-47).

Labor Crews. 8:7-10. **7-8.** Solomon reduced to slavery the descendants of the non-Israelite peoples who remained in the land (cf. 1 Kings 9:21; see I. Mendelsohn, *Slavery in the Ancient Near East,* p. 97). **9.** However, he did not make slaves of any of the Israelites for that work. They served as **men of war** (soldiers), chiefs of his adjutants, and **captains** (chiefs) **of his chariots and horsemen. 10.** These were the heads of the king's labor battalions, numbering 250 (cf. 1 Kings 9:23, where the number is 550, the chronicler's number being due to a copyist's error). Those **who bore rule** were taskmasters, literally, those "who had dominion over" the Canaanite remnant (v. 7), who were working in the forced-labor battalion.

A House Built for Pharaoh's Daughter. 8:11. **11.** Solomon did not consider it proper that his Egyptian wife should dwell in the house of David, because the places (the total complex of buildings) to which the ark of the LORD had come, had been made sacred by the symbol of God's presence and were not to be defiled by the idolatries and vanities of a foreign wife, which eventually led to apostasy in Israel (cf. 1 Kings 11:1, 8; cf. Ezra 9:1). At this juncture Solomon's conscience was still tender enough to remove her residence from the places that were **holy.** J. Myers posits that the move was due to the queen's ritualistic uncleanness (Lev. 15:19-33) as Solomon's wife (AB, p. 49), but that was scarcely the real reason for the change of her residence.

Completion of the Work on the House of God. 8:12-16. **12-16.** In line with his priestly slant, the mere building of the Temple edifice did not constitute the completion of this holy work for the chronicler. Not until all the prescribed sacrifices and worship had been duly established and performed could the house of the LORD be said to be **perfected,** that is, "completed in every detail."

Accordingly, Solomon continued the holy sacrifices there, following the Mosaic Law. All the sacrifices, as in the tabernacle, pointed to the coming Redeemer and His great redemption. He also continued the ministry of music and song, as instituted by David, who is called **the man of God,** as was Moses, because he was instructed and authorized by God to establish those procedures. Solomon was solicitous to see all of them observed **as the duty of every day required** (cf. 1 Chron. 23-26).

Solomon's Maritime Ventures. 8:17-18. **17-18.** Solomon went to Eziongeber near the north end of the Gulf of Aqaba (apparently known as Elath or Eloth at the time of the kings (1 Kings 9:26; see Nelson Glueck, BASOR 72 [1938]:2-13, present-day Tell el-Kheleifeh, west of Aqaba. There Solomon had a large copper and iron works and a naval yard. Refined copper and iron were the products traded with South Arabia and Ophir (see 1 Kings 9:26-28). Tyrian seamen assisted as shipbuilders and sailors in the maritime undertaking. Enormous quantities of gold (over fifteen tons) were procured.

I. THE QUEEN OF SHEBA, SOLOMON'S REVENUE, AND HIS DEATH. 9:1-31.

The Visit of the Queen of Sheba. 9:1-12. See 1 Kings 10:1-13, with which this account is almost verbally identical. **1-7.** The queen's visit to Solomon to test his wisdom and see his glory was basically in the nature of a trade and diplomatic mission to establish a modus vivendi with the great merchant prince of Palestine. Doubtlessly this episode appears immediately after the reference to Solomon's commercial activities on the Red Sea because his traffic with Ophir threatened the lucrative overland trade of the south Arabians.

Sheba (Saba, Sabaeans) is mentioned prominently in the Old Testament, especially with reference to its caravans and spice trade (cf. Isa. 60:6; Jer. 6:20; Ezek. 27:22; Joel 3:8). Excavations at Marib, the ancient capital of Sheba, reveal that it was an imposing center of activity (R. L. Bowen and F. P. Albright, *Archaeological Discoveries in South Arabia;* and W. F. Albright, *Eretz Israel,* 5:7-9). **8.** Amazing are the queen's words (cf. 1 Kings 10:9), which refer to Solomon occupying the LORD's throne **to be king for the Lord** (1 Chron. 17:14; 28:5; 29:23; 2 Chron. 13:8).

Solomon's Wealth. 9:13-28. **13-14.** The weight of the gold that Solomon received annually (666 talents of gold) was equivalent to over 25⅛ tons. That was **beside that which traders** (lit., "men of the caravans") **and merchants brought,** and the Arabian kings and the governors brought. **15-17.** Having an abundance of gold, Solomon used it lavishly on **bucklers** (large shields covering the body) and **shields** (the *māgēn,* a small oval shield about half the size of the target), which adorned **the house of the forest of Lebanon,** called that because it was built and adorned with cedar wood from the Lebanon region.

18-20. The great throne of ivory overlaid with gold is minutely described to accentuate Solomon's wealth and splendor. A **footstool** (footrest) made of gold was attached to the throne. The **lions** with which it was decorated bespoke Solomon's kingly majesty in government over Israel (the twelve tribes), but they envision the greater Solomon in His Kingdom rule as "the Lion of the tribe of Judah" (Rev. 5:5).

21. Solomon's ships **went to Tarshish** (lit., "were goers to Tarshish"), the name of the fleet, not the destination, the designation being adopted from Solomon's similar Mediterranean fleet. They were large ships that could transport heavy cargoes of refined copper as the stock in trade for exotic wares from far-off Ophir or Punt, such as **ivory** and two different varieties of monkeys (*qôpîm* and *tûkkîyîm;* cf. W. F. Albright, ARI, p. 212, n. 16). Parts of two years and one full year were reckoned as three years for the trip. **25-28.** For Solomon's horses and chariot cities and his horse and chariot trade, compare 1 Kings 10:28-29.

Conclusion of Solomon's Reign. 9:29-31. **29-31.** The chronicler omits the dark side of Solomon's life. His priestly emphasis lay in the idea of a theocratic kingdom that pointed toward a great redemptive future and the consummation of the divine promises vouchsafed to David and his successors in the Davidic Covenant. Hence, extraneous matters, such as Solomon's apostasy, were avoided.

II. THE HISTORY OF JUDAH.
10:1—36:14.

A. The Division of the Kingdom.
10:1-19.

Rehoboam's Folly. 10:1-15. **1-2.** And Rehoboam went to Shechem, the old amphyctionic (association of neighboring states) center of Israel, thirty miles north of Jerusalem. Seemingly, no question existed concerning Rehoboam's accession in Judah, but he had to receive the crown from the northern tribes at the hands of the elders of Israel. The old Davidic idea of a double crown, one of Judah and the other of Israel, now came to the fore, especially in the light of the fact that Jeroboam had already been divinely anointed for kingship over ten tribes (1 Kings 11:26-40), which was the reason for his flight to Egypt from Solomon's presence.

3. When Jeroboam returned from Egypt, **they sent and called him** to the assembly (cf. 1 Kings 12:20). **4.** When Jeroboam and all Israel arrived, they asked Rehoboam to ease **the grievous servitude,** saying they would **serve** him. **6-11.** Foolishly, Rehoboam rejected the counsel of **the old men,** who had served Solomon, and listened to **the young men who were brought up with him,** the insolent aristocracy raised under Solomon's luxurious regime. **13-15.** So Rehoboam answered the people **roughly** (harshly) and haughtily, **for the cause** (*nesibbâ,* "the turn of events") **was of God,** who had ordained the nation's dismemberment in punishment for Solomon's idolatrous lapse (1 Kings 11:29-33).

Israel's Division. 10:16-19. **16-19.** The shout of secession came easily under such extreme provocation. The chronicler does not even mention Jeroboam's accession. He considered the Northern Kingdom apostate from the start and dismissed its history from this point on. For him, only those elements of Israel that remained loyal to the dynasty of David were the true Israel (cf. v. 17; 11:3).

B. REHOBOAM FORTIFIES JUDAH.
11:1-23.

Rehoboam Forbidden to War Against Israel. 11:1-4. **1-4.** The divine directive to avoid war came through the prophet Shemaiah (cf. 12:5-8, 15). God's message was that everyone was to return to his own house **for this thing** (lit., "from Me became [arose] this matter," namely, the secession of the ten tribes; cf. 10:15).

Rehoboam's Fortifications. 11:5-12. **5-12.** Excavations at Azekah, Mareshah, Lachish, Bethzur, and elsewhere show fortifications apparently dating from this period (931-913 B.C.). These defenses were apparently directed mainly against foreigners (Egyptians and Philistines) and Edom (cf. 1 Kings 11:14-22, 25). Rehoboam either regarded Jerusalem as its own defense or else as an imperative defense against Israel and foreign attack.

Migration of Priests and Levites. 11:13-17. **13-14.** The chronicler reports the separation of priests and Levites from the Northern Kingdom and its apostasy, since Jeroboam in diametrical disobedience to the Law of Moses had rejected them and appointed incumbents who were non-Levites (cf. 1 Kings 12:31-32; 13:33).

15. From the priestly point of view, the chronicler assesses Jeroboam's wickedness (cf. 2 Chron. 13:9) in appointing alien priests for the idolatrous high places, and the **he-goats** (satyrs or goat idols) and the **calves** (bulls), which he had made. The "goat idols" had demonic affiliations, as did the bulls (cf. Isa. 13:21; 1 Cor. 10:19-20), therefore, the King James Version's rendering, "devils," that is, demons. **16-17.** Evidently a large defection to Judah is indicated, which made the Southern Kingdom representative not only of the true Israel, but of all the tribes (cf. 15:9).

Rehoboam's Family. 11:18-23. **18-21.** The chronicler as usual dilates upon genealogical affiliations of the Davidic dynasty as being important to the outworking of the divine redemptive plan and purpose to be wrought out through it. Rehoboam **took eighteen wives,** willfully flouting God's Law (Lev. 18:18; Deut. 17:17) and following the disastrous precedent of his father. **22-23.** Wisely, however, he delegated authority to his sons in the defense of the kingdom and provided well for them in order to avoid unrest and possible revolt. Also, he made ample provision for the undisputed succession of Ahijah as his heir.

C. REHOBOAM'S APOSTASY AND SHISHAK'S INVASION. 12:1-16.

Shishak's Invasion. 12:1-12. **1.** When Rehoboam's rule was established and was strong, he gratified fleshly indulgence (cf. 11:21) and plunged into apostasy. **He forsook the law of the Lord, and all Israel with him,** by becoming contaminated with Canaanite polytheism and immorality (cf. v. 14; 1 Kings 14:23-24; 15:12). Judah was the true Israel for the chronicler. Israel and her king had abandoned the Law of the LORD.

2-4. Divine chastening followed in the invasion of Shishak (Sheshonq I, the energetic founder of the twenty-second dynasty in Egypt). Shishak's campaign has been confirmed by his inscription on the walls of the temple of Amon at Karnak, revealing the fact that he overran northern Israel as well as Judah. His invasion took place in the fifth year of Rehoboam (c. 926 B.C.). Shishak's army consisted of Lubim (Libyans of North Africa), Sukkiim (foreign mercenaries; cf. W. F. Albright, *The Old Testament and Modern Study,* p. 18), and Ethiopians. **5-7.** The prophet Shemaiah's message was heeded, and the repentance of the king and his princes brought some relief to Jerusalem. **8-12.** But the people had to learn the difference between serving the LORD and the hard bondage of the world (cf. Matt. 11:28-30) through Shishak's plunder of the golden shields of Solomon and other exactions.

Rehoboam's Death. 12:13-16. **13-14. He did evil, because he prepared not his heart to seek the Lord.** Heart preparation by prayer, faith, and obedience is the only preventive against spiritual decline (cf. 1 Sam. 7:3; 1 Chron. 29:18; 2 Chron. 27:6). **15.** Besides the ordeal of Shishak's invasion, there were hostilities constantly between Rehoboam and Jeroboam, infidelity and compromise always occasioning chastening and trouble.

D. ABIJAH'S REIGN. 13:1-22.

Accession of Abijah. 13:1-3. **1-2.** Abijah is called Abijam (1 Kings 15:1, KJV), and Abijahu, the longer form of his name (2 Chron. 13:21, lit. Heb.). His brief reign from 913 to 910 B.C. (Thiele's dates) was occupied principally with a war with Jeroboam (cf. 1 Kings 15:6-7), which actually represents the struggle between true worship and apostasy in all times. **3.** The size of Abijah's army of four hundred thousand and Jeroboam's of eight hundred thousand is entirely plausible in the light of David's census figures (2 Sam. 24:9), though modern scholarship is inclined to interpret these numbers on the unit basis (four hundred to eight hundred units, with the number of each unit unspecified).

Abijah's Address. 13:4-12. **4.** The king gave a stirring challenge to the northern tribes from Mount Zemaraim, located somewhere in the vicinity of Bethel to the northeast (F. M. Abel,

Géographie de la Palestine, 2:454), in a scene reminiscent of Jotham's fable (Judg. 9:7). Abijah's address demonstrates faith in God and His promises to David's line in seven ways:

5. (1) It refers to the LORD's giving **the kingdom over Israel to David forever** (2 Sam. 7:8-16), that is, giving "eternal dominion over Israel to David and his sons" (AB), the divine promise rising above the human failure and to be realized in Christ (Luke 1:32-33; Acts 1:6), who at His second advent will establish the millennial Kingdom (Rom. 11:26-36; Rev. 19:11-16; 20:3-6). After that the thousand years will merge into the everlasting Kingdom of the eternal state (Rev. 21-22).

(2) The perpetuity of the kingdom was assured **by a covenant of salt,** salt's preservative qualities making it an apt figure of perpetuity (Num. 18:19). In antiquity, salt was indispensable at formal meals for the ratification of friendship treaties and alliances, and such a "salt treaty" alone was considered secure. Hence, salt accompanied sacrifices, being considered as so many renewals of the agreement between God and man (Lev. 2:13; Ezek. 43:24; cf. H. C. Trumbull, *The Covenant of Salt*).

6. (3) The ten tribes under Jeroboam were thus in rebellion against the LORD and His redemptive plans and purposes for the world through the Davidic line, not simply against Rehoboam (and his successor) as a man (cf. 1 Kings 11:26). **7.** (4) The rebels were therefore **worthless men** ("the children of Belial," "scoundrels"; see notes on 1 Sam. 1:16; 2:12) to dare to fight against God and take advantage of His human representative when he was **young** (immature in experience; Rehoboam was forty-one years old), **tenderhearted** (timid), and unable to hold his own against them. **8-9.** (5) How then, despite their material superiority, could they expect to resist God and win? Would their apostate cult of golden calves (originally pedestals for the enthronement of "the glory of God," supposedly fulfilling the same function for Israel as the ark with the cherubs did for Judah) give them victory? Would their illegitimate priesthood in the service of **no gods** come to their rescue?

10-11. (6) Will not the LORD aid His people who have not defected from Him and who remain loyal to His priesthood and system of sacrifice in Jerusalem, the place He has chosen? Does not all this look forward to the divine redemptive plans and purposes for the world? **12.** (7) Let the rebels (still referred to as **children of Israel**) not fight against the LORD God of their fathers, for they **shall not prosper.**

The Outcome of the Conflict. 13:13-22. **13-14.** Despite Jeroboam's brilliant strategy (cf. Josh. 8:4-5), it was no match against the LORD, who fought for His people as of old. **15-17.** The victory was His. **19.** Abijah took Bethel (modern Beitin, ten miles north of Jerusalem), Jeshanah (Burj el-Isaneh, four miles south of Shiloh), and Ephrain (Ephron-Ophrah, et-Taiyibeh, four miles northeast of Bethel). **20.** That victory broke the back of Jeroboam's strength, which he never regained, the chronicler revealing that God smote him and he died (cf. 1 Sam. 2:6; 25:38; Acts 12:23). **21.** Reference to the wives and progeny of Abijah indicates the blessing of the LORD upon him. **22. The story** (Midrash, commentary) **of the prophet Iddo** was a source available to the chronicler.

E. ASA'S EARLY REIGN. 14:1-15.

Asa's Accession and Reforms. 14:1-5. **1-2.** Abijah's son Asa ruled from 911 to 870 B.C. Peace crowned the first decade of his reign, resulting from Judah's great victory over the northern tribes and Asa's fidelity to the LORD, shown by his religious reforms. **3.** His efforts to root out illegitimate worship included removing **the altars of the foreign gods** (lit., "*altars* of the alien," cf. 1 Kings 15:12*b*) and the **high places** (Judg. 3:7; 2 Kings 3:2). He also **broke down the images** (*măṣṣēḇôṯ*, "rough, unhewn stones" set up for cultic worship; see 17:6; K. Galling, BRL, cols. 368-71), and **cut down the idols** (*ašērîm*, "cult objects" representing the original Canaanite sea-goddess).

4. He also **commanded** Judah **to seek** the LORD and **to do** (observe) His commandments. **5.** He removed **the images** (*hămmānîm*, "incense altars"; K. Elliger, ZAW 57[1939]:256-65; W. F. Albright, ARI, p. 215, n. 58). And **the kingdom was quiet before him** (cf. 14:1), that is, until the invasion of Zerah in 896 B.C. (but cf. 15:19). The chronicler presents Asa as a man like David, great in religious zeal and battle, devoting three chapters (14-16) to him in contrast to the relatively brief passage devoted to him in Kings (1 Kings 15:9-24).

Asa's Building Activities. 14:6-8. **6-8.** This section is added by the chronicler from another source (cf. 1 Kings 15:23; Jer. 41:9). The proportionally large number of Benjamites in Asa's army seems to indicate that he held on to the territory Abijah had wrested from the Northern Kingdom.

The Ethiopan War. 14:9-14. **9.** Zerah, the Ethiopian (the Cushite), invaded Asa's realm from the southwest. This may have been an attempt of Osorkon I, the second pharaoh of the twenty-second dynasty of Egypt, to duplicate the pillaging expedition of Shishak (Sheshonq), his predecessor (cf. 12:2). The invading horde **set the battle in array ... at Mareshah** (Tell Sandahannah), some twenty-five miles southwest of Jerusalem.

10-12. Asa prayed to the LORD to vanquish the overwhelming host, and the LORD routed the Ethiopians. **13-14.** They were pursued as far as Gerar (Tell Abu Hureira, about nine miles southeast of Gaza; cf. Y Aharoni, "The Land of Gerar," IEJ 6[1956] :26-32). Zerah's rout is related by the chronicler to illustrate graphically what could be expected by those who put their trust in the LORD. **15.** Asa's army also struck down **the tents of cattle** (i.e., encampments of the cattle herders in the area).

F. ASA AND THE PROPHET AZARIAH. 15:1-19.

Azariah's Sermon. 15:1-7. **1.** **Azariah, son of Oded,** is otherwise unknown. His effective sermon was Spirit-indited, empowered, and had three points: **2.** (1) The sermon declares that the LORD will be with the people as long as they are with Him (cf. 2 Chron. 20:14-17). **3-6.** (2) The sermon illustrates that truth from history, especially from the book of Judges (cf. Judg. 2:11-19; 3:7-10). Verse 3 should read, "And for many days Israel was without the true God and without a teaching priest [Lev. 10:8-11; 2 Chron. 17:8-9] and without law [a *tôrâ*, i.e., a body of instruction]" (NASB).

The priests instructed the people in the divine Law. When the people in their **trouble** (straits) returned to the LORD and sought Him, **he was found** by them (Judg. 4:3; 6:6; Psalms 106:44; 107:6). In those times of apostasy **there was no peace** (Judg. 10:54) ... **but great vexations** (*mᵉhûmôṯ,* "confusions, disturbances, tumults," Amos 3:9; cf. Deut. 28:20). Verse 6 describes the feuds between rival tribes (as in Judges 8 and 12; cf. Isa. 9:18-21; 19:2). **7.** (3) The sermon contains an exhortation.

Asa's Reformation. 15:8-15. **8.** Azariah's sermon was effective in stirring up Asa to conduct a thorough religious housecleaning. He removed **the abominable idols** (*hăshshīqqûṣîm,* "abominations," detestable pagan idolatries), which evidently included the purging out of the male cult prostitutes (*hăqqᵉdēshîm;* 1 Kings 15:12). At the same time he repaired the LORD's altar that had been desecrated by illicit offerings.

9. His reformation extended to the whole land as well as the cities taken from the Northern Kingdom in Mount Ephraim (cf. 13:19). The divine purpose in dividing Solomon's kingdom appears in the fact that many from Israel deserted to Judah in order that a remnant might be preserved (cf. 11:3, 14) through which God's purposes might be carried out.

10-11. Asa called a great assembly to celebrate what was apparently the Feast of Weeks (Pentecost) **in the third month, in the fifteenth year** (May/June 895 B.C.; see Lev. 23:15-21), evidently the year following Zerah's invasion (2 Chron. 15:19). **12-13.** The people entered into a covenant (Heb., "the covenant," meaning a renewal of the covenant of Exod. 19:5-8) **to seek the Lord ... with all their heart,** under pain of death for those who refused to do so. **14-15.** They sealed their decision with a solemn **oath** and received the **rest** (cessation from war) that the LORD gave them.

The Removal of Maacah. 15:16-19. **16.** Asa even removed Maacah, his mother (i.e., grandmother) from her status as queen grandmother because of her idolatry (cf. 13:2; 1 Kings 15:13), commendably placing faith in God above family devotion (cf. Deut. 33:9; Matt. 10:37). She had made **an idol in a grove** (i. e., "a horrible thing for Asherah"; cf. 14:3). Whatever this idolatrous symbol was, Asa burned it **at the brook, Kidron,** in the moderately steep valley on the east of Jerusalem below the Mount of Olives. **17.** But the **high places** (illegitimate places of worship) were not removed.

18. The spoils of Jeroboam (13:19) and of Zerah and his allies (14:13-15) were deposited in the Temple (cf. 1 Chron. 18:11; 26:26-28). **19.** This verse should read: "There had not been war until the thirty-fifth year that had reference to Asa's reign." The war alluded to is that with Zerah in 896 B.C., which took place in the thirty-fifth year after the breakup of the kingdom (cf. 16:1).

G. The Later Years of Asa's Reign. 16:1-14.

Baasha's Move Against Asa. 16:1-6. **1.** In the thirty-sixth year of Asa's reign (895 B.C.) Baasha of Israel fortified Ramah, located ten miles north of Jerusalem on the main north-south highway. That was a hostile move to cut off travel and communication and to prevent the defection of northerners to Judah, as well as to cut off worshipers from access to Jerusalem. **2-3.** Not in a position to wage an offensive campaign against Baasha, Asa sacrificed the results of his own piety and God's blessing (15:18) to buy the intervention of the Aramaean, Benhadad I of Damascus, against Baasha.

4. Asa's wily move succeeded. Benhadad broke his alliance with Baasha and invaded northern Israel, destroying Ijon (Merj Ayyun); Dan at the headwaters of the Jordan, about nine miles south-southeast of Ijon; and Abel-maim, four miles west-northwest of Dan, as well as all the **storage cities** of Naphtali. The invaders moved as far south as the district of Chinneroth, in the vicinity of the Lake of Galilee (1 Kings 15:20). **5.** Baasha was forced to

abandon his project at Ramah. **6.** Then Asa conscripted his fellow countrymen to dismantle the fortifications and constructed fortifications of his own at Geba (Jeba? or Tell el Ful?) and Mizpah (probably Tell el Nasbeh).

Hanani's Prophecy. 16:7-10. **7.** Hanani the seer (*hārōʾēh*) boldly faced Asa with his unbelief in relying on the king of Syria (Aram) instead of on the LORD. Had Asa trusted the LORD, **the host** (army) **of the king of Syria** ("of Israel," LXX) would have been encountered in battle and defeated (the LXX reading apparently being the correct one). **8.** How differently it was when Asa relied on the LORD. Vast hordes of Ethiopians and Libyans had been delivered into his hand (14:9-13).

9. Asa foolishly took things into his own hands, forgetting that the **eyes of the Lord run to and fro throughout the whole earth, to show himself strong in the behalf of them whose heart is perfect** (blameless) **toward him** (cf. Zech. 4:10). **10.** Asa's anger and stern punishment of the seer and some of his partisans show the low level of his spiritual life at that time.

Asa's Sickness and Death. 16:11-14. **12.** Doubtlessly as chastisement for his unbelief in relying on the king of Syria instead of on the LORD and his rejection of the word of God through Hanani the seer, Asa became afflicted with sickness (cf. 1 Cor. 11:30-32). His unbelief also was displayed in consulting only the physicians, without consulting the LORD at all. This incident must not be construed as a condemnation of physicians and the healing ministry as such. There are hints of approval of them in the Old Testament (Exod. 21:19; Isa. 38:21; Jer. 8:22), although generally the LORD did not use any human instrumentality when He healed His people (Exod. 15:26; Psalm 103:3). Human means alone are not enough if the matter involves sin and chastening on the part of the patient, for then confession and restoration to fellowship are essential. **13-14.** Asa's death and burial show the esteem in which he was held and reveal an expanded source unknown to or not used by the writer of Kings.

H. Jehoshaphat's Early Reign. 17:1-19.

Character and Rule of Jehoshaphat. 17:1-6. **1.** Asa's son Jehoshaphat (873-848 B.C., coregency included) evidently was associated in the kingship with his father in the last three or four years of his sick father's reign. Chapters 17 through 20 are devoted to the reign of this king, showing, as in the case of Asa, a considerable expansion of source material from that found in 1 Kings 15:24; 22:1-35, 41-49. The chronicler frequently expands the account of most good kings to show their rewards for their good deeds, as well as their chastisement for the bad things they did. This passage (vv. 1-6) is such an expansion, evidently from sources now lost.

2. Jehoshaphat began his reign by fortifying himself against Israel, stationing troops in all the fortified cities of Judah and placing garrisons throughout the kingdom, especially in the cities of Ephraim that Asa, his father, had taken (15:8), the reference either being to Abijah, Asa's father (13:19), or to some otherwise unrecorded accession of Israelite territory, perhaps just after Asa's victory over Zerah.

3. The chronicler's assessment of Jehoshaphat is given. He followed in **the first** (earlier) **ways of his father,** David (the chronicler tacitly acknowledging that David's later ways were less exemplary; cf. 2 Sam. 11-12), and **sought** (consulted) **not Baalim,** meaning the great Baal of Canaan, the plural being parallel to Elohim (God). **4.** He sought

the God of his father (Asa) and followed His commandments **and not after the doings of Israel** (cf. 1 Kings 12:28-33), his fidelity being contrasted to the apostasy of Israel (the northern tribes).

5. The rewards of Jehoshaphat's faithfulness are outlined, and further evidences of it are listed. **6. He took heart in the ways of the Lord and went on to remove the high places and shame images in Judah** (BV). The "shame images" (*'ašērîm*) were the Asherahs, that is, wooden poles or tree trunks sacred to the worship of the nature goddess, Astarte (Asherah), carved with the female pudenda. Stone pillars carved with the male counterpart (cf. 14:3) stood to one side, with an altar to Baal between the two.

Jehoshaphat as an Educator. 17:7-9. **7-9.** In the third year of his reign (i.e., his sole reign, 866 B.C.), Jehoshaphat sponsored a teaching mission, another example of his zeal for the LORD. The purpose was to instruct the people in **the book of the law** (Torah) **of the Lord,** the Mosaic Torah, the Pentateuch, including Deuteronomy, contrary to critical claims. To accomplish that task he sent out four princes accompanied by eight Levites and two priests.

The perceptive king saw that the teaching of God's Word is the business of *all* leaders who are of the faith (the laity), not just the so-called "clergy" (professional priests and Levites, Lev. 10:11; Deut. 33:10). These instructors filled the role of itinerant preachers and teachers (cf. 3 John 7-8).

Jehoshaphat's Power and Prosperity. 17:10-12. **10-11. The fear of the Lord** fell upon surrounding kingdoms; so instead of provoking war with Jehoshaphat, they placated him with presents and tribute, particularly was this true of the Philistines and the Arabians. Not all five cities of the Philistines were subject to Jehoshaphat (cf. 2 Sam. 8:1). The Arabians were perhaps the nomad Bedouin conquered by Asa (14:15). **12.** Jehoshaphat's greatness is further illustrated by the **fortresses** (fortified towns) **and cities for storage** (store cities) he built to contain his growing wealth.

Jehoshaphat's Military Officials. 17:13-19. **13-19.** This passage furnishes another illustration of Jehoshaphat's blessing because of his loyalty to the LORD. His military organizations in Jerusalem and the defense of his kingdom are described. His central command was located at Jerusalem. The organization focused on the tribal association of Judah and Benjamin, the former directed by a chief of staff and two assistants, and the latter by one chief and one assistant.

I. JEHOSHAPHAT'S ALLIANCE WITH AHAB. 18:1-34.

Jehoshaphat's Visit to Ahab. 18:1-27. **1-27.** See 1 Kings 22:1-35a, from which this chapter is taken almost word for word, except for verses 1 and 2. It constitutes by far the largest body of material from the Northern Kingdom employed by the chronicler. Since he studiously ignores the northern tribes as apostate and not the true Israel, he obviously had cogent reasons for including this extract in his work. Three reasons are:

(1) The story concerned a true prophet of the LORD, Micaiah, photographed against the dark background of the false hireling prophets of Ahab. Moreover, this prophet prophesied to a king of Judah and had some important lessons to teach that were very appropriate to the chronicler's overall message. The chronicler displays a strong leaning toward prophets and their messages that are not mentioned elsewhere

(e.g., 1 Chron. 21:18-19; 2 Chron. 12:5-6; 15:1-7; 16:7-9). He does not include Elijah or Elisha because their activity and message did not touch Judah.

(2) Undoubtedly the chronicler desired to strongly contrast the insistence upon the orthodox faith by the king of Judah with the lawless religion of the north. (3) The story was recounted here to highlight Ahab's wickedness and prepares the way for the timely rebuke administered to Jehoshaphat by the prophet Jehu, the son of Hanani, in the next chapter (19:2-3).

Jehoshaphat's Brush with Death. 18:28-34. **28-32.** Jehoshaphat's compromise with evil almost cost him his life (cf. 2 Cor. 6:14—7:1). Hobnobbing with Ahab, he was mistaken for that wicked king and narrowly escaped death. Only Jehoshaphat's shout to the LORD for help saved him. In the hour of need among such bad companions, he found the LORD did not forsake him. There was an immediate answer, vividly illustrating the power of prayer and God's care for His own.

33-34. Just as Jehoshaphat's life was miraculously spared, so Ahab's was miraculously taken. Since the chronicler had no direct interest in wicked Ahab, only the barest outline of his misfortune is presented and the gory details of his death are passed over. The lesson drawn is vividly presented. Why should Jehoshaphat, blessed by the LORD with great wealth and honor (v. 1), foolishly imagine that he needed a marriage alliance with the apostate Ahab?

Thus, the folly of such an alliance is depicted and its sad results stressed in the succeeding narratives to warn God's people of the peril of helping the evil and loving those who hate the LORD (cf. 19:2), a warning greatly needed in the compromising atmosphere that appears to be deluding God's people as age-end apostasy deepens.

J. THE PROPHETIC REBUKE AND JEHOSHAPHAT'S REFORMS. 19:1-11.

Jehu Rebukes the Compromising King. 19:1-3. **1.** Jehoshaphat's safe return home to Jerusalem is recounted to reflect the LORD's goodness to him despite his compromising folly. **2-3.** The prophet Jehu is pictured going out dramatically to meet the king and rebuking him pointedly, but not with undue severity, softening the condemnation with a word of commendation. Helping the evil and loving those who hate the LORD will necessitate chastening from the LORD (cf. 1 Cor. 5:5; 11:30-32; Heb. 12:3-11). **Nevertheless, there are good things found in thee,** the divine wrath will not pursue to death or destruction (cf. 1 John 5:16). **Thou hast taken away** (swept away) **the idols** (Asherahs; cf. Deut. 13:6; 2 Kings 23:24; see note on 2 Chron. 17:6) **and hast prepared** (determined in your mind) **to seek God,** the contrary of that declared of Rehoboam (12:14).

Reforms Instituted by the King. 19:4-11. **4. He went out,** not necessarily in person, but representatively through the former royal commission for the instruction of the people in the sacred Law (17:7-9). His entire realm was his goal, from the southern extremity, Beersheba, and the northern limit, Mount Ephraim (cf. 13:19-20). His purpose was to bring back the people **unto the Lord God of their fathers** by freeing them of the contamination of Baal worship and Canaanite influence, under which they had fallen. **5-7.** He appointed judges in all the fortified cities of Judah, imbuing them with the truth that they were judging in God's place and therefore were to loathe dishonesty, partiality, and bribery, even as the LORD did.

8-9. Crucial was Jehoshaphat's appointment of priests, Levites, and family heads to handle cases **for the judgment of the Lord** (lit., "for every matter of the LORD"), that is, for all ecclesiastical or religious causes as opposed to civil causes, called **controversies** (*rîb,* "strife, litigation," and in verse 11, "for all the king's matters"). The Jerusalem court was thus composed of priests, civil officials (elders), and Levites. Scholars see Egyptian parallels (cf. W. F. Albright, AMJV, pp. 74-82).

10. In all cases coming before the judges, whether capital or civil, and concerning the interpretation of commandments, statutes, or judgments, the all-important thing was that guilt before the LORD and His consequent wrath be not incurred, manifested in some calamity overtaking the offender. **11.** Amariah, the chief priest, presided over religious cases, and Zebadiah, the leader of the house of Judah, had oversight of civil cases. The Levites were official bailiffs. Decisive action was encouraged, with the LORD invoked on the side of the right.

K. THE LATTER PART OF JEHOSHAPHAT'S REIGN. 20:1-37.

The Invasion of Judah. 20:1-2. **1. It came to pass after this,** that is, after Jehoshaphat's unhappy alliance with Ahab and his religious and civil reformation, that his kingdom was invaded by Moabites, Ammonites, and Meunites (Heb., *Me'ûnîm;* cf. 1 Chron. 4:41-42; 2 Chron. 26:7). **2.** Intelligence reports indicated the invaders had already advanced around the southern end of the Salt (Dead) Sea to Hazazon-tamar in the vicinity of Engedi, midway on the western coast of the Dead Sea. The chronicler stresses a great victory over the enemies of the true faith and features the reward of Jehoshaphat as a king of faith.

596

Jehoshaphat's Great Prayer. 20:3-12. **3.** In fear, the king set himself to seek the LORD and proclaimed a fast as an act of self-humiliation and admission of guilt (cf. Judg. 20:26; 1 Sam. 7:6; Joel 2:12-17). **4.** The nation joined in seeking the LORD. **5.** Jehoshaphat offered a prayer **before the new court,** probably designating the "great" or outer court (4:9) of the Temple, called "new" perhaps because it had recently been repaired or enlarged. **6-12.** The prayer cast the nation upon God's sovereign power, as Asa had done (14:11-12). It recalled the requests made by Solomon at the dedication of the Temple (cf. 1 Kings 8:33-53).

God's Direction Through Jahaziel. 20:13-17. **13-15.** The Spirit of the LORD came upon **Jahaziel ... of the sons of Asaph** with the heartening message: **Thus saith the Lord ... Be not afraid ... of this great multitude ... the battle is not yours, but God's. 16.** The Spirit of God through Jahaziel described exactly where the enemy was to be encountered and defeated on the morrow, namely, in the **wilderness of Jeruel,** southeast of Tekoa on the steep ascent to Engedi. **17.** Fighting would be unnecessary. They were merely to **stand ... still, and see the salvation of the Lord** (cf. Exod. 14:13; Psalm 46:8).

The Victory. 20:18-30. **18-21.** The king, priests, Levites, and people worshiped and praised God, and the next morning they advanced southward to the Tekoa area, urged on to faith in the LORD by the king, who appointed singers to advance before the army, praising the LORD. **22-23.** When they began to sing and praise God, the LORD set ambushes against the invaders; in the ensuing confusion, their enemies fought and killed one another, as in Gideon's wonderful deliverance (Judg. 7:22). **24.** When Judah came to the eminence

overlooking the wilderness in quest of the invading armies, there were only corpses lying on the ground. **25.** It took Jehoshaphat and his people three days to claim the booty. **26.** On the fourth day they assembled in **the Valley of Beracah** ("Valley of Blessing"), where they praised the LORD. **27-28.** Thus, they returned with great joy to Jerusalem and the Temple with harps, zithers, and trumpets. **29.** Fear fell upon all the neighboring nations (cf. Josh. 5:1). **30.** After that God gave Jehoshaphat a peaceful reign, that is, **rest** ("cessation from war") on all sides.

Final Observations on Jehoshaphat's Reign. 20:31-34. **31-33.** Read 1 Kings 22:41-47, which is an adaptation of this section. **34.** The reference to the **book** (word, oracle) **of Jehu, the son of Hanani,** said to contain other acts of Jehoshaphat, is not mentioned in Kings. **The book of the kings of Israel** apparently is the same as "the chronicles of the kings of Judah" (1 Kings 22:45), the variation in name likely due to the chronicler's view that Judah was really the true Israel.

Jehoshaphat's Unsuccessful Maritime Venture. 20:35-37. **35.** The king **did ... join himself** (*'eṯḥabbǎr,* an Aramaism, "formed a partnership or trading syndicate") with Ahaziah, of the apostate Omride dynasty, who reigned in Israel from 853 to 852 B.C. **Who did very wickedly,** that is, Jehoshaphat (the pronoun is emphatic) did (acted) very wickedly, though some scholars apply the pronoun to Ahaziah, implying that Jehoshaphat's association with him was wrong.

36. And he joined himself with him (*wayeḥabberēhû,* "and he joined him with himself," i.e., "formed a maritime partnership with him) **to make ships to go to Tarshish,** that is, of the type that could go to Tarshish (see notes on 8:17-18;

9:21), their destination, of course, being Ophir, and their operation on the Red Sea (Gulf of Aqaba) was out of the port of Ezion-geber.

37. The prophet Eliezer, who denounced Jehoshaphat's association with Ahaziah, is otherwise unknown, but furnishes another instance of the chronicler's use of prophetic warnings (cf. 19:2, etc.). **The Lord hath broken** (a prophetic perfect), the LORD will surely break (wreck) **thy works. The ships were broken** (shattered to pieces) by a gale, for a holy God cannot tolerate unholy alliances. Verse 1 of chapter 21, relating the death of Jehoshaphat, logically terminates this chapter.

L. JEHORAM'S REIGN. 21:1-20.

Jehoram's Removal of Possible Opposition to the Throne. 21:1-4. **1.** Jehoshaphat left the kingdom to his oldest son, Jehoram, who reigned from 848 to 841 B.C., actually being coregent from 853 B.C. (cf. 2 Kings 3:1 with 2 Kings 8:16-17). **2-4.** This chapter reveals the character of the man who married Athaliah, the daughter of Ahab and Jezebel, and who followed their wicked life-style (v. 6).

His cruelty is exemplified in the brutal liquidation of his six brothers, two of whom are referred to by the same name, **Azariah,** although their names are different in Hebrew *(Azaryah* and *Azaryahu).* Although the practice of rooting out possible claimants to the throne was not uncommon, it was no less vicious than in previous cases (cf. Judg. 9:5; 2 Kings 11:1; 2 Chron. 22:10-11). In Jehoram's case it included suspicious Jerusalem officials. Following the policy of his great-grandfather, Rehoboam (11:23), Jehoshaphat had placed his six younger sons in fortified cities of Judah and had made lavish provisions for them.

The Character of Jehoram's Reign. 21:5-7. **5-6.** Jehoram's reign was godless and utterly out of keeping with the divine redemptive purposes through the Davidic dynasty. **7.** Yet the LORD would not destroy the house of David because through it would come what Isaiah later called "the sure mercies of David" (Isa. 55:3), the glorious and unforfeitable salvation that Christ would bring, and the eternal Kingdom of righteousness He would establish in fulfillment of the Davidic Covenant (2 Sam. 7:16; 1 Chron. 17:14; Psalm 89:3-4; Luke 1:31-33).

The Davidic Covenant was guaranteed by the divine promise **to give a light** (lamp) to David and his successors in the royal Messianic line **forever** (2 Sam. 7:12-13; 1 Kings 11:36; 2 Kings 8:19). Evil men and their dark deeds in this line (like Jehoram) could not extinguish that light; it would eventually be realized in the greater David, "the light of the world" (John 8:12).

Revolt of Edom and Libnah. 21:8-11. **8.** Jehoram's punishment for his wickedness first appears in the revolt of Edom from **the dominion of Judah** (cf. 2 Kings 8:20). Evidently the Edomites threw off the authority of the deputy or viceroy who ruled Edom for Judah (cf. 1 Kings. 22:47). **9-10.** Verse 9 does not relate a victory of Jehoram, but rather his desperate escape from enemy encirclement and his total failure to quell the rebellion in **Edom. Libnah** likewise revolted against him because God was punishing him for his apostasy (see notes on 2 Kings 8:22). Further examples of Jehoram's apostasy are given.

11. He (emphatic), in contrast with Asa and Jehoshaphat, his worthier predecessors (14:2-3; 17:6), **made high places in the mountains** ("cities," LXX, Vulgate) of Judah for the worship of pagan gods as well as the worship of the

LORD. He caused the inhabitants of Jerusalem **to be unfaithful** (spiritually untrue to the LORD; cf. Hos. 2:5, 7, 13; 1 Chron. 5:25) and **led** ("seduced") **Judah astray** (Deut. 13:6, 11).

Elijah's Letter to Jehoram. 21:12-15. **12-15.** Elijah's ministry, insofar as recorded activity is concerned, ended in 852 B.C. (2 Kings 1:3, 17). However, his translation may not have taken place until after Jehoram's foul crime of slaying all his brothers, following his accession to the throne in 848 B.C. In any case, Elijah had received the divine message concerning Jehoram's fate and had written it down. By the time of the delivery of his written communication, he had already gone, and so its message of judgment came almost as a voice from heaven, to which the venerable prophet and foe of the house of Ahab had been translated.

The Fulfillment of Elijah's Predictions. 21:16-19a. **16-19a.** Elijah's two predictions were fulfilled: (1) **The Lord stirred up ... the spirit of the Philistines, ... Arabians,** and the **Ethiopians** (Cushites) who were nearby, apparently the settlers around Gerar from the time of Shishak (see 14:8-14). They invaded Jehoram's kingdom and plundered the king's house, together with his sons and his wives, leaving only Jehoram's youngest son, **Jehoahaz,** in fulfillment of verse 14. (2) The LORD afflicted Jehoram with **an incurable disease** of the bowels so that **his intestines fell out** (i.e., "protruded") and he died of **severe diseases** ("in terrible pain," cf. Deut. 29:21), in fulfillment of verse 15.

Jehoram's Ignoble End. 21:19b-20. **19b.** The usual honors at the interment of a king were denied Jehoram. His people did not provide for him a **burning** in the form of a kindling of fragrant spices about the royal corpse, as in the case of his fathers (cf. 16:14). **20.** He passed away **without being desired** (unlamented) and was denied burial in the cemetery of the kings.

M. THE REIGN OF AHAZIAH, AND ATHALIAH'S USURPATION. 22:1-12.

Ahaziah's Brief Reign. 22:1-9. **1.** The Jerusalem citizenry **made Ahaziah ... king** (841 B.C.). Apparently the succession was disputed (cf. 2 Kings 23:30), perhaps by the ruthless Athaliah, the king's own mother (cf. 2 Chron. 22:10), so the people intervened. **The band of men,** the freebooters who had come with the Arabs against the Israelite camp, had murdered all the older sons of Jehoram, leaving only Ahaziah, the youngest, as claimant to the throne.

2. Ahaziah was forty and two years old (a copyist's error for twenty-two; cf. 21:5; 2 Kings 8:26) **and he reigned one year,** only for part of it (cf. 2 Kings 8:25; 3:1). **3.** His mother, **Athaliah,** is said to be **the daughter** (i. e., the granddaughter) of Omri, the usage linking her to the wicked Omride dynasty. The notice that Ahaziah's **mother was his counselor** emphasizes the baneful influence that evil woman exerted as a patron of Baalism and all its concomitant immoralities and pollutions. **4.** Little wonder **he did evil ... like the house of Ahab,** and **they were his counselors ... to his destruction.**

5. Following their advice, Ahaziah went with Jehoram, Ahab's son, to fight against Hazael at Ramoth-gilead. This was some dozen years after Ahab's mortal wounding suffered in fighting against the city in 853 B.C. (18:34). Meanwhile, Ahab's second son, Joram, had retaken the town. Hazael, the new king of Aram, reattacked the city (2 Kings 9:14-15) and in the fighting wounded Joram. **6.** It was while Joram was recuperating at Jezreel, at the head of the Valley of Esdraelon, the site of Ahab's summer palace (1 Kings 21:1),

that Ahaziah went down to see him. **7.**
All that was God's doing, to effect
Ahaziah's downfall that he might be cut
down by Jehu, the divinely anointed
exterminator of Ahab's house (2 Kings
9). **8.** Jehu also slew the sons of
Ahaziah's brothers (v. 1; cf. 2 Kings
10:12-14; 2 Chron. 21:4).

9. After Joram, the king of Israel, was
killed, his nephew Ahaziah fled to
Samaria, but was overtaken by Jehu,
who fatally wounded him near Ibleam,
on the way to Jezreel. He fled northwest
to Megiddo and died (see notes on 2
Kings 9:27). His servants carried his
corpse to Jerusalem for burial (2 Kings
9:28). The chronicler thus details how
sin brings its own punishment. **So the
house of Ahaziah had no power** (lit.,
"had none to retain strength for kingship"), that is, no one capable of assuming rule over the kingdom. This
marks the transition to the notice of
Athaliah's usurpation.

Athaliah Seizes Power. 22:10-12. **10.**
Learning her son was dead, Athaliah
immediately exterminated all the royal
seed of the Davidic line, a bold stroke of
satanic power working through this
wicked woman to destroy the Messianic
line, which almost succeeded; it was
similar to the satanic attempt through
King Herod to destroy the seed itself
(Gen. 3:15; Matt. 2).

11. But Joash, the sole surviving son
of Ahaziah, was hidden by Jehosha-
beath (Jehosheba, 2 Kings 11:1-3), the
daughter of King Joram and sister of
Ahaziah, and the wife of Jehoiada, the
high priest. She illustrates the marriage
and blood ties between the royal and
high-priestly families. Jehosheba
stowed Joash away **in a bedchamber**
(lit., "in the chamber of the beds," i.e.,
where the bedding was stored; see notes
on 2 Kings 11:2), from Athaliah, thus
preserving the rightful heir to the

Davidic throne. This preservation of the
sole heir was extremely important to the
divine redemptive plan and the chronicler's purpose in writing his religious
"history."

12. For six years Joash remained hidden with the high priest and his wife in
the Temple while **Athaliah reigned over
the land.** Meanwhile, the queen thought
she was ruling in her own name because
she believed all the royal issue had been
wiped out, but that was not the official
view. She was really a usurper, or at
most, a regent, because Joash was living. Then, too, no queen ruled in her
own name, either in Israel or Judah,
though at times one was regent.

N. THE DEPOSITION OF ATHALIAH. 23:1-21.

The Crowning of Joash. 23:1-11. **1.**
The high priest Jehoiada in the seventh
year **strengthened himself** ("showed
himself courageous") to bring matters
to a head. He determined to make a pact
with **the captains of hundreds** ("the Ca-
rians," the royal bodyguard) "and the
runners, couriers or royal messengers"
(cf. 2 Kings 11:4). **2.** Secretly, he assembled **the Levites . . . and the heads of
the fathers** (cf. v. 13).

3. The assembled company **made a
covenant with the king,** that is, "[Je-
hoiada] made a covenant with them" (2
Kings 11:4) and imposed a solemn
agreement upon them, making them
swear fidelity to the young prince (cf. 2
Sam. 3:21; 5:3). **The king's son shall
reign** (better, "Behold, the king's son!
Let him be king!"), **as the Lord hath
said,** as stipulated in the Davidic Covenant (2 Sam. 7:4-17).

4-6. Jehoiada outlined the strategy for
the crowning of Joash and the overthrow of Athaliah. On the Sabbath,
when there was a changing of the Levitical courses (1 Chron. 24:3,19), of those

coming on duty one-third were to be stationed at the gates of the Temple "behind the guard" to "keep the watch of the house" (2 Kings 11:6) to prevent the entrance of unauthorized non-Levitical personnel.

7. Another third were to surround the king and guard him when he entered and departed. The remaining third were to oversee the gate of Sur (2 Kings 11:6), **the gate of the foundation.** Apparently Jehoiada combined the royal guard with the Levitical workers so that the united body might be coordinated under the direction of the royal bodyguard.

8. All Jehoiada's directions were carefully followed in the case of those who came on as well as those who went off Sabbath duty, for he did not release any division (Levitical course) from duty. **9-10.** He armed the bodyguard with King David's spears and shields, which were in the Temple, stationing all the people to guard the king, each with his weapon in hand.

11. Then **they brought out the king's son ... put upon him the crown** (Exod. 29:6; 2 Sam. 1:10) **and gave him the testimony** (*hā-'ēdūt*), a scroll of the ten words (Exod. 25:21-22; 31:18). Perhaps the latter was placed on the king's shoulder or wrapped around his diadem. **And Jehoiada and his sons anointed him** (cf. 1 Kings 1:39), the chronicler emphasizing the fact that it was the priests who performed the anointing.

The Execution of Athaliah. 23:12-15. See 2 Kings 11:13-20. **12-13.** When Athaliah heard "the noise of the people, the couriers, and those who were acclaiming the king" (lit. Heb. trans.), she came into the house of the LORD and saw the king standing **at his pillar at the entrance ... then** Athaliah tore her clothes in fear and rage, crying, **Treason! Treason!** (the repetition signifying intensification, *base treason!*).

14. Jehoiada gave orders to **have her forth between the ranks,** that is, "make her go out between the ranks of guards." **15.** She was slain outside the holy Temple precincts at the entrance of the horse gate of the king's house.

The Religious Reformation. 23:16-21. **16.** The theocratic covenant was renewed and Baal worship extirpated as the Davidic dynasty was purged of association with evil Athaliah. In making the covenant, the chronicler regards Jehoiada, the high priest, as the LORD's representative in the transaction to avoid the irreverence of making deity a direct co-partner with men in the transaction. The Kings passage adds, "and between the king and the people" (2 Kings 11:17), an important item relating to certain limitations of the kingly prerogative, which were customarily defined and agreed upon at the commencement of a reign (2 Sam. 3:21; 5:3).

17. The house of Baal and the priest of Baal were wiped out. **18-19.** Jehoiada ordained a return to the Law of Moses and the observance of the orders established by David, and appointed porters for the gates of the Temple so its sacred holiness might not be violated. **20.** Then the king was conducted to the palace and enthroned there. **21.** So **the people of the land rejoiced; and the city was quiet.** The greatest impediment to their joy and peace (Athaliah, the wicked queen) had been removed, **slain ... with the sword.**

O. JOASH'S REIGN. 24:1-27.

Joash's Early Reign. 24:1-16. **1-2.** Joash reigned from 835 to 796 B.C. His early reign under the guiding hand of Jehoiada was good. **3.** Jehoiada selected two wives for him, a detail not mentioned in 2 Kings 12. **4.** The repair of the Temple was the chief work of the early period of Joash's reign. Renovation was needed because of the vandalism in the sacred precincts perpetrated by Athaliah's sons (perhaps Ahaziah and his older brothers), no doubt to gratify the queen's detestation of the exclusive worship of the LORD.

5. Joash's plan was for the priests and Levites to go out annually to the cities of Judah and collect money. But the Levites dallied. 6. Joash suggested **the collection** (tax) that Moses and the Israelites had imposed for the tent of testimony. Compare 2 Kings 12:4, which specifies the three sources of revenue: (1) "the dedicated things" of "every one that passeth the account," namely, the half shekel collected at the census (Exod. 30:14); (2) the evaluation at which every man is set in substitutionary redemptions (Lev. 22:1-8; Num. 18:15-16); and (3) voluntary gifts.

8-11. Joash's successful method for collecting funds is given (cf. 2 Kings 12:9-11). 13-14. The money was used only for repairs until the renovation was completed (cf. 2 Kings 12:13-14). As in 2 Kings 12:15, the honesty and faithfulness of the workmen are stressed. Thus, Joash honored the LORD in caring for the Temple and its priestly and sacrificial ritual, depicting God's great plan of salvation by grace through faith. 15-16. But Jehoiada's death, with the loss of his good influence, was to have a bad effect upon the king.

The Later Reign of Joash. 24:17-22. 17-18. Under Jehoiada's strong, godly hand, Joash honored the LORD, at least outwardly. But when that beneficent influence was removed, the king reversed the policy of the late high priest. He yielded to pressure to compromise with Baalism, serving the Asherahs and pagan images, so that wrath came upon Judah and Jerusalem for their guilt. 19. The LORD sent prophets, but the people threatened them and turned a deaf ear. 20-21. When **the Spirit . . . came upon** ("clothed Himself with") **Zechariah,** the son of the great and faithful Jehoiada (cf. 1 Chron. 12:18), and he prophesied against the king and his officials because of their defection from the LORD, they conspired against him, and at the king's order, stoned him in the LORD's house.

22. When he was dying, Zechariah cried, **The Lord look upon it, and require it.** Contrast his dying words to those of Stephen (Acts 7:60). Zechariah represents the Tribulation martyrs, who will give testimony concerning the coming King at the end of this age, and whose blood will cry out for vengeance (Rev. 6:9-11), as in the imprecatory psalms, which depict the same scenes (cf. Psalms 35, 69, 109, 139; see Merrill F. Unger, *Unger's Guide to the Bible,* p. 176). Our Lord referred to this incident (Matt. 23:35), calling the martyr the "son of Barachiah" ("blessed of the LORD"), apparently another name for the God-blessed Jehoiada.

Joash's Severe Chastisement and End. 24:23-27. **23-24.** A small detachment of the Syrian army invaded Judah and Jerusalem and defeated a large army of Joash, taking away great spoil to Hazael. This included all the wealth accumulated since the reign of Asa (cf. 16:2; 2 Kings 12:18), whose sin reaped a belated harvest (cf. 2 Chron. 16:10). That a large Judean army should fall to a small company of the enemy dovetails with what Moses foretold (Lev. 26:17).

25. The Aramaean invaders left Joash **in great diseases** (*māḥᵃlūyim,* a rare word occurring only here, which many construe as "wounds," the probable meaning being "pains" or "suffering"). **His own servants conspired against him** and slew him in his sickbed. Second Kings 12:21 specifies his burial "with his fathers in the city of David," but with the note that it was **not in the sepul-**

chers of the kings (cf. v. 16).

26. His conspirators are listed. **27. The greatness of the burdens ... upon him** refers to "the many prophetic oracles against him" (*măśśā'*, "burden"), is common as a weighty, threatening prophecy (2 Kings 9:25; Isa. 13:1; Hab. 1:1, etc.). **27. The story of the book of the kings** is "the commentary [*mĭdrăsh*] on the chronicle of the kings," *midrash* being a study or presentation of an earlier work.

P. AMAZIAH'S REIGN. 25:1-28.

Accession of Amaziah. 25:1-4. **1-2.** Amaziah reigned from 796 to 767 B.C. **He did that which was right ... but not with a perfect heart**—not wholeheartedly. **3-4.** When the sovereignty was confirmed to him, he executed his father's murderers, but not their children (see 2 Kings 14:6), in accordance with the Mosaic Law (Deut. 24:16).

Amaziah's Conquest of Edom. 25:5-13. This section, expanding on Amaziah's military strength, is largely peculiar to Chronicles and only mentioned in a single verse in Kings (2 Kings 14:7). **5.** He **gathered Judah together** (lit., "made them stand," marshaled them) according to families, that is, according to the **captains over thousands, ... and hundreds.** He also **numbered** (registered, mustered them) from **twenty years old,** the military age (Num. 1:2-3; 1 Chron. 27:23), totaling three hundred thousand select warriors, considerably less than the army of Asa or Jehoshaphat (cf. 14:8; 17:14-18).

6-9. His hiring an army out of Israel for 100 talents of silver (about 3¼ tons) provoked prophetic rebuke. **10.** Fortunately, the king listened and dismissed the army, placing his trust in God instead of man, as had his fathers (cf. 14:11; 20:12), but the men of the Northern Kingdom returned home in a rage. In his campaign against Seir (Edom), he reconquered a people with terrible cruelty who had enjoyed a half century of independence from Judah (cf. 21:8).

11. The Valley of Salt is identified with Wadi el-Milh, east of Beersheba, by Abel (*Géographie de la Palestine,* 1:407), and by Grollenberg and others with the Arabah, south of the Salt Sea. **12.** The rock from which the Judahites hurled ten thousand prisoners to their death is identified with Umm el Biyarah (AASOR 14 [1934] :77; and 15 [1935] :49).

13. In their anger, the troops he had hired and then sent back from accompanying him to battle, plundered the frontier cities of Benjamin to compensate for their exclusion from the victory over Edom. Thus, Amaziah's attempt to lure these mercenaries, proof of his unbelief in the LORD, brought about its own punishment (v. 5), the chronicler displaying particular interest in exhibiting the principle that "God is not mocked; for whatever a man sows, this he will also reap" (Gal. 6:7, NASB).

Amaziah's Idolatrous Defection. 25:14-16. **14.** Evidently the victory over Edom inflated Amaziah's pride and vanity, shown in his bringing **the gods** (images) **of the children of Seir** and setting them up to be **his gods.** Assyrian kings often carried off the idols of conquered peoples to add to the deities they worshiped.

15. Amaziah fell into ungodly syncretism, utterly obnoxious to the LORD, kindling the divine wrath and provoking prophetic rebuke. How utterly unreasonable to adopt gods that had proven themselves utterly powerless to **deliver their own people,** furnishing an example of the blind, demonic deception that settles upon idolaters (cf. 1 Cor. 10:20). **16.** At least Amaziah's wickedness did not approach Joash's murder of

Zechariah, and went no farther than threats (cf. 24:20-21). Amaziah's conduct was evidence enough that God had **determined** ("counseled," the prophet graphically employing the king's own word) to **destroy** him, that is, cut off his physical life prematurely because of the "sin unto [physical] death" (1 John 5:16; cf. 1 Cor. 11:30-32).

Amaziah's Tragically Foolish War with Israel. 25:17-24. **17.** Amaziah's victory over Edom inflated his ego and emboldened his vanity and pride to attack a far stronger power than Edom (see notes on 2 Kings 14:8-14). **18-19.** The northern ruler, Joash (Jehoash; 798-782 B.C.), sensibly pointed that out in his graphic fable. **21-24.** The clash at Beth-shemesh, located west of Bethlehem in Judah, resulted in utter rout for the insolent Amaziah and due punishment for his idolatries, especially the rifling of Jerusalem and its treasures and the taking of hostages.

Amaziah's Tragic End. 25:25-28. **25.** Amaziah's defection from the LORD eventuated in conspiracy against him and death. **28.** He was buried in **the city of Judah** (2 Kings 14:20; "the city of David," Jerusalem). But the chronicler's terminology is correct, for Jerusalem is called that in the Babylonian Chronicle (D. J. Wiseman, *Chronicles of Chaldean Kings (626-556 B.C.) in the British Museum*, p. 73).

Q. UZZIAH'S REIGN. 26:1-23.

The Beginning of Uzziah's Reign. 26:1-5. **1-5.** Amaziah's son, Uzziah (792 to 739 B.C., coregencies included) was also named Azariah, his personal name, while Uzziah was evidently his throne name. This section corresponds with 2 Kings 14:21—15:4, except that the chronicler omits any reference to Uzziah's failure to remove the high places and that the king **sought God** as long as

Zechariah, his religious adviser, lived (cf. Joash, 24:2, 17-22).

In line with his theological viewpoint, he stresses that as long as **he sought the Lord, God made him prosper.** He rebuilt Eloth, the seaport founded by Solomon at the head of the Gulf of Aqaba (8:17-18; 1 Kings 9:26-28), and restored it to Judah about sixty years after it had fallen under Edomite control under Jehoram of Judah (2 Kings 8:21-22).

Uzziah's Conquests. 26:6-8. **6-8.** These victories were possible since both Judah under Uzziah and Israel under Jeroboam II enjoyed freedom from the Syrian threat on the north because of Assyrian expansion there, but Assyria was not yet readied for her later destruction of the Hebrew states (cf. 2 Kings 15:19-22). So Israel enjoyed an "Indian summer" for expansion from about 790 to 750 B.C.

Uzziah had signal success in reducing the Philistine power and the Arabs residing on the southwestern borders of Judah, constructing fortresses in the occupied territory. Gur-baal is unknown. The Meunites (mentioned in 1 Chron. 4:41; Ezra 2:50; Neh. 7:52) were probably Maonites, with their original center at Maʿan, southeast of Petra.

Public Works and Internal Development. 26:9-10. **9.** Uzziah fortified the walls and gates of Jerusalem at the northwest, west, and east points of the wall (Neh. 3:19-25). **10.** He erected **towers in the desert** (the grazing country) to protect the royal herdsmen against predatory Bedouin (cf. Mic. 4:8). He **digged many wells** ("carved out many cisterns") to catch rain water for his herds in the Shephelah and in the plains. He had **husbandmen** ("farmers," I. Mendelsohn, BASOR 167 [Oct. 1962]:34) **... for he loved husbandry** (lit., "the land").

Abundant evidence for these activities of Uzziah abound in numerous excavated sites in the Negev around Beersheba, where cisterns, farms, and artifacts have been located (cf. Nelson Glueck, *Rivers in the Desert,* pp. 174-79; and R. L. Schiffer, "The Farms of King Uzziah," *The Reporter* 23 [Sept. 1, 1960] :3 4-38). Important persons during that period identified themselves as his "servants," as evidenced by recovered seals, especially the Azariah seal found in a cistern at Tell Beit Mirsim (W. F. Albright, AASOR 21-22[1943] :63-65, 73).

Armed Forces and Military Power. 26:11-15. **11-13.** Uzziah's conquests naturally required a strong military organization. His army of 307,500 is comparable in size to Amaziah's fighting force (25:5; but see G. E. Mendenhall, JBL 77[1958] :52-66, for an interpretation of these numbers on the basis of *'ĕlĕp,* "thousand," denoting a unit and thus yielding 600 chiefs for 7,500 men in 300 units). **14.** It is noteworthy that no longer did the soldiers supply their own arms, but were armed by the king. **15.** Uzziah also had a military research department, setting up skillfully invented devices on the towers of Jerusalem (cf. v. 9), from which to shoot arrows and hurl large stones. The defense of Lachish illustrates Uzziah's type of military innovations (ANET, pp. 130-31). The chronicler connects Uzziah's great fame to his being miraculously assisted by the LORD.

Uzziah's Sin and Downfall. 26:16-21. **16.** This section is mainly unique to the chronicler, 2 Kings 15:5-7 corresponding only to verses 21-23. Uzziah's great prosperity became his undoing. **His heart was lifted up** (with pride) even to his destruction, (lit., "to acting perversely, wickedly"). He was unfaithful to the LORD in intruding into the holy place and burning incense on the golden

altar, contrary to the Law, which rigidly restricted activity to the priesthood (v. 18; Num. 18:1-7; cf. Exod. 30:7-8).

Inflated with pride, Uzziah appears to have desired to become supreme pontiff as well as king, implying his claim to the Canaanite office of divine king-priest (see Gen. 14:18; cf. Num. 12:1-2, 10). It was not that he merely revived a precedent of David and Solomon, as some think, for it can scarcely be proved that these monarchs ever actually performed the distinctive priestly functions, as Uzziah did. Saul's conduct and its consequences (1 Sam. 13:9) point to the same conclusion.

17-19. Azariah, the high priest, and **valiant men** ("sons of valor") are so described because they had the moral courage to oppose (*'āmăḏ 'ăl,* "stand against") the king. Uzziah **was angry** (*zā'ăp,* "enraged"). His punishment was the same as that which befell Miriam (Num. 12:10) and Gehazi (2 Kings 5:27).

20. The priests **thrust** (*hiḇhîl,* "hustled") him out. He **hastened** (thrust himself) **out,** for it was plain to all that the **Lord had smitten** (struck) him in judgment (2 Kings 15:5). **21.** As a leper to the day of his death, Uzziah dwelt in **a separate house** (*bêṯ hăḥŏpshîṯ,* "quarantine ward," a term occurring in the Ugaritic texts as *btḥptṯ,* "house of pollution"; see John Gray, *The Legacy of Canaan,* p. 46, n. 1). **Jotham,** his son, assumed control as regent from about 751 to 739 B.C.

Uzziah's Death. 26:22-23. **22.** Notation is made that Isaiah, son of Amoz, wrote the remainder of Uzziah's history. **23.** Uzziah was interred in the field beside the cemetery of the kings, because he was a leper. His pride, and the sin in which it led him, followed him even in death.

R. JOTHAM'S REIGN. 27:1-9.

General Observations. 27:1-2. **1.** Uzziah's son Jotham (750-732 B.C., coregencies included) continued the attitude and policies of his father. The seal of Jotham was found at Ezion-geber, giving evidence of the continuity of administrative activity at the seaport on the Gulf of Aqaba (N. Glueck, BASOR 79[Oct. 1940]:13-15; and N. Avingnad, BASOR [Oct. 1961]:18-22).

2. Jotham **did . . . right in the sight of the Lord . . . howbeit** (however) **he entered not into the temple of the Lord,** perhaps because of resentment for the severe punishment inflicted upon his father in those holy precincts. Also the people **did . . . corruptly** (acted perversely; cf. 2 Kings 15:35).

Jotham's Building Activity. 27:3-4. **3.** He constructed the upper gate of the Temple and built extensively **on the wall of Ophel,** the citadel hill, the southern slope of the Temple hill, comprising a line of fortifications connecting Zion with Moriah, on which Uzziah had already worked (26:9), and which fortified the city from attacks from the south and east.

4. He also built cities in the hill country of Judah (cf. 26:10). On wooded heights he erected **fortresses** (*bīrāniyôt*) and **towers** for defense. Contemporary prophets looked askance at such trust in the arm of flesh instead of the LORD (cf. Psalm 18:1-2; Isa. 2:12-15; 12:2; 17:3-4; Hos. 8:14).

War Against the Ammonites. 27:5-6. **5.** Jotham prevailed in the Ammonite campaign and the Ammonites paid him high tribute for three years—100 talents of silver; 10,000 measures (about 105,000 bushels) of wheat, and the same amount of barley. **6.** Jotham became mighty because he established his ways before God.

Jotham's Obituary. 27:7-9. **7-9.**

Verse 8 repeats verse 1. Jotham's burial was in the city of David. His son Ahaz coreigned with him from 743 B.C. (cf. 26:21) and succeeded him.

S. AHAZ'S REIGN. 28:1-27.

Character of Ahaz. 28:1-4. Ahaz (736-716 B.C., coregencies included) was one of the weakest and most apostate incumbents of the Davidic throne. Both the parallel account in 2 Kings 16 and the chronicler present his reign in two stages. The first deals with his religious declension and resultant subjection to attack by the Syro-Ephraimite coalition (2 Chron. 28:1-7). The second involves his bowing to Assyria and his implication in the idolatries of his new overlords (vv. 16-27). Sandwiched between these accounts the chronicler has new material not recorded in Kings concerning the prophecy of Oded (vv. 8-15).

1-4. Ahaz's weak character is summarized: (1) He did not do what was right in the LORD's sight; (2) **he walked in the ways of the kings of Israel,** the worst thing that could be said of a king of Judah; (3) he **made . . . melted . . . images for Baalim** (the plural form of "Baal," being parallel to Elohim; cf. 27:3); (4) he **burned incense** in the valley of Hinnom, at the southeast corner of Jerusalem, where children were sacrificed (cf. 2 Kings 23:10; Jer. 7:31-32), *gê'-hinnōm* ("valley of Hinnom") giving rise to later "Gehenna," designating eternal separation from God (hell); (5) thus, Ahaz was polluted with all the **abominations** (customs associated with gross idolatry) **of the nations;** and (6) he desecrated the worship of the LORD with foul and cruel pagan rites.

The Syro-Ephraimite War. 28:5-8. **5-8.** This war was a calamity presented as a divine judgment upon Ahaz for his defection. The cause of the war is given in 2 Kings 15:37; 16:5; Isaiah 7; and

Hosea 5:8—6:6, where it is stated that Judah was invaded and Jerusalem besieged. Nothing is said here about the attack on Jerusalem, but the ferocious cruelty of Pekah, king of Israel, and Rezin, king of Syria (Aram), vented on Judah is stressed as an introduction to Oded's prophecy. Ahaz's army was cut to pieces, large numbers of captives were taken to Damascus and to northern Israel, prominent citizens were slain, and huge quantities of booty were taken. It is stressed that it happened **because they had forsaken the Lord God of their fathers** (cf. v. 2).

The Prophecy of Oded. 28:9-15. **9.** Oded, the otherwise unknown prophet of the Northern Kingdom, went out to meet the returning army that had devastated Judah (like Azariah ben Oded, 15:1-2). The fearless man of God warned that the victory over Judah was due to the LORD's punitive wrath, not to their own valor or superiority.

For that reason, compassion, not savage hatred, should have been shown the victims of divine displeasure, whom they frightfully massacred **in a rage** that literally **reacheth up unto heaven** (cf. Gen. 28:12; Ezra 4:6), in a guilty excess of cruelty calling for heaven's vengeance, like the blood of Abel (Gen. 4:10) or Sodom's sin (Gen. 18:20-21; Ezra 9:6).

10. In their plan to subjugate the Judeans as their slaves, he told them to consider whether they themselves were wholly guiltless when their anger was so intense against their brethren (cf. Gen. 20:11; Job 1:15). **11.** The prophet's strong advice was that they return the captives; otherwise **the fierce wrath of the Lord** would be upon them (lit., "the heat of anger"), since the Mosaic Law strictly forbids the permanent enslavement of Israelites by Israelites (Lev. 25:39).

12-13. The prophet's message was effective. The Ephraimite chiefs, specifically named, appealed to the army to relent, stressing the fact that they had already **offended against** the LORD and must not add guilt to that which was already sufficient to bring fierce wrath **against Israel. 14-15.** The result was a beautiful demonstration of love, even to the enemy (Exod. 23:4; Prov. 24:17; Matt. 5:44).

Ahaz's Appeal to Assyria. 28:16-21. **16.** Rejecting the LORD, in 734 B.C. Ahaz put his faith instead in the king of Assyria, Tiglath-pileser III (c. 744-727 B.C.) and sought his aid. **17.** He was desperate because the Edomites had invaded his realm on the southeast and carried away captives. **18-19.** The Philistines also had invaded the Shephelah west of Jerusalem and the Negev on the southwest and taken the cities enumerated in that area, for the LORD had humbled Judah because of Ahaz's unrestrained sin against Him.

20-21. Ahaz's idolatry had befuddled and made a fool of him, for Tiglath-pileser was to prove a poor substitute for the help of the LORD. Isaiah had vainly attempted to avert Ahaz from his folly, which was a breach of trust in the LORD (Isa. 7:4-9). Ahaz's move was not only unnecessary; it reduced Judah to the status as a tributary to Assyria, causing Israel's deportation—three and one-half tribes in 733 B.C. (2 Kings 15:29), and the rest in 722 B.C. (17:6). Moreover, it led to Judah's own devastation under the iron heel of Sennacherib's army in 701 B.C. (18:13). Foolishly, Ahaz impoverished himself materially as well as spiritually, but received no help from Assyria.

Ahaz's Further Apostasy and End. 28:22-27. **22.** Ahaz was of a peculiar stripe of wickedness. At the very time he was oppressed, he continued to wrong the LORD. **23.** He was a royal donkey in whose case divine chastisement beat no sense into his head but, rather, beat out of it what little sense that may have been there. His spiritual idiocy is seen in his offering sacrifices to **the gods of Damascus, which smote him** (through Resin), reasoning that if these gods helped his foes, they would now help him.

But they served only to cause him to stumble into ruin and all **Israel** (meaning Judah, as usual) with him, illustrated by what he did. **24-25.** He stripped the Temple of its equipment, sealed up its doors, made altars for himself to offer sacrifices to pagan gods in every corner of Jerusalem, and made **high places** for pagan worship throughout Judah. **27.** Ahaz was buried in Jerusalem, but his ignominy kept him from a sepulcher in the royal cemetery.

T. HEZEKIAH'S REIGN. 29:1-36.

Introductory Remarks Concerning Hezekiah's Reign. 29:1-2. **1.** Hezekiah reigned from 715 to 686 B.C. (including coregencies; on the complex problems involved, see Edwin R. Thiele, *The Mysterious Numbers of the Hebrew Kings,* pp. 118-40). **2.** Hezekiah **did ... right ... according to all that David his father had done.**

Call to Cleanse the House of God. 29:3-11. **3.** He began his good reign by cleansing the Temple **in the first month** (Nisan) of the sacred year. He **opened the doors,** which his wicked father, Ahaz, had closed (28:24), **and repaired them** by overlaying them with gold (cf. 2 Kings 18:16). **4.** He convened the priests and Levites on **the east street** (the plaza or open place apparently in front of the eastern gate of the sacred enclosure). **5.** There the king solemnly charged them to cleanse the house of God, which involved six things: (1) It was to be done

by sanctifying themselves first (cf. 1 Chron. 15:12, 14), and then by (2) cleansing the house of God by removing all traces of idolatry and carrying forth **the filthiness** (*nĭddâ,* "personal impurity," Lev. 12:2; Ezek. 18:6), that is, anything loathsome (Ezek. 7:9) connected with idolatrous worship. **6.** This condition of God's house was due to the the fact that their **fathers** (ancestors) had **trespassed** (acted faithlessly) and **turned their backs** on God's house, instead of their faces toward it.

7. (3) They had to reinstate the holy sacrifices and priestly worship. It was not enough merely to cleanse away the defiling debris of idolatry; they had to open **the porch** of the holy place, or nave, and provide access to the two holy chambers. They had to light the seven-branched lampstand, prefiguring God's gracious gospel light through the coming Messiah. They had to rekindle the sacred incense, bespeaking prayer and praise rising to God, and offer the burnt offering, looking forward to vicarious atoning sacrifice to bring sinful man to God. Ahaz's perverted ritual was counted worthless (2 Kings 16:14-15).

8-9. (4) They had to turn away God's wrath, delivering them **to trouble, to astonishment, and to hissing** (cf. Deut. 28:25, 37; Jer. 25:9, 18). What they saw with their own eyes was evidence enough—the cruel invasions of Syria (Aram), Israel, and Edom, and the terrible specter of the Assyrian menace. **10.** (5) They had to join their king in making a covenant with **the Lord God of Israel** to turn back to God. **11.** (6) They could not be remiss in rising to their high calling as God's servants and ministers in holy priestly and Levitical tasks.

The House of God Cleansed. 29:12-17. **12-14. Then the Levites arose ...** (their names are given according to the Kohath [Kehath] , Merari, and Gershon families, showing their importance and the dignity of their calling). **15. They gathered ... and sanctified themselves ... to cleanse the house of the Lord.**

16. The priests went into the inner part of the Temple, which the Levites were not allowed to enter, **and brought out all the uncleanness,** not just dirt, the accumulation of neglect, but Ahaz's filthy idolatries and their paraphernalia (cf. 2 Kings 16:15). And the Levites carried them out to the brook (wadi) Kidron, where Asa had burned the idolatrous abominations of the queen grandmother (2 Chron. 15:16). **17.** The consecration of the Temple, begun in the first day of the month, was completed in sixteen days.

Rededication of the Temple. 29:18-30. **18-19.** The report of the completed work of cleansing was made to Hezekiah. **20-22.** The king assembled the chiefs of the city, and they brought animals for a sin offering for the royal house, the sanctuary, and Judah, instructing the priests to offer them on the LORD's altar, which was done with the prescribed sprinkling of blood. **23-24.** Then the goats were offered for the sin offering and a burnt offering and sin offering for all Israel (see Lev. 1 for the burnt offering; and Lev. 4 for the sin offering, pointing to God's plan for human redemption).

25-29. The Levitical choirs and musicians performed while the priests blew trumpets in connection with the offering of the burnt offering, as the whole congregation and the king worshiped. **30.** The Levites praised the LORD with the words of David and Asaph the seer.

Offerings Brought for the Occasion. 29:31-36. **31-34.** All these offerings speak of the believer's consecration to God and his gratitude and praise for such a great salvation as that which God's grace provides. **35-36.** In this manner the service of the LORD's house was reinstituted and everyone rejoiced because the matter had been carried out so expeditiously.

U. HEZEKIAH'S PASSOVER CELEBRATION. 30:1-27.

Preparations for the Celebration. 30:1-12. **1.** Hezekiah sent out an invitation to **all Israel and Judah** (i.e., "from Beersheba to Dan," v. 5) and **wrote letters ... to Ephraim and Manasseh,** specifically inviting the northern tribes (cf. v. 10) **to keep the passover unto the Lord** (cf. Exod. 12:48). The Northern Kingdom had fallen and, without capital and king, the northern tribes were free to comply with Hezekiah's invitation and royal order (v. 6).

2-3. The king **had taken counsel** (determined) in consultation with his officials and the popular representatives, apparently *before* the fourteenth of Nisan, to keep the feast **in the second month** (not the first month as the Law prescribes, Num. 9:1-5) because of (1) the legal impurity of many of the priests, (2) the nonarrival of the people at the proper time, and (3) the fact that the Temple had been in the process of being cleansed and had just been reopened (cf. 29:3, 17).

5. For they had not done it (kept the Passover) **for a long time** (*lārōḇ,* "in multitude"). The people had not been accustomed to "coming in their numbers" (cf. vv. 13, 24). Apparently the obligation to observe the Passover was universal and at Jerusalem, **as it was written** (Exod. 12:1-20; Deut. 16:1-8), since the capital was the only legitimate place for it to be celebrated (cf. 2 Kings 23:22).

6-9. The **posts** (runners, couriers) carried the letters with the king's message throughout the tribes of those who had **escaped out of the hand of the kings** of

Assyria and were still left after the fall of Samaria (722/721 B.C.). Hezekiah implored the remnant to humble themselves, **yield** to the LORD, and **serve** Him, **that the fierceness of his wrath** might turn away from them. He reminded them that the LORD is **gracious and merciful** (cf. Exod. 34:6). If they would **turn again** to Him, He would not **turn away** from them.

10-11. Many derided and scorned Hezekiah's invitation, but some humbled themselves and came to Jerusalem. **12.** The hand of God was also at work in Judah to give a common mind to obey the command of Hezekiah and his officials, consistent with the word of the LORD.

Celebration of the Feast. 30:13-22. **13.** The great concourse celebrated the festival. **The feast of unleavened bread** followed the Passover (Lev. 23:5-6). It was a memento of Israel's hasty Exodus from Egypt (see notes on Exod. 12:11, 34; 1 Cor. 5:7). **14.** They purged out the leaven of idolatry. **15.** Killing the Passover lamb on the fourteenth day was a memorial of the divine plan of redemption to be wrought out by the future substitutionary death of Christ, the true Lamb of God, who would take away the sin of the world (John 1:29).

16. The priests sprinkled the blood as they received it from the Levites, for without the shedding and appropriation of the blood there can be no forgiveness. **17-20.** The **Levites** had to kill and sanctify the lambs, because many of the people **were not sanctified**—ritually cleansed (Num. 9:6). The efficacy of the sacrifice as a divine propitiation depended on its symbolizing the perfect ransom of Christ (Heb. 9:14). Yet the people ate, Hezekiah's prayer making it possible for them to share in the Passover. Their heart attitude, if right, made it possible for them to be **healed** (par-

doned) for a lapse in outward conformity (cf. Isa. 6:5, 10 with Lev. 15:31).

The Second Seven-Day Celebration. 30:23-27. **23-27.** The whole congregation resolved to celebrate for an additional seven days with great joy. Joy always abounds when God's people walk in His ways and separate themselves from sin, which was the truth featured in the Feast of Unleavened Bread.

V. HEZEKIAH'S FURTHER REFORMS. 31:1-21.

Cleansing of the Land. 31:1. **1.** The cleansing of Jerusalem and the Temple (30:14) and the celebration of the Passover with the Feast of Unleavened Bread filled the people with zeal to cleanse the land, which needed to be swept clean of the idolatrous impurities left over from Ahaz's wicked regime. Therefore, all Israel who were present at the feast set out to do this after the extended celebrations were over.

The people broke to pieces the **images** (pillars) and cut down **the idols** (Asherahs, see 14:3 for meaning). This iconoclastic fervor not only swept Judah clean, but also Ephraim and Manasseh, the northern tribes, where with the fall of Samaria and the central government, little serious political opposition was encountered.

Assignment of Priests, Levites and Offerings. 31:2-4. **2.** Hezekiah **appointed** (reestablished) the twenty-four Levitical courses in rotation (cf. 8:14), each according to its service, both for the priests and Levites to offer burnt and peace offerings (see Lev. 1, 3 for meaning), and to minister in praise and thanksgiving **in the gates of the camps of the Lord** (lit., "thresholds of the camps of the LORD," cf. 1 Chron. 9:18-19, an old designation reminiscent of the early tabernacle).

3. The reestablishing of the orderly worship first set up by David (cf. 1 Chron. 24-25) entailed provision for the national worship in the **set feasts.** Verse 3 should read: "And the king's portion [i.e., the part he contributed] from his property was for the burnt offerings ... of the morning and the evening ... the sabbath ... new moons, the set feasts. The king, therefore, gave the victims prescribed for the sacrifices prescribed in the Law [Num. 28-29], out of his own income" (cf. 32:27-29). **4.** He also commanded the giving of **the portion of the priests and Levites,** consisting of the firstfruits and tithes (Exod. 23:19; Lev. 27:30-33; Num. 18:12, 20-24), so they could devote themselves to God's work, unencumbered by secular pursuits (cf. Neh. 13:10). The king's purpose was **that they might be encouraged in** (stick fast to) **the law** of Moses.

The Generous Response of the People. 31:5-19. **5-6. As soon as the commandment** (order) **came abroad** (was broadcast), the tithe, in produce, was brought in **abundance** (in great quantities) and placed **by heaps** (lit., "heaps, heaps," the repetition denoting "many piles"). **7-10. In the third month** (May/June, ending the wheat harvest) they began to pile up the heaps, and by the seventh month they had completed them, evoking the gratitude of the king and the high priest. **11-19.** They also began the preparation of storage chambers to receive the gifts, and they set Levites to oversee and manage them and to distribute the gifts to the priests and everyone included in the official genealogy of the Levites.

Characterization of Hezekiah. 31:20-21. **20.** Hezekiah did what was good, right, and true **before the Lord, his God** (the expression hinting at his firm faith in God). **21.** He honored the Law of Moses and sought **his God ... with all his heart** (cf. Deut. 6:5; 1 Chron. 28:9).

W. HEZEKIAH AND THE ASSYRIAN INVASION. 32:1-33.

Hezekiah's Preparations Against Attack. 32:1-8. The chronicler deals less fully than the writer of Kings with the political involvements of this period; so the events are not comprehensible without reference to Kings, Isaiah, and the Assyrian records. This contrasts with the great fullness of his recital of Hezekiah's religious reforms (two whole chapters as compared to only four verses in 2 Kings 18:3-6).

According to 2 Kings 18:13 (cf. Isa. 36:1), Sennacherib invaded Judah in Hezekiah's fourteenth year (701 B.C.). The chronicler relates only the Assyrian king's *thought* of conquering the fortified cities of Judah. He does not mention that they were actually captured. According to the so-called Taylor Prism, Sennacherib captured forty-six cities of Judah and a huge number of prisoners; he handed over some of Hezekiah's territory to the kings of Ashdod, Ekron, and Gaza, and imposed a heavy tribute upon him (ANET, pp. 287-88).

1-8. To meet this colossal threat, Hezekiah did four things: (1) He stopped up all water sources outside Jerusalem, and at the same time he sought to use the available water supply for Jerusalem's defenders (cf. 2 Kings 20:20; 2 Chron. 32:30). (2) He strengthened Jerusalem's defenses, repairing the weak spots in the wall, erecting towers, building an outside wall, and strengthening the Millo (a fortress; cf. Isa. 22:9-10). **6.** (3) He also reorganized the army and mobilized the nation. (4) He addressed the nation, urging the people to be courageous and trust the LORD their God. (On Sennacherib's campaign in Palestine, see J.

Bright, *A History of Israel,* pp. 282-87.)

The Blasphemous Taunts of Sennacherib. 32:9-19. **9.** Through his servants, Sennacherib dispatched an insulting message from Lachish. **10-11.** He challenged Hezekiah's trust in the LORD and His ability to save Judah from Assyrian power. **12-14.** He derided Hezekiah's religious reforms and classified the LORD as just another impotent god, like the peoples' gods who had proved unable to deliver their devotees from his power.

15. He urged the people not to be misled and deluded by Hezekiah. He boasted vauntingly that no god of any nation had been able to deliver anyone from his hand or that of his fathers. **How much less shall your God deliver you . . . ? 17-19.** He also wrote **letters to rail on** (insult) the LORD God of Israel.

God's Reply Through Hezekiah's and Isaiah's Prayer. 32:20-23. **20.** Hezekiah and Isaiah, men of God, **cried to heaven** (cf. 2 Kings 19:15-19; Isa. 37:2-4, 15-20), meaning their petitions reached God's throne (2 Chron. 30:27; cf. 1 Sam. 5:12). **21. And the Lord sent an angel** (2 Kings 19:35-36; cf. Psalms 46-48; Isa. 37:36-37), the executor of God's wrath against the Assyrians' insolent blasphemy and to perform the LORD's will in answer to prayer.

So Sennacherib had to return home **with shame of face** (shamefacedly; Psalm 44:15; cf. Ezra 9:7), his offspring striking him down with the sword as he entered the house of his god (2 Kings 19:37). **22-23.** The LORD's deliverance resulted in Hezekiah's blessing and exaltation, for the Assyrian invasion was more of a testing to refine him than a chastening to punish him.

Hezekiah's Sickness. 32:24-26. **24. In those days** (2 Kings 20:1-11) **Hezekiah was sick to the death** (became critically ill). In answer to his prayer, God gave him a sign of the sundial (see 2 Kings 20:8-11; Isa. 38:7-8). **25-26.** Hezekiah's pride and his failure to respond adequately to the benefits received are stressed by the chronicler, who only hints at the manifestation of it in the reception of the envoys from Babylon, when he declares, "God left him to test him, to find out all that was in his heart" (v. 31, BV). His folly of proudly displaying his wealth to the foreign envoys revealed what was in his heart and drew forth Isaiah's prophetic rebuke and the woe that Hezekiah's indiscretion would bring to Judah in future years.

Summary of Hezekiah's Reign. 32:27-33. **27-29.** (1) Hezekiah's wealth, which was the result of his godliness, is stressed. **30.** (2) His great engineering feat was in damming up the upper outlet of the waters of the Gihon Spring and, through the rock-hewn conduit, connecting the Virgin's Well with the Pool of Siloam for water storage within the city. **33.** He was buried with great honor in the upper section of the graves of David's posterity.

X. THE REIGNS OF MANASSEH AND AMON. 33:1-25.

Manasseh's Idolatrous Orgy. 33:1-10. **1.** Manasseh's long reign of fifty-five years (696-642 B.C., coregencies included) tops the list (with Ahaz) of wicked rulers who occupied the Davidic throne. **2.** He followed the **abominations of the nations, whom the Lord had cast out** of Canaan to give the land to Israel (cf. Deut. 18:9-14).

It was Manasseh who contributed most to the downfall of the kingdom of Judah (2 Kings 23:26; 24:3). It is an anomaly that such an evil son of such a godly father was granted the longest reign of any Hebrew king. Like Ahaz, part of the price of his apostasy was subservience to Assyria (2 Kings

21:1-18). His later repentance, told only by the chronicler, did little to arrest the plunge to national ruin (vv. 11-20).

Manasseh's idolatrous binge included eight offenses: **3.** (1) He rebuilt the high places that Hezekiah, his father, had finally smashed, reviving a godless syncretism of Yahwism mixed with Baalism. (2) He erected altars for Baal, and made Asherahs, representations of the Canaanite fertility goddess.

(3) He lapsed into astrology, the cosmic fatalism that gripped the Assyrians as a prominent manifestation of the practice of occultism. **5.** (4) He polluted the house of the LORD with Baal altars, as Ahaz had done, as well as altars for astral worship in the sacred courts, violating the sanctity of the Temple (Deut. 12:11; 1 Kings 8:29; 9:3).

6. (5) He revived Molech worship and its cruel practice of child sacrifice (Deut. 18:9-10), and he ran the gamut of occult practices of idol-ridden paganism—soothsaying, divination, sorcery, necromancy (spiritistic mediumship, alleged conversation with the spirits of the deceased, but really deceptive dialogue with demonic spirits, or the familiar spirits, who work through the medium, the human agent). (6) He went the limit in inciting the LORD's wrath.

7-8. (7) He set up **a carved image** (*sĕmĕl,* "a slab-image"; W. F. Albright, ARI, p. 221, n. 121, a particularly offensive representation of Asherah, 2 Kings 21:7) in the Temple, which the LORD had sanctified as the place where He would place His name **forever** and bless His people with a permanent abode in the land He had given them, as long as they were obedient to His Law and covenant.

9. Manasseh's crime was in seducing God's people to commit greater evils than the nations the LORD destroyed before them to give them their land and to lapse into a terrible state of spiritual torpor. **10. And the Lord spoke to Manasseh** "by his servants, the prophets" (2 Kings 21:10-15), but he and his people paid no attention. Kings adds that Manasseh "shed [very much] innocent blood" (21:16). Bloody massacre ensued when those faithful to the LORD and Hezekiah were brutally done away with.

Manasseh's Captivity and Repentance. 33:11-17. This notice about Manasseh by the chronicler used to be scoffed at as utterly unhistorical. But such an attitude is now no longer possible historically and archaeologically. The climax of Assyrian intervention in the west came during this period when Esarhaddon (680-661 B.C.) was occupied with a protracted crisis in Egypt. In a list of twenty-two kings of the west who were summoned to Nineveh appears the name of Manasseh of Judah.

Caught in the stream of world politics, Manasseh was pressured into subservience to Assyria, like Ahaz, his weak forbear. That meant, in part, the adoption of the Assyrian religion. No doubt Manasseh appeared more than once in Nineveh, in view of the vassal treaties of Esarhaddon, dated 672 B.C., and centering around the induction of the crown prince Ashurbanipal (669-631 B.C.) into the kingship. Representatives of all countries under Assyrian sway were assembled at the royal palace and were bound with fearful oaths to support the new ruler.

11. Late in Manasseh's reign a rebellion broke out against Ashurbanipal (648-647 B.C.) in favor of his brother, the viceroy in Babylon. Whether Manasseh was actually involved or merely suspected, he was taken **in chains, and bound with fetters ... to Babylon** (cf. 2 Kings 19:28), where Ashurbanipal apparently was, because of the recently suppressed rebellion there. Seemingly, some time elapsed before he could return home, and his subsequent reign must have been very short. **12-17.** That is undoubtedly the reason why repentance and reformation are passed over in Kings and made no lasting impression. **18-19.** Manasseh's prayer finds an echo in *The Prayer of Manasseh,* an apocryphal book that has no claim to canonicity.

Amon's Reign. 33:21-25. **21-22.** Amon's short reign is a tragic repetition of that of Manasseh, with its apostasy and evils. **23.** He did not humble himself like his father had done, but rather, increased his crimes and guilt. **24-25.** The upshot was he was assassinated by his own servants, who in turn were put to death by the people of the land.

Y. JOSIAH'S REFORMATION. 34:1-33.

Record of Josiah's Reign. 34:1-2. **1-2.** Josiah, one of Judah's best kings, reigned from 640 to 608 B.C. He **walked in the ways of David,** not deviating to the right or to the left (cf. Deut. 5:32; 17:20; 28:14).

Josiah's Early Reformations. 34:3-7. **3.** Josiah began early **to seek after the God of David, his father** (15:2; 17:3-4), being about sixteen years of age. In the twelfth year of his reign, when he was about twenty and perhaps began to govern alone, he **began to purge** the land of the high places, idols, and images (cf. 23:16-17), the accumulation of idolatrous rubbish that had piled up during the long reign of Manasseh (33:3-7). Compare the similar reform movements under Asa (15:8-15) and Hezekiah (chap. 29).

4. Josiah's zeal was intense. He smashed to pieces the Baal altars as well as the incense altars that were above them, reduced the Asherahs and the images to dust, and strewed them upon the graves of the deceased idolaters. **5.** He burned the bones of their priests (cf. 2

Kings 23:13-16), which he disinterred and defiled, the horror with which such violation of the dead was then regarded (see Amos 2:1) being an index to his hatred of idolatry. **6-7.** He likewise zealously desecrated the northern sanctuaries and high places (2 Kings 23:20).

Josiah's Repair of the Temple. 34:8-13. **8-9.** Compare 2 Kings 12:4-7 and the similar account of the Temple's restoration by Joash (24:11-13). The repair took place between 622 and 621 B.C., in Josiah's eighteenth year, after the purging of the land and the Temple. The undertaking was necessary because the house of God had been neglected and abused under Manasseh and Amon (cf. 29:3, which records a similar activity following Ahaz's reign).

Three top officials were dispatched to make arrangements with the religious authorities and to deliver the money for the work, both that donated in the Temple as well as that collected by the Levites throughout the country. **10-12.** Then the money was delivered to the workmen. **13.** The Levites, who were Temple musicians, had charge of supervising the workmen. Some served as scribes, officials, and porters.

The Recovery of the Book of the Law. 34:14-21. **14-15.** Hilkiah the high priest found the book of the Law in the course of bringing out the funds gathered during the Temple's repair. He called it **a** *(the)* **book of the law of the Lord given by Moses ... the book of the law,** meaning "the law of the LORD communicated through the agency of Moses" (cf. 33:8); it was also called "the book of the covenant" (v. 30; Exod. 19-24), the curses it contained (2 Chron. 34:24) and the law of the central sanctuary (2 Kings 22:8-9) presupposing Leviticus 26 and Deuteronomy 12:5-13; 28:1-68.

Apparently the book was the official scroll of the Pentateuch, kept beside the ark (Deut. 31:25-26), but no doubt hidden away during one of the wicked reigns (such as Ahaz's or Manasseh's) to preserve it from destruction. **Given ... by Moses** means that all the contents of the Pentateuch are historical and originated from the time of Moses (Deut. 4:2; 12:32) and were composed under his direction and authority. Compare our Lord's own convictions (Luke 24:44; John 7:19). As if anticipating the widespread denial of the Mosaic authorship in modern times, Christ stated emphatically that those who balked at Moses' words could not consistently accept His declarations (John 5:47).

18-21. When the book was read to the king, he tore his garments in grief and fright over God's curses, which hovered over him and his people for their infraction of God's Law (cf. Lev. 26:32-33; Deut. 28:36-37).

The Prophecy of Huldah. 34:22-28. **23-25.** Huldah's prediction was twofold: (1) All the curses recorded in the book would come upon the sinning people. **26-28.** (2) The king, because his heart had become tender and he had humbled himself before God, would not see the calamity, but go in peace to his grave.

The Response of the King and People. 34:29-33. **29-30.** The king called a solemn assembly in the Temple and read **all the words of the book of the covenant** (Exod. 19-24). **31-32. And the king stood in his place** (on his stand, platform, or dais, 23:13) and entered into a solemn covenant before the LORD that both he and the people would carry out the terms of the covenant. **33.** He then continued his thoroughgoing reformation throughout all the territories belonging to the Israelites.

Z. JOSIAH'S PASSOVER AND DEATH. 35:1-27.

Josiah's Great Passover Celebration. 35:1-6. **1.** Josiah kept the greatest Passover of any held up to his time, according to the writer of Kings (2 Kings 23:21-23), but he gives no details. The chronicler agrees, at least "from the days of Samuel" (v. 18), and proceeds to give the details (vv. 1-17). Josiah kept the feast **on the fourteenth day of the first month,** in strict accord with the Law (cf. Hezekiah's observance, 2 Chron. 30:2, 13). **2. He set the priests in their charges** (i.e., "over their wards," cf. 8:14) that they might discharge their proper duties in the Passover ritual.

3. He then addressed the Levites who **taught all Israel** (cf. 17:8-9; Neh. 8:7), **who were holy unto the Lord,** that is, separated to His service (Exod. 28:36). The king's injunctions to **put the holy ark in the house which Solomon ... did build** implies that the ark had been removed and carried elsewhere to guard it from profanation under Manasseh's idolatrous orgy (33:7-17; cf. Ahaz, 28:24). **It shall not be a burden** ("bearing on the shoulder is not for you," i.e., "you need no longer carry it on your shoulders").

4. The king urged the Levites to serve the LORD in their courses according to the decree of David and Solomon. **6.** Thus, they were to kill the Passover so that all might be done according to the word of the LORD through Moses.

Provision of the Sacrificial Animals. 35:7-9. **7.** The king and his officials presented the animal sacrifice victims (cf. 30:24). Josiah gave to the people (the laity) thirty thousand **of the flock** (small cattle, lambs, and goats) for the Passover offerings. The **bullocks** were for the peace offerings and the sacrificial feasting (v. 13). **8-9.** Josiah's officials also made voluntary contributions for the people, the priests, and the Levites, as did the chiefs of the house of God, together with the Levitical chiefs.

The Passover Ritual. 35:10-19. **10. So the service was prepared,** that is, the preparations completed (cf. vv. 4, 16).

The priests and Levites occupied their stations—the former at the altar, the latter to assist families celebrating the feast. **11.** The Levites killed the paschal animals, passing the blood to the priests, who sprinkled it upon the altar (for the redemptive symbolism, see Exod. 12). Meanwhile, the Levites **flayed** (skinned) the victim and separated the parts for the burnt offering (cf. v. 14; see Lev. 1; 3:9; 4:31).

12. After separating the proper pieces, the Levites gave them to sections of the families of the people they were serving, to be handed over in turn to the priests for burning at the altar, as **written in the book of Moses** (Lev. 3:16). **And so did they with the oxen,** the proper parts of these also were separated for burning on the brazen altar. The rest of the animal parts served for food (symbolizing fellowship of the redeemed) for the Paschal festivities.

13. And they roasted the passover ... according to the ordinance (Exod. 12:8-9). They boiled the consecrated offerings and brought them speedily to the people so that the meat did not get cold. **14.** After serving the people, they **made ready** the Passover **for themselves, and for the priests** (Luke 22:8-13), because the latter were busy with other duties.

15. The singers and musicians were **in their place** (position), **according to the commandment** of David (cf. 1 Chron. 25:1-6), and did not have to leave their station, for their brethren, the Levites, prepared the Passover and brought it to them. **17. The feast of unleavened bread** was kept seven days, symbolizing the redeemed soul's separation from the leaven of sin in his walk before God. The Passover was killed on the fourteenth of Nisan in the evening, and the Feast of Unleavened Bread (*măṣṣôt*) was kept from the fifteenth to the twenty-first of the month.

18-19. The feast was a unique celebration (cf. 2 Kings 23:21-22; 2 Chron. 30:26). It was held in Josiah's eighteenth year (621 B.C.) as the capstone of Josiah's reformation and included **Israel** that was present, that is, the remnant who came from the ruined kingdom of the ten tribes (cf. 34:33).

Josiah's Death. 35:20-27. Compare 2 Kings 23:29-30. **20. After all this** (i.e., the account of Josiah's faithfulness, from which one might naturally have expected a different end for him—now recounted) **... Neco ... came up to fight against** (at) Carchemish in 608 B.C. This was Neco II of the twenty-sixth dynasty, whose rulers tried to succeed to the rule of the decadent Assyrian Empire after the collapse of Nineveh in 612 B.C.

Neco advanced on the Upper Euphrates River Country to challenge Babylon "on behalf of [not 'against'] the king of Assyria" (2 Kings 23:29). Carchemish was situated strategically at the westernmost point of the Euphrates at the big bend of the river. Josiah's big mistake was meddling in an affair that was none of his business. He **went out against** Neco, not by God's direction, but in bluster and self-will.

21. Neco's warning was explicit enough. **What have I to do with thee** (lit., "What to me and to thee"; cf. Mark 5:7; Luke 8:28). **I come ... against the house with which I have war,** namely, the Babylonians under Nebuchadnezzar. Neco's words, **God commanded me ... forbear ... from meddling with God,** certainly do not represent mere diplomatic double talk, but point out the fact that the one true, sovereign God overrules the oracles of pagan prophets to accomplish His own plans and purposes; so even demonic powers become the servants of God to chasten His erring people (cf. 1 Cor. 5:5). **22-24.** Josiah's disregard of the LORD's insistent message to Judah to rely upon Him and to avoid entanglement in international power politics (cf. 16:9; 28:16; 32:1, 5) was to cost the godly king dearly. Megiddo, where Josiah was slain, is the valley of the Kishon where Deborah and Barak fought against Sisera and where the last great conflict of the age will center. **25.** Jeremiah lamented the king (Jer. 22:10).

AA. FROM JOSIAH TO THE CAPTIVITY. 36:1-23.

Jehoahaz's Reign. 36:1-3. **1.** After Josiah's untimely death, **the people of the land** (the free citizenry) took Jehoahaz (Shallum), who was not the firstborn (1 Chron. 3:15), and made him king (see 2 Kings 23:30). **2-3.** Pharaoh Neco allowed him to reign **three months,** until he found opportunity to replace him (cf. 35:20-21), taking him to Egypt, where he died. The Egyptian king, after deposing Jehoahaz, **fined the land** (laid it under tribute) to the extent of 100 talents of silver (3¾ tons) plus **a talent of gold** (about 75½ pounds).

Jehoiakim's Reign. 36:4-8. **4.** Neco made Eliakim, Jehoahaz's brother, king and changed his name to Jehoiakim. **5. Jehoiakim . . . reigned eleven years** (608-598 B.C.) and **did evil.** He lived in luxury (Jer. 22:14-15), put the land under heavy taxes (2 Kings 23:35), oppressed the people, and perverted justice (Jer. 22:13-17). He persecuted the prophets who denounced his tyranny and cruelty (cf. 2 Kings 23:36-37; Jer. 22:13-19; 26:21-24).

6. Against him came Nebuchadnezzar II (605-562 B.C.), son of Nabopolassar, who had founded this dynasty by successful revolt against Assyria. In the spring of 605 B.C. the Babylonians won a decisive victory over Neco at Carchemish; as a result, the Egyptians were ousted from Asia, and Palestine was left a prey to Babylonian domination.

Jehoiakim was severely humbled, for Nebuchadnezzar **bound him in fetters, to carry him to Babylon.** But it is not said that his intention was carried out; he was merely threatened with deportation.

7. Nebuchadnezzar also carried off plunder from the Temple at this time, not mentioned in Kings, but confirmed by Daniel 1:2 and by two Babylonian tablets of Nebuchadnezzar's reign, in which he states that in the summer of 605 B.C. he conquered "the whole land of Hatti" (the western Fertile Crescent, including Palestine) and took "heavy tribute of Hatti to Babylon" (cf. J. B. Payne, *Bulletin of the Evangelical Theological Society* 1, no. 1 [Winter 1958]:14-18). In 602 B.C. Jehoiakim rebelled against Babylon (2 Kings 24:1-2), but he died before Nebuchadnezzar could punish him.

Jehoiachin's Reign. 36:9-10. **9. Jehoiachin was eight** (rather, "eighteen years old," 2 Kings 24:8), reigning only three months and ten days from December 598 to March 16, 597. **10.** He was taken to Babylon in 597 B.C. in a second deportation that included the prophet Ezekiel and ten thousand of the chief citizens (cf. 2 Kings 24:10-16). The list of Jehoiachin's seven sons (1 Chron. 3:17-18) is corroborated archaeologically in the Weidner texts, which enumerate five of them. These texts also verify the fact of Jehoiachin's captivity in Babylon in general.

Zedekiah's Reign. 36:11-16. **11.** Zedekiah was Jehoiachin's uncle (cf. 2 Kings 24:17; Jer. 52:1). He reigned **eleven years** (597-586 B.C.). **12.** He was weak, yet vicious, and in his evil he did not humble himself **before Jeremiah** (cf. Jer. 22:24-30), the LORD's mouthpiece. **13. He . . . rebelled against King Nebuchadnezzar.** He listened to Hophra (588-567), the pharaoh of the twenty-sixth Egyptian dynasty, and broke his solemn oath of vassalage to the Babylonians. Thus, he exposed himself and Jerusalem to Nebuchadnezzar's fury and paved the way for Judah's fall. His perfidy became his own undoing and also Judah's (Ezek. 17:13-19).

14. The sins of the ruling classes also brought divine judgment (cf. 2 Kings 17:7-23). They committed repeated offenses, like the abominations of the nations, and rendered the house of the LORD unclean (cf. Jer. 32:32-44; Ezek. 8:15-18). **15.** God faithfully sent **his messengers** (the prophets, 2 Kings 17:13), **rising up early and sending** (i.e., constantly and seasonably; Jer. 25:3-4; 26:5; 29:19), because He had compassion on (had compassionately been forbearing with) His people and on His **dwelling place** (*mā'ôn*, "habitation"; cf. 30:27; Psalm 26:8; Jer. 25:5-6). **16.** The final pitch of Judah's sin is graphically portrayed. **They mocked** God's messengers, **despised** His words, and **misused** His prophets until **there was no remedy** ("healing").

The Exile. 36:17-21. **17. Therefore, he brought upon them the king of the Chaldeans.** Literally, "He caused to come up" Nebuchadnezzar, alluding to the divine wrath that "arose" or went up (v. 16; *'ālâ*, "ascended" like smoke, Psalm 18:8; cf. 2 Sam. 11:20). All classes were delivered into the hand of the Babylo-

nians; none were spared. **18.** All the treasures of the LORD's house and the treasures of the king and his officials were seized. **19.** The Temple was burned, Jerusalem's walls were broken down, and the city was burned.

20. Those who escaped the sword were exiled to Babylon, where they became slaves until the rise of the Persian Empire. This catastrophe was to vindicate God's word through Jeremiah, who predicted the seventy years of Babylonian Exile (Jer. 25:11-12; 29:10). The seventy years are reckoned from the fourth year of Jehoiakim (606 B.C.), when the prophecy was uttered (Jer. 5:1, 12), to Cyrus's first year and the return under Zerubbabel in 536 B.C.

The Decree of Cyrus. 36:22-23. **22-23. In the first year of Cyrus** (538 B.C.), **... the Lord ... stirred up the spirit of Cyrus** (cf. 1 Chron. 5:26; 2 Chron. 21:16), since he was God's providential instrument to fulfill His Word and restore His people (Isa. 44:28—45:5), furnishing an illustration of God's working out His plans in and through history and prophecy. Cyrus conquered Nabonidus and his son Belshazzar and laid the foundation for the mighty Persian Empire (536-332 B.C.). Cyrus's inscriptions fully illustrate his policy of religious conciliation and of restoration of exiles to their native lands.

EZRA

INTRODUCTION

Title, Author, and Date. The book of Ezra takes its name from its chief character, as do the books of Ruth, Job, Nehemiah, Esther, and others. The author is not stated, though many scholars (e.g., W. F. Albright, *The Biblical Period from Abraham to Ezra,* p. 95) hold that Ezra himself was the author. The traditional view is that Ezra arrived in Jerusalem in 458 B.C. under Artaxerxes I, so that Ezra preceded Nehemiah. It is quite possible that Ezra himself wrote the book, using various original sources, such as letters, decrees, and genealogies.

Since Ezra lived to the time of Nehemiah (Neh. 8:1-9; 12:36), he could well have written the work by 444 B.C., when Nehemiah arrived. The Hebrew of Ezra is much more closely akin to that of Daniel, Haggai, and Chronicles than to that of Ecclesiasticus from a later period (c. 180 B.C.). Moreover, the Aramaic parts of Ezra (4:7—6:18; 7:12-26) display great similarity to the Elephantine papyri of the period.

However, most present-day students of the complicated problem of the authorship of the book distinguish between Ezra and the nameless compiler of the books of 1 and 2 Chronicles, Ezra, and Nehemiah, who is commonly designated "the chronicler." In the Septuagint, the books of Ezra and Nehemiah are designated Esdras B to distinguish them from an apocryphal book (Esdras A), which contains 2 Chronicles 35:1 through Ezra, together with Nehemiah 8:1-12, with some additions and variations.

Historical Setting. The book spans about eighty years of the Persian period from the fall of the Neo-Babylonian Empire by Cyrus the Persian in 539 B.C. to about 450 B.C., the first part of the reign of Artaxerxes I (464-423 B.C.). However, the period between 515 B.C. and 457 B.C., which is coeval with the background of the book of Esther and the Persian attempts to subdue Greece, is left unnoticed. The Persian rulers of this period are: Cyrus, 559 to 530 B.C.; Cambyses, 530 to 522; Darius I (Hystaspes), 522 to 486 B.C.; Xerxes I (Ahasuerus), 486 to 465; Artaxerxes I (Longimanas), 465 to 424; Xerxes II, 424 to 423; Darius II (Nothus), 423 to 404; and Artaxerxes II (Mnemon) 404 to 358.

Purpose. The events recounted in this book (1) illustrate the fulfillment of God's Word spoken through Jeremiah concerning the return of the Jews from Babylon at the end of seventy years (Jer. 25:10-12; cf. Lev. 26:33-35; 2 Chron. 36:21); and (2) they attest God's faithfulness to His nationally elect nation, despite their unfaithfulness. Although with the fall of Jerusalem in 586 B.C. the Davidic line and the kingdom as such virtually came to an end and the Temple was destroyed, God graciously caused a remnant to return to the land to rebuild the Temple, to reestablish worship, and to give His restored people a new focal point of unity in allegiance to the Mosaic Covenant, with its attendant symbols of Sabbath observance and circumcision.

The rebuilt Temple furnished a rallying point for the small theocratic community.

But the years intervening between 515 B.C., when the Temple was completed, and 458 B.C., when Ezra arrived, were characterized by mediocrity. It was Ezra, the "ready scribe in the law of Moses" (Ezra 7:6), who initiated a new era when the Pentateuch became a vital force as a manual of instruction governing every aspect of life, and awakening in the remnant a sense of a Messianic call and mission of this tiny nation restored to its land and capital city after the long years of the Exile, causing it to look forward to eventual fulfillment of the covenants, especially the Abrahamic Covenant (Gen. 12:1-3) and the Palestinian Covenant (Deut. 30:1-12). Ezra molded Jewish life from that point on in his insistence on unswerving fidelity to the Law of Moses. He thereby enabled the nation to survive the searching historical crisis it would be called upon to

ce in succeeding centuries, especially the cruel struggle against Greek paganism in the Maccabean period.

OUTLINE

COMMENTARY

I. THE REBUILDING OF THE TEMPLE. 1:1—6:22.

A. THE DECREE OF CYRUS AND THE RETURN. 1:1-11.

The Decree of Cyrus. 1:1-4. **1.** When Cyrus conquered Babylon in 539 B.C., one of his first acts was to permit deported peoples to return to their native lands. The wording of the decree does not mean that Cyrus was a worshiper of the LORD; it merely reflects his policy of conciliating the various religions of his empire.

The Cyrus Cylinder offers an archaeological parallel. In that inscription, Cyrus attributes his victories to Marduk, while in a text from Ur it is the moon-god Sin, worshiped there, who grants him victory. **The first year of Cyrus** was 539 B.C., the year Babylon fell to him (he had been king of Persia since 559 B.C.). Cyrus was the God-ordained instrument to fulfill the word spoken **by the mouth of Jeremiah** (Jer. 25:11-12; 29:10).

2-4. He (the LORD) **hath charged me to build him an house at Jerusalem.** Almost two centuries earlier Isaiah had not only predicted that Cyrus would be God's instrument for setting the Jewish captives free and instituting the rebuilding of the Temple in Jerusalem (Isa. 44:28—45:7; 45:13), but actually had specified him by name. Cyrus even decreed that his non-Jewish subjects should aid the Jewish exiles and send freewill offerings for the Temple. God is truly sovereign in the affairs of men.

The Response to the Decree. 1:5-11. **5. Then rose up the heads of the fathers of Judah . . . with all those whose spirit God had raised** (aroused). **6.** The same divine power that had prompted Cyrus was necessary to overcome the indifference of the exiles. **And all they that were about them** (their neighbors and friends, both their fellow-Jewish exiles, who preferred to remain in Babylonia, and non-Jewish neighbors), **strengthened their hands,** vigorously supported them with silver, gold, goods, cattle, and **precious things** (choice gifts) in addition to all they contributed voluntarily.

7. Cyrus's magnanimity (the result of God's Spirit stirring him) was manifest in his release of the Temple vessels taken away by Nebuchadnezzar. (cf. 2 Kings 24:13; 25:13-16; 2 Chron. 36:10; Jer. 52:17-19). Those that were not sent back at this time by Cyrus were later restored by Darius I about 518 B.C. (Ezra 6:5).

8. Sheshbazzar, the prince of Judah, was apparently Zerubbabel, who laid the foundation of the Temple (Ezra 3:8; 5:2; Zech. 4:9). Evidently he was known by his official Babylonian name, as Daniel was by his (Dan. 1:7). He is rightly referred to as **the prince** (*hănnāsî'*), since he was the grandson of King Jehoiachin (Jeconiah, 1 Chron. 3:17-19; cf. Matt. 1:12). He is called the son of Pedaiah instead of Shealtiel (Ezra 3:2), because Shealtiel probably died childless and his brother Pedaiah married his widow. **9-11.** The 5,400 articles include the 2,499 in verses 9 and 10, which may represent only the largest or more important ones.

B. The Remnant That Returned. 2:1-70.

Introduction to the List of Returnees. *2:1-2.* **1. The children of the province** are the Israelites of the captivity (Dan. 2:2-3) who went up from the captivity of the Exile and returned to the Judean province of Persia. They (about fifty thousand in number, cf. 2:64-65) returned to Jerusalem and Judah, each one to his own city. **2.** They came with Zerubbabel, the governor; Jeshua, the high priest (3:2); and other leaders. The **Nehemiah** here is, of course, not the famous governor of a later era.

The Enumeration of the Returnees by Families. 2:3-63. **3-19.** The list, besides Zerubbabel and his official leaders (vv. 1-2), includes Jewish families. Many of these names reappear in Ezra 8 and Nehemiah 10 and represent households that were old and well established. Some members of these families returned with Zerubbabel in 536 B.C., others with Ezra at a later date. **20-35.** The list includes returnees from Palestinian towns, such as Gibbar (Gibeon; v. 20) and Bethlehem, *most* of which are familiar from other parts of the Old Testament. **36-42.** The **priests** are enumerated, as are the **Levites,** these classes being indispensable to the reestablishment of the Temple service and the Mosaic institutions. The number of the priests (4,289) is large in proportion to each of the other classes. Only three of David's priestly courses are represented (1 Chron. 24:7-8, 14). The expression **the house of Jeshua** apparently indicates that the present high priest belonged to the family head of **Jedaiah,** who sprang from the high-priestly family of Eleazar. Only 341 Levites returned (cf. Ezra 8:15).

43-54. The Nethinim ("those given")

were Temple servants, the lowest order of the ministry who performed the more laborious sanctuary tasks (cf. Num. 31:47; Josh. 9:23). **55-58. The children of Solomon's servants** were doubtless descendants of his war prisoners, put in a servant class like the Nethinim, and counted with them.

59-62. A group with uncertain genealogies is included, with three families of common people (vv. 59-60) and three priestly families (vv. 61-62). They were permitted to accompany true Jews on this journey, but they were officially excluded since they could not prove their relationship to the nation through genealogical records. The priests **as polluted** (levitically disqualified) were **put from the priesthood,** not allowed to function ecclesiastically. **63.** The **Tirshatha,** a Persian title used interchangeably with "governor" (*pĕḥâ*; cf. Ezra 5:14; Neh. 7:65, 70; 8:9), and evidently meaning "his excellency, the one to be respected and feared," declared they should not **eat of the most holy things** (enjoy priestly privileges), **till there stood up a priest with Urim and with Thummim** to inquire of the LORD concerning them (cf. Exod. 28:30). These sacred lots were used to ascertain the divine will. But since the departure of the Shekinah glory in 592 B.C. (Ezek. 10:1-22), this feature of Israel's ancient worship vanished, never to return. Hence, the quandary in which these six families found themselves was never resolved.

The Number of the Returnees, Their Substance and Offerings. 2:64-70. **64.** The total of the **whole congregation** is given as 42,360, the same number given in Nehemiah 7:66. However, there are problems in the subtotals, probably due to mistranscription and other factors. **65.** The male and female singers (not Temple musicians), together with their large number of slaves, suggest some degree of affluence of the returnees.

68-69. The contributions by family heads, given for the construction of the Temple (cf. 1:6; Neh. 7:70), were sixty-one thousand **drams** (darics) of gold and five thousand **pounds** of silver (see Neh. 7:70-71). The unlikely figure of 530 priests' garments in Nehemiah 7:70 should be read textually as five hundred silver minas and 30 priests' garments. **70.** The location of the returnees is given, and the remnant is called **all Israel,** for it was representative of *all* the tribes, not just Judah and Benjamin.

C. THE TEMPLE BEGUN AND THE FEASTS ESTABLISHED. 3:1-13.

The Altar and the Foundation Laid. 3:1-7. **1. When the seventh month** (Sept. 536 B.C.) **was come** (approached) after the Israelites had been located **in the cities,** they assembled **as one man,** that is, as a body, at Jerusalem to keep the sacred festivals of the season, the Feast of Trumpets (v. 6; Num. 29:1-6), foreshadowing Israel's final regathering at the end of the age for Kingdom blessing.

The laying of the foundation of the Temple the following spring officially brought to an end the seventy-year Exile, 605 to 535 B.C. They first **builded the altar,** the Temple being built around it as the center of everything. On it was to be offered the **burnt offerings,** typifying Christ's redemptive work, as outlined **in the law of Moses, the man of God** (Deut. 12:5). **3.** The altar was set **upon its bases,** upon its old site uncovered among the ruins. Until their offerings went up, **fear** was upon the people who did not feel confident of the LORD's protection against their enemies until the tokens of their faith in God were manifest.

4-6. The Israelites also kept **the feast of tabernacles,** commemorative of their redemption from Egypt and future es-

tablishment in Kingdom blessing (see Lev. 23:33-44), **according to the custom,** stress being laid on the purpose to renew completely the Mosaic economy (see Lev. 23; Num. 29; Deut. 16). **7. Cedar trees** from Lebanon were to be floated by sea to Joppa, as in the case of Solomon centuries previously (2 Chron. 2:16). This was to be done **according to the grant . . . of Cyrus,** recorded in 6:3-5.

The Restoration of the Temple Begun. 3:8-13. **8. In the second year . . . in the second month** (May/June 535 B.C.; cf. v. 1), the Levites were appointed to superintend and set forth the work of Temple restoration, in strict harmony with the original ordinances of David (1 Chron. 23). Since the first offerings on the altar were strictly in accord with the Mosaic Law, the musical ceremonial was according to the precedent of David (1 Chron. 6; 16:25). **9.** Special Levitical families were placed in charge of the Temple workmen.

10. The priests with trumpets and the Levites with cymbals represent the same order used when the Ark was brought to Jerusalem in the time of David (1 Chron. 16:5-6; cf. Num. 10:8). **11. They sang together** ("one to another," i.e., antiphonally). Joy abounded as they realized the dark days of captivity lay behind. **12. But many . . . wept with a loud voice,** the old men contrasting the size and grandeur of the former Temple destroyed some fifty years previously (cf. Hag. 2:3). The contrast, too, with the glorious Temple prophesied by Ezekiel (Ezek. 40:1—47:12) was known only too well by the Jews of this period.

D. THE OPPOSITION OF THE SAMARITANS. 4:1-24.

The Temptation to Compromise. 4:1-5. **1.** The laying of the Temple's foundation was the signal for the beginning of trouble with Israel's enemies.

First came the temptation to compromise. When that was resisted, open opposition developed. **The adversaries** were the Samaritans (cf. Neh. 4:11). They were a mixed race consisting of an original Israelite nucleus, which was almost lost as the result of various importations of foreigners by Sargon, Sennacherib, and Esarhaddon (see 2 Kings 17:24-34; Isa. 7:8).

2. These foreigners, fused with the Israelites and their descendants, now approached the Israelite governor, Zerubbabel, with the protestation: **We seek your God, as ye do.** But the proposal was a subtle bid to form an alliance with corrupt religion and so break down the separateness of the LORD's people (cf. 2 Cor. 6:17; 11:15).

3-4. Zerubbabel saw the incongruity of joining with semipagans in the work of building God's house. **We ourselves, the people of the LORD, ... will build** was the reply to **the people of the land.** Had the Israelite leaders consented at this vital point, the whole design of the restoration movement would have been jeopardized. They also would have violated Cyrus's decree, the provisions of which were absolute and exclusive.

Opposition to the Rebuilding of the City. 4:6-23. This is probably a parenthetical section also dealing with opposition to Jewish rebuilding projects. However, if so taken, it must not be viewed as a misplacement or blunder by the author, as critics commonly do. The Temple was completed in 515 B.C.; thus, this episode apparently deals with later more general opposition in the reigns of Xerxes I (Ahasuerus, 485-464 B.C.) and of Artaxerxes (464-423 B.C.).

6. The reign of Xerxes I (**Ahasuerus**) is not known outside of the reference here. If this view of a parenthesis is correct, the author inserted the lengthy parenthesis to confirm and illustrate his

conviction that the lack of progress in building the Temple from 535 to 520 B.C. was due (among other reasons, cf. Zech. 8:9-10) to the opposition from the peoples of the land.

7-8. This section (4:8—6:18), consisting to a large degree of official correspondence linked by brief narrative, is **written in Aramaic,** the lingua franca of the Persian Empire. **Bishlam, Mithredath,** and **Tabeel** evidently were prominent Samaritans who hired two high Persian officials, **Rehum,** the chancellor, and **Shimshai,** the secretary, to write the letter of verses 11 to 16 to Artaxerxes. **9-10.** The imposing list was meant to add authority to the complaint. **The great and noble Osnapper** is the Aramaic equivalent of Ashurbanipal (669-630 B.C.).

11-16. The appeal to the Persian monarch was threefold: (1) the king would incur financial loss (v. 13); (2) his honor would be threatened (v. 14); and (3) his empire would be decreased (v. 16). Spiteful craft and exaggeration are stamped on every sentence of the letter. **Beyond the River** (v. 16, RSV) as a proper name refers to the official designation of the fifth Persian satrapy comprising Palestine and Syria, situated across the Euphrates west of the heartland of Persia.

17-19. The Persian monarch answered the charges made against the Jews. After receiving the letter, the king had instituted a search into the former history of Jerusalem, confirming the allegations of insurrection and rebellion, probably with reference to revolts under Jehoiakim and Zedekiah against Nebuchadnezzar.

20. He also made special mention of powerful kings in Jerusalem (like David, Solomon, Asa, and Uzziah) to whom taxes of various kinds were made by conquered people. **22.** Therefore, he decreed that the building of Jerusalem was to cease until further notice. **23.** When the decree was read to his officials in Palestine-Syria, they at once went up to Jerusalem and **by force and power** compelled the Jews to quit building.

The Work on the Temple Ceases. 4:24. **24.** Older expositors, assuming that 4:24 of necessity had to follow 4:23, chronologically interpreted Ahasuerus in 4:6 as Cambyses II (530-522 B.C.) son of Cyrus the Great, and Artaxerxes (4:7) as Gaumata (Smerdis), a usurper. It must be confessed that verse 24, as it stands in the text and as it is worded, would certainly suggest such a conclusion; and the older view is not to be dismissed as untenable, especially as Ahasuerus is apparently a royal title and not a proper name. Moreover, Persian princes often had more than one name.

E. THE BUILDING OF THE TEMPLE RESUMED. 5:1-17.

Ministry of Haggai and Zechariah. 5:1-2. **1-2.** The prophets Haggai and Zechariah had a powerful effect upon the people, and the building of the Temple was resumed after fifteen years of lethargy. Haggai's ministry began on August 29, 520 B.C. (Hag. 1:1), and work on the Temple was recommenced three weeks later on September 20, 520 B.C. (Hag. 1:14-15). Zechariah began his remarkable ministry in October/November of the same year.

Both Zerubbabel, the civil governor, and Joshua, the high priest, were not only honored by Zechariah, but they are prophetically seen as prefiguring the Messiah as Priest and King-Priest in the future Kingdom over Israel (Zech. 3, 6). Haggai glimpses Zerubbabel as a prefigurement of the Messiah at His second advent (Hag. 2:21-23). Then **rose up Zerubbabel . . . and Jeshua . . . and began to build,** the prophetic voices of Haggai

and Zechariah stirring them up to proceed with the Temple's construction without the formal permission of Darius (522-486 B.C.) in the monarch's second year (520 B.C.) Thus, **the prophets of God** helped the people by encouraging them from day to day in every stage of their work.

Investigation by the Persian Officials. 5:3-5. **3-4.** **Tatnai** (Tatenai) was the royal representative (Persian satrap) **on this side of the river,** being mentioned in a contemporary business document as "the governor of Trans-Euphratia," which included Syria-Palestine. He and Shethar-bozenai, his secretary, and their assistants were naturally quite concerned about the Jews' apparent delay to declare their loyalty to the new Persian government under Darius (who had just quelled a rebellion). So they took steps to clarify the situation by investigating the state of affairs at Jerusalem.

There they found the returned captives busily occupied in building the Temple. Hence, they demanded to know who had given them permission to build and the names of those responsible for this venture. **5.** Divine providential interposition kept the work from being interrupted during the investigation. Had not the LORD spoken His word through Haggai and Zechariah? Would that word fall to the ground? Tatnai, therefore, decided to refer the matter to the king.

Tatnai's Report to the King. 5:6-17. **6-8.** Tatnai's letter stressed four main points: (1) He and his associates had discharged their mission, that is, they had conducted an investigation at Jerusalem at **the house of the great God** (a solemn tribute to the God of the Jews, even though it was to be understood in the light of the decree of Cyrus and in the context of an official document). The house was being reconstructed with **great stones** (i.e., "huge stones"; lit., "stones of rolling") so massive that they had to be transported on rollers and with **timber** (beams) being laid **in the** (Temple's) **walls,** all of which work was reported as being carried on energetically and prospering (proceeding rapidly).

9-10. (2) They had requested evidence of authorization of the project and a list of the names of the builders. **11-17.** (3) They had brought a report from the Jewish authorities justifying their building activity. The Jews claimed to be servants of **the God of heaven and earth,** doubtless a diplomatic way of appealing to the Persians, who referred similarly to their god. (4) They mentioned the original builder of the Temple, **a great king of Israel** (Solomon), and specified the reason for its destruction by Nebuchadnezzar (they had **provoked the God of heaven unto wrath);** so in no sense was the tragic event to be thought of as the defeat of the God of the Jews.

Moreover, Cyrus had **made a decree to build** the Temple and ordered the return of all the holy vessels through **Sheshbazzar** (cf. 1:8, 11). He was the fourth son of Jehoiachin (1 Chron. 3:17), and was **governor** (*pĕḥâ,* cf. 6:7) and had something to do with the laying of the Temple's foundation (cf. Ezra 5:14-16). Apparently he died and was succeeded by Zerubbabel, who undoubtedly was a different person, although many scholars identify the two as one person (cf. P. R. Ackroyd, JNES 17[1958]:13-27).

Evidently Zerubbabel also participated in laying the foundation, but he alone brought the building to consummation, and so he was credited with both. The Jews stressed the fact that there had been no official cease-work decree from the Persian court and pleaded that a search be made for Cyrus's decree for the rebuilding of the Temple and that the king's decision be forwarded to Jerusalem. Tatnai likely hoped for a reversal from Darius, the founder of a new branch of the Achaemenid dynasty, even if Cyrus's decree was located.

F. THE COMPLETION OF THE TEMPLE. 6:1-22.

Darius's Decree Concerning the Temple. 6:1-12. **1.** Darius not only succeeded in locating Cyrus's decree, but issued an order of his own, directing Tatnai to assist the Jews in their work of building, and even threatening those who might try to circumvent. **Search** (investigation) **was made in the house of the archives ... in Babylon. 2.** But the official memorandum of Cyrus's decree was found at **Achmetha** (i.e., Ecbatana), the Median capital of Cyrus. Apparently the usurper Smerdis had destroyed the original roll of parchment, and the one recovered was a copy.

3-5. These verses contain the details of the memorandum of Cyrus's official oral decree, providing (1) that the Temple be reconstructed, its foundations retained, its specified measurements and manner of construction followed, and its cost to be met from the royal treasury; and (2) that the holy vessels of the Temple, which Nebuchadnezzar had taken from the Temple in 586 B.C., be returned and deposited in their place in **the house of God.**

6-12. These verses present five details of Darius's decree reinforcing that of Cyrus: (1) He warned Tatnai and his official assistants of the province **beyond** (across) **the river** to be ... **far from there** (i.e., "Keep away from there!" or "Hands off the Temple and the Temple's builders!"). **Let the work of this house of God alone,** that they may complete the task unhindered.

(2) He directed Tatnai how to

assist—the cost of the Temple's construction was to be paid fully from the royal treasuries out of the tax from the province beyond the river **that they be not hindered,** that is, without interruption, these words referring to payment of cost and not to the work of reconstruction. (3) He even was to provide animals for sacrifices, as well as wheat, salt, wine, and anointing oil required in the Temple ritual, that the Jews, as they offered their **sacrifices ... unto the God of heaven,** might pray for **the king, and ... his sons** (cf. Jer. 29:7; 1 Macc. 7:33; 12:11; Rom. 13:1-7).

(4) He somberly warned any who might flout the decree. This was no idle threat. Darius, according to Herodotus (*History* 3. 159), impaled three thousand Babylonians who dared to scorn his decrees. One's house **made a dunghill** is a strong figure, not only for complete destruction but also for shameful extinction (cf. 2 Kings 9:37; Dan. 2:5; 3:29). (5) He invoked the curse of **the God who ... caused his name to dwell** in the Jerusalem Temple against anyone who would dare to **alter** (the terms of the decree) or to **destroy this house of God.**

Consummation of the Temple Construction. 6:13-18. **13.** Tatnai and his official assistants executed **with all diligence what Darius the king had ordered** (RSV), that is, they carried out Darius's order precisely, though doubtlessly they would have preferred to have done otherwise.

14. Although Cyrus, Darius, and the Jewish elders had their part in the rebuilding of the Temple, even greater importance is to be accorded to the ministries of Haggai and Zechariah (cf. Hag. 1:1—2:19; Zech. 1-4), and more especially, of course, because of **the God of Israel,** the Inspirer of the restoration prophets and the ultimate Initiator of the whole project and the divine redemptive

plan toward which it pointed. Artaxerxes' name is added to those of Cyrus and Darius by Ezra, apparently because his own king had a significant part in beautifying the Temple at a later date (cf. Ezra 7:15-16, 21).

15-16. The Temple was finished **the third day of the month Adar** (March 12, 515 B.C.), the house being dedicated **with joy. 17.** Solomon offered more than two hundred times as many oxen and sheep at the dedication of his splendid edifice (1 Kings 8:63), but, of course, he had a powerful and rich kingdom to draw from in contrast to this tiny satellite of the mighty Persian overlord.

Celebration of the Passover. 6:19-22. **19. The children of the captivity** (i.e., the returned exiles) celebrated the Passover, according to the Mosaic Law (Exod. 12:5-6), **upon the fourteenth day of the first month,** which was April 21, 515 B.C. Recording this solemn event, Ezra returned to the Hebrew language after the extended portion in Aramaic (4:7—6:18).

20. Priests and Levites **were purified together,** that is, as one man, without exception. The Levites, having replaced the family heads (Exod. 12:6), killed the Passover lambs for both the people (who might be unclean) and the priests (who were occupied otherwise, cf. 2 Chron. 35:11).

21. Besides the returned exiles there were the Jews who had remained in the land (2 Kings 17:33). They had to separate themselves from the impurity of the surrounding peoples in order to eat the Passover. **22.** The **feast of unleavened bread** was followed for seven days. The Persian Darius is loosely alluded to as the king of Assyria because he was ruling the territories that formerly had been ruled by Assyria (cf. Herodotus 1. 178, who refers to Babylon as the capital of Assyria).

II. THE MINISTRY OF EZRA.
7:1—10:44.

A. Ezra Introduced. 7:1-28.

Ezra's Genealogy and Journey to Jerusalem. 7:1-10. The traditional date of Ezra's return to Jerusalem (vv. 7-8) is 458 B.C., in the seventh year of the reign of Artaxerxes I (Longimanus, 465-424 B.C.), although some scholars place him under Artaxerxes II (Mnemon, 404-358 B.C.). Following the traditional date, almost sixty years separate chapters 6 and 7 of the book of Ezra, constituting a period of almost complete obscurity, illuminated only by the book of Malachi, dating about 465 B.C. There are intimations, however, that the period was characterized by disorder and instability, which were brought to an end only by the arrival of Ezra and later by Nehemiah, who lifted the despised Jewish community out of its mediocrity.

1-5. These verses give Ezra's genealogy, selectively tracing back his descent to Aaron himself. This genealogical feature was important since Ezra was to become "the father of Judaism" in bringing the nation back to a way of life that centered in unswerving allegiance to the Torah of Moses.

6. Having thus introduced him by his priestly lineage, the summary statement is "That was the Ezra who came from Babylon" (AB). He is further introduced as a **ready** (skilled) **scribe in the law of Moses,** that is, a proficient guardian and expositor of the Mosaic Torah. The hand of **the Lord, his God** (bespeaking his piety), was **upon him. 7-10.** His journey and arrival in Jerusalem are noted, and the fact is stressed that he **prepared his heart** (set his mind on) studying the Law in order to teach it proficiently.

Ezra's Credentials and Commission. 7:11-26. **11.** This section consists of a copy of the official document in Aramaic that King Artaxerxes gave to Ezra, who is described as the **priest, the scribe, even a scribe.** In Ezra's case the function of scribe was more pivotal than that of priest, for it consisted principally in expounding and applying the general moral commandments and ceremonial statutes of the Mosaic Law, which were so needed in the restored community.

12-13. The three provisions of the decree were: (1) It gave permission for Ezra, and any of the people of Israel in the Persian kingdom who desired to accompany him, to go to Jerusalem. **14-20.** (2) It specified the purpose of the mission assigned Ezra by Artaxerxes' supreme court (**his seven counselors,** cf. Esther 1:14) to inquire into the condition of the city and province with regard to their relation to the divine Law and to transport the silver and gold donated voluntarily for the God of Israel together with the money from the entire province of Babylon and the voluntary offerings of the people and priests, freely given for the Jerusalem Temple, directing specifically how these gifts were to be spent.

21-22. Artaxerxes recorded the formal order issued to all the treasuries of the province "beyond [across] the river" to give to Ezra whatever he might need and request to fulfill his mission, even naming the prescribed limit. **23-24.** Everything demanded by **the God of heaven** was to be provided meticulously from government funds, and not by any tribute, tax, or duty placed upon any Temple personnel. **25.** (3) Ezra was empowered to appoint magistrates and judges to enforce the laws of his God and to teach those laws to any who might not know them. **26.** He also was directed to punish anyone who refused to comply with the Law of his God or **the law of the king.**

Ezra's Doxology. 7:27-28. **27-28.** In this solitary expression of Ezra's private devotion, he praised the LORD God of his fathers for so wonderfully influencing the Persian king to adorn the LORD's house in Jerusalem and for extending to him **mercy ... before the king** and his advisers. He ascribed the honor done him to the mercy of God and rejoiced that the **hand of the Lord** his God was upon him to undertake the journey and fulfill the great mission assigned him.

B. EZRA'S JOURNEY TO JERUSALEM. 8:1-36.

The List of the Returnees. 8:1-14. **1-14.** The priestly and lay clans who returned with Ezra totaled 1,496; the counterpart to this appears in 1 Esdras, where the total is 1,690. In view of Artaxerxes' magnificent decree and liberality, the company that responded was not large. Since the dangers and privations that lay ahead were too great, the majority elected to remain at ease in Babylon. But God took notice of the faithful, whose names are perpetually recorded in His Word as a memorial to their faith. **Those who came later** (v. 13, RSV) seems to infer that other smaller groups left later after Ezra's company.

Enlistment of Temple Personnel. 8:15-20. **15.** Ezra assembled the company of returnees at the canal Ahava, apparently named after a town, otherwise unknown. After three days' inspection, he learned that no Levites were in the group. They seem to have been a neglected group in the exilic period and had engaged in other work. Their disengagement is why a special appeal had to be made to them here (R. Kittel, GVI, p. 394).

16-17. To compensate for this lack, Ezra appointed nine leaders and two teachers to confer with Iddo, the head of the community at Casiphia (precise location unknown), where the Levitical families resided or were concentrated for other purposes (R. deVaux, IAT, 2:187). **18-19.** In response to Ezra's plea, and **by the good hand** of God, a Levitical chief by the name of Sherebiah and two others of the Merari line agreed to go with thirty-eight of their colleagues.

20. Also, of the Nethinim (the Temple servants, descendants of the Temple slaves, whom David and the princes had appointed for the service of the Levites) there were **two hundred and twenty** who joined the company. **All of them were mentioned** (designated) **by name,** though Ezra does not record them, but had them in his files. It is likely that the decision of such a large number of Temple slaves to accompany Ezra helped to influence the Levites to go.

The Farewell Prayer Meeting. 8:21-23. **21.** Ezra proclaimed a fast for his encampment at the Ahava canal that the returnees might **afflict** (humble) themselves before their God and seek His protection from the perils that would naturally beset them on their long journey. **22.** Ezra confessed he was **ashamed** to request a contingent of cavalry from the king to protect them en route, since he had testified before him of God's faithfulness in watching over and protecting those who **seek him** and that **his power and wrath are against all them who forsake him. 23.** So they **fasted and besought** their God about this matter. **And he was intreated by us** (listened to us).

Selection of Treasure Bearers. 8:24-30. **24-27.** Ezra selected priests and Levites to be in charge of transporting the dedicated contributions to Jerusalem. This procedure followed the Mosaic regulations, which specified that the priests were to be charged with the sacred objects of the tabernacle, while the Levites were to transport them (Num. 3:8, 31; 4:7-15).

28-30. Ezra's address to the priests and Levites, reminding them of their sacred mission and the sacredness of the contributions entrusted to their care, and the careful weighing of all the treasure (worth about $3 million) is not to be thought of in any sense as casting suspicion on their honesty. It was done to avoid suspicion (cf. 2 Cor. 8:21) and as a warning to possible robbers on the way that these valuables were not only under the LORD's protection, but also that molestation of the bearers or theft of the sacred objects would bring fearful punishment to the guilty.

The Journey and Arrival at Jerusalem. 8:31-36. **31-32.** Verse 31 records the answer to the prayer in verses 21 to 23. The caravan left Ahava on April 8, 457 B.C., and arrived in Jerusalem on July 9 (7:9). Approximately nine hundred miles were covered in parts of four months, averaging almost ten miles per day. The three days at the end of the journey correspond to the three days at its beginning (8:15). **33-34.** On the fourth day the silver and gold were weighed out and recorded. **35.** What praise the exiles must have offered to God when they saw the beloved city and offered their sacrifices of gratitude to the LORD. **36.** The exiles also delivered the orders of the king to the royal satraps and governors of the province "beyond [across] the river," who then supported the Jews and the house of their God.

C. EZRA'S CALL TO REFORMATION. 9:1-15.

The Sin of the Returned Exiles. 9:1-5. **1-2.** After Ezra had been in Jerusalem about 4½ months (cf. 8:31; 10:9), he was confronted with the serious problem of intermarriage with the pagan peoples of the land. The whole nation was involved in this breakdown of separation from sin and ungodliness that threatened **the holy seed** (i.e., the "holy nation," Exod. 19:6; or "peculiar people," Deut. 14:1; cf. Isa. 6:13) with contamination and eventual destruction.

The **princes** (civil leaders) had led in this sin; so they came first to acknowledge it with the confession, "the holy race has mixed itself with the peoples of the lands. And in this faithlessness the hand of the officials and chief men has been foremost" (RSV). Intermarriage with five of the seven Canaanite nations is noted (cf. Deut. 7:1; Acts 13:19), plus three others, constituting a flagrant infraction of the Torah (Exod. 34:12-16; Deut. 7:1-5; cf. 2 Cor. 6:14; James 4:4; 1 Pet. 1:15-16; 1 John 2:15).

God's people are a **holy seed** [race] because they belong to God and are separated from evil and evildoers (cf. Isa. 62:12). That the returned remnant should so grossly violate their pilgrim character after so brief a time following their gracious and remarkable deliverance from Babylon and the restoration of the Temple, shows the deceitfulness of the human heart.

3. Ezra realized the pernicious effects of mixed marriages in Israel's history; hence, he took a firm stand. The same position was taken by Nehemiah (Neh. 13:23-28) and Malachi (Mal. 2:11, 13-14), showing that this was a recurring problem, probably aggravated by the preponderance of men among the returnees. Rending the garments and shaving the hair (Job 1:20) were customary ways of showing anguish or grief, but plucking out a portion of the hair or beard was a manifestation of violent moral indignation (Neh. 13:25; Isa. 50:6) in the face of the gravity of the trespass and the guilt it entailed. Such sin could only lead to being again plucked up out of the land and again carried away into captivity.

4. Then all those who **trembled at the words of the God of Israel,** in fear of the divine judgments, gathered about Ezra, who sat **appalled** (*m*e*shômem,* "stunned"; lit., "destroyed or devastated," i.e., emotionally) until the afternoon. **5.** Then, amid the solemnities of the sacrifice, which pointed to God's grace to be manifested in redemption toward a sinful race, he uttered the prayer on which he had been meditating.

Ezra's Prayer of Intercession. 9:6-15. **6.** Ezra pleaded, **O my God** in the first person. But inasmuch as he was an intercessor on behalf of the people, and hence their representative, he proceeded, "O our God" (v. 10), without once returning to the first person. **7.** **Since the days of our fathers have we been in a great trespass,** Ezra prayed, regarding the race of Israel as one and the national sin as one **great trespass.** This brought national guilt, entailing punishment by **sword ... captivity ... spoil** (plunder), and **confusion of face** (open shame).

8. The **little moment** (short time) in which the **grace** (favor) of the LORD their God had been shown them (actually less than eighty years) had seemed like a moment compared to the centuries of suffering under the Assyrians and Babylonians (cf. Neh. 9:32). During this period God had given them **a nail** (the restored Temple) upon which their hopes hung (cf. Isa. 22:23), that their God might **lighten** their eyes (cf. 1 Sam. 14:27, 29; Psalm 13:3).

9. They needed to see that they were actually **slaves,** and only God's mercy gave them favor with their masters (the Persian kings), a fact that should have humbled them and brought them to repentance and confession of sin in the matter of mixed marriages. God had also given them **a wall** in Judah and Jerusalem. Like the "nail" in verse 8, the "wall" (of protection) was figurative, the literal wall having not yet been rebuilt.

10-11. After this (meaning the demonstration of God's grace) there was no adequate recompense to the LORD, but rather a shocking forsaking of His commandments. **12-15.** So Ezra pleaded for a breaking off from marriage alliances and affinity with idolatrous people of the land and a cessation of that which angered their righteous God.

D. THE ABANDONMENT OF MIXED MARRIAGES. 10:1-44.

Response to Ezra's Plea. 10:1-5. **1.** Ezra's intercession and genuine distress, as he prostrated himself **before the house of God,** that is, in the court where all the people saw him, had its salutary effect. **2-3. Shechaniah,** the son of Elam, one of the transgressors (v. 26), came as a representative of the people, to confess his sin and to propose making a covenant with God to put away all the foreign wives and their offspring, according to Ezra's counsel and those who **tremble at the commandment of ... God,** and this was to be done **according to the law,** prescribing the terms of divorce (Deut. 24:1-4). **4.** Ezra was urged to proceed with vigor and was assured by Shechaniah, as the people's representative, that they all would be with him in rooting out the evil.

The Procedure for Dealing with the Situation. 10:6-17. **7.** A proclamation was circulated in Judah and Jerusalem, directing all the exiles involved to assemble at Jerusalem. **8.** Failure to comply with the order within three days after hearing the summons entailed forfeiture of property and exclusion from the congregation of the exiles.

9. Those implicated were not more

than could assemble **in the street,** that is, the plaza or open court of the Temple. The specified time was in the month Chisleu (Nov./Dec.), the period of the winter **rain** (*gĕshĕm*), and the people were **trembling** (*mărʿiḏiḏim*, "shake, shiver"). They were shivering from the cold rain and quivering emotionally because of the gravity of the situation.

10-11. Ezra's address to the people underscored the fact that: (1) they had **transgressed** (the Law of God); (2) they had implicated the nation (Israel); (3) they had to confess to the LORD and do His will by obeying His Word; and (4) that meant a clean-cut separation and divorcing **the foreign wives.**

12-13. The people responded with unanimous consent, but the difficulties in the way of a quick correction of the matter were pointed out — the rainy sea-

son and the impossibility of standing in the open, in addition to the large number of people involved in the transgression. **14-17.** The upshot was that Ezra selected family chiefs to investigate the matter. They took three months, from Tebet (Dec./Jan.) to Nisan (March/April), to bring in their report, which apparently contained the list of those who had sinned and were prepared to comply with Ezra's directions.

The List of Those Who Had Married Foreign Wives. 10:18-44. **18-44.** A total of 111 men (17 priests, 10 Levites, and 84 men of Israel) are listed (RSV), an emendation of verse 38, reducing by 2 the list as recorded in the King James Version. The process was an agonizing one, but the separation was absolutely essential to the purified people of God and the realization of God's purposes of redemption.

NEHEMIAH

INTRODUCTION

Title and Author. The book of Nehemiah, like the book of Ezra, is entitled after its main character. See Introduction to Ezra for the relation of the book of Nehemiah to the book of Ezra and their relationship to the apocryphal book of Esdras A. That Nehemiah wrote the book himself is indicated by the fact that the narrative is penned in many places in the first person singular. The places where Nehemiah is alluded to in the third person (8:9; 10:1; 12:26, 47) do not rule out his authorship, for he may have written the material after he had left the governorship and was viewing his regime retrospectively. He also may have been aiming at uniformity of style, as in 12:26, where he is listed with a number of other persons, all in the third person.

Date of the Book. The problem of the relationship of Nehemiah to Ezra has evoked a great deal of controversy. The date of Nehemiah's return, however, is best dated in the reign of Artaxerxes I (465-424 B.C.) rather than under Artaxerxes II (404-358 B.C.). Nehemiah was at Jerusalem from the twentieth year of Artaxerxes I (2:1) to the thirty-second year (13:6), that is, 445 to 433 B.C. He came back for a second term after an indeterminate period of absence from the Persian court (13:6). A date for Nehemiah under Artaxerxes II seems precluded by one of the Elephantine papyri, dated 407 B.C., which refers to Johanan (Jonathan?) the grandson of Eliashib, the contemporary of Nehemiah (3:1; 12:10-11, 22) and to Delaiah and Shelemiah, the sons of Sanballat, Nehemiah's enemy.

Historical Setting. Nehemiah was cupbearer to Artaxerxes I, the son of Ahasuerus (Xerxes), who took Esther as his queen. In the spring of 457 B.C. Ezra had led an expedition of Jews back to Jerusalem and initiated a reformation. Apparently one of the results of this spiritual movement under Ezra was an attempt to rebuild the walls of Jerusalem, provoking the opposition of the Persian officials of the province "beyond the river," who dispatched an accusation against them to Artaxerxes (Ezra 4:7-16). The Persian monarch issued an order for the work to cease until a further decree should be issued (4:21).

Upon receiving this royal edict, Rehum and Shimshai made the Jews cease their work "by force and power" (4:23). Evidently they demolished the walls that had been repaired and burned the gates (Neh. 1:3). The news of this new calamity shocked Nehemiah and brought him low before God in prayer for Jerusalem. His expedition to Jerusalem was made in the spring of 444 B.C., and his career extends to about 425 B.C., when he returned from Babylon to conduct a reformation similar to Ezra's, cleansing away various evils that had crept in since his absence in 432 B.C.

Spiritual Value of the Book. No portion of the Word of God offers greater incentive to dedicated service for God than the book of Nehemiah. Nehemiah's love for the truth of God and his discerning zeal for the work of

NEHEMIAH

God, no matter what the cost or consequences, present an example very much needed in a day of apostasy and easy compromise.

OUTLINE

COMMENTARY

I. NEHEMIAH'S RETURN AND THE BUILDING OF THE WALL. 1:1—7:73.

A. NEHEMIAH'S PRAYER FOR JERUSALEM. 1:1-11.

Nehemiah Learns of Jerusalem's Plight. 1:1-3. **1.** The opening phrase of the book, **the words of Nehemiah, the son of Hacaliah,** introduces the "memoirs of Nehemiah," one of the famous auto-biographical masterpieces of antiquity. In this personal narrative Nehemiah in chapters 1 through 6 describes his soul exercise and how the LORD enabled him to return to Jerusalem to build its walls. Nehemiah was a palace servant of Artaxerxes I at **Shushan** (Susa) in Elam, the winter residence of the kings of Persia (Esther 1:2, 5; Dan. 8:2). **In the month Chislev** (Chisleu; i.e., December) in the twentieth year of Artaxerxes' reign (445 B.C.), Nehemiah had visitors.

2. Hanani, apparently his own blood brother (7:2), and **certain men of Judah** came to see him. Nothing is suggested concerning the purpose of the visit, nor is there any indication that they had been sent by the returned exiles on account of recent disturbances. Nehemiah displayed his deep concern and interest in the returned exiles (1) by inquiring diligently of their welfare, and (2) by the deep pathos characterizing the terms he used in referring to them—**the Jews who had escaped, who were left of the captivity.**

3. The reply of the visitors contained pathetically tragic news—**the remnant ... are in great affliction ... the wall of Jerusalem also is broken down ... its gates are burned with fire.** Though many scholars refer this to the destruction in 586 B.C., it is difficult to see why Nehemiah should be shocked at what happened almost a century and a half before. It is much more probable that the walls of Jerusalem had been partially restored and again demolished (see Ezra 4:17-23).

Nehemiah's Response to the News. 1:4-11. **4-11.** Nehemiah showed his complete identification with his distressed compatriots. He prayed to God **day and night** (v. 6) for four months (2:1) on behalf of those with whom he counted himself one. In the great prayer he utters (vv. 5-11), note these features: (1) He did not look for help from the king, with whom he was closely associated as **cupbearer** (v. 11), but to the **Lord God of heaven,** whom he formally invoked as He who keeps covenant and mercy (v. 5). (2) He, as God's servant, interceded for the nation in its sin and unfaithfulness in full and earnest confession (vv. 6-7).

(3) He adduced the covenant warnings and promises (vv. 8-10; cf. Deut. 28:63-67; 30:1-10). (4) He pleaded the redemptive status of the Israelites (v. 10; cf. Exod. 14:30), and as such, "a people" for God's "own possession" (Exod. 19:5, literal Heb.; cf. Deut. 7:6; 14:2; 26:18; Titus 2:14; 1 Pet. 2:9). (5) He supplicated a present answer to his prayer (v. 11).

B. NEHEMIAH'S MISSION TO JERUSALEM. 2:1-20.

Nehemiah's Request to the King.

639

2:1-8. This section is a remarkable illustration of the power of persistent, faithful prayer. Nehemiah's protracted intercession of the previous four months had a climactic and exciting answer in the month Nisan (March/April). **1.** It was still Darius's twentieth year (cf. 1:1), because his official year began in Tishri, the seventh month (Sept./Oct.). **2.** Nehemiah's sad countenance, evoking the king's comment, was reason enough for his being **very much afraid** (exceedingly alarmed). Such sadness in the king's presence might arouse suspicions of a plot, thus meriting instant death (cf. Esther 4:2) at the hands of an absolute monarch.

3-4. Even the explanation might anger the king, or even the request for which the king graciously presented an open door. **So I prayed to the God of heaven.** This short petition was bolstered by four months' intercession (1:4-11) and was answered in a most astonishing way by one of the most remarkable reversals of royal policy in history (cf. Ezra 4:17-23), at the same time highlighting Nehemiah's unusual prayer life (cf. 1:4-11; 2:4; 4:4-5, 9; 5:19; 6:9, 14; 13:14, 22, 29, 31). **5.** Emboldened by God's presence, Nehemiah seized the opportunity presented and made his request that the king would send him to **the city** of Jerusalem that he might **build it.** His subsequent appointment as governor (cf. v. 14) meant the separation of Judah from Samaria. Shortly before this period there is historical evidence of a revolt by Megabyzos, the satrap of the district ''beyond the river.'' It would, therefore, appear that the creation of an independent Judah with a loyal governor would have a strong appeal to Artaxerxes. **6. So it pleased the king to send me; and I set him a time.** Whatever that was, circumstances later prolonged it. **7-8.**

The letters that the king issued to the western governors and to Asaph, **the keeper of the king's forest** (park), doubtlessly included his appointment as governor of Judah, as well as authority to rebuild Jerusalem and its walls. This is apparently the decree commencing Daniel's prophecy of the seventy weeks (Dan. 9:24-27).

Nehemiah's request specifically included (1) permission to pass through until he reached Judah; (2) an order for Asaph to furnish him with timber for **the palace which is near to the house** (the castle or citadel) that guarded the Temple on the northwest corner of its courts (cf. Neh. 7:2), in Herod's time called Antonia; and (3) timber for the city wall and the governor's palace.

Nehemiah's Journey to Jerusalem. 2:9-10. **9.** The trip, requiring perhaps three months, is largely passed over in silence, except it is said that Nehemiah was supplied with a military escort, as befitted his official position. These soldiers remained in Jerusalem to guard him (4:23).

10. Sanballat, the Horonite (apparently from Upper or Lower Beth-horon, some eight miles northwest of Jerusalem), was satrap of Samaria under the Persians, and **Tobiah, the servant, the Ammonite,** was an official in the service of the Persian king, whose jurisdiction apparently was in Transjordan. An Elephantine papyrus refers to Sanballat's sons as being governors of Samaria in 408 B.C. **It grieved them exceedingly** (*yēra' lāhĕm*), that is, it was displeasing (irritating) to them that someone had come on the scene to espouse the welfare of the Israelites.

Nehemiah's Arrival and Tour of Inspection. 2:11-20. **11-13.** After a three-day rest, Nehemiah and a few companions made a preliminary survey of the walls by night, employing every precaution and secrecy because of enemies and opposition (cf. v. 16). **14-15.** The itinerary seems to have been planned to complete the circuit of the walls, but was impeded by debris. **The gate of the valley,** from which Nehemiah went out, issued from the northwest sector of the city of David (IEJ 4 [1954] :240).

From that point he moved southward past the Dung port (gate) at the southern extremity. There he passed onto the wall of the Siloam Pool at the southeast extremity and then up the Kidron Valley to the nearby Fountain Gate. At this point, however, his movement toward Gihon and the Water Gate up the Kidron Valley was impeded by rubble (v. 14), and apparently he had to proceed on foot, viewing the ruined walls from the Kidron Brook. Then he returned by the way he had come (v. 15).

17-18. Nehemiah then recited the events that had brought him to Jerusalem, and the plan to build was adopted. **19-20.** Enemy opposition was again aroused, this time taking the form of scorn and misrepresentation. **Geshem, the Arabian** (cf. 6:1-2, 6), completed the triumvirate opposing Nehemiah's mission. Perhaps he was governor of a nearby Arab state.

C. REBUILDING THE CITY WALLS. 3:1-32.

Reconstruction of the Walls. 3:1-32. The work was carefully planned, with some forty sections assigned to various willing groups after negotiation (cf. M. Burrows, AASOR 14[1934] :115-40, who posits forty-one sections). Eight different gates and adjacent sections of the wall are listed, together with the workmen who repaired them. The descriptive list commences at the north wall of the city and moves counterclockwise.

1. The **sheep gate** was located north of the Temple and was so named because through it were brought the sacrificial animals for the Temple sacrifices. This portion of the wall, repaired by the priests, extended to **the tower of Hammeah** (correctly, "Tower of Meah," i.e., "the Tower of the Hundred") on the northwest corner, contiguous to **the tower of Hananel.**

3. The **fish gate,** which got its name from the fact that fish from the Mediterranean, the Lake of Galilee, and the Jordan were brought in through it, was located between the flanking towers of Meah and Hananel. **6.** The **old gate** (uncertain) was apparently in the northwestern sector of the wall.

13. The **gate of the valley** is where Nehemiah began his tour (see 2:13). **14.** The **dung gate** was on the south in the wall, enclosing the Siloam Pool. **15-19.** The **gate of the fountain** (see 2:14) and the other places mentioned in these verses describe the wall on the east, facing the Valley of Kidron, south of the Temple area and Ophel, at **the turning** (corner of the wall).

20-27. These verses describe repairs on the eastern wall in the area of the houses of the priests south of the Temple and Ophel. **28-32.** These verses describe the wall east, southeast, and northeast of the Temple, in which position the **horse gate** was located. **The ascent of the corner** (v. 31) was the turn in the wall as it merged into the northern wall. The words **the ascent of the corner unto the sheep gate** (v. 32) note the completion of the circuit of the entire wall.

D. OPPOSITION TO THE WORK. 4:1-23.

Opposition by Ridicule. 4:1-3. **1. Sanballat ... was angry** and **felt great indignation** (became furiously angry), his anger finding vent in scornful derision. His opposition was doubtlessly partly stirred by jealousy at the favor shown Nehemiah by the Persian king.

2. His words were bitterly sarcastic: **What are these feeble** (miserable) **Jews doing? Will they fortify themselves?** (lit., "Will they [the surrounding people] leave them to themselves?") **Will they sacrifice?** (an affront and challenge to God, referred to in v. 5). **Will they finish in a day?** This is a sarcastic comment on the prodigious activity and success of the builders. **Will they revive the stones ...** (that) **are burned?** (cracked and weakened, as they were, by fire). **3.** Tobiah's sarcasm was even more biting in its spite.

Nehemiah's Prayer. 4:4-6. **4-6.** The imprecatory prayers of the Old Testament are not inconsistent with Christian standards, but they express the will of God when the sin of man so violates the honor of God that summary punishment becomes necessary. Prayer, faith, industry, and determination assured the success of the work.

Opposition by the Threat of Military Attack. 4:7-9. **7-8.** When all else had failed, the enemies of the Jews tried the threat of concerted attack. They **conspired all of them together to come and to fight against Jerusalem, and to hinder it** (better, "to do it harm"). Their rage blinded them to the peril thus to be incurred in offending their Persian overlords. Calmer reflection made them abandon such an audacious maneuver, which from the start may have been nothing more than a desperate but impractical threat. **9.** Wisely, Nehemiah and the Jews combined prayer with practical action. They, as it were, "praised the LORD and passed the ammunition."

Opposition from Their Own Brethren. 4:10. **10. Judah** ("the Jews"), of all people, fell into complaining and discouragement. They lost heart because the strength of the burden bearers was

drooping and the **rubbish** (debris) was so vast that they were not able **to build the wall,** especially when so many were diverted to the watches.

Adoption of Protective Measures. 4:11-23. **12.** There was also pressure upon the wall builders from Jews living outside the city (3:2, 5, 7) to abandon the building of the walls and help them defend themselves against the threats of their enemies. **They said unto us ten times** (expressing persistent repetition), **from all places, Ye must return unto us** (ASV). **13.** It appears that Nehemiah brought these families into the city and armed them to defend themselves and at the same time defend the city.

14-15. Meanwhile, he encouraged all the workers and defenders so that the work was resumed after the enemies were frustrated in their plans. **16.** From that day on, half the workers continued building while the other half stood guard with spears, shields, bows, and coats of mail. **17-18.** People worked with one hand while holding a spear in the other. **19-20.** Provision was also made to sound an alarm in case of sudden attack.

22. A plan was put into effect for all to lodge in the city instead of returning to their homes outside the city. This increased the protective guard in case of a night attack. **23.** So diligent was the effort that no one took off his clothes to sleep, except to have them washed. What a lesson serving God often requires, fighting for God against fierce enemies of every sort (Eph. 6:10-20).

E. NEHEMIAH'S SOCIAL AND ECONOMIC MEASURES. 5:1-19.

Social Injustices Remedied. 5:1-13. **1.** Nehemiah's troubles were not only from enemies from without. Internal difficulties also plagued him, resulting from hard treatment of Jew by Jew. **There was a great cry** (outcry) from the people, especially from their **wives,** against fellow Jews.

2-4. Three classes of the aggrieved are listed: (1) large landless families with insufficient income to feed themselves; (2) families with property who were being forced to mortgage it to buy food to eat; (3) those who were forced to borrow money at exorbitant interest rates to pay the royal tax levied against their fields and vineyards by their Persian overlords.

5. The plaint of this verse was likely that of all three groups. They were not only losing their farms and vineyards, but were being compelled to sell their sons and daughters into bondage. Although Hebrew debt slaves had to be released after six years or at the year of jubilee (cf. Exod. 21:2-11; Lev. 25:10-17; Deut. 15:7-18), the suffering of the people was acute.

6-7. Righteous indignation welled up in Nehemiah when he heard of these inequities, and he severely reprimanded the nobles and officials (the people with money to lend) for exacting **interest, everyone of his brother.** Charging interest was forbidden between one Israelite and another (Exod. 22:25; Lev. 25:35-36; Deut. 23:19-20). But the practice itself was permitted in normal commerce with foreigners and was not in itself accounted evil (Deut. 23:20; Matt. 25:27). Greed and inhumanity had intruded.

8. Will ye even sell your brethren? Nehemiah and his colleagues who respected the Mosaic Law had redeemed their fellow Israelites who had been sold to foreigners. But these covetous usurers had sold their brothers to the pagans in open transgression of the Law. When confronted in the convocation called by Nehemiah, the guilty offenders remained silent because they could find no reply. **9.** Nehemiah pointedly appealed

to the national conscience and testimony to the enemy nations. **10.** He implicated himself as well as his brothers in the matter of lending to the needy.

11. He further proposed the *immediate* return of property taken in pledge, as well as the rescinding of claims involving interest (the **hundredth** representing 1 percent per month), and the advance of tax money and produce to meet the barest needs of the borrowers. Action was needed at once. There could be no delay until the year of release (cf. Deut. 15:1-18). **12. Then said they, We will restore . . . and will require nothing of them.** The assembly supported Nehemiah, and the lenders could do nothing less than agree.

13. The governor had still some question about the sincerity of their agreement and had them take an oath before the priest to give it legal validity and the highest religious sanction. **Also I shook out my lap,** a gesture symbolic of imprecating on every man who broke the covenant the appropriate penalty, namely, that he be emptied of all his possessions, even as the *lap* (pocket) of Nehemiah's outer garment was emptied of its contents. **13.** The assembly responded with a loud **Amen** of confirmation, since most of them doubtlessly benefited from this overdue reform.

Nehemiah's Defense of His Own Conduct. 5:14-19. **14.** Nehemiah presented an apologia for his twelve-year governorship. His regime had been honest and unselfish. He could say, **I and my brethren have not eaten the food** (the food allowance) **of the governor.** Neither he nor his colleagues had demanded their rightful salaries from the people. Rather, he had expended his own wealth.

15. By contrast, the former governors **laid heavy burdens upon the people, and**

took from them **food and wine, besides forty shekels of silver** (RSV), whether reckoned per day or per month is not specified. Nehemiah pointed out that even their servants **bore rule over** ("lorded it over," RSV) **the people.** Out of fear of God, Nehemiah averred that he did not conduct himself in such a manner. **16.** Instead, he applied himself to the work of building Jerusalem's walls, although he acquired no land through mortgages by loaning money and grain (v. 10) to the needy.

17. He regularly entertained 150 table guests, besides those Jews who returned from foreign lands and still had no place to live in the city. **18.** Though his food expenses were heavy, he put in no claim for the normal governor's food allotment because **the bondage** (service) **was heavy upon this people.** He meant the work requirement on the walls was great and the financial stringency of so many was severe. Therefore, he was willing to sacrifice with the people and conduct his governorship in an unselfish manner.

19. He closed his reminiscences in this present prayer in a humble request that his recompense be not from the people, but from God. Nothing was farther from his thoughts than the fame of his good deeds. See notes on 2:4 concerning Nehemiah's remarkable prayer life.

F. NEHEMIAH AND FURTHER ENEMY PLOTS. 6:1-19.

Opposition by Intrigue. 6:1-4. **1-2.** All previous attempts to stop God's work (ridicule, threat, conspiracy) having failed, the enemy then tried to lure Nehemiah to Ono near Lydda to do him harm, probably to assassinate him. **Come, let us meet together in ... the villages** (since the meaning of this is obscure, the Anchor Bible construes the expression "the villages" as a place name, "at Hakkephirim."

3-4. Wisely, Nehemiah saw through the enemy's intrigue. Ono was located in neutral territory, between the provinces of Ashdod and Samaria, but it was nineteen miles from Jerusalem. Nehemiah's reply shows the discernment of this great man, as well as his uncompromising separation from evildoers, even under great pressure. They sent unto him **four times in this way,** and he answered them each time in the same manner, refusing to be diverted from **a great work** for God. The best way to avoid compromise and spiritual disaster is to keep busy in the God-appointed work that the LORD in His will has committed to us.

Opposition by Blackmail. 6:5-9. **5.** After that failure, the enemy tried to intimidate Nehemiah. **Sanballat** (a Babylonian name, Sin-uballit, "sin has called into life") resorted next to blackmail. He sent an **open letter,** that is, an unsealed document that could be read by anyone who handled it, the purpose being to broadcast the innuendo and frighten Nehemiah by the thought that its contents had been read by the people.

6-7. The contents of the letter maliciously accused Nehemiah and the Jews of planning a rebellion. Sanballat sent Tobiah in his own name and claimed that **Gashmu** (a dialectical variation of Geshem) was circulating a report that, reaching the distant king, would be construed as rebellion.

7. Sanballat reached a moral low in twisting Messianic prophecies to fit his false allegations against Nehemiah, even insinuating that Nehemiah had **appointed** these **prophets to proclaim concerning** himself in Judah. Finally, the letter suggested the desirableness of a friendly conference to avert the danger. **8-9.** Nobly, Nehemiah refused to bow to this pressure, maintaining his complete integrity and committing the matter to

God in prayer, which was so characteristic of this wise and godly leader (cf. notes on 2:4).

Opposition by Terrorism. 6:10-14. **10.** Shemaiah was the enemy within the camp, secretly hired by Tobiah, who took the lead in this plot (cf. vv. 12, 14) to play the role of a hired prophet (cf. Zech. 13:2-6). So Shemaiah invited Nehemiah to his home under the pretext of having a divine revelation of a plot against the governor's life. Shemaiah was **shut in** (confined) to his house, probably acting as if he were threatened by the common enemy. He predicted that on the following night an attempt would be made to kill Nehemiah. Therefore, he proposed that he and the governor should meet **within the temple,** that is, in the holy place, for security.

11-12. All but the priests were excluded from those holy precincts on penalty of death (cf. Num. 18:7). Thus, the suggestion exposed Shemaiah's treachery. Nehemiah at once perceived that God could not have led him to break the stipulation of the Mosaic Law forbidding laymen from entering the Temple (Num. 1:51). **13.** Such cowardice and sacrilege on Nehemiah's part would have given ground for **an evil report** against him so that the enemy would have cause to **reproach** (taunt) him.

14. Other false prophets and even one **Noadiah,** the prophetess, tried to terrorize him. Shemaiah's plot was only one of perhaps many involving false prophetism, which soon would lift its ugly head in the postcaptivity period. Nehemiah's spontaneous prayer was characteristic of this great man of intercession (cf. 2:4).

The Completion of the Wall. 6:15-16. **15.** The wall was finished on Elul 25 (Aug./Sept.) and required fifty-two days. It was, therefore, begun about the fourth of Ab (July/Aug.). **16.** The work was carried through by the LORD's help through His willing people; so God and His people were exalted while the enemies of the project were diminished in their self-esteem.

The Reason for the Intrigues Described. 6:17-19. **17.** In those days there was an interchange of letters between the nobles of Judah and Tobiah, the Ammonite, because many in Judah were bound to him by oath. **18.** This was due to the fact that Tobiah had married the daughter of Shechaniah (cf. 3:29). His son Johanan (Jehohanan), in turn, had married a daughter of Meshullam, the leader of one of the repair groups (3:4, 30). These intermarital relationships put Tobiah in close contact with the prominent families of Judah and gave an opening for enemy intrigue. **19.** They lauded Tobiah before Nehemiah and relayed Tobiah's replies and reactions to him. Such worldly alliances are always a source of trouble to God's people.

G. DEFENSE PROVISIONS FOR JERUSALEM AND GENEALOGIES. 7:1-73.

Security Guards and Service Officials Appointed. 7:1-4. **1.** The completion of the wall and the placement of the doors in the gates made Jerusalem a complete fortress, but those things did not of themselves secure full protection against enemies. Special precautions had to be adopted against possible treachery, since numerous Jews were related in one way or another to Tobiah and Sanballat.

Gatekeepers were set and the **singers and the Levites,** who normally guarded only the Temple, were appointed to act as sentries over the city, because these organized bodies formed a large part of the inhabitants. **2.** The city itself was placed in charge of Hanani, Nehemiah's brother (see 1:2), and Hananiah, **the ruler of the palace,** that is, the commander of the citadel or fortress on the north side of the Temple (2:8). Both these men were loyal to Nehemiah and to the Persian government.

3-4. The unsettled conditions of the times, as well as Nehemiah's alertness, are reflected in the unusual order to shut the gates before the guards went off duty and to open them only when the sun was high. A citizen patrol was put in operation in addition to the security police. The duty of the former was to keep watch around their own houses. This was a wise move on Nehemiah's part, since they might be expected to be more alert where their own homes were directly concerned, and the move served to protect the city itself, which was sparsely populated. People had avoided building their homes in an unwalled city (see 11:1-2).

Nehemiah's Plan to Repopulate Jerusalem. 7:5-73. **5-73.** Reference has just been made to the small and scattered population of the city due to its unprotected condition (vv. 1-4). When the wall was completed and guards and sentries had been placed in the city, Nehemiah laid immediate plans for populating the capital with racially pure stock.

The register of the returnees with Zerubbabel became the basis for determining purity of genealogy. This register is practically identical with that of Ezra 2:1-70 (see notes there), except for verses 70 to 72, which deal with the gifts of the people. Verse 73*b* logically belongs with chapter 8 and is a connecting verse based on Ezra 3:1.

II. THE SPIRITUAL REVIVAL.
8:1—10:39.

A. THE READING OF THE LAW AND REVIVAL. 8:1-18.

The Exposition of the Law. 8:1-8. **1-2.** The people assembled in the seventh month (Tishri, Sept./Oct.; see 7:73*b*),

the **first** day of this month being a day of convocation (Num. 29:1). All the people gathered **as one man** (stressing unanimity rather than the number) **into the street** (rather, "square" or "plaza") before the water gate, which was in the vicinity of the southeast corner of the Temple near the Gihon spring. **And they spoke unto Ezra,** who had probably been absent at the Persian court, since this is the first time he is mentioned in this book.

Ezra was the appropriate person to read **the book of the law of Moses,** since he was a civilian leader. This was the Pentateuch, contrary to the higher-critical view that regards it as the so-called "priestly code" brought by Ezra from Babylon, and which later supposedly became the framework of the completed Pentateuch. It is highly unlikely that the Samaritans, who detested Ezra, would ever have received anything (such as a priestly code) from him. Ezra brought forth the Pentateuch and read it on the occasion of the Feast of Trumpets (Sept. 27, 444 B.C.), the festival prefiguring Israel's final regathering (see Lev. 23:23-25; Num. 29:1-6).

3-4. From **morning until midday** (about six hours) Ezra read from the **book of the law,** standing upon **a pulpit** (Heb., "tower") **of wood,** which evidently was a high platform or dais accommodating at least fourteen persons. Beside him stood six persons on his right hand and seven on his left, who may have been priests (cf. v. 7, where Levites are named as those who "caused the people to understand the law").

5-8. When Ezra **opened the book,** all the people stood up out of reverence for the Word of God; and Ezra **blessed** (fervently praised) **the Lord,** the people giving their solemn assent with a double **Amen** and with faces bowed to the ground in humble adoration. **8.** They read in the book of the Law **distinctly**

(*mᵉp̄ōrāsh,* "in a manner made clear"), suggesting not only the translation of the Hebrew into the vernacular Aramaic but also the exposition of the sense of the passage, as the rest of the verse emphasizes (cf. Ezra 4:18; Neh. 13:24).

Revival Through God's Word. 8:9-12. **9.** Ezra and the people revered the Word, believed it, and received it, with the result that true repentance was produced as they became conscience-stricken for their individual and national sins. This was manifested in the weeping of the people as **they heard the words of the law.** Their godly sorrow was expressed by tears. But the occasion was really one of rejoicing, for the Day of Atonement (the tenth day of this same month) alone was set aside specifically for weeping and sorrow (cf. Lev. 23:26-32).

10. The true strength of the penitent people was to be found in the joy the LORD gives to those who confess their sin and turn to Him. Fellowship with God brings joy, not sorrow, because true revival releases the floodgates of spiritual joy. The joy of the people was to be expressed in God's blessing. **Eat the fat, and drink the sweet** (wine; cf. Isa. 55:1) **and send portions** to them **for whom nothing is prepared;** thus, they would experience the truth that "it is more blessed to give than to receive" (Acts 20:35; cf. Luke 14:12).

Revival in Obeying God's Word. 8:13-18. **13-15.** The reading of God's Word produced a love for it and a keen desire to obey it, making the people aware that this very month of Tishri (Sept.-Oct.) was the time for the Feast of Tabernacles (see Lev. 23:33-44 for its observance and its typical significance). Hence, they had a holy compulsion to keep it *exactly* as its observance was specified in the Law.

16-17. So they constructed booths or brush arbors and dwelt in them, a manner in which the feast had not been kept since the days of Joshua. The result of such obedience to God's Word meant **there was very great gladness** (rejoicing), as there always is in true revival when the Word of God is obeyed.

B. HUMILIATION AND CONFESSION OF SIN. 9:1-38.

The Great Confession. 9:1-5. **1.** This scene followed closely after the Feast of Tabernacles ("booths" 8:18). The people's mood of penitence and sorrow, which had been interrupted (8:9-12), was resumed in order to acknowledge the depths of their national sins (cf. Joel 2:15-17). **Fasting** denoted self-denial, **sackcloth** denoted penitential sorrow, and **earth** put on the head denoted deep mourning (1 Sam. 4:12).

2. Israelites **separated themselves from all strangers** (cf. Neh. 13:3; 2 Cor. 6:17) because the confession was something in which non-Jews might not share, for they were not of the promised seed. **3. And they ... read** (i.e., listened to the reading of) **the book of the law** (see 8:1) **one fourth part of the day** (three hours). In another one-fourth of the day **they confessed** (their sins) **and worshipped.** Again the Word of God produced a spirit of revival. **4. The stairs** evidently refers to the steps of ascent to Ezra's pulpit (see 8:4). **5.** The Levites called the people to join in the praise that followed.

The Great Confession. 9:6-37. **6-37.** The Septuagint makes this Ezra's prayer by inserting, "And Ezra said." The Masoretic text, however, makes it the praise and confession of the Levites. The ode of praise and confession recalls the major events in Israel's checkered history: (1) the call of Abraham (vv. 7-8); (2) the Exodus and the giving of the Law (vv. 9-14); (3) the wilderness wandering (vv. 15-23), God's graciousness set in stark contrast to Israel's stubbornness; (4) the conquest of Canaan (vv. 24-25), emphasizing God's goodness to His people; (5) the defection of Israel in the land and their chastisements (vv. 26-31); (6) the servile state of the people, even in the postexilic period (vv. 32-37), the result of their sin.

The Covenant Made and Sealed. *9:38.* This verse belongs to the following chapter, 9:38—10:39.

C. THE PLEDGE OF REFORM. 10:1-39.

The Sealed Document with Its Signatories and Subscribers. 10:1-29. Verse 38 of chapter 9 gives the basis of the written agreement that was made. This was the great confession uttered (9:6-37). To prove their sincerity, the princes, Levites, and priests executed a written agreement and set their names to the sealed document. **1-27.** Upon the sealed document the name of **Nehemiah,** the **Tirshatha** (Persian word for governor), headed the list, followed by the names of twenty-two priests, seventeen or more Levites (vv. 9-13), and forty-four heads of the people (vv. 14-27).

28-29. The rest of the people, together with other priests, Levites, and the gatekeepers, singers, and Nethinim (Temple servants), in fact, **all** those who had separated themselves from the pagan and semipagan peoples of the land and enjoined themselves to cleave to **the law of God,** including their wives and children who had reached the age of accountability, joined the signers in a solemn oath to follow the Mosaic Law.

The Provisions of the Solemn Pledge. *10:30-39.* There were five stipulations of the covenant: **30.** (1) Mixed marriages were prohibited. **31.** (2) There was to be a sacred observance of the Sabbath day (cf. Exod. 20:9-10) and any other holy day, foregoing of the produce of the seventh (Sabbatic year; Lev. 25:4; Jer.

34:14), and the exacting of any debt in that year (Deut. 15:1-2). These provisions, which would have avoided recent economic woes (cf. Neh. 5:1-4), apparently had been ignored in Israel's history up to this time, largely through pressures from vested economic interests (cf. 2 Chron. 36:21).

32-33. (3) Faithful support was to be made for the Temple service by the payment of an annual sum of money—one-third shekel yearly (cf. Exod. 30:11-16; 38:25-26; 2 Chron. 24:6; Matt. 17:24). This was less than the recognized amount (cf. Exod. 30:13; Matt. 17:24), apparently dictated by the stringent economic conditions.

The Temple service is detailed, pointing out how the recent revival, initiating a reformation, had produced a love for the service of God, all of which points so instructively and illustratively to God's purposes and provisions for human redemption in Christ.

34. (4) A determination by lot was to be made for the supply of wood that was to be brought by priests, Levites, and people at appointed times of the year to the house of God to be burned upon the LORD's altar in connection with the sacrificial system, **as it is written in the law** (cf. Lev. 6:12, which prescribes that the fire on the altar be kept burning by wood).

35-36. (5) The LORD was to be presented various firstfruits and tithes, fully specified in the Mosaic Law and also, in this instance, suggesting that serious neglect of this natural expression of piety had crept in. **The first-born of our sons, and ... cattle** (cf. Lev. 27:26-27 for a similar collocation; there the cattle are defined as "unclean animals," NASB) and **the firstlings of our herds and of our flocks.** The latter were to be presented to the priests for sacrifice. The former, with "the sons," were to be redeemed by money, according to the priests' valuation.

37-39. The tithes, like the firstfruits, were to be deposited in the store chambers (cf. 1 Kings 6:5-6; 2 Chron. 31:11-12). **And the priest . . . shall be with the Levites, when the Levites take tithes.** In receiving the tithes, the Levites (as well as other Israelites) were responsible to support the priests (Num. 18:26-29) and the porters and singers (from among the Levites), who participated in Temple ministries. Such a gracious system was subject to human failure and had to be restored not long afterward (Neh. 13:10-14).

III. OTHER EVENTS OF NEHEMIAH'S FIRST TERM AS GOVERNOR. 11:1—12:47.

A. POPULATION OF JERUSALEM AND ITS ENVIRONS. 11:1-36.

Campaign for More Residents. 11:1-2. **1.** Jerusalem was underpopulated due to its unprotected condition before the repair of the walls (7:4), especially after the disaster alluded to in 1:3. The history here picks up the narrative interrupted by the events of the festival month with its revival and reformation (chaps. 8-10), preventing the immediate carrying out of the governor's purpose. The plan to repopulate Jerusalem called for the casting of lots for the transfer of one-tenth of the people of Judah to the capital.

Jerusalem is for the first time in Scripture called **the holy city** (cf. Isa. 48:2; Dan. 9:24), an appropriate designation in the light of the "separation" that had been effected (chap. 9) as a result of revival and reformation and the covenant of loyalty to the Word of God subscribed to (chap. 10; cf. Joel 3:17).

2. And the people blessed all the men who willingly offered themselves, apparently volunteers in addition to those selected by lot, their patriotism praised by all. Jerusalem was a post of danger, and it was not easy to leave their country possessions for a city that was still mostly in ruins.

A List of Jerusalem's Inhabitants. 11:3-24. **3-19.** This list includes the rulers (vv. 3-9), priests (vv. 10-14), Levites (vv. 15-18), and gatekeepers (v. 19), besides those conscripted by lot (v. 1) and an unspecified number of volunteers (v. 2). **20-21. The Nethinim** (Temple slaves) also dwelt in Jerusalem, but the remainder of the priests and Levites resided in all the towns of Judah.

23-24. In the oversight of the Temple personnel, two items of special interest are noted: (1) an imperial provision for certain classes, and (2) the fact that a representative of the Jews was stationed at the court of Persia, both arrangements being in agreement with what is known extrabiblically concerning Persian rule, particularly in interest shown in religious affairs.

Towns Occupied by the Jews. 11:25-36. **25-36.** Those in the former territories of Judah are enumerated (vv. 25-30) and in Benjamin (vv. 31-36). Why important places mentioned elsewhere in Ezra-Nehemiah are omitted is not stated; for example, Tekoa (Neh. 3:5); Bethlehem (7:26); and Jericho (7:36). **From Beersheba unto the valley of Hinnom** (v. 30) expresses the southern and northern boundary of Judah.

B. LISTS OF INHABITANTS AND DEDICATION OF THE WALLS. 12:1-47.

The Priests and Levites Who Returned with Zerubbabel. 12:1-9. These are the names of twenty-two priests and eight Levites who apparently returned with Zerubbabel. Fifteen of these priests sealed the covenant in Nehemiah's day. These and the numerous lists in Ezra-Nehemiah show how important pure Jewish descent was to the LORD's chosen covenant people, who had a special God-given task to perform and the honor of giving birth to the Messiah-Savior on the human plane.

The Genealogy of the Postexilic High Priests. 12:10-11. This is a continuation of the list of 1 Chronicles 6:3-5. **Jonathan** or Johanan (cf. v. 22) or Jehohanan (cf. Ezra 10:6, NASB) is mentioned in the Elephantine papyri dated 411 and 408 B.C.

A List of Priests and Levites. 12:12-26. **12-26.** A list of priests in the time of Joiakim (vv. 12-21) is followed by a list of Levites at the same time and later (vv. 22-26).

The Dedication of the Walls. 12:27-43. This section resumes the Nehemiah memoirs. The date is not given, but inference is made from 2 Maccabees 1:18 that it was three months after the completion of the project. **27.** The **Levites** were sought because the dedication was to be processional, musical as well as sacrificial. **28-29.** The **singers,** therefore, assembled for the ceremonies from their homes, located chiefly north of Jerusalem. **30.** Both the priests and Levites purified themselves by ablutions and offerings (cf. 2 Chron. 29:15; Ezra 6:20), the gates and wall also being sprinkled.

31-37. Two companies assembled at the southwest on part of the wall. The first company was led by Ezra and moved on to the right, that is, eastward and then northward along the eastern wall, past the Fountain Gate to the Water Gate east of the Temple, **with the musical instruments of David** accompanying every part of the ceremony conducted according to sacred precedent.

Levitical singers **gave thanks** (v. 31), followed by princes (vv. 32-34),

then came priests with trumpets (v. 35), and finally Levites with stringed instruments (v. 36). The order of processionals on the walls can be visualized by a comparison with the location of the various gates as discussed in chapter 3.

38-39. The second company included Nehemiah and proceeded left in a clockwise direction from the Dung Gate on the extreme southwest along the western wall past the Valley Gate and the Tower of Furnaces southeast of the Temple and on past the Broad Wall, the Hananel Tower, the Fish Gate, the Meah Tower past the Sheep Gate on the north, coming to a halt at the Prison Gate. **40-43.** Then the two choirs took their place in the house of God, where sacrificial ceremonies were conducted, attended with intense rejoicing.

Provision for Temple Services. 12:44-47. **44-47.** Men were appointed to take charge of the offerings of firstfruits and tithes to sustain the Temple services, according the the Mosaic Law and the institutions of David and Solomon.

IV. NEHEMIAH'S SECOND TERM AS GOVERNOR. 13:1-31.

A. REFORMS OF NEHEMIAH'S SECOND TERM. 13:1-31.

The Exclusion of Foreigners. 13:1-3. The connection of this section is obscure. It appears to belong to Nehemiah's second term as governor and the clash between him and Tobiah, the Ammonite (13:4-9; cf. 2:19). **1. They read** ("it was read") **in the book of Moses ... that the Ammonite and the Moabite should not come into the congregation of God forever** (Num. 22:4-5; Deut. 23:3). This law needed to be stressed urgently at that time, for Tobiah was an Ammonite (2:19) and was forging strong ties of friendship and influence through marriage alliances with prominent Jewish families (6:18; cf. 13:4-9).

2. The Moabites not only did not aid Israel in her distress when she came up out of Egypt, but they hired Balaam to curse her (Num. 22-24). The Ammonites also refused to aid her. But more liberal treatment was accorded the Edomites and Egyptians (Deut. 23:7-9). However, the pressure of foreign contamination of God's people in Nehemiah's day apparently demanded a more stringent application of the law, especially in the light of Tobiah's growing influence. **3.** The **mixed multitude,** which played a prominent part in Jewish history (cf. Exod. 12:38), always presented a danger, but the peril was now accentuated as the small and weak postexilic community struggled for survival to fulfill its divine redemptive mission for humanity.

The Scandal Concerning Tobiah the Ammonite. 13:4-9. This incident arose during Nehemiah's temporary absence from the Persian court in accordance with his agreement with Artaxerxes (cf. 2:6; 13:6-7). Liaison between the Jerusalem officials and leaders of the neighboring provinces was well known and bad enough, constituting a vexation Nehemiah had to face continually.

4-5. But the extreme gravity of the situation is illustrated by the alliance between Eliashib, the high priest, and Tobiah, the Ammonite, one of Nehemiah's most relentless enemies. As a result of this ungodly friendship, **before this** (i.e., before Nehemiah's return from Persia), Eliashib **had prepared ... a great chamber** in the forecourt of the Temple (cf. vv. 7-9), where the tithes and offerings of the people were supposed to be stored (12:44), and turned it over to the use of Tobiah whenever he visited Jerusalem.

6. Nehemiah explained this disorderly state of things by the fact that he had

been absent from the city when it took place. This absence was in 433 B.C., in Artaxerxes' thirty-second year. The monarch is called **king of Babylon** because that city was the administrative center of the Persian Empire and a residence of the Persian kings. **8-9.** This sacrilege and priestly desecration **grieved** Nehemiah intensely, and he **cast forth all the household stuff of Tobiah** out of the chamber, ordering the sacred precincts to be cleansed formally.

Provision for the Levites. 13:10-14. **10.** Nehemiah soon saw that Eliashib's defection was only the beginning of the need for reforms to be enforced in the Temple (cf. 10:35-39). Tithes and firstfruits had been withheld, and **the portions of the Levites had not been given them.** Those who performed the work of the Temple had **fled every one to his field.** They were compelled to earn their daily bread by returning to cultivate the land apportioned to them in the Levitical cities (Num. 35:2).

11. Nehemiah **contended ... with the rulers,** reprimanding them for violating the covenant they had entered into (cf. 10:39), thus indulging their covetousness at the expense of God's house. At the same time he **gathered** the Levites **together,** summoning them back from their fields. **12.** Meanwhile, the people responded and brought in their tithes **unto the storehouses** (the storerooms of the Temple designed for that purpose).

13. Nehemiah made his reforms permanently effective by appointing faithful treasurers (Eliashib having been derelict in his duty, v. 4). One of the appointees was **Hanan,** a layman, mentioned in connection with the building of the wall (10:22), but most of them were priests and Levites who faithfully distributed the tithes **unto their brethren.** **14.** Once more Nehemiah's refreshing prayer life surfaces (see 2:4). He beseeched God not to forget his **good deeds** ("kindnesses") that he had performed in behalf of God's house and for His service.

Abolition of Sabbath Desecration. *13:15-22.* **15.** Nehemiah observed the grossest violation of the Sabbath (cf. Exod. 20:8-11), both in the country districts as well as in Jerusalem. **I testified against** (warned) **them** on the day when they **sold provisions** (food). **16.** He saw Tyrians selling fish and many other products. They had brought timber for the construction of the Temple (Ezra 3:7), and apparently had settled down as tradesmen. Their offense was in causing the LORD's people to break the Sabbath.

17-18. Nehemiah remonstrated with the **nobles of Judah** and warned them of the evils they had endured as a nation as the result of Sabbath desecration (cf. Jer. 17:27). **19.** He ordered the gates shut on the Sabbath and stationed his servants there to prevent any burden from being brought into the city on the Sabbath day. The tradesmen sought to nullify this restriction by trading **outside** the wall, lodging there **once or twice,** that is, several times.

21. The evidence shows they were only waiting to evade the law until the governor vigorously threatened the use of force to evict them. **22.** Then Nehemiah ordered the Levites to cleanse themselves ceremonially from past neglect, which was a sin needing forgiveness. Nehemiah breathed another of his spontaneous prayers, committing his fidelity in reformation to God's merciful estimation (see 2:4).

The Recurrent Problem of Mixed *Marriages. 13:23-29.* Mixed marriages had been dealt with almost three decades previously (Ezra 9-10), with incidents prompting legislation during Nehemiah's first term of governorship (e.g., Neh. 9:2; 10:28-31), demonstrating that it had been a perennially vexing issue. Now, between Nehemiah's first and second term as governor, it had become a lively problem again, encouraged undoubtedly by an example within the family of the high priest himself (v. 28).

23-24. Nehemiah was scandalized when he **saw ... Jews ... had married** Philistines of Ashdod, and that their children spoke a mixture of Philistine and Aramaic. **25-27.** Nehemiah **cursed them,** in the sense of echoing the covenant sanction on this practice (10:29-30), and dealt firmly with the offenders, selecting some for special punishment and humiliation. Ezra, on a similar occasion, had humbled himself by plucking off his own hair (Ezra 9:3). Nehemiah made them **swear by God** to abandon the evil practice of marrying foreigners, warning them of Solomon's downfall for the same sin (cf. 1 Kings 11:1-13).

28-29. Eliashib, the high priest, who had furnished such a bad example (vv. 4-10), had this evil repeated in his own descendants, his grandson having married Sanballat's daughter. Vested with royal authority as governor, Nehemiah expelled this gross offender, sending him into exile, and committed this case of priestly violation of the Law and **the covenant of the priesthood** (Lev. 21:6-8) to God alone for punishment.

Conclusion. 13:30-31. **30-31.** A brief recapitulation of Nehemiah's reforms in his second term and his disciplinary measures are followed by mention of his provisions for the sacrificial ritual. Nehemiah closed with a prayerful committal of himself and his reforms to God, the righteous Judge (cf. 2:4).

ESTHER

INTRODUCTION

Title. The book of Esther, like the books of Ezra, Nehemiah, Job, and numerous other biblical books, takes its name from its principal character. The name Esther is Persian and means "star." Her Hebrew name, Hadassah, means "myrtle" (2:7). She has the role of a godly Jewish heroine in the story.

Date of the Events Narrated. The date of the events recounted in the book depends upon the identification of Ahasuerus (1:2). That he is Xerxes I (485-464 B.C.) is shown by the following considerations: (1) Ahasuerus represents the Hebrew transliteration of the Persian name Khshayarsha, more popularly known by the Greek form, Xerxes. (2) The extent of his empire was "from India even unto Ethiopia" (1:1). India (the area drained by the Indus River) was not included in the empire of previous Persian kings. (3) The character of Ahasuerus is strikingly similar to that of Xerxes, as reported by ancient historians (see Herodotus *History* 7. 35; and Juvenal 10. 174-87). Therefore, the events related in the book transpired between 483 B.C. (1:3), the third year of Ahasuerus's reign to the thirteenth year, 470 B.C., when the plan to exterminate the Jews was broached, after the casting of lots before Haman in the twelfth year (3:7).

Author and Date of Composition. The author was certainly a Jew, but he is otherwise unknown and intentionally anonymous. Attempts to specify who he was are futile and only pious guesses, whether he was Mordecai (Clement of Alexandria), Ezra (Augustine), or "the men of the great synagogue" (the Talmud). The fact that the book is early and to be assigned to the first part of the reign of Artaxerxes (464-425 B.C.) is supported by the following considerations: (1) The opening verse of the book shows that Ahasuerus (Xerxes) was no longer king.

(2) Internal evidence indicates that the writing took place not long after the reign of Ahasuerus. The writer had access to the documents to which he refers (e.g., 9:32; 10:2); so the book most assuredly was penned in Persia, and by an eyewitness (cf. 1:6; 8:10, 14-15), who displays intimate and accurate knowledge of Persian life, customs, geography, and history, now familiar from archaeology.

(3) The writer's reserve concerning the Jewish faith and life argues for an early date. The name of God in any form is entirely absent from the book. There is not the slightest allusion to the Jewish nation as exiled from its fatherland, or to that land itself, or to the newly rebuilt Jewish Temple, or in fact to any established Jewish custom. (4) Moreover, the Hebrew of the book closely resembles that of the books of Ezra, Nehemiah, and Chronicles, which belong to the same general period. A date for the composition of the book that conforms well with the known facts would be somewhere between 455 and 450 B.C.

Purpose of the Book. The book has a twofold aim: (1) to illustrate God's sovereign providence in all the affairs of men; and (2) to demonstrate it especially in the case of His elect people, Israel (the Jews), in their amazing deliverance from threatened extinction in the reign of Artaxerxes, and to preserve the memory of this great event for later generations by the institution of the annual festival of Purim.

But the deliverance of the book of Esther is a reminder that it is but a phase of the amazing miracle, not only of the preservation of Jewish identity through the centuries amid various cultures and ethnic groups, but the still more amazing wonder of Jewish survival in the face of fierce outbursts of anti-Semitism throughout the course of history. The book itself is a reminder that "God hath not cast away his people whom he foreknew" (Rom. 11:2) but will preserve a remnant of them to realize His covenants and promises made to them (cf. Rom. 9:4-5). As such, the book is a powerful attestation of God's sovereignty as well as His covenant faithfulness to His own in all ages.

Text and Position in the Canon. Because of the popularity of Esther, abundant copies have survived. Yet, early translations contain a variety of readings that differ from the Hebrew text, thus raising problems concerning the original text. The Septuagint actually contains about a hundred verses not found in the Hebrew. These are found in the Apocrypha, where they are called *The Rest of* (Additions to) *the Book of Esther*. But the Masoretic text, on which our English translations are based, "unquestionably represents the purest form of the text ... and must be taken as the basis for all critical discussion of the book" (L. B. Paton, *Esther,* ICC, p. 47). In English Bibles, Esther follows Ezra and Nehemiah, and shares the common historical background of the Persian period. The position of Esther in the Hebrew Bible as the last of the five Megilloth, or scrolls, is clearly artificial and obviously due to liturgical usage, the book being read at Purim, the last festival of the Jewish year.

OUTLINE

COMMENTARY

I. THE DETHRONEMENT OF QUEEN VASHTI. 1:1-22.

Ahasuerus's Feast. 1:1-9. **1-2.** Ahasuerus was Xerxes I (486-465 B.C.; see Introduction), the son of Darius I, who attempted to conquer Greece. **This is Ahasuerus who reigned from India** (the region west of the Indus River, today's Punjab district of West Pakistan) **even unto Ethiopia** or Cush, present-day north Sudan, conquered by Cambyses (530-522), and tributary to Xerxes (Herodotus 3. 97). This parenthesis in verse 1 is inserted to distinguish this sovereign from the father of Darius the Mede, who had the same name (Dan. 9:1). He ruled from Shushan (Susa), apparently the winter capital, Ecbatana and Babylon being other royal residences. He ruled over 127 provinces ($m^e d \hat{\imath} n \hat{a}$), which were the smaller racial divisions within the larger satraps, twenty of the latter being listed for Darius I by Herodotus (3. 89-94). **3. In the third year of his reign** (483 B.C.) Ahasuerus **made a feast** (Herodotus *History* 7. 8), evidently in connection with a six-month convocation of his nobles and military officers to plan an invasion of Greece. **4-5.** He used the occasion to display his immense wealth and regal glory. The feast evidently took place at the conclusion of the six-month period to celebrate the finalizing of the plans for invasion of the unconquered lands on the western frontier of his immense empire. **6.** The author colorfully depicts the splendor of the great feast in the spa-

cious courtyard of the palace. The **blue** and **white** cotton (muslin) curtains (the national colors of Persia), the marble pillars, the gold and silver couches, and the varicolored mosaic floor were all tokens of the king's wealth and splendor. **7.** The unique design of each goblet and the unlimited supply of the finest wine (**royal wine,** perhaps from Helbon, Ezek. 27:18) are notations that furnish the details of this grand display of royal splendor. **8.** The royal order on this occasion was to permit all to do as they pleased in the matter of drinking, instead of compelling them to drink—a later custom that became a degrading practice in the nation.

9. Also Vashti, the queen, made a feast for the women, the large numbers present probably necessitating a separate feast for the women guests. Vashti's identity is a problem. Was she Amestris of secular history, Vashti being a title, and was the deposition temporary? *Was* she Esther? A decisive answer is not yet forthcoming from evidence at hand.

But Vashti was evidently *the* queen par excellence before her deposition, according to Persian custom that one wife of the sovereign was supreme over the other wives. Her name seems to be a denominative from Avestan *vashita,* meaning "the best" (P. Haupt) or "the beloved, the desired one" (H. S. Gehman), which conceivably could have been applied to Amestris.

Vashti's Deposition. 1:10-22. **10-11.** By the seventh day **the heart** (the center of thinking and sensation) of the king

was merry with wine (i.e., he was intoxicated). In this drunken condition he ordered his **seven chamberlains** (eunuchs) who personally served him to bring Vashti into his presence wearing **the crown royal** (lit., "the turban of the kingdom"). This was made of blue and white and likely contained the royal tiara (cf. 2:17). It is evident from the way this incident is introduced that had Ahasuerus been sober, he would never have asked his queen to do such a cheap and humiliating thing.

12. Naturally Vashti had serious misgivings concerning her dignity in the midst of such an intoxicated crowd (Herodotus 5. 18). Unless she was to appear to condone this shameful scene, she could only refuse to obey the summons. **13-15.** Yet the king's dignity (by his own folly) was publicly affronted, and he found himself practically forced to take stern measures to enforce his authority. The royal privy council of seven members, whose duty was to advise the king, is noted by Herodotus (cf. Ezra 7:14). These seven men seem to have been a combination of astrologers and lawyers. Their names are Persian.

16-18. Memucan expressed the opinion of the seven, which breathes the folly of the king's original act that called it forth. It is almost ludicrous that they should have concluded that the king's honor was at stake when he had acted so irresponsibly, and that male supremacy was threatened when that institution was so strongly entrenched in Oriental life and could scarcely be affected by any who knew the real cause of Vashti's refusal to obey her husband. Some hidden reason must have lain behind the council's decision to cause it to blow up a private affair into a public and national crisis. Perhaps the council had had a serious clash with the queen, and this action was a means of revenge.

19-20. The council members were, therefore, particularly solicitous that the **king's decree** (royal edict) be made as irrevocable as possible by being recorded among the laws of the **Persians and the Medes** (cf. 8:8; Dan. 6:9). Certainly they did not want Vashti to return to power to punish them.

21-22. The king followed the council's advice through Memucan and **sent letters** through the national postal system (Herodotus 7. 98), the first "pony express," **to every people after their language.** Although Aramaic was the lingua franca of the empire, a multiplicity of peoples meant that many languages were spoken. The message was **that every man should bear rule in his own house, and** (literal Heb.) "be speaking according to the language of his own people," which means he was to show his domestic headship by preserving his native tongue in a household where two or more foreign languages were spoken due to the presence of foreign wives.

II. ESTHER MADE QUEEN. 2:1-23.

The Search for a New Queen. 2:1-14.
1. After these things evidently comprehends a lapse of time from the great feast at Susa in 483 B.C. and the spring of 481 B.C., when Xerxes embarked on his campaign against Greece. However, the marriage with Esther (v. 16) did not take place till after his return. The king had afterthoughts concerning Vashti.

2-3. So the king's **servants** ("pages," lit., "young men who ministered unto him"; cf. 6:3, 5), in a position to note the king's discontent and feel the brunt of it, suggested a plan to replace Vashti. Beautiful young virgins were to be selected for the king and brought together at Susa by commissioners in all the provinces of the empire. These prospects for the queenship were to be placed under **the custody** (authority) of

Hegai, **the king's chamberlain** (eunuch) in charge of the royal harem. **And let their beautifying ointments** (lit., "their massage," i.e., their beauty treatment; cf. v. 12) **be given them. 4.** The girl who most pleased the king was to be queen in Vashti's place. The plan pleased the sensuous, self-indulgent monarch, and he followed it.

5-6. In the acropolis of Susa resided **a ... Jew, whose name was Mordecai,** a descendant of a Benjamite named Kish, who some 117 years previously, in 597 B.C., had been carried away to Babylon; thus, the *four* generations listed here are readily accounted for. The term *Jew,* a name derived from Judah (Judahite), from the exilic period onward came to denote any Israelite.

7. Mordecai, upon the decease of his uncle Abihail (2:15), had adopted Abihail's orphaned daughter, Hadassah (Heb., "Myrtle"), **that is, Esther** (Pers., "star"), evidently following a practice, which later became common, of giving a child two names, one Hebrew and the other Gentile (e.g., Simon Peter, John Mark).

8-9. Living in the fortress or citadel of Susa, it was practically impossible to hide his adoptive daughter from those commissioned to supply the royal harem. So Esther was brought to the harem and placed under Hegai, with whom she found favor and who promptly gave her **ointments for beautification** (beauty treatment), **with such things as belonged to her** ("her delicacies"; lit., "her portions"; cf. 2:18; 9:19, 22; Neh. 8:10).

Unlike Daniel, Esther did not refuse the foods and other things banned by Jewish law (cf. Dan. 1:5, 10). Hegai gave Esther **seven maidens** (lit., "the delicate ones"), that is, seven special attendants, apparently deliberately reserved for the most likely successor to Vashti.

Hegai also transferred Esther and her attendants to the best quarters of the harem.

10. Why Mordecai had forbidden Esther to reveal her Jewish origin (lit., "her people and her descent," a chiasm for her origins) is not stated. **11. And Mordecai walked every day,** apparently as one of the royal doorkeepers (cf. 2:21; 5:13), before the court of the harem **to know how Esther did** (lit., "to ascertain the peace, or welfare, of Esther"), and **what should become of her** ("what was done with her," i.e., her progress in her twelve-month beauty treatment).

12-14. These verses describe the procedure by which the king was to make his selection of Vashti's successor. If a maid found no special favor with the king, she went to "the second harem," reserved for the king's concubines, and never again went to the king, unless summoned by name.

Esther Chosen as Queen. 2:15-18. **15.** When Esther's turn came to go to the king, she asked for nothing except what Hegai had advised. **16.** She went to the king in the month **Tebeth** (Jan./Feb.) 478 B.C., the seventh year of Xerxes' reign. The long delay in replacing Vashti was apparently due to the king's long absence in Greece.

17-18. Xerxes not only chose Esther and **set the royal crown upon her head,** but gave a great banquet in Esther's honor and **made a release** ($h^a n\bar{a}\d{h}\hat{a}$, "a causing to rest"), perhaps freedom from taxation and military service, as the False Smerdis did for a period of three years when he ascended the throne (Herodotus *History* 3. 67). The king also **gave gifts** ("portions"; cf. Jer. 40:5).

Mordecai Foils a Royal Plot. 2:19-23. **21.** As one of the royal gatekeepers (cf. 2:11; 5:13), Mordecai had every opportunity to overhear conspiracies. The motive for this scheme to assassinate

659

Xerxes is not given in the Masoretic text, but Xerxes was ultimately murdered by Artabanus, captain of the guard, and Mithridates, a eunuch. **22.** Mordecai told Esther of the plot, and Esther **informed the king . . . in Mordecai's name.** This incident was to prove to be an important event in the outcome of the story (6:1—7:10).

III. HAMAN'S PLOT AGAINST THE JEWS. 3:1-15.

Mordecai's Refusal to Do Obeisance to Haman. 3:1-4. **1.** The unmerited rewards of Haman are presented, in contrast to the unrewarded merit of Mordecai. The latter had saved the monarch's life; yet his faithfulness was for all intents and purposes forgotten. Nevertheless, God (who is not once mentioned personally in the entire book) was ordering every detail, and working out His sovereign plan in this instance, as well as in Haman's promotion (5:11) to the position of grand vizier, to whom all inferior officials were required to bow in homage.

Mordecai, as a Benjamite, would not do obeisance to an Amalekite of the family of Agag, Saul's enemy (cf. Num. 24:7; 1 Sam. 15:8), who descended from Esau, Jacob's brother, and was the perennial, bitter foe of Israel. He is specifically called "the Jews' enemy" (v. 10) and foreshadows their final foe, the Antichrist, the beast of Revelation 13:1-10, who will demand divine worship (2 Thess. 2:3-4). Like Mordecai, the godly Jewish remnant of the end time will refuse to worship him. The result will be that he will attempt to exterminate them before Christ's second advent in glory to set up His Kingdom over Israel (Acts 1:6).

2-4. Jews customarily bowed before their kings as God's servants (2 Sam. 14:4; 18:28; 1 Kings 1:16), but they refused to bow before a king who claimed to be God, as the Persian monarchs did. As Xerxes' representative, this worship was extended to Haman. To bow down to him would signify the recognition of a false god and be a violation of the first commandment of God (Exod. 20:3-6). Pressure to prostrate himself before Haman from **the king's servants** elicited from Mordecai the admission that he was **a Jew** (see note on 2:5), and that his refusal was mainly on religious grounds, that is, giving a man divine honors.

Probably Mordecai also rebelled against the ignominious character of the obeisance accorded to such an unprincipled person as Haman. Divulging his Jewish ancestry must have appeared disastrous and assuredly was the product of a sterling faith in God, such as Daniel had earlier manifested when he refused to pay divine honors to Darius, the Persian king (Dan. 6:1-28). Plans were laid to test whether Mordecai's **words would stand,** that is, whether the fact that he belonged to a nation that could only pay such reverence to God, as was paid to Haman, would hold good.

Haman's Plan to Destroy the Jews. 3:5-7. **5-6.** Haman's colossal pride and self-centeredness are highlighted in his great anger against Mordecai and his disdain to **lay hands on** him **alone.** His wrath embraced all Jews everywhere when he learned that this people, in abhorrence of idolatry, would not bow down to him. Hence, his insensate and diabolical decision to take vengeance on the whole people.

Similar acts of vengeance with wholesale slaughter are recounted by Herodotus (*History* 1. 106; 3. 79) and have been repeated in the twentieth century in equally irrational onslaughts on Israel, preparatory to the climactic age-end attack of the Antichrist. The separateness espoused by the Jews of Judah had aroused resentment (cf. Ezra 4; Neh. 4, 6). But anti-Semitism appears in bold relief in Haman's express intent to exterminate the Jews as a race and thus nullify God's plan for human redemption, which guarantees Satan's eventual undoing. Therefore, this incident foreshadows the age-end satanic attempt to set aside the divine program.

7. In the first month ... Nisan ... they cast Pur, that is, the lot. This was 474 B.C., Xerxes' twelfth year. How ironical that in the first month of the year, which marked the Passover and the Egyptian deliverance, Haman began his plot to destroy Israel. *Pur* is an ancient Akkadian word meaning "lot." Casting lots was practiced in Yahwism, where "the whole disposing thereof [was] of the LORD" (Prov. 16:33), but it was also a custom in pagan religion; so Haman had the astrologers and magicians cast the lot to decide what day of the year to bring destruction upon Israel. Little did Haman realize God's wonderful overruling providence in this instance. As they cast the lot for each subsequent day of the year, it fell upon the **thirteenth day of Adar** (NASB margin), the last month, giving time for the nefarious plan to be counteracted and the issuance of a counterdecree.

Haman's Accusation Against the Jews and Its Success. 3:8-11. **8.** Cleverly, Haman appealed to the king's deep-seated egotism through a subtle blend of truth and error. He deftly avoided naming the Jews when he accused them before the king of having their own law, which was true, and of failing to keep **the king's laws,** which was not true, except in the isolated detail that concerned his own status. The charge of disloyalty, a favorite weapon of persecutors (cf. Ezra 4:13, 16), brought Haman's conclusion, that it was

not for the king's profit to tolerate the Jews.

9. They must be liquidated. To clinch his evil plan Haman offered a bribe of **ten thousand talents of silver** (about $18 million) to be paid to **those in charge of the royal treasury** (BV). Either Haman was to pay this out of his own fortune or it was to be raised from the plunder of Jewish life and property. So cruel is revengeful hate that men will pay any price to vent it upon their victims.

10. The king ... gave his signet ring **unto Haman,** it being equivalent to his personal signature. With it he was able to dispatch decrees in the king's name (3:12), thereby being invested with royal authority. **11.** In addition, the king with incredible callousness made Haman a present of the enormous sum he had offered the king and in cold blood turned over a people, whom he did not even bother to identify by name, to wholesale annihilation in true Hitler-like fashion.

The Decree of Death. 3:12-15. **12-14.** With all possible speed, the edict was formulated, translated into the various languages of the realm, and dispatched to all parts of the far-flung empire by means of the Persian postal system introduced by Cyrus. There was ample time from the **thirteenth day of the first month** (Nisan) to the **thirteenth day of the twelfth month** (Adar), not only for the decree to reach the most distant parts of the empire, but months to spare to arrange for the liquidation of the Jews and the confiscation of their property.

15. The planning of the terrible pogrom closed with a dramatic scene in which is pictured the nonchalant king and the callously cruel courtier enjoying their wine against the somber background of the inhabitants of Shushan, confused and apprehensive at the promulgation of such a frightfully cruel and unjust edict. Not only were the

Jews in the capital city stunned, but their many friends (cf. 8:15), among whom they had earned great respect, were equally nonplussed at this shocking exhibition of irresponsible despotism.

IV. ESTHER'S MOMENTOUS DECISION. 4:1-17.

The Lamentation of the Jews. 4:1-3.
1-3. Mordecai and the Jews, in tearing their clothes, putting on **sackcloth** (a coarse cloth of goat's hair) and **ashes,** and their bitter wailing and loud mourning, prefigure prophetically the earnest turning to the LORD of the Jewish remnant during the end of this age (Joel 2:12; Zech. 12:10—13:1). At that time their very existence will be threatened again and their final deliverance, foreshadowed by the deliverance of the book of Esther, consummated. Because these traditional Oriental manifestations of intense grief and mourning rendered one ritually unclean, Mordecai could not enter **the king's gate.** Since the king was regarded as divine, his palace was looked upon as a holy place into which sorrow and tragedy were not to intrude (cf. Neh. 2:1-2).

Esther Learns of the Decree. 4:4-9.
4. The queen was informed of Mordecai's grief by her maids and **chamberlains** (eunuchs), but apparently she was not told the details. Quite upset, she dispatched clothing for Mordecai to wear so he could take off his sackcloth, but he refused it. How could he do so when it was not a matter of personal sorrow but of dire public calamity and nothing had as yet been done to avert it? **5.** So Esther dispatched Hathach, one of the royal eunuchs appointed to wait on her, to go to Mordecai **to learn what it was, and why it was** (i.e., "to learn the full particulars," AB). **6.** Hathach met

Mordecai in **the street of the city** (the city square), which was **before** (in front of) **the king's gate.**

7-8. Mordecai then informed him of all the details of the decree to exterminate the Jews, giving him a written copy of the edict of destruction, which had been posted in Shushan, to show Esther and that he might instruct her to go to the king to intercede with him on behalf of her people. **9.** So Hathach went and reported to Esther all that Mordecai had said.

Esther's Dilemma. 4:10-14. **10-12.** Esther reminded Mordecai through Hathach of the death penalty that faced anyone who approached the king without having been summoned, the only exception being that person to whom the king might extend his gold scepter. But the queen's quandary lay in the fact that she had not been summoned to come to the king for the past thirty days. The king's temporary lack of interest in her might jeopardize even her life, not to mention her formal request for an audience and the granting of her request.

13-14. Mordecai's reply to Esther contains a boldly fearless warning of the queen's perilous position if she refused to come to the aid of her people, the Jews, in their hour of terrible crisis. Such a course of action would incur divine judgment upon her and her family. Meanwhile, God would send **relief and deliverance** to His people from some other quarter.

Mordecai knew the history of God's people and the promises of God's Word concerning them too well to doubt God's help even for a moment. **Who knoweth whether thou art come to the kingdom for such a time as this?** These words of Mordecai furnish the key to the basic meaning of the book, namely, to show the unfailing providence of God for His people, Israel, even though they were out of the promised land and scattered among the nations. Mordecai's eloquent appeal was irresistible.

Esther's Decision. 4:15-17. **15-16.** Esther's reply to Mordecai requested fasting (inseparably connected with prayer, Joel 1:13) for three days on the part of all the Jews in Shushan. She and her maidens (perhaps Jewish proselytes whom the queen had taught to pray) also would fast. **If I perish, I perish.** These words express yieldedness to God's will and faith in His sovereign purpose (cf. Job 13:15; Dan. 3:17-18). Esther bravely faced death and was ready to give her life to save her people. Mordecai's faith and Esther's noble decision foreshadow the trust and confidence of that godly remnant of the Jewish people who will pass through "the time of Jacob's trouble," but will be "saved out of it" (Jer. 30:7).

V. ESTHER'S INTERCESSION BEFORE THE KING. 5:1-14.

Esther's Request. 5:1-8. **1-3. On the third day** after Esther's fasting and agony, in which she faced the issue of death and actually in a sense passed through a death experience (4:16), she, adorned in her royal apparel, appeared before the king and was graciously received. **And the king held out ... the golden scepter that was in his hand. So Esther drew near, and touched the top** (tip) **of the scepter.** The third day, speaking of resurrection in Scripture (Gen. 22:4-5; Jonah 1:17; 2:10; Hosea 6:2; Matt. 12:40; Heb. 11:19), looks forward to the time when the Jewish remnant, having passed through the agony of the Great Tribulation, shall be revived and live before the LORD in Kingdom blessing (Hos. 6:1).

The third day will surely come when Israel will arise out of the dust of na-

tional death of persecution and suffering. Then the *golden scepter* of the true King of kings, bespeaking His divine power and grace, will be extended to His earthly people to hear their cry and grant their petition, **even ... to the half of the kingdom.** Even though hyperbolic in Oriental fashion, the expression was never considered a frivolous promise (cf. v. 6; 7:2; Mark 6:23; Herodotus *History* 9. 109). How wonderfully illustrative it is of that future day of Israel's deliverance and entrance into Kingdom blessing, when the King shall say to those who merely befriended the persecuted Jewish remnant, "Come, ye blessed of my Father, inherit the kingdom prepared for you" (Matt. 25:34). What then will be the King's words to the Jewish remnant itself?

4-5. Instead of asking a large favor, Esther merely requested that the king and Haman be present at a dinner she had prepared. Her purpose was to accuse Haman of plotting the colossal pogrom to wipe out her people (cf. 7:6). **6-8.** But, evidently sensing that she did not yet have sufficient influence with the king to make such a bold accusation, she deferred her request and invited the king and Haman to another dinner the next evening. This was clearly the divine leading, for the intervening events (recorded in chap. 6) furnished the necessary foundation for her accusation at the second dinner. Then, too, on the human plane, Esther was acting very discreetly. She was subtly arousing the king's curiosity and expectancy and at the same time building up Haman's ego and bold pride as a prelude to his ruin.

Haman's Self-Delusion. 5:9-14. **9.** Haman left Esther's dinner in high spirits, congratulating himself on his favor, not only with the king, but with Queen Esther. But his rage flamed when Mordecai in the royal gate neither rose nor changed position for him. **10-12.** It was all he could do to control himself in the face of this rude but well-earned insult. However, he allayed his smoldering wrath in a spree of self-indulgent boasting before his wife and friends, regaling them with a recital of his great wealth, the number of his sons, the honor the king had showered upon him, and particularly the special invitation from Queen Esther twice accorded him to a private banquet at the palace.

13. Yet all was poisoned by Haman's hatred of Mordecai and his people, the Jews. For the proud, a fly is always to be found even in the finest ointment, and their steps are stalked by delusion. So Haman made the sad confession, **Yet all this does me no good, so long as I see Mordecai the Jew sitting at the king's gate** (RSV). **14.** So blinded was Haman by hate that he listened to the foolish advice of his wife and friends, **Let a gallows fifty cubits** (seventy-five feet) **high be made, and in the morning tell the king to have Mordecai hanged upon it** (RSV).

In his self-deluding pride, Haman did not realize that he was constructing the gallows for himself. Construction of the gallows in his own courtyard began that very moment, so confident was Haman that the king would grant his request and he could enjoy Queen Esther's second banquet in complete relaxation. He would build it high so it might be seen from a distance, likely from the palace itself. How dramatically does Haman illustrate the arrogant pride of the man of sin, the beast, the final enemy of the Jewish people, who will seek to destroy them before Christ sets up the Kingdom over them (Acts 1:6) at His second advent in glory (Rev. 19:16—20:6).

VI. MORDECAI HONORED. 6:1-14.

The King's Sleepless Night. 6:1-3.

1-2. Although the name of God does not occur in the book of Esther (see Introduction), no part of God's Word displays so remarkably the veiled providential control of God over the events of human history to accomplish the divine purposes. Humanly speaking, upon the king's sleeplessness and the reading of **the book of records of the chronicles** hung the survival of the Jewish people, the fulfillment of prophecy, the coming Redeemer, and consequently the whole divine redemptive plan. Yet God was sovereignly in control and the outcome was never in doubt for a moment.

Even events so apparently trivial as those recounted here are not mere coincidences and literary devices, employed as common motifs in Oriental tales, as higher critics view them (see *Oxford Annotated Bible*). They are examples of God's working in history. God ordered the king's insomnia and directed in the reading of the record of Mordecai's uncovering of the plot against the king and the account of his saving the king's life (2:21-23).

3. God also undertook that the king should inquire, **What honor and dignity hath been bestowed upon Mordecai for this?** Royal benefactors were enrolled on an honor list and were to be suitably rewarded, though not necessarily at the moment. The reward, however, was something to which the benefactor theoretically had a distinct claim that almost amounted to a legal right. Herodotus records how Persian kings maintained records of notable services rendered (*History* 8. 85, 90).

The Outcome of Haman's Delusion. 6:4-10. **4-5.** The king's inquiry, **Who is in the court?** meant "What official is currently in attendance?" Haman's fierce urge for revenge and his abysmal self-deluding pride had driven him to early attendance to official business, and his superior rank accorded him precedence. His official business on this occasion was to engineer the hanging of Mordecai **on the gallows that he had prepared for him** (5:14; 7:10).

What a dramatic moment! The king in the inner court was pondering what reward to bestow upon Mordecai, while Haman in the outer court planned to enter the king's presence primed with an ardent request that he be hanged. It seems the king wanted to consult any statesman available, and Haman happened to be the one on hand at the moment, furnishing another extraordinary example of divine providential working.

6. Then followed the remarkable contrast between Haman's self-deluding pride and Mordecai's self-effacing humility and exaltation, brought out by the king's question, **What shall be done for the man the king delighteth to honor?** Then Haman **thought in his heart** (reasoned to himself), **Whom would the king especially want to honor besides me!** (AB).

What an illustration of the truth that "pride goeth before destruction, and an haughty spirit before a fall" (Prov. 16:18; cf. 18:12). The honors Haman's pride would bestow upon himself were to be bestowed upon his enemy, Mordecai, the Jew, hatred for whom had deprived him of all sense and reason, and like all his ilk, made him a colossal megalomaniac.

7-8. The honors Haman glibly named involved all the outward trappings of royalty, so that, in the case of the one on whom they were bestowed, one would think the king himself was arriving. He requested a royal robe that the king himself had worn, a horse that the king himself had ridden, and a royal crown for the horse's head. Persian horses with crowns may be seen in the reliefs of

Xerxes' *apadana* at Persepolis and on Assyrian monuments.

9. Then Haman excitedly suggested that the robe and the horse be handed over to one of the king's favorite princes to robe the man whom the king especially wanted to honor, and lead him on horseback through the city square in token of royal favor upon that man. **10.** How thunderstruck Haman must have been when he was jolted out of his proud self-delusion upon hearing the king's order, "Hurry up . . . take the robe and the horse, and do exactly as you have advised to Mordecai the Jew . . . do not omit a single detail that you have suggested!" (AB).

Mordecai's Exaltation. 6:11. **11.** What a moment of dramatic irony! While Haman envisioned his own honor and greatness, he was suddenly awakened out of his delusive dream and rudely faced with the unalterable command of the king, whose word was law, to do all he had spoken to the man whom he despised, and whose death sentence he so confidently expected to be signed by the king. He could not wait or parley, but with all speed he had to do that which he hated to do above all things. And Mordecai in his exaltation prefigures the happy lot of Israel when, in that future day, they will be delivered out of the hands of their enemies.

Haman's Anticipation of Doom. 6:12-14. **12-13.** Life continued as before for Mordecai. He went back to his regular place at the king's gate, for his elevation awaited the moment the king would learn of his relationship to Esther (8:1). But life had taken a tragic turn for Haman. Covering his head as a sign of deep distress and grief (cf. 2 Sam. 15:30; 19:4; Jer. 14:3-4), he went home to lick his wounds and seek solace, which was not to be granted him, from his wife and friends. They now sensed a change of fortune and superstitiously recalled that no one who plotted against the Jews ultimately prospered. **14.** Again dramatically, at that very moment the royal eunuchs arrived and hastened to take Haman to Esther's banquet, according to Oriental custom (Luke 14:17) and according to his official importance.

VII. HAMAN HANGED. 7:1-10.

Haman Unmasked. 7:1-6. **1-2.** At the second banquet the following day, the king, knowing that Esther's invitation did not constitute her real request but merely provided the occasion to broach it, was certainly very curious to find out the queen's petition. Arousing the monarch's curiosity was an important part of her sagacious plan to expose Haman's wickedness. **3.** Since the first banquet the situation had changed so drastically that when the king urged Esther to state her petition, she was able to do so boldly. How amazed was the king to find Esther begging for her life and the life of her people.

4. For we are sold, I and my people, to be destroyed (cf. 3:9, 13). Boldly, but of necessity, Esther made full confession of her nationality and risked her own fate and that of her race on the momentary impulse of the fickle monarch, despite his recent gratitude to one of her race and his present mood of cordiality to her. Had not divine providence been operating so wonderfully all along, even these favorable tokens would have proved insufficient grounds of reliance for safety and deliverance.

Esther protested that if her people had been sold as slaves, she would have kept quiet and not mentioned the matter to the king, for that would have resulted in financial profit for him. However, in the annihilation of the Jews **the enemy could not compensate the king's damages** (lit.,

"the enemy is not equal to the damage of the king"), probably meaning that Haman's punishment would entail far less financial loss to the king than the liquidation of tens of thousands of Jews.

5. Esther's brave plea produced the desired response from the king, **Who is he ... who would** [dare] **presume in his heart to do so?** The king was overwhelmed that his queen and her people had been sold to destruction. This was his punishment for his callousness and carelessness in consenting originally to Haman's plot with little or no deliberation (3:10-11). But is hard to imagine that he did not know or had entirely forgotten who had been responsible for instituting this nefarious pogrom barely two months previously (cf. 3:7; 8:9). Apparently he had not cared until the horror of it boomeranged and touched him by touching his queen.

6. The dramatic moment had come for Esther's accusation. **An enemy! An adversary!** (AB) was her impassioned reply to the king's first question ("Who is he?") and **This wicked Haman!** was her answer to his second question (Carey Moore, *Esther,* AB, p. 71). **Then Haman was afraid** ("dumbfounded," in the sense of being completely "taken by surprise"; 1 Chron. 21:30; Dan. 8:17).

Haman Condemned and Executed. 7:7-10. **7-8.** While the king arose in anger from his wine and went out into the palace garden, Haman remained behind to cast himself as a suppliant before Esther to plead for his life. **For he saw that there was evil** ("the evil" in the sense of "the doom," i.e., death) **determined against him** by the king. When the king returned to **the place of the banquet of wine,** he found Haman prostrate at Esther's feet, as she reclined at the banquet upon a couch, according to ancient Oriental custom (cf. 1:6; John 13:23).

The king vented his anger to show how he now felt toward Haman, attributing to him the worst of motives in his approach toward the queen. It is utterly inconceivable that the king thought that Haman would **force** (violate) the queen under those impossible conditions. His preposterous accusation was meant to be a death sentence pronounced against Haman. The king's servants so interpreted the king's word and so **covered Haman's face,** indicating that he was to be executed and never again see the king's face.

9. Then **Harbonah,** one of the royal eunuchs (1:10) who specially attended the king, suggested that there was the gallows at Haman's house, which he had made for Mordecai, who saved the king's life. The great height (seventy-five feet, 5:14) is ironically mentioned. Tersely and dramatically, the king gave the order, **Hang him on that!** (AB). **10.** The climax of the story is now reached. **They hanged Haman on the gallows that he had prepared for Mordecai.** Again, divine providence shines out resplendently in the book. Not only does the LORD deliver His people, but brings upon their enemy the very destruction that he had plotted against them.

Moreover, Haman, as the Jews' enemy, illustrates the ignominious end of the Antichrist, the last great foe of the Jewish people. As Haman almost succeeded in annihilating God's people, so also will the coming man of lawlessness (Dan. 12:9-12). As Haman's end came by royal decree, so will the Antichrist by the word out of the mouth of the coming King of kings (Rev. 19:20).

VIII. THE EDICT OF DELIVERANCE. 8:1-17.

Mordecai Made Prime Minister. 8:1-2. **1.** On the same day that Haman was executed, the king gave Esther Haman's **house,** that is, his entire estate, including all his property, both real estate and other holdings (cf. Gen. 39:4; 44:1; 1 Kings 13:8; Job 8:15). All of this automatically reverted to the crown, since Haman was a traitor (Herodotus 3. 128-29); so it was the king's to give to Esther, probably in consideration of the suffering she had undergone because of Haman's perfidy. **And Mordecai came before the king** (i.e., "became his right-hand man"), replacing Haman as grand vizier, **for Esther had told what he was unto her,** "not only their blood relationship but also the quality of that relationship and the character of the man" (Moore, AB, p. 77).

2. Then the king took the signet ring, which he had recovered from Haman, and in presenting it to Mordecai, invested him with powers of the prime minister, which he had previously conferred on Haman (3:10). In order that Mordecai might have wealth commensurate with his new post (cf. 8:15; 10:3), **Esther set** (appointed) **Mordecai over the house** (the estate) **of Haman.** He was the queen's cousin, and since he had on one occasion been the means of saving the king's life, he began his high official career under extremely favorable circumstances.

Esther's Second Petition. 8:3-8. **3.** Then Esther again spoke to the king, **and fell down at his feet and besought** (implored) **him . . . to put away the mischief** ("frustrate the wicked plot," BV) of Haman. Esther's work was not yet complete, despite the fact that she had witnessed the fall of the foe of her race and the elevation of her cousin as prime minister. The royal edict authorizing the annihilation of the Jews still stood; and since it was unalterable, it was not a case where Mordecai's newly acquired power could interfere. Esther, therefore, encouraged by her successes, made a fresh appeal to the king. **4. The king held out the golden scepter,** in this instance as a sign of encouragement rather than of clemency (cf. 4:11; 5:2).

5-6. Her request that a decree be written to revoke Haman's edict, involving the extermination of all the Jews in the king's empire, was theoretically beyond the king's power. In asking it, Esther displayed unfamiliarity with the complexities of Persian law, probably attributable in part to the deep emotion she was experiencing for the safety of her people. **How can I endure to see the destruction of my kindred?** (Better, "Oh, how could I bear the ruin of my race!" BV.) However, Esther showed considerable skill in presenting her petition. She sagaciously avoided implicating the king, calling **the letters devised by Haman, . . . which he wrote,** and wisely hinted that injury was done the king in the projected destruction of the Jews **in all the king's provinces.**

7-8. In answering the queen's request, the king reviewed his gestures of goodwill in executing Haman and handing over his estate to Esther, **because he would lay hands on the Jews** (RSV). But he shrank from attempting to recall an irrevocable decree and thus overturn established Persian law. He lit upon a plan to meet the difficulty and save the Jews without reversing the decree. Esther and Mordecai, as prime minister, were to write an order concerning the Jews, as they might think best. It was to be issued **in the king's name, and sealed with the king's ring,** making it irreversible.

Haman's letter, also so sealed, could not be countermanded. But the king was permitting them to issue any orders, short of repealing the former order, that might seem good to them to deliver the Jews under the sentence of extermination. The result was that authority was given to the Jews to defend themselves. Whether this plan of counteraction was suggested by the king or Esther and Mordecai is not stated.

The Second Decree. 8:9-15. **9.** Great activity ensued as the royal scribes (secretaries) were summoned on the twenty-third day of Sivan (Bab., *simanu*), which began at the new moon in May (Baruch 1:8), showing that two months and ten days had elapsed since Haman's edict had been issued (3:12). At Mordecai's orders, the dispatch was addressed to the Jews, **deputies** (satraps, see 3:12), **governors and princes** (officials) **of the provinces . . . from India unto Ethiopia** (cf. 1:1), 127 provinces, to each province in its own script, and to each of the many ethnic groups in its own language.

10. The letters, sealed with the royal signet ring, were dispatched **by mounted couriers riding on swift horses, the royal coursers bred from the mares** (AB). The precise meaning of the technical terms in this passage have not as yet been fully clarified by research. However, the general meaning is clear, and the reference is to the Persian postal system, which employed fleet horses to bring Shushan (Susa), the capital, into communication with the far-flung empire (see note on 1:22; cf. 8:14).

11. The new decree was to the effect that royal permission had been granted the Jews throughout the empire to defend themselves and annihilate those who were their enemies, **both little ones and women,** evidently measure-for-measure retaliation, patterned after the sanguinary terms of Haman's original decree (3:13), and perhaps recalling the ancient ban (*ḥĕrĕm*) vowed against all Amalekites (cf. 1 Sam. 15:3). Haman and his supporters would receive what they had planned to give, according to the concept of retributive justice. The Jews were also authorized to take over the property of their vanquished foes for spoil.

12-13. The appointed day was the date that Haman had set (the thirteenth day of the month Adar, i.e., February). Hence, there was need of haste to make prevention sure. **14. So urged on by the king's command, the couriers riding on swift horses, the royal coursers, galloped away. Meanwhile, the decree had been published in the acropolis of Susa** (AB; see 8:10).

15. After the decree was issued, Mordecai left the king's presence attired **in royal apparel** (a royal robe) **of blue and white** (see 1:6) and with **a great crown** (ʻaṭĕrĕṯ, "turban or headdress"; cf. 2 Sam. 12:30) **of gold** (not to be confused with the royal crown [kĕṯĕr] of 1:11; 2:17; 6:8). He was also attired with **a garment** (tăkrîk, "cloak") **of fine linen and purple. The city of Shushan** (Susa) **rejoiced** ("cheered, shouted exultingly"), including the Gentile majority and not just the Jews, rooting evidently with the winning side.

The Joy of the Jews. 8:16-17. **16. The Jews** (cf. 2:5) **had light,** symbolic of spiritual prosperity (Psalms 27:1; 36:9) and well-being (Job 22:28; 30:26; Psalms 97:11; 139:12). **17.** Especially in every province and city where the royal edict came, **the Jews had joy and gladness, a feast and a good day** (i.e., "a holiday"), indicating, as in later Jewish usage, a religious festival.

And many of the people of the land (ʻ$a$mmê hā ʼ$ā$rĕṣ, "pagans," a technical term for non-Jews or Gentiles; cf. Deut. 28:10; Josh. 4:24; 1 Kings 8:53; Ezra 10:2) **became Jews** (mīṯyăh^{a}ḏîm, "professed themselves Jews," a hithpaʻal denominative of y^{e}hûḏî, "Jew"). Apparently they embraced the Hebrew faith as proselytes, submitting doubtlessly to circumcision (according to the Septuagint and Old Latin).

Some scholars, however, interpret the passage to mean that the Gentiles merely identified themselves with the cause of the threatened Jews and pretended to be Jews (C. H. Gordon, *Introduction to Old Testament Times,* p. 279), **for the fear of the Jews fell** (had fallen) **upon them.** In the light of the subsequent statistics concerning the slaughter of the enemies of the Jews, their fear of the Jews was quite justified.

IX. THE FEAST OF PURIM INSTITUTED. 9:1-32.

The Jews Resist and Are Victorious. 9:1-10. **1.** On the fatal day, the thirteenth of Adar (see 8:12; 3:7), when the time for the enforcement of the royal mandate, **drew near** (arrived, came; cf. 8:17), the Jews' enemies expected to overpower them. Instead, it turned out to be a day in which the Jews themselves **had rule** (gained the upper hand) **over them that hated them.**

2. Jewry united throughout the empire **to lay hand on** (lit., "to send the hand against" in the sense of "kill," 2:21; 3:6; 9:16) **such as sought their harm** (ruin), doubtlessly taking the offensive in some instances rather than waiting to be attacked. And no one **could withstand them** (lit., "stood before them," in the sense of being "successful against them"). The reason given is **for the fear of them** had fallen upon all the peoples.

3. Moreover, because the Jews were in favor at court, **all the princes of the provinces, and the deputies** (satraps), **and the governors, and officers of the king** (lit. Heb., "those who did the business that belonged to the king") **helped** (aided or supported; cf. Ezra 1:4) **the Jews,** morally and perhaps also financially and militarily. They stood in fear of Mordecai.

4. For Mordecai was great, since his power as prime minister made him very influential **in the king's house,** in the sense of the entire capital (cf. 2:8), not merely in the palace or acropolis of Shushan. He **grew greater and greater** (lit., "was growing and was great," i.e., "grew more and more powerful"). **5.** The result was that the Jews vanquished all their foes, slaughtering and destroying them, and **did what they would** (pleased) to those who hated them, a clear example of "do unto others as they would have done to you."

6-10. In Shushan (Susa), **the palace** (the acropolis or stronghold), the Jews slew five hundred men, doubtlessly because Haman had had many friends and supporters there (including his ten sons) who were deadly enemies, as he had been, of Mordecai. That this thorough purge of the enemy was considered absolutely necessary to guarantee the Jews' permanent safety and not mere retributive hatred, is suggested by the appended notice—**but on the spoil** (plunder) **laid they not their hand,** which they might have done according to the decree (8:11), showing that restraint in killing was exercised, despite appearance to the contrary. The Jews would demonstrate the purity of their motives by refraining to take advantage of their rightful privilege.

Esther's Petition and Its Result. 9:11-19. **11.** The king apparently rejoiced with Esther and Mordecai when the number of those slain in the acropolis (stronghold) of Shushan **was brought** to him. **12.** He surmised how great the victory of the Jews must have been in the royal provinces. Evidently Esther had been informed of some new plot against the Jews. Thus, the king, detecting her deep concern, sensed she was burdened to make another petition in behalf of her people, and he promised to grant it.

13. Her request, certainly dictated by necessity and not by a desire for needless butchery, was that an additional day be added for the Jews to defend themselves in the capital, and that the ten sons of Haman be hanged (exposed) on the gallows, as a stern warning of a similar fate to be meted out to those who hated and would harm the Jews.

14-16. Esther's petition was granted and the decree issued, and three hundred more enemies of the Jews were put to death in Shushan (Susa), and the dead bodies of Haman's sons were exposed (cf. Deut. 21:22-23). But again it is noted that the Jews did not lay hand on any plunder (cf. v. 10), although throughout the empire they **gathered themselves together** (organized), **and defended their lives,** and **had rest** (relief, respite) from their enemies, slaying seventy-five thousand of them. **17.** That took place on the thirteenth day of Adar. Thus, they rested on the fourteenth day, making it a day of feasting and rejoicing. **18.** But the Jews in the capital had organized themselves and fought their foes on both the thirteenth and fourteenth days. Therefore, they rested on the fifteenth day and observed it as a day of feasting and rejoicing. **19.** Accordingly, Jews in the country districts celebrated the fourteenth day of Adar as a holiday.

The Establishment of the Feast of Purim. 9:20-32. Having the historical setting for the first celebration of Purim on the fourteenth and fifteenth of Adar (vv. 1-19), there were three major steps by which this feast became an established celebration of the Jewish religious calendar: **20-22.** (1) Mordecai's festal letter made them days of feasting, rejoicing, and for sending **portions** (delicacies) as well as **gifts** (alms) **to the poor. 23-28.** (2) The Jews deliberately intended to celebrate annually the events of Purim (vv. 23, 27-28). **The Jews**

undertook to do as they had begun, that is, they "made customary what they had started doing" (AB).

29-32. (3) The confirmatory letter of Esther and Mordecai established the feast. Esther wrote with full authority **to confirm this second letter of Purim,** lending all her prestige as queen and heroine to ratify Mordecai's festal letter. The reference to "this second letter" is probably to Esther's own message, reaffirming Mordecai's (v. 20). **The matters of the fastings and their lamentations** suggest that the Jews throughout the empire had instituted abstention from food and lamentations in addition to what Mordecai's letter had stipulated and is likely to be connected with the fast now observed by Jews on the thirteenth of Adar.

The book of Esther, recording a great outburst of hatred against God's people, Israel, furnishes an illustration of the final age-end outburst of anti-Semitism that will aim, as this one did, at the Jews' total annihilation (Jer. 30:5-7; Zech. 12:1-9; 14:1-6; Rev. 13:1-16). The fate of the end-time enemies of the Jews will be similar to what happened to the enemies of the Jews in Shushan (Susa) and the far-flung Persian Empire (Num. 24:7-8; Deut. 32:41). Haman's miserable end illustrates the fall of the Antichrist (Rev. 19:20), the most terrible hater and persecutor the Jews will ever have, and the person to whom all preceding anti-Semitic leaders point. The ten sons of Haman, so closely associated with their father in his infamy and fate, prefigure the Antichrist's ten-kingdom confederation (Dan. 2:41; 7:20-28), which will crash with him in ruin at his fall and terrible end (Dan. 2:34-35).

X. MORDECAI'S GREATNESS. 10:1-3.

The Greatness of the Persian King. 10:1-2. **1-2.** The writer of the book of Esther began by narrating the greatness of Ahasuerus (Xerxes), and he ends the book on the same note (cf. 1:1-8 with 10:1-2). His purpose is to picture the Jew Mordecai's exaltation to become the savior and deliverer of his people against this background of royal power.

The king **laid a tribute** (lit., *măs,* "a forced payment" or "taxes") on his realm, doubtlessly to fill the royal coffers exhausted by the disastrous expedition to Greece. The **seacoasts** are mentioned. The chief island remaining to Persia in the Mediterranean, after Persian losses in the Aegean, was Cyprus. In indicating Xerxes' greatness, the author not only cites his source of information, **the chronicles** (annals) **of the kings of Media and Persia,** but also invites his readers to check the facts for themselves to establish the veracity and trustworthiness of his account of the origin of the feast of Purim.

The Greatness of Mordecai. 10:3. **3.** This exaltation of Mordecai is emphasized by his being **next unto King Ahasuerus** and his being **great among** the Jews, his own kinsmen, as their hero and deliverer. The events of the book reach to 470 B.C., at which time Mordecai attained the zenith of his power. How long he retained it is unknown, for at the end of Xerxes' reign his chief adviser was Artabanus, the captain of the guard, by whom he was assassinated in 464 B.C. Mordecai passed off the scene **seeking the welfare** (best interests) of his people, and concerned for **all his seed,** that is, all the stock of Israel.

JOB

INTRODUCTION

Title of the Book. The book of Job takes its title from its chief character, Job (*'iyyôb*), a common west-Semitic name in the second millennium B.C., attested by the Egyptian Execration Texts, the Mari and the Amarna letters, and the Alalakh and Ugaritic documents. In the light of this new evidence, the original form of the name seems to have been *Ayyab(um)*, meaning either "Where is [my] father?" or simply "no father," possibly suggesting orphancy or illegitimacy (see AB, pp. 5-6).

Uniqueness and Nature of the Book. The book is unique despite the fact that numerous documents from the ancient biblical world touch upon the question of theodicy (the defense of God's goodness and omnipotence in the light of the existence of evil and the suffering of the righteous). The uniqueness of the biblical book derives from the satisfying depth and thoroughness with which it handles this problem, owing to its divine inspiration and monotheism. Extrabiblical parallels from Sumer, Babylonia, Egypt, and other places are polytheistic and, hence, hamstrung at the start to deal adequately with the problem of theodicy.

Not only the literary genre but also the overall format of the book stem from the world of which it was a part. It is commonly called Wisdom literature, which was well known in the biblical world (cf. Proverbs and Ecclesiastes and some of the psalms). This genre of Hebrew literature not only comes to grips with the practical problems of life, as in Proverbs, but also with great moral and spiritual issues, like the prosperity of the wicked (Psalm 37), materialism, pessimism, fatalism (cf. Ecclesiastes), and the suffering of God's people (Job). In dealing with everyday living, it reflects a clear-sighted practicality, free from speculative philosophy, that finds its center in "the fear of the LORD," which is considered "the beginning of knowledge [wisdom]" (Prov. 1:7).

But the book of Job cannot be forced into any single classification in its literary form. Besides features of Wisdom literature, it contains other elements, such as drama and epic, being a magnificent dramatic poem acknowledged as one of the great literary masterpieces of world literature.

Authorship and Literary Unity. The book is anonymous, as all admit, but the heated question is whether it is of single or composite authorship. Higher criticism typically considers the book a gradual aggregation of materials on an original base (the prologue and epilogue). Additions are claimed to be the dialogues, the poem on divine wisdom (chap. 28), the speeches of Elihu (chaps. 32-37), and the divine discourses (chaps. 38-41).

The common contention is that the prologue-epilogue represents an ancient epic tale, which was employed by the author of the dialogues. This alleged tale about a "legendary" figure named Job (Ezek. 14:14, 20) is claimed to have been used to set forth later more advanced concepts of theodicy under a proper hoary antiquity. Under such a critical view, the book is considered an artistic masterpiece skillfully fabricated by a great poet at a much later date, using sources available to him.

Although the book makes no claim of Jobine authorship (the prologue-epilogue being *about* him), such a view tends to deny that Job was a real person (cf. Ezek. 14:14, 20; James 5:11) and undermines the authenticity of the book. The discourses do claim to be spoken by a definite individual, who lived in a definite place, at a definite time, and had certain definite experiences. If all of this is mere fiction or allegory, it is difficult to imagine that the integrity of the book would not be impaired.

Higher critics allege incongruities between the prologue, epilogue, and the dialogues. In the former, Job is presented as a saint of God, while in the latter he is set forth as an extremely embittered man, filled with shocking complaints, while his friends, who seem to be saying what is right, are rebuked, and Job is commended in the epilogue. These and other alleged incongruities are much more satisfactorily explained under the view of literary unity of the book and under the interpretation that Job's "friends" were mouthing mere pious platitudes and empty clichés, while Job had challenged God, impelled by a moral duty to speak only the truth before Him (cf. Y. Kaufmann, *The Religion of Israel,* p. 135).

Date and Canonicity. Vast disagreement prevails concerning the date of the composition from the Solomonic era and before to the second century B.C. But these late dates have been discredited by the recovery of fragments of Job written in palaeo-Hebrew script among the Dead Sea manuscripts. Apparently Job himself lived in the second millennium B.C., not far removed from the patriarchal age. His longevity and the picture of him as a man, whose wealth was measured in cattle and who contended with marauding Sabaean and Chaldean tribesmen, fit the early patriarchal period.

It is possible the story may have existed in oral form or even in partially written form until an anonymous Israelite author under divine inspiration put it into its present literary form. If so, this would account for the non-Israelite tone of the book and also explain its unquestioned place in the Hebrew canon. That a book with nothing distinctively Israelite about it should be accepted into the Hebrew canon and never be seriously challenged is truly remarkable. Certainly the Hebrews recognized the superior spiritual message of this book from earliest times. Since inspiration was the test of canonicity, and the acceptance of a book by the community of God's people was a major test for inspiration and admission to the canon, the Hebrews adjudged the book God-breathed and placed it in the third section of their inspired books called the Writings.

The Language of the Book. The book is written in Hebrew with a strong Aramaic tinge, with Hebrew and Aramaic words frequently juxtaposed as synonyms in the poetic parallelism. The book also contains more *hapax legomena* (words occurring only once—110 according to W. B. Stevenson, *The Poem of Job*) and rare words than any other biblical book, many of which have been explained from the cognate Semitic languages. Others remain as yet obscure or unknown. The recovery of the Ugaritic poetical literature has added considerably to knowledge of early northwest Semitic poetry, and hope is held out that further discoveries will help to elucidate many obscure passages in the book.

The Theme of Job. The book deals with the perplexing question, Why do the righteous suffer, and how can their suffering be squared with the all-powerful and infinitely holy God? Theologically, this subject is called theodicy — a justification of God's righteous character and omnipotence in the face of sin and evil in the world and the suffering of His saintly people as a result of it.

Job's three friends found the answer in Job's sinfulness. They reasoned that suffering is always the result of sin (chaps. 3-31). Job desperately protested his innocence, and in his dilemma was driven to assume that God must be dealing unjustly with him. At this point, Elihu appeared on the scene as the

LORD's messenger and forerunner in declaring the balancing truth that afflictions are frequently chastenings of a loving Father, not in any sense the expressions of an angry and implacable Deity (chaps. 32-37).

God's speech to Job out of the whirlwind (chaps. 38-41) was meant not only to humble Job in bringing him to the place of abhorring himself before the divine majesty, but was also intended to show that the ultimate answer to the problem of the suffering of the righteous lies in the infinite wisdom of God, which to a degree at least and in its final essence, must remain inscrutable to sinful finite creatures. Accordingly, Job's self-abnegation and spiritual refining (42:1-6), opened the way for his restoration and blessing (42:7-17).

OUTLINE

I. PROLOGUE: JOB'S TESTING. 1:1—2:13.
  A. Job's Integrity and Satan's First Accusation. 1:1-22.
  B. Job's Integrity and Satan's Second Accusation. 2:1-13.
II. JOB'S THREE FRIENDS SPEAK. 3:1—31:40.
  A. The First Cycle of Speeches. 3:1—14:22.
    1. Job's Despairing Lament. 3:1-26.
    2. Eliphaz's First Speech—God Is Pure. 4:1-21.
    3. Eliphaz's First Speech Continued—His Views of Suffering. 5:1-27.
    4. Job's First Speech—He Answers Eliphaz. 6:1-30.
    5. Job's First Speech Continued—Effects of Bad Counseling. 7:1-21.
    6. Bildad's First Speech—God Is Just. 8:1-22.
    7. Job's Reply to Bildad—Does God Love Him? 9:1-35.
    8. Job's Reply to Bildad Continued—He Struggles with God. 10:1-22.
    9. Zophar's First Speech—God Is All-Wise. 11:1-20.
    10. Job's Reply to Zophar—He Asserts His Innocence. 12:1-25.
    11. Job's Reply to Zophar Continued—He Resents His Friends. 13:1-28.
    12. Job's Reply to Zophar Concluded—The Brevity of Life. 14:1-22.
  B. The Second Cycle of Speeches. 15:1—21:34.
    1. Eliphaz's Second Speech—The Wicked Do Not Prosper. 15:1-35.
    2. Job's Reply—His Friends Are Miserable Comforters. 16:1-22.
    3. Job's Reply Continued—He Cries for Vindication. 17:1-16.
    4. Bildad's Second Speech—The Doom of the Wicked. 18:1-21.
    5. Job's Reply to Bildad—My Redeemer Lives. 19:1-29.
    6. Zophar's Second Speech—The Misery Awaiting the Wicked. 20:1-29.
    7. Job's Reply—The Sovereign God Will Deal with the Wicked. 21:1-34.

C. The Third Cycle of Speeches. 22:1—31:40.
  1. Eliphaz's Third Speech—Agree with God. 22:1-30.
  2. Job's Reply to Eliphaz—Good People Often Suffer. 23:1-17.
  3. Job's Reply to Eliphaz Continued—Bad People Often Go Unpunished. 24:1-25.
  4. Bildad's Third Speech—God and Man in Contrast. 25:1-6.
  5. Job's Reply to Bildad—He Acknowledges God's Greatness. 26:1-14.
  6. Job's Reply Continued—He Maintains His Integrity. 27:1-23.
  7. Job's Poem on Wisdom. 28:1-28.
  8. Job's Reminiscence upon His Earlier Prosperity. 29:1-25.
  9. Job's Present Sufferings. 30:1-31.
  10. Job's Final Protestation of Innocence. 31:1-40.
III. ELIHU SPEAKS TO JOB. 32:1—37:24.
  A. Elihu's First Speech—His Anger at Job's Self-Justification. 32:1-22.
  B. Elihu's First Speech Continued—He Defends God's Righteousness. 33:1-33.
  C. Elihu's Second Speech—God Is Not Unjust. 34:1-37.
  D. Elihu's Third Speech—God Is Not Indifferent to Virtue or Vice. 35:1-16.
  E. Elihu's Fourth Speech—God's Ways Are Just but Inscrutable. 36:1—37:24.
IV. THE LORD SPEAKS TO JOB. 38:1—42:6.
  A. The Lord's First Discourse—He Challenges Job. 38:1—39:30.
  B. The Lord's Second Discourse—Job Brought to Repentance. 40:1-24.
  C. The Lord's Second Discourse Continued—Job's Heart Bared. 41:1-34.
  D. Job's Confession and Restoration. 42:1-6.
V. EPILOGUE: JOB'S RESTORATION AND BLESSING. 42:7-17.

COMMENTARY

I. PROLOGUE: JOB'S TESTING. 1:1—2:13.

A. JOB'S INTEGRITY AND SATAN'S FIRST ACCUSATION. 1:1-22.

Job's Character and Prosperity. *1:1-5.* **1. There was a man in the land of Uz**—a real person, who resided in a definite place (Jer. 25:20; Lam. 4:21), just as definite as Tema (Job 6:19), Sheba (6:19), Ethiopia (28:19), or the Jordan River (40:23). Jewish, Christian, and Muslim traditions point to a real flesh-and-blood Job who lived in history (F. Delitzsch, *Commentary on the Book of Job,* 2:395-447). The existence of extrabiblical parallels in other ancient Near Eastern cultures does not nullify the historicity of the biblical Job (see Introduction).

The most likely location of Uz is Syria (Aram), rather than Edom, Idumea, or another area. The Uz of Genesis 10:23 is apparently the only person who could have established an area bearing his name by the time Job lived, apparently in the Abrahamic or pre-Abrahamic age. If this is so, the other two men named Uz (Gen. 22:20-24; 36:28) were not even born by the time Job lived, based upon matching his long life-span with other biblical patriarchs (cf. Gen. 25:7).

Whose name was Job (for meaning of the name, see Introduction). Job is described as being **perfect** (*tām*, "blameless") and **upright** (*yāshār*, from a root meaning "to be straight" or "go straight"). Noah similarly is said to have been "perfect" (Gen. 6:9), and Abram was enjoined to be so (Gen. 17:1; cf.

Matt. 5:48). The connotation is, of course, not sinless perfection, but consistent integrity, for Job was quite cognizant of his sins (e.g., Job 7:20; 13:26). He **feared God,** had deep reverence for Him who was infinitely holy, hence, **shunned** ("turned away from") **evil,** exhibiting the character in which wisdom is declared to consist (28:28; Prov. 1:7).

2-3. Job was not only godly, he was God-blessed domestically with a large family, **seven sons and three daughters,** as well as materially, **his substance** (lit., "cattle," since wealth was so measured in the patriarchal age in which he lived) being seven thousand sheep, three thousand camels, five hundred yoke of oxen, and five hundred female donkeys. He also had **a very great household,** meaning he possessed many servants. Job was **the greatest of all the men** ("sons") **of the east,** meaning "Easterners," the tribal chieftains inhabiting the country northeast of Palestine, which the Arabs still call the land of Job.

4. Job's domestic blessing was enhanced by the social conviviality of his children, for **his sons used to go and hold a feast in the house of each one on his day** (NASB), apparently indicating a round of festivities on certain special occasions, such as birthdays, sheepshearing, or spring and harvest festivals.

5. When the days of their feasting **were finished** ("had completed their cycle," NASB), **Job sent and sanctified them,** acting patriarchally as family priest. He offered burnt offerings as symbolic of the Messianic expiation of sin, to make atonement for sins his children might have committed. In this manner he "sanctified" them, that is, dedicated them afresh to God. He thus showed his faith in the one true gospel of salvation by grace through faith, after the manner of Abraham and the patriarchs (Gen. 8:20; 22:7; 31:54), according to early custom before the institution of the Mosaic Law restricting sacrifice to the Levitical priests.

It may be that my sons have . . . cursed God in their hearts. No formalist or ritualist, Job perceived the exceeding sinfulness of sin and its root in the human heart (cf. Job 31; Jer. 17:5, 9). Nor was he a mere moralist, for he was keenly aware, as special revelation had emphasized, that without the shedding of sacrificial blood there is no remission of sins.

Satan's First Accusation Against Job. 1:6-12. **6.** The scene is dramatically transported to heaven, the world of the spirits. **The sons of God** are angels, so called because they are creatures of God, partaking of His spiritual nature and intimately associated with Him (Gen. 6:2; Psalms 29:1, NASB margin; 89:6; Dan. 3:25). Hence, they **came to present themselves before the Lord** as His ministers and agents in the conduct of human affairs.

And Satan (the adversary) **came also among** (lit., "in the midst of") **them.** The revelation of Satan in the Bible is progressive, beginning with his original sinless state in eternity past, followed by his fall (Ezek. 28:11-19; Isa. 14:12-14). It continues in time with his appearance to tempt man under the guise of the Edenic serpent (Gen. 3:1-5), and proceeds with his operation in the heavenlies (Job 1:6), his future casting out of heaven upon the earth during the Great Tribulation (Rev. 12:7-10), his incarceration in the abyss

during the Kingdom age (20:1-3), and concludes with his final doom in gehenna for eternity (20:10).

7. Satan is presented in this passage as not only having access to the earth but the heavenly realm as well (cf. Eph. 6:10-20). He is introduced as **going to and fro,** that is, "roaming about" **in the earth** (1 Pet. 5:8), as "the accuser of our brethren" (Rev. 12:10). **8.** In this, his common role since the Fall of man and the divine redemptive program was instituted, Satan accused Job before God, despite the LORD's high commendation of His child.

9. Doth Job fear God for nothing? Satan's accusation was dastardly. **10-11.** The material prosperity hedging Job's life, Satan insinuated, was the reason why he served God. Remove the hedge and Job's piety would vanish. The charge was that Job served God only for what he got out of such service.

12. Satan's challenge was accepted by God, and the stage was set for the examination of the validity of Satan's ugly insinuation. Satan was given permission to test Job, but strictly under the divine direction and for the divine purpose, an illustration that Satan and all his evil forces, as well as sin and wicked men, are in the final analysis but agents of the omnipotent and absolutely sovereign God to accomplish His plan and purposes for the ages.

Job's Testing–Loss of Property and Family. 1:13-19. **13.** On the day when a new round of feasting began in the house of Job's firstborn son, Satan, under the permissive will of God working through human agency, swept away Job's possessions. **14-15. The Sabeans,** nomads from the Arabian Desert, took his oxen and donkeys and slew his servants. **16. The fire of God,** doubtlessly lightning (cf. Gen. 19:24; 2 Kings 1:10-14), a natural phenomenon viewed as directed by supernatural power, **burned up the sheep, and the servants.**

17. The Chaldeans, desert marauders, originally from southern Mesopotamia, carried away the camels and slew the servants. One disaster following upon another points to the conclusion that all the calamities were the distinct work of Satan, according to the permission allowed him (cf. v. 12). **18-19. A great wind** came across the desert and struck the house where Job's children were feasting (cf. v. 13), killing all of them.

Job's Integrity. 1:20-22. **20-21.** In the face of his great loss, Job displayed genuine wisdom in holding fast to true wisdom itself—man's faithful Creator-Redeemer. He displayed absolute dedication of himself to God as his world flew apart and calamity stunned him almost to insensibility. He worshiped with tokens of deepest penitence, submission, and humility as a wise man—wise not because he understood the reason for his suffering, but because, not understanding, he maintained unswerving faith in God.

Wisely he reasoned that as a naked baby born into the world, he brought nothing with him and likewise he would make his exit from this material world. He realized at least in degree the great truth the apostle Paul emphasized: "For our light affliction, which is but for a moment, worketh for us a far more exceeding and eternal weight of glory, while we look not at the things which are seen, but at the things which are not seen; for the things which are seen are temporal, but the things which are not seen are eternal" (2 Cor. 4:17-18).

The Lord gave . . . the Lord hath taken away; blessed be the name of the Lord. Job even found in his deep adversity an occasion for praise, employing the covenant name of grace and redemption, which also is an indication of the early date of these events. How completely was Satan foiled as Job declared the Lord's name **blessed,** the very word Satan employed in a contrary sense ("curse") in verse 11.

B. Job's Integrity and Satan's Second Accusation. 2:1-13.

Satan's Second Accusation. 2:1-6. **1-3.** This, the second scene in heaven (see 1:6-11), was followed, as was the first scene, by a series of happenings on earth, which resulted from the encounters between the Lord and Satan. In this appearance Satan avoided any report on Job, so the Lord openly declared the fact of the tried and true integrity of His servant, repeating for emphasis the very words of commendation spoken in the first session (cf. 1:8).

However, this time the Lord reminded the adversary of Job's steadfastness. **And still he holdeth fast his integrity, although thou movedst** (incited) **me . . . to destroy** (swallow up or consume) **him without cause** (ḥinnām). This is the same Hebrew word of Satan's question in 1:9, "Doth Job fear God *for nothing?*" that is, gratuitously, freely, without thought of return benefit or recompense? The Lord employed the same term to show the utter falsity of Satan's base insinuation. Now it had become apparent that Job did fear God *for nothing,* that is, gratuitously, without thought of recompense, and therefore, it was *for nothing* ("without cause," a slightly different shade of meaning of the word) that Satan had accused him.

4-5. Satan, however, persistent and undaunted by failure in the first round of temptation, proceeded to attack Job with a more extreme form of the initial accusation of 1:9. **Skin for skin,** "hide for hide," a proverb probably employed by Bedouin tradesmen, **yea, all that a man hath will he give for his life. But . . .**

touch his bone and his flesh, and he will curse thee to thy face.

Satan insinuated that even Job's praise to God, born in the anguish of bereavement of his family, was nothing more than the phony performance of a shrewd bargainer, selfishly concerned only about his own physical well-being, and offering God feigned love as the fee of a sort for a health insurance policy. Satan suggested if he were allowed to touch his **bone and his flesh** (his physical body), and there was no possible profit to be realized from "the religious game," Job would openly and defiantly curse God.

6. Behold, he is in thine hand (power). Compare the New Testament parallel of being delivered unto Satan (1 Cor. 5:5; 1 Tim. 1:20). Once more God permitted the mystery of the suffering of the righteous, but He again restricted Satan. **But save his life.** Even if Job failed and did curse God, God would remain faithful (2 Tim. 2:13). The LORD cared for Job and the life of His servant more than Job himself cared for it. He could not deny Himself.

Job's Integrity in the Loss of Physical Health. 2:7-10. **7. Satan ... smote Job with sore boils.** Was Job's disease elephantiasis, an extreme form of leprosy in which the skin becomes rough and hard like an elephant's hide, with painful cracks and sores? **8.** Whatever it was, it was extremely loathsome and itchy, so that he took pieces of broken pottery to scrape himself and sat down in ashes, as an outcast from human society.

9. But Job had not yet faced his greatest trial. His worst temptation of all was when his wife, like Eve, succumbed to Satan's lie: **Curse God, and die.** The blasphemous apostasy, to which she urged her suffering spouse, was precisely what Satan had predicted of Job.

It is calamity indeed when a man's foes become those of his own household (Mic. 7:6; Matt. 10:36) and, instead of strengthening our faith in God, join with Satan to destroy it. Her rash advice fanned Job's torment to its fiercest pitch and brought a decisive rebuke of her folly, for she was acting in diametrical contrast to true wisdom (Prov. 1:7).

10. The folly of her behavior brings into clearer focus the godly "patience" (endurance) of Job (cf. James 5:11). **Shall we not receive** (meekly, patiently) **evil?** His words are fuller than his thought, for his faith told him that calamities become blessings in disguise.

The Coming of the Counselors. 2:11-13. **11.** These **three friends,** like Job's wife, we are tempted to believe, were reserved by Satan for further employment in his spiritual war against Job's soul. **Eliphaz, the Temanite,** came from Teman (Tawilan) in northern Edom (cf. Gen. 36:11; Jer. 49:20; Ezek. 25:13; Amos 1:12). The inhabitants of Teman were famed for their wisdom (Jer. 49:7).

Bildad, the Shuhite, probably was descended from Shuah, Abraham's son by Keturah who was the brother of Midian and the uncle of Sheba and Dedan (Gen. 25:2-3). Bildad came from the east country, the land of wise men (cf. 1 Kings 4:30), as did **Zophar, the Naamathite.** They were renowned sages and great men of their tribes since they were friends and counselors of "the greatest of all the men of the east" (1:3). They arranged to meet together to go **to mourn with** (condole) Job **and to comfort him.**

12. When they saw Job from afar, they could not recognize him, for his sickness and suffering had so disfigured him (cf. Isa. 53:3). Weeping, each of the sheikhs tore his **mantle,** that is, his robe, which was a badge of his nobility (cf. 1:20), and sprinkled dust upon his head as a sign of extreme grief (Josh. 7:6; 1 Sam. 4:12; Lam. 2:10).

13. Their stunned, week-long silence was like mourning for the dead (cf. Gen. 50:10; 1 Sam. 31:13), in which the comforters were not allowed to utter a word until the mourner opened the conversation. Evidently they were sincerely affected and aimed to console and comfort. But their subsequent interpretation of Job's suffering showed they had become duped by Satan, as Job's wife had been, and become his agents, and as such had more success than any previous means used by the adversary against Job to cause him to sin with his lips, in contrast to 1:22 and 2:10.

II. JOB'S THREE FRIENDS SPEAK. 3:1—31:40.

A. THE FIRST CYCLE OF SPEECHES. 3:1—14:22.

1. JOB'S DESPAIRING LAMENT. 3:1-26.

He Curses the Day of His Birth. *3:1-10.* **After this** (the seven-day silence, the style being classical; cf. Gen. 15:14; 23:19; 25:26) **opened Job his mouth, and cursed his day.** This chapter is evidently quoted by Jeremiah (20:14-18), applying to his own life the well-known expression of a patriarchal experience. But the vexing question is, What caused the drastic change in Job from godly, patient submission to his sufferings to impatient imprecations? Although many natural causes for this alteration may be surmised, such as the erosion of his spiritual resistance by the unrelenting bout with his physical affliction, and the sight of his distinguished companions, which recalled too vividly his own splendid past now vanished, the underlying cause was satanic inroad through his would-be comforters. The brooding presence of these wise men set Job philosophizing about his own sad state.

But the more intently Job sought an answer, the more subtly it vanished behind a curtain of mystery. In seeking to know why he was afflicted, he strayed from the narrow path of wisdom. Instead of holding fast to the confidence that God had not abandoned him, he cursed not God, as Satan would have had him do, but his own miserable existence, which was a step at least in the direction of Satan's goal. For, in doing so, he was daring to argue with God, who had so ordered it. In not submitting to his sovereign LORD, he was not acting in faith, which was sin. Hence, in the final analysis, Job needed to repent (cf. 42:1-6).

3. Job not only cursed **the day** he was born (vv. 3-5) but **the night** in which he was conceived (vv. 6-10). The report of a birth to a father, especially that of a boy, was always a momentous event and accounted a great blessing. Yet, Job cried out, "Damn the day I was born, the night that said, 'A boy is begot' " (AB).

8. Job poetically invoked those who **curse the day** to curse his day, conceivably referring to pagan magicians in a mythological allusion, since it is parallel to "those ... prepared to rouse Leviathan" (NASB), cognate with Ugaritic *lotan,* "the sea monster." Many scholars see a reference to an eclipse, leviathan in ancient mythology being looked upon as devouring sun and moon in the celestial phenomenon. The Balaam story (Num. 22-24) furnishes an example of the importance of procuring someone skilled in this occult art (cf. Num. 22:6-7). **9. The stars of its twilight** are Venus and Mercury, which he wished had remained dark so that the day of his birth might never have dawned nor seen, literally, "the eyelids of the morning" (RSV), the first bright streaks that herald the sun.

He Inquires Why He Did Not Die. **3:11-19. 11-12. Why died I not from the womb? Why did the knees receive me?** The knees of the father or grandfather received the child as a token of legitimation (cf. Gen. 50:23). The knees of the mother in Beduoin society also received the newborn child (cf. B. Stade, ZAW 16 [1886]:153). **13-19.** Cursing life, Job welcomed death as the greatest boon, which he viewed as a state of quietness and rest, with mighty men and princes as his companions.

He Cries out in His Agony. **3:20-26. 20-22.** Why does God give life to the bitter of soul, who yearns in vain for death and seeks it like a treasure trove? **23.** Why does God give light to a man **whose way is hidden, and whom God hath hedged in?** Job now employed the same word **hedged in** of himself, as one hemmed in by God with darkness and disfavor, as Satan had used of Job having a "hedge about" (1:10) him on every side by divine favor. This intimates how far Job had opened himself up to satanic suggestion. **25-26.** Job's fears displayed his faltering faith and showed the reason for his inner disquietude and agony.

2. ELIPHAZ'S FIRST SPEECH—GOD IS PURE. 4:1-21.

God Does Not Punish the Righteous. **4:1-11. 1-2.** Eliphaz took the lead in the discussion, perhaps because of seniority. He began apologetically, **If one ventures a word with you, will you be offended?** (RSV). Job, it appears (29:9-10), was held in high esteem by everyone, and Eliphaz also regarded him with such awe as would have constrained him to be silent. But he was so certain that Job was wrong and merited reproof that he was compelled to speak. Perhaps it is not right to argue with a sick man; yet, how can one not do so when he harbors such thoughts as Job did?

Eliphaz, in opening up the long cycle of speeches, struck a note that all the friends sounded, with variations: it is the wicked who suffer, and therefore all who suffer must be wicked. But the basic thesis of the three friends was not true, and—even more unfortunate—their deductions from it were not applicable to Job's case, for he was not being punished for any secret sin he had committed, as they implied. As a result, their intended comfort turned into spiritual torment and harassment as Satan, so visibly and really active in the heavenly scene of the world of the spirits (1:6-12; 2:1-7), now operated invisibly but just as really in the earthly scene of the world of men in the flesh.

Job's three friends, in holding and propagating doctrinal error (truth subtly blended with untruth), or misapplying truth unmixed with error, exposed themselves to evil spiritual powers (cf. 1 Tim. 4:1-5; 1 John 4:1-4) ready to operate through them to attack Job to make him sin with his lips (Job 1:22; 2:10). What Satan failed to do previous to the arrival of Job's friends, he evidently succeeded in doing through their mere presence (chap. 3), and particularly by means of their words.

3-6. Eliphaz reproved Job for his impatience after he had upheld and strengthened others. **8-9.** His suffering was explained by the maxim that a man reaps what he sows. **10-11.** If the wicked exhibit the violent savagery of the lion, they may expect the lion's fate—to be hunted down, their teeth broken, and their young wandering without food to perish.

Sinful Man Must Perish. **4:12-21. 12-15.** Eliphaz claimed special revelation as the result of a "hair-raising" night vision. He gave the message vouchsafed to him in the vision (vv. 17-21). **17. Can man be righteous before**

God? Can a mortal be pure before His Maker? (BV). The answer is obviously no, and the theology is perfectly orthodox. But at the same time, the argument was utterly inadequate to deal with Job's problem.

Job's dilemma was How can God be just if He punishes the righteous with the unrighteous (those justified by faith over against those not justified by faith; Gen. 15:6; Hab. 2:4), those who take their place as frail mortal lost sinners, who approach the infinitely holy God? Eliphaz discoursed about the *one* prescribed way of sprinkling blood of a sacrificial animal, and the one who comes in his own merits apart from shed blood, without which is no remission of sin.

18-21. Job as a justified believer did not fit the general undifferentiated category Eliphaz dilated upon so eloquently. He found access to God in the forgiveness of sins, and so his sinfulness—in contrast to that of the fallen angels and unjustified men—was dealt with by God not only in a different category but for a different purpose. This mishandling and misapplication of truth, so widespread in religious circles, is an inlet to Satan's working, as it was in the case of Eliphaz and Job's other would-be comforters.

3. ELIPHAZ'S FIRST SPEECH CONTINUED—HIS VIEWS OF SUFFERING. 5:1-27.

Man's Only Refuge Is God. 5:1-16.
1-2. Job had to seek God as his refuge, for no **holy ones,** that is, the good, elect, unfallen angels (Dan. 4:23; 8:13; Zech. 14:5), not the fallen angels (Job 4:18), would answer his cry for help. Eliphaz's words insinuated that Job was a **foolish man** and a **silly one,** and that no intercession of spiritual beings could avert from man the wrath of an offended God (33:23, 24, NASB; Zech. 1:11-12). Let

Job take warning that he who harbors resentment at misfortune will perish through his passionate anger. **3-5.** Eliphaz once witnessed the destruction of such a fool. **I cursed** (declared the evil that must inevitably fall upon) **his habitation.**

6-7. Affliction and **trouble** do not come accidentally, but are regulated by the hand of God, manifest in human history, to work out His plan and purpose, and come to man with the regularity of a physical law. **8-16.** Therefore, Job should wisely submit himself to Him who **doeth great things and unsearchable, marvelous things without number,** described in verses 10 to 16.

Yet Eliphaz did admit that **man is born unto trouble, as the sparks fly upward** (lit., "as the sons of the burning coal," *rešep,* lift up "to fly"; "the sons of Resheph," the northwest Semitic god of pestilence, apparently being used poetically to denote "sparks"). Another interpretation is that "the various forms of pestilence may have been thought of as Resheph's children . . . just as Death had a first-born, 18:13" (Marvin Pope, *Job,* AB, p. 43).

Eliphaz's Explanation of Suffering of the Righteous. 5:17-27. This superlative passage shows that the divine aim in the suffering of the righteous is educatory and disciplinary, as a father chastens his son to improve him (cf. Heb. 12:3-11). **17.** Such suffering eventuates in happiness and is not to be despised.

18-27. God not only blesses His people in suffering, but He also delivers them out of it. In fact, the whole magnificent passage is applicable to the final outcome in Job's case. The wrong is not in the doctrine, but in the misguided application of the doctrine, just as Eliphaz's advice (vv. 1-16) was good but was applied to the wrong person. Job was not an ungodly sinner, reaping what he had sown. He was a "perfect" and "upright" child of God (1:4) who was being refined and purified for more useful and God-blessed sainthood. Satan not only works through unsound doctrine. He also operates through the soundest and most elevated doctrine that is, as here, misdirected and misapplied.

4. JOB'S FIRST SPEECH—HE ANSWERS ELIPHAZ. 6:1-30.

He Justifies His Despair. 6:1-7. Eliphaz had chided Job for his **grief** (anguish, vexation; cf. 5:2). Now the sufferer wished his anguish could be **thoroughly weighed** over against his pain; then it would not seem so excessive (cf. 31:6). **3.** Therefore, he declared, his **words are swallowed up** ("have been rash," RSV, NASB). Job addressed this chapter not only to Eliphaz, but to all the friends, as the plural forms indicate. By their silent conduct they had doubtlessly concurred, as would soon become evident in their own words.

4. He spoke of **the arrows of the Almighty** (El Shaddai, the name by which God revealed Himself to the patriarchs, Gen. 17:1-8; 28:3-4; 43:14; 49:25; Exod. 6:3, as the all-sufficient One who enriches and makes fruitful through chastisement). Hence, El Shaddai is the characteristic name of God in Job (cf. 5:17-25). The figure of God as an archer is common in the Old Testament (Deut. 32:23; Psalm 7:13; Lam. 3:12-13; Ezek. 5:16), the lightning being represented as the divine arrows (Psalm 144:6).

The present passage refers to poisoned arrows. "For Shaddai's barbs pierce me, my soul sucks in their venom" (AB); compare the venom of the deaf cobra; Psalm 58:4. Fiery arrows (cf. Eph. 6:16) were employed in ancient warfare, and arrowheads have been found with perforations for threading oil-soaked tow. **The terrors of God,** like a hostile army (cf. Psalm 88:15-16), are pictured as being arrayed against him (cf. Job 30:15).

5. Doth the wild ass bray when he hath grass? He would not complain if the commonest creature comforts were granted him (39:5). **6-7.** Instead, he was chided for not relishing unsalted, flat food and flavorless, slimy cream cheese, which his soul disdained to touch, and it was unnatural for him to resign himself to such a fate.

He Longs for Death. 6:8-12. **8-9.** Job's request and earnest desire was that it would **please God to destroy** (crush) him in death, and **let loose his hand** and **cut** him **off** (7:16; 9:21; 10:1; cf. Num. 11:15; 1 Kings 19:4; Jonah 4:3, 8). **10.** Such would be his comfort and he would "exult" (RSV), that is, "revel" or "leap for joy in unsparing pain" (BV). Why? **For I have not concealed** ("hidden," in the sense of "denied") **the words of the Holy One** (cf. 32:18; Exod. 4:15; 2 Tim. 3:16). He had not rejected the inspiration and authority of God's Word, nor denied the Holy One; therefore, he could face death fearlessly as a true believer (cf. comments on 1:5).

11. What prospects did he have to bolster his spirit to go on living? **12.** Was his strength **the strength of stones?** Was his flesh bronze? **13.** He confessed he had no help within himself, since any resource had been driven from him.

He Reproaches His Friends. 6:14-30. **14. For the despairing man** [cf. 4:5] **there should be kindness from his friend** (NASB). Job had not received such sympathetic understanding from those who should have given it. Therefore, they ran the risk of abandoning **the fear of the Almighty,** that is, "reverence for El Shaddai" (see comments on 6:4). "The fear of the LORD" is an expression of Old Testament pietistic wisdom meaning reverential trust coupled with aversion to evil (Psalm 19:9; cf. Job 1:1).

15-18. Job called his friends **brethren** (cf. Psalms 38:11; 41:9), but declared they **have dealt** (acted) **deceitfully like a brook** (wadi). They were like mountain torrents, swollen with turbid waters in winter, when nobody needs them, but dried up in the heat of summer. **The troops** (caravans) **of Tema** (Tawilan in northern Edom, the very place Eliphaz came from) and **the companies** (travelers) **of Sheba** in southwest Arabia looked to these wadis and changed their courses in travel to ascend the steep slopes in search of water. **20.** Disappointingly, like Job who expected refreshment and understanding from his friends, they find none and perish.

21. Job's friends saw his calamity but, obsessed with the false notion that he had to be a great sinner, they found it very difficult to sympathize with him. They had become waterless wadis. Now they looked upon him upon whom the chastening hand of God had fallen heavily, and they turned aghast from the horrible sight.

22-23. Yet, he confided to his friends, he expected so little from them! No gifts, no bribes, no requests to be ransomed by their wealth or rescued from an enemy or redeemed from brigands. Only, he did ask for understanding and pity! **24-26.** They considered him an evildoer. Let them prove it. Not by condemning him for rash words—for what but wind are the words of a despairing man driven to the wall and overwhelmed with calamity—but let them pass judgment upon him for his deeds.

27. Yet Job despaired of fair treatment from them. Judging by the callousness they had shown his case thus far, they were capable of casting lots for an orphan or bartering over a friend (selling him into slavery). **28-30.** He pleaded with them to look at him to see if he lied to them or that there was injustice on his tongue, and then desist from their hardhearted condemnation of him as a guilty sinner punished for his wickedness.

5. JOB'S FIRST SPEECH CONTINUED — EFFECTS OF BAD COUNSELING. 7:1-21.

The Misery of Despair. 7:1-6. The dark shadow of the adversary, who had so wrongfully accused Job (1:10-11; 2:4-5), momentarily enshrouded the man of God. As a result of Job's terrible testing, particularly through his friends, the foe was able to cast him into deep despair and depression. Satan's strategy is to go as far as he can. He could not get Job to curse God or impugn his integrity, but he was able through Job's weakness to enter his mind and fill his heart with seemingly hopeless despair.

1. Job bemoaned the fact that man is **forced to labor on earth** (NASB; 5:7; 10:17) and **his days** [are] **like the days of a hireling. 2.** He is **as a slave who pants for the shade ... as a hired man** (cf. 14:6) **who eagerly waits for his wages** (NASB). **3.** So he declared he was **made to possess** (was allotted) **months of vanity** (emptiness), and **wearisome nights** were **appointed** him. **4.** When he lay down, he said, **When shall I arise ... ?** And all night long he tossed restlessly till dawn.

5. His sickness had entered an advanced stage, when the skin became putrid, exuding ill-smelling puslike matter, and his loathsome sores were infested with worms (cf. Isa. 14:11). **6.** He lamented that his days (9:25; 16:22; 17:11; Psalm 90:5; Isa. 38:12; James 4:14) "go swifter than a weaver's shuttle, they run out without hope" (AB). There is a wordplay on *tiqwâ* in the sense of "hope" and "thread," the same word used of the scarlet thread marking Rahab's house (Josh. 2:18, 21).

Job's life had run out of hope, like a weaver's shuttle runs out of thread. Certainly no one but Satan could have filled his mind with such heartrending hopelessness.

Job's Prayer to God. 7:7-21. **7.** He requested that God remember that his life was **a breath.** He lamented that he would **not again see good** (NASB). **8-10.** He would go to Sheol, the place of the dead, the unseen world, the intermediate abode of the immaterial part of man (the soul and spirit) until the resurrection, the grave with reference to the material part of man (the body). At death he would vanish like a cloud and would not return to this present life. In his present state of despair he saw no hope beyond death.

11. Job then proceeded to remonstrate with God; impelled by the weight of human misery and his own dire suffering, he boldly gave vent to bitter complaint. **12. Am I the sea, or the sea-monster, that Thou dost set a guard over me?** (NASB). The imagery is poetical and mythological, relating the conflict between the sea-god Yamm and the weather-god Baal, in which the former is soundly defeated (cf. the Ugaritic texts, pp. 68, 129, 137; and AB, p. 61). God's dealing with him might almost appear to imply that he was like the sea, to be kept under restraint, or like the sea monster (dragon), endangering an orderly universe (cf. 40:24).

13-16. Job complained of the continued harassment and surveillance God maintained (cf. vv. 18-20). Prisoners have been driven mad by the incessant watchfulness of their guards. When Job would ease his complaint by sleep, he charged God with dismaying him with dreams and terrifying him with nightmares, till his throat would choose strangling and his bones death, recalling Eliphaz's description of a disturbing vision (4:12-16). Though Job longed for death, he did not plan suicide.

17-18. What is man, that thou shouldest magnify him ... that thou shouldest set thine heart upon him ... ? The words recall Psalm 8, where the question is, How can God in His majestic greatness stoop so low to take cognizance of insignificant, sin-cursed man? Here the emphasis is quite in contrast. If God is so great, why can't He leave man alone? **19. Wilt Thou never look away from me, or leave me alone till I swallow my spittle?** (BV), that is, "for a single moment," an expression still in use among Arabs.

20. In God's unceasing surveillance, Job called Him a "watcher of men" (NASB). **Why hast Thou set me as Thy target, so that I am a burden to myself?** (NASB). What depths of despondency to think of Him, whose love had been so fully demonstrated in the past, as his enemy who guarded him and watched every move he made. **21.** If he had sinned, why did not God pardon him and take away his iniquity? But this was not a confession of sin. He had more of the dark valley to traverse before he finally cried from his heart, "Therefore I despise myself, and repent in dust and ashes" (42:6, RSV).

6. BILDAD'S FIRST SPEECH—GOD IS JUST. 8:1-22.

Can God Pervert Justice? 8:1-7. **1-2.** Evidently scandalized by Job's remarks about God, which were rapidly approaching the verge of charging Him with being unjust, Bildad branded the words of Job's mouth as **a strong wind,** as tempestuous as they were empty. He made no allowance for the fact that Job was driven to his immoderate declarations by the cold and dogmatic assertions of Eliphaz and his misapplication of truth. How far can you press the utterances of a man who is overwrought not only as the result of physical pain, but even more so by mental anguish produced by his peers, who miscomprehend his spiritual condition and rub salt into his wounds instead of the mollifying oil of truth correctly applied?

3. But Bildad's outspoken discourtesy and unfeeling incivility suggest that he was a younger, more immature, individual. He declared a foundational truth: that God cannot be unrighteous. **Doth God pervert justice? Doth the Almighty** (El Shaddai; see comment on 6:4) **pervert righteousness** (what is right)? **4.** But then, he recklessly (with the apparent assurance of youth), misapplied a great truth to the death of Job's children, thrusting this poisoned dagger into the pain-surfeited heart of the father.

5. With the harshness of inexperience and callously oblivious of the pain he inflicted, he suggested that Job take warning from the fate of his family, even having the effrontery to piously use the tender and merciful name of God, "El Shaddai" (see above and comment on 6:4), to bolster his cruel and false insinuations.

6. He proceeded to insist that if Job was **pure and upright,** surely now God would arouse Himself for him and restore his righteous estate (cf. 5:17-27). **7.** But Bildad held out the possibility of some hope. Job could not have been quite as sinful as his children, since he was only overtaken by sickness rather than death. If he repented, there was a chance God might abundantly restore him.

Bildad was completely unaware that although in the main he was declaring truth, he was mixing it with error by reasoning from erroneous premises. That God is just is true. But it is not true that all of God's dealings with men flow exclusively from the motive of retributive justice. Bildad, like his fellow "Job comforters" and all teachers of error, was quite oblivious that in all such cases Satan gains entrance and becomes the unseen operator, causing much damage and havoc among God's people, just as Job's friends caused in Job (1 Pet. 5:8; 1 John 4:1-4; cf. Job 1:9-12; 2:4-8).

Consider the Experience of Past Generations. 8:8-22. **8-9.** Assuming an attitude of more modest restraint, Bildad bade Job to **inquire of past generations. ... For we are only of yesterday and know nothing** (NASB). **10.** He meant that one's own experience is not alone the best teacher, but that the experience of our forbears, the experience of history, is invaluable as well.

11-13. He reduced the problem to the simple terms of natural law and compared **the paths of all who forget God** (Psalm 9:17) and **the hypocrite's hope** (Job 11:20; 18:14; Psalm 112:10; Prov. 10:28) to the growth of plants. Just as the **rush** (papyrus) cannot grow apart from the wet, miry ooze of the marsh, nor **the flag** (reeds) flourish **without water,** and even while still fresh and uncut, if deprived of its natural habitat, would wither quicker than grass, such is the fate of **all** (and Bildad would not exclude Job) **who forget God** and the hope of the impious, who will perish.

14. Their confidence shall be cut off, and their **trust shall be a spider's web,** so flimsy and unsubstantial that it collapses at a touch. **15.** He who forgets God leans against his house, but like a spider's web (house), it does not stand; **he lays hold of it, but it does not endure** (RSV). **16-17.** He is like a trailing vine, sending its shoots to the housetop, penetrating the stone heap, and for a short interval showing signs of vitality, but then fading and dying as fast as it grew. **18.** When pulled out from his place, it disowns him, saying, **I never saw you** (NASB).

19. Behold, this is the joy of his way; it is short-lived and momentary (cf. 20:5).

There May Still Be Hope. 8:20-22. Bildad, with mental processes enslaved in the shackles of a rigid syllogism, discovered his prejudices were contradicted by the undeniable facts of experience. In the resulting spiritual tension, he found himself the subject of a mixture of self-assurance and uncertainty that half-heartedly comforted while it harshly condemned and held out a flicker of hope after it had already passed sentence.

20-22. Behold, God will not cast away a perfect man. But his dogmatic prejudice compelled him to categorize Job as a sinner, stamped as such by his grievous suffering. So the only way he could escape his dilemma was by resorting to ambiguity. "If thou wert ... upright" (v. 6). He had no faith in his provisional predictions. **He will yet fill your mouth with laughter and your lips with shouting** (NASB). This is plainly exhibited in that he interrupted his consolatory statements with what he really thought was applicable to Job: **Neither will he help the evil doers ... and the dwelling place of the wicked shall come to nothing.** Satan most assuredly was able to use Bildad, like Eliphaz, against Job to cause him to speak ill-advisedly with his lips (contrast 1:22; 2:10).

7. JOB'S REPLY TO BILDAD—DOES GOD LOVE HIM? 9:1-35.

The Justice of God. 9:1-12. **1. Then Job ... said, I know it is so of a truth,** namely, what Bildad had insisted upon: that God is just (cf. 8:3). But the question is, How can man (*'enôsh*, "man in his weakness and sin-sickness") be just (*yĭṣdăk*, "be right") before Him? **2-3.** No matter how right a man's cause, he is too imperfect and frail to defend it successfully in court before the divine omnipotence and omniscience.

4-9. Who could answer Him once in a thousand? Who could resist Him with impunity; He who overturns mountains in His anger, convulses the earth so that her pillars tremble, commands the sun that it does not rise, seals up the stars from sight, stretches out the heavens, treads on the back of the sea, and is the Maker of the Bear, Orion, the Pleiades, and the chambers of the south (the great sky spaces of the southern hemisphere)? **10.** He is the Doer of great deeds and marvels beyond number. **11-12.** As the eternal Spirit, He is invisible and all-powerful.

The Plight of the Man Who Doubts God's Love. 9:13-24. **13.** God will not turn back His anger, and Job envisioned Him as remote and inaccessible, beneath whom **crouch the helpers of Rahab** (NASB; cf. 26:12; Psalm 89:10; Isa. 30:7; 51:9). Rahab (*rāhăḇ*, "pride, arrogance") is a mythological figure used poetically, meaning the female monster of chaos (cf. Tiamat), closely associated with leviathan. The curbing of the forces of chaos (preeminently the unruly sea) at creation is poetically referred to as God's smiting through Rahab (cf. Job 26:12; 38:8-11).

14. How could Job answer such a God? **15.** Even though he were right, he could not answer. **16.** Even if God called and answered him, he could not believe that he was listening to His voice. **17-19.** He came to the dangerous place where he posed the question, Why should frail man (*'enôsh*) bother to contend with God? Satan had worked subtly through his friends to undermine his sense of God's loving-kindness.

20-24. Job viewed the Almighty (El Shaddai) as a giant adversary, instead of Satan, the real opponent. As a result, he resumed his complaint to God in a mood of reckless defiance and plunged into the darkest depths of imagined alienation from God, succumbing to one of Satan's most successful wiles—to get God's people to doubt that God loves them and that they are secure in His love.

When this lie is believed, God is transformed from a Friend into a fiend, from an unfailing Deliverer into an untrustworthy tyrant, declaring the guiltless guilty (v. 20), destroying the guiltless with the wicked (v. 22), mocking the despair of the innocent (v. 23), giving the earth into the control of the wicked, and even covering the faces of its judges (v. 24).

The Plaint of the Man Who Doubts God's Love. 9:25-31. Job complained about four things: (1) He complained about the brevity and evil of life. **25.** His days were **swifter than a post** (runner; cf. 7:6); **they see no good** (cf. 7:7). **26. They are passed away** (slip by) **as the swift ships** (reed boats; Isa. 18:2), **as the eagle that hasteneth to the prey** (Job 39:29; Hab. 1:8).

(2) **28-29.** He complained about the sadness and fear that beset him, believing (the devil's lie!) that God would not acquit him (cf. 7:21), but accounted him **wicked** (cf. 10:2; Psalm 37:33).

(3) **29.** He complained about the futility of life and its normal work. (4) **30-31.** He complained about the dread of unforgivable sin and the peril of being plunged into the pit as a result (another deception of Satan, into which he was goaded by the wrong counsel of his friends).

The Cry for an Umpire. 9:32-35. **32.** Job, in his anguish because of the distance, unapproachability, and unavailability of God, in his deep distress expressed the great need that was in due time to be supplied the sin-ridden and suffering race in the incarnation of Christ. **For he is not a man, as I am, that I should answer him, and we should come together in judgment** (cf. Isa. 45:9; Jer. 49:19; Rom. 9:20).

33. In his cry for a **daysman between**

us, **that might lay his hand upon us both** appears a prophetic reaching out for the "one mediator between God and men, the man, Christ Jesus" (1 Tim. 2:5). A "daysman" (*môkîăḥ*, "judge, a decider") is an umpire, an arbiter, or mediator in the sense of a go-between to reconcile two conflicting parties.

It is remarkable that at the lowest ebb of Job's faith there arose in this complaining negative form the first concept of the Mediator, which was to become for him a positive conviction (cf. 13:21-22; 16:21; 23:3), attaining its high-water mark in the speech in chapter 19 (v. 25). **34-35.** For lack of a daysman, Job was frightened before the omnipotent One, who seemed bent on terrifying him into utter despair and pronouncing him guilty, as his friends did.

8. JOB'S REPLY TO BILDAD CONTINUED— HE STRUGGLES WITH GOD. 10:1-22.

Job Conjures up a Phantom Deity. 10:1-7. **1.** Mentally and spiritually tormented, more by the anguish inflicted on him by his friends than by the pain of his own afflictions, Job continued his complaint. **My soul is** (i.e., I am) **weary of my life** (cf. 7:16); so he was determined to give full vent to the bitterness in his heart. With the bravado of despair, he did not challenge the God he knew, who loved him and blessed him, but a phantom God that Satan, through the wrong counsel of his friends, had conjured up in his mind and which his own overwrought thoughts had transformed into an obsession.

2-3. He accused this phantom deity of condemning him, contending with him, oppressing him, rejecting the labor of his hands, and looking favorably on (lit., "shining on") the schemes of the wicked. **4.** Did this phantom deity have **eyes of flesh** or did he see as **man seeth? 5.** Were his days **as the days of man,** a mere human being? **6-7.** Otherwise, asked Job, why did he **seek for my guilt, and search after my sin** when he knew that **I am ... not guilty** and **there is no deliverance** (NASB) from his power?

Job Struggles Between God and the Phantom Deity. 10:8-13. **8-9.** God (the real God) **fashioned and made** him **altogether** (NASB), literally, "together round about." Yet the phantom god, he imagined, would **destroy** him and bring him **into dust again** (cf. Gen. 2:7; 3:19). **10.** Evidently the phantom God was imagined as pouring him out **as milk** and curdling him **like cheese.**

11-12. Imperceptibly Job moved to the real God, who clothed him **with skin and flesh, and ... fenced** him (knit him together) with **bones and sinews,** granting him life and favor, and whose visitation ("care") had preserved his spirit. **13.** In his distraction, however, the sufferer imagined that God had **hidden** these things in His heart, as if He were trying to be someone other than He really was to Job. **14.** He confessed that if he sinned, God would mark (take note of) him and would not acquit him.

15. But again reverting to the phantom deity, Job concluded, **If I be righteous, yet will I not lift up my head.** Apparently, this was no godly, restful, and faith-inspired resignation to a loving God, but fatalistic, fearful cowering before an all-powerful, merciless being, not a God of love and justice, but an enemy. Job spoke realistically when he declared at this point: **I am full of confusion.** The reason was that his thinking oscillated between the true God and a god of his fabrication, manufactured by the wrong doctrine and misapplication of a right doctrine by false teachers and counselors. This is the context of all of Job's utterances (vv. 16-22), as correctly rendered in the *New American Standard Bible.*

18-19. Job questioned his birth and

dared to tell his phantom deity what he should have done about it. Would that he had died at birth, **borne from the womb directly to the tomb!** (BV). **20-22.** Viewing God as a guard, incessantly watching a prisoner, Job cried out for God to leave him alone. **Leave me alone, so I may ... go whence I shall not return, to the land of darkness and blackness** (BV).

What an illustration of the inlet to Satan (cf. 1:12; 2:6) and of the ravages of false doctrine or the misapplication even of true doctrine among the people of God—a theme that is prominent in the New Testament, where the satanic and demonic aspects of it are developed (cf. 1 Tim. 4:1-6; 1 John 4:1-4). The wisdom of Job's friends was "not that which comes down from above," but that which was "earthly, natural, demonic" (James 3:15, NASB). The fruit of it is seen in Job's confusions and rantings, sometimes almost bordering on the ravings of a madman, instead of the man of God he really was.

9. ZOPHAR'S FIRST SPEECH—GOD IS ALL-WISE. 11:1-20.

God Exacts Less Than Job's Iniquity Merits. 11:1-6. **1-2.** Zophar was the weakest of Job's counselors, as well as the bluntest and most tactless. Evidently Job's speeches had taxed his patience to the limit and irritated him. **Should not the multitude of words be answered? ... Should a man full of talk** (*'îsh śepātayim*, lit., "a man of lips," i.e., "a glib talker") **be justified** (*yiṣdāk*, "be right")?

3a. Should thy lies (better, "babblings") **make men hold their peace** (i.e., "silence" them)? **3b. When thou mockest** (deride, scorn; evidently Zophar means that Job has all but blasphemously taunted God), **Shall no man make thee ashamed? 4.** What especially upset Zophar and the other friends was primarily what Job had been saying, namely, that he was innocent, thus implying that God was unjust. Therefore, Zophar reminded Job of what he had said, namely, that his **doctrine** was **pure,** and that he was **clean** in God's sight.

5-6. But Zophar was sure Job must be guilty, and if God would speak He would show him **the secrets of wisdom,** which lie hidden in Him and **are double to that which is**—literally, "for sound wisdom is double," that is, "has two sides." God knows both sides, the manifest as well as the hidden, and it is the hidden side He would make known to Job.

Zophar's summary and blunt analysis of Job were given with terse dogmatism. **Know, therefore, that God exacteth of thee** (lit., "causes to be forgotten for you") **less than thine iniquity deserveth** (lit., "some" or "part of your iniquity"). Job had complained that God searched out and mercilessly marked his every sin (cf. 10:6, 14), afflicting him out of proportion to his sins. Eliphaz and Bildad had concluded a direct ratio. Zophar was more stringent in his judgment, concluding the first cycle of speeches in a climax of condemnation of Job.

God's Omniscience and Man's Stupidity. 11:7-12. **7.** God is all-knowing—no one can discover (fathom) **the deep things of God** or **the limit of the Almighty** (RSV), that is, El Shaddai, the all-sufficient One (see comments on 6:4). **8.** His infinity reaches to "the height of heaven" (lit. Heb.) and extends **deeper than sheol;** so what can man do, or how can man know?

10. Thus, He is absolutely sovereign; so who can restrain Him if He cuts off, shuts up, or gathers together (lit., "calls an assembly"), that is, for the purpose of condemning a culprit (cf. Prov. 5:14; Ezek. 16:40; 23:46)? **11. For he knoweth vain** (fake) **men.** Zophar implied that Job

was wicked and God knew it, even though man may have been unaware of his wickedness. **12.** Zophar's sarcasm and smoldering resentment against Job surfaced when he declared that **vain man** "will get sense, when the wild ass is born tame" (AB).

Job Called upon to Repent. 11:13-20. **13.** Job was invited to **prepare** his **heart** (i.e., order his mind) by stretching out his hands toward God in confession, supplication, and prayer. **14.** If **iniquity** (guilt) was in his hand, he was to **put it far away** and not let evil **dwell in** his **tents.**

15. Then the glittering rewards of repentance (cf. 5:17-27) were presented. Job would be able to look the world in the face fearlessly and unashamedly (cf. 10:15). **16-17.** The misery of the past would be forgotten, life would rise brighter than noon, and darkness would become as morning. **18.** Job would **be secure,** because there would be **hope,** and he would **rest in safety. 19.** He would **lie down,** and none would disturb; **many** would **make suit unto** "him" (i.e., "court him").

20. But, like Eliphaz and Bildad, Zophar had little faith that Job would repent; so he ended his speech with a somber warning concerning **the wicked,** in which category he tacitly consigned Job. As a narrow dogmatist, Zophar appealed neither to mysticism (Eliphaz), nor experience and study (Bildad), but to his own conviction of right and wrong. He was a legalist, presuming to know what God would do in any case, why He would do it, and what His thoughts were about it.

10. JOB'S REPLY TO ZOPHAR—HE ASSERTS HIS INNOCENCE. 12:1-25.

Job Denies the Accusations. 12:1-6. Job denied three things: (1) He denied the insinuations that he was ignorant or inferior to his friends. Zophar had hinted broadly that Job was stupid (11:2). All had assumed he was ignorant of his real sinfulness and guilt. He resorted to biting sarcasm (and excusably so) in the face of the rough (and one might even say irresponsible) treatment he was getting from his would-be comforters.

2. No doubt but ye (cf. 16:1-2; 17:10; Prov. 3:7) **are the people** (*'am*), in the sense of "gentry," the "people of the land," the effective male citizenry, the upper-class landowners (cf. 34:20). **And wisdom shall die with you. 3. But I have understanding as well as you** (cf. Zophar's implicit comparison of Job with a wild ass, 11:12).

They all facilely assumed that they had a right to talk down to him. Out of sheer exasperation, Job declared, **I am not inferior to you** (cf. 13:2). Who does not know all they say? Their platitudes were true enough, but everyone knew them (9:2; 13:2), nor did they shed light on Job's problem, because they were misapplied.

(2) He denied the contention that the innocent do not suffer and that, because suffering comes from sin, he had to be a great sinner, inasmuch as he was suffering so acutely. **4.** By contrast, he was a godly praying man whose prayers were answered (cf. Psalm 91:15), a **just** (righteous) and **upright man** (cf. 1:1, 5, 8, 22; 2:3, 10) who was made an object of scorn and a laughingstock by the accusations of his would-be comforters (21:3).

5. He who is at ease holds calamity in contempt, as prepared for those whose feet slip (NASB). Misfortune is so frequently treated with contempt by those who are enjoying good fortune. Instead of offering aid, Job's friends were ready to give the final shove to those whose feet were slipping.

(3) He denied the false premise that outward prosperity and health are nec-essarily indexes of godliness or wickedness. **6. The tents of the destroyers prosper.** God-provokers, **whom God brings into his power** (NASB), are often secure. These are the wicked who flourish for a while, but their payday is certain and their judgment sure.

Job Rejects False Teaching. 12:7-12. **7-8.** Nature and history reveal God. Let the beasts of the earth, the birds of the heaven, and the fish of the sea **teach thee.** As Wordsworth later expressed it: "Let Nature be your teacher." With this pedagogue at hand, surely Job was not in need of the unbalanced instruction of his would-be comforters.

9. Who does not realize (even plants and animals are given God-implanted instincts to guide them) **that the hand of the Lord hath wrought this?** (revealed Himself through His creation, particularly through animate creatures). **10.** In His **hand is the soul of every living thing, and the breath of all mankind** (cf. Gen 2:7; Job 33:4; Eccles. 12:7). Job had discovered the let-nature-teach-you principle, which he had to allow to conduct him in his quest for truth.

11. If his **palate** (NASB) could be relied on to guide him in the selection of food, his **ear** (a metonymy for his conscience and powers of reason) would not fail him in the discernment of truth and error in regard to the pompous verbalizings of his friends. **12. With the ancient** (aged) **is wisdom,** better taken as a question, "Do the aged have wisdom . . . ?" (JPS). In Job's mind, his friends were living proof that wisdom does not necessarily come with years (cf. 32:9).

Job Argues from History and Experience. 12:13-25. **13.** The friends had contended that the deeds of the Almighty are always transparently clear. He does not cause the innocent—only sinners—to suffer, normally in proportion to their sin. But is this true with Him with whom are all **wisdom and strength?** **14.** Is He not absolutely sovereign — breaking down, and there is no rebuilding; imprisoning, and there is no release?

15. What about natural calamities such as droughts and floods? Do not the righteous as well as the unrighteous suffer in these disasters? **16-22.** Does not the omniscient, omnipotent Sovereign of the universe and history employ both good and evil, the **deceived** and **the deceiver,** overruling evil powers and evil men for His honor to bring to pass His glorious purposes? **23.** Is it not He who makes nations great, then destroys them?

24-25. Does He not, as Lord of history and Consummator of His plan for time and eternity, deprive human leaders of intelligence and make them wander in pathless waste, to grope in gross darkness, making them **stagger like a drunken man?** Do not whole nations suffer for the sins of godless rulers, leaving men in perplexity concerning whether the power that operates providentially in these events is a power that makes for righteousness?

11. JOB'S REPLY TO ZOPHAR CONTINUED — HE RESENTS HIS FRIENDS. 13:1-28.

Job Expresses Resentment for His Friends. 13:1-12. Job resented four things: (1) He resented their claim of superior knowledge. **1.** In biting *argumentum ad hominem* he declared that he **understood** the matter they dwelt on continually, namely, the greatness, glory, and sovereignty of God, and did not need to be taught by them.

2. What ye know ... I know ... I am not inferior unto you, that is, in wisdom. Job repeated what he had said before (12:3) to emphasize his strong convic-

tion on the matter. **3.** Rather, he would **speak to the Almighty** (El Shaddai, the all-sufficient One; cf. comment on 6:4), who would not be so hard on him as his friends were. He would **desire to reason** ("remonstrate," a juridical term meaning "to argue") **with God.**

(2) He resented their unjust and uncharitable dealing with him. **4.** He branded them **forgers of lies** (*ṭōpᵉlê šĕqĕr*, lit., "daubers, painters, smearers of deceit, falsehood"), glossing over the ugly truth and attempting, as it were, to whitewash God — bungling artists who painted a smeared or blurred picture of Job. They were **physicians of no value,** fake healers, who wrongly diagnosed Job's case and gave him the wrong treatment. They framed a wrong hypothesis concerning divine Providence, and misapplied it, as if God never did seriously afflict any but wicked people. And from this they drew the false conclusion that Job was wicked and, in denying it, a hypocrite.

(3) He resented their vain and misdirected loquacity. **5-6.** His sharp-barbed retort showed how much this irked him: **Oh, that ye would altogether hold your peace.** That is, "I wish you would just shut up!" That would be the greatest display of their wisdom! They had pleaded that they could not keep from speaking (4:2; 11:2-3). They needed the advice of a genuine wise man. "Even a fool, when he holdeth his peace, is counted wise" (Prov. 17:28). He thought it only fair that they heard what he had to say: **Hear, now, my reasoning.**

(4) He resented the dishonor they did God, while pretending to plead for His honor. **7-8.** Would they dare to **speak wickedly for God?** Talk unfairly and deceptively for Him and thus misrepresent Him? Would they **accept his person,** that is, show partiality for Him, literally, "lift

up the face," as for a bribe (Deut. 10:17; Prov. 18:5) or with a desire to curry favor (Job 32:21; 34:19)? Would they be like those who have no right on their side but carry their cause by the partiality of the judge in favor of their persons? **Will ye contend for God,** as if His justice were questionable and needed to be cleared up?

Job warned his friends of God's inevitable judgment that would come upon their duplicity (vv. 9-12). Would it be well with them when God searched them out (probed them)? Could they deceive God as one deceives a man—trick Him as men are tricked? **10. He will surely reprove** them ("rebuke them severely") if they **secretly accept persons** ("covertly curry favor"), the same idiom as 8*a*, "show partiality" (NASB), "accept one's person."

11. Shall not **his excellency** (*śe'ēt,* "majesty," from *nāśā',* "lift up, carry") **make** them **afraid, and his dread** (dread of Him) **fall upon** them? **12.** He declared to them: **Your remembrances** ("memorable sayings" or "maxims"), time-honored but bankrupt notions are **proverbs of ashes** (NASB; *mishlê-'ēpĕr,* "ashen aphorisms"), preachings devoid of life and usefulness, like ashes from which all the good has been consumed. **Your defenses are defenses of clay** (NASB).

Job Stoutly Maintains His Integrity. 13:13-19. **13.** At this point Job's friends evidently tried to interrupt him, but he insisted on being heard to the end. He pleaded his cause before God Himself, not unaware of the boldness of the step, but thoroughly confident that he would be exonerated. **14.** When he declared that he would take his flesh in his teeth and put his life in his hands, he simply meant he would risk his life (cf. Judg. 12:3; 1 Sam. 19:5; 28:21; Psalm 119:109). **15.** This he reiterated: **Though he slay**

me, yet will I trust (hope) in him, a truly godly attitude, indubitably proving that Job had not lost his integrity. A hypocrite and man of guilty conscience would rather try to hide from God and not boldly defend his ways **before him** ("in His face"). **16.** Nor would he declare: **He also shall be my salvation.** This is not the language nor the action of a guilty man, but of a man who takes a fresh hold on his integrity, as one resolved not to let it go, or permit it to be wrested from him.

17. Job then directed his remarks to God. **18.** He had prepared his case and was certain he would be vindicated (cf. 6:29). **19. Who is he that will plead** (contend) **with me?** These are the words of a plaintiff challenging his adversary to come into court (cf. Isa. 1:18). If an opponent appeared with just cause, then Job would be silent and die.

Job's Prayer to God. 13:20-28. **20-22.** Before presenting his case, Job made a twofold request: (1) that God would withdraw His hand so that he might speak freely and not be terrified into silence at the dread of Him; and (2) that when he did speak, God would reply instead of continuing His crushing silence.

Job presented God seven questions and requests: (1) **23a. How many are mine iniquities and sins?** He made it transparently clear that he was maintaining his integrity (his innocence), not sinlessness. He admitted the faults of his youth (v. 26). (2) **23b.** He asked God to make him know his **transgression** and **sin** (cf. 22:5-10), evidence enough that he was not a hypocrite, trying to hide his sins.

(3) **24.** He bitterly inquired why God had withdrawn His presence from him, holding him as His enemy? To a gracious soul, valuing God's lovingkindness better than life (Prov. 18:14),

this was a grievous burden (cf. Psalms 77:7-9; 78:7, 15-16). (4) **25.** He pleaded his own utter inability to stand before God. **Wilt thou break a leaf ... pursue** (chase) **dry stubble**—trample upon one already prostrate, crush one who does not have or pretend to have any strength to resist you? (5) **26.** He commiserated on God's severe dealings with him, writing **bitter things against** him in outward afflictions and inner disquiet to humble him and bring him to good in the latter end.

(6) **27.** He complained of God's strict surveillance and severe check on his conduct, fettering his feet and making prints on the soles of his feet to mark each step he took. Slaves were thus variously marked, designs on the feet making it easier to track down a runaway servant. (7) **28.** He found himself wasting away under the heavy hand of God, **decaying like a rotten thing, like a garment that is moth-eaten** (NASB).

12. JOB'S REPLY TO ZOPHAR
CONCLUDED—THE BREVITY OF LIFE.
14:1-22.

The Brevity and Trouble of Life. 14:1-6. **1.** Job had reminded his friends of their frailty and mortality (13:12). Now he reminded himself of his own, and pleaded to God for some mitigation of his miseries. The very frailty of human nature was adduced by Job to enlist the divine compassion. **Man ... born of a woman is of few days, and full of trouble,** because he is born in sin, as Eve succumbed to temptation and fell, so that her progeny and that of every other woman of a fallen race is born in sin (Psalm 51:5), under death (Gen. 2:17), and doomed to trouble (3:16).

2. Man is like a flower that appears and soon withers; like a shadow, he is fleeting and does not remain. **3. Upon such an one** (cf. 7:17-18), who is frail,

ephemeral, strife-sated, **dost thou open thine eyes** (do You bother to turn Your gaze), to bring him into judgment with Yourself? Is such a one really significant enough for You to take his faults so seriously? Ought he not rather be an object of Your pity? And why bring man (Job) into judgment when he was born in sin, a part of the race corrupted in the Fall?

4. Who can bring a clean thing out of an unclean? Not one (except God). **5-6.** And why single out Job for such heavy sufferings and guard him as a jailer watches the prisoner (13:27)? Since man's life is so brief, his days so narrowly circumscribed, why not permit him to enjoy his short existence and grant him the small respite that is not even withheld from the lowliest hireling?

The Certainty of Death and Yearning for an Afterlife. 14:7-22. **7.** Job contrasted the fate of things with the fate of persons. **There is hope for a tree, if it be cut down, that it will sprout again, and that its tender branch will not cease. 8-9. Though its root grow old in the earth, and its stock** (stump) **die in the ground; yet at the scent** (smell) **of water it will bud.**

10. By contrast, **man dieth ... and where is he?** "If a man die, shall he live?" (v. 14). Here Job broached one of the three great problems raised by the book of Job, each of which Old Testament saints struggled with in haziness and uncertainty, because they were unanswered and unanswerable until God became incarnate in the Lord Jesus Christ: (1) the invisibility and unapproachability of God—"Oh, that I knew where I might find him!" (23:3), answered by the appearing of Christ; (2) human sin—How can a man be justified with God? (9:2; 25:4), answered by the death of Christ; and (3) death and immortality—"If a man die, shall he live again?" (14:14), answered by the resurrection of Christ.

11-12. In this passage, Job wrestled with the last problem. He did not expect annihilation, but his outlook was pessimistic and uncertain. As water fails from a lake and vanishes, and as a river parches and dries up, so a man lies down and never rises. **13.** Job earnestly desired that God would hide him **in sheol** and **remember him.**

14. If beyond this intermediate state there were a resurrection, such a happy prospect would enable Job to endure his weary days and would transform his whole outlook, till his change came. **15.** The prospect of resurrection did not provide a key to unlock the mystery of Job's present suffering, but it offered a wonderful hope to make it bearable. His earnest desire subsequently became a living conviction (19:25-27).

16-17. But from that mountain height Job descended once again into the valley. His crescendo was followed by an emotional and spiritual decrescendo. Momentarily, and doubtless as the result of the faulty counsel of his friends, his hope flickered low as he was overwhelmed by his bitter thoughts of the unsparing severity of God, whom he conjured up as a divine detective, counting his every step and watching over his sin with ceaseless and terrifying scrutiny, as a miser, hoarding up his transgressions and sealing them up in a bag to gloat over them as a treasure.

18-19. In his emotional letdown Job pictured God as a destroyer of man's hope, moving as relentlessly as a mountain crumbles, as water wears away stone, and torrents sweep away the soil. **20-21.** He declared that God forever overpowers man, and **he departs** this life. God changes man's appearance and sends him away (NASB), so that he does not see the good or bad that might occur even in his own family, because of the brevity of life. **22.** Even while man

lives his **body pains him, and he mourns only for himself** (NASB), for in Job's case, his children had been swept away before his eyes.

B. THE SECOND CYCLE OF SPEECHES. 15:1—21:34.

1. ELIPHAZ'S SECOND SPEECH—THE WICKED DO NOT PROSPER. 15:1-35.

Job Denounced as Godless and Blasphemous. 15:1-19. **1-2.** With his pride wounded by Job's treading underfoot the pearls of wisdom dropped by his friends, Eliphaz denied that Job was in the category of a wise man, and venomously branded him as a windbag who was irreligious at heart. **Should a wise man,** as Job claimed to be (12:3; 13:2), **utter vain knowledge, and fill his belly with the east wind?** The wind was the searing sirocco blowing from the desert, an expression equivalent in our parlance to "hot air." Thus, Eliphaz was simply and bluntly calling Job a bag of hot air.

The attempt of the friends to make Job bow as a guilty sinner before the all-wise and all-powerful God had been unsuccessful. Perhaps he would be warned in time by a dissertation upon the divine judgment falling upon wicked hypocrites like Job. That was the spearhead of the friends' attack in the second cycle of speeches. **3.** Should Job, said Eliphaz, **reason** (argue) **with unprofitable** (useless) **talk,** with **speeches** (words) that are utterly worthless?

4. He also accused Job of irreverence—casting off (annulling, destroying) **fear** (that is, "fear of the LORD" or religion) and restraining (deprecating) **prayer** (*śîḥâ,* "musing or meditation"; Psalm 119:97, 99), but in this context approaching our term *devotion* in reference to God. **5-6.** Eliphaz declared that Job's protestations of innocence were nullified by his words.

Thy mouth uttereth (teaches) **iniquity. ... Thine own mouth condemneth thee.** Eliphaz was saying that the manner in which Job presumed to defend himself really condemned him, and his crafty tongue exposed him as a wily hypocrite.

7. The main accusation against Job was that he set himself against the traditions of the fathers (vv. 7-19). Was he the **first man** (*'ādām*), Adam, the primeval man, who in his innocence before the Fall had unobstructed communion with God, hence, unusual wisdom (Gen. 3:8)? **8.** Was he from dim antiquity (cf. Psalm 90:2; Prov. 8:25), hearing **the secret counsel of God** (NASB) and holding a monopoly on wisdom?

9-10. He demanded to hear what Job knew and understood that they did not, pointing out that the **grayheaded** and the **very aged,** older even than Job's father, were still living. Would Job scorn the widsom of age and tradition? Eliphaz used the fallacy so common in heresy: that because a belief is hoary with age and tradition, it is necessarily the truth.

11. Are the consolations of God too small for you? (NASB), asked Eliphaz, apparently referring to his attempt to console Job with the unsound doctrine that says suffering is always deserved (cf. 13:7-12; 16:2). **12-13. Why doth thine heart carry thee away?** That is, "What has taken away your mind and bereaved you of common sense?" **What do thine eyes wink at** (lit., "Why do your eyes flash") with angry excitement **that you should turn your spirit against God, and allow such words** (as Job had spoken under grueling harassment from his friends) **to go out of your mouth?** (NASB; cf. vv. 5-6).

14. Again reference is made to human corruption, as a result of the Fall, but showing no comprehension of faith and Old Testament salvation (Gen. 3:15; 15:6; cf. Job 14:4; 25:4). **15.** Again Eliphaz went to God's defense (cf. 4:17), employing arguments concerning the angels that have no relevance to Job's case nor to His redemptive promises to the fallen race. **16.** He proved how unbalanced and distorted his analysis of Job's condition was by his cruel insinuation that Job was **detestable and corrupt** and **drinks iniquity like water!** (NASB).

Job Warned of the Terrible Fate of the Wicked. 15:20-35. Eliphaz then proceeded to depict the terrible fate of the wicked, which apparently was intended as a description of Job's deserved sufferings, as well as a stern warning of greater afflictions awaiting him unless his attitude changed. **20. The wicked man travaileth** (writhes) **with pain all his days** (v. 24; 24:1; 27:3), even in his prosperity.

21. A dreadful sound (lit., "a sound of fears") **is in his ears.** Even **in prosperity,** while at peace, **the destroyer shall come upon him** (evidently a studied allusion to Job; cf. v. 24; 18:11; 20:25; 21:20; 1 Thess. 5:3). **22.** He despairs of being able to return from the darkness (14:10-12) and **is destined for the sword** (NASB). **23.** He wanders about for food, saying, **Where is it? He knows that a day of darkness is at hand** (NASB). **24-25.** Distress and anguish **make him afraid** because **he stretcheth out his hand against God . . . against the Almighty** (El Shaddai; see comment on 6:4).

26. Eliphaz represented Job rushing headlong at God with his massive shield, defending his innocence. **27-30.** The wicked man will come to misery and poverty, and at the breath of God's mouth he will pass away. **31-32.** Emptiness shall be the reward of his self-deception before his time. His palm branch will not be green. **33.** He will be like an unripe grape that falls off the vine, like the blossom cast off by the olive tree. **34.** His company is barren, and fire consumes his tents. **35.** Such wicked people (like Job) **conceive mischief, and bring forth vanity . . . their heart** (mind) **prepareth deceit** (Psalm 7:14; Isa. 59:4; Hos. 10:13).

2. JOB'S REPLY—HIS FRIENDS ARE MISERABLE COMFORTERS. 16:1-22.

Job Finds Himself Forsaken by Man. 16:1-6. **2.** Eliphaz's second speech was harsh and absolutely comfortless. As a result, Job was deeply wounded by the utter callousness of a man from whom he had expected understanding and sympathy, and resentment burned in his heart like a volcano ready to erupt. **I have heard many such things.** "I have heard plenty of this! (AB). **Miserable** (*'āmāl*, "wearisome"; better, "galling") **comforters are ye all**, rubbing salt in open wounds.

3. Shall vain (windy) **words have an end?** Evidently this was a scornful retort to Eliphaz's remark (15:2). **Or what emboldeneth** (*yāmrîṣ*, "excites" or "moves") **thee that thou answerest?**, used here with a derisive connotation, "to prattle on" (AB). **4. I also could speak as ye do. If your soul** (i.e., you) **were in my soul's stead** (in my place). Job was saying it would be easy, if the tables were turned, to admonish his friends with artificial speeches. **I could heap up words against you,** "join words together against you" (RSV), but better taken from the root *hbr,* with the basic meaning of "sound, noise." "I could also speak to you with mere noise" or "could harangue you with words" (AB; see J. Finkelstein, JBL 75[1956]:328-31).

And shake my head at you. Shaking the head would probably denote feigned or mock sympathy in this context, elsewhere suggesting mockery or derision (2 Kings 19:21; Psalm 22:7; Lam. 2:15; Matt. 27:39). **5.** On the other hand, if he were in his friends' place, he could strengthen and comfort understandingly and sympathetically. **6.** But in his present impasse, whether he spoke or remained silent, his pain was not lessened.

Does He Find Himself Forsaken by God Too? 16:7-17. **7.** Job's fear of being forsaken by God, as the result of the pressure that the false comfort of his friends had imposed upon him, was like a frightful nightmare in which he envisioned an angry God, who was his enemy and tormenter. Reviewing again the long chain of his afflictions, he declared that God had made him **weary** (cf. 7:3) and **desolate. 8.** His woe had **filled** him **with wrinkles** (wizened or shriveled him). His **leanness** (physical as well as spiritual) testified **to his face** (10:17).

9. He again conjured up a phantom deity whose anger tore him and raged against him like a wild beast (Hos. 6:1), gnashing at him with his teeth. His enemy was not God, as he might have imagined, but Satan operating through his friends. **He . . . sharpeneth** (whets) **his eyes** against me (13:24; 33:10). **10.** His foes (Satan-influenced friends) **gaped** at him **with their mouth** (Psalms 22:13; 35:21), they slapped his face scornfully, and they assembled against him. Job's suffering is a reminder of the suffering of our Lord (Psalm 22); but what a contrast Job's imperfections were to the perfections and loveliness of our Lord.

11. Job imagined that God had delivered him to the ungodly—into the custody of the vicious. **12.** He declared, **I was at ease, but he hath broken me asunder** ("crushed me"; cf. 9:17). He was so wrought up that he depicted himself grabbed by the neck and **shaken . . . to pieces** (mangled), with God setting him up as **his mark** (target) of torture (7:20; Lam. 3:12). **13.** He phantomized that the divine **archers** compassed him (made a ring around him), cleaving (stabbing) his **kidneys** (i.e., vitals) without pity, pouring out his **gall** (lit., "gallbladder"; metaphorically, "guts"; cf. 2 Sam. 20:10; Lam. 2:11).

14. He breaketh me with breach upon breach (lit., "he tears [rends] me rift on rift"). The underlying figure is an attack on a fortified town and the breaking through of its walls (cf. 30:14; Isa. 5:5; Amos 4:3). **He runneth upon me like a giant** (*gĭbbôr,* "a warrior"). **15.** Job said, **I have sewed sackcloth over my skin** (as a sign of mourning), **and thrust my horn** (19:9; Lam. 2:3) **in the dust** (NASB), the symbol of power and pride (Psalms 75:5; 92:10). Job was felled by his misfortunes, even as the wounded bull sinks his horn in the dust and collapses.

16a. My face is foul (flushed) **with weeping,** not only a symptom of leprosy (elephantiasis, when the skin becomes hard and rough like an elephant's hide and the eyes readily secrete tears), but also as an indication of his troubles in general.

16b. On my eyelids is the shadow of death (i.e., deep darkness; cf. Psalm 23:4). Progressive impairment of vision is also common with leprosy.

17. All this woe was not because of any **violence in** his **hands. Also** his **prayer** was **pure.** Once again Job categorically denied the guilt his friends would connect with his sufferings. His anguish was without any justification (Isa. 53:9). Had God then forsaken him?

Job Changes His Appeal from His Phantom God to the Real God. *16:18-22.* Job had been abandoned by the God that he had conjured up in his mind as the result of Satan working through his false comforters (1:12; 2:6).

Now his anguished spirit changed its appeal from the phantom God, whom he imagined was oppressing him like a bloodthirsty foe, to the true picture of God as his only Defender and Advocate, who in the end would establish his right.

18. O earth, cover not thou my blood, which when shed cries out from the ground for vengeance (Gen. 4:10). To cover it with dust (Gen. 37:26; Isa. 26:21; Ezek. 24:8) would signify passing over the thought of vindication. Job wished his blood to remain uncovered as a permanent protest and plea for vindication. And he cried, **Let my cry find no resting place** (RSV).

19. Behold, my witness is in heaven, the preincarnate Redeemer to be anticipated (19:25-27; cf. Rom. 1:9). He appealed to God, the omniscient One, concerning his integrity. The witness in his heart was corroborated by the Witness in heaven. God is greater than our hearts, and we are not our own judges.

21. Job grasped a bit of comfort when he realized, if only momentarily, that there is One who pleads for man with God **as a man pleadeth for his neighbor** — another cry for a daysman or intercessor (mediator; see comment on 9:33; cf. 10:4-5; 13:21-22; 23:3). This coming Mediator would solve Job's dilemma and reconcile the two aspects of God — His infinite holiness on one hand, and His infinite love and grace toward sinners on the other hand — and would provide Someone who would understand both God and man, and draw them together.

22. In the light of the prospect of death, Job had confidence, for he had cast himself upon God after being rejected by men (v. 20), and he knew his heavenly Advocate would not let him die the death of a sinner. Here was faith conquering death. Just at the moment when Job saw himself rebuffed by man and forsaken by God (he thought), he risked a leap into the dark and knew he would land in God's arms.

3. JOB'S REPLY CONTINUED—HE CRIES FOR VINDICATION. 17:1-16.

Job Implores God to Vindicate Him. 17:1-5. **1.** Looking upon himself as a dying man, Job reflected on the harsh censures heaped upon him by his friends. He appealed to God to justify him, because they had wronged him, and he did not know how to justify himself. He cried, **My spirit is broken** (AB; NASB), **my days are extinct** (spent), **the grave is ready for me. 2.** He referred to his friends as **mockers** and complained that his **eye** gazed (lit., "lodged") **on their provocation** (NASB).

3. He asked that God would **lay down ... a pledge** for him and inquired as to who would be guarantor, signified by the gesture of striking hands (Prov. 6:1; 17:18). The practice of pledge-taking was a common commercial and juridical custom (Gen. 38:17-20; Exod. 22:26; Deut. 24:6-17; Neh. 5:3). Away with all hopes offered by men! Only God could undertake suretyship for him. Let God covenant to establish his integrity and be his Guarantor. **4-5.** These verses explain that God had to supply Job's pledge, because human friends refused to do so.

Job Utters a Bitter Lament. 17:6-9. Job mournfully surveyed his public humiliation. **6. He** (God, not Eliphaz, etc.) **hath made me also a byword of the people** (KJV), "one in whose face they spit" (AB). **7. Mine eye also is dim by reason of sorrow, and all my members are like a shadow,** Job said, so emaciated and frail had he become.

8. Upright (righteous) **men** would be astonished at this sight, and the **innocent shall stir up himself** (be aroused) **against the hypocrite** (the impious). **9.** But they

(Job included) would dauntlessly persevere in righteousness (lit., "hold to their way") and the clean-handed **shall be stronger and stronger** (grow in strength), undeterred by the incomprehensible dealings of Providence or the calumnies of men. This is certainly a triumphant confessing, giving the lie to Satan's charges (cf. 2:5).

Job Changes His Mood. 17:10-16. Like frail humanity, especially under extreme tension and suffering, Job's changes in mood were sudden and at times shocking. **10.** Suddenly, almost like a man demented, he disdainfully invited the wisdomless wise men to resume their tortuous counsel. "Come back," he cried, "but I shall not find a wise man among you" (AB). **11.** Then the tried saint plunged into a pitiful description of his pathetic plight: "My days are done, my plans shattered." **14-16.** Where was his hope? If he said to the pit, "You are my father," and to the maggots, "You are my mother and sister," where was his happiness?

4. BILDAD'S SECOND SPEECH—THE DOOM OF THE WICKED. 18:1-21.

Would Job Set Aside the Moral Order? 18:1-4. **1.** Bildad the Shuhite (cf. 8:1) did not have anything new to say to Job, or anything that would help him. He assumed that Job was wicked, but what he said of the fate of the wicked could have no relevance to Job's real state or need. He addressed Job in the plural, probably to ignore him as an individual and categorize him as belonging to the class of the impious.

2. He accused him of setting "word snares" (*qinṣê;* cf. Arab. *qanaṣa,* "hunt," and Akk. *qinṣu,* "trap," not a variant of *qeṣ,* "end," KJV, following Jewish commentators). So the verse should be translated, **How long will you hunt for words?** (NASB), or better,

"How long will you set word snares?" (AB). **Show understanding** (be sensible) **and then we can talk** (NASB).

3. Bildad was enraged that he and his companions were **counted** (regarded) **as beasts** and **vile** (stupid) by Job (cf. 12:7; 17:10; Psalm 73:22). 4. So he angrily retorted: **Thou that tearest thyself in thine anger** (ASV), like an insensate animal, bellowing all the while and blaming God (cf. 16:9). Was Job so senseless and stubborn as to think the divine order in creation and providence was to be set aside for him, especially with reference to the law of retribution expounded by the friends? Let him remember God's laws are immutable.

Let Him Be Warned by the Fate of the Godless. 18:5-21. **5-6.** The **light of the wicked shall be put out, and the spark** (flame) **of his fire shall not shine** (give light). "The light (lamp) of the wicked" is a common proverbial expression in the Wisdom literature (Prov. 13:9; 20:20; 24:20). **7.** Like an aging man, whose strong stride is reduced to a feeble hobble (cf. Psalm 18:36; Prov. 4:12), the fortunes of the wicked wane. **His own scheme brings him down** to ruin (NASB). **8.** His own feet lead him into the trap as he **walketh upon a snare,** that is, "steps on the webbing" (NASB), a reference to an interwoven net or to a trapdoor over a pit.

9-10. Bildad elaborated on the figure of the wicked man ensnared in his own trap. **11. All around terrors frighten him, and harry him at every step** (NASB), possibly a figurative representation of demonic onslaughts. **12. His strength shall be hunger-bitten** (famished), and **destruction** (calamity) stands ready beside him to attack him. **13a. His skin is devoured by disease** (NASB; *biḏwăy,* peculiarly applicable to Job if this obscure passage is so read; see M. Pope, *Job,* AB, p. 135). **13b. The first-born of**

death (possibly a metaphor for a deadly disease or the specific malady that afflicted Job) **devours his limbs** (NASB; lit., "parts, members").

14. He is torn (snatched) from his tent, and **they march him** (i.e., he is marched) **before the king of terrors** (NASB), an epithet of death, a deity in contemporary Semitic mythology now well known from the Ugaritic religious literature. Rashi probably understood the term correctly as "the chief of demons." Poetically, the god "Death" (Mot) is termed the shepherd of the occupants of the netherworld in Psalm 49:14, "shepherd" being an ancient kingly title.

15. In the light of the Ugaritic epics, this hitherto undecipherable verse may now be read: "Fire is set in his tent, on his abode is scattered brimstone" (see M. Dahood, *Biblica* 38 [1957]:312-13). **16.** Compared to a plant, the wicked man's roots dry up below, and above his branch withers. Destruction of root and branch is proverbial (cf. v. 19; Amos 2:9). **17. The remembrance of him** (Psalm 34:16) **shall perish from the earth ... he shall have no name in the street** (abroad).

18-19. He shall be driven from light into darkness and deprived of kith and kin, evidently studied references to Job. **20.** Both easterners and westerners were appalled at the fate of the wicked man (Job) and were seized with horror at his end. **21.** Bildad summarized his evaluation of Job's condition: **Surely such are the dwellings of the wicked ... the place of him that knoweth not God.**

5. JOB'S REPLY TO BILDAD—MY REDEEMER LIVES. 19:1-29.

Job Again Reproves His Friends. 19:1-6. Job charged his friends with five things: (1) **1.** He charged them with vexing (tormenting) and crushing him by their counsel. Their cruel innuendoes reached a peak as Bildad insinuated that Job deserved the loss of health, happiness, and children (cf. 18:13, 19). (2) **3b.** He charged them with reproaching him in the sense of taunting and deriding him with insults **these ten times** (a round number denoting many times, as in Gen. 31:7; Num. 14:22; Neh. 4:12; Dan. 1:20).

(3) **3b.** He charged them with shamelessly abasing him, making themselves **strange** to him, that is, wronging him. (4) **4.** He charged them with assuming God's prerogative in pronouncing guilt and prescribing punishment. "And if I have really erred, my error remains with me" (F. Delitzsch), that is, I shall have to expiate it without your taking upon yourselves the office of God to treat me uncharitably. Moreover, my transgression **remaineth** (*tālîn*, "lodges") **with myself** without leading others astray or involving you in guilt.

(5) **5-6.** He charged them with propounding a God of injustice and oppression. If they really maintained that he was suffering under retributive justice as a wicked person, then the God they propounded had wronged him, and they had conjured up an unjust tyrant of their own making, not the true God who is absolutely fair, righteous, and infinitely holy. "If ye will really magnify yourselves against me, and prove my reproach to me, know then that Eloah hath wronged me, and hath compassed me with His net" (Delitzsch).

Job Struggles for a Right Concept of God. 19:7-12. The relentless persistence of the friends in insisting that all suffering is the result of divine punishment, coupled with the unshakable consciousness of his innocence, had forced Job to the conclusion that God is arbitrary and unjust. He faced a dilemma. Could he still trust in a God who—if his friends were right—is malignancy personified?

The bold invectives of this section of the book are not aimed at the God of Job, but in Job's utter frustration at the God in whom his friends professed to believe. If you are right, then know that not I but God is the culprit (vv. 7-12).

7. "I cry violence! But He does not answer. I shout for help, but there is no redress." **8.** Job alleged that God had blocked his way so he could not **pass** and had **set darkness in** his **paths. 9-10. He hath stripped me of my glory** (Psalm 89:44), **and taken the crown from my head ... destroyed me ... mine hope hath he removed like a tree** (cf. 17:15-16). **11. He hath ... kindled his wrath against me ... counteth me ... as one of his enemies** (13:24; 33:10).

12. "His troop come massed against me, set seige against me, camp around my tent" (AB). At this pivotal point Job's heart, with its keen, burning desire for God, showed him in this famous chapter (often called the heart of the book) the way of escape from his intolerable plight. He had to struggle toward a concept of the God who would send His servants suffering that was not punishment for sin, and who would do so because He is animated by grace and love, not anger (cf. E. Brennecke, OTC, p. 507).

Job Taught Not to Place Confidence in Man. 19:13-22. Job was to be taught to see God as He really is, not as his friends had imagined Him to be, or as he, contaminated and thrown into a dilemma by their wrong concept, had also thought Him to be. He was also to be instructed to see men as they really are—fallen, erring creatures. The divine purpose in all of this was that he might turn away from man and put His confidence in God alone, the God about whom he was struggling to get a proper concept, and the God who was patiently dealing with him to reveal His true self to him. Accordingly, in verses 13 to 20 the props were knocked out (by God) from under Job as far as kith and kin were concerned.

13. His kin had abandoned him, and his acquaintances were alienated from him. **14.** His relatives and intimates had deserted, and the inmates of his house had forgotten him. **15.** His slave girls treated him **as a stranger. 16.** Even his slave did not respond, though Job entreated him humbly. **17-18.** Even his breath was offensive to his loved ones, and street urchins despised and reviled him. **19.** All his bosom friends detested him. **20.** His flesh rotted on his bones, and he had **escaped** (death) only by the skin of his teeth. **21-22.** He cried out for pity from his friends and wailed, **Why do you persecute me as God does, and are not satisfied with my flesh?** (NASB).

Job Made Ready to Cast Himself Solely upon God. 19:23-29. **23-24.** Since his contemporaries rejected his personal witness to his integrity, Job devoutly wished that his words might be **inscribed in a book . . . with an iron stylus and lead . . . engraved in the rock forever!** (NASB). Then, he concluded, it might merit a hearing and a kinder verdict from future generations. **25.** However, as quickly as a desire for a record of his innocence struck him, so he summarily dismissed it. For why should he appeal at all to men, who had so signally failed him? Why look toward the future? The present already had the answer! With the impact of a sudden revelation, the truth flashed upon his harassed spirit: "I now have a Vindicator in heaven!"

Dispelling the gloomy specter of a hostile God, hounding him and hedging him in with calamity upon calamity, he cried out in victorious faith: I *know* (*'anî*, emphatic). **As for me, I know that my Redeemer lives** (NASB; *ḥai*, "is alive"). All along Job had been longing

for "a daysman," or mediator, to come between him and God (see comments on 9:32-35). All along he had emphatically declared his innocence and appealed to God, who he was sure was conscious of it (10:7; 13:15-19). He also had affirmed that he had a "witness" in the heavens (16:19) and looked for an advocate to plead his cause (16:21). He had called upon God to be surety for him (17:3). It is apparent, therefore, that he had already recognized God as his Judge, Umpire, Advocate, Witness, and Surety.

Here, then, the suffering saint went a step farther in expressing his faith and declared five things: (1) *Job declared that he knew he had a Redeemer, a gō'ēl.* This *gō'ēl* was the next of kin, whose duty it was to redeem, ransom, or avenge the one who had fallen into debt or bondage, or who had been slain in a family vendetta (Lev. 25:48; Deut. 19:6-12). The term is often applied to the LORD as the Deliverer from Egyptian bondage (Exod. 6:6; 15:13). Job was convinced that God in the varied conditional functions of the *Gō'ēl*, would take it upon Himself to avenge his quarrel, be surety for him, act as an umpire, and vindicate him—in short, do what his professed friends would not do, even if they could.

(2) *Job declared that he knew that his Gō'ēl-Redeemer was alive,* presently as a reality, existing at that time, and not someone to come into existence later, though His manifestation in human flesh was to be an event in the future. His Redeemer was alive as the eternally existing One, the preincarnate Christ, the eternal Word who was with God and was God (John 1:1-3), and in the future was to become incarnate (John 1:14).

25c. (3) *Job declared that at the last his Redeemer would take His stand on the earth (yākûm,* "appear, rise up, stand"), particularly in a juridical sense as a Witness in a trial (cf. 16:8; 31:14; Deut. 19:16) to vindicate Job in the sense of a *Gō'ēl* ("one who ransoms, releases, delivers, avenges"). "God himself will avenge Job's blood, i.e. against his accusers, who say that it is the blood of one guilty" (Delitzsch, *Job,* 1:354). This, of course, could only be accomplished ultimately through the incarnation of Christ, as the New Testament shows.

The *Gō'ēl* will stand **upon the earth** (*'ăl-'āpār,* lit., "upon dust"); the word is used in this sense in Job 41:33, where the meaning "earth" is clear, arguing against a reference with mythological implications to the netherworld and to Job's death (cf. M. Dahood, *Biblica* 52 [1971]:346). Says Delitzsch, "Over the dust of the departed God will arise, and by His majestic testimony put to silence those who regard this dust of decay as the dust of a sinner" (Delitzsch, *Job,* 1:354).

The *Gō'ēl* shall stand at the latter day (*'aḥărôt,* "at last"), the period Paul designated as "the fullness of the time" when "God sent forth his Son" (Gal. 4:4). But some construe the term as a divine epithet, "the last" (Isa. 44:6) in parallelism with *gō'ēl,* "I know that my Redeemer lives, and that the Ultimate upon the dust will stand" — "The Ultimate" or "the Last" in the sense of "Guarantor" (M. Pope, *Job,* AB, p. 146).

26. (4) *Job definitely referred to life beyond death in a resurrection body.* A great change will occur at death involving compensation for the inequalities of life. God, who had seemed to be the enemy of the innocent sufferer, will then reveal His true character and range Himself on Job's side.

And after my skin (doubtless a metonymy for "body") **has been . . . destroyed, then from my flesh I shall see God** (RSV). This is a better translation of the Hebrew than "without my flesh" and "makes the doctrine of the resurrection of the body more explicit" (H. Lindsell, *Harper Study Bible*). Here latent in the Old Testament is the doctrine of the resurrection of the body (cf. Gen. 22:5; Psalms 16:10; 49:15; Isa. 26:19; Dan. 12:2; Hos. 13:14). At the time of Christ, Jews generally believed in the resurrection of the body, based on their knowledge of the Old Testament Scriptures (John 11:24; Acts 23:6-8; Heb. 6:1-2), and they had not fabricated the doctrine.

27. But even if "from my flesh" is rendered "without my flesh" (NASB), which is linguistically weak, the words **My eyes shall behold** intimate the use of a body after death!

(5) *Job's faith struck the joyful note of hope that the truth of the resurrection of the body always inspires* (cf. 1 Thess. 4:13; 1 John 3:2-3). He exulted: "I, even I, shall see [God] for myself . . . and not as a stranger" (ASV margin), whom God had become (even an enemy) when Job had previously viewed death as a hopeless ending of life. His **heart** ("reins, kidneys," considered the seat of the emotions) was **consumed** within him as he waited in hope.

Job Warns His Friends. 19:28-29. **28-29.** Job charged his counselors with prejudice and a desire to persecute him (cf. 6:14-30; 13:7-11; 17:4-5; 19:1-5), warning them of that condign punishment of which they regarded him as a glaring example.

6. ZOPHAR'S SECOND SPEECH — THE MISERY AWAITING THE WICKED. 20:1-29.

Zophar's Angry Reply to Job. 20:1-3. **1-2.** Zophar exploded with exasperation at Job's charges against God and his friends. **Therefore, my disquieting thoughts make me respond . . . because of my inward agitation** (NASB). **3.** He confessed that he had listened to Job's insulting reproof, and he declared, **the spirit of my understanding** (*mibbînāṯî,* "from my intellect") **makes me answer** (NASB).

The Fate of the Wicked Man. *20:4-29.* **4-5.** Zophar added nothing new, harping on the same note as his two colleagues—the prosperity of the wicked is short-lived, and their downfall is certain. Was Job really cognizant of this fact, known **from of old** (NASB; 8:8; 15:10)—**the triumphing of the wicked is short** (Psalm 37:35-36), the joy of the hypocrite (godless) but for a moment (Job 8:13; 13:16; 27:8)?

6-11. No matter how highly he is exalted, he shall **perish forever like his own dung** (excrement), flying away **like a dream** (Psalms 73:20; 90:5), **chased away like a vision of the night,** so that he, as well as his riches, vanishes (cf. v. 18) and suffers a premature death (cf. Psalm 55:23).

12-14. The evil he practices is like a tasty tidbit that turns to rank poison in his body (cf. Prov. 20:17). **15-16.** He vomits the riches he gorges, God not administering an emetic, but forcing him to disgorge his ill-acquired gains, which turn to poison, metaphorically, **the poison of asps. 17.** In contrast to the righteous, he shall see no streams of oil, no torrents of honey or curds. Oil, butter, milk, and honey are symbolic of plenty (cf. 29:6; Exod. 3:8, 17), amply illustrated extrabiblically in the Ugaritic literature.

18-19. He shall return his ill-gotten gain unused and shall not enjoy his wealth that was amassed dishonestly (cf. v. 10). **20-21.** His oppression and plunder of the poor give him no **quietness in his belly.** His godless greed rewards him with a nervous stomach, and so **he does not retain anything he desires,** while at the same time, anomalously, **nothing remains for him to devour** (NASB). **22.**

At the peak of plenty he is cramped and becomes the victim of every miserable **hand** (force; cf. 6:23).

23. God will **cast the fury of his wrath upon him,** when he is **about to fill his belly** (KJV). **24-25.** If he escapes the iron weapon, the bronze bow will pierce him, the shaft coming out of his back and the gleaming sword from his **gall** (gallbladder), used broadly for his entrails or guts (cf. 16:13). **26.** Total darkness is reserved for him, and an unfanned flame, literally, **a fire not blown** [by man], perhaps meaning lightning (cf. 1:16; 2 Kings 1:12), shall **consume him,** and those left in his tent shall fare ill (cf. 18:14-15).

27. Heaven and earth will testify against him (cf. Deut. 32:1; Isa. 1:2). Such an invocation as sanctioning witnesses goes back to an ancient form of covenant (treaty) oath (cf. the sanctions of the Hittite treaties, ANET, pp. 202-6). **28.** The increase of his household shall go into exile (cf. Deut. 28:31); Septuagint: "the offspring of his house shall be exposed" (*yāḡōl,* instead of *yîḡel,* MT).

29. Zophar summarized the topic of his speech. This is the **portion** (*ḥēleq,* "inheritance, lot, destiny") of the **wicked man** (*'āḏām rāshā'*) **from God** (*'elōhîm*) and his *nǎḥ^alǎṯ 'imrô mē'ēl,* "the heritage of his command from God" (*El*), that is, **the heritage appointed unto him by God.** But Job was not a "wicked man"; neither was he being punished for wickedness, so Zophar's whole grand dissertation, while true and eloquent, was completely misapplied, giving Satan leeway to torment Job (cf. 1:12; 2:6).

7. JOB'S REPLY—THE SOVEREIGN GOD WILL DEAL WITH THE WICKED. 21:1-34.

His Plaint Is Directed Toward God. *21:1-6.* **1. But Job answered,** his answer demonstrating that he now had the upper hand in the controversy, in a masterful manner meeting the arguments of his accusers. **2.** He implored them to **hear diligently** (listen closely) to his **speech** (what he had to say), for their thoughtfulness would bring him consolation (lit., "your consolation," with subjective not objective force, "the solace you give to me," not I to you). **3. Bear with me that I may speak**—"Allow me to have my say, and after I have spoken, go on mocking" (BV), specifically addressed to Zophar (the singular form of the verb in the Hebrew), who had taunted Job for being wicked and sharing the fate of the godless man (chap. 20).

4. Job asked, **Is my complaint regarding my fellow man?** (BV). No, it was now of a different kind, for he had long since abandoned hope of human sympathy. "His complaint concerns not men but God" (Delitzsch). He had already said, "While my friends are my scorners, my eyes turn weepingly to God" (16:20, BV). Job reminded his friends of this fact by asking further, **Why** [then] **should I not be impatient?** (NASB).

5. He was saying, my complaint to God concerns the ways of God, why His justice is so tardy. This is the problem, the unsolved riddle, which, when I face it, I am troubled, and horror lays hold of my flesh. And you, my friends, should be troubled too, **and lay** (put) **your hand upon** (over) **your mouth,** a gesture of awe and stupefaction (cf. 29:9; 40:4; Mic. 7:16), illustrated in a Mesopotamian cylinder seal of the late third millennium B.C., depicting gaping onlookers clapping their hands over their mouths as the goddess Etana mounts heavenward on eagle's wings (cf. ANET, pp. 695, 333).

He Notes the Frequent Prosperity of the Wicked. 21:7-16. **7-9.** Job asked why the wicked often go on living to old age,

getting richer as they advance in age—their progeny established securely before them, their homes free from fear, no **rod** (scourge) **of God** upon them. **10.** The wicked man's **bull** often **gendereth** (sires unfailingly), and his cow calves with no loss.

11. They send forth their little ones (produce a flock of offspring), and their children happily and merrily **dance** about them. **12.** They sing to the timbrel and lyre and **rejoice** (revel) to the tune of the flute. **13. They spend their days in wealth, and in a moment go down to sheol,** the place of departed spirits in the Old Testament (Hab. 2:5; Luke 16:23, "grave" only with reference to the material part of man).

14. They say to God, **Depart from us!** (cf. 22:17). **We do not even desire the knowledge of Thy ways** (NASB). **15. What is the Almighty** (El Shaddai; see comment on 6:4) **that we should serve him? And what profit** (34:9; cf. Exod. 5:2) **should we have, if we pray unto him? 16. Lo, their good** (prosperity, wealth) **is not in their hand** (control); **the counsel of the wicked** (their ways of thinking and doing), he had renounced, Job declared, and it was far from him (22:18; Psalm 1:1; Prov. 1:10).

God Is Sovereign with Both Righteous and Wicked Alike. 21:17-26. **17. How often is the lamp of the wicked put** (snuffed) **out!** And destruction comes upon them. God **distributeth** (apportions) them **sorrows** (pains) **in his anger. 18.** Like **stubble** and **chaff** (Psalm 1:4), the tempest snatches them away. Yet other people, just as wicked and conceivably even more so, by contrast live on to old age in undisturbed prosperity (vv. 7-16).

19. Job refuted the contention of the friends that God stores up the iniquity of wicked men for their children. **20. Let their own eyes see their calamity,** said

Job, **let them drink of the indignation of the Almighty** (El Shaddai; BV; cf. Jer. 31:29-30; Ezek. 18:2-4). **21.** A man who is dead has no contact or interest in his family. In these matters God is absolutely sovereign. **22.** Can anyone presume to teach Him knowledge, He who judges **those on high?** (NASB; cf. 4:17-18; 15:15; Psalm 82:1).

Job cited two contrasting cases (vv. 23-26). **23-24.** The first case is of one who dies in full strength and health. **24-25.** Another dies **with a bitter soul, never even tasting anything good. Together they lie down in the dust . . . worms cover them** (NASB). It is not a question of one being more wicked than the other, nor even that either was wicked. God is sovereign in His dealing. Accounts will be settled in the life to come, concerning which Job was gradually being given revelatory light (cf. 19:25-27).

Human Experience Demonstrates That Suffering Is Not Always the Result of Sin. 21:27-34. **27.** Job was clearly far ahead of his opponents in the debate. He let them know that the thrust of their argument was not lost on him. **Behold, I know your thoughts and the devices** (wiles) **which ye wrongfully imagine** (plot) **against me.** You reason: the wicked are ruined; Job is ruined; therefore, Job is wicked! (cf. 4:7). But is this true? Of course, honesty, integrity, and diligence as a rule bring prosperity. God wills it so, to encourage good conduct. But when people came to conclude that misfortune must be due to bad behavior, as Job's friends did, God undertook to teach the falsity of these conclusions through Job as His agent.

28. The scheming thoughts of Job's friends were revealed, for they said, **Where is the house of the prince** (i.e., of the virtuous princely man) and "the tent of the tabernacle of the wicked?" (lit.

Heb.). That is, "How can we tell who is virtuous and who is wicked? And, consequently, we do not know to which category you belong." That was the big blunder of Job's counselors; they put him in the wrong category. All along they had been insinuating that, though he seemed to be righteous, he was really wicked.

Though the friends paraded their observations as primeval law (cf. 20:4), they were ivory-tower theorists, totally out of line with common everyday experience (vv. 30-33; cf. comments on 4:2-11): (1) **29-30.** *There was the experience of travelers.* **Have ye not asked them that go by the way** (i.e., the wayfarers)? **And do ye not know their evidences** (i.e., the marks of their experience, and the conclusions at which they have arrived)? "Do you not recognize their witness?" (NASB).

Verse 30 can only be correctly translated by rendering the preposition *le* ("to"/"for") in the passage with separative force as "from," which it frequently has in Ugaritic (cf. C. H. Gordon, *Ugaritic Handbook,* 10:1). Thus, "that the wicked is kept *from* the day of disaster" and "delivered *from* [not 'to'] the day of wrath." Certainly Job was not corroborating what the friends have been constantly insisting on (15:20-24; 18:14-15; 20:11): that the wicked always suffer. Often when a band of travelers was attacked by robbers, the good were killed and the wicked spared.

(2) **31-33.** *There was the experience of the despot* who died without anyone having dared to oppose him or tell him about his true character to his face. He died in peace, had a grand funeral, and his body was guarded in a mausoleum. He was an illustration from life that flatly contradicted what the friends had asserted.

Job Draws a Final Conclusion. 21:34. **34.** Having punctured the bubble of airtight retribution, Job left his accusers clinging to a burst balloon that could offer him only vain comfort, which was no comfort at all, but only misery. **Seeing that in your answers there remaineth falsehood,** literally, "all that is left of them is transgression," that which is not only worthless, but worse still, that which is harmful and wrong.

C. THE THIRD CYCLE OF SPEECHES.
22:1—31:40.

1. ELIPHAZ'S THIRD SPEECH—AGREE
WITH GOD. 22:1-30.

Can a Man Be Profitable to God? 22:1-5. Again opening a new cycle of speeches, Eliphaz proceeded to reply in a far more offensive tone than before, irresponsibly accusing Job of specific crimes and, what is perhaps even more inexcusable, not even referring to, much less dealing with, Job's mental and spiritual dilemma created by the apparent incongruities of God's moral government in the world. Instead, he restricted himself to further exposition of the one warped idea that had dominated his thinking and that of his colleagues— Job's suffering was evidence of sinfulness. If Job would only agree with God on that point and repent of his rebellion, Eliphaz held out to him the prospect of recovery. But the God that Eliphaz presented was a heartless automaton, whose absoluteness divorced Him from practically all interest in man. **2. Can a man be profitable unto God?** No. He who is wise is profitable only to himself. **3a. Is it any pleasure to the Almighty** (El Shaddai, the all-sufficient One; see comment on 6:4) **that thou art righteous?** The answer before Eliphaz's automaton God would be no! **3b.** No, He as the absolute One sees no **gain** to Him-

self **that thou makest thy ways perfect** (blameless). **4. Will he reprove thee for fear of thee,** that is, because He stands in awe of thee? **Will he enter with thee into judgment,** that is, justify His dealings with you? Eliphaz's God would leave Job in the lurch. He was the antithesis of the God of Job, who is the God of the Bible—a living, loving God concerned for the lowliest and neediest of His creatures.

5. In the presence of this heartless, loveless, senseless deity of Eliphaz's manufacture—a divine monster; an absolute, infinite tyrant—Eliphaz's pronouncement upon Job was as monstrous as the phony deity he imagined he was defending, and whose sentence upon Job he was pronouncing—**thy wickedness** is **great ... thine iniquities endless.** What an illustration of the havoc and damage false doctrine and heresy can work, even in good men with the highest motives and sincerest attitude of defending God Himself (although it is questionable whether Eliphaz fits in this higher category). What an open door such a warped teaching gives to Satan (1:11; 2:6)!

Job's Alleged Sins. 22:6-11. Driven by the force of a narrow syllogism (that suffering is the result of sin; Job is a great sufferer; therefore, Job is a great sinner, v. 5), Eliphaz proceeded to charge Job with a number of unproved and unprovable crimes that were as outrageous as his distorted view of God and his analysis of Job's problem. (1) **6.** *He accused him of the crime of oppressing* and *plundering the poor of his own clan.* **Thou hast taken a pledge from thy brother for nothing** (ḥinnām, "without cause"). Without reason he had required pawn of his brothers, the Law stipulating that a garment taken in pledge be returned before sundown (Exod. 22:26; Deut. 24:10-13; cf. Amos

2:8). **And stripped the naked of their clothing.**

(2) **7-9.** *He accused him of the crime of inordinate greed and pitiless avarice,* withholding bread and water from the destitute, and neglecting and even abusing the widow and orphan, as an arrogant land-grabber, who dispossessed his weaker neighbors to become a **mighty man** who owned the earth, and a privileged inhabitant of it. **10-11. Therefore,** Eliphaz concluded, **snares are round about thee, and sudden fear** (dread) **troubleth thee . . . darkness, that thou canst not see . . . abundance of waters** (figure of tribulation) **cover thee.**

Job's Alleged Basic Sin. 22:12-20. Eliphaz concluded that the underlying cause of Job's alleged ruthless selfishness was disbelief in the omniscience of God. **12-14.** Because **God** is **in the height of heaven,** throning above the **height of the stars,** would Job deny His omniscience by saying, "What does God know? Can He judge through the thick darkness? Clouds are a hiding place for Him, so that he cannot see; and He walks on the vault of heaven" (NASB). Job had not given the slightest provocation for such an absurd charge, which was actually merited by Eliphaz's own concept of a robot deity, a heartless automaton (cf. vv. 2-4), who is not affected by or interested in the weal or woe of his creatures.

15-16. Had Job **marked** (noted) the **old way** (better, "dark" path, from Ugaritic *ġlm*, "grow dark," M. Dahood, NWSPJ, pp. 65-66), **which wicked men have trod,** who **were untimely snatched away** (BV), their **foundation . . . overflown with a flood** (a torrent), like the sudden destruction of the house the foolish man built on the sand in Jesus' parable (Matt. 7:26)?

17. They said to God, **Depart from us** (i.e., "let us alone!"). **What can the Al-**

mighty (El Shaddai; see 6:4) **do for them?** (better, "us," following the LXX and Syriac). Here again Eliphaz attributed to Job the very thoughts Job had ascribed to the wicked (21:14-15). **18-20.** In his declaration that **the counsel of the wicked is far from me,** Eliphaz again appropriated the very words of Job (21:16), and not only separated himself from these open transgressors, but also from Job, whom he classified among them.

Eliphaz's Advice for Job's Restoration. 22:21-30. While these exhortations were all proper, even eloquently beautiful, they were basically inapplicable to Job's dilemma. For if Job had acted upon this advice and had repented according to Eliphaz's demands, by doing so he would have confessed sins he had not committed and assented to the friends' false accusations. He would have acknowledged himself as the wicked man they had made him out to be.

21-23. The exhortations to yield, submit, accept instruction, and return to El Shaddai were all proper. But the injunction to **put away iniquity very far from thy tents** would be for Job to acknowledge as true Eliphaz's horrible accusations (vv. 6-20). **24-30.** These verses are elevated and truly wonderful when correctly applied, especially verses 29 and 30, which Job could well have profited from.

2. JOB'S REPLY TO ELIPHAZ—GOOD PEOPLE OFTEN SUFFER. 23:1-17.

Job's Longing for Converse with God. 23:1-7. It is noteworthy that Job did not deny Eliphaz's unfounded accusations. Apparently he viewed them as so preposterous and irresponsible as not to merit serious attention, maintaining meanwhile an attitude of dispassionate calm that had pervaded his words since the reassuring truth that God was his Friend had broken upon his consciousness. But he still struggled with the problem of the perplexing absence of discernible justice in God's behavior toward him, a righteous man (chap. 23), and toward the wicked (chap. 24).

2. Even today my complaint is rebellion (NASB). The patriarch was defiant toward any exhortation to penitence that would imply that his sufferings were justly merited. **3-4.** As he complained that the divine hand was heavy upon him despite his groanings, he cried, **Oh, that I knew where I might find him** to **come** to **his seat** (tribunal) to lay his case before Him with ample argument. **5.** Since now he had the conviction that God was his Friend, he was eager to know what He would say to him.

6a. With His **great** (legal) **power,** would He as a divine Attorney **plead against me? 6b. No, ... He would pay attention to me** (NASB). **7. There an upright man could reason with him, and I should be acquitted for ever by my judge** (RSV). Since Job now had the firm conviction that his divine Avenger lived (19:25), his keen desire to appear before His tribunal was more ardent than ever before, and his expectation of his vindication firmer.

Job's Faith Struggles with Doubt. 23:8-17. **8-9.** Still in the dark as to the reason for his suffering, Job nevertheless gave clear evidence that he was not the defiant man his friends would paint him, but one who longed for God and had faith that He would hear his cause and vindicate him. But he complained of God's distance, or rather, his distance from God. This riddle of undeserved suffering and the intolerable problems it had evoked had interposed as a frightful wall between him and God. so that he had lost the sense of fellowship and comfort of His presence.

10. Yet, despite this apparent unavailability of God, trust becomes resplendent in the beautiful exclamation: **But he knoweth the way that I take; when he hath tested me, I shall come forth** (emerge) **as gold** (Psalms 1:6; 139:1-3), or possibly, "shine as gold" (*yṣ'*, related to Arab. *wadu'a,* "be clean, fair," and *ḍa'a,* "shine"; cf. Psalm 37:6; Isa. 62:1; Hos. 6:5). This was certainly a high point in Job's search for a solution to his vexing problem.

In verses 11 to 13, Job gave unswerving testimony to his loyalty to God and His Word, which by its calm sincerity reveals the utter falsity of Eliphaz's charges of greed, doing so without giving the impression that he has those base accusations even in the background of his thoughts. **12. I have esteemed** (treasured) **the words of his mouth more than my necessary food** (lit., "my appointed portion"; 6:10; 22:22). Yet God inexorably executed against the patriarch all that He had foreordained, in apparent disregard of merit or demerit. **13.** "He chooses and who can turn him? What he wishes, he does" (AB).

15-17. "Therefore," declared the harried saint, "I am dismayed before him; I think of it, and recoil from him" (AB), not because of **the darkness nor deep gloom which covers me,** but because of God's apparent failure to reconcile in my mind His providential rule with His justice. What an illustration of the suffering and confusion caused by exposure to false doctrine or misapplied or misinterpreted truth.

3. JOB'S REPLY TO ELIPHAZ CONTINUED—BAD PEOPLE OFTEN GO UNPUNISHED. 24:1-25.

Why Is God Sometimes Slow to Punish the Wicked? 24:1-12. Job defined the perplexing problem. **Why, seeing times** (and events) **are not hidden from the Almighty, do they that know him** (i.e., believe in Him and love Him) **not see his days?** (i.e., His days of retribution and punishment of the wicked). Even those who know and love God, as well as those who do not know Him, are nonplussed concerning His principles of the government of the moral universe.

In verses 2 to 12 Job adduced instances of the crimes of the wicked and their evildoing, at which the Almighty (El Shaddai; cf. 6:4) seemed to wink (overlook; cf. Acts 17:30; 2 Pet. 3:9). **2a.** Removing **landmarks** (boundaries) was a detestable crime to Semites, and it was expressly prohibited by the Mosaic Law (Deut. 19:14; 27:17). **2b.** Seizing flock and shepherd apparently went along with plundering pasturage.

3-4. Plundering the property of the orphan and widow was particularly heinous, for these helpless people were to be objects of special protection. **5.** These rapacious plunderers went to their job of finding food like **wild asses** (onagers) **in the desert** (steppe). They reaped and gleaned in the field of the villain and in the vineyard of the wicked. **7-8.** Evidently their victims are described. **9-11.** Their rapacity is further delineated.

12a. From the city men groan ... the wounded cry out. 12b. The conclusion: **Yet God does not pay attention to folly** (NASB). He acted as if nothing were amiss. Here Job turned the argument on Eliphaz, who had accused Job of acting as if God did not know or care about the wickedness of sinners (22:12-13). Job suggested that God seemed to act in that manner.

Those Who Love Darkness. 24:13-17. **13-17.** Job described those who **rebel against the light; they know not its ways** (cf. Rom. 13:12; John 3:20; 1 John 1:7).

They walk and operate in darkness to murder, plunder, rob, and commit adultery (cf. 1 Thess. 5:4-8).

Let These Evildoers Perish! 24:18-25. **18-25.** These verses seem to represent a curse upon the wicked men described in this chapter, at whom Job, in his struggle with the problem of the apparent absence of discernible justice in the divine dealing with evildoers, imagined God looked at in silence from His high heaven. Many critics regard this section as belonging to the third speech of Bildad and misplaced from the following chapter.

4. BILDAD'S THIRD SPEECH—GOD AND MAN IN CONTRAST. 25:1-6.

The Greatness of God. 25:1-3. **2-3.** God is almighty, infinite, absolute. How can any man contend with Him, or claim to be pure in His sight? **Dominion and fear** (awe) **are with him** (i.e., "belong to Him," NASB). He maintains peace and harmony **in his high places,** the heavenlies of Ephesians 1:3, and among His **armies,** that is, His numberless celestial hosts that reflect His infinite glory and majesty, the light radiated by Him who is Himself light and the source of all light (cf. John 1:4; 8:12; 9:5; 12:35; 1 John 1:5).

The Puniness and Sinfulness of Man. 25:4-6. **4. How then can man be justified with God? ... Or ... be clean that is born of a woman?** Bildad did not attempt to reply formally to Job's arguments that the righteous, as well as the wicked, often suffer in God's inscrutable providence. **6.** As if all his arguments had become exhausted, he merely fell back upon the position twice set forth by Eliphaz (4:17-21; 15:14-16) and already allowed by Job (14:4), namely, the impossibility of man, who is a maggot and a worm, being righteous with God. Therefore, he adhered to the contention of all the friends, that Job was impious in holding to his righteousness before God. Bildad practically owned that he and his companions had been defeated in argument, since he attempted no answer, but repeated truisms that were irrelevant to Job's case and the real question at issue.

5. JOB'S REPLY TO BILDAD—HE ACKNOWLEDGES GOD'S GREATNESS. 26:1-14.

Job Again Rebukes His Friends. 26:1-4. **2-3.** Once again with biting irony, Job reprimanded his friends for giving no help. **What a help you are to the weak! How you have saved the arm without strength!** (6:11; Psalm 71:9). **What counsel . . . to one without wisdom! What helpful insight you have abundantly provided!** (NASB; manifested; lit., made known). **4. To whom hast thou uttered words?** That is, "Is it not to one [to me] who has declared the very same thing himself?" **And whose spirit came from thee?** "Was it not my own breath, my own teaching, that issued from your mouth?"

Job Celebrates the Power and Wisdom of God. 26:5-14. In contrast to his friends' powerlessness and lack of wisdom, Job extolled the power and wisdom of God in a magnificent soliloquy. Not only do the starry heavens display God's glory, as his friends had pointed out so frequently, but so do the underworld (vv. 5-6) and the universe as a whole (vv. 7-14).

5a. The departed spirits (*rĕp̄ā'îm,* "shades or denizens of the netherworld"; Psalm 88:10; Prov. 2:18; 9:18; 21:16; Isa. 14:9) **tremble** (NASB). **5b. The waters, and their inhabitants** are apparently not marine life, but spirit residents of the lower world, conceived as a watery abyss (cf. 2 Sam. 22:5; Psalms 42:7; 88:3-7; Jonah 2:2), with the earth resting on a watery foundation (Psalms 104:6; 124:5). **6. Sheol is naked before him,** and **destruction** (*'ăḇaddôn,* "perdition, ruin"), another designation of the netherworld (cf. 28:22; 31:12; Prov. 15:11; Rev. 9:11), **hath no covering** (cover).

7. He stretcheth out the north over the empty place (void), **and hangeth the earth upon nothing,** a remarkable illustration how the inspired Word of God anticipated the discoveries of modern science in describing with scientific accuracy the condition of our planet, and setting forth the facts as a proof of divine power. **8.** This verse is another remarkable instance of God's power, embodying the idea of the waters being bound up in the clouds and, although of immense weight, yet apparently defying gravity. **The cloud is not torn** (does not burst) under the great weight of water. How did the ancient poet, not knowing that water vapor is lighter than air, express this fact so beautifully and accurately?

9. He holdeth back (covers) **the face of his throne,** that is, "He veils the heavens with clouds" in poetic language. "He obscures the face of the full moon" (NASB and AB, reading *kĕsĕ',* "full moon," instead of *kĭssē',* "throne"). **10.** This verse should read, "He has described a circle upon the face of the waters, unto the confines of light and darkness" (lit. Heb. trans.), referring to the perfect circle of the horizon at sea, which is the apparent limit of light, and beyond which was thought to be darkness, because it was the sphere of the invisible. Indeed, darkness *is* beyond, for the other side of the earth is draped in night.

11. The pillars of heaven are apparently mountains, whose tops are hidden in clouds. **12.** By His power He **quieted** (stilled) **the sea** and **shattered Rahab** (NASB), literally "pride," but here having a mythological connotation referring to the sea (see 9:13; 38:8-11). **13. By his Spirit he hath garnished the heavens** (9:8). **His hand hath formed** (pierced) **the crooked** (fleeing) **serpent,** evidently a poetical mythological reference to God's control of both the terrestrial and celestial waters to assure favorable climatic order (cf. Isa. 27:1; Ugaritic text, Cyrus Gordon, *Ugaritic Handbook,* 67. 1. 1-2). Although Job employed terminology common in Canaanite mythology (*Yam,* "the sea"; and *Rahab,* "the fleeing serpent"), his usage is *strictly unmythological* and his reference is to natural phenomena, with which these names were identified (cf. E. Smick, *Job,* ZPEB, 3:609).

14. Lo, these are parts (lit., "ends"; i.e., "outskirts, fringes") **of his ways; but how little a portion** ("faint word" or "whisper") **is heard of him!** Job's exalted praise of God was at variance with his friends' assessment of him as wicked and ungodly. Had they recognized the limitations of their knowledge, they would not have so grossly misinterpreted his case and given such poor counsel.

6. JOB'S REPLY CONTINUED—HE MAINTAINS HIS INTEGRITY. 27:1-23.

Job Steadfastly Maintains His Integrity. 27:1-6. With his counselors apparently silenced, Job addressed all the friends (indicated by the plural tense, vv. 11-12), assuming the role of a teacher (v. 11). **2-5a.** Once again he averred his righteousness with a strong oath. **As God liveth, who hath taken away my** (judicial) **right; and the Almighty** (El Shaddai; see 6:4), **who hath vexed my soul** ("made me bitter").

In the oath Job's dilemma appears in clear view. With the same breath he proclaimed God as the God of truth, while at the same time he charged that His treatment of him was unjust. It is a

graphic portrayal of a man whose faith remained with him throughout the emotional and spiritual storm that raged in his heart. He could not forsake God, whom he was tempted to imagine was forsaking him. Yet he could not utter falsehood or deceit and justify his friends (say that they were right) in insisting that he was being punished for his sins.

5b. Till I die (6:9), he declared, **I will not remove** (put away, renounce) **mine integrity. 6. My righteousness** (innocence) **I hold fast, and will not let it go** (relinquish it). **My heart** (denoting his conscience and thinking powers) **shall not reproach me as long as I live** (lit., "from my days"; i.e., "my life long").

Job Contrasts Himself with the Wicked. 27:7-12. Job named five ways in which he differed from the wicked: (1) **7.** He utterly repudiated the godless, in which class his friends categorized him. (2) **8.** The wicked are hopeless when God takes away their life, in contrast to Job himself, who had hope (cf. 19:25-27). (3) **9.** They have no communication with God when trouble comes, but Job did, although he longed for a mediator, a daysman (9:32-33; 10:4-5; 13:21-22), to make the interchange easier. (4) **10.** They have no delight in the Almighty (El Shaddai; see 6:4), nor do they call upon God at all times as Job did. (5) **11.** The wicked do not know God, in contrast to Job, who not only knew Him, but would teach his friends concerning God's hand (power) and His will. **12.** Job declared that his friends had seen these things, so the question was, Why had they acted so foolishly, and spoken so vainly and pointlessly?

Job Underscores the Destiny of the Wicked. 27:13-23. Job agreed with his friends that the fate of the wicked is terrible, but only after contrasting himself with those who belong to that category. Many critics claim that verses 8 to 23 are really Zophar's third speech and that an introductory line was lost at this point or removed by an overzealous scribe, who wanted to tone down Job's argument. But the order of the Hebrew Bible is ably defended by many scholars and, we believe, represents the original scheme of the poem.

7. JOB'S POEM ON WISDOM. 28:1-28.

The Achievements of Man. 28:1-11. Still without a satisfactory solution to the fierce internal conflict raging within his soul concerning the problem of reconciling his sufferings with his own integrity of life, Job, at his wit's end, turned his attention to the wisdom of God. But how could a man so mentally and spiritually disturbed produce a poem so full of meditative tranquillity? Besides taking into account the influence of the Spirit of God upon him on the divine side, it is well known on the human plane that people in a state of great perturbation sometimes, in a moment of calm, author poems or hymns of deep tranquillity.

1-3. Man's ability to mine precious metals and gems from the earth is amazing. He extracts silver, gold, iron, and copper, conquering the blackness of the earth's bowels and searching out the ore of the earth in **darkness, and the shadow of death** (deep gloom). **4a-b.** He sinks (lit., "breaks open") **a shaft far from habitation,** that is, away from where people live, **forgotten by the foot** (NASB; lit. Heb.), where travelers do not go and man's foot does not touch. **4c. They swing to and fro** (RSV) is an allusion to the suspension of miners by ropes and doubtlessly refers to the lowering of them in baskets or cages. **5.** This verse refers to the surface of the earth producing food; **but underneath it is turned up as by fire** (RSV).

This reference may be to the igneous appearance of the rocks, or possibly the process of making the stone brittle by fire to facilitate the digging of the precious metal, a practice mentioned by Diodorus Siculus in connection with the gold mines of Nubia.

6. Job said **the stones** of the earth **are the place of sapphires,** and **it hath dust of gold,** that is, dust containing gold. **7-8.** The poet stressed the remoteness and inaccessibility of the mines (cf. v. 4). The Nubian mines worked by the Egyptians were over a week's journey into the inhospitable desert. The turquoise mines at Serabit el Khadem in the Sinaitic Peninsula were also remote and hard to get to.

9. Man **putteth forth his hand upon the rock** and **overturneth the mountains by the roots** (at the base), and that happened before the advent of the bulldozer and modern earth-moving equipment. **10.** He carves out channels in the rocks so his eye can see the precious metal and precious stones hidden there. **11. He bindeth the floods** (streams) "so that they do not trickle" (RSV), a possible reference to damming up a river to conserve water for irrigation.

The Wisdom of the Almighty. 28:12-27. **12.** Man is reminded that his true wisdom is to fear (reverence) the LORD and obey Him. So the poet asks, **But where shall wisdom be found?** Although man is clever and inventive (vv. 1-11), is it to be found in him? **13. Man knoweth not its price** (its value). **Neither is it found in the land of the living,** the sphere of natural life as opposed to the netherworld of disembodied spirits (cf. v. 22; Isa. 38:11; 53:8; Jer. 11:19).

14. The depth (deep) **... and the sea** refer to the primeval oceans that spring from the depths of the earth. Though man may explore the watery abyss, as he does in searching for gold and precious gems (v. 11), wisdom will not be found there. **15.** Neither gold nor silver can purchase it ("weighed as its price"; cf. Gen. 23:16; Zech. 11:12). **16. It cannot be valued with the gold** (*kĕṯĕm,* derived from the Egyptian designation of the country from which the gold was obtained, doubtlessly Nubia) **of Ophir** (cf. 1 Kings 9:26-28; 10:11), probably in east Africa or India.

17-19. The price of wisdom is above gold and any precious stone. **20-21. Whence, then, cometh wisdom?** concealed, as it is, from the **eyes of all living. 22. Abaddon** ("destruction, ruin," another name of Sheol) **and Death** can say they have heard only a **rumor** (report) of it (RSV). The question broached in verse 20: "Whence, then, cometh wisdom?" is answered in verses 23 to 28. **23.** God is the source of wisdom. **God understands its way ... He knows its place** (NASB; cf. 9:4; Prov. 8:22-36). **24.** He is omniscient, **for He looks to the ends of the earth, and sees everything under the heavens** (NASB; cf. Psalms 11:4; 33:13; 66:7; Prov. 15:3).

25-26. By His wisdom **He imparted weight to the wind** (Psalm 135:7) **and meted out the waters by measure** (Job 12:15; 38:8-11), **when He set a limit for the rain** (37:6, 11-12; 38:26-28), **and a course for the thunderbolt** (NASB; cf. 37:3; 38:25). **27.** He made His mighty and glorious creation in wisdom and through wisdom, the eternal Word, the preincarnate Christ (Prov. 8:22-36; John 1:1-3; Col. 1:15-17; Heb. 1:2-3).

28. To man He has given a revelation of wisdom that in the Old Testament was prophetic of the coming Christ (1 Cor. 1:30), and was defined in its practical outworking in human experience as (1) **fear of** (reverence for) **the Lord** in acknowledging His infinite holiness, man's utter lostness, and sin's exceeding sinfulness, and binding man to come

by a grace-through-faith approach through redemptive sacrifice; and (2) departure from evil, demanding separation from sin and sinners to serve an infinitely holy God (cf. 2 Cor. 6:14—7:1).

8. JOB'S REMINISCENCE UPON HIS EARLIER PROSPERITY. 29:1-25.

He Recalls His Former Happy Condition. 29:1-10. **1.** Job **continued his parable** (*māshāl,* "poetic discourse, poem," as in 27:1). **2.** He fervently wished that he **were as in months past** (of old) **when God preserved** (*shmr,* "guarded, watched over") him (Jer. 31:28). Was this a healthy desire (Eccles. 7:10)? Was God not now watching over him, perhaps even more solicitously (cf. Num. 6:24; Psalms 16:1; 91:11)?

3. Then, he recalled, God's **lamp** (light) shone over his head, and by **his light** Job **walked through darkness** (cf. Psalms 18:28; 36:9; 97:11). **4.** He was in his **prime of life** (BV) (*ḥōrĕp,* from the basic meaning of *ḥrp,* "be early, young," connecting it originally with the paschal celebration in the spring (cf. Exod. 13:2, 13). **The secret** (counsel) **of God** was upon his **tent** (in the sense of "household" or "family," as in Exod. 16:16).

5. The Almighty (El Shaddai; see 6:4) **was yet with** him when his **children were about** him (cf. 1:2; 8:4), numerous progeny being regarded as a token of divine favor (Psalms 127:3-5; 128:3-4). **6.** His prosperity is symbolized by these statements: **I washed my steps with butter** (cream), **and the rock poured me out rivers of oil** (cf. Deut. 32:13; 33:24; Psalm 81:16). In the Ugaritic myth of Baal, "The heavens rain oil, the wadies run honey" (49. 3. 6-9) as tokens of restoration of fertility to a barren earth. **7-10.** Job reflected on the honor shown him when he went out to the gate of the city and the public square, the scene of judicial proceedings and public business. All ages and classes of society honored him and showed him deference.

He Remembers His Charities. 29:11-17. **11-13.** Job was called blessed because he championed the cause of the poor, the orphan, and the widow (cf. Psalm 72:12), giving the lie to Eliphaz's baseless calumny (22:6-9). The sage Danel of the Ugaritic epic of Aqhat "judges the cause of the widow, adjudicates the case of the orphan."

14-16. Job **put on righteousness** and **justice** as a **robe and a diadem** (turban), being **eyes to the blind ... feet ... to the lame ... a father to the poor,** championing the cause of the stranger (cf. Psalm 68:5; Isa. 22:21). Hammurabi, in the epilogue of his code of laws, represents himself as "a ruler who is to the people like the father who bore [them]" (cf. ANET, p. 178, rev. 25, ll. 20-21). The king of Zenjirli, from the ninth century B.C., boasts of his fidelity to his royal duty, "I was father to some, and to some I was mother" (cf. ANET, p. 500). **17.** Job also resisted the wicked. Likening the wicked to a ravening beast, he declared, **I broke the fangs of the unrighteous, and made him drop his prey from his teeth** (RSV; cf. 4:10; Psalms 3:7; 58:6; 124:6-7).

He Anticipates a Prosperous Ripe Old Age. 29:18-20. **18-19.** Job looked forward to dying in his **nest** (cf. Deut. 32:11; Isa. 16:2), and multiplying his days as **sand,** flourishing like a tree whose roots spread out to water and in whose branches the dew lodged (cf. Job 8:16-17; 18:16; Psalm 1:3; Jer. 17:8; Ezek. 31:7). **20.** He foresaw his glory ever **fresh** with him, and his bow **renewed in** his **hand** (cf. Gen. 49:24). To break one's bow reduced him to impotence (Jer. 49:35; Hos. 1:5). **21-25.** Job

also envisioned the continuation of the honor men accorded him and his beneficent ministry and kingly status.

9. JOB'S PRESENT SUFFERING. 30:1-31.

Present Insults Heaped on Him. 30:1-15. **1.** Instead of a ripe old age of honor and prosperity, Job found himself surrounded by shame and misery. Boys whose fathers were beneath him, whom he would have **disdained to put with the dogs of** his **flock,** now **mock** (*śḥq,* "laugh at, deride, jeer, scorn") him (NASB; cf. 19:18). The dog in Bible times was looked upon as a filthy and vicious scavenger (Exod. 22:31; 1 Kings 14:11; 21:19, 23; Prov. 26:11; Jer. 15:3). To be called a dog was a grievous affront (1 Sam. 24:14; 2 Sam. 9:8; 2 Kings 8:13) or an extreme form of self-abasement (cf. Matt. 7:6; 15:26).

2-3. Those who made sport of Job were men whose strength and vigor had been dissipated by famine and dire scarcity and who **gnaw the dry ground by night in waste and desolation, who pluck mallow** (saltwort, a plant of the salt marshes, cf. 24:24, RSV) **by the bushes** (NASB), that is, among the scrub. **5-7.** They were riffraff driven from the community, "shouted at like a thief" (AB), dwelling in wadi gullies and in holes of the earth and rocks, "braying" (*nhq,* attested in Aramaic and Ugaritic) like a donkey, perhaps suggesting senselessness, huddling under **nettles** (*ḥārûl* is uncertain; cf. Prov. 24:31, where the word is parallel to "thorns").

8-9. They were **children of fools** (lit. "sons of a fool") **... children of base men** ("sons of no name"). Job had become the jest of this ignoble, nameless brood, which has been **scourged** (whipped) out of the land, who taunted him in scornful ditty and **byword** (jibe; NASB). **10.** Job declared, **They abhor me, they flee far from me** (keep aloof from me), **and spare**

not (do not hesitate) **to spit in my face** (lit. Heb., "and withhold not spittle from my face").

11. Because God has loosed Job's **cord** (bowstring; cf. 29:20), that is, afflicted him, his taunters had cast off restraint in his presence. **12-15.** The rabble was harassing Job like an army besieging a city, making escape impossible and then overrunning the town when the wall has been breached, inflicting terrors and pursuing Job's dignity **like the wind.** All the while Job lamented, **My prosperity has passed away like a cloud** (NASB; cf. 7:9; Hos. 13:3; James 4:14).

Job Imagines Himself Completely Forsaken by God. 30:16-23. **16.** Job's soul within him was **poured out** (emptied); the emotional strain had drained him of all zest for life. **Days of affliction** had **taken hold** of (*'hz,* "grabbed, seized") him. **17-18.** The night **pierced** (racked, tortured) his **bones,** and the gnawing pain that vexed him never rested (relaxed), violently seizing his garment and binding him about like the collar of his tunic.

19. He imagined that God had thrown him into the mire (Psalm 69:2, 14), reducing him to dust and ashes. **20.** God, he thought, ignored his cry for help and his plea for justice. **21.** He charged God with becoming cruel (cf. 14:10-14; Isa. 63:10) and persecuting him (Job 10:3; 16:9; 19:6, 22). **22.** God is pictured as lifting him up bodily on tornadic wind and tossing him about in the roar of the tempest. **23.** Job pessimistically could only foresee imminent death, the meeting place of all the living.

Job Expresses His Utter Perplexity at His Condition. 30:24-31. **24-25.** Job had not turned his hand against the needy when he cried for help, nor had he put

away compassion for the poor. Yet, he complained, **when I waited for light, there came darkness.** It is as if Job were saying, "If only God had dealt with me as generously as I have dealt with others, I wouldn't be in this deplorable condition!" It was faltering faith, to be sure, but faith nevertheless, reaching out through the storm and the night of affliction for a Deliverer he could not yet firmly trust, because he was looking to a savior he had conjured up in his own thoughts, dictated by the pressures of his suffering, not the real Deliverer whom God was preparing him to see.

27. Little wonder Job's **bowels boiled** (KJV), that is, his emotions were in constant turmoil (cf. Lam. 1:20; 2:11), the intestines being considered the seat of the feelings. **The days of affliction** that **prevented** (KJV; confronted, came to meet) him kept him perpetually upset. **28.** He cried, **I go about mourning** (or blackened, but not by the heat of the sun; cf. v. 30; Psalms 38:6; 42:9; 43:2). He stood up in the public assembly and cried vainly for help (19:7).

29. He was isolated from society as a desert dweller, the companion of the jackal, whose mournful howl disturbs the desert night (cf. Mic. 1:8); and the ostrich, another doleful denizen of the desert (Isa. 13:21; 34:13), whose hideous hissing and cackling break the wilderness silence. **30.** Job complained that his skin had turned black, and his bones burned with fever (lit., **heat;** cf. 7:5; 18:13; Psalm 102:3; Lam. 4:8). **31a. My harp** (lyre, an instrument of rejoicing) **is turned to mourning** (cf. 21:12; Psalm 150:4; Lam. 5:15). **31b.** His **flute** (*'ûgāḇ,* "pipe," used to celebrate auspicious occasions; apparently the single pipe or true flute, not the double pipe, *ḥālîl*), was turned into **the voice of them that weep.**

10. JOB'S FINAL PROTESTATION OF
INNOCENCE. 31:1-40.

*Job Names the Sins of Which He Is
Innocent. 31:1-40.* Job protested his innocence of ten sins: (1) **1.** *He protested
his innocence of the sin of lust* —the lust
of the eyes. **I made a covenant with mine
eyes,** as the inlet to sinful desires. **Why
then should I think upon** (look upon) **a
maid** (a virgin)? His external conduct
had been blameless, but not more so
than his heart (cf. Matt. 5:8, 28).

2. Being cognizant of the omniscience
of God, he declared, **And what is the
portion of God from above?** (NASB; cf.
Joseph, "How then can I do this great
wickedness, and sin against God?"
Gen. 39:9). **3.** What could I expect as a
recompense from God for wrongdoing?
Should I not expect calamity to befall
the wrongdoer? **4. Doth not he see my
ways,** that is, does not *He* (emphatic)
observe my path **and count all my steps?**

After this general introduction
stressing the fact that God sees and
punishes wrongdoing, sixteen clauses
are introduced by "if," in which Job
employs a form associated with ancient
Near Eastern oaths of covenant allegiance to highlight his final protestation of innocence. In extrabiblical vassal
treaties, a vassal would employ a formulation in which he called down curses
on himself as proof that he was free from
violating any of the stipulations laid
down by his sovereign. Such oaths were
held in high respect and were regarded
as having great potency, and hence were
held to be the ultimate test of integrity
(cf. Exod. 22:10-11; Num. 5:20-22;
Deut. 27:11-26; 1 Kings 8:31-32).

The same principle is seen in the oath
of Hittite soldiers (ANET, pp. 353-54).
An extrabiblical parallel also appears in
the Egyptian Book of the Dead, where
the deceased at the final judgment lists
the sins he has not committed (ANET,
p. 34). By taking such oaths, Job closed
the argument and silenced his counselors, for either he had to suffer the
sanctions or be acquitted (cf. E. Smick,
Job, ZPEB, 3:609).

(2) *He protested his innocence of the
sin of falsehood.* This was especially in
the form of insincerity, deceit, and fraud
directed toward despoiling his fellowman by unfair dealing. **6.** Therefore, he
said, **Let me be weighed in an even** (just)
balance, that God may know mine integrity. 8. If he were guilty, he listed the
sanctions: **Then let me sow, and let
another eat.**

(3) *He protested his innocence of the
sin of adultery.* The sin is specified (v.
9), the sanctions given (vv. 10-12). **10.
Then let my wife grind unto another**
(*ṭḥn*), used here indisputably with sexual
connotations, as the rabbis recognized
(Soṭah 10*a*; cf. 2 Sam. 12:11; Jer. 8:10),
the term being parallel to the words: **And
let others bow down upon her,** that is, in
sexual embrace.

11. Adultery is called **an heinous crime**
(*zimmâ,* "licentiousness, indecency,
shameful sexual conduct," a cognate of
this word occurring in Ugaritic *tdmmt,*
meaning "lewdness"). It is an **iniquity to
be punished by the judges** (i.e., criminal
iniquity; cf. v. 28; Gen. 38:24; Lev.
20:10; Deut. 22:22). **12.** It is **a fire that
consumeth to destruction** (*'aḇăddôn,*
"destruction in Sheol," 26:6) **and would
root out all mine increase** (yield; cf.
20:28; 31:8).

(4) *He protested his innocence of the
sin of injustice.* **13-14.** The sin of injustice
is described—he did not despise the
claim of his slaves when they complained; and the sanction mentioned —
what could he do if God should rise
against him for wrongdoing in this matter, or how could he answer if God took
him to task? **15.** Is not God the Creator of
all mankind? This is not the fake doctrine
of the fatherhood of God and the

brotherhood of all mankind (this is undercut by the fact of the Fall of man and the necessity of salvation), but it does stress that every human being—as a creature of God—is to be respected as God's creature, having equal claim to justice (cf. Prov. 17:5; 22:2; Eph. 6:9).

(5) *He protested his innocence of the sin of hardheartedness.* Job displayed tender concern for the orphans and widows, who are the special charges of the loving-kindness of God, as well as the poor and defenseless of every sort. He listed the sins of which he was accused but of which he was guiltless (vv. 16-21), then enumerated the sanctions, if he were guilty (vv. 22-23). **22. Let mine arm fall from my shoulder blade, and . . . be broken from the bone** (of the upper arm). **23. For calamity from God is a terror to me, and because of His majesty I can do nothing** (NASB).

(6) *He protested his innocence of the sin of idolatry.* **24-28.** If he made **gold** his god (cf. 22:27; Mark 10:24), or the heavenly bodies, the sanction is stated: **This also** would have been **an iniquity to be punished by the judge** (calling for judgment, 31:11; Deut. 17:2-7). For it meant a denial of the **God . . . above** (Josh. 24:27; Isa. 59:13). Idolatry is a perfidious sin that betrays God above, criminal iniquity indeed. The expression **my mouth hath kissed my hand** apparently refers to throwing the inaccessible heavenly bodies a kiss, since kissing was an ancient form of adoration, and idols were kissed by worshipers in the pagan fertility cult (1 Kings 19:18; Hos. 13:2).

(7) *He protested his innocence of the sin of malicious joy at an enemy's downfall.* **29-30.** Job had kept himself free from gloating in delight over the misfortune of others, or exulting when trouble befell his enemy, or speaking slanderously and **wishing a curse to** (on) **his soul,** that is, on him. Evidently the

thought that he had been guilty of this sin or the following was so preposterous that he did not mention any sanctions.

(8) *He protested his innocence of the sin of hatred of foreigners.* **31.** If his tent fellows had not so witnessed, there never was a man he did not generously supply with food, not did he ever allow a stranger to lodge in the street. **32.** He always opened his doors to wayfarers. It was customary in Job's country, Uz, as well as throughout the pagan world, to regard a member of another clan or nation as a potential enemy and to treat him accordingly. Job had displayed love for foreigners and showed them hospitality.

(9) *He protested his innocence of the sin of hypocrisy.* **33-34.** None who knew Job could ever stand up against him and charge him with any of the sins enumerated, or of hiding them in his bosom, or under a veil of secrecy, because he feared anyone.

(10) *He protested his innocence of the sin of murder for robbery.* **38-40.** If his land cried out against him because he had acquired it by violence and rapacity, or its furrows wept because of his greed, if he ate its yield **without money,** without paying for what he got, or caused the owners (or tenants) to lose their lives, he listed the sanctions for his misdeeds: **let thistles grow instead of wheat, and weeds instead of barley.** Job ended his argument.

The importance of the steps Job was taking must not be missed by the Western mind. In his culture the oath of covenant allegiance was more meaningful than swearing before a judge or jury in our society, where perjury has far less terrifying sanctions. His cry was "Oh that I had one to hear me! Behold, here is my signature" (*tāw,* "mark"), the final letter of the Hebrew alphabet that had the ancient form of a cross mark (×

or +), seemingly used as a signature by illiterates; but, in any case, it showed that Job was validating the oath and its sanctions by signature. Accordingly, after signing, he immediately cried out to his divine Sovereign to hear him and impose the sanctions if his protestation of innocence was not valid.

35. Let the Almighty (El Shaddai, 6:4) **answer me** (19:7; 30:20; 35:12-13)! **And the indictment which my adversary has written** (NASB; cf. 27:7). Job represented the defense he had just offered as a signed and sealed legal document. **36.** Then, with consummate conviction of his integrity, he declared how he would wear it on his shoulder and bind it on his head **as a crown. 37.** He would tell God **the number** of his **steps** (give a complete account of his walk), and **like a prince approach Him** (NASB), crowned with the very scroll of his indictment, transformed into an emblem of honor, because it had been refuted charge by charge.

Certainly, despite the fact that Job honestly maintained his integrity, inescapably there was the taint of self-righteousness. Job's final words may be epitomized, "I am clean!" The next time he spoke, the gist of his remarks was "I am vile"—"I abhor myself!" (42:6). Elihu, who speaks in the next six chapters, was evidently appointed by God to rebuke Job for this attitude of self-righteousness. God Himself then speaks to solve the riddle of why the righteous suffer and to effect the great change in Job that opened the way for his restoration and subsequent blessing.

III. ELIHU SPEAKS TO JOB. 32:1—37:24.

A. ELIHU'S FIRST SPEECH—HIS ANGER AT JOB'S SELF-JUSTIFICATION. 32:1-22.

Elihu Introduced. 32:1-5. Elihu ("my

God is He") is presented as the son of Barachel ("God has blessed") of the tribe of Buz and the family of Ram. Buz is the eponymous ancestor of this Aramaean tribe, being represented as Abraham's nephew (Gen. 22:20-21) and brother of Uz, the presumed founder of Job's tribe (cf. Gen. 10:22-23). Accordingly, Elihu is presented like the other characters of the book, as a real historical person. The Targum speaks of Elihu as a relative of Abraham.

If the life of Elihu is placed so early, the whole position and surroundings of Job's history become the more probable, because the revelation of God Almighty (El Shaddai, cf. 6:4) and other internal evidence fit the patriarchal era and the character of Job. If the book of Job ended at this point, the last word would be Job's, with the enigma of suffering unexplained and God's character impeached. Someone was needed to exercise a mediatorial function to bridge the impasse that aroused Elihu's anger.

2-3. Elihu was incensed at Job **because he justified himself rather than God** (27:5; 30:21) and at his three friends, **because they had found no answer, and yet had condemned Job** (declared him to be in the wrong). Elihu's task was to furnish a partial answer to the question of why the righteous suffer and to prepare the way for the LORD Himself to appear and to knock Job's self-righteousness out of him to ready him for reinstatement into prosperity and blessing. **4-5.** Elihu's deference to Job's friends, because they were older than he, shows that he was not exactly the brash, conceited person many expositors make him out to be.

He Speaks. 32:6-14. **6.** Elihu confessed that he was timid and afraid to declare his opinion. **7.** He thought **days should speak, and multitude of years** (many years) **should teach wisdom. 8.**

Man's spirit (1 Cor. 2:11) aided by **the breath of the Almighty** (God's Spirit) enabled him to understand (NASB; 1 Cor. 2:12). Elihu's silence, although sealed by his respect for age, was now unsealed by a greater respect for divine revelation, which can come to young men as well as to old. **9-10.** Men **great** in age are not always great in comprehension of spiritual wisdom; so Elihu bade them to listen to him, saying he would show his opinion (lit., "knowledge," which he claimed had been revealed to him).

11. He explained that he had paid close attention to them and their **reasons** (arguments), while they **searched out what to say. 12.** But he upbraided the friends, for not one of them had **convinced** (refuted, confuted) Job. Not one of them **answered his words** (reasonings). **13.** Let them beware lest they say, **We have found wisdom; God will rout** [vanquish] **him, not man** (NASB). Apparently Elihu meant that the friends were unjustified in dropping the argument, as if no answer to Job's problem were possible on the human plane, and it had to remain a divine humanly inscrutable secret. **14.** Inasmuch as Job had not **directed his words** against him, Elihu declared he would not **answer** him with their **speeches** (lit., "words," in the sense of "arguments").

He Confesses His Impelling Constraint to Speak. 32:15-22. **15.** Dramatically, Elihu described the friends as they were silenced by Job's discourses. **They are dismayed, they answer no more; words have failed them** (NASB). Their verbosity had vanished; they were squelched. **16. Shall I wait ... because they stop and answer no more?** (NASB).

17-18. Elihu decided to declare his opinion, to speak his piece, confessing he was full of words, the spirit (his human spirit) within him impelling him, although in the light of verse 8 and 33:4

he may have meant that the Spirit of God within him constrained him. **19.** His **belly** was like unvented wine, bloated with air, **ready to burst like new wineskins.** The wine, as well as the skins, was new and threatened to burst the container unless the pressure was released (cf. Jer. 20:9; Matt. 9:17). **20. I will** (must) **speak, that I may be refreshed** (get relief).

21. Let me not ... accept any man's person ("be partial"; lit., "lift up the face"; cf. 13:8; 34:19; Lev. 19:15). **Neither let me give flattering titles unto man** (*kny* means exactly as the KJV translates it, "to give flattering titles unto man"; cf. Isa. 44:5; 45:4). Was Elihu insinuating that the friends had dealt too politely and gently with Job, for there was scarcely anything in the long argumentation that could be called flattery. In the Babylonian theodicy the parties shower one another with lofty titles, but then proceed to trade hard verbal punches. **22. For I know not how to give flattering titles ... my maker would soon take me away** (*ns'*, "put an end" to me). Elihu espoused the role of an umpire, not that of a partisan. Job had wished for an arbiter (cf. 9:33-34).

B. ELIHU'S FIRST SPEECH
CONTINUED—HE DEFENDS GOD'S
RIGHTEOUSNESS. 33:1-33.

Elihu Challenges Job. 33:1-7. **1-4.** Elihu treated Job with dignity and respect, yet with firmness, speaking as one who was sure of the whole matter. He challenged Job to listen to what he had to say in all the sincerity of his heart, acknowledging himself to be a creature of God and utterly dependent upon his Creator for his very breath. **5.** Let Job answer him and take his stand. **6. Behold, I belong to God like you; I, too, have been formed out** (cut out) **of the clay** (NASB; cf. 4:19; Gen. 2:7).

7. He said that no fear of him needed to terrify Job, for his **hand** (that is, the pressure of his hand) would not be **heavy** upon him, apparently alluding to Job's charge that God was an enemy and a tyrant, intimidating him with violence and terror (9:34; 13:21). Ironically, Elihu was suggesting that such an accusation could not now be made, since Job's opponent was a mere mortal.

Elihu Denounces Job's Charges Against God. 33:8-18. **8.** Elihu had heard a charge Job had made against God, evidently as a bystander and auditor of the whole preceding debate. He clearly defined the charge Job had made, based on his mistaken claim to his own righteousness. **9. I am clean without transgression ... innocent; neither is there iniquity in me** (6:29; 9:17; 10:7; 11:4; 16:17; 23:10-11; 27:5; 29:14; 31:1). Although Job was a good man, he had lost sight of the fact (see 1:5) that all mere human righteousness is as filthy garments in the light of the infinite holiness of God, and that he was shut up solely to the redemptive grace of God.

Job's erroneous notion of self-righteousness led him to make two accusations: **10-11.** (1) *Job accused God of being a persecutor.* He claimed God found pretexts against him and counted him as an enemy (13:24; 19:6, 11), putting his feet in fetters, and watching (like a detective) his every step (cf. 13:27). **12a.** Elihu declared boldly to Job that he was **not just** (right) in this attitude toward God, erected upon a wrong view of himself. **12b. God is greater than man.** This latter fact Job had certainly not denied, for he had magnified God's infinite power and wisdom (cf. 9:1-13; 12:13-25). Apparently Elihu meant to point out that God is mightier; so it is pointless for man to argue with Him, which fact Job also had duly emphasized (9:14-20; 13:13-16). **13.** Yet Job did contend with God in spite of what he had said was useless. In this connection, (2) *Job accused God of not answering any of his words (cf. 23:5).* **14.** Elihu refuted this charge by insisting that God has spoken to Job, for He speaks to man in one of two ways— although man (like Job) often **perceiveth it not**—through dreams and visions in the night (vv. 15-18), or through sickness and pain (vv. 19-28).

16-17. Through dreams and visions God **openeth** (uncovers) **the ears of men** (36:10, 15) **and sealeth their instruction,** to leave the impress of it upon their minds, in this way affirming the warnings to them to withdraw man (*hăsîr,* "make him turn away") **from his purpose, and hide** ("cover, conceal, in the sense of keeping") **pride from man,** hitting home at Job's besetting sin of spiritual self-esteem (cf. 35:12; 36:9).

18. By this means God **keepeth back** (*hsk,* "hold back, stop, check") **his soul** (him) **from the pit** (*shāḥăṯ,* "the pit, or the netherworld of ruin and corruption"), **and his life from the sword** (MT; NASB: "from passing over into Sheol"; *shālăḥ,* not here "missile" or "dart," 2 Sam. 18:14, but "a water conduit or channel," Akk., *šalḥu;* cf. Neh. 3:15, "the pool of Shelah," referring poetically to the world of departed spirits and the river of the nether regions; cf. the river Hubur of Mesopotamian mythology and the Styx of the Greeks). However, the poetic language, as always in the Bible, is divested of its pagan mythological connotations (see Introduction).

Elihu Expounds God's Speaking to Man Through Sickness and Pain. 33:19-28. **19.** Man is **chastened** (reproved, corrected; cf. Heb. 12:6) by physical affliction **upon his bed** of sickness (30:17) "with ceaseless agony in his bones" (AB), probably caused by arthritis. **20. His life** (in the sense of appe-

724

tite, as in 38:39; Psalm 107:18) **abhorreth bread** (loathes food), **and his soul** (again in the sense of "appetite") **dainty food.** In the Ugaritic epic of Keret (127:10-12), when the ailing monarch is healed, his "soul" (*npš*) for food returns. **21.** As a result, the chastened person's flesh wastes away and his bare bones stick out.

22. His soul (i.e., he) draws near the **pit** (*shāḥāt,* see v. 18) and his life **to the destroyers** ("those who bring death"; *memîtîm,* "killers," possibly referring to destroying angels or perhaps to demonic powers; Akk., *mušmîtûti,* infernal demons), since Satan has power to kill the body (cf. 2:6; Matt. 10:28*a*) in cases where God allows the ultimate in His chastening to come into play, namely, when the believer commits "the sin unto [physical] death" (1 John 5:16; cf. 1 Cor. 5:5; 11:30-32).

23. Elihu spoke of **an angel** of mercy, a **mediator** (*mēlîṣ,* "an interpreter"; cf. Zech. 1:9, 13), **one out of a thousand** (NASB), a prominent spirit among many who thus serve God (Heb. 1:7), and who may act as a go-between between man and God, interpreting to man's beclouded mind the Word of God to conduct him to sincere confession of sin (1 John 1:3-9). **24.** Then, by God's gracious permission, he would say to Satan, who has the power of physical death (Heb. 2:14), **Deliver him from going down to the pit** (see v. 18); **I have found a ransom** (NASB; cf. 36:18; Psalm 49:7). The term *ransom* (*kōpĕr*) literally denotes a "covering" of sin in the sight of the infinite holiness of God in the sense of pretermitting it or passing over it in prospect of the future atoning work of Christ (Rom. 3:25).

Elihu presented that aspect of God so sorely bypassed by Job's counselors and so vaguely groped after by Job—the grace and love of God. The intervention of an angel of mercy to cheat the agents of Satan of their prey by interpreting to the sufferer the meaning of divine chastening and the proper reaction to it, represents an advance toward the final solution of the enigma of the suffering of the righteous. Their suffering is from the hand of God, who loves them and is graciously dealing with them on the basis of mercy in view of redemption (ransom) to be effected in time.

Then Elihu set forth the results that follow a right response to the overtures a gracious loving God makes to the sufferer (vv. 24-30): (1) the body of the sufferer is spared untimely physical death (v. 24), (2) restored to physical vitality (v. 25), (3) spiritual health (v. 26) with fellowship with God in prayer reinstated and consequent fruit of peace and joy manifested in testimony to men concerning God's salvation and victorious singing of praise to God for redemption and blessing (vv. 27-28).

Elihu's Exhortation to Job. 33:29-31. All these gracious things God does twice, even three times, to demonstrate His persistent love toward man, seeking his salvation and the highest welfare of those who, like Job, are His own! How deeply, then, Job had wronged God in viewing Him as a divine detective, seeking pretext to accuse him (13:27) and, as an enemy (13:24), intimidating him with violence and terror (cf. 33:10-11; 19:6, 11). Elihu's touching upon the divine love and grace in his main thought—that Job's suffering was really not so much punishment for sin, but the disciplinary dealing as an end to spiritual refinement—represents a real advance toward the solution of the conundrum that had tormented God's afflicted, and at times, wildly distraught saint.

31-32a. Evidently conscious of the validity of the truth he was expounding,

Elihu, with bold assurance, had Job be silent and listen, or, if Job could reply with just cause, he should do so. **32b.** He assured Job that his desire was to **justify** him, that is, to see him cleared of the false charges of his friends. **33.** If Job had nothing to say, let him listen and be silent. Elihu declared, **I will teach you wisdom** (BV), that is, the disciplinary value of suffering come upon you as a righteous person.

C. ELIHU'S SECOND SPEECH—GOD IS NOT UNJUST. 34:1-37.

Elihu Calls for a Hearing. 34:1-4. The structure of chapter 32 is repeated—an introductory call to hear (vv. 2-4), a listing of some of Job's complaints (vv. 5-9), an answer to them (vv. 10-28), and a concluding challenge (vv. 29-37). Apparently Elihu invited the audition of a larger circle of listeners than Job and the three friends (cf. v. 34).

Elihu Quotes from Job's Complaints. 34:5-9. Verses 5 and 6 contain the quotations in summary form. **5a. I am innocent** (RSV; cf. 13:18; 23:10; 27:6). **But God has taken away my right** (NASB; cf. 27:2). **6. Should I lie concerning my right? My wound is incurable, though I am without transgression** (NASB; cf. 6:4). **7.** Elihu, somewhat intoxicated by the importance of the *role* he was playing of a self-assumed defender of the divine righteousness, exclaimed indignantly, **What man is like Job, who drinketh up scorning** (scoffing) **like water,** literally, "gulps up mockery like water" (cf. 15:16), a vivid figure in lands where water is a precious commodity.

8. Despite his superior counsel, Elihu descended to exaggerated (not to say irresponsible) charges in this and the following accusation that Job hobnobbed with evildoers and consorted with wicked men (cf. 11:11; 22:15; 31:5; Psalm 1:1). **9.** Such words as came from

Job's lips, alleging that God had wronged an innocent man, inflicting wounds on him quite capriciously, only go to show that Job had been keeping faulty company. If this were not so, would he have been complaining that "it is no use for man to be the friend of God" (Moffatt; cf. 21:15; 35:3; Psalm 50:18)?

Refutation of Job's First Complaint. 34:10-33. **10-12.** Job had voiced the accusation that God had shown unfairness in His dealings with him. Elihu maintained that God is just because He is Almighty. Man reaps what he sows, whether he sows good or evil. Elihu supported his thesis with three arguments: (1) *Absolute authority belongs to God alone (vv. 13-15).* **13. Who gave Him authority ... who has laid on Him the whole world?** (NASB; cf. 38:4-5). **14-15.** If He should determine to withdraw to Himself His spirit and breath, **all flesh** (humanity) **would perish** and **return to dust** (9:22; 10:9; Gen. 3:19; 7:21). As Creator and sole Owner of the world (not a vicegerent ruling for another), there is no reason for injustice, which would spoil His handiwork.

(2) *Injustice on God's part would initiate a reign of worldwide lawlessness (vv. 16-20).* Can good government be based on injustice? **17. Shall one who hates justice rule?** (NASB; 34:30; 2 Sam. 23:3). The very continuance of the divine government implies justice in that administration. **18-20.** The charge of injustice is grave enough against earthly rulers; how much graver against the Creator and Ruler of the world, who is absolutely impartial in His dealings with all men and inexorably controls their lives and destiny.

(3) *God's omniscience directing His absolute power precludes injustice (vv. 21-29).* **21-22.** God sees all, knows all, and operates in infinite light; so there is

no darkness **where the workers of iniquity may hide themselves** (cf. Psalm 139:11-12; Amos 9:2-3). **23.** "He sets no man a date" (AB) to appear before Him in judgment, this same idiom "to set a date" occurring in Exodus 9:5. This was Elihu's answer to Job's plaint for an appointment for a hearing (14:13; cf. 24:1). God was not bound to regulate His government according to Job's little appointment book.

24-25. He shatters mighty men without inquiry or investigation, because He knows the very heart of men, not merely their outward conduct. He sets up other men in their place, as His omniscience may deem proper. **26-28.** He strikes down the wicked **in the open sight of others,** that is, in a public place, so everyone can see, because **they turned back from him** (cf. 1 Sam. 15:11), and their misconduct and misrule brought the cry of distress from the poor and the afflicted before Him (Job 35:9; James 5:4). Those who turn from God are callous to human suffering; so the oppressed have no resort but God.

29a. If God remains quiet, who can condemn Him (1 Chron. 22:9)? If He hides His face, who can get a glimpse of Him? **29b.** In His omniscience, He watches over nations and individuals, and so no godless man may reign except when the divine justice will be vindicated, either in time or eternity. God's justness is never compromised. If God permits a wicked ruler to continue to reign, can finite man read the ruler's thoughts, much less God's? **32-33.** Suppose the wicked ruler repents, would Job arrogate to himself the divine prerogative of choice and dare to lay down the terms upon which the omniscient God must operate?

Job Needs Testing to the End. 34:34-37. **34-35.** Elihu charged that Job spoke **without knowledge** and his words

are **without wisdom** (*hăśkêl,* "discernment"; NASB; cf. v. 10*a;* 35:16), since he had evidently failed to show proper "fear of [reverence for] the LORD" (28:28) in his wild and distraught accusations. **36-37.** He discerned that Job had not yet been sufficiently refined in the furnace of affliction. Therefore, he declared, Job ought to be **tested unto the end** (to the limit) for answering like wicked men, adding rebellion (7:11; 10:1; cf. 1 Sam. 15:23) to his sin, **clapping** (better, "clasping") **his hands** (NASB), perhaps in gesture of victory over his opponents, or in anguish over the impasse in the solution of his problem.

D. ELIHU'S THIRD SPEECH—GOD IS NOT INDIFFERENT TO VIRTUE OR VICE. 35:1-16.

Do Not Lose Sight of God's Greatness. 35:1-8. **1-3.** Elihu, continuing the exposition of the truth that God is infinitely exalted above any temptation to be unjust, cited Job's complaints that imply the contrary. Did Job think such an implication **to be right** in that he said, **My righteousness is more than God's** (cf. 19:6-7)? Job had not said this in so many words, but what he did say was capable of being so interpreted (9:22; 10:15). He also said, **What advantage will it be unto thee?** (cf. 34:9), or "How am I better off than if I had sinned?" (RSV; cf. 9:30-31). To criticize the consequences of righteousness is a subtle form of spiritual pride that assumes a righteousness superior to the divine righteousness.

In an effort to answer Job, Elihu employed an argument already used by Eliphaz (22:2-4): that man cannot add or detract from God by his righteousness or evil. **5. Look at the heavens and see** (cf. Gen. 15:5; Job 22:12; Psalm 8:3); **and behold the clouds—they are** higher than you (NASB). **6-8.** So God is higher than man, and man's sin or righteousness cannot affect God; therefore, under this deistic reasoning, God's administration of justice is always fair. Elihu's conclusion was true, but his presuppositions were wrong. The supramundane exaltation of God does not mean He is indifferent toward man, or that He does not love man. In this argument Elihu accommodated himself to Job's wrong reasoning concerning the unchangeableness of the self-contained Creator (cf. 7:20-21).

Why God Appears to Be Indifferent to Human Virtue or Vice. 35:9-13. **9.** Sufferers too often confine themselves to pitiful complaining instead of real repentance and turning to God in sincere prayer. In great oppression and distress **they cry for help because of the arm** (power) **of the mighty** (NASB; cf. 12:19). But they do it with a wrong motive and for a selfish reason (cf. James 4:2-3).

10. No one says, Where is God my Maker ... ? They do not seek God for Himself, nor for the blessing He gives to such genuine seekers, namely, **songs in the night** (8:21; Psalms 42:8; 77:6; 149:5; Acts 16:25). They do not seek God aright, to know Him as God and the Giver of songs in the night, but they present a mere selfish request for deliverance from the night and its dark experiences of pain. That had been Job's failure. He wanted to get out of the night, and he forgot to ask for the song to tide him over the night. It is pride in man's heart (and this was Job's great sin, cf. v. 12; cf. 33:17) that makes it appear to sinful man that God is indifferent to human virtue or wickedness.

11. Evidently Elihu suggested that since even the animal creatures in their need and distress cry to God (Psalms 104:21; 147:9; Joel 1:20), Job should

have learned a lesson from them and called upon God, too, instead of railing against Him. **13.** God seems far off and indifferent to prayer because He will **not hear vanity** (Isa. 1:15; Jer. 11:11; cf. Job 27:8-9). He does not listen to deceit.

14. Job claimed he could not see God; **yet justice** (the case involving the execution of justice) was before Him (36:17); **therefore, trust** (wait for) **him** (cf. 13:24; 23:8-9; 24:1; 30:20). Job had presented his case like a lawyer (cf. 13:18; 23:4). **15-16.** Elihu reminded him that the decision rested on the Judge, and concluded with a stern rebuke. **And now, because He has not visited in His anger, nor has He acknowledged transgression well, so Job opens his mouth emptily; he multiplies words without knowledge** (NASB; cf. 34:35), that is, "he jabbers on without knowing what he is saying."

E. ELIHU'S FOURTH SPEECH—GOD'S WAYS ARE JUST BUT INSCRUTABLE. 36:1—37:24.

Elihu Claims Inspiration from God. 36:1-4. In this, Elihu's final speech (36:1—37:24), he made his chief contribution to the solution of Job's dilemma—why the righteous suffer—and prepared the dramatic stage for the appearance of the LORD. Elihu was inspired with the truth that, in the case of the righteous, affliction is not always punitive, but disciplinary; often it is to refine and purify. **2.** Conscious of having something of great importance to say, he called for continued attention: **Bear with me a little** (longer). **I have yet to speak on God's behalf.**

3-4. He said he would **fetch** his **knowledge from afar,** meaning ostensibly by inspiration from God, as he ascribed righteousness to his Maker (8:3; 37:23), and claimed to speak the truth (33:3), inasmuch as God Himself, he asserts, was with them, whom he describes as perfect in knowledge (37:16). Scarcely would he appropriate such a claim to himself (as the KJV and RSV might seem to suggest). The remainder of Elihu's final speech shows that his claims were not empty. He presented a fitting introduction to the LORD's appearance to place the capstone on the structure of truth Elihu here laid down.

Suffering as a Purifying and Refining Agent. 36:5-16. **5.** God is all-powerful and all-knowing, **mighty in strength of understanding** (NASB), despising none of His creatures. **6.** He punishes the wicked (8:22; 34:26), **but gives justice to the afflicted** (NASB; 5:15). **7a.** He has perpetual interest in and **does not withdraw His eyes from the righteous** (NASB; Psalms 33:18; 34:15).

7b-9. He sets up kings on the throne and puts them down, even in chains and cords of affliction, if they transgress and magnify themselves against Him (15:25). **10.** Through their affliction He instructs and disciplines them to **return from evil** (NASB). **11-12.** If they hear and serve Him, He restores them to prosperity. If they scorn chastening and go on sinning, they die prematurely **by the sword** or some other calamity, illustrating the New Testament teaching of committing the "sin unto [physical] death" (1 John 5:16; cf. 1 Cor. 5:5; 11:30-32).

13. The godless in heart, however, treasure up divine wrath (cf. Rom. 2:5). Suffering hardens and confirms them in sin. **14.** They die in their youth, and their lives end in misery and disgrace **among the cult prostitutes** (NASB), the devotees of polluted pagan cults, harnessed by debilitating sexual immorality (Deut. 23:17).

15. Elihu anticipated (by inspiration, cf. vv. 1-4) the difference between God's chastening or disciplining His own for sin and His punishment of the wicked, a truth later developed in the New Testament. Accordingly, He delivers **the afflicted** saints, like Job (NASB; cf. v. 8), and "opens their ear" (v. 10, NASB) in time of affliction to teach them His gracious concern and love for them, and His desire to purify and refine them as His own through the adversity they pass through.

16. He also would have **enticed** (allured) His own out of **the mouth of distress** (NASB; Hos. 2:14), wooing them by His love **into a broad place, where there is no restraint** (constraint, cramping). Thus, He prepares a table for them (Psalm 23:5) **full of fatness** (prosperity, plenty). What a lesson for Job! What a lesson for Job's friends!

How evident it is that, so far from God dealing capriciously with His own, as Job contended, their sufferings are permitted in order to achieve beneficial results in life and faith. So far from suffering in a saint being purely punitive, the result of serious sin, as Job's friends contended, it is the blessed corrective discipline of a loving God with paternal concern for His children, to wean them from sin or to refine and purify them for finer living and serving.

A Solemn Warning to Job. 36:17-23. **17.** Job was to be solicitous to see God's chastening in the right light and react toward His disciplinary hand in the right spirit. In contrast, he was full of a spirit of **judgment of the wicked** and seized by an attitude of **judgment and justice** that made him sit in condemnation on God and man. **18.** With such an outlook he needed to watch out lest wrath allure him into scoffing both at God and man (34:33; Jonah 4:4, 9). He also was to be careful that **the greatness of the ransom** did not turn **him aside** (NASB; cf. 33:24) from the right road to restoration and blessing. He was warned against being "allured from the right way by the ransom which is required of him as the price of restoration to happiness, viz. humble submission to the divine chastisement, as though this ransom were exceeding great" (F. Delitzsch, *Job*, 2:283).

19. Would Job's cry avail to keep him from distress? **20.** He was not to long for the night (34:20, 25), "which shall remove people from their place" (F. Delitzsch). **21.** He was to be careful and keep away from evil, for he had "desired this [i.e., separation from evil] more than affliction" (F. Delitzsch). **22.** He was to realize that **God is exalted in His power; who is a teacher like Him?** (NASB). **23. Who has appointed Him His way,** whoever has corrected this omniscient Pedagogue, who is ready to teach Job, with the charge, **Thou hast done wrong?** (NASB). Teach him what? That God in His greatness revealed in nature deals with men according to their works.

God's Presence and Power in Nature. 36:24-28. **24.** God is great! Job was never to blame Him (v. 23), but to join those who sing the great Creator's doxologies. From here on Elihu extolled the greatness of God in hymnic stanzas as the Maker and Controller of all earth's meteorological forces (E. Smick, ZPEB, 3:610)—the rain and the evaporation cycle (vv. 27-28), the thunderstorm (vv. 29-33; 37:1-5, etc.). All nature is an open book recounting God's glory. **25-26. All men have seen it** (NASB), declaring His timelessness and unsearchability (11:7-9; Psalms 90:2; 102:24, 27). **27-28.** How wonderful is Nature (another name for the Creator)! He drives up the water to form the clouds, then distills it to **drip upon man abundantly** (NASB). All this proclaims God's glory (Psalm 19:1-6; Rom. 1:19-20).

God's Greatness Depicted in the Storm. 36:29–37:5. **29-30. Can anyone understand the spreading of the clouds**

... the thundering of His pavilion (37:11, 16) and how He disperses **His lightning about Him** (NASB)? "On his palm the lightning prances, He directs it with sure aim" (AB). **31. By these phenomena He judges peoples** (37:13; cf. Exod. 9:18, 23; 1 Sam. 12:18-19; Ezra 10:9), and through the rain upon the ground **gives food in abundance** (NASB; Psalms 104:27; 136:25; Acts 14:17). **32. He covers His hands with the lightning** (lit., "light") **and commands it to strike the mark** (NASB; 37:11-12, 15). **33.** The thunder declares His presence. Even the cattle are apprized by the storm concerning what is about to happen.

1. At the sight of God's glory revealed in the tempest, Elihu declared, **my heart trembles, and leaps** (NASB), reminding one of Wordsworth's "My heart leaps up when I behold/A rainbow in the sky;/So was it when my life began;/So is it now I am a man;/ . . . Or let me die!" **2-5.** Poetically, Elihu closely identified the Creator with the natural world of His creation. The thunder is God's voice, **the rumbling . . . goes out from His mouth** (NASB), letting it loose to the ends of the earth (v. 12; 28:24; 38:13), His thunderings being a token of the great things He does, which to us are incomprehensible.

God's Greatness Portrayed in Other Natural Wonders. 37:6-13. **7.** The **snow** (38:22) and the **rain** (36:27) often reduce man to a state of helplessness before the severity of the weather, serving as a timeless reminder that man is but a creature, not the Creator, as **He seals** (NASB), "puts a seal on" (F. Delitzsch, *Job*), **the hand of every man** (i.e., cuts off his human ability). **8.** In the storm or blizzard even the beast recognizes the greatness of the Creator and goes to his lair for protection (Psalm 109:27).

9a. Out of the south comes the storm (NASB). "Out of the south" is literally "chamber," perhaps an abbreviation of the term "chambers of the south" (wind; 9:9; cf. Psalm 135:7). **9b. Out of the north** (comes) **the cold** (NASB; *mezārîm,* "scatter-winds," probably in the sense of scatterers of cold air from the north). **10. From the breath of God ice is made** (NASB; 38:29; Psalm 147:17). **11-13.** God controls the clouds and lightning, guiding them for His purposes on the earth, whether for disciplinary correction of man's sin or to manifest His loving-kindness (Exod. 9:18, 23; 1 Sam. 12:18; 1 Kings 18:45; Job 38:26).

Elihu's Challenge to Job. 37:14-24. **14.** Job was asked to listen to this weight of testimony of God's glorious operations in His creation, which is now brought to focus upon Job's case. He was summoned to **stand still, and consider the wondrous works of God** (Psalm 111:2). **15-18.** Elihu directed a series of staggering questions to Job to impress him dramatically with man's frailty and nothingness before God's infinite greatness and glory, in order to stop him short in the way of insubmission, along which he had been rushing headlong.

Only God is **perfect in knowledge** (36:4), and man (let Job take note!) must confess the imperfection of his knowledge before such a God and humbly submit to Him and listen to what He says. Elihu's speeches thus prepared the way for God to speak to Job. **20. Shall it be told Him that I would speak?** No! Let a man (like Job) rather say that **he would be swallowed up** (NASB) before God, who has such power and greatness.

21-24. As clouds cover the light of the sun in the skies so that men cannot see **the light which is bright in the skies** until the wind **has passed and cleared them,** even so Job's vision of **God in awesome majesty** is to be made possible only as the dark clouds of spiritual pride and self-righteousness are dissipated, in order that he may envision **the Almighty** (El Shaddai; cf. 6:4). Moreover, Job needed to see God as He really is, not as his distraught spirit made Him out to be—**exalted in power,** not doing **violence to justice and abundant righteousness** (NASB), realizing that because God is such a God **men fear** (reverence) **Him.**

But Elihu ended on a note of stern warning to Job, which was eminently preparatory to his impending confrontation with the LORD: **He respecteth not** (*rā'â,* "does not regard, look at," in the sense of paying attention to) **any that are wise of heart.** The clever-minded, those wise in their own conceit—as Elihu considered Job—God does not "see," in the sense of regarding with favor (cf. 9:4).

IV. THE LORD SPEAKS TO JOB. 38:1—42:6.

A. THE LORD'S FIRST DISCOURSE—HE CHALLENGES JOB. 38:1—39:30.

The Lord Confronts Job. 38:1-3. **1. Then the Lord answered Job.** The divine name, Jehovah (Yahweh), the name of redemptive revelation (Exod. 6:3-4) used in the prologue and epilogue, but not in the dialogue, reappears here (as in 40:1, 3, 6; 42:1). The infinitely holy God can hold converse with fallen, sinful man only in prospect or retrospect of redemptive grace, either looking forward to or back to the sacrifice of Christ. It is notable that the LORD broke the silence of heaven in the face of Job's challenging cries and spoke directly to him who had so vehemently cried out for an answer (31:35), taking up the vehement appeal with which the patriarch had concluded his final monologue.

But did the LORD simply ignore Elihu and pass over him, as if he had made no

731

contribution to the question of why the righteous suffer? Although some critics tend to downgrade Elihu and view his speeches as ungenuine interpolations, this is scarcely defensible. In fact, Elihu represented the LORD, speaking by inspiration through His human agent (36:3-4) as the theophany presents the LORD speaking directly **out of the whirlwind** (*s^e'āṛâ*, "storm, tempest, hurricane," from the root *s'r*, "rage, storm, be agitated"), a common concomitant of a theophany (Exod. 13:22; 19:16; Psalm 18:8-16; Hab. 3:5-6; Nah. 1:4; Zech. 9:14).

Actually God, through Elihu, gave the answer to the question of why the righteous suffer, insofar as finite man can fathom the problem (36:5-16); and having done so, he solemnly warned Job to see suffering in its proper purpose and perspective (36:17-23) and then left the scene. Hence, the LORD took over to show Job his finite frailty and proud audacity to question His actions and government, and to demonstrate to all mankind that the suffering of the righteous has an unfathomable element that finite man cannot understand any more than Job could answer the questions put to him by the Almighty. So the LORD answered Job out of the whirlwind or tempest, that is, the tempest that had long been gathering, the subject of Elihu's remarks.

2. Who is this that darkens (obscures) **counsel ... ?** (NASB). It is an enfeebled, dying man, one persecuted and exhausted as Job himself (cf. 14:1), one therefore altogether unequal to the task he has undertaken. Moffatt paraphrases aptly: "Who darkens my design with a cloud of thoughtless words." By the term *counsel* (*'ēṣâ*, "plan, scheme, purpose") the LORD would impress Job with the fact that in His dealings with him, He was not acting capriciously or haphazardly (as Job had charged), but according to consistent intelligent design. Job also had been charged by Elihu with speaking out of ignorance (34:35), as the LORD Himself similarly charged him.

3. Gird up now thy loins (figuratively an expression for "prepare for a strenuous undertaking"; Exod. 12:11; 1 Kings 18:46; Isa. 11:5) **like a man** (*gĕbĕr*, denoting a man not in frailty but in strength). **For I will demand of thee ... answer thou me,** that is, "*you* instruct Me!" (irony). Job had demanded to argue his case with God (9:32; 13:3, 15), but the LORD turned the tables on him. The LORD declined to submit to questioning. However, instead of levying charges, as Job had challenged Him to do (13:23; 31:35), He overwhelmed Job with sublime interrogations that lay bare Job's utter ignorance and his folly in impugning God's wisdom and justice.

The Creator's Wisdom Displayed in Creation. 38:4-11. **4. Where wast thou when I laid the foundations of the earth?** (15:7; Psalm 104:5; Prov. 30:4). **Declare, if thou hast understanding** (i.e., "Tell me, if you know so much!"). Eliphaz had broached similar ironic questions (15:7-8), as well as Elihu (37:18).

5. Who hath laid (set) **the measures** (drafted its dimensions)? **If thou knowest** (emphatic *kî,* as in Ugaritic, "Surely you know!" with another instance of the divine irony exposing Job's cocky ignorance). Where was Job when God laid the foundation of the earth (vv. 4-7), which is compared to a building set on foundations (v. 4*a*; cf. Psalms 24:2; 102:25; Prov. 3:19), constructed according to plans and specifications, with the employment of a measuring line.

6. Its pillars are set in sockets, and its cornerstone (perhaps the capstone rather than the cornerstone; cf. Psalm

118:22; Isa. 28:16; Jer. 51:26) laid. Evidently this is the original creation of the earth in the illimitable past before the fall of Lucifer (Isa. 14:12-17; Ezek. 28:11-19) and the entrance of sin into a hitherto sinless universe (see comments on Gen. 1:1-3).

7. When the morning stars sang together. Creation morning is especially associated with the "morning stars," including Lucifer, which are especially beautiful. The stars are figuratively said to sing God's praises (Psalms 19:1; 148:3) and here, in lofty poetry, are symbolic of the angels, answering to **the sons of God** or angels in the parallelism of this verse (see comments on Gen. 6:2-4; Job 1:6; 2:1). The fall of Lucifer, and a great host of angels with him (Ezek. 28:11-19), occurred subsequent to this blissful scene when all these jubilant, sinless creatures **shouted for joy** when the cornerstone (capstone), signaling completion of earth's creation, signalized the intense joy among all God's creatures (angels), as this scene evidently antedates the renovation of a chaotic earth for the late-comer man.

The laying of the foundation (Ezra 3:10-11), and especially the capstone (the crowning stone at the summit, marking the completion of the building), was an occasion of rejoicing and singing (Zech. 4:7). This passage from the lips of the Creator Himself sweeps away the curtain of time and presents a vista of eternity past and the scene of sinless bliss that marked the creation of the earth ex nihilo, apparently for the habitation of the pristine holy angelic hosts.

8-9. Where was Job when God thus founded the earth and subdued the sea, enclosing (confining) it within doors (floodgates; Gen. 7:11) when it is poetically conceived as gushing from the womb and the Creator made **the cloud its garment, and thick darkness a swaddling band for it? 10-11.** The Creator is pictured having **placed boundaries on** the sea (NASB), and setting **bars and doors** (cf. 7:12; 9:13; 26:12) to confine it, saying to it: **Thus far shalt thou come, but no farther . . . here shall thy proud waves be stayed** (yāshît, "stop, halt"). In the Mesopotamian creation epic, Marduk placed a bar and guard to keep back the waters of the primeval seas when they were created from the slain sea monster Tiamat (cf. ANET, p. 67, ll. 139-40).

The Creator's Wisdom Displayed in the Inanimate World. 38:12-38. **12.** Could Job control the coming of dawn? Had he ever commanded a morning to break in all its splendor or **caused the dayspring** (shāḥār, "dawn") **to know its place** (i.e., tell dawn to get to its post in its daily assignment ordained by divine decree)? **13.** Dawn is pictured as taking hold of **the ends** (lit., "wings" or "skirts") **of the earth** and snatching off the covering with which night cloaks it and under which the wicked perpetrate their crimes (24:13-17), and shaking out these evildoers as one would shake dust or vermin from his clothing (34:25-26; 36:6).

14. Dawn is further depicted as **turned like clay to the seal,** changing the earth like soft clay into which a cylinder seal is rolled. Wrapped in darkness, the earth is devoid of all form; but when illuminated by dawn, it presents an infinite variety of forms and scenery, and **they** (the endless forms of beauty unfolded by the dawn) **stand** out **like a garment** in which the earth is clad. **15. And from the wicked their light** (which is really darkness) **is withheld,** and their **high arm** (arm uplifted for murder or theft) is **broken** by dawn.

Did Job know anything about the depths beneath the earth or the expanse above it? **16.** Had he ever **entered into the springs** (under-ocean fountains) **of** the sea (Psalm 95:4) or **walked in . . . search of the depth** (deep; cf. 28:11), that which is only discovered by searching the deep (*tᵉhôm*) and whose vast secrets the modern science of oceanography is only beginning to unfold? **17.** How about the netherworld? Had the **gates of death** been opened to him? Had he **seen the doors of the shadow of death** (deep darkness)? Man during his lifetime does not even "see" the gates of the realm of departed spirits (cf. 10:21), much less are they "opened" to him. But these are "naked before" God (26:6). In Mesopotamian mythology, Ishtar has to pass seven gates in her descent into the netherworld (ANET, p. 107).

18. Did Job understand **the breadth** (expanse) **of the earth? 19-20.** Did he know where light and darkness come from and dwell? **21.** This verse is ironical, or perhaps interrogative in sense (as the KJV). **22-24.** What did Job know about storehouses of **snow** and **hail,** which are instruments of God to effect His purposes on earth? **28-30.** What could he comprehend about the production of **rain** and **ice?**

31. What could Job do about the movement of the constellations? Could he **bind** (tie) the chains (fetters) of the Pleiades (9:9; Amos 5:8), a compact cluster of seven stars in Taurus, visible just before sunrise in spring? The translation **sweet influences** construes *mā'ᵃdǎnnôt* from *'dn,* "to be delightful," and is construed as indicating their supposed effect on the burgeoning of spring. Could Job bind or loose the closely knit stellar tie? Could he loose the bands (cords) of Orion, "the Hunter"? This is a prominent southern constellation composed of first magnitude stars, represented in the East as a wicked giant chained to the sky. **32.** Could Job lead forth a constellation (**Mazzaroth,** possibly denoting the

twelve zodiacal signs) on time, and **guide the Bear** (RSV, NASB) with her sons (cubs, probably the Little Bear)? **Arcturus with his sons** designates the constellation Boötes that appears to follow the Great Bear (see G. R. Driver, JTS 4[1953]:208-12; and JTS 7[1956]:1-11).

34-35. Could Job command the clouds to give rain or the lightning to strike? **36.** Who had **put wisdom in the inward parts? Or . . . understanding to the heart** (mind; 9:4; Psalm 51:6; Eccles. 2:26)? **37-38. Who can count the clouds . . . or tip** (tilt) **the water jars of the heavens** (NASB; "bottles of heaven," KJV), the moisture-filled clouds, when the parched earth needs rain to break the drought?

The Creator's Wisdom Displayed in the Animate World. 38:39–39:30. **39-40.** Could Job hunt the lion's prey or satisfy the appetite of the young lions (Psalm 104:21)? **41.** Who prepares the raven's meals when its young **cry** to God (Psalms 104:27-28; 147:9; Matt. 6:26; Luke 12:24)?

1. Did Job know when the **wild goats of the rock,** the mountain goats (ibex), deliver their young, or did he watch the calving of the **hinds** (does), the wild goats being especially shy? **2-4.** Could he number the months they fulfill, the time of their gestation, and the process of giving birth to their young, which thrive and grow so rapidly, and leave their mother and do not return?

5-6. Who set the **wild ass free** and loosed from his bonds the onager (6:5; 11:12; 24:5; Psalm 104:11), to whom God gave the wilderness as a **house** (home) and the **barren land** (salt land) for his dwelling place (24:5; Jer. 2:24; Hos. 8:9)? **7.** Poetically, the wild ass is pictured as scorning the **multitude** (better, "tumult") **of the city,** not hearing the **crying** (shouting) **of the driver. 8.**

He is seen exploring the mountains for his pasture, searching for anything green to eat.

9-12. The wild ox (*rᵉ'ēm, Bos primigenius*) roamed Syria in antiquity (cf. Num. 23:22; 24:8; Psalms 22:21; 29:6; 92:10; Isa. 34:7). Hunting this dangerous buffalolike beast was a faorite sport of Assyrian kings, and Baal appears hunting this animal in one of the Ugaritic myths. Could Job control this fierce animal, or think of domesticating it to serve him?

13. Even animals such as the dumb ostrich scorn the might of man! She waves her wings proudly, but they are not **the pinions and plumage of love** (RSV). **14-15.** She abandons her eggs to the earth, forgetting they may be trampled upon by man or beast. **16-18.** Even when her young are hatched, she treats them cruelly, as if they did not belong to her, for God made her foolish; but when she flees, she can outrun a horse and his rider.

19-20. The snorting war horse also scorns man's might. Could Job **clothe his neck with a mane** or make himself **leap like a locust** (NASB)? **21-23.** He paws in the valley and rejoices before entering the battle, laughing at fear and danger, as **the quiver rattles against him** (NASB) and the spear and javelin flash. **25. He scents the battle** (NASB) from a distance and rushes headlong into the fray. **26-30.** As a final touch portraying man's humiliation (that Job might see himself in his human limitation!), God pictures the hawk and eagle triumphing over man as their young ones suck up the blood of those killed in battle (Matt. 24:28; Luke 17:37).

B. THE LORD'S SECOND DISCOURSE—JOB BROUGHT TO REPENTANCE. 40:1-24.

Job's Penitent Submission. 40:1-5.

1-2. The LORD ended His first discourse by calling on Job to abandon his contention with Him. **Will the faultfinder** (*yĭssôr,* "reprover, blamer") **contend** (strive) **with the Almighty** (El Shaddai; see 6:4; NASB; 9:3; 10:2; 33:13). **He that reproveth God, let him answer** (for) **it,** vindicate himself for such a daring act (13:3; 23:4; 31:35).

3-4. But all self-vindication had vanished as Job was humbled in the dust before the voice of the LORD revealing His infinite greatness to his frail and erring creature. **Job answered ... and said, Behold, I am vile** (*qll,* "be small, insignificant, be of small account"). **What shall I answer thee?** ("What can I say?) **I will lay mine hand upon my mouth** (21:5; 29:9), in token that I have nothing more to say, no plea to offer (Judg. 18:19). **5. Once have I spoken ...** (against God) **yea, twice, but I will proceed no further** (Job 9:3, 15; Psalm 62:11), that is, "I will not do so again." Job has been brought to silence, but not quite to full repentance. Therefore, the concluding speech was necessary to bring him to see his real self.

The Lord Continues to Question Job. 40:6-24. **6-7.** Again the LORD answered Job **out of the whirlwind** (storm; see 38:1), instructing him once more to **gird up** his **loins** (cf. 38:3; 42:4). **I will ask you ... you instruct Me** (NASB). Underlying the divine challenge is the figure of the ancient belt-wrestler (2 Sam. 2:14-16). Job was called on to resume his grappling with the Almighty. He had not yet been completely vanquished, and so the contest continued. The LORD adopted a tone of strong irony to bring Job to his senses.

8. Would Job **annul** God's judgment? Would he dare to condemn God (10:3, 7; 16:11; 19:6; 27:2) in order to justify himself (13:18; 27:6)? **9.** Did Job have **an arm like God?** Could Job **thunder** at all, much less with a **voice like** God's? **10.** If Job arrogated to himself the divine prerogatives, let him then put on God's glorious garments. Let him ascend the throne of the universe.

11-13. Let him **cast abroad the rage** of his wrath to send the thunderbolts of his wrath against the proud and the wicked. **14.** Then, and only then, could he sit in judgment upon the divine government and earn the divine commendation.

15-24. Otherwise, let Job consider **behemoth,** which, the LORD reminded Job, **I made as well as you** (NASB). Behemoth is an apparent plural of the common noun $b^e h\bar{e}m\hat{a}$, "beast, cattle," and is evidently an intensive plural, indicating "the beast" par excellence, variously interpreted as the elephant, the hippopotamus, the monstrous bullock of the Ugaritic myths—the Akkadian "bull of heaven" slain in the Gilgamish Epic (ANET, pp. 83-85). If it is the hippopotamus, this formidable creature does feed on both river plants and on land (cf. vv. 21-24), eats grass (v. 15), and is noted for the strength of his loins and the power of his massive belly (v. 16). But the tail of the hippopotamus is not that described in verse 17. Instead, it is almost absurdly small in proportion to its massive body.

Would Job dare to grasp this creature (whatever it is!) by his eyes or pierce his nose with **barbs** (NASB)? Behemoth is a powerful, uncontrollable beast. How weak is man in contrast to this beast possessing such marvelous strength. Yet behemoth is only a beast, and Job is a man! How despicable must Job's proud boasting appear in the sight of the Almighty!

C. THE LORD'S SECOND DISCOURSE CONTINUED — JOB'S HEART BARED. 41:1-34.

God's Glorious Power and Levia-

than. 41:1-11. **1-9.** Alongside behemoth, **leviathan** is introduced, another awesome animal creature of God (cf. 40:15*b*). If Job could not vanquish these creatures of God, how could he hope to win in contest with the Creator-God Himself? In his verbal forays Job was made to realize that God is God, not only in His omnipotence, but in all phases of His deity. Leviathan has frequently been identified with the crocodile, but the representation in this passage must be highly symbolic since the description goes beyond a mere crocodile.

It seems that after the description of the crocodile an unannounced transition occurs because God would remind Job of those cosmic forces that leviathan symbolizes and against which no human strength or ingenuity can prevail. The Old Testament often speaks figuratively of great evil powers, whether cosmic or political, in terms of monstrous creatures. In the day that the LORD punishes earth's inhabitants for their iniquity, He also will slay leviathan, the swift, crooked serpent (Isa. 27:1; cf. 51:9-10). **10.** Since Job was powerless before God's creature leviathan, God said, **Who then ... can stand before Me?** (NASB). **11. Who has given to Me that I should repay him? Whatever is under the whole heaven is Mine** (NASB).

Leviathan Further Described. *41:12-34.* **12-29.** The LORD described leviathan — **his limbs ... his mighty strength ... his orderly frame,** his hide, **outer armor ... double mail,** his terrible **teeth,** his **sneezes** that **flash forth light** (vv. 12-18, NASB), and his fiery breath (v. 21) and his invulnerability (vv. 26-29). **33. Nothing on earth is like him** (NASB).

34. He is king over all the sons of pride (NASB; cf. 28:8, NASB margin), evidently symbolizing the power of darkness (Isa. 27:1). It seems the description goes beyond that of a mere beast and envisions Satan in his character and rule (cf. the "beast" of Rev. 13). This symbolic presentation was intended to bring vividly to Job's consciousness that if he was proud, he belonged to leviathan, the king who rules over "the sons of pride," that is, "the proud." Deftly, the LORD had probed the secret of Job's trouble and searched out the depths of his heart. Pride, Satan's sin, had been lodged there and subtly cherished. Now, however, with the beast laid bare by the LORD's dealing, Job was prepared for a full and open confession and restoration.

D. JOB'S CONFESSION. 42:1-6.

Job's Full Repentance. 42:1-6. These words of confession are not misplaced from 40:3-5, as many critics contend, but were just as necessary as the additional words of the LORD to bring Job abjectly into the dust and to elicit from his lips the confession that alone could satisfy the LORD and free Him to restore and bless Job.

The divine purpose in the suffering of the saints is often to refine and purify them. In Job's case a subtly entrenched spiritual pride needed to be purged out. Job's confession, which contains the following six elements, demonstrates that this was accomplished: (1) He confessed God's omnipotence was not only a concept of his intellect, but of his heart as well. **2a. I know that thou canst do every thing.** (2) He confessed the same concerning God's omniscience. **2b. And that no thought** (purpose) **can be withheld from thee** (lit., "no thought of Thine can be hindered").

(3) He confessed that he had obscured counsel without knowledge (38:2). **3.** Job here repeated the question

previously put to him by the LORD and thus freely admitted the validity of the divine indictment. He had talked of things he did not know, wonders beyond his ken. (4) He confessed that he had truly turned about face (repented). **4.** Instead of **Hear, now, and I will speak** (NASB), we hear, "I will ask You, and You instruct me [Job]." (5) He confessed his lack of experiential knowledge of the LORD. **5.** He had heard of the LORD by hearsay. **But now my eye sees Thee** (Isa. 6:5).

(6) He professed full repentance. **6. Wherefore I abhor myself** (*m's*, "recant, retract, repudiate," that is, "that which I have previously thought and said"). However, the root *m's* also means to "despise, abhor," so the King James Version's "I abhor (i.e., despise) myself" constitutes a deeper description of the spiritual transformation in Job's heart, as he repudiated his self-justifying pride, evidencing his deep repentance, outwardly indicated by heaping dust and ashes on his head. Job was already sitting in ashes (2:8; cf. Isa. 58:5; Jer. 6:26; Jonah 3:6; Mic. 1:10).

V. EPILOGUE: JOB'S RESTORATION AND BLESSING 42:7-17.

7. The epilogue returns to prose, as in the prologue. The first thing mentioned is the divine rebuke of Job's three friends through Eliphaz. They are reprimanded for not speaking the truth about the LORD, as did Job, whom God owns as His servant (four times, vv. 7-8). They are ordered to present seven rams, which Job was to offer as a burnt offering for them, looking forward to cleansing through Christ's sacrifice (see Lev. 1).

8. Job was to intercede for them, who in his restoration reminds us of the suffering servant of Isaiah 53. **For I will**

accept him so that I may not do with you according to your folly, because you have not spoken of Me what is right, as My servant Job has (NASB). Job's mistakes were overruled by his intrepid honesty. He clung to God, though he criticized. He trusted, although almost blindly at times, even thinking of God as an enemy bent on killing him.

In contrast, Job's friends clung to ideas that were familiar and comfortable in the teeth of evidence to the contrary. Intrepid honesty in facing the facts of existence—no matter how upsetting and disturbing—is found to be much more pleasing to God than denying those facts through prejudice and smug complacency. It is noteworthy that Elihu was not reprimanded. The reason is that he presented a full-orbed picture of God that included the divine love and grace, and so he answered the question of the purpose of the suffering of the righteous, insofar as God has answered it through a human channel.

11-17. These verses present Job's restoration. While Job prayed for others, his own prosperity was restored, including restoration of friendship (v. 11),

property (v. 12), and family (vv. 13-17). This magnificent dramatic poem and spiritual saga fittingly ends with that which betokens God's love and faithfulness to His own: **And Job died, an old man and full of days** (NASB; cf. Gen 25:8; 35:29).

"Whom the Lord loveth he chasteneth. ... Now no chastening for the present seemeth to be joyous, but grievous; nevertheless, afterward it yieldeth the peacable fruit of righteousness unto them who are exercised by it" (Heb. 12:6-11). Moreover, the book of Job not only answers the problem of why the righteous suffer and why God chastens and tests His own, it also shows the role of Satan and the powers of darkness as God's agents in this testing process. Many Bible students have assumed that the spiritual conflict outlined in Ephesians 6:10-20 was confined to New Testament times and that Satan and his hosts did not so operate in Old Testament times. The book of Job shows the same conflict raged from the beginning of man's Fall (Gen. 3:15) and underlies all Old Testament history and prophecy.

PSALMS

INTRODUCTION

Title. In Hebrew the book of Psalms is called *Tehillim* ("Songs of Praise"), or in fuller form, *Sefer Tehillim* ("Book of Psalms"). The English title Psalms is derived from the Greek *psalmoi*, meaning "music of a stringed instrument," or more generally, "songs adapted to such music."

The Psalms and Ancient Near-Eastern Poetry. Although the editors of our present Hebrew Bible (the Masoretes) recognized only three poetical books (Psalms, Proverbs, and Job), the study of Hebrew versification in the last two or more centuries has demonstrated that large sections outside these books, particularly in the prophetical writings, share the poetical form. Moreover, poetical principles, lost for many centuries, not only have been recovered, but Hebrew poetry has been greatly illuminated by the recovery of Egyptian, Babylonian, and Assyrian (Akkadian) literature, particularly the Canaanite religious epic poetry from ancient Ugarit in north Syria. These discoveries have placed Hebrew poetry in the illuminating background of general Near Eastern prosody and demonstrated that it shares many of the forms and features of its neighbors and that many poetical forms and expressions, although unmythological in their biblical use, have their poetical Canaanite parallels in the current polytheistic literature of the times (cf. M. Dahood, *The Psalms*, AB).

The Psalms and Hebrew Poetry. (1) *Hebrew poetry employs parallelism*, sometimes called "sense rhythm," which consists of thought arrangement rather than word arrangement; it is the basic structure of Hebrew verse. Three principal types of parallelism exist—synonymous, antithetic, and synthetic. *Synonymous parallelism* occurs when the thought of the first line (stich) is substantially repeated and reinforced in equivalent terms in the second line, giving a distich, or couplet. "Day unto day uttereth speech, and night unto night showeth knowledge" (Psalm 19:2). *Antithetic parallelism* is the repetition of a contrasting thought in the second line to emphasize or confirm the thought of the first. "They are brought down and fallen; but we are risen, and stand" (Psalm 20:8).

Synthetic parallelism is the progressive flow of thought in which the second or following lines amplify or explain the first line. "And he will be like a tree firmly planted by streams of water, which yields its fruit in its season, and its leaf does not wither; and in whatever he does, he prospers" (Psalm 1:3, NASB). This is a quatrain, or tetrastich, but parallelisms may consist of two (distichs, Psalm 36:5) or three (tristichs, Job 3:9). This basic device of Hebrew poetry produces a musical effect that is pleasing to the ear and satisfying to the mind. It is subject to many variations and combinations, which help explain the beauty and appeal of the Psalms and Hebrew poetry in general (cf. G. B. Gray, *Forms of Hebrew Poetry*).

(2) *Hebrew poetry possesses rhythm.*

739

It is not quantitative in the sense of counting syllables, but depends upon the number of accents. Lyric meter (2 + 2, Song of Solomon), dirge (3 + 2, Lamentations) and epic or didactic (3 + 3, Job and Proverbs) may be distinguished. Studies seem to show that Hebrew poetry is rhythmical but not strictly metrical (cf. E. Sievers, *Studies in Hebrew Metre*).

(3) *Hebrew poetry is highly figurative.* It is rich in word pictures and numerous rhetorical devices (simile, metaphor, metonymy, synecdoche, alliteration, personification, hyperbole). The Hebrew language itself, even in the form of prose, has a rhythmic and musical quality that is admirably adapted to noble poetry.

The Titles and Authorship. All but thirty-four of the psalms bear some title as a superscription. Seventy-three of them employ the inscription *l^e Dāwîd*, rendered, "A Psalm of David" (KJV, RV, ASV, RSV, NASB). This expression normally suggests authorship "*by* David," but the Hebrew usage may indicate "connected with, belonging to, concerning, or, for David," or "in the style of David," and by no means must these titles be required in every instance to indicate authorship, whether with reference to David or others.

Yet, that David is the principal author of the Psalter is suggested by five facts: (1) The historical books of the Old Testament give ample evidence of David's poetic and musical gifts (2 Sam. 1:19-27; 23:1; cf. 1 Sam. 16:16-18; 18:10; Amos 6:5). (2) David is everywhere closely associated with the origin, composition, and publication of liturgical song (2 Sam. 6:5-15; 1 Chron. 16:4; 2 Chron. 7:6; 29:30). (3) David was especially anointed by God's Spirit as a musician and devotional singer (2 Sam. 23:1-2; Mark 12:36; Acts 2:25-31; 4:25-26). (4)

The Psalter itself furnishes substantial evidence of Davidic authorship. In most of the psalms ascribed to him, events in his life are clearly mirrored (e.g., Psalms 23, 51, 57). (5) Both the Old Testament and New Testament cite certain psalms as Davidic in origin (Psalm 2, cf. Acts 4:25-26; Psalm 16, cf. Acts 2:25-28; Psalm 18, cf. 2 Sam. 22:1-2; Psalm 32, cf. Rom. 4:6-8; Psalm 69, cf. Acts 1:16-20; Rom. 11:9-10; Psalm 109, cf. Acts 1:20; Psalm 110, cf. Matt. 22:44; Mark 12:36-37; Luke 20:42-44; Acts 2:34).

The titles or superscriptions, anciently prefixed to the psalms, antedate the LXX and reflect very old Hebrew tradition. They may not reasonably be rejected, except where indubitable proof may be adduced that they are not genuine. Besides David, other psalms are assigned to Asaph (Psalms 50, 73-80); Korah's sons (Psalms 42, 44-49, 84, 85, 87); Solomon (Psalms 72, 127); Moses (Psalm 90); Heman (Psalm 88); and Ethan (Psalm 89). Forty-nine psalms are anonymous, according to the Masoretic text.

The Message of the Psalms. While the devotional message of praise, thanksgiving, and worship, reflecting the experience of the Old Testament believer, constitutes the predominant note of the Psalter, the underlying theme is prophetic. The book of Psalms is preeminently a prophetic volume, attested by the fact that its frequent quotation in the New Testament is overwhelmingly on prophetic lines. There are about a hundred direct references or allusions to the Psalter in the New Testament, evidencing the truly marvelous prophetic scope of this portion of Scripture.

Three great prophetic themes run through the book: (1) *The first theme is the Messiah's humiliation and exaltation.* The Lord Jesus Christ is revealed uniquely in this book, as He Himself emphasized (Luke 24:44). Psalm 2 discloses His eternal divine sonship; Psalm 8 predicts His incarnation as the Son of Man; and Psalms 16 and 22 predict His death and resurrection, while each of these psalms looks forward to His glory. (2) *The second theme is the experiences of the godly Jewish remnant during the coming Tribulation period, and their deliverance and blessing at the second advent of Christ* (e.g., Psalms 3-7, 46-48, 55-57, 116). (3) *The third theme is the future glories reserved for restored Israel, for the nations, and for creation itself* (e.g., Psalms 72, 89, 110). The book ends with mighty hallelujahs in the glorious consummation when heaven and earth will sing His praises, as in the great closing "Hallelujah Chorus" in Handel's *Messiah* (Psalms 146-50).

The Division of the Psalms. The collection of the book of the Psalms was a gradual process, and the final arrangement into a fivefold division, we conclude, was the work of the Holy Spirit. Accordingly, it is spiritually significant, especially in a prophetic sense, adumbrating the redemptive ways and purposes of God with the fallen race, and particularly with His elect nation, Israel. Many scholars have failed to see this. As a result, their interpretations of the book have often missed the full prophetic sweep of the Psalter. They tended to treat each psalm as a separate gem instead of viewing many of them as clusters of gems with a mutual connection, each individual jewel contributing its sparkle. In line with this view of the psalms, the five divisions from ancient Jewish times to the present have been seen to bear a remarkable correspondence to the Mosaic Pentateuch.

1. *The Genesis Section (Psalms 1-41).* Like the book of Genesis, this section has much to say about man—the righteous man versus the wicked man (Psalm 1); the rebellious man versus the God-man Messiah (Psalm 2); the first man, Adam, versus the second Man, Christ, who was made a little lower than the angels (Psalm 8); the wicked man, Antichrist (Psalms 9-10); and the Tribulation to come upon wicked man (Psalms 11-15). The obedience of Christ, the last Adam, unto the death of the cross and His salvation and glory are previewed (Psalms 16-41), the section ending with a blessing and a double amen.

2. *The Exodus Section (Psalms 42-72).* Like the book of Exodus, where the LORD redeems an enslaved people in Egypt, an oppressed and suffering people is presented, envisioning the deliverance of the future Jewish remnant during the Great Tribulation (Psalm 42), whose prayers are answered by the coming of the King (Psalm 45). Redemption by power in Kingdom blessing is revealed in many of the following psalms, concluding with the great Kingdom psalm (Psalm 72), picturing Christ's millennial reign. This book likewise concludes with a double amen and the appropriate declaration: "And let the whole earth be filled with his glory" (Psalm 72:19), recalling the end of the book of Exodus with the glory of the LORD filling the tabernacle (Exod. 40:34-38).

3. *The Leviticus Section (Psalms 73-89).* As Leviticus strikes the keynote "Holiness unto the LORD," so in this section we are conducted into the sanctuary to glimpse the holiness of the LORD in dealing with His people, almost every psalm having some connection with the sanctuary, Zion, and approach to the LORD. It also ends with a benediction and double amen.

4. *The Numbers Section (Psalms 90-106).* Significantly, the first psalm of this

section is ascribed to Moses, evidently inspired as he witnessed the terrible pall of death in the wilderness wandering. Psalm 91 in its full sweep encompasses the second Man, and the succeeding psalms show that the times of unrest and wandering will end only when the Messiah reigns and the nations worship and serve Him. Like the others, this section ends with an amen and a hallelujah.

5. *The Deuteronomy Section (Psalms 107-50).* As in Deuteronomy, the Word of God is magnified in this section, and Christ is seen as the living Word in the beginning of this section—in His rejection, exaltation, and second advent. The times of praise to the LORD that follow are once more revealed in a cluster of psalms (109-13), followed by the grand consummation of redemption redounding to God's praise and glory in the closing hallelujah psalms (146-50).

OUTLINE

III. BOOK THREE: THE LEVITICUS SECTION.
73:1—89:52.
  A. The Problem of the Suffering of the Righteous.
      73:1-28.
  B. The Enemy Invades the Sanctuary. 74:1-23.
  C. God's Answer to the Desecration of His Sanctuary.
      75:1-10.
  D. The Messiah's Kingdom Established. 76:1-12.
  E. The Saint in the Day of Distress. 77:1-20.
  F. God's Working in History. 78:1-72.
  G. Jerusalem's Desolation—Past and Future. 79:1-13.
  H. Ultimate Restoration of Israel. 80:1-19.
  I. Revival of Israel's Hope. 81:1-16.
  J. The Messiah's Judgment at His Second Advent.
      82:1-8.
  K. Israel's Enemies Overthrown. 83:1-18.
  L. The Blessedness of True Worship. 84:1-12.
  M. Faith Appropriates Promised Blessings. 85:1-13.
  N. Prayer of a True Servant of God. 86:1-17.
  O. Jerusalem's Kingdom Exaltation. 87:1-7.
  P. The Cry of an Afflicted Saint. 88:1-18.
  Q. God's Faithfulness and the Davidic Covenant.
      89:1-52.

IV. BOOK FOUR: THE NUMBERS SECTION.
90:1—106:48.
  A. God's Greatness and Man's Frailty. 90:1-17.
  B. The Redeemed Man's Security. 91:1-16.
  C. The Victorious Believer. 92:1-15.
  D. The Messiah's Millennial Reign. 93:1-5.
  E. God's Judgment upon the Wicked. 94:1-23.
  F. The Advent of Israel's King Anticipated. 95:1-11.
  G. The Advent of Israel's King Realized. 96:1-13.
  H. The King's Glorious Reign. 97:1-12.
  I. The New Song. 98:1-9.
  J. The Righteous Rule of the King. 99:1-9.
  K. Universal Praise in the Kingdom. 100:1-5.
  L. The Davidic Ideal of a King. 101:1-8.
  M. Humiliation Is a Prelude to the King's Glory.
      102:1-28.
  N. Israel's Praise in Kingdom Blessing. 103:1-22.
  O. Creation's Praise of the Creator. 104:1-35.
  P. Celebration of the Lord's Covenant Faithfulness.
      105:1-45.
  Q. Israel's Confession of Sin and Restoration.
      106:1-48.

COMMENTARY

I. BOOK ONE: THE GENESIS SECTION. 1:1—41:34.

A. THE RIGHTEOUS AND THE WICKED IN CONTRAST. 1:1-6.

*The Righteous and Their Reward.
1:1-3.* This psalm is introductory to the entire Psalter, presenting the trenchant difference stressed throughout the Word of God between the believer and the unbeliever, the saved and the lost, the saint and the sinner. But since in a fallen race of universally lost, undone sinners, sinful man can become righteous purely on the basis of faith in God's redemptive plan centering in the righteous One to come, the righteous man in Psalm 1 in final analysis can be none other than God incarnate, the Savior Jesus Christ, who by virtue of His person and work opened the way for *any sinner* to be called righteous.

Hence, the righteous man also denotes a person in any age who, believing he was an utterly lost sinner shut up to God's grace for salvation, trusted God for that salvation (Gen. 15:6; Rom. 4:1-5). Such faith, resting in types and shadows in the Old Testament, was prospective with respect to the cross in the case of the Old Testament believer and is retrospective in the case of New Testament believers (Rom. 3:25).

1. Blessed (happy) **is the man** (lit., "Oh the happinesses of the man") who does three things: (1) He separates himself from sin and sinners. He avoids the first step in sin's downward pull and unavoidable deterioration. He **walketh not in the counsel of the ungodly,** nor is he tempted to stand **in the way of sinners,** so as to be reduced to a low and dangerous state where he **sitteth in the seat of the scornful** to scoff at God and revile good men and goodness itself.

2. (2) He delights himself in God's Word and "meditates" on it (*hāgâ,* "ruminates," chews it as an animal chews its cud, enjoying and digesting delightedly every morsel of it). He does this constantly **day and night. 3.** (3) He is spiritually prosperous. **Whatsoever he doeth shall prosper** (*yăṣlīăḥ,* he is happy and successful, in the sense of carrying worthwhile projects to completion). Hence, the godly man is compared to **a tree planted by the rivers** (streams or canals) **of water** (92:12-14; Jer. 17:8; Ezek. 19:10), whose foliage is perennially fresh, indicative of unceasing productivity.

The Wicked and Their Doom. 1:4-6.
4. The ungodly are not so. The Hebrew is emphatic in the contrast—"Not so! are the ungodly," that is, the ungodly are *not* like the godly. The "ungodly" (*rāšā'*) denotes fundamentally the unjustified, unsaved, unrighteous man (cf. Gen. 15:6) encompassing all degrees of his lawlessness or wickedness.

Every man without faith in God's grace to save sinners has two characteristics: (1) He is like **chaff which the wind driveth away** (i.e., into Sheol; 35:5; Job 21:18; Isa. 17:13). He is characterized by uselessness, vanity, and purposelessness, or at best, misdirected purpose. The picture is that of a threshing floor atop a hill, with the wind blowing away the chaff and leaving the wheat.

5a. (2) **Therefore** (because not justified by faith in God's redemptive grace), **the ungodly shall not stand** (cf. 5:5; be acquitted) **in the judgment** (89:5, 7). This anticipates the judgment of the unsaved for their deeds at the end of time, preluding eternity (Rev. 20:11-15), when they will be cast into eternal hell (gehenna, the lake of fire, Rev. 20:15).

5b. Nor shall **sinners** (the unsaved) stand **in the congregation of the righteous** (the saved), anticipating the New Testament revelation that the first resurrection (in stages) is exclusively for the saved and is unto eternal life, while the second resurrection (exclusively for the unsaved) is unto judgment (condemnation) and eternal death in gehenna. This is based upon divine omniscience. **6. The Lord knoweth the way** (destiny) of the **righteous.** By contrast, the way (doom) of the ungodly (the unsaved) **shall perish** (come to nought) in eternal death (separation from God).

B. THE REJECTED KING. 2:1-12.

The Rebellion Against Earth's Rightful King. 2:1-3. **1. Why do the nations rage** (*rāgăsh*, "band together with evil intent"; 64:2). This is applied to the rejection of the perfect Man, the Lord Jesus Christ, by man at His first advent (Acts 4:25-26), a hostility that has continued throughout this present age and will find its climax at the second advent. Then the nation will tumultuously assemble and **imagine** (meditate, devise) **a vain thing** (*rîq*, "an empty, senseless scheme"), namely, the insensate plan to banish the name of God and His Christ from the earth and take possession of it. This evil will find fruition in Satan working through the beast and the demon-blinded and demon-energized armies at Armageddon (Rev. 16:13-16; 19:19).

2. The nations with their kings and apostate Israel **set themselves** in hostile opposition and **take counsel together** against the LORD and His Anointed (His Messiah, Christ). **3.** They express in plain language their evil intent to **break** (snap) the bonds and throw off the yoke of the LORD and His Christ over them and over the earth, which they are demonically deluded into thinking belongs to them, when all the while the earth and its inhabitants belong to Him, both by creation (24:1; 100:3; 139:13-14) and by redemption (Eph. 1:13-14; Rev. 5:7-9).

Heaven's Silence Is Broken. 2:4-6. **4.** Rebellious man's foolish plan is so preposterous that the One who sits in heaven, the Lord (*'ădōnāy,* "Sovereign"), laughs. His position, enthroned at the right hand of the Father and sharing His Father's throne as the Overcomer par excellence through death, resurrection, and ascension (Rev. 3:21), gives Him such confidence in the face of man's impious opposition as to make it ridiculously pathetic.

In infinite patience He has been waiting during the interlude between His first and second advents, silent to all the calumnies and insults of rebellious man. But as man's final rebellion reaches its peak, He breaks His long silence with laughter as He holds His enemies in derision (cf. Psalms 37:13; 59:8). Are they so deluded to believe that they could set aside His covenant with David (2 Sam. 7:8-17) and His oath (Psalm 89:34-37)?

5. Then He who has so long spoken in love will speak in **wrath** (21:8-9; 76:7) and **vex** (terrify) in His **great displeasure** (fury) (78:49-50; Rev. 19:15) as He strikes death to His foes (19:19-21). **6.** This is His answer as He informs the flagrant rebels that He has already installed His King with full divine approval. **But as for Me** (very emphatic), **I have installed My King upon Zion, My**

holy mountain (NASB; Psalms 45:6; 48:1-2; Rev. 19:16; 20:4).

The Anointed Declares His Charter of Kingship. 2:7-9. **7.** The Anointed proclaims God's counsel concerning Himself and announces it as the divine decree: **Thou art my son; this day have I begotten thee.** He appears announcing His right to the kingship on the basis of sonship. His eternal sonship is implied, but it is His sonship attested in the incarnation, resurrection, and ascension that comes into focus here (Acts 13:33; Heb. 1:5; 5:5), in which capacity His increasing rejection will grow till it issues in climactic rebellion at His second advent.

8. Although the psalmist doubtlessly had in mind a contemporary chosen ruler (2 Sam. 7:14), the Messiah is previsioned in the light of the New Testament. Thus, His sonship in incarnation, resurrection, and ascension to glory becomes the basis for His asking the Father for the **nations** as His inheritance and **the uttermost parts of the earth** for His possession (Psalms 21:1-2; 22:27; 65:2; 67:7), and so in the Kingdom age He will rule as KING OF KINGS, AND LORD OF LORDS (Rev. 19:16), the *one* absolute and sole Sovereign of the earth. **9.** His unflinching sternness in dealing with recalcitrants is depicted in His breaking offenders with **a rod of iron** (Psalm 110:5-6; Rev. 2:27; 12:5; 19:15), shattering them **like a potter's vessel** (earthenware) (Psalms 28:5; 52:5; 72:4).

His Solemn Warning to Dissidents. 2:10-12. **10-11.** He calls upon kings and judges in the Kingdom to **be wise** (show discernment) and to **be instructed** (take warning; cf. 32:8; Prov. 8:15; 27:11), to **serve the Lord with fear** (with reverence; Psalm 5:7), and to **rejoice with trembling** (119:119-20). The choice of wisdom goes beyond mere outward acceptance of the decree of the Anointed's kingship; they are to reverence His divine right to rule. **12.** They are to **kiss the Son** in token of homage, according to common custom of showing fidelity. Even as the way of the wicked spells doom in Psalm 1:6, so shall be the end of those who refuse to submit to the LORD's anointed King. However, millennial bliss will accrue to all who **put their trust** (*ḥāsâ*, "flee to, take refuge") in Him.

C. MORNING PRAYER OF TRUST IN GOD. 3:1-8.

Psalms 3 to 7 present the trials of God's saints that are applicable to any age, but they focus prophetically upon the sorrows of the godly Jewish remnant during the coming Tribulation as they wait for their Redeemer-King. These five psalms form a bridge connecting Psalm 2 (the King-Messiah in rejection) with Psalm 8, when He will have all things put under His feet. David represents in the prophetic sense the Jewish remnant called out during the Tribulation period when the enemies of God will be many and fierce (Rev. 12:13—13:18).

The Psalmist's Plight. 3:1-2. **1.** The occasion was David's cry to God when he fled during Absalom's rebellion (2 Sam. 15:13-17, 29). He reminded the LORD how his adversaries and troublers had increased (Psalm 69:4; 2 Sam. 15:12). **2.** Many were saying of David's soul (i.e., of David), **There is no help** (salvation, deliverance) **for him in God** (Psalms 22:7; 71:11), or, following the Ugaritic meaning of the preposition *b*, "from God" (Cyrus Gordon, *Ugaritic Texts, 10:1*).

The Psalmist's Trust. 3:3-6. **3.** David quickly turned from his troubles to the LORD, claiming Him as his **shield** (*māgēn*, "protection, Protector"; cf. 5:12; 62:7), his **glory** (62:7) to restore his dignity, and **the lifter up of** his **head** to give him new courage (9:13; 27:6). **4.** In full voice he called to the LORD, who answered (4:3) from His **holy hill** (cf. 2:4; 15:1; 43:3).

5. He expressed his quiet confidence. **I laid down and slept.** After waking from restful slumber, he realized that it was God who had sustained him (4:8; Prov. 3:24). **6.** With faith thus nourished in relaxed trust in God, he was buoyed up by the confidence that no number of foes could terrify him (Psalms 23:4; 27:3; cf. 118:10-13).

The Psalmist's Petition. 3:7-8. **7. Arise, O Lord.** He invoked God's power and deliverance. He was either recalling what God had done on previous occasions, or what he was confident God would do for him now (prophetic perfect, forseeing an event as so certain that it is spoken of as complete already). Smiting the enemy on the **cheekbone** (jaw; Job 16:10) and shattering the teeth of the wicked (Psalms 57:4; 58:6) poetically depict divine intervention.

8. David confessed **salvation** (*yᵉshûʻâ*, "deliverance, help"; cf. v. 2) **belongeth to the Lord** (28:8; 35:3; cf. Jer. 3:23; Jonah 2:9, the theme of the Bible). He invokes God's blessing (Psalms 28:8; 35:3) upon His people (29:11). **Selah,** employed three times in this psalm (vv. 2, 4, 8), is a musical term, apparently indicating a pause, crescendo, or interlude.

D. EVENING PRAYER OF TRUST IN GOD. 4:1-8.

The background of this psalm is similar to that of Psalm 3 (see the introduction to that ode). Here, however, the lament becomes a song of trust. It is "to [better, 'for'] the chief Musician," that is, the choir director, "on Neginoth" (stringed instruments).

Urgent Appeal to God. 4:1. **1. Answer me ... be gracious ... hear my prayer** (NASB). In his trouble the saint addressed the LORD as **O God of my righteousness** ("vindication"; for this connotation of *ṣĕḏĕq*, see 17:2; 35:28; Isa. 50:8). He meant God who maintained his right. He remembered past deliverances and cried, **Thou hast enlarged** (expanded) **me** spiritually, relieving me by Your presence and deliverance **in distress.** The trials of God's people often minister to their spiritual enlargement, which will be eminently true of the saints during the coming Tribulation period, especially the godly Jewish remnant (Rev. 7:1-8).

Sage Advice and Warning. 4:2-5. **2.** He warned wicked, unregenerate mankind, particularly proud men of rank who turn God's glory into shame by loving **vanity** (*rîq*, "what is empty and worthless"), in connection with idolatry, and of seeking avidly after **falsehood** (*kāzāḇ*, "deception"), in particular that connected with idolatry, which will be rampant during the coming Tribulation period (Matt. 24:11-12; Rev. 9:20-21; cf. 2 Thess. 2:4-12).

3. But let these lawless idolaters and rebels **know that the Lord hath set apart him who is godly** (*ḥāsîḏ*, "the pious, devoted man") **for himself,** or with another reading, "Yahweh will work wonders for the one devoted to him" (AB) and hear his prayer (cf. James 5:16-18).

4. Stand in awe (*rgz*, "be disquieted") occurs in this sense in the Phoenician Tabnit Inscription, this meaning concurring with Ephesians 4:26, "Be ye angry, and sin not." Be upset and "tremble" with anger or fear at the fierce persecutions of your enemies, but do not sin by distrusting the LORD to come to your aid. Nurse your faith in Him by "communing with your own heart" (lit., "looking into your heart," in the sense of "examining your conscience"; for *'āmar* in the sense of "see, look,'' see M. Dahood, ''Hebrew-Ugaritic Lexicography I,'' *Biblica* 44 [1963] :295-96) **and be still** in faithfully trusting in God.

5. Offer sacrifices of righteousness (51:19; Deut. 33:19), legitimate sacrifices, as opposed to sacrifices to idols (Psalm 51:19), that genuinely prevision Christ's redemptive work, eventuating in providing us God's perfect righteousness (1 Cor. 1:30) and demonstrating our trust in the Lord (Psalms 37:3; 62:8).

Peaceful Trust in God. 4:6-8. **6.** Many were saying, **Who will show us any good?** (cf. Job 7:7; 9:25). Dark times of wickedness and persecution come to all of God's own when pessimists would have us believe that evil has conquered and God is either dead or in abeyance. Such will be the state of things in the dark days of the Tribulation. But the cry of the godly Jewish remnant in the ''gross darkness'' of that hour (Isa. 60:2) will be: **Lord, lift thou up the light of thy countenance upon us** (Num. 6:26; Psalm 80:3, 7, 19).

7. Their testimony, as well as that of all of God's people rescued out of desperate plight, will be **Thou hast put gladness in my heart** (97:11-12) surpassing the joy of abundant harvesting and harvest festivals (119:14, 72). **8.** Submissive trust in the Lord enabled God's child to lie down and sleep (Job 11:19; Psalm 3:5) in the midst of dangers and foes, conscious of the fact that the Lord alone made him **dwell in safety** (Lev. 25:18-19; Deut. 12:10; Psalm 16:9).

E. PRAYER FOR PROTECTION FROM FOES. 5:1-12.

For the prophetic scope of this psalm and its connection with the great ''Messianic Psalms'' (2 and 8), see the introduction to Psalm 3. The background of strife and dangerous foes was connected with the psalmist's experiences, but it looks forward to saints in every age, with special application to those in the heyday of man's rebellion (Psalm 2) preceding Kingdom establishment (Psalm 8).

God Is Invoked. 5:1-3. **1-2.** The troubled saint pleaded for God to hear and to consider his **meditation** (groaning; 4:1) and heed his **cry** for help. He appropriately claimed the Lord as his **King** and his **God** in the light of the soon expected return of the Messiah to establish the Kingdom promised to David's Son and Lord (110:1-3; 2 Sam. 7:8-17; cf. Psalm 84:3). **3.** He began the day in eager anticipation of the coming of divine deliverance. **In the morning will I direct my prayer unto thee, and will look up** (eagerly watch; 88:13; 130:6).

The Righteous and the Wicked Are Contrasted. 5:4-7. As the troubled saint faced wickedness and wicked men (in full manifestation in the Great Tribulation), he presented a double contrast—the attitudes and actions of the righteous and the wicked, as well as the different responses of God toward the two groups.

4. God cannot tolerate sin, nor can any evil dwell with Him (92:15; cf. Isa. 6:3). **5a. The foolish** (boastful, arrogant) **shall not stand** (acquitted) in His presence (Psalms 1:5; 73:3; 75:4). **5b.** God hates all **workers of iniquity** (cf. 11:5; 45:7), those who perpetrate vanity by trafficking in idolatry and the demonized religion connected with it, which will reach its apex in the Great Tribulation (Rev. 9:20-21; 13:11-13).

6. The Lord will **destroy those who speak falsehood** (lies; cf. Psalm 52:4). The Lord will **abhor** (detest) the man of bloodshed and deceit (Rev. 13:1-18), who will predominate in the unbridled lawlessness of the end times (Rev. 9:21). In contrast, the psalmist (representing

753

the Jewish remnant) will worship in God's house, relying upon the multitude (abundance) of God's mercy springing from faith in His redemptive grace. **7.** In reverence for God, he would worship toward His holy Temple, to be rebuilt in Jerusalem in Tribulation times (cf. 2 Thess. 2:4).

Prayer for Leading Because of Enemies. 5:8-9. **8.** Surrounded by persecutors and foes, the cry of God's servant was **Make thy way straight before my face.** If this was not done, he would be swallowed up and destroyed by his persecutors, who will—under the last-day Antichrist and his followers—mercilessly persecute the saints (Rev. 13:15), particularly the Jewish remnant, who will be looking for the King and His Kingdom when the Antichrist is bent on establishing his own worldwide rule.

9. Then human depravity will reach its acme and attest what the unregenerate man really is. Paul quoted this passage to show the utter sinfulness of the unregenerate heart (Rom. 3:13)—(1) **no faithfulness in their mouth** (i.e., "there is nothing reliable in what they say," NASB; Psalm 52:3); (2) **their inward part** (7:14) **is very wickedness** (destruction itself); (3) **their throat is an open sepulcher** (Rom. 3:13), giving vent to the corruption of their heart; and (4) **they flatter with their tongue.**

A Prayer for Retribution. 5:10. **10.** Here occurs the first imprecatory prayer recorded in the Psalms. It is not that the psalmist, living in a semibarbaric age, knew no better, as some critics maintain, nor are such prayers evidence against their divine inspiration, as others maintain. Nor would it be right for a Christian to pray these prayers during this age, in which the church is to suffer and endure rejection with Christ. But seen in the light of correct interpretation, they are fully inspired and perfectly in order when the time comes for them to be answered, namely, when man's iniquity in his rejection of the LORD's anointed King has come to the full (Psalm 2) and God's judgments are ripe and ready to be unloosed on the earth (Rev. 6:1—19:11).

Our Lord refers to this subject in the parable of the unjust judge (Luke 18:1-8): "And shall not God avenge his own elect [Israel], who cry day and night unto him, though he bear long with them? I tell you that he will avenge them speedily." When the LORD rends the heavens and comes down (Isa. 64:1), then the Spirit of God will move through His persecuted saints on earth to call upon a righteous God to deal with the earth's rebels according to His righteousness.

The Assurance of Faith. 5:11-12. **11-12.** The first imprecatory outburst was followed by an exhortation to the faithful to **rejoice ... shout for joy ... be joyful.** Why? **Thou defendest** Thine own. **Thou ... wilt bless tne righteous ... with favor ... compass him ... with a shield** of protection (3:3; 25:4-5; 27:11; 31:3).

F. PRAYER IN TIME OF TROUBLE. 6:1-10.

For the scope and connection of this psalm with Psalms 1 to 8, see the introduction to Psalm 3. It is superscribed by the notation "To the chief Musician [better, 'For the precentor or choir director'] on Neginoth [stringed instruments] upon Sheminith ['upon an eight-stringed lyre,' or perhaps, 'according to a lower octave']."

A Prayer for Relief from Suffering. 6:1-5. **1-2. Rebuke me not ... neither chasten.... Have mercy upon me ... heal me.** The saint was passing through great trial, as in Psalms 3 to 7. The LORD's **hot displeasure** was being manifested. **3. My soul is ... very vexed** (greatly dismayed; 88:3; John 12:27). Passing through Tribulation anguish, the harried child of God cried out in his distress, **But thou, O Lord, how long?** (Psalm 90:13). **4.** He called upon the LORD to **deliver** (rescue) and save him from his troubles (Dan. 12:1; Matt. 24:20-21), which for the Tribulation saints will be harrowing. **5.** He faced imminent death, with its forboding aspects and the grave (Sheol), which he conceived as a place he would not enjoy.

He Describes His Suffering. 6:6-7. **6.** He was **weary** with his **groaning** (sighing). He wept so profusely that he spoke hyperbolically of making his **bed to swim**, watering his couch with his tears (42:3). **7.** He declared that his **eye** was **consumed** (had wasted away) **because of grief;** it had grown old because of enemies and persecutors. This terrible suffering has often faced the LORD's people, but it will confront the godly Jewish remnant in fullest manifestation during "the time of Jacob's trouble" (Jer. 30:5-7), at the end of the age preceding Christ's second advent to deliver them.

He Expresses Confidence in Divine Interposition. 6:8-10. **8-9.** He dismissed his foes in anticipation of the LORD's undertaking in answer to his prayers, branding them **workers of iniquity** (119:115). **10.** He envisioned a new era about to dawn, prophetically pointing to the second advent and the setting up of the Kingdom, when all his and the LORD's enemies will be destroyed (Rev. 19:11—20:4).

G. PRAYER FOR DEFENSE AGAINST THE WICKED. 7:1-17.

See the introduction to Psalm 3 for the scope and connection of this psalm with Psalms 1 to 8. It is called "a Shiggaion of David," probably signifying a dithyrambic rhythm indicating a wild,

passionate song, which he sang to the LORD concerning Cush, a Benjamite. Who Cush the Benjamite was is not certain. He must have been a wicked, lawless supporter of Saul who became an intense persecutor of David, and thus reflected, in the full contextual relationship of Psalms 3 to 7, the coming lawless one par excellence, the man of sin, the diabolical persecutor of God's saints during the Great Tribulation (Rev. 6:10-11; 13:7; 14:9-13).

A Prayer for Deliverance. 7:1-2. **1.** The persecuted saint averred that in the LORD his God he placed his **trust** (took refuge; 31:1; 71:1). He cried out to be delivered from **all those** who were persecuting him (pursuing and hounding him)! **2.** So terrible was the pressure that the wicked persecutor tried to **tear** (rend) his **soul** (him) **like a lion** (cf. 57:4; 1 Pet. 5:8), with no one to deliver unless the LORD intervened (cf. Rev. 13:6-7; 19:11-21).

A Protestation of Innocence. 7:3-5. **3-5.** David was convinced he was not deserving of his persecution: If there was **iniquity** (injustice) in his hands (1 Sam. 24:11), if he had **rewarded** (requited) evil for good to him who was at peace with him (Psalm 109:4), or **plundered him who without cause was my adversary** (NASB; cf. 1 Sam. 24:7), he declared, "Let the enemy pursue my soul [i.e., me] and overtake it [me] . . . let him trample my life down to the ground, and lay my glory in the dust" (NASB). Likewise, the saints of the Tribulation shall be undeserving of the violent persecutions inflicted upon them by the beast and his followers (Rev. 6:10-11).

A Prayer for Judgment. 7:6-10. **6. Arise, O Lord . . . lift up thyself . . . awake for me to the judgment . . . thou hast commanded.** A bold figure of arousing God is employed to emphasize the need of immediate judgment, both in a personal sense and in an eschatological sense (cf. 3:7; 35:23; 94:2; 138:7; Zech. 2:13). The terrible hatred depicted against the LORD's Anointed in Psalm 2 will be attached to all those identified with Him in the end time, both the godly Jews (Rev. 7:1-8) and the Gentiles (7:9-17). Many will have suffered martyrdom under the Antichrist; others will have faced the constant threat of torture and death because of their devotion to the rightful King and their opposition to the pretensions of the false king (Matt. 25:34-46).

8. Prayer arose for the LORD to return to vindicate His own who had been subjected to such gross injustices. **9.** Man's wickedness (Psalm 2) had come to the full, and so the Spirit-indited prayer was, **O let the evil of the wicked come to an end** (34:21; 94:23), **but establish the righteous** (i.e., in Kingdom blessing; NASB; 37:23; 40:2). Trouble in any age tries and tests God's people, but the Tribulation will in a special sense try the nation Israel and bring forth a saved remnant refined as gold for Kingdom blessing. **10.** Then God's people will have the glorious conviction that their **defense** (shield; 3:3; 18:2, 30) **is with God,** for Christ's second advent will be a splendid vindication and victory for them, saving the **upright in heart** (97:11).

God's Government and the End of the Wicked. 7:11-16. **11.** In prospect of imminent deliverance, the psalmist proclaimed God **a righteous judge** (NASB; 50:6), who **is angry** ("has indignation," NASB) against sinners **every day** (90:9). **12-13.** He is pictured as a warrior whetting His sword, making His bow ready, and turning His arrows into fiery shafts against the wicked (64:7; cf. 18:14; 45:5). Compare the New Testament depiction (Rev. 19:11-20).

Verses 14 to 16 prophetically glimpse the last day's lawless one, the man of sin, evidently prefigured by Cush the Benjamite. **14.** He **travails with wickedness ... conceives mischief** (Job 15:35; Isa. 59:4; James 1:15), **and brings forth falsehood** (NASB; cf. 2 Thess. 2:9-10; Rev. 13:12-14). **15-16.** He is presented as digging a pit and hollowing it out for the innocent to fall into, but he falls **into the ditch** (hole) himself (Psalm 57:6; cf. Rev. 19:19-20), his mischief returning upon his own head (Psalm 140:9), and **his violent dealing** (cf. Rev. 13:7-8) will descend upon his own pate (Psalm 140:11).

The Coming Praise. 7:17. **17.** The psalmist, as identified particularly with the saints of the Tribulation era, gave **thanks to the Lord according to His righteousness** (NASB; 71:15-16) so clearly manifested in bringing down the lawless one and punishing him. He sang **praise to the name of the Lord Most High** (NASB), "possessor of heaven and earth" (Gen. 14:19), who has entered into His possession by setting up His Kingdom rule (Psalm 8), which spells the end of the wicked (cf. Zech. 4:2-3, 14; Rev. 11:4; see comments on these texts).

H. THE MESSIAH (SON OF MAN) IN KINGDOM DOMINION. 8:1-9.

This psalm contrasts to Psalm 2. There the King is rejected in man's full rebellion against Him and His earth rule. Here the King is presented as the Son of Man (incarnate Deity), who has quelled all rebellion and put all things under His feet as He rules in complete dominion over man and the earth. For the scope and relation of Psalms 2 to 8 to one another, see the introduction to Psalm 3. The psalm is "To [for] the chief Musician [choir director, precentor] upon Gittith," perhaps a stringed instrument, the precise force of the word (occurring also in the headings of Psalms 81 and 84), being unknown.

The Son of Man in Kingdom Sovereignty. 8:1-2. **1a.** The psalmist addressed the LORD (Jehovah, Yahweh) as *Adonai* ("Sovereign") because this second great Messianic psalm begins and ends with the declaration: **How excellent** (*'ăddîr*, "glorious, majestic, great") **is thy name in all the earth** (vv. 1, 8). Therefore, it relates to the coming Kingdom age when the entire creation will be in subjection to the crucified, risen Lord, whose glorious name as Creator-Redeemer will then be worshiped and exalted universally. That blessed time has not yet come. In fact, the colossal rebellion and the events of Psalm 2 are still future and must precede the glorious prophecy of Psalm 8.

1b. Who hast set (57:5, 11; 148:13) **thy glory above the heavens!** The heavens declare the glory of God (19:1), and the celestial splendors are the work of His fingers. But His glory far exceeds the merely reflected glory of His marvelous creation. His is a glory that is *above* the heavens. This outburst of praise will flow from the hearts of His redeemed people, Israel, at His second advent. Redeemed by the blood of Him whom they once cast out, delivered from their oppressors, restored to their land and their covenanted blessings, they will utter these praises (see 66:1-4). The nations of the earth will join in the paean, when His name will be gloriously splendid in the earth.

2a. Out of the mouth of babes and sucklings hast thou ordained (established) **strength.** The little children in the Temple, who sang their hosannahs when Jesus appeared there (Matt. 21:15-16), foreshadow this coming praise, which also will be born of similar childlike faith in the newborn souls, who will then enter the Kingdom of heaven (cf. Psalm 110:3).

2b. The enemy and the avenger (cf. Psalm 2) will be silenced (made to cease) as the result of the **strength** (power) of God manifested in response to this childlike faith of the future remnant (29:1; 118:14; cf. 44:16). Then the sinners, both of Israel (Matt. 25:1-10) and the nations, will be purged out (25:31-46), as well as Antichrist and his hordes at Armageddon, with Satan and demons remanded to the abyss (Rev. 19:11—20:3).

The First Man (Adam) Prefiguring the Second Man (Christ). 8:3-8. Many expositors have confined **the son of man** to Adam, the first and representative man. He is, of course, included, but the passage goes beyond the first Adam to the second Adam, the Son of Man, the Lord Jesus Christ, as Hebrews 2:6-9 so clearly points out. In prophetic perspective, the author of Hebrews sees Him "made a little lower than the angels for the suffering of death" and as the risen, glorified, ascended Lord in heaven "crowned with glory and honor" (2:9). But he is careful to note: "now we see not yet all things put under him" (2:8), as Psalm 8 predicts will be the case one day (cf. 1 Cor. 15:27).

6-8. The first man (Adam, Gen. 1:26) lost his dominion through sin. The second Man has brought it back by His death and resurrection. When He returns as the Son of Man, all things will be put under His feet. **9.** Then He will reign till all enemies are subdued, and the praise voiced here (and in v. 1) will rise like a mighty crescendo from His redeemed people, both of Israel and the nations (cf. 1 Cor. 15:24-28; Rev. 19:1-8).

I. THANKSGIVING FOR GOD'S JUSTICE. 9:1-20.

Psalms 9 to 15, while reflecting the experiences of the psalmist himself and troubled and persecuted saints in every age, in their ultimate scope, continue the great prophetic themes of the book. They portray the end-time godly Jewish remnant in its conflict with the wicked one (the Antichrist) and his followers, and its eventual enjoyment of God's deliverance and administration of justice in Kingdom blessing. The superscriptions: "To the chief Musician [for the precentor] upon Muth-labben [i.e., death to the Son], A Psalm of David."

Praiseful Thanks to the Most High. 9:1-2. **1-2.** Thanksgiving and praise filled the heart of the psalmist as he showed forth ("told") all of God's **marvelous works** (*niplā'ôt,* "deeds that are miraculous and supernatural"), which find their ultimate reference to acts of the LORD by which He in Kingdom rule assumes His role as the **Most High** (*'elyôn,* "possessor of heaven and earth," Gen. 14:19; Zech. 4:2-3; Rev. 11:4).

Millennial Deliverances and Glories. 9:3-6. **3.** What happens when the Most High reigns is reflected prophetically in experiences David personally had. As he had seen his **enemies . . . turned back,** so will the godly remnant at Christ's advent and the setting up of the Kingdom of the Messiah promised in the Davidic Covenant (2 Sam. 7:8-17) behold their foes **fall and perish** at the presence of the returning Christ (Zech. 12:1-9; 14:1-3; Rev. 19:11—20:3).

4. Then the people of God, relentlessly persecuted by the Antichrist (the beast of Rev. 13:1-10), who will try to blot out their existence in the final and most terrible outburst of anti-Semitism the world has ever seen, will be able to say after the beast and the false prophet have been taken and cast alive into gehenna (Rev. 19:20): **For thou hast maintained my right.**

5. Then the King will sit upon the throne of His glory and judge the wicked persecutors of His people (Matt. 25:31-46), rebuking the nations and destroying the wicked at Armageddon (Rev. 19:11—20:3). **6.** Then it will be said, **The enemy has come to an end in perpetual ruins** (Psalm 40:15). **And Thou hast uprooted the cities; the very memory of them has perished** (NASB; 34:16).

The Kingdom Established. 9:7-12. **7a.** (1) the LORD shall **endure** (abide; "sit") as King **forever** (102:12, 26; Heb. 1:11). **7b-8.** (2) **He hath prepared** (established) **his throne for judgment,** the throne of His glory (Matt. 25:31), from which He will administer absolute justice in the Kingdom age. **9.** (3) He will then be **a refuge for the oppressed** (Psalms 32:7; 46:1; 91:2).

10. (4) Then His own who know His name will put their trust (cf. John 10:14) in Him, who never forsakes His own. **11.** This will call forth praise and testimony in Kingdom blessing. **12.** (5) Then **he maketh inquisition for blood** (i.e., avenges bloodshed; Gen. 9:5; cf. 1 Kings 21:17-19; cf. Rev. 6:9-11) by punishing those who will slaughter the LORD's people during the Great Tribulation. Then He will not forget the **cry of the humble** ("the afflicted"; v. 18).

Events Preceding the Establishment of the Kingdom. 9:13-20. Six events will precede the Kingdom's establishment: (1) **13a.** The godly remnant in their great ordeal will cry to the LORD for deliverance from death at the hands of their persecutors and troublers (38:19; Rev. 6:9-11). **13b.** They will address the LORD as He **who liftest . . . up from the gates of death** (Psalms 30:3; 86:13), the domain of the dead being pictured as a walled city ruled over by death (Matt. 16:18), contrasting **the gates of death** with "the gates of the daughter of Zion" (v. 14).

(2) **14.** They in faith anticipate deliverance and the consequent praise they will **show forth** (tell; 106:2) in Jerusalem, then to become the capital of

the millennial earth (Isa. 2:1-3). **14b.** Then they will rejoice in God's salvation (Psalms 13:5; 20:5; 35:9; 51:12; Isa. 12:1-6; 35:1-10). (3) **16a.** The LORD will execute His judgments upon the wicked one, the Antichrist and his hordes (cf. Rev. 6:1—19:10).

(4) **16b.** The wicked will be snared in their crimes of violence against the LORD's own (cf. Rev. 9:15; 11:18; 14:14-20; 16:21; 19:20-21). **17.** They will be **turned into sheol** (cf. Job 24:19; Psalm 49:14), the intermediate realm of the wicked dead, where the soul and spirit go at death until after the judgment of the great white throne, when they in their resurrected bodies will be cast into eternal hell (gehenna; Rev. 20:11-15). (5) **18.** The LORD will then administer mercy to the poor and needy (Psalm 62:5).

(6) **19a.** The godly will be inspired to pray for the LORD to **arise** to judgment to prevent wicked man under the Antichrist from prevailing and taking over the earth. **19b.** This is the judgment of the **nations** (Matt. 25:31-46), when the wicked (goats) will be consigned to "everlasting fire, prepared for the devil and his angels" (25:41). **20.** In answer to prayer of the righteous remnant, God will strike His (and their) enemies with **fear** so that they will **know themselves to be but men** (Psalm 62:9), daring to wage war (at Armageddon) against God (Rev. 19:19).

J. PRAYER FOR THE OVERTHROW OF THE WICKED. 10:1-18.

See the introduction to Psalm 9 for the scope of this psalm.

The Prayer. 10:1-2. **1-2.** A renewed cry went up to the LORD, because He had appeared to withdraw Himself, to **stand afar off** and **hide** Himself in the terrible **times of trouble** (NASB), occasioned by the wicked one (*rāshā'*, "the

Antichrist"), who will then persecute the saints with diabolical fury (Rev. 13:7), torturing and putting to death many of them. In his pride this wicked (lawless) one will **persecute the poor** (afflicted). The lawless one's followers are included in the prayer: **let them be taken** (caught) **in the devices** (plots) **that they have imagined** (Psalms 2:1-3; 9:16). See comment on the imprecatory prayers (5:10).

That Wicked One. 10:3-11. **3.** The final terrible persecutor of God's saints is now prophetically revealed in his arrogant pride. He **boasteth of his heart's desire** (49:6; 94:3; 112:10). He **curses and spurns the Lord** (NASB; 10:13; cf. Rev. 13:6). **4.** In the **haughtiness of his countenance** he sets aside God (Psalms 10:13; 36:2); like an atheist, he rules Him out of his thoughts (14:1; 36:1; 2 Thess. 2:4; Rev. 13:5).

5. His ways are always grievous (lit., "strong"); God's judgments are on high, out of his sight (Psalm 28:5; cf. Dan. 11:36; Rev. 13:6). He **puffeth** (snorts) at his enemies. **6.** He says **in his heart** (to himself), **I shall not be moved ... never be in adversity** (Psalm 49:11). But this boasting hides his real feeling of insecurity, for he persecutes those who still maintain faith in God, as a threat to his rule. These are the waiting, praying remnant of Israel and the Gentiles who believe the gospel of the Kingdom preached among the nations (Matt. 24:14).

7-11. Additional features of the wicked one are outlined. Verse 7 is quoted by Paul in Romans 3:14, showing that what develops in Christ's chief opponent among men is but the ripe development of what is in the fallen nature of every man. In his wickedness he says **in his heart** (to himself; v. 6): **God hath forgotten; he hideth his face; he will never see it.**

The Heart-Cry of the Remnant. 10:12-15. **12.** The remnant cry out for the LORD to **arise,** to **lift up** his hand (17:7; Mic. 5:9), that is, to interpose in behalf of His own and **forget not the humble** (the afflicted). **13.** They ask why the wicked should presume to **despise** God, and think that God will **not require it. 14.** But they are convinced God will **requite** it. He will help the helpless. **15.** They pray an imprecatory prayer (see 5:10): **Break . . . the arm of the wicked** (37:17). **Seek out his wickedness** (i.e., to punish it) **till thou find none** (to punish; 140:11).

The Gracious Answer of the Lord. 10:16-18. **16.** God replies to His people's anguished cry. He is **King forever and ever** (cf. Matt. 25:31-46; Rev. 19:16; 20:6). He judges the nations that have afflicted His people (Matt. 25:40, 45). **17.** He has heard **the desire of the humble** (the afflicted). He has heard their prayer. **18.** He undertakes for the oppressed, **that the man of the earth** (Antichrist and his followers) **may no more oppress** (terrify; Isa. 29:20-21; Rev. 19:20-21).

K. FLEEING TO GOD FOR REFUGE. 11:1-7.

This is a psalm of David penned in a time of persecution, probably at the hand of Saul or Absalom. For the scope of this psalm, see the introduction to Psalm 9.

The Lord Is a Refuge and Defense. 11:1-3. **1. In the Lord put I my trust** (*ḥāsîṯî,* "I take refuge"), the phrase "in the LORD" being emphatic by its position in the Hebrew (2:12). Faith's refuge in time of trouble is in divine aid. Here the prophetic scope comprehends the final time of trouble for the godly in the period of "Jacob's trouble" (Jer. 30:5-7; Dan. 12:1; Matt. 24:21-22; Rev. 6:1— 19:11). Since he is putting confidence in the LORD, how can anyone say to his

soul (i.e., to him), **Flee as a bird to your mountain** (Psalm 121:1; i.e., fly away to a place of safety in your own self-confidence).

2. The activity of the enemy presents a real peril. They bend the bow and make ready the arrow **that they may secretly** (lit., in darkness) **shoot at the upright in heart. 3.** The time comprehends the Tribulation era, when **the foundations** of morality and godliness will be **destroyed** (Rev. 9:20-21) in the unbridled lawlessness, apostasy, and rampant demonism of that time. What can **the righteous** (the justified, faithful people of God of that dark day) **do,** except be viciously persecuted and suffer wholesale martyrdom (Rev. 6:9-11; 7:14-17; 13:7, 16-17)?

The Lord Chastens His Own and Punishes the Wicked. 11:4-7. **4a.** The LORD is in His holy temple in heaven (18:6; Mic. 1:2; Hab. 2:20; Rev. 15:5, 8), ready to pour out His plagues upon sinners whose iniquity has come to the full (Gen. 15:16; Lev. 18:24). **4b.** His **throne,** from which He as Sovereign of the universe will issue His commands to punish evildoers, **is in heaven** (Psalm 2:4; Isa. 66:1; Matt. 5:34; 23:22; Acts 7:49; Rev. 4:2). **4c. His eyes behold, his eyelids test the children of men** (mankind; cf. Psalm 17:3; Gen. 22:1; James 1:12, 14). **5.** He tests the **righteous** (the justified) and the **wicked** (the unjustified), and He detests **him who loveth violence.**

6. Upon the wicked He will **rain snares, fire and brimstone** (Rev. 6:1 — 19:11). **This shall be the portion of their cup** (Psalm 75:8; Rev. 8:7-8; 16:8-9). **7. For the Lord is righteous; He loves righteousness** (Psalm 7:9). Therefore, He will punish those who have persecuted and wronged His people, and especially when their iniquity has come to the full (cf. Gen. 15:16) in the Great Tribulation. By contrast, **the upright will behold His**

face (NASB; Psalms 16:11; 17:15; Rev. 7:9, 11; 14:4). He chastens them to refine and purify them, but all the while He is giving them tokens of His grace and favor.

L. DELIVERANCE FROM THE ARROGANCE OF THE WICKED. 12:1-8.

This is a psalm of David for the choir director (precentor) upon Sheminith (probably reference to an eight-stringed lyre). For the scope of the psalm, see the introduction to Psalm 9.

The Arrogance of the Wicked. 12:1-4. **1. Help, Lord.** A renewed cry for help arose because of a time of departure from the LORD, resulting in terrible wickedness and persecution of the righteous. **For the godly man ceaseth** (ceases to be) . . . **the faithful fail** (disappear) **from among the children of men** (i.e., mankind; Isa. 57:1; Mic. 7:2). Sin and iniquity have come to the full (see comments on Psalm 11:3).

2. Especially coming into focus is the corruption of the earth at the end of the age (cf. Rev. 9:20-21), with particular emphasis on the evil of man's heart as expressed through his lips. **They speak vanity** (emptiness, falsehood), what is consonant with the idolatry and rampant occultism of the day, with **flattering lips** and a **double heart** (i.e., mind; cf. "a double-minded man is unstable in all his ways," James 1:8).

3. This verse is evidently a prayer, **May the Lord cut off all flattering lips, the tongue that speaks great things** (NASB), which will find its ultimate answer in the destruction of the Antichrist (Dan. 7:8; Rev. 13:5). **4.** The arrogant and lawless spirit that dominates the wicked, particularly the blasphemers of the end time (16:11), is shown in their claim, **our lips are our own; who is lord over us?** (cf. Psalm 2:2-3).

Faith Envisions God's Help. 12:5-8. **5.** Because of the awful oppression and devastation of the poor and needy, the LORD declares He will **arise** (cf. Zech. 2:13), that is, pour out His judgments upon the wicked, vindicate the sufferings of His own (Isa. 33:10), and set His own **in the safety for which he longs** (NASB; Psalms 34:6; 35:10).

6. The psalmist's faith in God's help is nurtured by the **words of the Lord**, which he declares to be **pure** (19:8, 10; 119:140), **like silver tested in a furnace . . . purified** (refined) **seven times**, that is, to the ultimate degree of purity (Prov. 30:5). **7.** The LORD will faithfully **keep them** (do what He promises to do in His Word). He will **preserve** (keep, protect) **him** (His own) **from this generation forever** (NASB), preserving him through his times of trouble, especially his dreadful foes during the Great Tribulation (Rev. 7:1-8, 14).

8. This "generation" is composed of **the wicked** who **walk** (strut about in impious arrogance) **on every side** (Psalm 55:10-11), at a time when **the vilest men are exalted** (Isa. 32:5; 2 Thess. 2:4; Rev. 13:4). What a frightening era, when **vileness is exalted among the sons of men** (NASB) and iniquity will come to the full (cf. Gen. 15:16), the same period when "the foundations" of morality and order "are destroyed" (Psalm 11:3, NASB).

M. THE TRIAL OF FAITH. 13:1-6.

This is a psalm of David that depicts the trial of his faith, and that of the saint of every age, but focuses upon the severe testing of Tribulation saints (see the introduction to Psalm 9).

The Psalmist Begins to Despair. 13:1-2. **1.** Prolonged suffering and persecution elicited the cry of distress, recorded four times: **How long . . . O Lord?** Patient endurance will be tested to the limit by the fierce persecution of the saints under the Antichrist (Rev. 13:1-18), and so in their anguish they will be tempted to think the LORD has forgotten them **forever** (Psalm 44:24; Rev. 6:10-11) and hidden His face in anger from them (Psalm 89:46). The psalmist's experience reflects the experiences of saints of every age, particularly those of the end time.

2. He asked how long he would **take counsel in** his **soul**, that is, ask himself concerning his dire sufferings, **having sorrow in** his **heart daily** (all day long). He inquired how long his enemies would be exalted over him. David knew such lively foes as Saul, and even his own son Absalom, but these prophetically prefigure the relentless and implacable enemies of the saints during the coming Tribulation.

The Psalmist Betakes Himself to Prayer. 13:3-4. **3-4.** He implored the LORD his God to consider and answer him (5:1), to enlighten his eyes (1 Sam. 14:29; Ezra 9:8; Job 33:30; Psalm 18:28), to show him His love and mercy, and to manifest His protecting care and concern, lest he **sleep the sleep of death**, that is, be slain by his enemies, or in the case of the Tribulation saints (Matt. 24:22), suffer martyrdom (Rev. 6:9-11; 7:14), lest his enemies conclude they **have prevailed against** him and **rejoice** over him as one **moved** from steadfast trust in God.

The Psalmist Gives His Testimony. 13:5-6. **5.** He protested his trust in God's mercy, despite the severe pressure his woes and foes had placed upon him to despair (cf. vv. 1-2; 52:8). **My heart shall rejoice in thy salvation** (9:14; 51:12). **6.** He was determined to **sing unto the Lord** because he realized that in spite of his temporary doubt, the LORD had **dealt bountifully** with him.

N. MAN'S WICKEDNESS REACHES ITS PEAK. 14:1-7.

Human Depravity in Full Manifestation. 14:1-6. This psalm describes the condition of the fallen race at large (Rom. 3:10-12). It reflects the moral conditions that will prevail at the time of Israel's great trouble before restoration to Kingdom blessing. The wickedness of that period will be characterized by four things: (1) **1a.** There will be vast rejection and rebellion against God. Society will be grossly secularized and permeated with **the fool**, who says **in his heart** (by his actions, if not by his lips), **There is no God** (Psalms 10:4; 53:1). He will not so much prate against the existence of God as he will atheistically bar Him from his actions and deeds.

(2) **1b.** There will be abysmal corruption, immorality, and abominable conduct (cf. Matt. 24:12, 37-38; Rev. 9:20-21). **1c.** So thorough is the moral and spiritual corruption that it is said, **There is none that doeth good** ("no, not one," v. 3*c*; cf. Psalm 130:3; Rom. 3:10-12). **2.** The LORD is graphically portrayed as looking down from heaven (Psalm 33:13-14) **upon the children of men, to see if there were any that did understand** (Rom. 3:11), **and seek God** (1 Chron. 22:19). **3.** All were found to have **turned aside** (NASB) and become universally corrupt.

(3) There will be relentless hatred and persecution of God's people. **4a.** The persecutors are called **workers of iniquity** (*pō'ălê 'āwĕn*, "practicers of vanity," traffickers in idolatrous occult religion; Rev. 9:20), who have **no knowledge** (Psalm 82:5) that they who touch the LORD's people touch "the apple of his eye" (Zech. 2:8) and incur the sternest divine displeasure. **4b.** Their violent treatment of the LORD's people is indicated graphically by the figure of eating

or devouring food: **Who eat up my people as they eat bread** (Jer. 10:25; Amos 8:4; Mic. 3:3).

At the same time their godlessness is underscored. **4c. And call not upon the Lord** (Psalm 79:6; Isa. 64:7). Their contempt for the Lord is reflected in their contempt for His people. **5.** This is going to result in their being **in great dread** (Rev. 6:15-17), when God's judgments are going to be poured out upon them (Rev. 8:1—19:21) for their misconduct toward His people, **for God is with the righteous generation** (NASB; Psalms 73:15; 112:2), that is, His justified people.

(4) The wicked will put to shame **the counsel of the poor** (the afflicted) by denying them equity and justice in their cause (42:3, 10). By contrast, the Lord is his (the afflicted one's) **refuge** (40:17; 46:1; 142:5).

Human Depravity Severely Curbed. 14:7. **7.** Will this eruption of human wickedness go on unchecked? Will not a better day than violence and wickedness dawn? It will come when **salvation will come out of Zion** (Rom. 11:26), when Israel's enemies are destroyed, the nation restored in Kingdom blessing, and the Messiah rules in righteousness with a rod of iron (Deut. 30:3; Psalm 2:7-9; Rev. 2:27; 19:15). Then **Jacob shall rejoice . . . Israel shall be glad** (Isa. 12:1-6; 35:1-10; Zeph. 3:14-20; Zech. 2:10-12).

O. THOSE WHO STAND BEFORE THE LORD. 15:1-5.

This is a psalm of David. For the scope of Psalms 9 to 15, see the introduction to Psalm 9.

The Question. 15:1. **1a. Lord, who shall abide in thy tabernacle?** (tent; 27:5-6; 61:4). **1b. Who shall dwell in** (on) **thy holy hill?** (Zion; 24:3). The question, accordingly, is: Who shall be permitted

to enter the Kingdom and enjoy the presence of the Lord when He appears in glory? The connection with the preceding psalm is obvious.

The Answer. 15:2-5. The character of the person here described, representative of all who enter the Messiah's Kingdom at His second advent, is that of a regenerated (born-again) person (John 3:3-5). No natural man could meet the six things that describe him: (1) **2a.** He **walketh** (lives) **uprightly** (with integrity; Psalm 24:4; Isa. 33:15). (2) **2b.** He **speaketh the truth in his heart** (not merely with his lips; Zech. 8:16; Eph. 4:25).

(3) **3.** He does not slander (Psalm 50:20) or do evil to his neighbor (Exod. 23:1; Lev. 19:18). (4) **4a-b.** In his estimation **a vile person** (a reprobate) **is despised** (Psalms 53:5; 73:20), but he honors those **who fear the Lord** (hold Him in godly reverence; Acts 28:10). (5) **4c-d.** He is absolutely honest, swearing to his own disadvantage if need be (Judg. 11:35), **and changeth not**, is not unstable or fickle in his moral convictions.

(6) **5a.** He is not covetous or greedy. He does not exact interest from his brother (Lev. 25:36-37), that is, a fellow Israelite (Exod. 22:25; Deut. 23:20). **5b.** Nor does he accept a **reward** (bribe) **against the innocent** (Exod. 23:8; Deut. 16:19). **He that doeth these things** manifests that he is saved and fit to enter the Kingdom and **shall never be moved** (shaken) from his integrity.

P. THE OBEDIENT ONE WHO PASSES THROUGH DEATH AND RESURRECTION. 16:1-11.

Psalms 16 to 24 form a cluster that constitutes a prophecy of the coming One, the Messiah-Savior. These odes are attributed to David, but David's experiences prefigure the greater David and His own as identified with Him. An interesting progression is also discernible in the Messianic revelation of this section, which culminates in the manifestation of the King, the LORD of glory in Psalm 24. Psalm 16 is a *Michtam* (cf. Psalms 56-60), perhaps meaning "a golden jewel" (Martin Luther).

The Obedient One. 16:1-3. In hearing David's voice there is discerned the greater voice of David's Son and Lord (110:1). This is indicated by Peter, who quoted this psalm and declared that David spoke of Christ (Acts 2:25-31). Therefore, Psalm 16 is the third specific Messianic psalm, Psalm 2 declaring the Messiah's sonship; Psalm 8 His future dominion as the Son of Man; and this psalm portraying His utter dependence upon God and His obedience to death, followed by His resurrection. David penned this portrayal as a prophet (Acts 2:30), and hence went beyond his own experience. Consequently, the voice heard in this ode is actually that of our Lord Himself in His deep humiliation and trust.

1. Preserve me, O God (Psalm 17:8), **for in thee do I put my trust** (*ḥāsîtî*, "I take refuge"; 7:1). **2-3. O my soul, thou hast said** means, "I said to the LORD," **Thou art my Lord** (Adonai); **my goodness is not to thee** ('*ăl*, "toward, unto thee," Heb. lit. trans.), meaning His obedience with all its self-abnegation as the incarnate One was not for Himself or His own profit, but for **the saints** (lit., "holy ones") **... in the earth ... the excellent** (noble) in whom was all His delight (Psalm 119:63).

His great love toward those who were to be constituted saints was the motive for His humiliation in becoming a servant and being obedient even to death. Those for whom He took the servant's place are already viewed as "saints" (i.e., saved; cf. Eph. 1:4) and "excellent," anticipating their certain glorification (Rom. 8:30).

4. They stand in contrast to those **who hasten after another god.** Despite the fact that there is only one God (1 Cor. 8:5-6), paganism had so-called "gods," such as Dagon and Baal. Then and now, whatever or whoever takes priority in the heart over the true God may be called a god (self, others, pleasure, etc.; 2 Tim. 3:2, 4). This verse describes the unsaved who reject Christ, either prospectively in Old Testament times by refusing to identify themselves as sinners shut up to God's salvation by bringing proper offerings, or retrospectively in New Testament times by failing to look back to Calvary and trust in Christ's death.

But specifically, in the prophetic context of the Psalms, it has special application to Israel in their rejection of Christ at His first advent (Matt. 27:25) and to the worst multiplication of their sorrows yet to come when they, during the Tribulation, will hasten **after another** (the beast; 2 Thess. 2:4; cf. Dan. 9:27). Those who reject Him have no share in His salvation and intercession.

The Path of the Obedient One. 16:5-8. **5a.** His voice again came to the fore: **The Lord is the portion of mine inheritance** (my assigned portion) **and of my cup.** In the LORD's case, His *portion*, what belonged to Him (73:26; 119:57; 142:5), and His *cup*, what He appropriated and made His own (23:5), were one—His joy was full. The LORD was the measure of both. He had and wanted nothing beside. How often in the case of His saints what we are in union with Him is so little realized in the measure of the cup of our enjoyment of it. How few really possess their possessions in Him. He, however, possessed fully His position of oneness with the Father.

5b. Thou maintainest my lot (125:3). He delighted in the truth that the Father was on His side and would maintain His right against all these wrongs of men. He had the abounding joy in the knowledge that His elect would be reserved for Him without the loss of one as His lot and eternal reward. So our joy should be full in contemplation of the fact that the Judge of all the earth will vindicate our righteous cause.

6. The lines are fallen unto me in pleasant places (78:55). The lines, the portion of land of the inheritance measured out by line, hence, "boundary lines," had fallen for Him in pleasant places, resulting in **a goodly heritage** (Jer. 3:19). Our Lord and all who have followed the way of obedience to God's will have found that it leads to pleasant places. No one was ever so thoroughly acquainted with grief yet experienced so much delight and joy in service as Christ (cf. Heb. 12:2). So His own in the pathway of obedience find light to illuminate the darkness and His presence to make the keenest suffering bearable. His "goodly heritage" lies in His redeemed, who will be with Him where He is and behold His glory (John 17:24). Our heritage will be to share His glory.

7. I will bless (extol) **the Lord, who hath given me counsel** (Psalm 73:24). He walked on earth in complete dependence upon the leading the LORD gave Him through His Word, which was His daily food (Matt. 4:4). **My heart** (lit., "reins, kidneys," figuratively used of the seat of the emotions and conscience; cf. Psalm 73:21-22) **instructs me in the night seasons.** These sessions alone with God in the desert appear prominently in Mark, the gospel of the Son of God, the

Servant (cf. Mark 1:12-13, 45; 6:31-32).

8. In retirement with God, He sought and found guidance in the Word of God, and so He could say, **I have set** (placed) **the Lord always before me** (Acts 2:25-28; Psalm 27:8). God's glory and will were His supreme goal and ever uppermost in His mind, ever at His **right hand**, the place of honor, because He always honored the Father. For this reason He could **not be moved** from His divine redemptive purpose and mission.

The Death and Resurrection of the Obedient One. 16:9-11. The four results of His complete devotion to God's will were: (1) **9a.** His heart was **glad**, and His **glory**, as the obedient Servant, rejoiced (4:7; 13:5). His was the shout of triumph over death and the grave (cf. 1 Cor. 15:51-56). (2) **9b.** His **flesh** (humanity, human body) rested (dwelt securely) **in hope** (Psalm 4:8). Faith in Christ's life, death, and resurrection not only imparts living joy, but bestows dying rest.

(3) **10.** His death was to be followed by the resurrection of His body. David's hope for eternity lay in Christ's resurrection, which he predicts here as a prophet (Acts 2:30-31). **For thou wilt not leave** (abandon) **my soul in sheol** (the realm of the dead where the soul and spirit of Christ went at His death; Psalms 49:15; 86:13), **neither wilt Thou allow Thy Holy One to see the pit** (NASB; undergo decay). "The pit" (*shāhăt*) is a synonym for Sheol, referring to the soul, and "corruption," referring to the body (Acts 13:35). "For David, after he had served his own generation . . . fell asleep . . . and saw corruption; but he, whom God raised again, saw no corruption" (13:36-37).

(4) **11.** Christ's resurrection was followed by His glorious ascension and installation at God's right hand. This was **the path of life** God made Him know

(Psalm 139:24; Matt. 7:14). This was God's **presence** of **fulness of joy** (Psalms 21:6; 43:4; Phil. 2:16-18; Heb. 12:2), which He would enjoy and make possible for all who would believe in His death and resurrection (1 Cor. 15:3-4) to enjoy also. This was the position of exaltation to which He was raised, at God's **right hand**, the place of supreme honor, where **there are pleasures for evermore** (Psalms 36:7-8; 46:4). And all who trust in Him follow Him through death and resurrection into God's own presence (Eph. 2:5-7).

Q. THE RIGHTEOUS INTERCESSOR. 17:1-15.

For the scope of this psalm, see the introduction to Psalm 16. It is entitled "a prayer of David," but it reaches beyond David's lips, or the lips of any saint, to the sinless lips of the greater than David. Jewish expositors detected the lofty moral claims of the intercessor and supposed that this psalm could not have been composed until after David's great sin. But at no time could David, even as a redeemed sinner, have claimed the full scope of this ode. It belongs to Another, who was "holy, harmless, undefiled, [and] separate from sinners" (Heb. 7:26), and who intercedes for the "saints ... in whom is ... [His] delight" (Psalm 16:3).

The Character of the Intercessor. 17:1-5. **1-2.** He called upon the LORD to **hear the right** (a just cause; 103:6), to **attend unto** (give attention to) His **cry** (61:1; 142:6), to **give ear unto** His **prayer**, **let** His **sentence** (judgment of vindication) come forth from the divine presence, and let God's eyes **behold the things that are equal** (what is equitable). Five things formed the basis upon which the One who prayed claimed that an answer be given: (1) He claimed perfection—His prayer went forth from

unfeigned lips, lips free of deceit (*mirmâ*, "falsehood, fraud"; cf. Isa. 29:13; John 8:46).

(2) **3a-c.** He claimed full testing and proof in trial (Psalm 26:1; cf. Matt. 4:1-10; Heb. 4:15; 12:3) and that God had **visited** Him (*pāqǎḏ*, dealt with Him in all the holy disciplines of sonship) and found **nothing** (i.e., sinful or lacking; Jer. 50:20; cf. Matt. 27:24; Luke 23:4, 14; John 18:38; 19:4, 6). (3) **3d.** He testified that He had purposed (determined) that His mouth should not transgress (Psalm 39:1; Isa. 53:7; Matt. 26:62-63; Mark 15:3-5; John 19:9; Acts 8:32-33).

(4) **4.** He declared that He walked in obedience to the Word of God, **the word of thy lips** (Psalm 119:9, 101), that is, that which came from the mouth and heart of God. (What a magnificent testimony to inspiration!) As a result, He **kept from** (kept guard against) **the destroyer** (course of the violent). (5) **5.** He maintained that His steps held fast to God's paths (lit., "tracks"), and so His **feet** had **not slipped** (NASB). Thus, David's prayer was prophetic of Christ's prayer, since he was a prophet (Acts 2:30).

His Prayer for Deliverance. 17:6-12. **6. I** (*'ǎnî*, emphatic, "As for me," such a One as described in vv. 1-5, David's Lord) **have called upon thee.** A marvelous prayer for His own, with whom He so perfectly identified Himself, follows. He prayed for three things: (1) **7.** He prayed for a demonstration of the Father's loving-kindness in delivering from their enemies those who put their trust in Him (cf. John 17:11, 14-15). (2) **8a.** He prayed to be kept **as the apple** (*'îshôn*, "little man, pupil"; Deut. 32:10; Zech. 2:8) **of the eye**, a most sensitive and precious part of the body. (3) **8b-11.** He prayed to be hidden (from harm and evil) **under the shadow of** His **wings** (Ruth 2:12; Psalms 36:7; 57:1; 61:4;

63:7; 91:1, 4; cf. John 17:15) from the wicked who despoil (Psalm 31:20), **deadly enemies** who **encompass** (surround) Him (27:12), who have **closed their unfeeling heart** (NASB), who **with their mouth . . . speak proudly** (1 Sam. 2:3; Psalms 31:18; 73:8), and who now surround **us** (pl., showing the identity of the LORD's own with their LORD) as the enemy is seen threatening God's people on earth, setting their eyes to cast them to the ground (Psalm 37:14).

12. The enemy is the evil one and those allied to him (cf. John 17:15). He is the adversary, the devil, and his own are those who go about **like a lion that is greedy of his prey** (eager to tear to pieces) and as a **young lion lurking in secret places** (waiting in ambush; cf. 1 Pet. 5:8). The Intercessor speaks as if praying for Himself, but actually His prayer is for the saints and their deliverance. And God hears and answers.

The Deliverance Assured. 17:13-15. **13.** The LORD is called upon to **arise** (3:7), **disappoint** (confront) the wicked, and **cast him down** (bring him low; 55:23). **14.** Contrasted is the portion of the saint (v. 15), who suffers at the hand of the wicked, and the portion of the wicked, who oppress the saint. Wicked men have **their portion in this life** (73:3-7; Luke 16:25). God fills their **belly** with His **treasure** (what He has stored up for them, Psalm 49:6). These worldlings are satisfied to leave their material wealth, which is all they have, to their posterity.

15a. In striking contrast, the saint has spiritual wealth that is imperishable, which comprehends not only fellowship with God in time, but God's presence in eternity (11:7; 16:11; 140:13; cf. 2 Cor. 3:18; Rev. 7:9, 15; 14:4). **15b.** He will be satisfied with God's likeness when he awakes (Num. 12:8), not excluding awakening from the sleep of death (Job 19:25-27; Psalm 16:10-11; Isa. 26:19;

Dan. 12:2; Hos. 13:14; 1 Cor. 15:51-53).

R. THE VICTORY SONG OF DAVID AND DAVID'S LORD. 18:1-50.

For the scope of this psalm (and Psalms 16-24), see the introduction to Psalm 16. While David's experiences are clearly seen, attested by the inscription itself, yet there are utterances and experiences reflected that can only be matched in the life of David's "seed" (posterity, v. 50) par excellence—the Lord Jesus Christ from heaven—His sufferings, His deliverances, His exaltation, and coming Kingdom. Those constitute the deeper prophetic meaning of this superb ode and link it contextually with Psalms 16 to 24. The psalm is also found with minor variations in 2 Samuel 22.

Persecutions and Sufferings to the Point of Death. 18:1-6. Looking back at those experiences from which the LORD had delivered him, David (and through him the greater David) protested his fervent love for the LORD for His great salvation (deliverance), which comprehended rescue from the jaws of death and exaltation to the throne by the power of God. **1-2.** Therefore, David called God his **deliverer . . . strength . . . the horn** of his **salvation**, and used metaphors emphasizing the LORD's protection—**rock . . . fortress . . . shield . . . high tower.**

3-4. David's prayer was directed toward the LORD, who is **worthy to be praised** (Rev. 5:12), and looked forward to the prayer of the Savior (Heb. 5:7), who similarly was encompassed by the **sorrows** (cords) **of death** (Psalm 116:3) and **the floods** (torrents) **of ungodly men** (Heb., *belial*, "ungodliness") that assailed him. **5.** The **sorrows** (cords) **of Sheol** surrounded him, and **the snares of death** confronted him. **6.** Both David and the greater David called upon the

767

LORD and were delivered from the jaws of death by God's power—David from physical death, and our Lord from the power of death through bodily resurrection (cf. Acts 2:24).

The Manifestation of God's Power. 18:7-15. These verses present a marvelous description of God's power exemplified in four ways: (1) in David's deliverance from death at the hands of his enemies, notably King Saul; (2) the deliverance of God's saints from their enemies in every age, particularly during the time of Jacob's fiercest suffering during the Great Tribulation (Jer. 30:5-7; Rev. 6:1—19:11); (3) the deliverance of the incarnate Son of God from death by His glorious conquest of it by resurrection (Acts 2:24); and (4) the deliverance of *all* saints from death at the translation or the first resurrection (1 Cor. 15:51-54; 1 Thess. 4:13-18).

The power of God is set forth in graphic figures like those describing the theophany at Mount Sinai when the Law was given (Exod. 19:16-18) and of that in Habakkuk's vision of the second advent of Christ (Hab. 3:3-15). **7-8.** Earthquake (Judg. 5:4; Psalm 68:7-8; Isa. 13:13; Hag. 2:6; cf. Matt. 27:45-51; Rev. 16:18-20) is expressive of the divine wrath (Psalm 114:4, 6; Rev. 16:1, 17-18), as are the **smoke** issuing from God's **nostrils** and **fire** out of His **mouth** (Psalm 50:3).

9-10. He is pictured bowing the heavens and coming down (144:5), with thick darkness under His feet (97:2), riding upon a **cherub** (80:1; 99:1), and speeding upon **the wings of the wind** (104:3). **11-15.** Darkness, clouds, storms, thunder, lightning, and hailstones are additional symbols of the divine indignation, which will be prominent in the apocalyptic judgments of the end of the age preceding Kingdom blessing (Rev. 6:1—19:16). While this part of the psalm illustrates the power that raised Christ from the dead (Eph. 1:19-21), it also carries the scene forward to the day of His visible manifestation in judgment of His enemies and His people, and His establishment in Kingdom glory.

Exaltation to Glory. 18:16-29. While David's conquest of all his enemies and his establishment on the throne of Israel furnish the historical background of this section, it in turn forms the backdrop of the Messianic prophecy that previsions the greater conquest by David's Lord and His exaltation at His second advent. That fact appears (1) from the context of this section of the psalm in relation to the psalm as a whole, and its connection with the other psalms (16-24), among which it is logically placed; and (2) from the internal evidence that transcends what could rightfully be applied morally and spiritually to David, even before his great sin (2 Sam. 11), and much more after it, when this psalm was most probably penned.

16-24. Accordingly, verses 16 to 19 speak prophetically of Christ's glorious victory over His enemies and His being brought **into a large** (broad) **place** (Psalms 31:8; 118:5) because God **delighted** in Him (cf. Matt. 3:17; Eph. 1:3-6). **20-27.** He **rewarded** Him **according to His righteousness; according to the cleanness of His hands** (cf. Phil. 2:9-11; Heb. 2:9; Rev. 5:13). Why did God give Him such glory? Because He rewards every man (the God-man as well) according to his works, that which He sees man to be. He recompensed Him because He was obedient, He was perfect, and He humbled Himself. **28-29.** Therefore, the LORD illuminated His darkness (Psalm 22:1) and caused Him to do exploits.

His Enemies Subdued. 18:30-42. As David's foes were utterly defeated, so the enemies of the greater David shall be utterly consumed (Rev. 19:11—20:3) because of seven reasons: (1) **30a.** Such subjugation is according to God's way and will, declared in His Word, which has been proved and tested by the Word incarnate and by generation upon generation of saints (Psalms 12:6; 119:140; Prov. 30:5). (2) **30b.** God is **a shield** to protect and give victory **to all those who trust in him** (take refuge in Him).

(3) **31.** God is the LORD, the only true God (Psalm 86:8-10; Isa. 45:5), and the only sure **rock** of protection and defense (v. 2; Psalm 62:2; Deut. 32:31). (4) **33.** God, who is omnipotent, girds His own with strength, makes their way perfect, and their feet like hinds' feet (Hab. 3:19), exalting them.

(5) **34.** He teaches His own to conduct warfare against his foes (Eph. 6:10-20; cf. Psalm 144:1; Rev. 19:11). (6) **35.** He gives His own the shield of His salvation (Psalm 33:20), His right hand upholds them, and His **gentleness** (condescension) makes them great. (7) **36.** He enlarges the steps of His own (18:33) so that their feet do not slip from His pathway of obedience.

37-42. David's lively portrayal of the destruction of his (and God's) enemies is graphically prophetic of the greater David, who will come to "judge and make war . . . with a vesture dipped in blood . . . out of [whose] mouth goeth a sharp [two-edged] sword, that with it he should smite the nations" (Rev. 19:11-15).

He Becomes Head of the Nations. **18:43-50. 43.** He is **delivered . . . from the strivings of the peoples** (2:1-3). He is made the **head of the nations** (2:8) as King par excellence and LORD par excellence (Rev. 19:16; 20:4). **44-45.** Homage and service, even from foreigners, shall be spontaneous, as was the case with David, but much more so

in the case of Christ at His second advent (Isa. 2:2-3; 66:23; Zech. 8:20-23; 14:16-21).

46-48. David praised and exalted **the God of** his **salvation** (deliverance) because He had executed vengeance for him and subdued the peoples under him. Again the prophetic foreview focuses on the victorious Christ, returning to slay the impious rebels of the military at Armageddon (Rev. 16:13-16) and the nonmilitary rebels of Israel (Matt. 25:11-12) and the nations before His millennial throne of glory (25:41-46).

49. This prospect calls for the highest praise to the LORD (2 Sam. 22:50; Rom. 15:9). **50. Great deliverance giveth he to his king . . . to David, and to his seed** (to all the justified of every age; Rom. 4:6-8), but principally and prophetically He gives it to the seed (posterity) of David (Matt. 1:1), the Son of David, the Lord Jesus Christ. He shows **mercy** (*ḥěsěd,* "loving-kindness, covenant grace") **to his anointed** (and to His Anointed) in fulfillment of the Davidic Covenant (see 2 Sam. 7:8-17).

S. THE REVELATION OF CHRIST THE CREATOR. 19:1-14.

By His Works. 19:1-6. **1. The heavens declare** (*mᵉsǎppᵉrîm,* are "telling, relating, making known, celebrating") **the glory of God** (*'ēl*), presenting Him as the mighty One in His role as Creator. The participle gives the sense of an emphatic present. The heavens present a continual witness to El, God of power and might, and to His "glory," which is the sum of His perfections. **The firmament** (*rāqîǎ',* "the expanse" of the sky stretching out above) **showeth** (*mǎggîd,* "makes known by declaring or announcing") **his handiwork**, literally, His "production," what He has made or created, His "work."

2. Day unto (after) **day uttereth** (*yǎb-*

bîă', "pours forth") **speech** as a stream of water flowing copiously for all humanity to know there is a Creator worthy of worship (Rom. 1:20-21). **Night unto (after) night showeth** (*yᵉhăwwĕh*, "announces, relates") **knowledge** concerning the Creator's "eternal power and Godhead" (Rom. 1:20) or deity (Col. 2:9).

3a. But the resplendently wonderful thing about the witness of the heavens, both in their nocturnal and daylight splendors, is that their speech is magnificently eloquent in its silence. They copiously pour forth **speech** (*'ōmer*), yet there is no audible "speech" (*'ōmer*). By day the sun rises and sets noiselessly, the clouds move and change hue imperceptibly. By night the moon and stars rise "silently one by one in the infinite meadows of heaven" (Longfellow). Yet what a grand symphony of praise they raise to the Creator.

3b. Their voice is not heard, yet how eloquently clear and loud their testimony goes forth to the power and glory of their Maker. **4a.** This proclamation of God's glory is universal. **Their line** (a measuring tape showing the extent of their influence) goes forth (*yṣ'*, "issues forth") **through all the earth** (cf. Rom. 10:18) **... to the end of the world,** for "God is concerned about the whole race of men, not simply a chosen few" (BBC, 3: 183). His book of natural revelation is therefore open and made plain to all men.

4b-5a. The **sun** is made prominent in this witness of creation, because it is symbolic of supreme authority ruling over the day (Gen. 1:16; cf. Rev. 12:1), and in its brightness is the source of light, its healing powers and splendor being used as a figure of Christ, "the sun of righteousness" who will "arise with healing in its [His] beams" to usher in the Kingdom age (Mal. 4:2, BV).

5b-6. Like a strong man to run a race, Christ will consummate God's plan and purpose for the ages (Heb. 12:1-2) and will realize the intense joy of His accomplishment (John 15:11). The heavens, which thus declare the glory of God, present a revelation of Christ in creation, for He created the celestial bodies (John 1:3; Col. 1:16; Heb. 1:3; 2:10).

By His Word. 19:7-11. Besides the witness of His works, there is the witness of God's Word, His written Word, here styled "the law of the LORD" (v. 7a), "the testimony of the LORD" (v. 7b), "the statutes of the LORD" (v. 8a), "the commandment of the LORD" (v. 8b), and "the judgments [ordinances] of the LORD" (v. 9, NASB). In David's day (c. 1011-971 B.C.), the Holy Scriptures consisted principally of the five books of Moses plus Joshua, Judges, Ruth, and some of the more ancient psalms, but the terms used anticipated the future *completed* canon.

The Word of God is described here in ten ways: (1) **7a.** It is **perfect** (*tāmîm*, "faultless," in the sense of being completely reliable as a moral and spiritual guide for God's people, and "complete" in the sense of being all we need to save us and lead us on in fellowship with God (119:160). (2) **7b.** It is **restoring to the soul** (NASB; 23:3; lit., "constantly drawing the soul back" from the incessant downward pull of sin).

(3) **7c.** It is **sure** (lit., "firm, faithful"; 93:5). (4) **7d.** It makes **wise the simple** (the foolishly credulous, the one susceptible to seduction to sin; 119:98-100; 2 Tim. 3:15). (5) **8a.** It is **right** (Psalm 119:128; *yāshār*, "straight, upright," in the sense of righteous, in line with God's will). (6) **8b.** It brings **rejoicing to the heart** (119:14; lit., "making the heart glad"). (7) **8c.** It is **pure** (*băr*, "clear, sincere," in the sense of being trans-

parently free of any taint to encourage sin).

(8) **8d.** It is **enlightening to the eyes,** imparting vision to see the worthwhileness of righteousness and goodness and to glimpse the unseen and the eternal (cf. 2 Cor. 4:18). (9) **9A.** It instills **the fear of the Lord**, godly reverence and reverential trust in the LORD, which abhors evil. (10) **9b.** It is **true and righteous altogether** (Psalm 119:138, 142). There is no admixture of error and, as given in the autographs, it is inerrant and absolutely trustworthy, being "inspired by God" (2 Tim. 3:16, NASB).

10a. God's Word is one of God's greatest gifts to mankind—more valuable and desirable than the finest gold (Psalm 119:72, 127). **10b.** It is **sweeter also than honey and** (the drippings of) **the honeycomb** (119:103).

Verses 11 to 14 indicate six aspects of the ministry of the Word of God: (1) **11a.** It warns God's **servant** against the treachery of sin (17:4). (2) **11b.** It encourages God's servant in righteous living by apprizing him of the **great reward** of such a life (24:5-6; Prov. 29:18; cf. 1 Cor. 3:11-16; 2 Cor. 5:10; Rev. 22:12).

(3) **12a.** It enables him to **understand** (discern) **his errors** (Psalms 40:12; 139:6), which otherwise would soon cause him to become callous to sin and fail to see his faults and mistakes. **12b.** In this ministry it reveals to God's servant his **secret** (hidden) **faults** (Heb. 4:12-13); thus, as a result of its "reproof" and "correction" (2 Tim. 3:16), the man of God may see his sin, confess it, and be cleansed (Psalm 51:1-2), that is, acquitted of the evil of which he might not otherwise even be cognizant (90:8; 139:23-24).

(4) **13.** It holds back God's servant from **presumptuous sins** (Num. 15:30), proud, impulsive sins that quickly be-

come habitual and gain **dominion** (mastery) **over** a believer, enslaving him so he can no longer serve God. Such sins, committed with a high hand as deliberate violations of God's Law, lead inevitably, if not faced and confessed, to **great transgression**, that is, the "sin unto [physical] death" (1 John 5:16), such as King Saul committed (1 Chron. 10:13-14; cf. 1 Cor. 5:5; 11:30). (5) **14a.** It enables **the meditation** of God's servant to be upon God's thoughts so that **the words** of his mouth as well as the thoughts of his heart (mind; Psalm 104:34) are **acceptable** in God's sight.

(6) **14b.** It causes him to appropriate all the redemptive grace and covenant love that the name "the LORD" (Jehovah, Yahweh) connotes (the name that appears six times in vv. 7-11), dealing with the revelation of Christ, the believer's **rock** (NASB; Psalm 18:2) and **redeemer** (*gō'ēl*; Psalm 31:5; Ruth 4:4, 6). Thus Psalm 19 is a presentation of Christ in creation (vv. 1-6) and in revelation through His Word (vv. 7-11). It serves as an introduction to the next five Psalms (20-24), which prophetically detail Christ more fully as Creator and Redeemer.

T. THE MESSIAH-KING AND HIS SALVATION. 20:1-9.

For the scope of this psalm, see the introduction to Psalm 16. The king (David) is presented in the sanctuary, offering there his sacrifices, while the people are assembled in the outer court, praying that the LORD will graciously accept the offerings and send him help and victory in battle. But prayer for King David ascends prophetically for the greater David, the coming Redeemer, King-Messiah, from the lips of the godly remnant of Israel.

A Prophetic Prayer for the King-Messiah. 20:1-4. **1a.** Petition ascends that the LORD would answer Him **in the day of trouble** as He faced "the power of darkness" (Luke 22:53), His persecutors and those who put Him to death (cf. 22:42). In Psalm 22:11 His own prayer is heard concerning that time of trouble—"Be not far from me; for trouble is near; for there is none to help."

1b. The answer to that prayer is recorded in the prophetic petition—**the name of the God of Jacob defend thee** (lit., "set you on high"), envisioning the Messiah-King's resurrection, ascension, and enthronement as the glorified Christ at God's right hand (Rom. 8:34; Eph. 1:20-21). The term "the God of Jacob" bespeaks God revealed in grace, which alone could take Jacob the supplanter and make of him an Israelite, a striver and prevailer with God (Gen. 32:27-28).

2. Send thee help from the sanctuary, where the Shekinah glory of God's presence was enthroned, and **strengthen thee** out of Zion, where the tabernacle was, both figures of the heavenly tabernacle of God's presence, whence the King-Messiah received His support.

3. His meal offerings and burnt offerings speak of that upon which His finished redemption rests, not only offering up prayer and tears (Heb. 5:7), but finally, His own sinless body as a sacrifice for sin. So God remembers as He surveys the eternally sufficient burnt offering and displays His infinite divine grace. **Selah** may mean "a pause, crescendo, or musical interlude." **4. Grant thee according to thine own heart** (i.e., "your heart's desire"; Psalm 21:2) **and fulfill all thy counsel** (purpose, plan), for in the case of the King-Messiah they will be in complete agreement with God's plan and redemptive purpose (40:8-9; 145:19).

Celebration of the Deliverance of the King-Messiah and His People. 20:5-6.

5a. We will rejoice in ("shout for joy over") **thy salvation,** here in the sense of "triumphant victory" (9:14; cf. 1 Cor. 15: 51-57). **5b. Banners,** symbols of victory, will be set up (Psalm 60:4). **5c. The Lord fulfill all thy petitions** (1 Sam. 1:17), including "Thy kingdom come, Thy will be done in earth, as it is in heaven" (Matt. 6:10) as the Kingdom is restored to Israel (Acts 1:6) at the second advent.

6a. Now know I that the Lord saveth his anointed, when He destroys earth's rebels (Psalm 2:1-5, 9) and sets "his anointed" (2:2) on His "holy hill of Zion" (2:6). **6b.** Then **he will hear from his holy heaven** (Isa. 58:9; Rev. 8:1; 15:5-8), **with the saving strength of his right hand** (Psalm 28:8), ushering in the cataclysmic judgments that will purge out sinners from Israel and the nations preparatory to setting up the Messiah's Kingdom (Matt. 25:1-46; Rev. 6:1—10:11).

Deliverance of the King-Messiah's People, Israel. 20:7-9. **7a. Some trust in chariots, and some in horses** (Deut. 20:1; Psalm 33:16-17; Prov. 21:31), describing the enemies of the LORD and His people. They gloried in the arm of flesh, as did even Israel when in the blindness of sin and unbelief. **7b.** But now all is changed. They will then have turned to the LORD (i.e., the believing sector of the nation) and will cry, **But we will remember** (lit., "make mention of"; i.e., "boast in") **the name of the Lord our God** (2 Chron. 32:8). They behold God's enemies and theirs brought down and fallen (Rev. 19:11—20:3).

8. They cry, **But we are risen, and stand upright** (Psalm 37:24; Ezek. 37:10-14; Mic. 7:8). The true believing Israel will rise out of the dust of their long spiritual and national death and stand upright in the presence of their Redeemer-Savior-King-Messiah. **9.**

Save, Lord; let the king hear us when we call. This will be a prayer of the godly Jewish remnant of the last days, when they anticipate "the time of Jacob's trouble" and cry to their King to soon appear so they will be "saved out of it" (cf. Jer. 30:5-7).

U. THE MESSIAH-KING'S GLORY ANTICIPATED. 21:1-13.

For the scope of this psalm, see the introduction to Psalm 16.

His Power and Glorious Salvation. 21:1-6. David's kingly glory furnishes the historical background of this psalm; but, like the preceding and succeeding psalms (16-24), it anticipates the greater David's reign as "KING OF KINGS" (Rev. 19:16), when He returns in glory to set up His Kingdom in fulfillment of the Davidic Covenant (2 Sam. 7:8-17). This ode immediately presents the King in six ways:

(1) **1.** He is presented as having entered "the joy" set before Him as a consequence of His enduring the cross (Heb. 12:1-2), and having passed through resurrection to glory on high and in public manifestation of power in His return to earth in Kingdom blessing. So the King is pictured prophetically as rejoicing in the LORD's **strength** as His Anointed (Psalm 59:16-17) and greatly rejoicing in His salvation ("triumphant victory" over His enemies; Rev. 19:11—20:3).

(2) **2.** He is presented as having been given **his heart's desire** (Psalms 20:4; 37:4), namely, the salvation and deliverance of His people, made possible by His incarnation and death and granted **the request of his lips** (Matt. 6:9-13; cf. John 17:1-26), especially the petition of Psalm 2:8, "Ask of me, and I shall give thee the nations for thine inheritance, and the uttermost parts of the earth for thy possession" (cf. 2 Sam. 7:26-29).

(3) **3.** He is presented as having been met with the **blessings of goodness** ("good things"), proceeding from the Davidic Covenant and culminating in the Messiah-King's coronation as "KING OF KINGS" (Rev. 19:16; 20:6), His **crown of pure** (fine) **gold** (cf. 2 Sam. 12:30) speaking of His right to rule by virtue of His glorified humanity forever joined to His deity (gold), as the Godman (cf. Psalm 2:6-7).

(4) **4.** He is presented as having been given life—eternal life. **He asked life of thee** (61:5-6), **and thou gavest it him, even length of days forever and ever.** He asked for life when He faced death "with strong crying and tears" of "him that was able to save him from death, and was heard" (Heb. 5:7) in that God raised Him from the dead, so that now He lives forever and ever (cf. 2 Sam. 7:29) in His glorified body. As the triumphant, divine-human sin-bearer, He received eternal life. As such, He is head of the new creation, and in Him all who are born again share eternal life, His very own life procured for fallen humanity under sentence of death.

(5) **5.** He is presented as having been given glory. **His glory is great** in the LORD's salvation. It is the result of His suffering and death to procure salvation. It is in addition to the glory He had with the Father from all eternity (John 17:5), or the glory He now possesses in the salvation of countless multitudes who have trusted Him and in whom He has His inheritance of glory (Eph. 1:7-11). It is the glory that will be His at His second advent "in his glory" to "sit upon the throne of his glory" (Matt. 25:31). The psalmist foresaw this coming glory and cried: **Honor and majesty hast thou laid upon him.**

(6) **6.** He is presented as having been

773

made **most blessed forever ... exceeding glad with thy countenance.** It is the full realization of "the joy ... set before him" as He faced the suffering and death of the cross (Heb. 12:2).

His Triumph over His Enemies. 21:7-13. Again the prominent prophetic theme appears, envisioning the complete overthrow of the Messiah's enemies when He returns to earth to set up His Kingdom (the theme of the book of the Revelation, 6:1—20:3; cf. Psalm 2:9-12). **7a.** This victory is assured because the Messiah-King completely **trusteth in the Lord** (*bṭḥ*, probably with the Arabic root idea of "casting oneself down upon the face" in the sense of "completely reposing oneself upon another," BDB, p. 105).

7b. And through the mercy (*ḥĕsĕḏ*, "covenant love," reflected in the Davidic Covenant of kingship, 2 Sam. 7:8-17) **of the Most High he shall not be moved** to doubt or turn aside from its gracious and glorious promises. "The Most High" presents the LORD as the "possessor of heaven and earth" (Gen. 14:19, 22), "the Lord of the whole earth" (Zech. 4:14; 6:5; Mic. 4:13; Rev. 11:4). This embraces "the revelation of Messiah as King-Priest of the Most High exercising the restored dominion of the earth ... by virtue of His finished redemption" (M. F. Unger, *Zechariah*, p. 81).

While verse 7 presents the reason for the victory, verses 8 to 13 detail its results. The enemies of the LORD's people will be completely exterminated. **8-9a.** The King's hand will **find out all** His **enemies**, destroying them as a fiery oven burns up what is placed in it. **9b.** The LORD will **swallow them up in his wrath** (Mal. 4:1; Luke 21:23; Rev. 6:16-17; 11:18; 16:19; 19:15). **9c. Fire shall devour them** (Psalm 50:3; Rev. 8:7; 9:17; 14:18; 16:8; 18:8; 19:12). **10. Their fruit** (offspring) **shalt thou destroy from the**

earth ... **their seed** (posterity) **from among** mankind (Psalm 37:28; Rev. 6:15-17; 9:18; 19:17-21).

11. Their evil intent against the LORD (Psalm 2:1-3) and their **mischievous device** are to dispossess the LORD and His Anointed from the earth, which is the LORD's by right, both of creation (Psalm 24:1-2; Rev. 4:11) and redemption (Eph. 1:14). Their folly will come to a head at Armageddon (Rev. 16:13-16), where the Antichrist and his armies will have the insensate notion of ousting God and taking over the earth (Rev. 19:19). **12.** The rebels will not succeed, for the LORD will **make them turn their back** and aim with His bowstrings at their faces, utterly destroying them (cf. Rev. 19:20-21).

13. This verse records a prophetic prayer that this great triumph will be consummated. **Be thou exalted, Lord, in thine own strength.** When he is exalted, redeemed, and restored, Israel will **sing and praise** His **power** (cf. Isa. 12:1-6; 35:10; 65:19), as will saved Gentiles who enter the Kingdom (Matt. 25:34-40; cf. Isa. 2:2-3; Zech. 8:21-23).

V. CHRIST'S SUFFERINGS AND COMING GLORY. 22:1-31.

For the scope of this psalm, see the introduction to Psalm 16. Psalms 22, 23, and 24 form a trilogy. Psalm 22 presents the *good* Shepherd giving His life for the sheep (John 10:11). Psalm 23 shows the *great* Shepherd, "brought again from the dead" (Heb. 13:20), tenderly caring for the sheep. Psalm 24 prophetically portrays the *chief* Shepherd coming as the King of glory to reward His sheep (1 Pet. 5:4). Psalm 22 is inscribed "To[for] the chief Musician [precentor] upon Aijeleth Shahar" (lit., "The Hind of the Morning"), referred in Jewish tradition to the Shekinah glory, symbolizing "the dawn of redemption."

The dawning of the morning is compared with the horns of a hind, since the first rays of dawn appear like horns. According to this ancient tradition, a lamb was sacrificed as soon as the sentinel on the pinnacle of the Temple glimpsed the first rays of the morning light. Whatever may be the precise significance of "The Hind of the Morning" (perhaps the title of a tune to which the song was to be sung, BBC, 3: 189), the blessed subject of this most marvelous prophetic ode is the dawning of redemption through Him who is the Lamb of God and is attributed to David, who was a prophet par excellence (Acts 2:30), but everything in it transcends David or any mere mortal.

Christ's Sufferings and Death Foretold. 22:1-21. Only the Holy Spirit speaking through David could reveal the unfathomable depths plumbed here of the sufferings of Christ and the glories to follow (cf. 1 Pet. 1:10-12) and present one of the completest portraits of Christ's passion as the pathway to His glory found anywhere in the Word. Our Lord's utterance from the cross of the solemn opening words: "My God, my God, why hast thou forsaken me?" (Matt. 27:46; Mark 15:34) gives the most conclusive evidence that He is the subject of this psalm. Moreover, the glory side of this prophetic gem (vv. 22-31) furnishes unmistakable proof that none other than the promised Messiah-Redeemer is meant.

First presented is the spiritual suffering of Christ (vv. 1-10), then His physical agonies (vv. 11-21). Christ's spiritual suffering involved five things: (1) **1a.** His suffering involved being forsaken (abandoned) by God. He who was God, being forsaken by God, comprehends the stupendous miracle of the incarnation of the Creator in order to become the Redeemer, when God "made him, who knew no sin, to be sin for us" (2 Cor. 5:21). He who on earth could say, "I am not alone" (John 8:16,

29) was left alone when He became our sin-bearer and as the spotless One bore the sins of the fallen race and the consequent wrath of the all-righteous God, who turned away His face from Him in that dark hour.

(2) **1b.** From God's side, the suffering the Savior endured was the heart of His atoning work. Hence, it occupies the foreground in the prophecy and involves the infinite aspect of His agony that He alone, as the sinless One, could experience. **Why ... so far from helping me, and from the words of my roaring?** This strong word suggests infinite depths of suffering, calling forth plaints like the roaring of a lion. Other men may have suffered as much (or more) physically as our Savior, but none could ever experience the quintessence of His pain, because none but He of Adam's fallen race was sinless, and none but He took upon His holy soul all the sin of the race and faced its horror as the spotless One when darkness overwhelmed Him as the Father turned away His face as He became the sin offering to be consumed by the fire of the wrath of the all-holy, sin-hating God.

(3) **2.** Despite His intense appropriation of God's presence and help ("My God" uttered three times), He was nevertheless abandoned and left completely bereft of the divine presence and aid in the terrible hours of suffering in Gethsemane (Luke 22:39-46) and on Golgotha's brow. **O my God, I cry in the daytime, but thou hearest not; and in the night season ... am not silent.**

(4) **3.** The answer to the *why* of the divine abandonment of the Sufferer is found in the infinite holiness of God. **But thou art holy** (Psalm 99:9; infinitely holy; Isa. 6:3; Rev. 4:8). As the sin-bearer of the world, the Substitute for sinners, the sin-abhorring God **who inhabitest** (*yshḇ*, "is seated," "enthroned upon") **the praises of Israel** (Psalm

775

148:14) as "the Holy One of Israel" (*qāḏôsh*, "separate" or "set apart" from sin, Isa. 1:4; 5:19, etc., many times in Isaiah), could only turn away from the One "made . . . sin for us, that we might be made the righteousness of God in him" (2 Cor. 5:21).

(5) **4-5.** His spiritual suffering was rendered more acute as He considered how His fathers (according to the flesh) **trusted** and God delivered them (Psalms 78:53; 107:6), while He, despite His intense faith (cf. *My* God, three times in vv. 1-2), faced not only God's silence, but also the jeering taunts of men concerning God's apparent abandonment of Him (vv. 6-9).

6-8. So distressful were this aloneness and the agony of separation from God's presence that He accounted Himself less than human, reduced to such depths of anguish that He considered Himself **a worm** (Job 25:6; Isa. 41:14), whom God would not answer or help, **a reproach . . . despised by the people** (Psalm 109:25; Matt. 27:39-44), who laughed Him to **scorn**, insolently deriding Him for His trust in God, and God's apparent abandonment of Him (Matt. 27:43).

(6) **9-10.** In this awful experience of darkest woe, as the face of God turned away from Him, He recalled the miracle of His birth (Psalm 71:5-6; Matt. 1:18-25; Luke 1:26-35; 2:1-7), and how God caused Him to trust even as a babe upon His mother's breast, and how He was cast on God from His birth (Isa. 46:3; 49:1; Matt. 2:13-23).

Having foretold Christ's spiritual suffering (vv. 1-10), the psalmist prophetically glimpsed in the most remarkable detail the physical sufferings of the coming Savior-Redeemer, who had been promised at the dawn of redemptive history (Gen. 3:15). As He faced the physical ordeal, the suffering One prayed for the divine presence, the loss of which had been the most terrible part of His passion. **11. Be not far from me; for trouble is near . . . none to help** (Psalm 71:12).

Then follows a detailed prophecy of the crucifixion scene, with the following features described: (1) **12.** The Sufferer was surrounded by enemies, metaphorically pictured as angry **bulls** ready to gore Him with their horns; **strong bulls of Bashan** were from the rich pastureland east of the upper Jordan, famed for its cattle (Deut. 32:14; Amos 4:1). **13.** By a change of figure the enemies are portrayed as ravening lions, roaring for prey (Psalms 10:9; 17:12).

(2) The Sufferer endured the agonies of crucifixion—excessive dehydration of the body by perspiration and loss of blood. **14a.** He was **poured out like water** (Job 30:16; Matt. 27:48). **14b.** All His **bones** were **out of joint** (Psalm 31:10; Dan. 5:6). His heart was **like wax** (Psalm 73:26; Josh. 7:5; Nah. 2:10), the action of the heart seriously affected.

15-17. His strength **dried up like a potsherd** (clay baked in an oven or dried in the sun) (Psalm 38:10). He was extremely thirsty, with His **tongue** sticking to His **jaws**, resulting in physical **death** (Psalm 104:29; Matt. 27:50), the piercing of **hands** and **feet** (Matt. 27:35; but cf. John 20:20), extreme emaciation (v. 17*a*), nudity, and shameful exposure (v. 17*b*).

18. The casting of lots (Matt. 27:35) is another striking feature of the scene at Calvary. How wonderful is the evidence of inspiration in this psalm, especially when it is remembered that crucifixion was a Roman, not a Jewish, form of execution. Yet the Spirit of prophecy previsioned the details of this most inhuman practice.

19-20a. Again the Sufferer called for God's presence (cf. v. 11) and help (Psalm 70:5), pleading deliverance **from**

the sword. This prayer was answered, for He willingly yielded up His spirit (Matt. 27:50; John 10:17-18), the Roman sword piercing Him only *after* He had already died for the sin of the world as an act of obedience to God's will; yet He had to be so pierced to fulfill God's Word (John 19:34-37).

20b. The Sufferer also prayed, **Deliver ... my darling** (KJV; "my lonely self," BV, referring to His aloneness in suffering) **from the power of the dog** (perhaps a figurative prophetic reference to pagan Rome, whose governor condemned Jesus and whose soldiers officiated at the crucifixion, since Gentiles were viewed as "dogs" by Jews (Matt. 7:6; 15:26). "The assembly of the wicked" (v. 16) refers to wicked Jews.

21. The Sufferer also prayed to be saved (delivered) **from the lion's mouth** (cf. 1 Pet. 5:8; 2 Tim. 4:17), that is, from death that would be by demonic power working through Jewish hate and Roman power instead of by the will of God. Then God's silence (vv. 1-10) was broken. He heard. He answered **from the horns of the wild oxen** (their strong horns are symbolic of the mighty power of God released to raise the Sufferer from the dead; Eph. 1:19-23).

Christ's Resurrection and Glory Foretold. 22:22-31. The Spirit of prophecy in David declared five things about the glory that would follow the sufferings and death of the Redeemer to come: (1) **22a.** In the foreview of this glory appears the forsaken One, answered by God in His resurrection from the dead, making known God's name (all that God is in grace, love, goodness, etc.) to His **brethren** (brothers), and praising God in the midst of the congregation (*qāhāl*, "assembly"), a reference to the New Testament church, which was a hidden truth in the Old Testament, not to be revealed till the

Messiah's death and resurrection (Eph. 3:1-10; cf. Heb. 2:11-12).

On the day of His resurrection, He gave the joyful message, "But go to my brethren, and say unto them, I ascend unto my Father and your Father, and to my God and your God" (John 20:17). Two great truths emerge. First, He speaks of His disciples as "my brethren" (in anticipation of His death and resurrection, Matt. 12:50, but actually only after these great events, Heb. 2:11). Second, He declared a new relationship to be effected in all who believe and who are brought into the blessings of His atoning work on the cross—"my Father ... your Father ... my God ... your God."

(2) **22b.** The glory includes His position **in the midst of the congregation** (the church) where the resurrected glorified One is (Rev. 1:13; 2:1), where He sings praises (Heb. 2:11-12), that is, through the Spirit's ministry. (3) His glory expands. **23.** All who **fear the Lord** will include Gentiles saved during the end-time Tribulation and the Kingdom. **The seed of Jacob** are Jews saved during that time of trouble, and the **seed of Israel** are saved Jews during the Kingdom age. (4) His glory will be enhanced by His matchless person and character. **24.** He has not **despised ... the affliction of the afflicted** nor **hidden his face** from the needy and the distressed.

(5) The glory embraces His receiving the Kingdom at His second advent (Rev. 20:4-9), guaranteed by the Davidic Covenant (2 Sam. 7:8-17; cf. Psalm 2:6-12) and realized by the glorified Son of Man (vv. 25-28). **25.** He declared that His **praise** (the praise given Him) was **of thee** (*mē'ēṯ*, "from Him," i.e., God) **in the great congregation** (assembly of millennial nations), where He says, **I will pay my vows,** the vows of praising God and making known

His name (cf. Psalm 109:30).

26-29. Closely connected with the paying of the vows is the declaration that **the meek** (Matt. 5:5) **shall eat** (Luke 22:16; John 6:51-58; 1 Cor. 11:26) until they are **satisfied.** Eating was connected with the peace offering (Lev. 7:11-20). Through Him who through death fulfilled every offering that foreshadowed His redemptive work and paid His vows, a feast is spread to which all may come and be satisfied (cf. Isa. 25:6-7; and the glory side of Isa. 53:10-12): **All they that are fat** (i.e., prosperous) **... shall eat and worship.**

There will be universal recognition of Christ's redemptive work, and **the ends of the earth shall ... turn unto the Lord**, for the **kingdom** will be His (Rev. 11:15), and He will rule over **the nations** (Psalm 47:7; Obad. 21; Zech. 14:9; Rev. 19:16; 20:4). In His exaltation, every knee shall bow before Him (Isa. 45:23; Phil. 2:5-11) in forced submission, even those who have gone down to the dust of death in unbelief and rebellion. They will have to acknowledge Him who Himself did not shun death to effect man's redemption. But this does not mean they will be saved; they merely must acknowledge Him as Savior and Lord. **30-31. A seed shall serve him** (cf. Isa. 53:10-11) **... shall declare his righteousness** to unborn generations **that he hath done this** —wrought the wonderful redemption and glory proceeding from it.

W. CHRIST THE GREAT SHEPHERD.
23:1-6.

For the scope of this psalm of David, see the introductions to Psalms 16 and 22. The great Shepherd of Psalm 23 is the Good Shepherd who passed through death and resurrection (Psalm 22) to make available the blessings of the psalm to all who trust in His completed redemption. The psalm, therefore, has application to (1) the redeemed of the precross era, like Abraham (Gen. 15:6; Rom. 4:1-5) and David (Psalm 32:1-2; Rom. 4:6-11), who believed God and were saved in view of the coming Redeemer (Rom. 3:24); (2) the New Testament church saints; (3) Tribulation and millennial saints; (4) and with particular emphasis upon future restored and converted Israel (cf. Gen. 48:15; 49:24; Psalms 80:1-12; 95:7; Isa. 40:11; Mic. 7:14; Ezek. 34:11-13), the Shepherd of Israel being rejected by His own people at His first advent (Zech. 13:7), thus nullifying any claim to the blessings of this psalm, as do all who do not believe in the death and resurrection of the Good Shepherd.

The Blessings the Believer May Claim. 23:1-3. The believer may claim six blessings: (1) He may claim the shepherdhood of the LORD. **1a. The Lord is my shepherd** (Psalm 78:52; Jer. 31:10; John 10:11; 1 Pet. 2:25). Unbelievers may have false shepherds or lay invalid claim to the one true Shepherd, but the psalmist had the deep-seated assurance that the LORD, the eternal One, the God of redemptive grace and covenant love, was *his* Shepherd, whom he appropriated as his very own with a deep, abiding faith.

(2) Therefore, he may claim, with confident and unwavering assurance, the full sufficiency of the Shepherd's tender care. **1b. I shall not want** (34:9-10), literally, "I shall not lack [be deficient in] anything." In His "so great salvation" (Heb. 2:3) and in His tender Shepherd's care, He fully provides for all the needs of His sheep. All we need is found in Him. When we say, "The LORD is *my* Shepherd," it means the end of all our cares and anxieties (Phil.

778

4:6-7) and the supply of all our needs (4:19), issuing in the happy testimony, "I lack nothing."

(3) The believer may claim rest and refreshment. **2a. He maketh me to lie down in green pastures** (*bin'ôt dĕshĕ'*, "in meadows of tender herbage" (65:11-13; Ezek. 34:14). While He supplies rest, not only physical and mental, but most important and crucial, spiritual rest (Matt. 11:28), both "peace with God" (Rom. 5:1) and the very "peace of God" surpassing all understanding (Phil. 4:7) will keep (guard or garrison) your hearts (emotional life) and minds (mental life) against worry, pressure, and tension.

(4) The believer may claim guidance. **2b. He leadeth me beside the still waters** (*me' mᵉnŭḥôt*, "waters of deep quietness"; 36:8; 46:4), with emphasis on deep tranquillity of these waters, thus stressing the matchless restfulness that results where the believer yields to the Shepherd's guidance (cf. 1 Tim. 2:2).

(5) The believer may claim spiritual renewal. **3a. He restoreth my soul** (19:7; 51:12; Gal. 6:1). He turns the sheep back to the green pastures and the still waters when it yields to its ever present proneness to wander away to a place of peril (cf. 1 John 1:9; 2:1-2).

(6) The believer may claim guidance. **3b. He leadeth** (guides) **me** (5:8; 31:3) **in the paths of righteousness** (85:13; Prov. 4:11; 8:20; cf. John 14:18; 16:12-13). So crucial is the matter of divine guidance that it is presented under two aspects. The Shepherd goes ahead to lead the sheep to the green pastures and still waters. But He is present to guide the sheep past the steep cliff or through the rushing torrent or through the narrow defile, where the helpless lamb might make the wrong turn and land in disaster (25:9; 32:8; 48:14; 73:24; Isa. 58:11).

The Comfort the Believer May Appropriate. 23:4-6. The believer may appropriate six things: (1) He may have the divine companionship. **4a. Yea, though I walk through the valley of the shadow of death** (Job 3:5; 10:21-22; 24:17; Psalm 44:19; cf. Rev. 1:18). **4b. I will fear no evil** (harm) (Psalm 27:1). **4c. For thou art with me** (Psalm 16:8; Isa. 43:2; cf. Matt. 28:20; John 14:18). "The valley of the shadow of death" includes not only the experience or the near-experience of death (1 Thess. 4:13-18; 1 Cor. 15:51-53), but any "valley of deep darkness," when God seems to be far away and fear is most likely to appear as a frightful specter. In such exigencies His presence is guaranteed the believer in order to rout fear.

(2) He may have the divine comfort. **4d. Thy rod** (Mic. 7:14) **and thy staff . . . comfort me.** The rod and staff were used in directing the sheep to pasture or water, and in fighting off attacking wild beasts; so they were symbols of comfort and assurance to the sheep.

(3) He may have the divine supply of food and fellowship. **5a. Thou preparest a table before me in the presence of mine enemies** (78:19; 104:15). This is reminiscent of the Lord's table with its bread and wine, mementoes of the love of the Good Shepherd, who died for the sheep and will return to claim them as His own and share His victory with them (1 Cor. 11:26; 2 Cor. 5:10). Thus, the table becomes a symbol of His victory over His and our foes (Rev. 19:11—20:3) as well as over our present enemies (Rom. 8:31-34).

(4) He may have the divine impartation of overflowing spiritual power and joy. **5b. Thou anointest my head with oil** (45:7; 92:10; Eccles. 9:8; Luke 7:46). **5c. My cup runneth over** (16:5). (5) He may have the divine provision for every

blessing in time. **6a. Surely goodness and mercy shall follow me** (*rdp*, "pursue me vigorously") **all the days of my life** upon earth (25:7). (6) He may have the divine provision for every blessing in eternity. **6b. And I will dwell in the house of the Lord forever** (lit., "for length of days"; 27:4-6; cf. John 14:2-3; Rev. 7:15-17; 14:4; 21:3-4; 22:3-5, 14).

X. CHRIST THE CHIEF SHEPHERD. 24:1-10.

For the scope of this psalm, see the introductions to Psalms 22 and 23. It is a psalm of David.

The Citizens of the Messiah's Kingdom. 24:1-6. Since this psalm portrays the chief Shepherd coming as the King of glory to set up His Kingdom of righteousness and peace, His title of ownership of the earth by creation (and redemption) is stressed. **1a. The earth is the Lord's.** His possession is emphasized in contrast to the claims of His foes, the rebellious hordes at Armageddon (2:1-3; Rev. 16:13-16; 19:19). **1b.** Not only the earth (1 Cor. 10:26, 28) is His, but also **the fullness thereof** (all it contains), **the world, and they who dwell therein** (Psalm 89:11).

2. The reason is that He made it and **founded it upon the seas . . . established it upon the floods** (rivers), creating it so that man's life upon it is sustained by the miracle of evaporation from the oceans and condensation from clouds to cause rain. The question in verses 3 to 6 is: Who is going to rule the earth—the Antichrist and his God-defying hordes (Psalm 2:1-3; Rev. 13:1-10; 16:13-16), or the true Christ, the Creator and Redeemer of the earth? It is a question of worthiness, and no one is worthy but the Lamb who redeemed the earth (Eph. 1:13-14) by His redemptive work (cf. Dan. 7:13-14; Matt. 25:31; Rev. 5:1-10). **3. Who shall ascend into the hill of the Lord?** Only He of whom God said, "Yet have I set my king upon my holy hill of Zion" (Psalm 2:6). Only He who is "holy, harmless, undefiled, separate from sinners" (Heb. 7:26) shall stand in His holy place (Psalm 65:4; Deut. 12:5) and exercise His millennial role of King-Priest (Psalm 110:4; Zech. 6:13).

But since His redeemed will be identified and glorified with Him (Rom. 8:30) and share His millennial rule and dominion, verses 4 and 5 also comprehend His own associated with Him in glory (Rev. 3:21; 20:4-6), as well as the saved and unglorified Jews and Gentiles who will survive the Tribulation and enter the Kingdom (7:1-17; 20:4). **Who shall stand in his holy place?** (Isa. 2:2-3). The reference is to the great millennial Temple to be built; it will be filled with the glory of the LORD (Ezek. 40:1—47:12), and be a mecca for worship in the millennial earth.

4-6. Clean hands . . . a pure heart (Matt. 5:8) belong only to the sinless Redeemer, whose own infinite righteousness is imputed to the redeemed by the God of His and their salvation when they are born again (John 3:3-5) and thus receive the credentials for Kingdom entry. These born-again saints of the Tribulation period will be **the generation of them** who will **seek** God as the God of Jacob, who in His redemptive grace will transform them from their scheming Jacob role into Israel, a contender and prince with God (Gen. 32:28), to be resplendent in God's salvation and worldwide blessing in their millennial role (cf. Zech. 8:20-23) when Jerusalem becomes the capital and religious center of the earth (Isa. 2:2-3; 66:23; Zech. 14:16-21).

The King in Glorious Manifestation in His Kingdom. 24:7-10. He who comes in glory as King and Lord (Rev. 19:16), to take possession of the earth

(vv. 1-2), is seen doing so as He enters His "holy hill of Zion" (Psalm 2:6), "the hill of the LORD," to assume His kingly office and to "stand in his holy place" (24:3) in the millennial Temple to assume His priestly role.

Tradition claims that this psalm was composed to celebrate the bringing of the ark from Kirjath-jearim to Mount Zion (2 Sam. 6:1-23) and doubtlessly sung antiphonally. Josephus says seven choirs preceded the ark and chanted the psalm. When the King of glory enters Zion as the great Conqueror (Isa. 63:1-3; Rev. 19:11-16), the entry of the greater David will be a fulfillment of the day when David conquered the ancient stronghold and the gates of Zion were opened to let him in.

7. Now the **King of glory** (1 Cor. 2:8), the all-conquering Christ, is to enter. The gates and doors, so long shut against Him, are now commanded to open wide and admit Him, for He has vanquished every foe (Rev. 19:11—20:3). **8.** Then the cry will ascend, **Who is this King of glory?** The antiphonal choir will respond, **The Lord strong and mighty** (Psalm 96:7; Deut. 4:34), **the Lord mighty in battle** (Psalm 76:3-6; Exod. 15:3, 6; Isa. 9:4-7; 11:4; Rev. 19:11, 13-16). **9.** Verse 7 is repeated to emphasize the crucial importance of the identity of the King, so long the bane of the critic, the jest of the scorner, and the object of hate and resistance of the unbeliever.

10. Who is this King of glory? (cf. Deut. 30:3-10; Psalm 50:3; Acts 1:11). The concluding answer comes: **The Lord of hosts** (Gen. 32:2; Josh. 5:14; 2 Sam. 5:10; Neh. 9:6), Jehovah (Yahweh), the eternally existing One, the Creator of all life, the Marshal of the armies of heaven (Rev. 19:14), **he is the King of glory**, who has vanquished His enemies (Isa. 9:4-5) and taken posses-

sion of the earth for His glorious Kingdom reign.

Y. PRAYER FOR DELIVERANCE FROM TROUBLE. 25:1-22.

Psalms 25 to 39 (except for Psalm 33) are attributed to David. They (1) reflect many of David's experiences of suffering as a child of God in a hostile world, (2) but these odes also express the trials of the godly in every age, (3) particularly the sufferings of the Jewish remnant of the end time of trouble preceding Israel's establishment in Kingdom blessing. (4) Also reflected in many instances are our Lord's experiences during the days of His flesh (cf. Heb. 5:7-8).

Trust in the Lord Expressed. 25:1-7. **1-2.** The psalmist in this acrostic directed his prayer to the LORD, for he was surrounded by **enemies** that threatened to **triumph** over him. **3.** He was in peril of being made **ashamed** (humbled and thrown into confusion and defeat) by those **who transgress without cause**, who in unprovoked rage and malice attacked him to ruin him.

He prayed for two things in his need: (1) **4-5.** He prayed for teaching and guidance in God's ways and truth, comprehending instruction concerning God and His great salvation (His deliverance of His own). So important was this that the psalmist said, **I wait** (*qiwwîtî*, "to wait for someone" in an attitude of expectancy and hope) **on thee** (God) **all the day** (constantly; cf. 40:1). (2) **6-7.** He prayed for merciful forgiveness, appealing to the LORD's **tender mercies and ... loving-kindnesses** (103:17; 106:1; cf. Isa. 63:15; Jer. 33:11) revealed in the history of His people, **for they have been ever of old.** In response to faith in divine grace to provide a Savior from sin, as signified by the blood sacrifice instituted at the Fall (Gen. 3:16, 21), the redeemed

781

from the beginning looked forward to Calvary, even as saints in the postcross era look backward to claim forgiveness on the basis of the shed blood of the Lamb of God, revealing God's goodness and grace (cf. Psalms 31:19; 51:1). Merciful forgiveness will be realized in a most wonderful way someday in the case of the Jewish remnant, when the Deliverer will come out of Zion and turn ungodliness from Jacob (Jer. 31:34; cf. Rom. 11:26-32).

Confident Assurance in the Lord Asserted. 25:8-15. The psalmist expressed confidence in five things: (1) **8a.** He expressed his confident assurance in the LORD Himself, in His character as good and upright (86:5; 92:15). (2) **8b-9.** He expressed his assurance in His consequent ability to **teach** (instruct) **sinners in the way** of salvation and righteousness (32:8), and to **guide the meek** (humble) **in justice** (9:16) and teach them **his way** (27:11). **10.** The LORD's *way* is described as **paths of ... mercy** (loving-kindness) **and truth** to those who **keep** (observe) **his covenant,** that is, the New Covenant in Christ's blood (Heb. 8:7-13), especially as it will be embraced by the saved remnant of Israel at the second advent (Jer. 31:31-34) **and his testimonies.**

11. Keeping the New Covenant will be a matter of faith, believing its gracious provisions of full forgiveness of sins, however great (Rom. 5:20), for the LORD's **name's sake** (Psalms 31:3; 79:9; 109:21; 143:11), that is, through the name of the Savior, Jesus Christ, and by virtue of His redemptive sacrifice.

(3) **12-13.** He expressed his assurance that the LORD would teach him who fears Him (holds Him in godly reverence) the way He shall choose, not his own way of self-will (v. 8), and that one so taught will **dwell at ease** (abide in prosperity; Prov. 1:33; Jer. 23:6), and

his descendants will **inherit the earth** (the land; Psalms 37:11; 69:36).

(4) **14.** He expressed his assurance that **the secret of the Lord** (His confidential counsel) **is with those who fear** (reverence) **him** (Job 29:4; Prov. 3:32) and that **he will show** (make them know) **his covenant**, that is, the New Covenant, according to which He writes His Law on the heart of those redeemed through the blood of Christ (Heb. 8:7-13; cf. Jer. 31:31-34). (5) **15.** He expressed his assurance that the LORD would **pluck** his **feet out of the net** laid for him by his enemies, and so his **eyes** were **ever toward** the LORD as his Helper and Deliverer.

A Cry for Redemption out of Trouble. 25:16-22. The psalmist's keen cry of distress focused prophetically on the terrible sufferings of the Jewish remnant in the time of Jacob's trouble (v. 22; cf. Jer. 30:5-7). **16.** The saint was **desolate and afflicted** (Psalm 143:4). **17-18. The troubles of** his **heart** were **enlarged** (40:12). He mentioned his **distresses ... affliction ... trouble** (NASB).

19. He spoke of his many **enemies** and those who hated him **with cruel** (violent) **hatred** (cf. Matt. 24:9-22; 25:34-41; Rev. 7:4-17; 13:15-18). **20.** He called upon the LORD to **keep** (preserve) his **soul** (i.e., "him") and **deliver** him (Psalm 82:2-4; Dan. 12:1; Matt. 24:21-22; Rev. 7:14), that he might not **be ashamed** (be humiliated and brought low) by his enemies (Psalm 25:2), for he had **put** his **trust in** ("taken refuge in") the LORD. **21.** He pleaded his **integrity and uprightness** (41:12) to preserve him from destruction at the hands of his foes, for he waited for the LORD (25:3).

22. That the prophetic focus is upon troubled Israel during the Great Tribulation is indicated by the closing petition: **Redeem Israel, O God, out of all his troubles** (130:8; Exod. 14:30; Isa. 59:20).

This will occur when "the Redeemer shall come to Zion, and unto those who turn from transgression in Jacob" (Isa. 59:20; Jer. 30:5-7; Zech. 12:10—13:1; Matt. 24:31; Rom. 11:26-32; Rev. 7:4-8).

Z. A PLEA FOR PROTECTION AGAINST FOES. 26:1-12.

Protestations of Integrity. 26:1-5. The voice of saints in every age is discerned, but the cry of the godly remnant of the dark days of the Tribulation comes to the fore. The plea is for vindication against the wicked. **1a. Judge** (vindicate) **me, O Lord; for I have walked in mine integrity** (7:8; Prov. 20:7; *tāmîm*, "uprightness, honesty"), walking being a common figure for living, taking one step at a time (cf. v. 3*a*). **1b.** He protested his unfaltering faith: **I have trusted ... I shall not slide** (Heb. 10:23).

2. Examine ... prove (try) **... test my heart and my mind** (cf. 139:23; 7:9). **3.** He opened his life to God, for he had separated himself from the sinners and apostates about him and joined himself to the LORD. **4.** He reminds us of the godly man of Psalm 1. He had not **sat with vain** (deceitful) **persons** or hobnobbed with **dissemblers** (pretenders, hypocrites; 28:3). **5.** He detested (31:6) **the congregation** (assembly) **of evildoers** and refused to **sit with the wicked,** practicing godly separation (cf. 2 Cor. 6:14—7:1).

6. He washed his hands **in innocence,** a Jewish custom (Deut. 21:6) of cleansing from defilement to approach God's altar, as the priests had to bathe hands and feet (Exod. 30:17-21; cf. Psalms 43:3-4; 73:13). **7.** Thus he maintained his integrity that his testimony might not be blemished, but that he might **make known** (God's glory) **with the voice of thanksgiving, and tell** of all the LORD's **wondrous works** (*nipl$^{e'}$ôt*, "miraculous doings").

Plea for Preservation. 26:8-12. His plea was based on two things: (1) **8.** His plea was based on his love for God's house, **the place where** His **honor** (glory) **dwelleth** (27:4; 84:1-4, 10), literally, "the place of the tabernacle of Thy glory," where the Shekinah presence was manifested. There will be a restored Temple in Jerusalem during the Tribulation period (2 Thess. 2:4), and a magnificent Temple during the Kingdom age (Ezek. 40:1—47:12).

(2) **9-11.** His plea was based on his walking in his integrity. Therefore, he prayed that his life would not be taken away along with **sinners** and **bloody men** ("men of blood"), murderers who have their hands stained with innocent blood (Psalm 139:19; Isa. 1:15; cf. Rev. 6:9-10; 9:21), in **whose hands is mischief** ("a wicked scheme"; Psalms 2:1-3; 37:7), and whose **right hand is full of bribes** (15:5). He implored redemption (44:26; 69:18) and the manifestation of the divine grace (Isa. 59:20; Zech. 12:10—13:1).

12a. He protested his sure footing **in an even** (level) **place** as he placed his trust in God (Psalm 27:11) and in His redemption. **12b.** He would **bless** (victoriously praise) the LORD **in the congregations** (22:22) as he looked for the risen, glorified Redeemer-King to appear in Kingdom glory (Rev. 19:11—20:6).

AA. FEARLESS TRUST IN GOD. 27:1-14.

For the scope of this psalm, see the introduction to Psalm 25.

Strong Confidence in the Lord. 27:1-3. The saint was beset by grievous troubles and enemies, but he expressed fearless trust in God. The voice is that of David and a host of the saints of every age, but again the focus comes to rest on the Tribulation saint, who will be faced by the greatest time of trouble God's people will ever encounter (2:5; Dan. 12:1; Matt. 24:13, 21-22; Rev. 7:14).

As his defense the psalmist owned the LORD as (1) **1a.** his **light** (Psalm 18:28; Isa. 60:20; Mic. 7:8; John 8:12); (2) **1b.** his **salvation** (Exod. 15:2; Psalms 62:7; 118:14; Isa. 33:2; Jonah 2:9); and (3) **1c.** the strength (*mā'ôz*, "defense, refuge, fortress") of his life (Psalm 28:8).

1d-2a. With his confidence in such a Protector, the psalmist scouted fear and dread (118:6) and **the wicked**, who attacked him viciously to devour his **flesh** (14:4; Jer. 10:25; Amos 8:4; Mic. 3:3), that is, to consume or destroy him. **2b.** In their onslaught **they stumbled and fell** (Psalm 9:3). **3.** He would not fear though a **host** (huge army) should encamp against him, or war rise against him (3:6); in spite of that, he declared, **I shall be confident** (NASB; Job 4:6; cf. Rom. 8:31).

Holy Longings and Anticipations. 27:4-6. The heart yearnings of the true Israelite, the Old Testament saint, come into view, as well as the godly remnant of the future (42:1-4). **4.** His one request of the LORD, which he would perseveringly seek, was to **dwell in the house of the Lord all the days of** his **life** (23:6; 26:8; 65:4; cf. Luke 2:37), **to behold the beauty** (*nō'ăm*, "loveliness, graciousness") **of the Lord** (Psalm 90:17) **and to inquire** (*bǐqqēr*, "to consider with pleasure, meditate") **in his temple** (18:6). Such yearnings for the earthly tabernacle, where God's glory resided in visible splendor, are found in other psalms.

The New Testament saint, however, beholds the glory of the incarnate, crucified, and risen Lord (2 Cor. 3:18), and no veil hides the divine glory, for the veil is rent and we enter into the very presence of God (Heb. 4:16). If the Is-

raelite entered the holy precincts "to inquire" and to "meditate," how much more ought we inquire into the far greater revelations of God's redeeming love vouchsafed to us in the Word.

5. In that holy sanctuary, God's pavilion, the Israelite knew God would **hide** (conceal) him from harm **in the time of trouble** (Psalm 50:15). **In the secret of his tabernacle** ("secret place of His tent") He would conceal him under the cover of His tent (31:20) and **set him upon a rock** (40:2), prefiguring Christ as the believer's rock of salvation and defense (18:2; 42:9; 71:3; Matt. 7:25; 16:18; 1 Cor. 10:4).

6. Exaltation above his enemies roundabout him (Psalm 3:3) prompted the believer to offer sacrifices in the LORD's tent (107:22) with shouts of joy (Isa. 9:3-5; 35:10; Rev. 19:5-6) and **sing praises unto the Lord,** his deliverer (Psalm 13:6; Isa. 12:1-6; Rev. 12:12; 18:20).

Faithful Prayer in Trials. 27:7-14. **7-8.** Again the cry of the persecuted suffering saint of the Tribulation period comes to the fore. His troubles are so great (Dan. 12:1; Matt. 24:21-22) that it seems God is not listening (Hab. 2:20; Zeph. 1:7; Zech. 2:13) and has forgotten to be gracious and answer him (Psalms 4:3; 13:3), despite his heartfelt seeking of God's face (34:4; 105:4; Amos 5:6).

9. The unprecedented wickedness and persecution of the end time (Rev. 13:1-18) cause the saint (Rev. 7:1-17) to conclude that God is hiding His face from him (Psalm 69:17) and turning away His servant in anger (6:1; Rev. 6:9-11; 7:14), abandoning and forsaking him (Psalms 37:28; 94:14), and not showing Himself as the God of his salvation (deliverance).

10. But in his dilemma the tried and harried saint expresses his faith in the fact that though his father and mother have forsaken him (Isa. 49:15; cf. Matt. 24:10), nevertheless **the Lord** will take him up, that is, in His tender arms of love and protection (Isa. 40:11). **11.** So difficult and distressing is the way of suffering and persecution he is treading that he cries out for God to **teach** him His way and **lead** him in a **plain** (level) **path** (Psalm 5:8), without the perils and steep climb that his present course of suffering entails (Psalms 25:4; 86:11), because of his enemies (those who lay in wait for him to harm him).

12. So terrible are his persecutions from his adversaries that it seems the LORD has delivered him over to their evil devices—false witnessing and the employment of violence and cruelty (35:11; Deut. 19:18; Matt. 24:9-13; 26:60; Acts 9:1). **13.** In the face of such diabolical conduct (cf. Rev. 9:20-21; 13:1-18), the distraught saint cries out: **I had fainted** (despaired), **unless I had believed to see the goodness of the Lord** (Psalm 31:19) **in the land of the living** (52:5; 116:9; 142:5; Job 28:13; Isa. 38:11; 53:8; Jer. 11:19), that is, see God's gracious deliverance in preserving from physical death those who survive the horrors of the Tribulation, "the land of the living" denoting the sphere of physical life.

14. The blessed results of confidence in the LORD are summarized. The psalmist determines to **wait on** (wait for) the LORD (Psalms 25:3; 37:34; 40:1; 62:5; 130:5). Then the blessed results follow. The saint can **be strong** (NASB), and see the LORD **strengthen** his **heart** with courage. So important is this waiting on the LORD that the psalmist repeats it: **Yes, wait for the Lord** (NASB).

BB. PRAISE FOR ANSWERED PRAYER. 28:1-9.

For the scope of Psalm 28, see the introduction to Psalm 25.

The Prayer for Help. 28:1-5. **1a. Unto thee will I cry,** O LORD, ... **be not silent** (deaf) **to me** (cf. 27:7-10; 35:22; 39:12; 83:1). **1b-c.** So extreme were the sufferings and persecutions from the wicked, which will reach their apex in "the time of Jacob's trouble" (Jer. 30:5-7), that the psalmist despaired of life itself (Matt. 24:22) if the LORD did not heed his prayer. **1c.** He would become **like those who go down** (descend) **into the pit** (*bôr*, lit., "a hole, well, or dungeon," metaphorically, "the grave"; Psalms 88:4; 143:7; Prov. 1:12), that is, like those who die physically, the body going to the grave, the soul and spirit to Sheol.

2-3a. If the LORD did not hear his prayer, he would suffer death at the hands of his enemies. **3b.** He would be drawn (dragged) away **with the wicked ... the workers of iniquity** (Psalm 5:5), **who speak peace** (12:2; 55:21; 62:4; Jer. 9:8), **but mischief** (evil) **is in their hearts.**

4. This verse constitutes an imprecatory prayer (see comment on Psalm 5:10 for the meaning of this kind of prayer). The psalmist petitioned: **Give** (requite, repay) **them** (the wicked) **according to their deeds** (62:12; 2 Tim. 4:14); **render to them their desert** ("repay them their recompense," NASB; "their dealings"). When the iniquity of the wicked is full, the Spirit of God prays according to the will of God for the merited punishment of the offenders (Gen. 15:16; Lev. 18:24; Rev. 6:10, 17).

Such deserved imprecations of doom were doubtless called forth during David's experiences, but they will be realized on a colossal scale in the endtime apostasy and revolt against God (Psalm 2:1-3; Rev. 6:1—19:10). **5.** The reason for the imprecation and its justification are presented, the iniquity reaching a pitch where the LORD in His righteousness and justice must **destroy** the evildoers, and the Spirit of God prays

785

through the saint to that end.

The Assurance of Answered Prayer.
28:6-9. **6-7.** The testimony of the psalmist was: The LORD has heard and answered my prayer (cf. v. 2) in showing Himself **my strength** (59:17) and **my shield** (3:3). **My heart trusted in him** (13:5; 112:7) **and I am helped** (40:3). As a result, his testimony was: **My heart greatly rejoiceth** (exults; 16:9), **and with my song will I praise** (thank) **him** (40:3; 69:30; cf. Isa. 12:1-6; 35:2; 51:11; 55:12; Zech. 2:10).

8. Final assurance of answered prayer will be realized when the LORD becomes the saving strength (defense) of His Anointed when He scatters His foes (Psalm 2:1-5) and installs Him as King upon His holy hill of Zion (2:6-12). **9a.** Then the prayer, **Save thy people** (Israel), **and bless thine inheritance** (33:12; 106:40; Deut. 9:29; 32:9; 1 Kings 8:51) will be fully answered.

9b. Then the Lord Jesus Christ will **feed them also** ("be their Shepherd"; Psalm 80:1; Isa. 40:11; Ezek. 34:12-15), ruling "with a rod of iron" (Psalm 2:8-9; Rev. 19:15). **9c.** Then the chief Shepherd of the sheep (Psalm 24) will **lift them up** (carry Israel) **forever** (Deut. 1:31; Isa. 40:11; 46:3; 63:9). Then Israel will be regathered home and saved (Isa. 11:11-16; Ezek. 37:1-28; Rom. 11:25-32) as a display of God's matchless wisdom and grace (11:33-36).

CC. THE GATHERING STORM OF JUDGMENT. 29:1-11.

For the context and scope of Psalm 29, see the introduction to Psalm 25.

The Prelude to the Coming Storm of Judgment. 29:1-2. **1.** The **sons of the mighty** ($b^e n\hat{e}$ $'\bar{e}l\hat{i}m$, "the powerful, the strong") are the rulers, the rich and influential who will be living on the earth at the time the Lord is about to be manifested in His Kingdom glory. **2.** They are addressed and exhorted to **give** (ascribe) to the LORD the worship and the glory due His name before the judgments, which are to be poured out before the Kingdom is set up, break like a terrible tempest upon the godless and rebellious world (cf. 2:1-12; 96:7-9; 1 Chron. 16:28-29).

The Storm of Judgment Described. 29:3-9. **3a. The voice of the Lord is upon the waters** (symbolizing the peoples upon the earth; 104:7; Rev. 17:15). "The voice" is the Word of God, the voice of Him into whose hands has been committed "all judgment" (John 5:22). The Day of the Lord, the time of worldwide Tribulation that will precede the Kingdom (Rev. 6:1—20:4), will come, and the LORD will begin to administer the long-predicted judgments, all poetically set forth under the figure of an onrushing tempest. **3b. The God of glory** (Acts 7:2; cf. Matt. 25:31) **thundereth** (Job 37:4; Psalm 18:13; cf. 1 Sam. 2:10; 7:10; Rev. 4:5; 6:1; 10:3; 16:18; 19:6). **3c.** He is called **the Lord ... upon many waters,** "waters" symbolizing peoples (Rev. 17:1; cf. 3a) because He is about to judge the nations (Matt. 25:31-46).

4a. The **voice of the Lord** (the Word of God uttered by Him who judges and triumphantly makes war against His foes, Rev. 9:11), is described as **powerful** ($b^e k\bar{o}\bar{a}h$, "strength itself"; Psalm 68:33; Jer. 23:29; Heb. 4:12), for out of His mouth issues the sharp sword of His Word, "that with it he should smite the nations" (Rev. 19:15). **4b-5.** It is also described as **full of majesty** ($b\check{e}h\bar{a}\underline{d}\bar{a}r$, "very splendor"), breaking to pieces with shafts of fire (lightning; cf. v. 7) **the cedars of Lebanon**, poetically alluding to "every one who is proud ... lofty, and ... lifted up" and who at that time "shall be brought low" (Isa. 2:12-13; 14:8; cf. Judg. 9:15; 1 Kings 5:6; Psalm 104:16; Rev. 19:11—20:3).

6. The LORD in judgment also makes the "cedars" (v. 5) **skip** (*yărqîd*, "cause to move up and down, to and fro") with the hills on which they stand by reason of an earthquake (JFB). He makes **Lebanon**, a mountain range of Syria, and **Sirion** (the Canaanite name of Mount Hermon, the highest peak of the Lebanon range) skip like **a young wild ox.**

8. The LORD's voice **shaketh** (convulses) **the wilderness . . . the wilderness of Kadesh** (Num. 13:26), the steppe bordering the southern extremity of Palestine, as Lebanon marks the northern boundary. The whole land of the LORD's people trembles to the very center at the LORD's voice as His judgments sweep the whole land preceding Kingdom blessing (cf. Joel 2:1-10).

9. But there will be more than judgment. In wrath the LORD will remember mercy (Hab. 3:2) while He is stripping the forest bare, purging out the sinners of both Israel and the nations. He **maketh the hinds to calve** (Job 39:1). He will bring forth a saved remnant of Israel. The nation will be born again and prepared for Kingdom blessing (Isa. 66:6-10; Ezek. 36:24-28; Rom. 11:26-32).

And **in his temple** (the heavenly temple, since the tribulational judgments prophetically come into focus; Psalm 11:4; Isa. 6:1; Rev. 11:19; 15:5-6; 16:1, 17) **doth everyone speak of his glory** (Psalm 26:8), or "in His temple everything says, 'Glory!'" (NASB). Even the terrible judgments upon sinful, rebellious man redound to the glory of God (Rev. 15:5-8; 16:5-7) since human iniquity has reached its full and calls for judgment (cf. Gen. 15:16; Rev. 15:1-3).

The Postlude to the Storm of Judgment. 29:10-11. **10a. The Lord sits enthroned over** (upon) **the flood** (RSV; Gen. 6:17; Job 38:8). The psalmist pic-

tures the LORD sitting in judgment as He sat in judgment "at" or "over" the Flood of Noah (Psalm 9:4, 7-8; Joel 3:12), vindicating His people and destroying the ungodly foe. Hence, the triumphal inference follows.

10b. Therefore, **the Lord sitteth** ("will sit") **King forever.** As the Deluge terminated an age, so this age will be terminated by the judgment of the Great Tribulation. Then the "KING OF KINGS" (Rev. 19:16) will be enthroned on the Davidic throne (2 Sam. 7:8-17; Matt. 25:31-46; Rev. 19:11—20:6). **11.** Then the King will give **strength** to His people (Psalm 28:8) and as "Prince of Peace" (Isa. 9:6-7, NASB) will bless His people with peace (Isa. 11:3-9; Dan. 2:44; Luke 1:32-33).

DD. SONG OF DELIVERANCE. 30:1-12.

See the introduction to Psalm 25 for the scope and context of Psalm 30. It is a psalm of David. "A . . . Song at the dedication of the house" (i.e., of God). The Hebrew *hᵃnŭkkâ* means the consecration of a *new* building, and the reference is probably to "the house of the LORD God" (1 Chron. 22:1-2), and the construction of the altar on the Temple site purchased from Araunah, when the LORD hallowed the spot by His answer by fire (2 Sam. 24:24).

Considered prophetically, this psalm constitutes a hymn of praise to be sung by the godly remnant of Israel at the dedication of the millennial Temple when that sacred edifice will be hallowed by the King-Priest, who will dedicate it by the glory of His presence (Ezek. 43:2-6).

Praise for Deliverance. 30:1-5. **1.** Some unknown experience of David is reflected in the deliverance recounted in this psalm, and David's rescue has been echoed by God's people through the ages. But the prophetic spotlight rests on the Israelite who will be preserved through the horrors of the Great Tribulation and extol the LORD for having delivered him (lit., drawing him up; 3:3) and not allowing his enemies to triumph over him (25:2; 35:19, 24; cf. Matt. 24:21-22; Rev. 7:3, 14).

2-3. He praised the LORD for His help and healing (Psalms 6:2; 103:3; cf. Exod. 15:26) when he faced certain death and was brought up, as it were, **from sheol**, that is, the nether world (Psalm 86:13), being kept alive, in that he did **not go down to the pit** (the infernal regions).

4. With the storm of judgment (Psalm 29) now past, the time of joyous singing His praise had come (149:1), and the LORD's **saints** (godly ones; 50:5; Rev. 7:3-8; 14:3-5) were exhorted to give thanks (Psalm 97:12) to the holy name of the LORD (Exod. 3:15; Psalm 135:13; Hos. 12:5; Rev. 4:8; 15:3-4), who has displayed His infinite holiness in His judgments upon Satan and wicked men (Rev. 4:1—20:3).

5a. His anger (Psalm 103:9; Isa. 26:20; 54:7; cf. 2 Cor. 4:17), here with special prophetic application to the terrible end-time judgments (cf. Rev. 8:5; 11:19; 16:1, 19), is said to last only for **a moment** (cf. Matt. 24:22). **In his favor** (redeemed by His grace) **is life**, physical life in being preserved from death in the end-time judgments, spiritual life to enter the Kingdom (John 3:3, 5), and eternal life as His free gift of faith (Gen. 15:6; John 3:16).

5b. Weeping—any anguish God's own may have to go through, but especially His own in the horrors of the time of Jacob's trouble (Jer. 30:5-7)—**may endure** (last) **for a night** (the dark time of worldwide woe (Dan. 12:1; Matt. 24:21). **But joy** (joyous singing) **cometh in the morning** of Kingdom rest and

gladness (Isa. 12:1-6; 35:10; 54:7-8; Zech. 9:16-17).

A Heartfelt Testimony. 30:6-12. **6.** The psalmist reviewed his experience in detail—his former **prosperity** tempted him to self-confidence. **7a.** He acknowledged that only by the LORD's favor did He make his **mountain** (figurative for what is sure and immovable) to **stand strong.** David and every saint, especially the Tribulation saint, has to learn that in God alone we stand firm.

7b. When the LORD hides His face by allowing painful chastisements and refining fires to test His own, as notably will be the case in the coming Tribulation (cf. Rev. 6:10-11), then the saint will discover that his only confident assurance is in the LORD if he would not be **troubled** (dismayed; Psalm 104:29; Deut. 31:17). **8-9a.** But the saint's testimony in time of trouble is, **To the Lord I made supplication** (NASB), the gist of which is, What profit would there be in martyrdom? (Psalm 28:1).

9b. Will death at the hands of enemies bring praise to God and advertise the LORD's faithfulness to His own? (6:5; Rev. 6:9-11; cf. 3:7; 19:11). **10.** The LORD hears and manifests His redemptive grace and mercy in becoming the **helper** of His own. **11.** In the case of His Tribulation saint, He will turn his mourning (Psalm 6:8; Isa. 61:3; Jer. 3:14) into dancing (2 Sam. 6:14) as He strips away his sackcloth of mourning (Zech. 12:10—13:1) and girds him with gladness in Kingdom blessing (Isa. 12:1-6; 35:10).

12. The purpose of this great change: **that my glory** (Psalms 2:3; 16:9; 57:8; 108:1), that is, the glory of God, manifested in his soul will cause him to **sing praise** and not be silent and to **give thanks** to God forever for His glorious deliverance from enemies and death itself.

EE. TRUST OF THE TROUBLED SAINT. 31:1-24.

For the scope of this psalm, see the introduction to Psalm 25.

Prayer and Expression of Confidence. 31:1-8. The troubled saint in every age here expresses his trust in the LORD, but prophetically the godly Israelite in the time of Jacob's trouble (Jer. 30:5-7) comes into view. The superscription ascribes the song to David; but because of similarity to Jeremiah, some have attributed the psalm to him (cf. v. 10 with Lam. 1:20; v. 11 with Jer. 20:8; v. 18 with Jer. 17:18; v. 23 with Lam. 3:64). That David and Jeremiah, as suffering saints, were led to use the same expressions, seems to be the best explanation.

1-5. The suffering saint takes refuge in the LORD and pleads for deliverance on the basis of (1) God's righteousness (v. 1; cf. Rev. 16:5-6); (2) His **strength**—a **strong rock ... an house of defense ... a fortress** (vv. 2-4); (3) His redemption (v. 5*a*; cf. Luke 23:46); and (4) His **truth** (v. 5*b*; Deut. 32:4).

6-8. He protests his detestation of idolaters, **those who regard lying vanities** (i.e., "vain idols"; Psalm 144:11; Jonah 2:8; cf. Rev. 9:20-21), which turn one away from trust in the LORD and His mercy and loving concern for His own, delivering him from the power of the enemy and setting his feet **in a large room** (place; Psalm 4:1; cf. Rev. 7:1-10).

Prayer for Deliverance. 31:9-18. The sufferings of the saint in an evil world in every age are depicted, but prophetically in view are the terrible woes of the coming time of trouble preceding the establishment of Christ's earthly Kingdom over Israel (Acts 1:6; Isa. 11:1-16;

Matt. 24:20—25:46; Rev. 6:1—20:6).

9. The saint is in **trouble** (distress; Psalms 66:14; 69:17), both in **soul and ... body** (NASB; 63:1). **10.** His life is spent in **sorrow and ... sighing** (NASB; contrast Isa. 35:10). **11-13.** He is a **reproach,** an object of dread to his neighbors and acquaintances (cf. Matt. 24:9-10), **forgotten as a dead man** (Psalm 88:5), slandered (50:12; Jer. 20:10), beset by **fear ... on every side,** and counsel and plottings against his life (cf. Matt. 27:1), the godly Israelite getting a taste of the sufferings his unbelieving countrymen afflicted upon the Messiah.

14-15. Protestations of trust in the LORD and that his times (destiny) are in the LORD's hands (Job 14:5; 24:1) cause the suffering one to cry to the LORD for deliverance from his enemies and persecutors (Psalm 143:9), that is, those who will hate the godly Israelites, and therefore the LORD, in that fearful day (Matt. 25:41-46).

16. He beseeches the LORD to make His **face to shine upon** His servant (Psalms 4:6; 80:3; Num. 6:25) and **save** him in His loving-kindness (Psalm 6:4), manifested through Christ's redemption (Zech. 12:10—13:1) then to become a glorious reality to the Jewish remnant (Rom. 11:26-33). **17-18.** The imprecatory prayer (see comment on Psalm 5:10) will be appropriately prayed when men's iniquity has come to the full and when the immediate destruction of the wicked is God's will; the saint's prayer fully expresses that will (cf. Gen. 15:16; cf. Rev. 15:1; 16:5-6).

Praise for Deliverance. 31:19-24. He praised God for three things: (1) **19.** He praised Him for His **goodness,** which alone sent deliverance. God has laid up His goodness as a treasure stored up (secretly, as it were), and brought forth for His people in their hour of greatest

789

need (27:13; 36:7-8) and **wrought (openly)** . . . **before the sons of men** (cf. Rev. 19:11-21; cf. 1:7; Psalm 23:5).

(2) **20.** He praised Him for hiding His people in the secret place of His presence (27:5) **from the pride of man** (2:1-3; Rev. 19:19) and **the strife of tongues** (Job 5:21; Psalm 31:13). (3) **21-22.** He praised Him for His marvelous display of His loving-kindness **in a strong** (besieged) **city** (Psalm 87:5; 1 Sam. 23:7; cf. Zech. 12:1-9), answering and delivering from a hopeless situation (Psalm 85:5; Isa. 38:11; Lam. 3:54; Rev. 19:11-16).

23-24. The saint burst forth in spontaneous exhortation (1) to **love the Lord**, who **preserveth** the faithful (Psalm 145:20; Rev. 2:10) and fully recompenses the proud doer (Psalm 94:2; Deut. 32:41; Rev. 19:11—20:3) and for (2) **all** who **hope** in ("wait for") **the Lord** (cf. Rev. 6:9-10) to be strong and courageous (Psalm 27:14).

FF. Blessedness of Sins Forgiven. 32:1-11.

See the introduction to Psalm 25. A "Maschil" is evidently a didactic ode giving instruction on an especially important subject. This is the first of thirteen such songs (Psalms 42, 44, 45, 52-55, 74, 78, 88, 89, 142) relating to the understanding of spiritual things that the godly in every age possess, but with particular reference to the godly in Israel at the end time (Dan. 12:3, 10).

The Blessedness of Forgiveness of Sins. 32:1-7. The foundation of this psalm is David's own experience of salvation by grace through faith (Rom. 4:7-8). **1. Blessed is he whose transgression is forgiven, whose sin is covered** (Psalms 85:2; 103:3). Literally, the Hebrew is exclamatory in force: 'O the blessings [benefits] of him," that is, "How blessed is he!" Old Testament

saints like Abraham (Gen. 15:6) and David were justified by faith in God's redemptive grace, reflected in the sacrificial ritual of shedding the blood of an animal, which was prospective of salvation to come. Hence, sins were pretermitted (*kesûy*, "covered, concealed") until expiated by the coming Redeemer's death (Rom. 3:25).

This inestimable benefit of being justified by faith and all it includes will become the experience of the godly remnant during the end of the age after the glorification of the church when they will believe in the crucified and risen Redeemer and come to enjoy "the sure mercies of David" (Isa. 55:3; Zech. 12:10—13:1; Rom. 11:25-26; cf. Rev. 7:1-8; cf. Matt. 25:1-13).

2a. Blessed is the man, literally, "O the blessings of the man" (*'āḏām*, "human being"), unto whom the Lord **imputeth not** (*ḥāshāḇ*, does not "reckon, account") **iniquity** (2 Cor. 5:19), that is, does not set down to the sinner's account sin in any of its variegated forms ("transgression," as commission of evil; "sin," as missing the divine mark or standard; and "iniquity," as inequity and unrighteousness).

2b. And in whose spirit there is no guile ("deceit"; John 1:47), manifested in *keeping silence* (v. 3) concerning one's sin, failing to acknowledge it by *hiding* it before God (v. 5). Guile refuses to face the sin problem honestly and therefore rules out the saving faith and blessedness that God's salvation brings. By contrast, the misery such "guile" produces is dramatically set forth (vv. 3-5).

When the psalmist kept silence about his sin (Psalm 39:2), three things happened: (1) **3.** His **bones** (body, substance), his physical powers, wasted away (31:10) through his **roaring** (deep groaning; 38:8) **all the day long.** (2) **4a.**

The **hand** of the LORD **was heavy upon** him (38:2; 39:10; 1 Sam. 5:6; Job 23:2) in chastisement. (3) **4b.** His **moisture** (life juices, vitality) was **turned into the drought of summer** (Psalm 22:15). Guile keeps one from being saved and, after one is saved, from enjoying the fellowship with God that salvation brings.

5. Such fellowship is restored as forgiveness is realized by confession (38:18; Prov. 28:13; 1 John 1:9). **6a.** Therefore, the forgiven saint exhorts fellow saints, **every one that is godly**, saved by grace through faith (vv. 1-2; Eph. 2:8-9), to enjoy the instant forgiveness that immediately follows guileless confession of sin that may have been committed. Such prompt confession means approaching God in a time in which He **[may] be found** (Psalm 69:13), literally, "in a time of finding out," namely, that in His redemptive grace He is gracious and propitious, and does not set down to the saved sinner's account sin in any of its forms (vv. 1-2), but has declared him fully righteous by virtue of His redemptive grace (cf. Rom. 4:7-8).

6b. The saint who thus confesses his sin and enjoys fellowship with God shall be spared **in the floods of great waters**, in overwhelming judgments for sin that destroy all others, as did the Flood in Noah's day, with a prophetic application to the Great Tribulation, when the Israelite remnant (Rev. 7:1-8) shall be sealed against death and destruction by "the seal of the living God" (7:2).

7. To His saints thus saved by faith and who walk by faith, the LORD is a **hiding place** (Psalms 9:9; 27:5; 31:20; Jer. 36:26; Col. 3:3), preserving them from trouble and compassing them about with **songs of deliverance**, with application prophetically to the godly in the time of "Jacob's trouble" (Jer.

30:5-7; cf. Isa. 26:20-21; Matt. 11:28-30; Rev. 6:1 — 19:21).

Exhortation to Trust the Lord for Forgiveness. 32:8-11. **8.** The psalmist, having experienced the forgiveness of sins and God's salvation, apparently recedes into the background as the LORD gives instruction on how to receive this blessing and on the **way** of faith one is to walk in to enjoy the fullest benefits of it (cf. 1 John 1:5-10). **I will instruct thee ... teach thee** (Isa. 48:17) **... guide,** "counsel you with My eye upon you" (NASB) (Psalm 33:18), which "implies the ideal bond between teacher and pupil, between father and son" (NBC, p. 471).

9. In contrast to the sensitive response of the heart that acknowledges its sin and looks by faith to divine redemptive grace for forgiveness is the stubborn will, like that of an animal devoid of a sense of right or wrong, that refuses to draw near to God, and must be disciplined and controlled by brute force rather than by the tender love and grace the LORD exemplifies (cf. Prov. 26:3).

Verses 10 and 11 present the conclusion of the spiritual "instruction," which as the title, *Maschil*, implies, is a leading object of the psalm (JFB). **10. The wicked** includes not only open transgressors, but all who are unbelieving and whose sin is unforgiven and to whom the LORD imputes iniquity (vv. 1-2). Their sorrows (Prov. 13:21; Rom. 2:9) are many in contrast to him **who trusteth in the Lord** (Psalms 34:8; 84:12; Prov. 16:20; Jer. 17:7), that is, to him to whom the LORD does not impute iniquity (vv. 1-2) but, as the New Testament reveals, imputes to him the very righteousness of God in Christ (James 2:23).

11. Such people (saved by faith) are designated **righteous** (Psalms 64:10; 97:12) and **upright in heart** (7:10; 64:10). Their portion, in contrast to the "many sorrows" (v. 10) of the wicked (unjustified), is gladness in the LORD (cf. Phil. 4:4), rejoicing, and shouting for joy. Most wonderfully will this be illustrated when the remnant of Israel finds "the way" (v. 8; John 14:6) and walks in it (Isa. 35:8-9; Zech. 12:10—13:1; Rom. 11:25-32). Then "the ransomed of the LORD shall return, and come to Zion with songs and everlasting joy ... and sorrow and sighing shall flee away" (Isa. 35:10; cf. 65:19).

GG. PRAISE OF THE REDEEMED. 33:1-22.

For the scope of Psalm 33, see the introduction to Psalm 25.

The Call to Praise the Lord. 33:1-3. **1.** The shout of joy issuing from the **righteous** of the preceding psalm (32:11), who know the blessedness of sins forgiven, is more fully unfolded in this ode. The call to praise is for all the redeemed of every age, but it looks forward with special emphasis to the Kingdom age, when all the earth will fear the LORD and "stand in awe of him" (v. 8), having been subdued by Him (v. 10; cf. 2:4-12). **Rejoice in the Lord ... praise is befitting** ("becoming, suitable"; cf. 32:11; 92:1; 147:1; Phil. 3:1; 4:4). **2.** Thanksgiving for salvation is to be rendered to God to the accompaniment of the **harp** (lyre) and with an instrument of ten strings. **3.** The call is to sing to the LORD **a new song** (Psalms 40:3; 96:1; 98:1; 144:9; Isa. 42:10). In the New Testament the redeemed sing a "new song" (Rev. 5:9; 14:3). This new song will be redemption's fullest song on earth by redeemed Israel and the nations—a mighty hallelujah chorus (cf. Psalms 146-50).

Praise the Lord as Creator. 33:4-9. **4a.** The grounds of praise are the Word, works, and character of the LORD. His Word is **right** (upright; 19:8) and it is His

promise to His people (105:42). **4b.** Like His "works," it represents His faithfulness and His truth (119:89-90; cf. Rev. 19:11, 13; John 14:6).

5. He is righteous; therefore, He loveth righteousness and justice (Isa. 9:7; 11:3-5; Rev. 19:11). **The earth is full of the goodness** (ḥĕsĕd, "loving-kindness, covenant-keeping love") **of the Lord.** The Kingdom will be a demonstration of this covenant-keeping love, particularly in the fulfillment of the Davidic Covenant (2 Sam. 7:8-17).

6-7. His all-powerful Word was the agent of creation (Gen. 1:3; John 1:1-3; Heb. 11:3; 2 Pet. 3:5), the heavens attesting His glorious power and wisdom (Gen. 2:1; Psalm 19:1-3), and the sea is a monument to His praise (cf. Job 38:8-11). **8.** One reason, among many others, why **all the earth** should **fear** (revere) the LORD and **stand in awe of him** (Psalms 67:7; 96:9) is His creatorship. **9.** His Word created and established the universe (Gen. 1:3; Psalm 148:5).

Praise the Lord as Ruler of Nations. 33:10-17. The LORD is to be praised because of five things: (1) **10.** He brings the **counsel of the nations to nought** ("frustrates" their evil designs and plottings; 2:4-12; Rev. 16:13-16; 19:11—20:3; cf. Isa. 8:10; 19:3; 40:15).

(2) **11.** His counsel and eternal purposes stand forever and cannot be overturned by puny man or rebellious nations (Job 23:13; Psalm 2:1-3; Prov. 19:21). His plans from eternity past to eternity future will be consummated despite all opposition (Psalms 40:5; 92:5; 139:17; Isa. 55:8; Rev. 21:1—22:21).

(3) **12.** He blesses the nation who recognizes His lordship (Psalm 144:15; cf. 9:15, 17) and His elect, **the people whom he hath chosen for his own inheritance,** the nation Israel specifically (Deut. 28:9; 1 Pet. 5:13), as well as all the elect of the ages.

(4) **13-15.** His loving concern is for the **sons of men**, all mankind. He did not create them to ignore them or leave them to themselves. Even when they fell into sin, He began to work for their redemption. With loving concern He looks **from heaven** (14:2; Job 28:24) and sees **all the sons of men** (Psalm 11:4) ... **all the inhabitants of the earth.** None is so sinful, so needy, that He in His love is not concerned—**He who fashions the hearts of them all, He who understands all their works** (NASB, 119:73; Job 10:8; 34:31; 2 Chron. 16:9).

(5) **16-17.** He lovingly interposes in the affairs of men. He saves the king, but not by the strong army of the king (Psalms 44:6; 60:11). He delivers the warrior, but not by the warrior's great strength. Without His providential help the horse is a false hope for victory, even in a day when cavalry was a prime military asset (20:7; 147:10; Prov. 21:31).

Praise to the Lord, the Keeper of His People. 33:18-22. **18-19.** **Behold** (what is a precious reason for praise is that) **the eye of the Lord** (cf. Psalm 32:8) is tenderly and with the most loving concern **upon those who fear him** and **hope in his mercy** to **deliver** them **from death** (physical, spiritual, and eternal death, the full provision of His mercy in redemptive grace). **20-22.** As Keeper of His people, the LORD is a **help** and **shield**, the all-worthy object of faith and joy.

HH. PRAISE FOR DELIVERANCE.
34:1-22.

For the full scope of Psalm 34, see the introduction to Psalm 25. This is a Davidic psalm and, according to the inscription, it reflects David's experiences when he feigned insanity before Achish, the king of Gath (1 Sam. 21:10-15), "Abimelech" being a royal title of Philistine kings, as "Pharaoh" was of Egyptian monarchs and "Agag" of Amalekite kings. After David had escaped death, he evidently saw his folly and the LORD's patient watch care over him, despite his defection, and so he burst into praise to the LORD for His faithfulness despite His servant's unfaithfulness (cf. 2 Tim. 2:13). This is an acrostic psalm, but one Hebrew letter is missing.

Praise for God's Goodness. 34:1-7. **1-4.** David's ecstatic praise echoes the praise of all afflicted saints (v. 2) as they experience answered prayer and deliverance from dangers and fears. This will be the experience of saints delivered out of the Great Tribulation to enter the Kingdom.

5. Then the remnant of Israel (and the nations) will look unto Him (Zech. 12:10—13:1), and their deep repentance will issue in glorious salvation when they are **radiant** (Psalm 36:9; Isa. 60:5) and **their faces** (countenances) shall nevermore be **ashamed** (cast down in fearful despair; Psalm 25:3). Because the LORD's face will shine upon them, their faces will shine as a result of His great salvation having been revealed (80:19).

6. This verse presents an illustration of answered prayer and deliverance. This **poor** (afflicted) **man cried, and the Lord heard him, and saved him out of all his troubles** (Psalm 34:4; cf. Dan. 12:1; Matt. 24:21). **7. The angel of the Lord** (the LORD Himself in theophanic form; cf. Josh. 5:13-15; 2 Kings 6:15-17) **encampeth round about those who fear** (revere) Him and delivers them (cf. Dan. 6:22).

Exhortation to Trust the Lord. 34:8-10. **8-9.** The call is (1) to experience the LORD's goodness (**taste and see**, 119:103; Heb. 6:5; 1 Pet. 2:12) and the blessedness He bestows on the one who **trusteth in him** ("takes refuge in Him"; Psalm 2:12); and (2) to **fear** (reverence) **the Lord** (31:19) and enjoy the sufficiency He supplies. **For there is no lack** (23:1).

10. The **young lions** with voracious appetites **do lack, and suffer hunger**, but those who manifest their faith by seeking Him **shall not lack any good thing** (84:11). They may lack many things they think are good, but not anything that is really good for them.

Warning Against Sin. 34:11-16. **11.** God's people are addressed as **children** who must listen and be taught **the fear of the Lord** and that He requires practical holiness of life (cf. 66:16; 111:10). **12-13.** Such practical godliness in Old Testament thought issued in long life and earthly blessings (34:12; 1 Pet. 3:10-12; Eccles. 3:13) and demanded separation from sin, such as an evil and deceitful tongue (Psalm 141:3; Prov. 13:3; James 1:26; 1 Pet. 2:22). The sins of the tongue are singled out, because this organ is a very sensitive barometer indicating the general spiritual climate of the heart (Matt. 12:34-37). **14.** Evil in any form is to be avoided (Psalm 37:27; Isa. 1:16-17), the negative **Depart from evil** opening the way for positive goodness—**do good; seek peace, and pursue it** (Rom. 14:19; Heb. 12:14).

Encouragement of Righteousness. 34:15-22. The encouragement of righteousness finds expression in four things: (1) **15.** It is in the LORD's attitude toward **the righteous**—those justified by faith, who live by faith in God's grace (Psalm 32:1-2). His **eyes ... are upon** them in loving concern to chasten them if they do wrong, and to bless and reward them when they do right (33:18). **His ears are open unto their cry.** He hears their prayer and delivers them, for they are justified (v. 17; 32:1-2) and therefore in right relation to Him as the infinitely

Holy One. He is near the brokenhearted and saves the crushed in spirit (v. 18; Isa. 57:15; 61:1).

(2) **16.** It is in the LORD's attitude toward the unrighteous (evildoers), those not justified by faith (Gen. 15:6; Psalm 32:1-2), whose unforgiven sin is manifest in their evil deeds. **The face of the Lord** is against such evildoers (Jer. 44:11; Amos 9:4) to **cut off the remembrance of them from the earth** (Psalms 9:6; 109:15; Job 18:17). "Evil shall slay the wicked ... they ... shall be desolate" (v. 21).

(3) **19.** It is in the fact that although the **afflictions of the righteous** are many (Psalm 71:20; 2 Tim. 3:11-12), they continually enjoy the LORD's deliverance out of them all (Psalm 34:4, 6, 17), David's own life, as well as the lives of the Tribulation saints, being dramatic examples. The latter will experience God's great deliverance, whether by being spared death or suffering martyrdom (Rev. 7:1-8; 7:9-17; 14:1-5); in fact, their martyrdom will bring them even greater glory and reward (6:11).

(4) **20.** It is in consideration of God's wonderful keeping power over His own. He **keepeth all his bones; not one of them is broken** (cf. Exod. 12:46; John 19:36). This divine guardianship is made exceedingly precious to the believer because it applies to the all-righteous One, our Savior, who through His unfathomable sufferings and death was still kept by the Father. **22.** The LORD redeems His own—not one of them **shall be desolate** (*'shm*, "be or be held guilty" or "condemned"; Psalm 37:40), because their sins are forgiven, and the LORD does not impute iniquity to them (see 32:1-2).

II. CRY FOR RESCUE FROM FOES. 35:1-28.

For the full scope of this psalm, see

the introduction to Psalm 25. The psalm is said to have been penned by David, probably at some time during his persecution by Saul. The whole ode is a powerful appeal to the all-righteous God to execute judgment upon the wicked persecutors of His people. Such vehement prayer has issued from the lips of persecuted and afflicted saints in every age, but it will find its prophetic fulfillment and full moral justification from the lips of the Jewish remnant during the end-time reign of Antichrist (Rev. 13:1-18), when human wickedness will have reached its apex (9:20-21) and will call for swift and irremediable execution of God's wrath (14:19-20; 15:7-8; 16:1-21; cf. comment on Psalm 5:10).

Prayer Appeal to the All-Righteous God. 35:1-16. **1.** The LORD was called upon to **plead** (contend) and **fight against** the enemies and persecutors of His people (cf. Exod. 14:25; Psalm 18:43; Isa. 49:25). The cause was put in the LORD's hands because the saint's enemies were His foes.

2-3. Dramatically, the psalmist summoned the LORD to arm Himself with **shield... buckler... spear** and **battle-axe** (NASB; Psalms 44:26; 91:4; cf. Rev. 19:15). He prayed the imprecatory prayer (see 5:10), in which he cried out for three things: (1) **4.** He prayed for the utter **confusion** of his enemies (cf. v. 26; 40:14-15; 129:5). (2) **5-6.** He prayed for their total destruction **as chaff before the wind** (1:4; 83:13; Job 21:18; Isa. 29:5; Dan. 2:35), with **the angel of the Lord,** the preincarnate Christ (Gen. 16:7; Judg. 2:1; Isa. 37:36), chasing and persecuting them, as they had done to His people (cf. Rev. 14:19). **7.** Their crime showed that their iniquity was ripe for judgment, for their persecution was completely without justification (cf. v. 12).

(3) **8.** He prayed that destruction would come upon the LORD's enemies without warning and that they would be taken in the very trap they had laid for God's people (Psalms 9:15; 55:23; 73:18; Isa. 47:11; 1 Thess. 5:3). **9.** Meanwhile, the saint having experienced the LORD's wonderful deliverance, rejoiced in Him (Isa. 61:10) and exulted in His salvation (Psalms 9:14; 13:5).

10-16a. All his **bones**, a poetic figure for the psalmist's innermost convictions, would declare the incomparableness of the LORD (Exod. 15:11; Psalm 86:8; Mic. 7:18) in delivering the afflicted and the needy from those who robbed him (Psalms 37:14; 109:16), maliciously witnessed against him (27:12; cf. Matt. 24:9-12), requited him evil, hatred, and betrayal for good and for loving concern (Psalms 38:20; 109:5; Jer. 18:20; John 10:32). They thus manifested the depth of their sin, its ripeness for judgment, and the consequent justness of the saint's imprecations that they be destroyed (Rev. 14:19; 19:15; cf. Isa. 63:3; Lam. 1:15).

16b. Like the enemies that crucified Christ—smiting, slandering, and deriding Him, and doubtlessly also gnashing at Him with their teeth (cf. Matt. 27:27-44)—so the enemies of His people treat them as they treated Him, and they especially will do so under the ruthless regime of the Antichrist (Rev. 13:7, 17).

Cry for Vindication. 35:17-28. **17. Lord, how long ... ?** (Psalm 13:1; Hab. 1:13; Rev. 6:9-10). **Rescue my soul** (i.e., "me") **... mine only one** ("my only life," NASB; "my face," AB) **from the lions** (Psalm 22:20-21), lionlike, fierce foes. **18.** The same spirit that animated Christ also seems to animate His own in their deep sufferings (22:22, 25). **19.** The prayer is that those who hate the LORD and His people shall not rejoice in victory or **wink with the eye** (i.e., "maliciously"; cf. Prov. 6:13; 10:10). **20-21.** They do not speak peace, but devise deceit and treachery.

23-26a. The psalmist cried to God to bestir Himself, to awake, as if He were sleeping and therefore unconscious of his plight (Zech. 2:13; cf. Hab. 2:20; Zeph. 1:7) and **judge** him (do him justice). Compare the widow and her prayer in Jesus' parable (Luke 18:1-8), "Avenge me of mine adversary," which gives another prophetic foregleam of the Israelite remnant and their cry for vindication to be answered at the Messiah's second advent and Kingdom (Matt. 25:31-46; Rev. 19:11—20:3).

26b-27. Let God's enemies be **clothed with shame and dishonor**, but in contrast, let God's people **shout for joy** (cf. Rev. 18:20). Let them say continually, **Let the Lord be magnified**, which they will do when established in Kingdom blessing (Isa. 12:1-6; 35:1-10). Then, too, the saint's **tongue shall speak** of His praise perpetually.

JJ. MAN'S WICKEDNESS AND GOD'S LOVING-KINDNESS. 36:1-12.

The central theme of this psalm is God's loving-kindness (vv. 5, 7, 10) sharply set in opposition to the wickedness of man (vv. 1-4), the latter prophetically reaching its heyday in the end-time revolt against God (2:1-3). The psalm concludes with a prayer for deliverance and the assurance of the overthrow of the wicked (vv. 10-12; cf. 2:4-12).

A *Picture of Human Depravity.* *36:1-4.* Three things are said about the wicked man: (1) **1a. Transgression** is pictured as speaking from the heart of a wicked man, who regards it as an oracle (lit. Heb., "The wicked man has an oracle of rebellion [*pĕshă'*] in his heart," following the Septuagint, the Syriac,

and Jerome, rather than "my" heart; Matt. 15:19). Sin deludes the sinner to project his evil thoughts from the seat of moral authority, from which God has been dethroned.

(2) **1b.** The wicked man has **no fear of God before his eyes** (Rom. 3:18). His rebellion against God deludes him into thinking he has no need to fear any consequences of his conduct as he shuts himself within himself and listens to his old fallen nature (his own oracle), which persuades him that he does not have to answer to his Creator for his deeds.

2. Transgression (as an oracle) flatters the wicked in his own eyes (Deut. 29:19; Psalms 10:11; 49:18), inflates his ego and self-righteousness, or glosses over his sins, even when his iniquity is hateful. (3) **3.** The wicked man's words are flagrant deceit itself (Deut. 29:19; Mark 7:21-23), and **he hath ceased to be wise ... to do good** (Psalm 94:8; Jer. 4:22), rapidly discovering that evil in the heart and thoughts soon expresses itself in evil conduct.

4. As a result, he plans wickedness **upon his bed** (Prov. 4:16; Mic. 2:1) and **setteth himself in a way** (on a course or path) **that is not good** (Isa. 65:2), and so he **abhorreth** (despises) not evil (Psalm 52:3; Rom. 12:9). Finally, man's day comes to full fruition in the Antichrist of the end time (Rev. 13:1-8), the "man of sin ... the son of perdition" (2 Thess. 2:3), in whom human depravity will be personified as "the wicked [lawless] one" (2:8).

A *Portrait of Divine Goodness and Mercy.* *36:5-9.* **5.** What a contrast to the wicked is the LORD, whom they do not fear! The **mercy** (*hĕsĕd*, "covenant love") and **faithfulness** of God are as limitless as the heavens and the endless perspectives of the **clouds** (Psalms 57:10; 103:11; 108:4). **6a-b.** His **righteousness** (71:19) is like the mountains of

God (mighty mountains); His **judgments** are metaphorically compared to a great deep (77:19; Job 11:8; Rom. 11:33). **6c.** He preserves man and beast (Psalms 104:14-15; 145:16; Neh. 9:6), both of whom are dependent upon Him.

7-9a. His loving-kindness is "precious" (Psalms 40:5; 139:17), and so mankind takes refuge in the shadow of His wings (57:1; Ruth 2:12; Matt. 23:37) and drinks to the full in His house of plenty (Psalm 63:5; Isa. 25:6; Jer. 31:12-14) and from the river of His delights (Psalm 46:4; Job 20:17; Rev. 22:1). In Him is **the fountain of life** (Jer. 2:13; John 4:10, 14), the source of all life—physical, spiritual, and eternal. **9b.** In His light, who is "the light of the world" (John 8:12), **we see light** (cf. 1 John 1:5-7; 1 Tim. 6:16).

A Prayer for the Divine Interposition. 36:10-12. **10.** He prayed for the continuance of God's **loving-kindness** to those who **know** Him, and the manifestation of His **righteousness** to the **upright in heart** (the forgiven; 32:1-2). **11.** He prayed that **the foot of pride**, the proud foot of the sinner (vv. 1-4), would not advance against him, and the hand of the wicked would not **remove** him (drive him away), particularly when the wicked one and his followers at the end time will attempt to exterminate every godly person (Rev. 13:1-18; 16:13-16; Psalm 2:1-3). **12.** He saw the final overthrow of the **workers of iniquity** (Rev. 9:21), then being cast down to rise no more (19:11—20:3).

KK. PROVIDENCE AND THE PROSPERITY OF THE WICKED. 37:1-40.

The major problem of the poet is the seeming inconsistency connected with the prosperity of the wicked and the suffering of the godly at their hands. How can that be reconciled with God's goodness? The problem has always been acute, but it will be much more so in the heyday of lawlessness at the end of the age when the righteous will suffer so greatly at the hands of the wicked that they will appear to be forsaken by God (cf. Rev. 13:7, 15). The psalm is alphabetical, similar to the acrostics in Psalms 9 and 10.

Faith in the Lord Is the Solution to the Problem. 37:1-11. **1. Fret not** (Prov. 23:17; 24:19) **... neither be envious** (Psalm 73:3; Prov. 3:31) against **evildoers** and **workers of iniquity.** Their doom is imminent and certain. **2.** They will **wither ... like the grass, and fade like the green herb** (NASB; Job 14:2; Psalms 90:6; 92:7; 129:6). Such vivid similes in Bible lands are very expressive since the hot sun so quickly scorches up the spring flowers and verdure.

The cure for fretting (becoming overwrought) over evildoers and becoming indignant at wrongdoers is to have faith in the LORD (vv. 3-11). **3-4.** This vital trust will produce good works (Psalm 62:8), insure residence **in the land** (the promised land; Deut. 30:20), guarantee being fed on the truth of God's faithfulness, cause one to give top priority to the LORD, manifested in delighting oneself in Him (Psalm 94:19; Job 22:26; Isa. 58:14), resulting in realizing the desires of one's heart (Psalms 21:2; 145:19; Matt. 7:8).

5a. It will also mean complete surrender to the LORD (Psalm 55:22; Prov. 16:3; Rom. 12:1-2; 2 Cor. 5:8; 1 Pet. 5:7) in committing (rolling) one's way on the LORD. **5b-6.** Such truth enlists the help and direction of the LORD and His vindication against the attacks and charges of the wicked (Job 11:17; Psalm 97:11; Isa. 58:8, 10; Mic. 7:9).

7-8. Such trust will also enable one to **rest in the Lord**, be quiet and submissive before Him (Psalm 62:5), patiently waiting for His aid and vindication (40:1), and to cease being disturbed or upset by the prosperity and apparent success of evil men (37:1; Jer. 12:1), thus avoiding anger and wrath (Eph. 4:31; Col. 3:8), which otherwise would be inevitable and poison the spirit of the saint.

9-11. Faith in the LORD and consequently in His Word will assure the suffering saint that the evildoer will shortly be cut off (v. 2); and that the earth, which the wicked design to take over (2:1-3), the **meek** (the afflicted) **shall inherit** (Matt. 5:5; Psalms 22:26; 147:6; 149:4; Isa. 29:19; Rev. 20:4-6). *The Way of the Wicked and Righteous in Contrast. 37:12-21.* **12. The wicked plotteth against the just** ("the righteous"; 32:1-2; cf. 2:1-3). **13.** The LORD shall laugh at him (2:4; 59:8) because He sees **his day** (of overthrow and punishment) is coming. **14-15.** The wicked fight against the poor and needy, but the sword shall enter their own heart, and their bow shall be broken (cf. 1 Sam. 17:50-51; Rev. 16:13-16; 19:11—20:3).

16-18. The little a true saint possesses of worldly goods (Prov. 15:16; 16:8; 1 Tim. 6:6) is better than the wealth of many wicked people, for the wicked shall be punished, but the righteous have an everlasting inheritance (cf. Eph. 1:11). **19-20.** The righteous shall not be put to confusion in an evil time, or perish in famine, as will the wicked, who will be **like the glory** (flowers) **of the pastures** that vanishes before the hot sun **like smoke** (NASB) before the wind. **21. The wicked borrows and does not pay back,** in contrast to the righteous, who is **gracious and gives** (NASB; Psalm 112:5). *The End of the Righteous and the Wicked. 37:22-40.* **22.** The **blessed** (cf. Matt. 25:34) inherit the Kingdom. The

cursed (25:41) are cut off in death (25:46). **23.** The good man and his step-by-step walk are ordered by the LORD; his delight is in His way. **24-29.** The LORD's unfailing sustenance and care of the good man and his separation from evil and his good works and reward (cf. v. 22) are described.

30-31. His mouth speaks wisdom, his heart contains the Word of God, and so his way is sure and his steps do not slide into sin. **32-33.** In contrast, the wicked watches the righteous in order to slay him (cf. Rev. 13:6-7, 17), but the LORD will not abandon His own to the wicked (Psalm 31:8; 2 Pet. 2:9) or let him be condemned when he is judged (Psalms 34:22; 109:31).

34. God's persecuted saints are exhorted to wait for the LORD (v. 9; 27:14), and He will exalt them to inherit the land (see vv. 9, 11) **when the wicked are cut off** (Rev. 19:11—20:3; cf. 1:7). **35-36.** The psalmist gave testimony of the transiency and evil of the wicked, spreading himself like a **green bay tree** ("a luxuriant tree in its native soil," NASB; Job 8:16), which dies and soon passes away (Psalm 37:10; Job 20:5).

37. The righteous man, however, **will have a posterity** (NASB), both physical and spiritual, to leave behind him. But the wicked will be cut off and utterly destroyed (Rev. 19:11—20:3; cf. Psalms 37:20; 73:17). **39. The salvation of the righteous** will be from the LORD, and He is their strength **in the time of trouble** (9:9; Dan. 12:1; Matt. 24:21-22; Rev. 7:1-17). **40.** He **shall help them, and ... deliver them from the wicked** (Rev. 12:13—13:18), because they (His own) trust in Him (Psalm 2:12).

LL. CRY OF A SUFFERING PENITENT. 38:1-22.

In this penitential psalm the disquietude caused by unbelief and sin can be discerned in the experience of the psalmist and in that of the saints of all ages. But, it will climax in the penitential confession of the remnant of Israel that will turn to the LORD at His second advent in Kingdom glory (Zech. 12:10—13:1). Then the great strains of Isaiah 53:1-10 will well up from Israel's heart and lips (Rom. 11:25-33).

Deep Conviction of Sin. 38:1-12. The physical and mental distress, metaphorically presented, accentuates the piercing contrition for sin experienced. **1.** The LORD rebuking and chastening in **wrath** and **hot displeasure** (anger; v. 3; 6:1; cf. Rev. 6:17; 11:18; 16:1; 19:15) led the psalmist to realize and own his sin. This is the purpose of the sufferings of saints in general, and it will be the specific purpose of "the time of Jacob's trouble," namely, that Jacob may be "saved out of it" (Jer. 30:7).

2. The divine agencies are pictured figuratively as **arrows** that **stick fast** in him (Job 6:4), with the divine **hand** relentlessly pressing down on him (Psalm 32:4). **3-4.** His sin is set forth figuratively as an infirm body (6:2; 31:10; Job 33:19; Isa. 1:5-6), with his iniquities going over his head (Psalm 40:12; Ezra 9:6) and constituting a heavy burden utterly weighing him down.

5-6. His **wounds** ("stripes") laid upon him in the divine chastening grow foul and fester because of his folly (Psalm 69:5), bending him down and reducing him to deep mourning (42:9; 43:2; Job 30:28). **7.** His loins were **filled with burning** (NASB; Psalm 102:3; cf. Jer. 30:6-7), and there was no soundness in his flesh (Psalm 38:3), for he saw his deep sin and abhorred it. **8.** The sense of his sin caused him to feel **feeble** and **very broken** (Lam. 1:13; 5:17). He **roared** (groaned loudly; Psalms 22:1; 32:3) because of the **disquietness of** his **heart.**

9-12. He laid his soul bare before the LORD (10:17; 102:5) as his strength failed (31:10; 69:3; 88:9). His friends and relatives avoided him (31:11; 88:18; Matt. 24:9-12; Luke 23:49) and his enemies sought his life (Psalm 54:3), laying snares (140:5) and threatening destruction (Mic. 7:3), constantly devising treachery (Psalm 35:20; Matt. 24:9-12; John 15:20-21; Rev. 2:10).

True Confession of Sin. 38:13-20. **13-15.** The psalmist was oblivious of his enemies and persecutors, like a **deaf** and **dumb man** (39:2, 9), because he placed his hope in the LORD and waited for Him (39:7), confident He would answer in help and deliverance (17:6). **16.** He was concerned that the godless persecutors would rejoice over him and magnify themselves against him when his foot slipped into unbelief and sin.

17-18. He realized his peril and sorrow and made full confession of his sin (32:5; Zech. 12:10—13:1), being wholly exercised because of it (2 Cor. 7:9-10). **19.** But his enemies were vigorous and strong (Psalms 18:17; 35:19; cf. Rev. 6:9-10; 7:14; 13:7, 17). **20.** They repaid him evil for good (Psalm 35:12) and opposed him, because he followed what was good (109:4; 1 John 3:12).

Genuine Prayer for Help. 38:21-22. **21. Do not forsake me . . . do not be far from me** (NASB; 22:19; 35:22). **22. Make haste to help me, O Lord, my salvation** (40:13; cf. 27:1; Rev. 6:9-10).

MM. FACING DEATH. 39:1-13.

This psalm (like Psalm 38) reflects the experience of the psalmist and the saint in every age who faces trouble and death. However, it has a climactic application to the suffering remnant of the time of Great Tribulation and widespread martyrdom under the Antichrist at the end of the age. Then the LORD's people will indeed learn the vanity of earthly things and wait for the LORD only. The superscription "to Jeduthun" refers to a famous leader of the tabernacle choir in David's day (cf. 1 Chron. 16:41, 42; 25:1-6; cf. titles of Psalms 62 and 77).

The Vanity of Life. 39:1-6. **1.** In the trouble that beset the psalmist, he resolved to **take heed** (*shmr*, "keep, guard") to his **ways** (his walk or conduct) that he might not **sin** (*hṭ'*, "miss the mark") with his **tongue** (34:13; Job 2:10; James 3:5-12), and to **keep** (guard) his **mouth** (Psalm 141:3) **with a bridle** (muzzle), while the **wicked** was before him (in his presence). Chastened by his trials, he would give no cause for others to stumble, nor would he give his foes reason for "reproach" (v. 8).

2a. Therefore, he was **dumb with silence** (38:13) and **held** his **peace** (refrained), **even from good**, evidently failing to testify to his faith to avoid further persecution from his enemies (cf. Dan. 12:10; Matt. 24:9-10; Luke 21:12). **2b-3.** Therefore, his **sorrow was stirred** ("grew worse") and his **heart** became **hot** and **the fire burned** (cf. Jer. 20:9).

4-6. His heart and lips burst out in prayer to the LORD, and he petitioned (1) for enlightenment concerning his **end** (Psalms 90:12; 119:84; Job 6:11), for tribulation and death stalked his steps (cf. Dan. 12:10; Matt. 24:9; Rev. 6:9-10; 7:14); and (2) that he might know the extent of his days (the length of his earthly life) that he might know **how frail** (*ḥāḏēl*, "ceasing, failing," i.e., "transient") he was (Psalms 78:39; 103:14).

5. He confessed the LORD had made his **days** (his earthly sojourn) **as an handbreadth** (*ṭĕpaḥ*, "the width of the hand at the base of the four fingers"); man's life is but "as a handbreadth," literally, "a few handbreadths in length" (cf. 89:47), and his **age** (lifetime, life-span) is as **nothing** in God's sight (144:4); and every man at best is **altogether vanity** (62:9; Job 14:2; Eccles. 6:12; James 4:14).

6. He walks **in a vain show** (as a shadow or phantom (1 Cor. 7:31; James 1:10-11; 1 Pet. 1:24) and makes an uproar for nothing (Psalm 127:2; Eccles. 5:17), amassing wealth (Psalm 62:9; Job 14:2; Eccles. 6:2), but not knowing who will gather it after his brief life is over.

Submission to God's Will. 39:7-13. **7.** Having surveyed the brevity of life and the vanity of man, the psalmist turned his case over to the LORD. **What wait I for?** His answer: **My hope is in thee** (38:15), because he found every other hope was futile as he faced foes and death itself. **8.** Accordingly, he prayed for spiritual blessings—deliverance from all his transgressions (51:9, 14; 79:9), and that the LORD would not permit him to be **the reproach** (scorn) **of the foolish** (*nāḇāl*), the godless, irreligious, and unbelieving man (44:13; 79:4; 119:22) of any age, the enemy of the godly man; quintessentially, the Antichrist, the lawless one of the end time (and his followers), the supreme exemplification of folly, the "foolish shepherd" (Zech. 11:15-17).

9. He demonstrated his submission by rigid silence concerning complaints against the LORD (Psalm 39:2). **Thou didst it** ("hast done it") became for him a sufficient justification for whatever affliction he might be called upon to endure (cf. 2 Sam. 16:10; Job 2:10). **10.** He saw in his sufferings the chastening hand of the LORD—the LORD's **stroke** (plague; Job 9:34; 13:21), **the blow** (opposition) of His hand in protest against his sin, by which he was **consumed**, became exhausted or spent (Psalm 32:4).

11. He realized that **with rebukes** (reproofs) God chastens His own **for iniquity** (Ezek. 5:15; 2 Pet. 2:16) and consumes man's **beauty** (*ḥᵃmûḏ*, "what is desirable or costly"), "what is precious to him" (NASB; cf. Psalm 90:7; Job 13:28; Isa. 50:9) **like a moth** consumes a splendid garment until it becomes useless. **Surely every man is vanity** (*'ăḵ*, "only," i.e., "nothing but vanity"; "vapor, mere breath"; Psalm 39:5).

12-13. These verses are a cry for divine response to the psalmist's **tears** (56:8; 2 Kings 20:5), for he said, "I am a passing guest with Thee" (BV). A guest in the Near East enjoyed childlike privileges of safety, food, and shelter, which the godly can claim from the LORD (cf. Lev. 25:23; 1 Chron. 29:15; Psalm 119:19; Heb. 11:13; 1 Pet. 2:11). He said he was **a sojourner** (transient), **as all** his **fathers** (ancestors) **were.** He prayed to be spared in order that the LORD might **turn** His scrutinizing **gaze away** (NASB) from him (in chastening) that he might **recover strength** (might "become cheerful," "smile again," NASB) before death overtook him (Psalm 102:24; Job 7:19; 14:6; cf. Matt. 24:13-22).

NN. CHRIST'S RESURRECTION SONG. 40:1-17.

That this psalm is Messianic (and goes beyond David's experiences and those of saints throughout the ages) is attested by the quotation of verses 6 to 8 as such in Hebrews 10:5-9. Moreover, the context of verses 1 to 5 is of a piece with verses 6 to 8 and 10 to 17, and so the *entire* psalm speaks prophetically of Christ and the result of His redemptive work.

The Messiah's Song of Triumph and the Results of His Redemption. 40:1-5. The subject of Psalm 40 is the Messiah, the LORD's Servant's obedience to death, which was crowned with resurrection and ascension and His "new song" of redemption (vv. 1-3). The psalm opens with Him "who, in the days of his flesh, when he had offered up prayers and supplications with strong crying and tears unto him that was able to save him from death . . . was heard" (Heb. 5:7).

Therefore, the Spirit of Christ spoke prophetically through the psalmist: **1. I waited patiently for the Lord, and he inclined unto me, and heard my cry** (Psalm 34:15). The answer to His cry was deliverance from death by resurrection. **2. He brought me up also out of an horrible pit** (*bôr shā'ôn*, "a deep roaring chasm"), "a vast deep cavity into which roaring waters rush" (JFB). The pit of "tumult, roar, rush, desolation, and destruction" (all these ideas are comprehended in the Hebrew *shā'ôn*; cf. Deut. 32:10), graphically symbolizes the Messiah's sufferings to death for us, bearing the thunders of the divine justice against our sins, the horror of the maledictory sentence of the Law, the mocking of men, and the rage of satanic powers.

The **miry clay** is the deep mud at the bottom of the pit (Psalm 69:2), into which one's feet sink, in contrast to the **rock**, an image of security (18:2, 33), upon which **He set my feet . . . making my footsteps firm** (NASB; 27:5; 37:23), embracing the ascension of our LORD and His being seated at the right hand of God.

3. The **new song** put in His mouth is the anthem of victory over sin, death, and hell, with redemption as its theme. It is led by Christ, the Prince-Leader of our salvation, and is taken up by His redeemed (Rev. 1:5-6; 5:9-10). The "new song" is one of **praise unto our God,** "our," not merely "my God," for many will constitute the vast choir of the redeemed that the Messiah will conduct. **Many shall see** God's deliverance of Christ, first from sin, death, and hell, and then of His redeemed, saved by Him.

This sight will create **fear** in many—fear of offending One who displayed His abhorrence of sin and redeemed His own from it at such dreadful cost, and so **trust** in Him is inseparably joined to it. Such fear begets faith (trust in the LORD), which in turn brings salvation. The passage is a prophecy of the great company of the elect who would believe on the One who would come into the world to die and rise again to bring them salvation by God's grace through faith (Gen. 15:6; Psalm 32:1-2; Eph. 2:8-9).

4. The psalmist then reviewed the blessedness of the person who subscribes to the one true gospel of salvation by grace through faith, **who maketh the Lord his trust** (Psalm 84:12) and **respecteth** (regards) **not the proud,** who rely upon their own goodness and parade their own self-righteousness and thus reject salvation by faith alone in the Savior and so **turn aside to lies** (125:5), lapsing into the falsehood of salvation by faith plus works, or salvation entirely by works (the basic error of all heresy and cultism).

5. When the psalmist considered the glorious salvation of the LORD his God (appropriating His blessing through the covenant, redemptive name, Jehovah), he doubtlessly considered it the quintessential wonder of all the **wonderful works** God has wrought (134:3; Job 5:9) and the supreme manifestation of His loving **thoughts ... toward us** (Psalm 139:17; Isa. 55:8), marking Him as incomparable. In attempting to declare these "wonders" ($nipl^{e\cdot} \hat{o}t$, "supernatural undertakings"), the believer found them uncounted and uncountable (Psalms 71:15; 139:18).

The Obedient One and His Sacrifice. 40:6-8. **6.** The speaker, as Hebrews 10:7-9 shows, is the preincarnate Son in the bosom of the Father. He declared the valuelessness of **sacrifice** ($z\check{e}\underbar{b}\bar{a}\underbar{h}$,

"blood sacrifice") and **offering** ($minh\hat{a}$, "bloodless sacrifice") apart from faith and obedience (1 Sam. 15:22; Psalms 50:5, 8-14; 51:16-17; Jer. 7:22-24; Hos. 6:6). God does not **desire** them, nor does He require **burnt offering** and **sin offering,** entailing the shedding of the blood of bulls and goats.

Rather, He desires the sacrifice of Christ, exemplifying perfect faith and obedience (Heb. 9:13-14), and hence efficacious to expiate sin. Therefore, the obedient One exclaims: **Mine ears hast thou opened** (lit., "dug" or "pierced for me," meaning, "Thou hast so constructed my ears that they have an open passage through which Thy Word reaches me"; or, in brief, "Thou hast given me ears to hear."

Hebrews 10:5, 7 quotes this passage from the Septuagint, "a body hast thou prepared me," that is, "fitted for me," for the way the Messiah attested His obedience was by the assumption of a human body, the ear being the physical member that symbolizes obedience. Bengel says the writer of Hebrews merely interprets the psalmist, using the ears as a part for the whole body. Others take the expression "to dig the ears" as equivalent "to open the ear" (Isa. 48:8; 50:4-5), "to uncover the ear" (1 Sam. 9:15; 20:2), in the sense of giving a divine communication that will be received and obeyed.

7. Then, when the sacrifices and offerings of the old economy proved not to be what God desired for the expiation of sin or even the perfect fulfillment of the Law of obedience, "when the fullness of the time was come" (Gal. 4:4) **said I, Lo, I come.** Christ was willing from eternity, but He openly evidenced His willing obedience at His advent into our fallen world. This was the perfect exhibition of His obedience to God's will expressed in verse 6, "Mine ears hast thou opened." **In the volume** (roll or scroll) **of the book** (of Scripture, which contained the Pentateuch) **it is written of me**, "prescribed to me" (Hengstenberg).

8. The Messiah is set forth as having come to fulfill all the will of God, expressed so fully in the warp and woof of the Pentateuch in prophecies, types, and promises (Luke 24:44; John 5:45). His one delight was to do God's will (John 4:34; 6:38; 17:4). He asserts God's Law was **within** His heart. Although Old Testament believers in a measure had the Law in their hearts (Deut. 6:6; Psalm 37:31; Prov. 3:3), yet the fullness of the Spirit, when the Law actually became inscribed on the hearts of God's people (Jer. 31:33), was reserved for the times of the Messiah, upon whose heart, as the God-man, the Law was first perfectly written (Matt. 5:17; Rom. 10:4). Christ alone (and no mere man such as David) fully reconciles the opposites and solves what would otherwise be self-contradictions — "delighting to do God's will" and having "the law within His heart," yet encompassed with "innumerable iniquities" (not His own, but ours, laid on Him by imputation, v. 12).

The Obedient One and His Preaching Ministry. 40:9-10. **9.** He **preached righteousness in the great congregation** (22:22, 25:35:18), that is, in the assembly of the redeemed. Both in His earthly ministry and after His death and resurrection, by the Holy Spirit through His followers, He declared to all mankind the salvation He purchased.

He preached (*bśr*, "announced good news," the good tidings of the gospel; Isa. 40:9; 61:1) that God not only would not impute iniquity, but also would reckon His very righteousness to the sinner who believes in Christ's redemptive sacrifice (Psalm 32:1-2; Dan. 9:24; Rom. 3:25-26), thereby vindicating the Law of God violated by fallen man (Isa. 42:21). Not merely did Christ have the Law of God within his heart (v. 8), but He proclaimed righteousness in a general sense as the essence of the Law.

10. Then He proceeded to speak of that righteousness as being peculiarly God's. **I have not hidden thy righteousness within my heart,** for God is the ultimate source of all good and righteousness. Christ through His servants has **declared** God's **faithfulness** and **salvation** and **not concealed** His **lovingkindness** (so wonderfully exhibited in Christ's obedient sacrifice of Himself) **... from the great congregation,** the whole vast assembly of the elect and the redeemed. This activity is so certain of fulfillment that it is viewed as already accomplished.

The Obedient One and His Sin-Bearing Ministry. 40:11-12. **11.** Once more (cf. vv. 6-8), the Messiah's substitutionary sacrifice comes into view. **Thou** is emphatic. "As for You, O LORD, You will not withhold Your mercies from me" (lit. Heb.). The passage is a steadfast assertion of faith (rather than a petition) based on the firm foundation of obedience and submission, even to death, laid in verses 1 to 10 (cf. Phil. 2:5-9). The Messiah could voice unswerving faith as He faced the supreme ordeal of bearing the sin of the world, that the Father's **loving-kindness and ... truth** would **preserve** Him (Psalms 23:6; 43:3; 57:3; 61:7; Heb. 5:7).

12. For innumerable evils surrounded Him (all the indignities and atrocities, especially during His trial and crucifixion). But the most terrible and painful was the supreme test of the obedience of the Holy One to become the sin offering for the whole world as He faced the issue of Calvary in Gethsemane's shadows (Luke 22:42, 44). **Mine iniquities,** the aggregate of both the sins of the whole world and their penal consequences (Isa. 53:4-6; Mark 15:28; 2 Cor. 5:21), **have taken hold upon me.** The obedient One had no sin, but He vicariously took our sins upon Himself; so the Father turned away His face from Him (Psalm 22:1; Matt. 27:46).

Not only was He engulfed on all sides by countless evils, but the mass of iniquities, which was *His* only vicariously, was laid upon His holy head; so He was unable to **look up,** for the heavens were black and the Father's face was turned away from the sinless One as the sin-bearer and His vicarious iniquities, infinite in their scope, since they were the sins of the entire fallen race. Their number was figuratively described as **more than the hairs** of His head.

This spiritual agony was absolutely unique, making our Lord's sufferings infinite in degree and unparalleled in the annals of human agony (Lam. 1:12). Therefore, His sinless **heart** failed when it bore this terrible load of sin, and it broke in anguish as the Holy One, by an act of His will, dismissed His spirit when His atoning sin-bearing work was completed (Matt. 27:50).

The Obedient One Identified with His Own Who Suffer. 40:13-17. **13-15.** The cry is from the persecuted and suffering saint of every age, but it has special relevance to the Lord's "brothers" (Matt. 25:40, 45), the pious Jewish remnant during the coming Great Tribulation (Dan. 12:1; Matt. 24:21; Rev. 7:1-8), who will undergo unparalleled anguish (Jer. 30:5-7) at the hands of the Antichrist and his followers. (For the imprecatory nature of these prayers, see comment on Psalm 5:10.) **16-17.** These verses express the prayer of His saints in the vortex of trouble (34:6; 41:7; Rev.

6:10-11). He who suffered so agonizingly (vv. 1-12) can identify and sympathize with His own who suffer.

OO. THE SUFFERINGS OF CHRIST AND THE GLORY TO FOLLOW. 41:1-13.

This is both a Davidic and a Messianic psalm, as the New Testament vouches (v. 9; John 13:18; cf. Acts 1:16). Like Psalm 40, it goes beyond David's experiences and those of saints throughout the ages and adumbrates "the sufferings of Christ, and the glory that should follow" (1 Pet. 1:11).

The Blessings of Faith in the Lowly One. 41:1-3. **1a. Blessed is he that considereth the poor** (*dăl,* "the one brought low, reduced to poverty and helplessness"), prefiguring our Lord when He "humbled himself ... even [to] the death of the cross" (Phil. 2:6-8). "O the blessings [benefits] of him who gives attention to [*măskîl 'ĕl,* 'acts circumspectly, responds prudently toward'] the lowly One [by believing in Him and thus evidencing saving faith]."

Such a genuine believer in any age enjoys many deliverances and the blessings of God's salvation. He shows his saving faith (Rom. 3:22) by his works (James 2:14-20), in his attitude toward the poor. **1b-2.** But the prophetic scope focuses upon the Jewish remnant of the future and its deliverance in the supreme **time of trouble** (Dan. 12:1; Matt. 24:21-22), and its preservation through the horrors of the Great Tribulation (Rev. 7:1-8).

3. The Lord will strengthen such a believer **upon the bed of languishing** (sickbed; Psalm 6:6) and in his illness **make all his bed,** like a tender nurse changing the bed of the patient to make him rest more comfortably. "All his bed" means figuratively that however great his affliction or however often he is afflicted, the LORD like a tender nurse watches lovingly over him and is concerned about his comfort.

The Curse of Unbelief in the Lowly One. 41:4-9. The speaker in this section is the lowly, rejected One, speaking prophetically of His rejection. He who can claim the promise of mercy to the lowly (vv. 1-3) pleads His distressed state before God and the malice of His foes as grounds for the fulfillment of the promise in His sufferings.

4. I (emphatic in the Hebrew) **said, Lord, be merciful** (gracious) **unto me, heal my soul ... I have sinned against thee.** David, the type, rightly looks upon sufferings as divinely permitted to bring the sufferer to confess his guiltiness and seek spiritual healing as preliminary to physical healing. The sufferings of the Antitype, the sinless One, by contrast, were the penalty of our sins, which He vicariously took upon Himself as our sin-bearer (cf. comments on Psalm 40:12).

Verses 5 to 9 outline the unbelief and consequent enmity of those who did not respond prudently toward the lowly One in faith. As a result they did five things: (1) **5.** They slandered Him and desired His death (Matt. 26:59-61; 27:20). (2) **6.** They spoke vanity (falsehood) against Him, hypocritically professing love while gathering material for malicious calumnies to broadcast against Him (John 13:30).

(3) **7.** They whispered against Him and devised His **hurt** ("planned harm against" Him; Matt. 27:28-31). (4) **8.** They declared **an evil disease** (lit., "a word or thing of Belial" was "poured upon him"; cf. Isa. 53:4, "We did esteem him stricken, smitten of God, and afflicted"). They concluded with fiendish joy that some fatal plague had been visited upon Him, and so when He lay down, He would never rise again.

(5) **9.** His **own familiar friend** (lit.,

"the man of my peace"), he who saluted Him with a kiss of peace, as Judas did (Matt. 26:49; cf. Jer. 20:10), **in whom I trusted, who did eat of my bread, hath lifted up his heel against me** (the figure of a horse kicking at his master; Acts 9:5). The historical background is Absalom's rebellion. Ahithophel, "David's counselor" (2 Sam. 15:12) who defected to Absalom, typifies Judas, as David does Christ. The careers and ends of Ahithophel and Judas are similar (2 Sam. 17:23; Matt. 27:5). Our Lord omitted the clause "whom I trusted," for the omniscient One knew Judas's heart and did not trust him.

The Triumph of the Lowly One. 41:10-13. **10-12.** His prayer (v. 4) was answered in His glorious resurrection — **And raise me up,** disappointing the malicious hope of His enemies ("he shall rise up no more," v. 8), **that I may requite** (repay) **them.** There was no personal revenge, but solely the vindication of God's honor and righteousness (Luke 19:27; 2 Thess. 1:8; Rev. 19:11—20:3).

The lowly One was raised from the dead that He might be King and Judge of all (Acts 17:31). To the risen One all judgment has been given (John 5:22). He will return and those who wisely acted toward Him in faith will be rewarded, but His enemies will be punished. Meanwhile, the risen One is in God's own presence. **13.** The first book of psalms concludes with praise, prophetic of the praise that will one day fill all the earth (cf. the ending also of Psalms 72, 89, 106, and all of Psalm 150).

II. BOOK TWO: THE EXODUS SECTION. 42:1—72:20.

This section of the Psalter corresponds to the book of Exodus. Like Exodus, which begins with the sufferings of a people enslaved in Egypt (cf.

Psalms 42-44) and after redemption ends with the glory of the LORD filling the newly completed tabernacle (cf. Psalms 45-72), the psalms of this second book are arranged in a similar order. The oppressed, persecuted people, who suffer at the hands of the ungodly, prefigure suffering saints in every age; but in a very special sense they focus upon the godly Israelite remnant of the end time. Their deliverance is effected by the advent of the Lord in glory, and the great Kingdom psalm (72), portraying the King reigning in His glorious Kingdom, concludes the section.

A. LONGING FOR GOD IN TIME OF TROUBLE. 42:1-11.

"To the chief Musician [precentor, director]." A *Maschil* ("instruction"; see the title of Psalm 32) for the sons of Korah (i.e., "by the Korahites"), who prevalently employ the name God (Elohim) in contrast to the name Jehovah (LORD), which predominates in the Davidic psalms of Book 1, the Genesis section. The Korahite Psalter (Psalms 42-49; 84-88) is thought by many scholars to have sprung from the sanctuary at Dan at the foot of Mount Hermon, the priesthood of which claimed its line went back to Moses through the Korahite family of Levites. Psalms 42 and 43 form a unit, joined by a common refrain (42:5, 11; 43:5).

Keen Desire for God. 42:1-8. **1-3. As the hart panteth after the water brooks, so panteth my soul after thee, O God** (119:131). The psalmist found himself somewhere east of Mount Hermon (v. 6), far from Jerusalem and the Temple of God. What the reason was, whether sickness or exile, the godless people about him taunted him and sneeringly inquired: **Where is thy God?** (Psalms 79:10; 115:2; Joel 2:17; Mic. 7:10).

Meanwhile, seeing a beleaguered deer

panting with thirst and far from its native waterbrooks, the psalmist found the afflicted animal a true companion in sorrow. As the deer whose body was drained of moisture panted for its native watercourses, so the psalmist **panteth** (*ᶜrg*, "had a keen, consuming desire") for **God** and [**thirsted**] **... for the living God** (Psalm 84:2; Josh. 3:10; Jer. 10:10; Dan. 6:26; Matt. 26:63; Rom. 9:26; 1 Thess. 1:9), that is, God manifested dynamically in power and blessing in the sacred feasts and services at the Jerusalem Temple (Psalms 43:4; 84:7; Exod. 23:17).

His **tears,** evidencing his sorrow in being deprived of seeing God's face in manifestation and fellowship at the sacred festivals, were running down his cheeks and entering his mouth as his daily food and drink (Psalms 80:5; 102:9). Meanwhile, his foes taunted him that his God had forsaken him (79:10; 115:2; Joel 2:17; Mic. 7:10).

Prophetically, the godly Jewish remnant is envisioned in the terrible time of Tribulation preceding Christ's advent when the Antichrist will desecrate their Temple, to be restored in Jerusalem (2 Thess. 2:4), and violently scatter and persecute them (Dan. 9:27; 12:11; Matt. 24:15; Rev. 13:5-8).

4. As the psalmist reminisced about how he used to lead the holy festal processions to the house of God (Psalms 55:14; 122:1; Isa. 30:29), he unburdened his saddened heart to God (Psalm 62:8; 1 Sam. 1:15; Job 30:16; Lam. 2:19) as he recalled the voice of joy and thanksgiving (Psalm 100:2) that welled up from the **multitude that kept holy day** (i.e., celebrated the sacred festivals).

5. Dramatically, he challenged his despairing soul (Psalm 38:6; Matt. 26:38) and the inner disturbance of his heart (Psalm 77:3) in his sufferings, and summoned up hope in God, manifested in patient waiting for Him to act on his behalf (71:14; Lam. 3:24), in lively anticipation of praising Him for the help and deliverance of His presence (Psalm 44:3).

6-7. In his deep suffering he cried to God **from the land of** the **Jordan** and . . . **the Hermons,** that is, "the peaks of Hermon" that look down on the headwaters of the Jordan River (Deut. 3:8; 2 Sam. 17:22). The thunder of the waterfalls fed by Hermon's melting snows seemed to answer the depths of his own sorrows.

8. But faith appropriated the divine loving-kindness by day and God's songs of joy by night as his prayer was directed to God, whom he called **the God of my life** (Eccles. 5:18; 8:15). Prophetically, the remnant of the Tribulation under Antichrist will face imminent death, and God alone will sustain in that awful nightmare of woe.

Renewed Cry to God. 42:9-11. **9.** Amid his sufferings the psalmist expressed faith in calling God his **rock** (cf. 18:2). Yet his trials were such that his faith wavered in imagining God had forgotten him. He went mourning (38:6) because of the **oppression of the enemy** (17:9; Rev. 12:13—13:18). **10.** His enemies reproached him and taunted him with the sneer, **Where is thy God?** (Psalm 42:3). **11.** This verse is a repetition of the refrain of 42:5; 43:5.

B. PRAYER FOR DELIVERANCE. 43:1-5.

Psalm 43 forms a unit with Psalm 42 (see the introduction to Psalm 42), actually constituting one psalm.

Prayer for Help and Vindication. 43:1-2. **1.** The persecuted and harassed saint pleaded that God would **judge** (vindicate) him (26:1; 35:24) and **plead** his **cause** (case; 1 Sam. 24:15) against **an ungodly nation** (his own unbelieving people, Israel, in the time of Jacob's

trouble, Jer. 30:5-7). This age will end with Jewish apostasy that will be as pronounced as Gentile apostasy. He pleaded also for deliverance from **the deceitful and unjust man** (Psalms 5:6; 38:12), the lawless one, the man of sin, the Antichrist, the beast (2 Thess. 2:4; Rev. 13:1-8), the product of the abysmal age-end apostasy, who will attempt to exterminate the godly remnant and nullify the divine plan for the Kingdom age (Rev. 7:1-8; 12:13-17; 13:7).

2. Faith alternated with doubt as the harassed one imagined in the awful sufferings of the period that God, though his "rock" (42:9) and his **strength** (Psalms 18:1; 28:7), had **cast** him **off** (rejected him; 44:9; 88:14). Therefore, he went sorrowing because of the terrible **oppression of the enemy** (cf. Rev. 13:7-18).

Prayer for Light and Truth. 43:3-5. **3.** The godly need light and truth, for they want to be led back to God's **holy hill,** Zion, the Temple site (2:6; 42:4; 46:4), and to His **tabernacles** (dwelling places; 84:1), where they can praise and worship the God of Israel. Then those sacred precincts will be desecrated by the Antichrist, who will set up his image in the Temple and demand worship (2 Thess. 2:4; cf. Dan. 9:27; 12:11; Matt. 24:15; Rev. 13:4).

In praying for light and truth, they were actually praying for Christ, the Shepherd of Israel (Psalm 80:1, 3), for He is both the "Sun of righteousness" (Mal. 4:2) to dispel Israel's darkness, and the truth (John 14:6) to end "*the lie*" (the Antichrist; 2 Thess. 2:11). Their prayer will be answered. Israel will be converted (Ezek. 36:26-28).

4. They will go to God's altar (Psalm 26:6), to God their **exceeding joy** (lit., "the gladness of my [their] joy"; Psalm 21:6; Isa. 12:1-6), and praise Him, *their* God (Psalms 33:2; 49:4; 57:8; 71:22). **5.**

Such a prospect and hope challenges despair (42:5, 11).

C. FORMER DELIVERANCES AND PRESENT TRIBULATION. 44:1-26.

The precise historical background of this psalm is unknown and need not be known, since it fits every one of the many times of trouble Israel has gone through. Its prophetic purview, however, is perspicuous. It peculiarly fits Israel's final and climactic era of woe—the Great Tribulation (Dan. 12:1), the time of Jacob's trouble par excellence (Jer. 30:5-7; Rev. 6:1—19:21).

God's Past Deliverances. 44:1-3. **1.** The psalmist reminded God of the work He did in behalf of their ancestors in **days ... of old** (78:3; Exod. 12:26-27; Deut. 6:20; Judg. 6:13; Isa. 51:9; 63:9). **2.** He drove out nations (Psalms 78:55; 80:8; Josh. 3:10; Neh. 9:24) and planted Israel (Exod. 15:17; 2 Sam. 7:10; Jer. 24:6; Amos 9:15), afflicting and scattering enemy peoples before them (Psalms 80:9; 135:10-12).

3. Emphatically, Israel did **not** possess Canaan by their **own sword**, nor did their **own arm save them** (Josh. 24:12). God's **right hand, and ... arm** (Psalm 77:15) and **the light** of His presence (4:6; 89:15) accomplished this, because His **favor** rested on them (106:4; Deut. 4:37; 7:7-8; 10:15).

Although the godly remnant of Israel will be surrounded by the apostate nation, who will have cast off God and no longer believe in the miraculous origins of their people nor their miraculous preservation, this faithful nucleus will believe that God is the same as yesteryear and will deliver them out of the horrors of their present tribulations.

Present Faith Becomes Vocal. 44:4-8. The vibrant faith of the godly broke through surrounding godlessness and unbelief and claimed the LORD as King (2:4-12), looking to Him to **command deliverances for Jacob**, particularly in his time of supreme trouble (Jer. 30:5-7). **5-8.** Faith boldly claimed the complete conquest of enemies and disclaimed trust in natural resources, claiming the example of past deliverances (Psalms 53:5; 136:24), making its boast in God alone (34:2), and thanking His name forever (30:12).

Present Severe Testings of Faith. 44:9-16. **9.** The present stress was so severe that it challenged the boldest faith. So the charge was made that God had rejected His people (43:2; 60:1; 74:1) and brought them to dishonor (69:19), not going out before their armies to give them victory (69:10; 108:11). **10-13.** Thus, they were defeated and despoiled by their foes, and scattered among the nations (44:22; 106:27; Lev. 26:33; Deut. 4:27; 28:64; Ezek. 20:23), sold to their enemies (Judg. 2:14; 3:8; Jer. 15:13), and made the object of scoffing and derision (Psalms 79:4; 89:41; Ezek. 23:32).

14. They were a **byword** (Psalm 69:11; Jer. 24:9) and a laughingstock (lit., "a shaking of the head") among the peoples (Psalm 109:25; 2 Kings 19:21). **15-16.** Dishonor and humiliation were suffered constantly from the enemy and the avenger around about (Psalms 8:2; 74:10). Particularly will this be true in the dark times of the coming Tribulation.

Protestation of Fidelity and Cry for Help. 44:17-26. **17.** Despite all their tribulation, the faithful cried, **Yet have we not forgotten thee** (78:7; 119:61) nor **dealt falsely in thy covenant** (Exod. 20:1-10). **18.** Nor had they backslidden (Psalm 78:57), or deviated from God's path (119:51; Job 23:11).

19. Yet, envisioning the horrors of the Great Tribulation, the psalmist imagined God had **broken** (crushed) them (Psalms 51:8; 94:5) in a **place of jackals** (Job 30:29; Isa. 13:22; Jer. 9:11) and **covered** them with the **shadow of death** (Job 3:5; cf. Isa. 60:2; Matt. 24:15-24). **20.** However, they had not forgotten God's name (Psalm 78:11) nor in false worship raised their hands to a strange god (81:9; Rev. 9:20-21), nor submitted to the worship of the Antichrist (Dan. 9:27; 2 Thess. 2:4; Rev. 13:15-18), whose image will then be set up in the restored Jewish Temple in Jerusalem.

21. The omniscient God will know His faithful remnant have kept themselves pure from that period's idolatry, which will be enforced on pain of death (Psalm 139:1-2; Jer. 17:10; Dan. 11:36-37). **22.** For that reason they are **killed all the day long** (Rom. 8:36) and accounted **as sheep for the slaughter** (to be slaughtered; Isa. 53:7; Jer. 12:3; cf. Rev. 6:9-10; 7:14; 13:15-18). To the suffering saints of that terrible time of unparalleled trouble (Dan. 12:1; Matt. 24:21-22; Rev. 12:12), it will appear that God has fallen asleep and is oblivious of His people's agony.

23. So the cry, **Awake, why sleepest thou, O Lord?** (Psalms 7:6; 78:65) **Arise** (cf. Zech. 2:13). **Cast us not off forever** (Psalm 77:7). **24.** **Why dost Thou hide Thy face...?** (88:14; Job 13:24). **25.** The agony of the Tribulation saints is graphically pictured. Their soul has sunk down **to the dust** (Psalm 119:25); their stomach cleaves to the ground. **26.** This verse gives the prayer that is soon answered by the return of Christ in glory to redeem His people (Zech. 12:10—13:1; cf. Psalms 6:4; 25:22; Rev. 19:11—20:6).

D. THE KING OF GLORY. 45:1-17.

This psalm was written for the precentor (choir director) according to *Shoshannim* ("lilies," perhaps a musical tune). It is a Maschil ("instruction")

of the Korahites, "A Song of loves."

The Beauty and Grace of the King. *45:1-2.* **1.** Under divine inspiration, the heart of the psalmist was **overflowing** (*rḥsh*, "bursting forth with") **a good matter** ("theme" or "subject"), the theme of all themes, the beauty and graciousness of the King-Messiah, crucified, risen, coming in glory to establish His earthly Kingdom. **I speak of the things which I have made** (i.e., "address my verses") **to the King** (NASB), a great king, perhaps Solomon, prefiguring the Messiah-King of kings. **My tongue is the pen of a ready** (*māhîr*, "quick, prompt," in the sense of "fluent" or "skillful") **writer** (Ezra 7:6).

2. The poet addressed the king and described him as **fairer** ("much more beautiful") **than the sons of men** (NASB; i.e., mankind as a whole), with **grace... poured upon** His lips (cf. John 7:46). Described is much more than the physical or outward beauty (cf. Isa. 53:2-3) of Christ. Rather, His moral and spiritual beauty is described; He is "altogether lovely" (Song of Sol. 5:16), and God has blessed Him forever (Psalm 21:6).

The King as a Mighty Conqueror. *45:3-5.* **3.** The poet pictures the King-Messiah as a great conquering Warrior, addressing Him as "O Mighty One" (NASB; Isa. 9:6) and dramatically enjoining Him to gird His sword on His thigh in His splendor and majesty. The Apocalypse says He will come to "judge and make war" (Rev. 19:11). On His head will be "many crowns" as "KING OF KINGS," and out of His mouth will issue "a sharp sword" with which He will "smite the nations" (19:12-16).

4a. The prophet-psalmist, of course, had some contemporary king in mind, but the Spirit of prophecy, who inspired him, envisioned the supreme King who in His majesty will one day **ride prosperously** ("ride on victoriously," NASB). John the seer glimpsed Him bestride "a white horse," symbolic of triumph (Rev. 19:11; cf. Matt. 21:2-5).

4b. His victorious career is **because of** (for the cause of) **truth and meekness and righteousness,** manifested in His first advent (Matt. 11:28-29; John 14:6; 1 Cor. 1:30; 2 Cor. 5:21). His name is "Faithful and True" and "in righteousness he doth judge and make war" (Rev. 19:11). **4c.** His right hand shall teach Him **awe-inspiring** ($n\hat{o}r\bar{a}'\hat{o}\underline{t}$, "awesome") **things** (Psalms 21:8; 2:4-12; Rev. 19:17-21).

5. His **arrows** will be **sharp** to pierce **the heart** of His enemies (Psalms 18:14; 92:9; Isa. 5:28; 7:13) as **the people fall** in defeat and death under Him (2 Sam. 18:14), as He "treadeth the winepress of the fierceness and wrath of Almighty God" (Rev. 19:15; cf. 14:20; Isa. 63:3-6; cf. Matt. 21:44).

The King on His Throne of Glory. *45:6-8.* **6. Thy throne, O God, is forever and ever** (93:2; Heb. 1:8). His throne is "the throne of his glory," which He will occupy as the risen, glorified Son of Man when He "shall come in his glory" (Matt. 25:31). Therefore, He is addressed as God, for He *is* God incarnate; God, the eternal Word, became man (John 1:1, 3, 14), who through death and resurrection has united deity and (glorified) humanity forever in His glorious person.

This passage is quoted in verses 8 and 9 of Hebrews 1, a chapter expounding the exaltation and future glory of the risen Christ. When He comes as the all-conquering Warrior (Psalm 45:3-5) dethroning unrighteousness, He will receive His throne (cf. Rev. 3:21), which will be eternal, not only lasting through the Millennium, the last age in time (4:4-6), but on into the endless ages of

eternity (22:1, 3). **The scepter** (Num. 24:17), the symbol of kingly rule, **is a right scepter** (lit. Heb., "a scepter of uprightness"; Psalm 98:9; Rev. 19:11, 15).

7. He **[loves] righteousness** and **[hates] wickedness,** exemplified so eloquently in His sinless life and vicarious death (Psalms 11:7; 33:5). In consequence, God, emphatically *His* God, **hath anointed** Him **with the oil of gladness** (21:6; Heb. 1:8-9) **above** His **fellows** (His brothers, His redeemed fellow human beings) through resurrection from the dead and exaltation far above all principalities and powers (Eph. 1:19-21).

8a. All the King's **garments** (royal robes) are described as being fragrant with **myrrh . . . aloes, and cassia,** sources of perfumes in antiquity (Song of Sol. 4:14; John 19:39), myrrh and cassia being ingredients of the holy anointing oil (Exod. 30:23-24). The perfection of the manhood of Him who was full of grace and truth and whose whole life was an unbroken fragrance to God is set forth poetically. But by His death, resurrection, and consequent exaltation He wears the robes of the King of kings, which as a consequence are redolent with righteousness and of fragrance to God (cf. 2 Cor. 2:15).

8b. Out of ivory palaces stringed instruments (NASB) have made Him glad (Psalm 150:4). His royal palaces are poetically described as being ivory, that is, built with, or at least sumptuously adorned with, ivory, as was Ahab's house (cf. 1 Kings 22:39; Amos 3:15). Remains of a palace of ivory inlay have been uncovered at Samaria.

Those Gathered Around the King's Throne. 45:9-15. **9.** The Kingdom has been set up. **Kings' daughters** (Song of Sol. 6:8) represent redeemed nations of the Kingdom. The queen at the King-

Messiah's **right hand** (the place of special honor; 1 Kings 2:19) is Israel, redeemed and restored to divine favor, symbolized by her being clad in **gold of Ophir**, a noted source of fine gold from either south Arabia or east Africa (cf. Job 22:24; 1 Kings 9:26-28). Many expositors make the queen the church, the Lamb's wife, and the marriage that of the Lamb (Rev. 19:7-9). But that marriage scene is in heaven and that relationship is a heavenly one. This scene, by contrast, is earthly, and the relationships symbolized are likewise earthly and millennial.

10-11. The term **daughter** (like "my son" in the book of Proverbs) is a common Oriental style of address. The person who employed it, either from age or authority, or as divinely commissioned, had a right to give instruction, as God would to His child or a father to his son (J. J. Stewart Perowne, *Psalms*).

So the queen (restored Israel, v. 9*b*) is addressed as "daughter" and urged to give careful attention to **forget** her **own people, and** her **father's house** (Deut. 21:13; Ruth 1:16) that the king may desire her beauty, as her lord, to whom she is to bow down in holy reverence (Gen. 18:12). **12. The daughter of Tyre,** that is, Tyre personified as a young woman, shall come with a gift; the rich shall entreat His (God's) favor, indicating that the millennial nations will bring their riches to the King and make suit to the Messiah.

13. The queen of verse 9 is further described (vv. 13-15) in her royal apparel in the inner apartments of the palace; *băt mĕlĕk* ("daughter of the king") should apparently be pointed *bŏt melek* ("royal garb") and verse 13 rendered, "All her robes are royal garb, inside brocaded with gold; her wardrobe comes from the women who weave threads of gold" (AB). **14. The virgins,**

the queen's companions (cf. Matt. 25:1-13), apparently refer to the Jewish remnant in Kingdom blessing, although some expositors understand them to be Gentile nations then brought to the King.

Praise to the King. 45:16-17. **16.** A princely and spiritual progeny shall be the fruit of Israel's restoration (Isa. 49:20-21; 54:1). David made his sons princes under him (2 Sam. 8:18), as the greater David will do in His Kingdom rule (Psalm 72:11; cf. Matt. 19:28; Rev. 5:10). **17.** The psalmist declared he would make the Messiah's **name to be remembered in all generations,** which has been realized in the publication of this psalm during three millennia. Then, too, the psalmist spoke representatively of all who will make the Messiah known to the world (Mal. 1:11), which will be Israel's millennial role so that the peoples shall praise Him **forever and ever** (Psalm 138:4).

E. GOD THE REFUGE OF HIS PEOPLE. 46:1-11.

Psalms 46 to 49 prophetically depict the glorious results of the advent of the King, whose second coming to establish His Kingdom (2 Sam. 7:8-17) is so vividly presented in Psalm 45. Addressed to the musician (precentor), this Korahite psalm is entitled "upon Alamoth" ("maidens"), evidently a song rendered by female (soprano) voices, recalling the first recorded song in the Bible, the song of redemption by Miriam and the women after the Red Sea deliverance (Exod. 15:20-21).

The Testimony of a Trusting People. 46:1-3. **1.** Although similar witness has arisen from the hearts of saints delivered out of severe trouble in every age, the prophetic element of this psalm points to the future remnant of Israel delivered out of the Great Tribulation (Dan. 12:1;

Matt. 24:21-22), when it will burst forth into singing and cry: **God is our refuge and strength** (Psalms 14:6; 62:7-8), **a very present help in trouble** (Deut. 4:7; Psalm 145:18; Rev. 7:1-8).

2. That coming "time of Jacob's trouble" (Jer. 30:5-7) will be fearful indeed. But the testimony of the faithful saints (both Jew and Gentile) of that terrible era of suffering and persecution under Antichrist and his forces will be because of their faith in God: **Therefore will not we fear** (Psalms 23:4; 27:1), **though the earth be removed** ("changed" or "displaced"; 82:5; cf. Rev. 8:8; 16:18-20), **and though the mountains be carried** (*mûṭ*, "totter, slip, slide") **into the midst** ("heart") **of the sea** (lit., "seas"; Psalm 18:7; Rev. 8:8; 16:18-20).

3. Though the waters (of the sea, symbolic of peoples) **roar and be troubled** (foam; Psalm 93:3-4; Luke 21:25-26; cf. Dan. 7:2, 7; Rev. 13:1). **Though the mountains** (symbolic of kingdoms) **shake** (quake; Mark 13:8; Luke 21:25-26; Rev. 16:18-20) at the **swelling** of the sea, doubtlessly indicating huge tidal waves (Luke 21:25). Not only are revolutions and commotions of the political world suggested (J. J. Stewart Perowne, *Psalms*), but in the natural world there will also be concomitant phenomena to augment the awful time of worldwide trouble (Psalm 2:5; Mark 13:19-20; Rev. 7:14).

The Messiah's Advent and Deliverance. 46:4-7. **4.** The floods of judgment had spent their force and receded. In their place there is **a river** (Ezek. 47:12), whose **streams . . . make glad** Jerusalem, the capital of the millennial earth (Isa. 2:2-3), here called **the city of God** (Psalms 48:1; 87:3; 101:8; Isa. 60:14; Rev. 3:12), because it will be the center of worship and the place where Ezekiel's Temple will be built in the

Kingdom age (Ezek. 40:1—47:12), consequently called **the holy place of the tabernacles of the Most High** (*'ĕlyôn*), the millennial name of the Messiah, as the Possessor of heaven and earth (Gen. 14:18-19), having entered into His possession.

The river whose streams gladden Jerusalem represents both spiritual and physical blessings, suggesting the Holy Spirit's operations in fullest blessing in the LORD's delivered and restored earthly people. Both Ezekiel (Ezek. 47:1) and Zechariah (Zech. 14:8) envisioned these refreshing waters, which John also saw in the eternal state (Rev. 22:1).

5. With the Temple of the Most High in the midst of the capital city of the Kingdom, **she** (Jerusalem) **shall not be moved** (Deut. 23:14; Isa. 12:6; Ezek. 43:7; Hos. 11:9; Joel 2:27; Zeph. 3:15; Zech. 2:5, 10-11; 8:3). **God shall help her, and that right early,** "when morning dawns," literally, "at the turning of the [millennial] morning." The dark night of Tribulation, when Jerusalem will be overrun and trodden down (Zech. 14:1-3), will be past, and the daybreak of the coming age will find the city as the beloved object of God's tender care and help (Psalm 37:40; Isa. 4:5-6; 60:1-14).

6. The first part of this verse pictures the great rebellion upon the earth just prior to the Messiah's advent in glory (Psalm 2:1-3; Rev. 16:13-16; 19:19), while the latter part depicts the second advent itself, when the returning King of kings will utter His voice (Rev. 19:15; cf. Psalms 18:13; 68:33; Jer. 25:30; Joel 2:11; Amos 1:2) **and the earth** will melt (dissolve; Amos 9:5; Mic. 1:4; Nah. 1:5).

7. The redeemed during this terrible age-end ordeal will give expression to their unfaltering faith in the presence of **the Lord of hosts** (Num. 14:9; 2 Chron.

13:12); He will be more than a match for the hosts of the Antichrist, which will be arrayed against them and God at Armageddon (Rev. 16:13-16; 19:19).

Messiah's Mighty Triumph and Exaltation. 46:8-11. **8.** Dramatically, the psalmist issued a call, **Come, behold the works of the Lord** (66:5), which are twofold: (1) There are works of judgment—**what desolations he hath made in the earth** at any time (Isa. 61:4; Jer. 51:43), but particularly the desolations caused by the opening of the seven seals (Rev. 6:1-17; 8:1), the blowing of the seven trumpets (8:2—9:21; 11:15-19), and the pouring out of the seven bowls, which will fill up the divine wrath against man's rebellion and sin (16:1-21).

(2) There are works of blessing, made possible by His preceding work of judgment during the Great Tribulation, making way for the millennium of peace and prosperity. **9.** The great work of blessing is His making **wars to cease unto the end of the** (millennial) **earth** (Isa. 2:4; Mic. 4:3) under the figure of the destruction of ancient armament, as employed in the psalmist's day of **bow . . . spear . . . chariot** (cf. Rev. 19:11—20:3).

10. The psalmist dramatically introduced God in direct exhortation to tumultuous humanity, which in the end time will be in open rebellion against Him. **Be still** (i.e., "cease [striving]" against Me). **Know** (realize) **that I am God** (Psalm 100:3) and what folly it is for puny man to fight against omnipotent Deity (2:4). Despite all your vain mutinous plottings (2:1-3), **I will be exalted among the nations** (the millennial nations). **I will be exalted in the earth** (Rev. 19:17; cf. 2 Sam. 7:16; Luke 1:31-33; Acts 2:29-32; 15:14-17). **11.** The psalm ends with an emphatic repetition of the unflagging faith of God's people in the LORD in every time of trouble (cf. v. 7),

notably in the time of Tribulation (Dan. 12:1; Matt. 24:21-22; cf. Jer. 30:5-7).

F. THE MOST HIGH KING OVER ALL THE EARTH. 47:1-9.

For the context of this psalm, see the introductions to Psalms 42 and 46.

Millennial Israel Speaks. 47:1-4. **1.** The redeemed and restored nation exhorts the nations gathered into the same kingdom to break forth in praise to God by clapping their hands (98:8) and shouting joyfully (106:47). **2.** The occasion is the establishment of the long-promised Kingdom over Israel (Acts 1:6), with the Messiah as King (2 Sam. 7:8-15; Psalm 2:5-12; Isa. 11:11—12:6; Rev. 20:4-6), and with Israel, so long "the tail," now becoming "the head" of the nations (Deut. 28:13); and the LORD, their Redeemer and Deliverer, now exercising His divine prerogative as the **Most High**, "possessor of heaven and earth" (Gen. 14:18-19; see Psalm 46:4; Mic. 4:13; Zech. 4:14; Rev. 11:4), now their **great King** over them, as well as **over all the earth** (Mal. 1:14).

This prophecy foresees Israel finally in the place assigned her in the divine purpose (Deut. 32:8), becoming the chief nation with all the other nations grouped in relation to her. In His kingly millennial role, the Most High is **awe-inspiring** (i.e., "to be feared, reverenced"), for He will rule with a rod of iron (Psalm 2:9-12; Rev. 19:15) and deal unsparingly with evildoers (Zech. 5:1-4).

3. He will subdue all Israel's foes (and the foes of His Kingdom rule) at His second advent (Rev. 19:11—20:3), as well as **the nations under** Israel's **feet,** in order that His elect nation might be the head nation. This is according to His gracious election of Jacob's posterity (Rom. 11:26-36; cf. Deut. 4:37; 7:7-8; Mal. 1:2).

813

Millennial Praise and Worship.
47:5-9. **5.** God has **gone up** (ascended;
'ālâ, "go up") **with** (amid) **a shout.** The
same verb is used in Psalm 68:18, referring to Christ's ascension in Ephesians
4:8. Here that blessed event is not in
view (as the context shows), but His
presence and appearance on earth in the
Kingdom age. He will descend in His
glorious second advent to deliver His
people, to destroy their enemies, to
claim His crown rights over the earth,
and to establish His throne rule.

But when that has been accomplished
He will ascend in visible glory, returning
to the New Jerusalem, for that is where
His glorified Body, the church, and His
glorious heavenly throne and dwelling
place will be. On earth His government
as King of kings will be delegated to
others. Very likely He Himself will descend and ascend (and doubtlessly His
glorified heavenly people with Him) at
stated seasons during the Kingdom age
to oversee and share in the earth rule.

6-8. The millennial peoples are
exhorted to **sing praises** (repeated four
times for emphasis) to their King
(Psalms 68:4; 89:18), for He is **King of all
the earth** (cf. v. 2*b*; Zech. 14:9), reigning
over the nations (Psalm 22:28; 1 Chron.
16:31), sitting on His holy throne
(Psalms 2:6; 97:2; Matt. 25:31).

9. The princes of the peoples who will
assemble will be those who will rule for
and in the King's name (Psalms 72:11;
102:22; Isa. 49:7, 23), **the people of the
God of Abraham**, those saved by grace
through faith (Rom. 4:11-12), who will
administer the King's earthly government for Him. "For to God [belong] the
shields of the earth" (J. J. Stewart
Perowne, *Psalms*), that is, the princes
as defenders of His people (cf. Psalm
89:18). In the Kingdom age He will be
greatly (highly) **exalted** (97:9), in contrast to the dishonor in which He is held
by so many in this age of His rejection.

**G. THE JUDGMENT OF THE NATIONS
AND MILLENNIAL JERUSALEM. 48:1-14.**

For the context of this psalm, see the
introductions to Psalms 42 and 46.

*Jerusalem as the City of the Great
King. 48:1-3.* The background of this
psalm is unknown, except that it may fit
into any number of historical events
under the Davidic line of kings. But its
fulfillment as a prophecy awaits the
Kingdom age when Jerusalem will become the political and religious capital
of the earth (Isa. 2:2-3). Then in universal worship the greatness of the LORD
will be celebrated in the millennial Temple to be erected there (Ezek. 40:1—
47:12).

1. Then Jerusalem will indeed be **the
city of our God** (Psalms 46:4; 87:3; Matt.
5:35), **the mountain of his holiness,** that
is, "His holy mountain" (Psalms 2:6;
87:1; Isa. 2:3; Mic. 4:1; Zech. 8:3). **2.** It
will be **the joy of the whole earth** (Lam.
2:15), **the city of the great King** (the Messiah ruling in Kingdom glory; Matt.
5:35). Jerusalem is said to be **beautiful
for situation** (elevation; Psalm 50:2) **on
the sides of the north** ("heart of
Zaphon"), "Mount Zion is the heart of
Zaphon" (AB), meaning Mount Zion is
to Yahwism what Mount Zaphon
("Mount North," present-day Mount
Casius) is to Canaanite religion, namely,
the dwelling place of God and the most
hallowed spot in the land (cf. M. Dahood, *Psalms*, AB).

3. In Jerusalem's palaces, God makes
Himself known as a **refuge** ("defense, a
high tower"; Psalm 46:7), which will
singularly be the case in the last and
most desperate attempt of her enemies
to utterly destroy her (cf. Zech. 12:1-9;
14:1-15).

*The Judgment of the Attacking Na-
tions. 48:4-7.* The psalmist envisioned
the numerous brutal attacks on
Jerusalem during the centuries by her

enemies—Assyrian, Babylonian, Egyptian, Greek, and Roman. **4. For, behold, the kings came together; they marched up together** (BV), that is, against the city. But the prophetic foreview centers on the last and most terrible attacks, the first by Russia and her allies of the last days (Ezek. 38:1—39:24; Dan. 11:40-45), evidently during the forepart of the Tribulation period, and later followed by the persecutions of the Antichrist and his hordes at the end of that period (Zech. 12:1-9; 14:1-15).

5-7. But the attackers are seen **amazed** (NASB) and **troubled** (terrified) and fleeing away, **fear** (panic) seizing them, **as of a woman in travail** (Isa. 13:8), the LORD breaking them as He breaks **the ships of Tarshish with an east wind** (Jer. 18:17; 1 Kings 10:22; 22:48; Ezek. 27:25). **8.** The psalmist had both heard from others and himself seen such deliverances of Jerusalem, **the city of the Lord of hosts . . . the city of our God,** that he was completely assured **God will establish it forever** (Psalm 87:5; Isa. 2:2; Mic. 4:1) throughout the Kingdom age and in eternity (Rev. 21:24) and utterly defeat her last and most terrible enemies (Ezek. 38:1—39:24; Zech. 12:1-9; 14:1-15; Rev. 19:11—20.3).

Millennial Joy and Worship. 48:9-14. **9.** The **loving-kindness** of God (26:3; 40:10) will become the object of thought and the great incentive to adoration in the midst of His Temple (Ezek. 40:1—47:12). **10.** As is God's **name** (Deut. 28:58; Josh. 7:9; Mal. 1:11), so will the praise be that is accorded Him **unto the ends of the** (millennial) **earth** (Psalms 65:1-2; 100:1; cf. Isa. 11:9). His **right hand** will be manifest worldwide as being **full of righteousness** (Isa. 41:10), for it symbolizes His all-righteous Kingdom rule.

11-13. Then Mount Zion and Jerusalem shall rejoice because of the divine **judgments** (Rev. 6:1—19:20),

which will purge out sinners and rebels, vindicating God's holiness and preparing the way for His righteous Kingdom administration. The walk about Jerusalem is a tour through the millennial period, when the city will be the capital of the millennial earth. **14.** Then the testimony of her inhabitants will be, **For this God**, who has kept His Word concerning His people and their city, **is our God forever and ever; he will be our guide** (Psalm 23:4) **even unto death** (Isa. 58:11).

H. WHY FEAR IN TIME OF TRIBULATION? 49:1-20.

This psalm concludes the series of psalms beginning with Psalm 42. Its purpose is to vindicate God's dealings in connection with men in general, but with special reference to His awful apocalyptic judgments upon the wicked in the Great Tribulation and His severe dealing with His own. But if the outcome and the goal of His purposes for His people are beneficent, why should they fear in the days of evil, which are but a prelude to coming glory?

The Call to Consider This Pivotal Question. 49:1-4. **1. Hear this, all ye peoples . . . all ye inhabitants of the world** (33:8; 78:1; Isa. 1:2; Mic. 1:2). So important and practical is the subject to be discussed and so universal in interest that all the peoples and the dwellers of a fleeting age are invited to give closest attention. **2.** Every person, no matter what his status in life (Psalm 62:9), is vitally concerned with it.

3-4. The psalmist (under divine inspiration) would **speak of wisdom** (37:30), and the **meditation** (thoughts, cogitations) of his heart would **be of understanding,** involving a **parable** (*māshāl*, "a proverb, a similitude, proverbial saying"—"a brief sentence of popular sagacity," BDB), and a **dark saying** (*ḥiḏâ*, "riddle, oracle, an enigma") of why the ungodly often prosper and the godly suffer persecution at their hands, and what the attitude of the latter ought to be.

The Question Considered. 49:5-15.
5-6. The question is stated: **Wherefore should I fear in the days of evil** (*rā'*, "adversity"), **when the iniquity of my heels** (*ᵃqēḇăy*, "treacherous foes, supplanters," from *'qḇ*, "to supplant" or "treacherously assail") **shall compass me about?** (23:4; 27:1; cf. Gen. 25:26; 37:36), even they who **trust in their wealth** and **boast themselves in the multitude of their riches** (Psalm 52:7; Job 31:24; Prov. 11:28; Mark 10:24).

The answer to the question Why should the suffering saint not fear in times of adversity and persecution by the ungodly rich? lies in four facts: (1) No human ransom can redeem the ungodly. **7. None of them** (the godless rich) **can by any means redeem his brother**—a brother in ungodliness and riches; **nor give to God a ransom** (lit., his ransom); that is, the ungodly rich man cannot even give (render) a **ransom** (*kōpĕr*, "covering") for himself, much less redeem his brother.

8. For the redemption of their soul is precious, too costly a price for any man to pay (1 Pet. 1:18-19), **and it** (the ransom money) **ceaseth** (fails) **forever. 9.** Consequently, that by which one can be redeemed from death can never be acquired, making it impossible that the unsaved should go on to **live forever** (Psalm 22:29), **and not see corruption** (*shāḥăt*, "the pit," the netherworld of departed spirits; "decay" with regard to the physical body; 16:10; 89:48).

(2) Death is universal, and worldly riches and power are fleeting. **10.** Death claims the **wise** as well as the **stupid** and senseless, and so *all* earthly wealth must be left behind to others (39:6; Eccles. 2:18, 21; Luke 12:20). **11.** Yet god-

less men act as if their possessions were immortal, and even the godly forget the impermanence of earthly possessions, the transiency of suffering, and the imminence of eternal glory.

12. However much men may dream of immortality and lasting earthly honor, they, in common with animals, must die (Psalm 49:20). **13.** Those who forget these truths **are foolish,** as well as those who **after them ... approve their words** (NASB; Psalm 49:18; Jer. 17:11). **14a.** They forget they are as helpless **sheep** appointed for **sheol** (the netherworld for the soul and spirit; Psalm 9:17). **Death shall feed on** (shepherd) **them** ("be their shepherd").

(3) **14b.** The **upright** shall eventually be victorious and **have dominion** (rule) **over them in the morning,** after the ungodly have been suddenly swept away during the night, as was Sennacherib's vast army when the LORD's people triumphed "in the morning" (Isa. 37:36; cf. Psalm 46:5). God's help will be manifested when Christ's "morning [of the millennial Kingdom] dawns" (NASB), when the saints possess the Kingdom (Dan. 7:22) and "shall tread down the wicked" (Mal. 4:3; Rev. 2:26; 20:4). Then the **beauty** of the wicked **shall consume in sheol from their dwelling,** that is, "so that they have no habitation" (NASB).

(4) **15a.** In contrast to the unredeemed and humanly unredeemable state of the wicked (vv. 7-9), God redeems the soul of His own **from the power of sheol** (i.e., from spiritual, physical, and eternal death through resurrection; Job 19:25-26; Psalms 16:10; 56:13; Isa. 26:19; Dan. 12:2; Hos. 13:14). **15b.** The reason: **He shall receive me** (Psalms 16:11; 73:24; Gen. 5:24; Matt. 11:28-30).

The Conclusion Summarized. 49:16-20. **16. Do not be afraid** (NASB; cf. v. 5, "Why should I be afraid?")

when the ungodly man becomes rich (cf. 37:7). **17.** When he dies he will take nothing with him (17:14; Job 1:21). His earthly **glory shall not descend after him. 18-19.** Though while he lived **he blessed his soul** (i.e., "congratulated himself"; Luke 12:19), and though people praised him when he did so well for himself—lauded him for being so successful in this life, as the world counts success—he shall nevertheless go **to the generation of his fathers** in unbelief and wickedness. He will **never see** the **light** of the sun that illuminates the world of the living, nor the better Sun of Righteousness, who shall arise in Kingdom glory (Mal. 4:2), nor the eternal light that gladdens the beatified saints in eternity (Rev. 21:23). **20.** This verse (cf. v. 12) epitomizes the whole discussion. The person who lacks spiritual understanding, however great his name or accomplishment in life, soon perishes in the midst of all, like irrational **beasts.**

I. THE MESSIAH'S SECOND ADVENT AS JUDGE. 50:1-23.

This is the first of a series of psalms attributed to Asaph (cf. Psalms 73-83). Heman, Asaph, and Ethan were chief musicians of David (1 Chron. 15:17, 19), and Asaph is called "the seer" (2 Chron. 29:30), pointing to the prophetic nature of these odes, in accord with the pronounced prophetic nature of the *entire* Psalter.

The Lord's Appearance as Judge. 50:1-6. **1.** The designation of Deity as **the mighty God**, the LORD (El, Elohim, Yahweh, as in Josh. 22:22) probably should be rendered with Perowne: "The God of gods, Jehovah." His appearance in theophanic form for judgment doubtless arose, as at Sinai (Exod. 19:16-19), out of a historical situation. But its prophetic fulfillment centers in the second advent of Christ to "judge and make

war" (Rev. 19:11). He breaks His long silence and speaks, summoning **the** whole **earth** (Psalm 113:3) to judicial accounting, not Israel alone, but all the nations as well—the saints, Israel, and the wicked (vv. 5, 7, 16, 23; Matt. 25:31-46).

2. Out of Zion (Jerusalem, the capital of the earth in the Kingdom age), **the perfection of beauty** (Psalm 48:2; Lam. 2:15), God will shine forth in the glory and splendor in which the Messiah will be revealed at His second advent (Psalms 80:1; 94:1; Deut. 33:2; Matt. 25:31; Rev. 19:11-16), when He will be "glorified" and "admired" in His saints (2 Thess. 1:10). Zion (Jerusalem) shall then be the place of His throne, whence He shall judge and reign (Psalm 2:6; Isa. 2:2-3; Zech. 2:10-13). Then in the Kingdom age the theocracy on earth will be realized on a worldwide scale and with a glory only dimly adumbrated in its temporary form in the Old Testament (Ezek. 43:7).

3. Our God shall come, because the returning Christ is the God and Deliverer of His waiting people (the Jews and Gentiles saved out of the Great Tribulation). He speaks in judgment (v. 1) and **shall not keep silence** any longer (Psalm 2:5; Hab. 2:3). He shall speak to His enemies in judgment through the "sharp sword" that issues from His mouth (Rev. 19:15), and to His own who have been sorely tried by His seeming silence and slowness in fulfilling His promise of vindicating them against their persecutors and foes.

As He returns **a fire shall devour before him** (Dan. 7:10; 2 Thess. 1:8-9; Heb. 10:27), and it will be **very tempestuous round about him** (Psalm 18:12-13), fire and storm symbolizing the divine anger against sinners (1 Kings 19:11-12; Ezek. 13:11; Heb. 12:29), who will then have reached the acme of wicked rebellion

(Psalm 2:1-3; Rev. 14:18-19; 16:13-16; 19:19).

4. The Judge calls the heaven and earth to witness the vindication of His righteousness in executing judgment for His people against their persecutors (Deut. 4:26; 31:28; 32:1; Isa. 1:2). **5.** This verse records the words the Judge utters: **Gather My godly ones to Me** (*ḥᵃsîḏîm*, "pious ones"; Psalms 30:4; 37:28; 52:9), **those who have made a covenant with Me by sacrifice** (NASB; Exod. 24:7; 2 Chron. 6:11). His people, Israel (v. 7), gathered for judgment, not for the execution of wrath, but that He may plead with them concerning the reality of their faith in His saving grace symbolized by their sacrifices. **6.** The proceedings open with a testimony by one of the witnesses to the righteousness of the divine Judge (Psalms 89:5; 96:13; 97:6).

The Judge's Testimony Against His People. 50:7-15. **7.** The Judge is the Messiah; He addresses His people, Israel, calling for their attention to testify against their empty ritualism that failed to recognize that He is God, even their God (Exod. 20:2; Isa. 53:1-12). When the prophetic aspects of this passage will be fulfilled, the remnant will be in the land with a restored (Tribulation) Temple (2 Thess. 2:4) and with the Mosaic sacrificial system reinstated (Rev. 11:1-2).

8. The Israelis will be piously offering **sacrifices** and **burnt offerings,** all of which point to the Messiah, their crucified and risen Savior, who is God, even their God (John 20:28). But many of them will not yet believe in God's grace now revealed, and without such faith the sacrifices are meaningless. So the LORD does not rebuke them for their sacrifices, but for their absence of faith in their Savior-God, toward whom the sacrifices pointed and toward whose

finished redemption work they directed the worshiper (v. 7). Such vain ritualism was excoriated in prospect of divine redemption (cf. Isa. 1:11-12; Jer. 7:22-23; Mic. 6:6-8). How much more in retrospect of the cross of Christ and a completed redemption.

9-11. Let them know that their Messiah-Redeemer is the Creator of all, to whom belong the world and all things, **every beast of the forest** (field) ... **the cattle on a thousand hills,** "upon the mountains by thousands" (J. J. Stewart Perowne, *Psalms*), and who knows every bird of the air. **12.** Does the infinite Creator-Redeemer, whose is the earth and its fullness, get hungry (Psalm 24:1; Exod. 19:5; Deut. 10:14)? **13.** Should He eat the flesh of bulls or drink the blood of male goats (Psalm 50:9)?

14. Instead of empty Christ-rejecting ritualism, they are to **offer to God a sacrifice of thanksgiving** (NASB; 27:6; 69:30; 107:22; 116:17; Hos. 14:2) for a completed redemption (Rom. 12:1; Heb. 13:15) and pay their **vows** (Psalms 22:25; 56:12; 61:8; 65:1; Num. 30:2; Deut. 23:21) **unto the Most High**—the millennial name of God (Gen. 14:18-19; see Psalm 46:4). This they can do (and will do!) by crying out in deep penitential confession (51:1-19) the wonderful strains of Isaiah 53:1-10. **15.** Then they shall call upon their crucified and risen Messiah **in the day of trouble** (the Great Tribulation; Dan. 12:1; Matt. 24:21-22; Zech. 12:10—13:1; 13:9), and He will rescue them when they honor Him as their God—their Messiah and Savior (Psalm 22:23; Zech. 14:9-11).

The Judge's Verdict Against the Wicked. 50:16-21. **16.** These verdicts (primarily at least) are against the wicked and apostate in Israel, who, having rejected even the outward observance of God's statutes, have no right to take His covenant in their mouth

(Isa. 29:13). **17.** They **hate discipline** (NASB; Prov. 5:12; 12:21; Rom. 2:21-22), despising the tribulations of the time of Jacob's trouble (Jer. 30:5-7), designed to bring them to faith in the Messiah. They likewise reject God's Word, which would bring them into fellowship with the Savior and Deliverer (1 Kings 14:9; Neh. 9:26).

18. They spurn God's moral Law (Exod. 20:1-17), evidenced by their condoning thievery (Rom. 1:32) and consorting with adulterers. **19-20.** They yield their mouth to evil speaking (Psalm 10:7), their tongue to framing deceit (36:3; 52:2) and slander, even against their own brother (Job 19:18; Matt. 10:21).

21. The LORD reminds them that they had **done** these things and He **kept silence** (Eccles. 8:11; Isa. 42:14; 57:11; contrast Psalm 2:5). So the wicked carelessly concluded that God was just like they were. But the Judge sternly announces, **I will reprove** (censure) **thee** and "put the case in order before your eyes" (BV; 90:8).

Summary and Conclusion. 50:22-23. **22a. Now consider this, ye who forget God** (Job 8:13; Psalm 9:17). The Judge issues a stern warning to the empty ritualists and apostates in Israel to bear in mind the approaching maelstrom of judgment to overtake Jacob (Israel) and the whole world (Dan. 12:1; Matt. 24:21-22; Rev. 6:1—19:20). The terrors of the Tribulation are graphically painted in the figure of a wild beast tearing its victim limb from limb with no one to deliver, because they have rejected the true and only Deliverer (Psalm 7:2).

22b. The Judge declares, **I will tear you in pieces,** but He does so only intermediately through the nations as His agents, who are likened to wild beasts (Dan. 7:4-7), especially the "little horn"

(7:8) that arises out of the dreadful and terrible fourth beast (the Roman Empire; cf. Rev. 13:1-8). **23.** This verse contains a wonderful promise to those latter-day Israelites in the time of Jacob's trouble who, through the restored Temple sacrifices in Jerusalem (2 Thess. 2:4; Rev. 11:1-2), will offer **praise** for a crucified and risen Savior and thus glorify the Messiah-Judge. Thus being saved, and ordering their manner of life in conformity to their faith, the Messiah-Judge will demonstrate to them God's deliverance in those terrible days of death and destruction (Psalm 91:16; Matt. 24:22; Rev. 7:1-8, 14).

J. ISRAEL'S GREAT PENITENTIAL CONFESSION. 51:1-19.

This psalm originated in King David's confession after his sin with Bathsheba and the murder of Uriah (2 Sam. 12:1-13), according to the superscription; but in its successive steps, it marks the mold of the experience of a sinning believer in any age who is restored to full fellowship and service to God. Prophetically, it outlines the pathway by which converted Israel will be restored to the Messiah-King in the day of His return, when they will look upon Him whom they have pierced (Zech. 12:10—13:1).

Conviction for Sin and Cry for Forgiveness. 51:1-13. David was a justified believer saved by grace through faith (Rom. 4:6-8; Eph. 2:8-9), who fell into deep sin (adultery and murder; 2 Sam. 11:1-27). As a result he lost fellowship with God and came under divine chastening and discipline. The way back to cleansing and fellowship for a believer is always by full and free confession of sin in total reliance upon (i.e., faith in) the grace and mercy of God. The believer saved by grace through faith is kept in fellowship in the same way—by grace through faith.

1. Hence, his cry, **Have mercy upon me ... according to thy loving-kindness; according unto ... thy tender mercies blot out my transgressions.** The sinning saint, to be forgiven, must never waver in his faith that God is not only light, but love as well, and that that love was manifested at Calvary. Old Testament saints through the sacrificial ritual looked forward and claimed that forgiving love prospectively. New Testament believers look back and claim that love retrospectively.

But without that manifested love at Calvary, there is no forgiveness available to justify the sinner or to restore the sinning saint to fellowship with the infinitely holy God. As a sinning saint David prayed for thorough washing from his iniquity. This involves that aspect of forgiveness that applies to a saint cleansed from the defilement of sin—the washing (with water) aspect (Num. 19:1-19).

2. So David prayed: **Wash me thoroughly from mine iniquity, and cleanse me from my sin** (John 13:10; Eph. 5:25-26). But the basis of this was the loving-kindness and grace of God centering in Christ's death (1 John 1:7).

3-4. Full confession is the one prerequisite for such cleansing (1:9), which involves the acknowledgment that we have sinned against God, who "is light, and in him is no darkness at all" (1:5). Crime is against man. Sin is against God. This must be acknowledged so that God may be justified in His sentence and blameless in His judging (Rom. 3:4).

5-6. The confession of sin in this great penitential psalm also faces forgiveness in the aspect of the cleansing of a sinner from the guilt of sin (original sin as well as actual sin). **Behold, I was shaped in iniquity... in sin did my mother conceive me** (Job 14:4; 58:3; John 3:6; Rom. 5:12; Eph. 2:3).

7. This aspect in the Old Testament required purging with hyssop, a small plant (1 Kings 4:33) with which the blood of the sacrificial animal (envisioning the blood of Christ) was applied (appropriated), making one **whiter than snow** (Exod. 12:22; Lev. 14:4; Isa. 1:18; Heb. 9:19), for the blood of Christ cleanses from *all* sin (1 John 1:7).

8-9. Cleansing from defilement causes the believer to **hear joy and gladness** (Isa. 35:10; Joel 1:16) so that **the bones which** God **hast broken** in His chastisement of His wayward child (Heb. 12:3-10) **rejoice** (12:11) and that God's face, hidden from the sinning believer (cf. Jer. 16:17), may again shine upon him, because all his iniquities have been blotted out—an image from erasing a debt out of an account book (as in v. 1).

10. The penitent soul also cries out for inner renewal from within (vv. 10-12)—for God to **create** in him **a clean heart** (Psalm 24:4; Matt. 5:8; Acts 15:9; Eph. 2:10) and **renew** (*ḥăddēsh*, "make new, restore") **a right** (*nākôn*, "steadfast, firmly established, faithful") **spirit within** [**him**] (Psalm 78:37), an attitude of mind steadfastly set and faithfully fixed on God.

11. As a saint under the Old Testament economy, David prayed not to be cast away from God's presence (2 Kings 13:23; 24:20; Jer. 7:15). Old Testament saints were saved by grace through faith, as New Testament saints are (Gen. 15:6; Rom. 4:1-8), but the grace shown them was anticipative of the death and resurrection of Christ and the consequent gift of the Spirit to indwell them perpetually and seal them. Hence, not possessing a permanently indwelling Spirit, they did not lack salvation, but the firm assurance of the salvation that New Testament believers have and which the ever indwelling, never departing Spirit imparts (John 14:16; Eph. 4:30). Therefore, when the Holy Spirit departed from Saul (1 Sam. 16:14), he did not lose his salvation, but the assurance of it. Hence, the psalmist could pray, **Take not thy holy Spirit from me** (Isa. 63:10-11).

Now, however, since the Holy Spirit has come and arrived to take up *permanent* residence in the saint (John 14:17; 16:12-13), no believer need ever pray such a petition, nor indeed could he intelligently pray such a prayer this side of Pentecost (Acts 2). But he may always scripturally pray that he may possess the faith in what Christ has done for him and what he is in Christ, in order that the necessary conditions for the filling of the Spirit (Eph. 5:18) may be forthcoming as the evidence of his faith.

12. Hence, David did not pray for the restoration of salvation, but **the joy** of it (Psalm 13:5; Eph. 5:18-19), and that God would **uphold** (sustain) him **with a willing spirit.** Restored Israel will have such a spirit (Psalm 110:3) when they experience the penitential depths of this great ode (Zech. 12:10—13:1), as they turn to their crucified, risen Messiah returning to deliver them and set up His earthly Kingdom over them (Acts 1:6). Then they will recite from deepest contrition the glorious strains of Isaiah 53:1-10 and the heart-searching cry of this the greatest of the penitential psalms, which is in fact a prayer precomposed for them by infinite wisdom when they realize that He whom they nailed to the cross was their Messiah-Savior. **13.** Then will the converted nation (Rom. 11:25-36) become a great evangelizing agency in the Kingdom, with the zeal of the great apostle to the Gentiles, who in this sense was a Hebrew prematurely born (1 Cor. 15:8).

Israel Faces Her Bloodguiltiness.

51:14-19. **14.** David's plea for deliverance from bloodguiltiness in the murder of Uriah (2 Sam. 11:1-27) foreshadows the heartrending cry of the Israelite remnant as Christ will be revealed to them at His second advent and they face their own terrible bloodguiltiness in the death of Christ, when their fathers shouted: "His blood be on us, and on our children" (Matt. 27:25). When that guilt is removed, they will be delivered and filled with joy and praise (v. 15; Psalms 35:28; 71:15; Isa. 12:1-6; 35:1-10).

15. Then the LORD (their covenant-keeping Savior) will open their lips (Exod. 4:15) so that they will be a nation that will declare God's praise (Psalm 9:14) and be emancipated from dead, ritualistic externalism. **16-17.** While the unbelieving part of the nation resumes the Temple worship and once more offers sacrifices (see comments on Psalm 50:7-14; cf. 2 Thess. 2:4; Rev. 11:1-2), the LORD will not desire them (1 Sam. 15:22; Mic. 6:6-8), but will look for the deep contrition of heart expressed in this great penitential ode (Psalm 34:18).

18-19. Then the LORD will **do good ... unto Zion** restored to His favor (69:35; Isa. 51:3); the walls of Jerusalem will be built (Psalms 102:16; 147:2) and the millennial Temple worship established, as foretold by Ezekiel in his great vision (4:5; 66:13, 15; Ezek. 40:1—44:31), the sacrifices being commemorative and retrospective of a finished redemption, as the Lord's Supper is today (cf. 1 Cor. 11:25).

K. THE LAWLESS MAN. 52:1-9.

Psalms 52 to 55 are Maschil ("instruction") psalms presenting deep spiritual teaching concerning the manifestation of depravity and lawlessness working in godless humanity and culminating in the lawless one (2 Thess.

2:4, 9-12), the Antichrist (Rev. 13:1-8) of the end time who will domineer over Israel. He is prefigured by Doeg the Edomite, the vicious and lawless chief herdsman of Saul (1 Sam. 21:7), who in an incredibly savage and blasphemous display of human depravity (which will come to full fruition in the end-time Antichrist), slew Ahimelech and the priests at Nob (eighty-five men) and massacred every living thing in a nearby village (1 Sam. 22:7-23; cf. Rev. 13:7, 15).

The Lawless Man Described. 52:1-4. The lawless man does four things: (1) **1a.** He boasts in evil (94:4; Isa. 14:13; Dan. 11:37; 2 Thess. 2:4; Rev. 13:6), in the face of the ever enduring **goodness of God** (Psalm 52:8). (2) **1b.** He is a **mighty man** (*gibbôr*, "powerful," in the evil sense of being godless, rich, and violent; Dan. 11:37-39; Rev. 13:7-8).

(3) **2a.** His tongue **deviseth mischiefs** ("destruction"; Psalm 5:9), the destruction of God's saints (Rev. 13:7, 15), like Doeg who slew the priests and servants of God (1 Sam. 22:18). **2b.** His tongue is **like a sharp razor** (Psalms 57:4; 59:7), revealing his cruelty and viciousness (Dan. 7:20, 25). (4) **2c-4.** He is a worker of deceit (Psalm 101:7; 2 Thess. 2:9-12; Rev. 13:13-14), loving evil, falsehood, and **all devouring words**, breaking his covenant with Israel and setting up "the abomination of desolation" (Dan. 9:27; 12:11; Matt. 24:15), his own image to be worshiped in the Jerusalem Temple.

The End of the Lawless Man Predicted. 52:5-7. **5. God shall ... destroy** (break, beat him down) **... forever ... take** (snatch) him away and **pluck** him from his **dwelling place** (tent; Isa. 22:18) and root him out of **the land of the living** (the sphere of physical life; Psalm 27:13; Prov. 2:22). As the lawless spirit comes to full fruition in the Antichrist (the

beast) and the false prophet (Rev. 13:1-18), it is brought to an abrupt end and made an example of the fate of all the lawless who despise God's moral Law. The two are caught red-handed in their wicked rebellion (19:19) and cast alive into the lake of fire (gehenna), without passing through hades or intermediate hell, as do all other lawless sinners (19:20; cf. 20:10).

6. The righteous (the regenerated) **also shall see** this public example of the destiny of the wicked, **and fear, and shall laugh at him** (Job 22:19; Psalm 37:34) as the epitome of the folly of sin. So God laughs at the insanity of puny man daring to try to oust Him from the ownership and rule of the earth (Job 22:19; Psalm 2:4). **7.** His derision centers in the foolhardiness of lawless mankind in refusing to make **God** its **strength,** but trusting **in the abundance of ... riches, strong** only in its evil desire (10:6; 49:6).

The Contrast of the Righteous Man. 52:8-9. **8a.** The psalmist (representative of all saints, particularly the Israelite remnant of the end time) flourished under God's blessings as a **green olive tree** (Psalm 128:3; Jer. 11:16), which is a symbol of Israel in covenant relation with the LORD. For a time they were the broken off branches of the good olive tree (Rom. 11:13-25), but at this period they are put back in their own olive tree (11:26-32), while Gentile Christendom will be cut out and cast away in its apostasy.

8b-9. Then saved Israel will **trust in the mercy of God** (centering in the death and resurrection of their Messiah) **forever and ever** (Psalm 13:5) and **praise** Him, for He has **done it** (performed all He promised; Deut. 30:1-10; 2 Sam. 7:8-17; Isa. 9:6-7; Rev. 20:4-6). Then restored Israel will **wait** on the name of Christ, the name above every other, and worship Him as their LORD and King.

What a picture of the man of lawlessness in general, but what a prophetic portrayal of *the* man of sin and his dethronement and the worship of the saved remnant in the Messiah's Kingdom.

L. THE ACME OF MAN'S LAWLESSNESS. 53:1-6.

For the scope of Psalm 53, see the introductions to Psalm 52 and Psalm 14, to which it is practically identical. This psalm (like Psalm 14) presents the moral conditions of the fallen race in a general sense (Rom. 1:20-32), but specifically and in a prophetic sense it portrays the complete apostasy of the end of the age preceding the second advent of Christ, that is, the apostasy under the lawless one, prophetically adumbrated in Psalm 52. It is said to be a psalm of David "upon ['ăl, 'after the manner of'] Mahalath ['sickness'] ," possibly meaning "that the Psalm was to be sung in a sad, mournful tone, as the addition of the verb in Psalm 88:1, and the whole character of that Psalm, which is the darkest in the Psalter, seems to imply" (J. J. Stewart Perowne, *Psalms*).

Man's Lawlessness Ripe for Judgment. 53:1-5. For the exposition of this psalm, see comments on Psalm 14. In both Psalm 14 and Psalm 53 the name of God occurs seven times (in Psalm 14, "Jehovah" four times and "Elohim" three times, while in Psalm 53 only "Elohim" occurs seven times), perhaps suggesting that the latter psalm was adapted from the former (apparently the original) to be slanted more directly toward Gentile apostasy and rebellion (cf. 2:1-3) for two reasons:

(1) **1-4.** Elohim is the divine name of the Creator, and the cry **There is no God** is a denial of His creatorship by the intellectual fool, who gravitates to atheism by substituting evolution for creationism. With no God the result is no divine law or morals (vv. 2-4; cf. Rev. 9:20-21).

(2) **5.** There is a significant change between 14:5 (contrast 14:6), where the emphasis is on the mistreatment of the LORD's people by the wicked, and Psalm 53:5, where it is on the punishment of the wicked for such mistreatment. The wicked are pictured in both psalms as being **in great fear** (dread), but in 53:5 the words **where no fear was** (cf. Lev. 26:17, 36; Prov. 28:1) are added, as when the hosts of Midian fled before Gideon's three hundred (Judg. 7:22). God is figured as scattering the bones of the enemy who encamps against His people (Psalm 141:7; Jer. 8:1-2; Ezek. 6:5; Zech. 12:3-5; 14:13-15). His people shall **put** their enemies **to shame** (Psalm 44:7), **because God hath despised** (rejected) **them** (2 Kings 17:20; Jer. 6:30; Lam. 5:22; Rev. 19:17—20:3).

The Faithful Ready for Divine Deliverance. 53:6. See the exposition on Psalm 14:7.

M. CRY FOR DELIVERANCE IN TROUBLE. 54:1-7.

This psalm is addressed to the "chief musician" (precentor), to be accompanied by *Neginoth* ("stringed instruments"). It is styled "Maschil" ("instruction"; see e.g., Psalms 4, 8, 32, 44) and is connected with David's experiences with the Ziphites (1 Sam. 23:19), but reflects similar experiences of danger of all saints at any time, particularly and prophetically the godly remnant in the midst of the fully ripened iniquity prevailing in the period of Jacob's (Israel's) end-time troubles (Jer. 30:5-7; Rev. 6:1—19:17; cf. Psalms 14 and 53).

Appeal for Vindication. 54:1-3. **1-2.** David's life was endangered by duplicity and false accusation, and he cried, **Save** (deliver) **me ... judge** (vindicate, exonerate, and avenge) **me, by Thy name** (NASB; 20:1), that is, "by Thyself," for the name means the person who bears the name. **Vindicate me by Thy power** (NASB; 2 Chron. 20:6). "The parallelism between 'name' and 'might' suggests that God's name is mighty to save" (LBC). **3.** The reason for the appeal is that ruthless men (such as those described in Psalms 14 and 53) were bent on destroying the psalmist's life. They were **strangers ... oppressors** (violent men), who had **not set God before them** (Psalms 14:1; 36:1; 53:1; Dan. 7:25; 11:36; Rev. 13:5-7; 19:19).

Testimony of Trust. 54:4-5. Confidence in God's interposition is expressed in declaring two things: (1) **4. God is my helper; the Lord** (Adonai, "Master") **is the sustainer of my soul** (NASB; 37:17; 41:12; 51:12; 145:14; Isa. 41:10). (2) **5.** God is the Punisher of the wicked. **He shall reward** (recompense) **evil unto mine enemies** (Psalm 94:23). The latter part of the verse is an imprecatory cry: **Cut them off** (destroy them) **in thy truth** (faithfulness; see Psalm 5:10 for the question of the morality of imprecatory prayers).

Vow of Thanksgiving. 54:6-7. **6-7.** God has answered, deliverance has been realized, and a sacrifice of thanksgiving (Num. 15:3; Psalm 116:17; Heb. 13:15) is forthcoming. The freewill offering presented was a type of peace offering for which there was no binding or legal requirement (Exod. 35:29; 36:3-5; Lev. 7:16); it was a free expression of heartfelt gratitude, in this case for deliverance (Psalm 34:6) from **all trouble** (distress; 59:10; 92:11; Matt. 24:22; Rev. 7:1-8) and for being enabled to see the punishment of godless and cruel persecutors (19:11—20:1-3).

N. IN THE VORTEX OF TRIBULATION. 55:1-23.

This, the last Maschil ("instruction") psalm of this series (Psalms 53-55), a psalm of David, reflects experiences of David and saints of every period who pass through great trouble. But again this Maschil presents deep prophetic instruction, introducing the reader to the darkest aspects of the Great Tribulation with full portrayal of the Antichrist (vv. 12-21). The person in David's life who foreshadowed this final oppressor of Israel was apparently Ahithophel, David's counselor, who so shamefully defected to Absalom (2 Sam. 16:20—17:23).

Appeal to God Because of Wicked Oppressors. 55:1-3. **1.** The cry was urgent and intense, God seeming to hide Himself from the persecuted saint's **supplication** (27:9; cf. Rev. 6:7-9; cf. Isa. 8:17; 64:7). **2-3.** He mourned (was restless) in his **complaint** (Psalm 64:1), and made **a noise** (moaned; Isa. 38:14; 59:11; Ezek. 7:16) because of the **voice of the enemy ... the oppression of the wicked** (Psalm 17:9), who troubled him and **in wrath** hated him (Matt. 24:9-10; Luke 21:12; John 15:20-21; Rev. 2:10).

Inner Turmoil and Outward Distress. 55:4-11. **4-5.** His heart was in anguish (38:8; Jer. 30:5-7), the **terrors of death** had **fallen upon** him (Psalms 18:4-5; 116:3), **trembling** (shuddering) had come upon him (119:120), horror had **overwhelmed** him (Job 21:6; Isa. 21:4; Ezek. 7:18). **6-8.** Like the psalmist, the godly in deepest distress in the vortex of the Tribulation, when the Antichrist will reign in Jerusalem (Matt. 24:15), will cry for **wings like a dove** to **fly away** (24:16-20) and **be at rest** (Job 3:13) and **remain** (lodge) **in the wilderness** (Rev. 12:13-17), hastening escape from the terrible whirlwind and tempest of persecution that will engulf Jerusalem and Judea under the Antichrist (beast; Isa. 25:4; 29:6; Rev. 12:15).

Verses 9 to 11 prophetically describe Jerusalem in the days when "the abomination of desolation" (Matt. 24:15; cf. Dan. 9:27; 12:11; 2 Thess. 2:4; Rev. 13:15-18) will be set up in the Tribulation Temple, which will have been erected on Mount Moriah. **9. Violence and strife** will fill **the city.**

10-11. Mischief (destruction) **... and sorrow** will be **in the midst of it** (Psalm 5:9), and oppression and deceit will not depart from her streets (10:7; 17:9; Matt. 24:23-26; 2 Thess. 2:9-12; Rev. 11:1-13; 13:13-18). The petition uttered—**Destroy** (swallow them up), **O Lord, ... confuse their tongues**—as at Babel (Gen. 11:7-9), is another imprecatory prayer, for iniquity is fully ripe and the winepress of God's wrath must be trodden (Rev. 14:18-20; cf. comment on Psalm 5:10; Gen. 15:16; Lev. 18:24).

The Source of the Trouble. 55:12-15. **12. It was not an enemy that reproached**—that could have been borne—nor **he that hated** the psalmist who exalted himself against him, for then he could have hidden himself from this dastardly traitor (35:26). **13.** But it was a man who was the psalmist's **equal** (in "rank" or "order," as in Exod. 40:23; Judg. 17:10), or "assessed as I am" (Calvin, as in 2 Kings 23:35) and therefore "of the same rank" (J. J. Stewart Perowne, *Psalms*), his **companion** (colleague) and his **familiar friend** (NASB; Psalm 41:9; Job 19:14; $m^e y\bar{u}\underline{d}\bar{a}'$, "one well known").

14. They had had sweet fellowship together ($s\bar{o}\underline{d}$, "counsel") and walked together to the house of **God in company** (in the throng; Psalm 42:4). Historically, this suggests Ahithophel (the Aramaic paraphrase inserting here the name of the renegade), David's counselor (1 Chron. 27:33). Prophetically, another Ahithophel is to rise and to head the end-time apostasy and revolt against God.

15. The imprecatory prayer (see comment on Psalm 5:10) is directed against the Antichrist and the false prophet, whose iniquity will be full and ripe for punishment, and they will be "cast alive" into gehenna (Rev. 19:20). Their followers will be slain (19:18-19, 21) recalling the fate of Korah, Dathan, and Abiram (Num. 16:30-31), and thus they went **down alive into sheol**, that is, "the netherworld," intermediate hell (Luke 16:19-31).

Prayer and Hope of the Godly Awaiting Salvation. 55:16-19. **16.** The psalmist, representing the saints, particularly in the supreme time of trouble (Dan. 12:1; Matt. 24:21-22), confidently turned to God in prayer for deliverance (Psalm 57:2-3). **17.** His prayer would be persevering at **evening** (141:2; Dan. 6:10; Acts 3:1; 10:3), **morning** (Psalms 5:3; 88:13), and at **noon** (Acts 10:9). The spirit of grace and supplication will be poured out upon God's people, Israel (Zech. 12:10—13:1).

18. They claim redemption in peace from the terrible battle that is against them (12:3-5; 13:8-9; 14:3-9), and from the many who strive against them (Psalm 56:2; Rev. 16:13-16; 19:11-20). **19.** God will hear and answer His people (Psalm 78:59), even He who **abideth** (sits enthroned) **of old** ("from of old [eternity]"; Deut. 33:27; Psalms 90:2; 93:2), **because in them** (the enemies and persecutors of God's people) **there has been no change and they do not revere God** (BV; Job 10:17; Psalm 36:1).

The Prophetic Portrayal of the Lawless One. 55:20-21. **20a. He hath put forth his hands against such as are at** peace with him (7:4; 120:7). Ahithophel's treachery against David in the historical setting (2 Sam. 16:20—17:23) furnishes the background for the Antichrist, the last-day traitor to the greater David. He, with the false prophet, will make a covenant with Israel at the beginning of the last seven years of this age (Dan. 9:27), allowing the Temple to be built in Jerusalem and the Temple worship resumed.

20b. He hath broken his covenant (Psalm 89:34; Num. 30:2; Dan. 9:27). In the middle of the period (Daniel's seventieth week) the Antichrist will suddenly break the treaty with Israel, set up his image in the Temple, and command worship upon pain of death (2 Thess. 2:4; Rev. 13:8, 15). **21.** His speech is **smoother than butter,** and by flattery and deception he will deceive Israel. **But war was in his heart. His words were softer than oil** (Psalm 12:2; Dan. 7:8, 11, 20, 25), **yet were they drawn swords** (Psalm 57:4; 59:7; Dan. 11:38; Rev. 13:6-8).

Comfort for the Tried and the Suffering. 55:22-23. **22.** In the awful Tribulation the LORD's people will be encouraged to cast their **burden upon the Lord, and he shall sustain** them (37:5; Matt. 6:25; Luke 12:22; 1 Pet. 5:7) and **never suffer** (allow) **the righteous** (the regenerated) **to be moved** (shaken; Psalm 15:5; 112:6; Matt. 24:22) from their faith in His faithfulness. **23.** By contrast, God will **bring ... down to the pit of destruction** the **bloody and deceitful men** (Psalm 73:18; Isa. 38:17; Ezek. 28:8; Rev. 19:20). They shall **not live out half their days** (Job 15:32; Prov. 10:27). But the psalmist and all tried and suffering saints cry out, **But I will trust in thee** (Psalm 25:2; 56:3).

O. COURAGEOUS TRUST. 56:1-13.

Psalms 56 to 60 constitute a series of

psalms called "Michtam," meaning "an inscription on a stone slab" (M. Dahood, *Psalms*, AB, pp. 2, 41). They present the soul exercise of troubled and persecuted saints throughout the ages. But, as in the other psalms of the Psalter, there is a prophetic aspect that envisions in a particular sense the godly remnant of Israel during the Tribulation, the time of worldwide trouble, which will be unparalleled in the history of the persecutions and sufferings of the people of God (Dan. 12:1; Matt. 24:20; Mark 13:19; Rev. 7:14; cf. Psalm 2:5).

According to the superscription, this is a psalm of David when the Philistines had taken him in Gath (1 Sam. 21:10-11). As he was hedged in by two enemies, his own people and the Philistines (Gentiles), so the godly Israelites of the end time will be beset by these enemies—the ungodly in Israel and the Gentiles who make their final stand under the Antichrist (beast) and his armies of the nations before Jerusalem. "Upon Jonath-elem-rehokim" means the psalm was sung to the tune of "The Silent Dove in Far-off Lands," evidently connecting it with Psalm 55:6-7, where the godly during the Tribulation will long for the flight from the troubled city. In this psalm the godly have fled the city (Matt. 24:15-21), and the expression of their trust in God's faithfulness is reflected in David's experiences.

Confident Trust in Time of Trouble. 56:1-7. **1.** The psalmist cried out for God's gracious interposition in his troubles, occasioned by the cruel oppression of enemies who would **swallow him up** (*sh'p*, "hound," AB; "harass unmercifully," "pant," "breathe" down his neck). **2. My enemies would daily swallow me up** (*sh'p*; i.e., "My defamers hound me all day long," AB). **Many ... fight** (battle) **against me, O thou Most High**, the millennial title of deity when

Christ assumes His title of "Possessor of heaven and earth" (cf. Gen. 14:18-19; Zech. 4:14; Rev. 11:4).

3. But faith calmly declares, **When I am afraid, I will trust in** (lean on) **thee** (Psalm 2:12). **4. In God, whose word I praise, in God I have put my trust** (56:10-11).... **What can mere man** (flesh) **do to me?** (NASB; 118:6; Heb. 13:6). **5.** The psalmist complained that **all day long** his slanderers vexed him, distorting (twisting) his words (NASB; 2 Pet. 3:16), and that all their thoughts were against him **for evil** (Psalm 41:7; Matt. 24:9-10; Luke 21:12; John 15:20-21; Rev. 2:10).

6. "Evilly they conspire, conceal themselves; see how my maligners watch! Lurking like a footpad for my life" (AB; cf. Mark 13:9-13; Rev. 12:13-17; 13:7-8, 15). **8.** This verse is an imprecatory prayer (see comment on Psalm 5:10). **7. Because of** their **wickedness, cast them forth** (NASB; 36:12; Prov. 19:5; Ezek. 17:15; Rom. 2:3; cf. Gen. 15:16; Lev. 18:24).

Praise for Anticipated Deliverance. 56:8-13. **8.** The psalmist's faith assured him that God was keeping a record of his **wanderings** ("tossings," RSV; 139:3) and his sorrows. **Put my tears in Thy bottle** (NASB; 39:12; 2 Kings 20:5), the skin bottle that is used in Eastern lands for keeping water, milk and other liquids; by a bold figure he was praying to God to treasure his tears (J. J. Stewart Perowne, *Psalms*). **Are they not in thy book?** (Mal. 3:16; *sĭprâ*, "reckoning, accounting," perhaps "register," Perowne).

9. He was assured his enemies would **turn back** in defeat in the day when he cried unto God, **for God** was **for** him (on his side; Psalms 41:11; 118:6; Rom. 8:31). God was for him, because he was for God, esteeming and praising the Word of God. **10.** The repetition of the

thought in this verse, echoing the same sentiment in verse 4, emphasizes his loyalty to the Word, and hence the will, of God.

11. His faith in the Word of God is again emphasized by repetition of the same thought in verse 4, as well as his deliverance from fear, especially the fear of man. **12.** The **vows** he had made to God (Psalm 50:14) he considered binding upon him, and he would render thank offerings in token of that fact.

13. He was thankful God had **delivered** him from **death** (33:19; 49:15; 86:13) and his feet from stumbling (116:8) so that he might walk before God (116:9) in the **light of the living** (Job 33:30), in contrast to the world of the dead. Moffatt renders it, "in the sunshine of life." Then, in Kingdom glory, Christ indeed will become "the light of the world" (John 8:12; cf. Matt. 25:31, 34), and those who survive the Great Tribulation will walk before God in His light.

P. TRUST IN TIME OF TROUBLE. 57:1-11.

"To the chief Musician [precentor], Al-tashheth ('do not destroy!')," is a title appropriate to this psalm, especially in its prophetic aspect portraying the remnant of Israel in the Great Tribulation, praying and trusting God to see them through the perils and trials of that time. It is also a "Michtam [see introduction to Psalm 56] of David," said to be uttered by him "when he fled from Saul in the cave" (probably at Adullam; 1 Sam. 22:1) or that at Engedi (24:1). David's sufferings reflect the trials of saints of every age, and prophetically the experiences of the godly Israelites during the time of "Jacob's trouble" (Jer. 30:7; cf. Dan. 12:1; Matt. 24:21; Rev. 4:1—19:20).

Appeal to the God of Grace. 57:1-3. **1a. Be merciful** (gracious)... **be merciful unto me,** the repetition emphasizes the intense earnestness of the petitioner and his complete trust in God's loving-kindness. **1b. My soul** (i.e., I) **trusteth** (takes refuge) **in thee** (2:12; 34:22) **... in the shadow of thy wings** (Ruth 2:12; see Psalms 17:8; 36:7; 63:7; 91:4; Matt. 23:37). The intensity of the appeal sprang from the severity of the **calamities** that threatened, and prayer was made until they were **passed by** (Isa. 26:20).

2. Cry was made to **God most high** (the millennial title of Christ as "Possessor of heaven and earth"; cf. Gen. 14:18-19; Rev. 11:4), who in a most wonderful sense will accomplish all things for the Tribulation saint by bringing him through the terrible time of trouble (Matt. 24:22) into Kingdom blessing (25:34).

3. He shall send from heaven (Isa. 25:9; Matt. 23:39; Rev. 19:11—20:4) **and save me** (Zech. 12:1-9; 14:1-15) **from the reproach of him** (Rev. 12:13-17; 13:6-8; 19:19) who would **swallow me up** ("hounds me," AB; Psalm 56:2), "unmercifully harasses" me (Rev. 12:13—13:18). God **shall send forth his mercy** (loving-kindness) **and his truth** (Psalms 25:10; 40:11; Mal. 4:2).

Fierce Foes of the Faithful. 57:4-6. **4a.** David and the believers of every age, especially the Tribulation saints, find themselves like Daniel in a lions' den (LBC), but the **lions** are men—wicked, lawless men—in the time of the Tribulation, the most wicked and lawless the fallen race has produced (Rev. 13:1-8). They will be "lions" because they will be energized by Satan (16:13), who "like a roaring lion" will go about seeking to devour the saints with a terribleness never before experienced (1 Pet. 5:8; cf. Rev. 12:13-17; 13:7, 15).

4b. The fierce wickedness of the beast, the false prophet, and their followers is further described figuratively

—they breathe forth **fire ... whose teeth are spears ... their tongue a sharp sword** (Prov. 30:14; Psalms 55:21; 59:7). **5-6.** The description of the wicked, interrupted by worship and praise to God in verse 5, is resumed in verse 6, which sets forth their evil purposes to trap and ensnare the believer, but they fall into their own pit themselves (Rev. 13:13-18; 19:15-21).

Complete Triumph of the Faithful. 57:7-11. The plotting enemy has gone. The LORD from heaven has dealt with him and plunged him into the pit (Rev. 19:17—20:3). **7.** The believer with steadfast heart sings God's praises (vv. 8-11; 108:1-5; Isa. 12:1-6; 35:1-10; Zech. 9:16-17). **8.** He calls his **glory** (his being preserved to be a citizen of the Messiah's glorious Kingdom; Psalms 16:9; 30:12) to awaken, as well as the harp and lyre to celebrate the triumph over all foes (150:3), for the morning of the Kingdom has dawned. **9-11.** The believer becomes an evangel to the millennial nations, celebrating God's loving-kindness and truth, and His exaltation in the Kingdom age.

Q. PLEA TO PUNISH THE WICKED. 58:1-11.

Like the preceding psalm, this psalm is also set to "Altashheth" ("do not destroy!"), a "Michtam [see introduction to Psalm 56] of David." Prophetically, it describes the fully developed wickedness of the end-time Tribulation. However, it echoes the cry of the Spirit of God through the saint in any age in the struggle against fully developed wickedness in men that calls for swift divine judgment (Gen. 15:16; Lev. 18:24; 2 Thess. 2:11-12).

Why God Must Act in Judgment. 58:1-5. These verses depict wicked men of every age, like Doeg and others of Saul's associates against David, and

828

Judas and the Sanhedrin against Christ, but it particularly portrays the outrages of the Antichrist and the false prophet and their followers of the Tribulation period. Here the Spirit of God through David inveighs against them and their depravity, manifested so saliently in their venomous hostility toward the righteous.

1a. This verse in the Hebrew reads literally, "Do you [i.e., you judges] indeed speak righteousness in silence," intimating that honest dealing is dumb and not heard amid the wickedness and violence on earth. **1b. Do you judge uprightly, O sons of men?** (NASB; 82:2). **2.** This verse emphatically answers "No!" to the questions broached in verse 1. **No, in heart you work unrighteousness** (Mal. 3:15); **on earth you weigh out the violence of your hands** (NASB; Psalm 94:20; Isa. 10:1).

3-5. Then follow six things in the divine analysis of the wicked: (1) They **are estranged** (from God) from birth (Psalm 51:5; Isa. 48:8). (2) They **go astray** from truth from the womb (Psalm 53:3). (3) They are venomous like a serpent (140:3; Deut. 32:33). (4) They are deaf to reproof, like a cobra that stops its ear so that it does not hear the voice of the charmer (Psalm 81:11; Eccles. 10:11; Jer. 8:17).

(5) These violent sinners are linked to the serpent, the devil, the liar from the beginning (John 8:44; Rev. 20:2). (6) Like the peculiarly dangerous cobra, which will not respond to the snake charmer, the wicked at the end of the age are hardening themselves against God; thus, nothing is left but judgment. *Imprecatory Prayer for Judgment. 58:6-9.* For the answer to the unbeliever's criticism, What kind of a God is He who gives such prayers?, see comments on Psalm 5:10. The destruction of the wicked is pleaded for under five figures: (1) **6.** The first figure is of the **teeth** (fangs) **of the young lions,** terrible to crush and tear. So the wicked have torn the righteous (cf. 1 Pet. 5:8; Rev. 13:7, 15-17); hence, God is besought to **break** (shatter) **their teeth ... in their mouth** (Psalm 3:7; Job 4:10).

(2) **7a.** The second figure is of a flash flood. **Let them flow away like water that runs off** (NASB; Psalm 112:10; Josh. 2:11; 7:5; Isa. 13:7; Ezek. 21:7). (3) **7b.** The third figure is of the arrows of the wicked (Psalm 64:3), headless shafts shall be aimed at the righteous. (4) **8a.** The fourth figure is of **a snail which melteth** (dissolves) **away** (i.e., secretes slime) as it crawls along, and certain species that actually dissolve in the heat of the sun.

(5) **8b.** The fifth figure is of the untimely miscarriage of a woman, the fetus passing away and never seeing the light of the sun (Job 3:16; Eccles. 6:3). By contrast, the godly Israelites of the end time shall be born again to see the glorious millennial "Sun of righteousness" (Mal. 4:2) and be zealous evangelists like Paul, who as an Israelite and representing his nation, was born prematurely (1 Cor. 15:8), that is, before the time for Israel's rebirth.

(6) **9.** The sixth figure is of the pots and the thorns. Before the **pots,** representing the godly, can feel the fire of **thorns**, representing the persecutions of the wicked (Psalm 118:12; Eccles. 7:6), He who hears the prayers of His own shall sweep the foe away with the whirlwind of His judgments (Rev. 19:11; 20:3), **both living, and in his wrath** (19:20), the beast and the false prophet being cast alive into gehenna.

Vindication of God and His People. 58:10-11. (1) **10.** *Vindication of God's people.* The **righteous** (justified) **shall rejoice** in deliverance (Rev. 19:1-5) when they see **the vengeance** (Psalms

32:11; 64:10; Rev. 18:20), that is, God's righteous wrath and judgment poured out upon those ripe for it (Deut. 32:35; Prov. 6:34; Isa. 34:8; 61:2; 2 Thess. 1:7-10). The righteous shall **wash his feet in the blood of the wicked** (Psalm 68:3) as he tramples in triumph upon their slain bodies gory with blood.

(2) **11.** *Vindication of God.* Men will see that God provides a **reward for the righteous** (Psalms 18:20; 19:11; Isa. 3:10; Luke 6:23; Rom. 2:6, 11; Rev. 22:12), and that He is righteous and rewards righteousness. Men will acknowledge that there **is a God** (cf. Psalms 14:1; 53:1), and that He **judgeth in the earth** (9:8; 67:4; 75:7; 94:2). Although the terrible injustices of the Tribulation period will cause some to doubt the fact of God's judgment, His second advent and Kingdom will be a glorious manifestation and vindication of His dealing with sinners (Isa. 9:7; 11:4-5; Rev. 19:15-16).

R. PRAYER FOR DELIVERANCE FROM FOES. 59:1-17.

This is the last of the series of psalms (57-59) superscribed with the phrase "Al-tashheth" ("do not destroy!"). It is another "Michtam [see the introduction to Psalm 56] of David," connected in the superscription with the incident when Saul sent, and they watched the house to kill him (1 Sam. 19:11-18). But not everything in this episode can be applied to David, and the psalm transcends the experiences of saints of every age and prophetically reflects the prayers of God's people hounded by fierce foes and engulfed in the terrible woes of Tribulation anguish (Zech. 12:3-5; 14:1-15; Mal. 4:1; Rev. 16:13-16).

The Cry for Help Against Foes. 59:1-8. Here the enemies of the Israelite remnant are not their apostate fellows, but the Gentiles, as the references to

"dog" (vv. 6, 14) and to "all the nations" (v. 8) indicate. **1-2.** Against these fiercely hostile people who rose up against the psalmist, practiced iniquity (lawlessness), and committed murder and violence as **bloody men** (cf. Rev. 9:20-21), he implored deliverance and protection (Psalm 26:9; Prov. 29:10).

3-4a. They lay in wait for him and set an ambush to kill him (Psalm 56:6); these fierce and violent men launched an attack against him, though he had done nothing wrong to provoke such hostility (7:3-4; 69:4; 1 Sam. 24:11). **4b.** So terrible was the psalmist's predicament that he imagined God had gone to sleep and forgotten him. So he cried for God to arouse Himself (Psalm 7:6; 35:23; Zech. 2:13), to see his anguish and come to his aid.

5a. He addressed his Helper as the **Lord God of hosts** (armies), who in the prophetic aspect will have the resources to rout the armies of the Antichrist and his followers (Rev. 16:13-16) and wage victorious war in behalf of His fiercely harassed saints (19:11), since He will marshal "the armies ... in heaven" (19:14) and have "a sharp sword" issuing from His mouth to "smite the nations" (19:15).

5b. He also employed the divine title **the God of Israel**, since He is the One to **awake to visit** (punish) **all the nations** (Psalm 9:5; Isa. 26:14; Rev. 19:15). **5c.** No one treacherous in iniquity and ripe for ruin is to be spared (Isa. 2:9; Jer. 18:23; Rev. 19:16—20:3). They are described (vv. 6-8). **6.** They go around **the city** (Jerusalem besieged; cf. Zech. 14:1-2) and howl **like a dog** (Psalm 22:16; Rev. 22:15).

7. They belch forth blasphemies and lies with their mouth (Psalm 94:4; Prov. 15:2, 28; Rev. 13:6). Swords are in their lips (Psalm 57:4; contrast Rev. 19:15). In their atheistic folly (Psalms 14:1; 53:1), they imagine that God is nonexistent and so they prate, "Who hears?" (10:11; 64:5; 73:11). **8.** But the LORD, the psalmist realized, will **laugh at them** (2:4; 37:13) and have **all the nations in derision**, for He will rule over them with a rod of iron (2:8-9; Rev. 19:15).

Faith Tested by Ferociously Cruel Foes. 59:9-15. **9.** "O my strength" (following the ancient versions and many manuscripts) "I will wait for Thee." The psalmist thus addressed God, for his faith laid hold of Him as his **defense** (stronghold; high place; tower; 9:9). **10.** Faith assured him God in grace would **meet** him and permit him to see his **desire upon** his **enemies**, that is, look triumphantly upon them in their utter defeat (54:7). **11.** He desired that they would not be killed, but scattered and brought low, as a lasting warning to His own people, lest they forget (God).

12-13. The prayer merges into imprecation (see comment on Psalm 5:10). Their sins of evil speaking, pride, cursing, and lying (Rev. 9:20-21) were fully ready for the harvest of judgment (Psalm 104:35; Rev. 14:15-20). Prophetically, the lawless nations and the military, envisioned gathered at Armageddon (Rev. 16:13-16) to fight against God (19:19), are to know that **God ruleth in Jacob** (Israel; Isa. 2:2-3) **unto the ends of the** (millennial) **earth** (Psalm 83:18; Isa. 11:9-10; 12:5-6).

14-15. The description of the wicked resumes, in which the enemy is pictured as returning at evening, howling **like a dog,** like a fierce scavenging animal, growling if it is not satisfied—a foregleam of the cruelly debased condition of the non-Jews under the Antichrist and false prophet (Rev. 9:20-21; 13:1-18).

Faith Triumphs in Answered Prayer. 59:16-17. **16.** The enemies were defeated, the grace of God manifested, and the saint (representative of all victorious saints) sang of God's strength and His manifested loving-kindness, for He had been the psalmist's stronghold (v. 9) and a refuge in the day of distress (46:1; 2 Sam. 22:3).

17. He called God his Helper and Deliverer, his **strength** (v. 9), his **defense** (stronghold), and "the God" of his "loving-kindness" (lit. Heb.), that is, "the God who shows redemptive mercy." Verses 16 and 17 will be sung by restored Israel as they enter the millennial Kingdom (Isa. 12:1-6; 35:1-10).

S. DELIVERANCE FROM ENEMIES AND RESTORATION. 60:1-12.

This psalm is for the "chief Musician" (precentor), according to "Shushan-eduth" ("lily of testimony"), perhaps a type of musical accompaniment, "a Michtam" of David (see Psalm 56), "to teach." The historical background is David's victory over the Aramaeans, particularly of Zobah, and Joab's subsequent triumph over Edom (2 Sam. 8:3, 13; 1 Chron. 18:12). In the larger prophetic scope of this psalm, these victories presage the great victory of the greater than David at His second advent, when He will deliver the waiting remnant of His people, Israel.

National Lament and Expressions of Hope. 60:1-5. **1.** Apparently David was surveying the past sad story of disobedient Israel. Yet how briefly and comprehensively he summed up prophetically the whole history of the nation. **O God, thou hast cast us off . . . scattered us . . . restore us** (NASB; 44:9; 2 Sam. 5:20; cf. Deut. 28:63-68; 30:1-10; Jer. 31:10).

2. This verse doubtlessly comprehends an earthquake in David's purview (Psalm 18:7); yet the prophetic scope goes beyond his times to find fulfillment in the disasters and convulsions of the Great Tribulation (Zech. 14:1-5;

Rev. 16:17-21). **3.** Then God will indeed show His **people**, Israel, **hard things** (Psalms 66:12; 71:20; Dan. 12:1; Matt. 24:21-22) and make them **drink the wine of astonishment** (staggering; Isa. 51:17, 22; Jer. 25:15; Rev. 14:19-20).

4. Yet in David's time, by the signal victories over the Aramaeans and Edomites, God gave **a banner** of hope and encouragement to those who feared Him, that it might **be displayed** (be lifted up) **because of the truth** (Psalm 20:5), that is, God's faithfulness to His promise "spoken in his holiness" (v. 6; cf. Rom. 15:8). His unfailing Word is the banner of His fidelity to His people in all ages and a pledge of hope in a special sense to His suffering, hard-pressed people during the Great Tribulation (Jer. 30:5-7).

5. As a result of their faith in His Word, they see themselves as His **beloved.** Benjamin, as the representative of the whole people, was called "the beloved of the LORD" (Deut. 33:12), and the cry **save with thy right hand** seems to refer to the meaning of Benjamin, "son of [my] right hand"; compare David's naming Solomon "Jedidiah," "beloved of Yah [God] " (2 Sam. 12:25).

Prospect of Restoration and Favor. 60:6-8. **6. God hath spoken** in His **holiness**—in His holy character infinitely removed from fickleness or deception (89:35; Num. 23:19). He has promised to deliver His beloved from their enemies (24:17-19) and regather and restore them from all their dispersions (Ezek. 37:1-14; Matt. 24:31; Rom. 11:26). So the title "Lily of testimony" seems to hint at God's lovely promises to Israel.

David's words of rejoicing over his conquests reflect the rejoicing of saints in their victories in all ages, but they prophetically reflect the utterances of the delivered remnant as they anticipate

entrance upon their inheritance of the land to be joyously apportioned by tribes, as in Joshua's day (Ezek. 47:13—48:35). **I will divide** (apportion; Josh. 13:7; 18:8) **Shechem** (west of Jordan), **and measure the valley of Succoth** (east of Jordan), hence indicating the whole of Canaan. Jacob's successive settlement at Succoth and Shechem on his return from the same region of Mesopotamia, from which the Israelite army of David's time had then returned, pointed to the occupancy of the whole land by his descendants (Gen. 33:17-18).

7. The claim to **Gilead . . . and Manasseh** (connected with east Jordan), echoing the very words of Jacob (48:5), and to **Ephraim** and **Judah** (connected with west Jordan) emphasize the claim to possession of all the promised land. Ephraim is called **the strength of my head,** that is, the fortress that protects the most vital part of the body (Psalms 27:1; 68:21). Judah is called **my lawgiver,** as Israel's ruling tribe (Gen. 49:10).

8. Moab is styled **my washpot** or tub, figuratively expressing the ignominious subjection to which David reduced her (2 Sam. 8:2), since washing others' feet was the task of a slave (John 13:8). The figure of casting a shoe over **Edom** signifies the victorious taking possession of the land, trampling down her pride, the shoe being a symbol of the transfer of possession (Ruth 4:7; cf. Josh. 10:24). **Philistia** is to raise a shout of triumph and "rejoice with trembling" (Psalm 2:11) at the remnant's possession of the land under Israel's King, ultimately her Messiah-King.

Anticipation and Prayer for Realization of Victory. 60:9-12. **9.** David had in mind the success of the expedition against Edom. **Who will bring me into the strong city** (Petra or Sela) the rock-built city of **Edom** (31:21; 2 Kings 14:7). **10. Wilt not thou, O God,** because of the promise (v. 6)? **11-12a.** When faith attests its reality by looking to God, despite human appearances, then the testimony of the saint will be, **Through God we shall do valiantly** (Psalm 118:16; Num. 24:18). **12b.** Then He will tread down the adversaries of His people (Psalm 44:5; Isa. 63:3). The grand prophetic fulfillment of this will be when the Messiah returns to fight for His people and establish them in Kingdom blessing (Rev. 19:11-20).

T. GOD THE SHELTER IN TIME OF TROUBLE. 61:1-8.

Psalms 61 to 68 form a new series that sets forth the faith and prayers of David and the saints of every age in extreme distress, with particular prophetic emphasis upon the sufferings of the Israelite remnant of the age-end period called "Jacob's trouble" (Jer. 30:5-7; Dan. 12:1; Matt. 24:21-22). All these psalms, except Psalms 66 and 67, are ascribed to David.

The Refuge of the Troubled Saint. 61:1-4. **1.** David (probably beyond Jordan during Absalom's rebellion) cried out to God to hear and answer his prayer (64:1; 86:6). **2.** He cried **from the end of the earth** (42:6), hyperbolic language to emphasize the deep feeling of homelessness that the Israelite experiences from separation from what is dear to him. His heart was **overwhelmed** (ʿṭp, "to be faint, exhausted, languish"; 77:3). He prayed to be led **to the rock** (18:2; 94:22) higher than he (Exod. 33:22; Deut. 32:4; 1 Sam. 2:2; 2 Sam. 22:3).

3. The psalmist figuratively referred to God as **a shelter,** a rock, **a strong tower** and spoke of the **shelter** of God's **wings** (Psalms 17:8; 36:7; 57:1; Mal. 4:2; Matt. 23:37). **4.** He prayed to dwell in God's tent forever (Psalm 23:6; 27:4; Rev. 21:3).

The Blessing and Glory of the King. 61:5-8. **5a.** David was assured that God had heard his **vows** (56:12; Job 22:27), his prayers being mixed with vows of thanksgiving (v. 8; cf. 2 Sam. 7:18-29). The basis of David's confidence was the prophetic Word of God (7:8-15), guaranteeing him eternal dominion through his son and Lord (Psalm 110:1).

5b-6. He declared that God had given him the **heritage** (inheritance) **of those who fear** His **name,** that is, the prolongation of the **king's life** and the abiding Kingdom of his posterity over Canaan, the land of Israel. The Israelites' feature of distinction from the Gentiles was their fear (reverence) of God's name.

Although it was David who spoke, his words envision the greater David, whose vows to do God's will, even to death in redeeming a lost world, were heard (Heb. 5:7) when God raised Him from the dead and gave Him an inheritance as "heir of all things" (1:2). Therefore, His days—His years as the glorified God-man—are prolonged from generation to generation (Isa. 53:10). **7-8.** He dwells with the redeemed in God's presence forever (Psalm 16:11). The King-Messiah not only shall reign in the restored Kingdom over Israel (Isa. 9:7-8; 11:11-16; Acts 1:6; Rev. 20:4-6), but "the throne of ... the Lamb" will continue (Rev. 22:1, 3) throughout eternity.

U. WAITING FOR GOD IN TIME OF TROUBLE. 62:1-12.

For the scope of this psalm, see Psalm 61. It is addressed "to the chief Musician [precentor]" that is, "to Jeduthun" (cf. Psalms 39, 77), the name of a member of a musical guild instituted by David (W. F. Albright, *Archaeology and the Religion of Israel*, p. 127). The special office of Jeduthun and his sons was to praise the LORD (1 Chron. 25:1, 3).

Looking to God Alone in Persecution. 62:1-2. **1a.** This verse in Hebrew is literally rendered, "Only unto God is my soul silent," that is, "is utterly silent" in His presence, in complete submission to expect all from Him, nothing from man, and to look away from self to Him. **1b.** The reason—**from him cometh my salvation** ("my deliverance") from persecutors. **2.** God alone was the psalmist's **rock** and **salvation** (18:2; 89:26) and his **defense** (*miśgāḇ*, "high place, fortress"). He said, **I shall not be greatly moved** (*'emmôṭ*, "stumble, totter, fall"; *răbbâ*, "unduly").

The Persecutors Confronted and Described. 62:3-4. **3. How long will ye imagine mischief against** (*hûṭ*, "assail, make an attack on") **a man** to **murder him** (NASB). These persecutors were compared to a **bowing** (leaning) **wall** and a **tottering fence** (Isa. 30:13), threatening the life and limb of anyone near them. They had only one purpose—to thrust down a man (i.e., the godly man) from his high position by falsehood (Psalm 4:2), blessing with their mouth (28:3; 55:21), but cursing inwardly. This is a description of the persecutors of God's people in every age, but particularly the wicked followers of the beast and the false prophet, who will hound the people of God with unparalleled cruelty (Rev. 13:7, 15).

Renewed Declaration of Trust in God Alone. 62:5-10. **5.** The psalmist exhorted himself (his soul) to **wait** in silence for God **only** (v. 1), because his hope sprang from Him. **6-7.** He repeated the figures of verse 2, God as his **rock** and **stronghold** (NASB). **8.** He urged his colleagues to **trust** God too and to **pour out** their **heart before him** (42:4; 1 Sam. 1:15; Lam. 2:19).

9. Man is unreliable and not to be trusted. Those of **low degree are vanity** (Psalm 49:2; Job 7:16; Isa. 40:17). Men of rank are a **lie** (Psalm 116:11). In the balances (Isa. 40:15), in the scales they go up, because they are **lighter than vanity** (breath or air). **10.** Riches acquired by oppression or robbery (30:12; 61:8; Ezek. 22:29; Nah. 3:1) not only are not to be trusted in, but to be viewed as a snare. Even material things that are acquired honestly can prove a terrible curse if the man of God sets his affection upon them (Psalms 49:6; 52:7; Mark 10:24; Luke 12:15; 1 Tim. 6:10).

God Is Worthy of All Trust. 62:11-12. God is worthy of trust for three reasons: (1) **11.** He is all-powerful. The psalmist declared this fact emphatically (Job 33:14; 40:5; Psalm 59:17; Rev. 19:1). (2) **12a.** He is gracious and loving. To Him also belongs **mercy** (loving-kindness; Psalms 86:5; 103:8; 130:7). (3) **12b.** He is righteous and impartial. He recompenses everyone **according to his work** (28:4; Job 34:11; Rom. 2:6; 1 Cor. 3:8; Rev. 22:12).

V. THE THIRSTING SOUL'S SATISFACTION IN GOD. 63:1-11.

This psalm is entitled "a Psalm of David" and is connected with his experiences "in the wilderness of Judah" (1 Sam. 23:14), separated from the sanctuary, a homeless refugee, though God's anointed king. His heart's desires, expressed in this sad, persecuted state, reflect the experiences through which the persecuted godly remnant will pass during the Tribulation.

Longing for the Joyous Fellowship of God. 63:1-8. **1.** Faith claimed God (118:28) and resolved to seek Him **early** (earnestly), expressing deep longing for God under the figure of thirst (42:2; 84:2; Matt. 5:6; cf. John 7:37; Rev. 21:6). He declared his **flesh longeth** (faints, pines) for Him in a dry, arid land, as the Judean wilderness is (Psalm 143:6).

2. Away from the sanctuary (27:4; Isa. 6:1), he longed to see God's power and glory, as manifested there. **3a.** His reason for his great desire (thirst) for God and His tabernacle was that God's loving-kindness was revealed there, since both priesthood and ritual pointed to divine redemptive grace to be revealed in something better than physical life (i.e., eternal life; Psalm 69:16).

3b-4. He was filled with praise because he sought spiritual blessings above material blessings or comforts, blessing God (104:33; 146:2) and lifting up his hands in God's name (28:2; 143:6). **5.** As a result, his soul was satisfied as **with marrow and fatness** (36:8), and his mouth offered joyful **praise** (71:23).

6. His thoughts were continually toward God, remembering Him upon his bed (42:8; 119:55; 149:5) and meditating (*hāgâ*, "muse, murmur," utter sounds expressive of the cogitations of one's mind) upon his bed and in the **night watches** (90:4; 119:48), the night being divided into four watches (6-9 P.M.; 9 P.M.-midnight; midnight-3 A.M.; 3-6 A.M.; cf. Mark 6:48). **7.** Faith recognized God as one's **help.** In the **shadow of** God's **wings** (Ruth 2:12; Psalms 17:8; 36:7; 57:1; 61:4; 68:13; 91:4; Matt. 23:37), faith rejoiced. **8.** Faith cleaved to God. **My soul** ("I") **followeth close behind** (*dḇq*, "sticks [clings] close to") **thee** (Num. 32:12; Deut. 1:36; Hos. 6:3). Faith appropriated God's sustaining power. **Thy right hand upholdeth** (*tmk*, "supports, sustains") **me** (Psalms 18:35; 41:12).

The Fate of the Persecutors. 63:9-10. **9.** Saul and his henchmen sought David's life to destroy it (1 Sam. 23:14). So will the willful king of the end time seek the life of the saints (Dan. 7:25;

Rev. 13:7, 15; cf. Matt. 24:15-24). But faith envisions the downfall of these wicked persecutors. They will be slain and go into the **lower parts of the earth,** that is, be killed, their bodies going to the grave, their souls and spirits to Sheol (cf. Rev. 19:11—20:3). **10.** They shall **fall by the sword** (Rev. 19:15-21). **They shall be a portion for foxes** (jackals; Lam. 5:18), which prey upon unburied carcasses (cf. 2 Sam. 18:7-8, 14, 17). Compare the prophetic fulfillment (Rev. 16:13-16; 19:17-18, 21).

The Exaltation of the King. 63:11. **11.** David, God's anointed king, rejoiced **in God,** as will the greater David when He returns as "KING OF KINGS" (Rev. 19:15-16), and as did everyone that swore by David, in token of loyalty (cf. Gen. 42:15-16), and as everyone who does likewise will **glory** in (share the glory of) the enthroned Messiah when He comes to rule on His throne (Matt. 25:31; Rev. 20:4-6). But the rebels and deceivers (the persecutors of God's people) shall have their lying mouths stopped (Job 5:16; Psalm 107:42; Rom. 3:19) by death (Rev. 19:21).

W. PRAYER FOR DELIVERANCE FROM ENEMIES. 64:1-10.

This psalm, ascribed to David, cannot with certainty be placed in its historical setting, but prophetically it fits in the context of Psalms 61 to 68. See the introduction to Psalm 61.

The Wicked Dominate over the Righteous. 64:1-6. The wicked dominated the righteous when David was hounded by Saul and his henchmen. It has been the story of the ages, but it will reach its height in man's rebellion at the end of the age (2:1-3), when the lawless one, the Antichrist, rules and persecutes the saints of God with unparalleled terror and violence (Dan. 7:25; Rev. 13:7, 15).

1. The cry of the psalmist, echoing the plea of the persecuted of every age, was that God would hear his prayer and preserve his life **from fear** (dread) of the enemy (Psalms 55:2; 140:1), who in the Tribulation period will indeed be a dreadful foe. 2. He pleaded to be hidden **from the secret counsel of the wicked** (2:1-3; 56:6) and **the insurrection** (*rĭgshâ*, "noisy, rebellious tumult") of **the workers of iniquity** (59:2), those who work vanity and operate under demonic dynamic as the result of the rejection of God and complicity in idolatry and demonized religion (Rev. 9:20-21; 13:13-18).

3-4. They **whet** (sharpen) **their tongue like a sword** (Psalm 140:3); they aim their bitter words like **arrows** (58:7) to **shoot in secret** (in concealment) at **the perfect** (blameless; 10:8; 11:2), meaning the godly man who has done nothing to incur their malignity. They do not fear the consequences of such heinous crimes (55:19), since they have rejected God and all sense of His eternal moral Law, reflected in the Mosaic Decalogue (Exod. 20:1-17).

5. They **encourage themselves** (lit., "make themselves firm") **in an evil matter** (purpose). They **speak of laying snares secretly** (Psalm 140:5) to entrap the blameless. They have denied God (14:1), and so they say, **Who can see them?** (NASB; 59:7; Job 22:13).

6. **They search out** (devise, invent) **iniquities** (injustices), asserting, **We are ready with a well-conceived plot** (NASB). Their depraved **inward thought** and **heart** are **deep** (i.e., unsearchable in wickedness). They will represent humanity in the full development of its lawlessness (Gen. 15:16) revealed in complete manifestation in the lawless one, the Antichrist (Rev. 13:18; 14:15-20).

God Acts in Judgment upon the Wicked. 64:7-10. **7a.** They shot their arrows at God's people (vv. 3-4). Now God shoots at them with His arrow of judgment (7:12-13). **7b. Suddenly shall they be wounded** to death (Rev. 19:21), prophetically at the hands of Christ at His second advent as a Warrior-Judge (19:11).

8. The **tongue,** which they designed to be the instrument of the destruction of God's people, proves the cause of their own undoing. **All that see them shall flee away,** lest they be destroyed in their punishment (cf. Num. 16:34; Jer. 51:6; Rev. 18:4-8)—a fitting retribution for their saying, "Who shall see them?" (v. 5), i.e., their wicked snares and those who set them.

9. **And all . . . shall fear** (Psalm 40:3) and **declare the work of God** and **wisely consider** what God has done, obtaining an insight into God's justice in judgment. 10. There will also be a salutary effect on the righteous. The **righteous** (man) will **be glad in the Lord** (32:11; Job 22:19; Rev. 18:20) and will **trust** (take refuge) in Him (Psalms 11:1; 25:20; Rev. 19:1-6). **All the upright . . . shall glory** in the LORD and His great deliverance wrought for them.

X. KINGDOM BLESSING REALIZED. 65:1-13.

"To the chief Musician [precentor]" indicates the ode is for the liturgy of the public worship of the nation. It is "A Psalm and Song of David" that prophetically glimpses the establishment of the Kingdom promised to David (2 Sam. 7:8-15) and comprehends the "restitution of all things . . . spoken by the mouth of all [God's] holy prophets" (Acts 3:21).

The Spiritual Blessings of the Kingdom. 65:1-4. There are seven spiritual blessings of the Kingdom: (1) **1a.** God will be praised, worshiped, and honored in Zion, for Jerusalem will then be the religious and political capital of the earth (Isa. 2:2-3). **Praise waiteth for thee ... in Zion** (lit., "for Thee [there is] the silence [of] praise in Zion," that is, silence is praise that springs from deep repose of the soul in God (cf. Psalm 42:1, 5). Such praise will be the response of those preserved out of the judgments of the Great Tribulation to enjoy the blessings of millennial rest.

(2) **1b.** God's vow involving the establishment of Christ's Kingdom and the conversion of the nations will then be performed: **Unto thee shall the vow be performed** (116:18). "I have sworn by myself ... that unto me every knee shall bow, every tongue shall swear" (Isa. 45:23).

(3) **2a.** God will then have heard (and answered) the Kingdom prayer—"Thy kingdom come" (Matt. 6:10)—**O thou who hearest prayer.** Also His gracious answer to prayer will have brought the survivors of the Great Tribulation through to Kingdom blessing, and their hearts will be filled with praise. (4) **2b. All flesh** (humanity in its totality) will then turn to God, and the earth will find peace and rest in Him who has chosen Zion (Jerusalem) for His rest (Psalm 132:13-14).

(5) **3.** Then iniquity and sin will be purged away—**As for our transgressions, thou shalt purge them away** (Zech. 12:10—13:1). Then Israel will have cried from the heart the great penitential strains of Psalm 51 and Isaiah 53:1-10. Romans 11:25-36 will have been fulfilled.

(6) **4a.** The electing love of God for Israel and the nations will be realized (Psalms 33:12; 84:4; Zech. 8:22-23). (7) **4b.** The great Kingdom Temple (Ezek. 40:1—44:31) will be the center of the spiritual life of the millennial age. **We**

shall be satisfied with the goodness of thy house ... thy holy temple.

Thanksgiving for God's Judgments on Sinners. 65:5-8. **5.** The psalmist envisioned God answering His people's prayers (Rev. 6:9-11) as the **God of** their **salvation,** their Deliverer from their enemies, by **awesome things in righteousness**—the fearful apocalyptic judgments of the Tribulation that will purge out sinners preceding the establishment of the Kingdom (Psalms 45:4; 66:3; Rev. 6:1—20:3). As a result of God's dealing with sinners (Psalm 2:4-12), He will be **the confidence of all the ends of the** (millennial) **earth** (22:27; 48:10) and **of the farthest sea** (NASB; 107:23; cf. Isa. 11:9).

6. He is described as the Creator and Sustainer of the universe. **By his strength** He **setteth fast** (establishes) **the mountains** and is **girded with power** (Psalms 93:1; 95:4). **7.** He **stilleth the noise** (roaring) **of the seas** (89:9; 93:3-4; 107:29; Matt. 8:26; cf. Dan. 7:2; Luke 21:25-26) **and the tumult of the people** (Psalms 2:1; 74:23; Isa. 17:12-13; Rev. 16:13-16; 19:21).

8. The people who **dwell in the uttermost parts** of the earth will be afraid of His **signs,** particularly the sign of Christ's second coming in glory (Matt. 24:30), the capstone of the signs and manifestations of His outpoured wrath during the Tribulation (cf. Luke 21:25). But God's judgments upon sin and sinners also inspire love and joy as well as fear. He makes **the outgoings of the morning** (i.e., the dawn) **and evening** (i.e., dusk, sunset) **to rejoice** (shout for joy).

Creation Sings. 65:9-14. Creation will sing because the curse that now rests upon it will be partially removed (cf. Rom. 8:19). The removal of the curse will not be complete because death will not be abolished until after the Millennium (1 Cor. 15:25-26; Rev. 20:14; 21:4). But the earth will apparently enjoy a wonderful approximation to Edenic conditions.

9. Christ's return to the earth will cause it to overflow with prosperity and enrichment (v. 10a; Psalms 72:6; 147:8; Deut. 32:2). He **visitest the earth, and waterest it** (causes it to overflow; Psalms 68:9; 104:13; 147:8; Lev. 26:4), greatly enriching it (Psalm 104:24) **with the river of God,** apparently referring to the fountain of fertilizing rain from above, which God has at His command, and which never, like earthly springs, runs dry (Deut. 11:11-12). The allusion recalls the rivers that watered Eden (Gen. 2:10-14), since paradise will be partially restored in the Kingdom age. Both Ezekiel (Ezek. 47:1-12) and Zechariah (Zech. 14:8) spoke of such a millennial stream, symbolically comprehending spiritual blessings as well as physical benefits. Christ is pictured as preparing **grain** (cf. 9:16-17).

10-11. He softens the earth with showers (Zech. 10:1; Joel 2:23; Hos. 6:3), crowns the year with His bounty (Psalm 104:28), and all His paths drip with fatness (prosperity; 147:14; cf. Amos 9:13-15). **12.** The hills are pictured as girding themselves with rejoicing (cf. Isa. 35:1-8). **13.** The meadows are clothed with flocks and the valleys covered with grain. They are personified as shouting for joy and singing. Everything sings—no more droughts, floods, no more destructive storms and calamities. Little wonder everything sings.

Y. PRAISE AND WORSHIP IN THE KINGDOM. 66:1-20.

Like the preceding, this psalm is "a Song" joyfully celebrating the coming Kingdom age. It is grounded in some unknown historical incident, but it goes beyond that, and its scope reaches prophetically into the blissful conditions of the Millennium.

The Glorious Rule of the Messiah. 66:1-7. **1-2.** All lands are apostrophized to **make a joyful noise,** "shout joyfully to" God (81:1; 95:1; 98:4; 100:1), to **sing forth the honor of his name** (79:9; Isa. 42:8) and **make his praise glorious** (12:1-6; 42:12). This call to the entire earth to praise God will be due to the fact the Lord has come (Rev. 19:11-16), destroyed the rebels and sinners (Psalm 2:4-12; Rev. 19:17—20:3), and set up His Kingdom (Isa. 9:7; 11:1; 12:6; 35:1-10; Rom. 11:25-36; Rev. 20:4-6).

3. These great undertakings will call forth the testimony of the entire millennial earth: **How awe-inspiring ... thy works!** — His work of judgment upon sinners (Rev. 6:1—19:11) in liberating the earth from their usurpation; His work of grace in setting up the Kingdom of righteousness and peace; and His work of power in ruling "with a rod of iron" (Psalm 2:8-9; Rev. 19:15) in order that His enemies will **submit themselves** to Him (lit., "feign submission to" Him; Psalms 18:44; 81:15). God's terrible deeds will constrain them so that if they will not render willing obedience, at the least it will be reluctant (cf. Exod. 8:8-15; Prov. 16:4).

4. Universal worship and praise to God will be the Kingdom order. **5-6.** An invitation is extended to review the classic demonstrations of God's awesome works in His deliverance of His people at the Red Sea and at the Jordan (Exod. 14:21; Josh. 3:16). **There let us rejoice in Him!** (NASB; Psalm 105:43).

7a. By this same omnipotent might He will rule in Kingdom glory forever (2 Sam. 7:16; Psalm 145:13), with His millennial throne, after the satanic revolt at the end of the Kingdom age (Rev. 20:7-10), merging into His eternal Kingdom and throne (22:1, 3) in the sinless eternal state (21:4, 8). **7b-c.** His millennial government will involve close scrutiny over the nations (Psalm 140:8; Zech. 5:1-4) and a rod-of-iron rule; so let not the rebellious **exalt themselves** (Psalms 2:8-9; 110:2; 140:8; Isa. 11:4; Dan. 7:13-14).

Praise of Those Delivered to Kingdom Blessing. 66:8-15. **8.** Their cry will be to **bless** their God and sound His praise abroad (lit., "cause the sound of His praise to be heard"; 98:4; Isa. 12:1-6; 35:10; 51:10-11; 54:1-3; Zech. 9:16-17). **9.** This verse gives the reason for praise. God will preserve them through the judgments preceding the Kingdom, keep them alive in those terrible times (Psalm 30:3; Matt. 24:21-22), and not allow their feet to slip (stumble) under the awful pressure from the Antichrist and his forces (Rev. 13:1-18).

10. They will confess that God has tried them through the Great Tribulation, through which they will have passed (Rev. 6:1—19:21), and through the trouble that had purified them (Isa. 48:10; Zech. 13:9; Mal. 3:3; cf. 1 Pet. 1:7). **11.** The terrible experience will be like being caught in a net (Lam. 1:13; Ezek. 12:13). It will involve deep suffering and acute affliction.

12-15. Men (*ᵉnôsh*, "mean men") will ride roughshod over their heads (Isa. 51:23), and they will go (pass) **through fire and ... water** (Psalm 78:21; Isa. 43:2), a graphic synopsis of the Tribulation anguish. But God, through this great trial, will bring them **into a wealthy place,** a place of abundance and spiritual prosperity (Psalm 18:19), shown (1) by their worship (v. 13*a*) in the millennial Temple (Ezek. 40:1—42:20) presenting burnt offerings, which in the Kingdom age will be commemorative of a finished redemption (46:1-24), as the Lord's Supper is in this age (1 Cor. 11:26); (2) by

their paying the vows (v. 13*b*; Psalms 22:25; 116:14), which they will have made during the great time of trouble preceding their deliverance by the coming of the Lord (v. 14; 18:6); and (3) by the abundance of their sacrifices in token of their gratitude and praise (v. 15). The psalmist, in using the singular tense, personified the restored nation Israel.

Testimony of Those Delivered to Kingdom Blessing. 66:16-20. **16.** The speaker continued in the singular number to personify the restored nation. An invitation was issued to all to hear what God has done for His restored people. **I will declare what he hath done for my soul** (71:15, 24). **17-19.** The psalmist extolled God and separated himself from wickedness, and so the LORD heard his prayer. **20.** God is to be **blessed** (highly praised). He has not turned away Israel's prayer, nor taken His lovingkindness from them (cf. Rom. 11:25-36).

Z. KINGDOM NATIONS EXHORTED TO PRAISE GOD. 67:1-7.

The designation "to the chief Musician [choir director] " indicates usage of this psalm in the liturgy of Israel's worship. It was to be accompanied by stringed instruments. Like Psalms 65, 66, and 68, it is a "Song" encompassing a joy that glimpses the establishment of "the kingdom over Israel" (Acts 1:6).

Prayer for God's Blessing upon Israel. 67:1-2. **1-2.** God is called upon to **be merciful** (gracious) to His people, Israel, and **bless** them (Num. 6:24-25), and cause His **face to shine** upon them (Psalms 4:6; 31:16; 80:3, 7, 19; 119:135), that through their testimony of God's delivering them from their enemies and establishing them in the millennial Kingdom, His **way** (cf. Acts 18:25; Psalms 25:10; 103:7) **may be known upon** (the millennial) **earth** (98:2; cf. Rom.

11:26-36), and His **saving health** (*y^eshû'â*, "salvation, deliverance") **among all nations**, that is, all the nations of the Kingdom (Psalm 66:4; Isa. 2:2-3; 45:14; 66:23; Zech. 8:20-23; 14:16-21).

Call to the Nations to Praise God. 67:3-7. **3-4.** The nations are to praise God and be glad and sing joyfully (100:1), because God will establish His just rule in righteousness and peace (9:8; 96:10, 13; Isa. 9:7) through the Messiah-King-Priest (Zech. 6:12-15). The blessedness of Israel in her Lord shall be a magnet to draw all nations to the same Savior (Isa. 2:2-4) when He will **govern** (guide; 58:11) the people of the Kingdom and **judge righteously** (lit., "in evenness"; i.e., with equity; Psalm 45:6).

5-6. When all the peoples praise God, then the millennial earth itself shall be delivered (at least to a degree) from the curse (Gen. 3:17-19; Isa. 9:6-9; Hab. 2:14) and **yield her increase** (Psalm 65:9-13; Isa. 35:1-10; Amos 9:13; Zech. 9:16-17; 10:1). God will bless Israel immediately and the nations intermediately through His restored people (Lev. 26:4; Psalm 65:5, 9-13). **7. All the ends of the** (millennial) **earth shall fear him** (22:27). God's blessing on the restored nation will be the forerunner of the conversion of the earth in the coming age.

AA. FULL KINGDOM BLESSING. 68:1-35.

This psalm was designated for "the chief Musician [precentor]" for the nation's liturgy. It is "A Psalm or Song of David," indicating that the time of Israel's singing has arrived (Isa. 30:19; 35:10; 65:19).

God Revealed in Victory. 68:1-6. **1. Let God arise, let his enemies be scattered** is taken from the Mosaic formula recited whenever the ark set forward (Num.

10:35). These great words of faith will be the answer to the prayer the remnant of Israel will pray when surrounded by their enemies during the Great Tribulation (Psalm 44:26).

2. The answer will be Christ's glorious manifestation (102:13) to deal with His and their enemies (Rev. 19:11—20:3). Their end will be sudden and catastrophic, **as smoke . . . driven away** by the wind (Psalm 37:20; Isa. 9:18), **as wax melteth before the fire** (Psalms 22:14; 97:5), **so . . . the wicked** will **perish at the presence of God** (9:3; 37:20; 80:16; Mal. 4:1; Rev. 19:19).

3-4. Then the **righteous** shall **exceedingly rejoice** (Psalms 32:11; 58:10; 64:10; Isa. 35:10) and **extol him who rideth upon the heavens** (clouds), literally, "cast up a highway for Him who rides through the deserts" (NASB; Isa. 57:14; 62:10). As the ark of old led God's people in the desert, so now again God rides forward, leading them safely through "the deserts" of conflict and trial (Deut. 33:26). The LORD is presented **by his name,** *Jah,* literally, "in Jah[is] his name," the concentrated essence of all that is comprehended by Jehovah (Yahweh; cf. Exod. 15:2) and the ground for His people to rejoice in Him (cf. Phil. 4:4).

5. God's compassionate love, for the distressed in particular, for the **fatherless** (orphans) and **widows** (Psalm 146:7-9; Deut. 10:18), emphasizes His concern for His troubled people. As a compassionate Judge, He vindicates His people's cause (Psalm 54:1), in contrast to the unjust judge in Luke 18:1-8. **His holy habitation**—the seat of His infinite holiness and righteousness—is contrasted with the earth, the seat of selfishness and iniquity (Psalms 11:4; 22:3).

6a. God setteth the solitary—those destitute of human help (25:16)—**in families** (lit. Heb., "in a home"). So Israel, after her final homeless wandering, will be placed in her homeland (Ezek. 37:1-28) in full restoration and blessing (Rom. 11:26-36). **6b. He bringeth out those who are bound with chains** (better, "He leads out the prisoners into prosperity," NASB; Psalm 66:12). **6c.** By contrast, **the rebellious**, the stiff-necked (Exod. 17:14, 16; Luke 19:14; John 19:15) **dwell in a dry land** (contrast v. 9).

A Historical Retrospect. 68:7-14. **7.** The psalmist reviewed Israel's past and recalled God's marching before His people in victory (Judg. 5:4-5; cf. Exod. 19:16; Num. 10:33; Deut. 33:2). **8.** The account is begun with the theophany on Sinai, because there the covenant with Israel was ratified (33:2-5) and there the manifestation of God was evidence of His special love for Israel (4:33).

9-10. God sent (shook out) **a plentiful rain** (lit., "rain of liberalities"), a very abundant rain, a most welcome boon to a thirsty people in the desert. But "the rain of gifts" (*nᵉḏāḇôt*) probably means God "shook out" in order to cause the rain of gracious gifts (including the manna and the quails) to fall on the whole congregation of His people, confirming (strengthening) His **inheritance** when it **was weary** (parched) and causing it to dwell in the promised land, providing in His **goodness for the poor**, that is, the homeless Israelites in the desert.

Verses 11 to 14 review God's working for His people from the time of their entrance into the land till the setting up of the sanctuary in Zion. **11. The Lord gave** (issued) **the word** (command) that insured victory for His people. "Great was the company of the female heralds *of* the *good* news" (lit. Heb.; Exod. 15:20-21; Judg. 5:12; 11:34; 1 Sam. 18:6-7). **12.** This verse refers to Sisera's defeat (cf. Judg. 5:30-31), in which the women shared in the spoil.

13. This verse presents the figure of Israel's degradation in Egypt (Lam. 4:8), where she is pictured as having "lain" **among the pots** (KJV), in the place where caldrons were set over the fire and where she was blackened by the smoke in servile labor. But in her deliverance she is pictured as a silver-winged dove (silver portraying redemption) reflecting the golden rays of the sun (gold portraying Israel's glory).

14. When the Almighty (El Shaddai) scattered kings **therein** (in the land; e.g., Cushan, Jabin, Agag), **it was white like snow in Zalmon** (shady, dark), a high mountain near the Jordan (Psalm 51:7; Mark 9:3). The brightness of victory, after the gloom of conflict, is likened to the snowy blanket covering Zalmon's black forests (Judg. 9:48). So will Israel appear when the LORD routs her final enemies and restores her to Kingdom blessing.

Jerusalem in Historical and Prophetic Perspective. 68:15-18. **15.** God has elected Zion upon which to dwell forever with His countless chariots, despite all the resistance of pagans. He indicated this by the victory vouchsafed to His people. **The hill of God** is a Hebraism for a "great [high] hill" and this verse should be rendered, "The hill of God is the hill of Bashan, an high hill is the hill of Bashan," that is, Mount Hermon on the extreme limit of Bashan and symbolizing the world's might (v. 22; 42:6; 89:12).

16. The original name of Hermon was Sion ("lofty"; Deut. 4:48), similar in sound to "Zion" and suggesting the contrast between the world's hills (vv. 15-16*a*) and the LORD's hill (Psalm 2:6), where His King will be installed in Kingdom rule (2 Sam. 7:8-15), and where the LORD will **dwell ... forever** (Psalm 2:7-12; 2 Sam. 7:16; 23:1-5; Matt. 25:31; Luke 1:31-33; Rev. 22:1, 3). **Why** (as in Psalm 2:1) **leap ye, ye high hills,**

namely, with eager, envious desire of setting at nought the hill of Zion, which God has chosen, and exalting yourselves above it. Let these "high hills" (lit., "mountain summits," i.e., mountain ranges) know that God has chosen Zion as His habitation, which ensures her eternal security against her foes.

17. His chariots are **twenty thousand** ("two myriads," Gen. 32:1-2), denoting a great number, **even thousands** ("thousands repeated") **of angels** (2 Sam. 10:18; cf. 2 Kings 6:16-17). What avail then are the enemies' war chariots against Zion (Psalm 2:1-3; Zech. 12:3-6; 14:3-4; Rev. 19:11—20:3)? The Lord (Adonai) **is among them as at Sinai, in holiness** (NASB; Deut. 33:2-3). The reference, although panoramic, focuses on Zion in the Kingdom age when Jerusalem will be the capital of the millennial earth (Isa. 2:2-5) and when all the angels who once ministered at the giving of the Law will be present on Mount Zion with the LORD among them. When Christ returns as Victor to rout His foes, He will come with myriads of angels, "the armies ... in heaven" (Rev. 19:14).

18. This verse in its historical context doubtlessly envisions a triumphant procession, headed by the warrior-king David, winding its way up the sacred hill of Zion, following the ark being carried into the tabernacle with the victorious monarch and leading **captivity** (i.e., a number of captives) **captive** in his triumph (Judg. 5:12), an emphatic way of expressing the utter prostration of his foes.

The prophetic aspect looks forward to two things: (1) It looks forward to the ascension of Christ, evidencing His triumph over sin and death by His resurrection, which attests His redemption of the earth and mankind (Eph. 1:14), thus securing His crown rights to it when He comes to possess it and dispossess His foes at His second advent. As the God-man He gave gifts to men, including the supreme gift of the Spirit, through whom the great salvation He purchased on Calvary was mediated and spiritual gifts were dispensed (4:8-10).

(2) It looks forward to the second advent of Christ, when He will descend from above to claim His crown rights over all, and dispense His gifts and gifted men to administer for Him in His Kingdom. Then He will again ascend on high, evidently visiting the millennial earth only at special times (Rev. 20:4-6). He **received gifts** to give (dispense) even **for the rebellious**, who, although they will not willingly bring gifts at His second advent, must nevertheless yield to His iron rule (Psalm 2:5-12; Rev. 19:15), when **the Lord God** (Yah) dwells in Jerusalem.

Victory and Restoration for Israel. 68:19-23. These verses look at David's historical victories over his foes, but they prophetically encompass Israel's testimony when she will be converted and reinstated in her national election (Rom. 11:26-36) at Christ's second advent. **19-20.** Christ will be delivered Israel's burden-bearer (Psalm 55:22; Isa. 46:4), her **salvation** (Psalms 49:15; 56:13), and her **God of deliverances** (NASB; 106:43) to whom belong **the issues** (escapes) **from death**, which will threaten to engulf her on every hand during the Great Tribulation. **21.** This verse presents the LORD's victory over His foes and those of His people, Israel — the **hairy scalp** (crown) **of such an one as goeth on still in his trespasses** envisions the Antichrist, who with his followers will be overthrown in the day of the King's glory (Rev. 19:11-21).

22-23. A glimpse is given of Israel's final age-end regathering from the ends of the earth (Deut. 30:1-9; Isa. 11:11-16;

35:8-10; Ezek. 37:1-28; Matt. 24:31) so the Israelites may see the destruction of their foes (Psalm 58:10; Isa. 63:1-6; Rev. 16:13-16; 19:17) and the tongues of their dogs may have portions from their enemies (Rev. 19:17-19, 21; cf. 1 Kings 21:19; Jer. 15:3).

The King's Triumphal Procession. 68:24-27. **24.** The figure of the triumphal procession is resumed from verse 18, the historical scene again pointing to the prophetic vista. As David headed the victorious march into the sanctuary after his great conquests, so the greater than David, the King-Messiah, will head the triumphal procession **into the sanctuary** (NASB), that is, the millennial Temple (Ezek. 40:5—43:12), in the day of His return in glory when He conquers His foes (Rev. 19:11—20:3).

25. Singers are first, then **players on instruments** and the **damsels** (maidens) **playing ... timbrels** (tambourines; cf. Exod. 15:20; Judg. 11:34; 1 Chron. 13:8; 15:16; Psalm 47:5). **26.** God is praised by those who are "of the fountain of Israel, referring apparently to Jacob, the fountain from which the whole nation issued as a stream" (Perowne). **27.** Then follows little Benjamin (Gen. 43:33; 1 Sam. 9:21) now made great, and a precursor of the greatness of all the tribes, making a great millennial nation (cf. Ezek. 47:13—48:29). Then follow other princes in the glorious procession.

Worldwide Conversion. 68:28-31. **28.** Restored Israel calls out to God to **strengthen** that which He has done for them in restoring and blessing them (29:11; 44:4; Isa. 26:12). **29.** Because of His Temple at Jerusalem (Ezek. 40:5—43:12; cf. Isa. 2:2-4), kings of the millennial earth will bring gifts to Him (Psalms 45:12; 72:10; 1 Kings 10:10; Isa. 18:7). **30.** The **rebuke** is administered to warlike peoples likened to wild animals, who would delight in war, since the King

will establish a warless world (Isa. 2:4; 9:6-7; 11:6-10). He will **scatter** (Psalms 18:14; 89:10) the peoples who delight in war (Rev. 19:11—20:3). **31.** Kingdom nations will court His favor (Isa. 19:19; 45:14; Zeph. 3:10; Zech. 8:20-23; 14:16-21).

Universal Praise in the Kingdom. 68:32-35. **32-33.** All the **kingdoms of the** (millennial) **earth** will **sing praises unto the Lord** (67:4; 102:21-22; Isa. 12:1-6), styled He **who rideth upon the heaven of heavens** (the highest heavens; Psalms 18:10; 104:3; Deut. 10:14; 33:26; 1 Kings 8:27) and who speaks with His mighty voice (Psalms 29:4; 46:6). **34.** Strength is ascribed to Him (29:1) whose majesty is over Israel, as the chief nation, His elect people in the Kingdom age. **35.** God is seen as awesome in His sanctuary (Isa. 2:2-4; Ezek. 40:5—43:12). **The God of Israel Himself** (NASB) will then give power to His people and will be **blessed** (extolled to the highest degree).

BB. FOREGLEAMS OF THE SUFFERING MESSIAH-SAVIOR. 69:1-36.

Psalms 69 to 72 form a series prophetically portraying the sufferings of Christ until the Kingdom glory to follow in Psalm 72 (cf. 1 Pet. 1:10-11). For the "chief Musician [precentor]," this psalm was "upon Shoshannim" (lilies; see the inscription to Psalm 45) and is ascribed to David. The psalm reflects (1) the sufferings of the psalmist when he penned it, foreshadowing (2) the sufferings of the suffering One, the rejected Messiah-Savior, at His first advent, as the numerous quotations and references to it in the New Testament amply attest, demonstrating it to be a great Messianic psalm, second only to Psalm 22 in New Testament quotations. (3) It also reaches out (vv. 22-28) to encompass the sufferings of Christ's own, particularly the Tribulation saints, who will be persecuted and rejected as He was, and who will endure for His sake (Matt. 24:13).

Hated Without Cause. 69:1-6. **1.** The psalmist, foreshadowing Christ, cried for God to **save** (deliver) him, for **the waters**, a figure of extreme peril (18:4, 16; 32:6; 42:7) had **come in unto** (*'ăḏ*, "up to") his **soul**, the danger threatening his physical life (Jer. 4:10; Jonah 2:6). **2.** He sank **in deep mire** (lit., "mud of the abyss"; cf. Psalm 40:2), **where there** was **no standing** ("standing place" or "foothold"). He was in **deep waters, where the floods** (lit., a flood; *shĭbbōlĕṯ*, "flowing stream") overflowed (*šṭp*, "overwhelmed, inundated") him (Jonah 2:3). **3.** He was **weary** with **crying** (Psalm 6:6; Heb. 5:7), his throat was parched, and his eyes failed (Deut. 28:32; Isa. 38:14).

4. Those who hated him **without a cause** (Psalm 35:19; John 15:25) were more than the hairs of his head (Psalm 40:12), and his enemies who wanted to destroy him were **mighty** (powerful) (Matt. 26:47, 57). He **restored** what he had not taken away, bringing into view the trespass offering (Lev. 5:1—6:7) and showing that in the vicarious sufferings of Christ more is restored than that which the enemy had taken away (7:1-7). He appealed to God's knowledge in support of his prayer that he suffered innocently (without a cause), but in men's eyes as if he were foolish and sinful. But he did so for the sake of God and his zeal for God's will and glory.

5. O God, thou (emphatic) **knowest my foolishness**—the sin imputed falsely by his enemies (Matt. 11:19; John 10:20). The subordinate sense seems also to be implied, *Thou* (emphatic) knowest how, as the sinner's Substitute, the sin of the world is laid upon Me (as vv. 7, 19 suggest). **6.** He prayed that those who

wait for **the Lord God of hosts** (armies) may not be ashamed or confounded through Him, for He is their Representative, and in such a case they would be put to shame and would conclude that waiting on God is valueless (Psalm 25:3).

Bearing Reproach. 69:7-12. **7.** For God's sake, He protested, He had **borne reproach** (Jer. 15:15). "For thy sake" echoes "for my sake" (v. 6). As the Messiah suffered for the sake of God's will, so He prayed that God for His sake would not let those who, like Himself, wait for God to wait in vain, which would be the case if God did not answer their prayers. He declared: **Shame** (dishonor) **hath covered my face** (Matt. 26:67; cf. Isa. 1:6). **8. I am become a stranger unto my brethren ... an alien** (Psalms 31:11; 38:11; Job 19:13-15; 1 Sam. 17:28; John 1:11; 7:5).

9. This verse is quoted in John 2:17, when Jesus cleansed the Temple: "And his disciples remembered that it was written, The zeal of [for] thine house hath eaten me up"—consumes me like an intense fire (Psalm 119:139). As a result of the Messiah's glowing ardor for God's honor, the reproaches aimed at God fell upon Him; this part of the verse is quoted in Romans 15:3 to demonstrate that Christ did not please Himself.

10. This ardent devotion for God drew the reproach of the wicked. Even when He wept and chastened His soul with fasting, that was turned to His reproach (cf. 2 Sam. 12:16, 21, in the case of David). The Messiah's fasting and weeping here are for the sins of the people, whose cause He advocates before God, and the approaching judgment that threatens to overtake them in consequence of their iniquities (cf. Matt. 23:37).

11. The Messiah's lamentation for them (Psalm 35:13), instead of moving them to repentance, led them to scoff, and so He became **a proverb** (44:13-14) and an idle jest. **12.** Those who sat **in the gate**, the place of public concourse and the conduct of business, spoke against Him, deliberately and with premeditation making Him the butt of their jokes. The drunkards made fun of Him in song (Job 30:9; Isa. 5:11-12; Lam. 3:14).

The Messiah's Prayer. 69:13-21. The Messiah's prayer for deliverance (renewed from vv. 1, 5) is on the ground already laid (vv. 1-12): that it was in God's will and for His sake that He had been brought into trouble. **13. But as for me** (emphatic), **my prayer is unto thee, O Lord, in an acceptable time** (Isa. 49:8; 55:6; 2 Cor. 6:2), literally, "a time of grace," "the acceptable year of the LORD" (the first advent) in contrast to "the day of vengeance of our God" (the second advent; Isa. 61:2). **14-15.** Therefore, He could pray for deliverance from the mire (cf. v. 2), his enemies (cf. v. 4), and the flood (cf. vv. 1-2).

16-20. He appealed to God's mercy and grace in His deep trouble, and to God's knowledge of His **reproach ... shame**, and **dishonor. Reproach,** He cried, **hath broken my heart.** As Calvin remarked, "Reproach is more bitter to an honorable man than a hundred deaths." The Savior apparently died of a broken heart, the result of the mental and spiritual agony in the garden, evidenced by the bloodlike sweat and the agonized cry on the cross, "My God, My God, why hast thou forsaken me?" and here, **I am full of heaviness** (*'nsh*, "sick unto death"). He looked in vain for **comforters**, but there were none.

21. They gave me ... gall for my food, "put poison in my food" (AB), preferable to "They gave me poison for food" (RSV). **In my thirst they gave me vinegar** (*ḥōmĕṣ*, "sour wine") **to drink.** Twice vinegar was offered to Christ on the cross, once mixed with gall (Matt. 27:34) and myrrh (Mark 15:23). Next, to fulfill this Scripture, He cried, "I thirst," and vinegar was given Him to drink (John 19:28; cf. Matt. 27:48).

Messiah's Judgment. 69:22-28. These words express God's righteous retribution in operation after His love and grace (Luke 23:34) have been spurned and the resulting iniquity has come to the full (see comment on Psalm 5:10 for the meaning of the imprecatory prayers). They are applied to the temporary setting aside of Israel during this age (Rom. 11:9-10), but will find full application to all the enemies of Christ and His people (Israel as well as the Gentiles) when their wickedness comes to full fruition under the Antichrist during the Great Tribulation and is ripe for judgment. Then Christ will not assume the character of the suffering Savior, but of the avenging Judge, and His people's prayers will reflect His just judgment upon sin and sinners (cf. Gen. 15:16; Lev. 18:24; Luke 18:7-8).

22. Let their table—the Jews' high religious privileges reflected in their sacrificial system (Psalm 23:5)—**become a snare** and **their welfare ...** ("peace") **a trap** (the Hebrew being plural *shelômîm*, "offerings that pertain to their peace," i.e., sacrificial peace offerings). Perversely rejecting the One and only sacrifice, the whole Jewish sacrificial system became a trap to ensnare them in ruin.

23. Judicial blindness overtook them (Isa. 6:10; Rom. 11:8, 25) and Israel's loins have shaken in fear and suffering throughout the ages (Deut. 28:63-68), but they will do so in a special sense in the time of Jacob's supreme trouble (Jer. 30:5-7). **24.** Then will the divine indignation be poured out on apostate Jewry (Dan. 12:1; Matt. 24:21) as well as on the rebellious Gentiles (Psalm 2:1-3;

Rev. 6:1—19:10), and the faithful remnant will echo the words of the Judge in this passage.

25. May their camp be desolate (NASB; Matt. 23:38; Luke 13:35; Acts 1:20). **26.** The reason for God's judicial wrath is that they persecuted Him (the Lord Jesus) whom God Himself **hast smitten** (Isa. 53:4, 10), and they **talk to the grief of** (i.e., derisively and exultingly), to the pain of the LORD's wounded ones. Such sin displays full development for judgment (Neh. 4:5; Rom. 1:28) and calls for speedy punishment.

27. Add iniquity (i.e., its penalty) **unto their iniquity,** assuring the quick doom of the reprobates (Rom. 2:5; Rev. 19:11—20:3). **Let them not come into thy righteousness,** which is the gift of divine grace to the penitent believer (Psalm 24:5; Rom. 10:3; Phil. 3:9). **28. Let them be blotted out of the book of the living,** that is, consigned to physical death (cf. Isa. 4:3; Rev. 19:17-21), and not be enrolled with the righteous (the saved, the elect), who can never be blotted out of the book of life (Rev. 20:12, 15; cf. John 10:28-29; Acts 13:48).

The Messiah's Exaltation and Victory. 69:29-33. **29. But I am poor and sorrowful . . . thy salvation** (deliverance) shall **set me up on high** (LXX). This is the ground of His exaltation (Eph. 1:19-23; Phil. 2:6-9). His humiliation to death in submission to God's will gives Him the confident anticipation of exaltation. **30-31.** The result is the free flow of joyous thanksgiving and praise. His redemption fulfills and supersedes animal sacrifices, however perfect (Lev. 11:2-4), which are of value only as expressions of faith and love. **32-33.** This redemption alone pleases God and results in the salvation of the humble, who come as guilty sinners to receive eternal life.

34-36. Universal praise is to rise up to Him in the Kingdom age, for **God will save Zion** (Psalm 51:18; Zech. 12:1-5; Rom. 11:26-35) and **build the cities of Judah** (Zech. 12:6-8; cf. Isa. 54:1-17; 60:1-22). That "the humble and the poor," the delivered godly remnant, **may dwell there** (permanently), **and have it in possession**, as well as their descendants (Isa. 65:9-10).

CC. PRAYER FOR DELIVERANCE FROM THE ENEMY. 70:1-5.

This psalm, like all 150 of the psalms is for the "chief Musician," the precentor, hence, for the public liturgy of the nation. It is a psalm of David "to bring to remembrance," that is, to hold before God, the righteous Sufferer, and His people. This ode is for anytime and anywhere when the believer is beset by troubles and God *seems* to have forgotten him (Isa. 43:26), which will be dramatically the case in the dark hours of Israel's coming supreme time of anguish (Dan. 12:1; Matt. 24:20). With minor variations, this psalm is a repetition of Psalm 40:13-17. For the scope of this ode and its connection with Psalms 69 to 72, see the introduction to Psalm 69.

The Cry of the Sufferer for Deliverance. 70:1-5. Springing from the experience of the psalmist that foreshadows the sufferings of the Messiah-Savior at His first advent, these verses in turn reflect the sufferings of His own, particularly in the Tribulation, when the believing Jewish remnant will be persecuted and rejected as He was. **Make haste** ("hasten," repeated three times for emphasis, vv. 1, 5, because the anguish experienced will be unparalleled; Dan. 12:1; Matt. 24:21-22). **Let them be ashamed and confounded . . . turned backward, and put to confusion** who seek the life of God's saints and desire their injury (see Psalm 69:22-28 and comment on Psalm 5:10 on the imprecatory psalms).

DD. ISRAEL'S SONG OF HOPE. 71:1-24.

There is no superscription to this psalm. For its scope and connection with Psalms 69 to 72, which form a series, see the introduction to Psalm 69. The psalm delineates the restoration and coming deliverance and glory of Israel, couched in the language of prayer, and ending in stanzas of joyful confidence and praise. While the psalm has direct reference to the past and future of Israel, it has lessons for saints of every age. The experience of the ancient psalmist, whoever he was, by inspiration reflects the past and future of his nation, Israel.

Declaration of Trust in the Lord. 71:1-6. **1-2.** In a severe time of trouble the psalmist (an elderly man) affirmed his trust in the LORD, in whom he had taken refuge, relying on divine righteousness to deliver and rescue him and to hear his prayer. **3.** He implored the LORD to be his **strong habitation** ("a rock of habitation"; 90:1; 91:9; Deut. 33:27), to which he could **continually resort** (come). He was assured that God had **given commandment** to save him (Psalms 7:6; 42:8) as his **rock** (18:2) and fortress, the basis of his prayer being the authoritative and efficacious Word of promise (44:4; 68:28). **4.** Prophetically, verses 1 to 3 reveal the confident trust of the Jewish remnant during Daniel's seventieth week (Dan. 9:27) and the cry of that godly nucleus to be rescued from **the hand of the wicked** (one), from **hand** (*mikkăp*, "grasp") **of the unrighteous and cruel man,** the lawless one (2 Thess. 2:4), the Antichrist (Rev. 13:1-8). **5-6.** The psalmist ardently declared that the Lord GOD had been his **hope** (Jer. 17:7) from his very conception in his mother's womb (Psalm 22:9), sustained by Him from infancy so that his praise

was continually centered in Him.

Miraculous Preservation in Retrospect and Prospect. 71:7-16. Through the psalmist's prayer, testimony is presented of the past national history of Israel, a story of miracle from its beginning. **7.** He was **as a wonder** (marvel; Isa. 8:18; 1 Cor. 4:9) **unto many** because of his miraculous birth and preservation to old age. Isaac's birth was a miracle (Gen. 21:1-3); so was Moses' preservation to be Israel's deliverer (Exod. 2:1-10) at the nation's birth at the Exodus (12:1-36; 14:29-31). Israel's preservation through the centuries is the standing miracle of history.

8-11. But during the final great trouble in the time of old age there will be an awakening and a calling upon the LORD, whom faithful Israelites know will not forsake them as their "strong refuge" (v. 7b) in their supreme hour of need (vv. 9-11), when their enemies will seek to exterminate them (Psalm 2:1-3). Verses 12 to 16 reflect the heart cry of the godly nucleus at the end time. **12.** Then God's presence and help will be most desperately needed. **13.** Their imprecatory prayer (see comment on Psalm 5:10 for explanation) will be seasonably uttered as the godless rejectors of God's grace now face His wrath as their sin comes to full harvest and is ready to be reaped (Rev. 14:14-20). **14-16.** In contrast to the wicked, the remnant will profess once again its ardent hope in the LORD and its confidence in His righteousness (15:4) and deliverance (17:14) through His mighty intervention (6:1—19:9).

Revival Song of Victory. 71:17-24. **17-18.** Prayer for help and deliverance in old age will be answered; the redeemed remnant, delivered into Kingdom blessing (Psalm 72), will burst forth in ecstatic praise. **19.** God's righteousness will be extolled (36:6; 57:10) for His terrible judgments upon His enemies. These are the **great things** He has done (Psalm 126:2; Luke 1:49; Rev. 6:1—19:21) to dispossess the earth's rebels and to set up the Messiah's Kingdom (20:4-6), making Him incomparable (Psalm 35:10; Deut. 3:24).

20. God, who has showed Israel **great and severe troubles** (Psalm 60:3; Jer. 30:5-7; Dan. 12:1; Matt. 24:21), will **revive** her again (Hos. 6:1; cf. Ezek. 37:1-14; Rom. 11:25-32) and bring her **from the depths of the earth** (Psalm 86:13; Dan. 12:2), her suffering, national death, and resurrection reflecting the suffering, death, and resurrection of her Messiah, by whose grace and power she will be restored into Kingdom blessing.

21. Then Israel's **greatness** (Psalm 18:35, RSV), her faith in God's grace revealed in the Messiah, shall be increased and God will **comfort** her (23:4; 86:17; Isa. 12:1; 49:13; Zech. 12:10—13:1). **22-23.** Then praise to God, the **Holy One of Israel** (Psalms 78:41; 89:18; Isa. 1:4), will issue from joyous lips and redeemed souls (Psalms 5:11; 32:11; 103:4; Isa. 35:10).

24. God's **righteousness** in destroying His enemies and taking over the redeemed earth (His by creation and redemption; Eph. 1:13-14; Rev. 5:1-7; 19:11—20:4) will be a perennial note of joyous praise, as Israel's enemies (13:1-18) and God's (Psalm 2:1-3) are ashamed and humiliated before the glorious "KING OF KINGS, AND LORD OF LORDS" (Rev. 19:11-16).

EE. THE DAVIDIC-MESSIANIC KINGDOM ESTABLISHED. 72:1-20.

The title "for Solomon" indicates authorship *by*, rather than *for* Solomon, whose great kingdom forms the background of the psalm and anticipates the Messiah's antitypical reign. Most ancient Jewish tradition correctly applies the psalm to the Messiah. It fur-

nishes a most fitting climactic note on which Book 2 of the Psalter ends.

The Messiah's Reign of Righteousness and Peace. 72:1-7. **1.** The psalm opens with a prayer to **give the king** (Solomon) God's **judgments** (legal sentences or decisions emanating from Him; Deut. 1:17; 2 Chron. 19:6), and righteousness, but the greater than Solomon is envisioned in His Kingdom rule. **2.** His just and righteous administration is stressed (Psalm 75:6-7; Isa. 9:7; 11:2-5; 32:1; Jer. 33:15; Rev. 19:11).

3. The mountains (symbolic of kingdoms; Dan. 2:35) **shall bring** (lift up, publish, proclaim) **peace** (Isa. 2:4; 9:7; Mic. 4:3-4; Zech. 9:10), to **the little hills** (smaller kingdoms) in **righteousness** (Isa. 40:9; 52:7-8). Peace shall prevail everywhere in righteousness (Psalm 85:11; Isa. 45:8), not as a compromise with unrighteousness (cf. Lev. 26:3-6). **4.** He shall **break in pieces** the wrongdoer and **the oppressor** (Isa. 9:4-5; cf. Psalm 2:9-12).

5. They shall fear (hold Thee in holy reverence) **as long as the sun and moon endure** because of Thy righteous rule and destruction of enemies and oppressors. The holding of God in highest reverence will continue **throughout all generations** (of the thousand-year reign) and on into the eternal state (Rev. 22:1, 3), when apparently the sun and moon in their present form will pass away, probably into new and brighter forms (Psalm 102:26; 2 Pet. 3:12-13).

6. He shall come down like rain . . . like showers that water the earth (Deut. 32:2; 2 Sam. 23:4; Psalm 65:10; Hos. 6:3). The Messiah's reign of righteousness and peace will revive the world as the showers do the grass. **7.** In His days **the righteous** will **flourish** (Psalm 92:12), and universal peace (Isa. 9:6-7) will prevail **as long as the moon endureth** (lit., "is no more"; cf. v. 5).

The Messiah's Universal Dominion.

72:8-15. Solomon's empire furnishes the typical background for the Messiah's antitypical reign. Then the Wadi el Arish south of Gaza, the Mediterranean, and the Euphrates formed the bounds of Israelite sway (1 Kings 4:21, 24; 2 Chron. 9:26, as promised in Gen. 15:18; Deut. 11:24). **8.** From those starting points the Messiah is to reign to the end of the earth (Isa. 9:5-6; Mic. 5:4; Zech. 9:10; cf. Psalm 2:8; Num. 24:19; Amos 9:11-12).

9. They that dwell in the wilderness (the wandering people of the desert) **shall bow before him** (Psalms 22:29; 74:14; Isa. 23:13) and **his enemies shall lick the dust**, a token of abject submission to an Oriental king (Isa. 49:23; Mic. 7:17). **10. The kings of Tarshish and of the isles** represent the millennial nations, which will bring tribute, as well as Sheba and Seba, wealthy kings to the south (cf. 1 Kings 4:21; 10:10, 24-25; cf. Psalm 68:29; Isa. 60:6-9).

11-14. As "King of kings" (i.e., *the* King par excellence; Rev. 19:16), all kings will **fall down before him; all nations ... serve him,** because of His just and equitable reign. **15. So may he live** (NASB), a universal and heartfelt "Long live the King!" He will be served and worshiped universally and continually.

The Messiah's Blessed Rule. 72:16-20. **16. There shall be an handful** (better, "abundance"; *pissâ*, "diffusion," from assumed root *pss*) **of grain in the earth upon the top of the mountains,** its fruit waving in the wind **like the cedars of Lebanon** (NASB; Psalm 104:16). Those from the city **shall flourish like grass** (vegetation) **of the earth** (Job 5:25). **17-18.** Blessing shall abound on earth. All nations will bless (ecstatically praise Him) as **the God of Israel** (Psalms 41:13; 89:52), who alone **doeth wondrous things** (works; *niplā'ôt*, "miracles, signs, supernatural feats";

Job 5:9; Psalms 77:14; 86:10; 136:4; Exod. 15:11).

19. His glorious name will be **blessed** (highly lauded) **forever** (Psalm 96:8; Neh. 9:5), and **the whole earth will be filled with his glory** (Num. 14:21; cf. Isa. 11:9; Hab. 2:14), when David's righteous Branch has set up the Kingdom (2 Sam. 7:8-16; Luke 1:31-33). Verses 18 to 20 form a doxology climactically concluding Psalms 1 to 72, comprising the first and second books of the psalms (cf. the shorter doxology closing Book 1, Psalm 41:13). The grand prayer prophecy is concluded with a double "amen." **20. The prayers of David ... are ended**, meaning only that most of the psalms of Book 2 are in the nature of prophetic prayers and that David was the chief author.

III. BOOK THREE: THE LEVITICUS SECTION. 73:1—89:52.

This section, corresponding to the book of Leviticus, consists of Psalms 73 to 89. Like Leviticus, whose theme centers in the holiness of the LORD and the sanctuary, this book of psalms has much to say about the same subject, particularly in connection with the remnant of Israel of the last days and its sufferings, trials, and deliverances to Kingdom blessing. Of the seventeen psalms of this book, the first eleven are called "Asaph psalms." Asaph, the chief of sacred music under David, was a psalmist (1 Chron. 16:5; 25:1-5) as well as a seer or prophet.

A. THE PROBLEM OF THE SUFFERING OF THE RIGHTEOUS. 73:1-28.

The Psalmist's Perplexity. 73:1-14. **1.** The psalmist was assured of the grand fact that **God is good to Israel** (86:5), **to such as are of a clean** (pure) **heart**, that is, He is good to true Israelites in whom there is no guile (v. 13; 24:6; John 1:47).

God's goodness to His people attests His absolute and universal goodness. He is "only [*'ăk*] good to Israel."

2-3. But the prosperity of the wicked had so shaken the psalmist that his **feet** had come close to stumbling, and he had almost **slipped** away from faith in God's goodness as he became **envious of the foolish** and **saw the prosperity of the wicked**, described in verses 4 and 5. The psalmist in his perplexity exaggeratedly concluded thirteen things about the wicked:

(1) **4a.** They have no **pangs** (pains) even up to their death; but contrast his mature judgment (vv. 17-20). (2) **4b. Their body is fat** (NASB; Psalm 10:5). (3) **5a. They are not in trouble as other men** (mortals; Psalm 73:12; Job 21:9). (4) **5b.** They are not **plagued like other men** (KJV; Psalm 73:14). (5) **6a.** As a result, "pride serves as their necklace" (AB; Gen. 41:42; Prov. 1:9). (6) **6b.** "The robe of injustice covers them" (AB; Psalm 109:18).

(7) **7a.** Their eyes protrude or bulge with fatness (Psalm 17:10; Job 15:27). (8) **7b. The imaginations of their heart run riot** (NASB; lit., "they exceed the imaginations of their heart"). (9) **8a.** They "scoff" (following the Aramaic and Syriac, *mǎyēq*) **and wickedly speak of oppression** (NASB). (10) **8b. They speak from on high** (NASB; lit. Heb.; Psalm 17:10; 2 Pet. 2:18; Jude 16), that is, "from the height to which they in their pride have elevated themselves."

(11) **9a. They set their mouth against the heavens.** (12) **9b. Their tongue walketh through the earth**, like their master, Satan (Job 1:7; 2:2), to maliciously accuse God's people (Rev. 12:10). (13) **10. Therefore, his** (God's) **people return here**, that is, forsake the LORD and take part with the wicked, **and waters of a full cup** are drunk (lit., "drained out") by them. Joining the wicked, they enjoy a full abundance, like a brimming cup (Job 15:16). **11. And they say, How doth God know?** (Psalm 10:11; Job 22:13).

12. Discovering that not only is there no punishment, but that prosperity ensues upon their defection, they soon renounce God's providential care completely (cf. Jer. 49:31; Ezek. 16:49). **13.** This posed a great problem for the psalmist, who concluded in his perplexity that surely **in vain** he had cleansed his heart (referring to v. 1, "such as are of a clean heart"; Job 21:15; 34:9; 35:3) and **washed** his **hands in innocency** (Psalm 26:6; cf. Mal. 3:14), maintaining his integrity spiritually and religiously (Prov. 20:9).

14a. He continued in this impatient and perplexed unbelieving spirit by complaining that **all the day long** he had been **plagued** (Psalm 38:6), in contrast to the wicked who are not "*plagued*" like other men (v. 5, KJV). **14b.** Rather, he found himself, as God's own, **chastened every morning**, constantly disciplined and whipped as a child of God (Psalm 118:18; Job 33:19; cf. 1 Cor. 11:30-32; Heb. 12:3-17), while the wicked are exempt from such divine dealing.

The Psalmist's Solution. 73:15-20. Then the psalmist aroused himself from his reverie of unbelief and spoke in faith as a true Israelite. **15.** If he said, **I will speak thus** (as in vv. 3-14), **behold, I should offend** (betray) **the generation of thy children** (14:5), be faithless to the pious of former generations. **16.** When he **thought** (pondered) to understand the problem of the prosperity of the wicked and the suffering of the righteous, **it was too painful for** him (lit., "it was labor in his eyes").

Verses 17 to 20 deal with the victory the psalmist won over his doubts in the sanctuary, where he came to comprehend the end of the godless (27:4; 77:13; cf. 37:38). God does three things to them: (1) **18a.** He sets them **in slippery places** (35:6). (2) **18b-19.** He throws them down into **destruction** (35:8; 36:12; cf. Rev. 19:20—20:3; 20:10, 14-15) and destroys them in a moment (lit., they "become a **desolation**"; Num. 16:21; Isa. 47:11; Rev. 9:18; 14:20; 19:21); they are utterly swept away by sudden **terrors** (Job 18:11; Ezek. 26:21).

(3) **20.** God despises **their image** (form), something remembered when awaking from a dream (Job 20:8). He seemed to be asleep as the wicked prospered, but He awakens to show His contempt for their imaginary prosperity by destroying them with it (cf. Psalm 39:6; Isa. 29:7-8; Hab. 2:20; Zeph. 1:7; Zech. 2:13; Rev. 6:1—19:21).

The Psalmist's Confession. 73:21-28. **21-22.** He confessed how wrong he had been (vv. 3-14). When his **soul** (heart) had been **grieved** (embittered; Judg. 10:16), and he was **pricked** (pierced) in his **heart** (kidneys; i.e., emotions; Acts 2:37) at his envy of the prosperous wicked, he realized how senseless, ignorant, and beastlike he had been before God (Psalms 49:10, 20; 92:6; Job 18:3; Eccles. 3:18).

His deep confession was followed by a remarkable testimony (vv. 23-28), in which faith shone forth triumphantly. He testified radiantly to eight things: (1) **23a.** He testified to God's continual presence and availability (Psalm 16:8). I am continually with Thee, because Thou art continually with me! (23:4). (2) **23b.** He testified to his eternal security. **Thou hast taken hold of my right hand** (NASB; John 10:28-29).

(3) **24a.** He testified to God's counsel and guidance (Psalms 32:8; 48:14; Isa. 58:11). (4) **24b.** He testified to his ultimate destiny in glory (Psalm 49:15; Gen. 5:24). (5) **25-26.** He testified to God as his only hope and desire for time and eternity (Psalm 16:2). All that was tem-poral would fail (38:10; 40:12; 84:2; 119:81), but God was his strength and eternal portion (16:5). (6) **27a.** He testified to the ultimate fate of the wicked. All **they that are far from thee** (the unsaved) **shall perish** (37:20; Rev. 20:14-15).

(7) **27b.** He testified to God's dealing with His unfaithful children (Exod. 34:15; Num. 15:39; Hos. 4:12; 9:1). They shall be **destroyed** prematurely by physical death. Compare King Saul's case (1 Chron. 10:13-14; cf. Acts 5:1-11; 1 Cor. 5:5; 11:30-32; 1 John 5:16-19), and contrast David's case (2 Sam. 12:13), because he sincerely confessed his sin.

(8) **28.** He testified that he (emphatic) had concluded it was **good ... to draw near to God** (Psalm 65:4; Heb. 10:22; James 4:8), and so he had made God his trust (refuge; Psalms 14:6; 71:7), that he might declare (publish) all His works (of creation, redemption, and providence; 40:5; 107:22; 118:17). This psalm in its prophetic aspect looks forward to the remnant of the Tribulation, who will have to wrestle with the problem of the prosperity of the wicked and the awful suffering of the righteous at their hands, which will be such as no previous generation of saints has ever endured (Dan. 12:1; Matt. 24:21-22; Rev. 6:1—18:24).

B. THE ENEMY INVADES THE SANCTUARY. 74:1-23.

A psalm of Asaph (see the introduction to Book 3, Psalm 73). One of Asaph's descendants seems to be meant (2 Chron. 35:15; Ezra 2:41; 3:10; Neh. 7:44), since the psalm is evidently late in date. "Maschil" means a didactic song, inculcating an important truth.

Prayer on Account of the Invading Foe. 74:1-11. **1.** The devastation was so great that the psalmist cried out to God, as though he imagined He had rejected His people **forever** (44:9; 77:7). It was as if God's anger smoked like a smoldering fire (18:8), the instrument of His judgment (Gen. 19:24; Exod. 9:23) against His people, Israel. Yet He tenderly and affectionately called them **the sheep of His pasture** (Psalms 95:7; 100:3; Jer. 23:1; Ezek. 34:8), evidencing His great love despite His severe chastisement of His covenant people.

2. God's grace of old, manifested in delivering His people from Egypt, and thereby "purchasing" them by "redeeming" (Exod. 15:13) them as His own (15:16; Deut. 32:6), was used as a strong plea for the present deliverance of His **congregation**, called **the rod** (tribe) of His **inheritance** (Deut. 32:9; Isa. 63:17; Jer. 10:16; 51:19), and **Mount Zion,** where He had dwelt (Psalms 9:11; 68:16), that is, in the tabernacle and later in the Temple.

In verses 3 to 9 the psalmist reminded God that the enemy had destroyed His sanctuary and "all the synagogues" (meeting places) in the land, leaving no traces of His presence anywhere. **3.** He beseeched God to **lift up** His **feet** (i.e., Himself) to come swiftly and majestically (7:6; 94:2) to restore what otherwise had to remain **perpetual desolation** (i.e., "eternal ruins"; Isa. 61:4).

There were eight features of the enemies' depredations: (1) **3b.** They had **done wickedly** (had done all evils) **in the sanctuary** (i.e., had "damaged everything within the sanctuary," NASB; Psalm 79:1). (2) **4a.** They roared (Lam. 2:7) like enraged animals in the **midst of** God's **congregations** (Heb. sing., "congregation," i.e., God's "meeting place," *mô'ēd*; Exod. 33:7), the sacred place of meeting between God and His people.

(3) **4b.** They set up their **banners,** "their own standards" for **signs** of their being conquerors and masters of the Temple instead of God (cf. v. 9), as in the days of Antiochus Epiphanes, who invaded Israel in 170 B.C., plundering the Temple and massacring the Jews, and again in 168 B.C., laying waste the city and burning the Temple gates, defiling the Temple with the worship of Olympian Zeus (Jupiter; 1 Macc. 1:45-54).

All of this foreshadows the Tribulation period when a Jewish Temple will be built and the ancient worship resumed, made possible through the covenant with the "prince that shall come," the Antichrist (Dan. 9:26-27). But in the middle of Daniel's seventieth week, the Antichrist will break his covenant with Israel and set up "the abomination of desolation," foreshadowed by what happened in the Maccabean period (cf. 1 Macc. 1:54; Rev. 13:13-18).

(4) **5-7.** The enemies destroyed the fine wood of the sanctuary with the indifference of a woodman chopping down trees in a forest (NASB), smashing all its **carved work ... with axes and hammers** and burning the sanctuary to the ground (2 Kings 25:9), which is applicable historically only to the Babylonian destruction of Solomon's Temple in 587 B.C. Before burning the Temple, the Babylonians removed all its precious metals (2 Kings 25:13; 2 Chron. 36:18; Jer. 52:12-17).

(5) **8a.** The enemies' purpose was **Let us destroy them** (the Jews) **together** (completely subdue, oppress them; Psalm 83:4; Rev. 12:13-17; cf. 7:1-8). (6) **8b.** They burned up **all the synagogues** (the meeting places) **of God in the land**, not the "synagogues" of the postexilic period, but the houses of sacred meeting, where the Law of God was read and prayer made (cf. 2 Chron. 17:7-9).

(7) **9a.** The enemies' signs had supplanted Israel's signs (cf. v. 4; see Dan. 11:31), such as the Passover (Exod. 12:13), the Sabbath (31:13), the

Temple, altar, sacrifices, and God's miraculous interpositions (Psalm 78:43). (8) **9b.** There was no **prophet** (Amos 8:11-12; cf. 1 Sam. 28:6, 15; Ezek. 7:26), for Jeremiah's prophetical career terminated with the fall of Jerusalem, and Daniel and Ezekiel were in Babylon. Jeremiah had foretold **how long** (Jer. 25:11), but the people reeled in such agony that they could not appropriate any comfort from it.

Verses 10 and 11 continue the intercession of verses 1 and 2, interrupted by the lengthy review of the enemies' destruction in verses 3 to 9. **10. O God, how long** (Psalm 13:2). . . . **Shall the enemy blaspheme thy name forever?** More concern was expressed regarding the dishonor done to God than concerning the suffering of the prophet-psalmist and his people. **11a.** In a bold anthropomorphism he asked why God had withdrawn His hand, even His right hand (the hand of strength and skill; Lam. 2:3). **11b.** He called upon God to pluck it from His bosom and destroy the enemy (Psalm 59:13).

Reflection upon God's Past Mighty Manifestations of His Power. 74:12-17. **12.** These retrospective references were to bring to mind to the Israelites the omnipotence of God, as their King, working deliverances in order to stir up faith in Him as their mighty and faithful God (44:4). *Thou* (vv. 13-17, repeated eight times) is emphatic: *Thou Thyself.* God did six mighty deeds for His people:

(1) **13-14.** He divided the Red (Reed) Sea (Exod. 14:21; Psalm 78:13), although in the light of the Ugaritic parallels, evidence suggests that these verses may describe primeval events (Gen. 1:1-2) rather than historical events (M. Dahood, *Psalms*, AB, pp. 17, 205), and thus would be translated: "It was you who shattered the Sea with your strength, who smashed the heads of

Tannin [the mythological seven-headed sea monster] . . . who crushed the heads of Leviathan" (the Hebrew *liwyāṯān* equals the Ugaritic *ltn*, one of the names of the primeval dragons the poet employed to dramatically represent the LORD's turning chaos into kosmos, Gen. 1:1-2, in connection with His re-creative, not creative, activity of Gen. 1:1-2). "Who gave him [Leviathan] as food to be gathered by desert tribes" (AB), the defeat of chaos (poetically represented) will be so complete that the ocean will become dry land (desert).

(2) **15a.** He brought water out of the rock (Exod. 17:5; Num. 20:11; Isa. 48:21). (3) **15b.** He dried up the Jordan River (Exod. 14:21-22; Josh. 2:10; 3:13; Psalm 114:3), although again this whole section (vv. 13-17) may possibly refer to primeval beginnings, as verses 16 and 17 would suggest. (4) **16.** He prepared **the light and the sun** (Gen. 1:14-18; Psalms 104:19; 136:7). (5) **17a.** He established **the borders** (boundaries) **of the earth** (Deut. 32:8; Acts 17:26). (6) **17b.** He made **summer and winter** (cf. Gen. 8:22; Psalm 147:16-18).

Plea to God for Present Manifestation of His Power. 74:18-23. The preceding retrospection concerning the mighty and faithful God (vv. 12-17) opens the way for this tender and beautiful prayer that was prayed by the psalmist and the suffering saints of his day, as well as by those who are in trouble at any time, but notably by the faithful remnant of the end time under the Antichrist's cruelty and mankind's filled-up lawlessness (2:1-3).

The psalmist presented the following four petitions: (1) **18.** He asked God to **remember** the enemy's reviling and blasphemy of His holy name (14:1; 39:8; Deut. 32:6). (2) **19.** He asked God not to deliver His **turtledove** (Israel; Song of

853

Sol. 2:14) **to the wild beast** (NASB; *ḥăyyâ*; cf. Dan. 7:1-8, where the persecuting Gentile nations are likened to wild beasts; Rev. 13:1-8) **nor forget the life of [His]** afflicted (people) **forever** (NASB; Psalm 9:18).

(3) **20.** He asked God to consider His **covenant** (Gen. 17:7; Psalm 106:45) to protect and preserve His people, **for the dark places of the earth** (land) **are full of the habitations of cruelty** (violence, 88:6; 143:3; Rev. 9:20-21; 13:1-18). (4) **21.** He asked God to vindicate His people so that the oppressed (Psalm 103:6) would not return dishonored and so the afflicted and needy might praise God's name for deliverance.

22-23. These verses form a climactic summary to the prayer. **Arise** (Zech. 2:13)**... plead thine own cause** (Psalm 43:1; Isa. 3:13); **remember how the foolish man reproacheth thee daily** (Psalms 14:1; 53:1; 74:18). **Do not forget the voice of Thine adversaries** (NASB; v. 10), **the tumult** (uproar; 2:1-3) **of those who rise up against thee** (65:7).

C. God's Answer to the
Desecration of His Sanctuary.
75:1-10.

For the scope and context of Psalm 75, see the introduction to Book 3, Psalm 73. "To the chief Musician [precentor], Al-tashheth ['destroy not']." (See comment on the title to Psalm 57.) This is a twin psalm to Psalm 76, where the victory anticipated in faith in this psalm is there actually gained and celebrated. It is a psalm of Asaph, a song anticipating deliverance.

The Messiah as the Righteous Judge. *75:1-5.* **1.** The people in faith joyfully thanked God for the anticipated salvation (79:13), because His **name** (i.e., He Himself revealed in saving power; 20:1) was **near** to deliver them (Deut. 4:7; Isa. 30:27; Matt. 24:33; Luke 21:28), as His

wondrous works displayed in His righteous judgments (Rev. 6:1—19:21) **declare** (cf. Psalm 46:8-11).

2. He will **select an appointed time** (NASB; lit., "take hold of a set time"). That will be the time of His manifestation in glory as Judge when He will declare, **I** (emphatic) **will judge with equity** (RSV; 9:8; 67:4; Isa. 11:4), when He comes to "judge and make war" as "the Faithful and True" (Rev. 19:11). **3.** Though **the earth and all the inhabitants thereof are dissolved** (melt; Psalm 46:6; Isa. 24:19), **it is I who have firmly set up its pillars** (NASB; lit. Heb.; 1 Sam. 2:8) and will be its Judge.

4-5. The Judge spoke to **the fools** (the boastful) and warned, **Deal not foolishly** (do not boast); **and to the wicked, Lift not up the horn** (Zech. 1:21), like a wild beast in which all its brute strength is concentrated in its horns (cf. Dan. 7:7; Rev. 13:1; cf. Deut. 33:17; 1 Sam. 2:1, 10). **Speak not with a stiff neck** (with insolent pride; Psalm 94:4; 1 Sam. 2:3; cf. Isa. 37:26), the uplifted neck indicating overweening haughtiness (Job 15:26).

The Messiah's Righteous Judgment. *75:6-8.* **6. Promotion** (exaltation) comes from God alone, not from any human source or natural direction (3:3; 113:7). **7a.** He as Judge will recompense to everyone (sinner and saint alike) according to his works (deeds; 50:6; Prov. 24:12; Jer. 17:10; Rom. 2:6, 11; Rev. 20:12-13; 22:12). **7b.** God puts down one (1 Sam. 2:7; Psalm 147:6; Dan. 2:21) and exalts another.

8a. He will most assuredly punish the wicked, for in His hand **is a cup, and the wine is red** (foams; Psalms 11:6; 60:3; Job 21:20; Jer. 25:15). **It is fully mixed** with spices, to increase its intoxicating power (Prov. 23:30; Song of Sol. 8:2; Isa. 5:22), the image expressing the stupefying effects of God's apocalyptic judgments upon the wicked (Psalm 60:3; Isa. 51:17, 22; cf. Rev. 14:19-20). **8b. But the dregs thereof all the wicked ... shall drain them** (Obad. 16). "But" (lit., "only"), that is, the wicked can do nothing else but drain out the whole cup of God's wrath to the dregs (Rev. 16:17-21), that is, drink it to the bitter end.

The Resolve of God's People. 75:9-10. **9.** God's people resolved to praise forever the God of Jacob for the anticipated destruction of the wicked (Rev. 6:1—19:21) and the exaltation of the righteous (19:7-10; 20:4-6). **But I** (emphatic, "as for me") **will declare** (it), that is, God's righteous judgments **forever** (vv. 7-8).

10. All the horns of the wicked (pictured as wild animals with their brute strength concentrated in their horns) **also will I cut off**, that is, I will announce as being cut off (Rev. 19:11—20:3), the prophets frequently being said to do that which they announced as being done, God being the real Doer (Jer. 1:10). In contrast, **the horns of the righteous** (the symbol of their power) **shall be exalted** (Rev. 20:4-6).

D. THE MESSIAH'S KINGDOM ESTABLISHED. 76:1-12.

For the scope of this psalm, see the introduction to Book 3 and Psalm 73 and its twin ode, Psalm 75. The psalm was for the choir director (precentor) for the Temple liturgy "on Neginoth [stringed instruments], A Psalm or Song of Asaph."

The King-Priest Enthroned. 76:1-3. **1. In Judah is God known** (48:3) by His wondrous acts, **his name is great in Israel** (99:3; Isa. 9:6-7). His people, Israel, are united (Ezek. 37:15-28). **2. His tabernacle** is **in Salem**, the ancient name of Jerusalem (Gen. 14:18; Heb. 7:1-2), **his dwelling place in Zion**, where the taber-

nacle stood in David's time and the Temple later was built. Jerusalem means "the foundation[*yeru*] of peace" (*salem*, Ur-Salimu, the city of peace of the Amarna Letters).

3. Now the greater than David is seen reigning in His Kingdom from His capital as the King-Priest, the true Melchizedek, who after His acts of righteousness in destroying His enemies and abolishing war, will reign as King of peace and as "the most high God, the possessor of heaven and earth" (Gen. 14:18, 22). He will break the weapons of war—the flaming arrows, the shield and the sword (Psalm 46:9), and universal peace will follow (Isa. 2:4), as restored and redeemed Israel sings the strains of Isaiah 12:1-6. Historically, the psalm springs out of the history of one of the kings of the Davidic line and his victory over his foes.

Humiliation and Defeat of His Foes. 76:4-10. **4.** The psalmist burst into ecstatic praise of the great Conqueror, now Prince of Peace: **Thou art ... glorious** (*na'ôr*, "resplendent, splendid") **more majestic** (NASB; *'addîr*, "noble, mighty, powerful") **than the mountains of prey**, that is, than the great plundering world kingdoms (cf. 46:2-3); in 68:16 the world kingdoms are figuratively described as towering "hills" (Song of Sol. 4:8).

5. The stouthearted are spoiled (plundered; Job 12:17, 19; Isa. 10:12; 46:12; Rev. 19:11-21); **they have slept their sleep**—their death-sleep (Psalm 13:3; Jer. 51:39; Nah. 3:18; Zech. 14:12-13). None of these self-vaunting **men of might**, who tried to turn their hands against Jerusalem, could "find" (use) their hands, for death had overtaken them.

6. At thy rebuke (Psalm 80:16), **...** both (war) **chariot and horse are cast into a dead** (deep) **sleep** (Exod. 15:1, 21;

Psalm 78:53), the war chariot poetically presented as asleep in death, its rattling having ceased, just as its rider is dead (Rev. 19:16-21). The **God of Jacob** administers the *rebuke* (from the root *g^cr*, "scold, threaten, address harshly"). Despite all of Jacob's faults and foibles, He will bring him into his true "Israel" role in Kingdom blessing (cf. Gen. 32:28).

7a. Thou, even thou, art to be feared (Psalm 2:9-12; 89:7; 96:4; 1 Chron. 16:25). **7b. Who may stand in thy sight** (presence) **when once thou art angry?** (Psalm 103:3; Ezra 9:15; Nah. 1:6; Mal. 3:2; Rev. 6:17; 15:7-8; 16:19). **8.** This verse is a synoptic description of the Apocalypse (Rev. 6:1—20:3): **Thou didst cause judgment to be heard from heaven; the earth feared, and was still.**

9. By the word of divine power spoken from heaven (Psalm 2:5-12; Rev. 18:1, 4), the tumultuous elements on earth (Psalm 2:1-3; 46:2-3; Matt. 24:7-12; Rev. 13:1-18; 16:13-16; 19:19) will be quelled at Christ's second advent in glory to judge and make war (Psalm 74:22; 82:8; Rev. 19:11), and **to save** (deliver) **all the meek of the earth** (Matt. 25:31, 34-40; Rev. 7:4, 14; 14:4-5; 20:4-6).

10a. Surely the wrath of man shall praise thee (Exod. 9:16; Rom. 9:17), whether against Old Testament enemies of the LORD's people, or Gog and His army of the end time (Ezek. 38:1—39:24), or the slaughter of Antichrist and his forces at Armageddon (Rev. 16:13-16; 19:11-21). Praise arises to God for these deliverances.

10b. The remainder of wrath shalt thou restrain, not permitting any further manifestation of man's wrath that would not eventuate in God's ultimate glory and praise or the eventual blessing of His people. The literal Hebrew reads: "And the remainder of the wrath

["wraths," plural intensifying the wrath] thou shalt gird Thyself" (*hgr*, "put on, bind about oneself"). The wrath of the enemies, even to its last remnants (Psalm 75:8), serve Thee as a weapon by which Thou girdest Thyself to accomplish their destruction (Hengstenberg).

The King-Priest Exalted. 76:11-12. **11.** In the light of the glory of the King, His subjects are exhorted to make vows to Him and **pay** (fulfill) them (50:14). The Gentile nations are also enjoined to **bring presents**, that is, tributary gifts (Psalm 68:29; cf. 2 Chron. 32:22-23 for a possible historical background). Such tributary gifts must be brought to Him who **ought to be feared** (Psalm 2:5-12). Why? **12. He shall cut off** (as a vinedresser, Rev. 14:18-19) **the spirit** (breath) **of princes** by death (Psalm 104:29). **He is fearsome** (awesome) **to the kings of the earth** (47:2), for He will reign as "King of kings," king par excellence (Rev. 19:15) and will rule "with a rod of iron" (Psalm 2:9; Rev. 19:15).

E. THE SAINT IN THE DAY OF DISTRESS. 77:1-20.

"To the chief Musician [precentor], to Jeduthun [see Psalms 39 and 62], A Psalm of Asaph." See the introduction to Book 3, Psalm 73 for the scope of Psalms 73-89, presenting a saint in deep distress of soul and his comfort in the LORD.

The Soul in Distress. 77:1-9. **1.** The saint cried out to God. His voice rose in prayer, and he was assured God would hear him. **2.** It was a **day of trouble** (50:15; 86:7), prophetically envisioning "the time of Jacob's trouble" (Jer. 30:5-7; Dan. 12:1; Matt. 24:21-22; Rev. 6:1—19:21). He sought the LORD (Isa. 26:9). **My sore ran,** "my hand was stretched out" (*yādî niggrâ*), graphically "flowed out" toward God, implying relaxation of the body in conscious weakness and helplessness. Yet, because of his deep trials, he **refused to be comforted** (Gen. 37:35; Jer. 31:15).

3. He **remembered God**, and **was troubled** (*hāmâ*, "groaned or moaned"; Psalm 55:2). He **complained** (meditatively prayed), but his spirit was **overwhelmed** (fainted), his powers of meditation failing him (61:2; 143:4). **4.** He complained of sleepless nights. **Thou holdest mine eyes waking**, and so he became accustomed to vigils. **I am so troubled that I cannot speak** (39:9).

5-6a. Then he considered **the days of old** (44:1; 143:5; Deut. 32:7; Isa. 51:9), and remembered his **song in the night** (Psalms 42:8; 92:2; Job 35:10), the happy past when he could sing even in the darkness. **6b.** He purposed to meditate and ponder, gaining comfort in trouble from recalling God's mighty deeds in the past (vv. 16-20).

7-9. The great trouble the psalmist was passing through arose from some historical situation now hidden, but it looks forward to the supreme time of Israel's testing in the crucible of the Great Tribulation, when her faith will be so severely tested that she will be tempted to conclude that the LORD has rejected His people forever (Psalm 44:9; contrast Rom. 11:25-32) and will never be favorable again (Psalm 85:1, 5). She will think that His loving-kindness has ceased forever (89:49), that His promise (Deut. 30:1-10; 2 Sam. 7:16) has failed (2 Pet. 3:9), that He has forgotten to be gracious (Isa. 49:15), and in anger has withdrawn His compassion (Psalms 25:6; 40:11; 51:1).

Faith Rises Above Infirmity. 77:10-15. **10. And I said, This is my infirmity** (lit., "my sickness, affliction"; 39:9; Jer. 10:19), appointed by God and to be submitted to with a yielded spirit. This is the transition point from doubt

and despondency to firm faith. **But I will remember** (these words are supplied from v. 11) **the years of the right hand of the Most High**, when God manifested His power and grace in behalf of His people. Those years of affliction were also from "the right hand," and hence the good hand, of God, and therefore were to be borne patiently (1 Pet. 5:6).

11. The psalmist took the sure path to regain faith and hope by also recalling **the works of the Lord** ("the deeds of Yah"; 1 Chron. 16:12; Psalm 143:5), His **wonders** (*pĭl'ĕkā*, "miraculous interpositions") **of old. 12. I will meditate** (*hāgâ*, "muse") **also of all thy work** (singular, viewing in the aggregate the whole gamut of God's wondrous undertakings in behalf of His people; 145:5) **and talk of** (muse or ponder) **thy doings** (deeds).

He concluded four things concerning God: (1) **13a.** God's **way** (His course of action) **is holy** (NASB; lit., "in holiness," Exod. 15:11; Psalms 63:2; 73:17), free from any wrong, since it is **in the sanctuary**, the heavenly holy place (11:4; 18:6; Hab. 2:20), His way being in heaven, far exalted above our ways (Isa. 55:9).

(2) **13b.** God Himself is incomparable in His greatness (Exod. 15:11; Deut. 3:24), far above the foolish nonentities that pagans call "gods," the worship of whom is demon-engineered (cf. 1 Cor. 10:20). (3) **14.** God is the God of miraculous wonders (Psalm 72:18), revealing His strength among "the peoples" (Exod. 9:16; 15:14). (4) **15.** He is the God of redemptive power (6:6; Deut. 9:29; Psalms 74:2; 78:42), redeeming His people, **the sons of Jacob and Joseph** (80:1).

Faith Gives Assurance of Deliverance. 77:16-20. Faith, having risen above infirmity (vv. 10-15), recalled to mind God's past wonders (vv. 16-20).

The remembrance of those great divine interpositions no longer aggravated the psalmist's pain, but filled his soul with assurance of deliverance. This will be eminently true of the Jewish remnant in the period of Jacob's (Israel's) supreme time of trouble. **16-18.** The psalmist recalled the Exodus, Israel's redemption from Egypt at the Red (Reed) Sea (Exod. 14:21; Psalm 114:3; Hab. 3:8, 10), although allusions to other great deliverances seem to be incorporated into the lively poetic presentation that exudes a vibrant faith (cf. Josh 3:15-17; 10:11, 14; Judg. 5:4).

19-20. The psalmist's conclusion was that God's **way is in the sea**, His **path in the great waters**, illustrated so dramatically in the case of Israel's redemption at the Red (Reed) Sea (cf. v. 13; Nah. 1:3). His way is open to Him alone, for only the Creator-Redeemer can make a path through the pathless sea (Isa. 51:10, 15; 63:11), encouraging His own to hope for deliverance, even in their deepest waters of trial (43:2; Dan. 12:1; Matt. 24:21-22; Rev. 6:9-10; 12:13-17).

And thy footsteps (footprints) **are not known**, as at the Red (Reed) Sea, where no traces were left of the divine footprints by which He led Israel, the waters having returned (Exod. 14:26-28). So transcendently wonderful are all God's ways with Israel (Rom. 11:33-35) and *all* His elect, even as He led them **like a flock by the hand of Moses and Aaron** (Isa. 63:11-12; Hos. 12:13; Mic. 6:4).

F. GOD'S WORKING IN HISTORY.
78:1-72.

For the context and scope of Psalm 78, see the introduction to Book 3, Psalm 73. This psalm is entitled a "Maschil [instruction] of Asaph." It is an inspired didactic poem embracing Israel's history from the Exodus to David. Against God's wonderful works and character is flashed the sorry picture of Israel's sin and failure.

Spiritual Instruction from History. *78:1-8.* **1.** The psalmist, identifying himself with the LORD, called on His people, Israel, to attend to His **law** (*tōrâ*, "instruction"; cf. Isa. 51:4; 55:3). **2. I will open my mouth in a parable** (*māshāl*, "a similitude, figurative comparison"; Psalm 49:4; Matt. 13:35). **I will utter** (*nb'*, causitive force "to cause to bubble forth, give vent to," as if the Spirit, being pent up, burst forth like a gushing fountain) **dark sayings** (enigmas), the historical events reviewed from Moses to David being enigmatic veils of spiritual truths or "instruction" (cf. *Maschil* in the superscription; as in 1 Cor. 10:6; Gal. 4:24).

3-4. These verses should be rendered, "What we have heard ... we will not hide from their children," meaning from *our* children, who are really *our father's* children. And our fathers transmitted to us these truths, not for our sakes only, but for all generations to come, to show them **the praises of the Lord, and his strength, and his wonderful works** (*niple'ôt,* "supernatural wonders") **he hath done** (*'āsâ,* "performed, worked").

5-7. He established ("erected, raised up") **a testimony in Jacob ... a law in Israel** (Psalms 19:7; 81:5; Isa. 8:20), namely, the Pentateuch, the record of God's laws and God's deeds to be taught each successive generation (vv. 6, 7, 10, 11) in order that they will put their trust in God and **keep his commandments**, avoiding the sins of their fathers (2 Chron. 30:7; Ezek. 20:18). **8.** This verse concerns the era of the Judges: **And might not be as their fathers** (of the Mosaic age), **a stubborn and rebellious generation** (cf. Deut. 9:6-7; 31:27).

The Disqualification of Ephraim. *78:9-20.* The didactic slant of this psalm is directed toward Judah, illustrating the divine choice of Jerusalem and the Davidic line as the recipients of the promises, instead of the tribe of Ephraim, the privileged tribe (cf. Jacob's prophecy, Gen. 48:14; 49:22-26), which disqualified itself by rebellion (vv. 9-11, 57, 60, 67-68).

9. The Ephraimites, representing all the tribes, were archers equipped with **bows** (1 Chron. 12:2), figuratively describing their noble call and destination. Yet they **turned back in the day of battle**, failing, when put to the test, to realize their high calling (cf. v. 57). Their unfaithfulness resulted in their defeat, the capture of the ark by the enemy (vv. 41-42, 56-60), followed by the rejection of Shiloh and the choice of Judah as the place of the sanctuary (vv. 67-69).

10-11. They did not keep **the covenant of God** (Judg. 2:20; 1 Kings 11:11; 2 Kings 18:12) and **refused to walk in his law** (Psalm 119:1; Jer. 32:23; 44:10) ... **forgot** God's **works** (deeds) and **his wonders** (miracles) ... **he had shown** them (Psalm 106:13), through their forefathers as the representatives of Israel to all succeeding ages.

Six of God's wonderful works and miracles were reviewed (vv. 12-20): (1) **12.** He wrought wonders in Egypt (Exod. 7:12; Psalm 106:22) **in the field of Zoan** (Avaris-Tanis, the Hyksos capital; Num. 13:22; Psalm 78:43; Isa. 19:11; 30:4; Ezek. 30:14). (2) **13.** He brought Israel across the Red (Reed) Sea (Exod. 14:21; Psalms 74:13; 136:13), miraculously making **the waters ... stand as an heap** (Exod. 15:8; Psalm 33:7).

(3) **14.** He conducted them by the pillar of fire and cloud (Exod. 13:21; 14:24; Psalm 105:39). (4) **15-16.** He brought water out of the rock (Exod. 17:6; Psalm 105:41; Isa. 48:21; 1 Cor. 10:4). (5) **17-19.** He gave quail out of heaven to feed the people (Num. 11:4, 18, 31-33; cf. Exod. 16:3). (6) **20.** He again brought

water from the rock (v. 15; Num. 20:8, 10-11).

Ephraim's (Israel's) Rebellion and God's Mercy. 78:21-39. **21-24.** The LORD **was angry** (Num. 11:1) at Israel's unbelief (Deut. 1:32; 9:23; Heb. 3:18); yet, in His love and mercy, He **commanded the clouds** and **opened the doors of heaven** (Gen. 7:11; Deut. 28:12; Mal. 3:10), raining down **manna,** the **grain of heaven,** to eat. **25. Man** (*every* man, Exod. 16:6) ate **angels' food,** food from the habitation of the angels, **to the full** (16:3).

26-28. God directed the winds and brought the quail (16:13; Psalm 105:40). **29-31.** Yet they displayed their lust, and the LORD chastened their stoutest ones with death and brought low **the chosen men of Israel. 32-33.** They persisted in their sin and unbelief (Num. 14:11); so He brought their days to an untimely end (14:29, 35) **in vanity** (futility) and terror.

34-35. When God chastened them with death, they repented and returned to seek Him (Num. 21:7; Hos. 5:15), remembering that **God was their rock** and their **redeemer** (Exod. 15:13; Deut. 9:26; 32:4; Psalm 74:2). **36-37.** But they lapsed into deception (Exod. 24:7-8; 32:7-8; Isa. 57:11; Ezek. 33:31), and in their fickleness (Psalm 78:8) and unfaithfulness forsook the covenant (Psalm 51:10). **38-39.** But in His compassion, God forgave them and did not destroy them (Exod. 34:6-7; Num. 14:20), remembering they were **but flesh** (Gen. 6:3; Job 10:9; Psalm 103:14; James 4:14).

God's Chastening Love. 78:40-53. **40-41.** Over and over again they rebelled in the wilderness (106:43), grieving Him (95:10; Isa. 63:10; Eph. 4:30), tempting Him, that is, putting Him to the test (Num. 14:22), and paining **the Holy One** of Israel by their unholiness (Psalm 89:18; 2 Kings 19:22).

The psalmist resumed the account of the Exodus (v. 12). **42-43.** God's people forgot His gracious mercy and redemptive power in redeeming them from Egypt (Judg. 8:34; Psalms 44:3; 106:10), and all the signs (Exod. 4:21; 7:3; Psalm 105:27) that He performed to rescue them from Egyptian bondage. **44-48.** He turned rivers (canals of the Nile) to blood (Psalm 105:29), sending swarms of flies (Exod. 8:24) and frogs (8:6), destroying their vines and cattle with hail (Exod. 9:19, 23).

49-51. He did that through the agency of a band of destroying angels, the executors of His wrath, literally, "a deputation of angels of evil," that is, good angels executing His punishments, especially death of the firstborn (Exod. 12:29-30), called **the first issue of their virility in the tents of Ham** (NASB; Psalms 105:23; 106:22), another name for Egypt. **52-53.** In His redemptive grace, however, He led forth His own people **like sheep** (Exod. 15:22; Psalm 77:20), safely and without fear (Exod. 14:19-20), while the sea engulfed the Egyptians (14:27-28).

Israel's Defection and Punishment in Canaan. 78:54-64. **54-55. And he brought them** (Exod. 15:13, 17) **to the border of his sanctuary** (*gᵉḇûl qŏdshô,* "His holy border [territory]," meaning, "His holy land," Palestine) **... this mountain,** the hill country (of Palestine), **which His right hand had gained** (NASB), driving out the Canaanite nations before them (Josh. 23:4), apportioning them an **inheritance by line** (a surveyor's line or measurement), and settled the Israelite tribes **in their tents** in the inheritance.

56-57. Yet they **tested** (v. 18) and rebelled against the Most High God (Psalm 78:40), turning traitors **like a de-** ceitful (treacherous) **bow** (Hos. 7:16; cf. v. 9), which disappoints the trust placed in it. **58-60.** For they angered the LORD with their **high places** (Lev. 26:30; 1 Kings 3:2) tainted by pagan cults (Deut. 4:25; 1 Kings 14:9; Isa. 65:3), arousing His jealous ire with their graven images (Exod. 20:4; Lev. 26:1; Deut. 4:25) to such an extent that God **greatly abhorred** His people, giving up Shiloh.

The removal of the ark by the Philistines shows that God had forsaken Shiloh, since the ark was never returned there (1 Sam. 21:1-2; 22:19; 1 Kings 3:4; Jer. 7:12, 14; 26:6), and it intimates that Shiloh was destroyed, evidently by the Philistines at the Battle of Ebenezer in about 1050 B.C., as archaeology also suggests.

61. God **delivered his strength,** that is, the ark, the symbol of His presence and power among His people, and what He used to rescue them from their foes (Psalm 132:8), **into the enemy's** (Philistines') **hand.** This meant that He also gave up **his glory,** the ark being the pledge of both God's strength and glory (1 Sam. 4:21-22; Psalms 29:1; 96:6-7), to the adversary.

62. He also delivered His people to the sword (Judg. 20:21; 1 Sam. 4:10). **63.** Fire devoured His young men (Num. 11:1; 21:28; Isa. 26:11; Jer. 48:45), and His virgins had no wedding songs (Jer. 7:34; 16:9; Lam. 2:21). **64.** His priests fell by the sword (1 Sam. 4:17; 22:18), and His widows could not weep (Job 27:15; Ezek. 24:23).

God's Sovereign Grace and Choice of David. 78:65-72. **65. Then the Lord awakened as one out of sleep** (44:23; 73:20), seeming to have been slumbering insofar as His people were concerned (Zech. 2:13), like a **mighty man** (*gibbôr,* "valiant man"). He **shouted** aloud joyfully **by reason of wine** (*mîyyăyĭn*), a bold figure of one whose natural strength is stimulated by that means (104:15).

66. "He smote them back," causing them to flee back, as in Psalm 9:3 (E. W. Hengstenberg), putting them to a **perpetual reproach** (1 Sam. 5:6). **67. He refused** (rejected) **the tabernacle of Joseph,** referring to "the tabernacle of [at] Shiloh" (v. 60), **and chose not the tribe of Ephraim,** the ruling tribe during the period of the Judges. The rejection comprehends only Ephraim's previous precedence and the presence of the tabernacle in that tribe. **68. But chose the tribe of Judah . . . Mount Zion which he loved** (Psalms 87:2; 132:13).

69-70. And he built his sanctuary like the heights (*rāmîm*); (NASB), the high mountains (1 Kings 6:1; 9:4; 2 Chron. 3:4), choosing David His servant (1 Sam. 16:12), taking him from the sheepfolds. **71-72. From following the ewes . . . he brought him to feed** (shepherd) **Jacob, his people, and Israel, his inheritance,** shepherding them **according to the integrity of his heart** (1 Kings 9:4; Psalm 75:2), guiding them **by the skillfulness of his hands.** Prophetically envisioned is the day when the greater than David, the true Shepherd of Israel, will appear and make Zion His spiritual and political capital in the Kingdom age, when as "the Lion of the tribe of Judah" (Rev. 5:5) He will take possession of the whole earth.

G. Jerusalem's Desolation—Past and Future. 79:1-13.

For the context and scope of Psalm 79, see the introduction to Book 3, Psalm 73.

The Lament. 79:1-7. **1.** A cry ascended to God that **the nations** had invaded His **inheritance** (74:2; Lam. 1:10) and defiled His holy Temple (Psalm 74:3) and laid Jerusalem in ruins (2 Kings 25:9-10; Jer. 26:18; Mic. 3:12).

Zion, the place God loves (Psalms 78:68; 87:2; 132:13), is here seen in desolation, both historically and prophetically. The inscription title, "Psalm of Asaph," evidently refers to the singers of the Asaph school, who regarded themselves as the mouthpiece of Asaph, who though long dead, yet spoke; thus, the Asaph psalms have a mutual affinity.

2-3. The nations had given **the dead bodies** of God's servants to be food to **the fowls of the heavens** and **the beasts of the earth** (Deut. 28:26; Jer. 7:33; 16:4; 19:7; 34:20), pouring out **their blood . . . like water round about Jerusalem** (14:16; 16:4). **4.** The people had become a **reproach . . . a scorn and derision** (Psalms 44:13; 80:6; Dan. 9:16). While Jerusalem more than once has experienced such desolations (under the Babylonians, Greeks, and Romans), these calamities in their prophetic aspect still point to that final and cataclysmic disaster that is yet to fall upon the city (Dan. 9:27; Zech. 14:1-2; Matt. 24:15; 2 Thess. 2:4; Rev. 11:1-13; 13:11-18). **5.** In that day of calamity the faithful will turn to the LORD, the God of covenant and salvation, and cry out, **How long, Lord?** They will call upon Him whose faithfulness has been attested in the past and is assured by the Davidic Covenant (2 Sam. 7:16).

6. They prayed an imprecatory prayer (see comment on Psalm 5:10) that God would pour out His **wrath upon the nations** (Rev. 15:7—16:21), for it was full (Gen. 15:16; Rev. 14:10, 15, 20); their prayer for the immediate judgment of the wicked was His Spirit praying through them, expressing *His* will. The nations had touched the apple of God's eye (Zech. 2:8) in devouring **Jacob** and **laying waste his dwelling place** (habitation; Psalm 53:4; 2 Chron. 36:19; Jer. 39:8).

The Prayer. 79:8-13. **8.** A plea was

861

made for God's grace and compassion (106:4-6; Isa. 64:9) because they were **brought very low** (Psalm 116:6; Deut. 28:43; Isa. 26:5). **9-10.** They cried for the God of their salvation (deliverance) to help them for **the glory** of His name (Psalm 31:3) and to forgive their sins (25:11; 65:3). The glory of His name, they reminded the LORD, had been tarnished by the taunt of the godless nations, who said, **Where is their God?** (115:2; Joel 2:17). What had become of His much-celebrated omnipotence and steadfast love for His own (Deut. 9:28)? "Let there be known among the nations in our sight [6:22] the revenging of the blood of thy servants which is shed" (lit. Heb.; cf. Deut. 32:43; Psalm 13:1-6; Rev. 6:10).

11. Let the sighing (groaning) **of the prisoner come before thee** (Psalm 102:20) ... **preserve** ... **those** ... **appointed** (doomed) **to die** (lit., "the children of the dying"; cf. 72:4; 102:19-20). **12. Render** (return) **unto our neighbors sevenfold** (Gen. 4:15; Lev. 26:21; Psalm 12:6; Prov. 6:31; Isa. 30:26) **into their bosom** (65:6-7), referring to the fold of the garment at the lap, which served as a receptacle for objects (Luke 6:38), **their reproach, wherewith they have reproached thee**, saying, "Where is their God?" (v. 10).

13. This verse presents a conclusion. In the confidence that God would answer the foregoing prayers, a vow of perpetual praise to God was made (Psalms 44:8; 89:1; Isa. 43:21), which envisions Kingdom blessing in its full sweep. The **sheep** of God's **pasture** (Psalms 74:1; 95:7; 100:3) will enjoy the care of the "Shepherd of Israel" (80:1; cf. 23:1).

H. ULTIMATE RESTORATION OF ISRAEL. 80:1-19.

For the context and scope of Psalm 80, see the introduction to Book 3, Psalm 73. "To the chief Musician [precentor] upon Shoshannim ['lilies'; cf. inscription titles for Psalms 45, 60, 69, referring to that which is lovely, i.e., the lovely salvation of the LORD, vv. 3, 7, 19] Eduth ['testimony,' Psalms 78:5; 81:5; or 'law,' pointing out to the godly the way of obtaining deliverance from trouble; cf. Psalm 78:1]."

Prayer for Help for Oppressed Israel. *80:1-3.* **1a. Give ear, O Shepherd of Israel** (23:1), the "LORD God of hosts" (v. 4), is a designation of Deity first used by Jacob, himself a shepherd (Gen. 48:15). **Thou who leadest Joseph like a flock** (Psalms 77:15; 78:67; Amos 5:15). The reference to "Joseph" (Ephraim and Manasseh, Gen. 48:3-5) doubtlessly fixes the captivity of the ten tribes in Assyria as the psalm's subject; so the LXX prefixes it with "concerning Assyria," with Judah offering prayer for her sister tribes (Calvin). "Asaph" would mean a descendant and member of that school, not David's actual contemporary. However, it is possible that the reference is to Asaph himself and that the psalmist was alluding to the order of march in the wilderness (Num. 2:17-24) and to servitude by Israel to invading enemies in the time of the Judges (cf. Judg. 3:8; 4:2).

1b. Whatever the time, Joseph (the northern tribes) was in dire distress and needed the help of Him who led Joseph like a flock and who **dwellest** (*yōshēḇ*, "sits" or "is enthroned") **above** (NASB; not "between") the cherubim, as is now known from archaeology. His enthronement *above* the cherubim (Exod. 25:22; 1 Sam. 4:4; 2 Sam. 6:2) points to His omnipotence and exalted supremacy above world powers, symbolized by the cherubim (Psalm 18:10).

1c. The petition **Shine forth** (Deut. 33:2) called upon the LORD to manifest

862

His loving grace and power in behalf of His oppressed people, the effulgent Shekinah glory symbolizing His manifested presence among them.

2-3. He was besought to **stir up** His power and come to **save** (deliver) His distressed people, to **restore** them (vv. 7, 19; Psalms 60:1; 85:4; 126:1; Lam. 5:21), to retrieve them from oppression and exile, **and cause** His **face to shine** (Num. 6:25; Psalm 31:16) that they might **be saved** (delivered).

The Terrible Oppression. 80:4-7. **4.** It is significant that when God was addressed for help against foes, He was called **the Lord** (Yahweh), expressing His covenant relation to Israel as "Shepherd" (v. 1) and as **God of hosts** (the infinite angelic army of heaven), revealing His omnipotent resources as the One enthroned *above* the cherubim (v. 1).

How long wilt thou be angry, literally, "smoke" (Deut. 29:20; Psalm 18:8), indicating the consuming fire of God's anger. Smoke also symbolizes prayer and the self-dedication indicated by the burnt offering (Isa. 6:4; Rev. 5:8; 8:3-4); the smoke of prayer should smother the fire of God's wrath (Lev. 16:13). But now God opposed the smoke of His anger against the smoke of His people's prayer (E. W. Hengstenberg).

Three features of the suffering people were: (1) **5.** God fed them with tears and gave them tears to drink (Psalms 42:3; 102:9), in contrast to the normal care of the Shepherd (23:5). (2) **6a.** He made them a **strife** ("an object of contention") to their **neighbors** (the Gentile nations surrounding them), who hassled over the spoils they took from them (44:13). (3) **6b-7.** He made them a laughingstock among their enemies, eliciting their heartrending cry (cf. vv. 3, 19).

The Vine out of Egypt. 80:8-13. The image springs from Jacob's prophecy concerning Joseph (Gen. 49:22; cf. Isa. 5:1-7; Hos. 14:7). **8-11.** The vine (Israel) was removed from Egypt (Jer. 2:21; 12:10; Ezek. 17:6). The LORD **cast out** (drove out) the nations inhabiting Palestine (Josh. 13:6; 2 Chron. 20:7; Acts 7:45), preparing room (clearing ground) **before it** (Exod. 23:28; Josh. 24:12; Isa. 5:2). The vine took deep root, filling the land (of promise; Hos. 14:5), covering the mountains of the southern extremity of Palestine "with its boughs of the cedars of God"(lit. Heb.), that is, **the goodly cedars** (of Lebanon) that marked the northern boundary (Psalms 29:5; 92:12; 104:16). The vine sent out its branches **unto the sea** (the Mediterranean; 72:8), the western boundary, and to the Euphrates, the eastern limit, according to the original promise to Jacob (Gen. 28:14; cf. Josh. 1:4).

12-13. Why hast thou ... broken down her hedges (walls, fences) intended to keep it from being trampled down (Psalm 89:40; Isa. 5:5), and so every passerby picks its fruit (Deut. 28:63) **and the boar out of the forest doth waste it** (Jer. 5:6), eating it up and trampling it down.

Prayer for the Vine. 80:14-19. **14-15.** The petition was that God would visit the vine (Israel) in mercy. **Return** ("turn again"; 90:13). God must first turn toward us that we may turn to Him (Lam. 5:21). **Look down from heaven** (Isa. 63:15) and **visit** (in mercy) **this vine**, which Thou hast **planted ... the branch** ("shoot"; Zech. 3:8), **and on the son** (figuratively, "sprout, branch") **whom Thou hast strengthened for Thyself** (NASB; Isa. 44:14; 49:5). The "son" is the spiritual **vine**, Israel, that is, "Israel ... my son" (Hos. 11:1), the poet passing from the figure to that which the figure represents (cf. v. 17). **16. They** (Israel) **perish,** the vineyard being cut down and burned **at the rebuke** of the

LORD'S **countenance**, which ceases to "shine" (v. 3) upon them.

17. The man of thy right hand encompassed Benjamin ("son of the right hand"), representing all Israel, now prostrate and needing to be strengthened by the LORD. The antitypical Israel, the Messiah, is ultimately referred to, of whom God said, "Mine arm ... shall strengthen him" (Psalm 89:21; JFB).

18. Israel, as a result of the Messiah, the Son of Man, "the BRANCH" (Zech. 3:8; 6:12) will not go back, if only the LORD will give them new life (Ezek. 37:1-28), which He will do at His second advent (Zech. 12:10—13:1). **19.** Then the **Lord God of hosts** (Rev. 19:11-12), coming with the armies of heaven to destroy their enemies (19:14), will cause His face **to shine** upon them. Then all Israel will be saved (Rom. 11:26-36).

I. REVIVAL OF ISRAEL'S HOPE. 81:1-16.

For the context and scope of Psalm 81, see the introduction to Book 3, Psalm 79. "To the chief Musician upon Gittith" (see the title to Psalm 8).

The Beginning of Israel's Promised Redemption. 81:1-5. **1-3.** The singing for joy, joyful shouting, raising a song, and the music of timbrel, lyre, and harp prefigure the blessedness Israel will enjoy when the Feast of Trumpets, which prophetically signifies the commencement of Israel's regathering and promised redemption (Lev. 23:23-25), is held. Celebrated on the first day of the seventh month, Tishri (October), it followed the harvest (the ingathering of the Gentiles of the church period, when "the fullness of the Gentiles [has] come in," Rom. 11:25).

This was followed by the Day of Atonement (Lev. 23:26-32), which looks forward to Israel's cleansing from sin, after which the prayer with which Psalm 80 ended will be answered (Psalm 80:19); therefore, these two odes, like all the psalms, display the marks of inspiration, not only in their composition, but also in their collection and arrangement in the psalter. **4.** Therefore, this feast (like all the feasts of Lev. 23) was established as a statute and ordinance of **the God of Jacob**, because they looked forward to the grace of God that would one day restore "Jacob" to his "Israel" character (Gen. 32:28) nationally.

5. Hence, they were ordained for **a testimony** in Joseph of Israel's redemption and future restoration, when he went **out through the land of Egypt** in the sight of their panic-striken oppressors (Exod. 14:8; Num. 33:3), **where I**, says Israel, in whose person the psalmist spoke (Psalm 114:1), **heard a language that I understood not** (Deut. 28:49; Jer. 5:15). Dwelling in servitude to an alien people whose language was not understood was peculiarly galling and was a feature that made deliverance from Egypt the more intensely desired.

God Reminds Israel of Her Past Deliverance. 81:6-10. **6. I** (the LORD, in whose person the psalmist now speaks) **removed** (relieved) **his shoulder from the burden** (Isa. 9:4; 10:27); **his hands were delivered** (freed) **from the basket** (burden baskets for carrying bricks, clay, and other things). **7a-b. Thou calledst in trouble, and I delivered thee** (Exod. 2:23; 14:10) **... I answered thee** (19:19; 20:18) **in the secret** (hiding) **place of thunder**, that is, in the thundercloud (Psalms 18:11-13; 77:17-18; Hab. 3:4). His lightninglike power, issuing from His secret place, responded to His people's plea for help (Exod. 14:24; 19:18-19; 20:18).

7c. I tested thee at the waters of Meribah (17:6-7; Psalm 95:8), this sudden reference to the first act of Israel's rebellion and unbelief preparing the way for God's complaint (vv. 11-16) follow-

864

ing His appeal to them (vv. 6-10). There God "proved" them, tested their faith, revealing their unbelief and provocation of His patience.

8-10a. God called upon His people to listen and be admonished, warning them against idolatry (Exod. 20:3; Deut. 32:12; Isa. 43:12); as His redeemed people, God had a double claim on their loyalty in creation and redemption (Exod. 20:2). **10b. Open thy mouth wide, and I will fill it**—I will fully satisfy all your desires (Rom. 10:12; Phil. 4:19)—you have no need to resort to other gods, for you have all you need in Me (Gen. 15:1; Psalm 16:5) so ask and expect of Me great blessings (37:4; 78:25; 107:9).

God Yearns over Israel Despite Her Perversity. 81:11-16. **11. But my people would not hearken** (listen) **to my voice** (106:25)... **Israel would none of me** (*'ābâ*, "acquiesce to me, obey me"). **12.** So God **gave them up** (Job 8:4; Acts 7:42; Rom. 1:24, 26) to **their own hearts' desire** (*sheʾrîrût*, "stubbornness, obstinacy" of their own hearts) to walk **in their own counsels** (devices; Isa. 65:2; Jer. 7:24; Rom. 11:1-25).

13-14. Had they responded rightly to God's goodness (Psalms 81:8; 128:1; Isa. 42:4; cf. Deut. 5:29; Jer. 7:23), He would have quickly **subdued their enemies** (Psalms 18:47; 47:3) and turned His hand against their foes (Amos 1:8). **15a. The haters of the Lord should have submitted themselves** (*yekāhʾshû*, "have yielded obedience, though feigned") **unto him** (Psalms 18:44; 66:3).

15b-16. But their (Israel's) **time** ("their time" of blessing in the land) should have been **forever** (2 Sam. 7:24), **fed ... with the finest** (fat) **of the wheat** (Deut. 32:14; Psalm 147:14); **and with honey out of the rock ... satisfied** (Deut. 32:13). However, in Israel's future restoration (vv. 1-5; Rom. 11:25-33), her

enemies will be subdued, and the blessings restored that they once forfeited.

J. THE MESSIAH'S JUDGMENT AT HIS SECOND ADVENT. 82:1-8.

For the context and scope of Psalm 82, see the introduction to Book 3, Psalm 73.

The Judge and His Righteous Judgment. 82:1-4. **1.** Asaph, the seer, glimpsed God standing up to plead and judge in His own **congregation** (lit., "the congregation of God"; Isa. 3:13; Matt. 25:31-46; Rev. 19:11; see Psalm 50, also an Asaph psalm, which commences with the appearance of God for judgment). The congregation of God ('El) will answer to **the gods** (*'elōhîm*, i.e., "judges or rulers"; Exod. 21:6; 22:8, 28; John 10:34), His vicegerents or representatives who bear His name and to whom His Word had come.

2. He will begin His judgment of those who, preceding His second advent, have been judges and rulers of the people. Since the congregation is God's (Psalm 74:2), He can tolerate no unrighteousness or power abuse on the part of those who will now be His representatives in the Kingdom age, namely, the Israelites of the end-time Tribulation period. Hence, His judgment must begin with His people, Israel (Matt. 25:1-10) before He can start His worldwide judgment of the nations (25:31-45).

Therefore, the psalmist proceeded to set forth how God (the Messiah) at His second advent will deal with the judges (*'elōhîm*) who have judged unjustly in showing partiality to people, either because of their wealth or poverty (Exod. 23:3; Lev. 19:15; Deut. 1:17; Psalm 58:1). **3-4.** He warned the judges to **defend** (judge) **the poor and fatherless,** instead of dismissing their appeals (cf. Isa. 1:17; Luke 18:3), and to **deliver the poor and needy** (Job 29:12).

The Judge Judges the Earth. 82:5-7.
5a-b. While those who judge (vv. 1-4) and who specifically are said not to **know** and **understand** (14:4; Jer. 4:22; Mic. 3:1) and **walk on** (about) **in darkness** (Prov. 2:13; Isa. 59:9; Jer. 23:12) belong to every age of the satanic world system, they prophetically focus upon the end time of gross darkness (Isa. 60:2*a*) and the acme of lawlessness (2 Thess. 2:4; Rev. 9:20-21), preceding the period when the LORD shall rise upon Zion and "his glory shall be seen upon [her]" (Isa. 60:2*b*) at the commencement of the Kingdom age.

5c. Then **all the foundations of the earth** will be **out of course** (*yĭmmôṭû*, "be moved or shaken"; Psalm 11:3) when the Lord of hosts, the returning Messiah, will "shake the heavens, and the earth" (Hag. 2:6-7, 21) in the catastrophic apocalyptic judgments (Rev. 6:1—20:3) preceding the setting up of the Kingdom (Isa. 9:6-7; 11:1—12:6; Rev. 20:4-6). Then everything out of place shall be shaken into its right place.

6. Then the returning Judge (19:11) will address those unscrupulous judges: **I** (emphatic) **have said, Ye are gods** (Psalm 82:1; John 10:34) **... all of you are children** (sons) **of the Most High** ('*ĕlyôn*), on the grounds that "the word of God came" to them (John 10:35), thus constituting them such. Even when the Judge is about to pass judgment on them, He will recognize their divinely appointed dignity in representing Him and His will, on which they will have presumed.

7. Their severe judgment (Job 21:32; Psalm 49:12; Ezek. 31:14) of dying like any ordinary man ('*āḏām*; Psalm 9:20), serves as a warning that those who rule with the Messiah in the righteous Kingdom about to be set up (Isa. 9:6-7; 11:3-4) must do so in absolute justice and equity, for He is God ('*ēl*) and "the Most High" (v. 6), "the possessor of heaven and earth" (Gen. 14:18-19), who is about to take possession of His millennial title (Zech. 3:14). His "sons" must judge and rule in the Kingdom with justice and righteousness that agree with Him in whom all the dignities of the kingship and judgeship, abused by others, shall be realized in their highest ideal (Psalm 2:6-12).

Call for the Judge to Appear. 82:8. **8. Arise, O God, judge the earth** (12:5; Rev. 19:11; cf. Zeph. 1:7; Hab. 2:20; Zech. 2:13). The prayer is that the prophetic intimations in the psalm will be accomplished, as prayer so often offered by God's oppressed people for the coming of the LORD to judge earth's wrongs (Psalm 12:5; Rev. 6:10; 11:5) is finally answered. That petition will be especially appropriate in the abounding wickedness of the end time (Matt. 24:12), which will precede the establishment of the Kingdom, when the Judge-King will **inherit all** (the millennial) **nations** (Psalms 2:8; 22:29; Rev. 11:15).

K. ISRAEL'S ENEMIES OVERTHROWN. 83:1-18.

This psalm is the last of the Asaph series (Psalms 73-83), all of which prophetically glimpse Israel's future trouble and deliverance into Kingdom blessing. However, no such comprehensive anti-Israel alliance, as is here depicted (vv. 6-8), is mentioned in the Old Testament, the nearest approach being the coalition in the days of Jehoshaphat (2 Chron. 20:1-12), when "Jahaziel ... a Levite of the sons of Asaph" prophesied "in the midst of the congregation" (20:14). It is still more difficult to fit this confederacy into the prophetic picture of either Russia's future invasion (Ezek. 38:1—39:24; Dan. 11:40-45), probably before the Tribulation, or that of Antichrist and his invading hordes at Armageddon at the end of the Tribulation (Rev. 16:13-16; 19:11-21). Probably its fulfillment will come in some pan-Arabic coalition and attack on the Israeli State before the church is taken out, or at least before Daniel's seventieth week begins.

Israel's Prayer in Face of the Attack. 83:1-8. **1.** The serious nature of the threat is reflected in the impetuous request, **Keep not ... silence ... hold not thy peace ... be not still** (28:1; 35:22; 109:1), which constitutes a desperate cry for God's open interposition. **2-3.** The confederate **enemies make a tumult** (uproar; 2:1; 74:4; Isa. 37:29; Jer. 1:19) in their hatred of God and **have lifted up the head** (exalted themselves; Judg. 8:28; Zech. 1:21) against Him and His people, Israel, taking **crafty counsel** (Psalm 64:2; Isa. 29:15) and consulting (conspiring) against His **hidden** (treasured) **ones** (Psalms 27:5; 31:20; cf. Exod. 19:5-6), His elect nation, being restored to its national election after its temporary setting aside during this age (Rom. 11:1-32).

4. They are viewed as concealed, protected, and treasured as God's own people to be preserved against the planned extinction of them by their adversaries (Psalm 74:8; Esther 3:6; Jer. 48:2), who have determined that **the name of Israel may be no more in remembrance** (Psalm 41:5). **5.** To this end **they have consulted** (conspired) **together with one consent** (mind; 2:2; Dan. 6:7; cf. Rev. 19:19). **They are confederate against thee** ("they have cut [or made] a covenant [or treaty] against thee"), in contrast to the LORD's people, who "have made [cut] a covenant" with the LORD "by sacrifice" (Psalm 50:5).

6-8. The enemy nations are listed. **The tabernacles** (tents) is a poetic designation for the whole nation (78:51; 120:5).

The foes enumerated were the semi-nomadic peoples whose petty kingdoms were located along the east side of the Dead Sea and southward and northward east of the Jordan; they included Edom, Moab, Ammon, and Amalek, as well as the Hagarites and Ishmaelites, who lived still farther east.

Gebal is probably not an Edomite clan, but the well-known Phoenician coastal town north of Sidon, while the Philistines and Tyrians represented nations located along the southwest and remote northwest areas of the Mediterranean coast. Assyria is listed last since it was the most remote and it engaged only indirectly in the confederacy. All the nations (not merely Assyria) had **helped**, literally, lent an arm of help to, **the children of Lot**, Moab and Ammon (Gen. 19:36-38), the prime movers in the coalition.

An Appeal to History. 83:9-12. **9-11.** Two astonishing deliverances by God's unmistakable intervention are cited: (1) the invasion of the Midianites (Judg. 6:1—8:35; 7:22) and (2) Sisera's attack and the enemy's debacle at the torrent of Kishon (4:22-23), including those destroyed at Endor, and their fleeing kings, **Oreb** and **Zeeb** (7:25), and **Zebah** and **Zalmunna** (8:21), put to death by Gideon. **12.** Boldly, then, Midianites declared, "Let us possess for ourselves the pastures of God" (NASB; 2 Chron. 20:11; Psalm 132:13).

Imprecatory Prayer. 83:13-18. This is a prayer inspired by God for the extinction of the foe, because his iniquity is filled up and the divine wrath must be outpoured. (See Psalm 5:10 for a discussion of imprecatory prayer.) **13.** God is besought to **make them like a wheel**, "a thing whirled round," "a tumbleweed" (AB), "the whirling dust" (NASB; Isa. 17:13). **Like the stubble** (chaff) **before the wind** (Exod. 15:7; Job 13:25; Psalms 1:4;

35:5; Isa. 40:24; Matt. 3:21). **14. As . . . fire burneth a forest** (Isa. 9:18), as the flame that sets the mountain on fire (Exod. 19:18; Deut. 32:22).

15-16. So the psalmist (who personates the godly remnant of the nation) called on his God to **persecute** (pursue) these enemies **with** His **tempest** and **make them afraid** (terrify them) **with** His **storm** (Job 9:17; Psalm 58:9), filling their faces with **shame** (109:29; 132:18; Job 10:15) that they might seek the LORD's name.

17. He implored that they might be **confounded** (ashamed), **troubled** (dismayed), humiliated, and perish perpetually so they might realize that God the LORD is the Most High ('*ĕlyôn*), His millennial name as "possessor of heaven and earth" (Gen. 14:18-19). **18.** In the Kingdom to be set up when the Most High's final enemies—toward which this psalm points prophetically—are put down, He will indeed be **the Most High over all the earth** as He takes possession of it (Psalm 2:4-12; Rev. 19:11-15).

L. THE BLESSEDNESS OF TRUE WORSHIP. 84:1-12.

The last six psalms of the Leviticus section of the Psalter (Psalms 84-89), ascribed to different authors, prophetically reveal the future blessing awaiting Israel at the Messiah's return in glory. The psalm is entitled, "To the chief Musician [precentor] upon Gittith" (see comment on the title of Psalm 8) and ascribed to (or perhaps "for") the Korahites, the posterity of the notorious rebel (Num. 16:1-50), whose descendants were shown great grace. They existed in David's time as an influential family of celebrated musicians and singers (1 Chron. 6:16-33) and guardians of the Tabernacle-Temple doors (cf. v. 10 with 1 Chron. 26:1-19).

The Blessedness of Vitalized Worship of God. 84:1-4. Note five things about the psalmist's worship: (1) **1.** The psalmist appreciated the beauty of God's house, the place of public worship. **How amiable** (*yādîḏ*, from *ydd*, Arab., *wadda*, "love," hence, "lovely, pleasant") **are thy tabernacles** (43:3; 132:5), that is, "your dwelling" (AB), plural in poetic form but singular in meaning, in line with Canaanite poetical parallels (M. Dahood, AB). The beauty of God's dwelling should not only be a material beauty but also a reflected glory, a borrowed glow from the splendor of Him who is worshiped there (27:4; 29:2; 90:17).

(2) **2.** The psalmist acknowledged that the essence of this beauty is the vision of the living God, for whom he yearned. **My soul longeth** (*niḵsᵉpâ*, lit., "is made pale like silver"; Arab., *kasapa*, "be pale," from intense longing; "pine for"; Gen. 31:30) . . . **fainteth** (*kālᵉṯâ*, "is exhausted, spent, come to the end of one's strength by longing") **for the courts of the Lord** (Psalms 42:2; 63:1). **My heart** (the inner man) and **my flesh** (the outer man) **cry out** piercingly (*rānăn*, "give a ringing cry," especially singing in joyful, ecstatic praise to God, 42:2; Jer. 31:12) **for the living God** (Deut. 5:26; Josh. 3:10; 1 Sam. 17:26; Heb. 3:12; 9:14; 10:31).

(3) **3.** He spontaneously gave evidence of the deep spirituality of his worship by envying the birds that had nested under the eaves of God's house, which he poetically called God's **altars** (Psalm 43:4). (4) He further gave evidence to his vitalized worship by the titles with which he addressed God—**The Lord of hosts** (cf. v. 1), the LORD (v. 2), "the living God" (v. 2), **my King** (v. 3) and **my God** (v. 3), the title "my King" looking toward the Kingdom age, when true spirituality, such as is reflected here,

will cover the earth (Isa. 11:9). (5) **4.** The psalmist's worship of "the living God" called forth praiseful consecration to God. How **blessed** are they who ever dwell in His house and sing God's praise near His altars (prophetically, Ezekiel's millennial Temple, Isa. 2:2-3; Ezek. 40:1—46:24).

The Blessedness of Vitalized Faith in God. 84:5-7. **5-6.** The psalmist declared that full joy comes only from heartfelt faith in God. **Blessed is the man** (*'ādām*) who realizes he is but a creature of the dust (Gen. 2:7) and **whose strength is in** God (Psalm 81:1) **in whose heart are the ways** of the LORD (perhaps "the highways to Zion," NASB). The picture is of a pilgrimage to the Temple at Jerusalem (vv. 6-7), passing on the way through **the valley** (23:4) **of Baca** ("weeping or balsam trees"), prefiguring some experience of deep sadness transformed by faith in God into **a well** ("spring, place of springs" or spiritual refreshment). **The rain** (the early or autumn showers) **also filleth the pools** (*berākôt*; Joel 2:23).

7. Vitalized faith assures sustained progress in any undertaking for God. Here the pilgrim band, on its way to worship in Zion, found itself going from **strength to strength,** getting larger and stronger as the result of new recruits as it journeyed on (Prov. 4:18; Isa. 40:31; John 1:16; 2 Cor. 3:18). Every pilgrim who started out **appeareth before God** in Zion (Exod. 34:23; Deut. 16:16; Psalm 42:2).

Blessedness of Vitalized Prayer and Service for God. 84:8-12. **8-9.** Vitalized worship and faith are linked with vitalized prayer (v. 1) and service (vv. 9-12). In prayer the plea is made on the grounds of covenant grace with the **God of Jacob,** who is His people's **shield** (Gen. 15:1; Deut. 33:29; Psalms 3:3; 28:7), the Hebrew word for "shield" standing first for emphasis, showing that all our hope of being protected from the foe rests in God. **And look upon the face of thine anointed** (2:2; 1 Sam. 16:6; 2 Sam. 19:21), prophetically encompassing the Kingdom age when God, looking upon the face of His anointed King (Psalms 2:2; 132:10), will in a particularly special sense be Israel's shield.

10. The psalmist declared the worthwhileness of service for God—a day in His house **is better than a thousand** spent elsewhere (27:4). **I had rather be a doorkeeper** (stand at the threshold of) **in the house of my God** (1 Chron. 23:5), **than to dwell in the tents of wickedness.** No matter how gorgeous or alluring, they are only impermanent "pavilions" in contrast to the permanency of God's "house," hinting at how emphemeral are the pleasures of the wicked.

11. The psalmist was thoroughly persuaded of the reward that comes from service to God. He is **a sun** to warm and invigorate, the Source of all life and energy (Isa. 60:19-20; Mal. 4:2; Rev. 21:23), and a **shield** to protect (v. 9). He will **give grace**—"grace" now, "glory" hereafter (Col. 3:3-4). **No good thing will he withhold from** those who **walk** (who go on walking, present participle, denoting continuous action) **uprightly** (*bătāmîm*, "in integrity, truth"). **12.** This verse is a summary in the form of a benediction. **Blessed** (oh the blessednesses, i.e., happy experiences) of the man (*'ādām*, "man of clay") who **trusteth** (*bth*, "reposes himself on") Another (Psalms 2:12; 40:4).

M. FAITH APPROPRIATES PROMISED BLESSINGS. 85:1-13.

For the scope of Psalm 85, see the introduction to Psalm 84.

Israel's Final Deliverance Anticipated. 85:1-3. Faith envisions the blessings accruing to Israel in this another "Psalm for [of] the sons of

Korah'' (cf. Psalms 42-48, 84, 85, 87, 88). Although other deliverances are not excluded, the psalm being designed for every time when by disobedience Israel forfeited the peace and prosperity promised for loyalty (Lev. 26:3-13), the final deliverance comes into prophetic focus, as the vast scope of verses 10 to 13 shows, as well as by the close resemblance of verse 4 to Psalm 80:3, 7, 19, where Israel's final restoration appears in clear perspective.

Faith's vision, springing from confidence in God's promises, includes four things: (1) **1a.** It includes favor to the land (77:7; 106:4; Isa. 35:1-2; Ezek. 36:9-10; Amos 9:13-15; Matt. 24:32-33). (2) **1b.** It includes blessing to the people Israel (Jacob). **Thou hast brought back the captivity of Jacob** ("reversed his state of distress"; Psalms 14:7; 126:1; Ezra 1:11; Jer. 30:18; Ezek. 39:25; Hos. 6:11; Joel 3:1; Matt. 24:31).

(3) **2.** It includes cleansing of Israel. **Thou hast forgiven** (Psalms 78:38; 103:3; Num. 14:19; Jer. 31:34) **the iniquity of thy people** (Zech. 12:10—13:1) ... **covered all their sin** (*nāśā'*, "hide from God through the atonement of Christ"; Gen. 3:15, 21). (4) **3.** It includes removal of all divine wrath (Exod. 32:12; Deut. 13:17; Jonah 3:9). **Thou hast turned thyself from the fierceness of thine anger** (displayed in Rev. 6:1—19:21; cf. Exod. 32:12).

Prayer Based upon Anticipated Deliverance. 85:4-7. **4.** It is precisely because of faith's appropriation of the promised deliverance (vv. 1-3), as if it has already been realized, that it is incited to pray more intensely for that which the spirit of prophecy in the psalmist reveals as an already accomplished fact. Present distress is faced in assured faith of future deliverance, with the present temporary national setting

aside (Rom. 11:1-25) and worldwide dispersion coming into view.

5. Wilt thou be angry ... forever? (Psalms 74:1; 79:5; 80:4; Zech. 2:6; cf. Rom. 11:25-32; Rev. 20:4-6). **Wilt thou draw out thine anger to all generations?** (Isa. 12:1). **6.** The psalmist pleaded for the national and spiritual revival of Israel (Psalms 71:20; 80:18; Hos. 6:2; 14:7; Matt. 24:32-33; cf. Ezek. 37:1-28), that God's people, Israel, may rejoice in the LORD (Psalms 33:1; 90:14; 149:2; Isa. 12:1-6; 35:10; 65:19). **7.** This will happen when God shows His lovingkindness to Israel and grants her His salvation (Psalm 106:4; Zech. 12:10—13:1; Rom. 11:25-32; Rev. 19:11—20:4).

God's Answer of Peace. 85:8-13. The divine reply comprehends Kingdom conditions, which include eight things: (1) **8a.** They include universal peace. The Messiah **will speak peace** (29:11; Hag. 2:9; Zech. 9:10), for He will then be in full manifestation as the Prince of Peace (Isa. 9:6-7; Mic. 5:5). He will "speak peace" to **his people ... his saints** (godly ones), but death and destruction to His foes (Rev. 19:15), for only by the war to end all war can peace be established in His Kingdom.

(2) **8b.** He will rule with inflexible justice (Psalm 2:9-10; Rev. 19:15), so let His people **not turn again to folly** (Psalm 78:57; 2 Pet. 2:21). (3) **9a.** He will reveal His great salvation in delivering His own (Psalm 34:18; Isa. 46:13; Rev. 19:11 — 20:4). (4) **9b.** Glory will dwell in Israel's land (Psalm 84:11; Hag. 2:7; Zech. 2:5).

(5) **10. Mercy and truth** will meet in perfect accord in the millennial Kingdom (Psalms 25:10; 89:14; Prov. 3:3), and **righteousness and peace** will kiss each other in perfect harmony (Psalm 72:3; Isa. 32:17). (6) **11. Truth** will spring

from the earth (Isa. 45:8) and righteousness look down from heaven.

(7) **12.** The LORD will dispense what is good (Psalm 84:11; James 1:17), and Israel's land (as well as all the earth) will yield prolifically (Lev. 26:4; Ezek. 34:27; Zech. 8:12; cf. Isa. 35:1-3; Amos 9:13-15). (8) **13.** Righteousness will go before the Messiah and make His footsteps into a way of life and blessing in the Kingdom age (Psalm 89:14).

N. PRAYER OF A TRUE SERVANT OF GOD. 86:1-17.

This is a prayer of David and the antitypical David and of every true servant of God in time of trouble and persecution, especially of the Jewish remnant in their supreme time of Tribulation before Kingdom blessing (v. 9). For the scope and context, see the introduction to Psalm 84.

God's Grace Is the Ground of Expecting Deliverance. 86:1-5. **1. Bow down** (incline) **thine ear ... hear me; for I am poor** (afflicted) **and needy** (17:6; 31:2; 71:2). Human need has a ready claim on God's mercy (40:17; 70:5). **2. Preserve my soul** (i.e., "me"; my life) **for I am holy** (*ḥāsîd*, "godly," "a godly or pious person"; 4:3; 50:5); **save** (deliver) **thy servant**—in the fullest sense applicable only to the antitypical David, "the Holy One of God" (Mark 1:24; cf. Psalm 16:10; Acts 2:27), the LORD's Servant, faultlessly holy in His humanity, constantly trusting the Father.

3-4. The earnest prayers are here answering to His "strong crying and tears unto him that was able to save him from death" (Heb. 5:7). Three times in three verses (vv. 2-4) He speaks of His soul—"preserve my soul," **rejoice** (my) **soul...unto thee, O Lord, do I lift up my soul. 5.** God's character is the basis of his prayer, for God is **good** (Psalm 25:8), **ready to forgive** (130:4), and **plenteous**

(abundant) **in mercy** (Exod. 34:6; Neh. 9:17; Psalm 103:8; Joel 2:13; Jonah 4:2).

God's Omnipotence to Help. 86:6-10. **6-7.** Though all-powerful, God hears prayer (55:1) in the day of trouble and distress (50:15; 77:2). **8a.** He is incomparable in His person among spirits (gods), because He is the Creator of all and, hence, uncreated Spirit (Exod. 15:11; 2 Sam. 7:22; 1 Kings 8:23; Psalm 89:6; Jer. 10:6). **8b.** He is incomparable in His works, both creative and redemptive (Deut. 3:24). **9.** Hence, **all nations whom** He has made **shall come and worship before** Him (Psalm 22:27; Isa. 66:23; Rev. 15:4) as a result of His creative and redemptive works, at last realizing in the Kingdom age that their idol-gods are false (Zeph. 2:11; Zech. 14:9; cf. Psalm 20:7-8).

10. For thou art great (77:13), **and doest wondrous things** (Exod. 15:11) in creation and redemption—**thou art God alone** (Deut. 6:4; 32:39; Isa. 37:16; Mark 12:29; 1 Cor. 8:4). God's miraculous deeds in the end time, especially the wonders He will perform in behalf of Israel against the Antichrist and his hordes (Psalm 2:1-12; Rev. 6:1—19:21; cf. Psalm 72:18-19), will so advertise God's greatness that they will be like a hammer to break the rock of the hearts of the millennial nations (Psalm 2:9-12).

Praiseful Prayer for Deliverance from Death. 86:11-13. **11.** David's petitions—**Teach me** (25:5) ... **unite my heart to fear thy name**—transcended his experiences and anticipate the antitypical David, as the Servant of the LORD. He prayed that reverence for God's name, already in his heart, might so fill and control him as to unite him wholly to the LORD in obedience and reverential love (Psalm 40:7-8; Mark 14:36). "Make my will one with thine, that I may not have a heart divided between fearing and loving Thee and the fear and love of the world."

12-13. Great is thy mercy toward me; and thou hast delivered my soul (me) **from the lowest sheol** (the depths of the nether world; 16:9), the unseen realm of disembodied spirits. Prophetically echoed is the Messiah's praise to the Father for having raised His body from the grave and His soul from hades, the great redemptive work that makes possible the vast millennial prophecy of verse 9, and for which all saints will magnify and **glorify** God's name forever.

Special Prayer for Deliverance from Assailants. 86:14-17. **14.** The immediate occasion was probably Absalom's revolt, but the petitions apply to the sufferings of saints in any age, especially the remnant of God's servants during the Great Tribulation, when the **proud** will rise up against them (2 Thess. 2:4; Rev. 13:1-18; 16:13-16), and violent godless men (Psalm 2:1-3; Rev. 9:20-21) will seek to destroy the righteous.

15-16. But God, merciful and gracious, will interpose on behalf of His own, as He did in behalf of His suffering Son (Psalms 25:16; 68:35; 116:16; Zech. 12:3-8; 14:3; Rom. 6:4; Phil. 2:9-11). **17.** He will show His own **a** (supernatural) **sign** for good (Judg. 6:17; Psalm 119:122) that those who hate God's people may see it and be ashamed (112:10; cf. Rev. 6:1—19:21) because the LORD has helped and comforted His people with glorious deliverance.

O. JERUSALEM'S KINGDOM
EXALTATION. 87:1-7.

See the introduction to Psalm 84 for the scope and context of Psalm 87. This Korahite-Elohim psalm is akin to Psalm 46 (another Korahite-Elohim ode). The historical occasion was possibly Jerusalem's escape from Sennacherib under Hezekiah, when Babylon and Egypt (Rahab; 89:10; Isa. 30:7; 51:9) were in power. Zion alone escaped and was accorded the favor above other cities of Judah (v. 2; cf. Isa. 37:38). But the historical setting prophetically anticipates a far grander and wider role for Zion.

The Glory of Zion. 87:1-3. Zion is a poetical name of Jerusalem, originally the hill on which a Jebusite fortress stood. The glory of the city consists of three things: (1) **1.** It is the "city of God" (v. 3), founded by God. **His** (God's) **foundation is in the holy mountains** (78:69; Isa. 28:16), established when it was selected as the seat of the sanctuary, its true foundation.

Zion, being part of a mountain range, is therefore described in the plural "mountains," which are called "holy" because God's sanctuary lent holiness to the city, and the "holy city" (Matt. 27:53; cf. Psalm 2:6) to the whole range. In turn, the sanctity of the mountains indicates their inviolable security, as long as the people did not forfeit God's presence by infidelity (68:16).

(2) **2.** It is the special object of divine love. **The Lord loveth the gates of Zion more than all the** (other) **dwellings of Jacob** (78:68-69; Isa. 28:16), the gates being taken as a part for the whole, since they were attacked first by an enemy, and their security was the badge of the city's safety.

(3) **3.** It is the special subject of history and prophecy. **Glorious things are spoken of thee, O city of God**—by God and man, by Israel and the nations (cf. Psalms 46 and 48), the grounds of her glory being that she was "the city of God" (46:4; 48:8). When that glory left, Ichabod ("the glory has departed") was her state (Luke 21:24), the sad testimony of history (Rom. 11:1-25). But her restoration is certain and glorious (Isa. 2:2-3; 54:11, 14; 60:1-22; Jer. 50:5;

Zech. 2:10-11; 8:21-23; 14:16-21; Rom. 11:26-35).

The Spiritual Birthplace of the Nations. 87:4-7. Zion (in the Kingdom age) will become a mother in which nations will be born. **4a. I will make mention of Rahab and Babylon** "among those" (NASB; i.e., personification "as persons") who **know me.** God, who is the Speaker, declares that He counts Rahab (Egypt; 89:10; Isa. 51:9), a symbol of human pride, and Babylon ("confusion") as His true worshipers, their pride and confusion to come to an end when Zion's Kingdom glory is realized, and these nations have become saved and are walking in the light of the LORD (Isa. 2:2-3; Zech. 2:11; 8:22; 14:19).

4b. Philistia, Israel's inveterate foe; Tyre (Psalm 45:12), rich and arrogant; and Ethiopia (Cush, "far off"), will then with other nations experience spiritual and national rebirth and "stretch out [their] hands unto God" (68:31). **4c. This man** (*zĕh*, "this one," with a depreciating tone) **was born there.**

5. But of Zion (emphatic) it shall be said, **This** (man, *'ish*) **and that man** (*'îsh*) **were born in her,** suggesting people of note and influence, consonant with the importance of Zion as the mother city of regenerated mankind and the capital of the earth in the Kingdom age (Isa. 2:2; Mic. 4:1-3). Moreover, Zion's primacy is also indicated by the fact that **the Most High Himself** (NASB) in His millennial role as the actual "possessor of heaven and earth" (Gen. 14:18-19; Josh. 3:13; Zech. 4:14; Rev. 11:4) **shall establish her** (Psalm 48:8).

6. The Lord shall count (22:30; 87:6), **when he writeth up** (registers) **the people** (69:28; Isa. 4:3), **that this man was born there.** God keeps a record (Psalms 56:8; 139:16) of all those whose spiritual birthplace is Zion (Gal. 3:26), whose

greatness is not temporary like other cities.

7. Singers and dancers, expressing joyous Israelite worship (Exod. 15:20; 2 Sam. 6:16; Psalms 30:11; 149:3; 150:4), will greet Zion, the source of spiritual life, rejoicing in her as the fountain of salvation and life (Isa. 12:3; Ezek. 47:1-12; Joel 3:18; Zech. 14:8; Rev. 22:1-2).

P. THE CRY OF AN AFFLICTED SAINT. 88:1-18.

For the context, see the introductions to Psalms 84 and 73. The title of this psalm, "A Song or Psalm for the sons of Korah... upon Mahalath Leannoth ['concerning the sickness of affliction']" apparently belongs also to Psalm 89, since the term *song* embraces joy, of which there is none in Psalm 88 (but cf. 89:1 and the joyous vein of that ode). The "Maschil" ("instruction"; cf. titles of Psalms 53, 54, and 55) is that mourners should pour out their griefs before God. Heman the Ezrahite (son of Zerah, 1 Chron. 2:6) and Ethan the Ezrahite were musicians in David's time into whose mouths the sons of Korah put their compositions (6:31-33, 44; 25:5). The psalmist's affliction is prophetic of the sufferings of the supreme Sufferer, the Messiah, and reflects the suffering saints of all ages, particularly the intense anguish of the saints of the Tribulation period (Jer. 30:5-7; Dan. 12:1; Matt. 24:21-22).

His Prayer. 88:1-2. **1a.** In his unrelieved anguish the sufferer demonstrated his faith by his direct plea to the **Lord God of** (his) **salvation** (24:5; 27:9). **1b-2.** His cry was persistent and continuous (22:2; 86:3; Luke 18:7), and he pleaded for a hearing (Psalms 18:6; 31:2; 86:1), as will the persecuted saints of the Tribulation (Luke 18:7).

His Terrible Sufferings unto Death.

88:3-9. **3.** The troubles of the sufferer were so numerous and serious that they clearly transcended those of any mere human sufferer and look forward to the afflictions of the divine-human Redeemer to come. **4-5a.** He was as good as dead—nothing was left him but the **pit** (another name for Sheol, the disembodied state between death and the resurrection; cf. v. 6) and **the grave** (where the body is laid). But this dark portrayal of Sheol and the grave is no scene for declaring God's praises.

5b-7a. God's honor was involved in deliverance from this pitiable state of being **cut off from** (God's) **hand** (31:22; Isa. 53:8), with His wrath (Psalm 22:1; Matt. 27:46) resting upon the Sufferer (Psalm 37:4; Isa. 53:4; 2 Cor. 5:21).

7b-8. He was afflicted with all God's waves of trouble (Psalm 42:7; Matt. 26:39, 42), with His **acquaintances** put far away from Him. He was delivered by His brothers; in His betrayal and crucifixion He was forsaken by His disciples (John 1:11; 7:5; 16:32); He was made an object of loathing to the world of sinners (Job 30:10); and He was **shut up** as a prisoner of God the Father for man's imputed sin, to suffering, abandonment, and death, so that there was no escape for Him consistent with man's salvation. **9.** His eye **mourneth** (wasted) **by reason of affliction** (Psalms 6:7; 31:9), and so his prayer was ceaseless (22:2; 86:3) and importunate (143:6; Job 11:13; Isa. 1:15).

His Appeal to God's Regard for His Own Honor. 88:10-12. **10.** This question is involved in delivering the suppliant: **Wilt thou show wonders to the dead? Shall the dead** (*r^epāim*, "ghosts, departed spirits, shades") **arise and praise thee?** (6:5; 30:9). **11-12.** Death is viewed in its unmitigated terrors totally apart from divine redemptive grace, and what it was to the Redeemer's soul. The dead (departed spirits) have not the requisite powers (apart from the resurrected body) to praise God; as for this passage being an argument against the resurrection, it is actually the Messiah's own powerful plea in defense of its necessity and the display of divine miraculous power ("wonders," v. 10; Rom. 6:4; Eph. 1:19-20) in effecting it.

His Sufferings Viewed as Unrelieved. 88:13-18. **13.** Prayer was followed by deep lamentation, which at first glance seems to express pain without consolation. But in reality unwavering faith and deep submission are underlying the anguish experienced, which reposes the issue with God in earnest, continuous prayer for help (30:2) to **come before** God, as if to surprise and anticipate Him **in the morning** (5:3; 57:8; Mark 1:35).

14. This verse anticipated the Messiah's cry on the cross (Psalm 22:1). Why did the LORD cast Him off and hide His face from Him? Because the penalty for our sins was not yet fully paid, and the time of the Sufferer's deliverance had not yet arrived.

15a. He declared, **I am afflicted and ready** (about to) **die from my youth up.** So the Messiah, born in a stable, was threatened by Herod's hate, and throughout His life was "a man of sorrows, and acquainted with grief" (Isa. 53:3). **15b. While I suffer thy terrors** ("horrors of stupefaction," Gesenius), the unfathomable agony of taking the sin of the whole world upon Himself and the Father's turning away His face from Him (Psalm 22:1; Matt. 27:46; 2 Cor. 5:21), **I am distracted** (overwhelmed) in His anguish (AB renders it: "I suffer the terrors of your [torture] wheel"; cf. Prov. 20:26).

16a. God's fierce wrath (burning anger) overwhelmed Him (2 Chron. 28:11; Isa. 13:13; Lam. 1:12), as the Messiah became the Lamb of God offered on the altar to bear away the sin of the world (John 1:29; Isa. 53:5; 1 Pet. 1:18-19). **16b. Thy terrors have cut me off** so utterly and completely (the Hebrew verb is reduplicated for emphasis) who am Thy property, that there can be no redemption of it, unless Thou dost speedily interpose (i.e., by raising my body from the dead).

17. God's terrors are pictured surrounding the Sufferer all day long like water, with **lover and friend** (companion) put from Him and His **acquaintances into darkness** (lit., "darkness"), that is, instead of an acquaintance, there was only gloomy blankness, the darkness of Sheol. Although this psalm ends on a rare negative note, it really does not end, but continues on in Psalm 89 (see title of Psalm 88), presuming the glorious fact of the resurrection of the Sufferer, the grounds of "the mercies of the LORD" (89:1) and the fulfillment of the Davidic Covenant outlined in Psalm 89.

Q. GOD'S FAITHFULNESS AND THE DAVIDIC COVENANT. 89:1-52.

For the scope and context of Psalm 89, see the introductions to Psalms 73 and 84. On the title, see the title of Psalm 88. It is a "Maschil" ("instruction"), inculcating faith in God's faithfulness to His covenants and promises. The occasion was the defeat and deposition of a king of the Davidic line (perhaps Jehoiachin, 2 Kings 24:8-17), which caused some to question God's fidelity of His promise to David (2 Sam. 7:8-16).

The Steadfast Love and Faithfulness of the Covenant Maker. 89:1-4. **1-2.** This short hymnic preface stresses the key words that recur throughout the psalm—God's steadfast *love* (*ḥěsěḏ*) and *faithfulness* ('*ĕmûnâ*, "steadfastness"). Love is rendered "mercies" and "mercy." **Mercy shall be built up** forever. Faithfulness occurs twice: **I will make known thy faithfulness to all generations** and **thy faithfulness shalt thou establish in the very heavens. 3-4.** Those attributes of God are placed in closest proximity to the LORD's declaration of His having **made a covenant** with David, His chosen **servant** (1 Kings 8:16; Psalm 132:11), that He would establish his **seed** (posterity) **forever** (2 Sam. 7:16) and **build up** (his) **throne forever** (Isa. 9:7; Luke 1:33; Rev. 22:1, 3).

Praise to the Incomparable Covenant-Maker. 89:5-14. **5a.** The heavens will praise His **wonders**, the central wonder being the incarnation (John 1:1-3, 14) of the virgin-born God-man and Redeemer, which resulted in His vicarious death and glorious physical resurrection (Rom. 6:4; Eph. 1:19-20).

5b-7. His **faithfulness** will be lauded in **the congregation of the saints** (holy ones; Psalm 149:1; Job 5:1), "the angels" of heaven (cf. Psalm 29:1-2; Deut. 33:2, NASB) attesting the fidelity of Him who is incomparably above them, inasmuch as the Creator is infinitely higher than the highest creature (v. 6) and worshiped and reverenced by them (v. 7).

The might and truth, or faithfulness, of the incomparable covenant-Maker are praised (vv. 8-14). **8-9.** His might is illustrated by His ruling the **raging** (swelling) **of the sea,** stilling its rising waves (Psalms 65:7; 107:29; Mark 4:39). **10a.** From the literal sea the psalmist passed to the figurative sea of the nations (Dan. 7:2-3), Rahab (Egypt) being **broken. . . in pieces** (Psalm 87:4; Isa. 30:7, NASB; 51:9), the first great world power to oppose the people of God, being reduced to corpselike helplessness at the Red Sea (*Yam sup*, "Sea of Reeds"; Exod. 14:28-30). **10b.** The LORD also scattered Israel's enemies with His mighty arm (Psalms 18:14; 68:1; 144:6).

11-13. As the all-powerful Creator, He possesses heaven and earth (Gen. 1:1; 1 Chron. 29:11; Psalm 96:5), the world and all it contains (24:1), the north and south. Tabor (Josh. 19:22; Judg. 4:6; Jer. 46:18) and Mount Hermon (Psalm 133:3; Deut. 3:8; Josh. 11:17; Song of Sol. 4:8) shout for joy at His powerful name and strong creative arm (Psalms 98:1; 118:16). **14.** The foundation of His throne is righteousness and justice (85:13; 97:2), and steadfast love and truth go before His face.

The Blessedness of Those Whose God Is This Incomparable Covenant-Maker. 89:15-18. **15.** Believers **know the joyful sound** of the trumpets at the great festivals (especially the first day of the seventh month, Lev. 23:24; and at the jubilee, 25:8-10) and who walk in the light of His **countenance** (Psalms 4:6; 44:3; 67:1; 80:3; 90:8). **16.** They rejoice in His name all the day (105:3) and in His righteousness are **exalted.**

17. He is **the glory of their strength** (28:8), and by His favor (*rāṣôn,* "grace, kindness") their **horn** (the symbol of their strength, taken from the figure of an animal whose strength is concentrated in its horn) **is exalted** (75:10; 92:10; 148:14). **18. For our shield** (a figurative name for our king) **belongs to the Lord, and our king to the Holy One of Israel** (NASB; 47:9; 71:22; 78:41).

The Incomparable Covenant-Maker's Promise to David. 89:19-37. The covenant with David, already mentioned briefly (vv. 3-4), is elaborated in detail (see 2 Sam. 7:8-17), especially as it will be realized in David's Son and Lord, the Lord Jesus Christ. **19.** This verse refers to the initial communication of the covenant in a **vision** through Nathan to David, called the Lord's **holy one** (*ḥāsîd,* "gracious, pious one"); 2

Sam. 7:17). Many manuscripts read "holy ones." In either case, whether the address is to "the holy ones," referring to the nation being "holy" by consecration to God (Exod. 19:6; Isa. 62:12), or to David, similarly holy by consecration and as representative of the nation, actually the Messiah, "the Holy One of God," is antitypically in view. He alone is holy in the fullest sense. And the **one who is mighty** and the **one chosen** (Psalm 78:70; 2 Sam. 17:10; 1 Kings 11:34) is likewise antitypically David's Lord.

20-26. Also, David typifies the Messiah in his anointing (v. 20; 1 Sam. 16:13); his establishment in the kingdom, v. 21; his conquest over his enemies (vv. 22-23; Psalm 125:3; 2 Sam. 7:9-10), the exaltation of his horn (power; v. 24; Psalm 132:17); his territorial expansion (v. 25; 72:8); and his trust in the Lord as his Father (v. 26; 2 Sam. 7:14; 1 Chron. 22:10; Jer. 3:19).

However, the type imperceptibly fades, and the antitype alone appears (vv. 27-29). Only Christ, the God-man, could be (1) **27a.** God's **first-born** (Psalm 2:7; Exod. 4:22; Col. 1:15, 18); (2) **27b. The highest of the kings of the earth** (NASB; Num. 24:7; Psalm 72:11), King par excellence and Lord par excellence (Rev. 19:16); (3) **28.** the Recipient of an eternal covenant based on divine loving-kindness and never-to-be-abrogated promises (Isa. 55:3); (4) **29a.** a posterity forever (Psalms 18:50; 89:4); (5) **29b.** a throne forever (Isa. 9:7; Jer. 33:17; Dan. 7:14; Rev. 22:1, 3), **as the days of heaven** (Deut. 11:21; Psalm 72:5).

30-32. These verses revert to King David and repeat the warning of 2 Samuel 7:14 concerning the chastening of sin in the Davidic dynasty. **33-37.** But the unconditional character and perpetuity of the covenant itself are stressed, guaranteed by the greater David (Psalm 72:5).

The Question of the Apparent Failure of the Covenant. 89:38-45. (For the occasion, see the introduction to the psalm.) The honor and power of God, extolled in verses 5 to 18, were reversed in the destruction God had wrought, the apparent abrogation of His promises, and the disgrace and shame that had befallen Israel (vv. 38-45). The psalmist also painted a deliberate parallel with the similar structure of verses 9 to 14.

38-43. The raging sea (v. 9) was replaced by anger toward the king (v. 38); the humiliation of "Rahab" by the degradation of the throne and the defiling of the crown (v. 39); the creation of the world (vv. 11-12) by the destruction of the Judean kingdom (vv. 40-41); the delivering right arm of God (vv. 13-16) by the destructive right hand of enemies (v. 42); the glory of their strength (vv. 17-18), now fighting for them only in pretense, His weapons being reversed and harmless (v. 43).

44-45. Instead of their king being their shield and representing the Holy One of Israel (v. 18), his splendor had ceased, his throne hurled to the ground, his physical life shortened, and he was **covered ... with shame.** Had God failed to keep His covenant promise to David?

Despite Appearances, Faith Becomes Vocal in Prayer. 89:46-51. The psalmist's plea was that the LORD would remember what He had sworn to David. **46-48.** The prayer assumed the form of a deliberate contrast, the thought of life's weakness and brevity standing in contrast to the strength and permanence of the promised Davidic dynasty (vv. 22-29), which ultimately would settle the vexing question of death and in doing so provide the ground for the fulfillment of the Davidic Covenant (i.e., the death and resurrection of Christ; cf. 22:22, 29; 49:9, 15).

49. The psalm concludes with the

question **Where are Thy former lovingkindnesses, O Lord, which Thou didst swear to David in Thy faithfulness?** (NASB; Jer. 30:9; Ezek. 34:23). **50-52. Remember ... the reproach of thy servants** (Psalms 69:9; 74:18, 22). As he thus summarized God's promises, he shaped them into prayers. All the while his faith was telling him that the adverse events of history do not present the last word, for that will be given in due time by God. His faithfulness and truth, now seemingly called into question, will still be triumphantly vindicated.

IV. BOOK FOUR: THE NUMBERS SECTION. 90:1—106:48.

This section of the Psalter corresponds to the book of Numbers. It opens with the only psalm attributed to "Moses, the man of God" (Deut. 33:1) and dealing with people dying on every hand because of unbelief, reflecting the situation in the wilderness wandering. The last two psalms (105-6) reflect this background also, which serves as the backdrop for numerous millennial psalms that relate to the glory of Israel when her wilderness experiences will come to an end and the Davidic Kingdom is set up.

A. GOD'S GREATNESS AND MAN'S FRAILTY. 90:1-17.

Moses' Meditation on God's Greatness. 90:1-6. God is great because of three things: (1) **1.** God is great because He is the home of man's soul. **Lord, thou hast been our dwelling place** ($m\bar{a}\hat{o}n$, "abode, home"), literally, "a house for us in all generations" (cf. Deut. 33:27; Psalms 71:3; 91:9), the counterpoise to our transitory life. How appropriate was the image of a fixed habitation to the Israelites in their homeless condition in the wilderness. God alone furnishes the home that man's soul so desperately needs. In Him alone can the soul find the rest, security, and permanence it craves.

(2) **2.** God is great because He is the eternal One, the Creator of all. **Before the mountains were brought forth ... from everlasting to everlasting, thou art God** (93:2; 102:24; Jer. 10:10). He existed before the universe; He created the world; He is eternal (Gen. 1:1; John 1:1-3; Col. 1:16-17; Rev. 1:8).

(3) **3-4.** God is great because He has absolute control over man's life. He controls the length of it. **Thou turnest man to destruction** (*dăkkā'*, "something crushed or pulverized, dust"), an evident allusion to Genesis 3:19: "Unto dust [*'āpār*] shalt thou return," as the reference to man's return to his original state shows: **Return, ye children of men** (Psalms 103:14; 104:29; Eccles. 12:7). How short is human life in the sight of God, to whom **a thousand years...are but as yesterday** (2 Pet. 3:8)...**as a watch in the night** (Exod. 14:24; Judg. 7:19). The first watch was from sunset to 10:00 P.M., the second from 10:00 P.M. till 2:00 A.M., the third from 2:00 A.M. till sunrise.

5-6. God sweeps away man's life with the suddenness of a flash flood that transforms a dry wadi into a raging torrent (Job 22:16; 27:20). "They become [or 'are' as] a sleep" (lit. Heb.; Job 14:12; 20:8; Psalm 76:5), **like grass which groweth up** (103:15; Isa. 40:6) and flourishes in the morning (Job 14:2) and by evening fades (Psalm 92:7; Matt. 6:30; James 1:11).

Moses' Meditation on Man's Frailty. 90:7-11. Man is frail because of three things: (1) **7.** Man is frail because he is a sinner under divine displeasure. He is **consumed by** (God's) **anger** (39:11), **troubled** by His **wrath.** The generation in the wilderness (except Caleb and

Joshua) died because of unbelief (Num. 11:31-35), ingratitude (16:41-50), and rebellion (21:4-6).

"Moses saw men dying all around him; he lived among funerals and was overwhelmed with the terrible results of the divine displeasure" (C. H. Spurgeon, *Treasury of David*). The sad fact of man's hastening mortality is traceable to its sadder cause in man's sin (Gen. 2:17; Rom. 5:12), even redeemed men facing death, but not eternal death—God's eternal wrath (1:18).

(2) Man is frail because he is subject to mental and physical sufferings and death (vv. 8-10). **8.** So far from the infinitely holy God overlooking sin, He has **set** (placed) **our iniquities** before Him (Psalm 50:21; Jer. 16:17) and set **our secret sins in the light of** (His) **presence** (NASB; Psalm 19:12; Eccles. 12:14). His infinite holiness searches out "our secret sin" (the singular is better supported textually than the plural "sins").

So deep-rooted is man's corruption that there are depths of sin in the human heart fathomed by God alone. Even the holiest and saintliest believer can only plead God's redemptive grace to be accepted in the light of His infinitely holy presence. Sin in the unbeliever entails eternal death (everlasting separation from God), with degrees of punishment in eternal hell according to his deeds and response to the eternal moral Law of God (Rom. 2:6; Rev. 20:6-7). Likewise, the believer, saved by grace alone through faith in redemptive grace, will suffer chastening in this life and loss of reward in heaven through sin and failure (1 Cor. 3:11-16; 2 Cor. 5:10).

9. The ungrateful and rebellious people of God, who were chastened in the wilderness to the point of premature physical death (1 Cor. 5:5; 11:30-32; 1 John 5:16), are described. Their days declined under God's anger (Psalm

78:33), and they finished their earthly career **as a tale**, rather, "a meditation" (*hĕgĕh*, "sigh," or "a half-uttered thought").

10. The days of our years (i.e., our life-span) **are threescore years and ten; and if, by reason of strength** (due to an unusually strong constitution), **they be fourscore years, yet is their strength** (*rāhāḇ*, "pride, boasting"), better rendered, "yet is their matter of pride [boasting] labor and vanity" (Eccles. 12:2-7; Jer. 20:18). This extended span of life is soon **cut off** (from *gzz*, "shear") like grass mown, or "it passes on" (from *gûz*, "pass by") and we **fly away** (Job 20:8; Psalm 78:39).

(3) **11.** Man is frail because he cannot comprehend the terribleness of the divine displeasure against sin. **Who knoweth the power of thine anger** (Psalm 76:7). **. . according to thy fear** (i.e., "the fear due Thee"; Neh. 5:9). "Thy awesomeness according to Thy indignation" (BV). This is a sad lament over man's slowness to perceive that in his brief and frail state lies the expression of God's just displeasure against his sin and its seriousness. How ready fallen man is to defend himself—his works, his morality, his own goodness! Only those who begin to revere God start to comprehend the seriousness of sin and their own helpless sinfulness apart from divine grace.

Moses' Supplication for God's Interposition in Behalf of Frail, Sinful Man. 90:12-17. (1) **12.** Moses implored God's aid to form a correct estimate of life. **So teach us to number** (*mānâ*, "count") **our days**, to reckon each one of them as a precious gift from the LORD to make us know the power of God's anger, as caused by our sin and manifested in our short-lived and frail existence.

The literal rendering is "to number our days, *so* teach us," that is, "*in this*

manner teach us, give us this kind of instruction" (J. J. S. Perowne). The "so" (*kēn*) stresses the infinite importance of this knowledge, which is to be learned only from God, not by natural ability. The purpose of this is **that we may apply our hearts unto wisdom**, literally, "cause to come [come by] a heart of wisdom" that discerns the brevity of life and our sin as the cause of God's anger against us (cf. Deut. 32:19), and so that, fearing God, we depart from evil (Deut. 4:6; Job 28:28).

(2) Moses pleaded for the manifestation of God's mercy (vv. 13-17). **13-15.** Only through divine redemptive grace (prefigured in Israel's priesthood and sacrificial system) can man's sinful frailty be overcome and his hopeless misery and dissatisfactions be transformed into joy and glad satisfaction with the removal of the divine anger and resulting chastisement (Heb. 12:11; cf. Isa. 61:7).

16. To this end Moses prayed that God's **work** of redemption (Deut. 32:4; Psalms 44:1; 77:12; 92:4) in bringing Israel out of Egypt and the wilderness into the land, typical of all redemption, might **appear** (be manifested) to His servants, and His redemptive **glory** to their posterity (1 Kings 8:11; Isa. 6:3), in which role the divine "majesty" appears most splendidly.

17. Only through redemptive grace can **the beauty** (*nō'ăm*, "favor, pleasantness, loveliness," from *n'm*, "be gracious or lovely") **of the Lord our God be upon us** (Psalm 27:4) and can the LORD **establish** (give permanence to) **the work of our hands** (Isa. 26:12; 2 Thess. 2:16-17; 3:3). **Yea, the work of our hands establish thou it.** How touching is Moses' case. He was to die without seeing the results of his great life's work. Yet God established it after his death. "The work of our hands" through grace becomes the work of His hands, which He is bound to accomplish, so that eternity, not time, becomes the real gauge of our life's work.

B. THE REDEEMED MAN'S SECURITY. 91:1-16.

Psalm 90 portrays man's fallen, lost estate in Adam, while Psalm 91 pictures redeemed man secure in fellowship with God and reflecting His Redeemer, the second Adam, our Lord from heaven.

The Basis of the Believer's Security. 91:1-8. Our security rests upon three things: (1) **1-2.** It rests upon faith in God's character—as **the Most High,** His millennial title as "possessor of heaven and earth" (Gen. 14:19), by virtue of creation and redemption (Eph. 1:14; Rev. 5:1-14; cf. Dan. 7:13-14), and whose plan for His redeemed and the earth will be most assuredly accomplished; as **the Almighty** (*El Shaddai,* "the all-sufficient One"), who intervenes in saving power when man's strength fades (Gen. 17:1; 28:3; 48:3; 49:25); as the LORD (*yhwh*), the covenant-keeping, eternally existing One; as *God,* the all-powerful Creator.

Faith in God is shown by the terms—**dwelleth in the secret place . . . abide** (lodge) **under the shadow** (protection) **of the Almighty . . . say** (declare) of the LORD, He is **my refuge . . . my fortress, my God,** indicating intense personal appropriation by faith— summarized in the final clause, **in him will I trust** (*'eḇṭāḥ,* "place my confidence"; Psalms 2:12; 25:2; 56:4).

(2) **3-4.** Our security rests upon faith in God's faithfulness. He delivers from **the snare of the fowler** (trapper; 124:7; Prov. 6:5), a figure of Satan's craftiness, **from the noisome** (deadly) **pestilence** (Psalm 91:6; 1 Kings 8:37; 2 Chron. 20:9). Like a mother bird (Deut. 32:11) covers her young with her feathers, under His

wings the believer finds refuge (Ruth 2:12; Psalms 17:8; 57:1; 61:4; Matt. 23:37). The **feathers** and **wings** represent the security the animal world knows, coupled with the **shield and buckler,** the security that man devises, which denotes the completeness of the safety to be found in trusting God's faithfulness.

(3) **5-8.** Our security rests upon faith in God's righteousness to safeguard integrity, implied by the contrasting fate of the wicked. God's protection touches all times, **night . . . day;** all circumstances, **darkness . . . noonday;** all perils, the **arrow** of the human foe, **pestilence** of the unseen foe, **destruction** (*qeṭeḇ,* "plague") **that wasteth** (lays waste) **at noonday** (Job 5:22); and all catastrophes, even the gravest calamities that might bring death to **a thousand,** or even **ten thousand . . . but it shall not come near thee** (Gen. 7:23; Josh. 14:10). The believer will only look on and **see the reward** (recompense) **of the wicked** (Psalms 37:34; 58:10).

This psalm in the *absolute* sense belongs only to the perfect Man, the second Adam, the Lord from heaven, who alone dwelt in the secret place of the Most High, and who as the sinless One could only be touched by sin and death as He willingly yielded up His life (John 10:17-18). As far as the believer is concerned, this psalm must not be understood to teach that he will be untouched by worldly calamities. Rather, it indicates that in God he merely possesses wealth and security that are completely unknown by the world.

The Blessings of Security. 91:9-16. **9a.** This verse is correctly rendered by J. J. S. Perowne: "For thou, O Jehovah, art my refuge" and viewed as a parenthesis from verse 2, expressing the psalmist's own trust in God and interrupting his flow of thought in verses 3 to 8, which is resumed in verse 9*b.* This opening phrase sets the course of the second part of the psalm as it describes the blessings of the security that become the portion of the one who has made the LORD his refuge and **the Most High** his **habitation** (cf. 90:1).

The first blessing is angelic surveillance and protection (vv. 10-12). **10.** "No harm shall befall you, nor shall any plague come near your tent" (BV; 121:7; Prov. 1:33; 3:25-26; 12:21; 2 Thess. 3:3; 2 Pet. 2:9; cf. Exod. 12:23-30). **11. For he shall give his angels charge over thee, to keep thee in all thy ways** (Matt. 4:6; Luke 4:10-11). God commissions the whole angelic host to "minister for them who shall be heirs of salvation" (Heb. 1:14; cf. Gen. 28:12; Psalms 34:7; 68:17; John 1:51).

12. They shall bear thee up ... lest thou dash (strike) **thy foot against a stone**, representing a danger such as meets a man of God without seeking it or running rashly or presumptuously into it (cf. Prov. 3:23). Satan omitted "in all thy ways" when he quoted this passage. All Christ's ways as man were God's ways of implicit reverent faith and filial obedience and dependence, and so God's angels guarded His sinless humanity. Satan attempted to make Christ act presumptuously, out of God's will, and thus tempt God by needlessly testing His power and faithfulness, as Israel did (Exod. 17:7; cf. Matt. 4:5-7). **13.** The second blessing of security is victory over the powers of darkness, the doubly mentioned **lion** prefiguring every opposition of satanic power (cf. 1 Pet. 5:8), and the doubly mentioned **serpent** every manifestation of demonic subtlety (Gen. 3:1). **14-16.** The third blessing of security is fellowship with God. This passage represents in its fullest meaning the address of the Father to Christ. "Because he hath set his love upon me ... I will set him on high, because he

hath known my name ... I will deliver him, and honor him. With long life will I satisfy him" (ASV, lit. Heb.; Psalm 21:4; Isa. 53:10; John 5:26; 10:28).

The perfect Man set His love upon God; He went into the jaws of death, was raised from the dead, exalted far above all principality and power (Eph. 1:19-21), and given "a name... above every name" (Phil. 2:9). In a secondary sense this passage is applicable to the believer who, through Christ, and identified with Him, dwells in the secret place of the Most High, as the God-man—Redeemer did.

C. THE VICTORIOUS BELIEVER. 92:1-15.

For the context and scope of Psalm 92, see the introduction to Book 4, Psalm 90. As a psalm or song for the Sabbath day, this ode describes any saint who has spiritually entered into the rest of the people of God (Heb. 4:9-11), but it focuses prophetically upon the Sabbath rest the saints in the Kingdom age will enjoy when the LORD arises to deliver them and all their enemies perish. "The application of the psalm is perennial. Its fulfillment, however, is millennial" (UBH, p. 285).

The Victorious Believer Is Filled with Praise. 92:1-4. The believer realized the value of praising God (vv. 1-3). **1.** He pronounced giving thanks to the LORD and singing praises to the name of the **Most High**, the millennial name of God when He takes possession of the earth (Gen. 14:18-19) as the rightful Possessor of it by virtue of creation and redemption (Rev. 5:1-10; Psalms 135:3; 147:1), to be **good.**

2. Foremost in his joyous thanksgiving was declaring God's **loving-kindness** (59:16) **in the morning.** In the Millennium, there will be rejoicing in the whole grand story of Christ's death, burial, resurrection, and glorious coming again, which will then be glorious facts of redemptive history. And His **faithfulness every night** (89:1). In Kingdom blessing there will be a full demonstration of God's faithfulness in keeping His covenants and promises made to Israel (Rom. 9:4-5; cf. Psalm 89:1-52).

3. The victorious saint was so filled with praise that he expressed his praiseful thanks in prayer, in song, and with instrumental music (33:2; 1 Sam. 10:5; 1 Chron. 13:8; Neh. 12:27), in striking contrast to thankless sinners (Rom. 1:21).

4. He confessed God as the Source of his joy and triumph. **For thou, Lord, hast made me glad through thy work** (lit., "Thy working"; i.e., "by what Thou hast done"; Psalms 40:5; 90:16) in redemption (Gal. 5:22; Phil. 4:4, 13). Victorious saints find the source of their joy in God, and freely testify to that fact. **I will triumph** ("sing for joy," Psalm 106:47) **in the works of thy hands** (8:6; 111:7; 143:5), that is, "Your working in me" (Phil. 2:12-13), as well as in other believers and in Your wonderful creation, and especially in effecting the final redemption of Your people.

The Victorious Believer Is Fortified by Faith. 92:5-11. **5a.** He believed in God's omnipotence, manifested especially in His **great...works** wrought for the deliverance of His people in destroying the wicked who are their enemies. These great doings come in panoramic view in Revelation 5:1—20:3, where the rebels and lawless (cf. Psalm 2:1-3) must be wiped out before the Kingdom can be set up (2:4-12; Rev. 20:4-6).

5b. Thy thoughts are very deep (Psalm 139:17; Isa. 28:29; 55:8-9; Jer. 23:20; Rom. 11:33). The psalmist also believed in God's omniscience. The "depth" of God's thoughts consists in their unfathomable riches of wisdom and good-

ness, not perceived by the ungodly, and only partially comprehended by believers (Psalm 40:5; Job 11:8). They cannot grasp the fact that when the unrighteous seem to triumph and the godly to be overwhelmed, the deliverance of the righteous and the overthrow of the wicked are suddenly effected in vindication of the righteousness of God. **6. A stupid man** ("a man—a brute") **knoweth not, neither doth a fool understand this** (Psalms 32:9; 73:22; 94:8; Prov. 30:32; Isa. 1:3; Jer. 10:14; 1 Cor. 2:14).

The victorious believer also believes in the inevitable doom of the wicked (vv. 7-9). **7.** No matter how quickly the ungodly spring up, like verdure on a Palestinian hill, or how luxuriantly they flourish (Job. 21:7; Jer. 12:1; Mal. 3:15), faith in God tells him that **it is that they shall be destroyed forever** (eternally; Rev. 20:11-15; John 3:36). The millennial saint will witness that truth on a colossal scale when the Great Tribulation, the time of the purging out of the wicked, becomes an event of history.

8. In the midst of the darkest hour of sin and the acme of lawlessness (Psalm 2:1-3; 2 Thess. 2:4; Rev. 16:13-16; 19:19), faith instructs the psalmist that even in that time when "darkness shall cover the earth, and gross darkness the peoples" (Isa. 60:2), the LORD will be exalted on high forever, unchanged and unchangeable in His eternal majesty and glory (Psalms 93:4; 113:5), while His enemies will have become ripe for ruin.

9. The repetition **lo, thine enemies** depicts their demonic energy and activity (Rev. 16:13-16), which in turn presaged their imminent destruction (Psalms 37:20; 68:1; 89:10; Rev. 19:11—20:3). **10-11.** Moreover, the psalmist believed in the vindication and reward of the righteous. The millennial saint will have been a witness of that truth, having been preserved through the Great Tribulation and having seen the destruction of the **wicked.**

But Thou hast exalted my horn (a symbol of strength; cf. Psalms 75:10; 89:17; 112:9) **like that of the wild ox** (NASB), an extinct animal appearing on Assyrian reliefs, with its vast strength concentrated in a huge frontal horn. **I shall be anointed with fresh oil** (23:5; 45:7), pointing prophetically to the outpouring of the Spirit in millennial times (Joel 2:28-29).

The Victorious Believer Is Favored with Prosperity. 92:12-14. **12.** He **shall flourish like the palm tree** (1:3; 52:8; 72:7), in contrast to the wicked who "spring like the grass" and flourish briefly, only to be destroyed (v. 7). The palm tree is an appropriate figure for a victorious saint because of its beauty—tall, straight, tufted with beautiful green fronds, itself a token of victory (Rev. 7:9) because of its utility. The Hindus list 360 uses of the palm. It shades, shelters, refreshes, furnishes delicious food (dates), etc.; and because of its vitality, it grows in the desert and semidesert regions, staying perennially green amid burning sands and scorching heat, with its large tap root going deep to draw upon sources of water. **He shall grow like a cedar in Lebanon.** Cedar trees were ancient monarchs of the mountains, weathering all sorts of storms and winds, and being prized by ancient kings in the construction of their palaces and temples.

13. He is **planted** in God's house (Psalm 80:15; Isa. 60:21) and **shall flourish in the courts of our God** (Psalms 100:4; 116:19), drawing his strength and blessing from the worship and service of God. **14.** As a result he will still yield fruit in old age, being full of sap and green because he will have his roots deep in God, as the palm and cedar have their roots deep in subterranean springs. **15.** Therefore, he is able to declare **that the Lord is upright.** His summary testimony is: **He is my rock** (18:2; 94:22)...**there is no unrighteousness in him** (Rom. 9:14).

D. THE MESSIAH'S MILLENNIAL REIGN. 93:1-5.

See the introduction to Psalm 90 (Book 4 of the Psalter) for the context and scope of Psalm 93. Psalms 47, 93, and 96 to 99 are often styled "enthronement psalms" (LBC, pp. 22-23) in which the kingship of the LORD is celebrated and His millennial reign predicted when He will actually exercise His worldwide rule. The author and the actual historical situation out of which the psalm sprang are unknown.

The Lord's Coming in His Kingdom. 93:1-2. **1a. The Lord reigneth,** that is, He has assumed kingship (96:10; 97:1; 99:1), the formula employed at the accession of earthly monarchs (2 Sam. 15:10; 1 Kings 1:11, 13), not a reference to the regular government of the king as God's representative. Hence, the prophetic view is of the King-Messiah assuming the long-predicted Kingdom over Israel (Acts 1:6; Rev. 11:15-18; 19:11-16).

If the historical background was the Assyrian threat against Jerusalem, the arrogant claim of the world power virtually was "the Assyrian reigneth" and his overthrow was the counterproclamation, "The LORD reigneth." The prophetic antitype is the world power under the Antichrist, which under Satan's energy (16:14; 17:12-14, 17) will make one last terrible attempt to defy and oust the LORD (2 Thess. 2:4-12). But Christ will return in glory to assume His kingship as He utterly decimates His foes (Isa. 24:23; Obad. 1:21; Zech. 14:9; Rev. 11:15-17; 19:6).

1b-c. Then He will visibly be **clothed**

with majesty (Job 40:10; Psalm 104:1; Isa. 59:17; 63:1) and with strength with which He will have girded himself (Psalm 96:10; Rev. 19:11-16), the antidote to the vaunting strength of the God-opposing satanic world system (2:1-3), utterly disordered with all its foundations of righteousness and morality put "out of course" (82:5; cf. 46:2-6).

Then the new world order will be "firmly established" (NASB) in the righteousness and peace that will be brought into the Kingdom that the Messiah will set up at His second advent (Isa. 9:6-7, 11; Dan. 2:44; Luke 1:32-33) as the result of the destruction of the satanic world system (Rev. 20:1-3). The will of the Messiah will be manifested in glorious power to renovate and reestablish the world (then disorganized by sin) so that it cannot be moved. In doing so He will manifest the same omnipotence He displayed in creating it (Psalms 96:10; 104:5).

2. God's throne, denoting His righteous rule and government, established from eternity (45:6; Lam. 5:19), will then be revealed in Christ's Davidic earthly throne (2 Sam. 7:16), "the throne of his glory" (Matt. 25:31), which He calls "my throne" (Rev. 3:21), and which will continue into eternity as "the throne of ... the Lamb" (22:1, 3), and which will be eternal, just as God is eternal (Psalm 90:2; cf. 2 Sam. 7:16).

Opposition to the Enthronement of the King. 93:3. 3a. The world's mighty, roaring floods are the seas (24:2; Jonah 2:3), figurative of the rebellious world powers opposing the enthronement of God's anointed King (Psalms 2:1-3; 46:2-3; Dan. 7:2, 7; Luke 21:25; Rev. 13:1). The psalmist viewed the threat of those forces arrayed against the righteous rule of the LORD "as more noise than power" (BBC, p. 3).

3b. They have lifted up their voice (Psalms 96:11; 98:7-8) ... their waves ("breakers"), waves dashing into collision with waves, metaphorically describing the awful lawlessness, rebellion, and violence of humanity gathered to oppose the enthronement of the earth's rightful King (Rev. 16:13-16; 19:19).

The Glorious Sovereignty of the King. 93:4. 4. The Lord on high upon His eternal throne as the eternal One (v. 2; cf. 76:4) is mighty, "More than the sounds of many waters, than the mighty breakers of the sea" (NASB; 65:7; 89:6, 9; 92:8). As King of creation, overcoming the forces of chaos (Gen. 1:1-2), He is all-powerful and sovereign as Ruler of the world order, over which He now assumes actual kingship by the double right of creation and redemption (Rev. 5:5-7). Therefore, His title is appropriately "KING OF KINGS AND LORD OF LORDS" (19:16).

The King in Manifestation. 93:5. 5. His royal majesty not only appears in the world of nature and government, but also in His revelation of Himself in His Word. His testimonies are very sure (fully confirmed; 19:7). The establishment of His millennial Kingdom, so amply predicted in His Word and so widely denied even by His people, shall then be completely authenticated. His house is to be located in Jerusalem, the millennial capital of the Kingdom (Isa. 2:2-3; Ezek. 40:1—44:31); it will have holiness as its mark (Zech. 14:20-21), since evil will be rooted out, Satan and demons bound (13:2; Rev. 20:1-3), truth vindicated, and the LORD Himself will be in visible manifestation as King.

E. GOD'S JUDGMENT UPON THE WICKED. 94:1-23.

Psalms 94 and 95 introduce Psalms 96 to 100 (five Kingdom psalms), which prophetically delineate the glorious manifestation of the Lord in His millennial reign as King. Psalm 94 deals with the problem of the awful wickedness of sinners in their persecution of God's people in the "time of Jacob's trouble" (Jer. 30:5-7) preceding that reign. See also the introduction to Book 4 and Psalm 90.

Prayer for Divine Vengeance upon the Wicked. 94:1-12. **1.** The Lord as Judge is addressed as **God, to whom vengeance belongeth** (lit., "God of avenging acts"). It is repeated for emphasis because, previous to Christ's enthronement upon His earthly Davidic throne, human wickedness will reach its climactic pitch. That will necessitate immediate judgment to recompense the terrible insult to God and the wrong done His people in the nightmare of lawlessness that bursts forth during the Tribulation (cf. Rev. 9:20-21; 13:1-18; 16:13-16; 19:19). "The God of avenging acts" is besought to **show** Himself (rather, "shine forth," make His epiphany, as in Psalms 50:2; 80:1; cf. Deut. 32:35) and recompense vengeance to those who trouble His people, and to give rest to His people, as the divine righteousness requires (2 Thess. 1:6-8).

2. As **judge of the earth** (Gen. 18:25), God is called upon to lift up Himself (Psalm 7:6), that is, set Himself on high on the throne of judgment (Matt. 25:31-46), and **render a reward** (a recompense) **to the proud** (Psalm 31:23), the God-defying, self-exalting, seemingly triumphant persecutors of the godly, who are described in more detail in verses 3 to 7. Their seeming impunity in violent deeds and words is the grounds of the prayer of verses 1 and 2. **3.** How long will they triumph? (Job 20:5). **4. They utter** (pour forth, spout) words; they **speak hard things** (*'ātāq*, "arrogantly, boldly"; Psalms 31:18;

75:5). These **workers of iniquity** ("doers of vanity," traffickers in occultism) **boast themselves** (speak impassionately). **5. They break in pieces** (crush) the Lord's people (Isa. 3:15) and **afflict** His heritage (Psalm 79:1; Rev. 7:1-15; 11:1-8; 13:1-18), atrocities and blasphemies that ripen them for ruin and call forth divine vengeance (vv. 1-2).

6-7. They show the depth of their depravity by slaying the widow and helpless stranger and murdering the defenseless orphan (Isa. 10:2), protesting that the Lord does not see or pay any attention, imagining God to be as wicked as they (Psalms 10:11; 59:7; 73:11).

So outrageous is the depravity of these lawless rebels ripened for ruin that the psalmist launches into a heated refutation of their insensate imagination that God does not see (vv. 8-11). **8.** He brands them **stupid** ("senseless" like the brute beast) as men become by severance from God, for he turns from pagan oppressors who utter cavils against God (v. 7) to those among God's professing people who secretly sympathize with them. He brands them **fools** (Exod. 4:11; Prov. 20:12). **9.** Can God give the faculties of hearing and seeing to His creatures and yet all the while not possess them Himself? **10.** Can He who chastens the nations (Psalm 44:2) not rebuke? Shall He who teaches man knowledge (Job 35:11; Isa. 28:26) not know?

11. Assuredly, the Lord **knoweth the thoughts of man** (Job 11:11; 1 Cor. 1:21; 3:20), **that they are vanity** (a mere breath), a truth that will be proved once and for all as the Lord returns to smite His enemies at Armageddon (Rev. 16:13-16) and root out rebels and sinners when He is enthroned in the power and glory of the kingdom.

The Answer to the Prayer for Divine Vengeance. 94:12-23. God answers in eight ways: (1) **12-13.** God answers by giving encouragement to those who do not misjudge God's long-suffering with the wicked oppressors, but profit by chastening, being assured that ultimately they shall be delivered and the wicked punished. The man whom God **chastenest...and teaches** out of His **law** (His Word) is pronounced **blessed** (happy; Job 5:17; Prov. 3:11; 1 Cor. 11:32; Heb. 12:5). He will be given **rest,** cessation from adversity and war in being preserved for the righteousness and peace of the Kingdom (Isa. 2:4; 9:6-7; 11:9). Meanwhile, **the pit** (cf. Psalms 9:15; 55:23) will **be digged for the wicked** (37:31-34; 2 Thess. 1:4-10).

(2) **14.** God, in His answer to the prayer of His people for divine vengeance upon their persecutors, gives the outright assurance that He **will not cast off** (abandon) **his people** (1 Sam. 12:22; Lam. 3:31; Rom. 11:2) or **forsake his inheritance** (Psalm 37:28). (3) **15.** He also promises that **judgment,** which will be so foully perverted by the sinners of the Tribulation period (vv. 3-7), **shall return unto righteousness** (lit. Heb.), that is, "will again be righteous" under the righteous King (97:2; Isa. 9:6-7; 11:3-4; 42:3; Mic. 7:9) and that **all the upright in heart** (the regenerate preserved out of the Tribulation to enter the Kingdom) **shall follow it** (i.e., righteousness).

(4) God also assures His people through His psalmist that He will espouse their cause (vv. 16-19). **16. Who will stand up for me against evildoers** (NASB) **... against the workers of iniquity?** (Num. 10:35; Isa. 28:21; 33:10). Who but the Lord (Psalm 35:1; Zech. 3:1-5), especially at His glorious coming (Rev. 19:11-16), when it is specifically declared that He will stand up for His people (Job 19:25; Dan. 12:1). The psalmist, in support of the divine assurance that God would undertake for them, gave his personal testimony (vv. 17-19).

17. He confessed that if the LORD had not been his help, he would soon have dwelt in **silence**—the stillness of death (Psalm 31:17). **18.** His foot had almost slipped in the fearful trials through which he passed (the psalmist speaks as a representative of all afflicted saints, but preeminently and prophetically of the godly remnant during the Tribulation).

(5) **19.** God also answers by granting His comfort and consolations to His own in the midst of their troubles and anxieties (Isa. 57:18; 66:13; 2 Cor. 1:3-5). (6) **20-21.** God answers by declaring that He will not allow enthroned iniquity to prevail. **Shall the throne of iniquity have fellowship with** (be allied to) **thee?** (Amos 6:3). "The throne that causes destruction"—**one which devises mischief by decree** (NASB; Psalms 50:16; 58:2). Under such a tribunal the wicked band themselves together against the life of the righteous (56:6; 59:3) and **condemn** the innocent to death (Exod. 23:7; Psalm 106:38; Prov. 17:15; Matt. 27:4).

(7) **22.** God answers by being the **defense** (stronghold) of His people (Psalms 9:9; 59:9) and the rock (Deut. 32:18; 1 Sam. 2:2; Psalms 18:2; 42:9; 71:3) of their refuge. (8) **23.** He will unfailingly recompense the wickedness of the wicked upon them (Psalms 7:16; 140:9) and **cut them off in their own wickedness** (Gen. 19:15). The thought is repeated to emphasize the absolute certainty of God's destruction of the wicked, which will be a welcome note for the Tribulation saints amid the horrors they will have to face in that dark period (Rev. 13:1-18).

F. The Advent of Israel's King Anticipated. 95:1-11.

For the context of this psalm, see the introduction to Psalm 94. Psalm 95 (like Psalm 94) constitutes a preface to the millennial psalms (96-100) that follow. The praise arises from the lips of the saved remnant of Israel as they warn their wavering brethren against unbelief, which will bar them from entrance into Kingdom rest.

Praise in Prospect of the Messiah's Soon Return. 95:1-7a. **1.** The saved remnant broke forth into joyful singing to the LORD (66:1; 81:1) and shouting in anticipation of the appearance of their Savior-Deliverer, whom they appropriately addressed as **the rock of our salvation** (18:2; 89:26). **2.** They exhorted one another to assemble **before his presence with thanksgiving** (100:4; 147:7; Jonah 2:9; Mic. 6:6) and joyfully shout to Him with psalms (Psalm 81:2; Eph. 5:19; James 5:13).

3. They praised and worshiped Him, whose right it is to rule, because (1) He is **the Lord** (Yahweh), the self-existent, covenant-keeping, faithful One, who will make good His covenants and promises made to His people, Israel (Rom. 9:4-5); and (2) He is a **great God** (Psalms 48:1; 135:5; 145:3) and **a great King above all gods**, because they are dead, but He is alive; they are nonexistent, but He is the eternally existing One; they are mere fabrications of man, but He made man and the earth and sea (vv. 4-5). **4.** His is the right to rule by virtue of His ownership of the earth—*all* the earth, the deepest depths of the earth as well as the loftiest peaks of the mountains (135:6). **5.** The sea is His also, as well as the dry land (Gen. 1:9-10; Psalm 146:6; Jonah 1:9). **6-7a.** Man is also His by creation (and redemption) and must

heed the call: **Come, let us worship and bow down** (Psalms 96:9; 99:5). **Let us kneel before the Lord our maker** (2 Chron. 6:13; Psalm 100:3; Isa. 17:7; Dan. 6:10; Hos. 8:14). For by redemption they can say, **We are the people of his pasture** (Psalms 23:1-3; 74:1).

Warning Against Disobedience in Prospect of Kingdom Rest. 95:7b-11. Let those who are about to be delivered by the returning "KING OF KINGS" (Rev. 19:16) take warning against unbelief and disobedience and the resulting peril of not entering Kingdom rest from those of old who forfeited the rest of Canaan for a similar reason (Heb. 3:7-11, 15; 4:7).

7b. Today (not "tomorrow"; Heb. 4:7) **if ye will hear his voice...** (followed by an ellipsis, such as, e.g., "you will be preserved through the Tribulation to Kingdom blessing"; Matt. 24:22; cf. Exod. 23:21-22; Psalm 80:8). **8. Harden not your heart, as in the provocation** (lit. Heb., "as at Meribah," Exod. 17:7, "place of strife") **... as in the day of temptation** (lit. Heb., "as in the day of Massah," temptation) **in the wilderness** (Exod. 17:5-7; Deut. 6:16).

9. The LORD, speaking by His Spirit through the psalmist, reminds the remnant of Israel² in the dark days of the Antichrist and his followers (Rev. 13:1-18) how their ancestors **tried** Him and **saw** His **work** (His miraculous undertaking in behalf of Israel). Yet in the face of all the manifestations of His power, they still did not believe and trust Him, but disobediently kept demanding fresh proof from Him that He was the God of Israel (Num. 14:22).

10. The LORD confesses, **Forty years ... was I grieved with** ('*āqûṭ*, "I loathed," "was disgusted with") **this generation** (Acts 7:36; 13:18; Heb. 3:17), the whole generation that died in the wilderness, except for Joshua and Caleb (Deut. 1:35; 2:14). God pronounced them "a people of erring heart" (lit. Heb.); **they have not known my ways**, having no spiritual comprehension of His dealing in grace and love with them.

11. Unto whom I swore in my wrath that they should not enter into my rest (Canaan; Num. 14:23, 28, 30; Deut. 1:34-35; Heb. 4:3). So future Israel in the wilderness of the world is warned against unbelief regarding their Messiah-Savior-King about to appear to deliver them from their persecuting enemies (Psalm 94) and establish them in Kingdom rest. But as in all the psalms, the application extends to God's people of every age, including our age, as the quotation in Hebrews 3:7-11, 15; 4:7 shows.

G. THE ADVENT OF ISRAEL'S KING REALIZED. 96:1-13.

This is a millennial psalm (see the introductions to Psalms 94 and 95 for its context and scope), the first of five singing psalms (96-100) that celebrate the King's reign when "the ransomed of the LORD shall return, and come to Zion with songs and everlasting joy upon their heads ... and sorrow and sighing shall flee away" (Isa. 35:10).

The New Song. 96:1-6. **1-2.** Three times the joyful exhortation arises: **Sing unto the Lord! All the earth**, comprehending the entire globe in the Kingdom age, is to "sing unto the LORD." The song is styled **a new song** (40:3), because it celebrates a new blessing never experienced before, namely, the realization of Christ's redemptive work as it affects the subjects of the earthly millennial Kingdom and those who in that age will "reign on the earth" (Rev. 5:9-10). The "new song" is attuned to **bless** ("highly extol") **his name** and **show forth** (*bśr*, "publish the good news of") **his salvation from day to day** (Psalm

71:15), that is, constantly, suited to an abiding deliverance.

3. The "new song" also celebrates the LORD's **glory** among the millennial nations and His **wonders** (wonderful deeds) among all the **peoples** (145:12). **4-5.** It also will rehearse the greatness of the LORD (48:1) and the reverence due Him as Creator (115:15; Isa. 42:5) in complete contrast to the impotent **idols** (nonexistent things; 1 Chron. 16:26).

6. It will also proclaim the **honor** (*hôḏ*, "splendor") and **majesty** of the King of kings (Rev. 19:16; Psalm 104:1) and the **strength and beauty ... in his sanctuary**—the restored Temple in millennial Jerusalem (Isa. 2:2-3; Ezek. 40:1—47:23). Then the LORD God Almighty and the Lamb will be the temple in the eternal perfect state (Rev. 21:22).

The Lord Reigns. 96:7-10. **7-8a.** All the **kindreds** (families) of the peoples are called to **give** (ascribe) to the LORD **glory and strength** due His name (1 Chron. 16:28-29; Psalms 22:27; 29:1-2). **8b-9.** They are exhorted to **bring an offering** (45:12; 72:10), for animal sacrifices, commemorative of Christ's finished redemptive work, will be offered in the millennial Temple (Isa. 2:2-3; Ezek. 43:19-27; Zech. 14:16-21), where the LORD in the Kingdom age is to be worshiped **in the beauty of holiness** (*hăḏrăṯ-qōḏĕsh*) and feared (held in reverence) by **all the earth.**

10. Say among the nations, "The LORD reigns" (NASB; Psalm 93:1). This is the announcement of His public enthronement, in fulfillment of the Davidic Covenant (2 Sam. 7:8-16), by those who have heard it to those who have not. Evidently this indicates that, although all Israel as a nation will be saved to enter the Millennium (Rom. 11:26-27), all Gentiles will not, and that the Israelites will be missionaries to the nations (cf. Isa. 40:9-10; Zech. 8:20-23;

14:16-21). Then the world will be firmly established (see Psalm 93:1) under the Messiah's righteous rule (Isa. 9:6-7). With enemies rooted out and Satan and demonic powers bound (Zech. 13:2; Rev. 20:1-3), the Messiah will judge the peoples with equity (Psalms 9:8; 58:11; 67:4; 98:9; cf. Isa. 11:3-5).

Full Kingdom Joy. 96:11-13. **11-12.** Then the heavens will **rejoice** (Isa. 49:13; Jer. 51:48; Rev. 12:12; 18:20), and the **earth** will **be glad** (Psalm 97:1), **the sea roar** (98:7) with happiness, **the field be joyful,** and **the trees of the forest rejoice** (Isa. 35:1; 55:12-13;). **13.** All creation "delivered from the bondage of corruption" (Rom. 8:21, 23; cf. Isa. 44:23) is poetically personified to express radiant exultation before the LORD in His advent **to judge the earth** (Psalm 67:4; Rev. 19:11).

H. THE KING'S GLORIOUS REIGN. 97:1-12.

For the context and scope of this psalm, see the introductions to Psalms 93, 94, and 95. The historical setting of Psalms 94 to 100 has been widely theorized upon (see LBC, pp. 24-25), but actually it is unknown, the Spirit of prophecy in the psalmist envisioning — through the actual enthronement or commemoration of the enthronement of some king of the Davidic line—the great climactic assumption of kingship by David's Son and Lord in fulfillment of the Davidic Covenant (2 Sam. 7:8-16).

The Lord Reigns. 97:1-5. **1.** This same exultant proclamation of the Messiah's anticipated assumption of Kingdom rule abruptly appears throughout this series of psalms (93:1; 96:10), suggesting it will overtake the earth by surprise (cf. Matt. 24:38-44). This climactic event will call forth intense joy from God's people (Isa. 25:9; Rev. 11:17); the earth and the coastlands,

poetically personified, represent the saints who inhabit them (Psalm 96:11; Isa. 42:10, 12).

2-4. Clouds ... darkness ... lightnings symbolize the divine wrath that will be manifested in the Tribulation judgments preceding the King's advent and reign (Exod. 19:9; Deut. 4:11; 1 Kings 8:12; Psalm 18:11; Rev. 6:1—19:21). **Righteousness and justice are the habitation** ($m^ek\hat{o}n$, "foundation, basis") **of his throne** (Psalm 89:14). The terrible seal, trumpet, and vial judgments (Rev. 6:1—16:21), which will dislodge and destroy sinners, will spring from the divine righteousness and justice and be so terrible that sinners will doubt this fact. But the saints, who will have gotten victory over the Antichrist and his forces, will sing, "Great and marvelous are thy works, Lord God Almighty; just and true are thy ways [16:7], thou King of saints" (15:3).

The judgments, which will decimate the rebellious, will be prefigured by **a fire that goeth before him** (Exod. 20:18; 24:17; Psalm 77:18; Dan. 7:10; Hab. 3:5) that **burneth up his enemies round about** (Mal. 4:1; Heb. 12:29), as His lightnings light up the world, lightnings being a common manifestation of the divine wrath in the Apocalypse (Rev. 4:5; 8:5; 11:19; 16:18) as well as accompanying earthquakes (Rev. 6:12; 8:5; 11:13; 16:18). **5.** The mountains will melt **like wax** (Psalm 46:6; Amos 9:5; Mic. 1:4) **at the presence of the Lord of the whole earth**, a millennial title when He, to whom the earth belongs both by creation and redemption, actually takes possession to reign over it (Gen. 14:19-20; Josh. 3:11; Mic. 4:13; Zech. 4:14; Rev. 11:4).

The Effect of His Reign. 97:6-9. There will be five results of the Lord's reign: (1) **6a. The heavens will declare his righteousness** (50:6), as the skies did when the LORD "rained upon Sodom and upon Gomorrah brimstone and fire from ... heaven" (Gen. 19:24), giving men severally their due. (2) **6b.** All the peoples who survive the Tribulation judgments will **see his glory** (Isa. 40:5; Rev. 1:7).

(3) **7a-b.** His coming will confound the idols and idolaters. All who serve **images** (Rev. 9:20-21), who **boast themselves of** (brag about) **idols** (*'elîlîm*, "nonentities, things of nought"; Psalm 106:36; Jer. 50:2; Hab. 2:18; Rev. 17:1—18:24).

(4) **7c.** The holy angels will attend the King (Rev. 9:13) and worship Him. The **gods** (*'elôhîm*, meaning the "angels," as Heb. 1:6 points out). If the angels worship the King, how much more must false gods give place to Him as King of kings (1 Cor. 15:24-25; Phil. 2:9)? (5) **8.** Zion, the capital of the earth Kingdom, will hear and be **glad** (Psalm 48:11; Zeph. 3:14), as will **the daughters of Judah** (i.e., the remaining cities of Judah), **because** of the LORD's **judgments** (v. 3).

9. The reason for the universal joy will be because the Messiah is the LORD **Most High over all the earth** (NASB; lit. Heb.), a millennial designation like "the Lord of the whole earth" (v. 5). As "the most high God" (*'ēl 'elyôn*), "possessor of heaven and earth" (Gen. 14:18-19), He originally allotted the earth to the human race (Deut. 32:8), and He will Himself rule over it by virtue of His redemptive work and covenant-keeping faithfulness (2 Sam. 8:7-16) as "LORD [*yhwh*] Most High over all the earth" in the Kingdom age, **exalted far above all gods** (earthly rulers and judges, Exod. 22:28; Psalm 82:6; John 10:34; and the angels, cf. v. 7, if they are also meant in this passage).

Exhortation to His Saints. 97:10-12. In the light of His reign as a manifestation of His grace, love, and right-eousness, the saints are exhorted to do two things: (1) **10.** They are exhorted to **hate evil** and thereby show they **love the Lord** (Prov. 8:13; Amos 5:15; Rom. 12:9). He is worthy of love, since He preserves His **saints** (godly ones; Psalms 31:23; 145:20; Prov. 2:8), having kept them through the Great Tribulation to enter the Kingdom (cf. Matt. 24:22), and delivering them from **the hand** (power) **of the wicked** (Psalm 37:40; Jer. 15:21; Dan. 3:28; 6:22).

11. He sows light like seed for the righteous (Job 22:28; Psalm 112:4; Prov. 4:18) **and gladness for the upright in heart** (Psalm 64:10). (2) **12.** The saints are also exhorted to **rejoice in the Lord** (32:11; Phil. 4:4) and **give thanks at the remembrance of** (for the memory of) **his holiness** (Psalm 30:4; cf. Rev. 15:4; cf. 4:8).

I. THE NEW SONG. 98:1-9.

See the introductions to Psalms 93, 94, and 95 for the context and scope of this psalm.

The Call to Sing. 98:1-3. **1a-b. Oh, sing unto the Lord a new song.** It is the same "new song" of Psalm 96:1; (*q.v.*; cf. 33:3). It is a new song because **the Lord hath done wonderful things** (Exod. 15:6; Psalms 40:5; 96:3) in rooting out the rebellious and sinful, destroying the Antichrist and his minions, imprisoning Satan and the demons, smashing the satanic world system, and setting up His glorious earthly Kingdom (Rev. 6:1—20:6).

1c-2. His right hand (Exod. 15:6) **and his holy arm** (Isa. 52:10), common anthropomorphisms expressing divine omnipotence, have **gotten** (gained) **him the victory** (Rev. 19:11—20:3), making known His salvation and revealing His righteousness (Rom. 3:25) in the sight of the heathen (nations), thereby showing them how fallen man can only be saved by faith in the Messiah's death and resurrection (1 Cor. 15:2-4), which as glorious events of past history, will furnish the basis for the establishment of the Kingdom in fulfillment of the Davidic Covenant (2 Sam. 7:8-16).

3. Thus, through His glorious redemption, it is said, **He hath remembered his mercy** (loving-kindness) **and his truth** (faithfulness; Rom. 15:8-9) **toward the house of Israel** (Luke 1:54, 72; Rom. 11:26-36). His salvation is first to be manifested to Israel, and through Israel to **all the ends of the earth.** Such was the case at His first advent (Luke 24:47; Rom. 1:16), and such will be the case at His second advent (Psalm 22:27; Isa. 2:2-3).

Universal Acclamation. 98:4-6. **4.** The occasion for this praise is so great and far-reaching that people are not only to sing, but also **make a joyful noise** ("shout joyfully") to the LORD (100:1). **All the earth** is to join, because the Kingdom is worldwide, and **make a loud noise** (*pis̱ẖû*, "break forth" in praise) and **rejoice** (*rănnᵉnû*, "cry out piercingly") and **sing praise** (*zămmērû*), words that ransack the Hebrew language to express the highest and most ecstatic joy that will prevail when Israel is in fellowship with God and the medium of blessing to the world.

5-6. Praise is to be rendered to the LORD with instrumental music—the lyre, trumpet, and horn, and with joyful shoutings **before the King, the Lord** (NASB; lit. Heb.), stressing the central glorious truth that the King, although human, *is* also divine *and* is none other than Jehovah, the LORD Himself, David's Lord, as well as his lineal Descendant (110:1).

The King, the Lord, as Judge. 98:7-9. **7. The sea** is to **roar** with joyous excitement (see 96:11), personifying **the** (millennial) **world and those who dwell in**

it (NASB; 24:1). **8-9. The floods** (rivers) are to **clap** their hands in joyous acclamation (93:3; Isa. 55:12), **the hills** (mountains) are to **be joyful** ("sing together for joy"; Psalms 65:12; 89:12) before the LORD as He appears **to judge the earth** (96:13; Rev. 19:11) **with righteousness ... and the peoples with equity** (Psalm 96:10; Isa. 9:7; 11:4-5).

J. THE RIGHTEOUS RULE OF THE KING. 99:1-9.

See the introductions to Psalms 93, 94, and 95 for the scope and context of this psalm.

The King's Millennial Throne. 99:1-5. **1. The Lord reigneth** ("sits enthroned"; 93:1; 96:10; 97:1). He whose advent is anticipated in Psalm 98 is reigning here. The people are pictured trembling before Him as He is enthroned **above** (NASB; not "between") **the cherubim** (2 Sam. 6:2), as is now known from Ancient Near Eastern iconography. He appears enthroned upon His millennial "throne of ... glory" (Matt. 25:31) in a manner antitypical to His ancient enthronement (cf. Exod. 25:22; 1 Sam. 4:4; Psalm 80:1). The people will **tremble** (Psalm 2:9-11), and the earth will **shake** (NASB; cf. Rev. 16:17-20).

2. The LORD will be **great in Zion** (Psalm 48:1; Isa. 12:6) because His throne will be there as the religious and political capital of the millennial earth (2:2-3; Zech. 2:10-13; 8:20-23; 14:16-21), as well as His Temple (Ezek. 40:1—43:5). It is not His greatness in general that is the particular theme of praise, but His greatness as Zion's King in Jerusalem, manifested as high above all the peoples (lit. Heb.), denoting the total population of the millennial earth.

3-4. Verse 3 is prophetic of what shall be. "All the peoples" (v. 2) will **praise** the LORD's **great** and **awe-inspiring**

name because of His fidelity to His ancient people, Israel, in keeping His covenants and promises to them, demonstrating that He is **holy** (Psalm 22:3; Lev. 19:2; Josh. 24:19; 1 Sam. 2:2; Isa. 6:3, 7), **loveth justice** (Psalms 11:7; 33:5), has established a rule of equity (17:2; 98:9), and has executed **justice and righteousness in Jacob** (103:6; 146:7; Jer. 23:5). How marvelous that God's interposition for Israel shall finally be the theme of praise of all the millennial nations, because they shall thereby become the recipients of the blessing flowing to them as the result of God's reinstating His ancient people in His favor (Psalm 98:3-4; Rom. 11:12, 15).

5. God's faithfulness to His Old Testament people is the basis of the outburst of praise from the peoples of the millennial earth: **Exalt ye the Lord our God** (Psalms 34:3; 107:32; 118:28), **worship at his footstool**—the Ark of the Covenant, which the LORD, sitting invisibly enthroned above the cherubim, as it were, touched with His feet (132:7; Lam. 2:1). **For he is holy**, repeated for emphasis from verse 3.

The King's Rule in Old Testament Times. 99:6-8. Admonitions are presented to Israel to be instructed from past history in preparation for the LORD's coming Kingdom. **6.** If Israel would be ready to enjoy in that Kingdom the intimate fellowship that, as His priests, Aaron and Moses (Exod. 24:6-8; 29:26; 40:23-27; Lev. 8:1-30) and Samuel (1 Sam. 7:9; 12:18; Psalm 99:6; Jer. 15:1) did, and have God answer their prayers as He did theirs (Exod. 15:25; 32:30-34), then Israel must, like them, keep God's testimonies and avoid sin.

7. He spoke to them in the pillar of cloud (Exod. 33:9; Num. 12:5). They kept His Word (Psalm 105:28). **8.** He answered them (106:44). He was a for-

giving God to them (Num. 14:20; Psalm 78:38); yet He was a punisher and an avenger of their **misdeeds** (Exod. 32:28; Num. 20:12; Psalms 95:11; 107:12).

The Lesson from History. 99:9. **9. Exalt the Lord, our God.** Appropriate Him in His grace and love, as well as revere Him as an avenger of sin (v. 8; Exod. 34:7). **Worship at his holy hill,** Zion, the place of His Temple and the seat of His worship and government (Psalm 2:6; Zech. 8:3; cf. Isa. 2:2-3; Ezek. 40:5—43:7). For **the Lord our God is holy** (cf. vv. 3, 5), an emphasis in this ode of the coming Kingdom, when "HOLINESS TO THE LORD" (Exod. 28:36; 39:30; Isa. 23:18; Jer. 2:3) will be a sign even on the most mundane things of life (Zech. 14:20-21).

K. UNIVERSAL PRAISE IN THE KINGDOM. 100:1-5.

See the introductions to Psalms 93, 94, and 95 for the scope of this psalm, the last in this cluster of Kingdom odes. "A Psalm of praise" (*tōḏah,* "thanksgiving").

The Call to Worship. 100:1-3. The invitation involves four things: (1) **1.** It involves acclaiming the King's accession. **Make a joyful noise** (*hārî'û,* "raise a joyful shout"; 98:4, 6), **all ye lands** ("all the earth," meaning the entire millennial earth). The blessings brought by the advent of "the King, the LORD" (98:6, NASB, lit. Heb.) will be so vast that praise will be excited and ecstatic. The "joyful noise" is the shout of acclamation that will be raised to greet the King at His accession to the throne, as at Solomon's coronation (1 Kings 1:39-40) and at the Messiah's personal and visible return to reign (Psalm 2:6, 8, 11-12).

(2) **2a.** The invitation involves serving the LORD **with gladness** (Deut. 12:11-12; 28:47), with true worship and spontane-

ous submission as King, not as in the case where rebels are warned, "Serve the LORD *with fear*" (cf. Psalm 2:1-3, 11, italics added). (3) **2b.** The invitation involved coming before **his presence** in true fellowship with Him, **with singing**, as the expression of spontaneous joy at His royal accession.

(4) **3.** The invitation involved realizing that the King is the LORD (*yhwh*) Himself, God (incarnate), in contrast to all the nonentity deities (gods) of the nations (Deut. 7:9; Psalm 46:10). He is the Creator of mankind (Job 10:3; Psalms 95:6; 119:73), our Redeemer-Deliverer by whose redemption we are His people (74:1-2; 95:7; Isa. 40:11; Ezek. 34:30-31) and the **sheep** of His pasture (Psalm 23:1-4).

The Call to Bless the Lord. 100:4-5. **4.** The call is to enter **his gates with thanksgiving**, and the courts of His millennial Temple (Isa. 2:2-3; Ezek. 40:5—43:7; Zech. 14:16-19) **with praise**, giving thanks to Him and blessing (exaltingly glorifying) His name (i.e., Him in His exalted majesty; Psalm 96:2). **5. For the Lord is good** (25:8; 86:5; Jer. 33:11; Nah. 1:7), demonstrated by His covenant-keeping faithfulness to His people, Israel, and through them to the whole world (Psalms 25:8; 34:8; 86:5).

His mercy will then be manifested as a fact of redemptive history in the crucified, risen, ascended LORD, returned to set up His Kingdom. His **truth** will be authenticated for all time in His keeping His Word to Israel concerning His covenants and promises to them. The result will be that all peoples of the Kingdom will have indubitable proof that His truth is not an ephemeral whim, but the essence of the very being of God and eternal as He Himself is eternal and enduring.

L. THE DAVIDIC IDEAL OF A KING. 101:1-8.

Psalms 101 to 104 form another series that prophetically glimpses the consecutive story of David's Son and Lord as the ideal King of righteousness and peace (Psalm 101), in humiliation as the prelude to His glory (Psalm 102), as the object of universal praise, especially of Israel in her restoration (Psalm 103), and as the object of creation's praise as Creator (Psalm 104). Psalm 101 is a mirror in which King David saw not so much what he actually was as what he ought to be and what the future King-Messiah, "the root and the offspring of David" (Rev. 22:16), in whom the Davidic Covenant will be fulfilled, will be in deed and truth.

The Celebration of God's Covenant Mercy. 101:1. **1.** King David resolved to extol the covenant **mercy** (*ḥĕsĕd*) and **justice** that through the Davidic Covenant (2 Sam. 7:8-16) will make possible the realization of the ideal kingship. David realized that the LORD is the source of this promised great blessing; therefore, he said, **Unto thee, O Lord, will I sing** (Psalms 51:14; 89:1; 145:7).

The King's Resolve of Exemplary Personal Conduct. 101:2-5. **2a.** King David's pledge to godly morality constitutes a prefiguration of the ideal King to come, the greater David, in whom the Davidic Covenant, and the steadfast love and mercy behind it, can be realized. **I will behave myself wisely in a perfect** (*tāmîm*, "blameless") **way** (1 Sam. 18:14-15; 2 Sam. 8:15; cf. John 8:46).

2b. Oh, when wilt thou come unto me? that is, to bless me, according to the promise recorded in Exodus 20:24, "In all places where I record my name I will come unto thee, and I will bless thee." David abruptly inserted this brief prayer because the Ark of the Covenant had been brought to Jerusalem, making it "the city of the LORD" (v. 8) and by its presence recording God's name there. So the Messiah's return to Jerusalem (Zech. 14:4; Acts 1:11) will by His presence record God's name there and assure the blessing of God upon the Holy City (Psalms 2:6; 48:1-3).

2c. I will walk within my house with a perfect heart (1 Kings 9:4; 11:4; 1 Tim. 2:4-5), literally, "in the integrity of my heart." **3-5.** He also vowed to **set no wicked** (worthless) **thing before** his **eyes** (Deut. 15:9), to abhor **the work of those who turn aside** (who practice apostasy (Psalm 40:4), to spurn **a perverse** heart and evil (1 Cor. 5:11; 2 Tim. 2:19), to destroy or silence slanderers (Psalm 50:20; Jer. 9:4), and not to tolerate him who had a **high look** (a haughty mien) or a **proud** (arrogant) **heart** (Psalms 10:4; 18:27; Prov. 6:17).

The King's Resolve of Exemplary Public Conduct. 101:6-8. **6-7.** David did not attempt to compartmentalize his ethics. He vowed the same lofty conduct in public administration as in private. He determined to seek out **the faithful of the land** to dwell with him as servants and counselors. He limited his ministers and servants to those who walked **in a perfect** (blameless) **way** (119:1), rejecting him who **worketh** (practices) **deceit** (43:1; 52:2) and demoting or "firing" him who **telleth lies** (52:4-5).

8. He resolved to **early** ("every morning") **destroy all the wicked doers from the city of the Lord,** indicating the unflagging zeal of the king to rule righteously and "with a rod of iron" (Psalm 2:9; Isa. 9:6-7; 11:4-5), putting himself under solemn obligation to root out all who were unworthy of citizenship in such a kingdom as the King-Messiah will set up at His second advent, for He

alone (not David or any other Davidic king) can meet the requirements of the ideal king and will be that King.

M. HUMILIATION IS A PRELUDE TO THE KING'S GLORY. 102:1-28.

For the scope and context of Psalm 102, see the introduction to Psalm 101. The inscription is significant: "A Prayer of the afflicted, when he is overwhelmed, and poureth out his complaint before the LORD" (cf. 142:2). That the afflictions of the afflicted one transcend the experience of the psalmist (David, we believe), or any other saints of any period, and prophetically glimpse the sufferings of Christ in His humiliation, is suggested by three things: (1) by the position of the psalm in the particular series in which it is found in the psalter; (2) by its being marked out in the New Testament as being Messianic by the Holy Spirit's applying verses 25 to 27 to the crucified, risen Christ (Heb. 1:10-12); and (3) by the internal evidence of the psalm itself. Through Christ's affliction, mercy shall yet come to Zion at His second advent, when all "nations shall fear . . . the LORD, and all the kings of the earth [His] glory" (vv. 13-15).

In the Place of Humiliation. 102:1-7. **1. Hear my prayer, O Lord** (cf. 18:6; 101:2). **2a. Hide not thy face from me** (69:17). So God the Father hid His face from the greater than David on the cross (13:1; 22:1; 27:9; Matt. 27:46). David (as a prophet) put into the mouth of his suffering seed (the Messiah) language that described but transcended his own anguish. **26. In the day when I call, answer me speedily.** Here in humiliation, facing His great work as sin-bearer, the LORD's Fellow (Zech. 13:7) is seen crying out with "prayers and supplications with strong crying and tears unto him that was able to save him from [out of] death" (Heb. 5:7).

3-5. This is a prophetic foregleam of Gethsemane (facing Calvary) when the sinless One was made sin for us (2 Cor. 5:21) and faced the agonies portrayed here that the finite mind can never really fathom—**days ... consumed like smoke** (Psalm 37:20) **... bones ... burned like an hearth** (Job 30:30; Lam. 1:13) **... heart ... smitten, and withered like grass** (Psalm 90:5-6; Isa. 40:7), forgetting to **eat ... bread** (1 Sam. 1:7; 2 Sam. 12:17; Ezra 10:6) **... bones** clinging to His flesh because of the **voice** (loudness) of His **groaning** (Job 19:20; Lam. 4:8). **6-7.** He was **like a pelican of the wilderness ... like an owl of the desert** (Isa. 34:11; Zeph. 2:14) **... like a sparrow alone upon the housetop.**

In the Throes of the Deepest Agony. 102:8-11. **8.** The sufferer (the greater David prefigured by David) was plunged into such a depth of anguish that His enemies employed it as a reproach or imprecation, wishing the same thing might happen to their enemies as had happened to Him (31:11; 42:10). Those who were angry at Him (Acts 26:11) boastfully derided Him and used His name as a curse (Num. 5:21; Isa. 65:16; Jer. 29:22).

9-10. He ate **ashes**, symbolizing the deepest sorrows and mourning, as His food, and He mingled His tears with His drink (Psalms 42:3; 80:5) because of the divine **indignation** and **wrath**, which fell upon Him, as the sin offering, the sinless Substitute for sinners, the Bearer of the sin of the world.

He was lifted up as the eternal God, the Word who was with God and was God (John 1:1-3), possessing the glory of the eternal God as one with God before the world was (17:5; Prov. 8:22-30). But in His redemptive purpose for the world, God **cast** Him **down** in the incarnation and in the humiliations that led to the death of the cross (Phil. 2:5-8). **11.**

The declining shadow and the withered grass symbolize the Savior's deep affliction.

In Anticipation of the Most Exhilarating Joy. 102:12-17. The sufferer, David, prefiguring David's Lord, found consolation in six things: (1) **12.** He found consolation in God's abiding character. **But thou, O Lord, shalt endure forever** (shall "sit," i.e., as a King forever; 9:7; 29:10; Lam. 5:19). However close to extinction the house of David may have seemed, as at the Babylonian Exile and especially when they nailed to the cross "THE KING OF THE JEWS" (Matt. 27:37), the LORD had promised its perpetuity (2 Sam. 7:8-16). The enduring permanence of His own throne guaranteed the continuance of David's posterity and the perpetuation of His memorial, the recorded manifestation of Himself in mighty deeds in behalf of His people. He can, therefore, never disown His glorious character **unto all generations** (Psalm 135:13; cf. Exod. 3:15).

(2) **13.** The sufferer also found consolation in the assurance and efficacy of God's promises. **Thou shalt arise, and have mercy upon Zion; for the time to favor her, yea, the set time, is come,** the time appointed by God in His unfailing Word (Isa. 40:2; Dan. 9:2; 12:9; Gal. 4:4), when Zion and the Davidic line are reduced to their lowest ebb (Psalms 12:5; 68:1). The "set time" is when "the times of the Gentiles" have run their course (Luke 21:24; Rom. 11:25) and Jerusalem reduced to her greatest misery (Zech. 12:1-9; 14:1-3).

(3) **14.** The sufferer also found consolation in the love the LORD has for Zion, manifested in the love and yearning sorrow His servants have for her in her desolation. **For thy servants take pleasure in her stones, and favor** (*y^eḥōnēnû*, "feel pity for") **the dust,** the stones and

dust being regarded as the materials for restoring the city of God (Psalm 69:35).

(4) **15.** The sufferer also found comfort in the blessed results that will result in the LORD's mercy upon Zion. The nations **shall fear** (reverence) **the name of the Lord.** God's glory is involved in the restoration of the city (68:29-32; Isa. 59:19-20).

(5) **16.** He found comfort in the fact that the Lord Himself shall appear in glory when the city is restored for its Kingdom role. **When the Lord shall build up** Zion (a prophetic perfect), **he shall appear** (prophetic perfect) **in his glory.** More is included than Jerusalem's ancient glory, for the glory here is inseparably connected with Christ's second advent in His glory. He shall **appear** (*nir'â*, "be manifested personally and visibly"; Gen. 48:3; Exod. 3:16; Lev. 9:4; cf. Titus 2:13).

(6) **17.** The sufferer lastly found solace in confident anticipation of answer to his prayer offered in verse 1. The LORD **will regard the prayer of the destitute**—His people, yes, but preeminently the prayer of His own beloved One, the Sufferer prefigured in this chapter. The restoration of Zion will be the result of His prayers, in a preeminent sense, and the prayers of His people (cf. v. 20; Isa. 62:6-7). God will **not despise their prayer** (Psalm 22:5).

In Realization of the Most Wonderful Blessings. 102:18-22. **18.** The prophecy of Zion's restoration for Kingdom glory will be consigned to writing for the record of the fact for future generations (Exod. 17:14; Deut. 31:10, 21; Psalms 22:30; 48:13; 78:4), in order that when its fulfillment takes place **a people yet to be created may praise the Lord** (NASB; 22:30-31; 48:13).

19. For he hath looked down (a prophetic perfect). At the appointed time the LORD will look down upon the groans of His people (Deut. 26:15; Psalm 14:2; Isa. 63:15; Zech. 2:13) **from the height of his sanctuary** (i.e., His holy height). **20-21.** Then He will set free those who are **appointed to death**, those on the point of death under the horrors of the Antichrist during the Great Tribulation, in order that both Israel and the nations converted through her may **declare** (make known) **the name of the Lord in Zion** (cf. v. 15; Psalm 26:7). **22.** That will be fulfilled in the millennial period **when the people** (peoples; "nations," v. 15), denoting all the citizens of the Kingdom, that is, **the kingdoms,** will be **gathered together. . . to serve the Lord** (Hos. 1:11; 3:5).

In the Place of Humiliation Once More. 102:23-27. Once again (cf. vv. 1-11) the great Sufferer and afflicted One, who suffered in our place and who paid the price of redemption for Israel and the world, comes into view, as is shown by the quotation of verses 25 to 27 in Hebrews 1:10-12, in connection with the incarnation, humiliation, death, and resurrection of our Lord.

23. The Sufferer renewed His plaint as a stepping-stone to confidence grounded in God's enduring character (vv. 24-27). This verse comprehends our Lord's humiliation and abasement in submission to the divine will and redemptive purpose. **He weakened** (humbled, afflicted) **my strength in the way,** the pathway marked out for David's Son and Lord from suffering and rejection to Kingdom glory (Exod. 18:8; 1 Pet. 1:11). **He shortened my days** (cf. vv. 3, 11; Psalm 39:5), painting this dark background to set in bright relief God's eternity and abiding faithfulness (vv. 25-27) as the basis of assurance.

24. O ... God, take me not away ("cause me not to ascend"), like smoke that vanishes (v. 3; Gen. 19:28; Jer. 48:15), **in the midst of my days** to share the doom of the wicked (Psalm 55:23), from whom He had separated Himself (101:4) and expressed faith that He would not be implicated in their fate. **25.** God's unchanging nature is emphasized by contrasting it with the most enduring of material things—the earth and the heavens.

26. Even those shall perish and change, but God never so (cf. Heb. 1:10-12, where what is here declared of the LORD is said of the Messiah). The thought is not of the new heavens and earth of the eternal state (Rev. 21:5), but the earth renovated by fire, which will precede it (2 Pet. 3:7, 10-11). **27. But thou art the same** (Heb. 1:12, lit., "But Thou art He"; Deut. 32:39), meaning "the imperishable One" (cf. Mal. 3:6; Heb. 13:8).

The Result of the King's Humiliation. 102:28. **28.** Israel shall be reborn and established in her land in Kingdom blessing. **The children of thy servants** constitute the nation Israel (Isa. 65:9), which through its forefathers—Abraham, Isaac, and Jacob—God made the covenant. As the children (descendants) of the patriarchs, they were the servants of God. They **shall continue** in ("dwell" or "inhabit") their own land (Psalms 37:27, 29; 69:35-36). **And their seed**, the true spiritually reborn seed (22:30-31; 89:36; Isa. 66:8-9; Rom. 11:25-36) **shall be established** before the LORD in Kingdom blessing (Gen. 17:1; Psalm 101:7; cf. Zeph. 3:13).

N. ISRAEL'S PRAISE IN KINGDOM BLESSING. 103:1-22.

For the context and scope of Psalm 103, see the introduction to Psalm 101. Although this beloved psalm of David expresses the heartfelt praise and thanksgiving of God's saints in every age, it finds its full meaning in its prophetic application to Israel restored to God's favor in Kingdom blessing.

Praise the Lord for Manifold Benefits. 103:1-6. **1.** The LORD answered the thrice-repeated **Bless the Lord, O my soul** (cf. vv. 2, 22), expressing blessing *from* the soul, to the thrice-repeated benediction from the LORD *to* the soul in the Mosaic formula (Num. 6:24-26). To "bless the LORD" is to delight Him with genuine heartfelt praise and thanksgiving. **All that is within me** (lit., "all my inward parts"; Psalm 5:9) denotes the entire inward man—emotions, will, and understanding—in contrast to the mere external lip service of the hypocritically thankful (62:4). God's **holy name** denotes God Himself in His infinitely holy character.

2. The human heart, even the regenerated heart, is so prone to **forget . . . all** His **benefits**, and so the warning is needed (Deut. 6:12; 8:11, 14). How ironic that the very prosperity God gives too often becomes the sad occasion of the heart becoming self-sufficient and forgetting the Giver and His "benefits," which are the gracious bounties He bestows as an expression of His love and goodness.

3. The *first benefit* is God's forgiving iniquities. This is what will happen when the nation (represented by the singular "you") turns to the LORD (Zech. 12:10—13:1; Rom. 11:25-26; cf. Exod. 34:7; Psalms 86:5; 130:8). The *second benefit* is God's healing all Israel's diseases (Exod. 15:26; Psalm 30:2; Jer. 30:17). When the Messiah returns and Israel is reinstated in her national election, her healing covenant will be renewed (Exod. 15:26; Isa. 35:4-6; 53:1-4; Heb. 6:5).

4. The *third benefit* is God's redeeming the nation's life **from destruction** ("the pit," another name for Sheol or the nether world) at the hands of the

Antichrist and his followers, under whose terrible reign of terror Israel will be all but obliterated (Psalm 2:1-3) from the earth (Zech. 11:15-17; 13:8-9; 14:2-3). The *fourth benefit* is God's crowning Israel with the **loving-kindness and tender mercies** that will flow from Calvary as the nation is converted and turns to the Lord at His second advent (Psalms 25:6; 40:11; Zech. 3:1-5; Rom. 11:25-33).

5. The *fifth benefit* is God's satisfying Israel with longevity and prosperity in the Kingdom. "Who satisfies you with good as long as you live" (RSV). "Who satisfies you throughout life with good things" (BV); "your years" (NASB). Both spiritually and temporally, Israel restored to Kingdom status will be greatly blessed with long life (Isa. 65:20; Zech. 8:4) and prosperity (Isa. 65:21-25; Ezek. 39:25-29; Amos 9:13-14; Zech. 9:16—10:1).

The result will be that in Kingdom blessing Israel's **youth** will be **renewed like the eagle's**, whose vigor was proverbial (Isa. 40:31); hence, the Greek proverb: "The eagle's old age is as good as the lark's youth." Neither this passage nor Isaiah 40:31 give any countenance to the fable of the eagle's renewing its youth; they simply mean that the LORD's millennial blessings upon restored Israel will make her as young and lusty as an eagle.

6. The *sixth benefit* is the King-Messiah's righteous and just millennial administration. **The Lord executeth righteousness and judgment**, literally, "righteousnesses and judgments," the plurals used intensively for emphasizing the various acts in which His righteous and just Kingdom rule will be realized (cf. Isa. 9:7; 11:3-4).

Praise the Lord for Himself. *103:7-18.* The LORD is to be praised because of two things: (1) **7.** He is to be praised for His self-revealing nature. **He made known** to His people **his ways ... his acts**, not in mere words, but in actual deeds and guidance (Exod. 33:13; Psalm 25:4). His mighty undertakings for Moses, His leader, and Israel, His people, displayed His gracious dealings (Exod. 34:10; Psalm 9:11; 78:11).

(2) **8.** The LORD is to be praised also because of His compassionate mercy and grace (vv. 8-18). **The Lord is merciful** (*rāḥûm*, "compassionate") and **gracious** (*ḥannûn*, "displaying unmerited favor" to repentant sinners; Exod. 34:6-7; Num. 14:18; Neh. 9:17; Jonah 4:2), **slow to anger, and plenteous** (abounding) **in mercy** (*ḥěsěd*, "covenant love and faithfulness").

9. He will not always chide (*yārîb*, "strive, contend, or dispute with," particularly in the sense of litigation or a suit in a court of law). "He will not always be contending" (J. J. S. Perowne; cf. Isa. 57:16). **Neither will he keep** (*nāṭar*, "maintain, retain") **[his anger] forever** (Jer. 3:5, 12; Mic. 7:18), the same ellipsis of "His anger" occurring in Leviticus 19:18 and Jeremiah 3:5. He does "keep" (reserve) wrath for the wicked, but not for His own.

10. His compassionate grace is also displayed in His not dealing with us (His people) **after our sins** (Ezra 9:13; Lam. 3:22), as He threatened in Leviticus 26:23-24, and as He does in the case of willful and persistent transgressors. **11.** The greatness of His **mercy** (loving-kindness) **toward them that fear him** (filially revere Him) is infinite, compared to the height of the heavens above the earth (Psalms 36:5; 57:10).

12. So completely has He acquitted believers of the guilt and penalty of sin (Mic. 7:18-19) that it is declared **as far as the east is from the west ... hath he removed our transgressions from us** (2 Sam. 12:13; Isa. 38:17; Zech. 3:9; Eph.

1:7; Heb. 9:26), through Christ's redemptive work, which will then be fulfilled and be retrospective with regard to Israel's paean of praise in full Kingdom blessing, as it was prospective through faith to Old Testament saints.

13. Just as a human father **pitieth** (has compassion on) his children, so the LORD **pitieth** (has compassion on) **them that fear him** (Mal. 3:17). **14. For he knoweth our frame** (our natural constitution; cf. Gen. 2:7, "The LORD God formed [framed] man of the dust"). Therefore, He is mindful of our sinful frailty (cf. Psalm 90:1-12) and the helpless misery of our state, which might seem to bar us from One so infinitely perfect. Instead, it proves to be divine incentive to display infinite compassion toward us (78:38-39; 89:47).

Man's sinful frailty is further described (vv. 15-18; cf. 90:1-5; Isa. 40:6-8). **15-16.** Man's days resemble **grass** (Psalm 90:5; Isa. 40:6; 1 Pet. 1:24). He flourishes like **a flower of the field** (Job 14:2; James 1:10-11), but is soon windblown (Isa. 40:7), withered, and gone (Job 7:10; 8:18; 20:9).

17. In striking contrast, the **mercy of the Lord**, especially as it will be fully manifested in the Kingdom (founded upon the finished redemptive work of David's Son and Lord, and viewed in its full perspective) will be seen to be **from everlasting to everlasting** (cf. Eph. 1:4) **upon those who fear him** (Psalm 25:6). Three times the warning "those who fear [revere] him" is issued against the presumption of transgressors appropriating this promise, which has no application to them (cf. vv. 11, 13).

And his righteousness, that is, His faithfulness to His promises (Exod. 20:6; Deut. 5:10; Psalm 105:8) **unto children's children**, to the fathers of Israel (v. 7) as well as the most distant descendants (Luke 1:72-74; Acts 2:39). Then

the ultimate basis of God's being righteous in displaying mercy (the Law-fulfilling righteousness of the Messiah) will be an accomplished fact of redemptive history. **18.** Those who fear (revere) the LORD are further defined as those who **keep his covenant** (Deut. 7:9; Psalm 25:10) and **remember his commandments** (precepts) **to do them** (Exod. 19:5; 24:8).

Praise the Lord for His Kingdom Rule. 103:19-22. **19.** The LORD has **prepared** (established) **his throne in the heavens** (11:4, 7; Heb. 1:11), **and his kingdom** (*mălkût*, "royal dominion, kingly sovereignty") **ruleth** (*māshăl*, "governs, reigns") **over all** (47:2; Dan. 4:17, 25). This divine rule refers to God's universal kingdom, including the entire creation, which is as eternal as God, exists without interruption, and never fails in its purpose. This kingdom is distinguishable from the mediatorial Kingdom of Christ, which issues from it (cf. 7:9-14) and will finally be merged with it (1 Cor. 15:24).

20. The mediatorial Kingdom that comes into view in verse 19*b* (cf. Matt. 25:31) elicits the praises of this entire psalm and calls the angelic realm to join (Psalm 148:2). The angels are ethereal spirits who **excel in strength** (*gĭbbōrê koāḥ*, "mighty ones") **that do his commandments** (lit. Heb., "perform His Word"; 29:1; 78:25; Matt. 6:10), **hearkening unto** (obeying) **the voice of his word** (Psalm 91:11; Heb. 1:14). They will accompany Christ at His second advent to set up His Kingdom (Matt. 25:31; Rev. 19:14). Then Jacob's vision (Gen. 28:12-15) will be fulfilled in the Davidic-Messianic Kingdom (John 1:51).

21-22a. The angelic host is augmented in its praise by the inanimate hosts, the heavenly bodies, sun, moon, stars, and planets that do His pleasure (Psalm

19:1). Thus *all* creation is called to **bless . . . the Lord—all ye his hosts** (Gen. 32:2; 1 Kings 22:19; Neh. 9:6; Psalm 148:2; Luke 2:13), who serve Him and do His will (Psalm 104:4), as well as **all his works—in all places of his dominion** (145:10).

22b. Bless the Lord, O my soul. How can the psalmist and every saint, especially the saints of the Kingdom age, to whom all of this will be realized in prophetic fulfillment when they receive such glorious tokens of God's favor, be silent when all the rest of creation praises Him?

O. CREATION'S PRAISE OF THE CREATOR. 104:1-35.

For the context of this psalm, which concludes a series (Psalms 101-4), see the introduction to Psalm 101. The Creator is depicted in His glory as Creator. When the Kingdom is set up and creation delivered from the bondage of corruption (Rom. 8:20-22), that glory will come into clear focus, as is set forth in this magnificent psalm (vv. 31-35). Franz Delitzsch entitles it a "Hymn in honor of the God of the Seven Days" and says it "is altogether an echo of the . . . history of the seven days of creation in Gen. 1:1—2:13" (*Psalms*, 3: 125, 127).

The First and Second Day–Natural Light and the Heavens. 104:1-5. **1.** The theme is announced. **Bless** (praise the LORD with genuine and spontaneous sincerity) **the Lord, O my soul**, that is, the psalmist, who speaks as the representative of the nation Israel prophetically, and particularly of her restoration to divine favor in Kingdom blessing. **O Lord my God, thou art very great**, evidenced by His creative powers and wonders. The LORD is to be blessed for His works, which reflect His majesty. **Thou art clothed with honor and majesty,**

the royal apparel with which You clothed Yourself at creation and still wear in continually preserving what You have created.

2. This verse poetically summarizes the first day of creation in calling forth light (Gen. 1:3)—covering **thyself with light as with a garment** (cloak; Dan. 7:9). This is not the eternal light of God's very being (1 Tim. 6:16; 1 John 1:5) but natural light proceeding from the sun, which had been obliterated by chaos and then began to penetrate earth's atmosphere as the result of the re-creative work (see comments on Gen. 1:1—2:3) of the second day, referred to in these words: **who stretchest out the heavens like a curtain** (tent cover), the Creator forming the sky and dry land (Gen. 1:6-9) with the same ease as a Bedouin spreads his tent (Isa. 40:22; 54:2).

3a. Who layeth the beams of his (upper) **chanbers in the waters.** The pavilion that God rears for His own abode is pictured with poetic artistry as resting on a floor of rain clouds, like a tent spread on a flat Eastern roof (Psalm 18:11; Amos 9:6-7). **3b-c.** He makes **the clouds his chariot** (Isa. 19:1), the Creator driving them at will like a king does his chariot, walking upon **the wings of the wind** (Psalm 18:10), directing the winged winds at His pleasure. The winds are naturally associated with the clouds, which they drive before them as fleet steeds.

4. In this manner **He makes the winds His messengers** (148:8; Heb. 1:7), **flaming fire** (lightning) **His ministers** (NASB; 2 Kings 2:11; 6:17). The quotation of this passage in Hebrews 1:4 demonstrates that (1) the glory of the risen Christ is revealed (then installed as King in millennial glory), and (2) that the angels of God, who in the Kingdom will ascend and descend upon the Son of Man (John 1:51) are meant. As God Himself "walketh upon the wings of the wind," so His angelic messengers and celestial servants manifest their agency in wind and fire, His celestial retinue in His mighty operations in nature (Deut. 33:2; Judg. 13:20; Psalm 103:20-21; Dan. 7:10).

5. Who laid the foundations of the earth, that it should not be removed forever (Job 38:4; Psalm 24:2), answering to what was said of the heavens (v. 3), the work of the second day of creation being still in the poet's mind. As the upper portion of the world's frame, the heavens, is firmly fixed, though it only has rain clouds for its beams, so the lower part, the earth, is solidly set by God's omnipotence, though it rests upon nothing (Job 26:7-8; 38:4-6).

The Third Day—The Earth Prepared for Man. 104:6-18. **6. Thou coveredst it** (the earth) **with the deep** ($t^e h \hat{o} m$, "primeval ocean"; Gen. 1:2; Prov. 8:27, BDB) **as with a garment; the waters stood above the mountains** before the separation of water and dry land, the Noahic Flood subsequently bringing back the earth to its earlier recreated state at that time (Gen. 7:19-20).

7. At thy rebuke they (the waters) **fled** (1:9), being removed from off the earth. The "deep," as it were, was viewed as chaos in opposition to the order (kosmos) that the Creator, as the God of order, was bringing into effect (cf. Mark 4:39). At the sound of the Creator's thunderlike voice, the waters **hastened** (hurried) away (Psalms 29:3; 77:18).

8. This verse admits grammatically of two translations: (1) "The mountains rose; the valleys sank down" (NASB, RSV, BV), the preferred rendering; and (2) **They** (the waters) **go up...they** (the waters) **go down** (KJV). The first rendering takes care of the phenomenon alluded to in the second rendering and explains the formation of oceans and dry

land (Psalm 33:7; 2 Pet. 3:5; cf. Job 38:10). **9.** It also explains the bounds God set upon the oceans that they should not return to inundate the earth again (Gen. 9:11).

Verses 10 to 14 celebrate the benefit that the shore-surrounded waters are to the animals and plants.

10-11. The Creator continuously sends forth **springs into the valleys** (Psalm 107:35; Isa. 41:18), which flow between the hills, giving drink to **every beast of the field** (see v. 13) so that **the wild asses quench their thirst** (Job 39:5). **12-14.** He depicts the birds of the air nesting beside the wild animals of the field and singing among the branches of the trees, while the Creator waters the hills **from his chambers** (see v. 3), the earth being richly nourished by the rain, causing **the grass to grow for the cattle** (Psalm 147:8) **and herb** (vegetation) **for the service** (labor) **of man** (Gen. 1:29) that he may through the cultivation of the soil **bring forth food out of** (from) **the earth** (Job 28:5). The grass grows spontaneously for the cattle, but man must cultivate his food by labor as a result of the curse of sin (Gen. 3:17-19), although what he produces is still due to the creative power and gracious concern of God.

15. The three chief agricultural products of Palestine are named: **wine** (Judg. 9:13; Prov. 31:6; Eccles. 10:19), (olive) **oil** (Psalms 23:5; 92:10; 141:5; Luke 7:46), and **bread** (food), made from grain, which **strengtheneth** (sustains) man's **heart** (Gen. 18:5; Judg. 19:5, 8), as distinguished from the gladdening effects of wine and oil, which are more luxuries than necessities.

16-17. The trees of the Lord (like the mighty cedars of Lebanon, which especially proclaim God's glory as Creator) **are full** (lit., "are satisfied"), that is, with the rain from the Lord's "upper chambers" (cf. v. 13), **where the birds**

901

make their nests (v. 12), as does the stork, whose home is the fir trees (Lev. 11:19). **18. The high hills** are for the **wild goats** (Job 39:1), and the cliffs a refuge for the (rock) **badgers** (Lev. 11:5).

The Fourth Day—Luminaries. 104:19-24. **19-23.** See comments on Genesis 1:14-19, which this section recalls. This, we believe, is not the creation ex nihilo of the sun and moon and stars, since natural light appeared on the first day, but the resolving of the chaotic celestial mass into cosmic atmosphere, allowing the light of these heavenly bodies to shine upon the earth, and appointing them for **seasons** and for time measurements (Psalm 19:6), regulating the activities and functions of man and beast (Gen. 3:19; Job 38:39; Joel 1:20). **24.** These provisions call forth a special doxology lauding the glorious creative variety (Psalm 40:5) and wisdom of the Creator, who has so lavishly stored the earth with His wealth, which man is continually discovering and appropriating.

The Fifth and Sixth Days—Birds, Fish, Animals—All for Man. 104:25-30. This section echoes Genesis 1:20-31. **25-26.** Pointed out is a special wonder of the Creator—the **great and wide** (broad) **sea** (Psalms 8:8; 69:34), swarming with animals both small and great, and with **ships** plying its surface, and in it **leviathan** (a huge marine animal; Job 3:8, NASB; 26:12-13; Isa. 27:1; 51:9). **27-28.** All these creatures wait for their Creator (Psalm 145:15) to give them **their food in due season** (136:25; 147:9) and satisfy them (145:16). **29.** God sustains all His creatures, dependent as they are upon Him for life (Job 34:14-15; Psalm 146:4; Eccles. 12:7), and facing death if He hides His face from them (Gen. 3:19; Job 10:9; Psalm 90:3). **30.** He creates all life and renews the face of the ground to support His creatures.

The Seventh Day—Sinners Consumed out of the Earth. 104:31-35. **31. The glory of the Lord** (such a Creator!) **shall endure forever** (86:12; 111:10), despite the Fall of man and the ensuing curse upon the Edenic re-creation described here, interrupting the Creator's rest (Gen. 2:2-3) by His work of redemption (John 5:17). His glory as Creator not only will be perpetuated but also enhanced as Redeemer. Then the LORD will **rejoice** (be glad) **in his works** (His work of creation and redemption) in the glorious consummation during the Kingdom age and on into a sinless eternity.

32a. But before that resplendent day He will look **on the earth** and it will tremble (Psalms 46:1-3; 97:4-5; 114:7; Rev. 16:17-20) in the terrible pouring out of the bowls of His wrath in destroying sinners from the earth in preparation for the setting up of His glorious millennial Kingdom. **32b.** He will touch the mountains, and they will **smoke** as at Sinai (Exod. 19:18) in the Tribulation judgments (Joel 2:30-31).

33-34. As the prophet-psalmist contemplated the glories of the Kingdom age after the storm of the Tribulation has passed, he burst out in ecstatic singing and praise to the Creator-Redeemer (Psalms 9:2; 19:14; 63:4; 146:2; cf. Rev. 19:7-9). **35.** But **sinners** will **be consumed out of the earth** (19:16—20:3) and **the wicked** will **be no more** (Psalm 37:10) before such unrestrained jubilation will be possible, calling forth the first "Hallelujah," that is, **Praise ... the Lord!** (105:45; 106:48), found in the Psalter; they become ever more frequent as one advances toward the close of the book of Psalms.

P. CELEBRATION OF THE LORD'S COVENANT FAITHFULNESS. 105:1-45.

Psalms 105 and 106 bring to a close the fourth section of the Psalter (Psalms 90-106), corresponding to the book of Numbers (see the introduction to Psalm 90). Psalm 105 prophetically glimpses restored Israel's celebration of the LORD's covenant faithfulness realized in Kingdom blessing. Psalm 106 presents a foregleam of Israel's repentance and national confession when the LORD will save them and with a new heart they will read their history aright in the light of divine grace and mercy, in fulfillment of Ezekiel 36:31, when they will "remember [their] ... *evil ways* ... and shall *loathe* [themselves] ... for [their] *iniquities*" (italics added).

Call to Restored Israel to Praise and Worship. 105:1-8. The first fifteen verses are found in 1 Chronicles 16:8-22 (with slight variation) as the first part of the festal song to celebrate the bringing of the ark to Zion. **1-3a.** Prophetically, the song will be sung when millennial Zion is graced by the presence of the Lord Jesus Christ at His second advent. The restored nation will be called upon to **give thanks** (Psalm 106:1), to call upon His name (99:6; Isa. 12:4), and as the LORD's reinstated elect nation (Rom. 11:25-32) to make known His deeds **among the peoples** (of the millennial earth; Psalm 145:12; Zech. 8:22-23; cf. Isa. 60:3) and **talk...of all his wondrous works** (Psalms 77:12; 119:27; 145:5) and **glory ... in his holy name** (34:2), by which they will have been delivered from their enemies and established in Kingdom blessing (Isa. 9:6-7; 11:10—12:6).

3b-6. Three times the **seed of Abraham**, the **children of Jacob**, are urged to **seek the Lord, his strength** (Psalm 63:2),

his face (27:8), and **remember his marvelous works** (wonders; 40:5; 77:11) **and the judgments of his mouth** (119:13). **7a.** Then in Kingdom blessing, as a reinstated elect nation, Israel's confession will be: **He is the Lord our God** (Zech. 12:10—13:1), repeating the confession of Thomas when he recognized the risen Lord by the prints of the nails in His hands and feet (John 20:27-28). **7b. His judgments are in all the earth** (Isa. 26:9; Rev. 6:1—20:6), a necessary prelude to the decimation of Israel's enemies (Psalm 2:1-3) and her own cleansing and conversion (Jer. 30:5-7).

The Lord's Faithfulness to His Covenant Through the Patriarchs. 105:8-25. **8-13.** When Israel is regathered to Palestine, **the land of Canaan, the lot of** (her) **inheritance** (Ezek. 37:1-28; Matt. 24:31), her people will be converted (Zech. 12:10—13:1), and established in Kingdom glory. They will joyfully cry out, **He hath remembered his covenant forever** (cf. v. 42; Gen. 12:1-3; Psalm 106:45; Luke 1:72-73), **the word which he commanded** (ordained) as an unalterable **law** (v. 10) that Israel should be His elect people and should inherit Canaan (vv. 11, 42).

He hath remembered his covenant forever ... to a thousand generations (Deut. 7:9; cf. Exod. 20:6), meaning to "all generations" (Luke 1:72-73). The Abrahamic Covenant (Gen. 12:1-3) was confirmed by oath to Isaac (26:3) and confirmed to Jacob **for a law ... and to Israel for an everlasting covenant** (28:13) **... when they were ... few ... very few** (34:30; Deut. 7:7), **and sojourners in it** (the land; Gen. 23:4; Heb. 11:9), going from **one nation to another** (the seven nations of Canaan, as well as Egypt, the Philistines, etc.). Though few in number, homeless, and wandering sojourners, they were protected by God from annihilation, and finally, in the person of their descendants, were given possession of the promised land.

14-15. The LORD **permitted** no one **to do them wrong** (oppress them; Gen. 20:7; 35:5), reproving kings **for their sakes** (12:17; 20:3, 7), saying, **Touch not mine anointed** (pl.), that is, **my prophets**, referring here to the patriarchs, Abraham (20:7), Isaac, Jacob, and Joseph (41:38), who had prophetic dreams, visions, and then divine communications by the Spirit. So in the Kingdom age there shall again be "anointed ones" (Zech. 4:14; cf. Isa. 54:13; Joel 2:28-29; Rev. 11:4). Being the LORD's anointed, no one dared touch these men endowed with the Holy Spirit with impunity, for in them God's fidelity to His promises was bound up (Gen. 26:11).

16. The LORD's faithfulness to His covenant through the patriarchs is continued (vv. 16-25) in His calling **for a famine upon the land** (41:54), breaking the **whole staff of bread** (Lev. 26:26; Isa. 3:1; Ezek. 4:16), in usage similar to our present-day expression referring to bread as "the staff of life."

17-19. With the covenant in mind, the LORD **sent a man** (Joseph) **before them** into Egypt (Gen. 45:5), who was **sold** as a slave (37:28, 36; Acts 7:9) and severely tested **until the time that his** (Joseph's) **word**, by which he interpreted to Pharaoh's servants their dreams in prison (41:11-20) **came** to pass. Joseph's word, in accentuating the divine faithfulness to the covenant, is more accurately called **the word of the Lord.**

20-23. Joseph's exaltation in Egypt is noted; he was there to greet his aged father when he arrived to sojourn in **the land of Ham**, so called poetically because Egypt is listed as one of the sons of Ham (10:6; cf. 46:6; Acts 7:15; 13:17). **24.** God worked sovereignly and provi-

dentially to make the people fruitful and stronger than their adversaries (Exod. 1:7, 9), always with His faithfulness to His covenant with Abraham in mind.

The Lord's Faithfulness to His Covenant Through Moses and the Exodus. 105:25-42. **25-26.** Again the LORD worked sovereignly to turn the heart of the Egyptians to hate His people (Exod. 1:8; 4:21) and deal craftily with them (1:10; Acts 7:19), sending Moses and Aaron as His deliverers (Exod. 3:10; 4:12-14; Num. 16:5; 17:5-8).

27-36. Through them He performed His wondrous acts and miracles (Psalm 78:43-51), sending the plagues upon the Egyptians (only eight of them are listed and their order differs from that found in Exod. 7-12; cf. Psalm 78:43-51), striking down **all the first-born in their land** (Exod. 12:29; 13:15; Psalm 135:8), called **the chief of all their strength**, meaning "the first fruits of all their vigor" (NASB).

37. He brought them forth (out) **with silver and gold** (Exod. 13:21; Neh. 9:12; Psalm 78:14; Isa. 4:5), with not one **feeble person among their tribes**, "not one who stumbled" (NASB; *kôshēl*, "stumbler"), unfit for the rigorous march (Exod. 13:18). **38. Egypt** (poetic for the Egyptians) **was glad, ... for the fear** (dread) **of them** had fallen upon them (11:1; 12:33; 15:16; Deut. 11:25).

The Lord's Faithfulness to His Covenant in the Wilderness. 105:39-42. **39. He spread a cloud for a covering** (Exod. 13:21; Neh. 9:12; Isa. 4:5), and **fire to give light** at night (Exod. 40:38), thus guiding and protecting His covenant people. **40.** In response to their request (Psalm 78:18), **he brought quails** (Exod. 16:13; Num. 11:31), satisfying (filling to repletion) His people **with the bread of heaven** ("angel's food"; Exod. 16:4). **41. He opened the rock** and water gushed out and ran like a river in the desert

(17:6; Num. 20:11; Isa. 48:21; 1 Cor. 10:4). **42.** All these mighty and gracious deeds He did for His people because He would keep His promises to Abraham His servant (v. 8; Gen. 15:14-18; Exod. 2:24).

The Lord's Faithfulness to His Covenant in the Conquest. 105:43-45. **43. He brought forth his people with joy** (*rĭnnâ*, "with a jubilant shout") and **gladness** (singing; Exod. 15:1; Psalm 106:12). **44.** He gave them **the lands of the nations** (the pagan nations of Canaan; Josh. 13:7; Psalm 78:55) that they might inherit (*yārăsh*, "take possession of, seize") **the labor of the peoples**, because the inhabitants, as a result of their moral debauchery, had forfeited any right to either the land or the fruit of their labor (toil) in the land (Gen. 15:16; Deut. 6:10; Josh. 13:7; 21:43; Psalms 44:2; 80:8).

45. By contrast, God gave it to His elect nation that **they might observe his statutes** (Deut. 4:40), **and keep his laws**, so completely violated by the Canaanites. The second "Hallelujah" (*hălᵉlû-yāh*), **Praise ye the Lord** (*yāh*), of the Psalter closes the psalm as it did Psalm 104, because, like it, it envisions the millennial celebration by Israel of the LORD's covenant faithfulness to His people.

Q. ISRAEL'S CONFESSION OF SIN AND RESTORATION. 106:1-48.

For the context and scope of Psalm 106, see the introduction to Psalm 105. As Psalm 105 celebrates the LORD's covenant blessing fully realized in Kingdom blessing, so Psalm 106 presents Israel's repentance for her unbelief and rebelliousness as she pours out her great lament in national confession when the nation is regathered to her homeland and saved at the Lord's second advent (Isa. 35:1-10; Ezek. 36:8-38;

37:1-28; Zech. 12:10—13:1; Rom. 11:25-36). Against the dark background of Israel's sin, God's grace shines out resplendently and elicits both an opening (v. 1) and closing "Hallelujah" (v. 48).

Introduction. 106:1-5. **1-3.** The introduction consists of a short call to praise (cf. 107:1; 118:1; 136:1) opening with **Praise** (*hălᵉlû*) **. . . the Lord** (*yāh*). Thanksgiving is rendered for (1) God's goodness; (2) His everlasting mercy (loving-kindness), as surveyed from the vantage point of Israel's final regathering and establishment in Kingdom blessing (cf. v. 47, which prophetic prayer will then have been answered); and (3) His **mighty acts** (deeds; 145:4, 12; 150:2) in preserving, regathering, and saving Israel for Kingdom blessedness as those who will then **observe justice** and do (practice) righteousness at all times (15:2). **4-5.** The brief call to praise (vv. 1-3) is followed by a personal petition of the psalmist that he may be permitted to share in the future restoration of the fortunes of his people.

Israel's Future Confession of Sin Predicted. 106:6. **6.** This verse states the theme developed in verses 7 to 46 and is rightly translated according to the Hebrew: **We have sinned with our fathers**, for in a sense all generations of Israelites came out of Egypt at the Exodus, just as all Christians were present when the Lord was crucified. So the nation at the time the psalmist wrote shared in the sins of the fathers, as the future nation regathered for Kingdom blessing will also share in the same. Israel—past, present, and future—has been perverse and deserved (and will deserve) to be cut off from the covenant—**have committed iniquity ... done wickedly**—and would be cut off except for God's grace and faithfulness (cf. 2 Tim. 2:13).

Israel's Future Confession of Sin Outlined. 106:7-46. This great penitential outpouring will include eight things: (1) **7.** It will include the sin of rebellion at the Red Sea (*yăm sûp,* "Sea of Reeds"; Exod. 14:11-12; Psalm 78:17), when the people did not understand God's wonders or His abundant grace and mercy. **8-10.** He nevertheless **saved them for his name's sake** (Ezek. 20:9) to demonstrate **his mighty power** (Exod. 9:16), rebuking the sea so that it dried up (14:21; Psalm 18:15; Nah. 1:4), leading them through the depths on dry ground (Isa. 63:11-13), saving and redeeming them in an episode that became the great type of divine salvation through Christ (Exod. 14:30; Psalm 107:2). **11-12.** Their deliverance was complete (Exod. 14:28; 15:5; Psalm 78:53) and elicited faith in God and joyful praise (Exod. 15:1-21).

(2) It will include the sin of murmuring for the flesh pots of Egypt (15:22—17:7; Num. 11:1-35). **13-14.** The people quickly forgot God's works (Exod. 15:24; 16:2; 17:2) and did not wait for His counsel (Psalm 107:11), lusting intensely (Num. 11:4; 1 Cor. 10:9), forgetting recent miracles (Psalm 78:42), and demanding new ones to satisfy their fleshly cravings. **15.** In giving them their request (Num. 11:31; Psalm 78:29), God sent spiritual **leanness into their soul** (Isa. 10:16).

(3) **16-18.** It will include the sin of jealousy toward God's leaders, Moses and Aaron (cf. Num. 16:1-3). Korah is not mentioned with the rebels, Dathan and Abiram, probably because his sons did not die (26:11). (4) **19.** It will include the sin of making and worshiping the golden calf (cf. Exod. 32:1-35; Deut. 9:8-21). **Horeb** is the designation of Sinai in Deuteronomy. **20.** In this manner **they changed their glory** (which is God) for the likeness of an animal (Psalm 3:3; Jer. 2:11; Rom. 1:23), the calf representing,

not displacing, God. But God would have no such representation, which violated the first commandment of the Sinaitic Covenant (Exod. 20:4-5).

21-23. It entailed forgetting God's great work of deliverance and merited the severest chastening, physical death; they would have died had not Moses' intercession availed as he stood before the LORD **in the breach** (Exod. 32:14; Ezek. 13:5; 22:30), the figure of a soldier covering the breach in a wall of a besieged fort, thus bearing the brunt of the enemy's attack.

(5) It will include the sin of unbelief and disobedience upon the return of the spies (vv. 24-27; Num. 13:25—14:38). **24a. They despised the pleasant land** (14:31; *'ĕrĕṣ ḥĕmḏâ,* "land of beauty [desire]"; Exod. 3:8; Deut. 11:11-15; Jer. 3:19; Ezek. 20:6; Dan. 8:9). **24-25. They believed not** (Deut. 1:32; 9:23) **... murmured** (grumbled; Num. 14:2; Deut. 1:27) **... hearkened** (listened) **not unto the voice of the Lord. 26.** As a result, God chastened them with death in the wilderness (Num. 14:28-35; Psalm 95:11; Ezek. 20:15; Heb. 3:11) and solemnly swore He would scatter their posterity among the nations (Deut. 4:27) in worldwide dispersion (28:63-68). It will be this final dispersion from which they will be gathered for Kingdom blessing (30:3; Ezek. 37:1-28; Matt. 24:31). (6) It will include the sin of idolatry at Baalpeor (vv. 28-31; Num. 25:1-18). This was extremely serious as it allied God's people with the grossly immoral worship of the Canaanite fertility cult of Baal, which involved sexual debauchery and utter moral degradation. **28.** Sexual union with the cult prostitute was supposed to constitute union with the god. Hence, the expression **joined themselves...unto Baal-peor** (or Baal of Peor; Num. 25:3; Deut. 4:3; Hos. 9.10) and **ate the sacrifices of the dead** (i.e.,

"the sacrifices offered to the dead"; Num. 25:2), offered to the dead (gods of Moab; Psalm 115:4-8). **29-31.** The result of such flagrant iniquity was a deadly **plague** (Num. 25:4), stopped only by the decisive act of judgment performed by Phinehas (25:7-8), reckoned to him as a righteous act to all posterity (25:11-13; cf. Gen. 15:6).

(7) **32-33.** It will include the sin of unbelief at Meribah (Num. 20:1-13). The sin at Meribah is probably placed unchronologically as the climax of the seven sins of Israel in the wilderness (vv. 7-33) because it involved even Moses (Deut. 1:37; 3:23-26) in an act of impatience (Num. 20:10; James 3:2) that cost him the privilege of leading the nation into Canaan.

(8) It will include the sin of complicity with Canaanite cults (vv. 34-39). **34-36.** Even possession of the promised land did not end Israel's sad history of unbelief. They failed to exterminate the Canaanites as God had commanded them (Deut. 7:2, 16; Judg. 1:21, 27-36); instead, they mingled with the religiously debauched nations (3:5-6), learned their occult practices (Deut. 18:9-14), and served their polluted deities (Judg. 2:12; 2 Cor. 6:10—7:1), which became a snare to them.

37. They even sacrificed their children to demons (Deut. 12:31; 32:17; 2 Kings 17:17; Ezek. 16:20-21), their idolatry being energized by demonism (1 Cor. 10:20), and the cruelty and debauchery of Canaanite religion empowered and propagated by demons (cf. Rev. 9:20-21). Divine wrath was incurred by this wicked complicity with demonized religion, which was an open and gross insult to God, violating particularly the first two commandments of the Mosaic Decalogue (Exod. 20:3-7).

38-39. Such demonized religion polluted the land with **innocent blood** (murder of innocent people; Num. 35:33; Deut. 18:20; Isa. 24:5; Jer. 3:1-2), debauched God's people (Lev. 18:24; Ezek. 20:18), and incurred base harlotry in brazen infidelity to the LORD, to whom Israel bore the relation as a husband (Lev. 17:7; Num. 15:39; Judg. 2:17; Hos. 4:12).

40-46. These verses allude to the cycles of oppression, repentance, and deliverance described throughout the book of Judges, sin incurring divine wrath and judgment through invasion and enslavement by foreign oppressors, followed by repentance and the LORD's deliverance and the display of His loving-kindness, remembering His covenant for their sakes (Lev. 26:41; Psalm 105:6; Luke 1:71-72), and making them objects of pity and compassion to their captors (Ezra 9:9; Jer. 42:12).

Closing Prayer and Doxology. *106:47-48.* **47.** This prayer for deliverance and gathering **from among the nations** (Jer. 32:37; Ezek. 36:24; Luke 1:74) will receive its final and decisive answer when the Messiah returns (Matt. 24:31) to set up His Kingdom over Israel (Acts 1:6; Rev. 19:11—20:6). Then the great confession of Israel's sin contained in this psalm will be made as they **give thanks unto** His **holy name** and **triumph in** His **praise** (Isa. 12:1-6; 35:10; 60:1-22; Ezek. 37:24-25; Zech. 2:10).

48. Then the joyful cry will arise: **Blessed be the Lord God of Israel from everlasting to everlasting**, and **all the** (millennial) **people** will say, **Amen.** The vision of this prophetic panorama elicits a glorious "Hallelujah"—**Praise ye the Lord** (*yāh*)!

V. BOOK FIVE: THE DEUTERONOMY SECTION. 107:1—150:6.

This last section of the Psalter bears

resemblance to the book of Deuteronomy. It shows God's dealings with His elect nation, Israel, and the consummation of these dealings not only for His people, but for their land, for the nations of the earth, and for all creation. The book ends with a mighty hallelujah chorus of redemption.

A. PRAISE OF REGATHERED AND RESTORED ISRAEL. 107:1-43.

This first psalm of the Deuteronomy section of the Psalter, in celebrating the regathering and restoration of Israel, appropriately develops the fulfillment of Moses' great prophecies in the book of Deuteronomy concerning the scattering of the nation on account of disobedience (Deut. 28:63-68) and the promised final great regathering and restoration to Kingdom blessing (30:1-10). Psalm 108 is closely allied to Psalm 107 and it, too, celebrates Israel's praise in the day of final regathering and restoration to Kingdom glory.

The Praise of Those Regathered and Redeemed. 107:1-3. Even as Moses reviewed God's gracious dealings with Israel in the Plains of Moab on the eve of their entrance into Canaan, so the remnant of the nation is prophetically envisioned as regathered and about to enter the land for Kingdom blessing. In doing so they retrospect on their age-long experiences of how the LORD led and preserved them.

1-2. In doing so, they break forth into a hymn giving thanks to the LORD for His goodness and His everlasting mercy, which **the redeemed of the Lord** (Isa. 35:9-10; 62:12; 63:4), those who turn to the Messiah (Zech. 12:10—13:1), will celebrate with ecstatic joy. Redemption **from the hand** (power) **of the enemy** (the adversary; Psalm 78:42; 106:10) focuses prophetically on deliverance from the beast and the false prophet (Rev. 13:1-18), their demon-driven followers (16:13-16; 19:11-21), and above all, from Satan (20:1-3) and his demon hordes (Zech. 13:2).

3. Redemption, springing from the death, resurrection, and return of the glorified Son of God for His millennial role as the King-Priest (3:8-10; 6:9-15), will also make possible Israel's final regathering from their worldwide diaspora to their homeland (Deut. 30:3; Neh. 1:9; Isa. 11:12; 43:5; 56:8; Ezek. 11:17; 20:34; 37:1-28; Matt. 24:31).

The Wandering Jews Regathered. 107:4-9. **4. They wandered in the wilderness in a solitary way** (in a desert region; Num. 14:33; 32:13; Deut. 2:7; Josh. 5:6; 14:10). **They found no city to dwell in,** that is, where they might settle down and establish a home (vv. 7, 36). Their wandering in the wilderness because of their unbelief and rebellion (Num. 15:1—20:29) presages their wandering in the wilderness of the nations throughout their history for the same reason.

5. Hungry...thirsty and faint (Psalm 77:3) describes their condition physically, morally, and spiritually. **6-7.** The LORD's faithfulness and covenant love appear in His hearing their cry of distress and delivering them out of their troubles and distresses (vv. 13, 19, 28; 50:15; cf. Jer. 30:5-7), leading them **by the right way** (Ezra 8:21; Isa. 63:12) **that they might go to a city of habitation** (v. 36) in contrast to verse 4, where they found no city where they might settle down and call home.

8. As a result of God's goodness in settling them at last in a permanent home (ultimately to be realized in Kingdom security), they will cry **that men would praise the Lord for his goodness, and for his wonderful works to the children of men!** (refrain of praise and gratitude repeated in vv. 15, 21, 31).

9. Then Israel's **longing** (parched,

thirsty) **soul** will be satisfied in the Messiah and His salvation (Isa. 55:1; John 4:14; 7:37; Rev. 21:6; 22:17), although "longing soul" (*nĕpĕsh sōqēqa*) literally means "running about restlessly in search of" something (Isa. 29:18), an incisive description of the Jew without Christ whose longing will be satisfied in Him alone (Psalms 103:5; 104:13, 16) and whose **hungry soul** will be satisfied **with goodness** (Zech. 9:16-17), who is the true "bread of life" (John 6:48; cf. Psalm 146:7; Matt. 5:6; Luke 1:53).

The Imprisoned Jew Released. 107:10-16. **10.** The extreme misery of Israel (Isa. 9:1; 42:7; 49:9) is set forth figuratively as those who **sit** (dwell) **in darkness and in the shadow of death,** that is, in the thickest gloom (Psalm 23:4), without knowledge of Christ's salvation (Isa. 9:2), judicially blinded and insulated against gospel truth (Rom. 11:7-10, 25), and **bound in affliction and iron** (with the iron fetters of affliction; Job 36:8; Psalm 102:20).

11. The reason for this sad spiritual state of Israel is her rejection of **the words of God** (Lam. 3:42) concerning the Messiah-Savior and His great salvation (Isa. 53:1-12) and despising **the counsel of the Most High** (Num. 15:31; 2 Kings 17:13-14; Prov. 1:25), the advice He gave His people for their welfare. They went even so far as to treat with contempt what was said in the Law and Prophets, especially concerning the theocratic position of Israel, in the sense of blasphemy (Num. 14:11, 23; 16:30; Deut. 31:20). They despised Israel's Kingdom glory under the Messiah, the millennial name "Most High" looking to "the times of restitution of all things, which God hath spoken by the mouth of all his holy prophets" (Acts 3:21; cf. Gen. 14:19-20).

12. Therefore, God **brought down** their proud, rebellious **heart with labor**

(affliction). **They,** who had hitherto been full of self-confidence, **fell down, and there was none to help** (Psalm 22:11). **13-14.** But the LORD showed His grace and mercy. When they cried out to Him **in their trouble,** He **saved** (delivered) **them out of their distresses** (v. 6), brought them out of their darkness (v. 10; 86:13), and broke their bands apart (116:16; Jer. 2:20; 30:8; Nah. 1:13; Luke 13:16; Acts 12:7).

15. Those gracious deliverances, despite the people's failure, call forth the recurring refrain of praiseful thanksgiving (cf. vv. 8, 21, 31). **16. For he hath broken the gates of bronze** (Isa. 45:1-2) and cut iron bars to pieces to free His people, as will be the case when He destroys their enemies (Rev. 8:1—20:3) as a prelude to setting them in Kingdom blessing (20:4-6).

The Foolish Jew Made Wise. 107:17-22. **17. Fools, because of ... transgression and ... iniquities, are afflicted** (Isa. 65:6; Jer. 30:14-15; Ezek. 24:23). This is what Moses, who knew the Israelites so well, called them: "O foolish people and unwise" (Deut. 32:6). Their folly was their unbelief and consequent rebellion. **18.** They became sick spiritually, abhorring all kinds of food (102:4), and drew near to the gates of (physical) death (88:3; Job 33:22; 1 Cor. 11:30; 1 John 5:16).

19-20. But when they repented and cried out to God in their distress, He sent His word (Psalm 147:15, 18; Matt. 8:8) and **healed them** (Exod. 15:26; Psalm 103:3), the very word they had rebelled against. Through its power He released them **from their destructions** (30:3; 49:15; 56:13; 103:4; Job 33:28, 30; lit., "from their pits," probably in the sense of the "pitfalls" involving the death to which their unbelief had exposed them.

21. Once again (vv. 8, 15, 31) the recurring refrain of praise is uttered, as the Israelites, regathered for the setting up of the millennial Kingdom, survey God's grace in the face of their past unbelief, which had brought them to the promised blessing.

22a. Let them sacrifice the sacrifices of thanksgiving (Lev. 7:12; Psalms 50:14; 116:17). This was done at the first Feast of Tabernacles after the return from the Babylonian Exile (Ezra 3:4-5) and prefigures the same celebration after Israel's worldwide regathering and establishment in the Kingdom, which the Feast of Tabernacles symbolizes (see Lev. 23:33-44). **22b.** Restored to the land from the final dispersion, saved Israel will declare the LORD's works **with rejoicing** ("singing"; cf. Isa. 12:1-6; 35:8-10).

The Restless Jew Brought to the Haven of Rest. 107:23-32. **23.** The Jew is presented figuratively as a storm-tossed mariner, transacting business in great waters (Isa. 42:10; Jonah 1:3-4). The sea symbolizes the unrest of the nations on which Israel is cast (Psalms 46:2-3; 93:3). **24. These** (who go down to the sea in ships) **see the works of the Lord, and his wonders in the deep**, that is, the deliverance He effects for His own of Israel from the waves of the nations' oppression (vv. 25-30).

25. He is sovereign. He raises the **stormy wind** (107:25) that **lifteth up the waves thereof** (better, "*His* waves," for He stirs them up to chasten and instruct His own). **26-27.** They **mount up to the heavens; they go down again to the depths** (104:8). Like the disobedient Jonah, who prefigures rebellious Israel, Israel's soul **melted** in anguish (22:14), the people reeling to and fro and staggering like a drunkard (Job 12:25; Isa. 24:20) and were **at their wits' end** (lit., "all their wisdom was swallowed up").

28-30. Again God's deliverance was

vouchsafed them as He stilled the storm as quickly as He had caused it to rise (Psalms 65:7; 89:9; Matt. 8:26; Luke 8:24), guiding His people to their desired haven, which in the prophetic scope of this psalm will be the Messianic-Davidic Kingdom.

31. Again God's wonderful acts of grace call forth the recurring refrain of praise (vv. 8, 15, 21). **32.** The exaltation of the Messiah **in the congregation of the people**—the public assembly for the worship of God after the Babylonian Exile (Ezra 3:1)—prefigures millennial worship. **And praise him in the assembly of the elders** (Ezra 1:5), the leaders of the people, prefiguring those who will reign with Christ during the Kingdom age (Rev. 20:4).

In Praise of God's Ways. 107:33-42. This is the response prophetically of regathered and restored Israel to the exhortation (vv. 31-32) to "praise the LORD for his goodness," then to be manifested in its full panoramic perspective. **33-34.** He **turneth** (changes) **rivers into a wilderness** (desert; 74:15; Isa. 42:15; 50:2)**...a fruitful land** (Gen. 13:10; 19:24-25; Deut. 29:23) **into barrenness** (a salt waste; Gen. 14:3; Job 39:6; Jer. 17:6) because of the wickedness of those who dwell in it.

35. He turns (changes) the desert **into a pool of water** (Psalm 105:41; Isa. 35:6-7; 41:18). **36-38.** He makes the hungry **to dwell** (resuming the thoughts of vv. 4, 5, 7), that they may establish an inhabited city and gather fruitful harvest and increase in wealth. **39-40.** When His people are **diminished and brought low through oppression. . . . He poureth contempt upon princes** (Job 12:21) and makes them **wander** (12:24) "in a pathless waste" (NASB; Deut. 32:10).

41. He sets the **poor** (needy) **on high** above their affliction in a place of security (1 Sam. 2:8; Psalms 59:1; 113:7-8) and makes their families **like a flock** (Job 21:11; Psalm 113:9). **42. The righteous shall see it, and rejoice** (Job 22:19; Psalm 52:6) **and all iniquity** will be silenced (63:11; Rom. 3:19). This will become a reality under the righteous Kingdom rule of the Messiah (Psalm 2:4-12).

The Conclusion. 107:43. The wise **will observe** (give attention to) **these things** (the LORD's dealings with His people, as set forth in this psalm). They will **understand the loving-kindness of the Lord** (pl., "loving-kindnesses," because they are so numerous and variegated). To be insensitive to them is sinful folly involving base ingratitude.

B. ISRAEL'S PRAISE IN KINGDOM BLESSING. 108:1-13.

For the scope and context of Psalm 108, see the introduction to Psalm 107. This psalm consists of portions of two other psalms (57 and 60), the first portion (vv. 1-5; Psalm 57:7-11) and the second part (vv. 6-13; Psalm 60:5-12). Both fragments are Davidic and are here combined under divine inspiration for a definite purpose in full harmony with Psalm 107, with which it is closely allied in prophetic scope. Psalm 108 also forms a trilogy with Psalms 109 and 110, setting forth historically and prophetically Israel's King's triumph over all foes. Hence, it is called "A Song." It would serve to console Jews during their periods of exile, including the Babylonian Exile and their present worldwide diaspora.

Praise for the Lord's Fidelity. 108:1-5. The psalmist (David) spoke prophetically, representing Israel's regathered and redeemed remnant praising the LORD in the Messiah's earthly Davidic Kingdom (2 Sam. 7:8-16). **3-4.** With steadfast heart, he set himself to praise the LORD **among the peoples** and **among the** (millennial) **nations** for His

mercy and **truth**, which are fully revealed in Christ's finished redemptive work, making possible the fulfillment of the Davidic Covenant and all the covenants and promises made through the holy prophets in "the restitution of all things" (Acts 3:21; cf. Gen. 12:2-3; Deut. 30:3; 2 Sam. 7:16; Rom. 11:26), which will then be realized. **5.** Such a demonstration of God's mercy and faithfulness in keeping His Word will call for the highest praise and exaltation of Him who will have proved Himself worthy of such from His redeemed and restored people, Israel.

Praise for the Lord's Deliverance and Victory. 108:6-13. **6.** The Israelite remnant (represented by King David and his people) will realize they are the LORD's **beloved** (pl.), and that it is God's glory to answer their prayers (Deut. 33:12; Jer. 31:3) and save with His **right hand** (the Messiah). **7. God hath spoken in his holiness**; so He cannot lie (Amos 4:2) or go back on His covenants and promises (Rom. 9:4-5), which promise victory and blessing for Israel in the Kingdom. Therefore, **I will rejoice, I will divide Shechem.**

Who is the speaker in verses 7 to 13? **8-9.** Historically, he is David; prophetically, he is the delivered Israelite speaking through David as a prophet (Acts 2:30), expressing the anticipations of victory over Israel's foes, of possessing their promised possessions and entering upon their inheritance when the land is divided among the tribes (Ezek. 47:13—48:29; see comments on Psalm 60:5-12).

10. Who will bring the remnant into **the strong city ... into Edom?** Historically, David will. Prophetically, it will be David's Lord (Psalm 110:1). **11.** Then Israel will have been **cast off** (temporally set aside in her national election, Rom. 11:1-24) and be ready to be restored

(Rom. 11:25-36). Then the LORD will **go forth** to battle for them (Zech. 12:3-4; 14:12-15). **12-13.** Their cry in that day will be, **Give us help from trouble** (14:1-2), **for vain is the help of man** (Isa. 30:3). **Through God we shall do valiantly** (Zech. 12:1-9), **for he ... shall tread down our enemies** (Isa. 25:10; 63:1-4; Lam. 1:15; Mal. 4:3; Rev. 19:11—20:3).

C. CHRIST FORESEEN IN REJECTION. 109:1-31.

Psalms 109 to 113 form a series prophetically glimpsing Christ in rejection (Psalm 109), exaltation (Psalm 110), and coming Kingdom glory (Psalms 111-12). Peter in Acts 1:20 includes Psalms 69 and 109 within the authorship of David and attributes the two "curses" he (Peter) selects as inspired by the Holy Spirit and declares that they were prophetic "concerning Judas" (Acts 1:16, 20). The apostle clearly identifies the psalmist with Jesus (vv. 1-5, 21-25) and sees in Judas the enemy who has requited hatred for love (vv. 6-20; cf. v. 8 and Acts 1:20). The voice of the rejected One (vv. 1-5, echoed in vv. 21-25) merges into the voice of the final Jewish remnant (vv. 26-31), identified with Him.

Despised and Rejected. 109:1-5. **1-3.** The psalmist in his experience prefigures Christ, who calls upon the **God of** His **praise** ("equivalent to God, who art my praise, Jer. xvii. 14; Deut. x. 21," F. Delitzsch, *Psalms*, 3: 177) not to be silent (Psalms 28:1; 83:1) when His enemies are so vocal, opening their wicked and deceitful mouths against Him with **lying tongue** (120:2), surrounding Him with words of hatred, and fighting against Him **without a cause** (69:4; John 15:25). **4-5.** Gratuitous as was His love (cf. Rom. 3:24), so gratuitous was their hate. **For my love they are my adversaries; but**

I give myself unto prayer (lit., "but I—prayer," i.e., "but I [am wholly taken up with] *prayer*," 2 Sam. 15:30; cf. Psalm 120:7, "I—peace," i.e., "I [am for] peace." Peace is my very being and element, as here prayer is, in the case of the Savior, Luke 6:12). **They have rewarded** (requited, repaid) me evil **for good ... hatred for my love** (Psalms 35:12; 38:20; John 7:7; 10:32).

The Rejectors and Their Doom. 109:6-20. This passage with its curses and imprecations refers to Judas as the rejector of Jesus (v. 8; Acts 1:20). Hence, it includes representatively *all* who reject Him and remain under the curse of sin (Gen. 3:14-19; Gal. 3:13). Of Judas, when he went out into the night to perpetrate His terrible act of betrayal, our Lord declared, "Good were it for that man if he had never been born" (Mark 14:21). Of all who reject Christ, who hate Him without a cause, it is also true that it would have been better if they had not seen the light of day.

What prompted our Lord to make such a declaration and for the Holy Spirit to inspire such terrible imprecations as fill this last of the imprecatory psalms (see comments on Psalm 5:10)? Only one answer can suffice. Behind the earthly curse lies the eternal curse—everlasting separation from God as "children of wrath" (Eph. 2:3) in an eternal night (Rom. 1:18; 2:5; 9:22). In infinite love and holiness God has provided a way of escape from His wrath in His Son, the curse-bearer (John 3:36).

6. If that remedy is rejected and that love spurned—"for my love they are my adversaries" (v. 4)—there is no other remedy. Such a Christ-rejecter is Satan-controlled and condemned. The adversary stands at his **right hand** (Zech. 3:1) to oppose him and condemn him to the ultimate penalty of the curse, which is the second death or eternal separation from God (Rev. 20:11-15). Satan was "set over" Judas in that he drove the traitor, after he had caused the Lord's murder, to murder himself (Matt. 27:5; Acts 1:18).

7. When he was judged, he came forth guilty (cf. Psalm 1:5; Matt. 27:6-10; Acts 1:18-20). As a Christ-rejecter he was also guilty of the one sin that shuts out divine forgiveness and seals the sinner in doom; so even **his prayer** becomes sin, since prayer without repentance and faith is sin in the sense of hypocrisy (Prov. 15:29; 28:9; Isa. 1:15; 66:18).

8. Even as he in wickedness plotted to shorten another's life, his own days were to be few, the wish according with the divinely appointed fact (Psalm 55:23; Matt. 27:5; Acts 1:18), and **another** was to **take his office** (Acts 1:20). **9-13.** The penalty descends upon the rejecter's children (Exod. 22:24; Jer. 18:21). Like wicked Cain, who rejected God's salvation and became a wanderer and outcast (Gen. 4:12), so his children are to be vagabonds and none is to show mercy to him or his posterity, which is to be blotted out (Psalm 21:10; 37:28; Prov. 10:7).

14-15. The visiting of the fathers' sins on the children has Exodus 20:5 in mind (cf. Num. 14:18; Isa. 65:6-7; Jer. 32:18), stressing the terribleness of human depravity and man's helpless cursed condition apart from divine redemptive grace.

16-20. The principle of sowing and reaping (Gal. 6:7) also appears; in the case of the Christ-rejecter, it becomes a frightening harvest of evil, engulfing him in ruin and drowning him in destruction and perdition. This is **the reward** (the recompense) from the LORD to all Christ-rejecters, of whom Judas is the prime example and warning (Psalm 54:5; 94:23; Isa. 3:11; Rom. 2:6, 11; Rev. 20:12-13), for all the unsaved (Christ-rejecters) will be judged according to their works (deeds) and be punished in Gehenna accordingly (20:12-13).

The Voice of the Rejected One. 109:21-25. **21a.** Again, as in verses 1 to 5, the voice of Christ, as the poor and needy One, is heard, prefiguring His wonderful prayer life on earth (Luke 6:12) and His complete trust and submission to the divine will (Psalms 23:3; 25:11; 79:9; 106:8). **21b-22.** He pleaded deliverance (69:14-16) in His humiliation as **poor** (afflicted) and **needy** (40:17; 86:1), His **heart** within Him **wounded** for our transgressions (143:4; Prov. 18:14; Isa. 53:5). **23.** His earthly life was like a lengthening shadow (Psalm 102:11), like a locust shaken off one's person (Exod. 10:19; Job 39:20). **24-25.** His **knees** were **weak from fasting**, His **flesh ... grown lean** (NASB; Heb. 12:12; Psalm 35:13), and He had become **a reproach** to those who rejected Him (Psalm 22:6-7; Jer. 18:16; Lam. 2:15), who looked upon Him and shook their heads (Matt. 27:39).

The Rejected One's Final Appeal. 109:26-29. **26-28a.** His prayer continued for deliverance from His foes, that they might know .**that this** (i.e., the work of delivering Him) **is** (the doing of) the LORD's **hand** (59:13; Job 37:7), and that despite their cursing, God will work out blessing (Num. 22:12; 2 Sam. 16:11-12). **28b-29. When they arise** (i.e., against Him), **let them be ashamed**, while God's Servant is made glad (Isa. 65:14). Let the Servant's false accusers be clothed with dishonor (Psalm 132:18), attired with their own confusion **as with a mantle** (a long garment reaching to the ankles), and so be clothed with vexation from head to foot (35:26; Job 8:22).

The Rejected One's Anticipation of Triumph. 109:30-31. **30.** He expressed thanksgiving and praise **among the mul-**

titude ("in the midst of many"; 22:22). **31.** His hope rested in Him who stands at **the right hand of the poor** (16:8; 73:23; 110:5), who through His anointed King (2:6) will reign and judge righteously (2:7-12; Isa. 9:6-7; 11:3-4; Rev. 19:11) **to save him from those that condemn his soul** (Psalm 2:8-9; Rev. 19:15) i.e., Him.

D. DOMINION GIVEN TO THE MESSIAH-KING-PRIEST. 110:1-7.

For the context of Psalm 110, see the introduction to Psalm 109. In Matthew 22:41-46 our Lord Himself attested four great facts concerning this psalm: (1) that it was written by David; (2) that it was given to David as an inspired revelation of God; (3) that it is a prophecy concerning Himself; and (4) that Christ is both David's Son (His humanity) and David's Lord (Deity)—God incarnate, God and man in one person.

The Messiah's Person and Present Session. 110:1. **1a. The Lord said unto my Lord** (*'ăḏōnî*; Matt. 22:44; Mark 12:36; Luke 20:42-43; Acts 2:34-35). That this is a prophecy of the incarnate Word, who was with God, was God, and became man (John 1:1, 3, 14), and as such was put to death, raised from the dead, and exalted to God's right hand, is evidenced by the Holy Spirit's employment of the psalm to show the exaltation of the glorified Christ (Acts 2:34-35; Heb. 1:13; 10:12-13).

The passage attests who Christ is— none other than the divine-human Savior (Matt. 22:43-45). The Hebrew word for "said" (*nᵉʾūm*) is consistently used of divine revelation, "to speak by inspiration" (2 Sam. 23:1-2). The expression "my Lord," of course, transcends merely personal application to David and assumes a representative character applicable to *all* saints.

1b. Sit thou at my right hand (Matt. 26:64; Eph. 1:20; Col. 3:1; Heb. 1:3; 8:1;

10:12; 12:2). The throne is the Father's throne (Rev. 3:21; cf. Dan. 7:13-14), the heavenly throne to which Jesus ascended after His resurrection (Matt. 26:64; 28:18) and which He is occupying in the interim between His ascension and His advent in Kingdom glory (Acts 2:34; Eph. 1:20-22; Heb. 1:13-14). The *right hand* is the place of honor and power (Exod. 15:6), not merely a position of honor, but a throne seat as Sharer in the divine power. This is apparent, for the conquest of the Messiah's foes is depicted as the result of this exalted session at the right hand of the LORD invested with His power over heaven and earth (Psalms 2:4; 29:10; 103:19), equal with the Father on the throne in respect to His Godhead, inferior only as touching His glorified manhood (cf. Zech. 13:7). The *sitting* points to settled dominion, the result of established sovereignty through death and resurrection (cf. Psalm 29:10; Eph. 1:19-23; Col. 3:1). The *seat* stands over against the *footstool*, which the LORD makes His adversaries become.

1c. Until I make thine enemies thy footstool ("a footstool for Thy feet"; Heb. 10:13). At His second advent in glory, His enemies shall be put down publicly and openly (Rev. 16:13-16; 19:11-21) and the satanic world system destroyed, including ecclesiastical (Rev. 17) and political Babylon (Rev. 18), as the result of the imprisonment of Satan and demon powers (Zech. 13:2; Rev. 20:1-3).

Then the Messiah will ascend His earthly throne (Matt. 25:31), on which He will reign till all enemies are put under His feet (1 Cor. 15:24-28). However, as God, no less then than now, He shall continue to sit on His heavenly throne, "the throne of God and of the Lamb" going on into the eternal state (Rev. 22:1, 3; cf. 2 Sam. 7:16).

The Messiah's Second Coming and Conquest of Foes. 110:2. **2. The Lord shall send** (*shlḥ*, "send forth, dispatch") **the rod of thy strength** ("Thy strong rod"). Springing from divine omnipotence and righteousness, it is a rod of slaughter and punishment (Jer. 48:17; cf. Isa. 9:4; 10:5; 14:5; Ezek. 7:11; 19:11-12), like the sharp sword out of the Messiah's mouth (Rev. 1:16; 19:15), called "the rod of his mouth" (Isa. 11:4), symbolizing not government, but conquest and punishment of foes (Psalm 2:9; Rev. 2:27).

This triumph will proceed **out of Zion**, the ancient capital of the Davidic dynasty and the future capital of the millennial Kingdom (Psalm 2:6; Isa. 2:3-4; Mic. 4:2-3; Luke 1:32-33). **Rule thou** (*rᵉdēh*, "lord it over, subdue, tread down," rather than "reign"), meaning "rule openly as supreme Lord over" all enemies "in the midst," not merely on the fringe (Num. 24:7; Psalm 72:7-8).

Israel's Conversion and Consecration. 110:3. **3a. Thy people shall be willing in the day of thy power** ("will volunteer freely," NASB; lit., will be "freewill offerings," *nᵉdābōt*). The King-Messiah's "people" are the Israelite remnant. Once Israel was not willing, but when He returns He will find a willing remnant. They will welcome Him in that day with the words which our Lord predicted they would use to welcome Him (Matt. 23:39), yielding their all in deep dedication to their Savior-King (Judg. 5:2, 9; 2 Chron. 17:16; Neh. 11:2). "A people of freewill gifts" is a people freely dedicating themselves to the LORD, an image taken from the freewill offerings in the Tabernacle (Temple; Exod. 25:2; 35:29).

3b. In the day of (the Messiah's) **power** (*ḥăyil*, "military prowess") is the time of the second advent in glory to war against His enemies and set up His Kingdom over Israel (Acts 1:6; Rev. 19:11—20:6), when He will openly manifest the power that He now wields unobserved by the world (11:17), and when He will send "the rod of [His] strength out of Zion" (v. 2; cf. 2 Pet. 1:16).

The Messiah's converted and consecrated people in the day of His power (military might) shall be attired **in the beauties of holiness**, a poetical expression for "in holy garments" or "array" such as those worn by the high priest on the great Day of Atonement (Lev. 16:4). Then Israel will have experienced the antitype (Zech. 12:10—13:1) and will wear as her priestly garb the beauties of holiness manifested in her through her Savior-Redeemer and King-Priest.

Then Israel, symbolized by Joshua the high priest, shall have her filthy garments of unbelief and sin removed (3:1-3) and be clothed with the rich priestly apparel referred to here (3:4-5). At the bringing of the ark to Zion, David wore priestly garments (2 Sam. 6:14), thereby foreshadowing the glorious garments of the Messiah and of His own at the future restoration of the Kingdom to Israel (Acts 1:6), which will mean the return of God's manifested presence in Christ, the antitypical ark, to Jerusalem.

3c. From the womb of the morning, thou hast the dew of thy youth possibly denotes the vigor and prowess of the King-Warrior "as the dew denotes fresh and early beauty" (J. J. S. Perowne). But the reference evidently refers to the Messiah's people, rather than to the Messiah, as the parallelism of the second clause shows: "From the womb of the dawn, Thy youth are to Thee as the dew" (NASB; cf. 2 Sam. 17:12; Mic. 5:7), construing "Thy youth" in a collective sense equivalent to "Thy young men," "Thy youthful warriors" (J. J. S. Perowne) The figure means "for the day of Thy battle Thy young men are to Thee [as] dew from the womb of the morning."

As the dew glitters when the sun rises, so the Messiah's redeemed people will reflect His glory as the night of this age ends in the "gross darkness" of the Tribulation (Isa. 60:2) and the Kingdom is born in the womb of the millennial morning. In each dewdrop there is a miniature sunbeam, and thus the Messiah's willing people will reflect Him when He arises as "the sun of righteousness ... with healing in ... [His] beams" (Mal. 4:2, BV).

The Messiah as the Eternal Priest. 110:4. **4.** Now comes the second word God speaks to His Son recorded in this psalm (cf. the first—"Sit ... at my right hand, until I make thine enemies thy footstool," v. 1*b*): **Thou art a priest forever after the order of Melchizedek** (Heb. 5:6, 10; 6:20; 7:17; Zech. 6:13), who in Zion (Salem, Heb. 7:1) united the priestly with the kingly office (see comments on Gen. 14:17-24). It is the everlasting priesthood of Israel's King that is the basis of the willing spirit, the holy attire, and the ever fresh youthfulness of the remnant described in this verse.

Although Christ is a Priest like Melchizedek now, the full display of that priesthood will not occur until He comes as King and unites the two offices in one Person. Not until the night visions of Zechariah (Zech. 1:4—6:8), which cover events that close this age, are completed will the symbolic action of the crowning of the high priest take place (6:9-15), prefiguring the Messiah upon "his throne" (6:13); so Christ must first receive His own throne before He can manifest the full glory of His eternal Melchizedek priesthood.

It was after the victorious battle with the invading foe that Melchizedek appeared to bless Abraham and reveal to him the name of the LORD as the "most high God" (Gen. 14:18). So it will not be until after Armageddon (Rev. 16:13-16) and the final age-end defeat of the wicked (19:11-21) that the true Melchizedek will appear to bless His people and show His glorious power. The extraordinary divine oath demonstrates that the King-Priesthood is unparalleled both in the Person who fulfills its requirements and the eternity of its duration (cf. Heb. 7:21; Num. 23:19).

The Messiah as Warrior and Judge. 110:5-7. **5. The Lord** (*Adonai*) **at** (God's) **right hand** is the King-Messiah. He was seated at God's right hand in verse 1; here God is at the King's right hand as His Protector (16:8; 109:31; 121:5) as He **shall strike through** (*mḥs*, "shatter, cleave, split, hew a way through") **kings** (68:14; 76:12) as "KING OF KINGS" (Rev. 19:16) **in the day of his wrath** (2:5, 12; Rev. 6:17; 15:7—16:21). Here the Messiah is seen coming to "judge and make war" (19:11).

6. He shall judge among the nations and peoples confederated against Him (Psalm 2:1-3; Rev. 16:13-16; 19:11-20; cf. Matt. 25:1-46). Literally, **He will fill them** (the nations, or earth, land) **with corpses** (NASB; Isa. 63:1-6; 66:24; Rev. 16:13-16; 19:17-21). **He shall wound** (*mḥs*, the same word as in 5*b*, meaning "shatter, hew a way through") **the heads** (lit. Heb., sing. "head") **over many countries** ("over a broad territory"), evidently referring to the literal "head" (cf. Gen. 3:15) of the Antichrist (Rev. 13:1-10), the Satan-dominated leader of the great end-time revolt against God and his attempt to take over the rule of the earth (Psalm 2:1-3; Rev. 13:7; cf. 19:20).

7. He (the Messiah-King-Conqueror) **shall drink of the brook in the way**, any brook or pool (*nāḥăl*, "stream, wadi, torrent") that may happen to be "in the way" of duty. But He does not turn aside from duty, even in the slightest degree, for self-refreshment, attesting His undeviating zeal for the honor of God. A parallel is Gideon's three hundred warriors, who in their eager zeal did not stoop to drink (Judg. 7:5-6).

Therefore (because of His unflagging zeal against God's foes, thus attested as the grounds of His exaltation) **shall he lift up the** (His) **head**, that is, in glorious triumph and sweeping victory (Psalm 27:6), in dramatic contrast to His previous humiliation (109:22-25), when on the cross Jesus "bowed his head, and gave up the spirit" (John 19:30).

E. PRAISE FOR THE LORD'S GOODNESS AND TRUSTWORTHINESS. 111:1-10.

For the context and scope of Psalm 111, see the introduction to Psalm 109. Psalm 111 is the first "Hallelujah Psalm" following Psalm 110. It expresses praise for what is there revealed concerning who the Messiah is and what He will do in attesting His goodness and faithfulness in establishing His people in Kingdom blessing. It is a complete alphabetical psalm, with not a letter of the Hebrew alphabet missing. It prophetically glimpses the perfect One and the praise He will receive on the throne as the King-Priest.

In Praise of the Lord's Works. 111: 1-6. **1. Praise ... the Lord** (*hălᵉlû,* "praise" *yāh,* "the LORD"), Hallelujah (112:1), strikes the keynote of this psalm, appropriate prophetically because the exploits of the Messiah in setting up the Kingdom in Psalm 110 come into view. **I will praise the Lord with my whole heart** (138:1) because of who He is and what He has done (Psalm 110), which demand the fullest and sincerest thanksgiving. **In the assembly** (*sôd,* "the secret, confidential gathering") **of the upright**, the "righteous" as distin-

guished from the general **congregation** (*'ēdâ*; 7:7; 25:14).

2-3a. The works of the Lord are singled out for praiseful thanksgiving. Both the work of creation, especially in view of a renewed millennial earth (Isa. 11:5-9; 35:1-2; Rom. 8:20-23), and the **work** of redemption, which will appear in full bloom with the Messiah on His throne of glory (Matt. 25:31) as the King-Priest (Zech. 6:9-15), will indeed be **honorable** (splendid) **and glorious** (majestic). These works, which will then be universally and enthusiastically realized as **great**, will be **sought out** (examined, investigated, minutely studied) by all who **have pleasure** (*ḥāpēṣ,* "delight in") in them, which will be universal in a day when "the earth shall be full of the knowledge of the LORD [lit., knowing the LORD], as the waters cover the sea" (Isa. 11:9).

3b. Then the LORD'S *righteousness,* both in justifying the believing sinner and at the same time maintaining His infinite holiness unimpeached (Rom. 3:25-26), as well as in keeping His Word in fulfilling His covenants and promises to Israel (9:4-5), will elicit the joyful acclaim: **his righteousness endureth** (*'md,* "continues, stands") **forever** (Psalms 112:3, 9; 119:142).

4a. The fact of God's infinite integrity will be attested to the whole earth in the Kingdom age. **He hath made his wonderful works** (wonders) **to be remembered** (as a memorial). In the prophetic fulfillment of this psalm the LORD'S wonderful acts recorded there will be gloriously supplemented by His most amazing wonder of salvation through Christ and its application to the deliverance of Israel and her restoration to blessing in the Kingdom at the second advent.

4b. The fact that **the Lord is gracious and full of compassion** will have a dimension and splendor that were not possible in Old Testament times (86:15; 103:8; 145:8), but they will be possible in the broader perspective of the salvation of the Gentiles (composing the church) and also the salvation of Israel and the nations at His advent in glory (Zech. 8:20-23; Rom. 11:25-36).

5a. Then He who redeemed them from Egypt and led them forth with the spoil of their captors (Exod. 12:36) in accord with the LORD's covenant with Abraham (Gen. 15:14), and on innumerable occasions gave them victory in battle and great booty and plunder from the conquered foe, will give **food** (*tĕrĕp*, "plunder, booty") unto **those who fear him** when He returns as a mighty conquering Warrior (Psalm 110:2, 5-7; Isa. 9:3-5) and will "divide the spoil with the strong" (53:12).

5b-6. Israel will be redeemed and restored to her homeland and established under the Messiah's Kingdom in blessing to all the nations of the earth, in fulfillment of the Abrahamic Covenant (Gen. 12:1-3), the Palestinian Covenant (Deut. 30:1-10), the Davidic Covenant (2 Sam. 7:8-16), and the New Covenant (Jer. 31:31-33). Then it will be proved that God **will ever be mindful of his covenant** (His overall covenant faithfulness; Psalm 105:8) in making known to **his people** (Israel) **the power of his works** (deeds) in giving them **the nations for their heritage** (BV; inheritance, possession), which will become a reality only through the Messiah's second advent and the conquests of Israel's enemies (Psalm 2:8-12; Rev. 19:11—20:4).

In Praise of the Lord's Trustworthiness. 111:7-9. **7. The works of his hands**, particularly in redeeming Israel out of Egypt and saving and restoring the nation at the end time into Kingdom blessing, **are verity** (truth, faithfulness to one's word) **and justice** (Rev. 15:3). **8.** They **stand fast** (are established) **for ever**

and ever (Psalm 119:160; Isa. 40:8; Matt. 5:18), upheld by His faithfulness, being **done** (performed) **in truth** (faithfulness) **and uprightness** (Psalm 19:9).

9. The LORD not only speaks His Word, but supports His Word by doing what He promised to do for Israel in commanding redemption for them (Luke 1:68; Rom. 11:26-32), in this manner commanding His covenant faithfulness forever, and so His name (Psalm 99:3; His essential character) is **holy and reverend** (awesome) to Israel and all citizens of the Kingdom who will witness the LORD's faithfulness to His Word.

Conclusion. 111:10. **10.** In view of the LORD's goodness and trustworthiness — His absolute fidelity to His Word — **fear** (godly reverence) of the LORD is **the beginning of wisdom** (Prov. 1:7; 9:10; cf. Deut. 4:6). This childlike reverential respect calls forth love that delights in His Word and His commandments (Psalm 112:1), imparting **a good understanding** (Prov. 3:4; 13:14-15) to the God-fearing person. This millennial psalm begins with praise, "Praise ... the LORD [Hallelujah]," and ends with the declaration, **His praise endureth** (continues) **forever** (Psalm 145:2). This is so because His trustworthiness is eternal and unfailing and will then be proved to be so.

F. THE RIGHTEOUS IN KINGDOM BLESSEDNESS. 112:1-10.

For the context and scope of Psalm 112, see the introduction to Psalm 109. Psalm 112, the second "Hallelujah Psalm" is closely allied with Psalm 111, the first "Hallelujah Psalm," and like it, is millennial in its prophetic scope as well as alphabetical in structure, both consisting of twenty-two letters, each prefixed by a letter of the Hebrew alphabet in successive order. Whereas Psalm 111 extols the LORD for what He is and what He has done to establish the Kingdom, Psalm 112 praises the LORD for the blessedness of the righteous in that glad day (but the blessedness is also applicable in a general sense to saints in every age).

Blessed Is the Man. 112:1-6. **1a. Praise ... the Lord** (Hallelujah) introduces the psalm, as in Psalm 111:1, for the mighty works of the LORD lauded there, particularly His redemptive work, are the basis of the blessedness described here. Three things are noted about such a blessed man: (1) **1b.** He **feareth** (reveres) **the Lord** (cf. 111:10; 128:1; Mal. 3:16).

(2) **1c-3.** He **delighteth greatly in his commandments** (Psalms 1:2; 112:1; 119:14), and **his seed** (descendants) **shall be mighty** in the Kingdom under the righteous rule of the Messiah-King-Priest, favored with **wealth and riches** (Prov. 3:16; 8:18), which is not always true of genuine believers in this age where the satanic world system operates and often results in injustice and wrong being done to the righteous. But, in the Kingdom, that system will have collapsed with the imprisonment of Satan and the demons (Zech. 13:2; Rev. 20:1-3), and Christ will rule absolutely and righteously (Psalm 2:4-12; Isa. 9:7; 11:4-5; Rev. 19:15).

(3) **4-6.** He **is gracious, and full of compassion, and righteous** (Psalm 37:26). For him light arises in darkness (97:11; Mal. 4:2), and his graciousness is manifested in his willingness to lend to the needy. His case shall be maintained judicially, and he will never be **moved** (shaken) from his integrity (Psalms 15:5; 55:22), while the memory of him will live on (Prov. 10:7).

The Blessed Man's Reward. 112:7-10. Two things are noted about the blessed man's reward: (1) **7-8.** He will be divested of fear of bad news

(Prov. 1:33), his steadfast faith in God giving him confidence that God's will is best and will work out for good (Rom. 8:28), as his heart is **established** and upheld so that it cannot fall into despair, knowing that the LORD will deal with his adversaries, which he knows are the LORD's also (Psalm 54:7).

(2) **9.** His consistent righteousness of life will be evidenced by his works (James 2:14-20). **He hath distributed** (scattered), **he hath given to** (i.e., "given liberally to") **the poor** (2 Cor. 9:9). **His horn** (symbolizing his general strength and prosperity) **shall be exalted**, for the Messiah-King shall rule righteously.

10. The wicked, unable to harm the righteous, shall see it and **be grieved** (vexed; Psalm 86:17). All the wicked man can do is futilely **gnash with his teeth** in total frustration (35:16; 37:12; Matt. 8:12; 25:30; Luke 13:28) and **melt away** (Psalm 58:7), his desire to do evil perishing because the righteous rule of the King will deal harshly with evildoers (Job 8:13; Psalm 2:5-6; Prov. 10:28; Zech. 5:3-5; Rev. 19:15).

G. MILLENNIAL PRAISE TO THE LORD. 113:1-9.

For the scope and context of Psalm 113, see the introduction to Psalm 109. This third "Hallelujah Psalm" (cf. 111:1; 112:1) begins and ends with "Hallelujah." Psalms 113 to 118 in Judaism are known as "Hallel, Hymn of Praise," or the "Egyptian Hallel" (114:1). This series is sung at the Passover, Weeks, Tabernacles, and Dedication (Hanukkah). At Passover, Psalms 113 to 114 are sung before the meal and Psalms 115 to 118 after it (cf. Matt. 26:30; Mark 14:26).

Exhortation to Praise the Lord. 113:1-3. **1-3. Praise ye the Lord. Praise, O ye servants of the Lord, praise the name of the Lord ... the Lord's name is**

to be praised. Such praise (although it springs from the heart of saints in every age) is altogether future and awaits the Kingdom age, when **from the rising of the sun unto the going down of the same** (Isa. 59:19; Mal. 1:11) the LORD's name will be praised. Now in man's day, under the satanic world system with Satan's forces abroad and wicked men in revolt, cursing, rather than blessing, God (cf. v. 2), is the general practice.

Apart from the true church, there is no praise of the Lord Jesus Christ in the earth today. But the day is coming when these words will be said and realized universally: **Blessed be the name of the Lord from this time forth** (the time of His glorious return and the establishment of His Kingdom) **and for evermore.** From the rising of the sun unto the going down of the same, the LORD's name will then be praised (Psalms 18:3; 48:1, 10; 50:1; cf. Isa. 11:9; 12:1-6; 35:10; Rev. 19:1-6).

The Greatness of the Lord. 113:4-5. **4a.** He is **high above all nations** (97:9; 99:2), meaning the Gentile nations, now so exalted in man's day under Satan's governmental system, and who so haughtily oppress His people, Israel (Rev. 12:13—13:18). But the LORD is high above them as the "great king over all the earth" (Psalm 47:2), as He now is; but in the Kingdom, when He assumes His earthly rule, He will be so indeed and in open manifestation.

4b. And his glory is **above the heavens** (8:1; 57:11; 148:13), the heavens declaring His glory, which far exceeds them (19:1), and the heavenly creatures ascribe all glory to Him (29:1; 103:20-21). **5. Who is like unto the Lord, our God** (Exod. 15:11; Deut. 3:24; Psalm 35:10; Isa. 40:18; 57:15), **who dwelleth** (sitteth), who makes Himself so sublimely exalted, "sitting," that is, "enthroned" **on high** (Psalm 103:19) "the heaven of the heavens," the highest or

"third heaven," the abode of God (2 Cor. 12:2; cf. 1 Kings 8:27).

The Condescension of the Lord. 113:6-9. **6. Who humbleth himself to behold** (lit., "he who maketh low to look" upon heaven and earth, BDB); "who stoopeth down to see [what is done] in heaven and in earth" (Perowne). He humbles Himself not only to behold the things in heaven (condescension enough for One so lofty), but also upon the earth.

7. He raiseth up the poor (afflicted) **out of the dust** (107:41; 1 Sam. 2:8), Israel's condition for so long (Psalm 44:25) in the dust of national death, scattered among the nations (Isa. 26:19; Ezek. 37:1-12; Dan. 12:2; cf. Isa. 52:2), and in the dunghill (refuse heap) of shame and rejection. **8.** But the LORD will raise His people from their shame (cf. Hannah's song, 1 Sam. 2:8) and set them **with princes** (Job 36:7), **with the princes** (nobles) **of his people,** Israel (Matt. 8:11).

9. He maketh the barren woman to keep house (lit., "to dwell in a house"; 1 Sam. 2:5; Psalm 68:6; Gal. 4:27) **as a joyful mother of children** (NASB; Isa. 54:1). Israel, the restored "wife" of the LORD (cf. Hos. 2:1—3:5), reinstated in her national election, shall be prolifically fruitful, both spiritually and materially, in Kingdom blessing. This grand vista of Israel's reinstatement in divine favor calls forth the spontaneous "hallelujah" with which this psalm ends as it begins.

H. WHEN THE EARTH TREMBLES BEFORE THE LORD. 114:1-8.

For the context and scope of Psalm 114, the second Hallel song, see the introduction to Psalm 113. Psalm 114 is more than a terse poetic survey of Israel's deliverance from Egypt (typical in her case of her final rescue from her worldwide scattering among the nations) into Canaan (a picture in her case of Kingdom rest and blessing). Underlying the history of her past rescue lies the glorious prophecy of her future deliverances from her enemies and oppressors into the Messiah's Kingdom promised through David (2 Sam. 7:8-16). Compare Jeremiah's great prophecy concerning this fact (Jer. 23:7-8).

Redemption out of Egypt into Canaan in Retrospect. 114:1-4. **1.** When Israel went out of Egypt (Exod. 13:3), she was called **the house of Jacob** as a reminder of her people's lowly condition there as slaves. Being rescued **from a people of strange language** enhances the joy of Israel's deliverance in recalling how alien in thought and life (indicated by language) were the people from under whose bondage she was delivered (cf. Psalm 81:5).

2a. Judah was (*hāyᵉṯâ lᵉ*, "became") **his** (i.e., God's) **sanctuary** or "holy dwelling place" (Exod. 15:17; 29:45; Psalm 78:69), denoting the elect nation's separation from the world and consecration as "holy people unto the LORD [her] God" (Deut. 7:6) being "a peculiar treasure" unto Him (lit., "a people for His own possession"; Exod. 19:5). Judah is the nation (construed as feminine in the Hebrew) viewed from the captivity of the ten tribes as being the surviving heir of the promises made to it (Psalm 76:1). Moreover, from David's time, Judah became the seat of the kingship and the national worship (78:68-71).

2b. And Israel his (God's) **dominion** (plural of amplification), His Kingdom, His specific sphere of rule (Num. 23:21; cf. Gen. 49:10), emphasizing the fact that through Judah would come the kingly reign that would embrace the *whole* nation of Israel. The LORD displayed His ownership and possession of

Israel as His own after her redemption out of Egypt by the demonstration of His mighty power to bring her into Canaan.

3-4. The lively poetic personification emphasizes God's power in deliverance. **The sea saw it, and fled** (Exod. 14:21; Psalm 77:16). **Jordan was driven back** (Josh. 3:13-16). The sea, river, mountains, and hills are symbolic of opposing overwhelming world powers and kingdoms (Psalms 45:2-3; 93:3-5; 107:23-30; Zech. 4:7; Rev. 13:1; 16:19-20). The poet skillfully used personification to conceal the name of God until verse 7. His purpose was to dramatize the greatness of God's delivering power to meet any situation.

Future Deliverance of Israel Implicit in Prospect. 114:5-8. **5-6.** The sea is asked why it **fled**, the Jordan River why it was **driven back**, the mountains why they **skipped like rams, and the little hills like lambs** (cf. Exod. 19:18; Judg. 5:4; cf. Psalm 68:8). **7-8.** The answer is given. **Tremble, thou earth, at the presence of the Lord** (96:9). The greater deliverance of Israel in the time of Jacob's trouble (Jer. 30:5-7) and her regathering to her homeland for Kingdom blessing come into prophetic view (Isa. 11:11-16; 35:10; Ezek. 37:1-28; Zech. 8:7-8; Matt. 24:31; Rom. 11:26-32). Then, not only the Red Sea, the Jordan, and Mount Sinai will respond to His omnipotence, but the entire earth will tremble before Him when He delivers and restores Israel in the Day of the Lord through the great apocalyptic judgments (Rev. 6:1—20:3).

Then it "shall no more be said, The LORD liveth, who brought up the children of Israel out of the land of Egypt, but, the LORD liveth, who brought up the children of Israel from the land of the north, and from *all the lands* where he had driven them; and I will bring them again into their land that I gave unto their fathers" (Jer. 16:14-15, italics added; cf. Ezek. 37:21-25). **The God of Jacob** will transform Jacob into Israel in that day by the same redemptive power by which He **turned the rock into a pool of water** (Exod. 17:6; Num. 20:11; Psalm 78:15-16), and **the flint into a fountain of waters** (Deut. 8:15).

I. WHEN THE WORSHIP OF THE LORD IS UNIVERSAL. 115:1-18.

Psalms 114 to 117 review God's ways with His people in the past with the implicit hint of His dealing with them in the future. For the scope of the Hallel Psalms (113-18), see the introduction to Psalm 113. As Psalm 114 reviews God's past deliverance in the light of future deliverance, so Psalm 115 looks back upon past idolatrous contamination to the future when the whole nation will be born again and trust the LORD, and through regenerated Israel the whole millennial earth will worship and serve the LORD.

Israel Acknowledges the Messiah-Savior-Lord. 115:1-8. Israel will acknowledge the Messiah at the second advent when the nation is converted (Zech. 12:10—13:1; Rom. 11:26-32). **1.** Then the cry of the restored nation will be, **Not unto us, O Lord, not unto us, but unto thy name give glory** (Psalms 29:2; 96:8), the repetition "not unto us" (Isa. 48:11; Ezek. 36:22) attesting the deep repentance for their Christ-rejection, which will sweep the nation (Isa. 53:1-12), and their acute sense of their sinfulness and utter unworthiness. Thus, the LORD is to be accorded *all* glory for His **mercy** (loving-kindness) displayed in the Messiah's redemption, worked out and made available to them in accord with His promises and for the sake of the truth (in the sense of "faithfulness" to His Word).

2. Then the whole converted nation will say that which the faithful remnant among them have always said, **Wherefore** (why) **should the nations say, Where is now their God?** (Psalms 42:3; 79:10). The sneer of pagan idolaters at the seeming inability of Israel's God to help her (due really to Israel's sin, which cut off God's aid) will then be a genuine concern of the restored nation because of the reflection on the character of the one true God.

3. But our (emphatic) **God is in the heavens** (103:19), infinitely exalted above the dead, earthly gods of the pagans. **He hath done** (does) **whatsoever he hath pleased** (pleases), being gloriously omnipotent and majestically sovereign (135:6; Dan. 4:35). Restored and converted Israel *as a nation* will see what the small remnant of them has always seen—the utter disparity between the LORD, the one true God, and heathen idols.

Three things are said of the idols: (1) **4.** They are mere material creations (Psalms 115:4-8; 135:15-18) of **gold**, bespeaking deity, but not gods, and **silver**, bespeaking redemption, but offering no salvation, purely the **work of men's hands** (Deut. 4:28; 2 Kings 19:18; Isa. 37:19; 44:10-20), in salient contrast to God, the Creator of all (John 1:1, 3; Col. 1:14-15). (2) **5-7.** They are mere lifeless nonentities, with bodily members that are powerless to function (Jer. 10:5). (3) **8.** They degrade and debauch all who make them or trust in them.

Call to the Nation to Trust the Lord. 115:9-13. **9-11.** Israel was told to **trust...in the Lord**, and then the nations were invited to note that, as a result, the LORD was **their help and their shield** (33:20). **12.** They were reminded of the LORD's aid and protection in the past, when they trusted Him and renounced all idolatrous taint: **The Lord hath been**

mindful of us (98:3), as when He restored them from the Babylonian Captivity, and later, as He will bring them back from the final worldwide scattering and place them in Kingdom blessing. **He will bless us:** (1) the house of Israel (prophetically, the whole reinstated and converted nation; cf. v. 9); (2) **the house of Aaron** (the ministers of the sanctuary; cf. v. 10); as the spiritual leaders of the nation, they should have led the way in trusting in the LORD; and (3) **13.** those **who fear the Lord**—all the true posterity of Jacob (22:23), **both small and great**, the faithful laity, as distinguished from "the house of Aaron," the priests.

Prayer for the Increase and Blessing of the Nation. 115:14-15. **14-15.** Historically, the restoration from Babylon is apparently in view. Prophetically, the final restoration and Kingdom status are envisioned.

Resolve of the Restored Nation. 115:16-18. **16.** The restored nation owns that **the heavens are the Lord's**, but that **the earth hath he given** to mankind to be man's heritage, in which He lavishes His blessings upon man and expects man's grateful praise (Gen. 1:28; 9:1). Therefore, He will not permit His elect people to be wiped out from the earth by their foes. **17.** In such a case, His gracious purpose for the earth would be frustrated. **The dead cannot praise God** on the earth (not denying that God can receive praise from discarnate souls). God will not allow His elect people, Israel (or any other elect group, such as the church), to be extirpated, that is, consigned to the **silence** of the grave, for then He would be robbed of the praise on earth, which only His people can accord Him. **18. But we** (ᵃnăḥnû, emphatic), the redeemed and restored nation (Rom. 11:26), **will bless the Lord from this time forth** (the Kingdom age) **and for evermore.** This glorious realiza-

tion elicits a closing Hallelujah.

J. RESTORED ISRAEL'S PRAISE FOR DELIVERANCE FROM DEATH. 116:1-19.

This is one of the Hallel Psalms (113-18; see the introduction to Psalm 113), which are linked together to present prophetically Israel's story of future deliverance and glory in the light of the history of their past deliverances, despite their failure. Psalm 116 foresees that deliverance and its gracious results for the God-fearing Israelite remnant. But the psalm (as is true of *all* the Psalter) has a beautiful application to *all* saints of every age and, like Psalm 23, is popular because it ministers to man in his deepest spiritual needs.

Deliverance from the Depths of Distress. 116:1-11. The first person "I" of the psalmist represents any suffering saint of any period, but it focuses prophetically upon the suffering Israelite saint in his dark experiences of unparalleled suffering and martyrdom during the Great Tribulation (Jer. 30:5-7; Dan. 12:1; Matt. 24:21-22) preceding Kingdom establishment (Rev. 12:9—13:18).

1-2. I love the Lord, because he hath heard... my supplications... therefore will I call upon him as long as I live. The LORD's hearing his cry of distress and preserving him alive during the nightmare of slaughter under the Antichrist (Matt. 24:22; Rev. 13:7) evokes the warm love of the saint spared for Kingdom blessing. **3.** This verse comprehends prophetically the terrible threat of death and martyrdom under the lawless one (2 Thess. 2:4; Rev. 13:17) and the **trouble** (distress) **and sorrow** of those terrible times (Dan. 12:1; Matt. 24:21-22; Luke 21:25).

4-6a. Then, in the vortex of tribulation, the saint recalled how he prayed and was delivered from physical death through the interposition of the grace and mercy of God, who **preserveth the simple** (those lacking worldly cleverness and expedients to preserve themselves, and who are easily overtaken by injuries; Psalm 19:7; Prov. 1:4). **6b.** Though brought low, the LORD delivered His praying child and brought him through the storm into Kingdom calm (Psalms 79:8; 142:6).

7. This is the **rest** to which the delivered saint (representing the restored nation) directs his **soul** (i.e., himself, his attention; Jer. 6:16; Matt. 11:29; Heb. 4:8), not only the spiritual rest of full trust in the LORD (3:18), but millennial rest in the land, in contrast to Israel's awful unrest among the nations (Deut. 28:65-66). **Return unto thy rest** (cf. Noah's dove that found no rest and returned to the ark, Gen. 8:9), and so Israel will find no rest from the floodwaters of the Tribulation till she returns to Christ, whom the ark prefigures.

8. This glorious rest will be made possible for Israel because of the LORD's bountiful dealing with her (Zech. 12:10—13:1; Rom. 11:26-32) through Christ (Isa. 53:1-12) by rescuing her **soul from death** (physical death) in preserving her through the Tribulation (spiritual death), in giving her spiritual life (Jer. 31:31-34; Ezek. 37:14, i.e., eternal life, John 3:16-18), and rescuing her from temporal woes.

9. Then restored Israel will be able to say, **I will walk before the Lord** (Christ in His millennial role as the King-Priest) **in the land of the living** (Psalm 56:13), that is, with physical life preserved to enjoy blessing in the Messiah's earthly Davidic Kingdom (27:13; Isa. 4:3-4).

10. Israel confesses that she **believed** (Gen. 15:6; 2 Cor. 4:13; cf. Isa. 53:1-12) "when" (*kî*, better, "therefore") she said, concerning her great time of trial during the Tribulation, **I was greatly afflicted** (cf. Jer. 30:5-7; Dan. 12:1; Rev. 12:13—13:18; cf. Deut. 28:63-68; Zech. 12:10—13:1), indicating that affliction will bring the nation to repentance and faith in Christ, confession with the mouth attesting faith in the heart (Rom. 10:9-10).

11. I said in my haste (*ḥpz*, "trepidation, alarm"), being harried by the persecutions of the wicked ripe for ruin (Rev. 9:20-21; 13:1-18), **All men** (*'aḏām*, "mankind") **are liars** (Psalm 62:9; Rom. 3:4), disappointing the hopes of those who trust in them (Psalm 108:12), and suggesting that Israel will thus be driven to faith in God alone, for one of the chief purposes of the Great Tribulation is to bring the nation to faith in Christ and salvation through Him alone.

Thanksgiving for Deliverance from Distress. 116:12-19. **12.** The grateful saint (prophetically prefiguring the saved remnant) asks what he may render unto the LORD (2 Chron. 32:25; 1 Thess. 3:9) for all His benefits (Psalm 103:2) in regathering the nation from worldwide dispersion, saving them and establishing them in the blessings of the Kingdom. **13-14.** He will **take** (lift up) **the cup of salvation** (16:5) to his lips and drink it (appropriate its blessings in Christ to the full) and **call upon the name of the Lord** (80:18; 105:1; Rom. 10:12-13), and **pay** his **vows** to the LORD (Psalm 50:14) **in the presence of all his people** (22:25).

15. Pausing in his thanksgiving, he again recalls the martyrs of the Tribulation and notes the LORD's zealous concern for His people's lives. Most **precious in His sight ... is the death of his saints** (*ḥᵃsîḏîm*, "godly ones," i.e., the Tribulation martyrs; cf. Rev. 6:9-11). **16.** Having been preserved out of the Great Tribulation, he protests his devotion to the LORD as His **servant** (Psalms 86:16; 119:125; 143:12; Isa.

61:1) loosed from the bondage of sin to be truly free serving God (Psalm 107:14; John 8:36).

17-18. To the LORD he therefore determines to offer a **sacrifice of thanksgiving . . . pay** his **vows** (cf. v. 14). **19.** He desires to do this publicly—**in the courts of the Lord's house** (the millennial Temple; Ezek. 40:5—44:31; cf. Isa. 2:2-3) **in the midst of thee, O Jerusalem**, then the religious and political capital of the millennial earth (Jer. 50:5; Zech. 8:21-23; 14:16-21). Again (cf. Psalms 113:9; 115:18), this glorious prophetic panorama calls for a hearty "Hallelujah!"

K. CALL TO UNIVERSAL PRAISE. 117:1-2.

One of the Hallel Psalms (Psalms 113-18; see the introduction to Psalm 113), this psalm is prophetic of the Kingdom age, when all nations and races will praise the LORD for His redemptive grace and faithfulness to His covenants and promises to Israel, and through that nation restored and redeemed, bringing salvation to the entire world. This psalm cannot be applied to any period of the Old Testament or the New Testament church period and will only be realized when Christ returns to the earth and sets up His Kingdom over Israel and "the earth shall be full of the knowledge of the LORD, as the waters cover the sea" (Isa. 11:9).

The Call. 117:1. **1.** The call is to **praise the Lord, all . . . nations . . . all . . . peoples** (148:11, 14; 150:6; Rev. 5:9). It is Israel's call to the whole millennial earth. Paul quotes this verse in Romans 15:11 to show "that Jesus Christ was a minister of the circumcision" (15:8), that is, to the circumcised (Jews), to show God's truthfulness, in order to confirm the promises given to the patriarchs and make possible the salvation of the Gen-

tiles not only in the church period, but, as in this psalm, in the Kingdom age. Thus, the apostle ends the Roman epistle proclaiming that God has a future for Israel as a nation in the Kingdom age, although it is often asserted that this truth is not taught in the New Testament.

The Reasons for the Call. 117:2. **2. His merciful kindness is great toward us** (that is, the nation Israel), and **the truth of the Lord** (His utter faithfulness in fulfilling His covenants and promises made to Israel, for He cannot lie) is **forever.** After Israel has been regathered, converted, and established in Kingdom blessing, she—with missionary zeal and because of the two reasons just enumerated—can offer all nations the same salvation that God has worked in her, for it is the salvation of the world. Then Jesus' word to the Samaritan woman will be fulfilled: "Salvation is of the Jews" (John 4:22).

L. THE PERPETUITY OF GOD'S COVENANT LOVE. 118:1-29.

This concluding Hallel Psalm (Psalms 113-18; see the introduction to Psalm 113) was sung at Passover and was the hymn sung by our Lord and His disciples before they went to the Mount of Olives (Matt. 26:30; Mark 14:26). Our Lord applied this psalm to Himself (cf. v. 22 and Matt. 21:42; v. 26 and Matt. 23:39). Whenever the psalm was written, whether in connection with the completion and dedication of the second Temple (Neh. 8:13-18) or some other occasion, it seems to have been sung in a triumphal procession culminating in sacrifice in the house of the LORD.

Thanks to the Lord for His Covenant Love. 118:1-4. **1-4.** The subject of thanksgiving is the LORD's goodness, manifested in the everlastingness of His **mercy** (*ḥěsěḏ*, "loving-kindness; His steadfast love''), shown in His gracious covenants and promises made to Israel (Rom. 9:4-5), grounded in sacrifice as the only approach of sinful man to the infinitely holy God. All Israel, particularly the house of Aaron (the priesthood as leaders and representatives of Christ's priesthood to come), and all that reverence the LORD are to celebrate the LORD's covenant love. No matter how or when that covenant love was manifested and celebrated in times past, this psalm looks forward to the ultimate celebration of it in the future Messianic Kingdom, when God's covenanted mercy will be completely attested in the fulfillments of His covenants and promises to Israel.

The Lord's Covenant Love Inspires Faith. 118:5-9. **5a.** The psalmist (as representative of suffering saints in every age, but from the prophetic aspect, of the Tribulation sufferers) declared: **In** (out of) **distress** (cf. Dan. 12:1; Matt. 24:21-22; Rev. 8:1—19:21) **I called upon the Lord. 5b.** He **answered me** (because of His covenant love), preserving me from destruction and death at the hands of the Antichrist and his violent anti-Semitic pogroms (Rev. 12:7—13:18). **And set me in a large place** (Psalm 18:19), that is, in Kingdom blessing (Rev. 20:4-6; cf. Isa. 35:10; Zech. 8:23).

6. The Lord is on my side (lit., ''is for me''; cf. Rom. 8:31; Psalm 56:9; Heb. 13:6). **I will not fear** (Psalm 23:4; 27:1; 46:1-3). The time of ''Jacob's trouble'' (Jer. 30:5-7) will be so fearful that it will be the supreme test of faith in the LORD's covenant love for His people. **What can man** (cf. Psalm 2:1-3; Rev. 16:13-16) **do unto me?** (Psalm 56:4, 11). But in the heyday of man's lawlessness (2 Thess. 2:4-12; Rev. 9:20-21) and power under the Antichrist and the flood tide of hatred of the Jew (Matt. 25:35-46; Rev. 12:13—13:18), this appears as a remarkable expression of confidence in the endurance of God's covenant love and faithfulness.

7. The Lord taketh my part (*li*, ''is for me''; Rom. 8:31; cf. v. 6) **... therefore shall I see my desire upon those who hate me**, a panorama of devil-inspired anti-Semitism through the centuries, culminating in its final and most horrible outburst under the Antichrist (Dan. 9:27; Luke 21:17; Rev. 12:13—13:18). Then, except for God's covenant love (7:3-8) and the faith it inspires in the remnant, Israel would be wiped out (Psalm 2:1-3), which is one of the objects of the Battle of Armageddon (Rev. 16:13-16).

As Israel looks with satisfaction upon the drowned army of Pharaoh, the first great anti-Semitist, at the Red Sea, so the believers in God's covenant love will look upon the doom of the Antichrist (19:20), the last great Jew-hater, and the destruction of his hordes at Armageddon (19:17-21). **8-9.** Then faith in God's enduring covenant love will be proved to be a far better refuge (Psalm 108:12; 2 Chron. 32:7-8; Isa. 31:1; Jer. 17:5) **than ... confidence in man**, even in the time of the acme of his power.

Faith in God's Covenant Love Under Its Severest Testing. 118:10-14. Although the testing that the LORD's saints have experienced through the centuries is not excluded, the final trial of faith during the Great Tribulation comes into clearest perspective. **10-12.** The thought repeated four times—**all nations compassed** (surrounded) **me**—has in view Israel's climactic latter-day invasion (Zech. 14:1-2; Matt. 24:15-22; Luke 21:20-24) in connection with Armageddon (Rev. 16:13-16, 19).

The thrice repeated **I will destroy them** (the invading enemies) demonstrates that the vibrant faith of the Jewish remnant will enlist God's almighty power for the destruction of their enemies and their deliverance against utterly overwhelming odds (Zech. 12:3-9; 14:3; Rev. 19:17-21). The invading foe is likened to swarms of **bees** (Deut. 1:44), and their defeat like a **fire of thorns** (Psalm 83:14-15; Nah. 1:10), flaring in a blaze with loud crackling, soon to be extinguished, the wicked often being compared to worthless briers and brambles (2 Sam. 23:6; Eccles. 7:6; Isa. 27:4; Heb. 6:8).

13. The enemy is directly addressed: **You pushed me violently so that I was falling** (Psalm 140:4; Matt. 24:22), **but the Lord helped me** (NASB; Psalm 86:7; Zech. 12:1-9; 13:8-9; 14:3-4; Rev. 19:17-21). **14.** The victory of faith will be celebrated as the remnant is saved physically out of the Tribulation (Matt. 24:13) and enters the Kingdom (cf. Exod. 15:2; Psalm 27:1; Isa. 12:2; Rev. 20:4-6).

Faith in God's Covenant Love Triumphant. 118:15-18. **15a. The voice of rejoicing** ("the sound of joyful shouting," NASB) **and salvation** heard throughout the centuries **in the tabernacles** (tents) **of the righteous**, who trusted in God's covenant love (and were not disappointed; John 3:16; Eph. 2:8-9), will reach its climactic crescendo in the saints who attain victory over the Antichrist and his wicked hordes (Rev. 13:1-18), surviving the horrors of the Tribulation (Matt. 24:13) to enter the blessed joys of the Kingdom (Isa. 12:1-6; Mic. 4:4-7; Zeph. 3:14-17; Zech. 2:10-12).

15b-16. The right hand (of power and favor) **of the Lord** (repeated three times) is exalted, because God's interposition (Rev. 19:11—20:3) has been the means of Israel's deliverances from death at the hands of her foes. **17a. I shall not die, but live** (Psalm 116:8; Hab. 1:12) is retrospective and presents the voice of

faith amid the lawlessness of the Antichrist and the constant threat of death under his anti-God, anti-Jew regime.

17b. Preservation through the Tribulation to **declare the works of the Lord** (Psalms 73:28; 107:22) in Kingdom blessing to all nations and people (117:1-2) will be joyfully celebrated. **18a.** The purpose of the Tribulation period, as realized by the surviving remnant, is clearly stated: **The Lord** has **chastened** (disciplined) **me very much** (severely; 73:14; Jer. 31:18; 1 Cor. 11:32; 2 Cor. 6:9). **18b. But he hath not given me over unto** (physical) **death** (Psalm 86:13), the ultimate in God's chastening of a sinning saint (1 Cor. 5:5; 11:30-32; 1 John 5:16).

The Salvation Offered Through Faith in God's Covenant Love Appropriated. 118:19-21. **19.** The psalmist, representative of all saints of every age (see above, vv. 5-9) here under the aspect of salvation as believing in and receiving the benefits of God's covenant love, called for **the gates of righteousness** to be opened to him (Isa. 26:2). Historically, perhaps the gates of Jerusalem, the holy city, are meant; prophetically, they are symbolic of the millennial Jerusalem, whose walls are salvation and whose gates are praise (60:10, 18); and again, of the heavenly Jerusalem, whose gates are of pearl and walls of jasper (Rev. 21:10-13, 18, 21), symbolizing the eternal abode and destiny of the redeemed of all ages.

Therefore, "the gates of righteousness" prefigure Christ, who alone gives access to God's righteousness, imputed to the sinner who reposes his faith in God's covenant love; He is "the door" to salvation (John 10:7) and "the way" to eternal life (14:6), and the only credential for the remnant of Israel to enter the millennial Kingdom of righteousness.

20. This gate is called **the gate of the Lord** because it was brought into existence through God's plan of salvation centering in Christ's sacrifice (1 Cor. 15:2-4) **into which the righteous shall enter** the millennial Kingdom (Psalms 15:1-2; 24:3-6). The righteous are those declared so on the basis of their faith in covenant love centering in Calvary and radiating from that center to validate all the covenants and promises made to Old Testament saints (117:1-2; cf. Rom. 15:8-14).

21. Twice **I will praise** (give thanks to) **thee** (cf. v. 19*b*) issued from the psalmist's lips as he joyfully envisioned Israel's salvation and entrance into the Kingdom of the Messiah. What a wonderful acknowledgment it will be when Israel says concerning Christ: **Thou ... art become my salvation** (Zech. 12:10—13:1; Rom. 11:25-32).

The Basis of God's Covenant Love. 118:22-29. **22.** This is **the stone which the builders refused**—our Lord Jesus Christ, the stone rejected by Israel and put to death, but through resurrection and exaltation to become **the head** (stone) **of the corner.** Historically, the stone is the foundation stone of the second Temple, an earnest of the completed structure when "the headstone" was brought to complete it "with shoutings ... Grace, grace unto it" (Zech. 3:9; 4:6-7).

The Messiah is the antitype, the foundation stone of the spiritual temple, the church (Eph. 2:20), rejected by men, but chosen by God and precious to believers (1 Pet. 2:6-7), first prophetically seen by Jacob as "the stone of Israel" (Gen. 49:24). Christ will be the headstone in exaltation and kingly glory at His second advent (Zech. 10:4; Matt. 21:42; Acts 4:11), in which exaltation Israel

will share nationally (Isa. 2:2-3; 60:1-22).

23. And when at last Israel has found this sure foundation stone, upon which the church is building, they will acknowledge with the deepest gratitude and praise: **This is the Lord's doing** (lit., "from the LORD"; cf. Zech. 4:6, "Not by might, nor by power, but by my Spirit, saith the LORD"). It will be **marvelous** in their eyes.

24. They will say, **This is the day which the Lord hath made,** that is, the day of the Feast of Tabernacles (Lev. 23:34-44), a rest to Israel commemorating the rest of creation and typifying the rest of Israel and the regenerated world in the Kingdom age. **We will rejoice and be glad in it** (Lev. 23:40; Psalm 31:7; Isa. 12:1-6; 35:10; Zech. 2:10).

25-26. This is a prayer of the remnant in view of the imminent return of the Lord in glory to consummate His covenant love to Israel. "Save now, Hosanna" was the cry of the palm-bearing crowd on the Sunday before the crucifixion, and it will be the cry of the penitent nation at His return, when the shout will arise, **Blessed is he that cometh in the name of the Lord** (Matt. 21:9; 23:39; Mark 11:9; Luke 13:35; 19:38; John 12:13).

The cry of the multitude on Palm Sunday (Matt. 21:9) was merely a harbinger of the fulfillment of this prophecy, for Christ told the Jews, "Ye shall not see me henceforth, till ye shall say, Blessed is he that cometh in the name of the Lord" (23:39), referring to His second advent in glory as King (Rev. 19:11-14). **We have blessed you out of the house of the Lord** is Christ's explanation of Himself coming as the manifestation of God's glory and bearing His name (Exod. 23:20; Rev. 19:12-13).

27. Then Israel will know that the

Lord Jesus Christ is God and that He has given them the **light** of salvation (1 Kings 18:39; Esther 8:16; Psalms 18:28; 27:1; 1 Pet. 2:9; cf. Mal. 4:2). **Bind the sacrifice** (lit., "feast," i.e., "the festive victim"; Exod. 23:18; 2 Chron. 30:22; i.e., at the Feast of Tabernacles) **... unto the horns of the altar,** symbolizing Christ's sacrifice, which ratified God's covenant love and is unchangeable. Since God has faithfully fulfilled all His covenants and promises through Christ, let us show our gratitude by sacrifices showing our spiritual love. **28.** This spiritual passion is expressed. **29. Oh, give thanks unto the Lord ... for his mercy** (covenant love) **endureth forever.** The psalm ends on the keynote with which it began, completing the great Hallel (Psalms 113-18).

M. RESTORED ISRAEL'S PRAISE OF THE WORD OF GOD. 119:1-176.

Psalm 119 is an alphabetic acrostic, each of its 22 sections of 8 verses, 176 verses in all, beginning with a different letter of the Hebrew alphabet, and each of the 8 verses of each section also beginning with the corresponding letter of that particular section, resulting in each letter of the alphabet being mentioned eight times in each section.

Two prominent features of the psalm emerge from these facts concerning its literary form: (1) *The first feature is the subject of the psalm —* praise of the Word of God. This longest and most perfect psalm of the whole collection is a marvelous evidence of verbal inspiration of the Word (cf. 2 Tim. 3:16). This is accentuated by highlighting the letters of the Hebrew alphabet in which (without vowels, which were not added until Christian times) the original Old Testament Scriptures were written. Since words are made from letters and—in the case of the original

Hebrew Scriptures—solely from consonants, those consonants are made very prominent in the psalm's literary form.

(2) *The second feature is the meaning of the psalm.* The remarkable prominence of the number eight (eight verses are located under each of the twenty-two letters of the alphabet mentioned in the psalm's sections) points to the specific slant of the psalm in dealing with resurrection. Jesus rose on the day after the Sabbath (seventh) day, that is, the eighth day (cf. Matt. 28:1). The solemn eighth day in connection with the Feast of Tabernacles (Lev. 23:36) prefigures Israel's Kingdom blessing, which springs out of Christ's death and resurrection.

Particularly, Psalm 119 deals with the spiritual resurrection of Israel as the context, following the Hallel Psalms (113-18) that connect Israel's past with her millennial future, shows. Of course, this great psalm has a far broader application to *all* saints of every age; yet *its precise and contextual* meaning centers in the time of trouble that will inaugurate Israel's coming spiritual and national resurrection (Jer. 31:31-34; Hos. 6:1-3; Zech. 12:10—13:1). The apostle Paul, in tracing Israel's future, calls this "receiving of them" back into divine favor "life from the dead" (Rom. 11:15), summarizing Ezekiel's vision of the dry bones (Ezek. 37:1-28).

Psalm 119 has specific application to Israel when the Great Tribulation produces a believing remnant that will embrace the Word when the once-rejected Messiah returns and the restored and converted nation with the divine law written "in their hearts" (Jer. 31:33) utters this paean of praise to the Word of God. Therefore, Israel brought through the Tribulation to be a restored and converted nation is the real speaker whom the psalmist represents.

ALEPH

The Blessing of Those Who Obey the Word. 119:1-8. **1-2.** The blessedness of obedience is emphasized by repetition, **Blessed** (lit., "Oh, the happinesses") that is, "How blessed are those whose way is undefiled" (cf. 1:1-2; 101:2; Prov. 11:20), because their **way** and their **walk** are **in the law of the Lord,** and they observe God's **testimonies** and seek Him **with the whole heart** (Deut. 6:5; 10:12; 11:13).

3-8. The result is that they **do no iniquity**; they obey what God has **commanded**; they enjoy direction and guidance; they are not **ashamed** or embarrassed because of a shabby life; they have a spirit of sincere praise to God as they learn of His **righteous judgments**; they develop a worthy determination to **keep** (observe) the divine **statutes**; and can boldly claim God's blessed presence (Psalms 38:21; 71:9, 18).

BETH

Cleansing Through the Word. 119:9-16. **9.** The cleansing power of the Word is able to keep pure the **way** of life of **a young man**, whose lusts are naturally strong and is prone to be defiled in thought and act (Prov. 1:4, 10; 4:10-17; 6:20; cf. 1 Kings 2:4; 8:25). Compare Jesus' words: "Now ye are clean through the word which I have spoken unto you" (John 15:3).

Such cleansing involves eight things: (1) **10a.** seeking the LORD with all of one's heart (1 Sam. 7:3; 2 Chron. 15:15; Psalm 78:37; Hos. 10:2); (2) **10b.** not straying from the LORD's commandments (Exod. 20:1-17); (3) **11.** hiding (treasuring) the Word in the heart (Psalms 37:31; 40:8; Luke 2:19, 51), for the thoughts of the heart determine the

conduct (Psalm 37:31; Prov. 7:1-3; Matt. 12:34); (4) **12.** appreciating the LORD's infinite purity and desiring to be taught in His holy statutes (v. 26; Psalm 25:4); (5) **13.** cleansing and freeing the lips to declare (tell of, relate) all the judgments of (God's) mouth (spoken by Him; v. 72; 40:9); (6) **14.** rejoicing in the observance of the LORD's testimonies (vv. 111, 162) as in all riches; (7) **15.** meditating on God's precepts (*śîaḥ*, "muse, ponder"; vv. 23, 48, 148), thereby developing a high regard for God's ways (Isa. 55:9-10; 58:2); (8). **16.** delighting in God's statutes (vv. 24, 35, 47) and not forgetting His Word (v. 93).

GIMEL

God's Generous Dealing Through the Word. 119:17-24. **17a. Deal bountifully with thy servant** (13:6). God's gracious manner of acting toward His servant through His Word involves seven things: (1) **17b.** It involves spiritual life (the abundant life Jesus mentioned; John 10:10); but in the prophetic context of the Psalms, it comprehends physical life spared through the Great Tribulation (Matt. 24:22), not to live for the flesh or self but to keep God's Word and live for Him.

(2) **18.** It involves spiritual insight, opening the believer's eyes that he may **behold** ("see with discernment") the deep truths of God's Word that are spiritually discerned (1 Cor. 2:14). Specifically, the Tribulation saint comes into the foreground and desires to see **wondrous things** (*niplā'ôt*, "the miracles of the Law," *tôrâ*), the mighty acts of the LORD against Israel's enemies, which will be reflected in the apocalyptic judgments of the book of the Revelation performed for Israel's deliverance and salvation.

(3) **19.** It involves spiritual guidance and direction because the believer is a

pilgrim and stranger on earth, inexperienced in the world and hence in special need of divine leading (Gen. 47:9; 1 Chron. 29:15; Psalm 39:12; 2 Cor. 5:6; Heb. 11:13). (4) **20.** It involves spiritual satisfaction for his soul, which **breaketh** (is crushed) with longing for God's ordinances (vv. 40, 131).

(5) **21.** It involves moral satisfaction, nurtured by the realization that God is the God of moral law and order, rebuking "the arrogant, the cursed" (NASB; 37:22; 68:30; Deut. 27:26) who **err** (wander) from His commandments, which reflect God's eternal moral being (vv. 10, 118). This will be especially appropriate during the Great Tribulation, the heyday of man's lawlessness and persecution of the saints (cf. Rev. 13:5-7).

(6) **22-23.** It involves social acceptance, yearned for in a time when the world's **reproach and contempt**, always heaped upon God's people (John 16:33; Acts 14:22; 1 Cor. 4:13), appear in climactic fury under the Antichrist (Jer. 30:5-7; Matt. 24:8-10; 25:35-40; Rev. 13:7-18) and his henchmen. (7) **24.** It involves spiritual and intellectual delight and counsel. The LORD's testimonies are his **delight** and **counselors** (lit., "men of my counsel").

DALETH

Revival Through the Word. 119:25-32. **25. Revive me according to thy word** (vv. 37, 40, 88, 93, 107, 149, 154, 156, 159). Spiritual revival through the Word produces ten great effects: (1) It lifts up the soul from the dust of sin, worldliness, and carnality, to which it so readily **cleaveth** (cleaves; 44:25), and restores it to spiritual health and vigor, erect and straight to walk as a man should, with his face heavenward.

(2) **26a.** It engenders deep heartfelt confession of sin with a full uncovering of one's (wicked) **ways**. (3) **26b.** It results

in renewed prayer life and power. (4) **26c-27a.** It causes a new learning experience of the power of the Spirit's teaching the Word (v. 12), making the revived saint understand the way of God's precepts. (5) **27b.** It imparts a new power in witness and testimony. (6) **28a.** It results in deep contrition for sin and failure (22:14; 107:26). (7) **28b.** It brings renewed strength and courage (20:2; 1 Pet. 5:10).

(8) **29-30a.** It causes a deep detestation of every false way of life, involving deceit or lying of any kind (Prov. 30:8; Isa. 44:20; Jer. 16:19; Eph. 4:22-25; 1 John 1:8; 2:4), and a definite choice to follow **the way** (path) **of truth.** (9) **30b-32a.** It enables the revived soul to lay (place) God's ordinances before him to honor and obey them, stick (cleave) to them, and to **run** with alacrity and joy in them, as a pathway that is a reflection of God's will. (10) **32b.** It results in enlargement of heart (1 Kings 4:29; Isa. 60:5; cf. 2 Cor. 6:11, 13), as the preceding benefits of revival are experienced.

HE

Teaching Through the Word. 119:33-40. **33a. Teach me,** O LORD, **the way of thy statutes** (vv. 5, 12). Such teaching of the Word does nine things: (1) **33b-34.** It makes for strict, complete, and spontaneous obedience to it as it is understood (vv. 2, 69, 73, 125, 144, 169; 1 Chron. 22:12; Ezek. 44:24). (2) **35a.** It makes (causes) the believer to live out the moral law of God in his conduct (Psalm 25:4; Isa. 40:14). (3) **35b.** It makes the believer delight in that law as he lives it out (v. 16; 112:1). (4) **36-37a.** It keeps the believer from the sin of **covetousness** (dishonest gain; Luke 12:15; Col. 3:5; Heb. 13:5) and **vanity** (Isa. 33:15). (5) **37b.** It promotes revival (v. 25)—quickening in God's ways (71:20).

38. It confirms God's **word** as that

which belongs to those who **fear** (revere) Him (2 Sam. 7:25), with specific application to Tribulation saints in establishing God's word of promise respecting the ultimate establishment of the Davidic kingdom (2 Sam. 7:8-16). (7) **39a.** It comforts the believer, particularly the Tribulation saint, who has reason to dread the **reproach** of the Antichrist and his followers, which threatens every believer in the Word with violent persecution and death (v. 22; cf. Matt. 24:9-10; Rev. 13:1-18).

(8) **39b.** It sustains the believer with the conviction that God's **ordinances** (judgments) **are good**—destructive to the wicked, as they should be, but savingly refining and corrective to His own people. In the case of those saved out of the Tribulation, it fits them for citizenship in the Kingdom of the Messiah. (9) **40.** It produces a yearning for God's Word and quickening in His righteousness, namely, the righteousness He accounts the believer in justifying him (Gen. 15:6) and experientially sanctifying him (Rom. 6:11), evidenced by a longing for God's commandments.

VAV

Ministering God's Grace Through the Word. 119:41-48. **41a. Let thy mercies come also unto me, O Lord** (v. 77). Such ministry of God's grace does nine things: (1) **41b.** It brings God's salvation according to His Word (vv. 58, 76), on the basis of faith (Gen. 15:6; Eph. 2:8-9), which, according to God's will, may include temporal deliverance from calamity and physical death (Matt. 24:13).

(2) **42.** It brings assurance and confidence in the Word and will of God; so the believer has a word to answer unbelievers who taunt and reproach him for his trust in God's Word (Prov. 27:11). (3) **43a.** It fills the mouth with the Word of God rather than taking the Word out of

it. (4) **43b.** It inspires hope in the Word of God "to wait for" its fulfillment (vv. 49, 74, 114, 147). (5) **44.** It gives faith to observe it continually (v. 33).

(6) **45.** It makes possible the enjoyment of true freedom (Prov. 4:12), in release from legalism, as God's precepts are sought and the one true gospel of salvation by grace through faith is believed and applied to one's walk (step-by-step conduct). Only then can the believer **walk at liberty** (i.e., "in a wide place" of blessing). (7) **46.** It gives boldness of testimony (Matt. 10:18; Acts 26:1-2) without shame or confusion. (8) **47-48a.** It generates delight in and love for God's commandments (vv. 16, 97, 127, 159). (9) **48b.** It furnishes an incentive to meditate on God's statutes (v. 15).

ZAYIN

Imparting Hope Through the Word. 119:49-56. **49. Remember the word unto thy servant, upon which thou hast caused me to hope.** Such imparting of hope through the Word does seven things: (1) **50.** It ministers to the comfort of the saint in his affliction (27:13; 28:7; 42:8, 11; Jer. 15:15-16; Rom. 5:3-5; Heb. 6:17-19; 12:11-12), the prophetic focus falling on the persecuted Tribulation saint (Rev. 12:13—13:18), who will pass through the vortex of trial (Jer. 30:5-7), but with the expectation of the return of the Messiah, the destruction of His enemies (Psalm 2:1-12), and the setting up of the Kingdom promised through David's Son and Lord (2 Sam. 7:8-16; Psalm 110:1-4). God's word of promise thus revives the suffering saint in giving him renewed faith instead of a lapse into despair (cf. vv. 65, 93).

(2) **51.** It gives enabling to face the derision of the arrogant (Job 30:1; Jer. 20:7) without declining (turning aside) from God's Law (v. 157; 44:18; Job

23:11). (3) **52.** It imparts ability to comfort oneself by recalling God's judgments of old—His past judicial vindications of His oppressed and persecuted people by mighty deliverances (Psalm 103:17-18). (4) **53.** It engenders horror ("burning indignation") against the lawless (Exod. 32:19; Ezra 9:3) who forsake God's Law, prophetically, against the lawless one (2 Thess. 2:4), the Antichrist, and his followers in their supreme attempt to set aside God's moral laws at the end of the age (Psalm 2:1-12; Dan. 11:36-39; Rev. 13:5-6; 19:19).

(5) **54.** It brings forth songs of joy in the saint in the house of his pilgrimage (v. 19; cf. Gen. 47:9), as a sojourner cheered in a foreign land by singing the native songs of his home. (6) **55.** It causes the saint to remember the LORD's name (Psalm 63:6) in the night (42:8; 92:2; Isa. 26:9; Acts 16:25), when sorrows press especially painfully upon us. (7) **56.** It causes the saint to keep (observe) the precepts of the Word. **This** (blessing) **has become mine, that I observe Thy precepts** (NASB; vv. 22, 69, 100).

HETH

Knowing God as Our Portion Through the Word. 119:57-64. **57a. Thou art my portion** (*ḥēlĕq*, "share, lot, inheritance"), an acquired possession of the psalmist (cf. 16:5; 73:26; 142:5; Lam. 3:24). Such knowledge of the LORD through His Word does nine things: (1) **57b.** It requires keeping God's words (Deut. 33:9). He who would claim God as his possession must first acknowledge that he is God's possession by obedience to His Word. (2) **58.** It stimulates entreating God's favor (1 Kings 13:6) with utter sincerity and dedication to God's will that can claim God's grace in fullest measure (Psalms 41:4; 56:1; 57:1; 119:2, 41). (3) **59.** It

encourages considering one's ways ("conduct, manner of life"; Mark 14:72; Luke 15:17) and turning one's feet in those ways to God's testimonies. (4) **60.** It stirs up zeal to keep the commandments of the LORD. (5) **61.** It stimulates recourse to God's Word (Law, *tôrâ*, "teaching") under persecution and attack by the wicked (Job 36:8; Psalm 140:5). (6) **62.** It calls forth earnest prayer and genuine thanksgiving (v. 55). (7) **63.** It inculcates separation from sinners and dedication to the society of God-fearers who keep God's precepts (101:6). (8) **64a.** It demonstrates the greatness and extent of God's mercy (loving-kindness, redemptive grace; 33:5). (9) **64b.** It craves the teaching ministry of God (the Holy Spirit; v. 12; cf. John 14:12-13).

TETH

Understanding God's Disciplinary Dealing Through the Word. 119:65-72. **65. Thou hast dealt well with thy servant, O Lord.** Historically, this is an apparent reference to release from the Babylonian Captivity; prophetically, it is a foreview of the Israelite remnant being brought through the Great Tribulation into Kingdom blessing **according unto** God's **word** (Jer. 30:5-7; Hos. 2:23; Zech. 13:8-9; Zeph. 3:12-13; Matt. 24:40-41; Rev. 7:1-8).

Comprehending that God deals well with His people (i.e., for their best interests) does four things: (1) **66.** It stirs up renewed desire to be taught **good judgment** (discernment) and **knowledge** from the Word (cf. Phil. 1:9), and to understand this great truth more clearly. To be thoroughly convinced that God is good and does good (v. 68; Deut. 8:16; 28:63; 30:5; Psalms 86:5; 100:5; 106:1) will be of the utmost importance to the Jewish remnant, which will undergo the greatest test of this great truth (cf. Rev.

15:3; 16:7) in all redemptive history in being called to pass through the horrors of the Great Tribulation (Jer. 30:5-7; Dan. 11:36-39; 12:1; Matt. 24:15-28; Rev. 8:1—20:3).

(2) **67.** It helps God's people to understand His purpose in affliction and suffering. Besides the omnitemporal application to saints of every era, the context and very structure of this psalm (see introduction) point to the special relevance of this truth to Tribulation saints, called to suffer in an unparalleled period of trouble and persecution (Dan. 12:1; Matt. 24:21-22; Rev. 12:13—13:18). With peculiar appropriateness, the Tribulation saint can say, **Before I was afflicted I went astray** (cf. v. 71; Deut. 32:15; Jer. 31:18-19; Heb. 12:5-11). The whole divine purpose of that period of the most intense suffering is revealed in the confession, **But now I keep Thy word** (NASB). "It is good for me that I have been afflicted (v. 71), for the remnant will realize that through this nightmare of anguish they have learned God's statutes.

(3) **69.** It enables God's people to be firm and steadfast in the midst of their testings, when the **proud** (arrogant), particularly the lawless Antichrist, false prophet, and their followers (Rev. 13:1-18), forge lies against the remnant (9:20-21). **70.** The hearts of these lawless renegades are **as fat as grease** (lit., "gross like fat"), utterly reprobate and ripe for ruin (cf. Gen. 15:16), completely insensitive to moral rectitude. (4) **72.** It enables God's people to see what a priceless treasure the Word of God is (v. 127; 19:10; Prov. 8:10, 11, 19).

YODH

Appreciating Through the Word the Creator at Work in His Own. 119:73-80. **73a. Thy hands have made me and fashioned** (established) **me** (Gen. 1:27;

2:7; Job 10:8; 31:15; Psalm 138:8; Eph. 2:10). The conviction of the Creator at work in His redeemed creatures does five things: (1) **73b-74.** It encourages prayer that God may grant His own people understanding to learn (to obey) His commandments (v. 34); so those who **fear** (revere) the LORD may be gladdened by their life and testimony (Psalms 34:2; 35:27; 107:42). This sort of testimony can only come about by "hoping in" ("waiting for") God's Word (v. 43).

(2) **75.** It gives understanding of God's judgments upon the wicked and His disciplinary dealings with His own. **I know ... thy judgments** upon the wicked **are right** (righteous; lit., "righteousness"; v. 138; cf. especially Rev. 15:3-4; 16:7). Therefore, he prays that the proud (arrogant) may "be ashamed" (v. 78) in frustration and defeat for their perverse dealing and causeless persecution. **And that thou in faithfulness hast afflicted me** (v. 138; Psalm 89:30-33; Heb. 12:10; Rev. 3:19; cf. Hos. 2:14-23; Mal. 4:2-3).

(3) **76.** It gives appreciation of redemptive grace as a comfort to God's suffering servants. (4) **77.** It grants boldness to ask for preservation of physical life amid persecutions and death (cf. Rev. 6:9-10; 7:14; 13:13-18). (5) **79-80.** It makes the LORD's own people conscious that through the Word they can be a help to other believers in times of distress; so they pray (through the psalmist) that they may be **sound** (blameless) in God's statutes (2 Chron. 15:17; Prov. 4:23; John 1:47), that they may not be ashamed (v. 46) before their enemies or other believers.

KAPH

Facing Persecutions in Reliance upon the Word. 119:81-88. **81a. My soul fainteth** (languishes) **for thy salvation** (13:1-6; Rev. 6:9-10), that is, "deliverance" from the terrible harassments of the wicked in the Tribulation period in the prophetic aspect. In the historical sense, it is from any persecution or affliction of the saints in any period. **81. I hope in** (wait for) **thy word** (v. 43). Such confrontation with persecutions, in steadfast confidence in the promises of the Word concerning salvation and deliverance (cf. Zech. 12:3 — 13:1; 14:3-14; Mal. 3:16-17), generates three things:

(1) **82-83.** It generates the expectation of God's help and comfort (v. 123; Isa. 38:14; Lam. 2:11; Rev. 6:9-10), even though the sufferer becomes **like a wineskin in the smoke** (Job 30:30). His skin is pictured as become parched and shriveled, like an Eastern wine bottle (made of skin) and dried in the fire (Psalms 32:4; 102:3-4; Prov. 17:22). Yet the help and comfort derived from God's Word do not allow the sufferer to forget its statutes (v. 61).

(2) **84.** It generates the expectation that God will vindicate His justice by judgments on the wicked persecutors of His people (Psalm 39:4; Rev. 6:10). The brevity of life is made the basis of the plea (cf. Job 7:6-21; 9:25; 16:22). **85-87. The proud** (arrogant), **which are not after** (in accord with) God's Law, are the lawlessly wicked of any age, with contextual prophetic focus upon the lawless one (the Antichrist; 2 Thess. 2:4) and his followers in the Great Tribulation (Psalm 2:1-3; Rev. 9:20-21; 19:19). They treacherously dig **pits** to entrap God's people (Psalms 7:15; 57:6; Jer. 18:22) and **persecute** them **wrongfully** ("with a lie") (vv. 78, 161; 35:19), their cruel duplicity and lying malignity eliciting a sudden, almost frantic, cry: **Help me!** (NASB; 109:26) and the sad comment on their relentless hatred: **They had almost consumed** (destroyed) **me upon earth** (lit., "in the earth" in its terrible

condition of lawlessness under the Antichrist; Dan. 11:36-37; Rev. 13:15; 19:19).

(3) **88.** It generates the expectation of gracious reviving from God, both physical and spiritual, with one desire in mind: to **keep** (observe) **the testimony** of God's Word, which he describes as **of thy** (God's) **mouth**, with real conviction that the Word of God is *theopneustos*, not only "divinely breathed in" but also "divinely breathed out," as God's inspired revelation (2 Tim. 3:16).

LAMEDH

The Eternal Steadfastness of the Word. 119:89-96. **89. Forever, O Lord, thy word is settled** (*nîṣāḇ*, "stands firm") **in heaven** (v. 160; Isa. 40:8; Matt. 24:35; 1 Pet. 1:25), eternal and unchangeable as the eternal One and His throne (Heb. 1:8; 13:8). This means seven things: (1) **90a.** The covenants and promises of God's Word are guaranteed by His **faithfulness** (His utter fidelity to perform all He said He would and to be all He said He would be), which continues unchangeably **unto all generations** (lit., "to generation and generation"), meaning not only throughout time, but eternity as well (Psalm 36:5; 89:1-2). **90b.** The Word, which is "settled in heaven," **established the earth**, spoke it into existence (33:9), maintains it, and causes it to remain (*'md*, "stand"; Eccles. 1:4).

(2) **91.** God may be counted on to execute His judgments to vindicate His people's cause against the enemy. "For [*lᵉ*] Thy judgments" (emphatic by position in the Hebrew), **they** (the forces and powers of the earth) **continue** (stand) **this day**, namely, for the purpose of executing God's judgments as obedient servants of the Creator. That interpretation is preferable, inasmuch as the psalmist frequently looks to God for His judg-

ments to vindicate Israel's cause against the enemy.

(3) **92.** The assurance of the utter reliability of God's Word preserves the afflicted through troubles (v. 50). The written Word is the vehicle through which the comfort and support of God flows in times of tribulation. The psalmist's **delight** in the Word (v. 16) kept him through such an experience, as will be the case of the godly Jewish remnant of the Great Tribulation (Matt. 24:22).

(4) **93.** This assurance concerning God's Word revives the afflicted saint (v. 25), the words **given me life** having the connotation of keeping one alive physically in the midst of fierce persecution and death (Matt. 24:22), as well as spiritually sustaining.

(5) **94.** This assurance gives confidence to claim God's salvation (deliverance) (v. 146), particularly when the saint realizes he belongs to God by creation (Gen. 1:27; Psalm 100:3) as well as by redemption (Eph. 2:10).

(6) **95.** This confidence drives the persecuted saint to diligent consideration of the Word in spite of foes (Psalm 40:14; Isa. 32:7), even as Daniel was not deterred by the plot of his enemies from praying three times a day (Dan. 6:10).

(7) **96.** This confidence gives a deep sense of the perfection of God's Word. **I have seen an end of** (limit to) **all** (human, finite) **perfection.** Thy Word alone is infinite, unchangeable, and boundless in its completeness, finality, and flawlessness, being **exceedingly broad**, its standards infinitely holy and righteous, in contrast to the narrow boundaries of human measurements.

MEM

Rewards for Loving the Word. *119:97-104.* **97a. Oh, how love I thy law!**

(vv. 47-48, 127, 163, 165). **97b.** His love was manifested by the Word being his **meditation all the day** (v. 15). There were four rewards of such love: (1) God's Word made him wise. **98.** He was wiser **than his enemies** (Deut. 4:6-8), with all their worldly shrewdness (Luke 16:8) as opposed to his simplicity (Psalm 116:6), for they were destitute of the true wisdom from God. **For they** (Thy commandments) **are ever with me**, guaranteeing his superiority to his foes in the wisdom that makes a believer wise to salvation (2 Tim. 3:15-17), the starting point of all true wisdom.

99. He was wiser than his teachers because God's **testimonies** were his **meditation** (v. 15). **100.** He was wiser than the **ancients** (aged; Job 32:7-9), who in the East, before the advent of many books, were held to be the repositories of knowledge. Theirs, however, was mere natural knowledge, while the psalmist's was supernatural revelation from God (vv. 22, 56).

(2) **101.** God's Word enabled him to avoid evil (Prov. 1:15), restraining his feet **from every evil way** in order that he might keep God's Word, illustrating the truth that either the Word keeps us from sin, or sin keeps us from the Word. **102.** So the psalmist could say, **I have not departed** (turned aside) **from thine ordinances** (Deut. 17:20; Josh. 23:6; 1 Kings 15:5), for the LORD Himself had taught him; therefore, the Word was ministered with power to affect the heart and thus the whole life.

(3) **103.** God's Word revealed its sweetness and preciousness (Psalm 19:10; Prov. 24:13-14). (4) **104.** God's Word showed him the wisdom of detesting every false way (vv. 128, 130). Not only did he get understanding in spiritual verities, but also discreet guidance in practical living.

NUN

The Word as a Guiding Light.
119:105-12. **105. Thy word is a lamp unto my feet, and a light unto my path** (Prov. 6:23). For the believer it is "a light that shineth in a dark place, until the day dawn" (2 Pet. 1:19). It is not the sun, but for the Tribulation saint it will be a precious guide through the "gross darkness" (Isa. 60:2) of that terrible time of trouble until "the Sun of righteousness" shall arise (Mal. 4:2). (1) **106.** The Word gives light, prompting saints to solemnly pledge their utmost loyalty to it. So the Jews swore under curse after their return from Babylon (Neh. 10:29), a repetition of their solemn promise at Sinai (Exod. 19:8; 24:3, 7), in dependence on the help of God's Spirit (Ezek. 11:19-20; 2 Cor. 3:5).

(2) **107.** The Word gives light, prompting prayer for reviving (v. 25), especially in times of persecution and trouble. This petition includes physical life and rescue from physical death in the Tribulation, when the martyrdom of God's people will be widespread (cf. Rev. 6:9-11; 13:15), as well as spiritual quickening.

(3) **108.** The Word gives light, prompting praise to God and the desire to be taught (Psalm 50:14; Hos. 14:2), "the sacrifice of praise to God ... the fruit of our lips" (Heb. 13:15). **And teach me** (v. 12). Light comes from being taught the Word, and such light produces a desire for more teaching, more light.

(4) **109.** The Word gives light to remember its guidance and help amid the perils of life. The psalmist's life was in peril, representative of all saints, especially Tribulation saints, whose lives will be continuously imperiled. So he said, **My soul** (i.e., I, my life) **is continually in my hand** (cf. 1 Sam. 19:5; Job

13:14), in danger, like those who carry anything precious in their hand, where it is not safe, and may readily be lost or stolen (Judg. 12:3). **110.** The psalmist faced the **snare** the wicked lay for him (Psalms 91:3; 140:5; 141:9).

(5) **111a.** The Word gives light that it is a precious heritage of the saint, an ever enduring inheritance, better than the literal Canaan flowing with milk and honey (Deut. 33:4). **111b.** The LORD's testimonies are **the rejoicing of** the **heart** (vv. 14, 162). (6) **112.** The Word gives light so that the heart is inclined to believe and practice it unto the end of life (v. 33).

SAMEKH

The Word in Relation to the Wicked.
119:113-20. **113. I hate vain thoughts** (*sēʿapîm*, "doubters, skeptics, double-minded men," those who are inconstant, whose heart is not wholly on God's side). The Word in relation to the wicked does seven things: (1) The Word engenders an attitude of detestation toward double-mindedness and vacillating doubt of unbelieving men, hating the sin not the sinner and developing love for God's Word (v. 47; 1 Kings 18:21; James 1:8; 4:8).

(2) **114.** The Word offers protection against the wicked, revealing the LORD as a **hiding place** in time of tribulation (Psalms 31:20; 32:7; 61:4; 91:1) and a **shield** against foes (84:9), that in which the beleaguered saint may take hope and courage.

(3) **115.** The Word separates the saint from evildoers (6:8; 139:19; Matt. 7:23) so the evildoers will not separate the saint from the Word (v. 22).

(4) **116.** The Word sustains the saint that he may live and not die at the hands of the wicked in order that he will **not be ashamed of** (disappointed in) his **hope** of deliverance (Psalm 25:2-3; Rom. 5:5;

9:33). This has special relevance to the Tribulation remnant, who will survive the Great Tribulation to enter the Kingdom (Matt. 24:13) and the great deliverance the returning Messiah will work for Israel (Rev. 19:11—20:3). Then Israel's "hope" will be realized (cf. Ezek. 37:11; Zech. 9:12).

(5) **117.** The Word upholds the saint in order that he may be safe from the attacks of the wicked (Psalm 12:5; Prov. 29:25), that he may **have respect** (regard) for the statutes of the LORD continually (vv. 6, 15).

(6) **118-19.** The Word rejects the wicked and shows the divine judgment the LORD will bring on them and that their deceptive course will end in utter defeat (vv. 10, 21). The book of the Revelation (8:1—20:3) is a prophetic illustration of the truth that the LORD will remove ("cause to cease") **all the wicked of the earth like dross** (Isa. 1:22, 25; Ezek. 22:18-19). At the second advent the flaming fire will separate the dross (the wicked) from the pure metal (the godly; Mal. 3:2-3). **Therefore, I love thy testimonies** (v. 47), because they shall be the seed of life, saving the godly from the apocalyptic judgments and removing sinners so that the millennial Kingdom may be set up.

(7) **120.** The Word instills trembling ("bristling" with fear) even in the godly, who will be untouched by the judgments that are to come upon the earth. How much more ought they to strike terror to the wicked, upon whom they will fall (cf. Rev. 6:15-17).

AYIN

Separation of the Godly from the Wicked Through the Word. 119:121-28. **121. I have done justice and righteousness; do not leave me to my oppressors** (NASB; 2 Sam. 8:15; Job 29:14). (1) The Word of God trenchantly distin-

guishes between the saved and the unsaved, the righteous and the wicked (Psalm 1:6).

(2) **122.** The Word furnishes a guarantee to the LORD's servant for good (Job 17:3). A **surety** (ʾ*rōḇ*) is an "exchanging, a giving of security or a pledge to assure the fulfillment of an undertaking" (Gen. 43:9; Heb. 7:22). Viewing the contest prophetically, it appears as a judicial trial in which the cause of the Jewish remnant is at issue, in which they want the LORD to make Himself responsible for them. The Messiah, as the Word assures us, has done this (Zech. 3:1-5; Heb. 7:22; 9:11-15). The result will be that **the proud** (the arrogant, lawless foes of Israel during the Great Tribulation) will not be allowed to **oppress** the remnant, who will be sealed and preserved from death (Rev. 7:1-8).

(3) **123.** The Word justifies the intense longing for deliverance on the part of the Tribulation saints, for according to God's **righteous word** their enemies will be destroyed (Rev. 19:11—20:3), and they will be preserved for Kingdom blessing (20:4-6). (4) **124-25.** The Word also promises the LORD's dealing with them in redemptive grace (Isa. 53:1-12; 55:1-12; Hos. 2:19, 23; 13:4-6; Zeph. 3:14-17); therefore, His people desire teaching of His Word that they might know of God's loving-kindness to be shown them.

(5) **126.** The Word indicates when it is time for the LORD to act in judgment against the lawless followers of Antichrist in the last days (Jer. 18:23; Ezek. 31:11; Rev. 6:17; 11:15). **For they**, the Antichrist and his lawless followers (2 Thess. 2:4; Rev. 13:1-18), who are ripe for ruin, **have made void** (broken) **thy law** (Dan. 11:36-37; cf. Psalm 2:1-3; Rev. 13:5-6, 15-18; cf. Gen. 15:16; Lev. 18:24).

127-28. Because of these wonderfully enheartening disclosures, the godly Jewish remnant will love God's **commandments above gold; yea, above fine gold** (Psalm 19:10; Prov. 3:13-18; 8:11; Matt. 13:45-46; Eph. 3:8), esteeming right all the LORD's **precepts concerning all things** and hating **every false way** (v. 104).

PE

Communion Through the Word. 119:129-36. Such communion with the LORD does eight things: (1) **129.** It comprehends the wonderfulness of God's Word and as a result observes its testimonies (vv. 18, 22). (2) **130.** It involves the entrance (*pētăḥ*, "opening, explanation, unfolding") of God's words, giving **light** (Prov. 6:23) and **understanding unto the simple** (Psalm 19:7; Prov. 1:4; 2 Pet. 1:19).

(3) **131.** It develops an intense longing for God's commandments (Job 29:23; Psalm 42:1). The psalmist **panted ... longed for** God's Word as a fainting person pants for air and as a thirsty person longs for water. For one in communion with God, the Word of God is the only thing that can really satisfy the deepest longings of the heart (84:2).

(4) **132.** It gives understanding of God's ways in grace. The psalmist pleaded for a manifestation of that grace to him (25:16) after the LORD's manner of dealing with those who **love** His name. (5) **133.** It orders the believer's life so that no iniquity overpowers him. Only when one's steps are ordered (established) in the Word (17:5) is the power of sin broken in the life (19:13), for the steps make a walk and that walk merges into a life.

(6) **134.** It purifies and exalts human motives. Deliverance from **the oppression of man** is that the LORD's precept might be observed, but not for selfish reasons (v. 84; 142:6). (7) **135.** It makes the favor and fellowship of God of paramount importance. God's **face** shining upon His **servant** (4:6; 31:16; 67:1; 80:3, 7, 19; Num. 6:25) is supreme bliss and the proper spiritual climate to be taught God's **statutes** (v. 12).

(8) **136.** It produces loving concern and care about the condition of the lost. The psalmist's eyes shed streams of tears (Jer. 9:1, 18; 14:17; Lam. 3:48) over those who did not keep God's Law (v. 158). In the Tribulation, when lawlessness under the lawless one (Psalm 2:1-3; Dan. 11:35-36; 2 Thess. 2:4; Rev. 13:1-18; cf. Gen. 15:16) reaches its highest tide, the saints of that period will have plenty of cause to weep **rivers of waters** (Ezek. 9:4).

TSADHE

Understanding God's Righteous Ways Through the Word. 119:137-44. **137-38. Righteous art thou, O Lord ... upright ... thy judgments** (Ezra 9:15; Jer. 12:1; Lam. 1:18; Dan. 9:7, 14). The Word of God does three things: (1) The Word of God imparts a firm conviction of the righteousness and fairness of God's dealings with mankind. God has commanded His testimonies in righteousness and 'very faithfulness (vv. 86, 90, 144, 172).

The terrible apocalyptic judgments of the Tribulation period will bring this issue to the fore (Rev. 15:3-4; 16:7). People who neglect or reject God's Word are apt to criticize the justice and fairness of God's ways in punishing evildoers or saving and rewarding sinners.

(2) **139-41.** The Word of God imparts a zeal for the truth of the holy oracles. **My zeal** (*qîn'â*, "jealousy, anger") for Thy Word **hath consumed me** (Psalm 69:9), devoured me emotionally, **because mine enemies have forgotten thy words**, will-

fully putting them out of their minds. This consumes me with jealous anger, more than the evils I suffer from the lawless, because **Thy word is very pure** (tried, refined) in the crucible of human experience, and proved to be absolutely free of the dross of unfaithfulness, deceit, or unrighteousness (12:6; 19:8). **Therefore, thy servant loveth it** (v. 47), and my jealousy for its honor is outraged by my adversaries, who ignore and despise it. Although **I am small and despised** (22:6), I do not despise Thy Word like my enemies, who willfully forget its precepts (v. 61; cf. v. 139).

(3) **142-44.** The Word of God demonstrates that God's righteousness and truth are eternal. God's Law is truth itself (vv. 151, 160). Though **trouble and anguish** had come upon the psalmist (as prophetically representative of the saints of the Tribulation period; Dan. 12:1; Matt. 24:21-22), those terrible testings had not turned him aside from the Word; rather, they made it his delight and gave him the unshakable faith that God's **testimonies are righteous forever** (NASB; Psalm 19:9).

Behind them is the all-righteous LORD, who will fulfill His covenants and promises to Israel (Rom. 9:4-5) and cause her to be regathered and converted, that she may **live** as a nation in Kingdom blessing (Ezek 37:1-28; Hos. 2:16-23; Joel 2:30-32; Zeph. 3:14-17), as well as "live" spiritually with the Word of God written on her heart (Jer. 31:31-33; Rom. 11:26).

QOPH

Prayer Through the Word. *119:145-52.* **145-48. I cried with my whole heart** (all my heart). **Hear** (answer) **me, O Lord ... I cried unto thee.** Observing the **statutes** and **testimonies** of the LORD does four things: (1) It pro-

duces a vigorous, dynamic prayer life. Since the psalmist represents all saints of any age (prophetically, Tribulation saints), he presented a foreview of the earnest, intense prayer in the time of Jacob's trouble (Jer. 30:5-7) that is utterly sincere and wholehearted, expects an answer, is directed toward salvation (deliverance) from the awful lawlessness of that period, and anticipates **the dawning of the morning**, that is, it was offered by one with such zeal that he rose before daylight to cry for help and hope (wait) for God's words (Psalms 57:8; 108:2). He anticipated **the night watches**; he was already awake and praying and meditating before the night watches came (63:6; 77:4; Lam. 2:19).

(2) **149a.** It gives the realization of how important God's redemptive grace is to efficacy in prayer. Then the remnant will have come to a knowledge of Christ (Isa. 53:1-12) and will be able to pray in Jesus' name, with all its connotation of God's **loving-kindness.** (3) **149b-50.** It imparts understanding to pray in accord with God's judicial dealing with the godly and the ungodly. **Revive me according to thy justice.** The future remnant will commit their spiritual and temporal life to God's hands, as well as **those who follow after wickedness** (NASB), who **draw near** to persecute and threaten (cf. Rev. 12:13—13:18). They are the lawless followers of the Antichrist (Psalm 2:1-3), who are aptly described as **far from thy** (God's) **law** (cf. 2 Thess. 2:4; Rev. 13:4-8, 14-18).

(4) **151.** It gives a sense of God's nearness and faithfulness. **Thou art near** (Deut. 4:7; Psalms 46:1; 75:1; Isa. 50:8). **All thy commandments are truth,** that is, truth itself (v. 142). **152. I have known of old that thou hast founded** (established) **them forever**, unchangeable and eternal (Luke 21:33).

RESH

Salvation Through the Word.
119:153-60. Salvation through the Word comprehends five things: (1) **153.** It comprehends rescue from affliction. But "deliverance" must be strictly according to God's Word, for such affliction may be chastening for sin (1 Cor. 11:30-32). In such a case, turning away from the sin is necessary for deliverance from it. Or it may be refining and purifying, the removal of the affliction not being in God's will (2 Cor. 12:7-10).

(2) **154-55.** It comprehends the LORD's pleading the cause of His own against the charges of the evil one and those enemies of the LORD's people under the evil one's power (1 Sam. 24:15; Psalm 35:1). Ultimately, Israel may confidently expect the LORD's pleading her cause (Mic. 7:9) when she is reinstated and restored as a high-priestly (millennial) nation (Zech. 3:1-10), and when the LORD rises to destroy her persecutors and enemies at Armageddon (Rev. 16:13-16; 19:11-21).

(3) **156.** It comprehends redeeming lost sinners. Israel, spiritually lost and scattered, will be regathered and saved on the basis of the greatness of God's **tender mercies**, that is, Christ's redemption wrought on Calvary (Isa. 53:1-12; 55:1-13; Ezek. 37:1-28; Hos. 14:4-7; Zech. 12:10—13:1; Matt. 25:1-11; Rom. 11:26-32).

(4) It comprehends granting life, quickening both spiritually and physically, giving (preserving) physical life amid terrible persecution and martyrdom (vv. 154, 156, 159), but strictly according to the Word (and will) of God. However, "salvation is far from the wicked" (v. 155), even as they are far from God's Law, a reference to the full ripening of human lawlessness in the

Tribulation (Psalm 2:1-3) and God's "giving up" (cf. Rom. 1:24, 26) these bold rebels to the full fruition of their wickedness (Rev. 14:18-20; 16:1-21). **157-58.** These are the **persecutors** and **enemies** singled out, and **the transgressors** at whose wicked lawlessness and rebellion the psalmist **was grieved** (better, whom he "loathed").

(5) **159-60.** The revelation of God's loving-kindness in salvation is a great impetus to quicken the love of God's redeemed for His Word, and give them deep conviction of the everlasting truth of it.

SHIN

The Perfection of the Word.
119:161-68. The perfection of the Word is seen in the eight effects it has on all who keep (observe) it; prophetically, on the Jewish remnant of the Tribulation period. (1) **161.** They stand in awe of it. Though **princes** ("great men") are persecuting them, without reason, they will only have deep reverence and humble submission before the Word of God (v. 120; cf. Rev. 12:13—13:18; 1 Sam. 24:11; 26:18).

(2) **162.** They rejoice at God's Word (vv. 14, 111; 1 Sam. 30:16) as one who finds **great spoil** (Isa. 9:3; Matt. 13:44). (3) **163.** They love God's Word (v. 47). Therefore, they hate and despise falsehood (vv. 104, 128; Psalm 31:6; Prov. 13:5), which will predominate in the gross deceptions of the Tribulation period (2 Thess. 2:4-12; Rev. 9:20-21; 13:13-18; 16:13-16).

(4) **164.** They praise God for His righteous judgments. So terrible will be the apocalyptic judgments (Rev. 8:1—18:24) that the wicked who hate the Word will curse God as unrighteous on account of them (6:15-17; 16:21), and even the righteous will need assurance

that those fearful manifestations of God's wrath are righteous (15:3; 16:7). The perfection of the Word in revealing the mind of God is hinted at in the fact that **seven times a day** the remnant will praise God for those **righteous** judgments, seven being the number for perfection.

(5) **165.** They get great peace. Even in the presence of potent enemies, the saints have an inner calm (v. 161; cf. Prov. 3:2; Isa. 57:21; John 14:27; Gal. 5:22; Phil. 4:7). As a consequence, **nothing shall offend them**, literally, "they shall have no stumbling block" (Prov. 3:23; Isa. 63:13; 1 John 2:10), neither the blasphemies of the Antichrist (Rev. 13:7-9) nor the deceptive miracles and murderous cruelty of the false prophet (Rev. 13:13-16).

(6) **166.** They are blessed with a vital hope of salvation (v. 81; Gen. 49:18). They will await the return of the King-Messiah (Zech. 2:10; Mal. 4:2) to set up His Kingdom (Matt. 25:31-46; Rev. 19:11—20:6). (7) **167.** They develop an ardent love for God's Word (v. 47). Keeping the Word begets a love for the Word (v. 129).

(8) **168.** They are favored with fearlessness under the scrutiny of God. They realize their lives are an open book before the omniscient One (Job 24:23; Psalm 139:3; Prov. 5:21; Jer. 23:24; Heb. 4:13; Rev. 2:23). Therefore, they obey His Word and do everything as in His presence, and so they have nothing to fear (cf. 2 Cor. 5:10-11).

TAV

Praiseful Prayer Inspired by the Word. 119:169-76. Praiseful prayer inspired by the Word does seven things: (1) **169-70.** It expresses assurance of being heard and answered. It is fervent prayer, a **cry** (*rǐnnâ*, "shout") of need that will **come near before** the LORD

(18:6; 102:1), **supplication**, earnest pleading. The first cry is for inner **understanding** (v. 27) in accord with God's Word (vv. 65, 154). The second cry is for outward deliverance, which follows obtaining understanding of God's ways in dealing with His own and their enemies (cf. 90:12-15; Rev. 6:9-10; 15:3; 16:7).

(2) **171.** Such prayer is filled with praise. It is the expression of a keen desire that the **lips shall utter praise** (Psalms 51:15; 63:3), literally, "shall pour forth praises as from a bubbling, overflowing fountain" (cf. 19:2), the result of the LORD's teaching the one who prays His **statutes** (v. 12; 94:12; Mic. 4:2; Rev. 19:1-6). (3) **172.** Such prayer is joyful and triumphant. **My tongue shall speak of thy word** (lit., "answer Thy Word, responding to it with praise"), **for all thy commandments are righteousness**, that is, righteousness itself (v. 138).

(4) **173.** Such prayer manifests complete dependence upon the LORD. **Let thine hand help me.** Saints have always needed such help, but the need will be intensified in the case of the Tribulation saints when confronted by the awful cruelty and lawlessness of the Antichrist, false prophet, and their wicked followers (Rev. 12:13—13:18). But the testimony of the godly will be, "We **have chosen thy precepts** in preference to worldly protection and gain" (13:15-18).

(5) **174.** Such prayer yearns for God's intervention and undertaking (vv. 131, 166), expecting God's deliverance as a result of delighting in (vv. 16, 24, 47, 77) God's **law** (Word), which explains and promises it (cf. Rev. 6:9-10). (6) **175.** Such prayer requests both physical and spiritual life, which his foes assail. His purpose is that he may serve and praise God. Also, he requests God's help by His inflicting judgment on his adver-

saries, for only then can wickedness be put down (Rev. 8:1—20:3) and the millennial Kingdom set up.

(7) **176.** Such prayer pleads for restoration. It realizes the frailty of the flesh and even redeemed man's proneness to err (Isa. 53:6; Jer. 50:6; Matt. 18:12; Luke 15:4). But it comprehends the Shepherd's love and willingness to restore (Psalm 23:3) and to seek the erring sheep, which the **servant** of God sometimes becomes. The basis for the pleas is **I do not forget thy commandments** (v. 16).

N. ISRAEL'S DISTRESS IN PANORAMIC VIEW. 120:1-7.

Psalms 120 to 134 bear the superscription, "A Song of degrees" correctly, "Song of Ascents" or "Goings-Up." Apparently the correct view is that these fifteen psalms were sung by worshipers as they went up to Jerusalem to celebrate the three great festivals (Deut. 16:16). An alternate view is that they were connected with the fifteen steps leading to the court of Israel in the Temple and that they were sung on those steps. The "I" of the psalmist goes beyond personal application to individual saints and comprehends the people Israel, for whom the LORD has planned a great future.

Israel's Cry of Distress and Its Answer. 120:1-4. **1. In my distress I cried unto the Lord, and he heard me.** Deliverance from Babylon, already an accomplished fact, is made the grounds of the prayer of faith, which envisions the establishment of the nation in Jerusalem. In turn, the historical setting furnishes the basis of the prophetic foreview that envisions the last great deliverance from worldwide scattering and the regathering for Kingdom blessing.

2. The cry is for deliverance **from lying lips, and from a deceitful tongue**,

with historical reference to the Samaritans, who by their slanders interrupted the work (cf. Ezra 4-6). The prophetic scope comprehends Israel's last great troubles, the lawless one (2 Thess. 2:4), the deceiver and liar par excellence (2:8-12).

3. What will his fate be? (Psalm 52:4; Dan. 7:8; Zeph. 3:13; Rev. 13:5-6). **4.** It is announced here: **Sharp arrows of the mighty** are those that are "sharp in the heart of the king's enemies" (Psalm 45:5). They are the arrows of "the mighty" (hero or warrior), that is, God, going to fight against His foes (Deut. 32:42; Psalm 7:13). In Revelation, Christ in His second advent returns as a mighty Warrior to slay His foes, notably the beast (Antichrist) and the false prophet, the preeminent lying tongues (Rev. 19:11-21).

Coals of juniper (the broom tree, regarded as a superior fuel wood by Arabs) are the red-hot embers. As the slanders of Israel's foes pierced like "sharp arrows" (Psalm 57:4) and burned like fiery embers, so retributively in kind, God will dispense to them "sharp arrows" and "coals of juniper" (18:12-13; 140:10).

Israel's Lament over Being Surrounded by Hostile Foes. 120:5-7. **5. Woe is me, that I sojourn in Meshech, that I dwell in the tents of Kedar!** "Meshech" was a descendant of Japheth (Gen. 10:2), from whom the Gentile nations sprang, and thus represents the Gentiles among Israel as a sojourner (1 Chron. 1:5; Ezek. 27:13; 38:2). "Kedar" (Gen. 25:13; Isa. 21:16; 60:7; Jer. 2:10), a descendant of Ishmael, is a people of Arabia, who love strife, like their father (Gen. 16:12).

How true this situation is today. The Jews are scattered throughout the world among the Gentiles, and the State of Israel is surrounded by overwhelming numbers of hostile Arabs (Ishmaelites), who plan their extinction. **6. My soul** (i.e., "I," the psalmist representing Israel) **hath long** ("too long") **dwelt with him** (representing Israel's enemies) **that hateth peace** (Psalm 35:20). **7. I am for peace; but when I speak, they are for war** (lit., "I peace"). My very nature is peace; but when I speak to foster peace, they breathe only war.

O. THE LORD AS ISRAEL'S KEEPER. 121:1-8.

For the superscription, see Psalm 120. The Hebrew is not as in the other "Psalms of Ascents" (120-34) but "for [*l^e*] ascents," suggesting that the object for which these odes were penned was the annual "goings up" to the great feasts at Jerusalem (Deut. 16:16). Tradition maintains this psalm was employed when pilgrims first caught sight of the mountains surrounding their beloved city.

Israel (Through the Psalmist) Speaks. 121:1-2. **1.** This verse is correctly rendered, **I will lift up my eyes to the mountains; from whence shall my help come?** (NASB; 87:1; 123:1; Isa. 40:26). It is *not* the hills that are looked to for help, but the LORD, whose seat is on Zion among them (Psalms 3:4; 14:7; 20:2; cf. Exod. 15:17). **2.** The answer to the question of verse 1b is given: **My help cometh from** the LORD (Psalm 124:8). He is well able to help as the Maker of **heaven and earth** (115:15).

Israel Is Addressed by the Psalmist. 121:3-8. The LORD, presented by the psalmist as Israel's Keeper (*shōmēr*, "Protector, Guardian") will watch over Israel in three ways: (1) **3.** He will not suffer Israel's **foot to be moved**, the negative *'al* expressing the hope of the speaker, because if Israel deliberately departs from God's pathway, she will forfeit His wonderful keeping power and

His sleepless and continuous watchcare over her (41:2; 127:1).

(2) **4.** He will never stop watching over Israel or abandon His purpose for her. **Behold** (pointing out a wonderful fact), **he who keepeth Israel shall neither** (*lō'*, the Hebrew negative, different from that of v. 3, is objective, declaring a fact not a subjective hope) **slumber nor sleep.** Therefore, He will never fail to be Israel's Keeper or fall short of fulfilling His covenants and promises made to her (Gen. 12:1-3; Deut. 30:1-12; 2 Sam. 7:8-16; Jer. 31:31-33), particularly His promise to Jacob, the father of Israel (Gen. 28:15), concerning which this psalm is a commentary.

(3) **5.** As their never failing **keeper** (Psalm 91:4), He is their **shade**, a protecting shelter from the merciless heat of the sun in Bible lands, **upon** the **right hand**, the position best adapted for the defense of the person being guarded. As Satan stands at the right hand of Israel (under the figure of Joshua, the high priest) to destroy her (Zech. 3:1), even so the LORD is at her right hand to save and deliver her (Psalms 16:8; 109:31), including her climactic deliverance from Satan's malignity, manifested in and through wicked men in the Tribulation period (Rev. 12:13-17; 13:2, 11).

6. With the LORD as Israel's "shade," **the sun shall not smite** them **by day** with heat (Isa. 49:10; Jonah 4:8; Rev. 7:16), **nor the moon by night** with cold. The moon, as "ruling the night" (Gen. 1:16), has all the influences connected with the night attributed to it; compare the words of Jacob (Gen. 31:40; Jer. 36:30), to whom verses 4 and 5 allude. **7-8.** In summary, the **Lord shall preserve** (same word as "keep") Israel **from all evil**, and their **soul** (i.e., "them") and their **going out and ... coming in** (Deut. 28:6), that is, every phase of their activity, perpetually, **for evermore** (Psalms 113:2; 115:18).

P. PRAYER FOR JERUSALEM'S PEACE.
122:1-9.

For the superscription, see Psalm 120. The internal evidence of the psalm supports Davidic authorship. David's purpose was to win over the northern tribes, who were more hesitant than the southern tribes to recognize him as king, and to make Jerusalem, the newly constituted capital, the religious center.

Introduction. 122:1-2. As the preceding psalm was sung when the hills of Jerusalem were sighted in the distance, so this psalm was chanted at the gates of the sanctuary. **1. I was glad when they said unto me, Let us go into the house of the Lord.** Each pilgrim Israelite told how glad he was to enter the LORD's house. Prophetically, this is what the nations will say to one another in the Kingdom age (Isa. 2:2-3; Jer. 50:5; Zech. 8:21-23; 14:16-21). **2. Our feet shall stand within thy gates, O Jerusalem** (Psalms 9:14; 87:2; 116:19; Jer. 7:2). A somewhat lengthy stay had to be made at the gates until all the pilgrims had come up, and the procession to the sanctuary arranged (cf. Psalm 42:4).

The Beauty and Excellence of Jerusalem. 122:3-5. **3-4. Jerusalem is builded as a city that is compact together** (lit., "Jerusalem, *the* built one," i.e., "*the* well-built one"; cf. Dan. 4:30, "Babylon, that I have built"), "built as a city which is bound together" (BV), as a closely knit unit (2 Sam. 5:9; 1 Chron. 11:8) for beauty and utility, a token of the LORD's favor (2 Sam. 5:9, 12), **whither** (to which) **the tribes go up** (Psalm 84:5, NASB; Deut. 16:16), called **the tribes of the Lord** (*yāh*), **unto the testimony of Israel**, the tabernacle, especially the ark, often being thus designated (Exod. 16:34; 25:16).

But the Hebrew may be taken in the sense of "the tribes go up [according to] the testimony for Israel," that is, "as

enjoined upon Israel" (BV) that all the males should appear three times a year before the LORD at the great feasts (Exod. 23:14-17; Deut. 16:16). **To give thanks unto the name**, that is, to the LORD in His revealed attributes (Psalm 54:6).

5. The reference to the **thrones of judgment** (i.e., "seats for judging"), **the thrones** (seats) **of the house of David**, implying Jerusalem's position as the civil and political capital (2 Sam. 5:9; 6:16), was a factor in its suitability to also be the religious capital. The plural "thrones" (seats) has in view the bench of judges whose authority derives from the king (cf. Isa. 32:1). In the millennial Kingdom these seats will be occupied by corulers of the Messiah (Matt. 19:28), the Davidic-Messianic rule being one of David's favorite themes (2 Sam. 7:11-13, 19, 25; Psalms 18:50; 21:4).

Prayer for the Peace of Jerusalem. 122:6-9. **6a.** Prayer (petition) was asked for **the peace** (the sign of prosperity and general welfare) **of Jerusalem** itself, its very name denoting "a peaceful possession." **6b-7.** The prayer was: (1) **6b.** "May they prosper who love you" (NASB; 102:14), and (2) **7.** "May peace be within your walls, and prosperity within your palaces" (NASB; 48:3; 51:18; Isa. 62:6; Jer. 17:27). **8.** Repeated was the prayer "May peace be within you" (NASB; 1 Sam. 25:6; John 20:19), a repetition made for the sake of all people under the redemptive covenant, whose welfare is bound up with that of Jerusalem.

9. In the Kingdom, prophetically envisioned in this psalm, **the house of the Lord our God** will be the glorious Temple foretold by Isaiah (Isa. 2:2-3) and Ezekiel (Ezek. 40:5—47:12). Then the tribes of Israel, as well as the saved nations, shall go up to Jerusalem to worship the LORD (Zech. 8:20-23; 14:16-21).

Q. PRAYER FOR THE LORD'S HELP. 123:1-4.

For the superscription, see Psalm 120. All these Psalms of Ascent (120-34), although they spring out of historical events, carry on the prophetic nature of the Psalter and present particularly the experiences of the Israelite saints during the coming Tribulation period and the Kingdom age.

Looking to the Lord for Help. 123:1-2. The historical setting is Israel beset by foes after her return from Babylon, when Samaria, Moab, Ammon, and Arabia (Neh. 2:19), favored by the ruling world power, Persia, were her bitter opponents. The psalmist is representative of Israel (cf. "I," v. 1, with "us," v. 3), both past and future, and in the broadest sense, of all saints of any age.

1-2. The psalmist's lifting up his eyes to the LORD **who dwellest** (is enthroned) **in the heavens** (Psalms 2:4; 11:4; Isa. 57:15) is compared to servants who patiently look for mercy from their **masters** (Prov. 27:18; Mal. 1:6), who have been punishing them, as the clause **Until he has mercy upon us** ("be gracious to us") suggests. The historic picture encompasses the humiliation and sufferings of the returned remnant from Babylon, while the prophetic scope bears on the Israelite remnant in the time of Jacob's trouble (Jer. 30:5-7; Rev. 12:13—13:18).

The Scoffing and Contempt of the Foe. 123:3-4. **3-4.** The threefold **have mercy upon us** ("be gracious to us," once in v. 2c, twice in v. 3; 4:1) arises to the LORD "enthroned in the heavens" when His beleaguered and persecuted people call upon Him in their desperate situation, being **exceedingly filled with contempt,** also repeated to stress the deep humiliation and suffering of Israel in Nehemiah's time (Neh. 4:4) in his-

torical perspective and in the Great Tribulation in the prophetic foreview (cf. Isa. 26:20-21; Rev. 6:9-10; 12:13—13:18). **Have mercy** ("be gracious") means for the LORD to manifest His delivering hand in rescuing and protecting His people from the **scoffing** (Neh. 2:19; Rev. 13:5-6) and **the contempt of the proud** (Neh. 4:4; Dan. 11:36-37; Rev. 13:15-18).

R. ISRAEL'S MIRACULOUS PRESERVATION. 124:1-8.

For the superscription, see Psalms 120 and 123. David is the author; historically, the psalm evidently represents the Aramaean-Ammonite war (2 Sam. 10:1-19); prophetically, it portrays "the time of Jacob's trouble" (Jer. 30:5-7; Dan. 12:1; Matt. 24:21-22; Rev. 12:13—13:18).

Israel's Extreme Peril. 124:1-5. **1-3.** **If it had not been the Lord who was on our side ... then they had swallowed us up alive** (cf. 55:15; Prov. 1:12), as Korah and his rebels were (Num. 16:32-33). The repetition of the clause "if it had not been the LORD who was on our side" stresses the fact that the danger Israel faced was so great and the power of her foes so formidable that no one except God in His miraculous power could have delivered the remnant (Matt. 24:22).

When men rose up against us (Psalm 2:1-3) prophetically glimpses the fiendish end-time anti-Semitism under the Antichrist (Dan. 9:27; Matt. 24:15-20; Rev. 12:13—13:18; 16:13-16). Then the **wrath** of the lawless one (2 Thess. 2:4; Rev. 13:1-8) will be kindled against the Jewish remnant, with the avowed purpose of destroying Israel from off the face of the earth in the Satan-engineered plan at Armageddon (Psalm 2:1-3; Rev. 16:13-16). With the Jewish remnant wiped out, God's promise to David in the Davidic Covenant (2 Sam 7:8-16) could not be fulfilled, or God's redemptive plan for the earth consummated.

4. Then the waters—symbolic of the floods of destruction (Psalms 18:16; 144:7)—and **the stream had gone over our soul** (18:4; 69:2), the very symbolism used in Revelation to portray the dragon's (Satan's) supreme attempt during the Tribulation to annihilate the Israelite remnant in his violent anti-Semitic pogrom (Rev. 12:15-17). **5. Then the proud waters,** symbolizing Israel's haughty enemies, the beast, false prophet, and their arrogant, God-despising followers (Psalm 89:9), **had gone over** (engulfed) **our soul** ("us").

Israel's Escape from the Snare. 124:6-8. **6. Blessed** ("extolled, praised ecstatically") **be the Lord, who hath not given us as a prey to their teeth**, that is, of their enemies—the beast and his followers being portrayed as wild beasts (Dan. 7:7-8; Rev. 13:1) thirsting for the blood of their prey.

7. Our soul (i.e., "we"), the hopelessly outnumbered and humanly doomed Israelite remnant (Zech. 13:8-9; cf. 14:1-2 with vv. 3-4; Rev. 19:11-21), **is escaped like a bird out of the snare of the fowlers,** a figure of the beast, the false prophet, and the demonized armies at Armageddon (16:13-16). **The snare is broken** (Zech. 14:3-4; Rev. 19:15-21), **and we are escaped** (Matt. 24:22) to enter Kingdom blessing (Rev. 20:4-6).

8. Israel confesses that her **help is in the name of the Lord.** He is her omnipotent Creator and will then have become her glorious Redeemer (Isa. 53:1-12; Zech. 12:10—13:1), and so there will be no barrier against the release of His power in behalf of His people.

S. ISRAEL'S MIRACULOUS PROTECTION. 125:1-5.

For the superscription and context,

see the introduction to Psalm 120. Psalm 125 forms a unit with Psalm 126. Both were born in the joy of deliverance from the captivity in Babylon and both look forward to the final restoration of Israel to Kingdom blessing.

The Security of Believers. 125:1-3. **1.** Those who **trust in the Lord** are compared to **Mount Zion, which cannot be removed** ($y\bar{\imath}mm\hat{o}\underline{t}$, "be shaken, dislodged") **but abideth** ($y\bar{e}sh\bar{e}\underline{b}$, "sits, dwells") **forever**, a symbol of spiritual permanency. The visible mountain, the seat of God's manifestation and government, portrays by its solid firmness the immovable spiritual Zion—those who ($b\bar{o}\underline{t}^e h\hat{\imath}m$) put their faith in the LORD (the emphasis being on the object of trust, not the firmness of the trust).

They who have the LORD as their object of trust, as will the remnant in the days of Antichrist (Rev. 12:13—13:18), will no more be dislodged from their loyalty to Him (cf. 13:13-18) than will the material Mount Zion, on which the city of David was built, the underlying imagery encompassing the certainty of fulfillment of the Davidic Covenant (2 Sam. 7:8-16). Not only are the certainty and permanency of the LORD's protection of His people stressed (v. 1), but also the all-encompassing nature of that protection (v. 2).

2. As the mountains are round about Jerusalem, so the Lord is round about his people; the LORD surrounds His own with His protecting love **from henceforth even forever** (Psalm 121:8; Zech. 2:5). Jerusalem itself, situated on a mountain range with surrounding higher hills and with deep valleys between, is a natural fortress, in a real sense protected by God. The city's geographical location is a badge of divine protection, especially of the faithful remnant of the Tribulation period, which will be delivered to be the nucleus of the Davidic-Messianic Kingdom.

3a. For the rod (scepter) **of the wicked** (world power; at that time, Persia) **shall not rest** (remain permanently) **upon the lot of the righteous**, that is, Palestine, which belongs by covenant agreement to Israel (Gen. 12:7; Deut. 30:5-10), here regarded in respect to her believing remnant, through whom her high calling as holy to the LORD will be realized. The Messiah's scepter (Rev. 19:11-16) shall at last destroy the pagan scepter (Psalm 2:9; 45:6; Zech. 14:4, 9).

3b. Lest the righteous put forth their hands (presumptuously and by unlawful means, cf. Gen. 3:22, to relieve themselves) **and thus commit iniquity.** If the ungodly and lawless were permitted indefinitely to harass the righteous, the faith of God's people might fail and they might be tempted to react toward God and their enemies in a sinful manner (cf. Psalm 73:13). Therefore, in pity for human frailty (103:9-17), God ceases to contend (Isa. 57:16).

Prayer for the Lord's Undertaking for Believers. 125:4-5. **Do good, O Lord, unto those who are good** (those described in vv. 1-3). Being "good" is closely connected with receiving "good," and the former means being **upright** in heart, "righteous," justified by faith in God's redemptive grace, according to the one and only true gospel of salvation by grace through faith (Gen. 3:15; 15:6; Eph. 2:8-9). All those "good" in God's eyes are justified by faith in His redemptive grace.

The remnant of the Tribulation will meet this qualification (Zech. 12:10—13:1; Rom. 11:26-32) and can boldly pray, "Do good, O LORD." And so can every truly justified believer. But to avoid God's chastisements, the upright in heart must exemplify their inner

goodness by their outer conduct (1 Cor. 11:30-32; Heb. 12:3-17).

5. But the unrighteous, the unsaved, who turn aside to **their crooked ways** (lit., "their tortuous crookednesses"; Prov. 2:15; Isa. 59:8), the LORD shall separate them from the righteous (Psalm 1:6) and **lead them forth** (away) **with the workers of iniquity** (92:7; 94:4), those in demonized paganism. **But peace shall be upon Israel**, that is, the true remnant after the unsaved Israelites have been removed in the judgments of the Tribulation (128:6; Rev. 20:4-6).

T. THANKSGIVING FOR RESTORATION TO ZION. 126:1-6.

For the superscription, see Psalm 120. For the scope of this psalm, see the introduction to Psalm 125.

Deliverance from Captivity. 126:1-3. **1a. When the Lord turned again the captivity of Zion**, that is, "brought back the captives of Zion," with the root from *shābâ*, "take captive," rather than with Perowne from *shûḇ*, "return," "brought back the returned of Zion" (cf. Psalm 85:1; Jer. 29:14; Hos. 6:11). **1b. We were like them that dream.** We could scarcely believe that it was a reality and not a mere dream. Isaiah 29:7-8 presents the same image with a different application (cf. Gen. 45:26; Acts 12:9).

2. Then was our mouth filled with laughter, and our tongue with singing (Job 8:21), with historical allusion to the return from Babylon, but with a prophetic view to the last-day regathering and restoration to Kingdom blessing (Isa. 35:10; 65:19). **2c-3.** Then the nations will say, **The Lord has done great things for them** (Psalm 71:19; 1 Sam. 12:24; Luke 1:49; cf. Joel 2:21). Then the saved remnant of Israel will concur most enthusiastically with what the Gentiles say and acknowledge and be glad for the great benefits the LORD has bestowed on them in establishing them in the joy of the Kingdom (Isa. 25:9; Zeph. 3:14) and will laud God's great goodness, as recounted in Psalm 103.

Blessed Establishment in the Land. 126:4-6. The prayer of the returned exiles is voiced in verse 4, and the hope that inspired it is expressed in verses 5 and 6. **4. Restore our fortunes, Lord, as streams in the Southland** (BV), that is, the Negev, the dry southern portion of Canaan. The "streams" are "channels" ("stream beds") that become brooks only as rain gladdens the arid country (cf. Job 6:15-20), otherwise a sad, barren region (Josh. 15:19; Psalm 68:9).

5. The psalmist, in referring to sowing **in tears**, historically saw the hard times attending the beginning of the second Temple (Zech. 4:10; cf. Ezra 6:16, 22; Neh. 8:9-17; 12:42-43). Prophetically, he glimpsed the final restoration of Israel (cf. Jer. 31:9, 14, 17, 31-34) when the remnant **shall reap in joy** (joyful singing).

6. He who is seen going forth and weeping, **bearing precious seed** (the draught of seed, i.e., seed to be drawn out from the seed basket; cf. Amos 9:13), shall **doubtless** (indeed) come again **with rejoicing** (a shout of joy), **bringing his sheaves with him** (cf. 2 Cor. 9:6; Gal. 6:8-9; James 5:7-8). Prophetically, the Jewish remnant is envisioned preaching the "gospel of the kingdom" (Matt. 24:14) and bringing in a harvest of converts (cf. Dan. 12:3). Anticipating these remarkable evangelists, the apostle Paul, as a converted Jew and a mighty evangelist, viewed himself as born prematurely (1 Cor. 15:8).

U. THE SAFETY AND SECURITY OF THE KINGDOM. 127:1-5.

See Psalm 120 for the comment on the inscription. Attributing the psalm "to" or "for Solomon," whose glorious reign typifies the peace and prosperity of the coming millennial Kingdom, and viewing the context of the psalm in its relationship to preceding psalms (120-26, which prophetically envision the same period, as do the "Psalms of Degrees" that follow, 128-34), the intimation is clear that this psalm also (besides its broader application) focuses prophetically on the Kingdom age.

Full Earthly Blessing. 127:1-2. These earthly benefits will not be realized in universal scope till the satanic world order is destroyed (Zech. 13:2; Rev. 20:1-3) and wicked men purged out at Christ's second advent (19:11-21). **1.** Then the LORD will **build the house** and **keep** (guard) **the city**, ending man's vain attempts to insure peace by his own ingenious inventions.

2. It is vain for you to rise up early, to sit up late, to eat the bread of sorrows (painful labors). Here the psalmist dramatically turns back and in a lively apostrophe addresses the vain worldlings of verse 1, who have no place for God in their plans or their work, as they rise early and retire late because of toil (Isa. 5:11), and eat **the bread of sorrows**, that is, food amid rigorous work (Gen. 3:17). **For so he** (the LORD) **giveth his beloved sleep** (better, "in sleep")— gives those who love and trust Him "in sleep" what vain worldlings work so hard to attain, as He did in Solomon's case (1 Kings 3:5-13), without sorrows and undue labor (Matt. 6:25, 34).

Complete Dependence upon God. 127:3-5. **3a.** The psalmist called attention to **children** as **an heritage of the Lord** (Gen. 33:5; 48:9; Josh. 24:4) as a basic illustration of the principle that all blessings ultimately flow from God. Comparatively few of earth's billions now sing, "Praise God from whom *all* blessings flow," and still fewer really believe it when they sing it.

However, in the Kingdom age, to which this psalm points, the belief in this great truth will be universal, as well as the spirit of complete dependence upon God as a corollary truth. As a father bequeathes an inheritance to his children (Prov. 19:14), so God gives sons to His children as their "heritage," a basic blessing illustrating all other blessings that come from Him.

3b. He also gives **the fruit of the womb** as His **reward** (Gen. 30:2; Deut. 7:13). So Leah regarded her son "Issachar" ("hire, reward"), because she looked upon him as a reward given her by God (Gen. 30:18). **4. Children of one's youth** are sons begotten when the father is in full strength (49:3; Isa. 54:6). They are like **arrows ... in the hand of a mighty man** (heroic warrior). When the parents decline in strength and need protection, the children become such a defense.

5. Happy is the man who hath his quiver full of them (Jer. 30:18-20; Zech. 8:5). They (such happy fathers) **shall not be ashamed** (be humiliated by being wronged or taken advantage of because of the infirmity of age). **But they shall speak with the enemies in the gate** (through the advocacy of their sons, who will take their place when they have a lawsuit with adversaries "in the gate," the place of justice; cf. Deut. 28:4-8).

V. WHEN THE LORD BLESSES OUT OF ZION. 128:1-6.

For the scope and context of this psalm, see the introductions to Psalm 120 and Psalm 127.

The Source of Blessedness. 128:1. **1. Blessed is every one that feareth the Lord** (112:1). Fearing the LORD is believing that He is who He reveals Himself to be and responding in reverential awe and obedience. The true manifestation of such godly reverence is walking (step-by-step living) **in his ways** (paths)

(119:3). Only such believers are entitled to the blessings enumerated, which apply to all saints in any age, but with special emphasis upon millennial saints, as the context and internal evidence of the psalm show.

The Elements of the Blessedness. 128:2-4. In the historical purview, Israel returned from Babylon and, persecuted by the Samaritan foes (cf. Neh. 4:1—6:19), was shown the way of comfort and blessing, as prophetically the returnees from the final diaspora will likewise be pointed to the way of comfort in Kingdom blessing. The blessings include two things: (1) They include general felicity and security. **2. Thou shalt eat of the labor of thine hands** (Isa. 3:10), instead of an invading enemy doing so (Deut. 28:33). **Happy shalt thou be ... it shall be well with thee** (Deut. 33:29; Amos 9:11-15; Zech. 8:10-13; cf. Isa. 60:21; Jer. 32:41; Ezek. 34:27-28; Joel 3:20).

(2) They include domestic bliss and tranquility. **3a. Thy wife shall be as a fruitful vine by the sides of thine house** (Prov. 5:18; Ezek. 19:10), "in the inner parts," the most comfortable and secure place of the house. The happy home was highlighted against the dark background of Israel's long and sad homeless state while scattered among the nations.

3b. Thy children like olive plants round about thy table (52:8; 144:12). A numerous and flourishing posterity is also promised to the hitherto husbandless and childless state of the nation in exile (Mic. 4:9-10; Zech. 8:5), a picture of the restored "wife" of the LORD (Hos. 2:1—3:5) reinstated and placed in Kingdom favor (Isa. 54:1-3; Ezek. 36:10-15).

4. The psalmist interrupted the enumeration of blessing to issue the solemn reminder that the enjoyment of these blessings is reserved for **the man ... who**

feareth (see v. 1) **the Lord.** The interjectional adverb **Behold** is like a sudden handclap to call attention to the sad fact that His people are often far too insensitive to His righteous and gracious ways.

Prayer for Realization of the Blessedness. 128:5-6. **5.** Prayerful reminder is issued that the enumerated blessings will be the result of the LORD's blessing out of Zion (the southeast hill of Jerusalem, poetically applied to the entire city), here historically applicable to the era of the return from the Babylonian Captivity, and prophetically to the Kingdom age, when Jerusalem will be the capital of the millennial earth (Isa. 2:2-3; Jer. 50:5; Zech. 8:21-23; 14:16-21).

The Lord bless you from Zion, and may you see the prosperity of Jerusalem all the days of your life (NASB; Psalm 122:6-9; lit., "See!"; it is an imperative denoting the certainty of the promise; cf. 37:27 for a similar imperative in the Hebrew). Jerusalem as the center of the national and spiritual life, envisioned both historically and prophetically, stands for the whole land; indeed, prophetically for the whole earth, for in the Kingdom age Israel's peace and blessing will be shared by the nations of the whole earth (122:1-3, 6; Isa. 2:2-3; Zech. 8:20-23). The Kingdom age will be an era of God's blessing upon the earth—immediately upon Israel, intermediately through the nation to the millennial earth.

6. Yea, thou shalt see thy children's children (Gen. 50:23; Job 42:16), because longevity will be restored (Isa. 65:20; Zech. 8:4), and **peace** will be **upon Israel** (and the world) because war will be banished, with Satan and demons (the real war makers, John 8:44; James 4:1-2) imprisoned (Rev. 20:1-3), and with armaments and arsenals done away

with (Isa. 2:4) under the rule of the Prince of Peace (9:6).

W. PAST DELIVERANCES OF ISRAEL PRESAGE FUTURE DELIVERANCE. 129:1-8.

For the context and scope of Psalm 129, see the introduction to Psalm 120.

Review of Israel's Past Persecutions. 129:1-4. **1.** Here the Jews appear after their return from Babylon, surveying their afflictions and recalling God's mercy and deliverance. **Many a time** have they (Israel's enemies) **afflicted** (persecuted) **me from my youth,** that is, from the time of Israel's national youth in Egypt (Jer. 2:2; Ezek. 23:3; Hos. 2:15; 11:1).

2. Many a time have they afflicted me from my youth; yet they have not prevailed against me. The repetition intensifies the vigor of the hostility shown by the enemy and connects it with Israel's invariable deliverance (Jer. 1:19; 15:20; 20:11; Matt. 16:18; 2 Cor. 4:8-9).

3. The plowers plowed upon my back (Isa. 50:6; Heb. 11:36). **They made long** (lengthened, extended) **their furrows.** The stripes of the smiter are compared to the furrow made by the plow (cf. 1 Sam. 14:14). The Messiah was to give His back to the smiters (Isa. 50:6). Israel caused her King to have His back furrowed by the floggers (Matt. 27:26), and retribution came in kind when Zion was, under the Roman Titus, "plowed as a field" (Mic. 3:12).

4a. The Lord is righteous. This is the ground of hope for deliverance. As the righteous One, He knows the righteous and espouses their cause and punishes the wicked (Psalm 1:4-6). When the Israelite remnant believes in the Messiah-Christ, God will declare them "righteous," and He has bound Himself to deliver them (Rom. 10:3-4).

4b. As He cut in pieces **the cords**

("ropes" by which the ox was yoked to the plow, a general figure of servitude) when He delivered His people from Babylon, so He will do on a far greater scale when He delivers His regathered people from the oppression of the Antichrist and his followers and binds all their enemies. The wicked will not be able to break those bands to pieces or cast those "cords from" them (Psalm 2:3; cf. Rev. 20:1-3).

Prayer for the Overthrow of Israel's Future Foes. 129:5-8. The Spirit of prophecy through the prayer of the psalmist announces the doom of the wicked, who manifest their hatred of God and His Word by their hatred of the Jew (cf. Matt. 25:34-45). **Let them all be confounded** (put to shame) **and turned back** (Psalms 70:3; 71:13; Ezek. 38:4; Dan. 11:40-45; Rev. 19:11-21).

6. Their end is compared to **grass upon the housetops** of flat-roofed Oriental homes, which readily takes root, but having no depth of soil, withers **before it groweth up** ("plucked up," Perowne; Psalms 37:2; 92:7; Jer. 17:5-6), the image portraying the sudden destruction of Israel's wicked foes by direct divine interposition (Dan. 2:34; Rev. 19:11-19). The wicked will be gone, just like the mower and the sheaf-binder do not fill their hands or bosoms with the harvest if it does not grow up or is plucked up before harvesttime. Neither is there the greeting and countergreeting, as in the normal picture of the harvest field (cf. Ruth 2:4), for the curse, not a blessing, will be on Israel's foes.

X. WHEN ISRAEL IS FORGIVEN AND RESTORED. 130:1-8.

This psalm is "A Song of degrees [ascents]," that is, "A Pilgrim Song" (Perowne). See the introduction to Psalm 120. Martin Luther classified this psalm with what he called "The Pauline Psalms" (Psalms 32, 51, 130, 143), so named by him because, Paul-like, they teach that forgiveness of sins is vouchsafed to all who believe totally by grace through faith completely apart from self-effort or works of the Law. Whereas the psalm has application to the whole fallen race, it has special prophetic reference to Israel when the nation will turn to the Messiah-Savior in connection with the Great Tribulation and the second coming to set up the Kingdom over Israel (Acts 1:6; Zech. 12:10—13:1).

Israel's Great Cry for Forgiveness. 130:1-4. **1. Out of the depths** (of sin, unbelief, and distress) **have I cried unto thee, O Lord** (18:4; 25:16; 40:2). Like Jonah in his anguish in the belly of the whale, "the belly of sheol [hell]" (Jonah 2:2), Israel in her deep distress in the Tribulation will through her suffering see her sin and unbelief in rejecting her Savior and Messiah (Isa. 53:1-12) and cry out to Him in deepest penitence for forgiveness.

2. Lord (*Adonai*), **hear my voice; let thine ears be attentive to the voice of my supplications** (Psalm 28:2). As LORD (Jehovah, Yahweh) denotes His unchangeable faithfulness to His promises to deliver His people, so *Adonai* points to His lordship over all obstacles in the way of His delivering them.

In verses 3 and 4, Israel prophetically comes into the knowledge of justification by faith after her long night of unbelief and rejection of the Messiah. **3. If thou, Lord, shouldest mark** (take strict account of) **iniquities** (Job 10:14; 14:16; Psalm 90:8), **O Lord** (*Adonai*), **who shall stand?** (Job 9:2-3; Rom. 3:20), a legal term for "be justified" or "declared righteous" (Psalms 1:5; 143:2). **4. But there is forgiveness with thee** (Exod. 34:7; Neh. 9:17; Psalm 86:5; Isa. 55:7; Dan. 9:9), **that thou mayest be** feared (1 Kings 8:39-40; Jer. 33:8-9; Heb. 12:28). The sense of God's gracious love and forgiveness gives sinners hope of acceptance with Him and deliverance from the penalty of sin, and it leads those who are forgiven to lovingly reverence Him and to shrink in fear from anything that would offend Him.

Israel's Keen Expectation of Redemption. 130:5-8. **5a. I wait for the Lord.** The psalmist's "waiting" for the LORD (the thought is repeated three times in verses 5 and 6 to emphasize the keenness of his faith and expectancy) prophetically represents the earnest attitude of the godly remnant of Israel awaiting the return of the Messiah-Redeemer to bring salvation and deliverance to the nation at His second advent (Zech. 14:3-4; Rom. 11:26-32). The LORD also will wait, that He may be gracious to those who wait for Him (Psalm 27:14; Isa. 30:18).

5b. And in his word do I hope, for His Word contains the way of salvation and the promise of deliverance (Rev. 8:1—20:3). Saints must not only hope, but wait patiently and perseveringly for the LORD's time for fulfilling their hope. The figure is used of watchmen of the night waiting for the dawn (cf. Isa. 21:11-12). **6.** The LORD's coming to dispel the gross darkness (60:2) of the Tribulation period as the Sun of Righteousness (Mal. 4:2) will result in the relief of His own as morning light dispels the darkness of the night.

7. The Spirit of God through the psalmist exhorted Israel to **hope in the Lord** as the remnant hopes in His Word (cf. v. 5). The reason: **For with the Lord ... is mercy** (loving-kindness) **and ... plenteous** (abundant) **redemption** (Psalms 103:4; 119:9; Rom. 3:24; Eph. 1:7). **8.** The believing Tribulation remnant will have hoped in the Word and have appropriated the salvation it tells

of through the crucified and risen Christ (1 Cor. 15:2-4), and so they will have abundant redemption to announce the "gospel of the kingdom" (Matt. 24:14). They will be able to proclaim it with glorious power and conviction, both from the promises of the Word and from their own experience, that the Messiah will **redeem Israel** (Ezek. 37:1-10, 21-28) **from all his iniquities** (Isa. 53:1-12; Zech. 13:1; Rom. 11:26-27).

Y. RESTORED ISRAEL HUMBLE BEFORE THE LORD. 131:1-3.

This psalm is "A Song of degrees" (see the introduction to Psalm 120), a song of David. Psalm 131 closely follows Psalm 130. In Psalm 130 Israel anticipates forgiveness and restoration, the ode ending with the confident assurance, "He shall redeem Israel from all *his iniquities* (v. 8, italics added). In this psalm the great redemption has been appropriated by faith, and the deep inner spiritual change is reflected in Israel's consequent humility and restfulness in the LORD.

The Testimony of the Redeemed. 131:1-2. The psalmist in the broadest sense represents all the redeemed of any age, but prophetically and contextually he represents the converted nation after its future national conversion at the Messiah-Savior's second advent and the establishment of the Davidic Messianic Kingdom.

1a. Lord, my heart is not haughty, nor mine eyes lofty (2 Sam. 22:28; Psalm 101:5; Isa. 2:12; 5:15; Jer. 45:5; Zeph. 3:11), the general attitude of those convicted of sin, particularly of the people of Israel convicted of their Christ-rejection and self-righteousness at the second advent. **1b-c. Neither do I exercise** (involve) **myself in great matters** (Jer. 45:5; Rom. 12:16), **or in things too high** (lit., "too wonderful") **for me,**

above my sphere and ability (Psalm 139:6; cf. Job 42:3), again a trait true of the soul convicted of sin, especially of the Christ-rejecting Jew when he turns to Christ.

2. Surely I have behaved (composed) **and quieted myself, like a child ... weaned of his mother** (Psalm 62:1; Matt. 18:3; 1 Cor. 14:20), as one who is still a child, though weaned (Isa. 11:8; 28:9), possessing all the humility of such a little one (Matt. 18:3-4). Though the child is still upon his mother's bosom, he no longer seeks his mother's milk. So the nation humbled before their Messiah-Savior (Isa. 53:1-12) will be occupied in such lowly contrition before the cross on which He died for them, that all their haughtiness and self-righteousness will have vanished.

Exhortation to the Redeemed Nation. 131:3. **3. Let Israel hope in the Lord** (130:7) **from henceforth and forever** (113:2). Now that the nation has realized its hope, long since accounted dead (Ezek. 37:11; Zech. 9:11), let them not abandon it, for it is the antidote against proud thoughts and haughty sins. If Israel desires to preserve the greatness she has acquired and have it continue permanently, she must commit herself humbly to the LORD and let Him magnify her in His own time and way (Matt. 23:12; James 4:10; 1 Pet. 5:6).

Z. THE FULFILLMENT OF THE DAVIDIC COVENANT ENVISIONED. 132:1-18.

Like the other anonymous pilgrim songs (see the introduction to Psalm 120), Psalm 132 seems to belong to the period of the return from Babylon, when the house of David and its fortunes were in a state of declension. However, numerous scholars have attributed the psalm to David or to his son Solomon or others. The important thing (no matter who wrote it) is that the psalm is prophetic-Messianic and looks forward to the time when David's Son and Lord will be King in Zion in fulfillment of the Davidic Covenant (2 Sam. 7:8-16).

Plea for the Lord to Remember His Covenant with David. 132:1-5. David's zeal for building the LORD's house is made the grounds for the prayer to remember him and his house now in affliction. **1. Lord, remember David** (i.e., "on David's behalf") ... **all his afflictions** (2 Sam. 16:12). David's personal affliction at the time centered in the tabernacle, which was almost forgotten in Kiriath-jearim (Psalm 78:60-61; 1 Chron. 13:3). His abortive effort to transport the ark to Jerusalem (2 Sam. 6:7-9) produced much anguish of soul, until his eager desire prevailed over his fear. Then he became obsessed with a new yearning to raise a temple to house the ark, the symbol of the presence of the LORD Himself.

Though the LORD denied his wish, He was so pleased with David's zeal for God's house that He made a covenant with him guaranteeing the perpetuity of his *own* house and kingdom (2 Sam. 7:8-16). Now the people and posterity of David plead the covenant when the LORD seemed to forget it and lose sight of David's zeal. Historically, the plea of the remnant from Babylon is heard; but prophetically, the voice of the remnant regathered from their final worldwide dispersion is discerned (Deut. 30:1-10; Ezek. 37:11-14; Amos 9:14-15; Matt. 24:31).

2. David's oath and vow to the **mighty God** (One) **of Jacob** (Gen. 49:24; Isa. 49:26; 60:16), He who will transform Jacob, the supplanter, into millennial Israel, a striver and prevailer with God (Gen. 32:28), is referred to in verses 3 to 5. **3-5.** David vowed not to enter **the tabernacle** of his house (viewing it as no more than a temporary abode, such as the ark lodged in; Job 21:28), or to **go up into** his **bed** (a raised Oriental couch approached by steps), or sleep (Prov. 6:4), until he found **a place for the Lord** (lit., "dwelling places"), **an habitation** (permanent abode) **for the Mighty God** (One) **of Jacob** (cf. v. 2). He determined to regard himself as homeless and without settled rest until he found a resting place for the ark of the LORD (2 Sam. 6; 7:2; cf. 1 Cor. 7:29-30).

David's Zeal in Bringing the Ark to Jerusalem. 132:6-9. **6.** When David was a lad at **Ephrathah** (the ancient name of Bethlehem; Gen. 35:19; 1 Sam. 17:12), he had heard of the ark at Kiriath-jearim and apparently had visited "the city of the woods," seeking it out **in the fields of the wood** (1 Sam. 7:1).

7. This verse rehearses the words of David and the people at the dedication of the ark on Zion. **We will worship at his** (the LORD'S) **footstool,** as the ark was (Psalm 99:5). **8.** The ark was the symbol of the LORD'S power, and hence it is called **the ark of** His **strength,** and its **rest** was its permanent abode on Mount Zion, its "resting place" (v. 14).

9. The manifestation of the Messiah on Mount Zion at His second advent will constitute the antitype. Then His priests will be **clothed with righteousness** (salvation, the imputed righteousness of God through Christ; cf. v. 16; Isa. 61:10; Rom. 13:14; Rev. 19:8) and His saints (godly ones) will sing for joy that will far surpass the scene on Mount Zion when King David brought the ark there.

Renewal of Plea to Remember the Covenant with David. 132:10-12. **10.** This verse reiterates the plea voiced in verse 1 (2 Chron. 6:42). **Thine anointed** is David (cf. v. 17; Psalm 84:9). Over and over it is said **for ... David's sake** the LORD spared Judah's kings and their kingdom (1 Kings 11:12-13; 15:4; 2 Kings 8:19). But it was not merely for

David's sake, but for the sake of God's covenant with him and his posterity (especially David's Son and Lord) and God's faithfulness tied up with it (v. 11; 1 Kings 8:24-26).

11. The LORD's oath, **sworn in truth** (2 Sam. 7:28) that **of the fruit** of David's body He would set upon his throne, has its ultimate fulfillment in the Messiah and His millennial reign (Luke 1:32-33, 69; Acts 2:30-31). **12.** Because the conditions of blessing for the Davidic royal line were broken, the Davidic dynasty was interrupted and the promise suspended; but it did not entail the abrogation of the promise, which will eventually be fulfilled when Israel turns to the LORD (2 Sam. 7:14-15).

Certainty of the Fulfillment of the Davidic Covenant. 132:13-18. The covenant's certainty is declared on the basis of seven things: (1) **13.** It is based on God's irrevocable choice of Zion (78:68), desiring it as His habitation (68:16). Its welfare is inseparably joined with David's throne, and so His choice involves the restoration of David's royal line and kingdom.

(2) **14.** It is based on God's unthwarted desire that Zion would be His resting place, as it was in the case of His symbolized presence in the ark, and as it will indeed be the habitation of the Messiah in His earthly Kingdom. The Messiah will answer the prayer of verse 8: "Arise, O LORD, into thy rest." (3) **15.** It is based on His promise of temporal blessing (147:14; Isa. 33:16, 20).

(4) **16.** It is based on His promise of salvation (Jer. 31:31-34; Ezek. 37:11-14; Rom. 11:26-32). (5) **17.** It is based on His promise of the Messiah's rule. He will make the horn (strength) **of David to bud** (sprout forth; Ezek. 29:21; Luke 1:69) and prepare a **lamp** (light) for His Anointed to flood the millennial Kingdom with light (Psalm 18:28; 1 Kings

11:36; 15:4; 2 Kings 8:19; Mal. 4:1). (6) **18a.** It is based on His promise of conquest of all enemies (Psalm 2:4-12; 35:26; 109:29). (7) **18b.** It is based on His promise of a resplendent Messianic reign (Psalm 21:3; Isa. 9:7; 11:1-9; Rev. 19:12, 16).

AA. ISRAEL'S BROTHERHOOD UNDER THE MESSIAH-KING-PRIEST.
133:1-3.

For the superscription, see Psalm 120. The theme of the excellence of brotherly unity first has a historical reference to the times in which the author (David) lived. Second, it has a prophetic application to the time when David's Son and Lord will be Priest upon His throne (Zech. 6:9-15) at His second coming and Kingdom. Then the entire redeemed nation of Israel (Rom. 11:26-32) will be united in a wonderful brotherhood.

The Excellence of Brotherly Unity Declared. 133:1. **1. Behold** draws attention historically to the meeting of the national brotherhood at the great feasts at Jerusalem. David glorifies the communion of the saints restored to Zion with the bringing of the tabernacle and the ark there, making it his religious capital. Compare Psalm 132, with which Psalm 133 is closely connected; both look forward to the wonderful unity that will be realized in the Kingdom age, when Israel under the Messiah-King-Priest will become in deed and in truth "a kingdom of priests, and an holy nation" (Exod. 19:6). **How good and how pleasant ... for brethren to dwell together in unity** (Gen. 13:8; Heb. 13:1).

The Source of Brotherly Unity Indicated. 133:2. **2a-b.** The Source of unity is the Holy Spirit flowing from and through the ministry of Him whom Aaron, the high priest of Israel, foreshadowed—our Lord Jesus Christ, particularly in reference to His King-

Priesthood office in the Kingdom age (Isa. 11:2-5). **It is like the precious ointment upon the head, that ran down upon the beard, even Aaron's beard** (Exod. 29:7; 30:25; Lev. 8:12). "The holy anointing oil," olive oil compounded with spices (Exod. 30:23-25), was poured upon the head of the high priest (29:7; Lev. 8:12; 21:10) so copiously that it flowed down upon his beard, bespeaking the anointing "without measure" of Christ as High Priest, with all the fragrance and sweet graces of the Holy Spirit (John 3:34; Acts 10:38) so that the oil is fittingly called "precious" (Exod. 30:25; Psalm 141:5; Song of Sol. 1:3; John 12:3).

2c. This copious effusion on the head, so that it **went down to the skirts** (came down upon the edge of Aaron's robes; Exod. 28:33; 39:24), bespeaks the Messiah's gloriously full anointing above His fellows; but their unity in Him is portrayed by the priests, who were merely streaked with oil upon their foreheads. This suggests that the unity of brothers (saints) in any age is in Him, and it is the "unity of the Spirit" (Eph. 4:3) that in the Kingdom age will bind the entire nation of Israel into a fellowship such as they have never enjoyed in all their national history.

The Blessing of Brotherly Unity Illustrated. 133:3. **3a-b.** The psalmist beautifully compares the blessing of unity to **the dew of Hermon** (Deut. 3:8-9; 4:48; Josh. 13:11) ... **that descended upon the mountains of Zion.** Brotherly unity in its "pleasant" aspect (v. 1) resembles the refreshing dew of Mount Hermon in the north, and it descends upon Zion, where this unity was manifested to a degree in Old Testament times, but is to be beautifully exemplified in Kingdom blessing.

3c. For there (where brotherly unity existed) **the Lord commanded the bless-**

ing (Lev. 25:21; Psalm 42:8). But the perfect tense is prophetic of the fulfillment of this in the Kingdom, when Israel will be converted to Christ and receive eternal life as a nation (Rom. 11:26-32) and enjoy the rich fellowship of Christ's salvation.

BB. ISRAEL'S PRAISE IN THE KINGDOM AGE. 134:1-3.

This is the last of the "Psalms of Ascent" or "Pilgrim Songs" (see the introduction to Psalm 120). The pilgrims have reached the consummation of their pilgrimage and are in the Temple worshiping; they watch as the priests and Levites praise the LORD. Prophetically, the Temple of Ezekiel (Isa. 2:2-3; Ezek. 40:1—47:12) comes into view, with the worship and perpetual adoration of the Creator, who became the incarnate Redeemer, and who will then be revealed as the true Melchizedek, King and Priest, in the midst of His redeemed people, Israel.

Call to Bless the Lord. 134:1-2. **1. Behold** calls attention to the joyful scene of Temple worship, characterized by sublime and heartfelt praising (blessing) the LORD (103:21). **All ... servants of the Lord, who by night stand** (serve) **in the house of the Lord** refers to the priests. **By night** (pl., "nights") seems to indicate that services were held for several nights in succession (cf. 1 Chron. 9:33), apparently during the Feast of Tabernacles in the autumn. Prophetically, this glorious scene looks forward to the Kingdom age, when the antitype of that feast will be realized. **2.** Lifting up the hands was a gesture signifying the participation of the heart in the worship (Psalm 28:2).

Entreaty for the Lord to Bless. 134:3. **3.** The priests responded with a priestly benediction (Lev. 9:22; Num. 6:22-26), which was a prayer that God might bless

His people from Zion (Psalm 128:5; cf. Isa. 2:2-3; Jer. 50:5; Zech. 8:21-23; 14:16-21). There are no limits to His blessing in the fulfillment of this psalm in Kingdom glory, because Israel will then be saved and in blessed fellowship with God in Christ (Rom. 11:26) and free to be a blessing to the nations, because the Blesser, as Creator of the universe, is boundless in His potentialities for blessing (Psalm 124:8; 128:5).

CC. HALLELUJAH FOR WHAT GOD HAS DONE FOR ISRAEL. 135:1-21.

Psalms 135 and 136 are psalms of praise. Both go beyond the historical and envision the prophetic future of Israel, when in Kingdom glory the nation will reminisce on God's wonderful works in their behalf in the past in preserving them for Kingdom blessing. The psalm opens and ends with "Praise ye the LORD" (Hallelujah!).

The Call to Praise. 135:1-4. **1-2.** Included in the call to **Praise ... the Lord** are not only the priests, as in Psalm 134:1, but also the Levites: **O ye servants of the Lord, ye who stand in the house of the Lord** and those who stand **in the courts of the house of our God**, that is, the people in general (92:13; Luke 2:37). **3.** Praise is to be rendered to the LORD for He is **good**, and to **his name; for it** (His name, i.e., Himself in the manifestation of His attributes) **is pleasant** (lovely; Psalm 147:1).

4. The reason for the call to praise (v. 1) is the LORD's (*yāh*, the concentrated essence of Jehovah, Yahweh) sovereign choice of Israel (Exod. 19:5; Deut. 7:6; 10:15) **for his peculiar treasure** ("His own possession," *s^egŭllâ*, not mere "property," but that which is rare, unique, and highly prized as one's choicest treasure; cf. Isa. 62:3; Mal. 3:17; Tit. 2:14; 1 Pet. 2:9).

Praise to the Lord for His Omnipo-

tence. 135:5-7. **5-7.** These verses mark the LORD's unique greatness (48:1; 145:3), placing Him **above all gods** (97:9), His omnipotent power enabling Him to consummate His holy will in every part of His created universe (115:3), absolutely controlling all phenomena in His creation (Jer. 10:13; Zech. 10:1; cf. Job 28:25-26; 38:25-26).

Praise to the Lord for His Redemptive Wonders. 135:8-12. **8-9.** The LORD redeemed Israel not only out of Egypt but also into their heritage of Canaan. His redemption from Egypt involved striking Egypt's firstborn (78:51; 105:36) and sending **signs and wonders** (78:43; Deut. 6:22) upon Pharaoh and his servants (Psalm 136:15). **10-12.** His redemption into the land involved striking **great nations** and slaying **mighty kings**, Sihon (Num. 21:21-24; Deut. 29:7) and Og (Num. 21:33-35), and all the kingdoms of Canaan (Josh. 12:7-24), giving their land as a **heritage unto Israel, his people** (Deut. 29:8; Psalm 78:55).

Praise to the Lord and Shame upon Idols. 135:13-18. The LORD is to be praised for (1) **13.** His everlasting **name** (i.e., His eternal being; Exod. 3:15; Psalm 102:12) and everlasting remembrance; (2) **14.** His compassionate judgment of His people (Deut. 32:16; Psalms 50:4; 90:13; 106:45); and (3) **15-18.** the infinite contrast between Him and the **idols of the nations**, which are gross, satanic counterfeits of Deity (gold) and redemption (silver); they are pure fabrications of the creature's hand, absolutely lifeless, making everyone who makes them or trusts in them like them (115:4-8; 135:15-18; Isa. 40:18-22; 41:7).

Full Expression of Praise to the Lord. 135:19-21. **19-21.** The psalm ends as it began, with the exhortation to bless the LORD. Not until the Messiah is received as Savior and King of Israel at His sec-

ond advent and the nation is converted will this paean of praise reach its climax (Rom. 11:26) and also call forth the doxology of praise of the apostle Paul (11:33-36) on the part of all Israel, indeed, of the entire earth—**ye who fear** (reverence) **the Lord** (cf. Psalm 2:4-12).

DD. THE EVERLASTING LOVING-KINDNESS OF THE LORD. 136:1-26.

This is a psalm of thanksgiving for the LORD's goodness to Israel. It is known as the Great Hallel ("praise"), both alone and associated with Psalm 135, to which it is very similar, and is to be distinguished from the Egyptian Hallel (Psalms 113-18). The psalm was probably sung responsively or antiphonally at the great feasts. Its prophetic meaning will not be realized until the everlastingness of God's *mercy* (*ḥĕsĕḏ,* "covenant love") is proved by Israel's future salvation and establishment in Kingdom blessing (cf. 2 Sam. 7:8-16).

Thrice-Repeated Thanks. 136:1-3. **1-3.** In the first **thanks** He is addressed as the **Lord** who is **good**; in the second **thanks**, as **the God of gods** (Exod. 18:11; Deut. 10:17; Josh. 22:22; 2 Chron. 2:5; Dan. 2:47); and in the third **thanks**, as **the Lord of lords** (1 Tim. 6:15; Rev. 17:14; 19:16), connecting Him prophetically with the Messiah at His second advent as Israel's Deliverer and all-conquering King of kings (Dan. 2:47; Rev. 17:14; 19:16). Then the constancy and perpetuity of His mercy will be demonstrated to His Old Testament people, who here celebrate it in past manifestation as a harbinger and guarantee of its future manifestation in consummation and perpetuation. The three times' repeated "thanks" recalls the thrice-repeated Mosaic benediction (Num. 6:24-26).

The Lord Thanked for His Crea-

tion Wonders. 136:4-9. **4-9.** The Lord is thanked for working great wonders (supernatural acts) (72:18; Deut. 6:22; Job 9:10)—creating the heavens by His wisdom (Psalm 104:24; Prov. 3:19; Jer. 10:12; 51:15), spreading out the earth above the waters (Psalm 24:2; Isa. 42:5; 44:24), and making the luminaries (Gen. 1:16; Psalm 74:16).

The Lord Thanked for His Redemptive Wonders. 136:10-22. **10-15.** The Lord redeemed Israel out of Egypt, smiting the firstborn (Exod. 12:29; Psalms 78:51; 135:8), bringing Israel out of Egypt **with a strong hand** (Exod. 6:1; 13:9) and **an outstretched arm** (6:6; Deut. 4:34; 5:15), making them pass through the midst of the sea (Exod. 14:22) and meanwhile overthrowing the Egyptians in it (14:27). **16-22.** The Lord's wonders continued till He got His people safely into the land, leading them through the wilderness (13:18; 15:22; Deut. 8:15), slaying Sihon and Og, and giving their land to Israel as a heritage.

The Lord Thanked for His Deliverances. 136:23-26. The Lord **remembered** Israel in her **low estate** (9:12; 103:14; 106:45). The historical reference is to the Babylonian Captivity, from which He had lately delivered her (113:7; 115:12). There is a prophetic foreview of the last great exile and regathering, when Israel will be in the lowest state (Jer. 30:5-7) to which she will be reduced in all her checkered history of suffering (Dan. 12:1; Matt. 24:21-22); the Lord will remember His people and deliver them from the worst and cruelest foes they have ever faced (Rev. 12:13—13:18).

25-26. Their Redeemer and Deliverer is none other than the gracious, provident God, who not only cares for His people, Israel, but also **giveth food to all flesh** (Psalms 104:27; 145:15). As **the God of heaven** (Gen. 24:3; Ezra 1:2;

Neh. 1:4), He will set up the Kingdom over Israel (Isa. 9:6-7; Dan. 2:44; 7:14, 27; Luke 1:32-53) that shall never be destroyed, since the Kingdom will be perpetuated in eternity in the new heaven and earth of the eternal state (Rev. 22:1-3; cf. 2 Sam. 7:16).

EE. Israel's Sad State in Captivity. 137:1-9.

This psalm is anonymous, but it was written by a poet who had endured the Babylonian Captivity. He must have been an old man since he had been spared to return to Jerusalem, although it is not impossible that he may have written the ode in Babylon and was never privileged to return home.

Israel Asked to Sing. 137:1-3. **1a. By the rivers of Babylon**, the lower Tigris-Euphrates basin, with its web of interlacing canals (cf. Ezek. 1:1; Dan. 8:2), **there we sat down**, doubtlessly in connection with worship, the Jews generally having their places of prayer beside a river (Acts 16:13), probably for the sake of water for ceremonial washings before prayer.

1b. Yea, we wept when we remembered Zion (Neh. 1:4). The dull flatness of Babylonia was a melancholy contrast to the hills, valleys, brooks, and generally charming scenery of Palestine. **2. Upon the willows** (or poplars), which abounded in the plain that was interlaced by rivers and canals, the captives hung their harps in sadness, the river streams an image of their tearful sorrow (Lam. 2:18; 3:48). They wept in remembering Zion, particularly the site of the Temple. Harps, normally used to accompany joyful songs (Gen. 31:27; 2 Sam. 6:5), were totally at variance with the sadness of the captives away from Zion, where God revealed Himself as the Source of His people's joy (Job 30:31; Isa. 24:8; Rev. 18:22).

3. Israel's captors **required** (demanded) of them **a song** ("the words of a song"), and **they that wasted** them (Aramaic Targum, "our depredators") demanded **mirth**, asking insistently of them what their treatment of their captives rendered impossible. Perhaps there was also an element of taunting in the pagans' demand, a suggestion of ridicule. Let them, the chosen people of God, making claim to a coming "son of David" who would reign over the nations, sing one of their famous songs written by David long ago.

Israel Answers the Request. 137:4-6. **4. How shall we sing the Lord's song in a foreign land?** (lit., "the land of a stranger"), a land steeped in idolatry (2 Chron. 29:27; Neh. 12:46). To do so would be virtually tantamount to renouncing their native land and spiritual home. **5. If I forget thee, O Jerusalem, let my right hand**, skillful in playing the harp, **forget her cunning** (skillfulness; cf. Job 31:22; Psalm 76:5), a fit retribution for its disloyalty to God (Isa. 65:11). **6. If I do not remember thee, let my tongue cleave to the roof of my mouth** (Psalm 22:15; Ezek. 3:26), that is, be struck dumb, for having misused the power of speech to sing joyful songs while forgetting Zion and not preferring (exalting) **Jerusalem above my chief joy** (Neh. 2:3).

Israel's Prayer of Imprecation. 137:7-9. For the imprecatory prayers, see the comments on 5:10. **7. Remember, O Lord, the children of Edom in the day of Jerusalem** (83:4-8; Isa. 34:5-6; Jer. 49:7-22; Lam. 4:21; Ezek. 25:12-14; 35:2; Amos 1:11; Obad. 10-14). **Who said, Raze it, raze it**, that is, completely decimate it, laying it absolutely bare to its very foundation (Psalm 74:7; Hab. 3:13).

As Hengstenberg says, "The psalmist only prays for that which the LORD had often declared was to be done, and which was grounded on His eternal retributive righteousness." Thus, the Spirit of God speaks according to the Word of God in the case of human wickedness reaching a fully ripened stage for God's judgment (see Gen. 15:16; Lev. 18:24), as will be the lawlessness and anti-Semitism under the beast and false prophet (Rev. 12:13—18:13), which will call for God's impending judgment (14:14-20; 16:7).

8. The same truth underlies the terribly severe pronouncement against Babylon. Doomed to destruction by God's Word (like Edom; Isa. 13:1-22; 47:1-15; Jer. 25:12; 50:1-46; 51:1-64), how blessed will be the one who executes God's will and repays her (Jer. 50:15; 51:24, 35-36, 49) with the same recompense with which that wicked power had repaid God's people.

9. This verse in its horror is meant to highlight the awful divine judgment (vengeance) that will fall upon human lawlessness, especially in the Great Tribulation, manifested in one important facet in its hatred of God's elect nation, Israel (Rev. 12:13—13:18; cf. Matt. 25:31-46).

FF. THANKSGIVING OF A REDEEMED PEOPLE. 138:1-8.

In Psalm 137 the harps of Israel hung silent on the willows of Babylon. In Psalm 138 they are in the hands of the people of God and used in praise and worship of Him. The superscription ascribes the psalm to David and historically represents joyful worship in the "temple" (i.e., the tabernacle). Prophetically, it describes Israel's praise for the fulfillment of God's Word in their deliverance through the judgments of God.

Thanksgiving for God's Magnifying His Word. 138:1-6. The full meaning of the thanksgiving expressed here will be revealed in the future in the Kingdom age, when God's "exalting" (magnifying) His Word will be attested by His faithfulness in fulfilling the covenants and promises made to Israel (Rom. 9:4-5), particularly the kingly covenant with David (2 Sam. 7:8-16).

1. Such fidelity will call forth heartfelt thanks (Psalm 111:1) and singing of praises to the LORD **before the gods**, best not taken to be "angels" (Calvin, Luther) or idols, but those who are "gods" (*'elōhîm*, "judges, men of authority"), called such (82:6; John 10:34) because they represent and stand in the place of God.

2-4a. Verse 2*b* is correctly rendered, "For Thou hast magnified Thy word [or promise] according to all Thy name" (NASB; Isa. 42:21). The heart of redeemed and reinstated Israel will be thrilled by God's **loving-kindness** ("covenant love") and **truth**, which will be fully demonstrated to them and the whole earth, because **all the kings of the earth** shall praise the LORD (Psalms 72:11; 102:15). This is entirely prophetic and will not occur until the second advent and the restoration of the Kingdom to Israel (Isa. 66:23; Zech. 8:20-23; 14:16-21).

4b-5. Then the kings of the earth and the millennial nations will **hear the words of** God's **mouth** through converted Israel (Isa. 40:9-11; 60:1; 61:10-11; cf. Psalms 72:10-11; 102:15, 22) and be so gloriously saved that **they shall sing in the ways of the Lord**, singing in them as they walk joyfully in them. The Hebrew can also be rendered "sing of the ways of the LORD" (NASB; 145:7), for with the return of the King of kings the **glory of the Lord** will be **great** in manifestation (21:5; cf. Isa. 11:9; Matt. 25:31). **6.** Although the LORD will be exalted in the millennial earth, He will regard the **lowly** (Isa. 11:4-5; 40:11; Luke 1:48; James

4:6). But the haughty He knows **afar off** (distantly; Psalms 40:4; 101:5).

Prayer of Assurance Based upon God's Word. 138:7-8. **7.** Israel will most assuredly **walk in the midst of trouble**—the Great Tribulation (Dan. 12:1; Matt. 24:21-22). Yet confidence in God's Word is declared because the Word promises to **revive** her (preserve her alive) through the trouble (Jer. 30:5-7) as a remnant for Kingdom blessing (Ezra 9:8-9; Psalm 71:20; Isa. 57:15; Matt. 24:22). He will do this by stretching forth His hand against the wrath of Israel's enemies (Rev. 8:1—19:21), and His right hand will **save** (deliver) them (Psalms 20:6; 60:5; Zech. 14:12-15).

8. Because the LORD magnifies His Word and places Himself and His honor behind it, Israel can say with deep assurance, **The Lord will accomplish what concerns me** (NASB; Psalm 57:2). Confident that the covenant love of God is everlasting (136:1), Israel's prayer can be raised expectantly: **Forsake not the works** (27:9; 71:9; 119:8) **of thine hands** (Job 10:3; 14:15; Psalm 100:3).

GG. PROTECTION OF ISRAEL'S GOD AGAINST ENEMIES. 139:1-24.

David shows that the character of God assures His protection of His people even in their darkest hour (vv. 19-22). For Israel that will be the time of her supreme trial (Jer. 30:5-7) during the Great Tribulation (Dan. 12:1; Matt. 24:21-22; Rev. 12:13—13:18).

God's Omniscience Assures Protection. 139:1-6. **1.** The LORD searches His people and knows all about them. **O Lord, thou hast searched me, and known me** (better, simply "known," i.e., all things), since in the Hebrew there is no object, and the omniscience of God is the attribute of God being set forth (17:3; 44:21; Jer. 12:3).

961

(1) The LORD's omniscience is seen in His knowing the most intimate details of the hearts and lives of His people. **2. Thou knowest my downsitting** (to rest) **and mine uprising** (to work; 2 Kings 19:27); **thou understandest my thought afar off** (Psalm 94:11; Isa. 66:18), that is, from Thy far-off throne in heaven, distance being no barrier to Thy omniscience.

3. Thou compassest (*zārâh*, "winnow, sift, scrutinize"; "investigate," LXX) **my path and my lying down** (Job 14:16; 31:4), and so the LORD is **intimately acquainted** (NASB) **with all my ways**, my outward conduct. **4.** But the LORD knows my inner thoughts, as well. **Even before there is a word on my tongue, behold, O Lord, Thou dost know it all** (NASB; Heb. 4:13). Apart from God, no one can speak out his thoughts (Prov. 16:1), and so God knows them before they are spoken.

(2) The LORD's omniscience means that His people are completely in His hands. **5. Thou hast beset me** (*ṣrr*, "enclosed me") **behind ... before** and from above—from every quarter Thou dost lay Thy hand upon me for blessing or chastisement (Psalms 34:7; 125:2). **6. Such knowledge is too wonderful for me** (Job 42:3; Rom. 11:33), the infinite vastness of God's knowledge calling forth praise. **It is high, I cannot attain unto it** (cf. Isa. 55:8-9).

God's Omnipresence Assures Protection. 139:7-12. **7.** Where can God's child go from His Spirit or **flee** from His **presence**, that is, if he had reason to fear judicial vengeance, where could he hide (Jer. 23:24; Amos 9:2; Jonah 1:3)? **8.** The omnipresent God is in heaven and in Sheol (the netherworld; Prov. 15:11). **9-10.** If he would **take the wings of the morning** (Psalms 18:10; 19:6; Mal. 4:2) to dart with the speed of light from east to west, desiring to escape from his enemies (cf. Psalm 55:6-8), and **dwell in the uttermost** (remotest) **parts of the sea**, even there the omnipresent hand of his protector would **lead** him (23:2-3) and His **right hand** would lay hold of him to protect him (27:11; 138:7).

11-12. If he thinks that surely **the darkness shall cover** ("overwhelm"; Job 9:7) him, then the night would become light around him, for even **darkness hideth not from thee**, the omnipresent, all-seeing One. Night to God is as bright as day and darkness, as far as His being able to see His own in all their needs, is the same as light (Job 34:22; Dan. 2:22; 1 John 1:5).

God's Creatorship Assures Protection. 139:13-16. **13.** God formed His own in the womb. **For thou** (emphatic, "Thou, the Creator of mankind") **hast possessed** (*qānâh*, "to acquire" by creating) **my inward parts** ("kidneys," i.e., "my inmost self," AB). **Thou hast covered me** (*skk*, "shelter, hide, weave") **in** ("from," AB) **my mother's womb** (119:73; Isa. 44:24). Forming me and sheltering me before birth, surely I may expect Thy protection now when I am threatened with dangers and enemies.

14. I will praise (give thanks to) **thee; for I am fearfully and wonderfully made**—an example of how **marvelous are thy works** (Psalm 40:5)—not only in creation, but in providence, and in keeping, sustaining, and protecting me as the product of Your creative skill. **My soul** (i.e., "I") knows this fact very well, and it gives me confidence in Your guarding and keeping me from dangers and death.

15. My substance (*'eṣem*, "bone, body, strength") **was not hidden from thee** (as the omniscient and omnipresent One, vv. 1-12), **when I was made in secret** (conceived and fashioned in the womb), **and intricately** (skillfully) **wrought**

(fashioned prenatally) **in the lowest parts of the earth** (63:9), a figure of the "dark" womb (v. 13; cf. Job 1:21; Isa. 45:19).

16. The omniscient eyes of the Creator **did see my substance** (Job 10:8-10; Eccles. 11:5), **yet being unformed** (i.e., being in the unshaped form of the embryo; *gōlĕm*, lit., "something rolled together"); **and in thy book** (the book of Thy foreordaining purpose; Psalm 56:8) **all my members** (implied in v. 15, "my substance") **were written** (56:8), namely, "The days that were ordained [for me], when as yet there was not one of them" (lit. Heb.; Job 14:5).

How can any child of God doubt the loving care and protection of God, the omniscient, omnipotent Creator, who takes such wonderful care of His creatures even before they are born, and foreordained our lives even when we were still unformed fetuses in the womb?

God's Loving Concern Assures Protection. 139:17-18. **17. How precious also are thy thoughts unto me, O God!** (40:5; Job 5:9; Isa. 55:8-9; Jer. 29:11). The emphasis in the Hebrew is on the phrase "unto me." God's concern is beautifully attested by His loving care even before we were born. **18.** More numerous **than the sand** (Hos. 1:10) are His tender and loving thoughts toward us (Psalm 40:5). So countless are they that they constantly fill the mind, being the last meditation before falling asleep and the first when the psalmist awakes. **When I awake, I am still with thee** (3:5) in delightful fellowship.

God's Protection Enlisted Against the Wicked. 139:19-22. The whole theme of the psalm to this point is that the character of God—the omnipotent, omniscient, omnipresent Creator and Sustainer—with loving concern for His people, constitutes their protection against their enemies, which are also

His enemies. The application is to foes of every age, but the prophetic aspect focuses specifically upon the lawless of the Tribulation era (Rev. 8:1—19:21), the Antichrist and his followers, who will especially persecute the godly Jewish remnant (12:13—13:18), and whose wickedness will be ripe for judgment (Gen. 15:16; Rev. 14:14-20).

19. That explains the imprecatory tone of this section (cf. Psalm 5:10), the prayer to **slay the wicked** (Isa. 11:4; Rev. 6:9-10), and the clear-cut separation from **bloody men**, murderous people guilty of shedding innocent blood, as will be notably true of the Antichrist and his lawless hordes of the Tribulation (13:1-18). **20-22.** Those wicked men are God's enemies and therefore the enemies of God's friends, and so the LORD's people detest them (i.e., their wicked ways).

Prayer for God's Searching. 139:23-24. **23-24.** The psalmist realized his strong language (vv. 19-22) bordered on sin. So he prayed that God would probe him (26:2) **and know** his **heart** and **try** him (7:9; Prov. 17:3; Jer. 11:20; 1 Thess. 2:4), and know his anxious **thoughts** to ascertain whether there was any **wicked** (hurtful) **way** ("way of pain or grief") in him (Psalm 146:9; Prov. 15:9; 28:10; Jer. 25:5; 36:3) and **lead** him (Psalms 5:8; 143:10) in **the way everlasting** (16:11), the pathway of eternal life.

HH. PRAYER FOR PROTECTION
AGAINST ENEMY ATTACK.
140:1-13.

Like Psalm 139, this psalm is Davidic and is closely associated with Psalms 139, 140, 141, and 142, which are also ascribed to David. While Psalm 139 presents the character of God as the assurance of His protecting His people in time of trouble and persecution from enemies, Psalm 140 contains the prayer that appropriates such protection. It finds its historical application in every age in time past, but prophetically envisions the wicked persecutors of the godly remnant of Israel during the Tribulation period.

The Wicked Described. 140:1-3. **1.** The cry is **Deliver** (rescue) **me ... preserve me** from **the evil ... violent man** ("man of violences," emphasizing his extreme violence; 17:13; 18:48; 59:2; 71:4; 86:14; 140:11). Prophetically, "the evil...violent man" is the lawless one (2 Thess. 2:4), the beast or Antichrist (Rev. 13:1-10), who after the church is taken (1 Thess. 4:13-17), will head up "the seed of the serpent" (cf. Gen. 3:15) and turn against the remnant of Israel and persecute them with diabolic fury (Rev. 12:13—13:18).

2. This verse switches to the plural, those **who imagine** (*hshb*, "devise, invent") **mischiefs** (evil things) **in their heart** (Psalms 2:1-3; 7:14; 36:4; 52:2; Prov. 6:14; Isa. 59:4; Hos. 7:15), the spirit of Antichrist (v. 1; cf. Dan. 11:36; 2 Thess. 2:4) permeating the followers of the Antichrist (Rev. 13:1-10) so that they will **continually stir up wars** (NASB; Psalm 56:6; Dan. 7:21; 11:38-39; Rev. 11:7; 13:7; 16:13-16; cf. Psalm 2:1-3; Rev. 19:19).

3. They have sharpened their tongues like a serpent (Psalms 57:4; 64:3), because they will follow Satan, "that old serpent, ... the Devil" (Rev. 20:2), and his henchman, the Antichrist, and **adders' poison is under their lips** (Psalm 58:4; Rom. 3:13; James 3:8; Rev. 13:5-6).

Prayer Offered for Preservation from the Wicked. 140:4-8. **4.** The request, **Keep me ... from the hands** (the plural pointing to the vast power of the Antichrist) **of the wicked** (*rāshā'*), **and preserve me from the violent man** ("man of violences," indicating the violent

man par excellence, as in v. 1), again the Hebrew merging into the plural, **who** (i.e., the Antichrist and his lawless hordes) **have purposed to overthrow** (trip up) **my goings** (lit., "my steps"; 36:11; cf. 2 Thess. 2:4-12).

5. The proud (arrogant; the same overweening enemies as in Psalm 138:6) **have hidden a snare** (trap) **for me ... cords ... a net ... traps** (Matt. 24:24; 2 Thess. 2:9-12; Rev. 12:9; 13:14; cf. 1 John 4:1-3). The end of the age will be a period of gross deception, demons working in mankind (Rev. 9:20-21), the Antichrist (13:1-10), and the false prophet, who will be the master deceivers of all time (13:11-18).

6. Amid the deception of the arrogant wicked, the saints (prophetically, the Tribulation saints) place their faith in the LORD, telling Him that He is their God (Psalms 16:2; 31:14) and addressing their believing prayer to Him (143:1). **7.** They address God, the Lord (*Adonai*), as **the strength of** their **salvation** (28:8; 118:14) and as the One who has **covered** their **head in the day of battle** (144:10), thus preserving the most vital part of their body from a deadly wound. So a king's bodyguard was called "the keeper of his head" (cf. 1 Sam. 28:2; Psalm 60:7).

The prayer request was for two things: (1) **8a.** He prayed that the LORD would not **grant ... the desires of the wicked** (112:10), which will culminate in the heyday and climax of lawlessness in the plan to oust God from the earth (2:1-3) and take over this planet in the name of Satan and wicked men (Rev. 19:11-21).

(2) **8b-c.** He prayed that the LORD would not **further** (promote) **his** (prophetically, the Antichrist's) **wicked device** (13:1-18; 19:19), **lest they** (Antichrist's followers) **exalt themselves** (Dan. 11:36-37; 2 Thess. 2:4; Rev.

13:5-6; cf. Psalm 2:1-3; Rev. 19:19).

Imprecation for the Destruction of the Wicked. 140:9-11. **9. As for the head of those who compass** (surround) **me** (namely, to annihilate me), **let the mischief of their own lips** (2:1-3), the harm they seek to perpetrate by their calumnies (cf. 7:16; Rev. 13:5-6), **cover them,** that is, with shame and destruction, in stark contrast to the covering with which God has covered His own "in the day of battle" (v. 7).

10. The imprecation that **burning coals fall** upon the wicked (Psalm 11:6) and that they **be cast into the fire** (21:9; Matt. 3:10), **into deep pits** from which they cannot **rise** (Psalm 36:12), are imprecatory prayers (see comments on 5:10), which will be in perfect order when, under the Antichrist, human lawlessness will reach its peak. Such prayers are out of order in the day of grace when God's patience persists and man's iniquity has not yet risen to the high tide of judgment (cf. Rom. 12:19-21). But they will be the very breathing of the Spirit of God through the Tribulation remnant when the sickle of divine judgment is ready to be applied to the ripened grain (Rev. 14:14-20). **11.** Then the cry, **Let not an evil speaker** (cf. 13:1-10) **be established in the earth** (13:11-18) will be answered, when **evil shall hunt the violent man to overthrow him** (16:13-16; 19:20).

Testimony of Faith in the Lord's Interposition. 140:12-13. **12.** The "I" of the psalmist represents every saint of every age in time of affliction, but it centers prophetically upon the godly Jewish remnant of the Tribulation expressing confidence that **the Lord will maintain the cause of the afflicted** amid the lawlessness and suffering under the Antichrist (Rev. 12:13—13:18; 19:11—20:3) **and the right of the poor** (Isa. 9:7; 11:4-5) in Kingdom blessing (Amos 9:13-15; Zech. 3:10). **13. The**

righteous (Rom. 11:26-32) **shall give thanks unto thy name** for Kingdom blessing (Isa. 12:1-6), and the **upright** (the saved) shall dwell in the presence of the Messiah returned in Kingdom glory (Psalms 16:11; 61:7).

II. PLEA FOR PROTECTION FROM ENEMY CONTAMINATION. 141:1-10.

Psalm 141, also a Davidic psalm, closely follows Psalms 139 and 140 (see the introductions to those psalms). Psalm 140 is a prayer for protection from attack from wicked enemies, while Psalm 141 is a plea for protection from contamination by fellowship with the wicked. The prophetic aspect looks forward to the perils of the godly Jewish remnant in the Tribulation to compromise with sinners in order to escape persecution.

Plea to Be Kept Separated from Sinners. 141:1-4. **1.** The psalmist, representing all saints in any age historically, but saints of the Tribulation period prophetically, pleaded for a speedy audience before the LORD (5:1; 22:19; 38:22; 70:5; 143:1). **2a.** He implored that his prayer might **be set forth** (regarded) **as incense**, a symbol of prayer accepted before God (Rev. 5:8; 8:3-4; cf. Mal. 1:11), being offered morning and evening (Exod. 30:7-8), indicating the general time for prayer (Luke 1:10).

2b. And the lifting up of my hands, as the evening sacrifice (*minḥâ*, "meal offering"), which had the chief place (2 Kings 16:15; cf. Exod. 29:39-41). The burnt offering was prominent in the morning sacrifice (see comments on Lev. 1), pointing to Christ's willing sacrifice of Himself that rose as fragrant incense to God. The evening offering symbolizes Christ's sinless humanity (see comments on Lev. 2) and the lifting up of the hands signifying the lifting up of the heart (Psalms 63:4; 86:4; Lam. 3:41; 1 Tim. 2:8).

There are two specific requests of the prayer: (1) The first is for preservation from sins of the mouth (Psalms 34:13; 39:1; Prov. 13:3). **3. Set a watch** (guard) **before** (over) **my mouth; keep the door of my lips** (Mic. 7:5; James 3:1-12). (2) The second is for preservation from sins of deed. **4. Incline not my heart to any evil thing, to practice wicked works** with the ungodly (Isa. 32:6; Hos. 6:8; Mal. 3:15), breaking down the wall of separation of the godly from the wicked (2 Cor. 6:11—7:1), and what is much more subtly alluring and deceptive, **let me not eat of their dainties** (delicacies; Prov. 23:6).

Determination to Accept Godly Discipline. 141:5-7. **5a.** In resisting the temptation to compromise his testimony by association with the wicked, the psalmist declared his conviction that the reproofs of the righteous are true kindness, as are God's chastisements (Prov. 9:8; 19:25; 25:12; 27:6; Eccles. 7:5; Gal. 6:1). He accounted such smiting and reproving by a justified believer walking sincerely in the LORD's will as a real **kindness** on the part of God, who causes the fellow believer to administer the divine discipline.

He would rather be associated by God with **the righteous** when they **smite** him than with the wicked who would allure him with their dainties. He viewed such smiting as **an excellent oil** (lit., "an oil for the head"), **which shall not break** his **head**, which "the dainties" of the wicked (v. 4) would inevitably do (Gen. 3:15; Psalms 68:21; 110:6; Hab. 3:13). Though the righteous smite, their smiting does not break the head, as do the delicacies of the wicked.

5b-c. For yet my prayer also shall be in their calamities, or "against their wicked deeds" (NASB; Psalm 35:14), "for I will still pray in the face of their wickedness" (BV). **6.** The psalmist envisioned

the corrupt **judges** (leaders) of the wicked hurled down on the rocks under God's retributive justice (cf. 2 Kings 9:33; Rev. 19:20). **They shall hear** (the psalmist's) **words** (of doom), **for they are sweet,** implying that the true sweetness is with the godly, not the wicked. Being hurled on rocks was a common mode of execution in antiquity and a method of execution used among the Jews (cf. 2 Chron. 25:12; Psalm 137:9; Luke 4:29). The rebellious world leaders of the end time shall be dashed to pieces "like a potter's vessel" (Psalm 2:9; cf. v. 10 for the "sweet" words of warning).

7. A doleful picture is presented of the scattering of Israel's bones. But the nation shall be resurrected (Isa. 26:19; Ezek. 37:1-10), and the dry bones of her national demise shall be turned up in resurrection for Israel to live as a nation again in millennial glory, even as the plow turns up what is buried in the earth. In the Tribulation, however, before Kingdom blessing, God will scatter the bones of him (the enemy) that encamped against Israel (Psalm 53:5; Rev. 16:13-16; 19:11—20:3).

Prayer for Preservation from the Wicked. 141:8-10. **8.** Israel's eyes are toward the LORD in complete trust (2:12; 25:15; 123:2) for defense (27:9) in the midst of her enemies. **9.** She prays to be kept from **the jaws of the trap** (NASB; 38:12; 64:5; 91:3) that the wicked (the beast, false prophet, and the violently lawless followers) have set for her (Rev. 12:13—13:18). **10.** The imprecatory prayer is completely consonant with the fully developed lawlessness of the end time in the light of the divine moral government (see comments on Psalms 5:10 and 140:9-10; cf. 7:15; 57:6; 124:7; Rev. 14:14-20).

JJ. SUPPLICATION IN DEEP DISTRESS. 142:1-7.

For this Maschil ("instruction")

psalm, see the introductions to these "Didactic Psalms": 4, 8, 32, 42, 44, 45, 52-55, 88, 89. David, in rejection and persecution, again appears as a representative, not only of suffering saints in every age, but particularly of the Tribulation saints. The inscription is: "A Prayer [*tepillâ*, 'supplication'] when he [David] was in the cave [of Adullam, 1 Sam. 22]. The psalm is suited to the people of God when they are in the cavelike darkness of trial and persecution, as the Tribulation remnant will be in a preeminent sense.

In Deep Distress. 142:1-4. **1.** The prayer of the heart finds expression in the voice, and the twice-repeated **with my voice** indicates the burning earnestness of David's **supplication** (30:8; 77:1). **2.** Also indicative of David's intensity is the expression **poured out** his complaint, and showing (declaring) the **trouble** he was in (77:2). **3-4a.** He also spoke of his spirit being **overwhelmed** (fainting) within him (77:3; 143:4). His intense supplication was called forth by his perilous position before his enemies and at the same time his conviction that God knew his **path**, and yet there was no one that would **know** (*makkîr*, "regard, understand") him (31:11; 88:8). **4b. Refuge** failed him, and in the cave he was shut up to the mercy of God alone, with all human escape taken away, and apparently no one caring for his soul (i.e., him; Jer. 30:7). Here David in deep humiliation and suffering also foresees the rejected King of Israel at His first advent.

In Fervent Supplication. 142:5-7. **5.** He cried out to the LORD, claiming the LORD as His **refuge** (*mãhsēh*, "shelter, a place to flee to"). This is preeminently what the saints under the cruel regime of Antichrist will need (Rev. 12:13—13:18). **My portion** (*hēlēq*, "inheritance, share") is **in the land of the living**, that is, the sphere of those physically alive, who

have not been put to death by their enemies (cf. 13:15), which seemed an imminent threat to David in the cave, surrounded and hounded by Saul and his men.

6. David supplicated the LORD to hear his **cry** of distress, for he was **brought very low**, hunted like a beast and shut up in the shadows of a cave, experiences of anguish that anticipate the awful suffering of Jewish saints in the Tribulation (Psalms 79:8; 116:6; Rev. 13:15-18). The cry was made for deliverance from persecutors, **for they are stronger than I** (i.e., "too strong for me," NASB; Psalm 18:17; Rev. 13:7).

7. A plea was made to be set free from **prison** (Psalms 143:11; 146:7; cf. Matt. 25:36-46). The psalm ends in glorious hope, prophetically reflecting Kingdom blessing with the **righteous** (saved) surrounding the Jewish remnant, and with the expression that the LORD will deal bountifully with His own (Psalm 13:6; Isa. 9:6-7; Amos 9:11-15).

KK. PENITENTIAL PRAYER FOR DELIVERANCE. 143:1-12.

Again David's sufferings at the hands of enemies presage the sufferings of all saints, particularly and prophetically the Jewish remnant of the end time preceding the setting up of the millennial Kingdom.

The Basis of the Prayer. 143:1-6. **1.** God's **faithfulness** and **righteousness** form the grounds for the double cry to the LORD (140:6; cf. 71:2; 89:1-2). God's faithfulness presupposes His fulfilling the covenants and promises made to Israel (Rom. 9:4-5), particularly the promise to David (2 Sam. 7:8-16). **2a.** His righteousness necessitates His vindicating His persecuted people (Rev. 6:9-10), punishing their enemies (cf. Psalm 36:5-6; Rev. 8:1—19:21), and not entering **into judgment with** His own (Job 14:3; 22:4). Prophetically, David envisions the fruition of the divine redemptive grace in Christ and the removal of all condemnation through faith from the believing sinner (Rom. 5:1; 8:1).

2b. The future Jewish remnant of the Tribulation will have come into the experience of the salvation that David looked forward to (Zech. 12:10—13:1) and realize what Paul set forth theologically in Romans: that in God's sight **shall no man living be justified** (Rom. 3:20), God declaring him righteous on the basis of the righteousness of God being imputed to him (1 Cor. 1:30; 2 Cor. 5:21).

3. The violence of the lawless enemy gives the reason urged for granting the petitioner's request and bringing God to the sufferer's aid, despite the shortcomings of the petitioner. Verses 4 and 5 prophetically shed light on the terrible cruelty of the Antichrist's forces in the coming Tribulation (cf. Rev. 12:13—13:18). They will smite (crush) the life of the believing remnant **to the ground** (Psalm 44:25; Rev. 6:9-10; 7:14; 13:15), making them **dwell in darkness** (dark places) (Psalm 88:6; Lam. 3:6) like **those that have been long dead.**

4. Under this terrible persecution, the believers are **overwhelmed** (Psalm 142:3) with suffering and woe, and their hearts are **desolate** (appalled; Lam. 3:11). **5.** To stir up their realization of God's faithfulness and righteousness (v. 1), the faithful remnant recalls former days and instances of God's dealing (Psalm 77:5, 10-11), meditates on His past acts of faithfulness and righteousness (77:12), and muses **on the work** of His hands (105:2). **6.** This gives encouragement to prayer (88:9; Job 11:13), deep thirst for God, and confidence in His deliverance (Psalms 42:2; 63:1).

Faith Assuring Answer to the Prayer. 143:7-12. **7.** Faith looks for a speedy answer, for his spirit is tried to the ut-

most (69:17; 73:26; 84:2; Jer. 8:18; Lam. 1:22). If the LORD hides His face (Psalms 27:9; 69:17; 102:2), the sufferer will be like those who **go down into the pit** (the grave), who are beyond hope of relief regarding the present order of things and will not be preserved for Kingdom blessing (Matt. 24:21-22; cf. Psalms 28:1; 88:4).

8. He prays to **hear** God's **lovingkindness in the morning** (90:14), that is, actually experience God's delivering mercy and being shown **the way** in which he should walk. **9-10.** Vicious lawlessness will prevail (Rev. 9:20-21), and diabolical pressure to renounce God (Psalm 2:1-3; Rev. 13:15) will be exerted by the Antichrist's forces, who will violently oppose God's will and slander His goodness (13:5-6).

11. Since wickedness will prevail and death will be a Damoclean sword hanging over the head of every believer (13:15), the prayer for quickening (preserving life physically and spiritually) will be in order (Psalm 25:11) for deliverance from the terrible trouble (Jer. 30:5-7; Dan. 12:1; Matt. 24:21).

12. Since human lawlessness will have reached its zenith, calling for immediate judgment (cf. Gen. 15:16; Rev. 14:14-20), this verse is a prayer consonant with God's righteousness (cf. 15:4-5; 16:7) and faithfulness, for this destruction of the enemies of God and His people (19:11—20:3) is essential for His establishment of the Davidic kingdom (2 Sam. 7:8-16) and for the fulfillment of all the covenants made with Israel (Gen. 12:1-3; Deut. 30:1-10; Jer. 31:31-33).

LL. PRAYER FOR RESCUE AND KINGDOM BLESSING. 144:1-15.

Psalm 144, like the preceding psalms of David (139-43), records the prayers of David, which will find answer prophetically in the deliverance of the Israelite remnant of the Tribulation from their enemies, and their subsequent establishment in the mediatorial Kingdom of the greater than David at His second coming.

What the Lord Is to His People. 144:1-4. David's eyes were upon the LORD. So will be the eyes of godly Israelites during the coming time of trouble that will prelude the Kingdom. **1-2.** They express their faith in Him as (1) their **rock** (NASB; 18:2), who **teacheth** (trains) their **hands to war** and their **fingers** to fight in battle (18:34; cf. Zech. 12:6-8); (2) their **goodness** ("lovingkindness," *ḥĕsĕḏ*, "covenant love"), for they will then believe on their Messiah (Zech. 12:10—13:1) and come into the knowledge of God's grace in salvation (Rom. 11:26-32); (3) their **fortress** (Psalms 18:2; 91:2); (4) their **stronghold** (NASB; 59:9); (5) **deliverer** (18:2); (6) their **shield** (18:2) and He in whom they **trust** (take refuge) and who subdues "peoples" (not "my people") under them (18:39; cf. Rev. 19:11-21).

3-4. In contrast to the mightiness of the LORD stands puny, helpless man. What is he that the LORD should take knowledge of him or make **account of** him ("think of him," NASB; Psalm 8:4)? He is **like to vanity** (like "a mere breath," 39:11, NASB), his days (life's span) like a passing shadow (102:11; 109:23; Job 8:9; 14:2).

Cry to the Lord for Deliverance from Foes. 144:5-8. **5. Bow thy heavens ... and come down** (18:9; Isa. 64:1). In Psalm 18 deliverance is celebrated in praise; here it is the subject of prayer in hopeful anticipation (cf. Rev. 19:11-14). A personal Deliverer is anticipated who will intervene miraculously by touching **the mountains** (symbolizing the God-opposing world kingdoms) so that **they ...smoke**, the token of fear and the pre-

lude to their being destroyed in the coming fire of God's wrath (Psalm 104:32).

6. Cast forth lightning, and scatter them (i.e., "aliens," vv. 7, 11, the enemies of God's people; 18:44-45; 54:3), aliens by blood and religion. **7. Rid me, and deliver me out of great waters** (18:16), great trouble. **8.** These aliens and enemies of God and Israel speak **vanity** (deceit) (12:2; 41:6; cf. 2 Thess. 2:8-12; Rev. 13:5-6; cf. Psalm 2:1-3), and their **right hand is a right hand of falsehood** (106:26; Gen. 14:22; Deut. 32:40; Isa. 44:20).

Singing a New Song. 144:9-11. **9.** A **new song** springs from the new mercies anticipated by faith (33:2-3), centering in the soon-fulfillment of the Davidic Covenant (2 Sam. 7:8-16; cf. Psalm 145:10) and springing from the New Covenant (Jer. 31:31-33), by the fulfillment of which Israel is born again as a nation (Ezek. 37:1-14; Rom. 11:26-31) as she turns to her Savior-Messiah at His second advent (Zech. 12:10—13:1).

10. He is called **he who giveth salvation unto kings** (Psalm 18:50) and rescues David His servant from **the hurtful** (evil) **sword** (2 Sam. 18:7), that is, those whom David represents in the prophetic aspect, namely, the Jewish remnant of the Tribulation period (cf. Rev. 19:11—20:3). **11.** This verse prophetically comprehends the Antichrist and his wicked followers of the end time (see v. 8).

Plea for Millennial Blessing. 144:12-15. The Tribulation saints pray for three things: (1) **12.** They pray for blessing on their children, that their sons in their youth may be **as grown-up plants** NASB; 92: 12-14; 128:3) and their daughters as **corner pillars fashioned as for a palace** (NASB; Song of Sol. 4:4; 7:4). (2) **13-14a.** They pray for temporal prosperity, for full garners and prosperous flocks (Prov. 3:9-10; Amos 9:13). (3) **14b.** They pray for civil and political justice (Isa. 24:11; Jer. 14:2; cf. Isa. 9:6-7; 11:3-5; Rev. 19:11). **15.** This closing verse surveys the happy condition of any people anywhere **whose God is the Lord** (Deut. 33:29; Psalms 33:12; 65:4; 89:15; 146:5), but it prophetically embraces the millennial age when Israel and the nations through Israel will be so situated.

MM. KINGDOM EXALTATION OF THE LORD. 145:1-21.

This is the last psalm mentioning David as author and is entitled "David's Psalm of praise." It is also the last alphabetical psalm, each of its twenty-one stanzas opening with a letter of the Hebrew alphabet, with one exception, the letter *nun* is missing. Since it is a Kingdom ode, some suggest that the omission suggests that the fullness of praise is not complete without other voices (those of the church and the heavenly saints in general). This may be true, since the prophetic horizon of the Psalms is Israelite, and concerns Israel's sufferings, redemption, and future earthly glory, the church and her destiny being unrevealed in the Psalter.

Praise for God's Wonderful Works. 145:1-7. **1-2.** Praise is to be given to God as King and it is to be perpetual (5:2; 30:1; 34:1; 66:17) and unceasing (71:6), this fact pointing prophetically to the Kingdom age (cf. Isa. 11:9; 12:1-6; Rev. 19:6). **3.** The LORD is to be praised for His greatness (Psalms 48:1; 86:10; 147:5) and its unsearchableness (Job 5:9; 9:10; 11:7; Isa. 40:28; Rom. 11:33). **4.** Then one generation to another shall praise the LORD's mighty works (Psalm 22:30-31; Isa. 38:19) and declare His mighty acts involved in regathering and restoring the nation Israel and blessing the nations of the earth through her (Rom. 11:26-36).

5-6a. All this will redound to **the glori-** **ous honor** (splendor) of His **majesty** (v. 12), and so His restored people will meditate upon and celebrate His **wondrous** (wonderful) **works** (Psalm 119:27). The nations of the Kingdom will speak of the power of His terrible (awesome) acts (Deut. 10:21; Psalms 66:3; 106:22), effected during the Great Tribulation to destroy the wicked and bring on a reign of righteousness, prosperity, and peace (Isa. 11:1-10). **6b.** This will give impetus to the righteous remnant to **declare** the LORD's **greatness** (Deut. 32:3).

7. Then Israel and the saved nations shall **abundantly utter** ("bubble over profusely in uttering," cf. Psalm 45:1) **the memory** of the LORD's **great goodness** (31:19; Isa. 63:7) and **sing of** (joyfully shout) His **righteousness** (Psalm 51:4), then plainly manifested to all that He has dealt with each in the manner consonant with His infinitely holy and just character—salvation to the righteous (justified), and destruction to wicked rebels and foes of His beneficent program for the earth.

Praise for God's Loving-kindness. 145:8-13. **8.** Then with the revelation of Christ's glorious redemption to Israel (Isa. 53:1-10) and the nation's restoration, the fact that the LORD is **gracious, and full of compassion, slow to anger, and of great mercy** (*ḥĕsĕḏ*, "covenant love, loving-kindness") will be a glorious experiential reality (Psalms 86:5, 15; 103:8; cf. Exod. 34:6; Zech. 12:10—13:1). **9.** Then it will be evident that **the Lord is good to all** (Psalm 100:5; Nah. 1:7; Matt. 5:45; Acts 14:17) and that **his tender mercies are over all his works** (v. 15).

10. All the divine works—creation, and redemption with the fulfillment of all the covenants and promises to Israel (Rom. 9:4-5), resulting in blessing her immediately and the nations of the earth intermediately—will redound in thanks to the LORD (Psalms 19:1; 103:22), and the **saints** (all the denizens of the kingdom) **shall bless** Him (68:26). **11.** They shall celebrate **the glory of [His] kingdom** (Isa. 2:2-3; Jer. 14:21) and **talk of** God's **power**, manifest in delivering the earth from the plots of lawless men (Psalm 2:1-12; Rev. 16:13-16; 19:11-21), Satan, and demonic powers (20:1-3; cf. Zech. 13:2).

12. These **mighty acts** are to be made known to mankind (Psalm 105:1) to advertise the **glorious majesty** of the Messiah's Kingdom (145:5; Isa. 2:10, 19, 21; Rev. 20:4-6). **13.** The Messiah's Kingdom is to be an **everlasting kingdom** ("a kingdom of all ages"; Dan. 2:44; cf. Isa. 7:14; 9:7; Mic. 4:7; 1 Tim. 6:15-16), the mediatorial phase of it (Rev. 20:4-10) merging into the eternal phase in the eternal state (20:11—22:5).

Praise for God's Sustaining Goodness. 145:14-16. **14. The Lord upholdeth** (sustains) **all that fall** (37:24) and **raiseth up** all who are **bowed down** (146:8; Isa. 11:4-5). **15-16.** In the Kingdom **the eyes of all** will **wait upon** (look for, hope for) Him (Psalm 104:27), to give them their **food in due season** (time); He opens His hand and satisfies **the desire of every living thing** (104:28), which has never really been the case in man's long history under the curse; it will not be the case till that curse is removed, at least partially (Rom. 8:22-23).

Praise for the Lord's Righteousness. 145:17-21. **17.** The LORD **is righteous in all his ways** (116:5), including His terrible judgments upon the wicked (Rev. 8:1—20:3; cf. 15:3; 16:7), and kind in all His deeds, because men may turn to Him and be saved. **18-20.** He is near to all who call upon Him (Deut. 4:7; Psalms 34:18; 119:151) **in truth** (John 4:24), and He will fulfill the desire of those who fear Him and keep all who love Him (Psalms 31:23; 97:10). **But all**

the wicked will he destroy (2:10-12; Rev. 19:15). **21.** Millennial Israel will praise the LORD (Psalm 71:8), and so will **all flesh**, the entire population of the globe (65:2; 150:6), perpetually (145:1-2).

NN. THE LORD WILL REIGN FOREVER. 146:1-10.

The Psalter is climaxed by five "Hallelujah Psalms," of which this is the first. Each begins and ends with *Hallelujah*, Hebrew for "Praise the LORD." The great paean of praise of these concluding five odes celebrates Kingdom blessing as a result of Christ's second advent, Israel's restoration, and the blessing of the whole world through the Messiah and His eternally elect nation.

Praise to the Lord. 146:1-2. **1-2.** These verses constitute the call to praise. **Praise the Lord** (Hallelujah). The invitation is to perpetual praise throughout one's lifetime (103:1; 104:33).

The Wisdom of Trusting the God of Jacob. 146:3-5. **3.** The psalmist warned of the folly of trusting in man for salvation. **Put not your trust in princes** (118:9), that is, great men of power and renown (118:8-9), **nor in the son of man** (lit., "a son of a man," i.e., a mere mortal), **in whom there is no help** (*t^{e}shû'â*, "salvation"; 60:11; 108:12).

4. Mortal man, even the greatest rulers of the God-opposing world powers, are here today, gone tomorrow. **His breath** (spirit) **goeth forth** (departs), **he returneth to his earth** (from which he was made; Gen. 3:19; Psalm 104:29; Eccles. 12:7). **In that very day his thoughts** ("shinings, polishings") **perish** (Psalm 33:10), implying how elaborately fabricated his plans were. How can he who is impotent to save himself bring salvation to others?

5. By contrast, **Happy** ("Oh the happinesses of," "how blessed") **is he that**

hath the God of Jacob for his help ('*ēzĕr*, "assistance"; Deut. 33:26; Psalm 144:15), the very name of God employed ('*ēl*, "the strong One") contrasts with human weakness, and the term "God of Jacob" suggesting His power to transform Jacob, the supplanter, into Israel, "striver with God" (Gen. 32:27-28), which epitomizes God's dealing with His elect nation throughout history to bring it to a princely place with Him in the millennial Kingdom. **Whose hope is in the Lord, his God** (Psalm 71:5).

The Reasons for Trusting Zion's God. 146:6-10. Five reasons are given for trusting God: (1) **6a.** He is to be trusted because He is the omnipotent Creator, Maker of heaven and earth (Gen. 1:1-25; Psalm 115:15; Acts 14:15). (2) **6b.** He is to be trusted because He is utterly faithful to His Word (Deut. 7:9; Dan. 9:4; Mic. 7:20; John 10:35; Tit. 1:2; Heb. 6:18). The Kingdom will be a grand attestation of His fidelity to His covenants and promises.

(3) He is to be trusted because He is infinitely righteous and gracious. **7.** He executes justice for the oppressed (Psalm 103:6; Isa. 11:3-4; Rev. 19:11). He gives food to the hungry (Psalms 107:9; 145:15). No one shall go hungry in the millennial Kingdom. He is the great Redeemer and Emancipator (68:6; Isa. 61:1). **8.** He is the great Reliever of human suffering and woe (Matt. 9:29-30; John 9:7), raising up those who are bowed down (Psalm 145:14). He loves the righteous (11:7). He loves the whole world (John 3:16), but His special love and care are lavished upon those who are justified by faith in Him and love Him because He first loved them (cf. 1 John 4:19). **9a-b.** He protects strangers (Exod. 22:21; Lev. 19:34) and supports the orphan and the helpless widow (Deut. 10:18; Psalm 68:5).

(4) **9c.** He is to be trusted because He punishes sin and sinners. He **turneth upside down** (lit., "makes crooked, thwarts") the way of the wicked (147:6), which in the Kingdom age (the theme of this psalm) will be seen in grand retrospect in the apocalyptic judgments of the Tribulation period (Rev. 8:1—20:3).

(5) **10.** He is to be trusted because His righteous rule will be eternal. He will **reign forever ... unto all generations** (Exod. 15:18; Psalm 10:16), the Kingdom age being the last of the ordered ages of time, merging eventually (Rev. 20:5—21:5) into the eternal Kingdom of the new heaven and earth (1 Cor. 15:24-28; Rev. 22:1, 3). Hallelujah, **Praise ye the Lord**, ends the psalm as it began it, because the time of singing for Israel and the nations has come (19:6-8).

OO. PRAISE FOR JERUSALEM
RESTORED. 147:1-20.

See the introduction to Psalm 146 for the scope of the Hallelujah Psalms (146-50), each of which begins and ends with "Hallelujah" ("Praise ye the LORD"). All combine the praises of God in creation, with praise for His redemptive grace. This cycle of psalms was apparently designed for the dedication of Jerusalem's walls in the time of Nehemiah (cf. Neh. 12:27-43) and look forward prophetically to the Kingdom age, when Jerusalem will be gloriously secure as the capital of the millennial earth (Isa. 2:2-3; 60:1-22; 66:10-14; Jer. 50:5; Zech. 8:21-23; 14:16-21).

Praise for the Lord's Wisdom, Grace, and Power. 147:1-11. **1. Praise ye the Lord** (Hallelujah!), **for it is good to sing praises unto our God** (135:3). Praise is **pleasant** for "He is gracious" **and praise is fitting** (*nā'â*, "becoming, lovely"). Six reasons are given for praise: (1) **2a.** The LORD should be praised for His goodness to Jerusalem, for building up the city (51:18; 102:16), historically after the Babylonian Captivity (Neh. 12:27-43), and prophetically as the capital of the Kingdom on earth (Zech. 1:17; 2:4-12; 8:21-23; 14:16-31).

(2) The LORD should be praised for His mercy to Israel (Deut. 30:3; Psalm 106:47; Isa. 11:12; 56:8; Ezek. 39:29). **2b.** He gathers the outcasts of Israel—historically from Babylon, and prophetically from the four corners of the earth in the end time (Isa. 26:19; 66:14; Ezek. 37:1-28; Joel 3:20; Amos 9:14-15). **3.** He will save the nation, which will turn to the LORD and be redeemed (Isa. 53:1-12; Zech. 12:10—13:1; Rom. 11:26). The LORD will heal the brokenhearted (Psalm 34:18; Isa. 61:1), bind up their wounds (Job 5:18; Isa. 30:26; Ezek. 34:16), and through converted Israel bring salvation to the nations of the Kingdom on earth (Isa. 2:2-3; 11:12; 45:14; 66:23; Zech. 8:20-23).

(3) The LORD should be praised for His infinite wisdom and power. **4-5. He appointeth** (counts) **the number of the stars** (Gen. 15:5) and calls them all by name (Isa. 40:26), the wonders of the heavens demonstrating God's greatness, infinite wisdom, and power in a most striking way (Psalms 48:1; 145:3). And the God of creation's wonders is the God of redemption, who knows His own by name as being peculiarly His own (Exod. 33:12; John 10:3; Rev. 2:17; 3:12).

(4) The LORD should be praised for His absolute justice and righteousness. **6.** He separates between the righteous and the wicked, the saved and the unsaved. He **lifteth up** (supports, relieves) **the meek**, the afflicted, His own who are persecuted (Psalms 37:24; 146:9). But He **casteth the wicked down to the ground** (Rev. 19:11—20:3), the judgments of

the Tribulation period being an instance of that for all eternity.

(5) The LORD should be praised for His providential care for all His creatures. **7.** This is a special cause for thanksgiving and joyful praise (Psalms 33:2; 95:1-2). **8-9.** To accomplish this glorious boon, He covers the heavens with clouds (Job 26:8) to provide rain for the earth (5:10; 38:26; Psalm 104:13) to make grass grow on the mountains (Job 38:27; Psalm 104:14), so that the animals and birds have food (Job 38:41; Psalms 104:27-28; 145:15).

(6) The LORD should be praised because His pleasure is in those who appropriate His saving grace. **10-11.** He does not delight in the strength of animals (33:17) or humans (1 Sam. 16:7), but showers His favor upon those who realize their absolute weakness and inability to save themselves, and who consequently **fear him**, that is, stand in awe and reverence before Him and His Word (Psalm 149:4) and who **hope** (believe that what He says concerning man's sin and His salvation is true and act upon it), and thus wait expectantly for the realization of His **mercy** (loving-kindness; *hĕsēd*, "never failing covenant love"; 33:18; Isa. 55:1).

Praise of Jerusalem and the Whole Earth. 147:12-20. **12.** A call is issued to Jerusalem and Zion to praise the LORD, their covenant-keeping Savior and God, their Creator. Four reasons for praise are listed: (1) Praise the LORD because He has blessed the city. **13. He hath strengthened the bars of** her **gates** (Neh. 3:3; 7:3), with historical reference apparently to Nehemiah's time and the building of the walls, and with prophetic view to the establishment and prosperity of the city and its inhabitants as the capital of the millennial earth (Isa. 2:2-3; 60:1-22; 66:10-12). **14.** Then Jerusalem shall indeed be the city whose border the

973

LORD **maketh peace** (Psalm 29:11; Isa. 54:13; 60:17-18) and be a city of plenty, her inhabitants being satisfied **with the finest** (lit., "fat") **of the wheat** (Deut. 32:14; Psalm 81:16).

(2) Praise the LORD because He has blessed the whole earth through the city. **15.** From "the throne of his glory" (Matt. 25:31) in the capital city of the Kingdom, the Lord, as "KING OF KINGS, AND LORD OF LORDS" (Rev. 19:16), will dispatch His **commandment** to the entire earth (Job 37:12; Psalm 148:5; Isa. 9:6-7; 11:3-5, 10), ruling recalcitrants with "a rod of iron" (Psalm 2:8-9; Rev. 19:15), and smashing all ungodly resistance through His **word** running **very swiftly** (Psalm 104:4) to execute His will, righteous rule, and government (Rev. 19:15).

(3) Praise the LORD because He who has blessed Israel and the earth is the Creator and Sustainer of the earth. **16-17.** The word that proceeds out of His mouth and runs swiftly to execute His righteous government in the millennial earth (v. 15) is the same word by which He gives **snow like wool** (Job 37:6; Psalm 148:8) and scatters **hoarfrost like ashes** (Job 38:29), by which He casts forth **his ice like morsels** (fragments; 37:10); thus, who can stand before His **cold** (37:9)? **18.** He dispatches His word and melts the icy fragments (v. 15; Psalm 33:9) and causes His wind to blow to melt the icy masses (107:25).

(4) Praise the LORD because He has given His words to Israel and made sovereign choice of her as His unique elect nation. **19.** Jacob's posterity has been the recipient and the custodian of His holy Word (Deut. 33:3) and Israel has been entrusted with His statutes and ordinances (Mal. 4:4; cf. Neh. 9:13-14; 10:29), the distinguishing glory of Israel. God's revelation to Israel at Sinai set apart the nation as the only one who knew the will of the one true God (Deut.

4:32-34; 33:2-4; Rom. 3:1-2). This will be the ground of the Lord's return in mercy to Israel (Rom. 11:26).

20. He made an original sovereign choice of her as His elect nation and the repository of His truth, having **not dealt so with any nation** (Deut. 4:32; Isa. 5:4-7; Matt. 21:3; Acts 14:16; 16:17-18; Rom. 3:1-2; Eph. 2:12; 1 Pet. 2:9). And as for the LORD's ordinances, **they** (the pagan nations) **have not known them** (Psalm 79:6; Jer. 10:25). No wonder restored Israel will say, "Hallelujah!"

PP. PRAISE OF ALL CREATION.
148:1-14.

For the scope of Psalm 148 among the Hallelujah Psalms (146-50), see the introductions to Psalms 146 and 147. In each of these concluding psalms of the Psalter, the Hallelujah chorus, like Handel's *Messiah*, rises in a grand crescendo to its final climactic outburst. In this ode the whole creation is invoked to praise the LORD for consummating His plan and purpose of the ages centering in His eternally elect nation, Israel.

Praise the Lord from the Heavens. 148:1-6. **1. Praise ye the Lord** (*yāh*; i.e., Heb., *hāl^elûyāh*) **from the heavens** (69:34; Rev. 19:1-6). The praise begins in the heavenly sphere **in the heights** (Job 16:19; Psalm 102:19; Matt. 21:9), the highest, or third, heaven (1 Kings 8:27), the abode of God (2 Cor. 12:2, 4), where the church (a New Testament revelation) will have been translated to glory and united to Christ, the Head, to become symbolically the Lamb's wife (Rev. 19:1-8), making known God's many-sided wisdom to the rulers and authorities in the heavenly spheres (Eph. 3:10).

2-3. What hallelujahs will ascend when He brings many sons to glory (Heb. 2:10). All His angels (Psalm 103:20; Dan. 7:10; Heb. 1:7), His heavenly **hosts** (Psalm 103:21), will praise Him, that is, His animate creation, as well as His inanimate creation personified. **4.** The **heavens of heavens** (1 Kings 8:27; 2 Cor. 12:2, 4), paradise, the abode of God, the highest heavens (Deut. 10:14; Psalm 68:33) will also, of course, praise Him. **And ye waters ... above the heavens** (Gen. 1:7; Psalm 104:3), the clouds, the *lowest* heaven in contrast to the highest or "heavens of heavens."

5-6. These (both animate and inanimate) are His creation, and therefore are to praise Him. **He commanded** and **they were created** (Heb. 11:3) ... **established them forever and ever** (Jer. 31:35-36; 33:20, 25); so they are actually bound as creatures to praise Him, having made **a decree** (the law of being and the order of existence eternally prescribed and assigned to all created things by the Creator's will) **which shall not pass** (is unchangeably set until God's purpose assigned them is fulfilled; Job 38:33).

Praise the Lord from the Earth. 148:7-12. **7. Serpents** (*tănnînîm*, "sea monsters"; Gen. 1:21; Psalm 74:13; Isa. 43:20) are especially singled out because they attest the infinite greatness of the divine creative power by their monstrous size. **And all deeps** (vast ocean depths; Deut. 33:13; Hab. 3:10). **8. Fire** (lightning) **and hail** (Psalm 18:12), **snow and vapor** (clouds; 103:20; 147:16), and **stormy wind** (135:7) **fulfilling his word** (103:20; Job 37:12; cf. Psalm 147:15-18). **9-10. Mountains and all hills** (Isa. 44:23; 49:13), **fruitful** (fruit) **trees and all cedars** (55:12), **beasts ... cattle** (43:20), **creeping things and flying** (winged) **fowl** (Hos. 2:18). Verses 7 to 10 call upon the animate lower creation and inanimate world of natural phenomena to praise the LORD, the Creator, and verses 11 and 12 call upon the human race to do so. **11-12. Kings ... and all peoples** (of the millennial earth; Psalm 102:15), as well as all princes and judges who will administer under the Messiah's rule (Isa. 11:1-10), and all classes of society are to praise Him.

The Reasons for Universal Praise. 148:13-14. Two reasons for praise are: (1) The LORD alone is worthy of such praise. **13.** His **name** (i.e., the LORD Himself in His attributes and actions) **alone is excellent** ("exalted"; 8:1; Isa. 12:4) by virtue of creation and redemption. Therefore, **His glory is above the earth and heaven** (Psalm 113:4).

(2) He is worthy of such praise because of His faithfulness to His Word concerning His people. **14.** He **exalteth** (lifts up) **the horn of his people ... the children of Israel** (lit. Heb., "He has raised up a horn for His people"; 1 Sam. 2:1; Psalm 75:10). Through the Messiah He has exalted them, who hitherto were so depressed, with salvation, power, prosperity, and preeminence (cf. Luke 1:69), thereby raising up a song of **praise of all his saints** (Deut. 10:21; Psalm 109:1; Jer. 17:14), namely, **the children of Israel, a people near unto him**, because they were permitted as a nation of priests (Exod. 19:6) to approach God (Lev. 10:3; Num. 16:10; Deut. 4:7; Psalm 147:19-20; Ezek. 42:13). Israel's conversion and reinstatement into divine favor (Rom. 11:26) will bring salvation and blessing to all mankind (11:27-36).

QQ. PRAISE THE LORD FOR JUDGMENT EXECUTED. 149:1-9.

This psalm is a call to Israel to praise the LORD for the establishment of the Kingdom, with the solemn reminder that the universal reign of righteousness and peace, which will have its seat in Jerusalem, will be brought about by judgment of sin, both with regard to Israel and the nations. Before the great hallelujah chorus is heard, the LORD must execute the predicted judgments.

Praise of the Messiah-Savior-King by Redeemed Israel. 149:1-4. **1-2.** The **new song** Israel will sing is the song of redemption (Rev. 5:9; 14:3), the result of their conversion at Christ's second advent (Isa. 42:10; 53:1-12; Zech. 12:10—13:1; cf. Psalms 33:3; 40:3; 96:1; 98:1; 144:9). The "new song" will be sung in praise of the LORD in **the congregation of saints** (the redeemed Israelite remnant, Rom. 11:26), the redeemed nation, the **children of Zion**, will be joyful in their King, that is, at His second advent when Christ will be manifested as Zion's King (cf. the prophetic type, Zech. 9:9; Matt. 21:5). Then the divine-human King—God's King—will be set upon the holy hill of Zion (Psalm 2:6). Then heaven and earth will join in Israel's joyful singing (Isa. 49:13; Zeph. 3:14-17).

3. His name will be praised with dancing (2 Sam. 6:14; Psalm 150:4), rhythmical movements to the accompaniment of music (timbrel and lyre) that were common on solemn occasions of joyful celebration (Exod. 15:20-21; Psalm 30:11; Jer. 31:4, 13). **4.** Here will be realized the supreme evidence of the LORD's pleasure in His nationally elect people, Israel (Psalms 35:27; 147:11; Zeph. 3:17; Rom. 11:26-36), having beautified His afflicted ones, who will have passed through the Great Tribulation (Rev. 7:1-10), **with salvation** (Psalm 132:16; Isa. 61:3).

Praise for Victory over God-opposing Nations. 149:5-9. **5.** Let the saints (godly ones) **be joyful** (exult) **in glory** (132:16). The "saints" are the godly, triumphant Israelite remnant, who having passed through the time of Jacob's trouble (Jer. 30:5-7; Rev. 8:1—19:21), will be saved out of it (Matt. 24:22). Their glory will be that of

their King-Messiah reigning in the midst of Zion (Psalm 2:6; Zech. 2:8-12; Matt. 25:31). So intense will be Israel's exultation that they will **sing aloud upon their beds**, where hitherto they have been afflicted with grief for their shame (Hos. 7:14). Now they will chant true "songs in the night" (Job 35:10; Psalm 42:8).

6. Let the high praises of God, praises extolling God on high, **be in their mouth** (66:17), and a **two-edged sword in their hand** (Neh. 4:17). While the remnant looks for the coming of Christ to "judge and make war" (Rev. 19:11) and to smite Israel's enemies (19:15), let them like Nehemiah hold a weapon in one hand while they do God's work with the other (Neh. 4:16-18).

7-8. They are **to execute vengeance upon the** (God-opposing) **nations** (under Antichrist; Ezek. 25:17; Mic. 5:15; Rev. 19:11—20:3), **to bind their kings with chains** (Job 36:8; Psalm 2:8-10) and **their nobles** (great men) with iron fetters (Nah. 3:10), **9. to execute upon them the judgment written** (Deut. 7:1-2; 32:42; Rev. 17:14; 19:11—20:3). **This honor** of sharing with the LORD in judging the world (Dan. 7:22; Luke 22:29-30; 1 Cor. 6:2-3; Rev. 3:21; 20:4) **have all his saints.** That the King-Messiah will use His restored people, Israel, in the execution of His judgments upon the God-opposing forces preceding Kingdom establishment is mentioned over and over again by the prophets (Isa. 54:14-17; 63:1-6; Mic. 4:11-13; Zech. 12:6, 8) in fulfillment of His word to Abraham, "I will . . . curse him that curseth thee" (Gen. 12:3).

RR. UNIVERSAL PRAISE. 150:1-6.

This is the majestically terse finale to the whole Psalter, a fulfillment of the words of the heavenly host at the birth of incarnate Deity: "Glory to God in the highest, and on earth peace" (Luke

2:14). The great hallelujah chorus rises to a grand crescendo and comes to an end in an outburst of universal praise.

Where the Lord Is to Be Praised. 150:1. **1. Praise God in his sanctuary** (73:17; 102:19), in His Temple on earth, referring to the great millennial Temple in Jerusalem (Isa. 2:2-3; Ezek. 40:5—47:12), in contrast to His also being praised **in the firmament** (heavenly expanse) **of his power** (Psalm 68:33-34), where He especially displays His glorious might (19:1).

Why the Lord Is to Be Praised. 150:2. **2.** Praise the LORD (1) because of His **mighty acts** in creation, in redemption, and particularly for His dealings with Israel in delivering, saving, and restoring her to the headship of the millennial nations (Deut. 28:13; Psalm 145:5-6); and (2) because of His **excellent greatness** revealed in His attributes (148:13).

How the Lord Is to Be Praised.

150:3-6. The LORD is to be praised with all sorts of musical instruments, **trumpet, psaltery, and harp** (cf. "and pipe," v. 4, NASB; Neh. 12:27, 35), with **timbrel** to accompany the **dance** ("dancing," see comment on Psalm 149:3; Exod. 15:20; Psalm 68:25). With **stringed instruments** (33:2; 92:3; 144:9; Isa. 38:20) **and flutes,** correctly, "pipes," mentioned here because they were evidently introduced at the feast dedicating the walls in Nehemiah's time for expressing great rejoicing (Neh. 12:27, 35). **5.** The **cymbals** were also used in Nehemiah's celebration (Neh. 12:27). **6.** The LORD is to be praised by whatever has sound or voice and breath (Psalms 103:22; 145:10; 148:7, 11; Rev. 5:13), including *all* the elect, with the church saints as well, who will then have been translated to heaven and will join in the mighty chorus of praise (Rev. 19:1-6). Hallelujah!

PROVERBS

INTRODUCTION

Nature of the Book. This writing is a compendium of moral and spiritual instruction and is most typical of the Wisdom Literature of the Old Testament (cf. Job and Ecclesiastes). The aim of the book is to present basic moral and spiritual principles to guide the young to realize a godly, happy life here and attain a reward in the life to come (Prov. 24:12). These terse, sententious sayings regulating conduct and life are called proverbs, from the Latin *proverbium* ("for a word"), that is, a group of words concisely setting forth or expanding the thought expressed by a single word, such as *morality, chastity, honesty, laziness, justice.* The proverb as a pithy saying centers in a comparison or an antithesis. The Hebrew word for proverb (*māšāl,* "to be like, represent") points to this basic meaning of a comparison or simile as underlying the moral maxim. The book is cast in poetic form with the common phenomenon of parallelism (see the introductions to Job and Psalms for the basic structure of Hebrew poetry). The terse maxims or epigrams constitute the distillation of the practical wisdom of the ages. The source of the biblical proverbs is "the fear of the LORD," which is "the beginning of knowledge" (1:7).

Authorship of the Book. Many of the proverbs stem from Solomon (1:1; 10:1; 25:1; cf. 1 Kings 4:32; 2 Chron. 1:10; Eccles. 12:9). Although numerous late nineteenth and early twentieth century critics denied the accuracy of the ascriptions of Solomonic authorship, more recent considerations of the book within the framework of Ancient Near-Eastern wisdom literature have resulted in a tendency to treat seriously the Solomonic inscriptions within the book (cf. W. Baumgartner, *Old Testament and Modern Study,* edited by H. H. Rowley, p. 213), since W. F. Albright has shown that the closest extrabiblical linguistic and literary analogies to Proverbs precede the Solomonic era by centuries (*Wisdom in Israel and in the Ancient Near East,* edited by M. Noth and D. W. Thomas, pp. 1-13).

Since many of the proverbs in 10:1—22:16 and 25:1—29:27 contain ideas and expressions that occur elsewhere in the Old Testament and contemporary Near Eastern wisdom literature, it is sensible to see Solomon as a compiler of his own and others' wise sayings and leaving upon them the impress of his own personality. In this sense the book of Proverbs is his own composition.

Collections of "the sayings of the wise [men]" occur in 22:17—24:22 and 24:23-34. It is not said that these were only Israelite wise men. Proverbs 22:17—23:11 bears close similarities with the Egyptian *Teaching of Amenemope.* But these likenesses do not mean that Solomon borrowed from Amenemope. Rather, both evidently arose out of the same literary and cultural milieu, but they differ radically in their underlying philosophy. The texts from Egypt and similar texts from Mesopotamia (e.g., *The Story of*

Ahikar) are a mixture of morality and pagan opportunism, such as is found among many nations of the world. However, in Proverbs the wisdom inculcated is a way of life that springs from reverence for the one true God and from loyalty to His revealed Word and will (1:7). This makes the book of Proverbs absolutely unique, the result of the inspiration of the Holy Spirit, and not a borrowing from a pagan culture immersed in polytheism.

Chapters 25 to 29 form a Solomonic collection that was published in Hezekiah's reign. Chapter 30 and 31:1-9 are attributed to "Agur, the son of Jakeh" and a certain "King Lemuel," both of whom are unknown. The portrait of the virtuous woman in 31:10-31 is an appendix.

OUTLINE

I. INTRODUCTION TO THE BOOK . 1:1-7.
  A. The Title, Purposes, and Motto. 1:1-7.
II. TWELVE LESSONS ON WISDOM VERSUS FOLLY.
  1:8—9:18.
  A. The First Lesson on Wisdom—The Rewards of
     Wisdom. 1:8-33.
  B. The Second Lesson on Wisdom—Its Benefits. 2:1-22.
  C. The Third Lesson on Wisdom—The Rewards of the
     Disciplined Life. 3:1-20.
  D. The Fourth Lesson on Wisdom—The Security and
     Duty of the Wise. 3:21-35.
  E. The Fifth Lesson on Wisdom—Wisdom as an
     Inheritance. 4:1-9.
  F. The Sixth Lesson on Wisdom—Wisdom as a Way of
     Life. 4:10-19.
  G. The Seventh Lesson on Wisdom—Wisdom as a
     Disciplinarian. 4:20-27.
  H. The Eighth Lesson on Wisdom—Sexual
     Relationships. 5:1-23.
  I. The Ninth Lesson on Wisdom—Warnings Against
     Various Follies. 6:1-19.
  J. The Tenth Lesson on Wisdom—Warning Against
     Adultery. 6:20-35.
  K. The Eleventh Lesson on Wisdom—The Peril of
     Adultery. 7:1-27.
  L. The Twelfth Lesson on Wisdom—Wisdom's Plea.
     8:1-36.
  M. Summary of the Twelve Lessons—Wisdom and Folly
     in Contrast. 9:1-18.
III. THE FIRST BOOK OF SOLOMON. 10:1—22:16.
  A. Right and Wrong Conduct in Contrast. 10:1-32.
  B. Right and Wrong Conduct in Contrast (cont.). 11:1-31.
  C. Right and Wrong Conduct in Contrast (cont.). 12:1-28.
  D. Right and Wrong Conduct in Contrast (cont.). 13:1-25.
  E. Right and Wrong Conduct in Contrast (cont.). 14:1-35.
  F. Right and Wrong Conduct in Contrast (cont.). 15:1-33.
  G. Right and Wrong Conduct in Contrast (cont.). 16:1-33.
  H. Right and Wrong Conduct in Contrast (cont.). 17:1-28.
  I. Right and Wrong Conduct in Contrast (cont.). 18:1-24.

COMMENTARY

I. INTRODUCTION TO THE BOOK. 1:1-7.

A. THE TITLE, PURPOSES, AND MOTTO. 1:1-7.

Title and Purpose of the Book. 1:1-6. This lengthy title of six verses is the longest of any Old Testament book. The Proverbs of Solomon 1 are "similitudes," pithy figurative sayings (see Introduction). The ascription of the book to Solomon indicates that the famous wise king (cf. 1 Kings 4:32) was the principal and most illustrious contributor to the book, and the greatest name in proverbial lore in antiquity.

There are six purposes of the book (set forth in vv. 2-6) for the reader: (1) The first purpose is to find out what God's will is and to be disciplined to do it. **2a. To know wisdom and instruction** (knowledge). Wisdom (*ḥŏkmâ*) is the knowledge (both doctrinal and experiential) of God and His ways; in the Hebrew mind it was inseparable from godliness and true piety. Wisdom is grounded in the fear of the LORD (1:7), that is, deep reverence for Him manifested in sincere and uniform obedience to His commandments. Instruction (*mûsar*, from *yāsăr*, "to chastise, to correct by discipline and admonition") means "discipline" in righteousness (cf. 2 Tim. 3:15-16; cf. Prov. 13:18; 22:15) and comprehends tutoring in the application of the principles of piety in the affairs of everyday living.

(2) The second purpose is to discern between good and evil and choose the good. **2b. To perceive** (discern) **the words of understanding** (*bînâ*, "insight") in order to differentiate between the useful and the hurtful, the true and the false, and to know what to do and not to do under every circumstance of life. (3) The third purpose is to impart instruction in a wise, honest way of life. **3. To receive the instruction of wisdom** (*hăśkēl*, "wise behavior, judicious dealing"), so that the reader may act with prudence and circumspect consideration and pursue **righteousness** (*ṣĕdĕq*, "righteousness exemplified in performing duties to God and man"), **justice** (*mishpāṭ*, "honesty" exercised toward men), and **equity** (*mēshārîm*, lit., "equities, uprightnesses"), the acts resulting from the cultivation of "righteousness" and "justice" (2:9).

(4) The fourth purpose is to put the naive and guilelessly simple on guard against the subtle snares of life. **4. To give prudence** (*ŏrmâ*, from the root "to make naked"; hence, "discernment" to see basic issues stripped of all false covering) **to the simple,** that is, "to give prudence to the naive" (NASB; cf. 8:5, 12), **to the young man** (credulous and inexperienced, and hence needing it most) **knowledge and discretion** (*mᵉzimmâ*, "practical prudence," distinguishing between what is honorable and dishonorable, choosing the former).

(5) The fifth purpose is to enable the prudent person to heed the warnings of the book and increase in learning and acquire wise counsel. **5. A wise man will hear, and ... attain unto wise counsels** (KJV), literally, "arts of seamanship"

to steer himself and others aright through the troubled waters of this life (9:9; 14:6; Eccles. 9:11). He will **increase learning** (*lĕqāḥ,* "what is received") and will use this as a basis for further advance in wisdom. So these proverbs are for the simple (v. 4) as well as the wise.

(6) The sixth purpose is to enable the wise to interpret in plain words the obscurity of parabolic sayings. **6. To understand a proverb** (*māshāl*) **and the interpretation** (*mᵉlîṣâ,* "a figure, a riddle"; "a saying requiring interpretation," BDB; "dark saying," LXX; cf. Hab. 2:6), **the words of the wise,** who interpret the obscurity of figurative sayings, **and their dark sayings** (lit., "knots"), intricate utterances or "riddles," like Samson's riddle (Judg. 14:12), puzzles propounded originally in a contest of wits (1 Kings 10:1).

The Motto of the Book. 1:7. The book's motto stands emphatically by itself between the preface (vv. 1-6) and the first of the admonitory discourses (1:8—9:18) and constitutes the grand summary and keynote of the whole book (cf. Psalm 111:10). **7a. The fear of the Lord is the beginning** (the first principle) **of knowledge** (Prov. 9:10; 15:33; Eccles. 12:13). "The fear of the LORD" is reverence for Him in recognition of who He is as the infinitely Holy One, of who we are as guilty sinners, and of what sin is— exceedingly sinful and offensive to Him. So it involves faith in God's grace to forgive sin and justify the believer, and separation from sin in worship and service to the LORD-Savior. **7b. But fools** (*'ĕwîlîm,* "the impious and headstrong") are those who **despise** (contemn, hold in contempt) **wisdom** (see v. 2) **and instruction** (godly discipline), which those who reverence the LORD must hold in high regard and obediently submit to.

II. TWELVE LESSONS ON WISDOM VERSUS FOLLY. 1:8—9:18.

A. THE FIRST LESSON ON WISDOM—THE REWARDS OF WISDOM. 1:8-33.

The Adornment of Virtue–The Seductions of Crime. 1:8-19. **8.** The source of virtue is found in following parental teaching. **My son** (see 3:11 for form of address), **hear the instruction** (discipline) **of thy father** (4:1) ... **forsake** (abandon) **not the law** (*tôrâ,* "teaching") **of thy mother** (6:20). The master is addressing the disciple, the teacher, the pupil. The home is the fountainhead of morality, the basic unit of society.

9. The adornment of virtue is described. **For they** (parental discipline and instruction) **shall be an ornament** (lit., "an adding, an ornamental accessory") **of grace** (*ḥēn,* "beauty, gracefulness") **unto thy head** (4:9), **and chains** (necklaces, ornaments) **about thy neck** (Gen. 41:42; Dan. 5:29). As jewels beautify a person's exterior, so true wisdom adorns the whole person.

10. Warning is issued not to yield to the threat perennially posed against virtue. **My son, if sinners entice thee** (lit., "make a fool of thee"), **consent thou not** (Deut. 13:8; Psalm 50:18). An illustration of the subtle allurement of a life of crime is presented (vv. 11-14). Sinners invite the unwary youth to join them to lie in **wait for blood** (Jer. 5:26), "make a bloody ambush" (AB), to **lurk secretly for the innocent without cause,** that is, to waylay some innocent person for pure sport and deviltry.

12-13. They would greedily **swallow them up alive ... and whole,** so as to leave no clue of their nefarious crime as they murder their victims for plunder in order to lay hands on all kinds of wealth and fill their homes with plunder.

14. Their appeal is, **Cast in** (throw in) **thy lot among** (with) **us; let us all have one purse** (a common treasury).

The solemn warning to rigidly avoid these criminals (vv. 15-19) is resumed from verse 10. **15-16. My son, walk not ... in the way with them; refrain thy foot from their path,** that is, "do not take the step they propose" (AB), **for their feet run** (rush) **to evil** (Isa. 59:7). **17.** This verse contains a popular adage: "It's no use setting a net so the birds can see it!" (AB), meaning the righteous escape but the wicked are caught in their own snare. **18.** Yet these wicked men are setting a bloody ambush for themselves and **lurk secretly for their own lives** (cf. Prov. 11:19). **19.** The summary warning is, **So are the ways of everyone who is greedy of gain** (2 Kings 5:20-27; Acts 8:19; 1 Tim. 6:10; 2 Pet. 2:3), the end of all criminals. Crime takes the life of all who engage in it (Prov. 15:27).

Wisdom's Admonition and Warning. 1:20-33. **20-21.** Wisdom personified is pictured shouting aloud in the city streets and making her voice heard in the open squares (8:1-3; 9:3), crying out from the top of the walls above the gates so that all who go in or out can hear. Wisdom's warning is given (vv. 22-33). **22.** She berates the naive, the foolish (8:5; 9:4; 22:3), and the scoffers (Psalm 1:1). She excoriates **fools** (*k^esîlîm,* "the crooked, immoral") who **hate knowledge** (Prov. 1:29; 5:12).

23. She warns the wicked to turn away from wickedness and crime and to heed her **reproof** so that she may **pour out** the **spirit** of wisdom, who is the Holy Spirit of God (Isa. 44:3; Zech. 12:10; John 7:38-39) in effecting a spiritual change. **I will make known my words unto you.** However, it is the Spirit-inspired message of grace, rather than the inward working of the Spirit, that comes into

the foreview, as the parallelism shows.

24-25. The fate of those who refuse this Spirit-indited message of grace (Isa. 66:4; Jer. 7:13; Zech. 7:11), and **set at nought** (neglect, spurn) wisdom's **counsel** (advice) and **would have none of** (did not want) her **reproof** (Prov. 15:10) is set forth (vv. 26-33). Since wisdom is here the Spirit of wisdom, God the Holy Spirit, God Himself is actually speaking; He indicates the fate of sinners whose iniquity has come to the full (cf. Gen. 15:16) and who are ripe for judgment and ruin under God's retributive wrath (cf. Lev. 18:24; Rev. 15:1-6).

God will then do four things: (1) **26-27.** He will laugh at the sinner's calamity (ruin; cf. Psalm 2:4; Prov. 6:15; 10:24), which will come like a storm and a whirlwind (10:25; cf. Jer. 30:5-7; Rev. 15:1—16:21). (2) **28-30.** God will then turn a deaf ear to the sinners' cry (1 Sam. 8:18; Job 27:9; Psalm 18:41; Isa. 1:15; Jer. 11:11; Ezek. 8:18; Mic. 3:4) and hide Himself from them (Prov. 8:17) because of their resistance of the truth (Job 21:14; Prov. 1:22; 2 Thess. 2:8-12) and refusal of the Spirit's overtures (Psalm 81:11; Prov. 1:25; John 16:8-11).

(3) **31.** God will punish them in kind. "They shall eat the fruit of their behavior and be gorged on their own devices" (Job 4:8; Prov. 5:22-23; Jer. 6:19; cf. Prov. 14:14). **32. For the turning away** (the waywardness) **of the simple** (witless) **shall slay them** (be their undoing and death), **and the prosperity** (complacency) **of fools shall destroy them** (Jer. 2:19). (4) **33.** God will grant salvation and security to those who heed His warnings. They shall **dwell safely** (live securely, assured in mind), **quiet from fear of evil** (untroubled by dread of calamity; cf. Psalm 25:12-13; Prov. 3:24-26).

B. THE SECOND LESSON ON WISDOM—ITS BENEFITS. 2:1-22.

Wisdom Introduces Us to God. 2:1-5. Wisdom produces faith that receives God's Word, here called wisdom's **words** (sayings; 4:10), and lays up (hides; treasures as great wealth) God's commandments in the heart (3:1). **2-4.** Such faith fastens attention of head and heart upon **understanding** (22:17), generates earnest prayer for discernment and knowledge, and prompts search for God's will and ways **as silver** (3:14) and **hidden treasures** (Matt. 13:44). **5.** This receiving (believing, v. 1) brings experiential **knowledge of God** (salvation) and discernment of the **fear** of (reverence for) the LORD (Prov. 1:7) as it perceives Him in His infinite holiness and sees the heinousness of sin as an offense to Him, and so it avoids it.

God Introduces Us to Wisdom. 2:6-10. **6.** As the Spirit of wisdom (1:23), God the Spirit gives wisdom (1 Kings 3:12; Job 32:8; James 1:5). From His mouth proceed **knowledge and understanding. 7.** He stores up sound wisdom for the **righteous** and so is the secret of their good judgment. He is a **shield** to those **who walk uprightly** (in integrity; Psalm 84:11; Prov. 30:5).

8. As the Giver of wisdom, its very source, **He keepeth** (guards) **the paths of justice** and preserves the way **of his saints** (1 Sam. 2:9; Psalm 37:23; Jer. 32:40-41; 1 Pet. 1:5), imparting to them instruction and warning to avoid the pitfalls of folly and sin.

9. Then (when God's people realize God as Wisdom itself and thus the very source of wisdom) they are enabled to understand (discerningly comprehend) **righteousness** (Prov. 8:20), both God's infinite righteousness and the grounds upon which it is reckoned or imputed to mankind on the basis of faith (Gen.

15:6), and the resultant righteousness God produces in the believing saint, enabling him to walk in justice and equity and **every good path** (course of conduct; Prov. 4:18).

10. This means that wisdom **entereth** the **heart** and becomes a vital experiential dynamic in the changed life (14:33), the **knowledge** of God and His Word and ways becoming **pleasant** to the person thus spiritually renewed, in contrast to the wicked and the fool, who hate that knowledge (1:29).

Wisdom Keeps Us from Evil. 2:11-20. **11.** Then, when God introduces us to wisdom, **discretion** (the perception of right and wrong and their consequence) **shall preserve** (guard) from all evil (Psalm 119:11, 104). **12.** The LORD, keeping His people "as the apple of his eye" (Deut. 32:10; Isa. 27:3), delivers **from the way of the evil man.** Such evil men do four things: (1) They speak **perverse things,** contrary to what is right, such as the utterances of the wicked quoted in 1:11-14 (cf. Prov. 6:12).

(2) **13.** They **leave** (abandon) **the paths of uprightness** (21:16) **to walk in the ways of darkness** (4:19; Psalm 82:5; John 3:19-20; Eph. 4:18). (3) **14.** They **rejoice** with diabolical glee **to do evil** and **delight** (exult, leap for joy) **in the perverseness of the wicked** (Prov. 10:23; Isa. 3:9), like Ahab, who sold himself to do wickedly (1 Kings 21:25; cf. Rom. 1:32). (4) **15.** Their **ways are crooked** (Prov. 21:8), better, "who are crooked in their ways," that is, in their manner of life (Psalm 125:5), and they are **perverse** (*'ĭkkᵉshîm,* "perverted") **in their paths.**

The LORD not only keeps from the way of the evil man (vv. 12-15), but also from the evil woman (vv. 16-19). (1) **16.** Such an evil woman is emphatically designated as **a strange woman** (*zārâ,* "alien, foreign," a euphemism for *zōnâ,* "harlot"), **a foreigner** (*nŏkrĭyyâ*) whose person belongs to someone else, and so the young man is solemnly warned from any relation with her (cf. Prov. 5:20), either in a spiritual or natural sense. It was foreign women worshiping alien gods that entrapped the once-wise Solomon (1 Kings 11:1-8). How possible for one to utter a warning that later on he disregards himself, as a result of weakening through yielding to lust and idolatry (cf. Neh. 13:26).

(2) **17.** Such an evil woman abandons God and her husband, **the guide** (*'ăllûp*, "companion, husband, friend") **of her youth** (Prov. 5:18; Jer. 3:4; Mal. 2:14-15), meaning her husband first in the literal sense, then God in the spiritual sense (Isa. 54:5-6; cf. Joel 1:8). What faithfulness can the youth expect from one who has turned traitor to her natural friend and true lover? **The covenant of her God** is primarily the marriage agreement and, in the spiritual sense, the Mosaic Covenant (Exod. 20:14; cf. 2 Chron. 15:12; Jer. 34:15), the breaking of which constituted spiritual adultery.

18-19. The greatness of deliverance from the seductions of this evil woman (v. 16) is indicated by the greatness of the peril she poses. **Her house** of ill-fame with its tapestry-bedecked bed (Prov. 7:16-18) promises exhilarating love, but proves to be a snare of death. **None,** except by a miracle of omnipotent grace, **that go unto her return again** from lust to chastity (Hos. 4:11). **20.** This verse connects with verse 11: "Discretion shall preserve thee" **that thou mayest walk in the way of good men,** escaping the evil man (vv. 12-16) and woman (vv. 17-19) and **keep the paths of the righteous** (Prov. 4:18).

Wisdom Rewards Piety. 2:21-22. **21. The upright** who receive wisdom into the heart and life **shall dwell in the land** (10:30; Psalm 37:9, 29), **and the perfect** (the blameless) **shall remain in it** (Prov.

28:10), in contrast to the wicked, who often die prematurely (vv. 18-19). The temporal rewards of piety in the Old Testament presage the millennial rewards of it here on earth in the coming age (Psalm 37:9, 11; Matt. 5:5), as well as the eternal rewards in the final state (Rev. 22:12). **22.** By contrast, the wicked are like trees that not only shall **be cut off from the earth** by the ax of the woodsman, but also pulled up by the roots (Matt. 15:13).

C. The Third Lesson on Wisdom—The Rewards of the Disciplined Life. 3:1-20.

The Rewards of the Disciplined Life. 3:1-10. Rewards are promised for following various admonitions of wisdom laid down. **1-2.** For fidelity to the teachings of wisdom (Psalm 119:61; Prov. 4:5) manifested in keeping God's **commandments** (Exod. 20:6; Deut. 30:16), a long life of **peace** (general blessing and welfare) is promised (Psalm 91:16; Prov. 3:16; 4:10; 9:11; 10:27).

3-4. For cultivating **mercy and truth** (2 Sam. 15:20; Prov. 14:22), binding them about the neck, not merely in an ornamental sense (1:9; 3:22), but as something always in view as a reminder (6:21; Deut. 6:8; 11:18), and writing them **upon the table** (tablet) of the heart (Prov. 7:3; Jer. 17:1; 2 Cor. 3:3), which is the work of the Spirit of God (Jer. 31:33), **favor and good understanding** (good success) are promised (1 Sam. 2:26; Psalm 111:10; Luke 2:52), both in **the sight of God and man.**

5-6. For trusting in the LORD wholeheartedly (Psalm 37:3, 5; Prov. 22:19), not leaning (relying) upon one's **own understanding** (23:4; Jer. 9:24), and acknowledging (recognizing) Him in all one's ways (in everything one does; 1 Chron. 28:9; Prov. 16:3), direction and guidance are assured (Isa. 45:13; Jer. 10:23) in all holiness and happiness.

7-8. For not priding oneself in one's own wisdom (Rom. 12:16), fearing (reverencing) the LORD in His infinite holiness, and thus departing from evil (avoiding what is sinful), there will be physical health, **health to thy navel** (Exod. 15:26; Prov. 4:22), denoting the softer parts of the anatomy, and **marrow,** "moistening" or vital moisture "refreshment" **to thy bones,** the harder parts, both denoting the whole body (Job 21:24).

9-10. For honoring the LORD with one's **substance** (possessions, wealth; Isa. 43:23) and with **the first fruits** (the first returns) of all one's **increase** (produce, revenue; Exod. 23:19; Deut. 26:2; Mal. 3:10), material prosperity is held out—**barns ... filled with plenty** and vats overflowing **with new wine** (Deut. 28:8; Joel 2:24).

Admonition to Submit to the Disciplined Life. 3:11-12. **11. My son** is the common address of master to pupil in Egyptian, Babylonian, Assyrian, and Jewish Wisdom books (ANET, pp. 412-21, 427-28; Tobit 4:4; Sirach 2:1; 3:1), the basic idea springing from the father's primary responsibility for moral instruction (Deut. 4:7-9; 1 Kings 2:1-9; Prov. 4:3-4), extending to teacher and prophet (2 Kings 2:12). **Despise not** (*m's,* "reject, refuse, repudiate, disdain") **the chastening** (*mûsăr,* "discipline, correction, instructive punishment") **of the Lord** (Job 5:17; Heb. 12:5-6). **Neither be weary of** (*qûş,* "feel displeasure and disgust," and so "resent") the LORD's **correction** (*tôkēḥâ,* "disciplinary punishment, reproof").

12. For whom the Lord loveth he correcteth, in similar fashion to an earthly father disciplining his son because he delights in him and desires the very best for him (Deut. 8:5; Prov. 13:24). Verses 11 and 12 are a necessary corrective of any wrong conclusion that might be mistakenly derived from verses 1 to 11 that piety assures a suffering-free life. The explanation of such suffering as a beneficent divine discipline (Job. 5:7; Psalm 94:12-13; Hos. 6:1) is a prominent theme of the New Testament (cf. 1 Cor. 11:30-32; Heb. 12:3-15).

Felicitation of the Man Who Finds Wisdom to Live a Disciplined Life. 3:13-20. There are six facts about the person who finds wisdom: (1) **13.** Such a person is **happy** (8:32, 34). (2) **14-15.** Such a person is truly prosperous and spiritually wealthy, for **the merchandise** (profit or gain) wisdom gives is **better than** the profit of **silver** and **fine gold** (Job 28:15-19; Prov. 8:10; 16:16), **more precious than rubies** (corals, the finest jewels), and the most desirable thing in life, to which nothing can be compared (vv. 8, 11). (3) **16.** Such a person is in line for a long life (3:2), wealth, and honor (8:18; 22:4). (4) **17.** Such a person walks in wisdom's pleasant ways and paths of peace (Psalm 119:165; Prov. 16:7).

(5) **18.** Such a person enjoys fullness of spiritual life as he lays hold upon wisdom with a tenacious grasp in order not to be separated from her. For wisdom **is a tree of life** (Gen. 2:9; Prov. 11:30; 13:12; 15:4). Wisdom brings life to those who take hold of her, as the tree of life in paradise would have done to Adam and Eve had they not forfeited it by falling prey to the devil's lie and folly of sin (Gen. 3:22-24). Those who retain her (hold her fast) are made **happy** (cf. v. 13), the repetition emphasizing the satisfaction and joy that wisdom brings.

(6) **19-20.** Such a person allows wisdom to discipline him and has the same omnipotence available to work in him that made and sustains the earth. **By wisdom** the LORD **hath founded the earth**

(Psalm 104:24; Prov. 8:27) and the heavens (8:27-28). By His knowledge the depths are **broken up** into rivers and streams for the refreshment of man (Gen. 1:9-10; Job 38:8-11; Psalm 104:8-13; Prov. 8:24-29), and the skies drip dew (here figuratively expressing soft, gentle rain (Deut. 33:13; Job 36:27-28), the evaporation of the oceans' waters making possible dew and rain, which in turn make possible the rivers and streams.

D. THE FOURTH LESSON ON WISDOM—THE SECURITY AND DUTY OF THE WISE. 3:21-35.

The Security of the Wise Man. 3:21-26. The secure tranquility of the wise man (who appropriates wisdom) is outlined (vv. 21-26). **21-22.** He keeps **sound wisdom and discretion** (see comments on Prov. 1:4; 2:7) ever before him (4:21), and they become spiritual life to his soul (Deut. 32:47; Prov. 4:22; 8:35; 16:22; 21:21) and an adornment to his neck (1:9), easily perceived by all. This enables the wise man to walk in his way **safely** (securely) (Prov. 4:12; 10:9), so that his **foot** does not **stumble** into temptation and sin (Psalm 91:12; Isa. 5:27; 63:13), his lying down to sleep is undisturbed by dread, and his **sleep** is **sweet** (Job 11:19; Psalm 3:5; Prov. 1:33; 6:22), unafraid of **sudden fear** (Psalm 91:5; 1 Pet. 3:14) or the **desolation** (lit., "storm, sudden onslaught") **of the wicked** when it occurs (Job 5:21). **26. For the Lord,** through the wisdom He imparts, will be the wise man's **confidence** and keep his foot from **being taken** in the snares of the enemy (Eccles. 7:26).

The Duty of the Wise Man. 3:27-35. The wise man has four duties: (1) **27-28.** He is not to **withhold . . . good from them to whom it is due** (lit., "its owners";

Rom. 13:7; Gal. 6:10), especially when it is in **the power of** his **hand to do it,** according to the law of love (Lev. 19:18; Rom. 13:8). This duty embraces not only material or physical help, but spiritual assistance as well. He is not to say to his neighbor, "Go, and come back, and tomorrow I will give it, when you have it with you" (NASB; Lev. 19:13; Deut. 24:15; James 2:15-16).

(2) **29.** He is to refrain from devising and doing evil to his neighbor (Prov. 6:14; 14:22), while he **dwelleth** (sits) securely by him (i.e., unsuspectingly in his company). If the wise man is to do good, how much more is he to refrain from doing evil. (3) **30.** He is not to dispute with a man **without cause,** that is, contend with him for no legitimate reason, avoiding all strife. Even if he has done you harm, reprove him, but love him (Lev. 19:17; Matt. 18:15; Luke 17:3).

(4) **31.** He is not to envy **the oppressor** ("the man of violence") or his ill-gotten gain. He is not to choose any of his ways by imitating them (Psalm 37:1; Prov. 24:1). The reason is simple. **For the perverse** (or crooked man) **is abomination** (utter detestation) **to the Lord** (Prov. 11:20). **But his secret** (*sôd,* "familiar intimacy," Job 29:4; Psalm 25:14) **is with the righteous** (the upright), a cogent enough reason why the crooked, violent man should not be envied, much less followed.

33. In addition, **the curse of the Lord is in the house of the wicked** (Deut. 11:28; Zech. 5:4; Mal. 2:2); by contrast, He **blesseth the habitation of the just** (righteous; Job 8:6), that is, the justified man who leads an upright life. **34. He scoffeth at the scoffers** (James 4:6) **but giveth grace unto the lowly** (1 Pet. 5:5). **35. The wise shall inherit glory, but shame** (dishonor) **shall be the promotion of fools** (lit., "but fools heighten [their] shame''). These are reasons enough (vv. 32-35) why the man of wisdom should not envy "the oppressor" (the violent man, v. 31).

E. THE FIFTH LESSON ON WISDOM— WISDOM AS AN INHERITANCE. 4:1-9.

Wisdom as an Inheritance. 4:1-9. **1.** This section is autobiographical. With intense desire for the moral and spiritual welfare of his pupils, **Hear, O sons** (NASB; cf. 3:11 for the address), the teacher related the experience of his own life under the tuition of his own father's wise instruction. His effort was directed to impress upon his students the importance of obtaining true wisdom. He implored his "sons" to carefully listen to his **instruction** (1:8) and pay attention that they might **know understanding** (1:2; 2:2).

2. He assured his pupils he was giving them **good doctrine**—sound teaching or advice (Deut. 32:2; Job 11:4); so he urged them not to **forsake** (abandon, treat with indifference) his **law** (*tôrâ*, "teaching"). **3.** He pointedly adduced his own childhood experience with his father, when he was **tender** (1 Chron. 22:5) and **the only son** (NASB; *yāḥîḏ*) of his mother, and hence her "darling" (*yāḏîḏ*, LXX; Zech. 12:10).

There his father taught him and said to him what is recorded in verses 4*b* to 9, presenting a teacher's testimony of how he was taught as a child. He testified to six things: (1) **4.** He testified how his father **taught** him, urging his **heart** (mind) to **retain** (hold fast, grasp firmly) his teachings (Psalm 119:168) and to **keep** (observe) his commandments if he would find life—fullness of life in this life, and eternal life to come (Prov. 7:2).

(2) **5a.** He testified how his father earnestly, even vehemently, urged him, **Get wisdom, get understanding,** that is,

"acquire" it (*qānâ*, "buy it"). Be like a merchant, sparing neither toil nor cost to get possession of the one pearl of great price. (3) **5b-6a.** He testified how he solemnly warned his son not to **forget** wisdom or **decline** (turn away, stray from) the words his father was teaching him concerning it, or **forsake** (abandon) it, **and she** would **preserve** (watch over) him.

(4) **6b.** He testified that if he would **love** and cherish her, she would **keep** (protect) him, to guard him from evil. (5) **7a.** He testified how his father stressed the primacy of wisdom. **Wisdom is the principal thing ... get** (acquire, buy) **wisdom.** The word order of the Hebrew emphasizes the importance of wisdom. "The primary thing [*rē'shîṯ*, 'the beginning' of everything] is wisdom—get wisdom." **7b. And with all thy getting** (acquiring), **get** (acquire) **understanding** (*bînâ*, "discernment, perception, insight to distinguish evil from good").

(6) **8.** He testified how his father was enthusiastic in praise of wisdom's rewards. **Exalt her** (prize, esteem highly, extol her; 1 Sam. 2:30; 1 Kings 5:3-13), **and she shall promote** (elevate) **thee. She shall bring thee to honor** if you **embrace her,** that is, take wisdom's injunctions to heart and practice them in conduct. **9.** She will **give to thine head an ornament of grace** (a graceful garland), **a crown of glory** (beauty; Prov. 1:9).

F. THE SIXTH LESSON ON WISDOM— WISDOM AS A WAY OF LIFE. 4:10-19.

Wisdom as a Way of life. 4:10-19. The two ways of life are presented—the way of wisdom (vv. 10-13) and the way of folly (evil; vv. 14-19), the latter to be sedulously avoided. **10. Hear, O my son** (see comment on 3:11), and **receive my sayings** (accept my advice; 2:1), **and the**

years of thy life shall be many (3:2).

11-12. The teacher stated what he was doing, namely, teaching (directing) his pupil **in the way of wisdom** and leading him in **right paths** (1 Sam. 12:23); so when he walked his **steps** would **not be hindered** (impeded; Job 18:7, 36), and when he ran he would **not stumble** (Prov. 3:23). **13.** Therefore, it would be necessary to **take fast hold of instruction** and not let her go (3:18). **Keep** (guard) **her; for she is . . . life** (3:22; John 6:63).

The way of the wicked (vv. 14-19) is described as a warning to the righteous man to beware of falling into that evil course of life. **14. Enter not . . . go not in the way of evil men** (Psalm 1:1; Prov. 1:15). **15. Avoid it, pass not by it, turn from it, and pass away** (on; cf. 2 Cor. 6:14—7:1). The reason is the extreme peril of being infected with the dangerous and contagious disease with which these evil men were afflicted.

16. They cannot fall asleep and rest until they **have done mischief** (evil; Psalm 36:4; Mic. 2:1) and **their sleep is taken away** ("they are robbed of sleep"), **unless they cause some to fall** (make someone stumble, or trip someone up). **17.** Their food is **the bread of wickedness** (Prov. 13:2), and their drink is **the wine of violence,** which intoxicates them in crime.

18. In striking contrast, **the path of the just** (righteous, the justified) **is like the shining light** (2 Sam. 23:4), "like the light of dawn" (NASB) **that shineth more and more,** "grows ever brighter until full day" (AB). **19. The way of the wicked is like darkness** (Job 18:5-6; Prov. 2:13; Isa. 59:9-10; Jer. 23:12; John 12:35); **they know not at what they stumble** (11:10); in the deep gloom in which they walk, "they cannot perceive what it is that trips them up" (AB).

G. THE SEVENTH LESSON ON WISDOM — WISDOM AS A DISCIPLINARIAN. 4:20-27.

The Self-Discipline of Wisdom. 4:20-27. Fervent appeal is made to heed the teacher's life-giving instructions. **20-22. My son** (see comment on 3:11), **attend to my words; incline thine ear** (listen carefully) **unto my sayings** (injuctions; 2:2; 5:1). **Let them not depart . . . keep** (guard) **them in . . . thine heart** (the mind) as a valuable treasure (3:21; 7:1-2), as **life . . . and health** (medicine) to the whole body (3:8, 22; 12:18).

23. Keep thy heart (your thoughts, your mind) **with all diligence** (utmost vigilance), **for out of it are the issues** (flow the springs) **of life** (Matt. 12:34; 15:18-19; Mark 7:21; Luke 6:45). **24. Put away from thee a crooked** (devious) **mouth, and perverse lips put far from thee** (Prov. 6:12; 10:32; 19:1), that is, "Avoid deceitfulness of speech. Let there be no trace of dishonesty in what you say" (AB).

25. Let thine eyes look right on, "directly ahead," like a dray horse with eye shades to keep his gaze straight ahead, not to be distracted or turned aside by what he might otherwise see transpiring around him. **And let your** (eyelids) **gaze be fixed straight in front of you** (NASB), so you will not see sin and be allured by its deception.

26. Ponder (consider, carefully watch) **the path of thy feet** in order that **all thy ways** may **be established** (Psalm 119:5; Prov. 5:21; Heb. 12:13). **27.** "Watch where you are going, so as to step only on firm ground" (AB), turning neither to the right or left hand from wisdom's path; so rather than walking into evil, you will walk away from it (Deut. 5:32; 28:14; Prov. 1:15; Isa. 1:16; Rom. 12:9).

H. THE EIGHTH LESSON ON WISDOM—SEXUAL RELATIONSHIPS. 5:1-23.

Appeal for Close Attention. 5:1-2.
1-2. My son (see comment on 3:11), **attend** (give attention) **unto my wisdom** (4:20) and **bow** (incline) **thine ear to my understanding** (insight; 22:17), that you may **regard** (observe) **discretion** (3:21) and your **lips may keep** (*nṣr*, "observe, preserve") **knowledge** (Mal. 2:7). Proper sexual relationships are of the highest importance to the happiness of the home, and they demand the most careful and discreet application of wisdom.

Warnings Against the Adulteress. 5:3-14. **3.** The adulteress is called **a strange woman** (cf. comment on 2:16). Her lips **drop** (drip) honey, **as an honeycomb** (Song of Sol. 4:11), **and her mouth** (lit., "palate," i.e., her speech) **is smoother than oil** (Psalm 55:21). **4.** But in the end she **is bitter as wormwood** (Eccles. 7:26), the flesh always promising delight, but eventually leaving only bitter dregs, which her dupes also share. She is **sharp as a two-edged sword,** and will mercilessly gash her victims. She can only be foiled with the Word of God, "sharper than any two-edged sword" (Heb. 4:12).

5. In lurid contrast to the men who follow wisdom and who "take hold of the paths of life" (Prov. 2:19), her feet descend **to death** and **her steps take hold on** (lay hold of) **sheol** (7:27). **6.** Her aim and tendency are toward death, and so her victim cannot **ponder the path of life** (4:26; 5:21). **Her ways are unstable** (*nûă‘*, "totter, move to and fro, wander"); they are as unreliable as she is unfaithful, and no confidence whatever can be put in her.

7-9. So dangerous was the adulteress that the teacher stopped to warn his sons (pupils; cf. comment on 3:11) solemnly again to listen to his admonitions and keep strictly away from her, and not to go near her house (7:25; 9:14), lest the one who went would give up his **honor** (*hôḏ*, "splendor"), that is, his chastity and purity, which are a man's true splendor before God and man. And give **thy years unto the cruel,** the adulteress, who is a heartless destroyer of both body and soul (6:32; 7:22-23, 26-27).

10. It is not her victim the adulteress wants, but his **wealth** and **labors,** that is, his hard-earned money, to lavish upon **an alien,** probably meaning the adulteress's favorite, rather than her husband and children. **11.** Then her victim will **mourn** (groan) **at the last** (at the latter end of his life), when the consequences of his sin overtake him and the powers of the body are consumed.

12-13. Then he will say regretfully, **How ... I hated instruction, and my heart despised reproof** (Prov. 1:7, 22, 29; 12:1); **and have not obeyed the voice of my teachers** (1:8), or listened to my instructors. **14. I was almost in all evil** (utter ruin) **in the midst of the congregation and assembly,** that is, there was scarcely any sin I did not commit openly and shamelessly in the assembly for worship, where of all places I should have refrained from evil (cf. Num. 25:6-8; Ezek. 8:15-16), like Eli's sons committing lewdness "at the door of the tabernacle of the congregation" (1 Sam. 2:22).

A Call to Cherish Holy Love. 5:15-23. **15.** The teacher turned to positive instruction on the joy and sacredness of a pure marital life and urged the learner to delight in his own wife as opposed to the adulteress. He cited an adage: **Drink waters out of thine own cistern, and running waters out of thine own well.** Since sexual desire is intense like thirst, to "drink waters" symbolizes sexual gratification, and the woman is compared to a "cistern" and a "well." Enjoy her loving embrace alone; permit no unlawful pleasures.

16. Should your springs be dispersed abroad (v. 18; 9:17; Song of Sol. 4:12, 15), **streams of water in the streets?** (NASB), "the springs" symbolizing the fountain of reproduction and physical life. **17.** Should you scatter your reproductive powers upon a harlot or an adulteress, "springs which should be yours only, not to be shared by strangers" (AB). **18. Let thy fountain be blessed** (Prov. 9:17; Song of Sol. 4:12, 15), by begetting a numerous progeny as you are faithful in your marital relationship and **rejoice with the wife of thy youth** (Eccles. 9:9; Mal. 2:14).

19. This verse gives instruction on how a husband should regard the wife of his youth **as a loving hind and a graceful doe** (NASB; Song of Sol. 2:9, 17; 4:5; 7:3). **Let her breasts satisfy you at all times; be exhilarated** (enraptured; lit., intoxicated) **always with her love** (NASB). **20. Why should you, my son** (cf. comment on 3:11), **be exhilarated with an adulteress** (lit., "a strange woman"; see comment on 2:16), **and embrace the bosom of a foreigner?** (NASB; Prov. 6:24; 7:5; 23:27). **21.** This sin may be committed in private, but it is open and public before the eyes of the Lord (Psalm 119:168; Prov. 15:3; Jer. 16:17; Hos. 7:2; Heb. 4:13), and He watches all the paths of a man (Prov. 4:26).

22. So the adulterer cannot escape the Lord's scrutiny or His punishment. Moreover, the **iniquities** of the wicked will take the sinner captive (1:31-32; Num. 32:23; Psalms 7:15; 9:15; 40:12), and he will be bound with the cords of his own sin. **23.** He will die both physically and spiritually for lack of **instruction** (discipline). **And in the greatness of**

his folly he will go astray and wander where there is no way (Job 12:24).

I. THE NINTH LESSON ON WISDOM—WARNINGS AGAINST VARIOUS FOLLIES. 6:1-19.

Warnings Against Various Follies. 6:1-19. There are four warnings against follies: (1) *The first warning is against suretyship (vv. 1-5).* **1-2. My son** (see comment on 3:11), **if thou be surety for thy neighbor ... thou art snared ... thou art taken.** The reference is to the custom of becoming a guarantor or a responsible party to stand good for the payment of an obligation incurred by someone else. The agreement to assume this responsibility was signalized by "striking the hand" into the hand of the creditor (11:15; 17:18; 20:16; 22:26; 27:13).

This precept does not forbid standing good for a relative or charitably for a friend in need (cf. Gen. 42:37; 43:9), but it forbids rashness in incurring obligations for strangers, or even friends, that cannot be fulfilled with honesty and due regard for the welfare of one's own family (1 Thess. 4:12; 1 Tim. 5:8). Such injudicious incurring of obligation ensnares a man and can reduce him and his family to poverty and financial slavery.

3. The procedure is outlined for a young man to deliver himself from involvement in such financial difficulty. He is to go and humble himself (lit., "present oneself to be trodden under foot") as a slave, inasmuch as he has passed from under his own power to that of another by virtue of the surety. He is to **importune** (NASB), implore release, either from the judge or the debtor. **4-5.** He is to do it at once, before taking rest in sleep (Psalm 132:4), extricating himself from his predicament **like a gazelle from the hunter's hand** (NASB) and like a bird from the hand of the fowler (91:3; 124:7).

(2) *The second warning is against laziness (vv. 6-11).* **6.** Indolence and sloth are to be avoided by the wise. The **sluggard** (Prov. 6:9; 10:26; 13:4; 20:4; 26:16) is challenged to go to the industrious **ant** and to **consider** (observe) **her ways** and receive a lesson in ambition and industry (30:24-25). This humble insect works incessantly to provide for its every need; so it neither begs nor borrows. **7-8.** The ant has no chief or ruler or leader of any kind; yet it **provideth** (prepares) its food in the summer, when food is grown, and does not let the heat deter its industry in gathering provision for the winter.

9-10. What a rebuke to the shiftless youth who lives only for the summertime of life and makes no preparation for the future, idling and sleeping his youth away. **11.** His punishment is poverty, which will advance to overtake him **like one that traveleth** (walks aimlessly and like a vagabond gets nowhere). His **want** (need, destitution) will be **like an armed man,** furnished with an offensive and defensive weapon, and irresistible, while the sluggard is completely unarmed and in a lazy stupor.

(3) *The third warning is against the crafty crook (vv. 12-15).* **12.** He is dubbed **a worthless person** (lit., "a man of Belial," meaning "a worthless scoundrel"), **a wicked man,** who **walketh** (a figure of step-by-step conduct) **with a perverse** (crooked) **mouth,** that is, someone whose speech is twisted and distorted from what is right. This describes a busybody.

13-14. He **winketh with his eyes ... speaketh with his feet ... teacheth with his fingers.** He shows by these signs and signals that he is a malignant, deceitful man (Psalm 35:19; Prov. 10:10), manifesting the **perversity** of his **heart** (his

mind), with which **he deviseth** (invents) **mischief** (evil) **continually** (Psalm 36:4; Isa. 32:7; Mic. 2:1; Matt. 26:4). That he is a trouble-making busybody is emphasized by his sowing **discord** (spreading strife) (Prov. 6:19; 16:28). **15.** His end is indicated: **His calamity** shall **come suddenly** (24:22). Instantly he will **be broken** (2 Chron. 36:16; Psalm 50:22; Jer. 19:11) like a potter's vessel (Psalm 2:9; Rev. 2:27).

(4) *The fourth warning is against six particularly detestable sins (vv. 16-19).* These sins are all prejudicial to one's neighbor: (*a*) **17a. a proud look** (lit., "haughty eyes"; Psalms 18:27; 101:5; Prov. 21:4; 30:13), so often a trait of the idle and the perverse, who have the least of anything to be proud of (cf. 26:16); (*b*) **17b. a lying tongue** (Psalms 31:18; 120:2; Prov. 12:22; 17:7); (*c*) **17c. hands that shed innocent blood** (Deut. 19:10; Prov. 28:17; Isa. 1:15; 59:7); (*d*) **18a. an heart** (mind) **that deviseth wicked imaginations** (Gen. 6:5; Prov. 21:8); (*e*) **18b. feet ... swift in running to mischief** (evil; 1:16); **19a. a false witness that speaketh lies** (Psalm 27:12; Prov. 12:17; 19:5; 21:28); (*f*) **19b. he that soweth discord among brethren** (6:14).

J. THE TENTH LESSON ON WISDOM—
WARNING AGAINST ADULTERY.
6:20-35.

Warning Against Adultery. 6:20-35. **20-23. My son** (see comment on 3:11), **keep thy father's commandment.** The exordium (vv. 20-23) deals with the guidance offered by sound parental teaching, which is to be strictly followed, to guard against the adulteress. **For the commandment is a lamp** (Psalm 119:105), **and the teaching** (*tôrâ*) **is light ... reproofs for discipline** (NASB), to point out **the way of life** to keep one from the **evil woman** (foreign woman;

5:3; 7:5, 21), whose ways are the ways of death (5:5; 7:27).

24. From the smooth tongue of the adulteress (NASB), who catches her victims with flattery and falsehood, the unwary youth must be guarded. **25. Lust not after her beauty in thine heart** (mind), giving birth to the inward desire of sin (Exod. 20:17; Matt. 5:28). Do not let the unlawful desire get a start. Do not let her **take** (catch) you with her seductive **eyelids** (2 Kings 9:30; Jer. 4:30; Ezek. 23:40). **26.** Be warned that **by means of an unchaste woman** (a harlot) a man is reduced **to a piece of bread** (Prov. 5:9; 10:29), and the adulteress hunts for **the precious life** (the life of youth), snatching it up to plunder and ruin it spiritually and physically (Prov. 7:23; Ezek. 13:18).

27-28. Flirting with the adulteress is as dangerous as playing with fire and walking on hot coals. Can a sensible person not expect to get burned? **29.** So every man who has sexual intercourse with his neighbor's wife is as foolish as a person who takes fire into his bosom or walks on red-hot embers. He is going to suffer the consequences and will not be held **innocent** and go unpunished, both by God and the woman's husband (cf. vv. 32-35; Num. 5:19; Job 9:28).

30. Men do not despise a thief, if he steal to satisfy himself when he is **hungry. 31.** Yet, if he is found, he must make sevenfold, or complete, restitution (cf. Exod. 22:1-4). **32-33.** How much more shall the adulterer not escape who gratuitously, and without any necessity of nature, violates his neighbor's wife. Accordingly, the adulterer is branded as lacking **understanding** (lit., "heart," i.e., "sense"; Prov. 7:7; 9:4; 10:13; 11:12; 12:11) and as one who would destroy himself (7:22-23), incurring wounds, disgrace, and ineradicable reproach.

34. The jealousy of the husband of the violated wife (27:4; Song of Sol. 8:6) fills him with murderous hate that will not allow him to spare the life of the guilty adulterer **in the day of vengeance** (Lev. 20:10; Prov. 11:4) when his opportunity comes to vindicate the gross wrong done to him and his family. **35.** He will not **regard** (consider, accept) **any ransom,** any sum, however large, paid to expiate the adultery (Exod. 21:30). No bribes will suffice to stop the husband from prosecuting the case, or the judge in handing down the full penalty.

K. THE ELEVENTH LESSON ON WISDOM—THE PERIL OF ADULTERY. 7:1-27.

Prefatory Exhortation. 7:1-5. **1-3. My son** (see comment on 3:11), **keep my words ... my commandments ... my law.** This introduces the customary exhortation to observe and keep in mind the paternal teaching, which is the way of life (cf. 6:1-5) and preserves from the harlot, whose way is that of death. **4-5.** The personal relations alluded to depict the close personal knowledge of wisdom that the teacher covets for his pupils, which will safeguard them from the wiles of the adulteress.

How the Adulteress Operates. 7:6-23. A graphic picture is presented of how the adulteress ensnares the naive and unwary youth. Wisdom, personifying itself in the first person, narrates the episode of the youth's seduction by a married woman.

6-7. Looking out from the window of her house through the lattice, which made one invisible from the street (Judg. 5:28; Song of Sol. 2:9), wisdom **discerned among the youths** (lit., "the simple ones," i.e., the inexperienced and naive) one **void of understanding** (lacking sense; 6:32).

8. He was passing through the street near the adulteress's corner, in violation of the precept not to go near her house (4:15). Instead, he **went the way** (*ṣ'd,* "walked with studied and affected gait") to impress the woman and flatter his own vanity by listening to her flatteries. He did not intend to defile himself with her, but he played with fire (6:27-28) and was to get burned. **9.** He chose the darkness, as lust hates the light (Job 24:15; John 3:20), thinking no one could see him. But God's eye is upon the transgressor (Psalm 139:12).

10. The harlot met him in her characteristic attire, which the youth recognized; it certainly should have been warning enough to him to flee the temptation (1 Cor. 6:18; 2 Tim. 2:22). But he did not have sense enough to do that. Nor did he have sense enough to discern that the woman was **subtle of heart,** "with secret plan in mind" (AB), to ensnare him.

11-12. The adulteress is described as **loud** (boisterous) and **stubborn,** rebellious against the laws of God and man, a never-at-home gadfly, now inside, now outside the house, lying in wait at every corner to catch her next unvigilant victim (Prov. 23:28). **13.** She **caught** (seized) **him** and **kissed him** boldly and brazenly, instead of waiting for him to make the first advance, as in the course of natural propriety. **With an impudent** (brazen) **face** (lit., "she strengthened her face"), she **said,** outdoing herself in brazenness and immodesty in the words she utters (vv. 14-20). With this fair speech she spread the net of temptation.

14. She courted him to dine with her and employed piety as a cloak for her sin. **I have peace offerings with me,** meaning she had sacrificial meat on hand for a feast, which she would make a prelude to lust. "It so happened that today I discharged my religious vows by

offering thank offerings for the prosperity given me." She virtually said, "I have a choice feast prepared," for the finest and most select victims were required for the peace offerings (Lev. 22:21), and of these the greatest share was returned to the offerer (2:3; 7:30; 19:6; 22:29-30). Subtle of heart ("with secret plan in mind" to seduce him, v. 10), she was well aware that the indulgence of the palate prepares for lust, and she would use this prelude to the full, even in the name of religion.

15. To strengthen the temptation, she pretended to have a very great affection for him, alleging that she had come out personally to meet him and to extend the invitation. Also, she gave the impression that Providence itself countenanced her choice of him, for how quickly she had found him whom she sought! The temptress appealed to three of the senses, starting with the sense of taste—with food.

16. She appealed to the sense of sight—she decked her bed with **coverings of tapestry** (with "coverlets" and "gaily colored linen from Egypt," AB). **17.** She appealed to the sense of smell—she **perfumed** her bed, "sprinkled" it with myrrh, aloes, and cinnamon. **18.** Then she suggested that they **take** their **fill of love,** by which she meant brutish lust.

19-20. She cleverly anticipated the objection he might make, since she was another man's wife. She explained that **her husband** (lit., "the man," by which term she spoke slightingly of him) was not at home. Their tryst would be safe enough, she suggested, because he had gone on **a long journey,** evidenced by the money bag taken with him, and he would not return until a specific time. **21.** She enticed him with alluring words and flattering lips (5:3; 6:24).

22. He succumbed to her blandishments. "All at once he is walking with her like an ox being led to the slaughter" (AB), full of alacrity, because he thought he was being led to the pastures or to the stall. Actually, he was being taken **as a fool to the correction of the stocks** (lit., "as the stocks— fetters—go to the correction of the fool"), a pitiable spectacle of a youth sporting with his chains as though they were an ornament or a clown's trick.

23. Till an arrow strike through his liver, a vital part of his body (Lam. 2:11), considered the seat of love. He was like a bird darting into a snare.

Concluding Summary of the Warning. 7:24-27. **24-25.** The dramatic picture of the foolish one tempted, of the wily temptress, and of the cunning temptation itself calls forth a renewed admonition to give solemn attention to the words of wisdom and to beware of turning aside to the adulteress's ways, and going astray in her paths (5:8). **26.** The reason is most compelling: **Many are the victims** [mortally wounded] **she has cast down, and numerous are all her slain** (NASB; cf. 9:18). **27.** Her house is described as **the way to sheol, going down** (descending) **to the chambers of death** (2:18; 5:5; 9:18).

L. THE TWELFTH LESSON ON WISDOM—WISDOM'S PLEA. 8:1-36.

Introduction by the Teacher. 8:1-3. The divine wisdom manifest in creation cries aloud and offers herself to mankind. Wisdom is vividly personified and, as in verses 22-31, appears as none other than God Himself in the person of the preincarnate Christ (John 1:1-3), the eternal Word who was with God and is God (Col. 1:15-17), and not a mere poetical personification.

1. Doth not wisdom cry (Prov.

1:20-21; 9:3; Isa. 49:1-6; 1 Cor. 1:21; Col. 2:3)? **2.** The precepts of wisdom may be known, for not only are they proclaimed aloud, but from on high. Wisdom **standeth** on the top of the heights where the roads meet and the paths cross, where the people throng (Prov. 9:3, 14). **3.** She cries aloud **at the gates** of the city, the place of business and assembly where the throngs gather (Job 29:7). She cries at the entrance of the doors of each house in the town.

The Invitation and Rewards of Wisdom. 8:4-21. **4-5.** Wisdom addresses herself to all members of the human race, to mankind as a whole as well as to the **simple** (the naive, the inexperienced; 1:4) and **fools** (1:22, 32; 3:35). **6-8.** Earnest attention is enlisted, for wisdom speaks **excellent** ($n^e \underline{g} \hat{\imath} d \hat{\imath} m$, "noble") **things** (22:20), **right things** (23:16), that is, concerning equity and **truth** (Job 36:4; John 1:17; 8:14; Rom. 15:8; Rev. 3:14), for **wickedness** is an **abomination** (an abhorrence, utter detestation) to wisdom. All the words wisdom speaks are **in righteousness ... nothing crooked or perverse** (distorted) **in them** (Deut. 32:5; Prov. 2:15; Phil. 2:15).

9. They are all **plain** (straight forward) to those apt for knowledge (Prov. 14:6), and **right** to those of a discerning mind (3:13). **10-11.** Accepting wisdom is urged as a wiser course than accepting silver and the choicest gold (3:14-15; 8:19), **for wisdom is better than** jewels (Job 28:15-19; Psalms 19:10; 119:127; Matt. 16:23; Phil. 3:8). In the realm of desirable things, wisdom is incomparable (Prov. 3:15).

12. Wisdom dwells with, that is, is inseparably associated with **prudence** (v. 5), and is found in company with **knowledge and discretion** (NASB). Christ, the fountain of wisdom (Col. 1:19; 2:3), is the source not only of spiritual knowledge, but of practical sagacity for the conduct of life as well. Wisdom enables her disciples to **find out knowledge of witty inventions** (i.e., "sagacious plans"), enabling them to order their lives with cautious prudence in accord with God's Word.

13. Wisdom inculcates **the fear of** (reverence for) **the Lord** (Prov. 3:7; 16:6), which involves hating what God hates—**evil** of every sort—**pride, and arrogance** (1 Sam. 2:3; Psalm 5:4; Prov. 6:17; Zech. 8:17; 1 Pet. 5:5), **... the evil way** (Prov. 15:9), that is, wicked behavior, and the **perverse mouth** (speech). **14.** Wisdom continues her plea to receive her and the treasures of her reward. She who is **understanding** imparts good counsel and has strength to grant power of achievement (Eccles. 7:19).

15-16. By her **kings reign ... princes decree justice** (Dan. 2:21; 7:14; Rom. 13:1). By her **princes rule, and nobles, even all the judges of the earth,** all who bear authority on the earth. **17.** She loves **those who love** her (Prov. 4:6; 1 Sam. 2:30; John 14:21), and declares **those who seek me early** (i.e., diligently) **... find me** (Prov. 2:4-5; James 1:5). Wisdom's rich rewards are particularly emphasized (vv. 18-21). **18. Riches ... honor ... durable** (enduring) **riches** (wealth) **and righteousness** (Matt. 6:33) are with her (Psalm 112:3; Prov. 3:16). She possesses them and lavishes them upon those who follow her.

19. Her **fruit**—the benefit derived from her (3:14)—is better than the purest gold, and her **revenue** (*tᵉbû'â,* "increase, income, profit, produce") than the choicest silver (10:20). **20-21.** Wisdom walks in the sense of leading **in the way** (path) of **righteousness** and **justice** to endow those who **love** her with **substance** (*yōshĕr,* "wealth") that she may fill all their **treasuries** with her benefits (24:4).

The Deity, Eternity, and Creatorship of Wisdom. 8:22-31. That the preincarnate Christ, the eternal Word who was with God and is God (John 1:1-3), is spoken of here is a fact because of six reasons: (1) An intelligent, divine Person with personal properties and actions is presented, and not a mere attribute of the divine nature. Even if the Spirit-inspired writer himself designed only the praise of wisdom as a divine attribute "of the creative action of God" (LBC, p. 45) in order to recommend to men the study of that wisdom, "yet the spirit of God, who indited what he wrote, carried him, as David often, to such expressions as could agree to no other than the Son of God" (Matthew Henry). Christ is the object of all divine revelation.

(2) The preincarnate Christ is envisioned because His personality and distinct subsistence—yet oneness with God and being of the same essence, while still being a person of Himself—appear. The LORD possessed (v. 22), was set up (v. 23), was brought forth (vv. 24-25), was by (beside) Him (v. 30) as "the express image of his person" (Heb. 1:3). (3) His eternity is declared (vv. 22-26). **22. The Lord possessed me** (not "created me," as in the LXX and in the Arian heresy) **in the beginning of his way, before his works of old** (Job 28:26-28; Psalm 104:24; Prov. 3:19). The "beginning of his way" is the beginning of His eternal counsels, which were before His works of creation and redemption and indeed had no beginning because God's purposes in Himself are eternal, as He Himself is eternal; in so speaking, He accommodates His infinity to our finiteness.

The LORD *possessed* (*qānâ,* "acquire, get," and so "possess," used of God in possessing by virtue of creating, Gen. 14:19, 22; Deut. 32:6; Psalm

139:13; or generating, Prov. 8:22). "The LORD possessed me," that is, by the right of paternity, as the same Hebrew word "gotten" or "possessed" occurs in Genesis 4:1: "I have gotten" a man by parentage (cf. Prov. 8:24-25, "I was brought forth" or "begotten," Psalm 2:7; Mic. 5:2; John 1:1-3). Paternity is indicated by the same Hebrew word in Deuteronomy 32:6: "Is not he thy father who hath bought thee" (*qānâ*, "possessed thee" in the sense of "created" thee (RSV).

23-26. That the eternal Word, the preincarnate Christ, the eternal Son **was brought forth** as to His being and **set up from everlasting** as to His office, before the world was made, is most emphatically declared in a great variety of expressions—**from the beginning, or ever the earth was,** before the **depths,** before the **fountains,** before the **mountains . . . the hills . . . the fields . . . the dust of the world** (the cultivable soil).

(4) **27-29.** His creatorship of the universe is asserted. He not only had a being before the material universe, but was present, not merely as a spectator but as the Architect and Maker of the worlds (Eph. 3:9; Col. 1:16; Heb. 1:2), "as a master workman" (*'āmmān*, v. 30*a*, with LXX, Syriac, Vulgate, RSV, NASB) who made the heavens as well as the earth and the sea (cf. Job. 38:4-11).

(5) The infinite delight that the Father had in Him and He in the Father is proclaimed. **30a. I was by him** (a distinct Personality, coeternal, coexistent; John 1:2-3), **as one brought up with him** (*'āmôn*, "pupil," or "nursling"), reflecting the idea of the Aramaic paraphrase, "I was nursed at His side," giving the thought of John 1:18, "the only begotten Son, who is in the bosom of the Father," inseparably one with Him. **30b. And I was daily his delight** (cf. Matt. 3:16-17; Col. 1:13), **rejoicing al-** **ways before him,** the image being of children who, playing in the sight of their nurses, are their delight.

(6) The gracious concern He had for mankind is declared. The eternal Son not only rejoiced in the Father's presence, but also in the world and His created earth and the creatures upon it. **31. Rejoicing in the habitable . . . earth** (Psalm 40:6-8). Wisdom rejoiced not so much in the material wealth of the earth, but her **delight was with the sons of men,** that is, in the creation (Gen. 1:26) and redemption of man to which great work the Son of God was "foreordained before the foundation of the world" (1 Pet. 1:20).

The Invitation of Wisdom. 8:32-36.
32-34. The call is to **hearken** (listen) and **hear . . . be wise, and refuse . . . not** (neglect not) wisdom. The emphasis is upon the happiness wisdom brings— **blessed** are they who keep the ways of wisdom (Luke 11:28), and **blessed** is the person who hears (listens to) wisdom (Prov. 3:13, 18), watching daily at her **gates,** perhaps as a lover at the door of his beloved one (Job 31:9)—**waiting at the posts** (doorposts) of wisdom, as the priests used to wait at the doors of the tabernacle for the Word of the LORD (Exod. 29:42).

35. Whoever **findeth** wisdom (although it is God who gives, we are said "to find" because we must exert all diligence, as if all depended on us) finds **life** (lit., "lives," i.e., that of the present world and that of the world to come). For life, eternal life, is obtaining (*pûq,* "drawing forth") as a continuous outflow of blessing, namely, the **favor of the Lord,** acceptance with Him by faith, bringing justifying grace (Gen. 15:6), including in it every other blessing (Deut. 33:23; Psalms 5:12; 145:16, 19). **36. But he that sinneth against** wisdom (who does not love and seek wisdom)

wrongeth his own soul (himself) in choosing eternal death instead of eternal life.

M. SUMMARY OF THE TWELVE LESSONS—WISDOM AND FOLLY IN CONTRAST. 9:1-18.

The Invitation of Wisdom. 9:1-12. **1. Wisdom** ("wisdoms," plural of excellence and dignity connecting with the plural *Elohim,* God, and wisdom's divinity) has built **her house** (1 Cor. 3:9; Eph. 2:20-22; 1 Pet. 2:5), hewing out her **seven pillars** (not the pillars of the house but of herself), suggesting the manifold and complete (seven the number of perfection) stays or supports upon which (divine) wisdom rests. Insofar as God bestows His sevenfold Spirit (Isa. 11:2-3; Rev. 1:4) upon His ministers, they become "pillars" (Gal. 2:9). Wisdom's house is the body of the believer in whom the Spirit dwells (1 Cor. 3:17), and the glorified body, the "house not made with hands, eternal in the heavens" is the consummation (2 Cor. 5:1).

2-3. Wisdom not only has prepared her house, but her banquet as well—food (Matt. 22:4) and **wine** (Song of Sol. 8:2), and set her **table** (Luke 14:16-17), publishing her invitation through her maidens (i.e., the ministers of the Word; Psalm 68:11; Matt. 22:3), calling from the **highest places of the city,** that all may hear.

Wisdom's invitation is to salvation by grace through faith (Isa. 55:1-12; Eph. 2:8-9), for it rests on sacrifice: **She hath killed her beasts** ("immolated her immolation"), for all the blessedness of the gospel invitation and the Lamb's marriage supper (Matt. 8:11; 22:2-3; Luke 14:15-16; Rev. 19:9) springs from previous sacrifice, in contrast to the harlot's hypocritical feast of "peace offerings"

(Prov. 7:14). Wisdom's mingled **wine** (i.e., mixed with spices and other exhilarating ingredients; Song of Sol. 8:2) speaks of the keen delights of God's salvation (Isa. 55:1; Eph. 5:18).

To Whom the Invitation Is Given. 9:4-5. **4. Whoso is simple** (naive, untutored, credulous), in whose reformation there is hope, being misled by his own inexperience and not by malice aforethought, **let him turn in** here (NASB). **5.** To the senseless (the ignorant) she says, **Come, eat of my bread** (feast on my food; Isa. 55:1) ... **drink of the wine,** partake of the exhilarating joy and comforts of the gospel (Matt. 26:29). **6.** This entails abandoning the society and ways of **the foolish** (Prov. 1:22) in order to **live** (8:35; 9:11), no longer the life of a beast, but that of a man (4:4), yea, a regenerated man (John 3:16), to enjoy eternal life. **And go** (proceed, go forward) **in the way of understanding** (Ezek. 11:20; 37:24; 2 Pet. 3:18).

The Prerequisite for Accepting the Invitation. 9:7-12. It is necessary to abandon the foolish, lest he become a scorner, upon whom reproof is wasted (vv. 6-9). **7.** He who **reproveth** (corrects) a scoffer gets dishonor for himself (23:9). He who **rebuketh** (reproves) **a wicked man** invites insults for himself (lit., "gets himself a blot or blemish"). **8.** To reprove or try to correct a scoffer merely incurs his hatred (15:12; Matt. 7:6), but reproving a wise man stirs up his love for you (Psalm 141:5; Prov. 10:8).

9. A wise man will become still wiser by instruction, and a justified man will increase his learning (1:5). **10.** Reverence for the LORD is the beginning of wisdom (1:7) and experiential knowledge of the Holy One (*qᵉdōshîm;* for its plural form cf. Josh. 24:19, in which the Trinity is implicit; cf. Lev. 11:44; 19:2;

Prov. 30:3; Hos. 11:12, and in which the infinite holiness of Deity is emphasized). **11.** Embracing and following wisdom tends to longevity (Prov. 3:16; 10:27).

12. If thou be wise, thou shalt be wise for thyself (Job 22:2; Prov. 14:14), the benefit will be all your own (Dan. 12:3); you will not work for nothing, as do those who live for self and amass great riches to leave to others (Eccles. 2:18-19; 4:8). By contrast, if you are a scoffer, you **alone shalt bear** the consequences (Gal. 6:5), hurting only yourself by refusing wisdom's invitation (Job 35:6-8; Prov. 8:36; 19:29).

The Invitation of Folly. 9:13-18. **13. A foolish woman** ("woman of folly") **is clamorous** (noisy, boisterous, loud) ... **simple** (ignorant), and **knoweth nothing,** fools frequently being the loudest talkers. As wisdom is personified as a woman (vv. 1-12), so is folly (sin). "Folly is [like] a woman" (AB), construing *'ēšeṯ* not as a construct, but the archaic Canaanite absolute form.

14-15. Folly is pictured as a wanton woman sitting in the doorway of her house or **on a seat in the high places of the city,** as Wisdom cries "upon the highest places of the city" (v. 3; 8:2) **to call those who pass by, who go right on their way** (lit., "who are making right [straight] their ways," i.e., going straight morally). **16a.** Folly's aim is to seduce men from their right course of life, and so she calls seducingly: **Whoever is naive, let him turn in here** (NASB; cf. v. 4).

16b-17. And to him who **lacketh understanding,** she says, **Stolen waters are sweet** (5:15) **and bread eaten in secret is pleasant** (20:17), a metaphorical reference to illicit sexual indulgence (30:20). Water might be stolen, because in a land of scant rainfall it might be a salable commodity (cf. Deut. 2:6). Folly's "waters" contrast sharply with

wisdom's spiced "wine" (vv. 2, 5).

18. But he (whoever turns in to folly, v. 16) **knoweth not that the dead** (morally and spiritually) **are there, and that her guests** (her invited ones) **are in the depths of sheol.** Ptah-hotep, an Egyptian sage and the principal minister of a king of the fifth dynasty in Egypt, speaks similarly of the penalty for adultery: "one attains death through knowing her" (i.e., "the adulteress"; ANET, p. 413B).

III. THE FIRST BOOK OF SOLOMON. 10:1—22:16.

This section of the book contains some 374 proverbs attributed to Solomon (cf. 1 Kings 4:32). Most of the aphorisms are of one type, consisting of two lines, the second emphasizing the first by contrast. The arrangement of these brief aphorisms follows no strict continuity in subject matter. (For a rearrangement, see R. B. Y. Scott, *Proverbs,* AB, pp. 130-31.) However, the arrangement is not as haphazard as might initially appear. Frequently a series on the same subject or a kindred subject, or demonstrating the same principle, are grouped together. The following titles introducing chapters are approximate guides to the contents for the sake of convenience.

A. RIGHT AND WRONG CONDUCT IN CONTRAST. 10:1-32.

Introduction: The Proverbs of Solomon. 10:1. **1.** (Cf. 1:1). This preface marks a new division of the book and in a sense marks the purpose of the proverbs to set the course of **a wise son,** who will make a **glad father** (15:20; 29:3), and warn against being **a foolish son ... the heaviness** (grief) of his mother (17:25; 29:15).

Warning Against Ill-Gotten Gains. *10:2.* **2.** Such **treasures** amassed dishonestly **profit nothing** (11:4; 21:6; Psalm 49:6-7; Ezek. 7:19; Luke 12:19-20). **But righteousness,** flowing from faith in God's saving grace (Gen. 15:6) and manifested by right conduct before men, delivers from spiritual and eternal death (Jer. 23:6), and often from physical death, tending to a long life on earth (Exod. 20:12; Psalm 128:5-6).

The Lord's Care of the Righteous. *10:3.* **3.** The LORD will not let His own starve (Psalm 37:25-26). Not that the righteous are exempt from hunger or want. David was hungry (1 Sam. 21:3); so were Paul and the apostles (1 Cor. 4:11; 2 Cor. 11:27) and the martyrs (Heb. 11:37). But God watches over His own to give them higher spiritual food, and ordinarily feeds His own, even supernaturally if necessary, as He did Elijah (1 Kings 17:4-6). By contrast, **he casteth away** (rebuffs) **the substance** (craving) of the wicked, rejecting their evil desire and lust (cf. Mic. 7:3).

Admonition to Industry. 10:4-5. **4.** He comes to poverty who **dealeth** (works) **with a slack** (negligent) **hand.** Such careless work makes a man poor, **but the hand of the diligent** (*ḥārûṣîm,* "cut short, decided, sharpened"; those who are sharp and decisive to move at the right moment) **maketh rich** (brings wealth; 13:14; 21:5). **5.** He who gathers when the crop is ready shows intelligence, but the son who sleeps in harvesttime **causeth shame** (acts disgracefully).

The Blessings of the Righteous. 10:6-7. **6.** Those who trust God's grace and demonstrate their faith in God to their fellowman have blessings called down **upon their head** by both God and men. **But violence covereth the mouth of the wicked,** that is, with shame, so that they are silenced before the charges of their enemies, whom they have wronged (Psalm 107:42; Mic. 7:10). **7. The memory of the just is blessed** (Psalm 112:6), **but the name of the wicked shall rot** (9:5-6; 109:13; Eccles. 8:10).

The Security of the Man of Integrity. *10:8-10.* **8.** The man of integrity is **wise in heart** (mind), that is, discreet and intelligent, demonstrated by his willingness to **receive commandments** (commands). As a sensible man, he will take orders (9:8; Matt. 7:24). But a **prating** (babbling) **fool** who talks back **shall fall** (*yillābēṭ,* "be thrown down"; "fall headlong," BV). **9. He that walketh** (figure for step-by-step living) **uprightly** (in integrity) **walketh surely** (confidently, securely; Psalm 23:4). **But he that perverteth his ways** (as a dishonest man) **shall be known** (i.e., found out), and have no sense of confidence.

10. He that winketh with the eye, with cunning and malicious intent (Prov. 6:13), feigning kindliness to his neighbor, but all the while giving a secret sign to his accomplices to cheat or rob him, **causeth sorrow** (makes trouble; Psalm 35:19). And a babbling fool, who talks back, shall fall headlong (repeated from v. 8*b*).

The Blessing of the Tongue of the Wise. 10:11-14. **11. The mouth of a righteous** (saved, justified) man, who has a renewed heart (13:14; 18:4; Psalm 37:30) **is a well** (fountain) **of life** (James 3:11-12; cf. Matt. 12:34; Luke 6:45). **But violence covereth the mouth of the wicked** (see v. 6*b*). **12. Hatred** in the heart, surfacing through the lips (Matt. 12:34; Luke 6:45), **stirreth up strifes** (provokes quarrels), **but love covereth all sins** (1 Cor. 13:4; James 5:20; 1 Pet. 4:8), the reference to concealing sins being not before God but before one's fellowmen. Love takes no notice of a friend's errors (cf. Lev. 19:17-18).

13. In (on) **the lips of him that hath**

understanding (who is discerning), **wisdom is found** (Luke 4:22), that is, "a discerning man talks sense" (AB). **But a rod** (stick) **is for the back of him that is void of understanding** (lit., "lacks heart," that is, is devoid of common sense), who needs to be struck as a mule to keep him in line. **14. Wise men lay up** (in store, store up) **knowledge** (Prov. 9:9) in order to bring it forth seasonably for the benefit of themselves and others (Matt. 12:35; 13:52). **But the mouth of the foolish is near destruction.** He always has ready at hand on his tongue the words that bring ruin; so when he speaks, trouble and confusion brew (v. 8; 13:3; 18:7; 21:15).

The Wealth of the Wise. 10:15-16. **15. The rich man's wealth is his strong city** (fortress); **the destruction** (ruin) **of the poor is their poverty** (18:11; Psalm 52:7). In their own estimation, the rich fancy their riches as their fort that will keep them safe from all evil; while the poor are so overwhelmed by their poverty as to fear "destruction" by it. Both forget that "the name of the LORD" is the only "strong tower" (Prov. 18:10-12; Isa. 26:1). **16. The labor** (wages) **of the righteous** (the justified believer), the fruit of faith in God, is **life** (Prov. 11:18-19). **The fruit** (*tᵉḇû'â,* "produce, income, increase") **of the wicked** (the unjustified sinner) is **sin** (condemnation before God). Even good works cannot justify him before an infinitely holy God; so certainly his godless riches cannot.

The Value of Self-Discipline. 10:17. **17. He is in the way of life** (on the right course to fullness of spiritual life and the fullest enjoyment of physical life) **that keepeth instruction** (*shōmēr mûsᾱr,* "observes self-discipline"; 6:23). **But he that refuseth reproof** (ignores correction) **erreth** (goes astray, gets lost in many bypaths, and loses the way to life and fullness of life).

The Wisdom of Restraining One's Lips. 10:18-21. **18. He that hideth** (conceals) **hatred has lying lips** (plays the part of a hateful hypocrite; 26:24), **and he who uttereth a slander is a fool,** a common rogue. Hatred is often concealed by the hypocrite in order that it may give vent to slander (false defamatory speech). **19. In the multitude of words** (too much talk) **there lacketh not sin** (transgression; 18:21; Eccles. 5:3). **But he that refraineth** (restrains, controls) **his lips** (tongue) is wise. Because in too much talk there is sure to be some sin, a shrewd man holds his tongue (Prov. 17:27; James 1:19; 3:2).

20. The tongue of the just (the justified-by-faith believer) **is like choice silver** (Prov. 8:19), because he is redeemed and testifies of redemption, of which silver is a symbol (Exod. 26:19; 30:16; 1 Pet. 1:18-19). **The heart of the wicked,** out of which his mouth speaks (Matt. 12:34; Luke 6:45) **is of little worth** at best, a terrible debit at worst.

21. The lips of the righteous (man) **feed many,** because he is justified before God (Gen. 15:6) and has the Bread of Life, the true manna from heaven, to dispense to the spiritually hungry (v. 11; cf. Exod. 4:15; Matt. 4:4). **But fools,** who have no concept of the value of God's Word and spiritual food, **die** (physically, spiritually, and as a result, eternally in Gehenna, Rev. 20:11-14) **for lack of wisdom** (lit., "heart," as the seat of understanding; Prov. 5:23; Hos. 4:6).

The Blessing of the Lord. 10:22. **22.** The LORD's **blessing ... maketh** a man **rich,** because it is not confined to temporal benefits (Gen. 24:35; 26:12), but includes redemption "without money and without price" (Isa. 55:1), not with such corruptible things as silver and gold (1 Pet. 1:18), bringing God's "unspeakable gift" of salvation (2 Cor. 9:15). **And he** (the LORD) **addeth no sor-**

row ('*ēṣĕḇ*, "anxiety, harassment") with it (His blessing), such as the covetous and the lustful experience (cf. Prov. 8:20-21; Gen. 26:12).

The Satisfaction and Stability of the Righteous. 10:23-25. 23. It is like sport (*śehōq*, "merrymaking, jestful laughter") to a fool to do mischief (wickedness), "just as wisdom is to a man of understanding" (BV). 24. What the wicked fears (dreads) shall come upon him. But the desire of the righteous shall be granted, because what they want is in line with what God wants for them, and their prayers in God's will are answered (Psalm 145:19; 1 John 5:14-15). 25. As the whirlwind passeth, so is the wicked no more (Job 21:18; Psalm 58:9; Prov. 12:7), no wind being shorter or more violent. In contrast, the righteous is an everlasting foundation because he is established upon the everlasting God and the firm rock of His salvation (Psalm 15:5; Prov. 12:3; Matt. 7:24-25; 16:18).

The Lazy Person. 10:26. 26. As vinegar (is) to the teeth, causing them to smart, and smoke (is) to (in) the eyes, causing extreme discomfort, so is the sluggard (laggard) to one who sends him on an errand. He causes pain to his employer by either not performing his assigned task at all or bungling it (cf. 6:6-11; 20:4; 26:13-16).

The Fear of the Lord. 10:27-30. 27. Such reverence and holy awe before the LORD and His Word (1:7) prolongeth days (life; 3:2; 9:11; 14:27); it tends to add years to one's physical life by avoiding the sins and excesses of the wicked that tend to undermine health and longevity (Job 15:32-33; 22:16; Psalm 55:23).

28. It gives hope, producing gladness (16:9; Rom. 5:2; 12:12; 1 John 3:2) and a happy optimism. But the expectation of the wicked shall perish (Job 8:13; 11:20; Prov. 11:7). The godless can have no hope, for they have no faith in God, on whom hope is founded. 29. The way of the Lord (His will and plan for their lives) is strength (a stronghold) to the upright because they walk in the LORD's way in obedience and submission to His Word (13:6). But destruction (ruin) shall be to the workers of iniquity, those who practice idolatrous demonized religion, because they follow the path that leads to death.

30. The righteous shall never be removed—shaken from his position of faith in God here, much less from his hope of the hereafter (Psalm 37:11; John 5:24). In antithesis, the wicked shall not inhabit the earth permanently, in contrast to the righteous meek, who will indwell the regenerated earth (Prov. 2:21; Matt. 5:5).

The Speech of the Righteous. 10:31-32. 31. His mouth bringeth forth (*nūḇ*, "flows with, produces") wisdom, but the perverse (malicious) tongue shall be cut out (off; 17:20). 32. The lips of the righteous know (discern) what is acceptable ("delights others," BV). But the mouth of the wicked, what is perverted (NASB; 2:12; 6:12).

B. RIGHT AND WRONG CONDUCT IN CONTRAST—(CONT.). 11:1-31.

Dishonesty. 11:1. 1. A false balance (dishonest scales) is an abomination ("utter detestation," as is idolatry) to the Lord, showing that God takes a personal interest in the honesty of business deals. But a just (true) weight (lit., "a perfect stone"), for stones in antiquity were employed as weights (20:10, 23; Lev. 19:35-36; Deut. 25:13-16; Mic. 6:11), is his delight (*rāṣôn*, "pleasure"; Prov. 16:11).

Pride. 11:2. 2. When pride cometh, then cometh shame (dishonor; 16:18; 18:12; 29:23). Compare the case of

Nebuchadnezzar of Babylon (Dan. 4:30-31). **But with the lowly** (the humble) **is wisdom** (issuing in honor). Pride is such a cardinal, debasing sin because it makes the victim set himself against God and against his neighbor (Prov. 13:10; 21:24).

Integrity. 11:3. **3. The integrity** (*tūmmāh,* "honesty, innocence") **of the upright shall guide them** (13:6) through trials and temptations to live a victorious life in time and to inherit felicity in eternity. By contrast, **the perverseness** (the falseness, hypocrisy) of **transgressors** (treacherous, those who deal secretly and deceptively) **shall destroy them,** just as one who has no guide goes astray and falls over a cliff or succumbs to some other peril (19:3; 22:12).

The Efficacy of Righteousness. 11:4-8. **4.** Riches are profitless to save, especially **in the day** of divine judicial vengeance (10:2; Ezek. 7:19; Zeph. 1:18). **But righteousness** that is savingly reckoned to the believer by virtue of his faith in God's grace (Gen. 15:6; Psalm 51:7), and which practically in conduct evidences the reality of that faith, **delivereth from death** (spiritual and eternal death, John 3:16; Rom. 6:23; cf. Gen. 7:1).

5. Such **righteousness of the perfect** (the upright, who evidence the reality of his faith-imputed righteousness by righteous conduct) **shall direct his way** (keep him on the right road; Prov. 3:6), but the wicked man, who never gets on the right road, will **fall by his own wickedness** (5:22). **6. The righteousness of the upright shall deliver** (rescue) them from all fatal dangers and from eternal death. **But transgressors** (deceivers, treacherous people) shall be caught (trapped) **in their own iniquity** (greed, cupidity; Psalms 7:15; 9:15-16; Eccles. 10:8).

7. When a wicked man (an unjustified sinner) **dieth, his expectation** of any future bliss perishes (Prov. 10:28); and **the hope** (faith as it claims future blessing) **of unjust** (unsaved) **men** vanishes because they have no faith in God to generate hope in the future (Job 8:13-14). **8. The righteous is delivered out of trouble, and the wicked** (the unsaved) **cometh in his stead,** that is, falls into that very trouble in his place, as happened to Daniel and his enemies (Dan. 6:24) and wicked Haman (Esther 5:14; 7:8-10; cf. Psalm 7:15).

The Blessing of the Righteous. 11:9-12. **9. An hypocrite** (a godless, profane person) **with his mouth** (by his talk) **destroyeth** (would ruin) **his neighbor** (16:29), **but through** (God-given) **knowledge, shall the just** (the righteous, the justified believer) **be delivered,** being enabled to see through the hypocrite's nefarious schemes and evade them (v. 6). **10. When it goeth well with the righteous, the city rejoiceth** (28:12), for the well-being of the righteous in a state furthers the well-being of the state as a whole (Gen. 30:27). But **when the wicked perish, there is shouting** (jubilation).

11. By the blessing of the upright the city is exalted, because God blesses it for the sake of the righteous in it, who intercede for it (Ezra 6:10; Jer. 29:7; 1 Tim. 2:1-2). But the city **is overthrown by the mouth of the wicked**—by their bad counsels, calumnies, lies, and treachery (Prov. 29:8). **12. He that is void** (devoid) **of wisdom** (lacks sense) **despiseth his neighbor**—shows contempt for him. **But a man of understanding** keeps silent and does not contemptuously taunt him. He keeps his opinions to himself.

The Talebearer. 11:13. **13. A talebearer** ("he who walks, being a talebearer"; Lev. 19:16) **revealeth secrets** (betrays confidence), the offense being aggravated by the fact that what the talebearer (lit., "scandal merchant'') goes about peddling far and wide (Jer. 6:28; James 4:11; 1 Pet. 2:1) is a "secret" (*sôd*) committed to him confidentially. **But he that is of a faithful spirit** (is trustworthy, loyal to his promise of secrecy) **concealeth the matter** (keeps it hidden), in contrast to the gossip.

The Importance of Adequate Counsel. 11:14. **14. Where no counsel is** (*tăḥbŭlôt*, "wise counsels"; 1:5, in the sense of able "leadership" to steer the ship of state), **the people fall** (15:22; 20:18; 24:6). God's punishment on a sinful state is to give it leaders devoid of wisdom (15:22; Isa. 3:4). Compare the case of Rehoboam, whose kingdom suffered tragic loss because of neglect of good counsel (1 Kings 12:13-17).

The Perils of Suretyship. 11:15. **15. He that is surety for** (goes bond for) **a stranger shall smart for it** (lit., "shall be broken with a breakage," i.e., be completely ruined). The folly of reckless **suretyship** (lit., "sureties") is emphasized when it is for a "stranger," for whom one has not the slightest obligation to run such a risk (cf. 6:1).

The Importance of Honor. 11:16. **16. A gracious woman retaineth** (*tmk*, "attains, holds, maintains") **honor,** whereas **strong men** ('*āriṣîm*, "violent, fierce men") **retain** ("attain," same word) **riches,** but with shame instead of honor. Riches are to be rejected apart from honor.

The Rewards of the Righteous. 11:17-21. **17.** "The merciful man" ('*îš ḥĕsĕd*, "man of mercy") does himself (as well as others) **good** (Psalms 41:1; 112:4, 9; Isa. 32:7-8; Matt. 5:7; Luke 6:38). On the other hand the **cruel** man **troubleth** himself (his flesh), does himself harm (as well as others).

18. The wicked worketh a deceitful work (earns deceptive wages), but the righteous man **soweth righteousness** and

gets **a sure reward** (Hos. 10:12; Gal. 6:8-9; James 3:18). **19.** As **righteousness** (the outgrowth of faith in God's redemptive grace) assures spiritual life now and eternal life hereafter, so he who **pursueth** (avidly follows) **evil pursueth it to his own death** (spiritual, physical, and eternal death).

20. They that are of a perverse heart (a perverted mind) **are an abomination** (intense detestation, like idolatry) **to the Lord.** By contrast, the righteous who are **upright in their way** (their step-by-step walk or conduct in God's will made possible because their minds are straight and not crooked or perverted like the wicked) are the LORD's **delight** (1 Chron. 29:17; Psalm 119:1; Prov. 13:6).

21. Though hand join in hand and the wicked swear mutual help against their adversaries, they shall not go **unpunished,** God visiting them for punishment to the third or fourth generation as those who hate Him and despise His commandments (Exod. 20:6). **But the seed** (progeny, descendants) **of the righteous shall be delivered** from calamities and punishments that overtake the wicked.

The Propriety of Discretion. 11:22. **22.** As unseemly as a gold jewel **in a swine's snout** is a **fair woman . . . without discretion** (lit., "turned aside from," bereft of "taste," i.e., moral perception of what is right or wrong," pure or impure; Psalm 119:66). In ancient times women wore "jewels" (Isa. 3:21) in their noses. The comparison is between the discreet, beautiful woman ("the jewels of gold") and the impure, indiscreet, lustful woman (the filthy sow; 2 Pet. 2:22).

The Issue of Right Desires. 11:23. **23. The desire of the righteous is only good,** since its chief object is God and His favor. **But the expectation of the wicked,** since they have no faith in God, and hence no hope, which springs out of faith, is the **wrath** of God (Rom. 2:8; Gal. 6:8) hanging like a Damoclean sword over *all* unsaved (unjustified) humanity (Rom. 1:18), and treasured-up wrath against the day of wrath (2:5) upon those who recklessly scout the moral law of God.

The Boon of Liberality. 11:24-27. **24.** There is the man who **scattereth,** liberally dispersing his wealth for the glory of God and the blessing of men, **and yet** he **increaseth** his true riches by it (13:7; 19:17). **And there is he that withholdeth more than is fitting** (proper), that is, keeping back what is justly due, according to God's Word, **but tendeth** toward **poverty,** not increase (Hag. 1:6, 9-11; 2:15-19; Heb. 13:16; cf. Matt. 13:12). The metaphor is that of sowing and reaping. We reap what we sow. **25.** So the **liberal soul** (the generous giver) **shall be made fat** (prosperous; Prov. 3:9-10; 2 Cor. 9:6-7). **He that watereth** (another's garden) **shall be watered also himself**—shall have his own (garden) watered.

26. An illustration is a dealer who **withholdeth grain** to raise the price and reap selfish profit. **The people shall curse** him (Amos 8:5), **but blessing shall be** (implored by the grateful people) **upon the head of him that selleth it** at a fair price (Job 29:13). **27.** That in turn furnishes an illustration: **He that diligently seeketh good procureth favor,** both from God and man. But he who **seeketh mischief** (evil), **it shall come unto him** (boomerang upon him; Esther 7:10).

Folly of Trust in Riches. 11:28. **28.** He who trusts in riches will be loath to part with them in giving to God and others (vv. 24-27) and shall **fall** like a plant that withers (Job 31:24; Mark 10:24; Luke 12:21; 1 Tim. 6:17). **But the righteous** (inasmuch as they do not put their confidence in wealth) **shall flourish like a**

branch ("burgeon like green leaves," AB; cf. Psalm 1:3; Jer. 17:8).

Folly of Troubling One's Own Family. 11:29. **29.** He who **troubleth his own house,** whether by complaints, improvidence, extravagance, etc., will **inherit the wind** (15:27; Eccles. 5:16), shall gain nothing but wind, which makes a bluster and vanishes as quickly as it comes (Prov. 10:25; Eccles. 1:6). He who in such a manner plays the fool in the management of his house and property will automatically be reduced to the position of a servant in the estimation of one who wisely manages his domestic affairs.

The Fruit of the Righteous. 11:30-31. **30.** Compared to a fruit tree, the justified believer's produce of life and testimony is like the **tree of life** (Gen. 2:9; 3:22; Prov. 3:18) in that it yields benefits to the bodies and souls of others that are salutary and life-giving. Chief among these fruits is soul-winning. He who is wise **winneth** (*lqḥ,* "takes") **souls,** like a fisherman catches fish, that he may bring these converts to God and heaven (Luke 5:10; cf. Prov. 14:25; Dan. 12:3; 1 Cor. 9:19-22; James 5:20). **31. Behold, the righteous shall be recompensed** (rewarded) **in the earth** (2 Sam. 22:21, 25; Prov. 13:21). How **much more** will **the wicked and the sinner** get their just deserts and be punished in this life (as well as the life to come).

C. Right and Wrong Conduct in Contrast (cont.). 12:1-28.

Appreciating Discipline. 12:1. **1.** Whoever **loveth instruction** (*mûsăr,* "discipline") **loveth knowledge. But he that hateth reproof is stupid** (*bă'ăr,* "beastlike, unreasoning"; 3:11-12; Heb. 12:6). He is like an animal that does not look beyond momentary pain or pleasure, like a wounded dog that bites the hand that would offer help and healing. The believer loves disciplinary chastening, not for itself but because of its effect in making him a partaker of divine holiness (Heb. 12:10-11).

Recognizing Rigid Divine-Moral Distinctions. 12:2-3. **2.** A good man **obtaineth favor** from the LORD (3:4; 8:35). But He will **condemn** (declare and hold guilty) the **man of wicked devices** (schemes). **3.** So under the divine government of the universe a wicked man may flourish for a time, but the God of moral law and order will not allow him to be permanently established by wickedness, not in this life, and certainly not in the life to come (11:5). **But the root of the righteous,** being grounded by faith in divine redemptive grace, **shall not be moved,** because it is firmly anchored in the immovable and unchangeable One. They are "trees of righteousness" (Isa. 61:3), "rooted" in the LORD (Isa. 27:6; Jer. 17:8).

The Virtuous Wife. 12:4. **4.** A **virtuous woman is a crown to her husband** (31:23; 1 Cor. 11:7) and, as such, his chief ornament. But a wife who shames him is like rot in his bones, a disease hard to cure, affecting the inmost vital powers of mind and body, a fitting figure of the plague of sin working in the private sanctum of the home, but affecting the whole life of the husband, public as well as private.

The Effects of Thoughts and Words. 12:5-8. **5. The thoughts of the righteous** (those justified by faith in God's grace; Gen. 15:6) **are right** (lit., "judgment," i.e., in accord with "justice"), because they are basically and properly oriented in relation to God, themselves, and the sin question. In contrast, **the counsels** (*tăhbŭlôt*, "cunning plans") **of the wicked** to steer their lives apart from God **are deceit** (i.e., "are deceptive").

6. Their **words** (the product of their bloodthirsty minds) lie in wait for blood

(Prov. 1:11, 18). **But the mouth of the upright shall deliver them** from the murderous plans of the wicked (11:9), and their wise replies from the words of the wicked aimed at ensnaring them, as in the case of Jesus (Luke 11:53-54; 20:1-40).

7. The wicked are overthrown, and are not (nothing is left of them; Prov. 10:25). **But the house of the righteous shall stand** because it is built upon the rock of faith in God (Matt. 7:24-27). **8. A man shall be commended** (praised, well spoken of) **according to his wisdom** (*sĕkĕl,* "insight, intelligence, prudence"), but one of **perverse heart** (twisted mind, i.e., "the muddle-headed," AB) will be **despised.**

Foolishness of Putting on Airs. 12:9. **9.** He who is **despised** (who has a commendable humble estimation of himself, manifested by absence of worldly display) **and hath a servant** (and so has some means of livelihood) **is better than he that honoreth himself** (puts on airs of self-importance) **and lacketh bread** (is starving).

The Wickedness of Heartless Cruelty. 12:10. **10.** The **righteous** (regenerated) man has regard for (*yd',* "knows, understands") the **life** (needs) **of his beast** (livestock), but even the **tender mercies of the wicked are cruel** (Deut. 25:4).

The Plea for Sensible Industry. 12:11. **11.** The man who **tilleth his land** (Gen. 3:19) **shall be satisfied with** food (have plenty to eat). But he who pursues vain things (chases rainbows) **is void** (devoid) **of understanding** (i.e., lacks common sense).

The Perils of Evil Desires and Words. 12:12-14. **12. The wicked desireth the net** (booty) **of evil men** (21:10). **But the root of the righteous yieldeth fruit** (11:30). The wicked always wants what belongs to somebody else, while the righteous man earns his own living.

13. The snare the wicked falls into is **the transgression of his lips,** thinking to harm others by the breaking of God's laws with his tongue by lying, slandering, and false witness. But God's retributive justice orders his own undoing by the very sins with which he tried to ruin others. But the righteous **shall come out of such trouble** if he has inadvertently been ensnared through infirmity.

14. A man shall be satisfied with good by the fruit of his mouth (13:2; 15:23; 18:20), reaping the most blessing from the kindly words that proceed from his lips. **And the recompense** (*gᵉmûl,* "desert, benefit, deed") **of a man's hands shall be rendered** to him, that is, he will be paid according to what he has done and deserves (Isa. 3:10; Matt. 10:41-42; 2 Thess. 1:6).

The Way of a Fool. 12:15-16. **15.** The **fool** is self-deceived (3:7; Isa. 5:21; Luke 18:11), and in his cocksureness listens to no one. But the **wise** person **hearkeneth unto** (listens to) **counsel,** for he realizes none is exempt from the need of good counsel, especially from the great Counselor par excellence (Isa. 9:6), the Messiah, who is made unto us "wisdom" (1 Cor. 1:30), to whom all who are discerning hearken (Prov. 1:33).

16. A fool's wrath (*kă'ăs,* "anger, vexation, annoyance") is soon known (14:33; 27:3; 29:11, being short-tempered and quick to show annoyance and plunge into a shameful display of anger. **But a prudent man covereth** (conceals) **shame**—the dishonor or insult put upon by others. He "covers" it with the mantle of loving patience instead of losing his head like "a fool."

The Wisdom of Speaking Truth. 12:17-22. **17.** He who speaks truth **showeth forth** (manifests) **righteousness,**

attests his justifying faith by his works (James 2:14-26) in telling what is right. **But a false witness** speaks **deceit** (he tells what is wrong or untruthful). **18.** There is one who **speaketh like the piercings of a sword;** it is the tongue of the fool (cf. Meri-ka-re of Egypt, c. 2100 B.C.) "the tongue is a sword" (ANET, p. 415*a*). **But the tongue of the wise is health** (Prov. 4:22; 15:4), not only healthy but also ministering healing.

19. The lips of truth shall be established forever, for words of truth have the quality of permanence (Zech. 1:5-6; Matt. 24:35). **But a lying tongue is but for a moment** (Psalm 52:4-5; Prov. 19:9). **20. Deceit ... in the heart** is the reason people **imagine** (*hrsh,* "devise, forge") **evil,** in the sense of "strife," the opposite of **peace** that produces **joy,** ministered by **counselors** of peace, who not only possess peace but also promulgate it.

21. No evil shall **happen to** (befall) **the just** (righteous) because they are in God's hands and, whatever befalls them, God will work out for good (Rom. 8:28; 1 Cor. 3:21-23; 2 Cor. 4:17; 2 Thess. 1:6; 1 Pet. 3:12-13; 2 Pet. 2:9). **But the wicked shall be filled with mischief** (trouble, have their hands full of woe). **22. Lying lips are an abomination** (utter detestation) to the LORD (Psalm 5:6; Isa. 9:15; Rev. 22:15). **But they that deal truly** (act honestly in integrity) not only speak truth, but live it out, and **are his delight.**

Warning Against Showing off Knowledge. 12:23. **23. A prudent man concealeth knowledge** (10:14; 11:13; 13:16; 15:2; 29:11). He keeps quiet about what he knows. **But the heart of fools proclaimeth foolishness.** They have no thought but to babble forth their folly.

In Praise of Diligence. 12:24. **24. The hand of the diligent** (*hārûṣîm,* lit., "the sharpened," so "zealous, assiduous") shall bear rule, that is, gain control over others in order to be a leader instead of one led. But the slothful (lit., "sloth, remissness") shall be put to forced labor (*măs*), shall be under tribute (the corvée). In other words, "the lackadaisical must be forced to work" (R. B. Y. Scott, *Proverbs,* AB, p. 90).

Against Anxiety. 12:25. 25. Heaviness (*de'āgâ,* "apprehension, uneasiness, anxiety") in the heart (the mind) maketh it stoop (*hēshāh,* "depress, make low, weigh down"). Anxiety and stress in the mind weighs a person down. But a good (encouraging) word will make him glad (happy; 25:11; Isa. 50:4).

Concerning Guidance. 12:26. 26. The righteous is more excellent (MT, *yāthēr,* "more richly abundant") than his neighbor. "The righteous is a guide to his neighbor, but the way of the wicked leads them astray" (NASB), because they have no certain guide or no true way to go. Their pathway is that of the wrongdoer and cannot fail to lead them in the wrong direction.

Concerning Sloth. 12:27. 27. The slothful (lit., "slackness, shiftlessness") will not "catch his prey" (RSV; cf. Gr., Syriac), the Masoretic text reading "does not roast its prey" (*hārăk,* "roast"). however, occurring only in this sense in Aramaic (Dan. 3:24), and so the reading is uncertain. "But the precious possession of a man is diligence" (NASB; Prov. 10:4; 13:4; cf. also v. 24 in praise of diligence).

Concerning Life. 12:28. 28. In the way (pathway) of righteousness, the righteousness God reckons or imputes to the man who reposes faith in His justifying grace (Gen. 15:6), is life (eternal) and fullness of spiritual life, as faith translates that life into a righteous life here and now (Deut. 30:15; 32:47; Jer. 21:8; Ezek. 18:9; Rom. 5:21; 6:22-23; 2 Cor. 4:17). And in its pathway (the

pathway of righteousness) is no death, either spiritual or eternal (John 3:16; 10:10).

D. RIGHT AND WRONG CONDUCT IN CONTRAST (CONT.). 13:1-25.

A Wise Son and Paternal Discipline. 13:1. 1. A wise son heareth (accepts, gladly submits to; the verb being absent in the Hebrew) his father's instruction (*mûsăr,* "disciplinary instruction accompanied by suitable chastisement"; 10:1; 15:20). Eli is an example of a father who failed to administer such discipline, with disastrous results (1 Sam. 2:22-25). But a scoffer (a scoffing, insolent son) heareth not (does not listen to) rebuke (reprimand, reproof; Prov. 9:7-8; 15:12).

The Importance of What One Says. 13:2-3. 2. A man shall eat good in the sense of enjoying bountifully the fruit of his mouth, reaping the result of the good words he speaks (12:14). He receives the good his words deserve. But the soul of the transgressors (treacherous)— their inmost appetite and desire in contrast to the mouth of the good man who feeds on good—is only for violence and crime (1:31; Hos. 10:13).

3. He that keepeth (guards) his mouth (is careful of what he says) keepeth (*shmr,* "preserves") his life by maintaining a vibrant spiritual life (Prov. 18:21; 21:23; James 3:2). But he that openeth wide (*pśq*) his lips (is loquacious) shall have destruction (*mehittâ,* "ruin, crushing, downfall"), that is, "shall come to ruin" (cf. Prov. 10:19; 12:23).

The Frustration of Laziness. 13:4. 4. The soul (the inner being and desire) of the sluggard (*'āşēl,* "the indolent, idle") desireth (*'āwâ,* "eagerly, craves strongly"), that is, he craves (food), literally, "and nothing!" or, "and [gets] none." But the soul of the diligent (industrious, ambitious) **shall be made fat,** be well supplied, in the sense of being amply fed (11:25).

The Sin of Lying. 13:5. **5. A righteous man** (a regenerated man who manifests his spiritual renovation in a new life) **hateth lying** (utterly detests falsehood, deceit, or fraud in any of its forms). But the spiritually unrenewed man, who breaks God's moral laws by breaking the commandment aganst lying (Exod. 20:16), **is loathsome** (lit., "causes a stench") and **cometh to shame** (lit., "causes dishonor and disgrace").

The Security of a Righteous Life. 13:6. **6. Righteousness,** which is the outworking of faith in God's justifying grace to save, **keepeth** (guards) just as a watchman keeps the city gates to prevent the enemy from entering (Psalm 141:3), the **upright in the way** of God's will and Word (Prov. 11:3). **But wickedness** (the outworking of the old, unregenerate nature) **overthroweth** (subverts, destroys) **the sinner** (lit., "sin," stressing sin as the very element of the sinner, to which he is bound as a slave, Rom. 6:23).

The Wealth of Liberality. 13:7. **7.** There is the poor-rich man. **He maketh himself rich** (cf. 11:24, "He ... withholdeth more than is fitting, but it tendeth to poverty"). He hoards his wealth and does not use it for the glory of God and the good of man. His increase is the increase of poverty. He is poor because he is not rich toward God. There is the rich-poor man who makes himself poor by spending for God's glory and mankind's good. His decrease is the increase of real wealth. He is rich in the things of true and abiding wealth (cf. Luke 12:21; 21:4; 1 Tim. 6:18; James 2:5; Rev. 2:9). The interpretation that translates this, "pretends to be rich ... poor" (RSV; NASB, following many commentators)

seems to miss the valuable lesson of the proverb.

The Advantages of Wealth and Poverty. 13:8. **8.** Wealth has the advantage of being a **ransom** for the rich man's life, if it is threatened by kidnappers or other criminals (10:15; 18:11). **But the poor** man never hears **rebuke** ($g^{e^c}\bar{a}r\hat{a}$, "threatening"); such threatening against his life for money is never made. The rich have the advantage of delivering themselves from danger by their wealth. But the poor have the advantage of being free from the danger itself.

The Beneficent Influence of the Righteous. 13:9. **9.** The testimony of the righteous for good is compared to **light** that **rejoiceth,** that is, shines brightly (4:18; Job 29:3; Matt. 5:16; Eph. 5:8; 2 Pet. 1:19). "God is light" (1 John 1:5), and His manifestation through His regenerated children is a reflected glow that advertises His glory. **But the lamp** (candle) **of the wicked,** the faint glimmer of prosperity they enjoy now, shall soon be put out, in contrast to the righteous, who shine permanently (Job 18:5; 21:17; Dan. 12:3; Matt. 13:43).

The Evil of Pride. 13:10. **10. Pride** ($z\bar{a}\underline{d}\bar{o}n$) generates nothing but **contention** (strife). The proud do not have the wisdom to take advice to avoid a clash or to confess they are in the wrong to end a quarrel. **But with the well-advised,** those who are humble enough to take advice or yield to the superior opinion of another, **is wisdom** (James 3:17).

The Curse of Ill-Gotten Gain. 13:11. **11. Wealth** obtained **by vanity** ($h\check{e}\underline{b}\check{e}l$, "emptiness," answering to "a slack, deceitful hand"; 10:4) **shall be diminished** (will dwindle). **But he that gathereth by labor** (lit., "with the hand"), who works for it, increases it. A free-enterprise system, with honest toil rewarded, is the economic system condoned, not a socialistic system of free handouts for people who are able but unwilling to work.

The Blessing of Hope Realized. 13:12. **12. Hope deferred** (drawn out) makes one sick at heart, but when **the desire** is realized, **it is a tree of life.** Wisdom teaches us to place our hopes in eternal realities (Col. 3:1-4); and though we wait long, when the desire becomes a glorious reality it will yield eternal life and rewards as a veritable "tree of life" (Gen. 2:9; 3:24; Hab. 2:3; Heb. 10:37; Rev. 2:7).

Reverence for the Word of God. 13:13. **13.** He who **despiseth the word shall be destroyed** (Num. 15:31; 2 Chron. 36:16). But he who **feareth the commandment** and obeys as a result, **shall be rewarded** (v. 21).

Value of Teaching Wisdom. 13:14. **14. The law** (*tôrâ,* "teaching") **of the wise** (the sage) **is a fountain of life**—the source of faith that makes us wise "unto salvation" (2 Tim. 3:15) to receive life and the fountainhead of all instruction to be followed in order to enjoy fullness of life and **to depart** (turn away from) **the snares of death** (deadly traps) that beset us on every hand in our pilgrimage to heaven (2 Sam. 22:6; Psalms 18:5; 116:3).

The Way to Favor. 13:15. **15. Good understanding** (good sense) produces **favor** (*ḥēn,* "loveliness, charm, grace") before God as well as before men. **But the way** (the pathway of life) chosen by **transgressors** (*bōg̱eḏîm,* "those who deal deceitfully and treacherously") **is hard** (rugged, rough, as soil unfit to be tilled; Deut. 21:4) and yields no fruit of favor with God or men.

The Prudent Man and Knowledge. 13:16. **16.** The **prudent** (clever) **man** (12:23) **dealeth** (acts) **with knowledge. But a fool layeth open** (spreads out) **his folly** in full view of everybody, display-

ing it abroad as something desirable to be proud of.

A Wicked Emissary. 13:17. **17. A wicked** (unprincipled) **messenger falleth into mischief** (*rā',* "evil, misfortune, adversity, trouble"). **But a faithful ambassador** (envoy) **is health** ("brings healing," NASB), instead of the political sickness and trouble the other causes.

The Necessity of Cultivating Discipline. 13:18. **18. Poverty and shame shall be** (will come) **to him that refuseth** (*pr',* "rejects, ignores, neglects") **instruction** (*mûsār,* "disciplinary instruction, correction"). **But he that regardeth reproof shall be honored,** both in this life and surely in that to come.

The Satisfaction of Achieving a Goal. 13:19. **19. Desire accomplished** (realized) **is sweet to the soul** (to oneself; cf. v. 12). But fools never attain high goals, for not only are they unwilling to depart from evil, which is a necessary prelude to such attainment, but such a course of action is an **abomination** to them—something they detest and loathe thoroughly.

The Need of Watching the Company We Keep. 13:20. **20.** He who **walketh with** (hobnobs, associates with) **wise men shall be wise** (2:20; 15:31). **But a companion of fools** (28:19) shall become like them and **shall be destroyed** (lit., "shall be broken"; "will suffer harm," NASB).

The Advantages of Being Righteous. 13:21. **21. Evil pursueth sinners** (Gen. 4:7; Num. 32:23; Psalms 32:10; 140:11), "disaster dogs their steps" (AB). **But, to the righteous** (those justified by faith in God's grace and who follow the obedience of faith in keeping His Word), **good shall be repaid.** "They will be rewarded with [*ṭôḇ*] that which is good" (cf. 34:10; 84:11).

The Prosperity of the Good Man. 13:22. **22. A good man leaveth an inherit-**

ance to his children's children (Psalm 37:25; Ezra 9:12). However, the material **wealth of the sinner is laid up** (stored up) by God's intervention **for the just** (Job 27:16; Eccles. 2:26).

The Cruelty of Injustice. 13:23. **23. Much food is in the fallow ground of the poor** (the newly cultivated land they have prepared for sowing crops; 12:11). But it is **destroyed** (swept away) **for lack of justice,** that is, "it is swept away by the injustice" of the unscrupulous rich.

The Necessity of Paternal Discipline. 13:24. **24.** The father who **spareth his rod** (will not punish his son) **hateth his son** (i.e., shows no love for him; 19:18; 22:15; 23:13-14; 29:15, 17). **But he that loveth him chasteneth** (disciplines) **him early** (diligently), as soon as the corruption of the old nature begins to crop out (Deut. 8:5; Prov. 3:12; Heb. 12:7).

The Self-Control of the Righteous. 13:25. **25.** He **eateth to the satisfying of his soul,** "has enough to satisfy his appetite" (RSV), and he is content with God's blessing and kind providence, assured that God will provide for him what is for his true good (10:3; Psalms 34:10; 103:5; 132:15). **But the belly of the wicked shall want.** They are never satisfied, because they live purely in the thraldom of the old nature and its gluttonous lusts. Also, the LORD will punish them by giving them up to their insatiable lust without the means of gratifying it (Rom. 1:24, 26).

E. RIGHT AND WRONG CONDUCT IN CONTRAST (CONT.). 14:1-35.

The Wise Woman and Her House. 14:1. **1. Every wise woman** (lit., "the wisdom of women") **buildeth her house, but the foolish** (lit., "folly") **plucketh** (pulls) **it down.** Actually, "wisdom" and "folly" are personified. Wisdom builds her house; folly pulls it down.

Wisdom adorns it and makes it a haven of happiness (Ruth 4:11). Folly makes it a shambles (Prov. 24:3-4; 31:10).

Fear of the Lord. 14:2. **2.** He who walks **in his uprightness** (integrity) **feareth** (reverences) the LORD. He holds Him in highest esteem and honor and demonstrates it in his life by keeping His Word. But he who is **perverse in his ways** (his everyday conduct) gives incontrovertible evidence that he **despiseth** Him (1 Sam. 2:30; 2 Sam. 12:9-10; Mal. 1:6-7).

Pride and Foolish Talk. 14:3. **3. In the mouth of the foolish is a rod of pride** (his tongue with which he lashes and assails others). But it boomerangs, so that it strikes back at him and does him untold injury. By contrast, **the lips of the wise shall preserve them** from the woes to which proud talk exposes fools (Job 12:4; Psalm 123:3-4; Prov. 12:6; Luke 16:14).

Recognition of Debt to Even Brute Beasts. 14:4. **4. Where no oxen are, the crib** (manger) **is clean** (*bār,* "empty, bare"). Without the labor of oxen, whose strength makes possible the cultivation of the soil, there is no food. **But much increase** (abundant crops) is the result of **the strength of the ox.**

The Crime of Perjury. 14:5. **5. A faithful witness** (lit., "a witness of fidelity, trustworthiness") **will not lie** (Rev. 1:5; 3:14). **But a false witness** (lit., "a witness of deceit," *shĕqĕr*) **will utter lies** (lit., "breathe or pour out falsehoods"; Exod. 23:1; Deut. 19:16; Prov. 6:19; 12:17; 19:5).

The Scorner and Knowledge. 14:6. **6.** He **seeketh wisdom** but does not find it. **But knowledge is easy** (an easy thing) to him who **understandeth** (has understanding and is perceptive). The scoffer does not discover knowledge because, in contrast to the man who does, he does not seek it seriously with a view of obeying God (cf. John 7:17), but merely to get God's sanction on his own carnal desires (Jer. 42:1-20; Ezek. 20:1-4). Nor does he seek it at the right time, when things are going smoothly, but only in times of danger; nor is it sought in the right spirit, but with pride and confidence.

How to Treat a Fool. 14:7-9. **7. Go from** (leave) **the presence of a foolish man** (23:9). Separate from him or you will be contaminated by his folly, "you will not discern words [lips] of knowledge" (NASB), you will lose the ability to distinguish between wisdom and folly. "For you will not discern words of knowledge there" (BV) in the fool's company.

8. The wisdom of the prudent is to understand his way (to have a goal in life and know where he is going). But since his way is God's way, it is not being "unwise but understanding what the will of the Lord is" (Eph. 5:17). The fool's **deceit** (opposed to the wise man's honest and sincere understanding) practiced on others is really self-deception, which blinds him to order his conduct or his life aright to achieve any intelligent goal or arrive at any rational destination.

9. Fools make a mock of sin (*'āshām,* "sin in the aspect of guilt"; 2:14; 10:23; Isa. 3:9). They laugh at the idea of sin, the sense of guilt and punishment. The Hebrew may be also rendered: "Sin [when it incurs guilt and punishment] mocks fools," even as they mock at sin. **But among the righteous,** those declared righteous before God by faith in God's grace (Gen. 15:6) and therefore *upright* in their conduct, inasmuch as they do not mock at sin, there is **favor** (*rāṣôn,* "acceptance, delight") with God, the sin barrier having been removed (Prov 3:34; 11:20) and goodwill manifested among men of kindred spirit.

The Individuality of the Soul. 14:10. **10. The heart knoweth its own bitterness** (*mārâ,* "grief, sorrow"), literally, "the bitterness of its own soul" (1 Sam. 1:10; Job. 21:25). **And a stranger** (*zār,* "an alien, foreigner") does not **intermeddle** (intermingle, share) its joy. No one can enter so fully into our sorrow or happiness as ourselves (1 Cor. 2:11). Each soul is a distinct individuality in its innermost being, and so no one except our Creator-Savior Himself, who made each one of us, can know our hearts and enter into our varied experiences.

The Permanency of the Upright. 14:11. **11. The house of the wicked**— built to last, and though in his opinion destined to "continue forever" (Psalm 49:11)—**shall be overthrown** (destroyed; Job 8:15; 15:34; Prov. 3:33; 12:7; 21:12). In contrast, the mere **tabernacle** (tent) of the upright, though meant to be set up today and taken down and moved on tomorrow, **shall flourish** (prosper), because it houses God's pilgrims, upon whom His blessing rests.

The Wrong Road That Seems Right. 14:12. **12. There is a way** (road) **which seemeth right unto a man** (12:15; 16:25; Matt. 7:13), **but the end thereof** (its termination) **are the ways** (road) **of death** (Rom. 6:21). The way that seems right to the natural man is the supposed road to heaven by human goodness, human merit, and good works, instead of by faith alone in the grace of God according to the one true gospel (John 3:16; Eph. 2:8-9). The end of that road is eternal death. In the general sense, any seeming "right way" in any undertaking must be rigidly searched in the light of God's Word to be sure that our good intentions do not become a justification for wrongdoing (2 Sam. 6:6-7), which will lead to spiritual catastrophe (Judg. 17:6-13).

The Emptiness of Mere Natural Joy. 14:13. **13. Even in laughter the heart is** sorrowful (*k'b*, "to be grieved" with penetrating sorrow), **and the end of that mirth** (joy) **is heaviness** (grief; Eccles. 2:1-2; 7:6). Worldly joys are neither solid nor permanent, and their insubstantial nature teaches us to seek the joys that only God can give (Phil. 4:4).

The Satisfaction of a Godly Life. 14:14. **14. The backslider** (*sûg*, "one going back, drawing back") **in heart** (Psalm 44:18), who knowingly and deliberately backslides from a godly life, **shall be filled** (*śb'*, "sated, filled to the full") **with his own ways** until he becomes so nauseated with them (cf. Num. 11:19-20; Prov. 1:31; 12:21) that he is ready to vomit (cf. Rev. 3:16). **And** (but) **a good man,** a godly man who walks in his God-reckoned and faith-bestowed righteousness (Gen. 15:6), shall be satisfied **from himself,** that is, "from that which is in himself" (God Himself, who satisfies him as his unfailing Source of joy).

The Danger of Incredulousness. 14:15. **15. The simple** (naive, credulous) **believeth every word,** everything he hears. **But the prudent man** (*'ārûm*, "smart, clever") **looketh well** (carefully considers) **his going** (his steps)—"the sharp-witted looks where he is going" (AB).

The Wise Man and Evil. 14:16-17. **16.** A wise man **feareth** (holds God in awe and reverences His Word) and so **departeth from evil** (3:7; 22:3; Job. 28:28; Psalm 34:14). **But the fool** (simpleton) **rageth** (*mit'abbēr*, "flies into a passion"), **and is confident** (*bth*, "trusts") in himself, not God. **17.** As one **soon angry** (quick-tempered), he **dealeth** (acts) foolishly and **is hated** as **a man of wicked devices** (schemes).

The Naive and the Prudent. 14:18-19. **18-19. The simple** (simpletons, the fatuous) **inherit folly,** automatically come into possession of foolhardiness and im-

prudence (cf. v. 15), while **the prudent are crowned with knowledge,** their chief ornament giving them a kingly status as leaders; so **the evil bow before the good; and the wicked, at the gates of the righteous.**

The Sin of Hating and Being Merciless to the Poor. 14:20-21. **20. The poor,** because of his poverty and helplessness, is hated even by his own **neighbor** (Job 19:13-14). **But the rich,** because he is rich and influential, and can help in many ways, **hath many friends** (lit., "many are the lovers," i.e., fair-weather lovers, "of the rich").

21. But he who **despiseth his neighbor sinneth** (cf. v. 20*a*). He sins grievously and the fact that he looks down on his neighbor, and despises him for his poverty, aggravates the sin he commits. Rather, he is to have **mercy on the poor.** But how can he, if he hates and despises him? In acting as he does, he forfeits happiness (Psalms 41:1; 112:5, 9; Eccles. 11:1-2; Isa. 58:7; Dan. 4:27; Luke 6:20).

Against the Wicked Schemers. 14:22. **22. Do they not err** (go astray; fall into error and deeper sin) **that devise** (invent, imagine) **evil?** As **mercy and truth** become the portion of those who **devise good,** so the opposite judgment and falsehood become the recompense of those who devise evil (3:29; 12:2; Psalm 36:4; Mic. 2:1).

The Profitableness of Industry. 14:23. **23. In all labor** (toil) **there is profit; but the talk of the lips** (mere words and promises without work) leads **only to penury** (poverty).

The True Wealth of the Wise. 14:24. **24.** Wisdom (the opposite of "folly") is **the crown of the wise** (v. 18; 4:9) and constitutes their true **riches,** both earthly and heavenly. But wisdom is the result of "the blessing of the LORD ... maketh rich" (10:22); so the true wealth of the wise is the blessing of the LORD upon them, making them wise. **But the foolishness of fools** is not wealth to them, but direst poverty, for it continues to be ever impoverishing folly.

The Valuable Ministry of a True Witness. 14:25. **25. A true witness** is he who tells the truth and is literally "a witness of truth" (*'ēḏ 'ĕmĕt,* "a testifier who has personal knowledge and experience of a matter," particularly of God's saving grace and favor). Such a witness is an instrument in God's hands and **delivereth** (saves, rescues) **souls** from physical death as well as spiritual and eternal death, and saves innocent souls who are falsely accused before judges. But a **deceitful witness speaketh** (lit., "breathes forth") **lies** in order to destroy innocent souls.

The Blessings of Fearing the Lord. 14:26-27. **26-27.** Reverencing God and His Word (1) imparts **strong confidence** (confident strength; 18:10; 19:23; Isa. 33:6); (2) gives His children **a place of refuge** (Psalm 73:15); (3) becomes a **fountain of life** issuing in spiritual life in its fullness, and eternal life in its fruition (Prov. 13:14; Rev. 21:6); and (4) helps one to avoid **the snares of death,** traps that ensnare the believer and keep him from fullness of spiritual life and catch him in "the sin unto [physical] death" (1 John 5:16; cf. 1 Cor. 11:30-32), cutting short his earthly life.

The Majesty of a King. 14:28. **28. In the multitude of people is the king's honor.** A monarch's majesty derives from a populous nation. **But in the lack of people is the destruction** (ruin) **of the prince.** Without his people, a prince is nothing.

The Folly of a Hot Temper. 14:29. **29.** A man **slow to wrath,** not easily angered, **is of great understanding** (Prov. 16:32; 19:11; Eccles. 7:9). **But he that is hasty of spirit** (lit., "short of spirit"; i.e.,

quick-tempered) **exalteth folly**—shows what a fool he is (Prov. 15:18; 16:32; James 1:19-20).

The Benefit of Mental Health. 14:30. **30. A sound heart** (a tranquil mind) **is the life of the flesh** (the physical body), meaning that "bodily health comes with a tranquil mind" (AB). **But envy** (passion, passionate feelings, anger) **"is"** (metaphor) "like" (simile) **the rottenness of the bones** (Job 5:2; Psalm 112:10; Acts 7:9; Rom. 1:29; James 4:5), "as rottenness in his bones" (Prov. 12:4; Hab. 3:16).

Oppression of the Poor. 14:31. **31. He that oppresseth** (maltreats, cheats) **the poor** (man; Job 31:15-16; 1 John 3:17) **reproacheth** (*ḥērēp,* "insults, despises") **his Maker** (Creator), who made the poor as well as the rich (1 Sam. 2:7; Prov. 22:2). Such an oppressor assumes that either God cannot or will not vindicate the weak and needy. **But he that honoreth him** (God) **hath mercy on** (is gracious to) **the poor** (needy).

The Hope of the Righteous. 14:32. **32. The wicked is driven away** (thrust or knocked down) **in his wickedness** (by his wrongdoing) when the penalty of his evildoing catches up with him. He lives a hopeless, insubstantial existence (Psalm 1:4). **But the righteous** (the regenerate; Gen. 15:6) **hath hope in his death**—the firm hope of eternal life (Job 19:26; Psalm 23:4, 6; 37:37; Titus 1:2)—and in life when deathlike distresses fall upon him.

Wisdom's Resting Place. 14:33. **33. The heart** (the mind, the mental faculties) **of him that hath understanding** (*nāḇôn,* "who is discerningly prudent") is the place where wisdom **resteth** (*nûaḥ,* "settles down, dwells"). **But that which is in the midst of fools** (i.e., their folly) **is made known,** which eloquently advertises the fact that wisdom is unknown among them.

Righteousness and National Greatness. 14:34. **34. Righteousness**—God's bestowment by faith in His grace and its outworking by faith in the believer's life—**exalteth a nation, but sin is a reproach** (*ḥĕsĕḏ*, in the rare sense of "disgrace"; Arab., *ḥasada*, "envy"; Aram., *ḥᵃsăḏ*, "be put to shame") to any people (pl., "peoples," i.e., "to nations"). The LXX, Syriac, and Arabic read: "sins diminish peoples" (*ḥĕsĕr*, "want, poverty" for *ḥĕsĕḏ*).

Kingly Favor Toward Servants. 14:35. **35. The king's favor is toward a wise servant, but his wrath is against him that causeth shame** (conducts himself shamefully).

F. Right and Wrong Conduct in Contrast (cont.). 15:1-33.

How to Deal with Anger. 15:1. **1. A soft** (*răq*, "thin"; of a voice, "gentle") **answer** (or "reply" to inflammatory words) **turneth away** (aside) **wrath** (*ḥēmâ*, "heated anger"), **but grievous words** (lit., "words of trouble, grievance") **stir up anger** (*'āp*, "make it ascend," like a flame leaps up when fanned by bellows).

The Blessing of Sound Speech. 15:2-4. **2. The tongue of the wise** (wise men) **useth knowledge aright** (lit., "makes it good"; "commends" it, AB; "makes knowledge acceptable," NASB; puts it in a good light, v. 7). **But the mouth of fools poureth out** (spouts forth) **foolishness** (folly; 12:23; 13:16; 15:28).

3. Sound speech is a necessity because **the eyes of the Lord are in every place** omnipresently (2 Chron. 16:9; Jer. 16:17; Zech. 4:10; Heb. 4:13) and see and know omnisciently the thoughts of the heart before they are framed into words, **beholding** (watching) **the evil and the good,** to punish the one and bless and reward the other.

4. A wholesome (lit., "healing" or "soothing") **tongue** (that is, health-giving words) **is a tree of life,** whose fruit ministers to life and is fullness of life to those who partake of it (Gen. 2:9; Prov. 3:18; 11:30; 13:12; Rev. 22:2, 14). **But perverseness** (perversion) in the tongue (speech) **is a breach in** (the crushing of) **the spirit,** and reveals a disturbed mind.

Submission to Paternal Discipline. 15:5. **5. A fool despiseth** (treats with contempt) **his father's instruction** (*mûsăr*, "disciplinary teaching, correction"). But he who **regardeth** (holds in esteem) **reproof is prudent.** The "father" is representative of monitors of every sort and is basic to all of them.

The Curse of Ill-Gotten Gain. 15:6. **6. In the house of the righteous** (the regenerated man) **is much treasure** (riches, wealth). First and foremost is the imperishable spiritual wealth of the justifying grace of God (Gen. 15:6) and its resultant blessings, but there are also normally and frequently temporal benefits (Prov. 8:21). Even though he may be poor economically, he has that which makes him rich spiritually and able to enrich others (2 Cor. 6:10). **But in the revenues** (income) **of the wicked is trouble,** a harbinger of their inevitable overthrow.

The Speech of the Wise. 15:7. **7. The lips of the wise** (men) **disperse knowledge** ("scatter" it like a sower sowing seed, their every word being good seed of truth and benefit). **But the heart** (mind) **of the foolish doeth not so** (that is, does not, because it cannot produce good seed to be sown by the mouth), because "out of the abundance of the heart the mouth speaketh" (Matt. 12:34-37).

The Abomination of the Worship and Ways of the Wicked. 15:8-9. **8. The sacrifice of the wicked,** no matter how costly or ostentatious, not only is not the LORD's *delight,* as is the upright man's simple prayer (v. 29), but is a positive **abomination,** a detestable insult to the LORD, because it degrades Him to the level of the polluted pagan deities of the nations (21:27; Eccles. 5:1; Isa. 1:11; Jer. 6:20; Mic. 6:6-7).

9. Even the very **way** (road, course of life) **of the wicked,** his everyday behavior, **is an abomination** (intense detestation) **unto the Lord,** because it violates God's moral laws (Exod. 20:1-17) and hence the eternal Being of God, which these laws reflect. In contrast to the LORD's utter detestation of "the way of the wicked," He **loveth** him who **followeth** (pursues diligently) **after righteousness,** that conduct which is in conformity with salvation by grace through faith in showing proper gratitude for it (Prov. 21:21; Isa. 51:1, 7; Hos. 6:3; Rom. 12:1-2; 1 Tim. 6:11).

Necessity of Chastisement. 15:10-12. **10a.** Correction (*mûsăr,* "divine disciplinary dealing") **is grievous** (*rā',* "unpleasant, severe"; Heb. 12:11) **unto him that forsaketh the way,** the right road (cf. Ahab, 1 Kings 18:17-18; 21:20; 22:8) and Jehoiakim (Jer. 36:23). But it is a necessity because of God's infinite holiness and the free gift of His salvation, when a believer turns away from God's will and falls into serious sin. That demands severe chastening (1 Cor. 5:5; 11:30-32; Heb. 12:3-15) by an all-righteous, loving God.

10b. He who **hateth reproof** and refuses to amend his wrong ways, going on in serious sin, invites the "sin unto [physical] death" (1 John 5:16; cf. 1 Cor. 5:5), which King Saul, as an example, finally committed and died prematurely (1 Chron. 10:13-14), God destroying the flesh that the spirit might be saved (1 Cor. 11:32).

11. Such chastisement is also a necessity because God is not only infinitely holy and loving but also omniscient. If

Sheol and destruction (Abaddon, gehenna, eternal perdition, Rev. 20:11-15) **are before the Lord** (Job 26:6; Psalm 139:8), are wide open to Him, **how much more, then, the hearts** of mankind (1 Sam. 16:7; 2 Chron. 6:30; Psalm 44:21; Acts 1:24). Let not those who "forsake the way" (v. 10) think that their secret thoughts, much less their evil ways, can escape divine detection and chastisement. **12.** The **scoffer** in a deeper depth of sin **loveth not** the one **that reproveth** him, and will rebel at God's chastisement. Neither will he go to the wise man for counsel or help for this same reason.

The Boon of Cheerfulnes. 15:13-15. **13. A merry** (joyful) **heart maketh a cheerful countenance**—lights up the face (17:22), **But by sorrow of the heart** (grief of mind) **the spirit is broken** (12:25), the face ceases to wear a sunny expression (17:22; 18:14). **14. The heart** (mind) **of him that hath understanding** (is intelligent) **seeketh knowledge** (18:15), producing, in turn, good mental health and a radiant face. **But the mouth of fools,** feeding on folly, does not produce either mental or physical health and happiness. **15. All the days of the afflicted** (the miserable) **are evil** (bad). But to him who has **a merry** (cheerful) **heart,** every day is good, and life is a **continual feast** (Judg. 14:10; Eccles. 9:7).

The Boon of Love. 15:16-17. **16. Better is little with the fear of the Lord,** reverence for Him and His Word (Psalm 37:16; Prov. 16:8; Eccles. 4:6; 1 Tim. 6:6) **than great treasure,** living in opulence, **and trouble** (turmoil) with it (Prov. 16:8; 17:1). **17. Better is a dinner** ('*ăruḥăṯ,* "portion, dish, serving") **of herbs** (vegetables) **where love is** (17:1), **than a stalled** (fattened) **ox and hatred** with it—"than prime rib [garnished] with hate" (AB).

The Asset of Being Even-Tempered.

15:18. **18. A wrathful** (hot-tempered) **man stirreth up** (incites) **strife** (2 Sam. 20:1; Prov. 10:12; 29:22). **But he who is slow to anger appeaseth strife** (Gen. 13:8-9; Judg. 8:1-3; 1 Sam. 25:24; Eccles. 10:4; Matt. 5:9).

The Curse of Slothfulness. 15:19. **19. The way of the slothful** (lazy, shiftless) **man is like an hedge of thorns.** So it seems to him, and the thorns block him when there is any work to be done, especially when he is urged to enter the pathway of the LORD's commandments (26:13). **But the way of the righteous** (the regenerate man; Gen. 15:6) **is made plain** (lit., is "raised up" as a causeway, a highway, above all difficulties and impediments).

Filial Duty to Parents. 15:20. **20. A wise son maketh a glad father,** "makes his father happy," since he honors him (Exod. 20:12; Prov. 10:1; 29:3). **But a foolish man** (*'ādām*) **despiseth** (*bûz,* "treats with contempt") **his mother** and so makes her sad, even as a wise son makes his father glad (cf. 10:1). No age is exempt from children either honoring or dishonoring their parents.

The Upright Life of the Prudent. 15:21, **21. Folly is joy,** a sort of fiendish fun, to him who is **destitute of wisdom,** literally, lacking in heart (mind, mentality), deficient in common sense. **But a man of understanding** (intelligence) **walketh uprightly,** forges straight ahead on the right road of duty to God and man (14:8; Eph. 5:15).

The Wisdom of Adequate Counsel. 15:22. **22. Without counsel** (proper consultation) **purposes are disappointed** (plans miscarry). **But in the multitude of** (with many) **counselors they are established** (succeed), inculcating the truth: "that in the advice of many lies success" (AB).

The Delight of a Timely Word. 15:23. **23. A man hath joy by the answer of his mouth** (in apt reply). **And a word spoken in due season** (at the right moment) **how good!** An apt answer always gives pleasure, and it is always a word at the right time for the occasion.

The Upward Path. 15:24. **24. The way** (path) **of life is above** (upward) **to** (for) **the wise** (*măśkîl,* "the discerning," who know and avoid the paths and precipices of sin that lead downward; Psalms 16:11; 139:24; Jer. 21:8; Phil. 3:20), **that he** by his upward course **may depart from sheol beneath** on an ascending road that takes him farther and farther from the netherworld.

Punishment of Oppressors. 15:25. **25. The Lord will destroy the house** of these **proud** (arrogant) oppressors of the defenseless **widow,** representing the orphan, the poor, and the helpless in general. The proud had driven the widow from the border of her property, although the moving of the landmark was especially forbidden (Deut. 19:14). But the seemingly strong "house" of the proud oppressor will be brought down in ruin, while the LORD will protect not only the house, but the widow's property boundary.

The Words of the Virtuous. 15:26. **26. The thoughts** (plans) **of the wicked are an abomination** (utter abhorrence) **to the Lord,** because they are against His Word and commandments, and thus dishonor and blaspheme the One whom His commandments reflect. **But pleasant words** (i.e., of the righteous) **are pure** (NASB; lit. Heb.), because they are in accord with the Word and will of God and spring out of pure thoughts and plans.

The Bane of Illicit Profiting. 15:27. **27.** He who is **greedy for gain,** that is, the covetous profiteer, **troubleth his own house** (Josh. 6:18; 1 Sam. 8:3, 5; Prov. 1:19; Isa. 5:8; Zech. 5:3-4). **But he that hateth bribes shall live** (in peace), free from the trouble the unscrupulous profiteer brings upon his household.

The Value of a Wise Answer. 15:28. **28. The heart** (the mind) **of the righteous** (*ṣăddîq,* "the justified believer") **studieth** (ponders, meditates) ... **to answer** (i.e., what to reply; 1 Pet. 3:15). **But the mouth of the wicked poureth out evil things,** whatever may "bubble forth" (*nḇᶜ*) from the polluted fountain of his heart.

The Blessing of Answered Prayer. 15:29. **29. The Lord is far from the wicked** (1:28; Psalm 18:41; Eph. 2:12) because the wicked in their unbelief and fallen state as unregenerate sinners are far from Him as the infinitely Holy One, their cultivated wickedness putting even a greater distance between God and them. **But he heareth the prayer of the righteous,** because He is near them as justified sinners (Gen. 15:6; Psalm 51:1-5), and He hears their petition since it is based upon faith in His saving grace revealed in His Word (34:15-16; John 9:31; Rom. 8:26; 1 Pet. 3:12).

The Gladdening Effect of a Bright Countenance. 15:30. **30. The light of the eyes** (of someone of importance or a friend; 16:15), especially the "light of [God's] countenance" lifted upon one (Psalms 4:6; 36:9) gladdens **the heart.** And a **good report** (good news) **maketh the bones fat** (puts fat on the bones).

The Wisdom of Welcoming Disciplinary Instruction. 15:31-32. **31. The ear that heareth** (metonymy for "He who listens to") **the reproof of life** (life-giving reproof, correction that leads to fullness of life) **abideth** (dwells, is at home) **among the wise** (wise men). **32.** But he who **refuseth** (neglects) **instruction** (*mûsăr,* "disciplinary, corrective education"; 1:7; 8:33) **despiseth** (lightly esteems, places little value on) **his own soul** (himself as a person; 8:36). But he who **heareth** (listens to) **reproof getteth**

(*qānâ,* "gains") **understanding** not to hold himself cheap (15:5).

The Basis of All Instruction Is Wisdom. 15:33. **33. The fear of the Lord** (reverential awe before Him and His Word) **is the instruction of wisdom** (disciplinary education that is founded upon and begins in wisdom). But **before honor** (the honor of being enrolled in the roster of the wise) **is humility.** One must humble himself to see God as infinitely high and holy, sin as exceedingly sinful and separating from God, and himself as a sinner completely shut up to faith in divine redemptive grace. Then, as he trusts God's grace alone for salvation, he becomes spiritually regenerated to fear (reverence) the LORD and to be enrolled in wisdom's school.

G. RIGHT AND WRONG CONDUCT IN CONTRAST (CONT.). 16:1-33.

Man Proposes, God Disposes. 16:1. The literal Hebrew reads: "The plans are man's, but from the LORD is the tongue's answer" (cf. 19:21, and especially the close parallel of 16:9). Whatever man may intend, that which actually takes place is God's decision (cf. v. 33; 19:21; 21:30-31; Matt. 10:19-20). Compare the *Words of Ahiqar,* an Assyrian sage: "From thee is the arrow but from God the guidance" (*Ahiqar* 9, ANET, p. 429*b*).

God Is the Judge, Not Man. 16:2. **2. All the ways of a man** (all he thinks or does) **are clean** (*zăq,* "pure, innocent, right") **in his own eyes** (in his own estimation, according to his finite, human standards of evaluation, 14:12; 16:25). **But the Lord weigheth the spirits** (1 Sam. 16:7; Dan. 5:27). The LORD alone is the Judge as to whether a man's ways are as clean as the man himself adjudges them (1 Cor. 4:4-5). He alone, as the "God of the spirits of all flesh" (Num. 16:22;

27:16), weighing man in His infinitely accurate balance, can judge the attitudes and intentions. Thus, many of men's ways, which appear right to them, are not so in His holy eyes. The thought of "weighing the heart" is prominent in Egyptian religion, where a man's heart is weighed against truth in the balance of the supreme god, Re (cf. J. B. Pritchard, *The Ancient Near East in Pictures,* p. 210).

The Import of Yieldedness to God. 16:3. **3. Commit thy works** (what *you* plan to do) **unto the Lord** (Psalms 37:5; 55:22), literally, "roll" (*gōl,* "turn over") them, as a burden upon the shoulders of one who is stronger and wiser than you, **and thy thoughts** (plans) **shall be established,** will come to happy fruition instead of mere human frustration.

God's Absolute Sovereignty. 16:4. **4. The Lord hath made** (*pā'ăl,* "created, prepared, done") **all** (everything), **for himself** (1) "for His purpose" or (2) "for its purpose" (RSV), "for its own purpose" (NASB), both translations being possible in the Hebrew. **Even the wicked, for the day of evil** (Job 31:30; Rom. 9:22). He did not create man a sinner, but man in His purpose and by his own choice became a sinner, all of which was in the sovereign decree and eternal plan of the Creator.

The Abomination of Pride. 16:5. **5.** Everyone who is **proud in heart** (*gᵉḇăh lēḇ,* "haughty, arrogant, high-minded, self-exalted in mind") **is an abomination** (utter detestation) **to the Lord,** because such pride has close affinity to idolatry and puts self before the LORD and others. So in germ it breaks the whole gamut of the moral Law (Exod. 20:1-17) and constitutes the first and primal sin (Isa. 14:12-14).

Like Satan, the first to be lifted up by pride, the haughty **shall not be un-**punished (held guiltless; Rev. 20:1-3, 10), **though hand join in hand** (Prov. 11:21), though the wicked join forces to prevent punishment (Psalm 2:1-3; Rev. 16:13-16; 19:19), the career of Satan being the most dramatic illustration of this confederacy of evil to attempt to thwart divine justice.

How Iniquity Is Purged. 16:6. **6. By mercy** (*ḥĕsĕḏ,* "covenant love" based upon atonement and expiation by blood) **and truth** (God's revealed Word concerning His infinite holiness, man's helpless sinfulness and lostness, and sin's exceeding sinfulness, excluding all pride, v. 5; Rom. 3:27, and shutting man up to the gospel of salvation by grace through faith, Gen. 15:6; 1 Cor. 15:2-4; Eph. 2:8-9), **iniquity is purged,** literally, "covered," pretermitted by faith under the Old Testament until the Redeemer could come and make actual reconciliation by His death and resurrection (Rom. 3:25-26). **And by the fear of the Lord** (reverential awe before Him and His Word) **men depart from evil** and stay away from it (Prov. 8:13; 14:16).

The Benefit of Living to Please the Lord. 16:7. **7. When a man's ways** (his conduct) **please the Lord** (Psalm 69:31; 2 Cor. 5:9; Col. 1:10), **he maketh even his enemies to be at peace with him,** insofar as this is consonant with God's highest glory and for our true good. Both Laban and Esau were constrained by the LORD to be at peace with Jacob (Gen. 27:41; 31:24, 29, 44-55; 33:1-4).

Honesty the Best Policy. 16:8. **8. Better is a little with righteousness,** that you have come by honestly, than to have **great revenues** (a large income) **without right** or moral rectitude, but acquired through injustice (Psalm 37:16; Prov. 15:16).

Man's Proposal, God's Disposal. 16:9. **9. A man's heart** (mind) **deviseth** (*yᵉḥăshshēḇ,* "plans by thinking and meditating") **his way,** what he intends to do. But **the Lord,** in contrast to man's anxious and independent devising of his own way, **directeth his steps.** If the man yields his will to God's will, then the result is always happy. If the man persists in self-will and self-direction, the Lord is still sovereign in the disposal of his steps, overruling—despite man's freedom of choice—by His all-ordering providence. Indeed, God has at His control our very thoughts (Exod. 34:24); so the wise course is always to "commit [our] way" to Him (Psalm 37:5, 23) and let Him bring to pass whatever is best.

The Ethics of a King. 16:10-15. Six things were to be true of a king: (1) The king was held to be endowed with a special measure of divine wisdom (8:14-16; Isa. 9:2). **10. A divine sentence** (*qĕsĕm,* "oracular decision") **is in the lips of the king** (cf. 2 Sam. 23:1-2; 1 Kings 3:28). **His mouth** (in pronouncing a verdict) **transgresseth not in judgment,** that is, when he renders judgment (dispenses justice), he does not err.

(2) The king was to be scrupulously honest. **11.** As the Lord's representative, he was to realize **a just weight and balance** (symbolic of business integrity in general), which were the Lord's concern (Prov. 11:1), as were **all the weights of the bag** (Deut. 25:13). (3) The king was to be uncontaminated with wrongdoing of any sort. **12.** Committing wickedness is an **abomination** (see comment on v. 5), because his **throne is established by** (on) **righteousness** (25:5), and it is really God's throne, who is all-righteous, and set up by Him, the human incumbent merely being His representative.

(4) The king was therefore to be righteous himself. **13. Righteous lips** were to be his **delight** and he was to **love** the person who **speaketh right** (uprightly). (5) The wrath of a king was to be re-

spected. **14.** His wrath was to be viewed as possibly being the **messengers of death,** the plural hinting at the varied forms of death at the king's order. The **wise man will pacify** royal wrath, but the fool will only exasperate it.

(6) The king's favor was to be courted. **15.** In the light of his **countenance** was **life** in contrast to "death," which was in his "wrath" (v. 14). In the absolute sense, this is only true of the King of kings (Rev. 19:16), the Sun of Righteousness who is to arise (Psalms 4:6; 44:3; Mal. 4:2). **His favor is like a cloud of the latter rain** (*mālqôsh,* "the spring rain shortly before the grain ripens"; Deut. 11:14; Jer. 5:24), giving hope of harvest.

Supreme Value of Wisdom. 16:16. **16. How much better to ... get** (obtain) **wisdom than gold** (Job 28:12-13; Psalm 119:127; Prov. 3:15, 18; 4:7; Eccles. 7:12; Matt. 16:26; Luke 12:21). **And to get understanding ... rather to be chosen than silver** (Prov. 8:10-11).

The Upright and Evil. 16:17. **17. The highway** (*mesillâ,* "a road raised above all impediments") **of the upright is to depart from evil** (4:24-27; Isa. 35:8; Acts 10:35). The freeway the wise take leads away from iniquity and wrongdoing. He who travels it **keepeth his way** (watches, keeps close watch of every step he makes), and accordingly, **preserveth his soul** (i.e., his life, both his physical life and spiritual health).

The Snare of Pride. 16:18-19. **18. Pride goeth before** (precedes) **destruction** (overthrow, ruin; 11:2; 18:12; Jer. 49:16; Obad. 3-4). **And an haughty spirit** (an arrogant air) **before a fall** (stumbling). **19. Better ... to be of an humble spirit with the lowly** (Prov. 3:34; 29:23; Isa. 57:15) **than to divide the spoil** (share plunder) **with the proud** (Exod. 15:9; Judg. 5:30; Prov. 1:13).

Prudent Acting and Humble Trust-

ing. 16:20. **20. He that handleth a matter** (of business) **wisely shall find good** (virtue, happiness). And whoever **trusteth in the Lord, happy is he.** He must not merely depend on his own acumen, but must also "trust in the LORD" (Psalms 2:12; 34:8) if he is both to "find good" and be "happy." And vice versa, his trust in the LORD must not be coupled with idle shiftlessness, but with prudent dealing. (The LXX and Arabic support the MT and AV. The Vulgate, Syriac, and Aramaic support the NASB: "He who gives attention to the word [the Word of God] shall find good"; cf. Prov. 19:8.)

Sweet Speech and Pleasant Words. 16:21-24. **21. The wise in heart** (mind) **shall be called prudent** (Hos. 14:9), and as a result they will manifest **sweetness of the lips** (speech) and **learning** ("persuasiveness," NASB), for the heart (mind) is the source or fountain from which the words of the lips flow (Matt. 12:34-37).

22. Understanding is thus an inner wellspring of life that affects the speech of the wise, who submit to necessary discipline, which to fools is utter folly. **23-24.** But the **heart** (mind) of the wise **teacheth his mouth** (Psalm 37:30; Prov. 15:28; Matt. 12:34) and adds **learning** ("persuasiveness," NASB) **to his lips** (speech) and produces **pleasant words ... sweet to the soul ... like an honeycomb** (Prov. 15:26; 24:13-14; cf. Psalm 19:10), and **health to the bones** (Prov. 4:22; 17:22).

The Wrong Road That Seems Right. 16:25. **25.** See the comment on 14:12, with which this proverb is identical.

The Goad to Honest Toil. 16:26. **26.** The literal Hebrew translation is: "The soul [appetite] of a worker works for him, for his mouth boweth itself unto him," that is, as a suppliant craving food, his hunger urging him on to work,

which is fallen man's appointed portion (Gen. 3:17-19; Eccles. 6:7).

The Wickedness the Evil Man Perpetrates. 16:27-30. Three things are said about the evil man: (1) **27.** He is **ungodly** ("man of worthlessness, good-for-nothingness," i.e., "a worthless scoundrel") and **diggeth up evil** (6:12, 14, 18), in the sense of "devising" it to hurt others. "And *in* [upon] his lips [there is that which is] like a burning fire [a scorching flame; lit. Heb.]," "his speech is like a searing flame" (BV).

(2) **28.** He is **perverse,** a man of falsehood, who **soweth** (sends forth, broadcasts) **strife,** and **a whisperer** (slanderer) separating (estranging) **chief friends** (*'ăllūp,* "a prince, husband, a leading one among the most trusted and intimate friends").

(3) **29.** He is **a violent man** (man of violence, oppression) who **enticeth his neighbor,** luring him **into the way that is not good,** that is, into a course of evil conduct. **30. He shutteth** (MT; *'ōṣâ,* "winks," RSV, NASB, AB) **his eyes to devise perverse things,** "hatching some villainy" (AB) and **moving** (pursing or compressing) **his lips,** indicating he has concocted some new evil (cf. 6:12-14; 10:10).

The Glory of the Sunset Years. 16:31. **31. The hoary** (gray) **head is a crown of glory** (20:29) **... found in the way of righteousness** (3:1-2), that is, won by a life of virtue (cf. 3:16; 4:22).

The Praiseworthiness of Emotional Control. 16:32. **32.** He who is **slow to anger** (lit., "long, patient of nostrils," since anger is the emotion that dilates the nose) **is better than** (superior to) **the mighty** man (*gĭbbôr,* "hero, mighty one"). **And he who ruleth** (controls) **his spirit** (masters himself) is better than (superior to) **he that taketh** (captures) a city. Self-conquest yields the greatest victories.

The Lord's Providential Working in History. 16:33. **33.** Under God there is no room for the pagan ideas of chance or luck. Whatever happens to man is by the LORD's appointment, as the practice in Bible times of casting lots illustrates. **The lot is cast into the lap** (Lev. 16:8; Num. 26:55; Jonah 1:7; Acts 1:26), **but the whole disposing thereof** (every decision it gives) **is of** (from) **the Lord** (Prov. 29:26).

H. RIGHT AND WRONG CONDUCT IN CONTRAST (CONT.). 17:1-28.

The Blessing of Domestic Tranquility. 17:1. **1. Better is a dry morsel** (crust) without butter or oil (Lev. 7:10), old and stale, **and quietness** with it (*shǎlwâ,* "peace, tranquility, rest"; see Prov. 15:17) **than a house full of sacrifices** (victims, part of which were offered in sacrifices, which required the choicest animals), **with strife** (lit., "sacrifices of strife").

The Asset of Wise Conduct. 17:2. **2. A wise servant** (who conducts himself in an astute manner) **shall have rule** (authority) **over a son that causeth shame** (*mēḇîsh,* "conducts himself shamefully"), **and shall have part of** (share in) **the inheritance among the brethren** (brothers; cf. Gen. 15:3). "Unto the servant that is wise shall they who are free do service" (Ecclus. 10:25). The precise situation contemplated here, where a slave takes the share of a renegade son, is not provided for in the Mosaic Law (cf. Num. 27:8-11; Deut. 21:15-17). Property, however, could go to an adopted son who might be a former slave (Gen. 15:2-3; cf. the custom in Nuzi, ANET, pp. 219*b*-220*a*).

Divine Refining Discipline. 17:3. **3. The refining pot** (refining crucible) **is for silver, and the furnace** (smelter) **for gold** (Psalm 26:2; Prov. 27:21; Jer. 17:10;

Mal. 3:3; 1 Pet. 1:7; Rev. 2:23). **But the Lord testest** (*bḥn,* "proves, purifies, examines") **hearts,** that is, "the thoughts" (of men), since the mind is the source from which both words and actions come. This phase of chastening is not punishment for sin, but purifying for spiritual enrichment.

Evildoers and Liars. 17:4. **4. A wicked doer** (evil doer) **giveth heed** (listens) **to wicked lips,** that is, to what "the wicked lips" say or propose in the way of crime (Prov. 14:15). **And a liar** (MT; *shĕqĕr,* "lying," metonymy for *mᵉshǎqqēr,* "liar") **giveth ear** (lends his ear) **to a mischievous tongue** (lit., "a tongue of destruction," *hǎwwâ,* "corruption, wickedness").

The Fate of Him Who Makes Sport of Human Suffering. 17:5. **5.** He who **mocketh** (*l'g,* "make fun of, deride") **the poor** (in their hardships, either callously or with fiendish delight, makes sport of their sufferings), **reproacheth** (insults) **his Maker,** for his Creator is theirs as well as his (cf. Ezek. 26:2; Obad. 12). He who makes fun of a work is making fun of the workman. And he who is **glad** (*śmḥ,* "rejoices") **at calamities** (i.e., of others) **shall not be unpunished** (be accounted innocent; Job 31:29; Prov. 24:17). Compare the Egyptian sage Amen-em-ope, who says, "Do not laugh at a blind man nor tease a dwarf" (ANET, p. 424*a*).

A Reciprocal Ornament – Parents and Children. 17:6. **6. Children's children** (grandchildren) **are the crown** (garland) **of old men** (Gen. 48:11; Prov. 13:22). **And the glory of children** (sons) **are their fathers** (Exod. 20:12; Mal. 1:6). By God's blessing, children are a "crown," the ornament, help, and delight of their parents in old age. Fathers are the pride of their sons because of their counsel, prayers, and help.

The Suitability of Excellent Speech.

17:7. **7.** High-type **excellent speech** (lit. Heb., "lips of excellence") **becometh not** (*nā'wâ,* is not "becoming," in the sense of being suitable to, being lovely, or comely for) **a fool** (*nābāl,* "a knave, a godless, irreligious, senseless person" like Nabal, "fool," 1 Sam. 25). **Much less do lying lips** ("lips of falsehood"; become) **a prince** (*nādîb,* "a noble, a person of honor and repute").

The Powerful Effect of a Bribe. 17:8.
8. A bribe (*shōhād*) **is** (metaphorically) **like a precious stone** (*hēn,* "a stone of beauty") **in the eyes of him that hath it** (i.e., who has accepted it, and possesses it, and so will be influenced by it). Whenever the person who has accepted it **turneth** (the sparkling jewel turns with him, and he sees it and is influenced by it), **he prospereth** (*yaskîl,* "has success") in carrying through the particular project for which he has accepted the bribe. The lure of the bribe is exposed here in order to be shunned, not followed. However, a gift to conciliate the angry, not to pervert justice, is right (18:16; Gen. 32:20; 1 Sam. 25:27).

Love Overlooks Faults. 17:9. **9.** He who **covereth a transgression,** overlooks a fault (*pĕshă',* "an offense"), **seeketh love** (10:12; James 5:20; 1 Pet. 4:8), that is, he does so for love's sake (1 Cor. 13:5). But he **that repeateth a matter,** brings it up over and over again, **separateth** (alienates) **friends** (intimate friends; Prov. 16:28) by so doing, breaking up long-lasting friendships.

The Wise Response to Reproof. 17:10-12. **10. A reproof** (*gĕ'ārâ,* "a rebuke, word of remonstrance") **entereth more** (sinks deeper) **into a wise man** (*mēbîn,* "an intelligent, understanding person") **than an hundred stripes** (blows) **into a fool. 11. An evil man** (so the LXX and the Arabic) **seeketh only rebellion.** "A rebellious man seeks only evil" (NASB, following Syriac and

Aramaic). "A cruel messenger shall be sent against him," (KJV), either translation being an illustration of verse 10. Therefore, **a cruel messenger** (an emissary with hard, terrible tidings) **shall be sent against him.**

12. It is better to meet an infuriated female bear robbed of her cubs (2 Sam. 17:8; Hos. 13:8) than to offer reproof or remonstrate with **a fool in his folly.** The fool, spurning reproof (v. 10), assails his faithful reprover with the irrationality of an enraged beast, or like a madman attacking his physician.

The Crime of Repaying Good with Evil. 17:13. **13.** Such a one who **rewardeth** (returns) **evil for good** (Jer. 18:20; Rom. 12:17), **evil** (*rā'â,* "trouble, misfortune, adversity") **shall not depart from his house** (2 Sam. 12:9-10; 1 Kings 21:22; Prov. 13:21).

How to Avoid Strife. 17:14. **14. The beginning of strife is like when one letteth out water,** opening a sluice gate, or like a small leak in an earth dam, which will grow larger, if not stopped, till the whole embankment is swept away. **Therefore, leave off contention, before it is meddled with** (lit., "before the quarreling"). Abandon (*ntsh,* "leave, give up") the dispute (*rîb,* "the bone of contention").

Injustice Is Hateful to the Lord. 17:15. **15.** He who **justifieth the wicked** (absolves, exonerates the guilty) and **condemneth the just** (the innocent; Exod. 23:7; Prov. 18:5; Isa. 5:23)— both are **an abomination to the Lord,** utter detestation to Him, because their actions insult His very being and holy attributes as Creator by blatantly wronging His creatures (cf. v. 5), the belief in retribution resting on the thought of God as Creator of all.

The Fool and Wisdom. 17:16. **16. Why is there a price in the hand of a fool to get** (*qānâ,* "to buy") **wisdom, seeing he hath no heart to it?** (i.e., seeing he has no sense; 23:23). The fool possesses the means to get wisdom, but he has no heart (sense) for it.

The Mark of a True Friend. 17:17. **17. A friend loveth at all times.** The original: "At all times [emphatic] a friend loves" (is devoted; Ruth 1:16; Prov. 18:24), **and a brother is born for adversity.** But it is "in adversity" (*ṣārâ,* "distress"), in time of trouble, that he shows himself a real brother born to you; a blood brother, as it were, just born for the emergency (cf. Prov. 18:24).

The Senseless Man and Rash Bargaining. 17:18. **18. A man void of understanding** (sense, heart) **striketh hands** (as a sign of pledging himself to be responsible for another), **and becometh surety,** mortgages himself **in the presense of his neighbor,** implying habitual rashness in making bargains, which of necessity would lead to improvidence with regard to taking care of one's own family (cf. 1 Tim. 5:8).

The Sin of Loving Strife. 17:19. **19.** He who **loveth transgression** (is fond of crime) **loveth strife** (must be fond of trouble; 29:22). And he who **exalteth his gate** (his door; "makes his door high" so a visitor must go up to meet him, a figure of arrogance) **seeketh destruction,** for destruction is the issue of pride (16:18), the basic transgression.

The Issue of Perversity of Heart and Speech. 17:20. **20. He that hath a perverse** (*'iqqēsh,* "crooked, twisted") **heart** (mind) finds **no good** in anything and will come to no good (24:20). Such a man of perverted mind will of necessity be a man of **perverse** (perverted) **tongue** (speech; Matt. 12:33-37), and such a man perverted in his language **falleth into mischief** (*rā'â,* "evil, misfortune, destruction"; James 3:8).

The Tragedy of Begetting a Fool. 17:21. **21.** He who **begetteth a fool** does so **to his sorrow** (*tûgâ,* "grief"; v. 25;

10:1; 19:13). And the **father of a fool** (*nābāl,* "an ill-natured knave") **hath no joy** (happiness).

A Prescription for Good Health. 17:22. **22. A merry heart** (a cheerful mind) **does good like a medicine** (lit., "causes good healing"), meaning, "A cheerful spirit is good for the health" (AB). **But a broken** (*nᵉkē'â,* "beaten, afflicted, grieved") **spirit,** producing a gloomy outlook, **drieth** (up) **the bones** and so affects the whole body with ill health.

The Corrupt Man and Bribery. 17:23. **23. A wicked man taketh a bribe** (*shōḥăḏ*) **out of the bosom** of a dishonest client clandestinely, that is, accepts a secret bribe as an unscrupulous judge **to pervert** (Exod. 23:8) **the ways of justice,** "to avert or turn aside" (*hăṭṭôṯ*) the due course of justice.

Wisdom and the Wise Man's Action. 17:24. **24. Wisdom is before** (right in the presence of) **him that hath understanding,** enabling him to see it and appropriate it in thought, deed, and word, and to discern the right choice right in front of him. **But the eyes of a fool** (*kᵉsîl,* "the stupid, impious person") are far away **in the ends of the earth** (Eccles. 2:14), crassly oblivious to the presence of wisdom and the opportunities and blessings it offers right at his doorstep.

Parental Grief and a Foolish Son. 17:25. **25. A foolish son is a grief** (*kă'ăs,* "vexation, provocation") **to his father, and bitterness** (*mĕmĕr,* "severe pain, sorrow, and regret") **to her that bore him, worse** apparently than the grief of the father, perhaps due to having spoiled her son by indulgence to a greater degree than did the father.

The Outrage of Punishing Innocent People. 17:26. **26. Also** (even) **to punish the just** (*'nsh,* "to impose a fine or penalty upon"), "the righteous man," he who is justified before God by faith

(Gen. 15:6) and before men by an irreproachable life, **is not good,** meaning it is downright reprehensible. **Nor** (is it good) **to strike** (flog) **princes** (*n*e*ḏîḇîm,* "noble men, men of renown and position") for **their equity** (*'ǎl yōshĕr,* "for [their] uprightness").

The Virtue of Controlling the Tongue. 17:27-28. **27.** The Hebrew reads, "He who spares [*ḥśk,* 'holds back, restrains'] his words, has knowledge" (lit., "knows knowledge"), that is, is a learned or educated man in wisdom's love (10:19; James 1:19). "And he who is cool of spirit [cool-headed] is a man of judiciousness" (*t*e*ḇûnâ*).

28. Even a fool (*'e*wîl,* "a nitwit, an ignoramus"), **when he holdeth his peace** (who remains silent, keeps his mouth shut) **is counted** (is reckoned or thought to be) **wise; and he that shutteth his lips is esteemed a man of understanding** (cf. Prov. 11:12; 13:3). The wise man's reserve and self-control are an ideal also appearing in Egyptian wisdom writings (*Ani 7, Amen-em-ope,* chaps. 4, 9; ANET, pp. 420*b,* 422*a,* 423*a*).

I. RIGHT AND WRONG CONDUCT IN
CONTRAST (CONT.). 18:1-24.

The Divisive, Selfish Man. 18:1. **1.** The literal Hebrew reads, "He who separates himself [from truth and orthodoxy] **seeketh** [cares only about his own] **desire** [selfish interests]. Against all sound wisdom, he picks a quarrel [*yiṯgǎllā'*]." The Pharisees were such rigidly wrong separatists, trusting in themselves and their wisdom, and despising others (Luke 16:15; 18:9; Jude 19). All heretics, more or less, fall into this snare of self-conceit, which leads men to separate from orthodoxy (Ezek. 14:7; Hos. 9:10; Heb. 10:25).

The Fool and the Display of Folly. 18:2. **2. A fool hath no delight in under-standing** (for its own sake), finding no pleasure in reasoning, **but that his heart** (mind) **may discover** (reveal) **itself,** that he may display self in airing his views, which can only be worthless in that they come from an empty mind (cf. 12:23; 13:16; Eccles. 10:3).

The Accompaniments of a Wicked Man. 18:3. **3. When the wicked cometh** (among the wise), **then cometh also contempt** (*bûz,* "scorn, derision"). **And, with ignominy** (*qālôn,* "shame, disgrace"; properly, "shameful nakedness") **reproach** (*ḥĕrpâ,* "shame, pudenda").

The Source of Sound Speech. 18:4. **4. The words of a man's mouth** (i.e., *'îsh,* "a good man," not *'āḏām,* "any man") **are like deep waters** (20:5). What he says is deep, not merely on the surface for display, like the fool (vv. 1-2). **The wellspring** (*m*e*qôr,* "fountain") **of wisdom,** which the good man has in his heart, is like **a flowing brook** (Psalm 78:2); therefore, he has an unlimited source of inspiration and good to draw from (Matt. 12:34-37; cf. James 3:11).

The Crime of Judicial Injustice. 18:5. **5. It is not good** (right) **to accept the person of the wicked** (to favor and show partiality to them for any reason whatsoever because of their wealth, position, etc.; Lev. 19:15; Deut. 1:17; 16:19; Psalm 82:2; Prov. 17:15; 24:23; 28:21), **to overthrow** (to thrust or turn aside) **the righteous** (here in the sense of one who is innocent of the charge placed against him) **in judgment** (in the legal proceedings of justice). This is a legal maxim.

The Bane of a Fool's Speech. 18:6-8. **6. A fool's lips** (his words) **enter into contention,** involve him in endless brawling and argument. His talk always lands him in a dispute. **And his mouth** (what he says) **calleth** (cries out) **for strokes** (blows, a good beating). **7.** His mouth is his destruction (ruin) and his lips are the snare of his soul, the trap that catches him (Psalms 64:8; 140:9; Prov. 10:14; 12:13; 13:3; Eccles. 10:12).

8. His words are those of a **talebearer** (whisperer, slanderer) and **are as wounds** (KJV; cf. Prov. 12:18). But others take *mĭt lăhᵃmĭm* from the root *lḥm*, "to swallow greedily"; Arabic, *lahima*; and render it, "bits greedily swallowed, dainties" (BDB; 26:22), as figurative of a talebearer's words; so "The words of a whisperer are like dainty morsels, and they go down into the innermost parts of the body [lit., 'belly']" (NASB). Slander, once given an audience, is not soon erased from the memory.

Shiftlessness and Its Outcome. 18:9.
9. Also (connecting this with v. 8) he who is **slothful** (*mĭṭrăppĕh*, "demonstrates himself lazy and indolent") **in his work** (business) **is brother to him that is a great waster** (destroyer; lit., "lord of wasting," one wholly given up to it), not producing, being kin to destroying. The slothful and the wasteful are twin brothers.

The Security of the Believer. 18:10-11. **10. The name of the Lord** (i.e., the LORD Himself, in all that His name stands for, particularly in His gracious love and concern for His own; Exod. 3:15) **is a strong tower** ("a tower of strength"; 2 Sam. 22:2-3; Psalms 18:2; 61:3; 91:2; 144:2). **The righteous** (*ṣăddîq*, "the believer justified by faith"; Gen. 15:6) **runneth into it** (in times of temptation and peril), **and is safe** (*nĭsgāb*, "set on high," out of the reach of foes; Prov. 29:25).

11. The real security of the believer is not in material wealth, as it is imagined to be by worldly minded people. The rich man's wealth **is his strong city** (10:15), and **as an high wall in his own conceit** (*măśkît*, "imagination,

thought"), in contrast to the righteous man's "strong tower," "the name of the LORD" in which he is "set on high" in a place of safety (v. 10). The verse is a warning to "trust . . . in the living God" rather than in "uncertain riches" (1 Tim. 6:17).

The Peril of Pride and the Reward of Humility. 18:12. **12. Before destruction the heart** (mind) **of man is haughty** (*gbh*, "to be highminded, proud"), **and before honor is humility** ("*ᵃnāwâ*, "condescension, a bowed-down spirit and lowly appraisal of oneself"; 15:33; 16:18).

The Stupidity of Replying Before Understanding What Is Said. 18:13. **13.** He who **answereth a matter** (returns a word, replies) **before he heareth it,** "understands" (as in Deut. 28:49) what is said (Prov. 20:25; John 7:51), **it is folly and shame unto him.** He shows himself stupid and egocentric, for self-importance is usually the underlying cause of such interruptions. "Do not answer until you have heard the cause, neither interrupt men in the midst of their talk" (Ecclus. 11:8).

The Sustaining Power of the Human Spirit. 18:14. **14. The spirit of a man** (*'îsh*, i.e., "a hale spirit") **will sustain his infirmity** (of body). As the governor of the body, it is the office of the immaterial part of man to sustain (*yᵉkălkēl*, "support, nourish, bear up") the material part (the body), but not vice versa. Hence, if the spirit is **wounded** (*nᵉkē'â*, "afflicted, beaten, grieved"), there is nothing to bear it up (15:13). When the body is ill, the spirit supports it; but when the spirit is sick, psychologically and spiritually, who can bear such a burden?

On Acquiring Knowledge. 18:15. **15. The heart** (mind) **of the prudent getteth** (*qānâ*, "acquires") **knowledge, and the ear of the wise seeketh knowledge.** Little wonder that with an alert ear combined with a discerning mind, wise men increase their knowledge (1 Kings 3:9; Psalm 119:97; Luke 8:10; James 1:5).

On Acquiring Success. 18:16. **16. A man's gift** (*măttān*, "present, donation, bribe") may mean either an endowment God has given one (Psalm 68:18; Dan. 1:17; 6:3; 1 Cor. 12:4-11; Eph. 4:7-12) or a "present," or even in the sense of "a bribe" (Esther 9:22; Prov. 15:27; Eccles. 7:7) man gives to a fellowman. This "gift" from God **maketh room for him,** paving the way to advancement, as in the case of Joseph (Gen. 39:2-6; 41:14, 38-44) and Daniel (Dan. 1:17, 19-20; 6:3), in the good sense of being a blessing and bringing him before **great men,** like the pharaoh of Egypt and the king of Babylon. But in the bad sense, as a gift to a fellowman, it states the way of the world, as things are, not as what they ought to be, where gifts and bribes pave the way to temporal success and "money talks" for sinful and selfish ends.

Hearing Both Sides of a Dispute. 18:17. **17.** He who is **first in his own cause** (*rîḇ*, "quarrel, dispute, legal suit, case of litigation in a court of law"), who presents his case first, (is) **seemeth right. But his neighbor** (the other party, or his representative in the suit) **cometh and searcheth** (cross-examines) **him.** Often the case then appears in a different light. Any rashness of decision by a judge without thoroughly investigating both sides is to be sedulously avoided.

The Practice of Casting Lots. 18:18. **18. The lot** (i.e., the casting of the lot) **causeth contentions to cease** (settles disputes and lawsuits), **and parteth** (divides, decides) **between the mighty** ("*ᵃṣûmîm*, "powerful, strong" contenders). The lot was resorted to in difficult cases where the verdict was sought from the supreme Arbiter (16:33).

Winning over an Offended Brother.

18:19. **19. A brother offended** (*nīpshā'*, "transgressed against") **is harder to be won than a strong city, and ... contentions** (quarrels) **are like the bars of a castle,** preventing entry. So quarrels with those who are near of kin generate the fiercest hatred, harder to be broken through than a stoutly fortified castle.

Eating the Fruit of One's Words. 18:20-21. **20. A man's belly** (stomach) **shall be satisfied** (*śḇ'*, "be filled to satiety, be surfeited") **with the fruit of his mouth,** the words that proceed out of his mouth from his heart (Matt. 12:33-35). **And with the increase** (the product, produce, result) **of his lips** (the words his lips utter) **he shall be filled** (*śḇ'*, same word as above). Everyone must "eat his words," whether good or bad (Prov. 13:2). **21. Death and life are in the power of the tongue** (12:13; 13:3; Matt. 12:37), **and they that love it** (death or life) **shall eat the fruit thereof** (of either death or life, whichever one he chooses; Prov. 13:2; Isa. 3:10; Hos. 10:13; James 1:19, 25; 3:6, 8).

Finding a Wife and the Lord's Favor. 18:22. **22.** He who **findeth a wife** (realizing what a wife ought to be) **findeth a good thing** (Gen. 2:18; Prov. 12:4; 19:14; 31:10-31) **and obtaineth favor from the Lord.** *Finding* implies a diligent search for a rare treasure (Eccles. 7:22-28) and discriminating choice, with consultation with wise parents—contrast the case of Samson (Judg. 14:2-3)—and earnest prayer to God (Gen. 24:12-42). The favor of the LORD is manifested through the right choice (God's choice) of a wife, and so prayer for the right woman had better be resorted to and God's guidance depended on.

Poverty and Humility Versus Wealth and Pride. 18:23. **23. The poor** (man) **useth** (utters, speaks) **entreaties** (supplications; 19:7), poverty producing a sense of selflessness and humility. **But**

1029

the rich (man) **answereth roughly** (lit., "hard things"; 1 Kings 12:13; 2 Chron. 10:13; James 2:3, 6).

A Man and His Friends. 18:24. **24. A man who hath friends** (John 15:14-15) **must show himself friendly; and there is a friend** (lit., "one who loves") who **sticketh closer than a brother.** This "loving friend" (*dbq*, "cleaving, adhering through thick and thin") is only realized absolutely in our Lord Jesus Christ (Matt. 12:50).

J. RIGHT AND WRONG CONDUCT IN
CONTRAST (CONT.). 19:1-29.

Honorable Poverty Versus Dishonorable Wealth. 19:1. **1. Better is the poor (man) that walketh in his integrity** (who lives virtuously; Psalm 26:11; Prov. 14:2; 20:7) **than he that is perverse in his lips** (*'iqqēsh*, "crooked, distorted, perverted in his speech"), **and is a fool.** He manifests himself as a fool (although rich) by the way he talks, which reveals the folly of his heart (Matt. 12:34-35), demonstrating that he does not walk in integrity.

Zeal Without Knowledge. 19:2. **2. Also** (likewise) **. . . soul** (*něpěsh*, "soul," in the sense of "zeal" or "enthusiasm"; cf. Rom. 10:2) **. . . without knowledge . . . is not good.** Thus, it is rendered, "Zeal without knowledge is not a good thing, for a man in a hurry makes a slip" (AB); or, **And he that hasteneth with his feet sinneth** (*hôtē'*, "misses the mark, errs"). "Hastening with the feet" is acting without knowledge, and such precipitancy misses the bull's-eye and goes astray of the goal in mind.

Blaming the Lord for the Outcome of One's Own Stupidity. 19:3. **3. The foolishness** (stupidity) **of man perverteth** (*sĭllēp*, "corrupts, destroys, subverts") **his way,** the course of his life, **and his heart fretteth** (*z'p*, "be angry, resentful") **against the Lord.** Yet "against the

LORD" (emphatic) he "rages" like the angry sea (Jonah 1:15). How often a man's own stupidity ruins his life; yet he is bitter and resentful against the LORD, as if the LORD was the cause of his calamity instead of himself.

Estimating Friendships by Self-Utility. 19:4. **4. Wealth maketh** (lit. Heb., "adds") **many friends** (14:20), because so many people gauge friendships on the basis of their usefulness in advancing self-interests. **But the poor (man) is separated from his neighbor** (friend), from the one friend he has, from him who once was and still ought to be a friendly neighbor. Both ought to see the Friend par excellence as the "brother born for adversity" who "sticketh closer than a brother" (17:17; 18:24).

The Certain Punishment of Liars. 19:5. **5. A false witness shall not be unpunished** (Exod. 23:1; Deut. 19:16-19; Prov. 19:9; 21:28). **And he that speaketh** (breathes out) **lies shall not escape** (repeated in v. 9).

The Stigma of Human Selfishness. 19:6-7. **6. Many will entreat the favor of the prince** (*nādĭb*, "a generous, noble person"; 29:26). **And every man is a friend to him that giveth gifts** (18:16; 21:14). Literally, "Every friend [is] to a man of gifts," meaning "a man of gifts [who gives gifts] has all the friends."

7. All the brothers of a poor man hate him; how much more do his friends go far from him! He pursues them with words, but they are gone (NASB; "they are not"; Psalm 38:11; Prov. 18:23). They evaporate into thin air when they see that their erstwhile friend, now poor and helpless, can be of little use to them to further their plans of self-interest (cf. v. 4).

The Reward of Developing One's Mind. 19:8. **8. He that getteth** (*qōnĕh*, "acquires") **wisdom** (lit., "heart," i.e., "mind," meaning he who develops his mind, his mental capacities) **loveth his own soul** (himself; i.e., he is his own best friend). **He that keepeth** (*shmr*, "guards, treasures, cherishes") **understanding shall find good** (shall succeed; 16:20).

The Certain Punishment of the Liar. 19:9. See comments on verse 5.

The Incongruity of the Exaltation of a Fool. 19:10. **10. Delight** (*tǎ'ᵃnûg*, "enjoyment of comfort and luxury") **is not fitting** (suitable) **for a fool** (17:7; 26:1; Eccles. 10:6-7). Luxurious living often turns wise men into fools, but it turns fools into self-destroying idiots. **Much less** (is it suitable) **for a servant** (essentially a "slave" in character) **to have rule over princes,** over those noble in mind and experience and princely in character (Prov. 30:22; Eccles. 10:6).

The Virtue of Gracious Forbearance. 19:11. **11. The discretion** (common sense) **of a man deferreth** (lit., "lengthens, prolongs, extends, delays") **his anger** to a distant time, making him long-suffering and patiently forbearing of wrongs. **And it is his glory** (his honor) **to pass over a transgression** (overlook a fault and put up with an affront; Gen. 50:15-21; Prov. 25:21; Matt. 5:44; 18:21-22; Rom. 12:19; Eph. 4:32). Christ is our great Example of long-suffering, though ultimately the impenitent must pay the penalty (Amos 7:8; Mic. 7:18).

The Anger of a King. 19:12. **12. The king's wrath is like the roaring of a lion, but his favor is like dew upon the grass** (Gen. 27:28; Deut. 33:28; Psalm 133:3; Hos. 14:5; Mic. 5:7). If this is true of an earthly king, how much more is it true of the heavenly King of kings, whose wrath men ought to fear (Psalm 2:5; Rev. 19:11—20:3) and whose favor they ought to seek (Psalms 2:12; 72:6).

The Tragedy of Domestic Infelicity. 19:13. **13.** Two things are mentioned that destroy a happy home: (1) **a foolish** (stupid) **son** who is **the calamity of his father**; and (2) **the contentions** (quarrelings, grumblings) **of a wife,** which are **a continual dropping,** dripping (of rain), literally, "pushing," one drop pushing another continually through the roof of the house.

The Lord's Gift of a Prudent Wife. 19:14. **14. House and riches are the inheritance of** (from) **fathers** (2 Cor. 12:14), inherited from one's forebears, **and** (but) **a prudent** (sensible, discreet) **wife is from the Lord** (Gen. 24:7; 28:1, 4; Prov. 18:22), God's special and direct gift. Prayer to the LORD is the way to get such a wife, not by a human matchmaking agency or natural sagacity.

The Bane of Laziness. 19:15. **15. Slothfulness** (idleness) **casteth into a deep sleep** (*tǎrdēmâ*, "lethargy, sleepy stupor"). Moderate work and physical exercise increase the vitality of mind and body. Laziness decreases both. **And an idle soul** (person), someone remiss and shiftless, who soon remits his efforts, **shall suffer hunger** as a just retribution (6:9-10; 24:33; 26:14).

The Reward of Keeping God's Law. 19:16. **16.** To keep (observe) **the commandment** (of God) is to keep one's **own soul,** that is, to keep oneself (*šmr*, "guard" against evil or despoilment; "watch" against enemy attack). But he who **despiseth his ways** (is careless about his behavior) **shall die** (*yāwmǔṯ, kethiv,* but *yāmûṯ, qere,* "shall be put to death"; cf. 1 Cor. 5:5; 11:30-32; 1 John 5:16).

The Reward of Helping the Poor. 19:17. **17.** He who has **pity upon the poor** (man), is gracious to him in helping him, **lendeth unto the LORD** (Deut. 15:7; Prov. 14:31; 28:27; Eccles. 11:1-2; Matt. 10:42; 2 Cor. 9:6-8; Heb. 6:10). **And that which he hath given** (lit., "his deed") **will he** (the LORD) **pay him again,** that is, "repay him for his good deed" (NASB; Prov. 12:14; Luke 6:38).

The Urgency of Child Discipline. 19:18. **18. Chasten** (discipline) **thy son while there is hope** of his being reformed and before he becomes incorrigibly hardened in sin. The literal Hebrew reads, "Do not set your desire on his dying [i.e., his destruction], which you will do by failing to discipline him while there is time, and by so doing indulging him to his own destruction [death]." **And do not desire his death** (NASB), which in essence you will do (or at least appear to do), if you fail to discipline him early.

The Consequence of Uncontrolled Anger. 19:19. **19. A man of great wrath** (a very angry man) **shall suffer punishment** (shall bear the penalty of his uncontrolled temper). For if you **deliver** (rescue) **him . . . thou must do it again,** for he will repeat his offense endlessly, having no control over his passion. If you intervene, you will merely embroil yourself in his folly.

Receiving the Counsel of the Lord. 19:20-21. **20-21.** The injunction is to **hear counsel** (listen to advice) and **receive** (accept) **instruction** (*mûsăr*, "disciplinary instruction"). The purpose: that you may **be wise in thy latter end** (the latter part of your life; 4:1; 8:33; 12:15) and that you may not fall for the **many devices** (plans) **in a man's heart** (Gen. 37:19-20; Esther 9:25; Eccles. 7:29; Heb. 6:17). That can only be accomplished by heeding **the counsel of the Lord, that shall stand** the test of time and eternity (Psalm 33:10-11; Isa. 14:26).

Honesty the Best Policy. 19:22. **22. The desire of a man** (what is desirable in a man) **is his kindness** (*hĕsĕd*, "faithfulness, loyalty"). His kindness is what makes him desirable. **And a poor man,** though severely limited as far as material means are concerned, but disposed

to acts of kindness, **is better than a liar,** a rich man who deceptively withholds his wealth with which he has promised to relieve the poverty-stricken. His deceptive stinginess places him far below the godly poor, who have little or nothing to give.

The Fear of the Lord. 19:23. **23.** Standing in awe of the LORD, in reverence for His Word, **tendeth to life** — spiritual life, leading to salvation of the soul; physical life in inculcating principles of healthful living that tend to longevity; and eternal life in rescue from eternal death (14:27; 1 Tim. 4:8), "so that one may rest satisfied, not visited [untouched] by evil" (lit. Heb.; Psalms 25:13; 91:10; Prov. 12:21).

The Pathetic Lassitude of the Lazy Person. 19:24. **24.** The **slothful man** (the sluggard) **hideth** (*ṭmn*, "buries, conceals") **his hand** in his **dish** (*sāllāḥăṭ*, "bowl"; cf. Matt. 26:23; Mark 14:20) and, because he is so lazy, **will not so much as bring it to his mouth again.** With sarcastic humor, he is pictured as being too lazy even to eat (Prov. 26:15).

The Wiser One Is, the Readier He Is to Accept Correction. 19:25. **25. Smite** (strike) **a scoffer, and the simple** (*pĕtî*, "the naive," who does not err from forethought), and he "may act prudently" (*yă'rîm*, in the sense of learning a lesson). **And reprove** (admonish) **one that hath understanding, and he will understand knowledge.** He will readily accept advice and correction and become wiser and better, verbal reproof being amply sufficient to accomplish the desired end.

A Shameful Son. 19:26. **26.** He who **wasteth** (assaults, maltreats, BDB) **his father, and chaseth away** (puts to flight) **his mother,** making the home an unbearable place to stay, **is a son that causeth shame, and bringeth reproach** (*māḥpîr*, "disgrace").

The Peril of Ceasing to Listen to Disciplinary Instruction. 19:27. **27.** "Cease listening, my son [see 1:8; 2:1] to disciplinary instruction [*mūsār*; and you will stray] from the words of knowledge," hence become ensnared by heresy and false doctrine and by enslavement to various sins.

The Wickedness of the Ungodly Tongue. 19:28. **28. An ungodly witness** ("a witness of Belial"; lit., "a witness of good-for-nothingness," i.e., good-for-nothing, or rascal of a witness) **scoffeth at** (makes a mockery of) **justice** (*mishpāṭ*). **And the mouth of the wicked devoureth** (*bl'*, "swallows, eats up, gulps) **iniquity** (Job 15:16, 20:12-13; 34:7).

The Punishment of Scoffers and Fools. 19:29. **29. Judgments** (punishments) **are prepared for scoffers,** and **stripes** (blows, flogging) **for the back of fools.** Just as they scorned judgment (v. 28), it is meted out to them in kind as a righteous retribution (9:12; Prov. 10:13; 18:6; 26:3).

K. RIGHT AND WRONG CONDUCT IN CONTRAST (CONT.). 20:1-30.

Warning Against Intoxicating Beverages. 20:1. **1. Wine is a mocker** (Gen. 9:21; Prov. 23:29-30; Isa. 28:7; Hos. 4:11). **Strong drink** (*shēkār*, including every kind of intoxicating beverage besides wine; cf. Lev. 10:9) is **raging,** "a rager, a brawler" (*hōmĕh*, "one agitated and noisy"; Prov. 31:4; Isa. 5:22; 56:12). **And whosoever is deceived** (intoxicated) **thereby is not wise** (the figure of litotes, emphatically, "is very foolish"). Why? Because intoxication dulls the mind, stirs up the passions, and exposes its victim to many sins and tragic sorrows.

Warning Against Provoking a King to Anger. 20:2. **2. The fear of a king** (terror he inspires when he is angry) **is like the roaring of a lion,** who growls as he pounces upon his victim. Whoever **provoketh him to anger sinneth against his own soul** (himself), in the sense of endangering or even forfeiting his own life (Num. 16:38; 1 Kings 2:23; Hab. 2:10).

The Wisdom of Avoiding a Dispute. 20:3. **3. It is an honor for a man to cease from strife** (Gen. 13:7), not merely not to begin an altercation (Prov. 17:14; 19:11), but to desist from it once it is started. The latter is more difficult, and hence more honorable. **But every fool**—an unwise, small-minded person in contrast to a man (*'ish,* "a wise, broad-minded person")—**will be meddling** (becoming involved in strife; 17:14).

The Plight of the Lazy, Shiftless Person. 20:4. **4. The sluggard** (idler) **will not plow by reason of the cold** at the onset of winter. The shiftless is never without ready excuses for his disinclination to work. **Therefore shall he beg** (lit., "ask" for food) **in harvest,** when it is most abundant, because he did not sow and so he does not reap, and hence has **nothing** (Gal. 6:7; cf. 1 Cor. 6:9-10).

The Utility of Plan and Purpose in Life. 20:5. **5. Counsel** (*'ēsâ,* "wisdom, in the aspect of producing plan and purpose for living") **in the heart** (mind) **of man is like deep water** (cf. 18:4). Man's mind is a wonderful endowment of the Creator, capable of vast design and wonderful projects, and compared to deep water in a well, whose depth is not easily plumbed. The foolish man never attempts to plumb the depths, **but a man of understanding will draw ... out** this inner sagacity and find a thrilling plan and purpose for living.

Self-Proclaimed Virtue. 20:6. **6.** "Many a man ['*ādām,* 'a common, undistinguished Adamite'] will proclaim his own goodness (*hĕsĕd,* 'kindness, fidelity'], but a faithful man ['a man,' *'îsh*, 'a distinguished man of faithfulness'] —a man you can really trust— who can find?" (lit. Heb.; Psalm 12:1; Eccles. 7:28; Jer. 5:1; Mic. 7:2; Luke 18:11; John 1:47). It is one thing to advertise one's own virtues, and quite another to be virtuous.

The Heritage of a Godly Life. 20:7. **7. The just** (righteous) **man** (man justified before God by faith) **walketh in his integrity,** manifesting the reality of his saving faith in his conduct before men (19:1). **His children are blessed after him**— spiritually, and often materially, his offspring are fortunate in their inheritance (Psalms 37:26; 112:2).

The King as a Judge. 20:8. **8. A king that sitteth in** (on) **the throne of judgment,** to administer justice, **scattereth away all evil with his eyes** (disperses, winnows it, as the wind separates the chaff from the wheat; 2 Chron. 15:16; Psalm 1:4; Matt. 3:12) with his own God-given powers of perception. So does "the King of kings" (Psalm 5:5; Dan. 10:6; Hab. 1:13; Rev. 1:14; 19:12).

The Hollow Claims of Self-Righteousness. 20:9. **9. Who can say** (with truth), **I have made my heart clean** (*zākâ*, "be pure, innocent"; or, "My heart *is* clean"), **I am pure** (*ṭhr*, "be clean, pure") **from my sin?** (*ḥăṭṭā'â*, "missing God's mark"). Fallen man can only make such a claim on the basis of God's grace through faith, either in connection with salvation or sanctification of life. Any such claim on any other basis is self-righteousness, which is as filthy garments (Isa. 64:6) before an infinitely holy God (1 Kings 8:46; 2 Chron. 6:36; Job 14:4; Eccles. 7:20; Rom. 3:9; Eph. 2:8-9; 1 John 1:8).

Hatefulness of Dishonesty Before the Lord. 20:10. **10. Diverse** (differing) **weights, and diverse** (differing) **measures** (lit., "a stone and a stone . . . an ephah and an ephah," the standard dry measure, three-fifths of a bushel) implies one weight used in buying, another in selling, representing crookedness in the common affairs and business of life. All such injustice is an **abomination** (utter detestation) to the LORD, insulting His holy character and fit only in polluted paganism.

Actions Speak Louder Than Words. 20:11. **11. Even a child** (*nă'ăr*, "a boy, lad") **is known by his doings** (his actions, conduct; Psalms 51:5; 58:3; Matt. 7:16; Luke 1:15; 2:46-47), **whether his work** (what he does) **be pure** (*zăq*, "morally clean") **and whether it be right** (*yāshār*, "upright, honest").

Employing the Senses of Sight and of Hearing Aright. 20:12. **12.** Since the LORD, the Creator, has made both the ear that hears and the eye that sees (Exod. 4:11; Rom. 11:36), He not only sees and hears all things (Psalm 94:9), but has given us these wonderful endowments and abilities to glorify Him—to hear His Word and perceive His will in it, and to see His glory in His works and Word, and so serve Him devotedly (Deut. 11:7; Prov. 3:21).

Encouragement to Industry. 20:13. **13. Love not sleep** (Rom. 12:11; 2 Thess. 3:10), **lest thou come to poverty; open thine eyes**—after necessary rest—and see the opportunities for work and achievement to glorify God and benefit mankind (cf. v. 12). **And thou shalt be satisfied with bread**—have plenty to eat.

The Wrong of Cleverly Dishonest Bargaining. 20:14. **14. It is nothing, it is nothing** (no good, no good), says the buyer. **But when he is gone** on his way after making the clever deal, **then he boasteth,** brags and congratulates himself on his sophisticated duplicity.

The Preciousness of Wise Speaking. 20:15. **15. There is gold, and an abundance of rubies** (jewels, corals). **But the**

lips of knowledge (discreet, godly speech) **are a precious jewel**, far more precious than gold or costly stones, however abundant (cf. 3:14-15; 8:10-11).

The Risk of Acting as Guarantor. 20:16. **16. Take a man's garment when he has given surety for a stranger, and hold him in pledge when he gives surety for foreigners** (RSV; repeated in 27:13). In 6:1-5 warning is issued of the danger of acting as guarantor. Here the lender is advised to be rigid in claiming the "garment" pledged on behalf of (or by) a foreigner (a traveling merchant) or "for a stranger" (*kethiv nākrîm*, "foreigners"). This injunction stands in contrast to the leniency toward fellow Israelites (Exod. 22:26-27).

The Sad End of Making a Living Dishonestly. 20:17. **17. Bread of deceit**—one's livelihood gained by lying or falsehood—**is sweet** (*'ārēb*, "pleasant, attractive"*) **to a man** (9:17). Getting one's daily food by crooked means at first may seem to be an easy and delightful substitute for honest toil. **But afterwards** the dishonest person's **mouth shall be filled with gravel,** because he shall be brought down so that he will be prostrate on the ground (cf. Lam. 3:16).

Value of Consultation and Good Advice. 20:18. **18. Every purpose** (lit., "plans") **is established by counsel** (through consultation). Although the LORD alone can "establish purposes" (1 Chron. 29:18), He often uses human consultation to reveal His plans (Prov. 11:14; 15:22). **And with good advice** (wise counsel) **make war** (Luke 14:31), where victory is often achieved more by skill than strength.

Give a Gossip a Wide Berth. 20:19. **19. He that goeth about as a talebearer** (*rākîl*, "a trafficker in slander"*) **revealeth secrets** (betrays confidences).

Therefore, meddle not with (do not associate or mingle with) **him who flattereth** (lit., "one who opens his lips," i.e., "a gossip"), who is nothing but an empty babbler (11:13; 18:8).

Cursing Parents. 20:20. **20.** Cursing one's father or mother was considered the height of wickedness, not only in Israel (Exod. 21:17; Lev. 20:9; Deut. 27:16; Matt. 15:4), but also in Egypt (*Ani* 7-8, ANET, pp. 420*b*-21*a*) and in Assyria (cf. *Ahiqar* 9, ANET, p. 429*b*). **His lamp** (candle) **shall be put out in obscure darkness,** that is, in the most extreme misery, outer darkness (Matt. 8:12; 22:13; 25:30) and everlasting darkness of eternal separation from God (Rev. 20:11-15).

Blessing or Curse upon an Estate. 20:21. **21. An inheritance** (estate) may be **gotten hastily** (gained hurriedly; *m^{e}bōhĕlĕt, Qere*, LXX, Syriac; *m^{e}bûhĕlĕt*, "cursed or abominated," *Kethiv*), that is, by the LORD. **But the end thereof** (of it) **shall not be blessed** (28:8; Hab. 2:6; Zech. 5:4).

Divine Retribution, Not Personal Revenge. 20:22. **22.** "Do not say, 'I will repay a wrong'" (AB; Deut. 32:35; Rom. 12:17; 1 Pet. 3:9). **But wait on the Lord,** leaving the cause in His keeping. It is the lack of patient waiting on (trusting in) God that causes men to impatiently try to avenge themselves. **And he** (the LORD) **shall save thee** (deliver you). Nonresistance and trust in the LORD are thus enjoined as the most effective response to any wrong suffered (Lev. 19:18; Prov. 25:21-22; Matt. 5:38-48).

Hatefulness of Dishonesty Before the Lord. 20:23. **23.** See comment on verse 10.

How You Can Know God's Will. 20:24. **24. Man's goings** (steps, ways) **are of the Lord**, in the sense that He is absolutely sovereign and controls both saved and unsaved humanity, evil as well as good, the great man (*gĕbĕr*) as well as the small man (*'ādām*). In this absolute sense, all men's steps are directed by the LORD as Sovereign of the universe. How else could the common man (*'ādām*, "a mere human being") **understand his own way?**—know what path to take? Yet for God's saved people, He has a special plan for their redeemed life (Eph. 2:10). How can His own find that plan and take that path? Only by complete yieldedness, initiating the continuous and ever widening revelation of that way as each step is taken by the yielded soul (Rom. 12:1-2).

The Peril of Rash Vows. 20:25. **25. It is a snare** (entailing severe penalties) **to the man who devoureth** (appropriates to his own use) **that which is holy** (dedicated to sacred uses), **and after vows to make inquiry** (Eccles. 5:4-5), to reflect on the matter and its repercussions. So Achan did (Josh. 6:17-18; 7:1; cf. Deut. 23:21; Mal. 3:8-10). Many in Malachi's day (1:13-14), after vowing, sought to circumvent the vow. Compare Ananias and Sapphira (Acts 5:1-11). The ancient Hebrew interpreters construe *yālă'* as "speaks rashly" (RSV, NASB, BV). "It is a snare for a man to say rashly, 'It is holy!' And after the vows to make inquiry" (NASB).

A Wise King's Treatment of the Wicked. 20:26. **26. A wise king scattereth** (winnows) **the wicked, and bringeth the wheel** (drives the threshing wheel over them; 20:8; Isa. 28:27). He sifts out the wicked with unrelenting zeal.

The Spirit of Man. 20:27. **27. The spirit of man** is the part of him that "knows" (1 Cor. 2:11) and is capable of God-consciousness and communication with God (Job 32:8; cf. Psalm 18:28). It is **the lamp of the Lord** through which He, who is light, illuminates and

searches **all the inward parts** of the belly (all man's inmost being).

The Preservation of the King. 20:28. **28. Mercy** (steadfast love and kindness) and **truth preserve** (keep) **the king** and balance his actions and decisions. He himself needs God's mercy, and so he must demonstrate mercy to others. The king, as God's earthly representative, is to reflect the King of kings, the Messiah, in whom mercy and truth meet together in perfect balance (Psalm 85:10).

The Glory of Youth and Old Age. 20:29. **29. The glory of young men is their strength** (rightly used). **And the beauty** (*hᵃdār*, "splendor") **of old men is the gray head**—when it is found in the way of godliness (16:31).

The Cleansing Ministry of Chastening. 20:30. **30. The blueness of a wound** (indicating severe chastisement) **cleanseth away evil; so do stripes** (lashes) **the inward parts** of the belly. To be chastened by the LORD saves one from being "condemned with the world" (1 Cor. 11:32), and serious sin demands "scourging" (severe whipping; Heb. 12:6; cf. Prov. 15:5, 31; 16:16; 17:16; 18:15; 19:8; 22:6).

L. RIGHT AND WRONG CONDUCT IN CONTRAST (CONT.). 21:1-31.

The Lord's Control of Men's Hearts. 21:1. **1.** "The king's heart [mind] is like water channels in the hand [under the control of] the LORD. He turns it [the heart] wherever he wishes" (lit. Heb.; Ezra 6:22). The LORD sovereignly controls all men's hearts (minds), but kings are singled out to represent mankind since their hearts seem especially difficult to manage; and, because of their high position, they are inclined to do whatever they desire. If the LORD controls them, He controls common men, all men with as much ease as gardeners turn irrigation streams into whatever channels they please (cf. Cyrus, Ezra 1:1-4), and wicked kings (Rev. 17:17).

Man Looks on the Outward; God Looks on the Heart. 21:2. **2. Every way of a man** (everything he does) **is right in his own eyes, but the Lord weigheth** (*ṭkn*, "regulates, measures, estimates") **the hearts** (men's minds in their inner motives and attitudes) according to His standard, not theirs (16:2; 24:12; Luke 16:15).

Spiritual Reality Versus Religious Ritual. 21:3. **3. To do** (practice) **righteousness** (*ṣᵉḏāqâ*, "right") **and justice is more acceptable to the Lord than sacrifice.** To substitute ceremonial obedience (the means to the end) for moral and spiritual integrity (the end) is not only cold externalism, but also rank hypocrisy (1 Sam. 15:22; Mic. 6:7-8). Witness the Pharisees of Jesus' day (Matt. 23:13-36).

Evidence of the Sin of Pride. 21:4. **4. An high look** (lit., "haughtiness, exaltation of eyes"; Psalm 10:4; Isa. 2:11, 17; 1 Pet. 5:6), **and a proud heart,** an insolent attitude of mind, **and the plowing** (*nîr*) **of the wicked,** even their commendable labor, **are sin.** The wicked are full of sin, shown by their pride, the primal and basic sin (Isa. 14:12-14). Their sin vitiates all they are and do, even their "lamp" (*nēr*, "light, candle," following the LXX, Vulgate, Arabic, Syriac, RSV, NASB). Unregenerate and lawless, the wicked are evil in seed, root, branch, and fruit (ACC, 3: 760). Their "lamp" (Job 21:17; Prov. 13:9; 24:20) symbolizes everything in which they glory—their prosperity, wealth, power—everything that is the basis of their pride.

The Reward of Diligent Planning. 21:5. **5. The thoughts** (plans) **of the diligent** (*ḥārûṣ*, "sharp, keen") **tend only to plenteousness** (abundance, profit). **But** (the plans) **of every one that is hasty** (*'āṣ*, "who is pressed"), who allows himself to be pressurized into immature or unwise ventures, **tend only to want** (10:4; 13:4). We are to "run with patience," not with haste (Heb. 12:1; cf. Matt. 13:5-6; Rom. 2:7).

The Snare of Acquiring Wealth Dishonestly. 21:6. **6. The getting of treasures** (acquiring of wealth) **by a lying tongue is a vanity tossed to and fro** (*hěběl niddāp*, "a vapor or cloud dispersed or suddenly scattered") of those who **seek** (court) **death** (Job 18:5; Prov. 13:9; 24:20).

The Outcome of Violence. 21:7. **7. The robbery** (*shōḏ*, "violence, oppression, ruin") **of the wicked shall destroy them** (drag them down to ruin), **because they refuse to do** (practice) **justice.** The plunder seized by them will be their own undoing. They shall be recompensed in kind (24:29; Matt. 5:39; Rom. 12:17; 1 Thess. 5:15; 1 Pet. 3:9).

Wrong Conduct in Contrast to Right Conduct. 21:8. **8.** This verse is correctly translated: "The way of man that is perverted is also strange. But as for the **pure** [*zāq*, 'sincere, morally clean'] **his work** is upright." The conduct of a man (*'ish*, "a man once good"; "froward," KJV; "crooked," NASB) implies his perversity by having abandoned the "right" (upright) way. He is also strange (alien). This predicates that he who is perverted from goodness becomes alien and alienated from God and the congregation of "the pure." By contrast, "the pure" manifests his upright conduct by "his work," his actions and deeds.

The Contentious Woman Excoriated. 21:9. **9. It is better to dwell** (live, reside) **in a corner of the housetop** (in a small room built on the flat roof of an Oriental home, cf. 2 Kings 4:10, exposed to the elements), **than with a brawling woman** (a woman of contentions, a shrew) **in a** wide house ("a house of community," i.e., a dwelling shared with her). What irony that the master of the household should be banished to the corner of the roof by his wife's tongue (cf. v. 19; 25:24).

The Inveterate Viciousness of the Wicked. 21:10. **10. The soul of the wicked,** the mind of the vicious man, **desireth** (*'iww^etâ,* "eagerly desires, yearns for, lusts after") **evil. His neighbor** (fellowman) **findeth no favor in his eyes** (Jer. 10:23). His love of evil outweighs every other consideration.

The Superior Learning Power of the Wise. 21:11. **11. When the scoffer** (the railer at godliness and virtue) **is punished,** he comes to grief for his aggravated sin. At the same time **the simple** (the naive; the naively, not blatantly, foolish) **is made wise** (learns a lesson; cf. 19:25). **When the wise** (man) **is instructed, he receiveth knowledge** readily, intelligently. It does not have to be enforced upon him by drastic demonstration.

The Sure Doom of the Wicked. 21:12. **12. The righteous one considers the house of the wicked, turning the wicked to ruin** (NASB; v. 8). Most commentators render it, "The righteous man deals considerately with the house of the wicked," his thoughtfulness and concern accentuating the evil of his neighbor (cf. Prov. 25:21-22). **But God overthroweth** (destroys) **the wicked for their wickedness** (Rom. 2:8), recompensing them for their aggravated sin.

Callous Unconcern for the Poor. 21:13. **13. Whoso** (he who) **stoppeth his ears at the cry of the poor** (Matt. 18:29-34; 1 John 3:17), **he also shall cry himself, but shall not be heard** (be answered; Matt. 18:29-34; James 2:13; *Amen-em-ope:* "Guard yourself against robbing the oppressed," chap. 7, ANET, p. 422*a*).

The Evil Power of a Bribe. 21:14. **14. A gift in secret**—the secrecy implying a guilty present (17:23), not honorable gifts, as was Jacob's to pacify Esau (Gen. 32:20)—**pacifieth anger** (Prov. 18:16; 19:6). **And a reward** (bribe) **in the bosom** (allays) **strong wrath**—the stronger passion of greed giving way to the weaker passion of anger.

The Execution of Justice. 21:15. **15. The doing of justice is a joy to the righteous, but to the workers of iniquity it is a calamity** (BV; 10:29), for that spells ruin for them.

The Penalty of Backsliding. 21:16. **16. The man that wandereth out of the way of understanding** (i.e., goes astray from the truth of God's Word) **shall remain** (dwell) **in the congregation of the dead** (departed spirits; Psalm 49:14), forfeiting fellowship with God and God's people (not salvation; 1 John 1:5-7), and incurring premature physical death for serious sin (1 Cor. 11:30-32; 1 John 5:16).

The Outcome of Loving Pleasure and Luxury. 21:17. **17.** A person who loves pleasure and luxury will end in poverty—material as well as spiritual. To enjoy pleasure and to use wine and oil is lawful. But to "love" them is incompatible with loving God, which alone makes one truly "rich" (1 Cor. 7:29-31; 1 John 2:15).

The Wicked as a Ransom for the Righteous. 21:18. **18. The wicked shall be a ransom** (*kōpĕr,* "a consideration paid for the redemption of a captured person"), **and the transgressor for the upright** (Isa. 43:3-4; 53:4-5; 55:8-9). God often cuts off the wicked in order to set free His people from their power; He causes the wicked to fall into the traps they have set for the righteous (Prov. 11:8; cf. Josh. 7:24-26; Esther 7:10).

The Bane of a Quarrelsome Wife. 21:19. **19. Better to dwell in the wilder-**

ness (desert) with all its inhospitable hardships, than with a **contentious and an angry woman** (see v. 9; 25:24).

The Spendthrift Fool. 21:20. **20.** The precious treasure and oil in the dwelling of the wise (8:21; 22:4; Psalm 112:3), the **foolish man spendeth** (swallows) **it up**—squanders what wise men have diligently amassed.

The Reward of the Pursuit of Righteousness. 21:21. **21.** He **followeth after** (*rdp*, "diligently pursues, earnestly seeks") what is right and kind (*ḥĕsĕḏ*, "mercy, kindness, loving fidelity"; 15:9; Matt. 5:6). His reward is fullness of spiritual **life**, practical outworking of his **righteousness** before God by faith (Gen. 15:6) in everyday conduct before men and **honor** (respect) before God and man.

Wisdom Is More Potent Than Human Strength. 21:22. **22. A wise man scaleth** (the walls of) **the city of the mighty** (24:5; 2 Sam. 5:6-9; Eccles. 7:19; 9:15-16), **and casteth down the strength of the confidence** (the strength of trust, i.e., the stronghold in which the townspeople trust), instead of their putting their confidence in the LORD.

Watching One's Speech Is a Guard Against Trouble. 21:23. **23.** He who **keepeth** (guards, carefully watches) **his mouth and his tongue** (what he says), **keepeth** (guards) **his soul** (himself) **from troubles** (trials; 12:13; 13:3; 18:21; James 3:2).

Names Given the Proud Man. 21:24. **24. Proud ... haughty** and **scoffer** are the names of him who **dealeth** (acts) **in proud wrath** (1:22; 3:34; 24:9; Psalm 1:1; Isa. 29:20) in arrogant fury, a conspicuous manifestation of pride (16:6; Jer. 48:29; cf. Exod. 5:2; 2 Kings 18:35; Esther 3:5).

The Sad End of the Sluggard. 21:25-26. **25. The desire of the slothful** (lazy)—all his frustrated hopes (13:12) ending in destitution (20:4)—**kills him**,

because **his hands refuse to labor. 26. He coveteth greedily all the day long, but the righteous giveth and spareth not.** So far from coveting what others have, like the sluggard, he has his needs abundantly satisfied and gives liberally to others (Psalms 37:25-26; 112:9; Matt. 5:42; Eph. 4:28).

The Abomination of Religious Hypocrisy. 21:27. **27. The sacrifice of the wicked is an abomination** (an idolatrous affront) to the true God (15:8; Psalm 50:8-9; Isa. 66:3; Jer. 6:20; Amos 5:22). **How much more when** the pretended worshiper **bringeth it with a wicked mind** (with an evil intent), with some shameful purpose, as did Balak and Balaam to curse Israel (Num. 23:1-3, 13); Absalom to rebel against David (2 Sam. 15:7-10); Jezebel to cover her treachery (1 Kings 21:9-12); and the adulteress to entice her dupe (Prov. 7:14-15).

The Endurance of Truth. 21:28. **28. A false witness shall perish, but the man that heareth,** who gives testimony only to what he has heard with his own ears, his testimony will endure. He will speak **constantly**—he shall not be silenced as a liar (19:5, 9), but go on speaking (as a witness).

The Shamelessness of the Wicked. 21:29. **29. A wicked man hardeneth** (*hēēz*, "makes bold") **his face** against admonition in order to continue in his wrong way of life. He must put on a bold face to persevere in wickedness (Eccles. 8:1). **But ... the upright** (Psalm 119:5; Prov. 11:5) "considers" (*yāḇîn*, *Qere*) **his way.** If he inadvertently falls into sin, he does not harden his face (and heart) against admonition, but "considers" his course and turns from his sin. The Kethiv reading is: **he directs** his way in the right course and does not deliberately and shamelessly adhere to it like the wicked man (7:13; Isa. 3:9; Jer. 5:3).

The Futility of Withstanding God.

21:30. **30. There is no wisdom** (pretended wisdom) **nor understanding, nor counsel against the Lord** (Isa. 8:9-10; Acts 5:39). Compare the issue of Ahithophel's wise counsel (2 Sam. 16:23; 17:1-14, 23).

The Lord Alone Is Savior and Deliverer. 21:31. **31. The horse is prepared for the day of battle** (Psalms 20:7; 33:17; Isa. 31:1). **But safety** (Syriac, Vulgate), better, "victory" (RSV, NASB, AB) rests with the LORD. External helps are not to be rejected, but the LORD alone is to be trusted to give the victory.

M. RIGHT AND WRONG CONDUCT IN
CONTRAST (CONCLUDED). 22:1-16.

The Desirability of a Good Reputation. 22:1. **1. A good name** (Eccles. 7:1) **is rather to be chosen** (*bḥr*, "preferred, loved, desired") **than great riches, and loving favor** (*ḥēn*, "kindness, graciousness, grace") **rather than silver and gold.** What you are (your name) is far more important than what you have (silver and gold). Character is a far more pivotal consideration than possessions.

The Common Bond of All Mankind. 22:2. **2. The rich and poor meet together** (29:13; cf. 1 Cor. 12:21). They have a common bond, not of economic status, race, creed, or sex, but of origin. **The Lord is the maker of them all** (Gen. 1:26-27; Job 31:15; Prov. 14:31). This is not the doctrine of "the fatherhood of God and the brotherhood of man" (because the Fall came in and wiped that out). Only regenerated men are "brothers." But the tie of creation binds *all* men together in a common bond of love and mutual concern for one another's welfare, especially concern on the part of the regenerated for the salvation of the unregenerate.

The Prudence of Foreseeing and Forestalling Danger. 22:3. **3. A prudent** (cleverly discerning) **man foreseeth the evil** (*rā'â*, "trouble, misfortune"), **and hideth himself** from it (avoids it) until it is gone (Isa. 4:6; 26:20; 32:2). **But the simple** (the inexperienced, headstrong, and foolish) **pass on** (go right ahead), **and are punished**—they suffer for their imprudence and naivete, paying the penalty for being simpletons.

The Issue of Godly Humility. 22:4. **4. By humility** ("as a result of" humility), better, "the reward [*'ēqĕḇ*, 'result, end, consequence'] of humility" and the **fear of the Lord** (reverence for Him and His Word) **are riches, and honor, and life** (Psalms 19:11; 112:3; Matt. 6:33). True humility is inseparable from reverence for the LORD and *always* gives spiritual wealth (often temporal riches), honor, and eternal life. Humility enables us to see ourselves as sinners and to appropriate God's grace for salvation.

The Pathway of the Perverse. 22:5. **5.** The way of the perverse is strewn with **thorns,** causing suffering and woe, and **snares** (temptations), causing the morally and spiritually twisted to fall into the bondage of sin. He who will **keep** (guard) **his soul** (i.e., himself)—is cautious how he lives—will be **far from them** (i.e., give the thorns and the snares a wide berth).

The Benefits of Proper Child Training. 22:6. **6. Train up** (*ḥnk*, "teach, initiate, dedicate") **a child in the way he should go,** that is, "initiate" or "dedicate" him as a house (Num. 7:10-11) or a temple (1 Kings 8:63) by giving him the training he needs for life. The child is to be introduced to the right way to live from the earliest period of comprehension (Deut. 6:7; 2 Tim. 1:5; 3:15). As a newly built temple, not yet profaned, is solemnly dedicated to the LORD, so a child is to be dedicated as a temple of the Holy Spirit (1 Cor. 6:19-20; cf. 1 Sam. 1:28) in his youthful innocence and pliability. **And** (even) **when he is old, he will not depart from it.** The seed sown in childhood is bound to come to harvest in adulthood.

Capitalism, a Blessing or a Curse. 22:7. **7. The rich ruleth over** (*māshăl*, "manages, governs") **the poor.** It involves the capitalist and the laborer, a necessary God-ordained arrangement in a free society. But let the capitalist's control be exercised in order and kindness, not in pride and oppression (James 2:6). Greed turns a capitalist into a heartless tyrant, and a *lender* into a cruel master, who abases those who fall into debt and become his slaves.

The Law of Sowing and Reaping. 22:8. **8.** He who **soweth iniquity shall reap vanity** (Job 4:8; Prov. 24:16; Hos. 10:13; Gal. 6:7; "calamity," RSV; *'āwĕn*, "emptiness, wickedness, distress, hardship"). **And the rod of his anger,** with which in his wrath he struck the poor, **shall fail** ("perish," Syriac; "shall be consumed," Isa. 14:5-6).

Blessing of Liberality. 22:9. **9.** He who has **a bountiful eye** (lit., "good of eye"; i.e., is generous, liberal) **shall be blessed.** The "bountiful eye" contrasts with an evil eye against a poor brother (Deut. 15:9). It looks on and sees a brother's need (Luke 10:32) and is moved to compassion to help, and **shall be blessed** by the LORD (2 Cor. 9:6-7), the poor (Job 31:20), and all good people. **For he giveth of his bread to** (shares his food with) **the poor** (indigent; Luke 14:13).

The Scoffer and Strife. 22:10. **10. Cast out** (drive out) **the scoffer, and contention shall go out** (Gen. 21:9-10; Prov. 18:6). **Yea, strife and reproach** (dishonor) **shall cease.**

Purity of Heart and Graciousness of Speech. 22:11. **11. He who loves purity of heart** (Psalm 24:4; Matt. 5:8) **and whose speech is gracious, the king is his friend** (NASB). The "heart" (mind) is the source of our words (12:33-35), and a

pure fountain gives forth gracious words (James 3:10-11). The rewards of such a person with clean mind and gracious lips are summarized in the words: "the king shall be his friend." He will eventually be promoted to power and honor before the King of kings.

The Lord's Blessing upon Knowledge. 22:12. **12.** The LORD'S **eyes ... preserve** (*nṣr*, "watch over, guard, keep, protect") **knowledge** (the godly, experiential knowledge of the truth). His "eyes" (His omniscience) regard with favor; so He preserves (keeps) those who possess saving knowledge of His grace, and He watches out that such saving knowledge is not lost to them. **And** (but) **he overthroweth the words of the transgressor,** who hopes by lies and flatteries to gain his ends, and who has no perception of or hope in God's grace.

The Lazy Man and His Empty Excuses for Shirking Work. 22:13. **13.** A ridiculous example of the lazy man's excuses to justify his shiftlessness is given. **A lion outside; I shall be slain in the streets,** where no lion would venture under any conceivable circumstances (cf. 10:26; 13:4; 15:19; 18:9; 20:4).

The Lure of the Harlot. 22:14. **14.** Her **mouth ... is a deep pit** (5:3). He who is **abhorred** (cursed) **by the Lord shall fall therein** (into it; Eccles. 7:26).

The Necessity of Child Discipline. 22:15. **15. Foolishness is bound** (up) **in the heart** (mind) **of a child,** that is, willful ignorance is ingrained in his fallen nature. **The rod of correction**—the teacher's cane—**shall drive it far from him** (rid him of it; 13:24; 23:14).

The Penalty of Oppressing the Poor. 22:16. **16.** He who **oppresseth the poor to increase his riches** (to aggrandize himself) **and giveth to the rich,** as a bribe to gain something for himself, **shall surely come to want,** if not in this world, in the world to come. He will lack the true riches in the coming judgment of a man's works (Luke 14:12-14).

IV. THE PRECEPTS OF THE WISE MEN. 22:17—24:34.

This section contains (1) sayings (the "Thirty Precepts of the Sages") allegedly paralleled in Egyptian Wisdom Literature (22:17—23:12), in the *Instruction of Amen-em-ope* (ANET, pp. 421*a*-24*b*); (2) sayings with no parallel in Egyptian (23:13—24:22); and (3) an appendix to the "Precepts of the Wise Men" (24:23-34). See the Introduction to Proverbs.

A. PREAMBLE TO THE PRECEPTS. 22:17-21.

Introduction. 22:17-21. **17-18.** The general call is issued to hear **the words** of the wise and apply the **heart** (mind) to them, for it is set forth as **a pleasant thing** if they are kept (observed) internally and heartily, that they may **be fitted in thy lips** (may be "ready on your lips," NASB). **19.** The purpose of the teaching is that **trust** of the reader or hearer **may be in the Lord.** Solomon represents himself as the inspired speaker for the godly wise of all ages to inculcate this grand lesson.

20-21. This involves writing **excellent things** (*sh*e*lōshîm*, "thirty precepts," now known from the publication of the *Instruction of Amen-em-ope*) **in counsels and knowledge** to make **thee,** his auditor (reader), **know the certainty of the words of truth** (Luke 1:3-4) and that he might correctly **answer** (lit., "return") answer to him who sent him (1 Pet. 3:15).

B. THIRTY PRECEPTS OF THE WISE MEN. 22:22—24:22.

Precept One: Against Exploiting the Helpless and Poor. 22:22-23. **22. Rob not the poor, because he is poor** (Exod. 23:6; Job 31:16; Prov. 23:10), for he is unable to ward off wrong and defend himself. **Neither oppress** (crush) **the afflicted in the gate** (the place of public court; Zech. 7:10; Mal. 3:5). **23. For the Lord will plead their cause** (Jer. 50:34) in the sacred court of justice and plead against you in their behalf, dealing out retribution in kind and **spoil the soul** (rob, take the life) of those who **spoiled** (despoiled, robbed) **them.** *Amen-em-ope:* "Guard yourself against robbing the oppressed and against overbearing the disabled" (chap. 2, ANET, p. 422*a*).

Precept Two: Against Associating with a Hot-Tempered Man. 22:24-25. **24. Make no friendship** (do not associate) **with an angry man** (*bă'ăl 'āp,* "a possessor of wrath; a man given to anger"); **and with a furious** (hot-tempered) **man thou shalt not go** (hobnob with one given to violent outbursts; 29:22). **25. Lest thou learn his ways** (fall into his habits; 1 Cor. 15:33), **and get a snare to thy soul** (yourself). Compare *Amen-em-ope:* "Do not associate to yourself the heated man" (chap. 9, ANET, p. 423*a*).

Precept Three: Against Making Rash Pledges. 22:26-27. **26. Be not ... one of those ... who strike hands** (6:1; 17:18), a custom signifying giving a pledge (see comments on 6:1), among those who become **sureties for debts,** who pledge themselves as surety for loans (11:15; 17:18; 20:16; 27:13). **27. If thou hast nothing to pay** the assumed obligations with, why should (the creditor) **take away thy bed from under thee?**

Precept Four: Against Removing a Boundary Stone. 22:28. **28.** The stones or cairns (Gen. 31:52), marking ancient boundary lines, which one's **fathers have set** (one's ancestors established), are not to be removed (moved back; Deut. 19:14; 27:17; Hos. 5:10). Compare

Amen-em-ope (chap. 6, ANET, p. 422*b*).

Precept Five: In Praise of Diligence and Industry. 22:29. **29. Seest thou a man diligent** (*māhîr*, "quick, prompt, skillful") **in his business** (at his work; 1 Kings 11:28; Prov. 10:4; 12:24; Eccles. 9:10; Rom. 12:11; 2 Tim. 4:2). He will stand **before kings ... not ... mean** (obscure) **men** (Gen. 41:46; 1 Kings 10:8).

Precept Six: Watching One's Table Manners. 23:1-3. **1. When thou sittest** (down) **to eat with a ruler, consider diligently what** (or who) **is before thee** (food or delicacies) so as not to eat greedily or carelessly and thus offensively. **2.** Watch your table manners and **put a knife to thy throat, if thou be a man given to appetite**, that is, to great appetite, to restrain any exhibition of gluttony.

3. Be not desirous of (do not desire) **his dainties** (delicacies), **for they are deceitful food**, tempting to overindulgence, drunkenness, and abandonment of the simple life of chastity and self-denial. Compare *Amen-em-ope*: "Do not eat bread before a noble. ... Look at the cup which is before thee" (ANET, p. 424*a*).

Precept Seven: Warning Against Ambition to Be Rich. 23:4-5. **4. Labor not** (*yg'*, "toil, exert, and weary oneself") **to be rich** (28:20; John 6:27; 1 Tim. 6:9). "Do not wear yourself out in pursuit of wealth" (AB). **Cease from thine own wisdom** (Prov. 3:5; 26:12; Rom. 12:16), from your own brand of wisdom by which you make acquiring wealth your goal in life and give money top priority.

5. Wilt thou set thine eyes upon that which is not? Literally, "Will you cause your eyes to fly upon [cf. 1 Sam. 15:19, 'fly upon the spoil'] that which is not?"—that is, that which has no solid existence and which suddenly vanishes away. Wealth "takes to itself wings,

flying like an eagle toward heaven" (RSV; Prov. 27:24; 1 Tim. 6:17). Compare *Amen-em-ope*: "Do not cast your heart in pursuit of riches ... they will have made themselves wings like geese and are flown away to the heavens" (ANET, p. 422*b*).

Precept Eight: Avoiding the Professed Hospitality of a Stingy Host. 23:6-8. **6. Do not eat the bread** (food) **of a selfish man** (NASB), literally, **of him who hath an evil eye** (28:22), in contrast to a "bountiful eye" (22:9), one who is stingy and niggardly. **Neither desire ... his dainty foods** (delicacies; Psalm 141:4; Prov. 28:21).

7. For as he thinketh (estimates) **in his heart** (mind), **so is he.** He "estimates" the cost of the food and begrudges you what you eat. He says, **Eat and drink ... but his heart is not with thee.** If you eat, he dislikes you; and the more you eat, the more he dislikes you. **8. The morsel** (portion) you have **eaten** you will **vomit up** when you find out it was given so grudgingly. **And lose** your **sweet words**, forfeiting the hoped for effect of your "pleasant words" exchanged with him at the table.

Precept Nine: Against Wasting Wisdom on a Fool. 23:9. **9. Speak not in the ears** (in the hearing) **of a fool**, that is, do not speak wise words, as in the instance of the stingy host just described (vv. 6-8; 9:7-8; 26:4-5; Isa. 36:21; Matt. 7:6). **For he will despise the wisdom of thy words.** Compare *Amen-em-ope*: "Do not empty your belly [inner thoughts] to everybody" (chap. 21, ANET, p. 424*a*).

Precept Ten: Against Removing a Boundary Line. 23:10. **10. Remove** (move back) **not an old** (ancient) **landmark** (boundary) to cheat a neighbor of part of his ancestral property, especially not **the fields** (the lands) of **the fatherless** (orphans), rightly belonging to those helpless and unprotected (cf. 22:28; Exod. 22:22; Deut. 24:7). **11. For their redeemer** (Exod. 22:22-24; Deut. 27:19; Psalm 12:5; Jer. 50:34; 51:36), the nearest of kin to the poor is the representative of God to plead their case and recover their lost inheritance (Lev. 25:25). Compare *Amen-em-ope*: "Do not carry off the landmark ... nor encroach upon the boundaries of the widow" (chap. 6, ANET, p. 422*b*). **12.** This verse is evidently a second preamble (cf. Prov. 22:17-21, especially v. 17), serving to introduce 23:13—24:22.

Precept Eleven: On the Necessity of Youth Discipline. 23:13-14. **13. Withhold not correction** (discipline) **from the child. For if thou** (emphatic; you, the parent) **beatest him with the rod** (a stick), so that he will hate sin, **he shall not die** eternally. **14.** In fact, you will **deliver his soul** (save him) **from sheol** (1 Cor. 5:5; 11:32). This precept has a close parallel in *Ahiqar* 6 (ANET, p. 428*b*).

Precept Twelve: A Wise Heart and Lips That Speak What Is Right. 23:15-16. **15-16. My son, if thine heart be wise, my heart shall rejoice ... thine heart** (thy inmost being) **shall rejoice, when thy lips speak right things** (what is right). This is a resumption of the appeal in the preamble to the "Precepts of the Sages" (22:17-21, especially v. 19).

Precept Thirteen: Encouragement to Faith in God and the Future Life. 23:17-18. **17. Do not let your heart envy sinners,** the ungodly in a state of prosperity, so as to be tempted to want what they want and have what they have (Psalms 37:1; 73:3; Prov. 24:1, 19). **But live in the fear of the Lord always** (NASB). **18. For surely there is an end** (lit., "latter end"; i.e., a future; Psalms 19:11; 58:11; Prov. 24:14). **And thine expectation** (hope; Psalm 9:18) **shall not be cut off.**

Precept Fourteen: Against Immoderation in Eating and Drinking. 23:19-21. **19. Hear thou** (emphatic), **my son, and be wise** (gain wisdom), **and guide thine heart** (direct your mind) **in the way,** that is, in the course of right conduct about to be outlined. Compare the preamble (22:17-21). **20. Be not among winebibbers** (heavy drinkers of wine; vv. 29-30; 20:1; Isa. 5:22; Matt. 24:49; Luke 21:34; Rom. 13:13; Eph. 5:18), among riotous **eaters of flesh** (meat), those who tear meat to pieces and devour it gluttonously (*gzl*) like a wild animal (Deut. 21:20; Prov. 28:7).

21. For the drunkard (*sōbē'*, "the heavy drinker") **and the glutton** (*zōlēl*, "one who debauches himself by gluttony") **shall come to poverty** (lit. Heb., "will be disinherited, dispossessed"), **and drowsiness** (*nûmâ*, "sleepiness, slumber, the natural result of excess in eating and drinking") **shall clothe a man with rags** (19:15). **22.** See below.

Precept Fifteen: On Acquiring and Treasuring Wisdom. 23:23. Verse 23 seems to belong after verse 21 and to form a separate precept. **23. Buy** (*qᵉnēh*) **the truth, and sell it not** (4:7; 18:15; Matt. 13:44). Such truth includes **wisdom** and **instruction** (*mûsār*, "disciplinary teaching") and **understanding** (*bînâ*, "insight, prudence"). Get wisdom, but do not get rid of it for any reason whatever. It is so valuable a possession, it is foolish to barter it at any price.

Precept Sixteen: Parental Respect and Its Happy Results. 23:22, 24-25. **22. Listen to your father who begot you, and do not despise your mother when she is old** (NASB). This theme is found in every division of Proverbs (cf. 1:8; 10:1; 15:20; 29:3, etc.), attesting its importance as a vital aspect of wisdom teaching. **24-25.** The result of such honoring of parents (Exod. 20:12; Matt. 15:4; 19:19; Mark 7:10; Eph. 6:2-3) is that **the father of the righteous will greatly rejoice, and he who begets a wise son will be glad in him** (NASB; Prov. 10:1; 29:3), as will his mother, who gave him birth.

Precept Seventeen: Warning Against the Harlot. 23:26-28. The harlot theme has been treated repeatedly (cf. chaps. 1-9). **26-28.** A youth needs to pay particular attention to the warning of this peril, for a **harlot is a deep ditch** (pit) **. . . a narrow well** (NASB), lurking as a robber (6:26; 7:12; Eccles. 7:26). She **increaseth the transgressors** against God's laws (Exod. 20:14) and those faithless to their wives.

Precept Eighteen: Warning Against the Folly of Drunkenness. 23:29-35. • **29-30.** *The drunkard described:* **Who hath woe? Who hath sorrow?** (Deut. 21:18-21; 27:16; Isa. 5:11, 22) **. . . contentions . . . babbling** (complaining) **. . . wounds without cause . . . redness of eyes** (bloodshot eyes)? **They that tarry** (linger) **long at** (over) **. . . wine** (1 Sam. 25:36; Prov. 20:1; Isa. 5:11; 28:7; Eph. 5:18), those who go to **seek** (search out) **mixed wine** (Psalm 75:8; *mīmsāk*, "wine mixed with other wines or with spices"; Isa. 65:11, NASB).

31. *The warning given:* Do not **look** (gloat on) the wine when **it is red** and **giveth its color** (sparkles) **in the cup**, to be lured by its beauty and appeal to the eye, **when it moveth itself aright**—goes down smoothly (easily; Song of Sol. 7:9, NASB).

The result of ignoring the warning (vv. 32-35). **32. At the last** (afterward) **it biteth like a serpent** (Job 20:16), and **stingeth like an adder** (viper; Psalm 91:13; Isa. 11:8). **33.** Your eyes see **strange things** (*zārôṯ*, "foreign things, alien to ordinary experience; 'strange apparitions, exciting lust one moment, fear the next"). **And thine heart** (mind) **shall utter perverse things** (things over-

turned, upset, or confused)—your mind and speech will speak confusion and perversity.

34. And you will be like one who lies down in the middle of the sea, or like one who lies down on the top of a mast (NASB), tossed up and down and to and fro in helter-skelter confusion. **35.** All the while the drunkard says, "They struck me, but I did not become ill [*ḥālâ*, 'feel pain, suffer']. They beat [*ḥlm*, 'flogged, lashed'] me, but I didn't know it! As soon as I can wake up, I'll go after another drink!" (lit. Heb.).

Precept Nineteen: Warning Against Envying Evil Men. 24:1-2. **1. Do not be envious** (jealous) **of evil men** (NASB; Psalm 37:1; Prov. 3:31; 23:17; 24:19), that is, do not imagine they have some advantage you do not have, and desire to possess that same advantage. **Neither desire to be with them**—wish for their company (Psalm 1:1; Prov. 1:15; 2 Cor. 6:17). **2. For their heart** (mind) **studieth** (meditates, devises) **destruction** (*shōḏ*, "violence"), **and their lips talk of mischief** (trouble; Job 15:35; Psalms 10:7; 38:12; Isa. 30:12; Jer. 22:17).

Precept Twenty: This Is the House That Wisdom Built. 24:3-4. **3. Through** (by) **wisdom is an house** (household) **builded, and by understanding it is established.** In surveying the seeming prosperity of the wicked (vv. 1-2), do not despair of true prosperity for the godly (Jer. 22:13-16; Amos 5:11; Mic. 3:10-12). But the house (household), like a life, must be founded and established upon true wisdom (Christ; cf. 1 Cor. 1:30; 3:10-15). **4. And by knowledge** (of true wisdom) **shall the household and the individual life be filled with all precious and pleasant riches** (in Christ, the true wisdom), the true riches that transcend time (Luke 12:33; 16:11; 1 Cor. 3:10-15).

Precept Twenty-one: Wisdom Will Give You Power. 24:5-6. **5. A wise man** (*gĕ̱ḇer*, "a man of strength") is not only **strong** (lit., "is in strength," the sphere of power), but **increaseth strength** in the position of might he has (cf. Eph. 6:10), as he realizes his position and by faith in God converts it into his experience. **6.** For the wise man listens to **wise counsel** (God's Word, etc.) and becomes victorious in war, both natural warfare and spiritual conflict (6:11-19). Victory in warfare follows after the wise advice of many counselors (the Word of God, as well as godly people).

Precept Twenty-two: Wisdom Beyond the Comprehension of the Fool. 24:7. **7. Wisdom is too high for** (beyond the understanding of) **a fool** (Job 5:3-4; Psalm 10:5; Prov. 14:6; 17:16). He dares not open **his mouth** for lack of wisdom **in the gate** (the place where court was held and justice dispensed; Psalm 127:5) as loose-tongued and babbling as he is elsewhere.

Precept Twenty-three: The Wicked Schemer—Master of Trickery. 24:8-9. **8.** He who **deviseth** (schemes) **to do evil** (6:14; 14:22; Rom. 1:30) **will be called a mischief-maker** (BV). **9. The thought of foolishness** (the devising of folly) **is sin** (Isa. 59:7). **And the scoffer is an abomination to men** (*'ā̱dām*, "mankind"). Fully developed folly gives birth to the scorner, who reaches a low state morally when he makes a mockery of everything sacred, even exciting the disgust of worldlings.

Precept Twenty-four: Strength Attested in a Crisis. 24:10. **10.** If you **faint** (*hĭtrăppĭtā*, "show yourself slack or feeble") **in the day of adversity** (distress, in a time of crisis), your **strength is small.** A man is no more than a crisis shows him to be. But he can be supernaturally strengthened (Isa. 40:29).

Precept Twenty-five: Concern About the Welfare of Others. 24:11-12. **11.** "Rescue those who are being taken away to death; hold back those who are stumbling to the slaughter" (lit. Heb.; Psalm 82:4; Isa. 58:6-7). **12. If you say, "See, we did not know this," does He** (the LORD) not consider it who weighs the hearts? (1 Sam. 16:7; Prov. 21:2; Eccles. 5:8). **And does He not know it** (Psalm 121:3-8) **who keeps** (guards) **your soul?** (94:9-11). **And will He not render to** (requite) **man according to his work?** (NASB, Job 34:11; Prov. 12:14; Rom. 2:6; Rev. 20:12-13; 22:12).

The response of many to a situation of need such as this, is that of Cain: "Am I my brother's keeper" (Gen. 4:9). "It's none of my business. I have enough to do minding my own business." But the LORD guards our soul. Shall we have no concern for the souls of others or forget that we will be judged for our actions or inaction at the judgment for our works?

Precept Twenty-six: Wisdom's Assurance of Hope for the Future. 24:13-14. **13. My son, eat ... honey**—a gracious invitation to partake of wisdom, which is spiritual honey (Psalms 19:10; 119:103; Prov. 25:16; Song of Sol. 5:1)—**because it is good** for the body and the soul. **And the honeycomb** (*nō̱p̱ĕt*, "its drippings," BV; "wild honey," AB) ... **is sweet to thy taste.**

14. So shall the knowledge of wisdom be unto thy soul (Prov. 16:24; 27:7; Song of Sol. 4:11). When you have **found it** (Matt. 13:44, 46; 1 Cor. 1:30), **then there shall be a reward** (*'ăhᵃrît*, "a latter end, a future"), **and thy expectation** (*tĭqwĕh*, "hope") **shall not be cut off** (Prov. 23:18; 1 Tim. 4:8) in disappointment. Those who find Christ, God's wisdom (1 Cor. 1:30), find eternal life and the realization of an eternity of bliss in which they shall not be disappointed.

Precept Twenty-seven: The Resilience of the Righteous Man. 24:15-16.

15. The wicked man is warned not to lie in wait (plot evil) **against the dwelling** (home) **of the righteous** (Psalm 10:9-10), the regenerate man who reposes faith in divine redemptive grace (Gen. 15:6) and lives a life consonant with his trust. **Spoil not** (do not despoil) **his resting place** (*rĕḇeṣ*, "a place of repose"). **16. For a just** (righteous, same word) **man falleth seven times** (ever so many times; Prov. 26:25) into calamities **and riseth up again** out of them all by God's help (Job 5:19; Psalm 37:24; Mic. 7:8). How futile then the evil plans and attacks of the wicked. "But the wicked stumble in calamity" (lit. Heb.) and do not rise up again.

Precept Twenty-eight: Warning Against Rejoicing in the Fall of an Enemy. 24:17-18. **17. Do not rejoice ... do not ... be glad when he** (your enemy) falls or **stumbles** (NASB) into calamity; do not even be glad inwardly, much less outwardly. **18. Lest the Lord see it, and it displease him,** who would have us love our enemies (cf. Rom. 12:19-21). This is not inconsistent with rejoicing over the overthrow of public enemies such as Pharaoh (Exod. 15) and mystical Babylon (Rev. 18:20; cf. 2 Sam. 1:17; contrast Obad. 12). Lest the LORD **turn away his wrath from him** to punish you for exulting in his calamity (Job 31:29; Ezek. 25:3; 26:2).

Precept Twenty-nine: Against Fretting Oneself Because of Evildoers. 24:19-20. **19. Fret not thyself** (get yourself upset or angry; Psalm 37:1) or **be ... envious of the wicked** (v. 1), of their present well-being, which seems to nullify the doctrine of divine rewards and punishment (cf. Prov. 3:31-32; 23:17; 24:1). **20.** Whatever prosperity they may seem to enjoy now, **there shall be no reward** (*'ăḥªrît*, "future, latter end"), nothing to look forward to; and the **lamp of the wicked** (13:9), a figure of their seeming prosperity and well-being, **shall** be put out in the darkness of Sheol (Job 18:5-6; 22:17). Why fret at or be envious of anyone with such a bleak future?

Precept Thirty: On Reverencing the Lord and the King. 24:21-22. **21.** The LORD is to be held in awe because He is the absolute Sovereign of the universe, and the king is to be reverenced because he is the LORD's earthly representative (Rom. 13:1-7; 1 Pet. 2:7). "Do not meddle [associate with] those who are given to change" (lit. Heb.), who are fond of innovations that lead away from loyalty to the LORD and the king, and so to rebellion and disobedience.

22. For their calamity (v. 16; cf. Jer. 2:36-37; Jude 8), that is, of these innovators or rebels, **shall rise suddenly, and who knoweth the ruin of them both?**—of those who do not fear the LORD and of those who do not fear the king (Psalm 35:8). Or the sense may be: "For disaster from them [the LORD and the king] will rise suddenly, and who knows the ruin that will come from them both?" (RSV).

C. Appendix to the Precepts of the Wise Men. 24:23-34.

Introduction to the Appendix. 24:23a. **23a. These also are sayings of the wise** (NASB; see comment on 22:17).

Against Partiality in a Judicial Decision. 24:23b-26. **23b. To show partiality in judgment is not good** (NASB). This short line seems to be a legal maxim (cf. 18:5; 28:21) and is expanded in verses 24 to 26. **24.** He who says to the wicked, **Thou art righteous** (Exod. 23:6-7; Prov. 17:15; Isa. 5:23; Jer. 6:13-14; Ezek. 13:22), who tells a guilty man he is innocent, **him shall the people** (peoples) **curse, nations shall abhor** (loathe) **him.**

25. But to those who rebuke him (the guilty man) **shall be delight**—will be well regarded, **and a good blessing** (blessing of prosperity) **shall come upon them** from the LORD. **26. He kisses the lips**, that is, shows his love for his fellowman (2 Sam. 15:5), **who gives a right** (honest) **answer** (NASB), who does not show partiality in a judicial decision (Deut. 1:17; 2 Chron. 19:7; Prov. 18:5; John 7:24; James 2:4-6; 1 Pet. 1:17).

Wisdom in Building a House. 24:27. **27. Prepare thy work outside**—do thoroughly what needs to be done outside—in choosing the right spot, which must then first be made suitable for building. **And make it fit** (ready) ... **in the field**—get everything ready in the field so that you have food to eat when you move into the completed house. **Afterwards build thine house.** Why have a new house to starve in or have insufficient money to finish it? (cf. Luke 14:28-30).

Against False Witnessing. 24:28-29. **28-29.** Do not be **a witness against thy neighbor without cause,** falsely or even frivolously, and certainly not spitefully without a sure basis for your accusation. And **deceive not with thy lips,** either with false accusations or insidious insinuations out of a desire for revenge (20:22; 25:21-22; Matt. 5:3; Rom. 12:17-21).

The Folly of the Sluggard. 24:30-34. **30-31. I went by the field of the slothful** ('*îsh 'āṣēl*, "a man, a sluggard"), **and by the vineyard of the man void of understanding** (dull-witted); **and, lo, it was all grown over with thorns** (thorn bushes), **and nettles** (a kind of weed; Job 30:7) and its wall broken down (Isa. 5:5).

32-34. The lesson to the wise man (v. 32) is given: **A little sleep, a little slumber, a little folding of the hands to rest** (NASB), then poverty will come gradually as a traveler and then more rapidly, and finally **want** (destitution) like **an armed man** to hold you up suddenly and take all you have at sword's point, leaving you penniless.

V. THE SECOND BOOK OF SOLOMON. 25:1—29:27.

A. VARIOUS SOLOMONIC PROVERBS. 25:1-28.

Introduction to This Section. 25:1. **1.** This part of the book contains a selection from the three thousand proverbs that Solomon spoke (1 Kings 4:32; Eccles. 12:9) and were copied out by **the men of Hezekiah** (715-687 B.C.) almost three centuries later (2 Kings 18). This activity was doubtless a part of that good king's great reformation and revival of the Word of God (2 Chron. 31:21).

God's Glory and a King's Honor. 25:2-3. **2.** God's glory is **to conceal a thing.** He reveals only enough of His blessed nature and purposes for faith to rest upon, for He is obligated to none to render an account of His ways. He would not be God if His counsels and works did not transcend human minds and creature intelligence (Psalm 77:19; Rom. 11:33-36). **But the honor of kings is to search out a matter** (1 Kings 3:9, 28; 4:29, 31; Ezra 4:15; 5:17; 6:1), in contrast to God, who knows all things without searching (Ezra 4:15-19; 5:17; 6:1). In the capacity of a judge, kings were bound in duty to search out a matter in order to decide aright in difficult cases (1 Kings 3:16-28; Job 29:16; cf. Deut. 17:18-19). The honor of a king also stems from his being God's representative to the people.

3. So standing in the place of the heavenly King, the king is exalted, and his **heart** (mind) is unsearchable (unfathomable), and his deeper counsels of state, viewed as God-given, cannot be searched out by his people in a true theocracy. Therefore, the governed must respect his rule and not "speak evil of the things that they understand not" (2 Pet. 2:10, 12; Jude 8, 10).

The Founding of a King's Throne in

Righteousness. 25:4-5. **4. Take away** (remove) **the dross** (impurities) **from the silver** (26:23; Ezek. 22:18), **and there shall come forth a vessel for the refiner** (the smelter, the silversmith). Smelting out the dross makes the silver beautifully bright for the artisan to work it into a lovely vessel (Mal. 3:2-3). **5.** So the dross of wicked men (Isa. 1:22) must be removed if the royal **throne** is to **be established in righteousness** — firmly founded in right — and shine with the luster it should (Prov. 20:8).

Folly of Putting on Airs at a Royal Court. 25:6-7. **6. Put not forth thyself** (do not put yourself forward, be pushy, put on airs) **in the presence of the king** — boasting or claiming honors for yourself. **And stand not in the place of great men** — do not take position where the great belong. **7. Far better it is that it be said unto thee, Come up hither, than that thou shouldest be put lower** (and be humiliated) **in the presence of the prince** (Luke 14:7-11), **whom thine eyes have seen** — whom you have so boldly placed yourself unduly near in order to see him at such close proximity, and thus suffer special embarrassment to be placed far from him, as he looks on.

Warning Against Hasty Litigation. 25:8. **8. Go not forth hastily to strive** (press a quarrel, to litigate in a judicial sense, go to court; 17:14; Matt. 5:5). **Otherwise, what will you do in the end, when your neighbor puts you to shame?** (NASB). Better be well assured of your case before you take it to law, or your quarrel before you press it to its end (2 Kings 14:8-14; 2 Chron. 35:20-24). Some construe the last clause of verse 7 with verse 8: "What your eyes have seen [v. 7] do not hastily bring into court" (RSV; also AB following Vulgate). This rendering would be an admonition to bear in mind that "things are not always what they seem."

On Settling a Dispute. 25:9-10. **9.** Rather than resorting to a court of law (v. 8), **debate thy cause** (argue your case) **with thy neighbor himself** (Matt. 5:25; 18:15). **And disclose not a secret**, including the offense itself, which ought to be kept such and not be revealed to a third party. The introduction of a third party arouses the pride of the first party not to yield (cf. Gen. 13:6-9; 21:25-32; Judg. 11:12-27). But secrecy should be kept in all aspects of the case, particularly in disclosing only what is to the point in the issue at stake, avoiding all that is or ought to be confidential and would tend to blacken the adversary's character to establish that you are right in the quarrel. **10. Lest** he who **heareth it** (your revealing your neighbor's "secret" in blackening his character) **put thee to shame** (as an infamous backbiter), and the secrets of your own shame be broadcast in retaliation (Prov. 11:13).

On Fitting Speech. 25:11. **11. A word fitly spoken** (lit. Heb., "spoken upon its two wheels," moving quickly to the end aimed at), the speaker being compared to a skillful charioteer commanding his steeds and whisking his chariot to its desired destination. **Is like apples of gold in pictures of silver** (filigree work, in which Orientals excel). Such a well-spoken word has a lovely effect and delights like the sight of a work of artistic charm (15:23).

A Sage's Reprimand to a Docile Listener. 25:12. **12. As an earring** (or nose ring) **of gold** (Exod. 32:2; 35:22; Ezek. 16:12), **and an ornament of fine gold** (2 Sam. 1:24; Job 28:17), **so is a wise reprover upon an obedient ear** (Prov. 15:31; 20:12). Accepting such correction, effecting improvement in the willing hearer, is equivalent to be adorned with the most exquisite jewels.

The Refreshment of a Reliable Messenger. 25:13. **13. As the cold of snow** from the heights of Lebanon is employed to cool the drink of hot, thirsty harvesters, so is a messenger who has faithfully fulfilled his mission, and thus relieves the mind of his master, who has dispatched him (10:26 presents the contrast).

The Disappointment of the Man of Empty Promises. 25:14. **14.** He who **boasteth himself of a false gift** ("a gift of falsehood," i.e., "of a gift he does not give") is compared to **clouds and wind without rain,** watched eagerly after the dry summer for much-needed precipitation (Jude 12; cf. Jer. 5:13; Mic. 2:11).

The Effectiveness of Patient Persistence. 25:15. **15. By long forbearing** (lit., "length or duration of anger"; being long-tempered; Gen. 32:4; 1 Sam. 25:23-24; Eccles. 10:4) **is a prince** (a ruler, high official) **persuaded** (cf. Prov. 15:1), **and a soft tongue breaketh the bone**—breaks a heart as obdurate as bone (Judg. 8:2-3).

Warning Against Immoderation. 25:16. **16. Have you found honey?** (NASB; Judg. 14:8; 1 Sam. 14:25). **Eat as much as is sufficient for thee** (only what you need). Honey symbolizes lawful pleasures of this world. Be moderate (Phil. 4:5). Immoderation will sicken one spiritually, eventually producing nausea.

Wearing out One's Welcome. 25:17. **17. Withdraw thy foot** (let your foot be rarely in) **thy neighbor's house, lest he be weary of** (*śb‘*, "become sated with") **thee, and ... hate thee.** Seeing too much of you, he will begin to detest you.

A False Witness. 25:18. **18.** A false witness is compared to a **club of war** (*mēpîṣ*, "mace"), a **sword**, and a **sharp arrow** (12:18; Psalm 57:4; Jer. 9:8). Bearing false witness (Exod. 20:16; Prov. 24:28) is a particularly heinous sin that does irreparable damage to the one against whom it is committed.

Undependability of a Faithless Person. 25:19. **19. Confidence** (trust) in an undependable person (Job 6:14-20; Isa. 31:1-3; 36:6; Ezek. 29:7; 2 Tim. 4:16) **in time of trouble** (adversity) **is like a broken** (bad) **tooth,** which may start to pain at any moment, and **a foot out of joint** (*mû‘āḏĕt*, "fixed, permanently set in a crippled condition"; "palsied," AB), which will cause you to stumble and injure yourself at any moment.

The Incongruity of Joyful Singing to a Heavy Heart. 25:20. **20.** Singing to a heavy heart is like taking away a person's outer **garment in cold weather** or adding **vinegar** (sour wine) to **soda,** causing it to effervesce and become neutralized. So joyous songs (certainly worldly ditties) are incongruous to a heavy heart (Psalm 137:4; Dan. 6:18). Psalms of praise to the LORD can and do have a marked healing power upon the depressed mind.

Wise Treatment of an Enemy. 25:21-22. **21.** If an **enemy** is **hungry, give him bread** (food) **to eat ... thirsty, give him water to drink** (Exod. 23:4-5; 2 Kings 6:22; 2 Chron. 28:15; Matt. 5:44; Rom. 12:20). **22. For thou shalt heap coals of fire** (hot embers) **upon his head,** a figure of beneficent torture. Your return of good for evil will fill his mind (brain) with thoughts of how mean and despicable he has been to be an enemy of such a person as you, and that will torment him into repentance and reconciliation. Hence, you will by this means "overcome evil with good" (Rom. 12:20-21). And whether that return accomplishes the desired result or not, the LORD will **reward** (recompense; 2 Sam. 16:12) you.

The Ill-Effects of a Slanderous Tongue. 25:23. **23. The north wind brings forth** (*tᵉḥôlēl*, "produces, gives birth to") **rain, and a backbiting tongue** (lit., "tongue of secrecy," i.e., a whispering tongue produces) **an angry** countenance (NASB; looks; Psalm 101:5; this is the correct reading, supported by the Aramaic, Syriac, and Septuagint, followed by RSV, AB, and BV).

The Bane of an Ill-Humored Spouse. *25:24.* **24.** The ill-humored spouse is a repeated theme. (See comments on 21:9). The Italian proverb says, "Three things drive a man out of his house: smoke, rain, and a scolding wife" (R. B. Y. Scott, *Proverbs*, AB, p. 156).

The Refreshing Nature of Good News. 25:25. **25.** Good news is like **cold waters** to a **thirsty** (*'āyēp̱*, "weary, exhausted, faint") **soul** (person). Especially refreshing is such **good news** (*sheᵐû'â*, lit., "something heard," a report, a message) from a (distant) **far country** (cf. Luke 2:10), especially if one is an exile and the country heard from is his native land.

The Sad Spectacle of a Compromising Believer. 25:26. **26. A righteous man** (justified by faith; Gen. 15:6; Rom. 4:1-12) **falling down** (*māṭ*, "wavering, tottering, quailing"; Mic. 7:8; Matt. 26:69-70) **before** (in the presence of) **the wicked** is compared to **a troubled fountain** (*nirpāś*, "made muddy by trampling" in it) and **a corrupt spring** (polluted well).

The Shame of Self-Glory. 25:27. **27.** Even as it is **not good to eat much honey** (v. 16), for men **to search** (out) **their own glory** is not **glory,** supplying the negative in the second clause from the first clause, as sometimes happens (cf. Psalm 9:18; Prov. 27:2; Luke 14:11). To attribute all glory to God, under any circumstances, is the only wise course.

The Virtue of Self-Control. 25:28. **28.** He who has no **rule** (control) **over his own spirit** (contrast 16:32)—not only over anger, but over all wrong desires and inclinations—is like **a city ... broken down** (into) and **without walls** to

protect it from complete despoilment. Prayerful, watchful self-control is the wall, and every precaution must be exercised in order that self-reliant spiritual indolence does not breach the wall (2 Chron. 32:5; Neh. 1:3; cf. Gal. 5:23; 2 Pet. 1:6).

B. VARIOUS SOLOMONIC PROVERBS (CONT.). 26:1-28.

The Incongruity of Honoring a Fool. 26:1. **1.** As unfitting as are **snow in summer** and **rain in harvest,** upsetting the normal order of things (Eccles. 3:1) and leading only to confusion and evil (1 Sam. 12:17), **so honor** (the dignity and respect accorded by society) **is not fitting** (suitable) **for a fool.** It is a calamity when such unprincipled men are appointed to posts of responsibility.

The Impossibility of a Causeless Curse. 26:2. **2. As the bird by wandering** (like a sparrow in its flitting), **as the swallow by flying** (in its flying) never lights upon us, **so the curse ... causeless** (for which we have given no just cause) **shall not come,** alight upon us to do us harm. So Balaam could not curse God's people (Deut. 23:5), nor could Shimei's invective harm David (2 Sam. 16:5-12; cf. Psalm 109:28).

The Fool and How to Deal with Him. 26:3-12. **3.** The fool can only be treated like an animal, for he is brutish—**a whip for the horse, a bridle for the ass** (donkey), **and a rod for the fool's back** (Psalm 32:9); Prov. 10:13; 19:29. **4.** He must not be answered **according to his folly** (in his own foolish terms), **lest you also be like ... him**—descend to his folly and put yourself on his level.

5. Although you must not lower yourself to his level, you must size him up, as the occasion warrants, and answer him in such a manner that his folly will be exposed (Matt. 16:1-4; 21:24-27) and so he will not think himself wise (Prov. 3:7;

28:11; Rom. 12:16). **6.** He is to be completely eliminated from consideration for any responsible job. He who **sendeth a message** by a fool **cutteth** (chops) **off** his own feet and **drinketh damage** (violence). **7.** A **parable** (a wise saying, proverb) in his mouth is like the dangling limbs of a crippled man—unsightly, unseemly, and utterly useless, because he applies the wise saying wrongly.

8. He who **giveth honor to a fool** (cf. v. 1) is like he who **bindeth a stone in a sling** (*ṣrr*, "ties or securely fastens it") so it will not leave the sling, and the sling is rendered useless. **9.** A **parable** in his mouth (cf. v. 7) is like **a thorn** (thorn stick) in **the hand of a drunkard,** who in his drunken stupor mistakes it for a staff and runs it through his hand. So fools misuse proverbs and subvert their meaning into occasion for idle laughter or positive sin.

10. The great God that formed all things ... rewardeth (recompenses) both **the fool** and the **transgressors.** "[Like] an archer [*răb*; Job 16:13] wounding all [wounding everybody] is he who hires a fool or who hires those who pass by" indiscriminately (lit. Heb.). Everyone will suffer at the hands of the fool thus employed. **11. As a dog returneth to his vomit, so a fool** returns to (repeats) his folly (2 Pet. 2:22; cf. Exod. 8:15). **12.** A man **wise in his own conceit**—in his own estimation (lit. Heb., "eyes")—is more hopeless than a fool, since self-conceit is a barrier to all progress.

The Pitiable State of the Sluggard. 26:13-16. **13. The slothful man** (to escape work) says, **There is a lion** (a young lion) **in the way** (the road); **a lion is in the streets** (the open square; a variant of 22:13). **14.** As a wooden door turns in a stone socket, around the same center, backward and forward, but not ahead, so the lazy person turns to this side and

that, but will not be torn from his bed.

15. The slothful hideth (buries) **his hand in his dish** (*ṣǎllēhat*, "bowl"; cf. Matt. 26:23; Mark 14:20), but he is so lazy that he will not so much as bring it to his mouth again; he is too lazy even to eat (see Prov. 19:24). **16.** He is **wiser in his own conceit** (his own eyes or self-estimation; 27:11; 1 Pet. 3:15) **than seven men that can render a reason** (give an apt answer to prove their sagacity).

The Folly of the Meddler. 26:17. **17.** The meddler is compared to **one that taketh a dog by the ears** (3:30) and gets bitten for his foolhardy act. This is in contrast to wise interposition as a mediator in behalf of peace.

The Harm Done by Foolish Jesting. 26:18-19. **18-19.** The man who deceives his neighbor under the guise of a joke (24:28) is like a madman who **casteth** (hurls) **firebrands, arrows, and death** (10:23; Isa. 50:11). Much of the world's jesting is deadly deception and evil (2 Sam. 2:14) and is totally unsuitable for a believer (Eph. 5:4). A lie in jest does real mischief.

The Havoc Wrought by the Talebearer. 26:20-22. **20.** Just as fire goes out for lack of fuel, **so where there is no talebearer** (*nírgān*, "whisperer, slanderer, malicious gossiper"), **the strife** (contention, quarreling) **ceaseth** (dies out in silence). **21. As coals ... to burning coals** (charcoal to embers), **and wood to fire, so is a contentious** (quarrelsome) **man to kindle** (rekindle) **strife** (a dispute). Compare *Meri-ka-re*, the Egyptian sage: "The contentious man is a disturbance to citizens" (ANET, p. 415a). **22. The words of a talebearer are like wounds** (better, "dainty morsels"; identical with 18:8, *q.v.*).

The Evil of a Wicked Heart and Lips. 26:23-28. **23-24.** Such a **wicked heart** (mind) and **burning lips** (simulating love), which are fed by the wicked mind

(Matt. 12:34-37), are likened to **a pot-sherd**, a cheap piece of earthenware, covered with silver to give it an expensive glazed look, but the silver is full of dross (impurity) to cover the deception. The burning lips (professing love) are really lips burning with hate, and he who **hateth** (Psalm 41:6-7; Prov. 10:18) **dissembleth** (disguises it) **with his lips, and layeth up deceit within him** (12:20).

25. When he speaketh pleasantly (graciously; lit., "makes his voice gracious"), **believe him not** (v. 23; Psalm 28:3; Jer. 9:8), **for there are seven abominations in his heart**—seven the number of fullness, indicating his heart is completely filled with detestable sins practiced in idolatry, and therefore it is utterly detestable to the LORD. **26.** Though his **hatred is covered by deceit** (with guile), as the earthenware is covered with mock glaze (v. 23), **his wickedness shall be revealed** (exposed) **before the whole congregation**, for all to see.

27. He shall experience divine retributive justice (Psalm 7:15-16). He will fall into the pit he dug for others, and the stone he would roll on another shall roll upon him. **28.** That will be the recompense of a **lying tongue** that **hateth** those **afflicted** (crushed) **by it** (cf. Amnon's hatred of Tamar after he had violated her, 2 Sam. 13:5-15), and a **flattering mouth** that **worketh ruin** (Psalms 5:9; 10:7-10).

C. VARIOUS SOLOMONIC PROVERBS (CONT.). 27:1-27.

Folly of Boasting About the Future or the Past. 27:1-2. **1. Boast not thyself of** (do not flatter yourself about) **tomorrow** (that is, brag about what you will do then), **for you do not know what a day may bring forth** (NASB; Luke 12:19; James 4:14), the figure of childbearing events being conceived of as "sons of time," time giving them birth. **2.** Not

only are we not to boast of tomorrow and what we shall do in it, but we should not boast of what we have already done. **Let another man praise thee** for what you have done, **a stranger** (who will be completely unbiased and impartial), **and not thine own mouth.**

The Trial of a Provoking Fool. 27:3. **3. A stone is heavy** (lit., "heaviness"), **and the sand weighty**—"stone is a burden and sand a dead weight" (NEB), **but a fool's wrath** (*kă'ăs*, "provocation, vexation") **is heavier than them both**, that is, "to be vexed [provoked] by a fool is more burdensome than either" (NEB). Compare *Ahiqar* 8, "I have lifted sand, and I have carried salt, but there is naught which is heavier than [rage]" (ANET, p. 429*a*).

The Implacability of Jealousy. 27:4. **4. Wrath is cruel** (lit., "cruelty"— "cruelty itself"), **and anger is outrageous** (an overflowing flood, inundation), **but who is able to stand before envy?** (jealousy; 6:34-35). While the angry man shows his anger, the envious or jealous man hides it and without warning vents it when the opportunity presents itself. Anger may possibly be appeased, but jealousy is incurable like a cancer.

Genuine Love in Manifestation. 27:5-6. **5. Better is open rebuke** (NASB; reprimand), outspoken and laid bare of all false restraint, **than secret love**—love concealed in the heart that fails to perform its outward duty in reprimanding a friend in error through cowardly fear of offending him (28:23; Gal. 2:14). **6.** Genuine love sometimes inflicts **wounds**, but such wounds are faithful to love because they are administered by **a friend** (lit., "a lover; one who truly loves"; Psalm 141:5; Prov. 20:30). **But the kisses of an enemy** (*śônē'*, "a hater") **are deceitful** (Matt. 26:49; lit., "bland, entreated"; "perfidious," NEB).

Blessed Are the Hungry. 27:7. **7. The full soul** (the person sated with food) **loatheth honey** (lit., "tramples it under foot"; Mic. 5:5-6). **But to the hungry soul** (a hungry person) **every bitter thing is sweet**—even bitter food tastes sweet to him (Job 6:7; Luke 15:16-17). Compare *Ahiqar* 12, "Hunger makes bitterness sweet" (ANET, p. 430*a*). Full-fed Israel loathed "angels' food" (Psalm 78:25; cf. Num. 11:18-20). Care must be taken that fullness of gospel privilege and truth does not result in a bad spiritual appetite.

On Homesickness. 27:8. **8. As a bird that wandereth from her nest** (26:2; Isa. 16:2), **so is a man that wandereth from his place** (of abode; his home; Gen. 21:14).

The Sweetness of a Friend's Advice. 27:9. **9. Ointment** (oil) **and perfume** (incense) **make the heart glad** (NASB; Psalms 23:5; 141:5)—gratify the senses—**so** (does) **the sweetness of a man's friend, by hearty counsel** (lit., "by counsel of the soul"; i.e., "sincere counsel"), offered especially in time of great affliction, when the sufferer's judgment is clouded by pain or grief. Then he is aided by the clearer perception of his friend to do what ought to be done.

The Wisdom of Cultivating Friends. 27:10. **10. Do not forsake** (*'zḇ*, "abandon, neglect") **your own friend or your father's friend** (NASB; 1 Kings 12:6-8; 2 Chron. 10:6-8). You never know when calamity may strike you, and you will need such a friend near at hand to whom you ought to go rather than pull up stakes and go to your **brother's house** far away. **For better is a neighbor that is near** (at hand) **than a brother** (a close relative) **far off** (far away).

A Wise Son Makes His Father Happy. 27:11. **11. My son, be wise, and make my heart glad** (10:1; 23:15; 29:3). **That I may answer him that reproacheth**

me (*ḥrp*, "to criticize scornfully and insultingly"; Psalm 119:42). People often criticize a good father for a bad son (cf. 1 Sam. 2:17, 23-24). By wise conduct a son enables his father to forestall such criticism.

The Prudent and the Imprudent and Trouble. 27:12. **12. A prudent** (*'ārûm*, "shrewd, clever") **man foreseeth the evil** (sees trouble coming) **and hideth himself** (lies low). **But the simple** (naive simpletons) **pass on** (go right on and walk into it), **and are punished**—must pay the penalty (cf. 22:3).

On Pledging for Strangers. 27:13. **13.** See comments on 20:16, which is almost identical.

On Greeting Friends. 27:14. **14.** He who **blesseth his friend with a loud voice** (affectedly and implied ulterior motives) **... early in the morning** (an unseemly time for such a grandiloquent display), **it shall be counted** (reckoned) **a curse to him,** instead of the blessing he pretends. Such exaggerated praise and compliment are always to be regarded with suspicion, especially under such circumstances.

The Bane of a Quarrelsome Wife. 27:15-16. **15.** A quarrelsome wife is likened to a **continual dropping** (dripping of water from a leaky roof) on **a very rainy day** (see 19:13). **16.** To try to "restrain" such a nagging wife (lit., "hide, hold her back") is to attempt to "restrain" (lit., "hide") **the wind.** "As well try to control the wind as to control her!" (NEB). "And his hand encounters oil" (lit. Heb.). He gets "butterfingers," his hand becoming slippery, so that he cannot hold on to anything. "As well try to pick up oil in one's fingers" (NEB) as try to control such a cantankerous woman.

The Good Effect of a Cheerful Countenance. 27:17. **17. Iron sharpeneth iron** (Eccles. 10:10). **So a man**

sharpeneth the countenance of his friend—he inspires with keen delight the mind of his friend by mutual fellowship, and his face glows in expression of it. The meeting of intelligent friends sharpens the intellect and warms the heart (Job 4:3-4). "The very sight of a good man delights" (Seneca; cf. Eccles. 4:9-12).

The Reward of Faithful Stewardship. 27:18. **18.** He who **keepeth** (guards) **the fig tree shall eat the fruit** (2 Kings 18:31; Song of Sol. 8:12; Isa. 36:16; 1 Cor. 3:8; 9:7; 2 Tim. 2:6). **So he that waiteth on** (*shmr*, "keeps, watches, faithfully guards the interests of") **his master** (Luke 12:42-44; 19:17) **shall be honored** (come to honor; John 12:26).

Man Is a Reflection of His Thoughts. 27:19. **19. As in water, face answereth to** (reflects) **face, so the heart** (mind) **of man to man**—so one man's mind is reflected in another man's mind. Your heart (mind) is a kind of mirror of your neighbor's mind. You see your feelings and thoughts reflected in his feelings and thoughts, just as he sees his thoughts and feelings reflected in you.

Insatiableness of Man's Desire. 27:20. **20. Sheol and destruction** (the netherworld; 15:11) **are never full** (are insatiable; 30:15-16; Eccles. 1:8; 4:8); **so the eyes of man are never satisfied** (Hab. 2:5). "The lust of the eyes" in fallen man (1 John 2:16) is unsatisfied and unsatisfiable, becoming more enslaving and fiercely demanding for gratification as it is indulged, but it is never satisfied.

Praise the Test of Character. 27:21. **21. As the refining pot** (crucible, melting pot) **for silver, and the furnace** (smelter) **for gold**, so **a man is tested** (Luke 6:26) **by the praise accorded him** (NASB; lit., "according to his praise"). The test is whether he remains humble and gives the glory to God, or becomes proud and arrogates glory to himself. Men are the

"silver," speaking of redemption, and "the gold," speaking of Deity—God's grace manifested in saving them. And "praise," which in redeemed sinners is due solely to God, is the crucible and the furnace, testing their character.

The Incorrigibility of the Fool. 27:22. **22.** Though you **pound a fool in a mortar with a pestle along with crushed grain** (NASB; 23:35; 26:11; Jer. 5:3), **yet will not his foolishness depart from him**—you will not be able to drub his folly out of him (lit., "from upon him," like the hard-to-be-removed husk upon a grain of wheat). Even the bruising in the mortar of trial fails to reform a fool (cf. Ahaz, 2 Chron. 28:22; and Judah, Isa. 1:5-6; 9:13).

Exhortation to Business Diligence and Industry. 27:23-27. **23.** *The injunction:* **Be ... diligent to know the state** (condition) **of your flocks** (John 10:3), and **look well** (lit., "set your heart"; Exod. 7:23; Prov. 10:4; 12:27; 13:4; 21:5; Rom. 12:11), that is, "pay close attention" **to thy herds.**

24. *The reason for the injunction:* **For riches** (lit., "strength") **are not** (do not last) **forever.** In Israel, wealth centered in flocks and herds; so they were carefully inspected (Gen. 30:32-42; 31:38-40; 33:13; 1 Chron. 27:29). **And doth the crown** (symbolic of honor and wealth) **endure to every generation?** (Job 19:9; Psalm 89:39; Jer. 13:18; Lam. 5:16; Ezek. 21:26).

25-27. *The result of heeding the warning:* When the grass disappears and the new growth is seen, and the herbs (crops) of the mountain have been gathered in, the lambs will furnish you clothing and the goats **the price of the field,** that is, profit from the land. Also there will be ample **goats' milk** to feed you and your household and for the **maintenance** (sustenance) of your maid servants.

D. Various Solomonic Proverbs (cont.). 28:1-28.

The Boldness of the Righteous. 28:1.
1. The **righteous,** justified by faith (Gen. 15:6) and walking in the light of the Lord's commandments (Exod. 20:1-17), are as **bold as a lion**; they have confidence and poise at all times, in contrast to **the wicked** man, who flees (runs away) when no one is pursuing (chasing) him (Lev. 26:17, 36; Psalm 53:5). A defiled conscience makes cowards of all the wicked; so they *all* flee as one man (plural verb with a singular subject in the Hebrew).

The Penalty for the Transgression of a Land. 28:2. **2. For the transgression** (*pĕshă'*, "wickedness, rebellion") **of a land many are the princes** (rulers) **thereof** (1 Kings 16:8-28; 2 Kings 15:8-15), that is, the land is in a state of revolt (Isa. 3:4-5; Hos. 8:4), as a punishment for having many would-be rulers. **But by a man of understanding and knowledge the state thereof shall be prolonged,** but only with wise and intelligent leadership will it be perpetuated (endure).

A Poor Man as an Oppressor. 28:3. **3. A poor man** (*gĕbĕr*, "yet a man of might") **that oppresseth the poor** (*dăllîm*, "the needy, weak") **is like a sweeping** (driving) **rain which leaveth no food** (Matt. 18:28). He sweeps away the food left to the poor by richer oppressors and becomes more merciless than they. He is like a devastating rain because it washes the seed away and denudes the earth of its fertility, so that no crop results.

The Law-abiding Men and the Wicked. 28:4-5. **4.** Those who **forsake the law** (the lawless who reject morality) **praise the wicked** (Psalm 49:18; Rom. 1:32). But those who **keep the law** (the law-abiding men) **contend with** (oppose) **them** (1 Kings 18:18; Neh. 13:11, 15; Matt. 3:7; 14:4; Eph. 5:11). **5.** Such

lawless, **evil men understand not justice** (Psalm 92:6; Isa. 6:9; 44:18). **But they that seek the Lord understand all things** (Deut. 4:6; 1 Cor. 2:14; 1 John 2:20, 27) relating to their duty and happiness in this life and the life to come.

Superiority of Moral Integrity over Wealth. 28:6. **6. Better is the poor** (man) **that walketh in his uprightness** (integrity)—conducts himself on unimpeachable principles of honesty and general morality—**than he that is perverse** (crooked) **in his ways** (lit., "two ways"), **though he be rich,** perversely halting between those "two ways" and hypocritically trying to walk in both ways at the same time (1 Kings 18:21; Matt. 6:24).

The Importance of Keeping Good Company. 28:7. **7. Whoso keepeth the** (moral) **law** of God **is a wise son,** in the sense of being "discerning" (*mēbîn*), and makes his father happy and proud of him. **But he that is a companion of gluttonous men shameth** (humiliates) **his father.**

Warning Against Extortion. 28:8. **8. He that by interest and unjust gain** (cf. Ezek. 18:8; 22:12) **increaseth his substance** (wealth; Exod. 22:25; Lev. 25:36), **he shall gather it for him that will pity** (have compassion on) **the poor** (Prov. 14:31). The Lord will overrule in retributive justice and see to it that a charitable man of wealth (cf. Job 27:17; Prov. 13:22) comes into possession of the wealth of the wicked rich man.

The Result of Turning a Deaf Ear to God's Law. 28:9. **9. Even** the **prayer** of a man who does not listen to God is **an abomination** (Psalms 66:18; 109:7; Prov. 15:8; 21:27). Apparently the best thing he does is an utter detestation to the Lord, because it represents nauseating hypocrisy, reducing prayer to the sordid level of pagan incantation.

The Peril of Misleading Others into

Evil. 28:10. **10. Whoso causeth the right-eous** (the upright) **to go astray in an evil way, he shall fall himself into his own pit** (Psalm 7:15; Prov. 26:27). **But the upright** (blameless) **shall have good things in possession** (will inherit good; Matt. 6:33; Heb. 6:12; 1 Pet. 3:9).

The Deceptiveness of Worldly Wealth. 28:11. **11. The rich man is wise in his own conceit** (in his own eyes, his own estimation). **But the poor, who hath understanding** (the discerning poor man), **searcheth him out**—sees through him. But the spiritually discerning poor man who is able to discriminate between true and false wealth "searches out" the rich man's egotistical and false pretensions to wisdom and is able to expose them (Job 32:9; Prov. 18:17; Ezek. 28:2-4).

The Danger When Wicked Men Come into Power. 28:12. **12. When righteous men** (see v. 1) **rejoice** (*'ls*, "exult triumphantly"), **there is great glory** (Esther 8:15-17) in every phase of society. **But when the wicked rise** (to power; v. 28; Eccles. 10:5-6), **a man** (*'āḏām*, "men, mankind") **is hidden** (i.e., men hide themselves; v. 28; Prov. 11:10; 29:2) through fear of oppression, instead of the triumphal rejoicing in the "glory" that results when good men are exalted (1 Kings 17:2-3; 18:4; 19:1-6).

Warning Against Concealing One's Transgressions. 28:13. **13.** A person who conceals his sins will **not prosper** (Job 31:33; Psalm 32:3). **But whoso confesseth and forsaketh them shall find mercy** (compassion both from God and man; 32:5; 1 John 1:9). The sincerity of the confession is attested by a person's turning away from his sins (1:8-10).

The Blessing of Sensitivity to Sin. 28:14. **14. Happy** (how blessed!) **is the man that feareth** (i.e., God; holds Him in reverential awe) **always** (constantly) and as a result has an attitude of caution

against sin as offending God, whom he loves too much to give offense to (1 John 4:18). But he who **hardeneth his heart** (against God and His Word by unbelief, especially concerning what He says about sin) **shall fall into mischief** (calamity; cf. Pharaoh, Exod. 14:5-8, 23-31; 1 Cor. 5:5; 11:30-32; 1 John 5:16).

The Scourge of a Wicked Ruler. 28:15-16. **15.** A wicked ruler is like **a roaring lion,** ready to pounce on his prey (19:12; 1 Pet. 5:8), and a **ranging bear**—ranging to and fro in hunger and ready to charge on a victim. So is **a wicked ruler over a poor people,** whom he knows he can grind to the dust with impunity, since they cannot resist. **16.** Such a wicked ruler is **a prince that lacketh understanding** and is **a great oppressor** (Eccles. 10:16; Isa. 3:12), because he is greedy and covetous. But a good leader **hateth covetousness** and **shall prolong his days** (as a ruler of repute).

The Penalty of Bloodguiltiness. 28:17. **17.** A man who **doeth** (perpetrates) **violence to the blood of any person** (and is burdened with the guilt of murder, charged with bloodshed) **shall flee to the pit,** that is, "will be a fugitive until death" (NASB), like Cain (Gen. 9:4-5). Let no man **sustain** (*tmk*, "support, help") **him** (cf. Prov. 24:11 with Num. 35:33-34; Psalm 109:7).

The Security of a Blameless Life. 28:18. **18.** He who **walketh** (lives, conducts himself) **uprightly** (blamelessly) **shall be saved** (delivered) from falling into sin and other calamities. **But he that is perverse** (crooked) **in his ways** ("his two ways"; see v. 6) **shall fall at once** (lit., "in one" of his "two ways," as a hypocrite), as judgment for his perfidious compromise.

The Inculcation of Industry. 28:19. **19. He that tilleth** (cultivates) **his land shall have plenty of bread** (food). **But he who followeth after vain persons**—

1057

better, "worthless pursuits" (RSV), "empty pursuits" (NASB) **shall have poverty enough** (i.e., "plenty of poverty" in the place of "plenty of food").

The Peril of Those Who Want to Be Rich. 28:20-22. **20. A faithful man** (lit., "a man of fidelity, honesty") **shall abound with blessings** (10:6; Matt. 24:45; 25:21). **But he that maketh haste to be rich** (v. 22; Prov. 20:21), who "wills" (wants) to be rich (1 Tim. 6:9), making that his aim in life, **shall not be innocent** (unpunished).

21. Such a get-rich-quick enthusiast will not only be tempted to be unfaithful and dishonest, but also **to have respect of persons** (cf. v. 5; Prov. 24:23). He will show partiality, which is **not good,** emphasizing that it is indeed "very bad," so bad that **for a piece of bread** (a mere trifle) a judge, who at first would be induced only by a great bribe to favor one side, now comes to subvert justice for a bauble (Ezek. 13:19; Mic. 3:5; 2 Pet. 2:3). **22.** Such a person has **an evil eye** (a grudging, covetous eye; see Prov. 23:6). **And considereth** (knows) **not that poverty shall come upon him** (v. 8; Job 27:16-17), as a real possibility in this life and as a certainty in the future life.

The Happy Outcome of Faithful Rebuke. 28:23. **23. He that rebuketh** (reproves, chides, takes to task) **a man afterwards shall find more favor**—win more thanks—**than he that flattereth with the tongue**—not to the good but to his injury of his friend. When the man taken to task discovers this fact, he will know who his true friend was.

The Crime of Robbing Parents. 28:24. **24.** He who commits the crime of robbing his parents and claims he does no wrong, **the same is the companion** (accomplice) **of a destroyer** ("a man of destroying"), no better than a wanton vandal, on a level with the most abandoned (Deut. 21:18-21).

The Arrogant and the Humble in Contrast. 28:25-26. **25.** The **proud of heart** (lit., "broad of soul," i.e., arrogant), and therefore he who trusts in himself, **stirreth up strife** (13:10) and shall be made lean spiritually, and frequently temporally. **But he that putteth his trust in the Lord shall be made fat** (prosperous; 16:20). Trust in self and unbelief toward the LORD spring from the polluted fountain of pride. The pure fountain is the source of humility. **26.** Such a proved person, who **trusteth in his own heart,** following his own will and impulses (3:5, 7; 23:4; Hos. 10:13) and consequently walking unwisely, **is a fool** and shall not be delivered, as the wise man is, but rather destroyed.

The Liberal and the Stingy in Contrast. 28:27. **27.** He who gives to **the poor shall not lack** (Deut. 15:7, 10; Psalm 41:1, 3; Prov. 19:17). **But he that hideth his eyes** (from their need) **shall have many a curse,** both from men and God (21:13). The unspiritual man imagines he will be in want by giving, not realizing the reverse is true.

Wicked and Good Rulers in Contrast. 28:28. **28. When the wicked rise** (to power), **men hide themselves** (take cover; 11:10; 29:2). **But when they perish, the righteous** (see v. 1) **increase.**

E. VARIOUS SOLOMONIC PROVERBS (CONCLUDED). 29:1-27.

The Ultimate in Divine Chastening. 29:1. **1.** Specifically, the backsliding believer, persisting in flagrant sin, is meant. **Being often reproved,** resenting and resisting the reproof, and hardening **his neck,** a figure of obdurate stubbornness of an animal who tries to toss off the yoke and will not be turned (Isa. 48:4; Jer. 17:23), he **shall suddenly be destroyed ... without remedy** by physical death, the ultimate in God's chastening (1 Cor. 5:5; 11:30-32; 1 John 5:16), like

Eli's sons (1 Sam. 2:25) and Israel (2 Chron. 36:16). Compare the case of David, whose genuine repentance saved him from the sin to physical death (2 Sam. 12:13).

Righteous and Wicked Rulers in Contrast. 29:2. **2. When the righteous are in authority** (lit., "in increase," in the majority and so "in power" and public office), **the people rejoice** (11:10; 28:12; Esther 8:15). **But when the wicked beareth rule** (*mshl*, "rule, hold office"), **the people mourn** (lament, sigh, groan).

A Good Son and a Bad Son in Contrast. 29:3. The son who **loveth wisdom rejoiceth his father** (makes him glad; 10:1; 15:20; 27:11; 28:7) by retaining and increasing the family estate. But the son who **keepeth company with harlots spendeth his substance** (consumes his patrimony; 5:10; 6:26; Luke 15:30).

A Good King and Bad King in Contrast. 29:4. **4.** A good king **by justice establisheth the land** (makes his land secure). But **he that exacteth gifts** (lit., a man of *t͑erûmôt,* "gifts, presents, heave offerings, tribute"; "forced contributions," NEB; "bribes," NASB) **overthroweth** (ruins) **it.** *T͑erûmôt* is the common word for sacred oblations and apparently indicates a man who desires sacred oblations to be offered to him, as if he were a priest (Ezek. 45:13-17).

The Snare of Flattery. 29:5. **5.** A man who **flattereth** (cajoles) **his neighbor** (Psalm 5:9; Prov. 26:24-25; 28:23), far from being his friend, is a concealed enemy, who actually **spreadeth a net for his feet,** for even the godly are tempted to turn aside from God's way by flattery and fall into Satan's snare (2 Tim. 2:26). Compare Darius, who was entrapped in a plot to destroy his godly favorite, Daniel (Dan. 6:6-7, 9, 14).

The Snare of Sin and the Joy of Deliverance from It. 29:6. **6. In the transgression of an evil man there is a snare**

(*môqēsh*). His sin entraps him in deeper sin and a more abysmal slavery to iniquity (22:5; Eccles. 9:12; 2 Pet. 2:19-20). "By transgression an evil man is ensnared" (NASB; Syriac, Targum *mūqăš* for MT *môqēsh*, "snare"). **But the righteous** (see Prov. 28:1) **sings and rejoices** (NASB; Exod. 15:1) in escaping the snare of transgression and in the victory over sin that such joyful triumph affords (Gal. 5:22; Eph. 5:18-19).

The Righteous and the Wicked Contrasted in Their Attitude Toward the Poor. 29:7. **7. The righteous** (see 28:1) **considereth** (knows, and so is concerned about) **the cause** (*dîn,* "the legal rights, the case") **of the poor** (the weak, the helpless). In contrast, **the wicked** man **regardeth not** (*bîn,* "does not understand") **to know it**—comprehends no such concern. He is selfishly callous. He does not care to know about the poor; or if he does know, he acts as if he did not.

Scoffers Versus Wise Men. 29:8. **8. Scornful men bring a city** (1) **into a snare** (*yāpîḥû,* derived from *pāḥ,* "snare"), (2) "set a city aflame" (BV, NASB), in order to reduce it to ashes (from *pîăḥ,* "spark, dust, ashes"), or (3) "put in an uproar" (AB), excite sedition (from *nāpăḥ,* "to blow"). **But wise men turn away wrath**—divine wrath, incurred by the city through scornful men, who rail at the laws of God and man (Exod. 32:10-14; Psalm 106:23; Ezek. 22:30-31).

Folly of Debating with a Foolish Man. 29:9. **9. If a wise man contendeth** (argues) **with a foolish man,** the fool will only **rage** (rant abusively) **or laugh** (immoderately), and **there is no rest** (quiet) for rational thought or sensible discussion (Matt. 11:17). If the argument takes the form of going to law, the wise man will meet only abuse and derision, getting no remedy or satisfaction.

Haters and Lovers of Men's Souls.

29:10. **10. The bloodthirsty** (lit., "men of bloods," guilty of actual murder or its equivalent of violent hatred; Gen. 4:5-8; 1 John 3:12, 15) **hate the upright** (*tām*, "the man of integrity"), **but the just seek the welfare of his soul.** They are concerned with both his temporal and eternal well-being (Psalm 142:4).

Babbling Fools Versus Reticent Wise Men. 29:11. **11. A fool uttereth all his mind** (lit. Heb., "spirit"; lit., "gives vent to all his spirit," which may mean "anger," RSV, NEB; "temper," NASB), **but a wise man holds it back** (NASB; 19:11; the KJV takes "spirit" in the sense of "mind" or "intellect"). A fool utters all his mind, rashly babbling out (lit., "sends forth") whatever is on his mind (which is never much), with senseless disregard of people, time, or place (Judg. 16:17; Prov. 12:23). **But a wise man keepeth it in till afterwards** until a proper time and occasion arrive.

The Evil Influence of a Deceitful Ruler. 29:12. **12. If a ruler hearkeneth** (listens) **to lies** (falsehood), he himself will soon be practicing injustice and dishonesty, and **all his servants** (ministers) will copy his ways and become **wicked** (1 Kings 12:14).

The Lord Governs All Classes of Men. 29:13. **13. The poor and the deceitful man** (lit., "man of oppression," usurer, creditor) **meet together** ("meet at this point," i.e., "have this in common"); **the Lord lighteneth** (illuminates, gives light to) **both their eyes** (the eyes of both; 1 Sam. 14:29; Ezra 9:8; Psalm 13:3). "God enables both to see" (Toy, ICC, p. 511), that is, "gives both the light of life" (cf. Job 33:30; Eccles. 11:7). God "creates both, permits them to exist, and controls them; there must be social classes, but God governs all."

Justice and the Stability of a Throne. 29:14. **14. The king that faithfully judgeth the poor**, that is, administers justice with equity (Psalms 45:6-7; 72:4; Isa. 11:4; 32:1; Rev. 19:11), **his throne shall be established forever** (2 Sam. 7:13-16; Psalm 89:36-37; Dan. 2:44; 7:14; Zech. 12:8; Luke 1:32-33; Rev. 19:15-16).

The Training of Children. 29:15. **15. The rod and reproof**, a hendiadys for "the rod of correction," **give wisdom** (13:24; 23:13). **But a child left to himself** (lit., "let go," i.e., "unrestrained") **bringeth his mother** (as the one who has most to do with the training of a young child) **to shame** (disgrace; cf. 17:21; 23:24-25).

The Triumph of the Righteous. 29:16. **16. When the wicked are multiplied, transgression increaseth.** Increased numbers of the wicked augment their boldness in sin because of the mutual example and greater solicitation to evil, and thus they decrease the risk of prosecution by the righteous (cf. v. 2; 11:10-11; 28:12, 28). **But the righteous** (see comment on 28:1) **shall see** (lit., "look in on" or "see in on," cf. Ezek. 28:17) **their fall** (downfall; Psalms 3:7; 5:10; 34:21; 37:36).

Filial Discipline and Its Happy Results. 29:17. **17. Correct** (*ysr*, "discipline, chastise, reprove") **thy son** (13:24; 19:18; 23:13-14; Heb. 12:5-11) and he will **give thee rest** from all the anxieties ungodly children give their parents (cf. Deut. 12:10; 2 Sam. 7:1; Lam. 5:5; Ezek. 5:13). **Yea,** not only comfort and relief from anxiety, but **delight unto thy soul** (i.e., "to you"), which will richly compensate for the passing pain caused you in chastising your son.

Ignorance or Knowledge of God's Word and the Result. 29:18. **18. Where there is no vision** (*ḥāzôn*, "revelation") of God's Word and will, whether by special revelation as in Bible times (Psalm 74:9; Lam. 2:9; Ezek. 7:26), or by the ministry of the written Word now through God's ministers, **the people perish** (*nifal* of *pāră'*, "are loosened, absolved") from the teachings of the Word. So they become lawless and unruly and perish in ruin and misery (1 Sam. 3:1; Hos. 4:6; Amos 8:11; Matt. 9:36; Rom. 10:13-15). By contrast, **happy is he** who **keepeth the law,** who has the revealed Word of God and observes its teaching (John 13:17; James 1:25), the Law standing in contrast to "no vision."

How to Manage a Slave. 29:19. **19. A servant** (slave) **will not be corrected by words,** that is, "by mere words a servant is not disciplined" (RSV). By "servant" is meant a slave in spirit, who performs no task from love, but only when driven by fear (John 8:34-35; Rom. 8:15; 1 John 4:18). Such a slavish person will not be corrected (disciplined) by words (but only by stripes; Prov. 19:29). **For, though he understand, he will not answer** to your call by obeying your command. Compare *Ahiqar*, "A blow for a bondman . . . and for all your slaves discipline" (ANET, p. 428*b*).

The Stupidity of Ill-Advised Speech. 29:20. **20. Do you see a man ... hasty** (*'āṣ*, "hurrying, hastening") **in his words?** (NASB; "over-eager to speak," NEB; "who speaks too soon," AB; cf. v. 11; 18:13; James 1:19). **There is more hope of a fool than of him.**

How to Manage a Slave. 29:21. **21.** This verse apparently deals with the same subject as verse 19. **He that delicately bringeth up** (pampers) **his servant** (*'ěḇěḏ*, "slave") **from a child** (lit., "childhood"), **shall have him become his son** (*mānôn*, meaning uncertain) **at the length** (in the end), at the conclusion of this mode of procedure. The servant will eventually expect to be treated like a son, even to being appointed heir (cf.

RSV, "will in the end find him his heir").

The Evil of a Hot Temper. 29:22. **22. An angry** (irascible) **man stirreth up strife, and a furious** (hot-tempered; lit., "master of wrath"; "a hot-head," NEB) **man aboundeth in transgression** (*pěshă'*, "rebellion, refractoriness"), daring, lawless sin, such as passionate oaths, cursing God's name (19:3).

The Outcomes of Pride and Humility Contrasted. 29:23. **23. A man's pride shall bring him low** (16:18; 18:12; Isa. 2:11-12; Luke 14:11; 18:14). "But he who is lowly in spirit will attain honor" (lit. Heb.; Prov. 15:33; 18:12; 22:4; Isa. 66:2; Luke 14:11; James 4:10).

The Accomplice of a Thief. 29:24. **24.** A thief's partner **hateth his own soul** (himself, his life); he acts as if he did not care about his own welfare. **He heareth cursing** (Lev. 5:1), that is, he hears himself put on oath, **and revealeth it not,** does not disclose the information he has concerning the thief, deliberately withholding the testimony he should give. By so doing, he puts his own life in jeopardy.

The Snare of Fearing Man Rather Than God. 29:25. **25. The fear of man**—being fearful of man and so manifesting lack of faith in God—**bringeth a snare.** Fear of man involves regulating one's conduct by the attitudes of unbelievers and failing to speak truth and do right lest it should provoke enmity. Ironically, Abraham, the father of the faithful, through fear of man, twice disowned his wife (Gen. 12:10-20; 20:1-18), as did Isaac (26:7). But he who **putteth** (places) **his trust in the Lord shall be safe** (lit. Heb., "set on high"), positioned far above the fear of man. The fear of God (28:14) banishes the fear (terror) of man.

The Wrong of Relying on Human Power Rather Than on God. 29:26. **26. Many seek the ruler's favor** to give sentence in their favor. **But every man's judgment** (justice) **cometh** (is) **from the Lord** (emphatic). He is the real Source of all judicial decisions, and He is the sovereign Judge, both for time and eternity; nothing occurs except by His permission (21:1). Therefore, look to Him for justice. Compare *Amen-em-ope*: "As for justice, the great reward of God, he gives it to whom he will" (chap. 20).

The Antipathy Between the Righteous and the Wicked. 29:27. **27. An unjust man** (*'îsh 'āwĕl*, "a man of perverseness, wickedness") **is an abomination to the just** (righteous) because such a man is an abomination to the God of the righteous, the righteous God (Psalm 15:1-5). And vice versa, the upright man **in the way** (God's way) is **an abomination to the wicked**, the mutual antagonism of the woman's posterity and the serpent's existing from the very beginning of the fallen race (Gen. 3:15; Psalm 139:21-22). However, the difference is, the righteous hate the sin but love the sinner, while the wicked hate both the person and the ways of the upright.

VI. THE FINAL APPENDIXES.
30:1—31:31.

The concluding chapters of the book (30-31) consist of three appendixes— the words of Agur (30:1-33); the words of Lemuel (31:1-9) and the alphabetical poem on the virtuous wife (31:10-31).

A. THE WORDS OF AGUR—NUMERICAL PROVERBS. 30:1-33.

Introduction to Agur's Confession. 30:1. **1. Agur, the son of Jakeh,** otherwise unknown, seems to have been a public teacher, and Ithiel and Ucal to have been his students (ACC). **The words** of Agur, which he delivered to his students, constitute **the prophecy** (*măssa'*, "a prophetic utterance, an

oracle, something directly communicated by the Holy Spirit for the benefit of mankind"; Isa. 14:28; Ezek. 12:10). It is not, we believe, a reference to *Massa'*, an Ishmaelite tribe of northern Arabia (cf. Gen. 25:13-14), as construed by many scholars (cf. R. B. Y. Scott, *Proverbs*, AB, p. 176).

The man (*gĕbēr*, "a strong man," is an evident reference to Agur as a great teacher) **spoke** (*ne'ŭm*), showing that he spoke by divine inspiration, enforcing the fact that what he uttered is a solemn oracle involving revelation of *deep and important spiritual truth*. The inspired teacher spoke to **Ithiel** ("with me is God"), **even unto Ithiel** ("with me is God"), repeated to emphasize a great truth, and **Ucal** ("I am strong"). The names of Agur's students were symbolic of spiritual truth, as were Isaiah's sons (Isa. 7:3, 16; 8:1). *Ithiel* is faith's appropriation of *Immanuel*, "God with us" (7:14). *Ucal* signifies the mighty One, "The Mighty God" (9:6). Since all prophecies bear witness to the Messiah, should it be considered strange that this one should also, especially when it is introduced in such a solemn prophetic context?

Attempts to do away with the proper names, making them the beginning of Agur's utterance, and rendering them: "I wore myself out, O God, I wore myself out, and, O God, I languish," have not been too convincing. Less convincing is the thesis that they do not represent Hebrew but Aramaic and that they are the confession of an atheist and are to be translated: "There is no God! There is no God, and I can [not know anything]" (Scott, *Proverbs*, AB).

Agur's Confession of Faith. 30:2-6. **2.** The prophet aimed at three things: (1) to abase himself (vv. 2-3); (2) to exalt God (v. 4); and (3) to exalt His Word (vv. 5-6). (1) *In abasing himself he ad-*

mitted his own lack of righteousness and his folly. **Surely I am more stupid** (*bā°ār*, "like a brute beast") **than any man, and have not the understanding of a man** (Psalm 73:22; Jer. 10:14). The way to wisdom is to be conscious of our folly, just as the way to salvation is to see our utter sinfulness and fallen lost estate before the infinitely holy God.

3. I neither learned wisdom, nor have the knowledge of the Holy One (*q°dōshîm*, plural, as "Elohim"), particularly knowledge of the infinitely high standard of holiness God demands for acceptance before Him. Agur realized a man must "become a fool, that he may be wise" (1 Cor. 3:18), and that as long as a man thinks he knows, he is unfit to be a recipient of the knowledge from above (Isa. 6:5; 1 Cor. 8:2).

(2) *In abasing himself, he aimed at exalting God.* **4. Who hath ascended up into heaven, or descended?** — to comprehend what transpires there, to report to mortal men what he has seen. No wonder Agur was acutely conscious that he did not possess the knowledge of the Holy One. But now the Christian can speak of such a One (John 3:13), and He is foreseen and predicted by the Holy Spirit in this grand, far-reaching "prophecy" (prophetic revelation, *māśśā'*, v. 1), which this whole passage is, in a most distinct sense.

Though we have not ascended into heaven or descended into the depth (Psalm 68:18), we still, through Him who has done both, have the Word made near to us (Deut. 30:12-13; Rom. 10:6-8). And we are brought near the Creator-Redeemer, who has **gathered the wind in his fists** (Exod. 15:10; Job 38:24; Psalm 135:7), **bound the waters** (of the oceans) **in a garment** (Job 26:8; 38:8-9), **established all the ends of the earth** (Psalm 24:2; Isa. 45:18). **What is his name, and what is his son's name . . . ?** (Judg.

13:17-18; Rev. 19:12). It is the eternal, preincarnate Messiah-Christ (Prov. 8:22-31), for it is the Son's name, as well as God the Father, that is here inquired after — magnified in Old Testament times as One concealed, and now as One revealed. How glorious that the name of God and that of His Son are here linked together, as both alike ineffable and incomprehensible, distinct and yet one in essence and operation.

(3) *In abasing himself and exalting God, the prophet at the same time exalted God's Word* (vv. 5-6), which overcomes the defect of mere natural human understanding that Agur complained of (vv. 2-4). **5. Every word of God is pure** (lit., "smelted" in the fire like silver, "purified" of all dross of human error or falsehood; Psalms 12:6; 119:140) so that we must rest in divinely revealed truth, which alone points the way of salvation from the brutishness of sin and imparts wisdom of the Holy One — His name and ways. He becomes a **shield** of protection from sin and folly (Gen. 15:1; Psalms 18:30; 84:11) to those who **put their trust** (*ħāsâ*, "take refuge in") **in him** (2:12). **6. Do not add to His words** (NASB; Deut. 4:2; 12:32; Rev. 22:18), "above that which is written" (1 Cor. 4:6).

Agur's Prayer for Sufficient Grace and Convenient Food. 30:7-9. **7-8.** Agur asked for two things before he died, for it is too late to change our lives once death strikes. One thing he asked was for the soul: **Remove far from me vanity and lies,** all the emptiness and deception of the world (Psalm 119:37). The other thing he asked was for the body: **neither poverty nor riches . . . food convenient,** "food of my portion or allowance," that is, sufficient for day-to-day sustenance, the "daily bread" (Matt. 6:11), like the manna ("a certain amount every day," Exod. 16:4; 2 Kings 25:30; Neh. 12:47;

Luke 12:42; 1 Tim. 6:8). His purpose in his request is to avoid sin, either by wealth or poverty.

9. Lest I be full (Deut. 8:12; Neh. 9:25; Hos. 13:6), **and deny thee, and say, Who is the Lord?** (Josh. 24:27; Job 31:28). **Or lest I be poor, and steal, and take** (lit., "seize on") **the name of my God,** either in perjury or in complaint of God and His dealings (Exod. 20:7). Stealing and perjury were closely joined (Zech. 5:3-4), as the thief was put on oath as to whether he had stolen or not (Exod. 22:8-11; Lev. 6:2).

Against Informing on a Servant. 30:10. **10. Accuse not** (do not slander, inform on) **a servant unto his master, lest he** (the slave, already in an afflicted state) **curse thee** (for adding to his affliction), **and thou be found guilty** (before God, in accusing a helpless person wrongly and unjustly). But when the conscience requires exposing actual sin, that is to be done (Gen. 21:25).

Four Varieties of Sinners. 30:11-14. There are four classes of people: (1) **11. There is a generation** (*dōr,* "class of men, kind of people") **that curseth their father, and doth not bless their mother** (20:20; Exod. 21:17), a heinous sin punished by death, as was blasphemy toward God (Deut. 21:18-21), in whose place parents stood.

(2) **12a.** Another class is people who **are pure in their own eyes** (estimation; Judg. 17:5; 1 Sam. 15:13; Job 33:9; Psalm 36:2; Isa. 65:5; Jer. 2:22; Luke 16:16). They are self-righteous, with no adequate idea of God's infinite holiness, the depth of fallen man's depravity, and the exceeding sinfulness of sin. **12b.** Yet these self-justifying people are **not washed** (cleansed) **from their filthiness** (lit., "excrement"; cf. Zech. 3:3-5), ritually (Lev. 15:1-15) or morally (Prov. 15:26; 20:9; Isa. 1:6). Cleansing is possible only by faith in God's grace

foreshadowed in the sacrifices and priesthood of the Old Testament and in the New Testament by faith in Christ's atoning work (John 3:16-18; 1 John 1:3-8).

(3) **13.** A third class is proud people, **lofty ... their eyes .... And lifted up** in self-importance (Prov. 6:17; Isa. 2:11; 5:15; James 4:6; 1 Pet. 5:5). (4) **14.** A fourth class is those **whose teeth are ... swords** (Psalm 57:4) whose **jaw teeth ... knives** (Job 29:17) **to devour the poor** (afflicted) **... and the needy** (Psalms 10:8; 12:5; 14:4; Eccles. 4:1; Amos 2:7; Mic. 3:13; Hab. 3:14), oppression being a type of cannibalism.

The Importunate Leech. 30:15a. **15a.** This is an anecdotal fable-proverb, sarcastic and half-humorous. The **horse-leach** represents covetousness. Because it sucks the blood of its victim until it is glutted, it fittingly describes the greed of the covetous exploiters of verse 14 and suitably introduces the four examples of insatiable things (vv. 15b-16).

Four Insatiable Things. 30:15b-16. **15b-16.** (See Amos 1:3 for the idiom.) **Three things ... are never satisfied ... yea, four things: Sheol,** the netherworld of departed spirits, ever craving for newcomers from this world, **the barren womb,** ever craving children and producing none (Gen. 30:1), **the earth,** the dry land of Palestine always ready to drink in more rain, and **fire,** ready to devour any amount of fuel heaped upon it.

The End of a Worthless Son. 30:17. **17. The eye** (Gen. 9:22; Lev. 20:9) that mocks his father and **despiseth to obey his mother, the ravens of the valley shall pick it out** of his corpse, **and the young eagles shall eat it** (Deut. 28:26). He shall suffer a shameful death and his carcass will become a prey of carrion-eating birds (Exod. 21:15-17; Prov. 20:20), which especially feast on the *eye.*

Four Wonderful Things. 30:18-19.
18-19. Three . . . too wonderful for me . . . four which I know not (do not understand)—**the way** (course) **of an eagle in the air** (how it soars in the sky; Deut. 28:49; Jer. 48:40; 49:22), **the way of a serpent upon a rock** (how it glides across it), **the way of a ship in the midst of the sea** (how a ship moves over the sea), **and the way of a man** (*gĕḇĕr*, "a strong or wanton man") **with a maid** (*'ălmâ*, "an unmarried woman, a virgin"). The scene is of a virile man passionately bent on gratifying his burning lust after a virgin and resorting to various inscrutable devices that cannot be traced out in detail. The movements of all four are noiseless, quick, light, gliding, and the precise mode unknown. There is no reason from this passage to deny that *'ălmâ* (Isa. 7:14) means a virgin.

The Adulteress. 30:20. **20.** The adulteress eats and wipes her mouth, as one who eats a meal and then wipes away all trace of eating, and denies she has eaten at all (cf. "bread eaten in secret," 9:17; 20:17), saying, **I have done no wickedness.**

Four Intolerable People. 30:21-23. **21-23. For** (*tăḥăṯ*, "under") **three things the earth is disquieted** (*rgz*, "shudders, trembles, quakes") **and under four, it cannot bear up** (NASB; lit. Heb.), that is, cannot tolerate: (1) "a slave . . . become king" (AB), utterly unfit to rule (19:10); (2) **a fool when he is filled with food,** that is, when he becomes prosperous and gives free rein to his lusts, so that he becomes unbearably insolent by elevation (cf. 1 Tim. 3:6); (3) **an odious** (hated) **woman when she is married,** and elevated to the dignity of a wife, by her bad temper and conduct makes herself obnoxious to her husband, her servants, and her neighbors; (4) **and an handmaid** (slave girl) who becomes **heir to** (supplants) **her mistress** (cf. Gen. 16:1-6).

Four Remarkable Small Creatures. 30:24-28. **24.** Four **little** (small) creatures are **exceedingly wise. (1) 25. The ants** (6:6) **are a people** (folk) **not strong, yet they prepare their food in the summer,** carrying large burdens for their size and transporting quantities of food to their nests, and showing much ingenuity and skill, demonstrated in their tireless industry and sagacious providence. (2) **26. The badgers** (rock badgers or marmots; Lev. 11:5; Psalm 104:18), which display their wisdom by their uncanny ability to make their homes among the rocks and, like all these small but wise creatures, can teach man a lesson.

(3) **27. The locusts** have no king or leader (Exod. 10:4; Psalm 105:34; Joel 1:4; Rev. 9:3); yet with remarkable instinctive wisdom they **go . . . forth all of them by bands,** "take the field in battalions" (AB), "sally forth in detachments" (NEB). See Joel 2:4-9 for the figure of locusts as an invading army. (4) **28. The lizard** (the gecko or house lizard) **you may grasp with the hands** (NASB) and is noted for its ability to climb walls and thus frequents palaces.

Four Stately Beings. 30:29-31. **29-31. Three . . . which go well** (in their gait) **. . . four . . . stately in** (their) **going,** "carry themselves with dignity when they walk" (AB), "as they move" (NEB): (1) "the lion, lord of beasts" (AB; Judg. 14:8; 2 Sam. 1:23), which **turneth not away** (retreats) from any; (2) the **greyhound** (better, "the strutting cock," AB, NEB, NASB), domesticated in Palestine at least by the seventh century B.C., and doubtless much earlier; (3) **an he goat** (male goat), the leader of the flock; and (4) **a king** firmly established on his throne, so that there is no rising up against his majesty.

Folly Breeds Trouble. 30:32-33. **32-33.** "If you have acted foolishly in exalting yourself" (lit. Heb.), "have been such a fool to give yourself airs," or "if you have thought evil [schemed] with your hand to your mouth" (lit. Heb., i.e., surreptitiously and cunningly), be sure trouble will follow just as certainly as **the churning of milk bringeth forth butter, and the wringing of the nose bringeth forth blood** (produces bleeding); **so the forcing of wrath,** the agitation of anger (provocation), produces **strife.**

B. THE WORDS OF LEMUEL. 31:1-9.

The Superscription. 31:1. This section of Proverbs gives solemn advice to a king. **1.** This verse constitutes a superscription. **King Lemuel** (or possibly "Muel," ACC, pp. 3, 370) is unidentified and conceivably a figurative designation for an ideal king, since the word means "devoted to God." **Massa** (RSV, NEB) is here (as in 30:1) not a place name but a word (*măśśā'*) meaning "an oracle" or "solemn charge" (Jer. 23:23-33), **that his mother taught him,** that is, "set him in the right way" (cf. Prov. 9:7; 19:18; 29:17, 19).

A Queen Mother's Counsel to Her Son. 31:2-9. **2. What** (i.e., "what shall I say to you"), **my son? And what, the son of my womb? And what, the son of my vows?** The threefold repetition also expresses the deep maternal love and concern behind the advice, which is emphasized in the terminology — "my son," "son of my womb" (for whom I have born intense birth agonies), and "the son of my vows," the son given in answer to my promises and prayers, like Samuel, and as the name Lemuel ("consecrated to God") suggests (cf. 1 Sam. 1:11, 27-28).

Two snares are warned against — women (v. 3) and wine (vv. 4-7), which rob a king of the ability to administer justice effectively (vv. 8-9). **3.** *The warning against women.* **Give not thy strength** (the vigor or virility of your manhood) **unto women** (i.e., spend all your energy on sex), **nor thy ways** (your activities) on that which **destroyeth kings** (lust and self-indulgence, a peculiar snare to kings because of their wealth and power, and a large harem opening wide the gates of temptation to unbridled, self-destroying indulgence). Solomon fell into this trap, resulting in the splitting up of his kingdom, which was only one of the many tragic results of his sin (1 Kings 11:1).

The warning against the snare of strong drink (vv. 4-7) points out its pitfalls. **5-6.** Kings or rulers should not **drink wine** or have a craving for alcohol (Prov. 20:1; Eccles. 10:17; Isa. 5:22; Hos. 4:11), because when they drink they **forget the law** (4:11; lit., "what is decreed," i.e., by God in His Law) and **pervert** (alter) **the justice** (*dîn*, "the rights of everyone in a court of law") **of any** (all) **of the afflicted** (Exod. 23:6; Deut. 16:19; Prov. 17:15).

6-7. Intoxicating beverages are for the man who is **ready to perish,** as a restorative where stimulants are needed medically (Judg. 9:13; Luke 10:34; 1 Tim. 5:23), or for those of heavy heart or in poverty, to drown out their miseries, certainly *not* for a king to drown out his sense of justice by forgetting the Law.

The warnings against lust, self-indulgence, and strong drink were given by the queen mother to clear the way for a righteous rule by her son, paying special attention to the poor and underprivileged. **8. Open thy mouth** ("speak up," BV) **for the dumb,** those who cannot speak for themselves, in behalf of **all such as are appointed to destruction** (lit., "sons of passing away," those ready to succumb to their unfortunate situation).

1066

9. Judge righteously by being vocal for social justice, so frequently voiced by Israel's prophets (cf. Isa. 10:1-2; Amos 2:6-7; 4:1; 5:15).

C. THE VIRTUOUS WIFE. 31:10-31.

This acrostic poem contains twenty-two stanzas or couplets, each introduced by a letter of the Hebrew alphabet and constituting an immortal tribute to the virtuous wife and mother. It fittingly closes the book of Proverbs, where much has been said to warn against the contentious woman (cf. 19:13; 21:9; 25:24; 27:15) and the harlot (1:1—9:18; 22:14; 23:27; 29:3; 31:3). Now the sage presents a noble portrait of commendable womanhood, climaxing the teaching throughout the book of the training of children and the sanctity of the home (1:8-9; 10:1; 17:25; 18:22; 19:14; 23:25; 28:24). At the same time he furnishes a beautiful example of the outworking of wisdom in human life, underscoring the purpose of the book of Proverbs to inculcate this wisdom in people so that they might model their lives after it.

Characteristics of the Virtuous Wife. 31:10-29. **10. Who can find a virtuous woman?** (lit., "a woman of honesty," *ḥăyĭl*, "moral excellence and general integrity"). The interrogative stresses nine facts about such a true lady: (1) She is a rare discovery and treasure (Eccles. 7:28). **Her price** (worth) **is far above rubies** (jewels, coral).

(2) She merits the full confidence of her husband and is an unalloyed asset to him. **11. His heart doth safety trust in her**, with complete confidence, **so that he shall have no need of spoil**—no need to go forth to war to get booty, for his wife supplies all that ministers to domestic comforts. **12. She does him good ... all the days of her life**, not merely the first month or year, as is so often the case.

(3) She is unceasingly industrious. **13. She seeks** (not shuns) **wool, and flax**, because she works willingly with her hands and is ambitious. **14-15. She is compared to merchants' ships** (Ezek. 27:25) as she brings her **food** (provisions) for her household **from afar**, rising from sleep (Prov. 20:13; Rom. 12:11) **while it is yet night** and **giveth** (provides) **food** (prepares meals; Luke 12:42) **to her household, and a portion** to (better, "prescribes tasks for") her maid servants.

(4) She has outstanding business ability. **16. She considereth** (examines) **a field, and buyeth it**, being ambitious and industrious, but not rash or precipitous. **With the fruit of her hands** (her earnings) **she planteth a vineyard. 17. She girdeth her loins ... and strengtheneth her arms**, that is, fastens her skirt and sleeves so that she is unhindered in her work, putting all her strength in what she does (Exod. 12:11; 1 Kings 18:46).

18. She perceiveth (senses; lit., "tastes") **that her merchandise** (*săḥăr*, "trade, gain, business") **is good**, "that her business goes well" (NEB). **Her lamp** (light) **goeth not out at night.** Just as she rises early, so she works late at night by candlelight. **19. She stretches out her hands to the distaff, and her hands grasp the spindle** (NASB), giving herself to activities that minister to the good of her home, rather than to her own selfish pursuits or personal vanities.

(5) She is charitable toward the needy and unselfish and provident toward her own household. **20. She stretcheth out** (extends, opens wide) **her hand to the poor, ... reacheth forth her hands to the needy** in liberal distribution to others, the opposite of shutting the hand (Deut. 15:7-8). She is ready to help with one "hand" (sing.) or both "hands" (pl.).

Even as her industry in acquiring shines forth splendidly, so does her charity in giving. However, her charity begins at home, although it does not end there, as is first emphasized.

21. She does not fear the cold and the **snow,** for **all her household are clothed with scarlet** (*shānîm*, "fine, costly garments," as evidence of her industry and providence; the LXX and Vulgate render it *sh^enăyîm*, "double-garments," as does the AB, "doubly-clothed," and NEB, "wrapped in two cloaks"). **22. She makes coverings for herself** (Prov. 7:16), and her own clothing is attractive and beautiful, **of fine linen** (Gen. 41:42; Rev. 19:8, 14) **and purple** (NASB; Judg. 8:26; Luke 16:19). She unselfishly puts herself last, but she does not neglect her own appearance; she keeps herself attractive and in good taste.

(6) **23.** She is a boon to her husband, who **is known in the gates**, the place of business and the dispensing of justice (Deut. 16:18; 21:19; Ruth 4:1), his wife's diligence and capability at home enabling him with undistracted mind to attend to public duties (Prov. 12:4).

(7) Her industry and economy bring prosperity and security to her family. **24. She makes linen garments and sells them, and supplies belts to the tradesmen** (NASB). **25. Strength and honor are her clothing**—they are still better moral and spiritual clothing than the material clothing she makes for the body. And because of her general industry **she shall rejoice in time to come**—she can optimistically face the future.

(8) She is wise and kind, yet firm. **26. The law of kindness** (kindly instruction) is manifested in her dealing with her children, servants, and friends. **27. She looketh well to** (acts as a watchman over) **the ways** (conduct) **of her household**, supervising all that goes on. Not eating the bread of idleness herself, she does not permit others to eat without working (Prov. 14:1; 2 Thess. 3:6, 12; Titus 2:4-5).

(9) **28-29.** She is loved and respected by her family. Her children pronounce blessings on her; her husband sings her praises. His testimony of her is: **Many daughters have done nobly, but you excel them all** (NASB).

Concluding Tribute to the Virtuous Wife. 31:30-31. **30. Favor** (charm) **is deceitful, and beauty is vain** (skin-deep, fleeting). **But a woman who feareth the Lord ... shall be praised** (see comment on 1:7). **31. Give her of the fruit of her hands** (the reward she has earned), **and let her own works praise her in the** (city) **gates** (see v. 23).

ECCLESIASTES

INTRODUCTION

Title and Genre. The name of the book of Ecclesiastes derives from the Greek version, which is entitled *ekklesiastes* ("assembly"). The Hebrew designation is *qōhĕlĕt,* "one who convenes or addresses an assembly," that is, a preacher or teacher, the feminine form signifying a title or office; in this case, one who held the position of an instructor in wisdom and a philosopher speculating on the meaning of life. Ecclesiastes is to be classified as Wisdom Literature or *Hokmah,* but it belongs to a special category of the philosophical discourse of which no other examples have survived.

Authorship and Date. Since the days of Martin Luther, who denied Solomonic authorship, the tendency has been to attribute the book to a much later writer or writers—to the fifth century B.C., by such conservatives as E. Hengstenberg, Franz Delitzsch, H. C. Leupold, and E. J. Young, and to the third century or later by liberal scholars A. L. Williams, *Ecclesiastes* (1922); H. L. Ginsberg, *Studies in Koheleth* (1950); R. Gordis, *Koheleth: The Man and His World* (1955); O. S. Rankin and G. G. Atkins, *Ecclesiastes* in *The Interpreter's Bible* (1956). However, certain evidence may be adduced that Solomon himself actually wrote the book as a product of his later years of declension, in about 940 B.C., since it consists of his lifelong search for the real meaning of life.

1. It is difficult to escape the fact that the title (1:1) clearly attributes the book to "the son of David, king in Jerusalem." Although Solomon is not named outright, he is clearly meant, as the first two chapters assume the form of a Solomonic autobiography and, if he is not meant, no other king in the Davidic line fits the bill. His authorship must then be considered fictional and that the author personates Solomon, as in the apocryphal book of Wisdom (cf. Wisdom 6-9).

2. The linguistic uniqueness of the book argues for Solomonic authorship rather than against it. The book differs from *all* other Old Testament books of whatever age, including the fifth-century productions, Zechariah, Ezra, Nehemiah, Esther, and Malachi, as well as the intertestamental Hebrew books and the Qumran sectarian literature. So it fits nowhere in a later period, and it is impossible to date it as late as the second century B.C., for fragments from Qumran date from that period.

3. The linguistic and stylistic peculiarities of this book are due to its genre, not to a supposed later date. In ancient Semitic and Egyptian circles (as in Greek literature) the style in which each genre (such as epic, elegiac, lyric, etc.) was initially brought to classic perfection became conventional for each genre. It happens that no examples of the philosophical disquisition, to which genre Ecclesiastes belongs, have survived with which to compare it. However, it is very possible that Solomon, if he was the actual author, wrote in a genre that had been cultivated in

Phoenicia and Canaanite areas, as affinity for early Canaanite and Phoenician characteristics would suggest. Compare M. J. Dahood ("Canaanite-Phoenician Influence in Koheleth," *Biblica* 33 [1952]), who draws upon the linguistic data of the Ugaritic tablets (fourteenth century B.C.) and Phoenician and Punic inscriptions. Dahood concludes that the author of Ecclesiastes "wrote in Hebrew but employed Phoenician orthography" and his "composition shows heavy Canaanite-Phoenician influence."

4. The linguistic peculiarities of the book are due to early Canaanite-Phoenician influence rather than much later Greek and other alleged influences. Dahood gives many examples under orthography, inflections, particles, syntax, and lexical affinities to show the Canaanite-Phoenician-Punic impress on Ecclesiastes. Yet Dahood anomalously supports an early postexilic date for the book on the fine-spun theory for which there is not a shred of evidence, that a substantial colony of Jews fled to Phoenicia after the fall of Jerusalem in 587 B.C., and that Ecclesiastes was composed there by an unknown author.

5. The alleged Persian influence on the book, arguing for a postexilic date, can more plausibly be explained as Solomonic. Solomon's port and navy at Ezion-geber certainly gave him ready access to India, from where he may have borrowed such terms as *pitgam* ("official decision"), Sanskrit, *pratigama*, and *pardēs* ("park"), Sanskrit, *paridhis*. It is quite gratuitous to insist that such words demand a date during (530-331 B.C.) or after the Persian period, since the Persian language was allied to the Sanskrit language of India.

6. Other internal evidences commonly adduced against Solomonic au- *thorship can readily be reconciled with the Solomonic era.* For example, the supposedly nonroyal viewpoint of the author (cf. 4:13; 10:17, 20), implying disapproval or even hostility toward the king, is said to militate against Solomon as the author. But it must be remembered that the author is writing as a philosopher, not as a head of state, much less as a propagandist on his own behalf. A parallel is offered by the Roman Emperor Marcus Aurelius, who at a later age penned his *Meditations*, not as a piece of government propaganda, but as a Stoic philosopher.

7. The alleged anachronisms in the book, urged to support its fictional authorship, by no means have to be so interpreted. For example, Qoheleth's claim that he had attained more wisdom than "all they that have been before me in Jerusalem" (1:16) doubtlessly includes a reference to Melchizedek (Gen. 14:18-20) and certainly includes "wise men" who cultivated wisdom literature, such as Heman, Chalcol, and Darda (cf. 1 Kings 4:31). Another alleged anachronism is supposed to be 1:12: "I ... was [*hāyîtî*] king ... in Jerusalem," as though Solomon were no longer king, and therefore deceased, at the time of the writing of the book. But the Hebrew can also mean "I became king," a perfectly natural explanation for an elderly king to employ when reminiscing on his earlier years as king (see G. L. Archer, *Ecclesiastes*, ZPEB, p. 187).

The Message and Teachings of the Book.

1. Ecclesiastes is a book that describes the natural, unregenerate man, without God and without hope in the world. It is included in the canon of Scripture for one purpose—to show the natural man the utter "vanity" (emptiness and futility) of all that is "under the sun" (1:2-3). These two thoughts embrace the quintessential message of the book—"vanity" (that which soon vanishes into nothingness) and "under the sun" (occurring twenty-nine times in the book), describing what is on the earth and transient, as opposed to what is above (above the sun; Col. 3:1-4) and is heavenly and eternal, the subject of God's revelation. Since a believer who seriously lapses into sin and worldliness (as Solomon did in the latter part of his reign, 1 Kings 11:1-10) experientially duplicates the feelings and sentiments of the unregenerate natural man, the message of the book is also directed as a warning to all such backsliders.

2. Ecclesiastes is a book, itself divinely inspired, that describes the natural, unregenerate man apart from divinely inspired truth and revelation. This is the reason why the name of Yahweh (Jehovah), His name as He enters into covenant relation with man, does not occur in the book, a fact that higher criticism has so often failed to recognize, and completely misapplies and uses as an argument against Solomonic authorship, namely, that it is inconceivable that Solomon could have written the book without mentioning the name of Yahweh even once. In connection with this inspired book it must be remembered that it is *not* revelation of that which is "above the sun," the heavenly and the eternal, as for example the books of Romans or Ephesians. Rather, it is the Holy Spirit's recording of Solomon's naturalistic reasoning and conclusions as the aged, disillusioned monarch "communed with his own heart" (an expression occurring seven times in the book) rather than with God. It is in the light of this fact that such verses as 9:5, 10 must be interpreted—not to teach soul sleep or annihilation, but to record man's naturalistic views on the subject.

3. Ecclesiastes, in demonstrating the utter vanity and futility of the natural, unregenerate man and all he trusts in and lives for, is the way or preparer for the gospel of Jesus Christ. Like every other Old Testament book, it points and leads to Christ, in whom all problems are solved, all questions answered, and all doubts resolved.

Place in the Hebrew Scriptures. Ecclesiastes is found in the third part of the Hebrew Bible called the Writings (*Kethubhim*) among the five Scrolls (Rolls) called Megilloth, which includes Song of Solomon, Ruth, Lamentations, Ecclesiastes, and Esther. These five Scrolls are short enough to be read on anniversaries—the Song of Solomon at Passover, Ruth at Pentecost, Ecclesiastes at the Feast of Tabernacles, and Esther at Purim.

Importance of the Book. There is a reason why this book providentially came to be read every year at the Feast of Tabernacles (a prefigurement of the millennial Kingdom). It contains a message of such transcendent importance that it must be proclaimed to mankind year after year, even during the wonderful period of peace and prosperity of righteousness and joy that will be realized on earth in the personal reign of Christ in the Millennium. It is the message that everything on earth, even at its best, is fleeting and unsatisfying, and that the heart of man was made for God and will not find rest and satisfaction till it finds realization in Him who is changeless, absolute, and permanent.

OUTLINE

COMMENTARY

I. THE THEME: THE VANITY OF EVERYTHING TEMPORAL. 1:1—6:12.

A. THE THEME INTRODUCED, ILLUSTRATED, APPLIED, AND SUBJECTED TO EXPERIMENTATION. 1:1-18.

The Theme Introduced. 1:1-2. **1. The words of the Preacher** (Heb., *qōhĕlĕṯ*, "a convener of assemblies"; Exod. 35:1; Lev. 8:3; Deut. 4:10), a symbolical name of Solomon (cf. 1 Kings 8:1), under which he impersonated the natural, unregenerate man, the man "under the sun," and set forth the observations and experiences of such an unsaved person and his reactions to life according to the wisdom of this world and the best it can offer to answer and solve the problems of the natural man. The Preacher (Koheleth) is said to be **the son of David, king in Jerusalem** and, we believe, he is the historical Solomon (see Introduction on date and authorship).
2. This verse gives the theme of chapters 1 to 6 and the basis of the natural man's conclusions, chapters 7 to 12. **Vanity of vanities** (Hebraism for "complete absolute vanity"; *hĕḇĕl*, "breath, air, nothingness"; cf. Psalm 39:5). **All is vanity** (the word occurring thirty-seven times in Ecclesiastes and only thirty-three times in all the rest of the Bible), stresses the fact that everything earthly and temporal is transitory, fleeting, and unsubstantial as the wind and disappointingly unsatisfactory because of the vanity to which the creation

has been subjected due to man's Fall (Rom. 8:20), and especially so when men accord the temporal and the transitory a place of priority over God.
The Theme—All Is Vanity—Illustrated. 1:3-7. (1) *The theme is illustrated from the history of the fallen race.* **3. What advantage does man have in all his work which he does under the sun?** (NASB). **4. One generation passeth away** (goes), **and another generation cometh but the earth abideth** (remains) **forever.** The word "man" (*'āḏām*, "man in Adam"), fallen, sinful, under the curse (Gen. 3:16-18), occurs forty times in the book and portrays the natural, unregenerate person. Part of man's curse is "toil" or "labor" (*'āmāl*), occurring twenty-three times, and the expression "under the sun," repeated twenty-nine times, denoting everything temporal and subject to the curse, in contrast to the eternal and unchangeable "above the sun."
By his labor man may seem to lighten the burden of the curse, but the curse persists and man's inventions and so-called progress only hatch new broods of trouble. Death reigns and one generation after another passes away in endless cycles. Yet the earth remains, but it too remains under the vanity of the curse (Rom. 8:20, 22).
(2) *The theme is illustrated from natural phenomena.* **5-7.** It is illustrated from astronomy—the rising and setting of the sun, the earth being subject to the curse, rotating endlessly on its axis "under the sun"; from meteorology—the wind currents following cer-

tain set patterns, a young science understood only in recent years; and from the water cycle, involving knowledge of evaporation, condensation, and precipitation, phenomena operating endlessly without variation.

The Theme–All is Vanity–Applied. 1:8-11. The thesis—All is vanity—is applied in three ways to man, the crown and goal of God's creation: (1) The thesis is applied to his language, showing the futility of even this wonderful capability that lifts man above the beast. **8a. All things** (lit., "words") **are full of labor** (are wearied, tired, exhausted); **man cannot utter it,** literally, "cannot speak," that is, words fail him because of the vanity of his mind, the source of his words, and the vanity of man himself because of the Fall and the curse of sin.

(2) The thesis is applied to man's desires. **8b. The eye** (used figuratively of human "desires," "the lust of the eyes," Gen. 3:6; 1 John 2:16) **is not satisfied with seeing,** arousing the insatiable cravings of the old fallen nature, **nor the ear** (used figuratively of the natural man's inlet to his sinful longings) **with hearing** (his response to sin). Fallen natural man's desires are wrong and stay wrong, and his bondage to sin is not loosened by natural means.

(3) The thesis is applied to man's intellect and activity. This, too, is under the curse of the Fall. **9. The thing that hath been, it is that which shall be; and that which is done, is that which shall be done; and there is no new thing under the sun.** Man may progress culturally and scientifically, but "under the sun," in the realm of the natural—the old creation under the bondage and curse of sin—there is "nothing new," only the endless cycle of sin and death. It is the wearisome treadmill of vain thought and endeavor, as the apostle Paul declares: "Therefore, if any man be in Christ, he

is a new creation; old things are passed away; behold, all things are become new" (2 Cor. 5:17).

10. In the old order there is nothing concerning which it **may be said, See, this is new** (*ḥādāsh*, "fresh, renewed in a spiritual and moral sense"). **11.** The Preacher (Koheleth) did not have in mind purely natural things, and certainly not scientific inventions. He was dealing with the moral and spiritual realm, where the natural man so readily remembers the bad and forgets the good.

The Theme Subjected to Experimentation. 1:12-18. **12.** This verse is a resumption of verse 1, the intervening verses constituting the introductory illustration and application of his thesis. Next (to 2:26) the Preacher (Koheleth) demonstrated the vanity of everything in the old creation ruined by sin from his own experience. **I, the Preacher, was king** ("have been king," NASB) because Koheleth was *still* king and was about to describe the results of his *past* experiences during his long reign. He employed the regular formula for beginning a royal declaration (cf. the Moabite Stone: "I am Mesha . . . king of Moab," ANET, p. 320*b*; cf. 7:27; 12:8-10).

13. And I gave my heart (set my mind) **to seek and search out by wisdom concerning all things that are done** (by the unregenerate, natural man) **under heaven** (in the old, unrenewed creation, subject to vanity "under the sun," v. 3). He called that **severe travail** ("a grievous task"; 2:23, 26; 3:10), namely, inquiring into wisdom, and being busy about merely temporal things and the natural man's observations and reactions, which bring only pain.

But God had assigned such a task to Solomon on behalf of **the sons of man** (mankind) **to be exercised** (i.e., afflicted, disciplined) with it that they might by this means see the utter futility of everything connected with the fallen, sin-cursed old order and be chastised and humbled to seek what is *in*—not **under heaven** and *above*—not "under the sun" (vv. 3, 9). Solomon, eminently equipped as a scientist and a statesman for such a task (1 Kings 3:9-13; 4:29-34; 10:3-8), then proceeded to his grand thesis on the futility of everything temporal by logical induction, employing (1) experimentation (Eccles. 1:12—2:26) and (2) observation (3:1—9:12).

14. After experiencing and observing **all the works** (the activities of unregenerate humanity) **done under the sun** (in the old sin-cursed creation), his conclusion (and that of many a present-day university student) was: **Behold, all is vanity** (futility; 2:11, 17; 4:4; 6:9) **and vexation of spirit** ("a preying upon the spirit," Vulgate, Syriac), or "the pursuit of wind"—feeding on or occupying oneself with wind (cf. 5:16; Hos. 12:1; "an empty striving"; cf. the LXX, "a purpose of wind").

15. Why is wise investigation into fallen man's "works" (such as Solomon was assigned to do) such a "severe travail" (v. 13)? Because fallen man himself is **crooked** and **cannot be made straight** (he is hopelessly unmendable by any natural or creature agency; cf. 7:13). **And that which is lacking** (namely, acceptance with God, forgiveness of sins, etc.) **cannot be numbered.** Where nothing is, nothing can be computed (Dan. 5:27). This is the explanation of the sad note of Ecclesiastes. It portrays man as he is in his fallen state—the natural, unregenerate man, apart from God's grace and salvation—like something bent that cannot be straightened, something missing that cannot be made up by anything or anybody "under the sun" (by anything or any but God, who is *above* the sun).

16. Solomon tried worldly wisdom. **I spoke to mine own heart** ("I said to myself"), **Behold, I have magnified and increased wisdom** (2:9; 1 Kings 3:12; 4:30; 10:23) **more than all who were over Jerusalem before me** (see Introduction); **and my mind has observed a wealth of wisdom and knowledge** (NASB). The wisdom in which Solomon excelled all of his contemporaries by God's gift was concerning earthly things (Eccles. 1:13), and it is this natural, earthly wisdom, viewed by itself, that results only in "severe travail."

17. Solomon also experimented with **madness and folly,** not only intellectually by comparing folly with wisdom, but experientially in his lapse into idolatry (1 Kings 11:1-13). He pronounced all of this luxurious and wanton experience of all that the world can offer, which only a king of his power and wealth could have commanded and afforded, **vexation of spirit** ("striving after wind," NASB; see v. 14). **18.** His conclusion after experimentation with purely worldly knowledge and learning was: **in much wisdom is much grief** (2:23; 12:12) and increasing worldly knowledge by itself (apart from divine knowledge and revelation) **increaseth sorrow** (*măk'ôḇ*, "suffering, pain").

B. THE VANITY OF PLEASURE, WEALTH, AND WORK. 2:1-26.

The Experiment with Pleasure. 2:1-3. Solomon as a scientist (1:12-14a) had employed experiments in the area of learning and knowledge and made his conclusions, finding all to be "vanity and vexation of spirit" (1:14b-18). Then, as a ruler and statesman (2:1-11), he turned to other means to find something satisfying and permanent in life, and he tried worldly pleasure.

1-2. I said in mine heart (i.e., "to myself") **Come now, I will test thee with**

mirth; therefore enjoy pleasure. "So enjoy yourself—have a good time" (7:3; Prov. 14:13; cf. Luke 12:19). His satisfaction with frivolity was so fleeting that he gave the result before moving on to other experiments: **And, behold, this also is vanity** (futility), turning out to be as unsubstantial as a vapor.

3. He tried wine: **I sought in mine heart** (explored with my mind) **to give myself unto wine** (lit., "to draw my flesh with wine," i.e., stimulate my body with wine), **yet acquainting mine heart with wisdom,** "while my mind was guiding me wisely" (NASB), "while my reason remained in control" (AB). This was not drunken debauchery, but a carefully controlled experiment with the use of wine to answer the claim of many worldlings that alcoholic beverages are what man needs to enjoy the full exhilaration of life. He did not find it so, but he waited until verse 11 to give the conclusion.

The Experiment with Accomplishing Great Works. 2:4-6. **4-5.** Solomon made for himself **great works,** built **houses** for himself (1 Kings 7:1-12), planted **vineyards** for himself (Song of Sol. 8:11-12), and made **gardens** (4:16; 5:1) and **orchards** (parks) for himself, planting **all kind of fruits** in them (fruit trees). **6.** He also made **pools** (ponds, reservoirs) to irrigate a forest of growing trees (2:14; 3:15-16).

The Experiment with Prosperity and Great Wealth. 2:7-10. **7.** He bought male and female slaves in addition to **servants born in** his **house** (household retainers; Gen. 14:14; 15:3). He also had enormous possessions of flocks and herds (1 Kings 4:23), a stable item of wealth in the Near East.

8. Also he collected for himself silver and gold (9:28; 10:10, 14, 21), and **the peculiar treasure of kings and of the provinces** (satrapies), that is, such private fortune as kings and satraps enjoy (20:14; Lam. 1:1). He provided for himself **men singers and women singers** (as David; 2 Sam. 19:35), one of the prominent pleasures of a royal court, **and the delights of the sons of men,** "many concubines" (NASB; lit., "a princess and princesses" from an Arabic root). The meaning is one regular wife or queen (Esther 1:9), Pharaoh's daughter (1 Kings 3:1) and other secondary wives, "princesses" distinct from the "concubines" (11:3; Psalm 45:10; Song of Sol. 6:8). Solomon gave himself voluptuously to every sexual pleasure and carnal gratification, the experiment showing to mankind once for all that sex, even in the ultimate, is not the answer to an empty life, as many worldlings imagine.

9. So I was great (opulent; Gen. 24:35; Job 1:3; cf. 1 Kings 10:23), **more than all that were before me in Jerusalem** (v. 7; 1:16). Only Solomon himself could possibly have written this truthfully. **Also my wisdom** (the natural, earthly wisdom with which he was divinely endowed; v. 3; 1:16) **remained with me.** Therefore, it would be expected of him that he would be fully satisfied, if earthly things could satisfy.

10. He declared also that he did not refuse himself any possible earthly pleasure (6:2), and he was eminently pleased in the labor it took to obtain these delights (3:22; 5:18; 9:9). He was no cynic with a bitter spirit, which would have nullified the experiment. He found his **portion** (reward) in the pleasure (while it lasted) of making the experiment valid.

The Conclusion of the Experiment. 2:11. **11.** When he **looked on** (carefully weighed) all the things he had done and **the labor** (energy) expended in doing them, he had to admit: **Behold, all was vanity** ("utter futility, an empty breath") **and vexation of spirit** ("a grasping after the wind,'' vv. 22-23; 1:14). **And there was no profit** (*yĭtrôn*, "gain") for man's life **under the sun**—no real satisfaction or fulfillment to the natural, unregenerate man of Adam's fallen race under the curse (1:3; 3:9; 5:16).

The Analysis of the Experiment. 2:12-23. Solomon then set forth a true appraisal and evaluation of his experience of the ultimate and best of life (apart from God's revealed grace and salvation), and what it can offer the natural, unregenerate man. He was qualified to do that because his wisdom (of natural things, 1:13, 17-18) remained with him (2:9), and so he had an intelligent purpose and true value for all he had done.

He first presented his analysis of the experiment with life as a scientist (vv. 12-17). **12. And I turned myself** (i.e., stopped my activity and experimentation to evaluate the results more thoroughly than in v. 11) **to behold** (consider) **wisdom, and madness** (stupidity), **and folly** (1:17). Solomon at the same time pointed out that all that his successors could do was what he as king had already done in his vast experiment comprehending *all* phases of the problem of the vain existence of the purely natural man. By virtue of his wisdom (of things and life) he was able to do three things: (1) He was able to truly comprehend the emptiness of the natural man's life, which the stupid man or the fool might not understand. Thus, worldly wisdom does have some advantages over "madness" (stupidity) and "folly."

(2) **13a.** Solomon also was able to see **that wisdom excelleth folly** (7:11-12, 19; 9:18; 10:10). By "wisdom" (as in the entire book) he meant man-centered science, understanding the mysteries of life and the universe; it is a different concept from "wisdom" in Proverbs, where the term is God-centered (Prov. 1:7; 9:10) and means opening the life to God in reverential trust and relating all to Him who is holy and wise.

13b. Wisdom excels (surpasses) folly **as light excelleth** (surpasses) **darkness. 14. The wise man's eyes are in his head**—he has the light of wisdom and may see and avoid the pitfalls. But folly is like darkness in which the fool walks so that he does not see the snares around him and deliberately walks into them. The stupid, naive man stumbles along in semidarkness and lands in the same ditch that the fool deliberately falls into.

(3) Solomon also was able to conclude that though wisdom may be useful in life and excels folly, it represents a vain cycle that accomplishes nothing and changes nothing permanently. Solomon perceived **that one event** (death; Psalm 49:10; Eccles. 9:2-3) **happeneth to them all** (wise man, the stupid man, and the fool). **15.** "I said to myself, 'Since I shall meet the same fate as the fool, how then is wisdom an advantage?' So I concluded that this, too, was futility" (AB). His conclusion was wise, for worldly wisdom saves no man (1 Cor. 1:21), rescues no man from the curse of death, and gives no man the hope of immortality and eternal life.

16. Not only will both the wise man and the fool die (spiritually, physically, and eternally), but the futility of the whole vain cycle is that both will **be forgotten** (Eccles. 1:11; 4:16). It is humiliating enough for a wise man to die, but knowing that he will soon be forgotten by a world of fools is even more sobering. **17.** No wonder Solomon said, **Therefore I hated** (detested) **life** (4:2), because it depressed him that all man's activities **under the sun** (see comments on 1:3; 2:11; 3:9; 5:16) were **vanity and vexation of spirit** ("striving after wind," NASB). Thus, Solomon concluded his analysis of his experience with life as a scientist.

Solomon then presented his analysis of his great experiment with life as a statesman (vv. 18-23). He came to three conclusions: (1) *He came to detest all the fruit of his labor for the material and the temporal (1:3; 2:11).* **18. Yea, I hated all my labor which I had taken** (lit., "labored") **under the sun.** He realized that at death he had to leave it to **the man that shall be after** him (Psalms 39:6; 49:10), his heir or successor. **19.** The futility lay in not knowing whether his heir would be a wise man or fool. **Yet shall he have rule** (control) **over all my labor wherein I have labored, and wherein I have shown myself wise** (acted wisely). **This is also vanity** (1 Tim. 6:10).

20-21. He fell into despair once again, since a man who has labored with wisdom, knowledge, and skill has to hand over his possessions to one who has not worked for them (v. 18; 4:4). He branded this not only as **vanity** but as **a great evil,** not in itself, for this is the ordinary course of things, but "evil" in the sense of the havoc that inheriting such unearned wealth often brings with it, and "evil" in regard to the chief good—that one should have toiled so fruitlessly.

(2) *He came to lament the disappointing return from his investment in earthly things.* **22.** He questioned what a man has (i.e., what benefit he gets; 1:3; 3:9) from **all his labor** (v. 11) and **vexation of his heart, wherein he hath labored under the sun** (as the natural man with his goals and purposes).

(3) *He posited positive liability rather than any assets from such labor for the earthly and the temporal.* **23.** Such a task became painful and grievous (1:18; 5:17; Job 5:7; 14:1). In such a pursuit man spends all his days in the pains and vexations of his business. **Yea, his heart** (mind) **taketh not rest in the night.** "Even in the night his mind has no rest" (AB). **This is also vanity** (futility).

The Final Conclusion to the Whole Experiment. 2:24-26. The analysis being complete, Solomon gave a general five-point conclusion as to how a man should live in a world of vanity and emptiness resulting from man's (Adam's) Fall. (1) *Man must cultivate an attitude of contentment.* **24a. There is nothing better for a man** (*'āḏām*), forced to live in a world of vanity and frustration, **than that he should eat and drink, and that he should make his soul enjoy** (lit., cause his soul, i.e., himself, to see) **good in his labor,** in the sense of "finding satisfaction in doing his work" (v. 3; 3:12-13, 22; 5:18; 6:12; 8:15; 9:7; 1 Tim. 6:17).

(2) *Such contentment enjoined is a condition of the heart and a blessing from God.* **24b. This also I saw** (perceived by experience) **... was from the hand of God** (Eccles. 3:13; Psalm 4:6; James 1:17). He alone can give contentment and deliver us from the vanity and the futility of the natural man in a fallen world (cf. Prov. 15:15-16; Matt. 6:25-34; Phil. 4:11; 1 Tim. 6:6-11; Heb. 13:5).

(3) *Apart from God there is no enjoyment in a world of vanity and futility.* **25. For who can eat and who can have enjoyment without Him?** (NASB; "apart from Him," following eight Hebrew manuscripts, LXX, the Syriac, and Jerome). God is to be in our lives in all our activities (1 Cor. 10:31).

(4) *God gives wisdom and joyous contentment to His own, but to the sinner He gives travail.* **26a. To a person who is good in His** (God's) **sight,** that is, the righteous man, justified by faith (Gen. 15:6), and exemplifying that righteousness before God in a righteous life

before men, **He has given wisdom** (reverence for Him and His Word; Prov. 1:7; 9:10) **and knowledge** (of what is right and wrong) **and joy** (NASB), contentment and satisfaction with our place in God's will and what we have (Job 32:8; Prov. 2:6).

26b. In contrast **to the sinner,** the natural, unregenerate man "under the sun," who lives in sin in a state where anxiety and problems are compounded in a world of futility, God **giveth travail,** the task of gathering and collecting what the sinner must then hand over to the righteous and right-living man, who is good in God's sight (Job 15:20; 27:16-17; Prov. 13:22). The parable of the rich fool (Luke 12:15-21) illustrates Solomon's deduction. **This also is vanity,** utter futility and **vexation of spirit,** mere wind-chasing, to be such a man— unregenerate and under the curse of sin—and to die so soon, never even enjoying what he has.

(5) *It is a boon to be shown a path through life's journey by which the empty things of the world may be so related to God that they may give us joy and provide contentment in grateful satisfaction for God's provision for us.*

C. VANITY AND GOD'S WORKING IN THE WORLD. 3:1-22.

God Has Established Order in the Universe. 3:1-8. **1-8.** Up to this point Solomon had resorted to experimentation to prove his thesis of the vanity of all things in the old creation under sin. Next he turned to observation. He had lived life to the full and seen many things. He then adduced well-known and proven facts to support his argument.

First, the orderly cycles show that although sin has entered the world, it has not abrogated the divine order.

There is a time for everything. **To every thing there is a season, and a time to every purpose under the heaven: a time to be born, and a time to die.** Twenty-eight times the word "time" is used, while fourteen pairs of opposites span the widest spectrum of life's activities, suggesting that although all is vanity in a fallen world, God is still working in it, operating through His established order of things. Since God has ordained order, it is incumbent upon man to observe it.

Man Has a Responsible Place in God's Order. 3:9-13. **9.** Man is held accountable for how he fits into God's order and reacts to it. Is he working at cross-purposes with God's order or operating out of line with His time schedule? If so, he may well inquire: **What profit hath he that worketh in that wherein he laboreth?** (1:3; 2:11; 5:16). What benefit does the workman derive from that for which he in pure self-effort exhausts himself and wears himself to a frazzle working at cross-purposes with God's order?

10. I have seen the travail, which God hath given to the sons of men to be exercised in it (1:13; 2:26). Solomon observed that whatever jobs men work at, labor and exertion attend them all because of the curse under which mankind labors in the sweat of his brow (Gen. 3:19). **11a.** Yet God has **made everything beautiful** (*yāpĕh*, "appropriate, good"; 1:31) **in its time,** for He has a time schedule in His ordered universe. If I am reaching out for something I want before His time for me to have it, that which He has made beautiful in His time will cease to be beautiful for me.

11b. God also has **set the world** (*'ōlām*, "eternity," as in 1:4; 2:16; 3:14; 9:6; 12:5) **in their** (men's) **heart.** It is this God-consciousness that the atheist futilely seeks to convince himself and others does not exist. Because God has set eternity in our hearts (minds), the transient things of time do not satisfy. This deep sense of life hereafter shows that God is working in this world of vanity. That fact is pivotal in the argument moving to the climax that man knows instinctively that a day of reckoning is coming.

11c. Solomon declared that God has "set eternity" in the human consciousness **so that** (but in such a manner that) **no man can find out the work that God maketh** (has done) **from the beginning to the end** (Job 5:9; Eccles. 7:13; 8:17; Rom. 11:33). It is fallen man's God-implanted ability to discern something of eternity behind the present transient world and to cling to it.

But because of his finiteness and the effects of the Fall, man apart from God's revelation, is incapable of "finding out" (comprehending) God's work (what it is that God has been doing) from beginning to end, much less his own destiny in the afterlife. Finite, fallen creature that he is, subject to death, man can glimpse a mere century at most of the drama of human history in its outworking in God's larger plan and purpose for eternity. This is the reason why no man can presume to sit in judgment upon God's actions. He can only see a part, and a tiny part at that, and man knows intrinsically that any part must be judged by the whole, which must be in the light of eternity.

12. I know that there is no good in them (fallen men under the curse apart from redemptive grace). Solomon was saying that he knew that the only satisfaction of such a natural man was to be happy and find pleasure in living. **13.** Indeed, when such a man can **eat and drink, and enjoy the good of all his labor, it is the gift of God** (Eccles. 2:24; 5:19), the work of God upon the life, because it is not within man's natural heart to be satis-

fied; so even unregenerate people, if they enjoy life, must realize it is due to God's goodness to them. That is anything but the philosophy of Epicureanism. Rather, it is earthly prosperity due to God's blessing upon right-living, unregenerate people (cf. Jer. 22:15).

God Will Judge Man for His Response to His Responsibility. 3:14-17. **14a.** But God alone is the answer to man's need of permanency and reality in a fallen world of vanity. **I know that, whatsoever God doeth ... shall be forever,** in contrast to the fleetingness of man's endeavor (cf. Rom. 11:29). What God does He does forever—nothing to add to or subtract from it. When He saves, He saves forever; when He calls, His call is irrevocable. **14b.** All that God does is in order that men should **fear before him** (Eccles. 5:7; 7:18; 8:12-13; 12:13), hold Him in godly reverence and holy awe.

15. With God, time is an eternal *now.* **That which hath been** in the divine counsels **is now, and that which is** (yet) **to be hath already been;** and God **requireth that which is past** (*nĭrdāp̱*, "that which is driven on"), "God summons each event back in its turn" (NEB). Man is thus held accountable to God and will answer for his actions. **16.** For in this world **under the sun** Solomon observed **wickedness** and **iniquity** where **justice** and **righteousness** ought to be. God knows all about this as an eternal now, and He will hold man responsible and require accounting for past wrongs and injustice.

17. He concluded that **God shall judge the righteous and the wicked** (11:9; Psalms 96:13; 98:9; Rom. 2:6-10; 2 Cor. 5:10; Rev. 20:12-13; 22:12). Since He is the God of order (vv. 1-8), man has a place of accountability in His ordered universe (vv. 9-17), **for there is a time**

there for every purpose and for every work (deed; v. 1; 8:6).

Man Abrogates Responsibility by Denial of a Future Existence. 3:18-21. Although God has placed "eternity" in man's heart (consciousness; v. 11), so that man knows there is a life after death and a day of accountability and likewise knows intrinsically that he is not a mere animal to die "like a dog," that being the end of him, yet God is testing man on this score through man's fallen nature and the outward appearance of things.

18. I said in mine heart (i.e., "to myself," Solomon setting forth a value judgment on the matter) **concerning the estate of the sons of men** (mankind). **God has surely tested them in order for them to see** (as would seem to be the case by specious outward appearances) **that they are but beasts** (NASB; Psalms 49:12, 20; 73:22).

19-20. The outward appearances, by which God proves man, are specified—physical death is common to both man and beast (Eccles. 9:12), both having the same breath (*rūăḥ*, "spirit, breath"). So that abandoning the God-implanted consciousness of "eternity" (v. 11), fallen, unregenerate man, looking merely at outward appearances, and failing God's test, concludes, **there is no advantage for man over beast.... All go to the same place. All came from the dust and all return to the dust** (NASB; Gen. 3:19; Psalm 103:14; Eccles. 12:7).

Although the natural man is ready to succumb to outward appearances and regard himself as purely an animal with no future existence to face judgment for his deeds on earth, Scripture reveals that man is trenchantly different from an animal. Man is not only a soul (*nĕpĕš*) with life, for the Creator Himself has breathed the breath of life into him (Gen. 2:7) and given him divine life and God-

consciousness. This clear-cut distinction between man and the brute, however, has been lost in the Fall.

21. Solomon is speaking of physical death and dealing only with what the natural man can observe to distinguish himself from the beasts. Hence, he does not speak of Sheol (cf. 9:10). **Who knows that the breath of man ascends upward** (12:7) **and the breath of the beast descends downward to the earth?** (NASB). In other words, can a natural man by outward appearances really tell whether there is any difference at death between a man and an animal? The answer is that outward observation is utterly unable to make that distinction, and God at the same time is testing and proving men concerning what they will believe.

Conclusion Concerning the Natural Man. 3:22. **22.** The best an unregenerate man can attain in this life of vanity is to **rejoice in his own works**—get satisfaction out of what he does. **For that is his portion** (lot) as an unsaved person. **For who shall bring him** (the man who does not believe in an afterlife) **to see what shall be after him?** (2:18; 6:12; 8:7; 10:14). He might as well enjoy himself here, for he may not enjoy what God will do with him in the life after death, when he is called to give account for his life on earth (cf. v. 17). It is useless to argue with such an unbeliever. He will not be convinced, for God has arranged the whole matter in such a way that He might test mankind on this score.

D. THE VANITY OF DISORDERED RELATIONSHIPS. 4:1-16.

The Few in Disordered Relationship to the Many. 4:1-3. The observation of orderly cycles (3:1-22) is followed by apparent disorder in the world, particularly in man's relationship to man in the social order (4:1-16). Men cannot live together and work together in harmony, as they should. The reason is because in a world of vanity under the curse of sin things are wrong within man's heart and therefore they are wrong in his relation to others.

1. Solomon observed **all the** (acts of) **oppressions . . . done under the sun** (Job 35:9; Psalm 12:5; Eccles. 3:16; Isa. 5:7); **and . . . the tears of . . .** (the) **oppressed**, and that they **had no comforter** (repeated for emphasis on the forlorn and unrelieved distress of those exploited by the **power** possessed by a few).

2. In view of so much oppression and suffering, Solomon concluded that the dead are better off than the living. **Wherefore, I praised** (congratulated) **the dead** (Eccles. 2:17; Job 3:11-26). **3. Yea, better is he than both** (the living and the dead) who is not yet born and who has not lived in this world of suffering and tears (Eccles. 6:3).

Man in Disordered Relationship to Man Through Rivalry. 4:4-6. **4. Again, I considered** (observed) **that all travail** (toil), **and every right work** (*kĭśrôn*, "skill, success, prosperity"), was that for which **a man is envied by his neighbor** (2:21; lit., "this is the jealousy of a man from his neighbor," meaning either, "all the toil and skill in activities bring envy between a man and his neighbor" (BV), or "every labor and every skill which is done is the result of rivalry [*qin'â*, 'jealousy, zealous competition'] between a man and his neighbor" (NASB). In either case, this is another example of **vanity and vexation of spirit**—emptiness, futility, and a clutching at the wind (see 1:14).

5. In contrast to the person who is selfishly competitive and envious of the success of another is **the fool** who **foldeth his hands** (Prov. 6:10; 24:33) and, like a sluggard, has no ambition whatever to achieve anything. He shrinks from the competition completely. The result is

that he eats **his own flesh,** that is, destroys himself (Isa. 9:20; 49:26). The right course is a balanced position between the two extremes.

6. Better is an handful (one open palm) **with** (full of) **quietness, than both the hands** (fists) **full with** (what seems wealth, but is really) **travail and vexation of spirit** (striving after wind; Prov. 15:16-17; 16:8). Tranquility emanating from labor that is free from the spirit of rivalry is the happy medium between ruinous indolence on one hand (v. 5) and competitive acquisitions of wealth on the other.

Man in Disordered Relationship to Himself Through Loneliness. 4:7-12. **7-8.** Solomon observed another instance of **vanity under the sun**—the utter futility of fallen man under the curse apart from God. It is the case of **one alone, and there is not a second** (a dependent), that is, a single solitary man, with no son or brother to be an heir (Deut. 25:5, 10), who toiled endlessly. Yet his **eye** ("his desire"; see Eccles. 1:8) was not **satisfied with riches** (cf. Prov. 27:20; Hab. 2:5-9; 1 John 2:16), neither did he ask himself: **For whom do I labor, and bereave** (deprive) **my soul** (myself) **of good?** (enjoyment, prosperity; Eccles. 2:21). **This is also vanity, yea, it is heavy** (grievous) **travail** (1:13).

9. Two are better than one, because they have a good (better) **reward** (return) **for their labor. 10.** For if either of them falls, the one **will lift up his fellow** (companion). **But woe to him that is alone when he falleth; for** he will have no one to lift him up. **11. Again, if two lie together, then they have heat** (keep warm); **but how can one be warm alone?** (1 Kings 1:1-4). **12.** Also, where one may be overpowered (by an enemy), two can resist attack. **And a threefold cord** (a rope of three strands) **is not quickly broken** (e.g., husband, wife, and children;

Prov. 11:14). Untie the cord and the separate strands are easily "broken."

The Many in Disordered Relationship to One. 4:13-16. **13. Better is a poor and a wise child** (*yĕlĕḏ*, "youth") **than an old and foolish king, who will no longer be admonished** (lit., "who does not know how to be advised—does not have the wits to heed a warning"; 7:19; 9:15). **14. For out of prison** (the prison of poverty) **he cometh to reign** (Gen. 41:14, 41-43), that is, to become king, even though the youth was born poor in the old king's kingdom; thus, he rose from prison to the throne in the very kingdom where he was born in poverty.

15. I considered (saw, viewed) **all the living,** that is, all the present generation of subjects **who walk under the sun, with** (i.e., throng to the side of) **the second child,** that is, the youth, the second, who **shall stand up in his stead** (succeed the old king on the throne). **16.** Although that generation then living flocked to the support of the new young king, and they were endless in numbers, yet the people after them will **not rejoice** (be happy) with him. This shows that fallen man is disordered, fickle, and changeable, and that his conduct with others and with himself gives ample evidence of **vanity and vexation of spirit** (striving after or chasing wind; see Eccles. 1:14).

E. THE VANITY OF INSINCERE WORSHIP AND TEMPORAL THINGS. 5:1-20.

The Vanity of Empty Worship. 5:1-7. In chapter 4 the sick state of society is evidenced in the disordered relationships of men to each other. Now it appears that man is also sick in relationship to God, manifested in his disordered worship of God. That fact becomes apparent in man's attitudes and words to God, portraying the inner condition of his heart (cf. Matt. 12:34; 15:18).

1. Keep thy foot (watch your step, be circumspect) **when** (as) **thou goest to the house of God** (Exod. 3:5; 30:18-20; Isa. 1:12), **and be more ready** (*qārôb*, rather, "draw near, approach") **to hear** (listen in the sense of hearing and obeying), **than to give** (offer) **the sacrifice of fools** (lit. Heb., "than to offer sacrifice like fools"), **for they consider not that** (do not know when) **they do evil.** "To be ready [to draw near with the desire] to hear [obey; 1 Sam. 15:22] is a better sacrifice than to offer an empty ritual like fools, who know nothing except how to do wrong and then gloss over their wrong with religious veneer" (cf. Psalm 50:8; Prov. 15:8; 21:27; Hos. 6:6).

2. The Egyptian *Instruction to Ani* 8 contains a warning that recalls Solomon's in this verse: "Make an offering to your god, and beware of sins against him. You should not inquire about his [affairs]. Do not be free with him" (ANET, p. 420*b*). Says Solomon: **Be not rash with thy mouth** (Prov. 20:25, NASB; precipitous in word, speaking impetuously), **and let not thine heart be hasty** (do not be impulsive) in the sense of uttering a hurried word **before God.**

God is in heaven (cf. Matt. 6:9); therefore, He ought to be approached with reverence and carefully weighed words by frail creatures of the dust. **Let thy words be few.** Be not as those who think to compensate for their lack of devotion by their wordiness (6:7-8; Mark 12:40). James comments on the theme of the right use of words (James 1:19-26; 3:2-10).

3. For a dream cometh through the multitude of business. That is, it follows much busyness and many worldly concerns and worries; so many words are spoken by a fool (a sinner) in his "dream" that God will hear him for his much speaking (Matt. 6:7). This appears from verse 7: "For in the multitude of dreams and many words ... are also many vanities; but [rather] fear [revere] ... God (Eccles. 3:14; 7:18; 8:12-13; 12:13).

Verses 4 to 6 contemplate empty worship considered from the aspect of making vows. **4.** When such a vow is made to God (Deut. 23:21-23), **defer not to pay it** (Num. 30:2; Psalm 50:14), do not be slow or late in paying it, for God **hath no pleasure** (takes no delight) **in fools,** who are hasty of word in prayer (vv. 2-3), suggesting the subject of hasty vows (cf. Jephthah's, Judg. 11:35; and Saul's, 1 Sam. 14:24). God keeps His word, and so man must keep his (Psalm 76:11). **5. Better ... not vow, than ... vow and not pay** (Deut. 23:21, 23; Prov. 20:25; cf. Acts 5:1-11). **6. Suffer not** (do not allow) **thy mouth** (tongue; Prov. 6:2) **to cause thy flesh** (body) **to sin** by making a vow (e.g., fasting), which your bodily appetites (cf. Ezek. 16:26; 23:20) may pressure you into breaking (Prov. 20:25). **Neither say ... before the angel** ("the messenger" of God; Job 33:23; Rev. 1:20), that is, the priest (Mal. 2:7), before whom a breach of a vow was to be confessed (Lev. 5:4-5), **that it** (the vow) **was an error** (mistake). Any commitment to God is a serious matter, and going back on it is not to be made good by empty excuses before a priest. It incurs God's anger and punishment. True reverence for God will obviate all the disorders connected with the vanity of empty worship (v. 7; cf. v. 3).

The Vanity of Oppressive Government. 5:8-9. **8.** As long as man is under the curse and its resultant vanity, he is not to be shocked when he witnesses **the oppression of the poor** (4:1) **and violent perverting** (denial; Ezek. 18:18) of justice and righteousness **in a province** (state). The rapacity of government officials is not to be wondered at, since each

in turn suffers under the official above him, all the way up to the king. But even over the king there is **he that is higher than the highest** ($g^e\underline{b}\bar{o}h\hat{i}m$, the plural intimating the triune God), who has not abandoned this world under the vanity of the curse, but **regardeth** (*shōmēr,* "keeps watch over") mankind in view of present and future judgment (2 Chron. 16:9; cf. Exod. 2:25; Psalm 94:3-10).

9. In view of a hierarchy of exploiters, men are to be reminded that **the profit of the earth is for all,** even **the king ... is served by the field,** or (with the ASV marg.): "But the profit *of a land* every way is a king that maketh himself servant to the field" (italics added). No economy is to be built upon oppressive practices, but rather upon sound principles of agriculture and fair provisions for all.

The Vanity of Materialism. 5:10-20. Seven things are said about materialism: (1) **10.** Materialism never satisfies. **He that loveth silver shall not be satisfied with silver** (2:10-11). "Silver" represents money and all it can buy. True wealth is spiritual and satisfies in time and eternity (cf. Luke 12:15). **Nor he who loves abundance** (will be satisfied) **with its income** (NASB), showing the emptiness of temporal things.

(2) **11.** Materialism brings with it no real benefit. **When goods increase,** so do those who consume them; thus, the only benefit accruing to the owner is that he can look on to watch his accumulations find their devourers. (3) **12.** Materialism brings care and sleeplessness, while **the sleep of a laboring man is sweet, whether he eat little or much ... the abundance of the rich** will not permit him to sleep, because his mind is often perturbed by worry and his body glutted with food and made sleepless by lack of exercise.

(4) **13.** Materialism is often evil and

detrimental. Things may turn out to be **a great** (grievous) **evil.** This happens when **riches** are hoarded by their possessors **to their hurt** (*rā'â*, "misfortune, destruction, wickedness"), doing them injury in making them selfish misers in this life and working toward their ruin in the life to come (Eccles. 6:2; Luke 12:20-21). (5) **14.** Materialism is fraught with uncertainty and loss. **Riches** often **perish** (are lost) **by evil travail** (a bad investment), and a man has nothing **in his hand** (in his possession) to support or leave to his son.

(6) **15-16.** Materialism is short-lived and death strikes its knell. A man comes **naked** from **his mother's womb** (Job 1:21); so he will leave this world as he came, utterly stripped of possessions (Psalm 49:17; 1 Tim. 6:7). Thus, in the long-range view, **what profit** (advantage) has he who merely **labored for the wind?** (Eccles. 1:3; 2:11; Prov. 11:29). (7) **17.** Materialism often brings with it many evils, including **darkness,** both moral and spiritual; great **sorrow** (vexation); fighting in a world of intense competition; **sickness,** mental, spiritual, and physical; and **anger** (NASB) at others' greed and rapacity, and subconsciously at one's own avarice.

Conclusion on the Vanity of Material Things. 5:18-20. **18.** Here is what I (Solomon) **have seen to be good and fitting:** (1) **to eat, to drink and enjoy oneself in all one's labor** (NASB; cf. 2:24). This is the **portion** (reward) of the natural, unregenerate man **under the sun,** who lives a life not vitiated by materialism and greed.

(2) **19.** To the man to whom God has given riches (6:2; 2 Chron. 1:12), not the one who has acquired wealth by himself through greed and dishonesty, God empowers him to enjoy his portion and rejoice in his labor (Eccles. 6:2). This blessing is **the gift of God** (3:13). **20.** Such

a man **shall not much remember** ("not often consider," NASB) **the days of his life,** in the sense of brooding over the brevity of his life, since God keeps his mind occupied with happy thoughts.

F. THE VANITY OF LIFE IN AN IMPERFECT WORLD. 6:1-12.

The Vanity of Wealth Without Enjoyment. 6:1-2. **1. There is an evil** (*rā'â*, "misfortune, adversity") **which I have seen under the sun**—in a fallen world filled with disorders (chap. 5) and imperfections (chap. 6)—**and it is common among men** (*'ādām*, "mankind" under the curse), literally "it is great upon men," that is, "it weighs heavy upon" them (NEB; 5:13).

2. This verse describes the "evil." It is the man who has wealth but no satisfaction in it. God grants riches, possessions, and an honored place in society, and so he **lacketh nothing** that his heart could desire (Psalms 17:14; 73:7), but "has not empowered him" (NASB; Luke 12:20), that is, has not enabled him **to eat thereof**—to enjoy his wealth. **But a stranger,** one not related to, perhaps even hostile to, him (Lam. 5:2), **eateth** (enjoys) it.

This man had everything material and temporal he could possibly desire, a life full of things, without the ability or opportunity to enjoy them. His was not the problem of dissipation of his wealth by foolish heirs (Eccles. 2:18-23) or of the loss of it (5:13-17). But his case is an illustration from another angle of the **vanity** and **evil disease** (sore affliction), which are so characteristic of everything temporal under the curse, "under the sun" (v. 1), even when God grants these temporalities.

The Vanity of Life Without Satisfaction. 6:3-6. **3.** A numerous progeny and a long life were regarded by the Hebrews as blessings. But even these can turn out to be worse than useless in this vain world. If a man fathers a hundred children and is **not filled** (satisifed) **with good** (the good things of life), **and he does not even have a proper burial** (Isa. 14:20; Jer. 8:2; 22:19), **then I say, "Better the miscarriage** (the still-born child) **than he"** (NASB; Job 3:16; Eccles. 4:3).

4-5. For he ("it," the still-born child) **cometh in with vanity**—"its coming is an empty thing" (NEB)—**and departeth in darkness**—goes into obscurity; and its **name** (as dead and meaningless as the still-born infant) **shall be covered with darkness,** since it never sees **the sun** or knows anything. **This** (still-born child) **hath more rest than the other**—is better off than the man who lives so long without satisfaction in a world of vanity.

6. Yea, though he live a thousand years twice told (more than twice the age of Methuselah), his long life—without satisfaction and enjoyment of real _good—is only prolonged misery. **Do not all go to one place?** (the grave or Sheol; cf. Luke 16:19-31), where all arrive completely bereft of all earthly goods (1 Tim. 6:7). The man in question was evidently soured on life, for although he had such a numerous family, he was not even given a proper burial.

Conclusions on the Vanity of Life. 6:7-12. In a vain world of disorders and imperfections, how shall a man live? Ten conclusions are given: (1) **7.** He must realize that he cannot be satisfied by the temporal and the material. All the toil of the natural man is **for his mouth, and yet the appetite** (_nĕp̆ĕsh_, "soul") **is not filled** (satisfied). Unregenerate man forgets that "Man shall not live by bread alone, but by every word that proceedeth out of the mouth of God" (Matt. 4:4; cf. Deut. 8:3). The "soul" of man can only be really satisfied with heavenly bread—the eternal Word of

God. Any other satisfaction is only temporary and relative.

(2) **8a.** He must realize he cannot be satisfied by the mental and the intellectual apart from God any more than the physical. Even human wisdom is not enough (cf. Eccles. 2:12-17; 1 Cor. 1:20-21). **For what hath the wise** (man) **more than the fool?** The wise man's worldly wisdom may direct him how to cope better with life in a vain, empty world, but it is no more efficacious than the folly of the fool to prepare him for the unchangeable and eternal.

(3) **8b.** He must realize that a man's life does not consist in the things he possesses. **What advantage does the poor man have, knowing how to walk before the living?** (NASB). Actually and practically, he has more than the rich man just by knowing how to conduct himself wisely and dutifully before his contemporaries in joyful contentment with his lot in life. He has the favor of God, the respect of man, and his own self-respect.

(4) **9.** He must realize the rationality of enjoying what he has rather than grabbing greedily for more. **Better is the sight of the eyes** (what the eye sees), making the best of that which is present in our sight, **than the wandering of the desire** ("what the soul goes after"), its uneasy stepping ahead after things at a distance, inventing a myriad of imaginary satisfactions. He who is content is happier with ever so little than the discontented with ever so much. Such wandering desire is **vanity**, at best, **vexation of spirit**—mere grasping after the wind (Eccles. 1:14).

(5) **10a.** He must realize that his lot in life is God-appointed, unalterable, and to be acquiesced to cheerfully. **That which hath been** (is, and shall be) **is named already,** foredetermined in the divine foreknowledge, and so must be

resigned to with joyous contentment. (6) **10b.** He must realize that he is but a man, no matter what attainments or position he may achieve; and, as such, he is not above the common ills of humanity, "that which hath been" and is (man) "is named already," his Maker having given him his name (*'āḏām*, "Adam; red earth"; Gen. 5:2), **and it is known that it is man** (*'āḏām*), a frail, fallen creature of the dust; "mean, mutable and mortal" (Matthew Henry). Let man, even in his highest elevation and power, remember this (Psalm 9:20).

(7) **10c.** He must realize that as a mere creature he cannot strive with divine Providence. If it is man, he may not **contend with him** (God) **that is mightier than he** (Job 33:12). It is wicked presumption to stand in judgment of God's dealings or to charge Him with iniquity or folly. (8) **11.** In light of the utter futility of living in a vain world, man may well inquire what profit and outcome there are for him.

(9) **12a.** He must realize the severe limitations of human wisdom as a guide in living life as it should be lived. **For who** (limited to human wisdom) **knoweth what is good for man in . . . his vain life which he spendeth as a shadow?** ("going through motions, but accomplishing nothing," Amp.). "How impressive throughout Ecclesiastes is the evidence that, while Solomon the prodigal is doing his utmost to prove that life is futile and not worth living, the Holy Spirit is using him to show that these conclusions are the tragic effect of living 'under the sun'—ignoring the Lord . . . yet face to face with the mysteries of life and nature!" (Amp., p. 749). (10) **12b.** He must realize the uncertainty of all life **under the sun** (Eccles. 3:22). **For who can tell a man what shall be** (what will happen to his plans, work, and wealth)

after him . . . ? (after he is gone from this earthly scene).

II. HOW TO LIVE IN A WORLD OF VANITY. 7:1—12:14.

A. ADVICE FOR COPING WITH LIFE IN A WORLD OF VANITY. 7:1-29.

1. HOW TO MAKE THE BEST OF A BAD SITUATION. 7:1-22.

Solomon has given many proofs and illustrations of the emptiness and futility of life apart from God in a fallen, sin-cursed world. Now he suggests ways and means to be employed to cope with the perils and temptations this sad state of things presents, in order to arm a man under the sun against the harm he may suffer from it. The best is to be made of this situation by doing eight things:

(1) By Cultivating Good Character. 7:1a. **1a. A good name** (character manifested in a godly mind and life, issuing in a good reputation before men, Prov. 22:1), **is better than precious ointment,** used widely in the Near East as perfume and deodorant. Character is internal and exudes a permanent fragrance, while the sweet scent of ointment is only external and evanescent (Isa. 56:5; Mark 14:3-9).

(2) By Looking Forward to Reward After Death. 7:1b. **1b. Death** is to him who has cultivated good character ("a good name") better ("far better," Phil. 1:23) **than the day of** his **birth** (Eccles. 4:2; 7:8), which ushers one into a world of so much sin and troubles. We were born to uncertainty, but a good man does not die in uncertainty. The day of his birth clogs the soul with the burden of the flesh, but the day of death will set it at liberty.

(3) By Cultivating Sobriety and Seriousness. 7:2-6. Only a solemn and serious attitude is consonant with life in a world of sin and suffering. **2.** So **it is**

better to go to the house of mourning (a funeral or place where misfortune and sadness abound; Matt. 5:4), **than . . . the house of feasting,** the former tending to remind us of the vanity of the world, and the latter often shutting out thoughts of God and eternity. **For that** (i.e., death lamented in "the house of mourning") **is the end** (Eccles. 2:16; 3:19-20; 6:6; 9:2) **of all men** (*'āḏām*, "frail and mortal mankind as descended from Adam"). And **the living** who visit "the house of mourning" will be caused to think seriously about their own "end" (cf. Psalm 90:10-12).

3. For the same reason **sorrow is better than laughter** (reckless mirth that is liable to drown out sober thoughts of the eternal, whereas sorrow weans the soul from the temporal and invites it to consider spiritual realities). **For by the sadness of the countenance** (Psalm 126:5-6; 2 Cor. 4:17; 6:10; 7:10; Heb. 12:10-11) brought about by honestly facing the vanities of the world **the heart is made better,** by drawing it away from its emptiness and setting its "affection on things above, not on things on the earth" (Col. 3:1-3). The thin happiness experienced in this vain world may light up the countenance like the sun momentarily peeping through dark clouds, but it soon vanishes and leaves the heart empty.

4. The inevitable deduction is: **The heart** (mind) **of the wise is in the house of mourning, but the heart** (mind) **of fools is in the house of mirth** (pleasure). **5.** In a fallen world where sin and folly abound, **it is better to hear** (listen to; Eccles. 9:17; Psalm 141:5; Prov. 6:23; 13:18; 15:31-32) **the rebuke of the wise** (their stern warning concerning the vanities of an empty world, castigating the flesh but benefitting the spirit), **than . . . to hear** (listen to) **the song of fools** "in the house of mirth" (v. 4), pampering the flesh and injuring the spirit.

6. For . . . the laughter of the fool (Eccles. 2:2) is compared to **the crackling of thorn bushes** *(sîrîm)* **under a pot** *(sîr;* NASB), a play upon words in the Hebrew, the very fire consuming the thorns effecting the seemingly merry noise (Joel 2:5). Slow-burning, dried cow dung was the common fuel in the ancient Near East, graphically making the quick, blazing fire of thorns a very apt figure of the sudden end of fools (Psalm 118:12).

(4) By Exercising Calmness of Spirit. 7:7-10. In a vain world of many wrongs and vexations of spirit a man must learn to control his emotions. **7a.** For **oppression** (of which the sin-cursed earth is full) **maketh a wise man mad** (4:1; 5:8), that is, arouses his righteous soul so that he is tempted to call in question God's dispensations and rave angrily against the social injustices perpetrated by "fools" (vv. 4-6; cf. 3:16; 5:8).

7b. And a gift (a base bribe, perverting justice) **destroyeth** (corrupts, vitiates) **the heart** (Exod. 23:8; Deut. 16:19; Prov. 17:8, 23). The sight of the perversion of justice in that wicked way is so obnoxious to a wise man that he is tempted to lose his wisdom by giving vent to wrath and violent reaction (Job 12:6).

8. Better is the end of a thing, the final outcome of "oppressions" and injustices, which in their incipient stages perplex the faith of the wise. In the end God will overrule for good. Therefore, one is to be **patient in spirit** (Rom. 5:3), which is so far superior to **the proud in spirit,** who are tempted to criticize God and become angry and bitter against men and life in general in a world of vanity (Psalm 73:2-3; James 1:19; 5:11).

9. Therefore, the injunction: **Be not hasty . . . to be angry** (Prov. 16:32), **for anger resteth** (resides) **in the bosom of fools**—like a cancer producing vindictiveness, hatred, spite, murder. To give way to anger is for the wise man to exchange places with the fool.

10. Such a spirit of murmuring tends to call in question God's dealings and to say, **Why is it that the former days were better than these?** (NASB). It is not wisdom that acts in this way (as Job did; Job 29:2-5; cf. Mal. 2:17; 3:14-15). Wisdom instructs us in the value and purpose of suffering in God's dealings with us and shows us that these disciplinary actions eventuate in both our temporal and eternal welfare.

(5) By Using Business Acumen. 7:11-12. **11. Wisdom is good with** ('*im,* "along with") **an inheritance, and ... profit** (advantage) **to them that see the sun,** that is, those living "under the sun" in this world of vanity (Job 3:16; Psalm 49:19; Eccles. 11:7). **12.** Wisdom helps one manage an estate profitably and advantageously (Prov. 8:10-11), **for** it **is a defense** (lit., "is under a shadow"), **and money is a defense** ("under a shadow"), the figure of shade from the scorching sun expressing the protection that the wise handling of one's business affairs affords man. **But the excellency of knowledge is, that wisdom giveth life to them that have it**—life in the highest sense, both in this life and in that to come (3:18; John 17:3; 2 Pet. 1:3).

(6) By Submitting to God's Will in Everything. 7:13-15. In the world of vanity, many unhappy events and trials will tempt us to complain. **13.** Let us **consider the work of God** (3:11; 8:17), that it is impossible to change His dispensations, and so we should submit to His ways (Lev. 10: 3; Psalm 39:9) and realize no one **can make ... straight** what He has **made crooked** (Eccles. 1:15).

14. Be happy **in the day of prosperity** (3:22; 9:7; 11:9), and **in the day of adversity consider** that God has made the one as well as the other, the straight as well as the crooked, and man is patiently to

submit to the divine plan, in order that man **should find nothing after him,** that is, be able to fathom anything that lies beyond his present condition, and so be stripped of pride to humbly yield to God and "consider [His] work" (v. 13). **15.** In such a world, under the curse of vanity and futility, we must not be surprised at the greatest prosperity of the wicked or the saddest calamities that sometimes befall the godly.

(7) By Living a Balanced Life. 7:16-18. In the world of fallen man, dangerous extremes are to be avoided. **16a.** Do not be **righteous overmuch** (Phil. 3:6), that is, "excessively righteous" (NASB), referring to pharisaical and legalistic self-righteousness, mere external religion, so frequently denounced by our Lord (cf. Matt. 5:20; Luke 5:32). This righteousness is self-made and ignores the sinfulness of sin, the utter lostness of man, and the infinite holiness of God. It denies salvation by grace through faith alone and injects some degree of human goodness and works.

16b. Neither make thyself overwise (Job 11:12; Rom. 12:3, 16), presumptuously self-sufficient, as if you know more than God has revealed to man in His Word, and are intolerant of any opinion that disagrees with your interpretation of Scripture. **16c. Why shouldest thou destroy** (ruin) **thyself?** Extremes of this sort destroy a regenerated man's testimony and influence and keep an unregenerated man from saving faith in God's grace and thus facing spiritual and eternal ruin.

17. Warning is issued concerning being **wicked overmuch** (excessively). Such presumptuous sin results in premature physical death for a regenerated person (e.g., Samson, Saul, Ananias, and Sapphira; Judg. 16:28-31; 1 Sam. 28:19; Acts 5:1-11; 1 Cor. 5:5; 11:30-32; 1 John 5:16), and frequently for an unregenerated person (cf. Jezebel, 2 Kings 9:30-37).

18. This verse summarizes the truth of the necessity of living a balanced life and avoiding extremes. A person is to **take hold of** (*'hz*, "grasp, lay hold of firmly and hold to") this truth. "It is good that you grasp one thing [v. 16], and also not let go of the other" (NASB; v. 17)—not go completely overboard on right-eousness and wisdom to the place where these good things are used for evil ends (as in pharisaism or Galatianism).

Or, seeing apparent injustices in a fallen world (v. 15), a person in his heart accuses God of wrong and therefore does not even aim to live uprightly, tacitly concluding that if God will question him for his actions, he in turn will question God for His actions of apparent injustice. But such extremism courts disaster. The only way to maintain a balance between these two extremes is to fear (reverence) God (Eccles. 3:14; 5:7; 8:12-13; 12:13), which principle alone will cause a man to "come out well in all respects" (Alexandrian LXX).

(8) By Facing the Reality of Sin and Sinners. 7:19-22. **19-20. Wisdom strengthens a wise man more than ten rulers who are in a city** (NASB) to see the sinfulness and lostness of all unregenerate men and that, as far as regenerate (just, righteous) humanity is concerned, there is not such a man **on earth who continually does good and who never sins** (NASB). Jesus Christ was the only righteous and sinless One, and therefore could be the Savior. All others are sinners (1 Kings 8:46; 2 Chron. 6:36; Psalms 14:1-3; 53:2-4; Rom. 3:9-19), unsaved or saved sinners, the latter sanctified and victorious over sin experientially only as faith is exercised moment by moment in their sinless position in Christ (Romans 6:1-11).

21. Realizing then the imperfection of humanity (even regenerate humanity apart from continuous faith in God's grace), it is wise to **take no heed** (lit., "give not your heart") to everything that is said, **lest thou hear thy servant curse thee.** In "giving the heart" you allow what the ear hears to affect you too deeply. That will vex you and generate in you a bitter spirit of revenge and reprisal that will poison you.

22. If you realize your own faults and that you yourself have many times **cursed** (reviled) others, you will see God is perhaps working with you in the exact way you deal with your servant. If you cannot forgive him, how can you expect the LORD to forgive you (Matt. 18:21-22; Mark 11:25-26; Luke 17:3-4)? Therefore, "fear God" and do right to your fellowman (cf. v. 18).

2. A WARNING FROM EXPERIENCE. 7:23-29.

Solemn Warning from Experience. 7:23-29. **23.** Solomon confessed and lamented the severe limits of natural wisdom. **All this** (the futility of the natural man and the vanity of all things temporal) he had **proved** (tested) by observation and experience. He had natural wisdom to apprehend "all this" (chaps. 1-7). But when he came to inquire concerning spiritual wisdom and to be truly "wise" concerning God's counsels, ways, and salvation (2 Tim. 3:15), despite his industrious searching, he found such knowledge was **far from** him (Eccles. 3:11; 8:17), and not the subject of human research but of divine revelation.

24. He could only helplessly declare that it was **far off, and exceedingly deep**, and cry out, **who can find it out?** (Rom. 11:33; cf. Job 11:7; 37:23). **25.** So he limited himself and **directed** his **mind to**

know, to investigate, and to seek wisdom and an explanation concerning the evil of folly and the foolishness of madness (NASB; Eccles. 1:17; 10:13). As a result, Solomon understandably found an apt illustration from his own experience of the "evil of folly and the foolishness of madness" in the woman who employs her charms to enslave a man (cf. 1 Kings 11:1-8). He tacitly concluded that of all his sinful follies, none had been so ruinous a trap in drawing him away from God as idolatrous women (11:3-4; Prov. 5:3-4).

26. He found **more bitter than death** (5:4) **the woman whose heart is snares and nets** (7:23) and whose hands are **bands** (chains). Only he who pleases God, as Joseph did (Gen. 39:2-3, 9), **shall escape from her, but the sinner** (a confession by Solomon) **shall be taken** (captured) **by her** (Prov. 22:14).

27-28. After **adding one thing to another to find an explanation** (NASB) and conducting a diligent search, Solomon found only **one man among a thousand**—upright and truly worthy of being a man, but not one woman, alluding to his three hundred wives and seven hundred concubines (1 Kings 11:3). Verse 28 connects with verse 26 in condemning the seducing woman; it is not a universal or unqualified appraisal or condemnation of the feminine sex (cf. Prov. 12:4; 31:10-31).

29. This verse summarizes Solomon's investigation of fallen man. God **made man upright** (Gen. 1:27, 31). But **they** (mankind, Adam and Eve and their posterity) **have sought out many devices**—reasonings and speculations of the natural mind, enticing the heart from the true heavenly wisdom (1 Tim. 6:20), especially the infraction of God's primeval order uniting one man to one woman (Gen. 2:3; Matt. 19:4-5).

B. WISDOM TO FACE VEXATIONS IN A WORLD OF VANITY. 8:1-17.

The Benefit and Praise of Wisdom. 8:1. **1.** This is true wisdom—genuine piety that trusts in God and reveres Him. **Who is . . . the wise man?** The man who possesses this heavenly wisdom, possesses grace, and is accepted by God. This wisdom lifts a man above his unbelieving neighbors and makes him useful and serviceable to them.

Who but the wise man **knoweth the interpretation of a thing?** (matter), that is, God's Word (Prov. 1:6) and divine providences (cf. Eccles. 7:8, 13-14), so that he can give wise counsel concerning what ought to be done (1 Chron. 12:32). Such wisdom beautifies a man and **maketh his face to shine** (like Moses', Exod. 34:29-30; and Stephen's, Acts 6:15) and causes **the boldness** ('ōz, "strength, austerity, severity") **of his face** to **be changed** (Deut. 28:50) into a benign expression as the result of true faith.

Wisdom in Practical Manifestation. 8:2-17. Wisdom is manifested in six ways: (1) *Wisdom is manifested in due subjection to the government God has set over us (vv. 2-4). (a)* **2.** It involves keeping **the king's commandment** (lit., "observe the mouth"; i.e., what the king says or directs) **in regard** (because) **of the oath of God** (Exod. 22:11; 2 Sam. 21:7; Ezek. 17:18), "the oath before God" (NASB), in order not to violate obligations to God, which transcend obligations to the king, who, however, rules as God's representative.

(b) It also entails loyalty and steadfastness to constituted government (cf. Rom. 13:1-5). **3a. Be not hasty** (in a hurry) **to go out of his sight** (presence) (Eccles. 10:4) when you are displeased with the king or he with you. There may be just cause to do so, but do not act so

precipitously, as later the Israelites did who seceded from the crown under Rehoboam (1 Kings 12:16).

(c) Such subjection to government means we must not persist in a fault when it is pointed out to us. **3b. Stand not** ('*md*, "persist, continue") **in an evil thing.** If you have given offense to the civil administration, do not try to justify yourself in the wrong and proceed in it, **for he** (the king) **doeth whatsoever pleaseth him** as God's representative.

4. Where the word of a king is, there is power, since his decisions are authoritative and final, **and who may say unto him, What doest thou?** (Job 9:12; Dan. 4:35). (d) Such subjection to constituted government requires that we prudently take advantage of opportunities for redress of any grievances, both our own and others.

(2) *Wisdom is manifested in preparing for future judgment (vv. 5-7)*. **5.** Whoever observes **the commandment** (the royal decision or edict) **shall feel** (experience) **no evil thing** (trouble; Eccles. 12:13; Prov. 12:21), for **a wise man's heart discerneth both time and judgment** (*mišpāṭ*, "an eventual accounting for one's deeds before the divine tribunal"). He knows there is a judgment day coming, even though today in a vain world men may be crushed under the king in misery (Rom. 2:6; Rev. 20:5-6).

6. Because to every purpose (*ḥēpěś*, "desire") **there is time and judgment** (Eccles. 3:17) when God shall judge the deeds of all men. The wise discern the coming time of judgment and take courage in their "desire" for the establishment of God's Kingdom and the downfall of the present order of sin and sorrow, "because" (*kî*, not "therefore") man's **misery ... is great upon him,** and apart from the hope of such a time of divine adjudication to come, the godly would be left without anything to sustain them in their present sufferings.

7. This verse gives the reason for man's "great misery." The sinner, by neglecting "the accepted time" of salvation (2 Cor. 6:2), will be taken by surprise by the judgment (Eccles. 3:22; 6:12; 9:12). The godly wise look for the judgment and will not be taken by surprise (1 Thess. 5:2-4). But both the sinner and the righteous will be judged for works (deeds), the quality of their life, as unregenerate or regenerate, and go to their respective spheres (hell or heaven).

Since in Old Testament times no one knew what this process of judgment would be like, it created certain apprehension, even on the part of the justified believer (contrast 1 Cor. 3:1-17; 2 Cor. 5:10-11; Rev. 20:11-15). Neither did Old Testament saints know precisely when this process of adjudication would take place, which added a further note of anxiety. So Solomon wrote, **For he knoweth not that which shall be; for who can tell him when it shall be?**

(3) *Wisdom is also manifested in preparing for death (v. 8)*. No man has power over his spirit to retain the breath of life and dodge death. **8. There is no man that hath power over the spirit to retain the spirit.** He is as powerless to do that as he is to restrain the wind with the wind (Psalm 49:7-9). **Neither hath he power in** (over) **the day of death,** God having numbered the days of each man (Eccles. 6:12), and no man can extend them. **Neither is there any discharge** (exemption) in that war, an allusion to liability to military service of all men above twenty years old (Num. 1:3); yet many were exempted (Deut. 20:5-8). **Neither shall wickedness deliver those that are given to it** (lit., "its masters, patrons"; Eccles. 8:13).

(4) *Wisdom is further manifested in*

arming ourselves against temptation occasioned by oppressive government and the prosperity of the wicked (vv. 9-13). In all this the conclusion must fortify us that justice will be carried out ultimately. **9.** Solomon had observed and applied wisdom to **every work that is done under the sun** in a world of sin and vanity. He focused attention on the time when **one man ruleth over another to his own hurt,** that is, the tyrannical ruler injures not merely his subjects, but himself as well, as Rehoboam did (1 Kings 12).

Such oppressions, which the godly suffer, offer a temptation to unbelief (Eccles. 7:15) if looked at superficially. But Solomon **applied** his **heart** (his understanding), indicating he considered the matter deeply. **10. And so** (he) **saw** (viewed) **the wicked buried** (Ezek. 32:23-24; 39:11; Luke 16:22), death ending their oppressive career—they **who had come and gone from the place of the holy** (the place of the Holy One). That was not the rightful place of the wicked; so in God's due time they must go from it forever and be forgotten (Prov. 10:7). This oppressive rule of man over his fellowman soon ends and is **vanity.** But the righteous are delivered forever.

11. This verse states a well-known fact: the ungodly go on sinning because punishment seems so long delayed and remote (Exod. 34:6; Psalm 86:15; Eccles. 9:3; Rom. 2:4; 2 Pet. 3:9). But wisdom manifests itself in following the way of faith in God's justice and impartiality. **12-13.** No matter how a sinner may prosper, **yet surely I know that it shall be well with them who fear God** (Deut. 4:40; Psalm 37:11; Prov. 1:33; Isa. 3:10) . . . **but it shall not be well with the wicked** (Eccles. 8:8; Isa. 3:11).

(5) *Wisdom is again manifested by refusing to allow the present prosperity* of *the wicked and the afflictions of the righteous to be a stumbling block to faith in God (vv. 14-15).* **14.** We are not to be upset by this apparent injustice, but we should see it as a **vanity which is done upon the earth** under the curse and man in his fallen state (Job 21:7; Psalm 73:14; Eccles. 7:15; Jer. 12:1; Mal. 3:15). We must not be tempted to charge God with iniquity, but rather we should charge the world with vanity.

15. Neither are we to fret about it, but we are to cheerfully enjoy what God has given us in the world, being content with it and making the best of it. **Because a man** (a natural, unregenerate man) **hath no better thing under the sun** (though a regenerate man has much better things above the sun), **than to eat, and drink,** that is, soberly and thankfully (Eccles. 2:24; 3:12-13; 5:18; 9:7). Let not a man foolishly deny himself the common joys of life out of a peevish discontent because the world does not go as he would have it.

(6) *Lastly, wisdom is manifested in a quiet acquiesence to the will of God, humbly adoring the depths of His unsearchable counsels (vv. 16-17).* Wisdom will show a man that there are questions no finite mind can answer. Yet the answers are found in getting God's perspective and looking through His revelation (3:11; 7:23; Rom. 11:33).

C. LIFE'S INEQUALITIES MUST BE LEFT TO GOD. 9:1-18.

The Natural Man Has No Explanation for Life's Inequalities. 9:1-3. **1a.** Godly wisdom, however, after wise deliberation, does manifest itself (cf. 8:1-17) by declaring **that the righteous, and the wise, and their works** (deeds) **are in the hand of God** (Deut. 33:3; Job 12:10). God controls their lives, and what happens to them comes from God Himself or from what He permits to happen to them. But then Solomon speaks from the naturalistic standpoint as things appear to unaided reason. **1b.** Men do not know **either** (divine) **love or hatred** (cf. Mal. 1:2-3) **by all that is before** (what awaits) **them** in this disordered, sin-ridden world of vanity (v. 9*b*; 9:6; 10:14).

2. All things come (happen) **alike to all ... one event to the righteous, and the wicked.** Sickness, pain, and death happen to sinner and saint alike, **the** (ceremonially) **clean** and **the unclean; to him that sacrificeth, and ... sacrificeth not.** God makes no trenchant distinction between the good and the bad (the sinner) in His providential working in a world of vanity. But the mystery is that God is working through these providences with a far-reaching purpose (cf. 2 Cor. 12:9-10). Through Christ we now need not speculate whether God loves us. We know He does (John 14:21), whether what He brings into our lives is prosperity or adversity. Both are a token of His love.

3. Considering life and death from the human viewpoint, with God out of the picture, the unregenerate, earth-bound man can only conclude that **this is an evil in all that is done under the sun, that there is one fate for all men** (NASB; v. 2). He can only conclude what he observes on such a colossal scale, that **the hearts of the sons of men are full of evil, and insanity is in their hearts throughout their lives. Afterwards they go to the dead** (NASB).

The Natural Man Has No Explanation for Death. 9:4-6. **4.** Whoever is **joined** with **the living**—he who is still alive physically—has **hope.** Compare the proverb, "While there's life, there's hope"—there is hope to repent, to be saved, to achieve, to glorify God, and so forth. Death seals a man's destiny. **For a living dog** (a despised, unclean animal in

ancient times) **is better than a dead lion** (the king of the beasts). "The meanest beggar alive has that comfort of this world and does that service to it which the greatest prince, when he is dead, is utterly incapable of" (Matthew Henry).

5. For the living know that they shall die; but the dead (insofar as life in this world is concerned) **know not anything** (Job 14:21; Psalms 6:5; 88:10-11). Death terminates all enjoyments in this world. The dead have no **more a reward** (*śākār*, "income" or "benefit" from their life of toil in this world of vanity). **For the memory of them is forgotten**—not of the righteous (Psalm 112:6; Mal. 3:16), but the ungodly, who, despite all their efforts to preserve their names (Psalm 49:11-12), soon sink into oblivion (Eccles. 8:10). There is also an end to their friendships and enmities, as well as their envy of the prosperity of others.

The Natural Man Can Offer Only a Hedonistic Philosophy of Life. 9:7-10. The hedonistic philosophy is the highest philosophy normally attainable by a man without faith in a righteous God and a future life (cf. 2:24; 3:12, 22; 5:18; 8:15). **7. Eat ... bread ... drink ... wine**—enjoy the accepted means of sustenance and natural pleasures. **God now accepteth thy works.** Since you as a natural man (1 Cor. 2:14) are incapable of knowing God's will and ways, make the most of God's natural blessings that you can enjoy temperately and gratefully. Remember that God judges *all* men (unregenerate as well as regenerate) for their deeds—the quality of their life here on earth (Rom. 2:6, 11; 2 Cor. 5:10; Rev. 20:12-13).

8. Let thy garments be always white (normal attire for festive occasions; 3:4), **and let thy head lack no ointment,** a symbol of joy (Psalms 23:5; 45:7). Verses 9 and 10 portray the "good life" of the moral and upright unregenerate man, who in outwardly keeping God's moral laws, can enjoy the temporal blessings of God—a happy marriage, a tranquil homelife (v. 9), interesting work, and rewarding hobbies (v. 10). But the "good life" apart from God has its severe limitations of vanity and futility, at its very best bringing limited satisfaction and enduring only for a circumscribed length of time.

The Natural Man Can Posit Only Luck or Fate. 9:11-12. **11. I returned, and saw** ("again I observed") **under the sun** (in this fallen, sin-cursed world), **that the race is not to the swift, nor the battle to the strong ... but time** (cut short by death) **and chance happeneth to them all**, meaning, "when the time comes, bad luck overtakes [*yĭqrĕh*, 'befalls, occurs to'] them all." That is the pessimistic, fatalistic outlook of the picture when God is left out and man's crookedness is emphasized.

But there are elements affecting human destiny that God has reserved to His own control, and there are also forces in life that are subject to human intelligence and power. The regenerate man learns which are which, and he learns to manage those placed within his control and to accept with reverent awe and submission the forces that a sovereign God has reserved for Himself.

12. The worst of the misfortunes (bad luck or fate) to the natural man is *time* (time cut short by death). Man, subject to death in a vain world, **knoweth not his time** (8:7), but is like a fish caught in a treacherous **net** and **birds** trapped in a snare (Prov. 7:23); human beings are **snared in an evil time** (29:6; Isa. 24:18; Hos. 9:8), **when it** (the evil time) **falleth suddenly upon them** (Luke 21:34-35).

The Natural Man Often Rejects Wisdom and Accords It Little Honor. 9:13-18. **13.** Solomon presented an illustration of how man rejects wisdom

(vv. 13-16) in an event that he had witnessed, which had made a great impression on him. **14. There was a little city, and few men within it; and there came a great king against it, and besieged it, and built great bulwarks against it. 15. A poor wise man**, who, **by his wisdom, delivered the city** was soon forgotten and never brought to a place of prominence in the life of the city. That was the startling thing to Solomon and he tells why in verse 16.

16. It showed him **wisdom** was superior to **strength; nevertheless, the poor man's wisdom** was subsequently **despised,** and his words were **not heard** because he went on exercising his wisdom in trying to correct problems and abuses within the city. But when he began upsetting the status quo, this poor man's wisdom was despised and his advice rejected. The reason no one remembered this poor man is that he lived in a city when fools were in political power and wanted to stay in power.

Solomon makes applications of his illustration in verses 17 and 18. **17. The words of wise men are heard in quiet more than the cry of him that ruleth among fools.** A wise man speaks words of wisdom in a tranquil, rational manner. A fool with loud demagoguery plays on the emotions of other fools (7:5; 10:12). **18.** Wisdom is superior to **weapons of war,** but one **sinner** at the helm of government can destroy **much good** (material as well as spiritual and moral good), which was evidently the case with the ruler of the city delivered by the poor wise man.

D. NATURAL WISDOM VERSUS FOLLY. 10:1-20.

It Is Wisdom to Maintain a Good Reputation. 10:1. **1.** A man's reputation is like precious, fragrant **ointment** (7:1; Gen. 34:30). The more excellent the ointment, the sadder it is that so little a thing as **dead flies** ("flies of death") should not only take away the fragrance but replace it with a stench. The tragedy is that the finer the fragrance, the worse the stench, which happens when he who is **in reputation for wisdom and honor** (as Solomon himself was) succumbed not to **a little folly,** but much (1 Kings 11:1-8; cf. David, 2 Sam. 12:14; Jehoshaphat, 2 Chron. 18:1-34; 19:2; Josiah, 35:22).

Bad odor is tolerable in common oil, but not in what professes to be compounded by the perfumer for fragrance. "Flies," being small answer to the "little folly" (sin; cf. 1 Cor. 5:6; Gal. 5:9), **send forth an evil odor,** that is, "cause a stench through putrefaction," each of the "flies of death" causing the foul odor, as the plural subject with singular verbs indicates.

It Is Wisdom to Conduct One's Affairs Discreetly. 10:2-3. **2a. A wise man's heart is at his right hand** (2:14). His heart (the seat of the will, and so the guide of the understanding) is (as we say) "in the right place." The "right hand" is more skillful than the left and indicates that the godly wise man is able to conduct himself and his business with strength, discretion, and honor. Among many peoples the right hand became associated with what is good and honorable (cf. Psalm 110:1; Matt. 25:33-40), while the left hand is associated with that which is evil and repugnant (25:31-46).

2b. But a fool's heart (is) **at his left.** His will and understanding are in the wrong place, and so he cannot conduct himself or his affairs with anything but folly, dishonor, and indiscretion. **3.** Even when a fool **walketh by the way** (along the road) in the ordinary course of life (Prov. 6:12-14), he advertises to everyone that **he is a fool** (13:16) by much talking and little thinking, by snap judgments and without considering all the facts, and by acting as though he was right and everyone else was wrong.

It Is Wisdom to Be Submissive to Governmental Powers. 10:4-11. Unless the wise man is vigilant, a little folly can quickly do him irreparable harm. **If the spirit** (temper) **of the ruler rise up against thee, leave not** (do not resign) **thy place** (position) (8:3); **for yielding** (*mărpēh*, lit., "healing, remedy, composure, calmness") **pacifieth** (allays, reduces in intensity or severity) **great offenses** (1 Sam. 25:24-33; Prov. 25:15). The advice is: Do not hastily resign a position of trust you feel you should keep. Weather the storm and leave the decision to others (10:12; 15:1; 25:15; cf. Matt. 5:5).

5. Solomon confessed that **there is an evil ... under the sun** in this world of vanity. It is **an error** (*shᵉgāgâ*, "mistake, transgression") **which proceedeth from the ruler** in catering to his personal desires rather than the public interest, and preferring men for reasons other than merit and ability.

6. The sad result is that **folly is set in great dignity,** that is, men of dissipated fortunes and erratic minds are placed in positions of trust and power, while wealthy men, who by prudence have proved their ability, sit in low places and get no preferment (Esther 3:1; Prov. 28:12; 29:2). **7.** This verse illustrates the sad spectacle: **I have seen servants** (sordid, servile, mercenary "slaves" scarcely fit to be slaves, much less masters) **upon horses,** a mark of prestige and honor (Esther 6:8; Prov. 19:10; 30:22), **and princes,** men of noble birth and character, **walking like servants** (slaves) **upon the earth** (land).

Although rulers are not to infringe upon their subjects' rights and liberties, their subjects are not to mutiny and revolt against them (Rom. 13:1-8). The danger of such insurrection on the part of subjects is set forth in verses 8 to 11. **8. He that diggeth a pit** for another (a government official) runs the high risk of falling into it himself, and violence will boomerang (Psalm 7:15; Prov. 26:27). He who **breaketh an hedge** (a fence or wall), with which God has surrounded rulers as His servants (Rom. 13:2-3), **a serpent shall bite him** (Amos 5:19; cf. Deut. 19:14; 27:17).

9. Whoever **removeth stones** or **splitteth wood** for any malicious purpose in revolt against constituted government, let him remember that deeds of violence imperil the violent themselves. **10. If the iron be blunt** in cleaving wood (v. 9), extra strength is needed, and the knotty wood (men of perverse ways) may prove too tough a job to hew to pieces. Instead of hewing them to pieces, it may turn out they will hew you to pieces. **But wisdom is profitable to direct** the question at issue to a prosperous solution instead of trying to force matters by a show of strength and violence to one's own hurt (Eccles. 9:16, 18). Wisdom will also direct us to enchant the serpent with whom we are to contend, "rather than think to out-hiss it" (Matthew Henry).

11. Surely the serpent will bite without enchantment (Psalm 58:4-5; Jer. 8:17). The serpent symbolically represents the evil of a bad ruler (v. 5), with whom the wise subject must deal (v. 4) and "charm," in the sense of talking calmly and sanely with him, so that he will not "bite" (destroy) him (Prov. 25:15). **And a babbler** ("master of the tongue," a slick talker) is no better. However expert with his tongue, it is useless for a subject to attempt to appease a ruler's wrath, especially when he did not try to charm the serpent in the first place.

It Is Wisdom to Govern the Tongue Well. 10:12-15. **12. The words of a wise man's mouth are gracious** (lit., "grace itself"), like "enchantment" (v. 11),

averting the bite of the "old serpent" (Rev. 20:2; cf. Prov. 22:11), in contrast to the **lips of a fool,** which **swallow up himself** in just retribution, whose thought was to swallow up others with his malicious speech (10:8, 14, 21, 32).

13. Fools begin by talking **foolishness** (nonsense) and end in **mischievous madness** (an evil frenzy; Eccles. 7:25). The ungoverned tongue is like an unchecked fire, growing in intensity and destructiveness (James 3:5). **14. A fool . . . is full of words,** full of empty boastings of what he will do or be (Eccles. 5:2). What folly this is appears from the fact that no one (including the wise man), much less the fool, can foresee the future (3:22; 6:12; 8:7; 11:2).

15. The labor (exertions) **of the foolish wearieth** (exhausts) **every one of them.** They wear themselves out in endless futile pursuits, never accomplishing anything worthwhile, because they know **not how to go to the city.** That is a proverb, like "they haven't sense enough to come in out of the rain." In a spiritual sense, fools have no faith in knowledge of the heavenly city, as Abraham did (Gen. 15:6; Heb. 11:10, 16; 13:14), and as do all the faithful wise.

It Is Wisdom for Rulers to Be Discreet and Temperate. 10:16-17. **16. Woe** (calamity) to the land when it has a childish, immature king (Isa. 3:4, 12) and whose princes are so intemperate and dissolute as to **eat** (feast) **in the morning,** which should be for working and not banqueting, the usual time for dispensing justice (Jer. 21:12). **17. Blessed** (happy) is the land **when thy king is the son of nobles** (is of true nobility), and whose princes **eat in due season** (at the proper time) for physical **strength, and not for drunkenness** (Prov. 31:4; Isa. 5:11).

It Is Wisdom to Be Diligent in Public as Well as in Private Business. 10:18-19.

Shiftlessness and laziness have tragic consequences, both in the state and in the home. **18. By much slothfulness** (indolence; Prov. 24:30-34) **the rafters sag** (NASB), that is, the roof beams sink, **and through idleness of the hands the house droppeth through** (leaks). **19.** The object of a **feast** is to produce laughter and merriment and to forget care and concern of every kind, which seems to refer to the luxuriously living king and courtiers (v. 16), who are remiss in their public duties, and the country suffers like the run-down building described in verse 18.

Money answereth all things is a saying that has prevailed everywhere in a vain, materialistic world and with man "under the sun." It conceivably refers to the pleasure-loving rulers, who think that with money they can have what they wish. So they accept bribes to support their luxury and perpetuate wrongs in government (vv. 5-6; cf. Isa. 1:23).

It Is Wise Not to Speak Evil of Rulers. 10:20. **20.** Do not allow yourself even to think evil of the king, lest you give expression to your thoughts and be charged with treason. For **a bird of the air shall carry the voice** (a proverb, like "a little birdie told me so"; cf. Luke 19:40). In Bible lands superhuman sagacity was attributed to birds.

E. HOW BEST TO LIVE IN A WORLD OF VANITY. 11:1-10.

Be Generous. 11:1-3. The selfish life is fruitless (5:10-12; 6:1-6). Therefore, live generously. The natural man "under the sun" can either live a self-centered existence or a life for others. Life in a world of vanity is uncertain and filled with frustration; yet generosity and helpfulness are better than selfishness.

1. Cast thy bread (grain, seed, food) **upon the waters** (figure of sowing seed by casting it from a boat into the overflowing waters of the Nile or in any marshy ground. When the waters receded, the grain in the alluvial soil sprang up (Isa. 32:20). (The "waters" prefigure multitudes of people (Rev. 17:15) and suggest the apparent hopeless character of the recipients of the alms. But in the end it will prove not thrown away (Isa. 49:4), as will no charity distributed in faith and love.

2. Give ... to seven, and also to eight graphically says, "Give to many! Be generous!" (Psalm 112:9; Matt. 5:42; Luke 6:30; 1 Tim. 6:18-19). **For thou knowest not what evil** (misfortune) **shall be upon the earth** (Eccles. 11:8; 12:1). "Such may be the change of times that thou mayest yet stand in need of similar help thyself. Do as thou wouldst be done by" (Adam Clark, *Commentary*; cf. Luke 16:9). Motives for a generous life are found in the generosity of God, who "sendeth rain on the just and on the unjust" (Matt. 5:45).

3. If the clouds be full of rain, they empty themselves upon the earth, a blessing in an arid land like Palestine. Another motive for generosity is the fixation of one's fate or eternal destiny at death. As the tree falls, so shall it lie. But the content of the chapter is dealing with the results of human choices and the kind of life that results, which affects the destiny of men. The kind of choices from youth onward, determining the quality of one's living, will face God's judgment (v. 9; 12:1), in the case of both the regenerate and the unregenerate; so verses 1 to 3 contain more than mere sage economic advice in a world of vanity.

Be Industrious. 11:4-6. The good life of the natural man (as well as the regenerate man) requires decision and action (cf. 10:8-9). This vain, empty world is filled with uncertainties and perils, but it is challenging to those who will dare to run the risks and accomplish what is worthwhile.

4. He that observeth the wind — waits till there is perfect calm and nothing to interfere with the even scattering of seed — **shall not sow, and he that regardeth** (looks at) **the clouds** — to be certain the harvested grain will not get wet — **shall not reap.** Achievement, rewards, and success in a world of vanity are not for the fainthearted and indecisive, certainly not for the indolent. But in any decision we make in this vain world, and any action following, there are always risks and uncertainties in factors known only to God.

5. We do not know **the way of the wind** (spirit; possibly, "how man's spirit animates his soul and body"), but perhaps simply "the path of the wind" (John 3:8) and "how bones are formed in the womb of the pregnant woman" (NASB; Psalm 139:13-16), and so the natural man under the sun (apart from divine revelation) **knowest not the works** (activity) **of God, who maketh all** things (Eccles. 3:10-11; 8:17).

6. The advice of this verse summarizes both the reasoning and the conclusion of verses 4 and 5 and urges unremitting industry. "In the morning sow your seed, and till the evening give your hand no rest; for you know not which shall prosper, this or that, or whether both alike shall be good" (Smith-Goodspeed).

Be Cheerful and Optimistic. 11:7-8. Much in this empty world, which is under the curse of sin, would tend to make us gloomy and pessimistic. Truly **light** (the light of life; 7:11; Psalm 49:19) **is sweet** (*māṯôq*, "lovely, pleasant"), and it is **pleasant** (*tôḇ*, "good") **for the eyes to behold the sun.** The vanity of the earth and man under the curse with his present trials should not blind us to the

fact that life is a blessing and an opportunity for receiving and doing good, an arena in which we have a chance to achieve and be victorious despite great odds, a sort of bad situation because of man's Fall, despite which we are to make good. **8.** Yet the sober warning: **if a man live many years, and rejoice in them all** (Eccles. 9:7), even such a man finds himself in a world of supreme vanity (1:2). Let him remember that even he will experience many **days of darkness** (12:1) and that **all that cometh is vanity** (1:2).

Live in the Light of the Coming Judgment. 11:9-10. **9. Rejoice, O young man** is a stern warning, not a piece of advice. The *Amplified Bible* brings out the original: "Rejoice, O young man, in your adolescence, and let your heart cheer you in the days of your full-grown youth, and walk in the ways of your heart, and in the sight of your eyes. But know that for all these things God will bring you into judgment" (3:17; 12:4; Rom. 2:6; 14:10; 2 Cor. 5:10; Rev. 20:12-13; 22:12). Life is to be enjoyed, but according to God's laws and God's words, not in "the pleasures of sin for a season" (Heb. 11:25).

10. Hence, the exhortation: **Therefore, remove** (the lusts that end in) **sorrow** (vexation) **from thy heart** (mind), **and put away evil from thy flesh**, your body by which the sensual thoughts of the "heart" (mind) are converted into acts. The true motive for self-restraint is that the time hastens on when the vigor of youth will fade like a flower, showing that it too is part of the "vanity of vanities" (1:2), the supreme vanity of the life of fallen, sinful man.

F. THE CREATOR IS TO BE REMEMBERED IN YOUTH. 12:1-8.

Remember Your Creator in Youth. 12:1a. **1a. Remember now thy Creator**

("Creators," pl. of excellence) **in the days of thy youth** (Deut. 8:18; Neh. 4:14; Psalm 63:6). This pivotal admonition follows closely without a break from chapter 11, especially 11:9-10. If you desire life's best, start life with God. Give God the life He gave you as Creator in the prime of your powers.

Remember Your Creator Before Old Age Comes. 12:1b-5. Forgetting one's Creator in youth will decrease the pleasurableness of old age. **1b. Evil days** (11:8) will come and the years will draw near when you will say, **I have no pleasure** (delight) **in them** (the sunset years; 2 Sam. 19:35). **2.** Remember your Creator **before the sun** (Isa. 5:30; 13:10; Ezek. 32:7; Joel 3:15; Matt. 24:29), **the light, the moon, and the stars are darkened, and clouds return after the rain** (NASB). This is a figurative, highly poetical description of one trouble following another in old age unilluminated by Him who is the "Sun of righteousness" (Mal. 4:2), "the light of the world" (John 8:12), and "the bright and morning star" (Rev. 22:16).

Verses 3 to 5 constitute a figurative description of old age itself. **3. The keepers of the house** (the hands and arms that protect the body) **tremble** from weakness and paralysis. **The strong men** (the legs) **bow themselves** (stoop; Psalms 35:14; 38:6). **And the grinders** (the molar teeth) **cease** (are idle) **because they are few,** inadequate to masticate food properly. **And those who look out of the windows** (the eyes, opening and shutting like a window) **are darkened,** growing dim and blind.

4. And the doors (the lips) **shall be shut in** (toward) **the streets** (141:3), for if old men's toothless mouths were not closely shut when eating, the food would drop out. **When the sound of the grinding is low,** almost toothless and with mouth closed in eating, the sound of mastication is practically nil. **He** (the sleepless oldster) **shall rise up at the voice of the bird,** the early crowing cock, the least noise arousing an elderly person. **And all the daughters of music** (the organs that produce and enjoy music, the voice and the ear) **shall be brought low** (2 Sam. 19:35).

5a. In old age people become afraid of height, and fearful of the road (travel on a highway). Then **the almond tree shall flourish** (blossom) on a leafless tree in winter, illustrating the dormant powers of old age and perhaps the hoary head, although the almond blossoms are slightly pinkish. The best interpretation, however, is to take the image as a figure of wakefulness of old age; so the word in Hebrew for almond tree comes from a root meaning "to be wakeful," because it is the first that awakes from the sleep of winter (Jer. 1:11-12), blooming in January.

5b. And the grasshopper (or locust, portraying a shriveled-up old man) **shall be a burden** (to himself), "drags himself along" (NASB). **And desire,** normal bodily appetites, **shall fail** ("the caper tree"; or, "caperberry is ineffective," NASB, LXX, Vulgate; i.e., to stir up appetite or sexual desire). **Man goeth to his long home** (death), **and the** (professional) **mourners** will soon **go about the streets** (Amos 5:16; Matt. 9:36).

Remember Your Creator Before Death Strikes. 12:6-8. Verses 6 and 7 euphemistically and poetically describe death, just as verses 3 to 5 describe old age. **6.** Remember your Creator **or ever the silver cord** (of life) **is loosed** (snapped), **or the golden bowl is broken,** portraying a lamp hung from the ceiling by an interwoven cord of silk and silver. Just as the lamp is dashed to pieces when the cord breaks, so a man's life—as it were, let down from above—is shattered at death.

The other image of death is of the water pitcher lowered into a fountain or well by a rope wound about a wheel. Just as when the **pitcher** and **wheel** are **broken,** water can no longer be drawn, so life ceases when the vital energies are gone. A good old age is a blessing to the godly (Gen. 15:15; Job 5:26; Prov. 16:31; 20:29), but this dismal portrayal of old age applies to those who forget their Creator in their youth and grow sour and morose with age.

7. At death **the dust** (Gen. 3:19; Job 19:26; Eccles. 3:20; Dan. 12:2) shall **return to the earth as it was** (Psalm 104:29), **and the spirit shall return unto God** (Eccles. 3:21; Job 34:14; Luke 23:46; Acts 7:59), **who gave it** (Gen. 2:7; Num. 16:22; 27:16; Isa. 57:16; Zech. 12:1). The spirit, surviving the body , implies its immortality and the fact that each soul owes its origin directly to God and not to human parents.

8. For the last time the book voices the verdict upon the life that the natural, unregenerate man believes to end at the grave. **Vanity of vanities** (supreme emptiness, utter futility is such a life); **all** (in it) **is vanity.** Thus Solomon reiterates the pervading theme of the book with which it began (1:2; 1 John 2:17).

III. AUTOBIOGRAPHICAL FOOTNOTE AND CONCLUDING SUMMARY. 12:9-14.

The Autobiographical Observation. 12:9-12. **9.** Koheleth was not only a sage but a teacher. **In addition to being a wise man, the Preacher also taught the people knowledge** (NASB). It is implied that he composed other teachings not included in this book. **And he pondered, searched out and arranged many proverbs** (NASB; 1 Kings 4:32). **10a.** He said he **sought to find delightful words** (Prov. 10:32) **and to write words of truth correctly** (NASB). He reflected a writer's concern for his work as a literary masterpiece, but as a true man of God he never let his style obscure his message.

10b-11. What he wrote were **words of truth** (Proverbs 22:20-21), **words of the wise** (Eccles. 7:5; 10:12; Prov. 1:6; 22:17), words inspired with heavenly wisdom. They are described as **goads** (Acts 2:37), or sharp pricks inserted in the ends of a long stick used to prod dray animals to their work, and **like nails fastened** (well driven; lit., "planted") **by the masters of assemblies** ("participants in the collection," i.e., "collected sayings"), hence, joint-authors of the collected canonical Scriptures **given by one shepherd,** the chief (Ezek. 37:24) Shepherd, the Lord Himself (1 Pet. 5:2-4; cf. Eph. 4:11). The goadlike and naillike (Isa. 22:23) power of the words of the authors of Scripture are due to their divine inspiration, issuing from the LORD of all power (2 Tim. 3:16).

12. Because those words are the inspired voice of God, the exhortation to be advised and warned by them is presented with full confidence. **By these . . . be admonished** (Eccles. 4:13; Ezek. 3:21). Of mere human **books** written on the meaning of life **there is no end** (1 Kings 4:32-33). But apart from divine revelation, these turn out to be only **a weariness of the flesh** (Prov. 22:20-21). The man of God, while recognizing the place of the intellect (Eccles. 9:17-18), is at the same time acutely conscious of its severe limitations.

The Conclusion in a Nutshell. 12:13-14. **13a-b. The conclusion** ($s\bar{o}p$, "end") **of the whole matter,** "even all that has been heard" (lit. Heb.), that is, up to this point, is: **Fear** (revere) **God** (God placed in an emphatic position), **and keep** (observe) **his commandments** (His commandments likewise emphasized). This grand inference of the whole book is the antidote to the supreme vanity and futility (1:2; 12:8) outlined throughout the discourse on the plight of the natural, sin-cursed man in a sin-cursed world "under the sun."

13c. This is the whole duty of man, literally, "this is the whole man," the full ideal of man, as originally contemplated, realized completely by Jesus Christ, the second Man, alone. And through Him it is realized partially by saints in time, and perfectly in eternity (1 John 3:4, 22-24; Rev. 22:14).

14. The book ends with a pivotal truth of revelation: *all* men—both the natural, unregenerate man under the sun, as well as the regenerate man who trusts in God (Gen. 15:6) and keeps His commandments—will be judged for their works, that is, for the quality of their lives in this world of vanity (Rom. 2:6, 11; 2 Cor. 5:10; Rev. 20:12-13; 22:12). But, like all Old Testament books, Ecclesiastes in a very special sense, since it deals with the vanity of fallen man, prepares the way for the gospel of Christ. The masterly conclusion of the royal searcher still leaves God and man poles apart. But it places man in the position where he is as the result of the Fall and where the grace of God stands ready to meet him with the glorious redemption Christ offers.

SONG OF SOLOMON

INTRODUCTION

Title. The designation "Song of Songs," a literal rendering of the Hebrew idiomatic name (1:1), means "the best or most exquisite Song" (1 Kings 4:32). "The Song of Solomon" (KJV) is taken from the data of 1:1, but it is not a translation.

Place in the Jewish Canon and Meaning. The Song of Solomon is found in the third part of the Hebrew Bible, called the Writings (*Kethubim*) as one of the five Rolls (Scrolls) called Megilloth. These books are brief enough to be publicly read on anniversaries. The Song of Solomon heads the list because it was used at the first and greatest feast of the year, the Passover, speaking of redemption. This usage, we believe, is providential and points to the deeper spiritual and typical meaning of the book, expressing the love of God for His redeemed people in general and the godly remnant of Israel in particular.

The book, we believe, also reflects the intense affection that the King-Messiah will arouse in the hearts of this Israelite remnant at the time of the reestablishment of their relationship to Himself, a blessed union that was enjoyed so long by the faithful in Old Testament times and severed so long by Israel's unbelief and rejection of their Messiah, resulting in worldwide dispersion during the interim period of the Christian church.

Here, then, in this superlative composition under the figure of human love, is a song of enchanting beauty and power, with exquisite imagery from field and garden, animal and plant life (e.g., 1:12—2:3; 4:12—5:1; 6:2-3). It conveys a blessed revelation, not only of the purity and sanctity of human love in courtship and marriage, but in mystical form it foreshadows Christ's great love for His redeemed, especially the remnant of His redeemed people, Israel, and their heart response as they will enter the glory of the millennial Kingdom, when all God's promises and purposes of love toward them will be fulfilled.

The Literary Form. Understanding the spiritual meaning of the Song of Solomon hinges on the view adopted of its form. The conservative (and we believe the correct) view sees it as a unified lyrical poem with the dramatic form of dialogue. A less conservative view makes it out to be a drama or melodrama (Origin, Ewald, Koenig, Strack, Driver, Renan, Godet). A more radical view sees in it an anthology of loosely connected individual love lyrics (Herder, Goethe, Reuss, Lods, Haupt, Oesterley, Robinson, Pfeiffer, etc.) recited during wedding festivities (Wetzstein, Budde, Cheyne, Goodspeed, Cassuto).

That the book is a unified lyric with plan and definite purpose is apparent for the following two reasons: (1) Identical imagery and local color appear throughout the book. The bride is styled "fairest among women" (1:8; 5:9; 6:1). The bridegroom feeds his flock "among the lilies" (2:16; 4:5; 6:2-3) and is compared to a young hart (2:9, 17; 8:14). Compare the similar figure of the doe (gazelle; 2:7; 3:5; 4:5).

(2) The same persons appear throughout: the bride (1:5; 2:16; 3:4; 6:9; 7:10-11; 8:2, 8); the bridegroom (1:7; 2:13; 4:8—5:1; 6:1; 7:11-13); and the daughters of Jerusalem (1:5; 2:7; 3:5, 10; 5:8, 16; 8:4). Such evidence of unity militates against the notion that the book is a detached collection of erotic love lyrics, besides the incompatability of such a view with the requirements of divine inspiration and canonicity. Moreover, the poem does not possess sufficient plot or action to be classified as drama or melodrama.

The Interpretation. Three common methods of interpreting this difficult book prevail: (1) the literal, (2) the allegorical, and (3) the typical. (1) *The literal interpretation* takes the poem as purely a representation of human love. For example, E. J. Young espouses a species of the literal view, vaguely bordering on the typical. He sees the Song of Solomon as didactic and moral, in that it exalts the purity and dignity of human love and seeks to justify its place in the sacred canon by construing it as a reminder that God, who "has placed love in the human heart, is Himself pure" (*Introduction to the Old Testament*, p. 327). But it is difficult to see how the book would ever have been received as canonical on such a view, especially when it was on a plane often considered unedifying, and was actually forbidden by the Jews to be read by persons under thirty years of age. Besides, history demonstrates that such a view was inadequate to cause the faithful to persist in regarding the book as divinely inspired through the centuries.

However, most modern scholars in adopting the literal interpretation justify the canonicity by resorting to the "shepherd hypothesis," in which a third main character is introduced as the shepherd-lover of the bride, whom Solomon, villainlike, tries to seduce from her lover. The poem thus becomes the triumph of pure love over lust, but under an obviously objectionable representation of Solomon. More serious, the shepherd is a mere phantom, nothing more than a shadow cast by Solomon, as F. Delitzsch points out (KD, p. 8).

(2) *The allegorical interpretation* resulted because the inadequacy of the purely literal view led the Jews from earliest times to see in the poem a figurative representation of Jehovah's (Yahweh's) love for Israel, and the Christian church from Origen's time to see in it a representation of Christ's love for His church. Extravagances and abuses by a few have led many modern critics to reject and even scornfully denounce the allegorical interpretation.

(3) *The typical interpretation* is a mediating view between the two extremes represented by the purely literal on one hand and the allegorical on the other. It is adopted in this commentary for the following reasons: *(a)* It avoids the objections against the allegorical in that it neither denies the book's historical background nor condones fantastic interpretations of details, since the type adumbrates the antitype in only a few salient points.

(b) The typical view avoids the inescapable secularity of the literal view and finds not only an adequate but a superlatively lofty and soul-inspiring purpose in the book. At the same time it by no means excludes its exaltation of the dignity and purity of human love.

(c) The typical view gives point to the divine inspiration and canonical recognition of the book in its higher spiritual meaning, as well as its acceptance as such by God's people as exceedingly

lofty and precious. It enabled one of its very first commentators, R. Akiba (c. A.D. 115) to say of it: "The whole world is not worthy of the day in which this sublime song was given to Israel; for all the Scriptures are holy but this sublime Song is most holy" (ECB, 3: 386).

(d) The typical view is given abundant scriptural support. Both in the Old Testament and the New Testament the relationship of the LORD's people to the LORD is illustrated under the figure of marriage. Israel is the wife of Jehovah (Hos. 2:19-23), in her sin and unbelief now divorced, but yet to be restored (Isa. 54:5; Jer. 3:1; Hos. 1-3) in most wonderful grace and glory, which we believe is the aspect of the mutual love that is highlighted in the book. On the other hand, the Christian church is presented as a virgin espoused to Christ (2 Cor. 11:2; Eph. 5:23-32; Rev. 19:6-8) and is also typically reflected as a part of the redeemed.

(e) The typical view is not posited on a merely assumed higher spiritual meaning of the poem, but on an innate Spirit-inspired and Spirit-inwrought purpose providentially concealed from the unspiritual mind. Matthew Henry aptly says of the book: "It is a parable, which makes divine things more difficult to those who do not love them, but more plain and pleasant to those who do (Matt. 13:14, 16). Experienced Christians here find a counterpart of their experiences, and to them it is intelligible, while those neither understand it nor relish it who have no part or lot in the matter" (*Commentary on the Whole Bible*, 3: 1053).

The Authorship. While the notice of 1:1, "The song of songs, which is Solomon's," may conceivably be rendered "the Song of songs," which is *about* or *concerning* Solomon (cf. 1:4; 3:7-11; 8:11), the normal rendering (as in the Psalms) is indicative of authorship. Solomonic authorship is supported (1) by various internal evidences such as local color, affluence, and indications of luxury, and references to places like Jerusalem, Engedi, Sharon, Gilead, Lebanon, Carmel, and Hermon. The poem illustrates Solomon's knowledge of trees and plants (1 Kings 4:33). Into the 116 verses of the poem, Solomon "introduces twenty-one varieties of plants and fifteen species of animals" (John Steinmueller, *A Companion to Scripture Studies*, 2: 206).

(2) The linguistic peculiarities of the book (the presence of one or two Persian or Greek words) need not rule out Solomonic authorship. At most, these features may indicate that the precise form in which we have the poem cannot be earlier than the third century B.C. (Otto Eissfeldt). But Solomonic influence and commerce were incredibly widespread. Solomon's court was so cosmopolitan that an influx of foreign words would not be inconceivable. Little can be made of the Aramaisms, as close affinities existed between Hebrews and Aramaeans from earliest times and inevitably in the Solomonic realm, which embraced Aramaic countries.

OUTLINE

COMMENTARY

I. THE MUTUAL LOVE OF THE SHULAMITE AND THE KING. 1:1-17.

Title and Significance. 1:1. See the Introduction on the book's title and authorship. The book is a **song**, a love song, an epithalamium, or nuptial song, consisting of many individual love lyrics literally expressing the pure love of one man for one woman, eventuating in their union in marriage. Taken in this literal sense, the poem constitutes the only book in the canon that deals exclusively with the subject of love in courtship and marriage and the loftiness and purity of it as God-ordained and blessed, in contrast to the curse of polygamy, concubinage, and sexual promiscuity.

But since King Solomon is the lover, this exquisite song innately possesses a higher typical quasi-allegorical meaning, recognized by the LORD's people from ancient times—both Jews and Christians. This typical meaning follows because King Solomon prefigures the Messiah-Christ as the Prince of Peace (Isa. 9:6-7) succeeding David, the warring king, and setting forth Christ's second coming to reign in the millennial Kingdom (Psalms 72:1-19; 89:1-52; Isa. 11:1—12:6).

Solomon (like David) in his official royal capacity (not in his person, in which he later on in his life was guilty of serious sin) is a type of Christ in Kingdom glory. The Shulamite maid (beloved of Solomon), picturing perhaps Solomon's first love as a youthful king, typically represents specifically the saved remnant of the Jewish people entering Kingdom blessing at Christ's second advent in glory. But the Shulamite in the broadest perspective comprehends typically *all* the people of God (the elect—Old Testament Israel as well as the New Testament church) and their love for the LORD and King. Solomon represents God's love for all His redeemed people.

The Song of Solomon is a pastoral. The king appears as a shepherd, since Christ has always been figuratively set forth as a Shepherd of His people (Psalm 23:1-3; Heb. 13:20-21) and will specifically appear as the King-Shepherd in His millennial role (Psalm 80:1; Ezek. 34:11-31). The daughters of Jerusalem (vv. 5-6), whom the Shulamite addresses, are those of the Jewish nation of the Tribulation period who as yet do not share the knowledge of the Messiah and do not have intense love for Him (5:9), which characterizes the Shulamite as the representative of the saved remnant of the nation.

The Shulamite Praises the King. 1:2-4b. **2a. Let him kiss me with the kisses of his mouth.** Kissing is a token of reconciliation and restoration to favor, as was the case of Esau kissing Jacob (Gen. 33:4) and the father of the prodigal kissing his returning son (Luke 15:20), and will be when the Jewish remnant and the Gentiles "kiss the Son" in Kingdom blessing (Psalm 2:12). **2b. For thy love** ("loves," tokens of thy love) **is better than wine,** the symbol of earthly joys and pleasures. The tokens of His love transcend any earthly delights.

3a. Because ("as regards") ... **the savor** (fragrance) **of thy good ointments** (cf. 4:10-11), **thy name,** Christ's manifested character and office as the "Anointed" (Isa. 9:6), **is like ointment poured forth,** diffusing its fragrance everywhere. As the only Lord and Savior, the Messiah's name will have a peculiar preciousness to the Israelite remnant of the Tribulation (cf. Acts 4:12), illustrated by the holy oil with which the high priest was anointed, entailing death for anyone who tried to duplicate it (Exod. 30:23-38), and looking forward to Christ's glorious fullness of divine grace and sweet fragrance (Eph. 5:2; Col. 1:19; 2:9). Wonderful as this is to all saints, it will be peculiarly precious to the remnant of Israel when it comes to know the Messiah-King through Tribulation anguish (Jer. 30:5-7; Rom. 11:25-33).

3b. Therefore do the virgins — Israelites who will be saved during the Tribulation (Matt. 25:1-10; Rev. 14:4) **—love thee.** What love will well up from the hearts of converted and restored Israel when they look upon the crucified One (Zech. 12:10—13:1) and repeat the great penitential strains of Isaiah 53:1-12!

4a. Draw me (lit., "draw me after you") expresses the heart cry of the awakened Israelite remnant in the last days, echoing the yearning of ancient Israel for the Messiah (e.g., Simeon and Anna, Luke 2:25-38), and representing the keen desire of the awakened nation to glimpse the loveliness of Christ through the drawing of the Spirit (cf. John 6:44; 12:32) after it has come to see its own sinfulness and the ugliness of its unbelief.

4b-c. We will make haste (lit., "let us run"). Christ's love will kindle a corresponding passion in His people, Israel. **The king hath brought me into his chambers** (Psalm 45:14-15). He does so as the anointed Priest (v. 3) and King (v. 4), and in His appearance He brings her into the inmost chambers, where Oriental monarchs permitted only the most intimate friends. The scene portrays the full communion of the love of saved Israel at Christ's second advent (Rom. 11:26-32).

In the latter part of verse 4 the Shulamite joins with "the virgins," who love the King (v. 3), and whom the King has also admitted into His chambers to celebrate the gladness and intense rejoicing that the establishment of the Kingdom over Israel (Acts 1:6) will precipitate. **We will remember** (*hīzkîr*, "commemorate with praises"; Isa. 63:7) **thy love** (the Lord's love manifested in His restoration of the nation in fulfillment of His covenants and promises) **more than wine,** the mere recalling of spiritual joys being far superior to the actual experiencing of natural joys.

The upright, "the virgins" (v. 3; Psalm 58:1), **love thee,** or "they rightly love thee," or impersonally, "rightly art thou loved." Some believe this protestation of vibrant love to be on the part of "the daughters of Jerusalem." But that is untenable, for they have not yet been introduced, do not share the consuming passionate adoration of the Shulamite (5:9), and—representing Jews of the Tribulation period—they have not yet been brought to a saving knowledge of the coming King-Messiah.

The Shulamite Reveals Something of Her Character. 1:5-7. The Shulamite reveals five things about her character: (1) *She reveals that she has been a patient sufferer and a hard worker.* **5a.** She is **black** ("sunburned, swarthy," because of hard labor in the sun), nevertheless **comely** (lovely; cf. 2:14; 4:3; 6:4). She relates this to the **daughters of Jerusalem** (2:7; 3:5, 10; 5:8, 16; 8:4), who appear to be "professors," like the five foolish virgins (Matt. 25:1-10), but not actual "possessors" of the saving knowledge of the King-Messiah, like the Shulamite and "the virgins."

They are close to the King and stand in good stead of finding Him (5:8), have a desire to seek Him (6:1), and the Shulamite's Beloved eventually becomes their Beloved; however, this is not true of all of them. Evidently they represent the nation Israel soon to be saved and enter the millennial Kingdom, or conceivably (with Hengstenberg) the Gentile nations about to be brought into the Kingdom.

5b-6a. She compares her swarthy complexion to **the tents of Kedar** (Psalm 120:5; Isa. 60:7), drawing the image from the black goatskins of the Arabs, but she asserts her beauty notwithstanding: black, but comely, **like the curtains of Solomon**—rich and beautiful.

(2) *She discloses the reason for her suffering.* **6b.** The blackness was not natural, but was due to her affliction and suffering, foreshadowing "the time of Jacob's trouble" (Jer. 30:5-7), through which she will pass and come forth with the beauty of the LORD her God upon her (cf. Psalm 90:17). She got the swarthiness by the heat and burden of the day, which she was forced to bear, scorched with tribulation and persecution (Matt. 24:9-24).

(3) *She discloses the severity of her suffering.* **6c. The sun hath looked upon me** (*shzp*, "scorch, burn, singe"; cf. Matt. 24:21-22; Rev. 6:1—18:24). **My mother's children were angry with me** (Psalm 69:8). She was in perils by false brethren; her foes were those of her own house (Matt. 10:36), her own brothers being angry with her and persecuting her, even as apostate Israelites of the Tribulation period (24:9-10) will perse-

cute the faithful remnant of the nation who will turn to the Messiah in the terrible time of trouble preceding His second advent (Dan. 12:10; Luke 21:16).

(4) *She reveals the harsh treatment she suffered from her brothers.* **6d.** They made her **the keeper** (caretaker) **of the vineyards** (Song of Sol. 8:11-12), the drudge of the family to perform laborious servile work (Isa. 61:5). They are called her "mother's children," apparently half brothers, children of the same mother but not the same father, whose father in a spiritual sense was Satan, not God.

The brothers portray the apostates (Luke 8:41-44) of the Jewish nation of the Tribulation period, who will be **angry** at the believing remnant and persecute it, siding with the Antichrist and his godless followers against the followers of the Messiah. They made their sister care for the vineyards of Solomon at Baal-hamon, which the king had leased to her brothers (Song of Sol. 8:11-12). Accordingly, she was not able to take care of her **own vineyard,** her own personal appearance.

(5) *She reveals the intensity of her love for the king.* **7.** This verse constitutes words of the Shulamite addressed in soliloquy to the shepherd-king, her lover. She wants to belong to him only, and to be with him whom she loves (3:1-4) so dearly, especially to be with him where he is as he **feedeth** (pastures) his flocks (2:16; 6:3) and makes them **rest** (lie down) **at noon,** during the burning heat of midday (Isa. 13:20; Jer. 33:12).

For why should I be like one that turneth aside (lit., "like one who is veiled" in the garb of a harlot; cf. Gen. 38:15). In such a state she would appear to be unfaithful to the one she loves so intensely. For her, the king is the Shepherd of Israel (Psalm 80:1), who has found His sheep (Israel; Isa. 49:10; Ezek. 34:13-16).

The Gracious Response of the King to the Shulamite. 1:8. **8.** The shepherd-king replies to the Shulamite's question. While his beloved is yet speaking, he hears and answers, speaking in tenderest affection: **O thou fairest among women.** Believing souls are fair, in the eyes of the Lord Jesus, especially those "black" through suffering for Him, and especially the remnant of His people, Israel, when they will return to Him out of the Great Tribulation (Rev. 7:1-8). He checks her lovingly for her ignorance: **If thou knowest not,** intimating that she might have known had it not been her fault (Rom. 11:1-25). "What! You do not know where to find Me and My flock?" (cf. John 14:9).

But with infinite tenderness He directs her where to find Him: **Go thy way in the footsteps** (tracks) **of the flock, and feed thy kids beside the shepherds' tents.** Her jealousy of allowing even "His companions" to take His place leads Him to direct her to follow them, as they follow Him (Heb. 6:12). Where they are, He is. "The shepherds' tents" are the place where He, through His ministers, may be found (Psalm 84:1).

Mutual Expression of Love Between the Lovers. 1:9-17. (1) *The shepherd-king speaks (vv. 9-11).* **9.** He compares his beloved **to a company of horses in Pharaoh's chariots** (lit., "to a mare of Pharaoh's chariots"; 1 Kings 10:23; 2 Chron. 1:16-17; Isa. 31:1). Egyptian chariots were pulled by several pairs of horses, "but the prize mare led the chariot all alone ... uniquely noble and beautiful among the rest" (S. Craig Glickman, *A Song for Lovers*, p. 35).

10. The king regarded the Shulamite maid like that mare. He saw her **cheeks ... comely** (lovely) with jewels and her **neck with chains** (strings) of beads. **11.**

He (switching to the plural) promises her that his jewelers will make her **ornaments of gold with beads of silver** (NASB). His deity (gold) and redemption (silver) will adorn her and make her splendidly beautiful in the (millennial) kingdom.

(2) *The Shulamite speaks (vv. 12-14).* **12.** While the king was at his **table** (couch) dining, her **spikenard** (nard, a fragrant ointment) exuded its fragrance (Song of Sol. 4:13-14; Mark 14:3; John 12:3). **13-14.** She compares her beloved to **a bundle** (pouch) **of myrrh,** an aromatic gum used in antiquity as a perfume, and to a **cluster of henna flowers in the vineyards of Engedi.** En-gedi ("spring of the goat") was an oasis on the west of the Dead Sea, a bit of fertile country in the midst of a desert wilderness (1 Sam. 23:19). The king-shepherd was like En-gedi to the Shulamite, an oasis of life in a desert of monotony, and like the gorgeous henna blossoms of the area.

(3) *The shepherd-king speaks (v. 15).* **15. Behold, thou art fair** (beautiful), **my love** (darling); **behold, thou art fair** (beautiful), the repetition stressing her beauty. "How exceedingly beautiful you are, my love" (*dôdî*, "my darling, my sweetheart"). **Thou hast doves' eyes** (lit., "your eyes are doves"), large and beautiful, as is the case of Oriental doves; gentle, innocent, and lovely, as the dove is emblematic of the Holy Spirit, who transforms us into the image of Christ (2 Cor. 3:18). Such will be Christ's love for Israel when the nation is restored in Kingdom glory.

(4) *The Shulamite speaks (vv. 16-17).* **16-17. Behold, thou art fair** (handsome), **my beloved, yea, pleasant** (Song of Sol. 2:3, 9, 17; 5:2, 5-6, 8). This "snapshot" photographs them in the country. Their couch is the grass, and the cedars and cypresses form the beams and rafters of

their house and the scene of their courtship.

II. THE SHULAMITE IN FULL EXPERIENCE OF THE KING'S LOVE. 2:1-17.

The Shulamite Speaks. 2:1. **1.** The Shulamite's speech is continued unbroken from 1:16-17. In the woodland setting she sees herself as **the rose of Sharon** (Isa. 35:1), a beautiful flower that grew luxuriantly in the fertile coastal plain in northern Palestine (33:9; 35:2), and as **the lily of the valleys** (Song of Sol. 5:13; 7:2; Hos. 14:5). Both "the rose of Sharon" and "the lily" occur in contexts that prefigure Israel's future blessing in the Kingdom, when the nation will be restored to divine favor and the love relationship to the LORD will be restored (Isa. 35:2; Hos. 14:5). The Shulamite is not pompously lauding herself, but humbly and joyfully envisioning a love union with the shepherd-king and the reflection of his beauty in her, which in turn has enhanced her view of herself (cf. 1:5-6).

The King Replies. 2:2. **2.** The king will not allow the Shulamite to stop at her evaluation of herself as a mere "lily of the valleys." To him, she is unique among all the rest. **As the lily among thorns, so is my love** (darling) **among the daughters** (*bānôṯ*, "the daughters of Jerusalem" in particular, and the unregenerate daughters of men in general). The "thorns," evidence of the curse of sin (Gen. 3:17-18), focusing here upon Israel's unbelief and national setting aside during the interval between the first advent and rejection of the Messiah (Rom. 11:1-25) and her reinstatement in divine favor at the second advent in Kingdom blessing (11:26-33).

The Shulamite Speaks in Praise to Her Beloved. 2:3-6. The Shulamite

makes five comments on her beloved: (1) *She praises him for his uniqueness.* He had complimented her on her uniqueness (v. 2), and now she compliments him on his. **3a. As the apple tree**—a generic term including the pomegranate, orange, apple, and citron (8:5; Prov. 25:11)—**among the trees of the wood, so is my beloved among the sons** (all the sons of men). He alone is ever fruitful among the fruitless wild trees (Heb. 1:9). His perpetual foliage is an endless succession of blossoms, perfume, and fruit throughout the year.

(2) *She praises him for his delightful fellowship and protection.* **3b.** Under his **shadow** (shade) she sat down **with great delight,** illustrating how Christ interposes the protection of His cross between the blazing rays of justice and the sinner (Lam. 4:20). **His fruit was sweet to my taste** (Song of Sol. 4:13, 16; 8:11-12), the fruit of the tree of life (Gen. 2:9; 3:24), which the first Adam lost and the second Adam regained for him, and which redeemed man eats in part now (Psalm 119:103; John 6:55, 57) and will eat fully hereafter (Rev. 2:7; 22:2).

(3) *She praises him for the joy he gives and the love he displays.* **4. He brought me to the banqueting house** (lit., "house of wine"; see comments on Song of Sol. 1:4), such as Solomon had in his palace, according to Josephus, and prefiguring Israel restored in Kingdom communion and blessing with Christ.

And his banner over me was love. She has in mind the wide, high military standard that could be seen by everyone, showing that the king's love for her is evident to everyone and centering in the fact that Christ, as the Captain of her salvation (Heb. 2:10), has rescued her from the fierce foes of the godly Jewish remnant during the Tribulation period (cf. Rev. 12:13—13:18). That banner advertises the covenant-keeping love of

God for Israel in His restoring the nation in Kingdom blessing.

(4) *She asserts her overpowering love for the king.* He is unashamed of his love for her, and she in turn is unashamed of her love for him and is ecstatically secure in it. **5.** She becomes love-sick, weak from her overpowering devotion to the king, just as the restored nation Israel, after she is brought through the fires of Tribulation anguish, will be in her burning devotion to her Messiah-Deliverer. **Stay** (sustain) **me with flagons** (KJV; cf. "the house of wine," v. 4), but others render it "raisin cakes" (2 Sam. 6:19; 1 Chron. 16:3; Hos. 3:1). **Refresh me with apples** (NASB; i.e., from the tree, v. 3), so sweet to her.

(5) *She desires complete identification with him in kingdom glory under the figure of physical union* (Song of Sol. 8:3; Prov. 4:8). **6.** In soliloquy she says, **Let his left hand be under my head, and let his right hand embrace me** (BV).

The Shulamite Speaks of Her Beloved. 2:7. **7.** The Shulamite charges (adjures) the daughters of Jerusalem (see comment on 1:5), **by the roes** (gazelles; vv. 9, 17; 8:14), **and by the hinds of the field** (Gen. 49:21; Psalm 18:33; Hab. 3:19), not to **stir ... up** (arouse) or **awake ... love** until **it** (love) **please** (lit. Heb.). She would be dishonest to pretend that she does not have a strong desire to consummate her love in physical union. But she herself urges restraint until marriage.

Trying to force love is like trying to force a flower to blossom—it would only tear the petals. Love, like a flower, must blossom naturally. So after experiencing the most intense longing of her courtship (v. 6), she urges patience. So the Jewish remnant, preceding Christ's advent in glory and Kingdom blessing, must exert restraint and pa-

tiently await the Lord's coming (James 5:7-8).

The Shulamite Soliloquizes on the King's Coming. 2:8-14. **8-9a.** In the excitement of her ardent love, she imagines she hears the **voice** (sound) of her beloved (cf. John 10:4) **leaping upon the mountains, skipping upon the hills,** bounding as the gazelle or **young hart** (stag) over the roughest obstacles.

9b. She imagines him standing behind the **wall,** gazing through the windows, peering through the lattice (Judg. 5:28). It is a picture of the coming of the King-Messiah, revealing Himself to His repentant people, Israel (Zech. 12:10—13:1; cf. Song of Sol. 3:6; 8:4-5). It is the time when the remnant of Israel will come to know Him as their long-awaited Messiah and enter into the enjoyment of the blessings and glories promised them in their great covenants—the Abrahamic (Gen. 12:3), the Palestinian (Deut. 30:3-10), the Davidic (2 Sam. 7:16), and the New (Jer. 31:31-34).

10. The Shulamite (6:13) hears her beloved responding and saying to her, **Rise up, my love, my fair one, and come away** (v. 13). It is a call to kingdom joy after the winter of tribulation and suffering (Jer. 30:5-7; Dan. 12:1; Matt. 24:21-22). **11. For, lo, the winter is past, the rain is over and gone. 12. The flowers appear on the earth** (Isa. 35:1-2; 41:19; 51:3); **the time of ... singing ... has come** (12:1-6; 14:7; 35:2; 44:23; 49:13; 51:11; 54:1; 55:12). **The voice of the turtledove** (the bird of love) **is heard in the land** (Gen. 15:9; Psalm 74:19; Jer. 8:7, NASB).

13a. The fig tree (a figure of the Jewish nation) **putteth forth** (*ḥnṭ*, "ripens") **her green figs,** by which we "know that summer [the Kingdom] is near" (Matt. 24:32). The cursed fig tree (21:19) now begins to bear fruit, signifying Israel's conversion and restoration of her national election (Rom. 11:1-25) in Kingdom blessing (11:26-33).

13b. And the **vines,** another figure of the nation Israel (Psalm 80:11; Isa. 5:1-7; Matt. 21:33-46), **with the tender grapes give forth fragrance,** symbolizing Israel's reinstatement into divine favor in the millennial Kingdom. The King-Messiah will then call His beloved people, Israel, saved out of the Great Tribulation, to enter the Kingdom. **13c. Arise, my love, my fair one, and come away** (v. 10).

14a. O my dove (5:12) . . . **in the clefts of the rock** (Jer. 48:28), **in the secret places of the stairs** (steep pathway, cliff), **let me see thy countenance** (lit., appearance), **let me hear thy voice.** Doves often hide in rocks and inaccessible cliffs. So the Israelite remnant of the end time, under the fury of Antichrist and his followers, will be compelled to flee his wrath and hide in the dens and caves of the mountains (Matt. 24:16, 21; Rev. 12:6, 13-17). But all the while that God's people are in the clefts of the rock, they are in Him, the true rock, who protects and preserves them.

14b. At His coming to deliver the remnant, Christ's consuming love will go out to them, His beloved people. He will hear their voice, for it will be sweet to Him, and see their countenance, for it will be exceedingly **comely** (beautiful) to Him (cf. Song of Sol. 1:5; 8:13).

The King's Resolve to Preserve a Very Precious Love. 2:15. **15.** The king resolves with her, **Take us** ("let us catch") **the foxes, the little foxes, that spoil** (ruin) **the vines** (vineyards); **for our vines have tender grapes** (are in blossom). Since the vine is a symbol of the nation Israel (see v. 13), the blossoming of the vineyard graphically portrays the conversion of the remnant for reinstatement in divine favor, and the beautiful love relationship established between the King-Messiah and the converted nation as a result. Neither the King nor the Shulamite, as true lovers, want any obstacle, represented by the foxes, to intrude to mar their love.

The Shulamite's Ecstasy in the Experience of Mutual Belongingness. 2:16-17. **16a.** The Shulamite cries joyfully, **My beloved is mine, and I am his.** The commitment is mutual. The king-shepherd and his beloved can say, "We belong to each other. We are counterparts; we complete each other." So it is in God-ordained love between a man and woman, eventuating in marriage. So it is between Christ and the redeemed; specifically, it will be so between the returning Christ and the saved Jewish remnant made ready for entrance into Kingdom blessing.

16b. He feedeth (tends his flock) **among the lilies** (6:3). In affirming that she belongs to him, the Shulamite explicitly alludes to his shepherd role and, by so doing, highlights his shepherd-like characteristics of gentleness and strength. Pasturing his flock among the lilies refers to Christ's millennial role as Shepherd-King (2:2; 4:5; Hos. 14:5).

17. The Shulamite, in her deep love for the beloved, pleads for his coming, not doubting that eventually the **day** will **break, and the shadows flee away** in the glorious (millennial) dawn. But her cry is for him to come soon. **Turn, my beloved, and be thou like a roe** (gazelle) **or a young hart** (stag), swift in thy coming **upon the mountains of Bether,** apparently the same as "the mountains of spices" (8:14; cf. Psalm 45:7-8), figuratively presenting the fragrance of the true King's advent.

III. THE SHULAMITE IN DISTRESS, AND THE COMING OF THE KING. 3:1-11.

The Shulamite's Dream About Her Beloved. 3:1-4. **1a. By night** on her bed she **sought him** whom she so dearly loved (1:7). Just before the great event of marriage, she dreamed her beloved was taken from her. So deep was her burning affection (four times in four verses she refers to her beloved as "him whom my soul loveth," vv. 1, 2, 3, 4) that the fear of losing him reacted in her what psychologists call a fear-fulfillment dream. Her search for him was fruitless.

1b. I sought him, but I found him not (repeated for emphasis in v. 2; 5:6). **2.** In the anguish of her subconscious mind she dreams that she arises and goes through the streets and squares of the city seeking him. **3.** The night **watchmen** of the city (5:7) come across her, and she inquires with the naiveté of deep emotion whether they have seen him whom she loves so passionately, as if everyone ought to love him as she does. (Compare 1:2, and Mary Magdalene, John 20:15: "If thou have borne him from here," meaning Christ, but not naming Him.) The watchmen have no answer for her, as the language of love is incomprehensible to nonlovers.

4a. But scarcely has she passed the watchmen when she finds her beloved. **I held on to him and would not let him go, until I had brought him to my mother's house, and into the room of her who conceived me** (NASB). It is natural in periods of stress to have an urge to go to the place where one has always felt secure. After fearing the loss of her loved one, it is not surprising that in her dream she takes him to her own home and, as in childhood, in her fancy she crawls, as it were, under the covers of her mother

until her lingering fears subside. All the while she clings to him, till her sense of security returns.

In this episode of lapsing into fear and uncertainty, there is a prophetic revelation of the anguish and deep soul exercise of the godly remnant of Israel (Dan. 12:1; Matt. 24:21-22) during the dark night of Tribulation (Rev. 6:1—20:3) preceding the dawn of the millennial day (20:4-6).

The Shulamite's Refrain. 3:5. **5.** When she is quieted and realizes that all is well after her ordeal and distress (Matt. 24:21-22), she wisely urges others and herself to be patient, repeating the identical advice she had previously given (see Song of Sol. 2:7): "I adjure you, O daughters of Jerusalem, by the gazelles and the hinds of the field not to arouse, nor to awaken love until it please" (lit. Heb.).

In others words, "Don't rush God's plan. Let the flower of love blossom under His hand in its proper season. He knows what it will take of tribulation and suffering to bring forth the wonderful love of the godly Jewish remnant for Himself (symbolized by the Shulamite) that will furnish the foundation upon which the millennial Kingdom will be founded." Each cycle of courtship leads to a higher experience of love, preparatory to the wedding itself, which is a prefigurement of Israel's association with the Messiah-King in the earthly Kingdom about to be set up.

The Coming of the King. 3:6-11. This scene is the answer to the Shulamite's anxiety and seeking for the king (vv. 1-4). The uncertainty and trial of the night of tribulation now give way to the glorious advent of the king (vv. 6-11). **6. Who** (or what) **is this that cometh** (ascends) **out of the wilderness** (cf. 8:5). A large cloud of dust is seen in the distance, revealing a royal wedding procession, the dust now discerned as ascending clouds of smoke from burning myrrh and incense, compacted from all the scented powders of the merchant (1:13; 4:6, 14; Matt. 2:11).

7. It proves to be the **bed** (the palanquin or traveling couch) **which is Solomon's** (who is a type of Christ in His Kingdom glory). Sixty mighty men from the **valiant of Israel** surround the bridal car, indicating that the scene presents a full-dress military wedding, with the king's top officers in their uniforms.

8. They all hold (handle) **swords, being expert in war** (Jer. 50:9), each man with a **sword** at his side (Psalm 45:3) **guarding against the terrors of the night** (NASB; 91:5). They display Christ the King's ability to protect and provide for His beloved, the Jewish remnant who through His gracious interposition will be saved through the horrors of the Great Tribulation (Matt. 24:22; Rev. 19:15).

9. King Solomon made himself a chariot (rather, a sumptuous "palanquin," different from the "couch" or "litter"; cf. v. 7), possibly a sort of portable throne. He had it made of the fine **wood of Lebanon** (1 Kings 5:6-11). **10.** The pillars were made of silver, speaking of the greater Solomon as the Redeemer (Rev. 19:13); and the inlaid top of gold, speaking of the greater Solomon as Deity, the King of kings and Lord of Lords (19:16), coming to be united to His converted and restored people, Israel, and to "rule" in righteousness and peace (Isa. 9:6-7; Rev. 19:15) in the royal line of David, symbolized by the "seat of purple" (RSV). The inside of the palanquin was "lovingly and intricately wrought in needlework by the daughters of Jerusalem" (Amp.), showing that they are coming into a deeper knowledge of the King and developing a tender love for Him (see

comments on 1:7; 2:7; 3:5; 5:8, 16; 8:4).

11. The daughters of Zion (Jerusalem; Isa. 3:16-17; 4:4) are invited to **go forth** and gaze on **King Solomon with the crown with which his mother crowned him** on the day of his wedding (Psalm 110:3; Isa. 62:5; Rev. 11:15), **on the day of his gladness of heart** (NASB). The mother of the greater Solomon is Israel (12:5-6). In that glad day when He ascends from the wilderness like pillars of smoke in the Shekinah cloud, in the glorious splendor and fragrance of His person, He will appear as the mighty Conqueror (19:11-16) and yet He is the true Solomon, the Prince of Peace.

On that great day "of the gladness of his heart," His mother, Israel, then converted and restored, will crown Him King of kings and Lord of all. But the relationship between the Shepherd-King and His restored people, Israel, will not be that of a mother and son, but the ecstatic love between two lovers, as is so deftly portrayed in this superlative poem.

IV. THE KING'S EXPRESSION OF LOVE FOR THE SHULAMITE. 4:1-16.

The King Celebrates His Beloved One's Beauty. 4:1-7. The King (Christ) sees His beloved as "perfect through [His] splendor ... put upon [her]" (Ezek. 16:14) as a result of His redemptive grace. The poet employs the imagery of physical beauty to portray the inner moral and spiritual beauty of the redeemed remnant of Israel about to enter the millennial Kingdom (Psalm 45:11), when the LORD will "heal their backsliding" and will "love them freely" and will be unto them as "the dew," and Israel "shall grow like the lily, and cast forth his roots like Lebanon" (Hos. 14:4-5).

Eight descriptions are given of restored Israel's beauty, when "the beauty of the LORD [their] God" shall be upon them (Psalm 90:17), when he who is "left in Zion, and he who remaineth in Jerusalem," as survivors of the Great Tribulation, "shall be called holy ... when the Lord shall have washed away the filth of the daughters of Zion" (Isa. 4:3-4) and bestowed the splendor of His salvation upon them.

1a. As the King surveys His blood-cleansed people (Zech. 13:1), He cries, **Behold, thou art fair, my love; behold, thou art fair** (Song of Sol. 1:15), the repetition being a rhetorical device to indicate her being "exceedingly beautiful." She is so as the result of His salvation and workmanship, which is the case of all His redeemed people (Eph. 2:8-10). In Him, *all* His redeemed people have their completeness and perfection (cf. 5:27), and He appears as an ardent Lover of *all* His own of every age. But here His wonderful love appears in focus upon His beloved Israel, cleansed from their age-long unbelief, and restored to Him in radiant fellowship.

(1) **1b.** He praises her eyes that are as **doves' eyes**, bright and alert, with their blindness removed to see Him as the Messiah-Savior (Isa. 53:1-12; Zech. 12:10; Matt. 23:39) from behind her *veil* (lit. Heb.), which will then be removed to behold His beauty (2 Cor. 3:15-16). (2) **1c.** Her **hair** (her "glory," 1 Cor. 11:15), is like a flock of goats descending from **Mount Gilead** (Song of Sol. 6:5; Mic. 7:14), beyond the Jordan in the highlands stretching toward the desert famous for its pastureland.

(3) **2.** Her **teeth** (Song of Sol. 6:6) in their evenness are like sheep "paired, and not one of them is alone" (lit. Heb.), their glistening whiteness **like a flock of newly shorn ewes which have come up from their washing**—their completeness and intactness—**all of which bear twins,**

and not one among them (the ewes) **has lost her young** (NASB).

(4) **3a.** Her **lips** are **like a scarlet thread** (NASB) because she is redeemed (Josh. 2:18). (5) **3b.** Her **mouth** (NASB; Song of Sol. 5:16) is lovely because she will confess and own Him now as Savior and Lord. (6) **3c.** Her **temples** (6:7) are compared to halves of a pomegranate, ruddy and flushed with excitement and beauty, speaking of the dome of thought that in the beloved one is fixed on the Beloved. (7) **4.** Her **neck** (7:4) **like the tower of David**, a military fortress housing all the shields of war, giving the people a sense of protection and describing the loved one holding up her head in confidence and assurance.

(8) **5.** Her **breasts** (7:3) are **like fawns ... which feed among the lilies** (NASB; 2:16; 6:2-3), the whole description being a figure of the delicate and chaste beauty of Israel as she comes to a saving knowledge of her Redeemer, and His beauty is reflected in her as she enters into millennial bliss.

6. This is when **the day** (the glad millennial day) will **break** (lit., "breathe"), **and the shadows** of the dark night of the Great Tribulation (Jer. 30:5-7; Dan. 12:1; Rev. 8:1—20:3) will **flee away** (see Song of Sol. 2:17). Until that time the King will betake Himself **to the mountain of myrrh** (2:17; cf. John 19:39), **and to the hill of frankincense** (v. 14), a poetic description of Calvary, presenting a prophetic glance at the great redemptive act of the Messiah to be wrought there, which makes possible the King's superlative declaration in verse 7.

7. Thou art all fair, my love; there is no spot in thee (Song of Sol. 1:15; cf. Eph. 5:27; 2 Pet. 3:14). "The mountain of myrrh" and "hill of frankincense" speak of the fragrance of the Messiah's death on Mount Calvary, where "through the eternal Spirit [He] offered himself" (Heb. 9:14) for man's redemption.

The King's Call to His Beloved. 4:8-15. **8.** The King (Christ) pleads with the Shulamite to leave her native hills in the Lebanon region north of Palestine and to come to Him (1 Kings 4:33; Psalm 72:16) **from the top** (summit) **of Amana,** one of the peaks of the Anti-Lebanon Mountains, near the course of the Abana (Amana) River (2 Kings 5:12), **from the top of Senir,** the Amorite name for Mount Hermon (Deut. 3:9), doubtlessly one of the three peaks of Mount Hermon. He calls her from the mountains, the place of earthly privilege, beauty, and worldly attraction, but also the place of danger.

Come with me from Lebanon ... from the lions' dens, from the mountains of the leopards. The King's invitation is to leave the world and its pleasures, beauties, and dangers and be united to Him in the joys and blessings of the millennial Kingdom. The wild beasts speak of the Antichrist (Rev. 13:1-2) and his followers, who will threaten the godly Jewish remnant of the Tribulation period with suffering and death (12:13-17).

In verses 9 to 12 the King once again pours out His heart of love for His redeemed people under the figure of the Shulamite. **9.** He assures her that she has **ravished** His heart with one glance of her eyes. He calls her His **sister** in anticipation of her union with Him in Kingdom blessing, as the term in that culture was one of endearment for one's spouse. The King is deeply in love with His redeemed people, and He tenderly and freely expresses His love to them under the figure of God-ordained, pure human love between man and woman. **10.** He calls her love for Him **better ... than wine,** as she had previously described His love for her (Song of Sol. 1:2), and the fragrance of His ointments better than all kinds of spices (1:3). **11.** Her lips **drip honey** (NASB; Psalm 19:10; Prov. 5:3), and He sees **honey and milk,** the glory of the land of Israel, under her tongue, evidencing the glorious transformation His salvation had brought to Israel, under whose lips, in their former state, had been "adders' poison" (Psalm 140:3). To Him the fragrance of her **garments** (the garments of His salvation) was **like the fragrance of Lebanon** (Gen. 27:27; Hos. 14:6), abounding in odoriferous plants and trees.

The King's Description of His Beloved as a Garden and a Fountain. 4:12-16a. **12.** Restored Israel (the beloved) is pictured as a **garden enclosed** (walled in) and therefore set apart for the King-Messiah to bring forth fruit for His delight (Isa. 58:11; Jer. 31:12) in the Kingdom about to be set up. The "enclosed or walled garden" and the "sealed fountain" appear to be established metaphors for a pure and chaste spouse (Prov. 5:15, 20). The godly Israelite remnant will be such while enjoying salvation and cleansing (Isa. 4:3-4; Zech. 12:10—13:1; Rom. 11:26-32).

13-14. The King envisions His beloved in the land of Israel and describes the charms of her person when settled down there in union and communion with Him and manifesting His graces. He sees her as **a pomegranate orchard with precious fruits, a garden of henna with spikenard, spikenard and saffron, calamus and cinnamon, with all the trees of frankincense, myrrh and aloes, with all the chief spices** (BV).

15. The King is delighted with His spouse as He views her productive and fragrant life. He has compared her to a garden (vv. 12-14). Now He likens her to

a garden fountain, a well of living water
(John 4:14; 7:37-39), **flowing streams
from Lebanon** (BV). Streams from
snow-capped Hermon sink into the
ground to form subterranean springs to
refresh the thirsty soil.

16a. After singing His beloved's
charms when settled down in the land,
the King calls for the north wind and the
south wind (typifying the Holy Spirit) to
blow upon His garden in order that the
fragrance may **flow out** to the whole
earth, for reinstated Israel will be a
blessing under the Messiah-King to the
whole millennial globe (cf. Rom. 11:12;
cf. Zech. 8:20-23).

*The Shulamite Invites the King to His
Garden. 4:16b.* **16b.** This is the Shulamite's reply to Christ the King's call to
the north wind and the south wind to
scatter the fragrance of the garden and
waft its spices abroad. This can only
happen as the Beloved comes into His
garden and eats its **pleasant** (choice)
fruits (v. 13), that is, as He is joined to
His beloved in physical union, prefiguring the establishment of the restored nation of Israel in full Kingdom
blessing in association with the King.
These "fruits" are His (7:13), because
He made the irrevocable choice of Israel
(Rom. 11:26, 29) and paid the price for
her redemption on Calvary, as the restored nation will freely acknowledge
(Isa. 53:1-8).

V. THE SHULAMITE'S LAPSE AND RESTORATION. 5:1-16.

The King Comes to His Garden. 5:1.
Christ the King's coming to the garden is
in answer to the Shulamite's invitation
(see 4:16b). He calls His beloved **my
sister** (4:9), **my spouse.** As "sister," He
acknowledges the national relationship,
disowned in Matthew 12:46-50, because
the offer of the Kingdom had then been
rejected. Now it is reestablished, and

the saved portion of Israel becomes both
"sister" and "spouse."

In His garden (restored Israel,
4:12-15), the product of His love and
death, He now finds His enjoyment and
satisfaction under the poetic figure of
gathering His **myrrh** (a symbolic reference to His death) with **spice** (the fragrance of His redemptive work), eating
His **honeycomb** with His **honey** (in fulfillment of the Word of God, Psalm
19:10) and drinking His **wine** (a figure of
the joy His salvation brings to His
people and to Him as Savior, Judg. 9:13)
and **milk** (the nourishment it brings, Isa.
55:1). He invites others to come and
partake: **Eat, O friends. Drink . . . abundantly, O beloved** (ones), extending to
the whole millennial earth the great gospel invitation of Isaiah 55:1-12.

*The Shulamite's Distressing Dream.
5:2-8.* This is the Shulamite's second
disturbing dream (3:1-4). **2.** She goes to
sleep, but her heart stays awake. She
dreams she hears **the voice** of her beloved knocking, apparently at the door
of her mother's cottage, saying, **Open to
me, my sister, my love, my dove, my undefiled.** He is wet with heavy night dew,
and his hair is drenched with it (v. 11; cf.
Judg. 6:38). In her dream she responds
with apathy and excuse.

3. Doubtlessly weary from a day's
work in the vineyard, she has taken off
her dress (Luke 11:7). Why should she
put it on again? She has washed her feet;
why should she get them dirty again
(Gen. 19:2)? **4.** Her beloved, with the
fullest display of tender love, **put in his
hand by the hole of the door** (KJV) to
unbolt it, as one weary of waiting, intimating a work of the Spirit by which
she is made willing, as the remnant of
Israel will be in that day (Psalm 110:3).

5. Then she realizes her slothfulness
and her neglect of loving service. **6.** But
it is too late. When she finally opens the

door, he has **withdrawn himself, and** (is) **gone** (Song of Sol. 6:1), her heart going out to him as he spoke (5:2). But he left a "love note" on the handles of the bolt of the door—liquid, sweet-smelling myrrh—a reminder that he had been there, a memento of Christ's undying love manifest in Calvary's redemption, the myrrh speaking of His death. Then she searches for him (3:1) and calls for him in vain (Prov. 1:28).

7. The watchmen (Song of Sol. 3:3), who guard the peace of Jerusalem, find her and strike and wound her, severely chastising her for her lapse. Her very affection exposes her to reproof and places her in a position that plainly shows she has slighted her beloved. **The keepers of the walls took away** (her) **veil** from her. This involved the greatest indignity to an Oriental woman, intimating she was a mere wandering wanton.

The Shulamite's Appeal to the Daughters of Jerusalem. 5:8. **8.** The Shulamite's lapse and chastisement sharpen her love for her beloved and give her opportunity for testimony to the **daughters of Jerusalem,** who represent the rest of the nation, which does not know and love her beloved as she does. She adjures them, if they find her beloved, that they tell him that she is **sick with love** (2:7; 3:5), that is, love-sick (2:5).

The Reply of the Daughters of Jerusalem. 5:9. **9.** The daughters want to know why she loves her beloved so intensely, perhaps tauntingly calling her **fairest among women** (1:8). The repetition of the words **What is thy beloved more than another beloved?** emphasizes and highlights their kindled interest in him and the very effective opportunity the occasion presents to give her glowing testimony concerning him, which was bound to stir up faith in him and love for him, showing that the

sufferings and chastenings of the saved remnant (6:1) will be overruled for the good of the nation Israel to prepare her for Kingdom blessing.

The Shulamite's Description of Her Beloved. 5:10-16. In superlative poetic language the Shulamite testifies to the beauty and glory of Christ the King, who at His second advent will "restore again the kingdom to Israel" (Acts 1:6). She adoringly testifies to salient features of His beauty. **10.** She depicts Him as **white** ($ṣāḥ$, "dazzling, bright"; cf. Matt. 17:2) and **ruddy** (1 Sam. 16:12), **the chiefest among ten thousand** (Psalm 45:2; John 1:14).

11. His head is like finest **gold** (speaking of the omniscience of Deity and the godhead of the King). **His locks are bushy** (curled), a token of His headship, in contrast to the Shulamite's flowing hair (Song. of Sol. 4:1), and **black,** implying perpetual youth (Psalms 102:27; 110:3). **12.** His eyes are **like ... doves** (Song of Sol. 1:15; 4:1; cf. Rev. 1:14), suggesting love and gentleness (Matt. 3:16), **fitly set** like the finest gem in a ring.

13. His cheeks are like a bed of spices (balsam; Song of Sol. 6:2), like **banks of sweet-scented herbs** (NASB). **His lips** are **lilies** (2:1), that is, bloodred anemones. They distill **sweet-smelling** liquid **myrrh,** telling of His redemptive love, manifested in His death for sinners (v. 5).

14. His hands are **rods of gold set with beryl** (NASB; Exod. 28:20; 39:13; Ezek. 1:16; Dan. 10:6). **His belly** (abdomen), perhaps speaking of "his bowels of mercy," is carved **ivory overlaid with sapphires** (lapis lazuli; Exod. 24:10; 28:18; Job 28:16; Isa. 54:11). **15. His legs are ... pillars of marble** (alabaster) **set upon sockets** (pedestals) **of fine gold** (again speaking of His divine-human person). His **countenance** (appearance) is like **Lebanon** (Song of Sol. 7:4), as choice as its **cedars** (1 Kings 4:33; Psalm 80:10; Ezek. 17:23; 31:8).

16. His mouth is most sweet (Song of Sol. 7:9). The Shulamite has exhausted herself in praise of her Beloved and cries out, as do multitudes in every generation, **Yea, he is altogether lovely** (2 Sam. 1:23). In rapturous testimony she concludes, **This is my beloved, and this is my friend, O daughters of Jerusalem.**

No wonder she stirs up interest in Him!

VI. THE KING PRAISES THE SHULAMITE. 6:1-13.

The Inquiry of the Daughters of Jerusalem. 6:1. **1.** The Shulamite's outburst of praise and glowing testimony concerning her Beloved (Christ) understandably creates a keen desire in the hearts of the daughters of Jerusalem to become His, as will be the case with the converted remnant as the Kingdom age dawns (Isa. 2:3-4; Zech. 8:20-23; cf. Rom. 11:25-26). Compare 1 Corinthians 15:8, where Paul views himself as a converted Jew, prematurely born, before the great period of world evangelization by Jewish evangelists in the Kingdom age. **Whither has thy beloved turned aside, that we may seek him with thee?** Meanwhile, her Beloved's beauty is upon her (Psalm 90:17), and so they now speak sincerely in calling her **fairest among women.**

The Shulamite's Reply. 6:2-3. **2.** Her answer reveals she knows very well where Christ her Beloved is. He had gone down from Jerusalem to **his garden** at a little distance in the valley below. "His garden" is a figure of His converted people, Israel, restored to the land of Palestine. **The beds of spices** depict poetically the fragrance of His restored people, Israel. He has gone to His garden **to feed** (*rā'â,* "pasture") His

flock as the Shepherd of Israel (Psalm 80:1), that is, "rule" and "govern" them as the King-Messiah in the millennial Kingdom **in the gardens** (His Shepherd care extending to the nations of the entire earth Kingdom) **and to gather lilies**—those redeemed from among all peoples.

3. The Shulamite not only knows where her beloved is, but she is very assured of her own interest in him. **I am my beloved's, and my beloved is mine** (Song of Sol. 2:16). The relationship is mutual. The knot of love is tied. So it will be with restored Israel, even as in the Spirit it is with all of Christ's redeemed. Though she had said the same thing before (2:16), now she inverts the order and declares His (Christ's) interest in her first: "I am my beloved's"; she is entirely devoted and dedicated to Him. **He feedeth** (pastures His flock) **among the lilies** (His redeemed; 2:16; 4:5).

The King Praises the Shulamite. 6:4-10. How beautiful and altogether lovely will the converted and restored remnant of Israel be to Christ the King on the eve of her restoration in Kingdom glory, conformed to His likeness in the beauty of His salvation! **4.** The King pronounces His loved one **beautiful ... as Tirzah,** a royal city of one of the ancient Canaanite kings (Josh. 12:24), the loveliness of which had become proverbial by Solomon's time (1 Kings 14:17).

Comely (lovely; Song of Sol. 1:5) **as Jerusalem** (Psalms 48:2; 50:2), **terrible** (awesome, awe-inspiring, formidable) **as an army with banners** (Exod. 17:14-15; Psalm 60:4; cf. v. 10), a victorious army overcoming the world, the flesh, and the devil (1 John 5:4), like Jacob having "power with God" and prevailing (Gen. 32:28; Exod. 32:9-14; Hos. 12:4), even overcoming the

Messiah-King Himself, with "eyes" (v. 5) fixed on Him (Psalm 25:15; Song of Sol. 4:9). "Messiah-King is pleased to borrow these expressions of a passionate lover only to express the tenderness of a compassionate Redeemer and the delight he takes in his redeemed . . . in the working of his grace in them" (Matthew Henry).

5-7. Almost word for word the King repeats part of the descriptions He had given of her beauty—her **hair** and **teeth** and **temples** (see 4:1-3). He does this deliberately to prove He still has the same high esteem for her since her lapse from Him and His withdrawal from her (see 5:2-8). He lauds her uniqueness and prefers her above all rivals, envisioning the beauties and perfections of others meeting and centering in her (vv. 8-9).

8-9. Though these may be **sixty queens and eighty concubines and maidens without number** (NASB; 1 Kings 11:3; Song of Sol. 1:3), **my dove, my undefiled, is . . . one** (is unique; Deut. 4:6-7; 33:29), cleansed and purified by faith (Zech. 13:1; Rom. 11:26), and as mine, she excels all, though they are ever so many. So will the redeemed remnant of Israel appear to the Messiah-King when she believes on Him and is cleansed and reinstated in her national election (11:1-24) to be His **undefiled.**

Then He will own that remnant as **the only one of her mother** (the nation Israel), **the choice one of her who bore her** (Israel). Christ views all His redeemed as unique. But in this context His redeemed people, Israel, come into focus. To her in due time, when the Messiah sets up His earthly Kingdom over Israel, the many queens and concubines—the Gentiles—will see her, bless her, and follow her call and example to "be joined to the LORD in that day" (Zech. 2:11; 8:20-23; cf. Isa. 2:2-3; 66:23; Zech. 14:16-21) and enter with her into Kingdom blessing (Isa. 45:14-25).

10. Then of her (the restored remnant of Israel) it shall be said, **Who is this, who shines forth as the morning dawn**—ushering in the millennial day—**fair as the moon**—still resplendent in the semidarkness from her shining in the night of the Tribulation just passed through by light borrowed from the sun—**radiant as the sun**—the Sun of Righteousness, the Messiah-King arising with healing in His beams to flood the millennial earth (Mal. 4:2)—**captivating** (awesome) **as an army with banners?** (BV; cf. v. 4).

God's redeemed are as an army, militant as the camp of Israel in the wilderness. That army (restored Israel) will be as awesome to its enemies as ancient Israel was in the wilderness (Exod. 15:14-16; Num. 24:5-6). It will have its banners. The love of God manifested in Christ's redemption (Song of Sol. 2:4) will be the "ensign" held up to the nations, under which the Messiah will regather converted Israel to Kingdom blessing (Isa. 11:12).

The Shulamite's Response to the King's Lavish Praise. 6:11-12. The Shulamite apparently presents a modest confession that she had fallen in love with the king at first sight. **11.** Evidently in this scene she had gone down into her quiet garden to resume her rustic labors. **12.** But the moment the king appeared, her soul was enraptured and carried away as in a swift chariot. "Before I was aware, my fancy set me in a chariot beside my prince" (RSV)—"seated me in a princely chariot of my people" (BV). "She was subdued by the power of love. It was love that raised her to the royal chariots of her people. She beholds in King Solomon the concentration and the acme of her people's glory" *(Pulpit Commentary).* So restored Israel will see in the King-Messiah the full realization of her glory at His second coming and Kingdom.

Request of the Daughters of Jerusalem. 6:13a. **13a. Return** (*šūḇ*, "turn, turn about"), **return** (repeated four times for emphasis), **O Shulamite, that we may look upon** (gaze at) **thee.** These ladies, who have come to appreciate the beauty of the Shulamite, are attracted to her loveliness. They represent the unsaved Israelites who will be attracted to the King and, through His beloved, be led into Kingdom blessing. Apparently the urgent request is not that the Shulamite might remain, but that they might behold her beauty.

Reply of the King. 6:13b. **13b. What will ye see in** (what do you see in) **the Shulamite? As at the dance** (Judg. 21:21) **of the two companies** (NASB; or Mahanaim; Gen. 32:2; 2 Sam. 17:24), perhaps a name for a particular dance in which the inhabitants of Mahanaim excelled, or one in which angels were thought to engage. Perhaps the Shulamite danced as a simple shepherdess or vinedresser before the daughters of Jerusalem; or the dance may have been symbolic of the joy that was hers because she was associated with the king and would enter into kingdom blessing with him. Her name, Shulamite (Shulamith, Shulammith), is apparently the feminine form in Hebrew of the name Solomon (like George and Georgia). In this case the name would connote that she was the feminine counterpart of Solomon. However, many derive the name from Shulem (Shunem, Josh. 19:18; 1 Kings 1:3; 2 Kings 4:8), meaning "maid of Shunem" (modern Solem in Issachar near Jezreel).

VII. THE SHULAMITE'S BEAUTY IS EXTOLLED. 7:1-13.

The Daughters of Jerusalem Extol the Shulamite. 7:1-5. This section apparently is an assessment of the Shulamite's beauty by the daughters of Jerusalem as they implore her to "return," (better, "turn about") in the dance they had called upon her to perform before them in order that they might play the role of judges in a beauty contest of a sort. Possibly this is the reason their description of the beauty of the Shulamite proceeds feet upward instead of head downward, because the feet of the dancer would attract their attention first (ECB).

This rapturous outburst in praise of the Shulamite (the saved remnant of Israel) does not come from the Messiah-King, but from those who now recognize her as beloved of the King and joined to Him. The five reasons for this are: (1) The context joining it with 6:13 suggests it.

(2) The term *prince's daughter* (Psalm 45:13) in its lofty formality suggests someone other than the King, whose terminology has been that of endearment and passionate love, and (3) the reference to "the king" (v. 5) does not suggest a speaker in the first person, but speakers in the third person. (4) The King's assessment of the Shulamite's beauty has already been given (4:1-6).

(5) The assessment by the daughters of Jerusalem expands the historical-prophetic background of the love story. Their praise of the Shulamite illustrates how restored Israel "in the beauties of holiness" (Psalm 110:3) will not only love the King herself but also will cause others to love Him and extol His beauty, as it will be so wonderfully reflected through her when she turns away from her unbelief and receives Him as her Messiah-Savior-Redeemer.

They praise her for nine things: *(a)* **1a.** Her **feet** are **beautiful** (graceful) as she dances in highly bejeweled sandals. She is called a **prince's daughter** (*bāṯ nāḏîḇ*, "queenly maiden, daughter of a noble-man"). *(b)* **1b.** Her **thighs** (hips) are like **jewels,** the work of an artist's hand. *(c)* **2a.** Her **navel** is compared to a never empty wine **goblet.** *(d)* **2b.** Her abdomen is like a **heap of wheat** encircled with lilies. *(e)* **3.** Her **breasts** are likened to fawns (Song of Sol. 4:5). *(f)* **4a.** Her **neck** is compared (4:4) to a **tower of ivory,** like the clear pools in Heshbon (Num. 21:26). *(g)* **4b.** Her **nose** is like the **tower of Lebanon,** protecting Israel's frontier against an unfriendly neighbor (1 Kings 11:23-25). *(h)* **5a.** Her **head** with its headdress, is like Carmel ("garden land"), the beautiful main ridge of the range of hills some thirty miles long, running northwest to southeast from the Bay of Acre to the plain of Dothan. *(i)* **5b.** Her flowing hair is **like purple** . . . the king **is captivated by your tresses** (NASB).

The King Extols the Shulamite. 7:6-9a. **6.** The language returns to the passionate, intimate converse between the lover and his beloved Shulamite. He tells her **how beautiful and how delightful** she is, calling her his **love** (abstract for the concrete "O loved one") with all her **charms** (NASB; 1:15-16; 4:10).

7-8. He compares her **stature** to a tall, straight **palm tree** (Psalm 92:12), a symbol of victory (Rev. 7:9) and beauty, which he will **climb** and **take hold of its fruit stalks** (NASB) or branches, a figurative way of portraying the physical union of two lovers, and symbolizing the ecstatic union of the Messiah-King and His redeemed people, Israel, in millennial victory and joy with all their enemies conquered.

This is the symbolic meaning also of the reference to her breasts being **like clusters of the vine.** Israel was "the vine out of Egypt" (Psalm 80:8), desolated so long because of unbelief (Isa. 5:1-7), but here restored in love and devotion to the

LORD in millennial luxuriance (Hos. 14:7). Then **the fragrance** of restored Israel's **breath** will be **like apples,** symbolic of romantic love in antiquity, and prefiguring the wonderful love of Christ for His redeemed, here His redeemed and restored people, Israel, in a full love relationship with Himself. **9a.** Then the exhilarating joy restored Israel's love will give the King-Messiah is likened to **the best wine** (Judg. 9:13; Song of Sol. 5:16).

The Shulamite Luxuriates in the King's Love. 7:9b-13. **9b.** The Shula-mite listens intently to her lover's romantic encomium, but suddenly in her effervescence she boils over, as it were, when he likens her mouth to "the best wine" (v. 9a) and takes up his train of thought, crying, **It goes down smoothly for my beloved** (Prov. 23:31), **flowing gently through the lips of those who fall asleep** (NASB).

10. Joyously secure in his love, she exclaims, **I am my beloved's** (Song of Sol. 2:16; 6:3), **and his desire is for me** (NASB; Psalm 45:11). **11-12.** This is the signal for her to suggest a trip to the **field** (the country) to **lodge** (spend the night) **in the villages,** when she will give him her love. This whole scene prophetically symbolizes the union of the Messiah-King with His redeemed and restored people, Israel, as they enter full King-dom fellowship.

Arising and going early **to the vine-yards to see if the vine flourishes** (has budded; Song of Sol. 6:11) speaks of the Messiah-King's presence with His re-deemed remnant at the dawn of the Millennium and their sallying forth to behold evidence of Israel's national restoration to divine favor in the King-dom age (Psalm 80:1, 3, 14, 19). The blooming of the pomegranates also speaks of the inauguration of the King-dom age in the outworking of the divine redemptive plan, symbols of this fruit being woven into the hem of the robe of the high priest's ephod (Exod. 28:33-34) and adorning the tops of the pillars in Solomon's Temple (1 Kings 7:18, 20), which prefigures millennial worship and communion.

13. The mandrakes, a plant considered in ancient times to have aphrodisiac properties (Gen. 30:14-16), in giving forth fragrance symbolize the ideal marital union of Solomon and the Shulamite and prophetically set forth the spiritual union of the King-Messiah and His redeemed people in millennial bliss, illustrated on the natural plane by the joys and delights of God-ordained conjugal felicity.

VIII. THE TRUE LOVE OF THE SONG OF LOVE IN REVIEW. 8:1-14.

The Model Romance in Its Maturity. 8:1-4. Continuing her words to the king (unbroken from 7:9*b*-13), the Shulamite describes the ideal marriage relationship, which existed between Solomon and her, as a composite of many relationships—the partner being a brother, teacher, husband, and lover. **1-2.** First she considers the brother relationship. **O, that thou wert as my brother,** a natural brother, so that if she found him outside, she could kiss him without being despised or looked down upon. In her culture it was not proper to express affection publicly to a lover; such action was strictly limited to members of one's family.

She makes it clear that she is referring to a real brother, for she adds, **that nursed at the breasts of my mother;** and evidently it was a younger brother, for she declares, **I would lead thee, and bring thee into my mother's house.** *You* (lit. Heb.) **would instruct me.** Ironically, the one whom she would lead is actually the one who would teach her. She is emphasizing the freedom of their ideal relationship in her playful show of authority over him, which quickly vanishes in her recognition of his leadership over her.

In loving recompense to her beloved instructor, she would give him **spiced wine** to drink and **the juice** of her pomegranate, evidently the ancient version of a shining apple for the teacher. But he is not only her brother and teacher; he is also her husband and lover. **3.** So she expresses her fervent desire: **Let his left hand be under my head, and his right hand embrace me** (NASB; 2:6).

4. No wonder that with such an ideal marriage having come to maturity the Shulamite repeats once again, **I charge** (adjure) **you, O daughters of Jerusalem, that ye stir not up** (arouse), **nor awake my love, until it please** (2:7; 3:5). Such a marriage union needs no artificial stimulation, for it is as beautiful and spontaneous as the budding springtime in which it was born. Such will be the relationship of converted restored Israel and the Messiah-King as they are joined in spiritual union in Kingdom bliss. Such will be the happy destiny of all the redeemed in their future relationship to their Redeemer.

A Portrait of True Love. 8:5a. **5a. Who is this who cometh up from the wilderness, leaning upon her beloved?** (3:6). The poet (employing the literary device of a chorus), about to present a definition of true love, recaptures a scene from the courtship of the couple who exemplify such true love in their relationship. He pictures them as they had gone to the country and recalls them strolling together in the distance. Her head is tenderly resting on his chest, and his hand gently holds her to himself.

The Awakening of True Love. 8:5b. **5b.** The king speaks to the Shulamite (following the Syriac): **Beneath the apple tree I awakened you; there your mother was in labor with you, there she was in labor and gave you birth** (NASB). "The bride would not speak of awakening Solomon, but it was he who had awakened her" *(Pulpit Commentary).* "I awakened thee," that is, "I stirred thee up to return the love I showed thee" (2:7).

The "apple tree" symbolizes love and has been called "the sweetheart tree of the ancient world"; it is a familiar symbol of romance in the culture of the Solomonic age. Typically, it speaks of Christ's love for all His redeemed (cf. 2:3), particularly (as here) His awakening His love in the Israelite remnant born as a result of her mother's (Israel's) travail during the Tribulation (Rev. 12:1-2; cf. Isa. 26:15-18; 66:7; Jer. 30:5-7). During that supreme time of trouble (Dan. 12:1; Matt. 24:21-22), the nation Israel will give birth to the godly Jewish remnant (symbolized by the Shulamite; cf. Mic. 5:2-3), which will be closely associated with Christ (Rev. 12:5), prefigured by Solomon and his beloved.

Thus, true love, exemplified by Solomon for the Shulamite and Christ for His own, is born in pain. Christ's love issued from the pain of Calvary. The Jewish remnant's love for Christ will be engendered by Israel's travail in the Tribulation, but the real source of it will be Christ's love for Israel flowing from Calvary. This is part of love's definition—it is born in pain.

A Description of the True Love Between the King and His Beloved. 8:6-7. It is best to take these words as spoken by the Shulamite to Solomon. **6a.** She wishes to be **set . . . as a seal** (signet) upon his **heart** (Exod. 28:9-12, 29-30) and upon his **arm** (Isa. 49:16; Jer. 22:24; Hag. 2:23). The seal was the signature of the owner, with which he identified all his possessions. She desires to be his possession alone, his heart's possession, utterly yielded and surrendered to him, nothing ever being able to separate her from his love (his heart) and his power (his hand). To enforce that petition, she describes and pleads the power of love, of her love to him, which drew her out to press for tokens of his love for her.

Five things are said about love: (1) Besides being *born in pain* (cf. v. 5), (2) **6b.** *love is strong,* **strong as death,** because death is like a victorious hero who conquers all in his path. Love, too, will overcome all obstacles. And as death is irreversible, so also is love.

(3) **6c.** *Love is possessive.* **Jealousy** (burning love) is **cruel** (*qāshâ*, "severe, relentless, inflexible") **as sheol,** the place of the dead (the grave for the body, Sheol for the soul and spirit). As the grave and Sheol do not give up their dead, so the ardent lover will not give up his loved one, whom he possesses with jealous vehemence and whom he protects, as the object of his love, from harm or danger.

(4) **6c-7a.** *Love is intense and enduring.* Its **coals** ("flashes") **are flashes of fire, the very flame** of the LORD (*Jah*; NASB). The intensity and enduringness of the love the Shulamite describes is of the same nature as the LORD's love for His people—an unquenchable fire that many waters cannot extinguish, or **floods** (rivers) drown.

(5) **7b.** *Love is priceless.* One who tries to buy love would be **utterly despised** (NASB). Why? Because he has violated the very nature of love. Love must be freely and spontaneously given. To attempt to buy a person's love is to violate his personality as a creature of God made in God's image, and so it is utterly reprehensible.

The love that is born in pain and is strong, possessive, intense, enduring, "the very flame of the LORD," and priceless, is the love the Shulamite pledges to the king as a seal upon his heart, the tokens of which she desires from him to prove that she is indeed the enduring object of his deep affection. This *is* the love that the Messiah-King will shower upon restored Israel, and which she, as a pledge upon His heart, will return in full measure to Him, her Savior and Deliverer.

A Manifestation of the True Love Between the King and His Beloved to Others. 8:8-9. **8a.** The speaker is evidently the Shulamite, closely identified with her lover, the king. She has **a little sister** (i.e., "little" in a sense of young, of tender age, as in Gen. 44:20; 2 Kings 5:2), **and she hath no breasts,** is not yet mature or of marriageable age (Ezek. 16:7). The Shulamite has been concerned about her little sister and probably the matter of the child's future was the occasion of this particular visit of Solomon to the country home of his queen. **8b. What shall we do for our sister in the day when she shall be spoken for?,** that is, the time when she reaches marriageable age and begins to attract the attentions of a suitor. This is obviously an illustration of love's expansion and the missionary outreach to others in spiritual need. Those who bask in divine love, as the Shulamite basks in Solomon's affection, have a keen desire born in them to see others brought into the same blessing. This is true of all the redeemed, individual or corporate, whether Israel converted and restored, or the church of this age.

However, in the typical context of the Song of Solomon dealing with Solomon, it is a type of our Lord in Kingdom blessing, the "little sister" com-

prehending the immature and young who will need to be led into faith in the Messiah-King and brought to spiritual maturity in the Kingdom era. Commentators rightly express great disgust at the endless theorizings of allegorists and their fancies. But this can largely be eliminated, removing much of the censure against the allegorical typical interpretation, by *strictly* adhering to the *time* context, which is the period just before and after the establishment of the Kingdom over Israel.

9. Solomon replies to his beloved's concerned request. He uses the plural style of majesty, which eminently suits royalty and also fits the corresponding position of his beloved as a suppliant for her sister. **If she be a wall, we will build upon her a palace** (turret) **of silver** and make the wall much more beautiful. We will do all we can to help her and shower our love upon her.

If she be a door, we will enclose her with boards of cedar, and make her a much lovelier door. It is the grace and love of the greater Solomon, manifested so wonderfully in converted Israel in the person of His beloved, going out to embrace others, younger and immature, to bring them into the Kingdom, even as He brought His beloved Shulamite.

A Special Manifestation of the Love of the Beloved for the King. 8:10-12. The ready response of grace and love from the king toward her sister inspires the Shulamite to reciprocate with thankful acknowledgments and grateful praise. **10a. Well, I am a wall with battlements, and my breasts like the towers of it** (Amp.), a totally unexpected allusion in a love song, if the author had only the subject of human love in view. But if he had a typical connotation too, it is an apt comparison to Jerusalem, "beautiful for situation, the joy of the whole [millennial] earth" (Psalm 48:2), the capital of the earth in the Kingdom age (Isa. 2:2-4).

10b. One that found favor (peace), as the Shulamite did in Solomon's **eyes** (sight), is one who became the object of his affection (cf. Deut. 24:1; Esther 2:17; Jer. 31:2). The word "peace" *šālōm)* is likely chosen as a play on the name Solomon. "The king of peace delights in me because I am peace in his eyes."

11. Then the Shulamite mentions Solomon's **vineyard at Baal-hamon** (cf. Judith 8:3), evidently designating a place near Shunem (cf. Song of Sol. 6:13) in the plain of Jezreel. The vineyard was obviously large, since he leased it to **keepers** (overseers), every one of whom was to bring him **a thousand pieces of silver.** The vineyard of Israel in Old Testament times had been transferred from the Jews to the Gentiles when the former failed to render its fruits to God (Matt. 21:33-43). Under restored Israel and the Messiah-King at His second advent, the vineyard will be restored to Israel, who will no longer complain of herself, "Mine own vineyard have I not kept" (Song of Sol. 1:6).

12. Under the greater Solomon and the restored vineyard of the Kingdom age, Israel—filled with love for and dedication to the King-Messiah, as the Shulamite was to Solomon—will cry, **Thou, O Solomon, must have a thousand, and those who keep** (tend) **the fruit** (thereof) **two hundred.** Prophetically and typically these words envision a state of things in the millennial Kingdom, "when the spiritual and the temporal shall be perfectly adjusted" *(Pulpit Commentary)* in the righteous earth rule of the Messiah-King (Isa. 9:7; 11:4-5).

Then restored Israel will say what the Shulamite said to Solomon: **My vineyard, which is mine, is before me.** It is mine by gift of the true Solomon, not merely "leased . . . unto keepers," as in the Jewish age of works, but "mine" by grace. "Before me ['in my power'] is all this delight, and my desire is to my Beloved, and all that I have is His." What a manifestation of the true love that breathes throughout this immortal love song!

The Parting Request of the King's Love. 8:13. **13.** As the lovers must part for a while, the king's love makes a final request: **O you who sit in the gardens, My companions are listening for your voice—Let me hear it!** (NASB; 2:8). She is to remain "in the gardens," a figurative expression for her place of testimony and service on the earth, till the lovers are reunited. He ardently desires that meanwhile the lines of communication between them be kept open. He would hear her voice even as her "companions" listen to her voice.

The Shulamite's friends (typically, the friends of the Jewish remnant), who are the King's friends, will speak "often one to another" (Mal. 3:16) in mutual encouragement during the dark times of Tribulation when the King is making up His "jewels," whom He will spare out of the trial and bring them into Kingdom blessing (3:17—4:3). Let not these, in their communion with one another, neglect communion with the Messiah-King. Let them see His countenance and let Him hear their voice. Let them be persistent in their prayer, like the widow who cried to the unjust judge and was avenged of her adversary (Luke 18:1-8), for they too will be avenged of their foes.

The Parting Request of the Shulamite's Love. 8:14. **14.** The Shulamite desires the king's speedy return. **Make haste, my beloved, and be thou like a roe** (gazelle) **or ... young hart** (stag) **upon the mountains of spices** (*beśāmîm*, "balsams, fragrant spices"). Christ is to make haste to return at His second advent and is portrayed figuratively as a fleet gazelle or stag bounding over the mountains of spices, overcoming all impediments (Psalm 2:1-12) to manifest His fragrance in Kingdom rule (see comments on 2:17), which will be a sweet aroma to Israel and the nations of the millennial earth.